# The
# Weather
# Almanac

ISSN 0731-5627

# The Weather Almanac

A Reference Guide to Weather, Climate, and Air Quality in the United States and Its Key Cities, Comprising Statistics, Principles, and Terminology. Provides Weather/Health Information and Safety Rules for Environmental Hazards Associated with Storms, Weather Extremes, Earthquakes, and Volcanoes. Also Includes World Climatological Highlights and Special Features on Weather, Climate, and Society

## SIXTH EDITION

**Frank E. Bair**
Editor

 **Gale Research Inc.** · DETROIT · LONDON

Frank E. Bair, *Editor*
Kelly Bowen, Thomas Bowen, and Lorraine Smith,
*Research and Production Assistants*

**Gale Research Inc. Staff**

Mary Beth Trimper, *Production Manager*
Shanna Heilveil, *Production Assistant*

Art Chartow, *Art Director*
C.J. Jonik *Keyliner*

∞™ This book is printed on acid-free paper that meets the minimum requirements of American National Standard for Information Sciences— Permanence Paper for Printed Library Materials, ANSI Z39.48-1984.

♻ This book is printed on recycled paper that meets Environmental Protection Agency standards.

Copyright © 1992
Gale Research Inc.
835 Penobscot Bldg.
Detroit, MI 48226-4094

ISBN 0-8103-2843-7
ISSN 0731-5627
Library of Congress Catalog Card Number 81-644322

Printed in the United States of America.
Published simultaneously in the United Kingdom
by Gale Research International Limited
(An affiliated company of Gale Research Inc.)

# CONTENTS

## RETIREMENT AND HEALTH WEATHER

## AIR POLLUTION

## WEATHER FUNDAMENTALS AND GLOSSARY

## WEATHER INFORMATION AND COMMUNICATIONS

*Fahrenheit-to-Celsius conversion, the Beaufort Scale of Wind Effect, and other handy aids to reading Nature's advance weather signals are provided.*

## WEATHER, CLIMATE, AND SOCIETY

*U.S. climatic diversity and its relation to American agriculture is discussed.*

*Weather variations and their effects on power production are examined.*

*Atmospheric effects of the by-products of energy production and use are analyzed.*

*A view of the complex global climate system and its long-term changes is provided.*

*The possible consequences of increased carbon dioxide in the atmosphere are analyzed.*

## RECORD-SETTING WEATHER

*Tables and maps portray "Highest, Lowest, Wettest," etc.*

## ROUND-THE-WORLD WEATHER

*The climate of each continent is discussed separately in this text, which is supplemented by world climate maps.*

*A table listing the cities and their normal temperatures for the four seasons. Monthly precipitation normals are also listed.*

## WEATHER OF 109 SELECTED U.S. CITIES (with 1951-1980 Climatic Normals and revisions of "Extremes," as well as climatic histories through 1985)

*These reports, comprising about half of this book, provide both narrative and statistical descriptions of the cities' climates and weather tendencies. Records of 30 years are included.*

# INTRODUCTION

When Hurricane Hugo thundered its way across the South Carolina coast and inland in 1989, the potential for human casualties was tremendous. This *Intensity Four* hurricane, which flooded and smashed out more than $8 billion (!) of property damage was so powerful and so aimed that it would have killed thousands, in an earlier era. Why didn't it[*]? One reason is that we Americans have become the most avid people in the world for soaking up weather information. (Probably a function of being the most curious...?) Questions of weather are cereal sweetner at our breakfast table; pickle on our lunch-time burger; the rival of sports talk at coffee-break; and handmaiden to antacids with eventide dessert. In short, America is tuning in to the weather ten times as intently as in the sixties, twenty times as intently as in the forties! We are demanding and getting deluges of data, carloads of commentaries, seas of statistics. We, Americans, are, indeed, becoming *weatherwise* as a nation.

*Weather Almanac* has observed, and continues to respond to, this surging interest — with the broadest basket of weather wisdom it is possible to assemble within one set of boards. Let us check, for a moment, the spectrum this book has assembled.

*Weather Almanac* is a handy and comprehensive complement to the usual sources of day-to-day weather information in newspaper, radio, and television reports. This newly revised edition of *Weather Almanac* places in your hands a wide range of maps, charts, and safety rules based upon past records and experience to inform you (as far as possible in a single volume) of what may be expected from the restless atmosphere. Explanatory narratives of many of the basic processes involved enhance the significance of the various bits of information.

In the section on tornadoes, for example, *Weather Almanac* tells you what actions the U.S. Weather Service urges you to take immediately to protect yourself from nature's most violent of storms. Weather Service scientists also tell you exactly what a tornado is, where and when tornadoes occur most often, their typical duration and distance of travel. And, this *Weather Almanac* feature also provides tornado statistics and lets you follow selected tornado paths on U.S. maps.

The section on tornadoes is but one of a series of such sections in *Weather Almanac*, edited from official Weather Service and Geological Survey pamphlets, to serve as a popular basic reference for severe weather and other extreme conditions. Similar facts are given for hurricanes, blizzards, heat waves, earthquakes, thunderstorms, lightning, floods, tidal waves, and volcanic eruptions. Official records and statistics are

---

[*] Twenty one deaths were charged to *Hugo* during its U.S. travel. No one can feel good about that — only that it was not twenty one hundred, as it might have been if our warning systems had not become so effective.

included wherever they are useful and available.

Take the time to read the full text portraying each of these severe conditions. It will help you to better adapt *yourself* and *your* activities to the weather and let you prepare for a weather emergency at the best time: *before it is upon you*. Even if you must postpone full reading, do try to familiarize yourself with the *scope* of the information and where things are located in the book. Then you can return to the text for quick, precise references, again and again.

Of course, reference on storms and weather extremes is only one feature of this book. Helping you to anticipate and understand day-in, day-out weather has been a main purpose in compiling it. *Weather Almanac* provides a glossary of weather terms, explains the underlying weather principles, and includes a brief cloud atlas and other guides to personal observation. Most significantly, however, *Weather Almanac* offers you a great storehouse of data from hundreds of sources, assembled and presented in forms to let you look up detailed facts *as you need them*.

**A Look at Details**

This information begins with weather and climate data for the country as a whole. It is contained mostly in charts which present the monthly and yearly averages. Individually, the charts tell key facts about the weather story for a given observation point, such as Denver, Mobile, or Beckley (West Virginia); but they are brought together on U.S. maps so you get a quick picture of the entire nation's weather varieties. The charts-on-a-map form lets you compare the range of monthly temperatures in one area against the range in another area. Temperature highs and lows for each of the twelve months are presented on separate maps. Similar gatherings of charts depict the nation's sunshine picture in area-by-area detail. Other charts tell the precipitation story. Meanwhile, with intent to serve the farmer and gardener, a table and map series combine to present freeze data and the length of the growing season lengths for various points in the U.S. The *last date for spring frosts* in the areas and for *first killing frosts* in the fall is an important list that's added.

*Weather Almanac* also takes you around the world. One compact section gives you facts on temperature and precipitation for over 550 key cities in every part of the globe.

**Changes in *Weather Almanac*, Sixth Edition**

All sections of the book have been revised as new data on particular subjects and phenomena have become available, but the greatest amount of change occurs in the 445 page section on "Weather of 109 Selected U.S. Cities." The tables are presented in a large format, more readable than those of editions one-through-five. Climatic extremes and other information have been updated through 1990. A general introduction defines terms and indicates the efficient use of the statistical tables. Finely detailed weather statistics for each city typically include *40 years, or more, of weather history* (e.g. measurements of temperatures, rainfall, etc. since 1951). The tables also include the recently revised Climatic Normals 1951-1990. The careful reader can gain an appreciation of how weather conditions vary from place-to-place and also sense the magnitude of changes that can be expected in the various places from month-to-month and from year-to-year. For each city the reader will find a clearly spoken description of the climate — as a native might tell you about it, *if* the native also happened to be a meteorologist.

Everyone's concern over the climb in fuel bills, with the need to conserve energy resources, has led to a renewed interest in energy/weather relationships. The need to develop substitute sources has grown out of that concern. Basic information on heating and cooling degree days is included in the data for the 109 cities. Thirty-year normals for these data are displayed on maps in a special section, along with detailed explanations and cautionary statements about their use.

Air quality, while not an aspect of weather, is so weather-related that it belongs in a definitive weather source book. *Weather Almanac* therefore includes a section on Air Pollution. The background of current federally mandated, state implemented air quality control programs is sketched. The National Ambient Air Quality Standards are summarized and the Pollutant Standards Index is explained. The section also provides insight into the way weather principles modify and control air pollution episodes. The chemical principles of the phenomenon known as acid rain are added to this chapter.

Earthquakes and tidal waves are not manifestations of the weather, of course, but the need of the general public to be informed about them and the precautions to be taken when and where they occur — and indeed *before* they occur — warrant a special section. Particular problems along the San Andreas fault in California are highlighted as a background to a summary report on the October 17, 1989 earthquake in the San Francisco Bay area, epicentered at Santa Cruz. The recent series of volcanic eruptions of Mount Saint Helens. after more than a century of inactivity, and the likelihood of continued activity there are portrayed through the eyes of the U.S. Geological Survey's data. To that report is appended information about renewed activity in other long-dormant volcanoes, most particularly activity in Hawaii, the Philippines, and Japan. Discussions of these major geotectonic phenomena, and their associated *Safety Rules*, serve to complement the various weather-related hazards and safety rules.

In addition to these major information features, *Weather Almanac* provides sections on *Weather and Health* (including tips on choosing a retirement climate), *Wind Chill Factor, Heating and Cooling Degree Days, The Summer Comfort Index, Livestock Safety Index, NOAA Weather Radio Warning Network,* obtaining and interpreting *Marine Weather Advisories,* how to forecast the weather for yourself, and a potpourri of other high-utility items. Also, since many users of *Weather Almanac* commonly travel by jet aircraft, there is a text which treats the sybject of jet-lag or time-zone travel fatigue. It lists tips for coping with time-zone travel fatigue.

A new section on *Weather, Climate, and Society,* instituted with the fourth edition, provides an authoritative look at weather and climate as they relate to two of our most important economic sectors -- agriculture and power production. Other discussions center on climatic fluctuations and climatic changes which are among the most vexing and least understood scientific questions of our day. Fluctuations are the stuff of news headlines about extremely hard winters, hot dry summers, and other severe anomalies that can occur several times in a human lifetime. *But, true changes of climate develop more slowly.* Few scientific subjects have been treated so sensationally in the popular media; few scientific subjects have such a significant bearing on the future direction of life on the planet called Earth.

A special feature section for this sixth edition *Weather Almanac* is devoted to the problem of upper-atmosphere ozone.


**General Note on Sources**

Much of the information in this book is quoted directly from reports and records prepared by various United States Government departments, agencies, and services which share parts of the nation's great weather and environmental science efforts. For example, you will find several sets of safety rules for responding to harsh or unusual weather. These rules have been transcribed directly from National Oceanic and Atmospheric Administration (NOAA) publications. Similarly, the United States Geological Survey is the source of comparable safety advice for earthquakes and volcanic activity. This means the rules were developed by the nation's best informed, most responsible storm and natural hazard analysts, drawing on thousands of observations of damage and injury. Such authoritative suggestions have helped dramatically to minimize the impact of these severe hazards, and they merit your fullest confidence.

The city-by-city weather records are worthy of the same confidence, for they come directly from the cumulative records developed by the United States Weather Service observers around the country and have been coordinated by the people of the National Climatic Center, under leadership of Dr. Kenneth Hadeen, were written by the climatologists located in the individual areas, so they spring from first-hand experience as well as carefully kept records.

The core sections of the information on weather principles; Air Pollution; and Weather, Climate, and Society have also been compiled from a wide variety of sources drawn from the Environmental Protection Agency, the President's Council on Environmental Quality, the Department of Agriculture, the Department of Energy, as well as NOAA. The section on Retirement and Health Weather and various introductions are original with *Weather Almanac*.

The *Weather Almanac* editorial staff hope that this new revised sixth edition, in the new, larger, more readable format (introduced with editon five) and with many servicable features will be increasingly useful as a first source of basic information about the vagaries of our canopy of air and a variety of environmental hazards.

Comments or suggestions from readers are not only welcome but are solicited in our quest to constantly improve the book.

*Frank E. Bair*

# U.S. WEATHER
## IN
# ATLAS FORMAT

## NORMAL DAILY MAXIMUM, AVERAGE, MINIMUM,

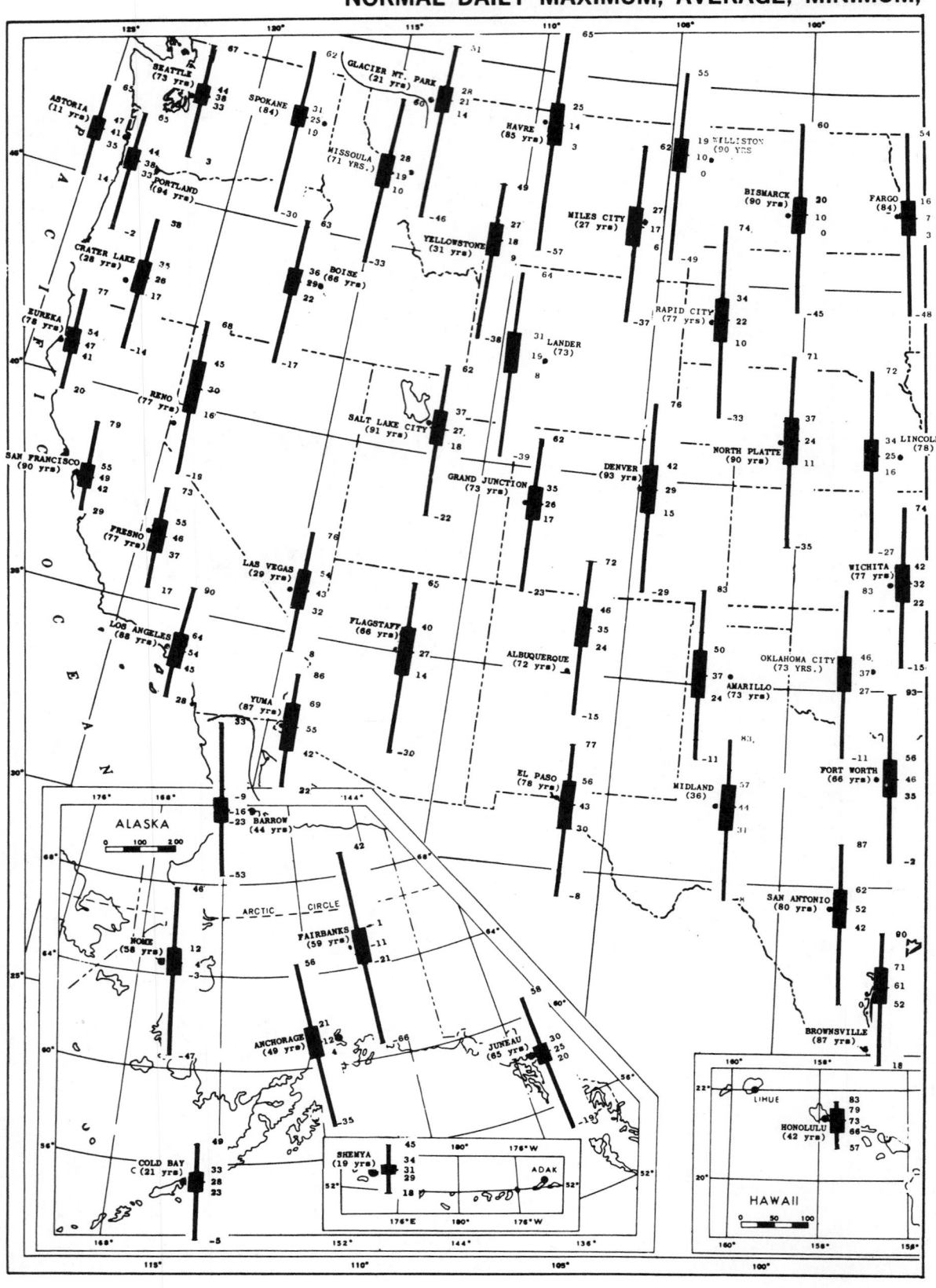

## AND EXTREME TEMPERATURES (°F), JANUARY

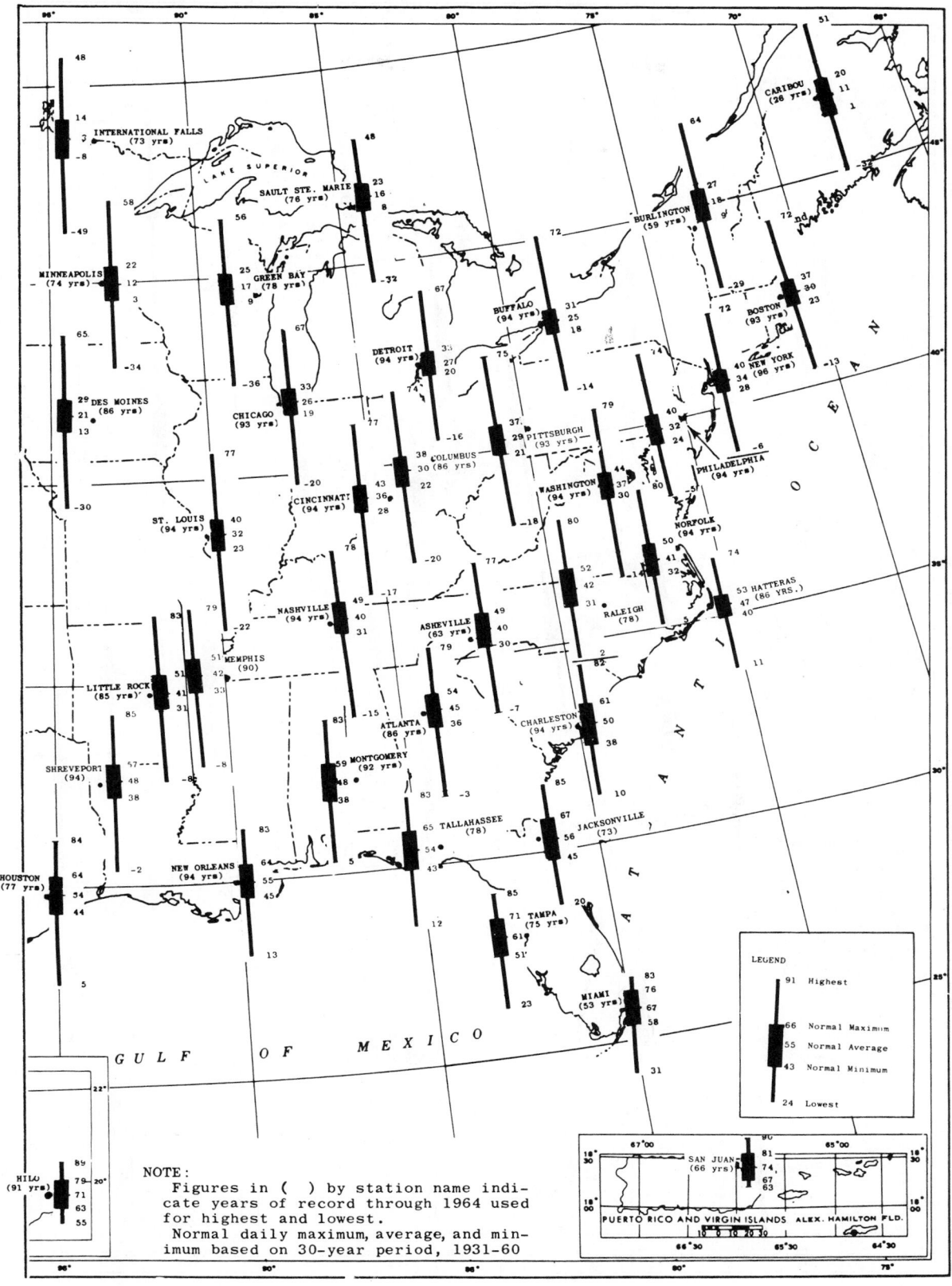

**See the "Weather of 109 selected U.S. Cities"** section at the back of this volume for
**1961-1990 adjustments to** Normals, Means, and Extremes.

## NORMAL DAILY MAXIMUM, AVERAGE, MINIMUM,

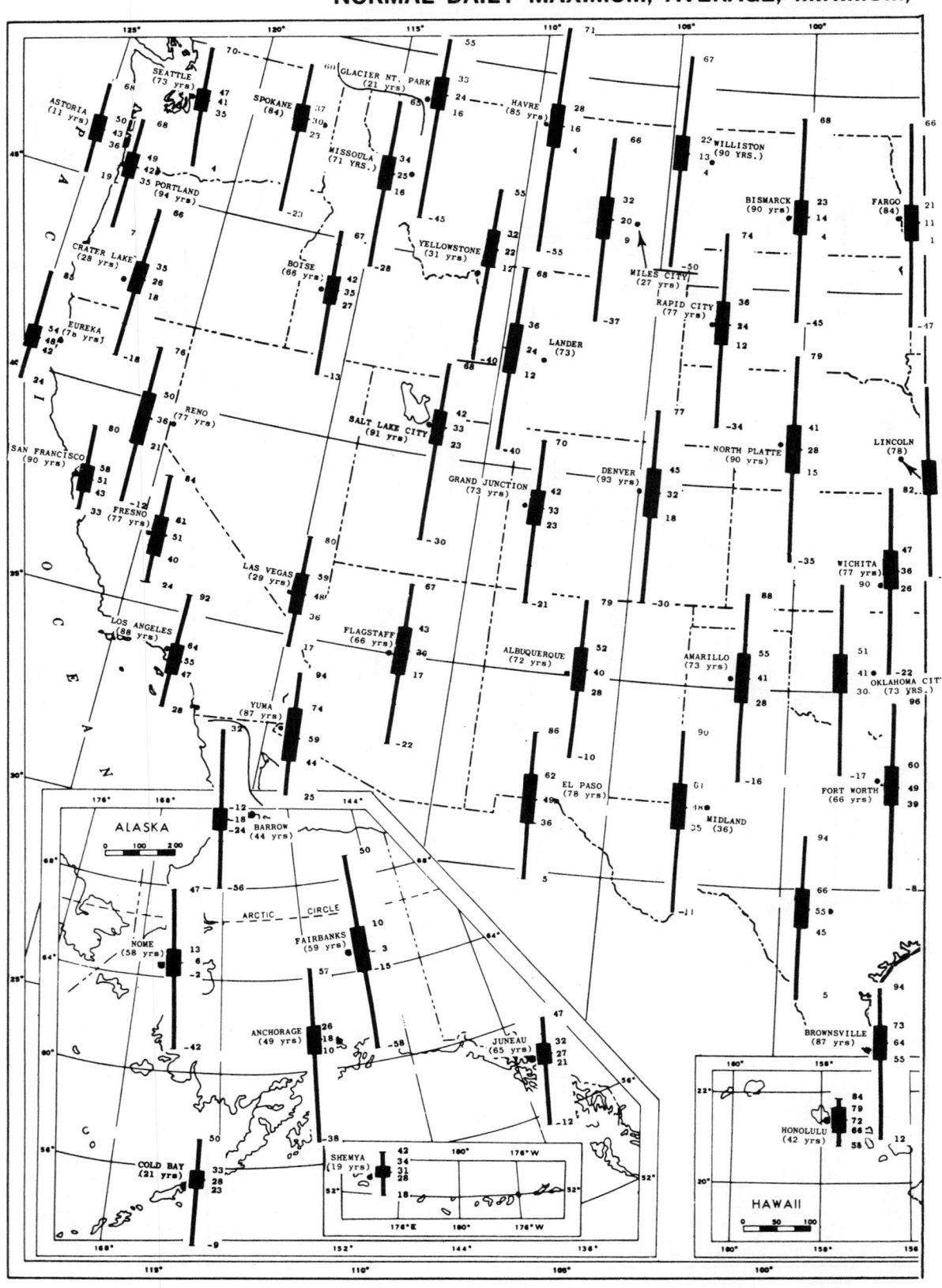

## AND EXTREME TEMPERATURES (°F), FEBRUARY

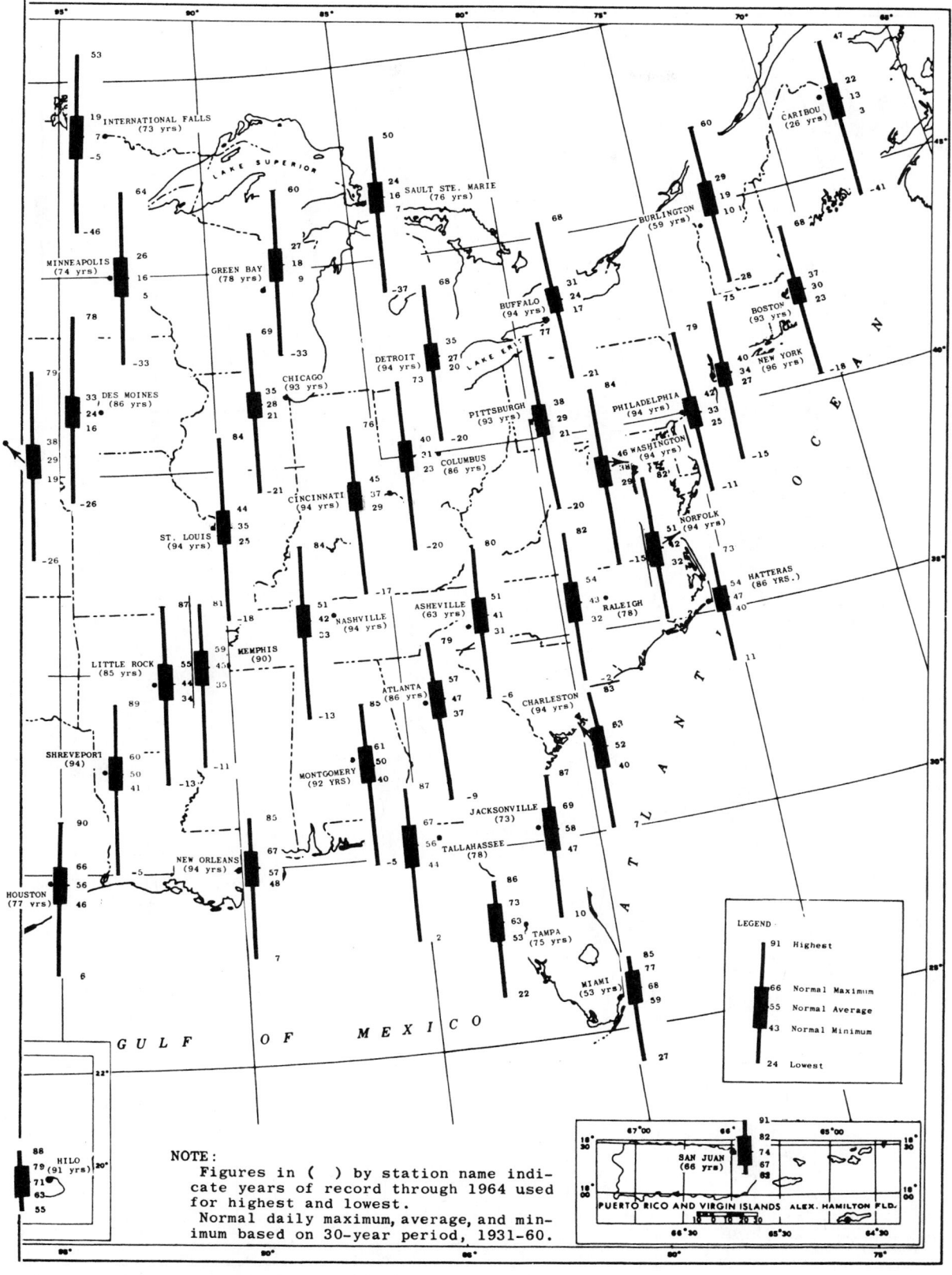

**See the "Weather of 109 selected U.S. Cities" section at the back of this volume for 1961-1990 adjustments to Normals, Means, and Extremes.**

## NORMAL DAILY MAXIMUM, AVERAGE, MINIMUM,

## AND EXTREME TEMPERATURES (°F), MARCH

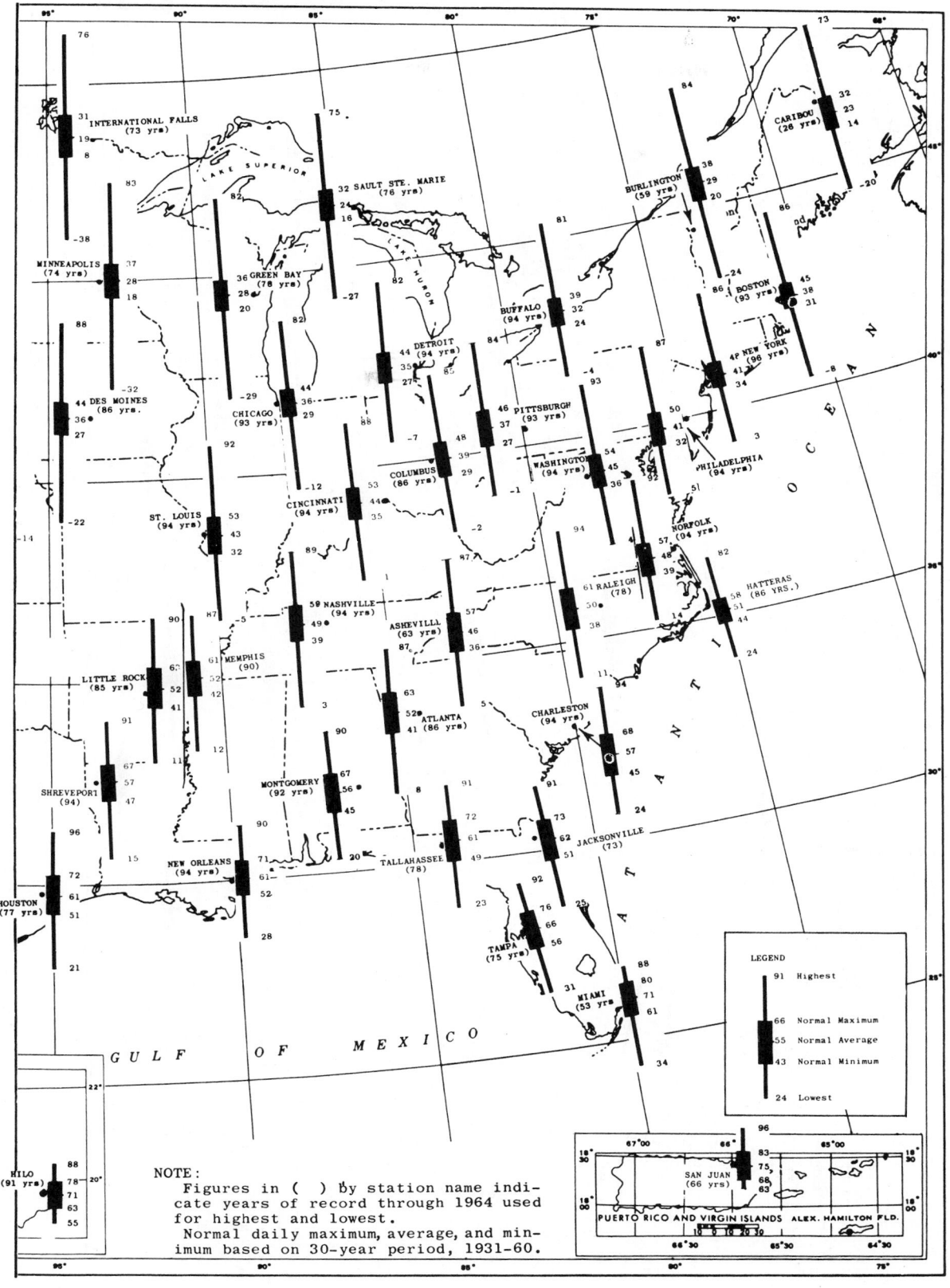

**See the "Weather of 109 selected U.S. Cities" section at the back of this volume for 1961-1990 adjustments to** Normals, Means, and Extremes.

NOTE:
Figures in ( ) by station name indicate years of record through 1964 used for highest and lowest.
Normal daily maximum, average, and minimum based on 30-year period, 1931-60.

LEGEND

91 Highest
66 Normal Maximum
55 Normal Average
43 Normal Minimum
24 Lowest

PUERTO RICO AND VIRGIN ISLANDS    ALEX. HAMILTON FLD.
SAN JUAN (66 yrs)

## NORMAL DAILY MAXIMUM, AVERAGE, MINIMUM,

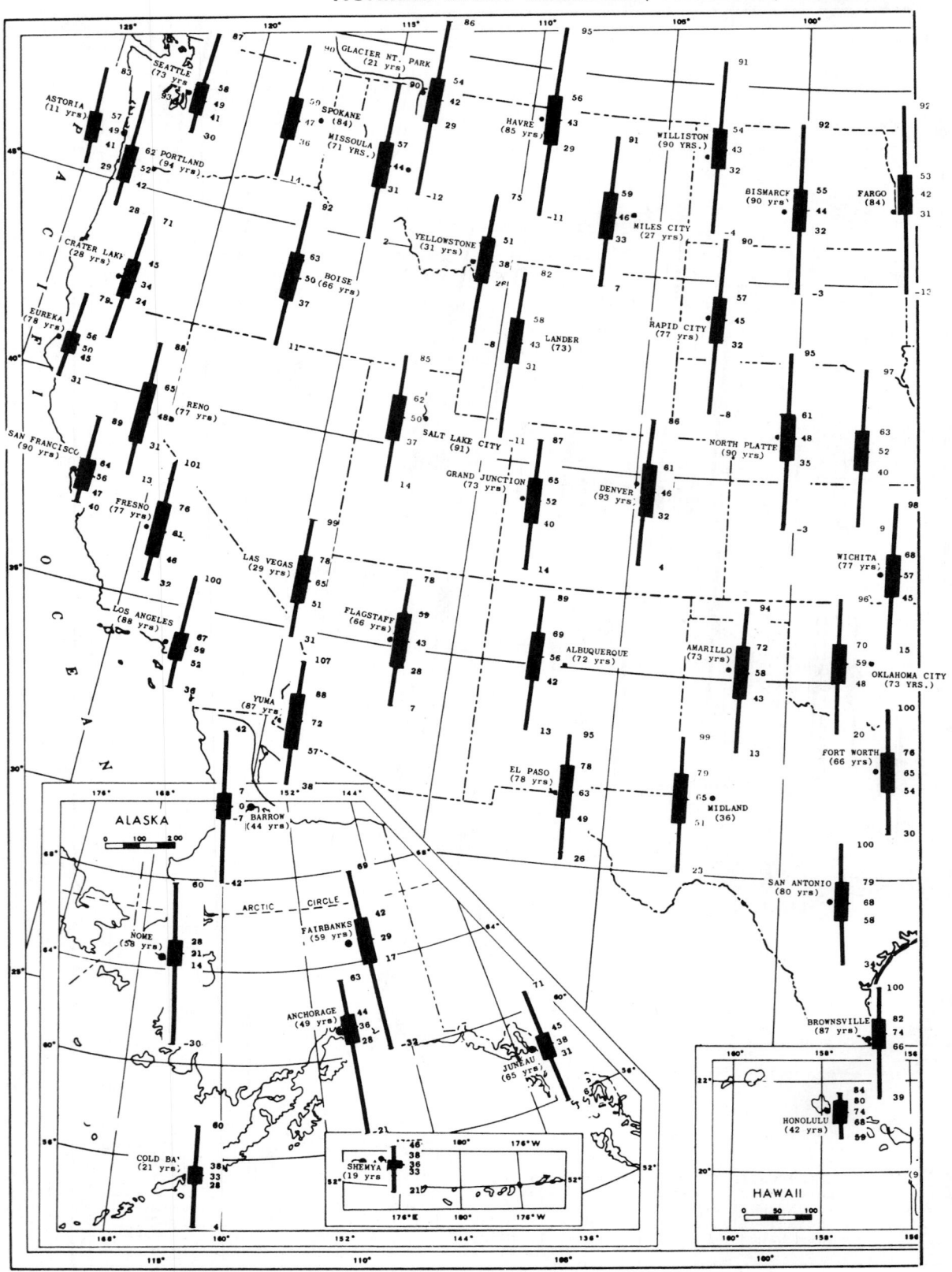

## AND EXTREME TEMPERATURES (°F), APRIL

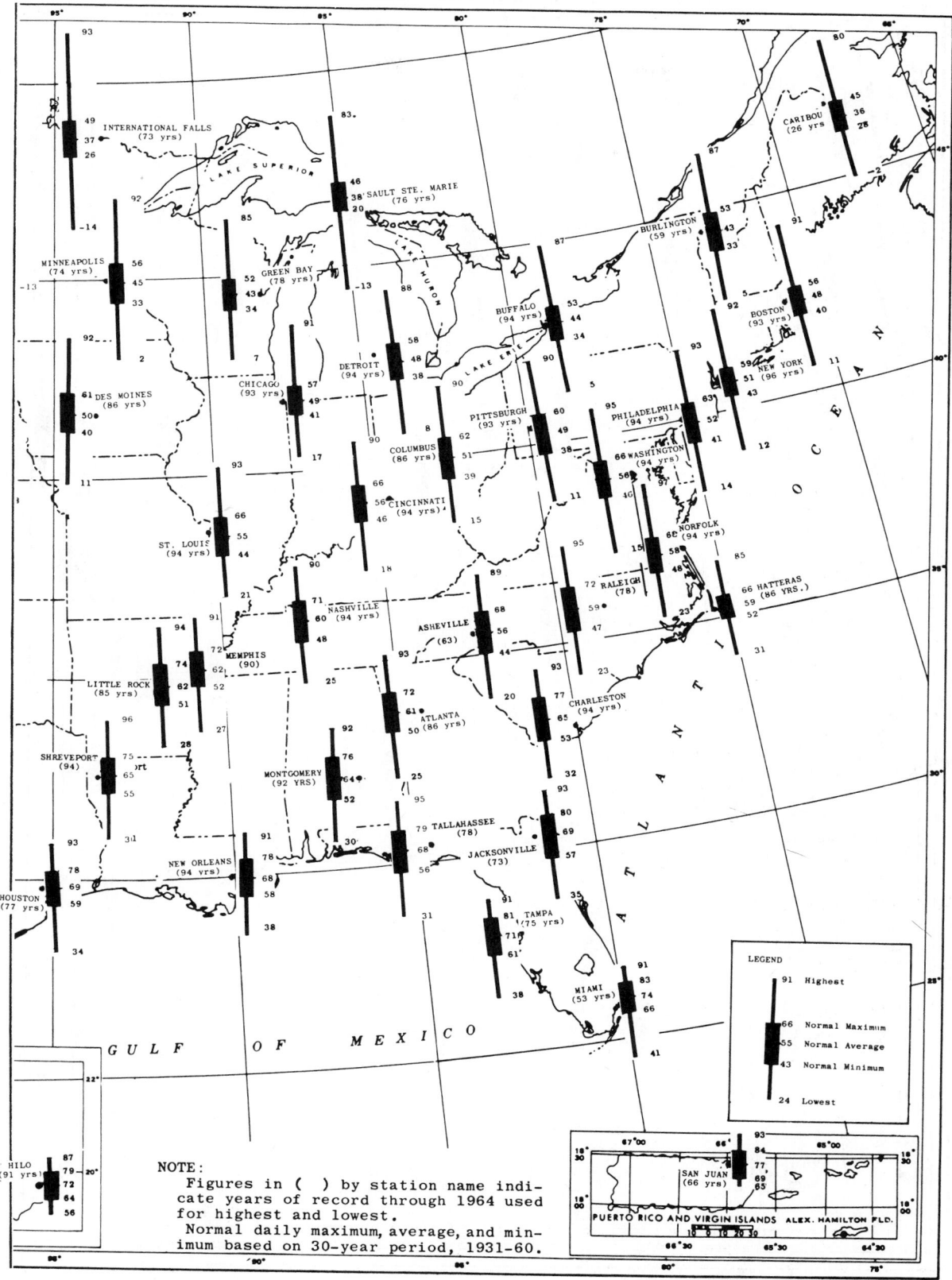

NOTE:
Figures in ( ) by station name indicate years of record through 1964 used
for highest and lowest.
Normal daily maximum, average, and minimum based on 30-year period, 1931-60.

**See the "Weather of 109 selected U.S. Cities" section at the back of this volume for
1961-1990 adjustments to** Normals, Means, and Extremes.

## NORMAL DAILY MAXIMUM, AVERAGE, MINIMUM,

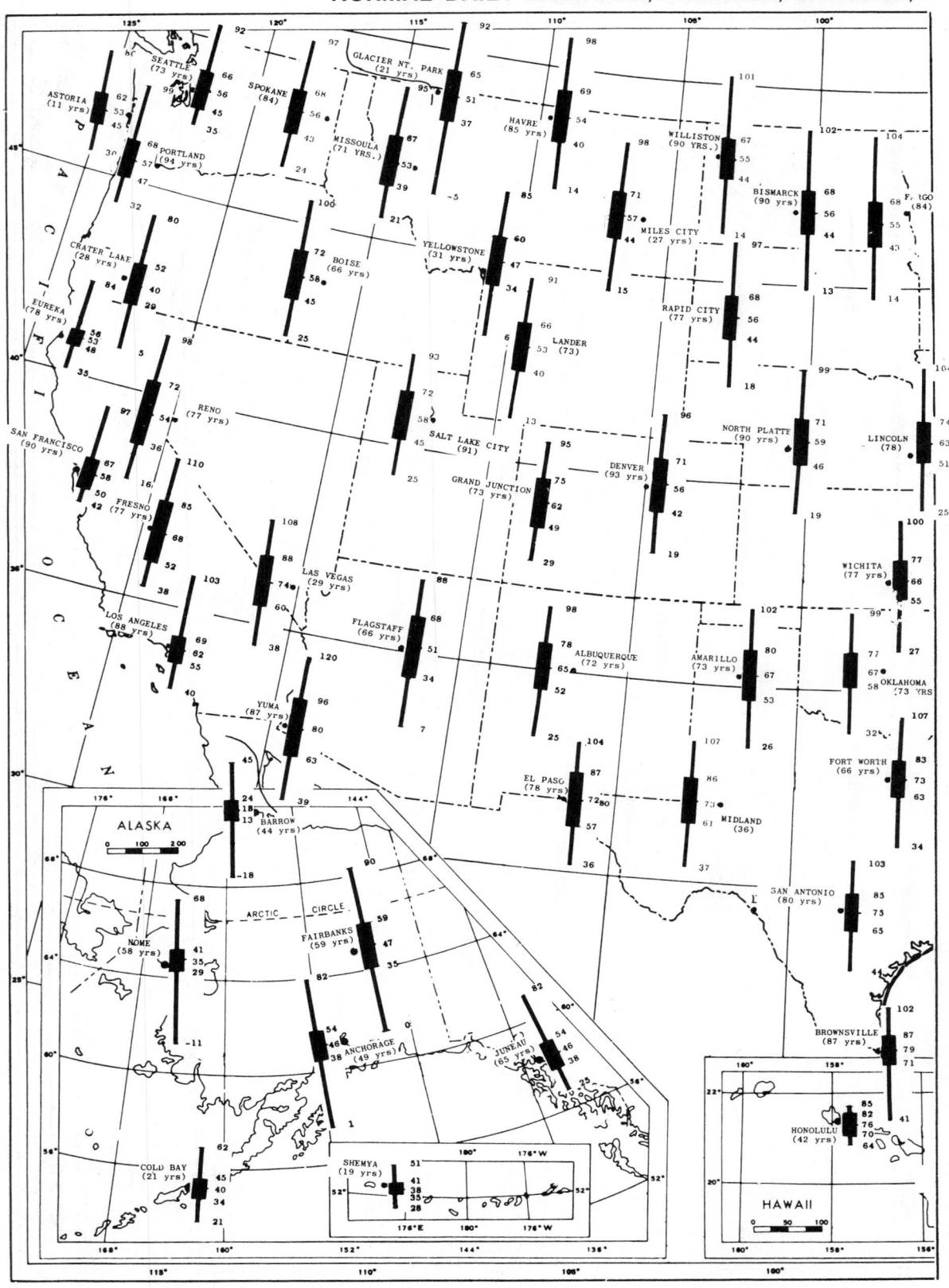

## AND EXTREME TEMPERATURES (°F), MAY

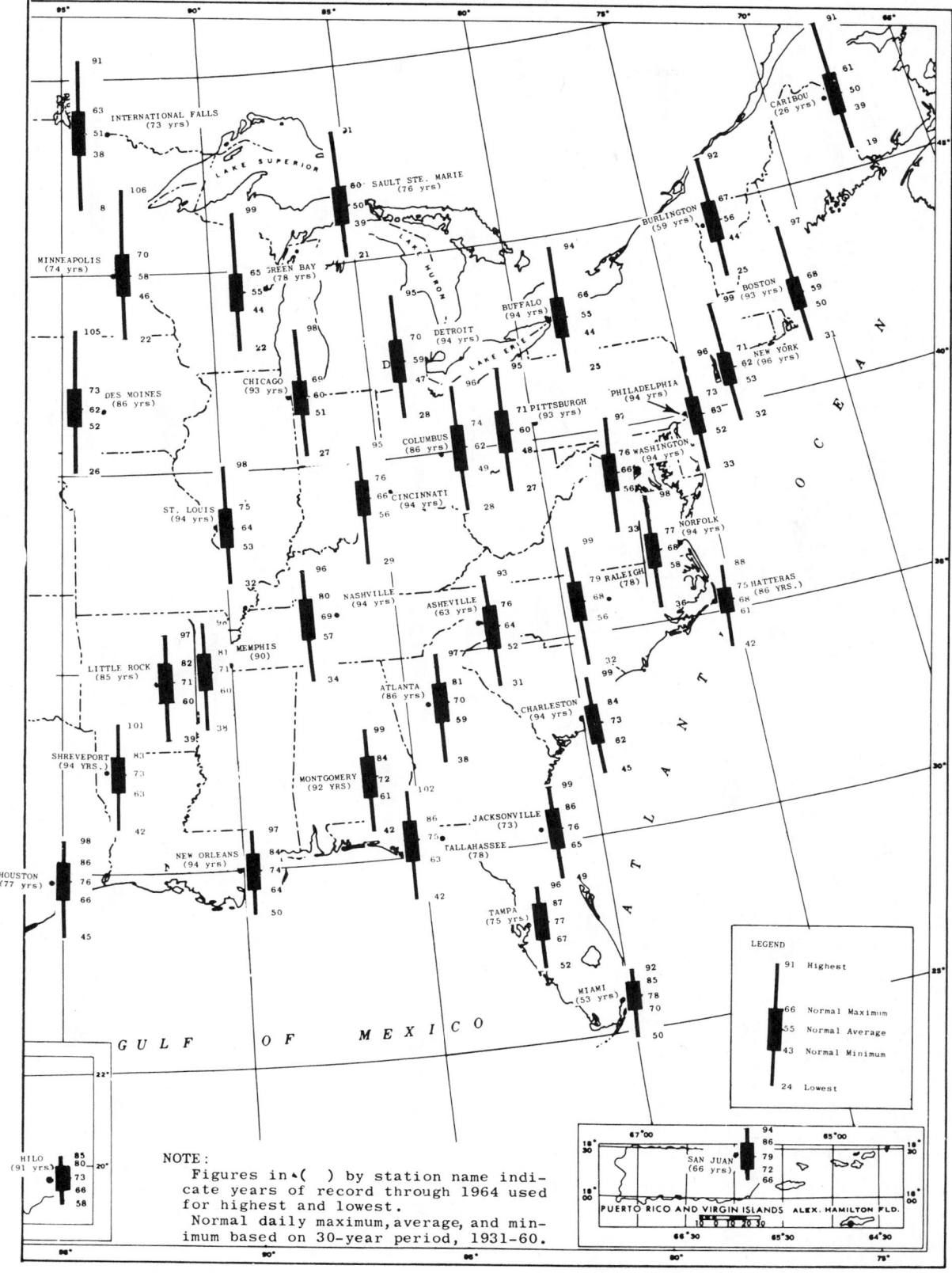

NOTE:
Figures in ( ) by station name indicate years of record through 1964 used
for highest and lowest.
Normal daily maximum, average, and minimum based on 30-year period, 1931-60.

**LEGEND**

| 91 | Highest |
| 66 | Normal Maximum |
| 55 | Normal Average |
| 43 | Normal Minimum |
| 24 | Lowest |

**See the "Weather of 109 selected U.S. Cities" section at the back of this volume for 1961-1990 adjustments to** Normals, Means, and Extremes.

## NORMAL DAILY MAXIMUM, AVERAGE,

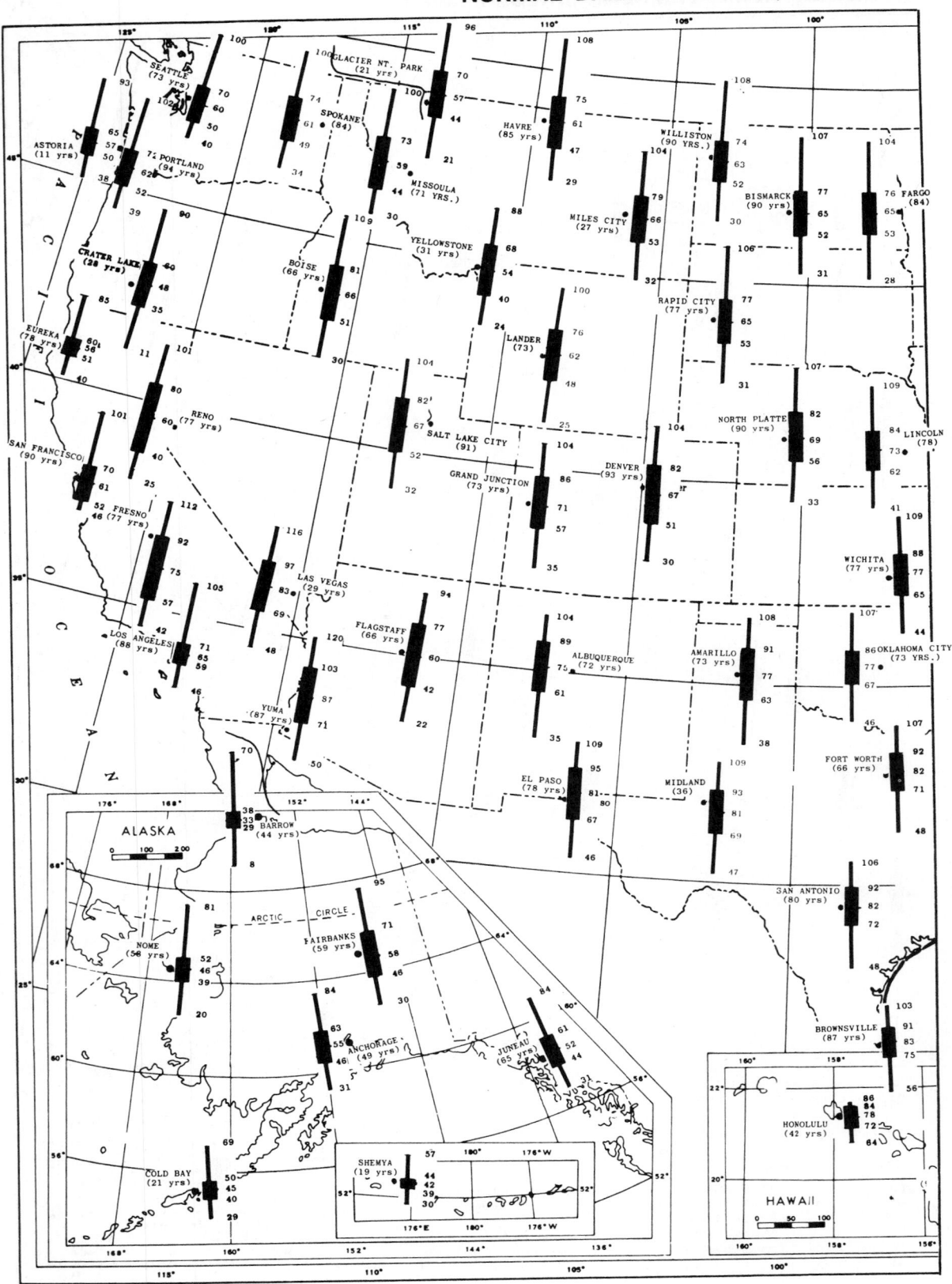

## MINIMUM, AND EXTREME TEMPERATURES (°F), JUNE

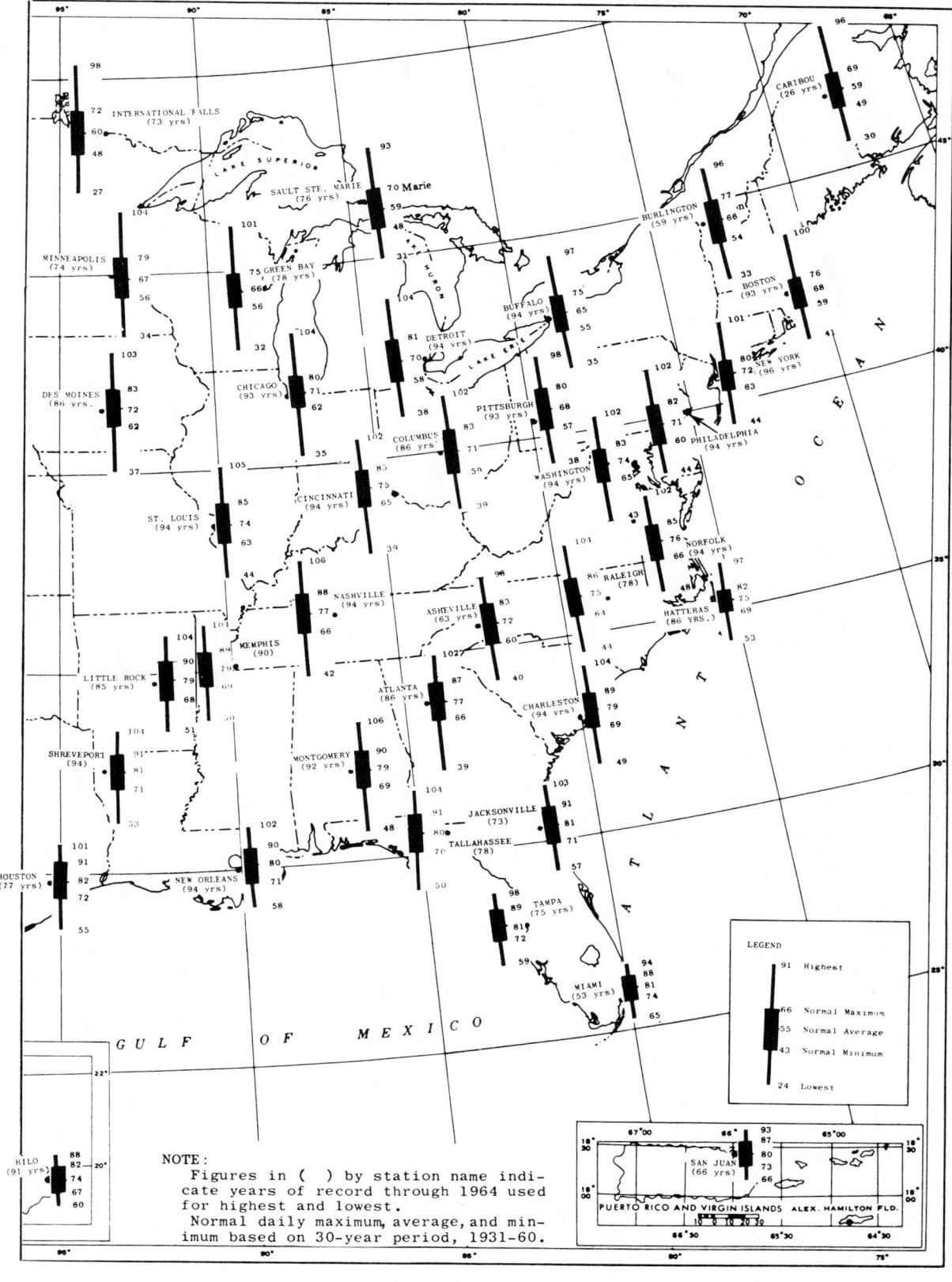

**See the "Weather of 109 selected U.S. Cities" section at the back of this volume for 1961-1990 adjustments to** Normals, Means, and Extremes.

## NORMAL DAILY MAXIMUM, AVERAGE,

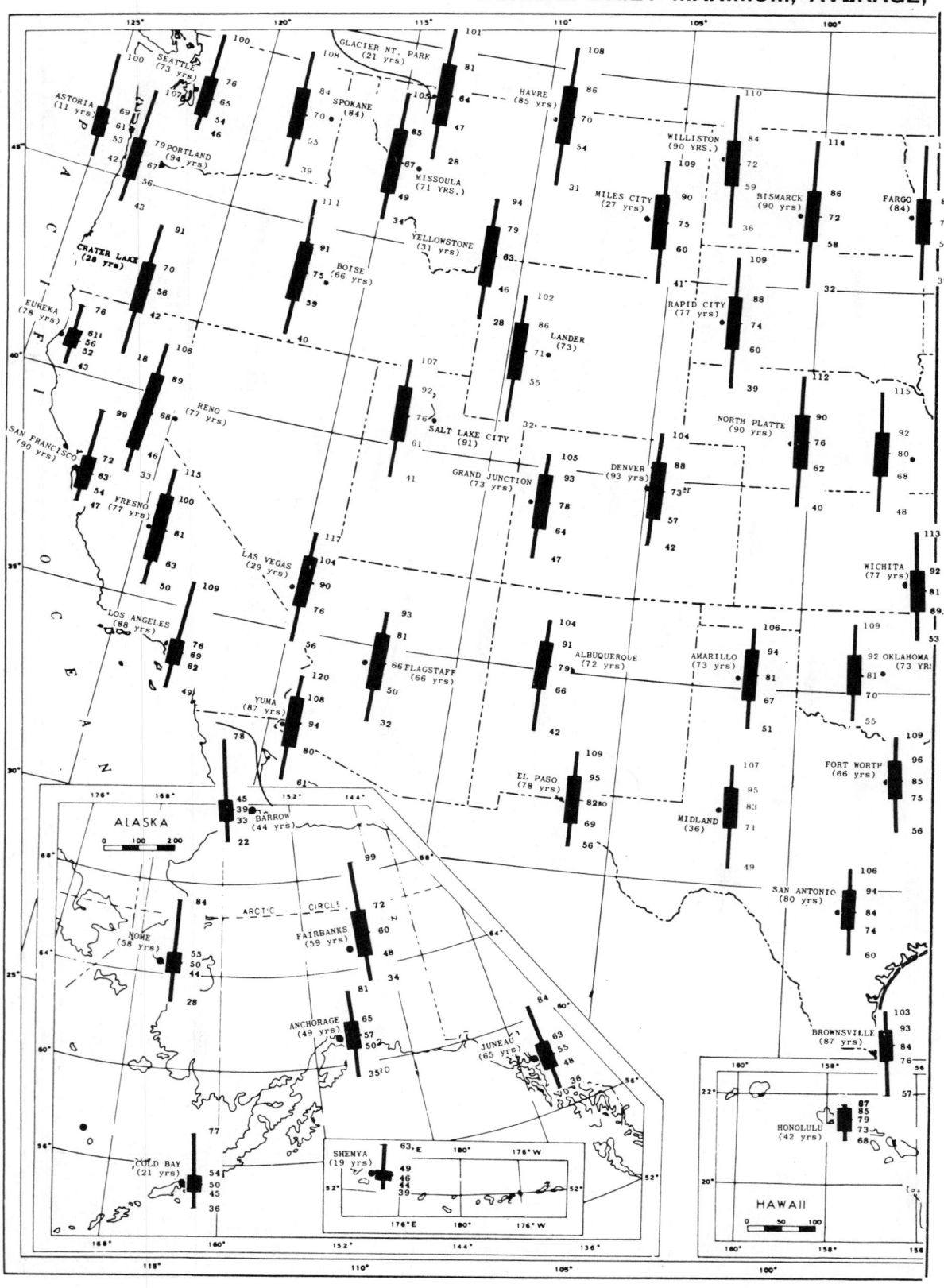

## MINIMUM, AND EXTREME TEMPERATURES (°F), JULY

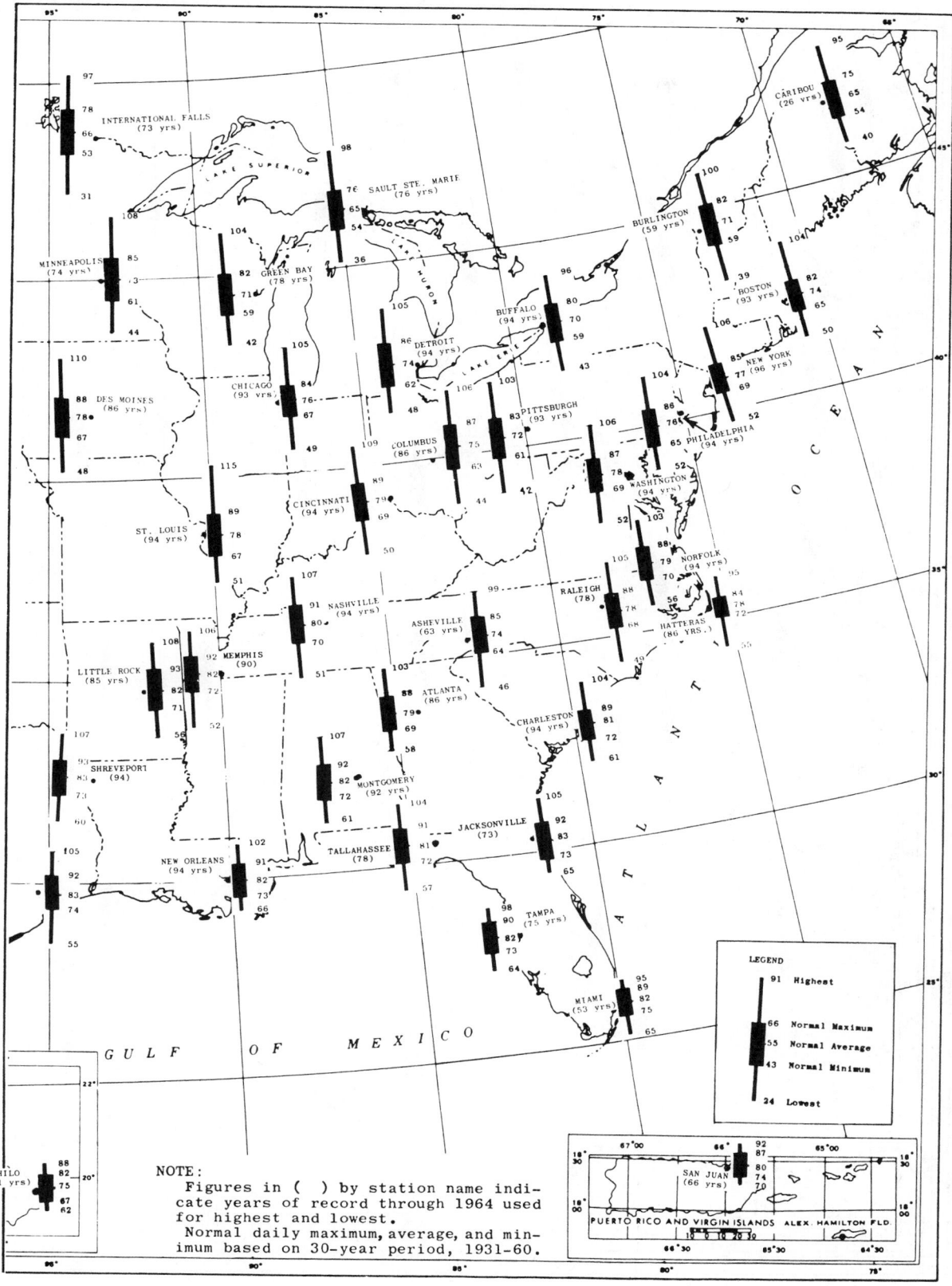

**See the "Weather of 109 selected U.S. Cities" section at the back of this volume for 1961-1990 adjustments to Normals, Means, and Extremes.**

## NORMAL DAILY MAXIMUM, AVERAGE, MINIMUM,

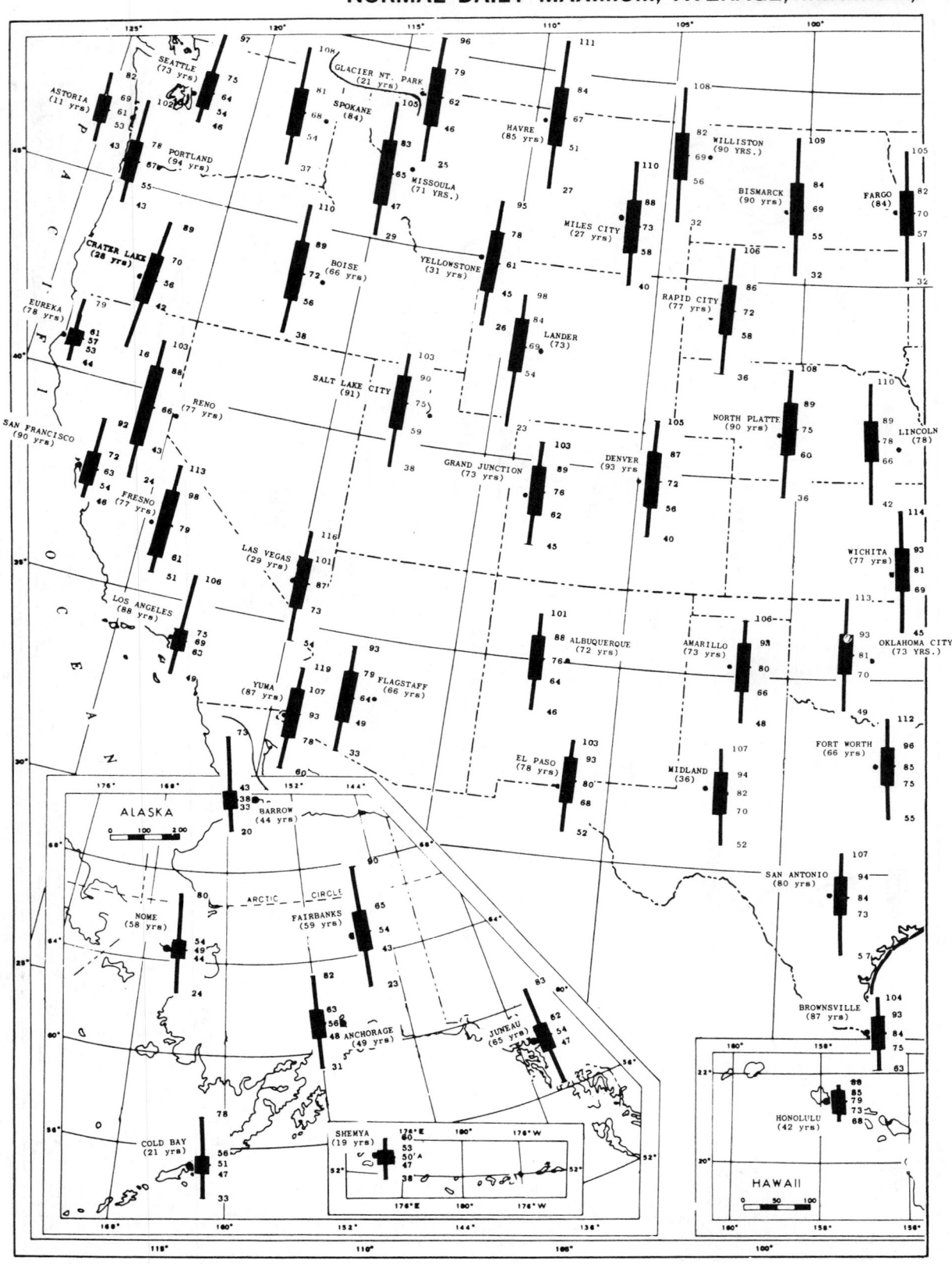

## AND EXTREME TEMPERATURES (°F), AUGUST

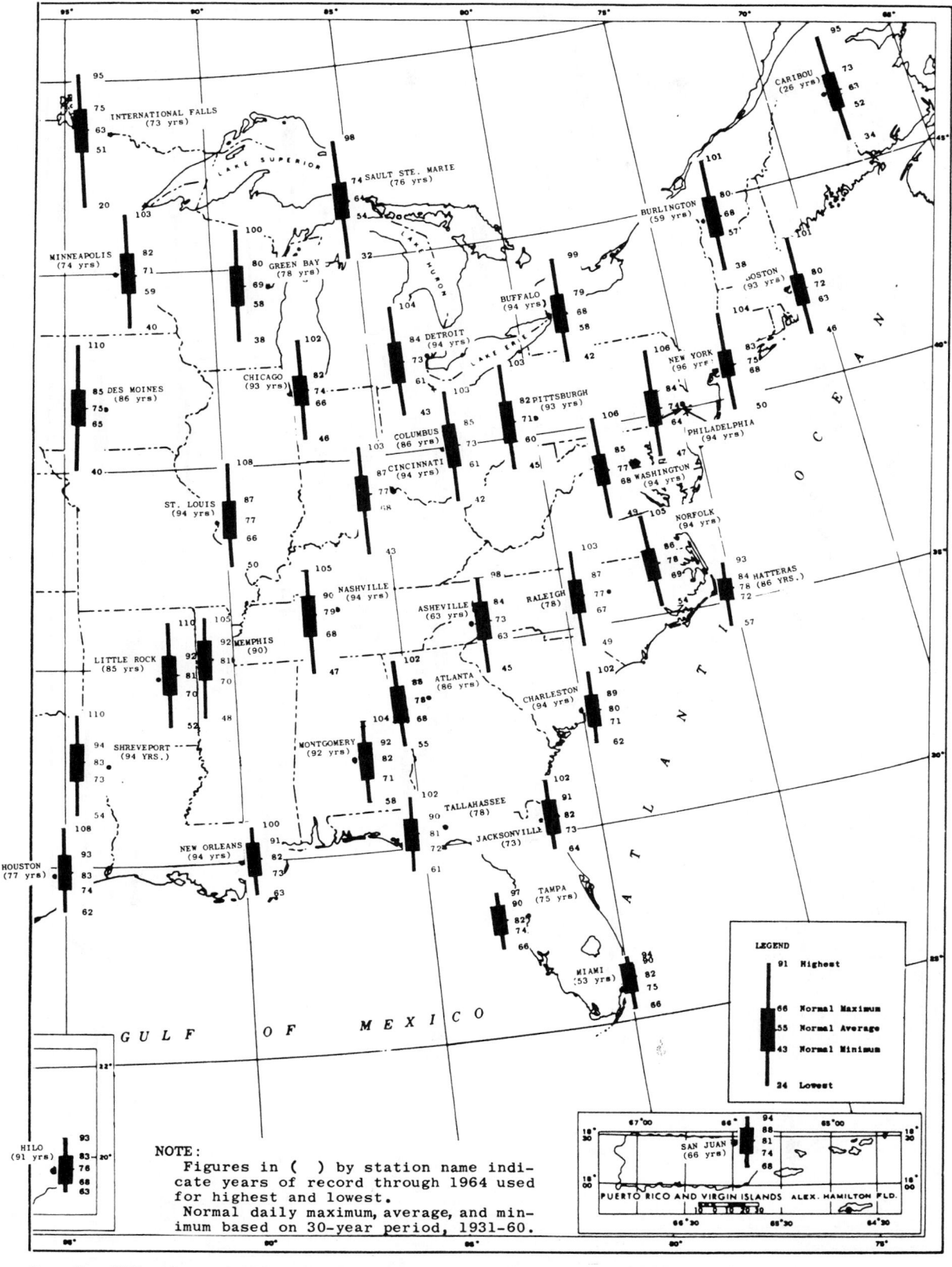

See the "Weather of 109 selected U.S. Cities" section at the back of this volume for 1961-1990 adjustments to Normals, Means, and Extremes.

## NORMAL DAILY MAXIMUM, AVERAGE, MINIMUM,

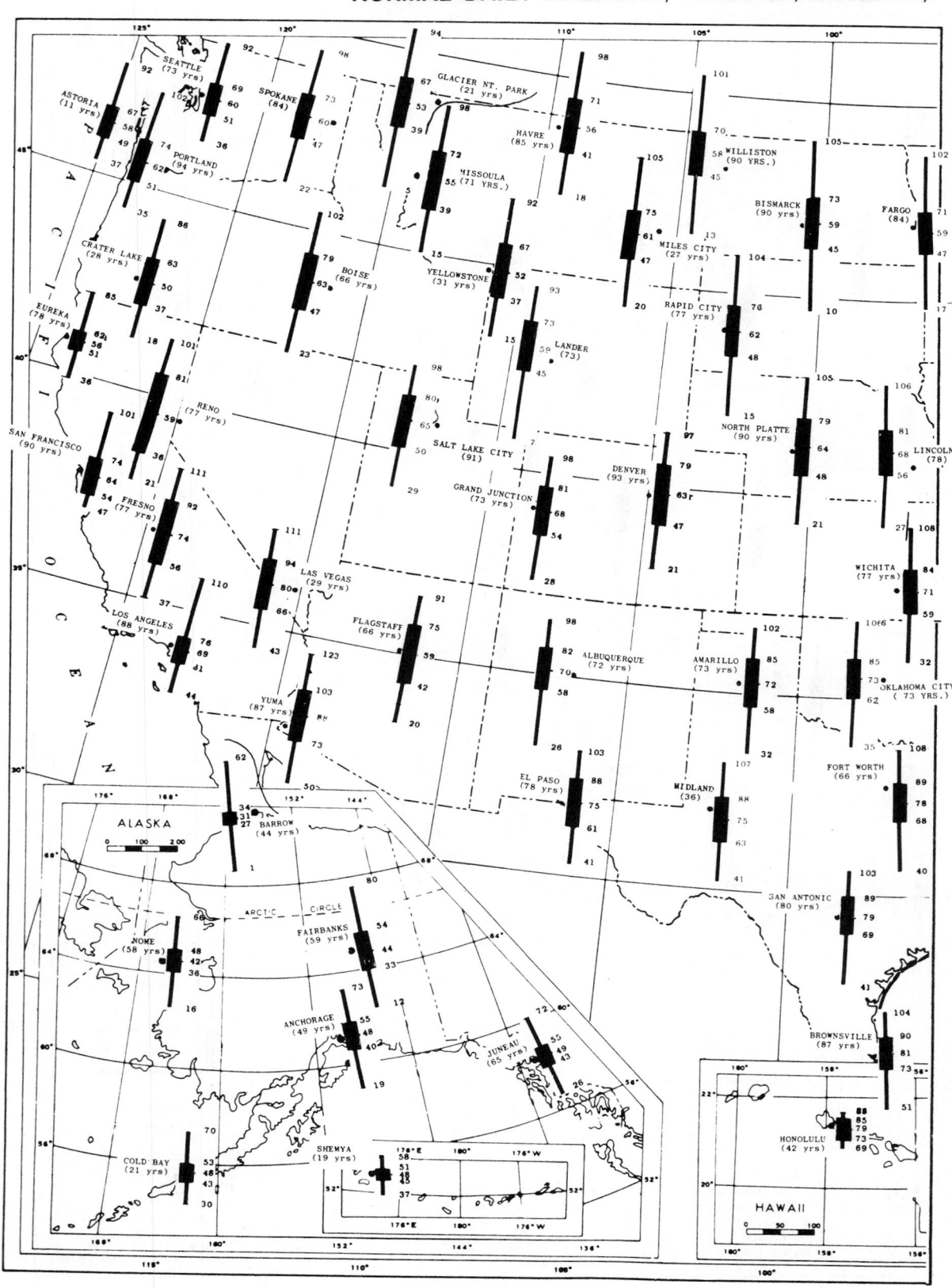

## AND EXTREME TEMPERATURES (°F), SEPTEMBER

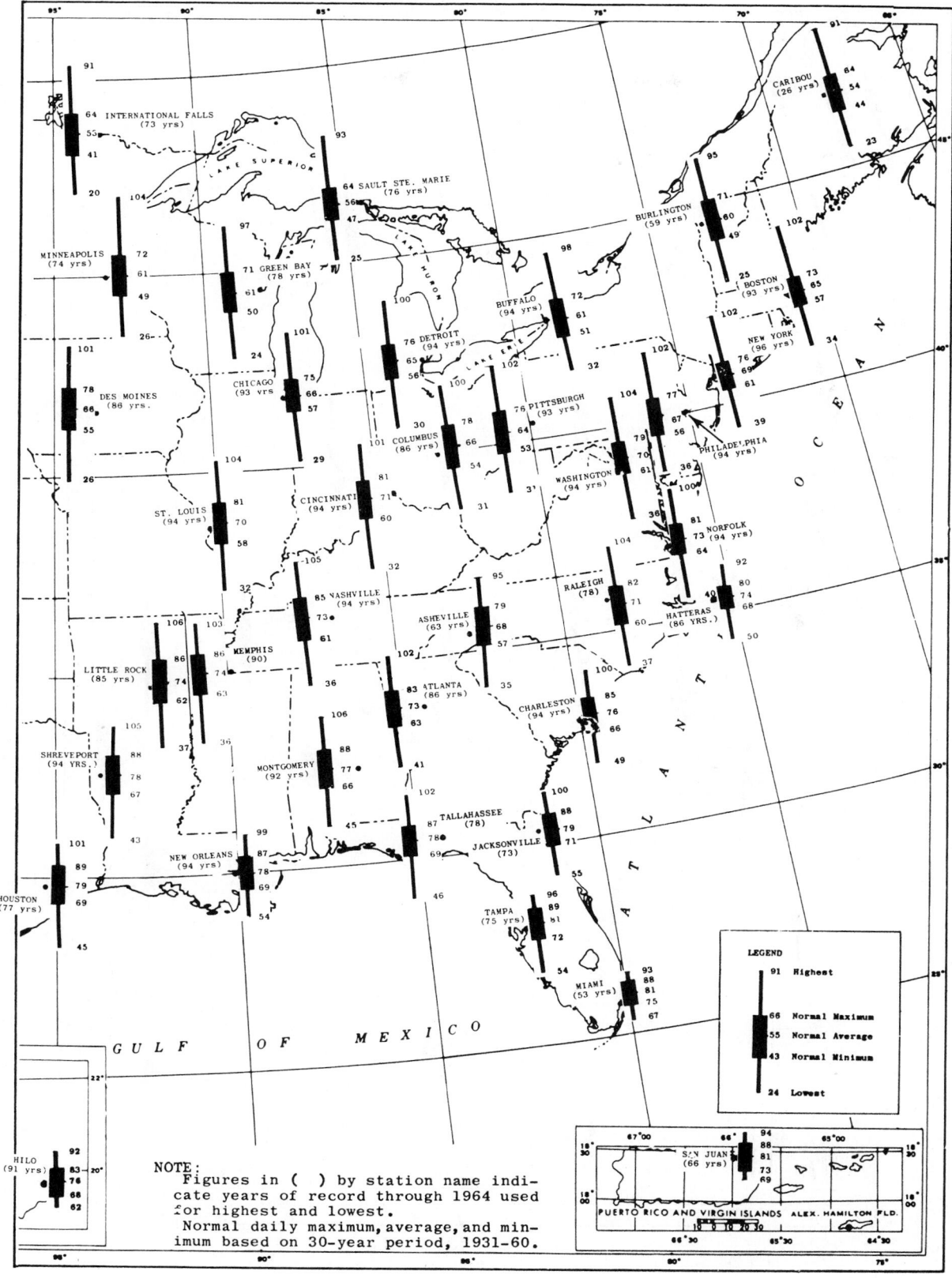

NOTE:
Figures in ( ) by station name indicate years of record through 1964 used
for highest and lowest.
Normal daily maximum, average, and minimum based on 30-year period, 1931-60.

**See the "Weather of 109 selected U.S. Cities" section at the back of this volume for 1961-1990 adjustments to Normals, Means, and Extremes.**

## NORMAL DAILY MAXIMUM, AVERAGE, MINIMUM,

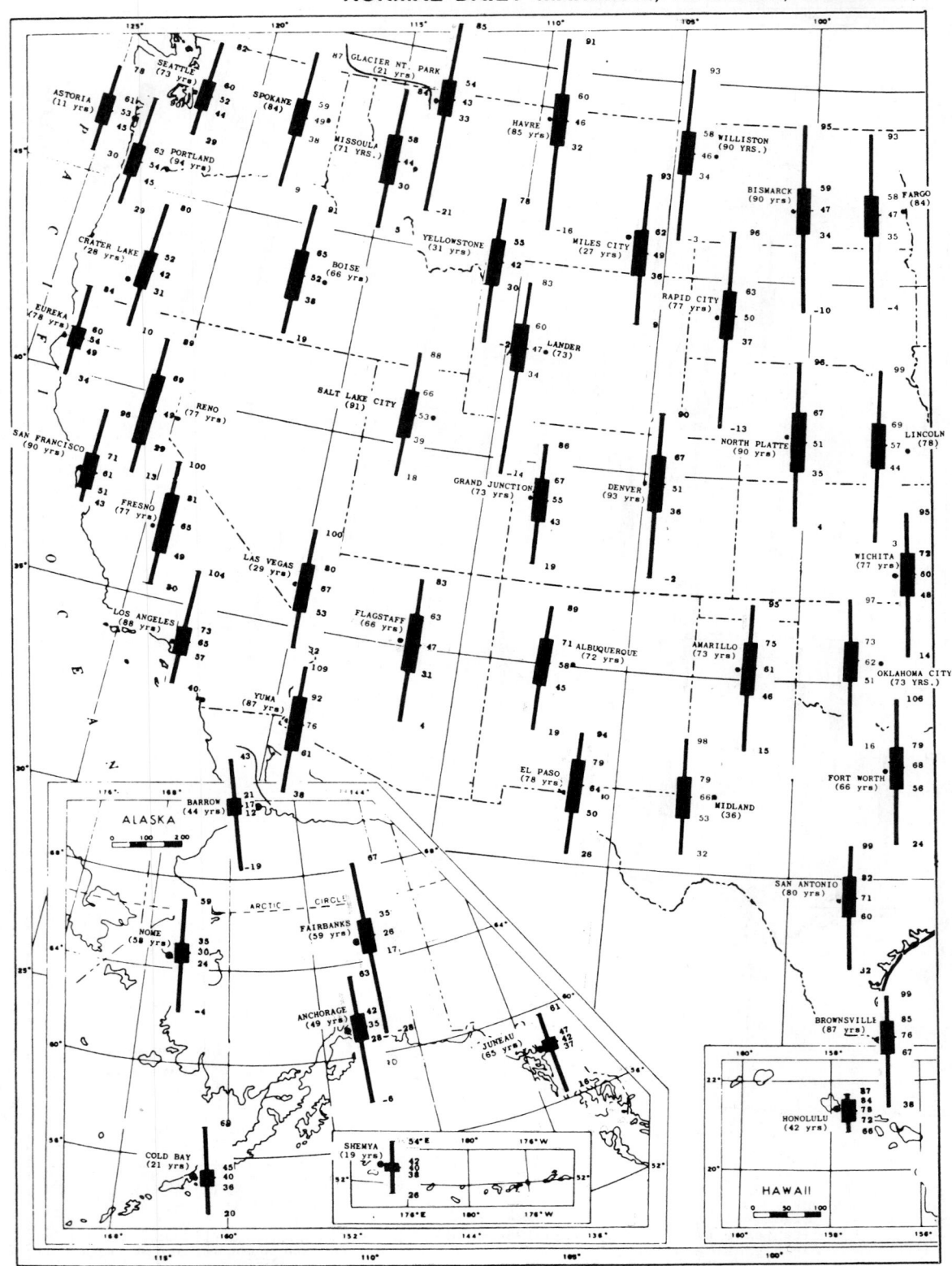

## AND EXTREME TEMPERATURES (°F), OCTOBER

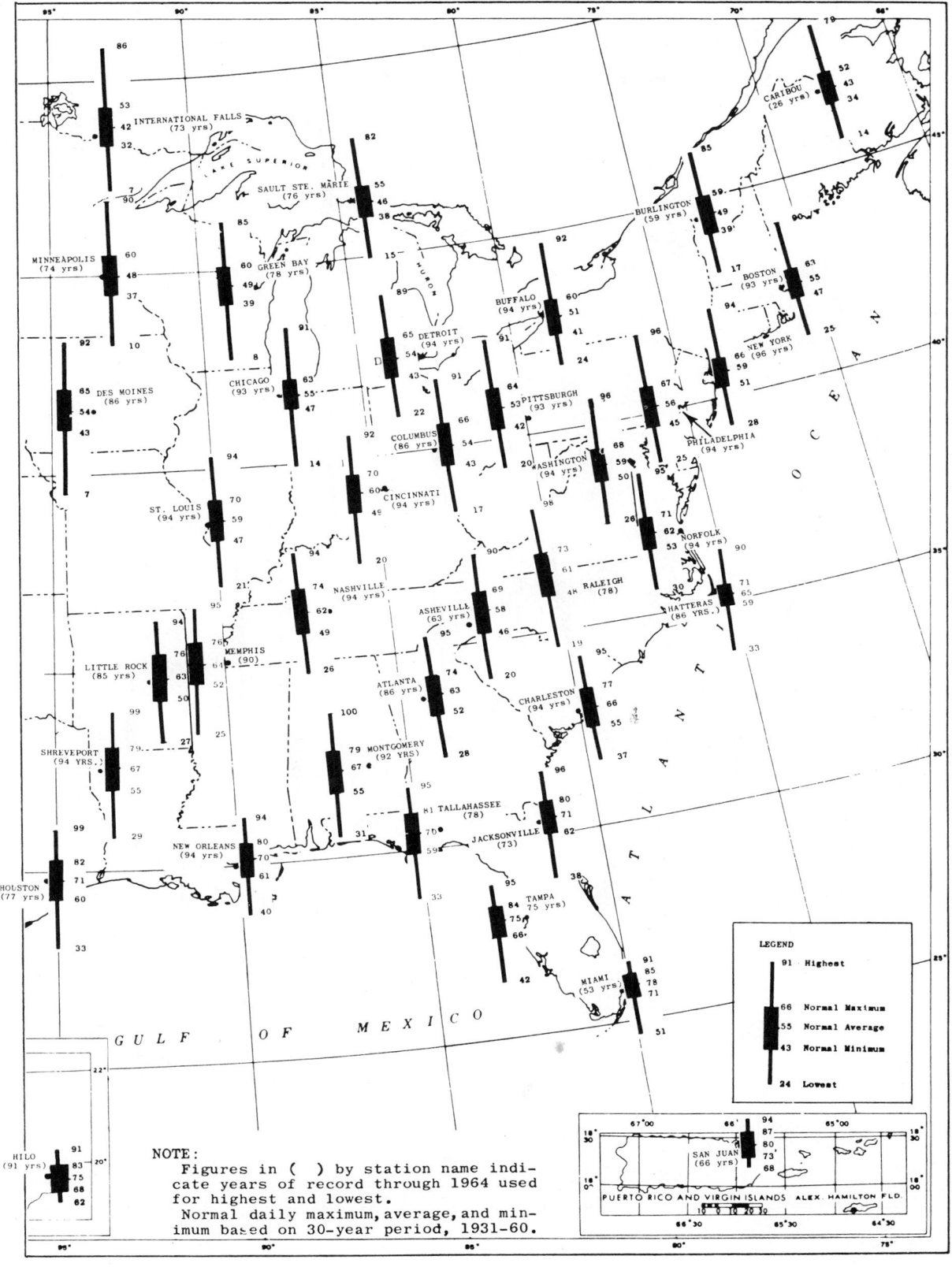

**NOTE:**
Figures in ( ) by station name indicate years of record through 1964 used for highest and lowest.
Normal daily maximum, average, and minimum based on 30-year period, 1931-60.

**LEGEND**

| | |
|---|---|
| 91 | Highest |
| 66 | Normal Maximum |
| 55 | Normal Average |
| 43 | Normal Minimum |
| 24 | Lowest |

PUERTO RICO AND VIRGIN ISLANDS    ALEX. HAMILTON FLD.

**See the "Weather of 109 selected U.S. Cities" section at the back of this volume for 1961-1990 adjustments to** Normals, Means, and Extremes.

## NORMAL DAILY MAXIMUM, AVERAGE, MINIMUM,

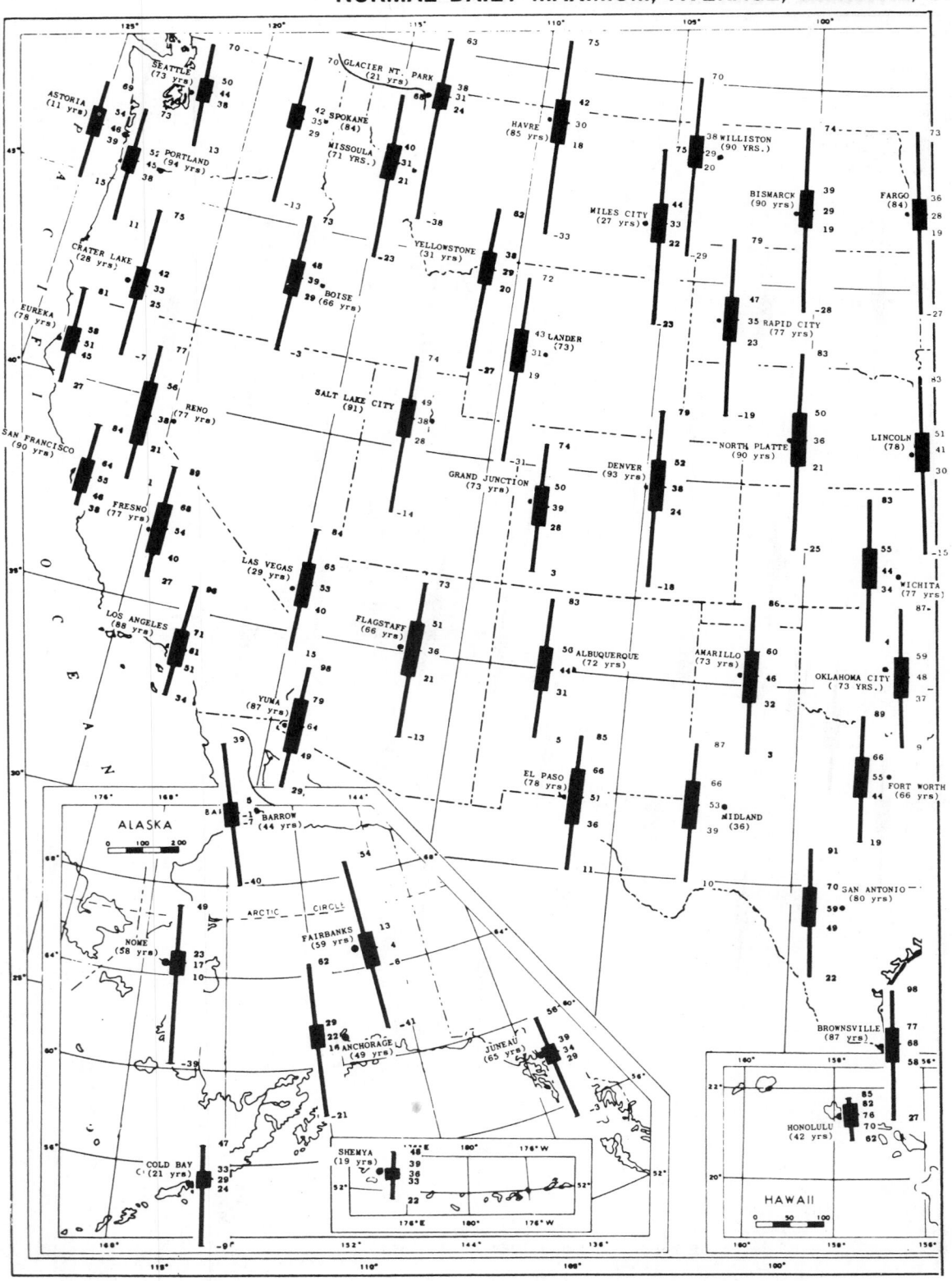

## AND EXTREME TEMPERATURES (°F), NOVEMBER

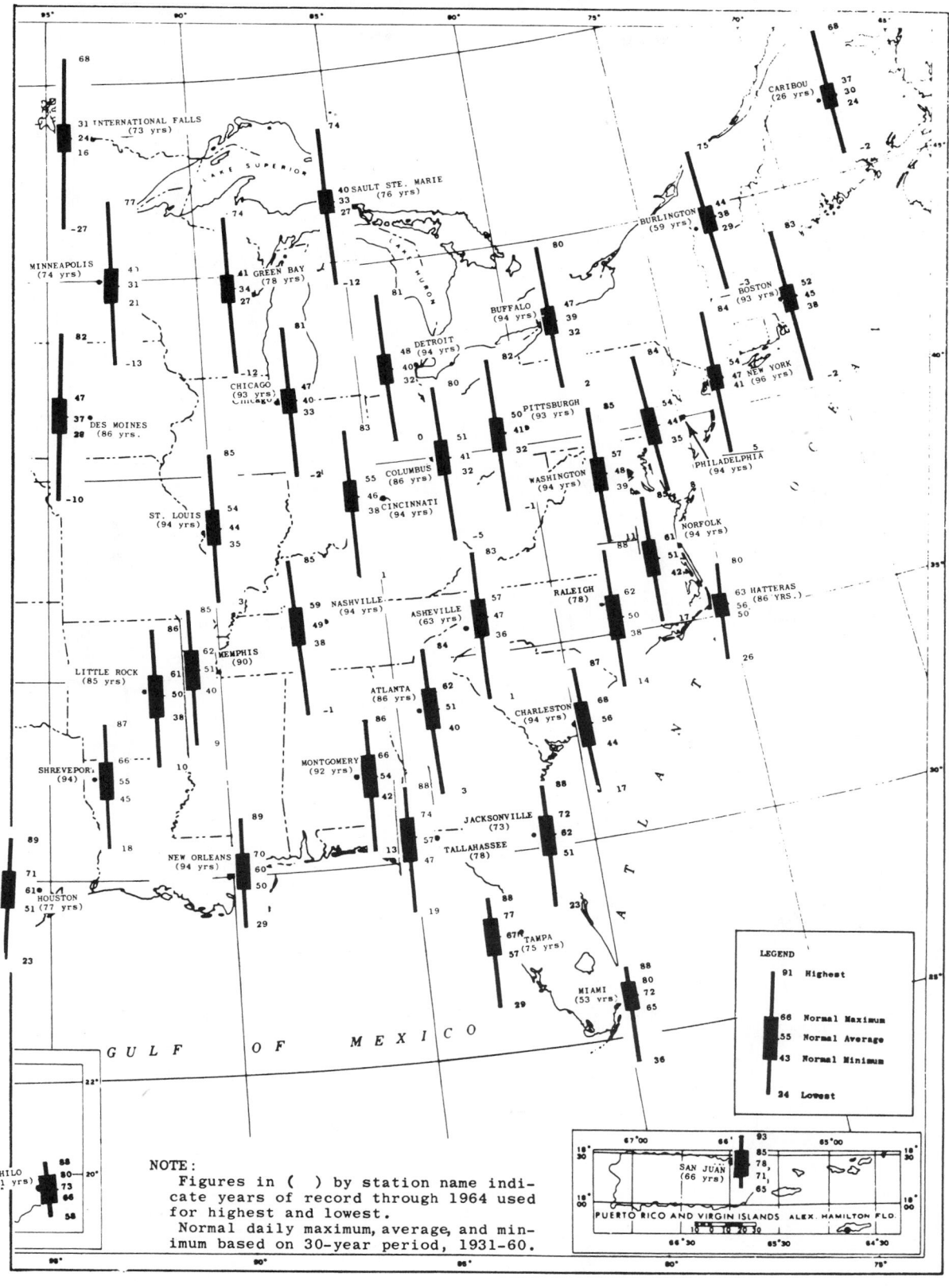

**See the "Weather of 109 selected U.S. Cities"** section at the back of this volume for **1961-1990 adjustments to** Normals, Means, and Extremes.

## NORMAL DAILY MAXIMUM, AVERAGE, MINIMUM,

## AND EXTREME TEMPERATURES (°F), DECEMBER

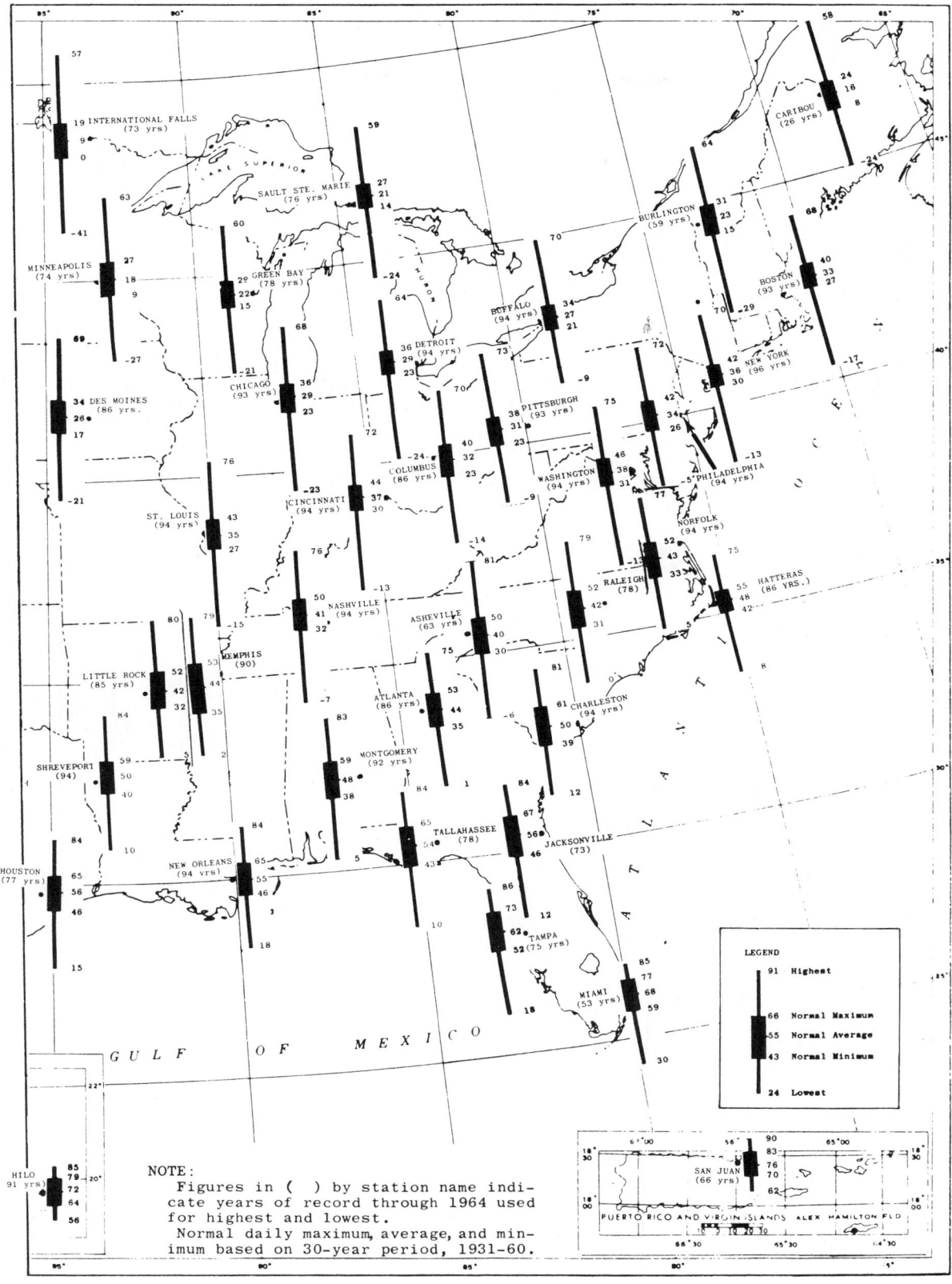

NOTE:
Figures in ( ) by station name indicate years of record through 1964 used for highest and lowest.
Normal daily maximum, average, and minimum based on 30-year period, 1931-60.

**See the "Weather of 109 selected U.S. Cities" section at the back of this volume for 1961-1990 adjustments to** Normals, Means, and Extremes.

## NORMAL MONTHLY TOTAL PRECIPITATION (Inches)

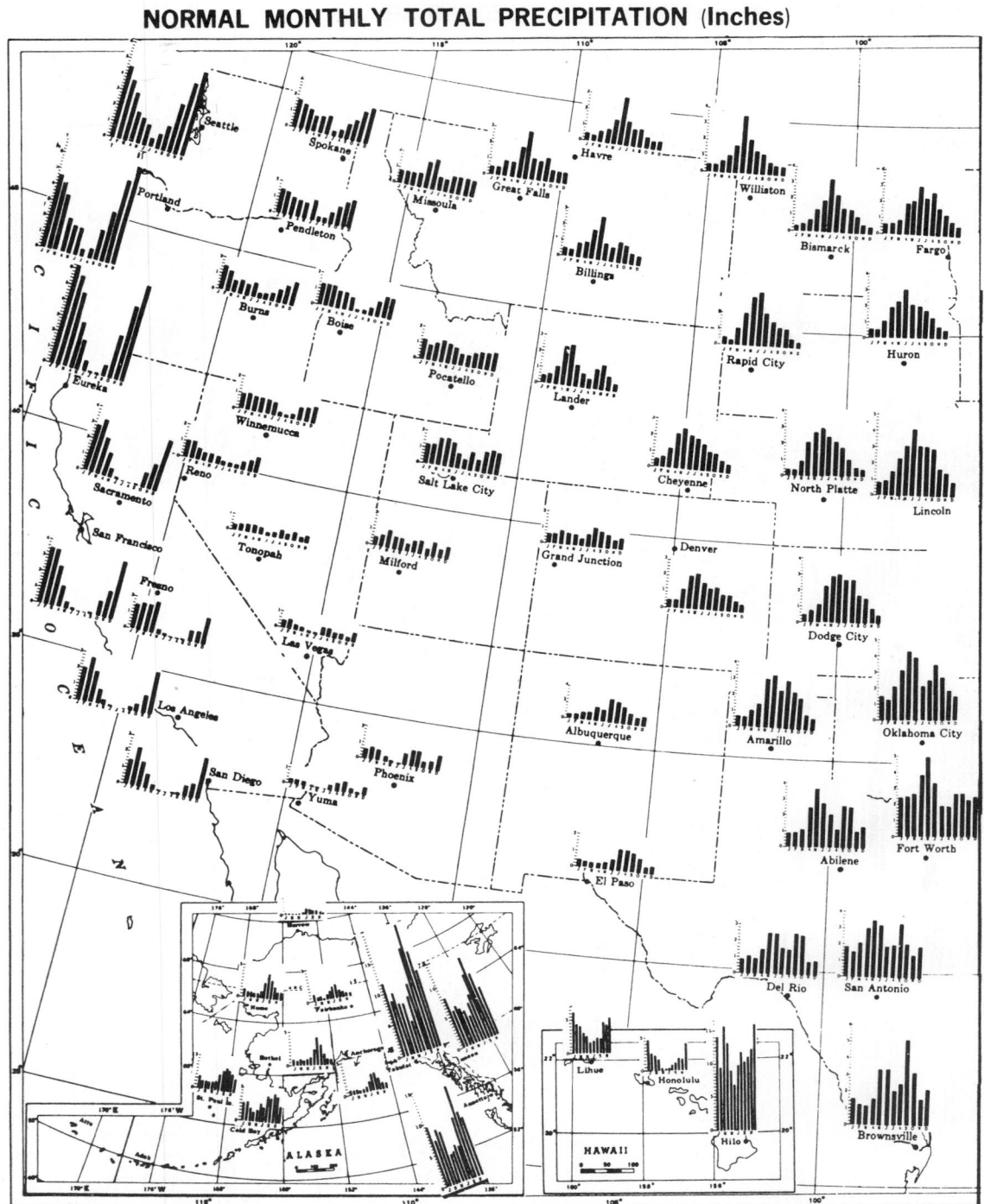

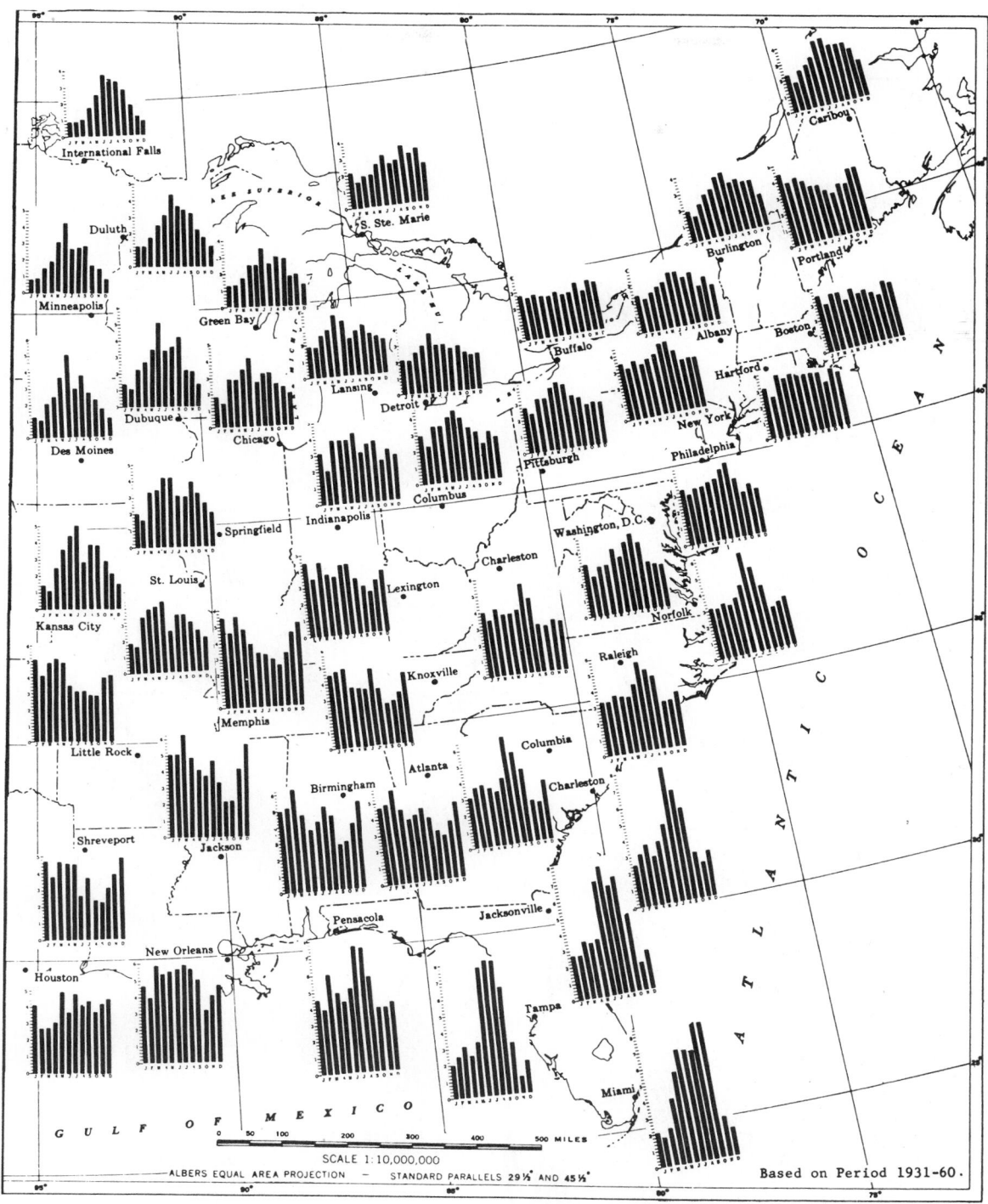

**See the "Weather of 109 selected U.S. Cities" section at the back of this volume for 1961-1990 adjustments to** Normals, Means, and Extremes.

## MEAN MONTHLY TOTAL SNOWFALL (Inches)
### For Selected Stations*

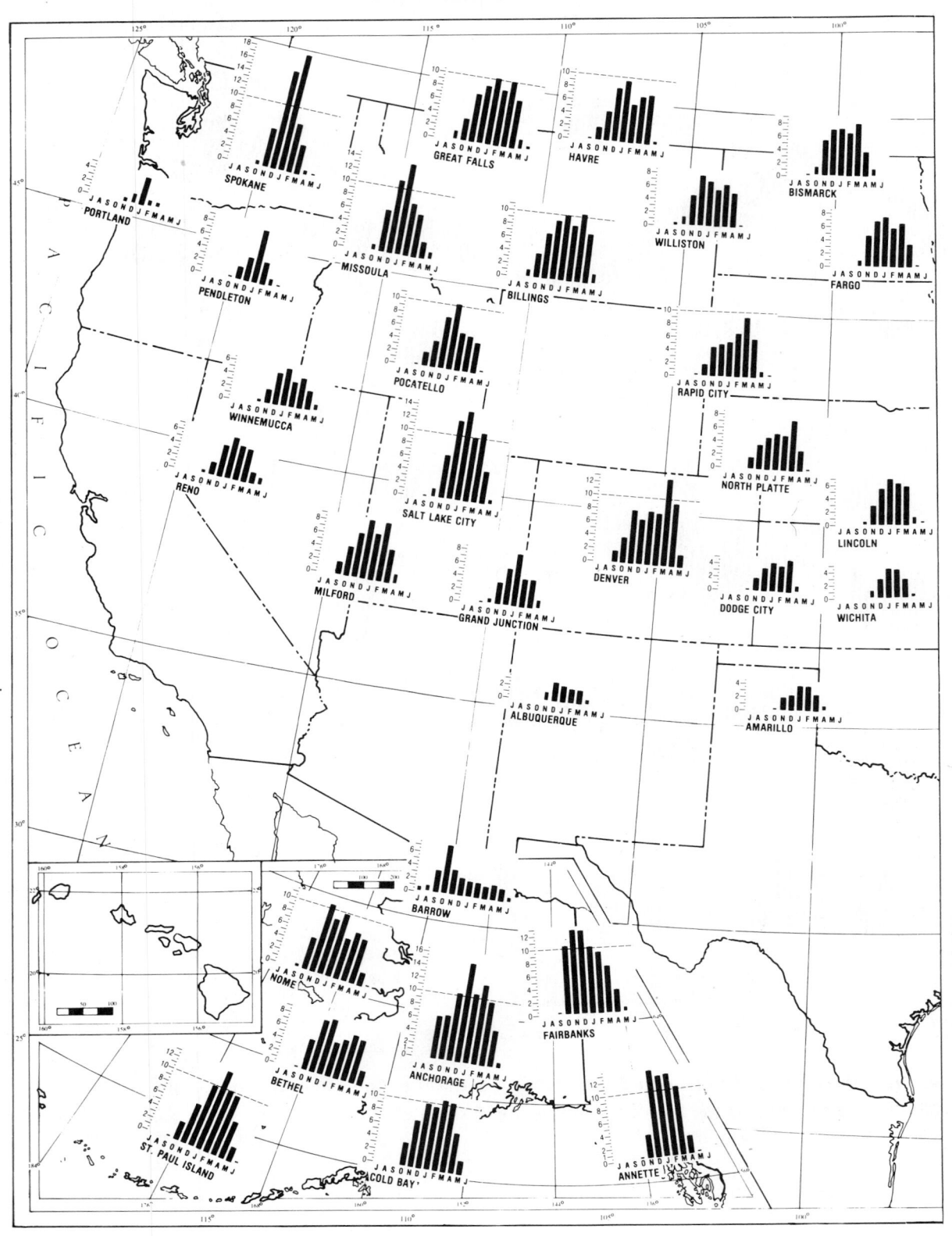

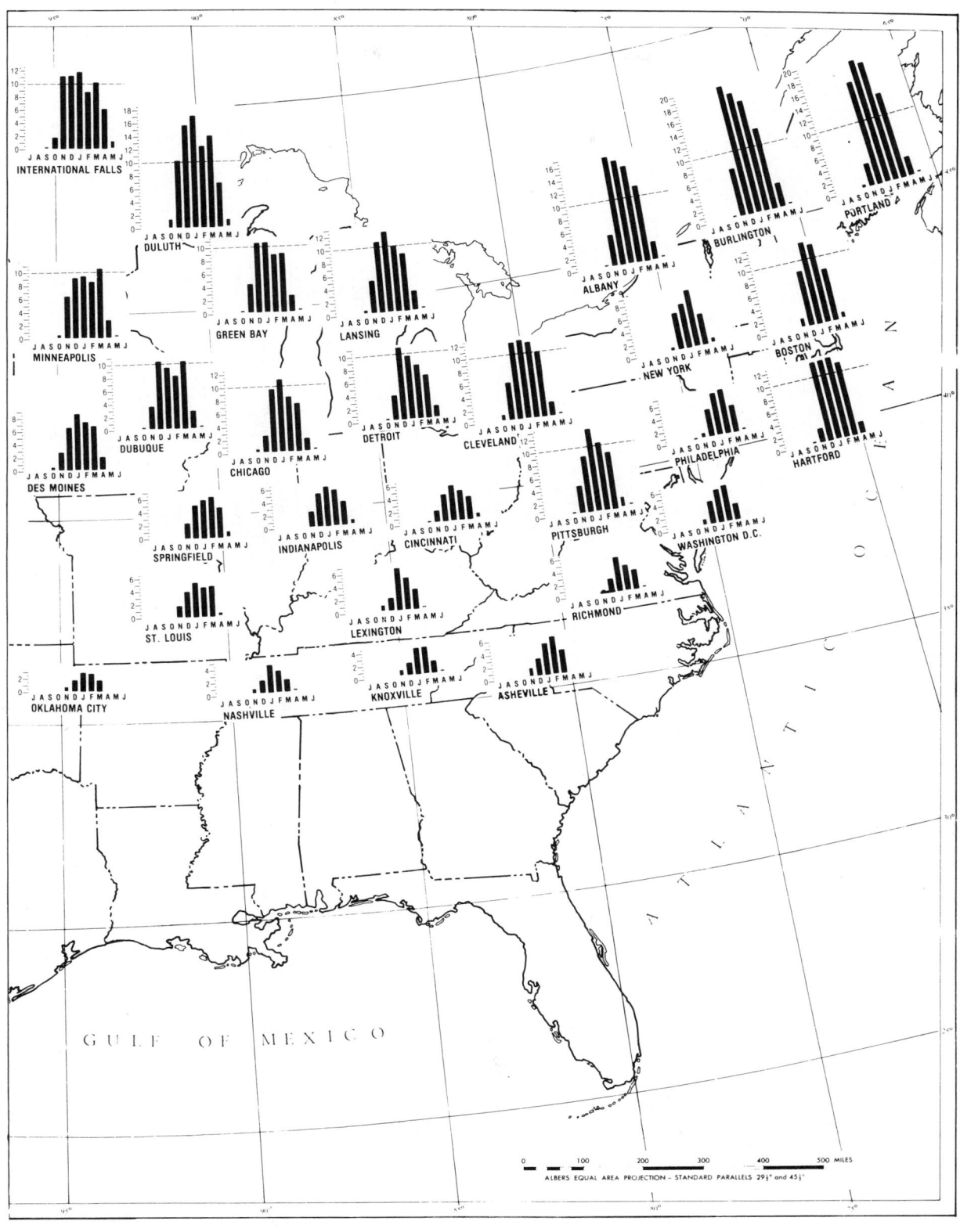

**Based on period, 1951-1980.**

## FREEZE DATA AND GROWING SEASON

### MEAN DATE OF LAST 32 F. TEMPERATURE IN SPRING, FIRST 32 F. IN AUTUMN, AND MEAN LENGTH OF FREEZE-FREE PERIOD (DAYS)

| State and Station | Mean date last 32°F. in spring | Mean date first 32°F. in fall | Mean freeze-free period (no. days) |
|---|---|---|---|
| ALA.Birmingham | Mar. 19 | Nov. 14 | 241 |
| Mobile U. | Feb. 17 | Dec. 12 | 298 |
| Montgomery U. | Feb. 27 | Dec. 3 | 279 |
| ALASKA.Anchorage | May 18 | Sept. 13 | 118 |
| Barrow | June 27 | July 5 | 8 |
| Cordova. | May 10 | Oct. 2 | 145 |
| Fairbanks. | May 24 | Aug. 29 | 97 |
| Juneau. | Apr. 27 | Oct. 19 | 176 |
| Nome. | June 12 | Aug. 24 | 73 |
| ARIZ.Flagstaff | June 8 | Oct. 2 | 116 |
| Phoenix. | Jan. 27 | Dec. 11 | 317 |
| Tucson. | Mar. 6 | Nov. 23 | 261 |
| Winslow. | Apr. 28 | Oct. 21 | 176 |
| Yuma U. | Jan. 11 | Dec. 27 | 350 |
| ARK.Fort Smith | Mar. 23 | Nov. 9 | 231 |
| Little Rock. | Mar. 16 | Nov. 15 | 244 |
| CALIF.Bakersfield. | Feb. 14 | Nov. 28 | 287 |
| Eureka U. | Jan. 24 | Dec. 25 | 335 |
| Fresno. | Feb. 3 | Dec. 3 | 303 |
| Los Angeles U. | * | * | * |
| Red Bluff. | Feb. 25 | Nov. 29 | 277 |
| Sacramento. | Jan. 24 | Dec. 11 | 321 |
| San Diego. | * | * | * |
| San Francisco U. | * | * | * |
| COLO.Denver U. | May 2 | Oct. 14 | 165 |
| Palisades. | Apr. 22 | Oct. 17 | 178 |
| Pueblo. | Apr. 28 | Oct. 12 | 167 |
| CONN.Hartford. | Apr. 22 | Oct. 19 | 180 |
| New Haven. | Apr. 15 | Oct. 27 | 195 |
| D.C.,Washington U | Apr. 10 | Oct. 28 | 200 |
| FLA.Apalachicola U | Feb. 2 | Dec. 21 | 322 |
| Fort Myers | * | * | * |
| Jacksonville U | Feb. 6 | Dec. 16 | 313 |
| Key West | * | * | * |
| Lakeland. | Jan. 10 | Dec. 25 | 349 |
| Miami. | * | * | * |
| Orlando. | Jan. 31 | Dec. 17 | 319 |
| Pensacola U. | Feb. 18 | Dec. 15 | 300 |
| Tallahassee. | Feb. 26 | Dec. 3 | 280 |
| Tampa. | Jan. 10 | Dec. 26 | 349 |
| GA.Atlanta U | Mar. 20 | Nov. 19 | 244 |
| Augusta. | Mar. 7 | Nov. 22 | 260 |
| Macon. | Mar. 12 | Nov. 19 | 252 |
| Savannah. | Feb. 21 | Dec. 9 | 291 |
| IDAHO.Boise. | Apr. 29 | Oct. 16 | 171 |
| Pocatello. | May 8 | Sept. 30 | 145 |
| Salmon. | June 4 | Sept. 6 | 94 |
| ILL.Cairo U. | Mar. 23 | Nov. 11 | 233 |
| Chicago U. | Apr. 19 | Oct. 28 | 192 |
| Freeport. | May 8 | Oct. 4 | 149 |
| Peoria. | Apr. 22 | Oct. 16 | 177 |
| Springfield U. | Apr. 2 | Oct. 30 | 205 |
| IND.Evansville. | Apr. 2 | Nov. 4 | 216 |
| Fort Wayne | Apr. 24 | Oct. 20 | 179 |
| Indianapolis U | Apr. 17 | Oct. 27 | 193 |
| South Bend | May 3 | Oct. 16 | 165 |
| IOWA,Des Moines U. | Apr. 20 | Oct. 19 | 183 |
| Dubuque U. | Apr. 19 | Oct. 19 | 184 |
| Koekuk | Apr. 12 | Oct. 26 | 197 |
| Sioux City | Apr. 18 | Oct. 12 | 167 |
| KANS,Concordia U | Apr. 16 | Oct. 24 | 191 |
| Dodge City | Apr. 22 | Oct. 24 | 184 |
| Goodland | May 2 | Oct. 9 | 157 |
| Topeka U | Apr. 9 | Oct. 26 | 200 |
| Wichita. | Apr. 5 | Nov. 1 | 210 |
| KY.Lexington U. | Apr. 13 | Oct. 28 | 198 |
| Louisville U | Apr. 1 | Nov. 7 | 220 |
| LA.Lake Charles. | Feb. 18 | Dec. 6 | 291 |
| New Orleans | Feb. 13 | Dec. 12 | 302 |
| Shreveport. | Mar. 1 | Nov. 27 | 272 |
| MAINE.Greenville | May 27 | Sept. 20 | 116 |
| Portland | Apr. 29 | Oct. 15 | 169 |
| MD.Annapolis | Mar. 4 | Nov. 15 | 225 |
| Baltimore U. | Mar. 28 | Nov. 17 | 234 |
| Frederick. | Mar. 24 | Oct. 17 | 176 |
| MASS.Boston. | Apr. 16 | Oct. 25 | 192 |
| Nantucket. | Apr. 12 | Nov. 16 | 219 |
| MICH.Alpena U. | May 6 | Oct. 9 | 156 |
| Detroit. | Apr. 25 | Oct. 23 | 181 |
| Escanaba U. | May 14 | Oct. 6 | 145 |
| Grand Rapids U | Apr. 25 | Oct. 27 | 185 |
| Marquette U. | May 14 | Oct. 17 | 156 |
| S. Ste. Marie. | May 18 | Oct. 3 | 138 |
| MINN.Albert Lee. | May 3 | Oct. 6 | 156 |
| Big Falls R.S. | June 4 | Sept. 7 | 95 |
| Brainerd. | May 16 | Sept. 24 | 131 |
| Duluth. | May 22 | Sept. 24 | 125 |
| Minneapolis. | Apr. 30 | Oct. 13 | 166 |
| St. Cloud. | May 9 | Sept. 29 | 144 |
| MISS.Jackson. | Mar. 10 | Nov. 13 | 248 |
| Meridian. | Mar. 13 | Nov. 14 | 246 |
| Vicksburg U. | Mar. 8 | Nov. 15 | 252 |
| MO.Columbia. | Apr. 9 | Oct. 24 | 198 |
| Kansas City. | Apr. 5 | Oct. 31 | 210 |
| St. Louis U. | Apr. 2 | Nov. 8 | 220 |
| Springfield. | Apr. 10 | Oct. 31 | 203 |
| MONT.Billings. | May 15 | Sept. 24 | 132 |
| Glasgow U. | May 19 | Sept. 20 | 124 |
| Great Falls. | May 14 | Sept. 26 | 135 |
| Havre U. | May 9 | Sept. 23 | 138 |
| Helena. | May 12 | Sept. 23 | 134 |
| Kalispell. | May 12 | Sept. 23 | 135 |
| Miles City. | May 5 | Oct. 3 | 150 |
| Superior. | June 5 | Aug. 30 | 85 |

* Occurs in less than 1 year in 10.  No freeze of record in Key West, Fla.
U indicates urban.

Charts and tabulation were derived from the Freeze Data tabulation in Climatography of the United States No. 60 – Climates of the States.

NOTE: Narrative descriptions of the climates of most of these cities are contained in the section, *"Weather of U.S. Cities"*. Check the narrative for the city of interest for further notes about the city's growing season and for any updating since this table's compilation.

## MEAN DATE OF LAST 32 F. TEMPERATURE IN SPRING, FIRST 32 F. IN AUTUMN, AND MEAN LENGTH OF FREEZE-FREE PERIOD (continued)

| State and Station | Mean date last 32°F. in spring | Mean date first 32°F. in fall | Mean freeze-free period (no. days) |
|---|---|---|---|
| NEBR.Grand Island | Apr. 29 | Oct. 6 | 160 |
| Lincoln | Apr. 20 | Oct. 17 | 180 |
| Norfolk | May 4 | Oct. 3 | 152 |
| North Platte | Apr. 30 | Oct. 7 | 160 |
| Omaha | Apr. 14 | Oct. 20 | 189 |
| Valentine Lakes | May 7 | Sept. 30 | 146 |
| NEV.Elko | June 6 | Sept. 3 | 89 |
| Las Vegas | Mar. 13 | Nov. 13 | 245 |
| Reno | May 14 | Oct. 2 | 141 |
| Winnemucca | May 18 | Sept. 21 | 125 |
| N.H.Concord | May 11 | Sept. 30 | 142 |
| N.J.Cape May | Apr. 4 | Nov. 15 | 225 |
| Trenton U. | Apr. 8 | Nov. 5 | 211 |
| N.MEX.Albuquerque | Apr. 16 | Oct. 29 | 196 |
| Roswell | Apr. 9 | Nov. 2 | 208 |
| N.Y.Albany | Apr. 27 | Oct. 13 | 169 |
| Binghamton U. | May 4 | Oct. 6 | 154 |
| Buffalo | Apr. 30 | Oct. 25 | 179 |
| New York U. | Apr. 7 | Nov. 12 | 219 |
| Rochester | Apr. 28 | Oct. 21 | 176 |
| Syracuse | Apr. 30 | Oct. 15 | 168 |
| N.C.Asheville U | Apr. 12 | Oct. 24 | 195 |
| Charlotte U | Mar. 21 | Nov. 15 | 239 |
| Greenville | Mar. 28 | Nov. 5 | 222 |
| Hatteras | Feb. 25 | Dec. 18 | 296 |
| Raleigh U | Mar. 24 | Nov. 16 | 237 |
| Wilmington U. | Mar. 8 | Nov. 24 | 262 |
| N.DAK.Bismarck | May 11 | Sept. 24 | 136 |
| Devils Lake U | May 18 | Sept. 22 | 127 |
| Fargo | May 13 | Sept. 27 | 137 |
| Williston U | May 14 | Sept. 23 | 132 |
| OHIO.Akron-Canton | Apr. 29 | Oct. 20 | 173 |
| Cincinnati (Abbe) | Apr. 15 | Oct. 25 | 192 |
| Cleveland | Apr. 21 | Nov. 2 | 195 |
| Columbus U. | Apr. 17 | Oct. 30 | 196 |
| Dayton | Apr. 20 | Oct. 21 | 184 |
| Toledo | Apr. 24 | Oct. 25 | 184 |
| OKLA.Okla.City U. | Mar. 28 | Nov. 7 | 223 |
| Tulsa | Mar. 31 | Nov. 2 | 216 |
| OREG.Astoria | Mar. 18 | Nov. 24 | 251 |
| Bend | June 17 | Aug. 17 | 62 |
| Medford | Apr. 25 | Oct. 20 | 178 |
| Pendleton | Apr. 27 | Oct. 8 | 163 |
| Portland U. | Feb. 25 | Dec. 1 | 279 |
| Salem | Apr. 14 | Oct. 27 | 197 |
| PA.Allentown | Apr. 20 | Oct. 16 | 180 |
| Harrisburg U. | Apr. 10 | Oct. 28 | 201 |
| Philadelphia U. | Mar. 30 | Nov. 17 | 232 |
| Pittsburgh | Apr. 20 | Oct. 23 | 187 |
| Scranton U. | Apr. 24 | Oct. 14 | 174 |
| R.I.Providence U. | Apr. 13 | Oct. 27 | 197 |
| S.C.Charleston U. | Feb. 19 | Dec. 10 | 294 |
| Columbia U. | Mar. 14 | Nov. 21 | 252 |
| Greenville | Mar. 23 | Nov. 17 | 239 |
| S.DAK.Huron U. | May 4 | Sept. 30 | 149 |
| Rapid City U. | May 7 | Oct. 4 | 150 |
| Sioux Falls U | May 5 | Oct. 3 | 152 |
| TENN.Chattanooga U. | Mar. 26 | Nov. 10 | 229 |
| Knoxville U. | Mar. 31 | Nov. 6 | 220 |
| Memphis U. | Mar. 20 | Nov. 12 | 237 |
| Nashville U | Mar. 28 | Nov. 7 | 224 |
| TEX.Albany | Mar. 30 | Nov. 9 | 224 |
| Balmorhea | Apr. 1 | Nov. 12 | 226 |
| Beeville | Feb. 21 | Dec. 6 | 288 |
| College Station | Mar. 1 | Dec. 1 | 275 |
| Corsicana | Mar. 13 | Nov. 27 | 259 |
| Dalhart Exp. Sta. | Apr. 23 | Oct. 18 | 178 |
| Dallas | Mar. 18 | Nov. 22 | 249 |
| Del Rio | Feb. 12 | Dec. 9 | 300 |
| Encinal | Feb. 15 | Dec. 12 | 301 |
| Houston | Feb. 5 | Dec. 11 | 309 |
| Lampasas | Apr. 1 | Nov. 10 | 223 |
| Matagorda | Feb. 12 | Dec. 17 | 308 |
| Midland | Apr. 3 | Nov. 6 | 218 |
| Mission | Jan. 30 | Dec. 21 | 325 |
| Mount Pleasant | Mar. 23 | Nov. 12 | 233 |
| Nacogdoches | Mar. 15 | Nov. 13 | 243 |
| Plainview | Apr. 10 | Nov. 6 | 211 |
| Presidio | Mar. 20 | Nov. 13 | 238 |
| Quanah | Mar. 31 | Nov. 7 | 221 |
| San Angelo | Mar. 25 | Nov. 15 | 235 |
| Ysleta | Apr. 6 | Oct. 30 | 207 |
| UTAH Blanding | May 18 | Oct. 14 | 148 |
| Salt Lake City | Apr. 12 | Nov. 1 | 202 |
| VT.Burlington | May 8 | Oct. 3 | 148 |
| VA.Lynchburg | Apr. 6 | Oct. 27 | 205 |
| Norfolk U | Mar. 18 | Nov. 27 | 254 |
| Richmond U. | Apr. 2 | Nov. 8 | 220 |
| Roanoke | Apr. 20 | Oct. 24 | 187 |
| WASH.Bumping Lake | June 17 | Aug. 16 | 60 |
| Seattle U. | Feb. 23 | Dec. 1 | 281 |
| Spokane | Apr. 20 | Oct. 12 | 175 |
| Tatoosh Island | Jan. 25 | Dec. 20 | 329 |
| Walla Walla U. | Mar. 28 | Nov. 1 | 218 |
| Yakima | Apr. 19 | Oct. 15 | 179 |
| W.VA.Charleston | Apr. 18 | Oct. 28 | 193 |
| Parkersburg | Apr. 16 | Oct. 21 | 189 |
| WIS.Green Bay | May 6 | Oct. 13 | 161 |
| La Crosse U | May 1 | Oct. 8 | 161 |
| Madison U | Apr. 26 | Oct. 19 | 177 |
| Milwaukee U | Apr. 20 | Oct. 25 | 188 |
| WYO.Casper | May 18 | Sept. 25 | 130 |
| Cheyenne | May 20 | Sept. 27 | 130 |
| Lander | May 15 | Sept. 20 | 128 |
| Sheridan | May 21 | Sept. 21 | 123 |

* Occurs in less than 1 year in 10. No freeze of record in Key West, Fla.
U Indicates urban.

Charts and tabulation were derived from the Freeze Data tabulation in Climatography of the United States No. 60 - Climates of the States.

**See the "Weather of 109 selected U.S. Cities" section at the back of this volume for 1961-1990 adjustments to Normals, Means, and Extremes.**

# MEAN PERCENTAGE OF POSSIBLE SUNSHINE

| STATE AND STATION | YEARS | JAN. | FEB. | MAR. | APR. | MAY | JUNE | JULY | AUG. | SEPT. | OCT. | NOV. | DEC. | ANNUAL |
|---|---|---|---|---|---|---|---|---|---|---|---|---|---|---|
| ALA. BIRMINGHAM | 56 | 43 | 49 | 56 | 63 | 66 | 67 | 62 | 65 | 66 | 67 | 58 | 44 | 59 |
| MONTGOMERY | 49 | 51 | 53 | 61 | 69 | 73 | 72 | 66 | 69 | 69 | 71 | 64 | 48 | 64 |
| ALASKA. ANCHORAGE | 19 | 39 | 46 | 56 | 58 | 50 | 51 | 45 | 39 | 35 | 32 | 33 | 29 | 45 |
| FAIRBANKS | 20 | 34 | 50 | 61 | 68 | 55 | 53 | 45 | 35 | 31 | 28 | 38 | 29 | 44 |
| JUNEAU | 14 | 30 | 32 | 39 | 37 | 34 | 35 | 28 | 30 | 25 | 18 | 21 | 18 | 30 |
| NOME | 29 | 44 | 46 | 48 | 53 | 51 | 48 | 32 | 26 | 34 | 35 | 36 | 30 | 41 |
| ARIZ. PHOENIX | 64 | 76 | 79 | 83 | 88 | 93 | 94 | 84 | 84 | 89 | 88 | 84 | 77 | 85 |
| YUMA | 52 | 83 | 87 | 91 | 94 | 97 | 98 | 92 | 91 | 93 | 93 | 90 | 83 | 91 |
| ARK. LITTLE ROCK | 66 | 44 | 53 | 57 | 62 | 67 | 72 | 71 | 73 | 71 | 74 | 58 | 47 | 62 |
| CALIF. EUREKA | 49 | 40 | 44 | 50 | 53 | 54 | 56 | 51 | 46 | 52 | 48 | 42 | 39 | 49 |
| FRESNO | 55 | 46 | 63 | 72 | 83 | 89 | 94 | 97 | 97 | 93 | 87 | 73 | 47 | 78 |
| LOS ANGELES | 63 | 70 | 69 | 70 | 67 | 68 | 69 | 80 | 81 | 80 | 76 | 79 | 72 | 73 |
| RED BLUFF | 39 | 50 | 60 | 65 | 75 | 79 | 86 | 95 | 94 | 89 | 77 | 64 | 50 | 75 |
| SACRAMENTO | 48 | 44 | 57 | 67 | 76 | 82 | 90 | 96 | 95 | 92 | 82 | 65 | 44 | 77 |
| SAN DIEGO | 68 | 68 | 67 | 68 | 66 | 60 | 60 | 67 | 70 | 70 | 70 | 76 | 71 | 68 |
| SAN FRANCISCO | 64 | 53 | 57 | 63 | 69 | 70 | 75 | 68 | 63 | 70 | 70 | 62 | 54 | 66 |
| COLO. DENVER | 64 | 67 | 67 | 65 | 63 | 61 | 69 | 68 | 68 | 71 | 71 | 67 | 65 | 67 |
| GRAND JUNCTION | 57 | 58 | 62 | 64 | 67 | 71 | 79 | 76 | 72 | 77 | 74 | 67 | 58 | 69 |
| CONN. HARTFORD | 48 | 46 | 55 | 56 | 54 | 57 | 60 | 62 | 60 | 57 | 55 | 46 | 46 | 56 |
| D. C. WASHINGTON | 66 | 46 | 53 | 56 | 57 | 61 | 64 | 64 | 62 | 62 | 61 | 54 | 47 | 58 |
| FLA. APALACHICOLA | 26 | 59 | 62 | 62 | 71 | 77 | 70 | 64 | 63 | 82 | 74 | 66 | 53 | 65 |
| JACKSONVILLE | 60 | 58 | 59 | 66 | 71 | 71 | 63 | 62 | 63 | 58 | 58 | 61 | 53 | 62 |
| KEY WEST | 45 | 68 | 75 | 78 | 78 | 76 | 70 | 69 | 71 | 65 | 65 | 69 | 66 | 71 |
| MIAMI BEACH | 48 | 66 | 72 | 73 | 73 | 68 | 62 | 65 | 67 | 62 | 62 | 65 | 65 | 67 |
| TAMPA | 63 | 63 | 67 | 71 | 74 | 75 | 66 | 61 | 64 | 64 | 67 | 67 | 61 | 68 |
| GA. ATLANTA | 65 | 48 | 53 | 57 | 65 | 68 | 68 | 62 | 63 | 65 | 67 | 60 | 47 | 60 |
| HAWAII. HILO | 9 | 48 | 42 | 41 | 34 | 31 | 41 | 44 | 38 | 42 | 41 | 34 | 36 | 39 |
| HONOLULU | 53 | 62 | 64 | 60 | 62 | 64 | 66 | 67 | 70 | 70 | 68 | 63 | 60 | 65 |
| LIHUE | 9 | 48 | 48 | 48 | 46 | 51 | 60 | 58 | 59 | 67 | 58 | 51 | 49 | 54 |
| IDAHO. BOISE | 20 | 40 | 48 | 59 | 67 | 68 | 75 | 89 | 86 | 81 | 66 | 46 | 37 | 64 |
| POCATELLO | 21 | 37 | 47 | 58 | 64 | 66 | 72 | 82 | 81 | 78 | 66 | 48 | 36 | 64 |
| ILL. CAIRO | 30 | 46 | 53 | 59 | 65 | 71 | 77 | 82 | 79 | 75 | 73 | 56 | 46 | 65 |
| CHICAGO | 66 | 44 | 49 | 53 | 56 | 63 | 69 | 73 | 70 | 65 | 61 | 47 | 41 | 59 |
| SPRINGFIELD | 59 | 47 | 51 | 54 | 58 | 64 | 69 | 76 | 72 | 73 | 64 | 53 | 45 | 60 |
| IND. EVANSVILLE | 48 | 42 | 49 | 55 | 61 | 67 | 73 | 78 | 76 | 73 | 67 | 52 | 42 | 64 |
| FT. WAYNE | 48 | 38 | 44 | 51 | 55 | 62 | 69 | 74 | 69 | 64 | 58 | 41 | 38 | 57 |
| INDIANAPOLIS | 63 | 41 | 47 | 49 | 55 | 62 | 68 | 74 | 70 | 68 | 64 | 48 | 39 | 59 |
| IOWA. DES MOINES | 66 | 56 | 56 | 56 | 59 | 62 | 66 | 75 | 70 | 64 | 61 | 53 | 48 | 62 |
| DUBUQUE | 54 | 48 | 52 | 52 | 58 | 60 | 63 | 73 | 67 | 61 | 55 | 44 | 40 | 57 |
| SIOUX CITY | 52 | 55 | 58 | 58 | 59 | 63 | 67 | 75 | 72 | 67 | 65 | 53 | 50 | 63 |
| KANS. CONCORDIA | 52 | 60 | 60 | 62 | 63 | 65 | 73 | 79 | 76 | 72 | 70 | 64 | 58 | 67 |
| DODGE CITY | 70 | 67 | 66 | 68 | 68 | 68 | 74 | 78 | 78 | 76 | 75 | 70 | 67 | 71 |
| WICHITA | 46 | 61 | 63 | 64 | 64 | 66 | 73 | 80 | 77 | 73 | 69 | 67 | 59 | 69 |
| KY. LOUISVILLE | 59 | 41 | 47 | 52 | 57 | 64 | 68 | 72 | 69 | 68 | 64 | 51 | 39 | 59 |
| LA. NEW ORLEANS | 69 | 49 | 50 | 57 | 63 | 66 | 64 | 58 | 60 | 64 | 70 | 60 | 46 | 59 |
| SHREVEPORT | 18 | 48 | 54 | 58 | 60 | 69 | 78 | 79 | 80 | 79 | 77 | 65 | 60 | 69 |
| MAINE. EASTPORT | 58 | 45 | 51 | 52 | 52 | 51 | 53 | 55 | 57 | 54 | 50 | 37 | 40 | 50 |
| MASS. BOSTON | 67 | 47 | 56 | 57 | 56 | 59 | 62 | 64 | 63 | 61 | 58 | 48 | 48 | 57 |
| MICH. ALPENA | 45 | 29 | 43 | 52 | 56 | 59 | 64 | 70 | 64 | 52 | 44 | 24 | 22 | 51 |
| DETROIT | 69 | 34 | 42 | 48 | 52 | 58 | 65 | 69 | 66 | 61 | 54 | 35 | 29 | 53 |
| GRAND RAPIDS | 56 | 26 | 37 | 48 | 54 | 60 | 66 | 72 | 67 | 58 | 50 | 31 | 22 | 49 |
| MARQUETTE | 55 | 31 | 40 | 47 | 52 | 53 | 56 | 63 | 57 | 47 | 38 | 24 | 24 | 47 |
| S. STE. MARIE | 60 | 28 | 44 | 50 | 54 | 54 | 59 | 63 | 58 | 45 | 36 | 21 | 22 | 47 |
| MINN. DULUTH | 49 | 47 | 55 | 60 | 58 | 58 | 60 | 68 | 63 | 53 | 47 | 36 | 40 | 55 |
| MINNEAPOLIS | 45 | 49 | 54 | 55 | 57 | 60 | 64 | 72 | 69 | 60 | 54 | 40 | 40 | 56 |
| MISS. VICKSBURG | 66 | 46 | 50 | 57 | 64 | 69 | 73 | 69 | 72 | 74 | 71 | 60 | 45 | 64 |
| MO. KANSAS CITY | 69 | 55 | 57 | 59 | 60 | 64 | 70 | 76 | 73 | 70 | 67 | 59 | 52 | 65 |
| ST. LOUIS | 68 | 48 | 49 | 56 | 59 | 64 | 68 | 72 | 68 | 67 | 65 | 54 | 44 | 61 |
| SPRINGFIELD | 45 | 48 | 54 | 57 | 60 | 63 | 69 | 77 | 72 | 71 | 65 | 58 | 48 | 63 |
| MONT. HAVRE | 55 | 49 | 58 | 61 | 63 | 63 | 65 | 78 | 75 | 64 | 57 | 48 | 46 | 62 |
| HELENA | 65 | 46 | 55 | 58 | 60 | 59 | 63 | 77 | 74 | 63 | 57 | 48 | 43 | 60 |
| KALISPELL | 50 | 28 | 40 | 49 | 57 | 58 | 60 | 77 | 73 | 61 | 50 | 28 | 20 | 53 |
| NEBR. LINCOLN | 55 | 57 | 59 | 60 | 80 | 63 | 69 | 76 | 71 | 67 | 66 | 59 | 55 | 64 |
| NORTH PLATTE | 53 | 63 | 63 | 64 | 62 | 64 | 72 | 78 | 74 | 72 | 70 | 62 | 58 | 68 |
| NEV. ELY | 21 | 61 | 64 | 68 | 65 | 67 | 79 | 79 | 81 | 81 | 73 | 67 | 62 | 72 |
| LAS VEGAS | 19 | 74 | 77 | 78 | 81 | 85 | 91 | 84 | 86 | 92 | 84 | 83 | 75 | 82 |
| RENO | 51 | 59 | 64 | 69 | 75 | 77 | 82 | 90 | 89 | 86 | 76 | 68 | 56 | 76 |
| WINNEMUCCA | 53 | 52 | 60 | 64 | 70 | 76 | 83 | 90 | 90 | 86 | 75 | 62 | 53 | 74 |

These charts and tabulation derived from "Normals, Means, and Extremes" table in U. S. Weather Bureau publication Local Climatological Data.

| STATE AND STATION | YEARS | JAN. | FEB. | MAR. | APR. | MAY | JUNE | JULY | AUG. | SEPT. | OCT. | NOV. | DEC. | ANNUAL |
|---|---|---|---|---|---|---|---|---|---|---|---|---|---|---|
| N. H. CONCORD | 44 | 48 | 53 | 55 | 53 | 51 | 56 | 57 | 58 | 55 | 50 | 43 | 43 | 52 |
| N. J. ATLANTIC CITY | 62 | 51 | 57 | 58 | 59 | 62 | 65 | 67 | 66 | 65 | 54 | 58 | 52 | 60 |
| N. MEX. ALBUQUERQUE | 28 | 70 | 72 | 72 | 76 | 79 | 84 | 76 | 75 | 81 | 80 | 79 | 70 | 78 |
| ROSWELL | 47 | 69 | 72 | 75 | 77 | 76 | 80 | 76 | 75 | 74 | 74 | 74 | 69 | 74 |
| N. Y. ALBANY | 63 | 43 | 51 | 53 | 53 | 57 | 62 | 63 | 61 | 58 | 54 | 39 | 38 | 53 |
| BINGHAMTON | 63 | 31 | 39 | 41 | 44 | 50 | 56 | 54 | 51 | 47 | 43 | 29 | 26 | 44 |
| BUFFALO | 49 | 32 | 41 | 49 | 51 | 59 | 67 | 70 | 67 | 60 | 51 | 31 | 28 | 53 |
| CANTON | 43 | 37 | 47 | 50 | 48 | 54 | 61 | 63 | 61 | 54 | 45 | 30 | 31 | 49 |
| NEW YORK | 83 | 49 | 56 | 57 | 59 | 62 | 65 | 66 | 64 | 64 | 61 | 53 | 50 | 59 |
| SYRACUSE | 49 | 31 | 38 | 45 | 50 | 58 | 64 | 67 | 63 | 56 | 47 | 29 | 26 | 50 |
| N. C. ASHEVILLE | 57 | 48 | 53 | 56 | 61 | 64 | 63 | 59 | 59 | 62 | 64 | 59 | 48 | 58 |
| RALEIGH | 61 | 50 | 56 | 59 | 64 | 67 | 65 | 62 | 62 | 63 | 64 | 62 | 52 | 61 |
| N. DAK. BISMARCK | 65 | 52 | 58 | 56 | 57 | 58 | 61 | 73 | 69 | 62 | 59 | 49 | 48 | 59 |
| DEVILS LAKE | 55 | 53 | 60 | 59 | 60 | 59 | 62 | 71 | 67 | 59 | 56 | 44 | 45 | 58 |
| FARGO | 39 | 47 | 55 | 56 | 58 | 62 | 63 | 73 | 69 | 60 | 57 | 39 | 46 | 59 |
| WILLISTON | 43 | 51 | 59 | 60 | 63 | 66 | 66 | 78 | 75 | 65 | 60 | 48 | 48 | 63 |
| OHIO, CINCINNATI | 44 | 41 | 46 | 52 | 56 | 62 | 69 | 72 | 68 | 68 | 60 | 46 | 39 | 57 |
| CLEVELAND | 65 | 29 | 36 | 45 | 52 | 61 | 67 | 71 | 68 | 62 | 54 | 32 | 25 | 50 |
| COLUMBUS | 65 | 36 | 44 | 49 | 54 | 63 | 68 | 71 | 68 | 66 | 60 | 44 | 35 | 55 |
| OKLA. OKLAHOMA CITY | 62 | 57 | 60 | 63 | 64 | 65 | 74 | 78 | 78 | 74 | 68 | 64 | 57 | 68 |
| OREG. BAKER | 46 | 41 | 49 | 56 | 61 | 63 | 67 | 83 | 81 | 74 | 62 | 46 | 37 | 60 |
| PORTLAND | 69 | 27 | 34 | 41 | 49 | 52 | 55 | 70 | 65 | 55 | 42 | 28 | 23 | 48 |
| ROSEBURG | 29 | 24 | 32 | 40 | 51 | 57 | 59 | 79 | 77 | 68 | 42 | 28 | 18 | 51 |
| PA. HARRISBURG | 60 | 43 | 52 | 55 | 57 | 61 | 65 | 68 | 63 | 62 | 58 | 47 | 43 | 57 |
| PHILADELPHIA | 66 | 45 | 56 | 57 | 58 | 61 | 62 | 64 | 61 | 62 | 61 | 53 | 49 | 57 |
| PITTSBURGH | 63 | 32 | 39 | 45 | 50 | 57 | 62 | 64 | 61 | 62 | 54 | 39 | 30 | 51 |
| R. I. BLOCK ISLAND | 48 | 45 | 54 | 47 | 56 | 58 | 60 | 62 | 62 | 60 | 59 | 50 | 44 | 56 |
| S. C. CHARLESTON | 61 | 58 | 60 | 65 | 72 | 73 | 70 | 66 | 66 | 67 | 68 | 68 | 57 | 66 |
| COLUMBIA | 55 | 53 | 57 | 62 | 68 | 69 | 68 | 63 | 65 | 64 | 68 | 64 | 51 | 63 |
| S. DAK. HURON | 62 | 55 | 62 | 60 | 62 | 65 | 68 | 76 | 72 | 66 | 61 | 52 | 49 | 63 |
| RAPID CITY | 53 | 58 | 62 | 63 | 62 | 61 | 66 | 73 | 73 | 69 | 66 | 58 | 54 | 64 |
| TENN. KNOXVILLE | 62 | 42 | 49 | 53 | 59 | 64 | 66 | 64 | 59 | 64 | 64 | 53 | 41 | 57 |
| MEMPHIS | 55 | 44 | 51 | 57 | 64 | 68 | 74 | 73 | 74 | 70 | 69 | 58 | 45 | 64 |
| NASHVILLE | 63 | 42 | 47 | 54 | 60 | 65 | 69 | 69 | 68 | 69 | 65 | 55 | 42 | 63 |
| TEX. ABILENE | 14 | 64 | 68 | 73 | 66 | 73 | 86 | 83 | 85 | 73 | 71 | 72 | 66 | 73 |
| AMARILLO | 54 | 71 | 71 | 75 | 75 | 75 | 82 | 81 | 81 | 79 | 76 | 76 | 70 | 76 |
| AUSTIN | 33 | 46 | 50 | 57 | 60 | 62 | 72 | 76 | 79 | 70 | 70 | 57 | 49 | 63 |
| BROWNSVILLE | 37 | 44 | 49 | 51 | 57 | 65 | 73 | 78 | 78 | 67 | 70 | 54 | 44 | 61 |
| DEL RIO | 36 | 53 | 55 | 61 | 63 | 60 | 66 | 75 | 80 | 69 | 66 | 58 | 52 | 63 |
| EL PASO | 53 | 74 | 77 | 81 | 85 | 87 | 87 | 78 | 78 | 80 | 82 | 80 | 73 | 80 |
| FT. WORTH | 33 | 56 | 57 | 65 | 66 | 67 | 75 | 78 | 78 | 74 | 70 | 63 | 58 | 68 |
| GALVESTON | 66 | 50 | 50 | 55 | 61 | 69 | 76 | 72 | 71 | 70 | 74 | 62 | 49 | 63 |
| SAN ANTONIO | 57 | 48 | 51 | 56 | 58 | 60 | 69 | 74 | 75 | 69 | 67 | 55 | 49 | 62 |
| UTAH. SALT LAKE CITY | 22 | 48 | 53 | 61 | 68 | 73 | 78 | 82 | 82 | 84 | 73 | 56 | 49 | 69 |
| VT. BURLINGTON | 54 | 34 | 43 | 48 | 47 | 53 | 59 | 62 | 59 | 51 | 43 | 25 | 24 | 46 |
| VA. NORFOLK | 60 | 50 | 57 | 60 | 63 | 67 | 66 | 66 | 66 | 63 | 64 | 60 | 51 | 62 |
| RICHMOND | 56 | 49 | 55 | 59 | 63 | 67 | 66 | 65 | 62 | 63 | 64 | 58 | 50 | 61 |
| WASH. NORTH HEAD | 44 | 28 | 37 | 42 | 48 | 48 | 48 | 50 | 46 | 48 | 41 | 31 | 27 | 41 |
| SEATTLE | 26 | 27 | 34 | 42 | 48 | 53 | 48 | 62 | 56 | 53 | 36 | 28 | 24 | 45 |
| SPOKANE | 62 | 26 | 41 | 53 | 63 | 64 | 68 | 82 | 79 | 68 | 53 | 28 | 22 | 58 |
| TATOOSH ISLAND | 49 | 26 | 36 | 39 | 45 | 47 | 46 | 48 | 44 | 47 | 38 | 26 | 23 | 40 |
| WALLA WALLA | 44 | 24 | 35 | 51 | 63 | 67 | 72 | 86 | 84 | 72 | 59 | 33 | 20 | 60 |
| YAKIMA | 18 | 34 | 49 | 62 | 70 | 72 | 74 | 86 | 86 | 74 | 61 | 38 | 29 | 65 |
| W. VA. ELKINS | 55 | 33 | 37 | 42 | 47 | 55 | 55 | 56 | 53 | 55 | 51 | 41 | 33 | 48 |
| PARKERSBURG | 62 | 30 | 36 | 42 | 49 | 56 | 60 | 63 | 60 | 60 | 53 | 37 | 29 | 48 |
| WIS. GREEN BAY | 57 | 44 | 51 | 55 | 56 | 58 | 64 | 70 | 65 | 58 | 52 | 40 | 40 | 55 |
| MADISON | 59 | 44 | 49 | 52 | 53 | 58 | 64 | 70 | 66 | 60 | 56 | 41 | 38 | 56 |
| MILWAUKEE | 59 | 44 | 48 | 53 | 56 | 60 | 65 | 73 | 67 | 62 | 56 | 44 | 39 | 57 |
| WYO. CHEYENNE | 63 | 65 | 66 | 64 | 61 | 59 | 68 | 70 | 68 | 69 | 65 | 63 | 63 | 66 |
| LANDER | 57 | 66 | 70 | 71 | 66 | 65 | 74 | 76 | 75 | 72 | 67 | 61 | 62 | 69 |
| SHERIDAN | 52 | 56 | 61 | 62 | 61 | 61 | 67 | 76 | 74 | 67 | 60 | 53 | 52 | 64 |
| YELLOWSTONE PARK | 35 | 39 | 51 | 55 | 57 | 56 | 63 | 73 | 71 | 65 | 57 | 45 | 38 | 56 |
| P. R. SAN JUAN | 57 | 64 | 69 | 71 | 66 | 59 | 62 | 65 | 67 | 61 | 63 | 63 | 65 | 65 |

Based on period of record through December 1959, except in a few instances.

**See the "Weather of 109 selected U.S. Cities" section at the back of this volume for 1961-1990 adjustments to** Normals, Means, and Extremes.

## MEAN MONTHLY PERCENTAGE OF POSSIBLE SUNSHINE,
### For Selected Stations

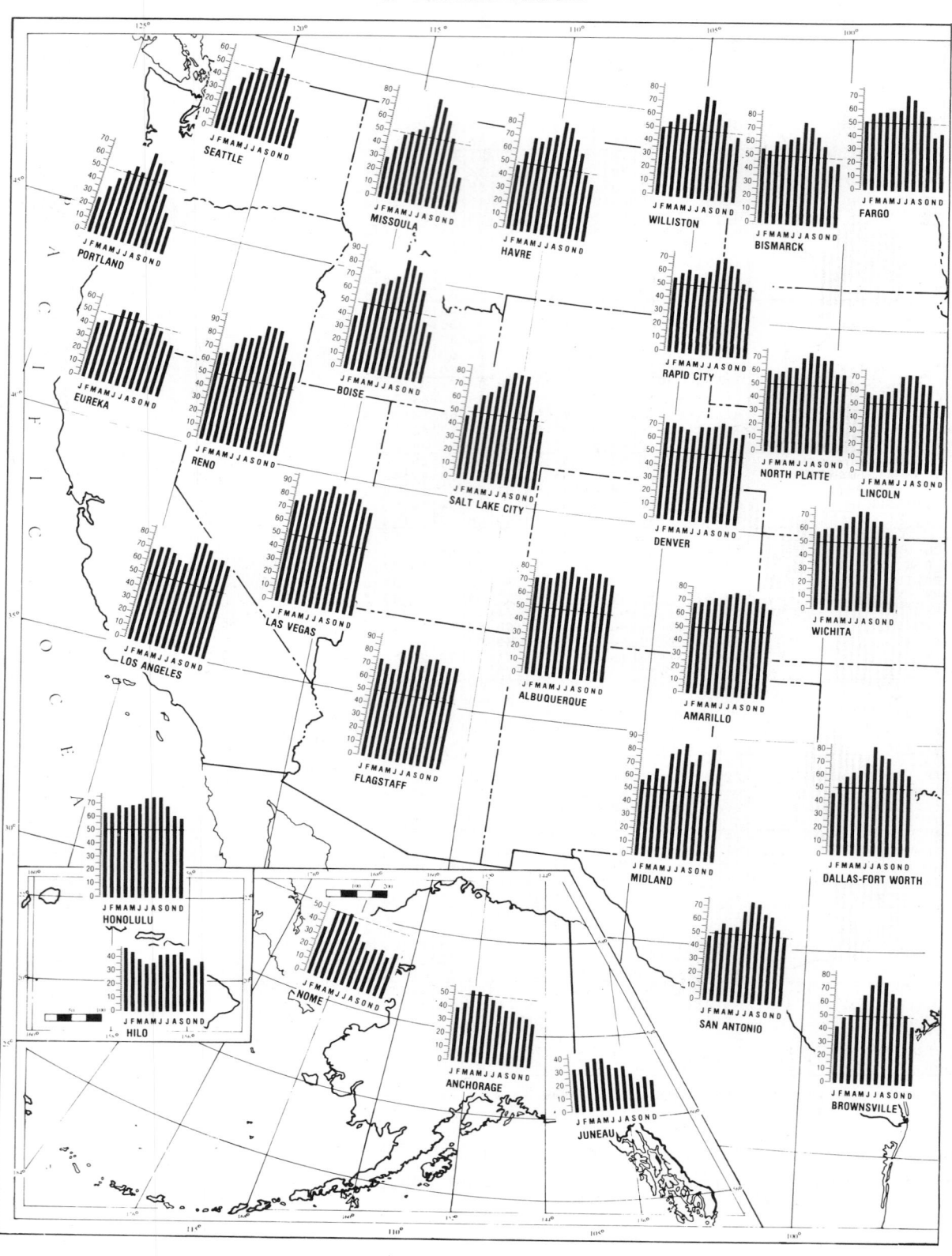

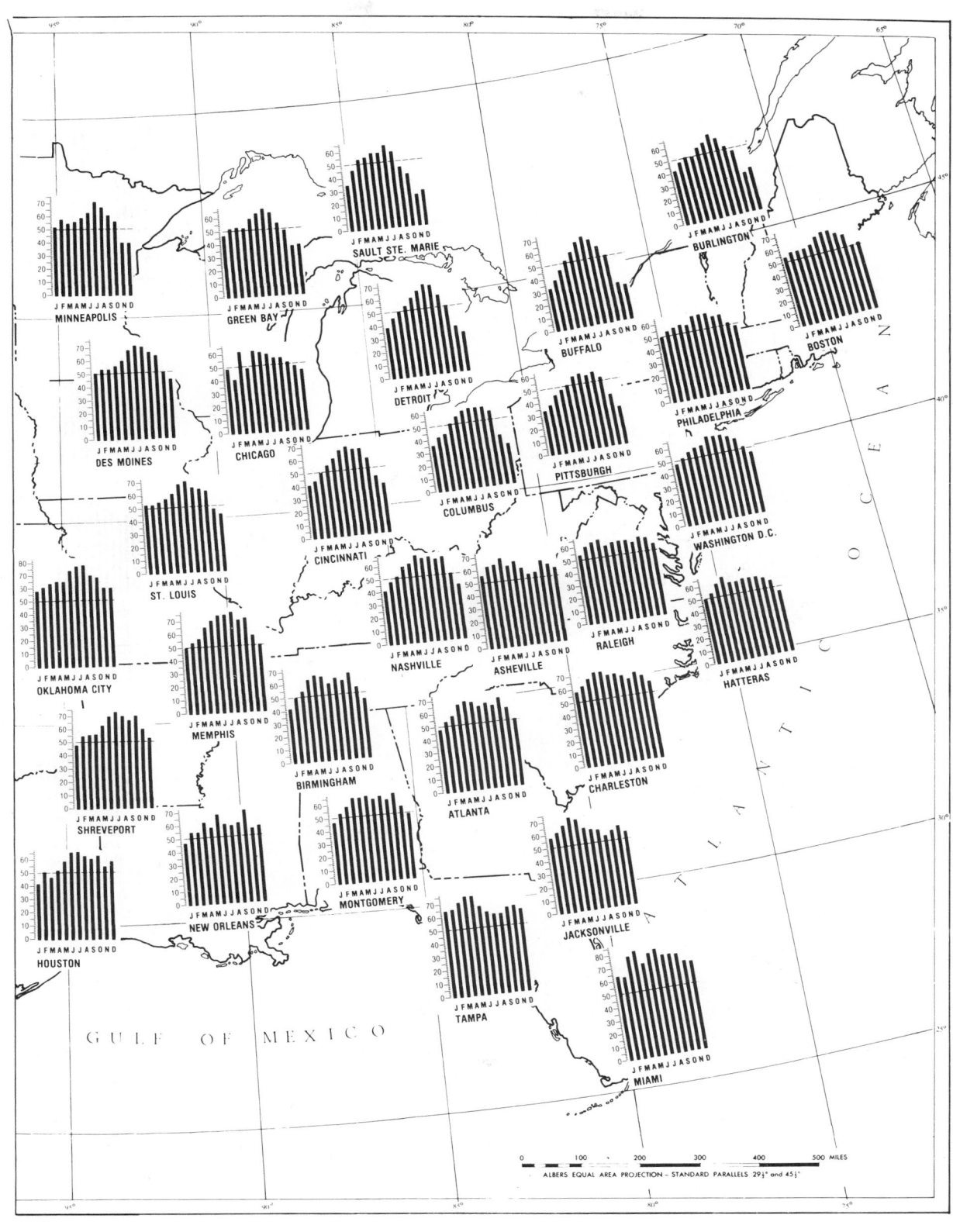

**Based on period, 1951-1980.**

## PREVAILING WIND DIRECTION

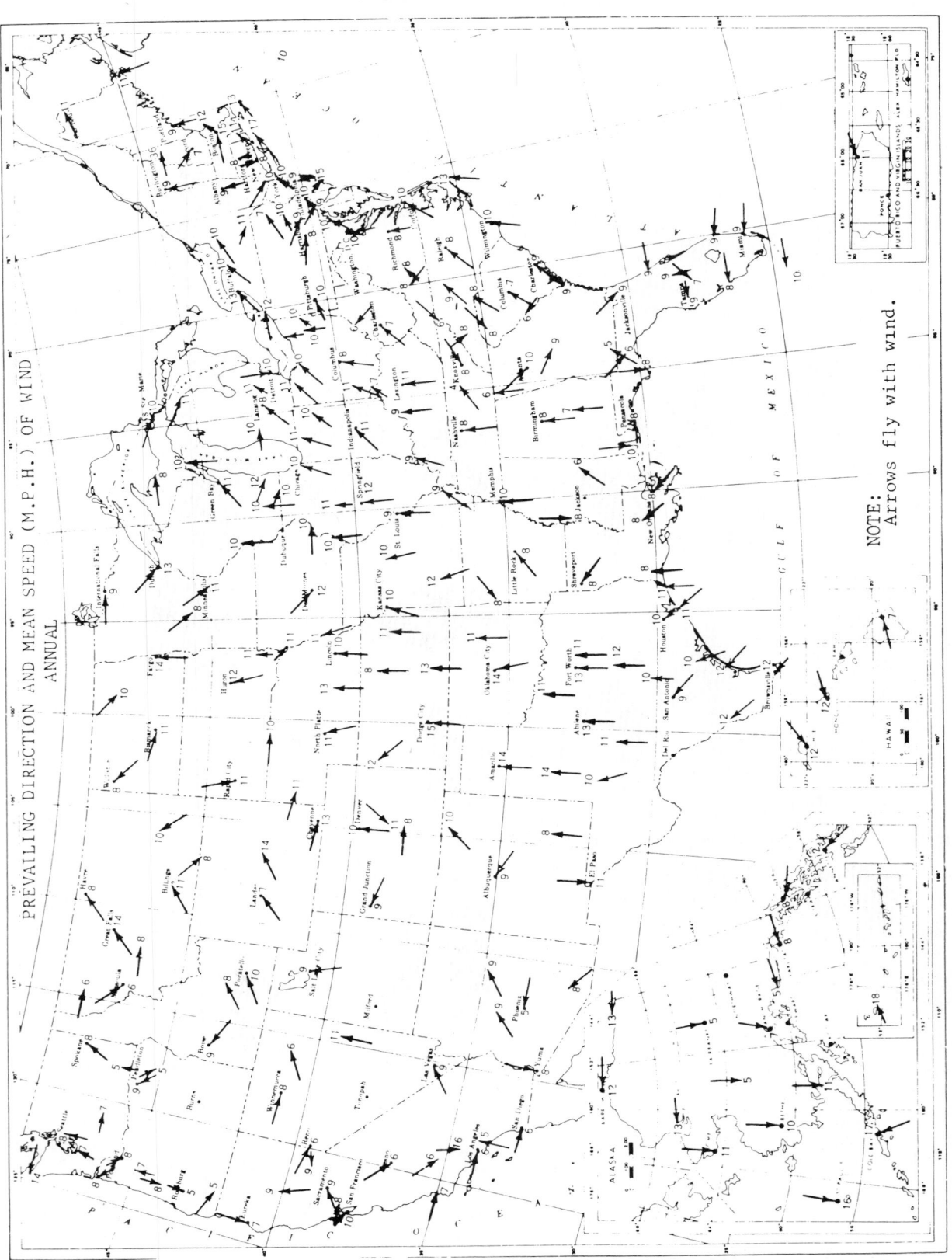

PREVAILING DIRECTION AND MEAN SPEED (M.P.H.) OF WIND
ANNUAL

NOTE:
Arrows fly with wind.

**See the "Weather of 109 selected U.S. Cities" section at the back of this volume for 1961-1990 adjustments to** Normals, Means, and Extremes.

# STORMS,
# SEVERE WEATHER,
## and
# GEOPHYSICAL PHENOMENA

# HURRICANES

## Hurricane Hugo tells us much about hurricanes in general—

Hurricane *Hugo* at 1001 EDT on September 21, 1989 when it was about 275 miles SE of the South Carolina coast. Photo was taken from the NOAA spacecraft known as GOES. The GOES spacecraft, which is maintained in a geosynchronous orbit, about 22,300 miles above the equator, routinely provides imagery every 30 minutes, day and night, using visible and infrared sensors. The craft's speed and altitude are precisely such that that the craft's motion exactly matches the earth's rotation, thus its position relative to the earth is always above the same point on the Equator. This means it acts as if it were a stationary platform. The GOES satellite provides full disk images and a variety of images depicting sections of the full disk. These images are available to weathercasters every half hour.)

Hurricane Hugo, crossing the coast of South Carolina on September 21, 1989, was the strongest storm to strike the United States since *Camille* pounded the Louisiana and Mississippi coasts in 1969*. At one point east of Guadeloupe, a NOAA research aircraft measured winds of 160 MPH and a central pressure of 27.11 inches (918mb) which rated Hugo as a Category #5 — the highest — storm on the *Saffir-Simpson Scale*. It was somewhat less fierce when it reached the U.S. mainland.

When Hugo struck the Virgin Islands, Puerto Rico and the Carolinas, it was classified as a Category #4 Hurricane. Storm tides of approximately 20 feet were experienced along part of the South Carolina coast, constituting record storm-tide heights for America's east coast. Although the highest surges struck sparsely populated areas north of Charleston, South Carolina, damage was extensive and lives were lost.

Forty-nine directly-related storm fatalities were recorded, 26 in the U.S. and its Caribbean Islands. Twenty-three died in other Leeward Islands. It is estimated that Hugo caused more than $9 billion in damage. The mainland of the U.S. alone accounted for $7 billion.

## HURRICANE — "The Greatest Storm On Earth"

There is nothing like the hurricane in the atmosphere.

Even seen by sensors on satellites thousands of miles above the earth, the uniqueness of these powerful, tightly coiled storms is clear. Hurricanes are not the largest storm systems in our atmosphere, or the most violent; but they combine those qualities as no other phenomenon does, as if they were designed to be engines of death and destruction.

In our hemisphere, they are called hurricanes, a term which echoes colonial Spanish and Caribbean Indian words for evil spirits and big winds. The storms are products of the tropical ocean and atmosphere, powered by heat from the sea, steered by the easterly trades and temperate westerlies, and their own fierce energy. Around their tranquil core, winds blow with lethal velocity and the ocean develops an inundating surge. What is more, as they move ashore, *tornadoes* may descend from the advancing bands of thunderclouds.

---

\* Some will ask, "What about *Gilbert* in 1988? Didn't that storm have the lowest barometer reading ever recorded in the Western hemisphere? Wasn't it just as deadly as this reading might imply? The answer is that *Gilbert* whose eye was was indeed the low barometer champ of recorded history, 26.22" Hg, (888 millibars), and maybe even two millibars lower while at sea, did not strike the U.S. mainland. It swept through the Caribbean with devastating effect, creating havoc on the Yucatan peninsula, where it made landfall on the morining of September 14, and causing a 20-foot storm surge at the resort of Cancun. *Gilbert* blew itself out over Mexico.

## Hurricane Names—

The National Hurricane Center near Miami, Florida, keeps a constant watch on oceanic storm-breeding areas for tropical disturbances which may herald the formation of a hurricane. If a disturbance intensifies into a tropical storm with rotary circulation and wind speeds above 39 miles per hour, the Center will give the storm a name from one of the six lists below. The tropical disturbance may never reach hurricane intensity, nevertheless it is given a name in anticipation that it may. A separate set of names is used each year beginning with the first name in the set. After the sets have all been used, they will be used again. The 1991 set, for example, will be used again to name storms in 1997. The letters Q, U, X, Y, and Z are not included because of the scarcity of names begining with those letters.

The name lists have an international flavor because hurricanes affect other nations and are tracked by countries other than the United States. Names for these lists are selected from library sources and agreed upon by nations involved during international meetings of the World Meteorological Organization (WMO).

### The Six-Year List of Names for Atlantic and Caribbean Storms

| 1991 | 1992 | 1993 | 1994 | 1995 | 1996 |
|------|------|------|------|------|------|
| Ana | Andrew | Arlene | Alberto | Allison | Arthur |
| Bob | Bonnie | Bret | Beryl | Barry | Bertha |
| Claudette | Charley | Cindy | Chris | Chantal | Cesar |
| Danny | Danielle | Dennis | Debby | Dean | Diana |
| Erika | Earl | Emily | Ernesto | Erin | Edouard |
| Fabian | Frances | Floyd | Florence | Felix | Fran |
| Grace | Georges | Gert | Gordon | Gabrielle | Gustav |
| Henri | Hermine | Harvey | Helene | Humberto | Horrtense |
| Isabel | Ivan | Irene | Isaac | Iris | Isidore |
| Juan | Jeanne | Jose | Joyce | Jerry | Josephine |
| Kate | Karl | Katrina | Keith | Karen | Klaus |
| Larry | Lisa | Lenny | Leslie | Luis | Lili |
| Mindy | Mitch | Maria | Michael | Marilyn | Marco |
| Nicholas | Nicole | Nate | Nadine | Noel | Nana |
| Odette | Otto | Ophelia | Oscar | Opal | Omar |
| Peter | Paula | Philippe | Patty | Pablo | Paloma |
| Rose | Richard | Rita | Rafael | Roxanne | Rene |
| Sam | Shy | Stan | Sandy | Sebastien | Sally |
| Teresa | Tomas | Tammy | Tony | Tanya | Teddy |
| Victor | Virginie | Vince | Valerie | Van | Vicky |
| Wanda | Walter | Wilma | William | Wendy | Wilfred |

(Names of particular individuals have not been chosen for inclusion in the list of hurricane names.)

## Hurricanes names cut death tolls—

Experience shows that the use of short, distinctive given names in written as well as in spoken communications is quicker, and less subject to error than the older more cumbersome latitude-longitude identification methods. These advantages 1are especially important in exchanging detailed storm information between hundreds of widely scattered stations, airports, coastal bases, and ships at sea. Hurricanes, as poorly understood as they are today, seem to have a single benefit — they are a major source of rain for those continental corners over which their unpredictible tracks carry them. Mostly they are seen as engines of tragedy, which still leave death and destruction in their paths, even though the effectiveness of warnings systems have doubled and redoubled in recent decades.

In Asia, the price in life paid the hurricane has had biblical proportions. As late as 1970, cyclone storm tides along the coast of what now is Bangladesh killed hundreds of thousands of persons. Eleven thousand people perished in a storm that struck that region in 1984, and even more in a storm seven years later.

Our hemisphere has not had such spectacular losses, but the toll has still been high. In August 1893, a storm surge drowned between one and two thousand people in Charleston, South Carolina. In October of that same year, nearly two thousand more perished on the Gulf Coast of Louisiana. The infamous Galveston storm of 1900 took more than six thousand lives. More than 1,800 perished along the south shore of Florida's Lake Okeechobee in 1928 when hurricane driven waters broached an earthen levee. Cuba lost more than two thousand to a storm in 1932. Four hundred died in Florida in an intense hurricane in September 1935 — The "Labor Day" hurricane that, until *Hugo* hit in 1989, shared with 1969's *Camille* the distinction of being the most severe to strike the U.S. mainland during the years of recordkeeping.

Floods from 1974's hurricane *Fifi* caused one of the Western Hemisphere's worst natural disasters in history, with an estimated five thousand persons dead in Honduras, El Salvador, Guatemala, and Belize.

In the United States, the hurricane death toll has been greatly diminished by timely warnings of approaching storms. But damage to fixed property continues to mount. *Camille,* in 1969, caused some $1.42 billion[*] in property damage. Floods from *Agnes* in 1972 cost an estimated $2.1 billion and damage from *Frederic* in 1979 totaled 2.3 billion dollars. Total damage for the 1985 season, when eight named storms (six hurricanes) hit our coastline, was in excess of $4 billion. *Hugo*, in 1989, our most expensive to date, wrought damage of more than $7 billion while coming ashore as a full-scale hurricane in South Carolina and moving hundreds of miles

---

[*] Dollars of hurricane damage prior to 1990 have been translated into 1990 dollar equivalents.

inland as a furious near-hurricane strength storm.

## The season of great storms—

It is the coming of summer to the northern hemisphere that ushers in conditions that spawn tropical storms and hurricanes. The movement of our sun — which is not really movement, of course, but a positional shift relative to the earth caused by our planet's year-long orbit — brings the peak power of the solar radiation northward. The sun's track moves first to the Equator, in March, then toward the Tropic of Cancer (23°,27' north latitude), as June, July and August unfold. Behind this solar track the sea and air grow warmer, and the polar airflows make a steady retreat.

This northward shift of the sun brings the season of tropical cyclones to the Northern Hemisphere. This means it is time to look seaward, along our coasts. This is as true for Asia as for the U.S. and the Caribbean.

Over the Western Pacific, the tropical cyclone season is never quite over, but varies greatly in intensity. Every year, conditions east of the Philippines send a score of violent storms howling toward Asia; but it is worse from June through October.

Southwest of Mexico, eastern Pacific hurricanes develop during the spring and summer. Most of these will die at sea as they move over colder ocean waters. But there are destructive exceptions when storms occasionally curve back toward Mexico.

Along our Atlantic and Gulf coasts, the nominal hurricane season lasts *from June through November.* Early in this season, the western Caribbean and Gulf of Mexico are the principal areas of origin. In July and August, this spawning center begins to shift eastward; by early September a few storms are being born as far east as the Cape Verde Islands off Africa's west coast. Again after mid-September, most storms begin in the western Caribbean and Gulf of Mexico.

In an average year, more than one hundred disturbances with hurricane potential are observed in the Atlantic, Gulf, and Caribbean; *but on an average only 10 of these reach the tropical storm stage, and only about six mature into hurricanes.* On average, *two* of these hurricanes strike the United States, where they are apt to kill from about 50 to 100 people, somewhere between Texas and Maine, and cause hundreds of millions of dollars in property damage. In a worse-than-average year, the same storms cause several hundred deaths, and property damage totaling *billions* of dollars.

For the National Oceanic and Atmospheric Administration (NOAA), the hurricane season means another hazard from the atmosphere, at a time when

20 JUNE 1972  TIME OF PHOTO 1800 GMT *

21 JUNE 1972  TIME OF PHOTO 1800 GMT

22 JUNE 1972  TIME OF PHOTO 1800 GMT

*Greenwich Mean Time

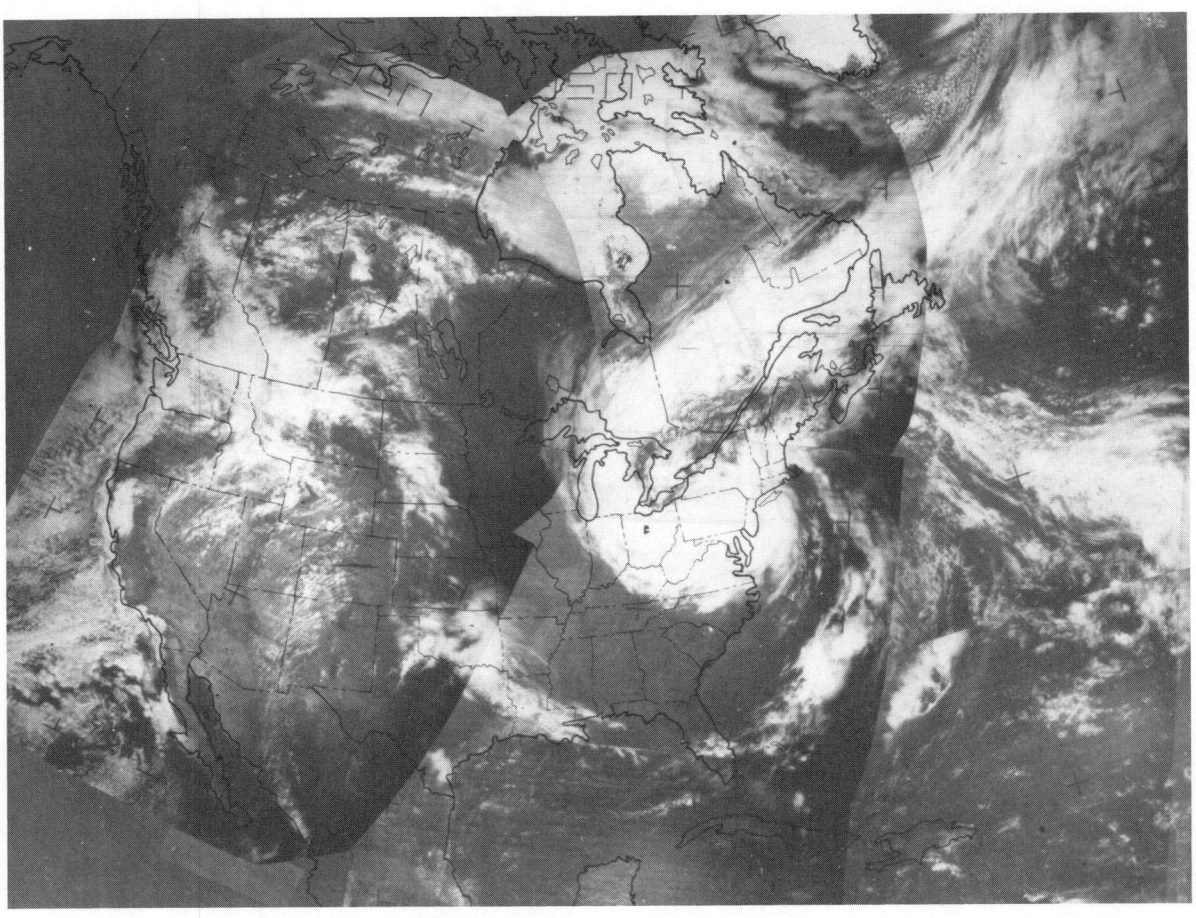

23 JUNE 1972

## TRACKING A HURRICANE FROM SPACE

*Tracking a tropical storm by means of satellites is one of the great life savers of the high-tech age. In the photos on the facing page and above, **Hurricane Agnes** is watched by an orbiting camera over a four-day span. Today, the satellite named GOES "hangs" at a fixed position over the equator and supplies progressive photos of the United States and our coast lines every 30 minutes. The vantage point is 22,300 miles in space (that is the altitude at which a satellite's movement in space exactly matches the earth's spin and therefore remains in the same position relative to the earth), a height from which ground observers can watch entire cloud systems, thousands of miles in scope. Since the cloud systems provide visual evidence of what is happening in the atmosphere up to about the 50,000 foot level, such vision permits forecasting of where and when a hurricane will come ashore. This means loss of life in U.S. hurricanes is now generally limited to persons who ignore the warnings, or for tragic reasons are unable to flee in time even with warning. Nine out of ten such deaths are due to the tidal-wave like storm surge (15 to 20 foot increases in water level at beaches) that accompanys the landfall of the storm.*

tornadoes, and floods, and severe storms are playing seasonal havoc elsewhere on the continent.

Meteorologists with NOAA's National Weather Service monitor the massive flow of data that might contain the early indications of a developing storm somewhere over the warm sea. Cloud images from satellites, meteorological data from hundreds of surface stations, balloon probes of the atmosphere, and information from hurricane-hunting aircraft are the tools of the Hurricane Forecaster.

In NOAA's Environmental Research Laboratories, scientists follow eagerly as nature furnishes additional specimens of the great storms — specimens they can probe and analyze to gather ever-greater understanding of the mechanics of the storms. Such analyses assist the forecaster with his warnings.

## Portrait of a hurricane—

Given that the hurricane, as an engine, is inefficient and hard to start and sustain, and given, further, that most tropical storms will never reach hurricane proportions, nevertheless some tropical storms will. A certain number every season will manage to accumulate the complex combination of natural forces required. When one does, it is an awesome natural event indeed.

The young storm stands upon the sea as a whirlwind of awful violence. Its hurricane-force winds (winds greater than 63 knots*) *cover thousands of square miles,* and tropical storm force winds — winds of 34 to 63 knots — *cover an   area ten times larger.* Along the twisting contours of its spiral are "rain bands" of dense clouds from which torrential rains fall. These spiral rain bands ascend in "decks" of cumulus and cumulonimbus clouds to the high upper-atmosphere. There condensing water vapor is swept off as ice-crystal wisps of cirrus clouds by high-altitude winds. Lightning glows in almost perpetual pulsations in the rainbands, and this cloudy terrain is whipped by turbulence.

In the lower few thousand feet, air flows *in* toward the center of the cyclone, and is whirled upward through ascending columns of air near the center. *Above 40,000 feet, this cyclone pattern is replaced by an anticyclonic** circulation — the high-level pump which functions as the "exhaust system" of the hurricane engine.*

At lower levels, where the hurricane is most intense, winds on the rim of the storm follow a wide pattern, like the slower currents on the rim of a whirlpool; like

---

* A knot is one nautical mile per hour; a nautical mile is about 1.15 statute miles. Winds of 63 knots (hurricane velocity) translate, roughly to about 74 statute miles per hour.
** Anti-cyclonic circulation means, in the Northern Hemisphere, a system of winds rotating in a clockwise direction about a center of relatively low barometric pressure. Contrast this to "cyclonic circulation" which has a counterclockwise pattern. Both of these definitions are reversed in the Southern Hemisphere.

those currents, these winds accelerate as they approach the central vortex. This inner band is the eye*wall*, where the storm's worst winds are felt, and where moist air entering at the surface is "chimneyed" upward releasing heat to drive the storm. In most hurricanes, these winds exceed 90 knots — in extreme cases they may double that velocity. Maximum winds run still higher in typhoons, the Pacific version of the same type of storm.

Hurricane winds are produced, as all winds are, by difference in atmospheric pressure, or density. The pressure gradient — the rate of pressure change with distance — produced in hurricanes is the sharpest pressure gradient in the atmosphere, excepting only the pressure change believed to exist across the narrow funnel of a tornado.

Atmospheric pressure is popularly expressed as the height of a column of mercury that can be supported by the weight of the overlying air at a given time.[*]

In North America, barometric measurements at sea level seldom go below 29 inches of mercury (982 millibars), and in the tropics the barometer reading is generally close to 30 inches (1,016 millibars) under normal conditions. *Hurricanes drop the bottom out of those normal categories.* The Labor Day hurricane that struck the Florida Keys in 1935 had a central pressure of only 26.35 inches (892 millibars). Hurricane *Gilbert*, which wrought havoc in the Caribbean and the Yucatan Penninsula during 1988, was measured at 26.22 inches in its eye. And the pressure change is swift: pressure may drop a full inch (34 millibars) per mile. Such pressure contrasts guarantee tremendous wind velocity.

At the center of the storm is a unique atmospheric entity, and a persistent metaphor for order in the midst of chaos — *the eye of the hurricane*. It is encountered suddenly. From the heated tower of maximum winds and thunderclouds, one bursts into the eye, where winds diminish to something less than 15 knots. Penetrating the opposite wall one is abruptly in the worst of winds again.

A mature hurricane orchestrates *more than a million cubic miles of atmosphere*. Over the deep ocean, waves generated by hurricane winds can reach heights of 50 feet or more. Under the storm center the ocean surface is drawn upward like water in a straw, forming a mound 1-3 feet or so higher than the surrounding ocean surface. This mound may translate into coastal surges of 20 feet or more. Besides this surge, massive swells pulse out through the upper levels of the sea. (It is not exaggerating to say that Pacific surfers often ride the oceanic memory of distant

---

[*] Weather maps show atmospheric pressure in *millibars,* units equal to a thousandth of a *bar*. The *bar* is a unit of measure equal to 29.53 inches of mercury in the English system; and to one million dydnes per square centimeters in the metric system.

typhoons, so pronounced are these energy releases of storms.)

Hurricane *Eloise*, which struck the Florida panhandle in September 1975, taught scientists something new about the influence of passing hurricanes on the marine environment. Expendable bathythermographs dropped from NOAA research aircraft ahead of, into, and in the wake of the storm showed that the ocean was disturbed to depths of hundreds of feet by a passing hurricane. Moreover the ocean "remembered" hurricane passage with internal waves that persisted for weeks after the storm had gone. The same storm also demonstrated that a passing hurricane can be felt deep in the sea-floor sediments.

While a hurricane lives, the transaction of energy within its circulation is immense. The condensation heat energy released by a hurricane in one day can be the equivalent of energy released by fusion of four hundred, 20-megaton hydrogen bombs. One day's released energy, converted to electricity, could supply the United States' electrical needs for about six months.

## The fatal thrust toward land

From birth, the hurricane lives in an environment that constantly tries to kill it — *and ultimately succeeds.*

The hurricane tends to survive while it is over warm water. But its movement is controlled by the forces which drive the storm ashore or over colder water beyond the tropics. In these non-nourishing enviroments it will fill and die. This thrust *away from the tropics* is the clockwise curve which propels Atlantic hurricanes into the eastern United States, and which takes eastern Pacific typhoons across the coastlines of Japan and into the Asian mainland.

Even before a hurricane forms, the embryonic storm has forward motion, generally driven by the *easterly flow* * in which it is embedded. As long as this westerly drift is slow — less than about 20 knots — the young hurricane may intensify. More rapid forward motion generally inhibits intensification in the storm's early stages. Entering the temperate latitudes (north of the Tropic of Cancer) some storms may move along at better than 50 knots; but such fast-moving storms soon weaken.

---

\* **Easterly flow is the metrological description of an air movement system of the tropic latitudes, featuring east to west flow of the atmosphere. While air movement in northern latitudes is generally west-to-east (e.g., Prevailing Westerly Winds), when the tropical latitudes are reached, south of the Tropic of Cancer and north of the Tropic of Capricorn, air movement is generally from the East, due to complex thermodynamic interactions and the earth's spin (i.e, Easterly flow is part of the wind system known as the Trade Winds). An Easterly Wave (air system) is generally associated with weather fluctuations which can resemble weather front action in the higher latitudes. .**

These diagrams show how hurricane watches and warnings and other advisories change as a hypothetical storm stalks Florida's northern Gulf coast.

First note the *extent* of the hurricane. Its dangerous core of high water and high winds is much larger than any of the communities in its path. When it comes ashore, its worst effects will be felt along some 50 miles of shoreline, with potentially dangerous heavy weather along a reach of coast several hundred miles long.

Then note that NOAA hurricane forecasters "overwarn"—that is, the areas covered by their watches and warnings are larger than the approaching storm. This reflects the state-of-the-art of hurricane forecasting, and the enormous complexity of predicting what a large, destructive, and inherently erratic weather system is going to do.

The hurricane warning area appears in the second panel. It generally covers a much smaller area than the hurricane watch. Beyond the warning area, peripheral gale warnings and small-craft cautionary statements are distributed around the predicted path of the hurricane.

In the third panel, the hurricane has moved ashore, and the watch and warning cycle ends; however, advisories continue to go out, until the ocean and atmosphere behind the hurricane have had a chance to settle down.

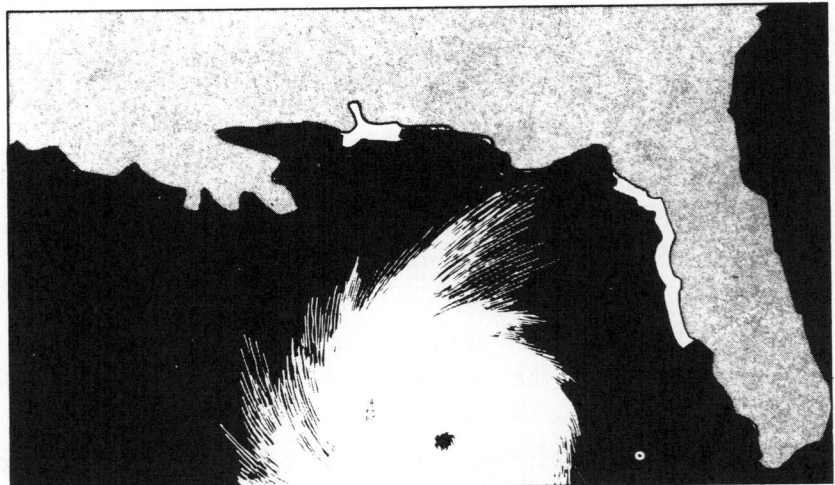

At middle latitudes, the hurricane's end usually comes swiftly. Colder air penetrates the cyclonic vortex; the warm core cools, and acts as a thermal brake on further intensification. Water below 80°F does not contribute much energy to a hurricane. Even though some large hurricanes may travel for days over cold North Atlantic water, **all storms are doomed once they leave the warm tropical waters which sustain them.** The farther they venture into higher latitudes, the less fuel they receive from the sea; this lack of fuel finally kills the storms. Over land, hurricanes break up rapidly. Cut off from their oceanic source of energy, and with the added effects of **frictional drag,** their circulation rapidly weakens and becomes more disorganized. Torrential rains, however, may continue even after the winds are much diminished. In the southeastern United States, about a fourth of the annual rainfall comes from dissipating hurricanes, and the Asian mainland and Japan suffer typhoons to get water from the sky.

Hurricanes are often resurrected into extratropical cyclones at higher latitudes, or their dynamic forces combine with existing temperate-zone disturbances. Many storms moving up our Atlantic coast are in the throes of this transformation when they strike New England, and large continental *Lows* are often invigorated by the remnants of storms born over the tropical sea.

## Destruction in a hurricane

Hurricanes are the unstable, unreliable creatures of a moment in our planet's natural history. But their brief life ashore can leave scars that never quite heal. In the mid-1970's, the hand of 1969's *Camille* could still be seen along the Mississippi Gulf Coast. *Most of a hurricane's destructive work is done by the general rise in the height of the seas which accompany the storm.* This quick, tidal-like rise in sea level is called *storm surge.*

Hurricane winds can be the least destructive of the hurricane's punches, although there are important exceptions like 1971's hurricane *Celia*, whose high winds did most of the storm's destructive work. These winds are a force to be reckoned with by coastal communities deciding how strong their structures should be. For example, normal atmospheric pressure at sea level is about two thousand pounds per square inch. As winds increase, pressure against objects is added at a disproportionate rate. Pressure mounts with the square of wind velocity, so that a tenfold increase in wind speed increases pressure one hundred-fold. Thus, 20-knot wind increases atmospheric pressure by about two pounds per square foot while a wind of 200 knots increases atmospheric pressure by more than 22.5 pounds(!) per square foot.

For some structures this added force is enough to cause failure. Tall structures

**HURRICANES BRING FLOODING**—Roads have disappeared in this area near Wilkes-Barre, Pennsylvania as the Susquehanna River pours over its banks after tropical storm *Agnes* dropped record rainfall. In some places waters reached 10 to 17 feet above flood level. This illustrates how tropical storms, even after they have lost hurricane intensity by passage over land, can still dominate the weather picture for hundreds of miles around their core. Flooding is the major cause of hurricane damage. (U.S. Coast Guard Photo)

**HURRICANE DAMAGE**—In Key West , Florida, 1960's Hurricane *Donna* converted many small boat docks into trash heaps. Boats that were not lashed down extremely well were soon pounded to pieces against the pilings. (American Red Cross photo)

like radio towers can be worried to destruction by gusty hurricane-force winds. Winds also carry a barrage of debris. Flying debris can be extremely dangerous.

All the wind damage does not necessarily come from the hurricane. As the storm moves shoreward, interactions with other weather systems can produce tornadoes, which work around the fringes of the hurricane. Although hurricane-spawned tornadoes are not the most violent form of these whirlwinds, they have added to the toll we pay the hurricane.

Floods from hurricane rainfall are quite destructive. A typical hurricane brings an awesome 6 to 12 inches of short-duration rainfall to the area it crosses, and some have brought much more. The resulting floods — often sudden flash floods — have caused great damage and loss of life, especially in mountainous area, where heavy rains can raise creek levels rapidly and send great surges of water down mountain draws. The most widespread flooding in United States history (through 1976) was caused by the remnants of hurricane *Agnes* in 1972. Rains from the dying hurricane brought disastrous floods to the entire Atlantic tier of states, causing 118 deaths and some $2.1 billion in property damage.

## Storm surge, the killer that slips in from the sea—

The hurricane's worst killing blow comes from the sea, in the form of storm surge. This subtly approaching smash of tidal wave immensity actually claims *nine of each ten victims* that fall to a hurricane.

As the storm crosses the continental shelf and moves close to the coast, mean water level may increase 15 feet or more. The advancing storm surge combines with the normal astronomical tide to create the hurricane storm tide. In addition, wind waves 5 to 10 feet high are superimposed on the storm tide. This buildup of water level can cause severe flooding in coastal areas — particularly when the storm surge coincides with normal high tides. Because much of the United States' densely populated coastline along the Atlantic and Gulf coasts lies less than 10 feet above mean sea level, the danger from storm surge is multiplied. Nearly every coastal location that is exposed to a hurricane is also a candidate for the smashing blow of storm surge.

Wave and current action associated with the surge also causes extensive damage. Water weighs some 1,700 pounds per cubic yard; extended pounding by frequent waves can demolish any structures not specifically designed to withstand such forces.

Currents set up along the coast by the gradient in storm surge heights and wind combine with waves to severely erode beaches and coastal highways. Many buildings withstand hurricane winds until, their foundations undermined by erosion, are

# STORM SURGE: HURRICANE'S KILLER BLOW

The storm surge is a great dome of water, *often 50 miles wide,* that comes sweeping across the coastline *near the area where the eye of the hurricane makes landfall.* The surge, aided by the hammering effect of breaking waves, acts like a giant bulldozer sweeping everything in its path. The stronger the hurricane, the higher the storm surge will be. This is unquestionably the most dangerous part of a hurricane. *Nine out of ten hurricane fatalities are caused by storm surge.* During the infamous *Hurricane Camille* in 1969, a 25 foot storm surge inundated Pass Christian in Mississippi. Lesser heights are more usual but still extremely dangerous.

    Many factors are involved in the formation and propagation of a storm surge, such as the strength of the storm, bottom conditions where the surge comes ashore, and the position of the storm center in relation to the shore. That means these pictorials cannot be representative of all storm surges for all coastal areas. The diagram, below, is typical of surges produced by a hurricane moving toward the lower-Atlantic or Gulf coastal areas.

## NORMAL TIDE - HIGH

It is a normal beach day. The sea rises and falls predictable with astronomical tidal action. There are the usual small waves. A hurricane has developed and a *Hurricane Watch* is in effect for the area.

\* MSL Mean Sea Level

## 12 HOURS BEFORE PEAK SURGE

The hurricane now poses a serious threat to this beach area and the *Watch* has been changed to a *Hurricane Warning.* The hurricane is 12 hours away. The tide is a little above normal; the water moves further up the beach. Swells are beginning to move in from the deep ocean and breaking waves—some as high as five to eight feet—crash ashore and run well up the beach. The wind is picking up.

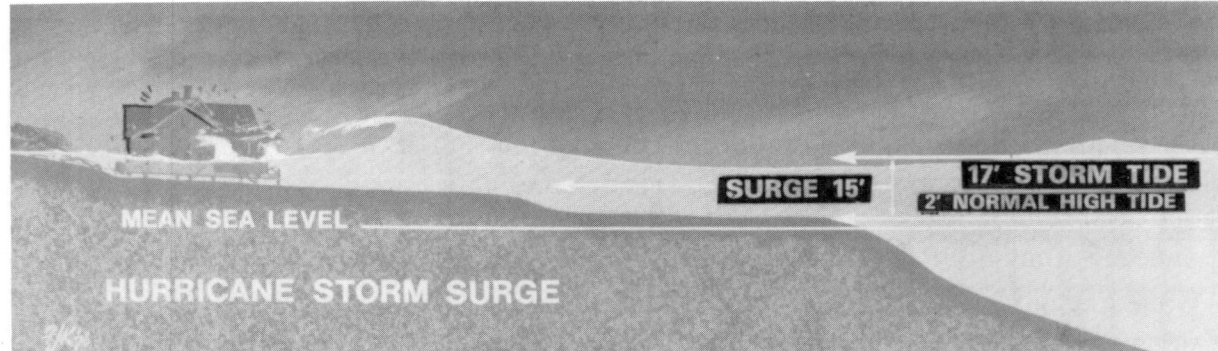

MEAN SEA LEVEL

SURGE 15'

**17' STORM TIDE**
2' NORMAL HIGH TIDE

HURRICANE STORM SURGE

The hurricane is moving ashore close to the beach area. It is high tide time again. This time, however, there is a 15-foot surge added to the normal 2-foot astronomical tide! This creates a 17-foot *storm tide*. This great mound of water, topped by battering waves, is moving slowly ashore along an area of coastline 50 to 100 miles wide. Winds are now over 130 miles an hour. Much ocean front property will be unable to withdtand this combined assault of wind and water.

*The combination of storm surge, battering waves, and high tide is the hurricane's most deadly killer.*

weakened and fail.

Storm tides, waves, and currents in confined harbors severely damage ships, marinas, and pleasure boats. In estuarine and bayou areas, intrusions of salt water endanger the public health — and can create bizarre effects, like salt-crazed snakes fleeing Louisiana's flooded bayous.

## Spotting a hurricane; and spreading the word—

The day is past when a hurricane could develop to maturity far out to sea and be unreported until it thrust toward land.

Earth-orbiting satellites operated by NOAA keep the earth's atmosphere under virtually continuous surveillance, night and day. Long before a storm has evolved even to the point of ruffling the easterly wave, scientists at NOAA's National Hurricane Center in Miami, Florida have begun to watch the disturbance.

In the satellite data coming in from both polar orbiting and geostationary spacecraft, and in reports from ships and aircraft they look for subtle clues that mark the development of hurricanes—cumulus clouds covered by the cirrostratus deck of a highly organized convective system; showers that become steady rains; dropping atmospheric pressure; intensification of the tradewinds, or a westerly wind component there.

Then, if this hint of a disturbance blooms into a tropical storm, a time-honored convention is applied: it receives a name. From there on the tracking process is nearly atomatic, with spotter aircraft being deployed and the entire Center going into the high alert mode.

## How the tracking traditions began—

The first hurricane warning in the United States was flashed in 1873, when the Signal Corps warned against a storm approaching the coast between Cape May, New Jersey, and New London, Connecticut. Today, naming a storm is a signal which brings a considerably more elaborate warning system to readiness. Long-distance communications lines and preparedness plans are flexed.

As an Atlantic hurricane drifts closer to land, it comes under surveillance by weather reconnaissance aircraft of the U.S. Air Force, the famous "Hurricane Hunters," who bump through the turbulent interiors of the storms to obtain precise fixes on the position of the eye, and measure winds and pressure fields. Despite the advent of satellites, the aircraft probes are the most detailed information hurricane forecasters receive.

The hurricanes are also probed by the "flying laboratories" from NOAA's Aircraft operations Center in Miami. Finally, the approaching storm comes within range of a radar network stretching from Brownsville, Texas to Boston, and from Miami to the Lesser Antilles.

Through the lifetime of the hurricane, advisories from the National Hurricane Center warning give the storm's position and what the forecasters in Miami expect the storm to do. As the hurricane drifts to within a day of two of its predicted landfall, these advisories begin to carry *watch* and *warning* messages, telling people *when* and *where* the hurricane is expected to strike, and what its effects are likely to be. Not until the storm has decayed over land and its cloud elements and great cargo of moisture have blended with other brands of weather does the hurricane emergency end.

This system works well. The death toll in the United States from hurricanes has dropped steadily as NOAA's hurricane tracking and warning apparatus has matured. Although the accuracy of hurricane forecasts has improved over the year any significant improvements must come from quantum leaps in scientific understanding.

The forecasters also know that science will never provide a full solution to the problems of hurricane safety. The rapid development of America's coastal areas has placed millions of people with little or no hurricane experience in the path of these lethal storms. For this vulnerable coastal population, the answer must be community preparedness and public education in the hope that education and planning before the fact will save lives and lessen the impact of the hurricane and its capacity to wreck havoc.

## The United States' hurricane problem—

*Editor's note: The following is a commentary on this nation's ability to cope with hurricanes of the future. It was issued by NOAA's National Hurricane Center, which bears large responsibility in saving our people from these sea-borne catyclysms.*

*The permanent populations of the hurricane-prone coastal counties of the United States continue to grow at a rapid rate. When weekend, seasonal, and holiday populations are considered, the number of people on barrier islands such as at Ocean City, Maryland, Gulf Shores, Alabama, and Padre Island, Texas increase by 10- to 100-fold or more. Also, these areas are subject to inundation from the rapidly rising waters known as the storm surge associated with hurricanes that generally result in catastrophic damage and potentially large losses of life. Over the past several years, the warning system has provided adequate time for the great majority of the people on barrier islands and along the immediate coast to move inland when hurricanes have threatened. However, it is becoming more difficult each year to evacuate people from these areas due to roadway systems that have not kept pace with the rapid population growth. This condition results in the requirement for longer and longer lead times for safe evacuation. Unfortunately, these extended forecasts suffer from increasing uncertainty. Furthermore, rates of improvements in forecast skills have been far out-paced by rates of population growth in areas vulnerable to hurricanes.*

*The combination of the growing populations on barrier islands and other vulnerable locations, and the uncertainties in the forecasts poses major dilemmas for forecasters and local and state emergency management officials alike, for example, how do you prevent complacency caused by "false alarms" and yet provide adequate warning times?*

*Preparations for hurricanes are expensive. When a hurricane is forecast to move inland on a projected path, the coastal area placed under warning is about 300 miles in length. The average cost of preparation, whether the hurricane strikes or not, is more than $50 million for the Gulf Coast. This estimate covers the cost of boarding up homes, closing down businesses and manufacturing plants, evacuating oil rigs, etc. It does not include economic losses due to disruption of commerce activities such as sales, tourists canceling reservations, etc.*

*In some locations, the loss for the Labor Day weekend alone can be a substantial portion of the yearly income of coastal businesses. An example of such losses were experienced along the Florida panhandle during Hurricane <u>Elena</u> in 1985.*

*If the width of the warned area has to be increased by 20% because of greater uncertainties in the forecast, the additional cost for each event would be $10 million. If uncertainties in the hurricane strength require warning for the next higher category of hurricane (Saffir/Simpson scale), then major increases in the number of people evacuated and preparation costs would be required.*

*Of course, if these uncertainties meant that major metropolitan areas such as Galveston / Houston, New Orleans, Tampa, Miami, or a number of other major coastal cities would or would not be included in the warning area, then the differences in preparation costs would be substantially more than the $10 million. What is more, the number of people evacuated would be substantially*

# HURRICANE TRACKING CHART

REMEMBER, hurricanes are large powerful storms that can suddenly change direction. Check frequently on the storm's progress until all Watches and Warnings for your area are canceled.

**HURRICANE WATCH:** hurricane may threaten within 36 hours
- Be prepared to take action if a warning is issued by the National Weather Service.
- Keep informed of the storm's progress.

**HURRICANE WARNING:** hurricane expected to strike within 24 hours
- Leave beachfront and low-lying areas
- Leave mobile homes for more substantial shelter
- Stay in your home if it is sturdy, on high ground, and not near the beach, but if you are asked to leave by authorities, Go!
- Stay tuned to radio, NOAA Weather Radio, or television for hurricane advisories and safety information.

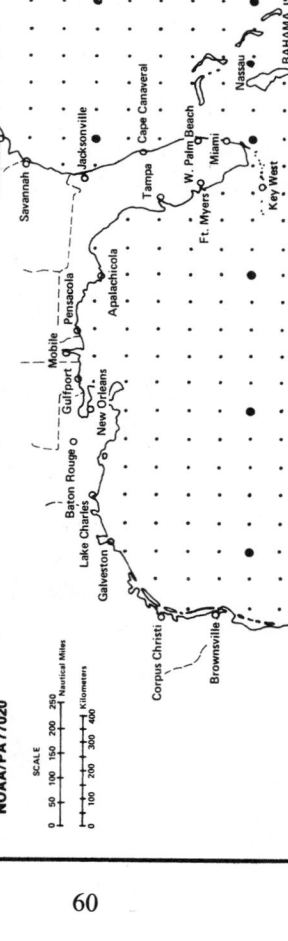

NOAA/PA 77020

SCALE
Nautical Miles
0  50  100  150  200  250
Kilometers
0  100  200  300  400

Plotting A Storm

Hurricane center positions are given by latitude and longitude. For example: "the storm's center is located near 41.5 degrees North and 63.0 degrees West." On the chart, read North to 41.5 degrees and then West to 63.0 degrees as shown below.

← 63.0° W
41.5° N

MARCH 1982

more than just tens of thousands of people. For instance, in the case of the Galveston/Houston area, an increase in storm strength of only 20 miles per hour (from a category #2 hurricane to a category #3 hurricane on the Saffir/Simpson scale) would require the evacuation of <u>an additional 200,000 people.</u> Likewise, if major industrial areas such as Beaumont/Port Arthur, Texas, or tourist areas such as Atlantic City, New Jersey were affected by these uncertainties, the financial impact would be huge.

Economic factors receive serious consideration from NHC, and local and state officials consider not only for direct but also for indirect effects on people response. **People will not continually take expensive actions which, afterwards, prove to have been unnecessary.** If we consistently **over-warn** by wide margins, people will not respond and such actions could result in large loss of life. To maintain credibility with the general public, NHC and local and state officials cannot treat all hurricanes as if they were **Camilles, Gilberts** or **Hugos!** Such an exaggerated approach may indeed provide maximum protection of life for a given event, but it endangers many more lives **the next time** when the threat may be even greater.

Finally, the hurricane problem is compounded by the fact that 80-to-90% of the people who now live in the hurricane-prone areas have never experienced the core of a major hurricane (Saffir/Simpson scale — category #3, or stronger). Many of these people have been through weaker hurricanes or been brushed by the fringe of a major hurricane. The result is a false impression of the damage potential of these storms. This frequently breeds complacency and delayed actions which could result in the loss of many lives. An example of the potential danger are those people living on barrier islands who might be reluctant to evacuate under "blue sky" conditions until they actually <u>see</u> the actual threat (water rising and winds increasing). The result could be people trapped in those areas as waters cut off escape routes. This situation nearly happened for about 200 people on western Galveston Island during Hurricane **Alicia** of 1983.

This type of response primarily results from three major factors. First, major hurricanes are infrequent events for any given location. Second for more than two decades, major hurricanes striking the United States coast have been less frequent than for the three previous decades (Fig. 1). Finally, it has been during this period of low hurricane activity that the great majority of the present coastal residents moved to the coast. The combination of these factors is illustrated in Fig. 2 which shows that property damage spiraled upward in tandem with the coastal populations until the last two decades when it leveled off. In fact if it had not been for the more than $7 billion loss caused by Hurricane Hugo in 1989, a significant decrease in losses would have been noted.

*Figure 3 shows the loss of life during this period. This figure clearly demonstrates the improvement in the effectiveness of hurricane forecast, warning, and response programs since the turn of the century. Those developments are described in the following sections of this paper. However, with the tremendous increase of populations in high-risk areas along our coastlines, the concern is that we may now not fare as well in the future when hurricane activity inevitably returns to the frequencies experienced during the 1940s-60s.*

## Hurricane warning service; a historical look-

The history of the weather service over the past century would be bland indeed without a detailed account of the growth of the Nation's hurricane warning service. Today, the hurricane forecast and warning service stands as the finest of its kind in the world, distinguished by its character, credibility and the confidence that our nation has in it. But that wasn't always the case.

The Weather Bureau was created as a civilian agency in 1890 mainly because of a general dissatisfaction with weather forecasting under the military. The hurricane of 1875 that destroyed Indianola, Texas without much warning was a contributing factor.

It was not until the Spanish American War of 1898 that an effort was made to establish a comprehensive hurricane warning service. President McKinley stated that he was more afraid of a hurricane than he was of the Spanish Navy. He extended the warning service to include warnings for shipping interests as well as the military. Before that, hurricane warnings were only issued for the U.S. coastal areas. Hurricane warning stations were established throughout the West Indies. A forecast center was established in Kingston, Jamaica and later moved to Havana, Cuba in 1899. The warning service was extended to Mexico and Central America. This recognition of the international responsibility for the U.S. hurricane warning service continues today under the auspices of the World Meteorological organization (WM0) of the United Nations.

In 1900, the infamous Galveston hurricane killed 6,000 people — the greatest natural disaster in U.S. history. There was no formal hurricane warning and this calamity prompted the transfer of the warning service to Washington, D.C., where it remained until 1935.

In the 1920's, there were several hurricanes that hit with little or no warning that led to dissatisfaction with the hurricane service operating out of Washington. The coastal communities felt that Washington was insensitive to the hurricane problem. In 1926, a very strong hurricane (Category #4 by today's standard) brought great devastation to Southeast Florida including Miami and Ft. Lauderdale, causing more than 200 deaths. The warnings for that storm were issued at night when most residents were asleep and unaware of the rapidly approaching hurricane. In 1928, another severe hurricane hit South Florida and killed an estimated 1800 people who drowned when Lake Okeechobee overflowed. In 1933, the largest number of tropical storms — 21 — developed. Nine of them were hurricanes and two that affected the East Coast of the U.S. including Washington were badly forecast and the public inadequately warned. In 1934, a forecast and warning for an approaching hurricane in the very sensitive Galveston area was badly flubbed by Washington.

Those incidents led Congress and the President to revamp and decentralize the Hurricane Warning Service. Improvements included 24-hour operations with teletypewriter hook-up along the Gulf and Atlantic coasts; weather observations at 6-hourly intervals; hurricane advisories at least four times a day; and a more adequate upper air observing network. New hurricane forecast centers were established at Jacksonville, Florida; New Orleans, Louisiana; San Juan, Puerto Rico; and Boston, Massachusetts (established in 1940).

In 1943, the primary hurricane forecast office at Jacksonville was moved to Miami where the Weather Bureau established a joint hurricane warning service with the Army Air Corps and the Navy under the Direction of Grady Norton. It was also in 1943 that Col. Joseph Duckworth made the first intentional plane reconnaissance into the eye of a hurricane. The following year, regular aircraft reconnaissance was begun by the military giving hurricane forecasters the location and intensity of the storms for the first time.

Grady Norton continued as head of the Miami Center until his death in 1954 during Hurricane *Hazel* that ravaged the east coast of the United States. Mr. Norton established a strong and popular reputation as an extraordinary forecaster with the tremendous ability to communicate with residents along the hurricane vulnerable coastlines. Gordon Dunn, who served as Norton's assistant in Jacksonville, was selected as Norton's successor and the Miami office was officially designated as the National Hurricane Center in 1955.

In the 1950's a number of hurricanes in addition to Hazel struck the East Coast causing much damage and flooding. Congress responded with increased appropriations to strengthen the warning service and intensify research into hurricanes. The Weather Bureau organized the National Hurricane Research Project under the direction of Dr. Robert H. Simpson. The Air Force and the Navy provided the first aircraft to be used by the Project to investigate the structure, characteristics, and movement of tropical storms.

In 1960, radars capable of "seeing" out to a distance of 200 to 250 miles from their coastal sites were established at strategic locations along the Atlantic and Gulf coasts from Maine to Brownsville, Texas. On April 1, 1960, the first weather satellite was placed in orbit giving hurricane forecasters the ability to detect storms before they hit land.

Gordon Dunn retired in 1967 and was succeeded by Dr. Simpson who placed a renewed emphasis on research and development activities at the Center through satellite applications and the development of statistical and dynamic models as forecast aids. Dr. Simpson retired after the 1973 hurricane season and was succeeded by his Deputy, Dr. Neil Frank who served until 1987. Dr. Frank's tenure was marked by great emphasis on the need for hurricane preparedness among the hurricane-prone communities in the U.S. as well as in the Caribbean. He and his staff created an increased national awareness of the hurricane threat through the cooperation of local and state emergency officials and the enlistment of the news media and other federal agencies in the campaign to substitute education and awareness for the lack of first-hand experience among the ever-increasing coastal populations.

Dr. Robert Sheets is the current Director of the National Hurricane Center, at a time where the future holds even greater promise to improve the hurricane warning capability of the National Weather Service. New technology and advances in the science under the weather service's modernization program now underway will lead to more improvement and effectiveness in the forecasting and warning of hurricanes.

## Improvements coming—

The next general GOES series of satellites, planned for 1991, is expected to provide more accurate and higher resolution sounding data than presently available from geosynchronous satellites, and similar improvements can be expected from the polar orbit satellite systems.

Major improvements in longer range hurricane forecasts (36-72 hours) will come through improved dynamical models. Global, hemispheric, and regional models show considerable promise.

Present operational reconnaissance aircraft provide invaluable data in the core of the hurricane. Doppler radar are now an integral part of NOAA's research aircraft operations providing entire data fields within several miles-of the aircraft's path.

NEXRAD, a new, more powerful radar system, capable of seeing deep into storm cells will add new dimensions to hurricane warning capabilities. The NEXRAD stations will, as they are progressively deployed around the nation, provide much needed information on tropical cyclone wind fields and the wind fields' changes as they move inland. Local offices will be able to provide more accurate short term warnings as rainbands, high winds and possible tornadoes move toward specific inland locations. Heavy rains and flooding frequently occur over widespread inland areas.

Improved observing systems and anticipated improvements in analysis, forecasting, and warning programs require efficient accessing, processing and analysis of large quantities of data from numerous sources. These data also provide the opportunity for improved numerical forecasts. The Class VII computer at the National Meteorological Center will permit operational implementation of next generation hurricane prediction models.

Products must be provided to users which optimize the desired response. AWIPS will be the primary tool for accomplishing this task. Critical hurricane information needed by local, state, and other federal agencies as well as the private sector will be displayed graphically and transmitted to the user faster and more complete than ever before making more effective warning and evacuation response.

The future of the Nation's splendid hurricane forecast and warning service is indeed brighter than ever before!

## Aerial Weather Reconnaissance—

Aerial weather reconnaissance is vitally important to the forecasters of the National Hurricane Center. Aircraft reports help the meteorologist determine what is going on inside a storm as it actually happens. This, along with the broader view provided by data from satellites, floating buoys, and land and ship reports, makes up the total "package" of information available to the hurricane forecasters who must make forecasts of the speed, intensity, and direction of the storm. Reconnaissance aircraft penetrate to the core of the storm and provide detailed measurements of its strengths as well as accurate location of its center, information that is not available from any other source.

The National Hurricane Center is supported by specially modified aircraft of the U.S. Air Force (USAF) and the National Oceanic and Atmospheric Administration's Aircraft Operations Center (NOAA/AOC) The USAF crews fly the Lockheed WC-130 "Hercules", a giant four-engine turboprop aircraft which carries a crew of six people and can stay aloft for up to 14 hours without refueling. Two squadrons of the USAF aircraft and their crews are based at Keesler Air Force Base near Biloxi, Mississippi, and can be deployed as needed for reconnaissance anywhere in the Atlantic Ocean, the Caribbean Sea, the Gulf of Mexico, and the Pacific Ocean from

**HURRICANE HUNTERS — NOAA and the U.S. Air Force cooperate closely in sending aircraft into tropical storms to probe their anatomy, and discover at the earliest possible time what intensity and breadth the storm is packing. Flying into the eye of of a hurricane was first accomplished by Col. Joseph Duckworth in 1943; and in 1944 the practice became one of the standard and most important efforts in providing early storm warnings for the mainland. The planes are equipped to keep their crew aloft up to 14 hours as they play hide and seek through the rainbands and violent wind shears. Since 1943, three planes, with crews, have been lost in hurricane tracking.**

the west coast of the U.S. to the international date line which is several hundred miles west of Hawaii. The two units at Keesler AFB are the famed "Hurricane Hunters" of the 53rd Weather Reconnaissance Squadron, and the equally renowned "Storm Trackers" of the 815th Weather Reconnaissance Squadron. NOAA's Aircraft Operations Center flies Lockheed P-3 "Orions", a four-engine turboprop aircraft which carries a crew of from 7 to 17 persons and can stay aloft for up to 12 hours at a time. The NOAA/AOC aircraft and crews are based at Miami International Airport.

Meteorological information obtained from aerial reconnaissance includes measurements of the winds, atmospheric pressure, temperature, and the location of the center of the storm. In addition, these aircraft also drop instruments called "dropsondes" as they fly through the storm's center. This device continuously radios back measurement of pressure, humidity, temperature, and wind direction and speed as it falls toward the sea. This information provides a detailed look at the structure of the storm and an indication of its intensity.

Aerial weather reconnaissance of nature's most powerful destructive force is not without risk. Since aircraft and crews first started flying into hurricanes and typhoons nearly 40 years ago, three have been lost, vanishing without a trace along with their crews. The first of these, A U.S. Navy P2V "Neptune" fell into the Caribbean Seas while flying into Hurricane *Janet* on September 26, 1955. Next came a U.S. Air Force WB-50 "Super Fortress" which crashed into the Pacific 0cean on January 15, 1958 while penetrating Typhoon *Ophelia*. Also lost was a WC-130 "Hercules" which disappeared in the vicinity of Typhoon Bess in the Philippine Sea south of Taiwan on October 12, 1974.

Flying into a hurricane is like no other experience. Crew members who have flown combat missions will tell you that their feelings before these flights and those involving hurricanes are very similar. There is a blend of excitement and apprehension that is difficult to describe. Adding to the tension is that no two hurricanes are alike. Some are nothing but gentle kittens while others seem like raging beasts. Preparations for flying into a hurricane are very precise; all crew members are fully trained by qualified instructors before being allowed to make a flight by themselves. Special precautions are taken by the crew as they enter the hurricane. All loose objects are tied down or put away and crew members slip into safety harness and belts. When radar picks up the storm, the crew then plans on how to get inside. The idea is to make the aircraft mesh with the storm rather than fight it. If it is a well defined storm, getting inside can be a real experience. The winds at flight altitude oftentimes exceed 100 miles an hour, and the wall cloud surrounding the center, or eye, can be several miles thick. Rain comes down in torrents, and the updrafts and downdrafts are usually strong and frequent. Inside the eye, however, the conditions are much different. The ocean is generally visible, and there is blue sky and sunshine. The flight level winds are nearly calm. After gathering all the information they need, the crew then exits the storm in the same manner they entered.

Making sure the National Hurricane Center gets the aerial weather reconnaissance it needs is the job of a small group of Air Force people assigned to a liaison office in the Center. This office, under a Chief, Aerial Reconnaissance Coordination, All Hurricanes (more commonly known as CARCAH) is responsible for coordinating requirements and arranging for the supporting flights. This office also records and monitors weather observations radioed back or received through direct satellite communication from the storm by the on-board meteorologists. These data are checked for accuracy and then transmitted to the world-wide meteorological community.

Aircraft meteorological reconnaissance is a team effort. A host of different organizations, tied together by CARCAH, is dedicated to providing the National Hurricane Center the vital information it needs to make accurate forecasts which help to ensure that communities in the path of a hurricane will be adequately warned. Warnings and forecasts help save countless lives and allow residents to take the necessary precautions to prevent enormous property damage each year.

# Terms To Know

By international agreement, **TROPICAL CYCLONE** is the general term for all cyclone circulations originating over tropical waters, classified by form and intensity as follows:

**TROPICAL WAVE:** A trough of low pressure in the trade-wind easterlies.

**TROPICAL DISTURBANCE:** A moving area of thunderstorms in the Tropics that maintains its identity for 24-hours or more. A common phenomenon in the tropics.

**TROPICAL DEPRESSION:** Rotary circulation at surface, highest constant wind speed 38 miles per hour (33 knots) or less.

**TROPICAL STORM:** Distinct rotary circulation, constant wind speed ranges 39-73 miles per hour (34-63 knots).

**HURRICANE:** Pronounced rotary circulation, constant wind speed of 74 miles per hour (64 knots) or greater.

**SMALL CRAFT CAUTIONARY STATEMENTS:** When a tropical cyclone threatens a coastal area, small craft operators are advised to remain in port or not to venture into the open sea.

**TROPICAL STORM WATCH:** Is issued for a coastal area when there is the threat of tropical storm conditions within 24-36 hours.

**TROPICAL STORM WARNINGS:** May be issued when winds of 39-73 miles an hour (34-63 knots) are expected. If a hurricane is expected to strike a coastal area, tropical storm warnings will not usually precede hurricane warnings.

**HURRICANE WATCH:** Is issued for a coastal area when there is a threat of hurricane conditions within 24-36 hours.

**HURRICANE WARNING:** Is issued when hurricane conditions are expected in a specified coastal area in 24 hours or less.

**STORM SURGE:** An abnormal rise of the sea along a shore as the result, primarily, of the winds of a storm.

**FLASH FLOOD WATCH:** Means a flash flood is possible in the area; stay alert.

**FLASH FLOOD WARNING:** Means a flash flood is imminent; take immediate action.

# The <u>deadliest</u> United States hurricanes this century
## (1900-1989 • 25 or more deaths)

| | HURRICANE | YEAR | CATEGORY | DEATHS |
|---|---|---|---|---|
| 1. | TX (Galveston) | 1900 | 4 | 6000 |
| 2. | FL (Lake Okeechobee) | 1928 | 4 | 1836 |
| 3. | FL (Keys)/S TX | 1919 | 4 | 600# |
| 4. | New England | 1938 | 3* | 600 |
| 5. | FL (Keys) | 1935 | 5 | 408 |
| 6. | AUDREY (SW LA/N TX) | 1957 | 4 | 390 |
| 7. | NE U.S. | 1944 | 3* | 390@ |
| 8. | LA (Grand Isle) | 1909 | 4 | 350 |
| 9. | LA (New Orleans) | 1915 | 4 | 275 |
| 10. | TX (Galveston) | 1915 | 4 | 275 |
| 11. | CAMILLE (MS/LA) | 1969 | 5 | 256 |
| 12. | FL (Miami) | 1926 | 4 | 243 |
| 13. | DIANE (NE U.S.) | 1955 | 1 | 184 |
| 14. | SE FL | 1906 | 2 | 164 |
| 15. | MS/AL/Pensacola | 1906 | 3 | 134 |
| 16. | AGNES (NE U.S.) | 1972 | 1 | 122 |
| 17. | HAZEL (SC/NC) | 1954 | 4* | 95 |
| 18. | BETSY (SE FL/SE LA) | 1965 | 3 | 75 |
| 19. | CAROL (NE U.S.) | 1954 | 3* | 60 |
| 20. | SE FL/LA/MS | 1947 | 4 | 51 |
| 21. | DONNA (FL/Eastern U.S.) | 1960 | 4 | 50 |
| 22. | GA/SC/NC | 1940 | 2 | 50 |
| 23. | CARLA (TX) | 1961 | 4 | 46 |
| 24. | TX (Velasco) | 1909 | 3 | 41 |
| 25. | TX (Freeport) | 1932 | 4 | 40 |
| 26. | S TX | 1933 | 3 | 40 |
| 27. | HILDA (LA) | 1964 | 3 | 38 |
| 28. | SW LA | 1918 | 3 | 34 |
| 29. | SW FL | 1910 | 3 | 30 |
| 30. | CONNIE (NC) | 1955 | 3 | 25 |
| 31. | LA | 1926 | 3 | 25 |

* Moving more than 30 miles per hour.
# Over 500 of these lost on ships at sea; 600-900 estimated deaths
@ Some 344 of these lost on ships at sea.

## ADDENDUM

| | | | |
|---|---|---|---|
| LA | 1893 | – | 2000 |
| SC/GA | 1893 | – | 1000-2000 |
| GA/SC | 1881 | – | 700 |
| SOUTHERN CALIFORNIA | 1939 | – | 45 |

## The <u>costliest</u> United States hurricanes this century
### (1900-1989 • More than $100 million in damage)

|     | HURRICANE               | YEAR | CATEGORY | DAMAGE (U.S.)    |
|-----|-------------------------|------|----------|------------------|
| 1.  | HUGO (SC)               | 1989 | 4        | $7,000,000,000   |
| 2.  | FREDERIC (AL/MS)        | 1979 | 3        | 2,300,000,000    |
| 3.  | AGNES (NE U.S.)         | 1972 | 1        | 2,100,000.000    |
| 4.  | ALICIA (N TX)           | 1983 | 3        | 2,000,000,000[1] |
| 5.  | JUAN (LA)               | 1985 | 1        | 1,500,000,000    |
| 6.  | CAMILLE (MS/AL)         | 1969 | 5        | 1,420,700,000    |
| 7.  | BETSY (SE FL/SE LA)     | 1965 | 3        | 1,420,500,000    |
| 8.  | ELENA (MS/AL/NW FL)     | 1985 | 3        | 1,250,000,000    |
| 9.  | GLORIA (Eastern U.S.)   | 1985 | 3*       | 900,000,000      |
| 10. | DIANE (NE U.S.)         | 1955 | 1        | 831,700,000      |
| 11  | ALLISON (N TX)          | 1989 | T.S.@    | 500,000,000      |
| 12  | ELOISE (NW FL)          | 1975 | 3        | 490,000,000      |
| 13. | CAROL (NE U.S.)         | 1954 | 3*       | 461,000,000      |
| 14. | CELIA (S TX)            | 1970 | 3        | 453,000,000      |
| 15. | CARLA (TX)              | 1961 | 4        | 408,000,000      |
| 16  | CLAUDETTE (N TX)        | 1979 | T.S.@    | 400,000,000      |
| 17. | DONNA (FL/Eastern U.S.) | 1960 | 4        | 387,000,000      |
| 18. | DAVID (FL/Eastern U.S.) | 1979 | 2        | 320,000,000      |
| 19. | New England             | 1938 | 3*       | 306,000,000      |
| 20. | KATE (FL Keys/NW FL)    | 1985 | 2        | 300,000,000      |
| 21. | ALLEN (S TX)            | 1980 | 3        | 300,000,000      |
| 22. | HAZEL (SC/NC)           | 1954 | 4*       | 281,000,000      |
| 23. | DORA (NE FL)            | 1964 | 2        | 250,000,000      |
| 24. | BEULAH (S TX)           | 1967 | 3        | 200,000,000      |
| 25. | AUDREY (LA/N TX)        | 1957 | 4        | 150,000,000      |
| 26. | CARMEN (LA)             | 1974 | 3        | 150,000,000      |
| 27. | CLEO (SE FL)            | 1964 | 2        | 128,500,000      |
| 28. | HILDA (Central LA)      | 1964 | 3        | 125,000,000      |
| 29. | FL (Miami)              | 1926 | 4        | 112,000,000      |
| 30. | SE FL/LA/MS             | 1947 | 4        | 110,000,000      |
| 31. | NE U.S.                 | 1944 | 3*       | 100,000,000+     |

* Moving more than 30 miles per hour.
@ Only of Tropical Storm intensity, but included because of high damage
  amount.

[1]Alicia was mistakenly listed as $200,000 in the previous version of this
Technical Memorandum.

# The <u>most intense</u> United States hurricanes this century
## (Intensity measured at time of landfall • Time span: 1900-1989)

| | HURRICANE | YEAR | CATEGORY | MILLIBARS | INCHES |
|---|---|---|---|---|---|
| 1. | FL (Keys) | 1935 | 5 | 892 | 26.35 |
| 2. | CAMILLE (LA/MS) | 1969 | 5 | 909 | 26.84 |
| 3. | FL (Keys)/S TX | 1919 | 4 | 927 | 27.37 |
| 4. | FL (Lake Okeechobee) | 1928 | 4 | 929 | 27.43 |
| 5. | DONNA (FL/Eastern U.S.) | 1960 | 4 | 930 | 27.46 |
| 6. | TX (Galveston) | 1900 | 4 | 931 | 27.49 |
| 7. | LA (Grand Isle) | 1909 | 4 | 931 | 27.49 |
| 8. | LA (New Orleans) | 1915 | 4 | 931 | 27.49 |
| 9. | CARLA (TX) | 1961 | 4 | 931 | 27.49 |
| 10. | HUGO (SC) | 1989 | 4 | 934 | 27.58 |
| 11. | FL (Miami) | 1926 | 4 | 935 | 27.61 |
| 12. | HAZEL (SC/NC) | 1954 | 4* | 938 | 27.70 |
| 13. | SE FL/LA/MS | 1947 | 4 | 940 | 27.76 |
| 14. | N TX | 1932 | 4 | 941 | 27.79 |
| 15. | GLORIA (Eastern U.S.) | 1985 | 3*& | 942 | 27.82 |
| 16. | AUDREY (LA/N TX) | 1957 | 4# | 945 | 27.91 |
| 17. | TX (Galveston) | 1915 | 4# | 945 | 27.91 |
| 18. | CELIA (S TX) | 1970 | 3 | 945 | 27.91 |
| 19. | ALLEN (S TX) | 1980 | 3@ | 945 | 27.91 |
| 20. | New England | 1938 | 3* | 946 | 27.94 |
| 21. | FREDERIC (AL/MS) | 1979 | 3 | 946 | 27.94 |
| 22. | NE U.S. | 1944 | 3* | 947 | 27.97 |
| 23. | SC/NC | 1906 | 3 | 947 | 27.97 |
| 24. | BETSY (SE FL/SE LA) | 1965 | 3 | 948 | 27.99 |
| 25. | SE FL/NW FL | 1929 | 3 | 948 | 27.99 |
| 26. | SE FL | 1933 | 3 | 948 | 27.99 |
| 27. | S TX | 1916 | 3 | 948 | 27.99 |
| 28. | MS/AL | 1916 | 3 | 948 | 27.99 |
| 29. | DIANA (NC) | 1984 | 3+ | 949 | 28.02 |
| 30. | S TX | 1933 | 3 | 949 | 28.02 |
| 31. | BEULAH (S TX) | 1967 | 3 | 950 | 28.05 |
| 32. | HILDA (Central LA) | 1964 | 3 | 950 | 28.05 |
| 33. | GRACIE (SC) | 1959 | 3 | 950 | 28.05 |
| 34. | TX (Central) | 1942 | 3 | 950 | 28.05 |
| 35. | SE FL | 1945 | 3 | 951 | 28.08 |

Continued on next page

*    Moving more than 30 miles per hour.
&    Winds and tides did not justify 4.
#    Classified 4 because of extreme tides.
@    Reached Cat. 5 intensity three times along its path through the Caribbean and Gulf of Mexico. The lowest pressure reported was 899 mb (26.55 in.) at 1742 UTC 8/7/80 off the northeastern tip of the Yucatan Peninsula.
+    Cape Fear, NC area only; was a 2 at final landfall.

## The <u>most intense</u> United States hurricanes this century (continued)
## (Intensity measured at time of landfall • Time span: 1900-1989)

| | HURRICANE | YEAR | CATEGORY | MILLIBARS | INCHES |
|---|---|---|---|---|---|
| 36. | FL (Tampa Bay) | 1921 | 3 | 952 | 28.11 |
| 37. | CARMEN (Central LA) | 1974 | 3 | 952 | 28.11 |
| 38. | EDNA (New England) | 1954 | 3* | 954 | 28.17 |
| 39. | SE FL | 1949 | 3 | 954 | 28.17 |
| 40. | ELOISE (NW FL) | 1975 | 3 | 955 | 28.20 |
| 41. | KING (SE FL) | 1950 | 3 | 955 | 28.20 |
| 42. | Central LA | 1926 | 3 | 955 | 28.20 |
| 43. | SW LA | 1918 | 3 | 955 | 28.20 |
| 44. | SW FL | 1910 | 3 | 955 | 28.20 |
| 45. | NC | 1933 | 3 | 957 | 28.26 |
| 46. | FL (Keys) | 1909 | 3 | 957 | 28.26 |
| 47. | EASY (NW FL) | 1950 | 3 | 958 | 28.29 |
| 48. | N TX | 1941 | 3 | 958 | 28.29 |
| 49. | NW FL | 1917 | 3 | 958 | 28.29 |
| 50. | N TX | 1909 | 3 | 958 | 28.29 |
| 51. | MS/AL | 1906 | 3 | 958 | 28.29 |
| 52. | ELENA (MS/AL/NW FL) | 1985 | 3 | 959 | 28.32 |
| 53. | CAROL (NE U.S.) | 1954 | 3* | 960 | 28.35 |
| 54. | IONE (NC) | 1955 | 3 | 960 | 28.35 |
| 55. | ALICIA (N TX) | 1983 | 3 | 962 | 28.41 |
| 56. | CONNIE (NC/VA) | 1955 | 3 | 962 | 28.41 |
| 57. | SW FL/NE FL | 1944 | 3 | 962 | 28.41 |
| 58. | Central LA | 1934 | 3 | 962 | 28.41 |
| 59. | SW FL/NE FL | 1948 | 3 | 963 | 28.44 |
| 60. | NW FL | 1936 | 3 | 964 | 28.47 |

* Moving more than 30 miles per hour.

### DIRECT HITS BY HURRICANES
### U.S. GULF & ATLANTIC COASTS
### 1900-1989

| | |
|---|---|
| Category 5: | 2 |
| 4: | 14 |
| 3: | 44 |
| 2: | 34 |
| 1: | 57 |
| TOTAL | 151 |

Major hurricanes (categories 3, 4, 5 )  :  60

This means that during the period 1900-1989, an average of 2 major
hurricanes every 3 years made landfall somewhere along the U.S.
Gulf or Atlantic coast. (All categories combined average about 5
hurricanes every 3 years for the same period.)

# Number of hurricanes (direct hits) affecting the U.S. and individual states, 1900-1989

(Measured on Saffir/Simpson scale. Updated from Hebert, Taylor, and Case, 1989)

| AREA | CATEGORY NUMBER | | | | | ALL | MAJOR HURRICANES (≥3) |
|---|---|---|---|---|---|---|---|
| | 1 | 2 | 3 | 4 | 5 | | |
| U.S. (Texas to Maine) | 57 | 34 | 44 | 14 | 2 | 151 | 60 |
| Texas | 12 | 9 | 9 | 6 | 0 | 36 | 15 |
| (North) | 7 | 3 | 3 | 4 | 0 | 17 | 7 |
| (Central) | 2 | 2 | 1 | 1 | 0 | 6 | 2 |
| (South) | 3 | 4 | 5 | 1 | 0 | 13 | 6 |
| Louisiana | 8 | 5 | 7 | 3 | 1 | 24 | 11 |
| Mississippi | 1 | 1 | 5 | 0 | 1 | 8 | 6 |
| Alabama | 4 | 1 | 5 | 0 | 0 | 10 | 5 |
| Florida | 17 | 15 | 16 | 5 | 1 | 54 | 22 |
| (Northwest) | 9 | 7 | 6 | 0 | 0 | 22 | 6 |
| (Northeast) | 1 | 7 | 0 | 0 | 0 | 8 | 0 |
| (Southwest) | 6 | 3 | 5 | 2 | 1 | 17 | 8 |
| (Southeast) | 4 | 10 | 7 | 3 | 0 | 24 | 10 |
| Georgia | 1 | 4 | 0 | 0 | 0 | 5 | 0 |
| South Carolina | 6 | 4 | 2 | 2 | 0 | 14 | 4 |
| North Carolina | 10 | 3 | 8 | 1* | 0 | 22 | 9 |
| Virginia | 2 | 1 | 1* | 0 | 0 | 4 | 1* |
| Maryland | 0 | 1* | 0 | 0 | 0 | 1* | 0 |
| Delaware | 0 | 0 | 0 | 0 | 0 | 0 | 0 |
| New Jersey | 1* | 0 | 0 | 0 | 0 | 1* | 0 |
| New York | 3 | 0 | 5* | 0 | 0 | 8 | 5* |
| Connecticut | 2 | 2* | 3* | 0 | 0 | 7 | 3* |
| Rhode Island | 0 | 1* | 3* | 0 | 0 | 4* | 3* |
| Massachusetts | 2 | 1* | 2* | 0 | 0 | 5 | 2* |
| New Hampshire | 1* | 1* | 0 | 0 | 0 | 2* | 0 |
| Maine | 5 | 0 | 0 | 0 | 0 | 5 | 0 |

* Indicates all hurricanes in this category were moving greater than 30 mph.

Note: State totals will not equal U.S. totals and Texas and Florida sectional totals will not necessarily equal state totals.

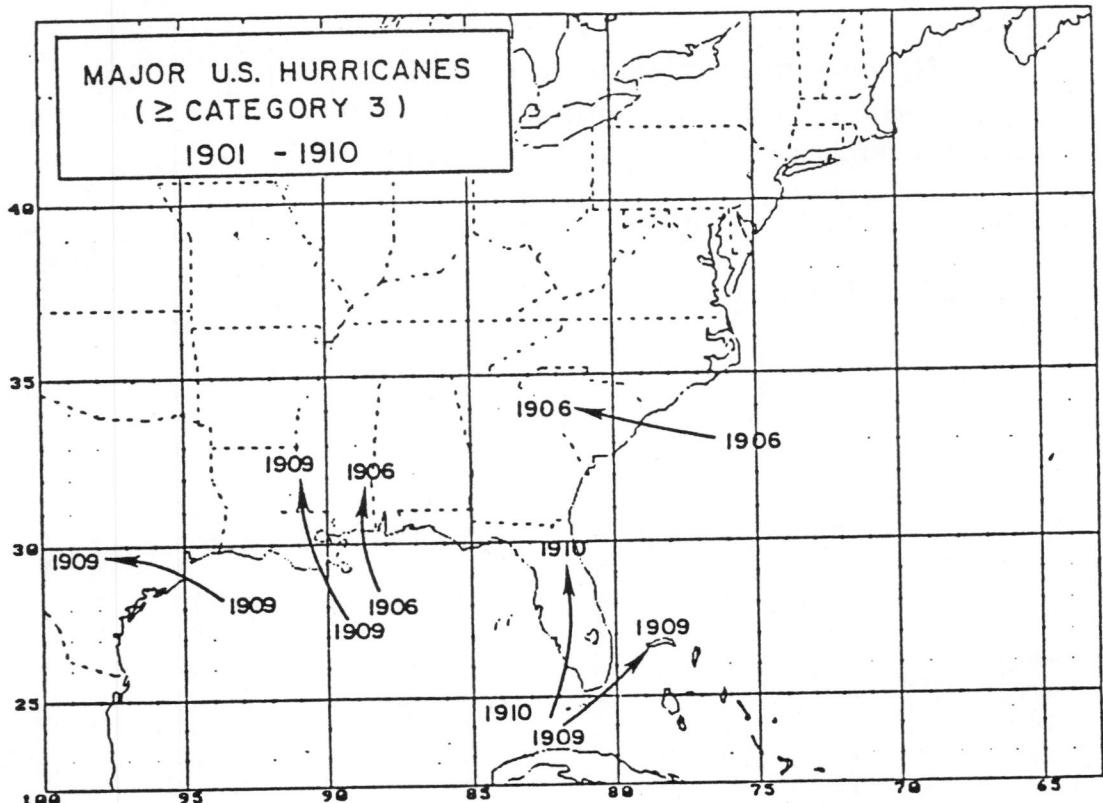

Figure 1. Major landfalling United States hurricanes (greater than or equal to a category 3) during the period 1901-1910.

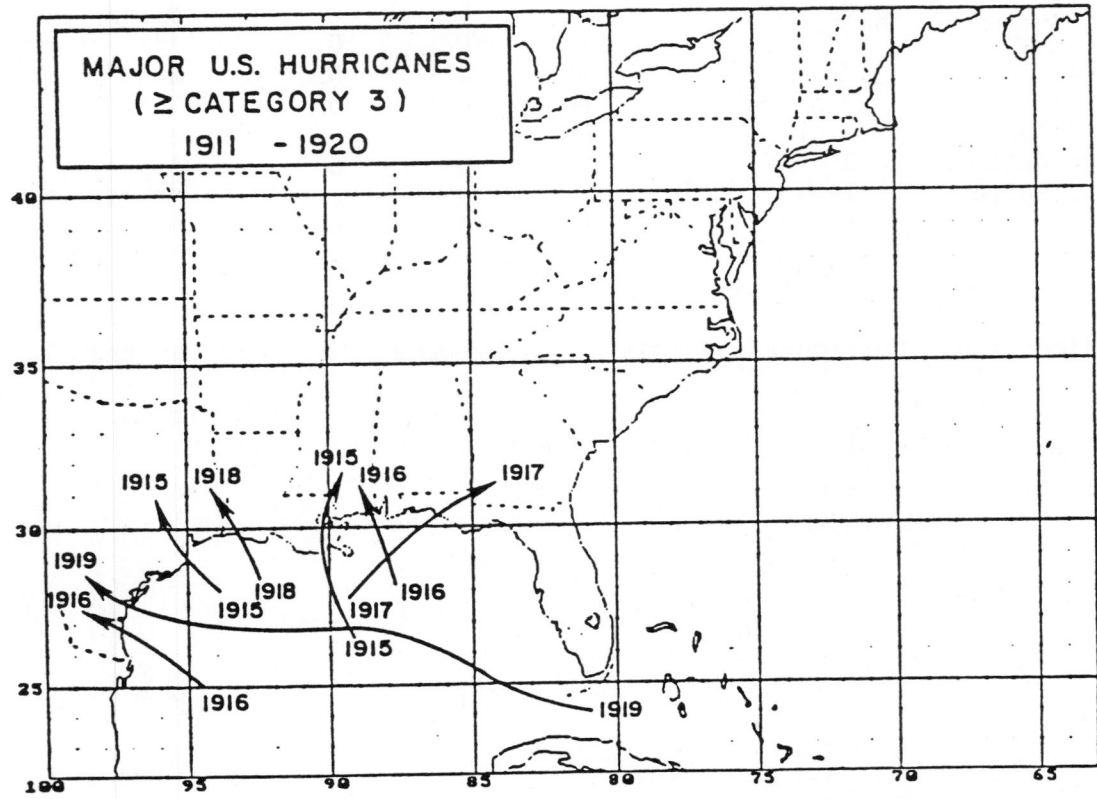

Figure 2. Major landfalling United States hurricanes (greater than or equal to a category 3) during the period 1911-1920.

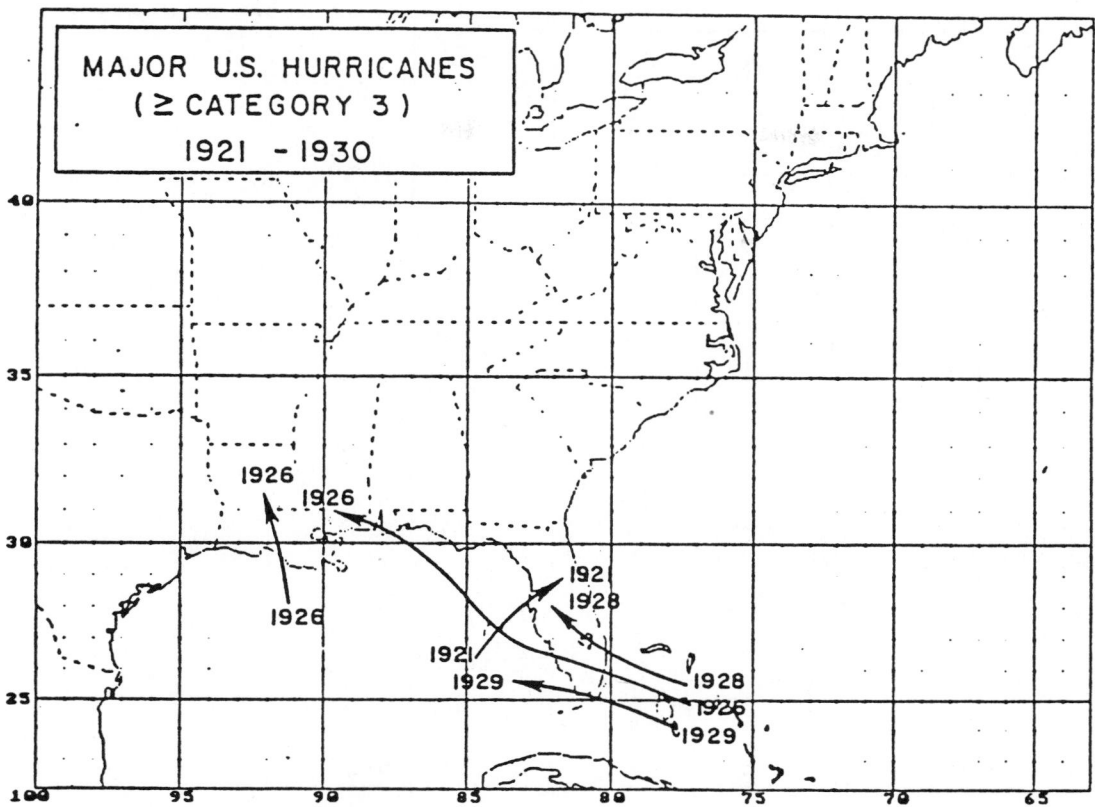

Figure 3. Major landfalling United States hurricanes (greater than or equal to a category 3) during the period 1921-1930.

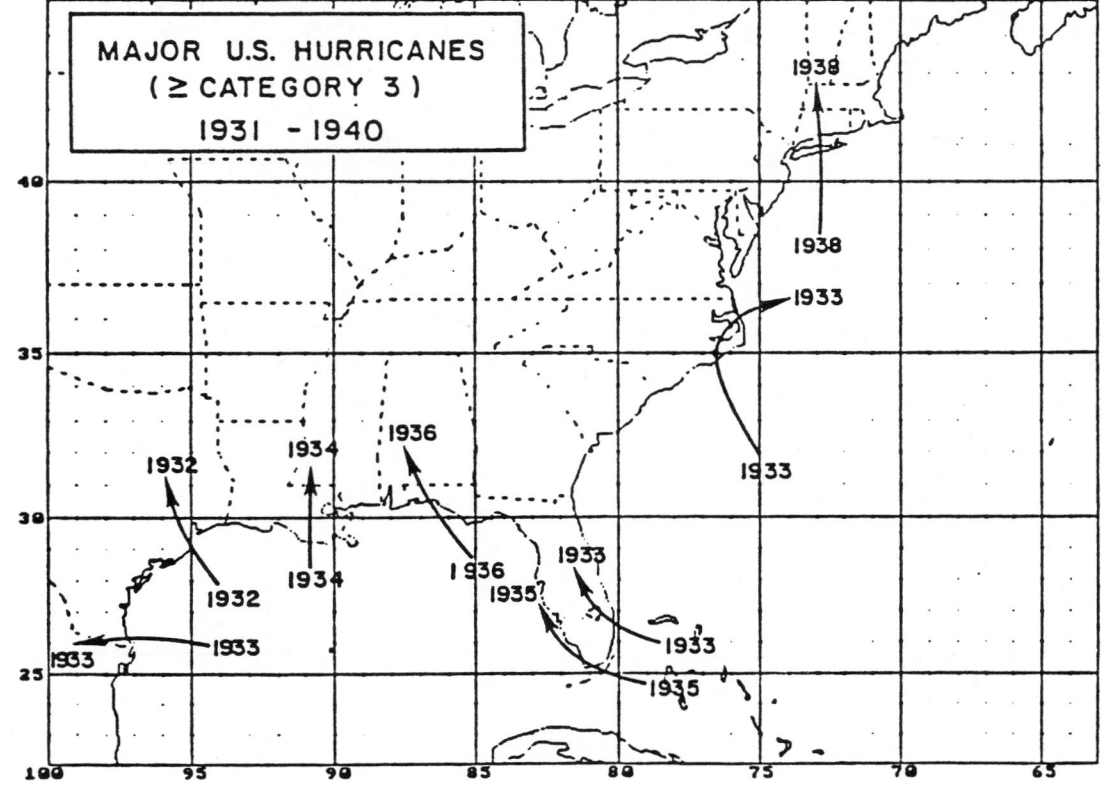

Figure 4. Major landfalling United States hurricanes (greater than or equal to a category 3) during the period 1931-1940.

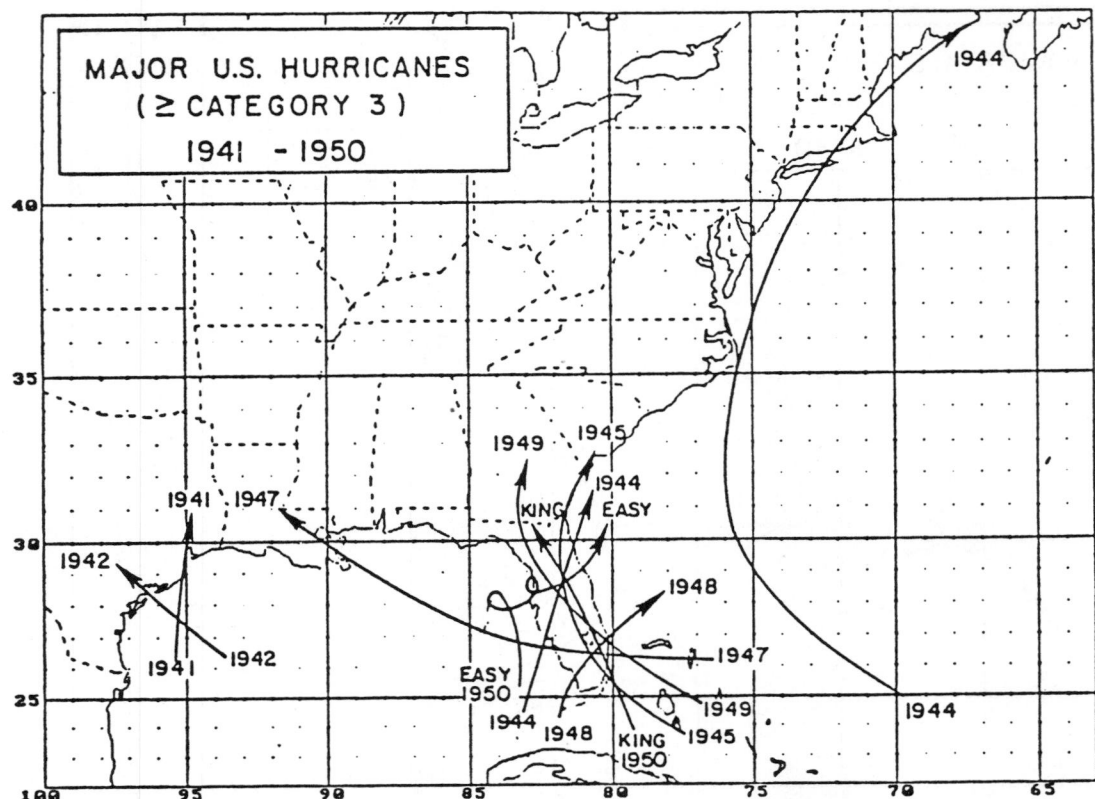

Figure 5. Major landfalling United States hurricanes (greater than or equal to a category 3) during the period 1941-1950.

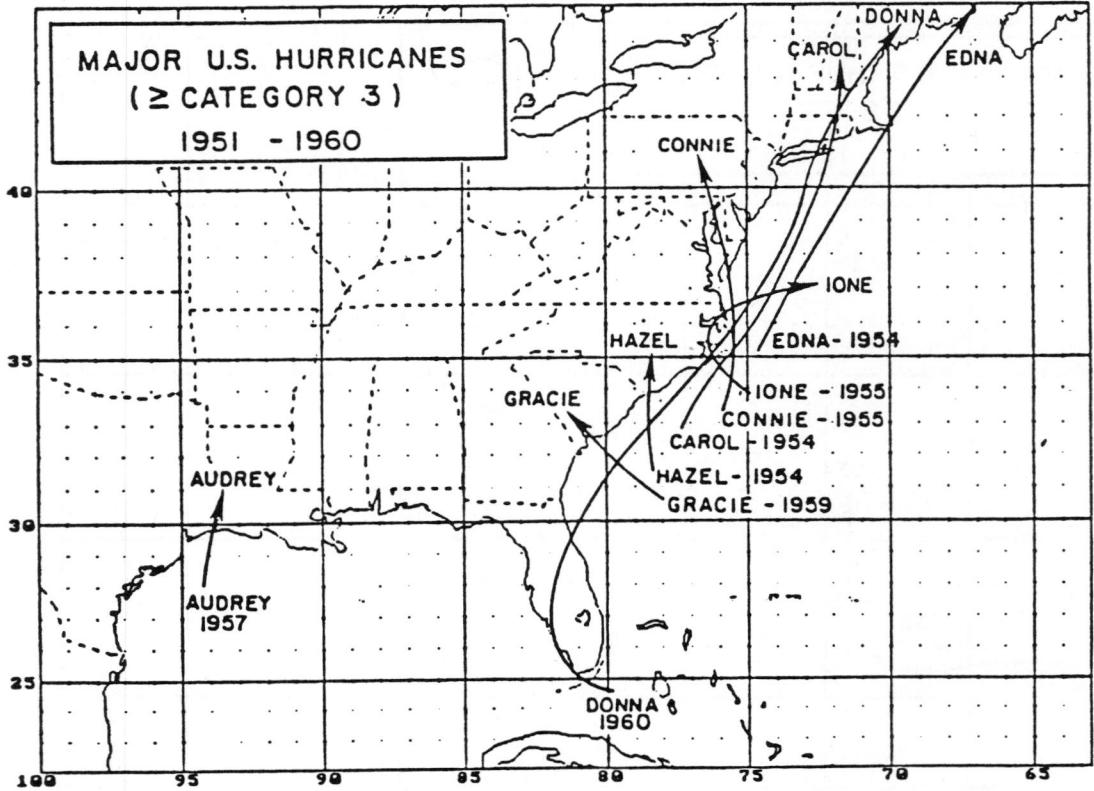

Figure 6. Major landfalling United States hurricanes (greater than or equal to a category 3) during the period 1951-1960.

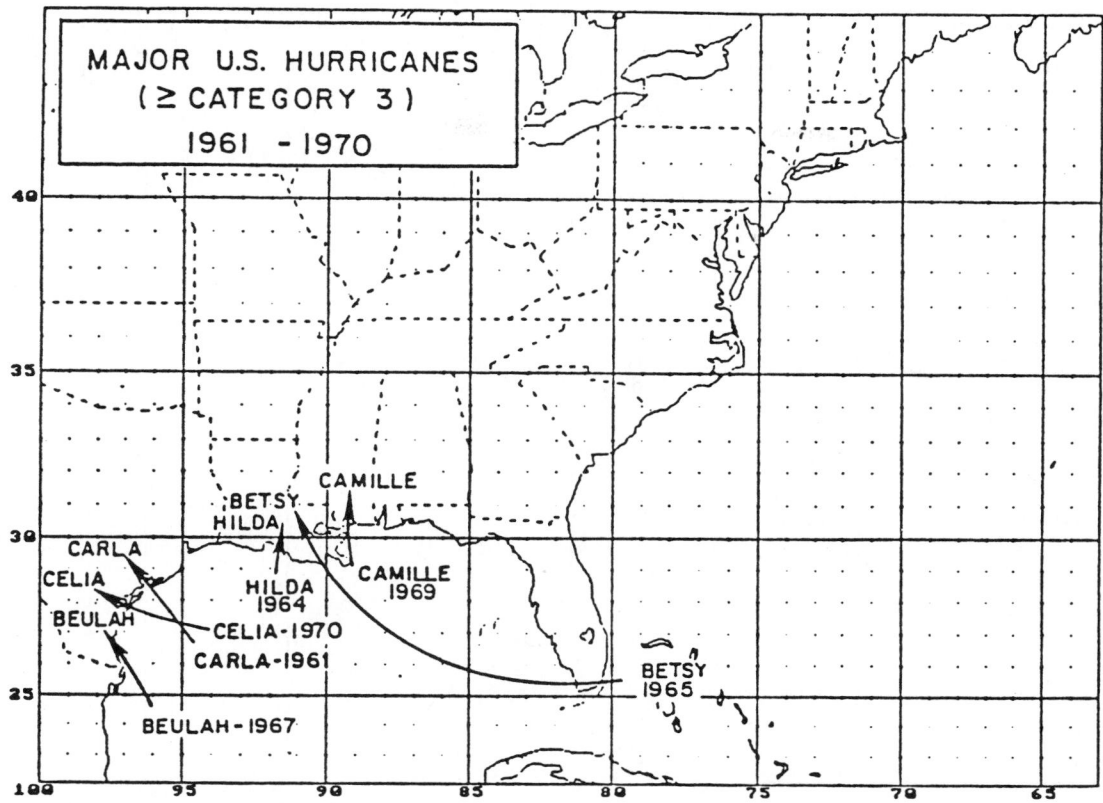

Figure 7. Major landfalling United States hurricanes (greater than or equal to a category 3) during the period 1961-1970.

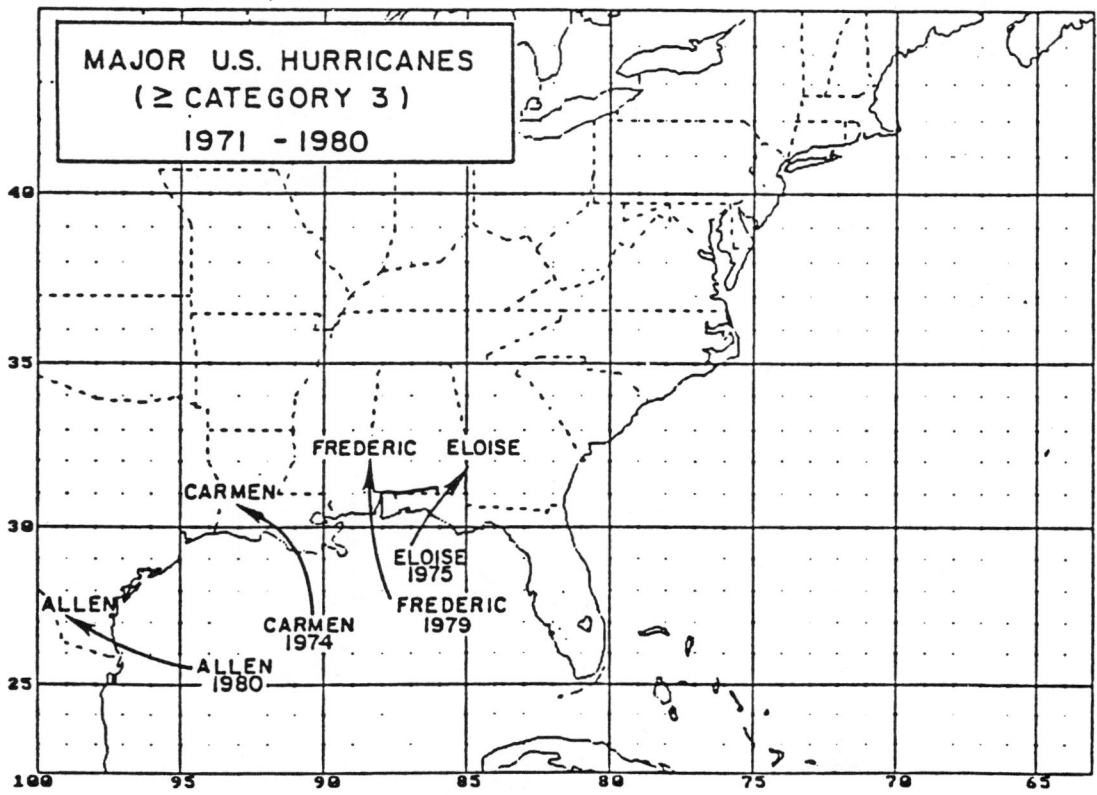

Figure 8. Major landfalling United States hurricanes (greater than or equal to a category 3) during the period 1971-1980.

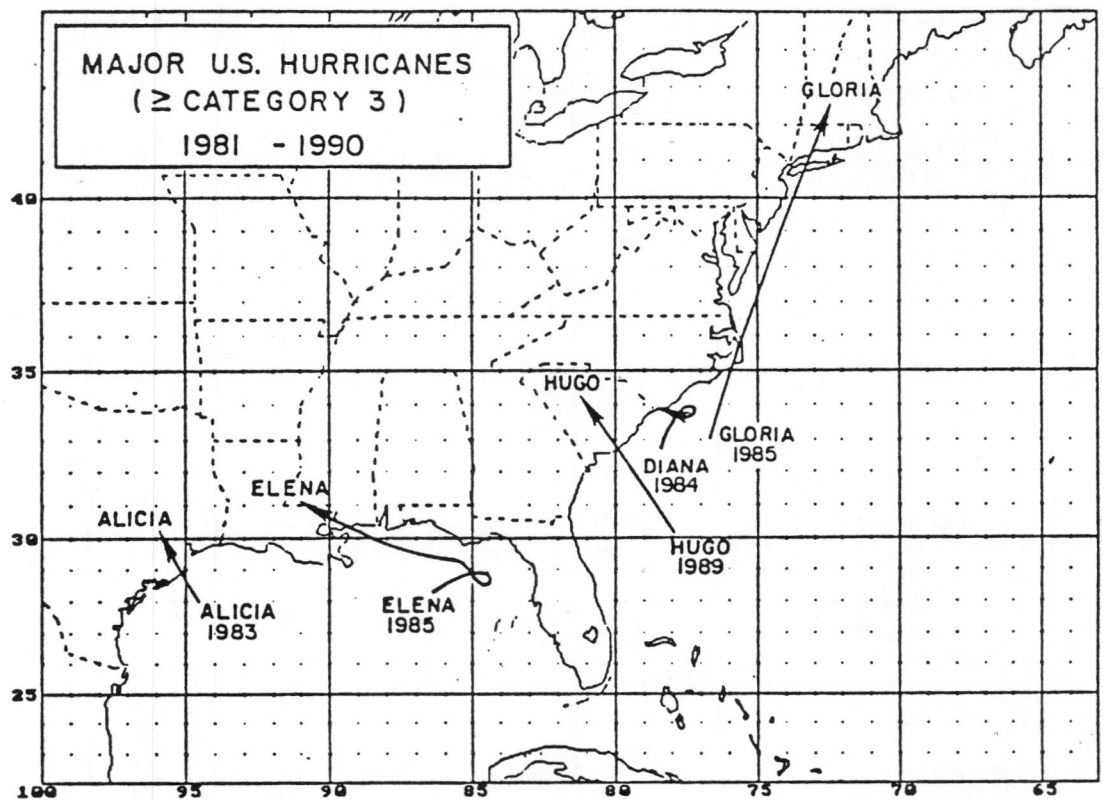

Figure 9. Major landfalling United States hurricanes (greater than or equal to a category 3) during the period 1981-1989.

# North Atlantic Tropical Cyclones

| | Tropical Storms and Hurricanes | | | | | | | | | | Hurricanes | | | | | | | | |
|---|---|---|---|---|---|---|---|---|---|---|---|---|---|---|---|---|---|---|---|
| | M | J | J | A | S | O | N | D | tot | Yr. | M | J | J | A | S | O | N | D | tot |
| | | 1 | 1 | 2 | 3 | 1 | 1 | | 9 | 1931 | | | | | 2 | | | | 2 |
| | 1 | | | 3 | 3 | 3 | 1 | | 11 | 1932 | | | | 3 | 1 | 1 | 1 | | 6 |
| | 1 | 1 | 3 | 7 | 5 | 3 | 1 | | 21 | 1933 | | 1 | 1 | 3 | 3 | 1 | | | 9 |
| | 1 | 1 | 1 | 2 | 2 | 3 | 1 | | 11 | 1934 | | 1 | 1 | 1 | 1 | 1 | 1 | | 6 |
| | | | | 3 | 1 | 2 | | | 6 | 1935 | | | | 2 | 1 | 2 | | | 5 |
| | | 3 | 2 | 6 | 4 | 1 | | | 16 | 1936 | | 1 | 1 | 3 | 2 | | | | 7 |
| | | | 1 | 2 | 6 | | | | 9 | 1937 | | | | | 3 | | | | 3 |
| | | | | 3 | 1 | 3 | 1 | | 8 | 1938 | | | | 2 | 1 | | | | 3 |
| | | 1 | | 1 | 1 | 2 | | | 5 | 1939 | | | | | 1 | 2 | | | 3 |
| | 1 | | | 3 | 2 | 2 | | | 8 | 1940 | | | | | 3 | 1 | | | 4 |
| | | | | 4 | 2 | | | | 6 | 1941 | | | | | 3 | 1 | | | 4 |
| | | | | 3 | 3 | 3 | 1 | | 10 | 1942 | | | | 3 | | | 1 | | 4 |
| | | | 1 | 2 | 4 | 3 | | | 10 | 1943 | | | 1 | 1 | 2 | 1 | | | 5 |
| | | | 3 | 2 | 4 | 2 | | | 11 | 1944 | | | 2 | 1 | 3 | 1 | | | 7 |
| | | 1 | 1 | 4 | 3 | 2 | | | 11 | 1945 | | 1 | | 1 | 1 | 2 | | | 5 |
| | | 1 | 1 | 1 | 1 | 2 | | | 6 | 1946 | | | 1 | | 1 | 1 | | | 3 |
| | | | 1 | 2 | 3 | 3 | | | 9 | 1947 | | | | 2 | 1 | 2 | | | 5 |
| | 1 | 1 | | 2 | 3 | 1 | 1 | | 9 | 1948 | | | | 1 | 3 | 1 | 1 | | 6 |
| | | | | 3 | 7 | 2 | 1 | | 13 | 1949 | | | | 2 | 4 | 1 | | | 7 |
| | | | | 4 | 3 | 6 | | | 13 | 1950 | | | | 4 | 3 | 4 | | | 11 |
| | 1 | | | 3 | 4 | 2 | | | 10 | 1951 | 1 | | | 2 | 3 | 2 | | | 8 |
| Feb 1 | | | | 2 | 2 | 2 | | | 7 | 1952 | | | | 2 | 2 | 2 | | | 6 |
| | 1 | | | 3 | 4 | 4 | 1 | 1 | 14 | 1953 | | | | 2 | 3 | 1 | | | 6 |
| | | 1 | 1 | 2 | 4 | 1 | 1 | 1 | 11 | 1954 | | 1 | | 2 | 3 | 1 | | 1 | 6 |
| | | | 1 | 4 | 5 | 2 | | | 12 | 1955 | | | | 3 | 5 | 1 | | | 9 |
| | | 1 | 1 | 1 | 4 | 1 | | | 8 | 1956 | | 1 | | 1 | 1 | 1 | | | 4 |
| | | 2 | | 1 | 4 | 1 | | | 8 | 1957 | | 1 | | | 2 | | | | 3 |
| | | 1 | | 4 | 4 | 1 | | | 10 | 1958 | | | | 3 | 3 | 1 | | | 7 |
| | 1 | 2 | 2 | 1 | 3 | 2 | | | 11 | 1959 | | 1 | 2 | 1 | 3 | | | | 7 |
| | | 1 | 2 | 1 | 3 | | | | 7 | 1960 | | | 1 | 1 | 2 | | | | 4 |
| | | | 1 | 6 | 2 | 2 | | | 11 | 1961 | | | 1 | | 5 | 1 | 1 | | 8 |
| | | | | 2 | 2 | 1 | | | 5 | 1962 | | | | 1 | 1 | 1 | | | 3 |
| | | | 1 | 1 | 5 | 2 | | | 9 | 1963 | | | 1 | 1 | 4 | 1 | | | 7 |
| | | 1 | 1 | 4 | 4 | 1 | 1 | | 12 | 1964 | | | | 2 | 3 | 1 | | | 6 |
| | | 1 | | 2 | 2 | 1 | | | 6 | 1965 | | | | 2 | 1 | 1 | | | 4 |
| | | 1 | 4 | 1 | 4 | | 1 | | 11 | 1966 | | 1 | 3 | 1 | 1 | | 1 | | 7 |
| | | | | 1 | 4 | 3 | | | 8 | 1967 | | | | 1 | 3 | 2 | | | 6 |
| | | 3 | | 1 | 3 | 1 | | | 8 | 1968 | | 2 | | 1 | 1 | 1 | | | 5 |
| | | | 1 | 5 | 6 | 5 | 1 | | 18 | 1969 | | | | 4 | 4 | 3 | 1 | | 12 |
| | 1 | | 1 | 3 | 3 | 2 | | | 10 | 1970 | 1 | | | 1 | 1 | 2 | | | 5 |
| | | | 1 | 4 | 6 | 1 | 1 | | 13 | 1971 | | | | 2 | 4 | | | | 6 |
| | 1 | 1 | | 2 | 2 | | 1 | | 7 | 1972 | | 1 | | 1 | 1 | | | | 3 |
| | | | 2 | 2 | 2 | 2 | | | 8 | 1973 | | | 1 | 1 | 1 | 1 | | | 4 |
| | | 1 | 1 | 4 | 4 | 1 | | | 11 | 1974 | | | | 2 | 2 | | | | 4 |
| | | 1 | 1 | 2 | 3 | 1 | | 1 | 9 | 1975 | | | 1 | 2 | 3 | | | | 6 |
| | 1 | | 1 | 5 | 2 | 1 | | | 10 | 1976 | | | | 4 | 1 | 1 | | | 6 |
| | | | | 1 | 3 | 2 | | | 6 | 1977 | | | | 1 | 3 | 1 | | | 5 |
| | | | 1 | 4 | 3 | 3 | | | 12 | 1978 | | | | 2 | 2 | 1 | | | 5 |
| Jan 1 | | 1 | 2 | 3 | 2 | 1 | | | 9 | 1979 | | | 1 | 2 | 2 | | | | 5 |
| | | | | 3 | 5 | 1 | 2 | | 11 | 1980 | | | | 3 | 3 | 1 | 2 | | 9 |
| | 1 | 1 | | 2 | 5 | 1 | 1 | | 11 | 1981 | | | | 1 | 5 | | 1 | | 7 |
| | | 1 | | 1 | 2 | 1 | | | 5 | 1982 | | 1 | | | 1 | | | | 2 |
| | | | | 2 | 2 | | | | 4 | 1983 | | | | 2 | 1 | | | | 3 |
| | | | | 4 | 6 | 1 | 1 | 1 | 13 | 1984 | | | | | 2 | 1 | 1 | 1 | 5 |
| | | | 2 | 3 | 3 | 2 | 1 | | 11 | 1985 | | | 1 | 3 | 1 | 1 | 1 | | 7 |
| | | 2 | | 1 | 2 | | 1 | | 6 | 1986 | | 1 | | 1 | 1 | | 1 | | 4 |
| | | | | 3 | 3 | 1 | | | 7 | 1987 | | | | 1 | 1 | 1 | | | 3 |
| J-1 F-1 | 12 | 31 | 43 | 143 | 194 | 99 | 23 | 4 | 551 | totals | 2 | 13 | 20 | 91 | 121 | 52 | 13 | 2 | 314 |

# Saffir / Simpson Hurricane Scale

ALL HURRICANES ARE DANGEROUS, BUT SOME ARE MORE SO THAN OTHERS. THE WAY STORM SURGE, WIND, AND OTHER FACTORS COMBINE DETERMINES THE HURRICANE'S DESTRUCTIVE POWER. TO MAKE COMPARISONS EASIER--AND TO MAKE THE PREDICTED HAZARDS OF APPROACHING HURRICANES CLEARER TO EMERGENCY FORCES--NOAA'S HURRICANE FORECASTERS USE A DISASTER-POTENTIAL SCALE, WHICH ASSIGNS STORMS TO FIVE CATEGORIES. CATEGORY 1 IS A MINIMUM HURRICANE; CATEGORY 5 IS THE WORST CASE. THE CRITERIA FOR EACH CATEGORY ARE SHOWN BELOW.

THIS CAN BE USED TO GIVE AN ESTIMATE OF THE POTENTIAL PROPERTY DAMAGE AND FLOODING EXPECTED ALONG THE COAST WITH A HURRICANE.

| CATEGORY | DEFINITION -- EFFECTS |
|---|---|
| ONE | WINDS 74-95 MPH OR STORM SURGE 4-5 FEET ABOVE NORMAL.* NO REAL DAMAGE TO BUILDING STRUCTURES. DAMAGE PRIMARILY TO UNANCHORED MOBILE HOMES, SHRUBBERY AND TREES. ALSO, SOME COASTAL ROAD FLOODING AND MINOR PIER DAMAGE. |
| TWO | WINDS 96-110 MPH OR STORM SURGE 6-8 FEET ABOVE NORMAL.* SOME ROOFING MATERIAL, DOOR AND WINDOW DAMAGE TO BUILDINGS. CONSIDERABLE DAMAGE TO VEGETATION, MOBILE HOMES AND PIERS. COASTAL AND LOW-LYING ESCAPE ROUTES FLOOD 2-4 HOURS BEFORE ARRIVAL OF CENTER. SMALL CRAFT IN UNPROTECTED ANCHORAGES BREAK MOORINGS. |
| THREE | WINDS 111-130 MPH OR STORM SURGE 9-12 FEET ABOVE NORMAL. SOME STRUCTURAL DAMAGE TO SMALL RESIDENCES AND UTILITY BUILDINGS WITH A MINOR AMOUNT OF CURTAINWALL FAILURES. MOBILE HOMES ARE DESTROYED. FLOODING NEAR THE COAST DESTROYS SMALLER STRUCTURES WITH LARGER STRUCTURES DAMAGED BY FLOATING DEBRIS. TERRAIN CONTINUOUSLY LOWER THAN 5 FEET ASL MAY BE FLOODED INLAND AS FAR AS 6 MILES. |
| FOUR | WINDS 131-155 MPH OR STORM SURGE 13-18 FEET ABOVE NORMAL. MORE EXTENSIVE CURTAINWALL FAILURES WITH SOME COMPLETE ROOF STRUCTURE FAILURE ON SMALL RESIDENCES. MAJOR EROSION OF BEACH AREAS. MAJOR DAMAGE TO LOWER FLOORS OF STRUCTURES NEAR THE SHORE. TERRAIN CONTINUOUSLY LOWER THAN 10 FEET ASL MAY BE FLOODED REQUIRING MASSIVE EVACUATION OF RESIDENTIAL AREAS INLAND AS FAR AS 6 MILES. |
| FIVE | WINDS GREATER THAN 155 MPH OR STORM SURGE GREATER THAN 18 FEET ABOVE NORMAL.* COMPLETE ROOF FAILURE ON MANY RESIDENCES AND INDUSTRIAL BUILDINGS. SOME COMPLETE BUILDING FAILURES WITH SMALL UTILITY BUILDINGS BLOWN OVER OR AWAY. MAJOR DAMAGE TO LOWER FLOORS OF ALL STRUCTURES LOCATED LESS THAN 15 FEET ASL AND WITHIN 500 YARDS OF THE SHORELINE. MASSIVE EVACUATION OF RESIDENTIAL AREAS ON LOW GROUND WITH 5-10 MILES OF THE SHORELINE MAY BE REQUIRED. |

*Actual storm surge values will vary considerably depending on coastal configurations and other factors.

# HURRICANE ACTION CHECKLIST

**Here is a list of the many things to consider before, during and after a hurricane. Some of the safety rules will make things easier for you during a hurricane. All are important and could save your life and the lives of others.**

## Should you stay or leave?

When a hurricane threatens your area, you will have to make a decision whether you should evacuate or whether you can ride out the storm in safety at your home.

**If local authorities recommend evacuation, you should leave!** Their advice is based on knowledge of the strength of the storm and its potential for death and destruction.

## In general :

- If you live on the coastline or offshore islands, **plan to leave.**
- If you live in a mobile home, **plan to leave.**
- If you live near a river or in a flood plain, **plan to leave.**
- If you live on high ground, away from coastal beaches, **consider staying.**

In any case, the ultimate decision to stay or leave will be yours. Study the following list and carefully consider the factors involved—especially the items pertaining to **storm surge** *(described on page 54).*

## At the beginning of the hurricane season (June) make plans for action

- Learn the storm surge history and elevation of your area
- Learn safe routes inland
- Learn location of official shelters
- Determine where to move your boat in an emergency
- Trim back dead wood from trees
- Check for loose rain gutters and down spouts
- If shutters do not protect windows stock boards to cover glass.

**(Continued on next page)**

**Safety Rules**

# HURRICANE ACTION CHECKLIST
**(Continued from previous page)**

## When a hurricane *watch* is issued for your area:

- Check often for official bulletins on radio, TV, or NOAA Weather Radio
- Fuel car
- Check mobile home tie-downs
- Moor small craft or move to safe shelter
- Stock up on canned provisions
- Check supplies of special medicines and drugs
- Check batteries for radio and flashlights
- Secure lawn furniture and other loose material outdoors
- Tape, board, or shutter windows to prevent shattering
- Wedge sliding glass doors to prevent their lifting from their tracks

## When a hurricane *warning* is issued for your area:

- Stayed turned to radio, TV, or NOAA Weather Radio for official bulletins
- Stay home if sturdy and on high ground
  —Board up garage and porch doors
  —Move valuables to upper floors
  —Bring in pets
  —Fill containers (bathtub) with several days supply of drinking water
  —Turn up refrigerator to maximum cold and don't open unless necessary
  —Use phone only for emergencies
  —Stay indoors on the downwind side of house away from windows
  —Beware of the eye of the hurricane
- Leave mobile homes
- Leave areas which might be affected by storm tide or stream flooding
  —Leave early—in daylight if possible
  —Shut off water and electricity at main stations
  —Take small valuables and papers but travel light
  —Leave food and water for pets (shelters will not take them)
  —Lock up house
  —Drive carefully to nearest designated shelter using recommended evacuation routes.

## After the all-clear is given:

- Drive carefully; watch for dangling electrical wires, undermined roads, flooded low spots
- Don't sight-see
- Report broken or damaged water, sewer, and electrical lines
- Use caution re-entering home
  —Check for gas leaks
  —Check food and water for spoilage

**Source: National Weather Service**

# TORNADOES

A tornado is a local storm of short duration formed of winds rotating at very high speeds, usually in a counter-clockwise direction. This storm is visible as a vortex, a whirlpool structure of winds rotating about a hollow cavity in which centrifugal forces produce a partial vacuum. As condensation occurs around the vortex, a pale cloud appears — the familiar and frightening tornado funnel. Air surrounding the funnel is also part of the tornado vortex; as the storm moves along the ground, this outer ring of rotating winds becomes dark with dust and debris, which may eventually darken the entire funnel.

These small, severe storms form several thousand feet above the earth's surface, usually during warm, humid, unsettled weather, and usually in conjunction with a severe thunderstorm. Sometimes a series of two or more tornadoes is associated with a parent thunderstorm. As the thunderstorm moves, tornadoes may form at intervals along its path, travel for a few miles, and dissipate. The forward speed of tornadoes has been observed to range from almost no motion to 70 miles per hour.

Funnels usually appear as an extension of the dark, heavy cumulonimbus clouds of thunderstorms, and stretch downward toward the ground. Some never reach the surface; others touch and rise again.

## Size, speed and duration

On the average, tornado paths are only a quarter of a mile wide and seldom more than 16 miles long. But there have been spectacular instances in which tornadoes have caused heavy destruction along paths more than a mile wide and 300 miles long. A tornado traveled 293 miles across Illinois and Indiana on May 26, 1917, and lasted 7 hours and 20 minutes. Its forward speed was 40 miles an hour, an average figure for tornadoes.

## Where do tornadoes occur?

Tornadoes occur in many parts of the world and in all 50 states. But no area is more favorable to their formation than the continental plains of North America, and no season is free of them. Normally, the number of tornadoes is at its lowest in the United States during December and January, and at its peak in May. The months of greatest total frequency are April, May, and June.

In February, when tornado frequency begins to increase, the center of maximum frequency lies over the central Gulf States. Then, during March, this center moves eastward to the southeast Atlantic states, where tornado frequency reaches a peak in April. During May, the center of maximum frequency moves to the southern plains states, and in June, northward to the northern plains and Great Lakes area as far east as western New York state. The reason for this drift is the increasing penetration of warm, moist air while contrasting cool, dry air still surges in from the north and northwest; tornadoes are generated with greatest frequency where these air masses wage their wars. Thus, when the Gulf states are substantially "occupied" by warm air systems after May, there is no cold air intrusion to speak of, and tornado frequency drops. This is the case across the nation after June. Winter cooling permits fewer and fewer encounters between warm and overriding cold systems, and tornado frequency returns to its lowest level by December.

The mathematical chance that a specific location will be struck by a tornado in any one year is quite small. For example, the probability of a tornado striking a given point in the area most frequently subject to tornadoes is 0.0363, or about once in 250 years. In the far western states, the probability is close to zero.

But tornadoes have provided many unmathematical exceptions. Oklahoma City has been struck by tornadoes 26 times since 1892. Baldwyn, Mississippi, was struck twice by tornadoes during a 25-minute period on March 16, 1942. A third of Irving, Kansas, was left in ruins by two tornadoes which occurred 45 minutes apart on May 30, 1879. Austin, Texas, had two tornadoes in rapid succession on May 4, 1922; and Codell, Kansas, was struck three times in 1916, 1917, and 1918—on May 20.

During the period 1953-1969, an average of 642 tornadoes per year occurred in the United States, about half of them during three months—April, May, and June. For the same period, the annual average number of tornado days—days on which one or more tornadoes were reported—was 159. Average annual frequency by states for this period ranges from 103 tornadoes in Texas to less than three in most of the northeastern and far western states.

Tornadoes may occur at any hour of the day or night, but, because of the meteorological combinations which create them, they form most readily during the warmest hours of the day. The greatest number of tornadoes—82 percent of the total—occurs between noon and midnight, and the greatest single concentration—23 percent of total tornado activity—falls between 4 and 6 p.m.

## Major tornadoes

The most death-dealing series of tornadoes on record occurred during the late afternoon on March 18, 1925, in portions of Missouri, Indiana, Illinois, Kentucky, and Tennessee. Eight separate and distinct tornadoes were observed. One of these killed 689 persons, injured 1,890 and caused more than 16 million dollars in property damage. The other seven tornadoes of the series increased the total loss of life to 740 and contributed significantly to the total casualty and property damage.

Another major series of tornadoes killed 268 people and injured 1,874 in Alabama on March 21, 1932. Property damage amounted to approximately 5 million dollars. More recently, in March, 1990, a series of four separate tornadoes occurred in central Kansas. Two of these tornadoes joined forces at one point and resulted in one of the three most intense to occur during the 1980s. This series cut a swath of over 100 miles in a two and one-half hour period.

## Trends

From 1916 through 1952, fewer than 300 tornadoes were reported in any one year. In 1953, when the U.S. Department of Commerce inititated its tornado forecasting effort, more than 437 tornadoes were observed and reported, beginning the first period of reliable statistical history. Since 1953, partly through improved equipment and techniques, partly through increasing public participation, essentially complete tornado records have been available.

In the United States, more tornadoes occurred in 1973 than any year from the beginning of firm records in 1916 through 1989. The year 1973 saw 1102 tornadoes strike in 46 states, kill 87 persons and cause property damage in the millions of dollars. A harsher year for tornado deaths, however, was 1953 when 515 people died from 421 recorded tornadoes.

*This sequence depicts the twelve minutes of a tornado in Ellswood, Kansas, which occurred from 7:20 p.m. to 7:32 on May 11, 1970. Winds surrounding a tornado's vortex are estimated at up to 300 miles per hour.*

The average tornado's life is usually measured in minutes, and its path is seldom more than 16 miles long. But one moved 293 miles, going on for seven hours and twenty minutes.

Over the ten-year period 1980-1989 an average of 820 tornadoes per year occurred in the U.S., resulting in approximately 62 deaths per year. The average for the forty-year period 1950-1989 was about 96 deaths per year. The overall decrease in tornado-related deaths can be attributed in part to improved early-warning systems.

## How a tornado is formed—

Tornado formation requires the presence of layers of air with contrasting characteristics of temperature, moisture, density, and wind flow. Complicated energy transformations produce the tornado vortex.

Many theories have been advanced as to the type of energy transformation necessary to generate a tornado, and none has won general acceptance. The two most frequently encountered visualize tornado generation as either the effect of thermally induced rotary circulations, or as the effect of converging rotary winds. Currently, scientists seem to agree that neither process generates tornadoes independently. It is more probable that tornadoes are produced by the combined effects of thermal and mechanical forces, with one or the other force being the stronger generating agent.

Numerous observations of lightning strokes and a variety of luminous features in and around tornado funnels have led scientists to speculate about the relationship between tornado formation and thunderstorm electrification. This hypothesis explores the alternative possibilities that atmospheric electricity accelerates rotary winds to tornado velocities, or that those high-speed rotary winds generate large electrical charges. Here, as in most attempts to understand complex atmospheric relationships, the reach of theory exceeds the grasp of proof.

## Tornado damage—

If there is some question as to the causes of tornadoes, there is none on the destructive effects of these violent storms. The dark funnel of a tornado can destroy solid buildings, make a deadly missile of a piece of straw, uproot large trees, and hurl people and animals for hundreds of yards. In 1931, a tornado in Minnesota carried an 83-ton railroad coach and its 117 passengers 80 feet through the air, and dropped them in a ditch.

Tornadoes do their destructive work through the combined action of their strong rotary winds and the partial vacuum in the center of the vortex. As a tornado passes over a building, the winds twist and rip at the outside at the same time that the abrupt pressure reduction in the tornado's "eye" causes explosive over-pressures inside the building. Walls collapse or topple outward, windows explode, and the debris of this destruction is driven through the air in a dangerous barrage. Heavy objects like machinery and railroad cars are lifted and carried by the wind for considerable distances.

Tornadoes do their destructive work through the combined action of their strong rotary winds and the impact of windborne debris. In the most simple case, the force of the tornado's winds push the windward wall of a building inward. The roof is lifted up and the other walls fall outward. Until recently, this damage pattern led to the incorrect belief that the structure had exploded as a result of the atmospheric pressure drop associated with the tornado. Mobile homes are particularly vulnerable to strong winds and windborne debris; they should be evacuated for more substantial shelter when tornado warnings are in effect.

## Tornado warnings—

Although it is not possible to predict exactly where and when severe thunderstorms and tornadoes will occur, it is possible to predict general areas where the probability of severe thunderstorm and tornado development is greatest by detecting the larger-scale events which are usually associated with such storms.

This important function is performed by the National Severe Storms Forecast Center in Kansas City, Missouri. The Kansas City facility is one of several environmental hazards centers of action operated by the National Weather Service (formerly the Weather Bureau), a major element of NOAA, the National Oceanic and Atmospheric Administration of the U.S. Department of Commerce.

Meteorologists at Kansas City monitor conditions in the North American atmosphere, using surface data from hundreds of points and radar summaries, satellite photographs, meteorological upper-air profile (obtained by sounding balloons), and reports from pilots. From these thousands of pieces of information, weathermen determine the area that is most likely to experience severe thunderstorms or tornadoes. Information on this area is then issued to National Weather Service offices and the public in the form of a **watch** bulletin.

A severe thunderstorm watch or tornado watch bulletin issued by the Center usually identifies an area about 140 miles wide by 240 miles long. Although the **watch** bulletin states approximately where and for how long the severe local storm threat will exist, it does not mean that severe local storms will not occur outside the **watch** area or time frame—the **watch** is only an indication of where and when the probabilities are highest.

**Watch** bulletins are transmitted to all National Weather Service offices. Designated offices prepare and issue a redefining statement which specifies the affected area in terms of counties, towns, and locally well-known geographic landmarks. These messages are disseminated to the public by all possible means, and are used to guide the activities of local government, law enforcement, and emergency agencies in preparing for severe weather.

**Watches** are not warnings. Until a severe thunderstorm or tornado warning is issued, persons in watch areas should maintain their normal routines, but watch for threatening weather and listen to the radio or television for further severe weather information.

A severe thunderstorm warning or tornado warning bulletin is issued by a local office of the National Weather Service when a severe thunderstorm or tornado has actually been sighted in the area or indicated by radar. **Warnings** describe the location of the severe thunderstorm or tornado at the time of detection, the area (usually the counties) that could be affected, and the time period (usually one hour) covered by the **warning.** The length of this area is equal to the distance the storm is expected to travel in one hour.

When a **warning** is received, persons close to the storm should take cover immediately, especially in the case of a tornado **warning.** Persons farther away from the storm should be prepared to take cover if threatening conditions are sighted.

Severe weather statements are prepared by local offices of the National Weather Service to keep the public fully informed of all current information, particularly when **watch** or **warning** bulletins are in effect. Statements are issued at least once each hour, and more frequently when the severe weather situation is changing rapidly. In this way, a close watch is kept on weather developments, and information is quickly disseminated to the counties for which the National Weather Service office has responsibility.

All-clear bulletins are issued whenever the threat of severe thunderstorms or tornadoes has ended in the area previously warned in a tornado or a severe thunderstorm **warning** bulletin. When a **warning** is cancelled, but a **watch** continues in effect for the same area or a **warning** is in effect for an adjacent area, a "Severe Weather Bulletin" is issued; this qualified message is also issued when a portion, but not all, of a **watch** area is cancelled. This permits a continuous alert in the path of the storm, with the alert being cancelled as the severe weather moves through the **watch** area.

# TORNADO-INTENSITY RATING SYSTEM

The intensity of tornadoes is defined according to the **Fujita Scale** (or F scale), which ranges from F0 to F6 as outlined below.

**F0**: 40 to 72 m.p.h. winds. Damage is light and might include damage to tree branches, chimneys and billboards. Shallow-rooted trees may be pushed over.

**F1**: 73 to 112 m.p.h. winds. Damage is moderate; mobile homes may be pushed off foundations and moving autos pushed off the road.

**F2**: 113 to 157 m.p.h. winds. Damage is considerable. Roofs can be torn off houses, mobile homes demolished, and large trees uprooted.

**F3**: 158-206 m.p.h. winds. Damage is severe. Even well constructed houses may be torn apart, trees uprooted, and cars lifted off the ground.

**F4**: 207-260 m.p.h. winds. Damage is devastating. Houses can be leveled and cars thrown; objects become deadly missiles.

**F5**: 261-318 m.p.h. winds. Damage is incredible. Structures are lifted off foundations and carried away; cars become missiles. Less than two percent of all tornadoes reach an intensity of this magnitude.

**F6**: The maximum tornado wind speeds are not expected to exceed 318 m.p.h

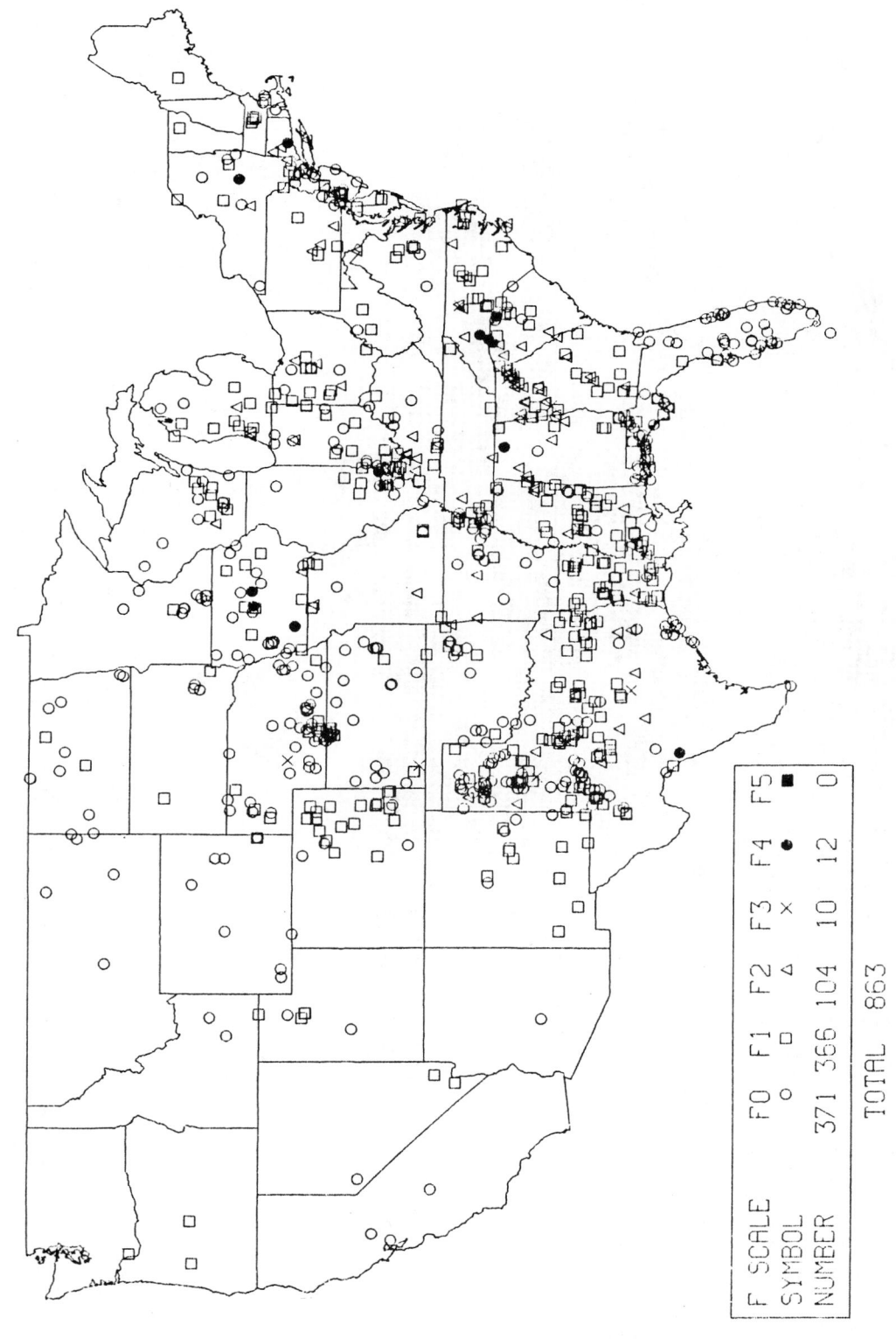

1989 CONFIRMED TORNADOES

| F SCALE | F0 | F1 | F2 | F3 | F4 | F5 |
|---------|----|----|----|----|----|----|
| SYMBOL | ○ | □ | △ | ✕ | ● | ■ |
| NUMBER | 371 | 366 | 104 | 10 | 12 | 0 |

TOTAL 863

*Tornado occurrence in the United States in 1989, with the intensity of each identified by the symbols in the box. By far the majority of tornadoes occur within the F0 and F1 ranges.*

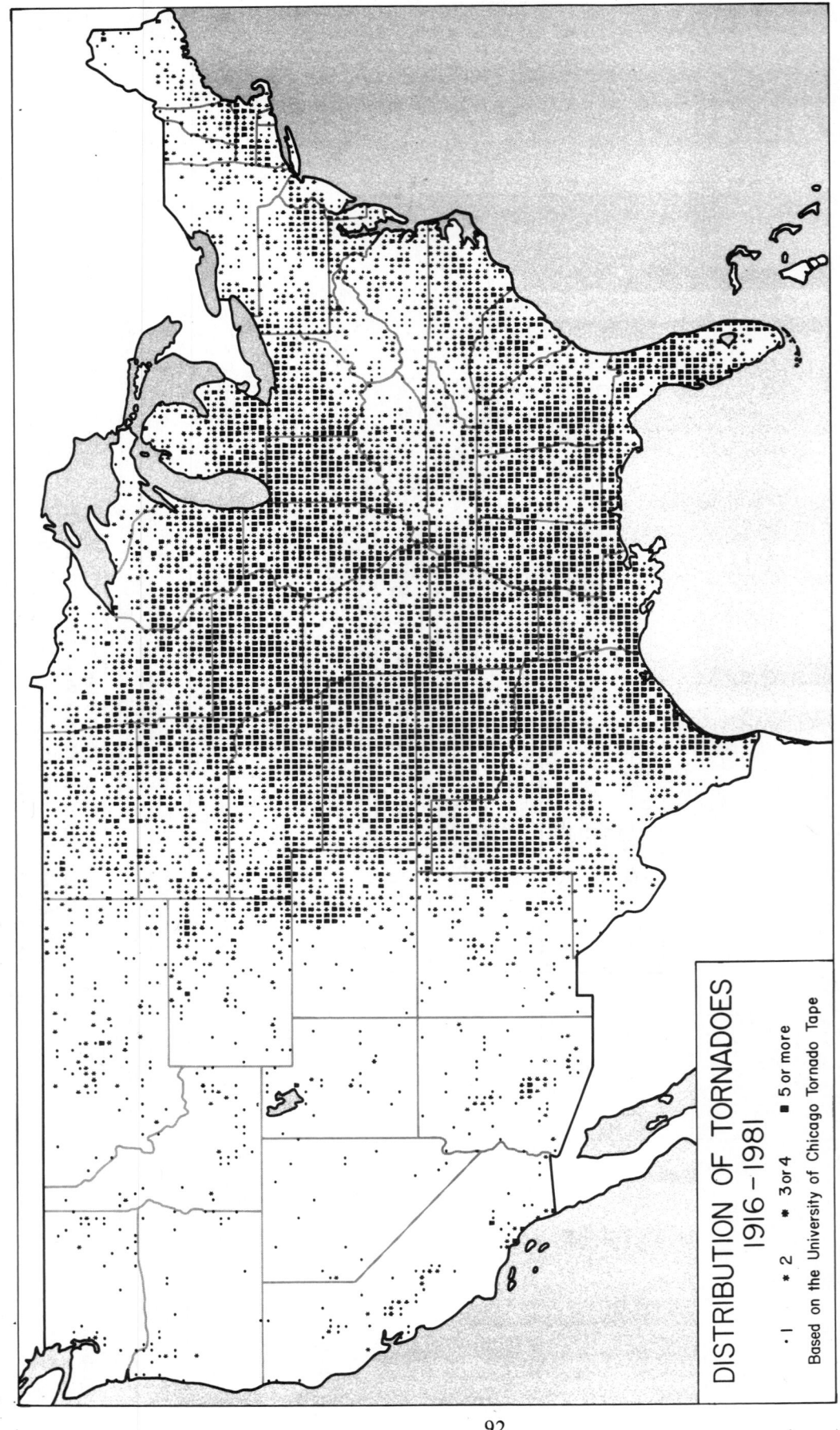

DISTRIBUTION OF TORNADOES
1916 – 1981

· 1   * 2   * 3 or 4   ■ 5 or more

Based on the University of Chicago Tornado Tape

This map includes 26,486 tornadoes between 1916 and 1981 archived in the University of Chicago Tornado Tape. In producing this map, the area of the contiguous United States was divided into 12,734 small subboxes of 15'x15' latitudes and longitudes. Then the number of tornado touchdowns in each subbox was counted by computer and printed on map coordinates. (Produced by T. Theodore Fujita, The University of Chicago.)

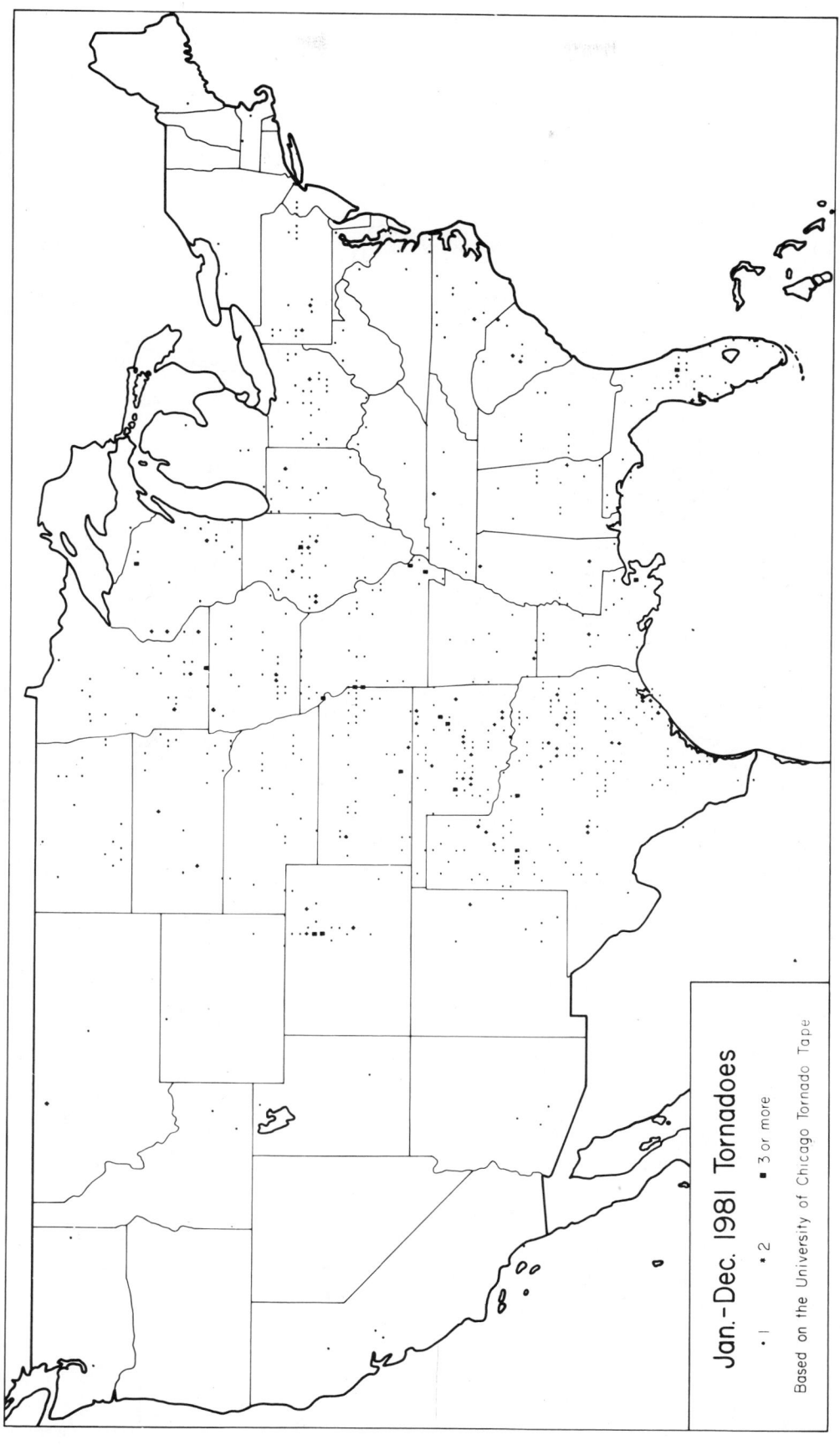

Jan.-Dec. 1981 Tornadoes

· 1    · 2    ■ 3 or more

Based on the University of Chicago Tornado Tape

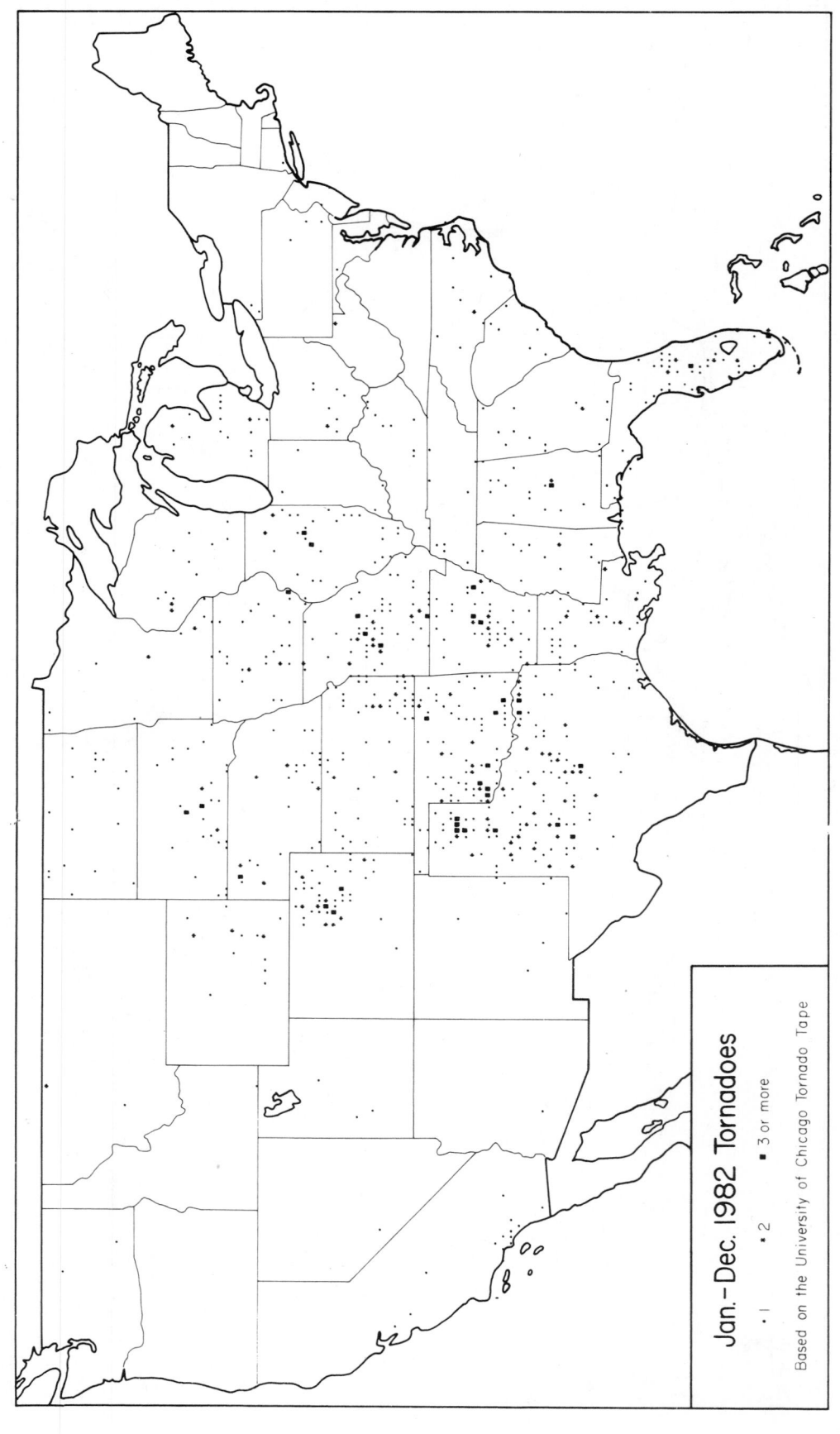

Jan.-Dec. 1982 Tornadoes

· 1    ■ 2    ■ 3 or more

Based on the University of Chicago Tornado Tape

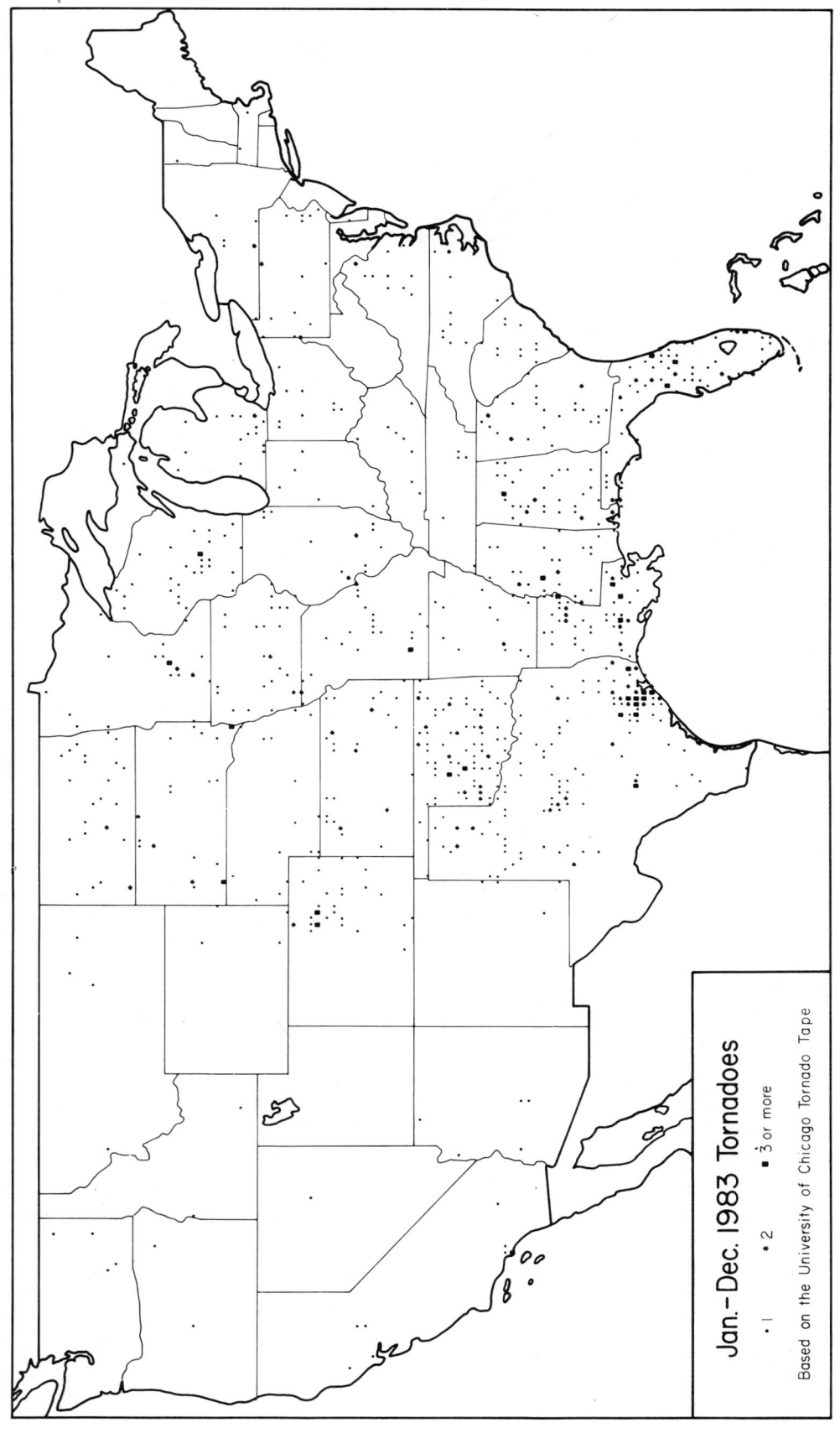

Jan.–Dec. 1983 Tornadoes

• 1    ■ 2    ■ 3 or more

Based on the University of Chicago Tornado Tape

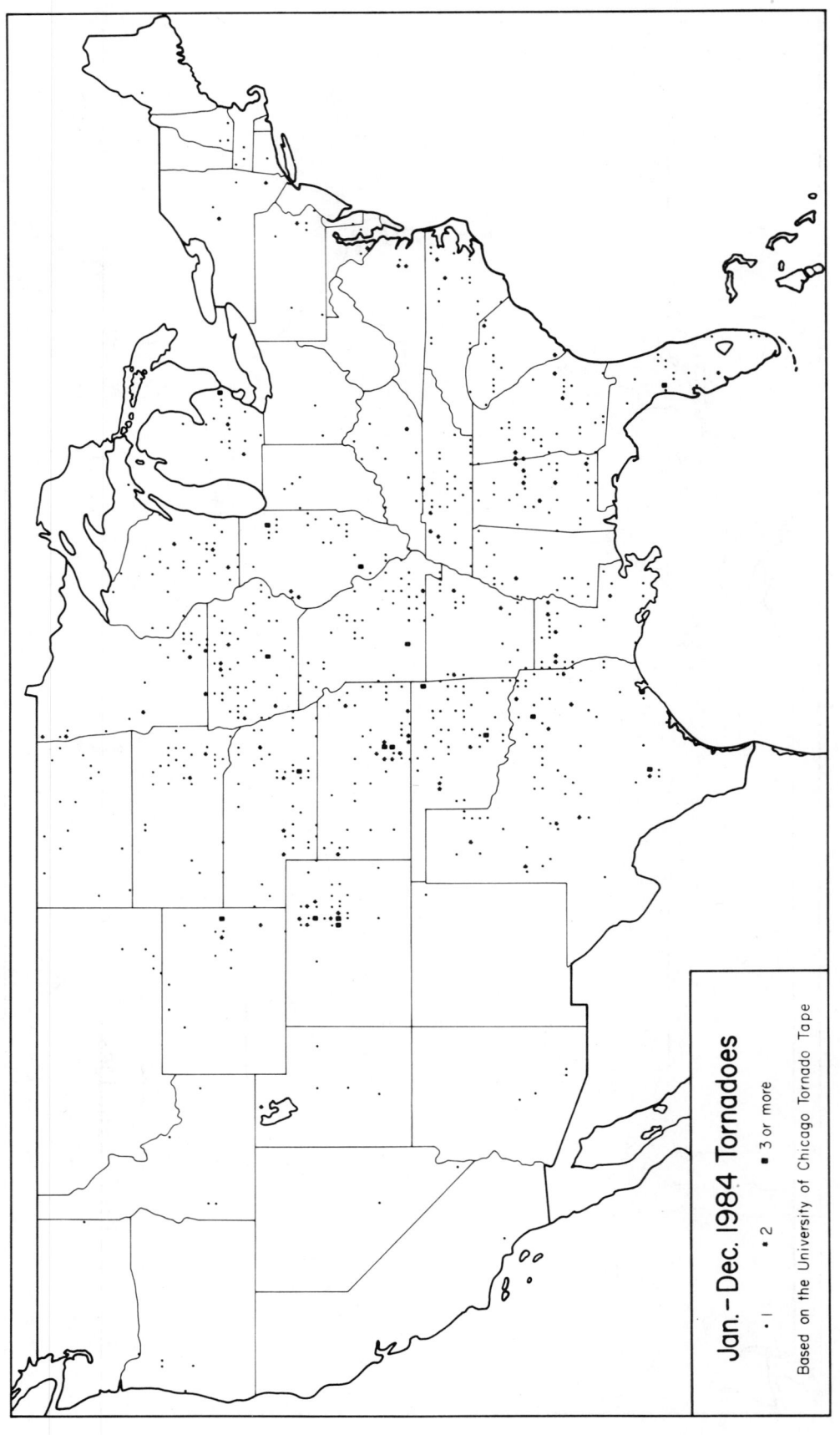

Jan.–Dec. 1984 Tornadoes

• 1
• 2
■ 3 or more

Based on the University of Chicago Tornado Tape

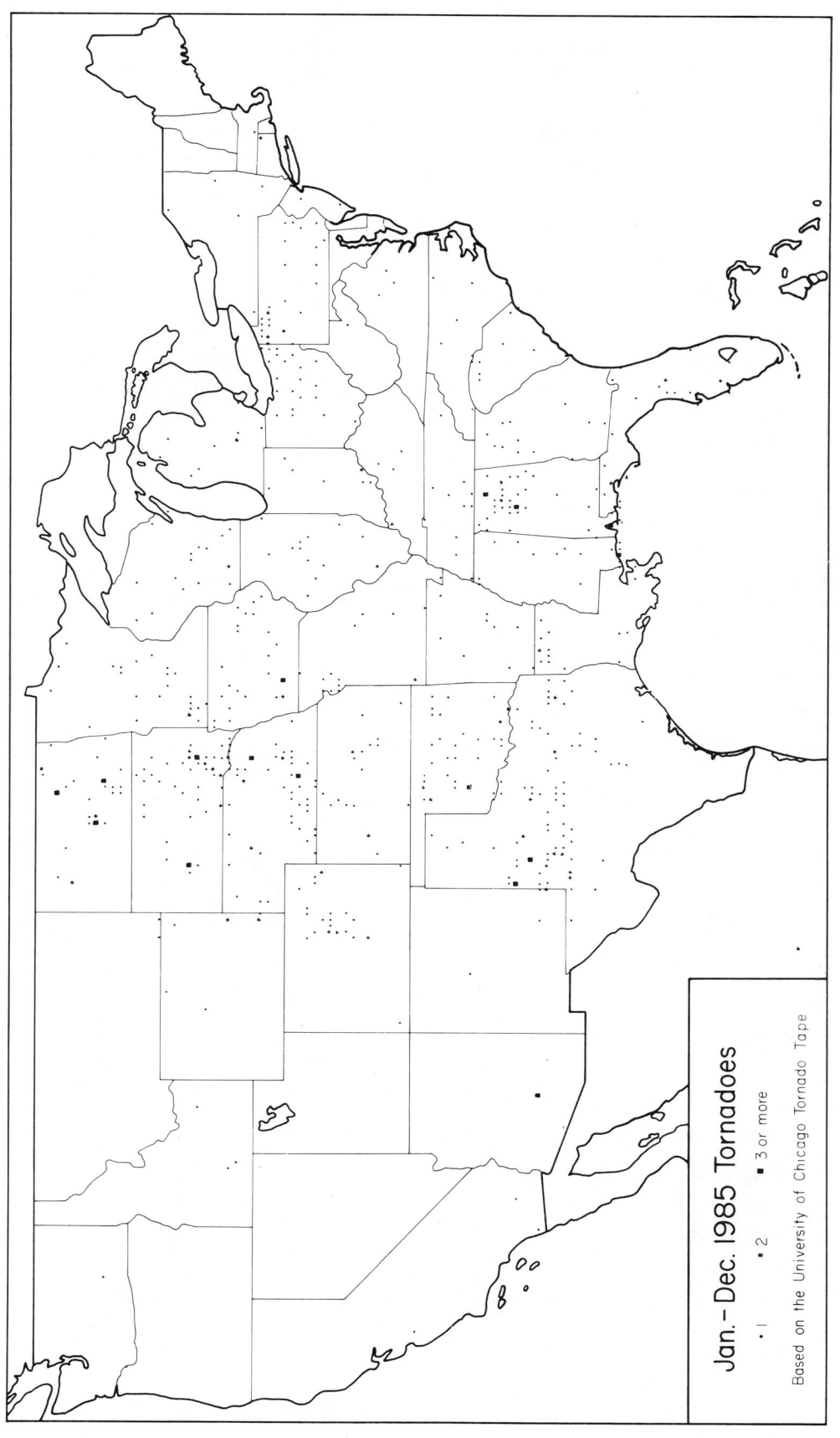

Jan.–Dec. 1985 Tornadoes

· 1    · 2    ■ 3 or more

Based on the University of Chicago Tornado Tape

# TORNADOES

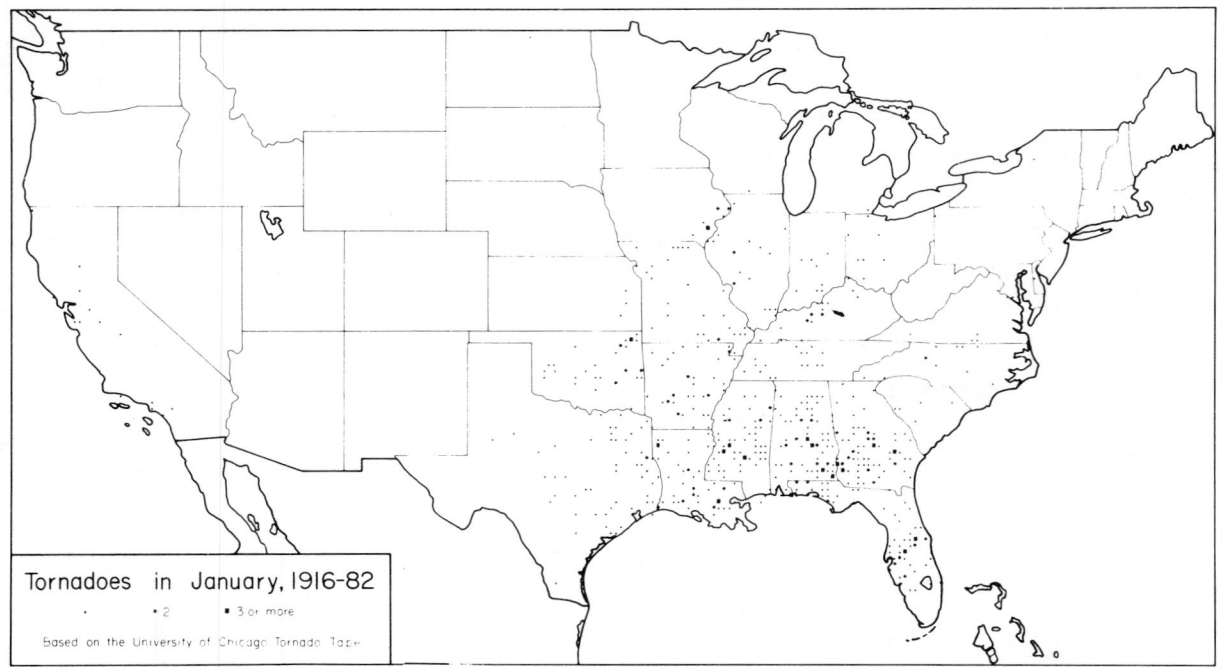

Tornadoes in January, 1916-82
· 1   · 2   ■ 3 or more
Based on the University of Chicago Tornado Tape

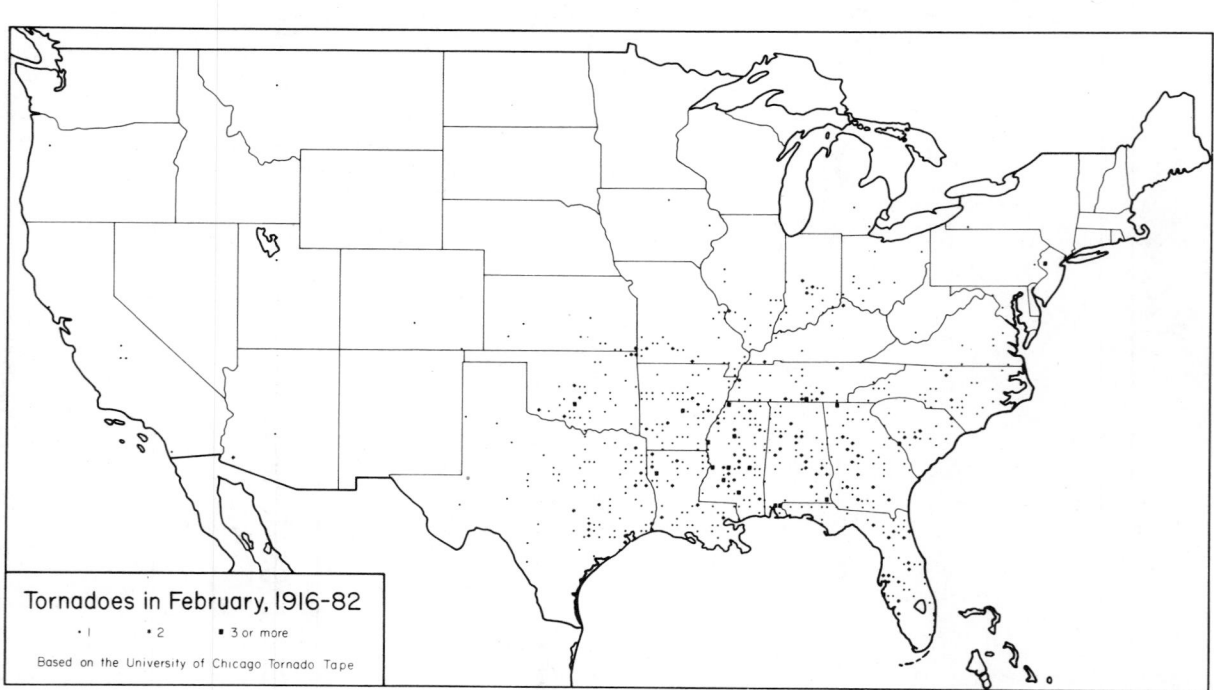

Tornadoes in February, 1916-82
· 1   · 2   ■ 3 or more
Based on the University of Chicago Tornado Tape

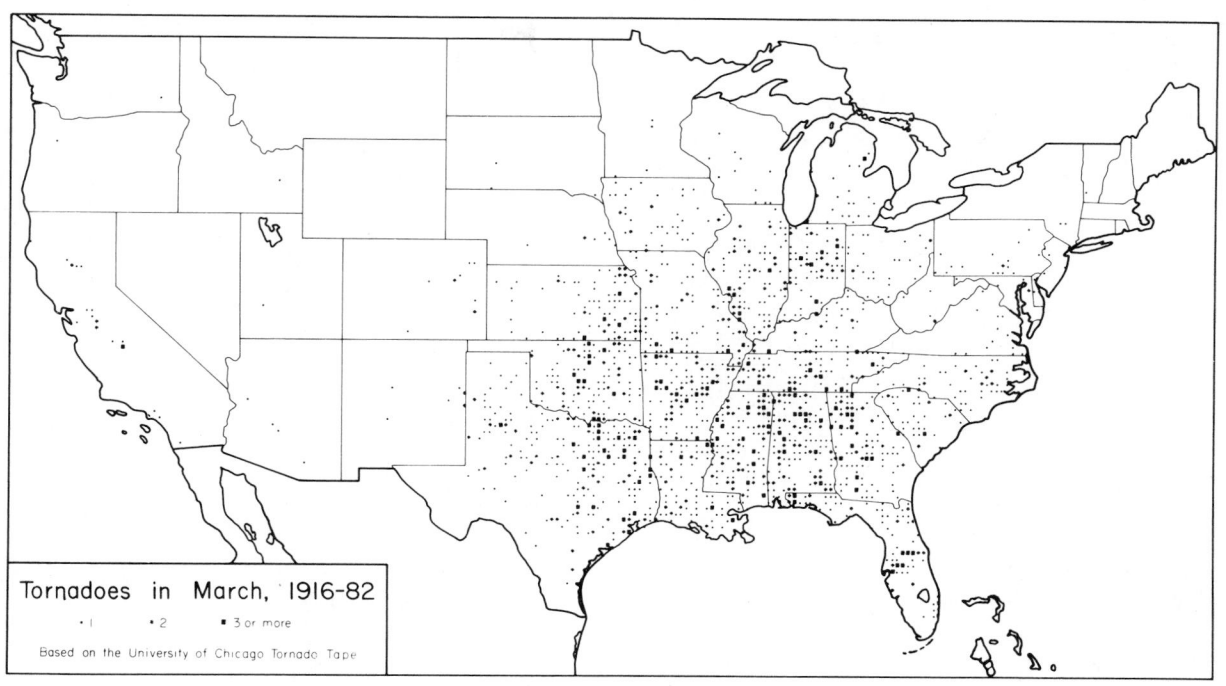

Tornadoes in March, 1916-82
• 1    • 2    ■ 3 or more
Based on the University of Chicago Tornado Tape

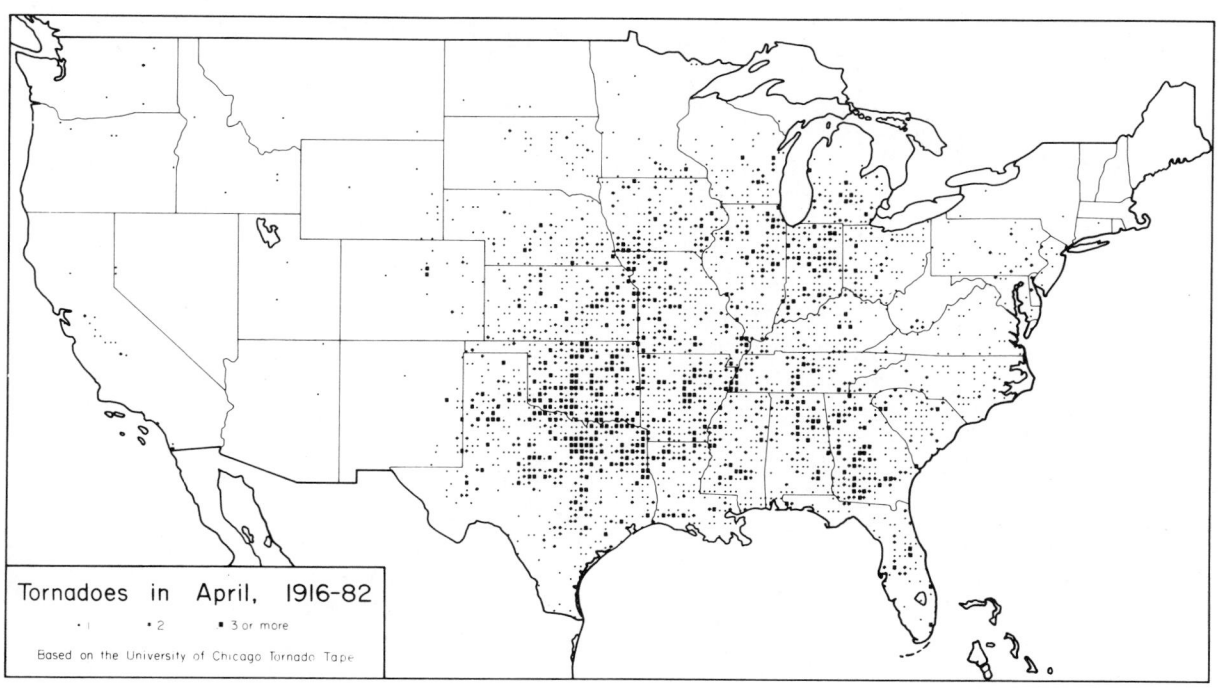

Tornadoes in April, 1916-82
• 1    • 2    ■ 3 or more
Based on the University of Chicago Tornado Tape

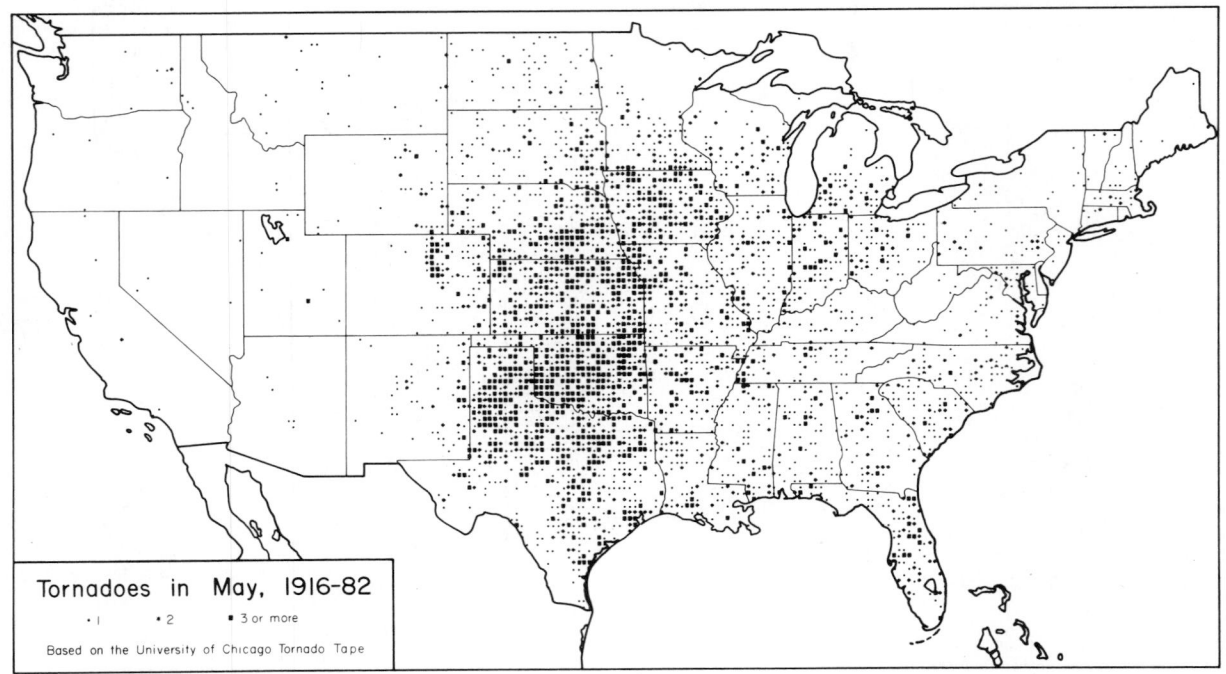

Tornadoes in May, 1916-82

· 1    · 2    ■ 3 or more

Based on the University of Chicago Tornado Tape

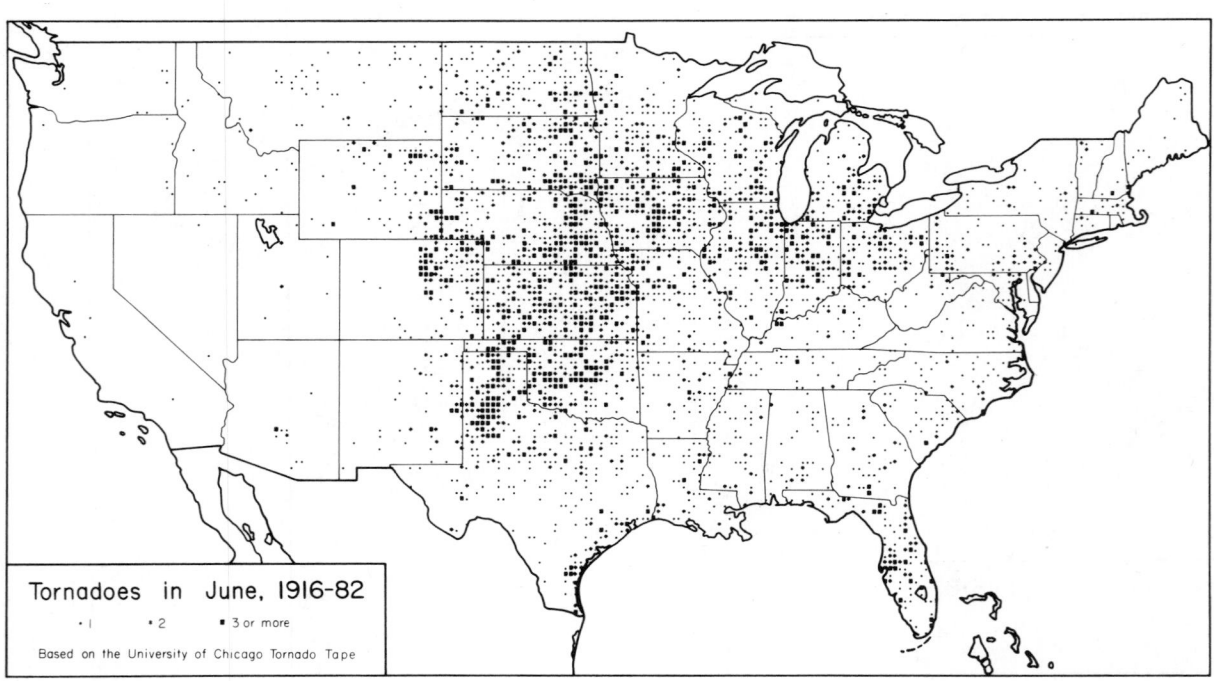

Tornadoes in June, 1916-82

· 1    · 2    ■ 3 or more

Based on the University of Chicago Tornado Tape

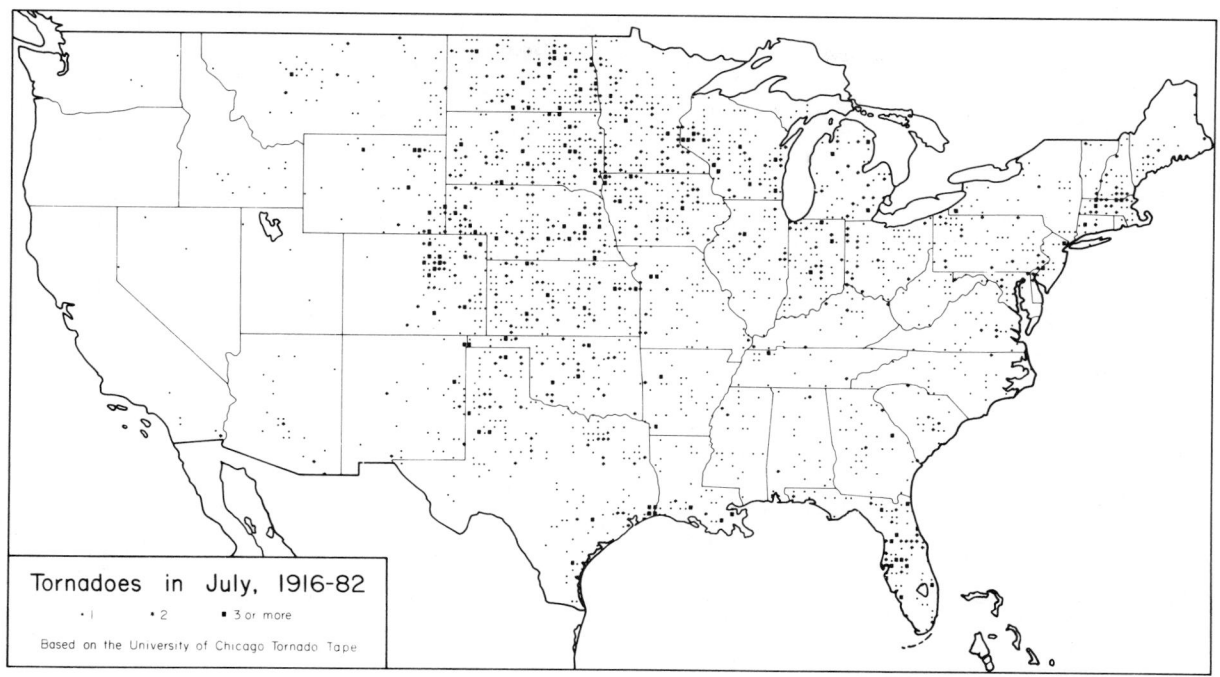

Tornadoes in July, 1916-82
· 1    · 2    ■ 3 or more
Based on the University of Chicago Tornado Tape

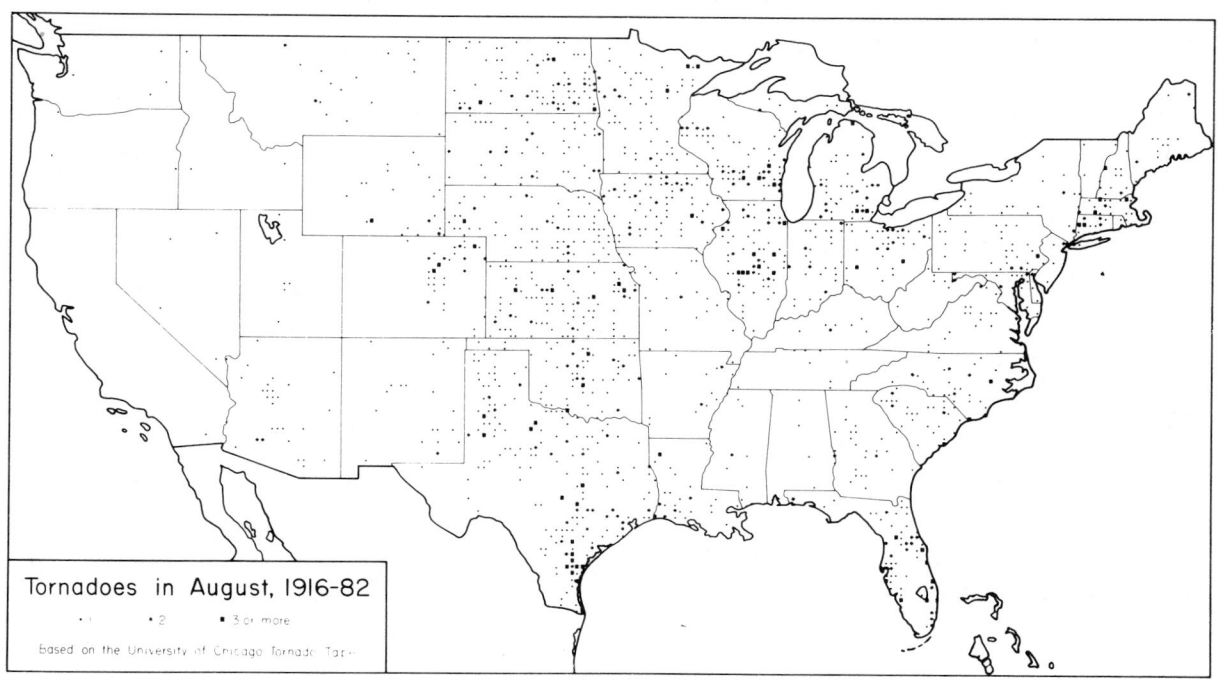

Tornadoes in August, 1916-82
· 1    · 2    ■ 3 or more
Based on the University of Chicago Tornado Tape

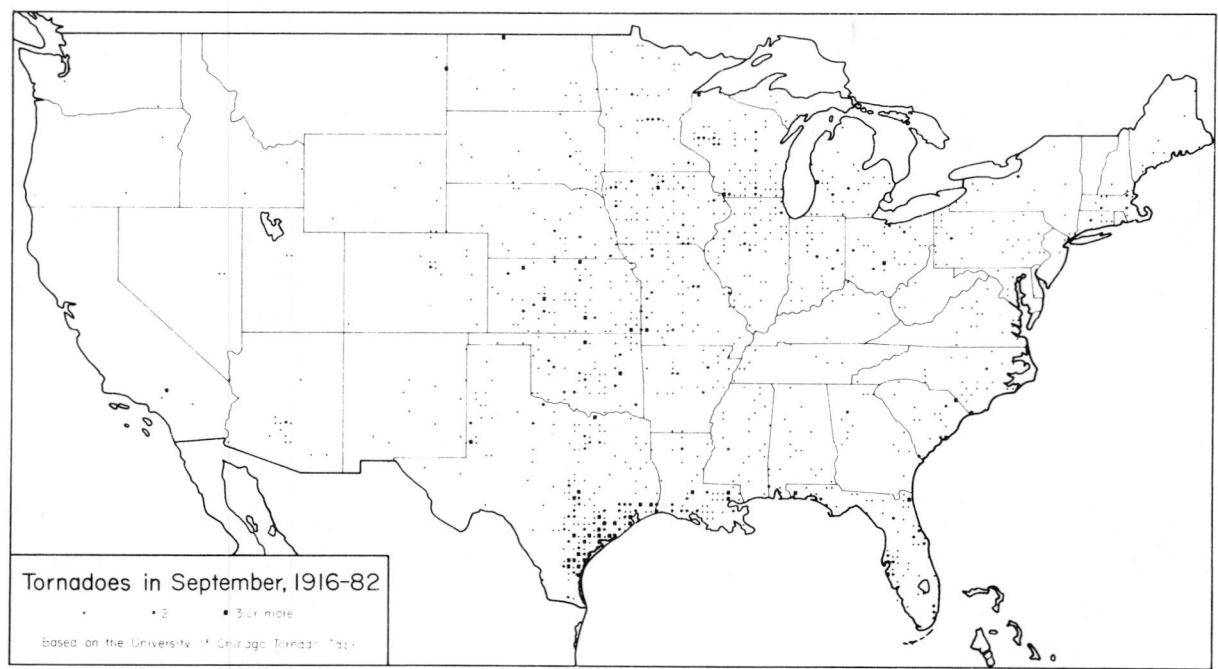

Tornadoes in September, 1916-82

• 1    • 2    ■ 3 or more

Based on the University of Chicago Tornado Tape

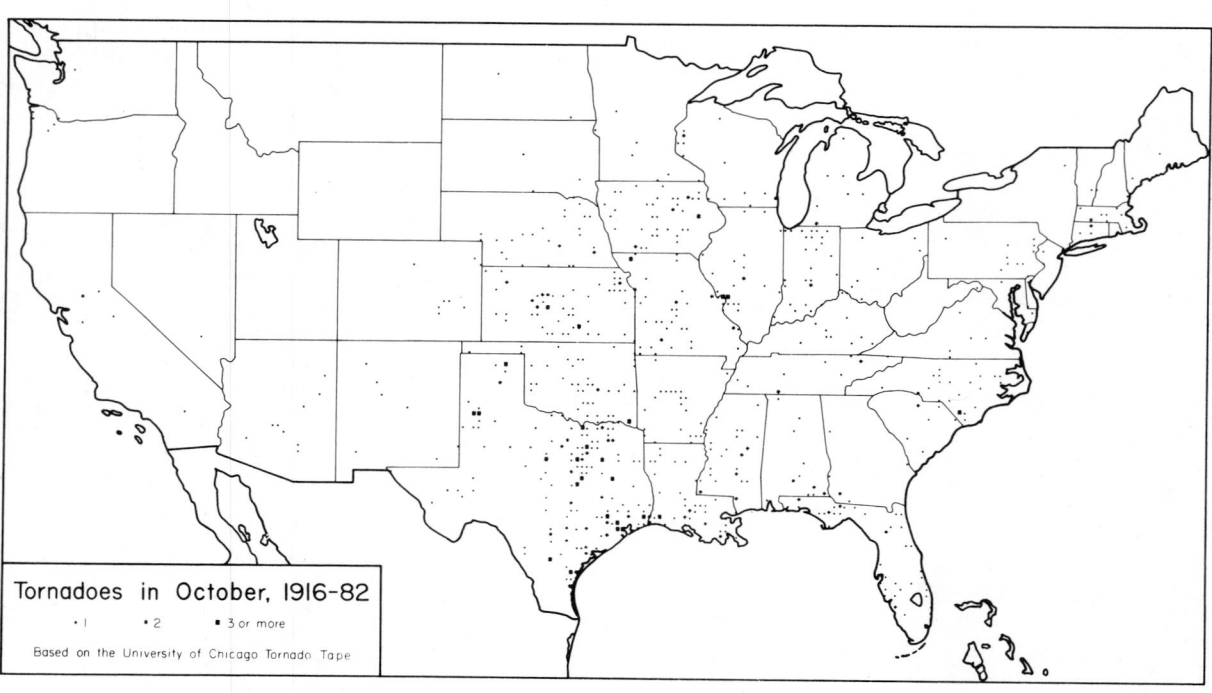

Tornadoes in October, 1916-82

• 1    • 2    ■ 3 or more

Based on the University of Chicago Tornado Tape

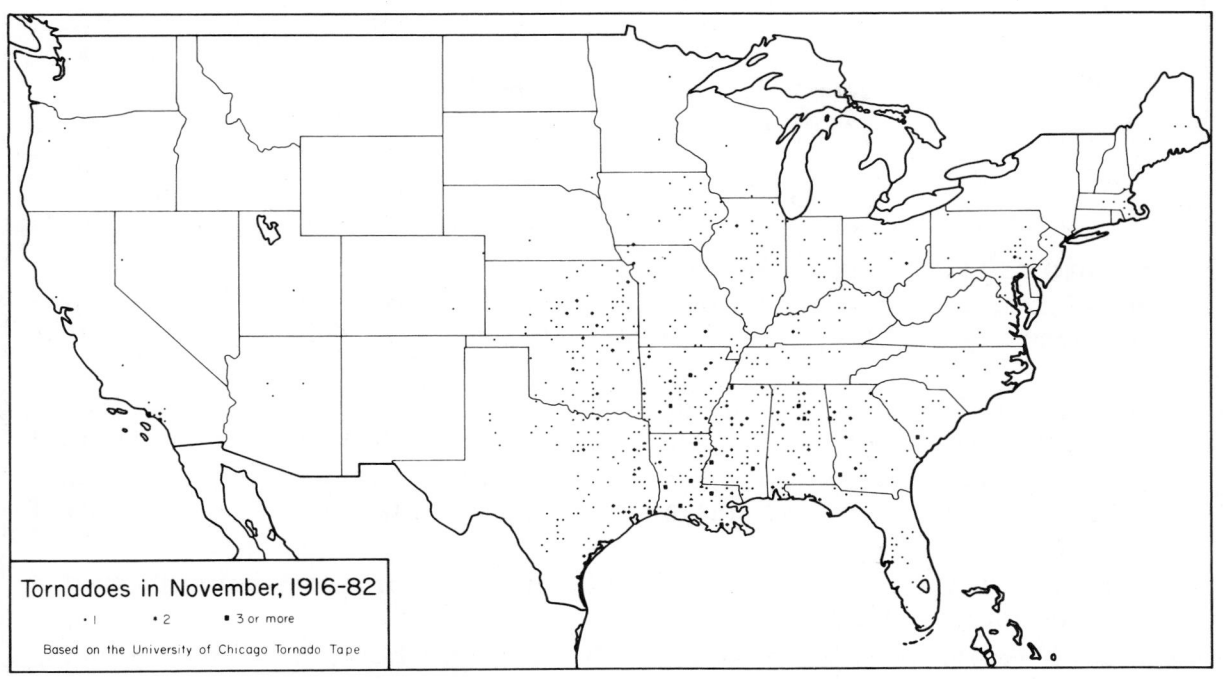

Tornadoes in November, 1916-82

• 1   • 2   ■ 3 or more

Based on the University of Chicago Tornado Tape

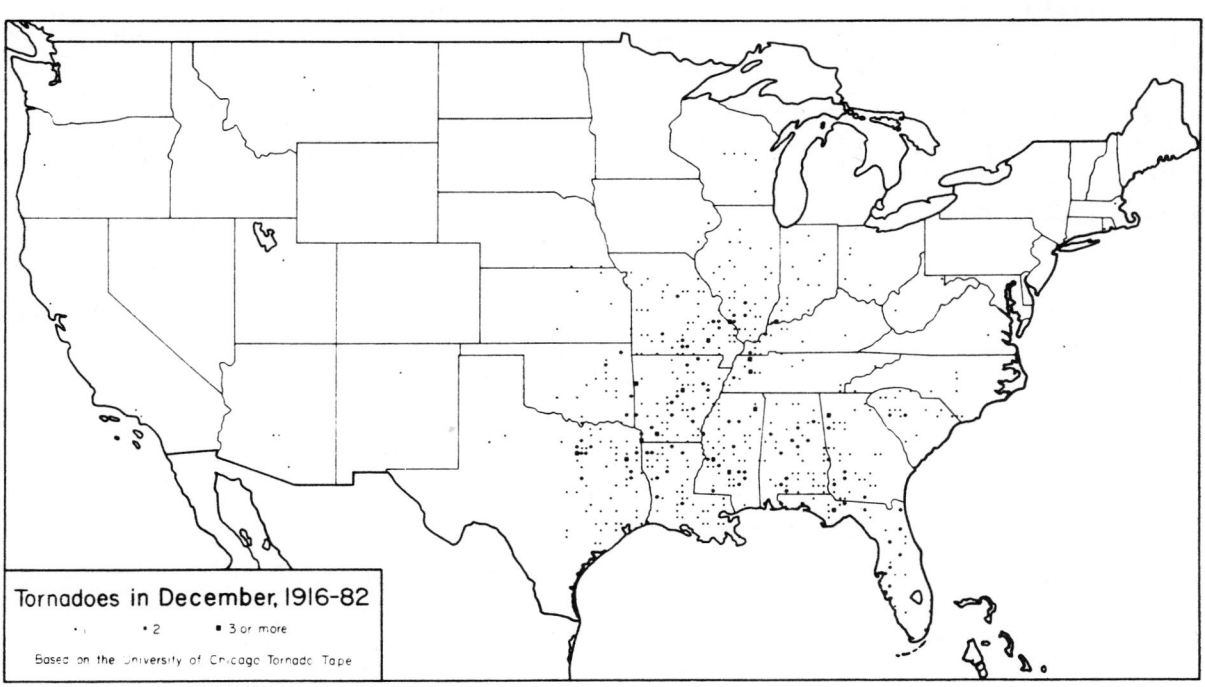

Tornadoes in December, 1916-82

• 1   • 2   ■ 3 or more

Based on the University of Chicago Tornado Tape

**Tornado Characteristics—**

**Time of Day** during which tornadoes are most likely to occur is mid-afternoon, generally between 3 and 7 p.m., but they have occurred at all times of day.

**Direction of Movement** is usually from southwest to northeast. (Note: Tornadoes associated with hurricanes may move from an easterly direction.)

**Length of Path** averages 4 miles, but may reach 300 miles. A tornado traveled 293 miles across Illinois and Indiana on May 26, 1917, and lasted 7 hours and 20 minutes.

**Width of Path** averages about 300 to 400 yards but tornadoes have cut swaths a mile and more in width.

**Speed of Travel** averages from 25 to 40 miles per hour, but speeds ranging from stationary to 68 miles per hour have been reported.

**The Cloud** directly associated with a tornado is a dark, heavy cumulonimbus (the familiar thunderstorm cloud) from which a whirling funnel-shaped pendant extends to the ground.

**Precipitation** associated with the tornado usually occurs first as rain just preceding the storm, frequently with hail, and as a heavy downpour immediately to the left of the tornado's path.

**Sound** occurring during a tornado has been described as a roaring, rushing noise, closely approximating that made by a train speeding through a tunnel or over a trestle, or the roar of many airplanes.

*The McKinley Elementary School in Xenia, Ohio, before a tornado
hit at 4:30 p.m. April 3, 1974.*

*The McKinley Elementary School and surrounding residences after
the tornado struck.*

# TORNADO SAFETY RULES

A tornado <u>watch</u> means tornadoes are expected to develop. Keep a battery-operated radio or television set nearby, and listen for weather advisories—even if the sky is blue. A tornado <u>warning</u> means a tornado has actually been sighted or indicated by weather radar. Seek inside shelter (in a storm cellar or reinforced building) and stay away from windows. Curl up so that your head and eyes are protected. Keep a battery-operated radio or television nearby, and listen for further advisories.

ON THE STREET OR IN A CAR, leave your car and take shelter in civil defense or other inside shelter areas with basements or storm cellars. Be sure to stay away from large glassed in areas. If no building is available or if caught out in the open countryside take shelter in a ditch or ravine or lie flat on the ground upwind of your parked car. If an overpass or concrete viaduct is available then take shelter behind the concrete pilings in such a way as to put the concrete between you and approaching tornado.

IN HIGH-RISE OFFICE BUILDINGS AND LARGE APARTMENT BUILDINGS, if possible post a trained spotter or lookout on the roof with a two-way radio. Go to the lower floors or the basement. Take shelter in small interior rooms such as rest rooms, closets and utility rooms as well as interior corridors. Be sure to cover and protect the head from flying and falling debris.

IN HOMES, take shelter in the basement under sturdy items. Concrete laundry tubs, heavy duty work benches, pool tables and staircases offer the greatest safety. If there is no basement take cover under heavily stuffed furniture in the center of the home or in a bathroom or interior closet. Open some windows on at least two different sides of the home, preferably those on the east and west side, but take shelter away from all windows. Caution: Avoid bathrooms with an out-side wall on the south or west side of the home. Also do not lock yourself in a closet that has no inside latch or door handle.

# TORNADO SAFETY RULES

IN SHOPPING CENTERS OR SHOPPING MALLS, **if possible post a trained security guard or lookout on the west or south side of the complex with a two way radio. Take shelter in the basement or in shops below ground level. If there is no basement take shelter in interior hallways, small interior rooms or shops on the east or north side of the center. If only one large building or room exists then take shelter in the north end of the room. Be sure to protect your head from flying or falling debris. Caution: Avoid large open malls or walkways with glass or plastic skylights as well as large glass signs and display cases.**

IN SCHOOLS, **go to a storm cellar or underground shelter if available. If there is no underground shelter area move the pupils into interior hallways or small interior rooms on the lowest floor and on the east or north side of the building. Caution: Avoid auditoriums, gymnasiums and other large rooms with long freespan roofs as well as southwest to northeast oriented corridors with exposed or unbaffled entrances on the south and west side of the building. Also avoid glass display cases, glassed in stairwells and all door ways.**

IN FACTORIES, **post a trained spotter or lookout on the roof with a two-way radio. Workers should move to sections of the plant that are below ground level. If this is not possible then have the workers take shelter in interior corridors or in small interior rooms such as rest rooms, closets and storage rooms on the east or north side of the building. Caution: Avoid the southwest corner of the plant as well as large rooms or work areas with long freespan roofs. Stay away from all windows.**

IN MOBILE HOMES, **leave your trailer and take shelter in an administration building with a basement or an approved community shelter area. If no shelter is available go to a ditch or ravine on the west or south side of the trailer park and lie down flat against the ground. Make sure you protect your head from flying debris.**

IN A BUS, TRUCK OR LARGE VAN, **try to move away from the storm by driving at right angles to its path. If this is not possible or if you experience strong cross winds then park the vehicle pointing into the wind, pull the hand break and unload your passengers. Open as many windows as time will allow on both sides of the vehicles then leave the vehicle and take shelter in a ditch, ravine or other depression in the ground that is upwind from your truck or bus.**

# CONSTRUCTING A SHELTER

IN parts of the country where tornadoes are comparatively frequent, a form of shelter is vital for protection from tornadoes. The shelter may never be needed; but during a tornado emergency, it can be worth many times the effort and cost of preparing it. One of the safest tornado shelters is an underground excavation, known as a storm cellar.

LOCATION — When possible, the storm cellar should be located outside and near the residence, but not so close that falling walls or debris could block the exit. If there is a rise in the ground, the cellar may be dug into it to make use of the rise for protection. The cellar should not be connected in any way with house drains, cesspools, or sewer and gas pipes.

SIZE — The size of the shelter depends on the number of persons to be accommodated and the storage needs. A structure 8 feet long by 6 feet wide and 7 feet high will protect eight people for a short time and provide limited storage space.

MATERIAL — Reinforced concrete is the best material for a tornado shelter. Other suitable building materials include split logs, 2-inch planks (treated with creosote and covered with tar paper), cinder block, hollow tile, and brick. The roof should be covered with a 3-foot mound of well-pounded dirt, sloped to divert surface water. The entrance door should be of heavy construction, hinged to open inward.

DRAINAGE — The floor should slope to a drainage outlet if the terrain permits. If not, a dry well can be dug. An outside drain is better, because it will aid ventilation.

VENTILATION — A vertical ventilating shaft about 1 foot square can extend from near the floor level through the ceiling. This can be converted into an emergency escape hatch if the opening through the ceiling is made 2 feet square and the 1-foot shaft below is made easily removable. Slat gratings of heavy wood on the floor also will improve air circulation.

EMERGENCY EQUIPMENT — A lantern and tools—crowbar, pick, shovel, hammer, pliers, screwdriver— should be stored in the cellar to ensure escape if cellar exits are blocked by debris. Stored metal tools should be greased to prevent rusting.

# NATIONAL TORNADOES, TORNADO DAYS, DEATHS AND RESULTING LOSSES BY YEARS, 1916-89

| YEAR | NUMBER TORNADOES | TORNADO DAYS | TOTAL DEATHS | MOST DEATHS IN SINGLE TORNADO | TOTAL PROPERTY LOSSES $ | PROPERTY LOSS FREQUENCY * | | |
|---|---|---|---|---|---|---|---|---|
| | | | | | | CATEGORY 5 | CATEGORY 6 | CATEGORY 7 AND OVER |
| 1916 | 90 | 36 | 150 | 30 | 6 | 7 | 1 | 0 |
| 1917 | 121 | 38 | 551 | 101 | 7 | 21 | 9 | 0 |
| 1918 | 81 | 45 | 136 | 36 | 7 | 20 | 5 | 0 |
| 1919 | 64 | 35 | 206 | 59 | 7 | 10 | 2 | 0 |
| 1920 | 87 | 50 | 499 | 87 | 7 | 14 | 10 | 0 |
| 1921 | 105 | 55 | 202 | 61 | 7 | 22 | 3 | 0 |
| 1922 | 108 | 64 | 135 | 16 | 7 | 27 | 5 | 0 |
| 1923 | 102 | 59 | 110 | 23 | 6 | 51 | 1 | 0 |
| 1924 | 130 | 57 | 376 | 85 | 7 | 26 | 11 | 0 |
| 1925 | 119 | 65 | 794 | 689 | 7 | 34 | 2 | 1 |
| 1926 | 111 | 57 | 144 | 23 | 6 | 28 | 0 | 0 |
| 1927 | 163 | 62 | 540 | 92 | 7 | 42 | 9 | 1 |
| 1928 | 203 | 79 | 95 | 14 | 7 | 40 | 7 | 0 |
| 1929 | 197 | 74 | 274 | 40 | 7 | 48 | 4 | 0 |
| 1930 | 192 | 73 | 179 | 41 | 7 | 38 | 6 | 0 |
| 1931 | 94 | 57 | 36 | 6 | 6 | 14 | 1 | 0 |
| 1932 | 151 | 67 | 394 | 37 | 7 | 23 | 1 | 1 |
| 1933 | 258 | 96 | 362 | 34 | 7 | 46 | 9 | 0 |
| 1934 | 147 | 77 | 47 | 6 | 6 | 10 | 3 | 0 |
| 1935 | 180 | 77 | 71 | 11 | 6 | 29 | 3 | 0 |
| 1936 | 151 | 71 | 552 | 216 | 7 | 17 | 5 | 1 |
| 1937 | 147 | 75 | 29 | 5 | 6 | 24 | 0 | 0 |
| 1938 | 213 | 76 | 183 | 32 | 7 | 29 | 6 | 0 |
| 1939 | 152 | 75 | 91 | 27 | 7 | 31 | 3 | 0 |
| 1940 | 124 | 62 | 65 | 18 | 7 | 13 | 2 | 0 |
| 1941 | 118 | 57 | 53 | 25 | 6 | 24 | 1 | 0 |
| 1942 | 167 | 66 | 384 | 65 | 7 | 42 | 10 | 0 |
| 1943 | 152 | 61 | 58 | 5 | 7 | 28 | 8 | 0 |
| 1944 | 169 | 68 | 275 | 100 | 7 | 50 | 9 | 0 |
| 1945 | 121 | 66 | 210 | 69 | 7 | 21 | 10 | 1 |
| 1946 | 106 | 65 | 78 | 15 | 7 | 29 | 7 | 0 |
| 1947 | 165 | 78 | 313 | 169 | 7 | 46 | 7 | 1 |
| 1948 | 183 | 68 | 139 | 33 | 7 | 62 | 11 | 2 |
| 1949 | 249 | 80 | 211 | 58 | 7 | 54 | 13 | 0 |
| 1950 | 200 | 88 | 70 | 18 | 7 | 47 | 9 | 2 |
| 1951 | 262 | 113 | 34 | 6 | 7 | 35 | 11 | 3 |
| 1952 | 240 | 98 | 229 | 57 | 7 | 53 | 19 | 2 |
| 1953 | 421 | 136 | 515 | 116 | 8 | 63 | 18 | 7 |
| 1954 | 550 | 160 | 36 | 6 | 7 | 63 | 9 | 1 |
| 1955 | 593 | 152 | 126 | 80 | 7 | 74 | 13 | 1 |
| 1956 | 504 | 155 | 83 | 25 | 7 | 83 | 24 | 1 |
| 1957 | 856 | 154 | 192 | 44 | 8 | 129 | 26 | 3 |
| 1958 | 564 | 166 | 66 | 19 | 7 | 70 | 8 | 1 |
| 1959 | 604 | 156 | 58 | 21 | 7 | 70 | 4 | 1 |
| 1960 | 616 | 172 | 46 | 16 | 7 | 65 | 11 | 1 |
| 1961 | 697 | 169 | 51 | 16 | 7 | 103 | 21 | 1 |
| 1962 | 657 | 152 | 28 | 17 | 7 | 51 | 10 | 0 |
| 1963 | 464 | 141 | 31 | 5 | 7 | 77 | 15 | 1 |
| 1964 | 704 | 156 | 73 | 22 | 7 | 113 | 17 | 5 |
| 1965 | 906 | 181 | 299 | 44 | 8 | 126 | 30 | 11 |
| 1966 | 585 | 150 | 98 | 58 | 8 | 79 | 13 | 4 |
| 1967 | 926 | 173 | 114 | 33 | 8 | 125 | 33 | 8 |
| 1968 | 660 | 171 | 131 | 34 | 8 | 82 | 26 | 6 |
| 1969 | 608 | 155 | 66 | 32 | 8 | 98 | 16 | 3 |
| 1970 | 653 | 171 | 72 | 26 | 8 | 97 | 24 | 5 |
| 1971 | 888 | 192 | 156 | 58 | 8 | 71 | 30 | 5 |
| 1972 | 741 | 194 | 27 | 6 | 8 | 100 | 28 | 1 |
| 1973 | 1102 | 206 | 87 | 7 | 8 | 219 | 67 | 9 |
| 1974 | 947 | 184 | 361 | 34 | 9 | 166 | 82 | 25 |
| 1975 | 920 | 204 | 60 | 9 | 9 | 189 | 31 | 11 |
| 1976 | 835 | 169 | 44 | 5 | 8 | 145 | 41 | 5 |
| 1977 | 852 | 189 | 43 | 22 | 8 | 173 | 40 | 6 |
| 1978 | 788 | 173 | 53 | 16 | 9 | 153 | 53 | 6 |
| 1979 | 852 | 186 | 84 | 42 | 9 | 169 | 62 | 11 |
| 1980 | 866 | 176 | 28 | 5 | 9 | 201 | 79 | 13 |
| 1981 | 783 | 175 | 24 | 5 | 9 | 144 | 43 | 12 |
| 1982 | 1046 | 182 | 64 | 10 | 9 | 254 | 79 | 13 |
| 1983 | 931 | 190 | 34 | 3 | 9 | 211 | 85 | 10 |
| 1984 | 907 | 166 | 122 | 16 | 9 | 193 | 90 | 35 |
| 1985 | 684 | 168 | 94 | 18 | 9 | 114 | 55 | 14 |
| 1986 | 764 | 168 | 15 | 3 | 9 | 157 | 66 | 9 |
| 1987 | 656 | 151 | 59 | 30 | 8 | 112 | 32 | 6 |
| 1988 | 702 | 156 | 32 | 5 | 9 | 148 | 48 | 17 |
| 1989 | 856 | 160 | 50 | 21 | 9 | 133 | 60 | 18 |
| MEAN | 748 | 169 | 95 | - | - | 125 | 38 | 8 |

NOTE: - THE ABOVE ESTIMATED LOSSES ARE BASED ON VALUES AT TIME OF OCCURRENCE.
MEAN WAS DERIVED FROM DATA FOR PERIOD 1953-1989.

$ STORM DAMAGES IN CATEGORIES:

    5. $50,000 TO $500,000         8. $50 MILLION TO $500 MILLION
    6. $500,000 TO $5 MILLION      9. $500 MILLION AND OVER
    7. $5 MILLION TO $50 MILLION

* NUMBER OF TIMES PROPERTY LOSSES REPORTED IN STORM DATA IN CATEGORIES 5, 6, 7, AND OVER.

# TORNADOES, TORNADO DAYS, AND DEATHS BY STATE AND NATION, 1953-89

| STATE | TORNADOES | | | | | | | DAYS | | DEATHS | | |
|---|---|---|---|---|---|---|---|---|---|---|---|---|
| | TOTAL | AVERAGE | GREATEST | YEAR | LEAST | YEAR | PER # 10,000 SQ. MI. | TOTAL | AVERAGE | TOTAL | AVERAGE | PER ' 10,000 SQ. MI. |
| ALABAMA | 788 | 21 | 45 | 1983+ | 5 | 1956 | 4.06 | 415 | 11 | 237 | 6 | 46 |
| ALASKA | 1 | 0 | 1 | 1959 | 0 | 1989+ | .00 | 1 | 0 | 0 | 0 | 0 |
| ARIZONA | 123 | 3 | 17 | 1972 | 0 | 1965 | .26 | 99 | 3 | 3 | 0 | 0 |
| ARKANSAS | 743 | 20 | 78 | 1982 | 2 | 1987+ | 3.76 | 339 | 9 | 163 | 5 | 31 |
| CALIFORNIA | 148 | 4 | 14 | 1983 | 0 | 1968+ | .25 | 110 | 3 | 0 | 0 | 0 |
| COLORADO | 771 | 21 | 58 | 1982 | 1 | 1959 | 2.02 | 460 | 12 | 2 | 0 | 0 |
| CONNECTICUT | 49 | 1 | 8 | 1973 | 0 | 1988+ | 2.00 | 43 | 1 | 4 | 0 | 8 |
| DELAWARE | 35 | 1 | 5 | 1975 | 0 | 1987+ | 5.00 | 32 | 1 | 2 | 0 | 10 |
| DISTRICT OF COLUMBIA | 0 | 0 | 0 | | 0 | | - - | 0 | 0 | 0 | 0 | 0 |
| FLORIDA | 1650 | 44 | 97 | 1975 | 10 | 1956 | 7.50 | 1052 | 28 | 70 | 2 | 12 |
| GEORGIA | 743 | 20 | 46 | 1974+ | 2 | 1987 | 3.40 | 408 | 11 | 78 | 2 | 13 |
| HAWAII | 27 | 1 | 4 | 1971 | 0 | 1987+ | 1.56 | 23 | 1 | 0 | 0 | 0 |
| IDAHO | 77 | 2 | 10 | 1986+ | 0 | 1977+ | .24 | 63 | 2 | 0 | 0 | 0 |
| ILLINOIS | 960 | 26 | 107 | 1974 | 4 | 1953 | 4.62 | 445 | 12 | 147 | 4 | 26 |
| INDIANA | 744 | 20 | 48 | 1973 | 4 | 1984 | 5.52 | 360 | 10 | 206 | 6 | 57 |
| IOWA | 1105 | 30 | 61 | 1984 | 7 | 1956 | 5.33 | 488 | 13 | 60 | 2 | 11 |
| KANSAS | 1532 | 42 | 97 | 1955 | 14 | 1976 | 5.07 | 714 | 20 | 168 | 5 | 20 |
| KENTUCKY | 304 | 8 | 34 | 1974 | 0 | 1953 | 1.98 | 181 | 5 | 102 | 3 | 25 |
| LOUISIANA | 841 | 22 | 64 | 1983 | 3 | 1955 | 4.60 | 496 | 13 | 90 | 3 | 20 |
| MAINE | 76 | 2 | 11 | 1971 | 0 | 1987+ | .60 | 67 | 2 | 1 | 0 | 0 |
| MARYLAND | 89 | 2 | 10 | 1975 | 0 | 1988+ | 1.90 | 69 | 2 | 2 | 0 | 2 |
| MASSACHUSETTS | 124 | 3 | 12 | 1958 | 0 | 1988+ | 3.61 | 87 | 2 | 99 | 3 | 114 |
| MICHIGAN | 611 | 17 | 39 | 1974 | 2 | 1959 | 2.91 | 353 | 10 | 236 | 7 | 40 |
| MINNESOTA | 652 | 18 | 34 | 1968 | 5 | 1988+ | 2.13 | 369 | 10 | 77 | 2 | 9 |
| MISSISSIPPI | 870 | 23 | 62 | 1988 | 1 | 1979 | 4.82 | 431 | 11 | 343 | 10 | 72 |
| MISSOURI | 996 | 27 | 79 | 1973 | 6 | 1987+ | 3.87 | 436 | 12 | 133 | 4 | 19 |
| MONTANA | 162 | 4 | 20 | 1988 | 0 | 1974+ | .27 | 114 | 3 | 1 | 0 | 0 |
| NEBRASKA | 1296 | 35 | 78 | 1975 | 10 | 1966 | 4.52 | 635 | 17 | 51 | 1 | 7 |
| NEVADA | 38 | 1 | 8 | 1987 | 0 | 1985+ | .09 | 34 | 1 | 0 | 0 | 0 |
| NEW HAMPSHIRE | 68 | 2 | 9 | 1963 | 0 | 1987+ | 2.15 | 59 | 2 | 0 | 0 | 0 |
| NEW JERSEY | 84 | 2 | 17 | 1989 | 0 | 1984+ | 2.56 | 61 | 2 | 0 | 0 | 0 |
| NEW MEXICO | 299 | 8 | 18 | 1972 | 0 | 1953 | .66 | 230 | 6 | 3 | 0 | 0 |
| NEW YORK | 163 | 4 | 15 | 1989 | 0 | 1953 | .81 | 122 | 3 | 18 | 0 | 4 |
| NORTH CAROLINA | 461 | 12 | 38 | 1973 | 2 | 1970 | 2.28 | 281 | 8 | 79 | 2 | 15 |
| NORTH DAKOTA | 669 | 18 | 52 | 1976 | 2 | 1961 | 2.55 | 364 | 10 | 21 | 1 | 3 |
| OHIO | 514 | 14 | 43 | 1973 | 0 | 1988 | 3.39 | 268 | 7 | 170 | 5 | 41 |
| OKLAHOMA | 1939 | 53 | 107 | 1957 | 17 | 1988 | 7.57 | 802 | 22 | 200 | 6 | 29 |
| OREGON | 33 | 1 | 4 | 1984 | 0 | 1988+ | .10 | 29 | 1 | 0 | 0 | 0 |
| PACIFIC ISLANDS | 2 | 0 | 1 | 1981+ | 0 | 1989+ | - - | 2 | 0 | 0 | 0 | 0 |
| PENNSYLVANIA | 325 | 9 | 33 | 1985+ | 0 | 1959 | 1.99 | 211 | 6 | 73 | 2 | 16 |
| PUERTO RICO | 9 | 0 | 2 | 1979 | 0 | 1989+ | .00 | 8 | 0 | 0 | 0 | 0 |
| RHODE ISLAND | 6 | 0 | 3 | 1986 | 0 | 1988+ | .00 | 5 | 0 | 0 | 0 | 0 |
| SOUTH CAROLINA | 335 | 9 | 23 | 1973 | 1 | 1986+ | 2.89 | 221 | 6 | 42 | 1 | 14 |
| SOUTH DAKOTA | 925 | 26 | 64 | 1965 | 1 | 1958 | 3.37 | 438 | 12 | 8 | 0 | 1 |
| TENNESSEE | 410 | 11 | 44 | 1974 | 1 | 1987+ | 2.61 | 222 | 6 | 82 | 2 | 19 |
| TEXAS | 4599 | 123 | 232 | 1967 | 32 | 1953 | 4.61 | 1767 | 48 | 446 | 12 | 17 |
| UTAH | 56 | 1 | 6 | 1984 | 0 | 1989+ | .12 | 47 | 1 | 0 | 0 | 0 |
| VERMONT | 31 | 1 | 5 | 1962 | 0 | 1985+ | 1.04 | 28 | 1 | 0 | 0 | 0 |
| VIRGINIA | 211 | 6 | 22 | 1975 | 1 | 1982+ | 1.47 | 143 | 4 | 16 | 0 | 4 |
| VIRGIN ISLANDS | 2 | 0 | 1 | 1979+ | 0 | 1989+ | - - | 2 | 0 | 0 | 0 | 0 |
| WASHINGTON | 49 | 1 | 4 | 1989+ | 0 | 1988+ | .15 | 42 | 1 | 6 | 0 | 1 |
| WEST VIRGINIA | 72 | 2 | 6 | 1980+ | 0 | 1988+ | .83 | 56 | 1 | 2 | 0 | 1 |
| WISCONSIN | 714 | 19 | 43 | 1980 | 3 | 1953 | 3.38 | 370 | 10 | 75 | 2 | 13 |
| WYOMING | 349 | 9 | 42 | 1977 | 0 | 1970 | .92 | 234 | 6 | 2 | 0 | 0 |
| TOTAL: UNITED STATES | 27688* | 748 | 1102 | 1973 | 421 | 1953 | 2.07 | 6259& | 169 | 3522 | 95 | 10 |

+ ALSO IN EARLIER YEAR(S).
* CORRECTED FOR BOUNDARY-CROSSING TORNADOES.
& TORNADO DAYS FOR COUNTRY AS A WHOLE.

# MEAN ANNUAL TORNADOES PER 10,000 SQUARE MILES.
' NUMBER OF DEATHS PER 10,000 SQUARE MILES.

# NATIONAL SUMMARY OF TORNADOES, TORNADO DAYS, AND DEATHS BY MONTH AND ANNUAL, 1953–89

| YEAR | JANUARY |||FEBRUARY |||MARCH |||APRIL |||MAY |||JUNE |||JULY |||AUGUST |||SEPTEMBER |||OCTOBER |||NOVEMBER |||DECEMBER |||ANNUAL |||
|---|---|---|---|---|---|---|---|---|---|---|---|---|---|---|---|---|---|---|---|---|---|---|---|---|---|---|---|---|---|---|---|---|---|---|---|---|---|---|---|
| | NUMBER | DAYS | DEATHS | NUMBER | DAYS | DEATHS | NUMBER | DAYS | DEATHS | NUMBER | DAYS | DEATHS | NUMBER | DAYS | DEATHS | NUMBER | DAYS | DEATHS | NUMBER | DAYS | DEATHS | NUMBER | DAYS | DEATHS | NUMBER | DAYS | DEATHS | NUMBER | DAYS | DEATHS | NUMBER | DAYS | DEATHS | NUMBER | DAYS | DEATHS | NUMBER | DAYS | DEATHS |
| POR | 491 | 160 | 98 | 734 | 203 | 203 | 1819 | 446 | 292 | 3852 | 645 | 1160 | 6131 | 917 | 813 | 5551 | 970 | 484 | 3104 | 927 | 46 | 2088 | 771 | 68 | 1418 | 518 | 64 | 855 | 285 | 70 | 973 | 237 | 109 | 679 | 180 | 115 | 27638 | 6259 | 3522 |
| MEAN | 13 | 4 | 3 | 20 | 5 | 5 | 49 | 12 | 8 | 104 | 17 | 31 | 166 | 25 | 22 | 150 | 26 | 13 | 84 | 25 | 1 | 56 | 21 | 2 | 38 | 14 | 2 | 23 | 8 | 2 | 26 | 6 | 3 | 18 | 5 | 3 | 748 | 169 | 95 |

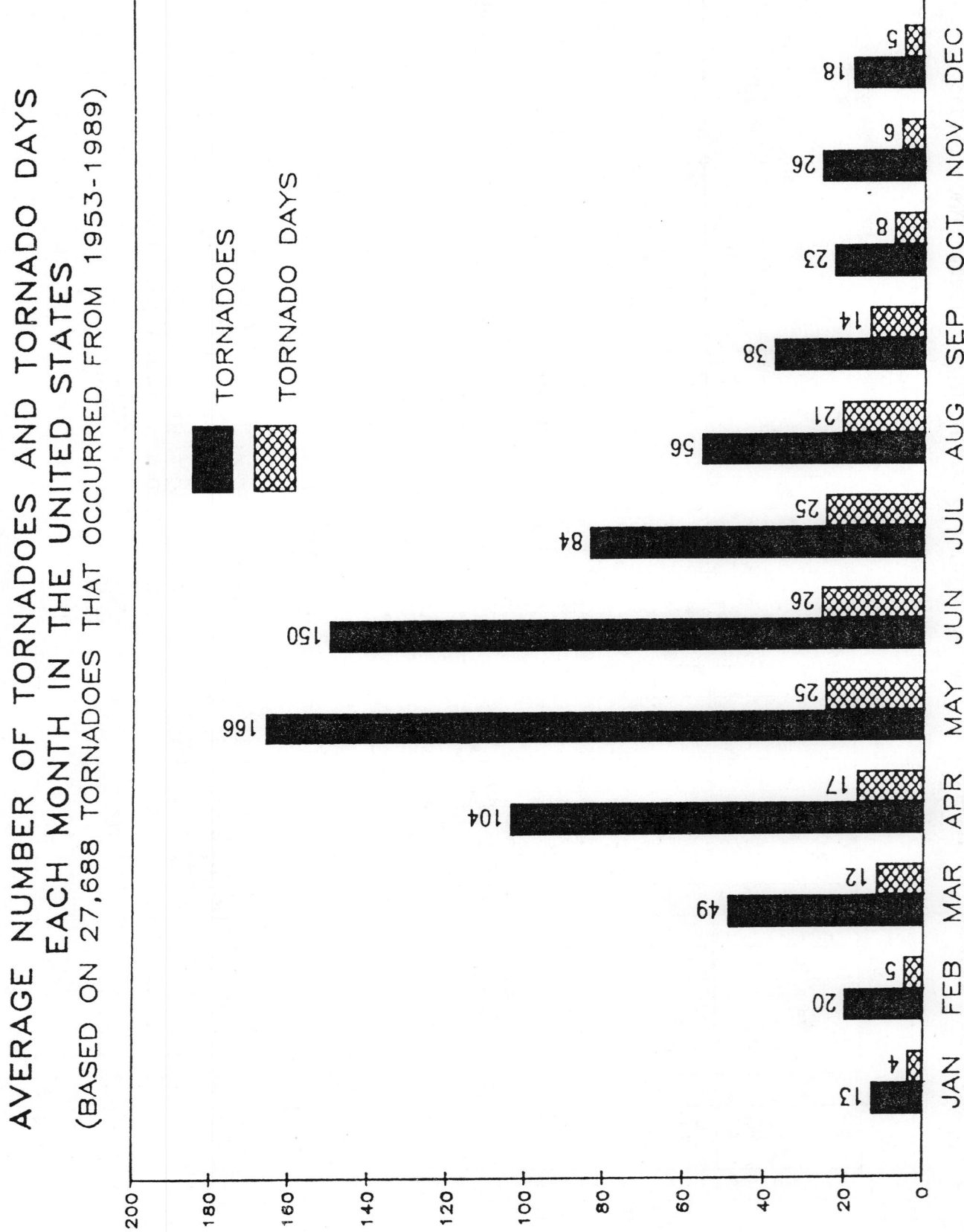

AVERAGE NUMBER OF TORNADOES AND TORNADO DAYS EACH MONTH IN THE UNITED STATES (BASED ON 27,688 TORNADOES THAT OCCURRED FROM 1953-1989)

## QUOTES FROM WEATHER FOLKLORE—

*A veering wind, fair weather;*
*A backing wind, foul weather.*
*If the wind back against the sun,*
*Trust it not, for back it will run.*

*Do business with men when the wind is*
*    from the westerly;*
*for then the barometer is high.*

*A severe autumn denotes a windy summer,*
*a windy winter a rainy spring,*
*A rainy spring a severe summer,*
*A severe summer a windy autumn;*
*So that the air in balance is*
*Seldom debtor unto itself.*          *– Bacon.*

*Fishes in general, both in salt and*
*fresh waters, are observed to sport most*
*and bite more eagerly before rain than*
*at any other time.*

*Go plant the bean when the moon is light,*
*And you will find that this is right;*
*Plant the potatoes when the moon is dark,*
*And to this line you always hark;*
*But if you vary from this rule,*
*You will find  you are a fool;*
*If you always follow this rule to the end,*
*You will always have money to spend.*

*Observe which way the hedgehog builds her*
*    nest,*
*To front the north or south, or east or west;*
*For if 'tis true what common peole say,*
*The wind will blow the quite contrary way.*
*If by some secret art the hedgehog knows,*
*So long before, the way in which the winds*
*    will blow,*
*She has an art which many a person lacks*
*That thinks himself fit to make our almanacks.*
*          – Poor Robin's Almanack, 1733.*

# THUNDERSTORMS

It is estimated that at any given moment, some 1800 thunderstorms are in progress over the earth's surface. The frequency with which these giant generators of local weather occur, the quantity of energy they release, and the variety of forms this energy may take, make thunderstorms great destroyers of life and property. For a single household, a single family, they can produce as much tragedy as a war.

The following paragraphs describe what thunderstorms are, how they form and how they die, and what you can do to prevent their doing violence to you.

## How thunderstorms develop—

Thunderstorms are generated by thermal instability in the atmosphere, and represent a violent example of convection—the vertical circulation produced in a fluid made thermally unstable by the local addition or subtraction of heat and the conversion of potential to kinetic energy. The convective overturning of atmospheric layers that sets up a thunderstorm is dynamically similar to convective circulations observed in the laboratory, where distinct patterns are generated in liquids by unequal heating.

The orderly circulations produced in the laboratory are rarely encountered in the atmosphere, where areas corresponding to the rising core of laboratory convective cells are marked by Cumulus and Cumulonimbus clouds. Clouds are parcels of air that have been lifted high enough to condense the water vapor they contain into very small, visible particles. These particles are too small and light to fall out as rain. As the lifting process continues, these particles grow in size, by collision and coalescence until they are large enough to fall against the updrafts associated with any developing convective clouds. Cumulus (for accumulation) clouds begin their towering movement in response to atmospheric instability and convective overturning. Warmer and lighter than the surrounding air, they rise rapidly around a strong, central updraft. These elements grow vertically, appearing as rising mounds, domes, or towers.

The atmospheric instability in which thunderstorms begin may develop in several ways. Radiational cooling of cloud tops, heating of the cloud base from the ground, and frontal effects may produce an unstable condition. This is compensated in air, as in most fluids, by the convective overturning of layers to put denser layers below less dense layers.

Mechanical processes are also at work. Warm, buoyant air may be forced upward by the wedge-like undercutting of a cold air mass, or lifted by a mountain slope. Convergence of horizontal winds into the center of a low-pressure area forces warm air near that center upward. Where these processes are sustained, and where lifting and cooling of the moist air continues, minor turbulence may generate a Cumulus cloud, and then a towering cumulonimbus system.

The history of the vertical movement of air in the center of the Cumulus or Cumulonimbus cloud system is the history of each convective cell. Most thunderstorms have, at maturity, a series of several cells, each following a life cycle characterized by changes in wind direction, development of precipitation and electrical charge, and other factors.

In the first stage of thunderstorm development, an updraft drives warm air up beyond condensation levels, where clouds form, and where continued upward movement produces Cumulus formations. The updraft develops in a region of gently converging surface winds in which the atmospheric pressure is slightly lower than in surrounding areas. As the updraft continues, air flows in through the cloud's sides in a process called entrainment, mixing with and feeding the updraft. The updraft may be further augmented by a chimney effect produced by high winds at altitude.

## Heat energy from water—

But a developing thunderstorm also feeds on another source of energy. Once the cloud has formed, the phase changes of water result in a release of heat energy, which increases the momentum of the storm's vertical development. The rate at which this energy is released is directly related to the amount of gaseous water vapor converted to liquid water.

As water vapor in the burgeoning cloud is raised to saturation levels, the air is cooled sufficiently to liberate solid and liquid particles of water, and rain and snow begin to fall within the cloud. The cloud tower rises beyond the level (3-5 kilometers) where fibrous streamers of frozen precipitation elements appear; this apparent ice phase is thought to be a condition of thunderstorm precipitation. The formation and precipitation of particles large enough and in sufficient quantity to fall against the updraft marks the beginning of the second, mature state of the thunderstorm cell.

A thunderstorm's mature stage is marked by a transition in wind direction within the storm cells. The prevailing updraft which initiated the cloud's growth is joined by a downdraft generated by precipitation. The downdraft is fed and strengthened, as the updraft was, by the addition of entrained air, and by evaporational cooling caused by interactions of entrained air and falling precipitation. The mature storm dominates the electrical field and atmospheric circulation for several miles around. Lightning—the discharge of electricity between large charges of opposite sign—occurs soon after precipitation begins, a clue to the relationship of thunderstorm electrification and formation of ice crystals and raindrops.

At maturity, the thunderstorm cloud is several miles across its base and may tower to altitudes of 40,000 feet or more. The swift winds of the upper troposphere shred the cloud top into the familiar anvil form, visible in dry regions as lonely giants, or as part of a squall line.

On the ground directly beneath the storm system, the mature stage is initially felt as rain, which is soon joined by the strong downdraft. The downdraft spreads out from the cloud in gusting, divergent winds, and brings a marked drop in temperature. Even where the rain has not reached the ground, the thunderstorm's mature stage can be recognized by this cold air stream flowing over the surface. This is nature's warning that the thunderstorm is in its most violent phase. It is in this phase that the thunderstorm unleashes its lightning, hail, heavy rain, high wind, and—most destructive of all—the tornado. But even as it enters maturity, the storm has begun to die. The violent downdraft initially shares the circulation with the sustaining updraft, then strangles it. As the updraft is cut off from its converging low-level winds, the storm loses its source of moisture and heat energy. Precipitation weakens, stops, and the cold downdraft ceases. And the thunderstorm, violent creature of an instant, spreads and dies.

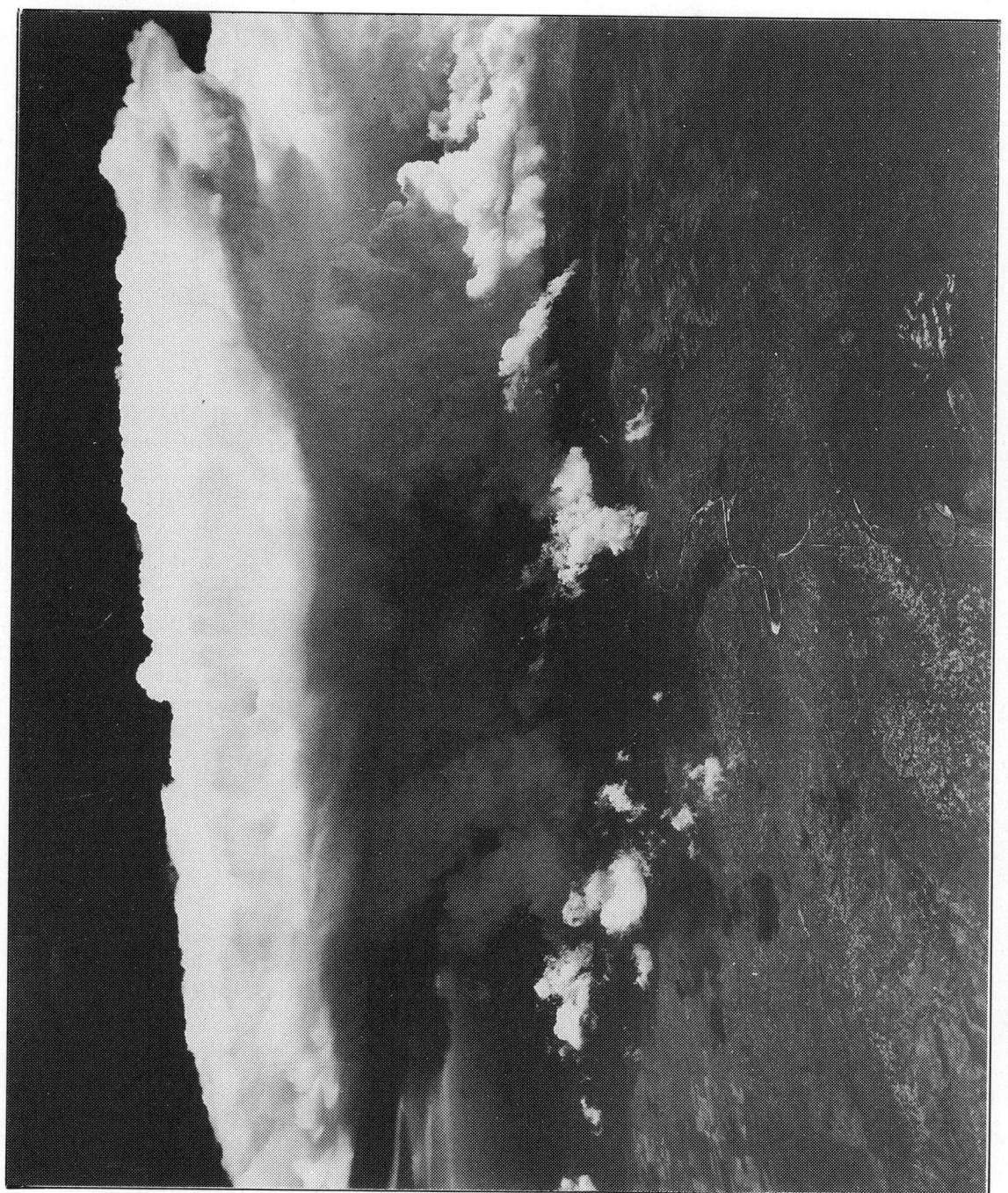

*Top: The dynamics of a classical cumulonimbus cloud (or thunderhead) with anvil top. Bottom: Thunderhead formation taken from an aircraft at approximately 30,000 feet. Note the cumulo-nimbus form with anvil top. Source: National Oceanic and Atmospheric Administration.*

# THUNDERSTORM SAFETY RULES

1. KEEP AN EYE ON THE WEATHER DURING WARM PERIODS AND DURING THE PASSAGE OF COLD FRONTS. **When Cumulus clouds begin building up and darkening, you are probably in for a thunderstorm. Check the latest weather forecast.**

2. KEEP CALM. **Thunderstorms are usually of short duration; even squall lines pass in a matter of a few hours. Be cautious, but don't be afraid. Stay indoors and keep informed.**

3. KNOW WHAT THE STORM IS DOING. **Remember that the mature stage may be marked on the ground by a sudden reversal of wind direction, a noticeable rise in wind speed, and a sharp drop in temperature. Heavy rain, hail, tornadoes, and lightning generally occur only in the mature state of the thunderstorm.**

4. CONDITIONS MAY FAVOR TORNADO FORMATION. **Tune in your radio or television receiver to determine whether there is a tornado watch or tornado warning out for your area. A tornado watch means tornado formation is likely in the area covered by the watch. A tornado warning means one has been sighted or radar-indicated in your area. If you receive a tornado warning, seek inside shelter in a storm cellar, below ground level, or in reinforced concrete structures; stay away from windows.**

5. LIGHTNING IS THE THUNDERSTORM'S WORST KILLER. **Stay indoors and away from electrical appliances while the storm is overhead. If lightning catches you outside, remember that it seeks the easiest—not necessarily the shortest—distance between positive and negative centers. Keep yourself lower than the nearest highly conductive object, and maintain a safe distance from it. If the object is a tree, twice its height is considered a safe distance.**

6. THUNDERSTORM RAIN MAY PRODUCE FLASH FLOODS. **Stay out of dry creek beds during thunderstorms. If you live along a river, listen for flash-flood warnings from the National Weather Service.**

# LIGHTNING

It is estimated that lightning strikes the earth 100 times each second. The average annual death toll for lightning is greater than for tornadoes or hurricanes.

According to data assembled by the National Center for Health Statistics, lightning kills about 150 Americans per year and injures about 250. Property loss—fire and other damage to structures, aircraft damage, livestock deaths and injuries, forest fires, disruption of electromagnetic transmissions, and other effects—is estimated at more than $100 million annually.

## What causes lightning?

Lightning is a secondary effect of electrification within a thunderstorm cloud system. Updrafts of warm, moist air rising into cold air can cause small cumulus clouds to grow into the large cumulonimbus cloud systems we associate with thunderstorms. These turbulent cloud systems tower about their companions, and dominate the atmospheric circulation and electrical field over a wide area. The transition from a small cloud to a turbulent, electrified giant can occur in as little as 30 minutes.

As a thunderstorm cumulonimbus develops, interactions of charged particles, external and internal electrical fields, and complex energy exchanges produce a large electrical field within the cloud. No completely acceptable theory explaining the complex processes of thunderstorm electrification has yet been advanced. But it is believed that electrical charge is important to formation of raindrops and ice crystals, and that thunderstorm electrification closely follows precipitation.

The distribution of electricity in a thunderstorm cloud is usually a concentration of positive charge in the frozen upper layers, and a large negative charge around a positive area in the lower portions of the cloud.

The earth is normally negatively charged with respect to the atmosphere. As the thunderstorm passes over the ground, the negative charge in the base of the cloud induces a positive charge on the ground below and several miles around the storm. The ground charge follows the storm like an electrical shadow, growing stronger as the negative cloud charge increases. The attraction between positive and negative charges makes the positive ground current flow up buildings, trees, and other elevated objects in an effort to establish a flow of current. But air, which is a poor conductor of electricity, insulates the cloud and ground charges, preventing a flow of current until large electrical charges are built up.

Lightning occurs when the difference between the positive and negative charges—the electrical potential—becomes great enough to overcome the resistance of the insulating air, and to force a conductive path for current to flow between the two charges. Potential in these cases can be as much as 100 million volts. Lightning strokes represent a flow of current from negative to positive (in most cases), and may proceed from cloud to cloud, cloud to ground, or, where high structures are involved, from ground to cloud.

The typical cloud-to-ground stroke we see most frequently begins as a pilot leader, too faint to be visible, advances downward from the cloud, and sets up the initial portion of the stroke path. A surge of current called a step leader follows the pilot, moving 100 feet or more at a time toward the ground, pausing, then repeating the sequence until the conductive path of electrified (ionized) particles is near the ground. There, discharge streamers extending from the ground intercept the leader path and complete the conductive channel between ground and cloud charges. When this path is complete, a return stroke leaps upward at speeds approaching that of light, illuminating the branches of the descending leader track. Because these tracks point downward, the stroke appears to come from the cloud. The bright light of the return stroke is the result of glowing atoms and molecules of air energized by the stroke.

Once the channel has been established and the return stroke has ended, dart leaders from the cloud initiate secondary returns, until the opposing charges are dissipated or the channel is gradually broken up by air movement. Even when luminous lightning is not visible, current may continue to flow along the ionized channel set up by the initial step leader.

Ground-to-cloud discharges are less frequently observed than the familiar cloud-to-ground stroke. In these cases, step leaders generally proceed from a tall conductive or semiconductive structure to the clouds; the initial leader stroke is not followed by a return stroke from the cloud, possibly because charges are less mobile in the cloud than in the highly conducting earth. Once the conductive path is established, however, current flow may set up cloud-to-ground sequences of dart leaders and returns.

## Thunder —

Thunder is the crash and rumble associated with lightning, and is caused by explosive expansion of air heated by the stroke. When lightning is close by, the thunder is a sharp explosive sound. More distant strokes produce the familiar growl and rumble of thunder, a result of sound being refracted and modified by the turbulent environment of a thunderstorm. Because the speed of light is about a million times that of sound, the distance (in miles) to a lightning stroke can be estimated by counting the number of seconds between lightning and thunder, and dividing by five.

The electromagnetic impulses of a lightning stroke produce whistlers— gliding tones which travel along lines of force in the earth's magnetic field from their lightning source in one hemisphere to a similar point in the opposite hemisphere, often echoing back and forth several times. Their sound is something like the whistle of World War II bombs, occasionally modified in a way that produces musical variations.

## Types of lightning —

Lightning comes in many forms. Streak lightning, a single or multiple line from cloud to ground, is the form seen most frequently. Forked lightning shows the conductive channel. Sheet lightning is a shapeless flash covering a broad area, often seen in cloud-to-cloud discharges. Heat lightning is seen along the horizon during hot weather, and is believed to be the reflection of lightning occurring beyond the horizon. Ribbon lightning is streak lightning whose conductive channel is moved by high winds, making successive strokes seem to parallel one another. Beaded lightning appears as an interrupted stroke.

Ball lightning is in some ways the most interesting—and most controversial—form. As reported, ball lightning appears as a luminous globe, toroid (doughnut-shape), or ellipsoid which hisses as it hurtles from cloud to earth, maneuvers at high speeds, rolls along structures, or hangs suspended in the air.

*Lightning over Tucson, Arizona, June, 1982.*

The dual character of lightning—it is a carrier of high currents and produces destructive thermal effects—makes it doubly dangerous. The current peaks, which may reach magnitudes of 200,000 amperes or more, produce forces which have a crushing effect upon conductors, and which can build to explosive levels in non-conducting or semiconducting materials like wood or brick. The continuous current produces heat, and is responsible for the numerous fires attributed to lightning.

## Work on the lightning problem—

At NOAA, the National Oceanic and Atmospheric Administration of the U.S. Department of Commerce, lightning is the subject of considerable scientific interest. The severe storm warnings of NOAA's National Weather Service carry implicit alerts that lightning can be expected—and avoided. Commerce Department scientists at NOAA's Environmental Research Laboratories are experimenting with lightning suppression techniques, measuring atmospheric electricity over the open ocean, and studying the apparent but elusive connections between lightning and other events in the atmosphere, ionosphere, earth, and geomagnetic field.

# LIGHTNING SAFETY RULES

THESE SAFETY RULES WILL HELP YOU SAVE YOUR LIFE WHEN LIGHTNING THREATENS.

1. Stay indoors, and don't venture outside, unless absolutely necessary.

2. Stay away from open doors and windows, fireplaces, radiators, stoves, metal pipes, sinks, and plug-in electrical appliances.

3. Don't use plug-in electrical equipment like hair dryers, electric tooth brushes, or electric razors during the storm.

4. Don't use the telephone during the storm—lightning may strike telephone lines outside.

5. Don't take laundry off the clothesline.

6. Don't work on fences, telephone or power lines, pipelines, or structural steel fabrication.

7. Don't use metal objects like fishing rods and golf clubs. Golfers wearing cleated shoes are particularly good lightning rods.

8. Don't handle flammable materials in open containers.

9. Stop tractor work, especially when the tractor is pulling metal equipment, and dismount. Tractors and other implements in metalic contact with the ground are often struck by lightning.

10. Get out of the water and off small boats.

11. Stay in your automobile if you are traveling. Automobiles offer excellent lightning protection.

12. Seek shelter in buildings. If no buildings are available, your best protection is a cave, ditch, canyon, or under high-high clumps of trees in open forest glades.

13. When there is no shelter, avoid the highest object in the area. If only isolated trees are nearby, your best protection is to crouch in the open, keeping twice as far away from isolated trees as the trees are high.

14. Avoid hill tops, open spaces, wire fences, metal clothes lines, exposed sheds, and any electrically conductive elevated objects.

15. When you feel the electrical charge—if your hair stands on end or your skin tingles—lightning may be about to strike you. Drop to the ground immediately.

Persons struck by lightning receive a severe electrical shock and may be burned, but they carry no electrical charge and can be handled safely. A person "killed" by lightning can often be revived by prompt mouth-to-mouth resuscitation, cardiac massage, and prolonged artificial respiration. In a group struck by lightning, the apparently dead should be treated first; those who show vital signs will probably recover spontaneously, although burns and other injuries may require treatment. Recovery from lightning strikes is usually complete except for possible impairment or loss of sight or hearing.*

*See Taussing, H. B. "Death From Lightning and the Possibility of Living Again." Annals of Internal Medicine, Vol. 68, No. 6 June 1968.

# LIGHTNING DEATHS BY STATE, RANK, AND LOCATION OF OCCURRENCE

### 1959-1989      1989

| STATE | RANK | 1959-1989 OPEN FIELDS NO. | % | UNDER TREES NO. | % | BOATING FISHING & WATER NO. | % | NEAR TRACTORS/HEAVY RD EQUIP NO. | % | GOLF COURSES NO. | % | AT TELEPHONES NO. | % | VARIOUS OTHER/UNKNOWN NO. | % | 1989 OPEN FIELDS NO. | % | UNDER TREES NO. | % | BOATING FISHING & WATER NO. | % | NEAR TRACTORS/HEAVY RD EQUIP NO. | % | GOLF COURSES NO. | % | AT TELEPHONES NO. | % | VARIOUS OTHER/UNKNOWN NO. | % |
|---|---|---|---|---|---|---|---|---|---|---|---|---|---|---|---|---|---|---|---|---|---|---|---|---|---|---|---|---|---|
| ALABAMA | 15 | 19 | 25 | 17 | 22 | 8 | 10 | 4 | 5 | 1 | 1 | 2 | 3 | 26 | 34 | | | | | | | | | | | | | 2 | 100 |
| ALASKA | 52 | | | | | | | | | | | | | | | | | | | | | | | | | | | | |
| ARIZONA | 26 | 21 | 43 | 6 | 12 | 5 | 10 | | | 3 | 6 | 3 | 6 | 11 | 22 | | | | | | | | | | | | | 2 | 100 |
| ARKANSAS | 8 | 34 | 33 | 19 | 18 | 11 | 11 | 8 | 8 | 3 | 3 | | | 29 | 28 | | | | | | | | | | | | | 2 | 100 |
| CALIFORNIA | 40 | 5 | 29 | 3 | 18 | 2 | 12 | 1 | 6 | | | | | 6 | 35 | | | | | | | | | | | | | 1 | 100 |
| COLORADO | 14 | 43 | 49 | 18 | 22 | 4 | 5 | 3 | 4 | 5 | 6 | | | 11 | 14 | | | | | | | | | | | | | 4 | 100 |
| CONNECTICUT | 42 | 3 | 23 | 2 | 16 | | | | | 3 | 23 | | | 5 | 38 | | | | | | | | | | | | | | |
| DELAWARE | 43 | 4 | 36 | | | 4 | 36 | 1 | 9 | | | | | 2 | 18 | | | | | | | | | | | | | | |
| DISTRICT OF COLUMBIA | 48 | 1 | 25 | 2 | 50 | | | | | 1 | 25 | | | | | | | | | | | | | | | | | | |
| FLORIDA | 1 | 84 | 28 | 38 | 13 | 74 | 25 | 20 | 7 | 9 | 3 | | | 73 | 24 | 1 | 11 | | | | | | | 1 | 11 | | | 7 | 78 |
| GEORGIA | 20 | 20 | 27 | 19 | 26 | 11 | 15 | 1 | 1 | 5 | 7 | 2 | 3 | 15 | 21 | | | | | | | | | | | | | | |
| HAWAII | 51 | | | | | | | | | | | | | | | | | | | | | | | | | | | | |
| IDAHO | 36 | 11 | 58 | 3 | 16 | 2 | 11 | 2 | 11 | 1 | 5 | | | | | | | | | | | | | 1 | 50 | | | 1 | 50 |
| ILLINOIS | 17 | 16 | 22 | 12 | 16 | 3 | 4 | 7 | 10 | 7 | 10 | 1 | 1 | 27 | 37 | | | | | | | | | | | | | | |
| INDIANA | 22 | 9 | 14 | 19 | 29 | 5 | 8 | 6 | 9 | 1 | 2 | 2 | 3 | 23 | 35 | | | | | | | | | | | | | 2 | 100 |
| IOWA | 23 | 8 | 13 | 8 | 13 | 1 | 2 | 5 | 8 | 2 | 3 | | | 37 | 61 | | | | | | | | | | | | | 2 | 100 |
| KANSAS | 25 | 15 | 28 | 1 | 2 | 4 | 7 | 10 | 19 | 2 | 4 | | | 22 | 41 | | | | | | | | | | | | | 5 | 100 |
| KENTUCKY | 16 | 21 | 28 | 10 | 13 | 4 | 5 | 3 | 4 | 1 | 1 | 1 | 1 | 35 | 47 | | | | | | | | | | | | | 6 | 100 |
| LOUISIANA | 7 | 15 | 14 | 30 | 29 | 34 | 32 | 8 | 7 | | | | | 20 | 19 | | | | | | | | | | | | | 1 | 100 |
| MAINE | 39 | | | 2 | 12 | 6 | 35 | | | | | | | 9 | 53 | | | | | | | | | | | | | | |
| MARYLAND * | 6 | 9 | 8 | 5 | 5 | 13 | 12 | | | | | | | 84 | 76 | | | | | | | | | | | | | 1 | 100 |
| MASSACHUSETTS | 33 | 4 | 17 | 3 | 13 | 1 | 4 | | | 1 | 4 | 1 | 4 | 14 | 58 | | | 3 | 75 | 1 | 25 | | | | | | | | |
| MICHIGAN | 11 | 24 | 27 | 23 | 26 | 10 | 11 | 2 | 2 | 10 | 11 | 2 | 2 | 17 | 20 | | | | | | | | | | | | | | |
| MINNESOTA | 27 | 16 | 31 | 14 | 27 | 3 | 6 | 6 | 12 | 1 | 2 | 2 | 4 | 9 | 18 | | | | | | | | | | | | | 3 | 100 |
| MISSISSIPPI | 12 | 29 | 35 | 19 | 23 | 9 | 11 | 5 | 6 | | | | | 21 | 25 | | | | | | | | | | | | | | |
| MISSOURI | 18 | 16 | 22 | 16 | 22 | 10 | 14 | 5 | 7 | 3 | 4 | 2 | 3 | 21 | 29 | | | | | | | | | | | | | | |
| MONTANA | 35 | 7 | 37 | 2 | 11 | 2 | 11 | 4 | 21 | | | | | 4 | 21 | | | | | | | | | | | | | | |
| NEBRASKA | 30 | 16 | 44 | 2 | 6 | 3 | 8 | 9 | 25 | | | | | 6 | 17 | | | | | | | | | | | | | | |
| NEVADA | 49 | | | | | 1 | 25 | | | | | | | 3 | 75 | | | | | | | | | | | | | 1 | 100 |
| NEW HAMPSHIRE | 46 | 2 | 33 | | | 1 | 17 | | | 1 | 17 | | | 2 | 33 | | | | | | | | | | | | | | |
| NEW JERSEY | 24 | 18 | 33 | 5 | 9 | 13 | 24 | 2 | 4 | 4 | 7 | 2 | 4 | 10 | 19 | | | | | | | | | | | | | | |
| NEW MEXICO | 19 | 35 | 47 | 13 | 18 | 6 | 8 | | | 1 | 1 | | | 19 | 26 | 1 | 33 | | | | | | | | | | | 2 | 67 |
| NEW YORK | 5 | 20 | 17 | 31 | 26 | 16 | 13 | 4 | 3 | 5 | 4 | 1 | 1 | 43 | 36 | | | 3 | 75 | | | | | | | | | 1 | 25 |
| NORTH CAROLINA | 2 | 34 | 22 | 20 | 13 | 20 | 13 | 6 | 4 | 5 | 3 | 1 | 1 | 68 | 44 | 1 | 25 | | | 1 | 25 | | | | | | | 2 | 50 |
| NORTH DAKOTA | 44 | 2 | 18 | | | | | 3 | 27 | | | | | 6 | 55 | | | | | | | | | | | | | | |
| OHIO | 9 | 33 | 32 | 19 | 18 | 15 | 14 | 4 | 4 | 7 | 7 | 1 | 1 | 25 | 24 | | | | | 1 | 50 | | | | | | | 1 | 50 |
| OKLAHOMA | 13 | 30 | 37 | 11 | 14 | 14 | 17 | 5 | 6 | 1 | 1 | 2 | 3 | 18 | 22 | | | | | | | | | | | | | | |
| OREGON | 45 | 3 | 50 | | | | | | | | | | | 3 | 50 | | | | | | | | | | | | | | |
| PENNSYLVANIA | 10 | 30 | 31 | 11 | 11 | 3 | 3 | 3 | 3 | 11 | 11 | 1 | 1 | 38 | 39 | | | | | | | | | | | | | | |
| PUERTO RICO | 31 | 11 | 39 | 8 | 29 | 1 | 4 | | | | | | | 8 | 29 | | | | | | | | | | | | | | |
| RHODE ISLAND | 47 | | | | | 1 | 25 | | | | | | | 3 | 75 | | | | | | | | | | | | | | |
| SOUTH CAROLINA | 21 | 15 | 22 | 14 | 20 | 6 | 9 | 7 | 10 | 1 | 1 | 3 | 4 | 23 | 33 | | | | | | | | | | | | | 2 | 100 |
| SOUTH DAKOTA | 38 | 5 | 28 | 1 | 6 | 2 | 11 | 8 | 44 | 1 | 6 | | | 1 | 6 | | | | | | | | | | | | | | |
| TENNESSEE | 4 | 32 | 28 | 31 | 27 | 8 | 7 | 9 | 8 | 7 | 6 | 2 | 2 | 27 | 23 | | | 1 | 50 | | | 1 | 50 | | | | | | |
| TEXAS | 3 | 62 | 44 | 24 | 17 | 20 | 14 | 5 | 4 | 4 | 3 | | | 26 | 18 | | | | | | | | | | | | | 2 | 100 |
| UTAH | 32 | 11 | 44 | 6 | 24 | 2 | 8 | | | 1 | 4 | 1 | 4 | 4 | 16 | | | | | | | | | 1 | 50 | | | 1 | 50 |
| VERMONT | 41 | 1 | 8 | 1 | 8 | 4 | 31 | | | | | | | 7 | 54 | | | | | | | | | | | | | | |
| VIRGINIA | 28 | 8 | 19 | 9 | 21 | 5 | 12 | 3 | 7 | 2 | 5 | | | 15 | 36 | | | | | | | | | | | | | | |
| WASHINGTON | 50 | 1 | 100 | | | | | | | | | | | | | 1 | 100 | | | | | | | | | | | | |
| WEST VIRGINIA | 37 | 6 | 33 | 2 | 11 | 2 | 11 | | | 1 | 6 | | | 7 | 39 | | | | | | | | | | | | | | |
| WISCONSIN | 29 | 7 | 16 | 3 | 7 | 9 | 21 | 4 | 9 | 6 | 14 | | | 14 | 33 | | | | | | | | | | | | | | |
| WYOMING | 34 | 11 | 52 | 2 | 10 | 3 | 14 | 1 | 5 | | | | | 4 | 19 | | | | | | | | | | | | | | |
| UNITED STATES | | 827 | 28 | 504 | 17 | 381 | 13 | 174 | 6 | 117 | 4 | 32 | 1 | 901 | 31 | 4 | 6 | 7 | 12 | 4 | 6 | 1 | 1 | 2 | 3 | | | 49 | 72 |

* ON DECEMBER 8, 1963 THE CRASH OF A JETLINER KILLING 81 PEOPLE NEAR ELTON, MARYLAND, WAS ATTRIBUTED TO LIGHTNING BY THE CIVIL AERONAUTICS BOARD INVESTIGATORS.

# LIGHTNING INJURIES BY STATE, RANK, AND LOCATION OF OCCURRENCE

1959-1989         1989

Columns are grouped into two periods (1959–1989 and 1989). Within each period the location categories are: Open Fields, Ball Parks, and Open Spaces; Under Trees; Boating, Fishing and Water Related; Near Tractors/Heavy Road Equipment; Golf Courses; At Telephones; Various Other and Unknown Locations. Each category lists NO. (number) and % (percent).

| STATE | RANK | 59-89 Open Fields No | % | 59-89 Under Trees No | % | 59-89 Boating No | % | 59-89 Near Tractors No | % | 59-89 Golf No | % | 59-89 Telephones No | % | 59-89 Various No | % | 1989 Open Fields No | % | 1989 Under Trees No | % | 1989 Boating No | % | 1989 Near Tractors No | % | 1989 Golf No | % | 1989 Telephones No | % | 1989 Various No | % |
|---|---|---|---|---|---|---|---|---|---|---|---|---|---|---|---|---|---|---|---|---|---|---|---|---|---|---|---|---|---|
| ALABAMA | 20 | 52 | 33 | 22 | 14 | 3 | 2 | 1 | 1 | 1 | 1 | 10 | 6 | 69 | 44 | | | | | | | | | | | | | 6 | 100 |
| ALASKA | 52 | | | | | | | | | | | | | | | | | | | | | | | | | | | | |
| ARIZONA | 32 | 48 | 59 | 5 | 6 | 2 | 2 | 5 | 6 | 1 | 1 | | | 20 | 25 | | | | | | | | | | | | | 2 | 100 |
| ARKANSAS | 16 | 42 | 22 | 25 | 13 | 12 | 6 | 7 | 4 | 4 | 2 | 11 | 6 | 90 | 47 | | | | | 2 | 12 | | | | | 1 | 6 | 14 | 82 |
| CALIFORNIA | 42 | 10 | 24 | 10 | 24 | 5 | 12 | | | | | | | 17 | 40 | | | | | | | | | | | | | | |
| COLORADO | 14 | 92 | 42 | 18 | 8 | 15 | 7 | 6 | 3 | 16 | 7 | 3 | 1 | 69 | 32 | | | 2 | 11 | | | | | | | 1 | 6 | 15 | 83 |
| CONNECTICUT | 34 | 6 | 9 | 22 | 34 | 4 | 6 | | | 3 | 5 | 3 | 5 | 26 | 41 | | | 1 | 20 | 3 | 60 | | | | | | | 1 | 20 |
| DELAWARE | 43 | 8 | 30 | 10 | 37 | 3 | 43 | | | 1 | 4 | 2 | 7 | 6 | 22 | | | 3 | 60 | | | | | | | | | 2 | 40 |
| DISTRICT OF COLUMBIA | 48 | 1 | 14 | 3 | 43 | | | 1 | 14 | 1 | 14 | | | 1 | 14 | | | | | | | | | | | | | | |
| FLORIDA | 1 | 276 | 34 | 83 | 10 | 115 | 14 | 23 | 3 | 30 | 4 | 21 | 3 | 265 | 33 | 2 | 5 | | | 5 | 12 | 2 | 5 | | | 1 | 2 | 31 | 76 |
| GEORGIA | 10 | 95 | 37 | 33 | 13 | 14 | 5 | 3 | 1 | 21 | 8 | 4 | 2 | 87 | 34 | | | | | | | | | | | | | 5 | 100 |
| HAWAII | 51 | 1 | 100 | | | | | | | | | | | | | | | | | | | | | | | | | | |
| IDAHO | 33 | 9 | 15 | 7 | 11 | 2 | 3 | 2 | 3 | 2 | 3 | 4 | 6 | 36 | 58 | | | | | | | | | | | | | 1 | 100 |
| ILLINOIS | 12 | 72 | 36 | 55 | 28 | 5 | 3 | 5 | 3 | 16 | 8 | 7 | 4 | 45 | 22 | | | 10 | 45 | | | 1 | 5 | 3 | 14 | 2 | 9 | 6 | 27 |
| INDIANA | 26 | 16 | 14 | 26 | 23 | 12 | 11 | 3 | 3 | 8 | 7 | 3 | 3 | 45 | 40 | | | | | | | | | | | | | 1 | 100 |
| IOWA | 21 | 27 | 17 | 20 | 13 | 1 | 1 | 1 | 1 | 2 | 1 | 2 | 1 | 102 | 66 | | | | | | | | | | | 1 | 17 | 5 | 83 |
| KANSAS | 19 | 26 | 16 | 14 | 8 | 2 | 1 | 7 | 4 | 10 | 6 | 7 | 4 | 101 | 60 | 3 | 43 | | | | | | | | | 2 | 29 | 2 | 29 |
| KENTUCKY | 18 | 55 | 29 | 23 | 12 | 7 | 4 | 3 | 2 | 11 | 6 | 7 | 4 | 81 | 43 | | | | | | | | | | | | | 1 | 100 |
| LOUISIANA | 17 | 94 | 49 | 30 | 16 | 18 | 9 | 4 | 2 | | | 2 | 1 | 41 | 22 | | | | | | | | | | | | | 2 | 100 |
| MAINE | 28 | 3 | 3 | 31 | 36 | 3 | 3 | | | | | 1 | 1 | 47 | 55 | | | | | | | | | | | | | 1 | 100 |
| MARYLAND | 25 | 45 | 39 | 16 | 14 | 15 | 13 | 4 | 3 | 3 | 3 | 1 | 1 | 31 | 27 | | | | | | | | | | | | | 1 | 100 |
| MASSACHUSETTS | 7 | 58 | 20 | 12 | 4 | 9 | 3 | 5 | 2 | 2 | 1 | 5 | 2 | 201 | 69 | | | | | | | | | | | | | 1 | 100 |
| MICHIGAN | 2 | 219 | 38 | 99 | 17 | 26 | 5 | 13 | 2 | 30 | 5 | 17 | 3 | 166 | 29 | | | 4 | 29 | | | | | | | 1 | 7 | 9 | 64 |
| MINNESOTA | 29 | 14 | 16 | 14 | 16 | 6 | 7 | 1 | 1 | 8 | 9 | 11 | 13 | 32 | 37 | | | | | | | | | | | | | | |
| MISSISSIPPI | 13 | 71 | 35 | 38 | 19 | 27 | 13 | 2 | 1 | 4 | 2 | 11 | 5 | 48 | 24 | | | | | | | | | | | 2 | 50 | 2 | 50 |
| MISSOURI | 31 | 23 | 30 | 16 | 21 | 1 | 1 | 1 | 1 | 1 | 1 | 3 | 4 | 31 | 41 | | | | | | | | | | | | | | |
| MONTANA | 41 | 14 | 38 | 5 | 14 | 3 | 8 | 1 | 3 | 3 | 8 | | | 11 | 30 | | | | | | | | | | | | | | |
| NEBRASKA | 36 | 21 | 38 | 1 | 2 | | | 5 | 9 | 5 | 9 | 5 | 9 | 19 | 34 | | | | | | | | | | | | | 1 | 100 |
| NEVADA | 49 | 2 | 40 | 1 | 20 | | | | | | | | | 2 | 40 | | | | | | | | | | | | | | |
| NEW HAMPSHIRE | 35 | 11 | 19 | 1 | 2 | | | | | | | 4 | 7 | 43 | 73 | | | | | | | | | | | | | | |
| NEW JERSEY | 27 | 49 | 47 | | | 8 | 8 | 1 | 1 | 5 | 5 | 2 | 2 | 39 | 38 | | | | | | | | | | | | | | |
| NEW MEXICO | 24 | 93 | 62 | 21 | 14 | 2 | 1 | 3 | 2 | 3 | 2 | 1 | 1 | 26 | 17 | | | | | | | | | | | | | 5 | 100 |
| NEW YORK | 6 | 44 | 12 | 81 | 21 | 20 | 5 | 22 | 6 | 6 | 2 | 9 | 2 | 200 | 52 | | | 5 | 16 | | | | | | | | | 26 | 84 |
| NORTH CAROLINA | 3 | 137 | 33 | 34 | 8 | 23 | 6 | 9 | 2 | 21 | 5 | 7 | 2 | 183 | 44 | 2 | 13 | 1 | 6 | 2 | 13 | | | | | | | 11 | 69 |
| NORTH DAKOTA | 47 | 5 | 38 | 1 | 8 | 1 | 8 | 2 | 15 | | | 1 | 8 | 3 | 23 | | | | | | | | | | | | | 2 | 100 |
| OHIO | 5 | 90 | 24 | 80 | 21 | 10 | 3 | 4 | 1 | 32 | 9 | 11 | 3 | 148 | 39 | | | | | 1 | 8 | | | 4 | 33 | 1 | 8 | 6 | 50 |
| OKLAHOMA | 11 | 78 | 38 | 12 | 6 | 9 | 4 | 10 | 5 | 5 | 2 | 16 | 8 | 78 | 38 | | | | | | | | | | | | | 3 | 100 |
| OREGON | 45 | 6 | 32 | | | | | 1 | 5 | | | 1 | 5 | 11 | 58 | 1 | 33 | | | | | | | | | | | 2 | 67 |
| PENNSYLVANIA | 4 | 153 | 35 | 19 | 4 | 5 | 1 | 2 | 1 | 9 | 2 | 4 | 1 | 243 | 56 | | | | | | | | | | | | | 4 | 100 |
| PUERTO RICO | 50 | 1 | 17 | 1 | 17 | | | | | | | | | 4 | 67 | | | | | | | | | | | | | | |
| RHODE ISLAND | 40 | 9 | 20 | 15 | 34 | | | | | 2 | 5 | | | 18 | 41 | | | | | | | | | | | | | | |
| SOUTH CAROLINA | 15 | 56 | 28 | 9 | 5 | 10 | 5 | 7 | 4 | 2 | 1 | 5 | 3 | 111 | 56 | | | 1 | 6 | | | | | | | | | 16 | 94 |
| SOUTH DAKOTA | 39 | 10 | 20 | 5 | 10 | 2 | 4 | 9 | 18 | | | 1 | 2 | 23 | 46 | | | | | | | | | | | | | | |
| TENNESSEE | 8 | 88 | 32 | 80 | 29 | 4 | 1 | 7 | 3 | 8 | 3 | 11 | 4 | 81 | 29 | | | | | | | | | 1 | 10 | 2 | 20 | 7 | 70 |
| TEXAS | 9 | 109 | 42 | 36 | 14 | 32 | 12 | 4 | 2 | 4 | 2 | 3 | 1 | 70 | 27 | | | | | | | | | | | | | 4 | 100 |
| UTAH | 38 | 24 | 40 | 11 | 18 | 3 | 5 | 1 | 2 | 4 | 7 | 3 | 5 | 14 | 23 | | | | | 1 | 100 | | | | | | | | |
| VERMONT | 46 | 4 | 25 | 1 | 6 | | | | | | | | | 11 | 69 | | | | | | | | | | | | | 1 | 100 |
| VIRGINIA | 22 | 14 | 9 | 35 | 23 | 7 | 5 | 1 | 1 | 7 | 5 | 3 | 2 | 84 | 56 | | | | | | | | | | | 1 | 3 | 38 | 97 |
| WASHINGTON | 44 | 3 | 13 | 4 | 17 | | | | | | | 2 | 9 | 14 | 61 | | | | | | | | | 1 | 100 | | | | |
| WEST VIRGINIA | 37 | 15 | 27 | 9 | 16 | 3 | 5 | 1 | 2 | 2 | 4 | 1 | 2 | 24 | 44 | | | | | | | 1 | 50 | | | | | 1 | 50 |
| WISCONSIN | 23 | 57 | 38 | 8 | 5 | 4 | 3 | 3 | 2 | 6 | 4 | 5 | 3 | 68 | 45 | | | 2 | 20 | | | | | | | | | 8 | 80 |
| WYOMING | 30 | 39 | 48 | 3 | 4 | 13 | 16 | 8 | 10 | 4 | 5 | | | 14 | 17 | | | | | | | | | | | | | | |
| UNITED STATES | | 2495 | 31 | 1105 | 14 | 458 | 6 | 198 | 2 | 308 | 4 | 226 | 3 | 3199 | 40 | 8 | 2 | 29 | 9 | 14 | 4 | 4 | 1 | 9 | 3 | 15 | 5 | 243 | 75 |

# FLOODS

## Flood danger—

The transformation of a tranquil river into a destructive flood occurs hundreds of times each year, in every part of the United States. Every year, some 75,000 American are driven from their homes by floods; on the average, 80 persons are killed each year. These destructive overflows have caused property damage in some years estimated at more than $1,000,000,000. Floods are also great wasters of water—and water is a priceless national resource.

## Why floods?

Floods begin when soil and vegetation cannot absorb falling rain or melting snow, and when water runs off the land in such quantities that it cannot be carried in normal stream channels or retained in natural ponds and manmade reservoirs. River Forecast Centers issue flood forecasts and warnings when the rain that has fallen is enough to cause rivers to overflow their banks, and when melting snow combines with rainfall to produce similar effects.

## Flood warnings—

Early flood warnings allow time for residents to leave low-lying areas, and to move personal property, mobile equipment, and livestock to higher ground. Sometimes valuable crops can be harvested in advance of a destructive flood. Emergency and relief organizations can prepare to handle refugees and to combat the inevitable health hazards caused by floods.

Flood warnings can be issued hours to days in advance of the flood peak on major tributaries. Main river flood forecasts can be issued as far as several days or even weeks in advance. In general, the time lapse between rainfall or snowmelt and the rise in river height increases with the size of the river.

Flood warnings are forecasts of impending floods, and are distributed to the public by radio and television, and through local emergency forces. The warning message tells the expected severity of flooding (minor, moderate, or major), the affected river, and when and where flooding will begin. Careful preparation and prompt response will reduce property loss and ensure personal safety.

Community sand bagging efforts tell more dramatically than river pictures of heavy rains and swelling streams. This Jack Shere, American Red Cross photo shows college and high school students preparing Minot, North Dakota to battle April 1969 flood waters.

# FLOOD SAFETY RULES

## BEFORE THE FLOOD:

1.  Become familiar with local flood areas and dams; know if flood waters might affect your home and property.
2.  Learn flood warning signals and community evacuation routes and shelters.
3.  Keep a stock of food that requires no cooking or refrigeration; electric and gas services may be interrupted.
4.  Keep a portable radio, emergency cooking equipment, lights and flashlights in working order.
5.  Keep first aid supplies and any medicines your family may need on hand.
6.  Store materials like sandbags, plywood, plastic sheeting and lumber to protect your house from flood waters and to make quick repairs.
7.  Keep your car fueled; in an emergency, filling stations may not be operating.
8.  Contact your insurance agent or local government to discuss flood insurance coverage.
9.  Install check valves in building sewer traps to prevent flood water from backing up in sewer drains.
10. Arrange for auxiliary electrical supplies for hospitals and other operations which are critically affected by power failure.

## WHEN YOU RECEIVE A FLOOD WARNING:

11. Store drinking water in clean bathtubs and in various closed containers; water service may be disrupted.
12. In coastal areas, board up windows or protect them with storm shutters or tape to prevent flying, broken glass.
13. Put sandbags or other protection in place, but away from outer walls. In the case of deep flooding you may opt to flood a basement with clean water.
14. If forced to leave your home and time permits, move essential items to safe ground or to upper levels of the house; turn off utilities at mainswitches but do not touch electrical equipment if you are wet or standing in water; fill tanks to keep them from moving away; grease immovable machinery; leave a note on your house to advise authorities that you have evacuated.
15. Move to a safe area before access is cut off by flood water. Watch for mud slides, downed electrical lines and areas with high or rising water levels.

FLOOD SAFETY RULES *continued*

## DURING THE FLOOD:

16. Avoid areas subject to sudden flooding.
17. Do not drive into flooded areas; if flood waters do rise around your car, abandon it and move to higher ground.
18. Do not swim or dive into the water.

## AFTER THE FLOOD:

19. Do not visit disaster areas; your presence might hamper rescue and other emergency operations.
20. If you have flood insurance, contact your agent that you have a loss.
21. Tune in to local radio and television for advice on where to obtain medical care and other assistance.
22. Do not enter structures if flood waters covered the first floor; seek expert advice to tell if the building is safe to enter.
23. Use battery-powered lanterns or flashlights (not oil or gas lanterns); if the building may have a gas leak, do not use any kind of light.
24. Flood waters may have swollen doors tightly shut; use windows or other openings.
25. Check with local authorities before using any water; wells should be pumped out and water tested before drinking.
26. Do not use fresh food that has come into contact with flood waters.
27. Do not handle live electrical equipment in wet areas; have an expert check all equipment before returning to service.
28. Pump water out of basements gradually (one-third of the water per day) to lessen damage to walls and foundation.
29. Report broken utility lines to appropriate authorities; have the gas company check for leaks and to turn the gas back on.
30. Watch out for poisonous snakes in previously flooded areas.

## Learn these flood terms:

**FLOOD FORECASTS** mean rainfall is heavy enough to cause rivers to overflow their banks or melting snow is mixing with rainfall to produce similar effects.

**FLOOD WARNINGS** or forecasts of impending floods describe the affected river, lake, or tidewater, the severity of flooding (minor, moderate or major), and when and where the flooding will begin.

*Flash floods are one of weather's most dangerous effects. Within minutes a nearly dry creek bed has become a roaring torrent totally submerging the road.*

# FLASH FLOODS

Flash flood waves, moving at incredible speeds, can roll boulders, tear out trees, destroy buildings and bridges, and scour out new channels. Killing walls of water can reach 10 to 20 feet. You won't always have a warning that these deadly, sudden floods are coming. But you can save yourself — your family — if you know what to expect and how to react.

On small streams, especially near the headwaters of river basins, water levels may rise quickly in heavy rainstorms, and flash floods can begin before the rain stops falling. There is little time between detection of flood crest. Swift action is essential to the protection of life and property.

NOAA's Weather Service has helped set up flash flood warning systems in about 100 communities. In these, a volunteer network of rainfall and river observing stations is established in the area, and a local flood warning representative is appointed to collect reports from the network. The representative is authorized to issue official flash flood warnings based on a series of graphs prepared by the Weather Service . These graphs show the local flooding that will occur under different conditions of soil moisture and rainfall. On the basis of reported rainfall, the representative can prepare a flood forecast from these graphs, and spread a warning within minutes. Communities within range of a Weather Service radar have the additional protection of advance warning when flood-producing storms approach.

Successful operation of a flash flood warning system requires active community participation and planning, but very little financial outlay. Still, the communities with cooperative flash flood warning systems are only a small fraction of the thousands of communities which need them.

Flash flood warnings are the most urgent type of flood warning issued, and are transmitted to the public over radio, television, and by sirens and other signals.

## Learn these flash flood terms used in forecasts and warnings:

**FLASH FLOOD** means the occurrence of a dangerous rise in water level of a stream or over a land area in a few hours or less caused by heavy rain, ice jam breakup, earthquake, or dam failure.

**FLASH FLOOD WATCH** means that heavy rains occurring or expected to occur may soon cause flash flooding in certain areas and citizens should be alert to the possibility of a flood emergency which will require immediate action.

**FLASH FLOOD WARNING** means that flash flooding is occurring or imminent on certain streams or designated areas and immediate precautions should be taken by those threatened.

# FLASH FLOOD SAFETY RULES

BEFORE THE FLOOD know the elevation of your property in relation to nearby streams and other waterways. Investigate the flood history of your area and how man-made changes may affect future flooding. Make advance plans of what you will do and where you will go in a flash flood emergency.

WHEN A FLASH FLOOD WATCH IS ISSUED listen to area radio and television stations for possible Flash Flood Warnings and reports of flooding in progress from the National Weather Service and public safety agencies. Be prepared to move out of danger at a moment's notice. If you are on the road, watch for flooding at highway dips, bridges, and low areas due to heavy rain not observable to you, but which may be indicated by thunder and lightning.

WHEN A FLASH FLOOD WARNING IS ISSUED for your area act quickly to save yourself. You may have only seconds:

1. Get out of areas subject to flooding. Avoid already flooded areas.

2. Do not attempt to cross a flowing stream on foot where water is above your knees.

3. If driving, know the depth of water in a dip before crossing. The road may not be intact under the water. If the vehicle stalls, abandon it immediately and seek higher ground — rapidly rising water may engulf the vehicle and its occupants and sweep them away.

4. Be especially cautious at night when it is harder to recognize flood dangers.

5. When you are out of immediate danger, tune in area radio or television stations for additional information as conditions change and new reports are received.

AFTER THE FLASH FLOOD WATCH OR WARNING IS CANCELLED stay tuned to radio or television for follow-up information. Flash flooding may have ended, but general flooding may come later in headwater streams and major rivers.

# WINTER STORMS

Winter storms can kill without breaking climatological records. Their **danger is** persistent, year to year. Since 1936 snowstorms have caused, directly and indirectly, about 100 deaths a year—and a year of 200 deaths is not unusual. Of such deaths, usually just over a third are attributed to automobile and other accidents; just less than a third to over-exertion, exhaustion, and consequent fatal heart attack; while only about 11 percent result from exposure and fatal freezing. The remaining number, 20-odd percent, are deaths due to home fires, carbon-monoxide poisoning in stalled cars, electrocution from downed wires, and building collapse. Large numbers of snow-related deaths—345 and 354—occurred in 1958 and 1960 respectively. About half of these deaths occurred in New England, New York and Pennsylvania.

## Winter storm impact—

Nearly everyone east of the Pacific coastal ranges remembers significant winter storms—days of heavy snow, interminable blizzard, inconvenience, economic loss, and sometimes, personal tragedy. Winter brings them all. For Wyoming or Kansas or Texas the blizzard of 1888 was one of the worst on record. The period January 11-13, in that year brought the most disastrous blizzard ever known in Montana, the Dakotas and Minnesota, combining gale winds, blowing snow, and extreme cold into a lethal, destructive push from the rockies eastward. The eastern seaboard got its big storm of the last century in the same year. March 11-14, 1888 saw the seaboard from Chesapeake Bay to Maine stricken with a blizzard that dumped an average of 40 inches of snow over southeastern New York and southern New England. The storm killed 200 in New York City alone; total deaths were over 400.

But every winter is a bad winter for someone. The 1966 season saw the eastern seaboard paralyzed by snow from Virginia to New England, with more than 50 deaths, and thousands marooned. A March storm buried the Dakotas, Minnesota, and Nebraska, with 30-foot drifts pushed up by winds gusting to more than 100 miles per hour. The 1967 winter storm season was not much better, and included a May Day blizzard in the Dakotas and a nor'easter which brought snow and hurricane-force winds to northern New England late in May. Snowfall across middle America was a much as four times normal in early 1968, and 1969 was called "the year of the big snows" in the midwest.

More recently, the winter of 1977-78 was unusually harsh, particularly in the midwest and east. Its most devastating punch was the "Northeast Blizzard of '78", one of the worst of this century. From February 5th to 7th it created havoc along the eastern seaboard. In New York City, the 17.7-inch snowfall was the sixth largest since records began in 1869. Boston had over 2 feet of snow, as did Providence, Rhode Island. Winds of more than 55 miles per hour caused massive snowdrifts, drove seas through seawalls, undermined homes, destroyed beaches (including Rockaway Beaches on Long Island), breached protective dunes, and left many areas from Cape May, New Jersey northward open to further damage from spring coastal storms. The American Red Cross reported 99 deaths and 4,587 injuries or illnesses attributable to the storm. Damage in Massachusetts exceded one-half billion dollars, while New York and New Jersey losses aggregated to about $94 million.

## Where and why winter storms occur—

The storms are generated, as are many of the thunderstorms of summer, from disturbances along the boundary between cold polar and warm tropical air masses, the fronts where air masses of different temperatures and densities wage their perpetual war of instability and equilibrium. The disturbances may become intense lowpressure systems, churning over tens of thousands of square miles in a great counter-clockwise sweep.

In the Pacific, these disturbances form along polar fronts off the east coast of Asia and travel northeastward toward Alaska. But some, particularly those forming along the mid-Pacific polar front, take a more southerly track, striking the United States as far south as southern California. Few Pacific disturbances cross the Rockies, but some do, redeveloping to the east. One region of such redevelopment lies east of the Colorado Rockies; the storms

*Red Cross volunteers look for persons trapped in their cars after a record snowfall in Buffalo, N. Y., February, 1977.*

which come out of that region are called Colorado Cyclones. Another region of storm redevelopment is east of the Canadian Rockies, from which come the so-called Alberta Cyclones. Both types take an eastward path, their most frequent ones converging over the Great Lakes. The Lakes themselves are generators of severe local winter storms, and forge others from northward-drifting disturbances originating over the Gulf of Mexico and our southern plains.

On our east coast, winter storms often form along the Atlantic polar front near the coast of Virginia and the Carolinas and in the general area east of the southern Appalachians. These are the notorious Cape Hatteras storms —nor'easters—which develop to great intensity as they move up the coast, then drift seaward toward Iceland, where they finally decay.

Because they form over water, these storms are difficult to forecast, and occasionally surprise the Atlantic megalopolis with paralyzing snows. In 1969, the U.S. Departments of Commerce, Transportation, and Defense tightened winter storm surveillance with reconnaissance aircraft, an ocean buoy, and a new weather ship. With better hour-to-hour information on the storms, weathermen ashore have begun to ease the burden of unexpected heavy snows in eastern cities.

For some parts of the United States—the Northern Rockies, for example—storms with snow followed by cold are a threat from mid-September to mid-May; during one of the colder months from November to March, it is not unusual for eight separate storms to affect some area across the continent. Intense winter storms are frequently accompanied by cold waves, ice or glaze, heavy snow, blizzards, or a combination of these; often, in a single winter storm, precipitation type changes several times as the storm passes. Their common feature is the ability to completely immobilize large areas and to isolate and kill persons and livestock in their path. In our northland, the severity of these storms makes their threat a seasonal one. Farther south, the occasional penetration of severe winter storms into more moderate climates causes severe hardship and great loss of warm-weather crops.

## Freezing rain (ice storms)—

Freezing rain or freezing drizzle is rain or drizzle occurring when surface temperatures are below freezing (32° Fahrenheit, F). The moisture falls in liquid form but freezes upon impact, resulting in a coating of ice glaze on all exposed objects. The occurrence of freezing rain or drizzle is often called an ice storm when a substantial glaze layer accumulates. Ice forming on exposed objects generally ranges from a thin glaze to coatings about an inch thick; but much thicker deposits have been observed. For example, ice deposits to eight inches in diameter were reported on wires in northern Idaho in January 1961, and loadings of 11 pounds per foot of telephone wire were found in Michigan in February 1922. It has been estimated that an evergreen tree 50 feet high with an average width of 20 feet may be coated with as much as five tons of ice during a severe ice storm. A heavy accumulation of ice, especially when accompanied by high winds, devastates trees and transmission lines. Sidewalks, streets, and highways become extremely hazardous to pedestrians and motorists—over 85 per cent of ice-storm deaths are traffic-related. Freezing rain and drizzle frequently occur for a short time as a transitory condition between the occurrence of rain or drizzle and snow, and therefore usually occur at temperatures slightly below freezing.

Some of the most destructive ice storms have occurred in the southern states, where neither buildings nor crops are designed with severe winter conditions in mind. The most damaging ice storm in the United States was

135

probably that which struck the southland from January 28 to February 4, 1951, causing some $50 million damage in Mississippi, $15 million in Louisiana, and nearly $2 million in Arkansas; this storm also caused 22 deaths. The region of greatest incidence, however, is a broad belt from Nebraska, Kansas, and Oklahoma eastward through the middle Atlantic and New England states.

## Ice storms are not sleet storms—

Ice storms are sometimes incorrectly referred to as sleet storms. Sleet can be easily identified as frozen rain drops (ice pellets) which bounce when hitting the ground or other objects. Sleet does not stick to trees and wires; but sleet in sufficient depth does cause hazardous driving conditions.

## Winter warnings—

The terms **watch** and **warning** are used for winter storms, as for other natural hazards. The **watch** alerts the public that a storm has formed and is approaching the area. People in the alerted area should keep listening for the latest advisories over radio and television, and begin to take precautionary measures. The warning means that a storm is imminent and immediate action should be taken to protect life and property.

The word **snow** in a forecast, without a qualifying word such as **occasional** or **intermittent,** means that the fall of snow is of a steady nature and will probably continue for several hours without letup.

**Heavy snow warnings** are issued to the public when a fall of four inches or more is expected in a 12-hour period, or a fall of six inches or more is expected in a 24-hour period. Some variations on these rules may be used in different parts of the country. Where four-inch snowfalls are common, for example, the emphasis on heavy snow is generally associated with six or more inches of snow. In other parts of the country where heavy snow is infrequent or in metropolitan areas with heavy traffic, a snowfall of two or three inches will justify a heavy snow warning.

**Snow flurries** are defined as snow falling for short durations at intermittant periods; however, snowfall during the flurries may reduce visibilities to an eighth of a mile or less. Accumulations from snow flurries are generally small.

**Snow squalls** are brief, intense falls of snow and are comparable to summer rain showers. They are accompanied by gusty surface winds.

**Blowing and drifting snow** generally occur together and result from strong winds and falling snow or loose snow on the ground. **Blowing snow** is defined as snow lifted from the surface by the wind and blown about to a degree that horizontal visibility is greatly restricted.

**Drifting snow** is used in forecasts to indicate that strong winds will blow falling snow or loose snow on the ground into significant drifts. In the northern plains, the combination of blowing and drifting snow, **after** a substantial snowfall has ended, is often referred to as a ground blizzard.

**Blizzards** are the most dramatic and perilous of all winter storms, characterized by low temperatures and by strong winds bearing large amounts of snow. Most of the snow accompanying a blizzard is in the form of fine, powdery particles of snow which are whipped in such great quantities that at times visibility is only a few yards.

**Blizzard warnings** are issued when winds with speeds of at least 35 miles per hour are accompanied by considerable falling or blowing snow and temperatures of 20°F or lower are expected to prevail for an extended period of time.

**Severe blizzard warnings** are issued when blizzards of extreme proportions are expected and indicate wind with speeds of at least 45 miles per hour plus a great density of falling or blowing snow and a temperature of 10°F or lower.

**Hazardous driving (travelers') warnings** are issued to indicate that falling, blowing or drifting snow, freezing rain or drizzle, sleet or strong winds will make driving difficult.

**Livestock (stockmen's) warnings** alert ranchers and farmers that livestock will require protection from a large accumulation of snow or ice, a rapid drop in temperature, or strong wind.

**A cold wave warning** indicates an expected rapid fall in temperature within a 24-hour period which will require substantially increased protection to agricultural, industrial, commercial, and social activities. The temperature falls and minimum temperatures required to justify cold wave warnings vary with the changing of the season and with geographic location. Regardless of the month or the section of the country, a cold wave warning is a red flag alert to the public that during a forthcoming forecast period **a change to very cold weather will require greater than normal protective measures.**

The terms **ice storm**, **freezing rain**, and **freezing drizzle** warn the public that a coating of ice is expected on the ground and on other exposed surfaces. The qualifying term **heavy** is used to indicate ice coating which, because of the extra weight of the ice, will cause significant damage to trees, overhead wires, and the like. Damage will be greater if the freezing rain or drizzle is accompanied by high winds.

# BLIZZARD SAFETY FOR CATTLE

**Blizzards take a terrible toll in livestock. For both humane and economic reasons, stockmen should take necessary precautions in advance of severe winter storms.**

MOVE LIVESTOCK, ESPECIALLY YOUNG LIVESTOCK, INTO SHELTERED AREAS. **Shelter belts, properly oriented and laid out, provide better protection for range cattle than shed type shelters, which may cause cattle to overcrowd, with consequent overheating and respiratory disorders.**

HAUL EXTRA FEED TO FEEDING AREAS **before the storm arrives. Storm duration is the largest determinant of livestock losses; if the storm last more than 48 hours, emergency feed methods are required. Range cattle are hardy and can survive extreme winter weather providing they have some non-confining type of shelter from the wind and are able to feed at frequent intervals.**

**Autopsies of cattle killed by winter storms have shown the cause of death to be dehydration, not cold or suffocation. Because cattle cannot lick enough snow to satisfy their thirst, stockmen are advised to use heaters in water tanks to provide livestock with water and feed after prolonged exposure to winter storm conditions.**

# WINTER STORM SAFETY RULES

Keep ahead of the winter storm by listening to the latest weather warnings and bulletins on radio and television.

CHECK BATTERY POWERED EQUIPMENT BEFORE THE STORM ARRIVES. A portable radio or television set may be your only contact with the world outside the winter storm. Also check emergency cooking facilities and flashlights.

CHECK YOUR SUPPLY OF HEATING FUEL. Fuel carriers may not be able to move if a winter storm buries your area in snow.

CHECK YOUR FOOD and stock an extra supply. Your supplies should include food that requires no cooking or refrigeration in case of power failure.

PREVENT FIRE HAZARDS due to overheated coal or oil burning stoves, fireplaces, heaters, or furnaces.

STAY INDOORS DURING STORMS and cold snaps unless in peak physical condition. If you must go out, avoid overexertion.

DON'T KILL YOURSELF SHOVELING SNOW. It is extremely hard work for anyone in less than prime physical condition, and can bring on a heart attack, a major cause of death during and after winter storms.

RURAL RESIDENTS: MAKE NECESSARY TRIPS FOR SUPPLIES BEFORE THE STORM DEVELOPS OR NOT AT ALL; arrange for emergency heat supply in case of power failure; be sure camp stoves and lanterns are filled.

DRESS TO FIT THE SEASON. If you spend much time outdoors, wear loose-fitting, lightweight, warm clothing in several layers; layers can be removed to prevent perspiring and subsequent chill. Outer garments should be tightly woven, water repellent, and hooded. The hood should protect much of your face and cover your mouth to ensure warm breathing and protect your lungs from the extremely cold air. Remember that entrapped, insulating air, warmed by body heat, is the best protection against cold. Layers of protective clothing are more effective and efficient than single layers of thick clothing; and mittens, snug at the wrists, are better protection than fingered gloves.

AUTOMOBILE PREPARATIONS. Your automobile can be your best friend—or worst enemy—during winter storms, depending on your preparations. Get your car winterized before the storm season begins. Everything on the checklist shown below should be taken care of before winter storms strike your area.

| | |
|---|---|
| ____ignition system | ____heater |
| ____battery | ____brakes perfectly |
| ____lights | adjusted |
| ____tire tread | ____wiper blades |
| ____cooling system | ____defroster |
| ____fuel system | ____snow tires installed |
| ____lubrication | ____chains |
| ____exhaust system tight | ____winter-grade oil |

Keep water out of your fuel by maintaining a FULL tank of gasoline.

138

BE EQUIPPED FOR THE WORST. Carry a winter storm car kit, especially if cross country travel is anticipated or if you live in the northern states.

Suggested Winter Storm Car Kit: blankets or sleeping bags, matches and candles, empty 3-pound coffee can with plastic cover, facial tissue, paper towels, extra clothing, high-calorie, nonperishable food, compass and road maps, knife, first aid kit, shovel, sack of sand, sand, flashlight or signal light, windshield scraper, booster cables, two tow chains, fire extinguisher, catalytic heater, axe.

## Winter auto travel safety—

Winter travel by automobile is serious business. Take your travel seriously.

If the storm exceeds or even tests your limitations, seek available refuge immediately.

Plan your travel and select primary and alternate routes.

Check latest weather information on your radio.

Try not to travel alone; two or three persons are preferable.

Travel in convoy with another vehicle, if possible.

Always fill gasoline tank before entering open country, even for a short distance.

Drive carefully, defensively.

# IF A BLIZZARD CATCHES YOU IN YOUR CAR

AVOID OVEREXERTION AND EXPOSURE. Exertion from attempting to push your car, shovel heavy drifts, and perform other difficult chores during the strong winds, blinding snow, and bitter cold of a blizzard may cause a heart attack—even for persons in apparently good physical condition.

STAY IN YOUR VEHICLE. Do not attempt to walk out of a blizzard. Disorientation comes quickly in blowing and drifting snow. Being lost in open country during a blizzard is almost certain death. You are more likely to be found, and more likely to be sheltered, in your car.

DON'T PANIC.

KEEP FRESH AIR IN YOUR CAR. Freezing wet snow and wind-driven snow can completely seal the passenger compartment.

BEWARE THE GENTLE KILLERS: CARBON MONOXIDE AND OXYGEN STARVATION. Run the motor and heater sparingly, and only with the downwind window open for ventilation.

EXERCISE by clapping hands and moving arms and legs vigorously from time to time, and do not stay in one position for long.

TURN ON DOME LIGHT AT NIGHT, to make the vehicle visible to work crews.

KEEP WATCH. Do not permit all occupants of car to sleep at once.

# WIND CHILL (EQUIVALENT TEMPERATURES)

### How cold will you feel?

The temperature of the air is not always a reliable indicator of how cold a person will feel outdoors. Other weather elements, such as wind speed, relative humidity and sunshine (solar radiation), also exert an influence. In addition, the type of clothing worn, together with the state of health and the metabolism of an individual also will have an influence upon how cold he will feel. Generally, "coldness" is related to the loss of heat from exposed flesh; it can be assumed to be proportional to the measured rate of heat loss from an object.

Figure 1 (Wind Chill Equivalent Temperature Table) gives equivalent temperatures for various combinations of wind and temperature. In the example shown, a combination of 20° F. and a 10 mph wind has the same cooling power as a temperature of 3° F. and a wind speed of 4 mph.

The next time you want to know how cold it is outdoors, go ahead and check that thermometer! But keep in mind that other things (wind speed, state of nourishment, individual metabolism and protective clothing) all help to determine how "chilly" you feel at a given time and place.

## WIND CHILL EQUIVALENT TEMPERATURE TABLE

### DRY BULB TEMPERATURE (°F)

| WIND VELOCITY (MPH) | 45 | 40 | 35 | 30 | 25 | 20 | 15 | 10 | 5 | 0 | −5 | −10 | −15 | −20 | −25 | −30 | −35 | −40 | −45 | |
|---|---|---|---|---|---|---|---|---|---|---|---|---|---|---|---|---|---|---|---|---|
| 4 | 45 | 40 | 35 | 30 | 25 | 20 | 15 | 10 | 5 | 0 | −5 | −10 | −15 | −20 | −25 | −30 | −35 | −40 | −45 | 4 |
| 5 | 43 | 37 | 32 | 27 | 22 | 16 | 11 | 6 | 0 | −5 | −10 | −15 | −21 | −26 | −31 | −36 | −42 | −47 | −52 | 5 |
| 10 | 34 | 28 | 22 | 16 | 10 | 3 | −3 | −9 | −15 | −22 | −27 | −34 | −40 | −46 | −52 | −58 | −64 | −71 | −77 | 10 |
| 15 | 29 | 23 | 16 | 9 | 2 | −5 | −11 | −18 | −25 | −31 | −38 | −45 | −51 | −58 | −65 | −72 | −78 | −85 | −92 | 15 |
| 20 | 26 | 19 | 12 | 4 | −3 | −10 | −17 | −24 | −31 | −39 | −46 | −53 | −60 | −67 | −74 | −81 | −88 | −95 | −103 | 20 |
| 25 | 23 | 16 | 8 | 1 | −7 | −15 | −22 | −29 | −36 | −44 | −51 | −59 | −66 | −74 | −81 | −88 | −96 | −103 | −110 | 25 |
| 30 | 21 | 13 | 6 | −2 | −10 | −18 | −25 | −33 | −41 | −49 | −56 | −64 | −71 | −79 | −86 | −93 | −101 | −109 | −116 | 30 |
| 35 | 20 | 12 | 4 | −4 | −12 | −20 | −27 | −35 | −43 | −52 | −58 | −67 | −74 | −82 | −89 | −97 | −105 | −113 | −120 | 35 |
| 40 | 19 | 11 | 3 | −5 | −13 | −21 | −29 | −37 | −45 | −53 | −60 | −69 | −76 | −84 | −92 | −100 | −107 | −115 | −123 | 40 |
| 45 | 18 | 10 | 2 | −6 | −14 | −22 | −30 | −38 | −46 | −54 | −62 | −70 | −78 | −85 | −93 | −102 | −109 | −117 | −125 | 45 |

VERY COLD · BITTER COLD · EXTREME COLD

WIND VELOCITY (MPH)

### EXAMPLE OF TABLE USE-

Suppose the temperature outside is 25°F, and wind velocity is 10 miles-per-hour. To determine wind-chill equivalent temperature, first scan across the top of the chart until 25°F is reached (5th vertical column of the chart). This is the vertical column to be checked. Now scan down the left side of the chart until 10 is reached. This numeral 10, which designates the 3rd horizontal column, is the wind velocity measured in miles-per-hour. Now follow these two vertical and horizontal columns until they intersect. **THE NUMBER IN THE SQUARE IN WHICH THE TWO COLUMNS INTERSECT IS THE WIND-CHILL EQUIVALENT TEMPERATURE YOU SEEK.**

| | 45 | 40 | 35 | 30 | **25** | 20 |
|---|---|---|---|---|---|---|
| 4 | 45 | 40 | 35 | 30 | 25 | 20 |
| 5 | 43 | 37 | 32 | 27 | 22 | 16 |
| **10** | 34 | 28 | 22 | 16 | **10** | 3 |
| 15 | 29 | 23 | 16 | 9 | | −5 |

VERY COLD

## Development of wind chill index —

A reasonably satisfactory solution to that elusive characteristic of weather known as "coldness" was first proposed by Dr. Paul Siple in 1939. The term "Wind Chill" was used to describe the relative discomfort resulting from combinations of wind and temperature. The method used was not applicable to temperatures above 0 °C. and high wind speeds caused exaggerated wind chill values. During the Antarctic winter of 1941, Siple and Passel developed a new formula to determine Wind Chill from experiments made at Little America. Measurements were made of the time required for the freezing of 250 grams of water in a plastic cylinder under a variety of conditions of wind and temperature. They assumed that the rate of heat loss was proportional to the difference in temperature between the cylinder and the temperature of the surrounding air. The results, expressed in kilocalories per square meter per hour per degree Celsius, were plotted against wind speed in meters per second.

Heat loss occurs by means of radiation, conduction and convection. Combining all effects, the general equation for heat loss "H" is:

$$H = (A + B\sqrt{v} + Cv)\,\Delta t$$

**Constants**

$$A = 10.45$$
$$B = 10.00$$
$$C = -1.00$$

where H = Heat loss (wind chill) in kg. cals/m$^2$/hr

v = Wind speed in meters per second

$\Delta t$ = Difference in degrees Celsius between neutral skin temperature of 33° and air temperature

The constant "A" includes the cooling caused by radiation and conduction. The value of the constants "A", "B", and "C" varies widely in formulae presented by different investigators. This is to be expected since "H" also depends on certain properties of the body being cooled. The above formula measures the cooling power of the wind and temperature in complete shade and does not consider the gain of heat from incoming radiation, either direct or diffuse. Under conditions of bright sunshine, the wind chill index should be reduced by about 200 kg/cals/m$^2$/hr.

The wind chill index, or equivalent temperature, is based upon a neutral skin temperature of 33 °C. (91.4 °F.). With physical exertion, the body heat production rises, perspiration begins, and heat is removed from the body by vaporization. The body also loses heat through conduction to cold surfaces with which it is in contact, and in breathing cold air which results in the loss of heat from the lungs. The index, therefore, does not take into account all possible losses of the body. It does, however, give a good measure of the convective cooling which is the major source of body heat loss.

Figure 2 (Wind Chill Index Nomogram) illustrates the amount of cooling produced by various combinations of wind and temperature. The line for 4 mph is accented because this is roughly the wind speed generated by someone walking briskly under calm conditions and is the generally accepted standard wind speed for calculating equivalent temperature. To obtain the temperature equivalent of 4 mph from the graph, move horizontally to the left from the intersection of a given wind and temperature until the 4 mph line is reached. The vertical line intersected is the equivalent temperature. In the example shown, a combination of **20°F.** temperature and a 10 mph wind has an equivalent temperature of **3°F.**

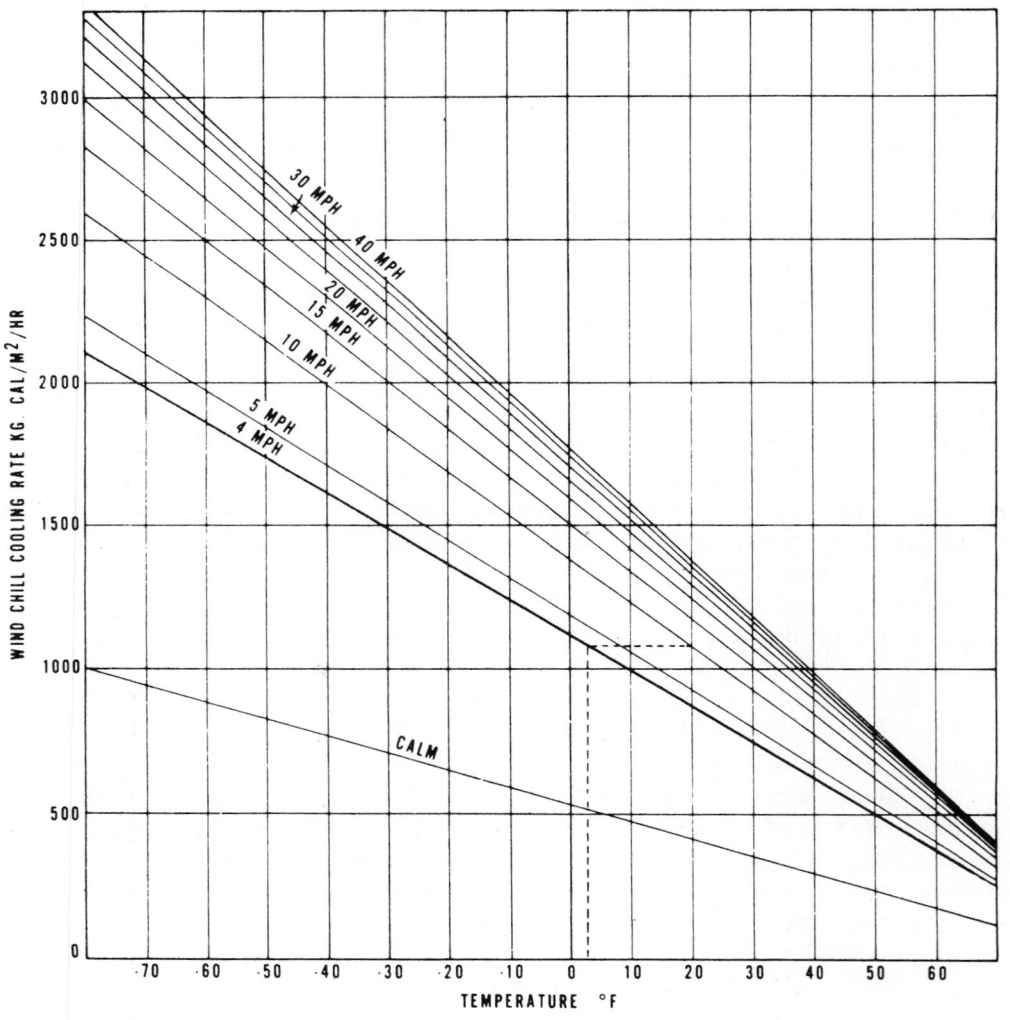

Figure 2

# HUMIDITY AND INDOOR WINTER COMFORT

Compared to summer when the moisture content of the air (relative humidity) is an important factor of body discomfort, the amount of moisture in the air in the winter has a lesser effect on the human body during outdoor winter activities. But moisture is a big factor for winter INDOOR comfort because of effects on health and energy consumption.

The colder the outdoor temperature, the more heat must be added indoors to be comfortable. That heat, however, drys the indoor air and lowers the indoor relative humidity. While a room temperature between 71 and 77 degrees Fahrenheit may be comfortable for short periods under very dry conditions, prolonged exposure to dry air has varying effects on the human body and usually causes discomfort.

Dry air has been shown to have four main effects on the human body:
1. Breathing dry air can cause such respiratory ailments as asthma, bronchitis, sinusitis, and nosebleeds or general dehydration since body fluids are depleted during respiration.
2. Skin moisture evaporation can cause skin irritations and eye itching.
3. Irritative effects, such as static electricity, which causes mild shocks when metal is touched, are common when moisture is low.
4. The "apparent temperature" of the air is lower than what the thermometer indicates, and the body "feels" colder.

These problems can be reduced by simply increasing the indoor relative humidity. By increasing the relative humidity to above 50 percent when the indoor temperature is between 71 and 77 degrees, most average dressed persons will feel comfortable. This can be done by using humidifiers, vaporizers, steam generators, or large pans of water. Even wet towels or water in a bathtub will help. The lower the room temperature the easier the relative humidity can be brought to its desired level. A relative humidity indicator (hygrometer) may be of assistance in determining the humidity in the house.

## How cold will you feel?

When the humidity is low, the body feels cooler than what the thermometer indicates. While the indoor temperature may read 75 degrees Fahrenheit, the apparent temperature (what is feels like) may be warmer or cooler depending upon the moisture content (relative humidity) of the air. Apparent temperature can vary as much as 8 degrees Fahrenheit when the relative humidity ranges between 10 to 80 percent. Why? The human body cools when exposed to dry air because skin moisture evaporates, and the sense of coolness increases as humidity decreases. The dryer the room the cooler the skin feels. With a room temperature of 70 degrees Fahrenheit, for example, a person will feel cooler if the humidity is low than if the humidity is high; this is especially noticeable when entering a dry room after bathing.

# APPARENT TEMPERATURE TABLE

This table provides apparent temperature (what the body feels the temperature to be) under various combinations of room temperature and relative humidity.

RELATIVE HUMIDITY (%)

| | 0 | 10 | 20 | 30 | 40 | 50 | 60 | 70 | 80 | 90 | 100 |
|---|---|---|---|---|---|---|---|---|---|---|---|
| 75 | 68 | 69 | 71 | 72 | 74 | 75 | 76 | 76 | 77 | 78 | 79 |
| 74 | 66 | 68 | 69 | 71 | 72 | 73 | 74 | 75 | 76 | 77 | 78 |
| 73 | 65 | 67 | 68 | 70 | 71 | 72 | 73 | 74 | 75 | 76 | 77 |
| 72 | 64 | 65 | 67 | 68 | 70 | 71 | 72 | 73 | 74 | 75 | 76 |
| 71 | 63 | 64 | 66 | 67 | 68 | 70 | 71 | 72 | 73 | 74 | 75 |
| 70 | 63 | 64 | 65 | 66 | 67 | 68 | 69 | 70 | 71 | 72 | 73 |
| 69 | 62 | 63 | 64 | 65 | 66 | 67 | 68 | 69 | 70 | 71 | 72 |
| 68 | 61 | 62 | 63 | 64 | 65 | 66 | 67 | 68 | 69 | 70 | 71 |
| 67 | 60 | 61 | 62 | 63 | 64 | 65 | 66 | 67 | 68 | 68 | 69 |
| 66 | 59 | 60 | 61 | 62 | 63 | 64 | 65 | 66 | 67 | 67 | 68 |
| 65 | 59 | 60 | 61 | 61 | 62 | 63 | 64 | 65 | 65 | 66 | 67 |
| 64 | 58 | 59 | 60 | 60 | 61 | 62 | 63 | 64 | 64 | 65 | 66 |
| 63 | 57 | 58 | 59 | 59 | 60 | 61 | 62 | 62 | 63 | 64 | 64 |
| 62 | 56 | 57 | 58 | 58 | 59 | 60 | 61 | 61 | 62 | 63 | 63 |
| 61 | 56 | 57 | 57 | 58 | 59 | 59 | 60 | 60 | 61 | 61 | 62 |
| 60 | 55 | 56 | 56 | 57 | 58 | 58 | 59 | 59 | 60 | 60 | 61 |

ROOM TEMPERATURE (°F)

**Examples of table use:** A room temperature of 70 degrees Fahrenheit combined with a relative humidity of 10 percent feels like 64 degrees Fahrenheit, but at 80% it feels like 71 degrees Fahrenheit. Although degrees of comfort vary with age, health, activity, clothing, and body characteristics, the table can be used as a general guideline when raising the level of comfort through an increase of room moisture rather than by an addition of heat to the room. This method of changing the apparent temperature can give the direct benefit of reducing heating costs because comfort can be maintained with a lower thermostat setting if moisture is added.

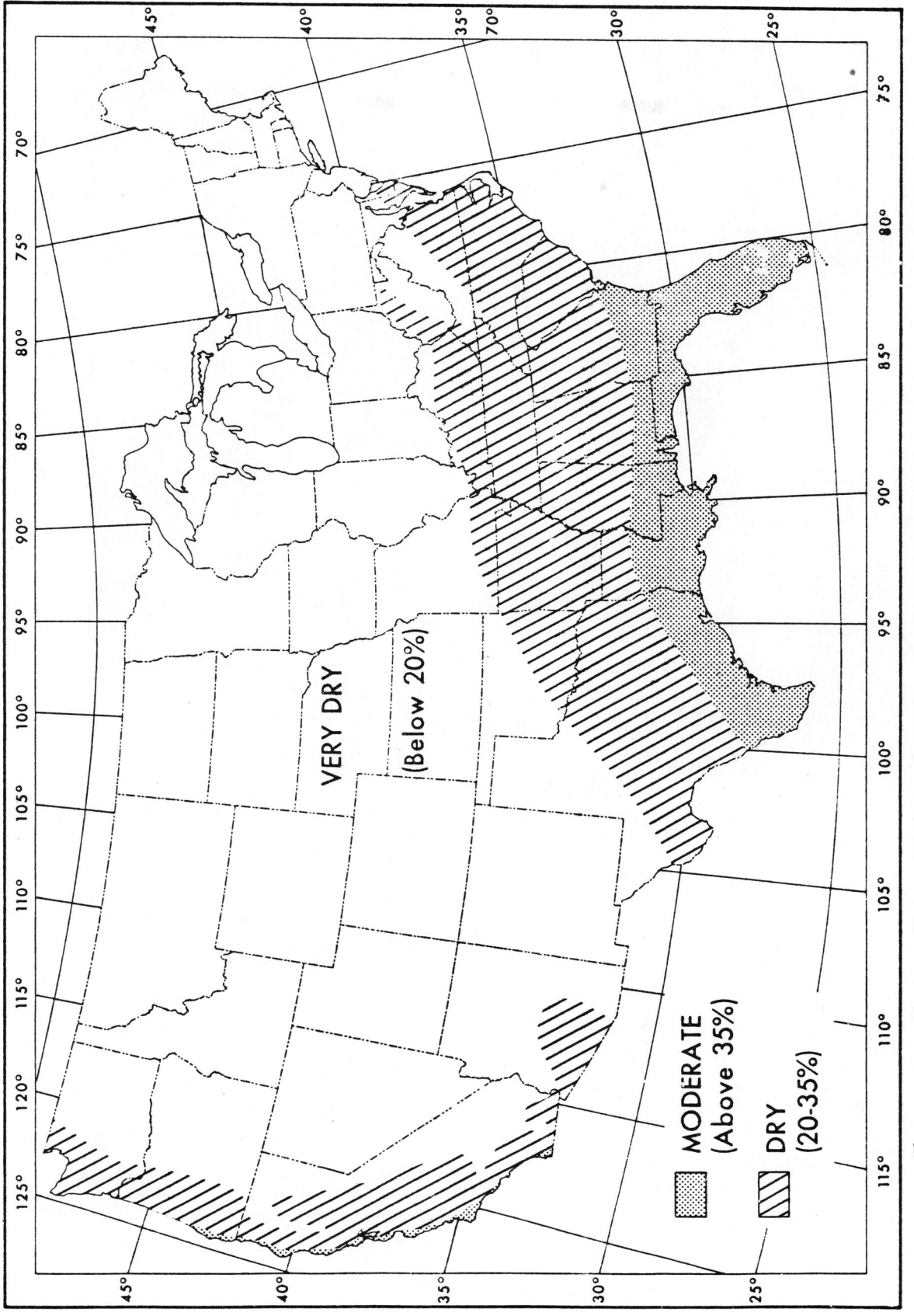

MODERATE
(Above 35%)

DRY
(20-35%)

VERY DRY

(Below 20%)

The average mid-winter (January) indoor relative humidity is noted on this map. (This assumes the thermostat setting is 70 degrees and no major indoor moisture sources are present.) As noted on the previous chart, if the average indoor relative humidity is 20% and the thermostat is set at 70 degrees Fahrenheit, the apparent temperature will be 65 degrees Fahrenheit. During periods of cold waves, the indoor relative humidity may be lower than values shown on the map.

*Scene from a February, 1977 snow storm in New York.*

# HEATING AND COOLING DEGREE DAYS

### Heating Degree Days

Early this century heating engineers developed the concept of heating degree days as a useful index of heating fuel requirements. They found that when the daily mean temperature is lower than 65 degrees, most buildings require heat to maintain an inside temperature of 70 degrees.* The daily mean temperature is obtained by adding together the maximum and minimum temperatures reported for the day and dividing the total by two. Each degree of mean temperature below 65 is counted as one heating degree day. Thus, if the maximum temperature is 70 degrees and the minimum 52 degrees, four heating degree days would be produced. (70 + 52 = 122; 122 divided by 2 = 61; 65 - 61 = 4). If the daily mean temperature is 65 degrees or higher, the heating degree day total is zero.

For every additional heating degree day, more fuel is needed to maintain a comfortable 70 degrees indoors. A day with a mean temperature of 35 degrees — 30 heating degree days — would require twice as much fuel as a day with a mean temperature of 50 — 15 heating degree days, assuming, of course, similar meteorological conditions such as wind speed and cloudiness.

**(Fuel conservation note:** *Each degree below 70°F that is called for as indoor temperature will conserve one* **heating-degree-day** *where the measure is used in calculating fuel unit requirements.*)

So valuable has the heating degree concept become that daily, monthly and seasonal totals are routinely computed for all temperature observing stations in the National Weather Service's network. Daily figures are used by fuel companies for evaluation of fuel use rates and for efficient scheduling of deliveries. For example, if a heating system is known to use one gallon of fuel for every 5 heating degree days, oil deliveries will be scheduled to meet this burning rate. Gas and Electric Company dispatchers use the data to anticipate demand and to implement priority procedures when demand exceeds capacity.

The amount of heat required to maintain a certain temperature level is proportional to the heating degree days. A fuel bill usually will be twice as high for a month with 1,000 heating degree days as for a month with 500. For example, it can be estimated that about four times as much fuel will be required to heat a building in Chicago, where the annual average is 6,100 heating degree days, as it would to heat a building in New Orleans, where the average is about 1,500. All this is true only if building construction and living habits in these areas are similar. Since such factors are not constant, these ratios must be modified by actual experience. The use of heating degree days has the advantage that consumption rates are fairly constant, i.e., fuel consumed for 100 degree days is about the same whether the 100 heating degree days were accumulated on only three or four days or were spread over seven or eight days.

Accumulation of temperature data for a particular location has resulted in the establishment of "normal" values based on thirty years of record. Maps and tables of heating degree day normals, are published by the National Oceanic and Atmospheric Administration's Environmental Data Service (EDS). The maps are useful only for broad general comparisons, because temperatures, even in a small area, vary considerably depending on differences in altitude, exposure, wind, and other circumstances. FIG. 11.1, NORMAL SEASONAL HEATING DEGREE DAYS, 1941-1970, illustrates the national distribution. Tables of normal monthly and annual heating degree days for U.S. cities provide a more accurate basis for comparison. The

---

\*   All temperatures are in degrees Fahrenheit unless otherwise specified.

tables show, for instance, that Washington, D.C. (National Airport) has a normal annual total of 4,211 heating degree days, while the normal for Boston, Massachusetts (Logan International Airport) is 5,621.

Heating degree day comparisons within a single area are the most accurate. For example, March heating degree day totals in the Midwest average about 70 percent of those for January. In Chicago, the coldest six months in order of decreasing coldness are January, December, February, March, November, and April. Annual heating degree day data are published by heating season which runs from July of one year through June of the next year. This enables direct comparison of seasonal heating degree day data and seasonal heating fuel requirements.

## Cooling Degree Days

The cooling degree day statistic — summer sister of the familiar heating degree day — serves as an index of air-conditioning requirements during the year's warmest months.

According to experts, the need for air-conditioning begins to be felt when the daily maximum temperature climbs to 80 degrees and higher. The cooling degree day is therefore a kind of mirror image of the heating degree day. After obtaining the daily mean temperature, by adding together the day's high and low temperatures and dividing the total by two, the base 65 is substracted from the resulting figure to determine the cooling degree day total. For example, a day with a maximum temperature of 82 degrees and a minimum of 60 would produce six cooling degree days. (82 + 60 = 142; 142 divided by 2 = 71; 71 - 65 = 6). If the daily mean temperature is 65 degrees or lower, the cooling degree day total is zero.

The greater the number of cooling degree days, the more energy is required to maintain indoor temperatures at a comfortable level. However, the relationship between cooling degree days and energy use is less precise than that between heating degree days and fuel consumption. There is considerable controversy among meteorologists, as well as air-conditioning engineers, as to what meteorological variables are most closely related to energy consumption by air-conditiong systems. Many experts argue that because high humidity levels make people feel more uncomfortable as temperatures rise, some measure of moisture should be included in calculating energy needs for air-conditioning. The Temperature-Humidity Index has been suggested as an alternative basis for calculating cooling degree days. In addition to humidity some experts feel there are other factors, such as cloudiness and wind speed, that should be included in computation of energy needs for air-conditioning. All agree, however, that there is a need for a more effective measure of the influence of weather on air-conditioning loads.

Until a definitive study of the problem is conducted, NOAA's EDS is continuing to use and publish statistics based on simple cooling degree day calculations, employing air temperatures measured at National Weather Service Offices and cooperating stations throughout the country. As with heating degree days, normals of cooling degree days have been established, based on thirty years of record. FIGURE 11.2, NORMAL SEASONAL COOLING DEGREE DAYS, 1941-1970, illustrates the national distribution.

PLEASE NOTE THAT HEATING AND COOLING DEGREE DAYS DO NOT CANCEL EACH OTHER OUT. TOTALS FOR EACH ARE ACCUMULATED INDEPENDENTLY.

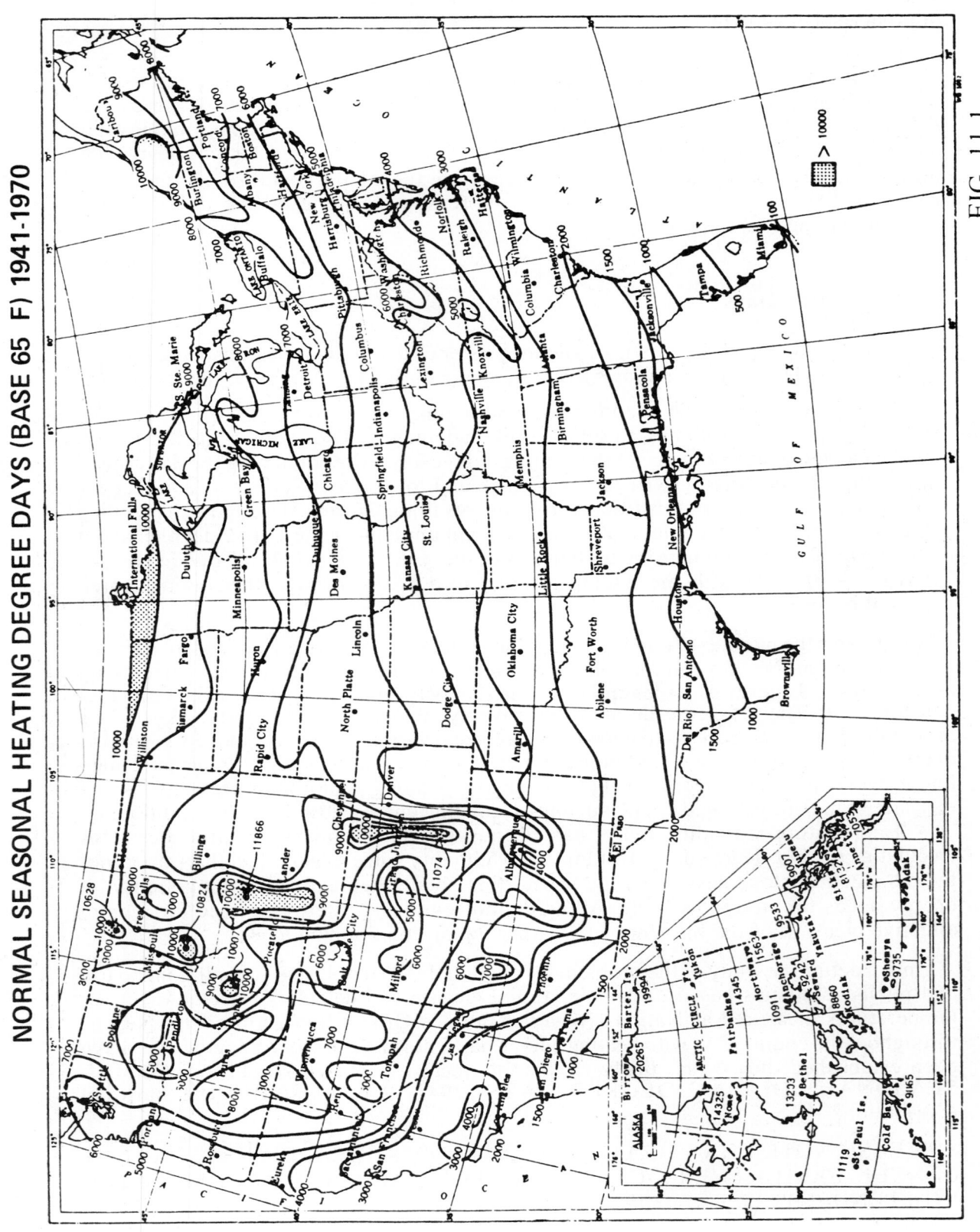

NORMAL SEASONAL HEATING DEGREE DAYS (BASE 65 F) 1941-1970

FIG. 11.1

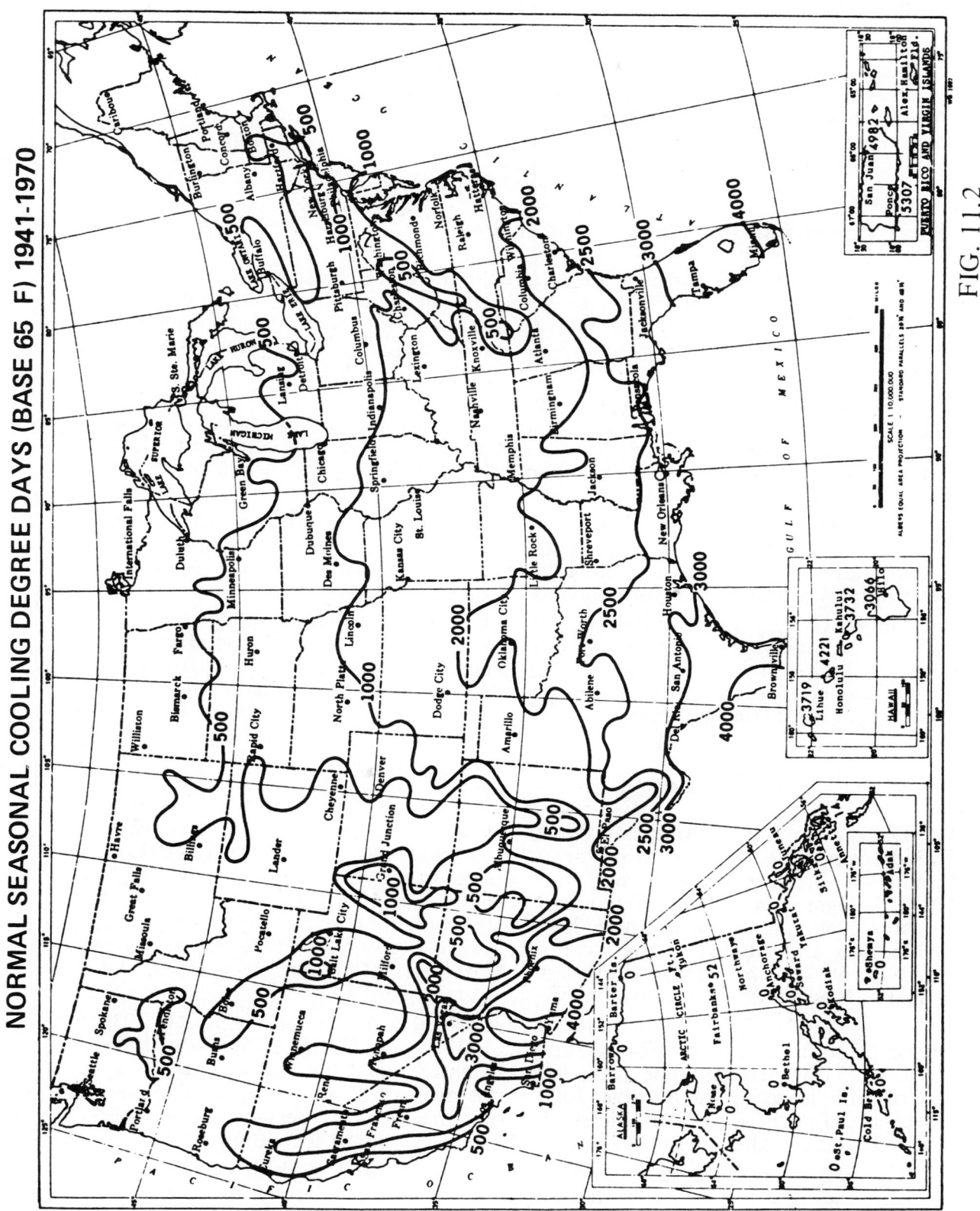

NORMAL SEASONAL COOLING DEGREE DAYS (BASE 65 F) 1941-1970

FIG. 11.2

# HEAT WAVE DANGERS

In a "normal" year, about 175 Americans die from summer heat and too much sun—"excessive heat and insolation" is the vital statistics category. Among our family of natural hazards, only the excessive cold of winter—not lightning, hurricanes, tornadoes, floods, earthquakes, or tsunamis—takes a greater average toll.

## Heat waves make a tragic difference—

In the period 1950 through 1967, more than 8,000 persons were killed in the United States by the effects of heat and solar radiation. The 1,401 dead in 1952, the 978 in 1954, and the several years with death tolls closer to 600 push the yearly average for this period to about 452 deaths, a high price to pay for warm weather.

These are direct casualties. It is not known how many deaths are encouraged by excessive heat or solar radiation—for example, how many diseased or aging hearts surrender that would not have under better conditions. Heat waves bring great stresses to the human body; among the aged or infirm are many who cannot run another summer race.

Most summers see heat waves in one section or another of the United States. East of the Rockies, they tend to be periods of high temperatures and humidities—those oppressive, muggy days when human comfort is just an expression—although the worst have been catastrophically dry.

Among the big ones are the hot summer of 1830, which scorched the north central interior, and that of 1860, which dried up the Great Plains. July 1901 may still be talked about by old timers in the middle west, remembering high temperatures, or thinking about someone the heat killed—there were 9,508 heat deaths in that year.

## Heat waves of the past—

There is nothing in American climatological annals to touch the heat waves which came with the Dust Bowl droughts of the 1930s. The years 1930, 1934, and 1936 brought progressively more severe summer weather. Record highs of 121 degrees in North Dakota and Kansas, and 120 degrees in South Dakota, Oklahoma, Arkansas, and Texas were observed in the ugly summer of 1936; July and August of that year saw record highs of 109 degrees or better tied or broken in Indiana. Louisiana, Maryland, Michigan, Minnesota, Nebraska, New Jersey, Pennsylvania, West Virginia, and Wisconsin.

These were cruel years in terms of heat deaths. From 1930 through 1936, ranging from a low of 678 deaths in 1932 to 4,768 in 1936, heat killed nearly 15,000 persons. The toll is consistently high, but tends sharply upward with increases in average July temperatures. This relationship between excessive July heat and significant jumps in heat deaths persists to the present day, despite the softening effects of modern consumer technology.

The first half of the 1950's was on the hot side, and its heat death toll is correspondingly high. Many states had their hottest summer of record in 1952; that year's death toll, 1,401, is the highest for the 1950-1967 period. The summer of 1954, a year when heat killed 978, was almost as bad.

The heat wave of July 1966 covered much of the eastern and middle continent with high temperatures and very high humidity. The portrait of a heat wave illustrated by charts with this text presents some of the meteorological and mortality particulars of the 1966 hot spell.

The highest death toll for a year since the 1930's belongs to 1980, according to the National Center for Health Statistics. That year unusually high temperatures held the central and southwestern United States in their grip for the best part of 15 weeks, and directly or indirectly caused 1700 deaths. This total, which also includes occupationally-related heat deaths, is more than nine times that of an ordinary year.

The 1980 heat wave, which is detailed on pages **160** through **168**, began about June 10, and except for remissions from about July 21 to about August 10, and August 17 to about September 1, lasted continuously through September's third week. As an example of its intensity, the first week of September saw temperatures of 9° above normal over much of the central and eastern states.

## How ordinary summer heat develops—

Given terrain and geographic situation, North American summers are bound to be hot. As the advancing sun drives back the polar air, the land is opened up to light and solar heat, and occupied by masses of moist warm air spun landward off the tropical ocean. With these rain-filled visitors come the tongues of dry desert air that flick northward out of Mexico, and, occasionally, the hot winds called chinooks which howl down the Rockies' eastern slopes.

Inequalities of atmospheric heating and cooling, of moistness and aridity, are regulated at middle latitudes by horizontal and vertical mixing. The mixing apparatus is the parade of cyclones (low-pressure centers, or Lows) and anticyclones (high-pressure centers, or Highs) which lie at the heart of most weather, good and bad.

The cyclones and anticyclones drift in the midlatitude westerlies, the prevailing eastward-blowing winds which follow a scalloped path around the northern hemisphere. The large-scale undulations of these winds may extend for thousands of miles, and are called planetary waves. Their high-speed core is the jet stream, which snakes across the continent some six to eight miles up, keeping mainly to the cool side of Highs and Lows as they form and spin and die below it.

The kind of weather predominating in an area over a period of time depends largely on the prevailing position and orientation of the jet stream. As the continent warms, the jet stream shifts northward, along with the tracks of surface weather disturbances. Cyclones like the ones which brought April rains to the Gulf states bring June thundershowers to the Plains; the humid spring of Georgia becomes the muggy summer of Illinois.

These semi-regular alternations of instability and equilibrium, hot and cool, moist and dry, combine year-in and year-out to generate the average June-to-September climate for North America.

## How heat waves occur—

When these alternating processes are somehow interrupted, the climatic "norm" of summer is marred by a heat wave. The anomaly is usually associated with a change in the planetary waves, so that the prevailing winds from the southwestern deserts sweep farther north than usual and blanket a large region with hot, often humid air at ground level. An upper-level High may settle over the mid-continent, destroying cloud cover with its descending, compression-heated currents, until the blessing of fair weather turns to the curse of drought. In addition, heat from the hot, dry ground feeds back into the atmosphere, tending to perpetuate the heat wave circulation.

Whatever the cause, the effect is uncomfortable and dangerous. Continental heat waves live in human memory the way fierce winters do.

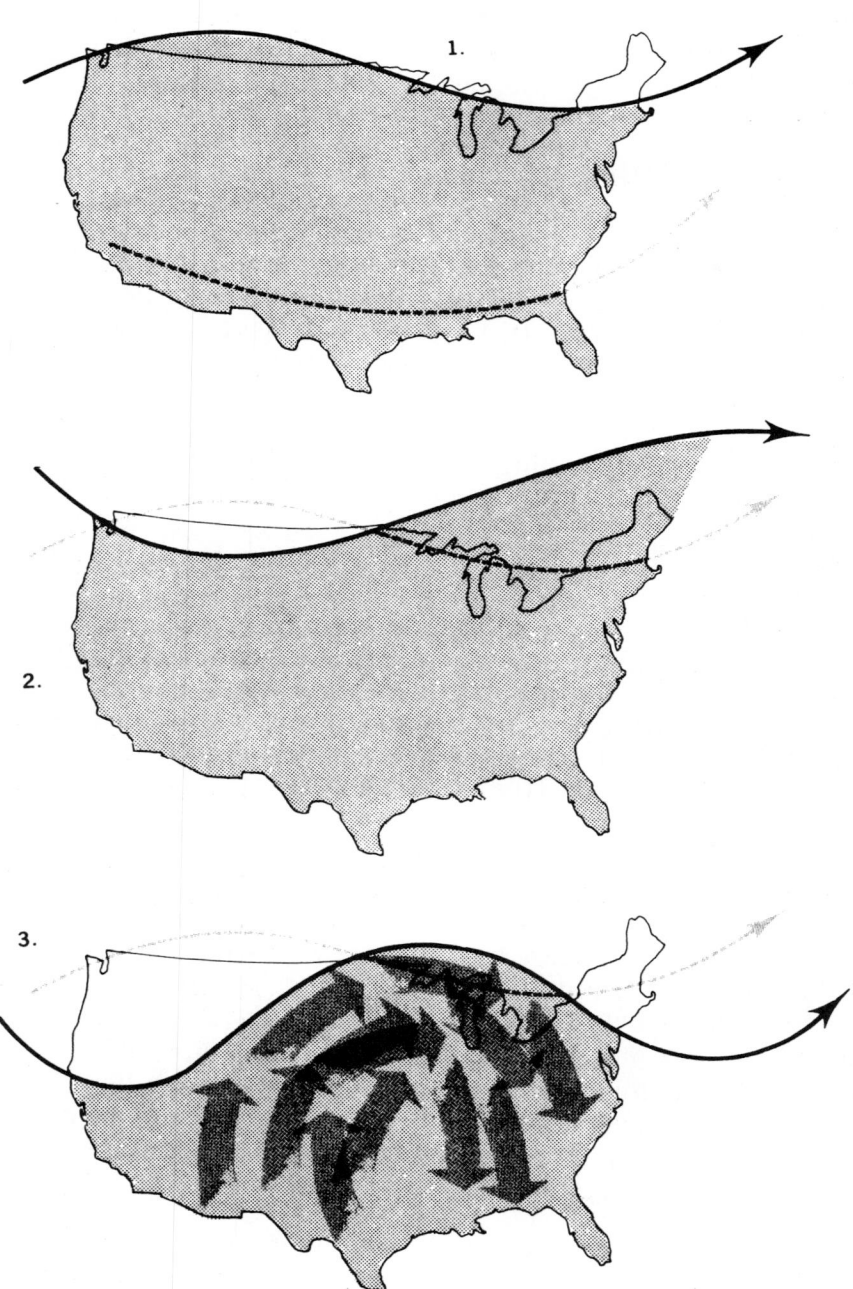

*In summer the jet stream can be an ill wind indeed. As the sun drives the polar front back into Canada, the jet stream keeps to the cool side of the boundary, and shifts northward (1).*
*The summer is a"normal" one—hot but not too hot; humid but not too humid.*
*But the polar front and jet stream may be oriented so that their eastern segment is displaced farther to the north (2), setting the stage for a midwestern and eastern heat wave. A persistent High can block the jet stream northward (3), its clockwise, sinking circulation drawing in hot dry air from the southwestern deserts, and dry air from the northwest. This classical Dust Bowl pattern brings hot, dry weather to the mid-continent, but often means cooler-than-normal conditions in New England and the far northwest. (Jet stream position at 500 mb level is shown here.)*

# The human body's reaction to heat—

To keep on the cool side of their upper thermal limits, our bodies dissipate heat by varying the rate and depth of blood circulation, by losing water through the skin and sweat glands, and, as the last extremity is reached, by panting. Under normal conditions, these reflex activities are kept in balance and controlled by the brain's hypothalamus, a comparatively simple sensor of rising and falling environmental temperatures, and a sophisticated manager of temperatures inside.

Like the hot light in a car, the hypothalamus responds to the temperature of coolant, in this case, blood. A surge of blood heated above 98.6 degrees sends the hypothalamus into action. As its orders go out, the heart begins to pump more blood, blood vessels dilate to accommodate the increased flow, and the bundles of tiny capillaries threading through the upper layers of the skin are put into operation. The body's blood is circulated closer to the skin's surface, and excess heat drains off into the cooler atmosphere. At the same time, water diffuses through the skin as insensible perspiration, so-called because it evaporates before it becomes visible, and the skin seems dry to the touch.

Heat loss from increased circulation and insensible perspiration is a comparatively minor correction. If the hypothalamus continues to sense overheating, it calls upon the millions of sweat glands which perforate the outer layer of our skin. These tiny glands can shed great quantities of water (and heat) in what is called sensible perspiration, or sweating. Between sweating and insensible perspiration, the skin handles about 90 percent of the body's heat-dissipating function.

As environmental temperature approaches normal body temperature, physical discomfort is replaced by physical danger. The body loses its ability to get rid of heat through the circulatory system, because there is no heat-drawing drop in temperature between the skin and the surrounding aid. At this point, the skin's elimination of heat by sweating becomes virtually the only means of maintaining constant temperature. Now it is not the heat but the humidity, as they say.

Most water enters the atmosphere via the process of evaporation, the jump from liquid to vapor phase; to do this, a water molecule must absorb enough energy to break the tenacious clutch of its fellow molecules. Evaporation, consequently, has the effect of absorbing large quantities of energy in the form of latent heat, which cools the parent body. This is familiar to anyone who has stepped from a bath into a dry room. The breakdown of the evaporation process when one steps from a bath into a hot, moist room is just as familiar.

Sweating, by itself, does nothing to cool the body, unless the water is removed by evaporation—and high relative humidity retards evaporation. Under conditions of high temperature (above 90 degrees) and high relative humidity (above 75 percent), the body is doing everything it can to maintain 98.6 inside. The heart is pumping a torrent of blood through dilated circulatory vessels; the sweat glands are pouring liquids—and essential dissolved chemicals, like sodium and chloride—onto the surface of the skin. And the body's metabolic heat production goes on, down in the vital organs.

Still, the thermal limits are there. When they are exceeded by very much or for very long, the warm-blooded organism does not doze, reptile fashion. It dies.

Much of the information on the human thermoregulatory system and heat syndrome is from Burch, G., and DePasquale, N., *Hot Climates, Man and His Heart.* Courtesy of Charles C. Thomas, Publisher

A study of three September heat waves in Los Angeles and Orange County, California, shows what excessive temperature alone can do. Without the complicating factors of high humidity or air pollution, the heat waves were accompanied by an increased mortality, especially among the elderly. The California study agreed with other researchers that increased mortality in a heat wave tends to follow maximum temperatures by about one day—the day it takes to overwork a tired circulatory system. The causes of "extra" deaths in September 1963 would seem to bear this out. Most were assigned to coronary and cerebrovascular disease. Heat syndrome was almost absent.

**Heat syndrome** refers to several clinically recognizable disturbances of the human thermoregulatory system. The disorders generally have to do with a reduction or collapse of the body's ability to shed heat by circulatory changes and sweating, or a chemical (salt) imbalance caused by too much sweating. Ranging in severity from the vague malaise of heat asthenia to the extremely lethal heat stroke, heat syndrome disorders share one common feature: the individual has overexposed or overexercised for his age and physical condition for the thermal environment.

## Portrait of a Heat Wave

*The summer of 1966 ended the mild period of the 1960s, and the relationship between heat deaths and summer temperatures repeated itself with a vengeance (1). In many States, high heat death tolls came with July temperatures several degrees above the average (2), and the monthly heat-death rate for the United States was dramatically different from that of milder 1965 (3).*

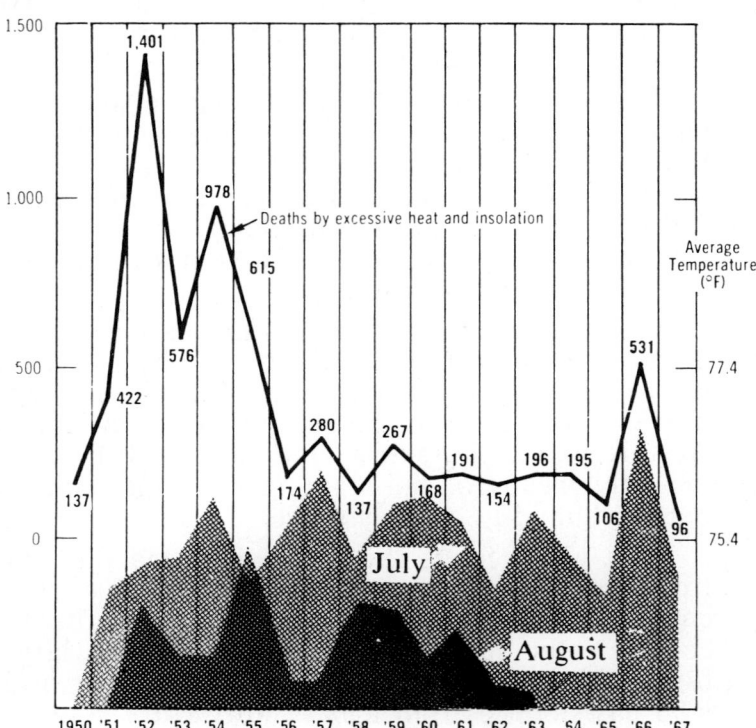

1. **HEAT DEATHS AND SUMMER TEMPERATURES**
1950-1967

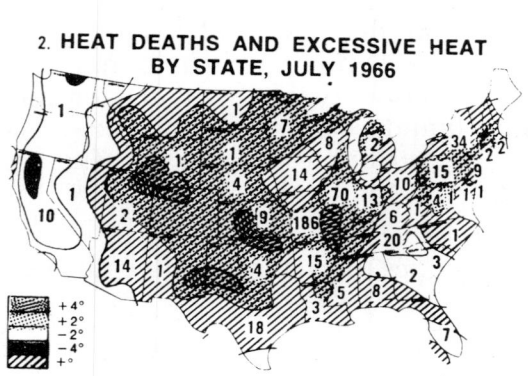

2. **HEAT DEATHS AND EXCESSIVE HEAT BY STATE, JULY 1966**

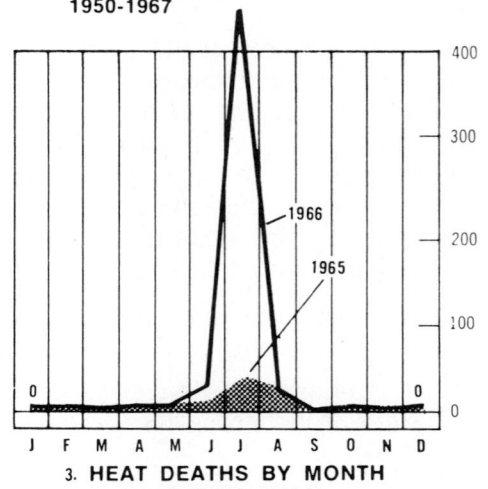

3. **HEAT DEATHS BY MONTH**
1965 VS. 1966

Sunburn, while not categorized as heat syndrome, is pertinent here, for ultraviolet radiation burns can significantly retard the skin's ability to shed excess heat.

Studies of heat syndrome and its victims indicate that it occurs at all ages of man, but, other things being equal, the severity of the disorder tends to increase with age—heat cramps in a 17-year-old may be heat exhaustion in someone 40, and heat stroke in a person over 60.

There is evidence that heat waves are worse in the airless, brick, and asphalt canyons of the "inner cities" than in the better lawned, more open suburbs. The July 1966 tragedy in St. Louis is a case in point.

Acclimatization has to do with adjusting sweatsalt concentrations, among other things. In winter and summer, this concentration changes, just as it does when one moves from Boston to Panama. The idea is to lose enough water to regulate body temperature, with the least possible chemical disturbance. Because females appear to be better at this than males—females excrete less sweat and so less salt—heat syndrome usually strikes fewer females.

For people with heart disease, climatic stress is worse than for others. In a hot, humid environment, impaired evaporation and water loss hamper thermal regulation, while physical exertion and heart failure increase the body's rate of heat production. The ensuing cycle is vicious in the extreme.

# HEAT WAVE SAFETY RULES

1. SLOW DOWN. **Your body can't do its best in high temperatures and humidities, and might do its worst.**

2. HEED YOUR BODY'S EARLY WARNINGS THAT HEAT SYNDROME IS ON THE WAY. **Reduce your level of activities immediately and get to a cooler environment.**

3. DRESS FOR SUMMER. **Lightweight, light-colored clothing reflects heat and sunlight, and helps your thermoregulatory system maintain normal body temperature.**

4. PUT LESS FUEL ON YOUR INNER FIRES. **Foods (like proteins) that increase metabolic heat production also increase water loss.**

5. DON'T DRY OUT. **Heat wave weather can wring you out before you know it. Drink plenty of water while the hot spell lasts.**

6. STAY SALTY. **Unless you're on a salt-restricted diet, take an occasional salt tablet or some salt solution when you've worked up a sweat.**

7. AVOID THERMAL SHOCK. **Acclimatize yourself gradually to warmer weather. Treat yourself extra gently for those first critical two or three hot days.**

8. VARY YOUR THERMAL ENVIRONMENT. **Physical stress increases with exposure time in heat wave weather. Try to get out of the heat for at least a few hours each day. If you can't do this at home, drop in on a cool store, restaurant, or theater—anything to keep your exposure time down.**

9. DON'T GET TOO MUCH SUN. **Sunburn makes the job of heat dissipation that much more difficult.**

10. KNOW THE HEAT SYNDROME SYMPTOMS AND FIRST AID.

## HEAT AND SUN FIRST-AID

| Heat Syndrome | Caused by | Symptoms | First Aid |
|---|---|---|---|
| **HEAT ASTHENIA (OR CALAS- THENIA)** | Excessively hot, humid environment. | Easy fatigue, headache, mental and physical inefficiency, poor appetite, insomnia, heavy sweating, high pulse rate, shallow breathing, and sometimes circulatory stress in the ill. | **Respite from heat and humidity, plenty of fluids, and, if sweating is heavy (and no dietary restrictions prevent it) a salt tablet and rest.** |
| **HEAT CRAMPS** | Strenuous activity under conditions of high heat and humidity, when evaporative cooling is impaired, stimulating excessive sweating and loss of salts from blood and tissue, causing cramps. | Painful spasms of voluntary muscles, contraction in flexor muscles in fingers, then larger muscles in legs and abdominal wall. Pupils dilate with each spasm, there may be heavy sweating, skin becomes cold and clammy. Unlike severe abdominal disease symptoms, heat cramps are intermittent. | **Usually respond better to firm pressure on cramping muscles than to vigorous kneading. Application of warm wet towels also gives relief. Three or four doses of salt solution (½ teaspoon dissolved in 4 fl. oz. water) administered at 15-minute intervals. Large quantities of water without salt may precipitate the disease.** |
| **HEAT EXHAUSTION** | Prolonged hot spell, excessive exposure, physical exertion cause thermoregulatory breakdown involving loss of vasomotor (blood-vessel diameter) control and circulatory shock. | Profuse sweating, weakness, vertigo, and sometimes heat cramps; symptoms similar to calasthenia may herald by several days. Skin is cold and pale, clammy with sweat; pulse is thready and blood pressure is low. Body temperature is normal or sub-normal. Vomiting may occur. Unconsciousness is rare. | **Move to cooler environment immediately. Provide bed rest, salt solution (see above); victims, sometimes nauseated at first, can usually take fluids after a period of rest. Seek medical help for severe heat exhaustion.** |

| Condition | Cause | Symptoms | Treatment |
|---|---|---|---|
| **HEAT STROKE** (or sunstroke, heat collapse, thermic fever, heat hyperexia) | Failure of thermoregulatory and cardiovascular systems brought about when intensive sweating under conditions of high heat and humidity restrict heat dissipation by sweating, which finally ceases. Advanced age and hot, humid, windless environment are factors. | Weakness, vertigo, nausea, headache, heat cramps, mild heat exhaustion, excessive sweating. Sweating stops just before heat stroke. Then temperature rises sharply, often to 106° or more, pulse is bounding and full, blood pressure elevated. Delirium or coma is common. Armpit and groin areas are dry (they are wet in heat exhaustion). Skin is flushed and pink at first; however, in later stages, it appears ashen or purplish. | **Heat stroke is a very serious emergency. Medical care is urgently needed.** Move the victim into cooler, indoor environment, remove his clothing, put him to bed. Primary objective is to reduce body temperature, preferably by iced bath (or by sponging the body with alcohol or lukewarm water) until a tolerable level (about 103° or a pulse rate below 110 per minute) is reached. Caution is necessary here. |
| **SUNBURN** | Overexposure to ultraviolet radiation. | Redness and pain caused by dilation of small blood vessels in skin. In more severe cases, tissue injury brings swelling of skin, blisters, and often fever and headache. Because it impairs thermoregulatory efficiency, sunburn may be accompanied by other heat syndrome disorders. | **Prevent severe sunburn by limiting the time of initial exposure, depending on comfort and conditions.** Treat mild sunburn with cold cream or certain oils or greases (e.g., salad oil, shortening). Wash hands before applying. Do not apply butter or oleomargarine. Dressing should be used if blistering appears, injured area should not be exposed to sunlight until healed. Medical care is needed for extensive or severe cases. |

HEAT STROKE IS A SEVERE MEDICAL EMERGENCY. SUMMON A PHYSICIAN OR GET THE PATIENT TO A HOSPITAL IMMEDIATELY. DELAY CAN BE FATAL.

SOURCE: U.S. Dept. of Commerce
National Oceanic and Atmospheric Administration

# THE GREAT HEAT WAVE AND DROUGHT OF 1980

*This special report on The Heatwave of 1980 was prepared by the Environmental Data and Information Service—Center for Environmental Assessment Services (CEAS), which is an organization within the Department of Commerce, NOAA. It is part of a continuing CEAS effort to provide current assessments of the effects of weather and climate on social and economic activities.*

## Description

Temperatures began exceeding 100°F in southwest Texas on June 10, and the ensuing string of hot days broke 16 daily maximum temperature records at El Paso. Beginning about June 23, 100°F temperatures encompassed the rest of Texas and intruded into surrounding states to the north and east. By the first week of July, the center of the heat wave had progressed northward into Oklahoma, and during the second week of the month, the center moved northeastward to Missouri, with most of the central third of the country experiencing 100°F temperatures. During mid-July the heat wave spread eastward to the Ohio Valley and mid-Atlantic region, but by July 21, a cold front had pushed southward into Texas, Oklahoma, and Missouri and eastward towards the East Coast, bringing rain and cooler air to much of the affected region. Temperatures in most of the heat-wave-affected area dropped to near or slightly above normal during the week ending July 27. However, these temperatures lasted only a short while, returning to their original levels and expanding throughout much of the eastern U.S. during the week ending August 10. A sharp temperature drop occurred during the week ending August 17, but it was short lived. The following 3 weeks (ending September 7) showed a return to the heat wave pattern. Average monthly temperatures for August were the hottest ever recorded at some locations, and the 1st week of September saw temperatures 9°F above normal over parts of the central and eastern states.

Temperature records were shattered in over a half-dozen states, with many cities setting all-time record highs. On one day (July 13), three cities in the Southeast simultaneously broke their all-time maximum temperature records, with Augusta, Atlanta, and Memphis recording 107°, 105°, and 108°, respectively. In Texas, Dallas reached 100° each day from June 23 through August 3, and no appreciable rain fell in the state from June 22 through July 19.

The drought situation in the central and southern U.S. changed considerably during August and early September. Rains which fell in Kansas, Nebraska, Montana, North and South Dakota, and southern Texas alleviated drought in these areas. However, drought still continued in Oklahoma, Arkansas, southern Missouri, northeastern Texas, and Louisana. Additionally, recent thunderstorms had not yet erased drought in southeastern states. Parts of Georgia, and South Carolina remained in critical need of rain, as did parts of the middle Atlantic and southern New England states.

**Cause**

A huge area of high pressure centered over the south-central U.S. and extending throughout most of the troposphere dominated the central U.S. from late June to mid-July. This system effectively blocked precipitation-bearing fronts and cooler air masses from penetrating the southern plains. Associated with the high was a large blocking high pressure system which stagnated over the North Pacific Ocean. The blocking, initiated by the Pacific high, stalled weather systems throughout the Northern Hemisphere, resulting in cool, wet weather over Europe and warm weather in central Asia, as well as the heat and dryness over the U.S. By the third week in July, the high over the south-central U.S. had moved eastward, merging with the Bermuda-Azores High. This allowed cooler air to penetrate the southern U.S. and provide at least a respite from the heat and drought. There were two major cold fronts during the first half of August which passed through the heat-wave-affected area. Both of these fronts swept southward and then eastward across the cental and eastern parts of the continent. Precipitation fell along the pathway of these fronts. Rainfall received in southern Texas was the result of Hurricane Allen's visit. Cold polar air masses which pushed southward through the heat-wave-affected area brought about the relief from the heat. A major shift in upper level circulation after September 7 suggested a possible end to the severe temperature anomalies.

**Fatalities**

As of September 7, 1980, the total count of fatalities related to the heat wave was estimated at 1,265, seven times the number in a near normal summer. Most of the victims were old and/or poor, living in non-air-conditioned homes and apartments.

The hardest hit state was Missouri, where 311 succumbed to the heat. Reasons suggested for this high toll, as compared to Texas and other states with higher temperatures over a longer period, are:

1. much higher humidity levels in St. Louis and Kansas City,
2. more elderly and poor in non-air-conditioned dwellings,
3. Missourians are not accustomed to heat waves, and
4. more brick (heat retaining) dwellings in Missouri than in Texas, where wooden structures predominate.

With respect to the 1954 heat wave (the last one resulting in nearly 1,000 deaths) 1980's heat wave has resulted in about 300 more fatalities, despite the prevalance of air-conditioning.

**Heat wave energy consumption**

The heat waves's major impact on energy use was through increased electricity consumption caused by air conditioning. On a given summer week, electricity used for cooling comprises approximately 15% of the national electricity bill. Unusually warm weather, therefore, can have a significant impact on total electric output.

## 1980 HEAT WAVE AND DROUGHT
(June 10 through July 27, 1980)

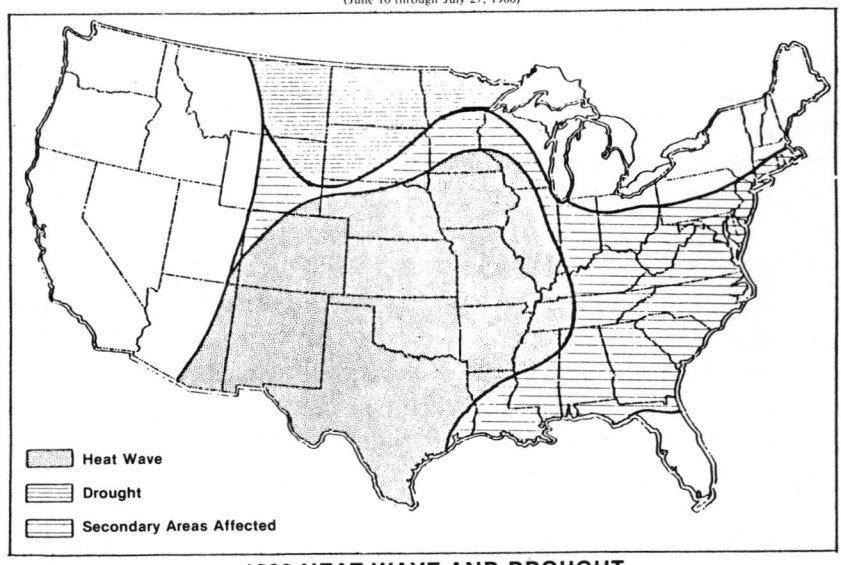

Heat Wave
Drought
Secondary Areas Affected

## 1980 HEAT WAVE AND DROUGHT
(July 28 through August 16)

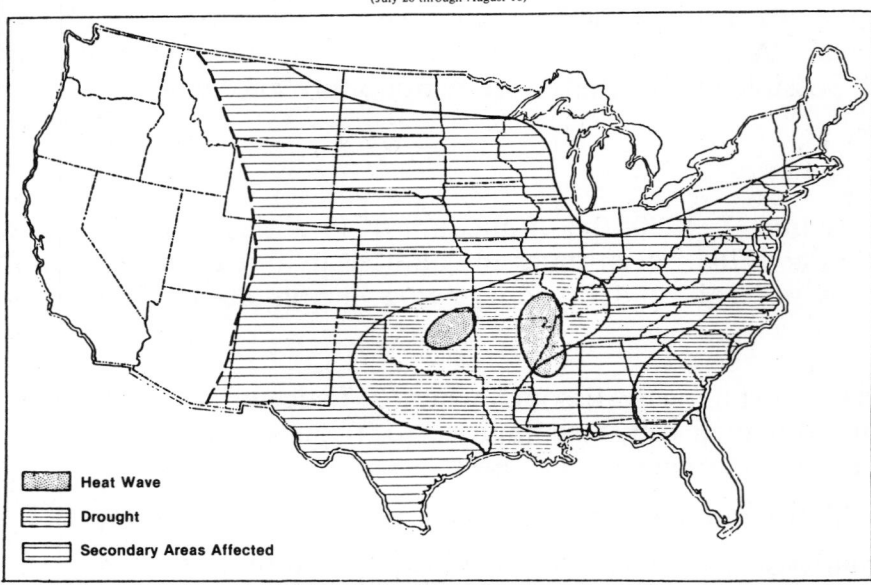

Heat Wave
Drought
Secondary Areas Affected

## 1980 HEAT WAVE AND DROUGHT
(August 17 through September 7)

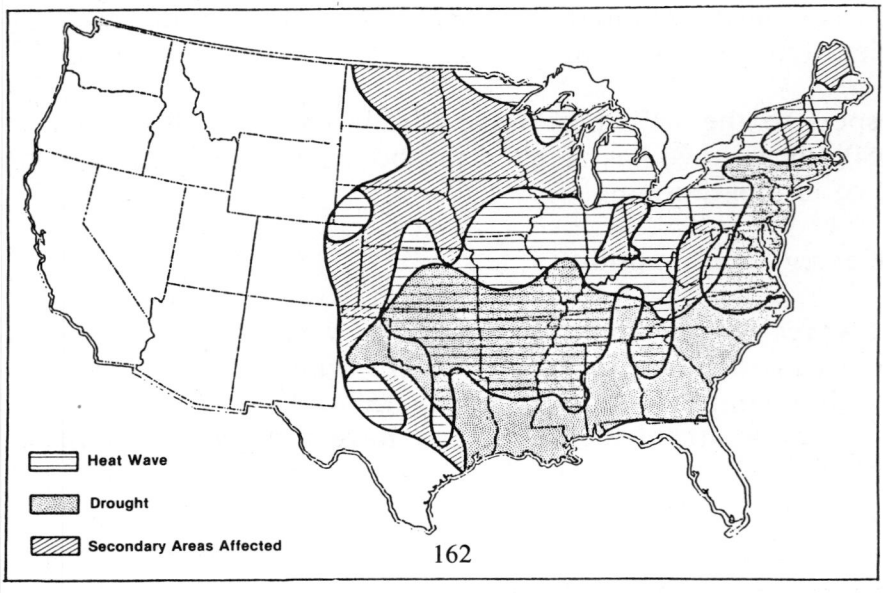

Heat Wave
Drought
Secondary Areas Affected

162

## WEEKLY EXPANSION OF THE 1980 HEAT WAVE SINCE MID-JUNE
(June 22 through July 20)

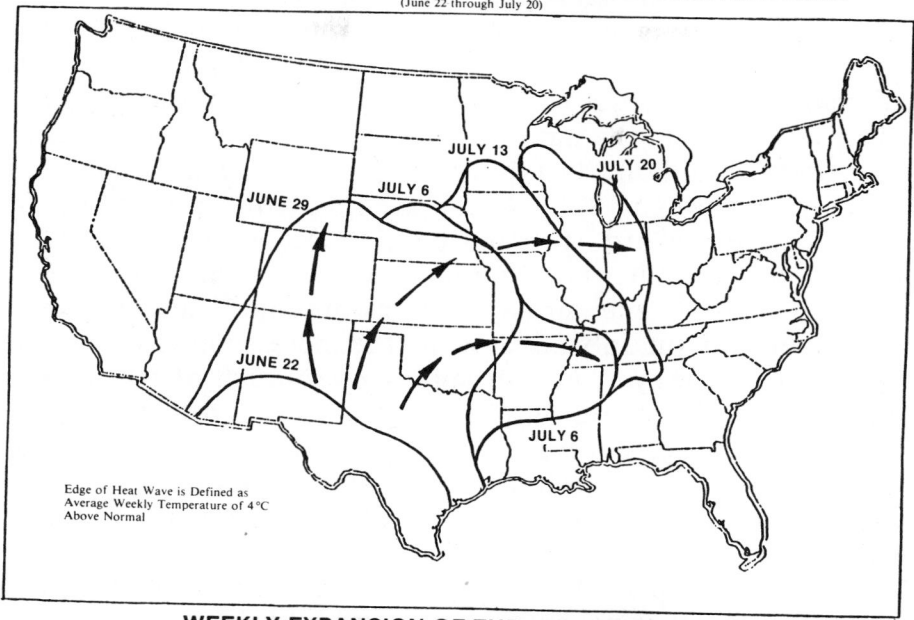

JULY 13
JULY 20
JUNE 29
JULY 6
JUNE 22
JULY 6

Edge of Heat Wave is Defined as
Average Weekly Temperature of 4°C
Above Normal

## WEEKLY EXPANSION OF THE 1980 HEAT WAVE
(July 27 through August 17)

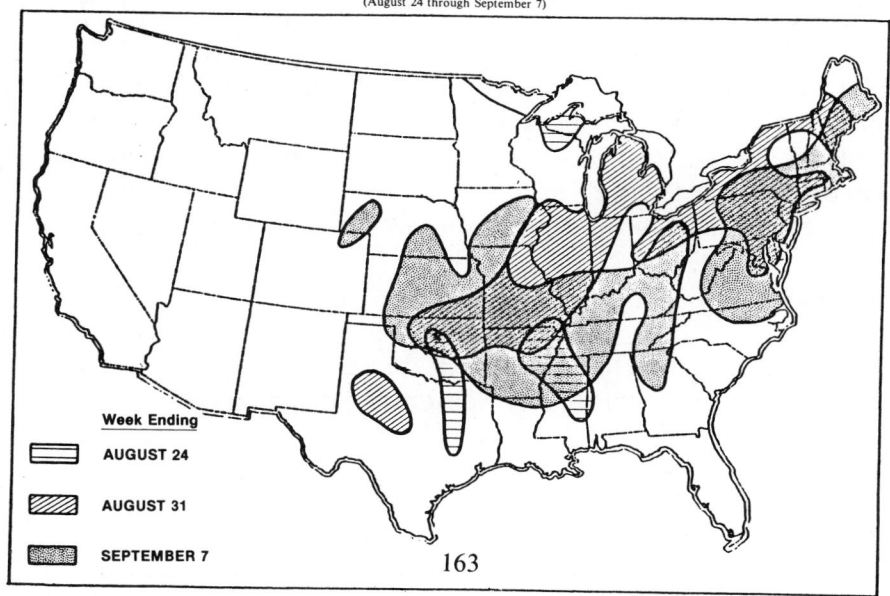

JULY 27
AUGUST 3
AUGUST 10
AUGUST 17

## WEEKLY EXPANSION OF THE 1980 HEAT WAVE SINCE LATE AUGUST
(August 24 through September 7)

**Week Ending**

AUGUST 24

AUGUST 31

SEPTEMBER 7

The heat wave began to substantially affect country-wide energy consumption and costs during the last week of June when unusually high temperatures spread northward from southern Texas to envelop much of the southern plains. By early July, the heat wave caused the nation's electric bill to surpass "normal" expenditures by nearly $100 million. By July 12, costs had reached $200 million. During the week of July 13 through 19, the heat wave reached its greatest spatial extent, setting an all-time record for national electric output (52.6 billion kilowatt-hours). As a result, the accumulated cost of the heat wave surpassed $400 million on July 19. Cooler air began spreading southward and eastward over much of the country about July 20, slowing the increase in electricity use during the next two weeks. However, hot air spread over much of the nation again in early August. The total electric output for August 3 through 9 of 51.8 billion kilowatt-hours was the second highest ever, and caused electicity costs to soar once again, bringing the accumulated cost since late June to over $1.3 billion. Total electric use from late June through early August was approximately 5.5% greater than would occur with "normal" temperatures, and 6.4% greater than during the corresponding period of 1979. Departures for the entire cooling season to-date, however, are somewhat smaller, as unusually low temperatures earlier in June offset later high temperatures.

For the entire cooling season, population-weighted cooling degree day (CDD) totals indicate this to be the warmest season since the 1930's. The seasonal CDD total ranks near the 90th percentile, suggesting that only one year in ten would be warmer.

Regional extremes were even greater than the national figures indicate. In northwest Missouri, for example, electricity use July 1 through 21 exceeded 1979's use by 47%. Electric output in the south-central states during July 13 through 19 exceeded 1979's output by 21%, and in the west-cental region that week, output was up 27%.

Power consumption after September 7 returned to more normal levels along with a major shift in atmospheric circulation.

### Notes on electricity discussion

Electricity consumption figures are based on weekly electric output data supplied by the Edison Electric Institute. Calculation of "normal" consumption was derived from a CEAS multiple regression equation which relates weekly national electric output to long-term mean population-weighted cooling degree days. Temperature lag factors, holiday factors, and base consumption estimates are also incorporated into the model. References to "normal" refer to the 1941-70 period. Percentile estimates are based on the 1931-78 period of record.

### Crops and livestock

— Corn production estimates indicate a decrease of 1.2 billion bushels nationally from 1979 levels (early September price was about $3.50 per bushel).

ECONOMIC ELEMENTS SERIOUSLY AFFECTED BY THE 1980 DROUGHT AND HEAT WAVE

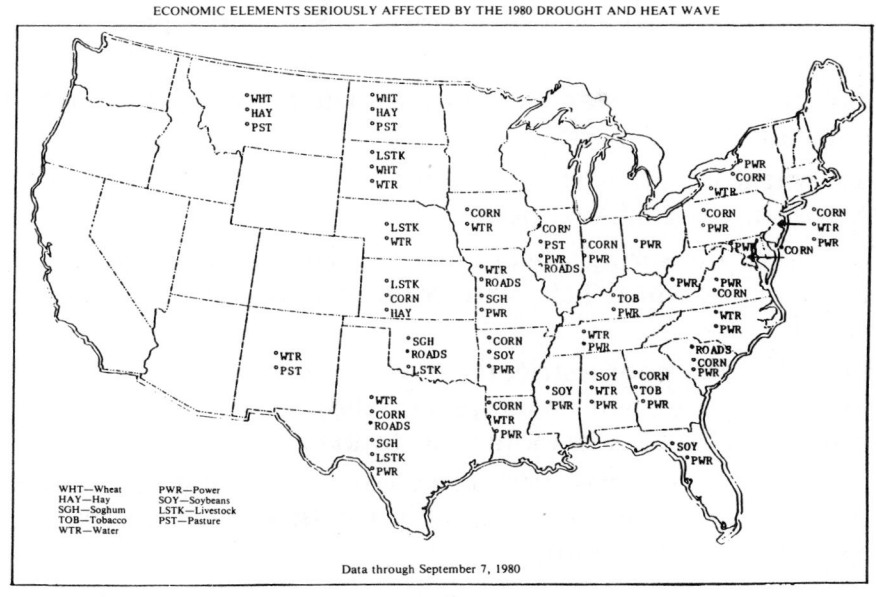

WHT—Wheat      PWR—Power
HAY—Hay        SOY—Soybeans
SGH—Soghum     LSTK—Livestock
TOB—Tobacco    PST—Pasture
WTR—Water

Data through September 7, 1980

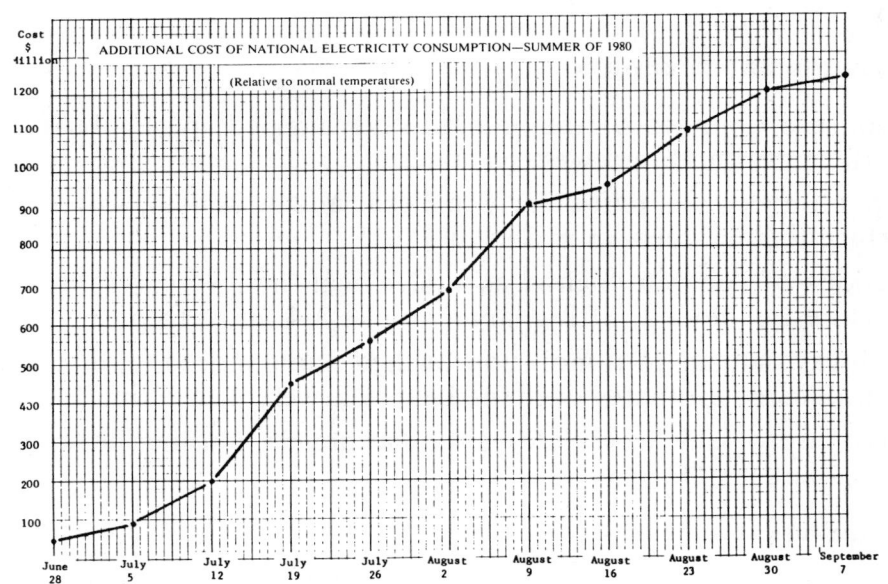

— Soybean production estimates indicate a decrease of 0.4 billion bushels nationally from 1979 levels (early September price was about $8.00 per bushel).

— The poultry industry was hard hit, with millions of birds perishing from Arkansas to Georgia.

— Winter wheat from Texas to Nebraska benefitted from hot, dry weather during the harvest period.

— Up to 90% of the spring wheat crop was damaged over large areas of the upper plains wheat belt, with Montana and North Dakota being hardest hit.

— Parched pastures, poor nutrients, and heat combined to slow and even reverse livestock growth. Widespread selloff of herds resulted, which diminished beef stocks in months to follow.

— Destruction of protective vegetative cover over many thousands of acres of midwest crop land probably resulted in severe soil erosion during future winter months.

— Prices for finished food items ready for sale to consumers rose by 4.4% in August alone.

— Prices for raw agricultural products rose 19% during the 2 months of July and August.

## Transportation and roadways

— Hundreds of miles of major highways buckled, particularly in the south central and mid-western states.

— Asphalt highways, particularly in Texas and Arkansas, softened with surface temperatures in excess of 150°F.

— Sections of concrete highways, under heat induced severe expansion pressures, exploded, lifting large chunks 3-4' into the air.

— Highway damage in Illinois approached one hundred million dollars; total damage estimates over the heat belt were 4 to 5 times as great.

— Wide spread vehicle breakdowns and a surge in automobile repair bills was experienced.

## Water resources

— Severe shortages and rationing were widespread, with Texas and Arkansas hardest hit.

— Drop in water table in Texas, Oklahoma and Arkansas forced farmers to dry farm formerly irrigated acreage. Water use in parts of Texas were mandatorily halved.

— In Arkansas pressure wells for rice farming failed. A sharp increase in pump wells with attendant power requirements and further stress on water table exacerbated the drought/heat problems.

— Drop in water table in sections of Arizona, Texas and Arkansas far exceeded yearly normals. The pronounced increase in the ground water consumption threatened not only agriculture, but the demographic shift and industrial development of the region.

# ESTIMATED COST OF THE HEAT WAVE AND DROUGHT

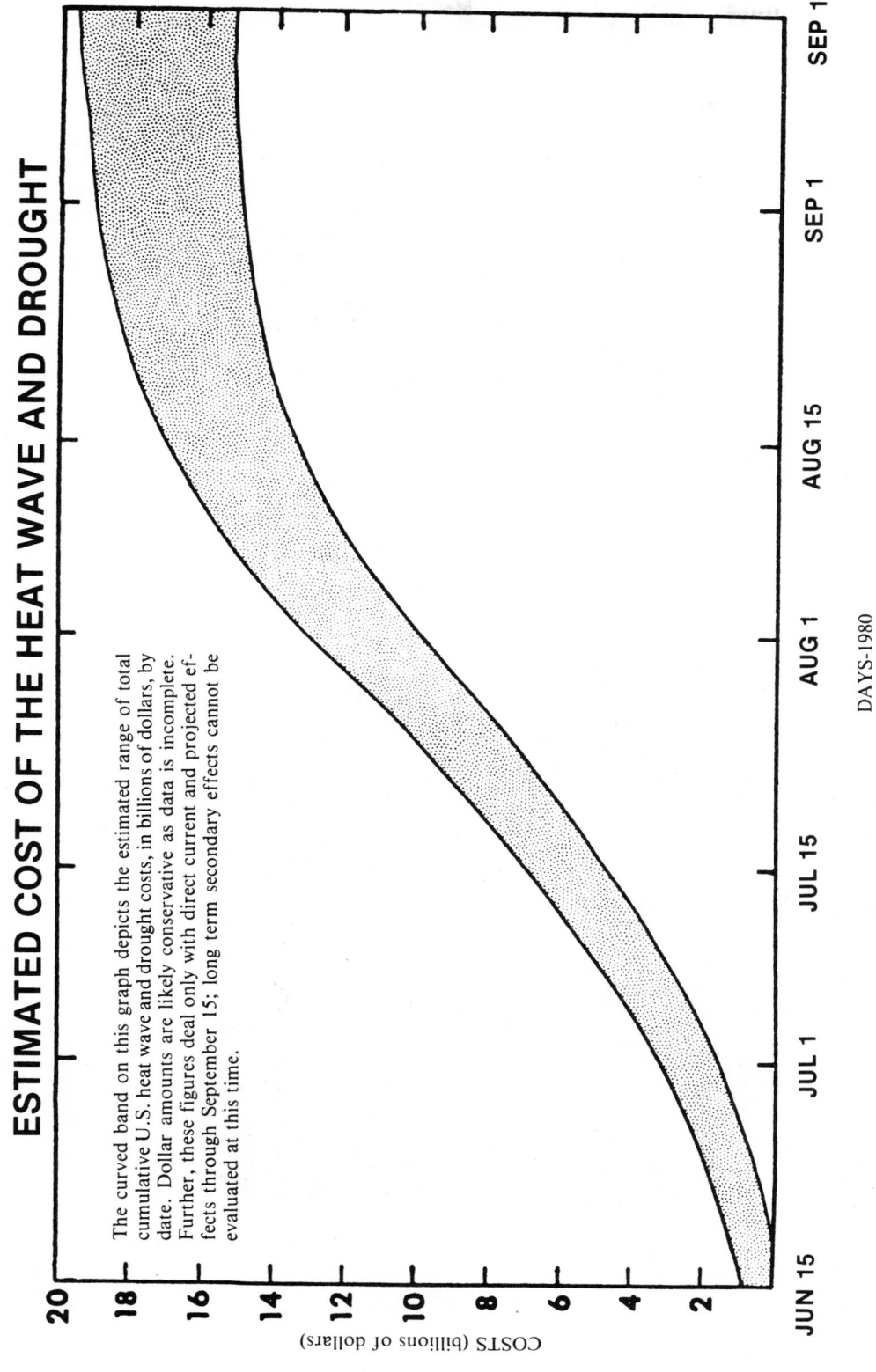

The curved band on this graph depicts the estimated range of total cumulative U.S. heat wave and drought costs, in billions of dollars, by date. Dollar amounts are likely conservative as data is incomplete. Further, these figures deal only with direct current and projected effects through September 15; long term secondary effects cannot be evaluated at this time.

DAYS-1980

The CEAS cost damage estimates constitute an assessment of those direct costs, attributable to the heat wave and drought, that can presently be evaluated. This measureable damage falls primarily into three major socio-economic categories:
1. loss of staple crops and livestock,
2. energy, particularly, electric power consumption,
3. damage to roads and highways.
The end of the principal period of crop and highway damage after August 15 is reflected in the flattening of the graph curve. Thereafter, the major

heat wave and drought costs is in added electric power consumption. Other serious losses which could not be cost-accounted at this time include heat-related health problems and a lowering of water tables in parts of the southern plains to a point where health was endangered and where irrigation could no longer be sustained. Also, secondary effects, such as pecuniary gains to agriculture interests outside stricken areas and corresponding losses to consumers from heat-induced raises in food prices, have not been considered.

### ESTIMATED ECONOMIC LOSSES FROM THE 1980 HEAT WAVE AND DROUGHT
#### (in millions of dollars)

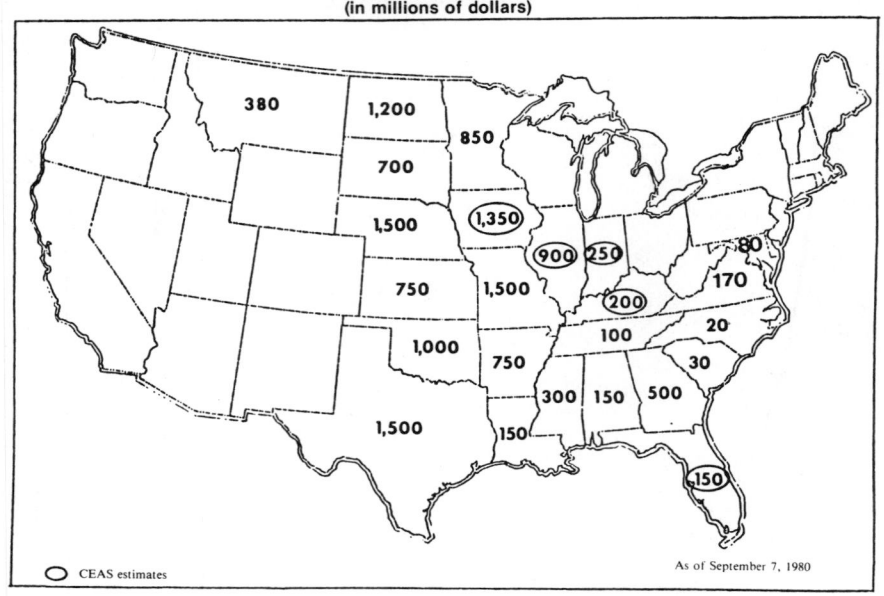

O  CEAS estimates

As of September 7, 1980

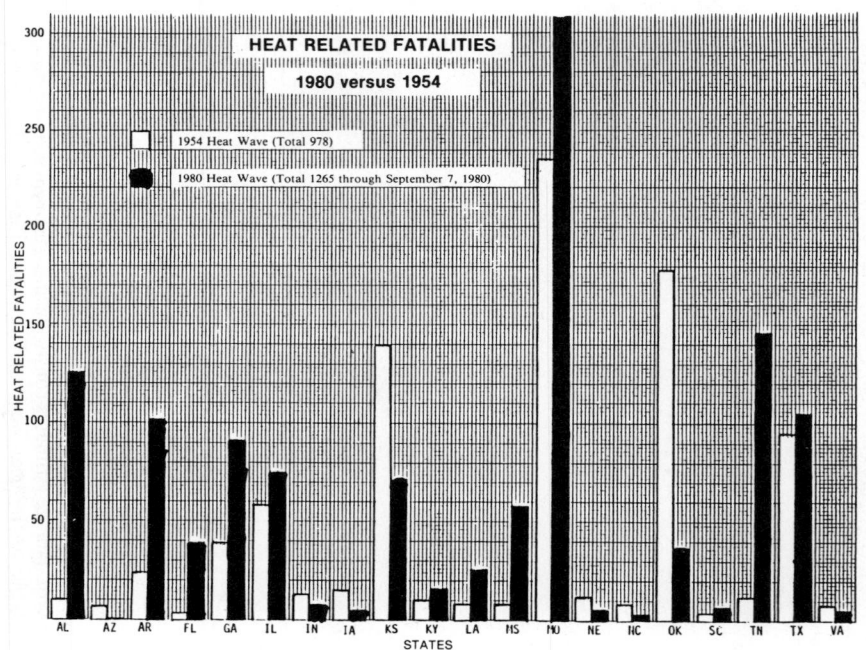

## *QUOTES FROM WEATHER FOLKLORE—*

*If the cock goes crowing to bed,*
*He'll certainly rise with a watery head.*


*If on Candlemas day (February 2) it is bright*
*and clear, the ground-hog will stay in his den,*
*thus indicating that more snow and cold are*
*to come; But if it snows or rains he will creep*
*out, as the winter is ended.          (German)*


*If Candlemas Day be fine and clear,*
*Corn and fruits will then be dear.*


*If the November goose bone be thick,*
  *So will the winter weather be;*
*If the November goose bone be thin,*
  *So will the winter weather be.*


                    *Human hair (red) curls and kinks at the*
                    *approach of a storm, and restraightens after*
                    *the storm.*


                    *When the moon lies on her back,*
                    *She sucks the wet into her lap.*
                                        *— Ellesmere.*


                    *The shepard would rather see the wolf*
                    *enter his fold on Candlemas Day than the sun.*


                    *March in January, January in March, I fear.*


                    *Who doffs his coat on a winter's day*
                    *Will gladly put it on in May.*

# TEMPERATURE-HUMIDITY INDEX

A useful guide to summer time comfort is the Temperature-Humidity Index. A single number can be used to approximately express the reaction of most people to the heat-humidity complex, although it is known that individual responses vary considerably from person to person and from time to time. Table 1 relates various degrees of sheltered air temperature and relative humidity to equivalent THI values. The table is read in the manner of some road map mileage tables and provides index values to the nearest whole number. A brief discussion of the index is also provided.

**Table 1    The Temperature-Humidity Index**

| TEMPERATURE | RELATIVE HUMIDITY | | | | | | | | | | |
|---|---|---|---|---|---|---|---|---|---|---|---|
| | 10% | 20% | 30% | 40% | 50% | 60% | 70% | 80% | 90% | 100% | |
| 66°F | 62 | 63 | 63 | 63 | 64 | 64 | 65 | 65 | 66 | 66 | |
| 67° | 63 | 63 | 64 | 64 | 65 | 65 | 66 | 66 | 67 | 67 | |
| 68° | 63 | 64 | 64 | 65 | 65 | 66 | 67 | 67 | 68 | 68 | |
| 69° | 64 | 64 | 65 | 65 | 66 | 67 | 67 | 68 | 68 | 69 | few people |
| 70° | 64 | 65 | 65 | 66 | 67 | 67 | 68 | 69 | 69 | 70 | feel uncomfortable |
| 71° | 65 | 65 | 66 | 67 | 67 | 68 | 69 | 70 | 70 | 71 | ↓ |
| 72° | 65 | 66 | 67 | 67 | 68 | 69 | 70 | 71 | 71 | 72 | |
| 73° | 66 | 66 | 67 | 68 | 69 | 70 | 70 | 71 | 72 | 73 | |
| 74° | 66 | 67 | 68 | 69 | 70 | 71 | 71 | 72 | 73 | 74 | about one-half of all |
| 75° | 67 | 67 | 68 | 69 | 70 | 71 | 72 | 73 | 74 | 75 | people feel uncomfortable |
| 76° | 67 | 68 | 69 | 70 | 71 | 72 | 73 | 74 | 75 | 76 | |
| 77° | 68 | 69 | 70 | 71 | 72 | 73 | 74 | 75 | 76 | 77 | ↓ |
| 78° | 68 | 69 | 70 | 71 | 73 | 74 | 75 | 76 | 77 | 78 | nearly everyone feels |
| 79° | 69 | 70 | 71 | 72 | 73 | 74 | 76 | 77 | 78 | 79 | uncomfortable |
| 80° | 69 | 70 | 72 | 73 | 74 | 75 | 76 | 78 | 79 | 80 | ↓ |
| 81° | 70 | 71 | 72 | 73 | 75 | 76 | 77 | 78 | 80 | 81 | |
| 82° | 70 | 72 | 73 | 74 | 75 | 77 | 78 | 79 | 81 | 82 | |
| 83° | 71 | 72 | 73 | 75 | 76 | 78 | 79 | 80 | 82 | 83 | |
| 84° | 71 | 73 | 74 | 75 | 77 | 78 | 79 | 81 | 83 | 84 | rapidly decreasing |
| 85° | 72 | 73 | 75 | 76 | 78 | 79 | 80 | 82 | 84 | 85 | work efficiency |
| 86° | 72 | 74 | 75 | 77 | 78 | 80 | 81 | 83 | 84 | 86 | |
| 87° | 73 | 74 | 76 | 77 | 79 | 81 | 82 | 84 | 85 | 87 | ↓ |
| 88° | 73 | 75 | 76 | 78 | 80 | 81 | 83 | 85 | 86 | 88 | |
| 89° | 74 | 75 | 77 | 79 | 81 | 82 | 84 | 86 | 87 | 89 | |
| 90° | 74 | 76 | 77 | 79 | 81 | 83 | 85 | 87 | 88 | 90 | |
| 91° | 75 | 76 | 78 | 80 | 82 | 84 | 85 | 87 | 89 | 91 | extreme danger |
| 92° | 75 | 77 | 79 | 81 | 83 | 85 | 86 | 88 | 90 | 92 | |
| 93° | 76 | 78 | 80 | 81 | 83 | 85 | 87 | 89 | 91 | | ⇩ |
| 94° | 76 | 78 | 80 | 82 | 84 | 86 | 88 | 90 | | | |
| 95° | 77 | 79 | 81 | 83 | 85 | 87 | 89 | 91 | 93 | | |
| 96° | 77 | 79 | 81 | 84 | 86 | 88 | 90 | 92 | 94 | | |
| 97° | 78 | 80 | 82 | 84 | 86 | 88 | 91 | | 95 | | |
| 98° | 78 | 80 | 83 | 85 | 87 | 89 | 91 | 94 | 96 | | |
| 99° | 79 | 81 | 83 | 85 | 88 | 90 | | | | | |
| 100° | 79 | 82 | 84 | 86 | 89 | 91 | | | | | |
| 101° | 80 | 82 | 84 | 87 | 89 | 91 | 94 | 96 | | | |
| 102° | 80 | 83 | 85 | 88 | 90 | 92 | 95 | | | | |
| 103° | 81 | 83 | 86 | 88 | 91 | 93 | 96 | | | | |
| 104° | 81 | 84 | 86 | 89 | 91 | 94 | 96 | | | | |
| 105° | 82 | 84 | 87 | 90 | 92 | 93 | | | | | |
| 106° | 82 | 85 | 87 | 90 | 93 | 96 | | | | | |
| 107° | 83 | 85 | 88 | 91 | 94 | 96 | | | | | |
| 108° | 83 | 86 | 89 | 92 | 95 | | | | | | |
| 109° | 84 | 87 | 89 | 92 | 95 | | | | | | |
| 110° | 84 | 87 | 90 | 93 | 96 | | | | | | |

The table progresses downward and to the right from a zone of comfort to a zone of dangerous heat stress. The values are for appropriately clothed persons engaged in sedentary activities in nearly calm air.

170

### Why a Temperature-Humidity Index?

"It isn't the heat; it's the humidity." As noted in the chapter entitled, "Heat Waves", the job of keeping the body cool falls increasingly upon the **evaporation of sweat** as the temperature rises. Meanwhile, the other forms of heat dissipation such as radiation and convection, which depend upon temperature differences between the skin and the surroundings, are reduced in effectiveness. In turn, the rate of evaporation of sweat is influenced by the humidity in the surrounding air. (Wind speed and thermal radiation are also factors.) Hence, the common assertion.

Discomfort is usually a complaint as soon as sweating begins, although to be sure the discomfort and heat stress on the body would be much greater if one could not sweat. "Politeness" aside, it is unfortunate that some people do not sweat as soon or as much as others. Clothing reduces the effectiveness of sweating, but it is needed for protection from the sun. In order to reflect heat and enhance circulation of air, hot weather clothing should be light colored, light weight, porous, and loose fitting. **Weather Almanac** believes that cotton or high cotton blends are still the best hot weather fabrics for most people.

A single number can be used to express the combined temperature-humidity effect and thereby provide a fairly good index of equivalent heat stress. In engineering, this combined index is referred to as "effective temperature." Briefly, in the Weather Bureau, it was referred to as the Discomfort Index or DI. Currently, in Weather Bureau practice, it is called simply the Temperature-Humidity Index or THI.

### What the Temperature-Humidity Index tells you

The THI represents the heat sensations reported by a panel of sedentary persons experimentally subjected to a series of temperature and humidity values, in comparison with a temperature of the same value in calm indoor air saturated with water vapor (relative humidity 100%). The "votes" of relative comfort or discomfort when tabulated showed considerable variation, as is to be expected. Among the factors in the variation are age, diet, exertion, type and amount of clothing, bodily functioning, state of health, state of mind, and past climatic experience especially within the previous several weeks. The results can be generalized as follows:

Relatively few people in summer will feel discomfort from heat and humidity at THI values of 70 or below.

**EXAMPLE OF USE:** Assume the outside temperature is 79°F and the relative humidity is 60 percent. Suppose you wish to know what Temperature-Humidity Index number this equals. Use the table like this to find out: 1. Look down the first vertical column of the chart (the column on the far left) until you reach "79°". A row of numbers appears to the right; remember that row for you will use it in the next step. 2. Now return to the top of the chart and move across until the caption "60%" is reached. (It heads the seventh column). Now let your eye travel down this vertical column until the column crosses the horizontal row which you located in step #1. **The number at this intersection is 74. It is the TH Index number for 79°F when the relative humidity stands at 60%.** Other values can be found by using the same method.

Air conditioning may be appropriate for THI values of 73 or higher.

About half of the people will be uncomfortable by the time the THI value reaches 75.

Nearly everyone feels uncomfortable by the time the THI value reaches 79, with some people experiencing acute discomfort. Restraint in exercise and care in the selection of clothing is very important.

With THI values rising into the 80s, discomfort becomes acute for everyone. Work efficiency begins to drop markedly. Mistakes and accidents increase.

THI values near 90 are in the danger zone for almost everyone. The THI values infrequently reach as high as 90 in some parts of the United States. A study several years ago found no THI values higher than 92. Higher values in the nation might be found under special local conditions or in poorly ventilated enclosed places.

Direct sunshine and hot radiating surfaces such as pavements, walls and windows decrease these tolerance limits somewhat. A light wind will increase them. Lacking detailed knowledge of local outdoor climates or special industrial conditions, the Temperature-Humidity Index and the limits given can serve as a rough guide.

Infants and old persons are generally comfortable at higher THI values than young healthy persons, but they probably have a lower tolerance for acute discomfort and dangerous heat stress. Persons of any age with cardiovascular problems also experience discomfort and dangerous heat stress at lower THI values than other people.

Everyone is more easily stressed in the first half of the hot season.

Light but active physical exertion may lower the various limits by about 5 units. Heavy work may reduce them by about 10 units.

Any of the following equations may be used to calculate THI values:

$$1) \quad THI = 0.4(td + tw) + 15$$

$$2) \quad THI = 0.55td + 0.2tdp + 17.5$$

$$3) \quad THI = td - (0.55 - 0.55RH).(td - 58)$$

Where THI is Temperature-Humidity Index; td is dry bulb temperature in °F; tw is wet bulb temperature in °F; tdp is dew point temperature in °F; RH is relative humidity expressed in decimal form, e.g., 60% is written as 0.60.

For convenience, Equation 3 relating temperature and relative humidity has been reduced to Table 1 above. If a wet-bulb temperature is available from a sling psychrometer or a ventilated thermometer whose bulb is kept wet with a saturated muslin sleeve, Equation 1 can be used.

# LIVESTOCK WEATHER SAFETY INDEX

Livestock, like human beings, are subject to heat stress that is variable not only with temperature but with different combinations of *temperature* **and** *relative humidity*. This is particularly true for animals that are confined or being loaded or transported. Thus, the Temperature-Humidity Index, as explained in the previous text, is a useful tool in animal care.

The research which established this connection was primarily focused on hogs; but the relationship for cattle and other animals was found to be very similar; so pet owners may also wish to consider adapting the TH Index in caring for their animals.

The same TH calculations shown in the preceeding table can be used when they are given the following meaning for animals:

**SAFETY INDEX (THI) READINGS OF 79–THROUGH–83 = LIVESTOCK DANGER!**

An index in this category is dangerous for confined livestock, particularly hogs. There is also a need for precautionary measures in anticipation of a higher index. In fact, disaster can strike at the upper level of this range unless proper safety steps are taken by stockmen. An increase of 25% or more can be expected in transit loss.

**SAFETY INDEX (THI) READINGS OF 84 OR HIGHER = LIVESTOCK EMERGENCY!**

An increase of 45% or more can be expected in transit loss.

**Additional hazard: the effect of calm, cloudless days**

Lack of cloud cover and little or no movement of air are additional hazards which can increase stress and should be considered. An emergency situation is most likely to develop when the temperature is 90 to 95 degrees early in the day, and higher temperatures are forecast for the period that the livestock will be in the marketing process. Additional stress created by handling livestock *should be kept at an absolute minimum*.

## Reduction of hazard: the effect of wind

The cooling effect of wind can lower the THI value a few degrees in open areas. However, when the air temperature approaches the skin temperature of the animal, the cooling effect of wind becomes minimal.

## Acclimatization

Hot, humid weather is more detrimental to livestock in the early summer than in mid- or late summer and during any season following an extended cool period. This heat tolerance has not been qualified but should be considered during periods of marginal danger or emergency categories.

## National Weather Service Warnings

Many Forecast Offices of the National Weather Service (U. S. Department of Commerce, National Oceanic and Atmospheric Administration) issue Danger and/or Emergency Warnings. If potential users are unaware of this program they should contact their local weather service office or agricultural extension agent for information on service in their region.

## What the index means

Most livestock do not adjust readily to high temperatures (heat stress). Hogs are especially vulnerable when *closely confined* in a vehicle, building, or pen. A careful study by Livestock Conservation Inc.* of the relationship of hog deaths during the marketing process shows that high temperatures, especially with high relative humidity, cause abnormally *high losses*.

When the outside temperature is above 80°, the high death loss is quite closely related to the National Weather Service "Temperature Humidity Index." Although this index was originally developed to indicate comfort ranges for humans, research by Livestock Conservation, Inc. points to similar ranges of comfort for animals. High values adversely influence efficiency of production, meat quality, health and survival.

## Why hogs are a special problem

Heat build up internally in the hog's body if it cannot be thrown off by the lungs or skin. If the internal temperature reaches 105-106°, heat exhaustion occurs and will be *followed by death* unless the situation is relieved.

Hogs lose about 80% of their body heat through the lungs when the environmental temperature is above 80°; only 20% is lost from the skin by radiation and air movement. Hogs must breathe approximately 20 times as much air at 100° as at 80° to maintain a safe internal body temperature (around 102° when their environmental temperature is 100°).

---

*19 West Chicago Avenue, Hinsdale, Illinois 60521

**Repair people, both land- and sea-borne work to remove and replace a section of the top tier of the San Francisco-Oakland Bay bridge following the October 17, 1989 earthquake. The shock wave elongated then contracted steel in the bridge, wrenching this top section from its anchors. The westbound roadway, along with cars on it at the time dropped precipitously. Drivers found themselves too stunned to drive away on the lower eastbound level, although they had been deposited there roller-coaster style.**

# EARTHQUAKES

### Bay Area's 1989 earthquake teaches basic lessons—

There is no substitute for experience in understanding an earthquake. Most of us will never have a significant earthquake experience, but millions had the next thing to it when television was uniquely deployed in San Francisco (for other reasons) and shifted its focus to tell us first-hand how the violent shaking there felt and looked. Since the situation provides a classic teaching demonstration, this article's description of earthquake morphology looks briefly at that event, and uses it as backdrop to the definive paragraphs which follow.

At 5:04 PM, on a quiet, autumnal afternoon — October 17, 1989 — the San Andreas fault upset life beyond description in the San Francisco-Oakland Bay area. It heaved its giant breast in the Santa Cruz Mountains and wrought havoc in widening circles that reached throughout the bay area and shook buildings as far as Reno, Nevada, 250 miles

**About 60 homes in the Marina district of San Francisco collapsed, with occupant injuries and deaths. The homes, mostly restored or rejuvenated structures, originally completed around 1900, were built on landfill, so felt the 15 second jolt more injuriously than any others in the area. Fires ignited in many almost immediately, as gas pipes broke open and severed electrical wires arced to ignite the explosive vapors. High rise office buildings, built to codes adopted after San Francisco's 1971 tremors, were typically unscathed by the earthquake, which had its epicenter in the Santa Cruz Mountains.**

*AP/Wide World Photos*

to the east, and quivered skyscrapers 400 miles south in Los Angeles. The internationally televised third game of baseball's "Worlds Series", about to begin, gave the world the word and picture as it was happening, beginning with views of apprehensive players and fans inside Candlestick Park stadium, and combining them with telephoto visuals of the fires and devastation some 8 to 10 miles to the north. However, virtually no one in the bay area needed the ABC television crew to tell them that the "big one" was happening. Fanning out in every direction from the epicenter, shock waves that reached 6.9 on the Richter scale were sundering the afternoon quiet of uncounted thousands of people — sundering it in a way that visited fright on the entire area, then destruction and, in the next minutes, death (estimates say more than 100 fatalities) as only an earthquake can. The injured persons count topped 3000, said authorities, with many being crippled for life.

As earthquakes go, the intensity, maintained for a short 15 seconds, was great. But it was nowhere near the 9.2 reading of the 1964 Alaskan quake that destroyed with tidal waves as much as with earth shaking. (Each whole number on the Richter scale equals ten times greater intensity than the previous whole number.) The toll in life and property of this 1989 cataclysm (third most lethal of all time) resulted because the epicenter was so close to very large concentrations of population and technology-laced living styles. In the cities of San Francisco, Oakland, and other edge communities, the urban lives of millions, densely packed into a few square miles, involves structures of all types and descriptions. Very important, it involves the penultimate in steel and concrete structure, a double-deck freeway connecting Oakland and the mainland to San Francisco's peninsula.

*AP/Wide World Photos*

**Nimitz Freeway, Interstate #80, linking the mainland, Oakland and San Francisco, provided some of the harshest of the quake, as the westbound top slab of steel and concrete broke its links with the ground supports and was dumped atop eastbound traffic on the lower tier. Deaths and damage here were the catyclysm's worst.**

## Structures that survived, and some that didn't—

Safest structures proved to be high-rise office buildings in San Francisco, constructed since a 1971 tremor had spurred new standards; most vulnerable were the restored single homes built 60 to 90 years ago on landfills in an area known as the Marina district of San Francisco. The former coped with the shocks with well planned engineering provisions, resulting in minimal damage. Meanwhile, more than 50 of the latter (wood and brick structures) collapsed into their foundations, and life loss was high as scores were trapped inside because things happened so fast. The really shocking element of the catastrophe was reserved however for that tribute to life in this half-century, *the ubiquitous freeway*. Due to reasoning that seems strange in retrospect, the lifeline traffic artery known as the Nimitz Freeway (Interstate Route 80) had been created years before as a *double decker* with its supports assumed to be, but never tested to be, *earthquake resistant*. The supports failed this test. Cars and drivers alike were crushed in mid-cruise as the upper deck first undulated with the shock wave then dropped its millions of tons of steel and concrete on the deck below. Drivers were pinned and vehicles crushed as if made of cardboard. The San Francisco-Oakland Bay bridge fared only slightly better, with one end of an upper section falling to meet the lower level, closing it for days.

As terrifying as this quake was, carnage was in one sense "light" because the early start of the ballgame had drained the streets of much rush hour traffic. That is small consolation to the families of those who died, but a Godsend to thousands of others whose route would have placed them directly under the collapsing concrete that repudiated its supports as fast as one could say "deathly inadequate."

## Understanding earthquakes and why they are always a surprise—

Most natural hazards can be detected before their threat matures. But seisms (from the greek *seismos*, earthquake) have no known precursors, and so they come without warning, like the vengeance of an ancient, lunatic god. For this reason, they continue to kill in some areas at a level usually reserved for wars and epidemics—the 68,000 dead in Peru died on May 31, 1970, not in antiquity. Nor is the horror of lethal earthquake completed with a heavy toll. The homeless living are left to cope with fire, looting, pestilence, fear, and the burden of rebuilding of what the planet so easily shrugs away.

Earthquakes have not been the killers in the United States they have in Eurasia and Africa. A 1972 study revealed that fewer than 1,600 deaths have been caused by earthquakes and tsunamis (so-called "tidal waves") in the U.S., and 700 of these came in the 1906 San Francisco earthquake and fire. Of more than 115,000 deaths from major earthquakes worldwide since 1960, fewer than 300 occurred in the United States.

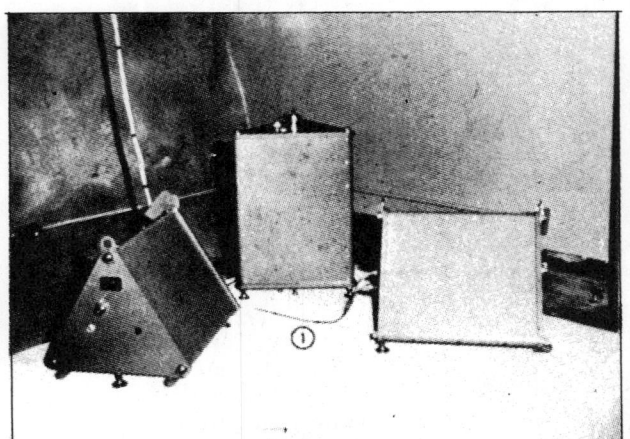 

*EARTHQUAKE LISTENING POST In the global network of standardized seismograph stations, three-component (vertical, north-south, east-west motion) seismometers (1) sense earthquake vibrations, and relay them in the form of electrical signals to galvanomenters (2) and recorders (3) installed in dark vaults. The seismogram is written by a light beam from the galvanometer, directed onto photo-sensitive paper on the recorder. As variations in seismometer signals deflect the galvanometer beam, the familiar ups and downs of an earthquake appear.*

Property damage is a different story. The San Francisco earthquake of 1906 did an estimated $24 million property damage, and the ensuring fire $500 million more. Between the time of that expensive tremor (imagine what $524 million translates to in 1991 dollars!) and the 1989 Bay area quake, about one billion dollars had been the cost of American earthquakes. Of that total, Alaska's 1964 quake cost about $400 million and $600 million was for 1971's seismic event in California's San Fernando area. Officials' estimates of the 1989's earthquake are more than $10 billion. And still experts say the worst is still ahead.

Alaska's 1964 earthquake measured 9.2 on the Richter scale, and was marked by great rends and offsets in the ground. This destroyed roadways, and left hundreds of businesses in ruins. The two scenes, top and bottom, attest to this severity. Although a 9.2 earthquake is more than two full orders of magnitude greater than the 6.9 upheaval in the bay area in 1989, its damage was far less because of the vast difference in population and building development of the two areas.

## Where earthquakes occur—

Our planet's most active earthquake-producing feature is the circum-Pacific seismic belt, which trends along the major geologic faults and the deep oceanic trenches of island arcs decorated here and there with the volcanic "Ring of Fire." The mid-Atlantic Ridge, with its fish-skelton figure of transverse cracks, is also quite active. Other major seismic belts branch from the circum-Pacific system and arc across southeastern and southern Asia into southern Europe, through the Indian Ocean up through the eastern Mediterranean, and up through southern Asia into China.

In an average year, these belts will generate several million tremors, ranging in severity from barely detectable wiggles to great earthquakes of the size which ravaged San Francisco in 1906, and tilted a third of Alaska in 1964. There is always an earthquake in progress somewhere.

Epicenters of damaging earthquakes are superimposed on a seismic risk map included with this article. That map divides the conterminous United States into four zones; zone 0, where there is no reasonable expectance of earthquake damage; zone 1, where minor earthquake damage can be expected; zone 2, where moderate damage can be expected; and zone 3, where major destructive earthquakes may occur. Similar maps for Alaski and Hawaii, and updated versions of this one are under development by the Environmental Research Laboratories. If you live in a high-risk area, check your homes' construction against your city's earthquake construction codes; build on solid ground, not fill; and use earthquake-resistant design.

# WHAT IS AN EARTHQUAKE?

## Earthquake conditions—

The planet Earth is believed to consist of a thin crust two or three miles thick under the oceans and as much as 25 miles thick beneath the continents that covers the large, solid sphere of the rock mantle, which descends to about 1800 miles. Below the mantle is the fluid outer core, and, at about 3200 miles' depth, the apparently solid inner core. The province of earthquakes recorded thus far is from the crust to a maximum depth of about 450 miles.

Conditions thought to prevail in this hot, dark, high-pressure land cannot be simulated in existing laboratories—at the base of the mantle, pressure is about 11,000 tons per square inch, temperature, 10,000 degrees Fahrenheit. These diamond-mashing pressures produce a rigidity in mantle rock about four times that of ordinary steel, with an average density about that of titanium.

This very solid mantle rock seems to behave, over periods of millions of years, like a very sluggish fluid. Something, perhaps the temperature difference between the white-hot region near the core and the cooler region near the crust, drives slow-moving cycles of rising and descending currents in the mantle rock itself.

Evidently, these currents rise beneath the thin-crusted ocean floor, thrust up the mid-ocean ridges, and generate the stresses which produce their spinelike transverse cracks and shallow earthquakes. This is believed to be the force which causes material to well up through the crust, replacing and spreading the old seafloor, and pushing drifting continents apart.

Where the currents begin their descent at the edges of continents, they produce compressive pressures, and massive folding in the form of trenches and mountain ranges. These regions are the sites of the deeper earthquakes, and of most volcanism.

## Earth stresses and strains and then releases—

Stresses generated in the crust and upper mantle by convective currents are stored in the form of strain—physical deformation of the rock structure. Under normal circumstances, the "solid" rocks deform plastically, releasing pent-up energy before it builds to catastrophic levels. But, when stresses accumulate too rapidly to be removed by plastic flow, some structural compensation is necessary. Large blocks of material are slowly forced into highly strained positions along faults, and held in place by a supporting structure of stronger materials. These energy- absorbing zones of weakness continue to shift, like longbows being pulled to the breaking point. Finally, more stress causes the supporting rocks to rupture, triggering the "cocked" fracture back toward equilibrium. The sides of the rebounding fault move horizontally with respect to one another (strike-slip), vertically (dip-slip), or in combinations of such motion, as in the large-scale tilting which accompanied the March 1964 Alaska earthquake.

## Foreshocks and aftershocks—

Sometimes all the energy to be released goes out in one large wrench, followed by trains of smaller tremors, or aftershocks, produced by continuing collapse and slippage along the fracture. Sometimes the fault shift is preceded by the small structural failures we detect as foreshocks. The magnitude 5.9 earthquake which shook Fairbanks, Alaska, on June 21, 1967, was preceded by a magnitude 5.6 foreshock, followed by a magnitude 5.5 aftershock, and then, over the next 24 hours, by more than 2,000 smaller aftershocks. Small tremors were detected for days after the initial event. But all small tremors or earthquake "swarms" do not necessarily indicate that a big one is on the way. The Matsushiro, Japan, swarm maintained an intermittent tremble for more than a year, probably doing more psychic than physical damage. Of more than 600,000 tremors recorded between August 3, 1965, and the end of 1966, 60,000 were strong enough to be felt, and 400 were damaging. During the most active period, in April and May 1966, Matsushiro felt hundreds of tremors daily, all under magnitude 5.

Whatever the time period involved, the energy of strain flows out through the shifted fault in the form of heat, sound, and earthquake waves. These last are the shakers and wreckers, the global messages sent out by earthquakes.

They are also man's only window to his planet's deep interior.

## How earthquake waves travel—

There are four basic seismic waves: two preliminary "body" waves which travel through the earth, and two which travel only at the surface. Combinations, reflections, and diffractions produce a virtual infinity of other types. The behavior of these is well enough understood that wave speed and amplitude have been the major means of describing the earth's interior. In addition, a large earthquake generates elastic waves which echo through the planet like vibrations in a ringing bell, and which actually cause the planet to expand and contract infinitesimally.

The primary (P) wave is longitudinal, like a sound wave, propagates through both liquids and solids, and is usually the first signal that an earthquake has occurred. Where the disturbance is near enough or large enough to be felt, the P wave arrives at the surface like a hammerblow from the inside. This is the swiftest seismic wave, its speed varying with the material through which it passes. In the heterogeneous crustal structure, P-wave velocity is usually less than 4 miles per second—nearly 15,000 miles per hour. Just below the crust, at a layer called the Mohorovicic discontinuity (popularly, the Moho), these speeds jump to 5 miles per second and subsequently increase to about 8½ miles per second (more than 30,000 miles per hour) through the core.

As the compressional phase of the P wave passes through the earth, particles are pushed together and displaced away from the disturbance. The rarefactional phase dilates the particles and displaces them toward the earthquake source. For an object imbedded in the ground, the result is a series of sharp pushes and pulls parallel to the wave path—motions similar to those which the passengers feel when a long train gets under way.

The secondary (S) wave is transverse, like a light or radio wave, and travels barely more than half as fast as the primary wave. Because S waves require a rigid medium to travel in coherent rays, their apparent absence below the mantle gives credence to the theory of a fluid core. About twice the period and amplitude of the associated P waves, these shear waves displace particles at right angles to the direction of wave travel. The vertical component of this movement is somewhat dampened by the opposing force of gravity; but side-to-side shaking in the horizontal can be quite destructive. Where the motion is perceptible, the arrival of the S waves marks the beginning of a new series of shocks, often worse than the P-wave tremor.

Surface waves, named for their discoverers, Love and Rayleigh, are of much greater length and period—e.g., 30 seconds or more, vs. less than one second for P waves. Love waves are shear in the horizontal dimension, and the Rayleigh wave induces a retrograde, elliptical motion, something like that in wind-driven ocean waves. The speed of the Love wave is about 2½ miles per second; the Rayleigh wave is about 10 percent slower. Despite the large proportion of earthquake energy represented by these waves, their long period smooths out the motion they impart, reducing their destructiveness.

Wave motion is not considered in describing the travel of seismic waves through the earth. Instead, the P and S body waves, and their large family of reflected, combined, or resonated offspring, are treated as rays. If the planet were homogeneous, like a ball of wax, these rays would be straight lines. But in the heterogeneous earth the rays describe concavely spherical paths away from the earthquake source, and from points of reflection at the surface.

Because they travel at different speeds, seismic waves arrive at a given point on the earth's surface at different times. Near the source, the ground will shake over a slightly longer interval of time than it took the fault to slip. At great distances, the same energy released by a single event may be detected instrumentally for days.

# Measuring an earthquake—

Intensity is an indication of an earthquake's apparent severity at a specified location, as determined by experienced observers. Through interviews with persons in the stricken area, damage surveys, and studies of earth movement, an earthquake's regional effects can be systematically described. For seismologists and emergency workers, intensity becomes an efficient shorthand for describing what an earthquake has done to a given area.

The Modified Mercalli Intensity Scale generally used in the United States grades observed effects into twelve classes ranging from I, felt only under especially favorable circumstances, to XII, damage total. The older Rossi-Forel Intensity scale, or R.F., has ten categories of observed effects, and is still used in Europe. Still other intensity scales are in use in Japan and the the U.S.S.R.

Rating earthquakes by intensity has the disadvantage of being always relative. In recent years, intensity ratings have been supplemented by an "objective" scale of earthquake magnitude.

Magnitude expresses the amount of energy released by an earthquake as determined by measuring the amplitudes produced on standardized recording instruments. The persistent misconception that the "Richter Scale" rates the size of earthquakes on a "scale of ten" is extremely misleading, and has tended to mask the clear distinction between magnitude and intensity.

Earthquake magnitudes are similar to stellar magnitudes in that they describe the subject in absolute, not relative, terms, and that they refer to a logarithmic, not an arithmetic, scale. An earthquake of magnitude 8, for example, represents seismograph amplitudes ten times larger than those of a magnitude 7 earthquake, 100 times larger than those of a magnitude 6 earthquake, and so on. There is no highest or lowest value, and it is possible here, as with temperature, to record negative values. The largest earthquakes of record were rated at magnitude 8.9; the smallest, about minus 3. Preliminary magnitude determinations may vary with the observatory, equipment, and methods of estimating—the Alaska earthquake of March 1964, for example, was described variously as magnitude 8.4, 8.5, 8.6 by different stations.

Magnitude also provides an indication of earthquake energy release, which intensity does not. In terms of ergs,[*] a magnitude 1 earthquake releases about one billionth the energy of a magnitude 7 earthquake; a magnitude 5, about one thousandth that of a magnitude 7.

———

[*] In the centimeter-gram-second system, an erg is the unit of work equal to a force of 1 dyne acting through a distance of 1 centimeter; a dyne is the force required to accelerate a freestanding gram mass 1 centimeter per second.

# Active faults of California

The most earthquake-prone areas in the conterminous United States are those that are adjacent to the San Andreas fault system of coastal California and the fault system that separates the Sierra Nevada from the Great Basin (see map, page 186). Many of the individual faults of these major systems are known to have been active during the last 150 to 200 years, and others are believed to have been active since the wane of the last great ice advance about 10,000 years ago. Parts of these earthquake-prone areas are among the most densely populated and rapidly urbanizing sections of the Western States. A knowledge of the location of these active faults and an understanding of the nature of the earthquake activity that is related to them is necessary for people to accomodate themselves and their work to these hazards.

Earthquakes in California are relatively shallow and clearly related to movement along active faults. During historical times at least 25 California earthquakes have been associated with movements that ruptured the Earth's surface along faults shown on the map. These earthquakes are briefly described in the accompanying table. On the San Andreas fault, eight moderate-to-severe earthquakes have been accompanied by movements on the fault at the Earth's surface since 1838, and other faults in the California region have also experienced repeated earthquakes.The magnitude of shallow earthquakes can generally be correlated with the amount and length of the associated fault movement. Thus, the largest episode of fault movement (or fault slip) recorded in California accompanied the three great earthquakes of 1857, 1872, and 1906—all of which had estimated magnitudes that were over 8 on the Richter Scale.

Many of the faults shown on the map have had one or more episodes of sudden slip or of slow movement, called creep, during historical time or a documented history of shallow earthquakes. For other faults, however, recent activity can only be inferred from geologic and topographic relations which indicate that they have been active during the past several thousand years. Such activity suggests that some of these faults will, and that any of them might, slip or creep again.

In parts of California where relatively little geologic work has been done, evidence of other recently active faults will undoubtedly be found as research progresses. This is particularly true of large areas in northern California where topographic features by which recent fault movements can be recognized are commonly obscured by dense vegetation and rapid erosion. Further study may also reveal that some of the faults not definitely known to have been recently active have actually been so, and that some parts of faults thought to be active are actually dead. There is, however, evidence which ranges from strongly suggestive to unequivocal for historical activity along the fault segments shown on the map by zigzag lines.

Most of the faults shown on the map are vertical or nearly vertical breaks, and movement along these breaks has been predominantly horizontal. The direction of ground movement along the faults is indicated on the map by arrows. If the block on the opposite side of the fault from the observer has moved to the right, the movement is termed *right-lateral*; movement of the opposite block to the left is termed *left-lateral*. Note that most of the faults trend northwesterly, and that the movement on these faults has been right-lateral. Notable exceptions to the predominantly northwesterly trend of faults are the west-trending Garlock and Big Pine faults; movement on these faults has been left-lateral.

A few reverse faults have also been active in California. The planes of such faults are inclined to the Earth's surface, and the rocks above the fault have been thrust upward over the rocks below the fault plane. The magnitude 7.7 Arvin-Tehachapi earthquake of 1952 (number 20 in the accompanying table) was associated with such movement along the White Horse reverse fault, and the magnitude 6.6 San Fernando earthquake of 1971 (number 25 in the table) was caused by a sudden rupture along a reverse fault at the foot of the San Gabriel Mountains.

Studies of historical fault movement have shown that they occur in two ways. The first and better known is the sudden displacement, or slip, of the ground along a fault. Such displacement is accompanied by earthquakes and occasionally produces spectacular offsets of topographic and even of man-made features. During the 1906 earthquake, the ground was displaced as much as 21 feet along the San Andreas fault in northern California. During the 1857 earthquake, displacement of the ground along this fault was possibly as much as 30 feet in southern California. The second type of fault movement, termed *creep*, is now taking place on portions of several faults in California. This type of movement was well documented for the first time in 1956, and has since been found to be commonplace. It is characterized by continuous or intermittent slight slip without noticeable earthquakes. Recent fault creep on portions of the Hayward, Calaveras, and San Andreas faults has produced cumulative offsets ranging from a fraction of an inch to almost a foot in curbs, streets, and railroad tracks, and has caused some damage to buildings.

Most of the faults shown on the map are, in reality, zones made up of a number of subsidiary faults or fault *strands*. These fault zones range in width from several feet to a mile or more. Slip along them during historical time and the recent geologic past has been found to recur repeatedly on only one or a few of the multiple strands that constitute these zones. Most of the strands commonly show no evidence of recent activity, although slip does at times recur on older strands or on entirely new ones. The strong tendency for fault slip and earthquakes to recur along the most recently active strands makes knowledge of the precise location of these strands essential to land-use planning.

The source of the stresses that cause the Earth's crust to break and slip in the California region is unknown, but the stresses appear to be related to crustal distortion on a global scale. Geologists have found abundant evidence that these stresses have been acting for millions of years. Whatever their source, the results is a continuing history of surface displacements and earthquakes along numerous faults in the California region.

# ACTIVE FAULTS OF CALIFORNIA

## MAP EXPLANATION

Recently active faults (believed to have been active within the past several thousand years.)

Fault segment along which slip has occurred during historical earthquakes or which is undergoing fault creep. Numbers show the location of earthquakes listed on the accompanying table.

Possible extension of recently active faults; also related faults that may have been recently active.

Inferred submarine faults that may have been recently active.

Parts of the San Andreas fault system in which fault slip, fault creep, and small-to-moderate earthquakes are most common.

Direction of relative horizontal slip along fault.

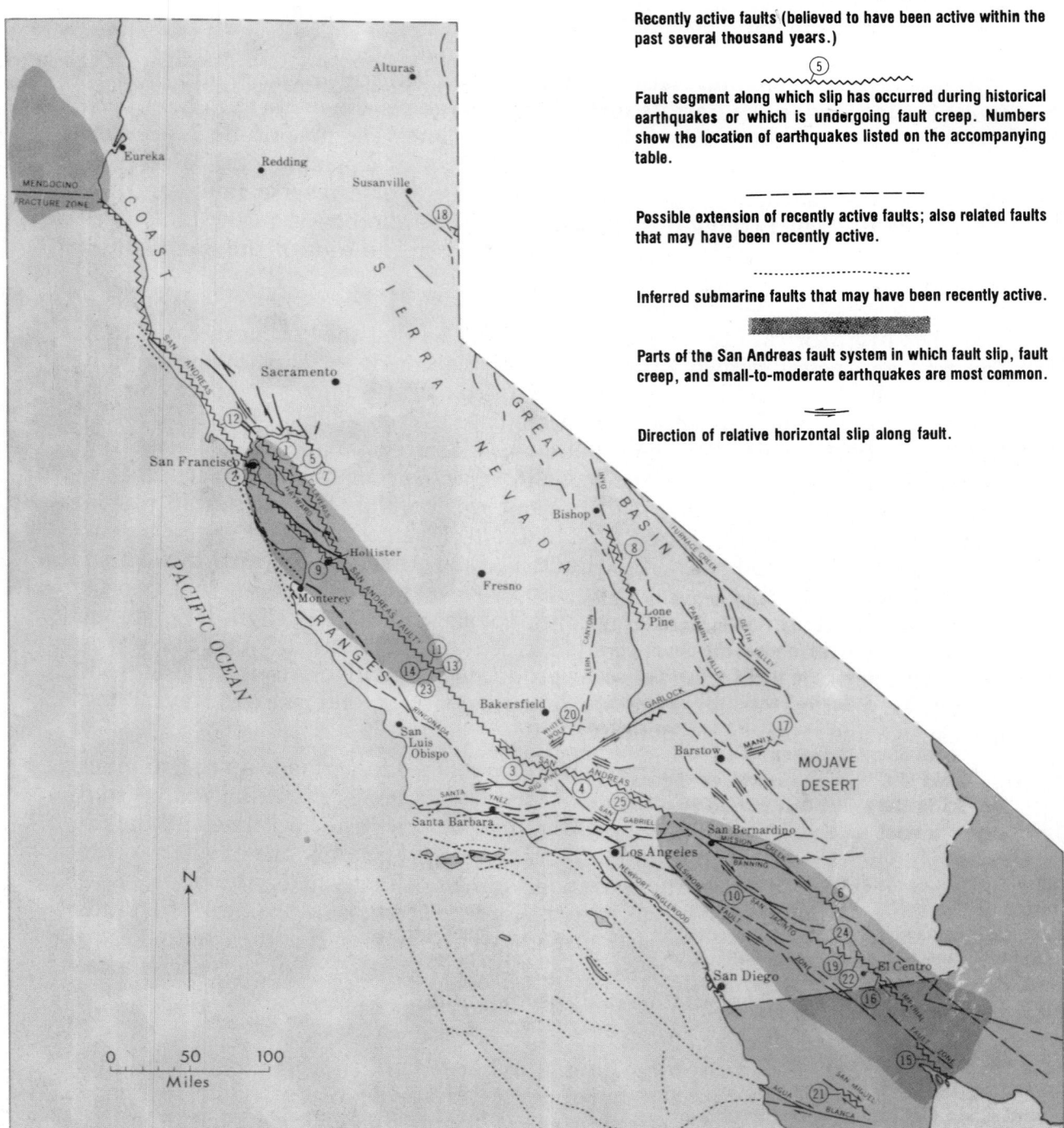

## The San Andreas Fault

The most important of California's faults is the San Andreas, which is the "master fault" of the intricate network of faults that cuts through rocks of the coastal region of California. It is a fracture in the Earth's crust along which two parts of the crust have slipped with respect to each other.

The presence of the San Andreas fault was dramatically brought to the attention of the world on April 18, 1906, when displacement along the fault resulted in the great San Francisco earthquake and fire. This, however, was but one of many, many earthquakes that have resulted from displacement along the fault throughout its life of possibly 100 million years.

**The San Andreas and other faults in the San Francisco Bay area** (after Geologic Map of California, 1961, by California Division of MInes and Geology.)

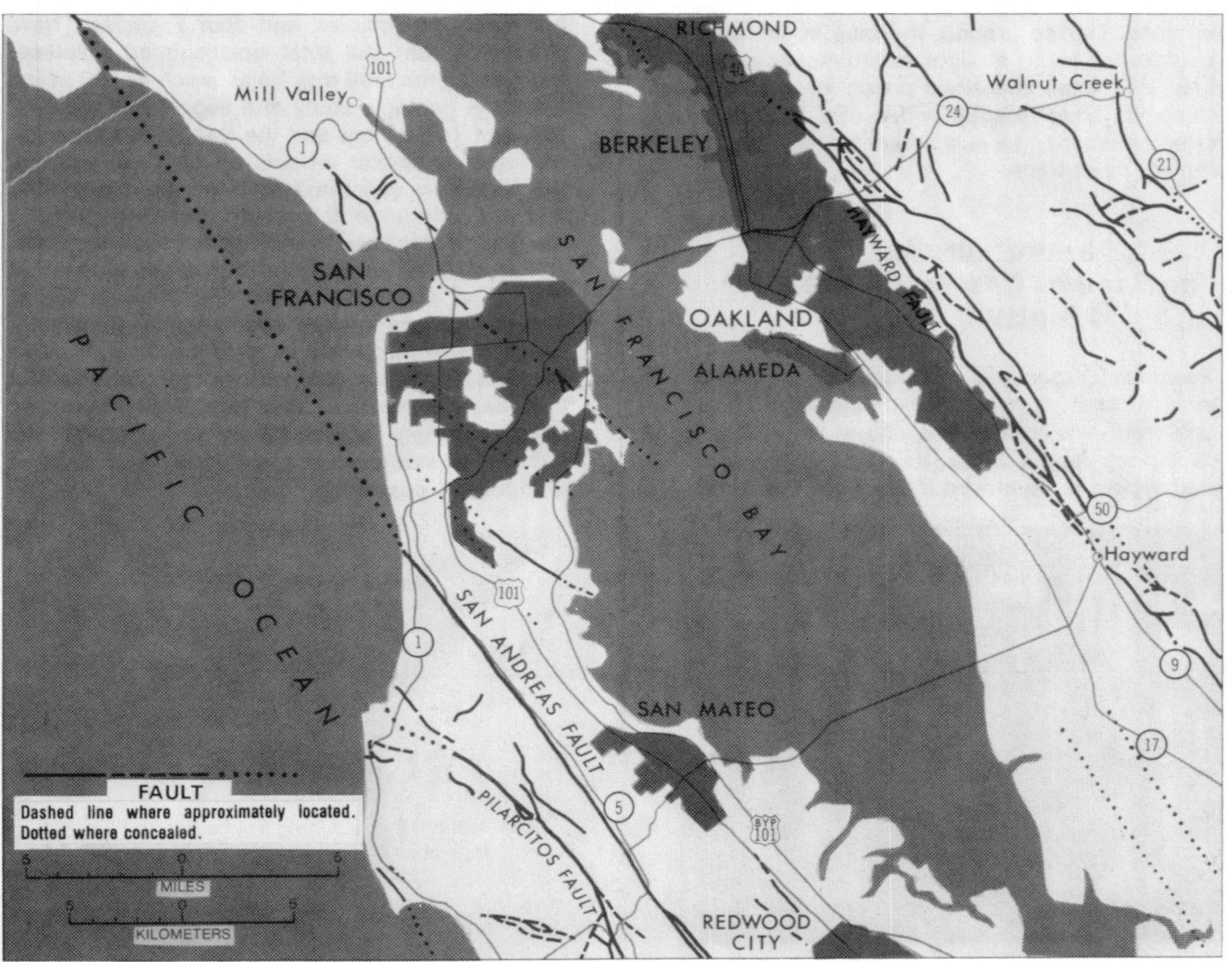

## SURFACE FAULTING DURING HISTORICAL EARTHQUAKES IN CALIFORNIA

| No. | Date | Fault | Magnitude (Richter Scale) | Surface Effects |
|---|---|---|---|---|
| 1. | 1836 | Hayward | 7.0* | Ground breakage |
| 2. | 1838 | San Andreas | 7.0* | Ground breakage |
| 3. | 1852 | Big Pine | No data | Ground breakage questionable |
| 4. | 1857 | San Andreas | 8.0* | Right-lateral slip, possibly as much as 30 feet |
| 5. | 1861 | Calaveras | No data | Ground breakage |
| 6. | 1868 | San Andreas | No data | Long fissure in earth at Dos Palmas |
| 7. | 1868 | Hayward | 7.0* | Strike slip |
| 8. | 1872 | Owens Valley fault zone | 8.3* | Right-lateral slip, 16-20 ft.; left-lateral movement may also have occurred; vertical slip, down to east, 23 ft. |
| 9. | 1890 | San Andreas | No data | Fissures in fault zone; railroad tracks moved; railroad bridge displaced |
| 10. | 1899 | San Jacinto | 6.6* | Surface evidence questionable |
| 11. | 1901 | San Andreas | 6.3* | Ground breakage |
| 12. | 1906 | San Andreas | 8.3 | Right-lateral slip, 21 ft. |
| 13. | 1922 | San Andreas | 6.5 | Ground breakage |
| 14. | 1934 | San Andreas | 6.0 | Ground breakage |
| 15. | 1934 | San Jacinto fault zone in Colorado River delta | 7.1 | Distinct fault trace on 1935 aerial photographs |
| 16. | 1940 | Imperial | 7.1 | Right-lateral slip, 19 ft. |
| 17. | 1947 | Manix | 6.4 | Left-lateral slip, 3 in. |
| 18. | 1950 | Unnamed fault along west edge Fort Sage Mtns. | 5.6 | Vertical slip, down to west, 5-8 in. |
| 19. | 1951 | Superstition Hills | 5.6 | Right-lateral slip, slight |
| 20. | 1952 | White Wolf | 7.7 | South-dipping reverse fault; left-lateral slip, 2 ft.; upthrown, 2 ft. |
| 21. | 1956 | San Miguel | 6.8 | Right-lateral slip, 3 ft.; vertical slip, down to southwest, 3 ft. |
| 22. | 1966 | Imperial | 3.6 | Right-lateral slip ½ in. |
| 23. | 1966 | San Andreas | 5.5 | Right-lateral slip, several inches |
| 24. | 1968 | Coyote Creek, Superstition Hills, Imperial, and San Andreas | 6.4 | Right-lateral slip up to 15 inches on Coyote Creek; slight right-lateral slip on Superstition Hills, Imperial, and San Andreas |
| 25. | 1971 | San Fernando | 6.6 | Left-lateral slip, up to 5 ft.; thrusting, up to 3 ft. (north side up); shortening 3 ft. |
| 26. | 1989 | Santa Cruz Mountains | 6.9 | (Data not avail.) |

\* Estimated

## FAULTS SHOWING CONTINUOUS OR INTERMITTENT CREEP

San Andreas fault from San Juan Bautista to Cholame
Hayward fault
Calaveras fault zone from near Dublin to Hollister
Imperial fault; possible creep after 1940 Imperial Valley earthquake
Manix fault
Garlock fault
Concord fault
Antioch fault

The fault is a huge fracture some 600 or more miles long, extending almost vertically into the Earth to a depth of at least 20 miles. In detail it is a complex zone of crushed and broken rock from a few hundred feet to a mile wide. Many smaller faults branch from and join the San Andreas fault zone, and if one examines almost any road cut in the zone, he will find a myriad of small fractures, fault gouge (pulverized rock), and a few solid pieces of rock.

## Where is the San Andreas fault?

The accompanying map shows the general location of the San Andreas fault and some other major faults in California.

The San Andreas fault forms a continuous break from northern California southward to Cajon Pass. From Cajon Pass southeastward the identity of the fault becomes confused, because several branching faults such as the San Jacinto, Mission Creek, and Banning faults have similar characteristics. Nevertheless, the San Andreas type of faulting continues unabated southward to and under the Gulf of Lower California.

Over much of its length a linear trough reveals the presence of the fault, and from an airplane the linear arangement of the lakes, bays, and valleys appears striking. Undoubtedly, however, many people driving near Crystal Springs Reservior, along Tomales Bay, through Cajon or Tejon Passes, do not realize they are on the San Andreas fault zone. On the ground, the fault zone can be recognized by long straight escarpments, narrow ridges, and small undrained ponds formed by the settling of small blocks within the fault zone. Characteristically, steam channels jog sharply along the fault trace.

## What type and amount of movement has there been along the fault?

Essentially, blocks on opposite sides of the San Andreas fault move horizontally, as suggested by the diagram below, and if one were to stand on one side of the fault and look across it, the block on the opposite side would appear to be moved to the right. Geologists refer to this as a *right-lateral strike-slip fault,* or *wrench fault*.

**Movement of blocks along the San Andreas fault.**

During the 1906 earthquake, roads, fences, and rows of trees and bushes that crossed the fault were offset several feet, and the road across the head of Tomales Bay was offset 21 feet, the maximum offset recorded. In each case the ground west of the fault moved relatively northward.

Geologists who have studied in detail the fault between Los Angeles and San Francisco have suggested that the total accumulated displacement along the fault may be as much as 350 miles. Similarly, geologic study of a segment of the fault between Tejon Pass and the Salton Sea revealed geologically similar terrains on opposite sides of the fault now separated by 150 miles, indicating that the separation is a result of movement along the San Andreas and branching San Gabriel faults.

It is difficult to imagine this great amount of shifting of the Earth's crust; yet the rate represented by these ancient offsets seems consistent with the rate measured in historical time. Precise surveying shows a slow drift at the rate of about 2 inches per year. At that rate, if the fault has been uniformly active during its possible 100 million years of existence, over 300 miles of offset is indeed a possibility.

Since 1934, earthquake activity along the San Andreas fault system has been concentrated in three areas shown by shading on the map. These are areas where historical earthquakes and fault displacements of the Earth's surface have been most common and where fault creep is taking place today. The two intervening segments, on the other hand, have had almost no earthquakes or known slip events since the great earthquakes of 1857 in the southernmost segment and 1906 in the northern segment. This implies to some earth scientists that these two segments of the San Andreas fault are temporarily *locked*, whereas in the other areas stress is being continually relieved by slip, which produces small to moderate earthquakes, and by creep. The lack of such activity in the locked segments could mean that these segments are subject to less frequent but larger fault movements and correspondingly more severe earthquakes.

The recorded history of earthquakes along the San Andreas fault is an extremely small sample from which, however, a clear pattern of behavior can be determined. Judging from this short history, great earthquakes seem to occur only a few times a century, but smaller earthquakes recorded only on sensitive seismographs occur much more frequently.

It is a popular misconception that once there has been a small earthquake along a segment of the fault, strain is released and further earthquakes are not to be expected for many years. Seismologists have pointed out, however, that the really great earthquakes have been preceded by numerous strong shocks and that large earthquakes seem to cluster in periods of 10 to 20 years long. Furthermore, the energy released during small earthquakes is insignificant compared to that in earthquakes having the same magnitude as the one in 1906.

Different segments of the fault also behave differently. For example, in the vicinity of Hollister, frequent small shocks are recorded, and slow movement at the rate of 12 mm per year has been recorded. In contrast, the segment near San Francisco, except for an earthquake of magnitude 5.3 in 1957, has been relatively quiet since 1906. Perhaps, as some believe, it is gradually bending or accumulating strain that will be adjusted all at once in one large "snap".

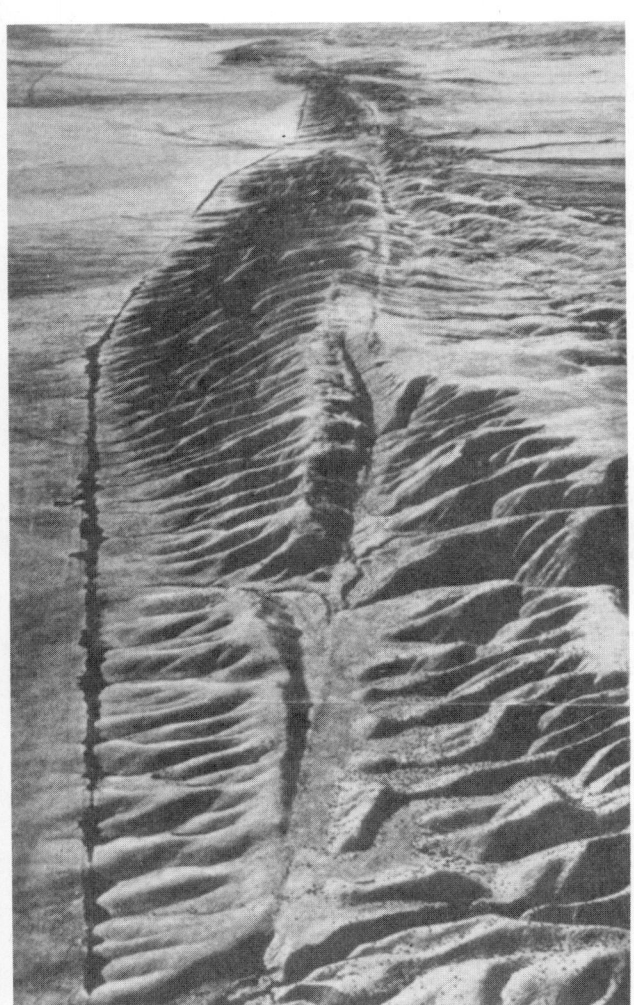

*Above*—The San Andreas fault is clearly evident in many areas of California.

*Right, above*—As a result of the historic San Francisco earthquake of April 18, 1906, the fence was offset 8½ feet.

*Right, below*—A housing development near San Francisco, California, that is sitting on the San Andreas fault.

## What can be done about the fault?

Much is yet to be learned about the nature and behavior of the San Andreas fault and the earthquakes it generates. Some questions geologists would like to answer are: How old is the fault? Has movement been uniform? What movement has there been on branching faults? What is the fundamental cause of the stresses that produced the San Andreas fault? Until these questions and others have been satisfactorily answered the question "what can be done about the fault?" is best responded to, says the U.S. Geological Survey, in this way:

*"Though man cannot stop earthquakes from happening, he can learn to live with the problems they cause. Of prime importance are adequate building codes, for experience shows that well-constructed buildings greatly lessen the hazards. In construction projects, greater consideration should be given to foundation conditions. Degree of damage will range widely between construction on bedrock, water-saturated mud, filled ground, or landslide terrain. For example, in 1906, most buildings on filled or "made" land near the foot of Market Street in San Francisco suffered particularly intense damage, whereas buildings on solid rock suffered little or no damage. Geologists are horrified to see land developers build rows of houses straddling the trace of the 1906 break...".*

Maps showing the most recently active strands or breaks along the San Andreas and related active faults are being prepared by the U.S. Geological Survey. Contact with this governmental agency can be made at 302 National Center, Reston, Virginia 22092, or 345 Middlefield Road, Menlo Park, California 94025. The Geological Survey also maintains Public Inquiries Offices in San Francisco, and Los Angeles.

# EARTHQUAKE SAFETY RULES

An earthquake strikes your area and for a minute or two the "solid" earth moves like the deck of a ship. What you do during and immediately after the tremor may make life-and-death differences for you, your family, and your neighbors. These rules will help you survive.

DURING AN EARTHQUAKE

1. Remain calm. Think through the consequences of any action you take. Try to calm and reassure others.

2. If indoors, watch for falling plaster, bricks, light fixtures, and other objects. Watch for high bookcases, china cabinets, shelves, and other furniture which might slide or topple. Stay away from windows, mirrors, and chimneys. If in danger, get under a table, desk, or bed; in a corner away from windows; or in a strong doorway. Encourage others to follow your example. Usually it is best not to run outside.

3. If in a high-rise building, get under a desk. Do not dash for exists, since stairways may be broken and jammed with people. Power for elevators may fail.

4. If in a crowded store, do not rush for a doorway since hundreds may have the same idea. If you must leave the building, choose your exit as carefully as possible.

5. If outside, avoid high buildings, walls, power poles, and other objects which could fall. Do not run through streets. If possible, move to an open area away from all hazards. If in an automobile, stop in the safest place available, preferably an open area.

AFTER AN EARTHQUAKE

1. Check for injuries in your family and neighborhood. Do not attempt to move seriously injured persons unless they are in immediate danger of further injury.

2. Check for fires or fire hazards.

3. Wear shoes in all areas near debris or broken glass.

4. Check utility lines and appliances for damage. If gas leaks exist, shut off the main gas valve. Shut off electrical power if there is damage to your house wiring. Report damage to the appropriate utility companies and follow their instructions. Do not use matches, lighters, or open-flame appliances until you are sure no gas leaks exist. Do not operate electrical switches or appliances if gas leaks are suspected. This creates sparks which can ignite gas from broken lines.

5. Do not touch downed powerlines or objects touched by the downed wires.

6. Immediately clean up spilled medicines, drugs, and other potentially harmful materials.

7. If water is off, emergency water may be obtained from water heaters, toilet tanks, melted ice cubes, and canned vegetables.

8. Check to see that sewage lines are intact before permitting continued flushing of toilets.

9. Do not eat or drink anything from open containers near shattered glass. Liquids may be strained through a clean handkerchief or cloth if danger of glass contamination exists.

10. If power is off, check your freezer and plan meals to use foods which will spoil quickly.

11. Use outdoor charcoal broilers for emergency cooking.

12. Do not use your telephone except for genuine emergency calls. Turn on your radio for damage reports and information.

13. Check your chimney over its entire length for cracks and damage, particularly in the attic and at the roofline. Unnoticed damage could lead to a fire. The initial check should be made from a distance. Approach chimneys with caution.

14. Check closets and storage shelf areas. Open closets and cupboard doors carefully and watch out for objects falling from shelves.

15. Do not spread rumors. They often do great harm after disasters.

16. Do not go sightseeing immediately, particularly in beach and water-front areas where seismic sea waves could strike. Keep the streets clear for passage of emergency vehicles.

17. Be prepared for additional earthquake shocks called "aftershocks." Although most of these are smaller than the main shock, some may be large enough to cause additional damage.

18. Respond to requests for help from police, fire fighting, civil defense, and relief organizations, but do not go into damaged areas unless your help has been requested. Cooperate fully with public-safety officials. In some areas, you may be arrested for getting in the way of disaster operations.

There are no rules which can eliminate all earthquake danger. However, damage and injury can be greatly reduced by following these simple rules.

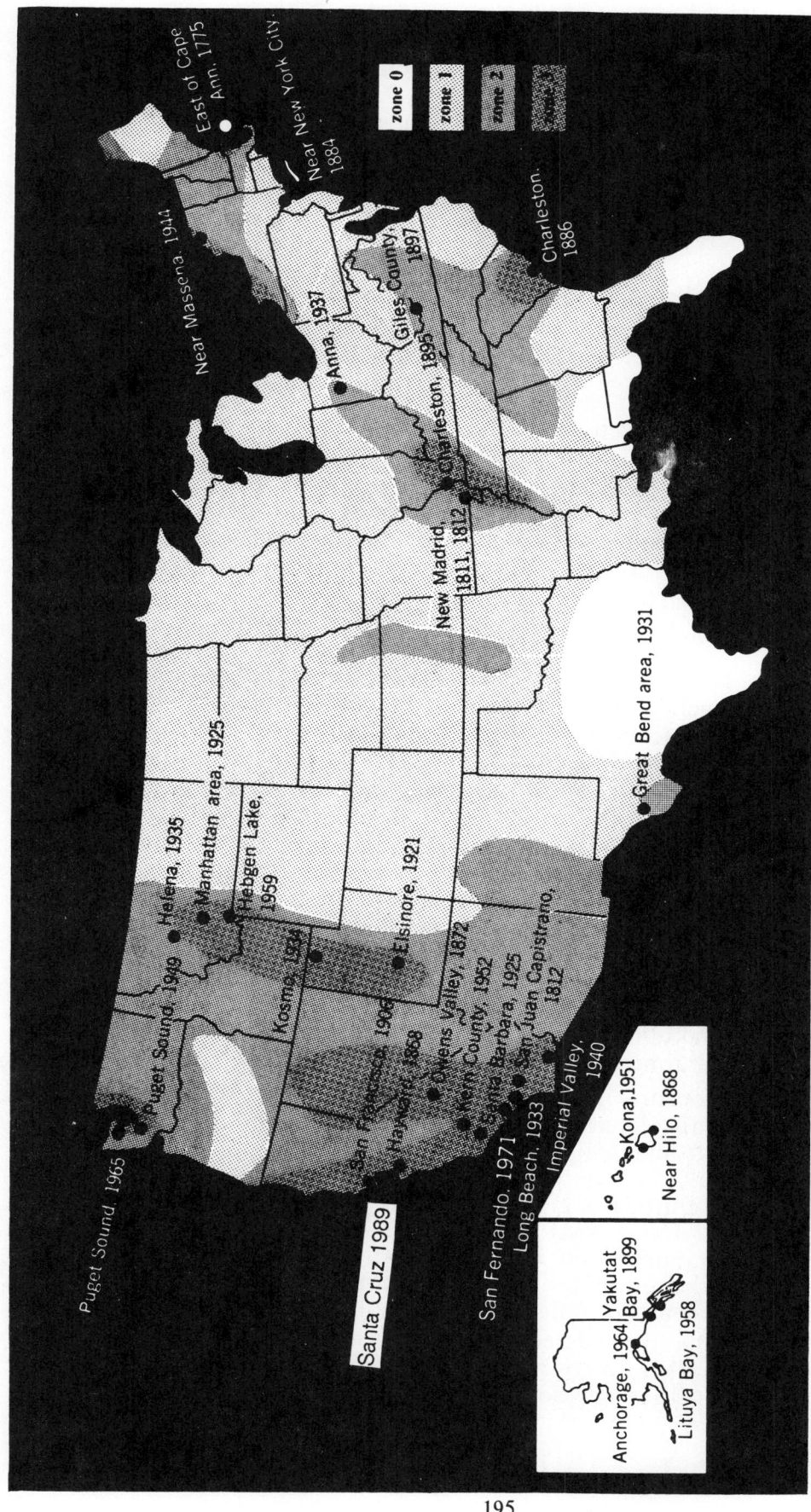

zone 0
zone 1
zone 2
zone 3

East of Cape Anm. 1775
Near New York City.
Near Massena. 1944
Anna. 1937
Giles County. 1897
Charleston. 1895
Charleston. 1886
New Madrid. 1811, 1812
Great Bend area, 1931
Helena, 1935
Manhattan area, 1925
Hebgen Lake, 1959
Elsinore, 1921
Kosmo. 1934
Owens Valley, 1872
Santa Barbara, 1925
Kern County, 1952
San Juan Capistrano, 1812
San Francisco. 1906
Hayward. 1868
Puget Sound, 1949
Puget Sound. 1965
Imperial Valley, 1940
Long Beach. 1933
San Fernando. 1971
Santa Cruz 1989

Kona,1951
Near Hilo, 1868

Anchorage, 1964
Yakutat Bay, 1899
Lituya Bay, 1958

*The four zones indicated by shadings on this map suggest the relative probability that earthquake damage may sometime occur in given areas. The epicenters of major earthquakes which have occured in the U.S. and the years of occurrence are also noted. Estimates of earthquake risk are based on the history of seismic disturbances, evidences of strain release and consideration of major geologic structures.*

# TSUNAMI (TIDAL WAVE)

## What is a tsunami?

The phenomenon we call "tsunami" is a series of traveling ocean waves of great length and long period, generated by disturbances associated with earthquakes in oceanic and coastal regions. As the tsunami crosses the deep ocean, its length from crest to crest may be a hundred miles or more, its height from trough to crest only a few feet. It **cannot** be felt aboard ships in deep water, and **cannot** be seen from the air. But in deep water, tsunami waves may reach forward speeds exceeding 600 miles per hour.

As the tsunami enters the shoaling water of coastlines in its path, the velocity of its waves diminishes and wave height **increases. It is in these shallow waters that tsunamis become a threat to life and property,** for they can crest to heights of more than 100 feet, and strike with devastating force.

## The warning system—

Development of the NOAA Coast and Geodetic Survey's Pacific Tsunami Warning System was impelled by the disastrous waves of April 1946, which surprised Hawaii and took a heavy toll in life and property. The locally disastrous tsunami caused by the March 1964 Alaska earthquake impelled the development of another type of warning apparatus—the Regional Tsunami Warning System in Alaska.

The Regional Tsunami Warning System is headquartered at the Coast and Geodetic Survey's Seismological Observatory at Palmer, Alaska. This is the nerve center for an elaborate telemetry network linking Palmer with remote seismic and tidal stations along the Alaska coast and in the Aleutian Islands. Seismograph stations in the network are at Palmer Observatory and its two remote stations 25 miles south and west, and at Biorka, Sitka, Gilmore Creek, Kodiak, and Adak. Tide stations are at Seward, Sitka, Kodiak, Cold Bay, Unalaska, Adak, Yakutat, and Shemya. Data from these stations are recorded continuously at Palmer, where a 24-hour watch is kept.

When an earthquake occurs in the Alaska-Aleutian area, seismologists at Palmer Observatory rapidly determine its epicenter (the point on the earth's surface above the underground source of the earthquake) and magnitude. If the epicenter falls in the Aleutian Island arc or near Alaskan coastal area, and if the earthquake magnitude is great enough to generate a tsunami, Palmer Observatory issues a TSUNAMI WARNING through the Alaska Disaster Office, Alaska Command, and Federal Aviation Administration (FAA) covering the area near the epicenter. A TSUNAMI WATCH is issued for the rest of the Alaskan coastline, alerting the public to the possibility of a tsunami threat. If a tsunami is detected by tide stations, Palmer Observatory extends the TSUNAMI WARNING to cover the entire coastline of Alaska. If no tsunami is observed, both the WATCH and WARNING bulletins are cancelled.

Subsidiary warning centers have been established at Sitka and Adak Ob-

*Tidal wave action caused much of the destruction when the 1964 earthquake hit Alaska. The surge ashore of a great wall of water is devastating, but its worst effects are often the result of the water's suddenly receding, carrying all manners of structures down the beach to their ruin. Above, boats have been tossed ashore from their moorings by the surprise wave.*

servatories. These facilities operate small seismic arrays and have a limited warning responsibility for local areas.

The Pacific Tsunami Warning System has its headquarters at the Coast and Geodetic Survey's Honolulu Observatory. There, seismologists monitor data received from seismic and tidal instruments in Hawaii and around the Pacific Ocean, and provide ocean-wide tsunami watches and warnings. The Pacific system works very closely with its regional counterpart in Alaska. Potentially tsunami-generating earthquakes in the Alaska-Aleutian area are detected and evaluated at Palmer Observatory, and the data relayed directly to Honolulu Observatory. Where there is tidal evidence of a tsunami, the warning is extended by Honolulu to cover the Pacific Ocean basin. For tsunamis generated elsewhere in the Pacific area, tsunami watch and warning bulletins are prepared at Honolulu Observatory and disseminated in Alaska by the Alaska Disaster Office, the military, and FAA.

# TSUNAMI (TIDAL WAVE) SAFETY RULES —

Tsunamis are the so-called "tidal waves" generated by some earthquakes. When you hear a tsunami warning, you must assume a dangerour wave is on its way. History shows that when the great waves finally strike, they claim those who have ignored the warning.

REMEMBER:

1. All earthquakes do not cause tsunamis, but many do. When you hear that an earthquake has occurred, stand by for a tsunami emergency.

2. A strong earthquake felt in a low-lying coastal area is a natural warning of possible, immediate danger. Keep calm and move to higher ground, away from the coast.

3. A tsunami is not a single wave, but a series of waves. Stay out of danger areas until an "all-clear" is issued by competent authority.

4. Approaching tsunamis are sometimes heralded by a noticeable rise or fall of coastal water. This is nature's tsunami warning and should be heeded.

5. A small tsunami at one beach can be a giant a few miles away. Don't let the modest size of one make you lose respect for all.

6. All tsunamis—like hurricanes—are potentially dangerous, even though they may not damage every coastline they strike.

7. Never go down to the beach to watch for a tsunami. When you can see the wave you are too close to escape it.

8. During a tsunami emergency, your local Civil Defense, police, and other emergency organizations will try to save your life. Give them your fullest cooperation.

Stay tuned to your radio or television stations during a tsunami emergency—bulletins issued through Civil Defense and NOAA offices can help you save your life!

# VOLCANIC ACTIVITY: GEOLOGICAL PHENOMENA WITH ENVIRONMENTAL, WEATHER, AND CLIMATIC IMPACT

Mount Unzen, in Shimbara, southern Japan — another of the volcanoes of the Pacific "Ring of Fire —" spews out a massive flow of hot gas, ash and molten rocks in a June 8th, 1991 eruption. In an eruption a week earlier 38 people were killed. A week later Mt. Pinatubo, overlooking Subic Bay, 60 miles northwest of Manila, another of the "Ring of Fire" chain, roared to life. U.S. Servicemen and women, stationed at Clark Air Force Base were evacuated. Damage was mostly to property as advance warnings were unusually effective. Kilauea on Hawaii continued its eruptions in 1991 which have occurred sparodically since 1983. Each of these volcanoes have belched millions of tons of ash and debris into the upper atmosphere, and in so doing altered the weather patterns in uncharted ways. Some scientists say cooler temperatures will result for many months; others figure the screening of sunlight by this ash will offset "greenhouse factors" which they say have been the reason the past decade was warmer than average.

199

*AP/Wide World Photos*

# Active Pacific volcanoes are cases in point; 1991 eruptions in Japan and the Philippines may offset warming trend of the eighties

*Since Mount St. Helens volcano, located in the State of Washington, erupted violently on May 18, 1980 volcanism has become a much talked about part of the weather and climate pictures of both the United States and the world. Much of the continuing importance of this spectacular eruption is owed to the fact that it lifted a great volume of ash and debris into the upper atmosphere. Some of the ash from a volcano eruption falls to earth quickly; but a large portion stays aloft, dispersed worldwide, for years. In that case it becomes a factor—as volcanic activity has always been—in meterological processes that shape weather events globally. For this reason* Weather Almanac *editors believe a discussion of volcanism, followed by a description of the eruption, is a logical inclusion in a broad-spectrum weather reference book.* Weather Almanac *is also a proper place to help publicize the VOLCANO SAFETY RULES prepared by the U.S. Geological Survey. They follow the volcano text material.*

Volcanic activity has played a dominant role in shaping the face of the Earth. Much of the natural beauty of the land, its mineral wealth, and the fertility of the soil is owed to volcanism, especially in the Western States. At one time or another during the last 70 million years, volcanic rocks covered nearly all of the Western States of Washington, Oregon, California, Nevada, Arizona, Utah, Idaho, and large parts of Montana, Wyoming, Colorado, New Mexico, and Texas. Still older volcanic rocks, now largely deformed and metamorphosed, are found in nearly every State.

## What are volcanoes?

Volcanoes are built by the accumulation of their own eruptive products: lava, bombs, ash, and dust. Usually the volcano is a conical hill or mountain built around a vent that connects with reservoirs of molten rock (known as magma) below the Earth's surface. Forced upward by the pressure of contained gas, the molten rock breaks through zones of weakness in the Earth's crust. It spews from the vent as lava flows or shoots into the air as dense coulds of lava fragments.

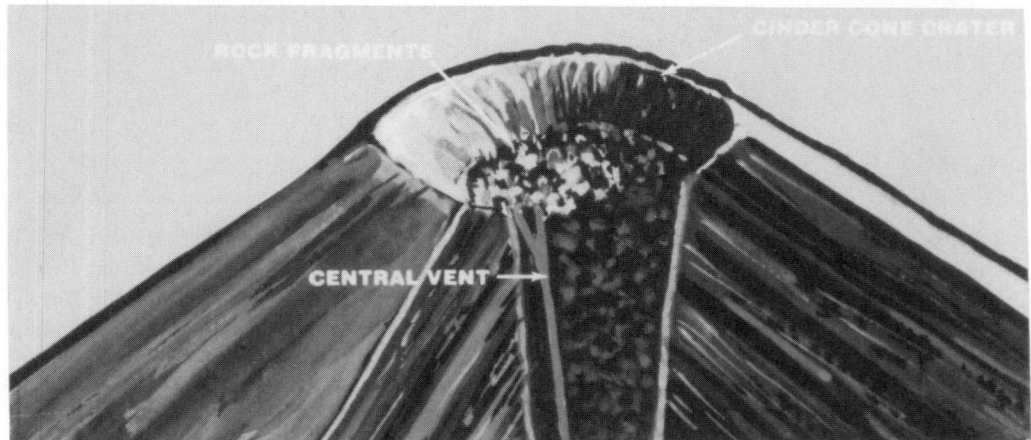

**Schematic representation of the internal structure of a typical cinder cone.**

Larger fragments (bombs and cinders) fall back around the vent. Some of the finer material (ash and dust) may be blown by the wind and eventually fall to the ground many miles away. Very fine particles reach the upper atmosphere (stratosphere) where they can circulate around the Earth for several years.

The gas in lava can be compared with the behavior of the gas in a soda bottle that is shaken and then the top released. The violent separation of gas from lava may produce rock froth known as pumice, which is so light that it floats on water.

## Kinds of volcanoes

There are four main kinds of volcanoes—*cinder cones, composite cones, shield volcanoes, and lava domes.*

1. **Cinder cones,** as the name suggests, are built of lava fragments. They are very numerous in the western United States; for example, Sunset Crater, Ariz., and Craters of the Moon National Monuments, Idaho.

2. **Composite cones** are built of alternating layers of lava flows, volcanic ash, and ash; they are sometimes called strato-volcanoes. Many of the world's large mountains are composite cones; for example, Mount Fuji, Japan, Mount Shasta, Calif., and Mount St. Helens and Mount Rainier, Wash.

⟶

**Volcanic areas of the Western United States, Alaska and Hawaii.**

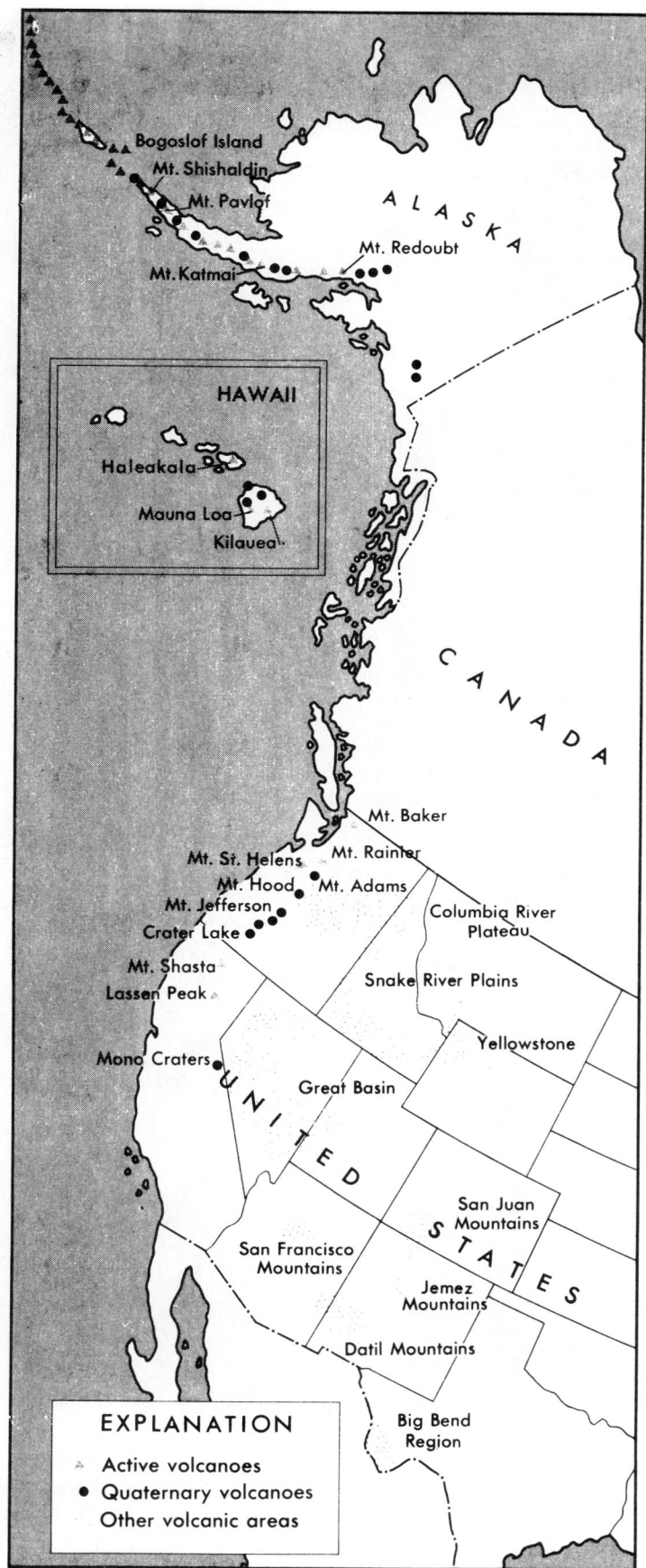

EXPLANATION
- ⚲ Active volcanoes
- • Quaternary volcanoes
- Other volcanic areas

Explosive erution of Mount Saint Helens Volcano, Washington, that occurred on May 18, 1980. Climatologists say much of the ash expelled will be dispersed worldwide in the upper atmosphere for years.

# The Pacific Ocean's "Ring of Fire"

There are more than 500 active volcanoes (those that have erupted within recorded history) in the world. More than half of them encircle the Pacific Ocean, forming the series known as the "Ring of Fire." Fifty active volcanoes are in the United States (Hawaii, Alaska, Washington, Oregon and California.) Many more volcanoes may be hidden beneath the seas.

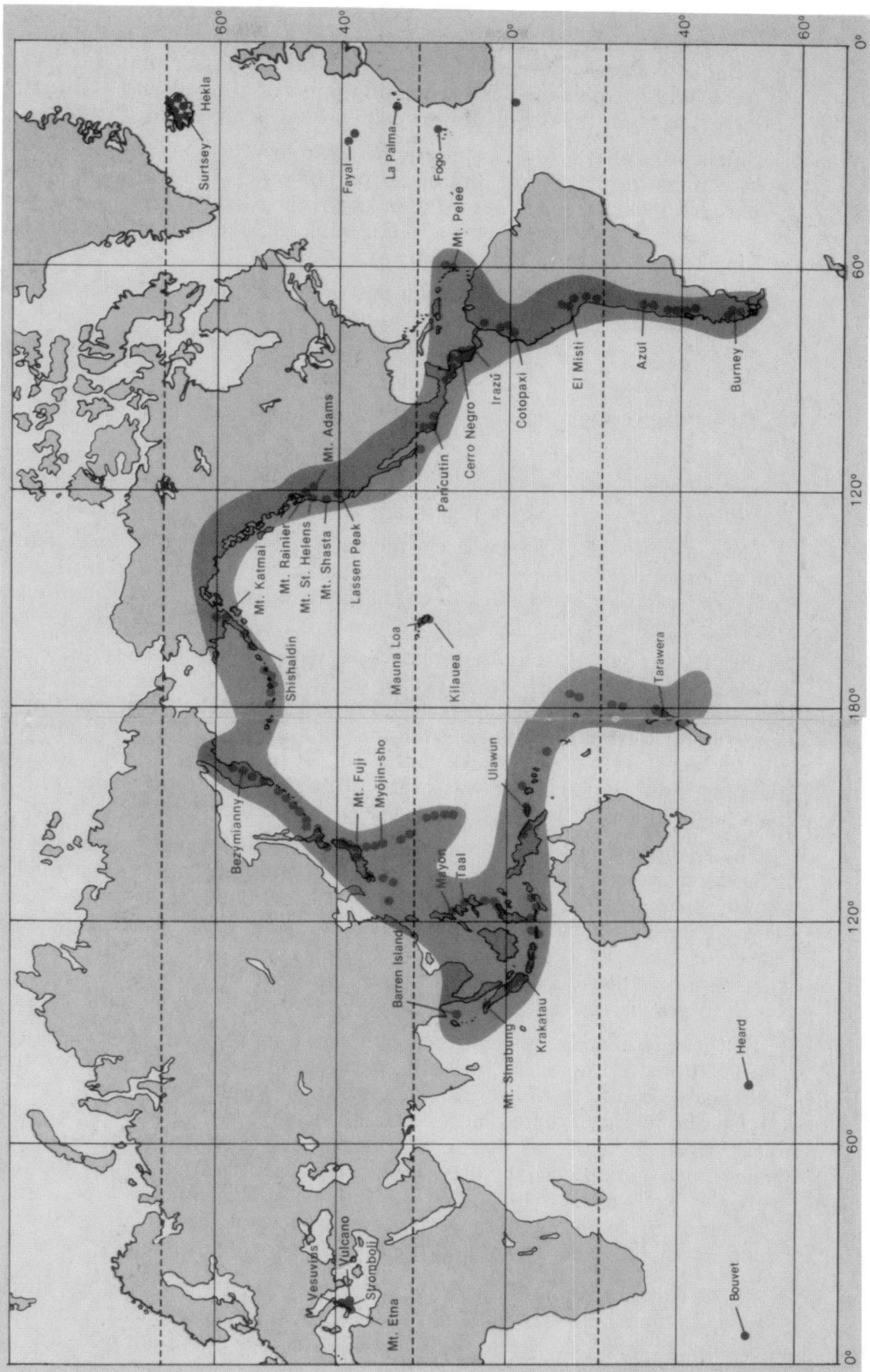

Crater Lake in Oregon is an interesting variation of a composite cone. Originally like Mount Rainier, the volcano lost its summit in a series of tremendous explosions; the remaining parts of the volcano eventually collapsed to form the depression or caldera that is now Crater Lake.

3. **Shield volcanoes** are built almost entirely of lava flows. These flow out in all directions from a central vent of a group of vents. The Hawaiian Islands are clusters of shield volcanoes (Mauna Loa is the world's largest active volcano and rises 13,653 feet above sea level). In Iceland, lava pours out quietly from long fissures to form broad plateaus.

4. **Lava domes** are built of viscous or pasty lava extruded like toothpaste from a tube. Lassen Peak and Mono Dome in California are examples of lava domes.

## Active volcanoes

Active volcanism in the United States is confined to the Hawaiian Islands, the Aleutian Islands, the Alaska Peninsula, and the Cascade Mountains.

The Hawaiian Islands consist entirely of volcanic rocks that form giant shield volcanoes; one rises nearly 30,000 feet from the ocean floor. By far the dominant rock type is dark gray to black *basalt* in the form of lava flows, cinders, pumice, ash, and bombs.

On the island of Hawaii are Mauna Loa, the largest volcano in the world, and Kilauea, one of the most active. During an eruption at Kilauea in 1959-60, great fountains of lava, some as high as 1,900 feet, were observed near the volcano summit. Lava from the fountains ran into an old pit crater and filled it to a depth of 365 feet, forming a lava lake. Late in 1963, nearly 4 years after the eruption, the crust on top of the lake was nearly 50 feet thick and the temperature of the lava below the crust was still about 2,000° Fahrenheit (1,100° Celsius).

The Aleutian Island Arc, including the Alaska Peninsula, is more than 2,000 miles long and contains about 36 historically active and many extinct volcanoes. Among them are some of the world's most beautiful but little-studied volcanoes. The composite volcanoes Pavlof, Shishaldin, and Pavlof Sister are examples. Bogoslof Island is a disapppearing volcano, having emerged and submerged in the sea more than once in historic time. Most of the Aluetian lavas consist of black to gray rocks called basalts and *andesites*.

Of the several active volcanoes on the Alaskan Peninsula, Mount Katmai (Katmai National Mounument) is the most notable. In 1912, one of the most remarkable eruptions of historic time occurred near its base. About 2 cubic miles of ash and pumice erupted in the form of incandescent ash flows or avalanches. The "river of sand," as the early explorers called it, flowed for more than 15 miles down a great glacial valley, filling it to a depth of more than 400 feet. This valley is known as the "Valley of Ten Thousand Smokes" because of the thousands of *fumaroles* (gas vents) that formed on the surface of the volcanic deposits and gave off steam and other vapors for many years.

In the Cascade Mountains of Washington, Oregon, and California are the well-known composite cones of Mounts Baker, Rainier, St. Helens, Adams, Hood, Mazama, and Shasta. These High Cascade volcanoes are built primarily of rocks called andesites, which are intermediate in chemical composition between basalts and rhyolites. Andesitic volcanoes are usually great cones of rubble consisting of interlayered lava flows and fragmented deposits called *mud flows*. These form when eruptions take place through crater lakes, when fragmented lavas and land-slides enter streams, or when water from melting snow or rain saturates and mobilizes previously erupted deposits. Volcanic mud flows may be hot or cold and may deposit boulders weighing many tons. Very young mud flow deposits are common on the flanks of Mount Rainier and other Cascade cones.

## Mud flows—a major cause of destruction

In some area of the world, mud flows have been the major cause of destruction and loss of life during volcanic catastrophes. Such an eruption in 1919 from Kelud Volcano in Java covered 50 square miles of land with mud and lava blocks. More than 5,000 human lives were lost and 100 villages completely or partly damaged. This great devastation was caused by the ejection of over 1 billion cubic feet of water from Kelud's lake.

Mount Mazama is the volcano that lost most of its top about 7,000 years ago during a tremendous explosive eruption. Nearly 12 cubic miles of ash and pumice erupted, producing under the volcano a void so large that the top caved in to form a great hole 6 miles across. Depressions formed in the top of volcanoes in this manner are known as *calderas*. They differ from craters that are produced by explosion rather than by collapse. the caldera of Mount Mazama is now filled with water to a depth of over 1,700 feet and is known as Crater Lake.

Lassen Peak is famous among volcanoes because it is one of the largest known *plug domes*. A plug dome is a part of a volcano formed by the vertical rise of a great sticky mass of lava which remains standing above the crater rim. Common-ly great vertical grooves are formed in the margin of the dome as the material oozes from the orifice. The mechanism may be compare to the squeezing of tooth paste from a tube. Subsequent eruptions from plug domes are among the most dangerous known. Gasses dissolved in the lava may burst forth violently, shatter the dome, and cause the formation of extremely mobile avalanches of hot blocks, rock dust, and gas. Such avalanches may travel at speeds up to 100 miles an hour and devastate everything in their paths. It was an eruption of this type in 1902 from Mount Pelee in the West Indies which destroyed the nearby town of St. Pierre and killed nearly 30,000 people.

## Mount St. Helens

Mount St. Helens is a symmetrical volcanic cone in southwestern Washington about 45 miles northeast of Portland Oregon. Most of the cone that can be seen now was formed within the last thousand years—but this overlies an older volcanic center that probably has existed for at least 40,000 years. Mount St. Helens has had a long history of spasmodic explosive activity. It is an especially dangerous volcano because of its past behavior and the high frequency of its eruptions during the past 4,500 years.

## Ancient volcanoes

There are several areas in the United States where, for many thousands of years, the only activity has been that of hot springs and *solfataras* (steam vents). Yellowstone National Park is the most famous of these areas. It is visited each year by thousands of people who come to see the geysers, mud pots, boiling hot springs, steam vents, and beautiful carbonate and silica deposits formed by precipitation from the hot waters. Such phenomena are vestiges of a former period of very active volcanism. We cannot be sure, however, that some day more violent volcanic activity may not begin again.

The youngest and most dominant volcanic eruptions in Yellowstone Park produced lavas called *rhyolite*. Chemically, rhyolite is high in silica and is the volcanic equivalent of granite. Among active volcanoes rhyolite is exceedingly rare. In the geologic past, however, rhyolite erutions were more common and among the most spectacular of natural phenomena. Over 600 cubic miles of rhyolite erupted from the Yellowstone volcanoes alone during their last active periods. Two-thirds of this amount erupted as ash flows like the "river of sand" that caused the "Ten Thousand Smokes" in Alaska in 1912. The remaining 200 cubic miles of material issued as great sticky lava flows.

So great was the volume of flows of ash and pumice that valleys were completely filled and the intervening ridges were covered. The ash flows merged to form flat-topped plateaus thousands of square miles in area. When deposited, these great sheets of ash were so hot that the particles fused together to form rocks knows as *welded tuffs*. Recent geologic studies have revealed that welded tuffs are perhaps the most abundant rhyolitis rocks in the Western United States. Tens of thousands of cubic miles are known in Nevada alone, and great volumes are also recognized in the San Juan Mountains of Colorado, southwestern New Mexico, the Big Bend region of Texas, and southwestern Arizona.

In the Jemez Mountains of New Mexico, about 1 million years ago, eruptions similar to those at Yellowstone produced nearly 50 cubic miles of welded tuffs. Removal of this large volume of material from the abyssal storage chamber caused a great circular block of the Earth's crust (more than 10 miles in diameter) to subside several thousand feet, producing a giant caldera at the surface. Formations of this, the Valles Caldera, was similar to that of Crater Lake, but of special interest to geologists is the subsequent, more complex history of the Valles Caldera. Renewed pressure from below uplifted and arched the subsided circular block so that its center rose even higher than its original elevation. During and after this uplift, new eruptions of rhyolitic lava broke out along the fracture system around the uplifted circular block and built a ring of 15 new volcanoes.

Detailed studies of the Valles Caldera have allowed geologists to relate this rhyolitic volcanism to more deeply seated processes of granite formation. Volcanism of this type is now known to have occurred in many other area of the United States. The San Juan Mountains of Colorado are an outstanding example, as are the Mono Craters in California. They, like Little Glass and Big Glass Mountains in northeastern California, are famous for black volcanic glass (obsidian) and for the large blocks of pumice that have recently become so popular as ornamental stones. The Mono Craters include some of the world's finest examples of rhyolitic pumice cones and lava domes. Their forms range from simple, almost perfectly symmetrical cones of pumice and ash, to cones whose craters are partly or completely filled or overflowing with lava. Some cones are completely covered with lava flows that have piled up to form steep-sided lava domes. Those cones containing lava that did not overflow the crater rim are similar to the plug dome of Lassen Peak but are much smaller and formed by more fluid lava.

Recurrently, throughout geologic time, very fluid basaltic lava has erupted from swarms of fissures to form vast lava plateaus. The Columbia River Plateau of Washington and Oregon and the Snake River Plains of Idaho are among the finest examples of this type of volcanism. The Columbia River Plateau has an area of 100,000 square miles, and the total volume of basaltic lava approximates 35,000 cubic miles. Individual lava flows can be traced for distances of more than 100 miles. Such lavas must have been almost as fluid as water to have covered such large areas so uniformly.

On the northern edge of the Snake River Plains is the Craters of the Moon National Monument. Here, basaltic lavas erupted perhaps less than 2,000 years ago. The vents from which the lavas issued are localized on great fissures and show a wide variety of forms, ranging from *cinder cones* built entirely on very frothy red and black lava cinders, to *spatter cones* formed by the piling up of liquid lava blobs and droplets around the vent. Both *aa* and *pahoehoe* lavas are found at "Craters of the Moon." Pahoehoe and aa are Hawaiian terms adopted the world over for two principal types of basaltic lavas. Pahoehoe is very fluid lava with smooth to ropy surface and the flows may travel long distances. Aa lava is more viscous lava that forms steep-sided flows seemingly composed only of craggy blocks, but usually containing a continuous fluid interior.

Occasionally the surface and sides of these basaltic lava flows solidify to form a thick outer crust. Yet the hot lava inside continues its forward movement and eventually drains out of its own crust to form *lava tunnels* or *lava tubes*. Water entering such tunnels may freeze in the winter and, because of the excellent insulation provided by the basalt crust, may not thaw in the summer even under desert conditions. Excellent examples of these ice caves and lava tunnels may be seen in the Modoc Lava Beds National Monument, California.

Basaltic lava fields in cinder cones are numerous in many parts of the West. Some of these are isolated volcanic vents, but basaltic vents are commonly clustered near or around large volcanoes composed of andesitic and similar lavas. Fine examples of the clustered types are the volcanic fields of the San Francisco Mountains, Arizona, and Mount Taylor, New Mexico.

Hundreds of other localities for volcanoes and volcanic rocks are known, and this very brief discussion simply serves to emphasize that the United States, particlarly the West, has been one of the most volcanically active areas in the world in recent geologic time. Because we do not yet know the real causes of volcanism, we cannot say whether eruptions will recur in areas like New Mexico, Arizona, or Nevada. We can be sure, however, that in our lifetime volcanoes in Hawaii and Alaska will erupt again.

## Volcanic hazards map of the United States

The map on the following page is abstracted from a preliminary map compiled by D. R. Mullineaux to indicate areas subject to potential volcanic hazard in the contiguous (48) States. The map shows general areas or zones that, over a long period of time, are relatively likely to be affected in one or more places by various kinds of hazardous volcanic events. These hazards include lava flows, mudflows, hot rock avalanches, ashfalls, and floods.

The map shows that volcanic hazards are limited to areas in the Western United States, principally in the Cascade Mountain Range in California, Oregon, and Washington; in Idaho's Snake River Plain; and in parts of Arizona, New Mexico, and Utah. No hazard areas are shown east of New Mexico.

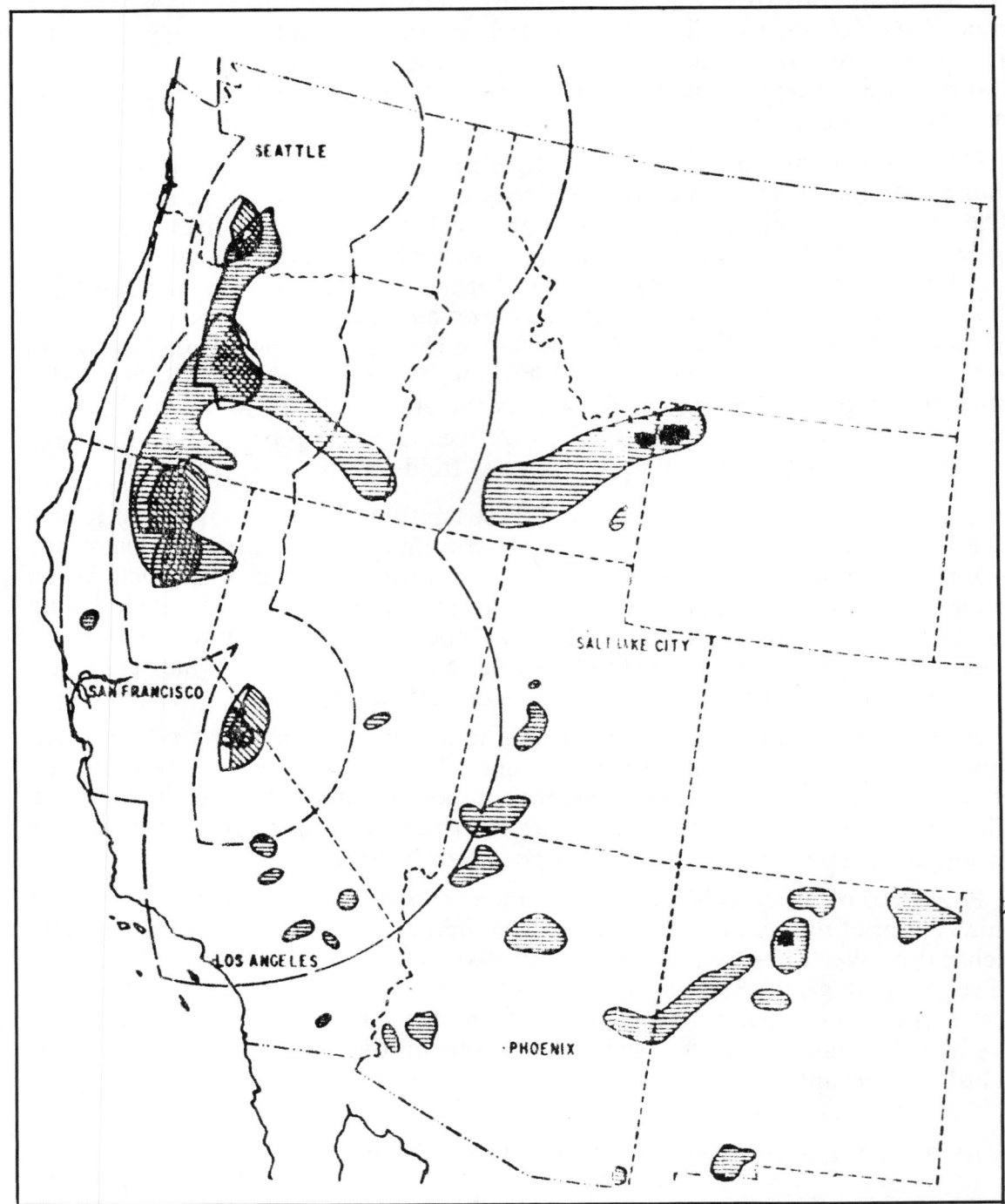

## Volcanic hazards map of the United States

U.S. Geological Survey map, prepared by D.R. Mullineaux, shows volcanic hazard zones in the Western United States. Solid black zones are volcanic vent areas that had one or more extremely explosive and voluminous eruptions within the last 2 million years. Zones with horizontal lines are subject to lava flows and small volumes of ash from groups of volcanic vents called "volcanic fields." Zones with diagonal lines would get most of the ashfall from nearby relatively active and explosive volcanoes. The inner dashed line encloses areas subject to 2 inches or more of ash from a large eruption and the outer dashed line encloses areas subject to 2 inches or more of ash from a very large eruption.

The immediate risk from volcanic hazards is low because eruptions are so infrequent. Severely destructive effects of eruptions, other than extremely rare ones of catastrophic scale, probably would be limited to areas within a few tens of miles downvalley or downwind from a volcano. Thus, the area seriously endangered by any one eruption would be only a very small part of the Western United States.

Except for Mount St. Helens' renewed activity in 1980, the only explosive volcanic eruption in the conterminous States since the area was settled was 10,457-foot-high Mount Lassen in northern California during a series of eruptions in 1914-15. The Mount Lassen eruption was moderate compared to major eruptions at other volcanos in the world during recorded history. No one was killed in the Mount Lassen eruption, and damage was minor.

Eruptions of moderate volume may occur somewhere in the Cascade Range as often as once every 1,000 to 2,000 years, but very large eruptions may occur no more than once every 10,000 years. A few large cataclysmic eruptions have occured during the last 2 million years in and near Yellowstone National Park, at Long Valley, Calif., and in the Jemez Mountains of New Mexico. These eruptions affected very large regions and deposited ash over much of the Western United States. The sites of these eruptions are shown on the map, but such cataclysmic eruptions were not considered in outlining potential hazard zones. These eruptions are so infrequent that it is not possible to judge whether one might occur during the time for which planning is feasible.

Risk from volcanic hazards decreases as distance from an erupting volcano increases. Lava flows are nearly uniformly destructive to their outer limits. Some other volcanic hazards, especially ashfalls, become less destructive and less frequent with increasing distance. The boundary of such a hazard is indefinite and often dependent upon land use. For example, an ashfall a centimeter or so thick might cause little damage to structures, yet destroy crops.

Copies of the full-size (28 x 36 inches) black-and-white map from which this map was taken, identified as MF-786, may be purchased at the U.S. Geological Survey Public Inquiries Offices or from the Branch of Distribution, U.S. Geological Survey, P.O. Box 25286, Federal Center, Denver, CO 80225.

# May 18th volcanic eruption at Mount St. Helens

On May 18, 1980 a powerful explosion occurred from Mount St. Helens at 8:32 a.m. that was heard 200 miles away. The explosion climaxed a series of activities which began with an earthquake shock of magnitude 4.1 on March 20th, 1980. Remarkable photographs, taken as the explosion began, show the north flank uplift peeling away from the volcano as a large vertical cloud began to rise from the summit. The tephra cloud rose very rapidly to more than 10 miles above

Two photographs of Mount St. Helens Volcano
The lower photo, which is a southwestern view, was made during the May 18 eruption.
209

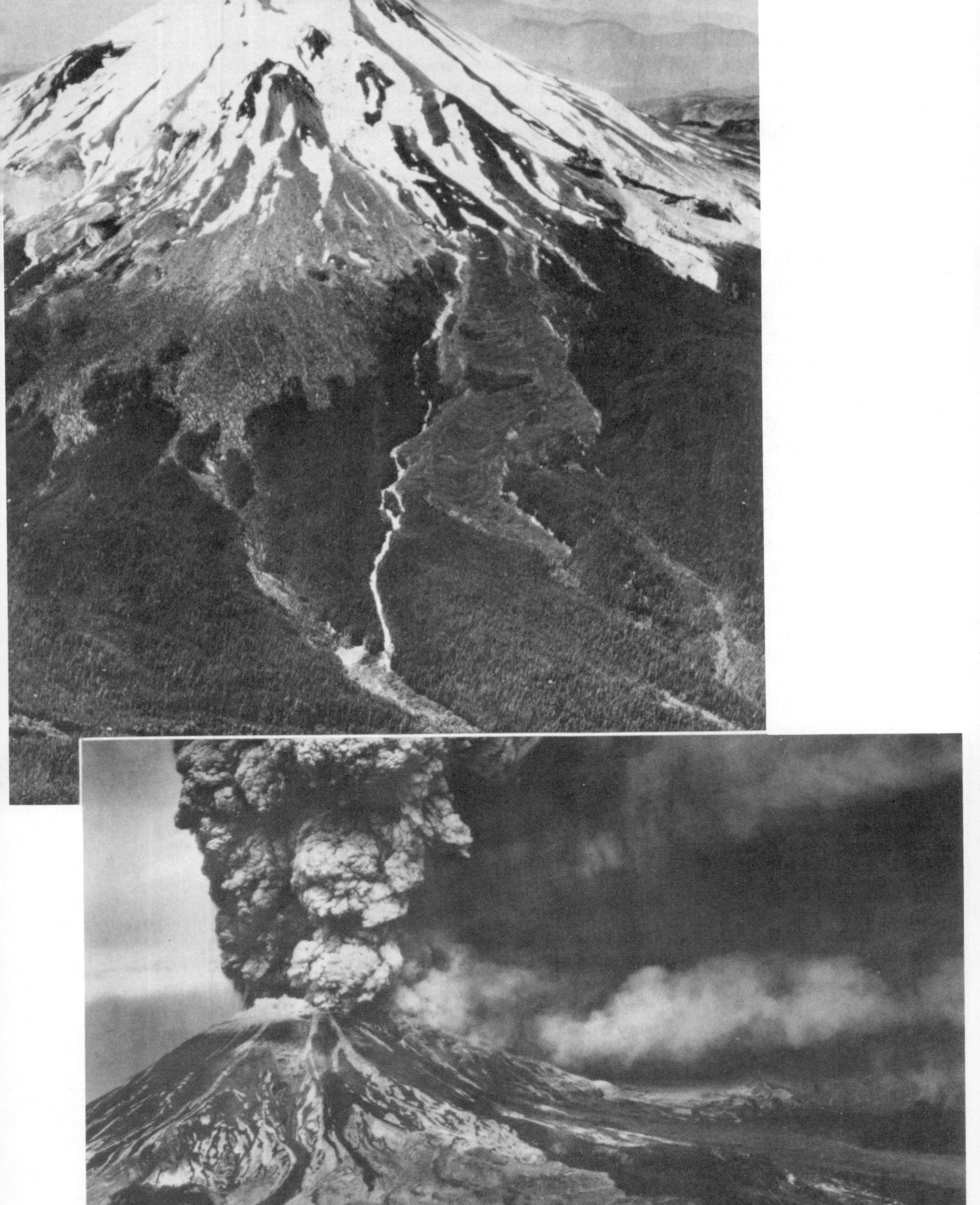

sea level, passing through the tropopause at 7 miles. Winds blew the cloud to the east. Ashfall at Yakima, 90 miles away, totaled as much as 4 to 5 inches and caused respiratory problems for some residents. By midafternoon, the ash had reached Spokane, reducing visibility to only 10 feet, although only half an inch was deposited there. Almost 2 inches of ash were reported from areas of Montana west of the Continental Divide, but only a dusting fell on the eastern slopes. Slight ashfall occurred in Denver on May 19. The ash blew generally eastward for the next several days, causing some problems for aircraft over the Midwest.

The U.S. Geological Survey identified three components of the initial eruptive event in addition to the vertical cloud:

**The first component** was a directed blast which leveled the forest on the north and northwest flanks for a distance of up to 15 miles from the former summit. The blast swept over ridges and flowed down valleys, depositing significant quantities of ash. Although the blast was hot, it did not char fallen or buried trees. Many persons are known to have been killed by the blast, and others in the devastated zone are missing.

**The second component** was a combined pyroclastic flow and landslide that carried the remnants of the north flank uplift across the lower slopes and about 17 miles down the Toutle River valley, burying it to depths as great as 180 feet. Large quantities of mud, logs, and other debris clogged several valleys around Mount St. Helens and rendered some shipping lanes impassible in the Columbia River.

**The third component** was a pumiceous pyroclastic flow, funneled northward through the breach formed by the destruction of the north flank bulge. This flow dammed the outlet of Spirit Lake, trapping a large quantity of water.

The volcano maintained an eruption column 10 miles high until a relatively sudden diminution of activity occurred in the early morning of May 19. The altitude of the top of the column declined to about 2.5 miles. Activity continued to weaken through May 22.

A new elliptical crater about a quarter mile deep had been formed by the explosion.

Preliminary analysis of seismic and deformation data indicates that there was no immediate warning of the imminence of a large explosion. A magnitude 5.0 earthquake occurred essentially simultaneously with the explosion at 8:32 a.m. Records of the only surviving tiltmeter, on the south flank, show that rapid inflation began at the same time as the explosion at 8:32 a.m.

Although volume estimates for this eruption are very rough, comparison with previous eruptions in the Smithsonian Institution's Volcano Reference File (a computer data file of the world's volcanoes and their eruptions) indicates that explosions of this size occur only about once a decade.

Climatology and weather experts reported early in 1981 that a considerable amount of Mount St. Helens ash was and will be for years to come distributed throughout the upper atmosphere of the entire world. Efforts to measure this atmosphere-borne ash are expected to go on for years to come; and understanding of its affect on world weather and climate will likewise be a continuing work with few definite answers available early.

Mount Saint Helens has erupted 22 times since it came to life on May 18, 1980. On 19 occasions the eruption has been predicted, as scientists use ever-more sensitive equipment to pick up ground vibrations and super-accurate lasers to detect the most minute "bulges" that occur in the slope of the mountain.

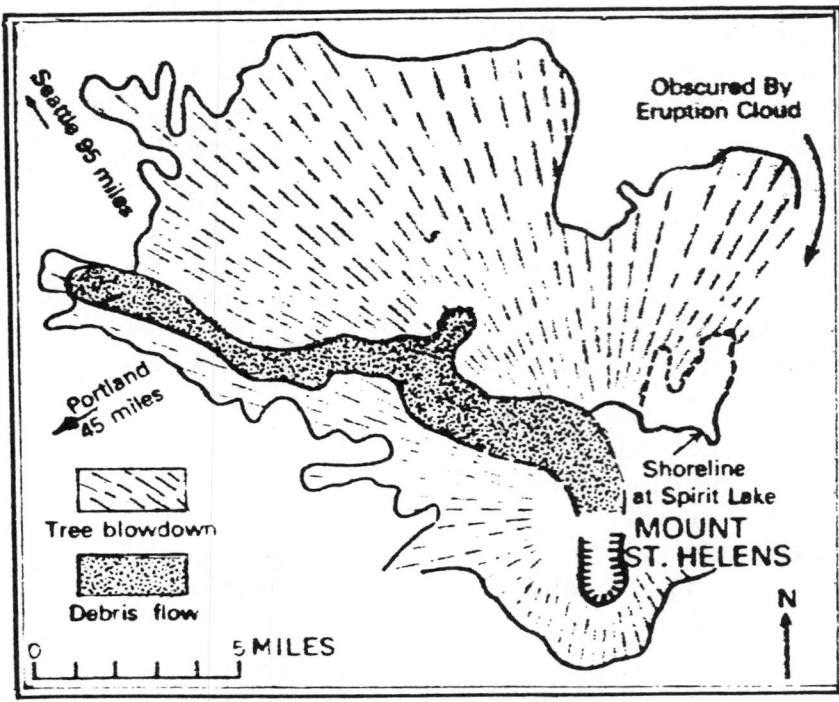

**Two of the effects
of Mt. Saint Helens
May 18, 1980 eruption**

**Top diagram shows
mudslides and tree falls
in 20 mile radius. Bottom
shows ash cloud movement**

**Map depicts damage caused on May 18, 1980 in the immediate vicinity
of Mount St. Helens.**

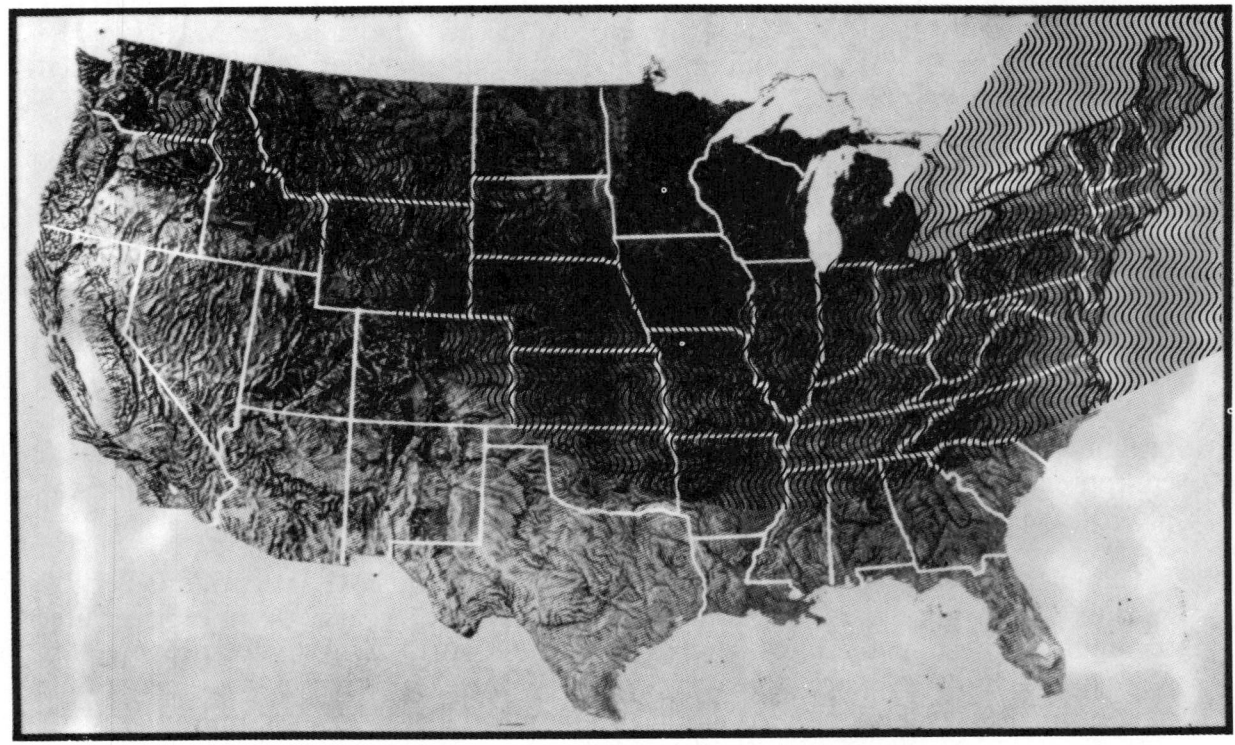

**Progress of ashfall after May 18, 1980, eruption at Mount St. Helens.**

# Hawaii has five volcanoes. One has been active periodically since 1983. Subdivisions fall to lava, streets disappear underneath its creep to the sea.

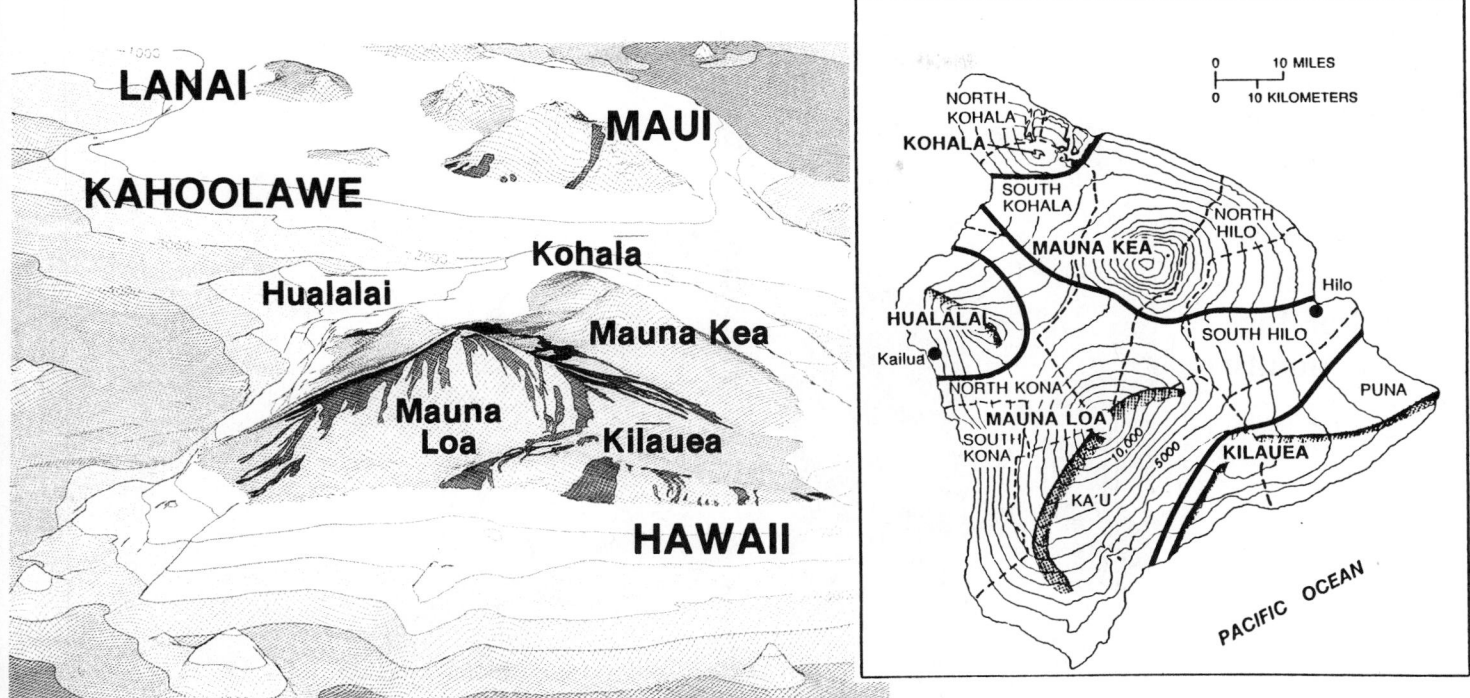

The island of Hawaii and its five volcanoes. The rift zones of the historically active volcanoes are indicated by the stippled gray pattern. Dashed lines indicate the boundaries of districts on the island.

Lava flowing from the Kapaianaha vent on Kilaue's east rift zone buries a street intersection in Kalapana Gardens subdivision. *(USGC photo by J.D. Griggs)*

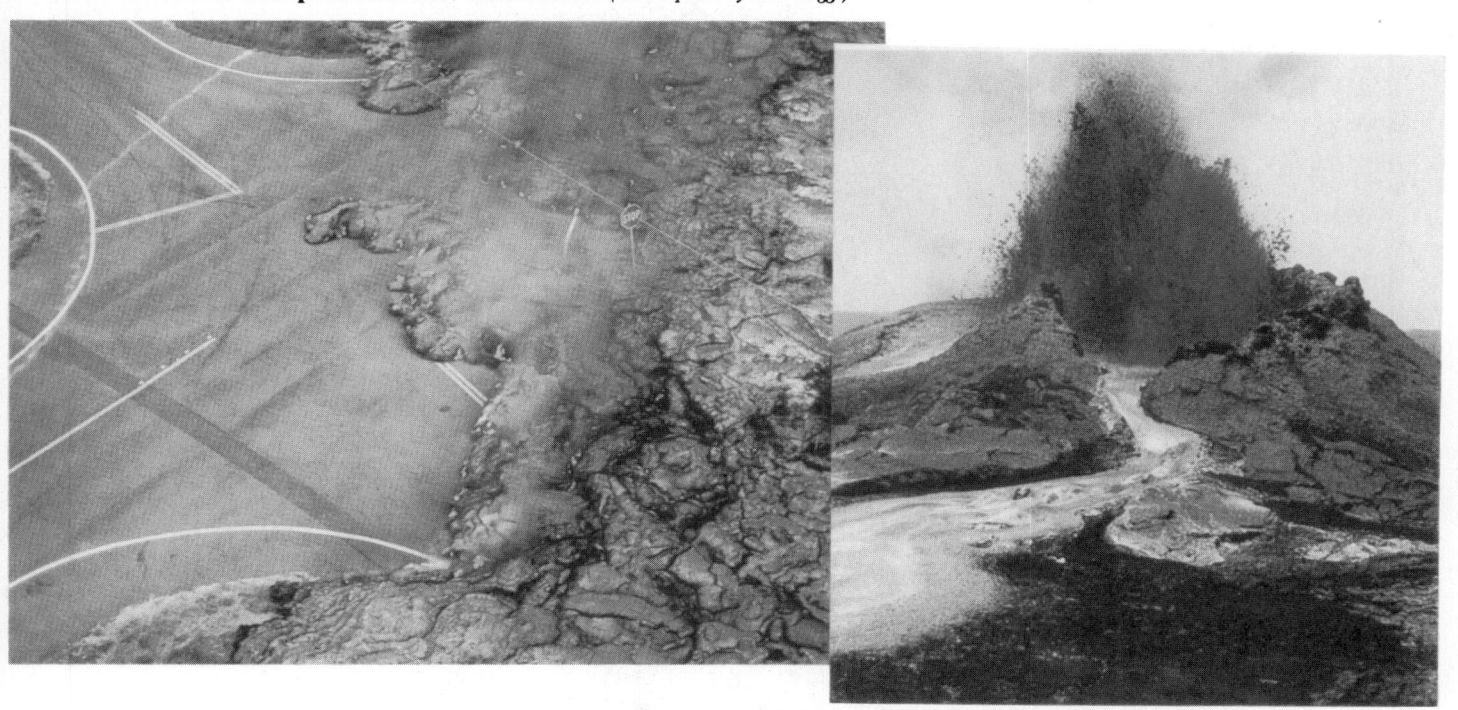

The Pu'u 'O'o vent began erupting in 1983 on Kilauea's east rift zone, 12 miles from the volcano's summit. *(National Park Service photo)*

**1991 volcano eruptions in Japan and the Philippines will affect weather for many months**

Japan's Mount Unzen, with its peak covered with volcanic ash, looms over local houses on this June 11, 1991 afternoon. The volcano in southwestern Japan, had claimed 38 lives to this point, and continued to threaten local residents. *(AP/Wide World Photos)*

A Filipino shovels ash off the roof of his hut following the June 16, 1991 eruption of Mount Pinatubo. A thundering storm struck at the same time as the eruption, increasing the ash problem by wetting it down and sharply increasing its weight. Personnel of nearby Clark Air Force base were evacuated to the hotel in the background of this picture. It is interesting to note that M. Pinatubo had been inactive for 600 years, and most residents did not even know the "grassy hill" was a volcano. Its name did not appear on the Smithsonian's registry of active volcanoes. *(AP/Wide World Photos)*

## SAFETY RULES

# WHAT TO DO WHEN A VOLCANO ERUPTS

**Most important, don't panic—keep calm.**

**If volcanic ash begins to fall:**

- **Stay indoors.**
- **If you are outside, seek shelter such as a car or a building.**
- **If you cannot find shelter, breathe through a cloth, such as a handkerchief, preferably a damp cloth to filter out the ash.**
- **When air is full of ash, keep your eyes closed as much as possible.**
  - . . .Heavy falls of ash seldom last more than a few hours—only rarely do they last a day or more.
  - . . .Heavy falls of ash may cause darkness during daylight hours and may temporarily interfere with telephone, radio, and television comunications.
  - . . .Do not try to drive a car during heavy fall of ash—the chance of accident will be increased by poor visibility.
  - . . .The thick accumulation of ash could increase the load on roofs, and saturation of ash by rain could be an additional load. Ash should be removed from flat or low-pitched roofs to prevent a thick accumulation.
  - . . .Valleys that head on the volcano may be the routes of mudflows which carry boulders and resemble wet flowing concrete. Mudflows can move faster than you can walk or run, but you can drive a car down a valley faster than a mudflow will travel. When driving along a valley that heads on a volcano, watch up the river channel and parts of the valley floor for the occurrence of mudflows.
- **Before crossing a highway bridge, look upstream.**
- **Do not cross a bridge while a mudflow is moving beneath it.**
- **The danger from a mudflow increases as you approach a river channel and decreases as you move to higher ground.**
- **Risk of mudflows also decreases with increasing distance from a volcano.**
- **If you become isolated, do not stay near a river channel, move upslope.**

**DURING AN ERUPTION MOVE AWAY FROM A VOLCANO, NOT TOWARD IT. (In the immediate vicinity of an eruption the hazards to life are much greater than those listed above.)**

Source: U.S. Geological Survey.

# RETIREMENT AND
# HEALTH WEATHER

# A REVIEW OF SOME ATMOSPHERIC FACTORS IN HEALTH AND DISEASE

*The illusion that perfect health and happiness are within man's possibilities has flourished in many different forms throughout history.*
*Rene Dubos in Mirage of Health*

Physicians since before the time of Hippocrates, the "father of medicine," have recognized the inexorable bond between the human organism and its physical environment. Hippocrates'[1] work *On Airs, Waters, and Places,* justly regarded as a medical classic and a source of philosophical inspiration in medical analysis, opens with this advice:

*Whoever wishes to investigate medicine properly, should proceed thus: in the first place to consider the seasons of the year, and what effects each of them produce (for they are not at all alike, but differ much in themselves and in their changes). Then the winds, the hot and the cold, especially such as are common to all countries, and then such as are peculiar to each locality. We must also consider the qualities of the waters, for as they differ from one another in taste and weight, so also do they differ much in their qualities. In the same manner, when one comes into a city to which he is a stranger, he ought to consider its situation, how it lies as to the winds and the rising of the sun; for its influence is not the same whether it lies to the north or the south, to the rising sun [east] or to the setting sun [west].*

Claude Bernard, the great pioneer of scientific medicine in the mid-nineteenth century, recognised that the conditions necessary to life are found neither in the organism nor in the outer environment, but in both at once. The germ theory of disease which is almost exactly one hundred years old did much however to focus medical research on micro-organisms and away from the weaker but more pervasive influences of diet and the physical environment. Nevertheless, a hardy and, indeed, at times even foolhardy band of scientists and physicians have continued to probe for an understanding of the vexing relationships between nature and nurture in health and disease.

Scientific disciplines such as Biometeorology and Medical Geography which cut across many research specialties have been developed with increasing success in recent years. The information retrieval problem in cross-disciplinary subjects such as these is difficult because relevant findings may be scattered widely among 50,000 or more scientific and medical publications. Yet, the greatest problems arise because of inherent difficulties in the subject matters of investigation.

The weather is noted for its restless variability. As Frederick Sargent II[2] points out the atmospheric ingredients of weather "are rarely present in exactly the same proportion, and, as a consequence, it has been exceedingly difficult to conceive exact models of the physical environment." Yet, he continues, "the variability of the organism is no less simple. The individual organism, be it plant or animal, has biochemical and physiological individuality. Biochemical, physiological, and behavioral events in plants and animals vary in time [and] are regulated by biological clocks." These clocks have multiple rhythms. Approximate periods vary from one day, to a week, a month, a season, a year, and longer. Given such multiple controls, the variation in factors such as the chemical properties of the blood, functions of important organs or body systems, and overt behavior may be greater in a single individual over a long period of time than between different individuals at the same time.

The theme of the biological and behavioral uniqueness of individuals is an important one. Nothing can be done with it in this review except to note the extraordinary difficulty in making sense of fluctuating series of unique environmental and organismic events. The resulting literature can be exceedingly confusing and contradictory. It is founded too often upon statistical correlations of doubtful significance with the physiological linkages poorly established, for as Nelson Dingle[3] indicates, "in the search for cause and effect relationship in bioclimatological work, one needs to give careful attention to the question whether the data actually contain the required information." As R.E. Munn[4] concludes, "there is a vast literature on medical climatology. In many cases the evidence is inductive and not very convincing." The task of the reviewer is to try to sort the wheat from the chaff.*

## Meteorotropisms

The Greek term "meteor" refers to atmospheric disturbances and "tropic" to turnings or changes. Hence, a scientific term has been coined to refer to a turn of events related to atmospheric disturbances: meteorotropism. The identification and analysis of such biological events is at the heart of the science of biometeorology. Having stated his ideas on the variability of living individuals, Sargent proceeds as follows:

> The main inquiry of biometeorology is to find out how much of this organismic variability is due to the changing atmospheric environment within which the organisms exist . . . When biological events are ordered in time, deviations from the expected aggregate about certain hours, days, months, etc. When sizable human populations are investigated, it has been found that sudden death, attacks of angina, joint pain, insomnia, and traffic accidents occur with unusual frequency on certain days, or in certain seasons. In some cases, it has been possible to demonstrate by appropriate statistical procedures that characteristic changes in the atmospheric environment are correlated with the biological aggregations. The biological event is then identified as a meteorotropism.

The convincing isolation of a weather related biological change from those related to some other form of environmental or internally induced stress is not an easy one, as Sargent is the first to acknowledge. Something of the problem can be seen by considering cases of aggravated duodenal ulcers.

## Duodenal ulcer aggravation

The monthly summary of the number of patients admitted to the Philadelphia General Hospital with hemorrhaging duodenal ulcers over the period 1949-1953 records cases in every month but shows a tendency to peak in March-April and October-November of any given year. The peak in the fall is somewhat greater than the spring peak. Francis K. Davis, Jr.[5] notes that "since hemorrhage from ulcers is intimately connected with the circulatory system and since this system definitely reacts to temperature changes, an attempt was made to find some relationship between temperature changes and ulcer hemorrhages." The greatest decrease in average temperature from one month to the next during the period under study did in fact occur from October to November, and the greatest increase occurred between March and April. One particular January-February period had a higher incidence of admission than the other comparable periods. This January was characterized by an unusually high monthly average temperature and was followed by an unusually cold February. Moreover, this particular January experienced 16 day to day changes of more than 10 F° in maximum temperature, nine of which were from warm to cold. Thus, the plausible suggestion that "the period of negative temperature change contributes more strongly to circulatory stresses than the period of positive temperature change" receives some support, but "more detailed data than are presently

---

\* A discussion of the effects of thermal stress on the body is found in the sections of this book dealing with "heat wave dangers" and "winter storms and wind chill."

available would be necessary to decide this point." Nevertheless, Davis concludes:

> *So, there is strong evidence that hemorrhage from duodenal ulcers may be brought on by marked variations in temperatures and the stress that such variations put on the body as it is forced to adjust. This fact, together with the observation that the number of cases is least in midsummer, would suggest that a warm climate with relatively little daily and seasonal variation in temperature would afford the most suitable residence for those prone to suffer from duodenal ulcers. Meanwhile, those northerners who are afflicted with duodenal ulcers might well be on the lookout for cold wave warnings in the fall. Such warnings cause construction workers to stop pouring concrete, prod farmers into taking special precautions to save crops, and serve to make fuel oil companies prepare for extra deliveries. They might be used to equal advantage by ulcer patients.*

Or, can they?

Another study in southern Australia found an increase of reported ulcer cases during May-June, the equivalent of Philadelphia's November-December, thereby seeming to confirm the latter study. Yet, as Munn[4] points out, still another study in Hawaii, where there is a climate like that described by Davis as most suitable for ulcer patients, revealed a variation in frequency of ulcer aggravation through the months similar to that found in Philadelphia. Does this latter finding indicate that the hemorrhages have nothing to do with the weather? Does it indicate that they are related to some weather or environmental circumstance common to both types of settings but as yet not detected? Or does it indicate that the body is somewhat sterotyped in its response to stress and that very different factors can help to bring about the same variation in clinical condition? The prudent person with ulcers may want to follow Davis's advice, at least in so far as it implies elimination of outside activities during periods when the temperature is forecast to change sharply. More properly, that person would also want to consult with a well-read specialist in internal medicine.

## Asthma and "Hay Fever"

The atmosphere is a carrier of countless gases and particles or droplets from natural and man-made sources. Some perons are extremely sensitive by way of allergic reactions to many substances that are quite common in the air. Different types of pollen and fungi spores are found in enormous numbers in various seasons. Asthma symptoms ranging from wheezes to near suffocation result from exposure to many of these substances. Various man-made air pollutants also seem to be implicated.

Fairly good correlations can be found between reported asthma attack rate and levels of air pollution measured variously by indices of sulfur dioxide, nitrates, suspended particulate, and total oxidant — the terms are treated further in the air pollution section of the book. Arlan A. Cohen, M.D. and co-workers[6] conducted an intensive study in New Cumberland, West Virginia where "significant correlations were found between . . . attack rate and pollution levels after the effects of temperature had been removed from the analysis. These temperature independent air pollution effects occurred at levels of pollution commonly found in large cities, and appeared greater at moderate than at low temperatures." The weather related effects, in themselves, are very interesting and fairly well established by independent investigators.

Sudden changes in the weather can be a very important trigger for the beginning of all types of asthma attacks whether characterized by an allergic reaction to air borne particles or by bronchial infections. Solco Tromp[7] of the Netherlands has concluded that the frequency of asthma increases rapidly after a sudden increase in the general turbulence of the air combined with rapidly falling temperature. In other words, the increase occurs during the advance and passage of an active fast-moving cold front. The increase is most striking after a long quiet period with moderate temperatures.

On a seasonal basis, the average asthma frequency is low during the winter and spring with significant increases, at least in the Netherlands, at the end of June. The maximum frequency generally occurs sometime between September and November. Studies in the United States seem to indicate that the effects are most pronounced in the early fall during the first or second invasion of cold air when indoor heating has to be reinitiated. Cold frontal passages later in the winter produce less spectacular increases in both the frequency and severity of asthma attacks. These meteorotropisms have been attributed variously to the stirring of allergenic substances in the house with the renewed heating and to the difficulty the body has in adjusting to cold stress after lengthy adaption to warm conditions. Either condition may be expected to decline over the winter months.

A sharp decrease in asthma frequency is observed during the influx of warm tropical air associated with an active warm front and during periods of mild but calm and settled weather. A rapid succession of cold and warm fronts can set up waves of increasing and decreasing asthma frequency. On the other hand, in warm climates, great heat stress is associated with an increase of asthma complaints. To further complicate the picture, Tromp notes that, contrary to patients suffering from non-infectious asthma, the bronchitic patients have the highest degree of complaints in winter, particularly in January and February, and a minimum in the summer.

"Hay fever" (seasonal vasomotor rhinitis) is neither caused by hay nor very often associated with fever. It is caused by seasonal allergens produced by plants that often flower around the hay season. The characteristic symptoms such as excessive sneezing, stuffiness, profuse nasal discharge, fatigue, itching eyes, nose, mouth and so forth may also occur on a non-seasonal basis as the result of allergies to substances such as house-dust, animal products, or foods. The weather factors associated with the production, release, and transport of various ragweed pollens of the "late season" from August until first frost have been studied in greater depth than those associated with the aeroallergens of other seasons.

The highest ragweed pollen indices are found in a triangular portion of the United States bounded by the eastern Great Plains, the Gulf of Mexico and the Appalachian Mountains, and the middle Great Lakes. In the southern part of Michigan, a particularly bad area for hay fever, it has been found that high May rainfall and low July rainfall promote the maximum annual yield of pollen. Dingle[3] reports that "on an average midsummer day, with dew at sunrise and sunny weather, the mature flowers begin to swell outward before the dew disappears . . . . As the relative humidity drops with solar warming, the anthers open in quick succession throughout the local ragweed population." He also notes that the openings take place quickly when the humidity is low, much more slowly when it is high, and perhaps not at all under steady rain.

The vast majority of ragweed pollen falls out within a few hundred feet of the source. Local up-drafts that produce fair weather or "bubble" clouds or the turbulence associated with thunderstorms or approaching cold fronts may, if timed properly with the release of pollen, carry large amounts of pollen to considerable heights. The grains may be swept along for hundreds of miles before falling out or being washed-out by precipitation. Dingle believes that the likelihood of the reflotation of pollen which has fallen out is small in comparison with the amount of fresh daily emissions.

## Heart diseases

According to the Department of Health, Education, and Welfare about 1,250,000 heart attacks (acute myocardial infarction) occur annually in the United States of which about 400,000 are deadly. Some 25,000,000 persons suffer from various forms of heart and vascular disease such as stroke and high blood pressure leading to more than 1,000,000 deaths each year. Many studies in Western Europe and various parts of the United States have shown significant correlations between these diseases and some form of temperature stress. It is said that persons with coronary artery disease cannot tolerate exposure to cold wind combined with high humidity without experiencing severe chest pain. Such sensitivity of course cannot explain the rather frequent occurrence of heart attacks during rest in a comfortable room or during sleep in a warm bed. Still, certain patterns emerge from the study of weather stresses that help to explain some of the seasonal variations, where they occur. An early study in Los Angeles before World War II could establish no significant seasonal variation in that mild climate. What the situation might be like today with many more social and environmental stresses added to the life of Angelenos would make the basis for an interesting study.

Solco Tromp,[7] who is perhaps the leading European biometeorologist, summarizes the major observed cardiovascular meteorotropic correlations as follows:

(1) In the Northern countries the mortality rate of coronary heart diseases, being considerably higher in males than in females, is almost every year highest in January-February and lowest around July-August.

(2) The mortality rate for stroke, being higher in females than in males, shows each year the same seasonal pattern as the coronary heart diseases.

(3) In very warm countries, such as the southern part of the United States, highest mortality incidence is observed in summer, lowest in winter.

Tromp notes further that winters with abnormally low temperatures are characterized by very high mortality and that during relatively warm winters mortality is relatively low. Similarly, during the summer, even in regions that have relatively low mortality rates in that season, the higher the temperature the more people seem to die from stroke and coronary heart disease. Studies in Philadelphia and Kentucky, where the seasonal extremes are fairly great, reveal a double peak in winter and in summer, at least in males.

One of the most suggestive studies was made in Dallas, Texas. The highest number of heart attacks occurred in the summer and the lowest during the winter season. But a more careful analysis conducted with an eye to strong frontal passages and sudden air mass changes rather than simply to average monthly temperatures revealed an increased frequency of heart attacks in any season during periods of sudden inflow of polar or tropical air masses. The winter cold waves may not last very long, but they can be quite severe, as can the summer heat waves. Thus, while the weather patterns in Dallas and Philadelphia are quite different, as are the patterns of heart disease, the correlations in both places with rapid changes toward hot or cold air masses show considerably unity of result.

Although the basic correlations between heart attacks and weather factors are not clearly established, the findings and opinions of different investigators do not have to be regarded as so widely divergent as they sometimes seem to be. Tromp notes that the findings of significant correlations between meteorological stress (particularly heat and cold) and increased incidence of diseases such as myocardial infarction, angina pectoris, and stroke have been confirmed in artifical climate chambers.

## Arthritis

Some persons have an almost legendary sensitivity to weather changes. They have been called variously, "cyclonopaths,' 'weather birds,' 'human barometers," and other terms suggesting sensitivity to changing conditions of the atmosphere. Twinges of gout and sciatica are popularly supposed to forecast rain. Most familiar is the conviction expressed in folklore that pains from scars and from arthritis sharpen during weather in the vicinity of a front separating one air mass from another type. For few indeed are those persons who doubt that

> *A coming storm our shooting corns presage*
> *Our aches will throb, our hollow tooth will rage.*

Such folk wisdom has received a great deal of medical support. Indeed, Hippocrates, or one of his followers, tried to relate atmospheric conditions and the personality of individuals in a treatise *On Temperaments and Humors.* The ideas survived in one form or another well past the time of Shakespeare. In the present day, some of the relations between mood or pain and the weather are being put on a fairly sound basis. Some of the more interesting results have been obtained in the Climatron or controlled climate chamber at the Hospital of the University of Pennsylvania.[8]

It should be clear by now that studies of human populations in their usual habitats are frustratingly difficult. Thus, many investigators have taken recourse to artificial chambers where experimental subjects can live for several weeks. Five or more factors can be varied singly or in various combinations. Some of the meteorotropic relations may be clarified in such chambers, although considerable difficulties remain in the attempt to generalize to the "real" world.

The Pennsylvania Climatron can control temperature, humidity, pressure, air flow, and ionization. Experiments with arthritic patients in which the environmental factors were varied one at a time in random order with a return to "standard" conditions in between resulted in no significant effect on the clinical index of well being and joint condition. Large effects however were produced in a group of eight patients with rheumatoid arthritis when they were subjected to simultaneous variations of pressure and humidity. Seven patients were afflicted with greatly increased arthritis in 57% to 100% of their trial exposures. One patient was insensitive to the same changes through six cycles. Typically, the effects occurred in a cycle when relative humidity was increased from 30% to 80% while the atmospheric pressure was simulataneously decreased by 10% over a six hour period. It should be noted that these rates of change are considerably higher than those that occur naturally in the atmosphere, except perhaps in rapidly moving hurricanes. The details of the clinical indices varied considerably from patient to patient and for different features of the programmed environmental changes, but the general effects were clear enough to justify the conclusion that

> *From these results, it would appear that at least one condition of changing weather factors – rising humidity with falling barometric pressure – fairly consistently exerts a detrimental effect on arthritic symptoms and signs. It would also appear that the changing conditions, rather than the high humidity or low barometric pressure, are responsible. It now seems reasonable to conclude that weather effect on arthritis is a definite phenomena, and not just another old wives' tale. It is not implied that climatic changes have any direct bearing on the cause of arthritis, nor is it believed that a constant climate would have any fundamentally curative effect.*

## On changing climate

The effects of many drugs change with changes in the weather. Digitalis, a drug widely used in heart disease, in experimental doses in animals is more toxic during storms than in stable atmospheric conditions. Its toxicity also rises with increased body temperature and increased elevations. It may be the case that these variations in toxicity as well as the variations in the effects of other drugs are related to the permeability of various membranes in the body and thereby to the ease with which the drugs can enter the blood stream. Weather may trigger the body responses that result in these changes, but little is known about the relevant biological mechanisms. At any rate, Helmut Landsberg[9] notes that some sleep inducing drugs have reduced effects at high temperatures, the response to insulin is apparently slowed by exposure to cold, atropine taken internally to relieve spasms also inhibits sweating and can thereby be dangerous in a hot environment, and some diuretics can cause excess loss of sodium leading to circulatory complications in persons not acclimated to a hot environment. Thus, in this era of high speed business and recreational travel from one climate zone to another, the traveler is well advised to check with a physician about possible changes in medication or dosage.

Jet-lag, or rapid time zone travel fatigue, has made people aware of the difficulties that even healthy individuals may experience in forcing their organism to adapt quickly to a new environment. Some persons can adapt fairly quickly with few ill effedts, but many individuals adjust only slowly and with considerable strain.

Many older persons as well as a few younger ones, who are otherwise healthy, may have organic responses to day to day weather changes that are slow enough so that their bodies are never quite "in balance" with the environment. Even though no particular disease may be present, feelings of dis-ease may result. On the other hand, there are schools of medical thought stemming from Hippocrates' time which do not draw sharp distinction between conditions of disease and feelings of dis-ease.

In trying to find an "ideal" climate, people frequently ask whether a move to a different area would be beneficial to their health. Vacations have traditionally been an attempt for many people to find a more ideal environment, at least for a short period of time. Yet, contemporary folk wisdom tells of the need to take a rest on returning from an otherwise delightful vacation. This bit of folk wisdom has some bearing on the question of moving to a different area. There are many reasons for this advice. One reason is the slowness with which human organisms adapt to major climatic changes. Acclimatization to a new area may take ten years or longer in the opinion of some investigators. It is certainly a process that can take weeks to occur. Clothing habits change quickly enough, and thirst brings about rapid changes in the amount of fluid intake — although to be sure the nature of the fluid imbibed in recreational settings is often inappropriate for a well functioning organism. The quantity and quality of food intake and physical exertion is even more frequently inappropriate to the new setting, and the process of acclimatization can be a long drawn out affair indeed. Motivation plays an important role in speeding the process.

An important consideration for the person thinking of making a "permanent" move to a new location is a possibility of a return to the original environment. Acclimatization is a two way process. After an experience of several years in a new environment, adaptation may be more or less complete. The process of readaptation to the original setting, however, may be even more difficult than the former process. The body is older and, for lack of a better term, may have less "elasticity" in the various vital systems. Also, there may have been adaptive changes that are in principle difficult to reverse. This latter point is highly speculative.

The search for an "ideal" climate may be a never ending one. Each person is affected in an individual way by his environment and no group could agree on the ideal. The process of acclimation is a complicated interplay of physiological, behavioral, and physological responses. A person has to feel "at home and wanted." The health and well-being of many persons may be served best by staying in the "native" setting even though it may be regarded as far from ideal. "Air conditioning" in both summer and winter can be a big help in making the old environment do. Of course, in the face of continued ecological decay and energy supplies that will be critical for some time to come and increasingly expensive, people need to consider the possibility of reducing their less essential demands in exchange for the goods and services that make for a healthier way of life.

## "Inadvertant" changes in climate

A major maladaption of modern societies concerns the disposition of industrial, commercial, transportation, and household wastes. Man has long disposed of these wastes into the air, water, and soil on the assumption that the vastness of these resources could cope adequately with the necessary dispersal, dilution, and assimulation of the waste products. Even before Hippocrates wrote *On Airs, Waters, and Places,* air, water, and soil have been known to be vital resources for all living things. It is now clear that these resources cannot continue to be polluted at the accelerating pace of modern society. The possible would wide effects on climate and environmental quality will not be discussed in this review, but the local and regional health effects of air pollutants will be treated briefly.

The large number of deaths in excess of seasonal normals associated with air pollution episodes in places such as Donora, Pennsylvania and London, England until as recently as ten or twenty years ago are hopefully things of the past. These earlier episodes involved changes in the expected death rates of 50% or more! They probably were triggered by extraordinarily high levels of pollutants such as sulfur dioxide and particulates: — the pollutants produced by uncontrolled heavy industrial processes and the burning of any but the highest grades of coal and fuel oil. In these earlier episodes, the pollutants accumulated to intolerably high levels when the weather pattern over the particular region stagnated for three or more days. Technological remedies of long standing (dating back 40 to 100 years or more!) and newer control techniques coupled with shifts from coal to gas and high grade fuel oil as energy sources finally have been instituted in most highly populated regions of the developed world. Some of the control techniques have not been adequately developed yet and the existing ones have not been universally adopted. With regard to the "old fashioned pollutants, most cities are in far better shape today than they were a decade ago. But the difficult improvements lie ahead.

The problem of urban air pollution by the old standby sulfer dioxide and respirable particles has by no means been solved. Out-patient and emergency ward counts in large cities continue to show low correlations with existing air pollution levels of these substances. The effects are truly marginal, and require very nice analytical techniques. Using the best studies available, the correlations involving the various measures of sulfur dioxide, suspended particulate, and total oxidant can be translated even today into thousands of excess hospital and doctor visits for respiratory ailments and associated cardiovascular problems. The dramatic death dealing episodes may be over, at least for a while, but air pollution related deaths continue to occur at lower levels where they tend to be hidden in the "noise of normal day-to-day and season-to-season variations in death rates.

Lester Lave and Eugene Seskin[10] believe they have developed techniques of analysis sensitive enough to isolate the proportion of deaths associated with air pollution described by indices of particulates and sulfates. The statistical significance of their findings remains even when climate, home heating, and various social or economic variables are added. They have available only crude measures of the various factors believed to be responsible for most of the observed variation, and one can question whether their air quality and other social and environmental data really contain the necessary information. Still, based on the best available measurements, they conclude that a 50% reduction in the urban levels of particulates and sulfates could cut the urban death rates by 4% and add one full year to life expectancy at birth. According to Lave and Seskin, the social and economic benefits of such a reduction in pollution, which is technologically feasible, would be comparable to the complete eradication of cancer, which is not medically possible at present. The economic cost of such reduction are varied according to different strategies economic management. With no offsetting governmental intervention, for example, the prices of manufactured goods — exclusive of automobiles — might be expected to rise between 0% and 5% for an average rise of about 2% and net unemployment might be expected to rise by about 0.2% during the first few years of such a phased abatement program.

The sickness and mortality effects of the types of air pollutants associated with automobile exhausts such as hydorcarbons, carbon monoxide, nitrogen oxides, and the oxides of heavy metal additives are more subtle and hence more difficult to isolate than similar effects in the case of heavy industrial effluents and the combustion products of raw coal and low grade oil. Even so, statistical analysis and prudent concern establishes well enough the need for new combustion technology and alternative forms of transportation. The goals set by the Clean Air Act of 1970 for the automobile industry to meet for the 1975 and 1976 model years are very stringent. The economic costs of meeting those standards are roughly twice those mentioned above and they include a significant penalty in consumption of limited fuel resources. Some people argue that the goals for the automobile industry are excessive, More realistically, it might be argued that those goals go somewhat beyond the level required for balanced progress in environmental management. The issue is not one of need, but one of priorities and strategy in achieving responsible environmental stewardship.

The truth is that only a brief respite will have been achieved from Man's habit of fouling his nest — someone's waste spaces are someone else's living spaces — unless the search for better technological palliatives is coupled with a less demanding way of life. The sad part of the picture is that the areas with the highest potential for air pollution episodes are precisely the areas with the most stable weather patterns and hence the areas most desirable for many health, recreational, and retirement living purposes. As the pressure mounts to continue the rapid subdivision and economic development of the desirable southeastern, southwestern and west coast areas of the United States, the high potential that they have for weather stagnation and serious air pollution episodes will be fullfilled with increasing frequency. The same conclusion applies to comparable areas in Europe. Existing social and technological mechanisms will have to be maintained even when the economic shoe begins to pinch a little, and new ones developed to make further significant cuts in the witches brew of chemicals that continue to degrade the quality of the air and other life resources. As an aid to the general public in thinking about these issues more deeply, this book draws together for the first time in a single convenient source the best judgments from members of the Environmental Protection Agency about the existing air quality in the various analysis regions of the nation.

## Spirit willing and pocketbook able

Americans have always been a mobile people. Freedom of movement for business, recreational, and retirement purposes is a valued privilege of the American way of life. It should not be treated lightly or abused. Knowledge of all the effects of any given movement is, of course, impossible to obtain. Nevertheless, considerable insight about the atmospheric conditions to be found in or near the major urban settings of the nation can be derived from this book. One of its purposes is to provide the basis for that insight in one convenient source. It is like an almanac, the more it is used, the more connections can be seen, and the more valuable the book becomes. On the basis of experience, conversation, and intuition, everyone has some idea of desirable, if not quite ideal, weather patterns. Everyone can extrapolate from known situations to plan for the visit or move that has to be made.

The various tables in this book summarize as far as possible in popular or semi-popular terms the recent weather and air quality history of more than 100 locations in the United States and many additional cities abroad. Each of the standard elements of the observed weather is presented in a way that indicates a great deal about the averages and the amount of deviation that may be expected to occur in any given month. The reader will want to pay attention especially to the information on temperature means and extremes,

the persistence of extreme conditions in any month, humidity, sky cover and sunshine. A complete guide to the information in the climatic summaries is found in the section, "How to get answers to your weather questions." Information is also presented to facilitate easy comparisons of the average air quality that may be expected.

It is impossible to make forecasts from this book. Not even the Farmer's Almanac (!) can do that in any meaningful way. The judicious examination of the various tables of the book, in comparison with the tables for an area known well from first hand experience, can be an aid in planning for both short term and longer term "changes of climate."

J.A.R.

**Suggestions for Further Reading**

The subject of biometeorology is treated simply and succinctly in
    Landsberg, Helmut E., *Weather and Health*, Doubleday Anchor Science Studies Series S 59 ($1.45), 1969

A very readable introduction to the philosophy of medicine and biological change is
    Dubos, Rene, *Mirage of Health*, Doubleday Anchor A258 ($1.25), 1959

The best elementary introduction to air pollution meteorology is
    Battan, Louis J., *The Unclean Sky*, Doubleday Anchor Science Studies Series S 46 ($1.25), 1966

A simple but more general approach to air pollution is
    [Corman, Rena], *Air Pollution Primer*, published in 1969 by the National Tuberculosis and Respiratory Disease Association (now, the American Lung Association) A copy can be obtained from the offices of your local chapter.

Somewhat more advanced treatments of these subjects can be found in the following books:

Dubos, Rene, *Man Adapting*, Yale University Press, 1965

Licht, Sidney, M.D., (Ed.), *Medical Climatology*, Elizabeth Licht, Publisher, 1965

Sulman, Felix G., M.D., D.V.M., *Short- and Long-Term Changes in Climate,* (two volumes), C.R.C. Press, 1983.

Tromp, Solco W., *Biometeorology*, Heyden & Son, 1980.

**Reference Notes**

1.  Hippocrates. A useful collection that includes *On Airs, Waters, and Places* along with other treatises or extracts is *The Theory and Practice of Medicine*, Citadel Press, 1964

2.  Sargent, Frederick, II, "The Nature and Nurture of Biometeorology," *Bulletin of the American Meteorological Society*, Vol. 44, No. 8 (August 1963), pp. 483-448.

3.  Dingle, A.N., comment, p. 148 in Tromp, S.W. (ed.), *Biometeorology*, Pergamon Press, 1962. Dingle's ideas on pollution by ragweed pollen are found in Licht, Sidney (ed.), *Medical Meteorology*, Licht, 1964, pp. 96-130.

4.  Munn, R.E., *Biometeorological Methods*, Academic Press, 1970, p. 255.

5.  Davis, Francis K., Jr., "Ulcers and Temperature Changes," *Bulletin of American Meteorological Society*, Vol. 39, No. 12 (December 1958), pp. 652-654

6.  Cohen, Arlan A., M.D., *et. al.*, "Asthma and Air Pollution from a Coal-Fueled Power Plant", *American Journal of Public Health*, Vol. 62, No. 9 (September 1972), pp. 1181-1188.

7.  Tromp, Solco W., "Biometeorological Aspects of Architectural and Urban Planning and Their Significance for the Thermoregulatory Efficiency, and Physico-Chemical State of the Blood of Human Subjects," Conference on Urban Environment and Second Conference on Biometeorology, 1972. *Preprint Volume* of papers available from the American Meteorological Society, 45 Beacon Street, Boston, Mass., 02108. Tromp's work is also reported extensively in two volumes he edited, *Biometeorology*, Pergamon Press, 1962 and *Medical Meteorology*, Elsevier, 1962. All three of these volumes are first rate.

8.  Hollander, Joseph L. and S.J. Yeostros, "The Effect of Simultaneous Variations of Humidity and Barometric Pressure on Arthritis," *Bulletin of the American Meteorological Society*, Vol. 44, No. 8 (August 1963), pp. 489-494.

9.  Landsberg, Helmut E., *Weather and Health*. Doubleday Anchor, 1969, pp. 126-128. Essential; the next book to be read.

10.  Lave, Lester B. and Eugene P. Seskin, "Air Pollution, Climate, and Home Heating: Their Effects on U.S. Mortality Rates," *American Journal of Public Health*, Vol. 62, No. 7 (July 1972), pp. 909-916.

# JET-LAG OR TIME-ZONE FATIGUE

The modern jet airplane makes it possible for a person to travel great distances in a few hours under conditions of great comfort and safety. An exception is the physiological and mental stress that most persons encounter if four or more time zones are crossed creating the effects of what is commonly called "jet-lag" or "time-zone fatigue."

More than 100 biological functions and human activities are geared to fluctuate between maximum and minimum values in about 24 hours, the so-called "circadian rhythms" (from the Latin words "circa" and "dies" for approximately one day) or "body clocks." After a jet flight of several hours across a continent or an ocean, a traveler's "body clocks" will be badly out of phase or "desynchronized" with respect to local time. The body rhythms will tend to be in phase with the time of the place of departure rather than the local time of the place of arrival.

The travel induced phase shift between "body time" and "local time" will cause some discomfort and, more dangerously, lapses in alertness, immediate memory, and impairment of normal judgments. Hunger, sleep, elimination patterns, and mental functioning may take several days to return to normal. Deep body temperatures, which are commonly highest around 5 PM and lowest around 4 or 5 AM, and the associated biochemical processes, may take a little longer to become resynchronized.

One easy to remember rule of thumb is that most travelers readjust to the new time zone at the rate of about one hour per day, although each function has its own rate of return and there is marked individual variability in the severity of desynchronization and the rate of recovery.

North-south flights produce few of these effects, although, for reasons to be made clear, such travel within a time zone can cause a high degree of subjective fatigue as well as certain physiological effects keyed to drugs, alcohol, and smoking that need attention by the wise traveler.

In nearly all cases, the effects increase with the age of the traveler.

## Social factors

Some studies of adaption to time zone shifts seem to show the importance of social and psychological factors in the readjustment process. Less deterioration seems to take place when persons travel in groups. Related observations reveal that fatigue seems to be less and resynchronization may occur more rapidly in relation to familiar surroundings. The problems may be reduced when the person experiences a high degree of motivation and generally feels "at home."

Anything that interferes with the oxygen up-take of body and brain cells produces an anemia, fatigue, and an impairment of mental functioning. Alcohol from drinking and carbon monoxide from smoking are two common sources of such deterioration. The reduced oxygen pressure at altitudes above 10,000 feet produces physiological effects similar to those of moderate drinking and smoking in persons acclimatized to near sea level pressures. Fatigue occurs rapidly in such persons at pressure altitudes above about 12,000 feet. With modern airplanes pressurized to between 6,000 and 8,000 feet, even though flying at altitudes well above 30,000 feet, fatigue and mental impairment are minimized. The various effects are additive, however. A person who drinks or smokes during, or for several hours prior, to a flight can experience a physiological altitude of 10,000 to 12,000 feet or more, with the alcohol and smoke having twice the effect of similar amounts at sea level. Thus, for example, two drinks immediately before and during flight might suddenly induce the effects of four drinks under normal circumstances. The effects of these habits on the cardio-vascular system and mental functioning are bad enough for north-sourth flights within a time zone. They aggravate considerably the jet-lag effects of easterly or westerly flights.

## Time-zone travel tips

Various common sense rules can be developed from these generalizations. Persons with chronic or acute respiratory and circulatory disorders should abstain from smoking and drinking during and for several hours before any air flight, even if they have not managed to change their behavior for the better in normal circumstances. Consultation with a physician is prudent. All persons should at least moderate their drinking and smoking habits, if not abstain altogether, in order to minimize fatigue and the other effects of long distance high speed travel.

A person should try to adjust sleeping and eating patterns over several days before departure. Eating smaller amounts, more frequently than usual, and, in any case, avoiding a heavy meal just before or just after the flight can be helpful. If possible, sleeping and awakening should be adjusted about an hour a day in each of several days before departure. Thus, before flying toward the east, bedtime and wakeup time can be set one hour earlier in each of several days, or set one hour later in preparation for a westbound flight. Flights of more than 10,000 miles should include a 24 hour stopover.

A flight can be selected profitably to arrive in the afternoon or evening rather than in the morning in order to move more quickly into the crucial sleep patterns of the new time zone. Evening entertainment or business activities should be avoided on the day of arrival. If adaption is to take place after arrival, important decisions or strenuous sight-seeing should be postponed for a day or two. Avoid sleep inducing medications, which reduce the most refreshing REM or rapid eye movement phase of sleep. Light meals, mild exercise such as walking, and warm baths should help to speed adaption to the new sleep cycle.

As a final suggestion, since the effects of many medications can change considerably with pressure altitude, it would be wise to check with your physician before departure about changes in schedule or dosage that might prove to be beneficial.

**Recommended further reading on body clocks and jet lag:**

Aschoff, J., "Circadian rhythms in man," *Science*, V. 148 (June 11, 1965), 1427-32.

Brown, F. A. Jr., "The 'clocks' timing biological rhythms," *American Scientist*, V. 60 (December 1972), 756-66.

McFarland, R. A., "Air travel across time zones," *American Scientist*, V. 63 (January-February 1975), 23-30.

Siegel, P. V., *et. al.*, "Time zone effects," *Science*, V. 164 (June 13, 1969), 1249-55.

Strughold, Hubertus, M.D., *Your Body Clock, its significance for the jet traveler*, Charles Scribner's Sons, New York, 1971.

# AIR POLLUTION

# AIR POLLUTION

(**Editor's note:** In 1990 President Bush signed into law additional amendments to the Clean Air Act of 1970. This new legislation left intact much of the program that implemented the 1977 amendments; thus, the following text, which focuses on that earlier program, remains valid. Whenever the new laws changed the 1977 amendments, the editors have tried to provide a note within the text to cue the reader to the changes. The 1990 Clean Air Act Amendments are summarized at the end of this section.)

We all are responsible for air pollution to some degree depending upon our economic demands and manner of living. We all are victims to some extent of its harmful consequences depending upon our physical state and where we live and work. Precise determination of these consequences, which vary considerably with time, place, and person, is not easy to make. It is certain, however, that no one completely escapes the ill effects of polluted air. The booklet, *A Citizen's Guide to Clean Air,* prepared by the Conservation Foundation under contract with the Environmental Protection Agency interpreted the seriousness of air pollution as follows:

> *Air pollution can kill. In London, New York, and Donora, Pennsylvania, polluted air—sustained and heavy for several days—has caused serious illness and death, especially among infants, the elderly, and people with weakened hearts or lungs.*

The examples are overworked and badly dated, but they remind us that one of the prices of clean air is continuing hard work. While the "death harvests" of the killer episodes have been greatly reduced since the 1950's and 60's, it is likely that thousands of preventable (pollution related) deaths per year remain in the national totals.

Other serious consequences of dirty air described in the *Citizen's Guide* can stand without comment:

> *Air pollution can impair health. Dirty air makes eyes water and smart; it stings the throat and upsets breathing. People with chronic lung or heart disease are particularly vulnerable to air pollution. We are just beginning to measure the adverse health effects that can result from continuous exposure to relatively low concentrations of pollutants. Epidemiological studies indicate that direct relationships exist between prolonged exposure to polluted air and the incidence of emphysema, bronchitis, asthma, and lung cancer.*

> *More obviously, of course, air pollution reduces visibility. It can spoil scenic vistas. It can ground planes and making driving hazardous. Its corrosive qualities cause vast economic losses and contribute to the deterioration of cities. It rots and soils clothes, discolors house paints, and rusts metals. By eating away stone and metal, it mars monuments and public buildings and increases housekeeping chores and costs for cities, families, and businesses. The Library of Congress says its books and manuscripts deteriorate more rapidly because of air pollution. The National Gallery of Art suspects that air pollution is damaging masterpieces.*

> *Damage from air pollution is not just an urban phenomenon. It affects rural areas, too, by injuring vegetation, stunting the growth of shrubs and flowers, severely damaging crops and trees, and causing illness among livestock. To many farmers, these costs are apparent and direct. But to most of us, they come indirectly—in the form of higher food bills and, from time to time, contaminated foods . . . . And there is growing evidence that air pollution may be having adverse effects on the growth and reproduction of some of our forests.*

Concern about air pollution in U.S. cities is at least a century old. Comprehensive control action began less than 20 years ago. The pioneer activities before World War II scored a few modest victories and probably can be credited with keeping many locally bad situations from getting worse. The early post war efforts, aided greatly by the rapid displacement of coal by oil and natural gas in small furnaces and boilers, showed that real, if limited, improvement was possible where local laws were enforced vigorously. The problem was one of using local "police" powers to force the widespread adoption and maintenance of known control remedies, many of which were of long standing development. These local approaches were directed mainly against dense smoke. They were fragmented, uneven in quality, and of limited effectiveness. The changing character of urban complexes, population distribution and mobility patterns, and the emergence of new emission problems or the more complete appraisal of old emission problems led to the development of increasingly comprehensive state and ultimately federal programs. Many forcing actions were required, as in the case of the automobile, to develop new or improved control techniques. Over the years, progress has been made, but many knotty technological, economic, and regulatory problems remain in the effort to clean up our air.

The first major attack on air pollution was mounted by the cities in the, so called, Progressive Era before World War I. One by one, cities inacted or upgraded laws governing their jurisdictions. The efforts at city and state levels were revitalized in the 1940's and 50's. Finally, in the years since 1955, the Congress has enacted a series of laws intended to encourage training, research, and development and to provide a framework for effective action coordinated by federal authorities, but implemented by state authorities. The most important of these federal laws were the Air Quality Act of 1967 and the Clean Air Act Amendments made of 1970, 1977, and 1990.

The Air Quality Act of 1967 provided for establishing air quality control regions with state-set standards of air quality based on federally established criteria. The Clean Air Act Amendments of 1970 required the U.S. Environmental Protection Agency (EPA) to establish national air quality standards to protect health and welfare, national standards for new facilities, and standards for facilities emitting hazardous substances. The 1970 Act also required states to develop implementation plans to bring their air quality to the levels set by national standards, and it required stringent national emission standards for new automobiles.

The Clean Air Act Amendments of 1977 incorporated a requirement for preventing the significant deterioration of air quality in areas where air already is cleaner than required by the national ambient air quality standards, set new deadlines for achieving them in areas that do not meet the standards, but also required the review of those existing standards by the EPA.

The clean air program was established, and reaffirmed in 1977, without regard for technological feasibility or economic costs. The primary concern was the attainment of air quality for various criteria pollutants in all parts of the nation better than that which would produce adverse health effects in the most sensitive segments of the population. By law these primary standards must have an "adequate" margin of safety to fully protect the public health. Secondarily, air quality should protect public welfare against loses to property, other living things, and aesthetics. It was the intention of the Congress to have the EPA establish stringent standards and enforce a definite timetable against tough economic and social sanctions for failure and that this program would finally unleash American technological ingenuity to solve long-standing air quality problems.

The 800-page Clean Air Act Amendments of 1990 carried the effort further by legislating what are considered innovative approaches to pollution control. By concentrating on "cost-effective, market-based programs," the EPA hopes to provide incentives for companies to seek environmental solutions on their own rather than waiting for the EPA to impose them. The overall goal is to enlist the power of the marketplace on behalf of the environment. In general, the EPA expects to achieve specific and ambitious environmental goals without unnecessarily damaging the nation's economic health or hampering its growth. (A summary of the 1990 Amendments appears at the end of this section.)

Control costs associated with the technologies developed for this clean air program during the 1980's were estimated to average about $30 billion annually in constant 1983 dollars. These control costs need to be set against social costs of far greater proportion that would be borne without the program. Estimated excess human health costs alone are assumed to be at least $40 billion annually. Significantly higher costs are associated with damage to property and other living things, and intangibles such as the loss of aesthetic value or the increase of suffering, anxiety, and grief. Given that there is no clear relationship between increased control costs and decreased social costs, and that there are additional social costs associated with factors such as bureaucratic interference, however, there is considerable uncertainty that the most "efficient" solution has emerged. Framers of the compromise involved in the 1990 Amendment feel that they are much closer to it than they have ever been before.

Meanwhile, whether efficient or not, and despite the persistence of problems such as those associated with acid precipitation described below, the nation enjoys higher air quality than it did at mid-century when the modern reform efforts began to take hold. Moreover, the EPA has developed as a part of the 1990 Amendments an emissions trading program, described below, intended to speed the achievement of clean air targets at lower costs. Highlights of the program follow.

## Air quality standards

NOTE: The following description of the Standards was written prior to enactment of the 1990 amendments but remains intact until various new deadlines arrive for tightening restrictions over the 1991-2000 decade. See the material at the end of this section for a summary of these 1990 amendments.

A national ambient **air quality standard** is the maximum level which will be permitted for a given pollutant. But there are two kinds of such standards: primary and secondary. **Primary standards** are to be sufficiently strigent to protect the public health; **secondary standards** must protect the public welfare including property and aesthetics. (See table 5.1).

EPA sets these standards after it issues a criteria document and a control-technology document on the pollutant in question.

Both the primary and secondary standards apply to all control regions.

The original Congressional deadline required that the primary or health-related standards be achieved throughout the nation by mid-1975, with allowances for a two year extension to 1977 in certain cases. The revised deadline for attainment was December 1982, but states with severe ozone or carbon monoxide problems were given until 1987 to achieve the standards for these largely automobile-related pollutants. State programs must also maintain air quality in areas where national standards have been met, and they must protect clean air areas from significant deterioration in air quality.

**Table 5-1** National Ambient Air Quality Standards (NAAQS)**

| Pollutant | Primary (Health Related) | | Secondary (Welfare Related) | |
|---|---|---|---|---|
| | Averaging Time | Concentration | Averaging Time | Concentration |
| TSP | Annual Geometric Mean | 75 ug/m³ | Annual Geometric Mean | 60 ug/m³* |
| | 24-hour | 260 ug/m³ | 24-hour | 150 ug/m³ |
| SO₂ | Annual Arithmetic Mean | (0.03 ppm) 80 ug/m³ | 3-hour | (0.50 ppm) 1300 ug/m³ |
| | 24-hour | (0.14 ppm) 365 ug/m³ | | |
| CO | 8-hour | (9 ppm) 10 mg/m³ | Same as Primary | |
| | 1-hour | (35 ppm) 40 mg/m³ | Same as Primary | |
| NO₂ | Annual Arithmetic Mean | (0.053 ppm) 100 ug/m³ | Same as Primary | |
| O₃ | Maximum Daily 1-hour Average | 0.12 ppm (235 ug/m³) | Same as Primary | |
| Pb | Maximum Quarterly Average | 1.5 ug/m³ | Same as Primary | |

*This annual geometric mean is a guide used in assessing implementation plans to achieve the 24-hour standards of 150 ug/m³.

Note: The standards are categorized for long- and short-term exposure. Long-term standards specify an annual or quarterly mean that may not be exceeded; short-term standards specify upper limit values for 1-, 3-, 8-, or 24-hour averages. The short-term standards are not to be exceeded more than once per year. For example, the ozone standard requires that the expected number of days per calendar year with daily maximum hourly concentrations exceeding 0.12 parts per million (ppm) be less than or equal to one.

** From 1977 Amendments to the Clean Air Act. See the explanation at the end of this section for comments on the effects the 1990 Amendments will have on the future of these standards.

## Definition of Pollutant Standard Index (PSI) Values*

Table 5.2

| PSI Index Value | Air Quality Level | Pollutant Level | | | | | Health Effect | General Health Effects | Cautionary Statements |
|---|---|---|---|---|---|---|---|---|---|
| | | TSP (24-hour), μg/m³ | SO₂ (24-hour), μg/m³ | CO (8-hour), mg/m³ | O₃ (1-hour), μg/m³ | NO₂ (1-hour), μg/m³ | | | |
| 500 | Significant Harm | 1000 | 2620 | 57.5 | 1200 | 3750 | | | |
| 400 | Emergency | 875 | 2100 | 46.0 | 1000 | 3000 | | Premature death of ill and elderly. Healthy people will experience adverse symptoms that affect their normal activity. | All persons should remain indoors, keeping windows and doors closed. All persons should minimize physical exertion and avoid traffic. |
| 300 | Warning | 625 | 1600 | 34.0 | 800 | 2260 | Hazardous | Premature onset of certain diseases in addition to significant aggravation of symptoms and decreased exercise tolerance in healthy persons. | Elderly and persons with existing diseases should stay indoors and avoid physical exertion. General population should avoid outdoor activity. |
| 200 | Alert | 375 | 800 | 17.0 | 400ᶜ | 1130 | Very Unhealthful | Significant aggravation of symptoms and decreased exercise tolerance in persons with heart or lung disease, with widespread symptoms in the healthy population. | Elderly and persons with existing heart or lung disease should stay indoors and reduce physical activity. |
| 100 | NAAQS | 260 | 365 | 10.0 | 240 | | Unhealthful ᵃ | Mild aggravation of symptoms in susceptible persons, with irritation symptoms in the healthy population. | Persons with existing heart or respiratory ailments should reduce physical exertion and outdoor activity. |
| 50 | 50% of NAAQS | 75ᵇ | 80ᵇ | 5.0 | 120 | 0 | Moderate ᵃ | | |
| 0 | | 0 | 0 | 0 | 0 | 0 | Good ᵃ | | |

ᵃ No Index values reported at concentration levels below those specified by "Alert Level" criteria.
ᵇ Annual primary NAAQS.
ᶜ 400 μg/m³ was used instead of the O₃ Alert Level of 200 μg/m³.

*From the 1977 Amendments to the Clean Air Act. See the explanation at the end of this section for the effects the 1990 Amendments may have on these values.

Source: U.S. Environmental Protection Agency, "Guidelines for Public Reporting of Daily Air Quality—Pollutant Standard Index."

## Pollutants Standards Index (PSI)

The Pollutant Standards Index is a health-related air pollution index designed for daily reporting of local air quality levels to the public through the new media. It is based generally on the primary short-term National Ambient Air Quality Standards (NAAQS) and the health-related Significant Harm Levels. Its main function is to inform the public of the potential health implications of currently observed air pollution levels. PSI has been in nation-wide use since late 1978.

The air pollutants covered by the index are carbon monoxide, sulfur dioxide, total suspended particulates, nitrogen dioxide, and ozone. An additional number— the product of the total suspended particulated concentration times the sulfur dioxide concentration—is included because it has been designated a Federal Episode Control Criterion. The 1990 Amendments will progressively add several more pollutants to the list over the next decade.

The index has a range of 0-500 and uses five descriptor words to identify progressively higher levels of air pollution: "good," "moderate," "unhealthful," "very unhealthful," and "hazardous." The designation of a "moderate" region recognizes the fact that although daily levels of a pollutant may never exceed its short-term standard, over the course of a year its average may violate its respective annual standard. As shown in Table 5.2 the zones of "unhealthful" and higher carry statements to advise people about possible effects of the various pollution levels on their well-being and about what preventive action they might take.

Each pollutant is examined individually by comparing its measured concentration with the index values. In some communities, the maximum index value for each pollutant is reported. In other communities, only the highest single index value computed for all the pollutants is reported to advise the public of the worst air pollution in the community or region. On days when two or more pollutants violate their respective standards (that is, have PSI values above 100), each pollutant may be mentioned. When the air pollution index indicates that the air quality is "unhealthful," "very unhealthful," or "hazardous," the media should report responsibly both the precautionary statements and the generalized health effects.

## Urban air quality

The air quality of many urban areas and several rural areas is still worse than the National Ambient Air Quality Standards for one or more of the "criteria" pollutants. Nevertheless, as indicated in the various *National Air Quality* reports of the Environmnetal Protection Agency and the *Environmental Quality* reports of the President's Council on Environmental Quality, published between 1978 and 1985, the overall trend in most areas is toward continued improvement.

The extreme variability of air pollution in time and space, the long lead time for published, nationally-assembled revised data, and the design of popular formats through which they can be presented to the public remain difficult problems. One of the most useful formats is that provided by the President's Council on Environmental Quality. Since 1978, CEQ has provided graphical information depicting the number of days that air quality was determined to fall within the various levels of violation of the Pollution Standards Index (PSI) for at least some small area of a reporting region.

Care must be taken to recognize the limitations of the data and not to read too much into them. Areas with air quality problems may be excluded because the monitors are placed outside of the zones of highest pollution while relying on computer modelling rather than direct measurement to determine violations of the standards. Progress in air pollution control usually consists in reducing any given pollution statistic by only a few days of violation per year, while year-to-year variation may be as large or larger than this overall trend due to the particular distribution of unfavorable weather conditions for the year. Thus, while the data presented have some utility in making comparisons between different geographical areas in a very broad sense, fuller and more current information should be sought as it become available. Some newspapers present preliminary PSI information as part of their daily weather map section.

## Status and trends for individual air pollutants

As previously stated, the national standards for $SO_2$, TSP, $NO_2$, and lead have been achieved almost everywhere in the nation. The Los Angeles Basin is the most notable exception with respect to $NO_2$. Therefore, this report will focus on the remaining $O_3$ and CO problems. Some EPA data will be presented relative to these other three criteria pollutants and lead, but the reader is referred to the 1982 CEQ Annual Report, which discusses the achievement of the national goals for the pollutants $SO_2$, TSP, and $NO_2$.

The $O_3$ problem is caused by volatile organic compounds (VOC) emissions from mobile and stationary sources. The predominant strategy that has been implemented nationwide to reduce $O_3$ levels is to reduce mobile source emissions of VOC through the Federal Motor Vehicle Control Program (FMVCP), which imposed progressively more stringent emission limits on new cars and trucks. Additionally, controls have been retrofitted on existing classes of industrial VOC emission sources, such as refineries, petrochemical manufacturing, and coating operations and printing. Some cities have also been required to implement auto inspection and maintenance programs and transportation control measures, both of which may be of incremental benefit. These latter programs will require further study to ascertain the continued need for these programs and their effectiveness in improving $O_3$ air quality.

The CO problem is totally related to mobile-source emissions and is confined to central city streets where vehicle congestion occurs during the morning and afternoon commute periods.

## Ozone ($O_3$) *

The NAAQS for $O_3$ or ozone is defined in terms of a daily maximum hourly value for the day and specifies that the expected number of days per year with observations greater than 0.12 parts per million (ppm) should not be greated than one day per year on the average. Because ambient ozone concentrations are usually higher during the summer when sunlight stimulates the production of ozone from the interaction with hydrocarbons and nitrogen oxides, some ozone monitors measure ozone concentrations only during the hotter months of the year. The length of this ozone season varies from one area of the country to another, but May through October is fairly typical. Southern and southwest states tend to monitor the entire year, while the northern states have a shorter monitoring season, May through September. The effects of meteorology and the year-to-year influence on ozone levels are discussed later.

EPA has reported the national ozone trends using the composite data from 62 trends sites from the official National Air Monitoring System (NAMS) network. These data, based on trends in both annual average concentration of $O_3$ and the number of days in which the 0.12 ppm standard was exceeded, are shown in Figure 5.3. EPA points out that some of the downward trend may be attributable to a change in calibration methods by some local agen-

* From the 1977 Amendments to the Clean Air Act. (See the summary of the 1990 Amendments at the end of this section for additional comments on ozone.)

**Figure 5.3**

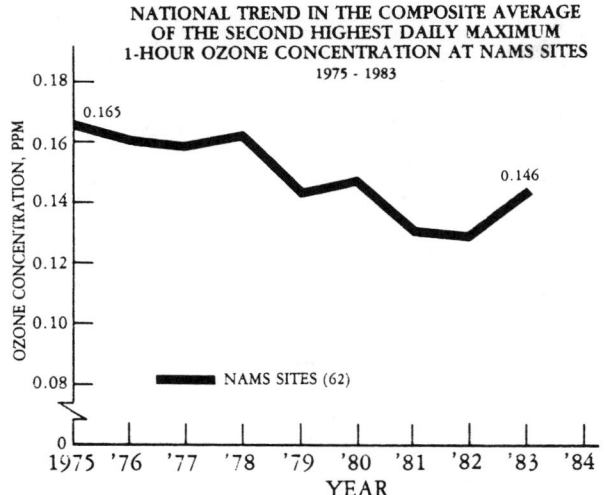

NATIONAL TREND IN THE COMPOSITE AVERAGE
OF THE SECOND HIGHEST DAILY MAXIMUM
1-HOUR OZONE CONCENTRATION AT NAMS SITES
1975 - 1983

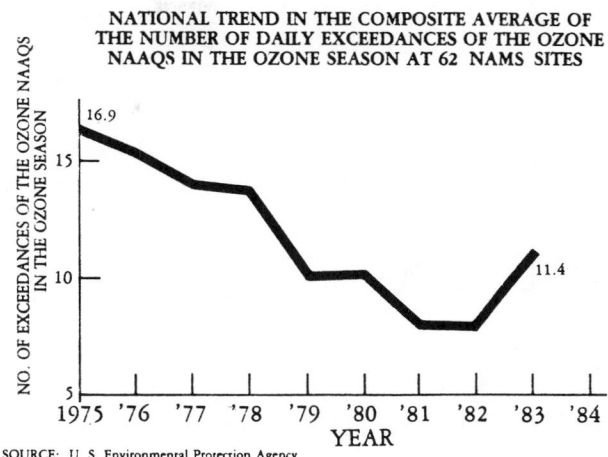

NATIONAL TREND IN THE COMPOSITE AVERAGE OF
THE NUMBER OF DAILY EXCEEDANCES OF THE OZONE
NAAQS IN THE OZONE SEASON AT 62 NAMS SITES

SOURCE: U. S. Environmental Protection Agency.

cies in 1978 and 1979, and that the reverse trend in 1983 may have been caused by the extremely hot weather experienced across the country in that year in combination with a projected nationwide increase in VOC emissions from 1982 to 1983.

CEQ examined the regional ozone trends using EPA's regional breakdown, but isolating the Los Angeles Basin, for the years 1976-1983. These 10 EPA regions are shown on the map in Figure 5.4. In order to remove the influence of Los Angeles, which dominates the ozone impact problem in Region IX, the six counties that make up the Los Angeles Basin were classified into Region 9B: Los Angeles Co., Ventura Co., Orange Co., San Bernadino Co., Santa Barbara Co., and Riverside Co. The data for the rest of California, Arizona, and Nevada were included in Region 9A. Region X (Washington, Oregon, Idaho, and Alaska) is excluded because this region does not experience any significant $O_3$ impacts. Figure 5.5 shows

**Figure 5.4**

# TEN REGIONS OF THE
## U. S. ENVIRONMENTAL PROTECTION AGENCY

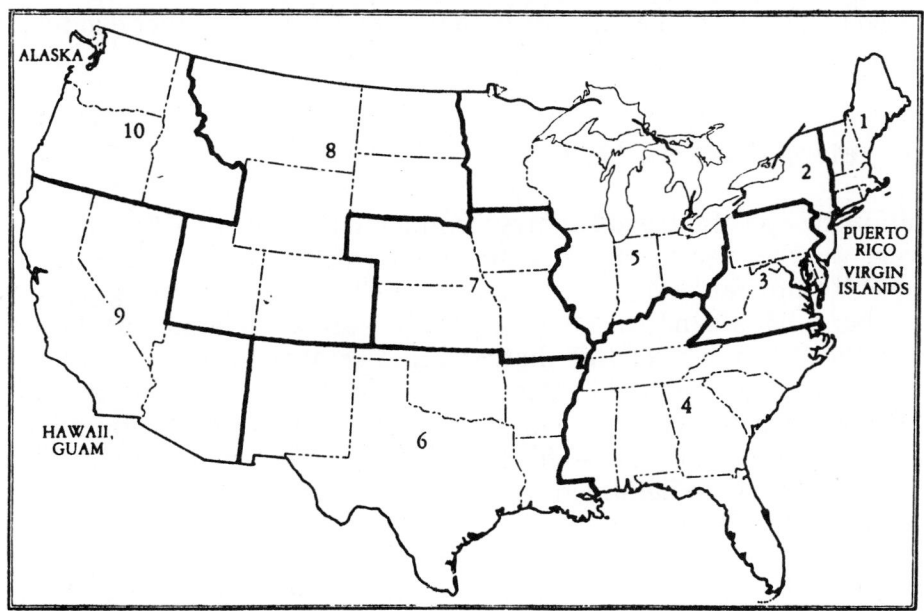

SOURCE: U. S. Environmental Protection Agency.

**Figure 5.5**

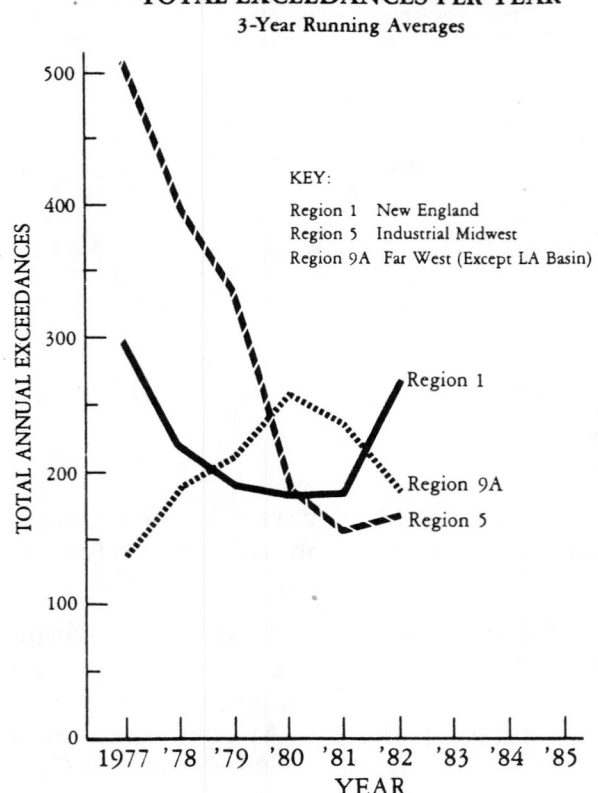

TRENDS IN REGIONAL O₃ AIR QUALITY
TOTAL EXCEEDANCES PER YEAR
3-Year Running Averages

KEY:

Region 1   New England
Region 5   Industrial Midwest
Region 9A  Far West (Except LA Basin)

**Figure 5.6**

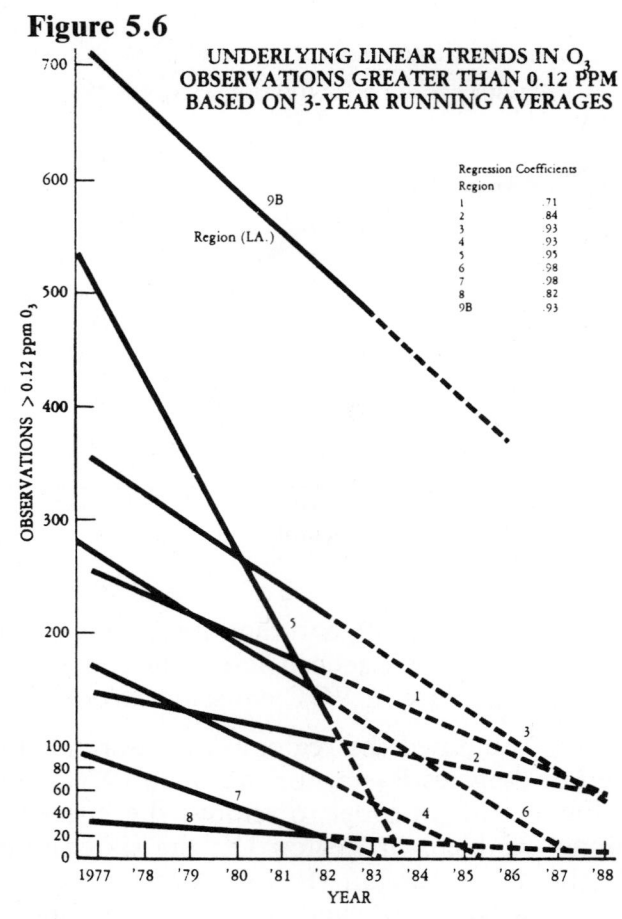

UNDERLYING LINEAR TRENDS IN O₃
OBSERVATIONS GREATER THAN 0.12 PPM
BASED ON 3-YEAR RUNNING AVERAGES

SOURCE: Roy F. Weston National Air Quality Data System (based on U.S. EPA SAROAD data).

the actual trends for three of the regions over the period 1977 through 1985. Figure 5.6 shows the underlying trends based on regression analysis. The correlations for the regions shown are excellent. Region 9A, which is not shown, is the only region not showing a significant downward trend among all of the regions analyzed. The inconsistent trend line for Region 9A in Figure 5.5 may be influenced by the fact that air quality data for San Diego and other regions surrounding the Los Angeles Basin are influenced by ozone transport from the Basin.

## Effects of meteorology on O₃ levels

The PSI and ozone-specific trends analysis conducted by both CEQ and EPA clearly show how year-to-year weather variations can affect the frequency of the exceedances of the ozone NAAQS or the PSI "unhealthful" index. High ozone levels occur during periods when the air mass over an urban area stagnates. Such stagnations are associated with large-scale weather patterns such as the "Bermuda High" that occurs several times per year off the East Coast. These cause stagnation conditions in cities throughout the East. the number of such weather patterns varies from year to year; in a similar fashion, the number of opportunities for high ozone days varies from year to year. Achievement of the ambient air quality standard, from a statistical point of view, is to demonstrate that the standard is not exceeded more than once per year *on the average*. This is to say that you could go for one or more years with no exceedances, but observe, in very hot years, several exceedances of the 0.12 ppm $O_3$ standard. EPA has chosen to use a three-year period as the basis for determining compliance with the ambient $O_3$ standard, as well as for establishing the baseline for planning purposes.

## Carbon monoxide (CO) *

Motor vehicles are the predominant source of carbon monoxide (CO) emissions in the United States. NAAQS for CO have been set for both 1-hour and 8-hour levels. The 1-hour standard specifies a level of 35 ppm not to be exceeded more than once per year, while the 8-hour standard specifies a level of 9 ppm not to be exceeded more than once per year. Because the 8-hour standard is generally more restrictive, this trend analysis focuses on the 8-hour data.

The 1975-83 trend for the second highest 8-hour CO value is shown in Figure 5.7a for data collected at 42 NAMS as reported by EPA. In that 9-year period the national composite average decreased by 33 percent. The median rate of improvement was approximately 5 percent per year, although there was little change between 1982 and 1983.

The composite average trend of the number of exceedances of the 8-hour CO NAAQS also declined sharply between 1975 and 1983, as shown in Figure 5.7b. This trend is consistent with the trend in ambient concentrations, although the decrease in exceedances is a more pronounced 81 percent decrease for the NAM sites.

**Figure 5.7a**

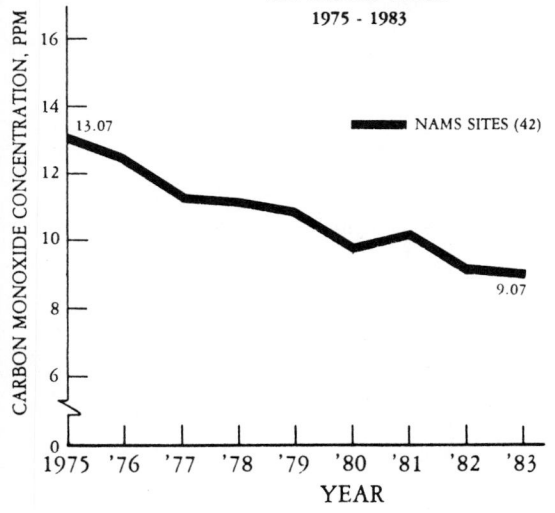

NATIONAL TREND IN THE COMPOSITE AVERAGE OF THE SECOND HIGHEST NONOVERLAPPING 8-HOUR AVERAGE CARBON MONOXIDE CONCENTRATION AT NAMS SITES

1975 - 1983

**Figure 5.7b**

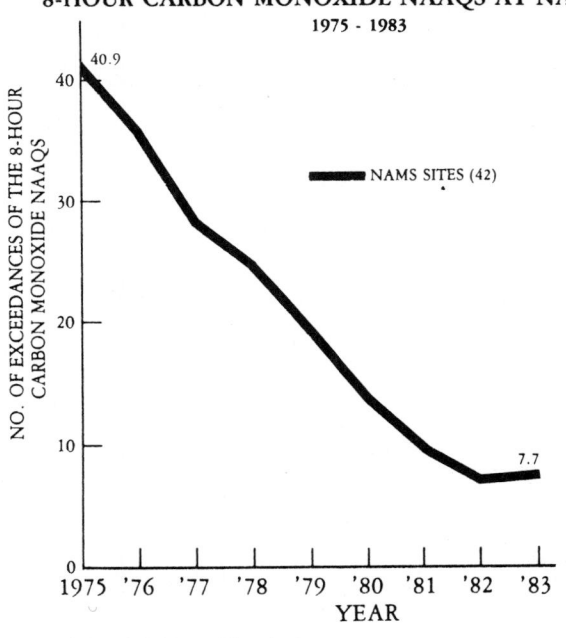

NATIONAL TREND IN THE COMPOSITE AVERAGE OF THE ESTIMATED NUMBER OF EXCEEDANCES OF THE 8-HOUR CARBON MONOXIDE NAAQS AT NAMS SITES

1975 - 1983

SOURCE: U. S. Environmental Protection Agency

* From the 1977 Amendments to the Clean Air Act. (See the summary of the 1990 Amendments at the end of this section for additional comments on carbon monoxide.)

**Table 5.3**
Pollutants Listed/Regulated Under Sections 112 and 111 of the Clean Air Act *

| Pollutant | Listed | | Proposal | Promulgated | Sources Regulated |
|---|---|---|---|---|---|
| | Date | Basis | | | |
| I. SECTION 112 | | | | | |
| Mercury | 3/31/71 | Central Nervous System damage | 12/71 | 4/06/73 | Mercury smelters Chlor-alkali plants |
| | | | 10/74 | 10/14/75 | Sewage sludge incinerators |
| Beryllium | 3/31/71 | Berylliosis | 12/71 | 4/06/73 | Extraction plants Foundries Ceramics Rockets |
| Asbestos | 3/31/71 | Cancer | 12/71 | 4/06/73 | Asbestos mills Roadways Manufacturing processes |
| | | | 10/74 | 10/14/75 | Demolition |
| Vinyl chloride (VC) | 12/24/75 | Cancer | 12/75 | 10/21/76 | Ethylene dichloride producers VC producers VC polymers |
| Benzene | 6/8/77 | Leukemia | 1/05/85 | 6/06/84 | Fugitive emission sources |
| | | | 6/16/84 | | Coke by-product plants |
| Radionuclides | 12/27/79 | Cancer | 4/06/83 | 2/06/85 | DOE facilities NRC-licensed facilities Elemental phosphorous plants |
| Inorganic arsenic | 6/05/80 | Cancer | 7/20/83 | — | High arsenic copper smelters Low arsenic copper smelters |
| Coke oven emissions | 9/18/84 | Cancer | — | — | |
| II. SECTION 111 | | | | | |
| Sulfuric acid | — | Lung damage | 11/76 | 10/77 | Sulfuric acid plants |

* From the 1977 Amendments to the Clean Air Act.

## Nitrogen dioxide (NO₂) *

Nitrogen dioxide ($NO_2$) is emitted by two main classes of sources: transportation vehicles and stationary fossil fuel combustors.

All urban areas of the U.S., except Los Angeles, are in compliance with the NAAQS for $NO_2$. Most cities are more than 10-20 percent below the standard.

## Sulfur dioxide (SO₂) *

Ambient sulfur dioxide ($SO_2$) levels result primarily from stationary source combustion of coal and oil and from nonferrous metal smelters. Trends in ambient $SO_2$ concentrations are derived from continuous monitoring instruments that measure as many as 8,760 hourly values per year. There are two primary NAAQS for $SO_2$: an annual standard is not to be exceeded, while the 24-hour standard is not to be exceeded more than once per year.

The $SO_2$ problem, from the standpoint of public health impacts, has essentially been eliminated in the nation.

## Total suspended particulates (TSP) *

Particulate emissions have declined primarily because of reductions in industrial emissions in all urban areas. The marginal problems of total suspended particulates (TSP), which exist in some areas, are due primarily to fugitive dust emissions from some industrial sources, such as mineral processing facilities, as well as from non-industrial sources, such as resuspended roadway and agricultural dust. A pending change in the particulate standard will focus on the inhalable fraction of the total particle concentration. Therefore, the remaining TSP problems must be reevaluated in terms of the new standard when and if it is established because the contributing sources may differ because of their emissions characteristics.

## Lead (Pb) *

Lead gasoline additives, nonferrous smelters, and battery plants are primary contributors to atmospheric lead (Pb) emissions. Transportation sources alone contribute about 80 percent of annual Pb emisssions.

Prior to promulgation of the lead NAAQS in October 1978, EPA implemented a gasoline phase-down program, which resulted in lower ambient lead levels. First, in the early 1970's, regualtions were issued to reduce the lead content in gasoline in order to protect the catalysts. The catalytic convertor is an important part of the current technology for controlling auto emissions. Second, as part of EPA's program to protect human health, further reductions in lead in gasoline were mandated in 1975. The overall effect of these two control programs has been a major reduction in ambient lead levels. The 1990 Amendments to the Clean Air Act carry the auto emissions controls to new dimensions. These are discussed in the 1990 Amendment summary at the end of this section.

Composite maximum quarterly averages for lead concentrations for 61 sites declined 67 percent between 1975 and 1983.

---

* From the 1977 Amendments to the Clean Air Act.

## Hazardous air pollutants

In addition to the regualtory programs established to attain and maintain the National Ambient Air Quality Standard (NAAQS), the Clean Air Act contains several provisions for regulating toxic or hazardous air pollutants from stationary sources. Section 112, the primary mechanism for dealing with such pollutants, requires EPA to list pollutants "which may reasonably be anticipated to result in an increase in mortality or increase in serious irreversible, or incapicatating reversible, illness." Within one year of listing, EPA must promulgate emission regulations for source categories of the listed pollutant causing a significant risk to the public. These regulations, applicable to both new and existing sources, must be met within two years of promulgation.

## Toxic air pollutants listed or regulated

To date, eight compunds have been listed under section 112, emission standards have been promulgated for five of these, and proposals are pending for two pollutants. The status of listings and regulations under section 112 is summarized in the first part of Table 5.3. Section 111 of the Act provides another mechanism for regulating non-criteria pollutants that may adversely affect public health or welfare. this mechanism involves EPA setting a new source performance standard (NSPS) for a pollutant not subject to the NAAQS or not listed under section 112. States are then required by section 111(d) to regulate existing sources of the same type covered by NSPS. The only health-based pollutant regulated to date under section 111(d) is sulfuric acid mist, as shown in the lower part of Table 5.3.

Section 122 of the Act requires EPA to determine whether four specified pollutants (arsenic, radionuclides, cadmium, and polycyclic organic matter (POM)) endanger public health and, if so, to take appropriate action to regulate those pollutants. As shown in Table 5.4, arsenic and radionuclides have been listed under section 112. In August 1984, EPA published a decision not to regulate POM as a specified air pollutant. This decision was based on a number of factors, including the great uncertainty as to the magnitude of the cancer risk to the public, the fact that many POM categories are being controlled under programs to attain and maintain the NAAQS for particulate matter, and difficulties in devising control programs for source categories not easily regulated. (e.g., existing wood stoves, forest fires, and agricultural burning). A decision on the final pollutant specified under section 122—cadmium—was expected in 1986. (**NOTE:** The 1990 Amendments to the Clean Air Act have some relevance to these pollutants' regulation. See the summary of the 1990 Amendments at the end of this section for additional comments.)

In addition to the POM decision, EPA published decisions on two other potential air toxics in 1984. EPA published a decision not to regulate toluene as a specified air pollutant under the Clean Air Act on the basis that current information does not indicate a threat to public health at concentrations found in the ambient air. Also, coke oven emissions were listed as a hazardous air pollutant under section 112 of the Clean Air Act. Assessments containing information on the sources, emissions, public exposure, health effects, current controls, and possible control improvements were completed for most of the substances shown in the "Regulatory Options Analysis" column of Table 5.4

Several actions involving the development of National Emissions Standards for Hazardous Air Pollutants (NESHAPS) under section 112 were also taken in 1984. These actions relied much more heavily on principles of risk assessment and risk management than previous

**Table 5.4**                    Toxic Air Pollutant Evaluation and Control Program[1] *

| Preliminary Health Screening | Detailed Assessment[2] | SAB Review[4] | Regulatory Options Analysis[5] | Regulatory Decisions[6] | NESHAPS Proposed | NESHAPS Promulgated |
|---|---|---|---|---|---|---|
| Copper | 1,3 Butadiene | Chloroform | Acrylonitrile | Toluene (N) | Benzene | Mercury |
| Phenol | Dibenzofurans | Dioxins | Methyl chloroform | Beryllium (L) | Arsenic | Beryllium |
| Propylene | | Nickel | Freon 113 | Asbestos (L) | Arsenic (L) | Asbestos |
| Propylene oxide | | Beryllium[3] | Carbon tetrachloride | Vinyl chloride (L) | | Vinyl chloride |
| Acetaldehyde | | | Methylene chloride | Coke oven emissions (L) | | Benzene |
| Acrolein | | | Manganese | | | Radionuclides |
| Hydrogen sulfide | | | Hexachlorocyclo pentadiene | Benzene (L) | | |
| Chlorine & HCl | | | Gasoline vapors | Radionuclides (L) | | |
| Ammonia | | | Chlorobenzenes | POM (N) | | |
| Zinc oxide | | | Epichlorohydrin | Mercury (L) | | |
| Styrene | | | Asbestos[3] | | | |
| | | | Vinylidene chloride | | | |
| | | | Ethylene dichloride | | | |
| | | | Chromium | | | |
| | | | Perchloroethylene | | | |
| | | | Trichloroethylene | | | |
| | | | Cadmium | | | |
| | | | Ethylene oxide | | | |
| | | | Chloroprene | | | |
| | | | Phosgene | | | |

[1] As of 2/14/85.
[2] Health and exposure assessment. Not yet submitted to SAB.
[3] Reassessment of original health effects information.
[4] Submitted to SAB. Recommendations not yet received.
[5] Recommendations received from SAB or no SAB review planned. Analysis underway to determine need for regulation.
[6] L = listed under Section 112; N = decision not to regulate.

\* From the 1977 Amendments to the Clean Air Act. (See the summary of the 1990 Amendments at the end of this section for additional comments on these regulatory decisions.)

rulemakings under section 112. In June 1984, EPA promulgated regulations for benzene equipment leaks (fugitive emission sources) and proposed regulations for benzene from coke oven by-product plants. The Agency also withdrew three earlier proposals on maleic anhydride manufacturing, ethyl benzene/styrene plants, and benzene storage, on the basis that the cancer risks to the public and the potential reduction in risk achievable with available control techniques did not warrant federal regulatory action for these source categories. For similar reasons, EPA also withdrew proposals for several source categories emitting rad ionuclides. Advance notices of proposed rulemaking were published for radon-222 emissions, a class of radionuclides, from underground uranium mines and from licensed uranium mills. The Agency was subsequently found in contempt of court for the radionuclides withdrawals, and in February 1985, final regulations were published for three source categories.

As part of the program for regulating benzene, EPA has been assessing the need to regulate sources in the gasoline marketing chain. This assessment was further spurred by data indicating that unleaded gasoline causes cancer in laboratory animals and should be considered a probable human carcinogen. An analysis of regulatory strategies for the gasoline marketing industry was published for public comment in August 1984. The options considered were: (1) no additional control, (2) control of vehicle refueling (Stage II) in ozone non-attainment areas, (3) control of gasoline marketing emissions nationwide via (a) Stage II controls, (b) on-board vehicle controls, and/or (c) controls on bulk terminals and plants (Stage I). A decision on the appropriate regulatory option is expected in late 1985.

## Establishment of National Air Toxics Information Clearinghouse

In the mid-eighties, substantial activities were undertaken to establish a National Air Toxics Information Clearinghouse in an effort to improve communication between the EPA and state and local agencies and among state and local agencies. The Clearinghouse is funded by the EPA and is a cooperative effort between EPA and the State and Territorial Air Pollution Program Administrators and Association of Local Air Pollution Control Officials. The goal of the Clearinghouse is to disseminate knowledge about activities underway to solve toxic air pollutant problems and to reduce duplication of effort. Some of the kinds of information included in the Clearinghouse are: (1) regulatory program activities, including acceptable ambient limits; (2) source information, such as pollutants emitted and required control technology; and (3) source test and ambient monitoring methods in use. Automation of the data base and publication of the first report compiling all the information contained in the Clearinghouse were completed in the late summer of 1985.

## Assessment of the magnitude and nature of the air toxics problem

EPA has recently completed the most comprehensive assessment to date of the scope of the air toxics problem in this country. However, the data available on air toxics significantly limited the scope of the analysis. For example, only cancer and direct inhalation were covered. It was not possible to consider quantitatively potential impacts caused by acute or chronic non-cancer effects; nor were the impact of indoor exposures, stratospheric contamination, and emissions from non-traditional sources such as hazardous waste disposal included. Conversely, many of the procedures and assumptions used were necessarily conservative. Carcinogenic potency (unit risk) values for the pollutants covered in the study assumed non-threshold effects, and generally only plausible upper-bound estimates were available for unit risk values. Some compounds were included for which carcinogenicity still is being debated.

Because of the large uncertainties inherent in quantitative risk assessment for environmental cancers, the result of this analysis must be intepreted with great care to avoid misuse of the study. With appropriate caveats that are detailed in the report, some of the more interesting findings presented in the study are:

1. Additive lifetime individual risks in urban areas due to simultaneous exposure to 10 to 15 pollutants ranged from one chance in 1000 to one chance in 10,000. These risks, which were calculated from monitoring data, did not appear to be related to specific point sources, but rather represented a portion of the total risks associated with the complex mixtures typical of urban ambient air.

2. Both "point" and "area" sources appear to contribute significantly to the air toxics problem. Large point sources are associated with many high individual risks; area sources appear to be responsible for the majority of aggregate incidence.

3. For the pollutants and sources studied and using unit risks that are plausible upper-bound values, annual national cancer incidence ranged from 1600 to 2000 per year. To place this figure in perspective, it should be noted that approximately 440,000 deaths from cancer occur annually in the United States from all causes.

4. The air toxics problem appears to be very diverse with no source category or specific pollutant appearing to dominate the analysis. Organic particulates (called Products of Incomplete Combustion and reresented by benzo-a-pyrene in the study) accounted for about 45 percent of the incidence; volatile organics, about 30 percent; and metals, about 25 percent.

5. For those cities with sufficient data for analysis, large city-to-city and neighborhood-to-neighborhood variation in pollutant levels and sources was found. However, our current data base is inadequate to characterize most local air toxics problems.

6. Criteria pollutant control programs (i.e., those related to pollutants covered by National Ambient Air Quality Standards) appear to have reduced air toxic risks over the past decade more than have programs for specific toxic compounds. This seems reasonable considering the widespread sources of air toxics, the multi-pollutant nature of the problem, and the relative intensity of regulatory programs for criteria pollutants, especially those for ozone and particulate matter.

## Strategic Implications

The findings of the study on the magnitude and nature of the problem suggest the need for a review of EPA's current program for hazardous air pollutants and an examination of potential new strategies. To facilitate this, the Administrator has established within EPA an Air Toxics Group to follow up on the assessment report. The group's activities include presentation and discussion of the findings of the study with a wide variety of affected organizations, including state and local air agencies, environmental and public health groups, industries that produce and use potentially toxic compounds, and other governmental agencies, including Congressional staff. (This and other study activities have been very influential in drafting and negotiating the 1990 Amendments to the Clean Air Act.)

Meetings with these groups include discussions of alternative national strategies and possible legislative changes. In addition, EFA has given a grant to the Center for Negotiation and Public Policy to promote more formally the exchange of opinions and information on air toxics strategies between diverse groups.

To aid in evaluating strategic options, EPA also has initiated several follow on analyses. These include:

- The controllability of the pollutants identified as associated with the highest incidence. This analysis will assess available technology and control costs.
- The impact on annual cancer incidence of pollution control achieved by 1995 through the implementation of regulatory programs for criteria pollutants.
- The impact on cancer incidence of the curent air toxics programs through 1995.
- The potential of including in a regulatory strategy non-cancer health implications, including effects on reproduction, mutagenesis, and acute effects.

The initital assessment report, the discussions, and the additional analyses were all being utilized in developing the comprehensive national air toxics strategy which was released by EPA in June 1985

## Revisions in state implementation plans

The original deadline for achieving the National Primary Ambient Air Quality standards was 1975, except where extensions had been granted. Strictly speaking, states could not legally allow growth in areas that failed to achieve the standards by that date. But in 1976 EPA issued an interpretative ruling which allowed new sources to be located in polluted areas if additional emission reductions in existing sources would more than offset the projected emissions from the new sources. The Congress adopted this "offset policy" in the 1977 Clean Air Act Amendments but also imposed new requirements for making further progress toward finally attaining national ambient standards in the 1980's.

## Prevention of significant deterioration

The state designations of attainment status identify areas where air quality is generally better than national standards require. For these areas (and also for clean pockets in non-attainment areas), states describe in their Implementation Plan revisions how they will enforce provisions of the 1977 amendments for prevention of significant deterioration (PSD).

## Controlling vehicle emissions

The most visible controversies on controlling automobile pollution have centered on standards for tailpipe emissions. Enforcing the standards, although less publicized, is complex. Enforcement begins with EPA certification of prototype engines to determine whether their design is adequate to meet standards. Based on this testing, EPA certifies engine families to be used in production. EPA also selectively tests vehicles on the assembly line to see whether production models also meet standards. Once the cars are on the road, EPA may recall entire fleets for major defects. EPA also limits the amount of lead in gasoline and encourages states to require regular inspection and maintenance to ensure that autos continue to meet standards. (**NOTE:** The 1990 Amendment to the Clean Air Act calls for development of "clean cars" and "clean fuels." See the summary of the 1990 Amendments at the end of this section for additional comments on vehicle emissions.)

Historically, the auto makers were able to submit vehicles for certification that were specially maintained during EPA tests. Production line cars would not receive the same attention during manufacturing or use, and performance frequently failed to meet emissions standards. EPA is addressing the problem by limiting the maintenance on the test vehicles, beginning to test vehicles on the assembly line, and accelerating the recall of automobiles with defective emission control components. EPA expects that these new efforts, along with state inspection and maintenance programs, will cut down some of the disparity between certification testing results and actual performance.

## State inspection and maintenance programs

Mandatory automobile inspection and maintenance (I/M) is one of the most controversial regulatory strategies currently being implemented. In terms of its impact on the general public, I/M has become a major environmental program. A large portion of the U.S. auto fleet is in 1991 subject to inspection annually or biennially. Inspection costs alone will total about a billion dollars per year. For about two-thirds of the inspections, the I/M program requires at least one special trip, and possibly two. (For the rest, the I/M test is combined with an existing safety check so an additional trip is rarely needed.)

Table 5.5 shows a listing of all I/M programs in effect in 1985, along with other information, such as the date the program was started. This list has grown significantly since it was originally compiled.

As time passes there is a significant shift in the age of the "population" of in-use vehicles and therefore in the relative emission contributions of newer versus older vehicles. thus even though the inspection of a pre-1975 vehicle may show higher failure rates (thus creditied with significant per-vehicle emission reductions when tuned up again) the contributions of this family of vehicles to the *total* mobile source emissions inventory is an urban area diminishes rapidly with fleet modernization.

## Permit requirements for new stationary sources

**NOTE:** Until enactment of the 1990 Amendments to the Clean Air Act, the previous version imposed its standard using a so-called "command-and-control" approach. The 1991 Amendments will gradually change that to a *Market-Based Allowance Trading System.* The following paragraphs describe the previously advocated "Command-and-control" approach which should be studied as background to the new philosophies. See the summary of the 1990 Amendments at the end of this section for a description of the market-based system.

The 1977 Amendments imposed somewhat different legal standards for controlling emissions from a few source, depending on the attainment status of the area where the source is to be located. Wherever they are, new sources are required to comply with the New Source Performance Standards if EPA has issued one for the industry involved. If a new plant would affect an area which exceeds national ambient standards for the pollutant involved, the Amendments impose a stricter control requirement—"lowest achievable emission rate." If the source is proposed for a site where it will affect an area whose air quality is significantly better than national standards a third requirement applies—"best available control technology" which cannot be less stringent than the New Source Performance Standards. In addition, the "offset policy" discussed below applies in nonattainmnet areas and requires a company with growth plans to find emission offsets from existing sources in the area.

## Existing sources

EPA estimates that more than 200,000 existing stationary sources are subject to emissions limitations in State Imptementation Plans. Approximately 15,000 of them are "major" sources (individually capable of emitting more than 100 tons of a pollutant per year). Because these major sources account for approximately 85 percent of all air pollution from existing stationary sources, enforcement efforts have centered on bringing these polluters into compliance, as of December 1982, about 6 percent of these major sources still were in violation of emission standards.

In efforts to reward past compliance and to give economic incentives to speed future compliance, EPA has developed a number of regulatory mechanisms, such as bubbles, offsetting, netting and banking, directed at lower costs of compliance. These "emissions trading" concepts are described briefly below and more fully in the *Federal Register* for April 7, 1982.

# AIR POLLUTION

## Table 5.5

**Inspection/Maintenance Program Summary \***

| EPA Region | State | City (SMSA) | No. of Counties | Program Started | Model Years Inspected | Emissions Test | Lead Test |
|---|---|---|---|---|---|---|---|
| I | CT | Statewide | – | 1/83 | 1968 + | Yes | No |
| | MA | Statewide | – | 4/83 | last 15 | Yes | No |
| | NH | Nashua | 2 | (9/87) | last 15 | (TBE) | (TBE) |
| | RI | Statewide | – | 1/79 | 1967 + | Yes | No |
| II | NJ | Statewide | – | 2/74 | all | Yes | No |
| | NY | NYC | 10 | 1/82 | all | Yes | No |
| III | DC | – | – | 1/83 | all | Yes | No |
| | MD | DC | 2 | 2/84 | last 12 | Yes | No |
| | VA | DC | 8 | 12/81 | last 8 | Yes | No |
| | MD | Baltimore | 5 | 2/84 | last 12 | Yes | No |
| | PA | Philadelphia | 5 | 6/84 | last 25 | Yes | No |
| | PA | Pittsburgh | 4 | 6/84 | last 25 | Yes | No |
| | PA | Allentown | 2 | 6/84 | last 25 | Yes | No |
| IV | GA | Atlanta | 4 | 4/82 | last 10 | Yes | No |
| | KY | Louisville | 1 | 1/84 | all | Yes | No |
| | NC | Charlotte | 1 | 12/82 | last 12 | Yes | No |
| | TN | Nashville | 1 | 1/85 | last 13 | Yes | No |
| | TN | Memphis | 1 | 8/83 | all | Yes | No |
| V | IL | Chicago | 3 | (10/85) | 1968 + | (TBE) | Yes |
| | IL | St. Louis | 2 | (10/85) | 1968 + | (TBE) | Yes |
| | IN | Chicago | 2 | 6/84 | last 12 | Yes | No |
| | IN | Louisville | 2 | 6/84 | last 12 | Yes | No |
| | WI | Milwaukee | 6 | 4/84 | last 15 | Yes | No |
| VI | OK | Tulsa | 5 | 1/86 | 1979 + | No | Yes |
| | LA | Baton Rouge | 2 | 9/85 | 1968 + | No | Yes |
| | TX | Houston | 1 | 7/84 | 1968 + | No | Yes |
| VII | MO | St. Louis | 4 | 1/84 | 1971 + | Yes | No |
| VIII | CO | Denver | 6 | 1/82 | 1968 + | Yes | No |
| | CO | Colorado Springs | 1 | 1/82 | 1968 + | Yes | No |
| | CO | Fort Collins | 1 | 1/82 | 1968 + | Yes | No |
| | UT | Salt Lake City | 1 | 4/84 | 1968 + | Yes | No |
| | UT | Davis | 1 | 4/84 | 1968 + | Yes | No |
| | UT | Provo | 1 | (7/86) | 1968 + | (TBE) | No |
| IX | AZ | Phoenix | 1 | 1/77 | last 13 | Yes | No |
| | AZ | Tuscon | 1 | 1/77 | last 13 | Yes | No |
| | CA | Los Angeles | – | 3/84 | last 20 | Yes | No |
| | CA | Ventura | – | 3/84 | last 20 | Yes | No |
| | CA | San Francisco | – | 3/84 | last 20 | Yes | No |
| | CA | Sacramento | – | 3/84 | last 20 | Yes | No |
| | CA | Fresno | – | 10/84 | last 20 | Yes | No |
| | CA | Bakersfield | – | 1/86 | last 20 | Yes | No |
| | NV | Las Vegas | 1 | 10/83 | 1965 + | Yes | No |
| | NV | Reno | 1 | 10/83 | 1965 + | Yes | No |
| X | AK | Anchorage | 1 | 7/85 | last 15 | Yes | Yes |
| | AK | Fairbanks | 1 | 7/85 | last 15 | Yes | Yes |
| | ID | Boise | 1 | 8/84 | 1970 + | Yes | No |
| | OR | Portland | 3 | 7/75 | last 20 | Yes | No |
| | OR | Medford | 1 | 1/86 | last 20 | Yes | No |
| | WA | Seattle | 2 | 1/82 | last 14 | Yes | No |
| | WA | Spokane | 1 | 7/85 | last 14 | Yes | No |

Source: Council on Environmental Quality, Washington, D.C., 1985.     \* This list was compiled circa 1985 and has since grown significantly.

## The bubble concept *

State implementation plans establish emissions limits for stationary, as well as mobile, sources of air pollution. These limits are calculated to assure that federal air quality standards are attained in that location. In making these decisions, states regularly take into account the nature and amount of emissions from each source, the control technology available, and the time required for its installation. However, SIPs are not necessarily as economically efficient as possible, nor are regulated companies prompted to seek innovations in control technology.

For this reason, EPA proposed on January 18, 1979 that states allow plants to reduce controls in that portion of a facility in which costs are high, in exchange for an equal increase in control in a part of the same facility where abatement is less expensive. Because it treats a facility in terms of its total emissions—as if it had a bubble over it—this has been called "the bubble concept." The policy statement recommends that the states inform facilities of the availability of the alternative emission-reduction approach, explain the advantages and conditions of use, and be receptive to proposals from facilities seeking to employ the more cost-effective mix of controls this policy allows. Under the proposed policy, facilities may obtain financial savings by employing more cost-effective mixes of control techniques than current process-by-process regulations allow, as long as total environmental benefits are not reduced.

Among the qualifications to the policy are: reductions in one class of pollutants cannot be "swapped" for increases in another class, especially toxic pollutants; all pollution from a plant cannot be "loaded" on one source in such a way that air quality standards are violated; and the concept cannot be used as an excuse to delay compliance with current air quality standards. If these qualifications can be met, use of the bubble concept will make source savings in air pollution abatement costs possible.

Firms that reduce emissions through approved programs below the minimum required for a "bubble," can gain "emission reduction credits" which may be held for the firm's own current or future expansion, or sold to another firm. Each firm thereby has economic incentives to reduce its pollution beyond the requirements of the law.

## The concepts of 'Offsetting', 'Netting', and 'Banking'

Once a participating firm has gained emission reduction credits by reducing its pollution below the legal ceiling, it can use those excess reductions as "offsets." "Offsetting" is the administrative procedure under development since 1976 that provides for trading of discharging permits among activities not in the same plant or not owned by the same firm. It requires a greater than one-for-one reduction to achieve net improvements in ambient air quality as a result of the transaction.

"Netting" is similar to "offsetting," with the difference that "netting" applies to firms that must reduce some pollutants from certain sources to enable them to expand the use of other sources of that same pollutant. Under present legal interpretation, "netting" can be used only in areas currently in attainment of National Ambient Air Quality Standards.

"Banking" of emission reduction credits is another concept introduced to encourage the maximum reduction of pollution from existing stationary sources. It would not be good environmental policy to induce continued operation of facilities at the maximum legal limit simply to retain future "offsets" or "nets." In January, 1979, the EPA proposed that states be allowed to include in their implementation plans schemes under which individual firms could "bank" or reserve for future use or sale actual emission reductions beyond those currently required. Final approval of appropriateness, of course, is retained by the federal agency.

## Visibility protection

NOTE: The 1977 Clean Air Act Amendments spawned the following arguments, which were decisively addressed by the 1990 Amendments. See the summary of the 1990 Amendments at the end of this section for additional comments on this topic.

When the 1977 Clean Air Act Amendments were debated, the air quality in and around National Parks, Wilderness Areas, and other unique areas was a subject of concerned congressional attention. For example, emissions from the Navaho Power Plant near Page, Arizona, sometimes fill the Grand Canyon with a layer of haze, reducing visibility to less than 15 miles and obscuring the opposite canyon rim. The Congress responded by stating as a national goal protection of visibility in mandatory Class I federal areas when the impairment results from manmade air pollution. Figure 5.10 shows the areas. Further, the Congress placed an affirmative responsibility on federal land managers to protect air quality values, including visibility, in all Class I areas through review of new sources before construction.

Impaired visibility is the most easily perceived effect of air pollution. Haze is especially objectionable when it makes a scenic vista less visible and less esthetically satisfying. Because visual air quality is sensitive to very small concentrations of pollutants in the form of fine particles, stringent control and planning may well be required to meet the visibility protection requirements of the Clean Air Act.

Impaired visibility may result from a decrease in visual range or from atmospheric discoloration. Visual range—the distance over which people can see objects—is one of the most variable of atmospheric properties. If pollutants are absent, the visual range at sea level is limited only by the scattering of naturally occurring gases or by topography. The visual range approaches 260 kilometers (162.5 miles) under such conditions. Humidity is also a factor. Both theory and measurements show that for relative humidities of less than 70 percent, the extinction coefficient is proportional to the concentration of fine particles in the air.

The addition of approximately 1.5 micrograms per cubic meter of fine particles to clean air decreases visual range by 30 percent, for example, from 260 to 200 kilometers (160-125 miles), and increases the haziness of dark objects (as near as 10 kilometers (6.25 miles).

Most fine particles in a polluted atmosphere are sulfate compounds, although nitrate compounds may also be significant. Most of the fine particles are formed in the air from sulfur dioxide and nitric oxide emitted from smelters and powerplants. The process of generating fine particles from gases takes place over several days, with extensive vertical mixing and horizontal transport. Because natural removal of fine particles is slow, visibility impairment from haze is relatively uniform over distances of perhaps 1,000 kilometers (625 miles). Thus haze is a regional problem, extending far beyond the source of fine particulate emissions. Plumes are exceptions to this regional problem: they can be traced to specific sources and substances and therefore are a more direct problem of control than haze covering an entire region.

Discoloration of the atmosphere results from absorption of light by particles or gases. For

**Figure 5.10**

Mandatory Class I Areas *

| 40. John Muir | 79. Mazatzal | 117. Mingo |
|---|---|---|
| 41. San Rafael | 80. Sierra Ancha | 118. Hercules-Glades |
| 42. Dome Land | 81. Mt. Baldy | 119. Upper Buffalo |
| 43. Cucamonga | 82. Superstition | 120. Caney Creek |
| 44. San Jacinto | 83. Galiuro | 121. Seney |
| 45. San Gabriel | 84. Saguaro | 122. Mammoth Cave |
| 46. San Gorgonio | 85. Chiricahua | 123. Great Smokey Mtns. |
| 47. Joshua Tree | 86. Mt. Zirkel | 124. Joyce Kilmer-Slickrock |
| 48. Agua Tibia | 87. Flat Tops | 125. Sipsey |
| 49. Selway-Bitterroot | 88. Rawah | 126. Cohotta |
| 50. Hell's Canyon | 89. Rocky Mtn. | 127. Okefenokee |
| 51. Sawtooth | 90. Eagles Nest | 128. St. Marks |
| 52. Craters of the Moon | 91. Maroon Bells Snowmass | 129. Chassahowitzka |
| 53. Jarbridge | 92. West Elk | 130. Breton |
| 54. Cabinet Mtns. | 93. Black Canyon | 131. Everglades |
| 55. Glacier | 94. La Garita | 132. Wolf Island |
| 56. Mission Mtn. | 95. Great Sand Dunes | 133. Cape Romain |
| 57. Bob Marshall | 96. Weminuche | 134. Shining Rock |
| 58. Medicine Lake | 97. Mesa Verde | 135. Linville Gorge |
| 59. Scapegoat | 98. Wheeler | 136. Swanquarter |
| 60. Gates of the Mountain | 99. San Pedro Parks | 137. James River Face |
| 61. UL Bend | 100. Pecas | 138. Shenandoah |
| 62. Anaconda Pintlar | 101. Bandelier | 139. Brigantine |
| 63. Red Rock Lake | 102. Bosque del Apache | 140. Dolly Sods |
| 64. North Absaroka | 103. Salt Ck | 141. Otter Creek |
| 65. Yellowstone | 104. White Mtn. | 142. Lye Brook |
| 66. Washakie | 105. Gila | 143. Great Gulf |
| 67. Grand Teton | 106. Carlsbad Caverns | 144. Presidential Range- |
| 68. Fitzpatrick | 107. Guadalupe | Dry River |
| 69. Bridger | 108. Big Bend | 145. Acadia |
| 70. Capitol Reef | 109. Lostwood | 146. Moosehorn |
| 71. Bryce Canyon | 110. Theodore Roosevelt | 147. Bering Sea |
| 72. Zion | 111. Badlands | 148. Simeonof |
| 73. Arches | 112. Wind Cave | 149. Mt. McKinley |
| 74. Canyonlands | 113. Witchita Mtns. | 150. Tuxedni |
| 75. Grand Canyon | 114. Voyageurs | 151. Haleakala |
| 76. Sycamore Canyon | 115. Boundary Waters | 152. Hawaii Volcanoes |
| 77. Petrified Forest | Canoe Area | 153. *Rainbow Lake* |
| 78. Pine Mt. | 116. Isle Royale | 154. *Brodwell Bay* |

| 1. Olympic | 14. Diamond Peak | 27. Yolla-Bolly-Niddle-Eel |
|---|---|---|
| 2. Pasayten | 15. Strawberry Mtn. | 28. Desolation |
| 3. North Cascades | 16. Crater Lake | 29. Pt. Reyes |
| 4. Glacier Peak | 17. Kalmiopsis | 30. Mokelumne |
| 5. Alpine Lakes | 18. Mountain Lakes | 31. Emigrant |
| 6. Mount Ranier | 19. Redwood | 32. Hoover |
| 7. Goat Rocks | 20. Gearhart Mtn. | 33. Yosemite |
| 8. Mt. Adams | 21. Marble Mtn. | 34. Pinnacles |
| 9. Mt. Hood | 22. Lava Beds | 35. Ventana |
| 10. Eagle Cap | 23. South Warner | 36. Kaiser |
| 11. Mt. Jefferson | 24. Thousand Lakes | 37. Kings Canyon |
| 12. Mt. Washington | 25. Lassen | 38. Sequoia |
| 13. Three Sisters | 26. Caribou | 39. Minarets |

¹Italicized names are areas not recommended where visibility is an important value.

Source: National Park Service.

* From the 1977 Amendments to the Clean Air Act.

example, the dun color of $NO_2$ is a result of its absorption of blue and ultraviolet light. Light passing through an $NO_2$ plume has the blue light removed, and the plume appears yellow or even brown.

Particles absorb light in a similar way. If the air is extremely clean (less than approximately 1 microgram per cubic meter of fine particles), dark objects are seen to be blue; with even a few micrograms per cubic meter change, the color is more neutral. Dark objects 10 kilometers (6.25 miles) or more away appear to be behind a haze; the color of the haze depends on the amount of scatter by fine particles.

Because most of the mass of fine particles inters the atmosphere in gaseous form, the technology to protect visibility will be designed to control $SO_2$, $NO_X$, and other reactant gases as well as emissions of fine particulates themselves. The regional load of fine particles and their precursors may well be the key regulatory issue in protecting visibility.

## Health and environmental effects of increased coal use

The President announced in the 1977 National Energy Plan that he would convene an advisory committee of medical, environmental, and engineering experts to study and report on the anticipated health and environmental effects of relying more heavily on coal to produce energy. (The 1990 Amendments to the Clean Air Act carry this methodology considerably further.)

The Committee reported to the President that in its judgement "it is safe to proceed with significantly increased use of coal in the U.S. to genrate energy, as proposed in the National Energy Plan through 1985, if strong environmental and safety policies are followed." But the Committee concluded that even with the best mitigation policies, adverse health and environmental effects would occur. It recommended rigorous adherence to the following policies:

- Compliance with federal and state air, water, and solid waste regulations
- Universal adoption and proper operation of best available control technology on new facilities
- Compliance with surface mine reclamation standards
- Compliance with mine health and safety standards
- Judicious siting of coal-fired facilities.

The Committee identified six issues which it said warrant "urgent attention" if the Nation is to minimize undesirable consequences of increased coal use:

- Air pollution health effect—Current standards may not provide adequate health protection from all coal combustion products. The evidence that some acidic particles have greater impact on public health than other particles increases our need to resolve the critical problems related to the transport, transformation, and health effects of the gas-aerosol complex.
- Coal mine worker health and safety—Strict enforcement of the Federal Coal Mine Safety and Health Act of 1977 should further reduce the risks to workers in the coal industry. Even with strict enforcement, in order to be certain that present standards provide adequate protection, effective health monitoring and assessment will be necessary. Continued improvement in miner safety will require increased education, especially for new miners. New developments, such as use of diesel-powered underground equipment, require further study of potential deleterious health effects.

- Global effects of carbon dioxide in the atmosphere—Combustion of fossil fuels, and especially coal, is increasing global atmospheric $CO_2$. This could induce climatic changes with potential for generating global sociopolitical disruption after 2025. It is urgent that we continue a strong research program to provide a sound basis for action no later than 1985. Because this problem is global in character, the United States should initiate a continuing international dialogue immediately.

- Acid fallout—Emissions of $SO_2$, particularly from coal, and $No_X$ from all fossil fuel combustion have increased the acidity of precipitation in the northeastern United States. This has decreased fish populations in many lakes and may already be reducing forest and agricultural productivity.

- Trace elements—Increased use of coal results in wastes that contain trace elements, many of which are toxic. These elements can leach and migrate into water or enter food chains in quantities which could impact public health and environmental quality. More data are needed to assess the extent to which these elements enter into the biosphere.

- Reclamation of arid lands—Enforcement of the Surface Control and Reclamation Act of 1977 will mitigate many adverse environmental effects of surface mining. However, it is not certain that some arid areas can be restored, even following full compliance. Prudence dictates that surface mining be deferred in these arid areas when information about their reclaimability is incomplete.

These issues were decisively addressed in the 1990 Amendments to the Clean Air Act.

## Non-criteria pollutants

It is becoming increasingly evident that the air pollutants upon which our standard and monitoring have been focusing do not represent all the important parameters of air quality. In some cases, they may not even represent the most important of informative ones.

Present ambient air quality standards and most monitoring of suspended particulates, for example, are concerned only with the total weight of airborne particulate matter, as measured by high-volume samplers. But total weight is at best only a crude indicator of trends in the kind of particulates that are most important to human health. By itself such a measurement is inadequate for many scientific purposes and therefore may be inadequate as a regulatory guide.

There are two major reasons for this inadequacy. First, the total weight of airborne particulates does not distinguish between tiny particles, which can penetrate the human respiratory system efficiently and thus pose considerable hazard to health, and the larger particles which generally do not. The proportion of respirable (small) particles—less than 3 microns in diameter—varies roughly from less than one-third to more than two-thirds of the total suspended particulates.

The second important reason is that most of the public health effects of particles in the air depend upon their chemical composition, which can also vary greatly. Toxic substances like a acid sulfates, nitrates, trace metals, and organic compounds are important and potentially harmful constituents of airborne particulate matter, but there are no ambient standards and there is very little monitoring for these consitiuents now.

## Particulate sulfates

Suspended sulfate aerosols are believed among the air pollutants most damaging to human health; and some of their estimated effects are listed in Table 5.6. A relatively small proportion of the sulfates in air is directly emitted as particulates, however. Worldwide, most sulfates are formed through secondary chemical reactions in the atmosphere from other kinds of sulfur compounds which originate from natural sources such as volcanic activity, ocean salts, and decomposition of dead plants and animals. In industrialized nations, the emission of sulfur in gaseous form may be a greater factor.

**Table 5.6**

Estimates of Adverse Health Effects of Aerosol Acid Sulfates

| Effect | Threshold concentration (micrograms per cubic meter) | Duration of exposure |
|---|---|---|
| Increased daily mortality (four studies) | 25 | 24 hours or longer |
| Aggravation of heart and lung disease in elderly (two studies) | 25 | 24 hours or longer |
| Aggravation of asthma (four studies) | 6–10 | 24 hours or longer |
| Increased acute respiratory diseases in children (four studies) | 13 | Several years |
| Increased risk of chronic bronchitis | | |
|   Cigarette smokers | 15 | Up to 10 years |
|   Nonsmokers | 10 | Up to 10 years |

Source: J. F. Finklea, et al., "Health Effects of Increasing Sulfur Oxides Emissions," Environmental Protection Agency (draft, 1975).

## Air pollution and weather

The atmospheric topographic factors that control the dispersal and hence affect the local ambient level for a given amount of pollutant emitted to the atmosphere are very complex and best reserved for advanced study by specialists. A few of these factors however can be described in easily understood terms. The following section was prepared originally for the orientation of urban planners with regard to the role of meteorology in the planning and air pollution control process. The section from *A Guide For Considering Air Quality in Urban Planning,* EPA, March 1974, provides a good general introduction to a complex subject. Information is provided also on the High Air Pollution Potential Advisory forecasts prepared by National Weather Service forecasters. Figure 5.11 illustrates the likely susceptibility of various large regions of the nation in any five year period to conditions favorable for the accumulation of air pollutants. The expected averages are derived from about ten years of forecast experience.

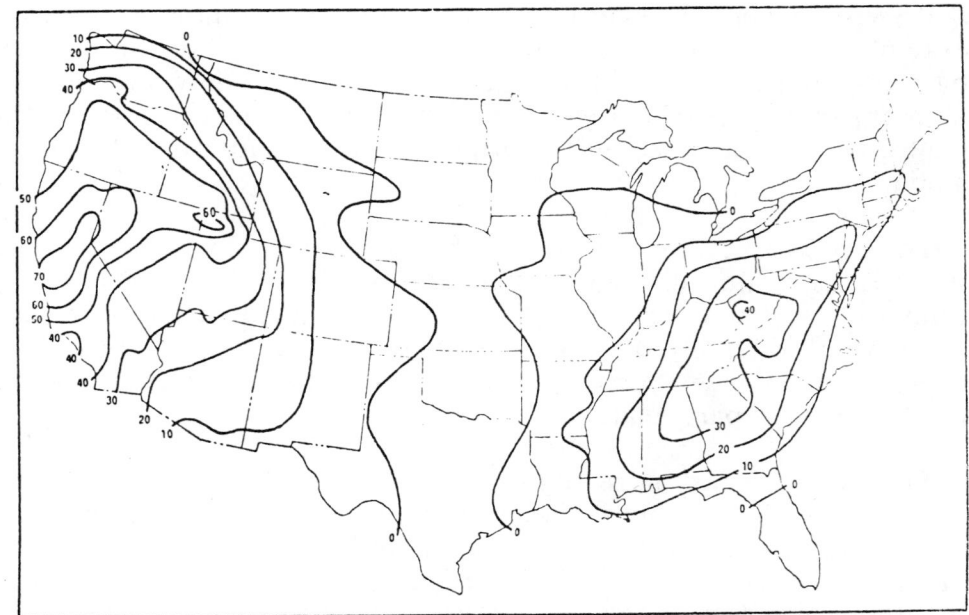

**Figure 5.11** Isopleths of total number of forecast-days of high meteorological potential for air pollution expected in a 5-year period. Data are based on forecasts issued since the program began, 1 August 1960 and 1 October 1963 for eastern and western parts of the United States, respectively, through 3 April 1970.

## Natural phenomena affecting air quality

The concentration of atmospheric pollutants observed at different locations depends on more than just the quantity of pollutants emitted at the various sources. The atmosphere is the agent that transports and disperses pollutants between sources and receptors. Consequently, the state of the atmosphere helps to determine the concentrations of pollutants observed at receptors. Unlike emissions sources, which can be controlled, the state of the atmosphere is not at present susceptible to man's control.

Some skill has been attained, however, in predicting the future state of the atmosphere. Since meteorological conditions that favor high concentrations of pollutants are known, severe air pollution episodes can therefore be forecast.

In general, three parameters are used to describe atmospheric transport and dispersion processes. These are wind speed, wind direction, and atmospheric stability. For emissions at a given source, a higher wind speed provides the pollutants with a greater air volume within which to disperse. This causes ground level pollutant concentrations, other things being equal, to be inversely proportional to wind speed.

Horizontally, the wind direction is the strongest factor affecting pollutant concentrations. For a given wind direction, nearly all the pollutant transport and dispersion will be downwind. Wind direction determines which sector of the area surrounding a source will receive pollutants from that source. The influences of wind speed and direction on pollution dispersion volumes and hence, on ground level concentratrions are illustrated in Figure 5.12a and Figure 5.12b

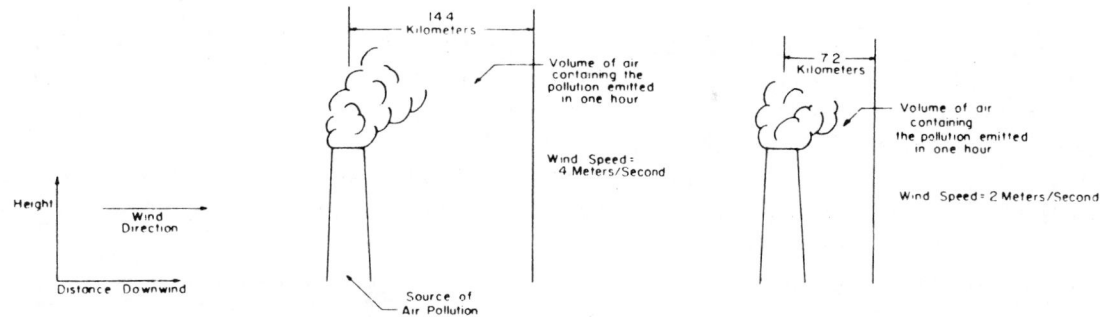

**Figure 5.12a    The influence of wind speed on ground level pollutant concentrations**

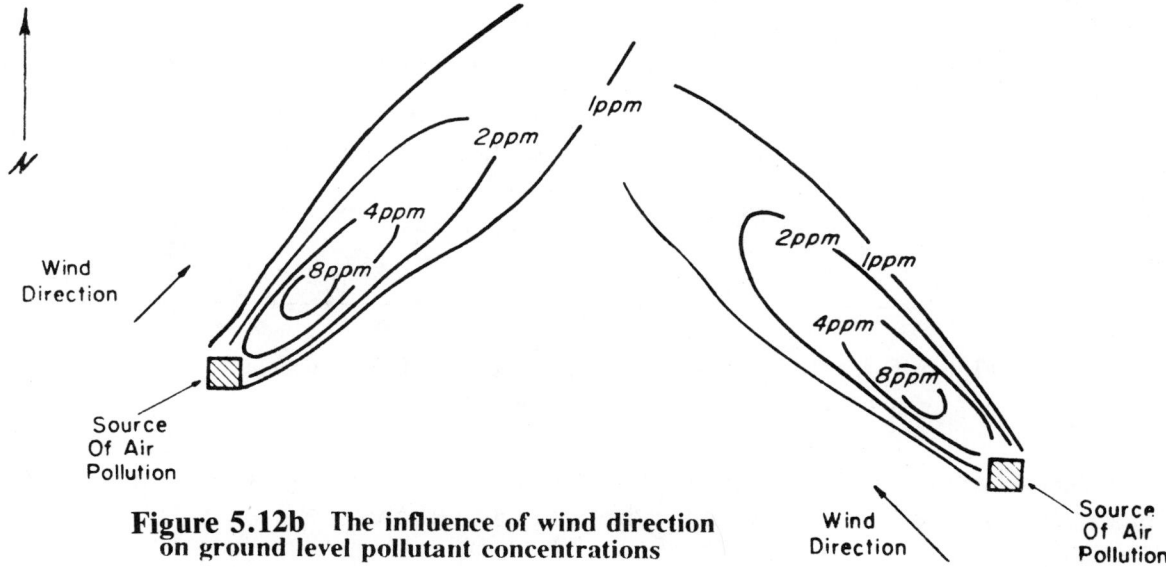

**Figure 5.12b   The influence of wind direction on ground level pollutant concentrations**

Atmospheric stability directly affects the vertical dispersion of atmospheric pollutants. Unlike wind direction and wind speed, atmospheric stability cannot be measured directly. Atmospheric stability is a measure of air turbulence and may be defined in terms of the vertical atmospheric temperature profile. When the temperature decreases rapidly with height, vertical motions in the atmosphere are enhanced, and the atmosphere is called unstable. An unstable atmosphere, with its enhanced vertical motions, is more effective for dispersing pollutants, and because of the large volume of air available for the spread of pollutants, ground-level concentrations can be relatively low. When the temperature does not decrease rapidly with height, vertical motions are neither enhanced nor repressed and the stability is described as neutral. Under these conditions, pollutants are also allowed to disperse vertically in the atmosphere, although not as rapidly as for the unstable case.

When the temperature decreases very little, remains the same, or increases with increasing height, the atmosphere is called stable. Under these conditions, the atmosphere inhibits the upward spread of pollutants. Upward-moving smoke, which rapidly assumes the temperature of the surrounding air, reaches a point where it is colder, and hence denser, than the air above it, so it can rise no further. This supression of upward motion effectively forms a lid beneath which pollutants can disperse freely. The weaker the temperature decrease with height, the higher is the lid. The extreme case is an inversion, when the temperature increases with height. Often, clouds are topped by a stable or inversion layer, which stops their vertical growth.

The well-mixed layer beneath a stable layer is called the mixing layer. When it extends to the ground its vertical extent is known as the mixing height or the mixing depth. Generally, turbulence is enhanced in the early moring hours as the sun heats the ground and temperature decreases with height causing unstable conditions. At night, as the earth cools, temperature increases with height causing less turbulence and stable atmospheric conditions. Figure 5.13 illustrates the influence of atmospheric stability on ground level pollutant concentrations.

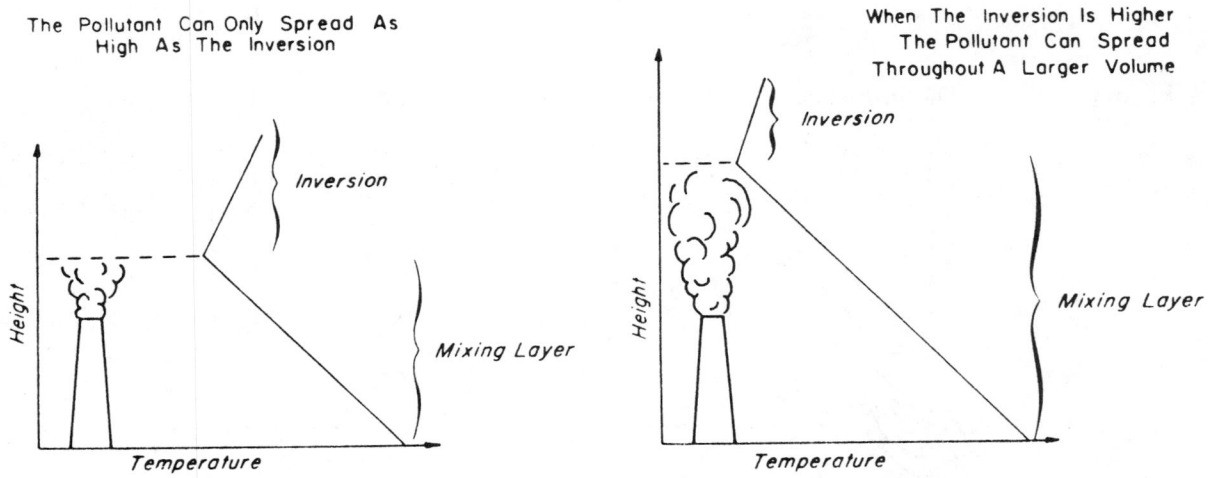

**Figure 5.13** The influence of atmospheric stability on ground level pollutant concentrations

Wind speed, wind direction, and atmospheric stability will vary greatly with time. For a certain location, some combinations occur more frequently than others.

Where detailed meteorological records have been kept for a year or more, a stability *wind rose* can be calculated. This wind rose is a set of tables, one for each stability class (ranging from very stable to very unstable), listing the frequency of occurence of all possible combinations of wind speed and wind direction. Such roses are available for many locations in the United States from the National Climatic Center in Asheville, North Carolina. It should be noted that topographical features such as mountains, hills, valleys, bodies of water, buildings, and other terrain features can change airflow patterns resulting in unexpected pollution effects.

Near a large body of water, local sea breezes influence the spread of pollutants. Early in the morning, when the air is still or the wind is off the land, pollutants can accumulate over their sources or downwind of them. Later in the day, when a local sea breeze develops, a fresh breeze blows in the direction from the water toward land. This breeze brings with it not only the pollutants emitted from the sources at this time of day, but also those accumulated earlier in the day, because they are carried back from water to land. Unexpectedly high pollutant concentrations can occur near the shore when the high pollutant loading blows past. In addition to this effect, which generally occurs close to land, the seabreeze itself can penetrate as far inland as 40 miles or more.

Mountains and valleys have characteristic airflow patterns, too. In the evening, as the earth cools, the coldest air will sink into the lowest part of the valley, as illustrated in Figure 5.14. This creates a stable inversion layer because lighter, warmer air stays above the valley. In this way, pollutants are trapped in the valleys all night. During the daytime when heating occurs, the air in the valley is warmed and rises, permitting the pollutants to escape (Figure 5.15). Unfortunately, this heating and upward motion does not always occur. During periods when high pressure settles over a region and the air is stagnant, the atmosphere is stable all day long, and pollutants continue to accumulate in the valley. Some of the worst episodes of air pollution have occured in mountain chains like the Appalachians, where industries are located in the valleys between adjacent hills.

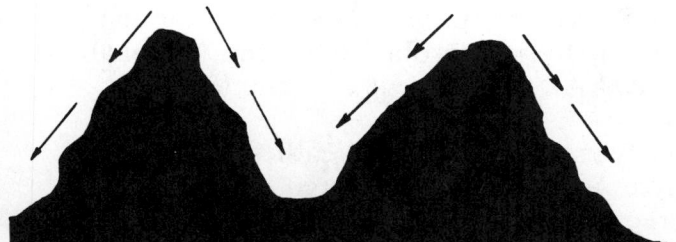

**Figure 5.14** Nighttime airflow into valleys      **Figure 5.15** Daytime airflow out of valleys

In cities, buildings form the topography. Where rows of tall buildings front on narrow streets the air flows through the streets as though they were canyons. Since ventilation is

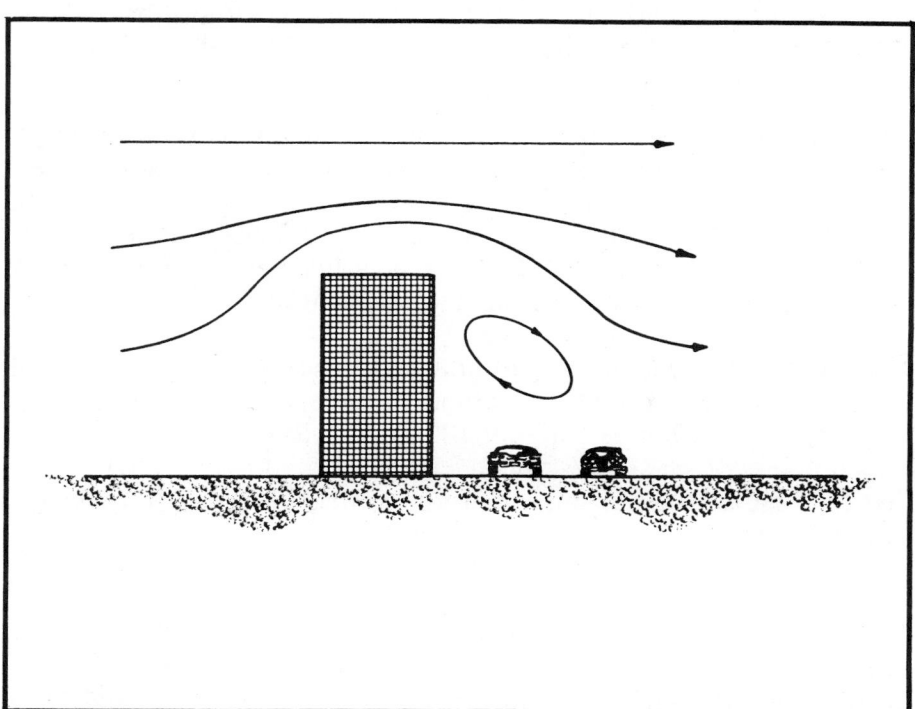

**Figure 5.16** Airflow around and in the wake of a building

determined by building configuration, many distortions in wind, and hence pollution flows, take place in a city. Figure 5.16 shows an example. Air flows over a building and into a street downwind of it. The lines show the direction of airflow. The building, because the air cannot flow through it, creates an obstruction in the pattern of the smooth airflow. Downwind of the building, an eddy, or circular movement of air at variance with the main airflow, is formed in its wake, such as the one shown in the figure. The eddy can trap pollutants emitted by cars in the street, and can cause concentrations of pollutants, for example, carbon monoxide, to be as much as three times higher on the side of the street further downwind than at the site of pollutant origin.

### High Air Pollution Potential Advisories

High Air Pollution Potential Advisories (HAPPA) are prepared at the National Meteorological Center (NMC) in Suitland, Maryland, by meteorologists of the National Oceanographic and Atmospheric Administration (NOAA), Department of Commerce.

Advisories are based both on reports received hourly via teletype from Weather Service stations in the United States and on numerous analyses and forecasts prepared by the NMC. With its electronic computer facilities, the NMC prepares mixing-depth and wind-speed data from all upper-air-observing stations in the contiguous United States (about 70 stations). These data are analyzed, intepreted, and integrated with other meteorlogical information.

National air pollution potential advisories based on these data are transmitted daily at 12:20 p.m., E.S.T., to Weather Service stations. When meteorlogical conditions do not warrant issuance of a HAPPA, the teletype message is "none today." When the forecast indicates that an advisory of high air pollution potential should be issued, the message designates the affected areas. The daily message indicates significant changes in the boundaries of advisory areas, including termination of an episode.

Because conditions of atmospheric transport and dispersion typically vary with location and time, the forecasting staff cannot prepare advisories for each city in the United States. For this reason, the NOAA metorologists limit their forecasts to areas at least as large as 75,000 square miles (roughly the size of Oklahoma), in which stagnation conditions are expected to persist for at least 36 hours. Individual Weather Service stations may modify these generalized forecasts on the basis of local meteorological conditions.

Users of the service should realize that boundaries of the forecast areas of high air pollution potential cannot be delineated exactly. For practical purposes, the lines defining the advisory area should be interpreted as bands roughly 100 miles wide.

To be notified of these advisories, air pollution control or research officials must inititate arrangements with the nearest Weather Service station.

# The 1990 Clean Air Act Amendments

The 1990 Clean Air Act Amendments were adopted in large part to address the concerns put forward by environmentalists and government regulators that real improvement in air quality could not be achieved without a substantial revision of the 1970 and 1977 Amendments. At the time, ninety-six cities still had not attained the national standard for ozone, forty-one had not met the requirements for reductions in carbon dioxide emissions, and seventy-two did not meet the standard for particulate matter. Indeed, since 1970, the EPA has successfully regulated only seven air pollutants out of possibly hundreds due to legal challenges to the 1970 act. The 1990 Clean Air Act Amendments, however, mark a significant departure from traditional governmental approaches to environmental protection, and may prove more effective.

Overcoming a host of regional and sectorial interests, the 1990 Clean Air Act Amendments are the product of unprecedented cooperation between the government and the private sector. Rather than relying on the traditional method of rule-making and regulation at the federal level, which often leads to expensive and time-consuming litigation, the EPA has committed itself to achieving a consensus on air-quality standards at the outset of the process. Local and state governments as well as industry, labor, and environmental groups will be actively consulted in the formulation of policies through advisory committees, informal meetings, and formal regulatory negotiations.

The 1990 Clean Air Act Amendments also acknowledge the economic constraints of environmental protection. The United States currently spends over $100 billion a year on environmental protection, and expenditures in this area are expected to reach 2.7 percent of the Gross National Product by the year 2000. With such figures in mind, legislators formulated the 1990 Clean Air Act Amendments according to stringent criteria regarding cost-effectiveness. As a result, the new laws, while setting specific standards concerning air quality, allow industry significant latitude in deciding how these goals will be met. The 1990 Clean Air Act Amendments also encourage business to assume a leadership role in environmental protection by providing incentives for companies to seek solutions to problems independent of government directives. Innovative, market-based programs such as tradable emissions allowances for sulfur dioxide, are integrated as well into the 1990 Amendments, as are reasonable time frames that make cost-effective approaches possible.

The 1990 Clean Air Act Amendments include over fifty-five new rules that must be integrated into the EPA's regulatory operations—a daunting task to which the agency has allotted 70 percent of its fiscal 1992 budget increase. Clean fuels, acid rain, and ozone depletion are among the many issues addressed by the new laws. Regulations concerning these and other major issues are outlined below:

## Urban Pollution

- **Ozone.** The 1990 Clean Air Act Amendments require that more rigorous controls be implemented for the most severe cases. States may have to initiate or upgrade inspection/maintenance programs; install vapor recovery systems at small stationary sources such as gasoline stations; and adopt transportation controls that would reduce vehicular emissions. Major stationary sources of nitrogen oxides will also have to reduce emissions.

• **Carbon Monoxide.** States may have to introduce or upgrade inspection/maintenance programs and/or institute transportation controls.

• **Particulate Matter.** States will have to implement Reasonably Available Control Technology (RACT), and use of wood-burning stoves and fireplaces would have to be reduced.

## Permits

The new act empowers the EPA and the states to enforce standards by requiring that all air-pollution-control obligations of an individual source be contained in a single, five-year operating permit. The states have three years to develop and submit their permit programs to the EPA for approval, which has one year to issue regulations describing the minimum requirements for such programs. Emission sources must then pay permit fees to the states to finance the operation of these programs.

## Motor Vehicles

• **Vehicle Emissions.** Beginning with the 1994 model year, tailpipe emissions of hydrocarbons, carbon monoxide, and nitrogen oxides must be significantly reduced and standards must be maintained over a longer vehicular life. On-board charcoal canisters to absorb evaporative emissions may also be required.

• **Fuels.** In 1995, reformulated gasolines containing less aromatics will be introduced in nine cities with the most severe ozone problems; this program will eventually be made available to other communities. In 1992, alternative fuels, such as ethanol and compressed natural gas, will be sold in winter in those cities with the worst carbon monoxide problems.

• **Clean Cars.** In 1996, a pilot program will introduce to California 150,000 cars that meet tighter emissions limits through a combination of vehicular and alternative-fuel technologies. This program will also in time be made available to other states.

## Air Toxics

Emissions of 189 toxics, including carcinogens, mutagens, and reproductive toxins, must be reduced in the next ten years. The EPA will compile a list of source categories within one year and issue a Maximum Achievable Control Standards (MACT) for each category.

## Acid Rain

A two-phase, market-based system will be implemented to reduce sulfur-dioxide emissions from power plants by half. Plants will receive emission allowances from the EPA and will be penalized if they exceed these allotments. However, plants in specified areas may bank or trade allowances with one another to achieve an overall reduction in emissions. In Phase I, high emission plants in the eastern and midwestern states will achieve reductions by 1995. In Phase II, which begins in the year 2000, limits will be enforced on smaller, cleaner plants, and tightened on Phase I plants. Nitrogen-oxide reductions will be achieved through performance standards set by the EPA.

## Ozone Depletion

The 1990 Clean Air Act Amendments exceed the requirements of the 1987 Montreal Protocol in restricting the use, emission, and disposal of ozone depleting substances. They phase out production of CFCs, carbon tetrachloride, and methyl chloride by the year 2000 as well as methyl chloroform by 2002; they freeze production of CFCs in 2015, phasing them out in 2030. Companies servicing air conditioning for cars will be required to purchase certified recycling equipment and train employees by 1992. By November, 1992, "nonessential" use of CFCs will be prohibited.

# ACID RAIN

"Acid rain" may be one of the most significant environmental problems of this decade. It poses new challenges to the full development of our forest, agricultural, and aquatic resources; and to the use of fossil fuels as an energy source.

The term "acid rain" first was used to describe environmental phenomena more than a century ago. Since then, and especially since 1970, the number of related studies carried out in Europe, Canada, and the United States has increased steadily. Because of that research, scientists are now beginning to speak with reasonable assurance about some of the elements of the acid rain problem.

It is now widely recognized that natural emissions of sulfur compounds may contribute approximately half of the global sulfur budget. Less is known about natural sources of nitrogen, but they probably contribute more to the global nitrogen budget than man-made sources. However, in some regions of concern like the northeastern United States and Europe, man-made pollutants are generally accepted as the primary contributors to acid deposition.

As a result of the combustion of tremendous quantities of fossil fuels such as coal and oil, the United States annually discharges approximately 40 million metric tons of sulfur and nitrogen oxides into the atmosphere. Through a series of complex chemical reactions these pollutants can be converted into acids, which may return to earth as components of either rain, snow, or dry deposition. This acid deposition, more commonly known as acid rain, may have severe ecological impacts on widespread areas of the environment.

Hundreds of lakes in North America and Scandanavia have become so acidic that they can no longer support fish life. More than 90 lakes in the Adirondack mountains in New York State are fishless because acidic conditions have inhibited reproduction. Recent data indicate that other areas of the United States, such as northern Minnesota and Wisconsin, may be vulnerable to similar adverse impacts.

While many of the aquatic effects of acid deposition have been well documented, data related to possible terrestrial impacts are just beginning to be developed. Yields from crops and forests can be changed as a result of both the direct effects of acids on foliage, and the indirect effects of altered soil chemistry. Preliminary field experiments with agricultural crops have shown a wide variety of relatively small responses, both positive and negative. According to most investigations, the effects on the health and productivity of forests are probably all negative.

In addition, acid deposition is contributing to the destruction of stone monuments and statuary throughout the world. The 2500 year old Parthenon and other classical buildings on the Acropolis in Athens, Greece, have shown much more rapid decay in this century as a result of the city's high air pollution levels. Research is underway to clarify the role of acid rain in the destruction.

In 1981, sulfur oxides accounted for 14 percent (22.5 million metric tons) of the total air pollution in the United States, while nitrogen oxides accounted for 12 percent (19.5 million metric tons). Although other pollutants also act as precursors to acid rain, it is believed that these two oxides are the major contributors to the problem.

Sulfur oxides ($SO_x$) are primarily emitted from stationary sources such as utility and industrial boilers burning coal as a fuel. However, nitrogen oxides ($NO_x$) are emitted from both stationary and transportation-related sources such as cars and trucks. Approximately 52 percent of the $NO_x$ discharged into the atmosphere in 1981 resulted from the combustion of fossil fuels by stationary sources, while 44 percent originated from transportation-related sources. Over the next twenty years the combustion of fossil fuels is expected to increase significantly. In particular, emissions of nitrogen oxides from stationary sources are likely to increase rapidly during this period.

## Fundamental chemistry

The most common sulfur and nitrogen oxides are sulfur dioxide ($SO_2$) and nitric oxide (NO). After being discharged into the atmosphere, these pollutants can be chemically converted into sulfuric ($H_2SO_4$) and nitric ($HNO_3$) acid through a process known as oxidation. There are several complicated pathways or mechanisms by which oxidation can occur. Which path is actually taken is dependent upon numerous factors such as the concentration of heavy metals, the intensity of sunlight, and the amount of ammonia present.

Again, one should keep in mind that other acids contribute to the acid rain problem. Hydrochloric acid (HCl), for example, may be emitted directly from coal-fired power plants and frequently is found relatively short distances downwind from the source.

The process by which acids are deposited through rain or snow is frequently called wet deposition. However, another atmospheric process known as dry deposition may also occur. Dry deposition is the process by which particles such as fly ash, or gases such as sulfur dioxide ($SO_2$) or nitric oxide (NO), are deposited, or adsorbed, onto surfaces. While these particles or gases are normally not in the acidic state prior to deposition, it is believed that they are converted into acids after contacting water in the form of rain, dew, fog, or mist following deposition. The precise mechanisms by which dry deposition takes place, and its effects on soils, forests, crops, and buildings, are not adequately understood. Much research will be undertaken in the coming years to clarify its contribution to the overall acid deposition problem.

## Long distance transport

Various sulfur compounds which may act as precursors to sulfuric acid are known to travel as far as several hundred kilometers per day while in the atmosphere. During transport these pollutants may easily cross geographical and political boundaries. This situation creates numerous national and international regulatory problems in that the air pollution standards of one state or country can have an indirect impact on the natural resources of another.

It is believed that other nitrogen-containing pollutants may be transported in a similar manner. Research is underway to clarify the transport processes associated with the major pollutants contributing to the acid deposition problem.

## pH scale and acidity of normal rain

The pH, a numerical value used to describe the strength of an acid, is determined by a mathematical formula based on a solution's concentration of hydrogen ions (H+). The pH scale ranges from a numerical value of 0 to 14. A value of pH 1 is very acid (battery acid), pH 7 is neutral, and pH 13 is very alkaline (lye). Because of the logarithmic nature of the scale, pH 4 is 10 times more acidic than pH 5, and 100 times more acidic than pH 6, and so on. Precipitation is defined as being acidic if the pH is less than 5.6, the pH of normal, unpolluted rain. The slight natural acidity of normal rain is due to the presence of carbonic acid ($H_2CO_3$), which is formed by the reaction of atmospheric carbon dioxide ($CO_2$) with water.

## Acidity of lakes

As was pointed out earlier, fish populations are especially sensitive to changes in the pH of their surroundings. A recent study of several hundred Norwegian lakes showed that of the lakes having a pH between 5.5 and 6.0, less than 10 percent contained no fish. At pH's of less than 4.5, more than 70 percent of the lakes were fishless. Acidic lake water not only affects fish directly. Low pH water frequently promotes the release of potentially toxic metals from the lake bed. Aluminum, for example, is frequently found in high concentrations in fishless lakes, and is released from soils at approximately pH 4.5. Rainfall runoff may carry aluminum from nearby soils into lakes, or into streams which empty into lakes and thus magnify the problem.

Most scientists today agree that reductions in the pH of water can lead to a decrease in the number and diversity of aquatic species. They also agree that in a few lakes and streams, especially in the northeastern United States, low pH levels have been associated with a virtual cessation of aquatic life. That man-made sources of $SO_2$ and $NO_X$ emissions have added to the acidity of rainfall is undeniable. Yet based on the research and monitoring data accumulated over the last decade, few scientists are willing to project what additional environmentalcosts would result if man-made air emissions continue into the future at the present rate, or what environmental benefits would accrue if man-made acid precursor emissions are reduced. The most important knowledge resulting from the accumulated acid rain research of the last 10 years probably is the realization that the causes and effects of acid rain are certainly more complicated than once believed.

# Acid Rain and Amendments to the Clean Air Act in 1990

Title IV of the 1990 Clean Air Act Amendments, which contains comprehensive provisions to control the emissions that cause acid rain, is the first legislation in U.S. history to directly address the problem of acid rain. It calls for reductions in sulphur dioxide emissions from the burning of fossil fuels—the principal cause of acid rain formation—and mandates significant reductions in nitrogen oxide and other toxic emissions.

The 1990 Amendments call for:

- reducing national sulphur dioxide emissions from the current level of 19 million tons to 9.1 million tons annually by the year 2000;

- placing a permanent cap on allowable sulphur dioxide emissions;

- reducing industrial nitrogen oxide emissions from six to four million tons annually by the year 2000;

- giving industry the freedom to choose the cheapest means of reducing emissions;

- reducing automobile tailpipe emissions of nitrogen oxide by 60 per cent and of hydrocarbons by 40 per cent by 1997;

- requiring polluters to switch to cleaner fuels, install emission-reduction equipment, and pay for cleanup; and

- eliminating 90 per cent of industrial emissions of benzine, mercury, and dioxin.

An innovative aspect of Title IV is the market-based allowance-trading system devised by the Environmental Protection Agency (EPA). Electrical power plants that burn fossil fuels—coal or oil—will be allocated allowances for sulphur dioxide emissions and must remain within these allowances to be in compliance with the law. Utilities that reduce their emissions below the number of allowances they hold may elect to trade allowances, bank them for future use, or sell them to other utilities. Allowance trading will be permitted nationwide. The EPA will record allowance transfers and monitor compliance.

Title IV of the 1990 Clean Air Act Amendments has been hailed around the world as a model of resourceful, inexpensive, and effective environmental policy. Officials of Canadian Prime Minister Brian Mulroney's government, in particular, have acclaimed Title IV and have suggested that it may pave the way for a joint U.S.-Canadian trans-boundary air-quality agreement.

*The NOAA weather research ship, the S.S. Malcolm Baldridge, watches weather trends in dozens of ways. Weather balloons launched from its deck provide early indications of impending tropical storms, while providing upper wind data for aviation safety. Provisions are carried for sampling ocean currents, including the sensing of long-duration after-effects of ocean storms or undersea volcanic eruptions and earthquakes.*

# WEATHER FUNDAMENTAL
## and
# GLOSSARY

# WEATHER FUNDAMENTALS

The following is intended to serve as a sort of "weather primer". It attempts to analyze in everyday language the fundamental factors and processes which are the components of weather.

## THE EARTH'S ATMOSPHERE

### Composition of our atmosphere

Air is a mixture of several gases. When completely dry, it is about 78% nitrogen and 21% oxygen. The remaining 1% is other gases such as Argon, Carbon Dioxide, Neon, Helium, and others. However, in nature, air is never completely dry. It always contains some water vapor in amounts varying from *almost* zero to about 5% by volume. As water vapor content increases, the other gases decrease proportionately.

### Vertical structure

We classify the atmosphere into layers, or spheres, by characteristics exhibited in these layers.

The TROPOSPHERE is the layer from the surface to an average altitude of about 7 miles. It is characterized by an overall decrease of temperature with increasing altitude. The height of the troposphere varies with latitude and seasons. It slopes from about 20,000 feet over the poles to about 65,000 feet over the Equator; and it is higher in summer than in winter.

At the top of the troposphere is the TROPOPAUSE, a very thin layer marking the boundary between the troposphere and the layer above. The height of the tropopause and certain weather phenomena are related, as will be explained later.

Above the tropopause is the STRATOSPHERE. This layer is typified by relatively small changes in temperature with height except for a warming trend near the top.

### Density

Air is matter and has weight. Since it is gaseous, it is compressible. Pressure the atmosphere exerts on the surface is the result of the weight of the air above. Thus, air near the surface is much more dense than air at high altitudes.

## TEMPERATURE

### Temperature scales

Two commonly used temperature scales are Celsius (Centigrade) and Fahrenheit. The Celsius scale is used exclusively for upper air temperatures and is rapidly becoming the world standard for surface temperatures also.

Traditionally, two common temperature references are the melting point of pure ice and the boiling point of pure water at sea level. The melting point of ice is 0° C or 32° F; the boiling point of water is 100° C or 212° F. Thus, the difference between melting and boiling is 100 degrees Celsius or 180 degrees Fahrenheit; the ratio between degrees Celsius and Fahrenheit is 100/180 or 5/9. Since 0° F is 32 Fahrenheit degrees colder than 0° C, you must apply this difference when comparing temperatures on the two scales. You can convert from one scale to the other using one of the following formulae:

$$C = \frac{5}{9}(F - 32) \qquad\qquad F = \frac{9}{5}C + 32$$

where C is degrees Celsius and F is degrees Fahrenheit.　　(See conversion chart, page 285)

Temperature is measured with a thermometer. But what makes a thermometer work? Simply the addition or removal of heat. Heat and temperature are not the same; how are they related?

## Heat and temperature

Heat is a form of energy. When a substance contains heat, it exhibits the property we measure as temperature—the degree of "hotness" or "coldness." A specific amount of heat absorbed by or removed from a substance raises or lowers its temperature a definite amount. However, the amount of temperature change depends on characteristics of the substance. Each substance has its unique temperature change for the specific change in heat. For example, if a land surface and a water surface have the same temperature and an equal amount of heat is added, the land surface becomes hotter than the water surface. Conversely, with equal heat loss, the land becomes colder than the water.

The Earth receives energy from the sun in the form of solar radiation. The Earth and its atmosphere reflect about 55 percent of the radiation and absorb the remaining 45 percent converting it to heat. The Earth, in turn, radiates energy, and this outgoing radiation is "terrestrial radiation." It is evident that the average heat gained from incoming solar radiation must equal heat lost through terrestrial radiation in order to keep the earth from getting progressively hotter or colder. However, this balance is world-wide; we must consider regional and local imbalances which create temperature variations.

## Temperature variations

The amount of solar energy received by any region varies with time of day, with seasons, and with latitude. These differences in solar energy create temperature variations. Temperatures also vary with differences in topographical surface and with altitude. These temperature variations create forces that drive the atmosphere in its endless motions.

## Day-to-night (diurnal) variation of temperature

*Diurnal variation is the change in temperature from day to night* brought about by the daily rotation of the Earth. The Earth receives heat during the day by solar radiation but continually loses heat by terrestrial radiation. Warming and cooling depend on an imbalance of solar and terrestrial radiation. During the day, solar radiation exceeds terrestrial radiation and the surface becomes warmer. At night, solar radiation ceases, but terrestrial radiation continues and cools the surface. Cooling continues after sunrise until solar radiation again exceeds terrestrial radiation. Minimum temperature usually occurs after sunrise, sometimes as much as one hour after. The continued cooling after sunrise is one reason that fog sometimes forms shortly after the sun is above the horizon.

## Seasonal variation of temperature

In addition to its daily rotation, the Earth revolves in a complete orbit around the sun once each year. Since the axis of the Earth tilts to the plane of orbit, the angle of incident solar radiation varies seasonally between hemispheres. The Northern Hemisphere is warmer in June, July, and August because it receives more solar energy than does the Southern Hemisphere. During December, January, and February, the opposite is true; the Southern Hemisphere receives more solar energy and is warmer.

## Temperature variation with latitude

The shape of the Earth causes a geographical variation in the angle of incident solar radiation. Since the Earth is essentially spherical, the sun is more nearly overhead in equatorial regions than at higher latitudes. Equatorial regions, therefore, receive the most radiant energy and are warmest. Slanting rays of the sun at higher latitudes deliver less energy over a given area with the least being received at the poles. Thus, temperature varies with latitude from the warm Equator to the cold poles.

## Temperature variations with topography

Not related to movement or shape of the earth are temperature variations induced by water and terrain. As stated earlier, water absorbs and radiates energy with less temperature change than does land. Large, deep water bodies tend to minimize temperature changes, while continents favor large changes. Wet soil such as in swamps and marshes is almost as effective as water in suppressing temperature changes. Thick vegetation tends to control temperature changes since it contains some water and also insulates against heat transfer between the ground and the atmosphere. Arid, barren surfaces permit the greatest temperature changes.

These topographical influences are both diurnal and seasonal. For example, the difference between a daily maximum and minimum may be 10° or less over water, near a shore line, or over a swamp or marsh, while a difference of 50° or more is common over rocky or sandy deserts. In the Northern Hemisphere in July, temperatures are warmer over continents than over oceans; in January they are colder over continents than over oceans. The opposite is true in the Southern Hemisphere, but not as pronounced because of more water surface in the Southern Hemisphere.

To compare land and water effect on seasonal temperature variation, consider northern Asia and southern California near San Diego. In the deep continental interior of northern Asia, July average temperature is about 50° F; and January average, about —30° F. Seasonal range is about 80° F. Near San Diego, due to the proximity of the Pacific Ocean, July average is about 70° F and January average, 50° F. Seasonal variation is only about 20° F.

Abrupt temperature differences develop along lake and ocean shores. These variations generate pressure differences and local winds which will be studied further on in this text.

Prevailing wind is also a factor in temperature controls. In an area where prevailing winds are from large water bodies, temperature changes are rather small. Most islands enjoy fairly constant temperatures. On the other hand, temperature changes are more pronounced where prevailing wind is from dry, barren regions.

Air transfers heat slowly from the surface upward. Thus, temperature changes aloft are more gradual than at the surface. The following looks at particulars of temperature changes with altitude.

## Temperature variation with altitude

Temperature normally decreases with increasing altitude throughout the troposphere. This *decrease of temperature with altitude* is defined as *lapse rate*. The average decrease of temperature—average lapse rate—in the troposphere is 2° C per 1,000 feet. But since this is an average, the exact value seldom exists. In fact, temperature sometimes increases with height through a layer. *An increase in temperature with altitude is* defined as *an inversion,* i.e., lapse rate is inverted.

An inversion often develops near the ground on clear, cool nights when wind is light. The ground radiates and cools much faster than the overlying air. Air in contact with the

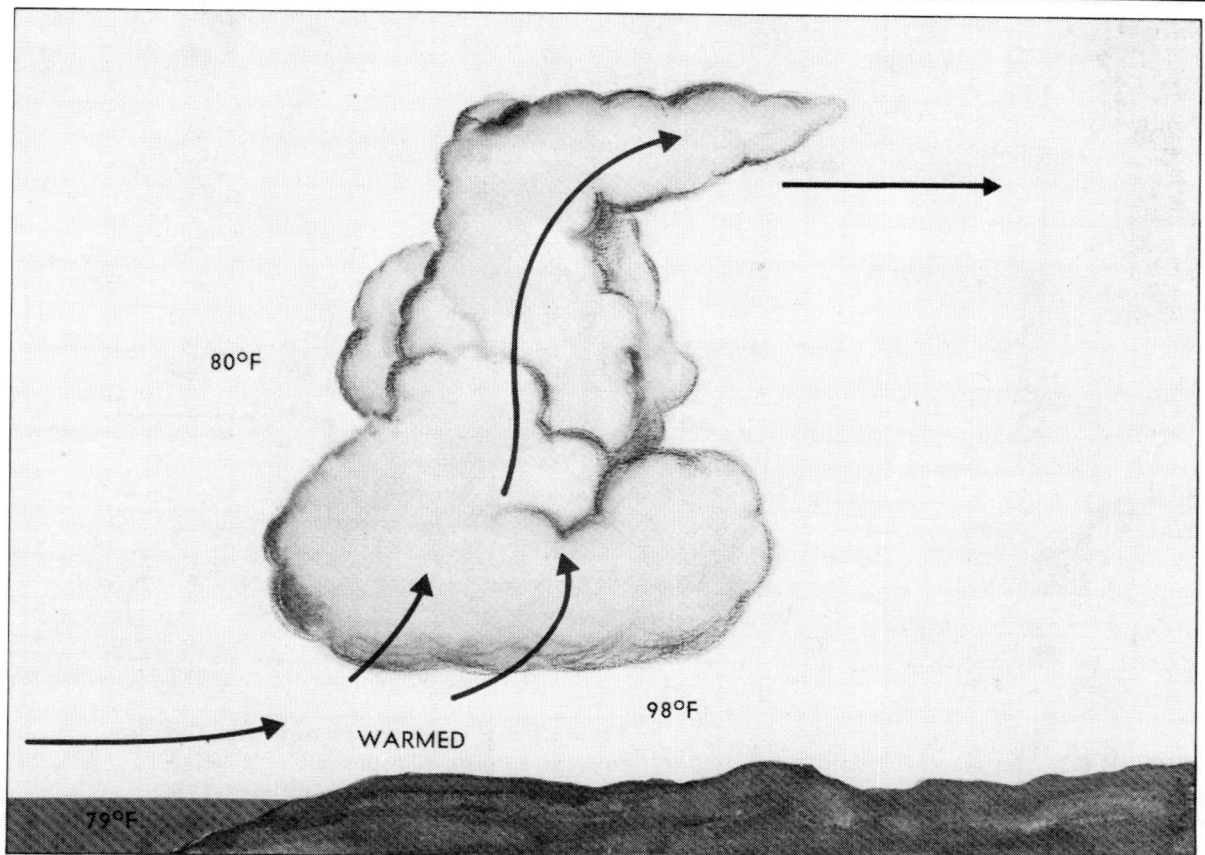

**FIGURE 6.1. Temperature differences create air movement and, at times, cloudiness.**

ground becomes cold while the temperature a few hundred feet above changes very little. Thus, temperature increases with height. Inversions may also occur at any altitude when conditions are favorable. For example, a current of warm air aloft overrunning cold air near the surface produces an inversion aloft. Inversions are common in the stratosphere.

## ATMOSPHERIC PRESSURE
## AND THE BAROMETER

### Atmospheric pressure

Atmospheric pressure is the force per unit area exerted by the weight of the atmosphere. Since air is not solid, we cannot weigh it with conventional scales. Yet, Toricelli proved three centuries ago that he could weigh the atmosphere by balancing it against a column of mercury. He actually measured pressure converting it directly to weight.

### Measuring pressure

The instrument Toricelli designed for measuring pressure is the barometer. Weather services and the aviation community use two types of barometers in measuring pressure—the mercurial and aneroid.

**The Mercurial Barometer**—The mercurial barometer, consists of an open dish of mercury into which we place the open end of an evacuated glass tube. Atmospheric pressure forces mercury to rise in the tube. At stations near sea level, the column of mercury rises on the average to a height of 29.92 inches or 760 millimeters. In other words,

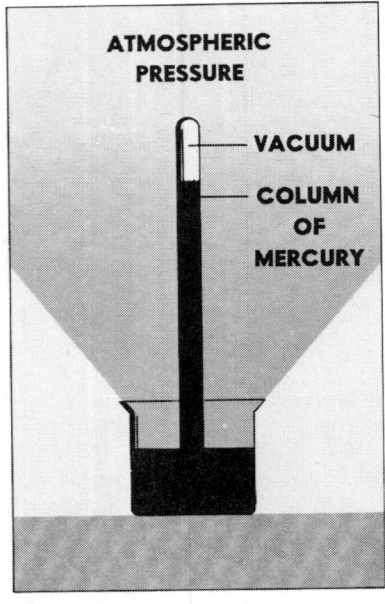

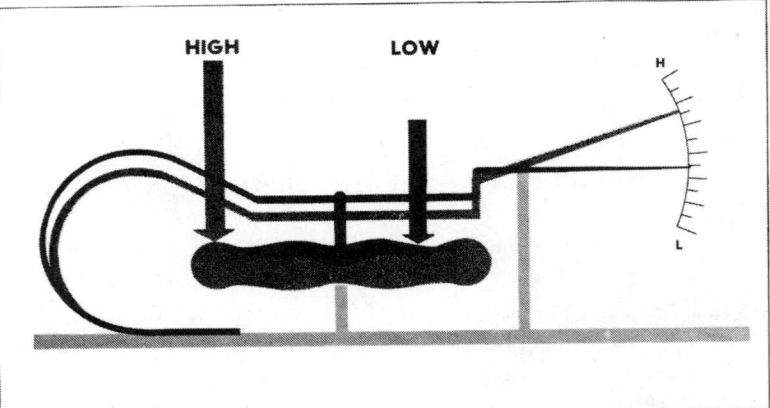

**FIGURE 6.2. The mercurial barometer.** Atmospheric pressure forces mercury from the open dish upward into the evacuated glass tube. The height of the mercury column is a measure of atmospheric pressure.

**FIGURE 6.3. The aneroid barometer. The aneroid consists of a partially evacuated metal cell, a coupling mechanism, and an indicator scale. The cell contracts and expands with changing pressure. The coupling mechanism drives the indicator along a scale graduated in pressure units.**

a column of mercury of that height weighs the same as a column of air having the same cross section as the column of mercury and extending from sea level to the top of the atmosphere.

Why is mercury used in the barometer? Mercury is the heaviest substance available which remains liquid at ordinary temperatures. It permits the instrument to be of manageable size. Water could be used but at sea level the water column would be about 34 feet high.

## The aneroid barometer

Essential features of an aneroid barometer are a flexible metal cell and the registering mechanism. The cell is partially evacuated and contracts or expands as pressure changes. One end of the cell is fixed, while the other end moves the registering mechanism. The coupling mechanism magnifies movement of the cell driving an indicator hand along a scale graduated in pressure units.

## Pressure units

Pressure is expressed in many ways throughout the world. The term used depends somewhat on its application and the system of measurement. Two popular units are "inches of mercury" or "millimeters of mercury." Since pressure is force per unit area, a more explicit expression of pressure is "pounds per square inch" or "grams per square centimeter." The term "millibar" precisely expresses pressure as a force per unit area, one millibar being a force of 1,000 dynes per square centimeter. The millibar is rapidly becoming a universal pressure unit.

## Station pressure

Obviously, pressure can be measured only at the point of measurement. The pressure measured at a station or airport is "station pressure" or the actual pressure at field elevation. For instance, station pressure at Denver is less than at New Orleans. Now look more closely at some factors influencing pressure.

## Pressure variation

Pressure varies with altitude and temperature of the air as well as with other minor influences.

**Altitude**—Moving upward through the atmosphere, weight of the air above becomes less and less. Within the lower few thousand feet of the troposphere, pressure decreases roughly one inch for each 1,000 feet increase in altitude.

**Sea Level Pressure**—Since pressure varies with altitude, it is not easy to compare station pressures between stations at different altitudes. To make them comparable, pressure readings must be adjusted to some common level. Mean sea level seems the most feasible common reference. Pressure measured at a 5,000-foot station is 25 inches; pressure increases about 1 inch for each 1,000 feet or a total of 5 inches. Sea level pressure is approximately 25 + 5 or 30 inches. The weather observer takes temperature and other effects into account, but this simplified example explains the basic principle of sea level pressure reduction.

Sea level pressure is usually expressed in millibars. Standard sea level pressure is 1013.2 millibars, 29.92 inches of mercury, 760 millimeters of mercury, or about 14.7 pounds per square inch.

**Pressure Analyses (Using Isobars)**—Sea level pressure are commonly plotted on a map and lines are drawn connecting points of equal pressure. These lines of equal pressure are *isobars*. Hence, the surface map is an *isobaric analysis* showing identifiable, organized pressure patterns. Five pressure systems are defined as follow:

1. LOW—a center of pressure surrounded on all sides by higher pressure; also called a cyclone. Cyclonic curvature is the curvature of isobars to the left when you stand with lower pressure to your left.

2. HIGH—a center of pressure surrounded on all sides by lower pressure, also called an anticyclone. Anticyclonic curvature is the curvature of isobars to the right when you stand with lower pressure to your left.

3. TROUGH—an elongated area of low pressure with the lowest pressure along a line marking maximum cyclonic curvature.

4. RIDGE—an elongated area of high pressure with the highest pressure along a line marking maximum anticyclonic curvature.

5. COL—the neutral area between two highs and two lows. It also is the intersection of a trough and a ridge. The col on a pressure surface is analogous to a mountain pass on a topographic surface. We simply contour the heights of the pressure surface. For example, a 700-millibar constant pressure analysis is a contour map of the heights of the 700-millibar pressure surface. While the contour map is based on variations in height, these variations are small when compared to flight levels, and for all practical purposes, you may regard the 700-millibar chart as a weather map at approximately 10,000 feet or 3,048 meters.

# WIND

## What causes wind?

Differences in temperature create differences in pressure. These pressure differences drive a complex system of winds in a never ending attempt to reach equilibrium. Wind also transports water vapor and spreads fog, clouds, and precipitation. To help the reader relate wind to pressure patterns and the movement of weather systems, this text explains *convection* and the *pressure gradient force*, describes the effects of the *Coriolis* and frictional forces, relates convection and these forces to the general circulation, discusses local and small-scale wind systems, introduces the concept of wind shear, and associates wind with weather.

## Convection currents cause wind

When two surfaces are heated unequally, they heat the overlying air unevenly. The warmer air expands and becomes lighter or less dense than the cool air. The more

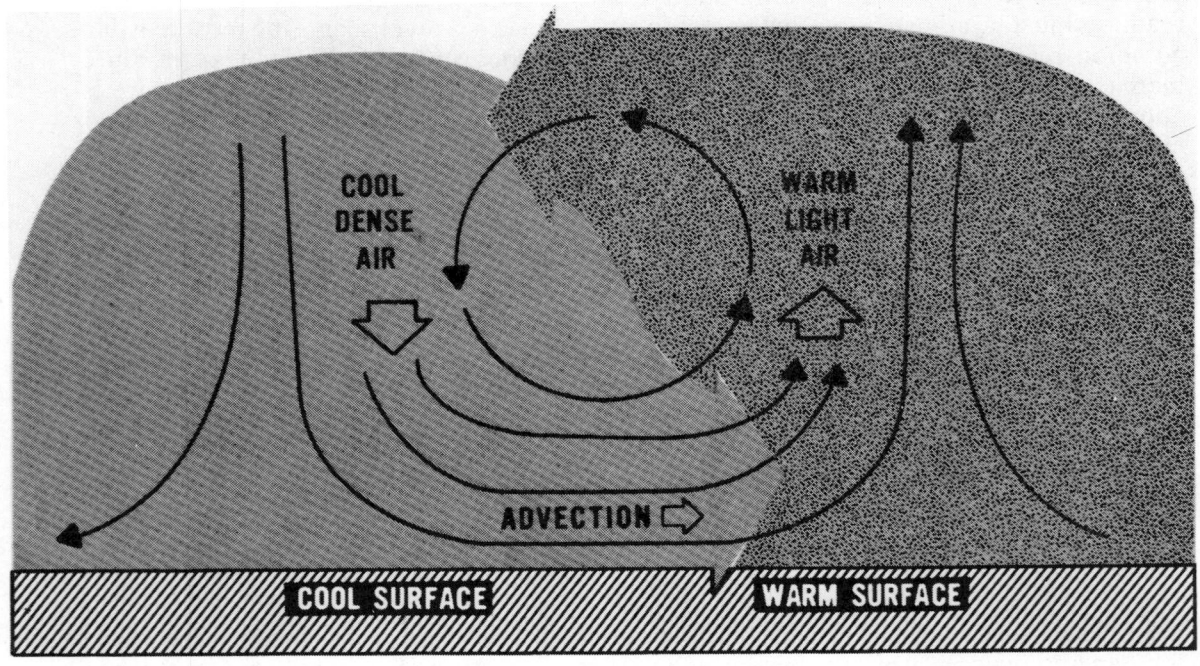

**FIGURE 6.4. Convective current resulting from uneven heating of air by contrasting surface temperatures. The cool, heavier air forces the warmer air aloft establishing a convective cell. Convection continues as long as the uneven heating persists.**

dense, cool air is drawn to the ground by its greater gravitational force lifting or forcing the warm air upward much as oil is forced to the top of water when the two are mixed. Figure 6.4 shows the convective process. The rising air spreads and cools, eventually descending to complete the convective circulation. As long as the uneven heating persists, convection maintains a continuous "convective current."

The horizontal air flow in a convective current is "wind." Convection of both large and small scales accounts for systems ranging from hemispheric circulations down to local eddies. This horizontal flow, wind, is sometimes called "advection." However, the term "advection" more commonly applies to the transport of atmospheric properties by the wind, i.e., warm advection; cold advection; advection of water vapor, etc.

## Pressure gradient force of wind

Pressure differences must create a force in order to drive the wind. This force is the *pressure gradient force*. The force is from higher pressure to lower pressure and is perpendicular to isobars or contours. Whenever a pressure difference develops over an area, the pressure gradient force begins moving the air directly across the isobars. The closer the spacing of isobars, the stronger is the pressure gradient force. The stronger the pressure gradient force, the stronger is the wind. Thus, closely spaced isobars mean strong winds; widely spaced isobars mean lighter wind. From a pressure analysis, the reader can get a general idea of wind speed from contour or isobar spacing.

Because of uneven heating of the Earth, surface pressure is low in warm equatorial regions and high in cold polar regions. A pressure gradient develops from the poles to the Equator. If the Earth did not rotate, this pressure gradient force would be the only force acting on the wind. Circulation would be two giant hemispheric convective currents. Cold air would sink at the poles; wind would blow straight from the poles to the Equator; warm air at the Equator would be forced upward; and high level winds would blow directly toward the poles. However, the Earth does rotate; and because of its rotation, this simple circulation is greatly distorted.

## Coriolis force: it modifies wind direction

A moving mass travels in a straight line until acted on by some outside force. However, if one views the moving mass from a rotating platform, the path of the moving mass relative to his platform appears to be deflected or curved. To illustrate, start rotating the turntable of a record player. Then using a piece of chalk and a ruler, draw a "straight" line from the center to the outer edge of the turntable. To you, the chalk traveled in a straight line. Now stop the turntable; on it, the line spirals outward from the center. To a viewer on the turntable, some "apparent" force deflected the chalk to the right.

A similar apparent force deflects moving particles on the earth. Because the Earth is spherical, the deflective force is much more complex than the simple turntable example. Although the force is termed "apparent," to us on Earth, it is very real. The principle was

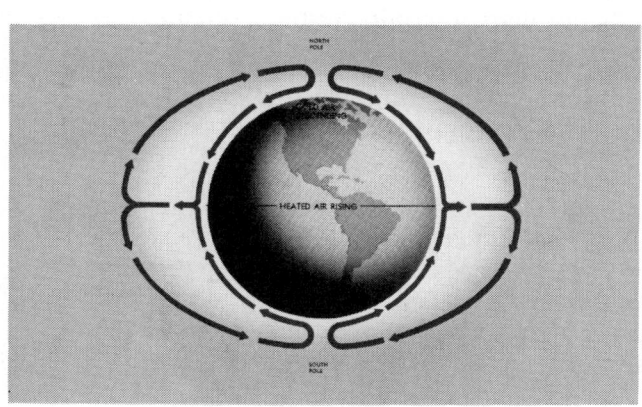

FIGURE 6.5 Circulation as it would be on a nonrotating globe. Intense heating at the Equator lowers the density. More dense air flows from the poles toward the Equator forcing the less dense air aloft where it flows toward the poles. The circulation would be two giant hemispherical convective currents.

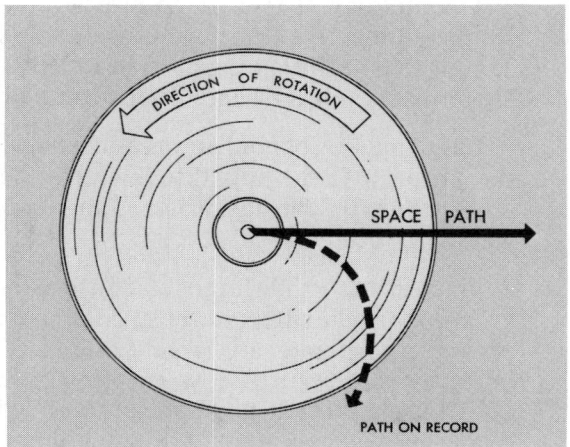

FIGURE 6.6. Apparent deflective force due to rotation of a horizontal platform. The "space path" is the path taken by a piece of chalk. The "path of record" is the line traced on the rotating record. Relative to the record, the chalk appeared to curve; in space, it traveled in a straight line.

277

first explained by a Frenchman, Coriolis, and carries his name—the Coriolis force.

The Coriolis force affects the paths of aircraft; missiles; flying birds; ocean currents; and, most important to the study of weather, air currents. The force deflects air to the right in the Northern Hemisphere and to the left in the Southern Hemisphere. This text concentrates mostly on deflection to the right in the Northern Hemisphere.

Coriolis force is at a right angle to wind direction and directly proportional to wind speed. That is, as wind speed increases, Coriolis force increases. At a given latitude, double the wind speed and you double the Coriolis force. Why at a given latitude?

Coriolis force varies with latitude from zero at the Equator to a maximum at the poles. It influences wind direction everywhere except immediately at the Equator; but the effects are more pronounced in middle and high latitudes.

Remember that the pressure gradient force drives the wind and is perpendicular to isobars. When a pressure gradient force is first established, wind begins to blow from higher to lower pressure directly across the isobars. However, the instant air begins moving, Coriolis force deflects it to the right. Soon the wind is deflected a full 90° and is parallel to the isobars or contours. At this time, Coriolis force exactly balances pressure gradient force. With the forces in balance, wind will remain parallel to isobars or contours. Surface friction disrupts this balance as we discuss later; but first let's see how Coriolis force distorts the fictitious global circulation.

## The general circulation of earth's air

As air is forced aloft at the Equator and begins its high-level trek northward, the Coriolis force turns it to the right or to the east. Wind becomes westerly at about 30° latitude temporarily blocking further northward movement. Similarly, as air over the poles begins its low-level journey southward toward the Equator, it likewise is deflected to the right and becomes an east wind, halting for a while its southerly progress. As a result, air literally "piles up" at about 30° and 60° latitude in both hemispheres. The added weight of the air increases the pressure into semipermanent high pressure belts. Maps of mean surface pressure for the months of July and January show clearly the subtropical high pressure belts near 30° latitude in both the Northern and Southern Hemispheres.

The building of these high pressure belts creates a temporary impasse disrupting the simple convective transfer between the Equator and the poles. The restless atmosphere cannot live with this impasse in its effort to reach equilibrium. Something has to give. Huge masses of air begin overturning in middle latitudes to complete the exchange.

Large masses of cold air break through the northern barrier plunging southward toward the Tropics. Large midlatitude storms develop between cold outbreaks and carry warm air northward. The result is a midlatitude band of migratory storms with ever changing weather.

Since pressure differences cause wind, seasonal pressure variations determine to a great extent the areas of these cold air outbreaks and midlatitude storms. But, seasonal pressure variations are largely due to seasonal temperature changes. It will be remembered that at the surface, warm temperatures to a great extent determine low pressure and cold temperatures, high pressure. It will also be recalled that seasonal temperature changes over continents are much greater than over oceans.

During summer, warm continents tend to be areas of low pressure and the relatively cool oceans, high pressure. In winter, the reverse is true—high pressure over the cold continents and low pressure over the relatively warm oceans. The same pressure variations occur in the warm and cold seasons of the Southern Hemisphere, although the effect is not as pronounced because of the much larger water areas of the Southern Hemisphere.

Cold outbreaks are strongest in the cold season and are predominantly from cold continental areas. Summer outbreaks are weaker and more likely to originate from cool water surfaces. Since these outbreaks are masses of cool, dense air, they characteristically are high pressure areas.

As the air tries to blow outward from the high pressure, it is deflected to the right by the Coriolis force. Thus, the wind around a high blows clockwise. The high pressure with its associated wind system is an *anticyclone*.

The storms that develop between high pressure systems are characterized by low pressure. As winds try to blow inward toward the center of low pressure, they also are deflected to the right. Thus, the wind around a low is counterclockwise. The low pressure and its wind system is a *cyclone*.

The high pressure belt at about 30° north latitude forces air outward at the surface to the north and to the south. The northbound air becomes entrained into the midlatitude storms. The southward moving air is again deflected by the Coriolis force becoming the well-known subtropical northeast trade winds. In midlatitudes, high level winds are predominantly from the west and are known as the prevailing westerlies. Polar easterlies dominate low-level circulation north of about 60° latitude.

There are three major wind belts. *Northeasterly trade* winds carry tropical storms from east to west. The *prevailing westerlies* drive midlatitude storms generally from west to east. Few major storm systems develop in the comparatively small Arctic region; the chief influence of the *polar easterlies* is their contribution to the development of midlatitude storms.

## Friction effect on wind

This discussion so far has said nothing about friction. Wind flow patterns aloft follow isobars or contours where friction has little effect. However, friction is a significant factor near the surface.

Friction between the wind and the terrain surface slows the wind. The rougher the terrain, the greater is the frictional effect. Also, the stronger the wind speed, the greater is the friction. One may not think of friction as a force, but it is a very real and effective force always acting opposite to wind direction.

As frictional force slows the windspeed, Coriolis force decreases. However, friction does not affect pressure gradient force. Pressure gradient and Coriolis forces are no longer in balance. The stronger pressure gradient force turns the wind at an angle across the isobars toward lower pressure until the three forces balance. Frictional and Coriolis forces combine to just balance pressure gradient force. Surface wind spirals outward from high pressure into low pressure crossing isobars at an angle.

The angle of surface wind to isobars is about 10° over water increasing with roughness of terrain. In mountainous regions, one often has difficulty relating surface wind to pressure gradient because of immense friction and also because of local terrain effects on pressure.

## The jet stream

A discussion of the general circulation is incomplete when it does not mention the "jet stream." Winds on the average increase with height throughout the troposphere culminating in a maximum near the level of the tropopause. These maximum winds tend to be further concentrated in narrow bands. A jet stream, then, is a narrow band of strong winds meandering through the atmosphere at a level near the tropopause. Further discussion of the jet stream is taken up later in this text.

### Local and small scale winds

Until now, this text has dealt only with the general circulation and major wind systems. Local terrain features such as mountains and shore lines influence local winds and weather.

### Mountain and valley winds

In the daytime, air next to a mountain slope is heated by contact with the ground as it receives radiation from the sun. This air usually becomes warmer than air at the same altitude but farther from the slope.

Colder, denser air in the surroundings settles downward and forces the warmer air near the ground up the mountain slope. This wind is a "valley wind" so called because the air is flowing up out of the valley.

At night, the air in contact with the mountain slope is cooled by terrestrial radiation and becomes heavier than the surrounding air. It sinks along the slope, producing the "mountain wind" which flows like water down the mountain slope. Mountain winds are usually stronger than valley winds, especially in winter. The mountain wind often continues down the more gentle slopes of canyons and valleys, and in such cases takes the name "drainage wind." It can become quite strong over some terrain conditions and in extreme cases can become hazardous when flowing through canyon restrictions.

### Katabatic wind

A katabatic wind is any wind blowing down an incline when the incline is influential in causing the wind. Thus, the mountain wind is a katabatic wind. Any katabatic wind originates because cold, heavy air spills down sloping terrain displacing warmer, less dense air ahead of it. Air is heated and dried as it flows down slope. Sometimes the descending air becomes warmer than the air it replaces.

Many katabatic winds recurring in local areas have been given colorful names to highlight their dramatic, local effect. Some of these are the Bora, a cold northerly wind blowing from the Alps to the Mediterranean coast; the Chinook, a warm wind down the east slope of the Rocky Mountains often reaching hundreds of miles into the high plains; the Taku, a cold wind in Alaska blowing off the Taku glacier; and the Santa Ana, a warm wind descending from the Sierras into the Santa Ana Valley of California.

### Land and sea breezes

As frequently stated earlier, land surfaces warm and cool more rapidly than do water surfaces; therefore, land is warmer than the sea during the day; wind blows from the cool water to warm land—the "sea breeze" so called because it blows from the sea. At night, the wind reverses, blows from cool land to warmer water, and creates a "land breeze."

Land and sea breezes develop only when the overall pressure gradient is weak. Wind with a stronger pressure gradient mixes the air so rapidly that local temperature and pressure gradients do not develop along the shore line.

### Wind shear

Rubbing two objects against each other creates friction. If the objects are solid, no exchange of mass occurs between the two. However, if the objects are fluid currents, friction creates eddies along a common shallow mixing zone, and a mass transfer takes place in the shallow mixing layer. This zone of induced eddies and mixing is a shear zone.

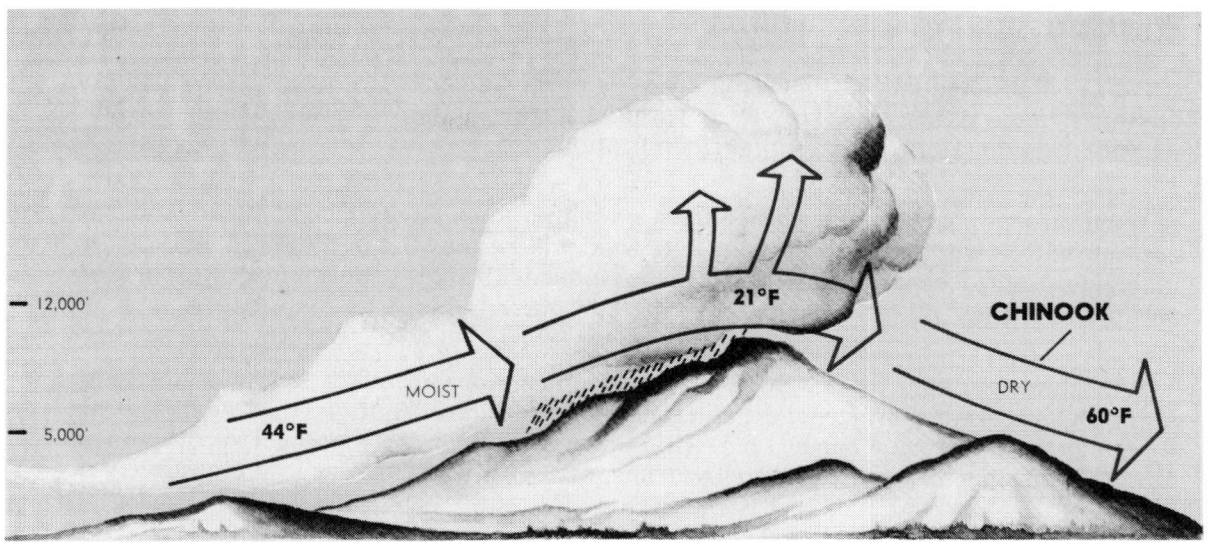

**FIGURE 6.7.** The "Chinook" is a katabatic (downslope) wind. Air cools as it moves upslope and warms as it blows downslope. The Chinook occasionally produces dramatic warming over the plains just east of the Rocky Mountains.

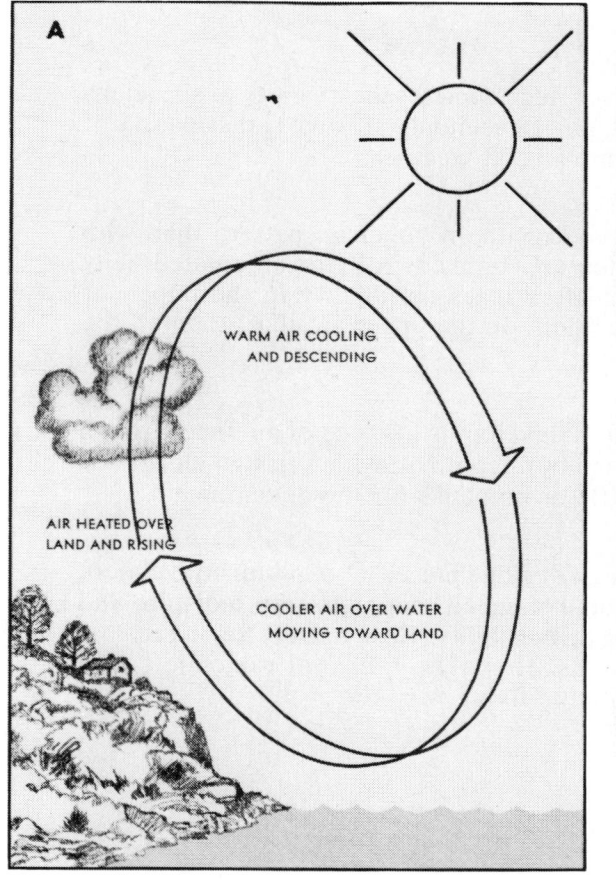

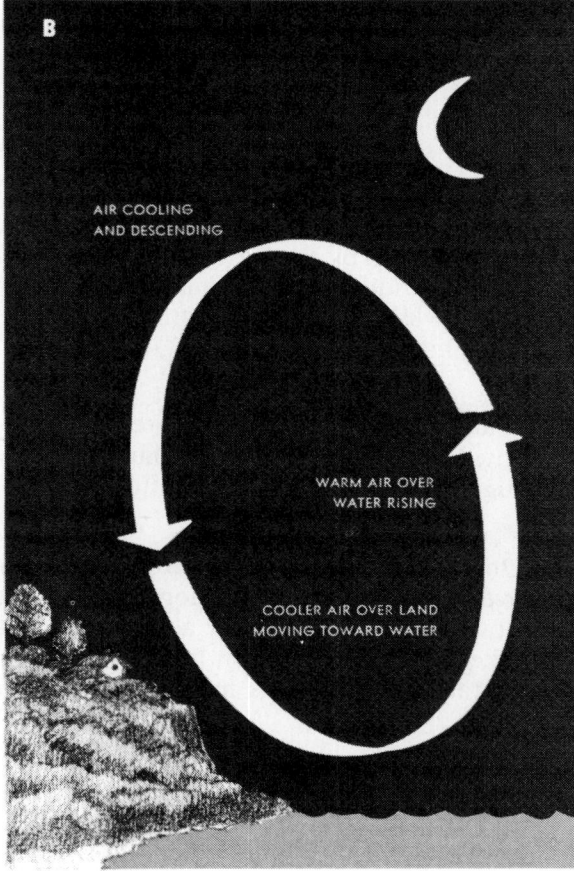

**FIGURE 6.8.** Land and sea breezes. At night, cool air from the land flows toward warmer water—the land breeze. During the day, wind blows from the water to the warmer land—the sea breeze.

## Wind, pressure systems, and weather

It has been noted earlier that wind speed is proportional to the spacing of isobars or contours on a weather map. However, with the same spacing, wind speed at the surface will be less than aloft because of surface friction.

Wind direction can be determined from a weather map. If you face along an isobar or contour with lower pressure on your left, wind will be blowing in the direction you are facing. On a surface map, wind will cross the isobar at an angle toward lower pressure; on an upper air chart, it will be parallel to the contour.

Wind blows counterclockwise (Northern Hemisphere) around a low and clockwise around a high. At the surface where winds cross the isobars at an angle, the transport of air from high to low pressure can be seen. Although winds are virtually parallel to contours on an upper air chart, there still is a slow transport of air from high to low pressure.

At the surface when air converges into a low, it cannot go outward against the pressure gradient, nor can it go downward into the ground; it must go upward.* Therefore, a low or trough is an area of rising air.

Rising air is conducive to cloudiness and precipitation; thus we have the general association of low pressure—bad weather. Reasons for the inclement weather are developed further on in this text.

By similar reasoning, air moving out of a high or ridge depletes the quantity of air. Highs and ridges, therefore, are areas of descending air. Descending air favors dissipation of cloudiness; hence the association, high pressure—good weather.

Many times weather is more closely associated with an upper air pattern than with features shown by the surface map. Although features on the two charts are related, they seldom are identical. A weak surface system often loses its identity in the upper air pattern, while another system may be more evident on the upper air chart than on the surface map.

Widespread cloudiness and precipitation often develop in advance of an upper trough or low. A line of showers and thunderstorms is not uncommon with a trough aloft even though the surface pressure pattern shows little or no cause for the development.

On the other hand, downward motion in a high or ridge places a "cap" on convection, preventing any upward motion. Air may become stagnant in a high, trap moisture and contamination in low levels, and restrict ceiling and visibility. Low stratus, fog, haze, and smoke are not uncommon in high pressure areas. However, a high or ridge aloft with moderate surface winds most often produces good flying weather.

---

\* Earlier it was stated that air "piles up" in the vicinity of 30° latitude increasing pressure and forming the subtropical high pressure belt. Why, then, does not air flowing into a low or trough increase pressure and fill the system? Dynamic forces maintain the low or trough; and these forces differ from the forces that maintain the subtropical high.

# MOISTURE, CLOUD FORMATION, AND PRECIPITATION

## Water vapor

Water evaporates into the air and becomes an ever-present but variable constituent of the atmosphere. Water vapor is invisible just as oxygen and other gases are invisible. However, water vapor can be readily measured and expressed in different ways. Two commonly used terms are (1) relative humidity, and (2) dew point.

## Relative humidity

Relative humidity routinely is expressed in percent. As the term suggests, *relative humidity* is "relative." It relates *the actual water vapor present to that which could be present*.

Temperature largely determines the maximum amount of water vapor air can hold. Warm air can hold more water vapor than cool air. Actually, relative humidity expresses the degree of saturation. Air with 100% relative humidity is saturated; less than 100% is unsaturated.

If a given volume of air is cooled to some specific temperature, it can hold no more water vapor than is actually present, relative humidity becomes 100%, and saturation occurs. What is that temperature?

## Dew point

Dew point is the temperature to which air must be cooled to become saturated by the water vapor already present in the air. Aviation weather reports normally include the air temperature and dew point temperature. Dew point when related to air temperature reveals qualitatively how close the air is to saturation.

## Temperature—dew point spread

The difference between air temperature and dew point temperature is popularly called the "spread." As spread becomes less, relative humidity increases, and it is 100% when temperature and dew point are the same. Surface temperature—dew point spread is important in anticipating fog but has little bearing on precipitation. To support precipitation, air must be saturated through thick layers aloft.

Sometimes the spread at ground level may be quite large, yet at higher altitudes the air is saturated and clouds form. Some rain may reach the ground or it may evaporate as it falls into the drier air. Our never ending weather cycle involves a continual reversible change of water from one state to another. A closer look at change of state follows in this text.

## Change of state

Evaporation, condensation, sublimation, freezing, and melting are changes of state. Evaporation is the changing of liquid water to invisible water vapor. Condensation is the reverse process. Sublimation is the changing of ice directly to water vapor, or water vapor to ice, bypassing the liquid state in each process. Snow or ice crystals result from the sublimation of water vapor directly to the solid state. The freezing and melting processes need no explanation.

### Latent heat

Any change of state involves a heat transaction with no change in temperature. Evaporation requires heat energy that comes from the nearest available heat source. This heat energy is known as the "latent heat of vaporization," and its removal cools the source it comes from. An example is the cooling of your body by evaporation of perspiration.

What becomes of this heat energy used by evaporation? Energy cannot be created or destroyed, so it is hidden or stored in the invisible water vapor. When the water vapor condenses to liquid water or sublimates directly to ice, energy originally used in the evaporation reappears as heat and is released to the atmosphere. This energy is "latent heat" and is quite significant as will be shown later. Melting and freezing involve the exchange of "latent heat of fusion" in a similar manner. The latent heat of fusion is much less than that of condensation and evaporation; however, each in its own way plays an important role in weather.

As air becomes saturated, water vapor begins to condense on the nearest available surface. What surfaces are in the atmosphere on which water vapor may condense?

### Condensation nuclei

The atmosphere is never completely clean; an abundance of microscopic solid particles suspended in the air are condensation surfaces. These particles, such as salt, dust, and combustion byproducts are "condensation nuclei." Some condensation nuclei have an affinity for water and can induce condensation or sublimation even when air is almost but not completely saturated.

As water vapor condenses or sublimates on condensation nuclei, liquid or ice particles begin to grow. Whether the particles are liquid or ice does not depend entirely on temperature. Liquid water may be present at temperatures well below freezing.

### Supercooled water

Freezing is complex and liquid water droplets often condense or persist at temperatures colder than 0° C. Water droplets colder than 0° C are supercooled. When they strike an exposed object, the impact induces freezing. For example, impact freezing of supercooled water can result in aircraft icing.

Supercooled water drops very often are in abundance in clouds at temperatures between 0° C and –15° C, with decreasing amounts at colder temperatures. Usually, at temperatures colder than –15° C, sublimation is prevalent; and clouds and fog may be mostly ice crystals with a lesser amount of supercooled water. However, strong vertical currents may carry supercooled water to great heights where temperatures are much colder than –15° C. Supercooled water has been observed at temperatures colder than –40° C.

### Dew and frost

During clear nights with little or no wind, vegetation often cools by radiation to a temperature at or below the dew point of the adjacent air. Moisture than collects on the leaves just as it does on a pitcher of ice water in a warm room. Heavy dew often collects on grass and plants when none collects on pavements or large solid objects. These more massive objects absorb abundant heat during the day, lose it slowly during the night, and cool below the dew point only in rather extreme cases.

Frost forms in much the same way as dew. The difference is that the dew point of surrounding air must be colder than freezing. Water vapor then sublimates directly as ice crystals or frost rather than condensing as dew. Sometimes dew forms and later freezes; however, frozen dew is easily distinguished from frost. Frozen dew is hard and transparent while frost is white and opaque.

To now, little has been said here about clouds. What brings about the condensation or sublimation that results in cloud formation?

## Cloud formation

Normally, air must become saturated for condensation or sublimation to occur. Saturation may result from cooling temperature, increasing dew point, or both. Cooling is far more predominant.

## Cooling processes

Three basic processes may cool air to saturation. They are (1) air moving over a colder surface, (2) stagnant air overlying a cooling surface, and (3) expansional cooling in upward moving air. Expansional cooling is the major cause of cloud formation.

## Clouds and fog

A cloud is a visible aggregate of minute water or ice particles suspended in air. If the cloud is on the ground, it is fog. When entire layers of air cool to saturation, fog or sheet-like clouds result. Saturation of a localized updraft produces a towering cloud. A cloud may be composed entirely of liquid water, of ice crystals, or a mixture of the two.

## Precipitation

Precipitation is an all inclusive term denoting drizzle, rain, snow, ice pellets, hail, and ice crystals. Precipitation occurs when these particles grow in size and weight until the atmosphere no longer can suspend them and they fall. These particles grow primarily in two ways.

## Particle growth

Once a water droplet or ice crystal forms, it continues to grow by added condensation or sublimation directly onto the particle. This is the slower of the two methods and usually results in drizzle or very light rain or snow.

Cloud particles collide and merge into a larger drop in the more rapid growth process. This process produces larger precipitation particles and does so more rapidly than the simple condensation growth process. Upward currents enhance the growth rate and also support larger drops. Precipitation formed by merging drops with mild upward currents can produce light to moderate rain and snow. Strong upward currents support the largest drops and build clouds to great heights. They can produce heavy rain, heavy snow, and hail.

## Liquid, freezing, and frozen

Precipitation forming and remaining liquid falls as rain or drizzle. Sublimation forms snowflakes, and they reach the ground as snow if temperatures remain below freezing.

Precipitation can change its state as the temperature of its environment changes. Falling snow may melt in warmer layers of air at lower altitudes to form rain. Rain falling through colder air may become supercooled, freezing on impact as freezing rain; or it may freeze during its descent, falling as ice pellets. Ice pellets always indicate freezing rain at higher altitude.

Sometimes strong upward currents sustain large supercooled water drops until some freeze; subsequently, other drops freeze to them forming hailstones.

## Precipitation versus cloud thickness

To produce significant precipitation, clouds usually are 4,000 feet thick or more. The heavier the precipitation, the thicker the clouds are likely to be.

## Land and water effects on clouds

Land and water surfaces underlying the atmosphere greatly affect cloud and precipitation development. Large bodies of water such as oceans and large lakes add water vapor to the air.

The greatest frequency of low ceilings, fog, and precipitation can be expected in areas where prevailing winds have an over-water trajectory. The aviator should be especially alert for these hazards when moist winds are blowing upslope.

In winter, cold air frequently moves over relatively warm lakes. The warm water adds heat and water vapor to the air causing showers to the lee of the lakes. In other seasons, the air may be warmer than the lakes. When this occurs, the air may become saturated by evaporation from the water while also becoming cooler in the low levels by contact with the cool water. Fog often becomes extensive and dense to the lee of a lake. Strong cold winds across the Great Lakes often carry precipitation to the Appalachians.

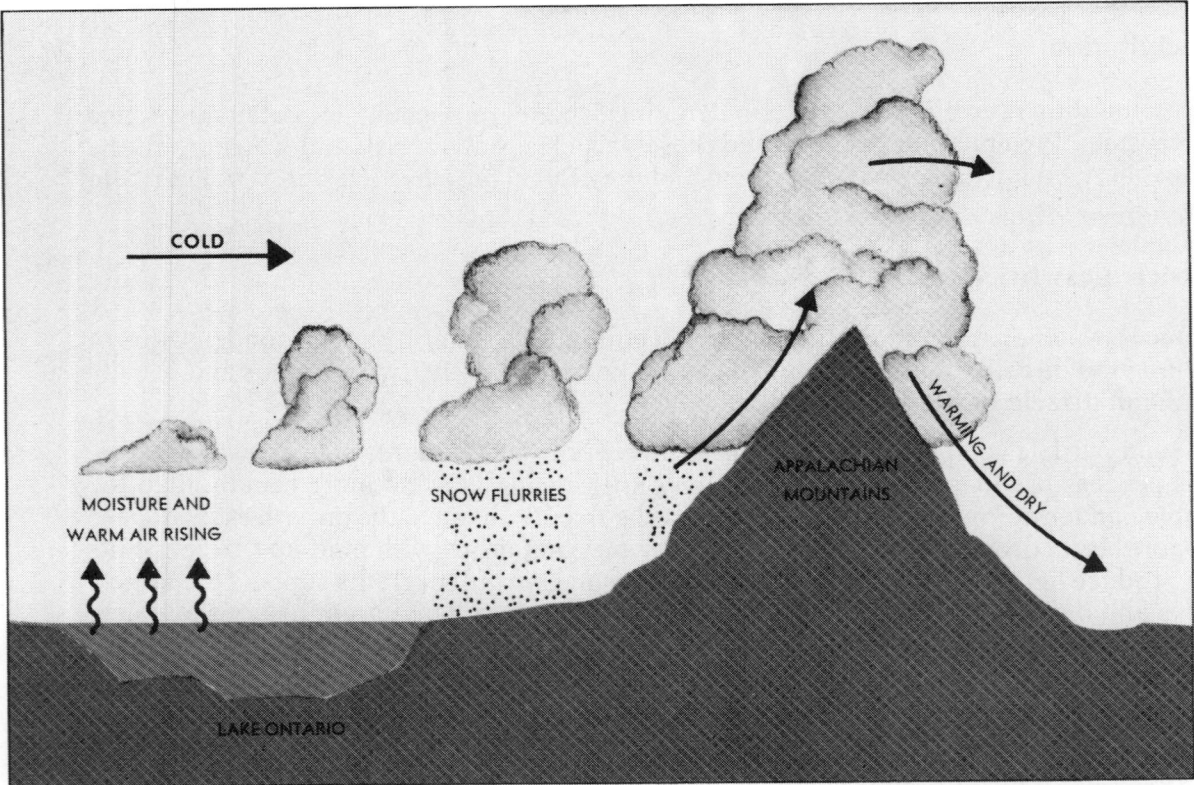

**FIGURE 6.9. Strong cold winds across the Great Lakes absorb water vapor and may carry showers as far eastward as the Appalachians.**

A lake only a few miles across can influence convection and cause a diurnal fluctuation in cloudiness. During the day, cool air over the lake blows toward the land, and convective clouds form over the land. At night, the pattern reverses; clouds tend to form over the lake as cool air from the land flows over the lake creating convective clouds over the water.

Water exists in three states—solid, liquid, and gaseous. Water vapor is an invisible gas. Condensation or sublimation of water vapor creates many common weather extremes. These things may be anticipated:

1. Fog when temperature-dew point spread is 5° F or less and decreasing.

2. Lifting or clearing of low clouds and fog when temperature-dew point spread is increasing.

3. Frost on a clear night when temperature-dew point spread is 5° F or less, is decreasing, and dew point is colder than 32° F.

4. More cloudiness, fog, and precipitation when wind blows from water than when it blows from land.

5. Cloudiness, fog, and precipitation over higher terrain when moist winds are blowing uphill.

6. Showers to the lee of a lake when air is cold and the lake is warm. Expect fog to the lee of the lake when the air is warm and the lake is cold.

7. Clouds to be at least 4,000 feet thick when significant precipitation is reported. The heavier the precipitation, the thicker the clouds are likely to be.

## STABLE AND UNSTABLE AIR

### Changes within upward and downward moving air

Anytime air moves upward, it expands because of decreasing atmospheric pressure. Conversely, downward moving air is compressed by increasing pressure. But as pressure and volume change, temperature also changes.

When air expands, it cools; and when compressed, it warms. These changes are *adiabatic*, meaning that no heat is removed from or added to the air. We frequently use the terms *expansional* or *adiabatic cooling* and *compressional* or *adiabatic heating*. The adiabatic rate of change of temperature is virtually fixed in unsaturated air but varies in saturated air.

### Unsaturated air

*Unsaturated* air moving upward and downward cools and warms at about 3.0° C (5.4° F) per 1,000 feet. This rate is *the "dry adiabatic rate of temperature change" and is independent of the temperature of the mass of air through which the vertical movements occur.* Figure 6.10 illustrates a "Chinook Wind"—an excellent example of dry adiabatic warming.

### Saturated air

Condensation occurs when *saturated* air moves upward. Latent heat released through

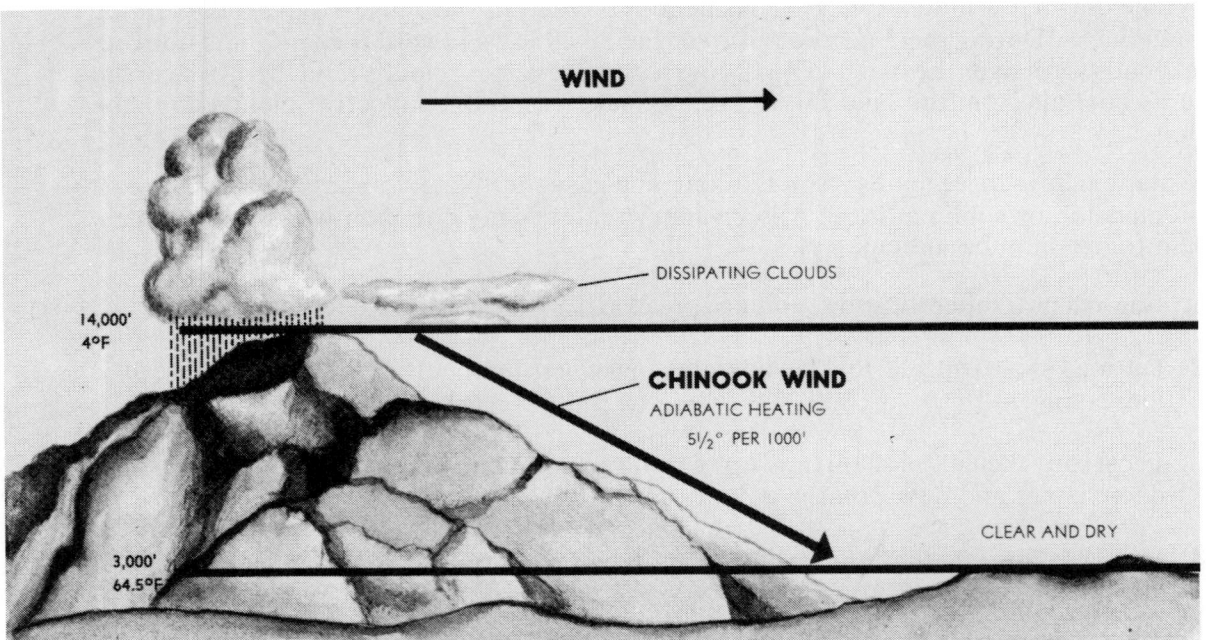

**FIGURE 6.10. Adiabatic warming of downward moving air produces the warm Chinook wind.**

condensation partially offsets the expansional cooling. Therefore, *the saturated adiabatic rate of cooling is slower than the dry adiabatic rate*. The saturated rate depends on saturation temperature or dew point of the air. Condensation of copious moisture in saturated warm air releases more latent heat to offset expansional cooling than does the scant moisture in saturated cold air. Therefore, *the saturated adiabatic rate of cooling is less in warm air than in cold air*.

When saturated air moves downward, it heats at the same rate as it cools on ascent *provided* liquid water evaporates rapidly enough to maintain saturation. Minute water droplets evaporate at virtually this rate. Larger drops evaporate more slowly and complicate the moist adiabatic process in downward moving air.

## Adiabatic cooling and vertical air movement

If a sample of air is forced upward into the atmosphere, two possibilities must be considered:

(1) The air may become colder than the surrounding air, or

(2) Even though it cools, the air may remain warmer than the surrounding air.

If the upward moving air becomes colder than surrounding air, it sinks; but if it remains warmer, it is accelerated upward as a convective current. Whether it sinks or rises depends on the ambient or existing temperature lapse rate.

Do not confuse existing lapse rate with adiabatic rates of cooling in vertically moving air.* The difference between the existing lapse rate of a given mass of air and the adiabatic rates of cooling in upward moving air determines if the air is stable or unstable.

---

\* Sometimes the dry and moist adiabatic rates of cooling will be called the dry adiabatic lapse rate and the moist adiabatic lapse rate. In this text, *lapse rate* refers exclusively to the existing, or actual, decrease of temperature with height in a real atmosphere. The dry or moist adiabatic lapse rate signifies a prescribed rate of expansional cooling or compressional heating. An adiabatic lapse rate becomes real *only* when it becomes a condition brought about by vertically moving air.

# CLOUDS

## Clouds—stable or unstable?

Earlier it was stated that when air is cooling and first becomes saturated, condensation or sublimation begins to form clouds. Further on in this text cloud types are explained along with their significance as "signposts in the sky." Whether the air is stable or unstable within a layer largely determines cloud structure.

**Stratiform Clouds**—Since stable air resists convection, clouds in stable air form in horizontal, sheet-like layers or "strata." Thus, within a *stable* layer, clouds are *stratiform*. Adiabatic cooling may be by upslope flow; by lifting over cold, more dense air; or by converging winds. Cooling by an underlying cold surface is a stabilizing process and may produce fog. If clouds are to remain stratiform, the layer must remain stable after condensation occurs.

**Cumuliform Clouds**—Unstable air favors convection. A "cumulus" cloud, meaning "heap," forms in a convective updraft and builds upward. Thus, within an *unstable* layer, clouds are *cumuliform*; and the vertical extent of the cloud depends on the depth of the unstable layer.

Initial lifting to trigger a cumuliform cloud may be the same as that for lifting stable air. In addition, convection may be set off by surface heating. Air may be unstable or slightly stable before condensation occurs; but for convective cumuliform clouds to develop, it must be unstable after saturation. Cooling in the updraft is now at the slower moist adiabatic rate because of the release of latent heat of condensation. Temperature in the saturated updraft is warmer than ambient temperature, and convection is spontaneous. Updrafts accelerate until temperature within the cloud cools below the ambient temperature. This condition occurs where the unstable layer is capped by a stable layer often marked by a temperature inversion. Vertical heights range from the shallow fair weather cumulus to the giant thunderstorm cumulonimbus—the ultimate in atmospheric instability capped by the tropopause.

When unstable air lies above stable air, convective currents aloft sometimes form middle and high level cumuliform clouds. In relatively shallow layers they occur as altocumulus and ice crystal cirrocumulus clouds. Altocumulus castellanus clouds develop in deeper midlevel unstable layers.

## Identification

For identification purposes, one needs to be concerned only with the more basic cloud types, which are divided into four "families." The families are: high clouds, middle clouds, low clouds, and clouds with extensive vertical development. The first three families are further classified according to the way they are formed. Clouds formed by vertical currents in unstable air are *cumulus* meaning *accumulation* or *heap*; they are characterized by their lumpy, billowy appearance. Clouds formed by the cooling of a stable layer are *stratus* meaning *stratified* or *layered*; they are characterized by their uniform, sheet-like appearance.

In addition to the above, the prefix *nimbo* or the suffix *nimbus* means raincloud. Thus, stratified clouds from which rain is falling are *nimbostratus*. A heavy, swelling cumulus type cloud which produces precipitation is a *cumulonimbus*. Clouds broken into fragments are often identified by adding the suffix *fractus*; for example, fragmentary cumulus is *cumulus fractus*.

## High clouds

The high cloud family is cirriform and includes cirrus, cirrocumulus, and cirrostratus.

They are composed almost entirely of ice crystals. The height of the bases of these clouds ranges from about 16,500 to 45,000 feet in middle latitudes.

### Middle clouds

In the middle cloud family are the altostratus, altocumulus, and nimbostratus clouds. These clouds are primarily water, much of which may be supercooled. The height of the bases of these clouds ranges from about 6,500 to 23,000 feet in middle latitudes.

### Low clouds

In the low cloud family are the stratus, stratocumulus, and fair weather cumulus clouds. Low clouds are almost entirely water, but at times the water may be supercooled. Low clouds at sub-freezing temperatures can also contain snow and ice particles. The bases of these clouds range from near the surface to about 6,500 feet in middle latitudes.

### Clouds with extensive vertical development

The vertically developed family of clouds includes towering cumulus and cumulonimbus. These clouds usually contain supercooled water above the freezing level. But when a cumulus grows to great heights, water in the upper part of the cloud freezes into ice crystals forming a cumulonimbus. The heights of cumuliform cloud bases range from 1,000 feet or less to above 10,000 feet.

## CLOUD RECOGNITION

**LOW-BASE CLOUDS**
**(Continued next page)**

**FIGURE 6.11. CUMULUS. Fair weather cumulus clouds form in convective currents and are characterized by relatively flat bases and dome-shaped tops. Fair weather cumulus do not show extensive vertical development and do not produce precipitation.**

**LOW-BASE
CLOUDS
(Continued)**

FIGURE 6.12. CUMULONIMBUS. Cumulonimbus are the ultimate manifestation of instability. They are vertically developed clouds of large dimensions with dense *boiling* tops when crowned with thick veils of dense cirrus (the anvil).

FIGURE 6.13. STRATUS. Stratus is a gray, uniform, sheet-like cloud with relatively low bases. When associated with fog or precipitation, the combination can become troublesome for visual flying.

FIGURE 6.14. NIMBOSTRATUS. Nimbostratus is a gray or dark massive cloud layer, diffused by more or less continuous rain, snow, or ice pellets.

FIGURE 6.15. STRATOCUMULUS. Stratocumulus bases are globular masses or rolls unlike the flat, sometimes indefinite, bases of stratus. They usually form at the top of a layer mixed by moderate surface winds. Sometimes, they form from the breaking up of stratus or the spreading out of cumulus.

## MIDDLE-BASE CLOUDS

FIGURE 6.16. ALTOSTRATUS. Altostratus is a bluish veil or layer of clouds. It is often associated with altocumulus and sometimes gradually merges into cirrostratus. The sun may be dimly visible through it.

FIGURE 6.17. ALTOCUMULUS. Altocumulus are composed of white or gray colored layers or patches of solid cloud. The cloud elements may have a waved or roll-like appearance.

## HIGH-BASE CLOUDS

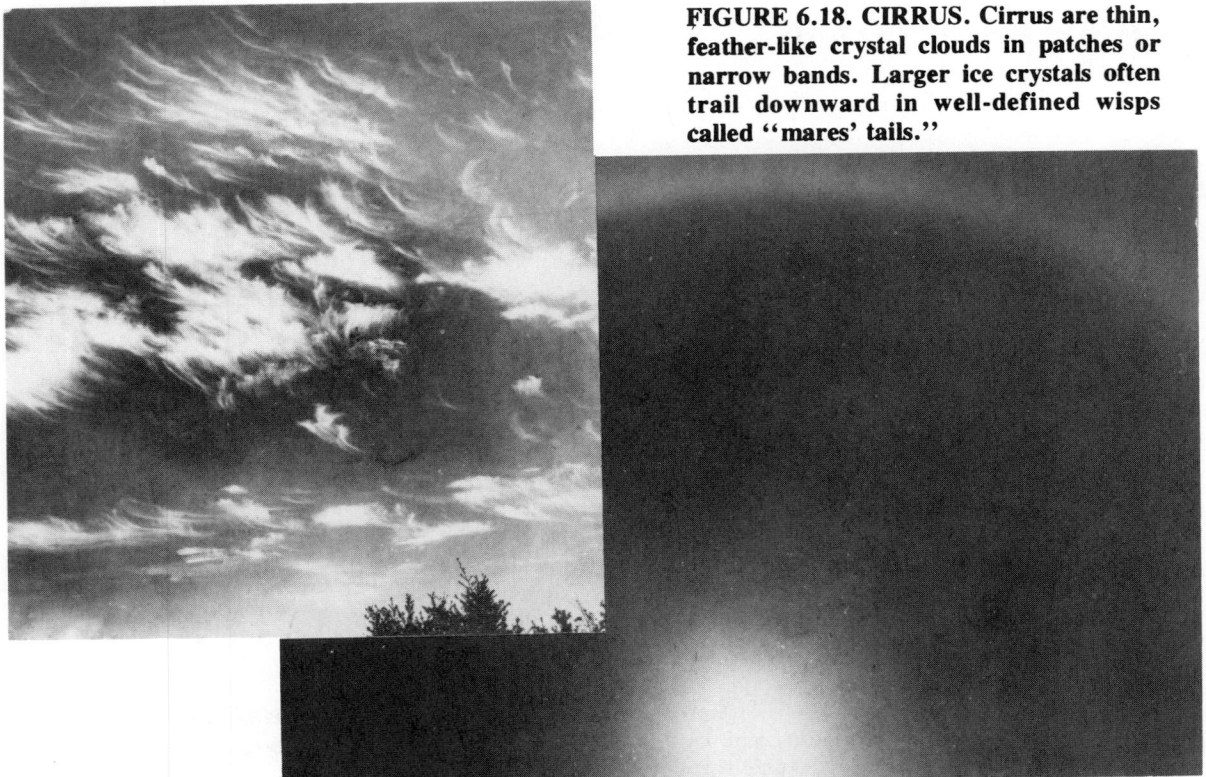

**FIGURE 6.18. CIRRUS.** Cirrus are thin, feather-like crystal clouds in patches or narrow bands. Larger ice crystals often trail downward in well-defined wisps called "mares' tails."

**FIGURE 6.19. CIRROSTRATUS.** Cirrostratus is a thin whitish cloud layer appearing like a sheet or veil. Cloud elements are diffuse, sometimes partially striated or fibrous. Due to their ice crystal makeup, these clouds are associated with halos—large luminous circles surrounding the sun or moon.

**FIGURE 6.20. CIRROCUMULUS.** Cirrocumulus are thin clouds, the individual elements appearing as small white flakes or patches of cotton. May contain highly supercooled water droplets.

# FOG

## Fog

Fog is a surface based cloud composed of either water droplets or ice crystals.

Small temperature-dew point spread is essential for fog to form. Therefore, fog is prevalent in coastal areas where moisture is abundant. However, fog can occur anywhere. Abundant condensation nuclei enhances the formation of fog. Thus, fog is prevalent in industrial areas where by-products of combustion provide a high concentration of these nuclei. Fog occurs most frequently in the colder months, but the season and frequency of occurrence vary from one area to another.

Fog may form (1) by cooling air to its dew point, or (2) by adding moisture to air near the ground. Fog is classified by the way it forms. Formation may involve more than one process.

## Radiation fog

Radiation fog is relatively shallow fog. It may be dense enough to hide the entire sky or may conceal only part of the sky. "Ground fog" is a form of radiation fog.

Conditions favorable for radiation fog are clear sky, little or no wind, and small temperature-dew point spread (high relative humidity). The fog forms almost exclusively at night or near daybreak. Terrestrial radiation cools the ground; in turn, the cool ground cools the air in contact with it. When the air is cooled to its dew point, fog forms. When rain soaks the ground, followed by clearing skies, radiation fog is not uncommon the following morning.

Radiation fog is restricted to land because water surfaces cool little from nighttime radiation. It is shallow when wind is calm. Winds up to about 5 knots mix the air slightly and tend to deepen the fog by spreading the cooling through a deeper layer. Stronger winds disperse the fog or mix the air through a still deeper layer with stratus clouds forming at the top of the mixing layer.

Ground fog usually "burns off" rather rapidly after sunrise. Other radiation fog generally clears before noon unless clouds move in over the fog.

## Advection fog

Advection fog forms when moist air moves over colder ground or water. It is most common along coastal areas but often develops deep in continental areas. At sea it is called "sea fog." Advection fog deepens as wind speed increases up to about 15 knots. Wind much stronger than 15 knots lifts the fog into a layer of low stratus or stratocumulus.

The west coast of the United States is quite vulnerable to advection fog. This fog frequently forms offshore as a result of cold water and then is carried inland by the wind. During the winter, advection fog over the central and eastern United States results when moist air from the Gulf of Mexico spreads northward over cold ground. The fog may extend as far north as the Great Lakes. Water areas in northern latitudes have frequent dense sea fog in summer as a result of warm, moist, tropical air flowing northward over colder Arctic waters.

Advection fog is usually more extensive and much more persistent than radiation fog. Advection fog can move in rapidly regardless of the time of day or night.

### Upslope fog

Upslope fog forms as a result of moist, stable air being cooled adiabatically as it moves up sloping terrain. Once the upslope wind ceases, the fog dissipates. Unlike radiation fog, it can form under cloudy skies. Upslope fog is common along the eastern slopes of the Rockies and somewhat less frequent east of the Appalachians. Upslope fog often is quite dense and extends to high altitudes.

### Precipitation-induced fog

When relatively warm rain or drizzle falls through cool air, evaporation from the precipitation saturates the cool air and forms fog. Precipitation-induced fog can become quite dense and continue for an extended period of time. This fog may extend over large areas, completely suspending air operations. It is most commonly associated with warm fronts, but can occur with slow moving cold fronts and with stationary fronts.

### Ice fog

Ice fog occurs in cold weather when the temperature is much below freezing and water vapor sublimates directly as ice crystals. Conditions favorable for its formation are the same as for radiation fog except for cold temperature, usually −25° F or colder. It occurs mostly in the Arctic regions, but is not unknown in middle latitudes during the cold season.

### Low stratus clouds

Stratus clouds, like fog, are composed of extremely small water droplets or ice crystals suspended in air. An observer on a mountain in a stratus layer would call it fog. Stratus and fog frequently exist together. In many cases there is no real line of distinction between the fog and stratus; rather, one gradually merges into the other. Stratus tends to be lowest during night and early morning, lifting or dissipating due to solar heating during the late morning or afternoon. Low stratus clouds often occur when moist air mixes with a colder air mass or in any situation where temperature-dew point spread is small.

### Haze and smoke

Haze is a concentration of salt particles or other dry particles not readily classified as dust or other phenomenon. It occurs in stable air, is usually only a few thousand feet thick, but sometimes may extend as high as 15,000 feet. Haze layers often have definite tops above which horizontal visibility is good. However, downward visibility from above a haze layer is poor, especially on a slant. Visibility in haze varies greatly depending upon whether the observer is facing the sun.

Smoke concentrations form primarily in industrial areas when air is stable. It is most prevalent at night or early morning under a temperature inversion but it can persist throughout the day.

## AIR MASSES AND FRONTS

### Air masses

When a body of air comes to rest or moves slowly over an extensive area having fairly uniform properties of temperature and moisture, the air takes on those properties. Thus, the air over the area becomes somewhat of an entity and has fairly uniform horizontal distribution of its properties. The area over which the air mass acquires its identifying distribution of moisture and temperature is its "source region."

Source regions are many and varied, but the best source regions for air masses are large snow or ice covered polar regions, cold northern oceans, tropical oceans, and large desert areas. Midlatitudes are poor source regions because transitional disturbances dominate these latitudes giving little opportunity for air masses to stagnate and take on the properties of the underlying region.

### Air mass modification

Just as an air mass took on the properties of its source region, it tends to take on properties of the underlying surface when it moves away from its source region, thus becoming modified.

The degree of modification depends on the speed with which the air mass moves, the nature of the region over which it moves, and the temperature difference between the new surface and the air mass. Some ways air masses are modified are: (1) warming from below, (2) cooling from below, (3) addition of water vapor, and (4) subtraction of water vapor:

1. Cool air moving over a warm surface is heated from below, generating instability and increasing the possibility of showers.

2. Warm air moving over a cool surface is cooled from below, increasing stability. If air is cooled to its dew point, stratus and/or fog forms.

3. Evaporation from water surfaces and falling precipitation adds water vapor to the air. When the water is warmer than the air, evaporation can raise the dew point sufficiently to saturate the air and form stratus or fog.

4. Water vapor is removed by condensation and precipitation.

### Stability

Stability of an air mass determines its typical weather characteristics. When one type of air mass overlies another, conditions change with height. Characteristics typical of an unstable and a stable air mass are as follows:

| *Unstable Air* | *Stable Air* |
|---|---|
| Cumuliform clouds | Stratiform clouds and fog |
| Showery precipitation | Continuous precipitation |
| Rough air (turbulence) | Smooth air |
| Good visibility, except in blowing obstructions | Fair to poor visibility in haze and smoke |

297

### Fronts

As air masses move out of their source regions, they come in contact with other air masses of different properties. The zone between two different air masses is a frontal zone or front. Across this zone, temperature, humidity and wind often change rapidly over short distances.

### Discontinuities

When you pass through a front, the change from the properties of one air mass to those of the other is sometimes quite abrupt. Abrupt changes indicate a narrow frontal zone. At other times, the change of properties is very gradual indicating a broad and diffuse frontal zone.

**Temperature**—Temperature is one of the most easily recognized discontinuities across a front. At the surface, the passage of a front usually causes noticeable temperature change.

**Dew Point**—Dew point temperature is a measure of the amount of water vapor in the air. Temperature—dew point spread is a measure of the degree of saturation. Dew point and temperature—dew point spread usually differ across a front. The difference helps identify the front and may give a clue to differences of cloudiness and/or fog.

**Wind**—Wind always changes across a front. Wind discontinuity may be in direction, in speed, or in both.

**Pressure**—A front lies in a pressure trough, and pressure generally is higher in the cold air. Thus, when a front is crossed directly into colder air, pressure usually rises abruptly. When a front is approached toward warm air, pressure generally falls until the front is crossed, and then remains steady or falls slightly in the warm air. However, pressure patterns vary widely across fronts.

### Types of fronts

The three principal types of fronts are the cold front, the warm front, and the stationary front.

**Cold Front**—The leading edge of an advancing cold air mass is a cold front. At the surface, cold air is overtaking and replacing warmer air. Cold fronts move at about the speed of the wind component perpendicular to the front just above the frictional layer. A shallow cold air mass or a slow moving cold front may have a frontal slope more like a warm front.

**Warm Front**—The edge of an advancing warm air mass is a warm front—warmer air is overtaking and replacing colder air. Since the cold air is denser than the warm air, the cold air hugs the ground. The warm air slides up and over the cold air and lacks direct push on the cold air. Thus, the cold air is slow to retreat in advance of the warm air. This slowness of the cold air to retreat produces a frontal slope that is more gradual than the cold frontal slope. Consequently, warm fronts on the surface are seldom as well marked as cold fronts, and they usually move about half as fast when the general wind flows is the same in each case.

**Stationary Fronts**—When neither air mass is replacing the other, the front is stationary. The opposing forces exerted by adjacent air masses of different densities are such that the frontal surface between them shows little or no movement. In such cases, the surface winds tend to blow parallel to the frontal zone. Slope of a stationary front is normally shallow, although it may be steep depending on wind distribution and density difference.

## Frontal waves and occlusion

Frontal waves and cyclones (areas of low pressure) usually form on slow-moving cold fronts or on stationary fronts. The life cycle and movement of a cyclone is dictated to a great extent by the upper wind flow.

In the initial condition of frontal wave development in figure 6.21, the winds on both sides of the front are blowing parallel to the front (A). Small disturbances then may start a wavelike bend in the front (B).

If this tendency persists and the wave increases in size, a cyclonic (counterclockwise) circulation develops. One section of the front begins to move as a warm front, while the section next to it begins to move as a cold front (C). This deformation is a frontal wave.

The pressure at the peak of the frontal wave falls, and a low-pressure center forms. The cyclonic circulation becomes stronger, and the surface winds are now strong enough to move the fronts; the cold front moves faster than the warm front (D). When the cold front catches up with the warm front, the two of them *occlude* (close together). The result is an *occluded front* or, for brevity, an *occlusion* (E). This is the time of maximum intensity for the wave cyclone. Note that the symbol depicting the occlusion is a combination of the symbols for the warm and cold fronts.

As the occlusion continues to grow in length, the cyclonic circulation diminishes in intensity and the frontal movement slows down (F). Sometimes a new frontal wave begins to form on the long westward-trailing portion of the cold front (F,G), or a secondary low pressure system forms at the apex where the cold front and warm front come together to form the occlusion. In the final stage, the two fronts may have become a single stationary front again. The low center with its remnant of the occlusion is disappearing (G).

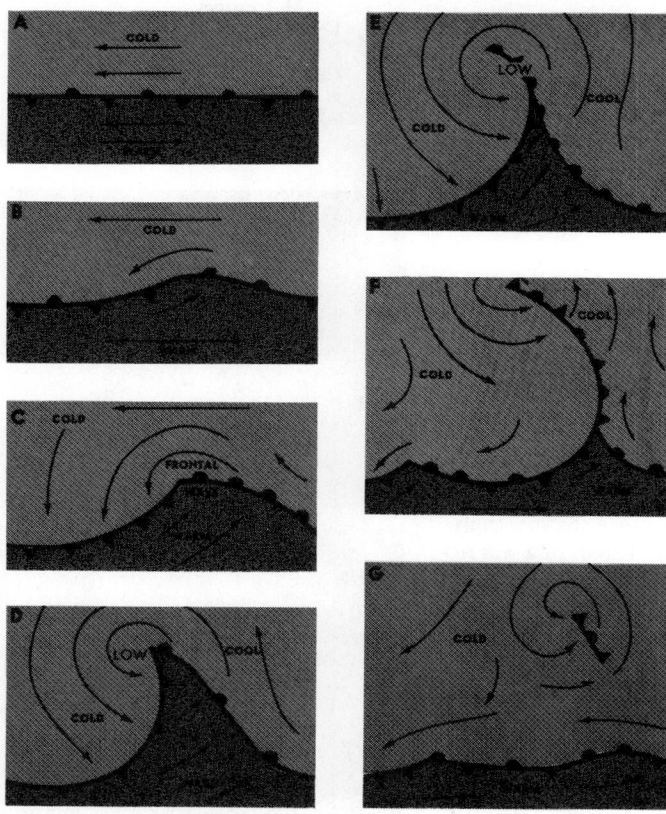

**FIGURE 6.21. The life cycle of a frontal wave.**

Figure 6.25 indicates a warm-front occlusion in vertical cross section. This type of occlusion occurs when the air is colder in advance of the warm front than behind the cold front, lifting the cold front aloft.

## Non-frontal lows

Since fronts are boundaries between air masses of different properties, fronts are not associated with lows lying solely in a homogeneous air mass. Nonfrontal lows are infrequent east of the Rocky Mountains in midlatitudes but do occur occasionally during the warmer months. Small nonfrontal lows over the western mountains are common as is

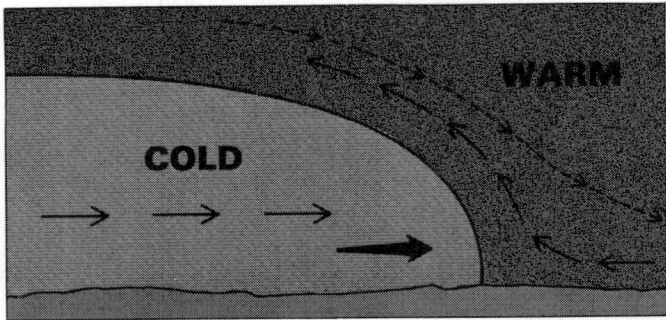

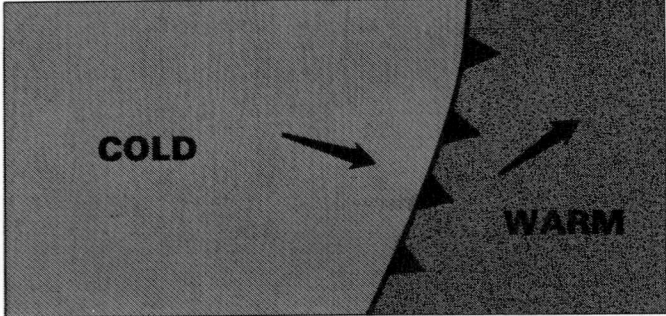

FIGURE 6.22. Cross section of a cold front (above) with the weather map symbol (below). The symbol is a line with pointed barbs pointing in the direction of movement. If a map is in color, a blue lines represents the cold front. The vertical scale is expanded in the top illustration to show the frontal slope. The frontal slope is steep near the leading edge as cold air replaces warm air. The solid heavy arrow shows movement of the front. Warm air may descend over the front as indicated by the dashed arrows; but more commonly, the cold air forces warm air upward over the frontal surface as shown by the solid arrows.

FIGURE 6.23. Cross section of a warm front (top) with the weather map symbol (bottom). The symbol is a line with rounded barbs pointing in the direction of movement. If a map is in color, a red line represents the warm front. Slope of a warm front generally is more shallow than slope of a cold front. Movement of a warm front shown by the heavy black arrow is slower than the wind in the warm air represented by the light solid arrows. The warm air gradually erodes the cold air.

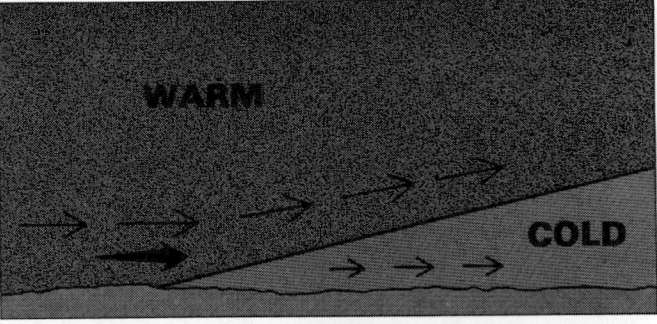

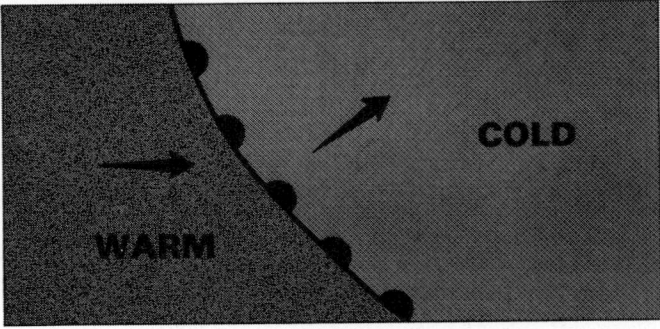

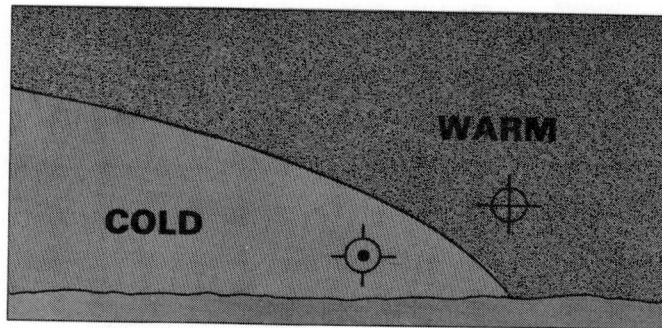

FIGURE 6.24. Cross section of a stationary front (top) and its weather map symbol (bottom). The symbol is a line with alternating pointed and rounded barbs on opposite sides of the line, the pointed barbs pointing away from the cold air and the rounded barbs away from the warm air. If a map is in color, the symbol is a line of alternating red and blue segments. The front has little or no movement and winds are nearly parallel to the front. The symbol in the warm air is the tail of a wind arrow into the page. The symbol in the cold air is the point of a wind arrow out of the page. Slope of the front may vary considerably depending on wind and density differences across the front.

FIGURE 6.25. Cross section of a warm-front occlusion (top) and its weather map symbol (bottom). The symbol is a line with alternating pointed and rounded barbs on the same side of the line pointing in the direction of movement. Shown in color on a weather map, the line is purple. In the warm front occlusion, air under the cold front is not as cold as air ahead of the warm front; and when the cold front overtakes the warm front, the less cold air rides over the colder air. In a warm front occlusion, cool air replaces cold air at the surface.

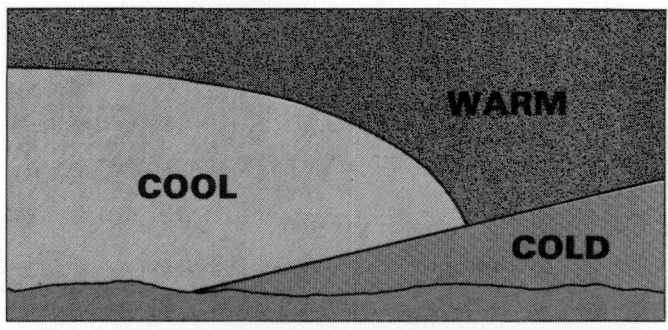

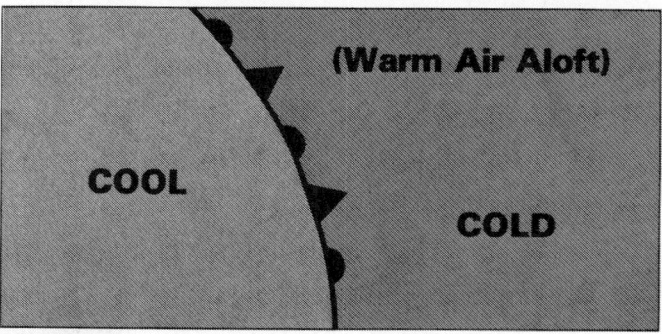

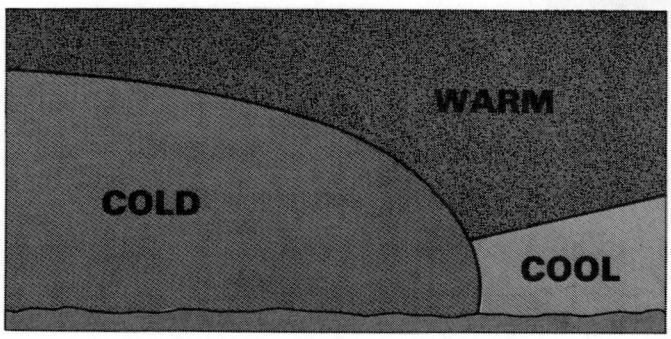

FIGURE 6.26. Cross section of a cold-front occlusion. Its weather map symbol is the same as for a warm-front occlusion shown in Figure 6.25. In the cold-front occlusion, the coldest air is under the cold front. When it overtakes the warm front, it lifts the warm front aloft; and cold air replaces cool air at the surface.

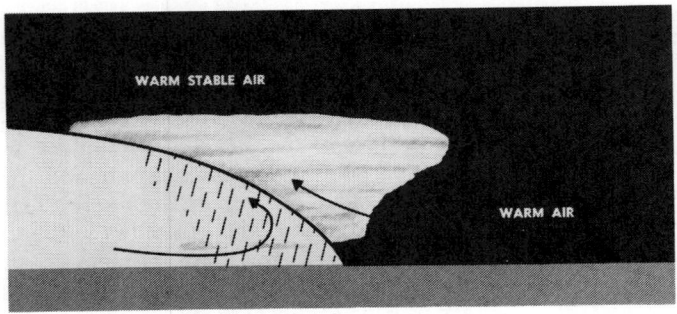

FIGURE 6.27. A cold front underrunning warm, moist, stable air. Clouds are stratified and precipitation continuous. Precipitation induces stratus in the cold air.

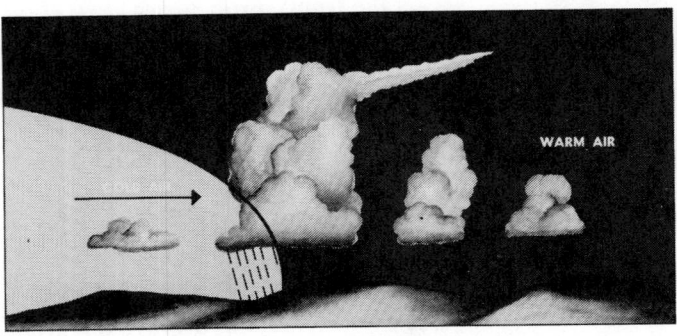

FIGURE 6.28. A cold front underrunning warm, moist, unstable air. Clouds are cumuliform with possible showers or thunderstorms near the surface position of the front. Convective clouds often develop in the warm air ahead of the front. The warm, wet ground behind the front generates low-level convection and fair weather cumulus in the cold air.

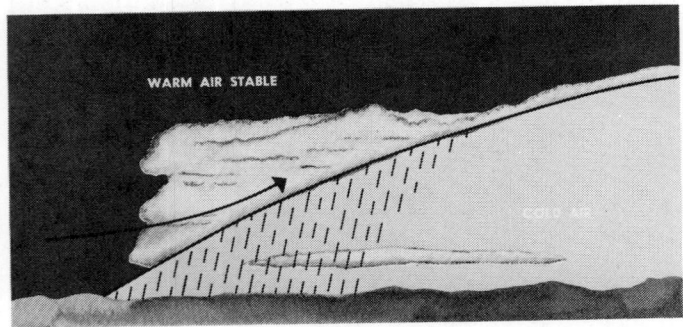

FIGURE 6.29. A warm front with overrunning moist, stable air. Clouds are stratiform and widespread over the shallow front. Precipitation is continuous and induces widespread stratus in the cold air.

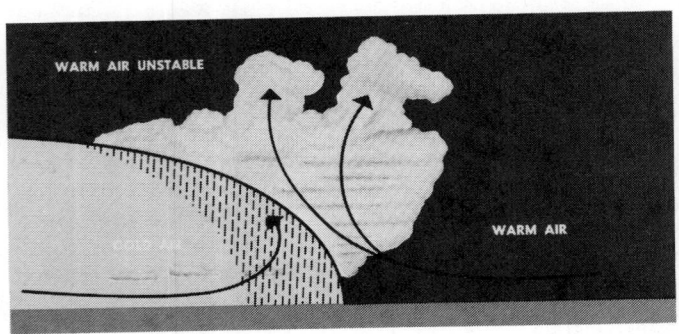

FIGURE 6.30. A slow-moving cold front underrunning warm, moist, unstable air. Note that the front is more shallow than the fast-moving front shown in figure 6.28. Clouds are stratified with embedded cumulonimbus and thunderstorms. This type of frontal weather is especially hazardous since the individual thunderstorms are hidden and cannot be avoided unless the aircraft is equipped with airborne radar.

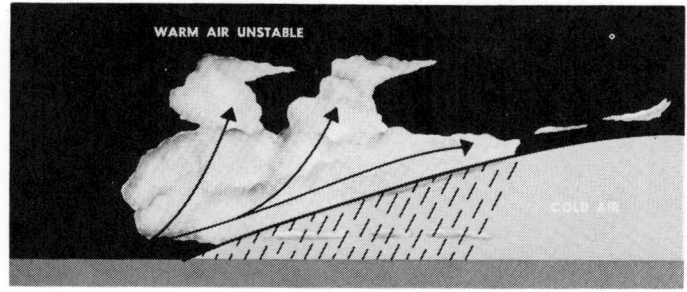

FIGURE 6.31. A warm front with over-running warm, moist, unstable air. Weather, clouds, and hazards are similar to those described in figure 6.30 except that they generally are more widespread.

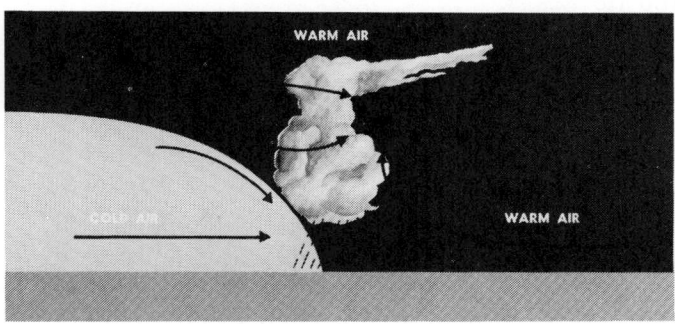

FIGURE 6.32. A fast moving cold front underrunning warm, moist, unstable air. Showers and thunderstorms develop along the surface position of the front.

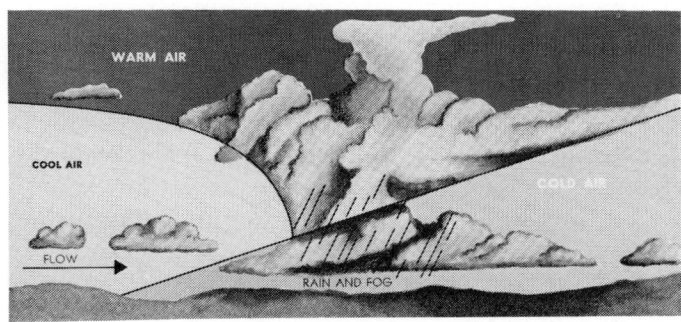

FIGURE 6.33. A warm front occlusion lifting warm, moist, unstable air. Note that the associated weather is complex and encompasses all types of weather associated with both the warm and cold fronts when air is moist and unstable.

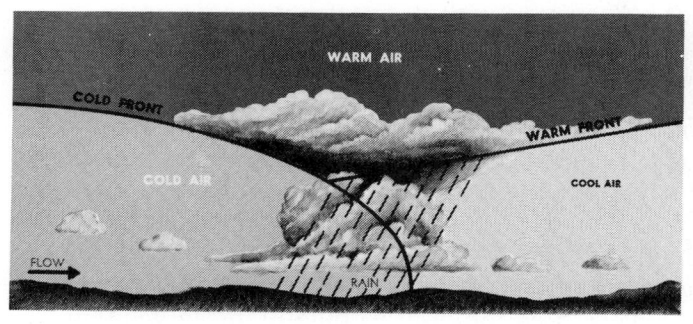

FIGURE 6.34. A cold front occlusion lifting warm, moist, stable air. Associated weather encompasses types of weather associated with both warm and cold fronts when air is moist and stable.

the semistationary thermal low in extreme Southwestern United States. Tropical lows are also nonfrontal.

## Frontolysis and frontogenesis

As adjacent air masses modify and as temperature and pressure differences equalize across a front, the front dissipates. This process is frontolysis, the generation of a front. It occurs when a relatively sharp zone of transition develops over an area between two air masses which have densities gradually becoming more and more in contrast with each other. The necessary wind flow pattern develops at the same time.

## Frontal weather

Weather occuring with a front depends on (1) the amount of moisture available, (2) the degree of stability of the air that is forced upward, (3) the slope of the front, (4) the speed of frontal movement, and (5) the upper wind flow.

Sufficient moisture must be available for clouds to form, or there will be no clouds. As an inactive front comes into an area of moisture, clouds and precipitation may develop rapidly. A good example of this is a cold front moving eastward from the dry slopes of the Rocky Mountains into a tongue of moist air from the Gulf of Mexico over the Plains States. Thunderstorms may build rapidly.

The degree of stability of the lifted air determines whether cloudiness will be predominately stratiform or cumuliform. If the warm air overriding the front is stable, stratiform clouds develop. If the warm air is unstable, cumuliform clouds develop. Precipitation from stratiform clouds is usually steady and there is little or no turbulence. Precipitation from cumuliform clouds is of a shower type and the clouds are turbulent.

Shallow frontal surfaces tend to give extensive cloudiness with large precipitation areas. Widespread precipitation associated with a gradual sloping front often causes low stratus and fog. In this case, the rain raises the humidty of the cold air to saturation. This and related effects may produce low ceiling and poor visibility over thousands of square miles. If temperature of the cold air near the surface is below freezing but the warmer air aloft is above freezing, precipitation falls as freezing rain or ice pellets; however, if temperature of the warmer air aloft is well below freezing, precipitation forms as snow.

When the warm air overriding a shallow front is moist and unstable, the usual widespread cloud mass forms; but embedded in the cloud mass are altocumulus, cumulus, and even thunderstorms. These embedded storms are more common with warm and stationary fronts but may occur with a slow moving, shallow cold front.

A fast moving, steep cold front forces upward motion of the warm air along its leading edge. If the warm air is moist, precipitation occurs immediately along the surface position of the front.

Since an occluded front develops when a cold front overtakes a warm front, weather with an occluded front is a combination of both warm and cold frontal weather.

A front may have little or no cloudiness associated with it. Dry fronts occur when the warm air aloft is flowing down the frontal slope or the air is so dry that any cloudiness that occurs is at high levels.

The upper wind flow dictates to a great extent the amount of cloudiness and rain accompanying a frontal system as well as movement of the front itself. Remember earlier it was said that systems tend to move with the upper winds. When winds aloft blow across a front, it tends to move with the wind. When winds aloft parallel a front, the front moves slowly if at all. A deep, slow moving trough aloft forms extensive cloudiness and precipitation, while a rapid moving minor trough more often restricts weather to a rather narrow band. However, the latter often breeds severe, fast moving, turbulent spring weather.

## Instability line

An instability line is a narrow, nonfrontal line or band of convective activity. If the activity is fully developed thunderstorms, the line is a *squall line*. Instability lines form in moist unstable air. An instability line may develop far from any front. More often, it develops ahead of a cold front, and sometimes a series of these lines move out ahead of the front. A favored location for instability lines which frequently erupt into severe thunderstorms is a dew point front or dry line.

## Dew point front or dry line

During a considerable part of the year, dew point fronts are common in Western Texas and New Mexico northward over the Plains States. Moist air flowing north from the Gulf of Mexico abuts the dryer and therefore slightly denser air flowing from the southwest. Except for moisture differences, there is seldom any significant air mass contrast across this "Front"; and therefore, it is commonly called a "dry line." Nighttime and early morning fog and low-level clouds often prevail on the moist side of the line while generally clear skies mark the dry side. In spring and early summer over Texas, Oklahoma, and Kansas, and for some distance eastward, the dry line is a favored spawning area for squall lines and tornadoes.

## TURBULENCE

### Convective currents

Convective currents are localized vertical air movements, both *ascending* and *descending*. For every rising current, there is a compensating downward current. The downward currents frequently occur over broader areas than do the upward currents, and therefore, they have a slower vertical speed than do the rising currents.

Convective currents are most active on warm summer afternoons when winds are light. Heated air at the surface creates a shallow, unstable layer, and the warm air is forced upward. Convection increases in strength and to greater heights as surface heating increases. Barren surfaces such as sandy or rocky wastelands and plowed fields become hotter than open water or ground covered by vegetation. Thus, air at and near the surface heats unevenly. Because of uneven heating, the strength of convective currents can vary considerably within short distances.

When cold air moves over a warm surface, it becomes unstable in lower levels. Convective currents extend several thousand feet above the surface resulting in rough, choppy turbulence. This condition often occurs in any season after the passage of a cold front.

## THUNDERSTORMS
### (See special text, page 114)

## TORNADOES
### (See special text, page 84)

## HIGH ALTITUDE WEATHER

### The tropopause

Earlier it was noted that the tropopause is a thin layer forming the boundary between the troposphere and stratosphere. Height of the tropopause varies from about 65,000 feet over the Equator to 20,000 feet or lower over the poles. The tropopause is not continuous but generally descends step-wise from the Equator to the poles. These steps occur as "breaks."

An abrupt change in temperature lapse rate characterizes the tropopause.

Maximum winds generally occur at levels near the tropopause. These strong winds create narrow zones of wind shear which often generate hazardous turbulence for aircraft.

## The jet stream

The jet stream is a narrow, shallow, meandering river of maximum winds extending around the globe in a wavelike pattern. A second jet stream is not uncommon, and three at one time are not unknown. A jet may be as far south as the northern Tropics. A jet in midlatitudes generally is stronger than one in or near the Tropics. The jet stream typically occurs in a break in the tropopause. Therefore, a jet stream occurs in an area of intensified temperature gradients characteristic of the break.

The concentrated winds, by arbitrary definition, must be 50 knots or greater to classify as a jet stream. The jet maximum is not constant; rather, it is broken into segments, shaped something like a boomerang.

Jet stream segments move with pressure ridges and troughs in the upper atmosphere. In general they travel faster than pressure systems, and maximum wind speed varies as the segments progress through the systems. In midlatitude, wind speed in the jet stream averages considerably stronger in winter than in summer. Also the jet shifts farther south in winter than in summer.

## Condensation trails

A condensation trail, popularly contracted to "contrail," is generally defined as a cloud-like streamer which frequently is generated in the wake of aircraft flying in clear, cold, humid air. Two distinct types are observed—exhaust trails and aerodynamic trails.

## Exhaust contrails

The exhuast contrail is formed by the addition to the atmosphere of sufficient water vapor from aircraft exhaust gases to cause saturation or super-saturation of the air. Since heat is also added to the atmosphere in the wake of an aircraft, the addition of water vapor must be of such magnitude that it saturates or supersaturates the atmosphere in spite of the added heat. There is evidence to support the idea that the nuclei which are necessary for condensation or sublimation may also be donated to the atmosphere in the exhaust gases of aircraft engines, further aiding contrail formation. These nuclei are relatively large. Recent experiments, however, have revealed that visible exhaust contrails may be prevented by adding very minute nuclei material (dust, for example) to the exhaust. Condensation and sublimation on these smaller nuclei result in contrail particles too small to be visible.

## Aerodynamic contrails

In air that is almost saturated, aerodynamic pressure reduction around airfoils, engine nacelles, and propellers cools the air to saturation leaving condensation trails from these

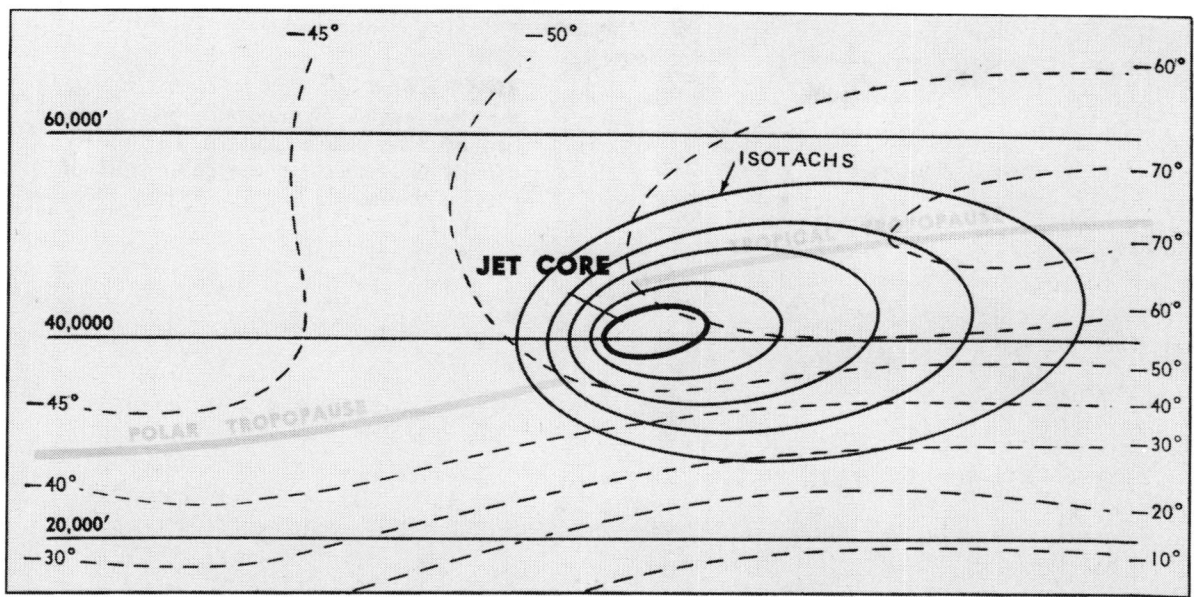

FIGURE 6.35. A cross section of the upper troposphere and lower stratosphere showing the tropopause and associated features. Note the "break" between the high tropical and the lower polar tropopause. Maximum winds occur in the vicinity of this break.

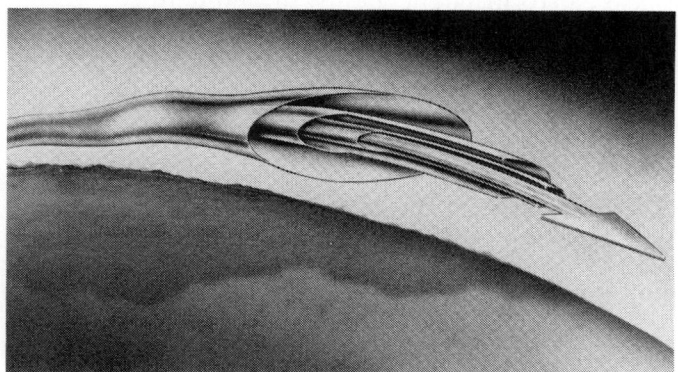

FIGURE 6.36. Artist's concept of the jet stream. Broad arrow shows direction of wind.

FIGURE 6.37. A jet stream segment.

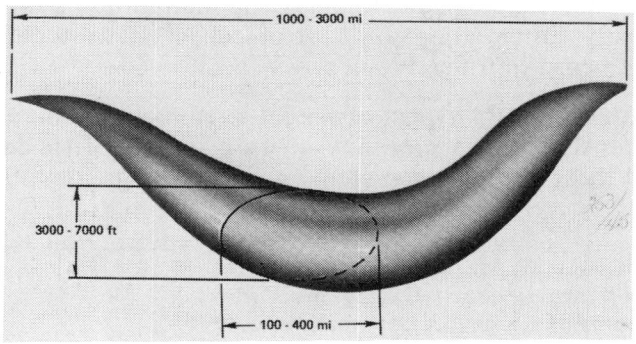

components. This type of trail usually is neither as dense nor as persistent as exhaust trails. However, under critical atmospheric conditions, an aerodynamic contrail may trigger the formation and spreading of a deck of cirrus clouds.

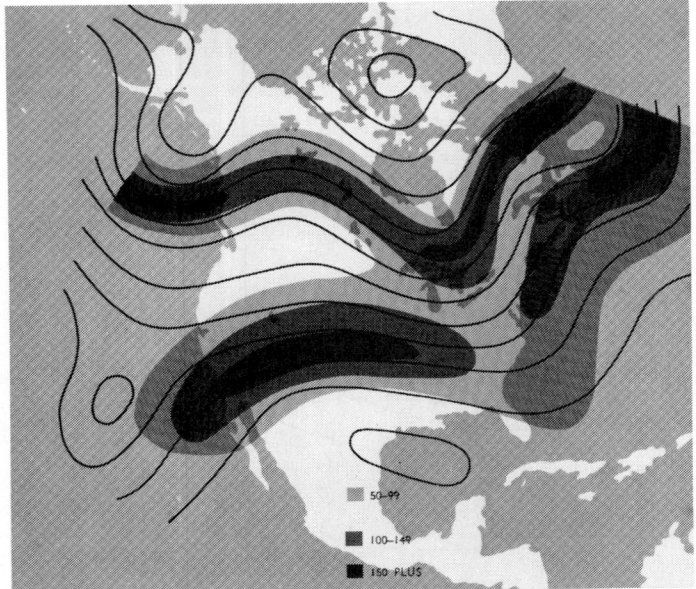

**FIGURE 6.38. Multiple jet streams. Note the ''segments'' of maximum winds embedded in the general pattern. Turbulence usually is greatest on the polar sides of these maxima.**

## Cirrus Clouds

Air travels in a ''corkscrew'' path around the jet core with upward motion on the equatorial side. Therefore, when high level moisture is available, cirriform clouds form on the equatorial side of the jet. Jet stream cloudiness can form independently of well-defined pressure systems. Such cloudiness ranges primarily from scattered to broken coverage in shallow layers or streaks. Their sometimes fish hook and streamlined, wind-swept appearance always indicates very strong upper wind usually quite far from developing or intense weather systems.

The most dense cirriform clouds occur with well-defined systems. They appear in broad bands. Cloudiness is rather dense in an upper trough, thickens downstream, and becomes most dense at the crest of the downwind ridge. The clouds taper off after passing the ridge crest into the area of descending air. The poleward boundary of the cirrus band often is quite abrupt and frequently casts a shadow on lower clouds, especially in an occluded frontal system.

The upper limit of dense, banded cirrus is near the tropopause; a band may be either a single layer of multiple layers 10,000 to 12,000 feet thick. Dense, jet stream cirriform cloudiness is most prevalent along midlatitude and polar jets. However, a cirrus band usually forms along the subtropical jet in winter when a deep upper trough plunges southward into the Tropics.

An important aspect of the jet stream cirrus shield is its association with turbulence. Extensive cirrus cloudiness often occurs with deepening surface and upper lows and these deepening systems produce the greatest turbulence.

**FIGURE 6.39. Mean jet positions relative to surface systems. Cyclogenesis (development) of a surface low usually is south of the jet as shown on the left. The deepening low moves nearer the jet, center. As it occludes, the low moves north of the jet, right; the jet crosses the frontal system near the point of occlusion.**

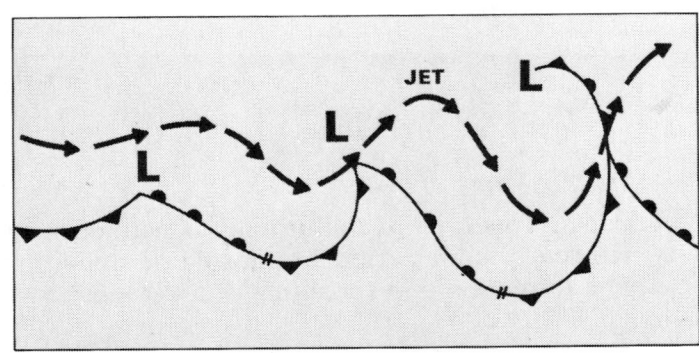

# GLOSSARY OF WEATHER TERMS

## A

**absolute instability**—A state of a layer within the atmosphere in which the vertical distribution of temperature is such that an air parcel, if given an upward or downward push, will move away from its initial level without further outside force being applied.

**absolute temperature scale**—*See* Kelvin Temperature Scale.

**absolute vorticity**—*See* vorticity.

**adiabatic process**—The process by which fixed relationships are maintained during changes in temperature, volume, and pressure in a body of air without heat being added or removed from the body.

**advection**—The horizontal transport of air or atmospheric properties. In meteorology, sometimes referred to as the horizontal component of *convection*.

**advection fog**—Fog resulting from the transport of warm, humid air over a cold surface.

**air density**—The mass density of the air in terms of weight per unit volume.

**air mass**—In meteorology, an extensive body of air within which the conditions of temperature and moisture in a horizontal plane are essentially uniform.

**air mass classification**—A system used to identify and to characterize the different *air masses* according to a basic scheme. The system most commonly used classifies air masses primarily according to the thermal properties of their *source regions*: "tropical" (T); "polar" (P); and "Arctic" or "Antarctic" (A). They are further classified according to moisture characteristics as "continental" (c) or "maritime" (m).

**air parcel**—*See* parcel.

**albedo**—The ratio of the amount of electromagnetic *radiation* reflected by a body to the amount incident upon it, commonly expressed in percentage; in meteorology, usually used in reference to *insolation* (solar radiation); i.e., the albedo of wet sand is 9, meaning that about 9% of the incident insolation is reflected; albedoes of other surfaces range upward to 80–85 for fresh snow cover; average albedo for the earth and its atmosphere has been calculated to range from 35 to 43.

**altimeter**—An instrument which determines the altitude of an object with respect to a fixed level. *See* pressure altimeter.

**altimeter setting**—The value to which the scale of a *pressure altimeter* is set so as to read true altitude at field elevation.

**altimeter setting indicator**—A precision *aneroid barometer* calibrated to indicate directly the altimeter setting.

**altitude**—Height expressed in units of distance above a reference plane, usually above mean sea level or above ground.

**altocumulus**—White or gray layers or patches of cloud, often with a waved appearance; cloud elements appear as rounded masses or rolls; composed mostly of liquid water droplets which may be supercooled; may contain ice crystals at subfreezing temperatures.

**altocumulus castellanus**—A species of middle cloud of which at least a fraction of its upper part presents some vertically developed, cumuliform protuberances (some of which are taller than they are wide, as castles) and which give the cloud a crenelated or turreted appearance; especially evident when seen from the side; elements usually have a common base arranged in lines. This cloud indicates instability and turbulence at the altitudes of occurrence.

**anemometer**—An instrument for measuring *wind speed*.

**aneroid barometer**—A *barometer* which operates on the principle of having changing atmospheric pressure bend a metallic surface which, in turn, moves a pointer across a scale graduated in units of pressure.

**anticyclone**—An area of high atmospheric pressure which has a closed circulation that is anticyclonic, i.e., as viewed from above, the circulation is clockwise in the Northern Hemisphere, counterclockwise in the Southern Hemisphere, undefined at the Equator.

**anvil cloud**—Popular name given to the top portion of a *cumulonimbus* cloud having an anvil-like form.

**Arctic air**—An air mass with characteristics developed mostly in winter over Arctic surfaces of ice and snow. Arctic air extends to great heights, and the surface temperatures are basically, but not always, lower than those of *polar air*.

**Arctic front**—The surface of discontinuity between very cold (Arctic) air flowing directly from the Arctic region and another less cold and, consequently, less dense air mass.

**astronomical twilight**—*See* twilight.

**atmosphere**—The mass of air surrounding the Earth.

**atmospheric pressure (also called barometric pressure)**—The pressure exerted by the atmosphere as a consequence of gravitational attraction exerted upon the "column" of air lying directly above the point in question.

**atmospherics**—Disturbing effects produced in radio receiving apparatus by atmospheric electrical phenomena such as an electrical storm. Static.

**aurora**—A luminous, radiant emission over middle and high latitudes confined to the thin air of high altitudes and centered over the earth's magnetic poles. Called "aurora borealis" (northern lights) or "aurora australis" according to its occurrence in the Northern or Southern Hemisphere, respectively.

## B

**backing**—Shifting of the wind in a counterclockwise direction with respect to either space or time; opposite of *veering*. Commonly used by meteorologists to refer to a cyclonic shift (counterclockwise in the Northern Hemisphere and clockwise in the Southern Hemisphere).

**backscatter**—Pertaining to radar, the energy reflected or scattered by a *target*; an *echo*.

**banner cloud (also called cloud banner)**—A banner-like cloud streaming off from a mountain peak.

**barograph**—A continuous-recording *barometer*.

**barometer**—An instrument for measuring the pressure of the atmosphere; the two principle types are *mercurial* and *aneroid*.

**barometric altimeter**—*See* pressure altimeter.

**barometric pressure**—Same as *atmospheric pressure*.

**barometric tendency**—The change of barometric pressure within a specified period of time. In aviation weather observations, routinely determined periodically, usually for a 3-hour period.

**Beaufort scale**—A scale of wind speeds.

**black blizzard**—Same as *duststorm*.

**blizzard**—A severe weather condition characterized by low temperatures and strong winds bearing a great amount of snow, either falling or picked up from the ground.

**blowing dust**—A type of *lithometeor* composed of dust particles picked up locally from the surface and blown about in clouds or sheets.

**blowing sand**—A type of *lithometeor* composed of sand picked up locally from the surface and blown about in clouds or sheets.

**blowing snow**—A type of *hydrometeor* composed of snow picked up from the surface by the wind and carried to a height of 6 feet or more.

**blowing spray**—A type of *hydrometeor* composed of water particles picked up by the wind from the surface of a large body of water.

**Buys Ballot's law**—If an observer in the Northern Hemisphere stands with his back to the wind, lower pressure is to his left.

## C

**calm**—The absence of wind or of apparent motion of the air.

**cap cloud (also called cloud cap)**—A standing or stationary cap-like cloud crowning a mountain summit.

**ceiling**—In meteorology in the U.S., (1) the height above the surface of the base of the lowest layer of clouds or *obscuring phenomena* aloft that hides more than half of the sky, or (2) the *vertical visibility* into an *obscuration*. *See* summation principle.

**Celsius temperature scale (abbreviated C)**—A temperature scale with zero degrees as the melting point of pure ice and 100 degrees as the boiling point of pure water at standard sea level atmospheric pressure.

**Centigrade temperature scale**—Same as *Celsius temperature scale*.

**change of state**—In meteorology, the transformation of water from one form, i.e., solid (ice), liquid, or gaseous (water vapor), to any other form. There are six possible transformations designated by the five terms following:

(1) **condensation**—The change of water vapor to liquid water.

(2) **evaporation**—The change of liquid water to water vapor.

(3) **freezing**—The change of liquid water to ice.

(4) **melting**—The change of ice to liquid water.

(5) **sublimation**—The change of (a) ice to water vapor or (b) water vapor to ice. *See* latent heat.

**Chinook**—A warm, dry *foehn* wind blowing down the eastern slopes of the Rocky Mountains over the adjacent plains in the U.S. and Canada.

**cirriform**—All species and varieties of *cirrus*, *cirrocumulus*, and *cirrostratus* clouds; descriptive of clouds composed mostly or entirely of small ice crystals, usually transparent and white; often producing *halo* phenomena not observed with other cloud forms. Average height ranges upward from 20,000 feet in middle latitudes.

**cirrocumulus**—A *cirriform* cloud appearing as a thin sheet of small white puffs resembling flakes or patches of cotton without shadows; sometimes confused with *altocumulus*.

**cirrostratus**—A *cirriform* cloud appearing as a whitish veil, usually fibrous, sometimes smooth; often produces *halo* phenomena; may totally cover the sky.

**cirrus**—A *cirriform* cloud in the form of thin, white feather-like clouds in patches or narrow bands; have a fibrous and/or silky sheen; large ice crystals often trail downward a considerable vertical distance in fibrous, slanted, or irregularly curved wisps called mares' tails.

**civil twilight**—*See* twilight.

**climate**—The statistical collective of the weather conditions of a point or area during a specified interval of time (usually several decades); may be expressed in a variety of ways.

**climatology**—The study of *climate*.

**clinometer**—An instrument used in weather observing for measuring angles of inclination; it is used in conjunction with a *ceiling light* to determine cloud height at night.

**cloudburst**—In popular teminology, any sudden and heavy fall of *rain*, almost always of the *shower* type.

**cloud cap**—*See* cap cloud.

**cold front**—Any non-occluded *front* which moves in such a way that colder air replaces warmer air.

**condensation**—*See* change of state.

**condensation level**—The height at which a rising *parcel* or layer of air would become saturated if lifted adiabatically.

**condensation nuclei**—Small particles in the air on which water vapor condenses or sublimates.

**condensation trail (or contrail) (also called vapor trail)**—A cloud-like streamer frequently observed to form behind aircraft flying in clear, cold, humid air.

**conditionally unstable air**—Unsaturated air that will become unstable on the condition it becomes saturated. *See* instability.

**conduction**—The transfer of heat by molecular action through a substance or from one substance in contact with another; transfer is always from warmer to colder temperature.

**constant pressure chart**—A chart of a constant pressure surface; may contain analyses of height, wind, temperature, humidity, and/or other elements.

**continental polar air**—*See* polar air.

**continental tropical air**—*See* tropical air.

**contour**—In meteorology, (1) a line of equal height on a constant pressure chart; analogous to contours on a relief map; (2) in radar meteorology, a line on a radar scope of equal *echo* intensity.

**contouring circuit**—On weather radar, a circuit which displays multiple contours of *echo* intensity simultaneously on the *plan position indicator* or *range-height indicator* scope. *See* contour (2).

**contrail**—Contraction for *condensation trail*.

**convection**—(1) In general, mass motions within a fluid resulting in transport and mixing of the properties of that fluid. (2) In meteorology, atmospheric motions that are predominantly vertical, resulting in vertical transport and mixing of atmospheric properties; distinguished from *advection*.

**convective cloud**—*See* cumuliform.

**convective condensation level (abbreviated CCL)**—The lowest level at which condensation will occur as a result of *convection* due to surface heating. When condensation occurs at this level, the layer between the surface and the CCL will be thoroughly mixed, temperature *lapse rate* will be dry adiabatic, and *mixing ratio* will be constant.

**convective instability**—The state of an unsaturated layer of air whose *lapse rates* of temperature and moisture are such that when lifted adiabatically until the layer becomes saturated, convection is spontaneous.

**convergence**—The condition that exists when the distribution of winds within a given area is such that there is a net horizontal inflow of air into the area. In convergence at lower levels, the removal of the resulting excess is accomplished by an upward movement of air; consequently, areas of low-level convergent winds are regions favorable to the occurrence of clouds and precipitation. Compare with *divergence*.

**Coriolis force**—A deflective force resulting from earth's rotation; it acts to the right of wind direction in the Northern Hemisphere and to the left in the Southern Hemisphere.

**corona**—A prismatically colored circle or arcs of a circle with the sun or moon at its center; coloration is from blue inside to red outside (opposite that of a *halo*); varies in size (much smaller) as opposed to the fixed diameter of the halo; characteristic of clouds composed of water droplets and valuable in differentiating between middle and cirriform clouds.

**corposant**—*See* St. Elmo's Fire.

**corrected altitude (approximation of true altitude)**—*See* altitude.

**cumuliform**—A term descriptive of all convective clouds exhibiting vertical development in contrast to the horizontally extended *stratiform* types.

**cumulonimbus**—A cumuliform cloud type; it is heavy and dense, with considerable vertical extent in the form of massive towers; often with tops in the shape of an *anvil* or massive plume; under the base of cumulonimbus, which often is very dark, there frequently exists *virga*, precipitation and low ragged clouds (*scud*), either merged with it or not; frequently accompanied by lightning, thunder, and sometimes hail; occasionally produces a tornado or a waterspout; the ultimate manifestation of the growth of a cumulus cloud, occasionally extending well into the stratosphere.

**cumulonimbus mamma**—A *cumulonimbus* cloud having hanging protuberances, like pouches, festoons, or udders, on the under side of the cloud; usually indicative of severe turbulence.

**cumulus**—A cloud in the form of individual detached domes or towers which are usually dense and well defined; develops vertically in the form of rising mounds of which the bulging upper part often resembles a cauliflower; the sunlit parts of these clouds are mostly brilliant white; their bases are relatively dark and nearly horizontal.

**cumulus fractus**—*See* fractus.

**cyclogenesis**—Any development or strengthening of cyclonic circulation in the atmosphere.

**cyclone**—(1) An area of low atmospheric pressure which has a closed circulation that is cyclonic, i.e., as viewed from above, the circulation is counterclockwise in the Northern Hemisphere, clockwise in the Southern Hemisphere, undefined at the Equator. Because cyclonic circulation and relatively low atmospheric pressure usually coexist, in common practice the terms cyclone and low are used interchangeably. Also, because cyclones often are accompanied by inclement (sometimes destructive) weather, they are frequently referred to simply as storms. (2) Frequently misused to denote a *tornado*. (3) In the Indian Ocean, a *tropical cyclone* of hurricane or typhoon force.

# D

**deepening**—A decrease in the central pressure of a pressure system; usually applied to a *low* rather than to a *high*, although technically, it is acceptable in either sense.

**density**—(1) The ratio of the mass of any substance to the volume it occupies—weight per unit volume. (2) The ratio of any quantity to the volume or area it occupies, i.e., population per unit area, *power density*.

**density altitude**—*See* altitude.

**depression**—In meteorology, an area of low pressure; a *low* or *trough*. This is usually applied to a certain stage in the development of a *tropical cyclone*, to migratory lows and troughs, and to upper-level lows and troughs that are only weakly developed.

**dew**—Water condensed onto grass and other objects near the ground, the temperatures of which have fallen below the initial dew point temperature of the surface air, but is still above freezing. Compare with *frost*.

**dew point (or dew-point temperature)**—The temperature to which a sample of air must be cooled, while the *mixing ratio* and barometric pressure remain constant, in order to attain saturation with respect to water.

**discontinuity**—A zone with comparatively rapid transition of one or more meteorological elements.

**disturbance**—In meteorology, applied rather loosely: (1) any low pressure or cyclone, but usually one that is relatively small in size; (2) an area where weather, wind, pressure, etc., show signs of cyclonic development; (3) any deviation in flow or pressure that is associated with a disturbed state of the weather, i.e., cloudiness and precipitation; and (4) any individual circulatory system within the primary circulation of the atmosphere.

**diurnal**—Daily, especially pertaining to a cycle completed within a 24-hour period, and which recurs every 24 hours.

**divergence**—The condition that exists when the distribution of winds within a given area is such that there is a net horizontal flow of air outward from the region. In divergence at lower levels, the resulting deficit is compensated for by subsidence of air from aloft; consequently the air is heated and the relative humidity lowered making divergence a warming and drying process. Low-level divergent regions are areas unfavorable to the occurrence of clouds and precipitation. The opposite of *convergence*.

# GLOSSARY

**doldrums**—The equatorial belt of calm or light and variable winds between the two tradewind belts. Compare *intertropical convergence zone*.

**downdraft**—A relative small scale downward current of air; often observed on the lee side of large objects restricting the smooth flow of the air or in precipitation areas in or near *cumuliform* clouds.

**drifting snow**—A type of *hydrometeor* composed of snow particles picked up from the surface, but carried to a height of less than 6 feet.

**drizzle**—A form of *precipitation*. Very small water drops that appear to float with the air currents while falling in an irregular path (unlike *rain*, which falls in a comparatively straight path, and unlike *fog* droplets which remain suspended in the air).

**dropsonde**—A *radiosonde* dropped by parachute from an aircraft to obtain *soundings* (measurements) of the atmosphere below.

**dry adiabatic lapse rate**—The rate of decrease of temperature with height when unsaturated air is lifted adiabatically (due to expansion as it is lifted to lower pressure). *See* adiabatic process.

**dry bulb**—A name given to an ordinary thermometer used to determine temperature of the air; also used as a contraction for *dry-bulb temperature*. Compare *wet bulb*.

**dry-bulb temperature**—The temperature of the air.

**dust**—A type of *lithometeor* composed of small earthen particles suspended in the atmosphere.

**dust devil**—A small, vigorous *whirlwind*, usually of short duration, rendered visible by dust, sand, and debris picked up from the ground.

**duster**—Same as *duststorm*.

**duststorm (also called duster, black blizzard)**—An unusual, frequently severe weather condition characterized by strong winds and dust-filled air over an extensive area.

**D-value**—Departure of true altitude from pressure altitude (*see* altitude); obtained by algebraically subtracting true altitude from pressure altitude; thus it may be plus or minus. On a constant pressure chart, the difference between actual height and *standard atmospheric* height of a constant pressure surface.

## E

**eddy**—A local irregularity of wind in a larger scale wind flow. Small scale eddies produce turbulent conditions.

**estimated ceiling**—A ceiling classification applied when the ceiling height has been estimated by the observer or has been determined by some other method; but, because of the specified limits of time, distance, or precipitation conditions, a more descriptive classification cannot be applied.

**evaporation**—*See* change of state.

**extratropical low (sometimes called extratropical cyclone, extratropical storm)**—Any *cyclone* that is not a *tropical cyclone*, usually referring to the migratory frontal cyclones of middle and high latitudes.

**eye**—The roughly circular area of calm or relatively light winds and comparatively fair weather at the center of a well-developed *tropical cyclone*. A *wall cloud* marks the outer boundary of the eye.

## F

**Fahrenheit temperature scale (abbreviated F)**—A temperature scale with 32 degrees as the melting point of pure ice and 212 degrees as the boiling point of pure water at standard sea level atmospheric pressure (29.92 inches or 1013.2 millibars).

**Fall wind**—A cold wind blowing downslope. Fall wind differs from *foehn* in that the air is initially cold enough to remain relatively cold despite compressional heating during descent.

**filling**—An increase in the central pressure of a pressure system; opposite of *deepening;* more commonly applied to a low rather than a high.

**first gust**—The leading edge of the spreading downdraft, *plow wind*, from an approaching thunderstorm.

**flow line**—A *streamline*.

**foehn**—A warm, dry downslope wind; the warmness and dryness being due to adiabatic compression upon descent; characteristic of mountainous regions. *See* adiabatic process, Chinook, Santa Ana.

**fog**—A *hydrometeor* consisting of numerous minute water droplets and based at the surface; droplets are small enough to be suspended in the earth's atmosphere indefinitely. (Unlike *drizzle*, it does not fall to the surface; differs from cloud only in that a cloud is not based at the surface; distinguished from haze by its wetness and gray color.)

**fractus**—Clouds in the form of irregular shreds, appearing as if torn; have a clearly ragged appearance; applies only to stratus and cumulus, i.e., *cumulus* fractus and *stratus* fractus.

**freezing**—*See* change of state.

**freezing level**—A level in the atmosphere at which the temperature is 0° C (32° F).

**front**—A surface, interface, or transition zone of discontinuity between two adjacent *air masses* of different densities; more simply the boundary between two different air masses. *See* frontal zone.

**frontal zone**—A *front* or zone with a marked increase of density gradient; used to denote that fronts are not truly a "surface" of discontinuity but rather a "zone" of rapid transition of meteorological elements.

**frontogenesis**—The initial formation of a *front* or *frontal zone*.

**frontolysis**—The dissipation of a *front*.

**frost (also hoarfrost)**—Ice crystal deposits formed by sublimation when temperature and dew point are below freezing.

**funnel cloud**—A *tornado* cloud or *vortex* cloud extending downward from the parent cloud but not reaching the ground.

## G

**glaze**—A coating of ice, generally clear and smooth, formed by freezing of supercooled water on a surface.

**gradient**—In meteorology, a horizontal decrease in value per unit distance of a parameter in the direction of maximum decrease; most commonly used with pressure, temperature, and moisture.

**ground fog**—In the United States, a *fog* that conceals less than 0.6 of the sky and is not contiguous with the base of clouds.

**gust**—A sudden brief increase in wind; according to U.S. weather observing practice, gusts are reported when the variation in wind speed between peaks and lulls is at least 10 knots.

## H

**hail**—A form of *precipitation* composed of balls or irregular lumps of ice, always produced by convective clouds which are nearly always *cumulonimbus.*

**halo**—A prismatically colored or whitish circle or arcs of a circle with the sun or moon at its center; coloration, if not white, is from red inside to blue outside (opposite that of a *corona*); fixed in size with an angular diameter of 22° (common) or 46° (rare); characteristic of clouds composed of ice crystals; valuable in differentiating between *cirriform* and forms of lower clouds.

**haze**—A type of *lithometeor* composed of fine dust or salt particles dispersed through a portion of the atmosphere; particles are so small they cannot be felt or individually seen with the naked eye (as compared with the larger particles of *dust*), but diminish the visibility; distinguished from *fog* by its bluish or yellowish tinge.

**high**—An area of high barometric pressure, with its attendant system of winds; an *anticyclone.* Also high pressure system.

**hoar frost**—*See* frost.

**humidity**—Water vapor content of the air; may be expressed as *specific humidity, relative humidity,* or *mixing ratio.*

**hurricane**—A *tropical cyclone* in the Western Hemisphere with winds in excess of 65 knots or 120 km/h.

**hydrometeor**—A general term for particles of liquid water or ice such as rain, fog, frost, etc., formed by modification of water vapor in the atmosphere; also water or ice particles lifted from the earth by the wind such as sea spray or blowing snow.

**hygrograph**—The record produced by a continuous-recording *hygrometer.*

**hygrometer**—An instrument for measuring the water vapor content of the air.

## I

**ice crystals**—A type of *precipitation* composed of unbranched crystals in the form of needles, columns, or plates; usually having a very slight downward motion, may fall from a cloudless sky.

**ice fog**—A type of fog composed of minute suspended particles of ice; occurs at very low temperatures and may cause *halo* phenomena.

**ice needles**—A form of *ice crystals.*

**ice pellets**—Small, transparent or translucent, round or irregularly shaped pellets of ice. They may be (1) hard grains that rebound on striking a hard surface or (2) pellets of snow encased in ice.

**indefinite ceiling**—A ceiling classification denoting *vertical visibility* into a surface based obscuration.

**indicated altitude**—*See* altitude.

**insolation**—Incoming solar *radiation* falling upon the earth and its atmosphere.

**instability**—A general term to indicate various states of the atmosphere in which spontaneous *convection* will occur when prescribed criteria are met; indicative of turbulence. *See* absolute instability, conditionally unstable air, convective instability.

**intertropical convergence zone**—The boundary zone between the trade wind system of the Northern and Southern Hemispheres; it is characterized in maritime climates by showery precipitation with cumulonimbus clouds sometimes extending to great heights.

**inversion**—An increase in temperature with height—a reversal of the normal decrease with height in the *tropo-*

*sphere;* may also be applied to other meteorological properties.

**isobar**—A line of equal or constant barometric pressure.

**isoheight**—On a weather chart, a line of equal height; same as *contour* (1).

**isoline**—A line of equal value of a variable quantity, i.e., an isoline of temperature is an *isotherm,* etc. *See* isobar, isotach, etc.

**isoshear**—A line of equal *wind shear.*

**isotach**—A line of equal or constant wind speed.

**isotherm**—A line of equal or constant temperature.

**isothermal**—Of equal or constant temperature, with respect to either space or time; more commonly, temperature with height; a zero *lapse rate.*

## J

**jet stream**—A quasi-horizontal stream of winds 50 knots or more concentrated within a narrow band embedded in the westerlies in the high *troposphere.*

## K

**katabatic wind**—Any wind blowing downslope. *See* fall wind, foehn.

**Kelvin temperature scale (abbreviated K)**—A temperature scale with zero degrees equal to the temperature at which all molecular motion ceases, i.e., absolute zero (0° K = −273° C); the Kelvin degree is identical to the Celsius degree; hence at standard sea level pressure, the melting point is 273° K and the boiling point 373° K.

**knot**—A unit of speed equal to one nautical mile per hour.

## L

**land breeze**—A coastal breeze blowing from land to sea, caused by temperature difference when the sea surface is warmer than the adjacent land. Therefore, it usually blows at night and alternates with a *sea breeze,* which blows in the opposite direction by day.

**lapse rate**—The rate of decrease of an atmospheric variable with height; commonly refers to decrease of temperature with height.

**latent heat**—The amount of heat absorbed (converted to kinetic energy) during the processes of change of liquid water to water vapor, ice to water vapor, or ice to liquid water; or the amount released during the reverse processes. Four basic classifications are:

(1) **latent heat of condensation**—Heat released during change of water vapor to water.

(2) **latent heat of fusion**—Heat released during change of water to ice or the amount absorbed in change of ice to water.

(3) **latent heat of sublimation**—Heat released during change of water vapor to ice or the amount absorbed in the change of ice to water vapor.

(4) **latent heat of vaporization**—Heat absorbed in the change of water to water vapor; the negative of latent heat of condensation.

**layer**—In reference to sky cover, clouds or other obscuring phenomena whose bases are approximately at the same level. The layer may be continuous or composed of detached elements. The term "layer" does not imply that a clear space exists between the layers or that the clouds or *obscuring phenomena* composing them are of the same type.

**lee wave**—Any stationary wave disturbance caused by a barrier in a fluid flow. In the atmosphere when sufficient moisture is present, this wave will be evidenced by *lenticular clouds* to the lee of mountain barriers; also called *mountain wave* or *standing wave*.

**lenticular cloud (or lenticularis)**—A species of cloud whose elements have the form of more or less isolated, generally smooth lenses or almonds. These clouds appear most often in formations of orographic origin, the result of *lee waves*, in which case they remain nearly stationary with respect to the terrain (standing cloud), but they also occur in regions without marked orography.

**level of free convection (abbreviated LFC)**—The level at which a *parcel* of air lifted dry-adiabatically until saturated and moist-adiabatically thereafter would become warmer than its surroundings in a conditionally unstable atmosphere. *See* conditional instability and adiabatic process.

**lifting condensation level (abbreviated LCL)**—The level at which a *parcel* of unsaturated air lifted dry-adiabatically would become saturated. Compare *level of free convection* and *convective condensation level*.

**lightning**—Generally, any and all forms of visible electrical discharge produced by a *thunderstorm*.

**lithometeor**—The general term for dry particles suspended in the atmosphere such as dust, haze, smoke, and sand.

**low**—An area of low barometric pressure, with its attendant system of winds. Also called a barometric depression or *cyclone*.

## M

**mammato cumulus**—Obsolete. *See* cumulonimbus mamma.

**mare's tail**—*See* cirrus.

**maritime polar air (abbreviated mP)**—*See* polar air.

**maritime tropical air (abbreviated mT)**—*See* tropical air.

**maximum wind axis**—On a constant pressure chart, a line denoting the axis of maximum wind speeds at that constant pressure surface.

**mean sea level**—The average height of the surface of the sea for all stages of tide; used as reference for elevations throughout the U.S.

**melting**—*See* change of state.

**mercurial barometer**—A *barometer* in which pressure is determined by balancing air pressure against the weight of a column of mercury in an evacuated glass tube.

**meteorology**—The science of the *atmosphere*.

**microbarograph**—An aneroid *barograph* designed to record atmospheric pressure changes of very small magnitudes.

**millibar (abbreviated mb.)**—An internationally used unit of pressure equal to 1,000 dynes per square centimeter. It is convenient for reporting *atmospheric pressure*.

**mist**—A popular expression for drizzle or heavy fog.

**mixing ratio**—The ratio by weight of the amount of water vapor in a volume of air to the amount of dry air; usually expressed as grams per kilogram (g/kg).

**moist-adiabatic lapse rate**—*See* saturated-adiabatic lapse rate.

**moisture**—An all-inclusive term denoting water in any o. all of its three states.

**monsoon**—A wind that in summer blows from sea to a continental interior, bringing copious rain, and in winter blows from the interior to the sea, resulting in sustained dry weather.

**mountain wave**—A *standing wave* or *lee wave* to the lee of a mountain barrier.

## N

**nautical twilight**—*See* twilight.

**negative vorticity**—*See* vorticity.

**nimbostratus**—A principal cloud type, gray colored, often dark, the appearance of which is rendered diffuse by more or less continuously falling rain or snow, which in most cases reaches the ground. It is thick enough throughout to blot out the sun.

**noctilucent clouds**—Clouds of unknown composition which occur at great heights, probably around 75 to 90 kilometers. They resemble thin *cirrus*, but usually with a bluish or silverish color, although sometimes orange to red, standing out against a dark night sky. Rarely observed.

**normal**—In meteorology, the value of an element averaged for a given location over a period of years and recognized as a standard.

**numerical forecasting**—*See* numerical weather prediction.

**numerical weather prediction**—Forecasting by digital computers solving mathematical equations; used extensively in weather services throughout the world.

## O

**obscuration**—Denotes sky hidden by surface-based *obscuring phenomena* and *vertical visibility* restricted overhead.

**obscuring phenomena**—Any *hydrometeor* or *lithometeor* other than clouds; may be surface based or aloft.

**occlusion**—Same as *occluded front*.

**occluded front (commonly called occlusion, also called frontal occlusion)**—A composite of two fronts as a *cold front* overtakes a *warm front* or *quasi-stationary front*.

**orographic**—Of, pertaining to, or caused by mountains as in orographic clouds, orographic lift, or orographic precipitation.

**ozone**—An unstable form of oxygen; heaviest concentrations are in the stratosphere; corrosive to some metals; absorbs most ultraviolet solar radiation.

## P

**parcel**—A small volume of air, small enough to contain uniform distribution of its meteorological properties, and large enough to remain relatively self-contained and respond to all meteorological processes. No specific dimensions have been defined, however, the order of magnitude of 1 cubic foot has been suggested.

**partial obscuration**—A designation of sky cover when part of the sky is hidden by surface based *obscuring phenomena*.

**pilot balloon**—A small free-lift balloon used to determine the speed and direction of winds in the upper air.

**pilot balloon observation (commonly called PIBAL)**—A method of winds-aloft observation by visually tracking a *pilot balloon.*

**plan position indicator (PPI) scope**—A radar indicator scope displaying range and azimuth of *targets* in polar coordinates.

**plow wind**—The spreading downdraft of a *thunderstorm;* a strong, straight-line wind in advance of the storm. *See* first gust.

**polar air**—An air mass with characteristics developed over high latitudes, especially within the subpolar highs. Continental polar air (cP) has cold surface temperatures, low moisture content, and, especially in its source regions, has great stability in the lower layers. It is shallow in comparison with *Arctic air.* Maritime polar (mP) initially possesses similar properties to those of continental polar air, but in passing over warmer water it becomes unstable with a higher moisture content. Compare *tropical air.*

**polar front**—The semipermanent, semicontinuous *front* separating air masses of tropical and polar origins.

**positive vorticity**—*See* vorticity.

**precipitation**—Any or all forms of water particles, whether liquid or solid, that fall from the atmosphere and reach the surface. It is a major class of *hydrometeor*, distinguished from cloud and *virga* in that it must reach the surface.

**precipitation attenuation**—*See* attenuation.

**pressure**—*See* atmospheric pressure.

**pressure altimeter**—An *aneroid barometer* with a scale graduated in altitude instead of pressure using *standard atmospheric* pressure-height relationships; shows indicated altitude (not necessarily true altitude); may be set to measure altitude (indicated) from any arbitrarily chosen level.

**pressure gradient**—The rate of decrease of pressure per unit distance at a fixed time.

**pressure jump**—A sudden, significant increase in *station pressure.*

**pressure tendency**—*See* barometric tendency.

**prevailing easterlies**—The broad current or pattern of persistent easterly winds in the Tropics and in polar regions.

**prevailing visibility**—In the U.S., the greatest horizontal visibility which is equaled or exceeded throughout half of the horizon circle; it need not be a continuous half.

**prevailing westerlies**—The dominant west-to-east motion of the atmosphere, centered over middle latitudes of both hemispheres.

**prevailing wind**—Direction from which the wind blows most frequently.

**prognostic chart (contracted PROG)**—A chart of expected or forecast conditions.

**pseudo-adiabatic lapse rate**—*See* saturated-adiabatic lapse rate.

**psychrometer**—An instrument consisting of a *wet-bulb* and a *dry-bulb* thermometer for measuring wet-bulb and dry-bulb temperature; used to determine water vapor content of the air.

**pulse**—Pertaining to radar, a brief burst of electromagnetic radiation emitted by the radar; of very short time duration. *See* pulse length.

**pulse length**—Pertaining to radar, the dimension of a radar pulse; may be expressed as the time duration or the length in linear units. Linear dimension is equal to time duration multiplied by the speed of propagation (approximately the speed of light).

## Q

**quasi-stationary front (commonly called stationary front)**—A *front* which is stationary or nearly so; conventionally, a front which is moving at a speed of less than 5 knots is generally considered to be quasi-stationary.

## R

**RADAR (contraction for radio detection and ranging)**—An electronic instrument used for the detection and ranging of distant objects of such composition that they scatter or reflect radio energy. Since *hydrometeors* can scatter radio energy, *weather radars*, operating on certain frequency bands, can detect the presence of precipitation, clouds, or both.

**radarsonde observation**—A *rawinsonde observation* in which winds are determined by radar tracking a balloon-borne target.

**radiation**—The emission of energy by a medium and transferred, either through free space or another medium, in the form of electromagnetic waves.

**radiation fog**—*Fog* characteristically resulting when radiational cooling of the earth's surface lowers the air temperature near the ground to or below its initial dew point on calm, clear nights.

**radiosonde**—A balloon-borne instrument for measuring pressure, temperature, and humidity aloft. Radiosonde observation—a *sounding* made by the instrument.

**rain**—A form of *precipitation;* drops are larger than *drizzle* and fall in relatively straight, although not necessarily vertical, paths as compared to drizzle which falls in irregular paths.

**rain shower**—*See* shower.

**range attenuation**—*See* attenuation.

**RAOB**—A *radiosonde* observation.

**rawin**—A *rawinsonde* observation.

**rawinsonde observation**—A combined winds aloft and radiosonde observation. Winds are determined by tracking the *radiosonde* by radio direction finder or radar.

**relative humidity**—The ratio of the existing amount of water vapor in the air at a given temperature to the maximum amount that could exist at that temperature; usually expressed in percent.

**relative vorticity**—*See* vorticity.

**ridge (also called ridge line)**—In meteorology, an elongated area of relatively high atmospheric pressure; usually associated with and most clearly identified as an area of maximum anticyclonic curvature of the wind flow (*isobars, contours,* or *streamlines*).

**rocketsonde**—A type of *radiosonde* launched by a rocket and making its measurements during a parachute descent; capable of obtaining *soundings* to a much greater height than possible by balloon or aircraft.

**roll cloud (sometimes improperly called rotor cloud)**—A dense and horizontal roll-shaped accessory cloud located on the lower leading edge of a *cumulonimbus* or less often, a rapidly developing *cumulus;* indicative of turbulence.

**rotor cloud (sometimes improperly called *roll cloud*)**—A turbulent cloud formation found in the lee of some large mountain barriers, the air in the cloud rotates around an axis parallel to the range; indicative of possible violent turbulence.

## S

**St. Elmo's Fire (also called corposant)**—A luminous brush discharge of electricity from protruding objects, such as masts and yardarms of ships, aircraft, lightning rods, steeples, etc., occurring in stormy weather.

**Santa Ana**—A hot, dry, *foehn* wind, generally from the northeast or east, occurring west of the Sierra Nevada Mountains especially in the pass and river valley near Santa Ana, California.

**saturated adiabatic lapse rate**—The rate of decrease of temperature with height as saturated air is lifted with no gain or loss of heat from outside sources; varies with temperature, being greatest at low temperatures. *See* adiabatic process and dry-adiabatic lapse rate.

**saturation**—The condition of the atmosphere when actual *water vapor* present is the maximum possible at existing temperature.

**scud**—Small detached masses of stratus *fractus* clouds below a layer of higher clouds, usually *nimbostratus*.

**sea breeze**—A coastal breeze blowing from sea to land, caused by the temperature difference when the land surface is warmer than the sea surface. Compare *land breeze*.

**sea fog**—A type of *advection fog* formed when air that has been lying over a warm surface is transported over a colder water surface.

**sea level pressure**—The *atmospheric pressure* at *mean sea level*, either directly measured by stations at sea level or empirically determined from the *station pressure* and temperature by stations not at sea level; used as a common reference for analyses of surface pressure patterns.

**sea smoke**—Same as *steam fog*.

**sector visibility**—*Meteorological visibility* within a specified sector of the horizon circle.

**shear**—*See* wind shear.

**shower**—*Precipitation* from a *cumuliform* cloud; characterized by the suddenness of beginning and ending, by the rapid change of intensity, and usually by rapid change in the appearance of the sky; showery precipitation may be in the form of rain, ice pellets, or snow.

**slant visibility**—For an airborne observer, the distance at which he can see and distinguish objects on the ground.

**sleet**—*See* ice pellets.

**smog**—A mixture of *smoke* and *fog*.

**smoke**—A restriction to visibility resulting from combustion.

**snow**—Precipitation composed of white or translucent ice crystals, chiefly in complex branched hexagonal form.

**snow flurry**—Popular term for snow *shower*, particularly of a very light and brief nature.

**snow grains**—*Precipitation* of very small, white opaque grains of ice, similar in structure to *snow* crystals. The grains are fairly flat or elongated, with diameters generally less than 0.04 inch (1 mm.).

**snow pellets**—*Precipitation* consisting of white, opaque approximately round (sometimes conical) ice particles having a snow-like structure, and about 0.08 to 0.2 inch in diameter; crisp and easily crushed, differing in this respect from *snow grains;* rebound from a hard surface and often break up.

**snow shower**—*See* shower.

**solar radiation**—The total electromagnetic *radiation* emitted by the sun. *See* insolation.

**sounding**—In meteorology, an upper-air observation; a *radiosonde* observation.

**source region**—An extensive area of the earth's surface characterized by relatively uniform surface conditions where large masses of air remain long enough to take on characteristic temperature and moisture properties imparted by that surface.

**specific humidity**—The ratio by weight of *water vapor* in a sample of air to the combined weight of water vapor and dry air. Compare *mixing ratio*.

**squall**—A sudden increase in wind speed by at least 15 knots to a peak of 20 knots or more and lasting for at least one minute. Essential difference between a *gust* and a squall is the duration of the peak speed.

**squall line**—Any nonfrontal line or narrow band of active *thunderstorms* (with or without *squalls*).

**stability**—A state of the atmosphere in which the vertical distribution of temperature is such that a *parcel* will resist displacement from its initial level. (*See also* instability.)

**standard atmosphere**—A hypothetical atmosphere based on climatological averages comprised of numerous physical constants of which the most important are:
(1) A surface *temperature* of 59° F (15° C) and a surface pressure of 29.92 inches of mercury (1013.2 millibars) at sea level;
(2) A *lapse rate* in the troposphere of 6.5° C per kilometer (approximately 2° C per 1,000 feet);
(3) A *tropopause* of 11 kilometers (approximately 36,000 feet) with a temperature of −56.5° C; and
(4) An *isothermal* lapse rate in the stratosphere to an altitude of 24 kilometers (approximately 80,000 feet).

**standing cloud (standing lenticular altocumulus)**—*See* lenticular cloud.

**standing wave**—A wave that remains stationary in a moving fluid. In aviation operations it is used most commonly to refer to a *lee wave* or *mountain wave*.

**stationary front**—Same as *quasi-stationary front*.

**station pressure**—The actual *atmospheric pressure* at the observing station.

**steam fog**—Fog formed when cold air moves over relatively warm water or wet ground.

**storm detection radar**—A weather radar designed to detect *hydrometeors* of precipitation size; used primarily to detect storms with large drops or hailstones as opposed to clouds and light precipitation of small drop size.

**stratiform**—Descriptive of clouds of extensive horizontal development, as contrasted to vertically developed *cumuliform* clouds; characteristic of stable air and, therefore, composed of small water droplets.

**stratocumulus**—A low cloud, predominantly *stratiform* in gray and/or whitish patches or layers, may or may not merge; elements are tessellated, rounded, or roll-shaped with relatively flat tops.

**stratosphere**—The atmospheric layer above the tropopause, average altitude of base and top, 7 and 22 miles respectively; characterized by a slight average increase of temperature from base to top and is very stable; also characterized by low moisture content and absence of clouds.

**stratus**—A low, gray cloud layer or sheet with a fairly uniform base; sometimes appears in ragged patches; seldom produces precipitation but may produce *drizzle* or *snow grains*. A *stratiform* cloud.

**stratus fractus**—*See* fractus.

**streamline**—In meteorology, a line whose tangent is the wind direction at any point along the line. A flowline.

**sublimation**—*See* change of state.

**subsidence**—A descending motion of air in the atmosphere over a rather broad area; usually associated with *divergence*.

**summation principle**—The principle states that the cover assigned to a layer is equal to the summation of the sky cover of the lowest layer plus the additional coverage at all successively higher layers up to and including the layer in question. Thus, no layer can be assigned a sky cover less than a lower layer, and no sky cover can be greater than 1.0 (10/10).

**superadiabatic lapse rate**—A *lapse rate* greater than the *dry-adiabatic lapse rate*. *See* absolute instability.

**supercooled water**—Liquid water at temperatures colder than freezing.

**surface inversion**—An *inversion* with its base at the surface, often caused by cooling of the air near the surface as a result of *terrestrial radiation*, especially at night.

**surface visibility**—Visibility observed from eye-level above the ground.

**synoptic chart**—A chart, such as the familiar weather map, which depicts the distribution of meteorological conditions over an area at a given time.

## T

**target**—In radar, any of the many types of objects detected by radar.

**temperature**—In general, the degree of hotness or coldness as measured on some definite temperature scale by means of any of various types of thermometers.

**temperature inversion**—*See* inversion.

**terrestrial radiation**—The total infrared *radiation* emitted by the Earth and its atmosphere.

**thermograph**—A continuous-recording *thermometer*.

**thermometer**—An instrument for measuring *temperature*.

**thunderstorm**—In general, a local storm invariably produced by a *cumulonimbus* cloud, and always accompanied by lightning and thunder.

**tornado (sometimes called cyclone, twister)**—A violently rotating column of air, pendant from a cumulonimbus cloud, and nearly always observable as "funnel-shaped." It is the most destructive of all small-scale atmospheric phenomena.

**towering cumulus**—A rapidly growing *cumulus* in which height exceeds width.

**tower visibility**—*Prevailing visibility* determined from the control tower.

**trade winds**—Prevailing, almost continuous winds blowing with an easterly component from the subtropical high pressure belts toward the *intertropical convergence zone;* northeast in the Northern Hemisphere, southeast in the Southern Hemisphere.

**tropical air**—An air mass with characteristics developed over low latitudes. Maritime tropical air (mT), the principal type, is produced over the tropical and subtropical seas; very warm and humid. Continental tropical (cT) is produced over subtropical arid regions and is hot and very dry. Compare *polar air*.

**tropical cyclone**—A general term for a *cyclone* that originates over tropical oceans. By international agreement, tropical cyclones have been classified according to their intensity, as follows:

(1) **tropical depression**—winds up to 34 knots (64 km/h);

(2) **tropical storm**—winds of 35 to 64 knots (65 to 119 km/h);

(3) **hurricane or typhoon**—winds of 65 knots or higher (120 km/h).

**tropical depression**—*See* tropical cyclone.

**tropical storm**—*See* tropical cyclone.

**tropopause**—The transition zone between the *troposphere* and *stratosphere*, usually characterized by an abrupt change of *lapse rate*.

**troposphere**—That portion of the *atmosphere* from the earth's surface to the *tropopause;* that is, the lowest 10 to 20 kilometers of the atmosphere. The troposphere is characterized by decreasing temperature with height, and by appreciable water vapor.

**trough (also called trough line)**—In meteorology, an elongated area of relatively low atmospheric pressure; usually associated with and most clearly identified as an area of maximum cyclonic curvature of the wind flow (*isobars, contours*, or *streamlines*); compare with *ridge*.

**true altitude**—*See* altitude.

**true wind direction**—The direction, with respect to true north, from which the wind is blowing.

**turbulence**—In meteorology, any irregular or disturbed flow in the atmosphere.

**twilight**—The intervals of incomplete darkness following sunset and preceding sunrise. The time at which evening twilight ends or morning twilight begins is determined by arbitrary convention, and several kinds of twilight have been defined and used; most commonly civil, nautical, and astronomical twilight.

(1) **Civil Twilight**—The period of time before sunrise and after sunset when the sun is not more than 6° below the horizon.

(2) **Nautical Twilight**—The period of time before sunrise and after sunset when the sun is not more than 12° below the horizon.

(3) **Astronomical Twilight**—The period of time before sunrise and after sunset when the sun is not more than 18° below the horizon.

**twister**—In the United States, a colloquial term for *tornado*.

**typhoon**—A *tropical cyclone* in the Eastern Hemisphere with winds in excess of 65 knots (120 km/h).

## U

**undercast**—A cloud *layer* of ten-tenths (1.0) coverage (to the nearest tenth) as viewed from an observation point above the layer.

**unlimited ceiling**—A clear sky or a sky cover that does not meet the criteria for a *ceiling*.

**unstable**—*See* instability.

**updraft**—A localized upward current of air.

**upper front**—A *front* aloft not extending to the earth's surface.

**upslope fog**—Fog formed when air flows upward over rising terrain and is, consequently, adiabatically cooled to or below its initial *dew point*.

## V

**vapor pressure**—In meteorology, the pressure of water vapor in the atmosphere. Vapor pressure is that part of the total atmospheric pressure due to water vapor and is independent of the other atmospheric gases or vapors.

**vapor trail**—Same as *condensation trail*.

**veering**—Shifting of the wind in a clockwise direction with respect to either space or time; opposite of backing. Commonly used by meteorologists to refer to an anticyclonic shift (clockwise in the Northern Hemisphere and counterclockwise in the Southern Hemisphere).

**vertical visibility**—The distance one can see upward into a surface based *obscuration;* or the maximum height from which a pilot in flight can recognize the ground through a surface based obscuration.

**virga**—Water or ice particles falling from a cloud, usually in wisps or streaks, and evaporating before reaching the ground.

**visibility**—The greatest distance one can see and identify prominent objects.

**visual range**—*See* runway visual range.

**vortex**—In meteorology, any rotary flow in the atmosphere.

**vorticity**—Turning of the atmosphere. Vorticity may be imbedded in the total flow and not readily identified by a flow pattern.

(a) **absolute vorticity**—the rotation of the Earth imparts vorticity to the atmosphere; absolute vorticity is the combined vorticity due to this rotation and vorticity due to circulation relative to the Earth (relative vorticity).

(b) **negative vorticity**—vorticity caused by anticyclonic

turning; it is associated with downward motion of the air.

(c) **positive vorticity**—vorticity caused by cyclonic turning; it is associated with upward motion of the air.

(d) **relative vorticity**—vorticity of the air relative to the Earth, disregarding the component of vorticity resulting from Earth's rotation.

## W

**wake turbulence**—*Turbulence* found to the rear of a solid body in motion relative to a fluid. In aviation terminology, the turbulence caused by a moving aircraft.

**wall cloud**—The well-defined bank of vertically developed clouds having a wall-like appearance which form the outer boundary of the *eye* of a well-developed *tropical cyclone*.

**warm front**—Any non-occluded *front* which moves in such a way that warmer air replaces colder air.

**warm sector**—The area covered by warm air at the surface and bounded by the *warm front* and *cold front* of a *wave cyclone*.

**water equivalent**—The depth of water that would result from the melting of snow or ice.

**waterspout**—*See* tornado.

**water vapor**—Water in the invisible gaseous form.

**wave cyclone**—A *cyclone* which forms and moves along a front. The circulation about the cyclone center tends to produce a wavelike deformation of the front.

**weather**—The state of the *atmosphere*, mainly with respect to its effects on life and human activities; refers to instantaneous conditions or short term changes as opposed to *climate*.

**weather radar**—Radar specifically designed for observing weather. *See* cloud detection radar and storm detection radar.

**weather vane**—A *wind vane*.

**wedge**—Same as *ridge*.

**wet bulb**—Contraction of either *wet-bulb temperature* or *wet-bulb thermometer*.

**wet-bulb temperature**—The lowest *temperature* that can be obtained on a *wet-bulb thermometer* in any given sample of air, by evaporation of water (or ice) from the muslin wick; used in computing *dew point* and *relative humidity*.

**wet-bulb thermometer**—A thermometer with a muslin-covered bulb used to measure wet-bulb temperature.

**whirlwind**—A small, rotating column of air; may be visible as a dust devil.

**willy-willy**—A *tropical cyclone* of hurricane strength near Australia.

**wind**—Air in motion relative to the surface of the earth; generally used to denote horizontal movement.

**wind direction**—The direction **from** which wind is blowing.

**wind speed**—Rate of wind movement in distance per unit time.

**wind vane**—An instrument to indicate wind direction.

**wind velocity**—A vector term to include both *wind direction* and *wind speed*.

**wind shear**—The rate of change of *wind velocity* (direction and/or speed) per unit distance; conventionally expressed as vertical or horizontal wind shear.

## X-Y-Z

**zonal wind**—A west wind; the westerly component of a wind. Conventionally used to describe large-scale flow that is neither cyclonic nor anticyclonic.

# WEATHER INFORMATION
## and
# COMMUNICATIONS

### (WEATHER RADIO,
### MARINE WEATHER,
### and
### BE YOUR OWN FORECASTER)

# NOAA WEATHER RADIO

The National Oceanic and Atmospheric Administration (NOAA) of the U.S. Department of Commerce provides the service known as *Weather Radio*. This service provides continuous broadcasts of the latest weather information directly from National Weather Service offices. Taped weather messages are repeated every four to six minutes and are routinely revised every one to three hours, or more frequently if needed. Most of the stations operate 24 hours daily.

The broadcasts are tailored to weather information needs of people within the receiving area. For example, stations along the sea coasts and Great Lakes provide specialized weather information for boaters, fishers, and others engaged in marine activities, as well as general weather information.

During severe weather, National Weather Service forecasters can interrupt the routine weather broadcasts and substitute special warning messages. The forecasters can also activate specially designed warning receivers. **Such receivers either sound an alarm** indicating that an emergency exists, alerting the listener to turn the receiver up to an audible volume; or, when operated in a muted mode, are **automatically turned on** so that the warning message is heard. "Warning alarm" receivers are especially valuable for schools, hospitals, public-safety agencies, and news media offices.

Under a January 1975, White House policy statement, NOAA Weather Radio was designated the sole Government-operated radio system to provide direct warnings into private homes for both natural disasters and nuclear attack. This capability is to supplement warnings by sirens and by commercial radio and TV.

NOAA weather Radio broadcasts are made on one of seven high-band FM frequencies as shown on the accompanying chart. The 162.475 MHz frequency is used only in special cases where required to avoid channel interference. These frequencies are not found on the average home radio now in use. However, a number of radios manufacturers offer special weather radios to operate on these frequencies, with or without the emergency warning alarm. Also there are now many radios on the market which offer standard AM/FM frequencies plus the so-called "weather band" as an added feature.

NOAA Weather Radio broadcasts can usually be heard as far as 40 miles from the antenna site, sometimes more. The effective range depends on many factors, particularly the height of the broadcasting antenna, terrain, quality of the receiver and type of receiving antenna. As a general rule, listeners close to or perhaps beyond the 40 mile range should have a good quality receiver system if they expect reliable reception.

If more information on NOAA Weather Radio is required, inquiry should be written to: National Oceanic and Atmospheric Administration, Silver Spring, Maryland 20910.

# NOAA WEATHER RADIO NETWORK

Legend—Frequencies are identified as follows:
(1)—162.550 MHz
(2)—162.400 MHz
(3)—162.475 MHz
(4)—162.425 MHz
(5)—162.450 MHz
(6)—162.500 MHz
(7)—162.525 MHz

Revised August 1983

| Location | Frequency |
|---|---|
| **Alabama** | |
| Anniston | 3 |
| Birmingham | 1 |
| *Columbia | 4 |
| Demopolis | 3 |
| Dozier | 1 |
| Florence | 3 |
| Huntsville | 2 |
| Louisville | 3 |
| Mobile | 1 |
| Montgomery | 2 |
| Tuscaloosa | 2 |
| **Alaska** | |
| Anchorage | 1 |
| Cordova | 1 |
| Fairbanks | 1 |
| Homer | 2 |
| Juneau | 1 |
| Ketchikan | 1 |
| Kodiak | 1 |
| Nome | 1 |
| Petersburg | 1 |
| Seward | 1 |
| Sitka | 2 |
| Valdez | 1 |
| Wrangell | 2 |
| Yakutat | 1 |
| **Arizona** | |
| Flagstaff | 2 |
| Phoenix | 1 |
| Tucson | 2 |
| Yuma | 1 |
| **Arkansas** | |
| Fayetteville | 3 |
| Fort Smith | 2 |
| Gurdon | 3 |
| Jonesboro | 1 |
| Little Rock | 1 |
| Mountain View | 2 |
| Star City | 2 |
| Texarkana | 1 |
| **California** | |
| Bakersfield (P) | 1 |
| Coachella (P) | 2 |
| Eureka | 2 |
| Fresno | 2 |
| Los Angeles | 1 |
| Merced | 1 |
| Monterey | 2 |
| Point Arena | 2 |
| Redding (P) | 1 |
| Sacramento | 2 |
| San Diego | 2 |
| San Francisco | 1 |
| San Luis Obispo | 1 |
| Santa Barbara | 2 |
| **Colorado** | |
| Alamosa (P) | 3 |
| Colorado Springs | 3 |
| Denver | 1 |
| Grand Junction | 1 |
| Greeley | 2 |
| Longmont | 1 |
| Pueblo | 2 |
| Sterling | 2 |
| **Connecticut** | |
| Hartford | 3 |
| Meriden | 2 |
| New London | 1 |
| **Delaware** | |
| Lewes | 1 |
| **District of Columbia** | |
| Washington, D.C. | 1 |
| **Florida** | |
| *Clewiston | 2 |
| Daytona Beach | 2 |
| Fort Myers | 3 |
| Gainesville | 3 |
| Jacksonville | 1 |
| Key West | 2 |
| Melbourne | 1 |
| Miami | 1 |
| Orlando | 3 |
| Panama City | 2 |
| Pensacola | 2 |
| Tallahassee | 2 |
| Tampa | 1 |
| West Palm Beach | 3 |
| **Georgia** | |
| Athens | 2 |
| Atlanta | 1 |
| Augusta | 1 |
| *Baxley | 7 |
| Chatsworth | 2 |
| Columbus | 2 |
| Macon | 3 |
| Pelham | 1 |

| Location | Frequency |
|---|---|
| Savannah | 2 |
| *Valdosta | 6 |
| Waycross | 3 |
| **Hawaii** | |
| Hilo | 1 |
| Honolulu | 1 |
| Kokee | 2 |
| Mt. Haleakala | 2 |
| Waimanalo (R) | 2 |
| **Idaho** | |
| Boise | 1 |
| Lewiston (P) | 1 |
| Pocatello | 1 |
| Twin Falls | 2 |
| **Illinois** | |
| Champaign | 1 |
| Chicago | 1 |
| Marion | 4 |
| Moline | 1 |
| Peoria | 3 |
| Rockford | 3 |
| Springfield | 2 |
| **Indiana** | |
| *Bloomington | 5 |
| Evansville | 1 |
| Fort Wayne | 1 |
| Indianapolis | 1 |
| Lafayette | 3 |
| South Bend | 2 |
| Terre Haute | 2 |
| **Iowa** | |
| Cedar Rapids | 3 |
| Des Moines | 1 |
| Dubuque (P) | 2 |
| Sioux City | 3 |
| Waterloo | 1 |
| **Kansas** | |
| Chanute | 2 |
| Colby | 3 |
| Concordia | 1 |
| Dodge City | 3 |
| Ellsworth | 2 |
| Topeka | 3 |
| Wichita | 1 |
| **Kentucky** | |
| Ashland | 1 |
| Bowling Green | 2 |
| Covington | 2 |
| Elizabethtown (R) | 2 |
| Hazard | 3 |
| Lexington | 2 |
| Louisville | 3 |
| Mayfield | 2 |
| Pikeville (R) | 2 |
| Somerset | 1 |
| **Louisiana** | |
| Alexandria | 3 |
| Baton Rouge | 2 |
| Buras | 3 |
| Lafayette | 1 |
| Lake Charles | 2 |
| Monroe | 1 |
| Morgan City | 3 |
| New Orleans | 1 |
| Shreveport | 2 |
| **Maine** | |
| *Caribou | 7 |
| *Dresden | 3 |
| Ellsworth | 2 |
| Portland | 1 |
| **Maryland** | |
| Baltimore | 2 |
| Hagerstown | 3 |
| Salisbury | 3 |
| **Massachusetts** | |
| Boston | 3 |
| Hyannis | 1 |
| Worcester | 1 |

| Location | Frequency |
|---|---|
| **Michigan** | |
| Alpena | 1 |
| Detroit | 1 |
| Flint | 2 |
| Grand Rapids | 1 |
| Houghton | 2 |
| Marquette | 1 |
| Onondaga | 2 |
| Sault Sainte Marie | 1 |
| Traverse City | 2 |
| **Minnesota** | |
| Detroit Lakes | 3 |
| Duluth | 1 |
| International Falls | 1 |
| Mankato | 2 |
| Minneapolis | 1 |
| Rochester | 3 |
| Saint Cloud (P) | 3 |
| Thief River Falls | 1 |
| Willmar (P) | 2 |
| **Mississippi** | |
| Ackerman | 3 |
| Booneville | 1 |
| Bude | 1 |
| Columbia (R) | 2 |
| Gulfport | 2 |
| Hattiesburg | 3 |
| Inverness | 1 |
| Jackson | 2 |
| Meridian | 1 |
| Oxford | 2 |
| **Missouri** | |
| Columbia | 2 |
| Camdenton | 1 |
| Hannibal | 3 |
| Hermitage | 5 |
| Joplin/Carthage | 1 |
| Kansas City | 1 |
| St. Joseph | 2 |
| St. Louis | 1 |
| Sikeston | 2 |
| Springfield | 2 |
| **Montana** | |
| Billings | 1 |
| Butte | 1 |
| Glasgow | 1 |
| Great Falls | 1 |
| Havre (P) | 2 |
| Helena | 2 |
| Kalispell | 1 |
| Miles City | 2 |
| Missoula | 2 |
| **Nebraska** | |
| Bassett | 3 |
| Grand Island | 2 |
| Holdrege | 3 |
| Lincoln | 3 |
| Merriman | 2 |
| Norfolk | 1 |
| North Platte | 1 |
| Omaha | 2 |
| Scottsbluff | 1 |
| **Nevada** | |
| Elko | 1 |
| Ely | 2 |
| Las Vegas | 1 |
| Reno | 1 |
| Winnemucca | 2 |
| **New Hampshire** | |
| Concord | 2 |
| **New Jersey** | |
| Atlantic City | 2 |
| **New Mexico** | |
| Albuquerque | 2 |
| Clovis | 3 |
| Des Moines | 1 |
| Farmington | 2 |
| Hobbs | 2 |
| Las Cruces | 2 |
| Ruidoso | 2 |
| Santa Fe | 1 |
| **New York** | |
| Albany | 1 |
| Binghamton | 3 |
| Buffalo | 1 |
| Elmira | 1 |
| Kingston | 3 |
| New York City | 1 |
| *Riverhead | 3 |

| Location | Frequency |
|---|---|
| Rochester | 2 |
| Syracuse | 1 |
| **North Carolina** | |
| Asheville | 2 |
| Cape Hatteras | 3 |
| Charlotte | 3 |
| *Fayetteville | 3 |
| New Bern | 1 |
| Raleigh/Durham | 1 |
| Rocky Mount | 3 |
| Wilmington | 1 |
| Winston-Salem | 2 |
| **North Dakota** | |
| Bismarck | 2 |
| Dickinson | 2 |
| Fargo | 2 |
| Jamestown | 2 |
| Minot | 2 |
| Petersburg | 2 |
| Williston | 2 |
| **Ohio** | |
| Akron | 2 |
| Caldwell | 3 |
| Cleveland | 1 |
| Columbus | 1 |
| Dayton | 3 |
| Lima | 2 |
| *Moscow | 4 |
| Sandusky | 2 |
| Toledo | 1 |
| **Oklahoma** | |
| Clinton | 3 |
| Enid | 3 |
| Lawton | 1 |
| McAlester | 1 |
| Oklahoma City | 2 |
| Tulsa | 1 |
| **Oregon** | |
| Astoria | 2 |
| Brookings | 1 |
| Coos Bay | 2 |
| Eugene | 2 |
| Klamath Falls | 2 |
| Medford | 2 |
| Newport | 1 |
| Pendleton | 2 |
| Portland | 1 |
| Roseburg | 3 |
| Salem | 3 |
| **Pennsylvania** | |
| Allentown | 2 |
| Clearfield | 1 |
| Erie | 2 |
| Harrisburg | 1 |
| Johnstown | 2 |
| Philadelphia | 3 |
| Pittsburgh | 1 |
| State College | 3 |
| Wilkes-Barre | 1 |
| Williamsport | 2 |
| **Puerto Rico** | |
| Maricao | 1 |
| San Juan | 2 |
| **Rhode Island** | |
| Providence | 2 |
| **South Carolina** | |
| Beaufort | 3 |
| Charleston | 1 |
| Columbia | 2 |
| Florence | 1 |
| Greenville | 1 |
| Myrtle Beach | 2 |
| Sumter (R) | 3 |
| **South Dakota** | |
| Aberdeen | 3 |
| Huron | 1 |
| Pierre | 2 |
| Rapid City | 1 |
| Sioux Falls | 2 |

| Location | Frequency |
|---|---|
| **Tennessee** | |
| Bristol | 1 |
| Chattanooga | 1 |
| Cookeville | 2 |
| Jackson | 1 |
| Knoxville | 3 |
| Memphis | 3 |
| Nashville | 1 |
| Shelbyville | 3 |
| Waverly | 2 |
| **Texas** | |
| Abilene | 2 |
| Amarillo | 1 |
| Austin | 2 |
| Beaumont | 3 |
| Big Spring | 3 |
| Brownsville | 1 |
| Bryan | 1 |
| Corpus Christi | 1 |
| Dallas | 2 |
| Del Rio (P) | 2 |
| El Paso | 3 |
| Fort Worth | 1 |
| Galveston | 1 |
| Houston | 2 |
| Laredo | 3 |
| Lubbock | 2 |
| Lufkin | 1 |
| Midland | 2 |
| Paris | 1 |
| Pharr | 2 |
| San Angelo | 1 |
| San Antonio | 1 |
| Sherman | 3 |
| Tyler | 3 |
| Victoria | 2 |
| Waco | 3 |
| Wichita Falls | 3 |
| **Utah** | |
| Logan | 2 |
| Cedar City | 2 |
| Vernal | 2 |
| Salt Lake City | 1 |
| **Vermont** | |
| Burlington | 2 |
| *Marlboro | 4 |
| Windsor | 3 |
| | |
| Heathsville | 2 |
| Lynchburg | 2 |
| Norfolk | 1 |
| Richmond | 3 |
| Roanoke | 3 |
| **Washington** | |
| Neah Bay | 1 |
| Olympia | 1 |
| Seattle | 2 |
| Spokane | 3 |
| Wenatchee | 3 |
| Yakima | 1 |
| **West Virginia** | |
| Beckley | 6 |
| Charleston | 2 |
| Clarksburg | 1 |
| Gilbert | 7 |
| Hinton | 4 |
| Romney | 7 |
| Spencer | 6 |
| Sutton | 5 |
| **Wisconsin** | |
| La Crosse (P) | 1 |
| Green Bay | 1 |
| Madison | 1 |
| Menomonie | 2 |
| Milwaukee | 2 |
| Wausau | 3 |
| **Wyoming** | |
| Casper | 1 |
| Cheyenne | 3 |
| Lander | 3 |
| Sheridan (P) | 3 |

**Notes:**

1. Stations marked with an asterisk (*) are funded by private interest groups.

2. Stations marked (R) are low powered experimental repeater stations serving a very limited local area.

3. Stations marked (P) operate less than 24 hours/day; however, hours are extended when possible during severe weather.

4. Occasionally the frequency of an existing or planned station must be changed because of unexpected radio frequency interference with adjacent NOAA Weather Radio stations and/or with other government or commercial operators within the area.

Warning display signals —

## SMALL CRAFT

**DAYTIME: Red Pennant.**
**NIGHTTIME: Red Light Over White Light.**
Indicates: Forecast winds as high as 33 knots and sea conditions considered dangerous to small-craft operations.

## GALE

**DAYTIME: Two Red Pennants.**
**NIGHTTIME: White Light over Red Light.**
Indicates: Forecast winds in the range 34-47 knots.

## STORM

**DAYTIME: Square Red Flag With Black Square Centered.**
**NIGHTTIME: Two Red Lights.**
Indicates: Forecast winds 48 knots and above no matter how high the wind speed. If the winds are associated with a tropical cyclone (hurricane), storm warnings indicate forecast winds of 48-63 knots.

## HURRICANE

**DAYTIME: Two Square Red Flags With Black Square Centered.**
**NIGHTTIME: White Light Between Two Red Lights.**
Indicates: Forecast winds of 64 knots and above, displayed only in connection with a hurricane.

## SAFE BOATING WEATHER RULES

BEFORE SETTING OUT

1. Check local weather and sea conditions.
2. Obtain the latest weather forecast for your area from radio broadcasts

When warnings are in effect, don't go out unless you are confident your boat can be navigated safely under forecast conditions of wind and sea. Be cautious when you see warning displays at U. S. Coast Guard stations, yacht clubs, marinas, and at other coastal points.

WHILE AFLOAT:

1. Keep a weather eye out for the approach of dark, threatening clouds, which may foretell a squall or thunderstorm; any steady increase in wind or sea; any increase in wind velocity opposite in direction to a strong tidal current. A dangerous rip tide condition may form steep waves capable of broaching a boat.

2. Heavy static on your AM radio may be an indication of nearby thunderstorm activity.

3. Check radio weather broadcasts for latest forecasts and warnings.

4. If a thunderstorm catches you afloat: —stay below deck if possible. —keep away from metal objects that are not grounded to the boat's protection system. —don't touch more than one grounded object at the same time (or you may become a shortcut for electrical surges through the protection system).

What about navigation? Do you have the NOAA National Ocean Survey charts and other publications covering your part of coastal or Great Lakes waters? Check your local office of the National Weather Service or National Ocean Survey and other essential aids to navigation.

# Temperature Conversion

## Fahrenheit to Celsius

| °F | °C | °F | °C | °F | °C |
|---|---|---|---|---|---|
| 120 | 48.9 | 63 | 17.2 | 6 | −14.4 |
| 119 | 48.3 | 62 | 16.7 | 5 | −15.0 |
| 118 | 47.8 | 61 | 16.1 | 4 | −15.6 |
| 117 | 47.2 | 60 | 15.6 | 3 | −16.1 |
| 116 | 46.7 | 59 | 15.0 | 2 | −16.7 |
| 115 | 46.1 | 58 | 14.4 | +1 | −17.2 |
| 114 | 45.6 | 57 | 13.9 | 0 | −17.8 |
| 113 | 45.0 | 56 | 13.3 | −1 | −18.3 |
| 112 | 44.4 | 55 | 12.8 | −2 | −18.9 |
| 111 | 43.9 | 54 | 12.2 | −3 | −19.4 |
| 110 | 43.3 | 53 | 11.7 | −4 | −20.0 |
| 109 | 42.8 | 52 | 11.1 | −5 | −20.6 |
| 108 | 42.2 | 51 | 10.6 | −6 | −21.1 |
| 107 | 41.7 | 50 | 10.0 | −7 | −21.7 |
| 106 | 41.1 | 49 | 9.4 | −8 | −22.2 |
| 105 | 40.6 | 48 | 8.9 | −9 | −22.8 |
| 104 | 40.0 | 47 | 8.3 | −10 | −23.3 |
| 103 | 39.4 | 46 | 7.8 | −11 | −23.9 |
| 102 | 38.9 | 45 | 7.2 | −12 | −24.4 |
| 101 | 38.3 | 44 | 6.7 | −13 | −25.0 |
| 100 | 37.8 | 43 | 6.1 | −14 | −25.6 |
| 99 | 37.2 | 42 | 5.6 | −15 | −26.1 |
| 98 | 36.7 | 41 | 5.0 | −16 | −26.7 |
| 97 | 36.1 | 40 | 4.4 | −17 | −27.2 |
| 96 | 35.6 | 39 | 3.9 | −18 | −27.8 |
| 95 | 35.0 | 38 | 3.3 | −19 | −28.3 |
| 94 | 34.4 | 37 | 2.8 | −20 | −28.9 |
| 93 | 33.9 | 36 | 2.2 | −21 | −29.4 |
| 92 | 33.3 | 35 | 1.7 | −22 | −30.0 |
| 91 | 32.8 | 34 | 1.1 | −23 | −30.6 |
| 90 | 32.2 | 33 | +0.6 | −24 | −31.1 |
| 89 | 31.7 | 32 | 0.0 | −25 | −31.7 |
| 88 | 31.1 | 31 | −0.6 | −26 | −32.2 |
| 87 | 30.6 | 30 | −1.1 | −27 | −32.8 |
| 86 | 30.0 | 29 | −1.7 | −28 | −33.3 |
| 85 | 29.4 | 28 | −2.2 | −29 | −33.9 |
| 84 | 28.9 | 27 | −2.8 | −30 | −34.4 |
| 83 | 28.3 | 26 | −3.3 | −31 | −35.0 |
| 82 | 27.8 | 25 | −3.9 | −32 | −35.6 |
| 81 | 27.2 | 24 | −4.4 | −33 | −36.1 |
| 80 | 26.7 | 23 | −5.0 | −34 | −36.7 |
| 79 | 26.1 | 22 | −5.6 | −35 | −37.2 |
| 78 | 25.6 | 21 | −6.1 | −36 | −37.8 |
| 77 | 25.0 | 20 | −6.7 | −37 | −38.3 |
| 76 | 24.4 | 19 | −7.2 | −38 | −38.9 |
| 75 | 23.9 | 18 | −7.8 | −39 | −39.4 |
| 74 | 23.3 | 17 | −8.3 | −40 | −40.0 |
| 73 | 22.8 | 16 | −8.9 | −41 | −40.6 |
| 72 | 22.2 | 15 | −9.4 | −42 | −41.1 |
| 71 | 21.7 | 14 | −10.0 | −43 | −41.7 |
| 70 | 21.1 | 13 | −10.6 | −44 | −42.2 |
| 69 | 20.6 | 12 | −11.1 | −45 | −42.8 |
| 68 | 20.0 | 11 | −11.7 | −46 | −43.3 |
| 67 | 19.4 | 10 | −12.2 | −47 | −43.9 |
| 66 | 18.9 | 9 | −12.8 | −48 | −44.4 |
| 65 | 18.3 | 8 | −13.3 | −49 | −45.0 |
| 64 | 17.8 | 7 | −13.9 | −50 | −45.6 |

## Celsius to Fahrenheit

| °C | °F | °C | °F |
|---|---|---|---|
| 50 | 122.0 | −7 | 19.4 |
| 49 | 120.2 | −8 | 17.6 |
| 48 | 118.4 | −9 | 15.8 |
| 47 | 116.6 | −10 | 14.0 |
| 46 | 114.8 | −11 | 12.2 |
| 45 | 113.0 | −12 | 10.4 |
| 44 | 111.2 | −13 | 8.6 |
| 43 | 109.4 | −14 | 6.8 |
| 42 | 107.6 | −15 | 5.0 |
| 41 | 105.8 | −16 | 3.2 |
| 40 | 104.0 | −17 | +1.4 |
| 39 | 102.2 | −18 | −0.4 |
| 38 | 100.4 | −19 | −2.2 |
| 37 | 98.6 | −20 | −4.0 |
| 36 | 96.8 | −21 | −5.8 |
| 35 | 95.0 | −22 | −7.6 |
| 34 | 93.2 | −23 | −9.4 |
| 33 | 91.4 | −24 | −11.2 |
| 32 | 89.6 | −25 | −13.0 |
| 31 | 87.8 | −26 | −14.8 |
| 30 | 86.0 | −27 | −16.6 |
| 29 | 84.2 | −28 | −18.4 |
| 28 | 82.4 | −29 | −20.2 |
| 27 | 80.6 | −30 | −22.0 |
| 26 | 78.8 | −31 | −23.8 |
| 25 | 77.0 | −32 | −25.6 |
| 24 | 75.2 | −33 | −27.4 |
| 23 | 73.4 | −34 | −29.2 |
| 22 | 71.6 | −35 | −31.0 |
| 21 | 69.8 | −36 | −32.8 |
| 20 | 68.0 | −37 | −34.6 |
| 19 | 66.2 | −38 | −36.4 |
| 18 | 64.4 | −39 | −38.2 |
| 17 | 62.6 | −40 | −40.0 |
| 16 | 60.8 | −41 | −41.8 |
| 15 | 59.0 | −42 | −43.6 |
| 14 | 57.2 | −43 | −45.4 |
| 13 | 55.4 | −44 | −47.2 |
| 12 | 53.6 | −45 | −49.0 |
| 11 | 51.8 | −46 | −50.8 |
| 10 | 50.0 | | |
| 9 | 48.2 | | |
| 8 | 46.4 | | |
| 7 | 44.6 | | |
| 6 | 42.8 | | |
| 5 | 41.0 | | |
| 4 | 39.2 | | |
| 3 | 37.4 | | |
| 2 | 35.6 | | |
| 1 | 33.8 | | |
| 0 | +32.0 | | |
| −1 | 30.2 | | |
| −2 | 28.4 | | |
| −3 | 26.6 | | |
| −4 | 24.8 | | |
| −5 | 23.0 | | |
| −6 | 21.2 | | |

| Barometer reduced to sea level. | Wind direction. | Character of weather indicated |
|---|---|---|
| 30.10 to 30.20 and steady | SW. to NW. | Fair with slight temperature changes for 1 to 2 days. |
| 30.10 to 30.20 and rising rapidly | SW. to NW. | Fair followed within 2 days by warmer and rain. |
| 30.10 to 30.20 and falling slowly | SW. to NW. | Warmer with rain in 24 to 36 hours. |
| 30.10 to 30.20 and falling rapidly | SW. to NW. | Warmer with rain in 18 to 24 hours. |
| 30.20 and above and stationary | SW. to NW. | Continued fair with no decided temperature change. |
| 30.20 and above and falling slowly | SW. to NW. | Slowly rising temperature and fair for 2 days. |
| 30.10 to 30.20 and falling slowly | S. to SE. | Rain within 24 hours. |
| 30.10 to 30.20 and falling rapidly | S. to SE. | Wind increasing in force with rain within 12 to 24 hours. |
| 30.10 to 30.20 and falling slowly | SE. to NE. | Rain in 12 to 18 hours. |
| 30.10 to 30.20 and falling rapidly | SE. to NE. | Increasing wind with rain within 12 hours. |
| 30.10 and above and falling slowly | E. to NE. | In summer with light winds, rain may not fall for several days. In winter rain within 24 hours. |
| 30.10 and above and falling rapidly | E. to NE. | In summer rain probable within 12 to 24 hours. In winter rain or snow, with increasing winds, will often set in, when the barometer begins to fall and the wind sets in from the NE. |
| 30 or below and falling slowly | SE. to NE. | Rain will continue 1 to 2 days. |
| 30 or below and falling rapidly | SE. to NE. | Rain with high wind, followed within 24 hours by clearing and cooler. |
| 30 or below and rising slowly | S. to SW. | Clearing within a few hours, and continued fair for several days. |
| 29.80 or below and falling rapidly | S. to E. | Severe storm of wind and rain or snow imminent, followed within 24 hours by clearing and colder. |
| 29.80 or below and falling rapidly | E. to N. | Severe northeast gales and heavy rain or snow, followed in winter by a cold wave. |
| 29.80 or below and rising rapidly | Going to W. | Clearing and colder. |

## BEAUFORT SCALE OF WIND EFFECTS

| Wind speed (miles per hour) | Beaufort Number | Wind Effects on Land | Official Description |
|---|---|---|---|
| Less than 1 | 0 | Calm; smoke rises vertically. | |
| 1 – 3 | 1 | Wind direction is seen in direction of smoke; but is not revealed by weather vane. | LIGHT |
| 4 – 7 | 2 | Wind can be felt on face; leaves rustle; wind vane moves. | |
| 8 – 12 | 3 | Leaves and small twigs in motion; wind extends light flag. | GENTLE |
| 13 – 18 | 4 | Wind raises dust and loose papers. Small branches move. | MODERATE |
| 19 – 24 | 5 | Small trees with leaves begin to sway; crested wavelets appear on inland waters. | FRESH |
| 25 – 31 | 6 | Large branches move; telegraph wires whistle; Umbrellas become difficult to control. | STRONG |
| 32 – 38 | 7 | Whole trees sway and walking into the wind becomes difficult. | |
| 39 – 46 | 8 | Twigs break off trees; cars veer on roads. | GALE |
| 47 – 54 | 9 | Slight structural damage occurs (roof slates may blow away, etc.) | |
| 55 – 63 | 10 | Trees are uprooted; considerable structural damage is caused. | WHOLE GALE |
| 64 – 72 | 11 | Widespread damage is caused. | |
| 73 or more | 12 | Widespread damage is caused. | HURRICANE |

## FOR THE ARMCHAIR FORECASTER

Above is the Beaufort Scale which permits the estimating of wind speeds from observations. It also gives the basis for converting wind descriptions used in weather reports to wind speed equivalents, and vice-versa.

Use your barometer and wind indicator to do your own forecasting. It's one of the most popular hobbies in the world. The opposite page gives you a chart combining the weather observations of both professionals and amateurs dating back to such observers as Ben Franklin.

# QUOTES FROM WEATHER FOLKLORE—

*Above the rest, the sun who never lies,*
*Foretells the change of weather in the skies;*
*For if he rise unwilling to his race,*
*Clouds on his brow and spots upon his face,*
*Or if through mists he shoot his sullen beams,*
*Frugal of light in loose and straggling streams,*
*Suspect a drizzling day and southern rain,*
*Fatal to fruits and flocks, and promised grain.*
*— Virgil.*

*A red morn, that ever yet betokened*
*Wreck to the seamen, tempest to the field,*
*Sorrow to shepherds, woe unto the birds,*
*Gust and foul flaws the herdmen and herds.*
*— Shakespeare.*

*Pipes for smoking tobacco become*
*indicative of the state of the air.*
*When the scent is longer retained than*
*usual and seems denser and more*
*powerful it often forebodes a storm.*

*Cats have the reputation of being weather*
*wise, an old notion which has given rise*
*to the most extensive folklore.*
*It is almost universally believed that*
*good weather may be expected when the*
*cat washes herself, but bad when she*
*licks her coat against the grain, or washes*
*her face over her ears, or sits with her tail*
*to the fire.*

*The moon and the weather*
*May change together;*
*But change of the moon*
*Does not change the weather.*
*If we'd no moon at all,*
*And that may seem strange,*
*We still should have weather*
*That's subject to change.*
*"Notes and Queries"*

*Evening red and morning gray*
*Will set the traveler on his way;*
*But evening gray and morning red*
*Will bring down rain upon his head.*

# WEATHER, CLIMATE, and SOCIETY

# WEATHER, CLIMATE, AND AGRICULTURE

### Climate

Climate is a composite of weather conditions over a period of time. It is a standard practice to relate climate in terms of statistical "Norms". But normal values do not adequately define the climatic risk. The frequency of occurrences among the various weather elements provides a more complete understanding of climate.

As a natural resource, climate is often overlooked in agricultural planning. Some reasons for this lack of concern are:
1. Climate, as a composite of weather events over a period of time, is very abstract,
2. It is not fixed in time and space like most other natural resource considerations, and
3. Climate is often viewed as given and uncontrollable, therefore nothing can be done anyway.

These erroneous views produce a lack of appreciation for climate information and its use in decisionmaking. This lack of use has in turn led to a lack of development in needed climatological data, their acquisition and analysis, in agricultural planning over the past several decades.

As a result, much of the current soil erosion, flood damage and land management problems in agriculture are traceable, in part, to lack of appreciation and understanding of climate as a manageable resource. The omission of climate information needs to be corrected in future agricultural systems planning.

### U.S. climatic diversity

An understanding of climate as a natural resource can be gained from examining the general climates in major food crop production regions of the world. The ten largest volume food crops, as well as almost all other crops, are adapted to certain latitude ranges and general climatic conditions.

Botanically, six of these ten major food crops are members of the grass family. They are wheat, rice, maize (corn), barley, sorghum and sugarcane. Five of the crops produce most of the world's food and feed grains, sugarcane being the only grass family crop not grown for grain production. Of the four remaining major food crops, three are staple root crops—potatoes, cassavas and sweet potatoes—and one is an oilseed-protein crop, soybeans. When grown under dryland or rain-fed cropping practices, all of these crops have some rather specific climatic *resource* requirements.

Eight out of ten of these world food and feed crops are successfully grown within the continental limits of the 48 contiguous States. Crops requiring true tropical climates, such as sugarcane and cassava, are not extensively grown within the contiguous States. But true tropical climates do exist in Hawaii and Puerto Rico. As a result, climatic resources of the 50 States and Puerto Rico are diverse enough to contain almost all crop-producing climates in the world.

These extensive and diverse crop-producing climatic resources are a central reason why the United States leads the world in food and feed production.

**Crop belts and climate**

A number of regions within the continental limits of the United States are named for their dominant topographic features and associated climatic conditions. Some of these regional labels are used in reporting weather crop-climate conditions.

These general topographic features and associated climates frequently determine the principal crops and cropping systems within a geographical area. This is particularly true for dryland (rain-fed or nonirrigated) cropping systems.

Within the continental United States, several geographical areas are devoted to growing one or two crops. These agricultural patterns or systems are known as "crop belts." Some examples are the Cotton Belt, Corn Belt, Spring Wheat Belt, and Winter Wheat Belt.

## Ten Major World Food Crops
(Source: U.N.-FAO 1980)

| Crop | Climate type (dryland or rain-fed croppings) | Latitudinal Range |
|---|---|---|
| Wheat | temperate humid, subhumid to semiarid | 25° to 55° |
| Rice | tropical-subtropical humid | 0° to 45° |
| Maize (Corn) | tropical-warm temperate humid | 0° to 45° |
| Potato | cool temperate | 30° to 60° |
| Barley | cool temperate | 35° to 60° |
| Sweet Potato | subtropical to warm temperate | 25° to 40° |
| Cassava | humid tropical | 0° to 30° |
| Soybeans | subtropical to warm temperate | 25° to 45° |
| Sorghum | semiarid tropics to semiarid warm temperate | 0° to 40° |
| Sugarcane | humid tropics | 0° to 30° |

Climate is usually the dominant natural resource which determines these principal crop production belts. An example of climate as the leading resource is the high latitude spring grain producing area in the United States, Canada and around the entire world. These spring grain belts of wheat, barley and oats are adapted to the high latitude subhumid temperate climates.

On a worldwide basis, the areas are known as cool-temperate grasslands. Spring grain production dominates these geographical areas largely because their annual growth cycle and grain-filling period climatic requirements are met in most years, while requirements of other possible competitive crops are not met in many years.

### Grasslands unique

The mid latitude cool-temperate grassland areas are unique the world over in their annual distribution of precipitation, temperature and solar energy. These climatic elements maximize in phase during late spring or early summer.

Precipitation usually reaches its annual maximum in late May, June and early July. Temperature reaches maximum levels in July and early August. Sunlight energy peaks in late June and early July during the longest days of the year.

Bismark, North Dakota, typifies the spring grain belt of the United States and Canada. The spring grain-cropping areas of North America normally receive between 12 and 18 inches of annual precipitation. Bismark receives an annual average of 16 inches. But the important feature from a climatic resource viewpoint is the annual distribution of precipitation. Over 60 percent occurs in the 3 months of May, June and July.

Annual Distribution of Mean
Monthly Precipitation and
Temperature, 1921-70

Annual Distribution of Mean
Monthly Precipitation and
Temperature, 1921-70

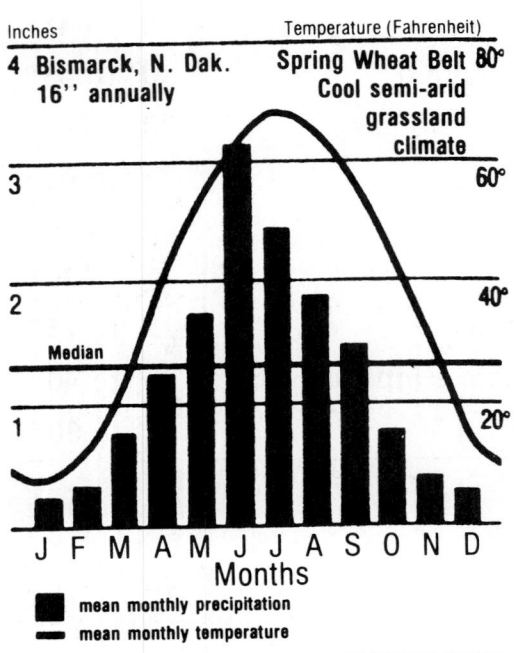

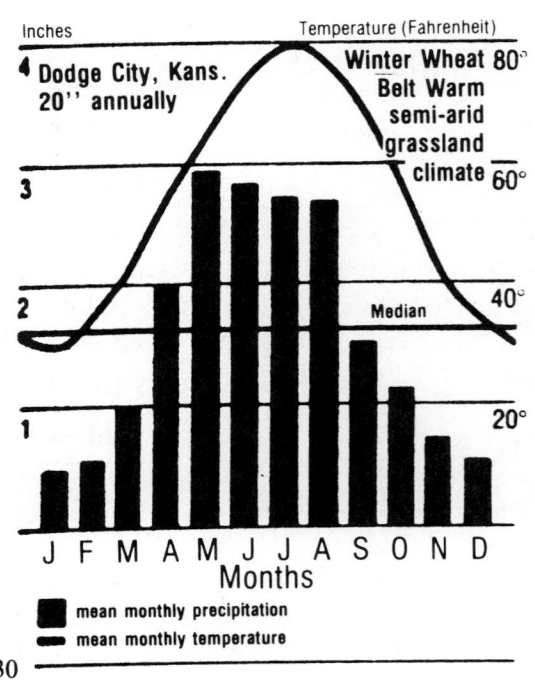

During this same period spring grain crops are growing rapidly, and crop water use in the form of evapotranspiration is greatest. As a result, the seasonal distribution of precipitation is in phase with annual spring grain crop needs.

The fact that precipitation, temperature and sunlight all reach their annual maximum values during the growth and grain-producing season of these annual spring grain crops is the key point of this unique climatic resource.

## Winter grain areas

The winter grain crops of wheat, rye, barley and oats are grown in the lower mid latitude grassland climates in all continents. In the United States, the hard red winter wheat belt lies in the southern half of the Great Plains from Nebraska to Texas.

Climatic resource features of these grassland winter grain areas are roughly similar to the higher latitude spring grain areas of the northern Great Plains. But there are some differences.

In the winter grain belts the warm season precipitation begins to increase about a month or more earlier. The mean annual maximum period occurs in late May or early June. Therefore, the growing season distribution of precipitation is about a month earlier in the winter grain areas when compared to those in the spring grain areas.

The mean monthly air temperatures are 5° to 10°F warmer during the warmest 6 months of the year in these winter grain areas. But there is a 10° to 20° or more difference between the spring and winter grain areas during the winter months within the Great Plains of North America. In fact the geographical division between spring grain and winter grain cropping belts of both North American and Eurasian continents is determined largely by winter seasonal minimum air temperatures and snow cover.

These specific crop-weather-climate relationships and their frequency of occurrence need more research emphasis in the future.

Normally, winter grains will outyield spring grains in these grassland climates. Therefore, farmers are willing to take some climatic risk of crop failure in favor of growing winter grains rather than spring grains.

In the Great Plains of the United States, the transition from winter grains to spring grains occurs in northern Nebraska and southern South Dakota. This transitional area has a climatic risk of winter grain crop failure due to winter kill of about 20 to 25 percent, or 1 year in 4 or 5. Winter kill in these transitional areas is caused by the normally dry winters with lack of snow cover and low winter minimum air temperatures.

## Corn belt uniformity

The Corn Belt of the North Central United States is the most valuable and extensive rain-fed cropland area in the world. It covers the three States of Iowa,

Illinois and Indiana completely, plus large portions of the nine surrounding States. Much of the value of this vast mid-continental cropland comes from its climate resource. On an annual basis the climate over the Corn Belt varies from subhumid tallgrass prairie in the western portions to a humid deciduous forest climate in the eastern portions.

From North to South it is a transition climate from a continental cool temperate to a continental warm temperate. The U.S. Corn Belt climate varies considerably when analyzed on an annual basis. But the uniqueness of that climate occurs during the crop-growing season. The precipitation amounts and temperature levels are amazingly uniform over the entire area from May through September.

Normal growing season rainfall during these 5 months is about 20 inches. This occurs with high frequency in both western and eastern portions. Des Moines, in central Iowa, receives an average of about 30 inches annually, but over 65 percent occurs during the warmest half of the year from April through September. At Indianapolis, Indiana, the warmest 7 months from March through September are all above the median. The annual seasonal maximum precipitation occurs in late May and early June at both locations.

The annual temperture change characteristics are slightly more continental in western portions of the Corn Belt. This means the winter temperatures are a little colder and the summer a little warmer in western than in eastern portions.

There are more days above 90°F in the western areas, primarily because of less carryover soil moisture from dry winters and hot dry winds from the High Plains in the West. Except for higher hail frequency in the western portion, most other forms of climatic risks are exceptionally uniform across the Corn Belt during the growing season.

## Dryland cotton

Dryland or rain-fed cotton is grown in most of the Southern and Southeastern States. The main dryland cotton belt begins in east Texas and continues eastward across the States of Louisiana, Mississippi, Alabama, Georgia and South Carolina. Lesser acreages of cotton are grown in several other Southern States. The climate varies from warm temperate subhumid in eastern Texas to warm temperate humid climate in the States further east.

Annual distribution of mean monthly precipitation and temperature at Jackson, Mississippi, provides a good example of the dryland cotton belt climate of the southern continental United States. Nearly 60 percent of the annual precipitation normally occurs from November through April. The Cotton Belt usually experiences wet winters which extend well into the early spring planting season. The late summer and early fall months of August, September and October are usually the driest period of the year.

On an annual basis the U.S. Cotton Belt has a humid warm temperate climate, but the annual distribution of precipitation is somewhat out-of-phase with the summer crop-growing seasonal water demands. This is particularly true for cotton.

Driest months occur in late summer and early fall toward the end of a long annual growing season. This explains why much of the dryland summer crop production in the South and Southeastern States experience drought in a high percentage of the years within a humid climate. The annual precipitation distribution, along with soil resources having limited water-retention capacities, produce crop water stress in most years.

**West coastal states**

The West Coastal States of Washington, Oregon and California are dominated by the winter precipitation climates. World-wide, these climates are known as the Mediterranean type. They are characterized by wet winters and dry summers. This type of climatic resource is illustrated by Portland, Oregon. Nearly 30 inches of the normal 42 inches of annual precipitation occurs during the coldest half of the year.

Annual Distribution of Mean Monthly Precipitation and Temperature, 1921-70

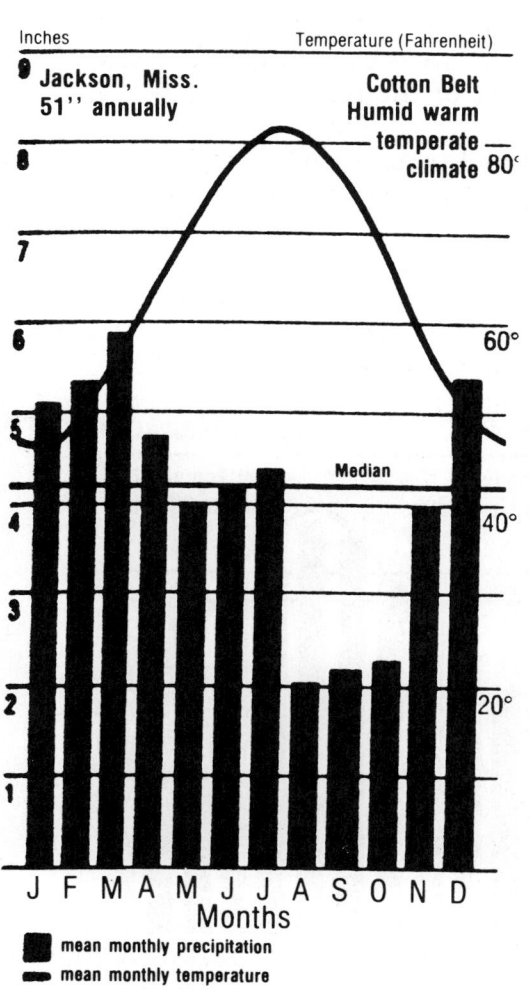

Annual Distribution of Mean Monthly Precipitation and Temperature, 1921-70

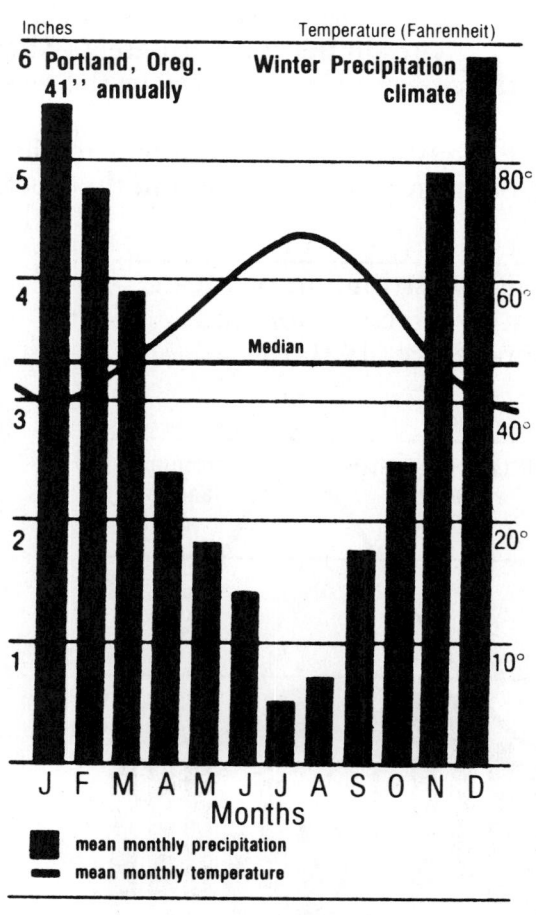

Annual winter grain crops and many perennial forage and tree crops are well adapted to these wet winter—dry summer climates. The well-adapted winter annual crops are planted in fall, become dormant in winter due to low temperatures, then complete their growth and reproduction phases before onset of the dry summer. Many perennial forage crops are well adapted to these climates for the same reasons. Forests and perennial tree crops can adapt or survive summer dry climates that are not too hot or too long.

These climates are well suited for irrigated agriculture. The low winter temperatures and relatively high effective precipitation produces water surpluses during the winter season. Therefore, management of stored water is necessary during the annual summer growing season.

Irrigation in these climates makes it possible to bring the surplus winter seasonal precipitation in phase with the summer seasonal temperatures and solar energy. That is why irrigated agriculture is so productive in these warm temperate and subtropical Mediterranean climates the world over.

**Intermountain areas**

The intermountain regions of the western United States are dominated by a complex of cool semiarid climates in the northern and central portions and arid desert climates in the southern areas. These climatic areas exist largely because of the effect of mountain ranges to the west and east of the region.

The Coastal and Sierra ranges to the west block sources of winter seasonal precipitation from the west, and the Rockies to the east are a barrier to the source

Annual Distribution of Mean
Monthly Precipitation and
Temperature, 1921-70

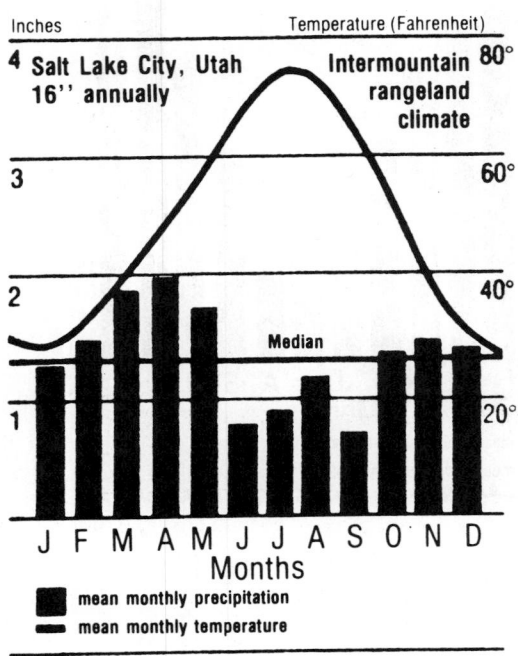

Annual Distribution of Mean
Monthly Precipitation and
Temperature, 1921-70

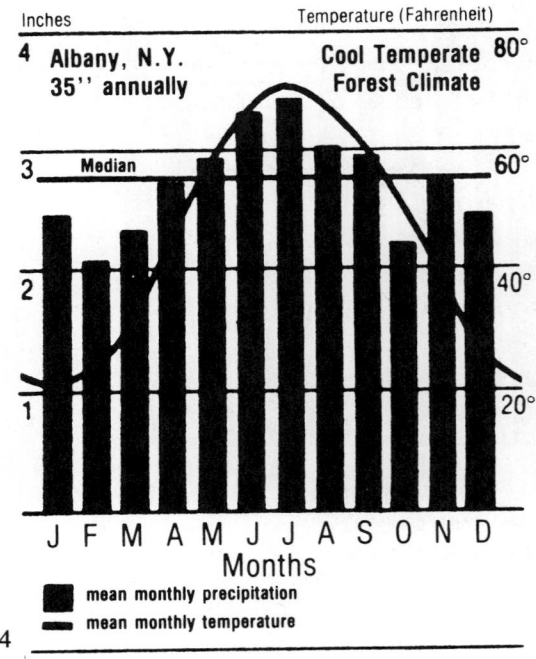

of the grassland summer seasonal precipitation from the east. As a result, the dryland agriculture of this intermountain region is largely confined to open range grazing.

The climatic record of Salt Lake City, Utah, provides a good example of these intermountain rangeland climates. The annual precipitation distribution reflects some of the Pacific Coast wet winter climates to the west as well as some lesser influences from the summer maximum precipitation climates to the east.

Irrigated croplands have been developed in many areas where water can be made available through water storage and management. Many different crops are grown with irrigation under highly varied growing season temperature zones in the intermountain regions. These varied growing season temperature conditions are caused by both elevation and latitude throughout the region.

## Northeast forest climates

Climatic conditions leading to forest vegetation of the Northeastern United States approach the ideal from the standpoint of annual and perennial crop moisture needed.

Mean monthly precipitation and temperature distributions are closely in phase with seasonal crop and forest growth. The highest mean monthly precipitation normally occurs in midsummer when crop and forest water demands are highest. A good example of these cool temperate humid forest climates of the northeast region is Albany, New York.

These climates exist from the upper Ohio Valley eastward across Pennsylvania into New Jersey, then northward through New York and the New England States. The northeast forest climates are characterized by a rather uniform mean monthly distribution of precipitation, with the highest amounts coming in midsummer in phase with the highest mean monthly temperature and evaporation.

Driest months of the year are February and October. The fact that the lowest annual mean monthly precipitation months do not occur consecutively is another unique feature of these climates. This is particularly true for large geographical regions.

Unfortunately, water supply systems in climates with relatively uniform and dependable precipitation are often underdesigned and overcommitted. As a result, when the inevitable drought occurs an acute water shortage develops. This has happened repeatedly in the densely populated northeast United States.

There are other unique climate regions within the continental United States, such as the Great Lakes region and those areas surrounding the Gulf of Mexico.

## Great Lakes region

Climate in and around the Great Lakes can best be described as humid and cool with snowy winters and cool pleasant summers. Annual precipitation is rather evenly distributed during the year.

Many small-scale climates exist in land areas surrounding the Great Lakes. There are several snow belts, fruit belts and other special small-scale climatic areas within the Great Lakes region, which are utilized to produce particular fruit or vegetable crops.

## Gulf coast region

Land areas surrounding the Gulf of Mexico are known as the Gulf Coast Region. The climate varies from humid warm temperate to humid subtropical. The frost-free crop growing season is 300 days or more in most of this region. Crops requiring long growing seasons such as sugarcane, cotton, and rice are produced.

The peninsular State of Florida is dominated by humid tropical, subtropical and warm temperate climates. The main crops are citrus, winter vegetables and sugarcane in the tropical and subtropical areas. The northern humid warm temperate areas are devoted to several special crops and cattle grazing.

Low desert areas of Arizona and California produce a number of tropical and subtropical crops requiring frost-free climates. Almost all crop production is under irrigation in these southwestern desert climates.

## Climatic niches

The large subcontinental land areas of Alaska have a variety of high latitude climates. They range from true Arctic to subarctic and cool marine climates. The agricultural worth of these high latitude climates is limited to certain climatic niches within this huge State.

Much of the true agricultural potential of Alaskan climate resources has not yet been exploited because of a mix of transportation, labor and energy cost considerations.

A wide diversity of crops are grown within the limits of the 50 States and Puerto Rico. Many of these crops require special climatic niches within the larger or more general climate type briefly discussed here. Some examples are pineapple, cranberries, tobacco, peanuts, and grapes.

These numerous climatic niches within the 50 States add much to the agricultural worth of the United States. Therefore, continued assessment of our collective climatic resources are of great economic value to all U.S. citizens.

# WEATHER AND CLIMATE: HOW THEY AFFECT POWER PRODUCTION

Variations in weather and climate affect many areas of society. Areas that are impacted include the productivity of farms, forests and fisheries; land and water resources; commercial, military and private transportation and communications; and the requirement for power generation and the means by which power is generated. Each area of society has a different tolerance to weather and climatic effects, depending on the institutional structure involved. Now that energy is in short supply, society has become more acutely aware of the interaction between weather and power production. Whether it be intense thunderstorms or intense heat, cold winters or dry winters, mountain runoff or valley winds—all effect how energy is supplied and used.

Weather can loosely be defined as the state of the atmosphere, including such conditions as rain, cloudiness, temperature and winds. Weather is highly variable and includes severe storms, hurricanes, downpours, and intense cold and hot spells. Weather forecasts deal with the near-term and the next few days, over which time relatively accurate descriptions of events can presently be made. Theory indicates that the forecasting time can probably be extended out to a week for weather events with scales of several hundred kilometers. It appears unlikely, however, that extreme local weather conditions can be foreseen much beyond a day, although, as described below, there is hope that anticipated monthly and seasonal average conditions can be forecast.

Beyond the few days over which weather can be forecast, reliance is usually placed on climatology, which is the average of the weather conditions in a region compiled, as a function of season, over a number of years. Climate is defined to include this set of average (or usual) conditions as well as the range of extreme conditions that can occur *and* the likelihood of their occurrence. In the U.S., the period of time used historically to develop averages or "normals" for a particular period (e.g., a month) has been 30 years with such averages being updated or recalculated every ten years. If climatic conditions were essentially constant, with only year to year fluctuations, the average would remain relatively constant. Climatic conditions are not constant, however and, in fact, it appears that climate has varied over all time scales. Both short (year to year) and long-term variations can be large, and both can be persistent. Thus there can be multiyear periods of drought and multimillenium periods of continental ice sheets. The former are perceived as a fluctuation; the latter (although very large) are often overlooked as being outside the range of consideration and because their presence would be evidenced in the short-term as a very small trend.

At present, there is only very limited improvement over climatology (skill) shown in NOAA forecasts of monthly and seasonal climates. Extensions of work using sea surface temperatures to forecast seasonal climates and incorporation of statistical correlations with solar-terrestrial activity (that may be anticipated several years in advance) offer hope that improvements eventually can be made in **the ability to forecast short- and intermediate-term climatic fluctuations.**

In describing the effects of weather and variations on power production, atmospheric behavior is divided into four time-scales.

337

- *Short term* is defined to mean that period of time over which detailed forecasting of specific atmospheric properties is reliable (currently up to 3-5 days) and over which responses to energy shortages are based on already in-place supplies. We will, however, restrict this domain to times of at least a day in the future, leaving to those actually producing the energy (as opposed to those planning and allocating it) the responsibility for responding to such shorter-term conditions as tornadoes, etc.
- *Intermediate term* is defined to mean that period of time over which short-term advance planning can alleviate potential problems of energy shortages, etc. Typically, this period ranges from weeks to a season or year.
- *Medium term* is defined as the period from one to ten years. This period corresponds to the time over which planning typically occurs to address questions of allocation of capital for energy generation facilities and resource utilization.
- *Long term* is defined as the period from ten to one-hundred years. This period corresponds to the time over which energy technologies typically can be introduced and become important contributors to national energy supplies or over which new national energy supplies or new technologies mature and their large-scale use may aggravate environmental problems.

The still longer time periods are not addressed here.

## The short term (days)

Providing the vast amounts of power needed for this country requires reliance on many modes of generation, including domestic and foreign energy supplies. Variations in the weather and climate can influence how energy resources are found, extracted, transported, transformed, distributed and consumed. To some extent the diversity of sources protects us from impacts of unusual weather on any one source or area. But, by being able to better understand what can be expected on a day to day basis and even a few days into the future (i.e., the "short-term"), energy-related activities can be planned so as to reduce overall consumption, and the daily comfort of people in their homes and the efficient functioning of industry can be made more certain.

The focal points in the short-term use of weather data for managing the operation of energy systems include: real-time contingency planning, responses to the impact of extremes of weather on the operation of energy systems or on energy demands, and fuel consumption reports. Problems of interest also include increased energy demands related to extreme cold or heat, icing or freezing rain impacting on the operation of transmission lines, freezing of rivers impeding the availability of barge transportation and normal cooling water, hurricanes interfering with the normal operation of natural gas wells in off-shore environments, precipitation rates in agricultural areas, and coastal forecasts required for liquified natural gas tanker unloading operations. Most of these examples require contingency planning and the identification of alternative supplies for either stand-by or current use.

## The intermediate term (weeks)

The past few years have provided examples of the impact monthly and seasonal variations in atmospheric behavior can have on energy supply and distribution.

The intense cold period in the eastern United States during December 1976 and January 1977 led to high demands for natural gas, the effects of which eventually spread to the west coast as gas supplies were diverted to the east. Although the winter as a whole in the east was not much colder than normal and total seasonal supplies were nearly adequate, the intensely cold months created such a large demand that the rate of delivering supplies was not adequate. Accurate forecasting of the weekly, monthly, and seasonal temperature patterns and the resulting energy demands would have permitted better planning of mitigating measures such as fuel switching.

Some impacts can affect the cost of energy. For example, the amount of water stored in mountain snow determines the amount of hydroelectric power that can be produced during the following year. Any shortfall in water supply must be made-up using more costly means of power generation. Accurate forecasts of spring rains and the rate of snow melt would permit more efficient (and therefore less expensive) use of available resources. Intermediate-term weather variations can also affect energy availability. For example, river or lake transport systems may be blocked by ice for extended periods, thus requiring the use of stockpiled fuels or provision of alternate means of delivery.

## The medium term (years)

In the design and planning of energy generation and supply facilities, account is already taken of the normal climate and a range of extremes (e.g., flood and hurricane frequency, etc.) that is based on past records. We have already discussed the need for short- and intermediate-term warning about such events.

For the medium term what is needed for energy planning purposes are predictions of trends and cycles of climate that might strain energy supplies in ways that make facilities uneconomical or inadequate to meet energy needs. For example, several years of drought in the western United States have heavily impacted hydroelectric supply capability and limited cooling water supply while at the same time increasing the power demands of some irrigation systems. These are not cases involving direct threats to public safety; rather the existing energy supplies are simply less abundant and plans must be made for augmenting them (e.g., gas turbines, etc.). An increase in the frequency of extreme hot spells during successive summers is an example where the demand for energy might change in a way not normally foreseen by energy planners. Unusually cold or lengthy winters in northern regions where river or sea ice might block access of ships to port facilities would limit the amount and period over which oil might be transported to the United States.

## Long term (decades)

The "normal" climate serves as the basis for planning energy needs (demands) and assessing the possibilities for energy supply. Thus, to even a greater extent than for the medium term, understanding trends, cycles and changes in variability of atmospheric behavior can affect the planning for energy supplies in the future in important ways. Shifts in circulation systems or ocean currents could cause changes in climate which affect energy demand, the availability of such resources as cooling water, and the ability to develop biomass as an energy source. All potential effects could be alleviated to some extent by improved understanding of future climatic events.

# HOW ENERGY TECHNOLOGIES AFFECT WEATHER AND CLIMATE

The by-products of energy production and consumption released to the atmosphere, namely waste heat, gases (including water vapor), and particles, can affect climate on a local or regional scale, usually by affecting the atmospheric radiation balance. In addition, any technology that alters the characteristics of the surface of the earth over extensive areas (such as the projected use of solar collectors) can also have climatic effects by altering the energy and moisture balances at the surface. The effects of energy use in large urban areas, and the resulting impacts on local and regional climate, have received considerable attention in recent years. Effects range from alteration of temperature to modification of precipitation.

Projecting energy use and consumption (and the resulting emission patterns) into the next century, reveals that several effects of energy production and consumption have the potential of extending beyond the regional scale, eventually out to the global scale. A primary source of these effects will be increased concentrations of $CO_2$ but heat, particles, and possibly other gases may also prove to be important considerations in evaluating future energy policy.

In the discussion of the effects of weather and climate variations on power production it was convenient to subdivide atmospheric behavior into various time-scales. Although energy production has diurnal, seasonal and annual cycles, it is more convenient to discuss the effects of energy technologies on weather and climate in terms of the spatial scale of the effect. Some effects of power production may be intermittent, but the most significant effects result from continuous or persistent emissions that either impact the region near the source (e.g., $H_2O$ and particles) or contribute to a build up of the global background concentration (e.g., $CO_2$, $^{85}Kr$).

The spatial scales of importance to power production and climatic effects are:

- local (to distances up to tens of Kilometers from the source)
- regional (to distances up to hundreds of kilometers)
- sub-continental (to distances up to thousands of kilometers)
- global (world-wide distribution).

Apart from very limited amounts of permanently stored energy, all energy that is generated is eventually dissipated and ends up as heat, regardless of the means of generation. The released heat may be concentrated at specific sites (e.g., waste heat at power plants) or it may be broadly distributed (e.g., space heating in business and residences). The climatic impact depends upon both the total amount of energy released and the amount released in a given area (flux per unit area).

The combined impact of population increases, changing patterns of population densities, and escalating per capita energy consumption has been to concentrate very large energy fluxes per unit area (flux density) in some regions of the world.

In 1971, for example, the world average energy consumption was approximately $1.5 \times 10^9$ Btu/km$^2$ of land area per year (0.05 W/m$^2$). In the same year, New York City's Manhattan Island had a total energy flux density of approximately $3 \times 10^{12}$ Btu/km$^2$ per year (100 W/m$^2$), which is very nearly equal to the global average net radiation (solar and longwave absorption minus longwave emission) at the earth's surface. Hence, current levels of energy consumption are insignificant in the global heat budget but can be significant on the local or regional scale.

Urban areas are typically warmer than the surrounding rural regions, thus leading to the term "urban heat island." A major portion of the urban heat island effect is caused by changes in the physical parameters of the area, namely radiative properties, moisture properties, evapotranspiration rates, and surface roughness. Another cause is anthropogenic heat rejection, which varies with season and latitude. In the cold northern climates during winter, anthropogenic heat in metropolitan areas may equal or exceed the amount of solar energy received. Energy conservation efforts may reduce the heat island effect.

In addition to waste heat, large-scale particulate and gaseous emissions can also affect the weather and climate. The major sources of atmospheric particles are: wind-raised dust and sea salt, direct products of combusion, volcanic particles, organic products of plant and animal life, and indirect products of combustion (resulting from chemical conversion in the atmosphere of gaseous emissions). The major anthropogenic sources of particles are industrial production and processing of materials such as metals and cement, agriculture, and combustion associated with industrial, commercial and domestic needs. The particles directly emitted tend to be large and are usually radiatively important only on the local and regional scales. Secondary particles, which form from vapors in the atmosphere, are usually sub-micron in size ($<10^{-6}$ m in diameter), have optical properties which induce strong scattering of solar radiation, and can be carried by the wind over sub-continental and global distances. Increased energy consumption relying on fuel conbustion without adequate controls may increase the atmospheric loading of both primary and secondary (indirect) particles. Atmospheric particles may also affect the nucleation and condensation of water vapor to form cloud droplets and, thus, the rates and pattern of precipitation. Hygroscopic particles may act as cloud condensation nuclei, thus affecting cloudiness and precipitation. Changes in cloudiness or atmospheric particle loading affect the transmission and scattering of solar radiation and the exchange of longwave radiation, thereby further perturbing the radiation balance, which in turn affects temperature patterns.

Gaseous emissions which are radiatively important, such as $CO_2$ and $H_2O$, may affect the climate directly by their radiative impact or indirectly by affecting the concentrations of other atmospheric constituents. $CO_2$ and $H_2O$ are both strong absorbers of infrared radiation, but they are relatively transparent to solar radiation. Consequently, an increase in the atmospheric concentration of these species would act to reduce the flux of infrared radiation emitted to space. To restore the balance with incoming solar radiation, there would be an increase in atmospheric temperature. Estimates of the increase in the global average surface temperature due to a doubling of $CO_2$ from 300 to 600 ppm range from 1.5 to 3.0 °C. Predictions of the future $CO_2$ increase due to combustion of fossil fuels suggest a doubling of the concentration before the middle of the next century.

Heat and moisture from cooling towers have been observed to affect the generation of cumulus clouds. Depending upon the stability of the prevailing air flow, the moisture and heat may lead to decreased stability increasing convective activity, and precipitation. Some have suggested this may lead to an increased frequency of thunderstorms and, possibly, tornadoes if employed on a large scale. Evaporation processes used to dissipate waste heat may also cause fogging and icing.

Other aspects of providing and distributing energy may also affect the weather or climate, but the magnitudes of many of the effects have not yet been assessed. Reservoirs behind hydroelectric dams alter important surface characteristics. Strip mining and similar processes of resource extraction cause vegetation to be removed, thereby exposing soil that has a reflectivity (albedo) different from the natural surface, thus altering the amount of solar radiation absorbed. The moisture retention properties are also altered, so energy that would have been dissipated as latent heat by evaporation is dissipated as sensible heat. In addition, particulate matter may be released to the atmosphere as wind-blown dust. These effects are likely to be local or regional in scale.

Transportation of crude oil and gasoline has the potential for inadvertent climatic effects. The use of supertankers offers the possibility of large oil spills or slicks at sea in the event of an accident. Very thin oil slicks extending over many square kilometers in higher latitudes or colder water would change the albedo of the ocean and reduce the amount of evaporation. These changes in surface energy balance would affect the ocean-atmosphere exchange rates for moisture and sensible heat.

Other examples of how providing and distributing energy may affect weather and climate are given below for various energy technologies.

## Fossil fuel combustion (coal, oil, gas)

Combustion of fossil fuels causes atmospheric emissions of primary particles and numerous gaseous species (SOx, NOx, COx, $H_2O$ and hydrocarbons). The species SOx, NOx and hydrocarbons may be converted to secondary particles that can contribute to acid rain on the sub-continental scale and affect radiative processes and precipitation patterns, as already noted above.

## Nuclear

Routine emissions of $^{85}Kr$, although at very small concentrations, are building up the global background concentration of this species. Ionization caused by $^{85}Kr$ decay increases the atmospheric conductivity. This increase in turn can affect the atmospheric electric field that is believed to be related to scavenging and precipitation processes in thunderstorms and severe convective activity.

## Solar

The technologies being developed to provide electrical power on a large scale using solar energy include photovoltaic, distributed collector, and central receiver systems. The interception and collection of solar radiation by large arrays of reflectors and absorbers will alter the regional radiation budget (solar and longwave) and change the moisture retention properties of the earth's surface. Natural surfaces absorb 70-90% of the incident solar radiation; deserts 70-75%, and vegetated surfaces 80-90%. Portions of the solar energy absorbed are convected away from the surface as heat, used for evaporation, radiated away as longwave radiation, or conducted into the ground. If arrays of mirrors or collectors were placed over soil with a significant moisture content, evaporation would be restricted, thus affecting the moisture and radiation budgets.

Solar thermal collector systems that use large arrays of mirrors or distributed collectors use the absorbed solar radiation to heat a working fluid that in turn powers a steam turbine generator. Cooling towers are used for disposal of the waste heat (approximately 60% of the thermal energy absorbed in the working fluid). The solar thermal collector system reduces the normal amount of energy absorbed at the surface and available for heating the atmosphere in the region. This deficiency would have an effect like a high desert albedo. Cooling towers concentrate the energy and moisture released to the atmosphere, effects that may impact on weather and climate as already noted above.

## Biomass

There are two approaches to the use of biomass as a source of energy. One is to cut down existing forests for firewood, such as is done on a large scale in South America and in other tropical locations. The second is to grow special crops for either their oil and rubber content or their combustible mass. Both aspects change the surface conditions (i.e., increase or derease albedo, affect the moisture flux by changing evaporation or evapotranspiration rates) in ways that may lead to local, regional, or even larger-scale climatic effects. Deforestation also contributes $CO_2$ to the atmosphere, and biomass crops contribute gaseous and particulate emissions.

## Wind

Individual wind turbine generators do not have a significant effect on the planetary boundary layer. However, many such wind turbine generators grouped together may extract energy from a region at a rate that is a significant fraction of the natural rate of kinetic energy replenishment (which averages about 2.5 W/m$^2$ over the U.S.). In this case there may be a significant change in the wind flow pattern of the planetary boundary layer, that may affect surface heat and moisture losses, temperature, and the precipitation rate on a regional scale.

## Geothermal

Among the various gaseous emissions resulting from the extraction of geothermal energy, $H_2S$ has the greatest potential for affecting weather and climate since it can be converted to sulfate aerosols (particles) through a chain of chemical reactions. As in the case of particles from other energy technologies, these aerosols may affect the regional climate by perturbing the radiation and condensation nucleii budgets.

## Hydroelectric

Reservoirs formed behind dams can alter important surface characteristics. For example, the evaporation rate is enhanced because of the increased water surface area, especially in the West during normally dry summer months. Changing from a vegetated surface to a lake surface also changes the albedo. The net effect is a change in the local and regional temperature and moisture distributions. Dams also help to reduce the effects of extreme weather by controlling flooding and by providing water for irrigation in times of drought.

## Ocean thermal energy conversion (OTEC)

These facilities extract energy from the temperature difference between the surface and deeper water. Bringing the cooler, deep water to near the surface will reduce the sea surface temperature and alter salinity gradients. The extent to which ambient surface temperatures are lowered will depend on plant design and site conditions. A 100-240 MW OTEC plant may lower the surface temperature 2-3 °C. Near the equator changes in the sea surface temperature can affect the development of tropical storms. The pumping of large amounts of deep, nutrient-rich ocean water to near the ocean surface may cause formation of large plankton blooms, that would change the ocean albedo.

The artificial upwelling of deep ocean water caused by OTEC plants also may have an effect on the concentration of $CO_2$ in the atmosphere. The forced upwelling of deep ocean waters (containing about 15% more dissolved carbon than the ocean surface layers) is a potential source of atmospheric $CO_2$ if the water is discharged from the plant near the ocean surface. The microclimate at OTEC sites could be affected further if open cycle systems are utilized. Degassing procedures needed to ensure operating efficiencies may lead to the venting of concentrations of oxygen, nitrogen, and $CO_2$. The potential climatic impacts of these changes need to be assessed.

## Summary

The examples given above for the various energy technologies highlight the climate related issues associated with primary and alternative sources of power. There is no assurance that all of the critical issues have been identified, nor have assessments of the possible climatic effects been completed. There is a need for constant awareness of potential climatic effects, continued development of improved assessment capabilities, and regular updating of assessments.

# THE CLIMATE SYSTEM AND PROCESSES OF CLIMATIC CHANGE

The atmosphere is a dynamic system powered by the sun. The differential heating caused by a surplus of solar radiation at low latitudes and a deficit at high latitudes serves as the forcing function for the varying behavior of the atmosphere. The atmosphere through its motions strives to return to a condition of static stability constrained by the requirements of conserving mass, energy and momentum. The atmospheric conditions as they vary from moment to moment and from place to place are referred to as weather. The term climate refers loosely to the weather averaged over both time and space as well as the statistical properties of the atmosphere, including weather extremes, joint frequency distributions, and many other measures of weather variability.

The climate at any location on the earth is determined by a combination of influences ranging from the global scale down to details of the local environment. The distribution of solar radiation, for example, affects climate on a global scale (the macroclimate), whereas geographic features may influence climate within smaller regions (the mesoclimate and microclimate).

## The global climate system

The global climate system is composed of several components: the atmosphere, oceans, land surfaces, snow and ice masses (the cryosphere), and the biosphere. These major physical components are coupled by the transport of mass, momentum, energy, and water. The coupling is further complicated by many feedback mechanisms, including the radiative effects of trace atmospheric constituents.

The oceans are large heat storage reservoirs that absorb, store and resupply to the atmosphere vast amounts of energy through the exchange of latent and sensible heat as well as longwave radiation. The energy which is lost to the atmosphere is replenished by absorption of solar radiation. The ocean currents play an important role in affecting the spatial distribution of the energy transferred to the atmosphere. The momentum exchange between the atmosphere and ocean due to wind stress affects both atmospheric and oceanic circulation patterns. Variations in the extent of sea-ice alter the global radiation and energy balances changing the albedo and thermal capacity of the earth's oceans. Factors affecting surface albedo include the amount of snow and ice on land surfaces, soil moisture, and the extent and type vegetation.

The atmospheric composition, including cloudiness, affects the transfer of solar and longwave radiation. The net flux of radiative energy at the earth's surface determines the amount of energy available for evaporation or transfer as sensible heat to the atmosphere. Since cloudiness depends upon temperature, humidity and wind circulation patterns in addition to convective activity, there is a coupling between atmospheric dynamics and the radiative and hydrological processes. The biosphere affects evapotranspiration of water and release of certain other trace constitutents to the atmosphere and is itself regulated by such growth-controlling factors as wind, temperature, moisture, and the solar energy available for photosynthesis.

This complex climate system has undergone many changes in the past, as reflected in the climatic record. In addition to the natural climatic variations to be expected in the future, it is possible that man can also affect the climate by disturbing the delicate balances of heat, radiation, and water on a regional and ultimately on a global scale.

## The climatic record

In interpreting and extrapolating the historical records, it is important to realize that the magnitudes of climatic averages themselves vary not only with the location but with the period and length of the record. Thus a particular 30-year period may not be representative. Indeed, the period 1931-1960, upon which many statistical analyses are based in defining "normal" climate, was abnormally warm compared to the average for the last thousand years. Further, the climatic record for the past million years shows that the climate has varied over all recorded time scales.

The variation in global mean surface temperature over the past 100 years is about 0.5°C. From the 1890's to the mid-1940's the global air temperature increased by about 0.5°C. Since 1940 global mean temperatures have fallen by about 0.3°C and appear to have leveled off. Every summer during the 1930's in the corn belt of the United States was warmer than the average for the century. The results of the recent cooling trend can be seen in agricultural records. For example, harvests in England were completed about 9 days later on the average during 1960-1973 than during the 1940's. Food production may be affected less by cooling or warming trends than by a trend associated with greater variability of the weather and more common occurrence of droughts, floods, hot summers, and severe winters.

The instrumental record of climatic change only spans the last 200-300 years. Climatic variations over much longer time scales have been deduced by analyses of tree rings; fossil flora pollen and fauna in deep ocean sediments and their isotopic composition; fossil pollen in soil and lake sediment layers (varves); isotopic composition in ice cores from Greenland and the polar ice caps; and sea-level changes. Although these data do not give a complete global picture, they do clearly show climatic trends and periods of significant climatic variations.

The variation during the last 1,000 years of the mean temperature for central England inferred from historical data is about 2.0°C. Fluctuations in temperature of this magnitude coincided with significant changes in agricultural practices that caused the migration of civilizations. Around the ninth century Norse settlers in Iceland seem to have flourished in a phase of rapid warming and were able to establish a colony in Greenland. However, within a few hundred years a deterioration in climate occurred that was a major contributing factor in the collapse of the Greenland colony. The Iceland colony barely survived through the Little Ice Age, which extended from the 15th to the 19th centuries.

# Mechanisms of climatic change

The causes of past climatic changes have not yet been adequately explained. There are three mechanisms, however, that seem to offer the greatest insight into patterns of climatic change on various time scales over the past 400,000 years. First, there are the long-term cyclic effects produced by subtle, regular variations in the earth's orbital path and inclination around the sun and in the orientation of the spin axis of the earth relative to the sun. These factors induce predictable, systematic changes in the amount of solar energy reaching the top of the atmosphere for different latitudes. In a cycle of approximately 23,000 years, the earth advances in its elliptical orbit so that its closest approach to the sun occurs at different times of the year. The earth and the sun are now closest in January, but in 10,000 years they will be closest in July (a period of approximately 20,000 years). There are also orbital changes affecting climate on time scales greater than 20,000 years. In a cycle of approximately 41,000 years, the orbit tilts so that the earth's axis is sometimes more nearly perpendicular to the planetary plane than at other times (more properly, the tilt changes with respect to the moving ecliptic). In a cycle of approximately 93,000 years, the eccentricity of the earth's orbit changes from nearly circular to more noticeably elliptical.

A second mechanism, which may cause climatic changes on the time scale of a few decades, is variation in the solar output. There is still considerable debate about the link between solar activity (e.g., the 11-year sunspot cycle) and weather. Nevertheless, many features of the observed record of temperature variations since 1600 have been reproduced with a model which incorporated an empirical dependence on solar activity as measured by the Wolf sunspot number. This dependence seems to imply that the solar output is more than 2% less when there is no sunspot activity than when there is moderate activity. More observations by either satellite or balloon-borne instrument systems are needed to confirm such a relationship.

A third mechanism for climatic change is increased atmospheric dust loading due to volcanic activity, which can affect climate on a time scale of years to decades. Intense volcanic eruptions can inject large amounts of dust into the stratosphere where the residence time may range from several months to several years. Dust produced by volcanoes can have a veiling effect that reduces the amount of solar radiation reaching the ground and scatters more incoming solar radiation back to space. The reduction in solar heating of the earth/atmosphere system results in cooler surface temperatures. Climate models including simulation of the effect of volcanic dust have duplicated the major features of the recent climatic record, including the cool temperatures of the Little Ice Age and the decades around 1800 along with the general warming trend between the 1890's and 1940's. None of the above mechanisms, however satisfactorily explains the decline in temperature observed since 1940.

Some have postulated that the cooling since 1940 is due to anthropogenic influences rather than natural climate variability. The suggestion that man has increased the amount of atmospheric dust through agricultural and industrial activities and that this is the cause of the recent cooling is not borne out in global measurements of atmospheric turbidity, although this may partially explain the observed changes in regional climates.

Climatic fluctuations involve processes on a range of spatial scales that can interact in a highly complex way so as to cause climatic anomalies affecting large geographic areas. The intermediate-term anomalies are the result of persistently recurrent weather systems of the same type. The fundamental question involves how and why particular events recur during a given season or sometimes recur for several seasons or years. To cause recurrent events like prolonged droughts or cold waves would seem to require some sort of memory. It is highly unlikely that the atmosphere alone can account for this persistent recurrence because of its highly variable nature and its relatively short thermodynamic relaxation time.

The oceans play a major role in the evolution of intermediate- and medium-term climatic fluctuations. The top three meters of the ocean contain as much heat as the entire atmosphere, and anomalies in ocean temperature have been observed to penetrate down to a few hundred meters. These temperature anomalies create vast heat reservoirs that may affect the course and behavior of storms and jet streams later on. The anomalies are in turn frequently responses to antecedent abnormal atmospheric conditions.

It appears that the abnormal winter of 1976-77 was the result of several factors that operated in a synergistic fashion so that positive feedback processes were amplified in the coupled ocean/air/land system. Extreme cold dominated the eastern half of the United States, record drought affected the far west, and equally abnormal warmth occurred over Alaska and much of the Canadian Arctic. Jerome Namias suggests that interactions between sea surface temperature anomalies in the Pacific, known as El Niño and the atmospheric flow pattern resulted in storms being diverted northward to Alaska rather than coming into the West. The storms moving up to Alaska then created a southward bulge in the jet stream in the eastern United States that moved arctic air masses southward producing snow. Snow-albedo feedback then intensified the cold and the temperature difference between the continent and the Gulf Stream, setting up another set of storms along the Eastern seaboard that created more snow and more cold air. The very strong El Niño of 1982-83 produced many new puzzles that require even more complex explanations, possibly involving the volcanic eruption of El Chicon and other poorly understood factors.

This simplified description illustrates the complex coupling of physical processes and events that can lead to climatic change. Understanding of these processes has not yet developed to the point, however, where scientific consensus on the causes, trends, and magnitudes of climatic variations has been achieved, let alone understanding to offer prospects for accurate quantitative predictions. Considerable debate still goes on within the scientific community about all these matters. The trends over the next 100 to 1,000 years may be toward warmer climates or the return of a major Ice Age. Or, perhaps, Planet Earth is in for a prolonged period of highly variable and very disruptive patterns of weather and short term climatic fluctuations. Another Ice Age cannot be ruled out, especially when one considers a time frame beyond a few hundred years. For the moment, however, a moderate degree of consensus has developed among climatological experts that the trends over the next hundred years or more will be toward warmer climates. Some of the thinking about this possibility is reviewed in the special section of this report entitled, "The Carbon Dioxide Problem." But keep an open mind. The problems of climatic fluctuation, variation, and change are among the most urgent open scientific questions of our Age.

# THE CARBON DIOXIDE PROBLEM

A recent analysis by the National Research Council of the potential climatic effects of the by-products of energy production and consumption (heat, particulate matter, and gases) showed that the combustion product carbon dioxide has the greatest apparent potential for disturbing the global climate over the next few centuries. The perception that there *might* be a serious $CO_2$ problem stems from the following:

- There has been a well-documented world-wide increase in atmospheric $CO_2$ concentrations since 1958; this growth has probably been occurring since the middle of the last century.

- An amount equivalent to about fifty percent of the $CO_2$ released from fossil-fuel burning has been accumulating in the atmosphere.

- $CO_2$ transmits solar radiation but absorbs some of the outgoing long-wave radiation from the earth, which is the so-called "greenhouse" effect. Thus, qualitatively, $CO_2$ should act to warm the lower atmosphere and, by radiating more outgoing energy, cool the stratosphere.

- Different calculations of the "greenhouse" warming indicate that doubling of the $CO_2$ content of the air could result in a 1.5-3 °C warming of the lower atmosphere. This global warming is sufficient to cause significant alteration of the present climate.

- While the climatic effects would be world-wide, they will likely not be uniform: some regions of the globe would experience greater changes from the present climate; others less.

- The doubling of atmospheric $CO_2$ could take place within the next 75 years. There are sufficient fossil-fuel reserves to raise the atmospheric $CO_2$ many-fold if they are consumed rapidly enough.

- Natural rates of removal of $CO_2$ from the air are calculated to be so slow that it might take many centuries before atmospheric $CO_2$ levels returned to "normal" after emissions ceased.

The crucial questions to be answered include:
1. What will be the potential future atmospheric concentrations of carbon dioxide?
2. What will be the climatic effects of these concentrations?
3. What will be the effect on the biological and physical environment of these changes?
4. What, if any, will be the effects on human societies?
5. What, if any, actions can be taken in order to diminish the climatic changes or mitigate their consequences?

## Sources of atmospheric carbon dioxide

The main source of the observed increase in $CO_2$ is thought to be combustion of fossil fuels. Recently, however, the possibility has been raised that world-wide land-use practices, particularly deforestation and oxidation of humus, could also be contributing to the buildup. It is not thought likely that natural sources, while important over the long history of the earth, are a significant factor in the recent rise.

Volcanoes and other natural venting of $CO_2$ from the earth's interior, as well as weathering of terristrial carbonates, is thought to be only a very small fraction of the current annual net input. Recent suggestions that venting of methane along fault lines, and subsequent oxidation, could represent an additional source may need to be checked. No specific study of natural sources is now planned but it should be borne in mind that no comprehensive theory exists to explain the natural cycle of $CO_2$ over the billions of years of the earth's history—or in fact what atmospheric concentrations of $CO_2$ actually occurred during this time.

There are three aspects to the problem that should be considered: estimation of the carbon content of fossil fuel reserves in the ground; determination of the annual rate at which these reserves are converted to fuel and used (also other industrial sources such as cement production); and projection of future demand for these fuels.

The available reserves are well enough known today to argue that, if burned rapidly enough, atmospheric $CO_2$ will continue to increase to several times its present value. Nevertheless, better assessement on a country-by-country bases will be needed to keep track of the potential supply.

A controversy exists whether the carbon in the atmosphere is increasing partly because of deforestation and other land-use practices, or whether the biosphere now acts as a net sink, absorbing a fraction of the fossil fuel $CO_2$. Current models of oceanic uptake of $CO_2$ allow, at most, only a small amount of extra non-fossil fuel $CO_2$ to come from the biosphere. Other investigators have claimed that amounts as great as the fossil-fuel contribution itself could be coming to the air from deforestation. If the latter is the case, then the understanding of the various sinks for atmospheric $CO_2$ must currently be seriously in error.

Regardless of current and past biospheric trends, it is clear that future levels of atmospheric $CO_2$ could be substantially increased by large-scale clearing of tropical rain forests followed by oxidation and associated disturbances of the soils. There are reasonably good estimates of past and current fossil fuel usage, but there is very poor knowledge of the current rate of conversion of one type of vegetation to another or to nonvegetated areas like cities and what this means in terms of the total biospheric mass of fixed carbon. These conversions can be deliberate, as with conversion of the forest to agriculture or incidental to other activities, or they may be natural as a result of local climatic shifts. It is desirable to estimate the current changes in the biosphere both to formulate and calibrate models of the carbon cycle as well as to determine the effects of future land-use changes on $CO_2$ levels.

## Sinks for atmospheric $CO_2$

The ocean is currently believed to be the major sink for atmospheric $CO_2$. To provide reliable predictions of future atmospheric $CO_2$ levels, one must thoroughly understand the dynamics of the $CO_2$ uptake and the transfer of $CO_2$ from the surface waters to deeper waters. Several important aspects are involved. The exchange rate of $CO_2$ between air and sea must be known as a function of temperature, sea state, and possibly wind speed and water chemistry. The thermodynamic distribution coefficient of $CO_2$ gas between air and sea water (the $CO_2$ buffer factor) must be known as a function of temperature, alkalinity and total dissolved inorganic carbon concentration. The patterns and rates of vertical transfer within the sea must be determined. The impact of climate changes on these rates must also be anticipated. The vertical flux of particles and organisms transporting carbon downward through the sea should be assessed. The possible influence of environmental changes induced by man's activities on these fluxes must be determined. The role of $CaCO_3$ in determining the uptake of $CO_2$ from the air should be examined. The dissolution of $CaCO_3$ in marine sediments enhances the capability of the ocean to absorb fossil fuel $CO_2$ from the air. For the shallow sediments, the critical mineral is high-magnesium calcite; for the deep sea sediments, the critical mineral is calcite.

Most scientists now believe that transfer of $CO_2$ from the surface waters to deeper waters will constitute the rate-limiting step for oceanic uptake of $CO_2$ for the next several hundred years. This transfer takes place both by turbulent mixing through the main thermocline and by organized circulations where water previously in contact with the air sinks, mainly at high latitudes. Much of our knowledge of the penetrations of $CO_2$ into the oceans stems from observations of man-made tracers, notably tritium and $^{14}C$, produced in nuclear weapons tests. Continued surveys of these and other transient tracers are likely to be our main tool to provide an understanding of oceanic circulation and mixing.

The rate of future increases in $CO_2$ concentrations are dependent on how much higher $CO_2$ levels would enhance the primary production potential of the vegetation and so increase the rate of carbon fixation by the biota. Such fixation would reduce the rate of increase in atmospheric $CO_2$ from new sources.

To acquire information on the plants' responses to higher $CO_2$ levels, it will be necessary to consider the effects of increased $CO_2$ on photosynthesis, nitrogen fixation, water-use efficiency of plants and, of course, actual growth. Photosynthesis is the central process governing the primary productivity of all green plants. The availability of nutrients and water are generally considered to be the major limiting factors to plant productivity, and it is not clear to what extent enhancement of photosynthesis by increased $CO_2$ will increase carbon fixation. Water use by plants is controlled largely by the stomata, which in turn may be influenced by the ambient $CO_2$ concentration. It is possible that increased atmopheric $CO_2$ could result in increased water-use efficiency by allowing the photosynthesis rate to remain unchanged while reducing the demand for water. On the other hand, plants may increase photosynthesis for the same water usage at elevated $CO_2$ concentrations. Note that increased primary productivity by itself is not sufficient to slow down the atmospheric $CO_2$ growth. Only if this increased productivity results in a year to year increase in *stored* biomass or detritus will it increase the strength of the sink for excess $CO_2$.

## Models of the carbon cycle

All the major components of the carbon dioxide research program involve model development as part of their efforts, but an additional component will be devoted to integrating the results of these studies into a global carbon cycle model. Its goal will be to predict the future atmospheric $CO_2$ concentrations from scenarios of fossil fuel use and land-use changes. To be valid, these models must be able to reproduce not only the currently available data on atmospheric $CO_2$ growth, but be compatible with the distribution of the isotopes of carbon in the atmosphere, oceans and biosphere.

Progress in this area will depend upon progress in determining the components of the carbon cycle and their reactions to increased atmospheric $CO_2$ coupled with any attendant climate changes. Attempts to model the carbon cycle will also likely disclose areas needing particular research emphasis in the other components. This effort must proceed, as with all modeling efforts, in close association with data gathering and analysis.

Some modeling of the carbon cycle is now going on both in the U.S. and abroad. Cooperation among the groups is essential. There is marked similarity in the assumptions and transfer rates among carbon reservoirs, but this may indicate the paucity of information upon which all of the modeled processes are based.

## Climate effects of increased $CO_2$

The consequences to the climate of increased atmospheric $CO_2$ have been estimated from computer simulations. These simulations, which indicate that a doubling of $CO_2$ concentrations would increase the global mean temperature of the lower atmosphere by between 1.5 and 3 °C, are crude even though they employ the most sophisticated techniques and machines available. Several factors not now included in simulation models are thought to be important and others not now known could also prove to be significant. In addition, none of the climate models applied to the $CO_2$ problem have contained a realistic topography or distribution of land and water. Thus, regional climatic changes cannot now be predicted, yet regional modifications of precipitation may be the most crucial consequence of $CO_2$ increases in the atmosphere.

Knowledge of the climatic history of the earth is important both to anticipate what might happen and to provide data to help validate the computer simulations. Emphasis can be put on periods where the earth was warmer than it is now—such as the hypsithermal. Abnormally warm years within the period when instruments were available can also be considered.

# Effects of climate change

It is necessary to translate the anticipated climate changes due to increased $CO_2$ into effects on the biosphere as well as on the cryosphere and ocean circulation. It is likely that some of these effects will feed back to the climate system itself and to the carbon cycle. In addition to the effects already mentioned, the following effects are also possible and in need of further study.

- Marine organisms could be affected by increases in dissolved $CO_2$. The slow lowering of oceanic pH and lowering of the supersaturation with respect to $CaCO_3$ of surface waters could affect the ability of organisms to form carbonate shells and skeletal structures.

- Changes in atmospheric circulation could produce changes in oceanic circulation. Marine productivity could be reduced if the rate of upwelling were decreased since the latter controls the supply of nutrients to certain surface waters.

- Greatly elevated $CO_2$ concentrations in the air may have effects on non-photosynthesizing organisms. It is unlikely that mammals would suffer, but possibly invertebrates and microorganisms would be affected.

- Ecosystem stability and the geographic distribution of plants, and the animals associated with them, could be affected. Shifts of temperature and precipitation patterns could rearrange the location of major biomes; some species could suffer, others might prosper.

- Special attention should be given to agricultural effects of climate changes. This, of course, is of current concern because climate changes occur naturally. The reaction of the world's food and fiber producing regions to the $CO_2$-induced climate changes warrants special consideration, however.

- Much concern has been expressed that warming would cause the polar ice sheets to melt and the sea level to rise. It is quite unlikely that this would happen in the next few centuries and the likelihood of its occurrance may have been overstressed. Climatically-induced surges of the ice sheets are possible, but the causes of surges are not well understood. It has been asserted, however, that West Antarctica could deglaciate if the ocean should warm. Because this could produce a 5 meter sea level rise, this possibility deserves some special attention. The recession of mountain glaciers also should be examined although total melting of them would only raise sea level about 1 m.

## Societal impacts

The ultimate issue is, of course, the impact of increased $CO_2$ on society. It must be stressed that impacts of climate change will not fall equally on all segments of the world's society despite their global nature. Indeed some regions or countries may find benefits in the altered climate, others may be relatively unaffected, while some could be harmed significantly. Such disparity of effects may make international agreements very difficult to achieve if they are ever needed.

Among the more obvious things to explore are the impacts of shifting agricultural regions and productivity, water availability due to changing precipitation regimes (e.g., can inter-basin transfer of water alleviate the problems of local drought), and impacts on energy demand itself (is there a positive or negative feedback on $CO_2$ production?).

The decision to curtail fossil fuel will be made only if and when society's costs are believed to exceed the benefits to continued fossil fuel combustion. Worldwide agreement on reduced consumption of fossil fuel will present very serious international problems. Thus, it seems worthwhile to explore how societies might cope with the climatic consequences of increased $CO_2$.

## Mitigating strategies

Besides reducing fossil-fuel use, one may consider other technological "solutions" should $CO_2$ increases be seen as undesirable. Certainly both more efficient use of energy and the development of non-fossil energy sources would help reduce the $CO_2$ growth and could conceivably delay the onset or even solve the problem.

No technical solution has been proposed so far that seems practicable, but this should not deter the search. One should still explore the possibilities of removing $CO_2$ from effluent streams or from the air, sequestering it in permanent or quasi-permanent reservoirs. Even if such studies fail to uncover a feasible method for doing so, they will serve to demonstrate that technological optimism will not be a substitute for a realistic assessment of the problem.

# RECORD-SETTING WEATHER

# HIGHS

# LOWS

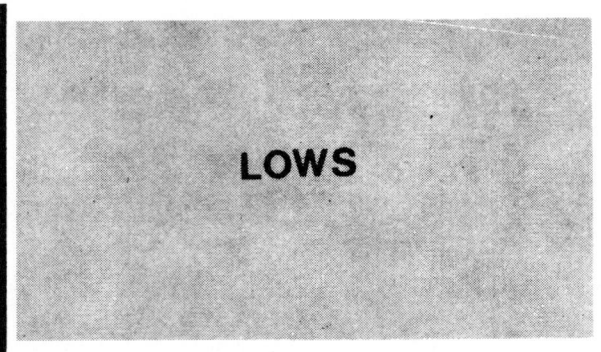

## RECORD HIGHEST TEMPERATURES BY STATION

| State | Temp. °F. | Date | Station | Elevation Feet |
|---|---|---|---|---|
| Ala. | 112 | Sept. 5, 1925 | Centerville | 345 |
| Alaska | 100 | June 27, 1915 | Fort Yukon | --- |
| Ariz. | 127 | July 7, 1905* | Parker | 345 |
| Ark. | 120 | Aug. 10, 1936 | Ozark | 396 |
| Calif. | 134 | July 10, 1913 | Greenland Ranch | -178 |
| Colo. | 118 | July 11, 1888 | Bennett | --- |
| Conn. | 105 | July 22, 1926 | Waterbury | 400 |
| Del. | 110 | July 21, 1930 | Millsboro | 20 |
| D. C. | 106 | July 20, 1930* | Washington | 112 |
| Fla. | 109 | June 29, 1931 | Monticello | 207 |
| Ga. | 112 | July 24, 1952 | Louisville | 337 |
| Hawaii | 100 | Apr. 27, 1931 | Pahala | 850 |
| Idaho | 118 | July 28, 1934 | Orofino | 1,027 |
| Ill. | 117 | July 14, 1954 | E. St. Louis | 410 |
| Ind. | 116 | July 14, 1936 | Collegeville | 672 |
| Iowa | 118 | July 20, 1934 | Keokuk | 614 |
| Kans. | 121 | July 24, 1936* | Alton (near) | 1,651 |
| Ky. | 114 | July 28, 1930 | Greensburg | 581 |
| La. | 114 | Aug. 10, 1936 | Plain Dealing | 268 |
| Maine | 105 | July 10, 1911* | North Bridgton | 450 |
| Md. | 109 | July 10, 1936* | Cumberland & Frederick | 623 - 325 |
| Mass. | 106 | July 4, 1911* | Lawrence | 51 |
| Mich. | 112 | July 13, 1936 | Mio | 963 |
| Minn. | 114 | July 6, 1936* | Moorhead | 904 |
| Miss. | 115 | July 29, 1930 | Holly Springs | 600 |
| Mo. | 118 | July 14, 1954* | Warsaw & Union | 687 - 560 |
| Mont. | 117 | July 5, 1937 | Medicine Lake | 1,950 |
| Nebr. | 118 | July 24, 1936* | Minden | 2,169 |
| Nev. | 122 | June 23, 1954* | Overton | 1,240 |
| N. H. | 106 | July 4, 1911 | Nashua | 125 |
| N. J. | 110 | July 10, 1936 | Runyon | 18 |
| N. Mex. | 116 | July 14, 1934* | Orogrande | 4,171 |
| N. Y. | 108 | July 22, 1926 | Troy | 35 |
| N. C. | 109 | Sept. 7, 1954* | Weldon | 81 |
| N. Dak. | 121 | July 6, 1936 | Steele | 1,857 |
| Ohio | 113 | July 21, 1934* | Gallipolis (near) | 673 |
| Okla. | 120 | July 26, 1943* | Tishomingo | 670 |
| Oreg. | 119 | Aug. 10, 1898* | Pendleton | 1,074 |
| Pa. | 111 | July 10, 1936* | Phoenixville | 100 |
| R. I. | 102 | July 30, 1949 | Greenville | 420 |
| S. C. | 111 | June 28, 1954* | Camden | 170 |
| S. Dak. | 120 | July 5, 1936 | Gannvalley | 1,750 |
| Tenn. | 113 | Aug. 9, 1930* | Perryville | 377 |
| Tex. | 120 | Aug. 12, 1936 | Seymour | 1,291 |
| Utah | 116 | June 28, 1892 | Saint George | 2,880 |
| Vt. | 105 | July 4, 1911 | Vernon | 310 |
| Va. | 110 | July 15, 1954 | Balcony Falls | 725 |
| Wash. | 118 | Aug. 5, 1961* | Ice Harbor Dam | 475 |
| W. Va. | 112 | July 10, 1936* | Martinsburg | 435 |
| Wis. | 114 | July 13, 1936 | Wisconsin Dells | 900 |
| Wyo. | 114 | July 12, 1900 | Basin | 3,500 |

\* Also on earlier dates at the same or other places.

## RECORD LOWEST TEMPERATURES BY STATES

| State | Temp. °F. | Date | Station | Elevation Feet |
|---|---|---|---|---|
| Ala. | -24 | Jan. 31, 1966 | Russellville | 880 |
| Alaska | -80 | Jan. 23, 1971 | Prospect Creek | 1,100 |
| Ariz. | -40 | Jan. 7, 1971 | Hawley Lake | 8,180 |
| Ark. | -29 | Feb. 13, 1905 | Pond | 1,250 |
| Calif. | -45 | Jan. 20, 1937 | Boca | 5,532 |
| Colo. | -60 | Feb. 1, 1951 | Taylor Park | 9,206 |
| Conn. | -32 | Feb. 16, 1943 | Falls Village | 585 |
| Del. | -17 | Jan. 17, 1893 | Millsboro | 20 |
| D. C. | -15 | Feb. 11, 1899 | Washington | 112 |
| Fla. | - 2 | Feb. 13, 1899 | Tallahassee | 193 |
| Ga. | -17 | Jan. 27, 1940 | CCC Camp F-16 | --- |
| Hawaii | 14 | Jan. 2, 1961 | Haleakala Maui Island | 9,750 |
| Idaho | -60 | Jan. 18, 1943 | Island Park Dam | 6,285 |
| Ill. | -35 | Jan. 22, 1930 | Mount Carroll | 817 |
| Ind. | -35 | Feb. 2, 1951 | Greensburg | 954 |
| Iowa | -47 | Jan. 12, 1912 | Washta | 1,157 |
| Kans. | -40 | Feb. 13, 1905 | Lebanon | 1,812 |
| Ky. | -34 | Jan. 28, 1963 | Cynthiana | 684 |
| La. | -16 | Feb. 13, 1899 | Minden | 194 |
| Maine | -48 | Jan. 19, 1925 | Van Buren | 510 |
| Md. | -40 | Jan. 13, 1912 | Oakland | 2,461 |
| Mass. | -34 | Jan. 18, 1957 | Birch Hill Dam | 840 |
| Mich. | -51 | Feb. 9, 1934 | Vanderbilt | 785 |
| Minn. | -59 | Feb. 16, 1903* | Pokegama Dam | 1,280 |
| Miss. | -19 | Jan. 30, 1966 | Corinth | 420 |
| Mo. | -40 | Feb. 13, 1905 | Warsaw | 700 |
| Mont. | -70 | Jan. 20, 1954 | Rogers Pass | 5,470 |
| Nebr. | -47 | Feb. 12, 1899 | Camp Clarke | 3,700 |
| Nev. | -50 | Jan. 8, 1937 | San Jacinto | 5,200 |
| N. H. | -46 | Jan. 28, 1925 | Pittsburg | 1,575 |
| N. J. | -34 | Jan. 5, 1904 | River Vale | 70 |
| N. Mex. | -50 | Feb. 1, 1951 | Gavilan | 7,350 |
| N. Y. | -52 | Feb. 9, 1934 | Stillwater Reservoir | 1,670 |
| N. C. | -29 | Jan. 30, 1966 | Mt. Mitchell | 6,525 |
| N. Dak. | -60 | Feb. 15, 1936 | Parshall | 1,929 |
| Ohio | -39 | Feb. 10, 1899 | Milligan | 800 |
| Okla. | -27 | Jan. 18, 1930* | Watts | 958 |
| Oreg. | -54 | Feb. 10, 1933* | Seneca | 4,700 |
| Pa. | -42 | Jan. 5, 1904 | Smethport | --- |
| R. I. | -23 | Jan. 11, 1942 | Kingston | 100 |
| S. C. | -13 | Jan. 26, 1940 | Longcreek (near) | 1,631 |
| S. Dak. | -58 | Feb. 17, 1936 | McIntosh | 2,277 |
| Tenn. | -32 | Dec. 30, 1917 | Mountain City | 2,471 |
| Tex. | -23 | Feb. 8, 1933* | Seminole | 3,275 |
| Utah | -50 | Jan. 5, 1913* | Strawberry Tunnel | 7,650 |
| Vt. | -50 | Dec. 30, 1933 | Bloomfield | 915 |
| Va. | -29 | Feb. 10, 1899 | Monterey | --- |
| Wash. | -48 | Dec. 30, 1965 | Mazama & Winthrop | 2,120 - 1,765 |
| W. Va. | -37 | Dec. 30, 1917 | Lewisburg | 2,200 |
| Wis. | -54 | Jan. 24, 1922 | Danbury | 908 |
| Wyo. | -63 | Feb. 9, 1933 | Moran | 6,770 |

\* Also on earlier dates at the same or other places.

## HIGHEST TEMPERATURES IN CONTERMINOUS UNITED STATES BY MONTHS

| Month | Temp. °F. | Year | Day | State | Place | Elevation Feet |
|---|---|---|---|---|---|---|
| Jan. | 98 | 1936 | 17 | Tex. | Laredo | 421 |
| Feb.* | 105 | 1963 | 3 | Ariz. | Montezuma | 735 |
| Mar.* | 108 | 1954 | 31 | Tex. | Rio Grande City | 168 |
| Apr. | 118 | 1898 | 25 | Calif. | Volcano Springs | -220 |
| May* | 124 | 1896 | 27 | Calif. | Salton | -263 |
| June*† | 127 | 1896 | 15 | Ariz. | Ft. Mohave | 555 |
| July | 134 | 1913 | 10 | Calif. | Greenland Ranch | -178 |
| Aug. † | 127 | 1933 | 12 | Calif. | Greenland Ranch | -178 |
| Sept. | 126 | 1950 | 2 | Calif. | Mecca | -175 |
| Oct.* | 116 | 1917 | 5 | Ariz. | Sentinel | 685 |
| Nov.* | 105 | 1906 | 12 | Calif. | Craftonville | 1,759 |
| Dec. | 100 | 1938 | 8 | Calif. | La Mesa | 539 |

\* Two or more occurrences, most recent given.

† Slightly higher temperatures in old records are not used owing to lack of information on exposure of instruments.

## LOWEST TEMPERATURES IN CONTERMINOUS UNITED STATES BY MONTHS

| Month | Temp. °F. | Year | Day | State | Place | Elevation Feet |
|---|---|---|---|---|---|---|
| Jan. | -70 | 1954 | 20 | Mont. | Rogers Pass | 5,470 |
| Feb. | -66 | 1933 | 9 | Mont. | Riverside R. S. | 6,700 |
| Mar. | -50 | 1906 | 17 | Wyo. | Snake River | 6,862 |
| Apr. | -36 | 1945 | 5 | N. Mex. | Eagle Nest | 8,250 |
| May | -15 | 1964 | 7 | Calif. | White Mountain 2 | 12,470 |
| June | 2 | 1907 | 13 | Calif. | Tamarack | 8,000 |
| July* | 10 | 1911 | 21 | Wyo. | Painter | 6,800 |
| Aug. * | 5 | 1910 | 25 | Mont. | Bowen | 6,080 |
| Sept. * | - 9 | 1926 | 24 | Mont. | Riverside R. S. | 6,700 |
| Oct. | -33 | 1917 | 29 | Wyo. | Soda Butte | 6,600 |
| Nov. | -53 | 1959 | 16 | Mont. | Lincoln 14 NE | 5,130 |
| Dec. * | -59 | 1924 | 19 | Mont. | Riverside R. S. | 6,700 |

\* Two or more occurrences, most recent given.

## TEMERATURE EXTREMES, HIGHEST

Temperature extremes depend upon a number of factors, important among which are altitude, latitude, surface conditions, and the density and length of record of observing stations.

The World's highest temperatures as well as the greatest range of extremes and the greatest and most rapid temperature fluctuations occur over continental areas in the Temperate Zones.

A reading of 136° F., observed at Azizia (elevation about 380 feet), Tripolitania, Libya, North Africa, on Sept. 13, 1922, is generally accepted as the World's highest temperature recorded under standard conditions.

The highest temperature ever observed in Canada was 115° at Gleichen, Alberta on July 28, 1903. A high of 120° or higher has been recorded on all the Continents except Antarctica where the high is only 58.3°.

Greenland Ranch, Calif., with 134° on July 10, 1913, holds the record for the highest temperature ever officially recorded in the United States. This station is located in barren Death Valley which is about 140 miles long and 4 to 16 miles wide and runs north and south in southeastern California and southwestern Nevada. The valley is below sea level and is flanked by towering mountain ranges with Mt. Whitney, the highest landmark in the 48 States, rising to 14,495 feet, less than 100 miles to the west. Death Valley has the hottest summers in the Western Hemisphere, and is the only known place in the United States where nighttime temperatures sometime remain above 100°.

The highest average annual temperature in the World is probably the 88° at Lugh, Somalia, East Africa. In the United States the station normally having the highest annual average is Key West, Fla., 77.7°; the highest summer average, Death Valley, Calif., 98.2° and the highest winter average, Key West, Fla., 70.2°.

Amazing temperature rises of 40° to 50° in a few minutes occasionally may be brought about by chinook winds. Some outstanding extreme temperature rises in short periods are:

12 hours:    83°, Granville, N. Dak., Feb. 21, 1918, from −33° to 50° from early morning to late afternoon.

15 minutes:    42° Fort Assiniboine, Mont., Jan. 19, 1892, from −5° to 37°.

7 minutes:    34°, Kipp, Mont., Dec. 1, 1896; observer also reported that a total rise of 80° occurred in a few hours and that 30 inches of snow disappeared in one-half day.

2 minutes:    49°, Spearfish, S. Dak., Jan. 22, 1943, from −4° at 7:30 a. m., to 45° at 7:32 a. m.

The range of temperature extremes over large bodies of water is much less than over land. The absolute extremes over the sea, as far as can be ascertained, range from 100° recorded by the SS TITAN on Aug. 8, 1920, in the Red Sea to −40° observed by the SS BAYCHINO, Jan. 27, 1932, when beset by ice at latitude 70° 50' N., longtitude 159° 11' W. In the Persian Gulf sea-surface temperatures average as high as 88° for July and August, and a high of 96° measured by the SS FRANKENFELS on Aug. 5, 1924, is at least among the highest if not the highest sea-surface temperatures ever observed.

## TEMPERATURE EXTREMES, LOWEST

Antarctica, a vast elevated, snow-covered continent at the South Pole is one of the most favorable regions in the World for extremely low temperatures. Several stations there now have records dating back through 1957. During the early part of this period, a new World record low temperature was observed on several occasions. The latest, −126.9° F (−88.3° C), was recorded at Vostok (Russian station) on August 24, 1960. At the Amundsen-Scott station (elevation 9,186 ft.) located on a snow plain within a few hundred yards of the geographical South Pole, the average annual temperature for the period 1957 - 1964 was −59°. For July the average maximum temperature was −69°, the minimum −80° and for January these values were −17° and −22°, respectively. The average temperature at Vostok for the 2-year period 1958 - 59 was −67°. Even colder locations may exist on the continent.

Other regions favorable for unusually low winter extremes include Greenland, a high snow-covered area located mostly in the north polar regions, and north-central Siberia, part of a great land mass at high latitudes. Minima of −90° (Verhoyansk −89.7° F, Feb. 5 & 7, 1892 and Oimekon −89.9° F, Feb. 6, 1933) in the latter region stood as the World's lowest temperatures prior to observations in Antarctica. The lowest temperature on the Greenland Icecap, −86.8° F (−66.0°C) was observed at Northice January 9, 1954. Canada's lowest temperature, −81° F, was observed at Snag, Yukon territory, near the border of Alaska at an altitude of 2,120 feet on February 3, 1947.

In the United States, the lowest temperature on record, −79.8°, was recorded at Prospect Creek Camp which is located in the Endicott Mountains of Northern Alaska at Latitude 66° 48' N. Longtitude 150° 40' W. The lowest temperature in the 48 States, −69.7°, occurred at Rogers Pass, in Lewis and Clark County, Montana. This location is in mountainous and heavily forested terrain, about 1/2 mile east of and 140 feet below the summit of the Continental Divide.

The lowest average annual temperature recorded in the United States is 9.6° at Barrow, Alaska, which lies on the Arctic coast. Barrow also has the coolest summers (June, July, August) with an average of 36.7°. The lowest average winter (December, January, February) temperature is −15.6° at Barter Island on the Arctic coast of northeast Alaska. In Hawaii, average annual temperatures range from 44.0° at Mauna Loa Slope Oberservatory (elevation 11,146 feet) on the island of Hawaii to 75.9° at Honolulu on the island of Oahu.

In the 48 States, Mt. Washington, N. H. (elevation 6,262 feet) has the lowest mean annual temperature, 27.0° F, and the lowest mean summer (June, July, August) temperature, 47.2°. A few stations in the North-east and upper Rockies have mean annuals in the high 30's, and at the same stations in the latter area summers may average in the high 40's. Winter (December, January, February) mean temperature are lowest in northeastern North Dakota where the average is 5.9° at the Langdon Experiment Farm and northwestern Minnesota where the average is 6.1° at Hallock.

In continental areas of the Temperate Zone, 40° to 50° temperature falls in a few hours caused by advection of cold air masses are not uncommon. Sometimes, following these large drops due to advection, radiation may cause a further temperature fall resulting in remarkable changes. Some outstanding extreme temperature falls are:

| | |
|---|---|
| 24 hours: | 100°, Browning, Mont., Jan. 23 - 24, 1916, from 44° to −56°. |
| 12 hours: | 84°, Fairfield, Mont., Dec. 24, 1924, from 63° at noon to −21° at midnight. |
| 2 hours: | 62°, Rapid City, S. Dak., Jan. 12, 1911, from 49° at 6 a. m ., to −13° at 8 a. m. |
| 27 minutes: | 58°, Spearfish, S. Dak., Jan. 22, 1943, from 54° at 9. a. m., to −4° at 9:27 a. m. |
| 15 minutes | 47° Rapid City, S. Dak., Jan. 10, 1911, from 55° at 7 a. m., to 8° at 7:15 a. m. |

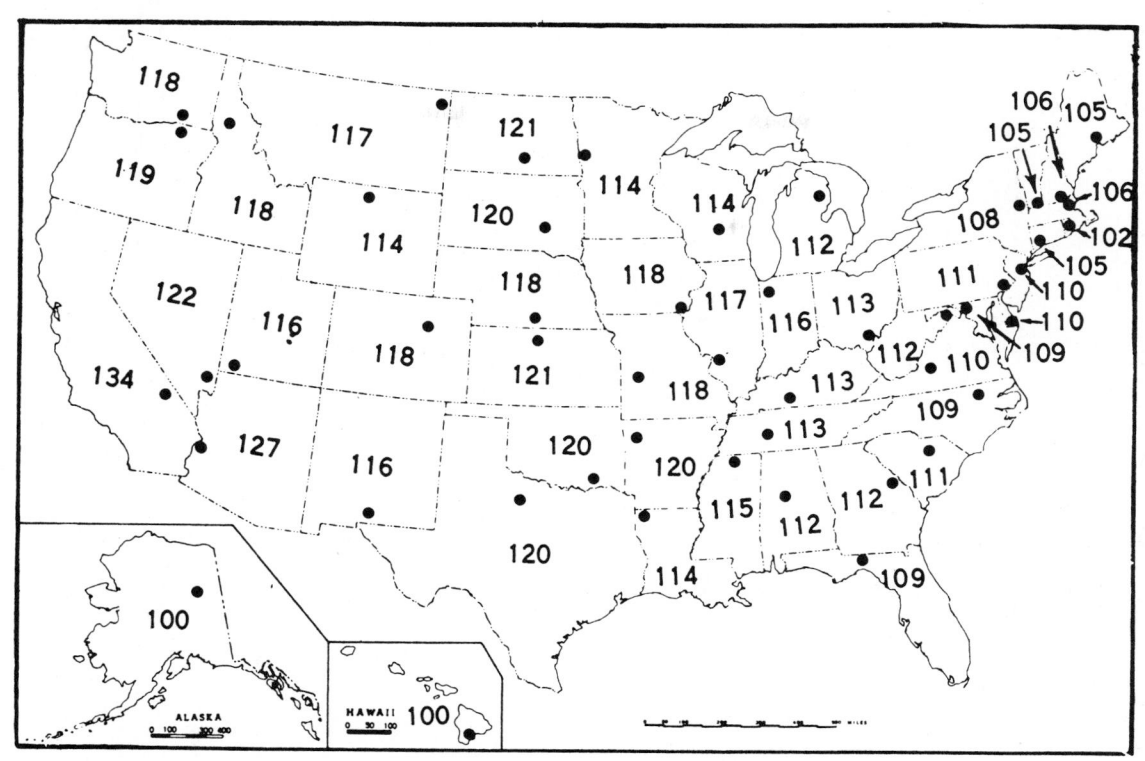

**HIGHEST TEMPERATURES OF RECORD
AND LOCATIONS, BY STATES**

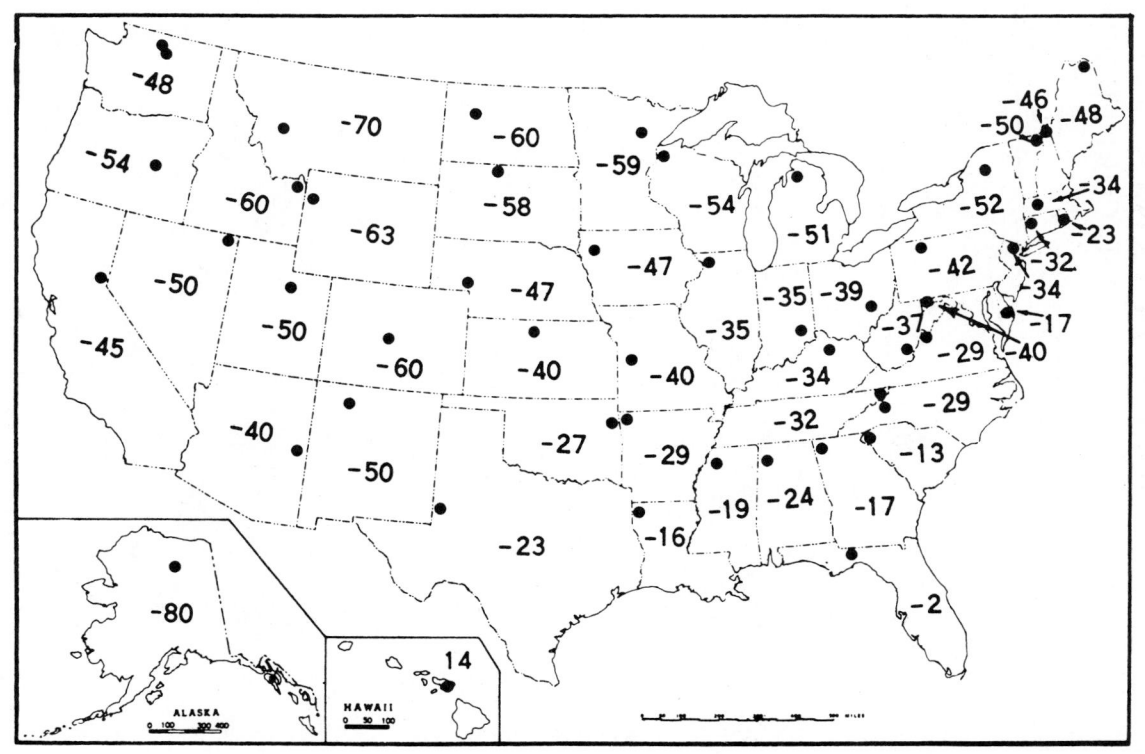

**LOWEST TEMPERATURES OF RECORD
AND LOCATIONS, BY STATES**

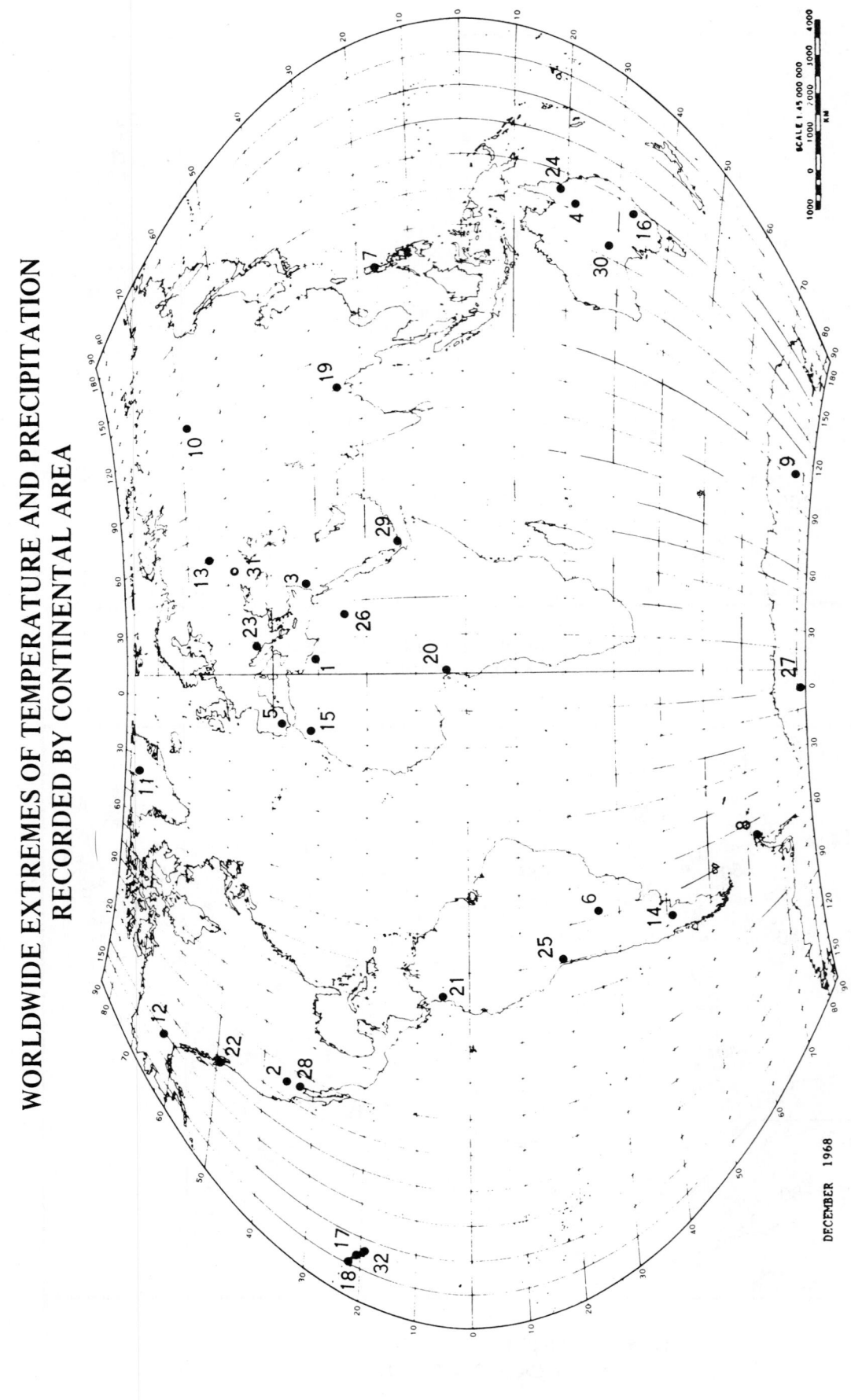

## WORLDWIDE EXTREMES OF TEMPERATURE AND PRECIPITATION RECORDED BY CONTINENTAL AREA

DECEMBER 1968

● Key numbers correspond to data entries on following page.

## TEMPERATURE EXTREMES

| Key No. | Area | Highest °F | Place | Elevation Feet | Date |
|---|---|---|---|---|---|
| 1 | Africa | 136 | Azizia, Libya | 380 | Sep. 13, 1922 |
| 2 | North America | 134 | Death Valley, Calif. | -178 | July 10, 1913 |
| 3 | Asia | 129 | Tirat Tsvi, Israel | -722 | June 21, 1942 |
| 4 | Australia | 128 | Cloncurry, Queensland | 622 | Jan. 16, 1889 |
| 5 | Europe | 122 | Seville, Spain | 26 | Aug. 4, 1881 |
| 6 | South America | 120 | Rivadavia, Argentina | 676 | Dec. 11, 1905 |
| 7 | Oceania | 108 | Tuguegarao, Philippines | 72 | Apr. 29, 1912 |
| 8 | Antarctica | 58 | Esperanza, Palmer Pen. | 26 | Oct. 20, 1956 |

| Key No. | Area | Lowest °F | Place | Elevation Feet | Date |
|---|---|---|---|---|---|
| 9 | Antarctica | -127 | Vostok | 11,220 | Aug. 24, 1960 |
| 10 | Asia | -90 | Oymykon, U.S.S.R. | 2,625 | Feb. 6, 1933 |
| 11 | Greenland | -87 | Northice | 7,690 | Jan. 9, 1954 |
| 12 | North America | -81 | Snag, Yukon, Canada | 1,925 | Feb. 3, 1947 |
| 13 | Europe | -67 | Ust'Shchugor, USSR | 279 | January + |
| 14 | South America | -27 | Sarmiento, Argentina | 879 | June 1, 1907 |
| 15 | Africa | -11 | Ifrane, Morocco | 5,364 | Feb. 11, 1935 |
| 16 | Australia | -8 | Charlotte Pass, N.S.W. | --- | July 22, 1947* |
| 17 | Oceania | 14 | Haleakala Summit, Maui | 9,750 | Jan. 2, 1961 |

+   exact date unknown; lowest in 15-year period  
*   and earlier date  
---   elevation unknown

## EXTREMES OF AVERAGE ANNUAL PRECIPITATION

| Key No. | Area | Greatest Amount Inches | Place | Elevation Feet | Years of Record |
|---|---|---|---|---|---|
| 18 | Oceania | 460.0 | Mt. Waialeale, Kauai, Hawaii | 5,075 | 32 |
| 19 | Asia | 450.0 | Cherrapunji, India | 4,309 | 74 |
| 20 | Africa | 404.6 | Debundscha, Cameroon | 30 | 32 |
| 21 | South America | 353.9 | Quibdo, Colombia | 240 | 10-16 |
| 22 | North America | 262.1 | Henderson Lake, B. C., Canada | 12 | 14 |
| 23 | Europe | 182.8 | Crkvica, Yugoslavia | 3,337 | 22 |
| 24 | Australia | 179.3 | Tully, Queensland | --- | 31 |

| Key No. | Area | Least Amount Inches | Place | Elevation Feet | Years of Record |
|---|---|---|---|---|---|
| 25 | South America | 0.03 | Arica, Chile | 95 | 59 |
| 26 | Africa | <0.1 | Wadi Halfa, Sudan | 410 | 39 |
| 27 | Antarctica | *0.8 | South Pole Station | 9,186 | 10 |
| 28 | North America | 1.2 | Batagues, Mexico | 16 | 14 |
| 29 | Asia | 1.8 | Aden, Arabia | 22 | 50 |
| 30 | Australia | 4.05 | Mulka, South Australia | --- | 34 |
| 31 | Europe | 6.4 | Astrakhan, USSR | 45 | 25 |
| 32 | Oceania | 8.93 | Puako, Hawaii | 5 | 13 |

* The value given is the average amount of solid snow accumulating in one year as indicated by snow markers. The liquid content of the snow is undetermined.

*Look closely. It's our planet, Earth. This is the way NASA's cameras see it from 22,300 miles in space. Such satellite photos have opened a new doorway to meteorology by allowing the global movement of weather to be tracked with precise accuracy.*

# ROUND-THE-WORLD WEATHER

# CLIMATES OF THE WORLD

## Temperature Distribution

The distribution of temperature over the world and its variations through the year depend primarily on the amount of distribution of the radiant energy received from the sun in different regions. This in turn depends mainly on latitude but is greatly modified by the distribution of continents and oceans, prevailing winds, oceanic circulation, topography, and other factors.

Maps showing average temperatures over the surface of the earth for January and for July are given in figures 1 and 2.

In the winter of the Northern Hemisphere, it will be noted, the poleward temperature gradient (that is, the rate of fall in temperature) north of latitude 15° is very steep over the interior of North America. This is shown by the fact that the lines indicating changes in temperature come very close together. The temperature gradient is also steep toward the cold pole over Asia —the area marked −50° In western Europe, to the east of the Atlantic Ocean and the North Atlantic Drift, and in the region of prevailing westerly winds, the temperature gradient is much more gradual, as indicated by the fact that the isotherms, or lines of equal temperature, are far apart. In the winter of the Southern Hemisphere, as shown on the map for July (a winter month south of the Equator), the temperature gradient toward the South Pole is very gradual, and the isothermal deflections from the east-west direction (that is, the dipping of the isothermal lines) are of minor importance because continental effects are largely absent.

In the summers of the two hemispheres—July in the north and January in the south— the temperature gradients poleward are very much diminished as compared with those during the winter. This is especially marked over the middle and higher northern latitudes because of the greater warming of the extensive interiors of North America and Eurasia than of the smaller land areas in middle and higher southern latitudes.

## Distribution of Precipitation

Whether precipitation (see the map, fig. 3) occurs as rain or snow or in the rarer forms of hail or sleet depends largely on the temperature climate, which may be influenced more by elevation than by latitude, as in the case of the perpetually snowcapped mountain peaks and glaciers on the Equator in both South America and Africa.

The quantity of precipitation is governed by the amount of water vapor in the air and the nature of the process that leads to its condensation into liquid or solid form through cooling. Air may ascend to great elevations through local convection, as in thunderstorms and in tropical regions generally; it may be forced up over topographical elevations across the prevailing wind direction, as on the southern or windward slopes of the Himalayas in the path of the southwest monsoon in India; or it may ascend more or less gradually in migratory low-pressure formations such as those that govern the main features of weather in the United States.

The areas of heaviest precipitation on the map (fig. 3) are generally located, as would be expected, in tropical regions, where because of high temperature the greatest amount of water vapor may be present in the atmosphere and the greatest evaporation takes place—although only where conditions favor condensation can rainfall occur. Outstanding exceptions are certain regions in high latitudes, such as southern Alaska, western Norway, and southern Chile, where relatively warm, moist winds from the sea undergo forced ascent over considerable elevations.

In marked contrast to the rainy regions just named are the dry polar regions, where the water-vapor content of the air is always very low because of the low

**AVERAGE JANUARY TEMPERATURE (Fº)**

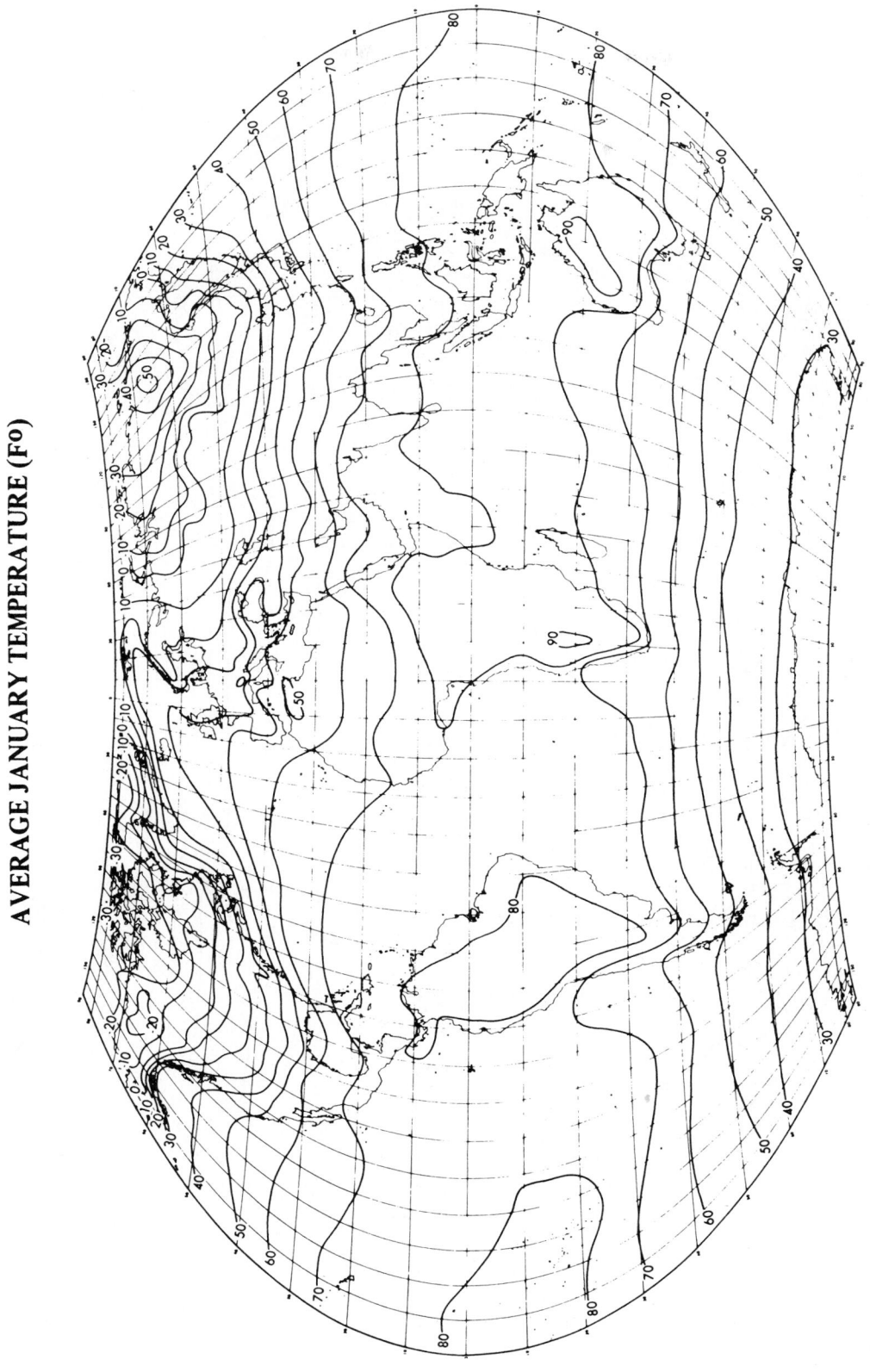

**Figure 1.**

**AVERAGE JULY TEMPERATURE (Fº)**

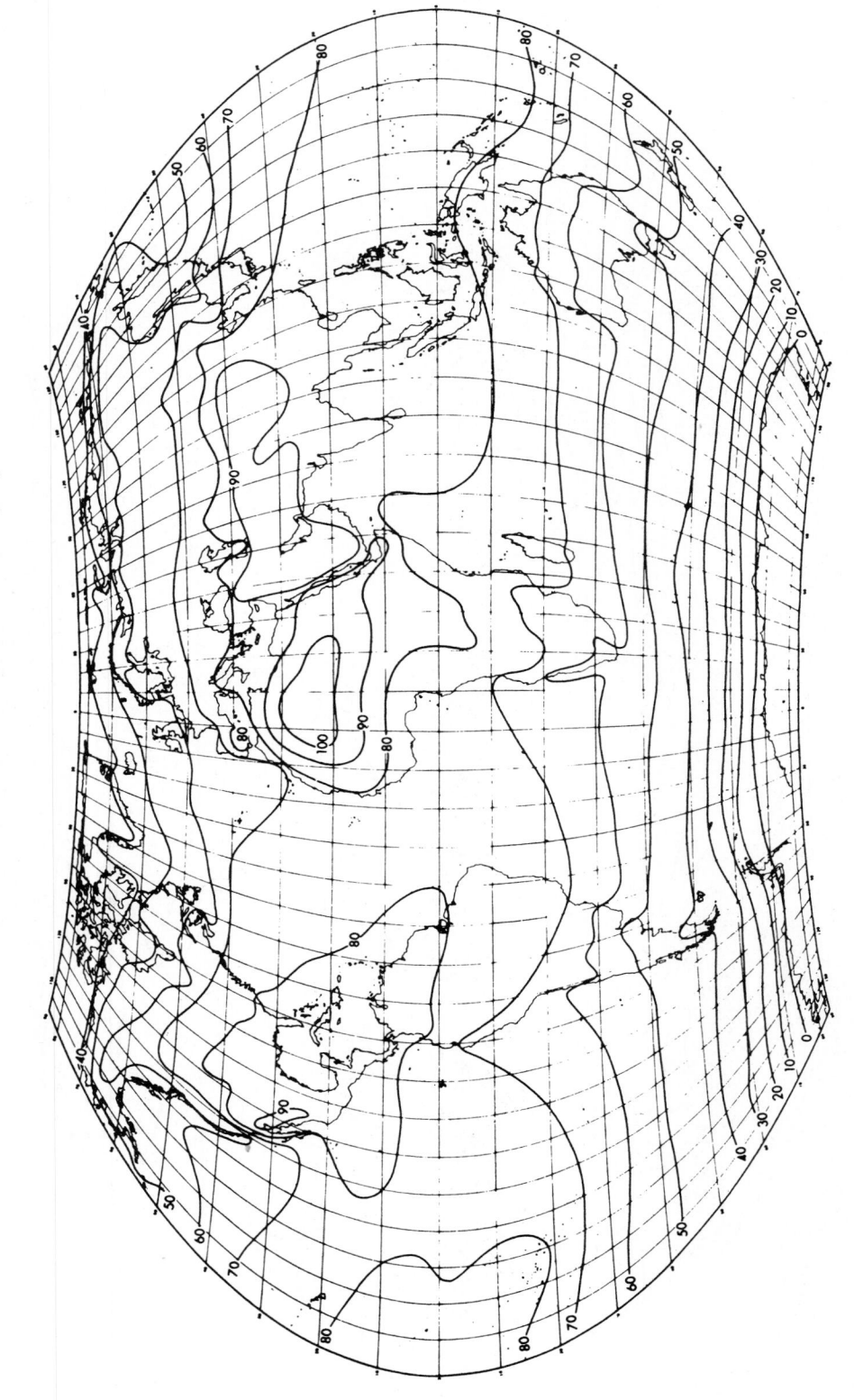

**Figure 2.**

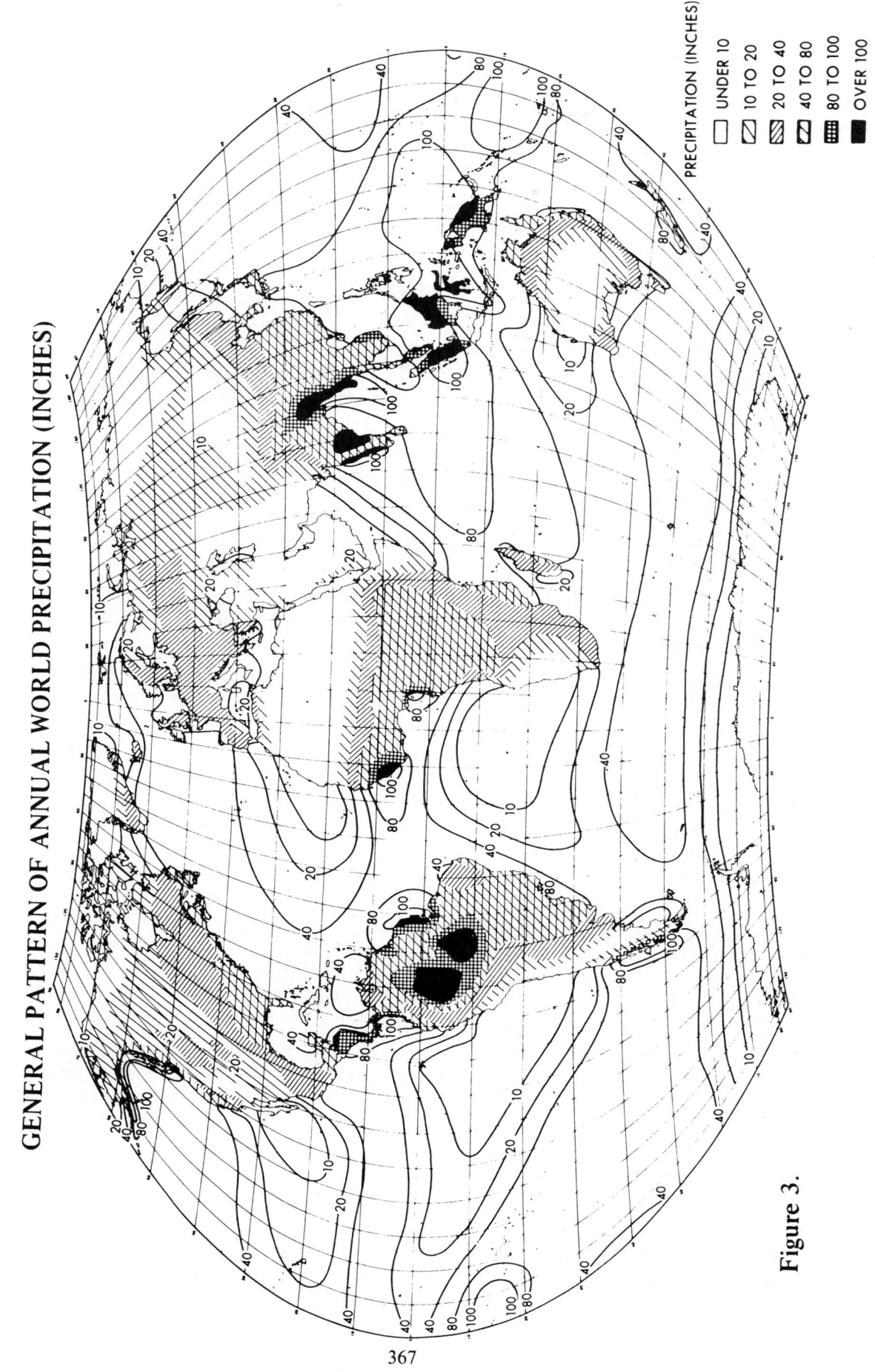

GENERAL PATTERN OF ANNUAL WORLD PRECIPITATION (INCHES)

PRECIPITATION (INCHES)
UNDER 10
10 TO 20
20 TO 40
40 TO 80
80 TO 100
OVER 100

Figure 3.

temperature and very limited evaporation. The dry areas in the subtropical belts of high atmospheric pressure (in the vicinity of latitude $30°$ on all continents, and especially from the extreme western Sahara over a broad, somewhat broken belt to the Desert of Gobi) and the arid strips on the lee sides of mountains on whose windward slopes precipitation is heavy to excessive, are caused by conditions which, even though the temperature may be high, are unfavorable to the condensation of whatever water vapor may be present in the atmosphere.

In the tables following are data on mean maximum and minimum temperatures for January, April, July, and October, with extremes recorded in the period of record, and monthly and annual precipitation for about 800 selected stations well distributed over the earth.

## North America

North America is nearly all within middle and northern latitudes. Consequently it has a large central area in which the continental type of climate with marked seasonal temperature is to be found.

Along the coasts of northern Alaska, western Canada, and the northwestern part of the United States, moderate midsummer temperatures are in marked contrast to those prevailing in the interior east of the mountains. (Note, for example, the great southward dip of the $60°$ isotherm along the west coast in fig. 2.) Again, the mild midwinter temperatures in the coastal areas stand out against the severe conditions to be found from the Great Lakes region northward and northwestward (fig. 1).

In the West Indian region, temperature conditions are subtropical; and in Mexico and Central America, climatic zones depend on elevation, ranging from subtropical to temperate in the higher levels.

The prevailing westerly wind movement carries the continental type of climate eastward over the United States, so that the region of maritime climate along the Atlantic Ocean is very narrow.

From the Aleutian Peninsula to northern California west of the crests of the mountains, there is a narrow strip where annual precipitation is over 40 inches; it exceeds 100 inches locally on the coast of British Columbia (see fig.3). East of this belt there is an abrupt fall-off in precipitation to less than 20 inches annually over the western half of the continent from Lower California northward, and to even less than 5 inches in parts of what used to be called the "Great American Desert." in the southwestern part of the United States.

In the eastern part of the continent—that is, from the southeastern part of the United States northeastward to Newfoundland—the average annual precipitation is more than 40 inches. Rainfall in the West Indies, southern Mexico, and Central America is generally abundant. It is very spotty, however, varying widely even within short distances, especially from the windward to the leeward sides of the mountains.

The northern areas are, of course, very cold; but the midwinter low temperatures fall far short of the records set in the cold-pole area of northeastern Siberia, where the vast extent of land becomes much colder than the partly ice-covered area of northern Canada .

## South America

A large part of South America lies within the Tropics and has a characteristically tropical climate. The remaining rather narrow southern portion is not subject to the extremes of heat and cold that are found where wide land areas give full sway to the continental type of climate with its hot summers and cold winters, as in North America and Asia. Temperature anomalies unusual for a given latitude are to be found mainly at the elevated levels of the Andean region stretching from the Isthmus of Panama to Cape Horn.

The Antarctic Current and its cool Humboldt branch skirting the western shores northward to the Equator, together with the prevailing on-shore winds, exert a strong cooling influence over the coastal regions of all the western countries of South America except Colombia. On the east the southerly moving Brazilian current from tropical waters has the opposite, or warming, effect except along southern Argentina.

In the northern countries of South America the sharply contrasted dry and wet seasons are related to the regime of the trade winds. In the dry season (corresponding to winter in the Northern Hemisphere) these winds sweep the entire region, while the wet season (corresponding to summer in the Northern Hemisphere) calms and variable winds prevail. In the basin of the Amazon River the rainfall is related to the equatorial belt of low pressure and to the trade winds, which give the maximum amounts of rainfall in the extreme west, where they ascend the Andean slopes.

The desert areas on the west coast of South America, extending from the Equator to the latitude of Santiago, are due primarily to the cold Humboldt or Peruvian Current and upwelling coastal water. The moist, cool ocean air is warmed in passing over the land, with a consequent decrease in relative humidity, so that the dew point is not reached and condensation of vapor does not occur until the incoming air has reached high elevations in the Andes, where temperatures are very much lower than along the coast.

In southern Chile the summer has moderate rainfall, and winters are excessively wet. The conditions that prevail farther north are not present here, and condensation of moisture from the ocean progresses from the shores up to the crests of the Andes. By the time the air passes these elevations, however, the moisture has been so depleted that the winds in the leeward slopes are dry, becoming more and more so as they are warmed on reaching lower levels. The mountains can be looked upon as casting a great "rain shadow"—an area of little rain—over southern Argentina.

## Europe

In Europe there is no extensive north-south mountain system such as is found in both the Americas, and the general east-west direction of the ranges in the south allows the conditions in the maritime west to change rather gradually toward Asia. Generally rainfall is heaviest on the western coast, where locally it exceeds 60 inches annually, and diminishes toward the east—except in the elevated Alpine and Caucasus regions—to less than 20 inches in eastern Russia. There is a well-defined rain shadow in Scandinavia, with over 60 inches of rain in western Norway and less than 20 inches in eastern Sweden.

Over much of Europe rainfall is both abundant and rather evenly distributed throughout the year. The chief feature of seasonal distribution of precipitation is the marked winter maximum and the extremely dry, even droughty, summers in most of the Mediterranean lands.

Isothermal lines have the general direction of the parallels of latitude except in winter, when the waters of the western ocean, warmed by the Gulf Stream, give them a north-south trend. Generally there are no marked dips in isotherms due to elevation and continental type of climate such as are found in North America. In Scandinavia, however, the winter map shows an abrupt fall in temperature from the western coast of Norway to the eastern coast of Sweden and thence a continued fall eastward, under a type of exposure more and more continental in contrast to the oceanic exposure on the west.

## Asia

The vast extent of Asia gives full opportunity for continental conditions to develop a cold area of high barometric pressure in winter and a low-pressure, hot area in summer, the former northeast of the Himalayas and the latter stretching widely from west to east in the latitude of northern India. (See the area marked 90° on the map, fig. 2.) These distributions of pressure give to India the well-known monsoon seasons, during which the wind comes from one direction for several months, and also affect the yearly distribution of rainfall over eastern Asia.

In winter, the air circulation is outward over the land from the cold pole, and precipitation is very light over the entire continent. In summer, on the contrary, there is an inflow of air from the oceans; even the southeast trade winds flow across the Equator and merge into the southwest monsoon which crosses India. This usually produces abundant rain over most of that country, with excessively heavy amounts when the air is forced to rise, even to moderate elevations, in its passage the land. At Cherrapunji (4,455 feet), on the southern side of the Khasi Hills in Assam, the average rainfall in a winter month is about 1 inch, while in both June and July it is approximately 100 inches. However, this heavy summer rainfall meets an impassable barrier in the Himalaya Mountains, while the much lighter summer monsoon rainfall over Japan and eastern Asia does not extend far into China because of lesser elevations. Consequently, while the southeast quadrant of Asia, including the East Indies, also with monsoon winds, has heavy to excessive annual rainfall, the remainder of the continent is dry, with vast areas receiving less than 10 inches annually.

North of the Himalayas the low plains are excessively cold in winter and temperatures rise rather high in summer. At Verkhoyansk in the cold-pole area, and north of the Arctic Circle, the mean temperature in January is about −59° F, and in July approximately 64°; the extreme records are a maximum of 98° from readings at 1 p.m., and a minimum of −90°.

In southwestern Asia the winter temperature control is still the interior high-pressure area, and temperatures are generally low, especially at high elevations; in summer at low elevations excessively high maxima are recorded, as, for example, in the Tigris-Euphrates Valley

## Africa

Africa, like South America, lies very largely within the Tropics. There too, temperature distribution is determined mainly by altitude. Moreover, along the southern portion of the western coast the cool Benguela Current moves northward, and on the eastern coast are the warm tropical currents of the Indian Ocean, which create conditions closely paralleling those found around the South American Continent. In the strictly tropical areas of Africa conditions are characterized by prevailing low barometric pressure, with conventional rainfall and alternate northward and southward movement of the heat equator, while in both the north and the south the ruling influences are the belts of high barometric pressure.

Except in the Atlas Mountains in the northwest where the considerable elevations set up a barrier in the path of trade winds and produce moderate rainfall, the desert conditions typified by the Sahara extend from the Atlantic to the Red Sea and from the Mediterranean southward well beyond the northern Tropic to about the latitudes of southern Arabia.

South of the Sahara, rainfall increases rapidly, becoming abundant to heavy from the west coast to the central lakes, with annual maxima of over 80 inches in the regions bordering the eastern and western extremes of the Guinea coast. This marked increase in precipitation does not extend to the eastern portion of the middle region of the continent, where the annual amounts received are below 40 inches and decrease to less than 10 inches on the coasts of Somalia. Also to the south of the central rainy area there is a rapid fall in precipitation toward the arid regions of Southwest Africa, where conditions are similar to those in Somalia.

The heavy rainfall over sections of Ethiopia from June to October, when more than 40 inches fall and bring the overflowing of the otherwise arid Nile Valley, is one of the earth's outstanding features of seasonal distribution of rainfall.

Moist equatorial climate is typified by conditions in the Democratic Republic of the Congo; arid torrid climate by those of the United Arab Republic and the Sahara; and moderate plateau climate by those found in parts of Ethiopia, Kenya and Tanzania.

## Australia

In the southern winter the high-pressure belt crosses the interior of Australia, and all except the southernmost parts of the continent are dry. In summer, on the other hand, this pressure belt has moved south of the continent, still giving dry conditions over the southern and western areas. Thus the total annual precipitation is less than 20 inches except in the extreme southwest and in a strip circling from southeast to northwest. The average annual precipitation is even less than 10 inches in a large south-central area.

In the south the winter precipitation is the cyclonic type; the heavy summer rains of the north are of monsoon origin; and those of the eastern borders are in large part orographic, owing to the presence of the highlands in the immediate vicinity of the coasts. In the outer border of the rainfall strip along the coastal region, the mean annual rainfall is over 40 inches and in many localities over 60 inches. This is true for the monsoon rains in the north.

Because of the location of Australia, on both sides of the southern Tropic, temperatures far below freezing are to be found only in a small part of the continent, in the south at high elevations. In the arid interior extreme maximum temperatures are very high, ranking with those of the hottest regions on the earth

---

**ROUND-THE-WORLD WEATHER** ⟶

Travel plans demand some research about climate and what weather to expect and prepare for along your route. The following pages let you check on weather expectations for all four seasons for more than 550 key cities of the world. Of course, one season's weather, or even one year's weather may, and often does deviate considerably from averages. That is true in Greece or Spain the same as in New York or Denver, meaning that averages can never serve as a guarantee that this year or this season mightn't be the exception. A traveler should assess that for himself, after determining what is "normal" for the area, and what he might ordinarily expect the weather there to be.

U.S. cities appear in these tables, but far more detailed studies of the weather and climate of more than 100 U.S. cities await the reader in a special section of this book.

## NORTH AMERICA

| Country and Station | Latitude | Longitude | Elevation (feet) | Temp. Length of Record (yr) | Jan Max (°F) | Jan Min (°F) | Apr Max (°F) | Apr Min (°F) | Jul Max (°F) | Jul Min (°F) | Oct Max (°F) | Oct Min (°F) | Extreme Max (°F) | Extreme Min (°F) | Precip. Length of Record (yr) | Jan (in.) | Feb (in.) | Mar (in.) | Apr (in.) | May (in.) | Jun (in.) | Jul (in.) | Aug (in.) | Sep (in.) | Oct (in.) | Nov (in.) | Dec (in.) | Year (in.) |
|---|---|---|---|---|---|---|---|---|---|---|---|---|---|---|---|---|---|---|---|---|---|---|---|---|---|---|---|---|
| **United States (Conterminous):** | | | | | | | | | | | | | | | | | | | | | | | | | | | | |
| Albuquerque, N. Mex. | 35 03N | 106 37W | 5,311 | 30 | 46 | 24 | 69 | 42 | 91 | 66 | 71 | 45 | 104 | -16 | 30 | 0.4 | 0.4 | 0.5 | 0.5 | 0.8 | 0.6 | 1.2 | 1.3 | 1.0 | 0.8 | 0.4 | 0.5 | 8.4 |
| Asheville, N.C. | 35 26N | 82 32W | 2,140 | 30 | 48 | 28 | 67 | 42 | 84 | 61 | 68 | 45 | 99 | -7 | 30 | 4.2 | 4.0 | 4.8 | 4.0 | 3.7 | 3.5 | 5.9 | 4.9 | 3.6 | 3.1 | 2.8 | 3.6 | 48.1 |
| Atlanta, Ga. | 33 39N | 84 26W | 1,010 | 30 | 52 | 37 | 70 | 50 | 87 | 71 | 72 | 52 | 103 | -9 | 30 | 4.4 | 4.5 | 5.4 | 4.5 | 3.2 | 3.8 | 4.7 | 3.6 | 3.3 | 2.4 | 3.0 | 4.4 | 47.2 |
| Austin, Tex. | 30 18N | 97 42W | 597 | 30 | 60 | 41 | 78 | 57 | 95 | 74 | 82 | 60 | 109 | -2 | 30 | 2.4 | 2.6 | 2.1 | 3.6 | 3.7 | 3.2 | 2.2 | 1.9 | 3.4 | 2.8 | 2.1 | 2.5 | 32.5 |
| Birmingham, Ala. | 33 34N | 86 45W | 620 | 30 | 57 | 36 | 76 | 50 | 93 | 71 | 79 | 52 | 107 | -10 | 30 | 5.0 | 5.3 | 6.0 | 4.5 | 3.4 | 4.0 | 5.2 | 4.9 | 3.3 | 2.8 | 3.5 | 5.0 | 53.1 |
| Bismark, N. Dak. | 46 46N | 100 45W | 1,647 | 30 | 20 | 0 | 55 | 32 | 86 | 58 | 59 | 34 | 114 | -45 | 30 | 0.4 | 0.4 | 0.8 | 1.2 | 1.3 | 3.4 | 2.2 | 1.7 | 1.2 | 0.9 | 0.6 | 0.4 | 15.2 |
| Boise, Idaho | 43 34N | 116 13W | 2,838 | 30 | 36 | 22 | 63 | 36 | 91 | 59 | 65 | 38 | 112 | -28 | 30 | 1.3 | 1.3 | 1.3 | 1.2 | 1.3 | 0.9 | 0.2 | 0.2 | 0.4 | 0.8 | 1.2 | 1.3 | 11.4 |
| Brownsville, Tex. | 25 54N | 97 26W | 16 | 30 | 71 | 52 | 82 | 66 | 93 | 76 | 85 | 67 | 104 | 12 | 30 | 1.4 | 1.5 | 1.3 | 1.6 | 2.4 | 3.0 | 1.7 | 2.8 | 5.0 | 3.5 | 1.3 | 1.7 | 26.9 |
| Buffalo, N.Y. | 42 56N | 78 44W | 705 | 30 | 31 | 18 | 53 | 34 | 80 | 59 | 60 | 41 | 99 | -21 | 30 | 2.8 | 2.7 | 3.2 | 3.0 | 3.0 | 2.5 | 2.6 | 3.1 | 3.1 | 3.0 | 3.6 | 3.0 | 35.6 |
| Cheyenne, Wyo. | 41 09N | 104 49W | 6,126 | 30 | 37 | 14 | 56 | 30 | 85 | 55 | 63 | 32 | 100 | -38 | 30 | 0.5 | 0.6 | 1.2 | 1.9 | 2.5 | 2.1 | 1.8 | 1.4 | 1.1 | 0.8 | 0.6 | 0.5 | 15.0 |
| Chicago, Ill. | 41 47N | 87 45W | 607 | 30 | 33 | 19 | 57 | 41 | 84 | 67 | 63 | 47 | 105 | -23 | 30 | 1.9 | 1.6 | 2.7 | 2.5 | 3.7 | 4.1 | 3.4 | 3.1 | 2.9 | 2.8 | 2.2 | 1.9 | 33.2 |
| Des Moines, Iowa | 41 32N | 93 39W | 938 | 30 | 29 | 11 | 59 | 38 | 87 | 65 | 66 | 43 | 110 | -30 | 30 | 1.3 | 1.1 | 2.0 | 2.5 | 3.7 | 4.7 | 3.4 | 3.7 | 3.2 | 2.1 | 1.8 | 1.1 | 30.5 |
| Dodge City, Kans. | 37 46N | 99 58W | 2,582 | 30 | 42 | 20 | 66 | 41 | 93 | 68 | 71 | 46 | 109 | -26 | 30 | 0.6 | 0.7 | 1.2 | 1.8 | 3.2 | 3.0 | 2.3 | 2.4 | 1.5 | 1.4 | 0.6 | 0.5 | 19.2 |
| El Paso, Tex. | 31 48N | 106 24W | 3,918 | 30 | 56 | 30 | 78 | 49 | 95 | 69 | 79 | 50 | 109 | -8 | 30 | 0.5 | 0.4 | 0.4 | 0.3 | 0.4 | 0.7 | 1.3 | 1.2 | 1.1 | 0.9 | 0.3 | 0.5 | 8.0 |
| Indianapolis, Ind. | 39 44N | 86 17W | 792 | 30 | 37 | 21 | 61 | 40 | 86 | 64 | 67 | 44 | 107 | -25 | 30 | 3.1 | 2.3 | 3.4 | 3.7 | 4.0 | 4.6 | 3.5 | 3.0 | 3.2 | 2.6 | 3.1 | 2.7 | 39.2 |
| Jacksonville, Fla. | 30 25N | 81 39W | 20 | 30 | 67 | 45 | 80 | 58 | 92 | 73 | 80 | 62 | 105 | 10 | 30 | 2.5 | 2.9 | 3.5 | 3.6 | 3.5 | 6.3 | 7.7 | 6.9 | 7.6 | 2.9 | 1.7 | 2.2 | 53.6 |
| Kansas City, Mo. | 39 07N | 94 36W | 742 | 30 | 40 | 23 | 66 | 46 | 92 | 72 | 72 | 49 | 113 | -22 | 30 | 1.4 | 1.4 | 2.5 | 3.6 | 4.4 | 4.6 | 3.2 | 3.8 | 4.4 | 3.0 | 1.8 | 1.5 | 34.2 |
| Las Vegas, Nev. | 36 05N | 115 10W | 2,162 | 30 | 54 | 32 | 78 | 51 | 104 | 76 | 80 | 53 | 117 | 8 | 30 | 0.5 | 0.4 | 0.4 | 0.2 | 0.1 | * | 0.5 | 0.5 | 0.3 | 0.2 | 0.3 | 0.4 | 3.8 |
| Los Angeles, Calif. | 33 56N | 118 23W | 97 | 30 | 64 | 45 | 67 | 52 | 76 | 62 | 73 | 57 | 110 | 23 | 30 | 2.7 | 2.9 | 1.8 | 1.1 | 0.1 | 0.1 | * | * | 0.2 | 0.4 | 1.1 | 2.4 | 12.8 |
| Louisville, Ky. | 38 11N | 85 44W | 477 | 30 | 44 | 27 | 66 | 43 | 89 | 67 | 70 | 46 | 107 | -20 | 30 | 4.1 | 3.3 | 4.6 | 3.8 | 3.9 | 4.0 | 3.4 | 3.0 | 2.6 | 2.3 | 3.2 | 3.2 | 41.4 |
| Miami, Fla. | 25 48N | 80 16W | 7 | 30 | 76 | 58 | 83 | 66 | 89 | 75 | 85 | 71 | 100 | 28 | 30 | 2.0 | 2.3 | 1.9 | 3.9 | 6.4 | 7.4 | 6.8 | 7.0 | 9.5 | 8.2 | 2.8 | 1.7 | 59.9 |
| Minneapolis, Minn. | 44 53N | 93 13W | 834 | 30 | 22 | 2 | 56 | 33 | 84 | 61 | 61 | 37 | 108 | -34 | 30 | 0.7 | 0.9 | 1.5 | 1.9 | 3.2 | 4.0 | 3.3 | 2.9 | 2.4 | 1.6 | 1.4 | 0.9 | 24.9 |
| Missoula, Mont. | 46 55N | 114 05W | 3,190 | 30 | 28 | 18 | 57 | 31 | 85 | 49 | 58 | 37 | 105 | -33 | 30 | 0.9 | 0.9 | 0.7 | 1.0 | 1.9 | 1.9 | 0.7 | 0.7 | 0.9 | 1.0 | 0.9 | 1.1 | 12.9 |
| Nashville, Tenn. | 36 07N | 86 41W | 590 | 30 | 49 | 31 | 71 | 48 | 91 | 70 | 74 | 49 | 107 | -15 | 30 | 5.5 | 4.5 | 5.2 | 3.7 | 3.7 | 3.3 | 3.7 | 2.9 | 2.9 | 2.3 | 3.3 | 4.2 | 45.2 |
| New Orleans, La. | 29 59N | 90 15W | 3 | 30 | 64 | 45 | 78 | 58 | 91 | 73 | 80 | 61 | 102 | 7 | 30 | 3.8 | 4.0 | 5.3 | 4.6 | 4.4 | 4.4 | 6.7 | 5.3 | 5.0 | 2.8 | 3.3 | 4.1 | 53.7 |
| New York, N.Y. | 40 47N | 73 58W | 132 | 30 | 40 | 27 | 60 | 43 | 85 | 68 | 66 | 50 | 106 | -15 | 30 | 3.3 | 2.8 | 4.0 | 3.4 | 3.7 | 3.3 | 3.7 | 4.4 | 3.9 | 3.1 | 3.4 | 3.3 | 42.3 |
| Oklahoma City, Okla. | 35 24N | 97 36W | 1,285 | 30 | 46 | 28 | 71 | 49 | 93 | 72 | 74 | 52 | 107 | -17 | 30 | 1.3 | 1.4 | 2.0 | 3.1 | 5.2 | 4.5 | 2.4 | 2.1 | 3.0 | 2.5 | 1.6 | 1.4 | 30.9 |
| Phoenix, Ariz. | 33 26N | 112 01W | 1,117 | 30 | 64 | 35 | 84 | 50 | 105 | 75 | 87 | 55 | 118 | 16 | 30 | 0.7 | 0.7 | 0.7 | 0.3 | 0.1 | 0.1 | 0.8 | 1.1 | 0.7 | 0.5 | 0.5 | 0.9 | 7.3 |
| Pittsburgh, Pa. | 40 27N | 80 00W | 747 | 30 | 40 | 25 | 63 | 42 | 85 | 65 | 65 | 45 | 103 | -20 | 30 | 2.8 | 2.3 | 3.5 | 3.4 | 3.8 | 4.0 | 3.6 | 3.5 | 2.7 | 2.5 | 2.3 | 2.5 | 36.9 |
| Portland, Maine | 43 39N | 70 19W | 47 | 30 | 32 | 12 | 53 | 32 | 80 | 57 | 60 | 37 | 103 | -39 | 30 | 4.4 | 4.2 | 4.3 | 3.7 | 3.4 | 3.2 | 2.9 | 2.4 | 3.5 | 3.2 | 4.2 | 3.9 | 42.9 |
| Portland, Oreg. | 45 36N | 122 36W | 21 | 30 | 44 | 33 | 62 | 42 | 79 | 56 | 63 | 45 | 107 | -3 | 30 | 5.4 | 4.2 | 3.8 | 2.1 | 2.0 | 1.7 | 0.4 | 0.7 | 1.6 | 3.6 | 5.3 | 6.4 | 37.2 |
| Reno, Nev. | 39 30N | 119 47W | 4,404 | 30 | 45 | 16 | 65 | 31 | 89 | 46 | 69 | 29 | 106 | -19 | 30 | 1.2 | 1.0 | 0.7 | 0.5 | 0.5 | 0.4 | 0.3 | 0.2 | 0.2 | 0.5 | 0.6 | 1.1 | 7.2 |
| Salt Lake City, Utah | 40 46N | 111 58W | 4,220 | 30 | 37 | 18 | 63 | 36 | 94 | 60 | 65 | 38 | 107 | -30 | 30 | 1.4 | 1.2 | 1.8 | 2.2 | 1.5 | 0.9 | 0.5 | 0.9 | 0.7 | 1.3 | 1.3 | 1.3 | 14.1 |
| San Francisco, Calif. | 37 37N | 122 23W | 8 | 30 | 55 | 42 | 64 | 47 | 72 | 54 | 71 | 51 | 106 | 20 | 30 | 4.0 | 3.5 | 2.7 | 1.3 | 0.5 | 0.1 | * | * | 0.2 | 0.7 | 1.6 | 4.1 | 18.7 |
| Sault Ste. Marie, Mich. | 46 28N | 84 22W | 721 | 30 | 23 | 8 | 46 | 30 | 76 | 54 | 60 | 37 | 98 | -37 | 30 | 2.1 | 1.5 | 1.8 | 2.2 | 2.8 | 3.3 | 2.5 | 2.9 | 3.8 | 2.8 | 3.3 | 2.3 | 31.3 |
| Seattle, Wash. | 47 27N | 122 18W | 400 | 30 | 44 | 33 | 58 | 40 | 76 | 54 | 60 | 44 | 100 | 0 | 30 | 5.7 | 4.2 | 3.8 | 2.4 | 1.7 | 1.6 | 0.8 | 1.0 | 2.1 | 4.0 | 5.4 | 6.3 | 39.0 |
| Sheridan, Wyo. | 44 46N | 106 58W | 3,964 | 30 | 34 | 9 | 56 | 31 | 87 | 56 | 62 | 33 | 106 | -41 | 30 | 0.6 | 0.7 | 1.4 | 2.2 | 2.6 | 1.5 | 1.2 | 0.9 | 1.2 | 1.1 | 0.8 | 0.6 | 15.9 |
| Spokane, Wash. | 47 38N | 117 32W | 2,356 | 30 | 31 | 19 | 59 | 36 | 86 | 55 | 60 | 38 | 108 | -30 | 30 | 2.4 | 1.9 | 1.5 | 0.9 | 1.4 | 1.5 | 0.4 | 0.4 | 0.8 | 1.6 | 2.2 | 2.4 | 17.2 |
| Washington, D.C. | 38 51N | 77 03W | 14 | 30 | 44 | 30 | 66 | 46 | 87 | 69 | 68 | 50 | 106 | -15 | 30 | 3.0 | 2.5 | 3.2 | 3.2 | 4.1 | 4.1 | 4.2 | 4.9 | 3.8 | 3.1 | 2.8 | 2.8 | 40.8 |
| Wilmington, N.C. | 34 16N | 77 55W | 28 | 30 | 58 | 37 | 74 | 51 | 89 | 71 | 76 | 55 | 104 | 5 | 30 | 2.9 | 3.4 | 4.0 | 2.9 | 3.5 | 4.3 | 7.7 | 6.9 | 6.3 | 3.0 | 3.1 | 3.4 | 51.4 |

(See footnotes at end of tables)

| COUNTRY AND STATION | LATITUDE | LONGITUDE | ELEVATION (FEET) | TEMP LENGTH OF RECORD (YEAR) | JAN MAX (°F) | JAN MIN (°F) | APR MAX (°F) | APR MIN (°F) | JUL MAX (°F) | JUL MIN (°F) | OCT MAX (°F) | OCT MIN (°F) | EXT MAX (°F) | EXT MIN (°F) | PRECIP LENGTH OF RECORD (YEAR) | JAN (IN.) | FEB (IN.) | MAR (IN.) | APR (IN.) | MAY (IN.) | JUN (IN.) | JUL (IN.) | AUG (IN.) | SEP (IN.) | OCT (IN.) | NOV (IN.) | DEC (IN.) | YEAR (IN.) |
|---|---|---|---|---|---|---|---|---|---|---|---|---|---|---|---|---|---|---|---|---|---|---|---|---|---|---|---|---|
| **United States, Alaska:** | | | | | | | | | | | | | | | | | | | | | | | | | | | | |
| Anchorage | 61 13N | 149 52W | 85 | 30 | 21 | 4 | 44 | 28 | 65 | 50 | 42 | 28 | 86 | -38 | 30 | 0.8 | 0.7 | 0.5 | 0.4 | 0.5 | 1.0 | 1.9 | 2.6 | 2.5 | 1.9 | 1.0 | 0.9 | 14.7 |
| Annette | 55 02N | 131 34W | 110 | 30 | 38 | 30 | 50 | 37 | 63 | 51 | 51 | 42 | 90 | -4 | 30 | 11.4 | 8.5 | 9.6 | 9.1 | 7.1 | 5.7 | 6.0 | 7.5 | 9.9 | 16.9 | 14.7 | 12.1 | 118.5 |
| Barrow | 71 18N | 156 47W | 31 | 30 | 9 | -23 | 7 | -7 | 45 | 33 | 21 | 12 | 78 | -56 | 30 | 0.2 | 0.2 | 0.1 | 0.1 | 0.1 | 0.4 | 0.8 | 0.9 | 0.6 | 0.5 | 0.2 | 0.2 | 4.3 |
| Bethel | 60 47N | 161 48W | 125 | 30 | 11 | -4 | 34 | 18 | 62 | 48 | 38 | 25 | 90 | -52 | 30 | 1.1 | 1.1 | 1.0 | 0.6 | 1.0 | 1.2 | 2.0 | 4.2 | 2.6 | 1.5 | 1.1 | 1.0 | 18.4 |
| Cold Bay | 55 12N | 162 43W | 96 | 30 | 33 | 23 | 38 | 28 | 54 | 45 | 45 | 36 | 78 | -9 | 30 | 2.3 | 3.2 | 1.8 | 1.5 | 2.3 | 2.0 | 1.8 | 4.3 | 4.3 | 4.6 | 3.8 | 2.6 | 34.5 |
| Fairbanks | 64 49N | 147 52W | 436 | 30 | -1 | -21 | 42 | 17 | 72 | 48 | 35 | 17 | 99 | -66 | 30 | 0.9 | 0.5 | 0.4 | 0.3 | 0.7 | 1.4 | 1.8 | 2.3 | 1.1 | 0.9 | 0.6 | 0.5 | 11.3 |
| Juneau | 58 22N | 134 35W | 12 | 30 | 30 | 20 | 45 | 31 | 63 | 48 | 47 | 37 | 89 | -21 | 30 | 4.0 | 3.1 | 3.3 | 2.9 | 3.2 | 3.4 | 4.5 | 5.0 | 6.7 | 8.3 | 6.1 | 4.2 | 54.7 |
| King Salmon | 58 41N | 156 39W | 49 | 30 | 21 | 6 | 41 | 25 | 63 | 47 | 43 | 29 | 88 | -40 | 30 | 1.1 | 1.0 | 1.0 | 0.6 | 1.0 | 1.4 | 2.1 | 3.4 | 3.1 | 2.2 | 1.5 | 1.0 | 19.4 |
| Nome | 64 30N | 165 26W | 13 | 30 | 12 | -3 | 28 | 14 | 55 | 44 | 35 | 24 | 84 | -47 | 30 | 1.0 | 0.9 | 0.9 | 0.8 | 0.7 | 0.9 | 2.3 | 3.8 | 2.7 | 1.7 | 1.2 | 1.0 | 17.9 |
| St. Paul Island | 57 09N | 170 13W | 22 | 30 | 30 | 23 | 33 | 28 | 49 | 44 | 41 | 33 | 64 | -26 | 30 | 1.8 | 1.2 | 1.1 | 1.0 | 1.3 | 1.2 | 2.3 | 3.3 | 3.1 | 3.2 | 2.5 | 1.8 | 23.8 |
| Shemya | 52 43N | 174 06E | 122 | 30 | 34 | 29 | 38 | 33 | 49 | 44 | 42 | 38 | 63 | 16 | 30 | 2.5 | 2.3 | 2.6 | 2.1 | 2.4 | 1.3 | 2.2 | 3.3 | 2.3 | 2.8 | 2.7 | 2.1 | 27.4 |
| Yakutat | 59 31N | 139 40W | 28 | 30 | 34 | 20 | 45 | 29 | 61 | 48 | 49 | 35 | 86 | -24 | 30 | 10.9 | 8.2 | 8.7 | 7.2 | 8.0 | 5.1 | 8.4 | 10.9 | 16.6 | 19.6 | 16.1 | 12.3 | 132.0 |
| **Canada:** | | | | | | | | | | | | | | | | | | | | | | | | | | | | |
| Aklavik, N.W.T. | 68 14N | 135 00W | 30 | 22 | -10 | -26 | 19 | -2 | 66 | 47 | 25 | 15 | 93 | -62 | 22 | 0.5 | 0.3 | 0.4 | 0.5 | 0.5 | 0.8 | 1.4 | 1.4 | 0.9 | 0.9 | 0.8 | 0.4 | 9.0 |
| Alert, N.W.T. | 82 31N | 62 20W | 95 | 9 | -19 | -29 | -8 | -18 | 44 | 36 | 2 | -7 | 67 | -53 | 30 | 0.2 | 0.3 | 0.3 | 0.5 | 0.3 | 0.6 | 1.1 | 1.1 | 1.0 | 0.9 | 0.4 | 0.4 | 6.3 |
| Calgary, Alta. | 51 06N | 114 01W | 3,540 | 55 | 24 | 2 | 53 | 27 | 76 | 47 | 54 | 29 | 97 | -49 | 55 | 0.5 | 0.5 | 0.8 | 1.0 | 2.3 | 3.1 | 2.3 | 2.1 | 1.5 | 0.7 | 0.6 | 0.6 | 16.7 |
| Charlottetown, P.E.I. | 46 17N | 63 08W | 181 | 65 | 26 | 10 | 43 | 30 | 73 | 58 | 54 | 41 | 98 | -27 | 65 | 3.8 | 3.0 | 3.2 | 2.8 | 2.7 | 2.6 | 3.0 | 3.4 | 3.4 | 4.1 | 3.8 | 4.0 | 39.8 |
| Chatham, N.B. | 47 00N | 65 27W | 109 | 50 | 23 | 2 | 47 | 28 | 77 | 56 | 55 | 37 | 102 | -43 | 65 | 3.4 | 2.7 | 3.3 | 3.0 | 3.2 | 3.6 | 3.9 | 4.0 | 3.1 | 4.0 | 3.4 | 3.2 | 40.8 |
| Churchhill, Man. | 58 45N | 94 04W | 94 | 71 | -11 | -27 | 24 | 2 | 64 | 43 | 34 | 20 | 96 | -57 | 50 | 0.5 | 0.6 | 0.7 | 1.0 | 0.9 | 1.9 | 2.2 | 2.7 | 2.3 | 1.4 | 1.0 | 0.7 | 16.0 |
| Edmonton, Alta. | 53 34N | 113 31W | 2,219 | 12 | 16 | 1 | 52 | 28 | 74 | 52 | 51 | 30 | 99 | -57 | 71 | 0.9 | 0.7 | 0.7 | 1.0 | 1.9 | 3.2 | 3.3 | 2.4 | 1.3 | 0.8 | 0.9 | 0.9 | 18.0 |
| Fort Nelson, B.C. | 58 50N | 122 35W | 1,253 | 42 | 1 | -15 | 47 | 25 | 74 | 51 | 43 | 25 | 98 | -61 | 13 | 0.9 | 1.2 | 0.5 | 0.8 | 1.4 | 2.5 | 2.0 | 2.4 | 1.3 | 1.4 | 1.2 | 1.2 | 16.3 |
| Fort Simpson, N.W.T. | 61 45N | 121 14W | 554 | 18 | -10 | -27 | 38 | 14 | 74 | 50 | 36 | 21 | 97 | -70 | 42 | 0.7 | 0.7 | 0.8 | 0.7 | 1.4 | 1.5 | 2.3 | 1.5 | 1.3 | 0.9 | 0.8 | 0.8 | 13.1 |
| Frobisher Bay, N.W.T. | 63 45N | 68 33W | 110 | 14 | -9 | -23 | 16 | -1 | 53 | 39 | 29 | 18 | 76 | -49 | 10 | 0.7 | 0.9 | 0.8 | 0.8 | 0.7 | 0.9 | 1.5 | 2.0 | 1.8 | 1.1 | 1.0 | 1.0 | 13.3 |
| Gander, Nfld. | 48 57N | 54 34W | 496 | 75 | 27 | 13 | 40 | 27 | 71 | 55 | 51 | 37 | 96 | -17 | 14 | 2.6 | 3.3 | 2.8 | 2.6 | 2.8 | 2.8 | 3.6 | 3.6 | 3.7 | 4.1 | 4.2 | 3.7 | 39.6 |
| Halifax, N.S. | 44 39N | 63 34W | 83 | 19 | 32 | 15 | 47 | 31 | 74 | 55 | 57 | 37 | 99 | -21 | 75 | 5.4 | 4.4 | 4.9 | 4.5 | 4.0 | 3.8 | 3.6 | 4.0 | 4.1 | 5.4 | 5.3 | 5.4 | 55.7 |
| Kapuskasing, Ont. | 49 25N | 82 28W | 743 | 30 | 10 | -14 | 43 | 19 | 75 | 50 | 47 | 31 | 101 | -53 | 23 | 2.0 | 1.1 | 1.6 | 1.8 | 2.1 | 2.3 | 3.3 | 3.5 | 3.5 | 2.4 | 2.4 | 1.9 | 27.5 |
| Knob Lake, Que. | 54 48N | 66 49W | 1,712 | 67 | 3 | -21 | 30 | 12 | 64 | 46 | 37 | 25 | 88 | -59 | 19 | 1.9 | 1.9 | 1.4 | 1.6 | 1.7 | 3.3 | 3.3 | 4.4 | 3.7 | 2.9 | 2.4 | 1.5 | 29.7 |
| Montreal, Que. | 45 30N | 73 34W | 187 | 17 | 21 | 6 | 50 | 33 | 78 | 61 | 54 | 40 | 97 | -35 | 10 | 3.8 | 3.0 | 3.5 | 2.6 | 3.1 | 3.4 | 3.7 | 3.5 | 3.4 | 3.4 | 3.5 | 3.6 | 40.8 |
| North Bay, Ont. | 46 21N | 79 25W | 1,216 | 65 | 22 | 3 | 48 | 31 | 78 | 56 | 48 | 36 | 99 | -46 | 77 | 2.9 | 2.2 | 1.8 | 2.6 | 2.5 | 3.2 | 3.2 | 2.7 | 3.7 | 3.2 | 2.7 | 2.1 | 30.8 |
| Ottowa, Ont. | 45 19N | 75 40W | 374 | 32 | 21 | 3 | 51 | 31 | 81 | 58 | 54 | 38 | 102 | -38 | 23 | 2.9 | 2.2 | 2.8 | 2.7 | 3.1 | 3.4 | 3.4 | 2.7 | 3.2 | 3.0 | 3.0 | 2.6 | 34.3 |
| Penticton, B.C. | 49 28N | 119 36W | 1,129 | 62 | 32 | 21 | 61 | 35 | 84 | 53 | 59 | 34 | 105 | -16 | 65 | 1.0 | 0.7 | 0.7 | 1.1 | 1.2 | 1.2 | 0.8 | 0.8 | 1.0 | 0.8 | 0.9 | 1.1 | 10.8 |
| Port Arthur, Ont. | 48 22N | 89 19W | 644 | 27 | 17 | -4 | 44 | 26 | 74 | 52 | 50 | 30 | 104 | -42 | 32 | 0.9 | 0.8 | 1.0 | 1.5 | 2.1 | 2.8 | 1.6 | 1.9 | 3.4 | 2.5 | 1.5 | 0.9 | 23.8 |
| Prince George, B.C. | 53 53N | 122 41W | 2,218 | 26 | 23 | 3 | 54 | 27 | 75 | 44 | 52 | 30 | 102 | -58 | 59 | 1.8 | 1.2 | 1.4 | 0.8 | 1.3 | 2.1 | 1.6 | 1.9 | 2.0 | 2.0 | 1.9 | 1.9 | 19.9 |
| Prince Rupert, B.C. | 54 17N | 130 23W | 170 | 72 | 39 | 30 | 50 | 37 | 62 | 49 | 53 | 40 | 97 | -3 | 27 | 9.8 | 7.6 | 8.4 | 6.7 | 5.3 | 4.1 | 4.8 | 5.1 | 7.7 | 12.2 | 12.3 | 11.3 | 95.3 |
| Quebec, Que. | 46 48N | 71 23W | 239 | 55 | 18 | 2 | 44 | 29 | 76 | 57 | 51 | 37 | 110 | -34 | 26 | 3.5 | 2.7 | 3.0 | 3.0 | 3.5 | 4.1 | 4.0 | 4.0 | 3.7 | 3.4 | 3.2 | 3.2 | 39.8 |
| Regina, Sask. | 50 26N | 104 40W | 1,884 | 13 | 10 | -11 | 50 | 26 | 79 | 51 | 51 | 27 | 93 | -56 | 72 | 0.5 | 0.3 | 0.7 | 0.7 | 1.8 | 3.3 | 2.4 | 1.8 | 1.3 | 0.9 | 0.6 | 0.4 | 14.7 |
| Resolute, N.W.T. | 74 43N | 94 59W | 220 | 61 | -20 | -33 | -1 | -16 | 45 | 35 | 11 | 0 | 61 | -61 | 49 | 0.1 | 0.1 | 0.2 | 0.2 | 0.5 | 0.8 | 0.9 | 1.1 | 0.8 | 0.5 | 0.2 | 0.1 | 5.5 |
| St. John, N.B. | 45 17N | 66 04W | 119 | 68 | 28 | 11 | 43 | 29 | 69 | 54 | 54 | 40 | 93 | -24 | 7 | 4.1 | 3.1 | 3.7 | 3.2 | 3.1 | 3.2 | 3.1 | 3.6 | 3.7 | 4.1 | 3.9 | 3.8 | 42.6 |
| St. Johns, Nfld. | 47 32N | 52 44W | 211 | 38 | 30 | 18 | 41 | 29 | 69 | 52 | 53 | 40 | 93 | -21 | 61 | 5.3 | 5.1 | 4.6 | 3.8 | 3.9 | 3.1 | 3.1 | 4.0 | 3.7 | 4.8 | 5.7 | 6.0 | 53.1 |
| Saskatoon, Sask. | 52 08N | 106 38W | 1,690 | 38 | 9 | -11 | 49 | 26 | 77 | 52 | 51 | 27 | 104 | -55 | 38 | 0.9 | 0.5 | 0.7 | 0.7 | 1.4 | 2.6 | 2.4 | 1.9 | 1.5 | 0.9 | 0.5 | 0.6 | 14.6 |

| COUNTRY AND STATION | LATITUDE | LONGITUDE | ELEVATION (FEET) | TEMP. LENGTH OF RECORD (YEAR) | JANUARY MAX °F | JANUARY MIN °F | APRIL MAX °F | APRIL MIN °F | JULY MAX °F | JULY MIN °F | OCTOBER MAX °F | OCTOBER MIN °F | EXTREME MAX °F | EXTREME MIN °F | PRECIP. LENGTH OF RECORD (YEAR) | JAN IN | FEB IN | MAR IN | APR IN | MAY IN | JUN IN | JUL IN | AUG IN | SEP IN | OCT IN | NOV IN | DEC IN | YEAR IN |
|---|---|---|---|---|---|---|---|---|---|---|---|---|---|---|---|---|---|---|---|---|---|---|---|---|---|---|---|---|
| The Pas, Man. | 53 49N | 101 15W | 890 | 27 | 1 | -18 | 45 | 21 | 75 | 54 | 45 | 26 | 100 | -54 | 27 | 0.6 | 0.5 | 0.7 | 0.8 | 1.4 | 2.2 | 2.2 | 2.1 | 2.0 | 1.2 | 1.0 | 0.8 | 15.5 |
| Toronto, Ont. | 43 40N | 79 24W | 379 | 105 | 30 | 16 | 50 | 34 | 79 | 59 | 56 | 40 | 105 | -26 | 105 | 2.7 | 2.4 | 2.6 | 2.5 | 2.9 | 2.7 | 3.0 | 2.7 | 2.9 | 2.4 | 2.8 | 2.6 | 32.2 |
| Vancouver, B.C. | 49 17N | 123 05W | 127 | 43 | 41 | 32 | 58 | 40 | 74 | 54 | 57 | 44 | 92 | 2 | 41 | 8.6 | 5.8 | 5.0 | 3.3 | 2.8 | 2.5 | 1.2 | 1.7 | 3.6 | 5.8 | 8.3 | 8.8 | 57.4 |
| Whitehorse, Y.T. | 60 43N | 135 04W | 2,303 | 10 | 13 | -3 | 41 | 22 | 67 | 45 | 41 | 28 | 91 | -62 | 10 | 0.6 | 0.5 | 0.6 | 0.4 | 0.6 | 1.0 | 1.6 | 1.5 | 1.3 | 0.7 | 1.0 | 0.8 | 10.6 |
| Winnipeg, Man. | 49 54N | 97 14W | 783 | 66 | 7 | -13 | 48 | 27 | 79 | 55 | 51 | 31 | 108 | -54 | 66 | 0.9 | 0.9 | 1.2 | 1.4 | 2.3 | 3.1 | 3.1 | 2.5 | 2.3 | 1.5 | 1.1 | 0.9 | 21.2 |
| Yellow Knife, N.W.T. | 62 28N | 114 27W | 674 | 13 | -8 | -23 | 29 | 9 | 69 | 52 | 36 | 26 | 90 | -60 | 13 | 0.8 | 0.6 | 0.7 | 0.4 | 0.7 | 0.6 | 1.5 | 1.4 | 1.0 | 1.3 | 1.0 | 0.8 | 10.8 |
| **Greenland:** | | | | | | | | | | | | | | | | | | | | | | | | | | | | |
| Angmagssalik | 65 36N | 37 33W | 95 | 30 | 23 | 10 | 35 | 16 | 54 | 37 | 35 | 25 | 77 | -26 | 38 | 2.9 | 2.4 | 2.6 | 2.1 | 2.0 | 1.8 | 1.5 | 2.1 | 3.3 | 4.7 | 3.0 | 2.7 | 31.1 |
| Danmarkshaven | 76 46N | 19 00W | 7 | 2 | -1 | -15 | 6 | -13 | 47 | 34 | 13 | 2 | 63 | -42 | 2 | 1.2 | 0.7 | 0.7 | 0.1 | 0.2 | 0.2 | 0.5 | 0.6 | 0.3 | 0.3 | 1.0 | 0.7 | 6.0 |
| Eismitte | 70 53N | 40 42W | 9,843 | 1 | -33 | -53 | -14 | -37 | 19 | 1 | -23 | -42 | 27 | -85 | 1 | 0.6 | 0.2 | 0.3 | 0.2 | 0.1 | 0.1 | 0.1 | 0.4 | 0.3 | 0.5 | 0.8 | 1.0 | 4.3 |
| Godthaab | 64 10N | 51 43W | 66 | 40 | 19 | 10 | 31 | 20 | 52 | 38 | 35 | 26 | 76 | -20 | 45 | 1.4 | 1.7 | 1.6 | 1.2 | 1.7 | 1.4 | 2.2 | 3.1 | 3.3 | 2.5 | 1.9 | 1.5 | 23.5 |
| Ivigtut | 61 12N | 48 10W | 98 | 48 | 24 | 12 | 38 | 24 | 57 | 42 | 40 | 29 | 86 | -20 | 50 | 3.3 | 2.6 | 3.4 | 2.5 | 3.5 | 3.2 | 3.1 | 3.7 | 5.9 | 5.7 | 4.6 | 3.1 | 44.6 |
| Jacobshavn | 69 13N | 51 02W | 104 | 32 | 8 | -7 | 24 | 6 | 51 | 42 | 31 | 20 | 71 | -46 | 52 | 0.8 | 0.4 | 0.5 | 0.5 | 0.6 | 0.8 | 1.2 | 1.4 | 1.3 | 0.6 | 0.7 | 0.5 | 9.2 |
| Nord | 81 36N | 16 40W | 118 | 8 | -15 | -28 | -5 | -18 | 44 | 35 | 3 | -6 | 61 | -60 | 8 | 0.8 | 0.8 | 0.5 | 0.3 | 0.1 | 0.3 | 1.0 | 1.4 | 1.2 | 0.9 | 1.4 | 0.5 | 8.9 |
| Scoresbysund | 70 29N | 21 58W | 56 | 12 | 12 | -3 | 22 | 6 | 49 | 36 | 25 | 15 | 63 | -42 | 12 | 1.8 | 1.4 | 0.9 | 1.4 | 0.4 | 0.8 | 1.5 | 0.7 | 1.7 | 1.4 | 1.1 | 1.9 | 15.0 |
| Thule | 76 31N | 68 44W | 251 | 12 | -4 | -17 | 10 | -7 | 46 | 38 | 19 | 8 | 63 | -44 | 12 | 0.4 | 0.3 | 0.2 | 0.2 | 0.3 | 0.2 | 0.7 | 0.6 | 0.6 | 0.7 | 0.5 | 0.2 | 4.9 |
| Upernivik | 72 47N | 56 07W | 59 | 40 | -1 | -13 | 15 | -1 | 48 | 35 | 29 | 21 | 69 | -44 | 50 | 0.4 | 0.5 | 0.7 | 0.6 | 0.6 | 0.5 | 0.9 | 1.1 | 1.1 | 1.1 | 1.1 | 0.6 | 9.2 |
| **Mexico:** | | | | | | | | | | | | | | | | | | | | | | | | | | | | |
| Acapulco | 16 50N | 99 56W | 10 | 8 | 85 | 70 | 87 | 71 | 89 | 75 | 88 | 74 | 97 | 60 | 40 | 0.3 | * | 0.0 | * | 1.4 | 12.8 | 9.1 | 9.3 | 13.9 | 6.7 | 1.2 | 0.4 | 55.1 |
| Chihuahua | 28 42N | 105 57W | 4,429 | 9 | 65 | 36 | 81 | 51 | 89 | 66 | 79 | 51 | 102 | 12 | 22 | 0.2 | 0.4 | 0.3 | 0.2 | 0.2 | 1.7 | 3.6 | 3.7 | 3.3 | 0.9 | 0.5 | 0.4 | 15.4 |
| Guadalajara | 20 41N | 103 20W | 5,194 | 26 | 73 | 45 | 85 | 53 | 79 | 60 | 78 | 56 | 101 | 26 | 33 | 0.4 | 0.2 | 0.2 | 0.2 | 1.1 | 8.8 | 9.4 | 8.5 | 7.2 | 2.2 | 0.8 | 0.7 | 39.7 |
| Guaymas | 27 57N | 110 55W | 58 | 9 | 74 | 57 | 84 | 65 | 96 | 82 | 91 | 75 | 117 | 41 | 41 | 0.5 | 0.2 | 0.2 | 0.1 | * | 0.1 | 1.7 | 2.7 | 2.1 | 0.7 | 0.3 | 0.8 | 9.4 |
| La Paz | 24 07N | 110 17W | 85 | 9 | 74 | 54 | 86 | 58 | 96 | 73 | 90 | 68 | 108 | 31 | 12 | 0.4 | 0.1 | 0.2 | 0.3 | 0.0 | 0.2 | 0.4 | 1.2 | 1.4 | 0.6 | 0.5 | 1.1 | 5.7 |
| Lerdo | 25 30N | 103 32W | 3,740 | 10 | 72 | 45 | 86 | 57 | 90 | 73 | 82 | 58 | 105 | 23 | 14 | 0.4 | 0.1 | 0.2 | 0.0 | 0.0 | 1.5 | 1.5 | 1.3 | 2.0 | 0.8 | 0.5 | 0.5 | 10.2 |
| Manzanillo | 19 04N | 104 20W | 26 | 17 | 86 | 68 | 87 | 67 | 93 | 76 | 91 | 76 | 103 | 54 | 17 | 0.1 | 0.2 | * | 0.0 | 0.1 | 4.7 | 5.7 | 6.4 | 14.5 | 5.1 | 0.9 | 1.8 | 39.5 |
| Mazatlan | 23 11N | 106 25W | 256 | 10 | 71 | 61 | 76 | 65 | 86 | 77 | 85 | 76 | 93 | 52 | 46 | 0.8 | 0.5 | 0.2 | 0.1 | 0.1 | 1.5 | 5.9 | 8.3 | 8.0 | 2.6 | 0.9 | 1.3 | 30.2 |
| Mérida | 20 58N | 89 38W | 72 | 22 | 83 | 62 | 92 | 69 | 92 | 73 | 87 | 71 | 106 | 51 | 40 | 1.2 | 0.9 | 0.7 | 0.8 | 3.2 | 5.6 | 5.2 | 5.6 | 6.8 | 3.8 | 1.3 | 1.3 | 36.5 |
| Mexico City | 19 26N | 99 04W | 7,340 | 42 | 66 | 42 | 78 | 52 | 74 | 54 | 70 | 50 | 92 | 24 | 48 | 0.2 | 0.3 | 0.5 | 0.7 | 1.9 | 4.1 | 4.5 | 4.3 | 4.1 | 1.6 | 0.5 | 0.3 | 23.0 |
| Monterrey | 25 40N | 100 18W | 1,732 | 11 | 68 | 48 | 84 | 62 | 90 | 71 | 80 | 64 | 107 | 25 | 33 | 0.6 | 0.7 | 0.8 | 1.3 | 1.3 | 3.0 | 2.3 | 2.4 | 5.2 | 3.0 | 1.5 | 0.8 | 22.9 |
| Salina Cruz | 16 12N | 95 12W | 184 | 10 | 85 | 72 | 87 | 76 | 89 | 76 | 87 | 75 | 98 | 62 | 22 | * | 0.2 | 1.0 | 1.5 | 3.3 | 11.6 | 4.5 | 5.5 | 7.1 | 4.0 | 0.9 | 0.1 | 38.5 |
| Tampico | 22 16N | 97 51W | 78 | 12 | 75 | 59 | 83 | 69 | 89 | 75 | 85 | 73 | 104 | 34 | 22 | 1.5 | 1.2 | 1.0 | 0.8 | 1.9 | 8.7 | 4.9 | 4.8 | 10.8 | 5.0 | 2.0 | 1.6 | 44.9 |
| Vera Cruz | 19 12N | 96 08W | 52 | 10 | 77 | 66 | 83 | 72 | 87 | 74 | 85 | 73 | 98 | 53 | 40 | 0.9 | 0.6 | 0.6 | 0.8 | 2.6 | 10.4 | 4.1 | 11.1 | 13.9 | 6.9 | 3.0 | 1.0 | 65.7 |
| **CENTRAL AMERICA** | | | | | | | | | | | | | | | | | | | | | | | | | | | | |
| **British Honduras:** | | | | | | | | | | | | | | | | | | | | | | | | | | | | |
| Belize | 17 31N | 88 11W | 17 | 27 | 81 | 67 | 86 | 74 | 87 | 75 | 86 | 72 | 97 | 49 | 33 | 5.4 | 2.4 | 1.5 | 2.2 | 4.3 | 7.7 | 6.4 | 6.7 | 9.6 | 12.0 | 8.9 | 7.3 | 74.4 |
| **Canal Zone:** | | | | | | | | | | | | | | | | | | | | | | | | | | | | |
| Balboa Heights | 08 57N | 79 33W | 118 | 34 | 88 | 71 | 90 | 74 | 87 | 74 | 85 | 73 | 97 | 63 | 46 | 1.0 | 0.4 | 0.7 | 2.9 | 8.0 | 8.4 | 7.1 | 7.9 | 8.2 | 10.1 | 10.2 | 4.8 | 69.7 |
| Cristobal | 09 21N | 79 54W | 35 | 36 | 84 | 76 | 86 | 77 | 85 | 76 | 86 | 75 | 97 | 66 | 73 | 3.4 | 1.5 | 1.5 | 4.1 | 12.5 | 13.9 | 15.6 | 15.3 | 12.7 | 15.8 | 22.3 | 11.7 | 130.3 |
| **Costa Rica:** | | | | | | | | | | | | | | | | | | | | | | | | | | | | |
| San Jose | 09 56N | 84 08W | 3,760 | 8 | 75 | 58 | 79 | 62 | 77 | 62 | 77 | 60 | 92 | 49 | 34 | 0.6 | 0.2 | 0.8 | 1.8 | 9.0 | 9.5 | 8.3 | 9.5 | 12.0 | 11.8 | 5.7 | 1.6 | 70.8 |

(See footnotes at end of tables)

| Country and Station | Latitude | Longitude | Elevation (feet) | Length of Record (yr) | Jan Max (°F) | Jan Min (°F) | Apr Max (°F) | Apr Min (°F) | Jul Max (°F) | Jul Min (°F) | Oct Max (°F) | Oct Min (°F) | Extreme Max (°F) | Extreme Min (°F) | Length of Record (yr) | Jan (in.) | Feb (in.) | Mar (in.) | Apr (in.) | May (in.) | Jun (in.) | Jul (in.) | Aug (in.) | Sep (in.) | Oct (in.) | Nov (in.) | Dec (in.) | Year (in.) |
|---|---|---|---|---|---|---|---|---|---|---|---|---|---|---|---|---|---|---|---|---|---|---|---|---|---|---|---|---|
| **El Salvador:** | | | | | | | | | | | | | | | | | | | | | | | | | | | | |
| San Salvador | 13 42N | 89 13W | 2,238 | 39 | 90 | 60 | 93 | 65 | 89 | 65 | 87 | 65 | 105 | 45 | 39 | 0.3 | 0.2 | 0.4 | 1.7 | 7.7 | 12.9 | 11.5 | 11.7 | 12.1 | 9.5 | 1.6 | 0.4 | 70.0 |
| **Guatemala:** | | | | | | | | | | | | | | | | | | | | | | | | | | | | |
| Guatemala City | 14 37N | 90 31W | 4,855 | 6 | 73 | 53 | 82 | 58 | 78 | 60 | 76 | 60 | 90 | 41 | 29 | 0.3 | 0.1 | 0.5 | 1.2 | 6.0 | 10.8 | 8.0 | 7.8 | 9.1 | 6.8 | 0.9 | 0.3 | 51.8 |
| **Honduras:** | | | | | | | | | | | | | | | | | | | | | | | | | | | | |
| Tela | 15 46N | 87 27W | 41 | 4 | 82 | 67 | 87 | 72 | 88 | 73 | 86 | 71 | 96 | 58 | 20 | 8.9 | 5.1 | 2.6 | 3.3 | 4.3 | 5.0 | 6.4 | 9.4 | 7.7 | 13.5 | 15.9 | 14.0 | 96.1 |
| **WEST INDIES** | | | | | | | | | | | | | | | | | | | | | | | | | | | | |
| Bridgetown, Barbados | 13 08N | 59 36W | 181 | 35 | 83 | 70 | 86 | 72 | 86 | 74 | 86 | 73 | 95 | 61 | 22 | 2.6 | 1.1 | 1.3 | 1.4 | 2.3 | 4.4 | 5.8 | 5.8 | 6.7 | 7.0 | 8.1 | 3.8 | 50.3 |
| Camp Jacob, Guadaloupe | 16 01N | 61 42W | 1,750 | 19 | 77 | 64 | 79 | 65 | 81 | 68 | 81 | 68 | 92 | 54 | 21 | 9.2 | 6.1 | 8.1 | 7.3 | 11.5 | 14.1 | 17.6 | 15.3 | 16.4 | 12.4 | 12.3 | 10.1 | 140.4 |
| Ciudad Trujillo, Dominican Rep. | 18 29N | 69 54W | 57 | 26 | 84 | 66 | 85 | 69 | 88 | 72 | 87 | 72 | 98 | 59 | 25 | 2.4 | 1.4 | 1.9 | 3.9 | 6.8 | 6.2 | 6.3 | 6.3 | 7.3 | 9.7 | 4.8 | 2.4 | 55.8 |
| Fort-de-France, Martinique | 14 37N | 61 05W | 13 | 22 | 83 | 69 | 86 | 71 | 86 | 74 | 87 | 73 | 96 | 56 | 22 | 4.7 | 4.3 | 2.9 | 3.9 | 4.7 | 7.4 | 9.4 | 10.3 | 9.3 | 5.8 | 7.9 | 5.9 | 80.4 |
| Hamilton, Bermuda | 32 17N | 64 46W | 151 | 59 | 68 | 58 | 71 | 59 | 85 | 73 | 79 | 69 | 99 | 40 | 31 | 4.4 | 4.7 | 4.8 | 4.1 | 4.6 | 4.4 | 4.5 | 5.4 | 5.2 | 5.8 | 5.0 | 4.7 | 57.6 |
| Havana, Cuba | 23 08N | 82 21W | 80 | 25 | 79 | 65 | 84 | 69 | 89 | 75 | 85 | 73 | 99 | 43 | 62 | 2.8 | 1.8 | 1.8 | 2.3 | 4.7 | 6.5 | 4.9 | 5.3 | 5.9 | 6.8 | 3.1 | 2.3 | 48.2 |
| Kingston, Jamaica | 17 58N | 76 48W | 110 | 59 | 86 | 67 | 87 | 70 | 90 | 73 | 88 | 73 | 104 | 56 | 72 | 0.9 | 0.6 | 0.9 | 1.2 | 4.0 | 3.5 | 1.5 | 3.6 | 3.9 | 7.1 | 2.9 | 1.4 | 31.5 |
| La Guerite, St. Christopher (St. Kitts) | 17 20N | 62 45W | 157 | 33 | 86 | 67 | 85 | 71 | 86 | 76 | 85 | 73 | 97 | 56 | 59 | 4.1 | 2.0 | 2.3 | 2.3 | 3.8 | 3.6 | 4.4 | 5.2 | 6.0 | 5.4 | 7.3 | 4.5 | 50.9 |
| Nassau, Bahamas | 25 05N | 77 21W | 12 | 19 | 80 | 71 | 83 | 71 | 88 | 75 | 85 | 75 | 91 | 61 | 21 | 1.4 | 1.5 | 1.4 | 2.5 | 4.6 | 6.4 | 5.8 | 5.3 | 6.9 | 6.5 | 2.8 | 1.3 | 46.4 |
| Port-au-Prince, Haiti | 18 33N | 72 20W | 121 | 35 | 77 | 68 | 89 | 71 | 94 | 74 | 90 | 72 | 94 | 41 | 57 | 1.3 | 2.3 | 3.4 | 6.3 | 9.1 | 4.0 | 2.9 | 5.7 | 6.9 | 6.7 | 3.4 | 1.3 | 53.3 |
| Saint Clair, Trinidad | 10 40N | 61 31W | 67 | 42 | 87 | 69 | 90 | 69 | 88 | 71 | 89 | 71 | 101 | 58 | 70 | 2.7 | 1.6 | 1.8 | 3.7 | 3.7 | 7.6 | 8.6 | 9.7 | 7.6 | 6.7 | 7.2 | 4.9 | 64.2 |
| Saint Thomas, Virgin Is. | 18 20N | 64 58W | 11 | 49 | 82 | 71 | 85 | 74 | 88 | 77 | 87 | 76 | 92 | 63 | 97 | 2.5 | 1.9 | 1.7 | 2.2 | 4.6 | 3.2 | 3.2 | 4.1 | 6.9 | 5.6 | 5.0 | 3.9 | 43.7 |
| San Juan, Puerto Rico | 18 26N | 66 00W | 13 | 30 | 81 | 67 | 84 | 69 | 87 | 74 | 87 | 73 | 94 | 60 | 30 | 4.7 | 2.9 | 2.2 | 3.7 | 7.1 | 5.7 | 6.3 | 7.1 | 6.8 | 5.8 | 6.5 | 5.4 | 64.2 |
| **SOUTH AMERICA** | | | | | | | | | | | | | | | | | | | | | | | | | | | | |
| **Argentina:** | | | | | | | | | | | | | | | | | | | | | | | | | | | | |
| Bahia Blanca | 38 43S | 62 16W | 95 | 33 | 88 | 62 | 71 | 51 | 57 | 39 | 71 | 48 | 109 | 18 | 46 | 1.7 | 2.2 | 2.5 | 2.3 | 1.2 | 0.9 | 1.0 | 1.0 | 1.6 | 2.2 | 2.1 | 1.9 | 20.6 |
| Buenos Aires | 34 35S | 58 29W | 89 | 23 | 85 | 63 | 72 | 53 | 57 | 42 | 69 | 50 | 104 | 22 | 70 | 3.1 | 2.8 | 4.3 | 3.5 | 3.0 | 2.4 | 2.2 | 2.4 | 3.1 | 3.4 | 3.3 | 3.9 | 37.4 |
| Cipolletti | 38 57S | 67 59W | 889 | 9 | 89 | 56 | 72 | 40 | 55 | 29 | 72 | 43 | 107 | 9 | 24 | 0.4 | 0.4 | 0.7 | 0.4 | 0.6 | 0.6 | 0.5 | 0.3 | 0.6 | 0.9 | 0.5 | 0.6 | 6.4 |
| Corrientes | 27 28S | 58 50W | 177 | 39 | 93 | 71 | 81 | 63 | 71 | 53 | 82 | 60 | 112 | 30 | 40 | 4.7 | 4.5 | 5.3 | 5.6 | 3.3 | 1.9 | 1.7 | 1.5 | 2.8 | 4.7 | 5.2 | 5.2 | 46.4 |
| La Quiaca | 22 06S | 65 36W | 11,345 | 23 | 90 | 41 | 73 | 32 | 69 | 16 | 76 | 32 | 95 | 0 | 25 | 3.5 | 2.6 | 1.8 | 0.3 | * | 0.0 | * | * | 0.1 | 0.3 | 1.0 | 2.7 | 12.3 |
| Mendoza | 32 53S | 68 49W | 2,625 | 23 | 90 | 60 | 73 | 47 | 59 | 35 | 76 | 50 | 109 | 15 | 46 | 1.1 | 1.2 | 1.1 | 0.6 | * | 0.3 | * | 0.3 | 0.5 | 0.7 | 0.7 | 0.7 | 7.5 |
| Parana | 31 44S | 60 31W | 210 | 12 | 91 | 67 | 77 | 58 | 62 | 45 | 75 | 54 | 113 | 21 | 23 | 3.1 | 3.1 | 3.9 | 4.9 | 2.6 | 1.2 | 1.2 | 1.6 | 2.4 | 2.8 | 3.7 | 4.5 | 35.0 |
| Puerto Madryn | 42 47S | 65 01W | 26 | 50 | 81 | 57 | 70 | 46 | 55 | 36 | 68 | 45 | 104 | 10 | 50 | 0.4 | 0.6 | 0.7 | 0.5 | 0.9 | 0.6 | 0.6 | 0.4 | 0.6 | 0.7 | 0.4 | 0.7 | 7.0 |
| Santa Cruz | 50 01S | 68 32W | 39 | 12 | 70 | 48 | 57 | 39 | 41 | 28 | 58 | 39 | 94 | 1 | 20 | 0.3 | 0.3 | 0.3 | 0.6 | 0.4 | 0.5 | 0.6 | 0.5 | 0.3 | 0.3 | 0.4 | 0.7 | 5.3 |
| Santiago del Estero | 27 46S | 64 18W | 653 | 28 | 97 | 69 | 82 | 59 | 70 | 44 | 87 | 59 | 116 | 19 | 20 | 3.4 | 3.0 | 3.0 | 1.3 | 0.6 | 0.3 | 0.2 | 0.2 | 0.5 | 1.4 | 2.5 | 4.1 | 20.4 |
| Ushuaia | 54 50S | 68 20W | 26 | 16 | 57 | 41 | 48 | 33 | 39 | 25 | 52 | 35 | 85 | -6 | 21 | 2.0 | 2.6 | 1.9 | 2.1 | 1.5 | 1.2 | 1.2 | 1.1 | 1.3 | 1.6 | 1.5 | 1.9 | 19.9 |
| **Bolivia:** | | | | | | | | | | | | | | | | | | | | | | | | | | | | |
| Concepcion | 16 15S | 62 03W | 1,607 | 5 | 85 | 66 | 86 | 62 | 81 | 54 | 88 | 62 | 101 | 32 | 16 | 7.2 | 4.7 | 4.4 | 1.8 | 2.0 | 1.5 | 1.1 | 0.9 | 1.2 | 2.9 | 5.0 | 5.9 | 38.6 |
| La Paz | 16 30S | 68 08W | 12,001 | 31 | 63 | 43 | 65 | 40 | 62 | 33 | 66 | 40 | 80 | 26 | 50 | 4.5 | 4.2 | 2.6 | 1.3 | 0.5 | 0.3 | 0.4 | 0.5 | 1.1 | 1.6 | 1.9 | 3.7 | 22.6 |
| Sucre | 19 03S | 65 17W | 9,344 | 5 | 63 | 48 | 63 | 45 | 61 | 37 | 65 | 46 | 88 | 25 | 52 | 7.3 | 4.9 | 3.7 | 1.6 | 0.2 | 0.1 | 0.2 | 0.3 | 1.0 | 1.6 | 2.6 | 4.3 | 27.8 |
| **Brazil:** | | | | | | | | | | | | | | | | | | | | | | | | | | | | |
| Barra do Corda | 05 35S | 45 28W | 266 | 9 | 89 | 71 | 89 | 71 | 92 | 64 | 94 | 72 | 103 | 45 | 9 | 6.7 | 8.7 | 8.0 | 6.1 | 2.3 | 1.0 | 0.7 | 0.7 | 1.0 | 2.5 | 3.9 | 5.7 | 47.2 |

Temperature in °F. Precipitation in inches. `*` = trace.

| Country and Station | Latitude | Longitude | Elev. (feet) | Temp. Length of Record (yr) | Jan Max | Jan Min | Apr Max | Apr Min | Jul Max | Jul Min | Oct Max | Oct Min | Extreme Max | Extreme Min | Precip. Length of Record (yr) | Jan | Feb | Mar | Apr | May | Jun | Jul | Aug | Sep | Oct | Nov | Dec | Year |
|---|---|---|---|---|---|---|---|---|---|---|---|---|---|---|---|---|---|---|---|---|---|---|---|---|---|---|---|---|
| Bela Vista | 22 06S | 56 22W | 525 | 13 | 91 | 67 | 85 | 61 | 77 | 49 | 87 | 61 | 108 | 20 | 20 | 6.6 | 4.9 | 4.4 | 4.3 | 5.0 | 2.8 | 1.3 | 1.8 | 2.9 | 5.4 | 5.8 | 7.0 | 52.2 |
| Belem | 01 27S | 48 29W | 42 | 16 | 87 | 72 | 87 | 73 | 88 | 71 | 89 | 71 | 98 | 61 | 20 | 12.5 | 14.1 | 14.1 | 12.6 | 10.2 | 6.7 | 5.9 | 4.4 | 3.5 | 3.3 | 2.6 | 6.1 | 96.0 |
| Brasilia | 15 51S | 47 56W | 3,481 | 3 | 80 | 65 | 82 | 62 | 78 | 51 | 82 | 64 | 93 | 46 | 5 | 9.0 | 7.8 | 4.8 | 3.4 | 1.4 | * | 0.0 | * | 1.3 | 4.9 | 9.7 | 11.7 | 54.0 |
| Conceicao do Araguaia | 08 15S | 49 12W | 53 | 8 | 88 | 73 | 91 | 68 | 95 | 64 | 93 | 68 | 106 | 55 | 11 | 14.9 | 12.1 | 10.8 | 4.6 | 1.9 | 0.4 | * | 0.5 | 1.5 | 6.6 | 4.9 | 8.0 | 66.2 |
| Corumba | 19 00S | 57 39W | 381 | 17 | 94 | 73 | 92 | 68 | 84 | 64 | 93 | 70 | 102 | 33 | 11 | 7.3 | 5.6 | 5.1 | 4.6 | 2.9 | 1.9 | 0.3 | 1.2 | 2.6 | 4.0 | 5.6 | 7.1 | 48.5 |
| Florianopolis | 27 35S | 48 33W | 96 | 11 | 83 | 72 | 74 | 64 | 68 | 57 | 73 | 63 | 102 | 32 | 25 | 7.6 | 4.9 | 6.3 | 4.1 | 3.6 | 3.5 | 2.2 | 3.7 | 4.3 | 5.1 | 3.5 | 4.3 | 53.1 |
| Goias | 15 58S | 50 04W | 1,706 | 10 | 86 | 63 | 91 | 63 | 89 | 56 | 94 | 63 | 104 | 41 | 11 | 12.5 | 10.2 | 10.2 | 4.6 | 0.4 | 0.3 | 0.0 | 0.3 | 2.3 | 5.3 | 9.4 | 9.5 | 64.8 |
| Guarapuava | 25 16S | 51 30W | 3,592 | 11 | 79 | 61 | 73 | 55 | 66 | 47 | 74 | 53 | 94 | 23 | 5 | 8.7 | 5.8 | 5.4 | 4.5 | 4.6 | 6.5 | 2.7 | 3.6 | 4.6 | 6.9 | 6.6 | 6.1 | 65.8 |
| Manaus | 03 08S | 60 01W | 144 | 25 | 88 | 76 | 87 | 75 | 89 | 69 | 92 | 76 | 101 | 63 | 25 | 9.8 | 9.1 | 10.3 | 8.7 | 7.1 | 3.6 | 2.7 | 1.5 | 1.4 | 4.2 | 5.6 | 8.0 | 71.3 |
| Natal | 05 46S | 35 12W | 52 | 18 | 87 | 76 | 86 | 73 | 82 | 69 | 85 | 75 | 105 | 61 | 18 | 1.9 | 3.9 | 9.4 | 8.7 | 7.1 | 8.7 | 7.7 | 2.1 | 1.1 | 0.8 | 0.7 | 1.1 | 54.2 |
| Parana | 12 26S | 48 06W | 853 | 19 | 90 | 58 | 90 | 58 | 91 | 48 | 94 | 58 | 105 | 37 | 19 | 11.3 | 9.3 | 9.4 | 4.0 | 0.5 | * | 0.1 | 0.2 | 1.1 | 5.0 | 9.1 | 12.2 | 62.3 |
| Porto Alegre | 30 02S | 51 13W | 33 | 22 | 87 | 67 | 78 | 60 | 66 | 49 | 74 | 57 | 105 | 25 | 22 | 3.5 | 3.2 | 3.9 | 4.1 | 4.5 | 5.1 | 4.5 | 5.0 | 5.2 | 3.4 | 3.1 | 3.5 | 49.1 |
| Quixeramobim | 05 12S | 39 18W | 653 | 9 | 92 | 79 | 86 | 76 | 88 | 74 | 93 | 77 | 100 | 63 | 13 | 0.7 | 5.0 | 6.6 | 5.0 | 7.0 | 1.7 | 0.7 | 0.6 | 0.4 | 0.6 | 0.7 | 0.6 | 29.6 |
| Recife | 08 04S | 34 53W | 97 | 27 | 86 | 77 | 85 | 75 | 80 | 71 | 84 | 66 | 94 | 50 | 56 | 2.1 | 3.3 | 6.3 | 8.7 | 10.5 | 10.1 | 10.0 | 2.6 | 2.5 | 1.0 | 1.0 | 5.4 | 63.4 |
| Rio de Janeiro | 22 55S | 43 12W | 201 | 38 | 84 | 73 | 80 | 69 | 75 | 63 | 77 | 66 | 102 | 46 | 84 | 4.9 | 4.8 | 5.1 | 4.2 | 3.1 | 2.1 | 1.6 | 1.7 | 2.6 | 3.1 | 4.5 | 5.4 | 42.6 |
| Salvador (Bahia) | 13 00S | 38 30W | 154 | 25 | 86 | 74 | 84 | 74 | 79 | 69 | 83 | 71 | 100 | 50 | 20 | 2.6 | 5.3 | 6.1 | 11.2 | 10.8 | 9.4 | 7.2 | 4.8 | 3.3 | 4.0 | 2.3 | 4.1 | 74.8 |
| Santarem | 02 30S | 54 42W | 66 | 22 | 86 | 73 | 85 | 73 | 87 | 71 | 91 | 73 | 99 | 65 | 22 | 6.8 | 10.9 | 13.2 | 9.4 | 11.3 | 6.9 | 4.1 | 1.7 | 1.5 | 1.9 | 2.2 | 8.0 | 77.9 |
| Sao Paulo | 23 37S | 46 39W | 2,628 | 44 | 77 | 63 | 73 | 59 | 66 | 53 | 68 | 57 | 100 | 32 | 24 | 8.8 | 7.8 | 5.4 | 2.2 | 3.0 | 2.4 | 1.5 | 2.1 | 3.5 | 4.6 | 5.1 | 7.5 | 57.3 |
| Sena Madureira | 09 04S | 68 39W | 443 | 12 | 92 | 69 | 91 | 68 | 91 | 63 | 93 | 69 | 100 | 41 | 17 | 11.2 | 11.3 | 10.2 | 9.4 | 4.1 | 2.2 | 1.1 | 1.5 | 4.0 | 7.0 | 7.5 | 11.7 | 81.2 |
| Uaupes | 00 08S | 67 05W | 272 | 15 | 88 | 72 | 88 | 72 | 85 | 70 | 89 | 71 | 100 | 52 | 10 | 10.3 | 7.7 | 10.0 | 10.6 | 12.0 | 9.2 | 8.8 | 7.2 | 5.1 | 6.9 | 7.2 | 10.4 | 105.4 |
| Uruguaiana | 29 46S | 57 07W | 246 | 15 | 91 | 69 | 78 | 59 | 66 | 48 | 77 | 55 | 108 | 27 | 12 | 3.6 | 3.6 | 5.6 | 5.1 | 3.7 | 4.2 | 3.2 | 2.8 | 3.6 | 4.1 | 2.9 | 4.1 | 46.6 |
| **Chile:** | | | | | | | | | | | | | | | | | | | | | | | | | | | | |
| Ancud | 41 47S | 73 52W | 184 | 30 | 62 | 51 | 57 | 47 | 50 | 42 | 55 | 45 | 82 | 30 | 46 | 3.1 | 3.7 | 5.3 | 7.4 | 9.9 | 11.0 | 10.3 | 9.4 | 6.5 | 4.2 | 4.7 | 4.6 | 80.1 |
| Antofagasta | 23 42S | 70 24W | 308 | 22 | 76 | 63 | 70 | 58 | 63 | 51 | 66 | 55 | 86 | 37 | 32 | 0.0 | 0.0 | 0.0 | * | * | 0.1 | 0.2 | 0.1 | * | 0.1 | * | 0.0 | 0.5 |
| Arica | 18 28S | 70 20W | 95 | 15 | 78 | 64 | 74 | 60 | 66 | 54 | 69 | 58 | 93 | 39 | 25 | * | 0.0 | 0.0 | 0.0 | 0.0 | 0.0 | 0.0 | * | 0.0 | 0.0 | 0.0 | * | * |
| Cabo Raper | 46 50S | 75 38W | 131 | 10 | 58 | 46 | 54 | 44 | 47 | 38 | 51 | 40 | 72 | 28 | 10 | 7.8 | 5.8 | 7.1 | 7.7 | 7.5 | 7.9 | 9.5 | 7.5 | 5.6 | 7.0 | 6.7 | 7.0 | 87.1 |
| Los Evangelistas | 52 23S | 75 07W | 190 | 16 | 50 | 44 | 48 | 41 | 43 | 36 | 45 | 39 | 66 | 19 | 27 | 11.7 | 10.0 | 11.3 | 11.4 | 9.6 | 9.4 | 10.3 | 8.6 | 9.2 | 8.8 | 9.9 | 10.1 | 119.4 |
| Potrerillos | 26 30S | 69 27W | 9,350 | 8 | 65 | 44 | 63 | 47 | 57 | 40 | 61 | 44 | 75 | 20 | 7 | * | * | * | 0.7 | 0.7 | * | 0.5 | 0.3 | 0.2 | 0.2 | * | * | 2.2 |
| Puerto Aisen | 42 24S | 72 42W | 33 | 8 | 63 | 50 | 55 | 43 | 45 | 37 | 55 | 42 | 75 | 18 | 11 | 7.8 | 7.8 | 8.3 | 7.5 | 14.7 | 10.4 | 11.1 | 11.1 | 6.5 | 7.8 | 7.0 | 7.9 | 107.9 |
| Punta Arenas | 53 10S | 70 54W | 26 | 15 | 58 | 45 | 50 | 39 | 40 | 31 | 51 | 38 | 86 | 11 | 15 | 1.5 | 0.9 | 1.3 | 1.4 | 1.3 | 1.6 | 1.1 | 1.2 | 0.9 | 1.1 | 0.7 | 1.4 | 14.4 |
| Santiago | 33 27S | 70 42W | 1,706 | 14 | 85 | 53 | 74 | 45 | 59 | 37 | 72 | 45 | 99 | 24 | 58 | 0.1 | 0.1 | 0.2 | 0.5 | 2.5 | 3.3 | 3.0 | 2.2 | 1.2 | 0.6 | 0.3 | 0.2 | 14.2 |
| Valdivia | 39 48S | 73 14W | 16 | 29 | 73 | 52 | 62 | 46 | 52 | 41 | 63 | 44 | 97 | 19 | 60 | 2.6 | 2.9 | 5.2 | 9.2 | 14.2 | 17.7 | 15.5 | 12.9 | 8.2 | 5.0 | 4.9 | 4.1 | 102.4 |
| Valparaiso | 33 01S | 71 38W | 135 | 30 | 72 | 56 | 67 | 52 | 60 | 47 | 65 | 50 | 94 | 32 | 41 | 0.1 | * | 0.3 | 0.6 | 4.1 | 5.9 | 3.9 | 2.9 | 1.3 | 0.4 | 0.2 | 0.2 | 19.9 |
| **Colombia:** | | | | | | | | | | | | | | | | | | | | | | | | | | | | |
| Andagoya | 05 06N | 76 40W | 197 | 8 | 90 | 75 | 90 | 75 | 89 | 74 | 90 | 74 | 97 | 62 | 15 | 25.0 | 21.4 | 19.5 | 26.1 | 25.5 | 25.8 | 23.3 | 25.3 | 24.6 | 22.7 | 22.4 | 19.5 | 281.1 |
| Bogota | 04 42N | 74 08W | 8,355 | 10 | 67 | 48 | 67 | 51 | 64 | 50 | 66 | 50 | 75 | 30 | 49 | 2.3 | 2.6 | 4.0 | 5.8 | 4.5 | 2.4 | 2.0 | 2.2 | 2.4 | 6.3 | 4.7 | 2.6 | 41.8 |
| Cartagena | 10 28N | 75 30W | 39 | 6 | 84 | 73 | 87 | 76 | 88 | 78 | 87 | 77 | 98 | 61 | 10 | 0.4 | 0.0 | 0.4 | 0.9 | 3.4 | 3.4 | 3.0 | 0.6 | 0.5 | 10.8 | 8.9 | 4.5 | 36.8 |
| Ipiales | 00 50N | 77 42W | 9,680 | 9 | 61 | 50 | 60 | 49 | 57 | 42 | 62 | 49 | 77 | 32 | 13 | 3.1 | 2.3 | 3.5 | 3.5 | 2.8 | 1.9 | 3.1 | 1.3 | 1.4 | 3.1 | 3.3 | 2.6 | 29.9 |
| Tumaco | 01 49N | 78 45W | 7 | 10 | 82 | 75 | 84 | 76 | 82 | 75 | 82 | 75 | 90 | 64 | 10 | 16.9 | 11.7 | 9.6 | 14.6 | 17.4 | 12.0 | 7.7 | 7.3 | 7.3 | 5.9 | 4.9 | 7.0 | 122.3 |
| **Ecuador:** | | | | | | | | | | | | | | | | | | | | | | | | | | | | |
| Cuenca | 02 53S | 78 39W | 8,301 | 7 | 69 | 50 | 69 | 50 | 65 | 47 | 70 | 49 | 81 | 29 | 10 | 2.0 | 1.8 | 3.2 | 4.3 | 4.3 | 1.7 | 0.9 | 1.1 | 1.6 | 3.1 | 1.8 | 2.5 | 28.3 |

(See footnotes at end of tables)

| Country and Station | Latitude | Longitude | Elevation (feet) | Temp. Length of Record (yr) | Jan Max | Jan Min | Apr Max | Apr Min | Jul Max | Jul Min | Oct Max | Oct Min | Extreme Max | Extreme Min | Precip. Length of Record (yr) | Jan | Feb | Mar | Apr | May | Jun | Jul | Aug | Sep | Oct | Nov | Dec | Year |
|---|---|---|---|---|---|---|---|---|---|---|---|---|---|---|---|---|---|---|---|---|---|---|---|---|---|---|---|---|
| Guayaquil | 02 10S | 79 53W | 20 | 5 | 87 | 72 | 88 | 72 | 84 | 67 | 86 | 68 | 98 | 52 | 10 | 8.3 | 11.4 | 11.5 | 8.1 | 2.1 | 0.4 | 0.2 | * | * | * | 0.1 | 1.1 | 43.2 |
| Quito | 00 08S | 78 29W | 9,222 | 54 | 67 | 46 | 69 | 47 | 71 | 44 | 71 | 46 | 86 | 25 | 33 | 3.9 | 4.4 | 5.6 | 6.9 | 5.4 | 1.7 | 0.8 | 1.2 | 2.7 | 4.4 | 3.8 | 3.1 | 43.9 |
| **French Guiana:** | | | | | | | | | | | | | | | | | | | | | | | | | | | | |
| Cayenne | 04 56N | 52 27W | 20 | 38 | 84 | 74 | 86 | 75 | 88 | 73 | 91 | 73 | 97 | 65 | 51 | 14.4 | 12.3 | 15.8 | 18.9 | 21.7 | 15.5 | 6.9 | 2.8 | 1.2 | 1.3 | 4.6 | 10.7 | 126.1. |
| **Guyana:** | | | | | | | | | | | | | | | | | | | | | | | | | | | | |
| Georgetown | 06 50N | 58 12W | 6 | 54 | 84 | 74 | 85 | 76 | 85 | 75 | 87 | 75 | 93 | 68 | 35 | 8.0 | 4.5 | 6.9 | 5.5 | 11.4 | 11.9 | 10.0 | 6.9 | 3.2 | 3.0 | 6.1 | 11.3 | 88.7 |
| Lethem | 03 24N | 59 38W | 270 | 3 | 91 | 73 | 91 | 74 | 87 | 73 | 92 | 73 | 97 | 63 | 9 | 1.2 | 1.4 | 1.3 | 5.7 | 11.5 | 11.9 | 14.8 | 9.4 | 3.4 | 2.3 | 4.3 | 1.3 | 68.5 |
| **Paraguay:** | | | | | | | | | | | | | | | | | | | | | | | | | | | | |
| Asuncion | 25 17S | 57 30W | 456 | 15 | 95 | 71 | 84 | 65 | 74 | 53 | 86 | 62 | 110 | 29 | 30 | 5.5 | 5.1 | 4.3 | 5.2 | 4.6 | 2.7 | 2.2 | 1.5 | 3.1 | 5.5 | 5.9 | 6.2 | 51.8 |
| Bahia Negra | 20 14S | 58 10W | 318 | 20 | 92 | 74 | 87 | 68 | 79 | 61 | 90 | 69 | 106 | 35 | 20 | 5.4 | 5.3 | 4.9 | 2.9 | 2.3 | 1.6 | 1.5 | 0.6 | 2.3 | 4.2 | 5.3 | 4.3 | 40.6 |
| **Peru:** | | | | | | | | | | | | | | | | | | | | | | | | | | | | |
| Arequipa | 16 21S | 71 34W | 8,460 | 13 | 67 | 49 | 67 | 48 | 67 | 47 | 68 | 47 | 82 | 25 | 37 | 1.3 | 1.8 | 0.7 | 0.2 | * | * | * | * | 0.0 | * | * | 0.4 | 4.4 |
| Cajamarca | 07 09S | 78 30W | 8,662 | 9 | 71 | 48 | 70 | 47 | 70 | 41 | 71 | 47 | 79 | 25 | 9 | 3.6 | 4.2 | 4.6 | 3.4 | 1.7 | 0.5 | 0.2 | 0.3 | 2.3 | 2.3 | 1.9 | 3.2 | 28.2 |
| Cusco | 13 33S | 71 59W | 10,866 | 13 | 68 | 45 | 70 | 40 | 70 | 31 | 72 | 43 | 72 | 16 | 12 | 6.4 | 5.9 | 4.3 | 2.0 | 0.6 | 0.2 | 0.2 | 0.4 | 1.0 | 2.6 | 3.0 | 5.4 | 32.0 |
| Iquitos | 03 45S | 73 13W | 384 | 5 | 90 | 71 | 87 | 71 | 88 | 68 | 90 | 70 | 100 | 54 | 5 | 9.1 | 10.4 | 9.3 | 13.6 | 10.7 | 5.7 | 6.4 | 5.2 | 10.5 | 7.3 | 9.1 | 10.3 | 107.7 |
| Lima | 12 05S | 77 03W | 394 | 15 | 82 | 66 | 80 | 63 | 67 | 57 | 71 | 58 | 93 | 49 | 15 | 0.1 | * | * | * | 0.2 | 0.2 | 0.3 | 0.3 | 0.3 | 0.1 | 0.1 | * | 1.6 |
| Mollendo | 17 00S | 72 07W | 80 | 10 | 79 | 66 | 76 | 63 | 67 | 57 | 70 | 59 | 90 | 50 | 10 | * | 0.1 | * | * | 0.1 | 0.1 | * | 0.2 | 0.2 | 0.1 | 0.1 | * | 0.9 |
| **Surinam:** | | | | | | | | | | | | | | | | | | | | | | | | | | | | |
| Paramaribo | 05 49N | 55 09W | 12 | 35 | 85 | 72 | 86 | 73 | 87 | 73 | 91 | 73 | 99 | 62 | 75 | 8.4 | 6.5 | 7.9 | 9.0 | 12.2 | 11.9 | 9.1 | 6.2 | 3.1 | 3.0 | 4.9 | 8.8 | 91.0 |
| **Uruguay:** | | | | | | | | | | | | | | | | | | | | | | | | | | | | |
| Artigas | 30 24S | 56 23W | 384 | 13 | 91 | 65 | 77 | 55 | 65 | 45 | 75 | 54 | 107 | 24 | 50 | 4.3 | 3.9 | 4.7 | 5.1 | 4.1 | 4.1 | 2.8 | 3.0 | 4.0 | 4.7 | 3.8 | 4.1 | 48.6 |
| Montevideo | 34 52S | 56 12W | 72 | 56 | 83 | 62 | 71 | 53 | 58 | 43 | 68 | 49 | 109 | 25 | 56 | 2.9 | 2.6 | 3.9 | 3.9 | 3.3 | 3.2 | 2.9 | 3.1 | 3.0 | 2.6 | 2.9 | 3.1 | 37.4 |
| **Venezuela:** | | | | | | | | | | | | | | | | | | | | | | | | | | | | |
| Caracas | 10 30N | 66 56W | 3,418 | 30 | 75 | 56 | 81 | 60 | 78 | 61 | 79 | 61 | 91 | 45 | 46 | 0.9 | 0.4 | 0.6 | 1.3 | 3.1 | 4.0 | 4.3 | 4.3 | 4.2 | 4.3 | 3.7 | 1.8 | 32.9 |
| Ciudad Bolivar | 08 07N | 63 32W | 197 | 10 | 90 | 72 | 93 | 75 | 90 | 75 | 93 | 75 | 100 | 64 | 10 | 1.4 | 0.8 | 0.7 | 1.0 | 3.8 | 5.5 | 6.3 | 7.1 | 3.6 | 4.0 | 2.8 | 1.3 | 38.3 |
| Maracaibo | 10 39N | 71 36W | 20 | 12 | 90 | 73 | 92 | 76 | 94 | 76 | 92 | 76 | 102 | 66 | 36 | 0.1 | * | 0.3 | 0.8 | 2.7 | 2.2 | 1.8 | 2.2 | 2.8 | 5.9 | 3.3 | 0.6 | 22.7 |
| Merida | 08 36N | 71 10W | 5,293 | 14 | 73 | 56 | 75 | 60 | 76 | 59 | 75 | 60 | 90 | 48 | 14 | 2.5 | 1.5 | 3.6 | 6.7 | 9.8 | 7.3 | 4.7 | 5.7 | 6.7 | 9.5 | 8.2 | 3.4 | 69.7 |
| Santa Elena | 04 36N | 61 07W | 2,976 | 10 | 82 | 61 | 82 | 63 | 81 | 61 | 84 | 61 | 95 | 48 | 10 | 3.2 | 3.2 | 3.2 | 5.7 | 9.6 | 9.5 | 9.1 | 7.6 | 5.3 | 4.9 | 4.9 | 4.5 | 70.7 |
| **PACIFIC ISLANDS** | | | | | | | | | | | | | | | | | | | | | | | | | | | | |
| Easter Is. (Isla de Pascua) | 27 10S | 109 26W | 98 | 4 | 77 | 64 | 78 | 63 | 70 | 58 | 73 | 58 | 88 | 46 | 10 | 4.8 | 3.7 | 4.6 | 4.2 | 4.6 | 4.3 | 3.5 | 3.0 | 2.7 | 3.7 | 4.6 | 4.9 | 48.6 |
| Mas a Tierra (Juan Fernandez) | 33 37S | 78 52W | 20 | 25 | 72 | 60 | 68 | 57 | 6C | 50 | 61 | 51 | 86 | 39 | 29 | 0.8 | 1.2 | 1.6 | 3.4 | 5.9 | 6.4 | 5.8 | 4.4 | 2.9 | 1.9 | 1.6 | 1.0 | 36.9 |
| Seymour Is. (Galapagos Is.) | 00 28S | 90 18W | 36 | 3 | 86 | 72 | 87 | 75 | 81 | 69 | 81 | 67 | 93 | 58 | 3 | 0.8 | 1.4 | 1.1 | 0.7 | * | * | * | * | * | * | * | * | 4.0 |
| **ATLANTIC ISLANDS** | | | | | | | | | | | | | | | | | | | | | | | | | | | | |
| Fernando de Noronha | 03 50S | 32 25W | 148 | 32 | 84 | 75 | 82 | 75 | 81 | 73 | 82 | 75 | 93 | 63 | 32 | 1.7 | 4.7 | 7.4 | 10.5 | 10.5 | 7.3 | 5.4 | 1.9 | 0.7 | 0.3 | 0.4 | 0.5 | 51.3 |
| Cumberland Bay, South Georgia | 54 16S | 36 30W | 8 | 23 | 48 | 35 | 42 | 29 | 34 | 23 | 41 | 28 | 84 | -3 | 24 | 3.3 | 4.3 | 5.3 | 5.4 | 5.2 | 4.9 | 5.5 | 5.3 | 3.5 | 2.6 | 3.4 | 3.0 | 51.7 |
| Laurie Is., South Orkneys | 60 44S | 44 44W | 13 | 48 | 35 | 29 | 31 | 21 | 20 | 4 | 30 | 19 | 54 | -40 | 46 | 1.4 | 1.5 | 1.9 | 1.6 | 1.2 | 1.0 | 1.3 | 1.3 | 1.1 | 1.1 | 1.3 | 1.0 | 15.7 |
| Stanley, Falkland Isles | 51 42S | 57 51W | 6 | 25 | 56 | 42 | 49 | 37 | 40 | 31 | 48 | 35 | 76 | 12 | 41 | 2.8 | 2.3 | 2.5 | 2.6 | 2.6 | 2.1 | 2.0 | 2.0 | 1.5 | 1.6 | 2.0 | 2.8 | 26.8 |

See footnotes at end of table.

EUROPE

| COUNTRY AND STATION | LATITUDE | LONGITUDE | ELEVATION FEET | TEMP. LENGTH OF RECORD YEAR | JAN MAX °F | JAN MIN °F | APR MAX °F | APR MIN °F | JUL MAX °F | JUL MIN °F | OCT MAX °F | OCT MIN °F | EXT MAX °F | EXT MIN °F | PRECIP LENGTH OF RECORD YEAR | JAN IN. | FEB IN. | MAR IN. | APR IN. | MAY IN. | JUN IN. | JUL IN. | AUG IN. | SEP IN. | OCT IN. | NOV IN. | DEC IN. | YEAR IN. |
|---|---|---|---|---|---|---|---|---|---|---|---|---|---|---|---|---|---|---|---|---|---|---|---|---|---|---|---|---|
| Albania: Durres | 41 19N | 19 28E | 23 | 10 | 51 | 42 | 63 | 55 | 83 | 74 | 68 | 58 | 95 | 21 | 10 | 3.0 | 3.3 | 3.9 | 2.2 | 1.6 | 1.9 | 0.5 | 1.9 | 1.7 | 7.1 | 8.5 | 7.3 | 42.9 |
| Andorra: Les Escaldes | 42 30N | 01 31E | 3,543 | 5 | 43 | 29 | 59 | 39 | 78 | 55 | 61 | 42 | 91 | 0 | 9 | 1.5 | 1.7 | 2.9 | 2.4 | 4.7 | 3.1 | 2.2 | 3.4 | 3.1 | 3.5 | 3.3 | 2.5 | 34.3 |
| Austria: Innsbruck | 47 16N | 11 24E | 1,909 | 34 | 34 | 20 | 60 | 39 | 78 | 55 | 58 | 40 | 97 | -16 | 35 | 2.1 | 1.8 | 1.5 | 2.2 | 2.9 | 4.1 | 5.1 | 4.5 | 3.1 | 2.4 | 2.2 | 1.9 | 33.8 |
| Vienna (Wien) | 48 15N | 16 22E | 664 | 50 | 34 | 26 | 57 | 41 | 75 | 59 | 55 | 44 | 98 | -14 | 100 | 1.5 | 1.4 | 1.8 | 2.0 | 2.8 | 2.7 | 3.0 | 2.7 | 2.0 | 2.0 | 1.9 | 1.8 | 25.6 |
| Bulgaria: Sofiya (Sofia) | 42 42N | 23 20E | 1,805 | 30 | 34 | 22 | 62 | 41 | 82 | 57 | 63 | 42 | 99 | -17 | 27 | 1.3 | 1.1 | 1.7 | 2.3 | 3.3 | 3.2 | 2.4 | 2.0 | 2.3 | 2.1 | 1.9 | 1.4 | 25.0 |
| Varna | 43 12N | 27 55E | 115 | 30 | 40 | 30 | 59 | 43 | 84 | 63 | 67 | 50 | 107 | -12 | 20 | 1.5 | 0.9 | 1.2 | 1.2 | 1.8 | 2.6 | 1.9 | 1.2 | 1.5 | 1.9 | 1.9 | 2.0 | 19.6 |
| Cyprus: Nicosia | 35 09N | 33 17E | 716 | 40 | 58 | 42 | 74 | 50 | 97 | 69 | 81 | 58 | 116 | 23 | 64 | 2.9 | 2.0 | 1.3 | 0.8 | 1.1 | 0.4 | * | * | 0.2 | 0.9 | 1.7 | 3.0 | 14.6 |
| Czechoslovakia: Praha (Prague) | 50 05N | 14 25E | 662 | 40 | 34 | 25 | 55 | 40 | 74 | 58 | 54 | 44 | 98 | -16 | 70 | 0.9 | 0.8 | 1.1 | 1.5 | 2.4 | 2.8 | 2.6 | 2.2 | 1.7 | 1.2 | 1.2 | 0.9 | 19.3 |
| Prerov | 49 27N | 17 27E | 702 | 20 | 34 | 25 | 57 | 38 | 77 | 55 | 56 | 40 | 100 | -23 | 21 | 1.3 | 1.1 | 1.1 | 2.0 | 2.4 | 2.9 | 3.5 | 3.2 | 2.0 | 2.4 | 1.5 | 1.4 | 24.8 |
| Denmark: Copenhagen (Kobenhavn) | 55 41N | 12 33E | 43 | 30 | 36 | 29 | 50 | 37 | 72 | 55 | 53 | 42 | 91 | -3 | 30 | 1.6 | 1.3 | 1.2 | 1.7 | 1.7 | 2.1 | 2.2 | 3.2 | 1.9 | 2.1 | 2.2 | 2.1 | 23.3 |
| Aarhus | 56 08N | 10 12E | 161 | 21 | 35 | 27 | 51 | 37 | 70 | 54 | 53 | 42 | 87 | -12 | 21 | 2.3 | 1.5 | 1.4 | 1.8 | 1.2 | 2.2 | 2.5 | 3.3 | 3.2 | 2.6 | 2.5 | 2.1 | 26.6 |
| Finland: Helsinki | 60 10N | 24 57E | 30 | 20 | 27 | 17 | 43 | 31 | 71 | 57 | 45 | 37 | 89 | -23 | 50 | 2.2 | 1.7 | 1.7 | 1.7 | 1.9 | 2.0 | 2.3 | 3.3 | 2.8 | 2.9 | 2.7 | 2.4 | 27.6 |
| Kuusamo | 65 57N | 29 12E | 843 | 20 | 17 | 2 | 35 | 18 | 68 | 50 | 36 | 27 | 90 | -40 | 20 | 1.1 | 1.1 | 1.1 | 1.1 | 1.4 | 2.3 | 2.8 | 3.0 | 2.1 | 2.1 | 1.6 | 1.1 | 20.8 |
| Vaasa | 63 05N | 21 36E | 13 | 18 | 26 | 16 | 41 | 28 | 69 | 55 | 44 | 36 | 89 | -29 | 19 | 1.1 | 0.8 | 0.8 | 1.0 | 1.4 | 1.8 | 2.4 | 2.5 | 2.7 | 2.3 | 1.7 | 1.1 | 19.6 |
| France: Ajaccio (Corsica) | 41 52N | 08 35E | 243 | 46 | 56 | 40 | 66 | 48 | 85 | 64 | 72 | 55 | 103 | 23 | 86 | 3.0 | 2.3 | 2.6 | 2.2 | 1.6 | 0.9 | 2.8 | 0.7 | 1.7 | 3.8 | 4.4 | 3.1 | 29.1 |
| Bordeaux | 44 50N | 00 43W | 157 | 51 | 48 | 35 | 63 | 44 | 80 | 58 | 66 | 47 | 102 | 9 | 47 | 2.7 | 2.8 | 2.9 | 2.6 | 2.5 | 2.3 | 2.0 | 1.9 | 2.2 | 3.0 | 3.9 | 3.9 | 32.7 |
| Brest | 48 19N | 04 47W | 56 | 56 | 49 | 40 | 57 | 44 | 70 | 56 | 61 | 49 | 95 | 7 | 56 | 3.5 | 3.0 | 2.5 | 2.5 | 1.9 | 2.0 | 2.0 | 2.2 | 2.3 | 3.6 | 4.2 | 4.4 | 34.1 |
| Cherbourg | 49 39N | 01 38W | 30 | 47 | 47 | 40 | 54 | 43 | 67 | 57 | 59 | 50 | 91 | 14 | 47 | 3.3 | 2.9 | 2.7 | 2.0 | 1.9 | 1.8 | 1.9 | 3.0 | 2.9 | 4.6 | 5.1 | 5.2 | 37.3 |
| Lille | 50 35N | 03 05W | 141 | 40 | 42 | 33 | 58 | 40 | 75 | 55 | 59 | 45 | 96 | 0 | 40 | 2.5 | 1.4 | 2.5 | 2.0 | 2.4 | 2.9 | 2.8 | 2.3 | 2.6 | 3.1 | 3.0 | 3.2 | 30.3 |
| Lyon | 45 42N | 04 47E | 938 | 70 | 41 | 30 | 61 | 42 | 80 | 58 | 61 | 57 | 105 | -13 | 70 | 1.4 | 1.4 | 1.8 | 2.1 | 2.8 | 2.9 | 2.8 | 2.9 | 3.1 | 3.1 | 2.6 | 1.9 | 28.8 |
| Marseille | 43 18N | 05 23E | 246 | 72 | 41 | 38 | 59 | 41 | 78 | 57 | 76 | 57 | 101 | 9 | 102 | 1.9 | 1.5 | 1.8 | 1.8 | 1.9 | 1.0 | 0.6 | 0.9 | 2.6 | 3.7 | 3.1 | 2.2 | 23.2 |
| Paris | 48 49N | 02 29E | 164 | 66 | 42 | 32 | 60 | 41 | 76 | 55 | 59 | 44 | 105 | 1 | 118 | 1.5 | 1.1 | 1.5 | 1.7 | 2.0 | 2.1 | 2.1 | 2.0 | 2.0 | 2.2 | 2.0 | 1.9 | 22.3 |
| Strasbourg | 48 35N | 07 46E | 465 | 20 | 40 | 31 | 59 | 41 | 78 | 57 | 58 | 43 | 101 | -8 | 20 | 1.6 | 1.4 | 1.7 | 2.6 | 2.6 | 3.1 | 3.4 | 3.4 | 3.1 | 2.7 | 2.0 | 1.9 | 29.5 |
| Toulouse | 43 33N | 01 23E | 538 | 47 | 47 | 35 | 62 | 43 | 82 | 59 | 66 | 48 | 111 | 1 | 47 | 1.7 | 1.7 | 2.3 | 2.7 | 2.9 | 2.4 | 1.5 | 2.1 | 2.3 | 2.2 | 2.4 | 2.3 | 26.7 |
| Germany: Berlin | 52 27N | 13 18E | 187 | 50 | 35 | 26 | 55 | 38 | 74 | 55 | 55 | 41 | 96 | -15 | 40 | 1.9 | 1.3 | 1.5 | 1.7 | 1.9 | 2.3 | 3.1 | 2.2 | 1.9 | 1.7 | 1.7 | 1.9 | 23.1 |
| Bremen | 53 05N | 08 47E | 52 | 50 | 37 | 30 | 53 | 38 | 71 | 55 | 54 | 43 | 94 | 7 | 80 | 1.9 | 1.6 | 1.8 | 1.5 | 2.1 | 2.6 | 3.2 | 2.8 | 2.1 | 2.2 | 2.0 | 2.2 | 26.0 |
| Frankfurt A/M | 50 07N | 08 40E | 338 | 50 | 37 | 29 | 58 | 41 | 75 | 56 | 56 | 43 | 100 | 7 | 80 | 1.7 | 1.3 | 1.6 | 1.5 | 2.0 | 2.5 | 2.8 | 2.6 | 1.9 | 2.2 | 2.1 | 2.0 | 24.1 |
| Hamburg | 53 33N | 09 58E | 66 | 50 | 35 | 28 | 51 | 39 | 69 | 56 | 53 | 44 | 92 | -4 | 80 | 2.1 | 1.4 | 2.0 | 1.8 | 2.1 | 2.7 | 3.4 | 3.2 | 2.5 | 2.6 | 2.5 | 2.5 | 28.9 |
| Munchen (Munich) | 48 09N | 11 34E | 1,739 | 50 | 33 | 23 | 54 | 37 | 72 | 54 | 53 | 40 | 92 | -14 | 80 | 1.7 | 1.9 | 2.2 | 2.7 | 3.7 | 4.6 | 4.7 | 4.2 | 3.2 | 2.2 | 1.9 | 1.9 | 34.1 |
| Munster | 51 58N | 07 38E | 207 | 50 | 39 | 29 | 56 | 38 | 73 | 54 | 56 | 41 | 96 | -17 | 80 | 2.6 | 1.9 | 2.2 | 2.0 | 2.2 | 2.2 | 3.3 | 3.1 | 2.5 | 2.7 | 2.4 | 2.9 | 30.5 |
| Nurnberg | 49 27N | 11 03E | 1,050 | 50 | 35 | 26 | 56 | 38 | 74 | 55 | 55 | 41 | 99 | -18 | 80 | 1.5 | 1.2 | 1.3 | 1.7 | 2.2 | 2.5 | 3.1 | 3.1 | 2.1 | 2.1 | 1.9 | 1.7 | 24.4 |

(See footnotes at end of tables)

| Country and Station | Latitude | Longitude | Elevation (feet) | Temp. Length of Record (yr) | Jan Max (°F) | Jan Min (°F) | Apr Max (°F) | Apr Min (°F) | Jul Max (°F) | Jul Min (°F) | Oct Max (°F) | Oct Min (°F) | Extreme Max (°F) | Extreme Min (°F) | Precip. Length of Record (yr) | Jan (in.) | Feb (in.) | Mar (in.) | Apr (in.) | May (in.) | Jun (in.) | Jul (in.) | Aug (in.) | Sep (in.) | Oct (in.) | Nov (in.) | Dec (in.) | Year (in.) |
|---|---|---|---|---|---|---|---|---|---|---|---|---|---|---|---|---|---|---|---|---|---|---|---|---|---|---|---|---|
| **Gibraltar:** | | | | | | | | | | | | | | | | | | | | | | | | | | | | |
| Windmill Hill | 36 06N | 05 21W | 400 | 12 | 58 | 50 | 64 | 55 | 77 | 66 | 70 | 61 | 97 | 35 | 12 | 4.6 | 3.4 | 3.7 | 2.5 | 1.4 | 0.2 | * | 0.1 | 0.8 | 3.5 | 4.1 | 5.4 | 29.7 |
| **Greece:** | | | | | | | | | | | | | | | | | | | | | | | | | | | | |
| Athinai (Athens) | 37 58N | 23 43E | 351 | 72 | 54 | 42 | 67 | 52 | 90 | 72 | 74 | 60 | 109 | 20 | 80 | 2.2 | 1.6 | 1.4 | 0.8 | 0.8 | 0.6 | 0.2 | 0.4 | 0.6 | 1.7 | 2.8 | 2.8 | 15.8 |
| Iraklion (Crete) | 35 20N | 25 08E | 98 | 21 | 60 | 48 | 70 | 54 | 85 | 72 | 77 | 62 | 114 | 32 | 22 | 3.7 | 3.0 | 1.6 | 0.9 | 0.7 | 0.1 | * | 0.1 | 0.7 | 1.7 | 2.7 | 4.0 | 19.2 |
| Rodhos (Rhodes) | 36 26N | 28 15E | 289 | 10 | 60 | 51 | 67 | 59 | 83 | 72 | 76 | 68 | 104 | 30 | 6 | 5.7 | 3.9 | 2.6 | 1.7 | 0.5 | 0.3 | 0.0 | * | 0.4 | 1.7 | 5.2 | 6.7 | 28.5 |
| Thessaloniki (Salonika) | 40 37N | 22 57E | 78 | 9 | 49 | 37 | 66 | 49 | 90 | 70 | 73 | 56 | 107 | 15 | 26 | 1.5 | 1.5 | 1.6 | 1.9 | 2.0 | 1.2 | 1.0 | 0.7 | 1.2 | 2.4 | 2.1 | 1.9 | 19.0 |
| **Hungary:** | | | | | | | | | | | | | | | | | | | | | | | | | | | | |
| Budapest | 47 31N | 19 02E | 394 | 50 | 35 | 26 | 62 | 44 | 82 | 61 | 61 | 45 | 103 | -10 | 50 | 1.5 | 1.5 | 1.7 | 2.0 | 2.7 | 2.6 | 2.0 | 1.9 | 1.8 | 2.1 | 2.4 | 2.0 | 24.2 |
| Debrecen | 47 36N | 21 39E | 430 | 50 | 33 | 21 | 61 | 39 | 81 | 57 | 60 | 41 | 102 | -22 | 80 | 1.2 | 1.1 | 1.4 | 1.8 | 2.4 | 2.8 | 2.5 | 2.3 | 1.8 | 2.2 | 2.0 | 1.6 | 23.1 |
| **Iceland:** | | | | | | | | | | | | | | | | | | | | | | | | | | | | |
| Akureyri | 65 41N | 18 05W | 16 | 23 | 34 | 26 | 40 | 30 | 57 | 47 | 43 | 34 | 83 | - 8 | 26 | 1.7 | 1.5 | 1.7 | 1.3 | 0.6 | 0.9 | 1.3 | 1.6 | 1.9 | 2.3 | 1.9 | 1.9 | 18.6 |
| Reykjavik | 64 09N | 21 56W | 92 | 25 | 36 | 28 | 43 | 33 | 58 | 48 | 44 | 36 | 74 | 4 | 30 | 4.0 | 3.1 | 3.0 | 2.1 | 1.6 | 1.7 | 2.0 | 2.6 | 3.1 | 3.4 | 3.6 | 3.7 | 33.9 |
| **Ireland:** | | | | | | | | | | | | | | | | | | | | | | | | | | | | |
| Cork | 51 54N | 08 29W | 56 | 27 | 48 | 38 | 55 | 41 | 68 | 53 | 58 | 44 | 85 | 15 | 35 | 4.9 | 3.6 | 3.3 | 2.6 | 2.9 | 2.0 | 2.9 | 3.1 | 2.9 | 3.9 | 4.5 | 4.7 | 41.3 |
| Dublin | 53 22N | 06 21W | 155 | 30 | 47 | 35 | 54 | 38 | 67 | 51 | 57 | 43 | 86 | 8 | 35 | 2.7 | 2.2 | 2.0 | 1.9 | 2.3 | 2.0 | 2.8 | 3.0 | 2.8 | 2.7 | 2.7 | 2.6 | 29.7 |
| Shannon Airport | 52 41N | 08 55W | 8 | 9 | 46 | 36 | 55 | 41 | 66 | 53 | 58 | 45 | 87 | 12 | 12 | 3.8 | 3.0 | 2.0 | 2.2 | 2.4 | 2.1 | 3.1 | 3.0 | 3.0 | 3.4 | 4.2 | 4.3 | 36.5 |
| **Italy:** | | | | | | | | | | | | | | | | | | | | | | | | | | | | |
| Ancona | 43 37N | 13 32E | 52 | 30 | 46 | 36 | 62 | 50 | 83 | 68 | 67 | 55 | 102 | 18 | 30 | 2.6 | 1.7 | 1.6 | 2.3 | 2.1 | 1.9 | 1.5 | 1.5 | 3.5 | 3.7 | 2.5 | 3.0 | 28.0 |
| Cagliari (Sardinia) | 39 15N | 09 03E | 3 | 30 | 56 | 43 | 66 | 50 | 86 | 67 | 72 | 58 | 102 | 25 | 25 | 2.2 | 1.5 | 1.5 | 1.2 | 1.5 | 0.5 | 0.1 | 0.4 | 1.0 | 3.0 | 1.8 | 2.3 | 17.0 |
| Genova (Genoa) | 44 24N | 08 55E | 318 | 10 | 50 | 41 | 65 | 53 | 82 | 70 | 73 | 58 | 100 | 18 | 10 | 3.9 | 4.0 | 3.3 | 3.4 | 4.6 | 1.4 | 1.6 | 2.3 | 4.7 | 6.1 | 7.2 | 4.1 | 46.6 |
| Napoli (Naples) | 40 51N | 14 15E | 82 | 30 | 54 | 40 | 65 | 52 | 84 | 66 | 71 | 60 | 101 | 24 | 30 | 3.7 | 3.2 | 3.0 | 2.6 | 1.8 | 1.8 | 0.6 | 0.7 | 2.8 | 5.1 | 4.5 | 5.4 | 35.2 |
| Palermo (Sicily) | 38 07N | 13 19E | 354 | 10 | 58 | 47 | 67 | 53 | 86 | 71 | 75 | 62 | 113 | 31 | 30 | 3.8 | 3.4 | 2.4 | 1.9 | 1.1 | 0.6 | 0.2 | 0.6 | 2.0 | 3.7 | 4.1 | 4.5 | 28.3 |
| Rome | 41 48N | 12 36E | 377 | 10 | 54 | 39 | 68 | 46 | 88 | 64 | 73 | 53 | 104 | 20 | 30 | 3.3 | 2.9 | 2.4 | 2.0 | 1.9 | 0.6 | 0.4 | 0.7 | 2.8 | 4.3 | 4.4 | 4.1 | 29.5 |
| Taranto | 40 28N | 17 17E | 56 | 10 | 55 | 43 | 66 | 50 | 89 | 70 | 73 | 58 | 108 | 26 | 10 | 1.6 | 0.9 | 1.3 | 1.8 | 1.0 | 0.6 | 0.4 | 0.7 | 1.0 | 2.2 | 1.8 | 1.9 | 14.2 |
| Venezia (Venice) | 45 26N | 12 23E | 82 | 10 | 43 | 33 | 63 | 49 | 82 | 67 | 65 | 52 | 97 | 14 | 30 | 2.0 | 2.1 | 2.4 | 2.8 | 3.2 | 3.3 | 2.6 | 2.6 | 2.6 | 3.7 | 3.5 | 2.6 | 33.4 |
| **Luxembourg:** | | | | | | | | | | | | | | | | | | | | | | | | | | | | |
| Luxembourg | 49 37N | 06 03E | 1,096 | 7 | 36 | 29 | 58 | 40 | 74 | 55 | 56 | 43 | 99 | -10 | 100 | 2.3 | 2.0 | 1.9 | 2.1 | 2.4 | 2.5 | 2.8 | 2.6 | 2.4 | 2.7 | 2.7 | 2.8 | 29.2 |
| **Malta:** | | | | | | | | | | | | | | | | | | | | | | | | | | | | |
| Valletta | 35 54N | 14 31E | 233 | 90 | 59 | 51 | 66 | 56 | 84 | 72 | 76 | 66 | 105 | 34 | 90 | 3.3 | 2.3 | 1.5 | 0.8 | 0.4 | 0.1 | * | 0.2 | 1.3 | 2.7 | 3.6 | 3.9 | 20.3 |
| **Monaco:** | | | | | | | | | | | | | | | | | | | | | | | | | | | | |
| Monaco | 43 44N | 07 25E | 180 | 60 | 54 | 46 | 61 | 53 | 77 | 70 | 67 | 60 | 93 | 27 | 60 | 2.4 | 2.3 | 3.1 | 2.2 | 2.1 | 1.4 | 0.7 | 1.1 | 2.3 | 4.7 | 4.3 | 3.5 | 30.1 |
| **Netherlands:** | | | | | | | | | | | | | | | | | | | | | | | | | | | | |
| Amsterdam | 52 23N | 04 55E | 5 | 29 | 40 | 34 | 52 | 43 | 69 | 59 | 56 | 48 | 95 | 3 | 29 | 2.0 | 1.4 | 1.3 | 1.6 | 1.8 | 1.8 | 2.6 | 2.7 | 2.8 | 2.8 | 2.6 | 2.2 | 25.6 |
| **Norway:** | | | | | | | | | | | | | | | | | | | | | | | | | | | | |
| Bergen | 60 24N | 05 19E | 141 | 49 | 43 | 27 | 55 | 34 | 72 | 51 | 57 | 38 | 89 | 3 | 75 | 7.9 | 6.0 | 5.4 | 4.4 | 3.9 | 4.2 | 5.2 | 7.3 | 9.2 | 9.2 | 8.0 | 8.1 | 78.8 |
| Kristiansand | 58 10N | 07 59E | 175 | 11 | 32 | 25 | 50 | 35 | 71 | 53 | 53 | 39 | 90 | -14 | 56 | 5.0 | 3.6 | 3.6 | 2.7 | 2.5 | 2.8 | 3.5 | 5.3 | 4.7 | 6.2 | 5.7 | 6.4 | 52.0 |
| Oslo | 59 56N | 10 44E | 308 | 44 | 30 | 20 | 50 | 34 | 73 | 56 | 49 | 37 | 93 | -21 | 56 | 1.7 | 1.3 | 1.4 | 1.6 | 1.8 | 2.4 | 2.9 | 3.8 | 2.5 | 2.9 | 2.3 | 2.3 | 26.9 |
| Tromso | 69 39N | 18 57E | 335 | 47 | 30 | 22 | 37 | 27 | 59 | 48 | 40 | 33 | 83 | -1 | 75 | 4.1 | 3.8 | 3.3 | 2.4 | 2.1 | 2.1 | 2.3 | 2.9 | 4.7 | 4.5 | 4.0 | 3.9 | 40.1 |
| Trondheim | 63 25N | 10 27E | 417 | 44 | 31 | 22 | 45 | 32 | 66 | 51 | 46 | 36 | 95 | -22 | 65 | 3.1 | 2.7 | 2.6 | 2.0 | 1.7 | 1.9 | 2.4 | 3.0 | 3.4 | 3.7 | 2.8 | 2.8 | 32.1 |
| Vardo | 70 22N | 31 06E | 43 | 40 | 27 | 19 | 34 | 26 | 53 | 44 | 38 | 32 | 80 | -11 | 56 | 2.5 | 2.5 | 2.3 | 1.5 | 1.3 | 1.3 | 1.5 | 1.7 | 1.9 | 2.5 | 2.1 | 2.4 | 23.5 |

| Country and Station | Latitude | Longitude | Elevation (feet) | Temp Length of Record (years) | Jan Max (°F) | Jan Min (°F) | Apr Max (°F) | Apr Min (°F) | Jul Max (°F) | Jul Min (°F) | Oct Max (°F) | Oct Min (°F) | Extreme Max (°F) | Extreme Min (°F) | Precip Length of Record (years) | Jan (in.) | Feb (in.) | Mar (in.) | Apr (in.) | May (in.) | Jun (in.) | Jul (in.) | Aug (in.) | Sep (in.) | Oct (in.) | Nov (in.) | Dec (in.) | Year (in.) |
|---|---|---|---|---|---|---|---|---|---|---|---|---|---|---|---|---|---|---|---|---|---|---|---|---|---|---|---|---|
| **Poland:** | | | | | | | | | | | | | | | | | | | | | | | | | | | | |
| Gdansk (Danzig) | 54 24N | 18 40E | 36 | 36 | 33 | 25 | 49 | 37 | 70 | 56 | 53 | 42 | 94 | -16 | 35 | 1.2 | 1.0 | 1.3 | 1.5 | 1.8 | 2.3 | 2.8 | 2.6 | 2.1 | 1.8 | 1.8 | 1.5 | 21.7 |
| Krakow | 50 04N | 19 57E | 723 | 35 | 32 | 22 | 55 | 38 | 76 | 57 | 56 | 41 | 97 | -28 | 35 | 1.1 | 1.3 | 1.4 | 1.8 | 2.8 | 4.0 | 4.5 | 3.8 | 2.7 | 2.2 | 1.7 | 1.3 | 28.6 |
| Warsaw | 52 13N | 21 02E | 294 | 25 | 30 | 21 | 54 | 38 | 75 | 56 | 54 | 41 | 98 | -22 | 113 | 1.2 | 1.1 | 1.3 | 1.5 | 1.9 | 2.6 | 3.0 | 3.0 | 1.9 | 1.7 | 1.4 | 1.4 | 22.0 |
| Wroclaw (Breslau) | 51 07N | 17 05E | 482 | 50 | 35 | 25 | 55 | 39 | 74 | 57 | 55 | 42 | 98 | -26 | 40 | 1.5 | 1.1 | 1.5 | 1.7 | 2.4 | 2.4 | 3.4 | 2.7 | 1.8 | 1.7 | 1.5 | 1.5 | 23.2 |
| **Portugal:** | | | | | | | | | | | | | | | | | | | | | | | | | | | | |
| Braganca | 41 49N | 06 47W | 2,395 | 11 | 46 | 31 | 59 | 39 | 80 | 54 | 62 | 42 | 103 | 10 | 11 | 11.9 | 6.9 | 7.7 | 3.7 | 3.0 | 1.6 | 0.5 | 0.6 | 1.5 | 3.0 | 6.3 | 7.1 | 53.8 |
| Lagos | 37 06N | 08 38W | 46 | 21 | 61 | 47 | 67 | 52 | 83 | 64 | 73 | 58 | 107 | 28 | 17 | 3.2 | 2.6 | 2.8 | 1.4 | 0.8 | 0.2 | * | * | 0.4 | 1.5 | 2.6 | 2.8 | 18.3 |
| Lisbon | 38 43N | 09 08W | 313 | 75 | 56 | 46 | 64 | 52 | 79 | 63 | 69 | 57 | 103 | 29 | 75 | 3.3 | 3.2 | 3.1 | 2.4 | 1.7 | 0.7 | 0.2 | 0.2 | 1.4 | 3.1 | 4.2 | 3.6 | 27.0 |
| **Romania:** | | | | | | | | | | | | | | | | | | | | | | | | | | | | |
| Bucuresti (Bucharest) | 44 25N | 26 06E | 269 | 41 | 33 | 20 | 63 | 41 | 86 | 61 | 65 | 44 | 105 | -18 | 41 | 1.5 | 1.1 | 1.7 | 1.6 | 2.5 | 3.8 | 2.3 | 1.8 | 1.5 | 1.6 | 1.9 | 1.5 | 22.8 |
| Cluj | 46 47N | 23 40E | 1,286 | 15 | 31 | 18 | 58 | 38 | 79 | 56 | 60 | 41 | 100 | -26 | 16 | 1.3 | 1.2 | 1.0 | 2.1 | 3.3 | 3.3 | 2.6 | 3.3 | 2.0 | 1.7 | 1.0 | 1.2 | 24.0 |
| Constanta | 44 11N | 28 39E | 13 | 20 | 37 | 25 | 55 | 42 | 79 | 63 | 62 | 49 | 101 | -13 | 39 | 1.2 | 1.2 | 1.1 | 1.1 | 1.3 | 1.7 | 1.3 | 1.1 | 1.1 | 1.4 | 1.2 | 1.4 | 15.1 |
| **Spain:** | | | | | | | | | | | | | | | | | | | | | | | | | | | | |
| Almeria | 36 51N | 02 28W | 213 | 20 | 61 | 47 | 69 | 54 | 85 | 69 | 76 | 62 | 108 | 34 | 20 | 0.9 | 1.0 | 0.7 | 0.9 | 0.7 | 0.2 | * | 0.1 | 0.6 | 0.9 | 1.5 | 1.1 | 8.6 |
| Barcelona | 41 24N | 02 09E | 312 | 20 | 56 | 42 | 64 | 51 | 81 | 69 | 71 | 58 | 98 | 24 | 30 | 1.2 | 2.1 | 1.9 | 1.8 | 1.8 | 1.3 | 1.2 | 1.7 | 2.6 | 3.4 | 2.7 | 1.8 | 23.5 |
| Burgos | 42 20N | 03 42W | 2,825 | 29 | 42 | 30 | 57 | 38 | 77 | 53 | 61 | 43 | 99 | 0 | 29 | 1.5 | 1.5 | 2.1 | 1.9 | 2.4 | 1.7 | 0.8 | 0.7 | 1.4 | 2.0 | 2.2 | 2.0 | 20.2 |
| Madrid | 40 25N | 03 41W | 2,188 | 30 | 47 | 33 | 64 | 44 | 87 | 62 | 66 | 48 | 102 | 14 | 30 | 1.1 | 1.7 | 1.7 | 1.7 | 1.5 | 0.9 | 0.4 | 0.3 | 1.2 | 1.9 | 2.2 | 1.6 | 16.5 |
| Sevilla | 37 29N | 05 59W | 98 | 26 | 59 | 41 | 73 | 51 | 96 | 67 | 78 | 57 | 117 | 27 | 26 | 2.2 | 2.9 | 3.3 | 2.3 | 1.3 | 0.9 | 0.1 | 0.1 | 1.1 | 2.6 | 3.7 | 2.8 | 23.3 |
| Valencia | 39 28N | 00 23W | 79 | 26 | 58 | 41 | 67 | 51 | 83 | 68 | 73 | 57 | 107 | 20 | 29 | 0.9 | 1.5 | 0.9 | 1.2 | 1.1 | 1.3 | 0.4 | 0.5 | 2.2 | 1.6 | 2.5 | 1.3 | 15.4 |
| **Sweden:** | | | | | | | | | | | | | | | | | | | | | | | | | | | | |
| Abisko | 68 21N | 18 49E | 1,273 | 11 | 20 | 6 | 33 | 19 | 61 | 45 | 35 | 24 | 82 | -30 | 11 | 0.7 | 0.6 | 0.5 | 0.5 | 0.7 | 1.8 | 1.6 | 1.8 | 1.2 | 1.0 | 0.6 | 0.6 | 11.7 |
| Goteberg | 57 42N | 11 58E | 55 | 39 | 35 | 27 | 48 | 36 | 69 | 56 | 51 | 42 | 88 | -13 | 61 | 2.5 | 2.0 | 2.0 | 1.7 | 1.9 | 2.2 | 2.8 | 3.7 | 3.1 | 3.1 | 2.7 | 2.8 | 30.5 |
| Haparanda | 65 50N | 24 09E | 30 | 20 | 22 | 10 | 38 | 23 | 73 | 53 | 39 | 30 | 89 | -34 | 20 | 2.2 | 1.6 | 1.2 | 1.5 | 1.4 | 1.7 | 2.1 | 2.8 | 2.6 | 2.8 | 2.5 | 2.0 | 24.4 |
| Karlstad | 59 23N | 13 30E | 164 | 30 | 30 | 20 | 49 | 28 | 69 | 56 | 49 | 38 | 93 | -21 | 28 | 1.9 | 1.2 | 1.2 | 1.4 | 1.9 | 1.9 | 2.6 | 3.1 | 2.9 | 2.4 | 2.4 | 1.9 | 24.8 |
| Sarna | 61 41N | 13 07E | 1,504 | 20 | 19 | 4 | 42 | 23 | 69 | 46 | 42 | 28 | 91 | -51 | 20 | 1.6 | 0.8 | 0.9 | 1.2 | 1.6 | 2.8 | 3.6 | 3.3 | 2.6 | 2.3 | 1.8 | 1.8 | 24.3 |
| Stockholm | 59 21N | 18 04E | 146 | 30 | 31 | 23 | 45 | 32 | 70 | 55 | 48 | 39 | 97 | -26 | 30 | 1.5 | 1.1 | 1.1 | 1.5 | 1.6 | 1.9 | 2.8 | 3.1 | 2.1 | 2.1 | 1.9 | 1.9 | 22.4 |
| Visby (Gotland) | 57 39N | 18 18E | 36 | 30 | 35 | 28 | 44 | 33 | 67 | 55 | 50 | 41 | 88 | 1 | 30 | 1.7 | 1.1 | 1.2 | 1.4 | 1.1 | 1.4 | 2.0 | 2.7 | 1.7 | 1.9 | 2.1 | 2.0 | 20.3 |
| **Switzerland:** | | | | | | | | | | | | | | | | | | | | | | | | | | | | |
| Berne | 46 57N | 07 26E | 1,877 | 30 | 35 | 26 | 56 | 39 | 74 | 56 | 55 | 42 | 96 | -9 | 77 | 1.9 | 1.9 | 2.6 | 3.0 | 3.7 | 4.4 | 4.4 | 4.3 | 3.5 | 3.5 | 2.7 | 2.5 | 38.5 |
| Geneve (Geneva) | 46 12N | 06 09E | 1,329 | 30 | 39 | 29 | 58 | 41 | 77 | 58 | 58 | 44 | 101 | -1 | 125 | 1.9 | 1.8 | 2.2 | 2.5 | 3.0 | 3.1 | 2.9 | 3.6 | 3.6 | 3.8 | 3.1 | 2.4 | 33.9 |
| Zurich | 47 23N | 08 33E | 1,617 | 23 | 38 | 28 | 57 | 39 | 76 | 55 | 57 | 42 | 98 | -12 | 23 | 2.3 | 1.9 | 2.9 | 3.4 | 4.0 | 4.9 | 5.0 | 4.6 | 3.3 | 3.2 | 2.5 | 2.9 | 40.9 |
| **Turkey:** | | | | | | | | | | | | | | | | | | | | | | | | | | | | |
| Edirne (Adrianople) | 41 39N | 26 34E | 154 | 18 | 41 | 28 | 66 | 44 | 88 | 63 | 70 | 49 | 107 | -8 | 18 | 2.2 | 1.9 | 1.7 | 1.9 | 1.7 | 2.1 | 1.5 | 1.1 | 1.1 | 2.1 | 2.9 | 3.0 | 23.2 |
| Istanbul (Constantinople) | 40 58N | 28 50E | 59 | 18 | 45 | 36 | 61 | 45 | 81 | 65 | 67 | 54 | 100 | 17 | 18 | 3.7 | 2.3 | 2.6 | 1.9 | 1.4 | 1.3 | 1.7 | 1.5 | 2.3 | 3.8 | 4.1 | 4.9 | 31.5 |
| **United Kingdom:** | | | | | | | | | | | | | | | | | | | | | | | | | | | | |
| Belfast | 54 35N | 05 56W | 57 | 7 | 42 | 34 | 53 | 38 | 65 | 52 | 55 | 44 | 82 | 14 | 30 | 4.2 | 2.8 | 2.3 | 2.4 | 2.3 | 2.5 | 3.5 | 3.5 | 3.4 | 3.8 | 3.6 | 3.9 | 38.2 |
| Birmingham | 52 29N | 01 56W | 535 | 30 | 42 | 35 | 53 | 40 | 69 | 54 | 55 | 45 | 92 | 11 | 30 | 2.9 | 2.1 | 1.7 | 2.2 | 2.5 | 1.8 | 2.8 | 2.7 | 2.3 | 2.9 | 3.2 | 2.6 | 29.7 |
| Cardiff | 51 28N | 03 10W | 203 | 30 | 45 | 36 | 55 | 41 | 69 | 54 | 57 | 45 | 91 | 2 | 30 | 4.6 | 3.0 | 2.3 | 2.5 | 3.0 | 2.2 | 3.4 | 3.9 | 3.6 | 4.5 | 4.6 | 4.3 | 41.9 |
| Dublin | 53 22N | 06 21W | 155 | 35 | 47 | 35 | 54 | 38 | 67 | 51 | 57 | 43 | 86 | 8 | 35 | 2.7 | 2.2 | 2.6 | 1.9 | 2.3 | 2.0 | 2.8 | 3.0 | 2.8 | 2.7 | 2.7 | 2.6 | 29.7 |
| Edinburgh | 55 55N | 03 11W | 441 | 30 | 43 | 35 | 53 | 39 | 65 | 52 | 53 | 44 | 83 | 15 | 30 | 2.5 | 1.6 | 1.6 | 1.6 | 2.2 | 1.9 | 3.1 | 3.1 | 2.6 | 2.9 | 2.4 | 2.1 | 27.6 |
| London | 51 29N | 00 00 | 149 | 30 | 44 | 35 | 56 | 40 | 73 | 55 | 58 | 44 | 99 | 9 | 30 | 2.0 | 1.5 | 1.4 | 1.8 | 1.8 | 1.6 | 2.0 | 2.2 | 1.8 | 2.3 | 2.5 | 2.0 | 22.9 |

380

(See footnotes at end of tables)

| COUNTRY AND STATION | LATITUDE | LONGITUDE | ELEVATION (FEET) | TEMP. LENGTH OF RECORD (YR) | JAN MAX °F | JAN MIN °F | APR MAX °F | APR MIN °F | JUL MAX °F | JUL MIN °F | OCT MAX °F | OCT MIN °F | EXTREME MAX °F | EXTREME MIN °F | PRECIP. LENGTH OF RECORD (YR) | JAN IN. | FEB IN. | MAR IN. | APR IN. | MAY IN. | JUN IN. | JUL IN. | AUG IN. | SEP IN. | OCT IN. | NOV IN. | DEC IN. | YEAR IN. |
|---|---|---|---|---|---|---|---|---|---|---|---|---|---|---|---|---|---|---|---|---|---|---|---|---|---|---|---|---|
| Liverpool | 53 24N | 03 04W | 198 | 30 | 44 | 36 | 52 | 41 | 66 | 55 | 55 | 46 | 87 | 15 | 30 | 2.7 | 1.9 | 1.5 | 1.6 | 2.2 | 2.0 | 2.8 | 3.1 | 2.6 | 3.0 | 3.0 | 2.5 | 28.9 |
| Perth | 56 24N | 03 27W | 77 | 30 | 43 | 32 | 53 | 38 | 68 | 51 | 55 | 41 | 89 | 0 | 30 | 3.1 | 2.2 | 1.9 | 1.7 | 2.3 | 2.0 | 3.1 | 2.9 | 2.8 | 3.3 | 2.7 | 2.7 | 30.7 |
| Plymouth | 50 21N | 04 07W | 87 | 30 | 47 | 40 | 48 | 43 | 66 | 55 | 58 | 49 | 88 | 16 | 30 | 4.3 | 3.0 | 2.6 | 2.3 | 2.5 | 2.0 | 2.6 | 2.9 | 2.8 | 3.8 | 4.6 | 4.4 | 37.8 |
| Wick | 58 26N | 03 05W | 119 | 30 | 42 | 35 | 48 | 38 | 59 | 50 | 52 | 43 | 80 | 8 | 30 | 2.9 | 2.1 | 1.8 | 2.1 | 1.8 | 2.0 | 2.6 | 2.6 | 2.9 | 3.2 | 3.1 | 2.9 | 30.0 |
| **U.S.S.R.:** | | | | | | | | | | | | | | | | | | | | | | | | | | | | |
| Arkhangelsk | 64 33N | 40 32E | 22 | 23 | 9 | 2 | 36 | 23 | 64 | 51 | 36 | 30 | 91 | -49 | 25 | 1.2 | 1.1 | 1.1 | 0.7 | 1.3 | 1.9 | 2.6 | 2.7 | 2.2 | 1.9 | 1.6 | 1.3 | 19.8 |
| Astrakhan | 46 21N | 48 02E | 45 | 10 | 23 | 14 | 57 | 40 | 85 | 69 | 56 | 40 | 99 | -22 | 25 | 0.5 | 0.5 | 0.4 | 0.6 | 0.6 | 0.7 | 0.5 | 0.4 | 0.6 | 0.4 | 0.6 | 0.6 | 6.4 |
| Dnepropetrovsk | 48 27N | 35 04E | 259 | 18 | 23 | 16 | 53 | 39 | 80 | 62 | 50 | 40 | 101 | -25 | 17 | 1.6 | 1.1 | 1.3 | 1.4 | 1.8 | 3.0 | 1.9 | 1.6 | 1.0 | 1.8 | 1.6 | 1.6 | 19.4 |
| Kaunas | 54 54N | 23 53E | 118 | 19 | 26 | 18 | 49 | 34 | 72 | 55 | 50 | 38 | 96 | -23 | 19 | 1.2 | 1.0 | 0.9 | 1.8 | 2.0 | 2.5 | 3.3 | 3.5 | 1.9 | 2.0 | 1.6 | 1.3 | 25.0 |
| Kirov | 58 36N | 49 41E | 594 | 20 | 6 | -2 | 41 | 27 | 72 | 58 | 37 | 29 | 92 | -43 | 29 | 1.5 | 1.0 | 0.9 | 0.9 | 1.9 | 2.5 | 3.2 | 2.9 | 2.3 | 1.8 | 1.6 | 1.7 | 20.6 |
| Kursk | 51 45N | 36 12E | 773 | 15 | 19 | 11 | 47 | 35 | 74 | 57 | 48 | 36 | 91 | -23 | 20 | 1.3 | 0.9 | 1.2 | 1.5 | 2.2 | 2.5 | 3.2 | 2.3 | 1.6 | 1.8 | 1.5 | 1.3 | 22.3 |
| Leningrad | 59 56N | 30 16E | 16 | 26 | 19 | 12 | 45 | 31 | 71 | 57 | 45 | 37 | 97 | -36 | 95 | 1.0 | 0.9 | 0.9 | 1.0 | 1.6 | 2.0 | 2.5 | 2.8 | 2.1 | 2.0 | 1.4 | 1.7 | 19.2 |
| Lvov | 49 50N | 24 01E | 978 | 12 | 31 | 22 | 47 | 38 | 77 | 54 | 45 | 43 | 92 | -29 | 35 | 1.3 | 1.5 | 1.8 | 2.0 | 2.8 | 3.7 | 4.1 | 3.1 | 2.4 | 1.5 | 0.8 | 1.2 | 28.2 |
| Minsk | 53 54N | 27 33E | 738 | 15 | 22 | 13 | 47 | 33 | 76 | 55 | 47 | 36 | 96 | -27 | 20 | 1.4 | 1.1 | 1.3 | 1.5 | 2.0 | 3.8 | 3.0 | 3.1 | 1.6 | 2.7 | 1.7 | 1.6 | 22.9 |
| Moskva (Moscow) | 55 46N | 37 40E | 505 | 20 | 21 | 9 | 52 | 41 | 79 | 65 | 57 | 47 | 99 | -27 | 11 | 1.0 | 0.7 | 1.1 | 1.5 | 2.0 | 2.9 | 3.0 | 2.9 | 1.9 | 1.4 | 1.7 | 1.6 | 24.8 |
| Odessa | 46 29N | 30 44E | 214 | 14 | 28 | 22 | 48 | 35 | 72 | 56 | 53 | 39 | 102 | -13 | 15 | 1.0 | 0.7 | 0.7 | 1.1 | 1.2 | 1.9 | 1.6 | 1.4 | 1.1 | 2.0 | 1.9 | 1.1 | 14.3 |
| Riga | 56 57N | 24 06E | 67 | 20 | 20 | 20 | 55 | 42 | 82 | 64 | 63 | 50 | 97 | -20 | 57 | 1.3 | 1.0 | 1.1 | 1.2 | 1.7 | 2.4 | 3.0 | 3.0 | 2.1 | 1.4 | 1.4 | 1.5 | 22.2 |
| Saratov | 51 32N | 46 03E | 197 | 14 | 15 | 7 | 52 | 36 | 79 | 65 | 53 | 37 | 106 | -27 | 15 | 1.0 | 1.0 | 0.8 | 0.9 | 1.2 | 1.8 | 1.2 | 1.3 | 1.1 | 1.5 | 1.2 | 1.2 | 14.5 |
| Sevastopol | 44 37N | 33 31E | 75 | 20 | 39 | 30 | 50 | 37 | 84 | 60 | 67 | 48 | 95 | -4 | 30 | 1.1 | 1.0 | 0.6 | 0.6 | 0.6 | 1.1 | 0.8 | 0.6 | 0.7 | 1.0 | 1.5 | 1.1 | 12.2 |
| Stalingrad | 48 42N | 44 31E | 136 | 8 | 15 | 4 | 61 | 44 | 76 | 55 | 47 | 38 | 89 | -30 | 12 | 0.9 | 1.0 | 0.6 | 0.6 | 1.0 | 1.9 | 0.8 | 0.8 | 2.5 | 1.0 | 1.8 | 1.3 | 12.2 |
| Stavropol | 45 02N | 41 58E | 1,886 | 18 | 26 | 17 | 35 | 17 | 65 | 49 | 33 | 23 | 95 | -22 | 41 | 1.4 | 1.1 | 1.5 | 2.4 | 3.0 | 4.1 | 3.0 | 2.0 | 2.3 | 2.1 | 1.9 | 1.8 | 26.9 |
| Tbilisi | 41 43N | 44 48E | 146 | 15 | 27 | 18 | 44 | 30 | 75 | 58 | 41 | 31 | 90 | -19 | 63 | 0.7 | 0.8 | 1.3 | 1.6 | 3.6 | 3.1 | 2.1 | 1.7 | 1.9 | 2.2 | 2.0 | 1.8 | 20.2 |
| Ust'Shchugor | 64 16N | 57 34E | 279 | 10 | 4 | -14 | | | | | | | 99 | -67 | 10 | 1.1 | 0.8 | 0.8 | 0.7 | 1.4 | 3.0 | 3.0 | 3.2 | 2.4 | 1.3 | 2.0 | 1.2 | 21.4 |
| Ufy | 54 43N | 55 56E | 571 | 15 | 6 | -3 | | | | | | | 99 | -42 | 15 | 1.6 | 1.3 | 1.2 | 0.9 | 1.6 | 2.4 | 2.6 | 2.2 | 1.8 | 2.3 | 2.2 | 2.3 | 22.5 |
| **Yugoslavia:** | | | | | | | | | | | | | | | | | | | | | | | | | | | | |
| Beograd (Belgrade) | 44 48N | 20 28E | 453 | 16 | 37 | 27 | 64 | 45 | 84 | 61 | 65 | 47 | 107 | -14 | 16 | 1.6 | 1.3 | 1.6 | 2.2 | 2.6 | 2.8 | 1.9 | 2.5 | 1.7 | 2.7 | 1.8 | 1.9 | 24.6 |
| Skopje | 41 59N | 21 28E | 787 | 10 | 40 | 26 | 67 | 42 | 88 | 60 | 65 | 43 | 105 | -11 | 10 | 1.5 | 1.2 | 1.3 | 1.5 | 1.9 | 1.9 | 1.3 | 1.1 | 1.1 | 2.6 | 2.3 | 1.8 | 19.5 |
| Split | 43 31N | 16 26E | 420 | 14 | 51 | 29 | 65 | 50 | 87 | 68 | 69 | 55 | 100 | 17 | 51 | 3.1 | 2.5 | 3.2 | 3.0 | 2.5 | 2.1 | 1.2 | 1.6 | 2.9 | 4.4 | 4.2 | 4.4 | 35.1 |
| **OCEAN ISLANDS** | | | | | | | | | | | | | | | | | | | | | | | | | | | | |
| Bjornoya, Bear Island | 74 31N | 19 01E | 49 | 10 | 26 | 17 | 27 | 16 | 44 | 36 | 36 | 29 | 71 | -25 | 25 | 1.6 | 1.3 | 1.3 | 0.9 | 0.8 | 0.7 | 0.8 | 1.2 | 1.8 | 1.7 | 1.4 | 1.6 | 15.1 |
| Gronfjorden, Spitzbergen | 78 02N | 14 15E | 23 | 19 | -4 | -4 | 31 | -3 | 46 | 38 | 25 | 17 | 60 | -57 | 15 | 1.4 | 1.3 | 1.1 | 0.9 | 0.5 | 0.4 | 0.6 | 0.9 | 1.0 | 1.2 | 0.9 | 1.5 | 11.7 |
| Horta, Azores | 38 32N | 28 38W | 200 | 30 | 62 | 54 | 64 | 55 | 76 | 65 | 69 | 62 | 88 | 38 | 30 | 4.5 | 4.1 | 4.2 | 3.0 | 2.9 | 2.0 | 1.4 | 1.9 | 3.2 | 4.4 | 4.1 | 4.5 | 40.3 |
| Jan Mayen | 71 01N | 08 28W | 131 | 5 | 31 | 21 | 31 | 22 | 46 | 38 | 39 | 29 | 71 | -18 | 29 | 2.1 | 3.4 | 1.6 | 0.9 | 0.9 | 0.9 | 1.4 | 1.8 | 3.2 | 4.3 | 4.2 | 4.5 | 21.2 |
| Lerwick, Shetland Island | 60 08N | 01 11W | 269 | 30 | 42 | 35 | 46 | 37 | 58 | 49 | 50 | 42 | 68 | 17 | 30 | 4.5 | 3.4 | 2.9 | 2.7 | 2.2 | 2.2 | 2.7 | 2.9 | 3.7 | 4.3 | 4.5 | 4.5 | 40.5 |
| Matochkin Shar, Novaya Zemlya | 73 16N | 56 24E | 61 | 9 | 8 | -6 | 13 | -1 | 47 | 36 | 30 | 21 | 85 | -41 | 9 | 0.6 | 0.6 | 0.6 | 0.4 | 0.3 | 0.4 | 1.4 | 1.5 | 1.5 | 0.6 | 0.6 | 0.4 | 8.9 |
| Ponta Delgada, Azores | 37 45N | 25 40W | 118 | 30 | 62 | 54 | 64 | 55 | 76 | 64 | 71 | 61 | 78 | 37 | 30 | 4.0 | 3.5 | 3.5 | 2.5 | 2.3 | 1.4 | 1.0 | 1.2 | 2.9 | 3.6 | 3.7 | 3.0 | 32.6 |
| Stornoway, Hebrides | 58 11N | 06 21W | 34 | 30 | 42 | 37 | 45 | 39 | 57 | 51 | 53 | 44 | 78 | 11 | 15 | 6.4 | 3.2 | 3.2 | 3.1 | 2.5 | 2.4 | 3.0 | 4.3 | 4.7 | 6.2 | 4.6 | 5.5 | 49.1 |
| Thorshavn, Faeroes | 62 02N | 06 45W | 82 | 50 | 42 | 33 | 45 | 36 | 56 | 47 | 58 | 40 | 70 | 8 | 50 | 6.6 | 5.2 | 4.8 | 3.6 | 3.4 | 2.5 | 3.1 | 3.5 | 4.7 | 5.9 | 6.3 | 6.6 | 56.2 |

## AFRICA

| Country and Station | Latitude | Longitude | Elevation (feet) | Temp Length of Record (yr) | Jan Max (°F) | Jan Min (°F) | Apr Max (°F) | Apr Min (°F) | Jul Max (°F) | Jul Min (°F) | Oct Max (°F) | Oct Min (°F) | Extreme Max (°F) | Extreme Min (°F) | Precip Length of Record (yr) | Jan (in.) | Feb (in.) | Mar (in.) | Apr (in.) | May (in.) | Jun (in.) | Jul (in.) | Aug (in.) | Sep (in.) | Oct (in.) | Nov (in.) | Dec (in.) | Year (in.) |
|---|---|---|---|---|---|---|---|---|---|---|---|---|---|---|---|---|---|---|---|---|---|---|---|---|---|---|---|---|
| **Algeria:** | | | | | | | | | | | | | | | | | | | | | | | | | | | | |
| Adrar | 27 52N | 00 17W | 938 | 15 | 69 | 39 | 92 | 60 | 115 | 82 | 92 | 63 | 124 | 25 | 15 | * | * | 0.1 | * | * | * | * | * | * | 0.2 | 0.2 | * | 0.6 |
| Alger (Algiers) | 36 46N | 03 03E | 194 | 25 | 59 | 49 | 68 | 55 | 83 | 70 | 74 | 63 | 107 | 32 | 25 | 4.4 | 3.3 | 2.9 | 1.6 | 1.8 | 0.6 | * | 0.2 | 1.6 | 3.1 | 5.1 | 5.4 | 30.0 |
| Bone | 36 54N | 07 46E | 66 | 25 | 59 | 46 | 67 | 49 | 85 | 69 | 75 | 61 | 115 | 32 | 26 | 5.6 | 4.1 | 2.9 | 2.2 | 1.5 | 0.6 | 0.1 | 0.3 | 1.2 | 3.0 | 4.3 | 5.2 | 31.0 |
| El Golea | 30 35N | 02 53E | 1,247 | 15 | 63 | 37 | 84 | 56 | 107 | 79 | 87 | 60 | 120 | 23 | 15 | 0.1 | 0.3 | 0.5 | * | * | * | * | * | * | 0.3 | 0.4 | 0.3 | 1.9 |
| Fort Flatters | 28 06N | 06 42E | 1,224 | 15 | 67 | 38 | 90 | 59 | 110 | 78 | 92 | 63 | 124 | 19 | 15 | 0.3 | 0.1 | 0.1 | 0.2 | 0.4 | 0.1 | 0.0 | * | 0.1 | * | * | 0.2 | 1.1 |
| Tamanrasset | 22 42N | 05 31E | 4,593 | 15 | 67 | 39 | 86 | 56 | 95 | 71 | 85 | 59 | 102 | 20 | 15 | 0.2 | * | * | 0.2 | 0.2 | 0.2 | 0.1 | 0.4 | 0.1 | 0.3 | * | * | 1.5 |
| Touggourt | 33 07N | 06 04E | 226 | 26. | 62 | 38 | 83 | 55 | 107 | 77 | 84 | 59 | 122 | 26 | 26 | 0.2 | 0.4 | 0.5 | 0.2 | 0.2 | * | * | * | 0.1 | 0.3 | 0.5 | 0.3 | 2.9 |
| **Angola:** | | | | | | | | | | | | | | | | | | | | | | | | | | | | |
| Cangamba | 13 41S | 19 52E | 4,331 | 6 | 84 | 62 | 89 | 58 | 82 | 46 | 87 | 59 | 109 | 20 | 7 | 8.9 | 7.4 | 6.8 | 1.8 | 0.1 | 0.0 | 0.0 | 0.2 | 0.2 | 1.6 | 5.1 | 8.5 | 40.6 |
| Luanda | 08 49S | 13 13E | 194 | 27 | 83 | 74 | 85 | 75 | 74 | 65 | 79 | 71 | 98 | 58 | 59 | 1.0 | 1.4 | 3.0 | 4.6 | 0.5 | * | * | * | 0.1 | 0.2 | 1.1 | 0.8 | 12.7 |
| Mocamedes | 15 12S | 12 09E | 10 | 15 | 79 | 65 | 82 | 66 | 68 | 56 | 74 | 61 | 102 | 44 | 21 | 0.3 | 0.4 | 0.7 | 0.5 | * | * | * | * | 0.6 | * | 0.1 | * | 2.1 |
| Nova Lisboa | 12 48S | 15 45E | 5,577 | 14 | 78 | 58 | 78 | 57 | 77 | 47 | 81 | 58 | 90 | 36 | 14 | 8.7 | 7.8 | 9.8 | 5.7 | 0.4 | 0.0 | * | * | 0.6 | 5.5 | 9.6 | 8.9 | 57.0 |
| **Botswana:** | | | | | | | | | | | | | | | | | | | | | | | | | | | | |
| Francistown | 21 13S | 27 30E | 3,294 | 20 | 88 | 65 | 83 | 56 | 75 | 41 | 90 | 61 | 107 | 24 | 28 | 4.2 | 3.1 | 2.8 | 0.7 | 0.2 | 0.1 | * | * | * | 0.9 | 2.3 | 3.4 | 17.7 |
| Maun | 19 59S | 23 25E | 3,091 | 20 | 90 | 66 | 87 | 58 | 77 | 42 | 95 | 64 | 110 | 24 | 20 | 4.3 | 3.8 | 3.5 | 1.1 | 0.2 | * | 0.0 | 0.0 | * | 0.5 | 1.9 | 2.8 | 18.2 |
| Tsabong | 26 03S | 22 27E | 3,156 | 10 | 94 | 65 | 83 | 51 | 71 | 34 | 88 | 54 | 107 | 15 | 14 | 2.0 | 1.9 | 1.9 | 1.3 | 0.4 | 0.4 | 0.1 | * | 0.2 | 0.7 | 1.1 | 1.5 | 11.5 |
| **Cameroon:** | | | | | | | | | | | | | | | | | | | | | | | | | | | | |
| Ngaoundere | 07 17N | 13 19E | 3,601 | 9 | 87 | 55 | 87 | 64 | 82 | 63 | 82 | 59 | 102 | 46 | 10 | * | * | 1.1 | 5.5 | 7.0 | 8.4 | 10.6 | 9.6 | 9.2 | 5.3 | 0.5 | * | 57.2 |
| Yaounde | 03 53N | 11 32E | 2,526 | 11 | 85 | 67 | 85 | 66 | 80 | 66 | 81 | 65 | 96 | 57 | 11 | 0.9 | 2.6 | 5.8 | 6.7 | 7.7 | 6.0 | 2.9 | 3.1 | 8.4 | 11.6 | 4.6 | 0.9 | 61.2 |
| **Central African Republic:** | | | | | | | | | | | | | | | | | | | | | | | | | | | | |
| Bangui | 04 22N | 18 34E | 1,270 | 5 | 90 | 68 | 91 | 71 | 85 | 69 | 87 | 69 | 101 | 57 | 5 | 1.0 | 1.7 | 5.0 | 5.3 | 7.4 | 4.5 | 8.9 | 8.1 | 5.9 | 7.9 | 4.9 | 0.2 | 60.8 |
| Ndele | 08 24N | 20 39E | 1,939 | 3 | 99 | 67 | 98 | 73 | 86 | 73 | 90 | 68 | 109 | 58 | 3 | 0.2 | 1.3 | 0.6 | 1.7 | 8.4 | 6.1 | 8.3 | 10.1 | 10.7 | 7.8 | 0.6 | 0.0 | 55.8 |
| **Chad:** | | | | | | | | | | | | | | | | | | | | | | | | | | | | |
| Am Timan | 11 02N | 20 17E | 1,430 | 3 | 98 | 56 | 105 | 68 | 89 | 70 | 96 | 67 | 113 | 43 | 3 | 0.0 | 0.0 | 0.1 | 1.2 | 4.3 | 5.0 | 7.3 | 12.3 | 5.8 | 1.2 | 0.0 | 0.0 | 37.2 |
| Fort Lamy | 12 07N | 15 02E | 968 | 5 | 93 | 57 | 107 | 74 | 92 | 72 | 97 | 70 | 114 | 47 | 5 | 0.0 | 0.0 | 0.0 | 0.1 | 1.2 | 2.6 | 6.7 | 12.6 | 4.7 | 1.4 | 0.0 | 0.0 | 29.3 |
| Largeau (Faya) | 18 00N | 19 10E | 837 | 5 | 84 | 54 | 104 | 69 | 109 | 76 | 103 | 72 | 121 | 37 | 5 | 0.0 | 0.0 | 0.0 | 0.0 | * | 0.0 | * | 0.7 | * | 0.0 | 0.0 | 0.0 | 0.7 |
| **Congo, Democratic Republic of the:** | | | | | | | | | | | | | | | | | | | | | | | | | | | | |
| Albertville | 05 54S | 29 12E | 2,493 | 5 | 85 | 66 | 83 | 67 | 82 | 58 | 87 | 67 | 92 | 50 | 20 | 4.2 | 4.7 | 6.3 | 8.4 | 3.3 | 0.3 | 0.1 | 0.3 | 0.8 | 2.8 | 7.9 | 6.3 | 45.4 |
| Kinspasa (Leopoldville) | 04 20S | 15 18E | 1,066 | 8 | 87 | 70 | 89 | 71 | 81 | 64 | 88 | 70 | 97 | 58 | 12 | 5.3 | 5.7 | 7.7 | 7.7 | 6.2 | 0.3 | 0.1 | 0.1 | 1.2 | 4.7 | 8.7 | 5.6 | 53.3 |
| Luluabourg | 05 54S | 22 25E | 2,198 | 3 | 85 | 68 | 86 | 68 | 85 | 63 | 85 | 68 | 94 | 57 | 14 | 5.4 | 5.6 | 7.7 | 7.6 | 3.3 | 0.8 | 0.5 | 2.3 | 4.6 | 6.5 | 9.1 | 8.9 | 62.3 |
| Stanleyville | 00 26N | 25 14E | 1,370 | 8 | 88 | 69 | 88 | 70 | 84 | 67 | 86 | 68 | 97 | 61 | 14 | 2.1 | 3.3 | 7.0 | 6.2 | 5.4 | 4.5 | 5.2 | 6.5 | 7.2 | 8.6 | 7.8 | 3.3 | 67.1 |
| **Congo, Republic of:** | | | | | | | | | | | | | | | | | | | | | | | | | | | | |
| Brazzaville | 04 15S | 15 15E | 1,043 | 15 | 88 | 69 | 91 | 71 | 82 | 63 | 89 | 63 | 98 | 54 | 18 | 6.3 | 4.9 | 7.4 | 7.0 | 4.3 | 0.6 | * | * | 2.2 | 5.4 | 11.5 | 8.4 | 58.0 |
| Ouesso | 01 37N | 16 04E | 1,132 | 4 | 88 | 69 | 91 | 71 | 85 | 69 | 87 | 69 | 106 | 60 | 4 | 2.4 | 3.6 | 6.4 | 3.2 | 5.8 | 4.6 | 2.9 | 3.7 | 7.9 | 10.0 | 5.7 | 2.4 | 58.6 |
| Pointe Noire (Loango) | 04 39S | 11 48E | 164 | 7 | 85 | 73 | 87 | 74 | 78 | 66 | 83 | 72 | 93 | 59 | 7 | 5.4 | 6.7 | 6.4 | 8.0 | 3.9 | 0.0 | 0.0 | 0.0 | 0.4 | 4.1 | 6.6 | 6.6 | 48.1 |
| **Dahomey:** | | | | | | | | | | | | | | | | | | | | | | | | | | | | |
| Cotonou | 06 21N | 02 26E | 23 | 5 | 80 | 74 | 83 | 78 | 78 | 74 | 80 | 74 | 95 | 65 | 10 | 1.3 | 1.3 | 4.6 | 4.9 | 10.0 | 14.4 | 3.5 | 1.5 | 2.6 | 5.3 | 2.3 | 0.5 | 52.4 |

(See footnotes at end of tables)

382

| COUNTRY AND STATION | LATITUDE | LONGITUDE | ELEVATION (FEET) | TEMP. LENGTH OF RECORD (YEAR) | JAN MAX °F | JAN MIN °F | APR MAX °F | APR MIN °F | JUL MAX °F | JUL MIN °F | OCT MAX °F | OCT MIN °F | EXTREME MAX °F | EXTREME MIN °F | PRECIP. LENGTH OF RECORD (YEAR) | JAN IN. | FEB IN. | MAR IN. | APR IN. | MAY IN. | JUN IN. | JUL IN. | AUG IN. | SEP IN. | OCT IN. | NOV IN. | DEC IN. | YEAR IN. |
|---|---|---|---|---|---|---|---|---|---|---|---|---|---|---|---|---|---|---|---|---|---|---|---|---|---|---|---|---|
| **Ethiopia:** | | | | | | | | | | | | | | | | | | | | | | | | | | | | |
| Addis Ababa | 09 20N | 38 45E | 8,038 | 15 | 75 | 43 | 77 | 50 | 69 | 50 | 75 | 45 | 94 | 32 | 37 | 0.5 | 1.5 | 2.6 | 3.4 | 3.4 | 5.4 | 11.0 | 11.8 | 7.5 | 0.8 | 0.6 | 0.2 | 48.7 |
| Asmara | 15 17N | 38 55E | 7,628 | 9 | 74 | 44 | 78 | 51 | 71 | 51 | 72 | 53 | 88 | 31 | 17 | * | * | 0.4 | 1.5 | 1.5 | 1.3 | 6.7 | 5.0 | 1.3 | 0.3 | 0.4 | * | 18.4 |
| Diredawa | 09 02N | 41 45E | 3,937 | 8 | 81 | 58 | 91 | 69 | 90 | 68 | 89 | 67 | 100 | 49 | 8 | 0.8 | 0.8 | 3.3 | 3.0 | 2.8 | 1.5 | 4.3 | 3.8 | 2.2 | 0.5 | 0.3 | 0.8 | 24.1 |
| Gambela | 08 15N | 34 35E | 1,345 | 26 | 98 | 64 | 98 | 71 | 87 | 69 | 92 | 67 | 111 | 48 | 30 | 0.2 | 0.4 | 1.4 | 3.2 | 5.9 | 6.7 | 8.5 | 9.5 | 7.3 | 3.5 | 1.8 | 0.4 | 48.8 |
| **French Territory of Afars and Issas (F.T.A.I.):** | | | | | | | | | | | | | | | | | | | | | | | | | | | | |
| Djibouti | 11 36N | 43 09E | 23 | 16 | 84 | 73 | 90 | 79 | 106 | 87 | 92 | 80 | 117 | 63 | 46 | 0.4 | 0.5 | 1.0 | 0.5 | 0.2 | * | 0.1 | 0.3 | 0.3 | 0.4 | 0.9 | 0.5 | 46.0 |
| **Gabon:** | | | | | | | | | | | | | | | | | | | | | | | | | | | | |
| Libreville | 00 23N | 09 26E | 115 | 11 | 87 | 73 | 89 | 73 | 83 | 68 | 86 | 71 | 99 | 62 | 21 | 9.8 | 9.3 | 13.2 | 13.4 | 9.6 | 0.5 | 0.1 | 0.7 | 4.1 | 13.6 | 14.7 | 9.8 | 98.8 |
| Mayoumba | 03 25S | 10 38E | 200 | 8 | 84 | 73 | 86 | 73 | 78 | 68 | 82 | 72 | 91 | 60 | 8 | 6.5 | 9.3 | 6.2 | 10.2 | 2.3 | 0.1 | 0.1 | 0.2 | 2.6 | 9.3 | 10.7 | 4.6 | 62.0 |
| **Gambia:** | | | | | | | | | | | | | | | | | | | | | | | | | | | | |
| Bathurst | 13 21N | 16 40W | 90 | 9 | 88 | 59 | 91 | 65 | 86 | 74 | 89 | 72 | 106 | 45 | 9 | 0.1 | 0.1 | * | * | 0.4 | 2.3 | 11.1 | 19.7 | 12.2 | 4.3 | 0.7 | 0.1 | 51.0 |
| **Ghana:** | | | | | | | | | | | | | | | | | | | | | | | | | | | | |
| Accra | 05 33N | 00 12W | 88 | 17 | 87 | 73 | 88 | 76 | 81 | 73 | 85 | 74 | 100 | 59 | 65 | 0.6 | 1.3 | 2.2 | 3.2 | 5.6 | 7.0 | 1.8 | 0.6 | 1.4 | 2.5 | 1.4 | 0.9 | 28.5 |
| Kumasi | 06 40N | 01 37W | 942 | 10 | 88 | 66 | 89 | 71 | 82 | 70 | 86 | 70 | 100 | 51 | 10 | 0.8 | 2.3 | 5.7 | 5.1 | 7.5 | 7.9 | 4.3 | 3.1 | 6.8 | 7.1 | 3.7 | 0.8 | 55.2 |
| **Guinea:** | | | | | | | | | | | | | | | | | | | | | | | | | | | | |
| Conakry | 09 31N | 13 43W | 23 | 7 | 88 | 72 | 90 | 73 | 83 | 72 | 87 | 73 | 96 | 63 | 10 | 0.1 | 0.1 | 0.4 | 0.9 | 6.2 | 22.0 | 51.1 | 41.5 | 26.9 | 14.6 | 4.8 | 0.4 | 169.0 |
| Kouroussa | 10 39N | 09 53W | 1,217 | 9 | 93 | 60 | 99 | 73 | 87 | 69 | 90 | 69 | 109 | 39 | 10 | 0.4 | 0.3 | 0.9 | 2.8 | 5.3 | 9.7 | 11.7 | 13.6 | 13.4 | 6.6 | 1.3 | 0.4 | 66.4 |
| **Ifni (now in Morocco):** | | | | | | | | | | | | | | | | | | | | | | | | | | | | |
| Sidi Ifni | 29 27N | 10 11W | 148 | 14 | 66 | 52 | 71 | 59 | 75 | 64 | 75 | 62 | 124 | 40 | 14 | 1.0 | 0.6 | 0.5 | 0.6 | 0.1 | 0.1 | * | * | 0.4 | * | 0.9 | 1.8 | 6.1 |
| **Ivory Coast:** | | | | | | | | | | | | | | | | | | | | | | | | | | | | |
| Abidjan | 05 19N | 04 01W | 65 | 13 | 88 | 73 | 90 | 75 | 83 | 73 | 85 | 74 | 96 | 59 | 10 | 1.6 | 2.1 | 3.9 | 4.9 | 14.2 | 19.5 | 8.4 | 2.1 | 2.8 | 6.6 | 7.9 | 3.1 | 77.1 |
| Bouake | 07 42N | 05 00W | 1,194 | 12 | 91 | 68 | 92 | 70 | 85 | 68 | 89 | 68 | 104 | 57 | 10 | 0.4 | 1.5 | 4.1 | 5.8 | 5.3 | 6.0 | 3.1 | 4.6 | 8.2 | 5.2 | 1.5 | 1.0 | 46.7 |
| **Kenya:** | | | | | | | | | | | | | | | | | | | | | | | | | | | | |
| Mombasa | 04 03S | 39 39E | 52 | 45 | 87 | 75 | 86 | 76 | 81 | 71 | 84 | 74 | 96 | 61 | 54 | 1.0 | 0.7 | 2.5 | 7.7 | 12.6 | 4.7 | 3.5 | 2.5 | 2.5 | 3.4 | 3.8 | 2.4 | 47.3 |
| Nairobi | 01 16S | 36 48E | 5,971 | 15 | 77 | 54 | 75 | 58 | 69 | 51 | 76 | 55 | 87 | 41 | 17 | 1.5 | 2.5 | 4.9 | 8.3 | 6.2 | 1.8 | 0.6 | 0.9 | 1.2 | 2.1 | 4.3 | 3.4 | 37.7 |
| **Liberia:** | | | | | | | | | | | | | | | | | | | | | | | | | | | | |
| Monrovia | 06 18N | 10 48W | 75 | 6 | 89 | 71 | 90 | 72 | 80 | 72 | 86 | 72 | 97 | 62 | 4 | 0.2 | 0.1 | 4.4 | 11.7 | 13.4 | 36.1 | 24.2 | 18.6 | 29.9 | 25.2 | 8.2 | 2.9 | 174.9 |
| **Libya:** | | | | | | | | | | | | | | | | | | | | | | | | | | | | |
| Banghazi (Benghazi) | 32 06N | 20 04E | 82 | 46 | 63 | 50 | 74 | 58 | 84 | 71 | 80 | 66 | 109 | 37 | 46 | 2.6 | 1.6 | 0.8 | 0.2 | 0.1 | * | * | * | 0.1 | 0.7 | 1.8 | 2.6 | 10.5 |
| Cufra | 24 12N | 23 21E | 1,276 | 7 | 69 | 43 | 90 | 62 | 101 | 75 | 90 | 64 | 122 | 26 | 7 | * | 0.0 | 0.0 | 0.0 | * | 0.0 | 0.0 | 0.0 | 0.0 | 0.0 | 0.0 | * | * |
| Sabhah | 27 01N | 14 26E | 1,457 | 3 | 64 | 41 | 89 | 60 | 102 | 74 | 91 | 64 | 120 | 24 | 10 | * | * | * | * | 0.1 | 0.1 | 0.0 | 0.0 | 0.0 | * | * | * | 0.3 |
| Tarabulus (Triopoli) | 32 54N | 13 11E | 72 | 47 | 61 | 47 | 72 | 57 | 85 | 71 | 80 | 65 | 114 | 33 | 56 | 3.2 | 1.8 | 1.1 | 0.4 | 0.2 | 0.1 | * | * | 0.4 | 1.6 | 2.6 | 3.7 | 15.1 |
| **Malagasy Republic:** | | | | | | | | | | | | | | | | | | | | | | | | | | | | |
| Diego Suarez | 12 17S | 49 17E | 100 | 11 | 88 | 75 | 88 | 75 | 84 | 69 | 86 | 72 | 98 | 63 | 31 | 10.6 | 9.5 | 7.6 | 2.2 | 0.3 | 0.2 | 0.3 | 0.3 | 0.3 | 0.7 | 1.1 | 5.8 | 38.7 |
| Tananarive | 18 55S | 47 33E | 4,500 | 44 | 79 | 61 | 76 | 58 | 68 | 48 | 80 | 54 | 95 | 34 | 62 | 11.8 | 11.0 | 7.0 | 2.1 | 0.7 | 0.3 | 0.3 | 0.4 | 0.7 | 2.4 | 5.3 | 11.3 | 53.4 |
| Tulear | 23 20S | 43 41E | 20 | 27 | 92 | 72 | 89 | 64 | 81 | 58 | 86 | 65 | 108 | 43 | 15 | 3.1 | 3.2 | 1.4 | 0.3 | 0.7 | 0.4 | 0.1 | 0.2 | 0.3 | 0.7 | 1.4 | 1.7 | 13.5 |
| **Malawi:** | | | | | | | | | | | | | | | | | | | | | | | | | | | | |
| Karonga | 09 57S | 33 56E | 1,596 | 8 | 86 | 71 | 85 | 70 | 81 | 59 | 91 | 66 | 99 | 51 | 8 | 7.1 | 7.0 | 10.8 | 6.2 | 1.7 | 0.1 | * | * | 0.0 | 0.3 | 0.3 | 4.7 | 38.3 |
| Zomba | 15 23S | 35 19E | 3,141 | 27 | 80 | 65 | 78 | 62 | 72 | 53 | 85 | 64 | 95 | 41 | 29 | 12.1 | 9.9 | 10.1 | 2.7 | 0.7 | 0.4 | 0.3 | 0.3 | 0.2 | 1.0 | 4.3 | 10.9 | 52.9 |

383

| COUNTRY AND STATION | LATITUDE | LONGITUDE | ELEVATION (feet) | TEMPERATURE Length of Record (yr) | JANUARY Max °F | JANUARY Min °F | APRIL Max °F | APRIL Min °F | JULY Max °F | JULY Min °F | OCTOBER Max °F | OCTOBER Min °F | EXTREME Max °F | EXTREME Min °F | PRECIP Length of Record (yr) | JAN (in.) | FEB (in.) | MAR (in.) | APR (in.) | MAY (in.) | JUN (in.) | JUL (in.) | AUG (in.) | SEP (in.) | OCT (in.) | NOV (in.) | DEC (in.) | YEAR (in.) |
|---|---|---|---|---|---|---|---|---|---|---|---|---|---|---|---|---|---|---|---|---|---|---|---|---|---|---|---|---|
| **Mali:** | | | | | | | | | | | | | | | | | | | | | | | | | | | | |
| Araouane | 18 54N | 03 33W | 935 | 8 | 81 | 48 | 110 | 67 | 111 | 79 | 103 | 70 | 130 | 37 | 10 | * | * | 0.0 | 0.0 | 0.0 | 0.2 | 0.2 | 0.5 | 0.6 | 0.1 | 0.1 | * | 1.7 |
| Bamako | 12 39N | 07 58W | 1,116 | 11 | 91 | 61 | 103 | 76 | 89 | 71 | 93 | 71 | 117 | 47 | 10 | * | * | 0.1 | 0.6 | 2.9 | 5.4 | 11.0 | 13.7 | 8.1 | 1.7 | 0.6 | * | 44.1 |
| Gao | 16 16N | 00 03W | 902 | 15 | 83 | 58 | 105 | 77 | 97 | 80 | 100 | 78 | 116 | 44 | 19 | * | 0.0 | * | 0.1 | 0.4 | 1.0 | 2.9 | 5.4 | 1.5 | 0.2 | * | 0.0 | 11.5 |
| **Mauritania:** | | | | | | | | | | | | | | | | | | | | | | | | | | | | |
| Atar | 20 31N | 13 04W | 761 | 7 | 84 | 54 | 97 | 67 | 106 | 81 | 98 | 72 | 117 | 39 | 10 | * | 0.0 | * | * | * | 0.1 | 0.3 | 1.2 | 1.1 | 0.1 | * | * | 2.8 |
| Nema | 16 36N | 07 16W | 883 | 9 | 86 | 62 | 105 | 79 | 99 | 78 | 101 | 79 | 120 | 47 | 10 | 0.1 | * | * | * | 0.7 | 1.1 | 2.3 | 4.7 | 2.1 | 0.7 | * | 0.1 | 11.6 |
| Nouakchott | 18 07N | 15 36W | 69 | 5 | 85 | 57 | 90 | 64 | 89 | 74 | 91 | 71 | 115 | 44 | 10 | * | 0.1 | * | * | * | 0.1 | 0.5 | 4.1 | 0.9 | 0.4 | 0.1 | * | 6.2 |
| **Morocco:** | | | | | | | | | | | | | | | | | | | | | | | | | | | | |
| Casablanca | 33 35N | 07 39W | 164 | 48 | 63 | 45 | 69 | 52 | 79 | 65 | 76 | 58 | 110 | 31 | 40 | 2.1 | 1.9 | 2.2 | 1.4 | 0.9 | 0.2 | 0.0 | * | 0.3 | 1.5 | 2.6 | 2.8 | 15.9 |
| Marrakech | 31 36N | 08 01W | 1,509 | 35 | 65 | 40 | 79 | 52 | 101 | 67 | 83 | 57 | 120 | 27 | 31 | 1.0 | 1.1 | 1.3 | 1.2 | 0.6 | 0.3 | 0.1 | 0.1 | 0.4 | 0.9 | 1.2 | 1.2 | 9.4 |
| Rabat | 34 00N | 06 50W | 213 | 35 | 63 | 46 | 71 | 52 | 82 | 63 | 77 | 58 | 118 | 32 | 29 | 2.6 | 2.5 | 2.6 | 1.7 | 1.1 | 0.3 | * | * | 0.4 | 1.9 | 3.3 | 3.4 | 19.8 |
| Tangier | 35 48N | 05 49W | 239 | 35 | 60 | 47 | 65 | 51 | 80 | 64 | 72 | 59 | 106 | 28 | 35 | 4.5 | 4.2 | 4.8 | 3.5 | 1.7 | 0.6 | * | * | 0.9 | 3.9 | 5.8 | 5.4 | 35.3 |
| **Mozambique:** | | | | | | | | | | | | | | | | | | | | | | | | | | | | |
| Beira | 19 50S | 34 51E | 28 | 37 | 89 | 75 | 86 | 71 | 77 | 61 | 87 | 71 | 109 | 48 | 39 | 10.9 | 8.4 | 10.1 | 4.2 | 2.2 | 1.3 | 1.2 | 1.1 | 0.8 | 5.2 | 5.3 | 9.2 | 59.9 |
| Chicoa | 15 36S | 32 21E | 899 | 8 | 96 | 65 | 93 | 63 | 86 | 55 | 101 | 68 | 117 | 32 | 8 | 7.8 | 5.7 | 4.4 | 0.6 | * | * | * | * | * | 1.1 | 2.6 | 5.2 | 27.4 |
| Lourenco Marques | 25 58S | 32 36E | 194 | 42 | 86 | 71 | 83 | 66 | 76 | 55 | 82 | 64 | 114 | 45 | 42 | 5.1 | 4.9 | 4.9 | 2.1 | 1.1 | 0.8 | 0.5 | 0.5 | 1.1 | 1.9 | 3.2 | 3.8 | 29.9 |
| **Niger:** | | | | | | | | | | | | | | | | | | | | | | | | | | | | |
| Agades | 16 59N | 07 59E | 1,706 | 8 | 86 | 50 | 105 | 70 | 104 | 75 | 101 | 68 | 115 | 40 | 10 | 0.0 | 0.0 | * | * | 0.2 | 0.3 | 1.9 | 3.7 | 0.7 | 0.0 | 0.0 | 0.0 | 6.8 |
| Bilma | 18 41N | 12 55E | 1,171 | 9 | 81 | 45 | 101 | 63 | 108 | 75 | 101 | 62 | 116 | 29 | 10 | 0.0 | * | 0.0 | * | * | 0.0 | 0.1 | 0.5 | 0.3 | 0.0 | * | 0.0 | 0.9 |
| Niamey | 13 31N | 02 06E | 709 | 10 | 93 | 58 | 108 | 77 | 94 | 74 | 101 | 74 | 114 | 47 | 10 | * | * | 0.2 | 0.3 | 1.3 | 3.2 | 5.2 | 7.4 | 3.7 | 0.5 | * | 0.0 | 21.6 |
| **Nigeria:** | | | | | | | | | | | | | | | | | | | | | | | | | | | | |
| Enugu | 06 27N | 07 29E | 763 | 11 | 90 | 72 | 91 | 74 | 83 | 71 | 87 | 71 | 99 | 55 | 33 | 0.7 | 1.1 | 2.6 | 5.9 | 10.4 | 11.4 | 7.6 | 6.7 | 12.8 | 9.8 | 2.1 | 0.5 | 71.5 |
| Kaduna | 10 35N | 06 26E | 2,113 | 18 | 89 | 59 | 95 | 72 | 83 | 68 | 89 | 66 | 105 | 46 | 34 | * | 0.1 | 0.5 | 2.5 | 5.9 | 7.1 | 8.5 | 11.9 | 10.6 | 2.9 | 0.1 | * | 50.1 |
| Lagos | 06 27N | 03 24E | 10 | 32 | 88 | 74 | 89 | 77 | 83 | 74 | 85 | 74 | 104 | 60 | 47 | 1.1 | 1.8 | 4.0 | 5.9 | 10.6 | 18.1 | 11.0 | 2.5 | 5.5 | 8.1 | 2.7 | 1.0 | 72.3 |
| Maiduguri | 11 51N | 13 05E | 1,162 | 15 | 90 | 54 | 104 | 72 | 90 | 73 | 96 | 68 | 112 | 43 | 40 | * | * | * | 0.3 | 1.6 | 2.7 | 7.1 | 8.7 | 4.2 | 0.7 | * | 0.0 | 25.3 |
| **Portuguese Guinea:** | | | | | | | | | | | | | | | | | | | | | | | | | | | | |
| Bolama | 11 34N | 15 26W | 62 | 31 | 88 | 67 | 91 | 73 | 84 | 74 | 87 | 74 | 106 | 59 | 37 | * | * | * | * | 0.8 | 7.8 | 23.1 | 27.6 | 16.9 | 8.0 | 1.6 | 0.1 | 85.9 |
| **Rhodesia:** | | | | | | | | | | | | | | | | | | | | | | | | | | | | |
| Bulawayo | 20 09S | 28 37E | 4,405 | 15 | 81 | 61 | 79 | 56 | 70 | 45 | 85 | 59 | 99 | 28 | 50 | 5.6 | 4.3 | 3.3 | 0.7 | 0.4 | 0.1 | * | * | 0.2 | 0.8 | 3.2 | 4.8 | 23.4 |
| Salisbury | 17 50S | 31 08E | 4,831 | 15 | 78 | 60 | 78 | 55 | 70 | 44 | 83 | 58 | 95 | 32 | 50 | 7.7 | 7.0 | 4.6 | 1.1 | 0.5 | 0.1 | * | 0.1 | 0.2 | 1.1 | 3.8 | 6.4 | 32.6 |
| **Senegal:** | | | | | | | | | | | | | | | | | | | | | | | | | | | | |
| Dakar | 14 42N | 17 29W | 131 | 25 | 79 | 64 | 81 | 65 | 88 | 76 | 89 | 76 | 109 | 53 | 26 | * | * | * | * | * | 0.7 | 3.5 | 10.0 | 5.2 | 1.5 | 0.1 | 0.3 | 21.3 |
| Kaolack | 14 08N | 16 04W | 20 | 9 | 93 | 60 | 103 | 68 | 91 | 75 | 93 | 74 | 114 | 48 | 10 | * | 0.0 | * | * | 0.3 | 2.6 | 6.9 | 10.7 | 7.0 | 2.7 | 0.1 | * | 30.3 |
| **Sierra Leone:** | | | | | | | | | | | | | | | | | | | | | | | | | | | | |
| Freetown/Lungi | 08 37N | 13 12W | 92 | 8 | 87 | 73 | 88 | 76 | 82 | 73 | 85 | 72 | 98 | 62 | 8 | 0.4 | 0.2 | 1.2 | 3.1 | 9.5 | 14.3 | 29.2 | 36.5 | 22.3 | 14.2 | 5.5 | 1.2 | 137.6 |
| **Somalia:** | | | | | | | | | | | | | | | | | | | | | | | | | | | | |
| Berbera | 10 26N | 45 02E | 45 | 30 | 84 | 68 | 89 | 77 | 107 | 88 | 92 | 76 | 117 | 58 | 30 | 0.3 | 0.1 | 0.2 | 0.5 | 0.3 | * | * | 0.1 | * | 0.1 | 0.2 | 0.2 | 2.0 |
| Mogadishu (Mogadiscio) | 02 02N | 45 21E | 39 | 13 | 86 | 73 | 90 | 78 | 83 | 73 | 86 | 76 | 97 | 59 | 21 | * | * | * | 2.3 | 2.3 | 3.8 | 2.5 | 1.9 | 1.0 | 0.9 | 1.6 | 0.5 | 16.9 |

(See footnotes at end of tables)

| COUNTRY AND STATION | LATITUDE | LONGITUDE | ELEVATION (FEET) | TEMP LENGTH OF RECORD (YEAR) | JAN MAX | JAN MIN | APR MAX | APR MIN | JUL MAX | JUL MIN | OCT MAX | OCT MIN | EXTREME MAX | EXTREME MIN | PRECIP LENGTH OF RECORD (YEAR) | JAN | FEB | MAR | APR | MAY | JUN | JUL | AUG | SEP | OCT | NOV | DEC | YEAR |
|---|---|---|---|---|---|---|---|---|---|---|---|---|---|---|---|---|---|---|---|---|---|---|---|---|---|---|---|---|
| **South Africa, Republic of:** | | | | | | | | | | | | | | | | | | | | | | | | | | | | |
| Capetown | 33 54S | 18 32E | 56 | 19 | 78 | 60 | 72 | 53 | 63 | 45 | 70 | 52 | 103 | 28 | 18 | 0.6 | 0.3 | 0.7 | 1.9 | 3.1 | 3.3 | 3.5 | 2.6 | 1.7 | 1.2 | 0.7 | 0.4 | 20.0 |
| Durban | 29 50S | 31 02E | 16 | 15 | 81 | 69 | 78 | 64 | 72 | 52 | 75 | 62 | 107 | 39 | 78 | 4.3 | 4.8 | 5.1 | 3.0 | 2.0 | 1.3 | 1.1 | 1.5 | 2.8 | 4.3 | 4.8 | 4.7 | 39.7 |
| Kimberley | 28 48S | 24 46E | 3,927 | 19 | 91 | 64 | 77 | 52 | 65 | 36 | 83 | 54 | 103 | 20 | 57 | 2.4 | 2.5 | 3.1 | 1.5 | 0.7 | 0.2 | 0.2 | 0.3 | 0.6 | 1.0 | 1.6 | 2.0 | 16.1 |
| Port Elizabeth | 33 59S | 25 36E | 190 | 14 | 78 | 61 | 73 | 55 | 67 | 45 | 70 | 54 | 104 | 31 | 84 | 1.2 | 1.3 | 1.9 | 1.8 | 2.4 | 1.8 | 1.9 | 2.0 | 2.3 | 2.2 | 2.2 | 1.7 | 22.7 |
| Port Nolloth | 29 14S | 16 52E | 23 | 20 | 67 | 53 | 66 | 50 | 62 | 45 | 64 | 49 | 107 | 31 | 64 | 0.1 | 0.1 | 0.2 | 0.2 | 0.3 | 0.3 | 0.3 | 0.3 | 0.2 | 0.1 | 0.1 | 0.1 | 2.3 |
| Pretoria | 25 45S | 28 14E | 4,491 | 13 | 81 | 60 | 75 | 50 | 66 | 37 | 80 | 55 | 96 | 24 | 12 | 5.0 | 4.3 | 4.5 | 1.7 | 0.9 | * | * | 0.1 | 0.8 | 2.2 | 5.2 | 5.2 | 30.9 |
| Walvis Bay | 22 56S | 14 30E | 24 | 20 | 73 | 59 | 75 | 55 | 70 | 47 | 67 | 51 | 104 | 25 | 20 | * | 0.2 | 0.3 | 0.1 | 0.1 | * | * | 0.1 | * | * | * | * | 0.9 |
| **Southwest Africa:** | | | | | | | | | | | | | | | | | | | | | | | | | | | | |
| Keetmanshoop | 26 35S | 18 08E | 3,295 | 17 | 95 | 65 | 85 | 57 | 70 | 42 | 87 | 55 | 108 | 26 | 45 | 0.8 | 1.1 | 1.4 | 0.6 | 0.2 | * | * | * | 0.1 | 0.2 | 0.3 | 0.4 | 5.2 |
| Windhoek | 22 34S | 17 06E | 5,669 | 30 | 85 | 63 | 77 | 55 | 68 | 43 | 84 | 59 | 97 | 25 | 60 | 3.0 | 2.9 | 3.1 | 1.6 | 0.3 | * | * | * | 0.1 | 0.4 | 0.9 | 1.9 | 14.3 |
| **Spanish Sahara:** | | | | | | | | | | | | | | | | | | | | | | | | | | | | |
| Semara | 26 46N | 11 31W | 1,509 | 6 | 73 | 47 | 88 | 58 | 99 | 66 | 88 | 61 | 121 | 37 | 6 | 0.1 | * | 0.0 | * | * | 0.0 | 0.0 | * | 1.0 | * | 0.4 | 0.0 | 1.5 |
| Villa Cisneros | 23 42N | 15 52W | 35 | 12 | 71 | 56 | 74 | 60 | 78 | 65 | 80 | 65 | 107 | 48 | 14 | * | * | * | * | 0.1 | 0.0 | * | 0.2 | 1.4 | 0.1 | 0.2 | 1.0 | 3.0 |
| **Sudan:** | | | | | | | | | | | | | | | | | | | | | | | | | | | | |
| El Fasher | 13 38N | 25 21E | 2,395 | 17 | 88 | 50 | 102 | 64 | 96 | 70 | 99 | 64 | 113 | 33 | 17 | * | 0.0 | * | * | 0.3 | 0.7 | 4.5 | 5.3 | 1.2 | 0.2 | 0.0 | 0.0 | 12.2 |
| Khartoum | 15 37N | 32 33E | 1,279 | 46 | 90 | 59 | 105 | 72 | 101 | 77 | 104 | 77 | 118 | 41 | 46 | * | * | * | * | 0.1 | 0.3 | 2.1 | 2.8 | 0.7 | 0.2 | * | 0.0 | 6.2 |
| Port Sudan | 19 37N | 37 13E | 18 | 30 | 81 | 68 | 89 | 71 | 106 | 83 | 93 | 76 | 117 | 50 | 40 | 0.2 | 0.1 | * | * | * | * | 0.3 | 0.1 | * | 0.4 | 1.7 | 0.9 | 3.7 |
| Wadi Halfa | 21 55N | 31 20E | 410 | 39 | 75 | 46 | 98 | 62 | 106 | 74 | 98 | 67 | 127 | 28 | 39 | * | * | * | * | * | 0.0 | * | * | * | * | * | 0.0 | * |
| Wau | 07 42N | 28 03E | 1,443 | 38 | 96 | 64 | 99 | 72 | 89 | 69 | 93 | 69 | 115 | 50 | 38 | * | 0.2 | 0.9 | 2.6 | 5.3 | 6.5 | 7.5 | 8.2 | 6.6 | 4.9 | 0.6 | * | 43.3 |
| **Tanzania:** | | | | | | | | | | | | | | | | | | | | | | | | | | | | |
| Dares Salaam | 06 50S | 39 18E | 47 | 44 | 83 | 77 | 86 | 73 | 83 | 66 | 85 | 69 | 96 | 59 | 49 | 2.6 | 2.6 | 5.1 | 11.4 | 7.4 | 1.3 | 1.2 | 1.0 | 1.2 | 1.6 | 2.9 | 3.6 | 41.9 |
| Iringa | 07 47S | 35 42E | 5,330 | 14 | 76 | 59 | 75 | 59 | 72 | 52 | 80 | 57 | 90 | 42 | 24 | 6.8 | 5.1 | 7.1 | 3.5 | 0.5 | * | * | * | 0.1 | 0.2 | 1.5 | 4.5 | 29.3 |
| Kigoma | 04 53S | 29 38E | 2,903 | 26 | 80 | 67 | 81 | 67 | 83 | 63 | 84 | 69 | 100 | 53 | 18 | 4.8 | 5.0 | 5.9 | 5.1 | 1.7 | 0.2 | 0.1 | 0.2 | 0.7 | 1.9 | 5.6 | 5.3 | 36.5 |
| **Togo:** | | | | | | | | | | | | | | | | | | | | | | | | | | | | |
| Lome | 06 10N | 01 15E | 72 | 5 | 85 | 72 | 86 | 74 | 80 | 71 | 83 | 72 | 94 | 58 | 15 | 0.6 | 0.9 | 1.9 | 4.6 | 5.7 | 8.8 | 2.8 | 0.4 | 1.4 | 2.4 | 1.1 | 0.4 | 31.0 |
| **Tunisia:** | | | | | | | | | | | | | | | | | | | | | | | | | | | | |
| Gabes | 33 53N | 10 07E | 7 | 50 | 61 | 43 | 74 | 54 | 89 | 71 | 81 | 62 | 122 | 27 | 50 | 0.9 | 0.7 | 0.8 | 0.4 | 0.3 | * | * | 0.1 | 0.5 | 1.2 | 1.2 | 0.6 | 6.7 |
| Tunis | 36 47N | 10 12E | 217 | 50 | 58 | 43 | 70 | 51 | 90 | 68 | 77 | 59 | 118 | 30 | 50 | 2.5 | 2.0 | 1.6 | 1.4 | 0.7 | 0.3 | 0.1 | 0.3 | 1.3 | 2.0 | 1.9 | 2.4 | 16.5 |
| **Uganda:** | | | | | | | | | | | | | | | | | | | | | | | | | | | | |
| Kampala | 00 20N | 32 36E | 4,304 | 15 | 83 | 65 | 79 | 64 | 77 | 62 | 81 | 63 | 97 | 53 | 15 | 1.8 | 2.4 | 5.1 | 6.9 | 5.8 | 2.9 | 1.8 | 3.4 | 3.6 | 3.8 | 4.8 | 3.9 | 46.2 |
| Lira | 02 15N | 32 54E | 3,560 | 14 | 91 | 61 | 86 | 64 | 81 | 61 | 86 | 61 | 100 | 50 | 14 | 0.7 | 1.0 | 3.5 | 6.9 | 7.9 | 4.9 | 6.4 | 10.0 | 8.3 | 6.1 | 3.2 | 1.8 | 60.7 |
| **United Arab Republic:** | | | | | | | | | | | | | | | | | | | | | | | | | | | | |
| Alexandria | 31 12N | 29 53E | 105 | 61 | 65 | 51 | 74 | 59 | 85 | 73 | 83 | 68 | 111 | 37 | 61 | 1.9 | 0.9 | 0.4 | 0.1 | * | * | * | * | * | 0.2 | 1.3 | 2.2 | 7.0 |
| Aswan | 24 02N | 32 53E | 366 | 46 | 74 | 50 | 96 | 66 | 106 | 79 | 98 | 71 | 124 | 35 | 11 | * | * | * | * | * | * | 0.0 | 0.0 | 0.0 | * | * | * | * |
| Cairo | 29 52N | 31 20E | 381 | 42 | 65 | 47 | 83 | 57 | 96 | 70 | 86 | 65 | 117 | 34 | 42 | 0.2 | 0.2 | 0.2 | 0.1 | 0.1 | * | 0.0 | 0.0 | * | * | 0.1 | 0.2 | 1.1 |
| **Upper Volta:** | | | | | | | | | | | | | | | | | | | | | | | | | | | | |
| Bobo Dioulasso | 11 10N | 04 15W | 1,411 | 11 | 92 | 58 | 99 | 71 | 87 | 69 | 90 | 70 | 115 | 46 | 10 | 0.1 | 0.2 | 1.1 | 2.1 | 4.6 | 4.8 | 9.8 | 12.0 | 8.5 | 2.5 | 0.7 | 0.0 | 46.4 |
| Ouagadougou | 12 22N | 01 31W | 991 | 10 | 92 | 60 | 103 | 79 | 91 | 74 | 95 | 74 | 118 | 48 | 15 | * | 0.1 | 0.5 | 0.6 | 3.3 | 4.8 | 8.0 | 10.9 | 5.7 | 1.3 | * | 0.0 | 35.2 |
| **Zambia:** | | | | | | | | | | | | | | | | | | | | | | | | | | | | |
| Balovale | 13 34S | 23 06E | 3,577 | 8 | 82 | 65 | 84 | 61 | 81 | 47 | 91 | 64 | 108 | 38 | 9 | 8.5 | 6.9 | 5.8 | 1.2 | * | 0.0 | 0.0 | * | 0.3 | 2.3 | 4.4 | 8.9 | 38.3 |

Average Precipitation and Temperature table (Atlantic Islands, Indian Ocean Islands, Asia – Far East)

| COUNTRY AND STATION | LATITUDE | LONGITUDE | ELEVATION (FEET) | TEMP. LoR (YEAR) | Jan Max (°F) | Jan Min (°F) | Apr Max (°F) | Apr Min (°F) | Jul Max (°F) | Jul Min (°F) | Oct Max (°F) | Oct Min (°F) | Extreme Max (°F) | Extreme Min (°F) | PRECIP. LoR (YEAR) | Jan (in.) | Feb (in.) | Mar (in.) | Apr (in.) | May (in.) | Jun (in.) | Jul (in.) | Aug (in.) | Sep (in.) | Oct (in.) | Nov (in.) | Dec (in.) | Year (in.) |
|---|---|---|---|---|---|---|---|---|---|---|---|---|---|---|---|---|---|---|---|---|---|---|---|---|---|---|---|---|
| Kasama | 10 12S | 31 11E | 4,544 | 10 | 79 | 61 | 79 | 60 | 76 | 50 | 87 | 62 | 95 | 39 | 10 | 10.7 | 9.9 | 10.9 | 2.8 | 0.5 | * | * | * | * | 0.8 | 6.4 | 9.5 | 51.5 |
| Lusaka | 15 25S | 28 19E | 4,191 | 10 | 78 | 63 | 79 | 59 | 73 | 49 | 88 | 64 | 100 | 39 | 10 | 9.1 | 7.5 | 5.6 | 0.7 | 0.1 | * | * | 0.0 | * | 0.4 | 3.6 | 5.9 | 32.9 |
| **ATLANTIC ISLANDS:** | | | | | | | | | | | | | | | | | | | | | | | | | | | | |
| Funchal, Madeira Island | 32 38N | 16 55W | 82 | 30 | 66 | 56 | 67 | 58 | 75 | 66 | 74 | 65 | 103 | 40 | 30 | 2.5 | 2.9 | 3.1 | 1.3 | 0.7 | 0.2 | * | * | 1.0 | 3.0 | 3.5 | 3.3 | 21.5 |
| Georgetown, Ascension Island | 07 56S | 14 25W | 55 | 29 | 85 | 73 | 88 | 75 | 84 | 72 | 83 | 71 | 95 | 65 | 45 | 0.2 | 0.4 | 0.7 | 1.1 | 0.5 | 0.5 | 0.5 | 0.4 | 0.3 | 0.3 | 0.2 | 0.1 | 5.2 |
| Hutts Gate, St. Helena | 15 57S | 05 40W | 2,062 | 30 | 68 | 60 | 69 | 61 | 62 | 55 | 61 | 54 | 82 | 50 | 30 | 2.1 | 3.1 | 4.2 | 3.1 | 2.8 | 3.2 | 4.3 | 2.6 | 2.2 | 1.7 | 1.2 | 1.6 | 32.1 |
| Las Palmas, Canary Islands | 28 11N | 15 28W | 20 | 45 | 70 | 58 | 71 | 61 | 77 | 67 | 79 | 67 | 99 | 46 | 48 | 1.4 | 0.9 | 0.9 | 0.5 | 0.2 | * | * | * | 0.2 | 1.1 | 2.1 | 1.6 | 8.6 |
| Porto da Praia, Cape Verde Is. | 14 54N | 23 31W | 112 | 25 | 77 | 68 | 79 | 69 | 83 | 75 | 85 | 75 | 94 | 56 | 25 | 0.1 | * | * | * | 0.0 | * | 0.2 | 3.8 | 4.5 | 1.2 | 0.3 | 0.1 | 10.2 |
| Santa Isabel, Fernando Po | 03 46N | 08 46E | ----- | 2 | 87 | 70 | 89 | 70 | 84 | 69 | 86 | 71 | 102 | 61 | 16 | 1.3 | 2.5 | 4.2 | 7.2 | 9.4 | 11.1 | 7.4 | 6.6 | 9.6 | 10.4 | 3.5 | 1.7 | 74.9 |
| Sao Tome, Sao Tome | 00 20N | 06 43E | 16 | 2 | 86 | 73 | 86 | 73 | 82 | 69 | 84 | 71 | 91 | 56 | 10 | 3.2 | 4.2 | 5.9 | 7.2 | 5.3 | 1.1 | * | * | 0.9 | 4.3 | 4.6 | 3.5 | 38.0 |
| Tristan da Cunha | 37 03S | 12 19W | 75 | 5 | 66 | 59 | 64 | 57 | 57 | 50 | 59 | 51 | 75 | 38 | 5 | 3.5 | 3.5 | 6.4 | 4.7 | 7.1 | 5.9 | 6.1 | 6.9 | 7.9 | 5.8 | 4.3 | 4.0 | 66.1 |
| **INDIAN OCEAN ISLANDS:** | | | | | | | | | | | | | | | | | | | | | | | | | | | | |
| Agalega Island | 10 26S | 56 40E | 10 | 3 | 86 | 77 | 87 | 77 | 83 | 75 | 84 | 75 | 91 | 69 | 2 | 5.9 | 10.1 | 4.9 | 6.9 | 13.2 | 8.9 | 8.7 | 3.2 | 1.8 | 4.2 | 7.0 | 10.0 | 84.7 |
| Cocos (Keeling) Island | 12 05S | 96 53E | 15 | 36 | 86 | 77 | 85 | 78 | 82 | 76 | 84 | 76 | 94 | 68 | 38 | 5.4 | 7.7 | 8.5 | 10.4 | 7.9 | 9.0 | 8.7 | 4.8 | 3.7 | 3.3 | 4.2 | 4.6 | 78.2 |
| Heard Island | 53 01S | 73 23E | 16 | 5 | 41 | 35 | 39 | 33 | 34 | 27 | 35 | 28 | 58 | 13 | 5 | 5.8 | 5.8 | 5.7 | 6.1 | 5.8 | 3.9 | 3.6 | 2.2 | 2.5 | 3.3 | 4.0 | 5.1 | 54.3 |
| Helburg, Reunion Island | 21 04S | 55 22E | 3,070 | 5 | 74 | 59 | 73 | 56 | 65 | 48 | 69 | 51 | 84 | 40 | 11 | 22.4 | 8.0 | 16.4 | 7.2 | 5.3 | 4.4 | 3.1 | 3.0 | 2.0 | 2.3 | 3.5 | 12.9 | 90.5 |
| Port Victoria, Seychelles | 04 37S | 55 27E | 15 | 60 | 83 | 76 | 86 | 77 | 81 | 75 | 83 | 75 | 92 | 67 | 64 | 15.2 | 10.5 | 9.2 | 7.2 | 6.7 | 4.0 | 3.3 | 2.7 | 5.1 | 6.1 | 9.1 | 13.4 | 92.5 |
| Royal Alfred Observatory, Mauritius | 20 06S | 57 32E | 181 | 40 | 86 | 73 | 82 | 70 | 75 | 62 | 80 | 64 | 95 | 50 | 43 | 8.5 | 7.8 | 8.7 | 5.0 | 3.8 | 2.6 | 2.3 | 2.5 | 1.4 | 1.6 | 1.8 | 4.6 | 50.6 |
| **ASIA – FAR EAST** | | | | | | | | | | | | | | | | | | | | | | | | | | | | |
| China | | | | | | | | | | | | | | | | | | | | | | | | | | | | |
| Canton | 23 10N | 113 20E | 59 | 26 | 65 | 49 | 77 | 65 | 91 | 77 | 85 | 67 | 101 | 31 | 36 | 0.9 | 1.9 | 4.2 | 6.8 | 10.6 | 10.6 | 8.1 | 8.5 | 6.5 | 3.4 | 1.2 | 0.9 | 63.6 |
| Chanasha | 28 15 | 112 58E | 161 | 14 | 45 | 35 | 70 | 56 | 94 | 78 | 75 | 59 | 111 | 16 | 26 | 1.9 | 3.7 | 5.3 | 5.7 | 8.2 | 8.7 | 4.4 | 4.3 | 2.7 | 3.0 | 2.7 | 1.5 | 52.1 |
| Chungking | 29 30N | 106 33E | 855 | 27 | 51 | 42 | 73 | 59 | 93 | 76 | 71 | 61 | 111 | 28 | 60 | 0.7 | 0.8 | 1.5 | 3.8 | 5.7 | 7.1 | 5.6 | 4.7 | 5.8 | 4.3 | 1.9 | 0.8 | 42.9 |
| Hankow | 30 35N | 114 17E | 75 | 29 | 46 | 34 | 69 | 55 | 93 | 78 | 74 | 60 | 108 | 9 | 55 | 1.8 | 1.9 | 3.6 | 5.8 | 7.0 | 9.0 | 7.0 | 4.1 | 3.0 | 3.1 | 1.9 | 1.2 | 49.4 |
| Harbin (Ha-erh-pin) | 45 45N | 126 38E | 476 | 35 | 7 | -14 | 54 | 31 | 84 | 65 | 54 | 31 | 102 | -43 | 38 | 0.2 | 0.2 | 0.4 | 0.9 | 1.7 | 3.7 | 6.6 | 4.3 | 2.1 | 1.2 | 0.5 | 0.2 | 22.6 |
| Kashgar | 39 24N | 76 07E | 4,296 | 27 | 33 | 12 | 71 | 48 | 92 | 68 | 71 | 43 | 106 | -15 | 18 | 0.6 | 0.1 | 0.5 | 0.2 | 0.3 | 0.2 | 0.4 | 0.3 | 0.1 | 0.1 | 0.2 | 0.3 | 3.2 |
| Kunming | 25 02N | 102 43E | 6,211 | 32 | 61 | 37 | 76 | 51 | 77 | 62 | 70 | 53 | 91 | 22 | 31 | 0.4 | 0.5 | 0.7 | 0.8 | 4.3 | 6.3 | 8.8 | 8.6 | 5.0 | 3.0 | 1.7 | 0.4 | 40.5 |
| Lanchow | 36 06N | 103 55E | 5,105 | 40 | 33 | 7 | 65 | 40 | 84 | 61 | 62 | 39 | 100 | -3 | 4 | 0.2 | 0.2 | 0.7 | 0.5 | 0.8 | 0.7 | 3.3 | 5.1 | 2.2 | 0.6 | 0.0 | 0.3 | 14.1 |
| Mukden (Shen-yang) | 41 47N | 123 24E | 138 | 56 | 20 | -2 | 60 | 36 | 84 | 69 | 62 | 39 | 100 | -28 | 42 | 0.2 | 0.2 | 0.7 | 1.2 | 2.6 | 3.8 | 7.0 | 6.3 | 2.9 | 1.7 | 0.9 | 0.3 | 28.2 |
| Shanghai | 31 12N | 121 26E | 16 | 24 | 47 | 32 | 67 | 49 | 91 | 75 | 75 | 56 | 104 | 10 | 81 | 1.9 | 2.4 | 3.3 | 3.6 | 3.8 | 7.0 | 5.8 | 5.5 | 5.2 | 2.9 | 2.1 | 1.5 | 45.0 |
| Tientsin | 39 10N | 117 10E | 13 | 6 | 33 | 16 | 68 | 45 | 90 | 73 | 68 | 48 | 109 | -3 | 25 | 0.2 | 0.1 | 0.4 | 0.5 | 1.1 | 2.4 | 7.6 | 6.0 | 1.7 | 0.6 | 0.4 | 0.2 | 21.0 |
| Urumchi | 43 45N | 87 40E | 2,972 | 50 | 13 | -7 | 60 | 36 | 82 | 58 | 50 | 31 | 112 | -30 | 6 | 0.6 | 0.3 | 0.5 | 1.5 | 1.1 | 1.5 | 0.7 | 1.0 | 0.6 | 1.7 | 1.6 | 0.4 | 11.5 |
| Hong Kong: | 22 18N | 114 10E | 109 | | 64 | 56 | 75 | 67 | 87 | 78 | 81 | 73 | 97 | 32 | 50 | 1.3 | 1.8 | 2.9 | 5.4 | 11.5 | 15.5 | 15.0 | 14.2 | 10.1 | 4.5 | 1.7 | 1.2 | 85.1 |
| Japan: | | | | | | | | | | | | | | | | | | | | | | | | | | | | |
| Kushiro | 43 02N | 144 12E | 315 | 41 | 30 | 8 | 44 | 31 | 66 | 55 | 58 | 40 | 87 | -19 | 41 | 1.8 | 1.4 | 2.8 | 3.6 | 3.8 | 4.1 | 4.4 | 4.9 | 6.6 | 4.0 | 3.1 | 2.0 | 42.9 |

386

(See footnotes at end of tables)

| Country and Station | Latitude | Longitude | Elevation (feet) | Temp. Record (yr) | Jan Max (°F) | Jan Min (°F) | Apr Max (°F) | Apr Min (°F) | Jul Max (°F) | Jul Min (°F) | Oct Max (°F) | Oct Min (°F) | Extreme Max (°F) | Extreme Min (°F) | Precip. Record (yr) | Jan (in) | Feb (in) | Mar (in) | Apr (in) | May (in) | Jun (in) | Jul (in) | Aug (in) | Sep (in) | Oct (in) | Nov (in) | Dec (in) | Year (in) |
|---|---|---|---|---|---|---|---|---|---|---|---|---|---|---|---|---|---|---|---|---|---|---|---|---|---|---|---|---|
| Miyako | 39 38N | 141 59E | 98 | 30 | 43 | 23 | 58 | 37 | 77 | 62 | 66 | 46 | 99 | 1 | 30 | 2.9 | 3.0 | 3.2 | 3.5 | 4.5 | 5.0 | 5.0 | 7.2 | 9.5 | 6.8 | 3.0 | 2.6 | 56.2 |
| Nagasaki | 32 44N | 129 53E | 436 | 59 | 49 | 36 | 66 | 50 | 85 | 73 | 72 | 58 | 98 | 22 | 59 | 2.8 | 3.3 | 4.9 | 7.3 | 6.7 | 12.3 | 10.1 | 6.9 | 9.8 | 4.5 | 3.7 | 3.2 | 75.5 |
| Osaka | 34 47N | 135 26E | 49 | 60 | 47 | 32 | 65 | 47 | 87 | 73 | 72 | 55 | 102 | 19 | 60 | 1.7 | 2.3 | 3.8 | 5.2 | 4.9 | 7.4 | 5.9 | 4.4 | 7.0 | 5.1 | 3.0 | 1.9 | 52.6 |
| Tokyo | 35 41N | 139 46E | 19 | 60 | 47 | 29 | 63 | 46 | 83 | 70 | 69 | 55 | 101 | 17 | 60 | 1.9 | 2.9 | 4.2 | 5.3 | 5.8 | 6.5 | 5.6 | 6.0 | 9.2 | 8.2 | 3.8 | 2.2 | 61.6 |
| **Korea:** | | | | | | | | | | | | | | | | | | | | | | | | | | | | |
| Pusan | 35 10N | 129 07E | 6 | 36 | 43 | 29 | 62 | 47 | 81 | 71 | 70 | 54 | 97 | 7 | 36 | 1.7 | 1.4 | 2.7 | 5.5 | 5.2 | 7.9 | 11.6 | 5.1 | 6.8 | 2.9 | 1.6 | 1.2 | 53.6 |
| P'yongyang | 39 01N | 125 49E | 94 | 43 | 27 | 8 | 61 | 38 | 84 | 69 | 65 | 43 | 100 | -19 | 43 | 0.6 | 0.4 | 1.0 | 1.8 | 2.6 | 3.0 | 9.3 | 9.0 | 4.4 | 1.8 | 1.6 | 0.8 | 36.4 |
| Seoul | 37 31N | 126 55E | 34 | 22 | 32 | 15 | 62 | 41 | 84 | 70 | 67 | 45 | 99 | -12 | 22 | 1.2 | 0.8 | 1.5 | 3.0 | 3.2 | 5.1 | 14.8 | 10.5 | 4.7 | 1.6 | 1.8 | 1.0 | 49.2 |
| **Mongolia:** | | | | | | | | | | | | | | | | | | | | | | | | | | | | |
| Ulan Bator | 47 54N | 106 56E | 4,287 | 13 | -2 | -27 | 45 | 18 | 71 | 50 | 44 | 17 | 97 | -48 | 15 | * | * | 0.1 | 0.2 | 0.3 | 1.0 | 2.9 | 1.9 | 0.8 | 0.2 | 0.2 | 0.1 | 7.7 |
| **Taiwan:** | | | | | | | | | | | | | | | | | | | | | | | | | | | | |
| Tainan | 22 57N | 120 12E | 53 | 13 | 72 | 55 | 82 | 67 | 89 | 77 | 86 | 70 | 95 | 39 | 13 | 0.7 | 0.7 | 1.1 | 3.2 | 6.3 | 15.6 | 16.0 | 15.8 | 8.4 | 1.2 | 0.9 | 0.6 | 70.5 |
| Taipei | 25 04N | 121 32E | 21 | 12 | 66 | 53 | 77 | 64 | 92 | 76 | 80 | 68 | 101 | 32 | 12 | 3.8 | 5.3 | 4.3 | 5.3 | 6.9 | 8.8 | 8.8 | 8.7 | 8.2 | 5.5 | 4.2 | 2.9 | 72.7 |
| **Union of Soviet Socialist Republics:** | | | | | | | | | | | | | | | | | | | | | | | | | | | | |
| Alma-Ata | 43 16N | 76 53E | 2,543 | 19 | 23 | 7 | 56 | 38 | 81 | 60 | 55 | 35 | 100 | -30 | 27 | 1.3 | 0.9 | 2.2 | 4.0 | 3.7 | 2.6 | 1.4 | 1.2 | 1.0 | 2.0 | 1.9 | 1.3 | 23.5 |
| Chita (Tchita) | 52 02N | 113 30E | 2,218 | 10 | -10 | -27 | 42 | 19 | 75 | 51 | 38 | 18 | 99 | -52 | 24 | 0.1 | 0.1 | 0.1 | 0.4 | 1.1 | 1.8 | 3.3 | 3.3 | 1.2 | 0.5 | 0.2 | 0.2 | 12.3 |
| Dubinka | 69 07N | 87 00E | 141 | 5 | -23 | -31 | 6 | -10 | 59 | 47 | 19 | 11 | 84 | -62 | 5 | 0.3 | 0.4 | 0.2 | 0.3 | 0.6 | 1.9 | 1.5 | 2.1 | 1.8 | 0.9 | 0.4 | 0.3 | 10.7 |
| Irkutsk | 52 16N | 104 19E | 1,532 | 10 | 8 | -15 | 42 | 20 | 71 | 50 | 41 | 21 | 98 | -58 | 38 | 0.5 | 0.4 | 0.3 | 0.6 | 1.3 | 2.2 | 3.1 | 2.8 | 1.7 | 0.7 | 0.6 | 0.6 | 14.9 |
| Kazalinsk | 45 46N | 62 06E | 207 | 10 | 16 | 5 | 58 | 27 | 90 | 65 | 57 | 35 | 108 | -27 | 19 | 0.4 | 0.4 | 0.5 | 0.5 | 0.6 | 0.2 | 0.2 | 0.3 | 0.3 | 0.4 | 0.5 | 0.6 | 4.9 |
| Khabarovsk | 48 28N | 135 03E | 165 | 7 | -2 | -13 | 41 | 28 | 74 | 63 | 48 | 34 | 91 | -46 | 8 | 0.3 | 0.2 | 0.5 | 0.7 | 2.0 | 3.5 | 4.1 | 3.3 | 3.0 | 0.7 | 0.6 | 0.5 | 19.2 |
| Kirensk | 57 47N | 108 07E | 938 | 18 | -14 | -28 | 38 | 15 | 75 | 51 | 10 | -4 | 95 | -71 | 19 | 0.1 | 0.5 | 0.5 | 0.5 | 1.0 | 1.8 | 2.1 | 2.1 | 1.7 | 0.9 | 1.0 | 1.0 | 14.0 |
| Krasnoyarsk | 56 01N | 92 52E | 498 | 18 | 3 | -10 | 34 | 23 | 67 | 55 | 34 | 26 | 103 | -47 | 8 | 0.2 | 0.2 | 0.1 | 0.1 | 1.0 | 1.4 | 1.2 | 2.1 | 1.7 | 0.9 | 0.5 | 0.4 | 9.8 |
| Markovo | 64 45N | 170 50E | 85 | 15 | -19 | -29 | 5 | -8 | 59 | 47 | 16 | 9 | 84 | -72 | 16 | 0.8 | 0.5 | 0.8 | 0.2 | 1.0 | 0.8 | 1.0 | 1.9 | 1.1 | 0.4 | 0.4 | 0.9 | 7.0 |
| Narym | 58 50N | 81 39E | 197 | 13 | -7 | -18 | 35 | 19 | 71 | 56 | 35 | 25 | 94 | -61 | 14 | 0.1 | 0.1 | 0.3 | 0.5 | 1.3 | 2.6 | 2.4 | 2.7 | 1.1 | 1.4 | 1.1 | 0.9 | 16.8 |
| Okhotsk | 59 21N | 143 17E | 18 | 19 | -6 | -17 | 29 | 10 | 57 | 48 | 33 | 21 | 78 | -50 | 25 | 0.6 | 0.5 | 0.3 | 0.1 | 0.9 | 1.6 | 1.9 | 2.6 | 2.4 | 1.0 | 1.1 | 0.9 | 11.8 |
| Omsk | 54 58N | 73 20E | 279 | 19 | -1 | -14 | 39 | 21 | 74 | 56 | 40 | 27 | 102 | -56 | 22 | 0.6 | 0.3 | 0.3 | 0.5 | 1.2 | 2.0 | 2.0 | 2.0 | 1.1 | 1.0 | 0.7 | 0.8 | 12.5 |
| Petropavlovsk | 52 53N | 158 42E | 286 | 7 | 23 | 11 | 35 | 25 | 56 | 47 | 46 | 34 | 84 | -29 | 35 | 3.0 | 2.2 | 3.4 | 2.5 | 2.2 | 2.0 | 3.1 | 3.2 | 3.8 | 3.9 | 3.6 | 3.0 | 35.9 |
| Salehkard | 66 31N | 66 35E | 60 | 18 | -13 | -21 | 35 | 4 | 61 | 49 | 26 | 20 | 85 | -65 | 27 | 0.3 | 0.3 | 0.5 | 0.6 | 0.7 | 1.3 | 1.9 | 1.3 | 1.5 | 0.7 | 0.5 | 0.5 | 10.2 |
| Semipalatinsk | 50 24N | 80 13E | 709 | 10 | 8 | -7 | 45 | 26 | 81 | 57 | 46 | 30 | 101 | -47 | 10 | 0.9 | 0.3 | 0.5 | 0.6 | 0.7 | 1.5 | 1.1 | 1.3 | 0.7 | 1.2 | 1.1 | 1.0 | 11.6 |
| Sverdlovsk | 56 49N | 60 38E | 894 | 21 | 6 | -5 | 42 | 26 | 70 | 54 | 37 | 28 | 94 | -45 | 29 | 0.5 | 0.4 | 0.5 | 0.7 | 1.9 | 2.7 | 2.6 | 2.7 | 1.6 | 1.2 | 1.5 | 0.8 | 16.7 |
| Tashkent | 41 20N | 69 18E | 1,569 | 19 | 37 | 21 | 65 | 47 | 92 | 64 | 65 | 41 | 106 | -19 | 19 | 2.1 | 1.1 | 2.6 | 2.3 | 1.4 | 0.5 | 0.2 | 0.1 | 0.1 | 0.3 | 1.5 | 1.6 | 14.7 |
| Verkhoyansk | 67 34N | 133 51E | 328 | 24 | -54 | -63 | 12 | -10 | 66 | 47 | 12 | -3 | 98 | -90 | 44 | 0.2 | 0.2 | 0.1 | 0.2 | 0.3 | 0.9 | 1.1 | 1.0 | 0.5 | 0.3 | 0.3 | 0.2 | 5.3 |
| Vladivostok | 43 07N | 131 55E | 535 | 14 | 13 | 0 | 46 | 34 | 73 | 60 | 41 | 41 | 92 | -22 | 53 | 0.3 | 0.4 | 0.7 | 1.2 | 2.1 | 2.9 | 3.3 | 4.7 | 4.3 | 1.9 | 1.2 | 0.6 | 23.6 |
| Yakutsk | 62 01N | 129 43E | 535 | 19 | -45 | -53 | 27 | 6 | 73 | 54 | 23 | 11 | 97 | -84 | 22 | 0.3 | 0.2 | 0.1 | 0.3 | 0.4 | 1.1 | 1.6 | 1.3 | 1.1 | 0.5 | 0.4 | 0.3 | 7.4 |

### ASIA - SOUTHEAST

| Country and Station | Latitude | Longitude | Elevation (feet) | Temp. Record (yr) | Jan Max (°F) | Jan Min (°F) | Apr Max (°F) | Apr Min (°F) | Jul Max (°F) | Jul Min (°F) | Oct Max (°F) | Oct Min (°F) | Extreme Max (°F) | Extreme Min (°F) | Precip. Record (yr) | Jan (in) | Feb (in) | Mar (in) | Apr (in) | May (in) | Jun (in) | Jul (in) | Aug (in) | Sep (in) | Oct (in) | Nov (in) | Dec (in) | Year (in) |
|---|---|---|---|---|---|---|---|---|---|---|---|---|---|---|---|---|---|---|---|---|---|---|---|---|---|---|---|---|
| **Brunei:** | | | | | | | | | | | | | | | | | | | | | | | | | | | | |
| Brunei | 04 55N | 114 55E | 10 | 5 | 85 | 76 | 87 | 77 | 87 | 76 | 86 | 77 | 99 | 70 | 12 | 14.6 | 7.6 | 7.8 | 9.8 | 10.9 | 9.5 | 9.0 | 7.3 | 11.8 | 14.5 | 15.2 | 13.0 | 131.0 |

387

| COUNTRY AND STATION | LATITUDE | LONGITUDE | ELEVATION (FEET) | TEMPERATURE | | | | | | | | | | AVERAGE PRECIPITATION | | | | | | | | | | | | | |
|---|---|---|---|---|---|---|---|---|---|---|---|---|---|---|---|---|---|---|---|---|---|---|---|---|---|---|---|
| | | | | LENGTH OF RECORD (YEAR) | JANUARY MAX | JANUARY MIN | APRIL MAX | APRIL MIN | JULY MAX | JULY MIN | OCTOBER MAX | OCTOBER MIN | EXTREME MAX | EXTREME MIN | LENGTH OF RECORD (YEAR) | JAN | FEB | MAR | APR | MAY | JUN | JUL | AUG | SEP | OCT | NOV | DEC | YEAR |
| **Burma:** | | | | | | | | | | | | | | | | | | | | | | | | | | | | |
| Mandalay | 21 59N | 96 06E | 252 | 20 | 82 | 55 | 101 | 77 | 93 | 77 | 89 | 73 | 111 | 44 | 20 | 0.1 | 0.1 | 0.2 | 1.2 | 5.8 | 6.3 | 2.7 | 4.1 | 5.4 | 4.3 | 2.0 | 0.4 | 32.6 |
| Moulmein | 16 26N | 97 39E | 150 | 43 | 89 | 65 | 95 | 77 | 83 | 77 | 88 | 74 | 103 | 52 | 60 | 0.2 | 0.2 | 0.5 | 3.0 | 19.9 | 37.1 | 47.5 | 44.2 | 27.1 | 8.5 | 1.7 | 0.3 | 190.2 |
| **Cambodia:** | | | | | | | | | | | | | | | | | | | | | | | | | | | | |
| Phnom Penh | 11 33N | 104 51E | 39 | 37 | 88 | 71 | 95 | 76 | 90 | 76 | 87 | 76 | 105 | 55 | 49 | 0.3 | 0.4 | 1.4 | 3.1 | 5.7 | 5.8 | 6.0 | 6.1 | 8.9 | 9.9 | 5.5 | 1.7 | 54.8 |
| **Indonesia:** | | | | | | | | | | | | | | | | | | | | | | | | | | | | |
| Batavia (Jakarta) | 06 11S | 106 50E | 26 | 80 | 84 | 74 | 87 | 75 | 87 | 73 | 87 | 74 | 98 | 66 | 78 | 11.8 | 11.8 | 8.3 | 5.8 | 4.5 | 3.8 | 2.5 | 1.7 | 2.6 | 4.4 | 5.6 | 8.0 | 70.8 |
| Manokwari | 00 53S | 134 03E | 10 | 5 | 86 | 73 | 86 | 74 | 86 | 74 | 87 | 74 | 93 | 68 | 40 | 12.0 | 9.4 | 13.2 | 11.1 | 7.8 | 7.2 | 5.4 | 5.6 | 4.9 | 4.7 | 6.5 | 10.3 | 98.1 |
| Mapanget | 01 32N | 124 55E | 264 | 21 | 85 | 73 | 89 | 73 | 87 | 73 | 89 | 72 | 97 | 65 | 63 | 18.6 | 13.8 | 12.2 | 6.4 | 6.4 | 6.5 | 4.8 | 4.0 | 3.3 | 4.9 | 8.9 | 14.7 | 106.1 |
| Penful | 10 10S | 123 39E | 335 | 21 | 87 | 75 | 89 | 75 | 88 | 70 | 92 | 75 | 101 | 58 | 63 | 15.2 | 13.7 | 9.2 | 2.6 | 1.2 | 0.4 | 0.2 | 0.0 | 0.0 | 0.7 | 3.3 | 9.1 | 55.7 |
| Pontianak | 00 00N | 109 20E | 13 | 20 | 87 | 74 | 89 | 74 | 89 | 74 | 89 | 75 | 96 | 68 | 63 | 10.8 | 8.2 | 9.5 | 10.9 | 11.1 | 8.7 | 6.5 | 8.0 | 9.0 | 14.4 | 15.3 | 12.7 | 125.1 |
| Tabing | 00 52S | 100 21E | 19 | 21 | 87 | 74 | 87 | 74 | 87 | 74 | 86 | 74 | 94 | 68 | 63 | 13.9 | 10.1 | 12.2 | 14.5 | 12.8 | 11.7 | 10.5 | 13.7 | 16.2 | 20.1 | 20.5 | 19.2 | 175.4 |
| Tarakan | 03 19N | 117 33E | 20 | 19 | 85 | 73 | 86 | 73 | 87 | 74 | 87 | 74 | 94 | 67 | 31 | 10.9 | 10.2 | 14.0 | 13.9 | 13.5 | 12.6 | 10.3 | 12.4 | 11.6 | 14.3 | 15.2 | 13.4 | 152.3 |
| **Laos:** | | | | | | | | | | | | | | | | | | | | | | | | | | | | |
| Vientiane | 17 58N | 102 34E | 559 | 13 | 83 | 58 | 95 | 73 | 89 | 75 | 88 | 71 | 108 | 32 | 27 | 0.2 | 0.6 | 1.5 | 3.9 | 10.5 | 11.9 | 10.5 | 11.5 | 11.9 | 4.3 | 0.6 | 0.1 | 67.5 |
| **Malaya, Fed.:** | | | | | | | | | | | | | | | | | | | | | | | | | | | | |
| Kuala Lumpur | 03 06N | 101 42E | 111 | 19 | 90 | 72 | 91 | 74 | 90 | 72 | 89 | 73 | 99 | 64 | 19 | 6.2 | 7.9 | 10.2 | 11.5 | 8.8 | 5.1 | 3.9 | 6.4 | 8.6 | 9.8 | 10.2 | 7.5 | 96.1 |
| Singapore | 01 18N | 103 50E | 33 | 39 | 86 | 73 | 88 | 75 | 88 | 75 | 87 | 74 | 97 | 66 | 64 | 9.9 | 6.8 | 7.6 | 7.4 | 6.8 | 6.8 | 6.7 | 7.7 | 7.0 | 8.2 | 10.0 | 10.1 | 95.0 |
| **North Borneo:** | | | | | | | | | | | | | | | | | | | | | | | | | | | | |
| Sanda Kan | 05 54N | 118 03E | 38 | 45 | 85 | 74 | 89 | 76 | 89 | 76 | 88 | 75 | 99 | 70 | 46 | 19.0 | 10.9 | 8.6 | 4.5 | 6.2 | 7.4 | 6.7 | 7.9 | 9.3 | 10.2 | 14.5 | 18.5 | 123.7 |
| **Philippine Islands:** | | | | | | | | | | | | | | | | | | | | | | | | | | | | |
| Davao | 07 07N | 125 38E | 88 | 15 | 87 | 72 | 91 | 73 | 88 | 73 | 89 | 73 | 97 | 65 | 34 | 4.8 | 4.5 | 5.2 | 5.8 | 9.2 | 9.1 | 6.5 | 6.5 | 6.7 | 7.9 | 5.3 | 6.1 | 77.6 |
| Manila | 14 31N | 121 00E | 49 | 61 | 86 | 69 | 93 | 73 | 88 | 73 | 88 | 74 | 101 | 58 | 75 | 0.9 | 0.5 | 0.7 | 1.3 | 5.1 | 10.0 | 17.0 | 16.6 | 14.0 | 7.6 | 5.7 | 2.6 | 82.0 |
| **Sarawak:** | | | | | | | | | | | | | | | | | | | | | | | | | | | | |
| Kuching | 01 29N | 110 20E | 85 | 5 | 85 | 72 | 90 | 73 | 90 | 72 | 89 | 73 | 98 | 64 | 19 | 24.0 | 20.1 | 12.9 | 11.0 | 10.3 | 7.1 | 7.7 | 9.2 | 8.6 | 10.5 | 14.1 | 18.2 | 153.7 |
| **Thailand:** | | | | | | | | | | | | | | | | | | | | | | | | | | | | |
| Bangkok | 13 44N | 100 30E | 53 | 10 | 89 | 67 | 95 | 78 | 90 | 76 | 88 | 76 | 104 | 50 | 10 | 0.2 | 1.1 | 1.1 | 2.3 | 5.2 | 6.0 | 6.9 | 9.2 | 14.0 | 9.9 | 1.8 | 0.1 | 57.8 |
| **Viet Nam:** | | | | | | | | | | | | | | | | | | | | | | | | | | | | |
| Hanoi | 21 03N | 105 52E | 20 | 12 | 68 | 58 | 80 | 70 | 92 | 79 | 84 | 72 | 108 | 41 | 12 | 0.8 | 1.2 | 2.5 | 3.6 | 4.1 | 11.2 | 11.9 | 15.2 | 10.0 | 3.5 | 2.6 | 2.8 | 69.4 |
| Saigon | 10 49N | 106 39E | 33 | 31 | 89 | 70 | 95 | 76 | 88 | 76 | 88 | 74 | 104 | 57 | 33 | 0.6 | 0.1 | 0.5 | 1.7 | 8.7 | 13.0 | 12.4 | 10.6 | 13.2 | 10.6 | 4.5 | 2.2 | 78.1 |
| **ASIA — MIDDLE EAST** | | | | | | | | | | | | | | | | | | | | | | | | | | | | |
| **Aden:** | | | | | | | | | | | | | | | | | | | | | | | | | | | | |
| Riyan | 14 39N | 49 19E | 83 | 13 | 82 | 67 | 88 | 74 | 92 | 77 | 88 | 72 | 111 | 57 | 13 | 0.3 | 0.3 | 0.6 | 0.2 | * | 0.1 | 0.1 | 0.1 | * | * | 0.7 | 0.3 | 2.5 |
| **Afghanistan:** | | | | | | | | | | | | | | | | | | | | | | | | | | | | |
| Kabul | 34 30N | 69 13E | 5,955 | 9 | 36 | 18 | 66 | 43 | 92 | 61 | 73 | 42 | 104 | -6 | 45 | 1.3 | 1.5 | 3.6 | 3.3 | 0.9 | 0.2 | 0.1 | 0.1 | * | 0.4 | 0.6 | 0.6 | 12.6 |
| Kandhar | 31 36N | 65 40E | 3,462 | 7 | 56 | 31 | 83 | 50 | 102 | 66 | 85 | 44 | 111 | 14 | 7 | 3.1 | 1.7 | 0.8 | 0.3 | 0.2 | * | 0.1 | * | 0.0 | * | * | 0.8 | 7.0 |
| **Ceylon:** | | | | | | | | | | | | | | | | | | | | | | | | | | | | |
| Colombo | 06 54N | 79 52E | 22 | 25 | 86 | 72 | 88 | 76 | 85 | 77 | 85 | 75 | 99 | 59 | 40 | 3.5 | 2.7 | 5.8 | 9.1 | 14.6 | 8.8 | 5.3 | 4.3 | 6.3 | 13.7 | 12.4 | 5.8 | 92.3 |
| **East Pakistan:** | | | | | | | | | | | | | | | | | | | | | | | | | | | | |
| Dacca | 23 46N | 90 23E | 24 | 60 | 77 | 56 | 92 | 74 | 88 | 79 | 88 | 75 | 108 | 43 | 61 | 0.3 | 1.2 | 2.4 | 5.4 | 9.6 | 12.4 | 13.0 | 13.3 | 9.8 | 5.3 | 1.0 | 0.2 | 73.9 |

(See footnotes at end of tables)

| Country and Station | Latitude | Longitude | Elevation (Feet) | Temp. Length of Record (Year) | Jan Max °F | Jan Min °F | Apr Max °F | Apr Min °F | Jul Max °F | Jul Min °F | Oct Max °F | Oct Min °F | Extreme Max °F | Extreme Min °F | Precip. Length of Record (Year) | Jan In. | Feb In. | Mar In. | Apr In. | May In. | Jun In. | Jul In. | Aug In. | Sep In. | Oct In. | Nov In. | Dec In. | Year In. |
|---|---|---|---|---|---|---|---|---|---|---|---|---|---|---|---|---|---|---|---|---|---|---|---|---|---|---|---|---|
| **India:** | | | | | | | | | | | | | | | | | | | | | | | | | | | | |
| Ahmadabad | 23 03N | 72 37E | 180 | 45 | 85 | 58 | 104 | 75 | 93 | 79 | 97 | 73 | 118 | 36 | 45 | * | 0.1 | 0.1 | * | 0.4 | 3.7 | 12.2 | 8.1 | 4.2 | 0.4 | 0.1 | * | 29.3 |
| Bangalore | 12 57N | 77 40E | 2,937 | 60 | 80 | 57 | 93 | 69 | 81 | 66 | 82 | 65 | 102 | 46 | 60 | 0.2 | 0.3 | 0.4 | 1.6 | 4.2 | 2.9 | 3.9 | 5.0 | 6.7 | 5.9 | 2.7 | 0.4 | 34.2 |
| Bombay | 19 06N | 72 51E | 27 | 60 | 88 | 62 | 93 | 74 | 88 | 75 | 93 | 73 | 110 | 46 | 60 | 0.1 | 0.1 | 0.1 | * | 0.7 | 19.1 | 24.3 | 13.4 | 10.4 | 2.5 | 0.5 | 0.1 | 71.2 |
| Calcutta | 22 32N | 88 20E | 21 | 60 | 80 | 55 | 97 | 76 | 88 | 79 | 89 | 74 | 111 | 44 | 60 | 0.4 | 1.2 | 1.4 | 1.7 | 5.5 | 11.7 | 12.8 | 12.9 | 9.9 | 4.5 | 0.8 | 0.2 | 63.0 |
| Cherrapunji | 25 15N | 91 44E | 4,309 | 35 | 60 | 46 | 71 | 59 | 72 | 65 | 72 | 61 | 87 | 33 | 35 | 0.7 | 2.1 | 7.3 | 26.2 | 50.4 | 106.1 | 96.3 | 70.1 | 43.3 | 19.4 | 2.7 | 0.5 | 425.1 |
| Hyderabad | 17 27N | 78 28E | 1,741 | 50 | 85 | 59 | 101 | 75 | 87 | 73 | 88 | 68 | 112 | 43 | 45 | 0.3 | 0.4 | 0.5 | 1.2 | 1.1 | 4.4 | 6.0 | 5.3 | 6.5 | 2.5 | 1.1 | 0.3 | 29.6 |
| Jalpaiguri | 26 32N | 88 43E | 272 | 50 | 74 | 50 | 90 | 68 | 89 | 77 | 87 | 70 | 104 | 36 | 50 | 0.3 | 0.7 | 1.3 | 3.7 | 11.8 | 25.9 | 32.2 | 25.3 | 21.2 | 5.6 | 0.5 | 0.2 | 128.7 |
| Lucknow | 26 45N | 80 52E | 400 | 60 | 74 | 47 | 101 | 71 | 92 | 80 | 91 | 67 | 119 | 34 | 60 | 0.8 | 0.7 | 0.3 | 0.3 | 0.8 | 4.5 | 12.0 | 11.5 | 7.4 | 1.3 | 0.2 | 0.3 | 40.1 |
| Madras | 13 04N | 80 15E | 51 | 60 | 85 | 67 | 95 | 78 | 96 | 79 | 90 | 75 | 113 | 57 | 60 | 1.4 | 0.4 | 0.3 | 0.7 | 2.6 | 3.6 | 3.6 | 4.6 | 4.7 | 12.0 | 14.0 | 5.5 | 50.0 |
| Mormugao | 15 22N | 73 49E | 157 | 30 | 70 | 70 | 88 | 78 | 83 | 79 | 86 | 75 | 98 | 59 | 30 | * | * | * | 0.7 | 2.6 | 29.6 | 31.2 | 15.9 | 9.5 | 3.8 | 1.3 | 0.2 | 94.8 |
| New Delhi | 28 35N | 77 12E | 695 | 10 | 71 | 43 | 97 | 68 | 95 | 80 | 93 | 64 | 115 | 31 | 75 | 0.9 | 0.7 | 0.5 | 0.3 | 0.5 | 2.9 | 7.1 | 6.8 | 4.6 | 0.4 | 0.1 | 0.4 | 25.2 |
| Silchar | 24 49N | 92 48E | 95 | 60 | 78 | 52 | 88 | 69 | 90 | 77 | 88 | 72 | 103 | 41 | 53 | 0.8 | 2.1 | 7.9 | 14.3 | 15.6 | 21.7 | 19.7 | 19.7 | 14.4 | 6.5 | 1.4 | 0.4 | 124.5 |
| **Indian Ocean Islands:** | | | | | | | | | | | | | | | | | | | | | | | | | | | | |
| Port Blair, Andaman Is. | 11 40N | 92 43E | 261 | 60 | 84 | 72 | 89 | 75 | 84 | 75 | 84 | 74 | 97 | 62 | 60 | 1.8 | 1.1 | 1.1 | 2.4 | 15.1 | 21.1 | 15.4 | 16.3 | 17.4 | 12.5 | 10.5 | 7.9 | 123.2 |
| Amini Divi, Laccadive Is. | 11 07N | 72 44E | 13 | 29 | 86 | 74 | 92 | 80 | 86 | 77 | 86 | 77 | 99 | 65 | 30 | 0.7 | * | * | 1.5 | 3.7 | 14.3 | 12.0 | 7.7 | 6.3 | 5.8 | 2.6 | 1.3 | 56.0 |
| Minicoy, Maldive Is. | 08 18N | 73 00E | 9 | 20 | 85 | 73 | 87 | 80 | 85 | 76 | 85 | 76 | 98 | 63 | 50 | 1.8 | 0.7 | 0.9 | 2.3 | 7.0 | 11.6 | 8.9 | 7.8 | 6.3 | 7.3 | 5.5 | 3.4 | 63.5 |
| Car Nicobar, Nicobar Is. | 09 09N | 92 49E | 47 | 13 | 86 | 77 | 90 | 77 | 86 | 77 | 85 | 75 | 95 | 66 | 30 | 3.9 | 1.2 | 2.1 | 3.5 | 12.5 | 12.4 | 9.3 | 10.2 | 12.9 | 11.6 | 11.4 | 7.8 | 98.8 |
| **Iran:** | | | | | | | | | | | | | | | | | | | | | | | | | | | | |
| Abadan | 30 21N | 48 13E | 10 | 12 | 64 | 44 | 90 | 62 | 112 | 81 | 98 | 63 | 127 | 24 | 10 | 1.5 | 1.7 | 0.6 | 0.8 | 0.1 | 0.0 | 0.0 | 0.0 | 0.0 | 0.1 | 1.0 | 1.8 | 7.6 |
| Esfahan (Isfahan) | 32 37N | 51 41E | 5,238 | 45 | 47 | 25 | 72 | 46 | 98 | 67 | 78 | 47 | 108 | -4 | 45 | 0.7 | 0.6 | 0.8 | 0.6 | 0.3 | * | 0.1 | * | * | 0.1 | 0.4 | 0.7 | 4.4 |
| Kermanshah | 34 19N | 47 07E | 4,331 | 15 | 45 | 23 | 68 | 38 | 99 | 56 | 79 | 38 | 108 | -13 | 15 | 2.6 | 2.3 | 2.8 | 2.2 | 1.6 | * | * | * | * | 0.4 | 2.0 | 2.4 | 16.4 |
| Rezaiyeh | 37 32N | 45 05E | 4,364 | 3 | 32 | 17 | 67 | 45 | 91 | 64 | 67 | 47 | 99 | -11 | 3 | 1.9 | 2.3 | 2.0 | 1.7 | 1.2 | 0.5 | * | 0.1 | 0.2 | 1.5 | 0.8 | 1.6 | 13.8 |
| Tehran | 35 41N | 51 19E | 3,937 | 24 | 45 | 27 | 71 | 49 | 99 | 72 | 76 | 53 | 109 | -5 | 33 | 1.8 | 1.5 | 1.8 | 1.4 | 0.5 | 0.1 | 0.1 | 0.1 | 0.1 | 0.3 | 0.8 | 1.2 | 9.7 |
| **Iraq:** | | | | | | | | | | | | | | | | | | | | | | | | | | | | |
| Baghdad | 33 20N | 44 24E | 111 | 15 | 60 | 39 | 85 | 57 | 110 | 76 | 92 | 61 | 121 | 18 | 15 | 0.9 | 1.0 | 1.1 | 0.5 | 0.1 | * | * | * | * | 0.1 | 0.8 | 1.0 | 5.5 |
| Basra | 30 34N | 47 47E | 8 | 10 | 64 | 45 | 85 | 63 | 104 | 81 | 94 | 64 | 123 | 24 | 10 | 1.4 | 1.1 | 1.2 | 1.2 | 0.2 | 0.0 | * | * | * | * | 1.4 | 0.8 | 7.3 |
| Mosul | 36 19N | 43 09E | 730 | 26 | 54 | 35 | 77 | 49 | 109 | 72 | 88 | 51 | 124 | 12 | 29 | 2.8 | 3.1 | 2.1 | 1.9 | 0.7 | * | * | * | * | 0.2 | 1.9 | 2.4 | 15.2 |
| **Israel:** | | | | | | | | | | | | | | | | | | | | | | | | | | | | |
| Haifa | 32 48N | 35 02E | 23 | 16 | 65 | 49 | 77 | 58 | 88 | 75 | 85 | 68 | 112 | 27 | 30 | 6.9 | 4.3 | 1.6 | 1.0 | 0.2 | * | * | * | 0.1 | 1.0 | 3.7 | 7.3 | 26.2 |
| Jerusalem | 31 47N | 35 13E | 2,654 | 19 | 55 | 41 | 73 | 50 | 87 | 63 | 81 | 59 | 107 | 26 | 50 | 5.1 | 4.7 | 2.9 | 0.9 | 0.1 | * | 0.0 | 0.0 | * | 0.3 | 2.2 | 3.5 | 19.7 |
| Tel Aviv | 32 06N | 34 46E | 33 | 10 | 64 | 50 | 70 | 57 | 82 | 72 | 79 | 65 | 102 | 34 | 10 | 4.9 | 2.7 | 2.0 | 0.7 | 0.1 | 0.0 | 0.0 | 0.0 | 0.1 | 0.4 | 4.1 | 6.1 | 21.1 |
| **Jammu/Kashmir:** | | | | | | | | | | | | | | | | | | | | | | | | | | | | |
| Srinagar | 33 58N | 74 46E | 5,458 | 50 | 41 | 24 | 67 | 45 | 88 | 64 | 74 | 41 | 106 | -4 | 50 | 2.9 | 2.8 | 3.6 | 3.7 | 2.4 | 1.4 | 2.3 | 2.4 | 1.5 | 1.2 | 0.4 | 1.3 | 25.9 |
| **Jordan:** | | | | | | | | | | | | | | | | | | | | | | | | | | | | |
| Amman | 31 58N | 35 59E | 2,547 | 25 | 54 | 39 | 73 | 49 | 89 | 65 | 81 | 57 | 109 | 21 | 25 | 2.7 | 2.9 | 1.2 | 0.6 | 0.2 | 0.0 | 0.0 | 0.0 | * | 0.2 | 1.3 | 1.8 | 10.9 |
| **Kuwait:** | | | | | | | | | | | | | | | | | | | | | | | | | | | | |
| Kuwait | 29 21N | 48 00E | 16 | 14 | 61 | 49 | 83 | 68 | 103 | 86 | 91 | 73 | 119 | 33 | 10 | 0.9 | 0.9 | 1.1 | 0.2 | * | 0.0 | 0.0 | 0.0 | 0.0 | 0.1 | 0.6 | 1.1 | 5.1 |
| **Lebanon:** | | | | | | | | | | | | | | | | | | | | | | | | | | | | |
| Beirut | 33 54N | 35 28E | 111 | 62 | 62 | 51 | 72 | 58 | 87 | 73 | 81 | 69 | 107 | 30 | 71 | 7.5 | 6.2 | 3.7 | 2.2 | 0.7 | 0.1 | * | * | 0.2 | 2.0 | 5.2 | 7.3 | 35.1 |

| COUNTRY AND STATION | LATITUDE | LONGITUDE | ELEVATION (FEET) | TEMP. LENGTH OF RECORD (YEAR) | JAN MAX | JAN MIN | APR MAX | APR MIN | JUL MAX | JUL MIN | OCT MAX | OCT MIN | EXTREME MAX | EXTREME MIN | PRECIP. LENGTH OF RECORD (YEAR) | JAN | FEB | MAR | APR | MAY | JUN | JUL | AUG | SEP | OCT | NOV | DEC | YEAR |
|---|---|---|---|---|---|---|---|---|---|---|---|---|---|---|---|---|---|---|---|---|---|---|---|---|---|---|---|---|
| **Nepal:** | | | | | | | | | | | | | | | | | | | | | | | | | | | | |
| Katmandu | 27 42N | 85 22E | 4,423 | 27 | 65 | 36 | 84 | 53 | 84 | 69 | 80 | 56 | 99 | 27 | 9 | 0.6 | 1.6 | 0.9 | 2.3 | 4.8 | 9.7 | 14.7 | 13.6 | 6.1 | 1.5 | 0.3 | 0.1 | 56.2 |
| **Oman and Muscat:** | | | | | | | | | | | | | | | | | | | | | | | | | | | | |
| Muscat | 23 37N | 58 35E | 15 | 23 | 77 | 66 | 90 | 78 | 97 | 87 | 93 | 80 | 116 | 51 | 38 | 1.1 | 0.7 | 0.4 | 0.4 | * | 0.1 | * | * | 0.0 | 0.1 | 0.4 | 0.7 | 3.9 |
| **Pakistan (West):** | | | | | | | | | | | | | | | | | | | | | | | | | | | | |
| Karachi | 24 48N | 66 59E | 13 | 43 | 77 | 55 | 90 | 73 | 91 | 81 | 91 | 72 | 118 | 39 | 59 | 0.5 | 0.4 | 0.3 | 0.1 | 0.1 | 0.7 | 3.2 | 1.6 | 0.5 | 0.1 | 0.1 | 0.2 | 7.8 |
| Multan | 30 11N | 71 25E | 400 | 60 | 68 | 42 | 95 | 68 | 102 | 86 | 94 | 64 | 122 | 29 | 60 | 0.4 | 0.4 | 0.4 | 0.3 | 0.3 | 0.6 | 2.0 | 1.8 | 0.5 | 0.1 | 0.1 | 0.2 | 7.1 |
| Rawalpindi | 33 35N | 73 03E | 1,676 | 60 | 62 | 38 | 86 | 59 | 98 | 77 | 89 | 57 | 118 | 25 | 60 | 2.5 | 2.5 | 2.7 | 1.9 | 1.3 | 2.3 | 8.1 | 9.2 | 3.9 | 0.6 | 0.3 | 1.2 | 36.5 |
| **Saudi Arabia:** | | | | | | | | | | | | | | | | | | | | | | | | | | | | |
| Dhahran | 26 16N | 50 10E | 78 | 10 | 69 | 54 | 90 | 70 | 107 | 86 | 95 | 73 | 120 | 40 | 10 | 1.1 | 0.6 | 0.4 | 0.2 | 0.1 | 0.0 | 0.0 | 0.0 | 0.0 | 0.0 | 0.2 | 0.9 | 3.5 |
| Jidda | 21 28N | 39 10E | 20 | 5 | 84 | 66 | 91 | 70 | 99 | 79 | 95 | 73 | 117 | 49 | 5 | 0.2 | * | * | * | * | 0.0 | * | * | * | * | 1.0 | 1.2 | 2.5 |
| Riyadh | 24 39N | 46 42E | 1,938 | 3 | 70 | 46 | 89 | 64 | 107 | 78 | 94 | 61 | 113 | 19 | 3 | 0.1 | 0.8 | 0.9 | 1.0 | 0.4 | * | 0.0 | * | 0.0 | 0.0 | * | * | 3.2 |
| **Syria:** | | | | | | | | | | | | | | | | | | | | | | | | | | | | |
| Deir Ez Zor | 35 21N | 40 09E | 699 | 5 | 53 | 35 | 80 | 52 | 105 | 78 | 86 | 56 | 114 | 16 | 8 | 1.6 | 0.8 | 0.3 | 0.8 | 0.1 | * | 0.0 | 0.0 | 0.0 | 0.2 | 1.5 | 0.9 | 6.2 |
| Dimashq (Damascus) | 33 30N | 36 20E | 2,362 | 13 | 53 | 36 | 75 | 49 | 96 | 64 | 81 | 54 | 113 | 21 | 7 | 1.7 | 1.7 | 0.3 | 0.5 | 0.1 | * | * | 0.0 | 0.7 | 0.4 | 1.6 | 1.6 | 8.6 |
| Halab (Aleppo) | 36 14N | 37 08E | 1,280 | 8 | 50 | 34 | 75 | 48 | 97 | 69 | 81 | 54 | 117 | 9 | 10 | 3.5 | 2.5 | 1.5 | 1.1 | 0.3 | * | 0.0 | 0.0 | * | 1.0 | 2.2 | 3.3 | 15.5 |
| **Trucial Kingdoms:** | | | | | | | | | | | | | | | | | | | | | | | | | | | | |
| Sharjah | 25 20N | 55 24E | 18 | 11 | 74 | 54 | 86 | 65 | 100 | 82 | 92 | 71 | 118 | 37 | 12 | 0.9 | 0.9 | 0.4 | 0.2 | 0.0 | 0.0 | 0.0 | 0.0 | 0.0 | 0.0 | 0.4 | 1.4 | 4.2 |
| **Turkey:** | | | | | | | | | | | | | | | | | | | | | | | | | | | | |
| Adana | 36 59N | 35 18E | 82 | 21 | 57 | 39 | 74 | 51 | 93 | 71 | 84 | 58 | 109 | 19 | 31 | 4.3 | 4.0 | 2.5 | 1.6 | 2.0 | 0.7 | 0.2 | 0.2 | 0.7 | 1.9 | 2.4 | 3.8 | 24.3 |
| Ankara | 39 57N | 32 53E | 2,825 | 26 | 39 | 24 | 63 | 40 | 86 | 59 | 69 | 44 | 104 | -13 | 24 | 1.3 | 1.2 | 1.3 | 1.3 | 1.9 | 1.0 | 0.5 | 0.4 | 0.7 | 0.9 | 1.2 | 1.9 | 13.6 |
| Erzurum | 39 54N | 41 16E | 6,402 | 16 | 24 | 8 | 50 | 32 | 78 | 53 | 69 | 37 | 93 | -22 | 16 | 1.4 | 1.6 | 2.0 | 2.5 | 3.1 | 2.1 | 1.3 | 0.9 | 1.1 | 2.3 | 1.8 | 1.1 | 21.2 |
| Izmir (Smyrna) | 38 27N | 27 15E | 92 | 39 | 55 | 39 | 68 | 49 | 92 | 69 | 76 | 55 | 108 | 20 | 58 | 4.4 | 3.3 | 3.0 | 1.7 | 1.3 | 0.6 | 0.2 | 0.2 | 0.8 | 2.1 | 3.3 | 4.8 | 25.5 |
| Samsun | 41 17N | 36 19E | 131 | 24 | 50 | 38 | 59 | 45 | 79 | 65 | 69 | 56 | 103 | 20 | 27 | 2.9 | 2.6 | 2.7 | 2.3 | 1.8 | 1.5 | 1.5 | 1.3 | 2.4 | 3.2 | 3.5 | 2.4 | 29.1 |
| **Yemen:** | | | | | | | | | | | | | | | | | | | | | | | | | | | | |
| Kamaran I. | 15 20N | 42 37E | 20 | 26 | 82 | 74 | 89 | 79 | 98 | 85 | 93 | 82 | 105 | 66 | 21 | 0.2 | 0.1 | 0.1 | 0.1 | 0.1 | * | 0.5 | 0.7 | 0.1 | 0.1 | 0.4 | 0.9 | 3.4 |

## AUSTRALIA & PACIFIC ISLANDS

| COUNTRY AND STATION | LATITUDE | LONGITUDE | ELEVATION (FEET) | TEMP. LENGTH OF RECORD (YEAR) | JAN MAX | JAN MIN | APR MAX | APR MIN | JUL MAX | JUL MIN | OCT MAX | OCT MIN | EXTREME MAX | EXTREME MIN | PRECIP. LENGTH OF RECORD (YEAR) | JAN | FEB | MAR | APR | MAY | JUN | JUL | AUG | SEP | OCT | NOV | DEC | YEAR |
|---|---|---|---|---|---|---|---|---|---|---|---|---|---|---|---|---|---|---|---|---|---|---|---|---|---|---|---|---|
| **Australia:** | | | | | | | | | | | | | | | | | | | | | | | | | | | | |
| Adelaide | 34 57S | 138 32E | 20 | 86 | 86 | 61 | 73 | 55 | 59 | 45 | 73 | 51 | 118 | 32 | 104 | 0.8 | 0.7 | 1.0 | 1.8 | 2.7 | 3.0 | 2.6 | 2.6 | 2.1 | 1.7 | 1.1 | 1.0 | 21.1 |
| Alice Springs | 23 48S | 133 53E | 1,791 | 62 | 97 | 70 | 81 | 54 | 67 | 39 | 88 | 58 | 111 | 19 | 30 | 1.7 | 1.3 | 1.1 | 0.4 | 0.6 | 0.5 | 0.3 | 0.3 | 0.3 | 0.7 | 1.2 | 1.5 | 9.9 |
| Bourke | 30 05S | 145 58E | 361 | 63 | 99 | 70 | 82 | 55 | 65 | 40 | 85 | 56 | 125 | 25 | 72 | 1.4 | 1.5 | 1.1 | 1.1 | 1.0 | 1.1 | 0.9 | 0.8 | 0.8 | 0.9 | 1.2 | 1.4 | 13.2 |
| Brisbane | 27 25S | 153 05E | 17 | 91 | 85 | 69 | 79 | 61 | 68 | 49 | 80 | 60 | 110 | 35 | 91 | 6.4 | 6.3 | 5.7 | 3.7 | 2.8 | 2.6 | 2.2 | 1.9 | 1.9 | 2.5 | 3.7 | 5.0 | 44.7 |
| Broome | 17 57S | 122 13E | 56 | 50 | 92 | 77 | 93 | 72 | 82 | 58 | 91 | 72 | 113 | 40 | 50 | 6.3 | 5.8 | 3.9 | 1.2 | 0.6 | 0.3 | 0.2 | 0.1 | * | * | 0.6 | 3.3 | 22.9 |
| Burketown | 17 45S | 139 33E | 30 | 31 | 93 | 77 | 91 | 69 | 82 | 55 | 93 | 70 | 110 | 40 | 53 | 8.2 | 6.3 | 5.2 | 1.0 | 0.2 | 0.3 | * | * | * | 0.2 | 1.5 | 4.4 | 27.5 |
| Canberra | 35 18S | 149 11E | 1,886 | 23 | 82 | 55 | 67 | 44 | 52 | 33 | 68 | 43 | 109 | 14 | 25 | 1.9 | 1.7 | 2.2 | 1.6 | 1.8 | 2.1 | 1.8 | 2.2 | 1.6 | 2.2 | 1.9 | 2.0 | 23.0 |
| Carnarvon | 24 53S | 113 40E | 13 | 43 | 88 | 72 | 84 | 66 | 71 | 51 | 78 | 61 | 118 | 37 | 57 | 0.4 | 0.7 | 0.7 | 0.6 | 1.5 | 2.4 | 1.6 | 0.7 | 0.2 | 0.1 | * | 0.2 | 9.1 |
| Cloncurry | 20 40S | 140 30E | 622 | 32 | 99 | 77 | 90 | 67 | 77 | 51 | 95 | 68 | 127 | 35 | 59 | 4.4 | 4.2 | 2.4 | 0.7 | 0.5 | 0.6 | 0.3 | 0.1 | 0.3 | 0.5 | 1.3 | 2.7 | 18.0 |
| Esperance | 33 50S | 121 55E | 14 | 44 | 77 | 60 | 72 | 54 | 62 | 45 | 68 | 50 | 117 | 31 | 60 | 0.7 | 0.7 | 1.2 | 1.8 | 3.3 | 4.1 | 4.0 | 3.8 | 2.7 | 2.2 | 1.0 | 0.9 | 26.4 |
| Laverton | 28 40S | 122 23E | 1,510 | 30 | 96 | 69 | 77 | 57 | 64 | 41 | 82 | 55 | 115 | 25 | 30 | 0.8 | 1.8 | 1.6 | 0.8 | 0.9 | 0.7 | 0.6 | 0.5 | 0.2 | 0.3 | 0.8 | 0.8 | 8.8 |
| Melbourne | 37 49S | 144 58E | 115 | 88 | 78 | 57 | 68 | 51 | 56 | 42 | 67 | 48 | 114 | 27 | 88 | 1.9 | 1.8 | 2.2 | 2.3 | 2.1 | 2.1 | 1.9 | 1.9 | 2.3 | 2.6 | 2.3 | 2.3 | 25.7 |
| Mundiwindi | 23 52S | 120 10E | 1,840 | 15 | 101 | 64 | 87 | 61 | 70 | 41 | 89 | 58 | 112 | 22 | 15 | 1.0 | 1.9 | 2.0 | 0.8 | 0.6 | 0.9 | 0.1 | 0.3 | 0.3 | 0.5 | 0.5 | 1.2 | 10.1 |

(See footnotes at end of tables)

| COUNTRY AND STATION | LATITUDE | LONGITUDE | ELE-VATION (FEET) | TEMP. LENGTH OF RECORD (YEAR) | JAN MAX | JAN MIN | APR MAX | APR MIN | JUL MAX | JUL MIN | OCT MAX | OCT MIN | EXTREME MAX | EXTREME MIN | PRECIP. LENGTH OF RECORD (YEAR) | JAN (IN.) | FEB (IN.) | MAR (IN.) | APR (IN.) | MAY (IN.) | JUN (IN.) | JUL (IN.) | AUG (IN.) | SEP (IN.) | OCT (IN.) | NOV (IN.) | DEC (IN.) | YEAR (IN.) |
|---|---|---|---|---|---|---|---|---|---|---|---|---|---|---|---|---|---|---|---|---|---|---|---|---|---|---|---|---|
| Perth | 31 56S | 115 58E | 64 | 44 | 85 | 63 | 76 | 57 | 63 | 48 | 70 | 53 | 112 | 31 | 63 | 0.3 | 0.4 | 0.8 | 1.7 | 5.1 | 7.1 | 6.7 | 5.7 | 3.4 | 2.2 | 0.8 | 0.5 | 34.7 |
| Port Darwin | 12 25S | 130 52E | 104 | 58 | 90 | 77 | 92 | 76 | 87 | 67 | 93 | 77 | 105 | 55 | 70 | 15.2 | 12.3 | 10.0 | 3.8 | 0.6 | 0.1 | * | 0.1 | 0.5 | 2.0 | 4.7 | 9.4 | 58.7 |
| Sydney | 33 52S | 151 02E | 62 | 87 | 78 | 65 | 71 | 58 | 60 | 46 | 71 | 56 | 114 | 35 | 87 | 3.5 | 4.0 | 5.0 | 5.3 | 5.0 | 4.6 | 4.6 | 3.0 | 2.9 | 2.8 | 2.9 | 2.9 | 46.5 |
| Thursday Island | 10 35S | 142 13E | 200 | 31 | 87 | 77 | 86 | 77 | 82 | 73 | 86 | 76 | 98 | 64 | 49 | 18.2 | 15.8 | 13.9 | 8.0 | 1.6 | 0.5 | 0.4 | 0.2 | 0.1 | 0.3 | 1.5 | 7.0 | 67.5 |
| Townsville | 19 15S | 146 46E | 18 | 31 | 87 | 76 | 84 | 70 | 75 | 59 | 83 | 71 | 110 | 39 | 67 | 10.9 | 11.2 | 7.2 | 3.3 | 1.3 | 1.4 | 0.6 | 0.5 | 0.7 | 1.3 | 1.9 | 5.4 | 45.7 |
| William Creek | 28 55S | 136 21E | 247 | 39 | 96 | 69 | 80 | 55 | 65 | 41 | 84 | 56 | 119 | 25 | 30 | 0.5 | 0.6 | 0.3 | 0.3 | 0.3 | 0.5 | 0.2 | 0.3 | 0.3 | 0.5 | 0.7 | 0.7 | 5.0 |
| Windorah | 25 26S | 142 36E | 390 | 29 | 101 | 74 | 86 | 59 | 70 | 43 | 91 | 61 | 116 | 26 | 50 | 1.4 | 1.6 | 1.6 | 0.9 | 0.8 | 0.8 | 0.5 | 0.4 | 0.5 | 0.6 | 0.9 | 1.4 | 11.4 |
| **Tasmania:** | | | | | | | | | | | | | | | | | | | | | | | | | | | | |
| Hobart | 42 53S | 147 20E | 177 | 70 | 71 | 53 | 63 | 48 | 52 | 40 | 63 | 46 | 105 | 28 | 100 | 1.9 | 1.5 | 1.8 | 1.9 | 1.8 | 2.2 | 2.1 | 1.9 | 2.1 | 2.3 | 2.4 | 2.1 | 24.0 |
| **New Zealand:** | | | | | | | | | | | | | | | | | | | | | | | | | | | | |
| Auckland | 37 00S | 174 47E | 23 | 36 | 73 | 60 | 67 | 56 | 56 | 46 | 63 | 52 | 90 | 33 | 92 | 3.1 | 3.7 | 3.2 | 3.8 | 5.0 | 5.4 | 5.7 | 4.6 | 4.0 | 4.0 | 3.5 | 3.1 | 49.1 |
| Christchurch | 43 29S | 172 32E | 118 | 52 | 70 | 53 | 62 | 45 | 50 | 35 | 62 | 44 | 96 | 21 | 64 | 2.2 | 1.7 | 1.9 | 1.9 | 2.6 | 2.6 | 2.7 | 1.9 | 1.8 | 1.7 | 1.9 | 2.2 | 25.1 |
| Dunedin | 45 55S | 170 12E | 4 | 77 | 66 | 50 | 59 | 45 | 48 | 37 | 59 | 42 | 94 | 23 | 77 | 3.4 | 2.8 | 3.0 | 2.8 | 3.2 | 3.2 | 3.1 | 3.0 | 2.7 | 3.0 | 3.2 | 3.5 | 36.9 |
| Wellington | 41 17S | 174 46E | 415 | 66 | 69 | 56 | 63 | 51 | 53 | 42 | 60 | 48 | 88 | 29 | 79 | 3.2 | 3.2 | 3.2 | 3.8 | 4.6 | 4.6 | 5.4 | 4.6 | 3.8 | 4.0 | 3.5 | 3.5 | 47.4 |
| **PACIFIC ISLANDS:** | | | | | | | | | | | | | | | | | | | | | | | | | | | | |
| Canton, Phoenix Is. | 02 46S | 171 43W | 9 | 12 | 88 | 78 | 89 | 78 | 89 | 78 | 90 | 78 | 98 | 70 | 30 | 2.6 | 2.2 | 2.5 | 3.6 | 4.3 | 2.6 | 2.6 | 2.5 | 1.2 | 1.1 | 1.6 | 2.6 | 29.4 |
| Guam, Marianas Is. | 13 33N | 144 50E | 361 | 30 | 84 | 72 | 86 | 73 | 87 | 72 | 86 | 73 | 95 | 54 | 30 | 4.6 | 3.5 | 2.6 | 3.0 | 4.2 | 5.9 | 9.0 | 12.8 | 13.4 | 13.1 | 10.3 | 6.1 | 88.5 |
| Honolulu, Hawaii | 21 20N | 157 55W | 7 | 30 | 79 | 66 | 80 | 68 | 85 | 73 | 84 | 72 | 93 | 56 | 30 | 3.8 | 3.3 | 2.9 | 1.3 | 1.0 | 0.3 | 0.4 | 0.9 | 1.0 | 1.8 | 2.2 | 2.9 | 21.9 |
| Iwo Jima, Bonin Is. | 24 47N | 141 19E | 353 | 15 | 71 | 64 | 77 | 69 | 86 | 78 | 84 | 76 | 95 | 46 | 17 | 3.2 | 2.5 | 2.1 | 3.7 | 4.9 | 4.0 | 6.4 | 6.5 | 4.6 | 5.9 | 4.8 | 3.0 | 52.8 |
| Madang, New Guinea | 05 12S | 145 47E | 19 | 19 | 87 | 75 | 88 | 74 | 88 | 74 | 88 | 75 | 98 | 62 | 20 | 12.1 | 11.9 | 14.9 | 16.9 | 15.1 | 10.8 | 7.6 | 4.8 | 5.3 | 10.0 | 13.3 | 14.5 | 137.2 |
| Midway Is. | 28 13N | 177 23W | 29 | 21 | 69 | 62 | 71 | 64 | 81 | 74 | 79 | 72 | 92 | 46 | 20 | 3.7 | 3.7 | 3.1 | 2.5 | 1.9 | 1.3 | 1.3 | 3.9 | 3.7 | 3.7 | 3.6 | 4.2 | 40.7 |
| Naha, Okinawa | 26 12N | 127 39E | 96 | 30 | 67 | 56 | 76 | 64 | 89 | 77 | 81 | 69 | 92 | 41 | 30 | 5.3 | 5.4 | 6.1 | 6.1 | 8.9 | 10.0 | 7.1 | 10.0 | 7.1 | 6.6 | 3.6 | 4.3 | 82.8 |
| Noumea, New Caledonia | 22 16S | 166 27E | 246 | 24 | 86 | 72 | 83 | 70 | 76 | 62 | 80 | 65 | 99 | 52 | 52 | 3.7 | 5.1 | 5.7 | 5.2 | 4.4 | 3.7 | 3.6 | 2.6 | 2.5 | 2.0 | 2.4 | 2.6 | 43.5 |
| Pago Pago, Samoa | 14 19S | 170 43W | 29 | 2 | 87 | 75 | 87 | 76 | 83 | 74 | 85 | 75 | 98 | 67 | 41 | 24.5 | 20.5 | 19.2 | 16.5 | 15.4 | 12.3 | 10.0 | 8.2 | 13.1 | 14.9 | 19.2 | 19.8 | 193.6 |
| Ponape, Caroline Is. | 06 58N | 158 13E | 123 | 30 | 86 | 75 | 86 | 75 | 87 | 73 | 87 | 75 | 96 | 67 | 30 | 11.1 | 9.7 | 14.6 | 20.0 | 20.3 | 16.7 | 16.2 | 16.3 | 15.8 | 16.0 | 16.9 | 18.3 | 191.9 |
| Port Moresby, New Guinea | 09 29S | 147 09E | 126 | 29 | 89 | 76 | 89 | 73 | 83 | 73 | 86 | 75 | 98 | 64 | 38 | 7.0 | 7.6 | 6.7 | 4.2 | 2.5 | 1.3 | 1.4 | 0.7 | 1.0 | 1.4 | 4.4 | 4.4 | 39.8 |
| Rabaul, New Guinea | 04 13S | 152 11E | 28 | 19 | 90 | 73 | 90 | 73 | 89 | 73 | 92 | 73 | 100 | 65 | 24 | 14.8 | 10.4 | 10.2 | 10.0 | 5.2 | 3.3 | 5.1 | 3.7 | 3.5 | 5.1 | 7.1 | 10.1 | 88.8 |
| Suva, Fiji Is. | 18 08S | 178 26E | 20 | 43 | 86 | 74 | 84 | 73 | 79 | 68 | 81 | 70 | 98 | 55 | 43 | 11.4 | 10.7 | 14.5 | 12.2 | 10.1 | 6.7 | 4.9 | 8.3 | 7.7 | 8.3 | 9.8 | 12.5 | 117.1 |
| Tahiti, Society Is. | 17 33S | 149 36W | 7 | 23 | 89 | 72 | 89 | 72 | 86 | 68 | 87 | 76 | 93 | 61 | 27 | 13.2 | 11.5 | 6.5 | 6.8 | 4.9 | 3.2 | 2.6 | 1.9 | 2.3 | 3.4 | 6.5 | 11.9 | 74.7 |
| Tulagi, Solomon Is. | 09 05S | 160 10E | 8 | 20 | 88 | 76 | 88 | 76 | 86 | 77 | 87 | 76 | 96 | 68 | 37 | 14.3 | 15.8 | 15.0 | 10.0 | 8.1 | 6.8 | 7.6 | 8.7 | 8.0 | 8.7 | 10.0 | 10.4 | 123.4 |
| Wake Is. | 19 17N | 166 39E | 11 | 20 | 82 | 73 | 83 | 74 | 87 | 77 | 86 | 77 | 92 | 64 | 30 | 1.1 | 1.4 | 1.5 | 1.9 | 2.0 | 1.9 | 7.6 | 7.1 | 5.3 | 5.3 | 3.1 | 1.8 | 36.9 |
| Yap., Caroline Is. | 9 31N | 138 08E | 62 | 30 | 85 | 76 | 87 | 77 | 88 | 75 | 88 | 75 | 97 | 69 | 30 | 7.9 | 4.6 | 5.4 | 6.4 | 9.5 | 10.7 | 13.8 | 14.7 | 14.0 | 13.2 | 11.2 | 10.2 | 121.6 |

## ANTARCTICA

| COUNTRY AND STATION | LATITUDE | LONGITUDE | ELEVATION (FEET) | TEMPERATURE | | | | | | | | | | | | AVERAGE PRECIPITATION | | | | | | | | | | | | | |
|---|---|---|---|---|---|---|---|---|---|---|---|---|---|---|---|---|---|---|---|---|---|---|---|---|---|---|---|---|---|
| | | | | LENGTH OF RECORD (YEAR) | AVERAGE DAILY | | | | | | | | EXTREME | | LENGTH OF RECORD (YEAR) | JANUARY (IN.) | FEBRUARY (IN.) | MARCH (IN.) | APRIL (IN.) | MAY (IN.) | JUNE (IN.) | JULY (IN.) | AUGUST (IN.) | SEPTEMBER (IN.) | OCTOBER (IN.) | NOVEMBER (IN.) | DECEMBER (IN.) | YEAR (IN.) |
| | | | | | JANUARY MAX (°F) | JANUARY MIN (°F) | APRIL MAX (°F) | APRIL MIN (°F) | JULY MAX (°F) | JULY MIN (°F) | OCTOBER MAX (°F) | OCTOBER MIN (°F) | MAXIMUM (°F) | MINIMUM (°F) | | | | | | | | | | | | | | |
| Byrd Station | 80 01S | 119 32W | 5,095 | 6 | 10 | -2 | -11 | -30 | -25 | -45 | -15 | -33 | 31 | -82 | 6 | 0.4 | 0.4 | 0.2 | 0.3 | 0.4 | 0.5 | 0.7 | 0.7 | 0.3 | 0.7 | 0.0 | 0.3 | 4.9 |
| Ellsworth | 77 44S | 41 07W | 139 | 6 | 22 | 12 | -10 | -25 | -21 | -35 | -2 | -15 | 36 | -70 | 6 | 0.3 | 0.2 | 0.3 | 0.6 | 0.2 | 0.2 | 0.2 | 0.2 | 0.3 | 0.4 | 0.5 | 0.2 | 3.6 |
| McMurdo Station | 77 53S | 166 48W | 8 | 10 | 30 | 21 | -1 | -13 | -9 | -24 | 2 | -12 | 42 | -59 | 10 | 0.5 | 0.7 | 0.4 | 0.4 | 0.4 | 0.3 | 0.2 | 0.3 | 0.4 | 0.2 | 0.2 | 0.3 | 4.3 |
| South Pole Station | 89 59S | 000 00W | 9,186 | 5 | -16 | -23 | -66 | -79 | -67 | -81 | -55 | -64 | 6 | -107 | 5 | * | 0.1 | 0.0 | 0.0 | 0.0 | 0.0 | 0.0 | 0.0 | 0.0 | * | 0.0 | * | 0.1 |
| Wilkes | 66 16S | 110 31E | 31 | 7 | 34 | 28 | 17 | 9 | 8 | -3 | 16 | 6 | 46 | -35 | 7 | 0.5 | 0.4 | 1.7 | 1.1 | 1.4 | 1.2 | 1.3 | 0.8 | 1.5 | 1.2 | 0.8 | 0.3 | 12.2 |

NOTES

1. "Length of Record" refers to average daily maximum and minimum temperatures and precipitation. A standard period of the 30 years from 1931-1960 had been used for locations in the United States and some other countries. The length of record of extreme maximum and minimum temperatures includes all available years of data for a given location and is usually for a longer period.

2. * - Less than 0.05"

3. Except for Antarctica, amounts of solid precipitation such as snow or hail have been converted to their water equivalent. Because of the frequent occurrence of blowing snow, it has not been possible to determine the precise amount of precipitation actually falling in Antarctica. The values shown are the average amounts of solid snow accumulating in a given period as determined by snow markers. The liquid content of the accumulation is undetermined.

# WEATHER OF
# SELECTED
# U.S. CITIES

# LOCATION OF CITY REPORTS IN THIS SECTION
## (Arranged by State)

# HOW TO READ THESE REPORTS

### Weather in various cities

The information about the weather history of key cities is easy to find. The reports were planned to be informative, yet simple to read. The terminology used and the various standard formats are explained below.

The climate of each city is first presented as a narrative description, prepared by a local climatologist, whose job puts him in an unequalled position to know the weather of the particular area as no one ese would.

### The narrative report

Typically, the report begins with a description of the local area in terms of terrain, water bodies, and other topographical features because these features exercise key influences on the local weather. They are usually the cause if an area's weather differs sharply from weather in areas only a few miles away. For example, if a lake is near a city it will always influence the city's weather, and, in fact, may even create climatic differences from one part of the city to another, Mountains, swamps, even plowed fields exercise their influences on air masses as these masses move toward a city. The climatologist generally will describe these features and their climatic effect as the opening statement of the narrative report.

The report will usually discuss the range of temperatures in the city, rainfall tendencies, snowfall history, and other points. It will typically close with notes about the area's agricultural adaptability. The history of first fall frost and last spring freeze is usually described, along with suggestions about the types of crops for which the area is climatologically suited. This narrative may answer all of your questions without requiring that you study the tables of statistics.

### Statistics

The statistics are of two different kinds. The first type distills many years of history to give you a profile of the city's weather (e.g., NORMALS, MEANS AND EXTREMES). The second group offers data for individual years, going back thirty years to allow the user to see what variances have tended to occur, as well as to see to what extent weather conditions have repeated themselves.

There are several meteorological terms used in the table, many of which have been reduced to symbols. The following 30 notes are designed to clarify the information included in the tables on an item-by-item basis:

## TAMPA, FLORIDA City report (page 1)

Tampa is on west central coast of the Florida Peninsula. Very near the Gulf of Mexico at the upper end of Tampa Bay, land and sea breezes modify the subtropical climate. Major rivers flowing into the area are the Hillsborough, the Alafia, and the Little Manatee.

Winters are mild. Summers are long, rather warm and humid. Low temperatures are about 50 degrees in the winter and 70 degrees during the summer. Afternoon highs range from the low 70s in the winter to around 90 degrees from June through September. Invasions of cold northern air produce an occasional cool winter morning. Freezing temperatures occur on one or two mornings per year during December, January, and February. In some years no freezing temperatures occur. Temperatures rarely fail to recover to the 60s on the cooler winter days. Temperatures above the low 90s are uncommon because of the afternoon sea breeze and thunderstorms. An outstanding feature of the Tampa climate is the summer thunderstorm season. Most of the thunderstorms occur in the late afternoon hours from June through September. The resulting sudden drop in temperature from about 90 degrees to around 70 degrees makes for a pleasant change. Between a dry spring and a dry fall, some 30 inches of rain, about 60 percent of the annual total, falls during the summer months. Snowfall is very rare. Measurable snows under 1/2 inch have occurred only a few times in the last one hundred years.

A large part of the generally flat sandy land near the coast has an elevation of under 15 feet above sea level. This does make the area vulnerable to tidal surges. Tropical storms threaten the area on a few occasions most years. The greatest risk of hurricanes both during the months of June and ... many hurricanes ... 

### HOW TO READ THESE REPORTS (continued)

1. **DATA** provides precise geographic location and elevation of weather stations.

2. **NORMAL** as applied to temperature, degree days, and precipitation refers to the value of that particular element averaged over the period from 1951-1980. When the station does not have continuous records from an instrument site with the same "exposure," a "difference factor" between the old site and the new site is used to adjust the observed values to a common series. The difference factor is determined from a period of simultaneous measurements. The base period is revised every ten years by adding the averages for the most recent decade and dropping them for the first decade of the former normals for 1951-1980. *Normal* does not refer to "normalcy" or "expectation," but only to the actual averages for a particular thirty-year period.

## TAMPA, FLORIDA City report (page 2)

### NORMALS, MEANS AN...

**TABLE 1**

| | JAN | FEB | MAR | APR |
|---|---|---|---|---|
| ① LATITUDE: 27°58'N ③ LONGITUDE: 82°32'W ELEVATION | | | | |
| ② TEMPERATURE °F: Normals | | | | |
| ⑤ —Daily Maximum | 70.0 | 71.0 | 76.2 | 81 |
| ⑥ —Daily Minimum | 49.5 | 50.4 | 56.1 | 61 |
| —Monthly | 59.8 | 60.7 | 66.2 | 7 |
| ⑦ Extremes —Record Highest (39) | 84 1975 | 88 1971 | 91 1949 | |
| ⑧ —Year (39) | 21 1985 | 24 1958 | 29 1980 | |
| ⑨ —Record Lowest / —Year | | | | |
| ⑩ NORMAL DEGREE DAYS: Heating (base 65°F) | 228 | 186 | 87 | |
| ⑪ Cooling (base 65°F) | 66 | 68 | 124 | |
| ⑫ % OF POSSIBLE SUNSHINE | 66 | 66 | 71 | |
| ⑬ MEAN SKY COVER (tenths) Sunrise–Sunset (38) | 5.6 | 5.5 | 5.4 | |
| ⑭ MEAN NUMBER OF DAYS: Sunrise to Sunset (39) | | | | |
| ⑮ —Clear (39) | 9.6 | 9.1 | 10. | |
| —Partly Cloudy (39) | 9.9 | 9.1 | 10. | |
| —Cloudy (39) | 11.5 | 10.1 | 10 | |
| Precipitation .01 inches or more (39) | 6.4 | 6.8 | | |
| Snow,Ice pellets 1.0 inches or more (39) | 0.0 | 0.0 | | |
| (39) | 1.0 | 1.6 | | |
| Thunderstorms (39) | 5.7 | 2.9 | | |
| Heavy Fog Visibility 1/4 mile or less | 0.0 | 0.0 | | |
| Temperature °F —Maximum | | | | |
| ⑯ —90° and above (22) | 0.0 | 0.8 | | |
| ⑰ —32° and below (22) | 2.3 | 0.0 | | |
| ⑱ —Minimum —32° and below (22) | 0.0 | | | |
| ⑲ —0° and below (22) | | | | |
| ⑳ AVG. STATION PRESS.(mb) | 12 | 1019.9 | 1019.1 | |
| ㉑ RELATIVE HUMIDITY (%) Hour 01 (22) | 84 | 83 | | |
| Hour 07 (22) | 86 | 85 | | |
| Hour 13 (Local Time) (22) | 59 | 5 | | |
| Hour 19 (22) | 73 | 6 | | |
| ㉒ PRECIPITATION (inches): Water Equivalent —Normal (39) | 2.17 | 3. | | |
| ㉓ —Maximum Monthly (39) | 8.02 1948 | 7. 1 | | |
| —Year | 1950 | 0 1 | | |
| ㉔ —Minimum Monthly —Year (39) | T 3.29 1953 | | | |
| ㉕ —Maximum in 24 hrs —Year | | | | |
| Snow,Ice pellets —Maximum Monthly (39) | 0.2 1977 | | | |
| —Year (39) | 0.2 1977 | | | |
| ㉖ —Maximum in 24 hrs —Year | | | | |
| ㉗ WIND: Mean Speed (mph) (39) | 8.7 | | | |
| Prevailing Direction through 1963 | N | | | |
| ㉘ Fastest Obs. 1 Min. —Direction (33) | 2 3 | | | |
| —Speed (MPH) (33) | 195 | | | |
| ㉙ —Year Peak Gust —Direction | 2 2 | 19 | | |

## HOW TO READ THESE REPORTS (continued)

3. (Note "a") MEANS AND EXTREMES are based on the period of years in which observations have been made under comparable conditions of instrument exposure. Data are included for dates through 1985 unless otherwise noted. The DATE OF AN EXTREME is the *most recent* one in cases of repeated occurences.

4. LENGTH OF OBSERVATIONAL RECORD for *Means and Extremes* is based on the length of January data for the present instrument site exposure (15 equal 15 years). The length of the record is through 1985. The table *does not* give the all time *high* or *low* value if it was recorded at a *different site* within the area. The *Mean* (or average) values for *Relative Humidity, Wind, Sunshine, Sky Condition,* and the *Mean Number of Days* with the various other weather conditions listed are also based on length of record noted in each instance, down through 1985. Check the first column for each of these rows to read this length of record for each item.

5. AVERAGE of the HIGHEST TEMPERATURE (°F) on each day of the month and year for the *period 1951-1980*. This value is obtained by taking the sum of the highest temperature for each day of the period (adjusted for site exposure if necessary) and dividing by the number of days included.

6. AVERAGE of the LOWEST TEMPERATURE (°F) on each day of the month and year for the *period 1951-1980*.

7. AVERAGE of ALL DAILY TEMPERATURES (°F) for the month and year for the *period 1951-1980*; computed as being the temperature one-half way between the average daily maximum and minimum values in items 5 and 6 above.

8. EXTREMES—HIGHEST TEMPERATURE (°F) ever recorded during any month at present site exposure.

9. EXTREMES—LOWEST TEMPERATURE (°F) ever recorded during any month at present site exposure.

10. AVERAGE number of HEATING DEGREE DAYS for each month and year for the *period 1951-1980*. The statistic is based on the amount that the *Daily Mean Temperature* falls below 65°F. Each degree of mean temperature below 65 is counted as one *Heating Degree Day*. If the *Daily Mean Temperature* is 65 degrees or higher, the *Heating Degree Day* value for that day is zero. Monthly and annual sums are calculated for each period and averaged over the appropriate thirty years of record to establish these "normal" values. Compare this with *Cooling Degree Days*.

11. AVERAGE number of COOLING DEGREE DAYS for each month and year for the *period 1951-1980*. The concept of this statistic is the mirror image of the concept of *Heating Degree Days* and is based on the amount that the *Daily Mean Temperature* exceeds 65°F. Each degree of mean temperature above 65 is counted as one *Cooling Degree Day*. If the *Daily Mean Temperature* is 65 degrees or below, the *Cooling Degree Day* is zero. PLEASE NOTE: *Heating and Cooling Degree Days* are calculated independently and do not cancel each other out. Both concepts are discussed at length in the paragraph headed *Energy Consumption Indices* which follows note 30.

12. SUNSHINE—The average percent of daytime hours subject to direct radiation from the sun at the present site. The percentage is given without regard for the intensity of sunshine. That is, thin clouds, light haze, or other minor obstructions to direct solar rays may be present but would not mitigate the full counting of an hour.

13. VERTICAL OBSERVATION—Average amount of daytime sky obscured by any type of cover expressed in tenths (e.g.,4.8 equal 48/10...or 48%).

14. ACTIVITY LIMITING WEATHER—Average number of days in month with specified weather conditions based on *present exposure*. An (*) indicates less than ½ day.

15. CLOUDINESS—Average number of days in month at the *present site* with various amounts of cloud cover. *Clear* indicates average daytime cloudiness of 0.3 or less; *partly cloudy* indicates average daytime cloudiness between 0.4 and 0.7; *cloudy* indicates average daytime cloudiness of 0.8 or more.

16. VERY HOT DAYS—Average number of days in month and year when the temperatures at the *present site* 90° or above. (70°F or above at Alaskan stations.)

17. COLD DAYS—Average number of days at the *present site* when the temperatures remained below 32°F at all times.

18. FREEZING DAYS—Average number of days at the *present site* when the temperature dropped to a minimum of 32°F or below.

19. VERY COLD DAYS—Average number of days at *present site* when the minimum temperature was 0°F or below.

20. AVERAGE STATION PRESSURE—given in millibars.

| | | | | | | | | | | | | | | |
|---|---|---|---|---|---|---|---|---|---|---|---|---|---|---|
| (20) AVG. STATION PRESS.(mb) | 12 | 1019.9 | 1019.1 | 1017.6 | 1017.0 | 1015.5 | 1016.2 | 1017.6 | 1017.1 | 1015.4 | 1016.6 | 1018.5 | 1020.1 | 1017.6 |
| **RELATIVE HUMIDITY (%)** | | | | | | | | | | | | | | |
| (21) Hour 01 | 22 | 84 | 83 | 82 | 82 | 81 | 84 | 85 | 87 | 86 | 85 | 85 | 84 | 84 |
| Hour 07 | 22 | 86 | 85 | 86 | 87 | 86 | 87 | 88 | 91 | 91 | 89 | 88 | 87 | 88 |
| Hour 13 (Local Time | 22 | 59 | 56 | 55 | 51 | 53 | 60 | 63 | 64 | 62 | 57 | 57 | 59 | 58 |
| Hour 19 | 22 | 73 | 69 | 67 | 62 | 62 | 68 | 73 | 76 | 75 | 71 | 74 | 74 | 70 |
| **PRECIPITATION (inches):** | | | | | | | | | | | | | | |
| Water Equivalent | | | | | | | | | | | | | | |
| (22) —Normal | | 2.17 | 3.04 | 3.46 | 1.82 | 3.38 | 5.29 | 7.35 | 7.64 | 6.23 | 2.34 | 1.87 | 2.14 | 46.73 |
| (23) —Maximum Monthly | 39 | 8.02 | 7.95 | 12.64 | 6.59 | 17.64 | 13.75 | 20.59 | 18.59 | 13.98 | 7.36 | 6.12 | 6.66 | 20.59 |
| —Year | | 1948 | 1963 | 1959 | 1957 | 1979 | 1974 | 1960 | 1949 | 1979 | 1952 | 1963 | 1950 | JUL 1960 |
| (24) —Minimum Monthly | 39 | T | 0.21 | 0.06 | T | 0.17 | 1.86 | 1.65 | 2.35 | 1.28 | 0.16 | T | 0.07 | T |
| —Year | | 1950 | 1950 | 1956 | 1981 | 1973 | 1951 | 1981 | 1952 | 1972 | 1979 | 1960 | 1984 | APR 1981 |
| (25) —Maximum in 24 hrs | 39 | 3.29 | 3.68 | 5.20 | 3.70 | 11.84 | 5.53 | 12.11 | 5.37 | 4.99 | 2.93 | 4.22 | 3.28 | 12.11 |
| —Year | | 1953 | 1981 | 1960 | 1951 | 1979 | 1974 | 1960 | 1949 | 1985 | 1985 | 1963 | 1969 | JUL 1960 |
| Snow,Ice pellets | | | | | | | | | | | | | | |
| (26) —Maximum Monthly | 39 | 0.2 | T | T | | | | | | | | | | 0.2 |
| —Year | | 1977 | 1951 | 1980 | | | | | | | | | | JAN 1977 |
| —Maximum in 24 hrs | 39 | 0.2 | T | T | | | | | | | | | | 0.2 |
| —Year | | 1977 | 1951 | 1980 | | | | | | | | | | JAN 1977 |
| **WIND:** | | | | | | | | | | | | | | |
| (27) Mean Speed (mph) | 39 | 8.7 | 9.4 | 9.6 | 9.5 | 8.9 | 8.1 | 7.3 | 7.1 | 8.0 | 8.6 | 8.5 | 8.6 | 8.5 |
| (28) Prevailing Direction through 1963 | | N | E | S | ENE | E | E | E | ENE | ENE | NNE | NNE | N | E |
| Fastest Obs. 1 Min. | | | | | | | | | | | | | | |
| (29) —Direction | 33 | 29 | 32 | 29 | 29 | 36 | 31 | 32 | 11 | 34 | 02 | 29 | 36 | 31 |
| —Speed (MPH) | 33 | 35 | 50 | 43 | 37 | 46 | 67 | 58 | 38 | 56 | 38 | 40 | 45 | 67 |
| —Year | | 1959 | 1954 | 1956 | 1961 | 1958 | 1964 | 1963 | 1961 | 1960 | 1953 | 1963 | 1953 | JUN 1964 |
| Peak Gust —Direction | 2 | N | NW | W | NW | E | NE | N | S | W | SW | N | NW | N |
| —Speed (mph) | 2 | 32 | 46 | 32 | 33 | | 48 | 52 | 45 | 45 | 41 | 37 | 32 | 52 |
| —Date | | 1985 | 1984 | 1985 | | | 1985 | 1984 | 1985 | 1984 | 1985 | 1984 | 1984 | 1984 |

City report (page3)

TAMPA, FLORIDA

TABLE 2 PRECIPITATION (inches)

TABLE 3 AVERAGE TEMPERATURE (deg F)

REFERENCE NOTES FOR TABLES 1, 2, 3 and 6

GENERAL

T - TRACE AMOUNT
BLANK ENTRIES DENOTE MISSING/UNREPORTED DATA.
# INDICATES A STATION OR INSTRUMENT RELOCATION.

SPECIFIC

TABLE 1
(a) - LENGTH OF RECORD IN YEARS ALTHOUGH INDIVIDUAL MONTHS MAY BE MISSING
* LESS THAN .05

NORMALS — BASED ON THE MOST RECENT OCCURRENCE.
EXTREMES — DATES ARE THE MOST RECENT OCCURRENCE.
WIND DIR. — NUMERALS SHOW TENS OF DEGREES
CLOCKWISE FROM TRUE NORTH
00 INDICATES CALM
RESULTANT WIND DIRECTIONS ARE GIVEN TO WHOLE DEGREES.

EXCEPTIONS

TABLES 2, 3, and 6
RECORD MEANS AS
BEGINNING IN

City report (page 4)

TAMPA, FLORIDA

TABLE 4 HEATING DEGREE DAYS Base 65 deg F

TABLE 5 COOLING DEGREE DAYS Base 65 deg F

TABLE 6 SNOWFALL (inches)

Reference Notes, relative to all above tables, on preceding page.

## HOW TO READ THESE REPORTS (continued)

**21. AVERAGE RELATIVE HUMIDITY** at various hours of the day. The time is expressed in terms of the 24 hour clock (00 is midnight, 06 is 6 a.m., 12 is noon, and 18 is 6 p.m.). Values are for present site only.

**22. AVERAGE PRECIPITATION** in inches of water equivalent for each month and year during the *period 1951-1980.* As in the other precipitation data, the values are expressed in inches of depth of the liquid water content of all forms of precipitation even if initially frozen. As in all "normal" values, when the station does not have continuous records from the same instrument site, a "ratio factor" between the new and old exposure is used to adjust the observed values to a common series.

(See also, *Precipitation*, **under item 14,** *Mean Number of Days*)

**23. GREATEST PRECIPITATION** in inches of water equivalent ever recorded during any month *at present site.*

**24. LEAST PRECIPITATION** in inches of water equivalent ever recorded during any month *at present site.*

**25. GREATEST PRECIPITATION** in inches of water equivalent ever recorded during any *day at present site.*

**26. Summaries for SNOW and ICE PELLETS** including *sleet* are similar to those for total precipitation. The values are expressed in inches of actual snow or ice fall. The water equivalent can be estimated roughly by using the rule-of-thumb that 10" of snow equals 1" of water.

**27. WINDINESS**—Average speed of wind is expressed in mile-per-hour without regard of direction.

**28. PREVAILING WIND DIRECTION**—The most common single wind direction without regard for wind speed or any minimum amount of persistence. The aggregate total of wind from the other directions may be very much greater than that from the "prevailing" direction. Direction is coded in two different ways, some reports use letters, some use numbers. When letters are used, they have the usual meaning, such as WSW indicating west-south-west. When numbers are used, they are given in tens of degrees clockwise from true north, so that 09 is 90° clockwise from north (*east*), 18 is 180° (*south*), 27 is 270° (*west*), and 36 is 360° (*north*). The statistic is based on *data through 1963 only.*

**29. HIGH WIND**—The greatest speed in miles per hour of any "mile" of wind passing the station. The accompanying direction and year of occurrence are also given. A mile of wind passing the station 1 minute has an average speed of 60 mph, 2 minutes—30mph, 5 minutes—12 mph, etc. The wind cups of the particular instrument involved operate much like the wheel of a car in actuating the car's odometer. The instrument does not record the strength of individual wind gusts which usually last less than 20 seconds and which may be very much greater than the value given here. The fastest mile however does give some idea of the *extremes* of wind that can be encountered.

**30. SPECIAL SYMBOLS** that appear on many of the individual summaries:
   * **Less than one-half**
   T **Trace, an amount too small to measure.**
   - **Below zero temperatures are preceded by a minus sign.**

### Weather averages year-by-year

**PRECIPITATION** refers to the inches of water equivalent in the total of all forms of liquid or frozen precipitation that fell during each month. *Snowfall* refers to the actual amount of snow in inches that fell during the month. T (trace) is a precipitation amount of less than 0.005 inches. (Note: in estimating the water equivalent of snow a ratio of 10" of snow equal 1" of water is customarily employed.)

**AVERAGE TEMPERATURE** equals the *average* of the *maximum* and *minimum temperatures* for each day of the month for the given year; afternoon temperatures were typically higher than these values and late night/early morning temperatures were typically *below* them.

**ENERGY CONSUMPTION INDICES.** See items 10 and 11 above. *Heating Degree Days* provide a well established index of *relative fuel consumption* for space heating in a given place—a month of 2000 *HDD* requires about twice the amount of space heating energy as one of 1000 *HDD*, while 100 *HDD* will require about the same fuel whether accumulated in 2 or 4 days. Regional differences in the *Heating Degree Day Index* are only partially useful in estimating comparative fuel requirements because the building construction and cultural expectations tend to be different in different parts of the country (e.g., subjective ideas of comfort in relation to temperature will vary). For example, the average standards of efficiency in heating equipment and insulation are generally lower in warmer climates so that fuel requirements tend not to decrease as rapidly as the *heating degree days* decrease.*

The complementary index of *Cooling Degree Days* provides only a rough guide to relative energy consumption in air conditioning. A proper air conditioning index will almost certainly require a factor for humidity variation and possibly factors for cloudiness or other weather variables. However, the *Cooling Degree Days Index* will have some usefulness in indicating relative outdoor comfort and relative indoor air conditioning requirements.

* See page 148 for discussion of Heating and Cooling Degree Days

Birmingham is located in a hilly area of north-central Alabama in the foothills of the Appalachians about 300 miles inland from the Gulf of Mexico. There is a series of southwest to northeast valleys and ridges in the area.

The city is far enough inland to be protected from destructive tropical hurricanes, yet close enough that the Gulf has a pronounced modifying effect on the climate.

Although summers are long and hot, they are not generally excessively hot. On a typical mid-summer day, the temperature will be nearly 70 degrees at daybreak, approach 90 degrees at mid-day, and level off in the low 90s during the afternoon. It is not unusual for the temperature to remain below 100 degrees for several years in a row. However, every few years an extended heat wave will bring temperatures over 100 degrees. July is normally the hottest month but there is little difference from mid-June to mid-August. Rather persistent high humidity adds to the summer discomfort.

January is normally the coldest month but there is not much difference from mid-December to mid-February. Overall, winters are relatively mild. Even in cold spells, it is unusual for the temperature to remain below freezing all day. Sub-zero cold is extremely rare, occurring only a very few times this century. Extremely low temperatures almost always occur under clear skies after a snowfall.

Snowfall is erratic. Sometimes there is a two- or three-year span with no measurable snow. On rare occasions, there may be a 2 to 4 inch snowstorm. The snow usually melts quickly. Even 1 or 2 inches of snow can effectively shut down this sunbelt city because of the hilly terrain, the wetness of the snow and the unfamiliarity of motorists driving on snow and ice.

Birmingham is blessed with abundant rainfall. It is fairly well distributed throughout the year. However, some of the wetter winter months, plus March and July, have twice the rainfall of October, the driest month. Summer rainfall is almost entirely from scattered afternoon and early evening thunderstorms. Serious droughts are rare and most dry spells are not severe.

The stormiest time of the year with the greatest risk of severe thunderstorms and tornadoes is in spring, especially in March and April.

In a normal year, the last 32 degree minimum temperature in the spring is in mid to late March and the first in autumn is in early November.

**TABLE 1**  **NORMALS, MEANS AND EXTREMES**

BIRMINGHAM (MUNICIPAL AIRPORT), ALABAMA

LATITUDE: 33°34'N  LONGITUDE: 86°45'W  ELEVATION: FT. GRND 620 BARO 622  TIME ZONE: CENTRAL  WBAN: 13876

| | (a) | JAN | FEB | MAR | APR | MAY | JUNE | JULY | AUG | SEP | OCT | NOV | DEC | YEAR |
|---|---|---|---|---|---|---|---|---|---|---|---|---|---|---|
| **TEMPERATURE °F:** | | | | | | | | | | | | | | |
| Normals | | | | | | | | | | | | | | |
| -Daily Maximum | | 52.7 | 57.3 | 65.2 | 75.2 | 81.6 | 87.9 | 90.3 | 89.7 | 84.6 | 74.8 | 63.7 | 55.9 | 73.2 |
| -Daily Minimum | | 33.0 | 35.2 | 42.1 | 50.4 | 58.3 | 65.9 | 69.8 | 69.1 | 63.6 | 50.4 | 40.5 | 35.2 | 51.1 |
| -Monthly | | 42.9 | 46.3 | 53.7 | 62.8 | 70.0 | 77.0 | 80.1 | 79.5 | 74.1 | 62.6 | 52.1 | 45.6 | 62.2 |
| Extremes | | | | | | | | | | | | | | |
| -Record Highest | 46 | 81 | 83 | 89 | 92 | 99 | 102 | 106 | 103 | 100 | 94 | 84 | 80 | 106 |
| -Year | | 1949 | 1962 | 1982 | 1987 | 1962 | 1954 | 1980 | 1947 | 1980 | 1954 | 1961 | 1951 | JUL 1980 |
| -Record Lowest | 46 | -6 | 3 | 11 | 26 | 35 | 42 | 51 | 51 | 37 | 27 | 5 | 1 | -6 |
| -Year | | 1985 | 1958 | 1980 | 1973 | 1944 | 1966 | 1967 | 1946 | 1967 | 1956 | 1950 | 1989 | JAN 1985 |
| **NORMAL DEGREE DAYS:** | | | | | | | | | | | | | | |
| Heating (base 65°F) | | 685 | 532 | 368 | 110 | 36 | 0 | 0 | 0 | 7 | 137 | 387 | 601 | 2863 |
| Cooling (base 65°F) | | 0 | 8 | 18 | 44 | 191 | 360 | 468 | 450 | 280 | 62 | 0 | 0 | 1881 |
| **% OF POSSIBLE SUNSHINE** | 34 | 42 | 50 | 55 | 63 | 66 | 65 | 59 | 63 | 61 | 66 | 55 | 46 | 58 |
| **MEAN SKY COVER (tenths)** | | | | | | | | | | | | | | |
| Sunrise - Sunset | 36 | 6.9 | 6.5 | 6.5 | 5.8 | 5.9 | 5.9 | 6.4 | 5.8 | 5.6 | 4.6 | 5.7 | 6.4 | 6.0 |
| **MEAN NUMBER OF DAYS:** | | | | | | | | | | | | | | |
| Sunrise to Sunset | | | | | | | | | | | | | | |
| -Clear | 36 | 6.8 | 7.2 | 7.4 | 8.9 | 8.1 | 7.0 | 4.6 | 6.8 | 9.5 | 14.0 | 10.2 | 8.4 | 98.8 |
| -Partly Cloudy | 36 | 6.2 | 6.5 | 7.9 | 7.9 | 10.9 | 12.6 | 14.4 | 14.5 | 9.3 | 7.6 | 6.8 | 6.6 | 111.3 |
| -Cloudy | 36 | 17.9 | 14.6 | 15.7 | 13.2 | 12.0 | 10.5 | 12.0 | 9.7 | 11.2 | 9.4 | 13.0 | 15.9 | 155.1 |
| Precipitation | | | | | | | | | | | | | | |
| .01 inches or more | 46 | 11.1 | 10.2 | 11.0 | 9.2 | 9.7 | 9.6 | 12.5 | 9.7 | 8.0 | 6.3 | 9.2 | 10.5 | 116.8 |
| Snow, Ice pellets | | | | | | | | | | | | | | |
| 1.0 inches or more | 46 | 0.3 | 0.1 | 0.1 | 0.* | 0.0 | 0.0 | 0.0 | 0.0 | 0.0 | 0.0 | 0.* | 0.1 | 0.5 |
| Thunderstorms | 46 | 1.6 | 2.2 | 4.5 | 5.1 | 6.9 | 8.4 | 11.6 | 9.1 | 4.2 | 1.3 | 1.8 | 1.2 | 58.0 |
| Heavy Fog Visibility | | | | | | | | | | | | | | |
| 1/4 mile or less | 46 | 1.3 | 0.7 | 0.7 | 0.3 | 0.3 | 0.7 | 0.5 | 0.5 | 0.5 | 0.8 | 1.1 | 1.2 | 8.5 |
| Temperature °F | | | | | | | | | | | | | | |
| -Maximum | | | | | | | | | | | | | | |
| 90° and above | 26 | 0.0 | 0.0 | 0.0 | 0.1 | 1.8 | 10.4 | 16.4 | 14.5 | 5.7 | 0.1 | 0.0 | 0.0 | 49.1 |
| 32° and below | 26 | 1.7 | 0.5 | 0.* | 0.0 | 0.0 | 0.0 | 0.0 | 0.0 | 0.0 | 0.0 | 0.* | 0.6 | 2.8 |
| -Minimum | | | | | | | | | | | | | | |
| 32° and below | 26 | 17.8 | 13.9 | 6.1 | 1.1 | 0.0 | 0.0 | 0.0 | 0.0 | 0.0 | 0.5 | 6.7 | 14.6 | 60.6 |
| 0° and below | 26 | 0.2 | 0.0 | 0.0 | 0.0 | 0.0 | 0.0 | 0.0 | 0.0 | 0.0 | 0.0 | 0.0 | 0.0 | 0.2 |
| **AVG. STATION PRESS. (mb)** | 17 | 998.3 | 997.0 | 994.5 | 994.1 | 993.2 | 994.1 | 995.1 | 995.2 | 995.3 | 997.3 | 997.3 | 998.4 | 995.8 |
| **RELATIVE HUMIDITY (%)** | | | | | | | | | | | | | | |
| Hour 00 | 26 | 76 | 72 | 72 | 77 | 84 | 84 | 86 | 86 | 85 | 84 | 80 | 77 | 80 |
| Hour 06 (Local Time) | 26 | 80 | 79 | 79 | 83 | 86 | 86 | 88 | 90 | 88 | 87 | 84 | 81 | 84 |
| Hour 12 | 26 | 61 | 56 | 52 | 51 | 55 | 56 | 60 | 60 | 60 | 55 | 58 | 60 | 57 |
| Hour 18 | 26 | 64 | 57 | 52 | 51 | 58 | 60 | 65 | 66 | 69 | 71 | 69 | 68 | 63 |
| **PRECIPITATION (inches):** | | | | | | | | | | | | | | |
| Water Equivalent | | | | | | | | | | | | | | |
| -Normal | | 5.23 | 4.72 | 6.62 | 5.00 | 4.53 | 3.61 | 5.39 | 3.85 | 4.34 | 2.64 | 3.64 | 4.95 | 54.52 |
| -Maximum Monthly | 46 | 11.00 | 17.67 | 15.80 | 13.75 | 11.10 | 8.44 | 13.70 | 10.85 | 10.43 | 7.52 | 15.25 | 13.98 | 17.67 |
| -Year | | 1949 | 1961 | 1980 | 1979 | 1969 | 1963 | 1950 | 1967 | 1977 | 1977 | 1948 | 1961 | FEB 1961 |
| -Minimum Monthly | 46 | 1.09 | 1.20 | 1.71 | 0.42 | 1.15 | 0.67 | 0.30 | 0.38 | T | 0.11 | 0.42 | 0.81 | T |
| -Year | | 1981 | 1968 | 1985 | 1986 | 1951 | 1968 | 1983 | 1989 | 1955 | 1963 | 1949 | 1980 | SEP 1955 |
| -Maximum in 24 hrs | 40 | 5.81 | 6.57 | 7.05 | 5.08 | 4.63 | 3.85 | 5.47 | 5.13 | 5.03 | 3.75 | 4.87 | 5.29 | 7.05 |
| -Year | | 1949 | 1961 | 1970 | 1966 | 1969 | 1957 | 1985 | 1952 | 1977 | 1977 | 1948 | 1961 | MAR 1970 |
| Snow, Ice pellets | | | | | | | | | | | | | | |
| -Maximum Monthly | 46 | 6.6 | 2.3 | 2.0 | 5.0 | 0.0 | 0.0 | 0.0 | 0.0 | 0.0 | T | 1.4 | 8.0 | 8.0 |
| -Year | | 1982 | 1960 | 1984 | 1987 | | | | | | 1955 | 1950 | 1963 | DEC 1963 |
| -Maximum in 24 hrs | 40 | 4.5 | 2.3 | 2.0 | 5.0 | 0.0 | 0.0 | 0.0 | 0.0 | 0.0 | T | 1.4 | 8.4 | 8.4 |
| -Year | | 1948 | 1960 | 1984 | 1987 | | | | | | 1955 | 1950 | 1963 | DEC 1963 |
| **WIND:** | | | | | | | | | | | | | | |
| Mean Speed (mph) | 46 | 8.2 | 8.8 | 9.2 | 8.3 | 6.8 | 6.1 | 5.7 | 5.5 | 6.4 | 6.1 | 7.3 | 7.8 | 7.2 |
| Prevailing Direction | | | | | | | | | | | | | | |
| through 1963 | | S | N | S | S | S | SSW | SSW | NE | ENE | ENE | N | NNW | S |
| Fastest Mile | | | | | | | | | | | | | | |
| -Direction (!!!) | 34 | W | SE | SW | SW | NW | SW | SW | NW | SE | W | N | SE | SW |
| -Speed (MPH) | 34 | 49 | 59 | 65 | 56 | 65 | 56 | 57 | 50 | 50 | 43 | 52 | 41 | 65 |
| -Year | | 1975 | 1960 | 1955 | 1956 | 1951 | 1957 | 1960 | 1956 | 1951 | 1955 | 1944 | 1954 | MAR 1955 |
| Peak Gust | | | | | | | | | | | | | | |
| -Direction (!!!) | | | | | | | | | | | | | | |
| -Speed (mph) | | | | | | | | | | | | | | |
| -Date | | | | | | | | | | | | | | |

See reference Notes to this table on the following page.

# BIRMINGHAM (Airport) ALABAMA

PRECIPITATION (inches)    BIRMINGHAM (MUNICIPAL AIRPORT), ALABAMA

**TABLE 2**

| YEAR | JAN | FEB | MAR | APR | MAY | JUNE | JULY | AUG | SEP | OCT | NOV | DEC | ANNUAL |
|------|-----|-----|-----|-----|-----|------|------|-----|-----|-----|-----|-----|--------|
| 1961 | 1.49 | 17.67 | 9.22 | 4.33 | 2.45 | 4.85 | 10.17 | 3.56 | 2.42 | 2.05 | 4.29 | 13.98 | 76.48 |
| 1962 | 8.64 | 4.39 | 5.21 | 2.99 | 1.26 | 3.59 | 3.89 | 3.49 | 3.69 | 2.03 | 6.41 | 2.55 | 48.14 |
| 1963 | 7.32 | 3.25 | 6.31 | 6.70 | 3.72 | 8.44 | 6.54 | 1.53 | 1.21 | 0.11 | 4.00 | 5.94 | 55.07 |
| 1964 | 5.37 | 4.11 | 9.44 | 9.90 | 3.20 | 4.08 | 4.34 | 2.78 | 3.26 | 2.95 | 3.24 | 5.09 | 57.76 |
| 1965 | 3.21 | 6.22 | 6.10 | 2.54 | 1.37 | 8.17 | 4.87 | 3.55 | 2.60 | 0.67 | 2.80 | 2.06 | 44.16 |
| 1966 | 4.74 | 8.67 | 3.77 | 8.37 | 3.30 | 2.87 | 4.99 | 6.48 | 5.12 | 3.13 | 2.28 | 2.34 | 56.06 |
| 1967 | 2.84 | 4.74 | 1.79 | 1.35 | 9.32 | 4.37 | 6.60 | 10.85 | 2.84 | 4.23 | 6.42 | 11.49 | 66.84 |
| 1968 | 5.56 | 1.20 | 6.17 | 6.23 | 3.51 | 0.67 | 9.39 | 1.81 | 3.42 | 1.20 | 4.66 | 7.38 | 51.20 |
| 1969 | 7.78 | 3.17 | 5.19 | 5.32 | 11.10 | 3.75 | 2.91 | 1.76 | 6.85 | 2.66 | 2.51 | 6.07 | 59.07 |
| 1970 | 2.47 | 2.35 | 11.36 | 5.56 | 2.27 | 3.55 | 3.37 | 7.01 | 1.05 | 7.04 | 2.31 | 3.32 | 51.66 |
| 1971 | 3.58 | 9.28 | 6.65 | 4.25 | 2.64 | 6.57 | 8.90 | 3.68 | 3.35 | 1.21 | 1.76 | 5.92 | 57.79 |
| 1972 | 9.30 | 2.15 | 4.79 | 2.56 | 3.82 | 2.70 | 3.55 | 2.01 | 8.09 | 3.35 | 4.47 | 5.76 | 52.55 |
| 1973 | 6.85 | 2.33 | 9.71 | 5.33 | 8.29 | 3.74 | 8.36 | 5.41 | 2.64 | 0.96 | 4.91 | 7.58 | 66.11 |
| 1974 | 6.85 | 4.94 | 2.43 | 5.43 | 5.43 | 1.42 | 4.69 | 8.28 | 4.94 | 1.49 | 4.13 | 5.97 | 56.00 |
| 1975 | 7.23 | 4.96 | 7.57 | 3.19 | 4.15 | 2.44 | 7.33 | 3.33 | 3.69 | 4.34 | 4.15 | 5.27 | 55.27 |
| 1976 | 4.12 | 1.80 | 14.15 | 1.99 | 9.00 | 2.75 | 4.92 | 3.34 | 4.91 | 1.59 | 2.23 | 4.35 | 55.15 |
| 1977 | 5.08 | 3.89 | 8.70 | 6.73 | 3.51 | 0.96 | 6.24 | 0.87 | 10.43 | 7.52 | 4.10 | 2.01 | 60.04 |
| 1978 | 4.54 | 1.31 | 3.07 | 2.64 | 8.51 | 5.04 | 5.09 | 2.09 | 1.14 | 0.22 | 2.71 | 5.43 | 41.79 |
| 1979 | 5.94 | 4.70 | 5.69 | 13.75 | 6.64 | 1.19 | 9.98 | 2.30 | 10.40 | 2.05 | 5.51 | 1.55 | 69.70 |
| 1980 | 6.63 | 2.36 | 15.80 | 9.10 | 7.30 | 3.01 | 2.11 | 2.84 | 5.26 | 3.21 | 3.04 | 0.81 | 61.47 |
| 1981 | 1.09 | 4.87 | 7.23 | 2.45 | 2.81 | 2.49 | 3.88 | 5.30 | 0.93 | 3.34 | 1.67 | 5.82 | 41.88 |
| 1982 | 5.19 | 6.29 | 2.71 | 7.86 | 3.19 | 5.39 | 3.53 | 2.68 | 0.66 | 3.73 | 7.11 | 9.51 | 57.85 |
| 1983 | 3.26 | 6.42 | 5.06 | 8.28 | 9.57 | 3.81 | 0.30 | 0.99 | 2.83 | 3.67 | 9.14 | 12.63 | 65.96 |
| 1984 | 3.96 | 2.79 | 4.07 | 8.61 | 6.07 | 1.41 | 5.06 | 3.86 | 0.16 | 3.91 | 5.42 | 2.30 | 47.62 |
| 1985 | 5.22 | 5.79 | 1.71 | 2.86 | 4.36 | 5.34 | 10.07 | 4.07 | 1.97 | 4.12 | 2.62 | 2.54 | 50.67 |
| 1986 | 1.21 | 1.79 | 2.45 | 0.42 | 3.66 | 3.87 | 1.61 | 5.56 | 2.52 | 5.24 | 9.66 | 3.08 | 41.07 |
| 1987 | 5.89 | 5.82 | 4.77 | 1.03 | 6.03 | 4.59 | 2.30 | 3.96 | 3.52 | 1.16 | 3.17 | 3.08 | 45.32 |
| 1988 | 5.55 | 2.52 | 3.18 | 3.18 | 1.22 | 0.79 | 2.95 | 3.43 | 8.57 | 3.41 | 6.33 | 2.84 | 43.97 |
| 1989 | 4.76 | 4.31 | 5.70 | 3.40 | 3.82 | 8.00 | 6.42 | 0.38 | 7.38 | 1.52 | 4.63 | 3.39 | 53.71 |
| 1990 | 7.38 | 7.43 | 5.81 | 2.38 | 4.12 | 2.08 | 3.16 | 0.59 | 2.04 | 2.98 | 4.02 | 5.47 | 47.46 |
| Record Mean | 4.96 | 4.85 | 6.02 | 4.74 | 4.24 | 3.93 | 5.31 | 4.15 | 3.50 | 2.77 | 3.76 | 5.04 | 53.26 |

**TABLE 3**   AVERAGE TEMPERATURE (deg. F)    BIRMINGHAM (MUNICIPAL AIRPORT), ALABAMA

| YEAR | JAN | FEB | MAR | APR | MAY | JUNE | JULY | AUG | SEP | OCT | NOV | DEC | ANNUAL |
|------|-----|-----|-----|-----|-----|------|------|-----|-----|-----|-----|-----|--------|
| #1961 | 39.0 | 52.1 | 57.3 | 59.2 | 67.3 | 75.0 | 78.4 | 78.7 | 76.4 | 64.2 | 55.9 | 46.9 | 62.6 |
| 1962 | 41.7 | 55.2 | 52.1 | 62.2 | 78.6 | 79.0 | 82.6 | 82.1 | 74.8 | 66.4 | 52.0 | 42.6 | 64.1 |
| #1963 | 38.2 | 40.8 | 58.4 | 65.2 | 70.5 | 77.3 | 78.7 | 80.0 | 73.5 | 67.5 | 53.5 | 36.8 | 61.7 |
| 1964 | 42.8 | 42.7 | 53.9 | 65.3 | 71.7 | 78.2 | 77.7 | 78.1 | 76.0 | 59.6 | 55.3 | 48.0 | 62.5 |
| 1965 | 45.8 | 44.6 | 49.8 | 64.8 | 71.8 | 75.0 | 77.7 | 78.0 | 73.7 | 60.0 | 54.8 | 46.0 | 61.9 |
| 1966 | 37.7 | 46.2 | 52.3 | 62.2 | 66.9 | 73.6 | 81.3 | 77.0 | 71.8 | 58.8 | 54.1 | 44.3 | 60.5 |
| 1967 | 44.0 | 41.8 | 58.3 | 67.2 | 67.7 | 76.2 | 75.7 | 74.2 | 68.4 | 60.7 | 48.4 | 48.5 | 60.9 |
| 1968 | 42.5 | 38.7 | 52.8 | 62.9 | 68.3 | 77.9 | 78.8 | 79.4 | 72.1 | 63.2 | 50.3 | 41.5 | 60.7 |
| 1969 | 42.6 | 44.5 | 46.6 | 62.7 | 69.0 | 76.2 | 81.7 | 77.8 | 70.9 | 63.9 | 50.1 | 43.3 | 60.8 |
| 1970 | 37.9 | 44.5 | 52.6 | 65.6 | 71.3 | 75.7 | 80.6 | 78.7 | 77.0 | 63.3 | 48.4 | 47.9 | 62.0 |
| 1971 | 43.6 | 44.2 | 48.5 | 60.2 | 65.3 | 77.9 | 77.5 | 77.8 | 75.0 | 67.2 | 50.7 | 54.8 | 61.9 |
| 1972 | 47.2 | 46.9 | 53.7 | 63.1 | 67.2 | 74.2 | 76.9 | 78.8 | 75.1 | 61.7 | 48.9 | 47.7 | 61.8 |
| 1973 | 40.7 | 42.3 | 58.6 | 58.1 | 67.5 | 75.9 | 79.4 | 77.2 | 77.2 | 66.6 | 56.2 | 45.0 | 62.1 |
| 1974 | 52.8 | 47.3 | 61.2 | 61.5 | 71.0 | 72.7 | 79.2 | 78.4 | 70.1 | 60.6 | 52.7 | 47.3 | 62.9 |
| 1975 | 49.1 | 50.1 | 53.9 | 60.5 | 72.4 | 76.4 | 78.1 | 79.1 | 70.2 | 63.5 | 54.1 | 44.6 | 62.7 |
| 1976 | 39.1 | 54.3 | 58.7 | 61.5 | 64.2 | 74.4 | 78.3 | 77.0 | 71.9 | 57.4 | 45.5 | 41.2 | 60.3 |
| 1977 | 31.6 | 44.8 | 57.3 | 65.2 | 72.4 | 79.8 | 83.4 | 82.1 | 75.7 | 59.9 | 55.0 | 44.1 | 62.6 |
| 1978 | 33.5 | 37.4 | 50.2 | 62.9 | 68.2 | 77.1 | 81.5 | 79.8 | 76.9 | 60.6 | 57.9 | 46.1 | 61.0 |
| 1979 | 37.7 | 44.0 | 55.2 | 63.4 | 69.8 | 75.1 | 79.9 | 78.4 | 71.4 | 63.9 | 52.8 | 45.9 | 61.5 |
| 1980 | 45.2 | 42.3 | 51.4 | 60.9 | 70.0 | 77.6 | 84.4 | 83.0 | 78.4 | 60.3 | 52.4 | 44.0 | 62.5 |
| 1981 | 39.2 | 48.2 | 51.3 | 67.1 | 67.8 | 80.6 | 82.2 | 79.2 | 71.9 | 61.8 | 54.6 | 42.7 | 62.2 |
| 1982 | 41.9 | 47.3 | 58.9 | 59.1 | 72.6 | 75.7 | 80.7 | 79.6 | 73.1 | 64.2 | 54.1 | 51.2 | 63.2 |
| 1983 | 40.6 | 44.8 | 50.8 | 56.6 | 67.3 | 74.1 | 80.3 | 81.7 | 71.7 | 63.0 | 51.9 | 39.8 | 60.2 |
| 1984 | 38.5 | 46.8 | 52.4 | 59.0 | 67.5 | 77.1 | 78.2 | 77.5 | 72.1 | 71.1 | 51.4 | 54.3 | 62.2 |
| 1985 | 35.5 | 43.2 | 56.7 | 63.7 | 69.5 | 76.2 | 78.1 | 78.2 | 72.0 | 67.3 | 61.0 | 40.2 | 61.8 |
| 1986 | 41.9 | 49.9 | 55.5 | 61.8 | 71.2 | 78.6 | 82.5 | 77.8 | 76.9 | 63.9 | 57.4 | 44.0 | 63.5 |
| 1987 | 42.1 | 46.9 | 54.6 | 59.5 | 73.8 | 76.7 | 80.5 | 82.0 | 73.1 | 56.8 | 54.5 | 49.1 | 62.5 |
| 1988 | 39.7 | 43.5 | 54.1 | 61.2 | 67.6 | 77.5 | 79.8 | 81.5 | 74.4 | 57.7 | 55.2 | 45.8 | 61.5 |
| 1989 | 48.9 | 45.7 | 56.4 | 60.3 | 67.7 | 75.5 | 79.2 | 79.5 | 72.5 | 61.9 | 52.9 | 38.0 | 61.5 |
| 1990 | 49.0 | 54.5 | 57.0 | 60.7 | 68.9 | 77.8 | 79.8 | 82.3 | 77.5 | 63.9 | 55.7 | 49.7 | 64.7 |
| Record Mean | 44.8 | 46.9 | 54.8 | 62.7 | 70.5 | 77.7 | 80.1 | 79.7 | 75.0 | 64.2 | 53.5 | 46.2 | 63.0 |
| Max | 54.1 | 56.8 | 65.7 | 74.1 | 81.4 | 88.2 | 90.0 | 89.7 | 85.4 | 75.6 | 64.3 | 55.6 | 73.4 |
| Min | 35.4 | 37.0 | 44.0 | 51.3 | 59.5 | 67.1 | 70.1 | 69.6 | 64.6 | 52.7 | 42.7 | 36.7 | 52.6 |

## REFERENCE NOTES FOR TABLES 1, 2, 3 and 6    (BIRMINGHAM, [MUN. AIRPORT] AL)

**GENERAL**

T - TRACE AMOUNT
BLANK ENTRIES DENOTE MISSING/UNREPORTED DATA.
# INDICATES A STATION OR INSTRUMENT RELOCATION.

**SPECIFIC**

TABLE 1

(a) - LENGTH OF RECORD IN YEARS. ALTHOUGH
INDIVIDUAL MONTHS MAY BE MISSING.
* LESS THAN .05

NORMALS — BASED ON THE 1951-1980 RECORD PERIOD.
EXTREMES — DATES ARE THE MOST RECENT OCCURRENCE.
WIND DIR. — NUMERALS SHOW TENS OF DEGREES
CLOCKWISE FROM TRUE NORTH.
"00" INDICATES CALM.
RESULTANT WIND DIRECTIONS ARE GIVEN TO WHOLE DEGREES.

TABLE 3
MAX AND MIN ARE LONG-TERM MEAN DAILY MAXIMUM
AND MEAN DAILY MINIMUM TEMPERATURES.

**EXCEPTIONS**

TABLE 1

1. PERCENT OF POSSIBLE SUNSHINE, MEAN SKY COVER,
AND DAYS CLEAR-PARTLY CLOUDY-CLOUDY ARE
THROUGH 1977.
2. MAXIMUM 24-HOUR PRECIPITATION AND SNOW, AND
FASTEST MILE WINDS ARE THROUGH SEPTEMBER 1978.

TABLES 2, 3, and 6

RECORD MEANS ARE THROUGH THE CURRENT YEAR,
BEGINNING IN    1896 FOR TEMPERATURE
1896 FOR PRECIPITATION
1944 FOR SNOWFALL

**TABLE 4**

HEATING DEGREE DAYS Base 65 deg. F     BIRMINGHAM (MUNICIPAL AIRPORT), ALABAMA

| SEASON | JULY | AUG | SEP | OCT | NOV | DEC | JAN | FEB | MAR | APR | MAY | JUNE | TOTAL |
|---|---|---|---|---|---|---|---|---|---|---|---|---|---|
| 1961-62 | 0 | 0 | 3 | 93 | 301 | 556 | 718 | 285 | 398 | 154 | 1 | 0 | 2509 |
| #1962-63 | 0 | 0 | 9 | 100 | 382 | 686 | 822 | 672 | 225 | 84 | 25 | 0 | 3005 |
| 1963-64 | 0 | 0 | 4 | 35 | 350 | 869 | 680 | 639 | 348 | 71 | 5 | 0 | 3001 |
| 1964-65 | 0 | 0 | 0 | 196 | 305 | 520 | 591 | 571 | 478 | 85 | 2 | 0 | 2748 |
| 1965-66 | 0 | 0 | 13 | 171 | 305 | 583 | 840 | 520 | 393 | 149 | 34 | 9 | 3017 |
| 1966-67 | 0 | 0 | 3 | 203 | 331 | 635 | 643 | 645 | 248 | 51 | 65 | 2 | 2826 |
| 1967-68 | 0 | 0 | 41 | 162 | 492 | 510 | 690 | 755 | 387 | 108 | 30 | 0 | 3175 |
| 1968-69 | 0 | 0 | 1 | 148 | 434 | 723 | 687 | 566 | 563 | 95 | 26 | 4 | 3247 |
| 1969-70 | 0 | 0 | 4 | 110 | 443 | 663 | 830 | 568 | 377 | 91 | 23 | 0 | 3109 |
| 1970-71 | 0 | 0 | 10 | 104 | 493 | 523 | 657 | 578 | 500 | 171 | 74 | 0 | 3110 |
| 1971-72 | 0 | 0 | 0 | 28 | 437 | 320 | 548 | 526 | 348 | 138 | 21 | 7 | 2373 |
| 1972-73 | 0 | 0 | 9 | 135 | 486 | 534 | 749 | 629 | 217 | 228 | 48 | 0 | 3035 |
| 1973-74 | 0 | 0 | 3 | 73 | 285 | 615 | 374 | 491 | 161 | 147 | 9 | 0 | 2158 |
| 1974-75 | 0 | 0 | 19 | 159 | 378 | 542 | 493 | 412 | 361 | 190 | 2 | 0 | 2556 |
| 1975-76 | 0 | 0 | 49 | 105 | 349 | 626 | 795 | 314 | 213 | 129 | 65 | 0 | 2645 |
| 1976-77 | 0 | 0 | 7 | 241 | 580 | 732 | 1026 | 566 | 252 | 73 | 5 | 0 | 3482 |
| 1977-78 | 0 | 0 | 0 | 176 | 292 | 640 | 967 | 768 | 318 | 120 | 42 | 0 | 3457 |
| 1978-79 | 0 | 0 | 0 | 160 | 220 | 578 | 839 | 584 | 303 | 83 | 33 | 0 | 2800 |
| 1979-80 | 0 | 0 | 0 | 101 | 365 | 588 | 604 | 655 | 417 | 144 | 14 | 0 | 2888 |
| 1980-81 | 0 | 0 | 7 | 181 | 372 | 642 | 795 | 464 | 428 | 46 | 51 | 0 | 2986 |
| 1981-82 | 0 | 0 | 19 | 138 | 314 | 682 | 711 | 490 | 250 | 199 | 4 | 0 | 2807 |
| 1982-83 | 0 | 0 | 16 | 134 | 331 | 449 | 751 | 558 | 437 | 262 | 39 | 0 | 2977 |
| 1983-84 | 0 | 0 | 26 | 108 | 388 | 774 | 817 | 519 | 392 | 202 | 68 | 2 | 3296 |
| 1984-85 | 0 | 0 | 10 | 27 | 410 | 330 | 907 | 604 | 278 | 123 | 16 | 3 | 2708 |
| 1985-86 | 0 | 0 | 14 | 62 | 165 | 761 | 711 | 415 | 305 | 132 | 21 | 0 | 2586 |
| 1986-87 | 0 | 1 | 0 | 112 | 239 | 644 | 705 | 500 | 320 | 201 | 0 | 0 | 2722 |
| 1987-88 | 0 | 0 | 5 | 248 | 315 | 488 | 777 | 616 | 347 | 134 | 18 | 0 | 2948 |
| 1988-89 | 0 | 0 | 0 | 234 | 289 | 589 | 492 | 545 | 289 | 200 | 65 | 0 | 2703 |
| 1989-90 | 0 | 0 | 27 | 140 | 363 | 834 | 491 | 299 | 265 | 172 | 32 | 0 | 2623 |
| 1990-91 | 0 | 0 | 16 | 138 | 282 | 474 | | | | | | | |

**TABLE 5**

COOLING DEGREE DAYS Base 65 deg. F     BIRMINGHAM (MUNICIPAL AIRPORT), ALABAMA

| YEAR | JAN | FEB | MAR | APR | MAY | JUNE | JULY | AUG | SEP | OCT | NOV | DEC | TOTAL |
|---|---|---|---|---|---|---|---|---|---|---|---|---|---|
| 1969 | 0 | 0 | 0 | 33 | 156 | 346 | 523 | 402 | 188 | 84 | 2 | 0 | 1734 |
| 1970 | 0 | 0 | 2 | 115 | 227 | 330 | 492 | 432 | 377 | 58 | 0 | 0 | 2033 |
| 1971 | 1 | 0 | 0 | 35 | 90 | 394 | 393 | 403 | 309 | 105 | 10 | 13 | 1753 |
| 1972 | 4 | 6 | 7 | 88 | 93 | 291 | 379 | 434 | 318 | 40 | 8 | 2 | 1670 |
| 1973 | 0 | 0 | 24 | 28 | 132 | 333 | 452 | 385 | 376 | 129 | 28 | 0 | 1887 |
| 1974 | 4 | 3 | 52 | 48 | 204 | 238 | 450 | 418 | 180 | 28 | 15 | 0 | 1640 |
| 1975 | 8 | 0 | 26 | 61 | 241 | 351 | 416 | 447 | 211 | 66 | 29 | 2 | 1858 |
| 1976 | 0 | 8 | 25 | 27 | 48 | 290 | 418 | 376 | 219 | 15 | 1 | 0 | 1427 |
| 1977 | 0 | 5 | 21 | 85 | 241 | 450 | 578 | 537 | 329 | 25 | 0 | 1 | 2272 |
| 1978 | 0 | 0 | 0 | 64 | 151 | 370 | 515 | 463 | 365 | 34 | 12 | 1 | 1975 |
| 1979 | 0 | 1 | 8 | 43 | 188 | 308 | 466 | 424 | 198 | 74 | 7 | 2 | 1719 |
| 1980 | 0 | 4 | 6 | 25 | 176 | 386 | 607 | 563 | 413 | 43 | 2 | 0 | 2225 |
| 1981 | 0 | 1 | 9 | 113 | 145 | 475 | 539 | 448 | 231 | 46 | 9 | 0 | 2016 |
| 1982 | 1 | 0 | 65 | 28 | 247 | 327 | 495 | 459 | 265 | 118 | 12 | 27 | 2044 |
| 1983 | 0 | 0 | 7 | 17 | 115 | 281 | 481 | 528 | 233 | 53 | 2 | 0 | 1717 |
| 1984 | 0 | 0 | 11 | 30 | 151 | 373 | 421 | 395 | 230 | 221 | 2 | 6 | 1844 |
| 1985 | 0 | 1 | 27 | 90 | 163 | 349 | 413 | 417 | 233 | 139 | 51 | 1 | 1884 |
| 1986 | 0 | 0 | 16 | 43 | 222 | 413 | 547 | 406 | 364 | 84 | 18 | 0 | 2113 |
| 1987 | 0 | 0 | 5 | 46 | 280 | 357 | 487 | 532 | 254 | 1 | 7 | 3 | 1972 |
| 1988 | 0 | 0 | 13 | 26 | 105 | 382 | 467 | 516 | 292 | 14 | 1 | 0 | 1816 |
| 1989 | 0 | 14 | 27 | 65 | 155 | 323 | 447 | 459 | 257 | 51 | 3 | 0 | 1801 |
| 1990 | 1 | 14 | 21 | 49 | 160 | 393 | 466 | 543 | 398 | 110 | 9 | 4 | 2168 |

**TABLE 6**   SNOWFALL (inches)     BIRMINGHAM (MUNICIPAL AIRPORT), ALABAMA

| SEASON | JULY | AUG | SEP | OCT | NOV | DEC | JAN | FEB | MAR | APR | MAY | JUNE | TOTAL |
|---|---|---|---|---|---|---|---|---|---|---|---|---|---|
| 1961-62 | 0.0 | 0.0 | 0.0 | 0.0 | 0.0 | T | 3.8 | 0.0 | T | 0.0 | 0.0 | 0.0 | 3.8 |
| 1962-63 | 0.0 | 0.0 | 0.0 | 0.0 | 0.0 | T | T | 0.5 | 0.0 | 0.0 | 0.0 | 0.0 | 0.5 |
| 1963-64 | 0.0 | 0.0 | 0.0 | 0.0 | 0.0 | 8.0 | 0.4 | T | 0.0 | 0.0 | 0.0 | 0.0 | 8.4 |
| 1964-65 | 0.0 | 0.0 | 0.0 | 0.0 | 0.0 | T | T | T | T | 0.0 | 0.0 | 0.0 | T |
| 1965-66 | 0.0 | 0.0 | 0.0 | 0.0 | 0.0 | 0.0 | 1.2 | T | T | 0.0 | 0.0 | 0.0 | 1.2 |
| 1966-67 | 0.0 | 0.0 | 0.0 | 0.0 | •T | T | T | 0.8 | T | 0.0 | 0.0 | 0.0 | 0.8 |
| 1967-68 | 0.0 | 0.0 | 0.0 | 0.0 | T | T | 1.0 | 0.7 | T | 0.0 | 0.0 | 0.0 | 1.7 |
| 1968-69 | 0.0 | 0.0 | 0.0 | 0.0 | T | T | T | T | T | 0.0 | 0.0 | 0.0 | T |
| 1969-70 | 0.0 | 0.0 | 0.0 | 0.0 | T | T | 1.7 | 0.1 | T | 0.0 | 0.0 | 0.0 | 1.8 |
| 1970-71 | 0.0 | 0.0 | 0.0 | 0.0 | T | 0.0 | T | 0.8 | T | T | 0.0 | 0.0 | 0.8 |
| 1971-72 | 0.0 | 0.0 | 0.0 | 0.0 | T | 0.0 | T | T | T | 0.0 | 0.0 | 0.0 | T |
| 1972-73 | 0.0 | 0.0 | 0.0 | 0.0 | 0.0 | 0.0 | T | 0.0 | 0.0 | 0.0 | 0.0 | 0.0 | T |
| 1973-74 | 0.0 | 0.0 | 0.0 | 0.0 | 0.0 | 0.0 | T | 0.0 | T | 0.0 | 0.0 | 0.0 | T |
| 1974-75 | 0.0 | 0.0 | 0.0 | 0.0 | 0.0 | 0.4 | T | T | T | 0.0 | 0.0 | 0.0 | 0.4 |
| 1975-76 | 0.0 | 0.0 | 0.0 | 0.0 | T | T | T | 0.0 | 0.0 | 0.0 | 0.0 | 0.0 | T |
| 1976-77 | 0.0 | 0.0 | 0.0 | 0.0 | T | T | 1.4 | T | 0.0 | 0.0 | 0.0 | 0.0 | 1.4 |
| 1977-78 | 0.0 | 0.0 | 0.0 | 0.0 | 0.0 | T | 1.9 | T | T | 0.0 | 0.0 | 0.0 | 1.9 |
| 1978-79 | 0.0 | 0.0 | 0.0 | 0.0 | 0.0 | 0.0 | T | T | 0.0 | 0.0 | 0.0 | 0.0 | T |
| 1979-80 | 0.0 | 0.0 | 0.0 | 0.0 | 0.0 | 0.0 | T | T | 0.3 | 0.0 | 0.0 | 0.0 | 0.3 |
| 1980-81 | 0.0 | 0.0 | 0.0 | 0.0 | 0.0 | T | T | T | 0.0 | 0.0 | 0.0 | 0.0 | T |
| 1981-82 | 0.0 | 0.0 | 0.0 | 0.0 | 0.0 | T | 6.6 | 0.0 | T | 0.0 | 0.0 | 0.0 | 6.6 |
| 1982-83 | 0.0 | 0.0 | 0.0 | 0.0 | 0.0 | T | 1.0 | T | 1.5 | 0.0 | 0.0 | 0.0 | 2.5 |
| 1983-84 | 0.0 | 0.0 | 0.0 | 0.0 | 0.0 | T | T | T | 2.0 | 0.0 | 0.0 | 0.0 | 2.0 |
| 1984-85 | 0.0 | 0.0 | 0.0 | 0.0 | 0.0 | T | T | 0.3 | 0.0 | 0.0 | 0.0 | 0.0 | 0.3 |
| 1985-86 | 0.0 | 0.0 | 0.0 | 0.0 | 0.0 | T | T | T | 0.0 | 0.0 | 0.0 | 0.0 | T |
| 1986-87 | 0.0 | 0.0 | 0.0 | 0.0 | 0.0 | T | 2.6 | 0.0 | T | 5.0 | 0.0 | 0.0 | 7.6 |
| 1987-88 | 0.0 | 0.0 | 0.0 | 0.0 | 0.0 | 0.0 | 1.0 | T | T | 0.0 | 0.0 | 0.0 | 1.0 |
| 1988-89 | 0.0 | 0.0 | 0.0 | 0.0 | 0.0 | 0.0 | 0.0 | T | T | 0.0 | 0.0 | 0.0 | T |
| 1989-90 | 0.0 | 0.0 | 0.0 | 0.0 | T | 0.4 | 0.0 | T | 0.0 | 0.0 | 0.0 | 0.0 | 0.4 |
| 1990-91 | T | 0.0 | 0.0 | 0.0 | 0.0 | T | | | | | | | |
| Record Mean | T | 0.0 | 0.0 | T | T | 0.3 | 0.6 | 0.2 | 0.1 | 0.1 | T | T | 1.4 |

**See Reference Notes, relative to all above tables, on preceding page.**

# MOBILE, ALABAMA

Mobile is located at the head of Mobile Bay and approximately 30 miles from the Gulf of Mexico. Its weather is influenced to a considerable extent by the Gulf.

The summers are consistently warm, but temperatures are seldom as high as they are at inland stations. Normally, in summer, the day begins in the low 70s and the temperature rises rapidly before noon to the high 80s or low 90s, when it is checked by the onset of the sea breeze. On the rare occasions when northerly winds prevail throughout the day, temperatures may reach the high 90s or rise slightly above 100 degrees.

Winter weather is usually mild except for occasional invasions of cold air that last about three days. January is the coldest month in the year. Unusual winters may produce readings that require extensive protective measures as some citrus fruit is grown in the area and outdoor nurseries are numerous.

Based on the 1951–1980 period, the average first occurrence of 32 degrees Fahrenheit in the fall is November 26 and the average last occurrence in the spring is February 27.

The yearly rainfall is among the highest in the United States. It is fairly evenly distributed throughout the year with a slight maximum at the height of the summer thunderstorm season and a slight minimum during the late fall. Rainfall is usually of the shower type and long periods of continuous rain are rare.

Frontal thunderstorms may occur in any month of the year. There may be a thunderstorm every other day in July and August. The summer storms are usually not too violent and seldom produce hail.

The area is subject to hurricanes from the West Indies, the western Caribbean, and the Gulf of Mexico.

**TABLE 1**

# NORMALS, MEANS AND EXTREMES

MOBILE, ALABAMA

LATITUDE: 30°41'N   LONGITUDE: 88°15'W   ELEVATION: FT. GRND 211 BARO 226 TIME ZONE: CENTRAL   WBAN: 13894

| | (a) | JAN | FEB | MAR | APR | MAY | JUNE | JULY | AUG | SEP | OCT | NOV | DEC | YEAR |
|---|---|---|---|---|---|---|---|---|---|---|---|---|---|---|
| **TEMPERATURE °F:** | | | | | | | | | | | | | | |
| Normals | | | | | | | | | | | | | | |
| -Daily Maximum | | 60.6 | 63.9 | 70.3 | 78.3 | 84.9 | 90.2 | 91.2 | 90.7 | 87.0 | 79.4 | 69.3 | 63.1 | 77.4 |
| -Daily Minimum | | 40.9 | 43.2 | 49.8 | 57.7 | 64.8 | 70.8 | 73.2 | 72.9 | 69.3 | 57.5 | 47.9 | 42.9 | 57.6 |
| -Monthly | | 50.8 | 53.6 | 60.1 | 68.0 | 74.9 | 80.5 | 82.2 | 81.8 | 78.2 | 68.5 | 58.6 | 53.1 | 67.5 |
| Extremes | | | | | | | | | | | | | | |
| -Record Highest | 48 | 84 | 82 | 90 | 94 | 100 | 102 | 104 | 102 | 99 | 93 | 87 | 81 | 104 |
| -Year | | 1949 | 1989 | 1946 | 1987 | 1953 | 1952 | 1952 | 1968 | 1980 | 1963 | 1971 | 1974 | JUL 1952 |
| -Record Lowest | 48 | 3 | 11 | 21 | 32 | 43 | 49 | 60 | 59 | 42 | 32 | 22 | 8 | 3 |
| -Year | | 1985 | 1951 | 1943 | 1987 | 1960 | 1984 | 1947 | 1956 | 1967 | 1957 | 1950 | 1983 | JAN 1985 |
| **NORMAL DEGREE DAYS:** | | | | | | | | | | | | | | |
| Heating (base 65°F) | | 469 | 342 | 191 | 43 | 0 | 0 | 0 | 0 | 0 | 50 | 218 | 382 | 1695 |
| Cooling (base 65°F) | | 29 | 23 | 39 | 133 | 307 | 465 | 533 | 521 | 396 | 158 | 26 | 13 | 2643 |
| **% OF POSSIBLE SUNSHINE** | | | | | | | | | | | | | | |
| **MEAN SKY COVER (tenths)** | | | | | | | | | | | | | | |
| Sunrise - Sunset | 41 | 6.5 | 6.2 | 6.1 | 5.7 | 5.7 | 5.8 | 6.6 | 6.0 | 5.7 | 4.4 | 5.4 | 6.2 | 5.9 |
| **MEAN NUMBER OF DAYS:** | | | | | | | | | | | | | | |
| Sunrise to Sunset | | | | | | | | | | | | | | |
| -Clear | 41 | 7.9 | 7.8 | 8.8 | 9.4 | 8.8 | 7.1 | 3.8 | 6.1 | 8.8 | 14.6 | 10.8 | 9.1 | 103.0 |
| -Partly Cloudy | 41 | 6.4 | 6.6 | 8.0 | 8.7 | 11.4 | 13.9 | 15.0 | 14.7 | 10.1 | 7.6 | 7.1 | 6.3 | 115.9 |
| -Cloudy | 41 | 16.8 | 13.8 | 14.3 | 12.0 | 10.8 | 9.0 | 12.1 | 10.2 | 11.0 | 8.8 | 12.0 | 15.6 | 146.4 |
| Precipitation | | | | | | | | | | | | | | |
| .01 inches or more | 48 | 10.6 | 9.7 | 10.5 | 7.4 | 8.4 | 11.4 | 16.2 | 14.0 | 10.2 | 5.7 | 7.8 | 10.4 | 122.3 |
| Snow, Ice pellets | | | | | | | | | | | | | | |
| 1.0 inches or more | 48 | 0.* | 0.1 | 0.* | 0.0 | 0.0 | 0.0 | 0.0 | 0.0 | 0.0 | 0.0 | 0.0 | 0.* | 0.2 |
| Thunderstorms | 48 | 1.8 | 2.3 | 5.0 | 4.8 | 7.1 | 11.9 | 18.1 | 14.2 | 7.3 | 2.2 | 2.2 | 2.3 | 79.1 |
| Heavy Fog Visibility | | | | | | | | | | | | | | |
| 1/4 mile or less | 48 | 6.0 | 4.6 | 5.4 | 4.5 | 2.7 | 0.9 | 1.0 | 1.4 | 1.9 | 2.5 | 4.5 | 4.9 | 40.2 |
| Temperature °F | | | | | | | | | | | | | | |
| -Maximum | | | | | | | | | | | | | | |
| 90° and above | 27 | 0.0 | 0.0 | 0.0 | 0.4 | 4.1 | 17.3 | 22.2 | 20.5 | 10.3 | 1.0 | 0.0 | 0.0 | 75.8 |
| 32° and below | 27 | 0.3 | 0.0 | 0.0 | 0.0 | 0.0 | 0.0 | 0.0 | 0.0 | 0.0 | 0.0 | 0.0 | 0.1 | 0.4 |
| -Minimum | | | | | | | | | | | | | | |
| 32° and below | 27 | 8.8 | 5.9 | 1.2 | 0.* | 0.0 | 0.0 | 0.0 | 0.0 | 0.0 | 0.0 | 1.2 | 6.0 | 23.1 |
| 0° and below | 27 | 0.0 | 0.0 | 0.0 | 0.0 | 0.0 | 0.0 | 0.0 | 0.0 | 0.0 | 0.0 | 0.0 | 0.0 | 0.0 |
| **AVG. STATION PRESS. (mb)** | 17 | 1012.9 | 1011.6 | 1009.2 | 1008.7 | 1007.3 | 1008.1 | 1009.2 | 1008.9 | 1008.3 | 1010.7 | 1011.3 | 1012.9 | 1009.9 |
| **RELATIVE HUMIDITY (%)** | | | | | | | | | | | | | | |
| Hour 00 | 27 | 78 | 77 | 80 | 82 | 84 | 85 | 86 | 88 | 85 | 82 | 82 | 80 | 82 |
| Hour 06 | 27 | 81 | 81 | 84 | 87 | 87 | 87 | 89 | 91 | 89 | 86 | 86 | 83 | 86 |
| Hour 12 (Local Time) | 27 | 60 | 56 | 55 | 52 | 54 | 55 | 60 | 61 | 60 | 53 | 57 | 61 | 57 |
| Hour 18 | 27 | 68 | 63 | 63 | 61 | 63 | 66 | 71 | 74 | 72 | 67 | 71 | 71 | 68 |
| **PRECIPITATION (inches):** | | | | | | | | | | | | | | |
| Water Equivalent | | | | | | | | | | | | | | |
| -Normal | | 4.59 | 4.91 | 6.48 | 5.35 | 5.46 | 5.07 | 7.74 | 6.75 | 6.56 | 2.62 | 3.67 | 5.44 | 64.64 |
| -Maximum Monthly | 48 | 10.40 | 11.89 | 15.58 | 17.69 | 15.08 | 13.07 | 19.29 | 15.19 | 14.04 | 13.20 | 13.65 | 11.38 | 19.29 |
| -Year | | 1978 | 1983 | 1946 | 1955 | 1980 | 1961 | 1949 | 1984 | 1988 | 1985 | 1948 | 1953 | JUL 1949 |
| -Minimum Monthly | 48 | 0.98 | 1.31 | 0.59 | 0.48 | 0.45 | 1.19 | 1.72 | 2.35 | 0.58 | T | 0.25 | 1.29 | T |
| -Year | | 1968 | 1948 | 1967 | 1954 | 1962 | 1966 | 1983 | 1972 | 1963 | 1978 | 1960 | 1980 | OCT 1978 |
| -Maximum in 24 hrs | 48 | 8.34 | 5.37 | 6.52 | 13.36 | 8.00 | 7.38 | 5.34 | 6.62 | 8.55 | 5.65 | 7.02 | 5.50 | 13.36 |
| -Year | | 1965 | 1981 | 1951 | 1955 | 1981 | 1961 | 1975 | 1969 | 1979 | 1985 | 1975 | 1968 | APR 1955 |
| Snow, Ice pellets | | | | | | | | | | | | | | |
| -Maximum Monthly | 48 | 3.5 | 3.6 | 1.6 | T | 0.0 | 0.0 | T | 0.0 | 0.0 | 0.0 | T | 3.0 | 3.6 |
| -Year | | 1955 | 1973 | 1954 | 1988 | | | 1989 | | | | 1966 | 1963 | FEB 1973 |
| -Maximum in 24 hrs | 48 | 3.5 | 3.6 | 1.6 | T | 0.0 | 0.0 | T | 0.0 | 0.0 | 0.0 | T | 3.0 | 3.6 |
| -Year | | 1955 | 1973 | 1954 | 1988 | | | 1989 | | | | 1966 | 1963 | FEB 1973 |
| **WIND:** | | | | | | | | | | | | | | |
| Mean Speed (mph) | 41 | 10.4 | 10.7 | 10.9 | 10.3 | 8.9 | 7.7 | 7.0 | 6.8 | 8.0 | 8.2 | 9.4 | 10.1 | 9.0 |
| Prevailing Direction | | | | | | | | | | | | | | |
| through 1963 | | N | N | N | S | S | S | S | NE | NE | N | N | N | N |
| Fastest Obs. 1 Min. | | | | | | | | | | | | | | |
| -Direction (!!!) | 31 | 18 | 23 | 10 | 01 | 32 | 22 | 18 | 14 | 09 | 36 | 36 | 32 | 09 |
| -Speed (MPH) | 31 | 44 | 46 | 40 | 44 | 51 | 44 | 46 | 63 | 63 | 46 | 37 | 38 | 63 |
| -Year | | 1959 | 1960 | 1985 | 1964 | 1963 | 1989 | 1960 | 1969 | 1979 | 1964 | 1959 | 1959 | SEP 1979 |
| Peak Gust | | | | | | | | | | | | | | |
| -Direction (!!!) | 6 | SW | S | E | NW | SW | SW | N | NW | SE | S | NW | S | SW |
| -Speed (mph) | 6 | 45 | 61 | 52 | 43 | 62 | 60 | 54 | 46 | 60 | 52 | 48 | 39 | 62 |
| -Date | | 1985 | 1987 | 1985 | 1989 | 1985 | 1989 | 1986 | 1989 | 1985 | 1985 | 1988 | 1989 | MAY 1985 |

**See reference Notes to this table on the following page.**

PRECIPITATION (inches)    MOBILE, ALABAMA

**TABLE 2**

| YEAR | JAN | FEB | MAR | APR | MAY | JUNE | JULY | AUG | SEP | OCT | NOV | DEC | ANNUAL |
|------|-----|-----|-----|-----|-----|------|------|-----|-----|-----|-----|-----|--------|
| 1961 | 6.14 | 6.61 | 10.35 | 6.86 | 4.62 | 13.07 | 4.80 | 5.69 | 6.63 | 1.47 | 5.57 | 10.92 | 82.73 |
| 1962 | 4.75 | 6.57 | 6.97 | 1.89 | 0.45 | 7.15 | 5.44 | 3.01 | 4.87 | 2.41 | 2.75 | 4.54 | 50.80 |
| 1963 | 7.14 | 4.11 | 1.48 | 1.83 | 2.02 | 7.16 | 8.25 | 9.26 | 0.58 | 0.06 | 4.48 | 6.46 | 52.83 |
| 1964 | 7.36 | 2.73 | 4.23 | 13.45 | 4.32 | 4.27 | 8.83 | 6.20 | 2.19 | 2.42 | 3.73 | 4.12 | 63.85 |
| 1965 | 9.35 | 4.94 | 4.97 | 0.60 | 4.33 | 3.70 | 8.13 | 4.72 | 10.45 | 1.59 | 0.73 | 3.97 | 57.48 |
| 1966 | 5.52 | 9.01 | 3.21 | 2.37 | 4.66 | 1.19 | 5.20 | 6.48 | 4.32 | 4.44 | 1.35 | 4.60 | 52.35 |
| 1967 | 5.46 | 6.13 | 0.59 | 2.26 | 5.05 | 2.88 | 7.80 | 8.86 | 7.76 | 6.69 | 0.36 | 7.50 | 61.34 |
| 1968 | 0.98 | 2.88 | 1.30 | 2.24 | 3.17 | 3.71 | 4.59 | 6.13 | 1.13 | 4.05 | 10.70 | 43.96 | |
| 1969 | 2.79 | 3.40 | 8.15 | 4.53 | 7.95 | 1.33 | 14.14 | 12.05 | 1.95 | 0.67 | 0.44 | 5.58 | 62.98 |
| 1970 | 3.85 | 5.32 | 8.60 | 1.67 | 8.84 | 7.68 | 9.19 | 9.20 | 2.56 | 5.71 | 1.54 | 5.77 | 69.93 |
| 1971 | 2.15 | 7.15 | 6.49 | 0.99 | 3.16 | 2.88 | 7.75 | 10.46 | 7.30 | 0.03 | 1.23 | 5.58 | 55.17 |
| 1972 | 5.94 | 4.46 | 5.87 | 1.81 | 7.72 | 2.16 | 2.35 | 3.28 | 1.26 | 5.67 | 5.59 | 49.76 | |
| 1973 | 1.96 | 3.40 | 11.63 | 9.91 | 2.97 | 5.33 | 6.24 | 5.46 | 12.68 | 2.15 | 4.52 | 4.57 | 70.82 |
| 1974 | 3.89 | 6.47 | 6.16 | 5.91 | 2.31 | 3.48 | 6.60 | 7.03 | 10.60 | 0.88 | 3.91 | 4.31 | 61.55 |
| 1975 | 3.43 | 3.75 | 7.45 | 9.05 | 7.12 | 3.76 | 11.82 | 8.50 | 7.37 | 6.72 | 12.63 | 4.98 | 86.58 |
| 1976 | 1.80 | 2.36 | 9.60 | 1.69 | 11.11 | 4.71 | 4.43 | 4.77 | 3.51 | 5.67 | 4.64 | 4.21 | 58.50 |
| 1977 | 5.54 | 1.86 | 6.06 | 2.73 | 5.30 | 1.26 | 7.77 | 5.42 | 9.61 | 4.57 | 9.51 | 4.94 | 64.57 |
| 1978 | 10.40 | 3.88 | 4.08 | 7.03 | 9.74 | 6.13 | 7.74 | 7.34 | 3.04 | T | 5.05 | 4.36 | 68.79 |
| 1979 | 5.14 | 9.14 | 8.37 | 4.05 | 7.02 | 3.70 | 10.80 | 6.10 | 11.73 | 2.80 | 6.46 | 3.94 | 79.25 |
| 1980 | 4.95 | 1.58 | 13.46 | 15.43 | 15.08 | 2.57 | 6.54 | 6.42 | 5.94 | 2.90 | 1.96 | 1.29 | 78.12 |
| 1981 | 1.23 | 8.75 | 3.00 | 0.96 | 12.51 | 6.50 | 6.53 | 5.06 | 3.97 | 0.94 | 0.85 | 6.82 | 57.12 |
| 1982 | 3.56 | 7.42 | 6.81 | 4.48 | 2.84 | 11.00 | 13.14 | 7.00 | 4.68 | 1.61 | 3.66 | 8.24 | 74.44 |
| 1983 | 5.82 | 11.89 | 6.89 | 12.53 | 1.53 | 8.09 | 1.72 | 11.57 | 5.97 | 3.81 | 5.30 | 8.34 | 83.46 |
| 1984 | 6.13 | 4.79 | 4.75 | 3.53 | 4.28 | 2.07 | 2.36 | 15.19 | 0.74 | 6.19 | 1.67 | 2.12 | 53.82 |
| 1985 | 5.06 | 6.39 | 5.49 | 1.22 | 5.77 | 3.94 | 8.31 | 4.32 | 10.32 | 13.20 | 1.61 | 4.34 | 69.97 |
| 1986 | 2.67 | 4.17 | 4.53 | 2.16 | 4.18 | 7.53 | 7.13 | 5.60 | 4.41 | 4.83 | 8.45 | 3.68 | 59.34 |
| 1987 | 5.81 | 8.64 | 6.18 | 0.83 | 10.69 | 7.68 | 4.18 | 10.33 | 3.62 | 0.02 | 5.54 | 3.60 | 67.12 |
| 1988 | 4.64 | 6.26 | 7.80 | 4.19 | 0.58 | 2.34 | 6.04 | 10.43 | 14.04 | 1.83 | 2.30 | 1.80 | 62.25 |
| 1989 | 2.13 | 1.47 | 5.57 | 3.55 | 6.47 | 9.82 | 7.16 | 3.82 | 4.55 | 0.90 | 11.33 | 7.23 | 64.00 |
| 1990 | 7.35 | 8.13 | 12.24 | 4.51 | 6.47 | 2.68 | 2.28 | 1.46 | 2.65 | 1.23 | 1.77 | 5.20 | 55.97 |
| Record Mean | 4.71 | 5.13 | 6.60 | 5.02 | 4.78 | 5.55 | 7.43 | 6.69 | 5.61 | 3.22 | 3.77 | 5.15 | 63.65 |

**TABLE 3**    AVERAGE TEMPERATURE (deg. F)    MOBILE, ALABAMA

| YEAR | JAN | FEB | MAR | APR | MAY | JUNE | JULY | AUG | SEP | OCT | NOV | DEC | ANNUAL |
|------|-----|-----|-----|-----|-----|------|------|-----|-----|-----|-----|-----|--------|
| 1961 | 45.4 | 57.9 | 62.2 | 62.5 | 72.3 | 77.0 | 80.6 | 80.2 | 78.1 | 67.5 | 60.5 | 54.9 | 66.6 |
| #1962 | 48.9 | 61.7 | 57.0 | 65.6 | 80.1 | 80.6 | 83.4 | 82.1 | 78.0 | 56.9 | 50.6 | 68.0 | |
| 1963 | 46.2 | 47.8 | 63.9 | 71.2 | 76.1 | 80.4 | 82.7 | 83.5 | 77.3 | 71.7 | 59.2 | 44.9 | 67.1 |
| 1964 | 49.2 | 48.1 | 58.1 | 69.6 | 74.9 | 80.4 | 80.5 | 81.5 | 78.2 | 64.3 | 61.1 | 54.2 | 66.8 |
| 1965 | 52.5 | 53.4 | 58.2 | 71.4 | 75.7 | 79.4 | 82.4 | 81.2 | 79.1 | 68.7 | 63.9 | 53.7 | 68.3 |
| 1966 | 47.2 | 52.8 | 58.8 | 68.4 | 75.1 | 79.1 | 83.8 | 81.2 | 77.9 | 68.0 | 60.7 | 55.3 | 67.2 |
| 1967 | 53.0 | 52.2 | 64.5 | 74.6 | 74.6 | 82.5 | 81.5 | 79.8 | 74.2 | 66.7 | 59.5 | 57.9 | 68.4 |
| 1968 | 50.3 | 46.7 | 58.1 | 70.3 | 76.0 | 83.2 | 82.7 | 83.1 | 78.1 | 70.1 | 56.3 | 49.5 | 67.0 |
| 1969 | 51.5 | 53.7 | 53.8 | 68.9 | 74.5 | 82.4 | 83.5 | 80.6 | 77.5 | 71.2 | 58.0 | 53.7 | 67.4 |
| 1970 | 45.0 | 51.4 | 59.2 | 71.9 | 75.3 | 80.2 | 83.0 | 83.0 | 81.7 | 70.5 | 55.9 | 57.4 | 67.9 |
| 1971 | 53.7 | 54.3 | 59.9 | 67.9 | 73.0 | 82.4 | 82.3 | 82.1 | 79.5 | 72.9 | 63.5 | 69.2 | |
| 1972 | 58.4 | 55.0 | 61.8 | 69.4 | 74.7 | 80.7 | 81.4 | 83.4 | 81.6 | 71.0 | 56.8 | 55.5 | 69.2 |
| 1973 | 50.5 | 51.7 | 64.6 | 65.6 | 74.6 | 81.6 | 84.1 | 81.4 | 80.2 | 73.6 | 65.3 | 52.9 | 68.9 |
| 1974 | 64.0 | 55.2 | 64.3 | 66.1 | 75.5 | 77.8 | 82.2 | 81.4 | 75.5 | 65.5 | 59.2 | 55.1 | 68.5 |
| 1975 | 56.6 | 59.8 | 60.7 | 66.2 | 76.5 | 80.7 | 81.8 | 81.7 | 75.3 | 70.3 | 60.5 | 52.1 | 68.5 |
| 1976 | 49.5 | 59.4 | 64.0 | 69.9 | 72.7 | 79.8 | 83.4 | 81.0 | 75.5 | 61.4 | 50.6 | 48.0 | 66.3 |
| 1977 | 40.9 | 52.2 | 62.6 | 68.2 | 75.6 | 82.9 | 83.5 | 83.4 | 80.9 | 65.2 | 60.9 | 50.8 | 67.3 |
| 1978 | 41.2 | 45.1 | 56.7 | 68.5 | 75.4 | 81.2 | 82.8 | 83.2 | 81.6 | 69.8 | 65.1 | 54.4 | 67.1 |
| 1979 | 45.1 | 50.7 | 60.8 | 69.3 | 73.3 | 79.7 | 81.3 | 81.1 | 76.8 | 68.1 | 57.2 | 51.3 | 66.2 |
| 1980 | 56.2 | 49.7 | 61.6 | 65.9 | 74.6 | 81.2 | 84.6 | 83.2 | 81.8 | 66.3 | 57.8 | 51.6 | 67.9 |
| 1981 | 46.0 | 53.4 | 59.5 | 71.0 | 71.6 | 82.6 | 84.0 | 82.7 | 76.8 | 69.4 | 63.0 | 49.9 | 67.5 |
| 1982 | 49.7 | 53.3 | 63.5 | 67.1 | 74.4 | 80.7 | 81.0 | 81.0 | 76.0 | 68.5 | 60.4 | 56.9 | 67.7 |
| 1983 | 47.1 | 51.1 | 55.0 | 61.8 | 72.1 | 76.4 | 81.8 | 81.4 | 73.6 | 67.4 | 57.7 | 47.7 | 64.4 |
| 1984 | 46.1 | 52.4 | 58.6 | 65.7 | 72.5 | 78.1 | 79.9 | 78.8 | 75.6 | 72.7 | 56.3 | 40.4 | 66.4 |
| 1985 | 43.5 | 50.7 | 64.5 | 67.7 | 73.7 | 79.9 | 79.7 | 81.0 | 76.0 | 71.4 | 66.1 | 48.8 | 66.9 |
| 1986 | 49.7 | 56.4 | 59.7 | 66.1 | 74.4 | 81.0 | 83.3 | 80.5 | 79.5 | 68.5 | 64.3 | 51.1 | 67.9 |
| 1987 | 48.8 | 53.6 | 59.2 | 64.6 | 75.7 | 78.9 | 81.8 | 82.2 | 77.2 | 62.5 | 59.2 | 56.5 | 66.7 |
| 1988 | 46.8 | 50.6 | 58.6 | 67.3 | 72.8 | 79.5 | 81.4 | 81.3 | 78.3 | 65.3 | 52.7 | 53.8 | 66.6 |
| 1989 | 57.1 | 54.0 | 61.7 | 65.9 | 74.1 | 79.0 | 81.0 | 81.6 | 76.7 | 66.1 | 59.1 | 44.4 | 66.7 |
| 1990 | 54.6 | 59.0 | 61.7 | 65.0 | 73.4 | 81.1 | 81.7 | 83.1 | 78.6 | 68.0 | 60.9 | 56.7 | 68.7 |
| Record Mean | 51.4 | 54.2 | 60.1 | 67.1 | 74.2 | 80.3 | 81.8 | 81.5 | 78.0 | 68.8 | 59.1 | 53.0 | 67.5 |
| Max | 60.3 | 63.2 | 69.2 | 76.2 | 83.2 | 88.9 | 90.1 | 89.8 | 86.4 | 78.5 | 68.8 | 61.9 | 76.4 |
| Min | 42.5 | 45.1 | 51.1 | 57.9 | 65.1 | 71.6 | 73.5 | 73.2 | 69.5 | 59.0 | 49.4 | 44.0 | 58.5 |

## REFERENCE NOTES FOR TABLES 1, 2, 3 and 6    (MOBILE, AL)

### GENERAL

T - TRACE AMOUNT
BLANK ENTRIES DENOTE MISSING/UNREPORTED DATA.
# INDICATES A STATION OR INSTRUMENT RELOCATION.

### SPECIFIC

#### TABLE 1

(a) - LENGTH OF RECORD IN YEARS. ALTHOUGH
INDIVIDUAL MONTHS MAY BE MISSING.

* LESS THAN .05

NORMALS — BASED ON THE 1951-1980 RECORD PERIOD.
EXTREMES — DATES ARE THE MOST RECENT OCCURRENCE.
WIND DIR. — NUMERALS SHOW TENS OF DEGREES
CLOCKWISE FROM TRUE NORTH.
"00" INDICATES CALM.
RESULTANT WIND DIRECTIONS ARE GIVEN TO WHOLE DEGREES.

#### TABLE 3
MAX AND MIN ARE LONG-TERM MEAN DAILY MAXIMUM
AND MEAN DAILY MINIMUM TEMPERATURES.

### EXCEPTIONS

#### TABLES 2, 3, and 6

RECORD MEANS ARE THROUGH THE CURRENT YEAR,
BEGINNING IN    1871 FOR TEMPERATURE
1871 FOR PRECIPITATION
1942 FOR SNOWFALL

**TABLE 4**

HEATING DEGREE DAYS Base 65 deg. F    MOBILE, ALABAMA

| SEASON | JULY | AUG | SEP | OCT | NOV | DEC | JAN | FEB | MAR | APR | MAY | JUNE | TOTAL |
|---|---|---|---|---|---|---|---|---|---|---|---|---|---|
| #1961-62 | 0 | 0 | 0 | 42 | 193 | 339 | 511 | 141 | 270 | 83 | 0 | 0 | 1579 |
| 1962-63 | 0 | 0 | 0 | 41 | 242 | 441 | 575 | 473 | 108 | 6 | 3 | 0 | 1889 |
| 1963-64 | 0 | 0 | 0 | 17 | 186 | 616 | 486 | 484 | 187 | 25 | 0 | 0 | 2001 |
| 1964-65 | 0 | 0 | 0 | 78 | 167 | 347 | 387 | 342 | 240 | 4 | 0 | 0 | 1565 |
| 1965-66 | 0 | 0 | 0 | 43 | 100 | 345 | 554 | 333 | 208 | 27 | 1 | 0 | 1611 |
| 1966-67 | 0 | 0 | 0 | 32 | 173 | 374 | 370 | 363 | 100 | 0 | 3 | 0 | 1415 |
| 1967-68 | 0 | 0 | 23 | 46 | 202 | 273 | 448 | 525 | 251 | 12 | 0 | 0 | 1780 |
| 1968-69 | 0 | 0 | 0 | 50 | 284 | 474 | 420 | 320 | 342 | 8 | 0 | 0 | 1898 |
| 1969-70 | 0 | 0 | 0 | 20 | 220 | 345 | 618 | 375 | 190 | 14 | 10 | 0 | 1792 |
| 1970-71 | 0 | 0 | 0 | 7 | 273 | 265 | 361 | 308 | 190 | 57 | 6 | 0 | 1467 |
| 1971-72 | 0 | 0 | 0 | 8 | 204 | 136 | 244 | 295 | 131 | 35 | 0 | 0 | 1053 |
| 1972-73 | 0 | 0 | 0 | 33 | 284 | 308 | 442 | 368 | 86 | 75 | 0 | 0 | 1596 |
| 1973-74 | 0 | 0 | 0 | 18 | 91 | 377 | 108 | 288 | 106 | 49 | 0 | 0 | 1037 |
| 1974-75 | 0 | 0 | 0 | 58 | 215 | 336 | 276 | 185 | 183 | 70 | 0 | 0 | 1323 |
| 1975-76 | 0 | 0 | 9 | 11 | 211 | 402 | 475 | 174 | 100 | 8 | 0 | 0 | 1390 |
| 1976-77 | 0 | 0 | 0 | 149 | 430 | 520 | 738 | 355 | 141 | 28 | 0 | 0 | 2361 |
| 1977-78 | 0 | 0 | 0 | 73 | 149 | 439 | 731 | 551 | 268 | 16 | 0 | 0 | 2227 |
| 1978-79 | 0 | 0 | 0 | 20 | 53 | 355 | 613 | 401 | 152 | 8 | 4 | 0 | 1606 |
| 1979-80 | 0 | 0 | 0 | 43 | 246 | 424 | 267 | 454 | 159 | 52 | 0 | 0 | 1645 |
| 1980-81 | 0 | 0 | 0 | 63 | 235 | 420 | 581 | 323 | 180 | 9 | 4 | 0 | 1815 |
| 1981-82 | 0 | 0 | 5 | 42 | 113 | 463 | 485 | 323 | 161 | 48 | 0 | 0 | 1640 |
| 1982-83 | 0 | 0 | 5 | 63 | 185 | 296 | 545 | 383 | 306 | 119 | 4 | 0 | 1906 |
| 1983-84 | 0 | 0 | 7 | 60 | 243 | 529 | 582 | 363 | 218 | 69 | 10 | 0 | 2081 |
| 1984-85 | 0 | 0 | 2 | 17 | 270 | 172 | 665 | 397 | 84 | 50 | 1 | 0 | 1658 |
| 1985-86 | 0 | 0 | 1 | 22 | 69 | 503 | 469 | 251 | 188 | 40 | 0 | 0 | 1543 |
| 1986-87 | 0 | 0 | 0 | 43 | 105 | 433 | 500 | 311 | 193 | 106 | 0 | 0 | 1691 |
| 1987-88 | 0 | 0 | 0 | 108 | 194 | 283 | 565 | 421 | 214 | 33 | 0 | 0 | 1818 |
| 1988-89 | 0 | 0 | 0 | 53 | 122 | 363 | 254 | 335 | 170 | 81 | 2 | 0 | 1380 |
| 1989-90 | 0 | 0 | 6 | 71 | 204 | 630 | 326 | 186 | 128 | 71 | 0 | 0 | 1622 |
| 1990-91 | 0 | 0 | 2 | 58 | 145 | 287 | | | | | | | |

**TABLE 5**

COOLING DEGREE DAYS Base 65 deg. F    MOBILE, ALABAMA

| YEAR | JAN | FEB | MAR | APR | MAY | JUNE | JULY | AUG | SEP | OCT | NOV | DEC | TOTAL |
|---|---|---|---|---|---|---|---|---|---|---|---|---|---|
| 1969 | 5 | 10 | 4 | 134 | 303 | 527 | 582 | 490 | 380 | 220 | 17 | 4 | 2676 |
| 1970 | 6 | 2 | 16 | 229 | 335 | 467 | 564 | 567 | 505 | 184 | 6 | 36 | 2917 |
| 1971 | 18 | 13 | 37 | 151 | 260 | 531 | 541 | 534 | 441 | 261 | 37 | 94 | 2918 |
| 1972 | 47 | 15 | 40 | 173 | 309 | 478 | 513 | 575 | 505 | 224 | 46 | 20 | 2945 |
| 1973 | 0 | 1 | 80 | 98 | 303 | 508 | 598 | 518 | 462 | 293 | 110 | 10 | 2981 |
| 1974 | 85 | 19 | 91 | 88 | 332 | 392 | 539 | 517 | 323 | 81 | 45 | 36 | 2548 |
| 1975 | 21 | 44 | 57 | 115 | 363 | 475 | 529 | 524 | 325 | 183 | 85 | 11 | 2732 |
| 1976 | 0 | 17 | 74 | 160 | 245 | 454 | 578 | 504 | 321 | 48 | 4 | 0 | 2405 |
| 1977 | 0 | 4 | 74 | 132 | 333 | 543 | 543 | 576 | 482 | 85 | 31 | 7 | 2846 |
| 1978 | 0 | 0 | 17 | 127 | 329 | 496 | 560 | 573 | 507 | 177 | 64 | 34 | 2884 |
| 1979 | 0 | 6 | 28 | 144 | 267 | 448 | 512 | 509 | 361 | 146 | 16 | 5 | 2442 |
| 1980 | 2 | 17 | 61 | 89 | 305 | 495 | 618 | 571 | 512 | 110 | 25 | 9 | 2814 |
| 1981 | 0 | 4 | 15 | 195 | 217 | 538 | 595 | 557 | 366 | 185 | 60 | 4 | 2736 |
| 1982 | 17 | 2 | 119 | 118 | 296 | 475 | 502 | 503 | 342 | 177 | 54 | 53 | 2658 |
| 1983 | 0 | 0 | 4 | 27 | 229 | 351 | 532 | 514 | 271 | 140 | 29 | 2 | 2099 |
| 1984 | 0 | 3 | 24 | 96 | 249 | 401 | 469 | 435 | 327 | 261 | 16 | 34 | 2315 |
| 1985 | 4 | 2 | 77 | 133 | 275 | 452 | 461 | 504 | 339 | 227 | 108 | 7 | 2589 |
| 1986 | 0 | 15 | 31 | 79 | 295 | 486 | 573 | 489 | 444 | 158 | 89 | 8 | 2667 |
| 1987 | 4 | 0 | 21 | 99 | 341 | 422 | 527 | 544 | 373 | 41 | 27 | 28 | 2427 |
| 1988 | 7 | 10 | 21 | 108 | 251 | 442 | 529 | 513 | 404 | 67 | 61 | 20 | 2433 |
| 1989 | 16 | 33 | 74 | 116 | 289 | 431 | 498 | 523 | 366 | 114 | 31 | 0 | 2491 |
| 1990 | 7 | 23 | 34 | 80 | 267 | 493 | 525 | 569 | 417 | 155 | 29 | 36 | 2635 |

**TABLE 6**

SNOWFALL (inches)    MOBILE, ALABAMA

| SEASON | JULY | AUG | SEP | OCT | NOV | DEC | JAN | FEB | MAR | APR | MAY | JUNE | TOTAL |
|---|---|---|---|---|---|---|---|---|---|---|---|---|---|
| 1970-71 | 0.0 | 0.0 | 0.0 | 0.0 | 0.0 | 0.0 | 0.0 | 0.0 | T | 0.0 | 0.0 | 0.0 | T |
| 1971-72 | 0.0 | 0.0 | 0.0 | 0.0 | 0.0 | 0.0 | 0.0 | 0.0 | 0.0 | 0.0 | 0.0 | 0.0 | 0.0 |
| 1972-73 | 0.0 | 0.0 | 0.0 | 0.0 | 0.0 | 0.0 | T | 3.6 | 0.0 | 0.0 | 0.0 | 0.0 | 3.6 |
| 1973-74 | 0.0 | 0.0 | 0.0 | 0.0 | 0.0 | T | 0.0 | 0.0 | 0.0 | 0.0 | 0.0 | 0.0 | T |
| 1974-75 | 0.0 | 0.0 | 0.0 | 0.0 | 0.0 | 0.0 | 0.0 | 0.0 | 0.0 | 0.0 | 0.0 | 0.0 | 0.0 |
| 1975-76 | 0.0 | 0.0 | 0.0 | 0.0 | 0.0 | 0.0 | 0.0 | 0.0 | 0.0 | 0.0 | 0.0 | 0.0 | 0.0 |
| 1976-77 | 0.0 | 0.0 | 0.0 | 0.0 | 0.0 | T | 1.9 | 0.0 | 0.0 | 0.0 | 0.0 | 0.0 | 1.9 |
| 1977-78 | 0.0 | 0.0 | 0.0 | 0.0 | 0.0 | 0.0 | 0.4 | T | 0.0 | 0.0 | 0.0 | 0.0 | 0.4 |
| 1978-79 | 0.0 | 0.0 | 0.0 | 0.0 | 0.0 | 0.0 | T | 0.0 | 0.0 | 0.0 | 0.0 | 0.0 | T |
| 1979-80 | ·0.0 | 0.0 | 0.0 | 0.0 | 0.0 | 0.0 | 0.0 | T | T | 0.0 | 0.0 | 0.0 | T |
| 1980-81 | 0.0 | 0.0 | 0.0 | 0.0 | 0.0 | 0.0 | T | T | 0.0 | 0.0 | 0.0 | 0.0 | T |
| 1981-82 | 0.0 | 0.0 | 0.0 | 0.0 | 0.0 | 0.0 | T | 0.0 | 0.0 | 0.0 | 0.0 | 0.0 | T |
| 1982-83 | 0.0 | 0.0 | 0.0 | 0.0 | 0.0 | 0.0 | 0.0 | 0.0 | 0.0 | 0.0 | 0.0 | 0.0 | 0.0 |
| 1983-84 | 0.0 | 0.0 | 0.0 | 0.0 | 0.0 | 0.0 | T | 0.0 | T | 0.0 | 0.0 | 0.0 | 0.0 |
| 1984-85 | 0.0 | 0.0 | 0.0 | 0.0 | 0.0 | 0.0 | T | T | 0.0 | 0.0 | 0.0 | 0.0 | 1 |
| 1985-86 | 0.0 | 0.0 | 0.0 | 0.0 | 0.0 | 0.0 | 0.0 | 0.0 | 0.0 | 0.0 | 0.0 | 0.0 | 0.0 |
| 1986-87 | 0.0 | 0.0 | 0.0 | 0.0 | 0.0 | 0.0 | T | 0.0 | 0.0 | T | 0.0 | 0.0 | T |
| 1987-88 | 0.0 | 0.0 | 0.0 | 0.0 | 0.0 | 0.0 | 0.0 | 1.7 | 0.0 | T | 0.0 | 0.0 | 1.7 |
| 1988-89 | 0.0 | 0.0 | 0.0 | 0.0 | 0.0 | 0.0 | 0.0 | 0.0 | T | 0.0 | 0.0 | 0.0 | T |
| 1989-90 | T | 0.0 | 0.0 | 0.0 | 0.0 | T | 0.0 | 0.0 | 0.0 | 0.0 | 0.0 | 0.0 | T |
| 1990-91 | 0.0 | 0.0 | 0.0 | 0.0 | 0.0 | 0.0 | | | | | | | |
| Record Mean | T | 0.0 | 0.0 | 0.0 | T | 0.1 | 0.1 | 0.2 | T | T | 0.0 | 0.0 | 0.4 |

**See Reference Notes, relative to all above tables, on preceding page.**

Anchorage is in a broad valley with adjacent narrow bodies of water. Cook Inlet, including Knik Arm and Turnagain Arm, lies approximately 2 miles to the west, north, and south. The terrain rises gradually to the east for about 10 miles, with marshes interspersed with glacial moraines, shallow depressions, small streams, and knolls. Beyond this area, the Chugach Mountains rise abruptly into a range oriented north-northeast to south-southwest, with average elevation 4,000 to 5,000 feet and some peaks to 8,000 or 10,000 feet. The Chugach Range acts as a barrier to the influx of warm, moist air from the Gulf of Alaska, so the average annual precipitation is only 10 to 15 percent of that at stations located on the Gulf of Alaska side of the Chugach Range. The Alaska Mountain Range lies in a long arc from southwest, through northwest, to northeast, approximately 100 miles distant from Anchorage. During the winter, this range is an effective barrier to the influx of very cold air from the north side of the range.

The four seasons are well marked in Anchorage. In the summer, high temperatures average about 60 degrees and low temperatures nearly 50 degrees. Temperatures in the 70s are considered very warm. On summer days, temperatures on the east side of Anchorage may be about 10 degrees warmer than the official airport readings. Rain increases after mid-June. About two-thirds of the days in July and August are cloudy and one-third have rain.

Autumn is brief, beginning in early September and ending in mid-October. Temperatures begin to fall in September with snow becoming more frequent in October.

Winter can be considered as mid-October to early April when streams and lakes are frozen. Temperatures steadily decrease into January when the highs are near 20 degrees and lows near 5 degrees. The coldest weather is normally in January, when very cold days have high temperatures below zero. Cold days generally have clear skies and calm wind. Mild days do occur with temperatures in the 30s. On cold winter nights, temperatures on the east side of Anchorage may be 10-20 degrees lower than airport readings on the west side. Most winter precipitation is snow, but rain may occur on a few days.

Annual snowfall varies from about 70 inches on the west side to about 90 inches on the east side of Anchorage at low elevations. Along the Chugach Mountains, snow totals increase steadily with increasing elevations and winter arrives a month earlier and stays a month longer at the 1,000 to 2,000 foot level. Most snow is light or dry, i.e., low in water content. Freezing rain is extremely rare. Fog, made of water droplets, occurs on about fifteen days. In general, ice-fog does not occur in Anchorage.

Spring begins in late April and May when days are warm and sunny, nights are cool, and precipitation is exceedingly small. Foliage turns green by late May.

The wind in Anchorage is generally light. However, on several days each winter, strong northerly winds, up to 90 mph, affect the entire Anchorage area. Also during the winter there are about eight occurrences of very strong southeast winds which affect only the east side of Anchorage and the slopes of the Chugach Mountains. These winds occur more often above the 800 feet elevation in the Chugach where winds are funneled thru creek canyons. On the east side of Anchorage, damaging winds of over 100 mph have been recorded.

The average occurrence of the first snow is mid-October, but has occurred as early as mid-September. The average date of the last snow is mid-April, but has occurred as late as early May. The growing season is about 125 days. Average occurrence of the last temperature of 32 degrees in spring is mid-May and the first in fall is mid-September. Daylight varies from about 19 hours in late June to 6 hours in late December with 12 hours of daylight occurring in late September and late March.

## TABLE 1 NORMALS, MEANS AND EXTREMES

ANCHORAGE, ALASKA

LATITUDE: 61°13'N    LONGITUDE: 149°53'W    ELEVATION: FT. GRND  114 BARO  157    TIME ZONE: YUKON    WBAN: 26451

| | (a) | JAN | FEB | MAR | APR | MAY | JUNE | JULY | AUG | SEP | OCT | NOV | DEC | YEAR |
|---|---|---|---|---|---|---|---|---|---|---|---|---|---|---|
| **TEMPERATURE °F:** | | | | | | | | | | | | | | |
| Normals | | | | | | | | | | | | | | |
| -Daily Maximum | | 20.0 | 25.5 | 31.7 | 42.6 | 54.2 | 61.8 | 65.1 | 63.2 | 55.2 | 40.8 | 27.9 | 20.4 | 42.4 |
| -Daily Minimum | | 6.0 | 10.3 | 15.7 | 28.2 | 38.3 | 47.0 | 51.1 | 49.2 | 41.1 | 28.4 | 15.4 | 7.1 | 28.2 |
| -Monthly | | 13.0 | 17.9 | 23.7 | 35.4 | 46.3 | 54.4 | 58.1 | 56.2 | 48.2 | 34.6 | 21.7 | 13.8 | 35.3 |
| Extremes | | | | | | | | | | | | | | |
| -Record Highest | 36 | 50 | 48 | 51 | 65 | 77 | 85 | 82 | 82 | 73 | 61 | 53 | 47 | 85 |
| -Year | | 1961 | 1977 | 1984 | 1976 | 1969 | 1969 | 1989 | 1978 | 1957 | 1969 | 1979 | 1985 | JUN 1969 |
| -Record Lowest | 36 | -34 | -26 | -24 | -4 | 17 | 33 | 38 | 31 | 20 | -5 | -21 | -30 | -34 |
| -Year | | 1975 | 1956 | 1971 | 1985 | 1964 | 1961 | 1964 | 1984 | 1956 | 1956 | 1956 | 1964 | JAN 1975 |
| **NORMAL DEGREE DAYS:** | | | | | | | | | | | | | | |
| Heating (base 65°F) | | 1612 | 1319 | 1280 | 888 | 580 | 318 | 214 | 273 | 504 | 942 | 1299 | 1587 | 10816 |
| Cooling (base 65°F) | | 0 | 0 | 0 | 0 | 0 | 0 | 0 | 0 | 0 | 0 | 0 | 0 | 0 |
| **% OF POSSIBLE SUNSHINE** | 34 | 39 | 46 | 55 | 54 | 53 | 49 | 44 | 40 | 42 | 39 | 36 | 31 | 44 |
| **MEAN SKY COVER (tenths)** | | | | | | | | | | | | | | |
| Sunrise - Sunset | 36 | 6.9 | 7.0 | 6.7 | 7.2 | 7.7 | 8.0 | 7.9 | 7.9 | 7.8 | 7.6 | 7.4 | 7.4 | 7.5 |
| **MEAN NUMBER OF DAYS:** | | | | | | | | | | | | | | |
| Sunrise to Sunset | | | | | | | | | | | | | | |
| -Clear | 36 | 7.5 | 6.7 | 7.7 | 5.3 | 3.8 | 2.4 | 3.4 | 3.4 | 3.9 | 5.1 | 5.4 | 6.2 | 60.6 |
| -Partly Cloudy | 36 | 4.6 | 3.8 | 5.4 | 6.4 | 6.8 | 6.8 | 5.7 | 6.0 | 5.4 | 4.8 | 4.8 | 4.0 | 64.6 |
| -Cloudy | 36 | 18.9 | 17.8 | 17.9 | 18.3 | 20.4 | 20.8 | 21.9 | 21.6 | 20.7 | 21.1 | 19.8 | 20.8 | 240.0 |
| Precipitation | | | | | | | | | | | | | | |
| .01 inches or more | 25 | 7.4 | 7.8 | 7.5 | 6.5 | 7.0 | 8.2 | 11.5 | 13.5 | 14.0 | 12.4 | 9.7 | 11.1 | 116.7 |
| Snow,Ice pellets | | | | | | | | | | | | | | |
| 1.0 inches or more | 25 | 2.6 | 2.9 | 2.6 | 1.8 | 0.0 | 0.0 | 0.0 | 0.0 | 0.2 | 2.4 | 3.2 | 4.6 | 20.2 |
| Thunderstorms | 36 | 0.0 | 0.0 | 0.0 | 0.0 | 0.1 | 0.1 | 0.4 | 0.3 | 0.1 | 0.0 | 0.0 | 0.0 | 1.0 |
| Heavy Fog Visibility | | | | | | | | | | | | | | |
| 1/4 mile or less | 36 | 6.1 | 4.2 | 1.3 | 0.7 | 0.3 | 0.1 | 0.1 | 0.9 | 1.4 | 2.0 | 3.8 | 5.3 | 26.0 |
| Temperature °F | | | | | | | | | | | | | | |
| -Maximum | | | | | | | | | | | | | | |
| 70° and above | 25 | 0.0 | 0.0 | 0.0 | 0.0 | 0.4 | 2.9 | 6.4 | 3.3 | 0.2 | 0.0 | 0.0 | 0.0 | 13.2 |
| 32° and below | 25 | 24.8 | 19.6 | 11.6 | 2.3 | 0.0 | 0.0 | 0.0 | 0.0 | 0.0 | 0.0 | 4.7 | 20.7 | 24.3 | 108.0 |
| -Minimum | | | | | | | | | | | | | | |
| 32° and below | 25 | 30.6 | 27.0 | 28.1 | 21.2 | 2.6 | 0.0 | 0.0 | 0.0 | 0.1 | 3.1 | 19.3 | 28.2 | 30.0 | 190.4 |
| 0° and below | 25 | 10.1 | 6.7 | 2.4 | 0.* | 0.0 | 0.0 | 0.0 | 0.0 | 0.0 | 0.0 | 0.1 | 3.0 | 7.6 | 30.0 |
| **AVG. STATION PRESS. (mb)** | 17 | 1000.3 | 1001.6 | 1001.2 | 1003.7 | 1005.6 | 1008.0 | 1010.0 | 1008.5 | 1004.2 | 998.4 | 998.7 | 999.8 | 1003.3 |
| **RELATIVE HUMIDITY (%)** | | | | | | | | | | | | | | |
| Hour 03 | 36 | 72 | 72 | 70 | 72 | 72 | 75 | 80 | 82 | 82 | 76 | 77 | 76 | 76 |
| Hour 09 (Local Time) | 36 | 73 | 72 | 69 | 66 | 63 | 67 | 73 | 77 | 80 | 77 | 77 | 76 | 73 |
| Hour 15 | 36 | 71 | 66 | 56 | 54 | 49 | 55 | 62 | 64 | 63 | 65 | 73 | 75 | 63 |
| Hour 21 | 36 | 72 | 70 | 67 | 64 | 58 | 61 | 68 | 75 | 77 | 75 | 76 | 76 | 70 |
| **PRECIPITATION (inches):** | | | | | | | | | | | | | | |
| Water Equivalent | | | | | | | | | | | | | | |
| -Normal | | 0.80 | 0.93 | 0.69 | 0.66 | 0.57 | 1.08 | 1.97 | 2.11 | 2.45 | 1.73 | 1.11 | 1.10 | 15.20 |
| -Maximum Monthly | 36 | 2.71 | 3.07 | 2.76 | 1.91 | 1.93 | 3.40 | 4.44 | 9.77 | 5.43 | 4.11 | 2.84 | 2.67 | 9.77 |
| -Year | | 1987 | 1955 | 1979 | 1977 | 1989 | 1962 | 1958 | 1989 | 1961 | 1986 | 1976 | 1955 | AUG 1989 |
| -Minimum Monthly | 36 | 0.02 | 0.07 | T | T | 0.02 | 0.18 | 0.42 | 0.33 | 0.76 | 0.35 | 0.08 | 0.11 | T |
| -Year | | 1982 | 1958 | 1983 | 1969 | 1957 | 1969 | 1972 | 1969 | 1973 | 1960 | 1985 | 1982 | MAR 1983 |
| -Maximum in 24 hrs | 36 | 1.19 | 1.16 | 1.25 | 0.78 | 1.18 | 1.84 | 2.06 | 4.12 | 1.92 | 1.60 | 1.66 | 1.62 | 4.12 |
| -Year | | 1961 | 1956 | 1986 | 1989 | 1980 | 1962 | 1956 | 1989 | 1961 | 1986 | 1964 | 1955 | AUG 1989 |
| Snow,Ice pellets | | | | | | | | | | | | | | |
| -Maximum Monthly | 36 | 21.1 | 48.5 | 31.0 | 27.6 | 3.9 | 0.0 | 0.0 | 0.0 | 4.6 | 27.1 | 32.4 | 41.6 | 48.5 |
| -Year | | 1955 | 1955 | 1979 | 1963 | 1963 | | | | 1965 | 1982 | 1956 | 1955 | FEB 1955 |
| -Maximum in 24 hrs | 36 | 10.5 | 12.4 | 14.5 | 9.1 | 3.9 | 0.0 | 0.0 | 0.0 | 3.5 | 9.6 | 16.4 | 17.7 | 17.7 |
| -Year | | 1955 | 1956 | 1959 | 1955 | 1963 | | | | 1965 | 1955 | 1964 | 1955 | DEC 1955 |
| **WIND:** | | | | | | | | | | | | | | |
| Mean Speed (mph) | 36 | 6.2 | 6.8 | 6.8 | 7.2 | 8.3 | 8.3 | 7.2 | 6.8 | 6.4 | 6.7 | 6.2 | 6.1 | 6.9 |
| Prevailing Direction through 1963 | | NNE | N | N | N | S | S | S | S | NNE | N | NNE | NNE | N |
| Fastest Obs. 1 Min. | | | | | | | | | | | | | | |
| -Direction (!!!) | 32 | 03 | 04 | 03 | 15 | 35 | 17 | 16 | 02 | 18 | 03 | 04 | 05 | 03 |
| -Speed (MPH) | 32 | 61 | 52 | 51 | 35 | 33 | 30 | 29 | 31 | 33 | 40 | 41 | 41 | 61 |
| -Year | | 1971 | 1979 | 1989 | 1964 | 1964 | 1971 | 1957 | 1987 | 1956 | 1966 | 1978 | 1964 | JAN 1971 |
| Peak Gust | | | | | | | | | | | | | | |
| -Direction (!!!) | 10 | E | N | NE | SE | S | SE | SE | N | S | S | SE | SE | NE |
| -Speed (mph) | 10 | 64 | 59 | 75 | 43 | 43 | 46 | 40 | 44 | 48 | 55 | 54 | 48 | 75 |
| -Date | | 1986 | 1987 | 1989 | 1987 | 1988 | 1985 | 1980 | 1987 | 1985 | 1987 | 1985 | 1982 | MAR 1989 |

**See Reference Notes to this table on the following page.**

# ANCHORAGE, ALASKA

PRECIPITATION (inches)    ANCHORAGE, ALASKA

**TABLE 2**

| YEAR | JAN | FEB | MAR | APR | MAY | JUNE | JULY | AUG | SEP | OCT | NOV | DEC | ANNUAL |
|---|---|---|---|---|---|---|---|---|---|---|---|---|---|
| 1961 | 1.51 | 0.46 | 0.34 | 1.38 | 0.47 | 1.12 | 2.22 | 1.94 | 5.43 | 2.81 | 0.64 | 0.95 | 19.27 |
| 1962 | 0.88 | 0.74 | 0.58 | 0.25 | 1.52 | 3.40 | 0.72 | 1.92 | 1.45 | 1.56 | 0.49 | 1.06 | 14.57 |
| 1963 | 2.09 | 1.35 | 1.48 | 1.78 | 0.44 | 1.82 | 2.75 | 2.80 | 0.98 | 1.01 | 0.12 | 1.49 | 18.11 |
| #1964 | 0.35 | 1.15 | 1.07 | 0.89 | 0.97 | 1.73 | 1.08 | 2.16 | 0.83 | 2.31 | 2.71 | 0.64 | 15.89 |
| 1965 | 0.57 | 0.67 | 0.83 | 0.30 | 0.51 | 0.96 | 1.74 | 1.58 | 4.60 | 1.44 | 1.86 | 1.44 | 16.50 |
| 1966 | 0.63 | 0.80 | 0.44 | 0.70 | 0.75 | 0.27 | 0.71 | 2.47 | 2.45 | 0.86 | 1.11 | 1.06 | 12.25 |
| 1967 | 1.25 | 1.01 | 0.98 | 0.49 | 1.07 | 1.44 | 2.47 | 2.96 | 2.86 | 0.51 | 1.72 | 2.40 | 19.16 |
| 1968 | 0.83 | 1.67 | 0.29 | 0.85 | 1.60 | 0.62 | 1.34 | 0.69 | 1.05 | 1.61 | 1.08 | 0.45 | 12.08 |
| 1969 | 0.28 | 0.73 | 0.10 | T | 0.86 | 0.18 | 2.14 | 0.33 | 0.78 | 0.90 | 0.84 | 0.94 | 8.08 |
| 1970 | 0.86 | 0.57 | 0.29 | 0.27 | 0.43 | 0.85 | 2.23 | 2.03 | 1.11 | 1.62 | 1.21 | 1.62 | 13.09 |
| 1971 | 0.24 | 1.49 | 0.70 | 0.63 | 0.52 | 0.37 | 2.86 | 2.58 | 1.79 | 2.16 | 0.67 | 0.87 | 14.88 |
| 1972 | 0.56 | 0.63 | 0.68 | 0.73 | 0.81 | 0.61 | 0.42 | 1.40 | 4.42 | 2.89 | 0.76 | 0.72 | 14.63 |
| 1973 | 0.72 | 0.11 | 0.65 | 0.33 | 0.14 | 1.07 | 0.60 | 3.40 | 0.76 | 1.74 | 0.78 | 0.38 | 10.68 |
| 1974 | 0.02 | 1.15 | 0.60 | 0.61 | 0.34 | 0.69 | 1.22 | 1.62 | 1.53 | 2.63 | 1.01 | 2.00 | 13.42 |
| 1975 | 0.43 | 0.77 | 0.54 | 1.71 | 0.40 | 0.47 | 1.33 | 1.19 | 4.52 | 0.69 | 0.10 | 0.89 | 13.04 |
| 1976 | 0.98 | 0.33 | 1.77 | 0.74 | 0.16 | 0.33 | 0.60 | 0.97 | 3.50 | 1.29 | 2.84 | 1.03 | 14.54 |
| 1977 | 1.35 | 0.52 | 0.84 | 1.91 | 0.46 | 0.49 | 1.37 | 1.35 | 4.08 | 1.92 | 0.53 | 0.69 | 15.51 |
| 1978 | 0.39 | 1.19 | 0.45 | 0.02 | 0.03 | 3.09 | 1.41 | 0.54 | 2.16 | 1.65 | 0.85 | 2.60 | 14.75 |
| 1979 | 0.23 | 0.69 | 2.76 | 0.94 | 0.15 | 1.79 | 3.84 | 1.56 | 2.73 | 2.54 | 2.77 | 1.15 | 21.15 |
| 1980 | 1.28 | 1.18 | 0.30 | 0.19 | 1.68 | 2.73 | 2.27 | 3.06 | 2.53 | 3.05 | 0.49 | 0.41 | 19.17 |
| 1981 | 0.93 | 0.97 | 0.41 | 0.19 | 0.81 | 0.83 | 4.39 | 4.96 | 2.15 | 3.49 | 1.85 | 0.36 | 21.34 |
| 1982 | 0.02 | 0.69 | 0.42 | 0.27 | 0.54 | 1.56 | 2.41 | 2.33 | 4.66 | 2.95 | 1.72 | 0.11 | 17.68 |
| 1983 | 0.21 | 0.23 | T | 1.36 | 0.59 | 0.66 | 0.55 | 2.89 | 2.29 | 2.67 | 0.23 | 0.48 | 12.16 |
| 1984 | 1.30 | 1.08 | 0.08 | 0.93 | 0.96 | 1.10 | 1.11 | 3.21 | 2.59 | 1.38 | 0.15 | 1.08 | 14.97 |
| 1985 | 0.70 | 0.67 | 0.86 | 0.50 | 1.45 | 1.01 | 0.99 | 3.54 | 3.17 | 1.07 | 0.08 | 1.47 | 15.51 |
| 1986 | 0.20 | 0.55 | 1.70 | 0.42 | 0.50 | 0.33 | 2.02 | 3.62 | 2.85 | 4.11 | 1.23 | 1.42 | 18.95 |
| 1987 | 2.71 | 0.20 | 0.17 | 0.24 | 0.67 | 1.09 | 1.89 | 0.43 | 1.91 | 2.60 | 1.90 | 1.12 | 14.93 |
| 1988 | 0.38 | 0.32 | 0.65 | 0.37 | 0.56 | 0.79 | 0.64 | 3.77 | 1.26 | 2.96 | 1.11 | 1.51 | 14.32 |
| 1989 | 0.26 | 0.17 | 0.22 | 0.98 | 1.93 | 1.14 | 2.89 | 9.77 | 3.92 | 3.63 | 1.01 | 1.63 | 27.55 |
| 1990 | 1.42 | 1.46 | 0.46 | 0.27 | 0.71 | 1.52 | 0.81 | 1.90 | 6.64 | 0.73 | 1.31 | 1.78 | 19.01 |
| Record Mean | 0.82 | 0.78 | 0.63 | 0.57 | 0.64 | 1.11 | 1.90 | 2.50 | 2.64 | 1.79 | 1.03 | 1.08 | 15.48 |

**TABLE 3**    AVERAGE TEMPERATURE (deg. F)    ANCHORAGE, ALASKA

| YEAR | JAN | FEB | MAR | APR | MAY | JUNE | JULY | AUG | SEP | OCT | NOV | DEC | ANNUAL |
|---|---|---|---|---|---|---|---|---|---|---|---|---|---|
| #1961 | 20.9 | 17.9 | 16.3 | 36.0 | 47.8 | 54.9 | 57.7 | 54.5 | 48.5 | 29.0 | 16.5 | 4.2 | 33.7 |
| 1962 | 13.5 | 19.5 | 19.9 | 36.9 | 44.7 | 53.5 | 58.4 | 56.8 | 45.6 | 37.8 | 22.3 | 16.6 | 35.4 |
| 1963 | 19.2 | 23.5 | 24.0 | 31.9 | 46.9 | 51.6 | 58.6 | 57.0 | 52.0 | 36.8 | 12.1 | 24.8 | 36.5 |
| #1964 | 14.1 | 20.1 | 17.3 | 33.7 | 41.2 | 55.9 | 57.1 | 54.6 | 48.7 | 35.0 | 21.3 | 1.0 | 33.3 |
| 1965 | 10.0 | 10.3 | 36.5 | 39.7 | 45.4 | 52.9 | 59.0 | 56.3 | 53.7 | 30.7 | 20.5 | 13.1 | 35.7 |
| 1966 | 9.7 | 14.7 | 16.7 | 35.3 | 44.2 | 55.4 | 57.9 | 54.4 | 46.3 | 32.3 | 17.5 | 10.8 | 32.9 |
| 1967 | 7.1 | 14.4 | 23.2 | 35.1 | 47.1 | 56.1 | 59.3 | 58.3 | 48.1 | 35.7 | 30.0 | 16.0 | 35.9 |
| 1968 | 12.5 | 23.1 | 28.4 | 35.0 | 48.2 | 54.8 | 59.9 | 58.2 | 47.1 | 33.1 | 22.1 | 6.3 | 35.7 |
| 1969 | 4.6 | 17.9 | 28.6 | 39.4 | 47.7 | 57.7 | 59.3 | 54.2 | 48.9 | 41.2 | 23.7 | 28.4 | 37.7 |
| 1970 | 9.2 | 29.6 | 35.4 | 36.4 | 48.1 | 54.8 | 57.1 | 54.6 | 46.4 | 32.5 | 24.9 | 14.9 | 37.0 |
| 1971 | 2.7 | 20.6 | 14.2 | 33.4 | 41.6 | 51.2 | 55.0 | 55.0 | 46.1 | 32.3 | 18.3 | 16.2 | 32.3 |
| 1972 | 6.4 | 13.5 | 15.7 | 26.8 | 43.3 | 51.9 | 59.0 | 56.6 | 44.5 | 31.7 | 21.3 | 12.4 | 31.9 |
| 1973 | 2.9 | 13.1 | 24.2 | 35.8 | 43.6 | 51.4 | 57.8 | 53.8 | 45.7 | 32.2 | 13.6 | 18.3 | 32.7 |
| 1974 | 6.8 | 14.1 | 23.3 | 37.9 | 47.9 | 55.5 | 57.3 | 56.3 | 49.8 | 34.5 | 22.6 | 18.8 | 35.4 |
| 1975 | 11.9 | 12.9 | 22.5 | 32.9 | 46.3 | 53.0 | 58.6 | 56.6 | 49.3 | 34.6 | 14.2 | 11.6 | 33.7 |
| 1976 | 17.1 | 12.8 | 24.1 | 34.8 | 44.9 | 53.7 | 58.9 | 56.3 | 47.4 | 33.4 | 30.6 | 23.1 | 36.4 |
| 1977 | 32.0 | 32.7 | 24.7 | 35.7 | 46.9 | 57.8 | 62.6 | 60.3 | 50.7 | 38.3 | 15.3 | 11.3 | 39.0 |
| 1978 | 21.2 | 26.3 | 29.3 | 39.1 | 49.0 | 54.5 | 58.8 | 59.8 | 51.5 | 39.3 | 26.3 | 21.4 | 39.7 |
| 1979 | 22.3 | 10.6 | 31.6 | 38.8 | 50.2 | 55.9 | 60.4 | 58.8 | 52.0 | 41.1 | 33.5 | 10.0 | 38.8 |
| 1980 | 14.3 | 27.4 | 27.2 | 39.3 | 45.8 | 53.2 | 57.0 | 54.4 | 46.7 | 37.2 | 27.6 | 0.8 | 35.9 |
| 1981 | 31.5 | 24.8 | 34.4 | 36.0 | 50.7 | 53.8 | 57.4 | 54.8 | 47.9 | 36.0 | 21.8 | 15.9 | 38.8 |
| 1982 | 6.4 | 15.5 | 26.3 | 33.1 | 44.5 | 52.9 | 56.2 | 54.7 | 47.5 | 26.6 | 21.0 | 21.5 | 33.8 |
| 1983 | 16.2 | 21.4 | 28.7 | 37.4 | 48.7 | 55.9 | 58.5 | 56.1 | 45.3 | 34.4 | 24.9 | 16.7 | 37.0 |
| 1984 | 18.8 | 19.4 | 36.4 | 38.8 | 49.6 | 58.8 | 60.8 | 56.6 | 49.3 | 35.5 | 19.8 | 18.9 | 38.6 |
| 1985 | 30.3 | 13.5 | 26.7 | 28.4 | 45.1 | 51.9 | 58.5 | 55.2 | 47.6 | 30.3 | 14.0 | 27.5 | 35.8 |
| 1986 | 25.6 | 21.8 | 24.1 | 31.0 | 46.6 | 54.6 | 58.0 | 54.3 | 48.6 | 39.0 | 25.0 | 28.3 | 38.1 |
| 1987 | 22.8 | 25.3 | 26.8 | 37.9 | 47.2 | 51.9 | 57.1 | 57.3 | 48.0 | 38.9 | 26.9 | 18.2 | 38.2 |
| 1988 | 18.0 | 22.7 | 31.3 | 37.1 | 48.5 | 55.2 | 58.8 | 56.0 | 48.0 | 33.3 | 20.5 | 22.0 | 37.6 |
| 1989 | 3.5 | 17.6 | 23.6 | 39.3 | 46.3 | 55.3 | 59.4 | 59.0 | 50.6 | 34.0 | 17.2 | 24.2 | 35.8 |
| 1990 | 15.5 | 3.8 | 28.6 | 39.9 | 49.9 | 57.1 | 58.6 | 57.8 | 49.6 | 32.3 | 9.9 | 14.8 | 34.8 |
| Record Mean | 13.6 | 17.7 | 24.5 | 35.2 | 46.3 | 54.3 | 58.0 | 55.9 | 47.9 | 34.7 | 21.3 | 15.1 | 35.4 |
| Max | 20.8 | 25.6 | 32.9 | 43.0 | 54.6 | 62.1 | 65.3 | 63.2 | 55.1 | 41.0 | 27.6 | 21.6 | 42.7 |
| Min | 6.5 | 9.8 | 16.1 | 27.3 | 38.0 | 46.4 | 50.7 | 48.6 | 40.7 | 28.4 | 14.9 | 8.6 | 28.0 |

## REFERENCE NOTES FOR TABLES 1, 2, 3 and 6    (ANCHORAGE, AK)

### GENERAL

T - TRACE AMOUNT
BLANK ENTRIES DENOTE MISSING/UNREPORTED DATA.
# INDICATES A STATION OR INSTRUMENT RELOCATION.

### SPECIFIC

TABLE 1

(a) - LENGTH OF RECORD IN YEARS. ALTHOUGH INDIVIDUAL MONTHS MAY BE MISSING.
* LESS THAN .05

NORMALS — BASED ON THE 1951-1980 RECORD PERIOD.
EXTREMES — DATES ARE THE MOST RECENT OCCURRENCE.
WIND DIR. — NUMERALS SHOW TENS OF DEGREES CLOCKWISE FROM TRUE NORTH.
"00" INDICATES CALM.
RESULTANT WIND DIRECTIONS ARE GIVEN TO WHOLE DEGREES.

TABLE 3

MAX AND MIN ARE LONG-TERM MEAN DAILY MAXIMUM AND MEAN DAILY MINIMUM TEMPERATURES.

### EXCEPTIONS

TABLES 2, 3, and 6

RECORD MEANS ARE THROUGH THE CURRENT YEAR, BEGINNING IN
1943 FOR TEMPERATURE
1943 FOR PRECIPITATION
1943 FOR SNOWFALL

**TABLE 4** — HEATING DEGREE DAYS Base 65 deg. F — ANCHORAGE, ALASKA

| SEASON | JULY | AUG | SEP | OCT | NOV | DEC | JAN | FEB | MAR | APR | MAY | JUNE | TOTAL |
|---|---|---|---|---|---|---|---|---|---|---|---|---|---|
| #1961-62 | 221 | 318 | 489 | 1112 | 1450 | 1884 | 1593 | 1267 | 1394 | 837 | 621 | 338 | 11524 |
| 1962-63 | 197 | 249 | 578 | 836 | 1274 | 1499 | 1415 | 1156 | 1266 | 986 | 557 | 393 | 10406 |
| #1963-64 | 192 | 242 | 383 | 866 | 1583 | 1237 | 1573 | 1297 | 1476 | 936 | 733 | 263 | 10781 |
| 1964-65 | 240 | 315 | 485 | 922 | 1303 | 1980 | 1701 | 1530 | 879 | 754 | 598 | 357 | 11064 |
| 1965-66 | 178 | 261 | 333 | 1055 | 1328 | 1603 | 1713 | 1402 | 1493 | 882 | 641 | 285 | 11174 |
| 1966-67 | 214 | 324 | 553 | 1008 | 1419 | 1674 | 1791 | 1411 | 1292 | 890 | 547 | 261 | 11384 |
| 1967-68 | 172 | 200 | 501 | 901 | 1042 | 1513 | 1625 | 1209 | 1129 | 894 | 510 | 301 | 9997 |
| 1968-69 | 153 | 208 | 530 | 982 | 1280 | 1816 | 1869 | 1312 | 1124 | 761 | 527 | 217 | 10779 |
| 1969-70 | 168 | 330 | 478 | 732 | 1235 | 1128 | 1722 | 983 | 910 | 852 | 515 | 298 | 9351 |
| 1970-71 | 239 | 312 | 552 | 1003 | 1201 | 1550 | 1934 | 1238 | 1574 | 940 | 717 | 410 | 11670 |
| 1971-72 | 291 | 302 | 561 | 1008 | 1396 | 1508 | 1814 | 1488 | 1521 | 1138 | 666 | 384 | 12077 |
| 1972-73 | 185 | 252 | 608 | 1025 | 1308 | 1627 | 1925 | 1448 | 1258 | 866 | 654 | 399 | 11555 |
| 1973-74 | 216 | 342 | 573 | 1012 | 1532 | 1440 | 1797 | 1416 | 1285 | 805 | 526 | 279 | 11223 |
| 1974-75 | 235 | 263 | 452 | 937 | 1263 | 1425 | 1454 | 1454 | 1313 | 954 | 575 | 354 | 10868 |
| 1975-76 | 192 | 252 | 463 | 937 | 1517 | 1654 | 1485 | 1511 | 1260 | 897 | 615 | 332 | 11115 |
| 1976-77 | 184 | 262 | 521 | 972 | 1028 | 1241 | 1017 | 897 | 1241 | 872 | 554 | 208 | 9050 |
| 1977-78 | 75 | 144 | 421 | 820 | 1486 | 1659 | 1349 | 1077 | 1100 | 771 | 491 | 308 | 9701 |
| 1978-79 | 186 | 160 | 400 | 792 | 1153 | 1344 | 1321 | 1515 | 1029 | 781 | 454 | 268 | 9403 |
| 1979-80 | 138 | 184 | 384 | 735 | 937 | 1704 | 1568 | 1083 | 1164 | 764 | 592 | 347 | 9600 |
| 1980-81 | 243 | 320 | 542 | 855 | 1115 | 1990 | 1032 | 1122 | 943 | 863 | 438 | 329 | 9792 |
| 1981-82 | 230 | 307 | 507 | 893 | 1290 | 1516 | 1813 | 1382 | 1191 | 949 | 625 | 356 | 11059 |
| 1982-83 | 261 | 313 | 520 | 1184 | 1315 | 1342 | 1507 | 1216 | 1117 | 821 | 500 | 267 | 10363 |
| 1983-84 | 194 | 269 | 585 | 945 | 1194 | 1491 | 1425 | 1319 | 880 | 778 | 471 | 179 | 9730 |
| 1984-85 | 129 | 254 | 464 | 906 | 1350 | 1423 | 1070 | 1437 | 1182 | 1091 | 610 | 388 | 10304 |
| 1985-86 | 193 | 298 | 516 | 1065 | 1523 | 1155 | 1215 | 1206 | 1260 | 1013 | 564 | 307 | 10315 |
| 1986-87 | 215 | 325 | 486 | 800 | 1194 | 1133 | 1303 | 1104 | 1176 | 805 | 543 | 386 | 9470 |
| 1987-88 | 243 | 232 | 506 | 801 | 1136 | 1444 | 1450 | 1221 | 1037 | 830 | 504 | 285 | 9689 |
| 1988-89 | 184 | 270 | 503 | 975 | 1331 | 1326 | 1908 | 1322 | 1277 | 765 | 573 | 286 | 10720 |
| 1989-90 | 173 | 181 | 423 | 956 | 1428 | 1255 | 1533 | 1715 | 1121 | 746 | 465 | 237 | 10233 |
| 1990-91 | 191 | 222 | 457 | 1006 | 1648 | 1552 | | | | | | | |

**TABLE 5** — COOLING DEGREE DAYS Base 65 deg. F — ANCHORAGE, ALASKA

| YEAR | JAN | FEB | MAR | APR | MAY | JUNE | JULY | AUG | SEP | OCT | NOV | DEC | TOTAL |
|---|---|---|---|---|---|---|---|---|---|---|---|---|---|
| 1969 | 0 | 0 | 0 | 0 | 0 | 5 | 1 | 2 | 0 | 0 | 0 | 0 | 8 |
| 1970 | 0 | 0 | 0 | 0 | 0 | 0 | 0 | 0 | 0 | 0 | 0 | 0 | 0 |
| 1971 | 0 | 0 | 0 | 0 | 0 | 0 | 1 | 0 | 0 | 0 | 0 | 0 | 1 |
| 1972 | 0 | 0 | 0 | 0 | 0 | 0 | 5 | 0 | 0 | 0 | 0 | 0 | 5 |
| 1973 | 0 | 0 | 0 | 0 | 0 | 0 | 0 | 0 | 0 | 0 | 0 | 0 | 0 |
| 1974 | 0 | 0 | 0 | 0 | 0 | 0 | 1 | 0 | 0 | 0 | 0 | 0 | 1 |
| 1975 | 0 | 0 | 0 | 0 | 0 | 0 | 2 | 0 | 0 | 0 | 0 | 0 | 2 |
| 1976 | 0 | 0 | 0 | 0 | 0 | 0 | 3 | 0 | 0 | 0 | 0 | 0 | 3 |
| 1977 | 0 | 0 | 0 | 0 | 0 | 0 | 8 | 3 | 0 | 0 | 0 | 0 | 11 |
| 1978 | 0 | 0 | 0 | 0 | 0 | 0 | 1 | 7 | 0 | 0 | 0 | 0 | 8 |
| 1979 | 0 | 0 | 0 | 0 | 0 | 0 | 4 | 0 | 0 | 0 | 0 | 0 | 4 |
| 1980 | 0 | 0 | 0 | 0 | 0 | 0 | 0 | 0 | 0 | 0 | 0 | 0 | 0 |
| 1981 | 0 | 0 | 0 | 0 | 0 | 0 | 0 | 0 | 0 | 0 | 0 | 0 | 0 |
| 1982 | 0 | 0 | 0 | 0 | 0 | 0 | 0 | 0 | 0 | 0 | 0 | 0 | 0 |
| 1983 | 0 | 0 | 0 | 0 | 0 | 0 | 0 | 0 | 0 | 0 | 0 | 0 | 0 |
| 1984 | 0 | 0 | 0 | 0 | 0 | 0 | 5 | 1 | 0 | 0 | 0 | 0 | 6 |
| 1985 | 0 | 0 | 0 | 0 | 0 | 0 | 0 | 0 | 0 | 0 | 0 | 0 | 0 |
| 1986 | 0 | 0 | 0 | 0 | 0 | 0 | 4 | 0 | 0 | 0 | 0 | 0 | 4 |
| 1987 | 0 | 0 | 0 | 0 | 0 | 0 | 2 | 0 | 0 | 0 | 0 | 0 | 2 |
| 1988 | 0 | 0 | 0 | 0 | 0 | 0 | 0 | 0 | 0 | 0 | 0 | 0 | 0 |
| 1989 | 0 | 0 | 0 | 0 | 0 | 0 | 5 | 2 | 0 | 0 | 0 | 0 | 7 |
| 1990 | 0 | 0 | 0 | 0 | 0 | 3 | 1 | 2 | 0 | 0 | 0 | 0 | 6 |

**TABLE 6** — SNOWFALL (inches) — ANCHORAGE, ALASKA

| SEASON | JULY | AUG | SEP | OCT | NOV | DEC | JAN | FEB | MAR | APR | MAY | JUNE | TOTAL |
|---|---|---|---|---|---|---|---|---|---|---|---|---|---|
| 1961-62 | 0.0 | 0.0 | 0.0 | 18.5 | 13.9 | 11.0 | 12.1 | 1.4 | 14.2 | 3.0 | 0.0 | 0.0 | 74.1 |
| 1962-63 | 0.0 | 0.0 | 0.0 | 3.0 | 3.0 | 4.9 | 15.5 | 19.8 | 11.4 | 27.6 | 3.9 | 0.0 | 89.1 |
| #1963-64 | 0.0 | 0.0 | 0.0 | 4.0 | 2.6 | 9.8 | 17.9 | 15.1 | 6.8 | 0.4 | 0.0 | 0.0 | 64.2 |
| 1964-65 | 0.0 | 0.0 | 0.0 | 10.6 | 25.8 | 16.2 | 8.5 | 11.5 | 3.0 | 2.8 | 0.2 | 0.0 | 78.6 |
| 1965-66 | 0.0 | 0.0 | 4.6 | 16.7 | 17.9 | 23.9 | 9.7 | 10.7 | 5.2 | 6.1 | T | 0.0 | 94.8 |
| 1966-67 | 0.0 | 0.0 | 0.0 | 1.9 | 13.5 | 13.4 | 16.7 | 16.3 | 8.8 | 4.0 | 0.0 | 0.0 | 74.6 |
| 1967-68 | 0.0 | 0.0 | 0.0 | 4.8 | 2.5 | 26.5 | 7.3 | 26.1 | 3.2 | 7.8 | T | 0.0 | 78.2 |
| 1968-69 | 0.0 | 0.0 | 1.3 | 15.1 | 14.7 | 7.9 | 6.5 | 10.6 | 1.1 | T | 0.0 | 0.0 | 57.2 |
| 1969-70 | 0.0 | 0.0 | 0.0 | 0.2 | 2.6 | 8.7 | 16.1 | 8.7 | 1.4 | 4.1 | 0.0 | 0.0 | 41.8 |
| 1970-71 | 0.0 | 0.0 | T | 4.2 | 4.2 | 4.2 | 1.2 | 18.5 | 11.1 | 8.3 | T | 0.0 | 58.7 |
| 1971-72 | 0.0 | 0.0 | 0.0 | 11.9 | 8.2 | 11.4 | 9.6 | 8.9 | 12.0 | 12.6 | T | 0.0 | 74.6 |
| 1972-73 | 0.0 | 0.0 | 1.5 | 3.3 | 10.7 | 6.5 | 8.1 | 1.0 | 16.1 | 1.3 | 0.0 | 0.0 | 48.5 |
| 1973-74 | 0.0 | 0.0 | 0.0 | 6.6 | 10.6 | 6.7 | 0.5 | 23.3 | 8.2 | 1.9 | 0.0 | 0.0 | 57.8 |
| 1974-75 | 0.0 | 0.0 | 0.0 | 4.4 | 8.4 | 29.2 | 5.7 | 15.4 | 8.3 | 16.1 | 0.4 | 0.0 | 87.9 |
| 1975-76 | 0.0 | 0.0 | 0.0 | T | 2.0 | 11.5 | 9.7 | 1.8 | 30.7 | 5.6 | T | 0.0 | 61.3 |
| 1976-77 | 0.0 | 0.0 | 0.0 | 11.4 | 11.1 | 13.8 | 6.1 | 2.1 | 9.5 | 14.0 | 0.0 | 0.0 | 68.0 |
| 1977-78 | 0.0 | 0.0 | 1.0 | 13.2 | 12.6 | 10.6 | 7.3 | 20.8 | 9.5 | T | 0.0 | 0.0 | 75.0 |
| 1978-79 | 0.0 | 0.0 | 0.0 | 3.9 | 8.5 | 35.2 | 3.6 | 6.2 | 31.0 | 2.8 | 0.0 | 0.0 | 91.2 |
| 1979-80 | 0.0 | 0.0 | 0.0 | 4.3 | 13.7 | 16.0 | 12.0 | 18.7 | 3.4 | 0.8 | 0.0 | 0.0 | 68.9 |
| 1980-81 | 0.0 | 0.0 | 0.0 | 10.2 | 4.2 | 1.4 | 5.0 | 6.6 | 4.4 | 1.1 | T | 0.0 | 32.9 |
| 1981-82 | 0.0 | 0.0 | 1.5 | 6.3 | 20.0 | 7.6 | 0.5 | 0.6 | 5.6 | 3.5 | 0.7 | 0.0 | 46.3 |
| 1982-83 | 0.0 | 0.0 | 0.0 | 27.1 | 23.4 | 1.9 | 3.7 | 4.3 | T | 11.0 | 0.0 | 0.0 | 71.4 |
| 1983-84 | 0.0 | 0.0 | T | 23.7 | 2.1 | 10.5 | 15.0 | 18.9 | 0.2 | 9.8 | 0.0 | 0.0 | 80.2 |
| 1984-85 | 0.0 | 0.0 | 0.0 | 3.3 | 1.8 | 18.0 | 9.7 | 7.9 | 12.8 | 7.3 | 1.3 | 0.0 | |
| 1985-86 | 0.0 | 0.0 | 0.0 | 0.8 | 1.5 | 5.1 | 5.1 | 6.1 | 21.0 | 5.4 | 0.1 | 0.0 | 46.1 |
| 1986-87 | 0.0 | 0.0 | 0.0 | T | 3.8 | 10.1 | 18.5 | 2.2 | 2.5 | 1.6 | 0.0 | 0.0 | 38.7 |
| 1987-88 | 0.0 | 0.0 | 0.0 | T | 29.2 | 26.3 | 4.7 | 9.2 | 8.5 | 2.0 | 0.0 | 0.0 | 79.9 |
| 1988-89 | 0.0 | 0.0 | 0.0 | 12.0 | 15.3 | 18.6 | 10.1 | 2.3 | 5.1 | T | 0.2 | 0.0 | 63.6 |
| 1989-90 | 0.0 | 0.0 | 0.0 | 16.3 | 10.1 | 20.0 | 27.5 | 23.0 | 4.7 | 0.8 | T | 0.0 | 102.4 |
| 1990-91 | 0.0 | 0.0 | 0.0 | 1.6 | 16.9 | 21.4 | | | | | | | |
| Record Mean | 0.0 | 0.0 | 0.2 | 7.1 | 10.5 | 14.9 | 10.4 | 11.3 | 9.1 | 5.1 | 0.5 | 0.0 | 69.1 |

**See Reference Notes, relative to all above tables, on preceding page.**

Fairbanks is located in the Tanana Valley, in the interior of Alaska. It has a distinctly continental climate, with large variation of temperature from winter to summer.

The climate in Fairbanks is conditioned mainly by the response of the land mass to large changes in solar heat received by the area during the year. The sun is above the horizon from 18 to 21 hours during June and July. During this period, daily average maximum temperatures reach the lower 70s. Temperatures of 80 degrees or higher occur on about 10 days each summer. In contrast, from November to early March, when the period of daylight ranges from 10 to less than 4 hours per day, the lowest temperature readings normally fall below zero quite regularly. Low temperatures of −40 degrees or colder occur each winter. The range of temperatures in summer is comparatively low, from the lower 30s to the mid 90s. In winter, this range is larger, from about 65 below to 45 degrees above. This large winter range of temperature reflects the great difference between frigid weather associated with dry northerly airflow from the Arctic to mild temperatures associated with southerly airflow from the Gulf of Alaska, accompanied by chinook winds off the Alaska Range, 80 miles to the south of Fairbanks.

Snow cover is persistent in Fairbanks, without interruption, from October through April. Snowfalls of 4 inches or more in a day occur only three times during winter. Blizzard conditions are almost never seen, as winds in Fairbanks are above 20 miles an hour less than 1 percent of the time. Precipitation normally reaches a minimum in spring, and a maximum in August, when rainfall is common. During summer, thunderstorms occur in Fairbanks on an average of about eight days. Thunderstorms are about three times more frequent over the hills to the north and east of Fairbanks. Damaging hail or wind rarely accompany thunderstorms around Fairbanks.

There are rolling hills reaching elevations up to 2,000 feet above Fairbanks to the north and east of the city. During winter, the uplands are often warmer than Fairbanks, as cold air settles into the valley. In some months, temperatures in the uplands will average more than 10 degrees warmer than Fairbanks. During summer, the uplands are a few degrees cooler than the city. Precipitation in the uplands around Fairbanks is heavier than it is in the city by roughly 20 to 50 percent. Fairbanks exhibits an urban heat island, especially during winter. Low lying areas nearby, such as the community of North Pole, are often colder than the city, sometimes by as much as 15 degrees.

During winter, with temperatures of −20 degrees or colder, ice fog frequently forms in the city. Cold snaps accompanied by ice fog generally last about a week, but can last three weeks in unusual situations. The fog is almost always less than 300 feet deep, so that the surrounding uplands are usually in the clear, with warmer temperatures. Visibility in the ice fog is sometimes quite low, and this can hinder aircraft operations for as much as a day in severe cases. Aside from the low visibility in winter ice fog, flying weather in Fairbanks is quite favorable, especially from February through May, when crystal clear weather is common and the length of daylight is rapidly increasing.

Hardy vegetables and grains grow luxuriantly. Freezing of local rivers normally begins in the first week of October. The date when ice will normally support a persons weight is October 27. Rivers remain frozen and safe for travel until early April. Breakup of the river ice usually occurs in the first week of May.

## TABLE 1     NORMALS, MEANS AND EXTREMES

FAIRBANKS, ALASKA

LATITUDE: 64°49'N    LONGITUDE: 147°52'W    ELEVATION: FT. GRND   436 BARO   452    TIME ZONE: YUKON     WBAN: 26411

| | (a) | JAN | FEB | MAR | APR | MAY | JUNE | JULY | AUG | SEP | OCT | NOV | DEC | YEAR |
|---|---|---|---|---|---|---|---|---|---|---|---|---|---|---|
| **TEMPERATURE °F:** | | | | | | | | | | | | | | |
| Normals | | | | | | | | | | | | | | |
| -Daily Maximum | | -3.9 | 7.3 | 21.7 | 40.8 | 59.2 | 70.1 | 71.8 | 66.5 | 54.4 | 32.6 | 12.4 | -1.7 | 35.9 |
| -Daily Minimum | | -21.6 | -15.4 | -4.8 | 19.5 | 37.2 | 48.5 | 51.2 | 46.5 | 35.4 | 17.5 | -4.6 | -18.4 | 15.9 |
| -Monthly | | -12.8 | -4.0 | 8.5 | 30.2 | 48.2 | 59.3 | 61.5 | 56.6 | 44.9 | 25.0 | 3.9 | -10.1 | 25.9 |
| Extremes | | | | | | | | | | | | | | |
| -Record Highest | 38 | 50 | 47 | 51 | 74 | 89 | 96 | 94 | 90 | 84 | 65 | 46 | 44 | 96 |
| -Year | | 1981 | 1987 | 1987 | 1960 | 1960 | 1969 | 1975 | 1976 | 1957 | 1969 | 1970 | 1985 | JUN 1969 |
| -Record Lowest | 38 | -61 | -56 | -49 | -24 | -1 | 31 | 35 | 27 | 10 | -27 | -43 | -62 | -62 |
| -Year | | 1969 | 1968 | 1956 | 1986 | 1964 | 1963 | 1959 | 1987 | 1983 | 1975 | 1964 | 1961 | DEC 1961 |
| **NORMAL DEGREE DAYS:** | | | | | | | | | | | | | | |
| Heating (base 65°F) | | 2412 | 1932 | 1752 | 1044 | 521 | 198 | 141 | 270 | 603 | 1240 | 1833 | 2328 | 14274 |
| Cooling (base 65°F) | | 0 | 0 | 0 | 0 | 0 | 27 | 33 | 10 | 0 | 0 | 0 | 0 | 70 |
| **% OF POSSIBLE SUNSHINE** | | | | | | | | | | | | | | |
| **MEAN SKY COVER (tenths)** | | | | | | | | | | | | | | |
| Sunrise - Sunset | 38 | 6.2 | 6.2 | 5.8 | 6.7 | 6.9 | 7.3 | 7.5 | 7.8 | 7.6 | 7.9 | 6.9 | 6.9 | 7.0 |
| **MEAN NUMBER OF DAYS:** | | | | | | | | | | | | | | |
| Sunrise to Sunset | | | | | | | | | | | | | | |
| -Clear | 38 | 9.2 | 8.3 | 10.2 | 6.4 | 4.3 | 2.6 | 3.3 | 3.0 | 4.3 | 3.8 | 7.0 | 7.0 | 69.5 |
| -Partly Cloudy | 38 | 6.0 | 5.7 | 6.9 | 7.6 | 10.8 | 10.1 | 8.7 | 6.7 | 6.1 | 5.3 | 5.2 | 5.8 | 84.9 |
| -Cloudy | 38 | 15.8 | 14.2 | 13.9 | 16.1 | 15.8 | 17.3 | 18.9 | 21.3 | 19.6 | 21.9 | 17.8 | 18.2 | 210.9 |
| Precipitation | | | | | | | | | | | | | | |
| .01 inches or more | 38 | 7.2 | 6.4 | 5.9 | 4.9 | 7.0 | 10.5 | 12.4 | 12.5 | 9.5 | 10.8 | 10.0 | 8.7 | 106.0 |
| Snow,Ice pellets | | | | | | | | | | | | | | |
| 1.0 inches or more | 38 | 3.1 | 2.3 | 2.2 | 1.1 | 0.2 | 0.0 | 0.0 | 0.0 | 0.3 | 4.1 | 4.2 | 4.0 | 21.6 |
| Thunderstorms | 38 | 0.0 | 0.0 | 0.0 | 0.* | 0.4 | 2.5 | 2.1 | 0.8 | 0.1 | 0.0 | 0.0 | 0.0 | 5.9 |
| Heavy Fog Visibility | | | | | | | | | | | | | | |
| 1/4 mile or less | 38 | 4.7 | 2.3 | 0.6 | 0.3 | 0.2 | 0.3 | 0.8 | 1.8 | 1.4 | 1.7 | 1.1 | 3.4 | 18.8 |
| Temperature °F | | | | | | | | | | | | | | |
| -Maximum | | | | | | | | | | | | | | |
| 70° and above | 26 | 0.0 | 0.0 | 0.0 | 0.* | 3.2 | 16.5 | 20.6 | 10.8 | 1.3 | 0.0 | 0.0 | 0.0 | 52.4 |
| 32° and below | 26 | 29.9 | 25.8 | 21.3 | 6.1 | 0.2 | 0.0 | 0.0 | 0.0 | 0.2 | 16.0 | 28.0 | 29.5 | 157.0 |
| -Minimum | | | | | | | | | | | | | | |
| 32° and below | 26 | 31.0 | 28.3 | 30.8 | 26.7 | 6.2 | 0.0 | 0.0 | 0.6 | 8.4 | 28.2 | 30.0 | 31.0 | 221.2 |
| 0° and below | 26 | 26.1 | 22.3 | 16.5 | 2.3 | 0.* | 0.0 | 0.0 | 0.0 | 0.0 | 3.9 | 18.7 | 24.1 | 114.0 |
| **AVG. STATION PRESS.(mb)** | 17 | 993.9 | 995.8 | 993.0 | 992.9 | 992.5 | 993.5 | 995.6 | 995.5 | 992.9 | 989.9 | 991.2 | 992.7 | 993.3 |
| **RELATIVE HUMIDITY (%)** | | | | | | | | | | | | | | |
| Hour 03 | 40 | 68 | 66 | 66 | 67 | 67 | 74 | 81 | 85 | 81 | 78 | 73 | 70 | 73 |
| Hour 09 | 40 | 68 | 66 | 65 | 60 | 53 | 61 | 69 | 77 | 78 | 78 | 73 | 71 | 68 |
| Hour 15 (Local Time) | 40 | 68 | 63 | 53 | 46 | 38 | 43 | 50 | 54 | 55 | 67 | 72 | 71 | 57 |
| Hour 21 | 40 | 68 | 66 | 62 | 55 | 47 | 50 | 60 | 70 | 71 | 76 | 73 | 70 | 64 |
| **PRECIPITATION (inches):** | | | | | | | | | | | | | | |
| Water Equivalent | | | | | | | | | | | | | | |
| -Normal | | 0.53 | 0.42 | 0.40 | 0.27 | 0.57 | 1.32 | 1.77 | 1.86 | 1.09 | 0.74 | 0.67 | 0.73 | 10.37 |
| -Maximum Monthly | 38 | 1.92 | 1.75 | 2.10 | 0.93 | 1.67 | 3.52 | 4.35 | 6.20 | 3.05 | 2.19 | 3.32 | 3.23 | 6.20 |
| -Year | | 1957 | 1966 | 1963 | 1982 | 1955 | 1955 | 1962 | 1967 | 1960 | 1983 | 1970 | 1984 | AUG 1967 |
| -Minimum Monthly | 38 | 0.01 | 0.01 | T | T | 0.07 | 0.19 | 0.40 | 0.40 | 0.15 | 0.08 | T | T | T |
| -Year | | 1966 | 1976 | 1987 | 1969 | 1957 | 1966 | 1957 | 1957 | 1968 | 1954 | 1953 | 1969 | MAR 1987 |
| -Maximum in 24 hrs | 38 | 0.58 | 0.97 | 0.92 | 0.47 | 0.88 | 1.52 | 1.63 | 3.42 | 1.21 | 2.22 | 0.84 | 1.25 | 3.42 |
| -Year | | 1968 | 1966 | 1963 | 1979 | 1955 | 1955 | 1962 | 1967 | 1954 | 1976 | 1970 | 1968 | AUG 1967 |
| Snow,Ice pellets | | | | | | | | | | | | | | |
| -Maximum Monthly | 38 | 26.3 | 43.1 | 29.6 | 11.4 | 4.7 | T | 0.0 | T | 7.8 | 25.9 | 54.0 | 50.7 | 54.0 |
| -Year | | 1957 | 1966 | 1963 | 1982 | 1964 | 1974 | | 1969 | 1972 | 1982 | 1970 | 1984 | NOV 1970 |
| -Maximum in 24 hrs | 38 | 9.4 | 20.1 | 12.6 | 5.8 | 4.5 | T | 0.0 | T | 7.0 | 10.4 | 14.6 | 14.7 | 20.1 |
| -Year | | 1968 | 1966 | 1963 | 1982 | 1964 | 1987 | | | 1969 | 1972 | 1974 | 1970 | 1968 | FEB 1966 |
| **WIND:** | | | | | | | | | | | | | | |
| Mean Speed (mph) | 38 | 3.1 | 4.0 | 5.3 | 6.6 | 7.8 | 7.2 | 6.7 | 6.2 | 6.1 | 5.4 | 3.8 | 3.1 | 5.4 |
| Prevailing Direction | | | | | | | | | | | | | | |
| through 1963 | | N | N | N | N | N | SW | SW | N | N | N | N | N | N |
| Fastest Obs. 1 Min. | | | | | | | | | | | | | | |
| -Direction (!!!) | 38 | 03 | 27 | 22 | 24 | 23 | 25 | 27 | 27 | 22 | 25 | 25 | 24 | 25 |
| -Speed (MPH) | 38 | 29 | 33 | 40 | 32 | 32 | 40 | 32 | 34 | 30 | 40 | 35 | 37 | 40 |
| -Year | | 1983 | 1955 | 1970 | 1983 | 1984 | 1974 | 1989 | 1954 | 1975 | 1958 | 1970 | 1970 | JUN 1974 |
| Peak Gust | | | | | | | | | | | | | | |
| -Direction (!!!) | 5 | SW | SW | SW | E | SW | E | W | S | W | SW | SW | SW | W |
| -Speed (mph) | 5 | 39 | 40 | 46 | 28 | 38 | 43 | 53 | 38 | 51 | 28 | 24 | 38 | 53 |
| -Date | | 1989 | 1989 | 1985 | 1988 | 1986 | 1985 | 1989 | 1985 | 1985 | 1986 | 1985 | 1985 | JUL 1989 |

**See Reference Notes to this table on the following page.**

# FAIRBANKS, ALASKA

## TABLE 2

### PRECIPITATION (inches)  FAIRBANKS, ALASKA

| YEAR | JAN | FEB | MAR | APR | MAY | JUNE | JULY | AUG | SEP | OCT | NOV | DEC | ANNUAL |
|---|---|---|---|---|---|---|---|---|---|---|---|---|---|
| 1961 | 0.25 | 0.17 | 0.11 | 0.37 | 0.24 | 0.66 | 2.61 | 2.85 | 1.91 | 1.17 | 0.47 | 0.59 | 11.40 |
| 1962 | 0.69 | 1.26 | 0.66 | 0.38 | 0.62 | 2.22 | 4.35 | 4.03 | 1.40 | 0.28 | 0.17 | 0.56 | 16.62 |
| 1963 | 1.78 | 0.27 | 2.10 | 0.49 | 0.11 | 2.00 | 1.36 | 3.60 | 0.19 | 1.51 | 0.18 | 0.38 | 13.97 |
| 1964 | 0.21 | 0.46 | 0.18 | 0.68 | 0.97 | 1.33 | 1.28 | 2.37 | 0.85 | 0.53 | 0.86 | 0.34 | 10.06 |
| 1965 | 0.07 | 0.32 | 0.27 | 0.47 | 0.14 | 1.16 | 1.39 | 1.48 | 2.11 | 0.74 | 1.21 | 1.92 | 11.28 |
| 1966 | 0.01 | 1.75 | 0.34 | 0.32 | 0.38 | 0.19 | 0.83 | 0.59 | 0.15 | 0.29 | 2.06 | 0.16 | 7.07 |
| 1967 | 0.40 | 0.25 | 1.90 | 0.84 | 0.43 | 1.13 | 3.34 | 6.20 | 0.25 | 0.32 | 0.93 | 1.34 | 17.33 |
| 1968 | 1.19 | 0.15 | T | 0.29 | 0.67 | 1.52 | 0.84 | 0.96 | 0.15 | 0.31 | 0.27 | 1.38 | 7.73 |
| 1969 | 0.55 | 0.10 | 0.60 | T | 0.95 | 0.39 | 1.33 | 2.04 | 0.28 | 0.10 | 0.54 | T | 6.88 |
| 1970 | 0.10 | 0.32 | 0.25 | 0.45 | 0.42 | 2.57 | 1.81 | 1.98 | 0.65 | 1.84 | 3.32 | 2.29 | 16.00 |
| 1971 | 0.33 | 0.63 | 0.20 | 0.11 | 0.16 | 0.31 | 2.08 | 2.32 | 2.45 | 1.35 | 0.54 | 1.83 | 12.31 |
| 1972 | 0.73 | 0.16 | 0.27 | 0.20 | 0.35 | 0.55 | 0.63 | 1.09 | 2.09 | 0.86 | 0.46 | 1.13 | 8.51 |
| 1973 | 0.44 | 0.11 | 0.40 | 0.05 | 0.97 | 0.97 | 1.92 | 2.19 | 0.19 | 0.91 | 0.80 | 0.15 | 9.12 |
| 1974 | 0.14 | 0.33 | 0.27 | 0.21 | 0.11 | 1.22 | 1.17 | 1.14 | 0.47 | 1.08 | 1.03 | 0.55 | 7.72 |
| 1975 | 0.60 | 0.04 | 0.22 | 0.47 | 0.49 | 0.99 | 1.81 | 2.10 | 0.20 | 0.79 | 0.44 | 0.31 | 8.46 |
| 1976 | 0.22 | 0.01 | 0.55 | 0.08 | 0.94 | 1.08 | 1.60 | 0.69 | 1.05 | 0.89 | 0.13 | 0.08 | 7.32 |
| 1977 | 0.31 | 0.81 | 0.26 | 0.36 | 1.63 | 3.01 | 1.58 | 0.41 | 2.51 | 1.11 | 0.19 | 0.80 | 12.98 |
| 1978 | 0.39 | 0.19 | 0.09 | 0.16 | 0.44 | 1.71 | 1.19 | 1.24 | 0.98 | 0.59 | 1.02 | 1.40 | 9.40 |
| 1979 | 0.58 | 0.02 | 0.47 | 0.83 | 0.88 | 1.54 | 2.54 | 1.22 | 0.19 | 0.94 | 0.63 | 0.49 | 10.33 |
| 1980 | 0.52 | 0.22 | 0.13 | 0.10 | 0.31 | 1.38 | 1.37 | 1.68 | 0.76 | 0.39 | 0.70 | 0.32 | 7.88 |
| 1981 | 0.31 | 0.78 | 0.07 | 0.32 | 0.73 | 1.91 | 2.41 | 1.35 | 0.80 | 0.91 | 0.91 | 0.58 | 11.08 |
| 1982 | 0.34 | 0.38 | 0.39 | 0.93 | 0.96 | 1.96 | 2.33 | 1.67 | 0.77 | 1.48 | 1.49 | 0.23 | 12.93 |
| 1983 | 0.24 | 0.18 | 0.09 | 0.27 | 0.14 | 0.57 | 1.71 | 3.33 | 0.92 | 2.19 | 0.08 | 0.65 | 10.37 |
| 1984 | 0.89 | 0.64 | 0.03 | 0.47 | 1.17 | 0.48 | 2.95 | 1.15 | 0.22 | 0.70 | 0.42 | 3.23 | 12.35 |
| 1985 | 0.52 | 0.48 | 0.57 | 0.36 | 0.41 | 1.80 | 1.13 | 1.88 | 2.59 | 1.00 | 0.90 | 0.08 | 11.72 |
| 1986 | 0.13 | 0.19 | 0.32 | 0.07 | 0.54 | 0.87 | 2.12 | 2.36 | 0.65 | 1.79 | 0.48 | 0.34 | 9.86 |
| 1987 | 0.68 | 0.10 | T | 0.05 | 0.21 | 1.02 | 1.70 | 0.56 | 0.57 | 0.39 | 0.64 | 0.51 | 6.43 |
| 1988 | 0.32 | 0.13 | 0.13 | 0.21 | 1.51 | 2.26 | 1.02 | 1.95 | 0.73 | 1.07 | 0.68 | 0.46 | 10.47 |
| 1989 | 0.52 | 0.98 | 0.13 | 0.05 | 0.99 | 2.53 | 0.91 | 0.78 | 0.72 | 1.28 | 0.97 | 0.57 | 10.43 |
| 1990 | 0.52 | 0.72 | 0.11 | 0.07 | 0.40 | 1.73 | 4.87 | 3.60 | 1.74 | 0.31 | 1.51 | 2.94 | 18.52 |
| Record Mean | 0.67 | 0.46 | 0.39 | 0.28 | 0.66 | 1.39 | 1.87 | 2.16 | 1.03 | 0.88 | 0.70 | 0.69 | 11.18 |

## TABLE 3

### AVERAGE TEMPERATURE (deg. F)  FAIRBANKS, ALASKA

| YEAR | JAN | FEB | MAR | APR | MAY | JUNE | JULY | AUG | SEP | OCT | NOV | DEC | ANNUAL |
|---|---|---|---|---|---|---|---|---|---|---|---|---|---|
| 1961 | -2.0 | -4.4 | 0.7 | 25.1 | 49.3 | 58.8 | 59.2 | 55.3 | 44.1 | 21.2 | -4.2 | -23.9 | 23.3 |
| 1962 | -7.8 | 7.1 | 8.0 | 30.1 | 44.9 | 58.6 | 63.5 | 58.0 | 41.5 | 30.8 | 4.4 | -6.5 | 27.7 |
| #1963 | 1.7 | -0.3 | 7.7 | 24.5 | 49.4 | 53.4 | 60.0 | 54.7 | 47.9 | 26.4 | -10.5 | 4.0 | 26.6 |
| 1964 | -15.7 | 0.7 | -2.2 | 25.8 | 38.6 | 60.1 | 59.7 | 56.5 | 44.9 | 28.4 | 2.4 | -26.5 | 22.8 |
| 1965 | -18.0 | -18.1 | 24.5 | 30.9 | 42.9 | 55.2 | 60.2 | 52.7 | 48.2 | 13.9 | 3.9 | -14.1 | 23.5 |
| 1966 | -27.4 | -7.6 | -2.5 | 27.1 | 45.4 | 63.3 | 62.5 | 57.1 | 50.1 | 24.3 | 0.6 | -20.1 | 22.7 |
| 1967 | -15.3 | -6.9 | 9.8 | 31.7 | 45.7 | 61.8 | 59.8 | 58.3 | 46.6 | 24.8 | 9.5 | -1.6 | 27.1 |
| 1968 | -11.0 | -5.0 | 12.8 | 29.2 | 47.6 | 59.5 | 65.8 | 58.5 | 42.8 | 22.1 | 2.3 | -17.7 | 25.6 |
| 1969 | -26.7 | -7.3 | 10.1 | 36.3 | 49.4 | 64.9 | 59.4 | 49.8 | 49.1 | 34.0 | 1.2 | 4.0 | 27.0 |
| 1970 | -16.2 | 8.0 | 20.9 | 32.0 | 51.8 | 58.0 | 62.4 | 56.9 | 40.8 | 18.9 | 10.7 | -9.8 | 27.9 |
| 1971 | -31.7 | -4.6 | -0.4 | 26.7 | 47.3 | 63.4 | 61.0 | 56.1 | 44.7 | 27.9 | 0.5 | -5.8 | 23.8 |
| 1972 | -16.3 | -10.1 | -2.8 | 20.8 | 47.4 | 59.4 | 64.5 | 58.9 | 40.1 | 26.8 | 7.0 | -2.5 | 24.5 |
| 1973 | -18.2 | -1.5 | 11.9 | 35.3 | 50.6 | 60.3 | 62.0 | 55.0 | 47.3 | 25.1 | -0.7 | -3.4 | 27.0 |
| 1974 | -16.7 | -17.8 | 7.6 | 34.9 | 51.4 | 58.7 | 63.5 | 59.1 | 51.4 | 21.4 | 0.6 | -11.3 | 25.2 |
| 1975 | -15.5 | -3.4 | 12.6 | 30.5 | 53.5 | 63.4 | 68.4 | 56.1 | 45.8 | 23.3 | -8.0 | -16.1 | 25.9 |
| 1976 | -11.5 | -13.7 | 12.1 | 36.0 | 47.8 | 59.6 | 61.8 | 59.2 | 45.4 | 23.9 | 15.9 | -3.9 | 27.7 |
| 1977 | 9.8 | 8.6 | 4.6 | 27.8 | 48.7 | 59.6 | 62.8 | 62.6 | 45.6 | 25.6 | -7.6 | -14.9 | 27.8 |
| 1978 | 0.1 | 3.9 | 14.0 | 34.8 | 50.2 | 54.6 | 63.5 | 59.5 | 46.8 | 23.3 | 8.6 | 3.3 | 30.2 |
| 1979 | -7.7 | -25.3 | 12.0 | 30.9 | 49.9 | 57.4 | 61.3 | 60.0 | 46.5 | 32.4 | 20.2 | -10.2 | 27.3 |
| 1980 | -9.5 | 16.0 | 17.3 | 35.9 | 50.7 | 56.5 | 60.9 | 53.6 | 43.0 | 33.0 | 11.5 | -24.0 | 28.7 |
| 1981 | 18.1 | 5.1 | 27.1 | 31.4 | 51.3 | 58.9 | 56.5 | 53.6 | 44.1 | 29.5 | 12.3 | -4.2 | 32.0 |
| 1982 | -18.0 | -3.9 | 13.1 | 27.7 | 46.8 | 58.5 | 63.1 | 56.6 | 49.3 | 18.5 | 4.4 | 2.2 | 26.6 |
| 1983 | -11.0 | 3.4 | 13.8 | 34.7 | 50.4 | 62.3 | 64.2 | 53.1 | 41.2 | 23.6 | 8.6 | -3.7 | 28.6 |
| 1984 | -5.9 | -13.3 | 21.6 | 30.3 | 47.2 | 61.6 | 60.9 | 53.8 | 46.8 | 25.9 | 0.1 | -3.1 | 27.2 |
| 1985 | 11.1 | -9.4 | 14.6 | 20.8 | 46.7 | 57.8 | 63.1 | 56.3 | 42.9 | 18.8 | -4.7 | 7.7 | 27.1 |
| 1986 | -2.1 | 4.7 | 6.0 | 24.0 | 47.8 | 62.6 | 63.6 | 54.7 | 46.3 | 27.1 | 0.2 | 7.3 | 28.5 |
| 1987 | 0.7 | 1.5 | 13.5 | 35.0 | 50.9 | 61.9 | 64.2 | 57.7 | 44.1 | 33.0 | 6.0 | -3.2 | 30.4 |
| 1988 | -5.3 | 3.9 | 17.8 | 33.6 | 52.8 | 62.9 | 65.8 | 58.4 | 44.4 | 17.4 | -3.1 | 4.2 | 29.4 |
| 1989 | -21.3 | 3.4 | 6.7 | 36.2 | 47.8 | 60.1 | 64.6 | 60.8 | 48.6 | 26.2 | -7.1 | 4.5 | 27.5 |
| 1990 | -12.9 | -21.7 | 18.5 | 38.1 | 55.1 | 61.6 | 65.3 | 60.0 | 44.8 | 24.1 | -4.9 | -6.3 | 26.8 |
| Record Mean | -10.4 | -3.5 | 9.9 | 30.2 | 47.9 | 59.2 | 61.2 | 55.6 | 44.6 | 25.6 | 3.0 | -7.9 | 26.3 |
| Max | -1.5 | 7.7 | 23.3 | 41.3 | 59.0 | 70.3 | 71.8 | 65.7 | 54.1 | 33.1 | 11.1 | 0.3 | 36.4 |
| Min | -19.3 | -14.6 | -3.5 | 19.1 | 36.8 | 48.0 | 50.6 | 45.6 | 35.1 | 18.2 | -5.2 | -16.1 | 16.2 |

## REFERENCE NOTES FOR TABLES 1, 2, 3 and 6  (FAIRBANKS, AK)

### GENERAL

T - TRACE AMOUNT
BLANK ENTRIES DENOTE MISSING/UNREPORTED DATA.
# INDICATES A STATION OR INSTRUMENT RELOCATION.

### SPECIFIC

#### TABLE 1

(a) - LENGTH OF RECORD IN YEARS. ALTHOUGH INDIVIDUAL MONTHS MAY BE MISSING.
* LESS THAN .05

NORMALS — BASED ON THE 1951-1980 RECORD PERIOD.
EXTREMES — DATES ARE THE MOST RECENT OCCURRENCE.
WIND DIR. — NUMERALS SHOW TENS OF DEGREES CLOCKWISE FROM TRUE NORTH. "00" INDICATES CALM.
RESULTANT WIND DIRECTIONS ARE GIVEN TO WHOLE DEGREES.

#### TABLE 3

MAX AND MIN ARE LONG-TERM MEAN DAILY MAXIMUM AND MEAN DAILY MINIMUM TEMPERATURES.

### EXCEPTIONS

#### TABLES 2, 3, and 6

RECORD MEANS ARE THROUGH THE CURRENT YEAR, BEGINNING IN
1930 FOR TEMPERATURE
1930 FOR PRECIPITATION
1952 FOR SNOWFALL

414

## TABLE 4 — HEATING DEGREE DAYS Base 65 deg. F  FAIRBANKS, ALASKA

| SEASON | JULY | AUG | SEP | OCT | NOV | DEC | JAN | FEB | MAR | APR | MAY | JUNE | TOTAL |
|---|---|---|---|---|---|---|---|---|---|---|---|---|---|
| 1961-62 | 179 | 294 | 622 | 1353 | 2078 | 2759 | 2258 | 1620 | 1765 | 1040 | 617 | 201 | 14786 |
| 1962-63 | 86 | 223 | 696 | 1055 | 1816 | 2218 | 1959 | 1830 | 1777 | 1208 | 482 | 342 | 13692 |
| #1963-64 | 169 | 312 | 505 | 1189 | 2267 | 1890 | 2509 | 1862 | 2085 | 1166 | 810 | 148 | 14912 |
| 1964-65 | 165 | 256 | 595 | 1133 | 1876 | 2841 | 2574 | 2334 | 1249 | 1019 | 680 | 287 | 15009 |
| 1965-66 | 152 | 374 | 496 | 1580 | 1833 | 2453 | 2872 | 2039 | 2092 | 1132 | 600 | 63 | 15688 |
| 1966-67 | 92 | 247 | 441 | 1255 | 1929 | 2643 | 2496 | 2014 | 1704 | 991 | 594 | 138 | 14544 |
| 1967-68 | 178 | 213 | 545 | 1239 | 1661 | 2064 | 2358 | 2029 | 1613 | 1069 | 533 | 169 | 13671 |
| 1968-69 | 50 | 208 | 657 | 1320 | 1881 | 2567 | 2849 | 2024 | 1698 | 855 | 475 | 80 | 14664 |
| 1969-70 | 170 | 467 | 472 | 955 | 1914 | 1892 | 2524 | 1595 | 1365 | 981 | 401 | 203 | 12939 |
| 1970-71 | 96 | 244 | 722 | 1425 | 1630 | 2318 | 3002 | 1948 | 2030 | 1141 | 542 | 117 | 15215 |
| 1971-72 | 134 | 271 | 600 | 1143 | 1932 | 2195 | 2524 | 2178 | 2102 | 1318 | 539 | 205 | 15141 |
| 1972-73 | 63 | 184 | 738 | 1177 | 1739 | 2091 | 2582 | 1637 | 1864 | 883 | 439 | 150 | 13547 |
| 1973-74 | 111 | 302 | 523 | 1231 | 1968 | 2124 | 2535 | 2322 | 1778 | 895 | 414 | 188 | 14391 |
| 1974-75 | 85 | 195 | 402 | 1342 | 1935 | 2370 | 2497 | 1918 | 1620 | 1028 | 347 | 69 | 13808 |
| 1975-76 | 33 | 270 | 570 | 1270 | 2195 | 2513 | 2372 | 2285 | 1631 | 861 | 527 | 156 | 14683 |
| 1976-77 | 116 | 188 | 583 | 1269 | 1466 | 2136 | 1709 | 1574 | 1871 | 1107 | 500 | 155 | 12674 |
| 1977-78 | 101 | 124 | 573 | 1216 | 2184 | 2480 | 2013 | 1712 | 1576 | 898 | 454 | 304 | 13635 |
| 1978-79 | 65 | 176 | 542 | 1286 | 1689 | 1912 | 2260 | 2533 | 1638 | 1018 | 463 | 220 | 13802 |
| 1979-80 | 124 | 143 | 548 | 1004 | 1336 | 2335 | 2312 | 1415 | 1475 | 868 | 436 | 248 | 12244 |
| 1980-81 | 127 | 351 | 654 | 985 | 1599 | 2766 | 1447 | 1676 | 1168 | 999 | 418 | 188 | 12378 |
| 1981-82 | 255 | 347 | 622 | 1094 | 1573 | 2150 | 2581 | 1929 | 1602 | 1113 | 555 | 216 | 14037 |
| 1982-83 | 86 | 252 | 465 | 1434 | 1816 | 1946 | 2356 | 1725 | 1581 | 823 | 451 | 133 | 13068 |
| 1983-84 | 62 | 351 | 705 | 1280 | 1688 | 2126 | 2201 | 2277 | 1338 | 1035 | 549 | 120 | 13732 |
| 1984-85 | 140 | 344 | 538 | 1205 | 1950 | 2111 | 1666 | 2086 | 1558 | 1321 | 558 | 215 | 13692 |
| 1985-86 | 72 | 267 | 654 | 1430 | 2095 | 1776 | 2079 | 1686 | 1825 | 1224 | 527 | 113 | 13748 |
| 1986-87 | 110 | 312 | 559 | 1169 | 1943 | 1787 | 1994 | 1776 | 1594 | 893 | 428 | 128 | 12693 |
| 1987-88 | 61 | 218 | 620 | 987 | 1768 | 2111 | 2185 | 1768 | 1455 | 934 | 371 | 96 | 12574 |
| 1988-89 | 39 | 202 | 611 | 1469 | 2045 | 1883 | 2676 | 1722 | 1804 | 859 | 529 | 149 | 13988 |
| 1989-90 | 73 | 134 | 484 | 1195 | 2164 | 1875 | 2420 | 2433 | 1431 | 798 | 310 | 127 | 13444 |
| 1990-91 | 74 | 178 | 600 | 1261 | 2097 | 2212 | | | | | | | |

## TABLE 5 — COOLING DEGREE DAYS Base 65 deg. F  FAIRBANKS, ALASKA

| YEAR | JAN | FEB | MAR | APR | MAY | JUNE | JULY | AUG | SEP | OCT | NOV | DEC | TOTAL |
|---|---|---|---|---|---|---|---|---|---|---|---|---|---|
| 1969 | 0 | 0 | 0 | 0 | 0 | 83 | 2 | 0 | 0 | 0 | 0 | 0 | 85 |
| 1970 | 0 | 0 | 0 | 0 | 0 | 0 | 22 | 0 | 0 | 0 | 0 | 0 | 22 |
| 1971 | 0 | 0 | 0 | 0 | 0 | 73 | 16 | 0 | 0 | 0 | 0 | 0 | 89 |
| 1972 | 0 | 0 | 0 | 0 | 0 | 40 | 55 | 0 | 0 | 0 | 0 | 0 | 95 |
| 1973 | 0 | 0 | 0 | 0 | 0 | 13 | 24 | 2 | 0 | 0 | 0 | 0 | 39 |
| 1974 | 0 | 0 | 0 | 0 | 1 | 9 | 44 | 20 | 0 | 0 | 0 | 0 | 74 |
| 1975 | 0 | 0 | 0 | 0 | 0 | 28 | 146 | 1 | 0 | 0 | 0 | 0 | 175 |
| 1976 | 0 | 0 | 0 | 0 | 0 | 2 | 23 | 14 | 0 | 0 | 0 | 0 | 39 |
| 1977 | 0 | 0 | 0 | 0 | 0 | 0 | 44 | 54 | 0 | 0 | 0 | 0 | 98 |
| 1978 | 0 | 0 | 0 | 0 | 0 | 0 | 27 | 10 | 0 | 0 | 0 | 0 | 37 |
| 1979 | 0 | 0 | 0 | 0 | 0 | 0 | 16 | 7 | 0 | 0 | 0 | 0 | 23 |
| 1980 | 0 | 0 | 0 | 0 | 0 | 0 | 8 | 6 | 0 | 0 | 0 | 0 | 14 |
| 1981 | 0 | 0 | 0 | 0 | 1 | 11 | 0 | 2 | 0 | 0 | 0 | 0 | 14 |
| 1982 | 0 | 0 | 0 | 0 | 0 | 27 | 36 | 0 | 0 | 0 | 0 | 0 | 63 |
| 1983 | 0 | 0 | 0 | 0 | 5 | 61 | 40 | 0 | 0 | 0 | 0 | 0 | 106 |
| 1984 | 0 | 0 | 0 | 0 | 0 | 22 | 21 | 2 | 0 | 0 | 0 | 0 | 45 |
| 1985 | 0 | 0 | 0 | 0 | 0 | 8 | 20 | 4 | 0 | 0 | 0 | 0 | 32 |
| 1986 | 0 | 0 | 0 | 0 | 0 | 46 | 74 | 0 | 0 | 0 | 0 | 0 | 120 |
| 1987 | 0 | 0 | 0 | 0 | 0 | 42 | 42 | 0 | 0 | 0 | 0 | 0 | 84 |
| 1988 | 0 | 0 | 0 | 0 | 0 | 41 | 72 | 2 | 0 | 0 | 0 | 0 | 115 |
| 1989 | 0 | 0 | 0 | 0 | 0 | 10 | 67 | 11 | 0 | 0 | 0 | 0 | 88 |
| 1990 | 0 | 0 | 0 | 0 | 11 | 32 | 91 | 35 | 0 | 0 | 0 | 0 | 169 |

## TABLE 6 — SNOWFALL (inches)  FAIRBANKS, ALASKA

| SEASON | JULY | AUG | SEP | OCT | NOV | DEC | JAN | FEB | MAR | APR | MAY | JUNE | TOTAL |
|---|---|---|---|---|---|---|---|---|---|---|---|---|---|
| 1961-62 | 0.0 | 0.0 | T | 24.2 | 9.4 | 6.3 | 8.9 | 26.4 | 12.6 | 7.6 | 2.4 | 0.0 | 97.8 |
| 1962-63 | 0.0 | 0.0 | 0.5 | 2.8 | 3.1 | 6.0 | 17.5 | 29.6 | 5.8 | T | 5.0 | 0.0 | 70.3 |
| 1963-64 | 0.0 | 0.0 | 0.0 | 11.6 | 4.6 | 8.8 | 4.8 | 9.9 | 3.5 | 8.8 | 4.7 | 0.0 | 56.7 |
| 1964-65 | 0.0 | 0.0 | 0.0 | 4.7 | 18.1 | 14.0 | 3.0 | 7.6 | 1.4 | 5.8 | 0.7 | 0.0 | 55.3 |
| 1965-66 | 0.0 | 0.0 | T | 15.7 | 18.8 | 33.5 | 0.7 | 43.1 | 8.9 | 1.5 | 1.7 | 0.0 | 123.9 |
| 1966-67 | 0.0 | 0.0 | 0.0 | 5.5 | 36.6 | 2.9 | 13.0 | 5.2 | 28.4 | 11.1 | T | 0.0 | 102.7 |
| 1967-68 | 0.0 | 0.0 | 0.0 | 5.8 | 14.4 | 16.8 | 22.6 | 4.8 | 0.1 | 5.0 | 2.7 | 0.0 | 72.2 |
| 1968-69 | 0.0 | 0.0 | 0.9 | 6.7 | 8.0 | 20.2 | 10.8 | 1.4 | 11.3 | 0.4 | T | 0.0 | 59.7 |
| 1969-70 | 0.0 | T | 0.0 | 3.7 | 11.4 | T | 3.6 | 6.4 | 4.2 | 7.1 | T | 0.0 | 36.4 |
| 1970-71 | 0.0 | 0.0 | 4.1 | 21.9 | 54.0 | 32.5 | 8.5 | 16.3 | 6.4 | 0.9 | 1.1 | 0.0 | 145.7 |
| 1971-72 | 0.0 | 0.0 | 3.5 | 20.4 | 9.8 | 29.6 | 12.6 | 4.5 | 5.7 | 4.3 | 0.0 | 0.0 | 90.4 |
| 1972-73 | 0.0 | 0.0 | 7.8 | 6.9 | 12.2 | 26.9 | 14.2 | 1.8 | 8.7 | 1.0 | T | 0.0 | 79.5 |
| 1973-74 | 0.0 | 0.0 | 1.2 | 8.2 | 17.5 | 2.5 | 3.0 | 8.7 | 7.0 | 1.3 | 0.0 | T | 49.4 |
| 1974-75 | 0.0 | 0.0 | 0.3 | 24.4 | 22.5 | 17.9 | 14.1 | 1.6 | 5.0 | 4.4 | T | 0.0 | 90.2 |
| 1975-76 | 0.0 | 0.0 | T | 14.4 | 11.4 | 6.7 | 6.4 | 10.4 | 1.2 | T | 0.0 | | 51.0 |
| 1976-77 | 0.0 | 0.0 | T | 14.7 | 4.3 | 2.6 | 6.7 | 19.0 | 5.5 | 6.8 | T | 0.0 | 59.6 |
| 1977-78 | 0.0 | 0.0 | 1.0 | 17.3 | 5.1 | 14.4 | 4.9 | 3.0 | 1.6 | 0.7 | 0.1 | 0.0 | 48.1 |
| 1978-79 | 0.0 | 0.0 | 0.3 | 7.6 | 15.1 | 21.7 | 9.7 | 0.5 | 7.7 | 3.1 | 0.0 | 0.0 | 65.7 |
| 1979-80 | 0.0 | 0.0 | T | 6.5 | 4.4 | 11.0 | 10.8 | 4.4 | 3.2 | 0.8 | 0.0 | 0.0 | 41.1 |
| 1980-81 | 0.0 | 0.0 | 3.4 | 5.1 | 10.6 | 4.8 | 6.2 | 10.2 | 0.9 | 1.9 | 0.0 | 0.0 | 43.1 |
| 1981-82 | 0.0 | 0.0 | 0.3 | 7.8 | 16.2 | 10.6 | 7.6 | 7.0 | 7.2 | 11.4 | 0.3 | 0.0 | 68.4 |
| 1982-83 | 0.0 | 0.0 | 0.6 | 25.9 | 27.8 | 3.8 | 4.8 | 3.6 | 2.1 | 1.9 | 0.4 | 0.0 | 70.9 |
| 1983-84 | 0.0 | 0.0 | 0.4 | 17.3 | 2.4 | 14.4 | 13.8 | 11.1 | 0.8 | 6.7 | T | 0.0 | 66.9 |
| 1984-85 | 0.0 | 0.0 | 0.6 | 11.3 | 8.5 | 50.7 | 8.1 | 8.0 | 7.4 | 5.9 | 1.0 | 0.0 | 100.9 |
| 1985-86 | 0.0 | 0.0 | 2.1 | 5.4 | 14.7 | 1.8 | 2.3 | 2.6 | 3.7 | 1.0 | 0.0 | 0.0 | 33.6 |
| 1986-87 | 0.0 | 0.0 | T | 11.8 | 7.4 | 6.0 | 12.0 | 1.5 | T | 1.0 | T | 0.0 | 39.7 |
| 1987-88 | 0.0 | 0.0 | T | 3.5 | 14.1 | 10.4 | 6.3 | 2.5 | 2.6 | 0.2 | 0.3 | 0.0 | 39.9 |
| 1988-89 | 0.0 | 0.0 | 0.2 | 12.9 | 15.2 | 10.5 | 10.8 | 13.4 | 3.9 | 0.4 | 0.8 | 0.0 | 68.1 |
| 1989-90 | 0.0 | 0.0 | 0.5 | 19.7 | 18.1 | 11.1 | 10.4 | 16.0 | 2.6 | T | 0.0 | T | 78.4 |
| 1990-91 | T | 0.0 | 1.6 | 6.9 | 37.3 | 47.5 | | | | | | | |
| Record Mean | T | T | 0.9 | 10.8 | 13.5 | 13.5 | 9.7 | 8.7 | 6.1 | 3.4 | 0.5 | T | 66.9 |

**See Reference Notes, relative to all above tables, on preceding page.**

Juneau lies well within the area of maritime influences which prevail over the coastal areas of southeastern Alaska, and is in the path of most storms that cross the Gulf of Alaska. Consequently, the area has little sunshine, generally moderate temperatures, and abundant precipitation. In contrast with the characteristic lack of sunshine there are greatly appreciated intervals, sometimes lasting for several days at a stretch, during which clear skies prevail. The rugged terrain exerts a fundamental influence upon local temperatures and the distribution of precipitation, creating considerable variations in both weather elements within relatively short distances.

Temperature variations, both daily and seasonal, are usually confined to relatively narrow limits by the dominant maritime influences. There are, however, periods of comparatively severe cold, which usually start with strong northerly winds, and are most often caused by the flow of cold air from northwestern Canada through nearby mountain passes and over the Juneau ice field. These are generally of brief duration. During such periods strong, gusty winds, known locally as Taku Winds, often occur especially in downtown Juneau, Douglas, and other local areas, but generally they are not felt in the Mendenhall Valley. At times these are strong enough to cause considerable damage. During periods of calm or light winds, temperature differences within short distances are frequently very pronounced. Variations in local sunlight and air drainage patterns produce wide differences in temperatures particularly between upland or sloping areas and areas of low, flat terrain. Juneau International Airport, located on low, flat terrain formed by the Mendenhall River delta, and in the path of drainage air from the Mendenhall Glacier, averages about 10 days a year with minimum readings below zero. Downtown Juneau, located on a sloping portion of a rugged mountain area, experiences on the average only about one day each year with minimum readings below zero. At the airport the growing season averages 146 days, from May 4 to September 28, while the downtown average is 181 days, from April 22 to October 21.

The months of February to June mark the period of lightest precipitation, with monthly averages of about 3 inches. After June the monthly amounts increase gradually, reaching an average of 7.71 inches in October. Due to the rugged topography, precipitation throughout the year tends to vary greatly within short distances. At the Juneau Airport, yearly precipitation is 53 inches while downtown, only 8 miles away, it is 93 inches. The maximum yearly amount received in the city is almost double the maximum received at the airport.

Although a trace of snow has fallen as early as September 9, first falls usually occur in the latter part of October, and sometimes not until the first part of December. On the average there is very little accumulation on the ground at low levels until the last of November, although at higher elevations, and particularly on mountain tops, a cover is usually established in early October. Snow accumulation usually reaches its greatest depth during the middle of February. Individual storms may produce heavy falls as late as the first half of May. However, snow cover is usually gone before the middle of April. Ice accumulations due to alternating thawing and freezing of snow or due to freezing precipitation are frequent problems in the Juneau area during the winter months.

## TABLE 1    NORMALS, MEANS AND EXTREMES

JUNEAU, ALASKA

LATITUDE: 58°22'N   LONGITUDE: 134°35'W   ELEVATION: FT. GRND 12 BARO 20   TIME ZONE: YUKON   WBAN: 25309

| | (a) | JAN | FEB | MAR | APR | MAY | JUNE | JULY | AUG | SEP | OCT | NOV | DEC | YEAR |
|---|---|---|---|---|---|---|---|---|---|---|---|---|---|---|
| **TEMPERATURE °F:** | | | | | | | | | | | | | | |
| Normals | | | | | | | | | | | | | | |
| -Daily Maximum | | 27.4 | 33.7 | 37.4 | 46.8 | 54.7 | 61.1 | 64.0 | 62.6 | 55.9 | 47.0 | 37.5 | 31.5 | 46.6 |
| -Daily Minimum | | 16.1 | 21.9 | 25.0 | 31.3 | 38.1 | 44.2 | 47.4 | 46.6 | 42.3 | 36.5 | 28.0 | 22.1 | 33.3 |
| -Monthly | | 21.8 | 27.8 | 31.2 | 39.1 | 46.5 | 52.7 | 55.7 | 54.6 | 49.2 | 41.8 | 32.7 | 26.8 | 40.0 |
| Extremes | | | | | | | | | | | | | | |
| -Record Highest | 45 | 57 | 55 | 59 | 71 | 82 | 86 | 90 | 83 | 72 | 61 | 56 | 54 | 90 |
| -Year | | 1958 | 1977 | 1981 | 1989 | 1947 | 1969 | 1975 | 1977 | 1989 | 1987 | 1949 | 1944 | JUL 1975 |
| -Record Lowest | 45 | -22 | -22 | -15 | 6 | 25 | 31 | 36 | 27 | 23 | 11 | -5 | -21 | -22 |
| -Year | | 1972 | 1968 | 1972 | 1963 | 1972 | 1971 | 1950 | 1948 | 1972 | 1984 | 1966 | 1949 | JAN 1972 |
| **NORMAL DEGREE DAYS:** | | | | | | | | | | | | | | |
| Heating (base 65°F) | | 1339 | 1042 | 1048 | 777 | 574 | 369 | 288 | 322 | 474 | 719 | 969 | 1184 | 9105 |
| Cooling (base 65°F) | | 0 | 0 | 0 | 0 | 0 | 0 | 0 | 0 | 0 | 0 | 0 | 0 | 0 |
| **% OF POSSIBLE SUNSHINE** | 33 | 32 | 32 | 37 | 39 | 39 | 34 | 31 | 32 | 26 | 19 | 23 | 20 | 30 |
| **MEAN SKY COVER (tenths)** | | | | | | | | | | | | | | |
| Sunrise - Sunset | 39 | 7.7 | 8.0 | 8.1 | 8.1 | 8.0 | 8.1 | 8.3 | 8.0 | 8.5 | 8.9 | 8.5 | 8.5 | 8.2 |
| **MEAN NUMBER OF DAYS:** | | | | | | | | | | | | | | |
| Sunrise to Sunset | | | | | | | | | | | | | | |
| -Clear | 39 | 5.7 | 4.3 | 4.2 | 3.4 | 3.6 | 3.4 | 3.0 | 4.0 | 2.8 | 2.1 | 3.4 | 3.5 | 43.3 |
| -Partly Cloudy | 39 | 2.6 | 2.9 | 2.9 | 4.1 | 4.0 | 3.9 | 4.6 | 4.5 | 3.2 | 2.1 | 2.2 | 1.8 | 38.8 |
| -Cloudy | 39 | 22.7 | 21.0 | 24.0 | 22.5 | 23.4 | 22.6 | 23.4 | 22.5 | 23.9 | 26.8 | 24.4 | 25.7 | 283.1 |
| Precipitation | | | | | | | | | | | | | | |
| .01 inches or more | 45 | 18.0 | 16.6 | 17.7 | 16.8 | 17.2 | 15.6 | 16.6 | 17.6 | 19.9 | 23.5 | 19.7 | 20.7 | 220.0 |
| Snow,Ice pellets | | | | | | | | | | | | | | |
| 1.0 inches or more | 45 | 6.9 | 5.1 | 4.3 | 1.0 | 0.0 | 0.0 | 0.0 | 0.0 | 0.0 | 0.3 | 3.4 | 5.9 | 26.8 |
| Thunderstorms | 45 | 0.* | 0.0 | 0.0 | 0.0 | 0.0 | 0.* | 0.1 | 0.* | 0.1 | 0.0 | 0.* | 0.0 | 0.3 |
| Heavy Fog Visibility 1/4 mile or less | 45 | 2.1 | 2.4 | 1.9 | 0.8 | 0.8 | 0.3 | 0.2 | 1.2 | 2.9 | 3.2 | 3.2 | 2.4 | 21.3 |
| Temperature °F | | | | | | | | | | | | | | |
| -Maximum | | | | | | | | | | | | | | |
| 70° and above | 45 | 0.0 | 0.0 | 0.0 | 0.* | 1.2 | 4.9 | 7.1 | 5.6 | 0.2 | 0.0 | 0.0 | 0.0 | 19.1 |
| 32° and below | 45 | 16.4 | 9.5 | 4.1 | 0.3 | 0.0 | 0.0 | 0.0 | 0.0 | 0.0 | 0.2 | 6.6 | 12.4 | 49.4 |
| -Minimum | | | | | | | | | | | | | | |
| 32° and below | 45 | 25.6 | 22.5 | 23.4 | 15.2 | 3.9 | 0.1 | 0.0 | 0.1 | 1.5 | 7.7 | 18.5 | 23.5 | 142.0 |
| 0° and below | 45 | 4.5 | 1.8 | 0.5 | 0.0 | 0.0 | 0.0 | 0.0 | 0.0 | 0.0 | 0.0 | 0.2 | 2.0 | 9.0 |
| **AVG. STATION PRESS.(mb)** | 12 | 1011.0 | 1011.4 | 1009.2 | 1012.2 | 1013.5 | 1014.5 | 1015.8 | 1014.7 | 1012.7 | 1008.0 | 1008.2 | 1008.9 | 1011.7 |
| **RELATIVE HUMIDITY (%)** | | | | | | | | | | | | | | |
| Hour 03 | 23 | 80 | 83 | 83 | 86 | 87 | 86 | 87 | 90 | 92 | 89 | 85 | 85 | 86 |
| Hour 09 | 23 | 79 | 83 | 82 | 81 | 79 | 80 | 83 | 87 | 91 | 89 | 85 | 84 | 84 |
| Hour 15 (Local Time) | 23 | 76 | 74 | 67 | 63 | 63 | 65 | 70 | 74 | 77 | 79 | 80 | 82 | 73 |
| Hour 21 | 23 | 79 | 81 | 78 | 75 | 71 | 71 | 75 | 80 | 86 | 87 | 85 | 84 | 79 |
| **PRECIPITATION (inches):** | | | | | | | | | | | | | | |
| Water Equivalent | | | | | | | | | | | | | | |
| -Normal | | 3.69 | 3.74 | 3.34 | 2.92 | 3.41 | 2.98 | 4.13 | 5.02 | 6.40 | 7.71 | 5.15 | 4.66 | 53.15 |
| -Maximum Monthly | 45 | 8.19 | 8.48 | 6.36 | 5.32 | 6.33 | 6.02 | 7.88 | 12.31 | 11.61 | 15.25 | 11.22 | 9.89 | 15.25 |
| -Year | | 1976 | 1964 | 1966 | 1980 | 1966 | 1987 | 1969 | 1961 | 1981 | 1974 | 1956 | 1956 | OCT 1974 |
| -Minimum Monthly | 45 | 0.94 | 0.07 | 0.59 | 0.27 | 1.25 | 1.08 | 1.15 | 0.56 | 2.34 | 2.71 | 1.15 | 0.49 | 0.07 |
| -Year | | 1969 | 1989 | 1983 | 1948 | 1946 | 1950 | 1972 | 1979 | 1965 | 1950 | 1983 | 1983 | FEB 1989 |
| -Maximum in 24 hrs | 45 | 2.74 | 2.46 | 1.81 | 1.57 | 1.65 | 1.92 | 1.92 | 2.62 | 3.17 | 4.66 | 3.40 | 3.56 | 4.66 |
| -Year | | 1948 | 1988 | 1948 | 1952 | 1981 | 1953 | 1984 | 1974 | 1952 | 1946 | 1988 | 1956 | OCT 1946 |
| Snow,Ice pellets | | | | | | | | | | | | | | |
| -Maximum Monthly | 45 | 69.2 | 86.3 | 52.6 | 46.3 | 1.2 | T | 0.0 | 0.0 | T | 15.6 | 32.5 | 54.7 | 86.3 |
| -Year | | 1982 | 1965 | 1948 | 1963 | 1964 | 1970 | | | 1974 | 1956 | 1989 | 1964 | FEB 1965 |
| -Maximum in 24 hrs | 45 | 20.1 | 23.7 | 31.0 | 24.2 | 0.7 | T | 0.0 | 0.0 | T | 8.8 | 16.5 | 25.6 | 31.0 |
| -Year | | 1975 | 1949 | 1948 | 1963 | 1945 | 1970 | | | 1974 | 1956 | 1963 | 1962 | MAR 1948 |
| **WIND:** | | | | | | | | | | | | | | |
| Mean Speed (mph) | 44 | 8.3 | 8.5 | 8.5 | 8.7 | 8.3 | 7.7 | 7.5 | 7.4 | 7.9 | 9.5 | 8.5 | 9.0 | 8.3 |
| Prevailing Direction through 1963 | | ESE | ESE | ESE | ESE | ESE | N | N | N | N | ESE | ESE | ESE | ESE |
| Fastest Obs. 1 Min. | | | | | | | | | | | | | | |
| -Direction (!!) | 19 | 12 | 13 | 11 | 11 | 12 | 13 | 12 | 12 | 12 | 12 | 11 | 11 | 11 |
| -Speed (MPH) | 19 | 38 | 44 | 40 | 40 | 40 | 32 | 32 | 35 | 48 | 49 | 58 | 55 | 58 |
| -Year | | 1968 | 1970 | 1963 | 1962 | 1965 | 1965 | 1970 | 1969 | 1967 | 1965 | 1968 | 1963 | NOV 1968 |
| Peak Gust | | | | | | | | | | | | | | |
| -Direction (!!) | | | | | | | | | | | | | | |
| -Speed (mph) | | | | | | | | | | | | | | |
| -Date | | | | | | | | | | | | | | |

**See Reference Notes to this table on the following page.**

## PRECIPITATION (inches) — JUNEAU, ALASKA

**TABLE 2**

| YEAR | JAN | FEB | MAR | APR | MAY | JUNE | JULY | AUG | SEP | OCT | NOV | DEC | ANNUAL |
|---|---|---|---|---|---|---|---|---|---|---|---|---|---|
| 1961 | 3.76 | 4.07 | 2.67 | 3.92 | 4.75 | 3.22 | 6.04 | 12.31 | 7.01 | 10.20 | 6.12 | 4.04 | 68.11 |
| 1962 | 6.99 | 0.96 | 5.00 | 1.99 | 2.85 | 4.75 | 4.75 | 5.21 | 9.75 | 7.39 | 4.03 | 8.16 | 61.83 |
| 1963 | 6.55 | 6.03 | 3.69 | 3.85 | 2.02 | 4.53 | 5.22 | 1.20 | 8.05 | 7.78 | 3.91 | 4.56 | 57.39 |
| 1964 | 3.19 | 8.48 | 4.38 | 4.04 | 4.35 | 3.37 | 6.94 | 3.48 | 2.59 | 7.35 | 4.89 | 5.22 | 58.28 |
| 1965 | 7.75 | 5.10 | 1.66 | 3.33 | 4.45 | 3.11 | 2.26 | 4.17 | 2.34 | 7.99 | 1.46 | 4.26 | 47.88 |
| 1966 | 4.34 | 3.13 | 6.36 | 2.08 | 6.33 | 1.74 | 3.91 | 6.37 | 8.20 | 6.97 | 4.39 | 4.48 | 58.30 |
| 1967 | 4.04 | 4.74 | 1.34 | 1.12 | 2.94 | 2.87 | 4.26 | 5.46 | 8.53 | 5.71 | 5.81 | 3.25 | 50.07 |
| 1968 | 3.25 | 5.30 | 3.85 | 3.25 | 1.45 | 1.95 | 4.60 | 2.39 | 10.14 | 4.60 | 5.34 | 1.90 | 48.02 |
| 1969 | 0.94 | 0.68 | 4.17 | 1.74 | 3.38 | 2.41 | 7.88 | 7.54 | 5.44 | 3.77 | 8.69 | 2.58 | 51.00 |
| 1970 | 2.37 | 3.35 | 4.08 | 3.69 | 3.92 | 2.44 | 5.01 | 7.47 | 9.86 | 5.87 | 2.01 | 2.58 | 53.18 |
| 1971 | 5.56 | 3.93 | 3.33 | 2.44 | 4.30 | 1.74 | 1.67 | 6.89 | 5.36 | 5.80 | 4.38 | 3.23 | 48.63 |
| 1972 | 3.73 | 2.71 | 4.19 | 3.62 | 4.03 | 3.98 | 1.15 | 8.62 | 6.24 | 8.49 | 3.35 | 3.56 | 53.67 |
| 1973 | 4.37 | 3.94 | 3.01 | 2.41 | 4.09 | 2.80 | 3.65 | 6.64 | 4.95 | 6.07 | 1.63 | 7.03 | 45.86 |
| 1974 | 2.37 | 6.23 | 1.15 | 2.59 | 1.66 | 4.92 | 3.12 | 5.78 | 5.96 | 15.25 | 7.79 | 5.81 | 63.85 |
| 1975 | 4.10 | 3.76 | 2.17 | 3.04 | 3.59 | 2.48 | 4.96 | 2.78 | 7.25 | 3.55 | 2.83 | 5.81 | 46.32 |
| 1976 | 8.19 | 4.82 | 3.61 | 2.14 | 3.42 | 3.37 | 2.48 | 3.16 | 8.32 | 6.15 | 5.15 | 5.56 | 56.41 |
| 1977 | 4.59 | 4.56 | 3.31 | 4.02 | 1.56 | 3.47 | 3.19 | 3.03 | 5.57 | 7.14 | 4.58 | 2.16 | 47.18 |
| 1978 | 1.71 | 1.50 | 1.84 | 2.19 | 2.86 | 2.74 | 3.98 | 4.39 | 3.07 | 13.00 | 3.90 | 4.46 | 46.08 |
| 1979 | 2.19 | 0.91 | 3.98 | 0.98 | 2.45 | 3.12 | 5.44 | 0.56 | 4.89 | 9.06 | 8.36 | 7.73 | 49.29 |
| 1980 | 3.44 | 2.83 | 2.75 | 5.32 | 2.53 | 4.37 | 6.49 | 5.61 | 7.91 | 11.26 | 7.10 | 2.27 | 61.88 |
| 1981 | 4.66 | 2.57 | 1.88 | 2.11 | 3.27 | 2.44 | 4.25 | 6.19 | 11.61 | 6.18 | 6.93 | 2.24 | 54.33 |
| 1982 | 3.74 | 1.42 | 2.52 | 2.44 | 5.10 | 1.86 | 1.73 | 5.97 | 5.10 | 7.97 | 2.10 | 1.17 | 41.12 |
| 1983 | 4.00 | 1.69 | 0.59 | 2.53 | 5.37 | 2.69 | 3.16 | 9.52 | 6.13 | 4.24 | 1.15 | 0.49 | 41.56 |
| 1984 | 6.06 | 5.40 | 3.75 | 2.11 | 1.84 | 4.17 | 6.92 | 6.26 | 3.39 | 6.69 |  |  | 46.59 |
| 1985 |  |  |  |  |  |  |  |  |  |  |  | 8.33 | 8.33 |
| 1986 | 7.00 | 3.25 | 6.08 | 2.98 | 2.54 | 2.76 | 2.38 | 6.89 | 2.40 | 12.33 | 5.96 | 6.42 | 60.99 |
| 1987 | 3.99 | 3.13 | 2.12 | 2.08 | 2.60 | 6.02 | 2.54 | 4.54 | 8.92 | 10.36 | 7.17 | 5.32 | 58.79 |
| 1988 | 2.58 | 6.55 | 4.15 | 2.25 | 3.91 | 2.05 | 5.21 | 5.53 | 5.46 | 9.71 | 8.62 | 4.75 | 60.77 |
| 1989 | 6.77 | 0.07 | 1.33 | 0.87 | 3.44 | 1.10 | 3.81 | 2.82 | 7.29 | 6.37 | 6.23 | 6.78 | 46.88 |
| 1990 | 3.72 | 4.54 | 4.86 | 1.06 | 1.72 | 3.32 | 4.65 | 5.35 | 10.63 | 6.59 | 4.89 | 6.03 | 57.36 |
| Record Mean | 4.03 | 3.42 | 3.36 | 2.75 | 3.33 | 3.01 | 4.25 | 5.18 | 6.66 | 7.89 | 5.36 | 4.43 | 53.68 |

## AVERAGE TEMPERATURE (deg. F) — JUNEAU, ALASKA

**TABLE 3**

| YEAR | JAN | FEB | MAR | APR | MAY | JUNE | JULY | AUG | SEP | OCT | NOV | DEC | ANNUAL |
|---|---|---|---|---|---|---|---|---|---|---|---|---|---|
| 1961 | 30.5 | 31.5 | 34.5 | 39.9 | 47.4 | 52.4 | 56.3 | 53.9 | 47.7 | 40.3 | 30.6 | 24.6 | 40.8 |
| 1962 | 26.7 | 25.7 | 29.4 | 39.6 | 44.5 | 49.9 | 56.7 | 54.8 | 52.2 | 44.6 | 28.3 | 32.7 | 40.5 |
| 1963 | 27.7 | 33.1 | 31.9 | 36.6 | 48.7 | 50.4 | 55.4 | 56.9 | 52.2 | 45.0 | 32.1 | 16.6 | 41.5 |
| 1964 | 29.3 | 35.9 | 28.8 | 38.6 | 45.1 | 53.6 | 54.3 | 53.6 | 49.7 | 45.0 | 29.9 | 26.6 | 40.2 |
| 1965 | 23.1 | 23.6 | 35.0 | 37.7 | 42.4 | 48.5 | 55.4 | 55.1 | 50.3 | 43.7 | 29.9 | 26.6 | 39.3 |
| 1966 | 8.6 | 25.9 | 30.2 | 38.1 | 43.3 | 52.9 | 56.2 | 52.4 | 49.2 | 38.6 | 25.1 | 26.5 | 37.2 |
| 1967 | 23.1 | 30.4 | 24.1 | 37.3 | 45.6 | 54.8 | 53.8 | 55.1 | 50.0 | 43.1 | 32.3 | 27.3 | 39.7 |
| 1968 | 18.7 | 28.8 | 33.1 | 37.9 | 48.4 | 52.2 | 56.8 | 55.7 | 47.6 | 39.0 | 34.1 | 19.4 | 39.3 |
| 1969 | 6.8 | 21.2 | 30.7 | 40.6 | 49.9 | 57.8 | 52.3 | 53.7 | 50.3 | 47.4 | 41.4 | 35.1 | 38.9 |
| 1970 | 22.0 | 35.1 | 36.5 | 39.1 | 45.3 | 50.7 | 52.3 | 51.7 | 46.3 | 39.6 | 27.8 | 21.6 | 39.0 |
| 1971 | 13.0 | 28.1 | 28.9 | 38.6 | 43.5 | 53.2 | 57.5 | 55.4 | 48.1 | 38.5 | 20.9 | 23.6 | 37.4 |
| 1972 | 15.8 | 19.5 | 26.5 | 34.6 | 44.8 | 50.4 | 53.7 | 51.8 | 48.0 | 41.2 | 23.0 | 28.0 | 38.2 |
| 1973 | 18.9 | 24.6 | 32.9 | 39.6 | 45.9 | 51.3 | 53.7 | 54.7 | 50.1 | 42.5 | 36.4 | 33.8 | 39.6 |
| 1974 | 14.8 | 28.8 | 24.7 | 39.3 | 46.8 | 50.2 | 53.5 | 53.9 | 51.4 | 41.8 | 28.5 | 24.7 | 39.3 |
| 1975 | 23.1 | 24.5 | 30.6 | 38.3 | 47.4 | 51.4 | 57.5 | 53.9 | 51.4 | 41.8 | 28.5 | 24.7 | 42.1 |
| 1976 | 28.3 | 25.8 | 32.4 | 41.1 | 45.5 | 52.0 | 55.7 | 55.9 | 50.6 | 42.8 | 40.9 | 34.4 | 42.1 |
| 1977 | 35.0 | 40.1 | 36.0 | 42.3 | 47.7 | 54.1 | 57.0 | 58.5 | 50.5 | 42.4 | 29.4 | 18.9 | 42.7 |
| 1978 | 25.1 | 31.8 | 33.9 | 42.0 | 47.8 | 54.2 | 55.2 | 56.3 | 50.6 | 45.1 | 30.3 | 28.3 | 41.7 |
| 1979 | 20.6 | 11.0 | 35.6 | 41.1 | 47.7 | 52.2 | 56.7 | 58.2 | 51.0 | 45.2 | 37.2 | 26.5 | 40.2 |
| 1980 | 19.5 | 33.8 | 34.1 | 42.2 | 49.4 | 55.6 | 55.6 | 54.7 | 49.0 | 44.6 | 38.7 | 21.7 | 41.6 |
| 1981 | 37.6 | 32.7 | 39.4 | 39.1 | 52.1 | 54.3 | 56.1 | 55.9 | 49.2 | 42.8 | 36.8 | 26.9 | 43.6 |
| 1982 | 13.8 | 21.3 | 31.8 | 37.1 | 45.4 | 56.3 | 57.7 | 54.8 | 50.3 | 42.2 | 30.6 | 31.6 | 39.4 |
| 1983 | 30.2 | 31.8 | 34.8 | 42.6 | 49.7 | 55.6 | 57.1 | 54.6 | 48.0 | 42.1 | 31.8 | 18.9 | 41.4 |
| 1984 | 32.0 |  | 39.6 | 43.1 | 49.1 | 53.5 | 55.5 | 55.5 | 50.0 | 40.5 |  |  | 45.5 |
| 1985 |  |  |  |  |  |  |  |  |  |  |  | 32.5 | 32.5 |
| 1986 | 34.3 | 28.7 | 35.3 | 37.3 | 46.6 | 54.3 | 56.8 | 54.4 | 50.7 | 45.8 | 30.5 | 36.0 | 42.6 |
| 1987 | 33.1 | 34.7 | 31.8 | 41.6 | 47.8 | 51.6 | 58.6 | 57.5 | 50.1 | 44.4 | 40.0 | 34.3 | 43.8 |
| 1988 | 27.0 | 32.6 | 37.6 | 41.7 | 48.5 | 54.0 | 53.8 | 53.9 | 48.2 | 44.1 | 36.2 | 31.3 | 42.4 |
| 1989 | 25.5 | 23.9 | 29.4 | 42.7 | 49.0 | 55.4 | 60.1 | 58.2 | 52.4 | 41.7 | 32.9 | 36.0 | 42.3 |
| 1990 | 26.4 | 25.1 | 36.4 | 42.7 | 49.7 | 55.0 | 59.3 | 58.1 | 51.2 | 40.7 | 26.4 | 23.7 | 41.2 |
| Record Mean | 23.9 | 27.7 | 32.3 | 39.3 | 47.0 | 53.2 | 55.9 | 54.8 | 49.4 | 42.0 | 32.5 | 27.5 | 40.4 |
| Max | 29.2 | 33.4 | 38.4 | 46.7 | 55.1 | 61.5 | 63.9 | 62.6 | 56.0 | 47.0 | 37.2 | 32.0 | 46.9 |
| Min | 18.5 | 21.9 | 26.2 | 31.8 | 38.8 | 44.8 | 47.8 | 46.9 | 42.7 | 36.9 | 27.9 | 22.9 | 33.9 |

## REFERENCE NOTES FOR ALL TABLES FOR THIS STATION  (JUNEAU, AK)

### GENERAL

T - TRACE AMOUNT
BLANK ENTRIES DENOTE MISSING/UNREPORTED DATA.
# INDICATES A STATION OR INSTRUMENT RELOCATION.

### SPECIFIC

#### TABLE 1

(a) - LENGTH OF RECORD IN YEARS. ALTHOUGH INDIVIDUAL MONTHS MAY BE MISSING.

* LESS THAN .05

NORMALS — BASED ON THE 1951-1980 RECORD PERIOD.
EXTREMES — DATES ARE THE MOST RECENT OCCURRENCE.
WIND DIR. — NUMERALS SHOW TENS OF DEGREES CLOCKWISE FROM TRUE NORTH. "00" INDICATES CALM.
RESULTANT WIND DIRECTIONS ARE GIVEN TO WHOLE DEGREES.

#### TABLE 3

MAX AND MIN ARE LONG-TERM MEAN DAILY MAXIMUM AND MEAN DAILY MINIMUM TEMPERATURES.

### EXCEPTIONS

#### TABLE 1

1. PERCENT OF POSSIBLE SUNSHINE, MEAN SKY COVER, AND DAYS CLEAR-PARTLY CLOUDY-CLOUDY ARE THROUGH 1978
2. FASTEST OBSERVED WIND IS THROUGH 1979.

#### TABLES 2, 3, and 6

RECORD MEANS ARE FOR THE ENTIRE PERIOD OF RECORD, REGARDLESS OF LOCATION.

**RECORD MEANS ARE THROUGH THE CURRENT YEAR, BEGINNING IN 1944 FOR TEMPERATURE, 1944 FOR PRECIPITATION 1944 FOR SNOWFALL**

**ALL JUNEAU TABLES:**

**STATION WAS TERMINATED FOR 13 MONTHS, BEGINNING 11/1/84; ENDING 12/1/85**

## TABLE 4 — HEATING DEGREE DAYS Base 65 deg. F — JUNEAU, ALASKA

| SEASON | JULY | AUG | SEP | OCT | NOV | DEC | JAN | FEB | MAR | APR | MAY | JUNE | TOTAL |
|---|---|---|---|---|---|---|---|---|---|---|---|---|---|
| 1961-62 | 262 | 339 | 511 | 760 | 1027 | 1246 | 1182 | 1097 | 1095 | 756 | 627 | 447 | 9349 |
| 1962-63 | 250 | 305 | 486 | 645 | 810 | 1132 | 1147 | 885 | 1023 | 846 | 500 | 431 | 8460 |
| 1963-64 | 288 | 244 | 375 | 625 | 1093 | 993 | 1098 | 1118 | 785 | 610 | 336 | | 8400 |
| 1964-65 | 324 | 347 | 453 | 614 | 980 | 1496 | 1291 | 1154 | 923 | 813 | 693 | 487 | 9575 |
| 1965-66 | 292 | 297 | 435 | 654 | 1045 | 1182 | 1746 | 1090 | 1071 | 805 | 667 | 355 | 9639 |
| 1966-67 | 265 | 382 | 466 | 812 | 1191 | 1188 | 1291 | 963 | 1261 | 824 | 592 | 300 | 9535 |
| 1967-68 | 340 | 303 | 444 | 671 | 973 | 1162 | 1432 | 1043 | 984 | 808 | 508 | 374 | 9042 |
| 1968-69 | 248 | 281 | 516 | 802 | 920 | 1405 | 1801 | 1219 | 1054 | 727 | 464 | 218 | 9655 |
| 1969-70 | 343 | 448 | 521 | 724 | 975 | 921 | 1329 | 830 | 876 | 770 | 601 | 422 | 8760 |
| 1970-71 | 387 | 405 | 553 | 783 | 1110 | 1343 | 1607 | 1112 | 1112 | 784 | 658 | 346 | 10117 |
| 1971-72 | 227 | 290 | 504 | 811 | 1001 | 1360 | 1519 | 1315 | 1186 | 906 | 618 | 432 | 10169 |
| 1972-73 | 207 | 293 | 535 | 810 | 907 | 1275 | 1423 | 1126 | 986 | 752 | 584 | 404 | 9302 |
| 1973-74 | 343 | 404 | 505 | 732 | 1253 | 1143 | 1550 | 1006 | 1242 | 765 | 556 | 437 | 9936 |
| 1974-75 | 349 | 315 | 437 | 690 | 851 | 957 | 1296 | 1129 | 1063 | 791 | 541 | 402 | 8821 |
| 1975-76 | 281 | 337 | 402 | 712 | 1088 | 1244 | 1132 | 1131 | 1006 | 706 | 597 | 384 | 9020 |
| 1976-77 | 280 | 275 | 427 | 679 | 717 | 938 | 918 | 690 | 893 | 673 | 531 | 320 | 7341 |
| 1977-78 | 243 | 196 | 428 | 695 | 1062 | 1423 | 1233 | 922 | 954 | 683 | 525 | 317 | 8681 |
| 1978-79 | 298 | 262 | 427 | 612 | 1037 | 1134 | 1370 | 1505 | 904 | 712 | 528 | 378 | 9167 |
| 1979-80 | 251 | 205 | 415 | 609 | 830 | 1187 | 1404 | 895 | 949 | 678 | 477 | 278 | 8178 |
| 1980-81 | 283 | 308 | 472 | 628 | 783 | 1333 | 843 | 899 | 786 | 772 | 392 | 316 | 7815 |
| 1981-82 | 269 | 275 | 469 | 682 | 841 | 1175 | 1579 | 1214 | 1021 | 830 | 601 | 257 | 9213 |
| 1982-83 | 220 | 310 | 435 | 699 | 1027 | 1029 | 1073 | 924 | 931 | 663 | 470 | 275 | 8056 |
| 1983-84 | 237 | 317 | 502 | 701 | 991 | 1423 | 1014 | | 780 | 649 | 486 | 338 | |
| 1984-85 | 286 | 291 | 444 | 754 | | | | | | | | | |
| 1985-86 | | | | | | 1001 | 943 | 1011 | 913 | 822 | 564 | 316 | |
| 1986-87 | 249 | 319 | 423 | 587 | 1028 | 891 | 982 | 841 | 1020 | 697 | 526 | 394 | 7957 |
| 1987-88 | 199 | 222 | 440 | 635 | 744 | 944 | 1169 | 935 | 844 | 691 | 508 | 324 | 7655 |
| 1988-89 | 338 | 338 | 497 | 641 | 855 | 1040 | 1217 | 1144 | 1097 | 663 | 491 | 283 | 8604 |
| 1989-90 | 159 | 210 | 370 | 713 | 959 | 890 | 1191 | 1109 | 879 | 661 | 467 | 295 | 7903 |
| 1990-91 | 180 | 210 | 407 | 748 | 1152 | 1274 | | | | | | | |

## TABLE 5 — COOLING DEGREE DAYS Base 65 deg. F — JUNEAU, ALASKA

| YEAR | JAN | FEB | MAR | APR | MAY | JUNE | JULY | AUG | SEP | OCT | NOV | DEC | TOTAL |
|---|---|---|---|---|---|---|---|---|---|---|---|---|---|
| 1969 | 0 | 0 | 0 | 0 | 0 | 7 | 0 | 0 | 0 | 0 | 0 | 0 | 7 |
| 1970 | 0 | 0 | 0 | 0 | 0 | 0 | 0 | 0 | 0 | 0 | 0 | 0 | 0 |
| 1971 | 0 | 0 | 0 | 0 | 0 | 0 | 0 | 0 | 0 | 0 | 0 | 0 | 0 |
| 1972 | 0 | 0 | 0 | 0 | 0 | 0 | 0 | 0 | 0 | 0 | 0 | 0 | 0 |
| 1973 | 0 | 0 | 0 | 0 | 0 | 0 | 0 | 0 | 0 | 0 | 0 | 0 | 0 |
| 1974 | 0 | 0 | 0 | 0 | 0 | 0 | 0 | 0 | 0 | 0 | 0 | 0 | 0 |
| 1975 | 0 | 0 | 0 | 0 | 0 | 0 | 7 | 0 | 0 | 0 | 0 | 0 | 7 |
| 1976 | 0 | 0 | 0 | 0 | 0 | 0 | 3 | 3 | 0 | 0 | 0 | 0 | 6 |
| 1977 | 0 | 0 | 0 | 0 | 0 | 0 | 0 | 1 | 0 | 0 | 0 | 0 | 1 |
| 1978 | 0 | 0 | 0 | 0 | 0 | 0 | 0 | 0 | 0 | 0 | 0 | 0 | 0 |
| 1979 | 0 | 0 | 0 | 0 | 0 | 0 | 0 | 0 | 1 | 0 | 0 | 0 | 1 |
| 1980 | 0 | 0 | 0 | 0 | 0 | 1 | 0 | 0 | 0 | 0 | 0 | 0 | 1 |
| 1981 | 0 | 0 | 0 | 0 | 0 | 0 | 0 | 0 | 0 | 0 | 0 | 0 | 0 |
| 1982 | 0 | 0 | 0 | 0 | 0 | 2 | 0 | 0 | 0 | 0 | 0 | 0 | 2 |
| 1983 | 0 | 0 | 0 | 0 | 0 | 0 | 0 | 0 | 0 | 0 | 0 | 0 | 0 |
| 1984 | 0 | | 0 | 0 | 0 | 0 | 0 | 0 | 0 | 0 | 0 | 0 | 0 |
| 1985 | | | | | | | | | | | 0 | | 0 |
| 1986 | 0 | 0 | 0 | 0 | 0 | 2 | 0 | 0 | 0 | 0 | 0 | 0 | 2 |
| 1987 | 0 | 0 | 0 | 0 | 0 | 0 | 5 | 0 | 0 | 0 | 0 | 0 | 5 |
| 1988 | 0 | 0 | 0 | 0 | 0 | 0 | 0 | 0 | 0 | 0 | 0 | 0 | 0 |
| 1989 | 0 | 0 | 0 | 0 | 0 | 0 | 14 | 0 | 0 | 0 | 0 | 0 | 14 |
| 1990 | 0 | 0 | 0 | 0 | 0 | 1 | 8 | 3 | 0 | 0 | 0 | 0 | 12 |

## TABLE 6 — SNOWFALL (inches) — JUNEAU, ALASKA

| SEASON | JULY | AUG | SEP | OCT | NOV | DEC | JAN | FEB | MAR | APR | MAY | JUNE | TOTAL |
|---|---|---|---|---|---|---|---|---|---|---|---|---|---|
| 1961-62 | 0.0 | 0.0 | 0.0 | 0.0 | 6.0 | 26.4 | 31.5 | 7.7 | 37.4 | 1.8 | T | 0.0 | 111.4 |
| 1962-63 | 0.0 | 0.0 | 0.0 | 0.0 | 6.5 | 41.3 | 12.2 | 15.7 | 28.9 | 46.3 | 0.0 | 0.0 | 150.9 |
| 1963-64 | 0.0 | 0.0 | 0.0 | T | 20.1 | 7.2 | 13.4 | 19.4 | 38.9 | 4.4 | 1.2 | 0.0 | 104.6 |
| 1964-65 | 0.0 | 0.0 | 0.0 | T | 3.1 | 54.7 | 45.2 | 86.3 | 4.0 | 0.8 | 0.2 | 0.0 | 194.3 |
| 1965-66 | 0.0 | 0.0 | 0.0 | 0.3 | 9.6 | 16.9 | 54.8 | 17.6 | 49.0 | 1.5 | T | 0.0 | 149.7 |
| 1966-67 | 0.0 | 0.0 | 0.0 | 4.3 | 20.0 | 19.6 | 38.2 | 32.0 | 6.6 | 3.0 | 0.0 | 0.0 | 123.7 |
| 1967-68 | 0.0 | 0.0 | 0.0 | 0.0 | 9.5 | 21.1 | 31.1 | 17.0 | 8.2 | 6.1 | T | 0.0 | 93.0 |
| 1968-69 | 0.0 | 0.0 | 0.0 | T | 8.7 | 35.6 | 28.2 | 17.1 | 27.9 | T | 0.0 | 0.0 | 117.5 |
| 1969-70 | 0.0 | 0.0 | 0.0 | 0.0 | 18.2 | 0.7 | 15.8 | 2.0 | 1.1 | 3.5 | 0.0 | T | 41.3 |
| 1970-71 | 0.0 | 0.0 | T | 0.4 | 24.3 | 26.2 | 51.0 | 21.5 | 50.6 | 1.1 | T | 0.0 | 175.1 |
| 1971-72 | 0.0 | 0.0 | 0.0 | 6.9 | 20.5 | 37.1 | 45.1 | 31.1 | 27.1 | 10.3 | 0.0 | 0.0 | 178.1 |
| 1972-73 | 0.0 | 0.0 | 0.0 | 2.2 | 2.8 | 31.6 | 63.8 | 20.9 | 9.6 | 0.5 | 0.0 | 0.0 | 131.4 |
| 1973-74 | 0.0 | 0.0 | 0.0 | T | 18.6 | 15.7 | 36.0 | 32.8 | 15.3 | 0.5 | 0.0 | 0.0 | 118.9 |
| 1974-75 | 0.0 | 0.0 | T | 0.9 | 3.5 | 17.3 | 41.5 | 16.5 | 18.9 | 4.5 | 0.0 | 0.0 | 103.1 |
| 1975-76 | 0.0 | 0.0 | 0.0 | 5.3 | 32.5 | 51.0 | 32.9 | 34.1 | 25.5 | 2.3 | 0.0 | 0.0 | 183.6 |
| 1976-77 | 0.0 | 0.0 | 0.0 | 1.2 | 1.1 | 26.3 | 5.0 | T | 12.7 | T | 0.0 | 0.0 | 46.3 |
| 1977-78 | 0.0 | 0.0 | 0.0 | T | 27.4 | 16.6 | 5.2 | 1.1 | 1.7 | 0.4 | 0.0 | 0.0 | 52.4 |
| 1978-79 | 0.0 | 0.0 | 0.0 | 0.0 | 14.9 | 21.6 | 24.2 | 21.4 | 5.4 | T | 0.0 | 0.0 | 87.5 |
| 1979-80 | 0.0 | 0.0 | 0.0 | 0.0 | 1.6 | 48.4 | 41.6 | 4.1 | 2.4 | T | 0.0 | 0.0 | 98.1 |
| 1980-81 | 0.0 | 0.0 | 0.0 | 0.0 | 0.5 | 40.5 | 2.4 | 16.4 | 0.5 | 2.2 | 0.0 | 0.0 | 62.5 |
| 1981-82 | 0.0 | 0.0 | 0.0 | 0.0 | 4.0 | 6.0 | 69.2 | 29.6 | 8.4 | 1.1 | T | 0.0 | 118.3 |
| 1982-83 | 0.0 | 0.0 | 0.0 | 2.0 | 0.4 | 10.8 | 40.1 | 15.7 | 0.2 | T | 0.0 | 0.0 | 69.2 |
| 1983-84 | 0.0 | 0.0 | 0.0 | 0.0 | 8.1 | 13.3 | 43.1 | 0.7 | 1.0 | T | T | 0.0 | 66.2 |
| 1984-85 | 0.0 | 0.0 | 0.0 | 0.0 | | | | | | | | | |
| 1985-86 | | | | | | 2.0 | 10.3 | 7.4 | 30.4 | 4.4 | T | 0.0 | |
| 1986-87 | 0.0 | 0.0 | 0.0 | T | 22.1 | 1.4 | 3.3 | 1.4 | 7.3 | T | 0.0 | 0.0 | 35.5 |
| 1987-88 | 0.0 | 0.0 | 0.0 | T | 4.6 | 6.8 | 3.5 | 8.0 | 1.0 | 0.5 | 0.0 | 0.0 | 24.4 |
| 1988-89 | 0.0 | 0.0 | 0.0 | 0.0 | 4.8 | 11.3 | 44.7 | 0.2 | 10.0 | T | 0.0 | 0.0 | 71.0 |
| 1989-90 | 0.0 | 0.0 | 0.0 | 0.6 | 32.5 | 6.4 | 36.5 | 39.4 | 0.6 | 0.0 | 0.0 | 0.0 | 116.0 |
| 1990-91 | 0.0 | 0.0 | 0.0 | 0.0 | 48.8 | 33.2 | | | | | | | |
| Record Mean | 0.0 | 0.0 | T | 1.0 | 12.3 | 22.2 | 25.9 | 18.8 | 15.5 | 3.7 | T | T | 99.6 |

**See Reference Notes, relative to all above tables, on preceding page.**

# FLAGSTAFF, ARIZONA

Flagstaff, elevation 7,000 feet, is situated on a volcanic plateau at the base of the highest mountains in Arizona. The climate may be classified as vigorous with cold winters, mild, pleasantly cool summers, moderate humidity, and considerable diurnal temperature change. Only limited farming exists due to the short growing season. The stormy months are January, February, March, July, and August.

Based on the 1951–1980 period, the average first occurrence of 32 degrees Fahrenheit in the fall is September 21 and the average last occurrence in the spring is June 13.

Temperatures in Flagstaff are characteristic of high altitude climates. The average daily range of temperature is relatively high, especially in the winter months, October to March, as a result of extensive snow cover and clear skies. Winter minimum temperatures frequently reach zero or below and temperatures of −25 degrees or less have occurred. Summer maximum temperatures are often above 80 degrees and occasionally, temperatures have exceeded 95 degrees.

The Flagstaff area is semi-arid. Several months have recorded little or no precipitation. Over 90 consecutive days without measurable precipitation have occurred. Annual precipitation ranges from less than 10 inches to more than 35 inches. Winter snowfalls can be heavy, exceeding 100 inches during one month and over 200 inches during the winter season. However, accumulations are quite variable from year to year. Some winter months may experience little or no snow and the winter season has produced total snow accumulations of less than 12 inches.

## TABLE 1 — NORMALS, MEANS AND EXTREMES

FLAGSTAFF, ARIZONA

LATITUDE: 35°08'N LONGITUDE: 111°40'W ELEVATION: FT. GRND 7006 BARO 6997 TIME ZONE: MOUNTAIN WBAN: 03103

| | (a) | JAN | FEB | MAR | APR | MAY | JUNE | JULY | AUG | SEP | OCT | NOV | DEC | YEAR |
|---|---|---|---|---|---|---|---|---|---|---|---|---|---|---|
| **TEMPERATURE °F:** | | | | | | | | | | | | | | |
| Normals | | | | | | | | | | | | | | |
| -Daily Maximum | | 41.7 | 44.5 | 48.6 | 57.1 | 66.7 | 77.6 | 81.9 | 78.9 | 74.1 | 63.7 | 51.0 | 43.6 | 60.8 |
| -Daily Minimum | | 14.7 | 16.9 | 20.4 | 25.9 | 32.9 | 40.9 | 50.3 | 48.7 | 40.9 | 30.6 | 21.5 | 15.9 | 30.0 |
| -Monthly | | 28.2 | 30.7 | 34.5 | 41.6 | 49.9 | 59.2 | 66.1 | 63.8 | 57.5 | 47.2 | 36.3 | 29.8 | 45.4 |
| Extremes | | | | | | | | | | | | | | |
| -Record Highest | 40 | 66 | 71 | 73 | 80 | 87 | 96 | 97 | 92 | 90 | 85 | 74 | 68 | 97 |
| -Year | | 1971 | 1986 | 1988 | 1989 | 1974 | 1970 | 1973 | 1978 | 1950 | 1980 | 1977 | 1950 | JUL 1973 |
| -Record Lowest | 40 | -22 | -23 | -16 | -2 | 14 | 22 | 32 | 24 | 23 | -2 | -13 | -23 | -23 |
| -Year | | 1971 | 1985 | 1966 | 1975 | 1975 | 1955 | 1955 | 1968 | 1971 | 1971 | 1958 | 1978 | FEB 1985 |
| **NORMAL DEGREE DAYS:** | | | | | | | | | | | | | | |
| Heating (base 65°F) | | 1141 | 960 | 946 | 702 | 468 | 194 | 34 | 76 | 229 | 552 | 861 | 1091 | 7254 |
| Cooling (base 65°F) | | 0 | 0 | 0 | 0 | 0 | 20 | 68 | 39 | 0 | 0 | 0 | 0 | 127 |
| **% OF POSSIBLE SUNSHINE** | 10 | 77 | 73 | 76 | 82 | 89 | 85 | 74 | 76 | 82 | 78 | 75 | 73 | 78 |
| **MEAN SKY COVER (tenths)** | | | | | | | | | | | | | | |
| Sunrise - Sunset | 38 | 5.3 | 5.2 | 5.2 | 4.6 | 4.0 | 3.0 | 5.4 | 5.0 | 3.6 | 3.7 | 4.2 | 4.7 | 4.5 |
| **MEAN NUMBER OF DAYS:** | | | | | | | | | | | | | | |
| Sunrise to Sunset | | | | | | | | | | | | | | |
| -Clear | 38 | 12.3 | 11.2 | 11.8 | 12.8 | 15.5 | 18.5 | 8.9 | 10.1 | 15.9 | 16.9 | 15.4 | 13.9 | 163.3 |
| -Partly Cloudy | 38 | 6.3 | 6.1 | 8.1 | 8.6 | 9.2 | 7.8 | 13.0 | 12.9 | 9.6 | 7.2 | 6.4 | 6.6 | 101.6 |
| -Cloudy | 38 | 12.4 | 11.0 | 11.2 | 8.6 | 6.4 | 3.7 | 9.1 | 8.0 | 4.6 | 6.9 | 8.1 | 10.5 | 100.4 |
| Precipitation | | | | | | | | | | | | | | |
| .01 inches or more | 40 | 7.4 | 6.7 | 8.3 | 5.7 | 4.3 | 2.8 | 11.6 | 11.4 | 6.3 | 4.8 | 5.3 | 6.2 | 80.7 |
| Snow, Ice pellets | | | | | | | | | | | | | | |
| 1.0 inches or more | 39 | 4.2 | 3.8 | 4.9 | 2.4 | 0.6 | 0.0 | 0.0 | 0.0 | 0.* | 0.5 | 1.9 | 3.4 | 21.8 |
| Thunderstorms | 30 | 0.* | 0.3 | 0.6 | 1.3 | 2.6 | 3.7 | 16.6 | 15.7 | 6.7 | 2.2 | 0.7 | 0.2 | 50.5 |
| Heavy Fog Visibility | | | | | | | | | | | | | | |
| 1/4 mile or less | 30 | 1.8 | 1.8 | 1.6 | 1.2 | 0.2 | 0.* | 0.1 | 0.3 | 0.5 | 0.9 | 1.1 | 1.8 | 11.4 |
| Temperature °F | | | | | | | | | | | | | | |
| -Maximum | | | | | | | | | | | | | | |
| 90° and above | 40 | 0.0 | 0.0 | 0.0 | 0.0 | 0.0 | 1.1 | 1.5 | 0.3 | 0.* | 0.0 | 0.0 | 0.0 | 3.0 |
| 32° and below | 40 | 4.6 | 2.6 | 1.7 | 0.2 | 0.0 | 0.0 | 0.0 | 0.0 | 0.0 | 0.1 | 1.1 | 4.5 | 14.9 |
| -Minimum | | | | | | | | | | | | | | |
| 32° and below | 40 | 30.4 | 27.6 | 30.0 | 25.2 | 14.0 | 3.0 | 0.1 | 0.1 | 2.9 | 18.4 | 27.9 | 30.3 | 209.7 |
| 0° and below | 40 | 3.4 | 1.5 | 0.7 | 0.1 | 0.0 | 0.0 | 0.0 | 0.0 | 0.0 | 0.* | 0.5 | 2.1 | 8.2 |
| **AVG. STATION PRESS.(mb)** | 5 | 786.7 | 786.9 | 783.0 | 784.8 | 786.4 | 789.2 | 791.7 | 791.6 | 790.6 | 789.7 | 788.2 | 787.6 | 788.0 |
| **RELATIVE HUMIDITY (%)** | | | | | | | | | | | | | | |
| Hour 05 | 32 | 73 | 73 | 71 | 66 | 63 | 55 | 69 | 76 | 73 | 71 | 70 | 71 | 69 |
| Hour 11 (Local Time) | 34 | 53 | 50 | 44 | 35 | 29 | 23 | 34 | 40 | 37 | 38 | 44 | 50 | 40 |
| Hour 17 | 26 | 50 | 45 | 40 | 31 | 26 | 21 | 39 | 43 | 36 | 36 | 43 | 51 | 38 |
| Hour 23 | 21 | 67 | 64 | 61 | 53 | 47 | 41 | 60 | 68 | 64 | 63 | 64 | 71 | 60 |
| **PRECIPITATION (inches):** | | | | | | | | | | | | | | |
| Water Equivalent | | | | | | | | | | | | | | |
| -Normal | | 2.10 | 1.95 | 2.13 | 1.35 | 0.75 | 0.57 | 2.47 | 2.62 | 1.47 | 1.54 | 1.65 | 2.26 | 20.86 |
| -Maximum Monthly | 40 | 6.52 | 7.81 | 6.75 | 5.62 | 2.16 | 2.92 | 6.62 | 8.06 | 6.75 | 9.86 | 6.64 | 7.30 | 9.86 |
| -Year | | 1980 | 1980 | 1970 | 1965 | 1979 | 1955 | 1986 | 1986 | 1983 | 1972 | 1985 | 1967 | OCT 1972 |
| -Minimum Monthly | 40 | 0.00 | T | T | 0.01 | T | 0.00 | 0.32 | 0.26 | T | T | T | T | 0.00 |
| -Year | | 1972 | 1967 | 1972 | 1989 | 1974 | 1971 | 1963 | 1962 | 1973 | 1952 | 1989 | 1958 | JAN 1972 |
| -Maximum in 24 hrs | 40 | 2.10 | 2.53 | 2.96 | 1.79 | 1.11 | 2.79 | 2.55 | 3.04 | 3.43 | 2.73 | 3.69 | 3.11 | 3.69 |
| -Year | | 1979 | 1980 | 1970 | 1985 | 1965 | 1956 | 1964 | 1986 | 1965 | 1972 | 1978 | 1951 | NOV 1978 |
| Snow, Ice pellets | | | | | | | | | | | | | | |
| -Maximum Monthly | 39 | 63.4 | 42.1 | 77.4 | 58.3 | 8.2 | T | 0.0 | T | 2.0 | 24.7 | 40.7 | 86.0 | 86.0 |
| -Year | | 1980 | 1969 | 1973 | 1965 | 1975 | 1955 | | 1989 | 1965 | 1971 | 1985 | 1967 | DEC 1967 |
| -Maximum in 24 hrs | 39 | 23.1 | 23.1 | 26.3 | 17.2 | 6.6 | T | 0.0 | T | 2.0 | 13.5 | 18.4 | 27.3 | 27.3 |
| -Year | | 1980 | 1987 | 1970 | 1977 | 1965 | 1955 | | 1989 | 1965 | 1974 | 1985 | 1967 | DEC 1967 |
| **WIND:** | | | | | | | | | | | | | | |
| Mean Speed (mph) | 22 | 7.1 | 7.0 | 7.6 | 8.0 | 7.6 | 7.2 | 5.7 | 5.4 | 6.1 | 6.2 | 7.2 | 7.1 | 6.8 |
| Prevailing Direction | | | | | | | | | | | | | | |
| through 1963 | | NE | S | SSW | SSW | SSW | SSW | SSW | S | S | N | NNE | NE | SSW |
| Fastest Mile | | | | | | | | | | | | | | |
| -Direction (!!!) | 11 | SW | SW | SW | SW | SW | SW | NW | SW | W | NW | SW | NE | SW |
| -Speed (MPH) | 11 | 38 | 34 | 37 | 40 | 46 | 35 | 39 | 30 | 33 | 34 | 39 | 38 | 46 |
| -Year | | 1975 | 1980 | 1974 | 1974 | 1975 | 1984 | 1976 | 1978 | 1974 | 1978 | 1978 | 1982 | MAY 1975 |
| Peak Gust | | | | | | | | | | | | | | |
| -Direction (!!!) | | | | | | | | | | | | | | |
| -Speed (mph) | | | | | | | | | | | | | | |
| -Date | | | | | | | | | | | | | | |

**See Reference Notes to this table on the following page**

PRECIPITATION (inches)   FLAGSTAFF, ARIZONA

**TABLE 2**

| YEAR | JAN | FEB | MAR | APR | MAY | JUNE | JULY | AUG | SEP | OCT | NOV | DEC | ANNUAL |
|---|---|---|---|---|---|---|---|---|---|---|---|---|---|
| 1961 | 1.15 | 0.12 | 2.89 | 0.35 | 0.28 | 0.37 | 2.03 | 3.37 | 1.92 | 1.89 | 1.43 | 3.15 | 18.95 |
| 1962 | 2.65 | 4.15 | 1.30 | 0.09 | 0.99 | 0.52 | 2.36 | 0.26 | 2.48 | 1.23 | 1.23 | 0.85 | 18.11 |
| 1963 | 0.96 | 1.28 | 1.03 | 2.13 | 0.05 | T | 0.32 | 4.96 | 0.79 | 1.25 | 1.33 | 0.36 | 14.52 |
| 1964 | 1.07 | 0.14 | 3.08 | 2.17 | 0.84 | 0.17 | 5.23 | 1.32 | 0.99 | 0.02 | 1.21 | 2.74 | 19.04 |
| 1965 | 3.05 | 2.34 | 3.33 | 5.62 | 1.88 | 0.30 | 2.34 | 1.01 | 4.85 | 0.27 | 4.97 | 6.63 | 36.59 |
| 1966 | 1.10 | 1.06 | 0.95 | 0.27 | T | 0.21 | 1.62 | 3.55 | 2.03 | 0.99 | 2.33 | 6.17 | 20.28 |
| 1967 | 0.93 | T | 1.11 | 1.90 | 0.41 | 1.05 | 3.80 | 2.68 | 2.25 | 0.30 | 0.54 | 7.30 | 22.27 |
| 1968 | 1.55 | 1.29 | 1.15 | 2.09 | 0.55 | 0.16 | 3.61 | 1.13 | 0.04 | 1.38 | 0.87 | 2.71 | 16.53 |
| 1969 | 4.63 | 3.91 | 3.00 | 0.11 | 1.06 | 0.01 | 3.81 | 1.90 | 1.34 | 1.14 | 2.04 | 0.46 | 23.41 |
| 1970 | 0.51 | 0.41 | 6.75 | 1.16 | T | 0.07 | 2.58 | 5.15 | 3.79 | 0.11 | 1.37 | 2.12 | 24.02 |
| 1971 | 0.08 | 1.48 | 0.25 | 0.55 | 1.23 | 0.00 | 1.97 | 4.48 | 2.02 | 4.37 | 0.40 | 4.18 | 21.01 |
| 1972 | 0.00 | 0.02 | T | 0.72 | 0.14 | 1.93 | 1.90 | 2.82 | 9.86 | 0.81 | 2.34 | 4.13 | 24.67 |
| 1973 | 1.89 | 3.69 | 6.18 | 1.21 | 1.17 | 0.40 | 1.87 | 1.25 | T | 0.03 | 1.90 | 0.12 | 19.71 |
| 1974 | 3.63 | 0.26 | 1.01 | 0.57 | T | T | 3.00 | 2.16 | 0.93 | 3.64 | 1.03 | 1.18 | 17.41 |
| 1975 | 1.76 | 1.90 | 2.92 | 2.20 | 1.16 | 0.05 | 2.24 | 0.74 | 1.89 | 0.33 | 2.35 | 1.95 | 20.10 |
| 1976 | 0.17 | 5.96 | 2.06 | 3.09 | 1.65 | T | 3.82 | 0.58 | 1.16 | 0.73 | 0.10 | 0.80 | 20.12 |
| 1977 | 1.85 | 0.84 | 0.92 | 1.47 | 0.96 | 0.91 | 3.60 | 3.72 | 1.52 | 1.04 | 0.75 | 1.18 | 18.77 |
| 1978 | 4.09 | 4.67 | 5.58 | 1.60 | 0.27 | 0.09 | 1.17 | 0.68 | 0.46 | 0.56 | 6.16 | 5.39 | 30.72 |
| 1979 | 5.54 | 1.73 | 2.52 | 0.31 | 2.16 | 0.18 | 0.79 | 2.38 | 0.13 | 1.30 | 1.14 | 1.50 | 19.68 |
| 1980 | 6.52 | 7.81 | 4.16 | 1.21 | 1.79 | 0.25 | 2.49 | 2.19 | 0.65 | 1.08 | - | 1.15 | 29.30 |
| 1981 | 1.31 | 1.16 | 4.04 | 1.50 | 0.72 | 1.09 | 2.87 | 3.73 | 2.54 | 1.81 | 2.43 | 0.17 | 23.37 |
| 1982 | 4.62 | 2.55 | 5.69 | 0.25 | 0.86 | T | 1.89 | 2.32 | 3.17 | 0.71 | 5.35 | 3.67 | 31.09 |
| 1983 | 1.61 | 3.04 | 4.36 | 2.18 | 0.06 | 0.28 | 2.86 | 3.53 | 6.75 | 0.75 | 1.53 | 2.52 | 29.47 |
| 1984 | 0.36 | 0.13 | 0.89 | 0.73 | 0.21 | 0.13 | 4.20 | 3.86 | 1.75 | 1.43 | 1.40 | 5.00 | 20.09 |
| 1985 | 2.38 | 1.67 | 2.54 | 3.39 | 0.26 | 0.09 | 2.36 | 1.07 | 3.68 | 2.44 | 6.64 | 0.15 | 26.67 |
| 1986 | 0.31 | 1.76 | 2.60 | 1.23 | 0.72 | 1.16 | 6.62 | 8.06 | 4.80 | 2.02 | 1.68 | 1.43 | 32.39 |
| 1987 | 2.51 | 2.54 | 1.69 | 0.21 | 0.70 | 0.25 | 1.93 | 3.74 | 1.49 | 4.64 | 2.37 | 1.37 | 23.98 |
| 1988 | 1.64 | 2.30 | 0.14 | 3.83 | 0.14 | 1.86 | 3.48 | 4.77 | 0.15 | 1.23 | 1.14 | 1.00 | 21.68 |
| 1989 | 1.84 | 1.35 | 2.08 | 0.01 | 0.62 | 0.23 | 2.28 | 3.40 | 0.30 | 1.28 | - | 1.05 | 14.44 |
| 1990 | 1.54 | 3.20 | 2.17 | 2.32 | 0.73 | 0.24 | 4.32 | 1.71 | 6.18 | 0.49 | 1.09 | 1.68 | 25.67 |
| Record Mean | 1.98 | 1.96 | 2.05 | 1.34 | 0.68 | 0.51 | 2.78 | 2.86 | 1.82 | 1.52 | 1.49 | 1.90 | 20.89 |

**TABLE 3**   AVERAGE TEMPERATURE (deg. F)   FLAGSTAFF, ARIZONA

| YEAR | JAN | FEB | MAR | APR | MAY | JUNE | JULY | AUG | SEP | OCT | NOV | DEC | ANNUAL |
|---|---|---|---|---|---|---|---|---|---|---|---|---|---|
| 1961 | 30.2 | 33.8 | 34.9 | 44.1 | 48.8 | 63.1 | 66.7 | 64.1 | 53.8 | 44.5 | 34.2 | 26.0 | 45.3 |
| 1962 | 27.1 | 30.3 | 28.1 | 47.6 | 48.0 | 58.2 | 64.6 | 64.9 | 58.7 | 47.5 | 39.9 | 31.6 | 45.5 |
| 1963 | 25.4 | 36.7 | 34.5 | 39.6 | 52.7 | 56.3 | 68.0 | 63.8 | 59.2 | 49.8 | 37.9 | 30.3 | 46.2 |
| 1964 | 25.3 | 26.6 | 30.5 | 39.7 | 49.4 | 57.4 | 66.9 | 63.3 | 56.7 | 51.3 | 31.3 | 30.3 | 44.1 |
| 1965 | 31.4 | 29.7 | 33.0 | 39.2 | 46.7 | 53.0 | 65.0 | 63.7 | 53.8 | 49.7 | 39.7 | 30.2 | 44.6 |
| 1966 | 23.5 | 25.1 | 37.2 | 44.7 | 53.7 | 59.1 | 66.4 | 65.2 | 58.6 | 46.9 | 39.5 | 29.7 | 45.8 |
| 1967 | 29.1 | 35.3 | 39.0 | 37.6 | 48.7 | 56.2 | 66.6 | 64.4 | 57.9 | 50.0 | 40.4 | 23.1 | 45.7 |
| 1968 | 25.5 | 35.8 | 37.0 | 40.3 | 50.2 | 59.9 | 64.9 | 59.5 | 55.9 | 46.9 | 35.7 | 25.0 | 44.7 |
| 1969 | 31.8 | 25.4 | 27.3 | 41.7 | 52.4 | 57.9 | 66.2 | 65.1 | 58.2 | 40.5 | 33.9 | 33.3 | 44.5 |
| 1970 | 30.9 | 37.1 | 33.7 | 37.5 | 52.6 | 60.4 | 67.7 | 66.3 | 54.4 | 43.9 | 39.5 | 28.5 | 46.1 |
| 1971 | 29.3 | 31.1 | 37.0 | 41.9 | 46.8 | 58.7 | 67.5 | 64.0 | 53.0 | 38.6 | 33.5 | 22.5 | 43.6 |
| 1972 | 28.4 | 31.8 | 40.0 | 39.8 | 46.4 | 57.6 | 66.5 | 62.9 | 56.7 | 45.9 | 29.5 | 21.9 | 43.9 |
| 1973 | 22.9 | 28.7 | 26.8 | 38.0 | 52.8 | 60.5 | 65.7 | 64.6 | 57.7 | 50.0 | 37.1 | 33.0 | 44.8 |
| 1974 | 27.8 | 30.6 | 40.4 | 43.2 | 54.8 | 66.5 | 66.3 | 64.7 | 58.7 | 47.9 | 36.8 | 26.8 | 47.0 |
| 1975 | 27.7 | 27.6 | 33.2 | 36.2 | 47.5 | 57.1 | 65.7 | 63.5 | 57.9 | 46.5 | 37.3 | 29.2 | 44.2 |
| 1976 | 30.6 | 35.1 | 35.4 | 41.4 | 52.8 | 58.9 | 66.5 | 62.8 | 57.1 | 47.0 | 39.5 | 31.6 | 46.5 |
| 1977 | 26.8 | 34.2 | 33.5 | 44.7 | 47.4 | 62.2 | 67.2 | 66.2 | 60.2 | 50.8 | 41.0 | 37.6 | 47.6 |
| 1978 | 31.5 | 30.7 | 40.3 | 42.2 | 49.4 | 61.4 | 66.6 | 63.7 | 57.3 | 49.8 | 34.6 | 24.3 | 46.0 |
| 1979 | 22.6 | 25.9 | 32.3 | 40.7 | 47.9 | 57.8 | 64.1 | 60.5 | 58.8 | 47.8 | 31.2 | 31.2 | 43.4 |
| 1980 | 30.7 | 32.8 | 32.3 | 41.9 | 45.6 | 60.9 | 69.0 | 66.3 | 59.7 | 49.0 | 41.4 | 39.9 | 47.5 |
| 1981 | 36.2 | 36.3 | 36.6 | 48.5 | 52.1 | 66.1 | 68.2 | 65.4 | 58.7 | 46.7 | 41.8 | 36.4 | 49.4 |
| 1982 | 28.3 | 30.5 | 35.3 | 43.5 | 49.9 | 57.1 | 63.8 | 65.6 | 57.6 | 44.0 | 35.2 | 28.1 | 44.9 |
| 1983 | 31.0 | 32.3 | 36.2 | 37.0 | 49.9 | 57.3 | 65.5 | 63.8 | 60.7 | 48.6 | 36.3 | 34.0 | 46.1 |
| 1984 | 31.7 | 32.8 | 38.3 | 40.7 | 56.8 | 58.5 | 65.7 | 63.8 | 59.3 | 42.4 | 35.3 | 29.0 | 46.2 |
| 1985 | 27.5 | 28.9 | 35.5 | 46.2 | 51.5 | 62.6 | 67.2 | 65.3 | 53.1 | 47.7 | 33.8 | 32.4 | 46.0 |
| 1986 | 37.0 | 34.2 | 39.7 | 44.1 | 52.0 | 61.2 | 64.0 | 65.7 | 53.0 | 43.5 | 37.6 | 30.2 | 46.9 |
| 1987 | 27.6 | 31.1 | 32.8 | 45.9 | 50.7 | 61.3 | 62.8 | 62.8 | 56.5 | 50.4 | 36.2 | 27.1 | 45.4 |
| 1988 | 29.1 | 34.2 | 37.4 | 44.0 | 50.8 | 61.5 | 67.4 | 64.3 | 55.9 | 52.5 | 36.9 | 27.9 | 45.8 |
| 1989 | 26.2 | 32.3 | 41.8 | 50.4 | 50.8 | 60.8 | 68.1 | 63.6 | 58.7 | 47.5 | 31.6 |  | 47.8 |
| 1990 | 28.6 | 29.3 | 38.3 | 46.1 | 50.3 | 64.4 | 66.9 | 62.6 | 59.8 | 48.9 | 37.6 | 25.1 | 46.5 |
| Record Mean | 28.1 | 31.0 | 35.8 | 42.8 | 50.3 | 59.4 | 65.8 | 63.9 | 57.3 | 47.1 | 36.9 | 29.7 | 45.7 |
| Max | 41.5 | 44.2 | 49.3 | 57.8 | 66.8 | 77.4 | 81.1 | 78.5 | 73.2 | 62.9 | 51.5 | 43.2 | 60.6 |
| Min | 14.6 | 17.7 | 22.3 | 27.8 | 33.8 | 41.3 | 50.5 | 49.2 | 41.5 | 31.2 | 22.1 | 16.1 | 30.7 |

## TABLE 4 — HEATING DEGREE DAYS Base 65 deg. F    FLAGSTAFF, ARIZONA

| SEASON | JULY | AUG | SEP | OCT | NOV | DEC | JAN | FEB | MAR | APR | MAY | JUNE | TOTAL |
|---|---|---|---|---|---|---|---|---|---|---|---|---|---|
| 1961-62 | 21 | 50 | 330 | 628 | 919 | 1203 | 1168 | 965 | 1135 | 517 | 518 | 213 | 7667 |
| 1962-63 | 32 | 38 | 184 | 536 | 747 | 1026 | 1218 | 788 | 940 | 757 | 372 | 255 | 6893 |
| 1963-64 | 0 | 49 | 168 | 467 | 804 | 1071 | 1225 | 1105 | 1061 | 752 | 477 | 224 | 7403 |
| 1964-65 | 9 | 72 | 245 | 417 | 1001 | 1070 | 1034 | 983 | 985 | 768 | 560 | 353 | 7497 |
| 1965-66 | 22 | 69 | 326 | 467 | 753 | 1071 | 1281 | 1109 | 854 | 603 | 343 | 171 | 7069 |
| 1966-67 | 14 | 32 | 185 | 556 | 757 | 1069 | 1111 | 824 | 799 | 816 | 498 | 265 | 6946 |
| 1967-68 | 11 | 33 | 207 | 461 | 733 | 1292 | 1218 | 839 | 861 | 733 | 453 | 172 | 7013 |
| 1968-69 | 38 | 164 | 267 | 554 | 872 | 1234 | 1021 | 1105 | 1164 | 693 | 383 | 207 | 7702 |
| 1969-70 | 21 | 37 | 200 | 753 | 926 | 978 | 1051 | 775 | 962 | 821 | 378 | 174 | 7076 |
| 1970-71 | 6 | 16 | 310 | 643 | 758 | 1125 | 1098 | 943 | 862 | 683 | 557 | 210 | 7211 |
| 1971-72 | 24 | 40 | 352 | 809 | 938 | 1310 | 1126 | 956 | 768 | 749 | 573 | 220 | 7865 |
| 1972-73 | 22 | 78 | 241 | 584 | 1055 | 1330 | 1297 | 1006 | 1176 | 801 | 370 | 164 | 8124 |
| 1973-74 | 39 | 45 | 212 | 458 | 829 | 987 | 1147 | 960 | 754 | 650 | 310 | 67 | 6458 |
| 1974-75 | 19 | 34 | 195 | 522 | 841 | 1178 | 1150 | 1041 | 978 | 856 | 536 | 231 | 7581 |
| 1975-76 | 23 | 66 | 207 | 566 | 821 | 1101 | 1059 | 862 | 912 | 702 | 370 | 190 | 6879 |
| 1976-77 | 17 | 71 | 230 | 553 | 757 | 1027 | 1177 | 858 | 970 | 603 | 540 | 102 | 6905 |
| 1977-78 | 9 | 19 | 157 | 432 | 715 | 843 | 1032 | 954 | 756 | 677 | 478 | 128 | 6200 |
| 1978-79 | 33 | 73 | 227 | 465 | 907 | 1254 | 1089 | 1005 | 722 | 524 | 219 |  | 7825 |
| 1979-80 | 68 | 157 | 186 | 526 | 1008 | 1042 | 1056 | 930 | 1009 | 684 | 596 | 158 | 7420 |
| 1980-81 | 6 | 43 | 153 | 491 | 703 | 774 | 886 | 794 | 873 | 486 | 398 | 50 | 5657 |
| 1981-82 | 1 | 39 | 182 | 558 | 689 | 880 | 1130 | 963 | 911 | 640 | 458 | 230 | 6681 |
| 1982-83 | 65 | 22 | 218 | 643 | 888 | 1136 | 1046 | 911 | 888 | 835 | 461 | 222 | 7335 |
| 1983-84 | 26 | 64 | 134 | 502 | 837 | 952 | 1025 | 929 | 820 | 722 | 247 | 204 | 6462 |
| 1984-85 | 21 | 51 | 165 | 695 | 884 | 1109 | 1155 | 1005 | 911 | 557 | 411 | 102 | 7066 |
| 1985-86 | 26 | 31 | 351 | 532 | 931 | 1005 | 862 | 855 | 777 | 619 | 392 | 119 | 6500 |
| 1986-87 | 58 | 28 | 353 | 661 | 816 | 1069 | 1150 | 942 | 990 | 566 | 435 | 114 | 7182 |
| 1987-88 | 82 | 86 | 246 | 447 | 859 | 1167 | 1103 | 885 | 848 | 621 | 434 | 124 | 6902 |
| 1988-89 | 9 | 41 | 266 | 381 | 836 | 1141 | 1196 | 910 | 710 | 432 | 330 | 139 | 6391 |
| 1989-90 | 7 | 67 | 184 | 540 | 792 | 1030 | 1124 | 996 | 822 | 558 | 449 | 84 | 6653 |
| 1990-91 | 10 | 93 | 167 | 494 | 816 | 1231 |  |  |  |  |  |  |  |

## TABLE 5 — COOLING DEGREE DAYS Base 65 deg. F    FLAGSTAFF, ARIZONA

| YEAR | JAN | FEB | MAR | APR | MAY | JUNE | JULY | AUG | SEP | OCT | NOV | DEC | TOTAL |
|---|---|---|---|---|---|---|---|---|---|---|---|---|---|
| 1969 | 0 | 0 | 0 | 0 | 0 | 1 | 64 | 48 | 0 | 0 | 0 | 0 | 113 |
| 1970 | 0 | 0 | 0 | 0 | 0 | 44 | 99 | 64 | 1 | 0 | 0 | 0 | 208 |
| 1971 | 0 | 0 | 0 | 0 | 0 | 28 | 108 | 17 | 0 | 0 | 0 | 0 | 153 |
| 1972 | 0 | 0 | 0 | 0 | 0 | 4 | 76 | 20 | 0 | 0 | 0 | 0 | 100 |
| 1973 | 0 | 0 | 0 | 0 | 0 | 34 | 69 | 40 | 0 | 0 | 0 | 0 | 143 |
| 1974 | 0 | 0 | 0 | 0 | 0 | 120 | 66 | 33 | 13 | 0 | 0 | 0 | 232 |
| 1975 | 0 | 0 | 0 | 0 | 0 | 0 | 60 | 28 | 0 | 0 | 0 | 0 | 88 |
| 1976 | 0 | 0 | 0 | 0 | 0 | 15 | 70 | 13 | 0 | 0 | 0 | 0 | 98 |
| 1977 | 0 | 0 | 0 | 0 | 0 | 28 | 82 | 61 | 20 | 0 | 0 | 0 | 191 |
| 1978 | 0 | 0 | 0 | 0 | 0 | 25 | 87 | 38 | 2 | 0 | 0 | 0 | 152 |
| 1979 | 0 | 0 | 0 | 0 | 0 | 10 | 47 | 24 | 4 | 0 | 0 | 0 | 85 |
| 1980 | 0 | 0 | 0 | 0 | 0 | 43 | 133 | 91 | 2 | 0 | 0 | 0 | 269 |
| 1981 | 0 | 0 | 0 | 0 | 0 | 91 | 108 | 58 | 0 | 0 | 0 | 0 | 257 |
| 1982 | 0 | 0 | 0 | 0 | 0 | 1 | 36 | 46 | 6 | 0 | 0 | 0 | 89 |
| 1983 | 0 | 0 | 0 | 0 | 0 | 0 | 45 | 31 | 12 | 0 | 0 | 0 | 88 |
| 1984 | 0 | 0 | 0 | 0 | 2 | 14 | 49 | 23 | 2 | 0 | 0 | 0 | 90 |
| 1985 | 0 | 0 | 0 | 0 | 0 | 36 | 102 | 47 | 0 | 0 | 0 | 0 | 185 |
| 1986 | 0 | 0 | 0 | 0 | 0 | 11 | 33 | 55 | 0 | 0 | 0 | 0 | 99 |
| 1987 | 0 | 0 | 0 | 0 | 0 | 13 | 21 | 26 | 0 | 0 | 0 | 0 | 60 |
| 1988 | 0 | 0 | 0 | 0 | 0 | 28 | 94 | 28 | 1 | 0 | 0 | 0 | 151 |
| 1989 | 0 | 0 | 0 | 0 | 0 | 22 | 111 | 29 | 0 | 0 | 0 | 0 | 162 |
| 1990 | 0 | 0 | 0 | 0 | 0 | 76 | 76 | 28 | 18 | 0 | 0 | 0 | 198 |

## TABLE 6 — SNOWFALL (inches)    FLAGSTAFF, ARIZONA

| SEASON | JULY | AUG | SEP | OCT | NOV | DEC | JAN | FEB | MAR | APR | MAY | JUNE | TOTAL |
|---|---|---|---|---|---|---|---|---|---|---|---|---|---|
| 1961-62 | 0.0 | 0.0 | 0.0 | 8.2 | 11.7 | 29.6 | 30.8 | 32.4 | 13.0 | 0.0 | 3.2 | 0.0 | 128.9 |
| 1962-63 | 0.0 | 0.0 | 0.0 | 0.0 | 2.9 | 3.8 | 9.9 | 10.9 | 8.0 | 11.8 | 0.0 | 0.0 | 47.3 |
| 1963-64 | 0.0 | 0.0 | 0.0 | 0.0 | 4.6 | 10.3 | 1.4 | 38.5 | 19.9 | 3.8 | 0.0 | 0.0 | 89.4 |
| 1964-65 | 0.0 | 0.0 | 0.0 | 0.0 | 14.3 | 13.7 | 15.1 | 23.9 | 34.4 | 58.3 | 7.0 | 0.0 | 166.7 |
| 1965-66 | 0.0 | 0.0 | 2.0 | 2.2 | 2.9 | 38.5 | 14.5 | 10.8 | 7.4 | 5.1 | 0.0 | 0.0 | 83.4 |
| 1966-67 | 0.0 | 0.0 | 0.0 | T | 11.3 | 13.4 | 9.8 | T | 10.9 | 17.7 | 0.0 | 0.0 | 63.1 |
| 1967-68 | 0.0 | 0.0 | 0.0 | 0.0 | 5.1 | 86.0 | 15.2 | 9.3 | 10.1 | 22.7 | 2.0 | 0.0 | 150.4 |
| 1968-69 | 0.0 | 0.0 | 0.0 | T | 4.3 | 27.5 | 12.0 | 42.1 | 43.6 | 0.6 | 4.6 | 0.0 | 134.7 |
| 1969-70 | 0.0 | 0.0 | 0.0 | 1.5 | 3.0 | 4.6 | 5.2 | 2.8 | 67.3 | 11.3 | 0.0 | 0.0 | 95.7 |
| 1970-71 | 0.0 | 0.0 | 0.0 | 0.0 | 2.0 | 24.5 | 0.8 | 15.1 | 3.1 | 5.0 | 6.1 | 0.0 | 56.6 |
| 1971-72 | 0.0 | 0.0 | T | 24.7 | 4.9 | 18.8 | 0.0 | 0.4 | T | 1.5 | 0.0 | 0.0 | 50.3 |
| 1972-73 | 0.0 | 0.0 | 0.0 | 11.8 | 23.2 | 28.9 | 21.0 | 33.8 | 10.9 | 3.0 | 0.0 | 0.0 | 210.0 |
| 1973-74 | 0.0 | 0.0 | 0.0 | T | 20.7 | 1.2 | 35.3 | 2.4 | 8.8 | 1.6 | 0.0 | 0.0 | 70.0 |
| 1974-75 | 0.0 | 0.0 | 0.0 | 16.6 | 8.2 | 15.6 | 20.1 | 18.2 | 29.1 | 25.1 | 8.2 | 0.0 | 141.1 |
| 1975-76 | 0.0 | 0.0 | 0.0 | T | 25.2 | 18.9 | 1.5 | 31.2 | 20.4 | 31.2 | 3.2 | 0.0 | 131.6 |
| 1976-77 | 0.0 | 0.0 | 0.0 | T | 0.7 | 9.0 | 21.1 | 11.2 | 17.8 | 8.8 | 1.6 | 0.0 | 70.2 |
| 1977-78 | 0.0 | 0.0 | 0.0 | 0.0 | 7.0 | 1.6 | 40.4 | 32.1 | 24.5 | 9.3 | 1.3 | 0.0 | 116.2 |
| 1978-79 | 0.0 | 0.0 | 0.0 | 0.0 | 16.5 | 19.8 | 59.4 | 18.1 | 22.8 | 4.1 | 4.8 | 0.0 | 145.5 |
| 1979-80 | 0.0 | 0.0 | 0.0 | 0.5 | 5.5 | 20.7 | 63.4 | 32.9 | 42.5 | 11.6 | T | 0.0 | 177.1 |
| 1980-81 | 0.0 | 0.0 | 0.0 | 6.9 | T | 6.8 | 11.7 | 11.9 | 45.6 | 9.5 | 0.0 | 0.0 | 92.4 |
| 1981-82 | 0.0 | 0.0 | 0.0 |  | 0.0 | 0.0 | 47.5 | 20.4 | 26.7 | 1.9 | 0.4 | 0.0 |  |
| 1982-83 | 0.0 | 0.0 | T | 22.6 | 27.1 | 15.3 | 25.0 | 38.5 | 13.6 | 0.5 | 0.0 |  | 142.6 |
| 1983-84 | 0.0 | 0.0 | 0.0 | 0.0 | 14.3 | 5.8 | 4.3 | 1.8 | 0.3 | 5.5 | 0.0 | 0.0 | 32.0 |
| 1984-85 | 0.0 | 0.0 | 0.0 | 0.6 | 9.4 | 28.7 | 26.2 | 31.3 | 21.3 | 18.5 | 0.0 | 0.0 | 136.0 |
| 1985-86 | 0.0 | 0.0 | 0.0 | 0.0 | 40.7 | 2.6 | 0.4 | 26.9 | 32.8 | 1.6 | 0.4 | 0.0 | 105.4 |
| 1986-87 | 0.0 | 0.0 | 0.9 | 0.6 | 4.8 | 9.5 | 38.6 | 40.7 | 25.0 | 1.5 | 0.0 | 0.0 | 121.6 |
| 1987-88 | 0.0 | 0.0 | 0.0 | 0.0 | 2.9 | 16.7 | 28.9 | 21.0 | 1.5 | 33.1 | 0.0 | 0.0 | 104.5 |
| 1988-89 | 0.0 | 0.0 | 0.0 | 0.0 | 11.9 | 15.0 | 21.7 | 12.0 | 16.6 | T | 0.5 | 0.0 | 77.7 |
| 1989-90 | 0.0 | T | T | T | T | 13.1 | 24.2 | 45.5 | 25.0 | 4.2 | 1.4 | 0.0 | 113.4 |
| 1990-91 | T | T | T | T | 9.6 | 22.3 |  |  |  |  |  |  |  |
| Record Mean | T | T | 0.1 | 2.0 | 9.3 | 15.2 | 20.2 | 17.8 | 20.7 | 10.1 | 1.9 | T | 97.3 |

**See Reference Notes, relative to all above tables, on preceding page.**

Phoenix is located in the Salt River Valley at an elevation of about 1,100 feet. The valley is oval shaped and flat except for scattered precipitous mountains rising a few hundred to as much as 1,500 feet above the valley floor. Sky Harbor Airport, where the weather observations are taken, is in the southern part of the city. Six miles to the south of the airport are the South Mountains rising to 2,500 feet. Eighteen miles southwest, the Estrella Mountains rise to 4,500 feet, and 30 miles to the west are the White Tank Mountains rising to 4,100 feet. The Superstition Mountains, over 30 miles to the east, rise to as much as 5,000 feet. The valley, though located in the Sonora Desert, supports large acreages of cotton, citrus, and other agriculture along with one of the largest urban populations in the United States. The water supply for this complex desert community is partly from reservoirs on the impounded Salt and Verde Rivers, and partly from a large underground water table.

Temperatures range from very hot in summer to mild in winter. Many winter days reach over 70 degrees and typical high temperatures in the middle of the winter are in the 60s. The climate becomes less attractive in the summer. The normal high temperature is over 90 degrees from early May through early October, and over 100 degrees from early June through early September. Many days each summer will exceed 110 degrees in the afternoon and remain above 85 degrees all night. When temperatures are extremely high, the low humidity does not provide much comfort.

Indeed, the climate is very dry. Annual precipitation is only about 7 inches, and afternoon humidities range from about 30 percent in winter to only about 10 percent in June. Rain comes mostly in two seasons. From about Thanksgiving to early April there are periodic rains from Pacific storms. Moisture from the south and southeast results in a summer thunderstorm peak in July and August. Usually the break from extreme dryness in June to the onset of thunderstorms in early July is very abrupt. Afternoon humidities suddenly double to about 20 percent, which with the great heat, gives a feeling of mugginess. Fog is rare, occurring about once per winter, and is unknown in the other seasons.

The valley is characterized by light winds. High winds associated with thunderstorms occur periodically in the summer. These occasionally create duststorms which move large distances across the deserts. Strong thunderstorm winds occur any month of the year, but are rare outside the summer months. Persistent strong winds of 30 mph or more are rare except for two or three events in an average spring due to Pacific storms. Winter storms rarely bring high winds due to the relatively stable air in the valley during that season.

Based on the 1951–1980 period, the average first occurrence of 32 degrees Fahrenheit in the fall is December 13 and the average last occurrence in the spring is February 7.

**TABLE 1**  **NORMALS, MEANS AND EXTREMES**

PHOENIX, ARIZONA

LATITUDE: 33°26'N    LONGITUDE: 112°01'W    ELEVATION: FT. GRND 1110 BARO 1109    TIME ZONE: MOUNTAIN    WBAN: 23183

| | (a) | JAN | FEB | MAR | APR | MAY | JUNE | JULY | AUG | SEP | OCT | NOV | DEC | YEAR |
|---|---|---|---|---|---|---|---|---|---|---|---|---|---|---|
| **TEMPERATURE °F:** | | | | | | | | | | | | | | |
| Normals | | | | | | | | | | | | | | |
| -Daily Maximum | | 65.2 | 69.7 | 74.5 | 83.1 | 92.4 | 102.3 | 105.0 | 102.3 | 98.2 | 87.7 | 74.3 | 66.4 | 85.1 |
| -Daily Minimum | | 39.4 | 42.5 | 46.7 | 53.0 | 61.5 | 70.6 | 79.5 | 77.5 | 70.9 | 59.1 | 46.9 | 40.2 | 57.3 |
| -Monthly | | 52.3 | 56.1 | 60.6 | 68.0 | 77.0 | 86.5 | 92.3 | 89.9 | 84.6 | 73.4 | 60.6 | 53.3 | 71.2 |
| Extremes | | | | | | | | | | | | | | |
| -Record Highest | 52 | 88 | 92 | 100 | 105 | 113 | 117 | 118 | 116 | 118 | 107 | 93 | 88 | 118 |
| -Year | | 1971 | 1986 | 1988 | 1989 | 1984 | 1979 | 1989 | 1975 | 1950 | 1980 | 1988 | 1950 | JUL 1989 |
| -Record Lowest | 52 | 17 | 22 | 25 | 32 | 40 | 50 | 61 | 60 | 47 | 34 | 25 | 22 | 17 |
| -Year | | 1950 | 1948 | 1966 | 1945 | 1967 | 1944 | 1944 | 1942 | 1965 | 1971 | 1938 | 1948 | JAN 1950 |
| **NORMAL DEGREE DAYS:** | | | | | | | | | | | | | | |
| Heating (base 65°F) | | 394 | 269 | 187 | 52 | 0 | 0 | 0 | 0 | 0 | 13 | 159 | 368 | 1442 |
| Cooling (base 65°F) | | 0 | 20 | 51 | 142 | 376 | 645 | 846 | 772 | 588 | 273 | 27 | 6 | 3746 |
| **% OF POSSIBLE SUNSHINE** | 94 | 78 | 80 | 84 | 88 | 93 | 94 | 85 | 85 | 89 | 88 | 83 | 78 | 85 |
| **MEAN SKY COVER (tenths)** | | | | | | | | | | | | | | |
| Sunrise - Sunset | 44 | 4.7 | 4.5 | 4.3 | 3.4 | 2.6 | 1.9 | 3.7 | 3.2 | 2.3 | 2.8 | 3.5 | 4.1 | 3.4 |
| **MEAN NUMBER OF DAYS:** | | | | | | | | | | | | | | |
| Sunrise to Sunset | | | | | | | | | | | | | | |
| -Clear | 52 | 13.9 | 12.7 | 14.7 | 17.2 | 21.0 | 23.3 | 16.4 | 17.6 | 21.7 | 20.3 | 17.6 | 15.3 | 211.7 |
| -Partly Cloudy | 52 | 7.0 | 6.8 | 8.0 | 7.1 | 6.4 | 4.6 | 10.4 | 9.6 | 5.3 | 6.2 | 6.3 | 6.3 | 84.0 |
| -Cloudy | 52 | 10.1 | 8.7 | 8.3 | 5.7 | 3.5 | 2.2 | 4.2 | 3.8 | 3.0 | 4.5 | 6.2 | 9.4 | 69.6 |
| Precipitation | | | | | | | | | | | | | | |
| .01 inches or more | 50 | 3.9 | 3.8 | 3.5 | 1.8 | 0.8 | 0.7 | 4.3 | 4.8 | 2.9 | 2.8 | 2.5 | 3.8 | 35.6 |
| Snow,Ice pellets | | | | | | | | | | | | | | |
| 1.0 inches or more | 52 | 0.0 | 0.0 | 0.0 | 0.0 | 0.0 | 0.0 | 0.0 | 0.0 | 0.0 | 0.0 | 0.0 | 0.0 | 0.0 |
| Thunderstorms | 50 | 0.3 | 0.5 | 0.8 | 0.7 | 0.9 | 1.0 | 6.2 | 7.2 | 3.5 | 1.3 | 0.5 | 0.7 | 23.7 |
| Heavy Fog Visibility | | | | | | | | | | | | | | |
| 1/4 mile or less | 52 | 0.5 | 0.2 | 0.1 | 0.0 | 0.0 | 0.0 | 0.0 | 0.0 | 0.0 | 0.* | 0.2 | 0.5 | 1.6 |
| Temperature °F | | | | | | | | | | | | | | |
| -Maximum | | | | | | | | | | | | | | |
| 90° and above | 29 | 0.0 | 0.1 | 2.0 | 9.6 | 22.8 | 29.2 | 30.9 | 30.8 | 27.3 | 14.5 | 0.5 | 0.0 | 167.8 |
| 32° and below | 29 | 0.0 | 0.0 | 0.0 | 0.0 | 0.0 | 0.0 | 0.0 | 0.0 | 0.0 | 0.0 | 0.0 | 0.0 | 0.0 |
| -Minimum | | | | | | | | | | | | | | |
| 32° and below | 29 | 3.8 | 1.4 | 0.4 | 0.0 | 0.0 | 0.0 | 0.0 | 0.0 | 0.0 | 0.0 | 0.2 | 2.0 | 7.8 |
| 0° and below | 29 | 0.0 | 0.0 | 0.0 | 0.0 | 0.0 | 0.0 | 0.0 | 0.0 | 0.0 | 0.0 | 0.0 | 0.0 | 0.0 |
| **AVG. STATION PRESS.(mb)** | 17 | 978.5 | 977.7 | 974.4 | 972.8 | 970.7 | 969.9 | 971.3 | 971.5 | 971.6 | 974.1 | 976.5 | 978.3 | 973.9 |
| **RELATIVE HUMIDITY (%)** | | | | | | | | | | | | | | |
| Hour 05 | 29 | 67 | 60 | 56 | 43 | 35 | 31 | 45 | 51 | 49 | 52 | 58 | 67 | 51 |
| Hour 11 | 29 | 45 | 39 | 34 | 23 | 18 | 16 | 28 | 33 | 31 | 31 | 37 | 46 | 32 |
| Hour 17 (Local Time) | 29 | 32 | 27 | 24 | 16 | 13 | 11 | 20 | 23 | 23 | 23 | 27 | 34 | 23 |
| Hour 23 | 29 | 56 | 48 | 42 | 29 | 22 | 20 | 33 | 38 | 38 | 41 | 49 | 57 | 39 |
| **PRECIPITATION (inches):** | | | | | | | | | | | | | | |
| Water Equivalent | | | | | | | | | | | | | | |
| -Normal | | 0.73 | 0.59 | 0.81 | 0.27 | 0.14 | 0.17 | 0.74 | 1.02 | 0.64 | 0.63 | 0.54 | 0.83 | 7.11 |
| -Maximum Monthly | 52 | 2.41 | 2.23 | 4.16 | 2.10 | 1.06 | 1.70 | 5.15 | 5.56 | 4.23 | 4.40 | 3.04 | 3.98 | 5.56 |
| -Year | | 1955 | 1944 | 1941 | 1941 | 1976 | 1972 | 1984 | 1951 | 1939 | 1972 | 1952 | 1967 | AUG 1951 |
| -Minimum Monthly | 52 | 0.00 | 0.00 | 0.00 | 0.00 | 0.00 | 0.00 | T | T | 0.00 | 0.00 | 0.00 | 0.00 | 0.00 |
| -Year | | 1972 | 1967 | 1959 | 1962 | 1983 | 1983 | 1947 | 1975 | 1973 | 1973 | 1980 | 1981 | MAY 1983 |
| -Maximum in 24 hrs | 52 | 1.31 | 1.49 | 2.04 | 1.38 | 0.96 | 1.64 | 2.75 | 3.07 | 2.43 | 2.32 | 1.14 | 1.89 | 3.07 |
| -Year | | 1951 | 1987 | 1983 | 1941 | 1976 | 1972 | 1984 | 1943 | 1970 | 1988 | 1978 | 1967 | AUG 1943 |
| Snow,Ice pellets | | | | | | | | | | | | | | |
| -Maximum Monthly | 52 | T | 0.6 | T | T | 0.0 | 0.0 | 0.0 | 0.0 | 0.0 | 0.0 | 0.0 | 0.1 | 0.6 |
| -Year | | 1987 | 1939 | 1976 | 1949 | | | | | | | | 1985 | FEB 1939 |
| -Maximum in 24 hrs | 52 | T | 0.6 | T | T | 0.0 | 0.0 | 0.0 | 0.0 | 0.0 | 0.0 | 0.0 | 0.1 | 0.6 |
| -Year | | 1987 | 1939 | 1976 | 1949 | | | | | | | | 1985 | FEB 1939 |
| **WIND:** | | | | | | | | | | | | | | |
| Mean Speed (mph) | 44 | 5.3 | 5.9 | 6.7 | 7.0 | 7.1 | 6.8 | 7.2 | 6.7 | 6.3 | 5.8 | 5.4 | 5.1 | 6.3 |
| Prevailing Direction | | | | | | | | | | | | | | |
| through 1963 | | E | E | E | E | E | E | W | E | E | E | E | E | E |
| Fastest Obs. 1 Min. | | | | | | | | | | | | | | |
| -Direction (!!!) | 4 | 27 | 14 | 27 | 27 | 02 | 03 | 08 | 10 | 14 | 21 | 28 | 09 | 10 |
| -Speed (MPH) | 4 | 32 | 24 | 32 | 28 | 35 | 31 | 35 | 35 | 30 | 28 | 28 | 26 | 35 |
| -Year | | 1988 | 1987 | 1989 | 1986 | 1986 | 1986 | 1988 | 1989 | 1987 | 1986 | 1988 | 1988 | AUG 1989 |
| Peak Gust | | | | | | | | | | | | | | |
| -Direction (!!!) | 52 | W | W | W | W | SSE | NE | SE | E | SW | W | W | W | SE |
| -Speed (mph) | 52 | 60 | 54 | 51 | 49 | 59 | 73 | 86 | 78 | 75 | 61 | 60 | 68 | 86 |
| -Date | | 1983 | 1980 | 1989 | 1981 | 1954 | 1978 | 1976 | 1978 | 1950 | 1981 | 1982 | 1953 | JUL 1976 |

**See Reference Notes to this table on the following page.**

PRECIPITATION (inches)  PHOENIX, ARIZONA

**TABLE 2**

| YEAR | JAN | FEB | MAR | APR | MAY | JUNE | JULY | AUG | SEP | OCT | NOV | DEC | ANNUAL |
|---|---|---|---|---|---|---|---|---|---|---|---|---|---|
| 1961 | 0.23 | 0.01 | 0.41 | | T | T | 0.40 | 2.11 | 0.22 | 0.08 | 0.12 | 0.85 | 4.43 |
| 1962 | 1.20 | 0.83 | 0.50 | 0.00 | | 0.12 | 0.10 | 0.25 | 0.39 | T | 0.03 | 0.48 | 3.90 |
| 1963 | 0.55 | 1.16 | 0.30 | 0.33 | T | 0.00 | 0.03 | 2.68 | T | 1.46 | 0.73 | T | 7.24 |
| 1964 | 0.22 | 0.01 | 0.37 | 0.10 | T | 0.00 | 0.60 | 1.29 | 1.80 | 0.17 | 0.35 | 1.09 | 6.00 |
| 1965 | 1.22 | 0.91 | 1.39 | 1.35 | 0.16 | 0.91 | 0.16 | 0.18 | 0.60 | 0.20 | 0.92 | 3.19 | 11.19 |
| 1966 | 0.35 | 0.95 | 0.34 | T | | 0.22 | 0.09 | 2.17 | 2.00 | 0.25 | 0.38 | 0.52 | 7.27 |
| 1967 | 0.25 | 0.00 | 0.43 | 0.08 | 0.05 | 0.47 | 0.99 | 0.02 | 0.13 | 0.67 | 1.27 | 3.98 | 8.34 |
| 1968 | 0.19 | 1.20 | 1.04 | T | | 0.00 | 1.70 | 0.59 | 0.00 | 0.35 | 0.91 | 0.69 | 6.67 |
| 1969 | 1.37 | 0.78 | 0.56 | 0.03 | 0.26 | 0.00 | 0.28 | 0.14 | 2.11 | 0.08 | 0.65 | 0.68 | 6.94 |
| 1970 | T | 0.30 | 2.26 | T | T | 0.00 | 0.48 | 1.02 | 2.85 | 0.44 | 0.02 | 0.26 | 7.63 |
| 1971 | 0.22 | 0.35 | T | 0.13 | T | 0.00 | 0.24 | 0.99 | 0.92 | 0.27 | T | 0.47 | 3.59 |
| 1972 | 0.00 | T | T | T | T | 1.70 | 0.72 | 1.20 | 0.28 | 4.40 | 1.01 | 1.56 | 10.87 |
| 1973 | 0.13 | 1.36 | 1.69 | 0.07 | 0.10 | T | 1.30 | T | 0.00 | 0.00 | 1.36 | 0.00 | 6.01 |
| 1974 | 0.57 | 0.02 | 1.37 | 0.01 | 0.00 | 0.00 | 0.84 | 1.15 | 1.07 | 2.12 | 0.44 | 0.59 | 8.18 |
| 1975 | 0.02 | 0.33 | 0.63 | 0.43 | | T | 0.38 | T | 0.82 | 0.23 | 0.55 | 1.12 | 4.51 |
| 1976 | T | 0.47 | 0.40 | 0.67 | 1.06 | 0.09 | 1.48 | 0.12 | 1.69 | 0.70 | 0.43 | 0.85 | 7.96 |
| 1977 | 0.35 | 0.27 | 0.06 | 0.06 | 0.16 | 0.10 | 0.30 | 0.18 | 0.53 | 0.61 | T | 0.54 | 3.16 |
| 1978 | 2.33 | 2.21 | 2.14 | 0.20 | T | 0.01 | 1.44 | 1.79 | 0.09 | 0.09 | 2.30 | 2.46 | 15.23 |
| 1979 | 2.16 | 0.09 | 1.78 | 0.02 | 0.76 | 0.04 | 0.34 | 1.18 | 0.09 | 0.09 | 0.12 | 0.13 | 6.80 |
| 1980 | 1.58 | 2.09 | 0.86 | 0.44 | 0.21 | 0.03 | 0.56 | 0.06 | 0.13 | 0.02 | 0.00 | 0.08 | 6.06 |
| 1981 | 0.71 | 1.08 | 0.98 | 0.20 | 0.03 | T | 1.14 | 0.11 | 0.18 | 1.34 | 0.95 | 0.00 | 6.72 |
| 1982 | 0.81 | 0.67 | 1.30 | T | 0.50 | T | 0.43 | 1.97 | 0.12 | T | 2.50 | 1.64 | 9.94 |
| 1983 | 0.70 | 1.17 | 3.17 | 0.18 | 0.00 | 0.00 | 0.38 | 2.48 | 2.43 | 0.71 | 0.43 | 1.16 | 12.81 |
| 1984 | 0.31 | 0.00 | 0.00 | 0.91 | 0.18 | 0.18 | 5.15 | 0.87 | 3.36 | 0.31 | 0.71 | 2.93 | 14.91 |
| 1985 | 0.95 | 0.18 | 0.46 | 0.17 | T | 0.00 | 0.98 | 0.21 | 1.60 | 0.92 | 1.59 | 0.86 | 7.92 |
| 1986 | 0.07 | 1.19 | 1.58 | 0.01 | T | 0.01 | 1.19 | 1.27 | 0.47 | 0.41 | 0.03 | 1.38 | 7.61 |
| 1987 | 0.67 | 2.06 | 0.28 | 0.09 | 0.06 | 0.01 | 1.08 | 0.45 | 0.57 | 0.47 | 1.04 | 1.62 | 8.40 |
| 1988 | 0.90 | 0.23 | 0.17 | 1.09 | 0.00 | 0.02 | 0.87 | 0.63 | 0.00 | 2.38 | 0.78 | 0.14 | 7.21 |
| 1989 | 1.19 | T | 1.25 | 0.00 | T | 0.00 | 0.13 | 1.11 | 0.47 | 0.46 | 0.14 | 0.19 | 4.94 |
| 1990 | 0.80 | 0.70 | 0.35 | 0.17 | 0.16 | 0.04 | 1.05 | 2.70 | 1.11 | 0.04 | 0.15 | 0.46 | 7.73 |
| Record Mean | 0.76 | 0.73 | 0.73 | 0.34 | 0.13 | 0.10 | 0.93 | 1.02 | 0.79 | 0.52 | 0.63 | 0.89 | 7.57 |

**TABLE 3** AVERAGE TEMPERATURE (deg. F)  PHOENIX, ARIZONA

| YEAR | JAN | FEB | MAR | APR | MAY | JUNE | JULY | AUG | SEP | OCT | NOV | DEC | ANNUAL |
|---|---|---|---|---|---|---|---|---|---|---|---|---|---|
| 1961 | 54.2 | 55.6 | 59.6 | 69.2 | 75.6 | 88.6 | 91.7 | 88.6 | 80.6 | 69.6 | 57.1 | 52.3 | 70.2 |
| 1962 | 51.5 | 55.7 | 56.0 | 72.3 | 73.5 | 83.1 | 90.2 | 91.7 | 84.3 | 71.6 | 61.9 | 55.0 | 70.6 |
| 1963 | 48.4 | 60.2 | 61.0 | 65.8 | 80.0 | 81.7 | 92.0 | 87.1 | 85.1 | 76.2 | 55.5 | 51.8 | 67.8 |
| 1964 | 46.7 | 49.3 | 56.5 | 65.2 | 73.7 | 82.6 | 90.6 | 86.2 | 80.9 | 73.8 | 62.1 | 52.9 | 68.6 |
| 1965 | 52.7 | 52.4 | 56.1 | 63.4 | 71.8 | 79.0 | 91.0 | 89.0 | 79.2 | 70.9 | 60.5 | 52.0 | 70.5 |
| 1966 | 48.2 | 49.7 | 61.2 | 69.8 | 80.1 | 86.8 | 93.0 | 90.9 | 82.9 | 70.9 | 60.5 | 52.0 | 70.5 |
| 1967 | 50.7 | 55.7 | 62.8 | 62.4 | 75.1 | 81.1 | 91.6 | 91.0 | 84.8 | 73.5 | 53.9 | 48.2 | 70.1 |
| 1968 | 52.4 | 59.7 | 59.9 | 66.7 | 76.6 | 86.2 | 90.2 | 86.5 | 83.6 | 72.7 | 62.1 | 54.8 | 70.3 |
| 1969 | 54.9 | 53.0 | 56.9 | 68.5 | 78.3 | 84.2 | 93.1 | 94.4 | 86.0 | 69.5 | 61.4 | 52.6 | 71.3 |
| 1970 | 52.1 | 60.2 | 59.5 | 64.7 | 79.6 | 88.1 | 95.0 | 92.5 | 82.2 | 69.1 | 61.4 | 52.6 | 71.4 |
| 1971 | 52.2 | 56.3 | 63.3 | 66.5 | 73.3 | 85.3 | 94.9 | 89.6 | 85.6 | 69.3 | 59.7 | 50.2 | 72.5 |
| 1972 | 51.4 | 59.1 | 70.6 | 71.4 | 78.3 | 87.8 | 94.4 | 89.9 | 84.8 | 71.9 | 58.1 | 55.4 | 72.0 |
| 1973 | 51.2 | 67.5 | 56.6 | 67.2 | 80.9 | 88.1 | 93.5 | 93.4 | 84.7 | 74.4 | 60.8 | 50.6 | 73.1 |
| 1974 | 54.0 | 56.7 | 64.5 | 70.6 | 80.2 | 92.2 | 92.4 | 91.2 | 87.2 | 75.9 | 61.5 | 54.8 | 71.0 |
| 1975 | 52.3 | 54.0 | 59.0 | 62.6 | 76.7 | 86.6 | 94.3 | 91.9 | 86.2 | 72.9 | 60.9 | 54.8 | 72.8 |
| 1976 | 55.4 | 60.7 | 61.5 | 68.7 | 80.7 | 87.9 | 91.6 | 90.7 | 83.0 | 74.0 | 64.1 | 55.6 | 72.8 |
| 1977 | 53.8 | 61.7 | 60.8 | 73.5 | 75.7 | 91.4 | 95.0 | 94.1 | 87.6 | 78.7 | 65.8 | 59.9 | 74.9 |
| 1978 | 56.6 | 58.7 | 65.6 | 69.2 | 78.5 | 90.9 | 94.6 | 91.4 | 86.3 | 78.6 | 61.5 | 55.9 | 73.6 |
| 1979 | 50.1 | 55.7 | 60.4 | 70.1 | 78.1 | 89.5 | 93.8 | 89.4 | 90.2 | 77.2 | 58.2 | 61.3 | 72.4 |
| 1980 | 56.6 | 60.6 | 60.7 | 69.8 | 76.0 | 88.9 | 95.6 | 92.2 | 87.3 | 75.6 | 64.1 | 61.3 | 74.0 |
| 1981 | 59.2 | 61.4 | 63.8 | 76.0 | 80.5 | 93.4 | 95.2 | 95.8 | 89.2 | 73.6 | 66.1 | 58.6 | 76.0 |
| 1982 | 53.9 | 60.1 | 62.4 | 72.5 | 80.4 | 88.1 | 93.7 | 93.7 | 86.7 | 73.5 | 54.1 | 54.1 | 73.4 |
| 1983 | 56.0 | 58.4 | 62.2 | 66.6 | 80.6 | 88.6 | 95.5 | 92.6 | 91.0 | 77.2 | 62.4 | 57.2 | 74.0 |
| 1984 | 57.4 | 60.1 | 67.6 | 70.7 | 87.0 | 88.9 | 91.7 | 91.2 | 87.5 | 71.4 | 61.9 | 53.7 | 74.1 |
| 1985 | 54.3 | 57.4 | 62.9 | 75.1 | 84.2 | 92.4 | 94.9 | 94.5 | 82.3 | 75.1 | 61.3 | 55.9 | 74.2 |
| 1986 | 61.4 | 61.0 | 69.3 | 74.2 | 82.3 | 92.8 | 92.3 | 94.5 | 84.1 | 74.7 | 65.0 | 56.4 | 75.7 |
| 1987 | 54.7 | 59.7 | 63.4 | 77.9 | 82.6 | 93.0 | 93.1 | 92.2 | 86.9 | 80.9 | 63.1 | 52.7 | 75.0 |
| 1988 | 55.1 | 62.5 | 66.3 | 73.0 | 81.4 | 93.1 | 96.2 | 93.9 | 87.4 | 82.4 | 64.4 | 55.7 | 75.0 |
| 1989 | 54.4 | 61.9 | 70.7 | 80.1 | 83.1 | 92.1 | 97.4 | 93.7 | 89.9 | 77.3 | 66.4 | 57.0 | 77.0 |
| 1990 | 55.6 | 56.6 | 67.2 | 76.2 | 81.1 | 93.8 | 93.6 | 90.8 | 87.6 | 78.7 | 65.9 | 53.6 | 75.1 |
| Record Mean | 52.2 | 56.1 | 61.0 | 68.5 | 76.8 | 86.1 | 91.4 | 89.6 | 84.1 | 72.4 | 60.4 | 53.0 | 71.0 |
| Record Max | 65.3 | 69.5 | 74.9 | 83.5 | 92.3 | 102.1 | 104.5 | 102.2 | 98.0 | 87.2 | 74.8 | 66.1 | 85.0 |
| Record Min | 39.1 | 42.7 | 47.1 | 53.5 | 61.2 | 70.1 | 78.3 | 76.9 | 70.2 | 57.7 | 46.0 | 39.8 | 56.9 |

## REFERENCE NOTES FOR TABLES 1, 2, 3 and 6   (PHOENIX, AZ)

### GENERAL

T - TRACE AMOUNT
BLANK ENTRIES DENOTE MISSING/UNREPORTED DATA.
# INDICATES A STATION OR INSTRUMENT RELOCATION.

### SPECIFIC

#### TABLE 1

(a) - LENGTH OF RECORD IN YEARS. ALTHOUGH INDIVIDUAL MONTHS MAY BE MISSING.

* LESS THAN .05

NORMALS — BASED ON THE 1951-1980 RECORD PERIOD.
EXTREMES — DATES ARE THE MOST RECENT OCCURRENCE.
WIND DIR. — NUMERALS SHOW TENS OF DEGREES CLOCKWISE FROM TRUE NORTH. "00" INDICATES CALM.
RESULTANT WIND DIRECTIONS ARE GIVEN TO WHOLE DEGREES.

#### TABLE 3

MAX AND MIN ARE LONG-TERM MEAN DAILY MAXIMUM AND MEAN DAILY MINIMUM TEMPERATURES.

### EXCEPTIONS

#### TABLE 1

1. PEAK GUST WINDS ARE AS OBSERVED JANUARY 1938 THROUGH OCTOBER 1953 AND FROM RECORDER THEREAFTER.
2. PERCENT OF POSSIBLE SUNSHINE IS FROM CITY OFFICE AUGUST 1895 THROUGH OCTOBER 1953 AND FROM SKY HARBOR AIRPORT THEREAFTER.
3. MEAN SKY COVER IS 1940, 1941, AND 1948 TO DATE

#### TABLES 2, 3, and 6

RECORD MEANS ARE THROUGH THE CURRENT YEAR, BEGINNING IN
1896 FOR TEMPERATURE
1896 FOR PRECIPITATION
1938 FOR SNOWFALL

**TABLE 4**    HEATING DEGREE DAYS Base 65 deg. F     PHOENIX, ARIZONA

| SEASON | JULY | AUG | SEP | OCT | NOV | DEC | JAN | FEB | MAR | APR | MAY | JUNE | TOTAL |
|---|---|---|---|---|---|---|---|---|---|---|---|---|---|
| 1961-62 | 0 | 0 | 0 | 51 | 233 | 388 | 414 | 255 | 277 | 2 | 0 | 0 | 1620 |
| 1962-63 | 0 | 0 | 0 | 1 | 115 | 301 | 507 | 148 | 151 | 50 | 0 | 0 | 1273 |
| 1963-64 | 0 | 0 | 0 | 0 | 133 | 403 | 558 | 450 | 277 | 69 | 23 | 0 | 1913 |
| 1964-65 | 0 | 0 | 0 | 0 | 281 | 396 | 375 | 346 | 269 | 133 | 14 | 0 | 1814 |
| 1965-66 | 0 | 0 | 4 | 7 | 116 | 370 | 516 | 423 | 145 | 12 | 0 | 0 | 1593 |
| 1966-67 | 0 | 0 | 0 | 8 | 139 | 397 | 437 | 256 | 102 | 93 | 10 | 0 | 1442 |
| 1967-68 | 0 | 0 | 0 | 6 | 72 | 512 | 384 | 151 | 167 | 39 | 0 | 0 | 1331 |
| 1968-69 | 0 | 0 | 0 | 0 | 173 | 473 | 306 | 327 | 265 | 12 | 13 | 0 | 1569 |
| 1969-70 | 0 | 0 | 0 | 12 | 95 | 307 | 393 | 134 | 166 | 60 | 0 | 0 | 1167 |
| 1970-71 | 0 | 0 | 0 | 19 | 119 | 376 | 396 | 241 | 123 | 53 | 0 | 0 | 1327 |
| 1971-72 | 0 | 0 | 0 | 79 | 185 | 455 | 414 | 174 | 22 | 12 | 0 | 0 | 1341 |
| 1972-73 | 0 | 0 | 0 | 38 | 205 | 395 | 422 | 200 | 254 | 39 | 0 | 0 | 1553 |
| 1973-74 | 0 | 0 | 0 | 2 | 156 | 291 | 333 | 229 | 77 | 5 | 0 | 0 | 1093 |
| 1974-75 | 0 | 0 | 0 | 21 | 112 | 439 | 388 | 301 | 191 | 107 | 4 | 0 | 1563 |
| 1975-76 | 0 | 0 | 0 | 15 | 159 | 310 | 296 | 123 | 134 | 52 | 0 | 0 | 1089 |
| 1976-77 | 0 | 0 | 0 | 2 | 112 | 285 | 339 | 122 | 149 | 33 | 0 | 0 | 1042 |
| 1977-78 | 0 | 0 | 0 | 0 | 42 | 155 | 254 | 172 | 67 | 25 | 0 | 0 | 715 |
| 1978-79 | 0 | 0 | 0 | 1 | 148 | 405 | 455 | 254 | 143 | 30 | 0 | 0 | 1436 |
| 1979-80 | 0 | 0 | 0 | 11 | 204 | 277 | 254 | 130 | 129 | 35 | 0 | 0 | 1040 |
| 1980-81 | 0 | 0 | 0 | 12 | 108 | 122 | 181 | 131 | 74 | 8 | 0 | 0 | 636 |
| 1981-82 | 0 | 0 | 0 | 1 | 56 | 196 | 335 | 151 | 99 | 4 | 0 | 0 | 842 |
| 1982-83 | 0 | 0 | 0 | 1 | 103 | 331 | 272 | 181 | 120 | 53 | 0 | 0 | 1061 |
| 1983-84 | 0 | 0 | 0 | 0 | 154 | 236 | 228 | 139 | 16 | 23 | 0 | 0 | 796 |
| 1984-85 | 0 | 0 | 0 | 7 | 126 | 345 | 328 | 222 | 102 | 5 | 0 | 0 | 1135 |
| 1985-86 | 0 | 0 | 0 | 0 | 149 | 274 | 110 | 158 | 66 | 2 | 1 | 0 | 760 |
| 1986-87 | 0 | 0 | 0 | 0 | 43 | 260 | 318 | 172 | 95 | 4 | 0 | 0 | 892 |
| 1987-88 | 0 | 0 | 0 | 0 | 98 | 375 | 311 | 100 | 60 | 20 | 2 | 0 | 966 |
| 1988-89 | 0 | 0 | 0 | 0 | 135 | 284 | 321 | 133 | 46 | 0 | 0 | 0 | 919 |
| 1989-90 | 0 | 0 | 0 | 1 | 36 | 243 | 291 | 253 | 76 | 0 | 0 | 0 | 900 |
| 1990-91 | 0 | 0 | 0 | 0 | 65 | 348 | | | | | | | |

**TABLE 5**    COOLING DEGREE DAYS Base 65 deg. F     PHOENIX, ARIZONA

| YEAR | JAN | FEB | MAR | APR | MAY | JUNE | JULY | AUG | SEP | OCT | NOV | DEC | TOTAL |
|---|---|---|---|---|---|---|---|---|---|---|---|---|---|
| 1969 | 0 | 0 | 22 | 123 | 433 | 582 | 878 | 918 | 638 | 158 | 16 | 0 | 3768 |
| 1970 | 0 | 4 | 4 | 58 | 459 | 700 | 938 | 862 | 527 | 151 | 18 | 0 | 3721 |
| 1971 | 7 | 2 | 76 | 107 | 265 | 614 | 934 | 773 | 623 | 220 | 30 | 0 | 3651 |
| 1972 | 0 | 11 | 200 | 212 | 419 | 691 | 919 | 780 | 599 | 259 | 4 | 0 | 4094 |
| 1973 | 0 | 0 | 0 | 109 | 499 | 701 | 894 | 885 | 598 | 302 | 36 | 0 | 4024 |
| 1974 | 0 | 2 | 69 | 182 | 477 | 825 | 858 | 821 | 673 | 365 | 13 | 0 | 4285 |
| 1975 | 0 | 0 | 12 | 42 | 374 | 654 | 913 | 839 | 640 | 265 | 45 | 1 | 3785 |
| 1976 | 6 | 4 | 34 | 169 | 495 | 692 | 833 | 804 | 548 | 289 | 91 | 0 | 3965 |
| 1977 | 0 | 36 | 25 | 295 | 334 | 797 | 936 | 907 | 683 | 434 | 73 | 1 | 4521 |
| 1978 | 3 | 1 | 92 | 158 | 422 | 787 | 928 | 828 | 644 | 431 | 49 | 0 | 4343 |
| 1979 | 0 | 0 | 11 | 191 | 411 | 741 | 901 | 763 | 764 | 397 | 7 | 0 | 4186 |
| 1980 | 0 | 5 | 2 | 187 | 344 | 724 | 956 | 852 | 675 | 346 | 88 | 13 | 4192 |
| 1981 | 5 | 36 | 40 | 345 | 489 | 857 | 943 | 961 | 731 | 277 | 95 | 5 | 4784 |
| 1982 | 0 | 21 | 24 | 234 | 481 | 697 | 899 | 897 | 658 | 272 | 12 | 0 | 4195 |
| 1983 | 2 | 1 | 38 | 112 | 489 | 715 | 951 | 861 | 787 | 388 | 85 | 0 | 4429 |
| 1984 | 0 | 2 | 107 | 203 | 688 | 724 | 836 | 821 | 681 | 208 | 41 | 0 | 4311 |
| 1985 | 0 | 17 | 40 | 316 | 603 | 826 | 934 | 920 | 525 | 319 | 47 | 0 | 4547 |
| 1986 | 3 | 52 | 209 | 282 | 543 | 844 | 853 | 921 | 582 | 307 | 51 | 1 | 4648 |
| 1987 | 3 | 30 | 51 | 396 | 553 | 846 | 879 | 850 | 665 | 499 | 48 | 0 | 4820 |
| 1988 | 10 | 31 | 108 | 265 | 520 | 851 | 972 | 904 | 678 | 543 | 124 | 3 | 5009 |
| 1989 | 1 | 49 | 210 | 459 | 566 | 820 | 1013 | 897 | 751 | 392 | 87 | 0 | 5245 |
| 1990 | 5 | 25 | 150 | 339 | 506 | 873 | 895 | 806 | 683 | 431 | 101 | 0 | 4814 |

**TABLE 6**    SNOWFALL (inches)     PHOENIX, ARIZONA

| SEASON | JULY | AUG | SEP | OCT | NOV | DEC | JAN | FEB | MAR | APR | MAY | JUNE | TOTAL |
|---|---|---|---|---|---|---|---|---|---|---|---|---|---|
| 1961-62 | 0.0 | 0.0 | 0.0 | 0.0 | 0.0 | 0.0 | T | 0.0 | 0.0 | 0.0 | 0.0 | 0.0 | T |
| 1962-63 | 0.0 | 0.0 | 0.0 | 0.0 | 0.0 | 0.0 | 0.0 | 0.0 | 0.0 | 0.0 | 0.0 | 0.0 | 0.0 |
| 1963-64 | 0.0 | 0.0 | 0.0 | 0.0 | 0.0 | 0.0 | 0.0 | 0.0 | 0.0 | 0.0 | 0.0 | 0.0 | 0.0 |
| 1964-65 | 0.0 | 0.0 | 0.0 | 0.0 | 0.0 | 0.0 | 0.0 | 0.0 | 0.0 | 0.0 | 0.0 | 0.0 | 0.0 |
| 1965-66 | 0.0 | 0.0 | 0.0 | 0.0 | 0.0 | 0.0 | 0.0 | 0.0 | 0.0 | 0.0 | 0.0 | 0.0 | 0.0 |
| 1966-67 | 0.0 | 0.0 | 0.0 | 0.0 | 0.0 | 0.0 | 0.0 | 0.0 | 0.0 | 0.0 | 0.0 | 0.0 | 0.0 |
| 1967-68 | 0.0 | 0.0 | 0.0 | 0.0 | 0.0 | 0.0 | T | 0.0 | 0.0 | 0.0 | 0.0 | 0.0 | T |
| 1968-69 | 0.0 | 0.0 | 0.0 | 0.0 | 0.0 | T | 0.0 | 0.0 | 0.0 | 0.0 | 0.0 | 0.0 | T |
| 1969-70 | 0.0 | 0.0 | 0.0 | 0.0 | 0.0 | T | 0.0 | 0.0 | 0.0 | 0.0 | 0.0 | 0.0 | T |
| 1970-71 | 0.0 | 0.0 | 0.0 | 0.0 | 0.0 | 0.0 | 0.0 | 0.0 | 0.0 | 0.0 | 0.0 | 0.0 | 0.0 |
| 1971-72 | 0.0 | 0.0 | 0.0 | 0.0 | 0.0 | 0.0 | 0.0 | 0.0 | 0.0 | 0.0 | 0.0 | 0.0 | 0.0 |
| 1972-73 | 0.0 | 0.0 | 0.0 | 0.0 | 0.0 | 0.0 | 0.0 | 0.0 | 0.0 | 0.0 | 0.0 | 0.0 | 0.0 |
| 1973-74 | 0.0 | 0.0 | 0.0 | 0.0 | 0.0 | 0.0 | 0.0 | 0.0 | 0.0 | 0.0 | 0.0 | 0.0 | 0.0 |
| 1974-75 | 0.0 | 0.0 | 0.0 | 0.0 | 0.0 | T | 0.0 | 0.0 | 0.0 | 0.0 | 0.0 | 0.0 | T |
| 1975-76 | 0.0 | 0.0 | 0.0 | 0.0 | 0.0 | 0.0 | 0.0 | 0.0 | T | 0.0 | 0.0 | T | T |
| 1976-77 | 0.0 | 0.0 | 0.0 | 0.0 | 0.0 | 0.0 | 0.0 | 0.0 | 0.0 | 0.0 | 0.0 | 0.0 | 0.0 |
| 1977-78 | 0.0 | 0.0 | 0.0 | 0.0 | 0.0 | 0.0 | 0.0 | 0.0 | 0.0 | 0.0 | 0.0 | 0.0 | 0.0 |
| 1978-79 | 0.0 | 0.0 | 0.0 | 0.0 | 0.0 | 0.0 | 0.0 | 0.0 | 0.0 | 0.0 | 0.0 | 0.0 | 0.0 |
| 1979-80 | 0.0 | 0.0 | 0.0 | 0.0 | 0.0 | 0.0 | 0.0 | 0.0 | 0.0 | 0.0 | 0.0 | 0.0 | 0.0 |
| 1980-81 | 0.0 | 0.0 | 0.0 | 0.0 | 0.0 | 0.0 | 0.0 | 0.0 | 0.0 | 0.0 | 0.0 | 0.0 | 0.0 |
| 1981-82 | 0.0 | 0.0 | 0.0 | 0.0 | 0.0 | 0.0 | 0.0 | 0.0 | 0.0 | 0.0 | 0.0 | 0.0 | 0.0 |
| 1982-83 | 0.0 | 0.0 | 0.0 | 0.0 | 0.0 | 0.0 | 0.0 | 0.0 | 0.0 | 0.0 | 0.0 | 0.0 | 0.0 |
| 1983-84 | 0.0 | 0.0 | 0.0 | 0.0 | 0.0 | 0.0 | 0.0 | 0.0 | 0.0 | 0.0 | 0.0 | 0.0 | 0.0 |
| 1984-85 | 0.0 | 0.0 | 0.0 | 0.0 | 0.0 | 0.0 | 0.0 | T | 0.0 | 0.0 | 0.0 | 0.0 | T |
| 1985-86 | 0.0 | 0.0 | 0.0 | 0.0 | 0.0 | 0.1 | 0.0 | 0.0 | 0.0 | 0.0 | 0.0 | 0.0 | 0.1 |
| 1986-87 | 0.0 | 0.0 | 0.0 | 0.0 | 0.0 | 0.0 | T | 0.0 | 0.0 | 0.0 | 0.0 | 0.0 | T |
| 1987-88 | 0.0 | 0.0 | 0.0 | 0.0 | 0.0 | 0.0 | 0.0 | 0.0 | 0.0 | 0.0 | 0.0 | 0.0 | 0.0 |
| 1988-89 | 0.0 | 0.0 | 0.0 | 0.0 | 0.0 | 0.0 | 0.0 | 0.0 | 0.0 | 0.0 | 0.0 | 0.0 | 0.0 |
| 1989-90 | 0.0 | 0.0 | 0.0 | 0.0 | 0.0 | 0.0 | 0.0 | 0.0 | 0.0 | 0.0 | 0.0 | 0.0 | 0.0 |
| 1990-91 | 0.0 | 0.0 | 0.0 | 0.0 | 0.0 | 0.4 | | | | | | | |
| Record Mean | 0.0 | 0.0 | 0.0 | 0.0 | 0.0 | T | T | T | T | T | 0.0 | 0.0 | T |

**See Reference Notes, relative to all above tables, on preceding page.**

Tucson lies at the foot of the Catalina Mountains, north of the airport. The area within about 15 miles of the airport station is flat or gently rolling, with many dry washes. The soil is sandy, and vegetation is mostly brush, cacti, and small trees. Rugged mountains encircle the valley. The mountains to the north, east, and south rise to over 5,000 feet above the airport. The western hills and mountains range from 500 to 4,000 feet.

The climate of Tucson is characterized by a long hot season, from April to October. Temperatures above 90 degrees prevail from May through September. Temperatures of 100 degrees or higher average 41 days annually, including 14 days each for June and July, but these extreme temperatures are moderated by low relative humidities. The temperature range is large, averaging 30 degrees or more a day.

More than 50 percent of the annual precipitation falls between July 1 and September 15, and over 20 percent falls from December through March. During the summer, scattered convective or orographic showers and thunderstorms often fill dry washes to overflowing. On occasion, brief, torrential downpours cause destructive flash floods in the Tucson area. Hail rarely occurs in thunderstorms. The December through March precipitation occurs as prolonged rainstorms that replenish the ground water. During these storms, snow often falls on the higher mountains, but snow in Tucson is infrequent, particularly in accumulations exceeding an inch in depth.

From the first of the year, the humidity decreases steadily until the summer thunderstorm season, when it shows a marked increase. From mid-September, the end of the thunderstorm season, the humidity decreases again until late November. Occasionally during the summer, humidities are high enough to produce discomfort, but only for short periods. During the hot season, humidity values sometimes fall below 5 percent.

Tucson lies in the zone receiving more sunshine than any other section of the United States. Cloudless days are commonplace, and average cloudiness is low.

Surface winds are generally light, with no major seasonal changes in velocity or direction. Occasional duststorms occur in areas where the ground has been disturbed. During the spring, winds may briefly be strong enough to cause some damage to trees and buildings. Wind velocities and directions are influenced by the surrounding mountains, and the general slope of the terrain. Usually local winds tend to be in the southeast quadrant during the night and early morning hours, veering to northwest during the day. Highest velocities usually occur with winds from the southwest and east to south.

While dust and haze are frequently visible, their effect on the general clarity of the atmosphere is not great. Visibility is normally high.

Based on the 1951–1980 period, the average first occurrence of 32 degrees Fahrenheit in the fall is November 29 and the average last occurrence in the spring is February 28.

**TABLE 1**          # NORMALS, MEANS AND EXTREMES

TUCSON, ARIZONA

LATITUDE: 32°07'N    LONGITUDE: 110°56'W    ELEVATION: FT. GRND 2584 BARO 2589    TIME ZONE: MOUNTAIN    WBAN: 23160

| | (a) | JAN | FEB | MAR | APR | MAY | JUNE | JULY | AUG | SEP | OCT | NOV | DEC | YEAR |
|---|---|---|---|---|---|---|---|---|---|---|---|---|---|---|
| **TEMPERATURE °F:** | | | | | | | | | | | | | | |
| Normals | | | | | | | | | | | | | | |
| -Daily Maximum | | 64.1 | 67.4 | 71.8 | 80.1 | 88.8 | 98.5 | 98.5 | 95.9 | 93.5 | 84.1 | 72.2 | 65.0 | 81.7 |
| -Daily Minimum | | 38.1 | 40.0 | 43.8 | 49.7 | 57.5 | 67.4 | 73.8 | 72.0 | 67.3 | 56.7 | 45.2 | 39.0 | 54.2 |
| -Monthly | | 51.1 | 53.8 | 57.8 | 65.0 | 73.2 | 82.9 | 86.2 | 84.0 | 80.4 | 70.4 | 58.7 | 52.0 | 68.0 |
| Extremes | | | | | | | | | | | | | | |
| -Record Highest | 49 | 87 | 92 | 99 | 104 | 107 | 114 | 114 | 109 | 107 | 101 | 90 | 84 | 114 |
| -Year | | 1953 | 1957 | 1988 | 1989 | 1958 | 1988 | 1989 | 1944 | 1983 | 1987 | 1988 | 1954 | JUL 1989 |
| -Record Lowest | 49 | 16 | 20 | 20 | 27 | 38 | 47 | 62 | 61 | 44 | 26 | 24 | 16 | 16 |
| -Year | | 1949 | 1955 | 1965 | 1945 | 1950 | 1955 | 1982 | 1956 | 1965 | 1971 | 1979 | 1974 | DEC 1974 |
| **NORMAL DEGREE DAYS:** | | | | | | | | | | | | | | |
| Heating (base 65°F) | | 431 | 326 | 246 | 86 | 8 | 0 | 0 | 0 | 0 | 30 | 204 | 403 | 1734 |
| Cooling (base 65°F) | | 0 | 12 | 22 | 86 | 262 | 537 | 657 | 589 | 462 | 198 | 15 | 0 | 2840 |
| **% OF POSSIBLE SUNSHINE** | 42 | 81 | 83 | 87 | 91 | 94 | 93 | 78 | 81 | 87 | 88 | 85 | 80 | 86 |
| **MEAN SKY COVER (tenths)** | | | | | | | | | | | | | | |
| Sunrise - Sunset | 48 | 4.6 | 4.5 | 4.4 | 3.4 | 2.8 | 2.3 | 5.2 | 4.5 | 2.9 | 2.9 | 3.5 | 4.4 | 3.8 |
| **MEAN NUMBER OF DAYS:** | | | | | | | | | | | | | | |
| Sunrise to Sunset | | | | | | | | | | | | | | |
| -Clear | 49 | 13.8 | 13.0 | 15.0 | 17.2 | 20.3 | 21.5 | 10.1 | 12.6 | 19.5 | 19.9 | 17.7 | 15.1 | 195.6 |
| -Partly Cloudy | 49 | 7.1 | 6.5 | 6.7 | 7.3 | 6.7 | 6.0 | 12.4 | 11.9 | 6.8 | 6.3 | 6.1 | 6.0 | 89.8 |
| -Cloudy | 49 | 10.1 | 8.8 | 9.3 | 5.6 | 4.0 | 2.4 | 8.5 | 6.5 | 3.7 | 4.8 | 6.2 | 9.9 | 79.8 |
| Precipitation | | | | | | | | | | | | | | |
| .01 inches or more | 49 | 4.4 | 3.6 | 4.1 | 2.1 | 1.4 | 1.7 | 10.6 | 9.3 | 4.7 | 3.4 | 3.0 | 4.4 | 52.7 |
| Snow, Ice pellets | | | | | | | | | | | | | | |
| 1.0 inches or more | 49 | 0.1 | 0.1 | 0.1 | 0.* | 0.0 | 0.0 | 0.0 | 0.0 | 0.0 | 0.0 | 0.* | 0.1 | 0.5 |
| Thunderstorms | 49 | 0.4 | 0.2 | 0.4 | 0.7 | 1.3 | 2.6 | 14.0 | 13.5 | 5.5 | 2.0 | 0.5 | 0.3 | 41.4 |
| Heavy Fog Visibility | | | | | | | | | | | | | | |
| 1/4 mile or less | 49 | 0.3 | 0.2 | 0.* | 0.0 | 0.0 | 0.0 | 0.0 | 0.0 | 0.* | 0.0 | 0.2 | 0.4 | 1.0 |
| Temperature °F | | | | | | | | | | | | | | |
| -Maximum | | | | | | | | | | | | | | |
| 90° and above | 49 | 0.0 | 0.* | 0.5 | 4.3 | 17.3 | 28.2 | 29.4 | 28.7 | 23.7 | 8.4 | 0.* | 0.0 | 140.5 |
| 32° and below | 49 | 0.0 | 0.0 | 0.0 | 0.0 | 0.0 | 0.0 | 0.0 | 0.0 | 0.0 | 0.0 | 0.0 | 0.0 | 0.0 |
| -Minimum | | | | | | | | | | | | | | |
| 32° and below | 49 | 6.4 | 4.2 | 1.1 | 0.* | 0.0 | 0.0 | 0.0 | 0.0 | 0.0 | 0.* | 1.4 | 5.1 | 18.2 |
| 0° and below | 49 | 0.0 | 0.0 | 0.0 | 0.0 | 0.0 | 0.0 | 0.0 | 0.0 | 0.0 | 0.0 | 0.0 | 0.0 | 0.0 |
| **AVG. STATION PRESS. (mb)** | 17 | 927.8 | 927.0 | 924.8 | 924.1 | 922.8 | 922.9 | 924.7 | 924.8 | 924.2 | 925.8 | 926.9 | 927.9 | 925.3 |
| **RELATIVE HUMIDITY (%)** | | | | | | | | | | | | | | |
| Hour 05 | 49 | 62 | 58 | 53 | 42 | 34 | 33 | 57 | 65 | 55 | 53 | 54 | 61 | 52 |
| Hour 11 | 49 | 40 | 35 | 29 | 21 | 17 | 17 | 33 | 38 | 32 | 31 | 32 | 39 | 30 |
| Hour 17 (Local Time) | 49 | 32 | 27 | 23 | 16 | 13 | 13 | 28 | 33 | 26 | 25 | 28 | 34 | 25 |
| Hour 23 | 49 | 57 | 49 | 42 | 31 | 24 | 23 | 47 | 53 | 44 | 44 | 48 | 56 | 43 |
| **PRECIPITATION (inches):** | | | | | | | | | | | | | | |
| Water Equivalent | | | | | | | | | | | | | | |
| -Normal | | 0.83 | 0.63 | 0.68 | 0.32 | 0.14 | 0.22 | 2.42 | 2.13 | 1.33 | 0.88 | 0.62 | 0.94 | 11.14 |
| -Maximum Monthly | 49 | 2.94 | 2.90 | 2.26 | 1.66 | 0.89 | 1.46 | 6.17 | 7.93 | 5.11 | 4.98 | 1.90 | 5.02 | 7.93 |
| -Year | | 1979 | 1980 | 1952 | 1951 | 1943 | 1954 | 1981 | 1955 | 1964 | 1983 | 1952 | 1965 | AUG 1955 |
| -Minimum Monthly | 49 | T | 0.00 | 0.00 | 0.00 | 0.00 | 0.00 | 0.27 | 0.23 | 0.00 | 0.00 | 0.00 | 0.00 | 0.00 |
| -Year | | 1970 | 1972 | 1956 | 1972 | 1974 | 1983 | 1947 | 1976 | 1953 | 1982 | 1980 | 1981 | JUN 1983 |
| -Maximum in 24 hrs | 49 | 1.40 | 1.49 | 1.19 | 0.91 | 0.89 | 1.27 | 3.93 | 2.48 | 3.05 | 3.58 | 1.86 | 1.54 | 3.93 |
| -Year | | 1946 | 1942 | 1952 | 1988 | 1943 | 1954 | 1958 | 1961 | 1964 | 1983 | 1968 | 1967 | JUL 1958 |
| Snow, Ice pellets | | | | | | | | | | | | | | |
| -Maximum Monthly | 49 | 4.7 | 3.9 | 5.7 | 2.0 | 0.0 | 0.0 | 0.0 | 0.0 | 0.0 | T | 6.4 | 6.8 | 6.8 |
| -Year | | 1987 | 1965 | 1964 | 1976 | | | | | | 1959 | 1958 | 1971 | DEC 1971 |
| -Maximum in 24 hrs | 48 | 4.3 | 3.9 | 5.7 | 2.0 | 0.0 | 0.0 | 0.0 | 0.0 | 0.0 | T | 6.4 | 6.8 | 6.8 |
| -Year | | 1987 | 1965 | 1964 | 1976 | | | | | | 1959 | 1958 | 1971 | DEC 1971 |
| **WIND:** | | | | | | | | | | | | | | |
| Mean Speed (mph) | 44 | 7.9 | 8.1 | 8.5 | 8.9 | 8.7 | 8.6 | 8.3 | 7.8 | 8.3 | 8.1 | 8.0 | 7.8 | 8.2 |
| Prevailing Direction | | | | | | | | | | | | | | |
| through 1963 | | SE | SE | SE | SE | SE | SSE | SE | SE | SE | SE | SE | SE | SE |
| Fastest Mile | | | | | | | | | | | | | | |
| -Direction (!!!) | 41 | E | E | SE | SW | SE | SE | SE | NE | SE | SE | E | W | SE |
| -Speed (MPH) | 41 | 40 | 59 | 41 | 46 | 43 | 50 | 71 | 54 | 54 | 47 | 55 | 44 | 71 |
| -Year | | 1962 | 1952 | 195F | 1986 | 1984 | 1961 | 1971 | 1969 | 1960 | 1948 | 1951 | 1949 | JUL 1971 |
| Peak Gust | | | | | | | | | | | | | | |
| -Direction (!!!) | 6 | SW | E | SE | SW | SE | S | SE | SE | N | NW | SW | SE | SE |
| -Speed (mph) | 6 | 45 | 46 | 53 | 55 | 55 | 47 | 66 | 71 | 52 | 47 | 46 | 47 | 71 |
| -Date | | 1988 | 1987 | 1986 | 1984 | 1984 | 1989 | 1985 | 1988 | 1987 | 1988 | 1987 | 1988 | AUG 1988 |

**See reference Notes to this table on the following page.**

PRECIPITATION (inches)          TUCSON, ARIZONA

**TABLE 2**

| YEAR | JAN | FEB | MAR | APR | MAY | JUNE | JULY | AUG | SEP | OCT | NOV | DEC | ANNUAL |
|------|-----|-----|-----|-----|-----|------|------|-----|-----|-----|-----|-----|--------|
| 1961 | 0.95 | 0.01 | 0.41 | T | 0.00 | 0.26 | 1.81 | 4.28 | 0.51 | 0.65 | 0.44 | 1.57 | 10.89 |
| 1962 | 1.39 | 0.33 | 0.25 | T | 0.00 | 0.25 | 1.38 | 0.48 | 2.86 | 0.22 | 0.49 | 0.93 | 8.58 |
| 1963 | 0.59 | 0.81 | 0.34 | 0.32 | T | T | 1.66 | 2.86 | 1.45 | 0.60 | 1.26 | 0.08 | 9.97 |
| 1964 | 0.14 | 0.13 | 0.81 | 0.67 | 0.00 | 0.01 | 4.82 | 3.90 | 5.11 | 0.91 | 0.68 | 0.81 | 17.99 |
| 1965 | 0.45 | 0.64 | 0.27 | 0.23 | T | 0.01 | 2.13 | 1.12 | 0.82 | 0.07 | 0.77 | 5.02 | 11.53 |
| 1966 | 1.74 | 2.25 | 0.19 | 0.12 | 0.11 | 0.02 | 2.57 | 3.31 | 3.53 | 0.32 | 0.06 | 0.19 | 14.41 |
| 1967 | 0.04 | 0.13 | 0.41 | 0.29 | 0.62 | 0.42 | 2.72 | 2.00 | 1.35 | 1.03 | 0.48 | 3.44 | 12.93 |
| 1968 | 0.18 | 0.99 | 1.79 | 0.62 | T | 0.00 | 1.97 | 1.12 | T | 0.09 | 1.86 | 0.32 | 8.94 |
| 1969 | 0.74 | 0.50 | 0.34 | 0.60 | 0.46 | 0.00 | 1.51 | 2.57 | 1.31 | 0.03 | 1.06 | 0.82 | 9.94 |
| 1970 | T | 0.34 | 1.13 | 0.45 | 0.03 | 0.33 | 2.53 | 1.43 | 3.58 | 1.73 | 0.00 | 0.43 | 11.98 |
| 1971 | 0.04 | 0.50 | T | 0.56 | 0.01 | T | 2.18 | 3.29 | 1.75 | 1.18 | 0.69 | 1.97 | 12.17 |
| 1972 | 0.00 | 0.00 | 0.01 | 0.00 | 0.24 | 0.68 | 3.49 | 2.93 | 1.09 | 4.51 | 1.30 | 0.61 | 14.86 |
| 1973 | 0.06 | 1.60 | 2.20 | 0.02 | 0.09 | 0.50 | 1.74 | 0.54 | T | 0.00 | 0.47 | 0.00 | 7.22 |
| 1974 | 0.93 | T | 0.55 | T | 0.00 | 0.01 | 4.44 | 1.04 | 1.69 | 2.12 | 0.81 | 0.33 | 11.92 |
| 1975 | 0.36 | 0.13 | 0.95 | 0.27 | 0.11 | 0.00 | 2.38 | 0.32 | 1.26 | T | 0.34 | 0.52 | 6.64 |
| 1976 | 0.06 | 0.53 | 0.38 | 0.57 | 0.23 | 0.10 | 1.18 | 0.23 | 1.68 | 0.37 | 0.48 | 0.47 | 6.28 |
| 1977 | 1.83 | 0.04 | 0.74 | 0.43 | 0.08 | 0.06 | 0.76 | 0.80 | 1.41 | 2.36 | 0.33 | 1.33 | 10.17 |
| 1978 | 2.05 | 1.75 | 0.89 | 0.01 | 0.61 | 0.22 | 0.78 | 1.59 | 1.66 | 1.86 | 1.58 | 2.73 | 15.73 |
| 1979 | 2.94 | 0.42 | 0.64 | 0.04 | 0.67 | 0.53 | 2.04 | 2.60 | 0.02 | 0.33 | 0.01 | 0.15 | 10.39 |
| 1980 | 0.73 | 2.90 | 1.22 | 0.08 | T | 0.23 | 1.78 | 1.95 | 2.93 | 0.22 | 0.00 | 0.19 | 12.23 |
| 1981 | 1.29 | 0.71 | 1.98 | 0.56 | 0.26 | 0.16 | 6.17 | 0.80 | 1.10 | 0.06 | 0.61 | 0.00 | 13.70 |
| 1982 | 1.56 | 0.06 | 1.26 | 0.05 | 0.51 | 0.13 | 2.13 | 2.51 | 2.69 | 0.00 | 1.30 | 1.59 | 13.79 |
| 1983 | 1.70 | 0.94 | 1.28 | 0.14 | T | 0.00 | 1.98 | 4.24 | 4.28 | 4.98 | 1.71 | 0.61 | 21.86 |
| 1984 | 0.62 | 0.00 | 0.00 | 0.36 | 0.06 | 1.05 | 2.92 | 4.19 | 1.81 | 0.77 | 0.45 | 3.30 | 15.53 |
| 1985 | 1.71 | 1.08 | 0.20 | 0.45 | T | 0.07 | 3.14 | 1.97 | 1.13 | 2.03 | 0.95 | 0.15 | 12.88 |
| 1986 | 0.98 | 1.13 | 1.30 | T | 0.44 | 0.06 | 1.82 | 3.56 | 0.31 | 0.50 | 0.42 | 1.28 | 11.80 |
| 1987 | 0.59 | 1.64 | 0.83 | 0.80 | 0.74 | 0.16 | 0.37 | 2.79 | 2.30 | 0.34 | 0.44 | 1.50 | 12.50 |
| 1988 | 0.41 | 0.53 | 0.35 | 1.15 | 0.02 | 0.15 | 1.69 | 3.64 | 0.90 | 2.09 | 0.75 | 0.05 | 11.63 |
| 1989 | 0.96 | 0.23 | 0.62 | 0.00 | 0.13 | 0.06 | 1.42 | 0.90 | 0.02 | 1.84 | 0.12 | 0.18 | 6.48 |
| 1990 | 0.96 | 0.71 | 0.38 | 0.10 | 0.03 | 0.64 | 5.45 | 2.70 | 1.63 | 0.58 | 0.23 | 1.54 | 14.95 |
| Record Mean | 0.85 | 0.81 | 0.72 | 0.35 | 0.19 | 0.26 | 2.25 | 2.17 | 1.32 | 0.72 | 0.75 | 1.01 | 11.40 |

**TABLE 3**    AVERAGE TEMPERATURE (deg. F)          TUCSON, ARIZONA

| YEAR | JAN | FEB | MAR | APR | MAY | JUNE | JULY | AUG | SEP | OCT | NOV | DEC | ANNUAL |
|------|-----|-----|-----|-----|-----|------|------|-----|-----|-----|-----|-----|--------|
| 1961 | 52.5 | 53.0 | 58.2 | 66.2 | 72.9 | 84.7 | 86.1 | 81.8 | 77.1 | 68.5 | 54.4 | 50.5 | 67.1 |
| 1962 | 49.0 | 54.7 | 53.3 | 70.1 | 71.7 | 80.3 | 84.9 | 87.0 | 81.3 | 70.6 | 54.0 | 54.0 | 68.2 |
| 1963 | 48.3 | 57.5 | 57.7 | 64.0 | 77.3 | 80.5 | 87.6 | 82.3 | 82.4 | 73.2 | 59.3 | 52.7 | 68.6 |
| 1964 | 47.5 | 47.7 | 54.8 | 63.2 | 73.2 | 82.0 | 86.2 | 81.6 | 76.3 | 72.1 | 55.2 | 52.4 | 66.0 |
| 1965 | 53.6 | 51.1 | 55.1 | 64.5 | 70.1 | 77.6 | 85.0 | 84.0 | 76.8 | 71.9 | 62.6 | 52.1 | 67.1 |
| 1966 | 47.7 | 47.8 | 60.1 | 66.8 | 76.1 | 82.8 | 85.3 | 82.9 | 78.3 | 68.1 | 51.2 | 52.4 | 67.4 |
| 1967 | 51.4 | 55.6 | 62.1 | 62.1 | 71.9 | 80.7 | 85.4 | 84.6 | 80.7 | 71.6 | 62.9 | 48.6 | 68.1 |
| 1968 | 52.4 | 59.1 | 58.7 | 63.2 | 73.3 | 83.5 | 84.9 | 81.3 | 80.7 | 71.7 | 58.3 | 50.6 | 68.1 |
| 1969 | 55.5 | 53.1 | 54.3 | 66.6 | 74.9 | 80.7 | 86.1 | 86.3 | 81.2 | 66.8 | 58.6 | 52.4 | 68.0 |
| 1970 | 57.0 | 55.9 | 55.9 | 61.1 | 75.2 | 83.4 | 87.2 | 84.8 | 76.4 | 65.1 | 60.1 | 51.8 | 67.3 |
| 1971 | 50.5 | 52.3 | 59.8 | 62.8 | 69.3 | 81.2 | 87.5 | 81.3 | 79.1 | 64.2 | 56.8 | 47.1 | 66.0 |
| 1972 | 50.4 | 55.8 | 65.0 | 65.8 | 72.3 | 81.6 | 86.6 | 82.9 | 78.6 | 66.5 | 53.0 | 49.0 | 67.3 |
| 1973 | 47.6 | 53.4 | 51.6 | 59.7 | 73.0 | 81.4 | 84.3 | 84.7 | 79.6 | 70.7 | 58.4 | 52.3 | 66.4 |
| 1974 | 50.2 | 51.9 | 60.1 | 66.1 | 74.3 | 86.9 | 83.5 | 83.0 | 77.8 | 69.1 | 57.5 | 47.0 | 67.3 |
| 1975 | 49.8 | 50.7 | 55.3 | 57.9 | 69.8 | 80.5 | 84.2 | 85.8 | 80.0 | 69.5 | 59.3 | 53.0 | 66.3 |
| 1976 | 52.6 | 58.4 | 58.2 | 64.8 | 74.5 | 83.4 | 83.9 | 85.3 | 77.7 | 67.8 | 60.0 | 52.2 | 68.3 |
| 1977 | 50.7 | 56.9 | 55.7 | 67.0 | 70.8 | 84.7 | 87.0 | 86.4 | 82.0 | 73.3 | 61.7 | 56.9 | 69.4 |
| 1978 | 53.1 | 53.6 | 61.8 | 65.2 | 73.1 | 85.8 | 88.1 | 84.7 | 80.9 | 73.8 | 58.5 | 49.7 | 69.0 |
| 1979 | 48.4 | 53.8 | 56.4 | 65.6 | 72.2 | 83.1 | 87.5 | 83.4 | 84.2 | 73.0 | 56.6 | 55.0 | 68.3 |
| 1980 | 54.3 | 57.9 | 57.5 | 65.6 | 71.5 | 84.9 | 88.6 | 84.6 | 80.5 | 69.6 | 59.5 | 58.1 | 69.4 |
| 1981 | 54.8 | 57.1 | 57.1 | 69.1 | 73.4 | 86.1 | 85.2 | 86.4 | 80.7 | 68.1 | 62.2 | 55.0 | 69.6 |
| 1982 | 50.7 | 54.7 | 57.7 | 66.1 | 72.3 | 80.5 | 84.8 | 83.9 | 79.2 | 67.0 | 57.7 | 50.1 | 67.0 |
| 1983 | 52.9 | 53.8 | 57.3 | 60.4 | 73.8 | 81.6 | 86.9 | 84.0 | 82.2 | 69.5 | 57.4 | 53.5 | 67.8 |
| 1984 | 51.8 | 50.5 | 60.5 | 64.0 | 79.9 | 83.1 | 84.2 | 82.9 | 81.5 | 66.3 | 57.8 | 51.5 | 68.1 |
| 1985 | 50.3 | 53.1 | 58.7 | 68.7 | 75.9 | 85.8 | 87.5 | 86.1 | 77.4 | 70.0 | 58.0 | 52.9 | 68.7 |
| 1986 | 58.7 | 56.9 | 63.8 | 69.0 | 76.8 | 86.6 | 85.5 | 86.0 | 79.0 | 69.6 | 59.8 | 52.3 | 70.3 |
| 1987 | 50.9 | 54.2 | 57.9 | 70.1 | 74.3 | 86.3 | 87.4 | 85.1 | 79.9 | 75.1 | 58.9 | 50.3 | 69.2 |
| 1988 | 53.0 | 59.4 | 61.4 | 68.0 | 76.4 | 86.8 | 87.9 | 85.9 | 80.4 | 75.3 | 59.2 | 51.9 | 70.5 |
| 1989 | 49.9 | 58.2 | 65.0 | 73.8 | 77.4 | 85.4 | 90.0 | 86.6 | 84.5 | 71.1 | 61.7 | 53.0 | 71.4 |
| 1990 | 51.8 | 52.8 | 61.8 | 69.7 | 75.2 | 88.7 | 85.0 | 82.6 | 82.2 | 73.1 | 61.6 | 51.1 | 69.6 |
| Record Mean | 50.5 | 53.5 | 58.0 | 64.8 | 72.9 | 82.3 | 86.1 | 84.1 | 80.1 | 69.6 | 58.3 | 51.4 | 67.6 |
| Max | 64.4 | 67.8 | 73.0 | 80.9 | 89.6 | 99.0 | 99.2 | 96.7 | 94.0 | 84.8 | 73.2 | 65.3 | 82.3 |
| Min | 36.6 | 39.1 | 42.9 | 48.7 | 56.2 | 65.7 | 72.9 | 71.4 | 66.1 | 54.3 | 43.5 | 37.5 | 52.9 |

## REFERENCE NOTES FOR TABLES 1, 2, 3 and 6          (TUCSON, AZ)

### GENERAL

T - TRACE AMOUNT
BLANK ENTRIES DENOTE MISSING/UNREPORTED DATA.
# INDICATES A STATION OR INSTRUMENT RELOCATION.

### SPECIFIC

#### TABLE 1

(a) - LENGTH OF RECORD IN YEARS. ALTHOUGH INDIVIDUAL MONTHS MAY BE MISSING.

 *   LESS THAN .05

NORMALS — BASED ON THE 1951-1980 RECORD PERIOD.
EXTREMES — DATES ARE THE MOST RECENT OCCURRENCE.
WIND DIR. — NUMERALS SHOW TENS OF DEGREES
          CLOCKWISE FROM TRUE NORTH.
          "00" INDICATES CALM.
RESULTANT WIND DIRECTIONS ARE GIVEN TO WHOLE DEGREES.

#### TABLE 3
MAX AND MIN ARE LONG-TERM MEAN DAILY MAXIMUM AND MEAN DAILY MINIMUM TEMPERATURES.

### EXCEPTIONS

#### TABLES 2, 3, and 6

RECORD MEANS ARE THROUGH THE CURRENT YEAR, BEGINNING IN    1900 FOR TEMPERATURE
                                                            1900 FOR PRECIPITATION
                                                            1941 FOR SNOWFALL

HEATING DEGREE DAYS Base 65 deg. F  TUCSON, ARIZONA

**TABLE 4**

| SEASON | JULY | AUG | SEP | OCT | NOV | DEC | JAN | FEB | MAR | APR | MAY | JUNE | TOTAL |
|---|---|---|---|---|---|---|---|---|---|---|---|---|---|
| 1961-62 | 0 | 0 | 0 | 61 | 312 | 444 | 491 | 285 | 357 | 5 | 7 | 0 | 1962 |
| 1962-63 | 0 | 0 | 0 | 3 | 137 | 336 | 515 | 215 | 234 | 79 | 0 | 0 | 1529 |
| 1963-64 | 0 | 0 | 0 | 2 | 186 | 372 | 533 | 497 | 321 | 107 | 27 | 0 | 2045 |
| 1964-65 | 0 | 0 | 0 | 5 | 293 | 383 | 348 | 383 | 305 | 114 | 21 | 0 | 1852 |
| 1965-66 | 0 | 0 | 8 | 33 | 110 | 396 | 532 | 473 | 166 | 26 | 0 | 0 | 1744 |
| 1966-67 | 0 | 0 | 0 | 20 | 126 | 386 | 416 | 256 | 115 | 113 | 20 | 0 | 1452 |
| 1967-68 | 0 | 0 | 0 | 4 | 89 | 502 | 384 | 170 | 200 | 91 | 0 | 0 | 1450 |
| 1968-69 | 0 | 0 | 0 | 4 | 204 | 440 | 288 | 328 | 339 | 34 | 35 | 0 | 1672 |
| 1969-70 | 0 | 0 | 0 | 55 | 188 | 384 | 455 | 224 | 274 | 132 | 8 | 0 | 1720 |
| 1970-71 | 0 | 0 | 0 | 58 | 143 | 403 | 445 | 350 | 200 | 111 | 12 | 0 | 1722 |
| 1971-72 | 0 | 0 | 0 | 120 | 249 | 548 | 444 | 259 | 73 | 50 | 0 | 0 | 1743 |
| 1972-73 | 0 | 0 | 0 | 96 | 358 | 489 | 533 | 320 | 410 | 174 | 19 | 0 | 2399 |
| 1973-74 | 0 | 0 | 0 | 23 | 216 | 390 | 451 | 362 | 161 | 49 | 5 | 0 | 1657 |
| 1974-75 | 0 | 0 | 0 | 53 | 218 | 552 | 465 | 393 | 299 | 217 | 29 | 0 | 2226 |
| 1975-76 | 0 | 0 | 0 | 38 | 191 | 365 | 378 | 180 | 221 | 88 | 5 | 0 | 1466 |
| 1976-77 | 0 | 0 | 0 | 45 | 178 | 390 | 435 | 221 | 287 | 65 | 9 | 0 | 1630 |
| 1977-78 | 0 | 0 | 0 | 1 | 117 | 242 | 365 | 313 | 144 | 64 | 24 | 0 | 1270 |
| 1978-79 | 0 | 0 | 0 | 5 | 213 | 470 | 511 | 311 | 260 | 76 | 20 | 0 | 1876 |
| 1979-80 | 0 | 0 | 0 | 26 | 252 | 302 | 323 | 202 | 227 | 84 | 3 | 0 | 1419 |
| 1980-81 | 0 | 0 | 0 | 66 | 197 | 210 | 310 | 220 | 244 | 31 | 0 | 0 | 1278 |
| 1981-82 | 0 | 0 | 0 | 34 | 106 | 304 | 437 | 291 | 223 | 46 | 10 | 0 | 1451 |
| 1982-83 | 0 | 0 | 0 | 41 | 211 | 456 | 371 | 309 | 239 | 168 | 6 | 0 | 1801 |
| 1983-84 | 0 | 0 | 0 | 0 | 232 | 348 | 402 | 323 | 140 | 110 | 0 | 0 | 1555 |
| 1984-85 | 0 | 0 | 0 | 49 | 221 | 413 | 448 | 328 | 200 | 41 | 0 | 0 | 1700 |
| 1985-86 | 0 | 0 | 0 | 9 | 217 | 369 | 193 | 244 | 117 | 22 | 6 | 0 | 1177 |
| 1986-87 | 0 | 0 | 0 | 11 | 154 | 387 | 429 | 299 | 225 | 24 | 0 | 0 | 1529 |
| 1987-88 | 0 | 0 | 0 | 0 | 188 | 452 | 366 | 171 | 161 | 46 | 12 | 0 | 1396 |
| 1988-89 | 0 | 0 | 0 | 0 | 220 | 402 | 461 | 199 | 82 | 9 | 4 | 0 | 1377 |
| 1989-90 | 0 | 0 | 0 | 25 | 107 | 361 | 402 | 340 | 156 | 16 | 3 | 0 | 1410 |
| 1990-91 | 0 | 0 | 0 | 5 | 152 | 427 | | | | | | | |

**TABLE 5**  COOLING DEGREE DAYS Base 65 deg. F  TUCSON, ARIZONA

| YEAR | JAN | FEB | MAR | APR | MAY | JUNE | JULY | AUG | SEP | OCT | NOV | DEC | TOTAL |
|---|---|---|---|---|---|---|---|---|---|---|---|---|---|
| 1969 | 0 | 0 | 15 | 87 | 348 | 477 | 658 | 669 | 493 | 118 | 1 | 0 | 2866 |
| 1970 | 0 | 5 | 0 | 25 | 333 | 561 | 693 | 620 | 347 | 68 | 4 | 0 | 2656 |
| 1971 | 6 | 0 | 45 | 51 | 152 | 493 | 706 | 514 | 430 | 101 | 12 | 0 | 2510 |
| 1972 | 0 | 1 | 82 | 82 | 236 | 506 | 678 | 563 | 414 | 150 | 1 | 0 | 2713 |
| 1973 | 0 | 0 | 0 | 21 | 272 | 495 | 603 | 615 | 445 | 206 | 26 | 2 | 2685 |
| 1974 | 0 | 0 | 18 | 87 | 301 | 664 | 581 | 564 | 387 | 185 | 1 | 0 | 2788 |
| 1975 | 0 | 0 | 4 | 11 | 184 | 471 | 604 | 651 | 458 | 182 | 27 | 0 | 2592 |
| 1976 | 2 | 0 | 14 | 89 | 306 | 557 | 597 | 636 | 386 | 139 | 34 | 0 | 2760 |
| 1977 | 0 | 5 | 5 | 133 | 198 | 597 | 691 | 669 | 517 | 266 | 23 | 0 | 3099 |
| 1978 | 0 | 0 | 54 | 76 | 283 | 630 | 721 | 616 | 483 | 293 | 28 | 0 | 3184 |
| 1979 | 0 | 0 | 1 | 101 | 249 | 551 | 706 | 576 | 580 | 282 | 6 | 0 | 3052 |
| 1980 | 0 | 4 | 1 | 109 | 211 | 606 | 742 | 615 | 474 | 216 | 37 | 3 | 3018 |
| 1981 | 0 | 8 | 4 | 159 | 267 | 639 | 633 | 670 | 476 | 137 | 27 | 2 | 3022 |
| 1982 | 0 | 4 | 4 | 82 | 244 | 471 | 622 | 594 | 437 | 112 | 0 | 0 | 2570 |
| 1983 | 0 | 0 | 8 | 36 | 288 | 503 | 688 | 600 | 523 | 145 | 10 | 0 | 2801 |
| 1984 | 0 | 1 | 6 | 87 | 469 | 549 | 601 | 562 | 503 | 96 | 12 | 0 | 2885 |
| 1985 | 0 | 1 | 7 | 159 | 345 | 633 | 704 | 660 | 379 | 173 | 14 | 0 | 3075 |
| 1986 | 2 | 23 | 88 | 150 | 378 | 653 | 643 | 657 | 431 | 158 | 3 | 0 | 3186 |
| 1987 | 0 | 2 | 12 | 184 | 297 | 644 | 702 | 630 | 452 | 325 | 12 | 0 | 3260 |
| 1988 | 2 | 13 | 58 | 142 | 374 | 658 | 716 | 657 | 471 | 327 | 51 | 1 | 3470 |
| 1989 | 0 | 16 | 89 | 281 | 397 | 619 | 780 | 676 | 592 | 221 | 16 | 0 | 3687 |
| 1990 | 0 | 6 | 63 | 164 | 327 | 719 | 625 | 553 | 522 | 262 | 56 | 0 | 3297 |

**TABLE 6**  SNOWFALL (inches)  TUCSON, ARIZONA

| SEASON | JULY | AUG | SEP | OCT | NOV | DEC | JAN | FEB | MAR | APR | MAY | JUNE | TOTAL |
|---|---|---|---|---|---|---|---|---|---|---|---|---|---|
| 1961-62 | 0.0 | 0.0 | 0.0 | 0.0 | 0.0 | 0.0 | 0.0 | T | 0.0 | 0.0 | 0.0 | 0.0 | T |
| 1962-63 | 0.0 | 0.0 | 0.0 | 0.0 | 0.0 | 0.0 | 0.0 | 0.0 | 0.0 | 0.0 | 0.0 | 0.0 | 0.0 |
| 1963-64 | 0.0 | 0.0 | 0.0 | 0.0 | 0.0 | 0.0 | 0.0 | 0.0 | 5.7 | 0.0 | 0.0 | 0.0 | 5.7 |
| 1964-65 | 0.0 | 0.0 | 0.0 | 0.0 | 0.1 | 0.0 | 0.0 | 3.9 | 0.0 | 0.0 | 0.0 | 0.0 | 4.0 |
| 1965-66 | 0.0 | 0.0 | 0.0 | 0.0 | 0.0 | 0.3 | T | 1.2 | 0.0 | 0.0 | 0.0 | 0.0 | 1.5 |
| 1966-67 | 0.0 | 0.0 | 0.0 | 0.0 | 0.0 | 0.0 | 0.0 | 0.0 | 0.0 | T | 0.0 | 0.0 | T |
| 1967-68 | 0.0 | 0.0 | 0.0 | 0.0 | 0.0 | 1.6 | 0.0 | 0.0 | 0.0 | 0.0 | 0.0 | 0.0 | 1.6 |
| 1968-69 | 0.0 | 0.0 | 0.0 | 0.0 | 0.0 | 0.4 | 0.0 | 0.0 | T | 0.0 | 0.0 | 0.0 | 0.4 |
| 1969-70 | 0.0 | 0.0 | 0.0 | 0.0 | 0.0 | 0.0 | 0.0 | 0.0 | T | T | 0.0 | 0.0 | T |
| 1970-71 | 0.0 | 0.0 | 0.0 | 0.0 | 0.0 | 0.0 | T | T | 0.0 | 0.0 | 0.0 | 0.0 | T |
| 1971-72 | 0.0 | 0.0 | 0.0 | 0.0 | 0.0 | 6.8 | 0.0 | 0.0 | 0.0 | 0.0 | 0.0 | 0.0 | 6.8 |
| 1972-73 | 0.0 | 0.0 | 0.0 | 0.0 | 0.0 | 0.0 | T | 0.0 | 0.0 | 0.0 | 0.0 | 0.0 | T |
| 1973-74 | 0.0 | 0.0 | 0.0 | 0.0 | 0.0 | 0.0 | 0.4 | 0.0 | T | 0.0 | 0.0 | 0.0 | 0.4 |
| 1974-75 | 0.0 | 0.0 | 0.0 | 0.0 | T | T | 0.0 | T | 0.5 | 0.0 | 0.0 | 0.0 | 0.5 |
| 1975-76 | 0.0 | 0.0 | 0.0 | 0.0 | T | T | 0.0 | 0.0 | 3.8 | 2.0 | 0.0 | 0.0 | 5.8 |
| 1976-77 | 0.0 | 0.0 | 0.0 | 0.0 | 0.0 | 0.0 | 0.0 | 0.0 | 0.0 | 0.0 | 0.0 | 0.0 | 0.0 |
| 1977-78 | 0.0 | 0.0 | 0.0 | 0.0 | 0.0 | 0.0 | 0.0 | 0.0 | 0.0 | 0.0 | 0.0 | 0.0 | 0.0 |
| 1978-79 | 0.0 | 0.0 | 0.0 | 0.0 | 0.0 | T | 1.2 | 0.0 | 0.0 | 0.0 | 0.0 | 0.0 | 1.2 |
| 1979-80 | 0.0 | 0.0 | 0.0 | 0.0 | 0.0 | 0.0 | 0.0 | 0.0 | T | 0.0 | 0.0 | 0.0 | T |
| 1980-81 | 0.0 | 0.0 | 0.0 | 0.0 | 0.0 | 0.0 | 0.0 | 0.0 | T | 0.0 | 0.0 | 0.0 | T |
| 1981-82 | 0.0 | 0.0 | 0.0 | 0.0 | 0.0 | 0.0 | T | 0.0 | T | 0.0 | 0.0 | 0.0 | T |
| 1982-83 | 0.0 | 0.0 | 0.0 | 0.0 | 0.0 | 0.0 | 0.0 | 0.0 | 0.0 | 0.0 | 0.0 | 0.0 | T |
| 1983-84 | 0.0 | 0.0 | 0.0 | 0.0 | 0.0 | 0.0 | 0.0 | 0.0 | 0.0 | 0.0 | 0.0 | 0.0 | 0.0 |
| 1984-85 | 0.0 | 0.0 | 0.0 | 0.0 | 0.0 | T | 0.0 | 2.2 | 0.0 | 0.0 | 0.0 | 0.0 | 2.2 |
| 1985-86 | 0.0 | 0.0 | 0.0 | 0.0 | 0.0 | 0.0 | 0.0 | T | 0.0 | 0.0 | 0.0 | 0.0 | T |
| 1986-87 | 0.0 | 0.0 | 0.0 | 0.0 | 0.0 | 0.0 | 4.7 | 0.0 | T | 0.0 | 0.0 | 0.0 | 4.7 |
| 1987-88 | 0.0 | 0.0 | 0.0 | 0.0 | 0.0 | 3.6 | 0.0 | 0.0 | 0.0 | 0.0 | 0.0 | 0.0 | 3.6 |
| 1988-89 | 0.0 | 0.0 | 0.0 | 0.0 | 0.0 | T | 0.0 | T | 0.0 | 0.0 | 0.0 | 0.0 | T |
| 1989-90 | 0.0 | 0.0 | 0.0 | 0.0 | 0.0 | 0.0 | 2.7 | 2.3 | T | 0.0 | 0.0 | 0.0 | 5.0 |
| 1990-91 | 0.0 | T | T | 0.0 | 0.0 | 0.6 | | | | | | | |
| Record Mean | 0.0 | T | T | T | 0.1 | 0.3 | 0.4 | 0.2 | 0.3 | 0.1 | 0.0 | 0.0 | 1.4 |

**See Reference Notes, relative to all above tables, on preceding page.**

Little Rock is located on the Arkansas River near the geographical center of the state. It is situated on the dividing line between the Ouachita Mountains to the west and the flat lowlands comprising the Mississippi River Valley to the east. Elevations range from 222 feet at the river level to 257 feet over much of the flat land, including the airport in the southeast, to near 600 feet in the hilly residential area of the western portions of the city. Two minor temperature variations are observed due to the terrain; somewhat lower minimum temperatures are observed in the airport vicinity and a slight downslope adiabatic heating effect accompanies airflow from the ridges and hills in the west and northwest.

The modified continental climate of Little Rock includes exposure to all of the North American air mass types. However, with its proximity to the Gulf of Mexico, the summer season is marked by prolonged periods of warm and humid weather. The growing season averages 233 days in which 62 percent of the normal precipitation occurs. Winters are mild, but polar and Arctic outbreaks are not uncommon.

Precipitation is fairly well distributed throughout the year. Summer rainfall is almost completely of the convective type. The driest period usually occurs in the late summer and early fall. Snow is almost negligible. Glaze and ice storms, although infrequent, are at times severe. Warm front weather in the winter and early spring, characterized by shallow surface cold air flow from the north under warm moist Gulf air, results in excellent conditions for the production of freezing precipitation.

**TABLE 1**     # NORMALS, MEANS AND EXTREMES

LITTLE ROCK, ARKANSAS

LATITUDE: 34°44'N   LONGITUDE: 92°14'W   ELEVATION: FT. GRND 257 BARO 260   TIME ZONE: CENTRAL   WBAN: 13963

| | (a) | JAN | FEB | MAR | APR | MAY | JUNE | JULY | AUG | SEP | OCT | NOV | DEC | YEAR |
|---|---|---|---|---|---|---|---|---|---|---|---|---|---|---|
| **TEMPERATURE °F:** | | | | | | | | | | | | | | |
| Normals | | | | | | | | | | | | | | |
| -Daily Maximum | | 49.8 | 54.5 | 63.2 | 73.8 | 81.7 | 89.5 | 92.7 | 92.3 | 85.6 | 75.8 | 62.4 | 53.2 | 72.9 |
| -Daily Minimum | | 29.9 | 33.6 | 41.2 | 50.9 | 59.2 | 67.5 | 71.4 | 69.6 | 63.0 | 50.4 | 40.0 | 33.2 | 50.8 |
| -Monthly | | 39.9 | 44.1 | 52.2 | 62.4 | 70.5 | 78.5 | 82.1 | 81.0 | 74.3 | 63.1 | 51.2 | 43.2 | 61.9 |
| Extremes | | | | | | | | | | | | | | |
| -Record Highest | 48 | 83 | 85 | 91 | 95 | 98 | 105 | 112 | 108 | 106 | 97 | 86 | 80 | 112 |
| -Year | | 1950 | 1986 | 1974 | 1987 | 1964 | 1988 | 1986 | 1980 | 1947 | 1963 | 1955 | 1956 | JUL 1986 |
| -Record Lowest | 48 | -4 | -5 | 11 | 28 | 40 | 46 | 54 | 52 | 37 | 29 | 17 | -1 | -5 |
| -Year | | 1962 | 1951 | 1951 | 1971 | 1971 | 1969 | 1972 | 1986 | 1942 | 1989 | 1976 | 1989 | FEB 1951 |
| **NORMAL DEGREE DAYS:** | | | | | | | | | | | | | | |
| Heating (base 65°F) | | 778 | 585 | 417 | 124 | 18 | 0 | 0 | 0 | 8 | 132 | 414 | 676 | 3152 |
| Cooling (base 65°F) | | 0 | 0 | 20 | 46 | 188 | 405 | 530 | 496 | 287 | 73 | 0 | 0 | 2045 |
| **% OF POSSIBLE SUNSHINE** | 32 | 46 | 54 | 57 | 62 | 68 | 73 | 71 | 73 | 68 | 69 | 56 | 48 | 62 |
| **MEAN SKY COVER (tenths)** | | | | | | | | | | | | | | |
| Sunrise - Sunset | 35 | 6.5 | 6.0 | 6.2 | 6.1 | 6.0 | 5.4 | 5.5 | 5.0 | 5.2 | 4.5 | 5.5 | 6.2 | 5.7 |
| **MEAN NUMBER OF DAYS:** | | | | | | | | | | | | | | |
| Sunrise to Sunset | | | | | | | | | | | | | | |
| -Clear | 35 | 8.6 | 9.1 | 8.6 | 8.7 | 8.0 | 9.5 | 8.8 | 11.6 | 11.2 | 14.4 | 11.0 | 9.2 | 118.7 |
| -Partly Cloudy | 35 | 6.1 | 5.7 | 7.0 | 7.5 | 10.8 | 11.6 | 12.9 | 10.9 | 8.6 | 7.1 | 5.9 | 5.9 | 99.9 |
| -Cloudy | 35 | 16.3 | 13.5 | 15.4 | 13.8 | 12.3 | 8.9 | 9.3 | 8.5 | 10.1 | 9.5 | 13.1 | 16.0 | 146.6 |
| Precipitation | | | | | | | | | | | | | | |
| .01 inches or more | 47 | 9.4 | 9.1 | 10.1 | 10.1 | 10.0 | 8.3 | 8.2 | 7.0 | 7.3 | 6.7 | 8.2 | 9.1 | 103.6 |
| Snow,Ice pellets | | | | | | | | | | | | | | |
| 1.0 inches or more | 47 | 1.0 | 0.5 | 0.2 | 0.0 | 0.0 | 0.0 | 0.0 | 0.0 | 0.0 | 0.0 | 0.1 | 0.2 | 2.0 |
| Thunderstorms | 47 | 1.8 | 2.4 | 4.9 | 6.4 | 7.4 | 7.6 | 8.7 | 6.4 | 3.7 | 2.4 | 3.0 | 1.9 | 56.6 |
| Heavy Fog Visibility 1/4 mile or less | 47 | 2.8 | 1.8 | 1.1 | 0.8 | 0.8 | 0.3 | 0.5 | 0.7 | 1.0 | 1.8 | 1.9 | 2.5 | 15.9 |
| Temperature °F | | | | | | | | | | | | | | |
| -Maximum | | | | | | | | | | | | | | |
| 90° and above | 29 | 0.0 | 0.0 | 0.* | 0.3 | 3.9 | 16.1 | 22.0 | 19.7 | 8.8 | 1.3 | 0.0 | 0.0 | 72.1 |
| 32° and below | 29 | 3.8 | 1.1 | 0.1 | 0.0 | 0.0 | 0.0 | 0.0 | 0.0 | 0.0 | 0.0 | 0.* | 1.6 | 6.6 |
| -Minimum | | | | | | | | | | | | | | |
| 32° and below | 29 | 21.0 | 14.2 | 4.6 | 0.5 | 0.0 | 0.0 | 0.0 | 0.0 | 0.0 | 0.2 | 5.4 | 15.6 | 61.4 |
| 0° and below | 29 | 0.1 | 0.0 | 0.0 | 0.0 | 0.0 | 0.0 | 0.0 | 0.0 | 0.0 | 0.0 | 0.0 | 0.1 | 0.2 |
| **AVG. STATION PRESS. (mb)** | 17 | 1012.2 | 1010.5 | 1006.6 | 1006.0 | 1004.8 | 1005.7 | 1006.7 | 1007.0 | 1007.8 | 1009.8 | 1009.7 | 1011.4 | 1008.2 |
| **RELATIVE HUMIDITY (%)** | | | | | | | | | | | | | | |
| Hour 00 | 29 | 76 | 74 | 71 | 74 | 82 | 82 | 83 | 84 | 85 | 82 | 78 | 76 | 79 |
| Hour 06 (Local Time) | 29 | 80 | 80 | 79 | 82 | 87 | 86 | 88 | 88 | 89 | 86 | 83 | 80 | 84 |
| Hour 12 | 29 | 61 | 59 | 56 | 56 | 57 | 55 | 57 | 56 | 58 | 53 | 59 | 62 | 57 |
| Hour 18 | 29 | 64 | 59 | 55 | 55 | 59 | 57 | 60 | 60 | 64 | 63 | 65 | 65 | 61 |
| **PRECIPITATION (inches):** | | | | | | | | | | | | | | |
| Water Equivalent | | | | | | | | | | | | | | |
| -Normal | | 3.91 | 3.83 | 4.69 | 5.41 | 5.29 | 3.67 | 3.63 | 3.07 | 4.26 | 2.84 | 4.37 | 4.23 | 49.20 |
| -Maximum Monthly | 48 | 12.53 | 11.02 | 9.49 | 14.20 | 12.74 | 7.82 | 7.95 | 14.46 | 10.17 | 15.35 | 13.14 | 16.48 | 16.48 |
| -Year | | 1950 | 1956 | 1953 | 1973 | 1968 | 1974 | 1988 | 1966 | 1978 | 1984 | 1988 | 1987 | DEC 1987 |
| -Minimum Monthly | 48 | 0.50 | 0.51 | 0.73 | 0.50 | 0.69 | T | 0.14 | 0.19 | 0.28 | 0.01 | 0.28 | 1.26 | T |
| -Year | | 1986 | 1947 | 1966 | 1987 | 1970 | 1952 | 1986 | 1980 | 1956 | 1944 | 1949 | 1958 | JUN 1952 |
| -Maximum in 24 hrs | 42 | 5.18 | 5.15 | 3.40 | 7.96 | 7.71 | 4.61 | 3.58 | 7.32 | 4.05 | 5.17 | 7.81 | 7.01 | 7.96 |
| -Year | | 1969 | 1950 | 1944 | 1974 | 1955 | 1960 | 1988 | 1966 | 1967 | 1984 | 1988 | 1987 | APR 1974 |
| Snow,Ice pellets | | | | | | | | | | | | | | |
| -Maximum Monthly | 48 | 13.6 | 9.8 | 7.0 | T | 0.0 | 0.0 | 0.0 | 0.0 | 0.0 | 0.0 | 4.8 | 9.8 | 13.6 |
| -Year | | 1988 | 1979 | 1971 | 1983 | | | | | | | 1971 | 1963 | JAN 1988 |
| -Maximum in 24 hrs | 42 | 12.1 | 9.6 | 6.7 | T | T | 0.0 | 0.0 | 0.0 | 0.0 | 0.0 | 4.8 | 9.8 | 12.1 |
| -Year | | 1988 | 1966 | 1971 | 1989 | 1988 | | | | | | 1971 | 1963 | JAN 1988 |
| **WIND:** | | | | | | | | | | | | | | |
| Mean Speed (mph) | 47 | 8.6 | 9.0 | 9.7 | 9.1 | 7.7 | 7.2 | 6.7 | 6.4 | 6.7 | 6.8 | 8.0 | 8.3 | 7.9 |
| Prevailing Direction through 1963 | | S | SW | WNW | S | S | SSW | SW | SW | NE | SW | SW | SW | SW |
| Fastest Mile | | | | | | | | | | | | | | |
| -Direction (!!!) | 36 | S | SW | SE | NW | NW | NE | NW | NW | NW | SSW | SW | SW | NW |
| -Speed (MPH) | 36 | 44 | 57 | 56 | 65 | 61 | 60 | 56 | 54 | 50 | 58 | 49 | 48 | 65 |
| -Year | | 1950 | 1971 | 1959 | 1961 | 1952 | 1953 | 1960 | 1956 | 1952 | 1956 | 1952 | 1971 | APR 1961 |
| Peak Gust | | | | | | | | | | | | | | |
| -Direction (!!!) | | | | | | | | | | | | | | |
| -Speed (mph) | | | | | | | | | | | | | | |
| -Date | | | | | | | | | | | | | | |

**See Reference Notes to this table on the following page.**

# LITTLE ROCK, ARKANSAS

PRECIPITATION (inches)   LITTLE ROCK, ARKANSAS

**TABLE 2**

| YEAR | JAN | FEB | MAR | APR | MAY | JUNE | JULY | AUG | SEP | OCT | NOV | DEC | ANNUAL |
|---|---|---|---|---|---|---|---|---|---|---|---|---|---|
| 1961 | 0.75 | 3.65 | 8.07 | 3.38 | 5.68 | 1.48 | 2.64 | 3.14 | 1.60 | 0.85 | 6.11 | 7.15 | 44.50 |
| 1962 | 6.84 | 7.19 | 5.17 | 2.90 | 2.31 | 6.26 | 3.10 | 2.40 | 3.83 | 3.54 | 1.69 | 1.65 | 46.88 |
| 1963 | 0.87 | 2.70 | 3.81 | 3.29 | 1.29 | 1.25 | 5.54 | 0.62 | 1.81 | 0.10 | 4.50 | 2.48 | 28.26 |
| 1964 | 0.98 | 2.87 | 8.22 | 11.06 | 1.40 | 0.31 | 3.79 | 3.71 | 5.46 | 0.37 | 3.70 | 4.37 | 46.24 |
| 1965 | 4.45 | 5.73 | 3.63 | 1.19 | 5.42 | 2.49 | 2.51 | 2.03 | 7.67 | 0.21 | 1.54 | 2.05 | 39.92 |
| 1966 | 3.03 | 5.02 | 0.73 | 7.29 | 2.23 | 0.69 | 3.54 | 14.46 | 1.42 | 1.95 | 3.08 | 4.21 | 47.65 |
| 1967 | 2.13 | 2.31 | 3.11 | 7.58 | 8.69 | 3.02 | 4.29 | 1.73 | 6.25 | 4.96 | 1.73 | 4.95 | 50.75 |
| 1968 | 4.76 | 1.08 | 5.55 | 4.85 | 12.74 | 6.77 | 5.98 | 0.26 | 5.99 | 2.81 | 5.30 | 4.56 | 60.65 |
| 1969 | 8.06 | 2.41 | 3.65 | 4.30 | 3.60 | 2.98 | 3.40 | 2.73 | 2.33 | 3.60 | 8.10 | 3.94 | 49.10 |
| 1970 | 1.05 | 4.57 | 4.87 | 7.99 | 0.69 | 2.30 | 3.02 | 2.15 | 2.82 | 7.68 | 2.09 | 3.85 | 43.08 |
| 1971 | 2.07 | 2.21 | 3.24 | 1.70 | 5.37 | 7.66 | 4.01 | 8.62 | 0.78 | 2.55 | 3.38 | 6.97 | 48.56 |
| 1972 | 1.71 | 1.55 | 3.32 | 1.81 | 2.07 | 2.62 | 1.77 | 3.58 | 6.43 | 7.63 | 7.38 | 5.14 | 45.01 |
| 1973 | 5.64 | 2.95 | 7.89 | 14.20 | 3.96 | 2.66 | 6.59 | 1.26 | 9.09 | 5.93 | 9.03 | 5.19 | 74.39 |
| 1974 | 5.77 | 2.60 | 2.07 | 9.76 | 6.26 | 7.82 | 4.09 | 3.20 | 4.31 | 3.36 | 5.73 | 2.99 | 57.96 |
| 1975 | 4.64 | 4.38 | 7.67 | 4.14 | 5.87 | 1.56 | 3.98 | 2.73 | 1.86 | 1.62 | 3.68 | 2.92 | 45.05 |
| 1976 | 3.00 | 5.12 | 5.43 | 1.06 | 4.88 | 5.69 | 1.97 | 0.70 | 1.82 | 6.04 | 1.79 | 2.30 | 39.80 |
| 1977 | 2.70 | 1.96 | 6.75 | 4.47 | 2.89 | 4.70 | 5.07 | 1.37 | 6.38 | 0.63 | 9.34 | 1.40 | 47.66 |
| 1978 | 5.44 | 1.52 | 3.56 | 4.22 | 6.27 | 5.39 | 2.70 | 6.38 | 10.17 | 1.01 | 6.64 | 11.56 | 64.86 |
| 1979 | 4.05 | 5.67 | 3.10 | 9.64 | 11.54 | 4.45 | 4.27 | 6.51 | 4.35 | 3.36 | 4.02 | 3.53 | 64.49 |
| 1980 | 2.73 | 0.89 | 6.60 | 5.85 | 4.57 | 0.53 | 0.99 | 0.19 | 5.09 | 2.64 | 6.28 | 1.86 | 38.22 |
| 1981 | 1.11 | 3.89 | 4.00 | 2.75 | 9.73 | 7.80 | 3.15 | 2.91 | 1.37 | 6.11 | 1.64 | 1.34 | 45.80 |
| 1982 | 8.74 | 3.37 | 2.87 | 9.32 | 5.63 | 4.10 | 1.01 | 4.52 | 1.47 | 2.26 | 8.28 | 9.72 | 61.29 |
| 1983 | 2.25 | 1.49 | 4.19 | 6.72 | 7.58 | 3.34 | 1.07 | 0.79 | 0.41 | 3.73 | 4.47 | 9.07 | 45.11 |
| 1984 | 1.31 | 3.52 | 5.58 | 3.77 | 8.22 | 1.06 | 4.15 | 5.69 | 3.28 | 15.35 | 8.49 | 3.54 | 63.96 |
| 1985 | 3.11 | 2.78 | 5.27 | 8.63 | 2.99 | 2.40 | 3.30 | 3.52 | 4.36 | 3.91 | 5.78 | 2.97 | 49.02 |
| 1986 | 0.50 | 3.45 | 3.68 | 7.33 | 4.07 | 6.42 | 0.14 | 4.56 | 1.94 | 6.05 | 5.67 | 3.86 | 47.67 |
| 1987 | 2.07 | 7.07 | 3.52 | 0.50 | 4.56 | 4.63 | 1.60 | 2.12 | 7.56 | 1.37 | 10.96 | 16.48 | 62.44 |
| 1988 | 3.71 | 3.41 | 3.50 | 3.82 | 2.05 | 1.04 | 7.95 | 2.19 | 2.54 | 1.95 | 13.14 | 2.91 | 48.21 |
| 1989 | 3.01 | 9.55 | 7.64 | 2.57 | 4.04 | 3.95 | 7.87 | 1.21 | 3.57 | 1.70 | 1.95 | 2.19 | 49.25 |
| 1990 | 6.50 | 4.82 | 10.40 | 7.73 | 7.71 | 0.80 | 4.63 | 1.57 | 4.08 | 8.75 | 3.29 | 6.79 | 67.07 |
| Record Mean | 4.51 | 3.93 | 4.71 | 5.14 | 5.04 | 3.66 | 3.42 | 3.29 | 3.39 | 3.08 | 4.39 | 4.30 | 48.83 |

**TABLE 3**  AVERAGE TEMPERATURE (deg. F)   LITTLE ROCK, ARKANSAS

| YEAR | JAN | FEB | MAR | APR | MAY | JUNE | JULY | AUG | SEP | OCT | NOV | DEC | ANNUAL |
|---|---|---|---|---|---|---|---|---|---|---|---|---|---|
| 1961 | 35.9 | 47.7 | 55.9 | 60.4 | 67.9 | 75.8 | 80.7 | 78.8 | 74.3 | 63.4 | 51.1 | 41.7 | 61.1 |
| 1962 | 37.2 | 49.2 | 49.5 | 59.5 | 75.3 | 77.7 | 81.9 | 82.8 | 73.2 | 66.3 | 53.3 | 33.4 | 62.1 |
| 1963 | 34.0 | 39.4 | 57.7 | 64.3 | 71.4 | 80.4 | 81.5 | 81.1 | 73.7 | 60.1 | 54.0 | 43.9 | 61.8 |
| 1964 | 40.8 | 41.6 | 52.7 | 64.7 | 72.3 | 78.2 | 82.9 | 81.7 | 74.3 | 61.6 | 56.5 | 46.7 | 62.7 |
| 1965 | 44.2 | 43.2 | 44.5 | 65.8 | 72.7 | 78.2 | 82.9 | 81.2 | 72.0 | 59.2 | 54.8 | 43.2 | 61.1 |
| 1966 | 35.4 | 42.9 | 54.6 | 62.4 | 68.4 | 78.0 | 84.2 | 77.9 | 72.0 | 59.2 | 49.1 | 42.7 | 60.9 |
| 1967 | 41.7 | 40.4 | 58.9 | 66.7 | 68.6 | 79.5 | 77.9 | 75.5 | 69.0 | 60.9 | 51.2 | 42.7 | 59.9 |
| 1968 | 37.7 | 38.0 | 50.8 | 60.9 | 67.6 | 77.8 | 77.8 | 79.0 | 72.9 | 62.4 | 49.4 | 40.7 | 60.9 |
| 1969 | 43.5 | 43.0 | 45.5 | 61.8 | 69.9 | 77.6 | 79.9 | 81.2 | 78.1 | 61.1 | 50.3 | 47.2 | 61.5 |
| 1970 | 35.7 | 42.1 | 48.2 | 63.1 | 71.9 | 78.7 | 79.9 | 81.2 | 78.1 | 50.5 | 49.9 | 49.9 | 62.0 |
| 1971 | 41.0 | 44.4 | 50.0 | 59.4 | 65.6 | 79.3 | 80.0 | 78.0 | 76.4 | 69.3 | 47.3 | 41.0 | 62.0 |
| 1972 | 43.6 | 46.7 | 53.3 | 62.5 | 69.8 | 79.4 | 80.4 | 81.1 | 75.8 | 62.6 | 47.8 | 42.8 | 62.6 |
| 1973 | 39.7 | 42.1 | 58.2 | 59.9 | 68.2 | 78.6 | 81.1 | 80.4 | 75.7 | 67.6 | 51.9 | 44.9 | 61.9 |
| 1974 | 42.4 | 45.7 | 58.1 | 60.7 | 71.3 | 74.3 | 83.2 | 79.0 | 69.0 | 62.3 | 51.4 | 42.9 | 61.3 |
| 1975 | 44.6 | 44.6 | 48.7 | 60.7 | 72.5 | 78.6 | 80.2 | 79.5 | 69.2 | 63.0 | 51.4 | 41.9 | 60.4 |
| 1976 | 39.7 | 52.5 | 56.5 | 61.1 | 64.6 | 74.4 | 80.2 | 78.7 | 72.1 | 57.8 | 45.9 | 41.9 | 60.4 |
| 1977 | 31.3 | 46.9 | 56.4 | 64.7 | 73.7 | 80.0 | 82.1 | 80.4 | 77.3 | 62.6 | 52.9 | 42.0 | 62.5 |
| 1978 | 31.7 | 34.0 | 51.0 | 65.9 | 71.4 | 78.9 | 84.1 | 83.0 | 76.7 | 62.0 | 54.6 | 43.3 | 61.4 |
| 1979 | 29.9 | 38.7 | 55.5 | 62.7 | 70.2 | 77.9 | 81.0 | 79.0 | 72.7 | 65.3 | 50.3 | 45.8 | 60.7 |
| 1980 | 44.0 | 40.9 | 50.3 | 61.5 | 70.6 | 79.4 | 88.1 | 87.0 | 78.6 | 60.4 | 50.4 | 43.1 | 62.9 |
| 1981 | 39.7 | 44.6 | 52.5 | 67.5 | 67.4 | 80.1 | 83.5 | 79.9 | 75.3 | 61.4 | 55.5 | 43.2 | 62.5 |
| 1982 | 37.5 | 41.3 | 57.1 | 58.0 | 72.7 | 76.6 | 83.1 | 82.1 | 74.2 | 64.7 | 53.2 | 48.3 | 62.4 |
| 1983 | 39.2 | 43.8 | 51.1 | 54.4 | 67.7 | 77.4 | 82.5 | 86.1 | 76.0 | 64.0 | 50.8 | 30.9 | 60.3 |
| 1984 | 36.7 | 46.6 | 50.1 | 59.7 | 68.0 | 79.8 | 79.7 | 78.1 | 71.0 | 65.0 | 49.0 | 52.1 | 61.3 |
| 1985 | 33.7 | 39.3 | 57.6 | 63.0 | 70.0 | 78.2 | 81.2 | 80.8 | 72.5 | 66.2 | 56.1 | 38.1 | 61.4 |
| 1986 | 42.5 | 48.2 | 55.4 | 63.6 | 71.4 | 79.7 | 86.3 | 78.1 | 77.6 | 63.1 | 49.7 | 42.4 | 63.2 |
| 1987 | 40.2 | 47.1 | 53.4 | 62.4 | 76.3 | 79.9 | 82.2 | 84.4 | 74.9 | 59.1 | 53.0 | 45.2 | 63.2 |
| 1988 | 35.6 | 42.9 | 52.2 | 61.5 | 70.4 | 78.8 | 81.7 | 82.4 | 75.8 | 60.4 | 53.3 | 44.4 | 61.6 |
| 1989 | 46.3 | 38.4 | 52.5 | 62.6 | 69.6 | 76.2 | 79.3 | 80.2 | 71.2 | 63.3 | 55.3 | 35.7 | 60.9 |
| 1990 | 48.1 | 51.3 | 55.4 | 62.0 | 68.1 | 80.6 | 83.2 | 82.2 | 77.5 | 61.5 | 56.3 | 43.1 | 64.1 |
| Record Mean | 41.3 | 44.6 | 53.0 | 62.4 | 70.2 | 78.3 | 81.5 | 80.6 | 74.3 | 63.6 | 51.9 | 43.7 | 62.1 |
| Max | 50.0 | 53.8 | 62.8 | 72.5 | 80.0 | 88.0 | 91.1 | 90.4 | 84.5 | 74.4 | 61.7 | 52.3 | 71.8 |
| Min | 32.5 | 35.4 | 43.2 | 52.3 | 60.3 | 68.5 | 71.8 | 70.8 | 64.0 | 52.8 | 42.1 | 35.0 | 52.4 |

## REFERENCE NOTES FOR TABLES 1, 2, 3 and 6   (LITTLE ROCK AR)

**GENERAL**

T - TRACE AMOUNT
BLANK ENTRIES DENOTE MISSING/UNREPORTED DATA.
# INDICATES A STATION OR INSTRUMENT RELOCATION.

**SPECIFIC**

**TABLE 1**

(a) - LENGTH OF RECORD IN YEARS. ALTHOUGH INDIVIDUAL MONTHS MAY BE MISSING.

* LESS THAN .05

NORMALS — BASED ON THE 1951-1980 RECORD PERIOD.
EXTREMES — DATES ARE THE MOST RECENT OCCURRENCE.
WIND DIR. — NUMERALS SHOW TENS OF DEGREES CLOCKWISE FROM TRUE NORTH. "00" INDICATES CALM.
RESULTANT WIND DIRECTIONS ARE GIVEN TO WHOLE DEGREES.

**TABLE 3**
MAX AND MIN ARE LONG-TERM MEAN DAILY MAXIMUM AND MEAN DAILY MINIMUM TEMPERATURES.

**EXCEPTIONS**

**TABLE 1**

1. PRECIPITATION DATA DECEMBER 15, 1975 THROUGH OCTOBER 1976 IS FROM NORTH LITTLE ROCK
2. WIND DATA FROM DECEMBER 15, 1975 THROUGH DECEMBER 1976 IS FROM NORHT LITTLE ROCK.
3. MAXIMUM 24-HOUR PRECIPITATION AND SNOW, FASTEST MILE WINDS, MEAN SKY COVER, AND DAYS CLEAR-PARTLY CLOUDY-CLOUDY ARE THROUGH 1977.
4. PERCENT OF POSSIBLE SUNSHINE IS THROUGH 1975.

**TABLES 2, 3, and 6**

RECORD MEANS ARE THROUGH THE CURRENT YEAR,
BEGINNING IN   1880 FOR TEMPERATURE
             1880 FOR PRECIPITATION
             1943 FOR SNOWFALL

**TABLE 4**

HEATING DEGREE DAYS Base 65 deg. F     LITTLE ROCK, ARKANSAS

| SEASON | JULY | AUG | SEP | OCT | NOV | DEC | JAN | FEB | MAR | APR | MAY | JUNE | TOTAL |
|---|---|---|---|---|---|---|---|---|---|---|---|---|---|
| 1961-62 | 0 | 0 | 10 | 120 | 425 | 719 | 857 | 445 | 471 | 198 | 5 | 0 | 3250 |
| 1962-63 | 0 | 0 | 17 | 78 | 421 | 714 | 954 | 709 | 258 | 97 | 35 | 0 | 3283 |
| 1963-64 | 0 | 0 | 4 | 26 | 350 | 973 | 742 | 673 | 376 | 71 | 9 | 0 | 3224 |
| 1964-65 | 0 | 0 | 14 | 175 | 336 | 646 | 639 | 604 | 629 | 70 | 0 | 0 | 3113 |
| 1965-66 | 0 | 0 | 19 | 137 | 257 | 561 | 916 | 611 | 327 | 115 | 42 | 0 | 2985 |
| 1966-67 | 0 | 0 | 3 | 198 | 309 | 679 | 717 | 682 | 240 | 52 | 33 | 0 | 2913 |
| 1967-68 | 0 | 0 | 39 | 162 | 472 | 685 | 840 | 778 | 440 | 147 | 30 | 0 | 3593 |
| 1968-69 | 0 | 0 | 3 | 124 | 412 | 700 | 665 | 611 | 595 | 108 | 16 | 1 | 3235 |
| 1969-70 | 0 | 0 | 0 | 175 | 458 | 745 | 905 | 636 | 516 | 124 | 23 | 0 | 3582 |
| 1970-71 | 0 | 0 | 4 | 153 | 442 | 554 | 737 | 571 | 470 | 182 | 55 | 0 | 3168 |
| 1971-72 | 0 | 0 | 9 | 6 | 437 | 466 | 659 | 525 | 360 | 149 | 20 | 0 | 2631 |
| 1972-73 | 0 | 0 | 8 | 142 | 530 | 736 | 777 | 637 | 216 | 186 | 28 | 0 | 3260 |
| 1973-74 | 0 | 0 | 2 | 61 | 261 | 680 | 690 | 533 | 255 | 163 | 4 | 0 | 2649 |
| 1974-75 | 0 | 0 | 23 | 111 | 401 | 634 | 630 | 566 | 499 | 196 | 5 | 0 | 3065 |
| 1975-76 | 0 | 0 | 48 | 130 | 414 | 681 | 777 | 359 | 284 | 146 | 70 | 0 | 2909 |
| 1976-77 | 0 | 0 | 1 | 257 | 567 | 710 | 1041 | 502 | 265 | 70 | 10 | 0 | 3423 |
| 1977-78 | 0 | 0 | 0 | 105 | 370 | 709 | 1025 | 862 | 436 | 68 | 48 | 0 | 3623 |
| 1978-79 | 0 | 0 | 0 | 118 | 321 | 667 | 1083 | 732 | 314 | 110 | 13 | 0 | 3358 |
| 1979-80 | 0 | 0 | 0 | 80 | 436 | 588 | 645 | 693 | 450 | 142 | 15 | 0 | 3049 |
| 1980-81 | 0 | 0 | 16 | 184 | 437 | 673 | 774 | 565 | 388 | 37 | 45 | 0 | 3119 |
| 1981-82 | 0 | 0 | 4 | 186 | 278 | 668 | 847 | 656 | 298 | 223 | 6 | 0 | 3166 |
| 1982-83 | 0 | 0 | 12 | 119 | 369 | 536 | 795 | 587 | 425 | 332 | 33 | 0 | 3208 |
| 1983-84 | 0 | 0 | 19 | 89 | 422 | 1050 | 872 | 530 | 460 | 190 | 24 | 0 | 3656 |
| 1984-85 | 0 | 0 | 44 | 81 | 476 | 408 | 962 | 713 | 251 | 101 | 8 | 0 | 3044 |
| 1985-86 | 0 | 0 | 31 | 82 | 283 | 825 | 691 | 467 | 298 | 91 | 7 | 0 | 2775 |
| 1986-87 | 0 | 1 | 0 | 112 | 454 | 694 | 762 | 496 | 353 | 145 | 0 | 0 | 3017 |
| 1987-88 | 0 | 0 | 0 | 182 | 358 | 609 | 904 | 637 | 388 | 123 | 4 | 0 | 3205 |
| 1988-89 | 0 | 0 | 1 | 163 | 358 | 633 | 573 | 738 | 395 | 156 | 39 | 0 | 3056 |
| 1989-90 | 0 | 0 | 23 | 112 | 313 | 898 | 516 | 380 | 316 | 152 | 31 | 0 | 2741 |
| 1990-91 | 0 | 0 | 8 | 173 | 260 | 675 | | | | | | | |

**TABLE 5**

COOLING DEGREE DAYS Base 65 deg. F     LITTLE ROCK, ARKANSAS

| YEAR | JAN | FEB | MAR | APR | MAY | JUNE | JULY | AUG | SEP | OCT | NOV | DEC | TOTAL |
|---|---|---|---|---|---|---|---|---|---|---|---|---|---|
| 1969 | 4 | 0 | 0 | 21 | 176 | 386 | 622 | 439 | 243 | 100 | 0 | 0 | 1991 |
| 1970 | 3 | 0 | 0 | 77 | 243 | 416 | 416 | 511 | 404 | 51 | 9 | 9 | 2194 |
| 1971 | 0 | 0 | 11 | 19 | 79 | 435 | 470 | 411 | 355 | 146 | 10 | 3 | 1939 |
| 1972 | 2 | 0 | 3 | 81 | 174 | 440 | 484 | 507 | 341 | 76 | 3 | 0 | 2111 |
| 1973 | 0 | 0 | 14 | 41 | 135 | 415 | 506 | 485 | 330 | 147 | 17 | 0 | 2090 |
| 1974 | 0 | 0 | 45 | 37 | 206 | 288 | 572 | 441 | 148 | 36 | 14 | 0 | 1787 |
| 1975 | 6 | 0 | 4 | 73 | 245 | 416 | 475 | 455 | 178 | 73 | 14 | 2 | 1941 |
| 1976 | 0 | 5 | 27 | 37 | 65 | 292 | 434 | 434 | 220 | 42 | 0 | 0 | 1602 |
| 1977 | 0 | 0 | 7 | 67 | 287 | 455 | 537 | 482 | 377 | 40 | 14 | 0 | 2266 |
| 1978 | 0 | 0 | 9 | 104 | 253 | 424 | 599 | 565 | 357 | 31 | 16 | 0 | 2358 |
| 1979 | 0 | 0 | 24 | 48 | 178 | 396 | 502 | 442 | 240 | 95 | 1 | 0 | 1926 |
| 1980 | 0 | 1 | 1 | 42 | 196 | 439 | 725 | 688 | 432 | 50 | 5 | 0 | 2579 |
| 1981 | 0 | 0 | 9 | 117 | 131 | 458 | 580 | 470 | 318 | 78 | 2 | 0 | 2163 |
| 1982 | 0 | 0 | 57 | 21 | 253 | 355 | 570 | 540 | 294 | 114 | 20 | 24 | 2248 |
| 1983 | 0 | 0 | 0 | 21 | 121 | 381 | 550 | 660 | 355 | 63 | 6 | 0 | 2157 |
| 1984 | 0 | 1 | 4 | 38 | 126 | 451 | 462 | 416 | 234 | 88 | 3 | 17 | 1840 |
| 1985 | 0 | 0 | 31 | 48 | 167 | 404 | 508 | 501 | 265 | 125 | 21 | 0 | 2070 |
| 1986 | 0 | 5 | 7 | 56 | 211 | 446 | 668 | 415 | 385 | 63 | 0 | 0 | 2256 |
| 1987 | 0 | 0 | 3 | 74 | 359 | 456 | 540 | 610 | 304 | 8 | 3 | 0 | 2357 |
| 1988 | 0 | 0 | 2 | 24 | 177 | 423 | 523 | 546 | 332 | 25 | 15 | 0 | 2067 |
| 1989 | 0 | 0 | 13 | 91 | 189 | 345 | 450 | 479 | 213 | 70 | 29 | 0 | 1879 |
| 1990 | 0 | 4 | 26 | 67 | 135 | 475 | 571 | 540 | 392 | 73 | 8 | 0 | 2291 |

**TABLE 6**

SNOWFALL (inches)     LITTLE ROCK, ARKANSAS

| SEASON | JULY | AUG | SEP | OCT | NOV | DEC | JAN | FEB | MAR | APR | MAY | JUNE | TOTAL |
|---|---|---|---|---|---|---|---|---|---|---|---|---|---|
| 1961-62 | 0.0 | 0.0 | 0.0 | 0.0 | T | 1.5 | 6.0 | T | T | 0.0 | 0.0 | 0.0 | 6.0 |
| 1962-63 | 0.0 | 0.0 | 0.0 | 0.0 | 0.0 | 0.7 | 0.7 | 0.4 | T | 0.0 | 0.0 | 0.0 | 2.6 |
| 1963-64 | 0.0 | 0.0 | 0.0 | 0.0 | 0.0 | 9.8 | T | 0.0 | T | 0.0 | 0.0 | 0.0 | 9.8 |
| 1964-65 | 0.0 | 0.0 | 0.0 | 0.0 | 0.0 | 0.2 | T | 2.9 | 4.3 | 0.0 | 0.0 | 0.0 | 7.4 |
| 1965-66 | 0.0 | 0.0 | 0.0 | 0.0 | 0.0 | 0.0 | 12.0 | 9.6 | 0.0 | 0.0 | 0.0 | 0.0 | 21.6 |
| 1966-67 | 0.0 | 0.0 | 0.0 | 0.0 | T | 0.2 | 1.6 | T | T | 0.0 | 0.0 | 0.0 | 1.8 |
| 1967-68 | 0.0 | 0.0 | 0.0 | 0.0 | T | 1.1 | 1.0 | 4.3 | T | 0.0 | 0.0 | 0.0 | 6.4 |
| 1968-69 | 0.0 | 0.0 | 0.0 | 0.0 | 0.0 | 0.0 | T | 2.3 | T | 0.0 | 0.0 | 0.0 | 2.3 |
| 1969-70 | 0.0 | 0.0 | 0.0 | 0.0 | T | T | 4.0 | T | T | 0.0 | 0.0 | 0.0 | 4.0 |
| 1970-71 | 0.0 | 0.0 | 0.0 | 0.0 | 0.0 | T | T | 0.7 | 7.0 | T | 0.0 | 0.0 | 7.7 |
| 1971-72 | 0.0 | 0.0 | 0.0 | 0.0 | 4.8 | 0.6 | 0.1 | 0.3 | 0.0 | 0.0 | 0.0 | 0.0 | 5.8 |
| 1972-73 | 0.0 | 0.0 | 0.0 | 0.0 | T | 0.7 | 2.6 | T | 0.0 | T | 0.0 | 0.0 | 3.3 |
| 1973-74 | 0.0 | 0.0 | 0.0 | 0.0 | 0.0 | T | 0.3 | T | 0.0 | 0.0 | 0.0 | 0.0 | 0.3 |
| 1974-75 | 0.0 | 0.0 | 0.0 | 0.0 | T | T | 1.4 | 0.4 | 2.4 | 0.0 | 0.0 | 0.0 | 4.2 |
| 1975-76 | 0.0 | 0.0 | 0.0 | 0.0 | 0.2 | 1.0 | T | 0.0 | 0.0 | 0.0 | 0.0 | 0.0 | 1.2 |
| 1976-77 | 0.0 | 0.0 | 0.0 | 0.0 | 1.0 | 0.0 | 3.8 | 0.0 | 0.0 | 0.0 | 0.0 | 0.0 | 4.8 |
| 1977-78 | 0.0 | 0.0 | 0.0 | 0.0 | 0.0 | 0.0 | 10.0 | 3.4 | T | 0.0 | 0.0 | 0.0 | 13.4 |
| 1978-79 | 0.0 | 0.0 | 0.0 | 0.0 | T | 0.0 | 1.4 | 9.8 | 0.0 | 0.0 | 0.0 | 0.0 | 11.2 |
| 1979-80 | 0.0 | 0.0 | 0.0 | 0.0 | 0.0 | 0.0 | 0.9 | 0.5 | T | T | 0.0 | 0.0 | 1.4 |
| 1980-81 | 0.0 | 0.0 | 0.0 | 0.0 | 1.8 | T | T | 0.0 | 0.0 | 0.0 | 0.0 | 0.0 | 1.8 |
| 1981-82 | 0.0 | 0.0 | 0.0 | 0.0 | 0.0 | 0.0 | 5.0 | 6.3 | T | 0.0 | 0.0 | 0.0 | 11.3 |
| 1982-83 | 0.0 | 0.0 | 0.0 | 0.0 | 0.0 | T | T | T | T | T | 0.0 | 0.0 | T |
| 1983-84 | 0.0 | 0.0 | 0.0 | 0.0 | 0.0 | 0.8 | 1.5 | 0.2 | 4.5 | 0.0 | 0.0 | 0.0 | 7.0 |
| 1984-85 | 0.0 | 0.0 | 0.0 | 0.0 | 0.0 | T | 6.3 | 5.0 | 0.0 | 0.0 | 0.0 | 0.0 | 11.3 |
| 1985-86 | 0.0 | 0.0 | 0.0 | 0.0 | 0.0 | T | 0.0 | 1.5 | 0.0 | 0.0 | 0.0 | 0.0 | 1.5 |
| 1986-87 | 0.0 | 0.0 | 0.0 | 0.0 | T | 0.0 | 1.0 | T | 0.8 | 0.0 | 0.0 | 0.0 | 1.8 |
| 1987-88 | 0.0 | 0.0 | 0.0 | 0.0 | 0.0 | 0.0 | 13.6 | 2.5 | T | 0.0 | 0.0 | 0.0 | 16.1 |
| 1988-89 | 0.0 | 0.0 | 0.0 | 0.0 | 0.0 | T | 2.0 | T | 1.0 | 0.0 | 0.0 | 0.0 | 3.0 |
| 1989-90 | 0.0 | 0.0 | 0.0 | 0.0 | 0.0 | T | T | 0.0 | 0.0 | 0.0 | 0.0 | 0.0 | T |
| 1990-91 | 0.0 | 0.0 | 0.0 | 0.0 | 0.0 | T | | | | | | | |
| Record Mean | 0.0 | 0.0 | 0.0 | 0.0 | 0.2 | 0.7 | 2.5 | 1.5 | 0.5 | T | 0.0 | 0.0 | 5.4 |

**See Reference Notes, relative to all above tables, on preceding page.**

Humboldt Bay is one-quarter mile north and one mile west of the station. There are no hills in Eureka of any consequence. The land slopes upward gently from the Bay toward the Coast Range, which begins about 3 miles east of the station and reaches the top of its first ridge approximately 10 miles to the east. The elevation of the ridge is 2,000 feet and extends in a semicircle from a point 20 miles north of Eureka to a point 25 miles south.

The climate of Eureka is completely maritime with high humidity prevailing the entire year. There are definite rainy and dry seasons. The rainy season begins in October and continues through April, accounting for about 90 percent of the annual precipitation. The dry season from May through September is marked by considerable fog or low cloudiness that usually clears in the late morning and sunny weather is generally the case during the early afternoon hours.

Temperatures are moderate the entire year. Although record highs have reached the mid 80s and record lows near 20 degrees, the usual yearly range is from lows in the mid 30s to highs in the mid 70s.

The principal industries are lumbering, fishing, tourism, and dairy farming. There is very little truck farming due to the low temperatures and lack of sunshine, however, the climate is nearly ideal for berries and flowers.

Based on the 1951-1980 period, the average first occurrence of 32 degrees Fahrenheit in the fall is December 10 and the average last occurrence in the spring is February 6.

**TABLE 1**     # NORMALS, MEANS AND EXTREMES

EUREKA, CALIFORNIA

LATITUDE: 40°48'N     LONGITUDE: 124°10'W     ELEVATION: FT. GRND     43 BARO     00079     TIME ZONE: PACIFIC     WBAN: 24213

| | (a) | JAN | FEB | MAR | APR | MAY | JUNE | JULY | AUG | SEP | OCT | NOV | DEC | YEAR |
|---|---|---|---|---|---|---|---|---|---|---|---|---|---|---|
| **TEMPERATURE °F:** | | | | | | | | | | | | | | |
| Normals | | | | | | | | | | | | | | |
| -Daily Maximum | | 53.4 | 54.6 | 54.0 | 54.7 | 57.0 | 59.1 | 60.3 | 61.3 | 62.2 | 60.3 | 57.5 | 54.5 | 57.4 |
| -Daily Minimum | | 41.3 | 42.6 | 42.5 | 44.0 | 47.3 | 50.2 | 51.9 | 52.6 | 51.5 | 48.3 | 45.2 | 42.2 | 46.6 |
| -Monthly | | 47.3 | 48.7 | 48.3 | 49.4 | 52.2 | 54.7 | 56.1 | 57.0 | 56.8 | 54.3 | 51.4 | 48.3 | 52.0 |
| Extremes | | | | | | | | | | | | | | |
| -Record Highest | 79 | 78 | 85 | 78 | 80 | 84 | 85 | 76 | 82 | 86 | 84 | 78 | 77 | 86 |
| -Year | | 1986 | 1930 | 1914 | 1989 | 1939 | 1945 | 1985 | 1968 | 1983 | 1987 | 1987 | 1963 | SEP 1983 |
| -Record Lowest | 79 | 25 | 27 | 29 | 32 | 36 | 41 | 45 | 44 | 41 | 32 | 29 | 21 | 21 |
| -Year | | 1937 | 1989 | 1917 | 1929 | 1954 | 1966 | 1924 | 1935 | 1946 | 1971 | 1935 | 1972 | DEC 1972 |
| **NORMAL DEGREE DAYS:** | | | | | | | | | | | | | | |
| Heating (base 65°F) | | 549 | 456 | 518 | 468 | 397 | 309 | 276 | 248 | 246 | 332 | 408 | 518 | 4725 |
| Cooling (base 65°F) | | 0 | 0 | 0 | 0 | 0 | 0 | 0 | 0 | 0 | 0 | 0 | 0 | 0 |
| **% OF POSSIBLE SUNSHINE** | 79 | 42 | 46 | 52 | 57 | 57 | 58 | 54 | 50 | 54 | 49 | 43 | 40 | 50 |
| **MEAN SKY COVER (tenths)** | | | | | | | | | | | | | | |
| Sunrise - Sunset | 47 | 7.2 | 7.4 | 7.3 | 7.0 | 6.7 | 6.6 | 6.5 | 6.9 | 6.0 | 6.6 | 7.2 | 7.2 | 6.9 |
| **MEAN NUMBER OF DAYS:** | | | | | | | | | | | | | | |
| Sunrise to Sunset | | | | | | | | | | | | | | |
| -Clear | 79 | 5.9 | 5.3 | 5.7 | 6.3 | 6.5 | 7.2 | 6.5 | 5.4 | 8.7 | 8.0 | 6.2 | 6.3 | 78.0 |
| -Partly Cloudy | 79 | 6.2 | 5.8 | 7.6 | 8.3 | 9.9 | 9.6 | 10.9 | 10.8 | 8.5 | 8.3 | 6.5 | 6.4 | 99.0 |
| -Cloudy | 79 | 18.9 | 17.2 | 17.6 | 15.4 | 14.6 | 13.3 | 13.6 | 14.8 | 12.7 | 14.7 | 17.3 | 18.3 | 188.3 |
| Precipitation | | | | | | | | | | | | | | |
| .01 inches or more | 79 | 16.0 | 14.2 | 15.5 | 11.7 | 8.3 | 5.3 | 2.1 | 2.5 | 4.5 | 8.7 | 13.3 | 15.5 | 117.5 |
| Snow,Ice pellets | | | | | | | | | | | | | | |
| 1.0 inches or more | 79 | 0.1 | 0.* | 0.0 | 0.0 | 0.0 | 0.0 | 0.0 | 0.0 | 0.0 | 0.0 | 0.0 | 0.* | 0.1 |
| Thunderstorms | 67 | 0.7 | 0.6 | 0.4 | 0.1 | 0.2 | 0.1 | 0.2 | 0.1 | 0.4 | 0.4 | 0.6 | 0.6 | 4.5 |
| Heavy Fog Visibility | | | | | | | | | | | | | | |
| 1/4 mile or less | 67 | 4.1 | 2.7 | 1.9 | 1.7 | 1.2 | 2.2 | 3.4 | 5.3 | 7.5 | 9.7 | 6.1 | 4.5 | 50.4 |
| Temperature °F | | | | | | | | | | | | | | |
| -Maximum | | | | | | | | | | | | | | |
| 90° and above | 79 | 0.0 | 0.0 | 0.0 | 0.0 | 0.0 | 0.0 | 0.0 | 0.0 | 0.0 | 0.0 | 0.0 | 0.0 | 0.0 |
| 32° and below | 79 | 0.0 | 0.0 | 0.0 | 0.0 | 0.0 | 0.0 | 0.0 | 0.0 | 0.0 | 0.0 | 0.0 | 0.0 | 0.0 |
| -Minimum | | | | | | | | | | | | | | |
| 32° and below | 79 | 2.0 | 0.8 | 0.2 | 0.* | 0.0 | 0.0 | 0.0 | 0.0 | 0.0 | 0.* | 0.2 | 1.3 | 4.6 |
| 0° and below | 79 | 0.0 | 0.0 | 0.0 | 0.0 | 0.0 | 0.0 | 0.0 | 0.0 | 0.0 | 0.0 | 0.0 | 0.0 | 0.0 |
| **AVG. STATION PRESS.(mb)** | | | | | | | | | | | | | | |
| **RELATIVE HUMIDITY (%)** | | | | | | | | | | | | | | |
| Hour 04 | | | | | | | | | | | | | | |
| Hour 10 (Local Time) | | | | | | | | | | | | | | |
| Hour 16 | | | | | | | | | | | | | | |
| Hour 22 | | | | | | | | | | | | | | |
| **PRECIPITATION (inches):** | | | | | | | | | | | | | | |
| Water Equivalent | | | | | | | | | | | | | | |
| -Normal | | 6.99 | 5.20 | 5.05 | 2.91 | 1.60 | 0.56 | 0.10 | 0.37 | 0.90 | 2.71 | 5.90 | 6.22 | 38.51 |
| -Maximum Monthly | 79 | 13.92 | 13.94 | 13.97 | 10.68 | 6.05 | 2.57 | 1.34 | 3.42 | 3.56 | 13.04 | 16.58 | 14.13 | 16.58 |
| -Year | | 1969 | 1938 | 1938 | 1963 | 1960 | 1954 | 1916 | 1983 | 1925 | 1950 | 1973 | 1983 | NOV 1973 |
| -Minimum Monthly | 79 | 0.66 | 0.50 | 0.07 | 0.31 | 0.03 | 0.00 | 0.00 | 0.00 | 0.00 | 0.00 | T | 0.52 | 0.00 |
| -Year | | 1985 | 1923 | 1926 | 1956 | 1955 | 1917 | 1967 | 1940 | 1929 | 1917 | 1929 | 1976 | JUL 1967 |
| -Maximum in 24 hrs | 79 | 4.42 | 4.88 | 4.02 | 2.56 | 2.23 | 1.73 | 1.18 | 2.21 | 1.54 | 5.83 | 4.55 | 4.17 | 5.83 |
| -Year | | 1912 | 1959 | 1975 | 1983 | 1943 | 1943 | 1916 | 1983 | 1977 | 1950 | 1926 | 1939 | OCT 1950 |
| Snow,Ice pellets | | | | | | | | | | | | | | |
| -Maximum Monthly | 79 | 3.0 | 3.5 | 1.0 | T | 0.0 | 0.0 | 0.0 | 0.0 | 0.0 | 0.0 | 0.1 | 1.9 | 3.5 |
| -Year | | 1935 | 1989 | 1966 | 1982 | | | | | | | 1977 | 1972 | FEB 1989 |
| -Maximum in 24 hrs | 79 | 3.0 | 2.0 | 1.0 | T | 0.0 | 0.0 | 0.0 | 0.0 | 0.0 | 0.0 | 0.1 | 1.9 | 3.0 |
| -Year | | 1935 | 1989 | 1966 | 1982 | | | | | | | 1977 | 1972 | JAN 1935 |
| **WIND:** | | | | | | | | | | | | | | |
| Mean Speed (mph) | 54 | 6.9 | 7.2 | 7.6 | 8.0 | 7.9 | 7.4 | 6.8 | 5.8 | 5.5 | 5.6 | 6.0 | 6.4 | 6.8 |
| Prevailing Direction | | | | | | | | | | | | | | |
| through 1964 | | SE | SE | N | N | N | N | N | NW | N | N | SE | SE | N |
| Fastest Mile | | | | | | | | | | | | | | |
| -Direction (!!!) | 79 | S | SW | SW | N | NW | NW | N | N | N | SW | S | S | SW |
| -Speed (MPH) | 79 | 54 | 48 | 48 | 49 | 40 | 39 | 35 | 34 | 44 | 56 | 55 | 56 | 56 |
| -Year | | 1955 | 1960 | 1953 | 1915 | 1955 | 1949 | 1986 | 1920 | 1941 | 1962 | 1981 | 1931 | OCT 1962 |
| Peak Gust | | | | | | | | | | | | | | |
| -Direction (!!!) | 5 | SE | N | S | S | N | N | N | N | N | SE | N | SE | SE |
| -Speed (mph) | 5 | 64 | 60 | 59 | 43 | 45 | 46 | 45 | 38 | 49 | 52 | 60 | 62 | 64 |
| -Date | | 1986 | 1987 | 1987 | 1988 | 1985 | 1989 | 1986 | 1985 | 1988 | 1988 | 1986 | 1987 | JAN 1986 |

**See Reference Notes to this table on the following page.**

PRECIPITATION (inches)    EUREKA, CALIFORNIA

**TABLE 2**

| YEAR | JAN | FEB | MAR | APR | MAY | JUNE | JULY | AUG | SEP | OCT | NOV | DEC | ANNUAL |
|---|---|---|---|---|---|---|---|---|---|---|---|---|---|
| 1961 | 4.54 | 7.53 | 7.90 | 3.49 | 3.97 | 0.50 | 0.03 | 0.30 | 0.53 | 2.28 | 5.65 | 3.44 | 40.16 |
| 1962 | 3.26 | 6.08 | 4.04 | 2.62 | 0.60 | 0.11 | T | 1.92 | 0.71 | 6.49 | 6.77 | 2.58 | 35.18 |
| 1963 | 1.70 | 4.74 | 6.28 | 10.68 | 1.74 | 0.33 | 0.11 | 0.07 | 0.68 | 5.41 | 6.91 | 3.20 | 41.85 |
| 1964 | 11.13 | 1.20 | 5.91 | 0.67 | 1.59 | 0.72 | 0.83 | 0.03 | 0.07 | 1.82 | 12.11 | 10.96 | 47.04 |
| 1965 | 5.82 | 1.36 | 1.23 | 5.60 | 0.44 | 0.35 | T | 0.36 | T | 0.70 | 5.20 | 5.22 | 26.28 |
| 1966 | 9.44 | 3.12 | 6.57 | 1.34 | 0.06 | 0.30 | 0.25 | 0.50 | 1.33 | 1.02 | 9.86 | 6.52 | 40.31 |
| 1967 | 8.87 | 1.47 | 7.44 | 5.29 | 1.52 | 0.32 | 0.00 | T | 1.32 | 2.15 | 4.40 | 4.34 | 37.12 |
| 1968 | 7.59 | 2.93 | 3.85 | 0.40 | 1.04 | 0.20 | 0.04 | 1.98 | 0.60 | 2.81 | 5.88 | 8.32 | 35.64 |
| 1969 | 13.92 | 7.82 | 1.56 | 3.22 | 1.01 | 0.34 | 0.05 | T | 0.36 | 3.20 | 3.49 | 9.60 | 44.57 |
| 1970 | 12.46 | 3.15 | 2.70 | 1.54 | 1.38 | 0.29 | T | T | 0.32 | 2.11 | 13.20 | 10.24 | 47.39 |
| 1971 | 5.41 | 3.28 | 7.91 | 2.92 | 1.28 | 1.51 | 0.16 | 0.55 | 2.08 | 0.92 | 6.36 | 6.38 | 38.76 |
| 1972 | 7.96 | 5.93 | 5.08 | 2.27 | 1.11 | 0.88 | 0.01 | 0.07 | 1.06 | 1.97 | 5.41 | 7.42 | 39.17 |
| 1973 | 6.47 | 3.85 | 7.10 | 0.35 | 0.85 | 0.23 | T | 0.08 | 2.35 | 4.14 | 16.58 | 7.02 | 49.02 |
| 1974 | 6.02 | 5.98 | 6.98 | 3.15 | 0.42 | 0.33 | 0.11 | 0.32 | T | 1.76 | 2.75 | 6.40 | 34.22 |
| 1975 | 5.20 | 7.68 | 10.73 | 3.29 | 1.05 | 0.58 | 0.10 | 0.58 | 0.01 | 6.77 | 4.72 | 5.38 | 46.09 |
| 1976 | 1.88 | 7.51 | 3.12 | 2.80 | 0.54 | 0.14 | 0.20 | 1.70 | 0.04 | 0.28 | 2.98 | 0.52 | 21.71 |
| 1977 | 1.90 | 2.24 | 4.33 | 1.20 | 2.10 | 0.07 | T | 0.20 | 3.35 | 2.79 | 4.51 | 6.60 | 29.29 |
| 1978 | 4.52 | 6.06 | 2.88 | 4.10 | 0.82 | 0.34 | 0.03 | 0.59 | 2.72 | 0.04 | 2.39 | 1.16 | 25.65 |
| 1979 | 3.82 | 6.26 | 1.70 | 3.94 | 2.25 | 0.05 | 0.31 | 0.13 | 1.15 | 6.14 | 6.19 | 3.75 | 35.69 |
| 1980 | 3.19 | 4.67 | 6.14 | 4.18 | 1.70 | 0.42 | T | 0.07 | 0.14 | 1.38 | 2.49 | 6.10 | 30.48 |
| 1981 | 7.67 | 3.72 | 4.64 | 0.71 | 2.02 | 0.57 | T | 0.01 | 0.97 | 3.71 | 9.39 | 9.88 | 43.29 |
| 1982 | 4.75 | 5.76 | 7.06 | 5.97 | 0.07 | 0.78 | 0.08 | 0.03 | 0.62 | 4.89 | 7.83 | 10.30 | 48.14 |
| 1983 | 8.48 | 9.18 | 10.73 | 5.47 | 1.12 | 0.65 | 0.89 | 3.42 | 0.87 | 1.87 | 10.40 | 14.13 | 67.21 |
| 1984 | 0.76 | 5.18 | 4.70 | 2.76 | 2.51 | 1.07 | 0.03 | 0.05 | 0.55 | 3.67 | 15.15 | 4.27 | 40.70 |
| 1985 | 0.66 | 3.69 | 4.68 | 0.45 | 1.14 | 0.89 | 0.15 | 0.52 | 1.06 | 4.07 | 2.98 | 2.78 | 23.07 |
| 1986 | 7.19 | 10.08 | 6.12 | 1.46 | 2.34 | 0.21 | 0.02 | T | 2.70 | 1.75 | 1.85 | 3.83 | 37.55 |
| 1987 | 6.48 | 3.38 | 6.10 | 1.15 | 0.41 | 0.26 | 0.20 | 0.06 | 0.02 | 1.05 | 4.23 | 10.92 | 34.26 |
| 1988 | 7.13 | 0.54 | 1.18 | 2.06 | 2.70 | 2.22 | 0.05 | T | 0.12 | 0.41 | 8.93 | 6.26 | 31.60 |
| 1989 | 4.71 | 2.88 | 7.63 | 2.01 | 1.67 | 0.21 | 0.08 | 0.13 | 0.85 | 2.90 | 1.60 | 0.80 | 25.47 |
| 1990 | 7.20 | 4.50 | 3.30 | 1.41 | 3.74 | 0.32 | 0.22 | 0.71 | 0.19 | 1.73 | 3.07 | 2.95 | 29.34 |
| Record Mean | 6.66 | 5.73 | 5.29 | 3.00 | 1.85 | 0.71 | 0.12 | 0.25 | 0.88 | 2.68 | 5.47 | 6.29 | 38.92 |

**TABLE 3**  AVERAGE TEMPERATURE (deg. F)    EUREKA, CALIFORNIA

| YEAR | JAN | FEB | MAR | APR | MAY | JUNE | JULY | AUG | SEP | OCT | NOV | DEC | ANNUAL |
|---|---|---|---|---|---|---|---|---|---|---|---|---|---|
| 1961 | 50.5 | 50.2 | 49.7 | 49.2 | 52.5 | 56.4 | 54.5 | 57.2 | 55.3 | 52.6 | 49.5 | 46.4 | 52.2 |
| 1962 | 45.2 | 47.7 | 48.1 | 50.4 | 52.3 | 53.2 | 53.8 | 57.7 | 57.1 | 54.6 | 52.3 | 49.7 | 51.8 |
| 1963 | 46.0 | 55.3 | 49.2 | 50.1 | 53.9 | 54.4 | 57.2 | 57.1 | 59.4 | 57.0 | 52.5 | 50.1 | 53.5 |
| 1964 | 46.6 | 47.0 | 45.7 | 47.1 | 50.4 | 54.8 | 56.6 | 57.0 | 55.2 | 54.9 | 50.0 | 48.5 | 51.1 |
| 1965 | 47.3 | 45.7 | 48.5 | 50.1 | 49.9 | 51.9 | 54.8 | 58.9 | 53.9 | 55.7 | 54.6 | 47.0 | 51.6 |
| 1966 | 47.7 | 46.5 | 48.0 | 50.4 | 50.4 | 55.5 | 56.6 | 55.9 | 58.0 | 53.2 | 52.6 | 49.5 | 52.0 |
| 1967 | 47.4 | 47.6 | 46.7 | 46.2 | 51.9 | 54.6 | 56.5 | 56.8 | 59.1 | 56.9 | 53.3 | 45.1 | 51.8 |
| 1968 | 46.6 | 53.2 | 50.6 | 48.1 | 52.4 | 55.5 | 56.3 | 59.3 | 57.5 | 53.3 | 51.8 | 46.5 | 52.6 |
| 1969 | 44.0 | 46.2 | 48.3 | 49.8 | 53.4 | 56.6 | 55.8 | 55.8 | 55.2 | 51.3 | 51.3 | 52.0 | 52.0 |
| 1970 | 52.1 | 51.4 | 49.9 | 47.4 | 52.3 | 54.3 | 54.8 | 55.3 | 55.7 | 52.6 | 53.5 | 47.4 | 52.2 |
| 1971 | 45.7 | 46.3 | 47.1 | 48.1 | 50.6 | 54.3 | 55.2 | 60.0 | 56.7 | 50.6 | 49.4 | 45.0 | 50.8 |
| 1972 | 44.6 | 49.0 | 51.2 | 49.1 | 51.2 | 54.6 | 57.8 | 58.2 | 55.8 | 54.2 | 51.8 | 45.7 | 52.0 |
| 1973 | 47.3 | 50.7 | 47.4 | 50.1 | 52.0 | 55.1 | 55.6 | 54.8 | 57.1 | 52.1 | 51.4 | 51.2 | 52.1 |
| 1974 | 46.7 | 46.1 | 50.1 | 49.7 | 51.1 | 54.1 | 57.7 | 57.7 | 55.6 | 53.2 | 51.2 | 48.7 | 51.8 |
| 1975 | 45.8 | 48.0 | 47.6 | 46.5 | 51.4 | 53.2 | 56.9 | 55.3 | 55.2 | 54.2 | 48.5 | 47.4 | 50.8 |
| 1976 | 46.4 | 46.9 | 45.7 | 48.4 | 51.1 | 52.8 | 57.5 | 57.9 | 56.2 | 54.4 | 52.2 | 47.4 | 51.4 |
| 1977 | 47.4 | 50.5 | 46.2 | 49.2 | 51.5 | 54.2 | 51.5 | 58.3 | 57.1 | 53.8 | 51.2 | 51.0 | 52.1 |
| 1978 | 51.8 | 50.3 | 53.5 | 51.0 | 53.3 | 56.0 | 55.9 | 57.0 | 57.6 | 54.9 | 48.0 | 43.3 | 52.7 |
| 1979 | 46.6 | 48.0 | 50.0 | 51.0 | 52.7 | 54.0 | 58.1 | 59.4 | 62.3 | 57.3 | 52.4 | 51.8 | 53.6 |
| 1980 | 48.3 | 53.5 | 48.6 | 51.9 | 52.3 | 55.5 | 57.3 | 55.0 | 56.6 | 54.3 | 51.3 | 51.2 | 53.0 |
| 1981 | 52.5 | 51.3 | 50.2 | 50.6 | 53.3 | 56.5 | 55.2 | 58.1 | 57.9 | 54.3 | 53.6 | 52.1 | 53.8 |
| 1982 | 44.9 | 49.5 | 48.3 | 50.8 | 52.8 | 56.3 | 58.3 | 59.6 | 58.7 | 57.3 | 52.1 | 49.6 | 53.2 |
| 1983 | 51.3 | 53.4 | 53.4 | 51.8 | 54.4 | 58.0 | 60.5 | 61.9 | 60.7 | 57.9 | 50.6 | 50.6 | 55.6 |
| 1984 | 49.4 | 50.0 | 52.8 | 51.3 | 55.0 | 55.2 | 57.6 | 60.2 | 58.3 | 55.3 | 52.1 | 46.8 | 53.7 |
| 1985 | 48.4 | 47.9 | 47.4 | 51.6 | 53.9 | 56.6 | 58.6 | 58.5 | 56.7 | 54.5 | 46.6 | 47.7 | 52.4 |
| 1986 | 54.3 | 52.7 | 53.1 | 50.7 | 53.9 | 59.0 | 57.4 | 57.2 | 57.2 | 55.6 | 53.5 | 51.3 | 54.7 |
| 1987 | 49.1 | 51.4 | 52.7 | 54.2 | 56.6 | 57.7 | 59.5 | 58.5 | 57.3 | 57.8 | 54.8 | 49.7 | 54.9 |
| 1988 | 50.4 | 50.2 | 50.3 | 52.8 | 56.3 | 57.7 | 58.8 | 57.7 | 55.8 | 55.2 | 53.3 | 47.7 | 53.9 |
| 1989 | 46.0 | 45.6 | 51.8 | 54.6 | 55.9 | 57.6 | 59.3 | 59.3 | 56.6 | 54.9 | 52.6 | 49.2 | 53.6 |
| 1990 | 48.3 | 45.5 | 50.2 | 52.8 | 54.0 | 58.2 | 59.9 | 59.8 | 60.4 | 61.6 | 54.3 | 49.7 | 53.1 |
| Record Mean | 47.4 | 48.2 | 48.7 | 50.2 | 52.5 | 55.1 | 56.3 | 56.9 | 56.3 | 54.2 | 51.4 | 48.3 | 52.1 |
| Max | 53.6 | 54.3 | 54.6 | 55.7 | 57.5 | 59.7 | 60.6 | 61.2 | 61.7 | 60.1 | 57.7 | 54.6 | 57.6 |
| Min | 41.2 | 42.1 | 42.8 | 44.6 | 47.6 | 50.4 | 51.9 | 52.5 | 50.9 | 48.2 | 45.0 | 42.0 | 46.6 |

## REFERENCE NOTES FOR TABLES 1, 2, 3 and 6          (EUREKA, CA)

### GENERAL

T - TRACE AMOUNT
BLANK ENTRIES DENOTE MISSING/UNREPORTED DATA.
# INDICATES A STATION OR INSTRUMENT RELOCATION.

### SPECIFIC

#### TABLE 1

(a) - LENGTH OF RECORD IN YEARS. ALTHOUGH INDIVIDUAL MONTHS MAY BE MISSING.

* LESS THAN .05

NORMALS — BASED ON THE 1951-1980 RECORD PERIOD.
EXTREMES — DATES ARE THE MOST RECENT OCCURRENCE.
WIND DIR. — NUMERALS SHOW TENS OF DEGREES CLOCKWISE FROM TRUE NORTH.
"00" INDICATES CALM.
RESULTANT WIND DIRECTIONS ARE GIVEN TO WHOLE DEGREES.

#### TABLE 3

MAX AND MIN ARE LONG-TERM MEAN DAILY MAXIMUM AND MEAN DAILY MINIMUM TEMPERATURES.

### EXCEPTIONS

#### TABLE 1

1. PRIOR TO 1965, THUNDERSTORMS AND HEAVY FOG MAY BE INCOMPLETE, DUE TO PART-TIME OPERATIONS.
2. THUNDERSTORMS AND HEAVY FOG DATA ARE MISSING FROM 1965 THROUGH 1976.
3. MEAN WIND SPEED IS THROUGH 1964.

#### TABLES 2, 3, and 6

RECORD MEANS ARE THROUGH THE CURRENT YEAR, BEGINNING IN 1887 FOR TEMPERATURE
1887 FOR PRECIPITATION
1911 FOR SNOWFALL

**TABLE 4**  HEATING DEGREE DAYS Base 65 deg. F   EUREKA, CALIFORNIA

| SEASON | JULY | AUG | SEP | OCT | NOV | DEC | JAN | FEB | MAR | APR | MAY | JUNE | TOTAL |
|---|---|---|---|---|---|---|---|---|---|---|---|---|---|
| 1961-62 | 250 | 234 | 281 | 377 | 459 | 567 | 607 | 478 | 517 | 431 | 388 | 347 | 4936 |
| 1962-63 | 339 | 219 | 229 | 312 | 375 | 469 | 579 | 266 | 484 | 440 | 336 | 312 | 4360 |
| 1963-64 | 234 | 239 | 163 | 241 | 366 | 456 | 564 | 515 | 591 | 529 | 446 | 299 | 4643 |
| 1964-65 | 256 | 243 | 288 | 306 | 444 | 505 | 544 | 533 | 505 | 441 | 459 | 385 | 4909 |
| 1965-66 | 309 | 183 | 324 | 285 | 305 | 551 | 531 | 510 | 519 | 433 | 443 | 280 | 4673 |
| 1966-67 | 254 | 275 | 209 | 358 | 368 | 472 | 541 | 482 | 561 | 560 | 399 | 307 | 4786 |
| 1967-68 | 257 | 249 | 170 | 243 | 345 | 611 | 565 | 337 | 441 | 498 | 384 | 279 | 4379 |
| 1968-69 | 260 | 179 | 220 | 354 | 388 | 566 | 644 | 519 | 508 | 449 | 352 | 246 | 4685 |
| 1969-70 | 284 | 282 | 247 | 295 | 404 | 419 | 392 | 374 | 462 | 521 | 385 | 313 | 4378 |
| 1970-71 | 308 | 292 | 274 | 379 | 338 | 539 | 590 | 518 | 548 | 502 | 438 | 318 | 5044 |
| 1971-72 | 299 | 154 | 242 | 440 | 463 | 612 | 624 | 456 | 422 | 472 | 423 | 306 | 4913 |
| 1972-73 | 217 | 204 | 269 | 328 | 389 | 590 | 542 | 395 | 537 | 439 | 393 | 293 | 4596 |
| 1973-74 | 287 | 308 | 230 | 393 | 399 | 419 | 559 | 523 | 455 | 454 | 423 | 321 | 4771 |
| 1974-75 | 222 | 220 | 274 | 360 | 407 | 501 | 587 | 469 | 532 | 547 | 417 | 347 | 4883 |
| 1975-76 | 244 | 290 | 286 | 328 | 486 | 542 | 516 | 516 | 590 | 490 | 424 | 360 | 5125 |
| 1976-77 | 226 | 213 | 258 | 324 | 375 | 535 | 537 | 400 | 577 | 468 | 415 | 317 | 4645 |
| 1977-78 | 302 | 200 | 231 | 342 | 408 | 427 | 403 | 404 | 347 | 415 | 357 | 264 | 4100 |
| 1978-79 | 274 | 241 | 215 | 307 | 503 | 667 | 562 | 467 | 459 | 412 | 374 | 323 | 4804 |
| 1979-80 | 208 | 165 | 92 | 231 | 369 | 404 | 511 | 330 | 500 | 386 | 388 | 280 | 3864 |
| 1980-81 | 230 | 303 | 246 | 328 | 402 | 422 | 384 | 377 | 451 | 423 | 357 | 249 | 4172 |
| 1981-82 | 299 | 205 | 203 | 324 | 339 | 396 | 616 | 430 | 512 | 419 | 373 | 258 | 4374 |
| 1982-83 | 204 | 158 | 181 | 232 | 381 | 468 | 415 | 317 | 355 | 391 | 320 | 203 | 3625 |
| 1983-84 | 133 | 90 | 129 | 215 | 336 | 443 | 475 | 429 | 369 | 403 | 301 | 285 | 3608 |
| 1984-85 | 222 | 142 | 195 | 295 | 378 | 556 | 507 | 472 | 532 | 396 | 338 | 243 | 4276 |
| 1985-86 | 195 | 194 | 244 | 316 | 546 | 533 | 329 | 337 | 365 | 422 | 338 | 169 | 3988 |
| 1986-87 | 227 | 236 | 227 | 290 | 341 | 417 | 487 | 372 | 377 | 316 | 260 | 213 | 3763 |
| 1987-88 | 163 | 196 | 226 | 221 | 302 | 470 | 446 | 423 | 453 | 358 | 265 | 215 | 3738 |
| 1988-89 | 187 | 218 | 274 | 297 | 345 | 529 | 582 | 535 | 403 | 309 | 278 | 214 | 4171 |
| 1989-90 | 164 | 171 | 243 | 306 | 365 | 482 | 513 | 541 | 453 | 356 | 332 | 198 | 4124 |
| 1990-91 | 154 | 141 | 95 | 325 | 451 | 680 |  |  |  |  |  |  |  |

**TABLE 5**  COOLING DEGREE DAYS Base 65 deg. F   EUREKA, CALIFORNIA

| YEAR | JAN | FEB | MAR | APR | MAY | JUNE | JULY | AUG | SEP | OCT | NOV | DEC | TOTAL |
|---|---|---|---|---|---|---|---|---|---|---|---|---|---|
| 1969 | 0 | 0 | 0 | 0 | 0 | 0 | 0 | 0 | 0 | 0 | 0 | 0 | 0 |
| 1970 | 0 | 0 | 0 | 0 | 1 | 0 | 0 | 0 | 1 | 0 | 0 | 0 | 2 |
| 1971 | 0 | 0 | 0 | 0 | 0 | 0 | 0 | 2 | 0 | 0 | 0 | 0 | 2 |
| 1972 | 0 | 0 | 0 | 0 | 0 | 0 | 0 | 1 | 0 | 0 | 0 | 0 | 1 |
| 1973 | 0 | 0 | 0 | 0 | 0 | 1 | 0 | 0 | 0 | 0 | 0 | 0 | 1 |
| 1974 | 0 | 0 | 0 | 0 | 0 | 0 | 0 | 0 | 0 | 0 | 0 | 0 | 0 |
| 1975 | 0 | 0 | 0 | 0 | 0 | 0 | 0 | 0 | 0 | 0 | 0 | 0 | 0 |
| 1976 | 0 | 0 | 0 | 0 | 0 | 0 | 0 | 0 | 0 | 0 | 0 | 0 | 0 |
| 1977 | 0 | 0 | 0 | 0 | 0 | 0 | 0 | 0 | 0 | 0 | 0 | 0 | 0 |
| 1978 | 0 | 0 | 0 | 0 | 0 | 0 | 0 | 0 | 0 | 1 | 0 | 0 | 1 |
| 1979 | 0 | 0 | 0 | 0 | 0 | 0 | 0 | 0 | 15 | 0 | 0 | 2 | 17 |
| 1980 | 0 | 2 | 0 | 0 | 0 | 0 | 0 | 0 | 0 | 3 | 0 | 0 | 5 |
| 1981 | 4 | 0 | 0 | 0 | 0 | 0 | 0 | 0 | 0 | 0 | 0 | 0 | 4 |
| 1982 | 0 | 0 | 0 | 0 | 0 | 3 | 0 | 0 | 0 | 2 | 0 | 0 | 5 |
| 1983 | 0 | 0 | 0 | 0 | 0 | 0 | 0 | 2 | 7 | 0 | 0 | 0 | 9 |
| 1984 | 0 | 0 | 0 | 0 | 0 | 0 | 0 | 0 | 4 | 1 | 0 | 0 | 5 |
| 1985 | 0 | 0 | 0 | 0 | 0 | 0 | 1 | 0 | 0 | 2 | 0 | 0 | 3 |
| 1986 | 0 | 0 | 0 | 0 | 0 | 0 | 0 | 0 | 0 | 0 | 0 | 0 | 0 |
| 1987 | 0 | 0 | 0 | 0 | 3 | 0 | 0 | 0 | 5 | 0 | 0 | 0 | 8 |
| 1988 | 0 | 0 | 0 | 0 | 0 | 0 | 0 | 0 | 4 | 0 | 0 | 0 | 4 |
| 1989 | 0 | 0 | 0 | 1 | 0 | 0 | 0 | 0 | 0 | 0 | 0 | 0 | 1 |
| 1990 | 0 | 0 | 0 | 0 | 0 | 0 | 0 | 4 | 0 | 0 | 0 | 0 | 4 |

**TABLE 6**  SNOWFALL (inches)   EUREKA, CALIFORNIA

| SEASON | JULY | AUG | SEP | OCT | NOV | DEC | JAN | FEB | MAR | APR | MAY | JUNE | TOTAL |
|---|---|---|---|---|---|---|---|---|---|---|---|---|---|
| 1970-71 | 0.0 | 0.0 | 0.0 | 0.0 | 0.0 | 0.0 | T | T | 0.0 | 0.0 | 0.0 | 0.0 | T |
| 1971-72 | 0.0 | 0.0 | 0.0 | 0.0 | 0.0 | 0.0 | 1.6 | 0.0 | 0.0 | 0.0 | 0.0 | 0.0 | 1.6 |
| 1972-73 | 0.0 | 0.0 | 0.0 | 0.0 | 0.0 | 1.9 | 0.0 | 0.0 | T | 0.0 | 0.0 | 0.0 | 1.9 |
| 1973-74 | 0.0 | 0.0 | 0.0 | 0.0 | 0.0 | 0.0 | T | 0.0 | 0.0 | 0.0 | 0.0 | 0.0 | T |
| 1974-75 | 0.0 | 0.0 | 0.0 | 0.0 | 0.0 | T | 0.0 | 0.0 | 0.0 | T | 0.0 | 0.0 | T |
| 1975-76 | 0.0 | 0.0 | 0.0 | 0.0 | 0.0 | 0.0 | 0.0 | 0.0 | 0.1 | 0.0 | 0.0 | 0.0 | 0.1 |
| 1976-77 | 0.0 | 0.0 | 0.0 | 0.0 | 0.0 | 0.0 | 0.0 | 0.0 | T | 0.0 | 0.0 | 0.0 | T |
| 1977-78 | 0.0 | 0.0 | 0.0 | 0.0 | 0.0 | 0.1 | 0.0 | 0.0 | 0.0 | 0.0 | 0.0 | 0.0 | 0.1 |
| 1978-79 | 0.0 | 0.0 | 0.0 | 0.0 | 0.0 | 0.0 | 0.0 | 0.0 | 0.0 | 0.0 | 0.0 | 0.0 | 0.0 |
| 1979-80 | 0.0 | 0.0 | 0.0 | 0.0 | 0.0 | 0.0 | 0.0 | 0.0 | 0.0 | 0.0 | 0.0 | 0.0 | 0.0 |
| 1980-81 | 0.0 | 0.0 | 0.0 | 0.0 | 0.0 | 0.0 | 0.0 | 0.0 | 0.0 | 0.0 | 0.0 | 0.0 | 0.0 |
| 1981-82 | 0.0 | 0.0 | 0.0 | 0.0 | 0.0 | 0.0 | T | 0.0 | T | T | 0.0 | 0.0 | T |
| 1982-83 | 0.0 | 0.0 | 0.0 | 0.0 | 0.0 | T | 0.0 | 0.0 | T | 0.0 | 0.0 | 0.0 | T |
| 1983-84 | 0.0 | 0.0 | 0.0 | 0.0 | T | 1.0 | 0.0 | 0.0 | 0.0 | 0.0 | 0.0 | 0.0 | 1.0 |
| 1984-85 | 0.0 | 0.0 | 0.0 | 0.0 | 0.0 | 0.0 | 0.0 | 0.0 | 0.0 | 0.0 | 0.0 | 0.0 | 0.0 |
| 1985-86 | 0.0 | 0.0 | 0.0 | 0.0 | 0.0 | 0.0 | 0.0 | 0.0 | 0.0 | 0.0 | 0.0 | 0.0 | 0.0 |
| 1986-87 | 0.0 | 0.0 | 0.0 | 0.0 | 0.0 | 0.0 | 0.0 | 0.0 | 0.0 | 0.0 | 0.0 | 0.0 | 0.0 |
| 1987-88 | 0.0 | 0.0 | 0.0 | 0.0 | 0.0 | T | 0.0 | 0.0 | 0.0 | 0.0 | 0.0 | 0.0 | T |
| 1988-89 | 0.0 | 0.0 | 0.0 | 0.0 | 0.0 | 0.0 | 0.0 | 3.5 | 0.0 | 0.0 | 0.0 | 0.0 | 3.5 |
| 1989-90 | 0.0 | 0.0 | 0.0 | 0.0 | 0.0 | 0.0 | 0.0 | 1.0 | 0.0 | 0.0 | 0.0 | 0.0 | 1.0 |
| 1990-91 | 0.0 | 0.0 | 0.0 | 0.0 | 0.0 | T |  |  |  |  |  |  |  |
| Record Mean | 0.0 | 0.0 | 0.0 | 0.0 | T | T | 0.2 | 0.1 | T | T | 0.0 | 0.0 | 0.3 |

**See Reference Notes, relative to all above tables, on preceding page.**

Fresno is located about midway and toward the eastern edge of the San Joaquin Valley, which is oriented northwest to southeast and has a length of about 225 miles and an average width of 50 miles. The San Joaquin Valley is generally flat. About 15 miles east of Fresno the terrain slopes upward with the foothills of the Sierra Nevada. The Sierra Nevada attain an elevation of more than 14,000 feet 50 miles east of Fresno. West of the city 45 miles lie the foothills of the Coastal Range.

The climate of Fresno is dry and mild in winter and hot in summer. Nearly nine-tenths of the annual precipitation falls in the six months from November to April.

Due to clear skies during the summer and the protection of the San Joaquin Valley from marine effects, the normal daily maximum temperature reaches the high 90s during the latter part of July. The daily maximum temperature during the warmest month has ranged from 76 to 115 degrees. Low relative humidities and some wind movement substantially lower the sensible temperature during periods of high readings. Humidity readings of 15 percent are common on summer afternoons, and readings as low as 8 percent have been recorded. In contrast to this, humidity readings average 90 percent during the morning hours of December and January.

Winds flow with the major axis of the San Joaquin Valley, generally from the northwest. This feature is especially beneficial since, during the warmest months, the northwest winds increase during the evenings. These refreshing breezes and the normally large temperature variation of about 35 degrees between the highest and lowest readings of the day, generally result in comfortable evening and night temperatures.

Winter temperatures are usually mild with infrequent cold spells dropping the readings below freezing. Heavy frost occurs almost every year, and the first frost usually occurs during the last week of November. The last frost in spring is usually in early March, however, one year in five will have the last frost after the first of April. The growing season is 291 days.

Although the heaviest rains recorded at Fresno for short periods have occurred in June, usually any rainfall during the summer is very light. Snow is a rare occurrence in Fresno.

Fresno enjoys a very high percentage of sunshine, receiving more than 80 percent of the possible amounts during all but the four months of November, December, January, and February. Reduction of sunshine during these months is caused by fog and short periods of stormy weather.

During foggy periods, at times lasting nearly two weeks, sunshine is reduced to a minimum. This fog frequently lifts to a few hundred feet above the surface of the valley and presents the appearance of a heavy, solid cloud layer.

Spring and autumn are very enjoyable seasons in Fresno, with clear skies, light rainfall and winds and mild temperatures.

## TABLE 1 — NORMALS, MEANS AND EXTREMES

FRESNO, CALIFORNIA

LATITUDE: 36°46'N   LONGITUDE: 119°43'W   ELEVATION: FT. GRND 328 BARO 330   TIME ZONE: PACIFIC   WBAN: 93193

| | (a) | JAN | FEB | MAR | APR | MAY | JUNE | JULY | AUG | SEP | OCT | NOV | DEC | YEAR |
|---|---|---|---|---|---|---|---|---|---|---|---|---|---|---|
| **TEMPERATURE °F:** | | | | | | | | | | | | | | |
| Normals | | | | | | | | | | | | | | |
| -Daily Maximum | | 54.2 | 61.2 | 66.5 | 73.7 | 82.7 | 91.1 | 97.9 | 95.5 | 90.3 | 79.9 | 65.2 | 54.4 | 76.1 |
| -Daily Minimum | | 36.8 | 39.7 | 42.0 | 46.5 | 52.7 | 58.9 | 64.1 | 62.2 | 57.8 | 49.7 | 41.1 | 36.3 | 49.0 |
| -Monthly | | 45.5 | 50.5 | 54.3 | 60.1 | 67.7 | 75.0 | 81.0 | 78.9 | 74.1 | 64.8 | 53.2 | 45.3 | 62.5 |
| Extremes | | | | | | | | | | | | | | |
| -Record Highest | 40 | 78 | 80 | 90 | 100 | 107 | 110 | 111 | 111 | 111 | 102 | 89 | 76 | 111 |
| -Year | | 1986 | 1988 | 1972 | 1981 | 1984 | 1964 | 1984 | 1981 | 1955 | 1980 | 1949 | 1958 | JUL 1984 |
| -Record Lowest | 40 | 19 | 24 | 26 | 32 | 36 | 44 | 50 | 49 | 37 | 27 | 26 | 20 | 19 |
| -Year | | 1963 | 1989 | 1966 | 1982 | 1975 | 1955 | 1955 | 1966 | 1950 | 1972 | 1975 | 1987 | JAN 1963 |
| **NORMAL DEGREE DAYS:** | | | | | | | | | | | | | | |
| Heating (base 65°F) | | 605 | 406 | 336 | 187 | 52 | 8 | 0 | 0 | 0 | 88 | 354 | 611 | 2647 |
| Cooling (base 65°F) | | 0 | 0 | 0 | 40 | 135 | 308 | 496 | 431 | 277 | 82 | 0 | 0 | 1769 |
| **% OF POSSIBLE SUNSHINE** | 40 | 48 | 65 | 78 | 85 | 90 | 95 | 96 | 96 | 94 | 88 | 65 | 45 | 79 |
| **MEAN SKY COVER (tenths)** | | | | | | | | | | | | | | |
| Sunrise - Sunset | 40 | 7.3 | 6.1 | 5.3 | 4.3 | 3.1 | 1.9 | 1.2 | 1.4 | 1.8 | 2.9 | 5.3 | 7.0 | 4.0 |
| **MEAN NUMBER OF DAYS:** | | | | | | | | | | | | | | |
| Sunrise to Sunset | | | | | | | | | | | | | | |
| -Clear | 40 | 5.3 | 7.8 | 11.2 | 14.2 | 19.0 | 23.1 | 26.8 | 26.1 | 23.7 | 20.1 | 11.2 | 6.6 | 195.1 |
| -Partly Cloudy | 40 | 7.0 | 7.9 | 8.2 | 7.9 | 7.3 | 4.5 | 2.9 | 3.5 | 3.9 | 6.1 | 7.3 | 6.0 | 72.5 |
| -Cloudy | 40 | 18.7 | 12.6 | 11.6 | 7.9 | 4.7 | 2.3 | 1.3 | 1.4 | 2.4 | 4.7 | 11.5 | 18.4 | 97.6 |
| Precipitation | | | | | | | | | | | | | | |
| .01 inches or more | 40 | 7.6 | 7.0 | 6.9 | 4.4 | 1.9 | 0.7 | 0.2 | 0.3 | 1.0 | 2.1 | 5.6 | 6.8 | 44.6 |
| Snow,Ice pellets | | | | | | | | | | | | | | |
| 1.0 inches or more | 40 | 0.* | 0.0 | 0.0 | 0.0 | 0.0 | 0.0 | 0.0 | 0.0 | 0.0 | 0.0 | 0.0 | 0.* | 0.1 |
| Thunderstorms | 40 | 0.3 | 0.4 | 0.8 | 0.6 | 0.5 | 0.5 | 0.3 | 0.3 | 0.7 | 0.6 | 0.3 | 0.3 | 5.5 |
| Heavy Fog Visibility | | | | | | | | | | | | | | |
| 1/4 mile or less | 40 | 11.8 | 6.2 | 1.8 | 0.4 | 0.1 | 0.0 | 0.0 | 0.* | 0.1 | 0.9 | 6.2 | 12.4 | 39.8 |
| Temperature °F | | | | | | | | | | | | | | |
| -Maximum | | | | | | | | | | | | | | |
| 90° and above | 26 | 0.0 | 0.0 | 0.* | 2.2 | 10.4 | 19.7 | 28.5 | 26.5 | 16.8 | 4.2 | 0.0 | 0.0 | 108.3 |
| 32° and below | 26 | 0.0 | 0.0 | 0.0 | 0.0 | 0.0 | 0.0 | 0.0 | 0.0 | 0.0 | 0.0 | 0.0 | 0.1 | 0.1 |
| -Minimum | | | | | | | | | | | | | | |
| 32° and below | 26 | 7.3 | 3.2 | 0.8 | 0.1 | 0.0 | 0.0 | 0.0 | 0.0 | 0.0 | 0.2 | 1.9 | 8.6 | 22.0 |
| 0° and below | 26 | 0.0 | 0.0 | 0.0 | 0.0 | 0.0 | 0.0 | 0.0 | 0.0 | 0.0 | 0.0 | 0.0 | 0.0 | 0.0 |
| **AVG. STATION PRESS.(mb)** | 17 | 1009.0 | 1007.6 | 1005.3 | 1004.3 | 1001.7 | 1000.5 | 1000.4 | 1000.4 | 1000.8 | 1004.2 | 1007.4 | 1009.3 | 1004.2 |
| **RELATIVE HUMIDITY (%)** | | | | | | | | | | | | | | |
| Hour 04 | 26 | 91 | 90 | 86 | 80 | 71 | 65 | 61 | 67 | 72 | 78 | 87 | 92 | 78 |
| Hour 10 | 26 | 85 | 77 | 65 | 51 | 42 | 39 | 37 | 42 | 45 | 52 | 72 | 85 | 58 |
| Hour 16 (Local Time) | 26 | 68 | 56 | 47 | 35 | 26 | 23 | 22 | 25 | 28 | 35 | 55 | 69 | 41 |
| Hour 22 | 26 | 88 | 83 | 75 | 62 | 49 | 44 | 40 | 46 | 52 | 64 | 82 | 89 | 65 |
| **PRECIPITATION (inches):** | | | | | | | | | | | | | | |
| Water Equivalent | | | | | | | | | | | | | | |
| -Normal | | 2.05 | 1.85 | 1.61 | 1.15 | 0.31 | 0.08 | 0.01 | 0.02 | 0.16 | 0.43 | 1.24 | 1.61 | 10.52 |
| -Maximum Monthly | 40 | 8.56 | 5.97 | 5.79 | 4.41 | 1.56 | 0.60 | 0.08 | 0.25 | 1.19 | 1.58 | 3.50 | 6.73 | 8.56 |
| -Year | | 1969 | 1962 | 1958 | 1967 | 1957 | 1972 | 1979 | 1964 | 1976 | 1982 | 1972 | 1955 | JAN 1969 |
| -Minimum Monthly | 40 | 0.04 | T | 0.00 | 0.02 | 0.00 | 0.00 | 0.00 | 0.00 | 0.00 | 0.00 | 0.00 | 0.00 | 0.00 |
| -Year | | 1976 | 1964 | 1972 | 1962 | 1982 | 1983 | 1983 | 1981 | 1981 | 1978 | 1959 | 1989 | DEC 1989 |
| -Maximum in 24 hrs | 40 | 2.59 | 1.99 | 1.63 | 1.39 | 0.96 | 0.60 | 0.08 | 0.25 | 0.97 | 1.55 | 1.35 | 1.76 | 2.59 |
| -Year | | 1969 | 1969 | 1958 | 1983 | 1957 | 1972 | 1979 | 1964 | 1978 | 1976 | 1953 | 1955 | JAN 1969 |
| Snow,Ice pellets | | | | | | | | | | | | | | |
| -Maximum Monthly | 40 | 2.2 | T | T | 0.0 | 0.0 | 0.0 | 0.0 | 0.0 | 0.0 | T | 0.0 | 1.2 | 2.2 |
| -Year | | 1962 | 1989 | 1979 | | | | | | | 1974 | | 1968 | JAN 1962 |
| -Maximum in 24 hrs | 40 | 1.5 | T | T | 0.0 | 0.0 | 0.0 | 0.0 | 0.0 | 0.0 | T | 0.0 | 1.2 | 1.5 |
| -Year | | 1962 | 1989 | 1985 | | | | | | | 1974 | | 1968 | JAN 1962 |
| **WIND:** | | | | | | | | | | | | | | |
| Mean Speed (mph) | 40 | 5.3 | 5.7 | 6.7 | 7.3 | 8.1 | 8.2 | 7.3 | 6.7 | 6.1 | 5.2 | 4.7 | 4.9 | 6.3 |
| Prevailing Direction | | | | | | | | | | | | | | |
| through 1963 | | SE | NW | NW | NW | NW | NW | NW | NW | NW | NW | NW | SE | NW |
| Fastest Obs. 1 Min. | | | | | | | | | | | | | | |
| -Direction (!!!) | 11 | 27 | 31 | 32 | 30 | 32 | 30 | 31 | 31 | 31 | 32 | 30 | 31 | 30 |
| -Speed (MPH) | 11 | 31 | 29 | 29 | 32 | 29 | 28 | 28 | 23 | 28 | 29 | 23 | 25 | 32 |
| -Year | | 1983 | 1977 | 1982 | 1984 | 1979 | 1983 | 1983 | 1984 | 1978 | 1982 | 1983 | 1984 | APR 1984 |
| Peak Gust | | | | | | | | | | | | | | |
| -Direction (!!!) | 6 | SE | S | SE | NW | NW | NW | NW | NW | N | NW | NW | NW | SE |
| -Speed (mph) | 6 | 55 | 46 | 43 | 41 | 37 | 33 | 26 | 36 | 32 | 35 | 32 | 38 | 55 |
| -Date | | 1987 | 1986 | 1987 | 1984 | 1986 | 1984 | 1984 | 1984 | 1987 | 1985 | 1986 | 1984 | JAN 1987 |

**See Reference Notes to this table on the following page.**

## PRECIPITATION (inches)  —  FRESNO, CALIFORNIA

**TABLE 2**

| YEAR | JAN | FEB | MAR | APR | MAY | JUNE | JULY | AUG | SEP | OCT | NOV | DEC | ANNUAL |
|------|-----|-----|-----|-----|-----|------|------|-----|-----|-----|-----|-----|--------|
| #1961 | 1.52 | 0.40 | 1.04 | 0.57 | 0.40 | 0.01 | T | 0.10 | T | T | 1.60 | 1.32 | 6.96 |
| 1962 | 1.12 | 5.97 | 1.04 | 0.02 | 0.20 | | T | 0.00 | T | 0.73 | 0.03 | 0.48 | 9.59 |
| 1963 | 2.16 | 2.01 | 2.10 | 3.66 | 0.39 | 0.03 | 0.00 | 0.01 | 0.15 | 0.95 | 2.54 | 0.27 | 14.27 |
| 1964 | 0.66 | T | 1.27 | 0.50 | 0.35 | 0.06 | T | 0.25 | 0.00 | 1.23 | 1.49 | 2.63 | 8.44 |
| 1965 | 1.05 | 0.43 | 2.38 | 1.74 | T | | T | 0.02 | 0.00 | 0.30 | 2.69 | 1.73 | 10.34 |
| 1966 | 0.53 | 0.54 | 0.01 | 0.15 | 0.10 | 0.07 | 0.03 | 0.00 | 0.03 | 0.00 | 1.57 | 3.04 | 6.07 |
| 1967 | 2.21 | 0.22 | 3.15 | 4.41 | 0.19 | 0.14 | T | T | 0.00 | 0.07 | 1.55 | 1.04 | 12.98 |
| 1968 | 1.05 | 1.10 | 1.49 | 0.70 | 0.24 | 0.00 | T | T | 0.04 | 0.06 | 1.94 | 1.14 | 10.50 |
| 1969 | 8.56 | 5.60 | 1.16 | 1.64 | 0.06 | 0.04 | 0.04 | 0.00 | 0.00 | 0.06 | 0.80 | 2.51 | 19.14 |
| 1970 | 3.83 | 1.27 | 1.65 | 0.21 | 0.00 | 0.08 | T | 0.00 | 0.00 | 0.01 | 2.30 | 2.51 | 11.86 |
| 1971 | 0.40 | 0.29 | 0.58 | 1.04 | 1.40 | 0.00 | T | | 0.04 | 0.03 | 0.65 | 2.56 | 6.99 |
| 1972 | 0.37 | 0.67 | 0.00 | 0.27 | 0.15 | 0.60 | 0.00 | | 0.29 | 0.22 | 3.50 | 1.40 | 7.47 |
| 1973 | 1.91 | 3.69 | 2.84 | 0.09 | T | 0.00 | T | | 0.00 | 1.02 | 1.39 | 1.74 | 12.68 |
| 1974 | 2.82 | 0.25 | 2.56 | 0.64 | 0.00 | 0.00 | T | | 0.00 | 1.44 | 0.34 | 1.26 | 9.31 |
| 1975 | 0.69 | 0.97 | 2.44 | 0.55 | T | 0.00 | T | 0.05 | 0.22 | 1.07 | 0.20 | 0.14 | 6.33 |
| 1976 | 0.04 | 4.72 | 0.44 | 0.93 | T | 0.37 | 0.01 | 0.21 | 1.19 | 1.55 | 0.87 | 0.71 | 11.04 |
| 1977 | 0.68 | 0.09 | 1.04 | 0.04 | 1.16 | 0.06 | T | T | T | 0.01 | 0.46 | 3.02 | 6.56 |
| 1978 | 3.16 | 4.41 | 4.25 | 2.85 | 0.00 | 0.00 | T | | 1.05 | 0.00 | 1.34 | 0.62 | 17.68 |
| 1979 | 2.71 | 2.53 | 2.27 | 0.07 | 0.06 | 0.00 | 0.08 | 0.00 | T | 0.48 | 1.01 | 0.74 | 9.95 |
| 1980 | 3.83 | 3.30 | 2.05 | 0.25 | 0.18 | | 0.01 | 0.00 | 0.00 | 0.03 | 0.14 | 0.49 | 10.28 |
| 1981 | 2.67 | 1.29 | 2.59 | 1.01 | T | 0.00 | 0.00 | 0.00 | 0.00 | 0.58 | 1.22 | 0.65 | 10.01 |
| 1982 | 2.11 | 0.58 | 4.76 | 0.89 | 0.00 | 0.31 | 0.00 | T | 1.10 | 1.58 | 3.16 | 1.59 | 16.08 |
| 1983 | 5.14 | 3.70 | 4.53 | 2.76 | 0.01 | 0.00 | 0.00 | 0.09 | 1.03 | 0.09 | 2.51 | 1.75 | 21.61 |
| 1984 | 0.15 | 1.05 | 0.48 | 0.25 | 0.02 | 0.20 | T | T | 0.00 | 0.70 | 1.94 | 0.72 | 6.77 |
| 1985 | 0.43 | 0.71 | T | 1.73 | 0.12 | 0.33 | 0.04 | 0.02 | 0.43 | 0.85 | 3.02 | 0.72 | 8.40 |
| 1986 | 2.12 | 3.66 | 3.42 | 0.36 | 0.16 | 0.00 | T | 0.00 | 0.38 | 0.00 | 0.01 | 2.30 | 12.41 |
| 1987 | 1.93 | 1.36 | 2.39 | 0.07 | 0.87 | 0.01 | 0.00 | 0.00 | T | 0.85 | 0.52 | 1.19 | 9.19 |
| 1988 | 1.52 | 0.83 | 0.27 | 2.41 | 0.45 | 0.03 | 0.00 | 0.00 | 0.00 | 0.00 | 1.42 | 2.46 | 9.39 |
| 1989 | 0.48 | 1.18 | 2.25 | 0.05 | 0.89 | 0.00 | 0.00 | 0.03 | 1.11 | 0.42 | 0.50 | 0.00 | 6.91 |
| 1990 | 2.82 | 1.33 | 0.67 | 0.92 | 1.65 | 0.00 | T | 0.00 | 0.15 | 0.05 | 0.46 | 0.68 | 8.73 |
| Record Mean | 1.81 | 1.63 | 1.68 | 0.96 | 0.36 | 0.10 | 0.01 | 0.01 | 0.18 | 0.53 | 1.02 | 1.54 | 9.83 |

**TABLE 3**  AVERAGE TEMPERATURE (deg. F)  —  FRESNO, CALIFORNIA

| YEAR | JAN | FEB | MAR | APR | MAY | JUNE | JULY | AUG | SEP | OCT | NOV | DEC | ANNUAL |
|------|-----|-----|-----|-----|-----|------|------|-----|-----|-----|-----|-----|--------|
| #1961 | 42.4 | 51.5 | 53.4 | 61.4 | 63.9 | 78.8 | 82.5 | 81.1 | 72.4 | 64.3 | 51.9 | 43.8 | 62.3 |
| 1962 | 41.4 | 48.3 | 52.1 | 64.8 | 65.0 | 75.9 | 80.9 | 78.8 | 74.7 | 64.0 | 50.3 | 47.4 | 62.4 |
| #1963 | 42.2 | 56.4 | 53.3 | 55.9 | 67.6 | 73.2 | 78.5 | 78.2 | 76.6 | 65.4 | 52.1 | 40.0 | 61.6 |
| 1964 | 43.8 | 47.4 | 51.3 | 58.8 | 64.9 | 73.3 | 81.0 | 78.9 | 71.0 | 68.3 | 51.3 | 49.0 | 61.6 |
| 1965 | 46.3 | 49.6 | 55.5 | 60.8 | 67.5 | 77.4 | 78.9 | 78.8 | 68.6 | 65.8 | 54.7 | 42.0 | 61.6 |
| 1966 | 43.4 | 47.2 | 56.3 | 65.5 | 70.9 | 76.3 | 78.2 | 81.0 | 72.8 | 64.8 | 56.9 | 45.2 | 63.2 |
| 1967 | 46.1 | 48.9 | 54.4 | 52.6 | 68.8 | 74.3 | 83.8 | 83.6 | 77.4 | 66.0 | 56.8 | 42.6 | 62.9 |
| 1968 | 44.8 | 55.8 | 55.8 | 61.5 | 68.1 | 79.0 | 82.4 | 77.2 | 73.7 | 63.3 | 51.9 | 43.3 | 63.0 |
| 1969 | 44.8 | 47.5 | 53.1 | 59.7 | 70.4 | 72.9 | 80.9 | 79.7 | 75.7 | 59.7 | 53.1 | 46.2 | 62.0 |
| 1970 | 49.1 | 52.7 | 55.3 | 57.0 | 70.8 | 76.5 | 83.3 | 79.9 | 73.0 | 63.4 | 55.4 | 46.3 | 63.5 |
| 1971 | 45.7 | 47.6 | 54.4 | 59.1 | 64.2 | 74.4 | 81.9 | 81.1 | 73.4 | 60.9 | 50.7 | 42.9 | 61.4 |
| 1972 | 40.6 | 52.5 | 60.7 | 61.1 | 69.9 | 77.5 | 81.5 | 79.7 | 71.8 | 62.6 | 50.2 | 40.9 | 62.4 |
| 1973 | 45.1 | 51.9 | 50.4 | 61.2 | 72.9 | 79.6 | 80.4 | 78.5 | 72.0 | 63.3 | 52.9 | 47.2 | 62.9 |
| 1974 | 47.9 | 49.1 | 56.3 | 60.0 | 69.5 | 77.7 | 81.3 | 79.3 | 77.5 | 66.0 | 53.1 | 44.5 | 63.5 |
| 1975 | 43.4 | 49.9 | 51.5 | 53.9 | 68.4 | 74.7 | 78.1 | 75.9 | 75.8 | 61.4 | 49.5 | 43.9 | 60.6 |
| 1976 | 44.3 | 49.6 | 52.4 | 57.2 | 69.7 | 72.9 | 79.4 | 72.7 | 72.2 | 65.1 | 53.4 | 46.5 | 61.3 |
| 1977 | 44.3 | 53.5 | 52.4 | 65.5 | 63.6 | 79.8 | 81.5 | 80.6 | 74.0 | 66.8 | 54.6 | 51.3 | 64.0 |
| 1978 | 51.4 | 52.6 | 60.3 | 58.9 | 69.9 | 76.3 | 82.4 | 81.4 | 73.0 | 70.0 | 52.1 | 42.8 | 64.2 |
| 1979 | 47.0 | 51.4 | 57.4 | 62.7 | 71.1 | 77.9 | 82.2 | 79.9 | 79.5 | 67.8 | 54.0 | 46.9 | 64.8 |
| 1980 | 49.4 | 53.8 | 53.7 | 61.8 | 67.2 | 73.7 | 84.0 | 80.7 | 75.6 | 68.4 | 54.2 | 46.8 | 64.1 |
| 1981 | 47.9 | 52.0 | 54.5 | 63.2 | 70.9 | 82.8 | 84.9 | 82.9 | 76.5 | 61.4 | 55.5 | 47.7 | 65.0 |
| 1982 | 41.7 | 50.5 | 51.4 | 58.0 | 69.3 | 72.9 | 81.0 | 80.4 | 72.3 | 65.0 | 51.1 | 45.4 | 61.6 |
| 1983 | 45.2 | 53.1 | 55.9 | 57.9 | 69.7 | 76.3 | 79.0 | 82.5 | 78.8 | 68.5 | 54.6 | 51.1 | 64.4 |
| 1984 | 47.8 | 50.7 | 58.4 | 60.8 | 74.8 | 77.5 | 87.0 | 83.5 | 81.0 | 62.4 | 53.6 | 46.5 | 65.3 |
| 1985 | 43.3 | 51.3 | 53.1 | 67.2 | 69.4 | 81.8 | 86.0 | 80.5 | 72.3 | 65.0 | 52.5 | 43.8 | 63.9 |
| 1986 | 53.6 | 55.7 | 60.3 | 62.7 | 71.2 | 79.4 | 81.9 | 84.2 | 71.3 | 66.9 | 56.7 | 47.5 | 66.0 |
| 1987 | 45.3 | 52.8 | 55.6 | 66.7 | 71.8 | 78.4 | 77.0 | 80.2 | 75.5 | 70.1 | 52.3 | 44.2 | 64.2 |
| 1988 | 46.0 | 52.2 | 56.8 | 61.6 | 67.0 | 75.6 | 85.5 | 81.2 | 76.4 | 68.7 | 54.3 | 44.5 | 64.2 |
| 1989 | 42.9 | 48.8 | 57.9 | 67.3 | 69.6 | 77.0 | 82.5 | 79.3 | 74.3 | 65.3 | 53.8 | 43.8 | 63.6 |
| 1990 | 45.5 | 48.0 | 57.3 | 65.7 | 68.1 | 76.8 | 84.0 | 80.6 | 75.8 | 67.7 | 52.9 | 41.5 | 63.7 |
| Record Mean | 45.9 | 51.0 | 55.1 | 61.1 | 67.9 | 75.5 | 81.8 | 79.9 | 74.1 | 64.9 | 54.2 | 46.3 | 63.2 |
| Max | 54.3 | 61.3 | 66.5 | 74.4 | 82.6 | 91.4 | 98.7 | 96.7 | 89.8 | 79.1 | 66.0 | 54.8 | 76.3 |
| Min | 37.4 | 40.8 | 43.7 | 47.8 | 53.3 | 59.6 | 64.8 | 63.2 | 58.3 | 50.7 | 42.4 | 37.7 | 50.0 |

## REFERENCE NOTES FOR TABLES 1, 2, 3 and 6  (FRESNO, CA)

### GENERAL

T - TRACE AMOUNT
BLANK ENTRIES DENOTE MISSING/UNREPORTED DATA.
# INDICATES A STATION OR INSTRUMENT RELOCATION.

### SPECIFIC

#### TABLE 1

(a) - LENGTH OF RECORD IN YEARS. ALTHOUGH INDIVIDUAL MONTHS MAY BE MISSING.

* LESS THAN .05

NORMALS — BASED ON THE 1951-1980 RECORD PERIOD.
EXTREMES — DATES ARE THE MOST RECENT OCCURRENCE.
WIND DIR. — NUMERALS SHOW TENS OF DEGREES CLOCKWISE FROM TRUE NORTH.
    "00" INDICATES CALM.
RESULTANT WIND DIRECTIONS ARE GIVEN TO WHOLE DEGREES.

#### TABLE 3

MAX AND MIN ARE LONG-TERM _MEAN DAILY MAXIMUM_ AND _MEAN DAILY MINIMUM_ TEMPERATURES.

### EXCEPTIONS

#### TABLES 2, 3, and 6

RECORD MEANS ARE THROUGH THE CURRENT YEAR, BEGINNING IN   1888 FOR TEMPERATURE
    1878 FOR PRECIPITATION
    1939 FOR SNOWFALL

HEATING DEGREE DAYS Base 65 deg. F     FRESNO, CALIFORNIA

**TABLE 4**

| SEASON | JULY | AUG | SEP | OCT | NOV | DEC | JAN | FEB | MAR | APR | MAY | JUNE | TOTAL |
|---|---|---|---|---|---|---|---|---|---|---|---|---|---|
| #1961-62 | 0 | 0 | 0 | 126 | 382 | 654 | 724 | 461 | 392 | 66 | 65 | 6 | 2876 |
| 1962-63 | 0 | 0 | 0 | 69 | 291 | 538 | 698 | 234 | 356 | 266 | 30 | 0 | 2482 |
| #1963-64 | 0 | 0 | 2 | 56 | 382 | 767 | 651 | 502 | 417 | 201 | 92 | 12 | 3082 |
| 1964-65 | 0 | 3 | 3 | 41 | 410 | 492 | 572 | 423 | 287 | 191 | 58 | 8 | 2488 |
| 1965-66 | 0 | 0 | 12 | 41 | 302 | 707 | 664 | 492 | 271 | 60 | 7 | 1 | 2557 |
| 1966-67 | 0 | 0 | 1 | 65 | 238 | 606 | 579 | 444 | 322 | 366 | 59 | 11 | 2691 |
| 1967-68 | 0 | 0 | 0 | 29 | 239 | 686 | 619 | 258 | 278 | 139 | 37 | 2 | 2287 |
| 1968-69 | 0 | 0 | 12 | 73 | 387 | 665 | 619 | 480 | 366 | 168 | 30 | 0 | 2800 |
| 1969-70 | 0 | 0 | 0 | 166 | 349 | 574 | 485 | 340 | 291 | 232 | 25 | 0 | 2462 |
| 1970-71 | 0 | 0 | 0 | 108 | 282 | 573 | 593 | 480 | 322 | 181 | 81 | 8 | 2628 |
| 1971-72 | 0 | 0 | 20 | 209 | 423 | 678 | 750 | 357 | 142 | 128 | 37 | 0 | 2744 |
| 1972-73 | 0 | 0 | 2 | 108 | 437 | 740 | 610 | 358 | 444 | 140 | 12 | 2 | 2853 |
| 1973-74 | 0 | 0 | 0 | 94 | 360 | 544 | 522 | 438 | 260 | 160 | 33 | 0 | 2411 |
| 1974-75 | 0 | 0 | 0 | 59 | 350 | 628 | 661 | 419 | 409 | 325 | 53 | 3 | 2907 |
| 1975-76 | 0 | 0 | 0 | 154 | 455 | 648 | 636 | 440 | 385 | 242 | 10 | 9 | 2979 |
| 1976-77 | 0 | 1 | 5 | 63 | 342 | 566 | 636 | 313 | 386 | 42 | 98 | 0 | 2452 |
| 1977-78 | 0 | 0 | 0 | 46 | 302 | 417 | 415 | 343 | 143 | 182 | 19 | 0 | 1867 |
| 1978-79 | 0 | 0 | 6 | 30 | 382 | 682 | 549 | 372 | 234 | 96 | 34 | 0 | 2385 |
| 1979-80 | 0 | 0 | 0 | 56 | 323 | 555 | 473 | 318 | 343 | 129 | 46 | 0 | 2243 |
| 1980-81 | 0 | 0 | 0 | 69 | 318 | 553 | 521 | 359 | 316 | 114 | 9 | 0 | 2259 |
| 1981-82 | 0 | 0 | 0 | 118 | 278 | 530 | 711 | 398 | 412 | 217 | 21 | 4 | 2689 |
| 1982-83 | 0 | 0 | 13 | 62 | 411 | 602 | 607 | 327 | 276 | 206 | 55 | 0 | 2559 |
| 1983-84 | 0 | 0 | 1 | 3 | 304 | 421 | 530 | 408 | 198 | 149 | 6 | 0 | 2020 |
| 1984-85 | 0 | 0 | 0 | 128 | 335 | 566 | 664 | 378 | 361 | 39 | 8 | 3 | 2482 |
| 1985-86 | 0 | 0 | 0 | 63 | 369 | 651 | 345 | 258 | 156 | 98 | 30 | 0 | 1970 |
| 1986-87 | 0 | 0 | 13 | 22 | 242 | 537 | 602 | 337 | 282 | 56 | 26 | 0 | 2117 |
| 1987-88 | 0 | 0 | 0 | 7 | 374 | 636 | 583 | 366 | 251 | 124 | 69 | 12 | 2422 |
| 1988-89 | 0 | 0 | 0 | 20 | 316 | 629 | 679 | 450 | 213 | 52 | 14 | 0 | 2373 |
| 1989-90 | 0 | 0 | 7 | 73 | 310 | 649 | 598 | 470 | 236 | 35 | 19 | 1 | 2398 |
| 1990-91 | 0 | 0 | 0 | 17 | 356 | 722 | | | | | | | |

**TABLE 5**     COOLING DEGREE DAYS Base 65 deg. F     FRESNO, CALIFORNIA

| YEAR | JAN | FEB | MAR | APR | MAY | JUNE | JULY | AUG | SEP | OCT | NOV | DEC | TOTAL |
|---|---|---|---|---|---|---|---|---|---|---|---|---|---|
| 1969 | 0 | 0 | 4 | 15 | 206 | 241 | 500 | 462 | 331 | 10 | 0 | 0 | 1769 |
| 1970 | 0 | 0 | 0 | 0 | 212 | 353 | 573 | 466 | 245 | 67 | 3 | 0 | 1919 |
| 1971 | 0 | 0 | 0 | 8 | 64 | 296 | 529 | 505 | 279 | 89 | 0 | 0 | 1770 |
| 1972 | 0 | 0 | 17 | 18 | 195 | 383 | 518 | 464 | 213 | 42 | 0 | 0 | 1850 |
| 1973 | 0 | 0 | 0 | 32 | 264 | 419 | 484 | 423 | 218 | 47 | 4 | 0 | 1891 |
| 1974 | 0 | 0 | 0 | 20 | 179 | 384 | 512 | 448 | 381 | 96 | 0 | 0 | 2020 |
| 1975 | 0 | 0 | 0 | 0 | 164 | 303 | 413 | 344 | 329 | 49 | 0 | 0 | 1602 |
| 1976 | 0 | 0 | 2 | 16 | 162 | 254 | 456 | 228 | 228 | 73 | 0 | 0 | 1437 |
| 1977 | 0 | 0 | 0 | 62 | 60 | 451 | 518 | 494 | 275 | 108 | 0 | 0 | 1968 |
| 1978 | 0 | 0 | 3 | 6 | 179 | 342 | 546 | 516 | 250 | 187 | 0 | 0 | 2029 |
| 1979 | 0 | 0 | 2 | 37 | 229 | 396 | 541 | 471 | 442 | 149 | 0 | 0 | 2267 |
| 1980 | 0 | 0 | 0 | 39 | 120 | 265 | 594 | 493 | 326 | 181 | 0 | 0 | 2018 |
| 1981 | 0 | 0 | 0 | 67 | 200 | 545 | 622 | 562 | 352 | 14 | 0 | 0 | 2362 |
| 1982 | 0 | 0 | 0 | 12 | 162 | 251 | 501 | 483 | 240 | 70 | 0 | 0 | 1719 |
| 1983 | 0 | 0 | 0 | 0 | 207 | 343 | 440 | 537 | 422 | 119 | 0 | 0 | 2068 |
| 1984 | 0 | 0 | 1 | 30 | 318 | 382 | 688 | 581 | 487 | 55 | 0 | 0 | 2542 |
| 1985 | 0 | 0 | 0 | 111 | 153 | 516 | 657 | 487 | 227 | 69 | 2 | 0 | 2222 |
| 1986 | 0 | 1 | 18 | 34 | 231 | 440 | 530 | 603 | 206 | 87 | 0 | 0 | 2150 |
| 1987 | 0 | 0 | 0 | 114 | 243 | 409 | 379 | 480 | 323 | 172 | 0 | 0 | 2120 |
| 1988 | 0 | 0 | 3 | 28 | 139 | 338 | 642 | 511 | 349 | 143 | 3 | 0 | 2156 |
| 1989 | 0 | 0 | 4 | 129 | 166 | 366 | 546 | 449 | 291 | 90 | 0 | 0 | 2041 |
| 1990 | 0 | 0 | 2 | 61 | 122 | 360 | 595 | 490 | 333 | 108 | 0 | 0 | 2071 |

**TABLE 6**     SNOWFALL (inches)     FRESNO, CALIFORNIA

| SEASON | JULY | AUG | SEP | OCT | NOV | DEC | JAN | FEB | MAR | APR | MAY | JUNE | TOTAL |
|---|---|---|---|---|---|---|---|---|---|---|---|---|---|
| 1970-71 | 0.0 | 0.0 | 0.0 | 0.0 | 0.0 | 0.0 | T | 0.0 | 0.0 | 0.0 | 0.0 | 0.0 | T |
| 1971-72 | 0.0 | 0.0 | 0.0 | 0.0 | 0.0 | 0.0 | T | 0.0 | 0.0 | 0.0 | 0.0 | 0.0 | T |
| 1972-73 | 0.0 | 0.0 | 0.0 | 0.0 | 0.0 | T | 0.0 | 0.0 | T | 0.0 | 0.0 | 0.0 | T |
| 1973-74 | 0.0 | 0.0 | 0.0 | 0.0 | 0.0 | 0.0 | 0.0 | 0.0 | 0.0 | 0.0 | 0.0 | 0.0 | 0.0 |
| 1974-75 | 0.0 | 0.0 | 0.0 | T | 0.0 | 0.0 | 0.0 | 0.0 | 0.0 | 0.0 | 0.0 | 0.0 | T |
| 1975-76 | 0.0 | 0.0 | 0.0 | 0.0 | 0.0 | 0.0 | 0.0 | T | 0.0 | 0.0 | 0.0 | 0.0 | T |
| 1976-77 | 0.0 | 0.0 | 0.0 | 0.0 | 0.0 | 0.0 | 0.0 | 0.0 | 0.0 | 0.0 | 0.0 | 0.0 | 0.0 |
| 1977-78 | 0.0 | 0.0 | 0.0 | 0.0 | 0.0 | 0.0 | 0.0 | 0.0 | 0.0 | 0.0 | 0.0 | 0.0 | 0.0 |
| 1978-79 | 0.0 | 0.0 | 0.0 | 0.0 | 0.0 | 0.0 | 0.0 | T | T | 0.0 | 0.0 | 0.0 | T |
| 1979-80 | 0.0 | 0.0 | 0.0 | 0.0 | 0.0 | 0.0 | 0.0 | 0.0 | 0.0 | 0.0 | 0.0 | 0.0 | 0.0 |
| 1980-81 | 0.0 | 0.0 | 0.0 | 0.0 | 0.0 | 0.0 | 0.0 | 0.0 | 0.0 | 0.0 | 0.0 | 0.0 | 0.0 |
| 1981-82 | 0.0 | 0.0 | 0.0 | 0.0 | 0.0 | 0.0 | 0.0 | 0.0 | 0.0 | 0.0 | 0.0 | 0.0 | 0.0 |
| 1982-83 | 0.0 | 0.0 | 0.0 | 0.0 | 0.0 | 0.0 | 0.0 | 0.0 | 0.0 | 0.0 | 0.0 | 0.0 | 0.0 |
| 1983-84 | 0.0 | 0.0 | 0.0 | 0.0 | 0.0 | 0.0 | 0.0 | 0.0 | 0.0 | 0.0 | 0.0 | 0.0 | 0.0 |
| 1984-85 | 0.0 | 0.0 | 0.0 | 0.0 | 0.0 | 0.0 | 0.0 | 0.0 | 0.0 | 0.0 | 0.0 | 0.0 | 0.0 |
| 1985-86 | 0.0 | 0.0 | 0.0 | 0.0 | 0.0 | 0.0 | 0.0 | 0.0 | 0.0 | 0.0 | 0.0 | 0.0 | 0.0 |
| 1986-87 | 0.0 | 0.0 | 0.0 | 0.0 | 0.0 | 0.0 | 0.0 | 0.0 | 0.0 | 0.0 | 0.0 | 0.0 | 0.0 |
| 1987-88 | 0.0 | 0.0 | 0.0 | 0.0 | 0.0 | 0.0 | 0.0 | 0.0 | 0.0 | 0.0 | 0.0 | 0.0 | 0.0 |
| 1988-89 | 0.0 | 0.0 | 0.0 | 0.0 | 0.0 | 0.0 | 0.0 | 0.0 | 0.0 | 0.0 | 0.0 | 0.0 | 0.0 |
| 1989-90 | 0.0 | 0.0 | 0.0 | 0.0 | 0.0 | 0.0 | 0.0 | 0.0 | 0.0 | 0.0 | 0.0 | 0.0 | T |
| 1990-91 | 0.0 | 0.0 | 0.0 | 0.0 | 0.0 | T | 0.0 | 0.0 | 0.0 | 0.0 | 0.0 | 0.0 | T |
| Record Mean | 0.0 | 0.0 | 0.0 | T | 0.0 | T | 0.1 | T | T | 0.0 | 0.0 | 0.0 | 0.1 |

**See Reference Notes, relative to all above tables, on preceding page.**

The climate of Los Angeles is normally pleasant and mild through the year. The Pacific Ocean is the primary moderating influence. The coastal mountain ranges lying along the north and east sides of the Los Angeles coastal basin act as a buffer against extremes of summer heat and winter cold occurring in desert and plateau regions in the interior. A variable balance between mild sea breezes, and either hot or cold winds from the interior, results in some variety in weather conditions, but temperature and humidity are usually well within the limits of human comfort. An important, and somewhat unusual, aspect of the climate of the Los Angeles metropolitan area is the pronounced difference in temperature, humidity, cloudiness, fog, rain, and sunshine over fairly short distances.

These differences are closely related to the distance from, and elevation above, the Pacific Ocean. Both high and low temperatures become more extreme and the average relative humidity becomes lower as one goes inland and up foothill slopes. Relative humidity is frequently high near the coast, but may be quite low along the foothills. During periods of high temperatures, the relative humidity is usually below normal so that discomfort is rare, except for infrequent periods when high temperatures and high humidities occur together.

Like other Pacific Coast areas, most rainfall comes during the winter with nearly 85 percent of the annual total occurring from November through March, while summers are practically rainless. As in many semi-arid regions, there is a marked variability in monthly and seasonal totals. Precipitation generally increases with distance from the ocean, from a yearly total of around 12 inches in coastal sections to the south of the city to over 20 inches in foothill areas. Destructive flash floods occasionally develop in and below some mountain canyons. Snow is often visible on nearby mountains in the winter, but is extremely rare in the coastal basin. Thunderstorms are infrequent.

Prevailing winds are from the west during the spring, summer, and early autumn, with northeasterly wind predominating the remainder of the year. At times, the lack of air movement, combined with a frequent and persistent temperature inversion, is associated with concentrations of air pollution in the Los Angeles coastal basin and some adjacent areas. In fall, winter, and early spring months, occasional foehn-like descending Santa Ana winds come from the northeast over ridges and through passes in the coastal mountains. These Santa Ana winds may pick up considerable amounts of dust and reach speeds of 35 to 50 mph in north and east sections of the city, with higher speeds in outlying areas to the north and east, but rarely reach coastal portions of the city.

Sunshine, fog, and clouds depend a great deal on topography and distance from the ocean. Low clouds are common at night and in the morning along the coast during spring and summer, but form later and clear earlier near the foothills so that annual cloudiness and fog frequencies are greatest near the ocean, and sunshine totals are highest on the inland side of the city. The sun shines about 75 percent of daytime hours at the Civic Center. Light fog may accompany the usual night and morning low clouds, but dense fog is more likely to occur during the night and early morning hours of the winter months.

## TABLE 1 NORMALS, MEANS AND EXTREMES

LOS ANGELES, CALIFORNIA CIVIC CENTER

LATITUDE: 34°03'N    LONGITUDE: 118°14'W    ELEVATION: FT. GRND    270 BARO    TIME ZONE: PACIFIC    WBAN: 93134

| | (a) | JAN | FEB | MAR | APR | MAY | JUNE | JULY | AUG | SEP | OCT | NOV | DEC | YEAR |
|---|---|---|---|---|---|---|---|---|---|---|---|---|---|---|
| **TEMPERATURE °F:** | | | | | | | | | | | | | | |
| Normals | | | | | | | | | | | | | | |
| -Daily Maximum | | 66.6 | 68.5 | 68.7 | 70.9 | 73.2 | 77.9 | 83.8 | 84.1 | 83.0 | 78.5 | 72.7 | 68.1 | 74.7 |
| -Daily Minimum | | 47.7 | 49.2 | 50.2 | 53.0 | 56.6 | 60.4 | 64.3 | 65.3 | 63.7 | 59.2 | 52.7 | 48.4 | 55.9 |
| -Monthly | | 57.2 | 58.9 | 59.5 | 62.0 | 64.9 | 69.2 | 74.1 | 74.7 | 73.4 | 68.9 | 62.7 | 58.3 | 65.3 |
| Extremes | | | | | | | | | | | | | | |
| -Record Highest | 50 | 95 | 94 | 98 | 106 | 102 | 112 | 107 | 105 | 110 | 108 | 100 | 91 | 112 |
| -Year | | 1971 | 1986 | 1988 | 1989 | 1967 | 1990 | 1985 | 1983 | 1988 | 1987 | 1966 | 1979 | JUN 1990 |
| -Record Lowest | 50 | 28 | 34 | 35 | 39 | 46 | 50 | 54 | 53 | 51 | 41 | 38 | 30 | 28 |
| -Year | | 1949 | 1989 | 1976 | 1975 | 1964 | 1953 | 1952 | 1943 | 1948 | 1971 | 1978 | 1978 | JAN 1949 |
| **NORMAL DEGREE DAYS:** | | | | | | | | | | | | | | |
| Heating (base 65°F) | | 252 | 191 | 190 | 129 | 62 | 27 | 0 | 0 | 0 | 27 | 108 | 218 | 1204 |
| Cooling (base 65°F) | | 10 | 21 | 20 | 39 | 59 | 153 | 282 | 301 | 256 | 148 | 39 | 11 | 1339 |
| **% OF POSSIBLE SUNSHINE** | 32 | 69 | 72 | 73 | 70 | 66 | 65 | 82 | 83 | 79 | 73 | 74 | 71 | 73 |
| **MEAN SKY COVER (tenths)** | | | | | | | | | | | | | | |
| Sunrise - Sunset | 34 | 4.4 | 4.7 | 4.7 | 4.7 | 4.8 | 4.3 | 2.7 | 2.6 | 3.0 | 3.8 | 3.7 | 4.2 | 4.0 |
| **MEAN NUMBER OF DAYS:** | | | | | | | | | | | | | | |
| Sunrise to Sunset | | | | | | | | | | | | | | |
| -Clear | 34 | 14.3 | 12.4 | 12.9 | 12.0 | 11.4 | 13.6 | 20.9 | 22.4 | 18.4 | 16.1 | 16.5 | 15.0 | 186.0 |
| -Partly Cloudy | 34 | 8.1 | 6.9 | 9.3 | 9.8 | 11.8 | 10.5 | 8.9 | 7.4 | 8.4 | 9.3 | 7.4 | 8.0 | 105.8 |
| -Cloudy | 34 | 8.5 | 9.0 | 8.7 | 8.2 | 7.8 | 5.9 | 1.1 | 1.2 | 3.3 | 5.6 | 6.1 | 8.0 | 73.5 |
| Precipitation | | | | | | | | | | | | | | |
| .01 inches or more | 50 | 5.8 | 5.3 | 6.2 | 3.7 | 1.3 | 0.6 | 0.1 | 0.7 | 1.3 | 1.9 | 3.6 | 4.8 | 35.0 |
| Snow,Ice pellets | | | | | | | | | | | | | | |
| 1.0 inches or more | 44 | 0.0 | 0.0 | 0.0 | 0.0 | 0.0 | 0.0 | 0.0 | 0.0 | 0.0 | 0.0 | 0.0 | 0.0 | 0.0 |
| Thunderstorms | 24 | 0.5 | 1.1 | 0.9 | 0.8 | 0.2 | 0.1 | 0.2 | 0.4 | 0.4 | 0.3 | 0.6 | 0.7 | 6.1 |
| Heavy Fog Visibility | | | | | | | | | | | | | | |
| 1/4 mile or less | 24 | 1.5 | 1.8 | 1.1 | 1.3 | 0.5 | 0.6 | 0.5 | 0.8 | 1.5 | 2.6 | 2.5 | 2.1 | 16.8 |
| Temperature °F | | | | | | | | | | | | | | |
| -Maximum | | | | | | | | | | | | | | |
| 90° and above | 50 | 0.1 | 0.1 | 0.2 | 0.9 | 1.1 | 1.5 | 4.0 | 4.3 | 5.9 | 3.1 | 0.7 | 0.* | 21.7 |
| 32° and below | 50 | 0.0 | 0.0 | 0.0 | 0.0 | 0.0 | 0.0 | 0.0 | 0.0 | 0.0 | 0.0 | 0.0 | 0.0 | 0.0 |
| -Minimum | | | | | | | | | | | | | | |
| 32° and below | 50 | 0.1 | 0.0 | 0.0 | 0.0 | 0.0 | 0.0 | 0.0 | 0.0 | 0.0 | 0.0 | 0.0 | 0.1 | 0.2 |
| 0° and below | 50 | 0.0 | 0.0 | 0.0 | 0.0 | 0.0 | 0.0 | 0.0 | 0.0 | 0.0 | 0.0 | 0.0 | 0.0 | 0.0 |
| **AVG. STATION PRESS.(mb)** | | | | | | | | | | | | | | |
| **RELATIVE HUMIDITY (%)** | | | | | | | | | | | | | | |
| Hour 04 | 17 | 63 | 71 | 74 | 78 | 81 | 85 | 84 | 84 | 78 | 76 | 61 | 62 | 75 |
| Hour 10 (Local Time) | 10 | 51 | 54 | 52 | 53 | 56 | 59 | 54 | 56 | 52 | 55 | 45 | 45 | 53 |
| Hour 16 | 23 | 50 | 52 | 52 | 54 | 55 | 56 | 53 | 55 | 54 | 56 | 49 | 50 | 53 |
| Hour 22 | 11 | 67 | 70 | 72 | 74 | 75 | 78 | 79 | 79 | 76 | 74 | 62 | 62 | 72 |
| **PRECIPITATION (inches):** | | | | | | | | | | | | | | |
| Water Equivalent | | | | | | | | | | | | | | |
| -Normal | | 3.69 | 2.96 | 2.35 | 1.17 | 0.23 | 0.03 | 0.00 | 0.12 | 0.27 | 0.21 | 1.85 | 1.97 | 14.85 |
| -Maximum Monthly | 50 | 14.94 | 12.75 | 8.37 | 6.02 | 3.03 | 0.32 | 0.18 | 2.26 | 2.82 | 2.37 | 9.68 | 6.57 | 14.94 |
| -Year | | 1969 | 1980 | 1983 | 1965 | 1977 | 1964 | 1986 | 1977 | 1976 | 1987 | 1965 | 1971 | JAN 1969 |
| -Minimum Monthly | 50 | 0.00 | 0.00 | 0.00 | 0.00 | 0.00 | 0.00 | 0.00 | 0.00 | 0.00 | 0.00 | 0.00 | 0.00 | 0.00 |
| -Year | | 1976 | 1951 | 1959 | 1979 | 1981 | 1982 | 1983 | 1982 | 1980 | 1980 | 1980 | 1990 | DEC 1990 |
| -Maximum in 24 hrs | 50 | 6.11 | 4.02 | 3.79 | 2.05 | 2.41 | 0.32 | 0.18 | 2.22 | 1.95 | 1.77 | 4.07 | 3.92 | 6.11 |
| -Year | | 1956 | 1944 | 1978 | 1956 | 1977 | 1964 | 1986 | 1977 | 1986 | 1983 | 1970 | 1965 | JAN 1956 |
| Snow,Ice pellets | | | | | | | | | | | | | | |
| -Maximum Monthly | 47 | 0.3 | T | 0.0 | 0.0 | 0.0 | 0.0 | 0.0 | 0.0 | 0.0 | 0.0 | 0.0 | T | 0.3 |
| -Year | | 1949 | 1951 | | | | | | | | | | 1947 | JAN 1949 |
| -Maximum in 24 hrs | 44 | 0.3 | T | 0.0 | 0.0 | 0.0 | 0.0 | 0.0 | 0.0 | 0.0 | 0.0 | 0.0 | T | 0.3 |
| -Year | | 1949 | 1951 | | | | | | | | | | 1947 | JAN 1949 |
| **WIND:** | | | | | | | | | | | | | | |
| Mean Speed (mph) | 24 | 6.8 | 6.9 | 7.0 | 6.6 | 6.3 | 5.7 | 5.4 | 5.3 | 5.3 | 5.7 | 6.4 | 6.6 | 6.2 |
| Prevailing Direction | | | | | | | | | | | | | | |
| through 1963 | | NE | W | W | W | W | W | W | W | W | W | W | NE | W |
| Fastest Mile | | | | | | | | | | | | | | |
| -Direction (!!!) | 36 | N | NW | NW | NW | NW | N | W | E | NW | N | N | SE | N |
| -Speed (MPH) | 36 | 49 | 40 | 47 | 40 | 39 | 32 | 21 | 24 | 27 | 48 | 42 | 44 | 49 |
| -Year | | 1946 | 1961 | 1964 | 1955 | 1945 | 1949 | 1947 | 1945 | 1941 | 1959 | 1946 | 1943 | JAN 1946 |
| Peak Gust | | | | | | | | | | | | | | |
| -Direction (!!!) | | | | | | | | | | | | | | |
| -Speed (mph) | | | | | | | | | | | | | | |
| -Date | | | | | | | | | | | | | | |

**See reference Notes to this table on the following page.**

PRECIPITATION (inches)  LOS ANGELES, CALIFORNIA CIVIC CENTER

**TABLE 2**

| YEAR | JAN | FEB | MAR | APR | MAY | JUNE | JULY | AUG | SEP | OCT | NOV | DEC | ANNUAL |
|---|---|---|---|---|---|---|---|---|---|---|---|---|---|
| 1961 | 1.28 | 0.15 | 0.57 | 0.29 | T | T | T | 0.03 | 0.05 | T | 2.02 | 1.44 | 5.83 |
| 1962 | 2.56 | 11.57 | 1.10 | T | 0.02 | T | 0.00 | 0.00 | 0.00 | 0.12 | T | T | 15.37 |
| 1963 | 0.52 | 2.88 | 2.78 | 1.94 | T | 0.14 | 0.00 | 0.02 | 1.31 | 0.57 | 2.15 | T | 12.31 |
| 1964 | 1.43 | T | 1.79 | 0.33 | 0.01 | 0.32 | T | 0.00 | 0.00 | 0.33 | 1.72 | 2.05 | 7.98 |
| 1965 | 0.84 | 0.23 | 2.49 | 6.02 | 0.00 | 0.01 | T | 0.01 | 1.80 | 0.00 | 9.68 | 5.73 | 26.81 |
| 1966 | 0.96 | 1.51 | 0.53 | 0.00 | 0.22 | 0.00 | | T | 0.30 | 0.06 | 4.07 | 5.26 | 12.91 |
| 1967 | 5.93 | 0.11 | 2.50 | 3.76 | 0.01 | 0.00 | 0.00 | T | 1.02 | 0.00 | 8.67 | 1.66 | 23.66 |
| 1968 | 0.90 | 0.49 | 3.34 | 0.49 | 0.00 | 0.01 | 0.01 | 0.11 | 0.03 | 0.55 | 0.37 | 1.28 | 7.58 |
| 1969 | 14.94 | 8.03 | 1.49 | 0.63 | 0.03 | T | 0.03 | 0.00 | T | 0.00 | 1.11 | 0.06 | 26.32 |
| 1970 | 1.59 | 2.58 | 2.35 | 0.00 | 0.00 | 0.04 | 0.00 | 0.00 | 0.00 | 0.00 | 5.05 | 4.92 | 16.54 |
| 1971 | 0.43 | 0.67 | 0.53 | 0.50 | 0.22 | 0.00 | T | 0.00 | T | 0.04 | 0.30 | 6.57 | 9.26 |
| 1972 | 0.00 | 0.13 | T | 0.03 | 0.03 | 0.07 | 0.00 | 0.35 | 0.02 | 0.29 | 3.26 | 2.36 | 6.54 |
| 1973 | 4.39 | 7.89 | 2.70 | 0.00 | T | 0.00 | 0.00 | 0.00 | 0.00 | 0.12 | 1.68 | 0.67 | 17.45 |
| 1974 | 8.35 | 0.14 | 3.78 | 0.10 | 0.08 | 0.00 | 0.00 | 0.00 | 0.00 | 0.58 | 0.07 | 3.59 | 16.69 |
| 1975 | 0.12 | 3.54 | 4.83 | 1.53 | 0.09 | 0.00 | 0.00 | 0.00 | 0.00 | 0.27 | 0.00 | 0.32 | 10.70 |
| 1976 | 0.00 | 3.71 | 1.81 | 0.84 | 0.05 | 0.22 | 0.00 | 0.08 | 2.82 | 0.24 | 0.49 | 0.75 | 11.01 |
| 1977 | 2.84 | 0.17 | 1.89 | 0.00 | 3.03 | 0.00 | 0.00 | 2.26 | 0.00 | 0.00 | 0.08 | 4.70 | 14.97 |
| 1978 | 7.70 | 8.91 | 8.02 | 1.77 | 0.00 | 0.00 | 0.00 | 0.00 | 0.39 | 0.05 | 2.28 | 1.45 | 30.57 |
| 1979 | 6.59 | 3.06 | 5.85 | 0.00 | 0.00 | 0.00 | 0.00 | 0.01 | T | 0.77 | 0.21 | 0.51 | 17.00 |
| 1980 | 7.50 | 12.75 | 4.79 | 0.31 | 0.13 | 0.00 | 0.00 | 0.00 | 0.00 | 0.00 | 0.00 | 0.85 | 26.33 |
| 1981 | 2.02 | 1.48 | 4.10 | 0.53 | 0.00 | 0.00 | 0.00 | 0.00 | 0.00 | 0.02 | 1.80 | 0.48 | 10.92 |
| 1982 | 2.17 | 0.70 | 3.54 | 1.39 | 0.12 | 0.00 | 0.00 | 0.00 | 0.84 | 0.19 | 4.41 | 1.05 | 14.41 |
| 1983 | 6.49 | 4.37 | 8.37 | 5.16 | 0.36 | 0.01 | 0.00 | 0.79 | 1.99 | 0.75 | 2.52 | 3.23 | 34.04 |
| 1984 | 0.17 | 0.00 | 0.28 | 0.69 | 0.00 | 0.01 | 0.00 | 0.40 | 0.23 | 0.15 | 1.44 | 5.53 | 8.90 |
| 1985 | 0.71 | 2.84 | 1.29 | 0.00 | 0.23 | 0.00 | 0.00 | 0.00 | 0.00 | 0.19 | 0.42 | 2.91 | 8.92 |
| 1986 | 2.19 | 6.10 | 5.27 | 0.45 | 0.00 | 0.00 | 0.18 | 0.00 | 1.97 | 0.53 | 0.94 | 0.37 | 18.00 |
| 1987 | 1.39 | 1.22 | 0.95 | 0.06 | 0.00 | 0.05 | 0.01 | 0.00 | 0.09 | 2.37 | 1.13 | 1.84 | 9.11 |
| 1988 | 1.65 | 1.72 | 0.26 | 3.41 | 0.00 | 0.00 | 0.00 | 0.05 | 0.04 | 0.00 | 0.70 | 3.80 | 9.98 |
| 1989 | 0.73 | 1.90 | 0.81 | 0.00 | 0.05 | 0.00 | 0.00 | 0.00 | 0.35 | 0.43 | 0.29 | 0.00 | 4.56 |
| 1990 | 1.24 | 3.12 | 0.17 | 0.58 | 1.17 | 0.00 | 0.00 | 0.02 | 0.00 | 0.00 | 0.19 | 0.00 | 6.49 |
| Record Mean | 3.02 | 3.09 | 2.60 | 1.07 | 0.31 | 0.06 | 0.01 | 0.06 | 0.25 | 0.50 | 1.37 | 2.50 | 14.82 |

**TABLE 3**  AVERAGE TEMPERATURE (deg. F)  LOS ANGELES, CALIFORNIA CIVIC CENTER

| YEAR | JAN | FEB | MAR | APR | MAY | JUNE | JULY | AUG | SEP | OCT | NOV | DEC | ANNUAL |
|---|---|---|---|---|---|---|---|---|---|---|---|---|---|
| 1961 | 62.0 | 61.0 | 60.1 | 64.0 | 63.4 | 68.8 | 74.2 | 74.3 | 71.0 | 67.9 | 60.2 | 56.9 | 65.3 |
| 1962 | 57.5 | 53.8 | 55.2 | 64.3 | 62.9 | 66.3 | 70.1 | 74.1 | 70.9 | 65.7 | 60.6 | 57.4 | 63.2 |
| 1963 | 55.6 | 62.7 | 58.3 | 59.6 | 64.1 | 66.4 | 72.1 | 73.7 | 77.3 | 69.1 | 62.3 | 60.6 | 65.1 |
| 1964 | 56.7 | 59.0 | 58.6 | 60.5 | 61.7 | 64.8 | 71.8 | 73.4 | 70.2 | 70.5 | 59.8 | 56.5 | 63.6 |
| 1965 | 58.3 | 58.0 | 59.0 | 61.7 | 63.4 | 64.1 | 70.1 | 75.6 | 69.6 | 73.1 | 62.0 | 56.9 | 64.3 |
| 1966 | 55.7 | 56.2 | 61.3 | 64.4 | 64.5 | 70.2 | 74.4 | 76.6 | 73.4 | 71.2 | 63.6 | 60.7 | 66.0 |
| 1967 | 59.2 | 62.9 | 61.0 | 56.1 | 67.3 | 66.3 | 75.7 | 79.2 | 75.2 | 72.5 | 66.6 | 55.6 | 66.5 |
| 1968 | 58.5 | 63.8 | 62.9 | 64.0 | 65.5 | 69.2 | 74.7 | 74.1 | 73.4 | 69.2 | 63.3 | 56.2 | 66.2 |
| 1969 | 58.3 | 54.9 | 59.7 | 63.8 | 66.6 | 67.2 | 73.8 | 77.0 | 71.7 | 67.3 | 65.2 | 59.2 | 65.4 |
| 1970 | 57.6 | 61.4 | 61.2 | 60.9 | 67.4 | 70.0 | 75.3 | 76.2 | 74.4 | 68.3 | 63.3 | 57.2 | 66.1 |
| 1971 | 58.8 | 59.2 | 60.3 | 62.0 | 64.0 | 68.8 | 74.2 | 78.9 | 74.6 | 67.4 | 60.2 | 52.8 | 65.1 |
| 1972 | 55.5 | 60.3 | 63.7 | 63.9 | 67.6 | 72.2 | 78.0 | 77.4 | 72.3 | 67.2 | 62.2 | 58.1 | 66.5 |
| 1973 | 56.4 | 60.0 | 57.9 | 63.1 | 65.8 | 72.0 | 72.4 | 73.6 | 70.0 | 68.8 | 60.0 | 59.9 | 65.0 |
| 1974 | 55.2 | 59.2 | 59.6 | 64.7 | 65.7 | 72.2 | 74.1 | 72.3 | 73.2 | 67.6 | 64.0 | 56.2 | 65.3 |
| 1975 | 57.6 | 55.8 | 55.7 | 56.0 | 62.7 | 65.7 | 72.5 | 71.9 | 74.0 | 66.4 | 61.2 | 57.0 | 63.0 |
| 1976 | 59.4 | 56.4 | 58.4 | 57.8 | 64.3 | 71.1 | 72.6 | 71.6 | 72.6 | 70.7 | 66.9 | 60.4 | 65.2 |
| 1977 | 58.1 | 63.1 | 56.9 | 63.7 | 61.9 | 69.2 | 74.2 | 75.6 | 71.8 | 69.0 | 66.3 | 60.8 | 65.9 |
| 1978 | 58.1 | 58.9 | 63.2 | 60.8 | 68.6 | 71.8 | 73.4 | 73.7 | 76.0 | 70.3 | 58.4 | 53.2 | 65.5 |
| 1979 | 53.3 | 55.0 | 57.9 | 62.7 | 65.4 | 71.5 | 72.1 | 72.1 | 77.4 | 68.7 | 64.6 | 63.2 | 65.4 |
| 1980 | 60.9 | 64.6 | 60.9 | 64.8 | 63.2 | 71.8 | 77.1 | 76.3 | 72.6 | 71.5 | 65.3 | 63.7 | 67.7 |
| 1981 | 61.8 | 64.3 | 62.0 | 62.0 | 68.9 | 77.4 | 77.2 | 78.3 | 75.0 | 68.5 | 65.0 | 62.1 | 68.9 |
| 1982 | 57.1 | 64.0 | 59.3 | 62.2 | 64.4 | 65.3 | 74.0 | 75.1 | 73.9 | 70.9 | 61.7 | 58.1 | 65.5 |
| 1983 | 61.9 | 63.0 | 63.9 | 62.3 | 70.7 | 70.7 | 75.9 | 80.8 | 79.1 | 74.2 | 63.5 | 59.8 | 68.9 |
| 1984 | 61.2 | 61.9 | 65.6 | 65.3 | 72.4 | 72.2 | 78.7 | 76.4 | 81.3 | 68.5 | 61.0 | 57.2 | 68.5 |
| 1985 | 57.5 | 60.4 | 59.3 | 66.8 | 66.3 | 73.5 | 79.2 | 75.7 | 71.8 | 71.3 | 60.4 | 61.7 | 67.0 |
| 1986 | 65.9 | 62.4 | 64.5 | 66.4 | 68.1 | 71.2 | 73.2 | 76.0 | 68.8 | 69.4 | 66.4 | 60.1 | 67.7 |
| 1987 | 57.2 | 60.3 | 61.2 | 67.8 | 68.1 | 69.7 | 70.8 | 73.0 | 75.2 | 71.9 | 62.9 | 54.4 | 66.0 |
| 1988 | 58.3 | 62.9 | 64.9 | 64.1 | 67.2 | 67.9 | 74.3 | 72.9 | 72.2 | 69.7 | 61.9 | 57.1 | 66.8 |
| 1989 | 56.3 | 56.4 | 62.4 | 67.9 | 66.2 | 69.8 | 75.1 | 72.8 | 74.5 | 69.2 | 66.7 | 62.7 | 66.7 |
| 1990 | 59.4 | 58.0 | 61.7 | 65.7 | 66.9 | 74.3 | 77.3 | 74.0 | 76.0 | 73.2 | 65.6 | 57.5 | 67.5 |
| Record Mean | 56.3 | 57.5 | 58.9 | 61.2 | 63.8 | 67.6 | 71.9 | 72.6 | 71.2 | 67.0 | 62.3 | 57.8 | 64.0 |
| Max | 65.5 | 66.7 | 68.0 | 70.4 | 72.6 | 76.9 | 82.2 | 82.8 | 81.5 | 77.1 | 72.7 | 67.2 | 73.6 |
| Min | 47.0 | 48.2 | 49.7 | 52.0 | 55.0 | 58.2 | 61.6 | 62.4 | 60.9 | 56.9 | 52.0 | 48.3 | 54.4 |

## REFERENCE NOTES FOR TABLES 1, 2, 3 and 6   LOS ANGELES, CA (CIVIC CENTER STA.)

### GENERAL

T - TRACE AMOUNT
BLANK ENTRIES DENOTE MISSING/UNREPORTED DATA.
# INDICATES A STATION OR INSTRUMENT RELOCATION.

### SPECIFIC

**TABLE 1**

(a) - LENGTH OF RECORD IN YEARS. ALTHOUGH INDIVIDUAL MONTHS MAY BE MISSING.

* LESS THAN .05

NORMALS — BASED ON THE 1951-1980 RECORD PERIOD.
EXTREMES — DATES ARE THE MOST RECENT OCCURRENCE.
WIND DIR. — NUMERALS SHOW TENS OF DEGREES CLOCKWISE FROM TRUE NORTH.
"00" INDICATES CALM.
RESULTANT WIND DIRECTIONS ARE GIVEN TO WHOLE DEGREES.

**TABLE 3**
MAX AND MIN ARE LONG-TERM MEAN DAILY MAXIMUM AND MEAN DAILY MINIMUM TEMPERATURES.

### EXCEPTIONS

**TABLE 1**

1. RELATIVE HUMIDITY IS THROUGH 1963.
2. THUNDERSTORMS AND HEAVY FOG ARE THROUGH 1964 AND MAY BE INCOMPLETE, DUE TO PART-TIME OPERATIONS.
3. MEAN WIND SPEED IS THROUGH 1964.
4. PERCENT OF POSSIBLE SUNSHINE, MEAN SKY COVER AND DAYS CLEAR-PARTLY CLOUDY-CLOUDY ARE THROUGH 1976.
5. FASTEST MILE WIND IS THROUGH NOVEMBER 1977.

**TABLES 2, 3, and 6**

RECORD MEANS ARE THROUGH THE CURRENT YEAR, BEGINNING IN 1878 FOR TEMPERATURE
1878 FOR PRECIPITATION
1941 FOR SNOWFALL

**TABLE 4**  HEATING DEGREE DAYS Base 65 deg. F     LOS ANGELES, CALIFORNIA CIVIC CENTER

| SEASON | JULY | AUG | SEP | OCT | NOV | DEC | JAN | FEB | MAR | APR | MAY | JUNE | TOTAL |
|---|---|---|---|---|---|---|---|---|---|---|---|---|---|
| 1961-62 | 0 | 0 | 2 | 32 | 161 | 243 | 240 | 309 | 298 | 66 | 97 | 38 | 1486 |
| 1962-63 | 0 | 0 | 0 | 33 | 138 | 228 | 286 | 101 | 202 | 161 | 37 | 24 | 1210 |
| 1963-64 | 0 | 0 | 0 | 1 | 103 | 145 | 250 | 169 | 211 | 169 | 113 | 36 | 1197 |
| 1964-65 | 0 | 0 | 0 | 5 | 186 | 256 | 224 | 196 | 183 | 168 | 70 | 38 | 1326 |
| 1965-66 | 0 | 0 | 0 | 1 | 98 | 264 | 281 | 244 | 126 | 58 | 34 | 0 | 1106 |
| 1966-67 | 0 | 0 | 0 | 0 | 88 | 145 | 179 | 81 | 133 | 260 | 43 | 25 | 954 |
| 1967-68 | 0 | 0 | 0 | 0 | 32 | 287 | 207 | 70 | 99 | 70 | 50 | 7 | 822 |
| 1968-69 | 0 | 0 | 0 | 4 | 76 | 267 | 219 | 277 | 186 | 68 | 25 | 1 | 1123 |
| 1969-70 | 0 | 0 | 0 | 22 | 52 | 182 | 222 | 106 | 128 | 134 | 27 | 1 | 874 |
| 1970-71 | 0 | 0 | 0 | 8 | 72 | 243 | 255 | 184 | 154 | 127 | 77 | 11 | 1131 |
| 1971-72 | 0 | 0 | 0 | 94 | 153 | 288 | 132 | 61 | 35 | 0 | | | 1193 |
| 1972-73 | 0 | 0 | 0 | 14 | 97 | 230 | 266 | 136 | 214 | 77 | 32 | 2 | 1068 |
| 1973-74 | 0 | 0 | 1 | 8 | 156 | 174 | 300 | 160 | 171 | 54 | 32 | 1 | 1057 |
| 1974-75 | 0 | 0 | 0 | 25 | 73 | 268 | 243 | 254 | 283 | 262 | 75 | 21 | 1504 |
| 1975-76 | 0 | 0 | 0 | 31 | 132 | 247 | 190 | 246 | 215 | 215 | 50 | 12 | 1338 |
| 1976-77 | 0 | 0 | 0 | 0 | 62 | 138 | 215 | 86 | 247 | 57 | 108 | 1 | 914 |
| 1977-78 | 0 | 0 | 0 | 14 | 51 | 132 | 209 | 174 | 102 | 122 | 24 | 0 | 828 |
| 1978-79 | 0 | 0 | 0 | 0 | 7 | 209 | 361 | 354 | 274 | 226 | 80 | 46 | 6 1563 |
| 1979-80 | 0 | 0 | 0 | 1 | 59 | 114 | 128 | 60 | 123 | 79 | 75 | 4 | 643 |
| 1980-81 | 0 | 0 | 0 | 2 | 41 | 85 | 103 | 91 | 97 | 43 | 1 | 0 | 463 |
| 1981-82 | 0 | 0 | 0 | 11 | 58 | 102 | 238 | 58 | 184 | 113 | 41 | 16 | 821 |
| 1982-83 | 0 | 0 | 0 | 0 | 3 | 117 | 205 | 134 | 73 | 68 | 2 | 0 | 670 |
| 1983-84 | 0 | 0 | 0 | 0 | 99 | 158 | 140 | 99 | 29 | 59 | 5 | 0 | 589 |
| 1984-85 | 0 | 0 | 0 | 4 | 129 | 239 | 225 | 162 | 179 | 40 | 21 | 0 | 999 |
| 1985-86 | 0 | 0 | 0 | 0 | 163 | 131 | 42 | 125 | 92 | 32 | 7 | 0 | 592 |
| 1986-87 | 0 | 0 | 8 | 2 | 14 | 151 | 241 | 140 | 131 | 31 | 19 | 0 | 737 |
| 1987-88 | 0 | 0 | 0 | 3 | 91 | 323 | 216 | 82 | 81 | 88 | 30 | 11 | 925 |
| 1988-89 | 0 | 0 | 1 | 2 | 98 | 258 | 270 | 271 | 104 | 36 | 27 | 5 | 1072 |
| 1989-90 | 0 | 0 | 0 | 2 | 27 | 102 | 173 | 206 | 130 | 26 | 16 | 2 | 684 |
| 1990-91 | 0 | 0 | 0 | 0 | 42 | 244 | | | | | | | |

**TABLE 5**  COOLING DEGREE DAYS Base 65 deg. F     LOS ANGELES, CALIFORNIA CIVIC CENTER

| YEAR | JAN | FEB | MAR | APR | MAY | JUNE | JULY | AUG | SEP | OCT | NOV | DEC | TOTAL |
|---|---|---|---|---|---|---|---|---|---|---|---|---|---|
| 1969 | 19 | 0 | 30 | 39 | 81 | 73 | 276 | 377 | 209 | 100 | 65 | 10 | 1279 |
| 1970 | 0 | 11 | 17 | 17 | 106 | 155 | 326 | 352 | 287 | 118 | 28 | 10 | 1427 |
| 1971 | 71 | 28 | 16 | 46 | 50 | 131 | 291 | 435 | 296 | 176 | 17 | 0 | 1557 |
| 1972 | 0 | 4 | 27 | 34 | 122 | 223 | 409 | 391 | 225 | 89 | 21 | 25 | 1570 |
| 1973 | 9 | 2 | 0 | 25 | 64 | 220 | 236 | 272 | 157 | 133 | 9 | 21 | 1148 |
| 1974 | 3 | 5 | 8 | 51 | 58 | 223 | 288 | 235 | 254 | 115 | 53 | 2 | 1295 |
| 1975 | 21 | 0 | 0 | 0 | 11 | 48 | 241 | 221 | 277 | 82 | 26 | 4 | 931 |
| 1976 | 22 | 3 | 20 | 10 | 32 | 203 | 245 | 212 | 233 | 185 | 123 | 2 | 1290 |
| 1977 | 7 | 39 | 3 | 23 | 18 | 135 | 293 | 334 | 210 | 148 | 96 | 8 | 1314 |
| 1978 | 0 | 8 | 52 | 2 | 145 | 212 | 269 | 277 | 338 | 177 | 17 | 0 | 1497 |
| 1979 | 0 | 0 | 14 | 17 | 67 | 209 | 229 | 252 | 379 | 124 | 53 | 62 | 1406 |
| 1980 | 10 | 54 | 3 | 82 | 26 | 215 | 380 | 357 | 233 | 210 | 56 | 53 | 1679 |
| 1981 | 12 | 75 | 13 | 81 | 132 | 380 | 387 | 422 | 306 | 124 | 67 | 17 | 2016 |
| 1982 | 0 | 36 | 15 | 36 | 33 | 32 | 286 | 322 | 275 | 194 | 25 | 0 | 1254 |
| 1983 | 44 | 23 | 41 | 21 | 185 | 174 | 342 | 495 | 432 | 292 | 60 | 4 | 2113 |
| 1984 | 29 | 14 | 56 | 73 | 240 | 222 | 433 | 360 | 496 | 123 | 13 | 6 | 2065 |
| 1985 | 0 | 41 | 10 | 100 | 68 | 264 | 447 | 339 | 254 | 210 | 31 | 35 | 1748 |
| 1986 | 77 | 56 | 83 | 80 | 110 | 194 | 261 | 349 | 132 | 145 | 65 | 6 | 1558 |
| 1987 | 6 | 18 | 21 | 120 | 121 | 147 | 186 | 257 | 312 | 221 | 36 | 1 | 1446 |
| 1988 | 13 | 30 | 84 | 68 | 107 | 107 | 297 | 252 | 223 | 154 | 14 | 20 | 1356 |
| 1989 | 8 | 37 | 31 | 131 | 73 | 154 | 318 | 251 | 290 | 139 | 85 | 41 | 1558 |
| 1990 | 10 | 16 | 36 | 54 | 81 | 291 | 388 | 287 | 336 | 262 | 68 | 20 | 1849 |

**TABLE 6**  SNOWFALL (inches)     LOS ANGELES, CALIFORNIA CIVIC CENTER

| SEASON | JULY | AUG | SEP | OCT | NOV | DEC | JAN | FEB | MAR | APR | MAY | JUNE | TOTAL |
|---|---|---|---|---|---|---|---|---|---|---|---|---|---|
| 1970-71 | 0.0 | 0.0 | 0.0 | 0.0 | 0.0 | 0.0 | 0.0 | 0.0 | 0.0 | 0.0 | 0.0 | 0.0 | 0.0 |
| 1971-72 | 0.0 | 0.0 | 0.0 | 0.0 | 0.0 | 0.0 | 0.0 | 0.0 | 0.0 | 0.0 | 0.0 | 0.0 | 0.0 |
| 1972-73 | 0.0 | 0.0 | 0.0 | 0.0 | 0.0 | 0.0 | 0.0 | 0.0 | 0.0 | 0.0 | 0.0 | 0.0 | 0.0 |
| 1973-74 | 0.0 | 0.0 | 0.0 | 0.0 | 0.0 | 0.0 | 0.0 | 0.0 | 0.0 | 0.0 | 0.0 | 0.0 | 0.0 |
| 1974-75 | 0.0 | 0.0 | 0.0 | 0.0 | 0.0 | 0.0 | 0.0 | 0.0 | 0.0 | 0.0 | 0.0 | 0.0 | 0.0 |
| 1975-76 | 0.0 | 0.0 | 0.0 | 0.0 | 0.0 | 0.0 | 0.0 | 0.0 | 0.0 | 0.0 | 0.0 | 0.0 | 0.0 |
| 1976-77 | 0.0 | 0.0 | 0.0 | 0.0 | 0.0 | 0.0 | 0.0 | 0.0 | 0.0 | 0.0 | 0.0 | 0.0 | 0.0 |
| 1977-78 | 0.0 | 0.0 | 0.0 | 0.0 | 0.0 | 0.0 | 0.0 | 0.0 | 0.0 | 0.0 | 0.0 | 0.0 | 0.0 |
| 1978-79 | 0.0 | 0.0 | 0.0 | 0.0 | 0.0 | 0.0 | 0.0 | 0.0 | 0.0 | 0.0 | 0.0 | 0.0 | 0.0 |
| 1979-80 | 0.0 | 0.0 | 0.0 | 0.0 | 0.0 | 0.0 | 0.0 | 0.0 | 0.0 | 0.0 | 0.0 | 0.0 | 0.0 |
| 1980-81 | 0.0 | 0.0 | 0.0 | 0.0 | 0.0 | 0.0 | 0.0 | 0.0 | 0.0 | 0.0 | 0.0 | 0.0 | 0.0 |
| 1981-82 | 0.0 | 0.0 | 0.0 | 0.0 | 0.0 | 0.0 | 0.0 | 0.0 | 0.0 | 0.0 | 0.0 | 0.0 | 0.0 |
| 1982-83 | 0.0 | 0.0 | 0.0 | 0.0 | 0.0 | 0.0 | 0.0 | 0.0 | 0.0 | 0.0 | 0.0 | 0.0 | 0.0 |
| 1983-84 | 0.0 | 0.0 | 0.0 | 0.0 | 0.0 | 0.0 | 0.0 | 0.0 | 0.0 | | | | 0.0 |
| 1984-85 | | | | | | | | | | | | | |
| Record Mean | 0.0 | 0.0 | 0.0 | 0.0 | 0.0 | T | T | T | T | 0.0 | 0.0 | 0.0 | T |

**See Reference Notes, relative to all above tables, on preceding page.**

# SACRAMENTO, CALIFORNIA

Sacramento, and the lower Sacramento Valley, has a mild climate with abundant sunshine most of the year. A nearly cloud-free sky prevails throughout the summer months, and in much of the spring and fall. The summers are usually dry with warm to hot afternoons and mostly mild nights. The rainy season generally is November through March. About 75 percent of the annual precipitation occurs then, but measurable rain falls only on an average of nine days per month during that period. The shielding effect of mountains to the north, east, and west usually modifies winter storms. The Sierra Nevada snow fields, only 70 miles east of Sacramento, usually provide an adequate water supply during the dry season, and an important recreational area in winter. Heavy snowfall and torrential rains frequently fall on the western Sierra slopes, and may produce flood conditions along the Sacramento River and its tributaries. In the valley, however, excessive rainfall as well as damaging winds are rare.

The prevailing wind at Sacramento is southerly every month but November, when it is northerly. Topographic effects, the north-south alignment of the valley, the coast range, and the Sierra Nevada strongly influence the wind flow in the valley. A sea level gap in the coast range permits cool, oceanic air to flow, occasionally, into the valley during the summer season with a marked lowering of temperature through the Sacramento-San Joaquin River Delta to the capital. In the spring and fall, a large north-to-south pressure gradient develops over the northern part of the state. Air flowing over the Siskiyou mountains to the north warms and dries as it descends to the valley floor. This gusty, blustery north wind is a local variation of the chinook. It apparently carries a form of pollen which may cause allergic responses by susceptible individuals.

As is well known, relative humidity has a marked influence on the reactions of plants and animals to temperature. The extremely low relative humidity that ordinarily accompanies high temperatures in this valley should be considered when comparing temperatures here with those of cities in more humid regions. The extreme hot spells, with temperatures exceeding 100 degrees, are usually caused by air flow from a sub-tropical high pressure area that brings light to nearly calm winds and humidities below 20 percent.

Thunderstorms are few in number, usually mild in character, and occur mainly in the spring. An occasional thunderstorm may drift over the valley from the Sierra Nevada in the summer. Snow falls so rarely, and in such small amounts, that its occurrence may be disregarded as a climatic feature. Heavy fog occurs mostly in midwinter, never in summer, and seldom in spring or autumn. An occasional winter fog, under stagnant atmospheric conditions, may continue for several days. Light and moderate fogs are more frequent, and may come anytime during the wet, cold season. The fog is the radiational cooling type, and is usually confined to the early morning hours.

Sacramento is the geographical center of the great interior valley of California that reaches from Red Bluff in the north to Bakersville in the south. This predominantly agricultural region produces an extremely wide and abundant variety of fruits, grains, and vegetables ranging from the semi-tropical to the hardier varieties.

Based on the 1951-1980 period, the average first occurrence of 32 degrees Fahrenheit in the fall is December 1 and the average last occurrence in the spring is February 14.

# TABLE 1 — NORMALS, MEANS AND EXTREMES

SACRAMENTO, CALIFORNIA

LATITUDE: 38°31'N   LONGITUDE: 121°30'W   ELEVATION: FT. GRND 17 BARO 20   TIME ZONE: PACIFIC   WBAN: 23232

| | (a) | JAN | FEB | MAR | APR | MAY | JUNE | JULY | AUG | SEP | OCT | NOV | DEC | YEAR |
|---|---|---|---|---|---|---|---|---|---|---|---|---|---|---|
| **TEMPERATURE °F:** | | | | | | | | | | | | | | |
| Normals -Daily Maximum | | 52.6 | 59.4 | 64.1 | 71.0 | 79.7 | 87.4 | 93.3 | 91.7 | 87.6 | 77.7 | 63.2 | 53.2 | 73.4 |
| -Daily Minimum | | 37.9 | 41.2 | 42.4 | 45.3 | 50.1 | 55.1 | 57.9 | 57.6 | 55.8 | 50.0 | 42.8 | 37.9 | 47.8 |
| -Monthly | | 45.3 | 50.3 | 53.2 | 58.2 | 64.9 | 71.2 | 75.6 | 74.7 | 71.7 | 63.9 | 53.0 | 45.6 | 60.6 |
| Extremes -Record Highest | 39 | 70 | 76 | 88 | 93 | 105 | 115 | 114 | 108 | 108 | 101 | 87 | 72 | 115 |
| -Year | | 1976 | 1988 | 1988 | 1988 | 1984 | 1961 | 1972 | 1978 | 1988 | 1970 | 1960 | 1989 | JUN 1961 |
| -Record Lowest | 39 | 23 | 23 | 26 | 32 | 36 | 41 | 48 | 49 | 43 | 36 | 26 | 20 | 20 |
| -Year | | 1979 | 1989 | 1971 | 1953 | 1974 | 1952 | 1983 | 1978 | 1978 | 1989 | 1961 | 1972 | DEC 1972 |
| **NORMAL DEGREE DAYS:** Heating (base 65°F) | | 611 | 412 | 366 | 229 | 83 | 21 | 0 | 0 | 7 | 82 | 360 | 601 | 2772 |
| Cooling (base 65°F) | | 0 | 0 | 0 | 25 | 80 | 207 | 329 | 301 | 208 | 48 | 0 | 0 | 1198 |
| **% OF POSSIBLE SUNSHINE** | 41 | 46 | 64 | 73 | 81 | 89 | 93 | 97 | 96 | 93 | 86 | 64 | 47 | 77 |
| **MEAN SKY COVER (tenths)** Sunrise-Sunset | 41 | 7.1 | 6.2 | 5.5 | 4.7 | 3.5 | 2.2 | 1.1 | 1.5 | 1.9 | 3.3 | 5.7 | 6.8 | 4.1 |
| **MEAN NUMBER OF DAYS:** Sunrise to Sunset -Clear | 41 | 6.4 | 8.0 | 10.4 | 12.3 | 17.6 | 21.6 | 26.9 | 25.6 | 23.4 | 19.2 | 9.8 | 7.7 | 188.8 |
| -Partly Cloudy | 41 | 5.9 | 6.9 | 8.1 | 9.5 | 8.3 | 5.9 | 3.1 | 4.0 | 4.3 | 6.1 | 7.0 | 5.9 | 75.0 |
| -Cloudy | 41 | 18.7 | 13.3 | 12.5 | 8.2 | 5.1 | 2.5 | 1.0 | 1.3 | 2.3 | 5.7 | 13.2 | 17.5 | 101.4 |
| Precipitation .01 inches or more | 50 | 10.0 | 8.6 | 8.6 | 5.3 | 2.6 | 1.1 | 0.3 | 0.4 | 1.4 | 3.4 | 7.1 | 9.1 | 57.8 |
| Snow,Ice pellets 1.0 inches or more | 41 | 0.0 | 0.* | 0.0 | 0.0 | 0.0 | 0.0 | 0.0 | 0.0 | 0.0 | 0.0 | 0.0 | 0.0 | * |
| Thunderstorms | 41 | 0.3 | 0.5 | 0.8 | 0.8 | 0.3 | 0.2 | 0.2 | 0.1 | 0.5 | 0.3 | 0.3 | 0.2 | 4.6 |
| Heavy Fog Visibility 1/4 mile or less | 41 | 10.1 | 5.2 | 1.6 | 0.4 | 0.2 | 0.0 | 0.0 | 0.* | 0.2 | 1.5 | 5.6 | 9.7 | 34.5 |
| Temperature °F -Maximum 90° and above | 39 | 0.0 | 0.0 | 0.0 | 0.4 | 5.4 | 12.0 | 22.3 | 19.4 | 12.2 | 2.5 | 0.0 | 0.0 | 74.1 |
| 32° and below | 39 | 0.* | 0.0 | 0.0 | 0.0 | 0.0 | 0.0 | 0.0 | 0.0 | 0.0 | 0.0 | 0.0 | 0.* | 0.1 |
| -Minimum 32° and below | 39 | 6.6 | 1.8 | 0.6 | 0.* | 0.0 | 0.0 | 0.0 | 0.0 | 0.0 | 0.0 | 1.2 | 6.2 | 16.4 |
| 0° and below | 39 | 0.0 | 0.0 | 0.0 | 0.0 | 0.0 | 0.0 | 0.0 | 0.0 | 0.0 | 0.0 | 0.0 | 0.0 | 0.0 |
| **AVG. STATION PRESS.(mb)** | 17 | 1019.5 | 1017.9 | 1015.8 | 1015.1 | 1012.7 | 1011.4 | 1011.2 | 1011.1 | 1011.3 | 1014.8 | 1017.8 | 1019.9 | 1014.9 |
| **RELATIVE HUMIDITY (%)** Hour 04 | 29 | 90 | 87 | 85 | 81 | 81 | 78 | 76 | 78 | 77 | 80 | 87 | 90 | 83 |
| Hour 10 | 29 | 85 | 78 | 69 | 58 | 50 | 47 | 47 | 50 | 51 | 58 | 75 | 85 | 63 |
| Hour 16 (Local Time) | 29 | 71 | 60 | 53 | 43 | 35 | 31 | 28 | 29 | 32 | 39 | 59 | 71 | 46 |
| Hour 22 | 29 | 86 | 81 | 77 | 73 | 69 | 64 | 61 | 63 | 65 | 71 | 82 | 87 | 73 |
| **PRECIPITATION (inches):** Water Equivalent -Normal | | 4.03 | 2.88 | 2.06 | 1.31 | 0.33 | 0.11 | 0.05 | 0.07 | 0.27 | 0.86 | 2.23 | 2.90 | 17.10 |
| -Maximum Monthly | 50 | 9.14 | 8.77 | 7.12 | 4.76 | 3.13 | 0.63 | 0.79 | 0.65 | 2.78 | 7.51 | 7.41 | 12.64 | 12.64 |
| -Year | | 1978 | 1962 | 1982 | 1941 | 1948 | 1953 | 1974 | 1976 | 1989 | 1962 | 1970 | 1955 | DEC 1955 |
| -Minimum Monthly | 50 | 0.16 | 0.15 | 0.14 | 0.00 | T | 0.00 | 0.00 | 0.00 | 0.00 | 0.00 | 0.02 | 0.00 | 0.00 |
| -Year | | 1984 | 1964 | 1966 | 1949 | 1987 | 1981 | 1983 | 1982 | 1980 | 1966 | 1959 | 1989 | DEC 1989 |
| -Maximum in 24 hrs | 41 | 3.41 | 3.01 | 2.30 | 2.22 | 0.78 | 0.63 | 0.78 | 0.65 | 1.79 | 5.59 | 2.95 | 3.64 | 5.59 |
| -Year | | 1967 | 1986 | 1982 | 1958 | 1957 | 1953 | 1974 | 1965 | 1989 | 1962 | 1970 | 1955 | OCT 1962 |
| Snow,Ice pellets -Maximum Monthly | 41 | T | 2.0 | T | 0.0 | 0.0 | 0.0 | 0.0 | 0.0 | 0.0 | 0.0 | 0.0 | T | 2.0 |
| -Year | | 1974 | 1976 | 1982 | | | | | | | | | 1988 | FEB 1976 |
| -Maximum in 24 hrs | 41 | T | 2.0 | T | 0.0 | 0.0 | 0.0 | 0.0 | 0.0 | 0.0 | 0.0 | 0.0 | T | 2.0 |
| -Year | | 1974 | 1976 | 1982 | | | | | | | | | 1988 | FEB 1976 |
| **WIND:** Mean Speed (mph) | 40 | 7.2 | 7.6 | 8.7 | 8.7 | 9.2 | 9.8 | 9.0 | 8.6 | 7.6 | 6.4 | 6.0 | 6.7 | 8.0 |
| Prevailing Direction through 1963 | | SE | SSE | SW | SW | SW | SW | SSW | SW | SW | SW | NNW | SSE | SW |
| Fastest Mile -Direction | 41 | SE | SE | S | SW | S | SW | SW | SW | NW | SE | SE | SE | SE |
| -Speed (MPH) | 41 | 60 | 51 | 66 | 45 | 35 | 47 | 36 | 38 | 42 | 68 | 70 | 70 | 70 |
| -Year | | 1954 | 1959 | 1952 | 1955 | 1957 | 1950 | 1956 | 1954 | 1965 | 1950 | 1953 | 1952 | NOV 1953 |
| Peak Gust -Direction | | | | | | | | | | | | | | |
| -Speed (mph) | | | | | | | | | | | | | | |
| -Date | | | | | | | | | | | | | | |

**See Reference Notes to this table on the following page.**

PRECIPITATION (inches)   SACRAMENTO, CALIFORNIA

**TABLE 2**

| YEAR | JAN | FEB | MAR | APR | MAY | JUNE | JULY | AUG | SEP | OCT | NOV | DEC | ANNUAL |
|---|---|---|---|---|---|---|---|---|---|---|---|---|---|
| 1961 | 3.47 | 1.25 | 2.02 | 0.46 | 0.18 | 0.01 | T | 0.03 | 0.17 | 0.03 | 3.13 | 2.47 | 13.22 |
| 1962 | 1.00 | 8.77 | 1.69 | 0.15 | 0.03 | 0.01 | 0.00 | 0.13 | 0.06 | 7.51 | 0.39 | 1.84 | 21.58 |
| 1963 | 4.71 | 2.09 | 4.25 | 3.54 | 0.69 | T | 0.00 | T | 0.47 | 1.09 | 4.35 | 0.45 | 21.64 |
| 1964 | 3.83 | 0.15 | 1.36 | 0.17 | 0.23 | 0.39 | 0.01 | 0.11 | 0.00 | 1.72 | 2.70 | 6.03 | 16.70 |
| 1965 | 3.01 | 0.41 | 1.47 | 2.70 | 0.09 | T | T | 0.65 | T | 0.11 | 2.93 | 2.44 | 13.81 |
| 1966 | 1.91 | 1.56 | 0.14 | 0.47 | 0.25 | 0.02 | 0.10 | T | 0.07 | 0.30 | 5.73 | 3.53 | 13.78 |
| 1967 | 8.42 | 0.41 | 3.91 | 3.40 | 0.13 | 0.60 | T | 0.00 | 0.04 | 0.24 | 1.18 | 1.29 | 19.62 |
| 1968 | 3.77 | 2.13 | 2.39 | 0.42 | 0.16 | 0.15 | T | 0.02 | 0.00 | 0.60 | 2.49 | 2.77 | 14.90 |
| 1969 | 8.50 | 6.98 | 0.94 | 1.63 | 0.04 | 0.08 | T | 0.00 | 0.02 | 0.72 | 0.60 | 4.41 | 23.92 |
| 1970 | 7.88 | 1.58 | 1.62 | 0.18 | T | 0.16 | 0.00 | 0.00 | 0.00 | 0.84 | 7.41 | 3.40 | 23.07 |
| 1971 | 0.90 | 0.56 | 2.05 | 0.44 | 0.77 | 0.01 | 0.00 | 0.00 | T | 0.13 | 0.87 | 4.05 | 9.78 |
| 1972 | 0.81 | 1.28 | 0.29 | 1.39 | 0.28 | 0.19 | 0.00 | 0.00 | 0.90 | 1.75 | 5.14 | 1.88 | 13.91 |
| 1973 | 6.87 | 5.64 | 2.76 | 0.05 | 0.13 | 0.00 | 0.00 | 0.00 | 0.33 | 1.64 | 6.27 | 2.79 | 26.48 |
| 1974 | 3.58 | 1.37 | 3.27 | 0.96 | 0.01 | 0.50 | 0.79 | T | 0.00 | 1.16 | 0.66 | 2.86 | 15.16 |
| 1975 | 0.73 | 4.59 | 4.28 | 0.81 | T | T | 0.04 | 0.23 | T | 2.03 | 0.29 | 0.18 | 13.18 |
| 1976 | 0.36 | 1.49 | 0.44 | 1.53 | 0.00 | 0.04 | 0.00 | 0.65 | 0.52 | 0.02 | 0.55 | 0.65 | 6.25 |
| 1977 | 1.17 | 1.17 | 1.27 | 0.30 | 0.73 | 0.00 | T | 0.00 | 0.76 | 0.12 | 1.92 | 4.27 | 11.71 |
| 1978 | 9.14 | 4.46 | 3.38 | 2.31 | T | T | 0.00 | T | 0.30 | T | 3.20 | 0.95 | 23.74 |
| 1979 | 5.66 | 4.55 | 2.47 | 0.76 | 0.14 | 0.00 | 0.25 | 0.00 | T | 1.62 | 1.48 | 3.41 | 20.34 |
| 1980 | 5.64 | 7.12 | 2.62 | 1.06 | 0.49 | 0.04 | 0.40 | 0.00 | 0.00 | 0.06 | 0.12 | 1.79 | 19.34 |
| 1981 | 4.56 | 0.87 | 3.55 | 0.66 | 0.50 | 0.00 | 0.00 | 0.00 | 0.25 | 2.57 | 6.09 | 3.28 | 22.33 |
| 1982 | 5.50 | 2.35 | 7.12 | 3.07 | T | 0.15 | 0.00 | 0.00 | 1.81 | 2.61 | 5.74 | 3.25 | 31.60 |
| 1983 | 4.92 | 5.56 | 6.75 | 4.21 | 0.25 | 0.40 | 0.00 | 0.11 | 0.66 | 0.40 | 4.91 | 5.26 | 33.43 |
| 1984 | 0.16 | 1.22 | 1.35 | 0.34 | 0.01 | 0.10 | T | 0.01 | 0.07 | 1.39 | 3.61 | 1.23 | 9.49 |
| 1985 | 0.66 | 1.52 | 2.01 | T | 0.01 | 0.15 | T | 0.06 | 0.56 | 0.53 | 3.72 | 2.34 | 11.56 |
| 1986 | 3.67 | 8.60 | 3.20 | 0.91 | 0.07 | 0.00 | 0.00 | 0.00 | 0.60 | 0.19 | 0.14 | 0.76 | 18.14 |
| 1987 | 2.29 | 3.23 | 3.05 | 0.20 | T | T | 0.00 | 0.00 | 0.00 | 1.28 | 2.53 | 3.25 | 15.83 |
| 1988 | 2.96 | 0.99 | 0.17 | 1.58 | 0.89 | 0.19 | 0.00 | 0.00 | 0.00 | 0.19 | 1.68 | 2.73 | 11.38 |
| 1989 | 0.71 | 1.25 | 6.29 | 0.31 | 0.06 | 0.43 | 0.00 | 0.20 | 2.78 | 1.76 | 1.32 | 0.00 | 15.11 |
| 1990 | 4.97 | 2.91 | 0.93 | 0.73 | 2.10 | 0.00 | T | 0.00 | 0.00 | 0.09 | 0.43 | 1.60 | 13.76 |
| Record Mean | 3.60 | 2.91 | 2.47 | 1.34 | 0.44 | 0.10 | 0.03 | 0.05 | 0.30 | 0.98 | 2.27 | 2.89 | 17.40 |

**TABLE 3**   AVERAGE TEMPERATURE (deg. F)   SACRAMENTO, CALIFORNIA

| YEAR | JAN | FEB | MAR | APR | MAY | JUNE | JULY | AUG | SEP | OCT | NOV | DEC | ANNUAL |
|---|---|---|---|---|---|---|---|---|---|---|---|---|---|
| 1961 | 42.4 | 51.8 | 53.0 | 59.6 | 62.4 | 76.4 | 79.2 | 77.2 | 70.4 | 64.0 | 52.1 | 44.1 | 61.1 |
| 1962 | 41.8 | 47.6 | 51.1 | 61.4 | 63.5 | 71.6 | 75.1 | 74.9 | 70.9 | 62.3 | 54.6 | 46.0 | 60.1 |
| 1963 | 41.1 | 55.9 | 51.0 | 53.6 | 62.1 | 70.1 | 73.9 | 75.1 | 73.9 | 64.2 | 51.6 | 41.1 | 59.5 |
| 1964 | 45.1 | 49.4 | 52.3 | 58.9 | 63.0 | 70.0 | 75.9 | 75.8 | 70.3 | 66.7 | 50.3 | 49.7 | 60.6 |
| 1965 | 45.4 | 49.2 | 53.0 | 57.3 | 64.4 | 67.0 | 74.4 | 75.7 | 67.6 | 65.9 | 54.7 | 41.0 | 59.6 |
| 1966 | 45.7 | 47.5 | 54.3 | 62.9 | 66.4 | 72.6 | 72.9 | 76.9 | 72.0 | 64.1 | 54.7 | 46.1 | 61.4 |
| 1967 | 45.9 | 48.4 | 50.8 | 49.6 | 65.2 | 69.4 | 78.0 | 79.0 | 74.9 | 65.5 | 56.2 | 44.0 | 60.6 |
| 1968 | 43.4 | 54.5 | 55.1 | 59.8 | 64.7 | 73.9 | 76.2 | 73.0 | 72.2 | 62.0 | 52.3 | 43.5 | 60.9 |
| 1969 | 44.0 | 47.4 | 52.4 | 57.1 | 66.9 | 69.0 | 76.3 | 77.9 | 74.0 | 61.0 | 53.9 | 48.0 | 60.7 |
| 1970 | 49.3 | 51.9 | 54.9 | 56.1 | 67.6 | 71.5 | 76.8 | 74.7 | 72.8 | 62.1 | 55.3 | 46.1 | 61.6 |
| 1971 | 45.3 | 48.2 | 52.6 | 56.4 | 61.8 | 70.5 | 76.2 | 76.8 | 72.2 | 61.2 | 52.7 | 43.0 | 59.8 |
| 1972 | 41.0 | 51.4 | 58.6 | 58.6 | 66.9 | 72.5 | 76.0 | 75.9 | 69.5 | 62.0 | 49.7 | 40.6 | 60.2 |
| 1973 | 44.3 | 53.1 | 51.1 | 60.8 | 69.4 | 74.6 | 76.8 | 74.2 | 70.8 | 63.4 | 51.9 | 46.9 | 61.5 |
| 1974 | 46.3 | 48.4 | 54.1 | 56.6 | 63.8 | 70.5 | 74.1 | 74.0 | 72.2 | 66.3 | 53.2 | 46.4 | 60.5 |
| 1975 | 43.4 | 49.2 | 50.3 | 51.8 | 68.2 | 73.2 | 77.3 | 76.9 | 77.4 | 65.1 | 54.6 | 47.4 | 61.2 |
| 1976 | 47.2 | 51.9 | 54.6 | 57.9 | 70.1 | 73.9 | 76.5 | 73.4 | 71.8 | 66.1 | 56.7 | 46.5 | 62.2 |
| 1977 | 43.8 | 52.4 | 51.0 | 62.2 | 59.4 | 72.2 | 74.2 | 73.9 | 68.8 | 63.9 | 54.5 | 49.6 | 60.5 |
| 1978 | 50.3 | 51.9 | 57.2 | 55.8 | 66.4 | 70.0 | 75.1 | 75.0 | 69.6 | 65.9 | 49.8 | 41.7 | 60.7 |
| 1979 | 45.3 | 48.8 | 51.6 | 56.9 | 66.7 | 71.9 | 75.6 | 73.1 | 74.6 | 64.0 | 51.7 | 46.7 | 60.9 |
| 1980 | 46.9 | 51.9 | 51.6 | 59.6 | 62.7 | 66.8 | 75.0 | 71.4 | 69.4 | 63.7 | 53.5 | 45.4 | 59.9 |
| 1981 | 46.8 | 50.4 | 51.2 | 57.9 | 64.7 | 74.8 | 75.1 | 74.5 | 69.7 | 63.5 | 60.3 | 48.6 | 61.5 |
| 1982 | 42.0 | 50.5 | 50.8 | 55.5 | 64.6 | 66.2 | 72.1 | 71.7 | 68.2 | 61.0 | 46.9 | 43.0 | 57.7 |
| 1983 | 43.1 | 52.2 | 53.4 | 54.7 | 64.2 | 70.8 | 72.2 | 76.6 | 74.9 | 67.5 | 53.7 | 51.0 | 61.2 |
| 1984 | 48.2 | 50.2 | 58.1 | 58.7 | 70.0 | 71.7 | 78.3 | 75.3 | 75.3 | 62.8 | 53.6 | 45.1 | 62.3 |
| 1985 | 42.4 | 51.4 | 50.8 | 61.5 | 63.2 | 75.1 | 77.0 | 72.9 | 68.5 | 63.3 | 49.8 | 42.6 | 59.9 |
| 1986 | 51.4 | 54.7 | 58.8 | 58.4 | 65.5 | 71.6 | 75.0 | 75.2 | 66.2 | 64.8 | 55.5 | 45.7 | 61.9 |
| 1987 | 44.9 | 51.3 | 53.8 | 62.7 | 69.1 | 72.4 | 71.8 | 74.9 | 71.8 | 67.6 | 53.4 | 47.2 | 61.7 |
| 1988 | 48.0 | 54.2 | 58.0 | 60.9 | 64.7 | 72.9 | 80.4 | 75.9 | 72.5 | 66.5 | 53.8 | 46.2 | 62.8 |
| 1989 | 44.1 | 47.1 | 55.6 | 63.2 | 65.8 | 71.7 | 76.2 | 73.8 | 69.6 | 62.4 | 54.3 | 44.3 | 60.7 |
| 1990 | 47.5 | 48.6 | 55.4 | 63.4 | 65.5 | 72.4 | 77.7 | 76.6 | 74.0 | 66.6 | 53.0 | 41.0 | 61.8 |
| Record Mean | 45.3 | 50.2 | 53.5 | 58.5 | 64.8 | 71.1 | 75.4 | 74.3 | 71.5 | 63.8 | 53.0 | 45.7 | 60.6 |
| Max | 53.0 | 59.6 | 64.2 | 71.3 | 79.5 | 87.1 | 92.9 | 91.3 | 87.4 | 77.5 | 63.4 | 53.3 | 73.4 |
| Min | 37.5 | 40.8 | 42.7 | 45.6 | 50.1 | 55.0 | 57.9 | 57.3 | 55.5 | 50.0 | 42.6 | 38.0 | 47.8 |

## REFERENCE NOTES FOR TABLES 1, 2, 3 and 6     (SACRAMENTO, CA)

### GENERAL

T - TRACE AMOUNT
BLANK ENTRIES DENOTE MISSING/UNREPORTED DATA.
# INDICATES A STATION OR INSTRUMENT RELOCATION.

### SPECIFIC

**TABLE 1**

(a) - LENGTH OF RECORD IN YEARS. ALTHOUGH
    INDIVIDUAL MONTHS MAY BE MISSING.
 * LESS THAN .05

NORMALS — BASED ON THE 1951-1980 RECORD PERIOD.
EXTREMES — DATES ARE THE MOST RECENT OCCURRENCE.
WIND DIR. — NUMERALS SHOW TENS OF DEGREES
        CLOCKWISE FROM TRUE NORTH.
        "00" INDICATES CALM.
RESULTANT WIND DIRECTIONS ARE GIVEN TO WHOLE DEGREES.

**TABLE 3**
MAX AND MIN ARE LONG-TERM MEAN DAILY MAXIMUM
AND MEAN DAILY MINIMUM TEMPERATURES.

### EXCEPTIONS

**TABLES 2, 3, and 6**

RECORD MEANS ARE THROUGH THE CURRENT YEAR,
BEGINNING IN     1941 FOR TEMPERATURE
         1940 FOR PRECIPITATION
         1949 FOR SNOWFALL

HEATING DEGREE DAYS Base 65 deg. F          SACRAMENTO, CALIFORNIA

**TABLE 4**

| SEASON | JULY | AUG | SEP | OCT | NOV | DEC | JAN | FEB | MAR | APR | MAY | JUNE | TOTAL |
|---|---|---|---|---|---|---|---|---|---|---|---|---|---|
| 1961-62 | 0 | 0 | 6 | 122 | 378 | 640 | 709 | 482 | 425 | 121 | 82 | 4 | 2969 |
| #1962-63 | 0 | 0 | | 97 | 303 | 581 | 736 | 249 | 428 | 333 | 115 | 2 | 2844 |
| 1963-64 | 0 | 0 | 0 | 65 | 398 | 734 | 612 | 448 | 389 | 194 | 99 | 22 | 2961 |
| 1964-65 | 0 | 4 | 10 | 49 | 436 | 469 | 602 | 434 | 363 | 246 | 86 | 21 | 2720 |
| 1965-66 | 0 | 0 | 19 | 32 | 303 | 738 | 591 | 485 | 326 | 96 | 36 | 14 | 2640 |
| 1966-67 | 1 | 0 | 4 | 60 | 303 | 580 | 584 | 461 | 435 | 456 | 98 | 34 | 3016 |
| 1967-68 | 0 | 0 | 0 | 33 | 259 | 643 | 663 | 296 | 171 | 80 | 2 | 2446 |
| 1968-69 | 0 | 3 | 2 | 97 | 374 | 662 | 644 | 486 | 384 | 230 | 41 | 6 | 2929 |
| 1969-70 | 0 | 0 | 1 | 129 | 323 | 519 | 478 | 359 | 258 | 56 | 9 | 2436 |
| 1970-71 | 0 | 0 | 4 | 129 | 286 | 578 | 603 | 466 | 379 | 249 | 114 | 14 | 2822 |
| 1971-72 | 0 | 0 | 33 | 191 | 363 | 673 | 731 | 390 | 197 | 190 | 63 | 11 | 2842 |
| 1972-73 | 0 | 0 | 6 | 115 | 451 | 749 | 636 | 325 | 424 | 141 | 15 | 1 | 2863 |
| 1973-74 | 0 | 0 | 0 | 77 | 384 | 553 | 571 | 456 | 332 | 251 | 93 | 9 | 2726 |
| 1974-75 | 7 | 0 | 0 | 44 | 347 | 569 | 661 | 435 | 449 | 389 | 69 | 1 | 2971 |
| 1975-76 | 0 | 0 | 0 | 72 | 306 | 539 | 547 | 374 | 315 | 211 | 1 | 3 | 2368 |
| 1976-77 | 0 | 0 | 1 | 44 | 252 | 567 | 650 | 345 | 424 | 92 | 187 | 9 | 2571 |
| 1977-78 | 0 | 0 | 17 | 68 | 309 | 472 | 451 | 362 | 235 | 269 | 46 | 0 | 2229 |
| 1978-79 | 0 | 0 | 11 | 51 | 449 | 715 | 606 | 446 | 313 | 236 | 57 | 2 | 2886 |
| 1979-80 | 0 | 0 | 0 | 100 | 391 | 558 | 551 | 373 | 408 | 164 | 107 | 29 | 2681 |
| 1980-81 | 2 | 0 | 4 | 134 | 339 | 596 | 557 | 405 | 420 | 229 | 81 | 2 | 2769 |
| 1981-82 | 0 | 0 | 9 | 66 | 145 | 498 | 708 | 398 | 434 | 282 | 70 | 40 | 2650 |
| 1982-83 | 3 | 0 | 31 | 125 | 532 | 675 | 670 | 353 | 354 | 303 | 99 | 4 | 3149 |
| 1983-84 | 3 | 0 | 0 | 7 | 333 | 425 | 514 | 421 | 206 | 191 | 22 | 11 | 2133 |
| 1984-85 | 0 | 0 | 0 | 115 | 335 | 611 | 693 | 377 | 433 | 122 | 89 | 11 | 2786 |
| 1985-86 | 0 | 2 | 15 | 95 | 450 | 689 | 411 | 284 | 192 | 200 | 73 | 0 | 2411 |
| 1986-87 | 0 | 0 | 53 | 47 | 277 | 593 | 614 | 377 | 340 | 95 | 37 | 0 | 2433 |
| 1987-88 | 1 | 0 | 0 | 11 | 339 | 544 | 522 | 307 | 212 | 138 | 94 | 27 | 2195 |
| 1988-89 | 0 | 0 | 3 | 38 | 329 | 576 | 640 | 496 | 285 | 106 | 50 | 3 | 2526 |
| 1989-90 | 0 | 0 | 11 | 107 | 316 | 634 | 536 | 453 | 289 | 71 | 53 | 6 | 2476 |
| 1990-91 | 0 | 0 | 0 | 24 | 356 | 739 | | | | | | | |

**TABLE 5**          COOLING DEGREE DAYS Base 65 deg. F          SACRAMENTO, CALIFORNIA

| YEAR | JAN | FEB | MAR | APR | MAY | JUNE | JULY | AUG | SEP | OCT | NOV | DEC | TOTAL |
|---|---|---|---|---|---|---|---|---|---|---|---|---|---|
| 1969 | 0 | 0 | 0 | 1 | 108 | 136 | 361 | 409 | 278 | 13 | 0 | 0 | 1306 |
| 1970 | 0 | 0 | 0 | 0 | 143 | 208 | 374 | 305 | 245 | 46 | 0 | 0 | 1321 |
| 1971 | 0 | 0 | 0 | 0 | 22 | 186 | 355 | 375 | 254 | 82 | 0 | 0 | 1274 |
| 1972 | 0 | 0 | 6 | 5 | 129 | 245 | 351 | 349 | 147 | 30 | 0 | 0 | 1262 |
| 1973 | 0 | 0 | 0 | 19 | 156 | 295 | 373 | 293 | 181 | 34 | 0 | 0 | 1351 |
| 1974 | 0 | 0 | 0 | 5 | 61 | 180 | 296 | 285 | 222 | 89 | 0 | 0 | 1138 |
| 1975 | 0 | 0 | 0 | 0 | 177 | 258 | 388 | 375 | 375 | 81 | 0 | 0 | 1654 |
| 1976 | 0 | 0 | 1 | 8 | 167 | 278 | 363 | 270 | 213 | 83 | 8 | 0 | 1391 |
| 1977 | 0 | 0 | 0 | 12 | 19 | 230 | 290 | 284 | 139 | 40 | 0 | 0 | 1014 |
| 1978 | 0 | 0 | 0 | 0 | 98 | 157 | 318 | 315 | 157 | 87 | 0 | 0 | 1132 |
| 1979 | 0 | 0 | 0 | 0 | 117 | 214 | 336 | 260 | 295 | 72 | 0 | 0 | 1294 |
| 1980 | 0 | 0 | 0 | 8 | 42 | 91 | 317 | 207 | 145 | 99 | 0 | 0 | 909 |
| 1981 | 0 | 0 | 0 | 26 | 78 | 303 | 318 | 301 | 155 | 28 | 7 | 0 | 1216 |
| 1982 | 0 | 0 | 0 | 0 | 2 | 67 | 230 | 213 | 133 | 9 | 0 | 0 | 737 |
| 1983 | 0 | 0 | 0 | 0 | 81 | 183 | 235 | 368 | 304 | 92 | 0 | 0 | 1263 |
| 1984 | 0 | 0 | 0 | 6 | 183 | 216 | 419 | 327 | 320 | 57 | 0 | 0 | 1528 |
| 1985 | 0 | 0 | 0 | 22 | 41 | 319 | 380 | 254 | 128 | 48 | 0 | 0 | 1192 |
| 1986 | 0 | 0 | 10 | 9 | 95 | 207 | 315 | 321 | 95 | 47 | 0 | 0 | 1099 |
| 1987 | 0 | 0 | 0 | 34 | 171 | 234 | 220 | 314 | 212 | 100 | 0 | 0 | 1285 |
| 1988 | 0 | 0 | 5 | 22 | 88 | 269 | 484 | 346 | 233 | 92 | 0 | 0 | 1539 |
| 1989 | 0 | 0 | 1 | 60 | 83 | 211 | 354 | 280 | 158 | 32 | 0 | 0 | 1179 |
| 1990 | 0 | 0 | 0 | 33 | 75 | 236 | 399 | 367 | 276 | 82 | 0 | 0 | 1468 |

**TABLE 6**          SNOWFALL (inches)          SACRAMENTO, CALIFORNIA

| SEASON | JULY | AUG | SEP | OCT | NOV | DEC | JAN | FEB | MAR | APR | MAY | JUNE | TOTAL |
|---|---|---|---|---|---|---|---|---|---|---|---|---|---|
| 1970-71 | 0.0 | 0.0 | 0.0 | 0.0 | 0.0 | 0.0 | 0.0 | 0.0 | 0.0 | 0.0 | 0.0 | 0.0 | 0.0 |
| 1971-72 | 0.0 | 0.0 | 0.0 | 0.0 | 0.0 | 0.0 | 0.0 | 0.0 | 0.0 | 0.0 | 0.0 | 0.0 | 0.0 |
| 1972-73 | 0.0 | 0.0 | 0.0 | 0.0 | 0.0 | T | 0.0 | 0.0 | 0.0 | 0.0 | 0.0 | 0.0 | T |
| 1973-74 | 0.0 | 0.0 | 0.0 | 0.0 | 0.0 | 0.0 | T | 0.0 | 0.0 | 0.0 | 0.0 | 0.0 | T |
| 1974-75 | 0.0 | 0.0 | 0.0 | 0.0 | 0.0 | 0.0 | 0.0 | 0.0 | 0.0 | 0.0 | 0.0 | 0.0 | 0.0 |
| 1975-76 | 0.0 | 0.0 | 0.0 | 0.0 | 0.0 | 0.0 | 0.0 | 2.0 | 0.0 | 0.0 | 0.0 | 0.0 | 2.0 |
| 1976-77 | 0.0 | 0.0 | 0.0 | 0.0 | 0.0 | 0.0 | 0.0 | 0.0 | 0.0 | 0.0 | 0.0 | 0.0 | 0.0 |
| 1977-78 | 0.0 | 0.0 | 0.0 | 0.0 | 0.0 | 0.0 | 0.0 | 0.0 | 0.0 | 0.0 | 0.0 | 0.0 | 0.0 |
| 1978-79 | 0.0 | 0.0 | 0.0 | 0.0 | 0.0 | 0.0 | 0.0 | 0.0 | 0.0 | 0.0 | 0.0 | 0.0 | 0.0 |
| 1979-80 | 0.0 | 0.0 | 0.0 | 0.0 | 0.0 | 0.0 | 0.0 | 0.0 | 0.0 | 0.0 | 0.0 | 0.0 | 0.0 |
| 1980-81 | 0.0 | 0.0 | 0.0 | 0.0 | 0.0 | 0.0 | 0.0 | 0.0 | 0.0 | 0.0 | 0.0 | 0.0 | 0.0 |
| 1981-82 | 0.0 | 0.0 | 0.0 | 0.0 | 0.0 | 0.0 | 0.0 | 2.0 | T | 0.0 | 0.0 | 0.0 | T |
| 1982-83 | 0.0 | 0.0 | 0.0 | 0.0 | 0.0 | 0.0 | 0.0 | 0.0 | 0.0 | 0.0 | 0.0 | 0.0 | 0.0 |
| 1983-84 | 0.0 | 0.0 | 0.0 | 0.0 | 0.0 | 0.0 | 0.0 | 0.0 | 0.0 | 0.0 | 0.0 | 0.0 | 0.0 |
| 1984-85 | 0.0 | 0.0 | 0.0 | 0.0 | 0.0 | 0.0 | 0.0 | 0.0 | 0.0 | 0.0 | 0.0 | 0.0 | 0.0 |
| 1985-86 | 0.0 | 0.0 | 0.0 | 0.0 | 0.0 | 0.0 | 0.0 | 0.0 | 0.0 | 0.0 | 0.0 | 0.0 | 0.0 |
| 1986-87 | 0.0 | 0.0 | 0.0 | 0.0 | 0.0 | 0.0 | 0.0 | 0.0 | 0.0 | 0.0 | 0.0 | 0.0 | 0.0 |
| 1987-88 | 0.0 | 0.0 | 0.0 | 0.0 | 0.0 | 0.0 | 0.0 | 0.0 | 0.0 | 0.0 | 0.0 | 0.0 | 0.0 |
| 1988-89 | 0.0 | 0.0 | 0.0 | 0.0 | 0.0 | T | 0.0 | 0.0 | 0.0 | 0.0 | 0.0 | 0.0 | T |
| 1989-90 | 0.0 | 0.0 | 0.0 | 0.0 | 0.0 | 0.0 | 0.0 | 0.0 | 0.0 | 0.0 | 0.0 | 0.0 | 0.0 |
| 1990-91 | 0.0 | 0.0 | 0.0 | 0.0 | 0.0 | | | | | | | | |
| Record Mean | 0.0 | 0.0 | 0.0 | 0.0 | 0.0 | T | T | T | T | 0.0 | 0.0 | 0.0 | T |

**See Reference Notes, relative to all above tables, on preceding page.**

# SAN DIEGO, CALIFORNIA

The city of San Diego is located on San Diego Bay in the southwest corner of southern California. The prevailing winds and weather are tempered by the Pacific Ocean, with the result that summers are cool and winters warm in comparison with other places along the same general latitude. Temperatures of freezing or below have rarely occurred at the station since the record began in 1871, but hot weather, 90 degrees or above, is more frequent.

Dry easterly winds sometimes blow in the vicinity for several days at a time, bringing temperatures in the 90s and at times even in the 100s in the eastern sections of the city and outlying suburbs. At the National Weather Service station itself, however, there have been relatively few days on which 100 degrees or higher was reached.

As these hot winds are predominant in the fall, highest temperatures occur in the months of September and October. Records show that over 60 percent of the days with 90 degrees or higher have occurred in these two months. High temperatures are almost invariably accompanied by very low relative humidities, which often drop below 20 percent and occasionally below 10 percent.

A marked feature of the climate is the wide variation in temperature within short distances. In nearby valleys daytimes are much warmer in summer and nights noticeably cooler in winter, and freezing occurs much more frequently than in the city. Although records show unusually small daily temperature ranges, only about 15 degrees between the highest and lowest readings, a few miles inland these ranges increase to 30 degrees or more.

Strong winds and gales associated with Pacific, or tropical storms, are infrequent due to the latitude.

The seasonal rainfall is about 10 inches in the city, but increases with elevation and distance from the coast. In the mountains to the north and east the average is between 20 and 40 inches, depending on slope and elevation. Most of the precipitation falls in winter, except in the mountains where there is an occasional thunderstorm. Eighty-five percent of the rainfall occurs from November through March, but wide variations take place in monthly and seasonal totals. Infrequent measurable amounts of hail occur in San Diego, but snow is practically unknown at the Weather Service Office location. In each occurrence of snowfall only a trace was recorded officially, but in some locations amounts up to or slightly exceeding a half-inch fell, and remained on the ground for an hour or more.

As on the rest of the Pacific Coast, a dominant characteristic of spring and summer is the nighttime and early morning cloudiness. Low clouds form regularly and frequently extend inland over the coastal valleys and foothills, but they usually dissipate during the morning and the afternoons are generally clear.

Considerable fog occurs along the coast, but the amount decreases with distance inland. The fall and winter months are usually the foggiest. Thunderstorms are rare, averaging about three a year in the city. Visibilities are good as a rule. The sunshine is plentiful for a marine location, with a marked increase toward the interior.

## TABLE 1     NORMALS, MEANS AND EXTREMES

SAN DIEGO, CALIFORNIA

LATITUDE: 32°44'N    LONGITUDE: 117°10'W    ELEVATION: FT. GRND   13 BARO   33   TIME ZONE: PACIFIC    WBAN: 23188

| | (a) | JAN | FEB | MAR | APR | MAY | JUNE | JULY | AUG | SEP | OCT | NOV | DEC | YEAR |
|---|---|---|---|---|---|---|---|---|---|---|---|---|---|---|
| **TEMPERATURE °F:** | | | | | | | | | | | | | | |
| Normals | | | | | | | | | | | | | | |
|  -Daily Maximum | | 65.2 | 66.4 | 65.9 | 67.8 | 68.6 | 71.3 | 75.6 | 77.6 | 76.8 | 74.6 | 69.9 | 66.1 | 70.5 |
|  -Daily Minimum | | 48.4 | 50.3 | 52.1 | 54.5 | 58.2 | 61.2 | 64.9 | 66.8 | 65.1 | 60.3 | 53.6 | 48.7 | 57.0 |
|  -Monthly | | 56.8 | 58.4 | 59.0 | 61.2 | 63.4 | 66.3 | 70.3 | 72.2 | 71.0 | 67.5 | 61.8 | 57.4 | 63.8 |
| Extremes | | | | | | | | | | | | | | |
|  -Record Highest | 49 | 88 | 88 | 93 | 98 | 96 | 101 | 95 | 98 | 111 | 107 | 97 | 88 | 111 |
|  -Year | | 1953 | 1954 | 1988 | 1989 | 1953 | 1979 | 1985 | 1955 | 1963 | 1961 | 1976 | 1963 | SEP 1963 |
|  -Record Lowest | 49 | 29 | 36 | 39 | 41 | 48 | 51 | 55 | 57 | 51 | 43 | 38 | 34 | 29 |
|  -Year | | 1949 | 1949 | 1971 | 1945 | 1967 | 1967 | 1948 | 1944 | 1948 | 1971 | 1964 | 1987 | JAN 1949 |
| **NORMAL DEGREE DAYS:** | | | | | | | | | | | | | | |
| Heating (base 65°F) | | 258 | 196 | 193 | 124 | 71 | 40 | 5 | 0 | 7 | 32 | 118 | 240 | 1284 |
| Cooling (base 65°F) | | 0 | 11 | 7 | 10 | 21 | 79 | 170 | 226 | 187 | 109 | 22 | 0 | 842 |
| **% OF POSSIBLE SUNSHINE** | 49 | 72 | 72 | 70 | 67 | 59 | 57 | 69 | 70 | 68 | 67 | 74 | 73 | 68 |
| **MEAN SKY COVER (tenths)** | | | | | | | | | | | | | | |
| Sunrise - Sunset | 49 | 5.0 | 5.2 | 5.2 | 5.2 | 5.7 | 5.5 | 4.5 | 4.1 | 4.2 | 4.4 | 4.2 | 4.7 | 4.8 |
| **MEAN NUMBER OF DAYS:** | | | | | | | | | | | | | | |
| Sunrise to Sunset | | | | | | | | | | | | | | |
|  -Clear | 49 | 12.5 | 10.6 | 11.2 | 10.3 | 8.6 | 9.1 | 13.4 | 15.2 | 14.8 | 13.7 | 14.6 | 13.7 | 147.7 |
|  -Partly Cloudy | 49 | 7.4 | 7.4 | 9.5 | 10.0 | 11.4 | 11.7 | 12.7 | 11.4 | 9.5 | 9.7 | 7.8 | 7.8 | 116.3 |
|  -Cloudy | 49 | 11.1 | 10.2 | 10.3 | 9.7 | 11.0 | 9.2 | 4.9 | 4.3 | 5.7 | 7.6 | 7.6 | 9.6 | 101.3 |
| Precipitation | | | | | | | | | | | | | | |
|  .01 inches or more | 49 | 6.6 | 6.0 | 6.9 | 4.6 | 2.2 | 1.0 | 0.3 | 0.5 | 1.2 | 2.5 | 4.7 | 5.7 | 42.1 |
| Snow,Ice pellets | | | | | | | | | | | | | | |
|  1.0 inches or more | 49 | 0.0 | 0.0 | 0.0 | * | 0.0 | 0.0 | 0.0 | 0.0 | 0.0 | 0.0 | 0.0 | 0.0 | 0.0 |
| Thunderstorms | 49 | 0.1 | 0.3 | 0.4 | 0.1 | 0.1 | 0.1 | 0.1 | 0.2 | 0.3 | 0.3 | 0.3 | 0.4 | 2.9 |
| Heavy Fog Visibility | | | | | | | | | | | | | | |
| 1/4 mile or less | 49 | 3.1 | 2.6 | 1.5 | 1.2 | 0.6 | 0.7 | 0.6 | 0.7 | 2.2 | 3.3 | 3.6 | 4.2 | 24.4 |
| Temperature °F | | | | | | | | | | | | | | |
|  -Maximum | | | | | | | | | | | | | | |
|   90° and above | 29 | 0.0 | 0.0 | 0.1 | 0.2 | 0.1 | 0.4 | 0.3 | 0.2 | 1.5 | 0.9 | 0.2 | 0.0 | 4.0 |
|   32° and below | 29 | 0.0 | 0.0 | 0.0 | 0.0 | 0.0 | 0.0 | 0.0 | 0.0 | 0.0 | 0.0 | 0.0 | 0.0 | 0.0 |
|  -Minimum | | | | | | | | | | | | | | |
|   32° and below | 29 | 0.* | 0.0 | 0.0 | 0.0 | 0.0 | 0.0 | 0.0 | 0.0 | 0.0 | 0.0 | 0.0 | 0.0 | * |
|   0° and below | 29 | 0.0 | 0.0 | 0.0 | 0.0 | 0.0 | 0.0 | 0.0 | 0.0 | 0.0 | 0.0 | 0.0 | 0.0 | 0.0 |
| **AVG. STATION PRESS.(mb)** | 17 | 1017.4 | 1016.9 | 1015.4 | 1014.7 | 1013.3 | 1012.4 | 1012.5 | 1012.2 | 1011.5 | 1013.9 | 1015.8 | 1017.2 | 1014.4 |
| **RELATIVE HUMIDITY (%)** | | | | | | | | | | | | | | |
| Hour 04 | 29 | 70 | 73 | 75 | 75 | 77 | 81 | 82 | 81 | 80 | 76 | 73 | 71 | 76 |
| Hour 10  (Local Time) | 29 | 55 | 58 | 60 | 59 | 65 | 69 | 69 | 68 | 66 | 61 | 57 | 54 | 62 |
| Hour 16 | 29 | 56 | 58 | 59 | 59 | 64 | 67 | 66 | 66 | 65 | 63 | 61 | 58 | 62 |
| Hour 22 | 29 | 70 | 72 | 72 | 72 | 75 | 78 | 80 | 79 | 77 | 75 | 73 | 71 | 75 |
| **PRECIPITATION (inches):** | | | | | | | | | | | | | | |
| Water Equivalent | | | | | | | | | | | | | | |
|  -Normal | | 2.11 | 1.43 | 1.60 | 0.78 | 0.24 | 0.06 | 0.01 | 0.11 | 0.19 | 0.33 | 1.10 | 1.36 | 9.32 |
|  -Maximum Monthly | 49 | 6.26 | 5.40 | 6.57 | 3.71 | 1.79 | 0.38 | 0.19 | 2.13 | 1.90 | 2.90 | 5.82 | 7.60 | 7.60 |
|  -Year | | 1943 | 1976 | 1983 | 1988 | 1977 | 1972 | 1984 | 1977 | 1963 | 1941 | 1965 | 1943 | DEC 1943 |
|  -Minimum Monthly | 49 | T | 0.00 | T | T | 0.00 | 0.00 | 0.00 | 0.00 | 0.00 | 0.00 | 0.00 | 0.02 | 0.00 |
|  -Year | | 1976 | 1967 | 1972 | 1966 | 1952 | 1981 | 1982 | 1981 | 1979 | 1967 | 1980 | 1979 | JUL 1982 |
|  -Maximum in 24 hrs | 49 | 2.65 | 2.61 | 2.40 | 1.98 | 1.50 | 0.28 | 0.13 | 2.13 | 1.00 | 1.39 | 2.44 | 3.07 | 3.07 |
|  -Year | | 1978 | 1979 | 1952 | 1988 | 1977 | 1972 | 1984 | 1977 | 1986 | 1986 | 1944 | 1945 | DEC 1945 |
| Snow,Ice pellets | | | | | | | | | | | | | | |
|  -Maximum Monthly | 49 | T | 0.0 | T | 0.0 | 0.0 | 0.0 | 0.0 | 0.0 | 0.0 | 0.0 | T | T | T |
|  -Year | | 1949 | | 1985 | | | | | | | | 1985 | 1967 | MAR 1985 |
|  -Maximum in 24 hrs | 49 | T | 0.0 | T | 0.0 | 0.0 | 0.0 | 0.0 | 0.0 | 0.0 | 0.0 | T | T | T |
|  -Year | | 1949 | | 1985 | | | | | | | | 1985 | 1967 | MAR 1985 |
| **WIND:** | | | | | | | | | | | | | | |
| Mean Speed (mph) | 49 | 5.9 | 6.5 | 7.4 | 7.8 | 7.9 | 7.7 | 7.3 | 7.3 | 7.0 | 6.5 | 5.9 | 5.6 | 6.9 |
| Prevailing Direction | | | | | | | | | | | | | | |
|  through 1963 | | NE | WNW | WNW | WNW | WNW | SSW | WNW | WNW | NW | WNW | NE | NE | WNW |
| Fastest Mile | | | | | | | | | | | | | | |
|  -Direction (!!!) | 45 | SE | S | SW | S | S | S | NW | NW | S | N | SE | NW | SE |
|  -Speed (MPH) | 45 | 56 | 45 | 46 | 37 | 30 | 26 | 23 | 23 | 31 | 31 | 51 | 39 | 56 |
|  -Year | | 1980 | 1980 | 1945 | 1958 | 1977 | 1948 | 1968 | 1982 | 1978 | 1961 | 1944 | 1982 | JAN 1980 |
| Peak Gust | | | | | | | | | | | | | | |
|  -Direction (!!!) | 6 | W | W | NW | SW | NW | NW | SW | SW | NW | SE | SW | NW | W |
|  -Speed (mph) | 6 | 64 | 37 | 41 | 40 | 40 | 28 | 30 | 24 | 31 | 32 | 37 | 40 | 64 |
|  -Date | | 1988 | 1987 | 1985 | 1988 | 1988 | 1988 | 1985 | 1985 | 1989 | 1987 | 1985 | 1984 | JAN 1988 |

**See Reference Notes to this table on the following page.**

PRECIPITATION (inches)  SAN DIEGO, CALIFORNIA

**TABLE 2**

| YEAR | JAN | FEB | MAR | APR | MAY | JUNE | JULY | AUG | SEP | OCT | NOV | DEC | ANNUAL |
|---|---|---|---|---|---|---|---|---|---|---|---|---|---|
| 1961 | 1.21 | 0.06 | 0.85 | T | 0.01 | T | T | 0.04 | T | 0.20 | 0.79 | 1.45 | 4.61 |
| 1962 | 2.71 | 3.08 | 0.64 | 0.01 | 0.62 | 0.09 | T | T | 0.00 | 0.01 | 0.22 | 0.10 | 7.39 |
| 1963 | 0.11 | 1.22 | 1.33 | 0.71 | 0.09 | 0.28 | 0.00 | T | 1.90 | 0.13 | 1.85 | 1.17 | 7.72 |
| 1964 | 1.30 | 0.37 | 0.97 | 0.20 | 0.15 | 0.08 | 0.00 | T | 0.00 | 0.02 | 1.01 | 1.17 | 5.27 |
| 1965 | 0.40 | 0.52 | 1.79 | 3.58 | T | 0.01 | 0.02 | T | 0.29 | T | 5.82 | 6.60 | 19.03 |
| 1966 | 1.29 | 0.86 | 0.17 | T | 0.02 | T | T | 0.00 | T | 0.80 | 0.82 | 3.22 | 7.18 |
| 1967 | 2.20 | 0.00 | 1.14 | 2.24 | 0.05 | 0.16 | 0.01 | 0.14 | 0.08 | 0.00 | 3.53 | 1.66 | 11.21 |
| 1968 | 0.35 | 0.22 | 1.55 | 0.34 | 0.08 | T | 0.13 | T | T | 0.04 | 0.36 | 0.61 | 3.68 |
| 1969 | 4.78 | 4.34 | 0.94 | 0.21 | 0.17 | 0.02 | T | 0.01 | T | 0.04 | 0.79 | 0.46 | 11.76 |
| 1970 | 0.86 | 2.58 | 1.50 | 0.09 | 0.01 | T | T | T | 0.00 | 0.07 | 2.05 | 2.22 | 9.38 |
| 1971 | 0.30 | 1.27 | 0.20 | 0.93 | 0.95 | 0.01 | T | 0.03 | T | 1.66 | 0.06 | 3.27 | 8.68 |
| 1972 | 0.07 | 0.10 | T | 0.02 | 0.10 | 0.38 | T | 0.02 | 0.44 | 0.58 | 3.16 | 1.61 | 6.48 |
| 1973 | 1.68 | 1.63 | 2.26 | 0.05 | T | T | T | T | 0.02 | 0.01 | 1.63 | 0.19 | 7.47 |
| 1974 | 2.96 | 0.04 | 1.70 | 0.02 | 0.01 | 0.02 | 0.01 | T | T | 1.03 | 0.14 | 2.20 | 8.13 |
| 1975 | 0.49 | 0.96 | 3.79 | 2.00 | 0.01 | 0.02 | T | T | T | 0.09 | 0.64 | 0.37 | 8.37 |
| 1976 | T | 5.40 | 0.99 | 1.33 | 0.27 | 0.02 | 0.02 | 0.01 | 1.00 | 0.38 | 0.75 | 1.06 | 11.23 |
| 1977 | 2.36 | 0.06 | 0.61 | 0.01 | 1.79 | 0.03 | T | 2.13 | T | 0.50 | 0.05 | 1.67 | 9.21 |
| 1978 | 5.95 | 2.64 | 5.00 | 0.73 | 0.04 | T | 0.00 | T | 0.72 | 0.05 | 2.09 | 2.19 | 19.41 |
| 1979 | 5.82 | 0.85 | 3.71 | 0.02 | 0.09 | 0.01 | 0.09 | 0.01 | 0.00 | 0.73 | 0.27 | 0.02 | 11.62 |
| 1980 | 5.58 | 4.47 | 2.71 | 1.18 | 0.65 | 0.01 | T | 0.00 | T | 0.05 | 0.00 | 0.31 | 14.96 |
| 1981 | 1.48 | 2.26 | 3.74 | 0.22 | 0.04 | 0.00 | T | 0.00 | 0.03 | 0.14 | 1.79 | 0.54 | 10.24 |
| 1982 | 2.71 | 0.88 | 4.74 | 0.62 | 0.01 | 0.04 | 0.00 | 0.00 | 0.38 | 0.05 | 2.10 | 1.43 | 12.96 |
| 1983 | 2.10 | 3.88 | 6.57 | 1.74 | 0.01 | T | 0.01 | 0.39 | 0.21 | 0.40 | 1.94 | 1.53 | 18.78 |
| 1984 | 0.46 | 0.09 | 0.04 | 0.62 | 0.00 | 0.04 | 0.19 | 0.06 | T | 0.29 | 2.37 | 4.55 | 8.71 |
| 1985 | 0.52 | 0.77 | 0.58 | 0.32 | T | T | 0.00 | T | 0.20 | 0.29 | 4.92 | 1.06 | 8.66 |
| 1986 | 0.75 | 2.59 | 3.12 | 1.17 | 0.00 | T | 0.01 | 0.00 | 1.04 | 1.39 | 1.16 | 0.95 | 12.18 |
| 1987 | 1.68 | 1.53 | 1.04 | 0.78 | 0.03 | T | 0.03 | 0.01 | 0.70 | 1.74 | 1.33 | 2.73 | 11.60 |
| 1988 | 0.89 | 1.37 | 0.59 | 3.71 | 0.08 | 0.00 | T | T | T | T | 1.39 | 2.23 | 10.26 |
| 1989 | 0.42 | 0.70 | 0.69 | 0.12 | 0.04 | 0.06 | 0.00 | T | 0.23 | 0.47 | 0.09 | 1.01 | 3.83 |
| 1990 | 2.52 | 1.13 | 0.25 | 0.76 | 0.51 | 0.87 | T | 0.01 | T | T | 0.65 | 0.59 | 7.29 |
| Record Mean | 1.87 | 1.87 | 1.57 | 0.72 | 0.27 | 0.06 | 0.04 | 0.09 | 0.14 | 0.42 | 1.00 | 1.83 | 9.87 |

**TABLE 3** AVERAGE TEMPERATURE (deg. F)  SAN DIEGO, CALIFORNIA

| YEAR | JAN | FEB | MAR | APR | MAY | JUNE | JULY | AUG | SEP | OCT | NOV | DEC | ANNUAL |
|---|---|---|---|---|---|---|---|---|---|---|---|---|---|
| #1961 | 60.7 | 59.0 | 58.9 | 61.9 | 61.5 | 64.7 | 70.1 | 72.6 | 69.6 | 66.7 | 60.3 | 56.1 | 63.5 |
| 1962 | 56.7 | 56.5 | 55.7 | 61.8 | 62.6 | 63.9 | 68.3 | 70.5 | 68.4 | 64.6 | 59.8 | 56.4 | 62.1 |
| 1963 | 55.1 | 61.2 | 57.5 | 58.7 | 63.6 | 64.7 | 68.2 | 72.1 | 74.3 | 67.7 | 61.2 | 58.5 | 63.6 |
| 1964 | 55.3 | 56.7 | 57.8 | 60.2 | 60.9 | 64.0 | 69.2 | 70.7 | 67.7 | 68.6 | 59.1 | 55.6 | 62.1 |
| 1965 | 56.0 | 55.9 | 58.6 | 60.7 | 62.5 | 63.7 | 67.7 | 72.0 | 68.5 | 69.4 | 60.9 | 55.1 | 62.6 |
| 1966 | 53.9 | 54.6 | 58.1 | 61.3 | 63.5 | 66.5 | 69.2 | 72.6 | 69.9 | 68.1 | 64.1 | 57.2 | 63.0 |
| 1967 | 55.0 | 57.8 | 59.0 | 56.5 | 63.5 | 63.6 | 70.4 | 73.1 | 72.0 | 68.1 | 61.7 | 54.9 | 63.2 |
| 1968 | 57.2 | 60.7 | 60.7 | 62.4 | 63.9 | 65.8 | 71.7 | 72.2 | 71.3 | 66.6 | 61.7 | 59.1 | 64.1 |
| 1969 | 58.1 | 54.9 | 56.8 | 61.7 | 62.9 | 65.5 | 69.4 | 72.8 | 69.9 | 66.0 | 64.1 | 55.4 | 63.4 |
| 1970 | 57.0 | 59.7 | 60.5 | 60.1 | 63.6 | 65.6 | 70.4 | 72.8 | 69.7 | 66.3 | 61.4 | 55.4 | 63.5 |
| 1971 | 54.3 | 55.4 | 57.8 | 60.7 | 61.5 | 64.9 | 69.4 | 75.4 | 72.2 | 65.7 | 59.5 | 54.2 | 62.6 |
| 1972 | 54.9 | 57.8 | 60.2 | 62.3 | 64.7 | 67.0 | 72.7 | 72.2 | 68.7 | 65.6 | 59.8 | 57.5 | 63.6 |
| 1973 | 55.6 | 59.9 | 58.1 | 61.5 | 63.4 | 68.0 | 69.1 | 70.5 | 68.8 | 66.8 | 60.6 | 58.2 | 63.4 |
| 1974 | 56.9 | 58.2 | 59.1 | 62.0 | 63.3 | 66.9 | 71.4 | 70.2 | 70.3 | 66.8 | 62.2 | 56.3 | 63.6 |
| 1975 | 56.1 | 56.4 | 57.5 | 58.7 | 62.2 | 65.0 | 69.4 | 68.9 | 71.5 | 65.9 | 60.4 | 56.9 | 62.4 |
| 1976 | 58.9 | 59.6 | 60.3 | 61.0 | 65.2 | 69.7 | 71.1 | 72.4 | 73.8 | 71.2 | 66.8 | 60.7 | 65.9 |
| 1977 | 60.3 | 61.7 | 57.5 | 61.4 | 61.9 | 65.8 | 71.6 | 73.1 | 72.2 | 68.5 | 64.3 | 63.3 | 65.2 |
| 1978 | 61.0 | 60.9 | 64.3 | 63.4 | 68.2 | 71.3 | 71.6 | 72.9 | 74.0 | 70.1 | 61.7 | 55.2 | 66.2 |
| 1979 | 56.9 | 56.9 | 60.1 | 63.4 | 65.6 | 70.2 | 71.8 | 73.9 | 76.3 | 68.7 | 62.4 | 60.6 | 65.6 |
| 1980 | 61.1 | 63.5 | 61.5 | 63.9 | 63.8 | 68.5 | 72.9 | 74.2 | 70.4 | 67.3 | 62.7 | 60.8 | 65.9 |
| 1981 | 61.3 | 62.2 | 61.1 | 64.4 | 67.3 | 72.9 | 75.6 | 75.8 | 73.7 | 67.1 | 63.5 | 60.3 | 67.1 |
| 1982 | 56.6 | 60.7 | 60.5 | 63.8 | 65.8 | 66.7 | 71.9 | 73.5 | 73.1 | 70.1 | 62.1 | 57.4 | 65.2 |
| 1983 | 60.7 | 60.9 | 62.0 | 62.4 | 66.2 | 68.1 | 72.6 | 77.4 | 76.8 | 72.2 | 64.4 | 60.6 | 67.0 |
| 1984 | 61.2 | 60.2 | 63.7 | 64.3 | 68.1 | 69.9 | 77.2 | 76.6 | 78.9 | 68.5 | 61.4 | 56.7 | 67.2 |
| 1985 | 57.0 | 57.2 | 58.9 | 63.6 | 64.8 | 69.0 | 75.3 | 72.4 | 69.8 | 67.9 | 60.1 | 58.0 | 64.5 |
| 1986 | 61.0 | 58.9 | 60.5 | 62.8 | 64.6 | 67.4 | 69.6 | 71.8 | 66.9 | 65.5 | 62.8 | 57.6 | 64.1 |
| 1987 | 55.4 | 58.0 | 59.1 | 63.4 | 64.7 | 65.8 | 67.1 | 69.9 | 69.9 | 69.5 | 61.8 | 53.9 | 63.2 |
| 1988 | 56.7 | 59.9 | 59.6 | 62.4 | 63.9 | 64.9 | 70.4 | 71.0 | 70.0 | 66.7 | 60.1 | 56.0 | 63.6 |
| 1989 | 54.7 | 56.7 | 59.8 | 65.6 | 63.7 | 66.0 | 70.1 | 71.0 | 70.4 | 66.3 | 63.1 | 58.7 | 63.8 |
| 1990 | 56.6 | 55.2 | 58.7 | 63.2 | 64.3 | 69.0 | 72.3 | 71.6 | 71.7 | 65.1 | 62.7 | 55.6 | 64.1 |
| Record Mean | 55.5 | 56.5 | 57.9 | 60.2 | 62.3 | 65.1 | 68.8 | 70.2 | 68.8 | 65.1 | 60.8 | 57.0 | 62.3 |
| Max | 63.8 | 64.3 | 65.1 | 66.6 | 67.7 | 70.3 | 74.1 | 75.5 | 74.9 | 72.1 | 69.3 | 65.5 | 69.1 |
| Min | 47.2 | 48.7 | 50.7 | 53.7 | 56.9 | 59.9 | 63.5 | 64.8 | 62.8 | 58.1 | 52.3 | 48.5 | 55.6 |

## REFERENCE NOTES FOR TABLES 1, 2, 3 and 6    (SAN DIEGO, CA)

### GENERAL

T - TRACE AMOUNT
BLANK ENTRIES DENOTE MISSING/UNREPORTED DATA.
# INDICATES A STATION OR INSTRUMENT RELOCATION.

### SPECIFIC

**TABLE 1**

(a) - LENGTH OF RECORD IN YEARS. ALTHOUGH
INDIVIDUAL MONTHS MAY BE MISSING.
* LESS THAN .05

NORMALS — BASED ON THE 1951-1980 RECORD PERIOD.
EXTREMES — DATES ARE THE MOST RECENT OCCURRENCE.
WIND DIR. — NUMERALS SHOW TENS OF DEGREES
CLOCKWISE FROM TRUE NORTH.
"00" INDICATES CALM.
RESULTANT WIND DIRECTIONS ARE GIVEN TO WHOLE DEGREES.

**TABLE 3**
MAX AND MIN ARE LONG-TERM MEAN DAILY MAXIMUM
AND MEAN DAILY MINIMUM TEMPERATURES.

### EXCEPTIONS

**TABLES 2, 3, and 6**

RECORD MEANS ARE THROUGH THE CURRENT YEAR,
BEGINNING IN    1875 FOR TEMPERATURE
1850 FOR PRECIPITATION
1941 FOR SNOWFALL

**TABLE 4**  HEATING DEGREE DAYS Base 65 deg. F    SAN DIEGO, CALIFORNIA

| SEASON | JULY | AUG | SEP | OCT | NOV | DEC | JAN | FEB | MAR | APR | MAY | JUNE | TOTAL |
|---|---|---|---|---|---|---|---|---|---|---|---|---|---|
| 1961-62 | 0 | 0 | 0 | 33 | 152 | 269 | 257 | 231 | 290 | 103 | 77 | 33 | 1435 |
| 1962-63 | 0 | 0 | 1 | 25 | 154 | 258 | 299 | 114 | 227 | 180 | 43 | 21 | 1322 |
| 1963-64 | 0 | 0 | 0 | 6 | 115 | 202 | 296 | 234 | 222 | 154 | 125 | 40 | 1394 |
| 1964-65 | 0 | 0 | 0 | 8 | 187 | 280 | 277 | 249 | 135 | 138 | 73 | 35 | 1442 |
| 1965-66 | 3 | 0 | 0 | 9 | 118 | 303 | 335 | 284 | 209 | 107 | 40 | 4 | 1412 |
| 1966-67 | 0 | 0 | 0 | 4 | 113 | 236 | 302 | 197 | 183 | 245 | 72 | 48 | 1400 |
| 1967-68 | 0 | 0 | 0 | 3 | 42 | 288 | 239 | 119 | 135 | 85 | 47 | 8 | 966 |
| 1968-69 | 0 | 0 | 0 | 9 | 104 | 306 | 214 | 274 | 249 | 101 | 63 | 9 | 1328 |
| 1969-70 | 0 | 0 | 0 | 14 | 44 | 178 | 240 | 142 | 133 | 143 | 58 | 12 | 964 |
| 1970-71 | 0 | 0 | 0 | 12 | 107 | 290 | 331 | 266 | 215 | 143 | 109 | 29 | 1502 |
| 1971-72 | 0 | 0 | 0 | 78 | 160 | 326 | 310 | 203 | 139 | 78 | 34 | 0 | 1328 |
| 1972-73 | 0 | 0 | 0 | 29 | 149 | 224 | 286 | 131 | 209 | 107 | 61 | 1 | 1196 |
| 1973-74 | 0 | 0 | 0 | 6 | 132 | 205 | 243 | 184 | 175 | 85 | 55 | 4 | 1090 |
| 1974-75 | 0 | 0 | 0 | 14 | 97 | 265 | 273 | 237 | 225 | 182 | 83 | 10 | 1386 |
| 1975-76 | 0 | 0 | 0 | 19 | 141 | 246 | 196 | 150 | 148 | 115 | 16 | 0 | 1031 |
| 1976-77 | 0 | 0 | 0 | 0 | 39 | 129 | 143 | 94 | 224 | 103 | 88 | 3 | 823 |
| 1977-78 | 0 | 0 | 0 | 0 | 37 | 55 | 117 | 117 | 117 | 43 | 8 | 0 | 429 |
| 1978-79 | 0 | 0 | 0 | 0 | 102 | 297 | 244 | 219 | 153 | 45 | 20 | 6 | 1086 |
| 1979-80 | 0 | 0 | 0 | 4 | 75 | 136 | 117 | 50 | 104 | 61 | 43 | 1 | 591 |
| 1980-81 | 0 | 0 | 0 | 6 | 75 | 133 | 113 | 101 | 116 | 40 | 1 | 0 | 585 |
| 1981-82 | 0 | 0 | 0 | 9 | 57 | 136 | 258 | 119 | 139 | 64 | 9 | 2 | 793 |
| 1982-83 | 0 | 0 | 0 | 1 | 93 | 228 | 137 | 110 | 88 | 83 | 9 | 0 | 749 |
| 1983-84 | 0 | 0 | 0 | 0 | 66 | 130 | 123 | 134 | 51 | 43 | 4 | 0 | 551 |
| 1984-85 | 0 | 0 | 0 | 4 | 104 | 250 | 238 | 219 | 183 | 60 | 18 | 2 | 1078 |
| 1985-86 | 0 | 0 | 0 | 3 | 145 | 211 | 118 | 173 | 132 | 85 | 29 | 0 | 896 |
| 1986-87 | 0 | 0 | 7 | 10 | 66 | 223 | 291 | 197 | 178 | 72 | 21 | 6 | 1071 |
| 1987-88 | 0 | 0 | 0 | 0 | 98 | 338 | 250 | 147 | 125 | 85 | 53 | 22 | 1118 |
| 1988-89 | 0 | 0 | 0 | 4 | 141 | 275 | 313 | 237 | 158 | 37 | 40 | 14 | 1219 |
| 1989-90 | 0 | 0 | 1 | 13 | 67 | 188 | 252 | 268 | 165 | 52 | 39 | 1 | 1066 |
| 1990-91 | 0 | 0 | 0 | 3 | 88 | 284 | | | | | | | |

**TABLE 5**    COOLING DEGREE DAYS Base 65 deg. F    SAN DIEGO, CALIFORNIA

| YEAR | JAN | FEB | MAR | APR | MAY | JUNE | JULY | AUG | SEP | OCT | NOV | DEC | TOTAL |
|---|---|---|---|---|---|---|---|---|---|---|---|---|---|
| 1969 | 5 | 0 | 1 | 9 | 3 | 31 | 144 | 247 | 154 | 53 | 26 | 5 | 678 |
| 1970 | 0 | 1 | 1 | 1 | 21 | 40 | 172 | 247 | 145 | 58 | 7 | 0 | 693 |
| 1971 | 5 | 3 | 0 | 19 | 7 | 31 | 142 | 327 | 223 | 107 | 1 | 0 | 866 |
| 1972 | 0 | 0 | 0 | 4 | 33 | 68 | 247 | 230 | 117 | 53 | 0 | 1 | 753 |
| 1973 | 0 | 0 | 0 | 10 | 17 | 97 | 133 | 176 | 121 | 70 | 8 | 1 | 633 |
| 1974 | 0 | 0 | 0 | 2 | 9 | 69 | 204 | 169 | 164 | 75 | 19 | 0 | 711 |
| 1975 | 0 | 0 | 0 | 0 | 1 | 18 | 142 | 124 | 201 | 54 | 8 | 0 | 548 |
| 1976 | 14 | 0 | 10 | 3 | 31 | 147 | 196 | 240 | 269 | 200 | 102 | 0 | 1212 |
| 1977 | 5 | 9 | 0 | 2 | 1 | 34 | 212 | 258 | 224 | 128 | 40 | 8 | 921 |
| 1978 | 1 | 7 | 38 | 4 | 115 | 194 | 213 | 251 | 275 | 166 | 11 | 0 | 1276 |
| 1979 | 0 | 0 | 10 | 6 | 46 | 169 | 216 | 283 | 348 | 124 | 5 | 8 | 1215 |
| 1980 | 2 | 13 | 3 | 35 | 15 | 110 | 253 | 289 | 170 | 86 | 15 | 7 | 998 |
| 1981 | 7 | 29 | 0 | 26 | 81 | 244 | 335 | 343 | 265 | 80 | 21 | 0 | 1431 |
| 1982 | 0 | 7 | 6 | 32 | 42 | 58 | 219 | 271 | 250 | 164 | 12 | 0 | 1061 |
| 1983 | 11 | 0 | 1 | 9 | 51 | 99 | 242 | 392 | 364 | 231 | 55 | 0 | 1455 |
| 1984 | 13 | 0 | 15 | 31 | 107 | 156 | 387 | 366 | 422 | 119 | 4 | 0 | 1620 |
| 1985 | 0 | 7 | 0 | 22 | 19 | 128 | 325 | 235 | 153 | 104 | 6 | 0 | 999 |
| 1986 | 2 | 11 | 4 | 29 | 23 | 78 | 152 | 218 | 173 | 31 | 9 | 0 | 630 |
| 1987 | 0 | 6 | 5 | 29 | 17 | 35 | 71 | 158 | 154 | 147 | 10 | 0 | 632 |
| 1988 | 0 | 5 | 28 | 16 | 25 | 26 | 176 | 193 | 166 | 64 | 0 | 5 | 699 |
| 1989 | 0 | 13 | 2 | 63 | 5 | 48 | 165 | 193 | 168 | 58 | 17 | 0 | 732 |
| 1990 | 0 | 0 | 2 | 6 | 21 | 127 | 233 | 211 | 203 | 123 | 25 | 0 | 957 |

**TABLE 6**    SNOWFALL (inches)    SAN DIEGO, CALIFORNIA

| SEASON | JULY | AUG | SEP | OCT | NOV | DEC | JAN | FEB | MAR | APR | MAY | JUNE | TOTAL |
|---|---|---|---|---|---|---|---|---|---|---|---|---|---|
| 1970-71 | 0.0 | 0.0 | 0.0 | 0.0 | 0.0 | 0.0 | 0.0 | 0.0 | 0.0 | 0.0 | 0.0 | 0.0 | 0.0 |
| 1971-72 | 0.0 | 0.0 | 0.0 | 0.0 | 0.0 | 0.0 | 0.0 | 0.0 | 0.0 | 0.0 | 0.0 | 0.0 | 0.0 |
| 1972-73 | 0.0 | 0.0 | 0.0 | 0.0 | 0.0 | 0.0 | 0.0 | 0.0 | 0.0 | 0.0 | 0.0 | 0.0 | 0.0 |
| 1973-74 | 0.0 | 0.0 | 0.0 | 0.0 | 0.0 | 0.0 | 0.0 | 0.0 | 0.0 | 0.0 | 0.0 | 0.0 | 0.0 |
| 1974-75 | 0.0 | 0.0 | 0.0 | 0.0 | 0.0 | 0.0 | 0.0 | 0.0 | 0.0 | 0.0 | 0.0 | 0.0 | 0.0 |
| 1975-76 | 0.0 | 0.0 | 0.0 | 0.0 | 0.0 | 0.0 | 0.0 | 0.0 | 0.0 | 0.0 | 0.0 | 0.0 | 0.0 |
| 1976-77 | 0.0 | 0.0 | 0.0 | 0.0 | 0.0 | 0.0 | 0.0 | 0.0 | 0.0 | 0.0 | 0.0 | 0.0 | 0.0 |
| 1977-78 | 0.0 | 0.0 | 0.0 | 0.0 | 0.0 | 0.0 | 0.0 | 0.0 | 0.0 | 0.0 | 0.0 | 0.0 | 0.0 |
| 1978-79 | 0.0 | 0.0 | 0.0 | 0.0 | 0.0 | 0.0 | 0.0 | 0.0 | 0.0 | 0.0 | 0.0 | 0.0 | 0.0 |
| 1979-80 | 0.0 | 0.0 | 0.0 | 0.0 | 0.0 | 0.0 | 0.0 | 0.0 | 0.0 | 0.0 | 0.0 | 0.0 | 0.0 |
| 1980-81 | 0.0 | 0.0 | 0.0 | 0.0 | 0.0 | 0.0 | 0.0 | 0.0 | 0.0 | 0.0 | 0.0 | 0.0 | 0.0 |
| 1981-82 | 0.0 | 0.0 | 0.0 | 0.0 | 0.0 | 0.0 | 0.0 | 0.0 | 0.0 | 0.0 | 0.0 | 0.0 | 0.0 |
| 1982-83 | 0.0 | 0.0 | 0.0 | 0.0 | 0.0 | 0.0 | 0.0 | 0.0 | 0.0 | 0.0 | 0.0 | 0.0 | 0.0 |
| 1983-84 | 0.0 | 0.0 | 0.0 | 0.0 | 0.0 | 0.0 | 0.0 | 0.0 | 0.0 | 0.0 | 0.0 | 0.0 | 0.0 |
| 1984-85 | 0.0 | 0.0 | 0.0 | 0.0 | T | 0.0 | 0.0 | 0.0 | T | 0.0 | 0.0 | 0.0 | T |
| 1985-86 | 0.0 | 0.0 | 0.0 | 0.0 | T | 0.0 | 0.0 | 0.0 | 0.0 | 0.0 | 0.0 | 0.0 | T |
| 1986-87 | 0.0 | 0.0 | 0.0 | 0.0 | 0.0 | 0.0 | 0.0 | 0.0 | 0.0 | 0.0 | 0.0 | 0.0 | 0.0 |
| 1987-88 | 0.0 | 0.0 | 0.0 | 0.0 | 0.0 | 0.0 | 0.0 | 0.0 | 0.0 | 0.0 | 0.0 | 0.0 | 0.0 |
| 1988-89 | 0.0 | 0.0 | 0.0 | 0.0 | 0.0 | 0.0 | 0.0 | 0.0 | 0.0 | 0.0 | 0.0 | 0.0 | 0.0 |
| 1989-90 | 0.0 | 0.0 | 0.0 | 0.0 | 0.0 | 0.0 | 0.0 | 0.0 | 0.0 | 0.0 | 0.0 | 0.0 | 0.0 |
| 1990-91 | 0.0 | 0.0 | 0.0 | 0.0 | 0.0 | 0.0 | | | | | | | |
| Record Mean | 0.0 | 0.0 | 0.0 | 0.0 | T | T | T | 0.0 | T | 0.0 | 0.0 | 0.0 | T |

**See Reference Notes, relative to all above tables, on preceding page.**

San Francisco is located at the northern end of a narrow peninsula which separates San Francisco Bay from the Pacific Ocean. It is known as the air conditioned city with cool pleasant summers and mild winters. Flowers bloom throughout the year and warm clothing may be needed at times during any month.

Precipitation averages about 20 inches a year with pronounced wet and dry seasons, characteristic of its Mediterranean climate. Little or no rain falls from June through September while about 80 percent of the annual total falls from November through March. Snow is extremely rare. Measurable amounts fall about once every 15 years. Freezing temperatures are also extremely rare. On average, thunderstorms occur on only two days each year. The average annual wind speed is about 9 mph with lighter winds, 6 to 7 mph, occurring in the winter and stronger winds, 10 to 11 mph, in the summer.

San Francisco probably has greater climatic variability by far with respect to temperature, cloudiness, and sunshine within its 49 square mile area than any other similarly sized urban area in the country. Likewise, the San Francisco Bay area has considerably more variability than San Francisco itself.

Sea fogs, and the low stratus clouds associated with them are most common in the summertime, but may occur at any time of the year. In the summer the temperature of the Pacific Ocean is much lower than the temperature inland, particularly in the Central Valley of California. This condition tends to enhance the sea breeze effect common to coastal areas. Brisk westerly winds blow throughout the afternoon and evening hours. The fog is carried inland by these westerly winds in the late afternoon and evening and then evaporates during the subsequent forenoon.

The complex topography of San Francisco causes complex patterns of fog and sun as well as temperature. A range of hills with elevations of nearly 1000 feet above sea level, bisects the city from north to south. This range partially blocks the inland movement of the fog, but gaps in the hills permit small masses of fog to pass through, further complicating the pattern. Occasionally, the fog will reach 50 miles south to San Jose, while the area just to the lee of the highest hills is still mostly clear.

Sunshine varies greatly from one part of the city to another, especially in the summer. Spring and fall are the sunniest seasons. In the summer the sunniest area is a triangular shaped area to the lee of the highest hills and extending to the bay. The least sunny area is along the ocean due to the high frequency of fog there. The percent of possible summer sunshine varies from an estimated 25 to 35 percent at the ocean to 70 to 80 percent in the sunniest area.

The extent and behavior of the summertime fog on a particular day depends on several factors. A typical day would find the fog covering the entire city at sunrise and little wind. During the forenoon the skies become sunny in the eastern part of the city with some partial clearing reaching the ocean for a couple of hours in the early afternoon. By early afternoon the winds pick up and by late afternoon the fog is rolling inland again. The wind usually reaches a maximum velocity in the early evening.

In the winter relatively little difference in the climate is observed from one part of the city to another. This is due to the lack of temperature contrast between the ocean and the land and to the relative frequency of passage of Pacific frontal systems. However, those areas near the ocean have more sunshine than areas further inland. The source region for fog is inland during winter, mainly in the Central Valley, rather than the ocean.

Temperature patterns in the city are the same as those of sunshine. In the winter there is little variation, with average maximums from 55 to 60 degrees and average minimums in the mid to upper 40s. Average temperatures rise until June and remain nearly constant through August with average maximums in the lower 60s near the ocean and upper 60s in the sunny eastern half of the city. Summer minimums range from 50 to 55. The warmest time of the year is September and October when the fog diminishes greatly and some of the warmth from the Central Valley flows westward. At this time of year the average maximums are in the mid 60s near the ocean and in the mid 70s in the warmest areas of the city. The average minimums are about the same as they are during the summer.

## TABLE 1     NORMALS, MEANS AND EXTREMES

### SAN FRANCISCO, CALIFORNIA MISSION DOLORES

LATITUDE: 37°46'N     LONGITUDE: 122°26'W     ELEVATION: FT. GRND     75 BARO     TIME ZONE: PACIFIC     WBAN: 23272

| | (a) | JAN | FEB | MAR | APR | MAY | JUNE | JULY | AUG | SEP | OCT | NOV | DEC | YEAR |
|---|---|---|---|---|---|---|---|---|---|---|---|---|---|---|
| **TEMPERATURE °F:** | | | | | | | | | | | | | | |
| Normals | | | | | | | | | | | | | | |
| -Daily Maximum | | 57.2 | 61.0 | 61.5 | 63.2 | 65.4 | 67.9 | 69.1 | 70.2 | 72.5 | 70.2 | 63.2 | 57.1 | 64.9 |
| -Daily Minimum | | 44.2 | 47.5 | 47.9 | 48.5 | 50.7 | 53.3 | 54.5 | 55.8 | 56.2 | 53.9 | 49.5 | 45.1 | 50.6 |
| -Monthly | | 50.7 | 54.3 | 54.7 | 55.9 | 58.1 | 60.6 | 61.8 | 63.0 | 64.4 | 62.1 | 56.4 | 51.1 | 57.8 |
| Extremes | | | | | | | | | | | | | | |
| -Record Highest | 54 | 79 | 81 | 83 | 94 | 96 | 101 | 103 | 96 | 101 | 102 | 86 | 76 | 103 |
| -Year | | 1962 | 1986 | 1952 | 1989 | 1976 | 1961 | 1988 | 1968 | 1971 | 1987 | 1966 | 1958 | JUL 1988 |
| -Record Lowest | 54 | 30 | 31 | 38 | 40 | 44 | 47 | 47 | 48 | 48 | 45 | 41 | 28 | 28 |
| -Year | | 1937 | 1989 | 1942 | 1967 | 1964 | 1955 | 1953 | 1969 | 1955 | 1949 | 1985 | 1990 | DEC 1990 |
| **NORMAL DEGREE DAYS:** | | | | | | | | | | | | | | |
| Heating (base 65°F) | | 443 | 300 | 319 | 273 | 216 | 140 | 104 | 82 | 72 | 112 | 258 | 431 | 2750 |
| Cooling (base 65°F) | | 0 | 0 | 0 | 0 | 0 | 8 | 5 | 20 | 54 | 22 | 0 | 0 | 109 |
| **% OF POSSIBLE SUNSHINE** | 38 | 56 | 62 | 69 | 73 | 72 | 73 | 66 | 65 | 72 | 70 | 62 | 53 | 66 |
| **MEAN SKY COVER (tenths)** | | | | | | | | | | | | | | |
| Sunrise - Sunset | | | | | | | | | | | | | | |
| **MEAN NUMBER OF DAYS:** | | | | | | | | | | | | | | |
| Sunrise to Sunset | | | | | | | | | | | | | | |
| -Clear | | | | | | | | | | | | | | |
| -Partly Cloudy | | | | | | | | | | | | | | |
| -Cloudy | | | | | | | | | | | | | | |
| Precipitation | | | | | | | | | | | | | | |
| .01 inches or more | 54 | 10.8 | 10.0 | 10.5 | 6.2 | 3.0 | 1.3 | 0.5 | 0.8 | 1.6 | 4.4 | 8.1 | 10.1 | 67.2 |
| Snow, Ice pellets | | | | | | | | | | | | | | |
| 1.0 inches or more | 37 | 0.0 | 0.0 | 0.0 | 0.0 | 0.0 | 0.0 | 0.0 | 0.0 | 0.0 | 0.0 | 0.0 | 0.0 | 0.0 |
| Thunderstorms | 29 | 0.3 | 0.2 | 0.1 | 0.3 | 0.2 | 0.1 | 0.2 | 0.* | 0.3 | 0.2 | 0.1 | 0.3 | 2.2 |
| Heavy Fog Visibility | | | | | | | | | | | | | | |
| 1/4 mile or less | | | | | | | | | | | | | | |
| Temperature °F | | | | | | | | | | | | | | |
| -Maximum | | | | | | | | | | | | | | |
| 90° and above | 54 | 0.0 | 0.0 | 0.0 | 0.1 | 0.2 | 0.3 | 0.1 | 0.1 | 0.9 | 0.3 | 0.0 | 0.0 | 2.1 |
| 32° and below | 54 | 0.0 | 0.0 | 0.0 | 0.0 | 0.0 | 0.0 | 0.0 | 0.0 | 0.0 | 0.0 | 0.0 | 0.0 | 0.0 |
| -Minimum | | | | | | | | | | | | | | |
| 32° and below | 54 | 0.1 | 0.* | 0.0 | 0.0 | 0.0 | 0.0 | 0.0 | 0.0 | 0.0 | 0.0 | 0.0 | 0.1 | 0.2 |
| 0° and below | 54 | 0.0 | 0.0 | 0.0 | 0.0 | 0.0 | 0.0 | 0.0 | 0.0 | 0.0 | 0.0 | 0.0 | 0.0 | 0.0 |
| **AVG. STATION PRESS.(mb)** | | | | | | | | | | | | | | |
| **RELATIVE HUMIDITY (%)** | | | | | | | | | | | | | | |
| Hour 04 | 7 | 81 | 83 | 81 | 82 | 89 | 89 | 92 | 93 | 87 | 81 | 82 | 80 | 85 |
| Hour 10 (Local Time) | 7 | 72 | 70 | 61 | 59 | 65 | 70 | 73 | 73 | 64 | 62 | 69 | 71 | 67 |
| Hour 16 | 7 | 63 | 63 | 61 | 61 | 68 | 72 | 74 | 73 | 66 | 60 | 63 | 63 | 66 |
| Hour 22 | 7 | 76 | 78 | 76 | 80 | 86 | 88 | 90 | 90 | 82 | 74 | 76 | 74 | 81 |
| **PRECIPITATION (inches):** | | | | | | | | | | | | | | |
| Water Equivalent | | | | | | | | | | | | | | |
| -Normal | | 4.48 | 2.83 | 2.58 | 1.48 | 0.35 | 0.15 | 0.04 | 0.08 | 0.24 | 1.09 | 2.49 | 3.52 | 19.33 |
| -Maximum Monthly | 54 | 10.69 | 8.49 | 9.04 | 5.47 | 3.19 | 1.42 | 0.62 | 0.78 | 2.06 | 5.51 | 8.20 | 11.47 | 11.47 |
| -Year | | 1952 | 1938 | 1983 | 1958 | 1957 | 1967 | 1974 | 1976 | 1959 | 1962 | 1983 | 1955 | DEC 1955 |
| -Minimum Monthly | 54 | 0.31 | 0.04 | 0.07 | T | 0.00 | 0.00 | 0.00 | 0.00 | 0.00 | 0.00 | T | 0.00 | 0.00 |
| -Year | | 1976 | 1953 | 1988 | 1949 | 1982 | 1983 | 1982 | 1982 | 1980 | 1980 | 1959 | 1989 | DEC 1989 |
| -Maximum in 24 hrs | 54 | 4.22 | 2.34 | 3.65 | 2.36 | 1.47 | 1.36 | 0.61 | 0.49 | 2.06 | 3.11 | 2.72 | 3.14 | 4.22 |
| -Year | | 1982 | 1940 | 1940 | 1953 | 1990 | 1967 | 1974 | 1965 | 1959 | 1962 | 1973 | 1945 | JAN 1982 |
| Snow, Ice pellets | | | | | | | | | | | | | | |
| -Maximum Monthly | 40 | T | T | T | 0.0 | 0.0 | 0.0 | 0.0 | 0.0 | 0.0 | 0.0 | 0.0 | T | T |
| -Year | | 1962 | 1951 | 1951 | | | | | | | | | 1972 | DEC 1972 |
| -Maximum in 24 hrs | 36 | T | T | T | 0.0 | 0.0 | 0.0 | 0.0 | 0.0 | 0.0 | 0.0 | 0.0 | T | T |
| -Year | | 1962 | 1951 | 1951 | | | | | | | | | 1941 | JAN 1962 |
| **WIND:** | | | | | | | | | | | | | | |
| Mean Speed (mph) | 28 | 6.7 | 7.5 | 8.5 | 9.5 | 10.4 | 10.9 | 11.2 | 10.5 | 9.1 | 7.6 | 6.3 | 6.5 | 8.7 |
| Prevailing Direction through 1963 | | N | W | W | W | W | W | W | W | W | W | W | N | W |
| Fastest Mile | | | | | | | | | | | | | | |
| -Direction (!!!) | 36 | SE | SW | S | W | W | W | W | W | W | SE | S | SE | SE |
| -Speed (MPH) | 36 | 47 | 47 | 44 | 38 | 38 | 40 | 38 | 34 | 32 | 43 | 41 | 45 | 47 |
| -Year | | 1965 | 1938 | 1948 | 1965 | 1965 | 1965 | 1939 | 1966 | 1956 | 1950 | 1953 | 1965 | JAN 1965 |
| Peak Gust | | | | | | | | | | | | | | |
| -Direction (!!!) | | | | | | | | | | | | | | |
| -Speed (mph) | | | | | | | | | | | | | | |
| -Date | | | | | | | | | | | | | | |

**See Reference Notes to this table on the following page.**

PRECIPITATION (inches)  SAN FRANCISCO, CALIFORNIA MISSION DOLORES

**TABLE 2**

| YEAR | JAN | FEB | MAR | APR | MAY | JUNE | JULY | AUG | SEP | OCT | NOV | DEC | ANNUAL |
|---|---|---|---|---|---|---|---|---|---|---|---|---|---|
| 1961 | 2.79 | 0.96 | 2.27 | 0.79 | 0.88 | 0.04 | T | 0.02 | 0.22 | 0.09 | 4.44 | 2.13 | 14.63 |
| 1962 | 1.08 | 6.58 | 2.76 | 0.36 | T | T | T | 0.07 | 0.22 | 5.51 | 0.60 | 2.81 | 19.99 |
| 1963 | 3.35 | 1.92 | 3.87 | 3.35 | 0.45 | T | T | T | 0.06 | 1.39 | 3.52 | 0.87 | 18.78 |
| 1964 | 3.37 | 0.19 | 2.12 | 0.01 | 0.22 | 0.57 | T | 0.01 | T | 1.90 | 3.99 | 5.35 | 17.73 |
| 1965 | 3.97 | 0.94 | 2.92 | 3.21 | T | T | 0.02 | 0.49 | T | 0.01 | 4.79 | 3.51 | 19.86 |
| 1966 | 3.27 | 2.72 | 0.80 | 0.36 | 0.19 | 0.17 | 0.06 | 0.10 | 0.10 | 0.01 | 4.80 | 3.87 | 16.45 |
| 1967 | 9.49 | 0.22 | 4.35 | 4.90 | 0.09 | 1.42 | 0.00 | T | 0.04 | 0.53 | 1.10 | 2.12 | 24.26 |
| 1968 | 4.54 | 2.28 | 3.15 | 0.48 | 0.22 | T | T | 0.03 | 0.06 | 0.62 | 2.67 | 3.91 | 17.96 |
| 1969 | 7.74 | 7.26 | 1.01 | 1.74 | T | 0.05 | T | T | 0.01 | 0.45 | 2.61 | 6.15 | 27.02 |
| 1970 | 7.81 | 0.56 | 1.55 | 0.06 | 0.03 | 0.57 | T | T | T | 0.84 | 6.44 | 5.39 | 24.25 |
| 1971 | 2.04 | 0.26 | 2.91 | 0.72 | 0.19 | T | 0.01 | 0.01 | 0.22 | 0.11 | 1.92 | 3.93 | 12.32 |
| 1972 | 1.32 | 2.13 | 0.23 | 1.07 | T | 0.11 | 0.01 | 0.04 | 0.54 | 5.41 | 6.40 | 3.53 | 20.79 |
| 1973 | 9.38 | 6.32 | 2.63 | 0.02 | 0.08 | 0.00 | 0.62 | 0.00 | 0.30 | 1.62 | 7.80 | 3.65 | 31.80 |
| 1974 | 3.40 | 1.53 | 4.49 | 2.34 | 0.00 | 0.10 | 0.04 | 0.00 | 0.00 | 0.85 | 0.40 | 1.53 | 15.26 |
| 1975 | 2.57 | 3.72 | 5.15 | 1.25 | 0.02 | 0.04 | 0.20 | 0.02 | 0.00 | 0.00 | 2.44 | 0.43 | 16.02 |
| 1976 | 0.31 | 1.83 | 1.01 | 0.70 | 0.01 | 0.03 | 0.00 | 0.78 | 0.51 | 0.38 | 1.04 | 2.13 | 8.73 |
| 1977 | 1.65 | 0.90 | 2.01 | 0.05 | 0.57 | 0.00 | 0.00 | 0.03 | 0.86 | 0.17 | 1.96 | 3.30 | 11.50 |
| 1978 | 6.20 | 3.54 | 5.20 | 3.82 | 0.00 | 0.00 | 0.00 | 0.00 | 0.20 | 0.00 | 1.67 | 0.89 | 21.52 |
| 1979 | 6.74 | 4.96 | 1.58 | 0.87 | 0.15 | 0.00 | 0.07 | 0.00 | 0.01 | 1.66 | 2.98 | 3.10 | 22.12 |
| 1980 | 3.77 | 4.84 | 1.25 | 0.97 | 0.23 | 0.02 | 0.04 | 0.00 | 0.00 | 0.00 | 0.14 | 2.95 | 14.21 |
| 1981 | 4.00 | 1.78 | 3.71 | 0.17 | 0.12 | 0.00 | 0.00 | 0.00 | 0.22 | 1.74 | 3.73 | 4.15 | 19.62 |
| 1982 | 6.84 | 3.26 | 7.65 | 3.03 | 0.00 | 0.06 | 0.00 | 0.00 | 0.72 | 2.79 | 5.62 | 2.22 | 32.19 |
| 1983 | 5.77 | 8.06 | 9.04 | 3.48 | 0.47 | 0.00 | 0.01 | 0.00 | 0.68 | 0.26 | 8.20 | 7.72 | 43.75 |
| 1984 | 0.50 | 2.34 | 1.32 | 0.92 | 0.16 | 0.30 | 0.00 | 0.24 | 0.10 | 2.94 | 7.45 | 2.10 | 18.37 |
| 1985 | 0.59 | 1.98 | 3.94 | 0.27 | 0.09 | 0.31 | 0.00 | 0.00 | 0.38 | 0.80 | 4.83 | 2.47 | 15.66 |
| 1986 | 4.77 | 8.29 | 6.25 | 0.76 | 0.13 | 0.00 | 0.03 | 0.01 | 1.32 | 0.11 | 0.20 | 1.64 | 23.51 |
| 1987 | 4.26 | 3.77 | 2.31 | 0.14 | 0.06 | 0.01 | 0.00 | 0.00 | 0.00 | 1.07 | 3.09 | 5.09 | 19.80 |
| 1988 | 4.93 | 0.40 | 0.07 | 1.73 | 0.66 | 0.70 | 0.00 | 0.00 | 0.00 | 0.64 | 3.70 | 4.23 | 17.06 |
| 1989 | 1.26 | 1.49 | 5.28 | 0.70 | 0.06 | 0.07 | 0.00 | 0.05 | 0.98 | 1.18 | 1.33 | 0.00 | 12.40 |
| 1990 | 4.02 | 2.45 | 1.34 | 0.58 | 2.38 | 0.01 | 0.00 | 0.04 | 0.12 | 0.20 | 0.52 | 1.94 | 13.60 |
| Record Mean | 4.55 | 3.52 | 3.05 | 1.48 | 0.59 | 0.15 | 0.02 | 0.03 | 0.28 | 1.00 | 2.51 | 4.10 | 21.29 |

**TABLE 3**  AVERAGE TEMPERATURE (deg. F)  SAN FRANCISCO, CALIFORNIA MISSION DOLORES

| YEAR | JAN | FEB | MAR | APR | MAY | JUNE | JULY | AUG | SEP | OCT | NOV | DEC | ANNUAL |
|---|---|---|---|---|---|---|---|---|---|---|---|---|---|
| 1961 | 49.1 | 55.4 | 54.3 | 56.9 | 55.7 | 60.2 | 60.0 | 61.0 | 63.4 | 61.2 | 56.5 | 50.0 | 57.0 |
| 1962 | 51.9 | 51.8 | 52.7 | 57.0 | 55.2 | 57.5 | 56.0 | 60.0 | 58.3 | 60.8 | 58.8 | 52.9 | 56.1 |
| 1963 | 50.4 | 58.4 | 54.1 | 54.4 | 57.2 | 58.1 | 59.7 | 59.8 | 64.7 | 62.9 | 56.7 | 48.3 | 57.1 |
| 1964 | 51.0 | 55.0 | 53.2 | 53.8 | 53.4 | 57.8 | 58.9 | 60.0 | 62.4 | 63.1 | 55.3 | 53.7 | 56.5 |
| 1965 | 51.4 | 54.0 | 54.4 | 55.7 | 54.9 | 56.2 | 57.4 | 61.2 | 61.2 | 65.0 | 58.3 | 48.3 | 56.5 |
| 1966 | 52.1 | 51.8 | 53.8 | 57.9 | 55.1 | 59.4 | 58.2 | 58.8 | 63.6 | 62.6 | 57.2 | 51.3 | 56.8 |
| 1967 | 52.6 | 53.2 | 52.7 | 50.8 | 57.9 | 57.1 | 58.9 | 59.2 | 63.5 | 65.5 | 60.0 | 51.9 | 57.0 |
| 1968 | 49.8 | 56.7 | 56.7 | 56.2 | 55.7 | 59.0 | 58.0 | 62.3 | 63.1 | 60.5 | 56.2 | 49.8 | 57.0 |
| 1969 | 48.6 | 50.1 | 54.3 | 54.2 | 57.0 | 58.7 | 57.6 | 59.4 | 60.9 | 61.9 | 59.3 | 55.8 | 56.5 |
| 1970 | 54.0 | 57.4 | 57.8 | 53.3 | 57.7 | 56.8 | 57.8 | 57.2 | 64.4 | 58.6 | 57.9 | 50.6 | 57.0 |
| 1971 | 50.8 | 51.9 | 55.0 | 53.1 | 54.6 | 57.3 | 57.5 | 61.1 | 64.7 | 57.8 | 55.6 | 49.0 | 55.6 |
| 1972 | 48.5 | 54.0 | 55.8 | 55.5 | 55.5 | 57.5 | 60.9 | 60.2 | 61.5 | 61.7 | 54.9 | 47.2 | 56.1 |
| 1973 | 50.1 | 54.9 | 52.5 | 57.2 | 56.3 | 60.7 | 58.6 | 57.1 | 61.3 | 61.0 | 53.3 | 52.0 | 56.4 |
| 1974 | 51.1 | 52.2 | 53.3 | 55.4 | 54.9 | 58.2 | 59.6 | 59.9 | 60.3 | 62.2 | 56.6 | 51.1 | 56.3 |
| 1975 | 51.0 | 53.3 | 53.1 | 51.9 | 57.2 | 56.9 | 58.9 | 59.5 | 59.5 | 59.7 | 55.6 | 53.4 | 55.8 |
| 1976 | 53.4 | 52.8 | 52.5 | 54.1 | 56.8 | 61.5 | 59.2 | 62.5 | 62.2 | 62.8 | 60.4 | 54.6 | 57.8 |
| 1977 | 49.9 | 56.1 | 53.2 | 56.1 | 55.3 | 57.1 | 59.0 | 61.6 | 62.0 | 60.6 | 58.6 | 54.9 | 57.0 |
| 1978 | 55.0 | 55.2 | 59.0 | 56.3 | 60.7 | 58.9 | 58.4 | 60.6 | 65.5 | 61.9 | 55.9 | 49.6 | 58.1 |
| 1979 | 51.0 | 52.9 | 55.7 | 56.5 | 59.2 | 58.6 | 60.2 | 60.8 | 66.3 | 63.2 | 57.7 | 55.4 | 58.1 |
| 1980 | 53.0 | 57.2 | 56.0 | 56.9 | 55.4 | 57.9 | 59.5 | 58.0 | 61.3 | 62.0 | 58.3 | 53.4 | 57.4 |
| 1981 | 52.4 | 56.1 | 54.9 | 55.8 | 56.8 | 62.2 | 57.8 | 59.2 | 60.4 | 59.3 | 54.0 | 54.0 | 57.3 |
| 1982 | 48.5 | 55.0 | 52.8 | 55.6 | 55.8 | 56.3 | 57.9 | 60.1 | 62.6 | 62.8 | 54.4 | 52.2 | 56.2 |
| 1983 | 49.4 | 54.6 | 55.3 | 56.8 | 59.7 | 61.8 | 63.4 | 65.9 | 67.1 | 64.0 | 56.1 | 52.8 | 58.9 |
| 1984 | 51.6 | 52.6 | 56.7 | 54.2 | 59.9 | 59.7 | 63.9 | 62.8 | 69.4 | 61.5 | 56.0 | 50.9 | 58.3 |
| 1985 | 50.0 | 56.0 | 53.2 | 59.8 | 58.1 | 63.9 | 64.1 | 64.1 | 64.1 | 63.2 | 55.0 | 51.3 | 58.6 |
| 1986 | 56.6 | 58.9 | 60.4 | 58.6 | 60.0 | 63.2 | 62.8 | 61.9 | 62.8 | 63.6 | 60.2 | 52.5 | 60.1 |
| 1987 | 51.8 | 56.4 | 57.1 | 60.5 | 61.1 | 60.5 | 61.5 | 63.5 | 63.8 | 65.1 | 58.8 | 52.3 | 59.4 |
| 1988 | 52.8 | 57.7 | 59.1 | 58.8 | 59.1 | 61.1 | 64.2 | 64.0 | 63.1 | 61.5 | 57.3 | 53.3 | 59.3 |
| 1989 | 51.3 | 50.0 | 55.4 | 60.9 | 59.3 | 61.6 | 62.4 | 63.0 | 61.8 | 62.0 | 58.8 | 52.6 | 58.3 |
| 1990 | 52.8 | 52.0 | 54.9 | 59.2 | 59.0 | 62.4 | 62.9 | 65.3 | 66.0 | 64.2 | 58.0 | 49.1 | 58.8 |
| Record Mean | 50.5 | 53.2 | 54.5 | 55.8 | 57.0 | 59.0 | 59.1 | 59.8 | 62.0 | 61.1 | 57.0 | 51.7 | 56.7 |
| Max | 55.6 | 58.9 | 60.6 | 62.2 | 63.3 | 65.5 | 65.1 | 65.6 | 68.9 | 68.2 | 63.0 | 56.7 | 62.8 |
| Min | 45.3 | 47.5 | 48.5 | 49.4 | 50.8 | 52.5 | 53.1 | 53.9 | 55.1 | 54.1 | 50.9 | 46.7 | 50.6 |

## REFERENCE NOTES FOR TABLES 1, 2, 3 and 6    SAN FRANCISCO, CA (MISSION DELORES STA.)

### GENERAL

T - TRACE AMOUNT
BLANK ENTRIES DENOTE MISSING/UNREPORTED DATA.
# INDICATES A STATION OR INSTRUMENT RELOCATION.

### SPECIFIC

#### TABLE 1

(a) - LENGTH OF RECORD IN YEARS. ALTHOUGH INDIVIDUAL MONTHS MAY BE MISSING.

* LESS THAN .05

NORMALS — BASED ON THE 1951-1980 RECORD PERIOD.
EXTREMES — DATES ARE THE MOST RECENT OCCURRENCE.
WIND DIR. — NUMERALS SHOW TENS OF DEGREES CLOCKWISE FROM TRUE NORTH. ''00'' INDICATES CALM.
RESULTANT WIND DIRECTIONS ARE GIVEN TO WHOLE DEGREES.

#### TABLE 3
MAX AND MIN ARE LONG-TERM MEAN DAILY MAXIMUM AND MEAN DAILY MINIMUM TEMPERATURES.

### EXCEPTIONS

#### TABLE 1

1. THUNDERSTORM DATA ARE THROUGH 1964 AND MAY BE INCOMPLETE, DUE TO PART-TIME OPERATIONS.
2. MEAN WIND SPEED ARE THROUGH 1964.
3. RELATIVE HUMIDITY, SNOW, AND DAYS SNOW 1.0 INCH OR MORE ARE THROUGH 1972.
3. FASTEST MILE WINDS ARE THROUGH MARCH 1973.
4. PERCENT OF POSSIBLE SUNSHINE IS THROUGH 1973.

#### TABLES 2, 3, and 6

**RECORD MEANS ARE THROUGH THE CURRENT YEAR, BEGINNING IN 1875 FOR TEMPERATURE, 1850 FOR PRECIPITATION 1939 FOR SNOWFALL**

HEATING DEGREE DAYS Base 65 deg. F    SAN FRANCISCO, CALIFORNIA MISSION DOLORES

**TABLE 4**

| SEASON | JULY | AUG | SEP | OCT | NOV | DEC | JAN | FEB | MAR | APR | MAY | JUNE | TOTAL |
|---|---|---|---|---|---|---|---|---|---|---|---|---|---|
| 1961-62 | 167 | 127 | 91 | 156 | 246 | 456 | 398 | 364 | 376 | 242 | 297 | 231 | 3151 |
| 1962-63 | 270 | 157 | 196 | 130 | 182 | 369 | 445 | 179 | 332 | 313 | 234 | 201 | 3008 |
| 1963-64 | 166 | 160 | 39 | 67 | 244 | 514 | 427 | 284 | 360 | 338 | 355 | 219 | 3174 |
| 1964-65 | 186 | 152 | 139 | 100 | 284 | 343 | 414 | 302 | 319 | 280 | 306 | 259 | 3084 |
| 1965-66 | 230 | 123 | 120 | 73 | 199 | 509 | 393 | 362 | 336 | 217 | 300 | 182 | 3044 |
| 1966-67 | 205 | 188 | 78 | 102 | 241 | 417 | 375 | 325 | 372 | 420 | 230 | 229 | 3182 |
| 1967-68 | 184 | 173 | 67 | 47 | 158 | 398 | 465 | 235 | 254 | 263 | 281 | 174 | 2698 |
| 1968-69 | 213 | 98 | 92 | 148 | 258 | 462 | 505 | 412 | 333 | 315 | 242 | 185 | 3263 |
| 1969-70 | 221 | 171 | 132 | 107 | 166 | 277 | 334 | 210 | 222 | 341 | 237 | 242 | 2660 |
| 1970-71 | 231 | 246 | 95 | 201 | 208 | 439 | 433 | 359 | 354 | 351 | 317 | 230 | 3464 |
| 1971-72 | 225 | 120 | 85 | 229 | 275 | 490 | 506 | 312 | 279 | 278 | 287 | 226 | 3312 |
| 1972-73 | 144 | 139 | 110 | 115 | 298 | 546 | 455 | 277 | 380 | 225 | 267 | 167 | 3123 |
| 1973-74 | 199 | 239 | 137 | 134 | 285 | 396 | 423 | 353 | 354 | 284 | 309 | 202 | 3315 |
| 1974-75 | 167 | 153 | 153 | 119 | 243 | 422 | 428 | 320 | 360 | 386 | 257 | 238 | 3246 |
| 1975-76 | 185 | 170 | 177 | 164 | 276 | 352 | 353 | 344 | 378 | 321 | 262 | 179 | 3161 |
| 1976-77 | 173 | 86 | 114 | 102 | 152 | 315 | 463 | 242 | 359 | 261 | 294 | 233 | 2794 |
| 1977-78 | 197 | 116 | 93 | 139 | 187 | 304 | 304 | 269 | 188 | 254 | 154 | 177 | 2382 |
| 1978-79 | 196 | 137 | 43 | 138 | 268 | 471 | 431 | 332 | 281 | 250 | 185 | 197 | 2929 |
| 1979-80 | 151 | 125 | 23 | 64 | 213 | 293 | 366 | 221 | 275 | 240 | 291 | 218 | 2480 |
| 1980-81 | 165 | 212 | 132 | 128 | 201 | 350 | 384 | 243 | 304 | 284 | 248 | 121 | 2772 |
| 1981-82 | 220 | 175 | 136 | 174 | 196 | 334 | 506 | 273 | 369 | 278 | 281 | 253 | 3195 |
| 1982-83 | 210 | 151 | 82 | 90 | 311 | 391 | 478 | 283 | 296 | 238 | 174 | 112 | 2816 |
| 1983-84 | 83 | 14 | 30 | 52 | 257 | 369 | 408 | 354 | 251 | 321 | 172 | 159 | 2470 |
| 1984-85 | 70 | 84 | 19 | 117 | 263 | 430 | 459 | 254 | 359 | 173 | 209 | 57 | 2494 |
| 1985-86 | 71 | 49 | 35 | 99 | 302 | 419 | 254 | 172 | 146 | 196 | 154 | 67 | 1964 |
| 1986-87 | 78 | 93 | 63 | 84 | 152 | 383 | 399 | 233 | 243 | 140 | 154 | 147 | 2169 |
| 1987-88 | 106 | 52 | 50 | 60 | 179 | 387 | 370 | 207 | 181 | 197 | 198 | 125 | 2112 |
| 1988-89 | 60 | 53 | 79 | 137 | 229 | 358 | 419 | 416 | 289 | 171 | 181 | 129 | 2521 |
| 1989-90 | 86 | 68 | 94 | 113 | 183 | 377 | 371 | 357 | 305 | 170 | 188 | 97 | 2409 |
| 1990-91 | 74 | 23 | 8 | 56 | 204 | 487 | | | | | | | |

**TABLE 5**   COOLING DEGREE DAYS Base 65 deg. F    SAN FRANCISCO, CALIFORNIA MISSION DOLORES

| YEAR | JAN | FEB | MAR | APR | MAY | JUNE | JULY | AUG | SEP | OCT | NOV | DEC | TOTAL |
|---|---|---|---|---|---|---|---|---|---|---|---|---|---|
| 1969 | 0 | 0 | 5 | 0 | 1 | 1 | 0 | 0 | 14 | 20 | 3 | 0 | 44 |
| 1970 | 0 | 0 | 5 | 0 | 19 | 1 | 17 | 8 | 82 | 10 | 0 | 0 | 142 |
| 1971 | 0 | 0 | 0 | 0 | 0 | 7 | 0 | 6 | 83 | 12 | 0 | 0 | 108 |
| 1972 | 0 | 0 | 3 | 0 | 1 | 4 | 22 | 0 | 13 | 20 | 0 | 0 | 63 |
| 1973 | 0 | 0 | 0 | 2 | 5 | 43 | 8 | 0 | 34 | 15 | 0 | 0 | 107 |
| 1974 | 0 | 0 | 0 | 3 | 4 | 3 | 4 | 3 | 19 | 41 | 0 | 0 | 77 |
| 1975 | 0 | 0 | 0 | 0 | 23 | 0 | 4 | 8 | 15 | 5 | 0 | 0 | 55 |
| 1976 | 0 | 0 | 0 | 0 | 16 | 82 | 0 | 15 | 37 | 41 | 15 | 0 | 206 |
| 1977 | 0 | 0 | 0 | 0 | 0 | 1 | 18 | 17 | 8 | 8 | 0 | 0 | 52 |
| 1978 | 0 | 0 | 8 | 2 | 30 | 0 | 0 | 6 | 65 | 46 | 3 | 0 | 160 |
| 1979 | 0 | 0 | 0 | 0 | 11 | 13 | 10 | 3 | 72 | 16 | 0 | 0 | 125 |
| 1980 | 0 | 0 | 0 | 5 | 0 | 12 | 2 | 3 | 29 | 43 | 3 | 0 | 97 |
| 1981 | 0 | 0 | 0 | 13 | 1 | 44 | 6 | 3 | 3 | 5 | 2 | 0 | 77 |
| 1982 | 0 | 0 | 0 | 7 | 1 | 0 | 0 | 8 | 16 | 27 | 0 | 0 | 59 |
| 1983 | 0 | 0 | 0 | 0 | 16 | 21 | 41 | 50 | 101 | 27 | 0 | 0 | 256 |
| 1984 | 0 | 0 | 0 | 5 | 20 | 5 | 42 | 20 | 158 | 14 | 0 | 0 | 264 |
| 1985 | 0 | 7 | 0 | 24 | 2 | 28 | 50 | 27 | 16 | 49 | 8 | 0 | 211 |
| 1986 | 0 | 7 | 10 | 8 | 6 | 22 | 17 | 1 | 4 | 49 | 12 | 0 | 136 |
| 1987 | 0 | 0 | 5 | 12 | 38 | 19 | 5 | 14 | 22 | 68 | 0 | 0 | 183 |
| 1988 | 0 | 3 | 6 | 18 | 20 | 12 | 42 | 27 | 30 | 34 | 0 | 0 | 195 |
| 1989 | 0 | 0 | 0 | 56 | 9 | 35 | 15 | 12 | 5 | 28 | 2 | 0 | 162 |
| 1990 | 0 | 0 | 0 | 5 | 8 | 25 | 18 | 39 | 45 | 40 | 1 | 0 | 181 |

**TABLE 6**   SNOWFALL (inches)    SAN FRANCISCO, CALIFORNIA MISSION DOLORES

| SEASON | JULY | AUG | SEP | OCT | NOV | DEC | JAN | FEB | MAR | APR | MAY | JUNE | TOTAL |
|---|---|---|---|---|---|---|---|---|---|---|---|---|---|
| 1961-62 | 0.0 | 0.0 | 0.0 | 0.0 | 0.0 | 0.0 | T | 0.0 | 0.0 | 0.0 | 0.0 | 0.0 | T |
| 1962-63 | 0.0 | 0.0 | 0.0 | 0.0 | 0.0 | 0.0 | 0.0 | 0.0 | 0.0 | 0.0 | 0.0 | 0.0 | 0.0 |
| 1963-64 | 0.0 | 0.0 | 0.0 | 0.0 | 0.0 | 0.0 | 0.0 | 0.0 | 0.0 | 0.0 | 0.0 | 0.0 | 0.0 |
| 1964-65 | 0.0 | 0.0 | 0.0 | 0.0 | 0.0 | 0.0 | 0.0 | 0.0 | 0.0 | 0.0 | 0.0 | 0.0 | 0.0 |
| 1965-66 | 0.0 | 0.0 | 0.0 | 0.0 | 0.0 | 0.0 | 0.0 | 0.0 | 0.0 | 0.0 | 0.0 | 0.0 | 0.0 |
| 1966-67 | 0.0 | 0.0 | 0.0 | 0.0 | 0.0 | 0.0 | 0.0 | 0.0 | 0.0 | 0.0 | 0.0 | 0.0 | 0.0 |
| 1967-68 | 0.0 | 0.0 | 0.0 | 0.0 | 0.0 | 0.0 | 0.0 | 0.0 | 0.0 | 0.0 | 0.0 | 0.0 | 0.0 |
| 1968-69 | 0.0 | 0.0 | 0.0 | 0.0 | 0.0 | 0.0 | 0.0 | 0.0 | 0.0 | 0.0 | 0.0 | 0.0 | 0.0 |
| 1969-70 | 0.0 | 0.0 | 0.0 | 0.0 | 0.0 | 0.0 | 0.0 | 0.0 | 0.0 | 0.0 | 0.0 | 0.0 | 0.0 |
| 1970-71 | 0.0 | 0.0 | 0.0 | 0.0 | 0.0 | 0.0 | 0.0 | 0.0 | 0.0 | 0.0 | 0.0 | 0.0 | 0.0 |
| 1971-72 | 0.0 | 0.0 | 0.0 | 0.0 | 0.0 | 0.0 | 0.0 | 0.0 | 0.0 | 0.0 | 0.0 | | 0.0 |
| 1972-73 | 0.0 | 0.0 | 0.0 | 0.0 | 0.0 | T | 0.0 | 0.0 | 0.0 | 0.0 | | | |
| 1973-74 | | | | | | | | | | | | | |
| 1975-76 | | | | | | | | | | | | | |
| 1976-77 | | | | | | | | | | | | | |
| 1977-78 | | | | | | | | | | | | | |
| 1978-79 | | | | | | | | | | | | | |
| 1979-80 | | | | | | | | | | | | | |
| 1980-81 | | | | | | | | | | | | | |
| 1981-82 | | | | | | | | | | | | | |
| 1982-83 | | | | | | | | | | | | | |
| 1983-84 | | | | | | | | | | | | | |
| 1984-85 | | | | | | | | | | | | | |
| Record Mean | 0.0 | 0.0 | 0.0 | 0.0 | 0.0 | T | T | T | T | 0.0 | 0.0 | 0.0 | T |

**See Reference Notes, relative to all above tables, on preceding page.**

At an elevation near 6,200 feet above sea level, Colorado Springs is located in relatively flat semi-arid country on the eastern slope of the Rocky Mountains. Immediately to the west the mountains rise abruptly to heights ranging from 10,000 to 14,000 feet but generally averaging near 11,000 feet. To the east lie gently undulating prairie lands. The land slopes upward to the north, reaching an average height of about 8,000 feet in 20 miles at the top of Palmer Lake Divide.

Colorado Springs is in the Arkansas River drainage basin. The principal tributary feeding the Arkansas from this area is Fountain Creek which rises in the high mountains west of the city and is fed by Monument Creek originating to the north in the Palmer Lake Divide area.

Other topographical features of the area, and particularly its wide range of elevations, help to give Colorado Springs the various and altogether delightful plains and mountain mixture of climate that has established the locality as a highly desirable place to live. The higher elevations immediately to the west and north of the city produce significant differences in temperature and precipitation. Precipitation amounts at these higher elevations are approximately twice those at nearby lower elevations and the number of rainy days is almost triple.

In Colorado Springs itself, precipitation is relatively sparse. Over 80 percent of it falls between April 1 and September 30, mostly as heavy downpours accompanying summer thunderstorms. Temperatures, in view of the station latitude and elevation, are mild. Uncomfortable extremes, in either summer or winter, are comparatively rare and of short duration. Relative humidity is normally low and wind movement moderately high. This is notably true of the west-to-east movement of the chinook winds, that cause rapid rises in winter temperatures and remind us that the Indian meaning of CHINOOK is SNOW EATER.

Colorado Springs is best known as a resort city, but is also important to the high-tech industry and military community. Several military installations, including the United States Air Force Academy and the Space Command are located within or near the city. The surrounding prairie is also important for cattle raising and a considerable amount of grazing land is used for sheep in the summer months. The growing season varies considerably in length but averages from the first week in May to the first week of October.

## TABLE 1     NORMALS, MEANS AND EXTREMES

COLORADO SPRINGS, COLORADO

LATITUDE: 38°49'N    LONGITUDE: 104°43' W    ELEVATION: FT. GRND 6145 BARO 6093    TIME ZONE: MOUNTAIN    WBAN: 93037

| | (a) | JAN | FEB | MAR | APR | MAY | JUNE | JULY | AUG | SEP | OCT | NOV | DEC | YEAR |
|---|---|---|---|---|---|---|---|---|---|---|---|---|---|---|
| **TEMPERATURE °F:** | | | | | | | | | | | | | | |
| Normals | | | | | | | | | | | | | | |
| -Daily Maximum | | 41.4 | 45.3 | 49.3 | 59.5 | 68.9 | 79.9 | 84.9 | 82.3 | 74.9 | 64.6 | 50.4 | 43.9 | 62.1 |
| -Daily Minimum | | 16.2 | 19.6 | 23.8 | 32.9 | 42.5 | 51.5 | 57.4 | 55.6 | 47.2 | 37.0 | 25.0 | 18.9 | 35.6 |
| -Monthly | | 28.8 | 32.5 | 36.6 | 46.2 | 55.7 | 65.7 | 71.2 | 69.0 | 61.1 | 50.8 | 37.7 | 31.4 | 48.9 |
| Extremes | | | | | | | | | | | | | | |
| -Record Highest | 41 | 72 | 76 | 81 | 83 | 93 | 100 | 100 | 99 | 94 | 86 | 78 | 77 | 100 |
| -Year | | 1974 | 1963 | 1971 | 1989 | 1984 | 1954 | 1954 | 1954 | 1960 | 1979 | 1981 | 1955 | JUN 1954 |
| -Record Lowest | 41 | -26 | -27 | -11 | -3 | 21 | 32 | 42 | 43 | 22 | 5 | -8 | -17 | -27 |
| -Year | | 1951 | 1951 | 1956 | 1959 | 1954 | 1951 | 1952 | 1978 | 1985 | 1969 | 1976 | 1983 | FEB 1951 |
| **NORMAL DEGREE DAYS:** | | | | | | | | | | | | | | |
| Heating (base 65°F) | | 1122 | 910 | 880 | 564 | 296 | 78 | 8 | 25 | 162 | 440 | 819 | 1042 | 6346 |
| Cooling (base 65°F) | | 0 | 0 | 0 | 0 | 8 | 99 | 200 | 149 | 45 | 0 | 0 | 0 | 501 |
| **% OF POSSIBLE SUNSHINE** | | | | | | | | | | | | | | |
| **MEAN SKY COVER (tenths)** | | | | | | | | | | | | | | |
| Sunrise - Sunset | 41 | 5.3 | 5.6 | 5.9 | 5.8 | 6.1 | 4.9 | 5.0 | 5.0 | 4.3 | 4.3 | 5.0 | 5.0 | 5.2 |
| **MEAN NUMBER OF DAYS:** | | | | | | | | | | | | | | |
| Sunrise to Sunset | | | | | | | | | | | | | | |
| -Clear | 41 | 11.4 | 9.1 | 8.8 | 8.0 | 6.9 | 10.2 | 9.5 | 10.2 | 14.4 | 15.1 | 11.6 | 12.2 | 127.5 |
| -Partly Cloudy | 41 | 8.2 | 8.3 | 8.9 | 10.3 | 12.0 | 12.2 | 14.8 | 12.8 | 8.2 | 7.5 | 8.3 | 8.0 | 119.6 |
| -Cloudy | 41 | 11.3 | 10.9 | 13.3 | 11.7 | 12.1 | 7.6 | 6.7 | 8.0 | 7.4 | 8.4 | 10.0 | 10.8 | 118.1 |
| Precipitation | | | | | | | | | | | | | | |
| .01 inches or more | 41 | 5.0 | 4.9 | 7.5 | 7.3 | 10.4 | 9.4 | 13.1 | 12.0 | 6.7 | 5.1 | 4.0 | 4.6 | 89.9 |
| Snow,Ice pellets | | | | | | | | | | | | | | |
| 1.0 inches or more | 41 | 1.6 | 1.7 | 2.9 | 1.5 | 0.3 | 0.* | 0.0 | 0.0 | 0.1 | 0.7 | 1.5 | 1.8 | 12.2 |
| Thunderstorms | 41 | 0.0 | 0.* | 0.5 | 2.2 | 8.2 | 11.0 | 15.8 | 13.3 | 4.7 | 0.8 | 0.* | 0.0 | 56.6 |
| Heavy Fog Visibility | | | | | | | | | | | | | | |
| 1/4 mile or less | 41 | 2.2 | 2.4 | 2.3 | 1.9 | 1.8 | 0.8 | 0.5 | 0.9 | 2.0 | 1.9 | 2.3 | 2.1 | 21.0 |
| Temperature °F | | | | | | | | | | | | | | |
| -Maximum | | | | | | | | | | | | | | |
| 90° and above | 29 | 0.0 | 0.0 | 0.0 | 0.0 | 0.1 | 3.7 | 9.1 | 3.3 | 0.5 | 0.0 | 0.0 | 0.0 | 16.8 |
| 32° and below | 29 | 7.7 | 5.6 | 3.9 | 0.7 | 0.0 | 0.0 | 0.0 | 0.0 | 0.* | 0.3 | 3.1 | 6.7 | 28.0 |
| -Minimum | | | | | | | | | | | | | | |
| 32° and below | 29 | 30.1 | 26.6 | 26.0 | 13.2 | 2.2 | 0.0 | 0.0 | 0.0 | 0.9 | 8.4 | 24.0 | 29.2 | 160.7 |
| 0° and below | 29 | 3.1 | 1.4 | 0.4 | 0.0 | 0.0 | 0.0 | 0.0 | 0.0 | 0.0 | 0.0 | 0.1 | 2.0 | 7.0 |
| **AVG. STATION PRESS.(mb)** | 17 | 809.0 | 808.8 | 806.6 | 808.4 | 809.5 | 812.4 | 814.9 | 814.9 | 813.9 | 812.9 | 809.8 | 809.4 | 810.9 |
| **RELATIVE HUMIDITY (%)** | | | | | | | | | | | | | | |
| Hour 05 | 29 | 56 | 59 | 61 | 61 | 65 | 66 | 67 | 70 | 66 | 58 | 60 | 56 | 62 |
| Hour 11 | 29 | 42 | 40 | 40 | 34 | 37 | 36 | 36 | 40 | 39 | 35 | 39 | 42 | 38 |
| Hour 17 (Local Time) | 29 | 46 | 40 | 38 | 33 | 36 | 35 | 38 | 41 | 37 | 36 | 44 | 48 | 39 |
| Hour 23 | 29 | 57 | 58 | 57 | 55 | 59 | 57 | 59 | 64 | 60 | 56 | 59 | 57 | 58 |
| **PRECIPITATION (inches):** | | | | | | | | | | | | | | |
| Water Equivalent | | | | | | | | | | | | | | |
| -Normal | | 0.27 | 0.31 | 0.78 | 1.35 | 2.28 | 2.02 | 2.85 | 2.61 | 1.31 | 0.78 | 0.54 | 0.32 | 15.42 |
| -Maximum Monthly | 41 | 1.17 | 2.45 | 2.38 | 5.90 | 5.67 | 8.00 | 5.27 | 6.06 | 4.28 | 5.01 | 2.21 | 1.05 | 8.00 |
| -Year | | 1987 | 1987 | 1979 | 1957 | 1957 | 1965 | 1968 | 1986 | 1976 | 1984 | 1957 | 1988 | JUN 1965 |
| -Minimum Monthly | 41 | T | 0.03 | 0.01 | 0.01 | 0.33 | 0.15 | 0.67 | 0.15 | 0.01 | T | T | T | T |
| -Year | | 1964 | 1950 | 1966 | 1964 | 1974 | 1968 | 1987 | 1962 | 1953 | 1980 | 1965 | 1970 | DEC 1970 |
| -Maximum in 24 hrs | 41 | 0.79 | 1.49 | 1.51 | 2.45 | 2.57 | 3.09 | 3.00 | 3.73 | 1.73 | 1.60 | 1.45 | 0.69 | 3.73 |
| -Year | | 1987 | 1987 | 1987 | 1957 | 1955 | 1954 | 1951 | 1976 | 1959 | 1960 | 1979 | 1981 | AUG 1976 |
| Snow,Ice pellets | | | | | | | | | | | | | | |
| -Maximum Monthly | 41 | 28.7 | 23.2 | 23.2 | 42.7 | 19.4 | 1.1 | T | T | 27.9 | 25.9 | 19.1 | 18.2 | 42.7 |
| -Year | | 1987 | 1987 | 1984 | 1957 | 1978 | 1975 | 1989 | 1989 | 1959 | 1984 | 1979 | 1983 | APR 1957 |
| -Maximum in 24 hrs | 41 | 22.0 | 14.8 | 13.3 | 18.0 | 17.4 | 1.1 | T | T | 17.1 | 14.6 | 14.5 | 9.6 | 22.0 |
| -Year | | 1987 | 1987 | 1964 | 1957 | 1978 | 1975 | 1989 | 1989 | 1959 | 1984 | 1972 | 1979 | JAN 1987 |
| **WIND:** | | | | | | | | | | | | | | |
| Mean Speed (mph) | 41 | 9.5 | 10.1 | 11.3 | 11.8 | 11.3 | 10.5 | 9.3 | 9.0 | 9.5 | 9.6 | 9.5 | 9.5 | 10.1 |
| Prevailing Direction through 1963 | | NNE | N | N | N | NNW | SSE | NNW | N | SSE | NNE | NNE | NNW | N |
| Fastest Obs. 1 Min. | | | | | | | | | | | | | | |
| -Direction (!!!) | 39 | 29 | 36 | 29 | 23 | 27 | 20 | 35 | 36 | 27 | 36 | 32 | 27 | 29 |
| -Speed (MPH) | 39 | 55 | 52 | 60 | 48 | 52 | 55 | 47 | 40 | 40 | 41 | 50 | 60 | 60 |
| -Year | | 1950 | 1954 | 1954 | 1963 | 1971 | 1954 | 1968 | 1972 | 1953 | 1975 | 1953 | 1953 | MAR 1954 |
| Peak Gust | | | | | | | | | | | | | | |
| -Direction (!!!) | 6 | W | W | SW | NW | S | SW | NW | SW | SW | SW | NW | W | SW |
| -Speed (mph) | 6 | 61 | 61 | 71 | 61 | 70 | 62 | 58 | 54 | 53 | 58 | 59 | 59 | 71 |
| -Date | | 1989 | 1986 | 1985 | 1986 | 1988 | 1986 | 1989 | 1987 | 1986 | 1985 | 1987 | 1987 | MAR 1985 |

**See Reference Notes to this table on the following page.**

PRECIPITATION (inches)    COLORADO SPRINGS, COLORADO

**TABLE 2**

| YEAR | JAN | FEB | MAR | APR | MAY | JUNE | JULY | AUG | SEP | OCT | NOV | DEC | ANNUAL |
|------|-----|-----|-----|-----|-----|------|------|-----|-----|-----|-----|-----|--------|
| 1961 | 0.14 | 0.65 | 1.21 | 0.55 | 0.84 | 3.86 | 2.14 | 2.26 | 1.91 | 0.98 | 0.44 | 0.43 | 15.42 |
| 1962 | 0.42 | 0.34 | 0.88 | 0.44 | 0.63 | 3.36 | 1.60 | 0.15 | 0.41 | 0.97 | 0.89 | 0.03 | 10.12 |
| 1963 | 0.53 | 0.20 | 0.62 | 0.02 | 0.77 | 1.22 | 1.35 | 5.22 | 1.84 | 0.39 | 0.46 | 0.62 | 13.24 |
| 1964 | T | 0.22 | 1.08 | 0.01 | 2.54 | 0.96 | 1.14 | 0.60 | 1.33 | 0.03 | 0.46 | 0.22 | 8.59 |
| 1965 | 0.14 | 0.72 | 1.12 | .61 | 1.81 | 8.00 | 5.02 | 3.83 | 2.24 | 0.49 | T | 0.45 | 25.43 |
| 1966 | 0.39 | 0.49 | 0.01 | 0.79 | 0.95 | 2.56 | 2.91 | 2.00 | 2.12 | 0.36 | 0.16 | 0.17 | 12.91 |
| 1967 | 0.31 | 0.15 | 0.18 | 2.04 | 2.18 | 2.74 | 5.26 | 3.09 | 0.73 | 1.68 | 0.25 | 0.67 | 19.28 |
| 1968 | 0.10 | 0.22 | 0.37 | 0.54 | 0.62 | 0.15 | 5.27 | 2.12 | 1.03 | 0.43 | 1.32 | 0.24 | 12.41 |
| 1969 | 0.11 | 0.12 | 0.77 | 1.63 | 4.46 | 2.72 | 3.90 | 2.38 | 1.13 | 2.86 | 0.39 | T | 20.99 |
| 1970 | 0.05 | 0.17 | 1.06 | 0.31 | 0.33 | 3.63 | 3.79 | 4.24 | 1.09 | 0.95 | 0.27 | T | 16.49 |
| 1971 | 0.34 | 0.53 | 0.34 | 1.36 | 2.24 | 0.39 | 2.82 | 1.99 | 1.36 | 0.23 | 0.03 | 0.23 | 11.86 |
| 1972 | 0.27 | 0.25 | 0.55 | 0.42 | 1.46 | 2.07 | 4.08 | 3.55 | 4.13 | 1.34 | 1.08 | 0.83 | 20.03 |
| 1973 | 0.06 | 0.06 | 1.16 | 1.72 | 4.27 | 0.47 | 3.31 | 0.89 | 1.03 | 0.35 | 0.15 | 0.64 | 14.11 |
| 1974 | 0.26 | 0.18 | 0.52 | 1.88 | 0.33 | 1.29 | 1.42 | 1.14 | 0.43 | 1.36 | 0.23 | 0.42 | 9.46 |
| 1975 | 0.13 | 0.29 | 0.24 | 0.68 | 1.00 | 2.97 | 2.65 | 2.06 | 0.16 | 0.52 | 1.00 | 0.07 | 11.77 |
| 1976 | 0.32 | 0.23 | 0.63 | 1.63 | 2.09 | 2.46 | 1.75 | 5.94 | 4.28 | 0.49 | 0.40 | 0.12 | 20.34 |
| 1977 | 0.29 | 0.20 | 1.18 | 2.57 | 1.12 | 3.87 | 3.02 | 5.11 | 0.45 | 0.19 | 0.60 | 0.18 | 18.78 |
| 1978 | 0.25 | 0.38 | 0.40 | 1.15 | 3.58 | 0.54 | 2.14 | 2.51 | 0.05 | 0.90 | 0.37 | 1.01 | 13.28 |
| 1979 | 0.53 | 0.04 | 2.38 | 1.83 | 3.13 | 1.58 | 2.73 | 2.50 | 0.92 | 0.55 | 1.82 | 1.02 | 19.03 |
| 1980 | 0.25 | 0.54 | 1.30 | 3.64 | 4.99 | 1.60 | 1.69 | 4.59 | 0.65 | 0.01 | 0.35 | 0.05 | 19.66 |
| 1981 | 0.07 | 0.12 | 0.93 | 0.13 | 3.14 | 1.98 | 3.64 | 5.24 | 0.52 | 0.37 | 0.03 | 0.82 | 16.99 |
| 1982 | 0.25 | 0.27 | 0.73 | 0.16 | 3.07 | 3.81 | 3.64 | 5.37 | 3.02 | 0.22 | 0.10 | 0.70 | 21.94 |
| 1983 | 0.43 | 0.09 | 1.79 | 0.97 | 3.08 | 2.41 | 0.99 | 2.59 | 0.37 | 0.28 | 1.09 | 0.70 | 14.79 |
| 1984 | 0.32 | 0.09 | 1.93 | 1.66 | 0.74 | 1.54 | 3.97 | 4.03 | 0.93 | 5.01 | 0.14 | 0.64 | 21.00 |
| 1985 | 0.42 | 0.24 | 1.68 | 2.07 | 3.36 | 0.78 | 4.92 | 1.56 | 1.49 | 0.52 | 0.42 | 0.55 | 18.01 |
| 1986 | 0.01 | 0.30 | 0.31 | 0.65 | 1.89 | 2.47 | 1.63 | 6.06 | 0.61 | 1.41 | 0.64 | 0.28 | 16.26 |
| 1987 | 1.17 | 2.45 | 1.79 | 0.50 | 3.82 | 2.89 | 0.67 | 2.77 | 0.55 | 0.54 | 0.44 | 0.64 | 18.23 |
| 1988 | 0.43 | 0.68 | 0.90 | 0.27 | 1.01 | 1.69 | 2.07 | 2.88 | 1.19 | 0.08 | 0.36 | 1.05 | 12.61 |
| 1989 | 0.23 | 1.23 | 0.49 | 1.06 | 1.11 | 3.42 | 2.26 | 2.63 | 2.30 | 0.28 | 0.02 | 0.41 | 15.44 |
| 1990 | 0.53 | 0.59 | 1.77 | 2.04 | 3.90 | 0.13 | 5.13 | 1.45 | 1.50 | 1.46 | 0.30 | 0.27 | 19.07 |
| #Record Mean | 0.30 | 0.37 | 0.88 | 1.23 | 2.28 | 2.09 | 2.92 | 2.72 | 1.30 | 0.82 | 0.47 | 0.38 | 15.75 |

**TABLE 3**  AVERAGE TEMPERATURE (deg. F)    COLORADO SPRINGS, COLORADO

| YEAR | JAN | FEB | MAR | APR | MAY | JUNE | JULY | AUG | SEP | OCT | NOV | DEC | ANNUAL |
|------|-----|-----|-----|-----|-----|------|------|-----|-----|-----|-----|-----|--------|
| 1961 | 30.1 | 32.9 | 36.2 | 43.6 | 54.7 | 63.4 | 68.2 | 68.4 | 54.3 | 48.6 | 34.9 | 24.7 | 46.6 |
| 1962 | 22.1 | 31.8 | 33.6 | 48.1 | 58.6 | 62.9 | 68.9 | 70.6 | 62.1 | 53.9 | 40.5 | 35.4 | 49.1 |
| 1963 | 21.9 | 38.7 | 38.4 | 51.0 | 60.2 | 69.0 | 75.5 | 69.8 | 65.4 | 58.2 | 42.1 | 27.2 | 51.5 |
| 1964 | 30.3 | 26.1 | 30.9 | 46.2 | 57.6 | 65.0 | 75.3 | 69.3 | 61.9 | 52.3 | 38.4 | 32.8 | 48.8 |
| 1965 | 35.4 | 27.8 | 25.6 | 48.3 | 54.9 | 62.1 | 69.4 | 65.8 | 55.0 | 52.9 | 43.8 | 34.7 | 48.0 |
| 1966 | 25.1 | 26.8 | 40.8 | 44.4 | 57.1 | 65.7 | 73.9 | 66.8 | 62.1 | 48.9 | 39.6 | 29.4 | 48.5 |
| 1967 | 33.1 | 33.0 | 42.9 | 48.2 | 52.4 | 62.0 | 69.3 | 66.1 | 60.6 | 52.3 | 39.6 | 25.3 | 48.8 |
| 1968 | 30.7 | 32.6 | 38.6 | 42.5 | 51.5 | 66.9 | 68.4 | 65.8 | 60.3 | 51.5 | 34.5 | 29.4 | 47.7 |
| 1969 | 33.4 | 33.8 | 29.6 | 48.9 | 56.8 | 59.7 | 71.7 | 70.2 | 61.9 | 41.5 | 37.0 | 30.8 | 48.0 |
| 1970 | 28.2 | 37.2 | 32.6 | 42.6 | 58.2 | 64.6 | 71.2 | 71.4 | 57.7 | 44.2 | 38.2 | 32.9 | 48.3 |
| 1971 | 29.8 | 29.8 | 37.7 | 45.3 | 53.3 | 67.8 | 68.8 | 69.1 | 56.7 | 49.3 | 37.9 | 30.4 | 48.0 |
| 1972 | 30.0 | 36.1 | 43.3 | 49.1 | 55.9 | 67.8 | 68.9 | 67.7 | 60.8 | 49.4 | 29.8 | 23.5 | 48.5 |
| 1973 | 25.4 | 32.3 | 36.5 | 40.9 | 53.3 | 65.6 | 68.4 | 70.6 | 58.8 | 52.6 | 39.6 | 31.2 | 48.0 |
| 1974 | 27.0 | 33.9 | 42.1 | 46.0 | 59.7 | 66.2 | 72.6 | 67.9 | 58.0 | 52.6 | 38.5 | 28.0 | 49.4 |
| 1975 | 29.1 | 29.8 | 35.6 | 44.4 | 53.4 | 63.8 | 71.0 | 70.2 | 59.4 | 52.3 | 36.4 | 35.3 | 48.4 |
| 1976 | 30.1 | 37.8 | 36.1 | 47.7 | 54.7 | 64.3 | 72.1 | 68.1 | 59.3 | 45.7 | 36.2 | 32.9 | 48.8 |
| 1977 | 26.8 | 35.0 | 37.1 | 48.3 | 58.6 | 68.0 | 71.4 | 68.6 | 64.0 | 51.5 | 38.6 | 34.6 | 50.2 |
| 1978 | 25.1 | 27.7 | 40.9 | 48.8 | 52.5 | 66.2 | 72.8 | 67.5 | 62.8 | 51.9 | 36.5 | 21.9 | 47.9 |
| 1979 | 16.9 | 32.5 | 38.1 | 48.3 | 54.0 | 64.3 | 70.6 | 67.5 | 64.4 | 51.7 | 31.2 | 33.5 | 47.7 |
| 1980 | 26.7 | 34.3 | 35.7 | 44.3 | 53.4 | 69.2 | 75.3 | 70.4 | 62.3 | 49.9 | 39.5 | 39.8 | 50.1 |
| 1981 | 34.9 | 34.4 | 39.3 | 53.8 | 54.5 | 69.4 | 71.9 | 67.3 | 63.4 | 50.8 | 43.3 | 32.7 | 51.3 |
| 1982 | 29.4 | 29.0 | 38.1 | 45.7 | 54.7 | 60.1 | 70.2 | 68.5 | 59.0 | 47.6 | 35.4 | 29.8 | 47.1 |
| 1983 | 32.5 | 34.4 | 35.7 | 40.1 | 50.5 | 61.1 | 72.3 | 71.9 | 63.8 | 51.3 | 37.7 | 18.4 | 47.5 |
| 1984 | 26.1 | 33.3 | 35.3 | 41.4 | 58.2 | 65.1 | 71.5 | 68.4 | 59.5 | 42.8 | 38.4 | 33.1 | 47.8 |
| 1985 | 25.1 | 26.3 | 37.9 | 48.7 | 57.2 | 65.0 | 70.3 | 69.8 | 58.0 | 49.0 | 32.1 | 27.9 | 47.3 |
| 1986 | 38.2 | 34.7 | 44.3 | 48.5 | 54.6 | 65.8 | 70.4 | 67.6 | 59.1 | 48.0 | 37.7 | 29.8 | 49.9 |
| 1987 | 29.4 | 33.0 | 35.3 | 48.5 | 56.0 | 65.1 | 70.7 | 66.1 | 60.0 | 50.4 | 39.2 | 29.0 | 48.6 |
| 1988 | 24.3 | 31.8 | 36.2 | 48.2 | 56.4 | 68.7 | 70.4 | 70.4 | 60.8 | 53.0 | 39.2 | 29.2 | 49.1 |
| 1989 | 32.8 | 21.8 | 43.7 | 49.0 | 57.6 | 62.1 | 71.8 | 68.4 | 61.0 | 49.7 | 41.5 | 27.3 | 48.9 |
| 1990 | 33.6 | 31.7 | 38.9 | 47.1 | 53.8 | 69.5 | 68.0 | 68.0 | 64.5 | 49.5 | 42.7 | 24.3 | 49.3 |
| Record Mean | 29.1 | 32.0 | 36.2 | 46.1 | 55.4 | 65.3 | 70.8 | 68.8 | 60.5 | 50.3 | 38.0 | 30.7 | 48.7 |
| Max | 42.1 | 44.9 | 49.6 | 59.5 | 68.5 | 79.4 | 84.7 | 82.2 | 74.5 | 64.1 | 51.1 | 43.6 | 62.0 |
| Min | 16.1 | 19.1 | 23.9 | 32.7 | 42.2 | 51.3 | 57.0 | 55.3 | 47.3 | 36.6 | 24.9 | 17.8 | 35.3 |

## REFERENCE NOTES FOR TABLES 1, 2, 3 and 6      (COLORADO SPRINGS, CO)

### GENERAL

T - TRACE AMOUNT
BLANK ENTRIES DENOTE MISSING/UNREPORTED DATA.
# INDICATES A STATION OR INSTRUMENT RELOCATION.

### SPECIFIC

#### TABLE 1

(a) - LENGTH OF RECORD IN YEARS. ALTHOUGH
INDIVIDUAL MONTHS MAY BE MISSING.
* LESS THAN .05

NORMALS — BASED ON THE 1951-1980 RECORD PERIOD.
EXTREMES — DATES ARE THE MOST RECENT OCCURRENCE.
WIND DIR. — NUMERALS SHOW TENS OF DEGREES
CLOCKWISE FROM TRUE NORTH.
"00" INDICATES CALM.
RESULTANT WIND DIRECTIONS ARE GIVEN TO WHOLE DEGREES.

#### TABLE 3
MAX AND MIN ARE LONG-TERM MEAN DAILY MAXIMUM
AND MEAN DAILY MINIMUM TEMPERATURES.

### EXCEPTIONS

#### TABLE 1

1.  MAXIMUM 24-HOUR PRECIPITATION IS BASED ON SIX
HOUR MEASUREMENTS THROUGH APRIL 1974.

#### TABLES 2, 3, and 6

RECORD MEANS ARE THROUGH THE CURRENT YEAR,
BEGINNING IN        1949 FOR TEMPERATURE
1949 FOR PRECIPITATION
1949 FOR SNOWFALL

HEATING DEGREE DAYS Base 65 deg. F     COLORADO SPRINGS, COLORADO

**TABLE 4**

| SEASON | JULY | AUG | SEP | OCT | NOV | DEC | JAN | FEB | MAR | APR | MAY | JUNE | TOTAL |
|---|---|---|---|---|---|---|---|---|---|---|---|---|---|
| 1961-62 | 29 | 5 | 321 | 503 | 898 | 1246 | 1324 | 924 | 967 | 503 | 202 | 96 | 7018 |
| 1962-63 | 6 | 11 | 124 | 335 | 728 | 910 | 1331 | 730 | 817 | 415 | 167 | 30 | 5604 |
| 1963-64 | 0 | 4 | 34 | 211 | 680 | 1165 | 1068 | 1119 | 1051 | 555 | 253 | 73 | 6213 |
| 1964-65 | 0 | 22 | 151 | 385 | 790 | 992 | 910 | 1034 | 1214 | 497 | 306 | 107 | 6408 |
| 1965-66 | 10 | 31 | 304 | 366 | 632 | 931 | 1232 | 1061 | 744 | 613 | 249 | 63 | 6236 |
| 1966-67 | 0 | 33 | 111 | 489 | 728 | 1099 | 981 | 889 | 679 | 496 | 401 | 95 | 6001 |
| 1967-68 | 6 | 52 | 138 | 397 | 758 | 1223 | 1057 | 932 | 812 | 669 | 411 | 49 | 6504 |
| 1968-69 | 22 | 52 | 149 | 409 | 906 | 1096 | 969 | 868 | 1090 | 477 | 260 | 180 | 6478 |
| 1969-70 | 1 | 8 | 104 | 720 | 833 | 1053 | 1135 | 772 | 998 | 664 | 218 | 95 | 6601 |
| 1970-71 | 2 | 3 | 235 | 637 | 797 | 987 | 1086 | 980 | 837 | 584 | 357 | 32 | 6537 |
| 1971-72 | 33 | 5 | 285 | 481 | 806 | 1067 | 1080 | 832 | 665 | 469 | 273 | 6 | 6002 |
| 1972-73 | 41 | 34 | 136 | 476 | 1049 | 1281 | 1221 | 912 | 877 | 715 | 359 | 76 | 7177 |
| 1973-74 | 32 | 1 | 194 | 378 | 754 | 1041 | 1172 | 866 | 700 | 566 | 176 | 88 | 5968 |
| 1974-75 | 1 | 17 | 229 | 376 | 789 | 1143 | 1102 | 980 | 904 | 608 | 350 | 88 | 6587 |
| 1975-76 | 0 | 10 | 200 | 391 | 852 | 916 | 1075 | 782 | 891 | 512 | 314 | 80 | 6023 |
| 1976-77 | 0 | 11 | 191 | 593 | 859 | 988 | 1181 | 837 | 858 | 494 | 192 | 5 | 6209 |
| 1977-78 | 2 | 22 | 73 | 413 | 784 | 938 | 1231 | 1036 | 741 | 479 | 386 | 98 | 6203 |
| 1978-79 | 3 | 44 | 119 | 400 | 848 | 1329 | 1484 | 906 | 825 | 494 | 336 | 97 | 6885 |
| 1979-80 | 6 | 41 | 88 | 407 | 1005 | 969 | 1180 | 883 | 901 | 615 | 351 | 32 | 6478 |
| 1980-81 | 0 | 7 | 113 | 463 | 759 | 776 | 928 | 850 | 789 | 335 | 321 | 38 | 5379 |
| 1981-82 | 5 | 30 | 70 | 433 | 643 | 993 | 1095 | 1001 | 827 | 571 | 374 | 163 | 6205 |
| 1982-83 | 8 | 11 | 198 | 532 | 880 | 1084 | 1001 | 851 | 904 | 742 | 444 | 159 | 6814 |
| 1983-84 | 2 | 0 | 101 | 417 | 811 | 1438 | 1198 | 911 | 912 | 700 | 220 | 58 | 6768 |
| 1984-85 | 0 | 6 | 200 | 684 | 790 | 982 | 1233 | 1077 | 830 | 481 | 242 | 77 | 6602 |
| 1985-86 | 5 | 8 | 253 | 487 | 978 | 1142 | 822 | 840 | 635 | 487 | 315 | 49 | 6021 |
| 1986-87 | 4 | 14 | 174 | 519 | 813 | 1081 | 1096 | 888 | 912 | 491 | 272 | 50 | 6314 |
| 1987-88 | 17 | 74 | 150 | 445 | 767 | 1108 | 1256 | 958 | 886 | 499 | 273 | 25 | 6458 |
| 1988-89 | 7 | 8 | 154 | 366 | 767 | 1099 | 989 | 1207 | 655 | 475 | 247 | 134 | 6108 |
| 1989-90 | 0 | 4 | 172 | 473 | 699 | 1164 | 966 | 928 | 805 | 526 | 345 | 24 | 6106 |
| 1990-91 | 28 | 21 | 83 | 473 | 663 | 1258 | | | | | | | |

**TABLE 5**    COOLING DEGREE DAYS Base 65 deg. F     COLORADO SPRINGS, COLORADO

| YEAR | JAN | FEB | MAR | APR | MAY | JUNE | JULY | AUG | SEP | OCT | NOV | DEC | TOTAL |
|---|---|---|---|---|---|---|---|---|---|---|---|---|---|
| 1969 | 0 | 0 | 0 | 0 | 11 | 27 | 216 | 177 | 18 | 0 | 0 | 0 | 449 |
| 1970 | 0 | 0 | 0 | 0 | 15 | 89 | 200 | 209 | 22 | 0 | 0 | 0 | 535 |
| 1971 | 0 | 0 | 0 | 0 | 1 | 126 | 158 | 138 | 41 | 0 | 0 | 0 | 464 |
| 1972 | 0 | 0 | 0 | 2 | 0 | 96 | 168 | 124 | 17 | 0 | 0 | 0 | 407 |
| 1973 | 0 | 0 | 0 | 0 | 0 | 104 | 145 | 180 | 13 | 0 | 0 | 0 | 442 |
| 1974 | 0 | 0 | 0 | 0 | 18 | 130 | 241 | 109 | 26 | 0 | 0 | 0 | 524 |
| 1975 | 0 | 0 | 0 | 0 | 0 | 59 | 195 | 180 | 41 | 5 | 0 | 0 | 480 |
| 1976 | 0 | 0 | 0 | 0 | 0 | 66 | 227 | 114 | 28 | 0 | 0 | 0 | 435 |
| 1977 | 0 | 0 | 0 | 0 | 0 | 103 | 204 | 142 | 49 | 0 | 0 | 0 | 498 |
| 1978 | 0 | 0 | 0 | 0 | 4 | 143 | 255 | 127 | 59 | 1 | 0 | 0 | 589 |
| 1979 | 0 | 0 | 0 | 0 | 1 | 84 | 185 | 124 | 77 | 2 | 0 | 0 | 473 |
| 1980 | 0 | 0 | 0 | 0 | 0 | 169 | 327 | 180 | 41 | 0 | 0 | 0 | 717 |
| 1981 | 0 | 0 | 0 | 4 | 2 | 176 | 226 | 105 | 27 | 0 | 0 | 0 | 540 |
| 1982 | 0 | 0 | 0 | 0 | 0 | 23 | 176 | 127 | 26 | 0 | 0 | 0 | 352 |
| 1983 | 0 | 0 | 0 | 0 | 1 | 48 | 236 | 219 | 71 | 0 | 0 | 0 | 575 |
| 1984 | 0 | 0 | 0 | 0 | 17 | 68 | 207 | 119 | 42 | 0 | 0 | 0 | 453 |
| 1985 | 0 | 0 | 0 | 0 | 5 | 83 | 179 | 163 | 51 | 0 | 0 | 0 | 481 |
| 1986 | 0 | 0 | 0 | 0 | 1 | 82 | 180 | 102 | 3 | 0 | 0 | 0 | 368 |
| 1987 | 0 | 0 | 0 | 0 | 0 | 62 | 199 | 113 | 6 | 0 | 0 | 0 | 380 |
| 1988 | 0 | 0 | 0 | 0 | 12 | 143 | 190 | 181 | 33 | 0 | 0 | 0 | 559 |
| 1989 | 0 | 0 | 0 | 3 | 25 | 54 | 220 | 117 | 57 | 3 | 0 | 0 | 479 |
| 1990 | 0 | 0 | 0 | 0 | 6 | 168 | 128 | 121 | 73 | 0 | 0 | 0 | 496 |

**TABLE 6**    HEATING DEGREE DAYS Base 65 deg. F     COLORADO SPRINGS, COLORADO

| SEASON | JULY | AUG | SEP | OCT | NOV | DEC | JAN | FEB | MAR | APR | MAY | JUNE | TOTAL |
|---|---|---|---|---|---|---|---|---|---|---|---|---|---|
| 1961-62 | 29 | 5 | 321 | 503 | 898 | 1246 | 1324 | 924 | 967 | 503 | 202 | 96 | 7018 |
| 1962-63 | 6 | 11 | 124 | 335 | 728 | 910 | 1331 | 730 | 817 | 415 | 167 | 30 | 5604 |
| 1963-64 | 0 | 4 | 34 | 211 | 680 | 1165 | 1068 | 1119 | 1051 | 555 | 253 | 73 | 6213 |
| 1964-65 | 0 | 22 | 151 | 385 | 790 | 992 | 910 | 1034 | 1214 | 497 | 306 | 107 | 6408 |
| 1965-66 | 10 | 31 | 304 | 366 | 632 | 931 | 1232 | 1061 | 744 | 613 | 249 | 63 | 6236 |
| 1966-67 | 0 | 33 | 111 | 489 | 728 | 1099 | 981 | 889 | 679 | 496 | 401 | 95 | 6001 |
| 1967-68 | 6 | 52 | 138 | 397 | 758 | 1223 | 1057 | 932 | 812 | 669 | 411 | 49 | 6504 |
| 1968-69 | 22 | 52 | 149 | 409 | 906 | 1096 | 969 | 868 | 1090 | 477 | 260 | 180 | 6478 |
| 1969-70 | 1 | 8 | 104 | 720 | 833 | 1053 | 1135 | 772 | 998 | 664 | 218 | 95 | 6601 |
| 1970-71 | 2 | 3 | 235 | 637 | 797 | 987 | 1086 | 980 | 837 | 584 | 357 | 32 | 6537 |
| 1971-72 | 33 | 5 | 285 | 481 | 806 | 1067 | 1080 | 832 | 665 | 469 | 273 | 6 | 6002 |
| 1972-73 | 41 | 34 | 136 | 476 | 1049 | 1281 | 1221 | 912 | 877 | 715 | 359 | 76 | 7177 |
| 1973-74 | 32 | 1 | 194 | 378 | 754 | 1041 | 1172 | 866 | 700 | 566 | 176 | 88 | 5968 |
| 1974-75 | 1 | 17 | 229 | 376 | 789 | 1143 | 1102 | 980 | 904 | 608 | 350 | 88 | 6587 |
| 1975-76 | 0 | 10 | 200 | 391 | 852 | 916 | 1075 | 782 | 891 | 512 | 314 | 80 | 6023 |
| 1976-77 | 0 | 11 | 191 | 593 | 859 | 988 | 1181 | 837 | 858 | 494 | 192 | 5 | 6209 |
| 1977-78 | 2 | 22 | 73 | 413 | 784 | 938 | 1231 | 1036 | 741 | 479 | 386 | 98 | 6203 |
| 1978-79 | 3 | 44 | 119 | 400 | 848 | 1329 | 1484 | 906 | 825 | 494 | 336 | 97 | 6885 |
| 1979-80 | 6 | 41 | 88 | 407 | 1005 | 969 | 1180 | 883 | 901 | 615 | 351 | 32 | 6478 |
| 1980-81 | 0 | 7 | 113 | 463 | 759 | 776 | 928 | 850 | 789 | 335 | 321 | 38 | 5379 |
| 1981-82 | 5 | 30 | 70 | 433 | 643 | 993 | 1095 | 1001 | 827 | 571 | 374 | 163 | 6205 |
| 1982-83 | 8 | 11 | 198 | 532 | 880 | 1084 | 1001 | 851 | 904 | 742 | 444 | 159 | 6814 |
| 1983-84 | 2 | 0 | 101 | 417 | 811 | 1438 | 1198 | 911 | 912 | 700 | 220 | 58 | 6768 |
| 1984-85 | 0 | 6 | 200 | 684 | 790 | 982 | 1233 | 1077 | 830 | 481 | 242 | 77 | 6602 |
| 1985-86 | 5 | 8 | 253 | 487 | 978 | 1142 | 822 | 840 | 635 | 487 | 315 | 49 | 6021 |
| 1986-87 | 4 | 14 | 174 | 519 | 813 | 1081 | 1096 | 888 | 912 | 491 | 272 | 50 | 6314 |
| 1987-88 | 17 | 74 | 150 | 445 | 767 | 1108 | 1256 | 958 | 886 | 499 | 273 | 25 | 6458 |
| 1988-89 | 7 | 8 | 154 | 366 | 767 | 1099 | 989 | 1207 | 655 | 475 | 247 | 134 | 6108 |
| 1989-90 | 0 | 4 | 172 | 473 | 699 | 1164 | 966 | 928 | 805 | 526 | 345 | 24 | 6106 |
| 1990-91 | 28 | 21 | 83 | 473 | 663 | 1258 | | | | | | | |

**See Reference Notes, relative to all above tables, on preceding page.**

Denver enjoys the invigorating climate that prevails over much of the central Rocky Mountain region, without the extremely cold mornings of the high elevations during winter, or the hot afternoons of summer at lower altitudes. Extremely warm or cold weather in Denver is usually of short duration.

Situated a long distance from any moisture source, and separated from the Pacific Ocean by several high mountain barriers, Denver enjoys low relative humidity, light precipitation, and abundant sunshine.

Air masses from four different sources influence Denver weather. These include arctic air from Canada and Alaska, warm, moist air from the Gulf of Mexico, warm, dry air from Mexico and the southwestern deserts, and Pacific air modified by its passage over mountains to the west.

In winter, the high altitude and mountains to the west combine to moderate temperatures in Denver. Invasions of cold air from the north, intensified by the high altitude, can be abrupt and severe. However, many of the cold air masses that spread southward out of Canada never reach the altitude of Denver, but move off over the lower plains to the east. Surges of air from the west are moderated in their descent down the east face of the Rockies, and reach Denver in the form of chinook winds that often raise temperatures into the 60s, even in midwinter.

In spring, polar air often collides with warm, moist air from the Gulf of Mexico and these collisions result in frequent, rapid and drastic weather changes. Spring is the cloudiest, windiest, and wettest season in the city. Much of the precipitation falls as snow, especially in March and early April. Stormy periods are interspersed with stretches of mild, sunny weather that quickly melt previous snow cover.

Summer precipitation falls mainly from scattered thunderstorms during the afternoon and evening. Mornings are usually clear and sunny, with clouds forming during early afternoon to cut off the sunshine at what would otherwise be the hottest part of the day. Severe thunderstorms, with large hail and heavy rain occasionally occur in the city, but these conditions are more common on the plains to the east.

Autumn is the most pleasant season. Few thunderstorms occur and invasions of cold air are infrequent. As a result, there is more sunshine and less severe weather than at any other time of the year.

Based on the 1951–1980 period, the average first occurrence of 32 degrees Fahrenheit in the fall is October 8 and the average last occurrence in the spring is May 3.

## TABLE 1    NORMALS, MEANS AND EXTREMES

DENVER, COLORADO

LATITUDE: 39°45'N    LONGITUDE: 104°52'W    ELEVATION: FT. GRND 5282 BARO 5287    TIME ZONE: MOUNTAIN    WBAN: 23062

| | (a) | JAN | FEB | MAR | APR | MAY | JUNE | JULY | AUG | SEP | OCT | NOV | DEC | YEAR |
|---|---|---|---|---|---|---|---|---|---|---|---|---|---|---|
| **TEMPERATURE °F:** | | | | | | | | | | | | | | |
| Normals | | | | | | | | | | | | | | |
| -Daily Maximum | | 43.1 | 46.9 | 51.2 | 61.0 | 70.7 | 81.6 | 88.0 | 85.8 | 77.5 | 66.8 | 52.4 | 46.1 | 64.3 |
| -Daily Minimum | | 15.9 | 20.2 | 24.7 | 33.7 | 43.6 | 52.4 | 58.7 | 57.0 | 47.7 | 36.9 | 25.1 | 18.9 | 36.2 |
| -Monthly | | 29.5 | 33.6 | 38.0 | 47.4 | 57.2 | 67.0 | 73.3 | 71.4 | 62.6 | 51.9 | 38.7 | 32.6 | 50.3 |
| Extremes | | | | | | | | | | | | | | |
| -Record Highest | 55 | 73 | 76 | 84 | 89 | 96 | 104 | 104 | 101 | 97 | 88 | 79 | 75 | 104 |
| -Year | | 1982 | 1963 | 1971 | 1989 | 1942 | 1936 | 1939 | 1938 | 1960 | 1947 | 1989 | 1980 | JUL 1939 |
| -Record Lowest | 55 | -25 | -30 | -11 | -2 | 22 | 30 | 43 | 41 | 17 | 3 | -8 | -21 | -30 |
| -Year | | 1963 | 1936 | 1943 | 1975 | 1954 | 1951 | 1972 | 1964 | 1985 | 1969 | 1950 | 1983 | FEB 1936 |
| **NORMAL DEGREE DAYS:** | | | | | | | | | | | | | | |
| Heating (base 65°F) | | 1101 | 879 | 837 | 528 | 253 | 74 | 0 | 0 | 135 | 414 | 789 | 1004 | 6014 |
| Cooling (base 65°F) | | 0 | 0 | 0 | 0 | 11 | 134 | 261 | 203 | 63 | 8 | 0 | 0 | 680 |
| **% OF POSSIBLE SUNSHINE** | 40 | 71 | 70 | 69 | 68 | 65 | 71 | 71 | 72 | 74 | 72 | 65 | 67 | 70 |
| **MEAN SKY COVER (tenths)** | | | | | | | | | | | | | | |
| Sunrise - Sunset | 41 | 5.6 | 5.9 | 6.2 | 6.1 | 6.2 | 5.1 | 4.9 | 5.0 | 4.4 | 4.5 | 5.4 | 5.3 | 5.4 |
| **MEAN NUMBER OF DAYS:** | | | | | | | | | | | | | | |
| Sunrise to Sunset | | | | | | | | | | | | | | |
| -Clear | 55 | 10.2 | 8.0 | 7.8 | 6.8 | 6.2 | 9.5 | 9.1 | 9.9 | 13.4 | 13.4 | 10.3 | 10.7 | 115.3 |
| -Partly Cloudy | 55 | 9.1 | 8.7 | 10.1 | 10.7 | 12.0 | 12.2 | 15.8 | 13.8 | 8.9 | 9.1 | 9.5 | 9.7 | 129.6 |
| -Cloudy | 55 | 11.7 | 11.5 | 13.2 | 12.5 | 12.8 | 8.3 | 6.1 | 7.3 | 7.7 | 8.5 | 10.2 | 10.6 | 120.3 |
| Precipitation | | | | | | | | | | | | | | |
| .01 inches or more | 55 | 5.7 | 6.0 | 8.5 | 8.6 | 10.7 | 8.8 | 9.0 | 8.7 | 6.2 | 5.3 | 5.3 | 5.3 | 88.3 |
| Snow,Ice pellets | | | | | | | | | | | | | | |
| 1.0 inches or more | 55 | 2.3 | 2.4 | 3.7 | 2.5 | 0.5 | 0.0 | 0.0 | 0.0 | 0.3 | 1.2 | 2.4 | 2.5 | 17.7 |
| Thunderstorms | 55 | 0.* | 0.1 | 0.2 | 1.5 | 6.3 | 9.8 | 10.9 | 8.2 | 3.4 | 0.9 | 0.1 | 0.0 | 41.5 |
| Heavy Fog Visibility | | | | | | | | | | | | | | |
| 1/4 mile or less | 49 | 1.1 | 1.6 | 1.0 | 0.8 | 0.5 | 0.4 | 0.4 | 0.6 | 0.7 | 0.6 | 1.2 | 1.0 | 9.8 |
| Temperature °F | | | | | | | | | | | | | | |
| -Maximum | | | | | | | | | | | | | | |
| 90° and above | 29 | 0.0 | 0.0 | 0.0 | 0.0 | 0.4 | 6.1 | 15.5 | 9.4 | 2.1 | 0.0 | 0.0 | 0.0 | 33.6 |
| 32° and below | 29 | 6.7 | 4.6 | 3.0 | 0.4 | 0.0 | 0.0 | 0.0 | 0.0 | 0.* | 0.3 | 2.3 | 5.3 | 22.7 |
| -Minimum | | | | | | | | | | | | | | |
| 32° and below | 29 | 29.8 | 26.1 | 24.9 | 11.8 | 1.6 | 0.0 | 0.0 | 0.0 | 0.9 | 8.5 | 24.3 | 29.1 | 157.0 |
| 0° and below | 29 | 4.0 | 1.8 | 0.5 | 0.* | 0.0 | 0.0 | 0.0 | 0.0 | 0.0 | 0.0 | 0.2 | 2.8 | 9.4 |
| **AVG. STATION PRESS.(mb)** | 17 | 834.7 | 834.5 | 832.0 | 833.6 | 834.3 | 836.7 | 838.9 | 838.9 | 838.4 | 837.9 | 835.2 | 835.0 | 835.8 |
| **RELATIVE HUMIDITY (%)** | | | | | | | | | | | | | | |
| Hour 05 | 29 | 63 | 67 | 67 | 67 | 70 | 69 | 68 | 69 | 68 | 65 | 68 | 65 | 67 |
| Hour 11 | 29 | 45 | 44 | 42 | 38 | 39 | 37 | 34 | 36 | 38 | 36 | 44 | 45 | 40 |
| Hour 17 (Local Time) | 29 | 49 | 44 | 40 | 35 | 38 | 35 | 34 | 35 | 34 | 35 | 48 | 51 | 40 |
| Hour 23 | 29 | 63 | 65 | 62 | 58 | 61 | 59 | 56 | 58 | 59 | 59 | 65 | 64 | 61 |
| **PRECIPITATION (inches):** | | | | | | | | | | | | | | |
| Water Equivalent | | | | | | | | | | | | | | |
| -Normal | | 0.51 | 0.69 | 1.21 | 1.81 | 2.47 | 1.58 | 1.93 | 1.53 | 1.23 | 0.98 | 0.82 | 0.55 | 15.31 |
| -Maximum Monthly | 55 | 1.44 | 1.66 | 4.56 | 4.17 | 7.31 | 4.69 | 6.41 | 5.85 | 4.67 | 4.17 | 2.97 | 2.84 | 7.31 |
| -Year | | 1948 | 1960 | 1983 | 1942 | 1957 | 1967 | 1965 | 1979 | 1961 | 1969 | 1946 | 1973 | MAY 1957 |
| -Minimum Monthly | 55 | 0.01 | 0.01 | 0.13 | 0.03 | 0.06 | 0.09 | 0.17 | 0.06 | T | 0.05 | 0.01 | 0.03 | T |
| -Year | | 1952 | 1970 | 1945 | 1963 | 1974 | 1980 | 1939 | 1960 | 1944 | 1962 | 1949 | 1977 | SEP 1944 |
| -Maximum in 24 hrs | 55 | 1.02 | 1.01 | 2.79 | 3.25 | 3.55 | 3.16 | 2.42 | 3.43 | 2.44 | 1.71 | 1.29 | 2.00 | 3.55 |
| -Year | | 1962 | 1953 | 1983 | 1967 | 1973 | 1970 | 1965 | 1951 | 1936 | 1947 | 1975 | 1982 | MAY 1973 |
| Snow,Ice pellets | | | | | | | | | | | | | | |
| -Maximum Monthly | 55 | 23.7 | 18.3 | 30.5 | 28.3 | 13.6 | 0.3 | 0.0 | 0.0 | 21.3 | 31.2 | 39.1 | 30.8 | 39.1 |
| -Year | | 1948 | 1960 | 1983 | 1935 | 1950 | 1951 | | | 1936 | 1969 | 1946 | 1973 | NOV 1946 |
| -Maximum in 24 hrs | 55 | 12.4 | 9.5 | 18.0 | 17.3 | 10.7 | 0.3 | 0.0 | 0.0 | 19.4 | 12.4 | 15.9 | 23.6 | 23.6 |
| -Year | | 1962 | 1953 | 1983 | 1957 | 1950 | 1951 | | | 1936 | 1969 | 1983 | 1982 | DEC 1982 |
| **WIND:** | | | | | | | | | | | | | | |
| Mean Speed (mph) | 41 | 8.7 | 8.9 | 9.8 | 10.2 | 9.4 | 8.9 | 8.3 | 8.0 | 8.0 | 7.9 | 8.3 | 8.5 | 8.7 |
| Prevailing Direction | | | | | | | | | | | | | | |
| through 1963 | | S | S | S | S | S | S | S | S | S | S | S | S | S |
| Fastest Obs. 1 Min. | | | | | | | | | | | | | | |
| -Direction (!!!) | 8 | 32 | 30 | 36 | 36 | 36 | 21 | 28 | 33 | 29 | 30 | 36 | 32 | 32 |
| -Speed (MPH) | 8 | 44 | 36 | 38 | 41 | 43 | 38 | 37 | 33 | 36 | 32 | 36 | 38 | 44 |
| -Year | | 1982 | 1989 | 1983 | 1987 | 1983 | 1987 | 1982 | 1989 | 1988 | 1985 | 1987 | 1981 | JAN 1982 |
| Peak Gust | | | | | | | | | | | | | | |
| -Direction (!!!) | 6 | NW | NW | W | NW | S | NW | SW | NW | W | SW | NW | NW | NW |
| -Speed (mph) | 6 | 54 | 51 | 59 | 62 | 53 | 60 | 46 | 52 | 56 | 48 | 49 | 47 | 62 |
| -Date | | 1987 | 1989 | 1989 | 1986 | 1988 | 1988 | 1988 | 1989 | 1984 | 1989 | 1988 | 1984 | APR 1986 |

**See Reference Notes to this table on the following page.**

# DENVER, COLORADO

**TABLE 2**  PRECIPITATION (inches)  DENVER, COLORADO

| YEAR | JAN | FEB | MAR | APR | MAY | JUNE | JULY | AUG | SEP | OCT | NOV | DEC | ANNUAL |
|---|---|---|---|---|---|---|---|---|---|---|---|---|---|
| 1961 | 0.07 | 0.66 | 2.51 | 1.06 | 4.12 | 1.11 | 1.60 | 1.21 | 4.67 | 0.77 | 0.93 | 0.30 | 19.01 |
| 1962 | 1.33 | 1.05 | 0.52 | 1.10 | 0.84 | 1.52 | 0.54 | 0.46 | 0.19 | 0.05 | 0.68 | 0.17 | 8.45 |
| 1963 | 0.71 | 0.21 | 1.42 | 0.03 | 0.68 | 3.59 | 0.55 | 2.52 | 1.25 | 0.31 | 0.45 | 0.51 | 12.23 |
| 1964 | 0.26 | 1.04 | 1.38 | 1.25 | 2.53 | 0.82 | 0.72 | 0.27 | 0.41 | 0.18 | 0.88 | 0.40 | 10.14 |
| 1965 | 1.00 | 1.27 | 1.20 | 1.05 | 1.82 | 4.14 | 6.41 | 1.06 | 2.58 | 0.45 | 0.36 | 0.53 | 21.87 |
| 1966 | 0.30 | 1.28 | 0.32 | 1.46 | 0.34 | 1.41 | 1.04 | 2.06 | 1.15 | 0.96 | 0.32 | 0.17 | 10.81 |
| 1967 | 0.84 | 0.39 | 0.79 | 3.95 | 4.77 | 4.69 | 3.25 | 0.83 | 0.60 | 1.13 | 1.01 | 1.06 | 23.31 |
| 1968 | 0.51 | 0.74 | 0.85 | 2.39 | 0.71 | 0.50 | 1.34 | 2.53 | 0.59 | 0.75 | 0.71 | 0.51 | 12.13 |
| 1969 | 0.17 | 0.43 | 1.10 | 1.33 | 6.12 | 2.99 | 1.81 | 0.79 | 1.67 | 4.17 | 0.62 | 0.32 | 21.52 |
| 1970 | 0.10 | 0.01 | 1.34 | 0.97 | 0.64 | 3.83 | 1.67 | 0.54 | 2.47 | 0.88 | 1.19 | 0.09 | 13.73 |
| 1971 | 0.35 | 0.78 | 0.53 | 1.98 | 1.34 | 0.23 | 1.20 | 0.85 | 2.85 | 0.44 | 0.16 | 0.25 | 10.96 |
| 1972 | 0.36 | 0.44 | 0.50 | 3.52 | 0.49 | 2.94 | 0.63 | 2.71 | 2.07 | 0.82 | 1.69 | 0.70 | 16.87 |
| 1973 | 1.31 | 0.16 | 1.76 | 3.73 | 5.06 | 0.20 | 2.47 | 1.28 | 2.85 | 0.47 | 0.83 | 2.84 | 22.96 |
| 1974 | 1.03 | 0.82 | 1.32 | 2.28 | 0.06 | 2.01 | 2.34 | 0.16 | 0.98 | 1.68 | 1.06 | 0.29 | 14.03 |
| 1975 | 0.23 | 0.37 | 1.19 | 1.14 | 2.80 | 2.11 | 2.78 | 2.00 | 0.24 | 0.30 | 1.88 | 0.47 | 15.51 |
| 1976 | 0.19 | 0.54 | 1.34 | 1.27 | 1.34 | 0.63 | 2.31 | 2.50 | 1.88 | 0.93 | 0.59 | 0.16 | 13.41 |
| 1977 | 0.16 | 0.27 | 1.24 | 2.13 | 0.34 | 1.02 | 2.98 | 1.00 | 0.10 | 0.48 | 0.59 | 0.03 | 10.34 |
| 1978 | 0.27 | 0.27 | 1.07 | 1.82 | 3.46 | 1.17 | 0.54 | 0.26 | 0.07 | 1.45 | 0.50 | 0.82 | 11.70 |
| 1979 | 0.34 | 0.42 | 1.25 | 1.41 | 3.53 | 2.39 | 0.81 | 5.85 | 0.36 | 1.28 | 1.66 | 1.06 | 20.36 |
| 1980 | 0.64 | 0.45 | 1.15 | 2.54 | 2.73 | 0.09 | 2.93 | 1.65 | 0.63 | 0.10 | 0.66 | 0.10 | 13.67 |
| 1981 | 0.29 | 0.35 | 2.27 | 1.01 | 3.76 | 0.63 | 0.90 | 1.16 | 0.35 | 0.79 | 0.42 | 0.66 | 12.59 |
| 1982 | 0.32 | 0.09 | 0.18 | 0.34 | 3.48 | 2.26 | 0.92 | 1.16 | 1.38 | 1.51 | 0.47 | 2.34 | 14.45 |
| 1983 | 0.15 | 0.07 | 4.56 | 2.10 | 3.62 | 2.65 | 1.75 | 1.51 | 0.13 | 0.39 | 2.63 | 0.63 | 20.19 |
| 1984 | 0.18 | 0.81 | 1.19 | 2.42 | 0.65 | 1.26 | 2.11 | 3.20 | 0.47 | 3.47 | 0.27 | 0.46 | 16.49 |
| 1985 | 0.68 | 0.59 | 0.69 | 2.61 | 1.33 | 1.46 | 3.71 | 0.28 | 2.33 | 0.77 | 1.20 | 0.66 | 16.31 |
| 1986 | 0.22 | 0.65 | 0.43 | 2.59 | 1.30 | 1.07 | 1.69 | 0.53 | 0.43 | 1.80 | 1.07 | 0.31 | 12.09 |
| 1987 | 0.69 | 1.21 | 1.34 | 1.03 | 4.64 | 3.50 | 0.76 | 2.00 | 0.70 | 1.24 | 1.62 | 1.30 | 20.03 |
| 1988 | 0.40 | 0.60 | 1.28 | 0.65 | 4.26 | 1.28 | 2.19 | 1.83 | 0.90 | 0.06 | 0.47 | 1.04 | 14.96 |
| 1989 | 1.14 | 0.66 | 0.56 | 1.00 | 3.83 | 2.04 | 1.64 | 1.28 | 1.55 | 0.81 | 0.15 | 0.81 | 15.47 |
| 1990 | 0.74 | 0.55 | 3.10 | 1.01 | 1.51 | 0.21 | 3.57 | 1.96 | 1.46 | 1.03 | 1.28 | 0.27 | 16.69 |
| Record Mean | 0.47 | 0.57 | 1.14 | 1.96 | 2.43 | 1.50 | 1.73 | 1.43 | 1.09 | 1.01 | 0.69 | 0.63 | 14.67 |

**TABLE 3**  AVERAGE TEMPERATURE (deg. F)  DENVER, COLORADO

| YEAR | JAN | FEB | MAR | APR | MAY | JUNE | JULY | AUG | SEP | OCT | NOV | DEC | ANNUAL |
|---|---|---|---|---|---|---|---|---|---|---|---|---|---|
| 1961 | 31.7 | 35.2 | 38.9 | 46.0 | 55.7 | 66.1 | 71.5 | 72.2 | 56.3 | 50.0 | 34.7 | 27.7 | 48.9 |
| 1962 | 19.5 | 29.9 | 34.6 | 50.3 | 59.8 | 65.5 | 72.9 | 72.5 | 62.4 | 53.4 | 41.3 | 33.8 | 49.7 |
| 1963 | 19.1 | 37.3 | 37.3 | 50.0 | 60.9 | 66.7 | 74.8 | 68.7 | 57.9 | 41.7 | 28.5 | 35.0 | 50.8 |
| 1964 | 30.6 | 27.4 | 33.0 | 46.6 | 58.8 | 65.0 | 75.8 | 70.4 | 62.5 | 52.7 | 40.0 | 33.2 | 49.7 |
| 1965 | 35.0 | 27.4 | 29.0 | 51.2 | 57.1 | 63.9 | 72.7 | 70.2 | 55.1 | 43.3 | 35.0 | | 49.6 |
| 1966 | 28.6 | 28.4 | 42.5 | 44.6 | 58.7 | 64.6 | 76.9 | 70.8 | 65.0 | 52.2 | 41.5 | 31.9 | 50.5 |
| 1967 | 34.0 | 35.1 | 42.9 | 48.2 | 52.6 | 60.6 | 69.1 | 68.2 | 62.1 | 52.5 | 40.5 | 26.5 | 49.4 |
| 1968 | 29.7 | 34.2 | 40.6 | 43.0 | 53.9 | 67.8 | 71.7 | 68.1 | 60.9 | 51.9 | 35.7 | 28.9 | 48.9 |
| 1969 | 35.0 | 35.4 | 32.2 | 52.2 | 59.3 | 61.5 | 71.4 | 73.9 | 64.5 | 39.0 | 39.1 | 32.5 | 49.9 |
| 1970 | 30.6 | 38.6 | 33.5 | 43.7 | 58.8 | 65.2 | 72.0 | 73.9 | 59.5 | 45.9 | 39.1 | 33.3 | 49.5 |
| 1971 | 32.1 | 30.6 | 38.5 | 47.8 | 54.2 | 69.0 | 70.6 | 72.8 | 57.5 | 49.4 | 39.1 | 31.9 | 49.5 |
| 1972 | 30.5 | 36.2 | 44.8 | 48.5 | 57.0 | 68.3 | 70.2 | 71.0 | 62.1 | 52.1 | 32.9 | 24.9 | 49.9 |
| 1973 | 27.3 | 35.5 | 39.9 | 43.2 | 55.6 | 67.5 | 71.0 | 73.5 | 59.9 | 54.5 | 39.5 | 31.6 | 49.9 |
| 1974 | 23.7 | 35.2 | 43.2 | 47.9 | 61.6 | 68.4 | 74.7 | 69.5 | 59.4 | 52.4 | 38.0 | 31.2 | 50.5 |
| 1975 | 31.7 | 30.6 | 37.3 | 44.1 | 54.3 | 64.3 | 72.7 | 70.8 | 59.5 | 53.2 | 36.8 | 37.5 | 49.4 |
| 1976 | 32.3 | 39.3 | 37.1 | 49.2 | 56.7 | 66.3 | 75.3 | 70.2 | 61.8 | 48.4 | 39.5 | 35.5 | 51.0 |
| 1977 | 29.2 | 38.0 | 39.9 | 51.1 | 60.7 | 71.9 | 74.3 | 70.2 | 66.6 | 53.3 | 40.3 | 35.1 | 52.5 |
| 1978 | 25.8 | 31.4 | 43.3 | 50.3 | 54.4 | 66.9 | 74.7 | 69.6 | 65.0 | 53.1 | 37.8 | 24.6 | 49.7 |
| 1979 | 18.0 | 34.2 | 40.5 | 49.1 | 54.8 | 65.8 | 73.7 | 69.5 | 66.3 | 53.8 | 33.3 | 34.5 | 49.5 |
| 1980 | 26.0 | 34.5 | 38.0 | 47.7 | 57.1 | 71.9 | 76.4 | 73.2 | 65.8 | 52.4 | 41.9 | 41.2 | 52.2 |
| 1981 | 37.3 | 36.2 | 41.2 | 56.4 | 57.1 | 70.4 | 75.9 | 72.0 | 68.2 | 52.6 | 35.8 | 35.8 | 54.1 |
| 1982 | 30.3 | 32.0 | 41.1 | 47.4 | 55.1 | 63.1 | 72.7 | 73.1 | 61.7 | 49.0 | 35.7 | 30.9 | 49.3 |
| 1983 | 31.9 | 36.6 | 36.2 | 41.0 | 51.4 | 62.8 | 73.3 | 74.4 | 64.9 | 52.7 | 37.0 | 17.5 | 48.3 |
| 1984 | 27.3 | 34.1 | 37.2 | 42.3 | 60.0 | 66.5 | 74.9 | 71.8 | 60.7 | 44.8 | 39.7 | 32.8 | 49.3 |
| 1985 | 25.6 | 27.7 | 40.8 | 51.0 | 60.0 | 68.0 | 73.0 | 72.4 | 58.8 | 50.7 | 29.8 | 29.4 | 48.9 |
| 1986 | 40.3 | 36.1 | 47.1 | 49.6 | 56.7 | 70.3 | 73.5 | 72.2 | 60.7 | 49.3 | 39.0 | 31.0 | 52.2 |
| 1987 | 32.2 | 36.1 | 38.8 | 51.9 | 59.7 | 69.2 | 74.4 | 70.7 | 62.4 | 51.7 | 40.0 | 28.4 | 51.3 |
| 1988 | 25.2 | 34.1 | 38.5 | 50.3 | 59.0 | 71.9 | 74.2 | 73.6 | 62.3 | 54.0 | 40.6 | 31.1 | 51.2 |
| 1989 | 33.5 | 22.4 | 43.3 | 51.1 | 59.0 | 65.4 | 75.9 | 71.7 | 62.5 | 51.3 | 42.8 | 27.3 | 50.5 |
| 1990 | 36.4 | 33.3 | 39.5 | 49.1 | 56.6 | 72.6 | 70.8 | 71.3 | 66.9 | 52.3 | 44.0 | 25.7 | 51.5 |
| Record Mean | 30.1 | 32.9 | 38.8 | 47.7 | 56.8 | 66.8 | 72.8 | 71.4 | 62.7 | 51.5 | 39.5 | 32.1 | 50.3 |
| Max | 42.8 | 45.4 | 51.4 | 60.4 | 69.5 | 80.7 | 86.7 | 85.1 | 76.9 | 65.5 | 52.5 | 44.8 | 63.5 |
| Min | 17.4 | 20.4 | 26.2 | 34.9 | 44.0 | 52.9 | 58.9 | 57.7 | 48.5 | 37.6 | 26.5 | 19.4 | 37.0 |

## REFERENCE NOTES FOR TABLES 1, 2, 3 and 6          (DENVER, CO)

### GENERAL

T - TRACE AMOUNT
BLANK ENTRIES DENOTE MISSING/UNREPORTED DATA.
# INDICATES A STATION OR INSTRUMENT RELOCATION.

### SPECIFIC

#### TABLE 1

(a) · LENGTH OF RECORD IN YEARS. ALTHOUGH
    INDIVIDUAL MONTHS MAY BE MISSING.
*   LESS THAN .05

NORMALS — BASED ON THE 1951-1980 RECORD PERIOD.
EXTREMES — DATES ARE THE MOST RECENT OCCURRENCE.
WIND DIR. — NUMERALS SHOW TENS OF DEGREES
            CLOCKWISE FROM TRUE NORTH.
            "00" INDICATES CALM.
RESULTANT WIND DIRECTIONS ARE GIVEN TO WHOLE DEGREES.

#### TABLE 3
MAX AND MIN ARE LONG-TERM MEAN DAILY MAXIMUM
AND MEAN DAILY MINIMUM TEMPERATURES.

### EXCEPTIONS

#### TABLE 1

1.  FASTEST MILE WINDS ARE THROUGH AUGUST 1981.

#### TABLES 2, 3, and 6

RECORD MEANS ARE THROUGH THE CURRENT YEAR,
BEGINNING IN      1872 FOR TEMPERATURE
                  1872 FOR PRECIPITATION
                  1935 FOR SNOWFALL

## TABLE 4 — HEATING DEGREE DAYS Base 65 deg. F — DENVER, COLORADO

| SEASON | JULY | AUG | SEP | OCT | NOV | DEC | JAN | FEB | MAR | APR | MAY | JUNE | TOTAL |
|---|---|---|---|---|---|---|---|---|---|---|---|---|---|
| 1961-62 | 14 | 0 | 273 | 459 | 902 | 1150 | 1411 | 976 | 934 | 437 | 175 | 72 | 6803 |
| 1962-63 | 0 | 19 | 112 | 352 | 703 | 961 | 1417 | 768 | 848 | 442 | 156 | 50 | 5828 |
| 1963-64 | 6 | 7 | 29 | 229 | 690 | 1125 | 1059 | 1082 | 982 | 545 | 230 | 72 | 6056 |
| 1964-65 | 0 | 16 | 123 | 375 | 743 | 981 | 1044 | 1108 | 921 | 411 | 245 | 63 | 6030 |
| 1965-66 | 6 | 7 | 296 | 302 | 645 | 924 | 1122 | 1017 | 691 | 604 | 204 | 82 | 5900 |
| 1966-67 | 0 | 9 | 61 | 391 | 699 | 1018 | 954 | 832 | 679 | 498 | 388 | 135 | 5664 |
| 1967-68 | 4 | 16 | 108 | 389 | 729 | 1186 | 1086 | 885 | 751 | 655 | 343 | 38 | 6190 |
| 1968-69 | 10 | 35 | 145 | 399 | 871 | 1114 | 925 | 821 | 1011 | 378 | 204 | 144 | 6057 |
| 1969-70 | 2 | 0 | 56 | 801 | 769 | 998 | 1061 | 734 | 969 | 632 | 200 | 78 | 6300 |
| 1970-71 | 0 | 0 | 198 | 584 | 770 | 977 | 1018 | 958 | 817 | 508 | 329 | 25 | 6184 |
| 1971-72 | 24 | 0 | 273 | 479 | 771 | 1019 | 1063 | 832 | 621 | 486 | 246 | 4 | 5818 |
| 1972-73 | 42 | 15 | 107 | 397 | 960 | 1239 | 1162 | 820 | 771 | 646 | 290 | 56 | 6505 |
| 1973-74 | 8 | 0 | 166 | 321 | 758 | 1029 | 1277 | 831 | 671 | 507 | 137 | 67 | 5772 |
| 1974-75 | 0 | 9 | 199 | 381 | 803 | 1043 | 1024 | 957 | 852 | 621 | 332 | 85 | 6306 |
| 1975-76 | 0 | 4 | 195 | 363 | 840 | 843 | 1006 | 740 | 859 | 469 | 254 | 64 | 5637 |
| 1976-77 | 0 | 7 | 142 | 509 | 759 | 907 | 1105 | 749 | 771 | 414 | 137 | 0 | 5500 |
| 1977-78 | 2 | 14 | 38 | 358 | 737 | 920 | 1206 | 936 | 665 | 435 | 335 | 87 | 5733 |
| 1978-79 | 0 | 20 | 96 | 366 | 811 | 1245 | 1450 | 854 | 751 | 473 | 313 | 81 | 6460 |
| 1979-80 | 0 | 20 | 58 | 347 | 941 | 939 | 1204 | 876 | 828 | 514 | 247 | 9 | 5983 |
| 1980-81 | 0 | 4 | 56 | 386 | 683 | 731 | 853 | 801 | 727 | 260 | 243 | 26 | 4770 |
| 1981-82 | 0 | 12 | 19 | 375 | 570 | 898 | 1071 | 918 | 733 | 522 | 306 | 92 | 5516 |
| 1982-83 | 3 | 0 | 151 | 487 | 875 | 1050 | 1017 | 789 | 885 | 712 | 419 | 129 | 6517 |
| 1983-84 | 3 | 0 | 87 | 372 | 833 | 1469 | 1163 | 889 | 854 | 673 | 183 | 51 | 6577 |
| 1984-85 | 0 | 1 | 183 | 622 | 753 | 990 | 1215 | 1041 | 742 | 412 | 167 | 42 | 6168 |
| 1985-86 | 0 | 1 | 241 | 435 | 1051 | 1094 | 758 | 802 | 548 | 456 | 260 | 22 | 5668 |
| 1986-87 | 0 | 0 | 145 | 477 | 775 | 1045 | 1012 | 803 | 805 | 392 | 170 | 22 | 5646 |
| 1987-88 | 11 | 21 | 110 | 410 | 743 | 1125 | 1227 | 889 | 811 | 437 | 215 | 14 | 6013 |
| 1988-89 | 7 | 0 | 129 | 333 | 723 | 1043 | 969 | 1193 | 665 | 432 | 213 | 76 | 5783 |
| 1989-90 | 0 | 0 | 153 | 424 | 658 | 1162 | 879 | 882 | 781 | 469 | 265 | 7 | 5680 |
| 1990-91 | 12 | 3 | 64 | 388 | 623 | 1211 | | | | | | | |

## TABLE 5 — COOLING DEGREE DAYS Base 65 deg. F — DENVER, COLORADO

| YEAR | JAN | FEB | MAR | APR | MAY | JUNE | JULY | AUG | SEP | OCT | NOV | DEC | TOTAL |
|---|---|---|---|---|---|---|---|---|---|---|---|---|---|
| 1969 | 0 | 0 | 0 | 0 | 35 | 44 | 312 | 284 | 46 | 0 | 0 | 0 | 721 |
| 1970 | 0 | 0 | 0 | 0 | 16 | 93 | 222 | 282 | 40 | 0 | 0 | 0 | 653 |
| 1971 | 0 | 0 | 0 | 0 | 0 | 149 | 203 | 248 | 53 | 0 | 0 | 0 | 653 |
| 1972 | 0 | 0 | 0 | 0 | 6 | 110 | 210 | 207 | 28 | 1 | 0 | 0 | 562 |
| 1973 | 0 | 0 | 0 | 0 | 2 | 138 | 199 | 270 | 21 | 1 | 0 | 0 | 631 |
| 1974 | 0 | 0 | 0 | 0 | 36 | 176 | 307 | 157 | 39 | 0 | 0 | 0 | 715 |
| 1975 | 0 | 0 | 0 | 0 | 3 | 69 | 246 | 192 | 39 | 5 | 0 | 0 | 554 |
| 1976 | 0 | 0 | 0 | 0 | 3 | 112 | 324 | 176 | 52 | 0 | 0 | 0 | 667 |
| 1977 | 0 | 0 | 0 | 2 | 11 | 214 | 297 | 182 | 93 | 0 | 0 | 0 | 799 |
| 1978 | 0 | 0 | 0 | 0 | 12 | 152 | 308 | 171 | 103 | 2 | 0 | 0 | 748 |
| 1979 | 0 | 0 | 0 | 0 | 2 | 112 | 275 | 163 | 102 | 7 | 0 | 0 | 661 |
| 1980 | 0 | 0 | 0 | 2 | 10 | 224 | 358 | 263 | 88 | 1 | 0 | 0 | 946 |
| 1981 | 0 | 0 | 0 | 7 | 6 | 195 | 346 | 236 | 121 | 1 | 0 | 0 | 912 |
| 1982 | 0 | 0 | 0 | 0 | 6 | 42 | 247 | 257 | 59 | 1 | 0 | 0 | 611 |
| 1983 | 0 | 0 | 0 | 0 | 7 | 69 | 264 | 301 | 91 | 0 | 0 | 0 | 732 |
| 1984 | 0 | 0 | 0 | 0 | 33 | 104 | 315 | 218 | 60 | 0 | 0 | 0 | 730 |
| 1985 | 0 | 0 | 0 | 1 | 19 | 137 | 256 | 238 | 63 | 0 | 0 | 0 | 714 |
| 1986 | 0 | 0 | 0 | 0 | 11 | 188 | 271 | 227 | 20 | 0 | 0 | 0 | 717 |
| 1987 | 0 | 0 | 0 | 3 | 12 | 153 | 309 | 205 | 36 | 2 | 0 | 0 | 720 |
| 1988 | 0 | 0 | 0 | 1 | 35 | 225 | 300 | 277 | 55 | 0 | 0 | 0 | 893 |
| 1989 | 0 | 0 | 0 | 19 | 34 | 96 | 345 | 214 | 83 | 5 | 0 | 0 | 796 |
| 1990 | 0 | 0 | 0 | 0 | 9 | 244 | 196 | 203 | 129 | 1 | 0 | 0 | 782 |

## TABLE 6 — SNOWFALL (inches) — DENVER, COLORADO

| SEASON | JULY | AUG | SEP | OCT | NOV | DEC | JAN | FEB | MAR | APR | MAY | JUNE | TOTAL |
|---|---|---|---|---|---|---|---|---|---|---|---|---|---|
| 1961-62 | 0.0 | 0.0 | 5.8 | 6.2 | 11.4 | 3.8 | 17.2 | 11.3 | 6.8 | 10.0 | 0.0 | 0.0 | 72.5 |
| 1962-63 | 0.0 | 0.0 | 0.7 | 0.0 | 5.0 | 1.2 | 9.1 | 2.1 | 18.0 | 0.2 | 0.0 | 0.0 | 36.3 |
| 1963-64 | 0.0 | 0.0 | 0.0 | 1.1 | 3.5 | 5.9 | 2.6 | 12.7 | 18.4 | 12.1 | 1.0 | 0.0 | 57.3 |
| 1964-65 | 0.0 | 0.0 | 0.0 | T | 6.0 | 4.4 | 13.2 | 17.1 | 14.9 | 0.3 | T | 0.0 | 55.9 |
| 1965-66 | 0.0 | 0.0 | 5.5 | 0.0 | 5.5 | 5.6 | 3.6 | 14.6 | 2.8 | 6.4 | 2.9 | 0.0 | 46.9 |
| 1966-67 | 0.0 | 0.0 | T | 8.3 | 3.0 | 1.9 | 9.9 | 4.4 | 6.6 | 3.6 | 3.0 | 0.0 | 40.7 |
| 1967-68 | 0.0 | 0.0 | 0.0 | 1.7 | 9.4 | 13.1 | 3.0 | 7.3 | 9.2 | 15.1 | T | 0.0 | 58.8 |
| 1968-69 | 0.0 | 0.0 | 0.0 | 0.4 | 5.8 | 6.9 | 2.8 | 4.2 | 13.2 | T | 0.0 | 0.0 | 33.3 |
| 1969-70 | 0.0 | 0.0 | 0.0 | 31.2 | 5.1 | 3.1 | 0.9 | 0.3 | 20.5 | 4.7 | T | 0.0 | 65.8 |
| 1970-71 | 0.0 | 0.0 | 4.6 | 5.9 | 9.2 | 0.9 | 8.6 | 11.9 | 9.6 | 6.0 | T | 0.0 | 56.7 |
| 1971-72 | 0.0 | 0.0 | 17.2 | 3.1 | 1.4 | 8.4 | 10.9 | 9.1 | 7.1 | 17.2 | 0.0 | 0.0 | 74.4 |
| 1972-73 | 0.0 | 0.0 | 0.0 | 9.7 | 19.4 | 9.8 | 12.1 | 3.0 | 15.1 | 24.8 | 1.0 | 0.0 | 94.9 |
| 1973-74 | 0.0 | 0.0 | 0.0 | 2.3 | 9.3 | 30.8 | 8.2 | 10.3 | 12.8 | 17.8 | 0.0 | T | 91.5 |
| 1974-75 | 0.0 | 0.0 | 1.8 | 1.0 | 11.9 | 2.1 | 3.6 | 4.0 | 14.3 | 10.9 | 6.1 | 0.0 | 55.7 |
| 1975-76 | 0.0 | 0.0 | 0.0 | 2.7 | 15.2 | 7.3 | 3.2 | 6.4 | 18.7 | 1.2 | 0.0 | 0.0 | 54.7 |
| 1976-77 | 0.0 | 0.0 | 0.0 | 7.2 | 4.5 | 3.1 | 2.4 | 3.1 | 9.6 | 4.7 | 0.0 | 0.0 | 34.6 |
| 1977-78 | 0.0 | 0.0 | 0.0 | 3.3 | 4.1 | 0.7 | 5.5 | 6.2 | 8.6 | 4.6 | 13.5 | 0.0 | 46.5 |
| 1978-79 | 0.0 | 0.0 | T | 2.7 | 6.9 | 14.2 | 9.1 | 5.8 | 18.2 | 8.1 | 8.2 | 0.0 | 73.2 |
| 1979-80 | 0.0 | 0.0 | 0.0 | 2.7 | 22.3 | 16.5 | 12.3 | 9.6 | 12.1 | 10.0 | T | 0.0 | 85.5 |
| 1980-81 | 0.0 | 0.0 | 0.0 | 1.5 | 7.1 | 1.2 | 4.1 | 4.3 | 24.0 | 2.9 | T | 0.0 | 45.1 |
| 1981-82 | 0.0 | 0.0 | 0.0 | 2.8 | 3.3 | 4.9 | 4.8 | 1.8 | 2.1 | 2.0 | T | 0.0 | 26.7 |
| 1982-83 | 0.0 | 0.0 | 0.0 | 1.2 | 1.8 | 27.1 | 1.3 | 0.8 | 30.5 | 11.3 | 7.6 | 0.0 | 81.6 |
| 1983-84 | 0.0 | 0.0 | T | T | 29.3 | 11.5 | 3.4 | 7.9 | 12.0 | 16.8 | T | 0.0 | 80.9 |
| 1984-85 | 0.0 | 0.0 | 5.2 | 13.1 | 2.3 | 5.0 | 12.5 | 8.7 | 7.6 | 0.8 | T | 0.0 | 55.2 |
| 1985-86 | 0.0 | 0.0 | 8.7 | 1.9 | 17.0 | 10.3 | 2.4 | 6.2 | 2.6 | 14.0 | 0.0 | 0.0 | 63.1 |
| 1986-87 | 0.0 | 0.0 | 0.0 | 4.3 | 11.5 | 4.9 | 17.0 | 12.2 | 11.5 | 9.9 | 0.0 | 0.0 | 71.3 |
| 1987-88 | 0.0 | 0.0 | 0.0 | T | 11.2 | 21.5 | 5.8 | 7.0 | 13.5 | 2.0 | 1.3 | 0.0 | 62.3 |
| 1988-89 | 0.0 | 0.0 | 0.0 | 0.0 | 2.8 | 12.3 | 13.0 | 8.2 | 4.8 | 9.0 | T | 0.0 | 50.1 |
| 1989-90 | 0.0 | 0.0 | 2.3 | 7.8 | 1.6 | 11.8 | 8.4 | 7.0 | 21.9 | 3.6 | 0.1 | 0.0 | 64.5 |
| 1990-91 | T | T | 0.0 | 7.6 | 12.0 | 4.7 | | | | | | | |
| Record Mean | T | T | 1.6 | 3.7 | 8.2 | 7.4 | 7.9 | 7.5 | 12.8 | 9.0 | 1.7 | T | 59.9 |

See Reference Notes, relative to all above tables, on preceding page.

# GRAND JUNCTION, COLORADO

Grand Junction is located at the junction of the Colorado and Gunnison Rivers. It is on the west slope of the Rockies, in a large mountain valley. The area has a climate marked by the wide seasonal range usual to interior localities at this latitude. Thanks, however, to the protective topography of the vicinity, sudden and severe weather changes are very infrequent. The valley floor slopes from 4,800 feet near Palisade to 4,400 feet at the west end near Fruita. Mountains are on all sides at distances of from 10 to 60 miles and reach heights of 9,000 to over 12,000 feet.

This mountain valley location, with attendant valley breezes, provides protection from spring and fall frosts. This results in a growing season averaging 191 days in the city. This varies considerably in the outlying districts. It is about the same in the upper valley around Palisade, and 3 to 4 weeks shorter near the river west of Grand Junction. The growing season is sufficiently long to permit commercial growth of almost all fruits except citrus varieties. Summer grazing of cattle and sheep on nearby mountain ranges is extensive.

The interior, continental location, ringed by mountains on all sides, results in quite low precipitation in all seasons. Consequently, agriculture is dependent on irrigation. Adequate supplies of water are available from mountain snows and rains. Summer rains occur chiefly as scattered light showers and thunderstorms which develop over nearby mountains. Winter snows are fairly frequent, but are mostly light and quick to melt. Even the infrequent snows of from 4 to 8 inches seldom remain on the ground for prolonged periods. Blizzard conditions in the valley are extremely rare.

Temperatures above 100 degrees are infrequent, and about one-third of the winters have no readings below zero. Summer days with maximum temperatures in the middle 90s and minimums in the low 60s are common. Relative humidity is very low during the summer, with values similar to other dry locations such as the southern parts of New Mexico and Arizona. Spells of cold winter weather are sometimes prolonged due to cold air becoming trapped in the valley. Winds are usually very light during the coldest weather. Changes in winter are normally gradual, and abrupt changes are much less frequent than in eastern Colorado. Cold waves are rare. Sunny days predominate in all seasons.

The prevailing wind is from the east-southeast due to the valley breeze effect. The strongest winds are associated with thunderstorms or with pre-frontal weather. They usually are from the south or southwest.

# TABLE 1     NORMALS, MEANS AND EXTREMES

GRAND JUNCTION, COLORADO

LATITUDE: 39°07'N    LONGITUDE: 108°32'W    ELEVATION: FT. GRND 4843 BARO 4836    TIME ZONE: MOUNTAIN    WBAN: 23066

| | (a) | JAN | FEB | MAR | APR | MAY | JUNE | JULY | AUG | SEP | OCT | NOV | DEC | YEAR |
|---|---|---|---|---|---|---|---|---|---|---|---|---|---|---|
| **TEMPERATURE °F:** | | | | | | | | | | | | | | |
| Normals | | | | | | | | | | | | | | |
|   -Daily Maximum | | 35.7 | 44.5 | 54.1 | 65.2 | 76.2 | 87.9 | 94.0 | 90.3 | 81.9 | 68.7 | 51.0 | 38.7 | 65.7 |
|   -Daily Minimum | | 15.2 | 22.4 | 29.7 | 38.2 | 48.0 | 56.6 | 63.8 | 61.5 | 52.2 | 41.1 | 28.2 | 17.9 | 39.6 |
|   -Monthly | | 25.5 | 33.5 | 41.9 | 51.7 | 62.1 | 72.3 | 78.9 | 75.9 | 67.1 | 54.9 | 39.6 | 28.3 | 52.7 |
| Extremes | | | | | | | | | | | | | | |
|   -Record Highest | 43 | 60 | 68 | 81 | 85 | 95 | 103 | 105 | 103 | 98 | 88 | 75 | 64 | 105 |
|   -Year | | 1971 | 1986 | 1971 | 1989 | 1956 | 1981 | 1976 | 1969 | 1977 | 1963 | 1977 | 1980 | JUL 1976 |
|   -Record Lowest | 43 | -23 | -18 | 5 | 11 | 26 | 34 | 46 | 43 | 29 | 18 | -2 | -12 | -23 |
|   -Year | | 1963 | 1989 | 1948 | 1975 | 1970 | 1976 | 1976 | 1982 | 1968 | 1978 | 1989 | 1976 | 1978 | JAN 1963 |
| **NORMAL DEGREE DAYS:** | | | | | | | | | | | | | | |
| Heating (base 65°F) | | 1225 | 882 | 716 | 403 | 148 | 19 | 0 | 0 | 65 | 325 | 762 | 1138 | 5683 |
| Cooling (base 65°F) | | 0 | 0 | 0 | 0 | 58 | 238 | 431 | 338 | 128 | 12 | 0 | 0 | 1205 |
| **% OF POSSIBLE SUNSHINE** | 43 | 61 | 64 | 64 | 69 | 73 | 80 | 78 | 77 | 79 | 74 | 63 | 60 | 70 |
| **MEAN SKY COVER (tenths)** | | | | | | | | | | | | | | |
| Sunrise - Sunset | 43 | 6.1 | 6.2 | 6.2 | 5.9 | 5.5 | 4.0 | 4.3 | 4.3 | 3.6 | 4.2 | 5.4 | 5.8 | 5.1 |
| **MEAN NUMBER OF DAYS:** | | | | | | | | | | | | | | |
| Sunrise to Sunset | | | | | | | | | | | | | | |
|   -Clear | 43 | 9.2 | 7.7 | 8.1 | 8.4 | 9.7 | 14.9 | 13.5 | 13.8 | 16.5 | 14.9 | 10.7 | 9.6 | 137.0 |
|   -Partly Cloudy | 43 | 7.2 | 7.2 | 8.4 | 9.1 | 10.8 | 9.3 | 11.9 | 11.2 | 8.0 | 7.9 | 7.4 | 7.9 | 106.2 |
|   -Cloudy | 43 | 14.7 | 13.4 | 14.5 | 12.5 | 10.5 | 5.8 | 5.6 | 6.0 | 5.5 | 8.1 | 11.8 | 13.5 | 121.9 |
| Precipitation | | | | | | | | | | | | | | |
| .01 inches or more | 43 | 7.0 | 6.0 | 7.7 | 6.4 | 6.3 | 4.2 | 5.3 | 6.6 | 5.7 | 5.5 | 5.5 | 6.2 | 72.3 |
| Snow,Ice pellets | | | | | | | | | | | | | | |
| 1.0 inches or more | 43 | 2.6 | 1.2 | 1.3 | 0.3 | 0.* | 0.0 | 0.0 | 0.0 | 0.* | 0.2 | 1.0 | 2.1 | 8.7 |
| Thunderstorms | 43 | 0.1 | 0.3 | 0.8 | 1.9 | 4.5 | 4.9 | 7.7 | 7.8 | 5.0 | 1.5 | 0.4 | 0.1 | 34.8 |
| Heavy Fog Visibility | | | | | | | | | | | | | | |
| 1/4 mile or less | 43 | 2.9 | 1.9 | 0.6 | 0.1 | 0.* | 0.0 | 0.0 | 0.0 | 0.0 | 0.1 | 0.8 | 1.9 | 8.3 |
| Temperature °F | | | | | | | | | | | | | | |
| -Maximum | | | | | | | | | | | | | | |
|   90° and above | 26 | 0.0 | 0.0 | 0.0 | 0.0 | 1.3 | 14.0 | 24.9 | 19.8 | 4.3 | 0.0 | 0.0 | 0.0 | 64.5 |
|   32° and below | 26 | 11.7 | 2.5 | 0.2 | 0.0 | 0.0 | 0.0 | 0.0 | 0.0 | 0.0 | 0.0 | 0.7 | 6.7 | 21.7 |
| -Minimum | | | | | | | | | | | | | | |
|   32° and below | 26 | 30.3 | 25.1 | 17.0 | 6.8 | 0.5 | 0.0 | 0.0 | 0.0 | 0.2 | 3.1 | 20.2 | 29.5 | 132.6 |
|   0° and below | 26 | 3.8 | 0.7 | 0.0 | 0.0 | 0.0 | 0.0 | 0.0 | 0.0 | 0.0 | 0.0 | 0.* | 0.9 | 5.5 |
| **AVG. STATION PRESS.(mb)** | 17 | 855.1 | 853.5 | 849.4 | 849.8 | 849.5 | 851.1 | 853.2 | 853.4 | 853.2 | 854.3 | 853.6 | 855.0 | 852.6 |
| **RELATIVE HUMIDITY (%)** | | | | | | | | | | | | | | |
| Hour 05 | 26 | 78 | 72 | 63 | 56 | 53 | 45 | 49 | 51 | 51 | 58 | 70 | 76 | 60 |
| Hour 11 | 26 | 65 | 54 | 42 | 34 | 31 | 25 | 29 | 32 | 33 | 39 | 51 | 62 | 41 |
| Hour 17 (Local Time) | 26 | 62 | 47 | 36 | 27 | 25 | 20 | 22 | 24 | 26 | 33 | 47 | 59 | 36 |
| Hour 23 | 26 | 76 | 67 | 56 | 46 | 42 | 33 | 37 | 39 | 41 | 51 | 65 | 74 | 52 |
| **PRECIPITATION (inches):** | | | | | | | | | | | | | | |
| Water Equivalent | | | | | | | | | | | | | | |
|   -Normal | | 0.64 | 0.54 | 0.75 | 0.71 | 0.76 | 0.44 | 0.47 | 0.91 | 0.70 | 0.87 | 0.63 | 0.58 | 8.00 |
|   -Maximum Monthly | 43 | 2.46 | 1.56 | 2.02 | 1.95 | 1.79 | 2.07 | 1.92 | 3.48 | 2.81 | 3.45 | 2.00 | 1.89 | 3.48 |
|   -Year | | 1957 | 1948 | 1979 | 1965 | 1957 | 1969 | 1983 | 1957 | 1982 | 1972 | 1983 | 1951 | AUG 1957 |
|   -Minimum Monthly | 43 | T | T | 0.02 | 0.06 | T | T | 0.03 | 0.04 | T | 0.00 | T | 0.01 | 0.00 |
|   -Year | | 1961 | 1972 | 1972 | 1958 | 1970 | 1980 | 1972 | 1956 | 1953 | 1952 | 1989 | 1976 | OCT 1952 |
|   -Maximum in 24 hrs | 43 | 0.71 | 0.69 | 0.96 | 1.33 | 1.13 | 1.57 | 1.42 | 1.21 | 1.35 | 1.24 | 0.83 | 1.16 | 1.57 |
|   -Year | | 1989 | 1989 | 1983 | 1965 | 1983 | 1969 | 1974 | 1953 | 1965 | 1957 | 1983 | 1951 | JUN 1969 |
| Snow,Ice pellets | | | | | | | | | | | | | | |
|   -Maximum Monthly | 43 | 33.7 | 18.4 | 14.9 | 14.3 | 5.0 | 0.0 | 0.0 | 0.0 | 3.1 | 6.1 | 12.1 | 19.0 | 33.7 |
|   -Year | | 1957 | 1948 | 1948 | 1975 | 1979 | | | | 1965 | 1975 | 1964 | 1983 | JAN 1957 |
|   -Maximum in 24 hrs | 43 | 9.1 | 9.0 | 6.1 | 8.9 | 5.0 | 0.0 | 0.0 | 0.0 | 3.1 | 6.1 | 8.4 | 6.0 | 9.1 |
|   -Year | | 1957 | 1989 | 1948 | 1975 | 1979 | | | | 1965 | 1975 | 1954 | 1967 | JAN 1957 |
| **WIND:** | | | | | | | | | | | | | | |
| Mean Speed (mph) | 43 | 5.6 | 6.6 | 8.4 | 9.5 | 9.6 | 9.7 | 9.3 | 9.0 | 9.0 | 7.9 | 6.7 | 5.9 | 8.1 |
| Prevailing Direction | | | | | | | | | | | | | | |
| through 1963 | | ESE | ESE | ESE | ESE | ESE | ESE | ESE | ESE | ESE | ESE | ESE | ESE | ESE |
| Fastest Obs. 1 Min. | | | | | | | | | | | | | | |
|   -Direction (!!!) | 10 | 18 | 30 | 28 | 29 | 20 | 27 | 08 | 25 | 27 | 30 | 31 | 27 | 27 |
|   -Speed (MPH) | 10 | 35 | 29 | 35 | 46 | 46 | 53 | 40 | 37 | 35 | 33 | 39 | 32 | 53 |
|   -Year | | 1982 | 1989 | 1985 | 1985 | 1989 | 1981 | 1988 | 1988 | 1982 | 1989 | 1982 | 1982 | JUN 1981 |
| Peak Gust | | | | | | | | | | | | | | |
|   -Direction (!!!) | 6 | W | NW | W | S | W | W | E | S | NW | W | W | NE | S |
|   -Speed (mph) | 6 | 37 | 40 | 52 | 78 | 62 | 53 | 60 | 74 | 54 | 54 | 49 | 37 | 78 |
|   -Date | | 1987 | 1989 | 1988 | 1985 | 1989 | 1985 | 1988 | 1984 | 1989 | 1985 | 1984 | 1987 | APR 1985 |

**See reference Notes to this table on the following page.**

PRECIPITATION (inches)  GRAND JUNCTION, COLORADO

**TABLE 2**

| YEAR | JAN | FEB | MAR | APR | MAY | JUNE | JULY | AUG | SEP | OCT | NOV | DEC | ANNUAL |
|---|---|---|---|---|---|---|---|---|---|---|---|---|---|
| 1961 | T | 0.18 | 1.47 | 0.85 | 1.11 | T | 0.03 | 1.63 | 2.22 | 0.70 | 0.66 | 0.63 | 9.48 |
| 1962 | 0.39 | 1.09 | 0.28 | 0.97 | 0.17 | 0.30 | 0.08 | 0.15 | 1.41 | 0.46 | 0.36 | 0.36 | 6.02 |
| 1963 | 0.99 | 0.47 | 0.55 | 0.12 | 0.01 | 0.61 | 0.93 | 1.75 | 0.48 | 0.60 | 0.36 | 0.45 | 7.32 |
| 1964 | 0.47 | 0.02 | 0.70 | 1.37 | 0.41 | 0.16 | 0.65 | 1.16 | 0.36 | T | 1.05 | 0.53 | 6.88 |
| 1965 | 0.66 | 0.94 | 0.87 | 1.95 | 1.35 | 1.33 | 0.89 | 0.67 | 2.52 | 1.40 | 0.82 | 0.76 | 14.16 |
| 1966 | 0.65 | 0.44 | 0.04 | 0.83 | 0.71 | 0.13 | 0.31 | 0.52 | 0.26 | 1.23 | 0.62 | 1.78 | 7.52 |
| 1967 | 0.25 | 0.22 | 0.18 | 0.08 | 1.52 | 1.34 | 1.03 | 0.59 | 0.37 | 0.63 | 0.33 | 1.14 | 7.68 |
| 1968 | 0.26 | 1.13 | 0.44 | 0.67 | 1.14 | 0.05 | 0.49 | 1.37 | 0.07 | 0.94 | 0.42 | 0.47 | 7.45 |
| 1969 | 1.03 | 0.40 | 0.67 | 0.33 | 0.45 | 2.07 | 0.21 | 0.88 | 1.45 | 0.45 | 0.45 | 0.36 | 10.31 |
| 1970 | 0.52 | 0.05 | 1.75 | 0.76 | T | 0.91 | 0.60 | 0.44 | 0.78 | 1.56 | 0.54 | 0.39 | 8.30 |
| 1971 | 0.19 | 0.13 | 0.02 | 0.42 | 1.10 | 0.03 | 0.15 | 1.02 | 0.58 | 1.13 | 0.56 | 0.67 | 6.00 |
| 1972 | 0.20 | T | 0.02 | 0.11 | 0.44 | 0.64 | 0.03 | 0.29 | 0.72 | 3.45 | 0.69 | 0.74 | 7.33 |
| 1973 | 0.79 | 0.12 | 0.65 | 0.86 | 1.45 | 0.87 | 0.52 | 0.62 | 0.33 | 0.20 | 0.91 | 0.62 | 7.94 |
| 1974 | 1.20 | 0.40 | 0.81 | 1.03 | 0.01 | 0.14 | 1.53 | 0.48 | 0.38 | 0.72 | 1.18 | 0.32 | 8.20 |
| 1975 | 0.53 | 0.49 | 1.74 | 1.38 | 1.23 | 0.43 | 1.39 | 0.09 | 0.16 | 0.85 | 0.39 | 0.50 | 9.18 |
| 1976 | 0.13 | 0.81 | 0.75 | 0.40 | 1.49 | 0.14 | 0.20 | 0.31 | 0.67 | 0.32 | 0.04 | 0.01 | 5.27 |
| 1977 | 0.37 | 0.06 | 0.50 | 0.54 | 0.59 | 0.04 | 0.89 | 0.59 | 0.52 | 0.50 | 0.70 | 0.38 | 5.68 |
| 1978 | 1.08 | 0.64 | 1.19 | 1.19 | 0.55 | 0.01 | 0.25 | 0.54 | 0.49 | 0.03 | 0.62 | 1.30 | 7.89 |
| 1979 | 1.36 | 0.63 | 2.02 | 0.42 | 1.45 | 0.78 | 0.08 | 0.61 | 0.01 | 0.25 | 1.02 | 0.27 | 8.90 |
| 1980 | 0.57 | 1.10 | 1.77 | 0.53 | 1.17 | T | 0.96 | 1.39 | 0.58 | 1.31 | 0.52 | 0.24 | 10.14 |
| 1981 | 0.44 | 0.16 | 1.35 | 0.56 | 1.49 | 0.17 | 0.41 | 0.82 | 0.25 | 2.06 | 0.47 | 0.60 | 8.78 |
| 1982 | 0.29 | 0.41 | 0.79 | 0.09 | 0.75 | 0.21 | 0.35 | 0.94 | 2.81 | 0.83 | 0.48 | 0.27 | 8.22 |
| 1983 | 0.50 | 0.64 | 1.59 | 0.90 | 1.68 | 1.54 | 1.92 | 0.73 | 1.11 | 0.36 | 2.00 | 1.85 | 14.82 |
| 1984 | 0.28 | 0.11 | 1.57 | 1.21 | 0.55 | 1.68 | 0.62 | 1.77 | 0.34 | 2.65 | 0.38 | 0.43 | 11.59 |
| 1985 | 0.51 | 0.26 | 0.92 | 1.78 | 1.09 | 0.39 | 1.21 | 0.24 | 1.67 | 2.32 | 1.10 | 0.73 | 12.22 |
| 1986 | 0.13 | 0.33 | 0.25 | 0.71 | 1.15 | 0.15 | 0.94 | 0.97 | 1.52 | 1.22 | 1.02 | 0.47 | 8.86 |
| 1987 | 0.30 | 1.21 | 1.95 | 0.46 | 1.51 | 0.23 | 1.51 | 0.83 | 0.13 | 0.65 | 1.92 | 0.83 | 11.53 |
| 1988 | 1.07 | 0.21 | 0.72 | 0.99 | 1.10 | 0.21 | 0.18 | 1.37 | 0.76 | 0.02 | 1.02 | 0.20 | 7.85 |
| 1989 | 0.98 | 1.33 | 0.51 | 0.23 | 0.39 | 0.24 | 0.27 | 1.01 | 0.33 | 0.14 | T | 0.08 | 5.51 |
| 1990 | 0.59 | 0.55 | 1.07 | 0.71 | 0.05 | 0.26 | 0.96 | 0.49 | 1.23 | 0.95 | 0.57 | 0.98 | 8.41 |
| Record Mean | 0.59 | 0.58 | 0.82 | 0.74 | 0.76 | 0.44 | 0.62 | 1.01 | 0.89 | 0.91 | 0.63 | 0.58 | 8.58 |

**TABLE 3**  AVERAGE TEMPERATURE (deg. F)  GRAND JUNCTION, COLORADO

| YEAR | JAN | FEB | MAR | APR | MAY | JUNE | JULY | AUG | SEP | OCT | NOV | DEC | ANNUAL |
|---|---|---|---|---|---|---|---|---|---|---|---|---|---|
| 1961 | 29.4 | 37.1 | 42.4 | 50.3 | 63.0 | 76.2 | 78.4 | 76.2 | 58.9 | 52.9 | 37.9 | 23.1 | 52.2 |
| 1962 | 22.9 | 37.9 | 38.4 | 55.5 | 61.7 | 71.3 | 76.9 | 75.9 | 67.4 | 56.6 | 44.1 | 29.3 | 53.2 |
| #1963 | 12.1 | 38.6 | 41.9 | 51.1 | 66.3 | 71.4 | 79.8 | 73.6 | 69.8 | 61.3 | 44.0 | 27.1 | 53.1 |
| 1964 | 25.5 | 29.5 | 37.0 | 50.3 | 62.3 | 70.2 | 81.3 | 74.1 | 66.6 | 58.0 | 38.1 | 30.4 | 51.9 |
| 1965 | 32.3 | 32.9 | 40.4 | 53.9 | 62.4 | 70.3 | 78.9 | 76.6 | 63.4 | 58.1 | 48.3 | 33.8 | 54.3 |
| 1966 | 24.5 | 30.6 | 46.1 | 53.6 | 65.4 | 72.0 | 80.9 | 77.0 | 69.1 | 56.5 | 43.9 | 29.5 | 54.1 |
| 1967 | 23.9 | 36.4 | 48.5 | 51.6 | 59.5 | 68.6 | 77.7 | 76.2 | 67.5 | 55.3 | 41.0 | 18.3 | 52.0 |
| 1968 | 15.4 | 37.0 | 43.8 | 46.3 | 59.1 | 72.8 | 78.0 | 70.3 | 64.2 | 53.8 | 38.0 | 22.7 | 50.1 |
| 1969 | 28.5 | 33.6 | 38.1 | 53.8 | 66.4 | 67.7 | 80.3 | 79.5 | 69.3 | 47.4 | 39.2 | 32.7 | 53.1 |
| 1970 | 29.3 | 40.9 | 39.8 | 45.9 | 63.3 | 71.4 | 79.1 | 78.7 | 64.1 | 48.8 | 41.0 | 31.9 | 52.9 |
| 1971 | 27.7 | 34.1 | 41.1 | 52.2 | 60.1 | 74.1 | 80.2 | 78.5 | 63.2 | 52.3 | 38.4 | 25.9 | 52.3 |
| 1972 | 30.0 | 36.6 | 46.6 | 53.3 | 63.1 | 74.3 | 80.2 | 77.1 | 68.1 | 54.0 | 37.1 | 22.7 | 53.6 |
| 1973 | 11.5 | 29.1 | 42.1 | 48.1 | 61.5 | 70.5 | 78.1 | 77.4 | 65.7 | 56.4 | 41.2 | 30.1 | 51.0 |
| 1974 | 16.9 | 19.9 | 48.2 | 51.0 | 65.0 | 74.9 | 78.3 | 75.6 | 66.4 | 56.2 | 39.6 | 27.1 | 51.6 |
| 1975 | 20.0 | 33.0 | 41.0 | 46.4 | 57.1 | 67.5 | 78.3 | 75.4 | 67.1 | 53.5 | 36.2 | 27.4 | 50.2 |
| 1976 | 21.7 | 38.2 | 38.7 | 51.9 | 61.8 | 70.4 | 79.6 | 75.3 | 66.9 | 52.1 | 39.1 | 27.6 | 51.9 |
| 1977 | 23.9 | 37.1 | 40.8 | 56.9 | 63.7 | 79.1 | 80.2 | 78.3 | 70.2 | 58.2 | 40.3 | 33.3 | 55.2 |
| 1978 | 29.4 | 34.4 | 46.7 | 52.3 | 58.8 | 73.0 | 78.4 | 74.5 | 65.7 | 54.7 | 40.2 | 16.0 | 52.0 |
| 1979 | 16.6 | 23.5 | 41.1 | 52.5 | 60.3 | 71.0 | 78.7 | 74.6 | 72.0 | 58.9 | 33.2 | 26.9 | 50.8 |
| 1980 | 32.6 | 39.2 | 40.9 | 51.4 | 59.1 | 74.0 | 78.6 | 76.3 | 67.9 | 53.8 | 42.3 | 40.1 | 54.6 |
| 1981 | 36.8 | 37.9 | 44.0 | 56.8 | 60.9 | 76.4 | 79.4 | 76.8 | 69.2 | 50.7 | 41.6 | 31.3 | 55.1 |
| 1982 | 26.0 | 34.7 | 46.0 | 51.3 | 61.4 | 72.2 | 79.0 | 78.2 | 67.5 | 51.9 | 41.2 | 33.0 | 53.5 |
| 1983 | 34.3 | 40.9 | 45.9 | 48.7 | 58.7 | 69.8 | 78.3 | 80.4 | 71.4 | 58.2 | 42.1 | 30.5 | 54.9 |
| 1984 | 20.7 | 31.7 | 44.4 | 49.0 | 66.2 | 70.1 | 78.0 | 76.6 | 68.3 | 52.0 | 32.6 | 32.6 | 52.4 |
| 1985 | 31.1 | 32.0 | 43.9 | 54.5 | 63.6 | 73.0 | 77.6 | 77.1 | 62.4 | 52.8 | 38.8 | 31.9 | 53.2 |
| 1986 | 34.2 | 40.4 | 49.0 | 52.5 | 60.6 | 74.3 | 76.0 | 75.6 | 63.2 | 51.5 | 40.8 | 32.4 | 54.2 |
| 1987 | 27.4 | 36.8 | 40.1 | 54.5 | 61.2 | 73.5 | 75.2 | 72.9 | 66.2 | 56.8 | 39.6 | 27.9 | 52.7 |
| 1988 | 17.4 | 29.2 | 41.0 | 53.1 | 60.9 | 76.5 | 80.6 | 76.2 | 64.5 | 58.0 | 40.7 | 30.0 | 52.4 |
| 1989 | 20.2 | 27.7 | 47.5 | 57.0 | 63.8 | 71.0 | 80.5 | 74.4 | 68.3 | 54.9 | 40.6 | 29.2 | 52.9 |
| 1990 | 28.5 | 35.4 | 46.8 | 55.7 | 61.3 | 75.2 | 78.0 | 76.6 | 69.7 | 53.2 | 39.5 | 20.6 | 53.4 |
| Record Mean | 25.9 | 33.5 | 42.9 | 52.3 | 61.8 | 72.0 | 78.3 | 75.7 | 66.9 | 54.2 | 39.8 | 28.6 | 52.7 |
| Max | 36.3 | 44.1 | 54.5 | 65.2 | 75.3 | 86.7 | 92.4 | 89.2 | 80.6 | 67.2 | 51.3 | 38.8 | 65.1 |
| Min | 15.4 | 22.8 | 31.2 | 39.4 | 48.3 | 57.3 | 64.2 | 62.1 | 53.2 | 41.2 | 28.4 | 18.5 | 40.2 |

## REFERENCE NOTES FOR TABLES 1, 2, 3 and 6   (GRAND JUNCTION, CO)

### GENERAL

T - TRACE AMOUNT
BLANK ENTRIES DENOTE MISSING/UNREPORTED DATA.
# INDICATES A STATION OR INSTRUMENT RELOCATION.

### SPECIFIC

#### TABLE 1

(a) - LENGTH OF RECORD IN YEARS. ALTHOUGH
INDIVIDUAL MONTHS MAY BE MISSING.
* LESS THAN .05

NORMALS — BASED ON THE 1951-1980 RECORD PERIOD.
EXTREMES — DATES ARE THE MOST RECENT OCCURRENCE.
WIND DIR. — NUMERALS SHOW TENS OF DEGREES
CLOCKWISE FROM TRUE NORTH.
"00" INDICATES CALM.
RESULTANT WIND DIRECTIONS ARE GIVEN TO WHOLE DEGREES.

#### TABLE 3
MAX AND MIN ARE LONG-TERM MEAN DAILY MAXIMUM
AND MEAN DAILY MINIMUM TEMPERATURES.

### EXCEPTIONS

**TABLES 2, 3, and 6**

RECORD MEANS ARE THROUGH THE CURRENT YEAR,
BEGINNING IN  1892 FOR TEMPERATURE
1892 FOR PRECIPITATION
1947 FOR SNOWFALL

### TABLE 4

HEATING DEGREE DAYS Base 65 deg. F    GRAND JUNCTION, COLORADO

| SEASON | JULY | AUG | SEP | OCT | NOV | DEC | JAN | FEB | MAR | APR | MAY | JUNE | TOTAL |
|---|---|---|---|---|---|---|---|---|---|---|---|---|---|
| 1961-62 | 0 | 0 | 196 | 367 | 809 | 1290 | 1295 | 752 | 819 | 286 | 148 | 18 | 5980 |
| 1962-63 | 0 | 2 | 39 | 255 | 620 | 1099 | 1633 | 733 | 708 | 411 | 32 | 3 | 5533 |
| # 1963-64 | 0 | 2 | 4 | 145 | 624 | 1166 | 1220 | 1022 | 861 | 437 | 168 | 18 | 5667 |
| 1964-65 | 0 | 2 | 39 | 219 | 800 | 1067 | 1004 | 893 | 758 | 334 | 158 | 8 | 5282 |
| 1965-66 | 0 | 0 | 138 | 209 | 496 | 960 | 1246 | 959 | 582 | 337 | 59 | 4 | 4990 |
| 1966-67 | 0 | 2 | 16 | 256 | 628 | 1092 | 1268 | 795 | 508 | 396 | 213 | 21 | 5195 |
| 1967-68 | 0 | 0 | 28 | 320 | 714 | 1442 | 1532 | 805 | 648 | 552 | 218 | 24 | 6283 |
| 1968-69 | 0 | 12 | 86 | 346 | 804 | 1302 | 1125 | 874 | 826 | 332 | 52 | 34 | 5793 |
| 1969-70 | 0 | 0 | 20 | 545 | 764 | 995 | 1100 | 671 | 772 | 564 | 115 | 39 | 5585 |
| 1970-71 | 0 | 0 | 93 | 495 | 714 | 1019 | 1152 | 858 | 734 | 378 | 182 | 4 | 5629 |
| 1971-72 | 0 | 0 | 134 | 389 | 792 | 1204 | 1076 | 813 | 563 | 346 | 139 | 0 | 5456 |
| 1972-73 | 0 | 0 | 31 | 335 | 832 | 1303 | 1651 | 999 | 705 | 499 | 139 | 49 | 6543 |
| 1973-74 | 0 | 0 | 72 | 266 | 708 | 1075 | 1487 | 1260 | 513 | 415 | 66 | 32 | 5894 |
| 1974-75 | 0 | 0 | 60 | 266 | 756 | 1167 | 1387 | 888 | 736 | 551 | 249 | 51 | 6111 |
| 1975-76 | 0 | 0 | 35 | 358 | 858 | 1161 | 1335 | 775 | 807 | 386 | 122 | 25 | 5862 |
| 1976-77 | 0 | 0 | 41 | 421 | 769 | 1153 | 1267 | 775 | 743 | 250 | 94 | 0 | 5513 |
| 1977-78 | 0 | 1 | 17 | 214 | 736 | 975 | 1098 | 852 | 561 | 373 | 210 | 9 | 5046 |
| 1978-79 | 0 | 6 | 95 | 313 | 737 | 1510 | 1493 | 1154 | 732 | 377 | 192 | 37 | 6646 |
| 1979-80 | 0 | 3 | 0 | 209 | 945 | 1175 | 999 | 741 | 740 | 405 | 195 | 4 | 5416 |
| 1980-81 | 0 | 2 | 21 | 359 | 674 | 765 | 864 | 754 | 645 | 247 | 153 | 15 | 4499 |
| 1981-82 | 0 | 0 | 12 | 439 | 696 | 1039 | 1203 | 841 | 581 | 405 | 136 | 6 | 5358 |
| 1982-83 | 2 | 0 | 61 | 397 | 704 | 983 | 946 | 668 | 586 | 482 | 238 | 22 | 5089 |
| 1983-84 | 0 | 0 | 27 | 208 | 678 | 1064 | 1366 | 959 | 631 | 474 | 89 | 44 | 5540 |
| 1984-85 | 0 | 0 | 54 | 452 | 719 | 996 | 1044 | 919 | 646 | 310 | 81 | 12 | 5233 |
| 1985-86 | 0 | 0 | 139 | 371 | 779 | 1018 | 949 | 685 | 489 | 366 | 168 | 3 | 4967 |
| 1986-87 | 0 | 0 | 130 | 414 | 718 | 1001 | 1159 | 785 | 765 | 314 | 143 | 0 | 5429 |
| 1987-88 | 0 | 6 | 34 | 248 | 754 | 1147 | 1469 | 1031 | 741 | 350 | 172 | 8 | 5960 |
| 1988-89 | 0 | 0 | 106 | 183 | 724 | 1078 | 1379 | 1038 | 534 | 258 | 113 | 8 | 5421 |
| 1989-90 | 0 | 0 | 40 | 316 | 729 | 1103 | 1124 | 820 | 557 | 271 | 139 | 20 | 5119 |
| 1990-91 | 0 | 0 | 28 | 360 | 759 | 1371 | | | | | | | |

### TABLE 5

COOLING DEGREE DAYS Base 65 deg. F    GRAND JUNCTION, COLORADO

| YEAR | JAN | FEB | MAR | APR | MAY | JUNE | JULY | AUG | SEP | OCT | NOV | DEC | TOTAL |
|---|---|---|---|---|---|---|---|---|---|---|---|---|---|
| 1969 | 0 | 0 | 0 | 3 | 104 | 124 | 481 | 458 | 158 | 1 | 0 | 0 | 1329 |
| 1970 | 0 | 0 | 0 | 0 | 67 | 238 | 442 | 430 | 72 | 0 | 0 | 0 | 1249 |
| 1971 | 0 | 0 | 0 | 0 | 36 | 284 | 479 | 425 | 86 | 3 | 0 | 0 | 1313 |
| 1972 | 0 | 0 | 0 | 0 | 86 | 288 | 479 | 381 | 130 | 3 | 0 | 0 | 1367 |
| 1973 | 0 | 0 | 0 | 0 | 35 | 222 | 410 | 393 | 101 | 6 | 0 | 0 | 1167 |
| 1974 | 0 | 0 | 0 | 1 | 73 | 335 | 420 | 335 | 109 | 0 | 0 | 0 | 1273 |
| 1975 | 0 | 0 | 0 | 0 | 9 | 133 | 419 | 328 | 106 | 9 | 0 | 0 | 1004 |
| 1976 | 0 | 0 | 0 | 0 | 32 | 195 | 460 | 324 | 103 | 0 | 0 | 0 | 1114 |
| 1977 | 0 | 0 | 0 | 16 | 60 | 429 | 477 | 420 | 180 | 10 | 0 | 0 | 1592 |
| 1978 | 0 | 0 | 0 | 0 | 25 | 258 | 420 | 308 | 123 | 1 | 0 | 0 | 1135 |
| 1979 | 0 | 0 | 0 | 6 | 52 | 225 | 428 | 310 | 215 | 27 | 0 | 0 | 1263 |
| 1980 | 0 | 0 | 0 | 1 | 16 | 280 | 427 | 325 | 115 | 19 | 0 | 0 | 1183 |
| 1981 | 0 | 0 | 0 | 9 | 31 | 367 | 456 | 375 | 143 | 0 | 0 | 0 | 1381 |
| 1982 | 0 | 0 | 0 | 0 | 33 | 229 | 443 | 415 | 144 | 0 | 0 | 0 | 1264 |
| 1983 | 0 | 0 | 0 | 0 | 49 | 171 | 421 | 483 | 226 | 3 | 0 | 0 | 1353 |
| 1984 | 0 | 0 | 0 | 0 | 134 | 200 | 408 | 368 | 159 | 0 | 0 | 0 | 1269 |
| 1985 | 0 | 0 | 0 | 4 | 45 | 261 | 396 | 382 | 67 | 0 | 0 | 0 | 1155 |
| 1986 | 0 | 0 | 0 | 0 | 39 | 289 | 348 | 334 | 82 | 0 | 0 | 0 | 1092 |
| 1987 | 0 | 0 | 0 | 5 | 30 | 262 | 324 | 256 | 76 | 2 | 0 | 0 | 955 |
| 1988 | 0 | 0 | 0 | 0 | 51 | 360 | 489 | 357 | 98 | 4 | 0 | 0 | 1359 |
| 1989 | 0 | 0 | 0 | 26 | 85 | 195 | 489 | 300 | 145 | 11 | 0 | 0 | 1251 |
| 1990 | 0 | 0 | 0 | 1 | 34 | 331 | 412 | 368 | 174 | 3 | 0 | 0 | 1323 |

### TABLE 6

SNOWFALL (inches)    GRAND JUNCTION, COLORADO

| SEASON | JULY | AUG | SEP | OCT | NOV | DEC | JAN | FEB | MAR | APR | MAY | JUNE | TOTAL |
|---|---|---|---|---|---|---|---|---|---|---|---|---|---|
| 1961-62 | 0.0 | 0.0 | 0.0 | T | 1.1 | 8.1 | 4.6 | 6.1 | 3.0 | 1.7 | 0.0 | 0.0 | 24.6 |
| 1962-63 | 0.0 | 0.0 | 0.0 | 0.0 | 3.3 | 4.9 | 17.7 | 0.2 | 4.3 | 0.2 | 0.0 | 0.0 | 30.6 |
| 1963-64 | 0.0 | 0.0 | 0.0 | 0.0 | T | 7.0 | 0.4 | 4.8 | 8.0 | 0.8 | T | 0.0 | 21.0 |
| 1964-65 | 0.0 | 0.0 | 0.0 | 0.0 | 12.1 | 3.0 | 5.9 | 7.5 | 3.8 | 0.2 | T | 0.0 | 32.5 |
| 1965-66 | 0.0 | 0.0 | 3.1 | 0.0 | 2.8 | 3.5 | 11.0 | 5.9 | 0.3 | 0.8 | T | 0.0 | 27.4 |
| 1966-67 | 0.0 | 0.0 | 0.0 | 1.9 | 4.2 | 6.3 | 2.8 | T | 0.2 | 0.4 | T | 0.0 | 15.8 |
| 1967-68 | 0.0 | 0.0 | 0.0 | T | 0.5 | 16.7 | 3.7 | 0.9 | 0.3 | 0.6 | T | 0.0 | 22.7 |
| 1968-69 | 0.0 | 0.0 | 0.0 | 0.0 | 0.2 | 7.8 | 3.4 | 3.8 | 9.5 | T | T | 0.0 | 24.7 |
| 1969-70 | 0.0 | 0.0 | 0.0 | 0.6 | 0.5 | 4.8 | 5.2 | T | 12.4 | 1.2 | 0.0 | 0.0 | 24.7 |
| 1970-71 | 0.0 | 0.0 | 0.0 | 3.1 | T | 4.1 | 3.2 | 1.5 | 0.2 | 1.1 | T | 0.0 | 13.2 |
| 1971-72 | 0.0 | 0.0 | 0.0 | 0.5 | 3.9 | 4.0 | T | 0.0 | T | 0.0 | 0.0 | 0.0 | 18.8 |
| 1972-73 | 0.0 | 0.0 | 0.0 | 5.7 | 1.3 | 9.7 | 12.8 | 1.2 | 1.3 | 2.0 | T | 0.0 | 34.0 |
| 1973-74 | 0.0 | 0.0 | 0.0 | 0.0 | 7.7 | 5.7 | 17.0 | 5.5 | T | 1.2 | 0.0 | 0.0 | 37.1 |
| 1974-75 | 0.0 | 0.0 | 0.0 | T | 0.1 | 4.6 | 7.9 | 4.4 | 8.8 | 14.3 | 1.3 | 0.0 | 41.4 |
| 1975-76 | 0.0 | 0.0 | 0.0 | 6.1 | 3.9 | 7.2 | 1.7 | 4.0 | 6.8 | 0.2 | 0.0 | 0.0 | 29.9 |
| 1976-77 | 0.0 | 0.0 | 0.0 | 0.0 | T | 0.1 | 4.2 | T | 2.3 | 1.7 | 0.0 | 0.0 | 8.3 |
| 1977-78 | 0.0 | 0.0 | 0.0 | T | 3.3 | 2.5 | 12.0 | 2.5 | 0.6 | T | T | 0.0 | 20.9 |
| 1978-79 | 0.0 | 0.0 | 0.0 | 0.0 | 2.9 | 11.8 | 18.7 | 9.6 | 3.4 | 1.1 | 5.0 | 0.0 | 52.5 |
| 1979-80 | 0.0 | 0.0 | 0.0 | 0.0 | 8.2 | 3.5 | 2.2 | 0.5 | 7.3 | 0.2 | 0.0 | 0.0 | 21.9 |
| 1980-81 | 0.0 | 0.0 | 0.0 | 0.0 | T | 3.9 | 0.8 | 1.2 | T | 0.0 | 0.0 | 0.0 | 5.9 |
| 1981-82 | 0.0 | 0.0 | 0.0 | 0.5 | 3.3 | 3.4 | 3.4 | 4.0 | 0.8 | T | 0.0 | 0.0 | 15.4 |
| 1982-83 | 0.0 | 0.0 | 0.0 | T | T | 1.9 | 6.1 | 3.1 | 1.5 | 2.2 | T | 0.0 | 14.8 |
| 1983-84 | 0.0 | 0.0 | 0.0 | 0.0 | 4.2 | 19.0 | 3.7 | 0.6 | 6.1 | 2.9 | 0.0 | 0.0 | 36.5 |
| 1984-85 | 0.0 | 0.0 | 0.0 | 0.7 | 2.0 | 5.0 | 2.7 | 5.6 | 0.1 | 0.0 | 0.0 | 0.0 | 18.8 |
| 1985-86 | 0.0 | 0.0 | 0.0 | 0.0 | 4.6 | 4.4 | 1.8 | 0.7 | T | 0.2 | T | 0.0 | 11.7 |
| 1986-87 | 0.0 | 0.0 | 0.0 | 2.2 | 1.2 | 1.0 | 3.0 | 5.5 | 9.4 | 0.6 | T | 0.0 | 22.9 |
| 1987-88 | 0.0 | 0.0 | 0.0 | 0.0 | 1.1 | 7.1 | 12.2 | 2.2 | 4.3 | 0.0 | 0.0 | 0.0 | 26.9 |
| 1988-89 | 0.0 | 0.0 | 0.0 | 0.0 | 0.9 | 3.1 | 10.2 | 16.0 | 1.1 | T | T | 0.0 | 31.3 |
| 1989-90 | 0.0 | 0.0 | 0.0 | 0.0 | 0.0 | 1.1 | 6.2 | 8.6 | 1.8 | 0.8 | 0.0 | 0.0 | 18.5 |
| 1990-91 | 0.0 | 0.0 | 0.0 | 0.0 | 1.5 | 5.1 | | | | | | | |
| Record Mean | 0.0 | 0.0 | 0.1 | 0.5 | 2.8 | 5.3 | 7.3 | 4.3 | 4.0 | 1.0 | 0.1 | 0.0 | 25.4 |

**See Reference Notes, relative to all above tables, on preceding page.**

Bradley International Airport is located about 3 miles west of the Connecticut River on a slight rise of ground in a broad portion of the Connecticut River Valley between north–south mountain ranges whose heights do not exceed 1,200 feet.

The station is in the northern temperate climate zone. The prevailing west to east movement of air brings the majority of weather systems into Connecticut from the west. The average wintertime position of the Polar Front boundary between cold, dry polar air and warm, moist tropical air is just south of New England, which helps to explain the extensive winter storm activity and day to day variability of local weather. In summer, the Polar Front has an average position along the New England–Canada border with this station in a warm and pleasant atmosphere.

The location of Hartford, relative to continent and ocean, is also significant. Rapid weather changes result when storms move northward along the mid–Atlantic coast, frequently producing strong and persistent northeast winds associated with storms known locally as coastals or northeasters. Seasonally, weather characteristics vary from the cold and dry continental–polar air of winter to the warm and humid maritime air of summer.

Summer thunderstorms develop in the Berkshire Mountains to the west and northwest, move over the Connecticut Valley, and when accompanied by wind and hail, sometimes cause considerable damage to crops, particularly tobacco. During the winter, rain often falls through cold air trapped in the valley, creating extremely hazardous ice conditions. On clear nights in the late summer or early autumn, cool air drainage into the valley, and moisture from the Connecticut River, produce steam and/or ground fog which becomes quite dense throughout the valley, hampering ground and air transportation.

The mean date of the last springtime temperature of 32 degrees or lower is April 22, and the mean date of the first autumn temperature of 32 degrees is October 15.

## TABLE 1     NORMALS, MEANS AND EXTREMES

HARTFORD, CONNECTICUT

LATITUDE: 41°56'N    LONGITUDE: 72°41'W    ELEVATION: FT. GRND 169 BARO 201    TIME ZONE: EASTERN    WBAN: 14740

| | (a) | JAN | FEB | MAR | APR | MAY | JUNE | JULY | AUG | SEP | OCT | NOV | DEC | YEAR |
|---|---|---|---|---|---|---|---|---|---|---|---|---|---|---|
| **TEMPERATURE °F:** | | | | | | | | | | | | | | |
| Normals | | | | | | | | | | | | | | |
|  -Daily Maximum | | 33.6 | 36.3 | 45.5 | 60.0 | 71.4 | 80.1 | 84.8 | 82.6 | 74.8 | 63.9 | 50.6 | 37.3 | 60.1 |
|  -Daily Minimum | | 16.7 | 18.8 | 28.0 | 37.6 | 47.3 | 57.0 | 61.9 | 60.0 | 51.7 | 40.9 | 32.5 | 20.9 | 39.5 |
|  -Monthly | | 25.2 | 27.6 | 36.8 | 48.8 | 59.4 | 68.6 | 73.4 | 71.3 | 63.3 | 52.4 | 41.6 | 29.1 | 49.8 |
| Extremes | | | | | | | | | | | | | | |
|  -Record Highest | 35 | 65 | 73 | 87 | 96 | 97 | 100 | 102 | 101 | 99 | 91 | 81 | 74 | 102 |
|  -Year | | 1967 | 1985 | 1977 | 1976 | 1979 | 1964 | 1966 | 1975 | 1983 | 1963 | 1974 | 1984 | JUL 1966 |
|  -Record Lowest | 35 | -26 | -21 | -6 | 9 | 28 | 37 | 44 | 36 | 30 | 17 | 1 | -14 | -26 |
|  -Year | | 1961 | 1961 | 1967 | 1970 | 1985 | 1986 | 1962 | 1965 | 1979 | 1978 | 1989 | 1980 | JAN 1961 |
| **NORMAL DEGREE DAYS:** | | | | | | | | | | | | | | |
| Heating (base 65°F) | | 1234 | 1047 | 874 | 486 | 197 | 20 | 0 | 8 | 102 | 391 | 702 | 1113 | 6174 |
| Cooling (base 65°F) | | 0 | 0 | 0 | 0 | 24 | 128 | 260 | 203 | 51 | 0 | 0 | 0 | 666 |
| **% OF POSSIBLE SUNSHINE** | 35 | 56 | 57 | 57 | 55 | 57 | 60 | 63 | 63 | 59 | 58 | 47 | 49 | 57 |
| **MEAN SKY COVER (tenths)** | | | | | | | | | | | | | | |
| Sunrise - Sunset | 35 | 6.4 | 6.5 | 6.7 | 6.7 | 6.8 | 6.6 | 6.4 | 6.3 | 6.1 | 5.9 | 6.9 | 6.7 | 6.5 |
| **MEAN NUMBER OF DAYS:** | | | | | | | | | | | | | | |
| Sunrise to Sunset | | | | | | | | | | | | | | |
|  -Clear | 35 | 7.8 | 6.6 | 6.7 | 6.4 | 5.4 | 5.5 | 5.8 | 6.6 | 8.4 | 9.1 | 5.7 | 6.9 | 80.9 |
|  -Partly Cloudy | 35 | 8.0 | 7.8 | 8.5 | 8.5 | 9.7 | 10.5 | 11.9 | 10.8 | 8.9 | 8.9 | 8.2 | 7.6 | 109.1 |
|  -Cloudy | 35 | 15.2 | 13.9 | 15.9 | 15.2 | 16.0 | 14.0 | 13.3 | 13.6 | 12.7 | 13.0 | 16.1 | 16.5 | 175.2 |
| Precipitation | | | | | | | | | | | | | | |
| .01 inches or more | 35 | 10.6 | 10.2 | 11.3 | 11.1 | 11.8 | 11.5 | 9.7 | 9.8 | 9.4 | 8.3 | 11.2 | 11.9 | 126.8 |
| Snow,Ice pellets | | | | | | | | | | | | | | |
| 1.0 inches or more | 35 | 3.0 | 2.7 | 2.4 | 0.5 | 0.* | 0.0 | 0.0 | 0.0 | 0.0 | 0.* | 0.6 | 3.4 | 12.5 |
| Thunderstorms | 35 | 0.1 | 0.2 | 0.7 | 1.2 | 2.3 | 4.0 | 4.5 | 3.9 | 2.1 | 1.0 | 0.4 | 0.1 | 20.6 |
| Heavy Fog Visibility | | | | | | | | | | | | | | |
| 1/4 mile or less | 35 | 2.1 | 2.5 | 2.2 | 1.3 | 1.8 | 2.4 | 2.0 | 2.3 | 3.3 | 3.6 | 2.2 | 2.9 | 28.6 |
| Temperature °F | | | | | | | | | | | | | | |
|  -Maximum | | | | | | | | | | | | | | |
|   90° and above | 30 | 0.0 | 0.0 | 0.0 | 0.2 | 1.1 | 3.5 | 7.9 | 4.7 | 1.4 | 0.* | 0.0 | 0.0 | 18.9 |
|   32° and below | 30 | 14.3 | 9.3 | 1.9 | 0.1 | 0.0 | 0.0 | 0.0 | 0.0 | 0.0 | 0.0 | 0.5 | 9.9 | 36.0 |
|  -Minimum | | | | | | | | | | | | | | |
|   32° and below | 30 | 29.0 | 25.5 | 21.7 | 8.5 | 0.8 | 0.0 | 0.0 | 0.0 | 0.3 | 6.5 | 16.5 | 27.1 | 135.9 |
|   0° and below | 30 | 3.2 | 1.7 | 0.* | 0.0 | 0.0 | 0.0 | 0.0 | 0.0 | 0.0 | 0.0 | 0.0 | 1.2 | 6.1 |
| **AVG. STATION PRESS.(mb)** | 17 | 1009.7 | 1010.4 | 1009.2 | 1007.2 | 1008.1 | 1008.0 | 1008.5 | 1010.2 | 1011.6 | 1012.1 | 1010.8 | 1010.9 | 1009.7 |
| **RELATIVE HUMIDITY (%)** | | | | | | | | | | | | | | |
| Hour 01 | 30 | 69 | 68 | 68 | 68 | 76 | 80 | 82 | 84 | 86 | 80 | 75 | 73 | 76 |
| Hour 07  (Local Time) | 30 | 71 | 72 | 71 | 69 | 73 | 77 | 78 | 83 | 86 | 83 | 79 | 75 | 76 |
| Hour 13 | 30 | 56 | 54 | 50 | 45 | 47 | 51 | 51 | 53 | 54 | 51 | 56 | 59 | 52 |
| Hour 19 | 30 | 62 | 60 | 56 | 52 | 56 | 60 | 61 | 65 | 71 | 67 | 67 | 67 | 62 |
| **PRECIPITATION (inches):** | | | | | | | | | | | | | | |
| Water Equivalent | | | | | | | | | | | | | | |
|  -Normal | | 3.53 | 3.19 | 4.15 | 4.02 | 3.37 | 3.38 | 3.09 | 4.00 | 3.94 | 3.51 | 4.05 | 4.16 | 44.39 |
|  -Maximum Monthly | 35 | 9.61 | 7.27 | 6.86 | 9.90 | 12.00 | 13.60 | 8.43 | 21.87 | 9.02 | 11.61 | 8.53 | 8.36 | 21.87 |
|  -Year | | 1978 | 1981 | 1983 | 1983 | 1989 | 1982 | 1988 | 1955 | 1975 | 1955 | 1972 | 1969 | AUG 1955 |
|  -Minimum Monthly | 35 | 0.38 | 0.45 | 0.27 | 1.38 | 0.73 | 0.67 | 1.07 | 0.54 | 0.84 | 0.35 | 0.51 | 0.78 | 0.27 |
|  -Year | | 1981 | 1987 | 1981 | 1966 | 1959 | 1988 | 1983 | 1986 | 1963 | 1976 | 1955 | 1955 | MAR 1981 |
|  -Maximum in 24 hrs | 35 | 2.56 | 2.16 | 2.62 | 3.01 | 4.90 | 6.14 | 3.48 | 12.12 | 5.28 | 4.45 | 2.90 | 3.12 | 12.12 |
|  -Year | | 1979 | 1965 | 1987 | 1979 | 1989 | 1982 | 1960 | 1955 | 1960 | 1959 | 1988 | 1973 | AUG 1955 |
| Snow,Ice pellets | | | | | | | | | | | | | | |
|  -Maximum Monthly | 35 | 37.0 | 32.2 | 43.3 | 14.3 | 1.3 | 0.0 | 0.0 | 0.0 | 0.0 | 1.7 | 8.7 | 35.4 | 43.3 |
|  -Year | | 1978 | 1969 | 1956 | 1982 | 1977 | | | | | 1979 | 1986 | 1956 | MAR 1956 |
|  -Maximum in 24 hrs | 35 | 14.7 | 21.0 | 14.0 | 14.1 | 1.3 | 0.0 | 0.0 | 0.0 | 0.0 | 1.7 | 8.6 | 13.9 | 21.0 |
|  -Year | | 1978 | 1983 | 1956 | 1982 | 1977 | | | | | 1979 | 1980 | 1969 | FEB 1983 |
| **WIND:** | | | | | | | | | | | | | | |
| Mean Speed (mph) | 35 | 9.0 | 9.4 | 10.0 | 10.0 | 8.8 | 8.1 | 7.5 | 7.2 | 7.3 | 7.7 | 8.5 | 8.6 | 8.5 |
| Prevailing Direction | | | | | | | | | | | | | | |
|  through 1963 | | NW | NW | NW | S | S | S | S | S | S | N | S | N | S |
| Fastest Mile | | | | | | | | | | | | | | |
|  -Direction (!!!) | 31 | NW | SW | NE | NE | NW | W | SW | NW | S | NW | W | NW | NW |
|  -Speed (MPH) | 31 | 50 | 53 | 50 | 47 | 41 | 48 | 42 | 49 | 63 | 64 | 51 | 49 | 64 |
|  -Year | | 1964 | 1967 | 1956 | 1956 | 1957 | 1981 | 1980 | 1979 | 1979 | 1979 | 1955 | 1955 | OCT 1979 |
| Peak Gust | | | | | | | | | | | | | | |
|  -Direction (!!!) | 6 | NW | NW | S | NW | S | W | SW | S | S | W | S | NW | SW |
|  -Speed (mph) | 6 | 45 | 49 | 62 | 48 | 47 | 48 | 89 | 47 | 66 | 47 | 60 | 49 | 89 |
|  -Date | | 1988 | 1989 | 1987 | 1988 | 1989 | 1989 | 1988 | 1988 | 1985 | 1986 | 1989 | 1988 | JUL 1988 |

**See Reference Notes to this table on the following page.**

**TABLE 2** — PRECIPITATION (inches) — HARTFORD, CONNECTICUT

| YEAR | JAN | FEB | MAR | APR | MAY | JUNE | JULY | AUG | SEP | OCT | NOV | DEC | ANNUAL |
|---|---|---|---|---|---|---|---|---|---|---|---|---|---|
| 1961 | 2.56 | 3.43 | 3.86 | 4.73 | 4.37 | 2.46 | 1.50 | 3.64 | 4.78 | 2.45 | 3.72 | 3.15 | 40.65 |
| 1962 | 3.87 | 4.04 | 1.89 | 3.33 | 2.25 | 3.04 | 1.64 | 6.27 | 4.63 | 4.24 | 2.59 | 2.61 | 40.40 |
| 1963 | 2.92 | 3.33 | 3.68 | 1.57 | 2.28 | 4.25 | 3.89 | 1.59 | 4.98 | 0.35 | 5.66 | 2.42 | 36.92 |
| 1964 | 5.54 | 3.43 | 3.63 | 3.76 | 0.87 | 1.68 | 3.07 | 2.46 | 1.42 | 1.98 | 2.20 | 4.51 | 34.55 |
| 1965 | 2.73 | 4.43 | 1.50 | 2.14 | 1.20 | 1.98 | 1.68 | 1.09 | 3.50 | 4.97 | 2.21 | 2.02 | 29.45 |
| 1966 | 3.05 | 4.40 | 3.15 | 1.38 | 3.01 | 2.72 | 3.96 | 1.90 | 6.05 | 4.23 | 3.82 | 3.60 | 41.27 |
| 1967 | 2.01 | 2.00 | 4.43 | 4.18 | 6.34 | 3.82 | 2.59 | 4.34 | 2.85 | 2.59 | 3.13 | 6.77 | 45.05 |
| 1968 | 1.92 | 1.14 | 4.55 | 2.74 | 3.93 | 6.65 | 1.58 | 2.53 | 2.88 | 2.03 | 5.46 | 5.22 | 40.63 |
| 1969 | 1.19 | 3.32 | 3.11 | 5.63 | 3.13 | 2.63 | 5.79 | 3.32 | 3.53 | 1.45 | 6.17 | 8.36 | 47.63 |
| 1970 | 0.39 | 5.15 | 4.28 | 4.12 | 3.59 | 2.49 | 1.49 | 3.18 | 3.20 | 2.08 | 4.31 | 4.15 | 38.43 |
| 1971 | 2.80 | 4.60 | 3.24 | 2.85 | 4.08 | 0.71 | 3.23 | 5.31 | 4.24 | 4.46 | 5.68 | 3.55 | 44.75 |
| 1972 | 2.02 | 5.12 | 6.71 | 4.61 | 7.49 | 9.66 | 3.84 | 3.45 | 1.84 | 4.20 | 8.53 | 7.08 | 64.55 |
| 1973 | 3.28 | 3.05 | 3.22 | 6.59 | 5.95 | 5.07 | 1.77 | 4.50 | 3.73 | 3.47 | 2.14 | 8.31 | 51.08 |
| 1974 | 4.10 | 1.95 | 3.64 | 3.64 | 3.03 | 2.38 | 2.39 | 3.36 | 8.57 | 2.34 | 2.62 | 4.52 | 43.39 |
| 1975 | 4.30 | 3.22 | 3.82 | 2.99 | 3.29 | 3.83 | 6.11 | 4.60 | 9.02 | 5.28 | 4.57 | 4.31 | 55.34 |
| 1976 | 5.57 | 3.11 | 2.86 | 3.93 | 4.45 | 2.86 | 3.51 | 5.76 | 2.55 | 4.10 | 0.51 | 2.97 | 42.18 |
| 1977 | 2.41 | 2.81 | 6.57 | 4.89 | 3.70 | 3.99 | 3.37 | 2.44 | 8.17 | 5.45 | 4.38 | 5.68 | 53.86 |
| 1978 | 9.61 | 1.42 | 3.63 | 1.51 | 4.61 | 2.94 | 2.51 | 3.61 | 2.67 | 1.75 | 2.12 | 4.23 | 40.61 |
| 1979 | 9.12 | 2.83 | 4.25 | 5.88 | 3.48 | 0.91 | 1.97 | 4.44 | 2.95 | 4.76 | 3.46 | 2.57 | 46.62 |
| 1980 | 0.72 | 0.98 | 5.87 | 5.39 | 1.65 | 3.81 | 2.65 | 1.60 | 1.40 | 2.58 | 4.22 | 0.82 | 31.69 |
| 1981 | 0.38 | 7.27 | 0.27 | 2.92 | 2.17 | 1.37 | 4.21 | 0.54 | 4.49 | 5.19 | 2.34 | 4.00 | 35.15 |
| 1982 | 4.76 | 2.83 | 2.23 | 4.12 | 3.30 | 13.60 | 2.60 | 4.41 | 2.41 | 3.31 | 3.12 | 1.32 | 48.01 |
| 1983 | 4.68 | 3.83 | 6.86 | 9.90 | 4.82 | 2.61 | 1.07 | 2.55 | 2.10 | 5.52 | 6.09 | 5.97 | 56.00 |
| 1984 | 1.80 | 4.72 | 3.93 | 4.24 | 11.55 | 2.16 | 4.22 | 1.32 | 1.20 | 2.76 | 2.49 | 2.46 | 42.85 |
| 1985 | 0.73 | 1.72 | 2.16 | 1.54 | 2.77 | 3.55 | 4.55 | 6.44 | 3.83 | 2.27 | 6.04 | 1.28 | 36.88 |
| 1986 | 5.34 | 3.02 | 2.72 | 1.55 | 2.28 | 6.79 | 4.44 | 3.44 | 0.84 | 2.18 | 5.57 | 6.15 | 44.32 |
| 1987 | 6.20 | 0.45 | 4.44 | 5.23 | 2.18 | 3.66 | 2.27 | 4.25 | 7.19 | 3.67 | 3.66 | 1.57 | 44.77 |
| 1988 | 3.36 | 3.99 | 2.06 | 2.35 | 3.46 | 0.67 | 8.43 | 2.12 | 1.88 | 2.29 | 7.84 | 1.35 | 39.80 |
| 1989 | 0.88 | 1.85 | 3.02 | 3.33 | 12.00 | 6.65 | 3.40 | 6.81 | 4.67 | 7.62 | 2.89 | 1.49 | 54.61 |
| 1990 | 4.03 | 3.37 | 2.46 | 4.55 | 6.38 | 3.59 | 2.09 | 8.32 | 2.13 | 7.63 | 3.76 | 4.86 | 53.17 |
| Record Mean | 3.53 | 3.20 | 3.69 | 3.7⌐ | 3.72 | 3.59 | 3.55 | 3.88 | 3.59 | 3.25 | 3.83 | 3.70 | 43.30 |

**TABLE 3** — AVERAGE TEMPERATURE (deg. F) — HARTFORD, CONNECTICUT

| YEAR | JAN | FEB | MAR | APR | MAY | JUNE | JULY | AUG | SEP | OCT | NOV | DEC | ANNUAL |
|---|---|---|---|---|---|---|---|---|---|---|---|---|---|
| 1961 | 16.9 | 27.4 | 35.3 | 45.1 | 56.0 | 69.0 | 72.8 | 71.8 | 68.7 | 54.4 | 41.3 | 28.9 | 49.0 |
| 1962 | 25.3 | 23.4 | 37.2 | 48.4 | 58.9 | 68.4 | 69.0 | 69.2 | 60.0 | 50.9 | 37.4 | 22.5 | 47.6 |
| 1963 | 23.6 | 21.6 | 36.1 | 48.3 | 58.1 | 68.9 | 72.9 | 68.0 | 60.0 | 57.1 | 46.5 | 21.5 | 48.6 |
| 1964 | 27.1 | 25.9 | 37.7 | 48.8 | 62.6 | 68.3 | 75.0 | 68.1 | 63.0 | 51.3 | 43.3 | 29.7 | 50.1 |
| 1965 | 22.5 | 26.6 | 36.1 | 47.5 | 64.4 | 68.9 | 72.4 | 71.7 | 64.1 | 51.1 | 39.6 | 33.8 | 49.9 |
| 1966 | 26.4 | 28.8 | 39.1 | 46.9 | 56.4 | 70.7 | 75.8 | 73.4 | 63.4 | 51.9 | 46.2 | 31.8 | 50.9 |
| 1967 | 32.8 | 24.5 | 33.3 | 47.1 | 53.7 | 70.6 | 74.0 | 70.2 | 62.8 | 52.8 | 38.0 | 32.1 | 49.4 |
| 1968 | 21.1 | 25.8 | 39.9 | 52.4 | 58.2 | 67.4 | 75.1 | 70.8 | 65.0 | 54.7 | 38.9 | 25.4 | 49.6 |
| 1969 | 24.0 | 26.8 | 34.5 | 51.1 | 58.8 | 68.2 | 70.6 | 73.3 | 63.8 | 51.7 | 41.2 | 26.9 | 49.2 |
| 1970 | 16.8 | 28.2 | 35.1 | 49.0 | 61.5 | 67.8 | 75.2 | 73.8 | 65.4 | 54.9 | 44.1 | 26.8 | 49.9 |
| 1971 | 19.4 | 29.0 | 35.4 | 46.3 | 58.1 | 71.0 | 73.7 | 72.2 | 67.7 | 58.3 | 39.6 | 32.8 | 50.3 |
| 1972 | 27.9 | 26.0 | 34.6 | 44.3 | 60.1 | 65.9 | 73.8 | 71.1 | 64.3 | 48.9 | 38.7 | 30.8 | 48.9 |
| 1973 | 29.4 | 27.2 | 43.3 | 50.4 | 58.0 | 71.8 | 75.0 | 76.4 | 64.7 | 54.7 | 43.6 | 32.9 | 52.3 |
| 1974 | 28.2 | 27.0 | 36.8 | 50.7 | 56.6 | 67.3 | 73.7 | 72.7 | 63.3 | 47.3 | 40.7 | 30.7 | 49.6 |
| 1975 | 31.2 | 29.7 | 35.9 | 45.8 | 64.6 | 68.3 | 76.1 | 71.8 | 61.7 | 55.7 | 48.2 | 28.5 | 51.4 |
| 1976 | 19.5 | 34.8 | 40.3 | 53.3 | 58.4 | 72.7 | 72.4 | 71.0 | 62.4 | 49.9 | 38.3 | 24.8 | 49.8 |
| 1977 | 18.7 | 27.6 | 42.9 | 51.2 | 63.6 | 68.0 | 74.5 | 72.8 | 64.0 | 52.0 | 44.4 | 28.0 | 50.6 |
| 1978 | 23.6 | 22.1 | 35.1 | 48.1 | 59.9 | 69.2 | 71.9 | 70.0 | 58.6 | 49.0 | 38.6 | 29.3 | 47.9 |
| 1979 | 26.6 | 18.0 | 41.2 | 49.0 | 64.1 | 69.0 | 74.6 | 70.8 | 61.6 | 50.7 | 45.5 | 33.6 | 50.4 |
| 1980 | 27.6 | 24.3 | 35.2 | 49.2 | 61.0 | 66.4 | 74.2 | 73.2 | 64.9 | 50.3 | 37.9 | 24.6 | 49.1 |
| 1981 | 17.8 | 35.3 | 38.1 | 52.0 | 61.6 | 69.6 | 74.8 | 70.6 | 62.5 | 49.3 | 43.7 | 31.0 | 50.6 |
| 1982 | 18.8 | 29.2 | 36.7 | 45.8 | 61.4 | 65.0 | 74.4 | 69.5 | 63.0 | 51.5 | 45.8 | 36.0 | 49.8 |
| 1983 | 27.1 | 29.1 | 39.2 | 48.9 | 56.8 | 69.9 | 74.9 | 72.7 | 66.5 | 52.5 | 42.7 | 28.1 | 50.7 |
| 1984 | 21.8 | 34.3 | 31.4 | 48.0 | 56.0 | 69.8 | 71.8 | 73.2 | 59.8 | 55.2 | 41.5 | 35.7 | 49.9 |
| 1985 | 21.5 | 29.9 | 39.7 | 50.7 | 60.6 | 63.7 | 72.4 | 70.2 | 63.4 | 51.9 | 43.2 | 27.5 | 49.6 |
| 1986 | 27.4 | 26.2 | 38.7 | 51.0 | 61.7 | 66.0 | 72.3 | 69.5 | 61.8 | 51.4 | 38.3 | 33.1 | 49.8 |
| 1987 | 25.0 | 26.7 | 39.8 | 49.7 | 60.8 | 68.8 | 74.2 | 69.0 | 62.9 | 49.2 | 41.4 | 33.2 | 50.1 |
| 1988 | 23.1 | 28.3 | 38.5 | 47.4 | 59.7 | 66.7 | 75.2 | 74.5 | 62.2 | 47.6 | 42.3 | 29.3 | 49.6 |
| 1989 | 30.8 | 28.6 | 37.4 | 46.5 | 60.4 | 68.3 | 72.6 | 71.4 | 63.9 | 53.4 | 40.9 | 18.1 | 49.4 |
| 1990 | 34.7 | 33.0 | 40.2 | 49.2 | 56.7 | 69.0 | 74.4 | 73.3 | 64.0 | 57.4 | 44.5 | 36.7 | 52.8 |
| Record Mean | 26.6 | 27.8 | 37.2 | 48.2 | 59.1 | 67.8 | 73.2 | 71.0 | 63.5 | 53.0 | 42.1 | 30.3 | 50.0 |
| Max | 34.8 | 36.3 | 46.1 | 58.5 | 70.2 | 78.6 | 83.7 | 81.4 | 74.1 | 63.7 | 50.7 | 38.1 | 59.7 |
| Min | 18.5 | 19.3 | 28.2 | 37.8 | 48.0 | 57.1 | 62.7 | 60.6 | 52.9 | 42.2 | 33.4 | 22.5 | 40.3 |

## REFERENCE NOTES FOR TABLES 1, 2, 3 and 6 (HARTFORD, CT)

### GENERAL

T - TRACE AMOUNT
BLANK ENTRIES DENOTE MISSING/UNREPORTED DATA.
# INDICATES A STATION OR INSTRUMENT RELOCATION.

### SPECIFIC

**TABLE 1**

(a) - LENGTH OF RECORD IN YEARS. ALTHOUGH INDIVIDUAL MONTHS MAY BE MISSING.
* LESS THAN .05

NORMALS — BASED ON THE 1951-1980 RECORD PERIOD.
EXTREMES — DATES ARE THE MOST RECENT OCCURRENCE.
WIND DIR. — NUMERALS SHOW TENS OF DEGREES CLOCKWISE FROM TRUE NORTH.
"00" INDICATES CALM.
RESULTANT WIND DIRECTIONS ARE GIVEN TO WHOLE DEGREES.

**TABLE 3**
MAX AND MIN ARE LONG-TERM MEAN DAILY MAXIMUM AND MEAN DAILY MINIMUM TEMPERATURES.

### EXCEPTIONS

**TABLES 2, 3, and 6**

RECORD MEANS ARE THROUGH THE CURRENT YEAR, BEGINNING IN
 1905 FOR TEMPERATURE
 1905 FOR PRECIPITATION
 1955 FOR SNOWFALL

**TABLE 4**  HEATING DEGREE DAYS Base 65 deg. F      HARTFORD, CONNECTICUT

| SEASON | JULY | AUG | SEP | OCT | NOV | DEC | JAN | FEB | MAR | APR | MAY | JUNE | TOTAL |
|---|---|---|---|---|---|---|---|---|---|---|---|---|---|
| 1961-62 | 5 | 8 | 78 | 322 | 706 | 1110 | 1225 | 1160 | 854 | 501 | 230 | 22 | 6221 |
| 1962-63 | 3 | 20 | 179 | 428 | 819 | 1310 | 1277 | 1209 | 890 | 494 | 222 | 43 | 6894 |
| 1963-64 | 11 | 11 | 179 | 246 | 551 | 1342 | 1169 | 1129 | 842 | 481 | 127 | 46 | 6134 |
| 1964-65 | 2 | 16 | 128 | 419 | 644 | 1084 | 1311 | 1068 | 888 | 518 | 99 | 45 | 6222 |
| 1965-66 | 2 | 34 | 110 | 426 | 753 | 961 | 1186 | 1008 | 792 | 534 | 275 | 31 | 6112 |
| 1966-67 | 0 | 0 | 98 | 398 | 554 | 1019 | 993 | 1126 | 976 | 530 | 349 | 18 | 6061 |
| 1967-68 | 0 | 10 | 112 | 380 | 803 | 1013 | 1353 | 1134 | 771 | 374 | 205 | 46 | 6201 |
| 1968-69 | 0 | 16 | 56 | 326 | 775 | 1219 | 1262 | 1063 | 938 | 415 | 221 | 27 | 6318 |
| 1969-70 | 8 | 7 | 116 | 409 | 707 | 1175 | 1485 | 1026 | 922 | 483 | 161 | 37 | 6536 |
| 1970-71 | 0 | 0 | 89 | 322 | 619 | 1177 | 1410 | 1001 | 911 | 556 | 215 | 17 | 6317 |
| 1971-72 | 2 | 11 | 55 | 214 | 756 | 992 | 1140 | 1125 | 935 | 619 | 172 | 50 | 6071 |
| 1972-73 | 6 | 9 | 82 | 494 | 782 | 1054 | 1097 | 1051 | 665 | 444 | 229 | 13 | 5926 |
| 1973-74 | 0 | 0 | 102 | 322 | 635 | 988 | 1134 | 1056 | 868 | 435 | 287 | 37 | 5864 |
| 1974-75 | 2 | 1 | 121 | 542 | 725 | 1057 | 1040 | 986 | 894 | 567 | 111 | 43 | 6089 |
| 1975-76 | 0 | 11 | 121 | 292 | 503 | 1125 | 1403 | 869 | 759 | 391 | 213 | 20 | 5707 |
| 1976-77 | 0 | 16 | 118 | 467 | 794 | 1242 | 1429 | 1038 | 684 | 419 | 130 | 45 | 6382 |
| 1977-78 | 1 | 8 | 112 | 399 | 610 | 1141 | 1276 | 1192 | 920 | 500 | 220 | 25 | 6404 |
| 1978-79 | 9 | 15 | 209 | 489 | 790 | 1102 | 1184 | 1310 | 730 | 473 | 81 | 26 | 6418 |
| 1979-80 | 16 | 30 | 152 | 442 | 578 | 965 | 1151 | 1174 | 916 | 466 | 146 | 68 | 6104 |
| 1980-81 | 0 | 0 | 99 | 449 | 808 | 1246 | 1456 | 824 | 828 | 380 | 149 | 10 | 6249 |
| 1981-82 | 0 | 9 | 115 | 481 | 635 | 1048 | 1427 | 996 | 871 | 569 | 128 | 64 | 6343 |
| 1982-83 | 1 | 30 | 96 | 416 | 575 | 894 | 1170 | 1002 | 793 | 483 | 261 | 24 | 5745 |
| 1983-84 | 0 | 7 | 106 | 404 | 662 | 1135 | 1332 | 884 | 1035 | 503 | 286 | 32 | 6386 |
| 1984-85 | 3 | 3 | 186 | 298 | 698 | 896 | 1341 | 975 | 776 | 428 | 167 | 76 | 5847 |
| 1985-86 | 0 | 14 | 119 | 401 | 648 | 1157 | 1159 | 1081 | 809 | 413 | 174 | 63 | 6038 |
| 1986-87 | 14 | 32 | 135 | 422 | 793 | 981 | 1230 | 1065 | 773 | 452 | 191 | 29 | 6117 |
| 1987-88 | 1 | 31 | 100 | 481 | 700 | 981 | 1292 | 1057 | 817 | 523 | 186 | 75 | 6244 |
| 1988-89 | 9 | 23 | 112 | 539 | 672 | 1101 | 1054 | 1012 | 847 | 553 | 175 | 31 | 6128 |
| 1989-90 | 0 | 22 | 103 | 354 | 715 | 1444 | 935 | 890 | 763 | 478 | 251 | 21 | 5976 |
| 1990-91 | 5 | 0 | 112 | 276 | 608 | 873 | | | | | | | |

**TABLE 5**  COOLING DEGREE DAYS Base 65 deg. F      HARTFORD, CONNECTICUT

| YEAR | JAN | FEB | MAR | APR | MAY | JUNE | JULY | AUG | SEP | OCT | NOV | DEC | TOTAL |
|---|---|---|---|---|---|---|---|---|---|---|---|---|---|
| 1969 | 0 | 0 | 0 | 4 | 35 | 131 | 189 | 273 | 88 | 5 | 0 | 0 | 725 |
| 1970 | 0 | 0 | 0 | 8 | 58 | 129 | 322 | 280 | 108 | 16 | 0 | 0 | 921 |
| 1971 | 0 | 0 | 0 | 0 | 7 | 201 | 274 | 243 | 142 | 11 | 4 | 0 | 882 |
| 1972 | 0 | 0 | 0 | 3 | 30 | 83 | 286 | 203 | 70 | 1 | 0 | 0 | 676 |
| 1973 | 0 | 0 | 0 | 11 | 19 | 221 | 318 | 362 | 99 | 8 | 0 | 0 | 1038 |
| 1974 | 0 | 0 | 0 | 11 | 34 | 110 | 282 | 247 | 77 | 0 | 3 | 0 | 764 |
| 1975 | 0 | 0 | 0 | 0 | 106 | 147 | 348 | 229 | 27 | 7 | 6 | 0 | 870 |
| 1976 | 0 | 0 | 0 | 47 | 18 | 257 | 236 | 208 | 47 | 6 | 0 | 0 | 819 |
| 1977 | 0 | 0 | 4 | 13 | 93 | 144 | 303 | 259 | 88 | 1 | 0 | 0 | 905 |
| 1978 | 0 | 0 | 0 | 0 | 71 | 159 | 228 | 173 | 26 | 0 | 0 | 0 | 657 |
| 1979 | 0 | 0 | 0 | 0 | 60 | 151 | 320 | 218 | 56 | 6 | 0 | 0 | 811 |
| 1980 | 0 | 0 | 0 | 0 | 31 | 117 | 296 | 263 | 107 | 1 | 0 | 0 | 815 |
| 1981 | 0 | 0 | 0 | 0 | 53 | 152 | 311 | 190 | 48 | 0 | 0 | 0 | 754 |
| 1982 | 0 | 0 | 0 | 0 | 22 | 70 | 298 | 176 | 45 | 2 | 3 | 0 | 616 |
| 1983 | 0 | 0 | 0 | 5 | 16 | 177 | 313 | 253 | 158 | 23 | 0 | 0 | 945 |
| 1984 | 0 | 0 | 0 | 0 | 11 | 182 | 218 | 265 | 38 | 4 | 0 | 0 | 718 |
| 1985 | 0 | 0 | 0 | 3 | 37 | 44 | 234 | 182 | 78 | 3 | 0 | 0 | 581 |
| 1986 | 0 | 0 | 0 | 0 | 79 | 103 | 249 | 179 | 48 | 7 | 0 | 0 | 665 |
| 1987 | 0 | 0 | 0 | 3 | 70 | 150 | 292 | 161 | 42 | 0 | 0 | 0 | 718 |
| 1988 | 0 | 0 | 0 | 0 | 27 | 134 | 331 | 326 | 37 | 6 | 0 | 0 | 861 |
| 1989 | 0 | 0 | 0 | 0 | 37 | 136 | 240 | 224 | 77 | 0 | 0 | 0 | 714 |
| 1990 | 0 | 0 | 0 | 13 | 1 | 146 | 305 | 263 | 89 | 48 | 1 | 0 | 866 |

**TABLE 6**  SNOWFALL (inches)      HARTFORD, CONNECTICUT

| SEASON | JULY | AUG | SEP | OCT | NOV | DEC | JAN | FEB | MAR | APR | MAY | JUNE | TOTAL |
|---|---|---|---|---|---|---|---|---|---|---|---|---|---|
| 1961-62 | 0.0 | 0.0 | 0.0 | 0.0 | 5.0 | 11.3 | 1.6 | 22.9 | 0.7 | T | 0.0 | 0.0 | 41.5 |
| 1962-63 | 0.0 | 0.0 | 0.0 | T | 2.4 | 15.9 | 7.7 | 14.5 | 13.8 | T | 0.0 | 0.0 | 54.3 |
| 1963-64 | 0.0 | 0.0 | 0.0 | T | T | 16.1 | 13.8 | 22.0 | 4.1 | T | 0.0 | 0.0 | 56.0 |
| 1964-65 | 0.0 | 0.0 | 0.0 | T | T | 12.3 | 28.7 | 6.0 | 7.8 | 1.7 | 0.0 | 0.0 | 56.5 |
| 1965-66 | 0.0 | 0.0 | 0.0 | 0.0 | T | 4.5 | 18.4 | 19.1 | 10.6 | T | 0.0 | 0.0 | 52.6 |
| 1966-67 | 0.0 | 0.0 | 0.0 | 0.0 | T | 20.0 | 3.0 | 25.2 | 33.2 | 1.4 | T | 0.0 | 82.8 |
| 1967-68 | 0.0 | 0.0 | 0.0 | 0.0 | 3.7 | 21.7 | 7.5 | 1.6 | 6.8 | 0.0 | 0.0 | 0.0 | 41.3 |
| 1968-69 | 0.0 | 0.0 | 0.0 | 0.0 | 7.9 | 13.9 | 3.4 | 32.2 | 4.4 | 0.0 | 0.0 | 0.0 | 61.8 |
| 1969-70 | 0.0 | 0.0 | 0.0 | T | T | 35.4 | 3.2 | 6.7 | 14.7 | 2.0 | 0.0 | 0.0 | 62.0 |
| 1970-71 | 0.0 | 0.0 | 0.0 | T | T | 27.0 | 17.7 | 8.4 | 12.8 | 4.0 | 0.0 | 0.0 | 69.9 |
| 1971-72 | 0.0 | 0.0 | 0.0 | 0.0 | 8.2 | 6.6 | 2.9 | 24.9 | 13.2 | 2.7 | 0.0 | 0.0 | 58.5 |
| 1972-73 | 0.0 | 0.0 | 0.0 | 0.4 | 2.1 | 12.0 | 14.1 | 5.9 | 0.4 | 0.3 | 0.0 | 0.0 | 35.2 |
| 1973-74 | 0.0 | 0.0 | 0.0 | 0.0 | T | 3.1 | 14.3 | 5.8 | 4.8 | 2.1 | 0.0 | 0.0 | 30.1 |
| 1974-75 | 0.0 | 0.0 | 0.0 | T | 0.8 | 8.5 | 10.2 | 16.0 | 2.5 | 0.3 | 0.0 | 0.0 | 38.3 |
| 1975-76 | 0.0 | 0.0 | 0.0 | 0.0 | 0.3 | 13.4 | 15.6 | 12.3 | 5.0 | 0.0 | 0.0 | 0.0 | 46.6 |
| 1976-77 | 0.0 | 0.0 | 0.0 | 0.0 | 0.4 | 7.3 | 20.0 | 9.1 | 11.0 | 0.3 | 1.3 | 0.0 | 49.4 |
| 1977-78 | 0.0 | 0.0 | 0.0 | 0.0 | 1.3 | 12.6 | 37.0 | 18.1 | 13.3 | T | 0.0 | 0.0 | 82.3 |
| 1978-79 | 0.0 | 0.0 | 0.0 | 0.0 | 4.3 | 10.3 | 8.6 | 9.2 | T | 3.6 | 0.0 | 0.0 | 36.0 |
| 1979-80 | 0.0 | 0.0 | 0.0 | 1.7 | 0.0 | 0.9 | 0.2 | 7.7 | 5.9 | T | 0.0 | 0.0 | 16.4 |
| 1980-81 | 0.0 | 0.0 | 0.0 | 0.0 | 8.6 | 3.9 | 4.1 | 0.9 | 0.2 | 0.0 | 0.0 | 0.0 | 17.7 |
| 1981-82 | 0.0 | 0.0 | 0.0 | T | T | 13.1 | 16.7 | 5.8 | 6.5 | 14.3 | 0.0 | 0.0 | 56.4 |
| 1982-83 | 0.0 | 0.0 | 0.0 | 0.0 | T | 5.7 | 10.2 | 29.4 | 0.2 | 0.9 | 0.0 | 0.0 | 46.4 |
| 1983-84 | 0.0 | 0.0 | 0.0 | 0.0 | T | 7.9 | 14.7 | 1.3 | 19.3 | T | 0.0 | 0.0 | 43.2 |
| 1984-85 | 0.0 | 0.0 | 0.0 | 0.0 | 0.1 | 3.8 | 6.9 | 9.4 | 2.1 | 1.4 | 0.0 | 0.0 | 23.7 |
| 1985-86 | 0.0 | 0.0 | 0.0 | 0.0 | 2.0 | 5.4 | 5.1 | 11.8 | 0.2 | 0.8 | 0.0 | 0.0 | 25.3 |
| 1986-87 | 0.0 | 0.0 | 0.0 | 0.0 | 8.7 | 4.9 | 34.0 | 1.6 | 1.7 | 0.4 | 0.0 | 0.0 | 51.3 |
| 1987-88 | 0.0 | 0.0 | 0.0 | T | 8.6 | 5.8 | 22.6 | 17.6 | 4.9 | T | T | 0.0 | 59.5 |
| 1988-89 | 0.0 | 0.0 | 0.0 | 0.0 | 0.0 | 6.3 | 0.6 | 4.6 | 3.4 | T | T | 0.0 | 14.9 |
| 1989-90 | 0.0 | 0.0 | 0.0 | 0.0 | 5.3 | 12.4 | 10.5 | 9.0 | 4.3 | 1.5 | 0.0 | 0.0 | 43.0 |
| 1990-91 | 0.0 | 0.0 | 0.0 | 0.0 | T | 8.1 | | | | | | | |
| Record Mean | 0.0 | 0.0 | 0.0 | 0.1 | 2.1 | 10.6 | 12.3 | 11.6 | 9.5 | 1.6 | T | 0.0 | 47.9 |

**See Reference Notes, relative to all above tables, on preceding page.**

Delaware is part of the Atlantic Coastal Plain consisting mainly of flat low land with many marshes. Small streams and tidal estuaries comprise the drainage of the State. Wilmington, at the northern end of the State, marks the beginning of low rolling hills extending northward and northwestward into Pennsylvania. The Delaware River, the Delaware Bay, and the Atlantic Ocean are along the eastern boundary of the State. The broad Chesapeake Bay lies 35 miles, or less, to the west of the western boundary of nearly the entire State. These large water areas considerably influence the climate of the Wilmington, Delaware region.

Summers are warm and humid, winters are usually mild. During the summer maximum temperatures are usually in the 80s. The temperature reaches 100 degrees on the average once in six years. During January, the coldest month of the year, the daily average temperature is 32 degrees. Temperatures of zero may be expected once in four years. Most of the winter precipitation falls as rain. Seasonal snowfall has been as little as 1 inch, and as much as 50 inches. Snow is frequently mixed with rain and sleet, and seldom remains on the ground more than a few days.

The proximity of large water areas and the inflow of southerly winds cause the relative humidity to be quite high all year. During the summer months the relative humidity is approximately 75 percent. Fog is relatively frequent and may occur in any month. Light southeast winds blowing up the Delaware Bay favor the formation of fog. Light north-northeast winds bring in smoke from Philadelphia and from the heavy industry area located along the Delaware River north of Wilmington.

Rainfall distribution throughout the year is fairly uniform, however, the greatest amounts normally come during the summer months. Mostly, the summer rainfall comes in the form of thunderstorms. Moisture deficiencies for crops occur occasionally, but severe droughts are rare. During the fall, winter, and spring seasons, much of the rainfall comes from storms forming over the southern states or the South Atlantic and moving northward along the coast. During the late summer and early fall, hurricanes occasionally cause heavy rainfall, but winds seldom reach hurricane force in Wilmington. Heavy rains occasionally cause minor flooding, but the streams and rivers of northern Delaware are not subject to major flooding. Strong easterly and southeasterly winds sometimes cause high tides in the Delaware Bay and the Delaware River, resulting in the flooding of lowlands and damage to bay front and river front properties.

Based on the 1951-1980 period, the average first occurrence of 32 degrees Fahrenheit in the fall is October 29 and the average last occurrence in the spring is April 13.

## TABLE 1    NORMALS, MEANS AND EXTREMES

WILMINGTON, DELAWARE

LATITUDE: 39°40'N    LONGITUDE: 75°36'W    ELEVATION: FT. GRND  74 BARO   96    TIME ZONE: EASTERN    WBAN: 13781

| | (a) | JAN | FEB | MAR | APR | MAY | JUNE | JULY | AUG | SEP | OCT | NOV | DEC | YEAR |
|---|---|---|---|---|---|---|---|---|---|---|---|---|---|---|
| **TEMPERATURE °F:** | | | | | | | | | | | | | | |
| Normals | | | | | | | | | | | | | | |
| -Daily Maximum | | 39.2 | 41.8 | 50.9 | 63.0 | 72.7 | 81.2 | 85.6 | 84.1 | 77.8 | 66.7 | 54.8 | 43.6 | 63.5 |
| -Daily Minimum | | 23.2 | 24.6 | 32.6 | 41.8 | 51.7 | 61.2 | 66.3 | 65.4 | 58.0 | 45.9 | 36.4 | 27.3 | 44.5 |
| -Monthly | | 31.2 | 33.2 | 41.8 | 52.4 | 62.2 | 71.2 | 76.0 | 74.8 | 67.9 | 56.3 | 45.6 | 35.5 | 54.0 |
| Extremes | | | | | | | | | | | | | | |
| -Record Highest | 42 | 75 | 78 | 86 | 94 | 95 | 99 | 102 | 101 | 100 | 91 | 85 | 74 | 102 |
| -Year | | 1950 | 1985 | 1948 | 1985 | 1962 | 1952 | 1966 | 1955 | 1983 | 1951 | 1950 | 1984 | JUL 1966 |
| -Record Lowest | 42 | -14 | -6 | 2 | 18 | 30 | 41 | 48 | 43 | 36 | 24 | 14 | -7 | -14 |
| -Year | | 1985 | 1979 | 1984 | 1982 | 1978 | 1972 | 1988 | 1982 | 1974 | 1976 | 1955 | 1983 | JAN 1985 |
| **NORMAL DEGREE DAYS:** | | | | | | | | | | | | | | |
| Heating (base 65°F) | | 1048 | 890 | 719 | 378 | 130 | 6 | 0 | 0 | 36 | 282 | 582 | 915 | 4986 |
| Cooling (base 65°F) | | 0 | 0 | 0 | 0 | 43 | 192 | 341 | 304 | 123 | 12 | 0 | 0 | 1015 |
| **% OF POSSIBLE SUNSHINE** | | | | | | | | | | | | | | |
| **MEAN SKY COVER (tenths)** | | | | | | | | | | | | | | |
| Sunrise - Sunset | 42 | 6.6 | 6.4 | 6.4 | 6.4 | 6.5 | 6.0 | 5.9 | 5.8 | 5.7 | 5.5 | 6.4 | 6.5 | 6.2 |
| **MEAN NUMBER OF DAYS:** | | | | | | | | | | | | | | |
| Sunrise to Sunset | | | | | | | | | | | | | | |
| -Clear | 42 | 7.5 | 7.3 | 7.8 | 7.3 | 6.4 | 7.8 | 8.0 | 9.0 | 10.0 | 10.7 | 7.6 | 7.7 | 96.9 |
| -Partly Cloudy | 42 | 7.0 | 6.8 | 8.2 | 8.4 | 9.9 | 10.5 | 11.3 | 10.3 | 8.1 | 8.3 | 8.2 | 7.5 | 104.6 |
| -Cloudy | 42 | 16.5 | 14.2 | 15.0 | 14.3 | 14.6 | 11.7 | 11.7 | 11.8 | 12.0 | 12.0 | 14.2 | 15.8 | 163.8 |
| Precipitation | | | | | | | | | | | | | | |
| .01 inches or more | 42 | 10.8 | 9.6 | 10.8 | 10.9 | 11.5 | 9.6 | 9.2 | 8.9 | 8.0 | 7.7 | 9.5 | 9.7 | 116.2 |
| Snow,Ice pellets | | | | | | | | | | | | | | |
| 1.0 inches or more | 42 | 2.2 | 1.5 | 0.9 | 0.1 | 0.0 | 0.0 | 0.0 | 0.0 | 0.0 | 0.* | 0.2 | 0.9 | 5.9 |
| Thunderstorms | 42 | 0.2 | 0.3 | 1.2 | 2.2 | 4.4 | 5.8 | 6.2 | 5.8 | 2.3 | 0.9 | 0.6 | 0.2 | 30.0 |
| Heavy Fog Visibility | | | | | | | | | | | | | | |
| 1/4 mile or less | 42 | 4.1 | 3.5 | 2.9 | 2.0 | 2.4 | 1.8 | 1.7 | 2.5 | 2.5 | 4.0 | 3.6 | 3.6 | 34.5 |
| Temperature °F | | | | | | | | | | | | | | |
| -Maximum | | | | | | | | | | | | | | |
| 90° and above | 42 | 0.0 | 0.0 | 0.0 | 0.1 | 0.7 | 3.8 | 8.0 | 5.1 | 1.7 | 0.* | 0.0 | 0.0 | 19.6 |
| 32° and below | 42 | 7.7 | 4.5 | 0.8 | 0.0 | 0.0 | 0.0 | 0.0 | 0.0 | 0.0 | 0.0 | 0.1 | 4.1 | 17.3 |
| -Minimum | | | | | | | | | | | | | | |
| 32° and below | 42 | 25.8 | 22.2 | 15.3 | 3.1 | 0.* | 0.0 | 0.0 | 0.0 | 0.0 | 1.6 | 10.3 | 22.5 | 100.8 |
| 0° and below | 42 | 0.5 | 0.2 | 0.0 | 0.0 | 0.0 | 0.0 | 0.0 | 0.0 | 0.0 | 0.0 | 0.0 | 0.1 | 0.8 |
| **AVG. STATION PRESS.(mb)** | 17 | 1015.6 | 1015.7 | 1014.0 | 1012.1 | 1012.4 | 1012.5 | 1013.1 | 1014.4 | 1015.7 | 1016.8 | 1016.0 | 1016.4 | 1014.6 |
| **RELATIVE HUMIDITY (%)** | | | | | | | | | | | | | | |
| Hour 01 | 42 | 73 | 72 | 71 | 72 | 79 | 82 | 82 | 84 | 84 | 82 | 77 | 74 | 78 |
| Hour 07 | 42 | 75 | 75 | 73 | 73 | 76 | 78 | 79 | 83 | 85 | 84 | 80 | 76 | 78 |
| Hour 13 (Local Time) | 42 | 60 | 57 | 52 | 50 | 53 | 54 | 54 | 56 | 56 | 54 | 56 | 59 | 55 |
| Hour 19 | 42 | 68 | 65 | 61 | 59 | 64 | 65 | 66 | 69 | 71 | 70 | 69 | 69 | 66 |
| **PRECIPITATION (inches):** | | | | | | | | | | | | | | |
| Water Equivalent | | | | | | | | | | | | | | |
| -Normal | | 3.11 | 2.99 | 3.87 | 3.39 | 3.23 | 3.51 | 3.90 | 4.03 | 3.59 | 2.89 | 3.33 | 3.54 | 41.38 |
| -Maximum Monthly | 42 | 8.41 | 7.02 | 6.84 | 6.80 | 7.38 | 7.49 | 12.63 | 12.09 | 9.53 | 6.41 | 7.84 | 7.90 | 12.63 |
| -Year | | 1978 | 1979 | 1983 | 1983 | 1983 | 1972 | 1989 | 1955 | 1960 | 1971 | 1972 | 1969 | JUL 1989 |
| -Minimum Monthly | 42 | 0.52 | 0.83 | 0.81 | 0.35 | 0.22 | 0.21 | 0.16 | 0.25 | 0.82 | 0.21 | 0.49 | 0.19 | 0.16 |
| -Year | | 1981 | 1980 | 1966 | 1985 | 1964 | 1988 | 1955 | 1972 | 1970 | 1963 | 1976 | 1955 | JUL 1955 |
| -Maximum in 24 hrs | 42 | 2.12 | 2.29 | 3.11 | 2.56 | 2.41 | 4.35 | 6.83 | 4.11 | 5.62 | 3.88 | 3.83 | 2.22 | 6.83 |
| -Year | | 1978 | 1966 | 1978 | 1961 | 1985 | 1972 | 1989 | 1971 | 1960 | 1966 | 1956 | 1969 | JUL 1989 |
| Snow,Ice pellets | | | | | | | | | | | | | | |
| -Maximum Monthly | 42 | 21.4 | 27.5 | 20.3 | 2.6 | T | 0.0 | 0.0 | 0.0 | 0.0 | 2.5 | 11.9 | 21.5 | 27.5 |
| -Year | | 1987 | 1979 | 1958 | 1982 | 1963 | | | | | 1979 | 1953 | 1966 | FEB 1979 |
| -Maximum in 24 hrs | 42 | 12.1 | 16.5 | 15.6 | 2.4 | T | 0.0 | 0.0 | 0.0 | 0.0 | 2.5 | 11.9 | 12.4 | 16.5 |
| -Year | | 1987 | 1979 | 1958 | 1987 | 1963 | | | | | 1979 | 1953 | 1966 | FEB 1979 |
| **WIND:** | | | | | | | | | | | | | | |
| Mean Speed (mph) | 41 | 9.9 | 10.4 | 11.2 | 10.6 | 9.1 | 8.4 | 7.7 | 7.5 | 7.8 | 8.2 | 9.2 | 9.4 | 9.1 |
| Prevailing Direction | | | | | | | | | | | | | | |
| through 1963 | | WNW | NW | WNW | WNW | S | S | NW | S | S | NW | NW | WNW | S |
| Fastest Obs. 1 Min. | | | | | | | | | | | | | | |
| -Direction (!!!) | 41 | 29 | 29 | 06 | 29 | 30 | 23 | 27 | 35 | 07 | 20 | 16 | 32 | 20 |
| -Speed (MPH) | 41 | 46 | 46 | 43 | 45 | 46 | 40 | 48 | 46 | 40 | 58 | 46 | 46 | 58 |
| -Year | | 1957 | 1956 | 1984 | 1963 | 1984 | 1960 | 1963 | 1971 | 1956 | 1954 | 1950 | 1988 | OCT 1954 |
| Peak Gust | | | | | | | | | | | | | | |
| -Direction (!!!) | 6 | NW | NW | NW | NE | NW | NW | NW | SE | NW | W | NW | NW | NW |
| -Speed (mph) | 6 | 51 | 51 | 58 | 45 | 71 | 52 | 66 | 51 | 64 | 58 | 59 | 69 | 71 |
| -Date | | 1986 | 1987 | 1985 | 1987 | 1984 | 1989 | 1987 | 1986 | 1985 | 1987 | 1989 | 1988 | MAY 1984 |

**See Reference Notes to this table on the following pages.**

PRECIPITATION (inches)   WILMINGTON, DELAWARE

**TABLE 2**

| YEAR | JAN | FEB | MAR | APR | MAY | JUNE | JULY | AUG | SEP | OCT | NOV | DEC | ANNUAL |
|------|-----|-----|-----|-----|-----|------|------|-----|-----|-----|-----|-----|--------|
| 1961 | 2.84 | 3.74 | 5.19 | 4.88 | 2.45 | 3.10 | 4.84 | 3.45 | 2.33 | .88 | 2.41 | 3.03 | 40.44 |
| 1962 | 2.51 | 3.26 | 4.30 | 3.50 | 1.61 | 3.05 | 1.78 | 1.87 | 3.65 | .51 | 4.87 | 2.50 | 34.41 |
| 1963 | 2.05 | 2.09 | 4.24 | 1.12 | 1.23 | 3.26 | 1.65 | 4.03 | 2.77 | .21 | 6.87 | 1.85 | 32.10 |
| 1964 | 4.13 | 3.37 | 2.20 | 5.97 | 0.22 | 1.02 | 3.70 | 1.83 | 2.04 | .29 | 1.62 | 4.70 | 32.83 |
| 1965 | 2.38 | 2.17 | 3.20 | 1.76 | 1.76 | 1.41 | 1.62 | 3.84 | 2.04 | 1.59 | .94 | 1.54 | 24.90 |
| 1966 | 2.82 | 4.90 | 0.81 | 3.16 | 3.35 | 0.70 | 3.09 | 1.42 | 8.53 | 5.17 | 1.75 | 3.81 | 39.51 |
| 1967 | 1.67 | 1.90 | 5.45 | 2.69 | 3.79 | 3.01 | 4.45 | 11.16 | 1.16 | 2.05 | 2.08 | 5.24 | 44.65 |
| 1968 | 2.29 | 1.52 | 4.75 | 1.57 | 4.78 | 2.81 | 1.83 | 1.17 | 1.50 | 3.28 | 3.92 | 2.33 | 31.75 |
| 1969 | 1.68 | 1.76 | 1.71 | 1.58 | 3.21 | 6.48 | 3.62 | 2.34 | 2.31 | 0.82 | 2.64 | 4.09 | 38.31 |
| 1970 | 1.00 | 2.13 | 3.61 | 5.56 | 0.94 | 6.16 | 6.03 | 2.31 | 6.99 | 6.41 | 5.52 | 1.33 | 52.24 |
| 1971 | 2.22 | 6.29 | 2.29 | 2.15 | 4.51 | 2.50 | 3.65 | 8.38 | .25 | 1.64 | 4.20 | 7.84 | 48.13 |
| 1972 | 2.50 | 5.43 | 2.40 | 4.47 | 3.85 | 7.49 | 2.07 | 2.44 | 3.02 | 2.22 | 0.67 | 7.31 | 47.05 |
| 1973 | 3.81 | 3.42 | 4.02 | 6.57 | 5.56 | 5.19 | 2.82 | 2.44 | 5.11 | 5.65 | .77 | 1.19 | 39.61 |
| 1974 | 2.92 | 1.73 | 4.56 | 3.08 | 3.96 | 3.97 | 1.49 | 2.55 | 6.19 | 3.06 | 2.63 | 4.18 | 39.61 |
| 1975 | 4.23 | 2.95 | 4.63 | 3.03 | 5.65 | 6.16 | 5.53 | 2.55 | 6.19 | 3.06 | 2.63 | 3.00 | 49.61 |
| 1976 | 4.21 | 1.70 | 2.25 | 1.40 | 5.05 | 2.14 | 4.33 | 2.00 | 2.11 | 6.12 | 0.49 | 1.79 | 33.59 |
| 1977 | 2.18 | 1.09 | 4.55 | 3.91 | 0.96 | 4.41 | 1.38 | 4.82 | 1.29 | 3.59 | 6.14 | 5.81 | 40.13 |
| 1978 | 8.41 | 1.77 | 5.59 | 2.16 | 6.94 | 3.00 | 5.53 | 5.97 | 2.18 | 1.48 | 2.69 | 5.56 | 51.28 |
| 1979 | 7.61 | 7.02 | 2.61 | 4.03 | 3.10 | 4.01 | 4.76 | 6.11 | 5.94 | 3.45 | 3.23 | 1.44 | 53.31 |
| 1980 | 2.44 | 0.83 | 6.22 | 4.55 | 2.40 | 4.23 | 3.49 | 1.09 | 1.44 | 3.99 | 2.41 | 0.83 | 33.92 |
| 1981 | 0.52 | 3.23 | 1.26 | 3.54 | 5.05 | 4.50 | 2.52 | 3.38 | 3.82 | 2.84 | 0.67 | 3.95 | 35.28 |
| 1982 | 3.75 | 2.71 | 2.87 | 5.41 | 3.72 | 4.70 | 2.70 | 4.68 | 2.30 | 1.97 | 3.87 | 2.39 | 41.07 |
| 1983 | 2.98 | 3.55 | 5.40 | 6.84 | 6.80 | 7.38 | 3.94 | 2.33 | 1.29 | 3.44 | 5.48 | 6.80 | 54.70 |
| 1984 | 1.25 | 4.27 | 5.40 | 4.24 | 4.55 | 4.54 | 1.56 | 6.53 | 2.02 | 3.31 | 1.63 | 1.94 | 41.72 |
| 1985 | 1.56 | 2.05 | 2.03 | 0.35 | 5.52 | 1.37 | 6.91 | 2.28 | 4.56 | 1.84 | 4.46 | 0.80 | 33.73 |
| 1986 | 4.21 | 2.77 | 1.19 | 2.77 | 1.69 | 4.05 | 3.99 | 2.88 | 2.75 | 4.04 | 3.50 | 1.90 | 35.98 |
| 1987 | 4.35 | 1.52 | 1.16 | 2.63 | 3.15 | 2.31 | 4.09 | 4.21 | 3.03 | 2.31 | 5.29 | 0.90 | 37.80 |
| 1988 | 2.46 | 4.14 | 1.82 | 2.59 | 4.95 | 0.21 | 8.29 | 2.18 | 1.97 | 4.31 | 1.99 | 1.27 | 49.77 |
| 1989 | 2.48 | 2.75 | 3.69 | 2.76 | 6.57 | 5.43 | 12.63 | 1.56 | 2.64 | 2.85 | 1.61 | 4.27 | |
| 1990 | 3.56 | 1.35 | 2.15 | 3.42 | 7.03 | 3.94 | 4.27 | 6.15 | 2.64 | 2.85 | 1.61 | 5.16 | 44.13 |
| Record Mean | 3.30 | 3.07 | 3.64 | 3.51 | 3.69 | 3.76 | 4.56 | 4.53 | 3.59 | 3.03 | 3.25 | 3.42 | 43.37 |

**TABLE 3**

AVERAGE TEMPERATURE (deg. F)   WILMINGTON, DELAWARE

| YEAR | JAN | FEB | MAR | APR | MAY | JUNE | JULY | AUG | SEP | OCT | NOV | DEC | ANNUAL |
|------|-----|-----|-----|-----|-----|------|------|-----|-----|-----|-----|-----|--------|
| 1961 | 25.6 | 34.7 | 42.6 | 48.9 | 58.9 | 70.5 | 75.6 | 74.0 | 72.5 | 56.9 | 46.7 | 33.2 | 53.3 |
| 1962 | 31.2 | 31.3 | 41.2 | 52.2 | 64.2 | 71.5 | 72.6 | 72.9 | 63.6 | 56.7 | 42.5 | 30.3 | 52.5 |
| 1963 | 28.4 | 27.5 | 44.1 | 52.6 | 60.3 | 70.8 | 76.3 | 71.7 | 63.7 | 58.4 | 48.0 | 28.4 | 52.5 |
| 1964 | 33.2 | 31.6 | 43.1 | 49.4 | 64.3 | 72.1 | 75.8 | 71.5 | 67.2 | 52.8 | 47.6 | 37.3 | 53.8 |
| 1965 | 29.0 | 33.6 | 38.4 | 49.3 | 66.0 | 70.2 | 74.5 | 73.3 | 69.4 | 53.6 | 45.0 | 37.7 | 53.3 |
| 1966 | 29.3 | 31.9 | 42.9 | 47.9 | 60.3 | 72.5 | 77.2 | 74.8 | 65.3 | 53.6 | 46.6 | 34.8 | 53.1 |
| 1967 | 36.2 | 29.4 | 39.4 | 51.5 | 55.4 | 71.2 | 74.4 | 72.8 | 65.1 | 54.7 | 40.7 | 36.8 | 52.3 |
| 1968 | 28.0 | 30.5 | 44.6 | 54.1 | 59.6 | 71.4 | 76.7 | 77.1 | 69.7 | 59.0 | 47.0 | 34.2 | 54.3 |
| 1969 | 30.8 | 33.6 | 39.6 | 55.1 | 64.2 | 73.4 | 75.7 | 75.4 | 68.2 | 56.0 | 44.6 | 32.7 | 54.1 |
| 1970 | 24.5 | 33.5 | 38.9 | 51.9 | 66.0 | 71.7 | 76.6 | 76.7 | 72.1 | 60.4 | 48.5 | 35.9 | 54.6 |
| 1971 | 27.4 | 35.5 | 40.7 | 51.1 | 60.4 | 73.4 | 75.9 | 74.0 | 71.1 | 62.9 | 45.7 | 42.1 | 55.0 |
| 1972 | 36.1 | 32.6 | 41.3 | 50.0 | 62.5 | 68.6 | 75.5 | 75.6 | 69.6 | 53.5 | 41.6 | 41.6 | 54.4 |
| 1973 | 35.6 | 35.5 | 49.4 | 54.7 | 61.4 | 75.8 | 78.1 | 78.1 | 70.4 | 59.9 | 49.1 | 37.7 | 57.2 |
| 1974 | 36.2 | 33.1 | 44.3 | 55.5 | 62.4 | 70.4 | 76.7 | 76.1 | 66.5 | 53.2 | 46.6 | 38.9 | 55.0 |
| 1975 | 37.5 | 35.9 | 40.6 | 47.5 | 65.2 | 71.5 | 75.7 | 76.3 | 65.4 | 60.0 | 51.0 | 36.2 | 55.2 |
| 1976 | 27.7 | 41.2 | 46.5 | 54.7 | 59.9 | 72.4 | 74.2 | 73.7 | 66.9 | 52.5 | 45.3 | 31.0 | 53.6 |
| 1977 | 20.8 | 33.3 | 47.2 | 54.4 | 63.9 | 68.9 | 76.4 | 75.4 | 69.3 | 53.4 | 46.6 | 33.4 | 53.6 |
| 1978 | 27.2 | 22.8 | 37.6 | 50.3 | 60.3 | 70.6 | 73.4 | 77.1 | 66.7 | 54.1 | 46.8 | 37.2 | 52.0 |
| 1979 | 31.4 | 22.1 | 45.4 | 50.6 | 63.8 | 67.9 | 75.3 | 75.0 | 68.2 | 55.0 | 49.6 | 38.1 | 53.5 |
| 1980 | 32.4 | 29.9 | 40.0 | 54.6 | 64.9 | 68.9 | 77.7 | 78.2 | 71.3 | 54.8 | 43.3 | 33.1 | 54.1 |
| 1981 | 25.4 | 37.9 | 40.2 | 55.0 | 62.5 | 72.3 | 77.1 | 73.5 | 66.9 | 53.0 | 45.3 | 34.2 | 53.6 |
| 1982 | 24.2 | 34.2 | 41.8 | 50.6 | 65.0 | 69.9 | 77.3 | 72.0 | 67.4 | 56.0 | 41.3 | 41.3 | 53.9 |
| 1983 | 35.2 | 35.3 | 45.9 | 53.1 | 61.0 | 71.8 | 77.6 | 77.0 | 69.3 | 56.9 | 46.7 | 32.1 | 55.2 |
| 1984 | 24.8 | 38.6 | 35.6 | 50.7 | 61.2 | 73.8 | 75.2 | 75.2 | 69.1 | 61.2 | 43.3 | 42.1 | 53.8 |
| 1985 | 27.5 | 37.4 | 47.1 | 58.0 | 65.9 | 70.6 | 76.6 | 74.4 | 69.1 | 58.3 | 51.0 | 32.9 | 55.7 |
| 1986 | 32.2 | 31.6 | 43.6 | 52.4 | 65.7 | 72.1 | 77.1 | 72.5 | 67.5 | 57.2 | 44.1 | 37.3 | 54.4 |
| 1987 | 31.4 | 31.9 | 44.6 | 52.3 | 63.1 | 73.5 | 79.1 | 74.3 | 68.3 | 51.7 | 47.4 | 38.6 | 54.7 |
| 1988 | 27.4 | 34.8 | 44.2 | 50.8 | 62.9 | 71.6 | 79.4 | 77.3 | 65.8 | 51.0 | 46.7 | 35.1 | 53.9 |
| 1989 | 36.0 | 34.3 | 42.1 | 51.6 | 62.1 | 74.3 | 75.9 | 74.4 | 68.4 | 57.6 | 44.6 | 25.0 | 53.9 |
| 1990 | 40.5 | 41.1 | 46.0 | 53.7 | 61.5 | 72.1 | 77.4 | 74.6 | 66.7 | 60.0 | 48.4 | 41.0 | 56.9 |
| Record Mean | 32.2 | 33.2 | 42.1 | 52.3 | 62.7 | 71.3 | 76.1 | 74.3 | 67.8 | 56.5 | 45.7 | 35.2 | 54.2 |
| Max | 40.0 | 41.5 | 51.6 | 62.8 | 73.3 | 81.6 | 85.7 | 83.7 | 77.6 | 66.5 | 54.5 | 43.0 | 63.5 |
| Min | 24.3 | 24.9 | 32.6 | 41.7 | 52.1 | 61.1 | 66.4 | 64.8 | 58.1 | 46.6 | 36.9 | 27.4 | 44.8 |

## REFERENCE NOTES FOR TABLES 1, 2, 3 and 6   (WILMINGTON, DE)

**GENERAL**

T - TRACE AMOUNT
BLANK ENTRIES DENOTE MISSING/UNREPORTED DATA.
# INDICATES A STATION OR INSTRUMENT RELOCATION.

**SPECIFIC**

**TABLE 1**

(a) - LENGTH OF RECORD IN YEARS. ALTHOUGH
      INDIVIDUAL MONTHS MAY BE MISSING.
 * LESS THAN .05

NORMALS — BASED ON THE 1951-1980 RECORD PERIOD.
EXTREMES — DATES ARE THE MOST RECENT OCCURRENCE.
WIND DIR. — NUMERALS SHOW TENS OF DEGREES
            CLOCKWISE FROM TRUE NORTH.
            "00" INDICATES CALM.
RESULTANT WIND DIRECTIONS ARE GIVEN TO WHOLE DEGREES.

**TABLE 3**
MAX AND MIN ARE LONG-TERM MEAN DAILY MAXIMUM
AND MEAN DAILY MINIMUM TEMPERATURES.

**EXCEPTIONS**

**TABLES 2, 3, and 6**

RECORD MEANS ARE THROUGH THE CURRENT YEAR,
BEGINNING IN    1895 FOR TEMPERATURE
                1894 FOR PRECIPITATION
                1948 FOR SNOWFALL

**TABLE 4**  HEATING DEGREE DAYS Base 65 deg. F    WILMINGTON, DELAWARE

| SEASON | JULY | AUG | SEP | OCT | NOV | DEC | JAN | FEB | MAR | APR | MAY | JUNE | TOTAL |
|---|---|---|---|---|---|---|---|---|---|---|---|---|---|
| 1961-62 | 0 | 0 | 36 | 250 | 553 | 976 | 1042 | 940 | 729 | 400 | 122 | 6 | 5054 |
| 1962-63 | 0 | 4 | 113 | 266 | 672 | 1072 | 1130 | 1044 | 641 | 370 | 180 | 10 | 5502 |
| 1963-64 | 0 | 3 | 104 | 199 | 502 | 1128 | 982 | 962 | 869 | 467 | 91 | 21 | 5128 |
| 1964-65 | 0 | 9 | 49 | 372 | 514 | 854 | 1108 | 873 | 816 | 467 | 63 | 27 | 5152 |
| 1965-66 | 0 | 12 | 40 | 349 | 593 | 839 | 1103 | 921 | 676 | 507 | 186 | 24 | 5250 |
| 1966-67 | 0 | 0 | 84 | 346 | 545 | 931 | 888 | 991 | 788 | 402 | 295 | 5 | 5275 |
| 1967-68 | 0 | 0 | 80 | 327 | 722 | 866 | 1139 | 994 | 626 | 319 | 171 | 6 | 5250 |
| 1968-69 | 0 | 0 | 7 | 205 | 532 | 949 | 1052 | 874 | 780 | 298 | 92 | 1 | 4790 |
| 1969-70 | 0 | 0 | 41 | 288 | 606 | 993 | 1250 | 876 | 803 | 389 | 95 | 1 | 5342 |
| 1970-71 | 0 | 0 | 25 | 175 | 487 | 895 | 1159 | 821 | 746 | 411 | 153 | 3 | 4875 |
| 1971-72 | 0 | 2 | 23 | 93 | 585 | 702 | 889 | 935 | 732 | 443 | 105 | 27 | 4536 |
| 1972-73 | 0 | 0 | 20 | 356 | 586 | 716 | 902 | 820 | 477 | 322 | 143 | 0 | 4342 |
| 1973-74 | 0 | 0 | 15 | 179 | 469 | 839 | 886 | 887 | 635 | 300 | 137 | 7 | 4354 |
| 1974-75 | 0 | 0 | 65 | 362 | 553 | 805 | 847 | 808 | 753 | 520 | 84 | 5 | 4802 |
| 1975-76 | 0 | 0 | 56 | 177 | 418 | 888 | 1149 | 681 | 567 | 341 | 178 | 31 | 4486 |
| 1976-77 | 0 | 4 | 44 | 387 | 734 | 1047 | 1361 | 884 | 546 | 333 | 107 | 32 | 5479 |
| 1977-78 | 0 | 1 | 31 | 353 | 550 | 975 | 1165 | 1179 | 842 | 433 | 191 | 17 | 5737 |
| 1978-79 | 6 | 0 | 60 | 337 | 542 | 854 | 1037 | 1197 | 605 | 424 | 89 | 28 | 5179 |
| 1979-80 | 4 | 7 | 31 | 318 | 458 | 827 | 1004 | 1009 | 768 | 307 | 83 | 35 | 4851 |
| 1980-81 | 0 | 0 | 20 | 322 | 645 | 985 | 1222 | 752 | 763 | 299 | 135 | 4 | 5147 |
| 1981-82 | 0 | 0 | 57 | 370 | 585 | 947 | 1259 | 855 | 715 | 426 | 69 | 12 | 5295 |
| 1982-83 | 0 | 14 | 29 | 305 | 519 | 724 | 919 | 822 | 587 | 368 | 163 | 7 | 4457 |
| 1983-84 | 0 | 0 | 74 | 275 | 542 | 1013 | 1240 | 758 | 904 | 422 | 162 | 5 | 5395 |
| 1984-85 | 0 | 2 | 113 | 149 | 641 | 701 | 1154 | 766 | 550 | 248 | 73 | 7 | 4404 |
| 1985-86 | 0 | 0 | 45 | 213 | 411 | 986 | 1011 | 930 | 653 | 373 | 99 | 11 | 4732 |
| 1986-87 | 0 | 27 | 36 | 276 | 619 | 848 | 1032 | 923 | 628 | 374 | 143 | 2 | 4908 |
| 1987-88 | 0 | 2 | 22 | 406 | 521 | 811 | 1159 | 869 | 637 | 419 | 121 | 38 | 5005 |
| 1988-89 | 3 | 0 | 52 | 434 | 541 | 923 | 893 | 854 | 710 | 395 | 142 | 0 | 4947 |
| 1989-90 | 0 | 2 | 54 | 236 | 605 | 1231 | 749 | 661 | 593 | 368 | 127 | 6 | 4632 |
| 1990-91 | 2 | 1 | 69 | 214 | 494 | 734 | | | | | | | |

**TABLE 5**  COOLING DEGREE DAYS Base 65 deg. F    WILMINGTON, DELAWARE

| YEAR | JAN | FEB | MAR | APR | MAY | JUNE | JULY | AUG | SEP | OCT | NOV | DEC | TOTAL |
|---|---|---|---|---|---|---|---|---|---|---|---|---|---|
| 1969 | 0 | 0 | 0 | 8 | 73 | 258 | 336 | 330 | 143 | 14 | 0 | 0 | 1162 |
| 1970 | 0 | 0 | 0 | 2 | 97 | 211 | 365 | 371 | 244 | 38 | 0 | 0 | 1328 |
| 1971 | 0 | 0 | 0 | 0 | 16 | 261 | 345 | 287 | 214 | 34 | 16 | 0 | 1173 |
| 1972 | 0 | 0 | 2 | 0 | 35 | 143 | 376 | 334 | 165 | 8 | 0 | 0 | 1063 |
| 1973 | 0 | 0 | 0 | 19 | 42 | 332 | 416 | 413 | 183 | 29 | 0 | 0 | 1434 |
| 1974 | 0 | 0 | 0 | 24 | 64 | 175 | 370 | 355 | 113 | 2 | 6 | 0 | 1109 |
| 1975 | 0 | 0 | 0 | 0 | 97 | 207 | 337 | 355 | 73 | 27 | 5 | 0 | 1101 |
| 1976 | 0 | 0 | 0 | 37 | 25 | 260 | 291 | 278 | 106 | 6 | 0 | 0 | 1003 |
| 1977 | 0 | 0 | 5 | 20 | 80 | 156 | 360 | 328 | 166 | 0 | 5 | 0 | 1120 |
| 1978 | 0 | 0 | 0 | 0 | 48 | 188 | 273 | 383 | 117 | 7 | 0 | 0 | 1016 |
| 1979 | 0 | 0 | 4 | 1 | 57 | 123 | 327 | 324 | 138 | 16 | 0 | 0 | 990 |
| 1980 | 0 | 0 | 0 | 0 | 83 | 159 | 400 | 417 | 214 | 10 | 0 | 0 | 1283 |
| 1981 | 0 | 0 | 0 | 9 | 62 | 228 | 381 | 270 | 120 | 3 | 0 | 0 | 1073 |
| 1982 | 0 | 0 | 0 | 2 | 75 | 163 | 238 | 391 | 107 | 32 | 1 | 0 | 1009 |
| 1983 | 0 | 0 | 0 | 17 | 47 | 218 | 398 | 378 | 209 | 29 | 0 | 0 | 1296 |
| 1984 | 0 | 0 | 0 | 0 | 50 | 276 | 321 | 327 | 80 | 34 | 0 | 0 | 1088 |
| 1985 | 0 | 0 | 4 | 47 | 106 | 181 | 366 | 300 | 174 | 13 | 0 | 0 | 1191 |
| 1986 | 0 | 0 | 0 | 0 | 129 | 227 | 379 | 267 | 116 | 40 | 0 | 0 | 1158 |
| 1987 | 0 | 0 | 0 | 3 | 91 | 264 | 446 | 295 | 129 | 0 | 0 | 0 | 1228 |
| 1988 | 0 | 0 | 0 | 0 | 62 | 242 | 455 | 389 | 80 | 5 | 0 | 0 | 1233 |
| 1989 | 0 | 0 | 6 | 0 | 61 | 287 | 345 | 299 | 162 | 17 | 0 | 0 | 1177 |
| 1990 | 0 | 0 | 10 | 36 | 23 | 227 | 395 | 304 | 127 | 66 | 0 | 0 | 1188 |

**TABLE 6**  SNOWFALL (inches)    WILMINGTON, DELAWARE

| SEASON | JULY | AUG | SEP | OCT | NOV | DEC | JAN | FEB | MAR | APR | MAY | JUNE | TOTAL |
|---|---|---|---|---|---|---|---|---|---|---|---|---|---|
| 1961-62 | 0.0 | 0.0 | 0.0 | 0.0 | 3.3 | 6.4 | 1.2 | 8.0 | 5.2 | T | 0.0 | 0.0 | 24.1 |
| 1962-63 | 0.0 | 0.0 | 0.0 | 0.3 | T | 8.6 | 5.2 | 4.6 | 0.3 | 0.0 | T | 0.0 | 19.0 |
| 1963-64 | 0.0 | 0.0 | 0.0 | 0.0 | T | 8.0 | 6.7 | 14.9 | 9.5 | 0.0 | 0.0 | 0.0 | 39.1 |
| 1964-65 | 0.0 | 0.0 | 0.0 | 0.0 | T | 1.6 | 8.4 | 1.7 | 5.8 | 0.6 | 0.0 | 0.0 | 18.1 |
| 1965-66 | 0.0 | 0.0 | 0.0 | 0.0 | 0.0 | 0.0 | 17.2 | 10.0 | T | T | 0.0 | 0.0 | 27.2 |
| 1966-67 | 0.0 | 0.0 | 0.0 | 0.0 | T | 21.5 | 0.6 | 18.7 | 2.7 | T | 0.0 | 0.0 | 43.5 |
| 1967-68 | 0.0 | 0.0 | 0.0 | 0.0 | 0.0 | 6.8 | 4.0 | 1.6 | 0.9 | 1.3 | 0.0 | 0.0 | 14.6 |
| 1968-69 | 0.0 | 0.0 | 0.0 | 0.0 | T | 0.6 | 2.9 | 5.5 | 7.8 | 0.0 | 0.0 | 0.0 | 16.8 |
| 1969-70 | 0.0 | 0.0 | 0.0 | T | 0.1 | 6.8 | 9.7 | 1.5 | 0.4 | 0.0 | 0.0 | 0.0 | 18.5 |
| 1970-71 | 0.0 | 0.0 | 0.0 | 0.0 | 0.0 | 3.2 | 5.8 | 0.2 | 2.4 | 0.6 | 0.0 | 0.0 | 12.2 |
| 1971-72 | 0.0 | 0.0 | 0.0 | 0.0 | T | T | 2.1 | 7.0 | 0.3 | 0.1 | 0.0 | 0.0 | 9.5 |
| 1972-73 | 0.0 | 0.0 | 0.0 | T | T | T | T | 1.2 | T | T | 0.0 | 0.0 | 1.2 |
| 1973-74 | 0.0 | 0.0 | 0.0 | 0.0 | 0.0 | 6.1 | 2.4 | 11.5 | T | 0.0 | 0.0 | 0.0 | 20.0 |
| 1974-75 | 0.0 | 0.0 | 0.0 | 0.0 | T | 5.1 | 4.8 | 1.1 | T | 0.0 | 0.0 | 0.0 | 11.0 |
| 1975-76 | 0.0 | 0.0 | 0.0 | 0.0 | 0.0 | 0.3 | 4.5 | 1.7 | 6.7 | T | 0.0 | 0.0 | 13.2 |
| 1976-77 | 0.0 | 0.0 | 0.0 | 0.0 | 0.1 | 3.2 | 14.5 | T | 0.0 | T | 0.0 | 0.0 | 17.8 |
| 1977-78 | 0.0 | 0.0 | 0.0 | 0.0 | 0.4 | 0.9 | 16.0 | 18.4 | 9.9 | T | 0.0 | 0.0 | 45.6 |
| 1978-79 | 0.0 | 0.0 | 0.0 | 0.0 | 4.5 | T | 12.0 | 27.5 | 0.2 | T | 0.0 | 0.0 | 44.2 |
| 1979-80 | 0.0 | 0.0 | 0.0 | 2.5 | 0.0 | 1.4 | 6.1 | 0.8 | 5.1 | 0.0 | 0.0 | 0.0 | 15.9 |
| 1980-81 | 0.0 | 0.0 | 0.0 | 0.0 | 0.5 | 1.4 | 6.5 | T | 3.7 | 0.0 | 0.0 | 0.0 | 12.1 |
| 1981-82 | 0.0 | 0.0 | 0.0 | 0.0 | T | 2.8 | 14.6 | 4.5 | 0.4 | 2.6 | 0.0 | 0.0 | 24.9 |
| 1982-83 | 0.0 | 0.0 | 0.0 | 0.0 | T | 5.8 | T | 18.5 | 0.3 | 0.5 | 0.0 | 0.0 | 25.1 |
| 1983-84 | 0.0 | 0.0 | 0.0 | 0.0 | T | T | 9.7 | T | 5.2 | T | 0.0 | 0.0 | 14.9 |
| 1984-85 | 0.0 | 0.0 | 0.0 | 0.0 | T | 0.3 | 14.2 | 0.7 | T | 0.4 | 0.0 | 0.0 | 15.6 |
| 1985-86 | 0.0 | 0.0 | 0.0 | 0.0 | 0.0 | 1.4 | 3.1 | 9.7 | T | T | 0.0 | 0.0 | 14.2 |
| 1986-87 | 0.0 | 0.0 | 0.0 | 0.0 | T | 0.3 | 21.4 | 15.7 | 0.2 | 2.4 | 0.0 | 0.0 | 40.0 |
| 1987-88 | 0.0 | 0.0 | 0.0 | 0.0 | 0.7 | 2.1 | 10.8 | 1.1 | T | T | 0.0 | 0.0 | 14.7 |
| 1988-89 | 0.0 | 0.0 | 0.0 | 0.0 | T | 0.2 | 6.7 | 2.9 | 1.2 | 0.0 | 0.0 | 0.0 | 11.0 |
| 1989-90 | 0.0 | 0.0 | 0.0 | 0.0 | 5.6 | 8.9 | 1.5 | 1.0 | 1.3 | 1.6 | 0.0 | 0.0 | 19.9 |
| 1990-91 | T | 0.0 | 0.0 | 0.0 | 0.0 | 6.4 | | | | | | | |
| Record Mean | T | 0.0 | 0.0 | 0.1 | 1.0 | 3.5 | 6.8 | 6.2 | 3.2 | 0.2 | T | 0.0 | 20.9 |

**See Reference Notes, relative to all above tables, on preceding page.**

# WASHINGTON (National Airport) DISTRICT OF COLUMBIA

Washington lies at the western edge of the mid Atlantic Coastal Plain, about 50 miles east of the Blue Ridge Mountains and 35 miles west of Chesapeake Bay, adjacent to the Potomac and Anacostia Rivers. Elevations range from a few feet above sea level to about 400 feet in parts of the northwest section of the city.

Observations have been kept continuously since November 1870. Since June 1941 the official observations have been taken at Washington National Airport.

National Airport is located at the center of the urban heat island. As a result, low temperatures are the highest for the area. Differences between the airport and suburban locations are often 10 to 15 degrees. There is less variation in the high temperatures.

Summers are warm and humid and winters are cold, but not severe. Periods of pleasant weather often occur in the spring and fall. The summertime temperature is in the upper 80s and the winter is in the upper 20s. Precipitation is rather uniformly distributed throughout the year.

Thunderstorms can occur at any time but are most frequent during the late spring and summer. The storms are most often accompanied by downpours and gusty winds, but are not usually severe.

Tornadoes, which infrequently occur, have resulted in significant damage. Severe hailstorms have occurred in the spring.

Tropical storms can bring heavy rain, high winds and flooding, but extensive damage from wind and tidal flooding is rare. Wind gusts of nearly 100 mph and rainfall over 7 inches have occurred during the passage of tropical storms and hurricanes.

Major flooding of the Potomac River can result from heavy rains over the basin, occasionally augmented by snowmelt, and above normal tides associated with hurricanes or severe storms along the coast. Flooding may also occur after a cold winter when the Potomac may be blocked with ice.

Although a snowfall of 10 inches or more in 24 hours is unusual, several notable falls of more than 25 inches have occurred. Normal snowfall during the winter season is 18 inches.

The average date of the last freezing temperature in the spring is April 1 and the average date for the first freezing temperature in the fall is November 10.

# TABLE 1      NORMALS, MEANS AND EXTREMES

WASHINGTON, D.C. NATIONAL AIRPORT

LATITUDE: 38°51'N   LONGITUDE: 77°02'W   ELEVATION: FT. GRND  10 BARO  75  TIME ZONE: EASTERN   WBAN: 13743

| | (a) | JAN | FEB | MAR | APR | MAY | JUNE | JULY | AUG | SEP | OCT | NOV | DEC | YEAR |
|---|---|---|---|---|---|---|---|---|---|---|---|---|---|---|
| **TEMPERATURE °F:** | | | | | | | | | | | | | | |
| Normals | | | | | | | | | | | | | | |
| -Daily Maximum | | 42.9 | 45.9 | 55.0 | 67.1 | 75.9 | 84.0 | 87.9 | 86.4 | 80.1 | 68.9 | 57.4 | 46.6 | 66.5 |
| -Daily Minimum | | 27.5 | 29.0 | 36.6 | 46.2 | 56.1 | 65.0 | 69.9 | 68.7 | 62.0 | 49.7 | 39.9 | 31.2 | 48.5 |
| -Monthly | | 35.2 | 37.5 | 45.8 | 56.7 | 66.0 | 74.5 | 78.9 | 77.6 | 71.1 | 59.3 | 48.7 | 38.9 | 57.5 |
| Extremes | | | | | | | | | | | | | | |
| -Record Highest | 48 | 79 | 82 | 89 | 95 | 97 | 101 | 104 | 103 | 101 | 94 | 86 | 75 | 104 |
| -Year | | 1950 | 1948 | 1945 | 1976 | 1987 | 1988 | 1988 | 1988 | 1980 | 1954 | 1974 | 1984 | JUL 1988 |
| -Record Lowest | 48 | -5 | 4 | 11 | 24 | 34 | 47 | 54 | 49 | 39 | 29 | 16 | 1 | -5 |
| -Year | | 1982 | 1961 | 1943 | 1982 | 1947 | 1972 | 1988 | 1986 | 1963 | 1969 | 1955 | 1942 | JAN 1982 |
| **NORMAL DEGREE DAYS:** | | | | | | | | | | | | | | |
| Heating (base 65°F) | | 924 | 770 | 595 | 257 | 68 | 0 | 0 | 0 | 13 | 197 | 489 | 809 | 4122 |
| Cooling (base 65°F) | | 0 | 0 | 0 | 8 | 99 | 285 | 431 | 391 | 196 | 20 | 0 | 0 | 1430 |
| **% OF POSSIBLE SUNSHINE** | 41 | 47 | 51 | 55 | 57 | 58 | 64 | 63 | 62 | 61 | 58 | 51 | 46 | 56 |
| **MEAN SKY COVER (tenths)** | | | | | | | | | | | | | | |
| Sunrise - Sunset | 41 | 6.6 | 6.5 | 6.4 | 6.4 | 6.4 | 5.9 | 6.0 | 5.8 | 5.6 | 5.5 | 6.2 | 6.5 | 6.1 |
| **MEAN NUMBER OF DAYS:** | | | | | | | | | | | | | | |
| Sunrise to Sunset | | | | | | | | | | | | | | |
| -Clear | 41 | 7.6 | 7.4 | 7.6 | 7.0 | 7.1 | 7.8 | 7.6 | 9.0 | 9.8 | 10.9 | 8.0 | 8.4 | 98.3 |
| -Partly Cloudy | 41 | 7.2 | 6.5 | 8.6 | 9.1 | 9.9 | 10.8 | 11.9 | 10.1 | 8.4 | 7.7 | 8.0 | 6.6 | 104.8 |
| -Cloudy | 41 | 16.2 | 14.4 | 14.9 | 13.9 | 14.0 | 11.4 | 11.5 | 11.9 | 11.8 | 12.4 | 13.9 | 16.0 | 162.2 |
| Precipitation | | | | | | | | | | | | | | |
| .01 inches or more | 48 | 10.3 | 8.9 | 10.8 | 9.7 | 11.1 | 9.5 | 9.8 | 9.1 | 7.7 | 7.3 | 8.5 | 9.0 | 111.7 |
| Snow, Ice pellets | | | | | | | | | | | | | | |
| 1.0 inches or more | 46 | 1.7 | 1.4 | 0.7 | 0.0 | 0.0 | 0.0 | 0.0 | 0.0 | 0.0 | 0.0 | 0.2 | 0.8 | 4.8 |
| Thunderstorms | 41 | 0.2 | 0.2 | 1.2 | 2.4 | 4.7 | 5.7 | 6.5 | 5.1 | 2.2 | 1.0 | 0.6 | 0.* | 29.8 |
| Heavy Fog Visibility | | | | | | | | | | | | | | |
| 1/4 mile or less | 41 | 1.9 | 1.5 | 0.8 | 0.8 | 0.4 | 0.2 | 0.2 | 0.1 | 0.4 | 1.3 | 1.2 | 1.8 | 10.5 |
| Temperature °F | | | | | | | | | | | | | | |
| -Maximum | | | | | | | | | | | | | | |
| 90° and above | 29 | 0.0 | 0.0 | 0.0 | 0.4 | 1.6 | 7.5 | 13.8 | 10.2 | 3.9 | 0.1 | 0.0 | 0.0 | 37.4 |
| 32° and below | 29 | 5.3 | 2.3 | 0.2 | 0.0 | 0.0 | 0.0 | 0.0 | 0.0 | 0.0 | 0.0 | 0.* | 2.2 | 10.1 |
| -Minimum | | | | | | | | | | | | | | |
| 32° and below | 29 | 22.6 | 18.9 | 8.4 | 0.8 | 0.0 | 0.0 | 0.0 | 0.0 | 0.0 | 0.4 | 4.3 | 15.9 | 71.4 |
| 0° and below | 29 | 0.1 | 0.0 | 0.0 | 0.0 | 0.0 | 0.0 | 0.0 | 0.0 | 0.0 | 0.0 | 0.0 | 0.0 | 0.1 |
| **AVG. STATION PRESS. (mb)** | 17 | 1016.9 | 1016.8 | 1014.9 | 1012.9 | 1013.1 | 1013.3 | 1014.0 | 1015.2 | 1016.4 | 1017.6 | 1017.1 | 1017.6 | 1015.5 |
| **RELATIVE HUMIDITY (%)** | | | | | | | | | | | | | | |
| Hour 01 | 29 | 66 | 65 | 64 | 66 | 74 | 76 | 76 | 79 | 79 | 77 | 71 | 68 | 72 |
| Hour 07 | 29 | 69 | 69 | 69 | 69 | 74 | 75 | 76 | 80 | 81 | 79 | 75 | 71 | 74 |
| Hour 13 (Local Time) | 29 | 55 | 52 | 49 | 48 | 52 | 52 | 53 | 55 | 55 | 53 | 54 | 56 | 53 |
| Hour 19 | 29 | 59 | 57 | 53 | 51 | 58 | 60 | 61 | 64 | 65 | 64 | 61 | 61 | 60 |
| **PRECIPITATION (inches):** | | | | | | | | | | | | | | |
| Water Equivalent | | | | | | | | | | | | | | |
| -Normal | | 2.76 | 2.62 | 3.46 | 2.93 | 3.48 | 3.35 | 3.88 | 4.40 | 3.22 | 2.90 | 2.82 | 3.18 | 39.00 |
| -Maximum Monthly | 48 | 7.11 | 5.71 | 7.43 | 6.88 | 10.69 | 11.53 | 11.06 | 14.31 | 12.36 | 8.18 | 6.70 | 6.54 | 14.31 |
| -Year | | 1978 | 1961 | 1953 | 1983 | 1953 | 1972 | 1945 | 1955 | 1975 | 1942 | 1963 | 1969 | AUG 1955 |
| -Minimum Monthly | 48 | 0.31 | 0.42 | 0.64 | 0.03 | 0.75 | 0.95 | 0.93 | 0.55 | 0.20 | T | 0.29 | 0.22 | T |
| -Year | | 1955 | 1978 | 1985 | 1985 | 1986 | 1988 | 1966 | 1962 | 1967 | 1963 | 1981 | 1955 | OCT 1963 |
| -Maximum in 24 hrs | 46 | 2.13 | 1.94 | 3.43 | 3.08 | 4.32 | 7.19 | 4.69 | 6.39 | 5.31 | 4.98 | 2.63 | 2.86 | 7.19 |
| -Year | | 1976 | 1983 | 1958 | 1970 | 1953 | 1972 | 1970 | 1955 | 1975 | 1955 | 1971 | 1977 | JUN 1972 |
| Snow, Ice pellets | | | | | | | | | | | | | | |
| -Maximum Monthly | 46 | 21.3 | 30.6 | 17.1 | 0.6 | T | 0.0 | 0.0 | 0.0 | 0.0 | 0.3 | 11.5 | 16.2 | 30.6 |
| -Year | | 1966 | 1979 | 1960 | 1972 | 1963 | | | | | 1979 | 1987 | 1962 | FEB 1979 |
| -Maximum in 24 hrs | 46 | 13.8 | 18.7 | 7.9 | 0.6 | T | 0.0 | 0.0 | 0.0 | 0.0 | 0.3 | 11.5 | 11.4 | 18.7 |
| -Year | | 1966 | 1979 | 1960 | 1972 | 1963 | | | | | 1979 | 1987 | 1957 | FEB 1979 |
| **WIND:** | | | | | | | | | | | | | | |
| Mean Speed (mph) | 41 | 10.0 | 10.3 | 11.0 | 10.5 | 9.2 | 8.9 | 8.2 | 8.1 | 8.3 | 8.7 | 9.3 | 9.5 | 9.3 |
| Prevailing Direction | | | | | | | | | | | | | | |
| through 1963 | | NW | S | NW | S | S | S | S | S | S | SSW | S | NW | S |
| Fastest Mile | | | | | | | | | | | | | | |
| -Direction (!!!) | 36 | NW | SW | E | N | NW | NW | E | NE | SE | SE | E | SW | SE |
| -Speed (MPH) | 36 | 56 | 57 | 60 | 56 | 52 | 57 | 54 | 49 | 56 | 78 | 60 | 62 | 78 |
| -Year | | 1957 | 1961 | 1951 | 1952 | 1984 | 1954 | 1951 | 1955 | 1952 | 1954 | 1952 | 1957 | OCT 1954 |
| Peak Gust | | | | | | | | | | | | | | |
| -Direction (!!!) | 6 | NW | NW | W | S | NW | N | S | NW | NW | NW | W | NW | NW |
| -Speed (mph) | 6 | 51 | 49 | 55 | 48 | 60 | 53 | 54 | 53 | 54 | 44 | 52 | 56 | 60 |
| -Date | | 1985 | 1987 | 1985 | 1988 | 1984 | 1986 | 1987 | 1988 | 1985 | 1985 | 1989 | 1985 | MAY 1984 |

**See Reference Notes to this table on the following page.**

**TABLE 2**    PRECIPITATION (inches)      WASHINGTON, D.C. NATIONAL AIRPORT

| YEAR | JAN | FEB | MAR | APR | MAY | JUNE | JULY | AUG | SEP | OCT | NOV | DEC | ANNUAL |
|------|-----|-----|-----|-----|-----|------|------|-----|-----|-----|-----|-----|--------|
| 1961 | 3.12 | 5.71 | 4.18 | 3.24 | 2.57 | 4.84 | 3.95 | 6.31 | 1.02 | 2.37 | 1.75 | 2.88 | 41.94 |
| 1962 | 1.59 | 3.65 | 3.83 | 2.90 | 3.46 | 2.44 | 1.63 | 0.55 | 2.64 | 1.93 | 5.12 | 3.33 | 33.07 |
| 1963 | 1.86 | 1.94 | 5.43 | 0.99 | 1.06 | 6.87 | 1.95 | 3.61 | T | 6.70 | 1.72 | 39.34 |
| 1964 | 3.98 | 3.38 | 2.53 | 4.37 | 1.46 | 1.30 | 1.87 | 1.89 | 3.07 | 1.34 | 1.42 | 2.87 | 29.48 |
| 1965 | 2.73 | 1.89 | 4.37 | 1.65 | 1.72 | 1.88 | 2.98 | 4.44 | 2.12 | 2.32 | 0.37 | 0.47 | 26.94 |
| 1966 | 3.95 | 3.57 | 1.44 | 3.33 | 2.74 | 2.02 | 0.93 | 1.67 | 6.87 | 4.72 | 1.50 | 3.28 | 36.02 |
| 1967 | 1.35 | 2.32 | 3.49 | 0.80 | 4.27 | 1.51 | 5.24 | 9.17 | 0.20 | 1.77 | 2.10 | 5.93 | 38.15 |
| 1968 | 1.97 | 0.80 | 3.66 | 1.53 | 4.23 | 7.40 | 1.31 | 3.95 | 2.97 | 3.17 | 3.62 | 2.22 | 36.83 |
| 1969 | 1.69 | 2.08 | 1.60 | 1.71 | 1.20 | 3.46 | 9.44 | 6.98 | 5.07 | 1.14 | 2.39 | 6.54 | 43.30 |
| 1970 | 1.24 | 2.69 | 2.82 | 5.35 | 2.79 | 2.80 | 8.12 | 1.09 | 1.57 | 2.05 | 5.77 | 3.33 | 39.62 |
| 1971 | 1.86 | 5.44 | 1.93 | 2.10 | 6.80 | 1.72 | 4.97 | 7.18 | 2.48 | 6.12 | 3.76 | 1.66 | 46.02 |
| 1972 | 2.45 | 5.27 | 2.27 | 3.99 | 4.78 | 11.53 | 3.43 | 2.82 | 1.27 | 3.56 | 6.05 | 4.55 | 51.97 |
| 1973 | 2.26 | 2.68 | 2.97 | 4.19 | 3.39 | 2.11 | 2.68 | 4.41 | 1.58 | 1.71 | 0.97 | 6.03 | 34.98 |
| 1974 | 2.66 | 0.95 | 4.21 | 2.26 | 4.37 | 3.40 | 1.15 | 5.77 | 4.39 | 1.13 | 1.24 | 4.43 | 35.96 |
| 1975 | 3.09 | 1.56 | 5.33 | 2.13 | 4.71 | 2.15 | 7.16 | 3.54 | 12.36 | 2.38 | 2.05 | 4.04 | 50.50 |
| 1976 | 3.56 | 1.55 | 2.51 | 1.17 | 3.57 | 1.21 | 4.54 | 2.13 | 7.23 | 7.76 | 0.85 | 1.99 | 38.07 |
| 1977 | 1.50 | 0.66 | 2.17 | 2.66 | 1.73 | 3.28 | 4.06 | 4.74 | 0.32 | 5.35 | 4.81 | 4.86 | 36.14 |
| 1978 | 7.11 | 0.42 | 4.48 | 1.38 | 5.13 | 2.43 | 4.28 | 5.85 | 1.01 | 1.16 | 2.31 | 4.00 | 39.56 |
| 1979 | 6.64 | 5.62 | 2.45 | 1.88 | 3.55 | 2.99 | 3.43 | 5.41 | 6.64 | 5.54 | 2.33 | 0.85 | 47.33 |
| 1980 | 2.85 | 1.16 | 5.04 | 3.28 | 2.64 | 1.68 | 3.86 | 1.11 | 1.90 | 2.59 | 2.56 | 0.65 | 29.32 |
| 1981 | 0.38 | 2.82 | 1.49 | 2.63 | 3.42 | 2.55 | 5.69 | 3.02 | 1.94 | 3.64 | 0.29 | 2.80 | 30.67 |
| 1982 | 2.27 | 3.33 | 2.64 | 3.19 | 5.11 | 5.41 | 2.98 | 2.68 | 1.71 | 1.75 | 2.96 | 1.74 | 35.77 |
| 1983 | 1.69 | 3.09 | 4.84 | 6.88 | 4.62 | 7.09 | 1.78 | 3.11 | 2.90 | 4.87 | 5.09 | 5.91 | 51.87 |
| 1984 | 1.71 | 3.43 | 6.14 | 3.71 | 3.80 | 2.01 | 4.09 | 2.30 | 2.51 | 3.18 | 3.66 | 1.19 | 37.73 |
| 1985 | 2.11 | 3.07 | 1.88 | 0.03 | 5.79 | 2.05 | 2.91 | 2.35 | 6.67 | 3.85 | 4.47 | 0.68 | 35.86 |
| 1986 | 2.38 | 3.49 | 0.74 | 1.98 | 0.75 | 1.29 | 3.79 | 5.33 | 0.60 | 2.01 | 5.23 | 4.98 | 32.57 |
| 1987 | 4.90 | 2.11 | 1.54 | 2.28 | 2.54 | 3.90 | 2.59 | 2.07 | 5.11 | 2.53 | 4.49 | 2.57 | 36.63 |
| 1988 | 3.14 | 2.52 | 2.27 | 2.00 | 4.50 | 0.95 | 3.74 | 2.39 | 1.85 | 1.75 | 5.33 | 1.30 | 31.74 |
| 1989 | 2.49 | 2.80 | 4.30 | 3.50 | 7.77 | 6.02 | 5.66 | 1.15 | 6.68 | 5.48 | 2.37 | 2.10 | 50.32 |
| 1990 | 2.95 | 1.30 | 2.57 | 4.09 | 5.20 | 3.14 | 3.78 | 6.74 | 0.87 | 3.30 | 2.17 | 4.73 | 40.84 |
| Record Mean | 2.73 | 2.57 | 3.25 | 2.83 | 3.94 | 3.39 | 4.01 | 4.32 | 3.30 | 3.03 | 3.05 | 3.04 | 39.48 |

**TABLE 3**

AVERAGE TEMPERATURE (deg. F)      WASHINGTON, D.C. NATIONAL AIRPORT

| YEAR | JAN | FEB | MAR | APR | MAY | JUNE | JULY | AUG | SEP | OCT | NOV | DEC | ANNUAL |
|------|-----|-----|-----|-----|-----|------|------|-----|-----|-----|-----|-----|--------|
| 1961 | 29.8 | 38.3 | 47.6 | 52.0 | 62.2 | 73.2 | 78.6 | 77.6 | 74.8 | 59.5 | 50.2 | 36.4 | 56.7 |
| 1962 | 34.6 | 34.6 | 44.2 | 56.3 | 68.7 | 73.8 | 75.3 | 76.8 | 67.0 | 60.3 | 44.9 | 33.2 | 55.8 |
| 1963 | 31.4 | 31.0 | 48.5 | 57.8 | 64.9 | 73.7 | 77.6 | 75.4 | 66.5 | 61.2 | 49.8 | 31.1 | 55.7 |
| 1964 | 36.3 | 36.9 | 47.5 | 54.1 | 68.1 | 76.0 | 79.1 | 75.5 | 69.9 | 55.1 | 39.9 | 57.5 |
| 1965 | 33.4 | 36.8 | 41.4 | 51.8 | 69.1 | 72.6 | 78.2 | 77.2 | 72.6 | 57.5 | 49.5 | 41.5 | 56.8 |
| 1966 | 32.4 | 36.2 | 47.5 | 52.7 | 65.0 | 76.0 | 80.9 | 78.7 | 68.6 | 57.0 | 49.5 | 37.6 | 56.8 |
| 1967 | 41.0 | 34.0 | 45.0 | 57.6 | 60.0 | 74.7 | 77.2 | 76.2 | 68.0 | 57.9 | 45.0 | 39.9 | 56.4 |
| 1968 | 31.4 | 34.3 | 49.7 | 58.0 | 63.7 | 74.1 | 79.9 | 79.2 | 72.0 | 61.3 | 50.0 | 36.6 | 57.5 |
| 1969 | 34.2 | 36.9 | 43.0 | 58.7 | 68.4 | 77.1 | 79.5 | 76.3 | 70.1 | 58.8 | 47.2 | 36.3 | 57.2 |
| 1970 | 30.0 | 37.1 | 41.9 | 55.3 | 68.3 | 75.2 | 79.2 | 79.0 | 75.0 | 62.5 | 49.3 | 39.7 | 57.7 |
| 1971 | 31.3 | 39.1 | 43.2 | 55.0 | 63.7 | 75.9 | 78.3 | 76.7 | 73.0 | 64.7 | 48.2 | 45.5 | 57.9 |
| 1972 | 38.5 | 36.5 | 45.6 | 54.1 | 64.6 | 70.2 | 77.5 | 75.9 | 71.0 | 56.0 | 46.8 | 43.6 | 56.7 |
| 1973 | 37.6 | 37.0 | 51.1 | 56.0 | 62.8 | 77.1 | 79.2 | 79.9 | 74.3 | 63.3 | 51.6 | 41.9 | 59.3 |
| 1974 | 42.9 | 39.2 | 49.2 | 58.3 | 65.1 | 71.5 | 79.0 | 78.4 | 70.2 | 57.3 | 50.0 | 43.1 | 58.8 |
| 1975 | 40.9 | 40.6 | 45.2 | 53.6 | 69.7 | 76.4 | 79.3 | 80.1 | 68.5 | 63.2 | 54.4 | 40.5 | 59.4 |
| 1976 | 33.9 | 46.9 | 51.3 | 59.9 | 65.0 | 77.6 | 78.4 | 76.7 | 70.4 | 55.4 | 43.0 | 35.5 | 57.9 |
| 1977 | 25.4 | 38.8 | 52.7 | 60.1 | 69.4 | 74.3 | 80.9 | 78.8 | 73.9 | 59.0 | 51.8 | 38.1 | 58.6 |
| 1978 | 32.5 | 31.4 | 44.4 | 57.7 | 65.8 | 76.7 | 78.8 | 81.3 | 73.6 | 59.4 | 52.2 | 43.1 | 58.1 |
| 1979 | 35.1 | 28.4 | 51.5 | 56.0 | 67.7 | 72.4 | 78.6 | 78.5 | 71.6 | 58.6 | 54.4 | 43.7 | 58.1 |
| 1980 | 37.2 | 36.1 | 46.2 | 60.1 | 66.1 | 79.5 | 77.4 | 82.3 | 82.8 | 77.1 | 59.9 | 39.8 | 59.5 |
| 1981 | 33.0 | 43.7 | 47.6 | 62.1 | 66.2 | 78.7 | 80.2 | 77.0 | 71.0 | 58.3 | 51.4 | 38.5 | 59.0 |
| 1982 | 28.1 | 38.3 | 45.7 | 54.0 | 69.0 | 72.8 | 80.3 | 75.4 | 70.6 | 60.2 | 51.8 | 45.5 | 57.7 |
| 1983 | 38.1 | 38.7 | 48.8 | 53.3 | 64.9 | 75.0 | 81.2 | 81.0 | 72.6 | 60.5 | 50.3 | 36.0 | 58.4 |
| 1984 | 32.2 | 43.8 | 41.8 | 54.9 | 64.9 | 76.9 | 76.5 | 77.8 | 68.3 | 65.2 | 46.0 | 45.6 | 57.8 |
| 1985 | 30.8 | 37.8 | 47.7 | 61.6 | 68.1 | 72.3 | 79.0 | 76.7 | 71.9 | 61.2 | 54.3 | 36.4 | 58.2 |
| 1986 | 35.4 | 35.3 | 47.4 | 56.2 | 68.1 | 76.6 | 81.1 | 74.6 | 70.9 | 61.1 | 46.5 | 39.8 | 57.8 |
| 1987 | 34.7 | 37.0 | 47.7 | 54.8 | 67.2 | 76.4 | 82.6 | 78.7 | 72.1 | 54.4 | 49.9 | 41.5 | 58.1 |
| 1988 | 31.0 | 37.3 | 47.2 | 54.4 | 65.8 | 74.4 | 81.9 | 80.7 | 68.9 | 54.4 | 49.9 | 38.7 | 57.1 |
| 1989 | 39.9 | 37.8 | 46.1 | 55.4 | 64.1 | 76.8 | 78.3 | 77.1 | 71.4 | 60.5 | 48.0 | 27.9 | 56.9 |
| 1990 | 43.6 | 45.2 | 50.2 | 56.8 | 64.3 | 75.9 | 79.4 | 76.5 | 69.6 | 62.8 | 52.0 | 44.5 | 60.0 |
| Record Mean | 35.5 | 37.9 | 46.3 | 56.3 | 66.0 | 74.6 | 78.9 | 77.3 | 70.7 | 59.6 | 48.9 | 38.7 | 57.6 |
| Max | 43.1 | 46.3 | 55.5 | 66.6 | 75.8 | 83.9 | 87.8 | 85.9 | 79.5 | 68.9 | 57.6 | 46.3 | 66.4 |
| Min | 27.9 | 29.5 | 37.1 | 46.1 | 56.2 | 65.3 | 70.0 | 68.7 | 61.8 | 50.2 | 40.2 | 31.1 | 48.7 |

## REFERENCE NOTES FOR TABLES 1, 2, 3 and 6   (WASHINGTON [National Airport] D.C.)

**GENERAL**

T - TRACE AMOUNT
BLANK ENTRIES DENOTE MISSING/UNREPORTED DATA.
# INDICATES A STATION OR INSTRUMENT RELOCATION.

**SPECIFIC**

**TABLE 1**

(a) - LENGTH OF RECORD IN YEARS. ALTHOUGH
     INDIVIDUAL MONTHS MAY BE MISSING.

  * LESS THAN .05

NORMALS — BASED ON THE 1951-1980 RECORD PERIOD.
EXTREMES — DATES ARE THE MOST RECENT OCCURRENCE.
WIND DIR. — NUMERALS SHOW TENS OF DEGREES
           CLOCKWISE FROM TRUE NORTH.
           "00" INDICATES CALM.
RESULTANT WIND DIRECTIONS ARE GIVEN TO WHOLE DEGREES.

**TABLE 3**
MAX AND MIN ARE LONG-TERM MEAN DAILY MAXIMUM
AND MEAN DAILY MINIMUM TEMPERATURES.

**EXCEPTIONS**

**TABLES 2, 3, and 6**

* RECORD MEANS ARE THROUGH THE CURRENT YEAR,
  BEGINNING IN    1872 FOR TEMPERATURE
                 1871 FOR PRECIPITATION
                 1944 FOR SNOWFALL

## TABLE 4

HEATING DEGREE DAYS Base 65 deg. F          WASHINGTON, D.C. NATIONAL AIRPORT

| SEASON | JULY | AUG | SEP | OCT | NOV | DEC | JAN | FEB | MAR | APR | MAY | JUNE | TOTAL |
|--------|------|-----|-----|-----|-----|-----|-----|-----|-----|-----|-----|------|-------|
| 1961-62 | 0 | 0 | 16 | 181 | 459 | 882 | 932 | 848 | 642 | 302 | 60 | 0 | 4322 |
| 1962-63 | 0 | 0 | 59 | 182 | 599 | 981 | 1034 | 946 | 505 | 245 | 87 | 1 | 4639 |
| 1963-64 | 0 | 0 | 70 | 129 | 449 | 1042 | 882 | 810 | 536 | 339 | 54 | 4 | 4315 |
| 1964-65 | 0 | 0 | 29 | 300 | 415 | 771 | 974 | 785 | 724 | 395 | 27 | 24 | 4444 |
| 1965-66 | 0 | 1 | 18 | 236 | 458 | 723 | 1001 | 800 | 535 | 374 | 99 | 11 | 4256 |
| 1966-67 | 0 | 0 | 41 | 246 | 462 | 843 | 735 | 859 | 611 | 249 | 178 | 3 | 4227 |
| 1967-68 | 0 | 0 | 34 | 240 | 592 | 773 | 1033 | 886 | 471 | 216 | 87 | 0 | 4332 |
| 1968-69 | 0 | 0 | 0 | 162 | 445 | 875 | 949 | 780 | 671 | 208 | 40 | 0 | 4130 |
| 1969-70 | 0 | 0 | 18 | 226 | 525 | 883 | 1077 | 773 | 713 | 294 | 56 | 0 | 4565 |
| 1970-71 | 0 | 0 | 17 | 131 | 464 | 777 | 1034 | 722 | 670 | 294 | 85 | 2 | 4196 |
| 1971-72 | 0 | 0 | 12 | 61 | 518 | 597 | 815 | 817 | 599 | 326 | 56 | 21 | 3822 |
| 1972-73 | 0 | 0 | 8 | 278 | 543 | 654 | 843 | 777 | 423 | 286 | 109 | 0 | 3921 |
| 1973-74 | 0 | 0 | 4 | 103 | 399 | 708 | 677 | 716 | 490 | 228 | 85 | 4 | 3414 |
| 1974-75 | 0 | 0 | 26 | 250 | 446 | 674 | 740 | 677 | 608 | 345 | 24 | 0 | 3790 |
| 1975-76 | 0 | 0 | 20 | 102 | 328 | 752 | 956 | 524 | 415 | 236 | 80 | 0 | 3413 |
| 1976-77 | 0 | 0 | 11 | 306 | 652 | 907 | 1221 | 729 | 389 | 188 | 32 | 3 | 4438 |
| 1977-78 | 0 | 0 | 1 | 196 | 406 | 829 | 1001 | 933 | 633 | 219 | 86 | 0 | 4304 |
| 1978-79 | 0 | 0 | 9 | 192 | 378 | 671 | 918 | 1019 | 425 | 273 | 30 | 0 | 3915 |
| 1979-80 | 0 | 0 | 5 | 231 | 313 | 654 | 857 | 830 | 573 | 149 | 28 | 0 | 3640 |
| 1980-81 | 0 | 0 | 4 | 189 | 487 | 774 | 984 | 592 | 536 | 133 | 75 | 0 | 3774 |
| 1981-82 | 0 | 0 | 19 | 219 | 399 | 818 | 1135 | 743 | 592 | 328 | 19 | 3 | 4275 |
| 1982-83 | 0 | 2 | 9 | 193 | 402 | 597 | 827 | 730 | 497 | 365 | 77 | 0 | 3699 |
| 1983-84 | 0 | 0 | 32 | 177 | 433 | 890 | 1009 | 610 | 710 | 302 | 95 | 4 | 4262 |
| 1984-85 | 0 | 0 | 54 | 59 | 561 | 594 | 1053 | 757 | 533 | 166 | 30 | 6 | 3813 |
| 1985-86 | 0 | 0 | 14 | 147 | 320 | 879 | 913 | 824 | 542 | 267 | 61 | 3 | 3970 |
| 1986-87 | 0 | 13 | 18 | 180 | 548 | 775 | 931 | 777 | 527 | 304 | 68 | 0 | 4141 |
| 1987-88 | 0 | 0 | 4 | 325 | 448 | 719 | 1047 | 796 | 544 | 317 | 69 | 25 | 4294 |
| 1988-89 | 0 | 0 | 18 | 330 | 442 | 807 | 771 | 755 | 596 | 297 | 112 | 0 | 4128 |
| 1989-90 | 0 | 0 | 35 | 167 | 507 | 1144 | 656 | 550 | 481 | 285 | 64 | 4 | 3893 |
| 1990-91 | 0 | 0 | 38 | 153 | 381 | 630 | | | | | | | |

## TABLE 5

COOLING DEGREE DAYS Base 65 deg. F          WASHINGTON, D.C. NATIONAL AIRPORT

| YEAR | JAN | FEB | MAR | APR | MAY | JUNE | JULY | AUG | SEP | OCT | NOV | DEC | TOTAL |
|------|-----|-----|-----|-----|-----|------|------|-----|-----|-----|-----|-----|-------|
| 1969 | 0 | 0 | 0 | 24 | 151 | 367 | 458 | 360 | 180 | 39 | 1 | 0 | 1580 |
| 1970 | 0 | 0 | 0 | 10 | 166 | 311 | 449 | 442 | 324 | 60 | 0 | 0 | 1762 |
| 1971 | 0 | 0 | 0 | 0 | 52 | 337 | 422 | 372 | 258 | 60 | 22 | 0 | 1523 |
| 1972 | 0 | 0 | 3 | 5 | 50 | 184 | 393 | 346 | 195 | 8 | 2 | 0 | 1186 |
| 1973 | 0 | 0 | 2 | 21 | 47 | 371 | 448 | 469 | 288 | 57 | 3 | 0 | 1706 |
| 1974 | 0 | 0 | 4 | 33 | 96 | 205 | 441 | 422 | 192 | 17 | 27 | 0 | 1437 |
| 1975 | 1 | 0 | 0 | 12 | 177 | 344 | 448 | 475 | 132 | 50 | 15 | 0 | 1654 |
| 1976 | 0 | 4 | 1 | 92 | 86 | 383 | 424 | 370 | 179 | 15 | 0 | 0 | 1554 |
| 1977 | 0 | 0 | 10 | 49 | 177 | 289 | 496 | 434 | 274 | 18 | 15 | 0 | 1762 |
| 1978 | 0 | 0 | 0 | 10 | 117 | 358 | 434 | 514 | 274 | 25 | 0 | 0 | 1732 |
| 1979 | 0 | 0 | 14 | 9 | 120 | 231 | 431 | 425 | 208 | 39 | 2 | 0 | 1479 |
| 1980 | 0 | 0 | 0 | 9 | 174 | 301 | 546 | 563 | 374 | 38 | 1 | 0 | 2006 |
| 1981 | 0 | 0 | 6 | 49 | 118 | 417 | 478 | 380 | 204 | 18 | 0 | 0 | 1670 |
| 1982 | 0 | 0 | 0 | 6 | 155 | 244 | 479 | 330 | 185 | 51 | 13 | 1 | 1464 |
| 1983 | 0 | 0 | 0 | 21 | 81 | 310 | 510 | 504 | 269 | 42 | 0 | 0 | 1737 |
| 1984 | 0 | 0 | 0 | 4 | 99 | 368 | 365 | 404 | 157 | 73 | 0 | 0 | 1470 |
| 1985 | 0 | 0 | 6 | 70 | 135 | 232 | 444 | 373 | 228 | 37 | 6 | 0 | 1531 |
| 1986 | 0 | 0 | 5 | 10 | 162 | 358 | 503 | 318 | 202 | 70 | 1 | 0 | 1629 |
| 1987 | 0 | 0 | 0 | 8 | 146 | 347 | 554 | 431 | 222 | 0 | 0 | 0 | 1708 |
| 1988 | 0 | 0 | 1 | 4 | 101 | 313 | 534 | 490 | 144 | 11 | 0 | 0 | 1598 |
| 1989 | 0 | 0 | 16 | 14 | 91 | 362 | 417 | 381 | 233 | 33 | 1 | 0 | 1548 |
| 1990 | 0 | 0 | 30 | 46 | 50 | 309 | 451 | 364 | 183 | 88 | 0 | 0 | 1521 |

## TABLE 6

SNOWFALL (inches)          WASHINGTON, D.C. NATIONAL AIRPORT

| SEASON | JULY | AUG | SEP | OCT | NOV | DEC | JAN | FEB | MAR | APR | MAY | JUNE | TOTAL |
|--------|------|-----|-----|-----|-----|-----|-----|-----|-----|-----|-----|------|-------|
| 1961-62 | 0.0 | 0.0 | 0.0 | 0.0 | 1.3 | 1.2 | 2.0 | 6.5 | 4.0 | 0.0 | 0.0 | 0.0 | 15.0 |
| 1962-63 | 0.0 | 0.0 | 0.0 | 0.0 | T | 16.2 | 2.1 | 2.0 | 1.1 | 0.0 | T | 0.0 | 21.4 |
| 1963-64 | 0.0 | 0.0 | 0.0 | 0.0 | T | 6.4 | 8.9 | 11.7 | 6.2 | 0.4 | 0.0 | 0.0 | 33.6 |
| 1964-65 | 0.0 | 0.0 | 0.0 | 0.0 | 0.2 | 0.5 | 9.1 | 1.9 | 5.4 | 0.0 | 0.0 | 0.0 | 17.1 |
| 1965-66 | 0.0 | 0.0 | 0.0 | 0.0 | 0.0 | 0.2 | 21.3 | 6.9 | T | 0.0 | 0.0 | 0.0 | 28.4 |
| 1966-67 | 0.0 | 0.0 | 0.0 | 0.0 | T | 16.1 | 1.3 | 19.0 | 0.7 | 0.0 | 0.0- | 0.0 | 37.1 |
| 1967-68 | 0.0 | 0.0 | 0.0 | 0.0 | 6.9 | 6.3 | 2.8 | 2.4 | 3.0 | 0.0 | 0.0 | 0.0 | 21.4 |
| 1968-69 | 0.0 | 0.0 | 0.0 | 0.0 | T | 0.2 | 0.2 | 2.2 | 6.7 | 0.0 | 0.0 | 0.0 | 9.1 |
| 1969-70 | 0.0 | 0.0 | 0.0 | 0.0 | T | 6.8 | 3.6 | 3.6 | T | 0.0 | 0.0 | 0.0 | 14.0 |
| 1970-71 | 0.0 | 0.0 | 0.0 | 0.0 | T | 5.2 | 4.8 | 0.3 | 1.4 | T | 0.0 | 0.0 | 11.7 |
| 1971-72 | 0.0 | 0.0 | 0.0 | 0.0 | 1.4 | 0.1 | 0.3 | 14.4 | T | 0.6 | 0.0 | 0.0 | 16.8 |
| 1972-73 | 0.0 | 0.0 | 0.0 | T | T | 0.0 | 0.0 | T | 0.1 | T | 0.0 | 0.0 | 0.1 |
| 1973-74 | 0.0 | 0.0 | 0.0 | 0.0 | 0.0 | 11.0 | 1.5 | 4.2 | T | T | 0.0 | 0.0 | 16.7 |
| 1974-75 | 0.0 | 0.0 | 0.0 | T | T | 0.1 | 6.6 | 5.8 | 0.3 | T | 0.0 | 0.0 | 12.8 |
| 1975-76 | 0.0 | 0.0 | 0.0 | 0.0 | 0.0 | 0.4 | 0.1 | 0.9 | 0.8 | 0.0 | 0.0 | 0.0 | 2.2 |
| 1976-77 | 0.0 | 0.0 | 0.0 | 0.0 | 0.8 | 0.6 | 9.7 | 0.0 | 0.0 | T | 0.0 | 0.0 | 11.1 |
| 1977-78 | 0.0 | 0.0 | 0.0 | 0.0 | 0.0 | 0.1 | 10.3 | 3.8 | 8.3 | 0.0 | 0.0 | 0.0 | 22.7 |
| 1978-79 | 0.0 | 0.0 | 0.0 | 0.0 | 3.1 | T | 4.0 | 30.6 | T | 0.0 | 0.0 | 0.0 | 37.7 |
| 1979-80 | 0.0 | 0.0 | 0.0 | 0.3 | 0.0 | T | 8.6 | 5.1 | 6.1 | 0.0 | 0.0 | 0.0 | 20.1 |
| 1980-81 | 0.0 | 0.0 | 0.0 | 0.0 | T | 0.3 | 4.2 | T | T | 0.0 | 0.0 | 0.0 | 4.5 |
| 1981-82 | 0.0 | 0.0 | 0.0 | 0.0 | T | 1.7 | 15.3 | 5.3 | 0.2 | T | 0.0 | 0.0 | 22.5 |
| 1982-83 | 0.0 | 0.0 | 0.0 | 0.0 | 0.0 | 6.6 | T | 21.0 | 0.0 | T | 0.0 | 0.0 | 27.6 |
| 1983-84 | 0.0 | 0.0 | 0.0 | 0.0 | 0.3 | T | 6.5 | T | 1.8 | T | 0.0 | 0.0 | 8.6 |
| 1984-85 | 0.0 | 0.0 | 0.0 | 0.0 | T | 0.3 | 10.0 | T | T | T | 0.0 | 0.0 | 10.3 |
| 1985-86 | 0.0 | 0.0 | 0.0 | 0.0 | 0.0 | 0.7 | 1.8 | 12.9 | T | T | 0.0 | 0.0 | 15.4 |
| 1986-87 | 0.0 | 0.0 | 0.0 | 0.0 | 0.0 | T | 20.8 | 10.3 | T | T | 0.0 | 0.0 | 31.1 |
| 1987-88 | 0.0 | 0.0 | 0.0 | 0.0 | 11.5 | T | 13.1 | T | 0.4 | T | 0.0 | 0.0 | 25.0 |
| 1988-89 | 0.0 | 0.0 | 0.0 | 0.0 | 0.0 | 1.2 | 2.9 | 1.2 | 0.4 | 0.0 | 0.0 | 0.0 | 5.7 |
| 1989-90 | 0.0 | 0.0 | 0.0 | 0.0 | 3.5 | 9.0 | 0.2 | T | 2.4 | 0.2 | 0.0 | 0.0 | 15.3 |
| 1990-91 | T | 0.0 | 0.0 | 0.0 | 0.0 | 3.0 | | | | | | | |
| Record Mean | T | 0.0 | 0.0 | T | 0.9 | 3.2 | 5.5 | 5.4 | 2.1 | T | T | 0.0 | 17.1 |

**See Reference Notes, relative to all above tables, on preceding page.**

Daytona Beach is located on the Atlantic Ocean. The Halifax River, part of the Florida Inland Waterway, runs through the city. The terrain in the area is flat and the soil is mostly sandy. Elevations in the area range from 3 to 15 feet above mean sea level near the ocean to about 31 feet at the airport and on a ridge running along the western city limits.

Nearness to the ocean results in a climate tempered by the effect of land and sea breezes. In the summer, while maximum temperatures reach 90 degrees or above during the late morning or early afternoon, the number of hours of 90 degrees or above is relatively small due to the beginning of the sea breeze near midday and the occurrence of local afternoon convective thunderstorms which lower the temperature to the comfortable 80s. Winters, although subject to invasions of cold air, are relatively mild due to the nearness of the ocean and latitudinal location.

The rainy season from June through mid-October produces 60 percent of the annual rainfall. The major portion of the summer rainfall occurs in the form of local convective thunderstorms which are occasionally heavy and produce as much as 2 or 3 inches of rain. The more severe thunderstorms may be attended by strong gusty winds. Almost all rainfall during the winter months is associated with frontal passages.

Long periods of cloudiness and rain are infrequent, usually not lasting over 2 or 3 days. These periods are usually associated with a stationary front, a so-called northeaster, or a tropical disturbance.

Tropical disturbances or hurricanes are not considered a great threat to this area of the state. Generally hurricanes in this latitude tend to pass well offshore or lose much of their intensity while crossing the state before reaching this area. Only in gusts have hurricane-force winds been recorded at this station.

Heavy fog occurs mostly during the winter and early spring. These fogs usually form by radiational cooling at night and dissipate soon after sunrise. On rare occasions sea fog moves in from the ocean and persists for two or three days. There is no significant source in the area for air pollution.

## TABLE 1     NORMALS, MEANS AND EXTREMES

DAYTONA BEACH, FLORIDA

LATITUDE: 29°11'N    LONGITUDE: 81°03'W    ELEVATION: FT. GRND    29 BARO    34    TIME ZONE: EASTERN    WBAN: 12834

| | (a) | JAN | FEB | MAR | APR | MAY | JUNE | JULY | AUG | SEP | OCT | NOV | DEC | YEAR |
|---|---|---|---|---|---|---|---|---|---|---|---|---|---|---|
| **TEMPERATURE °F:** | | | | | | | | | | | | | | |
| Normals | | | | | | | | | | | | | | |
| -Daily Maximum | | 68.4 | 69.3 | 74.6 | 80.0 | 84.8 | 87.8 | 89.6 | 89.0 | 86.9 | 81.2 | 74.8 | 69.8 | 79.7 |
| -Daily Minimum | | 47.4 | 48.2 | 53.6 | 59.1 | 65.3 | 70.5 | 72.5 | 72.8 | 72.1 | 65.1 | 55.5 | 49.2 | 60.9 |
| -Monthly | | 57.9 | 58.8 | 64.1 | 69.6 | 75.1 | 79.2 | 81.1 | 80.9 | 79.5 | 73.2 | 65.2 | 59.5 | 70.3 |
| Extremes | | | | | | | | | | | | | | |
| -Record Highest | 46 | 86 | 89 | 91 | 96 | 100 | 102 | 102 | 100 | 99 | 95 | 89 | 86 | 102 |
| -Year | | 1985 | 1985 | 1977 | 1968 | 1953 | 1944 | 1981 | 1989 | 1944 | 1959 | 1948 | 1978 | JUL 1981 |
| -Record Lowest | 46 | 15 | 24 | 26 | 35 | 44 | 52 | 60 | 65 | 52 | 41 | 27 | 19 | 15 |
| -Year | | 1985 | 1958 | 1980 | 1950 | 1971 | 1984 | 1981 | 1984 | 1956 | 1989 | 1950 | 1983 | JAN 1985 |
| **NORMAL DEGREE DAYS:** | | | | | | | | | | | | | | |
| Heating (base 65°F) | | 264 | 214 | 116 | 14 | 0 | 0 | 0 | 0 | 0 | 0 | 83 | 209 | 900 |
| Cooling (base 65°F) | | 44 | 41 | 88 | 152 | 313 | 426 | 499 | 493 | 435 | 259 | 89 | 39 | 2878 |
| **% OF POSSIBLE SUNSHINE** | | | | | | | | | | | | | | |
| **MEAN SKY COVER (tenths)** | | | | | | | | | | | | | | |
| Sunrise - Sunset | 41 | 5.7 | 5.7 | 5.6 | 5.0 | 5.3 | 6.2 | 6.3 | 6.2 | 6.4 | 5.6 | 5.3 | 5.8 | 5.8 |
| **MEAN NUMBER OF DAYS:** | | | | | | | | | | | | | | |
| Sunrise to Sunset | | | | | | | | | | | | | | |
| -Clear | 46 | 9.5 | 8.9 | 9.6 | 11.0 | 10.0 | 5.8 | 4.4 | 4.8 | 5.2 | 9.4 | 10.1 | 9.3 | 98.2 |
| -Partly Cloudy | 46 | 9.3 | 8.0 | 9.7 | 10.6 | 11.4 | 12.5 | 14.6 | 15.5 | 12.7 | 10.7 | 10.1 | 9.0 | 134.0 |
| -Cloudy | 46 | 12.2 | 11.3 | 11.7 | 8.4 | 9.5 | 11.6 | 12.0 | 10.7 | 12.1 | 10.9 | 9.8 | 12.7 | 133.0 |
| Precipitation | | | | | | | | | | | | | | |
| .01 inches or more | 46 | 7.0 | 7.8 | 7.9 | 5.7 | 8.2 | 12.1 | 13.4 | 13.7 | 13.2 | 10.4 | 7.2 | 7.3 | 114.0 |
| Snow, Ice pellets | | | | | | | | | | | | | | |
| 1.0 inches or more | 46 | 0.0 | 0.0 | 0.0 | 0.0 | 0.0 | 0.0 | 0.0 | 0.0 | 0.0 | 0.0 | 0.0 | 0.0 | 0.0 |
| Thunderstorms | 45 | 1.0 | 1.8 | 3.3 | 3.5 | 7.8 | 13.1 | 17.4 | 15.4 | 8.6 | 3.1 | 1.2 | 1.1 | 77.4 |
| Heavy Fog Visibility | | | | | | | | | | | | | | |
| 1/4 mile or less | 45 | 5.3 | 3.3 | 3.3 | 1.9 | 1.5 | 1.0 | 1.1 | 1.3 | 0.7 | 1.5 | 2.9 | 4.5 | 28.3 |
| Temperature °F | | | | | | | | | | | | | | |
| -Maximum | | | | | | | | | | | | | | |
| 90° and above | 46 | 0.0 | 0.0 | 0.2 | 1.7 | 5.0 | 10.7 | 16.3 | 14.3 | 6.1 | 0.8 | 0.0 | 0.0 | 55.0 |
| 32° and below | 46 | 0.0 | 0.0 | 0.0 | 0.0 | 0.0 | 0.0 | 0.0 | 0.0 | 0.0 | 0.0 | 0.0 | 0.0 | 0.0 |
| -Minimum | | | | | | | | | | | | | | |
| 32° and below | 46 | 2.5 | 1.2 | 0.3 | 0.0 | 0.0 | 0.0 | 0.0 | 0.0 | 0.0 | 0.0 | 0.2 | 1.7 | 5.8 |
| 0° and below | 46 | 0.0 | 0.0 | 0.0 | 0.0 | 0.0 | 0.0 | 0.0 | 0.0 | 0.0 | 0.0 | 0.0 | 0.0 | 0.0 |
| **AVG. STATION PRESS. (mb)** | 17 | 1018.8 | 1018.0 | 1016.5 | 1015.9 | 1014.7 | 1015.2 | 1016.7 | 1016.0 | 1014.8 | 1016.1 | 1017.5 | 1019.0 | 1016.6 |
| **RELATIVE HUMIDITY (%)** | | | | | | | | | | | | | | |
| Hour 01 | 45 | 85 | 83 | 83 | 83 | 85 | 88 | 89 | 90 | 88 | 85 | 86 | 85 | 86 |
| Hour 07 | 45 | 87 | 86 | 86 | 85 | 85 | 87 | 88 | 91 | 90 | 87 | 87 | 87 | 87 |
| Hour 13 (Local Time) | 45 | 59 | 57 | 55 | 53 | 57 | 63 | 65 | 67 | 67 | 63 | 60 | 60 | 61 |
| Hour 19 | 45 | 77 | 72 | 70 | 68 | 71 | 76 | 78 | 80 | 80 | 77 | 79 | 79 | 76 |
| **PRECIPITATION (inches):** | | | | | | | | | | | | | | |
| Water Equivalent | | | | | | | | | | | | | | |
| -Normal | | 2.37 | 3.11 | 2.99 | 2.25 | 3.38 | 6.41 | 5.52 | 6.34 | 6.68 | 4.62 | 2.59 | 2.20 | 48.46 |
| -Maximum Monthly | 46 | 7.16 | 9.13 | 7.94 | 7.12 | 12.33 | 15.19 | 14.58 | 19.89 | 15.20 | 13.00 | 10.96 | 11.98 | 19.89 |
| -Year | | 1986 | 1960 | 1987 | 1949 | 1976 | 1966 | 1944 | 1953 | 1979 | 1950 | 1972 | 1983 | AUG 1953 |
| -Minimum Monthly | 46 | 0.15 | 0.29 | 0.25 | T | 0.08 | 1.03 | 1.07 | 2.01 | 0.42 | 0.19 | T | 0.06 | T |
| -Year | | 1950 | 1944 | 1956 | 1967 | 1965 | 1981 | 1976 | 1963 | 1972 | 1967 | 1967 | 1956 | APR 1967 |
| -Maximum in 24 hrs | 46 | 5.73 | 4.39 | 5.74 | 4.03 | 4.22 | 6.28 | 4.21 | 4.76 | 6.34 | 9.29 | 5.83 | 5.22 | 9.29 |
| -Year | | 1989 | 1971 | 1953 | 1982 | 1947 | 1966 | 1986 | 1974 | 1964 | 1953 | 1979 | 1983 | OCT 1953 |
| Snow, Ice pellets | | | | | | | | | | | | | | |
| -Maximum Monthly | 46 | T | T | 0.0 | 0.0 | 0.0 | T | 0.0 | 0.0 | 0.0 | 0.0 | 0.0 | T | T |
| -Year | | 1977 | 1951 | | | | 1989 | | | | | | 1989 | JUN 1989 |
| -Maximum in 24 hrs | 46 | T | T | 0.0 | 0.0 | 0.0 | T | 0.0 | 0.0 | 0.0 | 0.0 | 0.0 | T | T |
| -Year | | 1977 | 1951 | | | | 1989 | | | | | | 1989 | JUN 1989 |
| **WIND:** | | | | | | | | | | | | | | |
| Mean Speed (mph) | 44 | 8.9 | 9.6 | 9.9 | 9.6 | 8.9 | 8.1 | 7.4 | 7.1 | 8.4 | 9.2 | 8.6 | 8.5 | 8.7 |
| Prevailing Direction | | | | | | | | | | | | | | |
| through 1963 | | NW | NNW | SSW | E | E | SW | SSW | E | E | NE | NW | NW | E |
| Fastest Obs. 1 Min. | | | | | | | | | | | | | | |
| -Direction (!!!) | 41 | 26 | 20 | 20 | 18 | 24 | 33 | 25 | 11 | 11 | 05 | 27 | 34 | 11 |
| -Speed (MPH) | 41 | 43 | 44 | 45 | 46 | 41 | 40 | 40 | 50 | 58 | 53 | 37 | 40 | 58 |
| -Year | | 1978 | 1960 | 1986 | 1953 | 1989 | 1989 | 1963 | 1949 | 1960 | 1950 | 1963 | 1954 | SEP 1960 |
| Peak Gust | | | | | | | | | | | | | | |
| -Direction (!!!) | 6 | W | SW | W | SW | SW | NW | SW | W | S | W | SW | NW | SW |
| -Speed (mph) | 6 | 52 | 51 | 63 | 49 | 69 | 67 | 59 | 68 | 48 | 56 | 47 | 43 | 69 |
| -Date | | 1986 | 1984 | 1986 | 1988 | 1989 | 1989 | 1989 | 1989 | 1984 | 1985 | 1988 | 1989 | MAY 1989 |

**See Reference Notes to this table on the following page.**

PRECIPITATION (inches)   DAYTONA BEACH, FLORIDA

**TABLE 2**

| YEAR | JAN | FEB | MAR | APR | MAY | JUNE | JULY | AUG | SEP | OCT | NOV | DEC | ANNUAL |
|---|---|---|---|---|---|---|---|---|---|---|---|---|---|
| 1961 | 1.96 | 3.70 | 1.17 | 2.16 | 2.39 | 6.81 | 5.16 | 7.68 | 3.20 | 2.25 | 2.85 | 0.73 | 40.06 |
| 1962 | 0.90 | 0.82 | 1.82 | 0.78 | 0.16 | 7.96 | 10.04 | 8.50 | 8.84 | 3.57 | 2.49 | 0.71 | 46.59 |
| 1963 | 2.91 | 5.83 | 1.46 | 1.40 | 6.82 | 7.42 | 6.89 | 2.01 | 5.43 | 2.71 | 7.98 | 2.17 | 53.03 |
| 1964 | 5.29 | 2.65 | 4.84 | 3.61 | 2.58 | 4.73 | 7.67 | 10.81 | 11.39 | 3.54 | 3.13 | 2.52 | 62.76 |
| 1965 | 2.22 | 3.00 | 3.05 | 1.00 | 0.08 | 9.00 | 3.72 | 2.97 | 4.33 | 3.65 | 0.97 | 2.14 | 36.13 |
| 1966 | 2.89 | 5.58 | 0.36 | 2.56 | 6.77 | 15.19 | 7.09 | 7.93 | 4.49 | 4.60 | 1.19 | 1.60 | 60.25 |
| 1967 | 1.26 | 3.98 | 0.31 | T | 0.73 | 7.51 | 9.04 | 3.02 | 5.56 | 0.19 | T | 2.98 | 34.58 |
| 1968 | 0.42 | 1.73 | 1.79 | 0.40 | 4.79 | 14.38 | 6.25 | 11.09 | 6.07 | 7.44 | 2.43 | 1.38 | 58.17 |
| 1969 | 1.53 | 2.03 | 2.74 | 0.12 | 6.47 | 2.47 | 2.61 | 9.40 | 8.89 | 6.97 | 1.96 | 5.03 | 50.22 |
| 1970 | 3.94 | 3.79 | 3.59 | 2.08 | 1.68 | 2.62 | 3.65 | 3.61 | 3.54 | 3.87 | 0.31 | 0.72 | 33.40 |
| 1971 | 0.61 | 5.48 | 2.00 | 2.57 | 3.12 | 4.73 | 3.20 | 3.97 | 7.20 | 9.53 | 1.33 | 2.49 | 46.23 |
| 1972 | 2.37 | 3.97 | 6.66 | 1.41 | 4.02 | 7.06 | 3.22 | 8.29 | 0.42 | 3.08 | 10.96 | 2.48 | 53.94 |
| 1973 | 4.66 | 2.02 | 2.63 | 3.09 | 2.41 | 4.32 | 4.69 | 7.58 | 5.14 | 4.40 | 0.75 | 2.54 | 44.23 |
| 1974 | 0.30 | 1.10 | 3.19 | 0.44 | 2.66 | 8.65 | 6.31 | 9.96 | 10.50 | 1.42 | 0.48 | 2.20 | 47.21 |
| 1975 | 1.66 | 2.27 | 1.52 | 2.96 | 2.99 | 9.00 | 6.89 | 3.16 | 6.61 | 5.84 | 1.46 | 0.83 | 45.19 |
| 1976 | 0.60 | 0.70 | 2.03 | 4.27 | 12.33 | 11.14 | 1.07 | 3.80 | 5.10 | 1.90 | 3.38 | 6.00 | 52.32 |
| 1977 | 4.69 | 2.45 | 1.43 | 0.41 | 4.61 | 1.15 | 2.23 | 7.91 | 6.55 | 1.46 | 3.04 | 4.74 | 40.67 |
| 1978 | 2.89 | 5.98 | 2.31 | 3.30 | 0.56 | 7.48 | 5.53 | 7.99 | 4.63 | 8.31 | 0.07 | 4.89 | 53.94 |
| #1979 | 7.10 | 1.94 | 4.08 | 3.96 | 6.13 | 3.03 | 11.69 | 5.24 | 15.20 | 2.13 | 7.96 | 0.56 | 69.02 |
| 1980 | 3.75 | 0.76 | 2.41 | 2.54 | 3.62 | 5.57 | 5.82 | 4.13 | 1.83 | 2.42 | 3.12 | 1.39 | 37.36 |
| 1981 | 0.32 | 5.54 | 3.00 | 0.29 | 1.74 | 1.03 | 4.69 | 7.19 | 7.59 | 1.08 | 2.57 | 4.64 | 39.68 |
| 1982 | 2.46 | 2.08 | 5.81 | 6.04 | 4.68 | 8.29 | 5.31 | 3.21 | 4.96 | 3.23 | 1.58 | 2.53 | 50.18 |
| 1983 | 2.51 | 5.96 | 7.71 | 6.17 | 3.86 | 6.37 | 1.92 | 6.82 | 8.57 | 10.11 | 2.01 | 11.98 | 73.99 |
| 1984 | 1.46 | 3.44 | 1.31 | 5.29 | 6.04 | 2.84 | 6.77 | 4.02 | 10.73 | 1.09 | 3.52 | 0.20 | 46.71 |
| 1985 | 0.79 | 0.58 | 1.49 | 3.14 | 3.42 | 6.81 | 2.01 | 9.83 | 10.62 | 4.08 | 0.41 | 2.05 | 45.38 |
| 1986 | 7.16 | 1.28 | 1.85 | 0.44 | 0.99 | 3.50 | 14.43 | 3.47 | 3.58 | 3.47 | 5.08 | 2.76 | 48.01 |
| 1987 | 2.21 | 6.64 | 7.94 | 0.28 | 2.65 | 3.81 | 2.78 | 4.89 | 5.63 | 2.77 | 5.87 | 0.25 | 45.72 |
| 1988 | 5.36 | 1.72 | 4.57 | 1.68 | 1.78 | 2.39 | 2.94 | 4.79 | 6.81 | 1.24 | 6.70 | 0.93 | 40.91 |
| 1989 | 6.82 | 0.64 | 2.01 | 2.92 | 2.02 | 1.84 | 2.44 | 4.47 | 5.04 | 11.64 | 0.88 | 3.93 | 44.65 |
| 1990 | 1.42 | 5.61 | 1.94 | 1.48 | 1.45 | 2.71 | 5.85 | 7.00 | 1.61 | 5.88 | 0.83 | 0.34 | 36.12 |
| Record Mean | 2.35 | 3.02 | 3.19 | 2.50 | 3.04 | 5.87 | 6.16 | 6.29 | 6.85 | 4.93 | 2.53 | 2.32 | 49.07 |

**TABLE 3**   AVERAGE TEMPERATURE (deg. F)   DAYTONA BEACH, FLORIDA

| YEAR | JAN | FEB | MAR | APR | MAY | JUNE | JULY | AUG | SEP | OCT | NOV | DEC | ANNUAL |
|---|---|---|---|---|---|---|---|---|---|---|---|---|---|
| 1961 | 54.0 | 60.5 | 67.1 | 65.6 | 73.5 | 76.8 | 79.9 | 80.5 | 78.7 | 71.9 | 67.4 | 61.1 | 69.8 |
| 1962 | 57.2 | 64.8 | 60.6 | 66.9 | 76.7 | 78.6 | 81.3 | 80.8 | 79.3 | 73.0 | 62.0 | 55.0 | 69.7 |
| 1963 | 54.7 | 66.5 | 66.5 | 71.6 | 75.8 | 81.2 | 80.6 | 81.3 | 78.7 | 71.8 | 63.3 | 54.8 | 69.8 |
| 1964 | 56.7 | 56.4 | 64.2 | 71.1 | 74.8 | 80.6 | 81.0 | 80.8 | 78.3 | 70.4 | 67.9 | 62.9 | 70.4 |
| 1965 | 57.5 | 61.3 | 63.6 | 70.8 | 72.3 | 77.3 | 78.7 | 79.9 | 79.1 | 71.6 | 65.5 | 59.7 | 69.8 |
| 1966 | 57.0 | 59.2 | 61.9 | 68.2 | 75.6 | 77.6 | 81.6 | 81.2 | 79.1 | 74.2 | 64.1 | 58.4 | 69.8 |
| 1967 | 60.6 | 58.5 | 67.0 | 72.4 | 75.5 | 78.0 | 79.4 | 78.7 | 76.0 | 71.3 | 64.5 | 63.2 | 70.5 |
| 1968 | 58.2 | 52.9 | 60.0 | 72.2 | 75.1 | 78.6 | 80.7 | 80.8 | 79.1 | 73.2 | 61.6 | 56.2 | 69.0 |
| 1969 | 58.0 | 55.2 | 57.9 | 70.5 | 74.4 | 80.5 | 82.8 | 80.4 | 79.7 | 77.1 | 63.5 | 56.5 | 69.7 |
| 1970 | 54.5 | 56.1 | 65.5 | 73.1 | 76.1 | 80.8 | 82.7 | 83.5 | 82.4 | 76.9 | 60.6 | 61.5 | 71.1 |
| 1971 | 58.6 | 59.9 | 60.0 | 68.0 | 73.3 | 78.7 | 80.5 | 80.7 | 79.6 | 76.1 | 65.9 | 67.8 | 70.7 |
| 1972 | 65.5 | 59.0 | 64.7 | 70.8 | 74.4 | 79.6 | 80.7 | 80.2 | 78.7 | 75.0 | 67.3 | 63.5 | 71.6 |
| 1973 | 58.9 | 56.3 | 68.2 | 68.7 | 75.2 | 79.8 | 81.9 | 80.3 | 80.8 | 75.0 | 69.6 | 58.4 | 71.1 |
| 1974 | 69.5 | 59.5 | 68.5 | 69.3 | 76.0 | 78.6 | 79.2 | 80.3 | 80.5 | 72.0 | 65.5 | 59.5 | 71.5 |
| 1975 | 63.6 | 65.7 | 65.6 | 70.1 | 77.2 | 79.5 | 80.5 | 80.5 | 79.6 | 75.2 | 66.8 | 58.6 | 71.9 |
| 1976 | 54.4 | 61.1 | 68.1 | 67.7 | 73.3 | 77.4 | 80.9 | 80.0 | 78.3 | 70.4 | 60.5 | 59.4 | 69.3 |
| 1977 | 50.6 | 55.5 | 68.9 | 70.0 | 74.8 | 82.3 | 82.6 | 82.6 | 80.8 | 70.8 | 67.1 | 58.3 | 70.3 |
| 1978 | 53.9 | 52.1 | 62.3 | 71.3 | 77.3 | 81.5 | 82.7 | 82.3 | 80.7 | 74.2 | 65.6 | 65.6 | 71.3 |
| #1979 | 56.7 | 57.1 | 64.4 | 72.3 | 75.5 | 78.7 | 82.1 | 80.0 | 80.2 | 72.9 | 66.1 | 59.6 | 70.4 |
| 1980 | 57.7 | 55.3 | 66.3 | 68.8 | 74.9 | 79.2 | 82.8 | 82.1 | 80.3 | 72.7 | 65.3 | 57.0 | 70.2 |
| 1981 | 48.8 | 59.2 | 60.4 | 70.5 | 73.5 | 82.0 | 82.0 | 81.5 | 77.7 | 73.8 | 62.7 | 57.1 | 69.2 |
| 1982 | 56.6 | 64.4 | 66.8 | 69.4 | 72.6 | 79.5 | 80.0 | 79.9 | 77.9 | 71.5 | 68.8 | 64.0 | 70.9 |
| 1983 | 53.9 | 57.2 | 60.2 | 64.3 | 72.4 | 77.0 | 81.7 | 81.1 | 77.8 | 73.5 | 62.6 | 58.1 | 68.3 |
| 1984 | 55.1 | 58.0 | 61.8 | 66.8 | 72.4 | 76.3 | 79.0 | 81.4 | 79.5 | 75.7 | 66.5 | 65.2 | 69.8 |
| 1985 | 53.7 | 61.0 | 66.6 | 69.4 | 76.1 | 81.7 | 80.6 | 81.4 | 78.3 | 76.8 | 71.2 | 56.1 | 71.1 |
| 1986 | 56.7 | 62.4 | 63.1 | 66.3 | 73.8 | 79.9 | 81.4 | 81.4 | 79.6 | 75.3 | 72.5 | 64.7 | 71.4 |
| 1987 | 55.8 | 59.7 | 63.3 | 65.1 | 74.3 | 79.7 | 81.9 | 82.3 | 79.6 | 70.0 | 66.5 | 61.9 | 70.0 |
| 1988 | 55.1 | 56.8 | 62.8 | 69.1 | 72.6 | 79.0 | 81.2 | 81.5 | 80.6 | 70.7 | 67.5 | 59.8 | 69.7 |
| 1989 | 64.8 | 61.9 | 67.8 | 69.5 | 75.4 | 80.3 | 82.7 | 81.8 | 80.5 | 73.4 | 65.9 | 53.3 | 71.4 |
| 1990 | 62.7 | 67.5 | 66.4 | 69.6 | 77.3 | 80.7 | 81.9 | 81.9 | 80.5 | 76.0 | 67.4 | 65.1 | 73.1 |
| Record Mean | 58.2 | 59.6 | 64.3 | 69.2 | 74.7 | 79.2 | 80.9 | 80.9 | 79.3 | 73.3 | 65.7 | 59.9 | 70.4 |
| Max | 69.0 | 70.3 | 75.0 | 79.9 | 84.7 | 88.3 | 89.8 | 89.4 | 87.0 | 81.5 | 75.4 | 70.3 | 80.0 |
| Min | 47.4 | 48.8 | 53.5 | 58.5 | 64.6 | 70.1 | 72.0 | 72.4 | 71.6 | 65.0 | 55.9 | 49.4 | 60.8 |

## REFERENCE NOTES FOR TABLES 1, 2, 3 and 6   (DAYTONA BEACH, FL)

### GENERAL

T - TRACE AMOUNT
BLANK ENTRIES DENOTE MISSING/UNREPORTED DATA.
# INDICATES A STATION OR INSTRUMENT RELOCATION.

### SPECIFIC

#### TABLE 1

(a) - LENGTH OF RECORD IN YEARS. ALTHOUGH INDIVIDUAL MONTHS MAY BE MISSING.
  * LESS THAN .05

NORMALS — BASED ON THE 1951-1980 RECORD PERIOD.
EXTREMES -- DATES ARE THE MOST RECENT OCCURRENCE.
WIND DIR. — NUMERALS SHOW TENS OF DEGREES CLOCKWISE FROM TRUE NORTH. "00" INDICATES CALM.
RESULTANT WIND DIRECTIONS ARE GIVEN TO WHOLE DEGREES.

#### TABLE 3

MAX AND MIN ARE LONG-TERM MEAN DAILY MAXIMUM AND MEAN DAILY MINIMUM TEMPERATURES.

### EXCEPTIONS

#### TABLES 2, 3, and 6

RECORD MEANS ARE THROUGH THE CURRENT YEAR, BEGINNING IN   1935 FOR TEMPERATURE
1935 FOR PRECIPITATION
1944 FOR SNOWFALL

**TABLE 4**

HEATING DEGREE DAYS Base 65 deg. F          DAYTONA BEACH, FLORIDA

| SEASON | JULY | AUG | SEP | OCT | NOV | DEC | JAN | FEB | MAR | APR | MAY | JUNE | TOTAL |
|---|---|---|---|---|---|---|---|---|---|---|---|---|---|
| 1961-62 | 0 | 0 | 0 | 8 | 33 | 192 | 259 | 88 | 179 | 55 | 0 | 0 | 814 |
| 1962-63 | 0 | 0 | 0 | 16 | 117 | 320 | 264 | 288 | 73 | 15 | 0 | 0 | 1093 |
| 1963-64 | 0 | 0 | 0 | 15 | 91 | 322 | 279 | 251 | 106 | 13 | 0 | 0 | 1077 |
| 1964-65 | 0 | 0 | 0 | 18 | 22 | 126 | 246 | 138 | 136 | 9 | 1 | 0 | 696 |
| 1965-66 | 0 | 0 | 0 | 10 | 57 | 173 | 263 | 192 | 120 | 26 | 0 | 0 | 841 |
| 1966-67 | 0 | 0 | 0 | 3 | 88 | 217 | 168 | 192 | 37 | 5 | 0 | 0 | 710 |
| 1967-68 | 0 | 0 | 0 | 6 | 72 | 108 | 227 | 344 | 185 | 0 | 0 | 0 | 942 |
| 1968-69 | 0 | 0 | 0 | 27 | 152 | 301 | 216 | 275 | 228 | 2 | 0 | 0 | 1201 |
| 1969-70 | 0 | 0 | 0 | 0 | 105 | 272 | 330 | 252 | 80 | 2 | 0 | 0 | 1041 |
| 1970-71 | 0 | 0 | 0 | 0 | 164 | 143 | 230 | 199 | 194 | 55 | 7 | 0 | 992 |
| 1971-72 | 0 | 0 | 0 | 0 | 71 | 19 | 85 | 182 | 69 | 15 | 0 | 0 | 441 |
| 1972-73 | 0 | 0 | 0 | 0 | 62 | 139 | 226 | 251 | 38 | 29 | 0 | 0 | 745 |
| 1973-74 | 0 | 0 | 0 | 10 | 15 | 239 | 0 | 197 | 30 | 24 | 0 | 0 | 515 |
| 1974-75 | 0 | 0 | 0 | 0 | 69 | 201 | 108 | 69 | 91 | 30 | 0 | 0 | 568 |
| 1975-76 | 0 | 0 | 0 | 0 | 102 | 222 | 334 | 143 | 34 | 16 | 0 | 0 | 851 |
| 1976-77 | 0 | 0 | 0 | 11 | 168 | 209 | 444 | 273 | 53 | 20 | 0 | 0 | 1178 |
| 1977-78 | 0 | 0 | 0 | 23 | 63 | 241 | 352 | 356 | 132 | 5 | 0 | 0 | 1172 |
| #1978-79 | 0 | 0 | 0 | 0 | 4 | 71 | 279 | 244 | 79 | 5 | 0 | 0 | 682 |
| 1979-80 | 0 | 0 | 0 | 0 | 75 | 183 | 234 | 297 | 84 | 16 | 0 | 0 | 889 |
| 1980-81 | 0 | 0 | 0 | 11 | 93 | 247 | 497 | 184 | 171 | 0 | 1 | 0 | 1204 |
| 1981-82 | 0 | 0 | 0 | 0 | 127 | 284 | 273 | 72 | 63 | 26 | 0 | 0 | 845 |
| 1982-83 | 0 | 0 | 0 | 24 | 21 | 125 | 345 | 220 | 167 | 74 | 2 | 0 | 978 |
| 1983-84 | 0 | 0 | 0 | 2 | 126 | 255 | 323 | 215 | 148 | 37 | 3 | 0 | 1109 |
| 1984-85 | 0 | 0 | 0 | 0 | 63 | 77 | 372 | 173 | 44 | 21 | 0 | 0 | 750 |
| 1985-86 | 0 | 0 | 0 | 0 | 24 | 303 | 261 | 119 | 141 | 30 | 0 | 0 | 878 |
| 1986-87 | 0 | 0 | 0 | 0 | 11 | 84 | 301 | 160 | 99 | 81 | 0 | 0 | 736 |
| 1987-88 | 0 | 0 | 0 | 10 | 74 | 146 | 316 | 259 | 120 | 23 | 0 | 0 | 948 |
| 1988-89 | 0 | 0 | 0 | 1 | 39 | 187 | 70 | 154 | 68 | 20 | 1 | 0 | 540 |
| 1989-90 | 0 | 0 | 0 | 31 | 59 | 369 | 120 | 47 | 37 | 14 | 0 | 0 | 677 |
| 1990-91 | 0 | 0 | 0 | 9 | 35 | 96 | | | | | | | |

**TABLE 5**

COOLING DEGREE DAYS Base 65 deg. F          DAYTONA BEACH, FLORIDA

| YEAR | JAN | FEB | MAR | APR | MAY | JUNE | JULY | AUG | SEP | OCT | NOV | DEC | TOTAL |
|---|---|---|---|---|---|---|---|---|---|---|---|---|---|
| 1969 | 7 | 4 | 17 | 173 | 300 | 473 | 559 | 483 | 447 | 383 | 66 | 13 | 2925 |
| 1970 | 13 | 9 | 101 | 253 | 351 | 478 | 557 | 580 | 532 | 373 | 37 | 40 | 3324 |
| 1971 | 39 | 65 | 45 | 150 | 270 | 420 | 484 | 495 | 445 | 348 | 106 | 113 | 2980 |
| 1972 | 107 | 16 | 67 | 193 | 299 | 447 | 494 | 477 | 415 | 317 | 138 | 98 | 3068 |
| 1973 | 45 | 14 | 148 | 148 | 324 | 450 | 527 | 482 | 483 | 326 | 156 | 40 | 3143 |
| 1974 | 147 | 50 | 145 | 159 | 349 | 414 | 447 | 480 | 469 | 223 | 90 | 40 | 3013 |
| 1975 | 71 | 95 | 118 | 191 | 386 | 441 | 488 | 487 | 445 | 325 | 163 | 29 | 3239 |
| 1976 | 12 | 36 | 136 | 104 | 264 | 378 | 497 | 471 | 406 | 186 | 39 | 40 | 2569 |
| 1977 | 4 | 12 | 181 | 177 | 310 | 527 | 553 | 554 | 478 | 212 | 131 | 41 | 3180 |
| 1978 | 14 | 0 | 56 | 198 | 388 | 499 | 553 | 543 | 477 | 295 | 192 | 94 | 3309 |
| #1979 | 26 | 28 | 68 | 231 | 332 | 419 | 538 | 471 | 462 | 252 | 111 | 23 | 2961 |
| 1980 | 12 | 21 | 131 | 135 | 315 | 435 | 559 | 538 | 467 | 258 | 109 | 5 | 2985 |
| 1981 | 0 | 25 | 37 | 172 | 269 | 516 | 559 | 521 | 385 | 282 | 65 | 47 | 2878 |
| 1982 | 19 | 61 | 127 | 166 | 240 | 440 | 472 | 470 | 392 | 234 | 141 | 97 | 2859 |
| 1983 | 6 | 6 | 28 | 57 | 238 | 369 | 521 | 504 | 391 | 270 | 62 | 46 | 2498 |
| 1984 | 22 | 20 | 55 | 96 | 238 | 345 | 442 | 515 | 441 | 338 | 114 | 91 | 2717 |
| 1985 | 29 | 67 | 101 | 160 | 348 | 506 | 490 | 511 | 405 | 373 | 217 | 35 | 3242 |
| 1986 | 13 | 50 | 89 | 79 | 280 | 452 | 516 | 515 | 444 | 324 | 246 | 82 | 3090 |
| 1987 | 20 | 17 | 52 | 92 | 297 | 449 | 530 | 543 | 442 | 171 | 125 | 58 | 2796 |
| 1988 | 17 | 27 | 62 | 155 | 242 | 425 | 509 | 518 | 474 | 185 | 121 | 32 | 2767 |
| 1989 | 71 | 74 | 162 | 162 | 331 | 468 | 553 | 530 | 474 | 299 | 94 | 11 | 3229 |
| 1990 | 55 | 124 | 85 | 161 | 385 | 478 | 531 | 528 | 470 | 355 | 114 | 107 | 3393 |

**TABLE 6**

SNOWFALL (inches)          DAYTONA BEACH, FLORIDA

| SEASON | JULY | AUG | SEP | OCT | NOV | DEC | JAN | FEB | MAR | APR | MAY | JUNE | TOTAL |
|---|---|---|---|---|---|---|---|---|---|---|---|---|---|
| 1970-71 | 0.0 | 0.0 | 0.0 | 0.0 | 0.0 | 0.0 | 0.0 | 0.0 | 0.0 | 0.0 | 0.0 | 0.0 | 0.0 |
| 1971-72 | 0.0 | 0.0 | 0.0 | 0.0 | 0.0 | 0.0 | 0.0 | 0.0 | 0.0 | 0.0 | 0.0 | 0.0 | 0.0 |
| 1972-73 | 0.0 | 0.0 | 0.0 | 0.0 | 0.0 | 0.0 | 0.0 | 0.0 | 0.0 | 0.0 | 0.0 | 0.0 | 0.0 |
| 1973-74 | 0.0 | 0.0 | 0.0 | 0.0 | 0.0 | 0.0 | 0.0 | 0.0 | 0.0 | 0.0 | 0.0 | 0.0 | 0.0 |
| 1974-75 | 0.0 | 0.0 | 0.0 | 0.0 | 0.0 | 0.0 | 0.0 | 0.0 | 0.0 | 0.0 | 0.0 | 0.0 | 0.0 |
| 1975-76 | 0.0 | 0.0 | 0.0 | 0.0 | 0.0 | 0.0 | 0.0 | 0.0 | 0.0 | 0.0 | 0.0 | 0.0 | 0.0 |
| 1976-77 | 0.0 | 0.0 | 0.0 | 0.0 | 0.0 | 0.0 | T | 0.0 | 0.0 | 0.0 | 0.0 | 0.0 | T |
| 1977-78 | 0.0 | 0.0 | 0.0 | 0.0 | 0.0 | 0.0 | 0.0 | 0.0 | 0.0 | 0.0 | 0.0 | 0.0 | 0.0 |
| #1978-79 | 0.0 | 0.0 | 0.0 | 0.0 | 0.0 | 0.0 | 0.0 | 0.0 | 0.0 | 0.0 | 0.0 | 0.0 | 0.0 |
| 1979-80 | 0.0 | 0.0 | 0.0 | 0.0 | 0.0 | 0.0 | 0.0 | 0.0 | 0.0 | 0.0 | 0.0 | 0.0 | 0.0 |
| 1980-81 | 0.0 | 0.0 | 0.0 | 0.0 | 0.0 | 0.0 | 0.0 | 0.0 | 0.0 | 0.0 | 0.0 | 0.0 | 0.0 |
| 1981-82 | 0.0 | 0.0 | 0.0 | 0.0 | 0.0 | 0.0 | 0.0 | 0.0 | 0.0 | 0.0 | 0.0 | 0.0 | 0.0 |
| 1982-83 | 0.0 | 0.0 | 0.0 | 0.0 | 0.0 | 0.0 | 0.0 | 0.0 | 0.0 | 0.0 | 0.0 | 0.0 | 0.0 |
| 1983-84 | 0.0 | 0.0 | 0.0 | 0.0 | 0.0 | 0.0 | 0.0 | 0.0 | 0.0 | 0.0 | 0.0 | 0.0 | 0.0 |
| 1984-85 | 0.0 | 0.0 | 0.0 | 0.0 | 0.0 | 0.0 | 0.0 | 0.0 | 0.0 | 0.0 | 0.0 | 0.0 | 0.0 |
| 1985-86 | 0.0 | 0.0 | 0.0 | 0.0 | 0.0 | 0.0 | 0.0 | 0.0 | 0.0 | 0.0 | 0.0 | 0.0 | 0.0 |
| 1986-87 | 0.0 | 0.0 | 0.0 | 0.0 | 0.0 | 0.0 | 0.0 | 0.0 | 0.0 | 0.0 | 0.0 | 0.0 | 0.0 |
| 1987-88 | 0.0 | 0.0 | 0.0 | 0.0 | 0.0 | 0.0 | 0.0 | 0.0 | 0.0 | 0.0 | 0.0 | 0.0 | 0.0 |
| 1988-89 | 0.0 | 0.0 | 0.0 | 0.0 | 0.0 | 0.0 | 0.0 | 0.0 | 0.0 | 0.0 | 0.0 | 0.0 | 0.0 |
| 1989-90 | 0.0 | 0.0 | 0.0 | 0.0 | 0.0 | T | 0.0 | 0.0 | 0.0 | 0.0 | 0.0 | T | T |
| 1990-91 | 0.0 | 0.0 | 0.0 | 0.0 | 0.0 | 0.0 | | | | | | | |
| Record Mean | 0.0 | 0.0 | 0.0 | 0.0 | 0.0 | T | T | T | 0.0 | 0.0 | 0.0 | T | T |

**See Reference Notes, relative to all above tables, on preceding page.**

Miami is located on the lower east coast of Florida. To the east of the city lies Biscayne Bay, an arm of the ocean, about 15 miles long and 3 miles wide. East of the bay is the island of Miami Beach, a mile or less wide and about 10 miles long, and beyond Miami Beach is the Atlantic Ocean. The surrounding countryside is level and sparsely wooded.

The climate of Miami is essentially subtropical marine, featured by a long and warm summer, with abundant rainfall, followed by a mild, dry winter. The marine influence is evidenced by the low daily range of temperature and the rapid warming of cold air masses which pass to the east of the state. The Miami area is subject to winds from the east or southeast about half the time, and in several specific respects has a climate whose features differ from those farther inland.

One of these features is the annual precipitation for the area. During the early morning hours more rainfall occurs at Miami Beach than at the airport, while during the afternoon the reverse is true. The airport office is about 9 miles inland.

An even more striking difference appears in the annual number of days with temperatures reaching 90 degrees or higher, with inland stations having about four times more than the beach. Minimum temperature contrasts also are particularly marked under proper conditions, with the difference between inland locations and the Miami Beach station frequently reaching to 15 degrees or more, especially in winter.

Freezing temperatures occur occasionally in the suburbs and farming districts southwest, west, and northwest of the city, but rarely near the ocean.

Hurricanes occasionally affect the area. The months of greatest frequency are September and October. Destructive tornadoes are very rare. Funnel clouds are occasionally sighted and a few touch the ground briefly but significant damage is seldom reported. Waterspouts are often visible from the beaches during the summer months, however, significant damage is seldom reported. June, July, and August have the highest frequency of dangerous lightning events.

## TABLE 1  NORMALS, MEANS AND EXTREMES

MIAMI, FLORIDA

LATITUDE: 25°49'N  LONGITUDE: 80°17'W  ELEVATION: FT. GRND 7 BARO 12  TIME ZONE: EASTERN  WBAN: 12839

| | (a) | JAN | FEB | MAR | APR | MAY | JUNE | JULY | AUG | SEP | OCT | NOV | DEC | YEAR |
|---|---|---|---|---|---|---|---|---|---|---|---|---|---|---|
| **TEMPERATURE °F:** | | | | | | | | | | | | | | |
| Normals | | | | | | | | | | | | | | |
| -Daily Maximum | | 75.0 | 75.8 | 79.3 | 82.4 | 85.1 | 87.3 | 88.7 | 89.2 | 87.8 | 84.2 | 79.8 | 76.2 | 82.6 |
| -Daily Minimum | | 59.2 | 59.7 | 64.1 | 68.2 | 71.9 | 74.6 | 76.2 | 76.5 | 75.7 | 71.6 | 65.8 | 60.8 | 68.7 |
| -Monthly | | 67.1 | 67.8 | 71.7 | 75.3 | 78.5 | 81.0 | 82.4 | 82.8 | 81.8 | 77.9 | 72.8 | 68.5 | 75.6 |
| Extremes | | | | | | | | | | | | | | |
| -Record Highest | 47 | 88 | 89 | 92 | 96 | 95 | 98 | 98 | 98 | 97 | 95 | 89 | 87 | 98 |
| -Year | | 1987 | 1982 | 1977 | 1971 | 1989 | 1985 | 1983 | 1987 | 1987 | 1980 | 1989 | 1989 | AUG 1987 |
| -Record Lowest | 47 | 30 | 32 | 32 | 46 | 53 | 60 | 69 | 68 | 68 | 51 | 39 | 30 | 30 |
| -Year | | 1985 | 1947 | 1980 | 1971 | 1945 | 1984 | 1985 | 1950 | 1983 | 1943 | 1950 | 1989 | DEC 1989 |
| **NORMAL DEGREE DAYS:** | | | | | | | | | | | | | | |
| Heating (base 65°F) | | 76 | 62 | 14 | 0 | 0 | 0 | 0 | 0 | 0 | 0 | 5 | 42 | 199 |
| Cooling (base 65°F) | | 141 | 140 | 222 | 309 | 419 | 480 | 539 | 552 | 504 | 400 | 239 | 150 | 4095 |
| **% OF POSSIBLE SUNSHINE** | 13 | 69 | 67 | 76 | 79 | 73 | 73 | 75 | 75 | 74 | 74 | 69 | 66 | 73 |
| **MEAN SKY COVER (tenths)** | | | | | | | | | | | | | | |
| Sunrise - Sunset | 41 | 5.2 | 5.3 | 5.3 | 5.2 | 5.8 | 6.7 | 6.5 | 6.5 | 6.8 | 5.9 | 5.5 | 5.4 | 5.8 |
| **MEAN NUMBER OF DAYS:** | | | | | | | | | | | | | | |
| Sunrise to Sunset | | | | | | | | | | | | | | |
| -Clear | 40 | 9.9 | 8.7 | 8.7 | 8.9 | 6.3 | 3.3 | 2.5 | 2.4 | 2.3 | 6.8 | 7.7 | 9.3 | 76.8 |
| -Partly Cloudy | 40 | 12.8 | 11.9 | 14.0 | 14.6 | 15.3 | 14.2 | 17.2 | 17.9 | 15.2 | 13.9 | 13.9 | 12.5 | 173.4 |
| -Cloudy | 40 | 8.3 | 7.8 | 8.3 | 6.6 | 9.5 | 12.5 | 11.2 | 10.7 | 12.4 | 10.3 | 8.4 | 9.2 | 115.1 |
| Precipitation | | | | | | | | | | | | | | |
| .01 inches or more | 47 | 6.5 | 5.9 | 5.9 | 5.8 | 10.3 | 14.8 | 16.1 | 17.2 | 17.3 | 14.1 | 8.5 | 6.5 | 128.8 |
| Snow,Ice pellets | | | | | | | | | | | | | | |
| 1.0 inches or more | 40 | 0.0 | 0.0 | 0.0 | 0.0 | 0.0 | 0.0 | 0.0 | 0.0 | 0.0 | 0.0 | 0.0 | 0.0 | 0.0 |
| Thunderstorms | 40 | 0.8 | 1.2 | 1.9 | 2.5 | 6.9 | 12.2 | 14.9 | 15.4 | 11.4 | 4.4 | 1.2 | 0.7 | 73.6 |
| Heavy Fog Visibility | | | | | | | | | | | | | | |
| 1/4 mile or less | 41 | 1.4 | 0.9 | 0.7 | 0.6 | 0.3 | 0.0 | 0.1 | 0.1 | 0.1 | 0.2 | 0.9 | 0.9 | 6.1 |
| Temperature °F | | | | | | | | | | | | | | |
| -Maximum | | | | | | | | | | | | | | |
| 90° and above | 25 | 0.0 | 0.0 | 0.2 | 1.5 | 3.2 | 8.4 | 13.3 | 13.0 | 9.1 | 1.8 | 0.0 | 0.0 | 50.4 |
| 32° and below | 25 | 0.0 | 0.0 | 0.0 | 0.0 | 0.0 | 0.0 | 0.0 | 0.0 | 0.0 | 0.0 | 0.0 | 0.0 | 0.0 |
| -Minimum | | | | | | | | | | | | | | |
| 32° and below | 25 | 0.1 | 0.0 | 0.* | 0.0 | 0.0 | 0.0 | 0.0 | 0.0 | 0.0 | 0.0 | 0.0 | 0.1 | 0.2 |
| 0° and below | 25 | 0.0 | 0.0 | 0.0 | 0.0 | 0.0 | 0.0 | 0.0 | 0.0 | 0.0 | 0.0 | 0.0 | 0.0 | 0.0 |
| **AVG. STATION PRESS.(mb)** | 17 | 1019.4 | 1018.6 | 1017.5 | 1016.7 | 1015.5 | 1016.4 | 1017.8 | 1016.7 | 1015.1 | 1015.6 | 1017.3 | 1019.3 | 1017.2 |
| **RELATIVE HUMIDITY (%)** | | | | | | | | | | | | | | |
| Hour 01 | 25 | 80 | 79 | 77 | 76 | 79 | 83 | 82 | 82 | 85 | 82 | 81 | 79 | 80 |
| Hour 07 (Local Time) | 25 | 84 | 83 | 82 | 80 | 81 | 85 | 84 | 86 | 88 | 86 | 85 | 83 | 84 |
| Hour 13 | 25 | 59 | 57 | 56 | 53 | 59 | 65 | 63 | 65 | 66 | 63 | 62 | 59 | 61 |
| Hour 19 | 25 | 68 | 66 | 65 | 63 | 69 | 74 | 72 | 74 | 77 | 73 | 72 | 70 | 70 |
| **PRECIPITATION (inches):** | | | | | | | | | | | | | | |
| Water Equivalent | | | | | | | | | | | | | | |
| -Normal | | 2.08 | 2.05 | 1.89 | 3.07 | 6.53 | 9.15 | 5.98 | 7.02 | 8.07 | 7.14 | 2.71 | 1.86 | 57.55 |
| -Maximum Monthly | 47 | 6.66 | 8.07 | 10.57 | 17.29 | 18.54 | 22.36 | 13.51 | 16.88 | 24.40 | 21.08 | 13.15 | 6.39 | 24.40 |
| -Year | | 1969 | 1983 | 1986 | 1979 | 1968 | 1947 | 1947 | 1943 | 1960 | 1952 | 1959 | 1958 | SEP 1960 |
| -Minimum Monthly | 47 | 0.04 | 0.01 | 0.02 | 0.05 | 0.44 | 1.81 | 1.77 | 1.65 | 2.63 | 1.25 | 0.09 | 0.12 | 0.01 |
| -Year | | 1951 | 1944 | 1956 | 1981 | 1965 | 1945 | 1963 | 1954 | 1951 | 1977 | 1970 | 1988 | FEB 1944 |
| -Maximum in 24 hrs | 47 | 2.68 | 5.73 | 7.07 | 16.21 | 11.59 | 8.20 | 4.55 | 6.92 | 7.58 | 9.95 | 7.93 | 4.38 | 16.21 |
| -Year | | 1973 | 1966 | 1949 | 1979 | 1977 | 1977 | 1952 | 1964 | 1960 | 1948 | 1959 | 1964 | APR 1979 |
| Snow,Ice pellets | | | | | | | | | | | | | | |
| -Maximum Monthly | | 0.0 | 0.0 | 0.0 | 0.0 | 0.0 | 0.0 | 0.0 | 0.0 | 0.0 | 0.0 | 0.0 | 0.0 | |
| -Year | | | | | | | | | | | | | | |
| -Maximum in 24 hrs | 47 | 0.0 | 0.0 | 0.0 | 0.0 | 0.0 | 0.0 | 0.0 | 0.0 | 0.0 | 0.0 | 0.0 | 0.0 | |
| -Year | | | | | | | | | | | | | | |
| **WIND:** | | | | | | | | | | | | | | |
| Mean Speed (mph) | 40 | 9.5 | 10.2 | 10.6 | 10.5 | 9.6 | 8.4 | 8.0 | 8.0 | 8.3 | 9.4 | 9.8 | 9.3 | 9.3 |
| Prevailing Direction through 1963 | | NNW | ESE | SE | ESE | ESE | SE | SE | SE | ESE | ENE | N | N | ESE |
| Fastest Obs. 1 Min. | | | | | | | | | | | | | | |
| -Direction (!!!) | 32 | 24 | 25 | 04 | 36 | 32 | 13 | 18 | 36 | 06 | 05 | 07 | 32 | 36 |
| -Speed (MPH) | 32 | 46 | 41 | 46 | 33 | 52 | 37 | 38 | 74 | 69 | 41 | 38 | 38 | 74 |
| -Year | | 1978 | 1983 | 1966 | 1980 | 1980 | 1967 | 1962 | 1964 | 1965 | 1966 | 1985 | 1967 | AUG 1964 |
| Peak Gust | | | | | | | | | | | | | | |
| -Direction (!!!) | 6 | SW | W | SE | NW | N | S | NW | SE | SW | N | E | W | S |
| -Speed (mph) | 6 | 45 | 41 | 51 | 55 | 46 | 58 | 49 | 51 | 44 | 38 | 48 | 37 | 58 |
| -Date | | 1987 | 1985 | 1987 | 1984 | 1984 | 1989 | 1987 | 1985 | 1988 | 1987 | 1985 | 1989 | JUN 1989 |

**See Reference Notes to this table on the following page.**

## PRECIPITATION (inches)    MIAMI, FLORIDA

**TABLE 2**

| YEAR | JAN | FEB | MAR | APR | MAY | JUNE | JULY | AUG | SEP | OCT | NOV | DEC | ANNUAL |
|---|---|---|---|---|---|---|---|---|---|---|---|---|---|
| 1961 | 5.12 | 0.63 | 1.91 | 0.56 | 6.81 | 10.48 | 1.91 | 4.68 | 3.40 | 3.92 | 2.15 | 0.13 | 41.70 |
| 1962 | 1.46 | 0.13 | 2.78 | 1.19 | 0.92 | 10.36 | 3.74 | 8.02 | 7.82 | 1.50 | 0.20 | 0.20 | 42.27 |
| 1963 | 0.65 | 3.45 | 0.73 | 0.33 | 6.34 | 6.80 | 1.77 | 4.77 | 11.12 | 4.43 | 1.43 | 4.26 | 46.08 |
| 1964 | 0.45 | 2.21 | 0.50 | 3.31 | 4.67 | 10.48 | 5.51 | 9.84 | 4.22 | 9.77 | 3.00 | 6.24 | 60.20 |
| 1965 | 1.98 | 2.98 | 3.97 | 1.20 | 0.44 | 6.55 | 6.56 | 4.97 | 11.38 | 16.79 | 0.96 | 0.62 | 58.40 |
| 1966 | 3.97 | 6.56 | 3.25 | 1.80 | 5.53 | 21.37 | 8.50 | 7.62 | 8.00 | 10.88 | 3.84 | 0.74 | 82.06 |
| 1967 | 2.75 | 1.14 | 3.60 | 0.15 | 1.68 | 15.98 | 5.55 | 8.13 | 9.18 | 12.88 | 3.81 | 1.37 | 66.22 |
| 1968 | 1.92 | 2.77 | 0.88 | 1.27 | 18.54 | 22.36 | 6.15 | 8.34 | 11.11 | 8.71 | 1.21 | 0.13 | 83.39 |
| 1969 | 6.66 | 2.02 | 1.98 | 4.63 | 8.02 | 11.42 | 8.48 | 4.31 | 8.24 | 3.01 | 1.01 | 1.15 | 71.49 |
| 1970 | 2.64 | 1.77 | 2.61 | 0.95 | 10.98 | 5.53 | 4.48 | 3.60 | 8.89 | 3.01 | 0.09 | 0.17 | 44.72 |
| 1971 | 0.51 | 0.80 | 0.40 | 0.07 | 4.13 | 11.65 | 4.72 | 6.02 | 9.63 | 7.48 | 0.98 | 4.33 | 50.72 |
| 1972 | 1.60 | 2.71 | 3.01 | 2.67 | 13.71 | 10.90 | 7.13 | 6.49 | 5.08 | 2.86 | 2.77 | 4.18 | 63.11 |
| 1973 | 3.41 | 2.21 | 1.76 | 2.24 | 1.08 | 8.93 | 6.14 | 14.60 | 6.59 | 3.36 | 0.46 | 2.46 | 53.24 |
| 1974 | 2.54 | 0.10 | 2.27 | 2.11 | 2.63 | 8.12 | 6.09 | 9.29 | 6.38 | 3.68 | 4.62 | 1.17 | 49.00 |
| 1975 | 1.39 | 0.90 | 0.61 | 0.53 | 4.94 | 6.37 | 4.99 | 5.19 | 4.69 | 6.25 | 2.80 | 0.44 | 39.10 |
| 1976 | 0.95 | 3.54 | 0.23 | 4.17 | 10.45 | 6.81 | 3.83 | 9.45 | 7.75 | 4.42 | 2.69 | 1.61 | 55.90 |
| 1977 | 1.44 | 2.10 | 0.91 | 1.97 | 15.82 | 12.42 | 5.23 | 8.28 | 7.04 | 1.25 | 2.55 | 5.94 | 64.95 |
| 1978 | 2.07 | 3.44 | 2.92 | 3.50 | 5.66 | 5.29 | 2.69 | 3.93 | 3.42 | 7.68 | 3.17 | 2.06 | 45.83 |
| 1979 | 1.28 | 0.57 | 0.30 | 17.29 | 5.29 | 4.06 | 5.06 | 4.81 | 13.36 | 3.63 | 1.62 | 2.84 | 60.11 |
| 1980 | 1.89 | 0.88 | 3.17 | 10.20 | 2.14 | 3.02 | 9.40 | 11.32 | 5.60 | 6.05 | 3.47 | 0.20 | 57.34 |
| 1981 | 0.61 | 4.66 | 1.32 | 0.05 | 4.94 | 5.49 | 2.78 | 12.25 | 14.79 | 1.62 | 2.14 | 0.14 | 50.79 |
| 1982 | 0.44 | 1.22 | 4.22 | 9.27 | 8.80 | 10.82 | 3.84 | 5.79 | 7.62 | 7.12 | 7.09 | 1.18 | 67.41 |
| 1983 | 5.36 | 8.07 | 2.82 | 1.79 | 1.44 | 8.66 | 6.20 | 5.88 | 7.48 | 3.52 | 2.01 | 4.19 | 57.42 |
| 1984 | 0.18 | 0.70 | 6.12 | 4.51 | 10.91 | 7.24 | 7.38 | 5.44 | 10.45 | 2.35 | 4.04 | 0.70 | 60.02 |
| 1985 | 0.35 | 0.06 | 1.35 | 3.27 | 3.19 | 6.33 | 11.23 | 11.88 | 8.59 | 5.17 | 1.37 | 3.47 | 56.26 |
| 1986 | 5.04 | 1.72 | 10.57 | 0.71 | 8.24 | 9.06 | 7.81 | 7.67 | 4.38 | 3.96 | 4.75 | 2.21 | 66.12 |
| 1987 | 0.87 | 2.62 | 3.82 | 0.38 | 4.99 | 5.48 | 5.17 | 3.24 | 10.17 | 4.33 | 4.92 | 4.28 | 50.27 |
| 1988 | 1.88 | 0.61 | 0.39 | 1.82 | 5.28 | 10.36 | 10.90 | 7.89 | 3.09 | 1.49 | 0.76 | 0.12 | 44.59 |
| 1989 | 0.67 | 0.71 | 0.89 | 2.14 | 0.99 | 10.83 | 3.53 | 12.78 | 5.83 | 2.65 | 0.99 | 0.62 | 42.63 |
| 1990 | 0.24 | 1.19 | 2.28 | 6.96 | 7.79 | 6.84 | 4.31 | 11.06 | 3.52 | 4.82 | 1.67 | 1.03 | 51.71 |
| Record Mean | 1.97 | 1.92 | 2.28 | 3.57 | 6.16 | 8.61 | 6.65 | 7.40 | 8.31 | 6.68 | 2.75 | 1.80 | 58.11 |

**TABLE 3**  AVERAGE TEMPERATURE (deg. F)    MIAMI, FLORIDA

| YEAR | JAN | FEB | MAR | APR | MAY | JUNE | JULY | AUG | SEP | OCT | NOV | DEC | ANNUAL |
|---|---|---|---|---|---|---|---|---|---|---|---|---|---|
| 1961 | 64.9 | 69.6 | 73.8 | 74.1 | 78.0 | 81.1 | 83.5 | 82.0 | 82.0 | 77.7 | 73.6 | 68.9 | 75.9 |
| 1962 | 68.1 | 71.4 | 70.2 | 73.1 | 77.0 | 80.0 | 83.3 | 82.9 | 81.1 | 77.5 | 68.1 | 63.7 | 74.7 |
| 1963 | 67.1 | 65.8 | 73.4 | 74.7 | 77.0 | 80.6 | 83.2 | 83.0 | 81.3 | 76.2 | 71.2 | 63.5 | 74.8 |
| #1964 | 67.4 | 65.7 | 74.6 | 77.1 | 77.6 | 81.2 | 82.8 | 83.6 | 82.3 | 76.9 | 74.9 | 72.2 | 76.4 |
| 1965 | 67.0 | 70.9 | 73.1 | 76.7 | 78.5 | 80.7 | 81.3 | 81.7 | 79.9 | 78.1 | 74.2 | 69.3 | 76.0 |
| 1966 | 66.0 | 68.9 | 69.2 | 72.8 | 77.6 | 78.2 | 81.1 | 81.7 | 81.2 | 77.9 | 70.2 | 66.6 | 74.3 |
| 1967 | 71.4 | 68.9 | 72.8 | 74.7 | 79.3 | 79.9 | 82.4 | 81.8 | 81.3 | 76.2 | 71.2 | 70.3 | 75.8 |
| 1968 | 66.1 | 62.7 | 67.0 | 75.9 | 77.6 | 79.6 | 81.6 | 83.9 | 82.2 | 77.8 | 71.0 | 66.6 | 74.3 |
| 1969 | 67.6 | 65.2 | 67.8 | 77.3 | 79.6 | 82.3 | 84.1 | 83.5 | 82.5 | 80.3 | 70.4 | 65.9 | 75.5 |
| 1970 | 63.8 | 64.7 | 71.8 | 79.0 | 79.1 | 82.0 | 82.7 | 84.0 | 82.2 | 79.5 | 69.6 | 70.9 | 75.8 |
| 1971 | 68.2 | 70.9 | 70.3 | 75.0 | 79.1 | 81.0 | 82.7 | 81.9 | 80.7 | 78.9 | 73.9 | 74.2 | 76.4 |
| 1972 | 73.0 | 68.4 | 72.1 | 75.0 | 77.6 | 79.9 | 80.9 | 81.7 | 80.4 | 77.9 | 73.3 | 70.8 | 75.9 |
| 1973 | 70.3 | 65.3 | 74.5 | 75.6 | 79.6 | 81.3 | 81.8 | 81.3 | 81.8 | 77.6 | 76.2 | 69.0 | 76.1 |
| 1974 | 74.3 | 68.9 | 75.6 | 76.2 | 80.0 | 82.1 | 82.6 | 84.0 | 84.1 | 78.1 | 72.9 | 69.0 | 77.3 |
| 1975 | 72.7 | 73.1 | 73.4 | 77.5 | 79.4 | 81.5 | 81.1 | 82.6 | 82.0 | 79.2 | 72.3 | 69.0 | 77.0 |
| 1976 | 64.7 | 68.8 | 75.8 | 75.1 | 78.5 | 79.1 | 83.1 | 81.9 | 80.4 | 76.3 | 71.5 | 68.2 | 75.3 |
| 1977 | 61.1 | 66.1 | 74.9 | 74.8 | 77.0 | 81.7 | 83.7 | 83.2 | 83.0 | 76.5 | 74.0 | 69.1 | 75.4 |
| 1978 | 64.0 | 63.2 | 68.9 | 74.0 | 79.2 | 81.9 | 82.5 | 82.6 | 82.0 | 78.8 | 75.7 | 73.0 | 75.5 |
| 1979 | 65.0 | 64.9 | 69.2 | 77.8 | 80.6 | 81.9 | 83.2 | 82.1 | 80.7 | 77.9 | 75.4 | 70.2 | 75.7 |
| 1980 | 67.5 | 64.0 | 73.2 | 75.4 | 79.0 | 81.4 | 82.6 | 82.8 | 82.1 | 80.1 | 74.3 | 67.3 | 75.8 |
| 1981 | 59.7 | 69.5 | 70.1 | 77.8 | 79.6 | 83.7 | 85.0 | 83.2 | 81.2 | 79.7 | 71.4 | 67.8 | 75.7 |
| 1982 | 67.8 | 74.4 | 74.7 | 77.9 | 77.2 | 82.0 | 84.3 | 84.0 | 82.7 | 77.9 | 75.0 | 72.6 | 77.6 |
| 1983 | 67.2 | 67.5 | 67.6 | 71.9 | 78.2 | 81.8 | 85.0 | 83.3 | 81.6 | 78.3 | 72.5 | 69.8 | 75.4 |
| 1984 | 67.0 | 68.6 | 70.4 | 73.2 | 77.1 | 79.8 | 81.9 | 82.6 | 80.1 | 78.2 | 71.5 | 71.1 | 75.1 |
| 1985 | 62.1 | 68.4 | 72.5 | 74.2 | 79.1 | 82.4 | 81.0 | 82.4 | 80.6 | 80.5 | 75.6 | 66.0 | 75.4 |
| 1986 | 65.2 | 69.4 | 68.6 | 71.7 | 77.5 | 81.3 | 83.1 | 83.5 | 83.3 | 80.3 | 79.3 | 73.6 | 76.4 |
| 1987 | 66.1 | 70.8 | 71.9 | 70.6 | 78.7 | 84.2 | 84.2 | 85.4 | 83.6 | 77.6 | 75.3 | 69.8 | 76.5 |
| 1988 | 67.9 | 67.7 | 70.7 | 76.1 | 77.9 | 82.0 | 83.1 | 83.6 | 84.0 | 79.1 | 76.9 | 70.5 | 76.6 |
| 1989 | 72.7 | 70.8 | 73.6 | 77.1 | 81.0 | 82.7 | 83.3 | 84.3 | 84.0 | 79.0 | 76.2 | 65.0 | 77.5 |
| 1990 | 73.6 | 74.0 | 73.7 | 75.2 | 80.3 | 83.0 | 83.5 | 83.7 | 83.1 | 80.4 | 74.4 | 72.9 | 78.2 |
| Record Mean | 67.1 | 68.1 | 71.4 | 74.8 | 78.2 | 81.2 | 82.5 | 82.8 | 81.7 | 78.1 | 72.9 | 68.8 | 75.7 |
| Max | 75.5 | 76.6 | 79.5 | 82.6 | 85.4 | 88.0 | 89.3 | 89.7 | 88.2 | 84.7 | 80.2 | 76.8 | 83.1 |
| Min | 58.7 | 59.5 | 63.3 | 67.1 | 70.9 | 74.3 | 75.6 | 75.9 | 75.2 | 71.4 | 65.7 | 60.8 | 68.2 |

## REFERENCE NOTES FOR TABLES 1, 2, 3 and 6    (MIAMI, FL)

### GENERAL

T - TRACE AMOUNT
BLANK ENTRIES DENOTE MISSING/UNREPORTED DATA.
# INDICATES A STATION OR INSTRUMENT RELOCATION.

### SPECIFIC

**TABLE 1**

(a) - LENGTH OF RECORD IN YEARS. ALTHOUGH
     INDIVIDUAL MONTHS MAY BE MISSING.
  * LESS THAN .05

NORMALS — BASED ON THE 1951-1980 RECORD PERIOD.
EXTREMES — DATES ARE THE MOST RECENT OCCURRENCE.
WIND DIR. — NUMERALS SHOW TENS OF DEGREES
            CLOCKWISE FROM TRUE NORTH.
            "00" INDICATES CALM.
RESULTANT WIND DIRECTIONS ARE GIVEN TO WHOLE DEGREES.

**TABLE 3**
MAX AND MIN ARE LONG-TERM MEAN DAILY MAXIMUM
AND MEAN DAILY MINIMUM TEMPERATURES.

### EXCEPTIONS

**TABLES 2, 3, and 6**

RECORD MEANS ARE THROUGH THE CURRENT YEAR,
BEGINNING IN    1940 FOR TEMPERATURE
               1940 FOR PRECIPITATION
               1940 FOR SNOWFALL

HEATING DEGREE DAYS Base 65 deg. F          MIAMI, FLORIDA

**TABLE 4**

| SEASON | JULY | AUG | SEP | OCT | NOV | DEC | JAN | FEB | MAR | APR | MAY | JUNE | TOTAL |
|---|---|---|---|---|---|---|---|---|---|---|---|---|---|
| 1961-62 | 0 | 0 | 0 | 0 | 0 | 64 | 58 | 7 | 30 | 2 | 0 | 0 | 161 |
| 1962-63 | 0 | 0 | 0 | 0 | 26 | 120 | 48 | 46 | 6 | 0 | 0 | 0 | 246 |
| 1963-64 | 0 | 0 | 0 | 0 | 25 | 85 | 67 | 67 | 4 | 0 | 0 | 0 | 248 |
| #1964-65 | 0 | 0 | 0 | 0 | 0 | 4 | 63 | 25 | 18 | 0 | 0 | 0 | 110 |
| 1965-66 | 0 | 0 | 0 | 0 | 0 | 16 | 70 | 41 | 16 | 0 | 0 | 0 | 143 |
| 1966-67 | 0 | 0 | 0 | 0 | 27 | 41 | 28 | 41 | 0 | 0 | 0 | 0 | 137 |
| 1967-68 | 0 | 0 | 0 | 0 | 0 | 25 | 56 | 101 | 57 | 0 | 0 | 0 | 239 |
| 1968-69 | 0 | 0 | 0 | 0 | 32 | 80 | 18 | 54 | 49 | 0 | 0 | 0 | 233 |
| 1969-70 | 0 | 0 | 0 | 0 | 21 | 53 | 117 | 58 | 19 | 0 | 0 | 0 | 268 |
| 1970-71 | 0 | 0 | 0 | 0 | 42 | 23 | 67 | 45 | 31 | 5 | 0 | 0 | 213 |
| 1971-72 | 0 | 0 | 0 | 0 | 0 | 0 | 2 | 39 | 0 | 0 | 0 | 0 | 41 |
| 1972-73 | 0 | 0 | 0 | 0 | 3 | 30 | 41 | 64 | 0 | 0 | 0 | 0 | 138 |
| 1973-74 | 0 | 0 | 0 | 0 | 1 | 93 | 0 | 37 | 0 | 0 | 0 | 0 | 131 |
| 1974-75 | 0 | 0 | 0 | 0 | 2 | 32 | 14 | 1 | 10 | 0 | 0 | 0 | 59 |
| 1975-76 | 0 | 0 | 0 | 0 | 33 | 49 | 93 | 27 | 0 | 0 | 0 | 0 | 202 |
| 1976-77 | 0 | 0 | 0 | 0 | 9 | 32 | 165 | 62 | 3 | 0 | 0 | 0 | 271 |
| 1977-78 | 0 | 0 | 0 | 0 | 6 | 58 | 123 | 99 | 34 | 0 | 0 | 0 | 320 |
| 1978-79 | 0 | 0 | 0 | 0 | 0 | 1 | 84 | 82 | 13 | 0 | 0 | 0 | 180 |
| 1979-80 | 0 | 0 | 0 | 0 | 6 | 10 | 50 | 95 | 39 | 0 | 0 | 0 | 200 |
| 1980-81 | 0 | 0 | 0 | 0 | 7 | 59 | 168 | 25 | 12 | 0 | 0 | 0 | 271 |
| 1981-82 | 0 | 0 | 0 | 0 | 1 | 80 | 65 | 1 | 3 | 0 | 0 | 0 | 150 |
| 1982-83 | 0 | 0 | 0 | 0 | 0 | 22 | 50 | 25 | 38 | 2 | 0 | 0 | 137 |
| 1983-84 | 0 | 0 | 0 | 0 | 4 | 69 | 54 | 37 | 17 | 0 | 0 | 0 | 181 |
| 1984-85 | 0 | 0 | 0 | 0 | 9 | 18 | 135 | 61 | 4 | 1 | 0 | 0 | 228 |
| 1985-86 | 0 | 0 | 0 | 0 | 2 | 78 | 76 | 22 | 54 | 0 | 0 | 0 | 232 |
| 1986-87 | 0 | 0 | 0 | 0 | 0 | 0 | 83 | 15 | 6 | 27 | 0 | 0 | 131 |
| 1987-88 | 0 | 0 | 0 | 0 | 3 | 29 | 49 | 38 | 26 | 0 | 0 | 0 | 145 |
| 1988-89 | 0 | 0 | 0 | 0 | 0 | 36 | 1 | 49 | 18 | 0 | 0 | 0 | 104 |
| 1989-90 | 0 | 0 | 0 | 1 | 0 | 110 | 7 | 4 | 0 | 0 | 0 | 0 | 122 |
| 1990-91 | 0 | 0 | 0 | 0 | 0 | 4 | | | | | | | |

**TABLE 5**   COOLING DEGREE DAYS Base 65 deg. F          MIAMI, FLORIDA

| YEAR | JAN | FEB | MAR | APR | MAY | JUNE | JULY | AUG | SEP | OCT | NOV | DEC | TOTAL |
|---|---|---|---|---|---|---|---|---|---|---|---|---|---|
| 1969 | 104 | 66 | 145 | 375 | 459 | 526 | 597 | 581 | 532 | 478 | 191 | 88 | 4142 |
| 1970 | 85 | 59 | 239 | 425 | 446 | 518 | 558 | 596 | 522 | 457 | 185 | 213 | 4303 |
| 1971 | 176 | 219 | 202 | 315 | 444 | 488 | 558 | 531 | 476 | 443 | 274 | 292 | 4418 |
| 1972 | 262 | 144 | 227 | 307 | 398 | 454 | 498 | 523 | 471 | 408 | 261 | 217 | 4170 |
| 1973 | 212 | 81 | 301 | 324 | 459 | 499 | 531 | 516 | 511 | 394 | 343 | 163 | 4334 |
| 1974 | 294 | 150 | 335 | 342 | 471 | 518 | 551 | 596 | 578 | 414 | 245 | 163 | 4657 |
| 1975 | 261 | 233 | 276 | 382 | 456 | 501 | 508 | 553 | 517 | 448 | 257 | 178 | 4570 |
| 1976 | 92 | 144 | 336 | 309 | 424 | 429 | 569 | 530 | 470 | 361 | 209 | 141 | 4014 |
| 1977 | 50 | 97 | 318 | 299 | 381 | 508 | 587 | 574 | 549 | 364 | 284 | 191 | 4202 |
| 1978 | 97 | 54 | 163 | 273 | 449 | 515 | 547 | 552 | 513 | 437 | 329 | 254 | 4183 |
| 1979 | 90 | 81 | 149 | 391 | 492 | 516 | 572 | 537 | 481 | 407 | 324 | 178 | 4218 |
| 1980 | 138 | 75 | 296 | 321 | 441 | 501 | 555 | 563 | 519 | 476 | 292 | 135 | 4312 |
| 1981 | 10 | 154 | 177 | 389 | 460 | 568 | 625 | 570 | 492 | 460 | 198 | 173 | 4276 |
| 1982 | 161 | 270 | 311 | 394 | 385 | 518 | 606 | 596 | 537 | 406 | 304 | 264 | 4752 |
| 1983 | 125 | 101 | 124 | 213 | 417 | 514 | 628 | 576 | 503 | 419 | 236 | 221 | 4077 |
| 1984 | 124 | 144 | 194 | 252 | 380 | 452 | 532 | 554 | 460 | 416 | 213 | 214 | 3935 |
| 1985 | 55 | 164 | 244 | 285 | 445 | 529 | 505 | 546 | 476 | 488 | 329 | 114 | 4180 |
| 1986 | 86 | 150 | 175 | 207 | 395 | 495 | 569 | 582 | 556 | 483 | 432 | 272 | 4402 |
| 1987 | 122 | 186 | 227 | 202 | 430 | 580 | 603 | 639 | 565 | 401 | 314 | 182 | 4451 |
| 1988 | 145 | 123 | 209 | 339 | 408 | 516 | 571 | 584 | 578 | 445 | 364 | 216 | 4498 |
| 1989 | 247 | 219 | 292 | 367 | 502 | 540 | 576 | 603 | 578 | 442 | 346 | 114 | 4826 |
| 1990 | 279 | 262 | 276 | 314 | 479 | 547 | 578 | 587 | 552 | 486 | 287 | 254 | 4901 |

**TABLE 6**   SNOWFALL (inches)          MIAMI, FLORIDA

| SEASON | JULY | AUG | SEP | OCT | NOV | DEC | JAN | FEB | MAR | APR | MAY | JUNE | TOTAL |
|---|---|---|---|---|---|---|---|---|---|---|---|---|---|
| 1970-71 | 0.0 | 0.0 | 0.0 | 0.0 | 0.0 | 0.0 | 0.0 | 0.0 | 0.0 | 0.0 | 0.0 | 0.0 | 0.0 |
| 1971-72 | 0.0 | 0.0 | 0.0 | 0.0 | 0.0 | 0.0 | 0.0 | 0.0 | 0.0 | 0.0 | 0.0 | 0.0 | 0.0 |
| 1972-73 | 0.0 | 0.0 | 0.0 | 0.0 | 0.0 | 0.0 | 0.0 | 0.0 | 0.0 | 0.0 | 0.0 | 0.0 | 0.0 |
| 1973-74 | 0.0 | 0.0 | 0.0 | 0.0 | 0.0 | 0.0 | 0.0 | 0.0 | 0.0 | 0.0 | 0.0 | 0.0 | 0.0 |
| 1974-75 | 0.0 | 0.0 | 0.0 | 0.0 | 0.0 | 0.0 | 0.0 | 0.0 | 0.0 | 0.0 | 0.0 | 0.0 | 0.0 |
| 1975-76 | 0.0 | 0.0 | 0.0 | 0.0 | 0.0 | 0.0 | 0.0 | 0.0 | 0.0 | 0.0 | 0.0 | 0.0 | 0.0 |
| 1976-77 | 0.0 | 0.0 | 0.0 | 0.0 | 0.0 | 0.0 | 0.0 | 0.0 | 0.0 | 0.0 | 0.0 | 0.0 | 0.0 |
| 1977-78 | 0.0 | 0.0 | 0.0 | 0.0 | 0.0 | 0.0 | 0.0 | 0.0 | 0.0 | 0.0 | 0.0 | 0.0 | 0.0 |
| 1978-79 | 0.0 | 0.0 | 0.0 | 0.0 | 0.0 | 0.0 | 0.0 | 0.0 | 0.0 | 0.0 | 0.0 | 0.0 | 0.0 |
| 1979-80 | 0.0 | 0.0 | 0.0 | 0.0 | 0.0 | 0.0 | 0.0 | 0.0 | 0.0 | 0.0 | 0.0 | 0.0 | 0.0 |
| 1980-81 | 0.0 | 0.0 | 0.0 | 0.0 | 0.0 | 0.0 | 0.0 | 0.0 | 0.0 | 0.0 | 0.0 | 0.0 | 0.0 |
| 1981-82 | 0.0 | 0.0 | 0.0 | 0.0 | 0.0 | 0.0 | 0.0 | 0.0 | 0.0 | 0.0 | 0.0 | 0.0 | 0.0 |
| 1982-83 | 0.0 | 0.0 | 0.0 | 0.0 | 0.0 | 0.0 | 0.0 | 0.0 | 0.0 | 0.0 | 0.0 | 0.0 | 0.0 |
| 1983-84 | 0.0 | 0.0 | 0.0 | 0.0 | 0.0 | 0.0 | 0.0 | 0.0 | 0.0 | 0.0 | 0.0 | 0.0 | 0.0 |
| 1984-85 | 0.0 | 0.0 | 0.0 | 0.0 | 0.0 | 0.0 | 0.0 | 0.0 | 0.0 | 0.0 | 0.0 | 0.0 | 0.0 |
| 1985-86 | 0.0 | 0.0 | 0.0 | 0.0 | 0.0 | 0.0 | 0.0 | 0.0 | 0.0 | 0.0 | 0.0 | 0.0 | 0.0 |
| 1986-87 | 0.0 | 0.0 | 0.0 | 0.0 | 0.0 | 0.0 | 0.0 | 0.0 | 0.0 | 0.0 | 0.0 | 0.0 | 0.0 |
| 1987-88 | 0.0 | 0.0 | 0.0 | 0.0 | 0.0 | 0.0 | 0.0 | 0.0 | 0.0 | 0.0 | 0.0 | 0.0 | 0.0 |
| 1988-89 | 0.0 | 0.0 | 0.0 | 0.0 | 0.0 | 0.0 | 0.0 | 0.0 | 0.0 | 0.0 | 0.0 | 0.0 | 0.0 |
| 1989-90 | 0.0 | 0.0 | 0.0 | 0.0 | 0.0 | 0.0 | 0.0 | 0.0 | 0.0 | 0.0 | 0.0 | 0.0 | 0.0 |
| 1990-91 | 0.0 | 0.0 | 0.0 | 0.0 | 0.0 | 0.0 | | | | | | | |
| Record Mean | 0.0 | 0.0 | 0.0 | 0.0 | 0.0 | 0.0 | 0.0 | 0.0 | 0.0 | 0.0 | 0.0 | 0.0 | 0.0 |

**See Reference Notes, relative to all above tables, on preceding page.**

Orlando is located in the central section of the Florida peninsula, surrounded by many lakes. Relative humidities remain high the year-round, with values near 90 percent at night and 40 to 50 percent in the afternoon. On some winter days, the humidity may drop to 20 percent.

The rainy season extends from June through September, sometimes through October when tropical storms are near. During this period, scattered afternoon thunderstorms are an almost daily occurrence, and these bring a drop in temperature to make the climate bearable. Summer temperatures above 95 degrees are rather rare. There is usually a breeze which contributes to the general comfort.

During the winter months rainfall is light. While temperatures, on infrequent occasion, may drop at night to near freezing, they rise rapidly during the day and, in brilliant sunshine, afternoons are pleasant.

Frozen precipitation in the form of snowflakes, snow pellets, or sleet is rare. However, hail is occasionally reported during thunderstorms.

Hurricanes are usually not considered a great threat to Orlando, since, to reach this area, they must pass over a substantial stretch of land and, in so doing, lose much of their punch. Sustained hurricane winds of 75 mph or higher rarely occur. Orlando, being inland, is relatively safe from high water, although heavy rains sometimes briefly flood sections of the city.

## TABLE 1     NORMALS, MEANS AND EXTREMES

ORLANDO, FLORIDA

LATITUDE: 28°26'N    LONGITUDE: 81°19'W    ELEVATION: FT. GRND 96 BARO 94    TIME ZONE: EASTERN    WBAN: 12815

| | (a) | JAN | FEB | MAR | APR | MAY | JUNE | JULY | AUG | SEP | OCT | NOV | DEC | YEAR |
|---|---|---|---|---|---|---|---|---|---|---|---|---|---|---|
| **TEMPERATURE °F:** | | | | | | | | | | | | | | |
| Normals | | | | | | | | | | | | | | |
|  -Daily Maximum | | 71.7 | 72.9 | 78.3 | 83.6 | 88.3 | 90.6 | 91.7 | 91.6 | 89.7 | 84.4 | 78.2 | 73.1 | 82.8 |
|  -Daily Minimum | | 49.3 | 50.0 | 55.3 | 60.3 | 66.2 | 71.2 | 73.0 | 73.4 | 72.5 | 65.4 | 56.8 | 50.9 | 62.0 |
|  -Monthly | | 60.5 | 61.5 | 66.8 | 72.0 | 77.3 | 80.9 | 82.4 | 82.5 | 81.1 | 74.9 | 67.5 | 62.0 | 72.4 |
| Extremes | | | | | | | | | | | | | | |
|  -Record Highest | 47 | 87 | 90 | 92 | 96 | 102 | 100 | 100 | 100 | 98 | 95 | 89 | 90 | 102 |
|  -Year | | 1963 | 1962 | 1970 | 1968 | 1945 | 1985 | 1961 | 1980 | 1988 | 1986 | 1986 | 1978 | MAY 1945 |
|  -Record Lowest | 47 | 19 | 28 | 25 | 38 | 49 | 53 | 64 | 64 | 56 | 43 | 29 | 20 | 19 |
|  -Year | | 1985 | 1970 | 1980 | 1987 | 1945 | 1984 | 1981 | 1957 | 1956 | 1957 | 1950 | 1983 | JAN 1985 |
| **NORMAL DEGREE DAYS:** | | | | | | | | | | | | | | |
| Heating (base 65°F) | | 212 | 172 | 68 | 0 | 0 | 0 | 0 | 0 | 0 | 0 | 47 | 157 | 656 |
| Cooling (base 65°F) | | 73 | 74 | 124 | 214 | 381 | 477 | 539 | 543 | 483 | 307 | 122 | 64 | 3401 |
| **% OF POSSIBLE SUNSHINE** | | | | | | | | | | | | | | |
| **MEAN SKY COVER (tenths)** | | | | | | | | | | | | | | |
| Sunrise - Sunset | 41 | 5.6 | 5.6 | 5.6 | 5.0 | 5.4 | 6.4 | 6.5 | 6.4 | 6.5 | 5.4 | 5.1 | 5.6 | 5.8 |
| **MEAN NUMBER OF DAYS:** | | | | | | | | | | | | | | |
| Sunrise to Sunset | | | | | | | | | | | | | | |
|  -Clear | 41 | 9.5 | 8.9 | 9.2 | 10.5 | 9.0 | 4.4 | 3.3 | 3.2 | 3.8 | 9.7 | 10.5 | 9.9 | 92.0 |
|  -Partly Cloudy | 41 | 10.3 | 8.6 | 10.6 | 11.2 | 13.4 | 14.2 | 16.8 | 17.2 | 14.5 | 11.4 | 10.3 | 9.2 | 147.6 |
|  -Cloudy | 41 | 11.2 | 10.8 | 11.2 | 8.3 | 8.6 | 11.4 | 11.0 | 10.6 | 11.7 | 10.0 | 9.1 | 11.9 | 125.7 |
| Precipitation | | | | | | | | | | | | | | |
| .01 inches or more | 47 | 6.2 | 7.0 | 7.6 | 5.4 | 8.5 | 13.7 | 17.2 | 15.9 | 13.7 | 8.4 | 5.6 | 6.0 | 115.3 |
| Snow,Ice pellets | | | | | | | | | | | | | | |
| 1.0 inches or more | 47 | 0.0 | 0.0 | 0.0 | 0.0 | 0.0 | 0.0 | 0.0 | 0.0 | 0.0 | 0.0 | 0.0 | 0.0 | 0.0 |
| Thunderstorms | 45 | 1.0 | 1.5 | 2.9 | 3.2 | 7.7 | 14.4 | 19.2 | 17.2 | 9.6 | 2.6 | 1.1 | 1.1 | 81.5 |
| Heavy Fog Visibility | | | | | | | | | | | | | | |
| 1/4 mile or less | 41 | 5.6 | 3.3 | 2.6 | 1.4 | 1.6 | 0.9 | 0.5 | 0.9 | 1 2 | 1.7 | 2.8 | 4.4 | 27.0 |
| Temperature °F | | | | | | | | | | | | | | |
|  -Maximum | | | | | | | | | | | | | | |
|   90° and above | 26 | 0.0 | 0.0 | 0.5 | 4.2 | 11.0 | 19.5 | 24.8 | 25.3 | 18.2 | 3.6 | 0.0 | 0.* | 107.1 |
|   32° and below | 26 | 0.0 | 0.0 | 0.0 | 0.0 | 0.0 | 0.0 | 0.0 | 0.0 | 0.0 | 0.0 | 0.0 | 0.0 | 0.0 |
|  -Minimum | | | | | | | | | | | | | | |
|   32° and below | 26 | 1.8 | 0.5 | 0.2 | 0.0 | 0.0 | 0.0 | 0.0 | 0.0 | 0.0 | 0.0 | 0.1 | 0.7 | 3.2 |
|   0° and below | 26 | 0.0 | 0.0 | 0.0 | 0.0 | 0.0 | 0.0 | 0.0 | 0.0 | 0.0 | 0.0 | 0.0 | 0.0 | 0.0 |
| **AVG. STATION PRESS.(mb)** | 17 | 1016.6 | 1015.8 | 1014.3 | 1013.6 | 1012.3 | 1013.0 | 1014.4 | 1013.7 | 1012.5 | 1013.6 | 1015.1 | 1016.7 | 1014.3 |
| **RELATIVE HUMIDITY (%)** | | | | | | | | | | | | | | |
| Hour 01 | 25 | 85 | 83 | 84 | 83 | 85 | 89 | 89 | 90 | 90 | 87 | 87 | 86 | 87 |
| Hour 07 | 26 | 87 | 87 | 88 | 88 | 88 | 89 | 90 | 92 | 91 | 89 | 89 | 88 | 89 |
| Hour 13 (Local Time) | 26 | 56 | 52 | 50 | 46 | 49 | 57 | 59 | 60 | 60 | 56 | 55 | 57 | 55 |
| Hour 19 | 26 | 68 | 63 | 61 | 57 | 62 | 72 | 75 | 77 | 77 | 73 | 73 | 72 | 69 |
| **PRECIPITATION (inches):** | | | | | | | | | | | | | | |
| Water Equivalent | | | | | | | | | | | | | | |
|  -Normal | | 2.10 | 2.83 | 3.20 | 2.19 | 3.96 | 7.39 | 7.78 | 6.32 | 5.62 | 2.82 | 1.78 | 1.83 | 47.82 |
|  -Maximum Monthly | 47 | 7.23 | 8.32 | 11.38 | 6.27 | 10.36 | 18.28 | 19.57 | 16.11 | 15.87 | 14.51 | 10.29 | 5.33 | 19.57 |
|  -Year | | 1986 | 1983 | 1987 | 1982 | 1976 | 1968 | 1960 | 1972 | 1945 | 1950 | 1987 | 1983 | JUL 1960 |
|  -Minimum Monthly | 47 | 0.15 | 0.10 | 0.16 | 0.14 | 0.43 | 1.97 | 3.53 | 2.92 | 0.43 | 0.35 | 0.03 | T | T |
|  -Year | | 1950 | 1944 | 1956 | 1977 | 1961 | 1948 | 1981 | 1980 | 1972 | 1967 | 1967 | 1944 | DEC 1944 |
|  -Maximum in 24 hrs | 47 | 4.19 | 4.38 | 5.03 | 5.04 | 3.18 | 8.40 | 8.19 | 5.29 | 9.67 | 7.74 | 5.87 | 3.61 | 9.67 |
|  -Year | | 1986 | 1970 | 1960 | 1984 | 1980 | 1945 | 1960 | 1949 | 1945 | 1950 | 1988 | 1969 | SEP 1945 |
| Snow,Ice pellets | | | | | | | | | | | | | | |
|  -Maximum Monthly | 17 | T | 0.0 | 0.0 | 0.0 | 0.0 | 0.0 | 0.0 | T | 0.0 | 0.0 | 0.0 | 0.0 | T |
|  -Year | | 1977 | | | | | | | 1989 | | | | | AUG 1989 |
|  -Maximum in 24 hrs | 17 | T | 0.0 | 0.0 | 0.0 | 0.0 | 0.0 | 0.0 | T | 0.0 | 0.0 | 0.0 | 0.0 | T |
|  -Year | | 1977 | | | | | | | 1989 | | | | | AUG 1989 |
| **WIND:** | | | | | | | | | | | | | | |
| Mean Speed (mph) | 41 | 9.0 | 9.6 | 9.9 | 9.4 | 8.7 | 8.0 | 7.4 | 7.1 | 7.6 | 8.6 | 8.6 | 8.6 | 8.5 |
| Prevailing Direction | | | | | | | | | | | | | | |
|  through 1963 | | NNE | S | S | SE | SE | SW | S | S | ENE | N | N | NNE | S |
| Fastest Obs. 1 Min. | | | | | | | | | | | | | | |
|  -Direction (!!!) | 40 | 25 | 25 | 29 | 02 | 17 | 32 | 14 | 32 | 24 | 05 | 26 | 07 | 32 |
|  -Speed (MPH) | 40 | 42 | 46 | 45 | 50 | 46 | 64 | 46 | 50 | 46 | 48 | 46 | 32 | 64 |
|  -Year | | 1953 | 1969 | 1955 | 1956 | 1981 | 1970 | 1961 | 1957 | 1969 | 1950 | 1968 | 1968 | JUN 1970 |
| Peak Gust | | | | | | | | | | | | | | |
|  -Direction (!!!) | 6 | NE | SW | W | SW | SW | W | SW | NW | NW | SW | NE | W | W |
|  -Speed (mph) | 6 | 45 | 47 | 45 | 44 | 43 | 62 | 54 | 48 | 54 | 38 | 41 | 43 | 62 |
|  -Date | | 1989 | 1988 | 1989 | 1988 | 1985 | 1985 | 1985 | 1989 | 1988 | 1988 | 1984 | 1984 | JUN 1985 |

**See reference Notes to this table on the following page.**

PRECIPITATION (inches)  ORLANDO, FLORIDA

**TABLE 2**

| YEAR | JAN | FEB | MAR | APR | MAY | JUNE | JULY | AUG | SEP | OCT | NOV | DEC | ANNUAL |
|---|---|---|---|---|---|---|---|---|---|---|---|---|---|
| 1961 | 1.75 | 2.82 | 2.21 | 0.28 | 0.43 | 8.08 | 9.93 | 6.99 | 4.84 | 2.87 | 0.92 | 0.66 | 41.78 |
| 1962 | 1.11 | 2.08 | 3.55 | 1.58 | 2.74 | 3.11 | 12.77 | 5.11 | 12.24 | 1.90 | 2.46 | 1.70 | 50.35 |
| 1963 | 3.17 | 4.76 | 2.69 | 1.23 | 3.56 | 6.67 | 3.83 | 3.54 | 6.72 | 0.46 | 6.39 | 2.26 | 45.28 |
| 1964 | 6.18 | 3.42 | 4.65 | 2.14 | 2.74 | 6.11 | 6.68 | 9.00 | 9.47 | 1.64 | 0.45 | 1.91 | 54.39 |
| 1965 | 1.79 | 3.67 | 3.02 | 0.66 | 0.52 | 7.36 | 11.55 | 5.49 | 5.99 | 4.06 | 1.06 | 2.23 | 47.40 |
| 1966 | 4.45 | 6.31 | 2.57 | 1.92 | 6.57 | 9.77 | 6.73 | 7.76 | 6.25 | 1.98 | 0.09 | 0.99 | 55.39 |
| 1967 | 0.84 | 5.49 | 1.31 | 0.28 | 1.69 | 11.16 | 4.63 | 6.83 | 5.88 | 0.35 | 0.03 | 2.42 | 40.91 |
| 1968 | 0.65 | 2.76 | 2.27 | 0.30 | 3.72 | 18.28 | 5.60 | 3.44 | 5.91 | 5.47 | 2.82 | 0.88 | 52.10 |
| 1969 | 2.22 | 3.30 | 5.52 | 2.38 | 1.40 | 5.04 | 6.73 | 7.17 | 6.44 | 9.45 | 0.87 | 4.66 | 55.18 |
| 1970 | 4.05 | 6.77 | 3.66 | 0.45 | 4.08 | 4.92 | 5.97 | 5.91 | 3.25 | 2.60 | 0.24 | 2.06 | 43.96 |
| 1971 | 0.45 | 2.98 | 1.46 | 1.52 | 4.31 | 4.39 | 8.29 | 7.51 | 2.98 | 3.06 | 1.21 | 1.93 | 40.09 |
| 1972 | 0.99 | 4.96 | 5.06 | 1.39 | 3.76 | 6.33 | 3.98 | 16.11 | 0.43 | 2.34 | 4.11 | 2.56 | 51.35 |
| 1973 | 4.82 | 2.73 | 4.13 | 2.82 | 4.74 | 6.63 | 6.24 | 7.33 | 11.53 | 1.10 | 0.74 | 2.56 | 55.37 |
| #1974 | 0.18 | 0.63 | 3.67 | 1.17 | 2.69 | 15.28 | 6.01 | 6.56 | 5.78 | 0.48 | 0.31 | 1.62 | 44.38 |
| 1975 | 0.98 | 1.49 | 1.10 | 1.36 | 7.52 | 9.70 | 9.26 | 4.75 | 4.97 | 4.74 | 0.66 | 0.51 | 47.04 |
| 1976 | 0.37 | 0.83 | 1.72 | 2.16 | 10.36 | 9.93 | 7.05 | 3.25 | 5.87 | 0.74 | 2.03 | 2.77 | 47.08 |
| 1977 | 1.81 | 1.76 | 1.82 | 0.14 | 1.47 | 4.47 | 6.61 | 6.28 | 7.03 | 0.43 | 2.60 | 3.70 | 38.12 |
| 1978 | 2.49 | 5.45 | 2.14 | 0.61 | 3.16 | 10.00 | 11.92 | 5.13 | 4.31 | 1.51 | 0.18 | 3.69 | 50.59 |
| 1979 | 6.48 | 1.45 | 3.24 | 1.08 | 7.66 | 4.00 | 7.95 | 5.88 | 9.19 | 0.43 | 1.93 | 0.94 | 50.23 |
| 1980 | 2.45 | 1.64 | 1.51 | 4.07 | 6.96 | 5.25 | 5.14 | 2.92 | 3.70 | 0.55 | 6.55 | 0.47 | 41.21 |
| 1981 | 0.21 | 4.36 | 1.85 | 0.18 | 2.02 | 12.49 | 3.53 | 5.60 | 8.26 | 3.13 | 2.50 | 2.97 | 47.10 |
| 1982 | 1.72 | 1.34 | 4.85 | 6.27 | 5.29 | 6.06 | 11.81 | 5.03 | 6.96 | 0.74 | 0.53 | 1.01 | 51.61 |
| 1983 | 2.08 | 8.32 | 5.37 | 3.21 | 1.77 | 7.82 | 6.49 | 4.83 | 5.16 | 3.78 | 1.36 | 5.33 | 55.52 |
| 1984 | 2.01 | 2.73 | 1.85 | 6.21 | 3.20 | 5.32 | 6.19 | 7.89 | 6.19 | 0.56 | 2.10 | 0.19 | 44.44 |
| 1985 | 0.91 | 1.27 | 4.59 | 1.69 | 3.00 | 4.54 | 7.28 | 11.63 | 5.45 | 2.55 | 0.82 | 3.46 | 47.19 |
| 1986 | 7.21 | 1.84 | 2.64 | 0.49 | 0.88 | 9.50 | 5.80 | 5.99 | 4.50 | 5.64 | 1.69 | 3.69 | 49.83 |
| 1987 | 1.27 | 1.74 | 11.38 | 0.59 | 1.40 | 3.54 | 4.17 | 7.94 | 5.67 | 1.42 | 7.44 | 1.00 | 52.49 |
| 1988 | 3.12 | 1.38 | 6.07 | 2.02 | 2.82 |  | 9.44 |  | 6.20 |  | 1.75 | 1.44 | 45.66 |
| 1989 | 3.80 | 0.15 | 1.35 | 2.28 | 2.38 | 6.79 | 4.74 | 6.20 | 10.29 | 1.75 | 1.44 | 4.49 | 45.66 |
| 1990 | 0.23 | 4.13 | 1.92 | 1.73 | 0.55 | 6.22 | 6.68 | 3.78 | 2.46 | 2.10 | 1.05 | 0.83 | 31.68 |
| Record Mean | 2.18 | 2.76 | 3.40 | 2.39 | 3.34 | 7.02 | 7.91 | 6.65 | 6.80 | 3.27 | 1.93 | 1.99 | 49.65 |

**TABLE 3**  AVERAGE TEMPERATURE (deg. F)  ORLANDO, FLORIDA

| YEAR | JAN | FEB | MAR | APR | MAY | JUNE | JULY | AUG | SEP | OCT | NOV | DEC | ANNUAL |
|---|---|---|---|---|---|---|---|---|---|---|---|---|---|
| 1961 | 56.9 | 64.7 | 70.6 | 69.4 | 77.0 | 80.6 | 83.3 | 82.9 | 81.1 | 73.6 | 69.4 | 63.9 | 72.8 |
| 1962 | 60.9 | 68.4 | 63.7 | 70.3 | 79.8 | 81.6 | 83.9 | 82.8 | 80.6 | 75.0 | 63.0 | 57.7 | 72.3 |
| #1963 | 59.5 | 57.2 | 69.5 | 73.6 | 77.9 | 82.4 | 82.9 |  | 80.5 | 73.8 | 65.4 | 56.5 | 71.9 |
| 1964 | 58.5 | 58.3 | 68.1 | 74.1 | 77.1 | 82.4 | 81.6 | 82.8 | 79.8 | 72.5 | 70.5 | 64.4 | 72.5 |
| 1965 | 60.0 | 64.1 | 67.0 | 74.8 | 77.1 | 79.0 | 80.5 | 82.2 | 80.8 | 74.2 | 69.5 | 62.6 | 72.7 |
| 1966 | 58.7 | 62.3 | 64.4 | 70.5 | 77.4 | 78.0 | 82.3 | 82.3 | 80.1 | 75.8 | 65.8 | 60.1 | 71.5 |
| 1967 | 63.2 | 60.0 | 68.3 | 74.3 | 78.3 | 80.2 | 82.4 | 82.0 | 79.7 | 74.0 | 67.5 | 65.3 | 73.0 |
| 1968 | 59.6 | 54.8 | 61.4 | 73.5 | 76.7 | 78.8 | 81.3 | 82.3 | 80.3 | 74.3 | 63.4 | 58.7 | 70.4 |
| 1969 | 59.8 | 57.8 | 67.0 | 72.5 | 76.9 | 82.9 | 84.4 | 82.2 | 81.2 | 77.9 | 64.0 | 58.7 | 71.6 |
| 1970 | 55.1 | 58.7 | 67.0 | 75.8 | 77.7 | 81.8 | 83.8 | 82.3 | 83.6 | 77.0 | 63.4 | 64.6 | 72.6 |
| 1971 | 62.0 | 64.1 | 64.8 | 72.1 | 78.2 | 81.7 | 83.1 | 83.3 | 81.8 | 79.0 | 69.5 | 71.4 | 74.2 |
| 1972 | 68.9 | 62.0 | 68.7 | 72.7 | 77.4 | 82.2 | 83.2 | 82.8 | 81.8 | 76.8 | 68.9 | 66.1 | 74.3 |
| 1973 | 62.4 | 59.7 | 71.1 | 71.1 | 78.3 | 83.1 | 84.2 | 81.8 | 81.4 | 75.6 | 70.9 | 60.4 | 73.3 |
| #1974 | 71.6 | 60.5 | 70.2 | 71.4 | 78.0 | 80.3 | 80.7 | 82.0 | 81.8 | 72.6 | 67.6 | 60.9 | 73.1 |
| 1975 | 65.8 | 67.6 | 67.4 | 72.4 | 79.1 | 80.8 | 80.5 | 82.3 | 80.7 | 76.6 | 67.4 | 60.2 | 73.4 |
| 1976 | 56.5 | 63.7 | 70.4 | 71.3 | 76.8 | 79.7 | 82.4 | 81.9 | 80.5 | 72.6 | 63.0 | 60.1 | 71.6 |
| 1977 | 50.6 | 57.4 | 69.7 | 70.6 | 75.2 | 82.6 | 82.0 | 81.5 | 82.6 | 72.9 | 69.6 | 61.0 | 71.3 |
| 1978 | 56.8 | 55.8 | 66.3 | 73.4 | 79.3 | 82.9 | 82.6 | 82.6 | 81.7 | 75.0 | 72.3 | 66.8 | 73.0 |
| 1979 | 58.2 | 58.4 | 64.6 | 73.4 | 75.4 | 80.7 | 83.3 | 82.4 | 81.3 | 74.4 | 68.3 | 62.6 | 71.9 |
| 1980 | 60.5 | 57.2 | 68.2 | 70.4 | 76.4 | 80.1 | 83.6 | 83.6 | 81.7 | 75.4 | 67.1 | 59.0 | 71.9 |
| 1981 | 51.3 | 61.7 | 64.0 | 73.1 | 76.7 | 83.2 | 84.1 | 82.9 | 80.0 | 76.4 | 65.3 | 60.5 | 71.6 |
| 1982 | 60.0 | 68.4 | 70.4 | 72.6 | 75.3 | 82.0 | 82.6 | 82.2 | 80.2 | 74.1 | 70.8 | 66.7 | 73.8 |
| 1983 | 58.0 | 59.9 | 63.5 | 68.6 | 76.4 | 80.5 | 83.2 | 83.5 | 80.6 | 76.5 | 65.8 | 61.2 | 71.5 |
| 1984 | 57.8 | 61.2 | 64.7 | 69.2 | 75.6 | 78.4 | 80.7 | 81.5 | 78.9 | 75.4 | 65.8 | 66.0 | 71.3 |
| 1985 | 54.7 | 62.2 | 68.4 | 70.7 | 77.2 | 82.4 | 82.1 | 82.3 | 79.8 | 79.4 | 73.0 | 58.8 | 72.6 |
| 1986 | 59.8 | 64.3 | 65.4 | 69.3 | 76.7 | 81.7 | 82.3 | 83.3 | 81.7 | 77.5 | 75.8 | 67.3 | 73.8 |
| 1987 | 58.8 | 62.7 | 65.9 | 66.8 | 76.8 | 83.1 | 83.5 | 85.0 | 82.7 | 72.2 | 69.0 | 64.2 | 72.6 |
| 1988 | 58.5 | 60.4 | 65.5 | 72.0 | 75.5 | 80.3 | 80.7 | 82.8 | 83.9 | 73.7 | 70.5 | 62.4 | 72.2 |
| 1989 | 66.9 | 64.5 | 69.3 | 71.9 | 77.9 | 81.9 | 83.2 | 83.3 | 82.2 | 75.3 | 69.0 | 55.5 | 73.4 |
| 1990 | 65.8 | 69.1 | 69.3 | 71.5 | 79.4 | 81.9 | 82.8 | 83.5 | 82.0 | 77.1 | 69.3 | 66.3 | 74.8 |
| Record Mean | 60.3 | 62.1 | 66.8 | 71.8 | 77.3 | 81.2 | 82.3 | 82.6 | 81.0 | 74.8 | 67.6 | 62.0 | 72.5 |
| Max | 71.4 | 73.4 | 78.1 | 83.2 | 88.2 | 91.0 | 91.7 | 91.6 | 89.6 | 84.1 | 77.9 | 72.8 | 82.8 |
| Min | 49.2 | 50.8 | 55.5 | 60.3 | 66.3 | 71.4 | 72.9 | 73.5 | 72.3 | 65.6 | 57.2 | 51.2 | 62.2 |

## REFERENCE NOTES FOR TABLES 1, 2, 3 and 6    (ORLANDO, FL)

### GENERAL

T - TRACE AMOUNT
BLANK ENTRIES DENOTE MISSING/UNREPORTED DATA.
# INDICATES A STATION OR INSTRUMENT RELOCATION.

### SPECIFIC

**TABLE 1**

(a) - LENGTH OF RECORD IN YEARS. ALTHOUGH INDIVIDUAL MONTHS MAY BE MISSING.

∗ LESS THAN .05

NORMALS — BASED ON THE 1951-1980 RECORD PERIOD.
EXTREMES — DATES ARE THE MOST RECENT OCCURRENCE.
WIND DIR. — NUMERALS SHOW TENS OF DEGREES CLOCKWISE FROM TRUE NORTH.
"00" INDICATES CALM.
RESULTANT WIND DIRECTIONS ARE GIVEN TO WHOLE DEGREES.

**TABLE 3**
MAX AND MIN ARE LONG-TERM MEAN DAILY MAXIMUM AND MEAN DAILY MINIMUM TEMPERATURES.

### EXCEPTIONS

**TABLES 2, 3, and 6**

RECORD MEANS ARE THROUGH THE CURRENT YEAR, BEGINNING IN     1943 FOR TEMPERATURE
1943 FOR PRECIPITATION
1943 FOR SNOWFALL

HEATING DEGREE DAYS Base 65 deg. F     ORLANDO, FLORIDA

**TABLE 4**

| SEASON | JULY | AUG | SEP | OCT | NOV | DEC | JAN | FEB | MAR | APR | MAY | JUNE | TOTAL |
|---|---|---|---|---|---|---|---|---|---|---|---|---|---|
| 1961-62 | 0 | 0 | 0 | 5 | 16 | 149 | 176 | 46 | 111 | 21 | 0 | 0 | 524 |
| 1962-63 | 0 | 0 | 0 | 4 | 98 | 255 | 209 | 232 | 33 | 2 | 0 | 0 | 833 |
| #1963-64 | 0 | 0 | 0 | 3 | 72 | 272 | 235 | 199 | 39 | 4 | 0 | 0 | 824 |
| 1964-65 | 0 | 0 | 0 | 7 | 14 | 84 | 178 | 89 | 82 | 0 | 0 | 0 | 454 |
| 1965-66 | 0 | 0 | 0 | 1 | 19 | 112 | 215 | 122 | 72 | 5 | 0 | 0 | 546 |
| 1966-67 | 0 | 0 | 0 | 2 | 70 | 169 | 119 | 157 | 25 | 0 | 0 | 0 | 542 |
| 1967-68 | 0 | 0 | 0 | 0 | 29 | 80 | 191 | 293 | 149 | 0 | 0 | 0 | 742 |
| 1968-69 | 0 | 0 | 0 | 19 | 120 | 237 | 168 | 206 | 169 | 0 | 0 | 0 | 919 |
| 1969-70 | 0 | 0 | 0 | 0 | 93 | 204 | 316 | 187 | 58 | 0 | 0 | 0 | 858 |
| 1970-71 | 0 | 0 | 0 | 0 | 120 | 79 | 165 | 115 | 92 | 20 | 0 | 0 | 591 |
| 1971-72 | 0 | 0 | 0 | 0 | 26 | 9 | 124 | 24 | 6 | | 0 | 0 | 240 |
| 1972-73 | 0 | 0 | 0 | 0 | 54 | 105 | 160 | 169 | 12 | 9 | 0 | 0 | 509 |
| #1973-74 | 0 | 0 | 0 | 6 | 13 | 193 | 0 | 173 | 15 | 8 | 0 | 0 | 408 |
| 1974-75 | 0 | 0 | 0 | 0 | 40 | 163 | 73 | 44 | 57 | 10 | 0 | 0 | 387 |
| 1975-76 | 0 | 0 | 0 | 0 | 85 | 174 | 278 | 104 | 18 | 1 | 0 | 0 | 660 |
| 1976-77 | 0 | 0 | 0 | 4 | 118 | 197 | 440 | 218 | 41 | 8 | 0 | 0 | 1026 |
| 1977-78 | 0 | 0 | 0 | 6 | 38 | 179 | 275 | 255 | 71 | 0 | 0 | 0 | 824 |
| 1978-79 | 0 | 0 | 0 | 0 | 0 | 56 | 230 | 214 | 71 | 0 | 0 | 0 | 571 |
| 1979-80 | 0 | 0 | 0 | 0 | 47 | 119 | 161 | 245 | 61 | 4 | 0 | 0 | 637 |
| 1980-81 | 0 | 0 | 0 | 1 | 67 | 190 | 416 | 119 | 76 | 1 | 0 | 0 | 870 |
| 1981-82 | 0 | 0 | 0 | 0 | 75 | 205 | 204 | 21 | 33 | 7 | 0 | 0 | 545 |
| 1982-83 | 0 | 0 | 0 | 14 | 16 | 94 | 233 | 148 | 105 | 13 | 0 | 0 | 623 |
| 1983-84 | 0 | 0 | 0 | 0 | 63 | 188 | 252 | 137 | 86 | 18 | 0 | 0 | 744 |
| 1984-85 | 0 | 0 | 0 | 0 | 68 | 71 | 340 | 146 | 22 | 12 | 0 | 0 | 659 |
| 1985-86 | 0 | 0 | 0 | 0 | 14 | 228 | 180 | 82 | 105 | 4 | 0 | 0 | 613 |
| 1986-87 | 0 | 0 | 0 | 0 | 0 | 42 | 216 | 97 | 48 | 66 | 0 | 0 | 469 |
| 1987-88 | 0 | 0 | 0 | 0 | 39 | 97 | 221 | 169 | 71 | 7 | 0 | 0 | 604 |
| 1988-89 | 0 | 0 | 0 | 0 | 11 | 135 | 32 | 119 | 59 | 4 | 0 | 0 | 360 |
| 1989-90 | 0 | 0 | 0 | 21 | 27 | 308 | 71 | 34 | 11 | 5 | 0 | 0 | 477 |
| 1990-91 | 0 | 0 | 0 | 6 | 14 | 69 | | | | | | | |

**TABLE 5**     COOLING DEGREE DAYS Base 65 deg. F     ORLANDO, FLORIDA

| YEAR | JAN | FEB | MAR | APR | MAY | JUNE | JULY | AUG | SEP | OCT | NOV | DEC | TOTAL |
|---|---|---|---|---|---|---|---|---|---|---|---|---|---|
| 1969 | 12 | 10 | 32 | 232 | 376 | 544 | 608 | 540 | 495 | 406 | 68 | 16 | 3339 |
| 1970 | 19 | 14 | 128 | 330 | 399 | 511 | 586 | 544 | 565 | 380 | 77 | 72 | 3625 |
| 1971 | 77 | 97 | 90 | 238 | 411 | 505 | 569 | 573 | 510 | 440 | 167 | 214 | 3891 |
| 1972 | 181 | 44 | 146 | 243 | 391 | 524 | 570 | 561 | 509 | 374 | 179 | 148 | 3870 |
| 1973 | 88 | 28 | 207 | 198 | 421 | 548 | 602 | 529 | 501 | 341 | 199 | 58 | 3720 |
| #1974 | 213 | 51 | 183 | 207 | 410 | 463 | 492 | 536 | 510 | 241 | 125 | 43 | 3474 |
| 1975 | 105 | 121 | 141 | 237 | 442 | 481 | 489 | 541 | 479 | 366 | 167 | 32 | 3601 |
| 1976 | 18 | 75 | 194 | 196 | 374 | 449 | 549 | 529 | 474 | 247 | 65 | 49 | 3219 |
| 1977 | 1 | 13 | 192 | 182 | 324 | 534 | 537 | 521 | 536 | 257 | 185 | 62 | 3344 |
| 1978 | 26 | 3 | 116 | 259 | 449 | 541 | 550 | 553 | 508 | 321 | 225 | 115 | 3666 |
| 1979 | 26 | 31 | 65 | 260 | 449 | 479 | 575 | 546 | 498 | 299 | 153 | 53 | 3315 |
| 1980 | 27 | 25 | 169 | 172 | 362 | 459 | 586 | 582 | 508 | 331 | 138 | 12 | 3371 |
| 1981 | 0 | 34 | 52 | 253 | 372 | 552 | 602 | 559 | 458 | 359 | 89 | 73 | 3403 |
| 1982 | 56 | 123 | 211 | 241 | 325 | 518 | 550 | 542 | 465 | 303 | 196 | 152 | 3682 |
| 1983 | 22 | 11 | 68 | 129 | 361 | 473 | 573 | 582 | 476 | 362 | 95 | 77 | 3229 |
| 1984 | 37 | 35 | 84 | 151 | 332 | 411 | 490 | 520 | 426 | 331 | 99 | 107 | 3023 |
| 1985 | 27 | 74 | 137 | 191 | 386 | 531 | 539 | 548 | 451 | 454 | 262 | 45 | 3645 |
| 1986 | 25 | 69 | 124 | 139 | 372 | 506 | 543 | 573 | 507 | 392 | 333 | 121 | 3704 |
| 1987 | 32 | 38 | 82 | 127 | 376 | 549 | 582 | 627 | 540 | 230 | 163 | 78 | 3424 |
| 1988 | 26 | 43 | 95 | 223 | 336 | 466 | 496 | 559 | 573 | 275 | 182 | 61 | 3335 |
| 1989 | 101 | 111 | 213 | 216 | 408 | 509 | 573 | 579 | 523 | 346 | 153 | 19 | 3751 |
| 1990 | 102 | 156 | 156 | 206 | 453 | 514 | 559 | 581 | 518 | 388 | 149 | 116 | 3898 |

**TABLE 6**     SNOWFALL (inches)     ORLANDO, FLORIDA

| SEASON | JULY | AUG | SEP | OCT | NOV | DEC | JAN | FEB | MAR | APR | MAY | JUNE | TOTAL |
|---|---|---|---|---|---|---|---|---|---|---|---|---|---|
| 1970-71 | 0.0 | 0.0 | 0.0 | 0.0 | 0.0 | 0.0 | 0.0 | 0.0 | 0.0 | 0.0 | 0.0 | 0.0 | 0.0 |
| 1971-72 | 0.0 | 0.0 | 0.0 | 0.0 | 0.0 | 0.0 | 0.0 | 0.0 | 0.0 | 0.0 | 0.0 | 0.0 | 0.0 |
| 1972-73 | 0.0 | 0.0 | 0.0 | 0.0 | 0.0 | 0.0 | 0.0 | 0.0 | 0.0 | 0.0 | 0.0 | 0.0 | 0.0 |
| #1973-74 | 0.0 | 0.0 | 0.0 | 0.0 | 0.0 | 0.0 | 0.0 | 0.0 | 0.0 | 0.0 | 0.0 | 0.0 | 0.0 |
| 1974-75 | 0.0 | 0.0 | 0.0 | 0.0 | 0.0 | 0.0 | 0.0 | 0.0 | 0.0 | 0.0 | 0.0 | 0.0 | 0.0 |
| 1975-76 | 0.0 | 0.0 | 0.0 | 0.0 | 0.0 | 0.0 | 0.0 | 0.0 | 0.0 | 0.0 | 0.0 | 0.0 | 0.0 |
| 1976-77 | 0.0 | 0.0 | 0.0 | 0.0 | 0.0 | 0.0 | T | 0.0 | 0.0 | 0.0 | 0.0 | 0.0 | T |
| 1977-78 | 0.0 | 0.0 | 0.0 | 0.0 | 0.0 | 0.0 | 0.0 | 0.0 | 0.0 | 0.0 | 0.0 | 0.0 | T |
| 1978-79 | 0.0 | 0.0 | 0.0 | 0.0 | 0.0 | 0.0 | 0.0 | 0.0 | 0.0 | 0.0 | 0.0 | 0.0 | 0.0 |
| 1979-80 | 0.0 | 0.0 | 0.0 | 0.0 | 0.0 | 0.0 | 0.0 | 0.0 | 0.0 | 0.0 | 0.0 | 0.0 | 0.0 |
| 1980-81 | 0.0 | 0.0 | 0.0 | 0.0 | 0.0 | 0.0 | 0.0 | 0.0 | 0.0 | 0.0 | 0.0 | 0.0 | 0.0 |
| 1981-82 | 0.0 | 0.0 | 0.0 | 0.0 | 0.0 | 0.0 | 0.0 | 0.0 | 0.0 | 0.0 | 0.0 | 0.0 | 0.0 |
| 1982-83 | 0.0 | 0.0 | 0.0 | 0.0 | 0.0 | 0.0 | 0.0 | 0.0 | 0.0 | 0.0 | 0.0 | 0.0 | 0.0 |
| 1983-84 | 0.0 | 0.0 | 0.0 | 0.0 | 0.0 | 0.0 | 0.0 | 0.0 | 0.0 | 0.0 | 0.0 | 0.0 | 0.0 |
| 1984-85 | 0.0 | 0.0 | 0.0 | 0.0 | 0.0 | 0.0 | 0.0 | 0.0 | 0.0 | 0.0 | 0.0 | 0.0 | 0.0 |
| 1985-86 | 0.0 | 0.0 | 0.0 | 0.0 | 0.0 | 0.0 | 0.0 | 0.0 | 0.0 | 0.0 | 0.0 | 0.0 | 0.0 |
| 1986-87 | 0.0 | 0.0 | 0.0 | 0.0 | 0.0 | 0.0 | 0.0 | 0.0 | 0.0 | 0.0 | 0.0 | 0.0 | 0.0 |
| 1987-88 | 0.0 | 0.0 | 0.0 | 0.0 | 0.0 | 0.0 | 0.0 | 0.0 | 0.0 | 0.0 | 0.0 | 0.0 | 0.0 |
| 1988-89 | 0.0 | 0.0 | 0.0 | 0.0 | 0.0 | 0.0 | 0.0 | 0.0 | 0.0 | 0.0 | 0.0 | 0.0 | 0.0 |
| 1989-90 | 0.0 | T | 0.0 | 0.0 | 0.0 | 0.0 | 0.0 | 0.0 | 0.0 | 0.0 | 0.0 | 0.0 | T |
| 1990-91 | 0.0 | 0.0 | 0.0 | 0.0 | 0.0 | 0.0 | | | | | | | |
| Record Mean | 0.0 | T | 0.0 | 0.0 | 0.0 | 0.0 | T | 0.0 | 0.0 | 0.0 | 0.0 | 0.0 | T |

**See Reference Notes, relative to all above tables, on preceding page.**

Tampa is on west central coast of the Florida Peninsula. Very near the Gulf of Mexico at the upper end of Tampa Bay, land and sea breezes modify the subtropical climate. Major rivers flowing into the area are the Hillsborough, the Alafia, and the Little Manatee.

Winters are mild. Summers are long, rather warm, and humid. Low temperatures are about 50 degrees in the winter and 70 degrees during the summer. Afternoon highs range from the low 70s in the winter to around 90 degrees from June through September. Invasions of cold northern air produce an occasional cool winter morning. Freezing temperatures occur on one or two mornings per year during December, January, and February. In some years no freezing temperatures occur. Temperatures rarely fail to recover to the 60s on the cooler winter days. Temperatures above the low 90s are uncommon because of the afternoon sea breezes and thunderstorms. An outstanding feature of the Tampa climate is the summer thunderstorm season. Most of the thunderstorms occur in the late afternoon hours from June through September. The resulting sudden drop in temperature from about 90 degrees to around 70 degrees makes for a pleasant change. Between a dry spring and a dry fall, some 30 inches of rain, about 60 percent of the annual total, falls during the summer months. Snowfall is very rare. Measurable snows under 1/2 inch have occurred only a few times in the last one hundred years.

A large part of the generally flat sandy land near the coast has an elevation of under 15 feet above sea level. This does make the area vulnerable to tidal surges. Tropical storms threaten the area on a few occasions most years. The greatest risk of hurricanes has been during the months of June and October. Many hurricanes, by replenishing the soil moisture and raising the water table, do far more good than harm. The heaviest rains in a 24–hour period, around 12 inches, have been associated with hurricanes.

Fittingly named the Suncoast, the sun shines more than 65 percent of the possible, with the sunniest months being April and May. Afternoon humidities are usually 60 percent or higher in the summer months, but range from 50 to 60 percent the remainder of the year.

Night ground fogs occur frequently during the cooler winter months. Prevailing winds are easterly, but westerly afternoon and early evening sea breezes occur most months of the year. Winds in excess of 25 mph are not common and usually occur only with thunderstorms or tropical disturbances.

Based on the 1951–1980 period, the average first occurrence of 32 degrees Fahrenheit in the fall is December 26 and the average last occurrence in the spring is February 3.

## TABLE 1      NORMALS, MEANS AND EXTREMES

TAMPA, FLORIDA

LATITUDE: 27°58'N    LONGITUDE: 82°32'W    ELEVATION: FT. GRND 19 BARO 41    TIME ZONE: EASTERN    WBAN: 12842

| | (a) | JAN | FEB | MAR | APR | MAY | JUNE | JULY | AUG | SEP | OCT | NOV | DEC | YEAR |
|---|---|---|---|---|---|---|---|---|---|---|---|---|---|---|
| **TEMPERATURE °F:** | | | | | | | | | | | | | | |
| Normals | | | | | | | | | | | | | | |
| -Daily Maximum | | 70.0 | 71.0 | 76.2 | 81.9 | 87.1 | 89.5 | 90.0 | 90.3 | 88.9 | 83.7 | 76.9 | 71.6 | 81.4 |
| -Daily Minimum | | 49.5 | 50.4 | 56.1 | 61.1 | 67.2 | 72.3 | 74.2 | 74.2 | 72.8 | 65.1 | 56.4 | 50.9 | 62.5 |
| -Monthly | | 59.8 | 60.8 | 66.2 | 71.6 | 77.1 | 80.9 | 82.2 | 82.2 | 80.9 | 74.5 | 66.7 | 61.3 | 72.0 |
| Extremes | | | | | | | | | | | | | | |
| -Record Highest | 43 | 84 | 88 | 91 | 93 | 98 | 99 | 97 | 98 | 96 | 94 | 90 | 86 | 99 |
| -Year | | 1989 | 1971 | 1949 | 1975 | 1975 | 1985 | 1964 | 1975 | 1972 | 1959 | 1971 | 1978 | JUN 1985 |
| -Record Lowest | 43 | 21 | 24 | 29 | 40 | 49 | 53 | 63 | 67 | 57 | 40 | 23 | 18 | 18 |
| -Year | | 1985 | 1958 | 1980 | 1987 | 1971 | 1984 | 1970 | 1973 | 1981 | 1964 | 1970 | 1962 | DEC 1962 |
| **NORMAL DEGREE DAYS:** | | | | | | | | | | | | | | |
| Heating (base 65°F) | | 228 | 186 | 87 | 0 | 0 | 0 | 0 | 0 | 0 | 0 | 65 | 173 | 739 |
| Cooling (base 65°F) | | 66 | 68 | 124 | 202 | 375 | 477 | 533 | 533 | 477 | 295 | 116 | 58 | 3324 |
| **% OF POSSIBLE SUNSHINE** | 42 | 64 | 66 | 71 | 75 | 75 | 67 | 62 | 60 | 60 | 65 | 65 | 61 | 66 |
| **MEAN SKY COVER (tenths)** | | | | | | | | | | | | | | |
| Sunrise - Sunset | 43 | 5.6 | 5.5 | 5.4 | 4.8 | 5.1 | 6.1 | 6.7 | 6.5 | 6.3 | 5.1 | 5.0 | 5.5 | 5.6 |
| **MEAN NUMBER OF DAYS:** | | | | | | | | | | | | | | |
| Sunrise to Sunset | | | | | | | | | | | | | | |
| -Clear | 43 | 9.8 | 9.3 | 10.5 | 11.4 | 10.7 | 5.4 | 2.5 | 3.1 | 5.0 | 11.6 | 11.7 | 10.1 | 101.1 |
| -Partly Cloudy | 43 | 9.8 | 9.0 | 10.0 | 10.9 | 12.4 | 14.1 | 16.2 | 16.5 | 13.6 | 10.4 | 9.5 | 9.6 | 142.1 |
| -Cloudy | 43 | 11.4 | 10.0 | 10.5 | 7.7 | 7.9 | 10.5 | 12.2 | 11.3 | 11.6 | 8.8 | 8.9 | 11.3 | 122.0 |
| Precipitation | | | | | | | | | | | | | | |
| .01 inches or more | 43 | 6.4 | 6.9 | 6.8 | 4.6 | 6.2 | 11.7 | 15.7 | 16.8 | 13.0 | 6.8 | 5.5 | 6.3 | 106.7 |
| Snow,Ice pellets | | | | | | | | | | | | | | |
| 1.0 inches or more | 43 | 0.0 | 0.0 | 0.0 | 0.0 | 0.0 | 0.0 | 0.0 | 0.0 | 0.0 | 0.0 | 0.0 | 0.0 | 0.0 |
| Thunderstorms | 43 | 0.9 | 1.6 | 2.6 | 2.6 | 5.5 | 13.7 | 21.0 | 20.7 | 11.8 | 2.9 | 1.3 | 1.3 | 85.9 |
| Heavy Fog Visibility | | | | | | | | | | | | | | |
| 1/4 mile or less | 43 | 5.6 | 3.0 | 2.8 | 1.1 | 0.5 | 0.3 | 0.* | 0.3 | 0.3 | 1.1 | 2.7 | 4.2 | 22.0 |
| Temperature °F | | | | | | | | | | | | | | |
| -Maximum | | | | | | | | | | | | | | |
| 90° and above | 26 | 0.0 | 0.0 | 0.0 | 0.6 | 7.8 | 15.7 | 20.3 | 21.1 | 15.0 | 2.3 | 0.* | 0.0 | 82.9 |
| 32° and below | 26 | 0.0 | 0.0 | 0.0 | 0.0 | 0.0 | 0.0 | 0.0 | 0.0 | 0.0 | 0.0 | 0.0 | 0.0 | 0.0 |
| -Minimum | | | | | | | | | | | | | | |
| 32° and below | 26 | 2.0 | 0.7 | 0.1 | 0.0 | 0.0 | 0.0 | 0.0 | 0.0 | 0.0 | 0.0 | 0.1 | 1.0 | 3.8 |
| 0° and below | 26 | 0.0 | 0.0 | 0.0 | 0.0 | 0.0 | 0.0 | 0.0 | 0.0 | 0.0 | 0.0 | 0.0 | 0.0 | 0.0 |
| **AVG. STATION PRESS.(mb)** | 16 | 1020.1 | 1019.1 | 1017.7 | 1016.7 | 1015.6 | 1016.2 | 1017.7 | 1016.9 | 1015.4 | 1016.8 | 1018.3 | 1020.1 | 1017.5 |
| **RELATIVE HUMIDITY (%)** | | | | | | | | | | | | | | |
| Hour 01 | 26 | 85 | 83 | 83 | 82 | 81 | 84 | 85 | 87 | 87 | 85 | 86 | 85 | 84 |
| Hour 07 | 26 | 86 | 86 | 87 | 87 | 86 | 87 | 88 | 91 | 91 | 89 | 88 | 87 | 88 |
| Hour 13 (Local Time) | 26 | 59 | 56 | 55 | 51 | 52 | 60 | 63 | 64 | 62 | 57 | 57 | 59 | 58 |
| Hour 19 | 26 | 73 | 69 | 67 | 62 | 62 | 69 | 73 | 76 | 75 | 72 | 74 | 74 | 71 |
| **PRECIPITATION (inches):** | | | | | | | | | | | | | | |
| Water Equivalent | | | | | | | | | | | | | | |
| -Normal | | 2.17 | 3.04 | 3.46 | 1.82 | 3.38 | 5.29 | 7.35 | 7.64 | 6.23 | 2.34 | 1.87 | 2.14 | 46.73 |
| -Maximum Monthly | 43 | 8.02 | 7.95 | 12.64 | 6.59 | 17.64 | 13.75 | 20.59 | 18.59 | 13.98 | 7.36 | 6.12 | 6.66 | 20.59 |
| -Year | | 1948 | 1963 | 1959 | 1957 | 1979 | 1974 | 1960 | 1949 | 1979 | 1952 | 1963 | 1950 | JUL 1960 |
| -Minimum Monthly | 43 | T | 0.21 | 0.06 | T | 0.17 | 1.86 | 1.65 | 2.35 | 1.28 | 0.09 | T | 0.07 | T |
| -Year | | 1950 | 1950 | 1956 | 1981 | 1973 | 1951 | 1981 | 1952 | 1972 | 1988 | 1960 | 1984 | APR 1981 |
| -Maximum in 24 hrs | 43 | 3.29 | 3.68 | 5.20 | 3.70 | 11.84 | 5.53 | 12.11 | 5.37 | 4.99 | 2.93 | 4.48 | 3.28 | 12.11 |
| -Year | | 1953 | 1981 | 1960 | 1951 | 1979 | 1974 | 1960 | 1949 | 1985 | 1985 | 1988 | 1969 | JUL 1960 |
| Snow,Ice pellets | | | | | | | | | | | | | | |
| -Maximum Monthly | 43 | 0.2 | T | T | 0.0 | 0.0 | 0.0 | 0.0 | 0.0 | 0.0 | 0.0 | 0.0 | T | 0.2 |
| -Year | | 1977 | 1951 | 1980 | | | | | | | | | 1989 | JAN 1977 |
| -Maximum in 24 hrs | 43 | 0.2 | T | T | 0.0 | 0.0 | 0.0 | 0.0 | 0.0 | 0.0 | 0.0 | 0.0 | T | 0.2 |
| -Year | | 1977 | 1951 | 1980 | | | | | | | | | 1989 | JAN 1977 |
| **WIND:** | | | | | | | | | | | | | | |
| Mean Speed (mph) | 43 | 8.6 | 9.2 | 9.5 | 9.3 | 8.7 | 8.0 | 7.3 | 7.0 | 7.8 | 8.5 | 8.4 | 8.5 | 8.4 |
| Prevailing Direction | | | | | | | | | | | | | | |
| through 1963 | | N | E | S | ENE | E | E | E | ENE | ENE | NNE | NNE | N | E |
| Fastest Obs. 1 Min. | | | | | | | | | | | | | | |
| -Direction (!!!) | 37 | 29 | 32 | 29 | 29 | 36 | 31 | 32 | 11 | 34 | 02 | 29 | 36 | 31 |
| -Speed (MPH) | 37 | 35 | 50 | 43 | 37 | 46 | 67 | 58 | 38 | 56 | 38 | 40 | 45 | 67 |
| -Year | | 1959 | 1954 | 195? | 1961 | 1958 | 1964 | 1963 | 1961 | 1960 | 1953 | 1963 | 1953 | JUN 1964 |
| Peak Gust | | | | | | | | | | | | | | |
| -Direction (!!!) | 6 | NW | NW | NW | W | N | E | E | S | W | SW | NE | N | E |
| -Speed (mph) | 6 | 41 | 46 | 37 | 39 | 51 | 61 | 60 | 45 | 45 | 41 | 47 | 36 | 61 |
| -Date | | 1987 | 1984 | 1988 | 1988 | 1986 | 1988 | 1988 | 1985 | 1984 | 1985 | 1988 | 1989 | JUN 1988 |

**See Reference Notes to this table on the following page.**

## TABLE 2 — PRECIPITATION (inches)   TAMPA, FLORIDA

| YEAR | JAN | FEB | MAR | APR | MAY | JUNE | JULY | AUG | SEP | OCT | NOV | DEC | ANNUAL |
|------|-----|-----|-----|-----|-----|------|------|-----|-----|-----|-----|-----|--------|
| 1961 | 1.45 | 3.81 | 2.23 | 1.44 | 2.14 | 2.64 | 7.69 | 6.22 | 2.43 | 0.25 | 0.94 | 3.80 | 35.04 |
| 1962 | 1.40 | 1.46 | 4.26 | 1.43 | 2.76 | 6.34 | 2.31 | 10.14 | 7.57 | 1.28 | 2.21 | 0.46 | 41.62 |
| 1963 | 2.25 | 7.95 | 2.31 | 0.21 | 1.56 | 4.34 | 9.75 | 10.73 | 5.89 | 2.86 | 6.12 | 2.31 | 43.42 |
| 1964 | 5.08 | 5.37 | 3.92 | 0.53 | 3.58 | 6.64 | 9.75 | 10.73 | 5.89 | 2.86 | 0.38 | 3.19 | 57.92 |
| 1965 | 1.56 | 2.57 | 2.28 | 1.10 | 0.67 | 7.30 |  |  |  | 1.43 | 0.88 | 2.34 | 42.78 |
| 1966 | 4.05 | 3.08 | 1.16 | 1.57 | 0.71 | 6.44 | 7.62 | 4.75 | 4.12 | 1.22 | 0.39 | 0.94 | 36.05 |
| 1967 | 1.32 | 4.30 | 0.66 | T | 0.63 | 4.70 | 10.30 | 10.34 | 2.20 | 2.42 | 0.45 | 2.04 | 39.36 |
| 1968 | 0.41 | 1.52 | 1.23 | 0.74 | 2.08 | 6.72 | 8.39 | 6.79 | 3.58 | 4.16 | 3.14 | 0.59 | 39.35 |
| 1969 | 1.78 | 2.11 | 5.33 | 0.05 | 6.23 | 4.39 | 7.39 | 11.88 | 4.09 | 3.12 | 2.68 | 5.17 | 54.22 |
| 1970 | 3.10 | 4.02 | 6.12 | 0.49 | 4.12 | 2.05 | 2.77 | 8.43 | 3.95 | 0.89 | 1.08 | 1.25 | 38.27 |
| 1971 | 0.86 | 4.25 | 0.54 | 1.80 | 4.09 | 2.54 | 7.74 | 7.46 | 10.16 | 4.70 | 1.40 | 0.79 | 46.33 |
| 1972 | 0.54 | 4.44 | 3.01 | 0.38 | 1.88 | 5.24 | 6.65 | 9.78 | 1.28 | 3.29 | 3.53 | 2.16 | 42.18 |
| 1973 | 3.75 | 2.54 | 4.21 | 2.42 | 0.17 | 4.19 | 4.77 | 9.43 | 8.91 | 0.98 | 2.82 | 5.52 | 49.71 |
| 1974 | 0.17 | 0.89 | 2.35 | 0.38 | 1.11 | 13.75 | 3.43 | 4.67 | 3.08 | 0.23 | 0.12 | 2.80 | 33.90 |
| 1975 | 0.91 | 1.56 | 1.09 | 0.91 | 2.07 | 8.73 | 6.65 | 4.24 | 11.25 | 4.94 | 0.22 | 0.87 | 43.44 |
| 1976 | 0.40 | 0.49 | 1.64 | 1.83 | 8.13 | 7.22 | 4.58 | 7.02 | 6.04 | 1.30 | 1.59 | 2.05 | 42.29 |
| 1977 | 2.75 | 2.41 | 0.73 | 0.86 | 0.73 | 2.66 | 5.36 | 5.98 | 4.28 | 0.42 | 1.89 | 3.40 | 31.47 |
| 1978 | 2.82 | 5.17 | 2.44 | 0.94 | 5.00 | 2.03 | 5.85 | 5.97 | 3.08 | 3.42 | 0.01 | 3.12 | 39.85 |
| 1979 | 5.72 | 2.87 | 2.43 | 0.55 | 17.64 | 2.07 | 5.93 | 12.76 | 13.98 | 0.16 | 0.83 | 1.52 | 66.46 |
| 1980 | 1.72 | 2.01 | 3.09 | 4.38 | 3.94 | 3.81 | 5.66 | 7.62 | 4.05 | 1.27 | 2.68 | 0.37 | 40.60 |
| 1981 | 0.44 | 5.34 | 1.70 | T | 1.68 | 9.37 | 1.65 | 7.71 | 5.87 | 0.87 | 0.43 | 3.58 | 38.64 |
| 1982 | 1.86 | 2.09 | 2.99 | 1.87 | 5.90 | 8.34 | 10.49 | 7.20 | 10.76 | 2.17 | 0.85 | 1.29 | 55.81 |
| 1983 | 1.25 | 7.35 | 7.59 | 2.76 | 4.10 | 7.17 | 6.37 | 8.89 | 6.61 | 1.74 | 2.33 | 4.71 | 60.87 |
| 1984 | 1.62 | 3.32 | 1.31 | 1.51 | 3.19 | 3.24 | 7.15 | 5.68 | 4.21 | 0.29 | 0.72 | 0.07 | 32.31 |
| 1985 | 2.06 | 2.07 | 1.80 | 0.96 | 0.22 | 6.43 | 6.48 | 8.65 | 9.04 | 4.77 | 0.99 | 1.13 | 44.60 |
| 1986 | 2.37 | 1.49 | 4.27 | 0.95 | 2.46 | 5.00 | 6.24 | 5.46 | 3.87 | 6.21 | 1.33 | 1.95 | 41.60 |
| 1987 | 3.29 | 1.50 | 12.01 | 0.39 | 2.86 | 3.39 | 6.06 | 8.50 | 4.76 | 1.46 | 4.36 | 0.50 | 49.08 |
| 1988 | 2.76 | 1.44 | 4.09 | 1.83 | 1.27 | 5.19 | 3.40 | 11.09 | 13.56 | 0.09 | 5.97 | 1.64 | 52.33 |
| 1989 | 1.54 | 0.41 | 1.79 | 0.71 | 0.24 | 7.41 | 8.86 | 7.90 | 6.11 | 1.89 | 2.05 | 4.72 | 43.63 |
| 1990 | 0.53 | 4.58 | 1.71 | 1.47 | 1.76 | 5.16 | 10.01 | 3.27 | 2.42 | 2.63 | 0.66 | 0.19 | 34.39 |
| Record Mean | 2.21 | 2.79 | 3.03 | 2.00 | 3.04 | 6.82 | 7.69 | 7.95 | 6.54 | 2.62 | 1.65 | 2.04 | 48.38 |

## TABLE 3 — AVERAGE TEMPERATURE (deg. F)   TAMPA, FLORIDA

| YEAR | JAN | FEB | MAR | APR | MAY | JUNE | JULY | AUG | SEP | OCT | NOV | DEC | ANNUAL |
|------|-----|-----|-----|-----|-----|------|------|-----|-----|-----|-----|-----|--------|
| 1961 | 57.7 | 65.0 | 70.4 | 68.6 | 76.7 | 80.9 | 82.9 | 82.7 | 81.8 | 74.4 | 69.8 | 64.2 | 73.0 |
| 1962 | 60.5 | 66.8 | 63.8 | 69.4 | 77.9 | 79.6 | 83.0 | 81.9 | 79.7 | 74.8 | 62.5 | 58.2 | 71.5 |
| #1963 | 58.6 | 56.8 | 68.4 | 72.3 | 76.5 | 80.7 | 81.7 | 82.8 | 80.1 | 73.7 | 65.6 | 54.9 | 71.0 |
| 1964 | 58.6 | 57.1 | 68.0 | 74.0 | 76.7 | 81.8 | 82.0 | 81.5 | 79.3 | 70.9 | 63.2 | 60.6 | 71.7 |
| 1965 | 58.6 | 63.8 | 66.4 | 72.7 | 76.3 | 79.5 | 80.3 | 81.5 | 80.5 | 72.5 | 67.0 | 60.6 | 71.7 |
| 1966 | 57.0 | 59.9 | 63.1 | 69.2 | 78.5 | 79.2 | 81.7 | 82.5 | 80.6 | 75.3 | 65.1 | 59.2 | 70.9 |
| 1967 | 62.3 | 59.5 | 67.8 | 73.2 | 77.3 | 79.9 | 80.8 | 80.3 | 79.2 | 73.5 | 65.3 | 64.8 | 72.0 |
| 1968 | 59.4 | 54.3 | 60.9 | 72.5 | 75.7 | 79.6 | 80.2 | 82.0 | 79.6 | 73.2 | 62.3 | 57.6 | 69.8 |
| 1969 | 58.5 | 55.8 | 58.2 | 72.3 | 76.2 | 82.1 | 83.1 | 80.9 | 80.5 | 76.9 | 62.9 | 58.1 | 70.5 |
| 1970 | 54.0 | 57.6 | 64.9 | 73.2 | 76.2 | 80.1 | 82.8 | 82.9 | 81.9 | 76.1 | 62.9 | 62.4 | 71.2 |
| 1971 | 60.0 | 63.1 | 62.2 | 69.4 | 75.8 | 81.2 | 82.3 | 81.8 | 80.3 | 77.5 | 67.7 | 69.4 | 72.6 |
| 1972 | 67.0 | 60.7 | 66.8 | 71.4 | 76.6 | 81.0 | 81.9 | 82.1 | 81.3 | 76.1 | 68.2 | 65.1 | 73.2 |
| 1973 | 61.9 | 57.4 | 70.2 | 69.3 | 76.8 | 81.8 | 83.2 | 81.8 | 81.7 | 75.8 | 70.8 | 60.1 | 72.6 |
| 1974 | 71.1 | 61.1 | 70.9 | 70.9 | 78.2 | 80.1 | 81.1 | 82.8 | 82.8 | 72.9 | 67.9 | 61.9 | 73.5 |
| 1975 | 65.1 | 66.6 | 67.6 | 74.0 | 81.5 | 82.6 | 83.2 | 83.7 | 81.9 | 77.9 | 68.3 | 60.2 | 74.4 |
| 1976 | 56.6 | 63.1 | 70.5 | 70.6 | 76.1 | 79.0 | 81.7 | 81.6 | 79.3 | 71.0 | 62.8 | 59.6 | 71.0 |
| 1977 | 51.2 | 57.5 | 70.9 | 71.5 | 76.5 | 83.7 | 82.9 | 83.0 | 82.3 | 72.5 | 67.7 | 58.7 | 71.6 |
| 1978 | 55.0 | 53.2 | 64.2 | 72.3 | 78.7 | 82.4 | 83.0 | 82.8 | 81.4 | 75.1 | 66.2 | 66.2 | 72.2 |
| 1979 | 57.8 | 59.3 | 65.4 | 74.2 | 75.9 | 80.8 | 83.9 | 82.2 | 81.9 | 75.2 | 68.7 | 63.0 | 72.3 |
| 1980 | 62.0 | 56.6 | 68.1 | 70.1 | 77.2 | 81.6 | 84.0 | 83.0 | 81.3 | 74.0 | 66.4 | 57.5 | 71.8 |
| 1981 | 50.4 | 61.4 | 62.8 | 72.4 | 75.4 | 81.5 | 82.5 | 81.7 | 78.6 | 74.5 | 64.4 | 59.2 | 70.4 |
| 1982 | 59.8 | 67.9 | 68.1 | 71.4 | 74.4 | 81.5 | 82.1 | 82.1 | 80.2 | 74.3 | 70.8 | 67.6 | 73.4 |
| 1983 | 58.9 | 60.3 | 63.3 | 68.6 | 76.8 | 80.9 | 82.2 | 82.2 | 79.4 | 75.8 | 65.9 | 59.9 | 71.2 |
| 1984 | 58.0 | 62.6 | 66.0 | 71.0 | 78.0 | 80.4 | 81.5 | 82.4 | 79.9 | 75.7 | 64.9 | 67.3 | 72.3 |
| 1985 | 55.9 | 63.6 | 69.4 | 72.5 | 79.8 | 83.7 | 82.4 | 83.1 | 80.5 | 79.2 | 73.6 | 59.0 | 73.6 |
| 1986 | 59.3 | 65.0 | 65.4 | 69.1 | 77.4 | 81.8 | 83.0 | 82.6 | 82.3 | 76.8 | 76.3 | 66.5 | 73.8 |
| 1987 | 59.2 | 63.2 | 66.4 | 66.4 | 77.8 | 82.7 | 83.1 | 83.7 | 81.4 | 71.3 | 68.9 | 64.3 | 72.4 |
| 1988 | 58.6 | 59.1 | 65.6 | 70.6 | 75.3 | 81.0 | 82.7 | 82.9 | 82.0 | 73.5 | 70.8 | 63.0 | 72.1 |
| 1989 | 67.1 | 64.9 | 69.8 | 72.0 | 78.4 | 82.4 | 83.3 | 83.0 | 82.4 | 75.4 | 68.9 | 56.2 | 73.7 |
| 1990 | 66.1 | 69.2 | 69.7 | 72.1 | 80.5 | 82.7 | 82.5 | 83.9 | 82.8 | 77.6 | 70.2 | 66.9 | 75.4 |
| Record Mean | 60.8 | 62.2 | 66.7 | 71.4 | 77.0 | 80.8 | 81.8 | 82.1 | 80.6 | 74.7 | 67.3 | 62.0 | 72.3 |
| Max | 70.2 | 71.6 | 76.2 | 81.1 | 86.4 | 89.2 | 89.7 | 90.0 | 88.6 | 83.3 | 76.7 | 71.4 | 81.2 |
| Min | 51.3 | 52.7 | 57.2 | 61.7 | 67.5 | 72.3 | 74.0 | 74.1 | 72.6 | 66.0 | 57.9 | 52.6 | 63.3 |

## REFERENCE NOTES FOR TABLES 1, 2, 3 and 6   (TAMPA, FL)

### GENERAL

T - TRACE AMOUNT
BLANK ENTRIES DENOTE MISSING/UNREPORTED DATA.
# INDICATES A STATION OR INSTRUMENT RELOCATION.

### SPECIFIC

#### TABLE 1

(a) - LENGTH OF RECORD IN YEARS. ALTHOUGH INDIVIDUAL MONTHS MAY BE MISSING.
* LESS THAN .05

NORMALS — BASED ON THE 1951-1980 RECORD PERIOD.
EXTREMES — DATES ARE THE MOST RECENT OCCURRENCE.
WIND DIR. — NUMERALS SHOW TENS OF DEGREES CLOCKWISE FROM TRUE NORTH. "00" INDICATES CALM.
RESULTANT WIND DIRECTIONS ARE GIVEN TO WHOLE DEGREES.

#### TABLE 3

MAX AND MIN ARE LONG-TERM MEAN DAILY MAXIMUM AND MEAN DAILY MINIMUM TEMPERATURES.

### EXCEPTIONS

#### TABLES 2, 3, and 6

RECORD MEANS ARE THROUGH THE CURRENT YEAR, BEGINNING IN
1890 FOR TEMPERATURE
1890 FOR PRECIPITATION
1947 FOR SNOWFALL

HEATING DEGREE DAYS Base 65 deg. F          TAMPA, FLORIDA

**TABLE 4**

| SEASON | JULY | AUG | SEP | OCT | NOV | DEC | JAN | FEB | MAR | APR | MAY | JUNE | TOTAL |
|---|---|---|---|---|---|---|---|---|---|---|---|---|---|
| 1961-62 | 0 | 0 | 0 | 5 | 15 | 137 | 175 | 55 | 106 | 19 | 0 | 0 | 512 |
| 1962-63 | 0 | 0 | 0 | 2 | 98 | 240 | 212 | 229 | 37 | 2 | 0 | 0 | 820 |
| #1963-64 | 0 | 0 | 0 | 15 | 75 | 316 | 216 | 227 | 37 | 4 | 0 | 0 | 890 |
| 1964-65 | 0 | 0 | 0 | 22 | 24 | 114 | 204 | 96 | 84 | 2 | 0 | 0 | 546 |
| 1965-66 | 0 | 0 | 0 | 5 | 37 | 160 | 267 | 172 | 93 | 18 | 0 | 0 | 752 |
| 1966-67 | 0 | 0 | 0 | 7 | 85 | 198 | 129 | 175 | 23 | 0 | 0 | 0 | 617 |
| 1967-68 | 0 | 0 | 0 | 0 | 69 | 95 | 193 | 306 | 157 | 0 | 0 | 0 | 820 |
| 1968-69 | 0 | 0 | 0 | 27 | 138 | 264 | 201 | 252 | 220 | 0 | 0 | 0 | 1102 |
| 1969-70 | 0 | 0 | 0 | 0 | 111 | 218 | 343 | 209 | 81 | 0 | 0 | 0 | 962 |
| 1970-71 | 0 | 0 | 0 | 0 | 145 | 115 | 201 | 134 | 139 | 36 | 0 | 0 | 770 |
| 1971-72 | 0 | 0 | 0 | 0 | 41 | 13 | 62 | 139 | 26 | 5 | 0 | 0 | 286 |
| 1972-73 | 0 | 0 | 0 | 0 | 65 | 130 | 166 | 223 | 18 | 21 | 0 | 0 | 623 |
| 1973-74 | 0 | 0 | 0 | 6 | 24 | 200 | 0 | 159 | 17 | 12 | 0 | 0 | 418 |
| 1974-75 | 0 | 0 | 0 | 0 | 39 | 138 | 84 | 64 | 61 | 5 | 0 | 0 | 391 |
| 1975-76 | 0 | 0 | 0 | 0 | 88 | 183 | 268 | 109 | 18 | 2 | 0 | 0 | 668 |
| 1976-77 | 0 | 0 | 0 | 11 | 122 | 208 | 422 | 214 | 28 | 6 | 0 | 0 | 1011 |
| 1977-78 | 0 | 0 | 0 | 18 | 53 | 222 | 320 | 323 | 99 | 4 | 0 | 0 | 1039 |
| 1978-79 | 0 | 0 | 0 | 0 | 2 | 75 | 245 | 190 | 53 | 0 | 0 | 0 | 565 |
| 1979-80 | 0 | 0 | 0 | 0 | 47 | 112 | 136 | 262 | 64 | 8 | 0 | 0 | 629 |
| 1980-81 | 0 | 0 | 0 | 1 | 65 | 233 | 447 | 127 | 103 | 2 | 0 | 0 | 978 |
| 1981-82 | 0 | 0 | 0 | 0 | 83 | 223 | 209 | 24 | 53 | 8 | 0 | 0 | 600 |
| 1982-83 | 0 | 0 | 0 | 12 | 18 | 95 | 218 | 148 | 103 | 20 | 0 | 0 | 614 |
| 1983-84 | 0 | 0 | 0 | 0 | 57 | 214 | 252 | 115 | 68 | 5 | 0 | 0 | 711 |
| 1984-85 | 0 | 0 | 0 | 0 | 87 | 61 | 306 | 119 | 77 | 5 | 0 | 0 | 595 |
| 1985-86 | 0 | 0 | 0 | 0 | 9 | 238 | 185 | 78 | 105 | 7 | 0 | 0 | 622 |
| 1986-87 | 0 | 0 | 0 | 0 | 0 | 53 | 202 | 88 | 42 | 64 | 0 | 0 | 449 |
| 1987-88 | 0 | 0 | 0 | 4 | 46 | 107 | 221 | 195 | 85 | 14 | 0 | 0 | 672 |
| 1988-89 | 0 | 0 | 0 | 0 | 9 | 127 | 41 | 116 | 45 | 7 | 0 | 0 | 345 |
| 1989-90 | 0 | 0 | 0 | 17 | 27 | 285 | 70 | 32 | 13 | 5 | 0 | 0 | 449 |
| 1990-91 | 0 | 0 | 0 | 7 | 11 | 70 | | | | | | | |

**TABLE 5**    COOLING DEGREE DAYS Base 65 deg. F          TAMPA, FLORIDA

| YEAR | JAN | FEB | MAR | APR | MAY | JUNE | JULY | AUG | SEP | OCT | NOV | DEC | TOTAL |
|---|---|---|---|---|---|---|---|---|---|---|---|---|---|
| 1969 | 8 | 2 | 14 | 224 | 353 | 521 | 568 | 498 | 471 | 377 | 55 | 10 | 3101 |
| 1970 | 12 | 10 | 85 | 255 | 352 | 464 | 557 | 563 | 514 | 353 | 58 | 40 | 3263 |
| 1971 | 54 | 86 | 58 | 174 | 342 | 490 | 541 | 526 | 463 | 396 | 128 | 155 | 3413 |
| 1972 | 131 | 20 | 90 | 204 | 365 | 487 | 528 | 536 | 497 | 352 | 168 | 141 | 3519 |
| 1973 | 75 | 15 | 188 | 158 | 374 | 510 | 529 | 517 | 497 | 348 | 205 | 55 | 3541 |
| 1974 | 196 | 55 | 204 | 197 | 413 | 460 | 506 | 562 | 540 | 250 | 130 | 48 | 3561 |
| 1975 | 93 | 115 | 151 | 282 | 521 | 536 | 572 | 585 | 512 | 407 | 191 | 39 | 4004 |
| 1976 | 17 | 63 | 199 | 175 | 348 | 424 | 525 | 517 | 440 | 202 | 63 | 45 | 3018 |
| 1977 | 2 | 9 | 218 | 210 | 364 | 567 | 559 | 565 | 526 | 258 | 139 | 36 | 3453 |
| 1978 | 18 | 0 | 79 | 232 | 431 | 529 | 565 | 557 | 500 | 319 | 208 | 121 | 3559 |
| 1979 | 28 | 36 | 73 | 283 | 344 | 482 | 592 | 543 | 515 | 322 | 164 | 55 | 3437 |
| 1980 | 45 | 22 | 164 | 165 | 386 | 506 | 598 | 564 | 493 | 284 | 115 | 7 | 3349 |
| 1981 | 0 | 32 | 43 | 230 | 331 | 501 | 552 | 525 | 414 | 303 | 71 | 49 | 3051 |
| 1982 | 56 | 114 | 156 | 208 | 299 | 499 | 537 | 537 | 467 | 311 | 197 | 182 | 3563 |
| 1983 | 36 | 24 | 57 | 137 | 369 | 487 | 540 | 541 | 439 | 342 | 91 | 64 | 3127 |
| 1984 | 42 | 52 | 104 | 190 | 410 | 468 | 517 | 546 | 454 | 337 | 92 | 135 | 3347 |
| 1985 | 30 | 88 | 163 | 237 | 464 | 569 | 547 | 566 | 475 | 445 | 275 | 58 | 3917 |
| 1986 | 15 | 85 | 123 | 139 | 391 | 510 | 565 | 551 | 526 | 374 | 348 | 107 | 3734 |
| 1987 | 27 | 43 | 91 | 114 | 405 | 538 | 567 | 583 | 497 | 207 | 169 | 91 | 3332 |
| 1988 | 30 | 32 | 110 | 188 | 326 | 489 | 554 | 562 | 517 | 271 | 191 | 74 | 3344 |
| 1989 | 112 | 120 | 202 | 224 | 425 | 528 | 575 | 564 | 517 | 271 | 191 | 63 | 3792 |
| 1990 | 107 | 154 | 164 | 225 | 487 | 537 | 549 | 592 | 541 | 406 | 176 | 139 | 4077 |

**TABLE 6**    SNOWFALL (inches)          TAMPA, FLORIDA

| SEASON | JULY | AUG | SEP | OCT | NOV | DEC | JAN | FEB | MAR | APR | MAY | JUNE | TOTAL |
|---|---|---|---|---|---|---|---|---|---|---|---|---|---|
| 1970-71 | 0.0 | 0.0 | 0.0 | 0.0 | 0.0 | 0.0 | 0.0 | 0.0 | 0.0 | 0.0 | 0.0 | 0.0 | 0.0 |
| 1971-72 | 0.0 | 0.0 | 0.0 | 0.0 | 0.0 | 0.0 | 0.0 | 0.0 | 0.0 | 0.0 | 0.0 | 0.0 | 0.0 |
| 1972-73 | 0.0 | 0.0 | 0.0 | 0.0 | 0.0 | 0.0 | 0.0 | 0.0 | 0.0 | 0.0 | 0.0 | 0.0 | 0.0 |
| 1973-74 | 0.0 | 0.0 | 0.0 | 0.0 | 0.0 | 0.0 | 0.0 | 0.0 | 0.0 | 0.0 | 0.0 | 0.0 | 0.0 |
| 1974-75 | 0.0 | 0.0 | 0.0 | 0.0 | 0.0 | 0.0 | 0.0 | 0.0 | 0.0 | 0.0 | 0.0 | 0.0 | 0.0 |
| 1975-76 | 0.0 | 0.0 | 0.0 | 0.0 | 0.0 | 0.0 | 0.0 | 0.0 | 0.0 | 0.0 | 0.0 | 0.0 | 0.0 |
| 1976-77 | 0.0 | 0.0 | 0.0 | 0.0 | 0.0 | 0.0 | 0.2 | 0.0 | 0.0 | 0.0 | 0.0 | 0.0 | 0.2 |
| 1977-78 | 0.0 | 0.0 | 0.0 | 0.0 | 0.0 | 0.0 | 0.0 | 0.0 | 0.0 | 0.0 | 0.0 | 0.0 | 0.0 |
| 1978-79 | 0.0 | 0.0 | 0.0 | 0.0 | 0.0 | 0.0 | 0.0 | 0.0 | 0.0 | 0.0 | 0.0 | 0.0 | 0.0 |
| 1979-80 | 0.0 | 0.0 | 0.0 | 0.0 | 0.0 | 0.0 | 0.0 | 0.0 | 0.0 | 0.0 | 0.0 | 0.0 | 0.0 |
| 1980-81 | 0.0 | 0.0 | 0.0 | 0.0 | 0.0 | 0.0 | 0.0 | 0.0 | T | 0.0 | 0.0 | 0.0 | T |
| 1981-82 | 0.0 | 0.0 | 0.0 | 0.0 | 0.0 | 0.0 | 0.0 | 0.0 | 0.0 | 0.0 | 0.0 | 0.0 | 0.0 |
| 1982-83 | 0.0 | 0.0 | 0.0 | 0.0 | 0.0 | 0.0 | 0.0 | 0.0 | 0.0 | 0.0 | 0.0 | 0.0 | 0.0 |
| 1983-84 | 0.0 | 0.0 | 0.0 | 0.0 | 0.0 | 0.0 | 0.0 | 0.0 | 0.0 | 0.0 | 0.0 | 0.0 | 0.0 |
| 1984-85 | 0.0 | 0.0 | 0.0 | 0.0 | 0.0 | 0.0 | 0.0 | 0.0 | 0.0 | 0.0 | 0.0 | 0.0 | 0.0 |
| 1985-86 | 0.0 | 0.0 | 0.0 | 0.0 | 0.0 | 0.0 | 0.0 | 0.0 | 0.0 | 0.0 | 0.0 | 0.0 | 0.0 |
| 1986-87 | 0.0 | 0.0 | 0.0 | 0.0 | 0.0 | 0.0 | 0.0 | 0.0 | 0.0 | 0.0 | 0.0 | 0.0 | 0.0 |
| 1987-88 | 0.0 | 0.0 | 0.0 | 0.0 | 0.0 | 0.0 | 0.0 | 0.0 | 0.0 | 0.0 | 0.0 | 0.0 | 0.0 |
| 1988-89 | 0.0 | 0.0 | 0.0 | 0.0 | 0.0 | 0.0 | 0.0 | 0.0 | 0.0 | 0.0 | 0.0 | 0.0 | 0.0 |
| 1989-90 | 0.0 | 0.0 | 0.0 | 0.0 | 0.0 | T | 0.0 | 0.0 | 0.0 | 0.0 | 0.0 | 0.0 | 0.0 |
| 1990-91 | 0.0 | 0.0 | 0.0 | 0.0 | 0.0 | T | | | | | | | |
| Record Mean | 0.0 | 0.0 | 0.0 | 0.0 | 0.0 | T | T | T | T | 0.0 | 0.0 | 0.0 | T |

**See Reference Notes, relative to all above tables, on preceding page.**

Atlanta is located in the foothills of the southern Appalachians in north-central Georgia. The terrain is rolling to hilly and slopes downward toward the east, west, and south so that drainage of the major river systems is generally into the Gulf of Mexico from the western and southern sections of the city and to the Atlantic from the eastern portions of the city.

The Gulf of Mexico and the Atlantic Ocean are approximately 250 miles south and southeast of the city, respectively. Both the Appalachian chain of mountains and the two nearby maritime bodies exert an important influence on the Atlanta climate. Temperatures are moderated throughout the year while abundant precipitation fosters natural vegetation and growth of crops. Summer temperatures in Atlanta are moderated somewhat by elevation but are still rather warm. However, prolonged periods of hot weather are unusual and 100 degree heat is rarely experienced.

With the mountains to the north tending to retard the southward movement of Polar air masses, Atlanta winters are rather mild. Cold spells are not unusual but they are rather short-lived and seldom disrupt outdoor activities for an extended period of time. Late March is the average date of the last temperature of 32 degrees in the spring and mid-November is the average date of the first temperature of 32 degrees in the fall, which gives an average growing season of about 234 days.

Minimum dry precipitation periods occur mainly during the late summer and early autumn. Maximum thunderstorm activity occurs during July, but severe local thunderstorms occur most frequently in March, April, and May, some spawning highly damaging tornadoes.

The average annual snowfall varies widely from year to year. A fall of 4 inches or more occurs about once every five years. Most snows melt in a short period of time due to the rapid warming which often follows the storm. Ice storms, freezing rain or glaze, occur about two out of every three years, causing hazardous travel and disruption of utilities. Severe ice storms occur about once in ten years, causing major disruption of utilities and significant property damage.

The Bermuda High pressure area has a dominant effect on Atlanta weather, particularly in the summer months. East or northeast winds produce the most unpleasant weather although southerly winds are quite humid during the summer. The generally light wind conditions contribute to the formation of an occasional early morning fog.

## TABLE 1 NORMALS, MEANS AND EXTREMES

ATLANTA, GEORGIA

LATITUDE: 33°39'N  LONGITUDE: 84°25'W  ELEVATION: FT. GRND 1010 BARO 1110  TIME ZONE: EASTERN  WBAN: 13874

| | (a) | JAN | FEB | MAR | APR | MAY | JUNE | JULY | AUG | SEP | OCT | NOV | DEC | YEAR |
|---|---|---|---|---|---|---|---|---|---|---|---|---|---|---|
| **TEMPERATURE °F:** | | | | | | | | | | | | | | |
| Normals | | | | | | | | | | | | | | |
| -Daily Maximum | | 51.2 | 55.3 | 63.2 | 73.2 | 79.8 | 85.6 | 87.9 | 87.6 | 82.3 | 72.9 | 62.6 | 54.1 | 71.3 |
| -Daily Minimum | | 32.6 | 34.5 | 41.7 | 50.4 | 58.7 | 65.9 | 69.2 | 68.7 | 63.6 | 51.4 | 41.3 | 34.8 | 51.1 |
| -Monthly | | 41.9 | 44.9 | 52.5 | 61.8 | 69.3 | 75.8 | 78.6 | 78.2 | 73.0 | 62.2 | 52.0 | 44.5 | 61.2 |
| Extremes | | | | | | | | | | | | | | |
| -Record Highest | 41 | 79 | 80 | 85 | 93 | 95 | 101 | 105 | 102 | 98 | 95 | 84 | 77 | 105 |
| -Year | | 1949 | 1989 | 1982 | 1986 | 1953 | 1952 | 1980 | 1980 | 1954 | 1954 | 1961 | 1971 | JUL 1980 |
| -Record Lowest | 41 | -8 | 5 | 10 | 26 | 37 | 46 | 53 | 55 | 36 | 28 | 3 | 0 | -8 |
| -Year | | 1985 | 1958 | 1960 | 1973 | 1971 | 1956 | 1967 | 1986 | 1967 | 1976 | 1950 | 1983 | JAN 1985 |
| **NORMAL DEGREE DAYS:** | | | | | | | | | | | | | | |
| Heating (base 65°F) | | 716 | 563 | 400 | 133 | 37 | 5 | 0 | 0 | 7 | 130 | 394 | 636 | 3021 |
| Cooling (base 65°F) | | 0 | 0 | 12 | 37 | 170 | 329 | 422 | 409 | 247 | 44 | 0 | 0 | 1670 |
| **% OF POSSIBLE SUNSHINE** | 54 | 49 | 53 | 58 | 66 | 68 | 67 | 62 | 64 | 63 | 67 | 58 | 51 | 61 |
| **MEAN SKY COVER (tenths)** | | | | | | | | | | | | | | |
| Sunrise - Sunset | 55 | 6.4 | 6.2 | 6.1 | 5.5 | 5.6 | 5.8 | 6.2 | 5.8 | 5.5 | 4.6 | 5.4 | 6.2 | 5.8 |
| **MEAN NUMBER OF DAYS:** | | | | | | | | | | | | | | |
| Sunrise to Sunset | | | | | | | | | | | | | | |
| -Clear | 55 | 8.4 | 8.0 | 9.0 | 10.1 | 9.2 | 7.8 | 5.9 | 7.4 | 9.7 | 14.1 | 11.5 | 9.3 | 110.4 |
| -Partly Cloudy | 55 | 6.5 | 6.2 | 7.3 | 8.2 | 10.5 | 12.0 | 13.3 | 13.2 | 9.7 | 7.2 | 6.0 | 6.4 | 106.5 |
| -Cloudy | 55 | 16.1 | 14.0 | 14.7 | 11.7 | 11.3 | 10.3 | 11.8 | 10.3 | 10.6 | 9.7 | 12.5 | 15.3 | 148.3 |
| Precipitation | | | | | | | | | | | | | | |
| .01 inches or more | 55 | 11.4 | 10.1 | 11.4 | 9.0 | 9.1 | 9.9 | 11.9 | 9.4 | 7.6 | 6.4 | 8.5 | 10.2 | 115.0 |
| Snow,Ice pellets | | | | | | | | | | | | | | |
| 1.0 inches or more | 55 | 0.3 | 0.2 | 0.1 | 0.0 | 0.0 | 0.0 | 0.0 | 0.0 | 0.0 | 0.0 | 0.* | 0.1 | 0.6 |
| Thunderstorms | 55 | 1.1 | 1.8 | 3.7 | 4.2 | 6.1 | 8.7 | 10.3 | 8.0 | 3.0 | 1.0 | 1.0 | 0.7 | 49.8 |
| Heavy Fog Visibility | | | | | | | | | | | | | | |
| 1/4 mile or less | 55 | 4.9 | 3.4 | 2.7 | 1.3 | 1.3 | 1.0 | 1.5 | 1.7 | 1.9 | 2.3 | 3.1 | 4.5 | 29.7 |
| Temperature °F | | | | | | | | | | | | | | |
| -Maximum | | | | | | | | | | | | | | |
| 90° and above | 29 | 0.0 | 0.0 | 0.0 | 0.1 | 0.9 | 7.8 | 11.6 | 8.9 | 2.8 | 0.0 | 0.0 | 0.0 | 32.2 |
| 32° and below | 29 | 1.7 | 0.3 | 0.* | 0.0 | 0.0 | 0.0 | 0.0 | 0.0 | 0.0 | 0.0 | 0.* | 0.5 | 2.6 |
| -Minimum | | | | | | | | | | | | | | |
| 32° and below | 29 | 17.0 | 13.2 | 5.2 | 0.6 | 0.0 | 0.0 | 0.0 | 0.0 | 0.0 | 0.2 | 5.0 | 13.5 | 54.7 |
| 0° and below | 29 | 0.2 | 0.0 | 0.0 | 0.0 | 0.0 | 0.0 | 0.0 | 0.0 | 0.0 | 0.0 | 0.0 | 0.* | 0.3 |
| **AVG. STATION PRESS.(mb)** | 17 | 982.5 | 981.5 | 979.8 | 979.4 | 979.0 | 979.9 | 981.0 | 981.3 | 981.2 | 982.6 | 982.4 | 982.9 | 981.1 |
| **RELATIVE HUMIDITY (%)** | | | | | | | | | | | | | | |
| Hour 01 | 29 | 73 | 69 | 69 | 69 | 77 | 80 | 85 | 85 | 83 | 78 | 76 | 74 | 77 |
| Hour 07 | 29 | 78 | 75 | 77 | 78 | 82 | 84 | 88 | 90 | 88 | 84 | 81 | 79 | 82 |
| Hour 13 (Local Time) | 29 | 59 | 54 | 51 | 49 | 53 | 56 | 60 | 60 | 60 | 53 | 55 | 58 | 56 |
| Hour 19 | 29 | 62 | 56 | 53 | 50 | 57 | 61 | 66 | 67 | 68 | 63 | 63 | 64 | 61 |
| **PRECIPITATION (inches):** | | | | | | | | | | | | | | |
| Water Equivalent | | | | | | | | | | | | | | |
| -Normal | | 4.91 | 4.43 | 5.91 | 4.43 | 4.02 | 3.41 | 4.73 | 3.41 | 3.17 | 2.53 | 3.43 | 4.23 | 48.61 |
| -Maximum Monthly | 55 | 10.82 | 12.77 | 11.66 | 11.86 | 8.37 | 9.34 | 11.26 | 8.69 | 11.64 | 7.53 | 15.72 | 9.92 | 15.72 |
| -Year | | 1936 | 1961 | 1980 | 1979 | 1980 | 1989 | 1948 | 1967 | 1989 | 1966 | 1948 | 1961 | NOV 1948 |
| -Minimum Monthly | 55 | 0.84 | 0.77 | 1.86 | 0.49 | 0.32 | 0.16 | 0.76 | 0.50 | 0.04 | T | 0.41 | 0.69 | T |
| -Year | | 1981 | 1978 | 1985 | 1986 | 1936 | 1988 | 1980 | 1976 | 1984 | 1963 | 1939 | 1979 | OCT 1963 |
| -Maximum in 24 hrs | 55 | 3.91 | 5.67 | 5.09 | 5.58 | 5.13 | 3.41 | 5.44 | 5.05 | 5.46 | 5.41 | 4.11 | 3.85 | 5.67 |
| -Year | | 1973 | 1961 | 1976 | 1979 | 1948 | 1943 | 1948 | 1940 | 1956 | 1989 | 1935 | 1961 | FEB 1961 |
| Snow,Ice pellets | | | | | | | | | | | | | | |
| -Maximum Monthly | 55 | 8.3 | 4.4 | 7.9 | T | 0.0 | 0.0 | 0.0 | 0.0 | 0.0 | 0.0 | 1.0 | 2.5 | 8.3 |
| -Year | | 1940 | 1979 | 1983 | 1989 | | | | | | | 1968 | 1963 | JAN 1940 |
| -Maximum in 24 hrs | 55 | 8.3 | 4.2 | 7.9 | T | 0.0 | 0.0 | 0.0 | 0.0 | 0.0 | 0.0 | 1.0 | 2.2 | 8.3 |
| -Year | | 1940 | 1979 | 1983 | 1989 | | | | | | | 1968 | 1963 | JAN 1940 |
| **WIND:** | | | | | | | | | | | | | | |
| Mean Speed (mph) | 51 | 10.5 | 10.9 | 10.8 | 10.1 | 8.7 | 8.0 | 7.6 | 7.2 | 8.1 | 8.4 | 9.1 | 9.8 | 9.1 |
| Prevailing Direction | | | | | | | | | | | | | | |
| through 1963 | | NW | NW | NW | NW | NW | NW | SW | NW | ENE | NW | NW | NW | NW |
| Fastest Obs. 1 Min. | | | | | | | | | | | | | | |
| -Direction (!!!) | 13 | 23 | 12 | 28 | 31 | 27 | 24 | 30 | 32 | 27 | 09 | 24 | 30 | 30 |
| -Speed (MPH) | 13 | 46 | 36 | 47 | 41 | 54 | 51 | 60 | 41 | 37 | 30 | 37 | 33 | 60 |
| -Year | | 1978 | 1985 | 1984 | 1989 | 1984 | 1989 | 1984 | 1986 | 1980 | 1985 | 1984 | 1984 | JUL 1984 |
| Peak Gust | | | | | | | | | | | | | | |
| -Direction (!!!) | 6 | NW | NW | W | W | W | SW | NW | NW | E | E | NW | NW | NW |
| -Speed (mph) | 6 | 46 | 47 | 55 | 61 | 72 | 60 | 77 | 48 | 45 | 45 | 56 | 41 | 77 |
| -Date | | 1989 | 1987 | 1984 | 1985 | 1984 | 1989 | 1984 | 1988 | 1985 | 1985 | 1986 | 1984 | JUL 1984 |

**See Reference Notes to this table on the following page.**

PRECIPITATION (inches)    ATLANTA, GEORGIA

**TABLE 2**

| YEAR | JAN | FEB | MAR | APR | MAY | JUNE | JULY | AUG | SEP | OCT | NOV | DEC | ANNUAL |
|---|---|---|---|---|---|---|---|---|---|---|---|---|---|
| 1961 | 1.74 | 12.77 | 7.33 | 5.01 | 3.18 | 7.38 | 2.19 | 4.94 | 1.68 | 0.07 | 2.39 | 9.92 | 58.60 |
| 1962 | 5.24 | 5.09 | 6.72 | 5.96 | 0.38 | 4.39 | 5.25 | 1.21 | 3.51 | 1.53 | 6.19 | 2.34 | 47.81 |
| 1963 | 5.10 | 3.24 | 5.92 | 5.85 | 4.66 | 6.68 | 8.12 | 0.88 | 1.38 | | 3.81 | 5.86 | 55.31 |
| 1964 | 6.01 | 4.17 | 9.51 | 8.68 | 2.59 | 2.88 | 7.14 | 4.10 | 5.63 | 5.63 | 3.11 | 4.93 | 60.13 |
| 1965 | 3.74 | 4.31 | 5.94 | 3.10 | 2.51 | 7.15 | 4.59 | 1.53 | 3.02 | 2.35 | 2.32 | 1.70 | 42.26 |
| 1966 | 5.94 | 7.04 | 4.02 | 4.19 | 5.84 | 2.95 | 3.32 | 3.94 | 2.15 | 7.53 | 4.82 | 4.60 | 56.34 |
| 1967 | 4.85 | 3.75 | 3.63 | 2.81 | 4.95 | 3.06 | 6.46 | 8.69 | 1.90 | 2.51 | 5.52 | 6.71 | 54.84 |
| 1968 | 4.07 | 1.40 | 4.54 | 6.33 | 6.42 | 2.65 | 5.34 | 4.13 | 1.29 | 2.99 | 4.81 | 4.89 | 48.86 |
| 1969 | 2.85 | 3.20 | 4.00 | 5.70 | 7.68 | 1.00 | 2.64 | 6.12 | 3.74 | 1.53 | 2.67 | 3.27 | 44.40 |
| 1970 | 2.95 | 2.99 | 6.94 | 3.24 | 3.01 | 2.62 | 3.59 | 3.26 | 1.82 | 6.29 | 1.86 | 3.68 | 42.25 |
| 1971 | 4.40 | 5.77 | 8.65 | 4.09 | 2.12 | 3.33 | 8.22 | 2.76 | 3.32 | 0.31 | 3.42 | 2.79 | 49.18 |
| 1972 | 9.26 | 3.16 | 4.49 | 2.31 | 4.28 | 4.04 | 3.81 | 2.78 | 1.86 | 3.04 | 3.96 | 7.62 | 50.61 |
| 1973 | 8.89 | 3.44 | 9.53 | 4.03 | 7.14 | 3.35 | 2.10 | 1.35 | 4.16 | 0.75 | 2.31 | 8.11 | 55.16 |
| 1974 | 5.36 | 6.37 | 2.44 | 3.72 | 3.83 | 3.20 | 4.64 | 6.26 | 1.06 | 1.22 | 3.89 | 5.31 | 47.30 |
| 1975 | 6.19 | 8.98 | 8.31 | 4.28 | 4.62 | 5.52 | 8.52 | 3.30 | 2.99 | 5.31 | 4.62 | 3.36 | 66.00 |
| 1976 | 5.15 | 1.84 | 10.95 | 1.49 | 6.99 | 2.36 | 4.29 | 0.50 | 0.72 | 3.55 | 4.11 | 4.01 | 45.96 |
| 1977 | 3.49 | 2.14 | 6.28 | 1.77 | 2.04 | 3.03 | 4.26 | 4.23 | 4.90 | 5.00 | 7.18 | 2.36 | 46.68 |
| 1978 | 7.03 | 0.77 | 2.63 | 3.49 | 7.28 | 2.86 | 2.56 | 5.66 | 0.94 | 1.42 | 2.96 | 3.75 | 41.35 |
| 1979 | 5.03 | 5.71 | 3.19 | 11.86 | 2.43 | 1.46 | 3.62 | 7.28 | 6.08 | 2.17 | 5.19 | 0.69 | 54.71 |
| 1980 | 5.69 | 2.69 | 11.66 | 1.88 | 8.37 | 4.49 | 0.76 | 4.77 | 1.61 | 1.61 | 2.14 | 1.29 | 46.94 |
| 1981 | 0.84 | 6.62 | 3.93 | 2.06 | 3.89 | 2.69 | 2.74 | 2.76 | 5.27 | 3.01 | 1.85 | 6.25 | 41.91 |
| 1982 | 4.75 | 6.99 | 3.79 | 6.02 | 2.60 | 6.09 | 6.31 | 1.45 | 3.00 | 5.83 | 4.15 | 5.23 | 56.21 |
| 1983 | 3.09 | 4.99 | 6.68 | 4.79 | 1.42 | 1.52 | 1.85 | 1.06 | 7.52 | 1.97 | 7.46 | 9.27 | 51.62 |
| 1984 | 4.66 | 5.97 | 5.83 | 6.62 | 6.57 | 0.74 | 11.21 | 6.46 | 0.04 | 1.54 | 2.10 | 3.65 | 55.39 |
| 1985 | 4.11 | 4.98 | 1.86 | 2.75 | 4.69 | 2.04 | 9.92 | 4.57 | 2.63 | 5.74 | 4.23 | 2.28 | 49.80 |
| 1986 | 0.88 | 2.46 | 4.13 | 0.49 | 2.95 | 2.18 | 3.27 | 6.08 | 3.68 | 5.15 | 6.20 | 3.03 | 40.50 |
| 1987 | 5.63 | 6.13 | 5.44 | 1.16 | 2.74 | 6.36 | 7.35 | 1.22 | 3.02 | 0.70 | 2.36 | 4.13 | 46.24 |
| 1988 | 4.64 | 3.32 | 2.57 | 6.06 | 1.71 | 0.16 | 5.04 | 4.92 | 6.35 | 5.00 | 4.87 | 1.21 | 45.85 |
| 1989 | 2.57 | 4.30 | 3.85 | 5.24 | 6.42 | 9.34 | 7.65 | 2.13 | 11.64 | 1.71 | 3.97 | 4.49 | 63.31 |
| 1990 | 8.47 | 9.75 | 8.36 | 2.76 | 5.26 | 1.39 | 3.49 | 4.64 | 3.01 | 6.12 | 1.27 | 3.04 | 57.56 |
| Record Mean | 4.74 | 4.71 | 5.55 | 4.04 | 3.69 | 3.71 | 4.78 | 3.94 | 3.27 | 2.67 | 3.26 | 4.43 | 48.79 |

**TABLE 3**  AVERAGE TEMPERATURE (deg. F)    ATLANTA, GEORGIA

| YEAR | JAN | FEB | MAR | APR | MAY | JUNE | JULY | AUG | SEP | OCT | NOV | DEC | ANNUAL |
|---|---|---|---|---|---|---|---|---|---|---|---|---|---|
| 1961 | 38.5 | 49.5 | 54.7 | 56.4 | 65.2 | 72.7 | 76.3 | 75.6 | 73.0 | 61.1 | 55.3 | 43.5 | 60.1 |
| 1962 | 41.0 | 50.1 | 47.8 | 57.7 | 74.1 | 75.5 | 78.6 | 76.6 | 70.0 | 62.7 | 49.1 | 40.3 | 60.3 |
| 1963 | 37.2 | 38.9 | 56.4 | 62.9 | 68.8 | 74.3 | 75.8 | 77.7 | 70.9 | 65.1 | 51.5 | 35.5 | 59.6 |
| 1964 | 40.8 | 40.3 | 51.2 | 60.6 | 68.9 | 77.8 | 76.5 | 76.0 | 72.6 | 58.8 | 55.6 | 46.5 | 60.4 |
| 1965 | 43.2 | 43.9 | 48.8 | 63.3 | 71.8 | 71.7 | 76.6 | 77.3 | 72.9 | 60.3 | 53.8 | 44.8 | 60.7 |
| 1966 | 36.6 | 43.2 | 50.2 | 60.6 | 67.6 | 73.4 | 78.2 | 75.4 | 70.6 | 59.4 | 52.1 | 43.4 | 59.2 |
| 1967 | 43.9 | 41.8 | 56.7 | 65.0 | 66.2 | 72.5 | 74.1 | 74.0 | 66.5 | 59.4 | 48.5 | 47.7 | 59.7 |
| 1968 | 39.2 | 38.3 | 52.3 | 60.9 | 67.4 | 75.7 | 77.7 | 79.0 | 71.5 | 61.7 | 50.1 | 40.2 | 59.5 |
| 1969 | 40.2 | 42.7 | 46.9 | 62.8 | 69.2 | 77.4 | 76.1 | 76.1 | 70.9 | 62.5 | 50.1 | 41.7 | 60.1 |
| 1970 | 35.9 | 43.9 | 52.9 | 64.4 | 70.1 | 74.6 | 78.7 | 79.1 | 77.0 | 65.2 | 49.5 | 47.4 | 61.6 |
| 1971 | 42.9 | 44.3 | 47.5 | 60.8 | 66.7 | 77.2 | 76.3 | 76.7 | 73.7 | 66.8 | 49.6 | 48.3 | 61.3 |
| 1972 | 46.8 | 42.6 | 52.4 | 61.3 | 66.5 | 72.2 | 76.8 | 77.7 | 74.6 | 61.1 | 55.6 | 44.2 | 60.8 |
| 1973 | 41.4 | 42.8 | 57.4 | 57.6 | 65.0 | 75.6 | 78.9 | 77.4 | 75.6 | 64.7 | 52.4 | 44.3 | 61.3 |
| 1974 | 53.2 | 45.8 | 57.8 | 61.1 | 71.0 | 72.5 | 77.9 | 76.7 | 70.2 | 61.3 | 54.0 | 43.4 | 62.0 |
| 1975 | 47.2 | 47.1 | 50.5 | 59.8 | 71.0 | 75.3 | 76.4 | 77.9 | 70.3 | 63.3 | 54.0 | 43.4 | 61.4 |
| 1976 | 38.5 | 51.5 | 56.4 | 61.7 | 65.4 | 73.8 | 76.4 | 76.0 | 69.8 | 56.2 | 44.2 | 39.8 | 59.1 |
| 1977 | 29.3 | 42.0 | 55.3 | 63.0 | 69.9 | 77.1 | 79.5 | 77.7 | 73.5 | 59.6 | 54.3 | 42.1 | 60.3 |
| 1978 | 33.7 | 39.3 | 51.6 | 61.5 | 67.6 | 76.3 | 78.6 | 78.3 | 76.3 | 62.5 | 58.5 | 46.1 | 60.8 |
| 1979 | 37.3 | 41.7 | 56.2 | 62.7 | 70.1 | 75.7 | 78.8 | 80.1 | 72.7 | 62.4 | 54.3 | 46.7 | 61.6 |
| 1980 | 44.9 | 41.9 | 52.1 | 62.6 | 72.0 | 79.1 | 85.1 | 83.8 | 78.9 | 61.5 | 51.9 | 44.9 | 63.2 |
| 1981 | 39.5 | 46.8 | 51.8 | 67.7 | 67.6 | 81.3 | 82.2 | 77.7 | 72.4 | 60.2 | 54.5 | 39.1 | 61.8 |
| 1982 | 38.5 | 47.4 | 56.5 | 58.4 | 72.5 | 76.3 | 79.1 | 77.5 | 70.5 | 62.7 | 53.7 | 49.9 | 61.9 |
| 1983 | 40.4 | 44.4 | 51.3 | 56.4 | 67.8 | 74.0 | 81.4 | 81.4 | 70.8 | 62.1 | 51.5 | 39.9 | 60.1 |
| 1984 | 39.6 | 47.5 | 51.7 | 58.1 | 67.5 | 78.3 | 76.8 | 77.5 | 71.3 | 69.8 | 50.6 | 53.7 | 61.9 |
| 1985 | 36.3 | 44.2 | 56.8 | 64.0 | 69.9 | 77.5 | 78.4 | 77.6 | 72.5 | 66.4 | 62.0 | 41.4 | 62.3 |
| 1986 | 43.4 | 49.8 | 54.4 | 62.9 | 71.0 | 80.0 | 84.1 | 77.4 | 74.6 | 64.0 | 57.9 | 45.1 | 63.7 |
| 1987 | 41.9 | 45.7 | 53.2 | 60.3 | 73.2 | 77.8 | 81.0 | 82.0 | 74.1 | 59.7 | 55.7 | 48.8 | 62.8 |
| 1988 | 39.2 | 45.5 | 54.9 | 63.0 | 70.0 | 78.6 | 80.5 | 81.0 | 73.4 | 59.3 | 55.0 | 46.6 | 62.3 |
| 1989 | 49.7 | 47.5 | 56.8 | 62.9 | 68.8 | 76.9 | 79.8 | 79.4 | 72.9 | 64.2 | 54.3 | 39.1 | 62.7 |
| 1990 | 49.8 | 54.4 | 57.7 | 61.9 | 70.4 | 78.6 | 80.6 | 80.6 | 75.7 | 64.4 | 56.5 | 49.1 | 65.0 |
| Record Mean | 43.0 | 45.6 | 52.8 | 61.3 | 69.6 | 76.5 | 78.7 | 78.0 | 73.1 | 62.8 | 52.3 | 44.7 | 61.5 |
| Max | 51.5 | 54.8 | 62.7 | 71.5 | 79.5 | 86.0 | 87.7 | 86.8 | 82.0 | 72.3 | 61.6 | 53.1 | 70.8 |
| Min | 34.5 | 36.4 | 42.9 | 51.1 | 59.6 | 66.9 | 69.6 | 69.1 | 64.2 | 53.2 | 43.0 | 36.2 | 52.2 |

## REFERENCE NOTES FOR TABLES 1, 2, 3 and 6    (ATLANTA, GA)

### GENERAL

T - TRACE AMOUNT
BLANK ENTRIES DENOTE MISSING/UNREPORTED DATA.
# INDICATES A STATION OR INSTRUMENT RELOCATION.

### SPECIFIC

#### TABLE 1

(a) - LENGTH OF RECORD IN YEARS. ALTHOUGH
    INDIVIDUAL MONTHS MAY BE MISSING.

* LESS THAN .05

NORMALS — BASED ON THE 1951-1980 RECORD PERIOD.
EXTREMES — DATES ARE THE MOST RECENT OCCURRENCE.
WIND DIR. — NUMERALS SHOW TENS OF DEGREES
    CLOCKWISE FROM TRUE NORTH.
    "00" INDICATES CALM.
RESULTANT WIND DIRECTIONS ARE GIVEN TO WHOLE DEGREES.

#### TABLE 3
MAX AND MIN ARE LONG-TERM MEAN DAILY MAXIMUM
AND MEAN DAILY MINIMUM TEMPERATURES.

### EXCEPTIONS

**TABLES 2, 3, and 6**

RECORD MEANS ARE THROUGH THE CURRENT YEAR,
BEGINNING IN    1879 FOR TEMPERATURE
                1879 FOR PRECIPITATION
                1934 FOR SNOWFALL

## TABLE 4

HEATING DEGREE DAYS Base 65 deg. F          ATLANTA, GEORGIA

| SEASON | JULY | AUG | SEP | OCT | NOV | DEC | JAN | FEB | MAR | APR | MAY | JUNE | TOTAL |
|---|---|---|---|---|---|---|---|---|---|---|---|---|---|
| 1961-62 | 0 | 0 | 12 | 150 | 310 | 658 | 736 | 410 | 525 | 235 | 4 | 0 | 3040 |
| 1962-63 | 0 | 0 | 40 | 132 | 471 | 759 | 857 | 724 | 272 | 100 | 42 | 0 | 3397 |
| 1963-64 | 0 | 0 | 19 | 55 | 398 | 907 | 743 | 713 | 423 | 160 | 32 | 0 | 3450 |
| 1964-65 | 0 | 0 | 2 | 201 | 288 | 567 | 669 | 586 | 500 | 110 | 0 | 3 | 2926 |
| 1965-66 | 0 | 0 | 3 | 176 | 332 | 619 | 874 | 605 | 451 | 171 | 26 | 5 | 3262 |
| 1966-67 | 0 | 0 | 5 | 177 | 379 | 663 | 645 | 642 | 270 | 67 | 78 | 20 | 2946 |
| 1967-68 | 0 | 0 | 52 | 193 | 490 | 530 | 792 | 769 | 389 | 154 | 31 | 0 | 3400 |
| 1968-69 | 0 | 2 | 0 | 157 | 441 | 760 | 761 | 620 | 555 | 93 | 28 | 0 | 3417 |
| 1969-70 | 0 | 0 | 13 | 125 | 445 | 719 | 895 | 586 | 371 | 95 | 15 | 0 | 3264 |
| 1970-71 | 0 | 0 | 3 | 64 | 457 | 537 | 681 | 572 | 533 | 156 | 56 | 0 | 3059 |
| 1971-72 | 0 | 0 | 0 | 36 | 436 | 390 | 559 | 643 | 387 | 161 | 21 | 5 | 2638 |
| 1972-73 | 0 | 0 | 3 | 136 | 465 | 511 | 725 | 617 | 240 | 230 | 72 | 0 | 2999 |
| 1973-74 | 0 | 0 | 1 | 86 | 295 | 639 | 357 | 531 | 241 | 155 | 5 | 0 | 2310 |
| 1974-75 | 0 | 0 | 26 | 148 | 381 | 633 | 547 | 493 | 451 | 192 | 2 | 0 | 2873 |
| 1975-76 | 0 | 0 | 28 | 113 | 342 | 665 | 814 | 384 | 265 | 124 | 48 | 4 | 2787 |
| 1976-77 | 0 | 0 | 10 | 277 | 618 | 775 | 1099 | 640 | 300 | 102 | 11 | 0 | 3832 |
| 1977-78 | 0 | 0 | 4 | 178 | 313 | 701 | 966 | 714 | 412 | 137 | 57 | 0 | 3482 |
| 1978-79 | 0 | 0 | 0 | 112 | 194 | 580 | 853 | 646 | 279 | 97 | 16 | 0 | 2777 |
| 1979-80 | 0 | 0 | 5 | 122 | 320 | 559 | 616 | 668 | 399 | 113 | 3 | 0 | 2805 |
| 1980-81 | 0 | 0 | 18 | 154 | 391 | 618 | 786 | 502 | 410 | 36 | 43 | 0 | 2958 |
| 1981-82 | 0 | 0 | 17 | 179 | 314 | 795 | 819 | 486 | 282 | 204 | 2 | 0 | 3098 |
| 1982-83 | 0 | 0 | 16 | 139 | 341 | 466 | 755 | 571 | 423 | 261 | 24 | 0 | 2996 |
| 1983-84 | 0 | 0 | 32 | 123 | 400 | 770 | 780 | 503 | 409 | 221 | 50 | 0 | 3288 |
| 1984-85 | 0 | 0 | 13 | 22 | 426 | 346 | 882 | 576 | 265 | 111 | 14 | 1 | 2656 |
| 1985-86 | 0 | 0 | 15 | 71 | 131 | 725 | 663 | 422 | 331 | 133 | 14 | 0 | 2505 |
| 1986-87 | 0 | 11 | 2 | 107 | 243 | 609 | 709 | 534 | 359 | 191 | 6 | 0 | 2771 |
| 1987-88 | 0 | 0 | 0 | 172 | 279 | 494 | 791 | 559 | 310 | 104 | 6 | 0 | 2715 |
| 1988-89 | 0 | 0 | 0 | 188 | 291 | 566 | 468 | 490 | 284 | 160 | 44 | 0 | 2491 |
| 1989-90 | 0 | 0 | 29 | 103 | 318 | 797 | 462 | 297 | 250 | 150 | 20 | 0 | 2426 |
| 1990-91 | 0 | 0 | 12 | 109 | 252 | 488 | | | | | | | |

## TABLE 5

COOLING DEGREE DAYS Base 65 deg. F          ATLANTA, GEORGIA

| YEAR | JAN | FEB | MAR | APR | MAY | JUNE | JULY | AUG | SEP | OCT | NOV | DEC | TOTAL |
|---|---|---|---|---|---|---|---|---|---|---|---|---|---|
| 1969 | 0 | 0 | 1 | 31 | 162 | 379 | 494 | 348 | 197 | 51 | 0 | 0 | 1663 |
| 1970 | 0 | 0 | 0 | 80 | 178 | 292 | 430 | 442 | 371 | 77 | 0 | 0 | 1870 |
| 1971 | 0 | 0 | 0 | 38 | 115 | 374 | 358 | 371 | 265 | 95 | 13 | 5 | 1634 |
| 1972 | 0 | 0 | 3 | 56 | 72 | 227 | 370 | 396 | 297 | 25 | 7 | 0 | 1453 |
| 1973 | 0 | 0 | 11 | 15 | 78 | 322 | 438 | 388 | 323 | 79 | 20 | 0 | 1674 |
| 1974 | 0 | 1 | 24 | 42 | 198 | 229 | 405 | 368 | 187 | 41 | 11 | 0 | 1506 |
| 1975 | 0 | 0 | 6 | 44 | 195 | 313 | 359 | 406 | 193 | 63 | 21 | 0 | 1600 |
| 1976 | 0 | 1 | 8 | 30 | 67 | 273 | 359 | 346 | 159 | 11 | 0 | 0 | 1254 |
| 1977 | 0 | 0 | 3 | 51 | 171 | 367 | 456 | 403 | 266 | 17 | 1 | 0 | 1735 |
| 1978 | 0 | 0 | 2 | 40 | 144 | 346 | 428 | 420 | 345 | 40 | 7 | 1 | 1773 |
| 1979 | 0 | 0 | 13 | 33 | 181 | 327 | 436 | 475 | 243 | 49 | 5 | 0 | 1762 |
| 1980 | 0 | 4 | 4 | 49 | 227 | 428 | 632 | 589 | 440 | 51 | 0 | 0 | 2424 |
| 1981 | 0 | 0 | 9 | 124 | 131 | 494 | 540 | 398 | 246 | 36 | 4 | 0 | 1982 |
| 1982 | 2 | 0 | 25 | 13 | 243 | 346 | 446 | 394 | 192 | 73 | 8 | 6 | 1748 |
| 1983 | 0 | 0 | 3 | 10 | 118 | 278 | 515 | 512 | 212 | 40 | 0 | 0 | 1688 |
| 1984 | 0 | 0 | 2 | 21 | 132 | 405 | 372 | 397 | 210 | 178 | 1 | 2 | 1720 |
| 1985 | 0 | 0 | 18 | 88 | 172 | 381 | 423 | 401 | 248 | 119 | 49 | 0 | 1899 |
| 1986 | 0 | 0 | 11 | 74 | 208 | 455 | 599 | 401 | 300 | 83 | 34 | 0 | 2165 |
| 1987 | 0 | 0 | 2 | 60 | 266 | 391 | 502 | 531 | 281 | 12 | 6 | 2 | 2053 |
| 1988 | 0 | 0 | 5 | 49 | 169 | 416 | 490 | 502 | 258 | 18 | 0 | 0 | 1907 |
| 1989 | 0 | 7 | 36 | 101 | 170 | 364 | 467 | 452 | 273 | 85 | 6 | 0 | 1961 |
| 1990 | 0 | 5 | 26 | 66 | 194 | 415 | 490 | 488 | 341 | 98 | 2 | 0 | 2125 |

## TABLE 6

SNOWFALL (inches)          ATLANTA, GEORGIA

| SEASON | JULY | AUG | SEP | OCT | NOV | DEC | JAN | FEB | MAR | APR | MAY | JUNE | TOTAL |
|---|---|---|---|---|---|---|---|---|---|---|---|---|---|
| 1961-62 | 0.0 | 0.0 | 0.0 | 0.0 | 0.0 | 1.0 | 3.5 | 0.0 | T | 0.0 | 0.0 | 0.0 | 4.5 |
| 1962-63 | 0.0 | 0.0 | 0.0 | 0.0 | 0.0 | 0.0 | T | T | T | 0.0 | 0.0 | 0.0 | T |
| 1963-64 | 0.0 | 0.0 | 0.0 | 0.0 | T | 2.5 | 0.8 | 0.3 | 0.0 | 0.0 | 0.0 | 0.0 | 3.6 |
| 1964-65 | 0.0 | 0.0 | 0.0 | 0.0 | 0.0 | T | 2.4 | 0.1 | 0.5 | 0.0 | 0.0 | 0.0 | 3.0 |
| 1965-66 | 0.0 | 0.0 | 0.0 | 0.0 | 0.0 | 0.0 | 0.7 | T | T | 0.0 | 0.0 | 0.0 | 0.7 |
| 1966-67 | 0.0 | 0.0 | 0.0 | 0.0 | T | 0.0 | 0.0 | 2.0 | 0.0 | 0.0 | 0.0 | 0.0 | 2.0 |
| 1967-68 | 0.0 | 0.0 | 0.0 | 0.0 | 0.0 | 0.0 | 0.7 | 3.5 | T | 0.0 | 0.0 | 0.0 | 4.2 |
| 1968-69 | 0.0 | 0.0 | 0.0 | 0.0 | 1.0 | T | T | 1.2 | 0.0 | 0.0 | 0.0 | 0.0 | 2.2 |
| 1969-70 | 0.0 | 0.0 | 0.0 | 0.0 | T | T | 0.6 | T | T | 0.0 | 0.0 | 0.0 | 0.6 |
| 1970-71 | 0.0 | 0.0 | 0.0 | 0.0 | 0.0 | T | T | T | 1.0 | T | 0.0 | 0.0 | 1.0 |
| 1971-72 | 0.0 | 0.0 | 0.0 | 0.0 | T | 1.0 | T | T | T | 0.0 | 0.0 | 0.0 | 1.0 |
| 1972-73 | 0.0 | 0.0 | 0.0 | 0.0 | 0.0 | 0.0 | 1.0 | T | 0.0 | 0.0 | 0.0 | 0.0 | 1.0 |
| 1973-74 | 0.0 | 0.0 | 0.0 | 0.0 | 0.0 | T | 0.0 | T | T | 0.0 | 0.0 | 0.0 | T |
| 1974-75 | 0.0 | 0.0 | 0.0 | 0.0 | 0.0 | 0.0 | T | T | T | 0.0 | 0.0 | 0.0 | T |
| 1975-76 | 0.0 | 0.0 | 0.0 | 0.0 | 0.6 | 0.0 | T | T | T | 0.0 | 0.0 | 0.0 | 0.6 |
| 1976-77 | 0.0 | 0.0 | 0.0 | 0.0 | 0.0 | 0.0 | 1.0 | 0.0 | 0.0 | 0.0 | 0.0 | 0.0 | 1.0 |
| 1977-78 | 0.0 | 0.0 | 0.0 | 0.0 | 0.0 | T | T | 0.3 | T | 0.0 | 0.0 | 0.0 | 0.3 |
| 1978-79 | 0.0 | 0.0 | 0.0 | 0.0 | 0.0 | 0.0 | 0.2 | 4.4 | 0.0 | 0.0 | 0.0 | 0.0 | 4.6 |
| 1979-80 | 0.0 | 0.0 | 0.0 | 0.0 | 0.0 | 0.0 | T | 1.7 | 2.7 | 0.0 | 0.0 | 0.0 | 4.4 |
| 1980-81 | 0.0 | 0.0 | 0.0 | 0.0 | 0.0 | 0.0 | T | T | 0.0 | 0.0 | 0.0 | 0.0 | T |
| 1981-82 | 0.0 | 0.0 | 0.0 | 0.0 | 0.0 | T | 7.0 | 0.7 | 0.0 | 0.0 | 0.0 | 0.0 | 7.7 |
| 1982-83 | 0.0 | 0.0 | 0.0 | 0.0 | 0.0 | 0.0 | 1.9 | 0.5 | 7.9 | 0.0 | 0.0 | 0.0 | 10.3 |
| 1983-84 | 0.0 | 0.0 | 0.0 | 0.0 | 0.0 | T | T | T | 1.3 | 0.0 | 0.0 | 0.0 | 1.3 |
| 1984-85 | 0.0 | 0.0 | 0.0 | 0.0 | 0.0 | T | 0.4 | 1.5 | 0.0 | 0.0 | 0.0 | 0.0 | 1.9 |
| 1985-86 | 0.0 | 0.0 | 0.0 | 0.0 | 0.0 | T | 0.4 | T | 0.0 | 0.0 | 0.0 | 0.0 | 0.4 |
| 1986-87 | 0.0 | 0.0 | 0.0 | 0.0 | 0.0 | 0.0 | 3.6 | T | 1.2 | T | 0.0 | 0.0 | 4.8 |
| 1987-88 | 0.0 | 0.0 | 0.0 | 0.0 | 0.0 | 0.0 | 4.2 | T | T | 0.0 | 0.0 | 0.0 | 4.2 |
| 1988-89 | 0.0 | 0.0 | 0.0 | 0.0 | 0.0 | T | 0.0 | 0.7 | 0.0 | T | 0.0 | 0.0 | 0.7 |
| 1989-90 | 0.0 | 0.0 | 0.0 | 0.0 | 0.0 | 1.3 | 0.0 | 0.0 | 0.0 | T | 0.0 | 0.0 | 1.3 |
| 1990-91 | 0.0 | 0.0 | 0.0 | 0.0 | 0.0 | 0.3 | 0.0 | | | | | | |
| Record Mean | 0.0 | 0.0 | 0.0 | 0.0 | T | 0.2 | 0.9 | 0.5 | 0.4 | T | 0.0 | 0.0 | 2.0 |

**See Reference Notes, relative to all above tables, on preceding page.**

Savannah is surrounded by flat terrain, low and marshy to the north and east, and rising to several feet above sea level to the west and south. About half the land to the west and south is cleared and the other half is wooded and swampy.

The area has a temperate climate, with a seasonal low temperature of 51 degrees in winter, 66 degrees in spring, 80 degrees in summer, and 66 degrees in autumn. The lowest temperatures are below 10 degrees and the highest temperatures are about 100 degrees.

The normal annual rainfall is about 49 inches. About half falls in the thunderstorm season of June 15 through September 15. The remainder, produced principally by squall-line and frontal showers, is spread over the other nine months with a minor peak in March. Considerable periods of fair, mild weather are experienced in October, November, April, and to a less extent, in May. Snow is a rarity and even a trace does not occur on an average of once a year. The heaviest snowfalls are under 5 inches. Severe tropical storms affect this area about once in ten years. Rainfall from these storms constitute the heaviest sustained precipitation. Accumulations exceeding 22 inches have occurred.

The present exposure of the thermometers gives readings more nearly commensurate with those of suburban street levels of Savannah than was the case of previous locations atop various buildings. During that time, especially on still, clear nights, temperatures near the ground and in lower inland areas were as much as 15 degrees lower than the official low temperature. Present differences on comparable nights range from 3 - 8 degrees.

Sunshine is adequate at all seasons and seldom are there two or more days in succession without it. Sea- and land-breeze effect is usually not felt in Savannah, though it is a daily feature on the nearby islands. Dry, continental air masses reach this area in summer mostly by sliding down the Atlantic coast and giving cooler northeast winds. Such masses reaching this area from the northwest or west in summer bring mostly clear skies and high temperatures.

Based on the 1951-1980 period, the average first occurrence of 32 degrees Fahrenheit in the fall is November 15 and the average last occurrence in the spring is March 10.

## TABLE 1 — NORMALS, MEANS AND EXTREMES

SAVANNAH, GEORGIA

LATITUDE: 32°08'N   LONGITUDE: 81°12'W   ELEVATION: FT. GRND 46 BARO 52   TIME ZONE: EASTERN   WBAN: 03822

| | (a) | JAN | FEB | MAR | APR | MAY | JUNE | JULY | AUG | SEP | OCT | NOV | DEC | YEAR |
|---|---|---|---|---|---|---|---|---|---|---|---|---|---|---|
| **TEMPERATURE °F:** | | | | | | | | | | | | | | |
| Normals | | | | | | | | | | | | | | |
| -Daily Maximum | | 60.3 | 63.1 | 69.9 | 77.8 | 84.2 | 88.6 | 90.8 | 90.1 | 85.6 | 77.8 | 69.5 | 62.5 | 76.7 |
| -Daily Minimum | | 37.9 | 40.0 | 46.8 | 54.1 | 62.3 | 68.5 | 71.5 | 71.4 | 67.6 | 55.9 | 45.5 | 39.4 | 55.1 |
| -Monthly | | 49.2 | 51.6 | 58.4 | 66.0 | 73.3 | 78.6 | 81.2 | 80.8 | 76.6 | 66.9 | 57.5 | 51.0 | 65.9 |
| Extremes | | | | | | | | | | | | | | |
| -Record Highest | 39 | 84 | 86 | 91 | 95 | 100 | 104 | 105 | 104 | 98 | 97 | 89 | 83 | 105 |
| -Year | | 1957 | 1989 | 1974 | 1986 | 1953 | 1985 | 1986 | 1954 | 1986 | 1986 | 1961 | 1971 | JUL 1986 |
| -Record Lowest | 39 | 3 | 14 | 20 | 32 | 39 | 51 | 61 | 57 | 43 | 28 | 15 | 9 | 3 |
| -Year | | 1985 | 1958 | 1980 | 1987 | 1963 | 1984 | 1972 | 1986 | 1967 | 1952 | 1970 | 1983 | JAN 1985 |
| **NORMAL DEGREE DAYS:** | | | | | | | | | | | | | | |
| Heating (base 65°F) | | 507 | 387 | 243 | 42 | 0 | 0 | 0 | 0 | 0 | 58 | 240 | 444 | 1921 |
| Cooling (base 65°F) | | 17 | 12 | 38 | 72 | 261 | 408 | 502 | 490 | 348 | 117 | 15 | 10 | 2290 |
| **% OF POSSIBLE SUNSHINE** | 39 | 55 | 58 | 62 | 70 | 68 | 64 | 63 | 62 | 57 | 64 | 61 | 55 | 62 |
| **MEAN SKY COVER (tenths)** | | | | | | | | | | | | | | |
| Sunrise - Sunset | 39 | 6.1 | 6.1 | 5.9 | 5.3 | 5.8 | 6.1 | 6.5 | 6.2 | 6.3 | 5.1 | 5.4 | 6.0 | 5.9 |
| **MEAN NUMBER OF DAYS:** | | | | | | | | | | | | | | |
| Sunrise to Sunset | | | | | | | | | | | | | | |
| -Clear | 39 | 9.5 | 8.5 | 9.0 | 10.8 | 9.3 | 6.9 | 5.1 | 5.8 | 6.5 | 12.2 | 11.0 | 9.4 | 103.9 |
| -Partly Cloudy | 39 | 6.1 | 6.3 | 8.6 | 8.5 | 10.0 | 11.1 | 13.5 | 13.6 | 10.6 | 7.9 | 6.9 | 7.1 | 110.1 |
| -Cloudy | 39 | 15.4 | 13.4 | 13.4 | 10.7 | 11.7 | 12.0 | 12.4 | 11.6 | 12.9 | 10.9 | 12.1 | 14.5 | 151.3 |
| Precipitation | | | | | | | | | | | | | | |
| .01 inches or more | 39 | 9.3 | 8.8 | 9.4 | 6.8 | 8.7 | 11.0 | 13.8 | 12.7 | 10.1 | 5.9 | 6.5 | 8.2 | 111.1 |
| Snow,Ice pellets | | | | | | | | | | | | | | |
| 1.0 inches or more | 39 | 0.* | 0.1 | 0.* | 0.0 | 0.0 | 0.0 | 0.0 | 0.0 | 0.0 | 0.0 | 0.0 | 0.* | 0.2 |
| Thunderstorms | 39 | 0.9 | 1.2 | 3.0 | 3.6 | 7.4 | 10.2 | 14.8 | 12.4 | 5.6 | 1.5 | 0.4 | 0.6 | 61.7 |
| Heavy Fog Visibility | | | | | | | | | | | | | | |
| 1/4 mile or less | 39 | 4.7 | 3.1 | 3.3 | 2.6 | 3.3 | 2.3 | 1.3 | 2.0 | 3.7 | 3.4 | 5.1 | 4.5 | 39.2 |
| Temperature °F | | | | | | | | | | | | | | |
| -Maximum | | | | | | | | | | | | | | |
| 90° and above | 25 | 0.0 | 0.0 | 0.1 | 1.6 | 4.9 | 13.9 | 21.1 | 17.8 | 7.2 | 0.7 | 0.0 | 0.0 | 67.2 |
| 32° and below | 25 | 0.2 | 0.0 | 0.* | 0.0 | 0.0 | 0.0 | 0.0 | 0.0 | 0.0 | 0.0 | 0.0 | 0.1 | 0.4 |
| -Minimum | | | | | | | | | | | | | | |
| 32° and below | 25 | 11.0 | 7.7 | 2.1 | 0.* | 0.0 | 0.0 | 0.0 | 0.0 | 0.0 | 0.* | 2.5 | 8.2 | 31.6 |
| 0° and below | 25 | 0.0 | 0.0 | 0.0 | 0.0 | 0.0 | 0.0 | 0.0 | 0.0 | 0.0 | 0.0 | 0.0 | 0.0 | 0.0 |
| **AVG. STATION PRESS.(mb)** | 17 | 1018.9 | 1018.0 | 1016.1 | 1015.2 | 1014.4 | 1014.9 | 1015.9 | 1015.9 | 1015.6 | 1017.5 | 1018.3 | 1019.4 | 1016.7 |
| **RELATIVE HUMIDITY (%)** | | | | | | | | | | | | | | |
| Hour 01 | 25 | 77 | 76 | 77 | 78 | 84 | 86 | 87 | 89 | 89 | 84 | 83 | 79 | 82 |
| Hour 07 | 25 | 81 | 80 | 83 | 83 | 85 | 87 | 89 | 91 | 91 | 87 | 86 | 82 | 85 |
| Hour 13 (Local Time) | 25 | 54 | 50 | 48 | 45 | 51 | 55 | 58 | 61 | 60 | 53 | 52 | 54 | 53 |
| Hour 19 | 25 | 65 | 60 | 60 | 57 | 63 | 68 | 72 | 75 | 76 | 72 | 72 | 68 | 67 |
| **PRECIPITATION (inches):** | | | | | | | | | | | | | | |
| Water Equivalent | | | | | | | | | | | | | | |
| -Normal | | 3.09 | 3.17 | 3.83 | 3.16 | 4.62 | 5.69 | 7.37 | 6.65 | 5.19 | 2.27 | 1.89 | 2.77 | 49.70 |
| -Maximum Monthly | 39 | 8.87 | 7.92 | 9.57 | 7.74 | 10.08 | 14.39 | 20.10 | 14.94 | 13.47 | 8.54 | 4.91 | 5.80 | 20.10 |
| -Year | | 1984 | 1964 | 1959 | 1961 | 1957 | 1963 | 1964 | 1971 | 1953 | 1959 | 1972 | 1977 | JUL 1964 |
| -Minimum Monthly | 39 | 0.45 | 0.67 | 0.18 | 0.38 | 0.51 | 0.84 | 1.35 | 1.02 | 0.36 | 0.02 | 0.15 | 0.12 | 0.02 |
| -Year | | 1989 | 1989 | 1985 | 1986 | 1953 | 1954 | 1972 | 1980 | 1972 | 1963 | 1966 | 1984 | OCT 1963 |
| -Maximum in 24 hrs | 39 | 3.58 | 3.46 | 4.65 | 5.62 | 5.67 | 4.06 | 6.36 | 7.04 | 6.80 | 3.57 | 5.02 | 3.47 | 7.04 |
| -Year | | 1984 | 1964 | 1959 | 1976 | 1976 | 1963 | 1957 | 1971 | 1979 | 1959 | 1969 | 1964 | AUG 1971 |
| Snow,Ice pellets | | | | | | | | | | | | | | |
| -Maximum Monthly | 39 | 2.0 | 3.6 | 1.1 | 0.0 | 0.0 | T | 0.0 | 0.0 | 0.0 | 0.0 | 0.0 | 3.6 | 3.6 |
| -Year | | 1977 | 1968 | 1986 | | | 1989 | | | | | | 1989 | DEC 1989 |
| -Maximum in 24 hrs | 39 | 1.3 | 3.6 | 1.1 | 0.0 | 0.0 | T | 0.0 | 0.0 | 0.0 | 0.0 | 0.0 | 3.4 | 3.6 |
| -Year | | 1977 | 1968 | 1986 | | | 1989 | | | | | | 1989 | FEB 1968 |
| **WIND:** | | | | | | | | | | | | | | |
| Mean Speed (mph) | 39 | 8.5 | 9.2 | 9.2 | 8.7 | 7.7 | 7.4 | 7.1 | 6.6 | 7.3 | 7.4 | 7.5 | 7.9 | 7.9 |
| Prevailing Direction through 1963 | | WNW | NE | WNW | SSE | SW | SW | SW | SW | NE | NNE | NNE | NE | SW |
| Fastest Obs. 1 Min. | | | | | | | | | | | | | | |
| -Direction (!!!) | 9 | 31 | 29 | 32 | 10 | 22 | 27 | 35 | 25 | 29 | 29 | 23 | 30 | 32 |
| -Speed (MPH) | 9 | 30 | 30 | 46 | 35 | 44 | 31 | 37 | 29 | 35 | 24 | 40 | 29 | 46 |
| -Year | | 1989 | 1981 | 1981 | 1983 | 1984 | 1989 | 1986 | 1986 | 1989 | 1989 | 1985 | 1982 | MAR 1981 |
| Peak Gust | | | | | | | | | | | | | | |
| -Direction (!!!) | 6 | NW | W | SW | E | SW | SW | N | NW | W | S | S | NW | SW |
| -Speed (mph) | 6 | 51 | 46 | 41 | 41 | 68 | 46 | 63 | 56 | 54 | 41 | 62 | 38 | 68 |
| -Date | | 1989 | 1985 | 1988 | 1988 | 1984 | 1985 | 1986 | 1989 | 1989 | 1986 | 1985 | 1987 | MAY 1984 |

**See Reference Notes to this table on the following page.**

**TABLE 2**    PRECIPITATION (inches)     SAVANNAH, GEORGIA

| YEAR | JAN | FEB | MAR | APR | MAY | JUNE | JULY | AUG | SEP | OCT | NOV | DEC | ANNUAL |
|------|-----|-----|-----|-----|-----|------|------|-----|-----|-----|-----|-----|--------|
| 1961 | 2.15 | 3.76 | 4.69 | 7.74 | 3.50 | 3.74 | 4.08 | 12.80 | 2.61 | 0.09 | 0.99 | 2.85 | 49.00 |
| 1962 | 5.11 | 1.73 | 5.90 | 3.02 | 1.36 | 10.19 | 8.05 | 7.69 | 6.56 | 0.92 | 1.85 | 1.70 | 54.08 |
| 1963 | 3.32 | 5.06 | 1.68 | 4.55 | 3.85 | 14.39 | 7.94 | 2.36 | 3.61 | 0.02 | 2.90 | 4.16 | 50.83 |
| 1964 | 6.29 | 7.92 | 2.71 | 2.64 | 4.66 | 2.55 | 20.10 | 8.37 | 3.93 | 6.94 | 2.90 | 2.99 | 73.17 |
| 1965 | 0.83 | 4.34 | 7.75 | 1.39 | 2.62 | 5.63 | 7.46 | 4.56 | 4.82 | 1.33 |  | 2.09 | 45.81 |
| 1966 | 6.05 | 3.66 | 3.79 | 1.88 | 6.73 | 6.61 | 7.89 | 3.73 | 1.78 | 1.19 | 0.15 | 1.93 | 45.39 |
| 1967 | 7.18 | 2.80 | 0.50 | 1.38 | 2.94 | 4.38 | 6.23 | 8.57 | 2.12 | 1.36 | 0.84 | 2.97 | 41.27 |
| 1968 | 1.79 | 1.16 | 0.89 | 2.09 | 4.80 | 5.86 | 6.35 | 3.83 | 0.48 | 3.53 | 2.59 | 3.97 | 37.34 |
| 1969 | 1.77 | 1.59 | 5.11 | 0.71 | 8.74 | 9.99 | 7.57 | 10.33 | 3.74 | 4.04 | 3.82 | 3.43 | 60.84 |
| 1970 | 3.11 | 2.32 | 8.51 | 0.95 | 5.41 | 5.21 | 5.76 | 10.61 | 5.88 | 2.29 | 0.42 | 3.37 | 53.84 |
| 1971 | 3.40 | 2.60 | 2.63 | 3.53 | 3.56 | 6.98 | 9.07 | 14.94 | 1.67 | 8.01 | 1.26 | 3.69 | 61.34 |
| 1972 | 3.99 | 4.61 | 3.84 | 1.20 | 5.84 | 6.54 | 1.35 | 12.62 | 0.36 | 0.54 | 4.91 | 2.77 | 48.57 |
| 1973 | 3.61 | 4.46 | 5.36 | 4.43 | 1.23 | 9.19 | 2.89 | 6.45 | 3.65 | 0.19 | 0.68 | 3.26 | 45.40 |
| 1974 | 1.37 | 2.79 | 1.93 | 2.75 | 7.25 | 6.00 | 6.48 | 7.90 | 2.61 | 0.10 | 0.96 | 1.85 | 41.93 |
| 1975 | 3.17 | 3.01 | 3.99 | 4.71 | 6.00 | 2.08 | 11.55 | 3.13 | 10.07 | 4.75 | 4.83 | 3.87 | 51.18 |
| 1976 | 2.19 | 1.24 | 2.51 | 5.62 | 6.33 | 7.49 | 7.56 | 7.28 | 6.52 | 1.16 | 2.07 | 5.80 | 63.74 |
| 1977 | 3.14 | 1.83 | 2.72 | 1.94 | 1.03 | 2.00 | 5.62 | 8.01 | 2.61 | 0.60 | 1.85 | 2.85 | 35.41 |
| 1978 | 4.02 | 3.14 | 1.93 | 3.68 | 4.50 | 2.19 | 3.61 | 4.43 | 12.20 | 0.70 | 2.70 | 2.68 | 61.92 |
| 1979 | 3.96 | 4.14 | 2.42 | 3.83 | 8.49 | 7.37 | 10.78 | 2.65 | 5.81 | 1.62 | 2.04 | 1.33 | 37.84 |
| 1980 | 2.95 | 1.29 | 1.77 | 3.68 | 4.50 | 3.47 | 2.38 | 1.02 | 5.81 | 1.26 | 1.09 | 3.19 | 40.06 |
| 1981 | 1.03 | 2.94 | 3.91 | 1.75 | 2.10 | 3.01 | 5.42 | 10.91 | 2.88 | 1.29 | 1.65 | 3.17 | 52.26 |
| 1982 | 3.47 | 2.94 | 1.64 | 6.25 | 4.18 | 9.15 | 6.70 | 9.18 | 2.98 | 1.74 | 0.40 | 3.63 | 54.51 |
| 1983 | 5.90 | 5.23 | 9.01 | 5.15 | 1.07 | 5.81 | 5.30 | 3.67 | 3.39 | 1.03 | 4.18 | 4.77 | 50.66 |
| 1984 | 8.87 | 3.21 | 5.13 | 3.41 | 5.29 | 1.48 | 7.88 | 3.46 | 7.43 | 1.23 | 3.15 | 0.12 | 38.64 |
| 1985 | 0.51 | 1.37 | 1.65 | 1.37 | 2.18 | 6.72 | 5.00 | 9.42 | 0.76 | 3.37 | 4.28 | 2.01 | 45.33 |
| 1986 | 2.03 | 5.28 | 2.85 | 0.38 | 2.06 | 2.98 | 5.49 | 12.31 | 0.49 | 1.99 | 4.40 | 5.07 | 56.48 |
| 1987 | 8.62 | 4.39 | 5.33 | 0.50 | 3.82 | 8.03 | 4.37 | 9.46 | 8.16 | 0.33 | 2.06 | 1.41 | 48.17 |
| 1988 | 3.44 | 4.09 | 2.11 | 5.05 | 3.52 | 2.63 | 1.80 | 10.68 | 9.62 | 2.81 | 1.43 | 0.99 | 46.87 |
| 1989 | 0.45 | 0.67 | 1.41 | 3.59 | 3.10 | 7.30 | 4.91 | 6.29 | 7.98 | 4.71 | 1.26 | 5.20 | 43.08 |
| 1990 | 3.91 | 3.08 | 3.79 | 1.75 | 2.07 | 0.97 | 1.92 | 7.25 | 1.26 | 12.50 | 2.48 | 2.10 |  |
| Record Mean | 2.88 | 3.16 | 3.55 | 2.89 | 3.40 | 5.50 | 6.64 | 7.09 | 5.59 | 2.78 | 2.02 | 2.82 | 48.30 |

**TABLE 3**    AVERAGE TEMPERATURE (deg. F)     SAVANNAH, GEORGIA

| YEAR | JAN | FEB | MAR | APR | MAY | JUNE | JULY | AUG | SEP | OCT | NOV | DEC | ANNUAL |
|------|-----|-----|-----|-----|-----|------|------|-----|-----|-----|-----|-----|--------|
| 1961 | 45.6 | 54.7 | 63.2 | 61.4 | 71.3 | 77.5 | 81.8 | 79.1 | 77.1 | 65.2 | 60.6 | 52.1 | 65.8 |
| 1962 | 49.0 | 57.8 | 55.0 | 63.3 | 77.0 | 77.6 | 81.9 | 80.2 | 75.3 | 68.3 | 54.4 | 47.2 | 65.6 |
| 1963 | 46.8 | 47.1 | 61.2 | 66.9 | 72.6 | 79.1 | 80.1 | 81.7 | 74.3 | 66.7 | 57.3 | 43.7 | 64.8 |
| #1964 | 48.2 | 47.8 | 58.4 | 58.4 | 73.2 | 81.4 | 79.6 | 79.7 | 74.7 | 63.1 | 60.1 | 50.1 | 65.5 |
| 1965 | 49.9 | 52.4 | 56.8 | 66.4 | 74.8 | 76.4 | 79.8 | 80.6 | 76.7 | 66.2 | 57.1 | 49.5 | 64.4 |
| 1966 | 44.9 | 51.2 | 55.6 | 64.7 | 71.6 | 74.6 | 80.9 | 79.6 | 76.4 | 67.3 | 55.3 | 49.5 | 65.7 |
| 1967 | 51.4 | 49.6 | 61.7 | 69.0 | 73.2 | 77.2 | 79.9 | 79.4 | 71.6 | 64.4 | 54.8 | 55.3 | 64.8 |
| 1968 | 45.7 | 44.6 | 57.0 | 68.0 | 72.5 | 79.1 | 81.6 | 82.1 | 76.5 | 68.7 | 53.9 | 47.7 | 64.3 |
| 1969 | 47.4 | 47.1 | 52.4 | 66.1 | 71.0 | 79.7 | 82.2 | 78.9 | 75.4 | 69.9 | 53.9 | 54.1 | 66.0 |
| 1970 | 42.4 | 49.2 | 59.2 | 68.3 | 73.0 | 78.2 | 81.6 | 81.8 | 78.9 | 70.2 | 60.6 | 54.1 | 67.0 |
| 1971 | 50.1 | 52.4 | 54.5 | 64.6 | 71.1 | 80.5 | 80.9 | 80.8 | 78.6 | 72.4 | 58.0 | 60.6 | 67.1 |
| 1972 | 57.5 | 51.3 | 59.3 | 66.7 | 71.6 | 75.7 | 81.0 | 81.0 | 77.3 | 68.1 | 58.1 | 51.2 | 66.9 |
| 1973 | 49.8 | 49.6 | 63.6 | 64.0 | 73.5 | 79.3 | 82.2 | 80.0 | 79.0 | 68.9 | 61.6 | 53.1 | 67.3 |
| 1974 | 62.9 | 53.0 | 63.8 | 65.6 | 74.5 | 76.8 | 79.2 | 79.6 | 76.3 | 64.6 | 57.7 | 50.5 | 67.5 |
| 1975 | 55.3 | 57.7 | 59.5 | 65.4 | 76.7 | 79.5 | 78.4 | 81.7 | 76.5 | 70.0 | 59.3 | 50.5 | 64.4 |
| 1976 | 45.9 | 56.4 | 62.6 | 64.3 | 69.7 | 75.8 | 81.7 | 78.2 | 74.9 | 62.5 | 51.5 | 49.0 | 66.1 |
| 1977 | 39.9 | 49.2 | 62.1 | 67.6 | 74.0 | 82.0 | 83.3 | 81.1 | 78.9 | 64.1 | 61.2 | 50.0 | 66.1 |
| 1978 | 43.9 | 43.6 | 56.3 | 68.0 | 73.7 | 80.0 | 82.2 | 82.3 | 78.2 | 67.0 | 53.4 | 50.7 | 66.0 |
| 1979 | 45.4 | 49.0 | 59.8 | 67.7 | 73.9 | 76.8 | 82.1 | 81.4 | 77.4 | 67.5 | 60.4 | 48.1 | 66.1 |
| 1980 | 50.7 | 48.5 | 57.1 | 66.2 | 73.3 | 79.7 | 84.4 | 83.4 | 80.4 | 65.4 | 56.7 | 48.3 | 65.7 |
| 1981 | 43.5 | 52.6 | 56.8 | 69.0 | 71.6 | 84.5 | 84.4 | 79.2 | 75.2 | 65.4 | 57.7 | 57.4 | 67.5 |
| 1982 | 48.7 | 55.9 | 62.1 | 64.8 | 74.3 | 80.2 | 81.3 | 81.0 | 75.5 | 67.6 | 61.8 | 48.5 | 65.6 |
| 1983 | 46.1 | 50.8 | 58.0 | 62.8 | 73.0 | 78.2 | 84.1 | 82.9 | 75.7 | 69.7 | 57.7 | 59.5 | 67.0 |
| 1984 | 47.7 | 53.7 | 59.3 | 65.7 | 72.9 | 79.2 | 82.0 | 81.5 | 75.0 | 73.2 | 55.7 | 48.9 | 67.6 |
| 1985 | 45.3 | 53.0 | 61.5 | 66.9 | 74.6 | 81.3 | 82.7 | 82.7 | 76.6 | 72.2 | 67.5 | 53.9 | 68.7 |
| 1986 | 47.6 | 56.9 | 59.1 | 66.8 | 75.0 | 82.5 | 85.7 | 81.6 | 79.7 | 70.0 | 65.0 | 54.7 | 66.6 |
| 1987 | 49.0 | 50.4 | 58.2 | 63.9 | 74.1 | 80.6 | 83.6 | 84.5 | 77.8 | 61.5 | 60.4 | 51.1 | 65.7 |
| 1988 | 45.0 | 50.2 | 58.2 | 66.1 | 72.4 | 77.7 | 82.7 | 82.5 | 77.4 | 64.2 | 61.3 | 43.7 | 67.0 |
| 1989 | 56.6 | 56.1 | 60.6 | 65.6 | 72.3 | 81.0 | 82.9 | 80.7 | 76.8 | 68.6 | 59.5 | 56.5 | 69.4 |
| 1990 | 55.7 | 60.0 | 62.6 | 65.0 | 74.3 | 81.5 | 84.4 | 82.4 | 78.9 | 70.7 | 60.8 | 52.3 | 66.8 |
| Record Mean | 51.3 | 53.3 | 59.4 | 66.1 | 73.5 | 79.4 | 81.6 | 81.0 | 77.0 | 67.8 | 58.8 | 52.3 | 66.8 |
| Max | 60.8 | 63.1 | 69.3 | 76.1 | 83.0 | 88.4 | 90.3 | 89.4 | 85.1 | 77.1 | 68.8 | 62.0 | 76.1 |
| Min | 41.7 | 43.6 | 49.5 | 56.1 | 64.0 | 70.3 | 72.9 | 72.6 | 68.8 | 58.6 | 48.8 | 42.6 | 57.5 |

## REFERENCE NOTES FOR TABLES 1, 2, 3 and 6     (SAVANNAH, GA)

### GENERAL

T - TRACE AMOUNT
BLANK ENTRIES DENOTE MISSING/UNREPORTED DATA.
# INDICATES A STATION OR INSTRUMENT RELOCATION.

### SPECIFIC

**TABLE 1**

(a) - LENGTH OF RECORD IN YEARS. ALTHOUGH INDIVIDUAL MONTHS MAY BE MISSING.

\* LESS THAN .05

NORMALS — BASED ON THE 1951-1980 RECORD PERIOD.
EXTREMES — DATES ARE THE MOST RECENT OCCURRENCE.
WIND DIR. — NUMERALS SHOW TENS OF DEGREES CLOCKWISE FROM TRUE NORTH.
      "00" INDICATES CALM.
RESULTANT WIND DIRECTIONS ARE GIVEN TO WHOLE DEGREES.

**TABLE 3**
MAX AND MIN ARE LONG-TERM MEAN DAILY MAXIMUM AND MEAN DAILY MINIMUM TEMPERATURES.

### EXCEPTIONS

**TABLE 1**

1. FASTEST MILE WIND IS THROUGH OCTOBER 1980.

**TABLES 2, 3, and 6**

RECORD MEANS ARE THROUGH THE CURRENT YEAR, BEGINNING IN   1874 FOR TEMPERATURE
                 1871 FOR PRECIPITATION
                 1951 FOR SNOWFALL

**TABLE 4**

HEATING DEGREE DAYS Base 65 deg. F          SAVANNAH, GEORGIA

| SEASON | JULY | AUG | SEP | OCT | NOV | DEC | JAN | FEB | MAR | APR | MAY | JUNE | TOTAL |
|---|---|---|---|---|---|---|---|---|---|---|---|---|---|
| 1961-62 | 0 | 0 | 3 | 66 | 217 | 414 | 502 | 223 | 316 | 122 | 0 | 0 | 1863 |
| 1962-63 | 0 | 0 | 5 | 79 | 317 | 543 | 557 | 494 | 168 | 44 | 21 | 0 | 2228 |
| 1963-64 | 0 | 0 | 1 | 42 | 232 | 653 | 514 | 493 | 221 | 50 | 4 | 0 | 2210 |
| #1964-65 | 0 | 0 | 0 | 116 | 157 | 355 | 463 | 359 | 282 | 66 | 0 | 0 | 1798 |
| 1965-66 | 0 | 0 | 0 | 92 | 204 | 454 | 612 | 387 | 294 | 88 | 11 | 0 | 2142 |
| 1966-67 | 0 | 0 | 0 | 50 | 259 | 480 | 413 | 428 | 159 | 26 | 12 | 1 | 1828 |
| 1967-68 | 0 | 0 | 12 | 82 | 269 | 306 | 592 | 582 | 270 | 34 | 3 | 0 | 2150 |
| 1968-69 | 0 | 0 | 0 | 73 | 309 | 533 | 539 | 498 | 395 | 48 | 3 | 0 | 2398 |
| 1969-70 | 0 | 0 | 0 | 38 | 332 | 530 | 698 | 437 | 199 | 57 | 8 | 0 | 2299 |
| 1970-71 | 0 | 0 | 1 | 20 | 303 | 340 | 458 | 359 | 338 | 100 | 15 | 0 | 1934 |
| 1971-72 | 0 | 0 | 0 | 10 | 236 | 187 | 256 | 400 | 183 | 74 | 1 | 0 | 1347 |
| 1972-73 | 0 | 0 | 0 | 25 | 239 | 261 | 462 | 423 | 98 | 85 | 4 | 0 | 1597 |
| 1973-74 | 0 | 0 | 0 | 47 | 148 | 435 | 107 | 340 | 124 | 73 | 1 | 0 | 1275 |
| 1974-75 | 0 | 0 | 2 | 79 | 243 | 368 | 315 | 232 | 212 | 86 | 0 | 0 | 1537 |
| 1975-76 | 0 | 0 | 0 | 25 | 228 | 446 | 586 | 256 | 134 | 69 | 11 | 0 | 1755 |
| 1976-77 | 0 | 0 | 0 | 142 | 405 | 490 | 771 | 437 | 152 | 42 | 2 | 0 | 2441 |
| 1977-78 | 0 | 0 | 0 | 96 | 165 | 457 | 645 | 594 | 283 | 35 | 2 | 0 | 2277 |
| 1978-79 | 0 | 0 | 0 | 45 | 53 | 378 | 602 | 448 | 181 | 17 | 1 | 0 | 1725 |
| 1979-80 | 0 | 0 | 0 | 41 | 183 | 438 | 436 | 489 | 257 | 43 | 7 | 0 | 1894 |
| 1980-81 | 0 | 0 | 0 | 72 | 252 | 518 | 659 | 342 | 263 | 25 | 8 | 0 | 2139 |
| 1981-82 | 0 | 0 | 3 | 59 | 231 | 513 | 501 | 258 | 149 | 76 | 0 | 0 | 1790 |
| 1982-83 | 0 | 0 | 0 | 73 | 139 | 266 | 579 | 392 | 228 | 115 | 0 | 0 | 1792 |
| 1983-84 | 0 | 0 | 2 | 19 | 232 | 513 | 531 | 320 | 200 | 68 | 7 | 0 | 1892 |
| 1984-85 | 0 | 0 | 1 | 8 | 299 | 185 | 615 | 360 | 157 | 60 | 2 | 0 | 1687 |
| 1985-86 | 0 | 0 | 1 | 16 | 51 | 504 | 531 | 240 | 215 | 59 | 4 | 0 | 1621 |
| 1986-87 | 0 | 5 | 0 | 48 | 101 | 349 | 491 | 401 | 231 | 110 | 5 | 0 | 1741 |
| 1987-88 | 0 | 0 | 0 | 122 | 185 | 332 | 612 | 426 | 218 | 52 | 1 | 0 | 1948 |
| 1988-89 | 0 | 0 | 0 | 84 | 141 | 423 | 268 | 289 | 193 | 110 | 13 | 0 | 1521 |
| 1989-90 | 0 | 0 | 1 | 59 | 191 | 653 | 286 | 175 | 135 | 81 | 0 | 0 | 1581 |
| 1990-91 | 0 | 0 | 0 | 55 | 143 | 279 | | | | | | | |

**TABLE 5**

COOLING DEGREE DAYS Base 65 deg. F          SAVANNAH, GEORGIA

| YEAR | JAN | FEB | MAR | APR | MAY | JUNE | JULY | AUG | SEP | OCT | NOV | DEC | TOTAL |
|---|---|---|---|---|---|---|---|---|---|---|---|---|---|
| 1969 | 0 | 4 | 8 | 86 | 194 | 450 | 539 | 438 | 320 | 199 | 8 | 1 | 2247 |
| 1970 | 4 | 0 | 26 | 163 | 262 | 403 | 521 | 528 | 423 | 188 | 4 | 9 | 2531 |
| 1971 | 1 | 13 | 18 | 92 | 210 | 474 | 502 | 495 | 414 | 248 | 34 | 56 | 2557 |
| 1972 | 28 | 8 | 14 | 130 | 214 | 328 | 505 | 503 | 379 | 125 | 38 | 23 | 2295 |
| 1973 | 0 | 0 | 63 | 63 | 275 | 434 | 540 | 473 | 429 | 177 | 52 | 13 | 2519 |
| 1974 | 52 | 9 | 96 | 99 | 302 | 360 | 448 | 462 | 347 | 74 | 32 | 8 | 2289 |
| 1975 | 20 | 33 | 48 | 104 | 374 | 439 | 423 | 528 | 351 | 187 | 65 | 2 | 2574 |
| 1976 | 0 | 12 | 68 | 53 | 164 | 331 | 526 | 416 | 306 | 70 | 7 | 1 | 1954 |
| 1977 | 0 | 1 | 71 | 130 | 289 | 517 | 574 | 508 | 421 | 74 | 58 | 0 | 2643 |
| 1978 | 0 | 0 | 22 | 132 | 281 | 456 | 538 | 543 | 403 | 115 | 51 | 29 | 2570 |
| 1979 | 0 | 5 | 28 | 105 | 282 | 360 | 537 | 516 | 378 | 126 | 51 | 2 | 2390 |
| 1980 | 0 | 16 | 19 | 87 | 270 | 449 | 607 | 579 | 468 | 90 | 8 | 2 | 2595 |
| 1981 | 0 | 1 | 14 | 150 | 219 | 589 | 609 | 444 | 319 | 80 | 17 | 4 | 2446 |
| 1982 | 6 | 10 | 67 | 79 | 292 | 463 | 514 | 503 | 323 | 158 | 48 | 42 | 2505 |
| 1983 | 0 | 0 | 16 | 55 | 253 | 400 | 598 | 562 | 332 | 171 | 18 | 6 | 2411 |
| 1984 | 0 | 0 | 31 | 94 | 261 | 431 | 486 | 517 | 309 | 270 | 24 | 19 | 2442 |
| 1985 | 11 | 31 | 58 | 123 | 307 | 496 | 557 | 496 | 355 | 248 | 133 | 7 | 2822 |
| 1986 | 0 | 18 | 40 | 121 | 321 | 532 | 651 | 525 | 449 | 212 | 107 | 13 | 2989 |
| 1987 | 0 | 0 | 26 | 85 | 292 | 474 | 583 | 611 | 392 | 22 | 50 | 21 | 2556 |
| 1988 | 0 | 3 | 11 | 92 | 238 | 386 | 555 | 547 | 378 | 66 | 35 | 1 | 2312 |
| 1989 | 13 | 45 | 64 | 135 | 248 | 488 | 563 | 493 | 362 | 177 | 33 | 0 | 2621 |
| 1990 | 4 | 41 | 69 | 90 | 296 | 503 | 608 | 549 | 422 | 237 | 25 | 24 | 2868 |

**TABLE 6**

SNOWFALL (inches)          SAVANNAH, GEORGIA

| SEASON | JULY | AUG | SEP | OCT | NOV | DEC | JAN | FEB | MAR | APR | MAY | JUNE | TOTAL |
|---|---|---|---|---|---|---|---|---|---|---|---|---|---|
| 1970-71 | 0.0 | 0.0 | 0.0 | 0.0 | 0.0 | 0.0 | T | 0.0 | 0.0 | 0.0 | 0.0 | 0.0 | T |
| 1971-72 | 0.0 | 0.0 | 0.0 | 0.0 | 0.0 | 0.0 | 0.0 | 0.0 | 0.0 | 0.0 | 0.0 | 0.0 | 0.0 |
| 1972-73 | 0.0 | 0.0 | 0.0 | 0.0 | 0.0 | 0.0 | T | 3.2 | 0.0 | 0.0 | 0.0 | 0.0 | 3.2 |
| 1973-74 | 0.0 | 0.0 | 0.0 | 0.0 | 0.0 | 0.0 | 0.0 | 0.0 | 0.0 | 0.0 | 0.0 | 0.0 | 0.0 |
| 1974-75 | 0.0 | 0.0 | 0.0 | 0.0 | 0.0 | 0.0 | 0.0 | 0.0 | 0.0 | 0.0 | 0.0 | 0.0 | 0.0 |
| 1975-76 | 0.0 | 0.0 | 0.0 | 0.0 | 0.0 | 0.0 | T | 0.0 | 0.0 | 0.0 | 0.0 | 0.0 | T |
| 1976-77 | 0.0 | 0.0 | 0.0 | 0.0 | 0.0 | 0.0 | 2.0 | T | 0.0 | 0.0 | 0.0 | 0.0 | 2.0 |
| 1977-78 | 0.0 | 0.0 | 0.0 | 0.0 | 0.0 | 0.0 | 0.0 | 0.0 | 0.0 | 0.0 | 0.0 | 0.0 | 0.0 |
| 1978-79 | 0.0 | 0.0 | 0.0 | 0.0 | 0.0 | 0.0 | 0.0 | T | 0.0 | 0.0 | 0.0 | 0.0 | T |
| 1979-80 | 0.0 | 0.0 | 0.0 | 0.0 | 0.0 | 0.0 | 0.0 | 0.0 | T | 0.0 | 0.0 | 0.0 | T |
| 1980-81 | 0.0 | 0.0 | 0.0 | 0.0 | 0.0 | T | 0.0 | 0.0 | 0.0 | 0.0 | 0.0 | 0.0 | T |
| 1981-82 | 0.0 | 0.0 | 0.0 | 0.0 | 0.0 | 0.0 | 0.0 | 0.0 | 0.0 | 0.0 | 0.0 | 0.0 | 0.0 |
| 1982-83 | 0.0 | 0.0 | 0.0 | 0.0 | 0.0 | 0.0 | T | 0.0 | 0.0 | 0.0 | 0.0 | 0.0 | T |
| 1983-84 | 0.0 | 0.0 | 0.0 | 0.0 | 0.0 | 0.0 | T | 0.0 | 0.0 | 0.0 | 0.0 | 0.0 | T |
| 1984-85 | 0.0 | 0.0 | 0.0 | 0.0 | 0.0 | 0.0 | 0.0 | 0.0 | 0.0 | 0.0 | 0.0 | 0.0 | 0.0 |
| 1985-86 | 0.0 | 0.0 | 0.0 | 0.0 | 0.0 | 0.0 | 0.3 | 0.0 | 1.1 | 0.0 | 0.0 | 0.0 | 1.4 |
| 1986-87 | 0.0 | 0.0 | 0.0 | 0.0 | 0.0 | 0.0 | T | 0.0 | 0.0 | 0.0 | 0.0 | 0.0 | T |
| 1987-88 | 0.0 | 0.0 | 0.0 | 0.0 | 0.0 | 0.0 | T | T | 0.0 | 0.0 | 0.0 | 0.0 | T |
| 1988-89 | 0.0 | 0.0 | 0.0 | 0.0 | 0.0 | 0.0 | T | 1.0 | 0.0 | 0.0 | 0.0 | T | 1.0 |
| 1989-90 | 0.0 | 0.0 | 0.0 | 0.0 | 0.0 | 3.6 | 0.0 | 0.0 | 0.0 | 0.0 | 0.0 | 0.0 | 3.6 |
| 1990-91 | 0.0 | 0.0 | 0.0 | 0.0 | 0.0 | 0.0 | | | | | | | |
| Record Mean | 0.0 | 0.0 | 0.0 | 0.0 | 0.0 | 0.1 | 0.1 | 0.2 | T | 0.0 | 0.0 | T | 0.4 |

**See Reference Notes, relative to all above tables, on preceding page.**

The city of Hilo is located near the midpoint of the eastern shore of the Island of Hawaii. This island is by far the largest of the Hawaiian group, with an area of 4,038 square miles, more than twice that of all the other islands combined. Its topography is dominated by the great volcanic masses of Mauna Loa (13,653 feet), Mauna Kea (13,796 feet), and of Haulalai, the Kohala Mountains, and Kilauea. In fact, the island consists entirely of the slopes of these mountains and of the broad saddles between them. Mauna Loa and Kilauea, which occupy the southern half of the island, are still active volcanoes.

Hawaii lies well within the belt of northeasterly trade winds generated by the semi-permanent Pacific high pressure cell to the north and east. The climate provides equable temperatures from day to day and season to season. In Hilo, July and August are the warmest months, with average daily highs and lows of 83 and 68 degrees. January and February, the coolest months, have highs of 80 degrees and lows of 63 degrees. Greater variations occur in localities with less rain and cloud, but temperatures in the mid-90s and low 50s are uncommon anywhere on the island near sea level.

Over the windward slopes of Hawaii, rainfall occurs principally as orographic showers within the ascending moist trade winds. Mean annual rainfall, except for the semi-sheltered Hamakua district, increases from 100 inches or more along the coasts to a maximum of over 300 inches at elevations of 2,000 to 3,000 feet, and then declines to about 15 inches at the summits of Mauna Kea and Mauna Loa. Leeward areas are topographically sheltered from the trades and are therefore drier, although sea breezes created by daytime heating of the land move onshore and upslope, causing afternoon and evening cloudiness and showers. The driest locality on the island, and in the State, with an annual rainfall of less than 10 inches, is the coastal strip just leeward of the southern portion of the Kohala Mountains and of the saddle between the Kohalas and Mauna Kea.

Within the city of Hilo, average rainfall varies from about 130 inches a year near the shore to as much as 200 upslope. The wettest part of the island, with a mean annual rainfall exceeding 300 inches, lies about 6 miles upslope from the city limits. Relative humidity at Hilo is in the moderate range, however, due to the natural ventilation provided by the prevailing winds, the weather is seldom oppressive.

The trade winds prevail throughout the year and profoundly influence the climate. The islands entire western coast is sheltered from the trades by high mountains, except that unusually strong trade winds may sweep through the saddle between the Kohala Mountains and Mauna Kea and reach the areas to the lee. But even places exposed to the trades may be affected by local mountain circulations. Except for heavy rain, really severe weather seldom occurs. During the winter, cold fronts or the cyclonic storms of subtropical origin may bring blizzards to the upper slopes of Mauna Loa and Mauna Kea, with snow extending at times to 9,000 feet or below and icing nearer the summit.

Storms crossing the Pacific a thousand miles to the north, low pressure or tropical storms, may generate seas that cause heavy swell and surf.

## TABLE 1     NORMALS, MEANS AND EXTREMES

HILO, HAWAII

LATITUDE: 19°43'N     LONGITUDE: 155°04'W     ELEVATION: FT. GRND     27 BARO     34     TIME ZONE: BERING     WBAN: 21504

| | (a) | JAN | FEB | MAR | APR | MAY | JUNE | JULY | AUG | SEP | OCT | NOV | DEC | YEAR |
|---|---|---|---|---|---|---|---|---|---|---|---|---|---|---|
| **TEMPERATURE °F:** | | | | | | | | | | | | | | |
| Normals | | | | | | | | | | | | | | |
| -Daily Maximum | | 79.5 | 79.0 | 79.0 | 79.7 | 81.0 | 82.5 | 82.8 | 83.3 | 83.6 | 83.0 | 80.9 | 79.5 | 81.2 |
| -Daily Minimum | | 63.2 | 63.2 | 63.9 | 64.9 | 66.1 | 67.1 | 68.0 | 68.4 | 68.0 | 67.5 | 66.3 | 64.3 | 65.9 |
| -Monthly | | 71.4 | 71.2 | 71.5 | 72.4 | 73.6 | 74.8 | 75.4 | 75.9 | 75.8 | 75.3 | 73.6 | 71.9 | 73.6 |
| Extremes | | | | | | | | | | | | | | |
| -Record Highest | 43 | 91 | 92 | 93 | 89 | 94 | 90 | 89 | 93 | 92 | 91 | 90 | 93 | 94 |
| -Year | | 1979 | 1968 | 1972 | 1978 | 1966 | 1969 | 1986 | 1950 | 1951 | 1979 | 1985 | 1980 | MAY 1966 |
| -Record Lowest | 43 | 54 | 53 | 54 | 56 | 58 | 60 | 62 | 63 | 61 | 62 | 58 | 55 | 53 |
| -Year | | 1980 | 1962 | 1983 | 1949 | 1947 | 1946 | 1970 | 1955 | 1970 | 1985 | 1985 | 1977 | FEB 1962 |
| **NORMAL DEGREE DAYS:** | | | | | | | | | | | | | | |
| Heating (base 65°F) | | 0 | 0 | 0 | 0 | 0 | 0 | 0 | 0 | 0 | 0 | 0 | 0 | 0 |
| Cooling (base 65°F) | | 198 | 176 | 202 | 222 | 267 | 294 | 322 | 338 | 324 | 319 | 258 | 214 | 3134 |
| **% OF POSSIBLE SUNSHINE** | 39 | 47 | 46 | 41 | 35 | 36 | 44 | 42 | 42 | 43 | 39 | 34 | 38 | 41 |
| **MEAN SKY COVER (tenths)** | | | | | | | | | | | | | | |
| Sunrise - Sunset | 43 | 6.3 | 6.6 | 7.5 | 8.1 | 7.9 | 7.5 | 7.6 | 7.3 | 7.0 | 7.2 | 7.2 | 6.7 | 7.3 |
| **MEAN NUMBER OF DAYS:** | | | | | | | | | | | | | | |
| Sunrise to Sunset | | | | | | | | | | | | | | |
| -Clear | 43 | 6.3 | 5.2 | 2.7 | 1.1 | 1.1 | 1.7 | 1.3 | 1.8 | 3.1 | 2.8 | 3.4 | 5.4 | 35.9 |
| -Partly Cloudy | 43 | 11.6 | 10.1 | 10.0 | 8.3 | 10.3 | 10.9 | 11.5 | 12.1 | 11.9 | 11.6 | 10.6 | 10.7 | 129.7 |
| -Cloudy | 43 | 13.0 | 12.9 | 18.2 | 20.6 | 19.7 | 17.4 | 18.2 | 17.1 | 15.0 | 16.6 | 16.0 | 14.9 | 199.7 |
| Precipitation | | | | | | | | | | | | | | |
| .01 inches or more | 47 | 17.3 | 17.3 | 23.4 | 25.4 | 25.4 | 24.2 | 27.4 | 26.4 | 23.4 | 23.9 | 23.0 | 21.1 | 278.1 |
| Snow,Ice pellets | | | | | | | | | | | | | | |
| 1.0 inches or more | 47 | 0.0 | 0.0 | 0.0 | 0.0 | 0.0 | 0.0 | 0.0 | 0.0 | 0.0 | 0.0 | 0.0 | 0.0 | 0.0 |
| Thunderstorms | 44 | 1.0 | 1.3 | 1.6 | 1.2 | 0.7 | 0.1 | 0.3 | 0.3 | 0.5 | 1.3 | 1.1 | 0.9 | 10.0 |
| Heavy Fog Visibility | | | | | | | | | | | | | | |
| 1/4 mile or less | 44 | 0.0 | 0.0 | 0.0 | 0.0 | 0.0 | 0.0 | 0.0 | 0.0 | 0.0 | 0.0 | 0.0 | 0.0 | 0.0 |
| Temperature °F | | | | | | | | | | | | | | |
| -Maximum | | | | | | | | | | | | | | |
| 90° and above | 44 | 0.1 | 0.1 | 0.* | 0.0 | 0.* | 0.* | 0.0 | 0.1 | 0.2 | 0.2 | 0.* | 0.1 | 0.8 |
| 32° and below | 44 | 0.0 | 0.0 | 0.0 | 0.0 | 0.0 | 0.0 | 0.0 | 0.0 | 0.0 | 0.0 | 0.0 | 0.0 | 0.0 |
| -Minimum | | | | | | | | | | | | | | |
| 32° and below | 44 | 0.0 | 0.0 | 0.0 | 0.0 | 0.0 | 0.0 | 0.0 | 0.0 | 0.0 | 0.0 | 0.0 | 0.0 | 0.0 |
| 0° and below | 44 | 0.0 | 0.0 | 0.0 | 0.0 | 0.0 | 0.0 | 0.0 | 0.0 | 0.0 | 0.0 | 0.0 | 0.0 | 0.0 |
| **AVG. STATION PRESS.(mb)** | 17 | 1014.6 | 1015.0 | 1016.8 | 1016.8 | 1016.6 | 1016.4 | 1015.8 | 1015.0 | 1014.3 | 1014.5 | 1014.7 | 1014.8 | 1015.4 |
| **RELATIVE HUMIDITY (%)** | | | | | | | | | | | | | | |
| Hour 02 | 40 | 83 | 84 | 86 | 88 | 88 | 87 | 88 | 88 | 87 | 87 | 86 | 85 | 86 |
| Hour 18 | 40 | 79 | 78 | 80 | 81 | 80 | 78 | 81 | 81 | 79 | 80 | 81 | 80 | 80 |
| Hour 14 (Local Time) | 40 | 66 | 66 | 67 | 69 | 68 | 65 | 68 | 69 | 68 | 69 | 70 | 69 | 68 |
| Hour 20 | 40 | 82 | 82 | 82 | 83 | 83 | 81 | 82 | 83 | 84 | 85 | 85 | 84 | 83 |
| **PRECIPITATION (inches):** | | | | | | | | | | | | | | |
| Water Equivalent | | | | | | | | | | | | | | |
| -Normal | | 9.42 | 13.47 | 13.55 | 13.10 | 9.40 | 6.13 | 8.68 | 10.02 | 6.63 | 10.01 | 14.88 | 12.86 | 128.15 |
| -Maximum Monthly | 47 | 32.24 | 45.55 | 49.93 | 43.24 | 25.01 | 15.50 | 28.59 | 26.42 | 14.36 | 26.10 | 35.72 | 50.82 | 50.82 |
| -Year | | 1979 | 1979 | 1980 | 1986 | 1964 | 1943 | 1982 | 1957 | 1986 | 1951 | 1986 | 1954 | DEC 1954 |
| -Minimum Monthly | 47 | 0.36 | 0.58 | 0.88 | 2.93 | 1.18 | 1.80 | 3.83 | 2.66 | 1.59 | 2.40 | 1.01 | 0.28 | 0.28 |
| -Year | | 1953 | 1986 | 1972 | 1962 | 1945 | 1985 | 1975 | 1971 | 1974 | 1962 | 1989 | 1980 | DEC 1980 |
| -Maximum in 24 hrs | 47 | 9.94 | 22.30 | 17.05 | 11.07 | 10.26 | 4.21 | 7.11 | 9.65 | 7.23 | 8.88 | 15.59 | 11.45 | 22.30 |
| -Year | | 1949 | 1979 | 1980 | 1971 | 1965 | 1978 | 1982 | 1970 | 1986 | 1951 | 1959 | 1987 | FEB 1979 |
| Snow,Ice pellets | | | | | | | | | | | | | | |
| -Maximum Monthly | | 0.0 | 0.0 | 0.0 | 0.0 | 0.0 | 0.0 | 0.0 | 0.0 | 0.0 | 0.0 | 0.0 | 0.0 | |
| -Year | | | | | | | | | | | | | | |
| -Maximum in 24 hrs | 47 | 0.0 | 0.0 | 0.0 | 0.0 | 0.0 | 0.0 | 0.0 | 0.0 | 0.0 | 0.0 | 0.0 | 0.0 | |
| -Year | | | | | | | | | | | | | | |
| **WIND:** | | | | | | | | | | | | | | |
| Mean Speed (mph) | 40 | 7.5 | 7.7 | 7.6 | 7.5 | 7.3 | 7.1 | 6.9 | 6.8 | 6.7 | 6.7 | 6.8 | 7.2 | 7.2 |
| Prevailing Direction | | | | | | | | | | | | | | |
| through 1963 | | SW | SW | SW | WSW | WSW | WSW | WSW | WSW | WSW | SW | WSW | SW | WSW |
| Fastest Obs. 1 Min. | | | | | | | | | | | | | | |
| -Direction (!!) | 10 | 36 | 35 | 35 | 34 | 35 | 11 | 05 | 10 | 04 | 34 | 02 | 36 | 36 |
| -Speed (MPH) | 10 | 35 | 35 | 28 | 26 | 29 | 25 | 25 | 23 | 25 | 29 | 28 | 29 | 35 |
| -Year | | 1987 | 1987 | 1987 | 1987 | 1987 | 1982 | 1984 | 1988 | 1987 | 1983 | 1987 | 1989 | JAN 1987 |
| Peak Gust | | | | | | | | | | | | | | |
| -Direction (!!) | 6 | N | W | NE | N | N | NE | SE | SE | NE | SE | S | NW | W |
| -Speed (mph) | 6 | 47 | 55 | 40 | 40 | 41 | 32 | 36 | 35 | 35 | 33 | 36 | 45 | 55 |
| -Date | | 1988 | 1986 | 1989 | 1989 | 1987 | 1987 | 1986 | 1988 | 1987 | 1988 | 1988 | 1989 | FEB 1986 |

**See Reference Notes to this table on the following page.**

## PRECIPITATION (inches) — HILO, HAWAII

**TABLE 2**

| YEAR | JAN | FEB | MAR | APR | MAY | JUNE | JULY | AUG | SEP | OCT | NOV | DEC | ANNUAL |
|---|---|---|---|---|---|---|---|---|---|---|---|---|---|
| 1961 | 2.34 | 20.50 | 5.75 | 5.52 | 8.12 | 5.78 | 5.47 | 7.63 | 6.76 | 22.95 | 12.84 | 16.04 | 119.70 |
| 1962 | 2.51 | 5.31 | 10.88 | 2.93 | 13.58 | 3.25 | 8.01 | 4.15 | 9.49 | 2.40 | 6.63 | 2.31 | 71.45 |
| 1963 | 1.14 | 1.70 | 15.85 | 12.60 | 10.91 | 12.40 | 7.66 | 7.33 | 12.62 | 11.56 | 23.39 | 9.65 | 166.44 |
| 1964 | 14.65 | 18.22 | 19.58 | 11.03 | 25.01 | 7.01 | 6.39 | 4.79 | 5.72 | 5.80 | 19.18 | 14.94 | 127.29 |
| 1965 | 9.28 | 3.71 | 8.33 | 18.49 | 21.05 | 8.85 | 7.15 |  |  |  |  |  |  |
| 1966 | 12.56 | 7.63 | 5.59 | 5.24 | 5.04 | 7.49 | 13.26 | 7.22 | 8.37 | 15.69 | 20.83 | 15.09 | 124.01 |
| 1967 | 8.04 | 10.35 | 9.46 | 21.26 | 9.84 | 6.26 | 14.03 | 19.55 | 6.78 | 10.08 | 21.25 | 17.10 | 154.00 |
| 1968 | 4.77 | 11.46 | 10.21 | 29.68 | 2.71 | 8.72 | 7.43 | 9.62 | 8.53 | 5.97 | 10.22 | 24.82 | 134.14 |
| 1969 | 19.66 | 43.66 | 30.64 | 14.57 | 7.83 | 2.76 | 11.75 | 17.50 | 7.24 | 3.19 | 6.33 | 8.10 | 173.23 |
| 1970 | 2.76 | 2.56 | 4.89 | 28.60 | 20.26 | 5.60 | 12.27 | 20.53 | 5.61 | 8.44 | 7.21 | 35.25 | 153.98 |
| 1971 | 13.47 | 5.31 | 12.04 | 27.82 | 6.49 | 2.79 | 4.13 | 2.66 | 8.63 | 7.28 | 17.88 | 32.19 | 140.69 |
| 1972 | 10.96 | 10.13 | 0.88 | 17.79 | 4.71 | 4.58 | 9.07 | 8.77 | 5.20 | 9.52 | 13.23 | 4.01 | 98.85 |
| 1973 | 3.45 | 5.51 | 18.84 | 7.34 | 8.34 | 3.69 | 4.40 | 3.54 | 8.07 | 9.72 | 26.88 | 8.19 | 107.97 |
| 1974 | 5.88 | 7.57 | 13.47 | 19.11 | 8.07 | 4.76 | 7.81 | 4.25 | 1.59 | 6.65 | 14.56 | 19.20 | 112.92 |
| 1975 | 19.62 | 9.28 | 10.40 | 10.23 | 3.01 | 4.20 | 3.83 | 8.13 | 2.73 | 8.88 | 11.15 | 8.47 | 99.93 |
| 1976 | 15.62 | 11.63 | 25.00 | 11.58 | 6.01 | 2.97 | 5.46 | 5.13 | 5.31 | 11.35 | 7.24 | 7.37 | 114.67 |
| 1977 | 1.22 | 9.56 | 15.49 | 10.90 | 10.86 | 2.46 | 6.36 | 7.60 | 4.19 | 10.30 | 8.78 | 2.66 | 90.38 |
| 1978 | 5.41 | 4.26 | 12.95 | 6.53 | 9.64 | 10.99 | 11.19 | 13.53 | 5.44 | 10.12 | 20.21 | 8.82 | 119.09 |
| 1979 | 32.24 | 45.55 | 5.32 | 9.90 | 4.10 | 10.45 | 6.54 | 7.04 | 3.64 | 5.03 | 21.56 | 7.40 | 158.77 |
| 1980 | 0.91 | 4.14 | 49.93 | 11.01 | 5.88 | 9.66 | 9.17 | 8.24 | 13.70 | 7.69 | 7.13 | 0.28 | 127.74 |
| 1981 | 1.51 | 4.95 | 5.66 | 4.63 | 4.16 | 2.43 | 4.32 | 8.97 | 12.79 | 10.23 | 11.73 | 18.53 | 89.91 |
| 1982 | 13.58 | 1.35 | 48.50 | 12.00 | 6.89 | 6.03 | 28.59 | 25.45 | 9.92 | 6.53 | 4.74 | 6.78 | 170.36 |
| 1983 | 0.90 | 0.83 | 1.98 | 10.31 | 9.60 | 3.94 | 7.21 | 7.48 | 12.08 | 8.06 | 2.33 | 3.37 | 68.09 |
| 1984 | 10.76 | 10.06 | 3.37 | 12.08 | 6.59 | 4.28 | 6.63 | 9.36 | 4.05 | 2.52 | 18.38 | 12.00 | 100.08 |
| 1985 | 2.25 | 16.14 | 21.28 | 10.61 | 17.04 | 1.80 | 9.86 | 6.71 | 11.78 | 8.19 | 4.71 | 2.59 | 112.96 |
| 1986 | 4.95 | 0.58 | 15.37 | 43.24 | 8.61 | 9.11 | 11.17 | 10.64 | 14.36 | 11.53 | 35.72 | 5.75 | 171.03 |
| 1987 | 9.02 | 5.06 | 4.79 | 9.24 | 15.65 | 12.91 | 18.26 | 3.69 | 11.56 | 14.21 | 15.83 | 22.19 | 142.41 |
| 1988 | 10.31 | 9.95 | 13.09 | 12.90 | 7.77 | 5.11 | 16.56 | 11.30 | 8.50 | 25.74 | 13.46 |  | 140.19 |
| 1989 | 27.46 | 6.54 | 7.33 | 37.19 | 19.80 | 7.03 | 22.93 | 8.82 | 9.73 | 13.16 | 1.01 | 5.71 | 166.71 |
| 1990 | 29.13 | 15.24 | 10.80 | 4.02 | 8.13 | 10.04 | 10.78 | 7.80 | 18.47 | 20.96 | 45.75 | 30.10 | 211.22 |
| Record Mean | 10.06 | 11.76 | 13.56 | 13.56 | 9.32 | 6.27 | 9.70 | 9.90 | 7.74 | 10.03 | 14.83 | 13.87 | 130.59 |

## AVERAGE TEMPERATURE (deg. F) — HILO, HAWAII

**TABLE 3**

| YEAR | JAN | FEB | MAR | APR | MAY | JUNE | JULY | AUG | SEP | OCT | NOV | DEC | ANNUAL |
|---|---|---|---|---|---|---|---|---|---|---|---|---|---|
| 1961 | 71.7 | 71.7 | 71.9 | 72.5 | 73.7 | 74.9 | 75.2 | 76.1 | 75.4 | 75.6 | 73.4 | 70.7 | 73.6 |
| 1962 | 72.1 | 70.7 | 70.7 | 73.2 | 73.0 | 74.3 | 74.3 | 75.6 | 74.6 | 75.0 | 72.6 | 70.8 | 73.0 |
| 1963 | 71.1 | 72.9 | 72.0 | 73.6 | 73.3 | 74.5 | 75.4 | 75.7 | 76.0 | 73.7 | 72.7 | 73.2 | 73.9 |
| 1964 | 72.1 | 70.2 | 70.8 | 71.7 | 72.0 | 75.0 | 75.2 | 75.4 | 76.8 | 75.4 | 73.7 | 69.9 | 73.1 |
| 1965 | 71.7 | 68.4 | 69.7 | 72.4 | 74.5 | 74.1 | 75.2 | 75.8 | 76.8 | 75.4 | 74.3 |  | 74.3 |
| 1966 | 69.7 | 69.9 | 71.6 | 71.8 | 75.0 | 75.1 | 76.6 | 77.1 | 77.0 | 75.4 | 73.3 |  | 75.6 |
| 1967 | 71.9 | 73.9 | 74.1 | 74.3 | 77.1 | 77.5 | 77.8 | 77.1 | 77.2 | 75.4 | 73.7 |  | 75.5 |
| 1968 | 72.9 | 74.9 | 74.5 | 73.8 | 75.7 | 76.6 | 76.8 | 76.5 | 76.8 | 75.0 | 71.5 |  | 73.8 |
| 1969 | 71.4 | 72.2 | 72.5 | 72.8 | 74.5 | 76.2 | 75.8 | 76.2 | 75.0 | 74.5 | 72.7 |  | 73.3 |
| 1970 | 72.0 | 71.1 | 71.1 | 72.4 | 73.7 | 73.7 | 74.2 | 74.9 | 74.8 | 75.3 | 70.9 |  | 73.4 |
| 1971 | 71.3 | 71.9 | 69.4 | 70.9 | 72.2 | 75.0 | 76.6 | 76.6 | 76.6 | 75.4 | 73.8 | 70.9 | 73.4 |
| 1972 | 70.1 | 70.7 | 73.8 | 72.7 | 73.0 | 75.3 | 75.4 | 76.5 | 76.4 | 76.0 | 73.3 | 71.4 | 73.7 |
| 1973 | 72.2 | 71.1 | 72.5 | 72.2 | 72.9 | 74.6 | 75.7 | 76.3 | 76.3 | 75.8 | 75.4 | 73.8 | 74.1 |
| 1974 | 74.5 | 72.6 | 73.1 | 73.5 | 73.8 | 75.3 | 76.1 | 76.9 | 77.3 | 76.9 | 73.6 | 72.3 | 74.6 |
| 1975 | 71.0 | 71.9 | 71.2 | 72.4 | 73.1 | 74.4 | 74.8 | 75.7 | 75.5 | 74.7 | 73.5 | 72.2 | 73.4 |
| 1976 | 71.3 | 71.2 | 71.6 | 72.1 | 73.0 | 73.6 | 74.5 | 76.2 | 76.9 | 76.2 | 75.2 | 73.2 | 73.7 |
| 1977 | 73.9 | 74.0 | 73.3 | 74.2 | 74.7 | 76.2 | 77.1 | 78.1 | 77.5 | 76.9 | 75.2 | 73.7 | 75.4 |
| 1978 | 71.7 | 72.5 | 73.2 | 74.2 | 76.2 | 76.5 | 77.1 | 76.8 | 76.2 | 75.5 | 74.1 | 71.1 | 74.6 |
| 1979 | 69.8 | 70.4 | 71.5 | 73.8 | 73.8 | 74.2 | 74.6 | 75.6 | 76.5 | 76.1 | 73.0 | 72.8 | 73.5 |
| 1980 | 71.6 | 72.6 | 72.3 | 74.5 | 77.3 | 77.6 | 77.8 | 75.0 | 75.7 | 74.8 | 73.8 | 74.2 | 74.8 |
| 1981 | 73.5 | 72.7 | 71.6 | 72.8 | 74.2 | 76.0 | 76.1 | 76.1 | 76.2 | 74.6 | 73.9 | 72.0 | 74.1 |
| 1982 | 71.9 | 71.8 | 70.3 | 71.2 | 72.9 | 76.3 | 76.7 | 76.9 | 76.1 | 74.9 | 74.6 | 71.8 | 73.8 |
| 1983 | 71.4 | 71.9 | 72.5 | 71.9 | 72.6 | 74.3 | 74.8 | 75.2 | 74.9 | 74.1 | 73.8 | 72.9 | 73.3 |
| 1984 | 72.4 | 71.5 | 73.8 | 73.0 | 74.0 | 74.7 | 75.2 | 75.3 | 75.4 | 76.5 | 73.9 | 71.1 | 73.9 |
| 1985 | 69.8 | 70.5 | 69.4 | 69.8 | 71.4 | 74.4 | 75.4 | 75.7 | 75.7 | 74.3 | 73.0 | 71.6 | 72.6 |
| 1986 | 71.1 | 73.6 | 74.7 | 73.6 | 75.4 | 76.6 | 77.8 | 78.5 | 77.9 | 76.4 | 75.1 | 72.8 | 75.3 |
| 1987 | 71.8 | 70.7 | 71.6 | 72.2 | 72.5 | 75.4 | 76.7 | 77.9 | 77.8 | 76.6 | 74.7 | 73.1 | 74.3 |
| 1988 | 71.9 | 72.2 | 72.2 | 72.6 | 74.2 | 75.7 | 77.7 | 76.0 | 76.6 | 77.9 | 74.9 | 74.6 | 73.3 |
| 1989 | 72.2 | 71.4 | 72.4 | 71.1 | 72.7 | 74.7 | 75.2 | 75.0 | 74.6 | 75.6 | 73.6 | 71.3 | 73.3 |
| 1990 | 72.1 | 70.4 | 71.2 | 73.5 | 74.1 | 74.7 | 76.0 | 77.0 | 77.2 | 76.2 | 75.7 | 72.5 | 74.2 |
| Record Mean | 71.3 | 71.2 | 71.5 | 72.3 | 73.4 | 74.8 | 75.5 | 75.9 | 75.8 | 75.3 | 73.7 | 71.9 | 73.6 |
| Max | 79.3 | 79.2 | 79.0 | 79.4 | 80.7 | 82.3 | 82.6 | 83.2 | 83.4 | 82.8 | 80.9 | 79.4 | 81.0 |
| Min | 63.3 | 63.2 | 63.9 | 65.1 | 66.1 | 67.3 | 68.3 | 68.7 | 68.2 | 67.7 | 66.4 | 64.4 | 66.1 |

## REFERENCE NOTES FOR TABLES 1, 2, 3 and 6          (HILO, HI)

### GENERAL

T - TRACE AMOUNT
BLANK ENTRIES DENOTE MISSING/UNREPORTED DATA.
# INDICATES A STATION OR INSTRUMENT RELOCATION.

### SPECIFIC

**TABLE 1**

(a) - LENGTH OF RECORD IN YEARS. ALTHOUGH INDIVIDUAL MONTHS MAY BE MISSING.
* LESS THAN .05

NORMALS — BASED ON THE 1951-1980 RECORD PERIOD.
EXTREMES — DATES ARE THE MOST RECENT OCCURRENCE.
WIND DIR. — NUMERALS SHOW TENS OF DEGREES CLOCKWISE FROM TRUE NORTH. "00" INDICATES CALM.
RESULTANT WIND DIRECTIONS ARE GIVEN TO WHOLE DEGREES.

**TABLE 3**
MAX AND MIN ARE LONG-TERM MEAN DAILY MAXIMUM AND MEAN DAILY MINIMUM TEMPERATURES.

### EXCEPTIONS

**TABLES 2, 3, and 6**

RECORD MEANS ARE THROUGH THE CURRENT YEAR, BEGINNING IN     1947 FOR TEMPERATURE
1943 FOR PRECIPITATION

**TABLE 4**  HEATING DEGREE DAYS Base 65 deg. F     HILO, HAWAII

| SEASON | JULY | AUG | SEP | OCT | NOV | DEC | JAN | FEB | MAR | APR | MAY | JUNE | TOTAL |
|---|---|---|---|---|---|---|---|---|---|---|---|---|---|
| 1983-84 | 0 | 0 | 0 | 0 | 0 | 0 | 0 | 0 | 0 | 0 | 0 | 0 | 0 |
| 1984-85 | 0 | 0 | 0 | 0 | 0 | 0 | 0 | 0 | 0 | 0 | 0 | 0 | 0 |
| 1985-86 | 0 | 0 | 0 | 0 | 0 | 0 | 0 | 0 | 0 | 0 | 0 | 0 | 0 |
| 1986-87 | 0 | 0 | 0 | 0 | 0 | 0 | 0 | 0 | 0 | 0 | 0 | 0 | 0 |
| 1987-88 | 0 | 0 | 0 | 0 | 0 | 0 | 0 | 0 | 0 | 0 | 0 | 0 | 0 |
| 1988-89 | 0 | 0 | 0 | 0 | 0 | 0 | 0 | 0 | 0 | 0 | 0 | 0 | 0 |
| 1989-90 | 0 | 0 | 0 | 0 | 0 | 0 | 0 | 0 | 0 | 0 | 0 | 0 | 0 |
| 1990-91 | 0 | 0 | 0 | 0 | 0 | 0 | | | | | | | |

**TABLE 5**  COOLING DEGREE DAYS Base 65 deg. F     HILO, HAWAII

| YEAR | JAN | FEB | MAR | APR | MAY | JUNE | JULY | AUG | SEP | OCT | NOV | DEC | TOTAL |
|---|---|---|---|---|---|---|---|---|---|---|---|---|---|
| 1969 | 207 | 209 | 240 | 239 | 298 | 341 | 344 | 351 | 308 | 300 | 253 | 208 | 3298 |
| 1970 | 223 | 173 | 195 | 229 | 273 | 270 | 290 | 313 | 303 | 325 | 276 | 246 | 3116 |
| 1971 | 203 | 201 | 142 | 185 | 232 | 306 | 366 | 367 | 354 | 328 | 271 | 188 | 3143 |
| 1972 | 163 | 171 | 281 | 236 | 256 | 316 | 330 | 365 | 349 | 348 | 256 | 207 | 3278 |
| 1973 | 233 | 180 | 239 | 222 | 253 | 294 | 341 | 358 | 345 | 340 | 321 | 278 | 3404 |
| 1974 | 299 | 219 | 261 | 263 | 276 | 315 | 351 | 375 | 375 | 376 | 262 | 235 | 3607 |
| 1975 | 192 | 201 | 197 | 232 | 257 | 288 | 311 | 339 | 323 | 309 | 262 | 233 | 3144 |
| 1976 | 201 | 186 | 214 | 222 | 255 | 268 | 302 | 355 | 364 | 357 | 291 | 261 | 3276 |
| 1977 | 280 | 260 | 264 | 281 | 307 | 343 | 379 | 415 | 382 | 374 | 312 | 274 | 3871 |
| 1978 | 216 | 215 | 263 | 283 | 353 | 351 | 383 | 375 | 341 | 332 | 279 | 195 | 3586 |
| 1979 | 155 | 160 | 210 | 271 | 278 | 280 | 302 | 338 | 351 | 350 | 246 | 248 | 3189 |
| 1980 | 213 | 227 | 234 | 293 | 390 | 385 | 405 | 316 | 328 | 313 | 269 | 295 | 3668 |
| 1981 | 271 | 220 | 210 | 242 | 293 | 338 | 350 | 348 | 345 | 302 | 274 | 225 | 3418 |
| 1982 | 220 | 196 | 170 | 194 | 252 | 348 | 369 | 379 | 340 | 317 | 293 | 219 | 3297 |
| 1983 | 207 | 200 | 239 | 214 | 240 | 287 | 313 | 324 | 303 | 288 | 272 | 250 | 3137 |
| 1984 | 236 | 194 | 282 | 247 | 284 | 298 | 324 | 326 | 320 | 363 | 261 | 195 | 3330 |
| 1985 | 154 | 161 | 142 | 152 | 204 | 290 | 329 | 339 | 329 | 294 | 248 | 211 | 2853 |
| 1986 | 196 | 246 | 308 | 264 | 329 | 356 | 404 | 423 | 396 | 363 | 309 | 250 | 3844 |
| 1987 | 218 | 163 | 212 | 226 | 241 | 319 | 369 | 407 | 389 | 365 | 299 | 259 | 3467 |
| 1988 | 221 | 216 | 233 | 238 | 293 | 298 | 338 | 349 | 353 | 405 | 345 | 315 | 3604 |
| 1989 | 227 | 188 | 238 | 189 | 248 | 297 | 327 | 315 | 294 | 335 | 264 | 202 | 3124 |
| 1990 | 227 | 157 | 200 | 260 | 290 | 308 | 349 | 379 | 376 | 353 | 317 | 237 | 3453 |

**TABLE 6**  SNOWFALL (inches)     HILO, HAWAII

| SEASON | JULY | AUG | SEP | OCT | NOV | DEC | JAN | FEB | MAR | APR | MAY | JUNE | TOTAL |
|---|---|---|---|---|---|---|---|---|---|---|---|---|---|
| 1971-72 | 0.0 | 0.0 | 0.0 | 0.0 | 0.0 | 0.0 | 0.0 | 0.0 | 0.0 | 0.0 | 0.0 | 0.0 | 0.0 |
| 1972-73 | 0.0 | 0.0 | 0.0 | 0.0 | 0.0 | 0.0 | 0.0 | 0.0 | 0.0 | 0.0 | 0.0 | 0.0 | 0.0 |
| 1973-74 | 0.0 | 0.0 | 0.0 | 0.0 | 0.0 | 0.0 | 0.0 | 0.0 | 0.0 | 0.0 | 0.0 | 0.0 | 0.0 |
| 1974-75 | 0.0 | 0.0 | 0.0 | 0.0 | 0.0 | 0.0 | 0.0 | 0.0 | 0.0 | 0.0 | 0.0 | 0.0 | 0.0 |
| 1975-76 | 0.0 | 0.0 | 0.0 | 0.0 | 0.0 | 0.0 | 0.0 | 0.0 | 0.0 | 0.0 | 0.0 | 0.0 | 0.0 |
| 1976-77 | 0.0 | 0.0 | 0.0 | 0.0 | 0.0 | 0.0 | 0.0 | 0.0 | 0.0 | 0.0 | 0.0 | 0.0 | 0.0 |
| 1977-78 | 0.0 | 0.0 | 0.0 | 0.0 | 0.0 | 0.0 | 0.0 | 0.0 | 0.0 | 0.0 | 0.0 | 0.0 | 0.0 |
| 1978-79 | 0.0 | 0.0 | 0.0 | 0.0 | 0.0 | 0.0 | 0.0 | 0.0 | 0.0 | 0.0 | 0.0 | 0.0 | 0.0 |
| 1979-80 | 0.0 | 0.0 | 0.0 | 0.0 | 0.0 | 0.0 | 0.0 | 0.0 | 0.0 | 0.0 | 0.0 | 0.0 | 0.0 |
| 1980-81 | 0.0 | 0.0 | 0.0 | 0.0 | 0.0 | 0.0 | 0.0 | 0.0 | 0.0 | 0.0 | 0.0 | 0.0 | 0.0 |
| 1981-82 | 0.0 | 0.0 | 0.0 | 0.0 | 0.0 | 0.0 | 0.0 | 0.0 | 0.0 | 0.0 | 0.0 | 0.0 | 0.0 |
| 1982-83 | 0.0 | 0.0 | 0.0 | 0.0 | 0.0 | 0.0 | 0.0 | 0.0 | 0.0 | 0.0 | 0.0 | 0.0 | 0.0 |
| 1983-84 | 0.0 | 0.0 | 0.0 | 0.0 | 0.0 | 0.0 | 0.0 | 0.0 | 0.0 | 0.0 | 0.0 | 0.0 | 0.0 |
| 1984-85 | 0.0 | 0.0 | 0.0 | 0.0 | 0.0 | 0.0 | 0.0 | 0.0 | 0.0 | 0.0 | 0.0 | 0.0 | 0.0 |
| 1985-86 | 0.0 | 0.0 | 0.0 | 0.0 | 0.0 | 0.0 | 0.0 | 0.0 | 0.0 | 0.0 | 0.0 | 0.0 | 0.0 |
| 1986-87 | 0.0 | 0.0 | 0.0 | 0.0 | 0.0 | 0.0 | 0.0 | 0.0 | 0.0 | 0.0 | 0.0 | 0.0 | 0.0 |
| 1987-88 | 0.0 | 0.0 | 0.0 | 0.0 | 0.0 | 0.0 | 0.0 | 0.0 | 0.0 | 0.0 | 0.0 | 0.0 | 0.0 |
| 1988-89 | 0.0 | 0.0 | 0.0 | 0.0 | 0.0 | 0.0 | 0.0 | 0.0 | 0.0 | 0.0 | 0.0 | 0.0 | 0.0 |
| 1989-90 | 0.0 | 0.0 | 0.0 | 0.0 | 0.0 | 0.0 | 0.0 | 0.0 | 0.0 | 0.0 | 0.0 | 0.0 | 0.0 |
| 1990-91 | 0.0 | 0.0 | 0.0 | 0.0 | 0.0 | 0.0 | | | | | | | |
| Record Mean | 0.0 | 0.0 | 0.0 | 0.0 | 0.0 | 0.0 | 0.0 | 0.0 | 0.0 | 0.0 | 0.0 | 0.0 | 0.0 |

**See Reference Notes, relative to all above tables, on preceding page.**

Oahu, on which Honolulu is located, is the third largest of the Hawaiian Islands. The Koolau Range, at an average elevation of 2,000 feet parallels the northeastern coast. The Waianae Mountains, somewhat higher in elevation, parallel the west coast. Honolulu Airport, the business and Waikiki districts, and a number of the residential areas of Honolulu lie along the southern coastal plain.

The climate of Hawaii is unusually pleasant for the tropics. Its outstanding features are the persistence of the trade winds, the remarkable variability in rainfall over short distances, the sunniness of the leeward lowlands in contrast to the persistent cloudiness over nearby mountain crests, the equable temperature, and the general infrequency of severe storms.

The prevailing wind throughout the year is the northeasterly trade wind, although its average frequency varies from more than 90 percent during the summer to only 50 percent in January.

Heavy mountain rainfall sustains extensive irrigation of cane fields and the water supply for Honolulu. Oahu is driest along the coast west of the Waianaes where rainfall drops to about 20 inches a year. Daytime showers, usually light, often occur while the sun continues to shine, a phenomenon referred to locally as liquid sunshine.

The moderate temperature range is associated with the small seasonal variation in the energy received from the sun and the tempering effect of the surrounding ocean. Honolulu Airport has recorded as high as the lower 90s and as low as the lower 50s.

Because of the trade winds, even the warmest months are usually comfortable. But when the trades diminish or give way to southerly winds, a situation known locally as kona weather, or kona storms when stormy, the humidity may become oppressively high.

Intense rains of the October to April winter season sometimes cause serious, flash flooding. Thunderstorms are infrequent and usually mild and hail seldom occurs. Infrequently, a small tornado or a waterspout may do some damage. Only a few tropical cyclones have struck Hawaii, although others have come near enough for their outlying winds, waves, clouds, and rain to affect the Islands.

## TABLE 1 — NORMALS, MEANS AND EXTREMES

HONOLULU, HAWAII

LATITUDE: 21°20'N  LONGITUDE: 157°56'W  ELEVATION: FT. GRND 7 BARO 18  TIME ZONE: BERING  WBAN: 22521

| | (a) | JAN | FEB | MAR | APR | MAY | JUNE | JULY | AUG | SEP | OCT | NOV | DEC | YEAR |
|---|---|---|---|---|---|---|---|---|---|---|---|---|---|---|
| **TEMPERATURE °F:** | | | | | | | | | | | | | | |
| Normals | | | | | | | | | | | | | | |
| -Daily Maximum | | 79.9 | 80.4 | 81.4 | 82.7 | 84.8 | 86.2 | 87.1 | 88.3 | 88.2 | 86.7 | 83.9 | 81.4 | 84.2 |
| -Daily Minimum | | 65.3 | 65.3 | 67.3 | 68.7 | 70.2 | 71.9 | 73.1 | 73.6 | 72.9 | 72.2 | 69.2 | 66.5 | 69.7 |
| -Monthly | | 72.6 | 72.9 | 74.4 | 75.7 | 77.5 | 79.1 | 80.1 | 81.0 | 80.6 | 79.5 | 76.6 | 74.0 | 77.0 |
| Extremes | | | | | | | | | | | | | | |
| -Record Highest | 20 | 87 | 88 | 88 | 89 | 93 | 92 | 92 | 93 | 94 | 94 | 93 | 89 | 94 |
| -Year | | 1987 | 1984 | 1987 | 1988 | 1988 | 1987 | 1987 | 1987 | 1988 | 1984 | 1986 | 1983 | SEP 1988 |
| -Record Lowest | 20 | 53 | 53 | 55 | 57 | 60 | 65 | 67 | 67 | 66 | 64 | 58 | 54 | 53 |
| -Year | | 1972 | 1983 | 1976 | 1985 | 1989 | 1982 | 1981 | 1984 | 1985 | 1981 | 1972 | 1962 | FEB 1983 |
| **NORMAL DEGREE DAYS:** | | | | | | | | | | | | | | |
| Heating (base 65°F) | | 0 | 0 | 0 | 0 | 0 | 0 | 0 | 0 | 0 | 0 | 0 | 0 | 0 |
| Cooling (base 65°F) | | 236 | 221 | 291 | 321 | 388 | 423 | 468 | 496 | 468 | 450 | 348 | 279 | 4389 |
| **% OF POSSIBLE SUNSHINE** | 37 | 63 | 65 | 70 | 67 | 69 | 71 | 74 | 75 | 76 | 68 | 61 | 59 | 68 |
| **MEAN SKY COVER (tenths)** | | | | | | | | | | | | | | |
| Sunrise - Sunset | 43 | 5.4 | 5.6 | 5.8 | 6.2 | 6.0 | 5.6 | 5.3 | 5.3 | 5.2 | 5.7 | 5.7 | 5.5 | 5.6 |
| **MEAN NUMBER OF DAYS:** | | | | | | | | | | | | | | |
| Sunrise to Sunset | | | | | | | | | | | | | | |
| -Clear | 40 | 9.4 | 7.9 | 7.2 | 5.3 | 6.3 | 5.9 | 7.5 | 7.9 | 7.8 | 7.3 | 7.0 | 8.5 | 88.0 |
| -Partly Cloudy | 40 | 13.1 | 12.5 | 14.2 | 14.3 | 15.2 | 17.4 | 18.2 | 17.0 | 16.2 | 15.2 | 13.9 | 13.4 | 180.5 |
| -Cloudy | 40 | 8.6 | 7.9 | 9.4 | 10.5 | 9.5 | 6.7 | 5.3 | 6.2 | 5.9 | 8.4 | 9.2 | 9.1 | 96.7 |
| Precipitation | | | | | | | | | | | | | | |
| .01 inches or more | 40 | 9.8 | 9.3 | 8.9 | 9.1 | 7.3 | 5.8 | 7.4 | 6.4 | 7.0 | 8.8 | 9.2 | 10.1 | 99.0 |
| Snow,Ice pellets | | | | | | | | | | | | | | |
| 1.0 inches or more | 40 | 0.0 | 0.0 | 0.0 | 0.0 | 0.0 | 0.0 | 0.0 | 0.0 | 0.0 | 0.0 | 0.0 | 0.0 | 0.0 |
| Thunderstorms | 40 | 0.8 | 1.1 | 0.9 | 0.6 | 0.3 | 0.1 | 0.2 | 0.1 | 0.5 | 0.8 | 0.9 | 0.8 | 6.9 |
| Heavy Fog Visibility | | | | | | | | | | | | | | |
| 1/4 mile or less | 40 | 0.0 | 0.0 | 0.0 | 0.0 | 0.0 | 0.0 | 0.0 | 0.0 | 0.0 | 0.0 | 0.0 | 0.0 | 0.0 |
| Temperature °F | | | | | | | | | | | | | | |
| -Maximum | | | | | | | | | | | | | | |
| 90° and above | 20 | 0.0 | 0.0 | 0.0 | 0.0 | 0.3 | 1.8 | 4.6 | 10.3 | 9.9 | 4.0 | 0.3 | 0.0 | 31.0 |
| 32° and below | 20 | 0.0 | 0.0 | 0.0 | 0.0 | 0.0 | 0.0 | 0.0 | 0.0 | 0.0 | 0.0 | 0.0 | 0.0 | 0.0 |
| -Minimum | | | | | | | | | | | | | | |
| 32° and below | 20 | 0.0 | 0.0 | 0.0 | 0.0 | 0.0 | 0.0 | 0.0 | 0.0 | 0.0 | 0.0 | 0.0 | 0.0 | 0.0 |
| 0° and below | 20 | 0.0 | 0.0 | 0.0 | 0.0 | 0.0 | 0.0 | 0.0 | 0.0 | 0.0 | 0.0 | 0.0 | 0.0 | 0.0 |
| **AVG. STATION PRESS. (mb)** | 17 | 1015.0 | 1015.5 | 1017.2 | 1017.2 | 1016.9 | 1016.7 | 1016.1 | 1015.3 | 1014.7 | 1014.9 | 1015.0 | 1015.2 | 1015.8 |
| **RELATIVE HUMIDITY (%)** | | | | | | | | | | | | | | |
| Hour 02 | 20 | 82 | 79 | 77 | 75 | 75 | 74 | 73 | 74 | 74 | 75 | 78 | 81 | 76 |
| Hour 18 | 20 | 81 | 79 | 73 | 70 | 67 | 66 | 67 | 68 | 68 | 70 | 75 | 79 | 72 |
| Hour 14 (Local Time) | 20 | 62 | 59 | 57 | 56 | 54 | 52 | 51 | 53 | 52 | 55 | 58 | 61 | 56 |
| Hour 20 | 20 | 74 | 71 | 71 | 70 | 69 | 68 | 68 | 69 | 68 | 70 | 72 | 74 | 70 |
| **PRECIPITATION (inches):** | | | | | | | | | | | | | | |
| Water Equivalent | | | | | | | | | | | | | | |
| -Normal | | 3.79 | 2.72 | 3.48 | 1.49 | 1.21 | 0.49 | 0.54 | 0.60 | 0.62 | 1.88 | 3.22 | 3.43 | 23.47 |
| -Maximum Monthly | 43 | 14.74 | 13.68 | 20.79 | 8.92 | 7.23 | 2.46 | 2.33 | 3.08 | 2.74 | 11.15 | 14.72 | 17.29 | 20.79 |
| -Year | | 1949 | 1955 | 1951 | 1963 | 1965 | 1971 | 1989 | 1959 | 1947 | 1978 | 1965 | 1987 | MAR 1951 |
| -Minimum Monthly | 43 | 0.18 | 0.06 | 0.01 | 0.01 | 0.05 | T | 0.03 | T | 0.05 | 0.11 | 0.03 | 0.06 | T |
| -Year | | 1986 | 1983 | 1957 | 1960 | 1949 | 1959 | 1950 | 1974 | 1977 | 1957 | 1962 | 1976 | AUG 1974 |
| -Maximum in 24 hrs | 40 | 6.72 | 6.88 | 17.07 | 4.21 | 3.44 | 2.28 | 2.20 | 2.35 | 1.40 | 7.57 | 9.15 | 8.25 | 17.07 |
| -Year | | 1963 | 1955 | 1958 | 1972 | 1965 | 1967 | 1989 | 1959 | 1963 | 1978 | 1954 | 1987 | MAR 1958 |
| Snow,Ice pellets | | | | | | | | | | | | | | |
| -Maximum Monthly | | 0.0 | 0.0 | 0.0 | 0.0 | 0.0 | 0.0 | 0.0 | 0.0 | 0.0 | 0.0 | 0.0 | 0.0 | |
| -Year | | | | | | | | | | | | | | |
| -Maximum in 24 hrs | 43 | 0.0 | 0.0 | 0.0 | 0.0 | 0.0 | 0.0 | 0.0 | 0.0 | 0.0 | 0.0 | 0.0 | 0.0 | |
| -Year | | | | | | | | | | | | | | |
| **WIND:** | | | | | | | | | | | | | | |
| Mean Speed (mph) | 40 | 9.6 | 10.3 | 11.4 | 12.0 | 11.9 | 12.7 | 13.3 | 12.9 | 11.4 | 10.6 | 10.8 | 10.4 | 11.4 |
| Prevailing Direction | | | | | | | | | | | | | | |
| through 1963 | | ENE | ENE | ENE | ENE | ENE | ENE | ENE | ENE | ENE | ENE | ENE | ENE | ENE |
| Fastest Obs. 1 Min. | | | | | | | | | | | | | | |
| -Direction (!!!) | 9 | 07 | 08 | 08 | 06 | 13 | 05 | 07 | 04 | 07 | 07 | 20 | 31 | 20 |
| -Speed (MPH) | 9 | 32 | 30 | 30 | 31 | 30 | 26 | 28 | 28 | 26 | 25 | 46 | 30 | 46 |
| -Year | | 1982 | 1981 | 1985 | 1980 | 1985 | 1981 | 1980 | 1982 | 1980 | 1981 | 1982 | 1989 | NOV 1982 |
| Peak Gust | | | | | | | | | | | | | | |
| -Direction (!!!) | 6 | NE | W | NE | NE | E | NE | NE | E | NE | NE | NE | NW | NE |
| -Speed (mph) | 6 | 41 | 39 | 46 | 41 | 39 | 35 | 40 | 35 | 32 | 32 | 40 | 41 | 46 |
| -Date | | 1987 | 1986 | 1985 | 1986 | 1985 | 1986 | 1984 | 1984 | 1986 | 1985 | 1986 | 1989 | MAR 1985 |

**See Reference Notes to this table on the following page.**

## PRECIPITATION (inches) — HONOLULU, HAWAII

**TABLE 2**

| YEAR | JAN | FEB | MAR | APR | MAY | JUNE | JULY | AUG | SEP | OCT | NOV | DEC | ANNUAL |
|---|---|---|---|---|---|---|---|---|---|---|---|---|---|
| 1961 | 4.17 | 0.93 | 0.43 | 0.71 | 0.23 | 0.87 | 0.28 | 0.47 | 0.48 | 2.40 | 2.05 | 1.24 | 14.26 |
| 1962 | 2.20 | 2.62 | 2.10 | 1.07 | 0.32 | 0.11 | 0.13 | 0.32 | 0.66 | 0.70 | 0.03 | 3.32 | 13.58 |
| 1963 | 10.58 | 1.11 | 8.39 | 8.92 | 3.36 | 0.33 | 1.01 | 0.03 | 1.47 | 1.08 | 0.20 | 1.43 | 37.91 |
| 1964 | 2.18 | 0.52 | 5.21 | 0.88 | 0.21 | 0.08 | 1.34 | 0.46 | 0.97 | 0.34 | 2.36 | 5.57 | 20.12 |
| 1965 | 3.02 | 0.80 | 0.99 | 1.48 | 7.23 | 0.25 | 1.37 | 0.87 | 0.52 | 3.56 | 14.72 | 7.97 | 42.78 |
| 1966 | 1.39 | 3.71 | 0.39 | 0.46 | 0.41 | 0.04 | 0.43 | 0.82 | 0.16 | 2.95 | 9.44 | 2.98 | 23.18 |
| 1967 | 0.79 | 2.53 | 6.78 | 1.29 | 2.12 | 2.43 | 1.21 | 2.53 | 0.42 | 1.53 | 2.78 | 9.93 | 34.34 |
| 1968 | 8.17 | 2.91 | 2.49 | 3.14 | 1.22 | 0.24 | 0.29 | 0.10 | 1.30 | 2.13 | 5.64 | 9.63 | 37.26 |
| 1969 | 8.20 | 0.48 | 3.00 | 0.10 | 0.81 | 0.23 | 0.63 | 0.11 | 0.87 | 0.96 | 5.77 | 1.34 | 22.50 |
| 1970 | 1.81 | 0.77 | 0.07 | 0.74 | 0.21 | 0.23 | 2.01 | 0.21 | 0.39 | 1.88 | 5.94 | 1.23 | 15.49 |
| 1971 | 6.19 | 2.37 | 5.57 | 2.19 | 0.43 | 2.46 | 0.04 | 0.26 | 1.03 | 2.27 | 0.95 | 2.88 | 26.64 |
| 1972 | 5.28 | 5.00 | 2.45 | 5.15 | 0.12 | 0.79 | 0.20 | 0.46 | 0.92 | 2.39 | 0.59 | 3.59 | 26.94 |
| 1973 | 0.67 | 0.60 | 0.40 | 0.72 | 0.89 | 0.09 | 0.46 | 0.32 | 0.64 | 1.78 | 3.73 | 3.94 | 14.24 |
| 1974 | 4.21 | 1.28 | 3.49 | 4.13 | 0.82 | 1.52 | 0.44 | T | 2.08 | 2.77 | 2.69 | 0.59 | 24.02 |
| 1975 | 6.42 | 2.36 | 2.02 | 0.51 | 0.19 | 0.03 | 0.04 | 0.03 | 0.11 | 0.18 | 11.54 | 0.60 | 24.39 |
| 1976 | 1.29 | 6.08 | 2.67 | 0.71 | 0.26 | 0.18 | 0.24 | 0.17 | 0.33 | 0.45 | 0.61 | 0.06 | 12.90 |
| 1977 | 0.52 | 0.32 | 2.36 | 1.81 | 4.76 | 0.11 | 0.14 | 0.08 | 0.05 | 0.15 | 0.61 | 1.45 | 12.36 |
| 1978 | 0.34 | 0.75 | 1.37 | 2.07 | 3.39 | 1.06 | 0.20 | 0.83 | 0.28 | 11.15 | 1.55 | 2.06 | 25.05 |
| 1979 | 4.57 | 7.21 | 0.77 | 0.55 | 0.21 | 0.32 | 0.13 | 0.15 | 0.47 | 0.53 | 0.52 | 1.50 | 16.93 |
| 1980 | 8.91 | 2.26 | 3.04 | 1.13 | 0.78 | 1.76 | 0.37 | 0.36 | 0.41 | 0.30 | 0.21 | 7.37 | 26.90 |
| 1981 | 0.81 | 0.97 | 0.71 | 1.01 | 0.94 | 0.14 | 0.42 | 0.70 | 0.39 | 1.84 | 1.01 | 4.47 | 13.41 |
| 1982 | 12.82 | 2.16 | 3.73 | 1.28 | 0.13 | 0.35 | 0.20 | 1.98 | 0.52 | 7.24 | 1.32 | 3.19 | 34.92 |
| 1983 | 0.32 | 0.06 | 0.53 | 0.42 | 0.35 | 0.26 | 0.22 | 0.29 | 1.16 | 0.23 | 0.13 | 1.06 | 5.03 |
| 1984 | 0.21 | 0.60 | 1.08 | 2.41 | 0.16 | 0.08 | 0.23 | 0.04 | 1.36 | 1.89 | 3.58 | 5.44 | 17.08 |
| 1985 | 1.46 | 3.87 | 1.26 | 0.20 | 1.11 | 0.13 | 0.53 | 0.16 | 1.28 | 5.08 | 2.11 | 0.19 | 17.38 |
| 1986 | 0.18 | 1.38 | 0.17 | 0.35 | 0.81 | 0.36 | 1.54 | 0.90 | 2.00 | 1.23 | 4.23 | 0.78 | 13.93 |
| 1987 | 0.42 | 0.86 | 0.31 | 0.65 | 0.73 | 0.46 | 0.33 | 0.22 | 1.13 | 0.20 | 0.93 | 17.29 | 23.53 |
| 1988 | 3.05 | 1.31 | 0.67 | 0.50 | 1.25 | 0.04 | 0.12 | 0.34 | 0.86 | 0.23 | 1.39 | 6.71 | 16.47 |
| 1989 | 2.07 | 6.48 | 2.58 | 1.23 | 0.29 | 0.11 | 2.33 | 0.08 | 0.15 | 10.37 | 0.51 | 1.32 | 27.52 |
| 1990 | 4.32 | 4.15 | 0.86 | 0.30 | 0.30 | 0.08 | 0.49 | 0.01 | 0.98 | 0.47 | 2.96 | 4.92 | 19.84 |
| Record Mean | 3.98 | 2.59 | 2.70 | 1.38 | 0.99 | 0.40 | 0.53 | 0.58 | 0.75 | 1.98 | 2.78 | 3.63 | 22.28 |

## AVERAGE TEMPERATURE (deg. F) — HONOLULU, HAWAII

**TABLE 3**

| YEAR | JAN | FEB | MAR | APR | MAY | JUNE | JULY | AUG | SEP | OCT | NOV | DEC | ANNUAL |
|---|---|---|---|---|---|---|---|---|---|---|---|---|---|
| 1961 | 73.6 | 74.6 | 75.7 | 75.9 | 78.0 | 78.4 | 79.1 | 80.4 | 79.8 | 79.2 | 76.3 | 75.0 | 77.2 |
| #1962 | 74.6 | 72.3 | 73.2 | 76.4 | 77.2 | 78.6 | 79.2 | 80.0 | 79.1 | 77.2 | 77.5 | 72.7 | 76.5 |
| 1963 | 71.1 | 72.2 | 72.3 | 75.3 | 76.4 | 79.2 | 80.7 | 81.5 | 81.0 | 79.7 | 77.1 | 74.0 | 76.7 |
| 1964 | 75.1 | 74.7 | 74.7 | 75.7 | 76.4 | 77.9 | 79.3 | 80.4 | 80.2 | 78.3 | 76.4 | 74.9 | 77.0 |
| 1965 | 71.9 | 69.8 | 72.1 | 75.0 | 77.0 | 79.1 | 79.9 | 79.7 | 80.0 | 78.2 | 77.1 | 73.3 | 76.1 |
| 1966 | 72.6 | 72.0 | 75.1 | 75.1 | 77.1 | 80.6 | 80.8 | 82.0 | 82.4 | 80.9 | 77.2 | 74.6 | 77.6 |
| 1967 | 72.5 | 73.9 | 73.8 | 74.7 | 78.2 | 79.7 | 81.5 | 82.1 | 82.4 | 80.6 | 77.6 | 74.0 | 77.6 |
| 1968 | 73.0 | 73.4 | 74.8 | 76.7 | 78.4 | 80.4 | 81.5 | 82.9 | 82.0 | 80.6 | 78.8 | 72.7 | 77.9 |
| 1969 | 69.1 | 73.9 | 73.6 | 74.7 | 76.7 | 79.1 | 80.9 | 83.2 | 82.0 | 80.5 | 78.7 | 76.5 | 77.4 |
| #1970 | 74.2 | 73.3 | 76.2 | 78.3 | 80.4 | 81.1 | 82.2 | 83.8 | 79.0 | 78.5 | 75.8 | 74.7 | 78.2 |
| #1971 | 71.7 | 74.4 | 73.9 | 75.6 | 76.2 | 77.3 | 78.9 | 79.5 | 79.1 | 78.0 | 75.7 | 73.3 | 76.1 |
| 1972 | 70.4 | 70.6 | 72.8 | 75.0 | 77.3 | 78.9 | 80.4 | 81.1 | 80.5 | 79.3 | 76.7 | 71.6 | 76.2 |
| 1973 | 72.9 | 72.6 | 76.1 | 75.5 | 77.1 | 79.2 | 80.5 | 81.2 | 81.0 | 79.4 | 77.0 | 73.8 | 77.2 |
| 1974 | 74.5 | 74.4 | 74.0 | 77.4 | 78.2 | 79.3 | 79.9 | 81.2 | 80.0 | 79.5 | 75.7 | 75.8 | 77.5 |
| 1975 | 72.4 | 72.8 | 73.0 | 74.5 | 75.7 | 78.1 | 79.0 | 80.1 | 79.4 | 79.1 | 77.1 | 73.0 | 76.2 |
| 1976 | 73.7 | 72.0 | 76.2 | 75.1 | 77.5 | 78.2 | 79.7 | 80.8 | 80.7 | 79.1 | 75.3 | 75.3 | 76.8 |
| 1977 | 73.7 | 75.6 | 76.2 | 76.3 | 77.6 | 79.5 | 80.9 | 82.2 | 81.6 | 81.1 | 78.6 | 75.1 | 78.2 |
| 1978 | 74.2 | 73.2 | 75.7 | 76.8 | 78.2 | 78.7 | 79.0 | 80.5 | 80.5 | 77.8 | 72.4 | | 76.8 |
| 1979 | 69.9 | 72.1 | 72.8 | 74.8 | 78.0 | 80.0 | 80.9 | 80.4 | 81.1 | 81.0 | 77.4 | 75.3 | 77.0 |
| 1980 | 71.9 | 72.4 | 75.0 | 76.1 | 78.3 | 79.5 | 80.0 | 81.0 | 81.6 | 80.1 | 78.0 | 74.4 | 77.5 |
| 1981 | 73.2 | 73.6 | 74.7 | 75.9 | 77.3 | 80.6 | 79.7 | 80.1 | 80.7 | 78.3 | 76.7 | 74.0 | 77.1 |
| 1982 | 73.2 | 71.7 | 74.0 | 75.4 | 78.3 | 79.6 | 80.6 | 81.4 | 81.4 | 79.4 | 75.7 | 72.0 | 76.9 |
| 1983 | 71.9 | 71.3 | 73.5 | 74.6 | 75.7 | 78.9 | 79.7 | 82.4 | 82.3 | 81.1 | 80.1 | 75.1 | 77.2 |
| 1984 | 74.6 | 74.6 | 75.8 | 77.0 | 78.7 | 79.3 | 81.0 | 81.7 | 81.3 | 80.2 | 79.0 | 74.1 | 78.1 |
| 1985 | 71.4 | 73.9 | 74.5 | 74.5 | 76.5 | 79.2 | 81.6 | 81.9 | 81.1 | 79.8 | 75.1 | 73.3 | 76.9 |
| 1986 | 72.8 | 72.6 | 76.5 | 77.5 | 78.3 | 80.0 | 81.6 | 82.9 | 82.1 | 80.6 | 79.2 | 75.1 | 78.3 |
| 1987 | 73.4 | 71.2 | 74.0 | 76.0 | 75.7 | 80.4 | 82.1 | 82.7 | 82.9 | 81.4 | 78.8 | 75.8 | 77.9 |
| 1988 | 73.1 | 74.7 | 76.0 | 77.3 | 78.9 | 80.8 | 81.8 | 82.1 | 82.1 | 80.1 | 79.9 | 75.6 | 78.5 |
| 1989 | 74.5 | 73.6 | 75.3 | 74.5 | 78.4 | 80.9 | 81.6 | 81.4 | 81.9 | 78.6 | 76.7 | 72.9 | 77.5 |
| 1990 | 74.7 | 71.5 | 73.1 | 76.6 | 78.1 | 80.0 | 80.8 | 82.3 | 82.3 | 80.9 | 77.3 | 74.1 | 77.6 |
| Record Mean | 72.7 | 72.7 | 73.8 | 75.2 | 76.8 | 78.7 | 79.7 | 80.5 | 80.5 | 79.0 | 76.6 | 73.9 | 76.7 |
| Max | 79.7 | 79.9 | 80.7 | 81.8 | 83.5 | 85.4 | 86.3 | 87.2 | 87.3 | 85.8 | 83.2 | 80.5 | 83.5 |
| Min | 65.6 | 65.5 | 66.9 | 68.5 | 70.0 | 71.9 | 73.1 | 73.8 | 73.3 | 72.1 | 69.9 | 67.3 | 69.8 |

## REFERENCE NOTES FOR TABLES 1, 2, 3 and 6     (HONOLULU, HI)

**GENERAL**

T - TRACE AMOUNT
BLANK ENTRIES DENOTE MISSING/UNREPORTED DATA.
# INDICATES A STATION OR INSTRUMENT RELOCATION.

**SPECIFIC**

TABLE 1

(a) - LENGTH OF RECORD IN YEARS. ALTHOUGH
INDIVIDUAL MONTHS MAY BE MISSING.
* LESS THAN .05

NORMALS — BASED ON THE 1951-1980 RECORD PERIOD.
EXTREMES — DATES ARE THE MOST RECENT OCCURRENCE.
WIND DIR. — NUMERALS SHOW TENS OF DEGREES
CLOCKWISE FROM TRUE NORTH.
"00" INDICATES CALM.
RESULTANT WIND DIRECTIONS ARE GIVEN TO WHOLE DEGREES.

TABLE 3
MAX AND MIN ARE LONG-TERM MEAN DAILY MAXIMUM
AND MEAN DAILY MINIMUM TEMPERATURES.

**EXCEPTIONS**

TABLES 2, 3, and 6

RECORD MEANS ARE THROUGH THE CURRENT YEAR,
BEGINNING IN     1947 THRU 1964 AND
1970 TO DATE  FOR TEMPERATURE
1947 FOR PRECIPITATION

HEATING DEGREE DAYS Base 65 deg. F     HONOLULU, HAWAII

**TABLE 4**

| SEASON | JULY | AUG | SEP | OCT | NOV | DEC | JAN | FEB | MAR | APR | MAY | JUNE | TOTAL |
|---|---|---|---|---|---|---|---|---|---|---|---|---|---|
| 1983-84 | 0 | 0 | 0 | 0 | 0 | 0 | 0 | 0 | 0 | 0 | 0 | 0 | 0 |
| 1984-85 | 0 | 0 | 0 | 0 | 0 | 0 | 0 | 0 | 0 | 0 | 0 | 0 | 0 |
| 1985-86 | 0 | 0 | 0 | 0 | 0 | 0 | 0 | 0 | 0 | 0 | 0 | 0 | 0 |
| 1986-87 | 0 | 0 | 0 | 0 | 0 | 0 | 0 | 0 | 0 | 0 | 0 | 0 | 0 |
| 1987-88 | 0 | 0 | 0 | 0 | 0 | 0 | 0 | 0 | 0 | 0 | 0 | 0 | 0 |
| 1988-89 | 0 | 0 | 0 | 0 | 0 | 0 | 0 | 0 | 0 | 0 | 0 | 0 | 0 |
| 1989-90 | 0 | 0 | 0 | 0 | 0 | 0 | 0 | 0 | 0 | 0 | 0 | 0 | 0 |
| 1990-91 | 0 | 0 | 0 | 0 | 0 | 0 |  |  |  |  |  |  |  |

**TABLE 5**     COOLING DEGREE DAYS Base 65 deg. F     HONOLULU, HAWAII

| YEAR | JAN | FEB | MAR | APR | MAY | JUNE | JULY | AUG | SEP | OCT | NOV | DEC | TOTAL |
|---|---|---|---|---|---|---|---|---|---|---|---|---|---|
| 1969 | 133 | 255 | 269 | 295 | 369 | 428 | 500 | 572 | 517 | 488 | 419 | 365 | 4610 |
| 1970 | 293 | 239 | 378 | 109 | 485 | 490 | 540 | 586 | 429 | 426 | 332 | 306 | 4913 |
| 1971 | 216 | 269 | 284 | 326 | 355 | 376 | 435 | 456 | 431 | 408 | 328 | 265 | 4149 |
| 1972 | 178 | 170 | 249 | 307 | 386 | 425 | 484 | 506 | 470 | 450 | 357 | 209 | 4191 |
| 1973 | 252 | 219 | 353 | 322 | 382 | 432 | 485 | 512 | 484 | 455 | 367 | 279 | 4542 |
| 1974 | 300 | 270 | 285 | 378 | 415 | 434 | 468 | 509 | 458 | 457 | 328 | 341 | 4643 |
| 1975 | 235 | 224 | 256 | 292 | 337 | 438 | 438 | 475 | 438 | 442 | 372 | 257 | 4166 |
| 1976 | 278 | 209 | 275 | 311 | 393 | 402 | 464 | 498 | 479 | 446 | 315 | 325 | 4395 |
| 1977 | 276 | 305 | 355 | 344 | 396 | 441 | 498 | 541 | 505 | 507 | 417 | 320 | 4905 |
| 1978 | 292 | 238 | 346 | 361 | 417 | 418 | 439 | 489 | 473 | 401 | 298 | 239 | 4401 |
| 1979 | 159 | 209 | 250 | 299 | 412 | 458 | 500 | 485 | 489 | 504 | 378 | 326 | 4469 |
| 1980 | 222 | 220 | 317 | 340 | 418 | 442 | 501 | 504 | 503 | 476 | 395 | 295 | 4633 |
| 1981 | 263 | 249 | 311 | 335 | 385 | 474 | 463 | 477 | 477 | 419 | 355 | 284 | 4492 |
| 1982 | 261 | 195 | 288 | 318 | 421 | 442 | 493 | 514 | 499 | 452 | 326 | 225 | 4434 |
| 1983 | 223 | 182 | 270 | 295 | 335 | 425 | 461 | 544 | 525 | 508 | 461 | 318 | 4547 |
| 1984 | 304 | 285 | 340 | 366 | 432 | 438 | 501 | 527 | 494 | 475 | 425 | 291 | 4878 |
| 1985 | 205 | 256 | 300 | 293 | 364 | 437 | 521 | 532 | 491 | 464 | 310 | 264 | 4437 |
| 1986 | 251 | 217 | 366 | 384 | 421 | 457 | 519 | 561 | 521 | 491 | 433 | 318 | 4939 |
| 1987 | 267 | 178 | 285 | 337 | 337 | 465 | 537 | 556 | 544 | 516 | 418 | 342 | 4782 |
| 1988 | 260 | 289 | 346 | 373 | 437 | 482 | 527 | 537 | 520 | 478 | 455 | 336 | 5040 |
| 1989 | 301 | 244 | 325 | 291 | 425 | 482 | 521 | 517 | 512 | 431 | 358 | 252 | 4659 |
| 1990 | 306 | 189 | 258 | 354 | 412 | 456 | 498 | 543 | 525 | 501 | 377 | 289 | 4708 |

**TABLE 6**     SNOWFALL (inches)     HONOLULU, HAWAII

| SEASON | JULY | AUG | SEP | OCT | NOV | DEC | JAN | FEB | MAR | APR | MAY | JUNE | TOTAL |
|---|---|---|---|---|---|---|---|---|---|---|---|---|---|
| 1971-72 | 0.0 | 0.0 | 0.0 | 0.0 | 0.0 | 0.0 | 0.0 | 0.0 | 0.0 | 0.0 | 0.0 | 0.0 | 0.0 |
| 1972-73 | 0.0 | 0.0 | 0.0 | 0.0 | 0.0 | 0.0 | 0.0 | 0.0 | 0.0 | 0.0 | 0.0 | 0.0 | 0.0 |
| 1973-74 | 0.0 | 0.0 | 0.0 | 0.0 | 0.0 | 0.0 | 0.0 | 0.0 | 0.0 | 0.0 | 0.0 | 0.0 | 0.0 |
| 1974-75 | 0.0 | 0.0 | 0.0 | 0.0 | 0.0 | 0.0 | 0.0 | 0.0 | 0.0 | 0.0 | 0.0 | 0.0 | 0.0 |
| 1975-76 | 0.0 | 0.0 | 0.0 | 0.0 | 0.0 | 0.0 | 0.0 | 0.0 | 0.0 | 0.0 | 0.0 | 0.0 | 0.0 |
| 1976-77 | 0.0 | 0.0 | 0.0 | 0.0 | 0.0 | 0.0 | 0.0 | 0.0 | 0.0 | 0.0 | 0.0 | 0.0 | 0.0 |
| 1977-78 | 0.0 | 0.0 | 0.0 | 0.0 | 0.0 | 0.0 | 0.0 | 0.0 | 0.0 | 0.0 | 0.0 | 0.0 | 0.0 |
| 1978-79 | 0.0 | 0.0 | 0.0 | 0.0 | 0.0 | 0.0 | 0.0 | 0.0 | 0.0 | 0.0 | 0.0 | 0.0 | 0.0 |
| 1979-80 | 0.0 | 0.0 | 0.0 | 0.0 | 0.0 | 0.0 | 0.0 | 0.0 | 0.0 | 0.0 | 0.0 | 0.0 | 0.0 |
| 1980-81 | 0.0 | 0.0 | 0.0 | 0.0 | 0.0 | 0.0 | 0.0 | 0.0 | 0.0 | 0.0 | 0.0 | 0.0 | 0.0 |
| 1981-82 | 0.0 | 0.0 | 0.0 | 0.0 | 0.0 | 0.0 | 0.0 | 0.0 | 0.0 | 0.0 | 0.0 | 0.0 | 0.0 |
| 1982-83 | 0.0 | 0.0 | 0.0 | 0.0 | 0.0 | 0.0 | 0.0 | 0.0 | 0.0 | 0.0 | 0.0 | 0.0 | 0.0 |
| 1983-84 | 0.0 | 0.0 | 0.0 | 0.0 | 0.0 | 0.0 | 0.0 | 0.0 | 0.0 | 0.0 | 0.0 | 0.0 | 0.0 |
| 1984-85 | 0.0 | 0.0 | 0.0 | 0.0 | 0.0 | 0.0 | 0.0 | 0.0 | 0.0 | 0.0 | 0.0 | 0.0 | 0.0 |
| 1985-86 | 0.0 | 0.0 | 0.0 | 0.0 | 0.0 | 0.0 | 0.0 | 0.0 | 0.0 | 0.0 | 0.0 | 0.0 | 0.0 |
| 1986-87 | 0.0 | 0.0 | 0.0 | 0.0 | 0.0 | 0.0 | 0.0 | 0.0 | 0.0 | 0.0 | 0.0 | 0.0 | 0.0 |
| 1987-88 | 0.0 | 0.0 | 0.0 | 0.0 | 0.0 | 0.0 | 0.0 | 0.0 | 0.0 | 0.0 | 0.0 | 0.0 | 0.0 |
| 1988-89 | 0.0 | 0.0 | 0.0 | 0.0 | 0.0 | 0.0 | 0.0 | 0.0 | 0.0 | 0.0 | 0.0 | 0.0 | 0.0 |
| 1989-90 | 0.0 | 0.0 | 0.0 | 0.0 | 0.0 | 0.0 | 0.0 | 0.0 | 0.0 | 0.0 | 0.0 | 0.0 | 0.0 |
| 1990-91 | 0.0 | 0.0 | 0.0 | 0.0 | 0.0 | 0.0 |  |  |  |  |  |  |  |
| Record Mean | 0.0 | 0.0 | 0.0 | 0.0 | 0.0 | 0.0 | 0.0 | 0.0 | 0.0 | 0.0 | 0.0 | 0.0 | 0.0 |

**See Reference Notes, relative to all above tables, on preceding page.**

Boise is situated in the Boise River Valley about 8 miles below the mouth of a mountain canyon where the valley proper begins. Sheltered by large shade trees and averaging 2,710 feet in elevation, the denser part of the city covers a gentle alluvial slope about 2 miles wide, stretching southwest from the foothills of the Boise Mountains to the river. The Boise Mountains immediately north of the city rise 5,000 to 6,000 feet above sea level in about 8 miles, the slopes partly mantled with sagebrush and then chaparral giving way near the summit to ridges of fir, spruce, and pine. Across the river, the land rises in two irregular steps, or benches, for several miles, finally reaching the low divide between the Boise and Snake Rivers. Downstream the valley widens, merging with the valley of the Snake about 40 miles to the northwest. Once semi−arid, the entire area is now irrigated from the upstream reservoirs.

Although air masses from the Pacific are considerably modified by the time they reach Boise, their influence, particularly in winter, alternates with that of atmospheric developments from other directions. The result is almost a typical upland continental type of climate in summer, while winters are usually tempered by periods of cloudy or stormy and mild weather. Autumns have prolonged periods of near ideal weather, while springtime is noted by changeable weather and varied temperatures. The Boise climate in general may be described as dry and temperate, with sufficient variation to be stimulating.

Summer hot periods rarely last longer than a few days. Temperatures of 100 degrees or higher occur nearly every year.

Winter cold spells with temperatures of 10 degrees or lower generally last longer than the summer hot spells. During cold weather, however, there is ordinarily little wind to add to the discomfort.

The normal precipitation pattern in the Boise area shows a winter high and a very pronounced summer low. Total amounts and intensity are generally greatest near the foothills, dwindling to westward and southward.

Tornadoes are very rare as are destructive force winds. Northwesterly winds, drying and rather raw in character, although of moderate velocity, are common from March through May. Diurnal southeasterly winds, descending from nearby foothills at night, frequently have a moderating effect on winter temperatures. There is an occasional, but moderate, duststorm during the warmer months, usually occurring at times of cold frontal passage.

Relative humidity is low but widespread irrigation maintains humidity several percent above the general dryness of western arid conditions in summer. Thunderstorms occur primarily during spring and summer, with less frequency during fall and occasionally during winter. December and January are the months of heavy fog or low stratus cloud conditions. Only a moderate amount of sunshine is received in the average winter, but protracted periods of clear, sunny weather are the rule in summer. Ice storms are practically unknown.

Based on the 1951−1980 period, the average first occurrence of 32 degrees Fahrenheit in the fall is October 9 and the average last occurrence in the spring is May 8.

## TABLE 1 NORMALS, MEANS AND EXTREMES

BOISE, IDAHO

LATITUDE: 43°34'N    LONGITUDE: 116°13'W    ELEVATION: FT. GRND 2838 BARO    2875    TIME ZONE: MOUNTAIN    WBAN: 24131

| | (a) | JAN | FEB | MAR | APR | MAY | JUNE | JULY | AUG | SEP | OCT | NOV | DEC | YEAR |
|---|---|---|---|---|---|---|---|---|---|---|---|---|---|---|
| **TEMPERATURE °F:** | | | | | | | | | | | | | | |
| Normals | | | | | | | | | | | | | | |
| -Daily Maximum | | 37.1 | 44.3 | 51.8 | 60.8 | 70.8 | 79.8 | 90.6 | 87.3 | 77.6 | 64.6 | 49.0 | 39.3 | 62.8 |
| -Daily Minimum | | 22.6 | 27.9 | 30.9 | 36.4 | 44.0 | 51.8 | 58.5 | 56.7 | 48.7 | 39.1 | 30.5 | 24.6 | 39.3 |
| -Monthly | | 29.9 | 36.1 | 41.4 | 48.6 | 57.4 | 65.8 | 74.6 | 72 ^ | 63.2 | 51.9 | 39.7 | 32.0 | 51.1 |
| Extremes | | | | | | | | | | | | | | |
| -Record Highest | 50 | 63 | 70 | 81 | 92 | 98 | 109 | 111 | 110 | 102 | 91 | 74 | 65 | 111 |
| -Year | | 1953 | 1986 | 1978 | 1987 | 1986 | 1940 | 1960 | 1961 | 1945 | 1963 | 1988 | 1964 | JUL 1960 |
| -Record Lowest | 50 | -17 | -15 | 6 | 19 | 22 | 31 | 35 | 37 | 23 | 11 | -3 | -23 | -23 |
| -Year | | 1950 | 1989 | 1971 | 1968 | 1982 | 1984 | 1986 | 1980 | 1970 | 1971 | 1985 | 1972 | DEC 1972 |
| **NORMAL DEGREE DAYS:** | | | | | | | | | | | | | | |
| Heating (base 65°F) | | 1088 | 809 | 732 | 492 | 253 | 83 | 0 | 23 | 134 | 406 | 759 | 1023 | 5802 |
| Cooling (base 65°F) | | 0 | 0 | 0 | 0 | 17 | 107 | 298 | 240 | 80 | 0 | 0 | 0 | 742 |
| **% OF POSSIBLE SUNSHINE** | 47 | 39 | 50 | 62 | 68 | 71 | 76 | 87 | 85 | 81 | 69 | 43 | 39 | 64 |
| **MEAN SKY COVER (tenths)** | | | | | | | | | | | | | | |
| Sunrise - Sunset | 50 | 7.7 | 7.3 | 6.9 | 6.4 | 5.8 | 4.8 | 2.8 | 3.2 | 3.6 | 5.0 | 7.0 | 7.5 | 5.7 |
| **MEAN NUMBER OF DAYS:** | | | | | | | | | | | | | | |
| Sunrise to Sunset | | | | | | | | | | | | | | |
| -Clear | 50 | 4.5 | 4.4 | 6.0 | 6.7 | 8.4 | 11.6 | 20.5 | 18.6 | 16.9 | 12.2 | 6.1 | 4.9 | 120.6 |
| -Partly Cloudy | 50 | 4.9 | 6.5 | 7.2 | 8.7 | 10.0 | 10.2 | 7.2 | 8.0 | 7.0 | 8.3 | 6.2 | 5.6 | 90.0 |
| -Cloudy | 50 | 21.6 | 17.4 | 17.9 | 14.5 | 12.3 | 8.2 | 3.3 | 4.4 | 6.2 | 10.6 | 17.6 | 20.5 | 154.6 |
| Precipitation | | | | | | | | | | | | | | |
| .01 inches or more | 50 | 12.0 | 10.3 | 9.8 | 8.1 | 7.8 | 6.1 | 2.4 | 2.6 | 3.8 | 6.0 | 10.2 | 11.3 | 90.3 |
| Snow,Ice pellets | | | | | | | | | | | | | | |
| 1.0 inches or more | 50 | 2.4 | 1.3 | 0.5 | 0.3 | 0.* | 0.0 | 0.0 | 0.0 | 0.0 | 0.1 | 0.9 | 2.2 | 7.7 |
| Thunderstorms | 50 | 0.* | 0.3 | 0.6 | 0.9 | 2.7 | 2.8 | 2.6 | 2.4 | 1.6 | 0.6 | 0.3 | 0.1 | 14.9 |
| Heavy Fog Visibility | | | | | | | | | | | | | | |
| 1/4 mile or less | 50 | 5.7 | 3.1 | 0.7 | 0.3 | 0.2 | 0.1 | 0.0 | 0.* | 0.1 | 0.5 | 2.9 | 6.0 | 19.7 |
| Temperature °F | | | | | | | | | | | | | | |
| -Maximum | | | | | | | | | | | | | | |
| 90° and above | 50 | 0.0 | 0.0 | 0.0 | 0.1 | 1.2 | 5.3 | 18.5 | 15.0 | 3.1 | 0.1 | 0.0 | 0.0 | 43.3 |
| 32° and below | 50 | 10.5 | 2.9 | 0.2 | 0.0 | 0.0 | 0.0 | 0.0 | 0.0 | 0.0 | 0.0 | 0.9 | 6.7 | 21.1 |
| -Minimum | | | | | | | | | | | | | | |
| 32° and below | 50 | 26.2 | 20.8 | 17.8 | 8.2 | 1.8 | 0.* | 0.0 | 0.0 | 0.5 | 5.5 | 17.8 | 25.3 | 124.0 |
| 0° and below | 50 | 1.8 | 0.4 | 0.0 | 0.0 | 0.0 | 0.0 | 0.0 | 0.0 | 0.0 | 0.0 | 0.1 | 1.0 | 3.3 |
| **AVG. STATION PRESS.(mb)** | 17 | 920.2 | 918.0 | 914.2 | 914.4 | 913.6 | 914.0 | 914.3 | 914.3 | 915.7 | 917.8 | 917.9 | 920.2 | 916.2 |
| **RELATIVE HUMIDITY (%)** | | | | | | | | | | | | | | |
| Hour 05 | 50 | 80 | 80 | 74 | 70 | 69 | 67 | 54 | 52 | 59 | 67 | 77 | 81 | 69 |
| Hour 11 (Local Time) | 50 | 74 | 68 | 55 | 47 | 45 | 41 | 33 | 33 | 39 | 48 | 65 | 74 | 52 |
| Hour 17 | 50 | 71 | 60 | 45 | 36 | 34 | 30 | 22 | 23 | 30 | 39 | 60 | 71 | 43 |
| Hour 23 | 50 | 79 | 77 | 68 | 60 | 59 | 52 | 39 | 40 | 50 | 61 | 75 | 80 | 62 |
| **PRECIPITATION (inches):** | | | | | | | | | | | | | | |
| Water Equivalent | | | | | | | | | | | | | | |
| -Normal | | 1.64 | 1.07 | 1.03 | 1.19 | 1.21 | 0.95 | 0.26 | 0.40 | 0.58 | 0.75 | 1.29 | 1.34 | 11.71 |
| -Maximum Monthly | 50 | 3.87 | 3.70 | 3.46 | 3.04 | 4.00 | 3.41 | 1.62 | 2.37 | 2.93 | 2.25 | 3.36 | 4.23 | 4.23 |
| -Year | | 1970 | 1986 | 1989 | 1955 | 1942 | 1941 | 1982 | 1968 | 1986 | 1956 | 1988 | 1983 | DEC 1983 |
| -Minimum Monthly | 50 | 0.12 | 0.19 | 0.18 | 0.09 | 0.01 | 0.00 | 0.00 | T | 0.00 | 0.00 | 0.14 | 0.09 | 0.00 |
| -Year | | 1949 | 1964 | 1944 | 1949 | 1940 | 1966 | 1947 | 1980 | 1987 | 1988 | 1976 | 1976 | OCT 1988 |
| -Maximum in 24 hrs | 50 | 1.48 | 1.00 | 1.65 | 1.27 | 1.51 | 2.24 | 0.94 | 1.61 | 1.74 | 0.76 | 0.88 | 1.16 | 2.24 |
| -Year | | 1953 | 1951 | 1981 | 1969 | 1942 | 1958 | 1960 | 1979 | 1976 | 1947 | 1971 | 1955 | JUN 1958 |
| Snow,Ice pellets | | | | | | | | | | | | | | |
| -Maximum Monthly | 50 | 21.4 | 25.2 | 11.9 | 8.0 | 4.0 | T | T | T | 0.0 | 2.7 | 18.6 | 26.2 | 26.2 |
| -Year | | 1964 | 1949 | 1951 | 1967 | 1964 | 1954 | 1970 | 1989 | | 1971 | 1985 | 1983 | DEC 1983 |
| -Maximum in 24 hrs | 50 | 8.5 | 13.0 | 6.4 | 7.2 | 4.0 | T | T | T | 0.0 | 1.7 | 6.5 | 6.7 | 13.0 |
| -Year | | 1950 | 1949 | 1952 | 1969 | 1964 | 1954 | 1970 | 1989 | | 1971 | 1964 | 1983 | FEB 1949 |
| **WIND:** | | | | | | | | | | | | | | |
| Mean Speed (mph) | 50 | 8.0 | 9.0 | 10.1 | 10.1 | 9.5 | 9.0 | 8.4 | 8.2 | 8.2 | 8.3 | 8.4 | 8.1 | 8.8 |
| Prevailing Direction | | | | | | | | | | | | | | |
| through 1963 | | SE | SE | SE | SE | NW | NW | NW | NW | SE | SE | SE | SE | SE |
| Fastest Mile | | | | | | | | | | | | | | |
| -Direction (!!!) | 50 | SE | W | W | W | W | SW | W | SE | SE | SE | NW | NW | W |
| -Speed (MPH) | 50 | 50 | 56 | 52 | 50 | 50 | 50 | 61 | 56 | 50 | 56 | 57 | 56 | 61 |
| -Year | | 1941 | 1954 | 1957 | 1942 | 1954 | 1948 | 1944 | 1963 | 1960 | 1950 | 1953 | 1950 | JUL 1944 |
| Peak Gust | | | | | | | | | | | | | | |
| -Direction (!!!) | 6 | N | W | NW | W | NW | NW | S | W | SE | SE | SW | S | S |
| -Speed (mph) | 6 | 59 | 45 | 48 | 58 | 48 | 54 | 71 | 54 | 43 | 40 | 54 | 39 | 71 |
| -Date | | 1986 | 1989 | 1984 | 1986 | 1986 | 1987 | 1987 | 1984 | 1985 | 1985 | 1984 | 1987 | JUL 1987 |

**See reference Notes to this table on the following page.**

## TABLE 2 — PRECIPITATION (inches)  BOISE, IDAHO

| YEAR | JAN | FEB | MAR | APR | MAY | JUNE | JULY | AUG | SEP | OCT | NOV | DEC | ANNUAL |
|------|-----|-----|-----|-----|-----|------|------|-----|-----|-----|-----|-----|--------|
| 1961 | 0.42 | 1.20 | 1.39 | 0.22 | 0.54 | 0.55 | 0.25 | 0.21 | 0.79 | 1.76 | 0.95 | 0.90 | 9.?? |
| 1962 | 1.00 | 0.77 | 1.27 | 0.92 | 2.90 | 0.12 | 0.04 | 0.12 | 0.40 | 1.22 | 1.67 | 0.25 | 10.6? |
| 1963 | 1.13 | 1.70 | 0.21 | 1.65 | 1.90 | | T | 0.64 | 0.75 | 0.99 | 2.41 | 1.02 | 13.4? |
| 1964 | 2.46 | 0.19 | 0.64 | 1.35 | 1.76 | 2.00 | 0.41 | 0.53 | 0.70 | 0.21 | 2.33 | 3.19 | 15.?? |
| 1965 | 2.89 | 0.31 | 0.43 | 2.81 | 0.80 | 1.20 | 0.25 | 0.88 | 0.55 | 0.28 | 1.51 | 0.61 | 12.5? |
| 1966 | 0.81 | 0.73 | 0.60 | 0.61 | 0.32 | 0.01 | 0.06 | 0.01 | 0.19 | 0.29 | 1.60 | 1.41 | 6.6? |
| 1967 | 1.49 | 0.35 | 0.37 | 1.47 | 0.49 | 1.07 | 0.05 | T | 0.58 | 0.42 | 0.89 | 0.50 | 7.6? |
| 1968 | 0.43 | 1.86 | 0.71 | 0.35 | 0.40 | 0.60 | T | 2.37 | 0.10 | 0.70 | 0.59 | 1.95 | 10.?? |
| 1969 | 3.50 | 1.00 | 0.26 | 1.35 | 0.50 | 2.00 | 0.02 | T | 0.68 | 0.64 | 0.59 | 1.77 | 12.?? |
| 1970 | 3.87 | 0.30 | 1.04 | 0.93 | 0.73 | 1.72 | 0.28 | 0.10 | 1.00 | 0.81 | 2.03 | 1.37 | 14.?? |
| 1971 | 2.04 | 0.65 | 1.50 | 0.40 | 0.25 | 1.58 | 0.12 | 0.18 | 0.64 | 0.53 | 2.32 | 1.63 | 11.6? |
| 1972 | 2.15 | 0.91 | 1.50 | 0.62 | 0.32 | 0.90 | 0.21 | 0.05 | 1.11 | 0.64 | 1.11 | 1.79 | 11.3? |
| 1973 | 1.14 | 0.42 | 0.65 | 1.49 | 0.74 | 0.19 | 0.07 | 0.03 | 0.82 | 1.15 | 2.44 | 2.23 | 11.3? |
| 1974 | 1.35 | 0.66 | 1.50 | 0.67 | 0.10 | 0.60 | 0.53 | 0.22 | T | 1.45 | 0.67 | 1.71 | 9.4? |
| 1975 | 0.59 | 2.62 | 1.92 | 1.53 | 0.88 | 0.78 | 0.82 | 0.48 | 0.01 | 1.99 | 0.78 | 1.29 | 13.6? |
| 1976 | 1.49 | 1.31 | 0.72 | 1.60 | 0.46 | 1.66 | 1.15 | 0.95 | 2.11 | 0.52 | 0.14 | 0.09 | 12.?? |
| 1977 | 0.65 | 0.57 | 0.86 | 0.19 | 1.80 | 1.26 | 0.41 | 0.73 | 1.20 | 0.21 | 1.86 | 2.46 | 12.?? |
| 1978 | 2.37 | 1.50 | 1.43 | 2.34 | 0.36 | 0.56 | 0.48 | 0.24 | 0.89 | T | 1.06 | 0.60 | 11.8? |
| 1979 | 1.93 | 1.20 | 0.48 | 1.60 | 1.28 | 0.18 | 0.01 | 1.81 | 0.04 | 1.50 | 1.30 | 0.74 | 12.?? |
| 1980 | 1.56 | 1.29 | 2.14 | 1.20 | 3.77 | 0.58 | 0.03 | T | 1.59 | 0.30 | 1.26 | 1.49 | 15.2? |
| 1981 | 1.20 | 1.02 | 2.76 | 1.93 | 0.95 | 0.77 | 0.23 | 0.13 | 0.36 | 0.97 | 2.24 | 2.72 | 15.2? |
| 1982 | 1.42 | 1.54 | 1.39 | 0.79 | 0.39 | 0.35 | 1.62 | 0.19 | 1.38 | 1.74 | 1.10 | 1.92 | 13.8? |
| 1983 | 1.67 | 1.26 | 2.70 | 2.29 | 1.93 | 0.17 | 1.16 | 0.28 | 0.65 | 0.56 | 1.87 | 4.23 | 18.?? |
| 1984 | 0.80 | 0.86 | 1.43 | 1.62 | 1.06 | 1.47 | 0.23 | 1.24 | 0.69 | 0.85 | 2.36 | 0.63 | 13.2? |
| 1985 | 0.20 | 0.55 | 0.97 | 0.90 | 1.52 | 0.37 | 0.85 | 0.04 | 1.81 | 0.84 | 1.85 | 1.24 | 11.?? |
| 1986 | 0.98 | 3.70 | 2.01 | 1.55 | 1.10 | 0.35 | 0.17 | 0.07 | 2.93 | 0.33 | 1.00 | 0.12 | 14.3? |
| 1987 | 0.73 | 1.24 | 2.01 | 0.38 | 0.69 | 0.58 | 0.70 | 0.11 | 0.00 | T | 1.00 | 1.05 | 8.?? |
| 1988 | 1.30 | 0.43 | 1.45 | 1.80 | 1.33 | 0.47 | 0.02 | 0.09 | 0.24 | 0.00 | 3.36 | 0.59 | 10.?? |
| 1989 | 1.14 | 1.15 | 3.46 | 0.46 | 0.21 | 0.08 | 0.03 | 0.78 | 1.20 | 1.24 | 0.59 | 0.10 | 10.4? |
| 1990 | 0.84 | 0.79 | 0.77 | 2.14 | 4.07 | 0.11 | 0.42 | 0.39 | 0.50 | 0.45 | 0.61 | 0.98 | 12.0? |
| Record Mean | 1.46 | 1.27 | 1.33 | 1.20 | 1.21 | 0.87 | 0.29 | 0.27 | 0.59 | 0.93 | 1.35 | 1.34 | 12.?? |

## TABLE 3 — AVERAGE TEMPERATURE (deg. F)  BOISE, IDAHO

| YEAR | JAN | FEB | MAR | APR | MAY | JUNE | JULY | AUG | SEP | OCT | NOV | DEC | ANNUAL |
|------|-----|-----|-----|-----|-----|------|------|-----|-----|-----|-----|-----|--------|
| 1961 | 32.9 | 41.2 | 44.4 | 48.1 | 57.9 | 72.9 | 76.3 | 77.8 | 57.2 | 49.1 | 37.0 | 30.9 | 52.? |
| 1962 | 21.1 | 32.2 | 38.6 | 52.4 | 56.0 | 65.5 | 72.2 | 70.7 | 65.2 | 53.1 | 41.4 | 35.4 | 50.? |
| 1963 | 23.3 | 43.3 | 44.3 | 48.3 | 60.9 | 63.9 | 72.2 | 73.5 | 70.9 | 57.8 | 43.7 | 28.1 | 52.? |
| 1964 | 26.0 | 26.3 | 37.6 | 45.3 | 55.1 | 62.5 | 74.9 | 69.2 | 59.6 | 52.9 | 36.9 | 35.2 | 48.? |
| 1965 | 34.1 | 36.9 | 39.2 | 50.2 | 54.9 | 64.7 | 73.3 | 71.1 | 57.1 | 56.4 | 44.3 | 30.1 | 51.? |
| 1966 | 32.4 | 33.3 | 43.2 | 49.2 | 61.5 | 65.0 | 73.2 | 72.1 | 66.2 | 49.4 | 43.0 | 31.3 | 51.? |
| 1967 | 36.2 | 38.3 | 42.0 | 43.9 | 56.5 | 66.1 | 78.5 | 78.0 | 68.6 | 50.7 | 40.7 | 27.8 | 52.? |
| 1968 | 29.5 | 41.1 | 45.9 | 46.3 | 57.8 | 67.9 | 77.3 | 68.7 | 63.0 | 52.4 | 42.0 | 35.1 | 52.? |
| 1969 | 34.3 | 36.2 | 42.5 | 50.5 | 61.1 | 66.3 | 72.9 | 72.4 | 64.2 | 45.9 | 39.7 | 34.6 | 51.? |
| 1970 | 36.2 | 41.2 | 41.4 | 43.8 | 57.5 | 68.9 | 76.3 | 75.8 | 57.8 | 47.5 | 43.2 | 33.5 | 51.? |
| 1971 | 33.9 | 37.5 | 40.2 | 49.2 | 60.0 | 64.9 | 74.7 | 78.6 | 59.2 | 49.0 | 39.7 | 30.2 | 51.? |
| 1972 | 30.9 | 36.5 | 45.5 | 46.7 | 60.6 | 67.6 | 73.5 | 74.5 | 58.8 | 51.7 | 40.5 | 23.8 | 50.? |
| 1973 | 30.7 | 39.4 | 43.0 | 49.1 | 60.5 | 67.6 | 75.6 | 73.0 | 63.1 | 52.4 | 41.7 | 38.4 | 52.? |
| 1974 | 29.4 | 38.7 | 42.6 | 49.7 | 55.4 | 71.7 | 73.8 | 71.7 | 65.3 | 52.2 | 41.7 | 33.2 | 52.? |
| 1975 | 28.2 | 36.9 | 41.5 | 44.5 | 56.2 | 64.4 | 78.3 | 70.0 | 65.5 | 52.3 | 39.5 | 31.4 | 50.? |
| 1976 | 32.2 | 34.2 | 37.1 | 47.3 | 59.3 | 62.6 | 73.1 | 67.7 | 64.1 | 50.8 | 40.9 | 29.3 | 49.? |
| 1977 | 19.0 | 33.8 | 39.8 | 54.1 | 53.7 | 70.2 | 72.7 | 73.6 | 62.0 | 53.2 | 39.6 | 37.3 | 50.? |
| 1978 | 37.0 | 38.2 | 48.7 | 48.5 | 54.3 | 64.5 | 72.8 | 69.9 | 61.4 | 52.8 | 36.7 | 27.0 | 51.? |
| 1979 | 16.2 | 34.3 | 43.2 | 48.7 | 57.8 | 66.7 | 74.1 | 71.2 | 67.3 | 54.4 | 34.7 | 35.8 | 50.? |
| 1980 | 30.3 | 39.8 | 41.1 | 52.6 | 57.2 | 62.6 | 72.9 | 67.2 | 62.6 | 51.6 | 39.8 | 33.1 | 50.? |
| 1981 | 33.9 | 36.8 | 44.5 | 50.3 | 54.7 | 63.2 | 71.0 | 74.2 | 63.7 | 48.7 | 44.0 | 35.3 | 51.? |
| 1982 | 24.8 | 30.0 | 41.3 | 45.2 | 54.9 | 65.8 | 70.1 | 72.7 | 60.4 | 50.9 | 36.0 | 31.5 | 48.? |
| 1983 | 35.9 | 41.5 | 44.6 | 47.1 | 56.5 | 63.8 | 69.4 | 74.9 | 60.8 | 53.8 | 42.0 | 23.2 | 51.? |
| 1984 | 21.2 | 30.2 | 41.9 | 45.9 | 54.8 | 61.7 | 74.2 | 75.5 | 60.1 | 46.9 | 39.1 | 22.9 | 47.? |
| 1985 | 19.1 | 25.8 | 36.0 | 51.6 | 58.5 | 67.2 | 77.7 | 69.2 | 56.2 | 48.4 | 27.7 | 12.6 | 45.? |
| 1986 | 29.4 | 41.0 | 48.0 | 48.3 | 59.1 | 72.0 | 69.6 | 75.9 | 57.4 | 52.6 | 40.4 | 28.0 | 51.? |
| 1987 | 27.8 | 37.6 | 44.2 | 56.0 | 62.2 | 70.2 | 71.2 | 70.0 | 65.6 | 54.9 | 40.7 | 32.9 | 52.? |
| 1988 | 26.1 | 37.8 | 42.6 | 52.7 | 57.9 | 70.7 | 74.6 | 71.6 | 61.7 | 59.9 | 40.7 | 27.0 | 51.? |
| 1989 | 24.7 | 23.2 | 43.7 | 53.1 | 56.3 | 68.5 | 77.0 | 70.0 | 63.3 | 51.2 | 39.4 | 30.4 | 50.? |
| 1990 | 34.2 | 34.1 | 44.3 | 54.7 | 55.7 | 66.9 | 76.2 | 74.0 | 69.9 | 51.0 | 41.2 | 18.1 | 51.? |
| Record Mean | 29.5 | 35.4 | 42.3 | 49.8 | 57.6 | 65.6 | 74.3 | 72.4 | 62.7 | 52.3 | 40.3 | 31.5 | 51.? |
| Max | 36.7 | 43.4 | 52.4 | 61.8 | 70.6 | 79.4 | 90.0 | 87.8 | 76.9 | 64.7 | 49.3 | 38.7 | 62.? |
| Min | 22.2 | 27.3 | 32.2 | 37.7 | 44.6 | 51.7 | 58.5 | 56.9 | 48.4 | 39.9 | 31.2 | 24.2 | 39.? |

### REFERENCE NOTES FOR TABLES 1, 2, 3 and 6   (BOISE, ID)

**GENERAL**

T - TRACE AMOUNT
BLANK ENTRIES DENOTE MISSING/UNREPORTED DATA.
# INDICATES A STATION OR INSTRUMENT RELOCATION.

**SPECIFIC**

TABLE 1

(a) - LENGTH OF RECORD IN YEARS. ALTHOUGH
      INDIVIDUAL MONTHS MAY BE MISSING.
  * LESS THAN .05

NORMALS — BASED ON THE 1951-1980 RECORD PERIOD.
EXTREMES — DATES ARE THE MOST RECENT OCCURRENCE.
WIND DIR. — NUMERALS SHOW TENS OF DEGREES
            CLOCKWISE FROM TRUE NORTH.
            "00" INDICATES CALM.
RESULTANT WIND DIRECTIONS ARE GIVEN TO WHOLE DEGREES.

TABLE 3
MAX AND MIN ARE LONG-TERM MEAN DAILY MAXIMUM
AND MEAN DAILY MINIMUM TEMPERATURES.

**EXCEPTIONS**

TABLES 2, 3, and 6

RECORD MEANS ARE THROUGH THE CURRENT YEAR,
BEGINNING IN     1900 FOR TEMPERATURE
                 1900 FOR PRECIPITATION
                 1940 FOR SNOWFALL

**TABLE 4**

HEATING DEGREE DAYS Base 65 deg. F          BOISE. IDAHO

| SEASON | JULY | AUG | SEP | OCT | NOV | DEC | JAN | FEB | MAR | APR | MAY | JUNE | TOTAL |
|---|---|---|---|---|---|---|---|---|---|---|---|---|---|
| 1961-62 | 0 | 0 | 239 | 485 | 833 | 1052 | 1354 | 912 | 812 | 377 | 275 | 85 | 6424 |
| 1962-63 | 8 | 32 | 56 | 369 | 703 | 908 | 1286 | 600 | 636 | 498 | 164 | 124 | 5384 |
| 1963-64 | 2 | 2 | 21 | 252 | 631 | 1138 | 1202 | 1113 | 843 | 583 | 323 | 127 | 6237 |
| 1964-65 | 0 | 62 | 166 | 370 | 835 | 916 | 951 | 781 | 793 | 435 | 317 | 82 | 5708 |
| 1965-66 | 7 | 30 | 234 | 266 | 613 | 1075 | 1004 | 884 | 668 | 467 | 172 | 97 | 5517 |
| 1966-67 | 7 | 18 | 68 | 476 | 654 | 1039 | 885 | 742 | 707 | 627 | 279 | 79 | 5581 |
| 1967-68 | 0 | 0 | 49 | 434 | 723 | 1146 | 1092 | 688 | 586 | 555 | 235 | 58 | 5566 |
| 1968-69 | 0 | 59 | 119 | 382 | 684 | 918 | 945 | 797 | 689 | 432 | 147 | 75 | 5247 |
| 1969-70 | 3 | 13 | 91 | 585 | 751 | 935 | 886 | 659 | 724 | 631 | 249 | 79 | 5606 |
| 1970-71 | 0 | 0 | 240 | 537 | 650 | 969 | 958 | 765 | 763 | 465 | 176 | 78 | 5601 |
| 1971-72 | 10 | 6 | 210 | 492 | 753 | 1069 | 1047 | 818 | 598 | 543 | 194 | 45 | 5785 |
| 1972-73 | 11 | 0 | 222 | 406 | 727 | 1270 | 1056 | 708 | 673 | 470 | 182 | 91 | 5816 |
| 1973-74 | 4 | 13 | 103 | 382 | 692 | 817 | 1099 | 728 | 687 | 452 | 304 | 42 | 5323 |
| 1974-75 | 10 | 11 | 53 | 391 | 689 | 983 | 1132 | 782 | 721 | 607 | 275 | 76 | 5730 |
| 1975-76 | 6 | 21 | 74 | 399 | 759 | 1035 | 1013 | 886 | 858 | 524 | 189 | 132 | 5896 |
| 1976-77 | 3 | 36 | 76 | 434 | 720 | 1097 | 1418 | 868 | 772 | 342 | 358 | 7 | 6131 |
| 1977-78 | 8 | 32 | 145 | 362 | 758 | 853 | 859 | 744 | 500 | 488 | 329 | 74 | 5152 |
| 1978-79 | 5 | 38 | 173 | 370 | 841 | 1171 | 1503 | 855 | 668 | 481 | 241 | 72 | 6418 |
| 1979-80 | 5 | 2 | 26 | 326 | 903 | 899 | 1070 | 725 | 736 | 367 | 257 | 133 | 5449 |
| 1980-81 | 0 | 41 | 104 | 409 | 750 | 983 | 957 | 783 | 631 | 432 | 315 | 97 | 5502 |
| 1981-82 | 15 | 5 | 137 | 497 | 624 | 1240 | 974 | 729 | 586 | 312 | 86 |  | 6120 |
| 1982-83 | 27 | 2 | 182 | 432 | 863 | 1030 | 897 | 653 | 622 | 530 | 309 | 82 | 5629 |
| 1983-84 | 38 | 0 | 145 | 338 | 682 | 1290 | 1353 | 1004 | 710 | 566 | 328 | 162 | 6616 |
| 1984-85 | 0 | 8 | 204 | 557 | 771 | 1299 | 1412 | 1093 | 895 | 398 | 226 | 53 | 6916 |
| 1985-86 | 0 | 26 | 259 | 509 | 1113 | 1619 | 1097 | 668 | 522 | 499 | 280 | 15 | 6607 |
| 1986-87 | 35 | 2 | 259 | 376 | 733 | 1141 | 1149 | 761 | 639 | 287 | 140 | 41 | 5563 |
| 1987-88 | 23 | 18 | 86 | 306 | 722 | 990 | 1198 | 780 | 686 | 355 | 261 | 59 | 5488 |
| 1988-89 | 4 | 5 | 157 | 178 | 724 | 1169 | 1242 | 1166 | 656 | 356 | 276 | 30 | 5963 |
| 1989-90 | 0 | 29 | 97 | 421 | 759 | 1064 | 951 | 858 | 633 | 303 | 286 | 82 | 5483 |
| 1990-91 | 6 | 10 | 26 | 430 | 710 | 1449 |  |  |  |  |  |  |  |

**TABLE 5**

COOLING DEGREE DAYS Base 65 deg. F          BOISE. IDAHO

| YEAR | JAN | FEB | MAR | APR | MAY | JUNE | JULY | AUG | SEP | OCT | NOV | DEC | TOTAL |
|---|---|---|---|---|---|---|---|---|---|---|---|---|---|
| 1969 | 0 | 0 | 0 | 0 | 32 | 121 | 256 | 251 | 75 | 0 | 0 | 0 | 735 |
| 1970 | 0 | 0 | 0 | 0 | 24 | 201 | 357 | 341 | 30 | 0 | 0 | 0 | 953 |
| 1971 | 0 | 0 | 0 | 0 | 31 | 81 | 320 | 435 | 42 | 2 | 0 | 0 | 911 |
| 1972 | 0 | 0 | 0 | 0 | 62 | 129 | 283 | 303 | 40 | 0 | 0 | 0 | 817 |
| 1973 | 0 | 0 | 0 | 0 | 51 | 177 | 341 | 269 | 51 | 1 | 0 | 0 | 890 |
| 1974 | 0 | 0 | 0 | 0 | 13 | 252 | 289 | 226 | 71 | 0 | 0 | 0 | 851 |
| 1975 | 0 | 0 | 0 | 0 | 10 | 64 | 426 | 182 | 96 | 11 | 0 | 0 | 789 |
| 1976 | 0 | 0 | 0 | 0 | 19 | 66 | 263 | 130 | 55 | 2 | 0 | 0 | 535 |
| 1977 | 0 | 0 | 0 | 20 | 10 | 170 | 255 | 306 | 61 | 0 | 0 | 0 | 822 |
| 1978 | 0 | 0 | 1 | 0 | 6 | 64 | 254 | 200 | 72 | 0 | 0 | 0 | 597 |
| 1979 | 0 | 0 | 0 | 0 | 27 | 129 | 293 | 199 | 101 | 3 | 0 | 0 | 752 |
| 1980 | 0 | 0 | 0 | 3 | 25 | 68 | 251 | 117 | 38 | 2 | 0 | 0 | 504 |
| 1981 | 0 | 0 | 0 | 1 | 3 | 52 | 205 | 296 | 101 | 0 | 0 | 0 | 658 |
| 1982 | 0 | 0 | 0 | 0 | 2 | 117 | 194 | 248 | 50 | 0 | 0 | 0 | 611 |
| 1983 | 0 | 0 | 0 | 0 | 55 | 50 | 180 | 313 | 26 | 0 | 0 | 0 | 624 |
| 1984 | 0 | 0 | 0 | 0 | 19 | 70 | 291 | 340 | 64 | 2 | 0 | 0 | 786 |
| 1985 | 0 | 0 | 0 | 2 | 28 | 125 | 402 | 165 | 4 | 0 | 0 | 0 | 726 |
| 1986 | 0 | 0 | 0 | 1 | 103 | 235 | 184 | 348 | 37 | 0 | 0 | 0 | 908 |
| 1987 | 0 | 0 | 0 | 23 | 61 | 202 | 223 | 180 | 111 | 0 | 0 | 0 | 800 |
| 1988 | 0 | 0 | 0 | 0 | 46 | 237 | 308 | 215 | 66 | 24 | 0 | 0 | 896 |
| 1989 | 0 | 0 | 0 | 6 | 14 | 140 | 376 | 191 | 56 | 0 | 0 | 0 | 783 |
| 1990 | 0 | 0 | 0 | 3 | 5 | 145 | 357 | 293 | 180 | 6 | 0 | 0 | 989 |

**TABLE 6**

SNOWFALL (inches)          BOISE. IDAHO

| SEASON | JULY | AUG | SEP | OCT | NOV | DEC | JAN | FEB | MAR | APR | MAY | JUNE | TOTAL |
|---|---|---|---|---|---|---|---|---|---|---|---|---|---|
| 1961-62 | 0.0 | 0.0 | 0.0 | T | 3.4 | 6.5 | 9.2 | 1.6 | 3.7 | T | 0.0 | 0.0 | 24.4 |
| 1962-63 | 0.0 | 0.0 | 0.0 | 0.0 | 0.3 | T | 10.1 | T | 0.4 | 1.7 | 0.0 | 0.0 | 12.5 |
| 1963-64 | 0.0 | 0.0 | 0.0 | T | 1.0 | 5.5 | 21.4 | 2.1 | 2.6 | 0.4 | 4.0 | 0.0 | 37.0 |
| 1964-65 | 0.0 | 0.0 | 0.0 | 0.0 | 7.3 | 8.7 | 18.4 | 0.4 | 0.4 | 1.3 | T | 0.0 | 36.5 |
| 1965-66 | 0.0 | 0.0 | 0.0 | T | 0.7 | 4.5 | 3.6 | 7.1 | 0.2 | 0.1 | 0.0 | 0.0 | 16.2 |
| 1966-67 | 0.0 | 0.0 | 0.0 | 0.1 | T | 9.0 | 2.0 | 1.9 | 0.3 | 8.0 | T | 0.0 | 21.3 |
| 1967-68 | 0.0 | 0.0 | 0.0 | 0.0 | 1.3 | 4.3 | 3.3 | 0.1 | 0.3 | T | 0.0 | 0.0 | 10.1 |
| 1968-69 | 0.0 | 0.0 | 0.0 | 0.0 | 1.3 | 11.4 | 14.4 | 5.5 | 1.3 | 7.2 | T | 0.0 | 41.1 |
| 1969-70 | 0.0 | 0.0 | 0.0 | 1.2 | 0.3 | 4.8 | 4.0 | 2.9 | 0.1 | 1.1 | 0.5 | 0.0 | 13.2 |
| 1970-71 | T | 0.0 | 0.0 | 0.3 | 0.1 | 4.4 | 4.0 | 2.1 | 1.6 | T | 0.0 | 0.0 | 12.5 |
| 1971-72 | 0.0 | 0.0 | 0.0 | 2.7 | 0.4 | 14.8 | 5.0 | 0.6 | 0.6 | 1.6 | 0.0 | 0.0 | 28.6 |
| 1972-73 | 0.0 | 0.0 | 0.0 | T | T | 12.6 | 7.3 | 0.3 | 0.6 | T | 0.0 | 0.0 | 20.8 |
| 1973-74 | 0.0 | 0.0 | 0.0 | 0.0 | 8.8 | 4.5 | 6.0 | 2.4 | 5.7 | T | 0.0 | 0.0 | 27.4 |
| 1974-75 | 0.0 | 0.0 | 0.9 | 0.0 | 0.9 | 4.6 | 5.4 | 6.3 | 2.2 | 2.6 | 0.9 | 0.0 | 22.9 |
| 1975-76 | 0.0 | 0.0 | 0.0 | T | 3.9 | 4.2 | 6.3 | 6.7 | 3.9 | 0.2 | 0.0 | 0.0 | 25.2 |
| 1976-77 | 0.0 | 0.0 | 0.0 | 0.0 | T | 1.1 | 7.2 | 3.5 | 2.9 | T | T | 0.0 | 14.7 |
| 1977-78 | 0.0 | 0.0 | 0.0 | T | 4.7 | 4.4 | 1.6 | 7.3 | T | T | T | 0.0 | 18.0 |
| 1978-79 | 0.0 | 0.0 | 0.0 | 0.0 | 0.2 | 3.1 | 11.9 | 4.3 | 0.8 | 0.2 | T | 0.0 | 20.5 |
| 1979-80 | 0.0 | 0.0 | 0.0 | 0.0 | 6.6 | 1.4 | 3.8 | 0.8 | 2.7 | T | 0.0 | 0.0 | 15.3 |
| 1980-81 | 0.0 | 0.0 | 0.0 | 0.0 | 3.2 | 1.7 | 3.6 | 0.7 | T | 0.5 | 0.0 | 0.0 | 9.7 |
| 1981-82 | 0.0 | 0.0 | 0.0 | 0.0 | 2.8 | 11.1 | 12.2 | 1.4 | 3.6 | 1.4 | 0.0 | 0.0 | 32.5 |
| 1982-83 | 0.0 | 0.0 | 0.0 | 0.0 | 2.1 | 6.4 | 1.6 | 0.9 | T | 0.8 | 0.0 | 0.0 | 11.8 |
| 1983-84 | 0.0 | 0.0 | 0.0 | 0.0 | 2.2 | 26.2 | 4.3 | 4.4 | T | 0.3 | T | 0.0 | 37.4 |
| 1984-85 | 0.0 | 0.0 | 0.0 | T | 0.2 | 7.7 | 2.6 | 5.3 | 1.5 | 1.0 | 0.0 | 0.0 | 18.3 |
| 1985-86 | 0.0 | 0.0 | 0.0 | T | 18.6 | 12.6 | 3.9 | 4.4 | 0.0 | T | 0.0 | 0.0 | 39.5 |
| 1986-87 | 0.0 | 0.0 | 0.0 | 5.9 | 0.9 | 0.5 | 0.6 | T | 0.0 | T | 0.0 | 0.0 | 7.9 |
| 1987-88 | 0.0 | 0.0 | 0.0 | 0.0 | 0.5 | 3.0 | 3.9 | 0.3 | 2.9 | 1.2 | 0.0 | 0.0 | 11.8 |
| 1988-89 | 0.0 | 0.0 | 0.0 | 0.0 | 2.5 | 10.8 | 8.0 | 0.7 | T | T | 0.0 | 0.0 | 22.0 |
| 1989-90 | 0.0 | T | 0.0 | T | 0.4 | T | 5.2 | 6.5 | 0.4 | T | 0.0 | 0.0 | 12.5 |
| 1990-91 | 0.0 | 0.0 | 0.0 | 0.0 | 0.1 | 15.7 |  |  |  |  |  |  |  |
| Record Mean | T | T | 0.0 | 0.1 | 2.2 | 6.0 | 6.8 | 3.6 | 1.8 | 0.7 | 0.1 | T | 21.3 |

**See Reference Notes, relative to all above tables, on preceding page.**

Chicago is located along the southwest shore of Lake Michigan and occupies a plain which, for the most part, is only some tens of feet above the lake. Lake Michigan averages 579 feet above sea level. Natural water drainage over most of the city would be into Lake Michigan, and from areas west of the city is into the Mississippi River System. But actual drainage over most of the city is artificially channeled also into the Mississippi system. Topography does not significantly affect air flow in or near the city except that lesser frictional drag over Lake Michigan causes winds to be frequently stronger along the lakeshore, and often permits air masses moving from the north to reach shore areas an hour or more before affecting western parts of the city.

Chicago is in a region of frequently changeable weather. The climate is predominately continental, ranging from relatively warm in summer to relatively cold in winter. However, the continentality is partially modified by Lake Michigan, and to a lesser extent by other Great Lakes. In late autumn and winter, air masses that are initially very cold often reach the city only after being tempered by passage over one or more of the lakes. Similarly, in late spring and summer, air masses reaching the city from the north, northeast, or east are cooler because of movement over the Great Lakes. Very low winter temperatures most often occur in air that flows southward to the west of Lake Superior before reaching the Chicago area. In summer the higher temperatures are with south or southwest flow and are therefore not influenced by the lakes, the only modifying effect being a local lake breeze. Strong south or southwest flow may overcome the lake breeze and cause high temperatures to extend over the entire city.

During the warm season, when the lake is cold relative to land, there is frequently a lake breeze that reduces daytime temperature near the shore, sometimes by 10 degrees or more below temperatures farther inland. When the breeze off the lake is light this effect usually reaches inland only a mile or two, but with stronger on-shore winds the whole city is cooled. On the other hand, temperatures at night are warmer near the lake so that 24-hour averages on the whole are only slightly different in various parts of the city and suburbs.

At the OHare International Airport temperatures of 96 degrees or higher occur in about half the summers, while about half the winters have a minimum as low as -15 degrees. The average occurrence of the first temperature as low as 32 degrees in the fall is mid-October and the average occurrence of the last temperature as low as 32 degrees in the spring is late April.

Precipitation falls mostly from air that has passed over the Gulf of Mexico. But in winter there is sometimes snowfall, light inland but locally heavy near the lakeshore, with Lake Michigan as the principal moisture source. The heavy lakeshore snow occurs when initially colder air moves from the north with a long trajectory over Lake Michigan and impinges on the Chicago lakeshore. In this situation the air mass is warmed and its moisture content increased up to a height of several thousand feet. Snowfall is produced by upward currents that become stronger, because of frictional effects, when the air moves from the lake onto land. This type of snowfall therefore tends to be heavier and to extend farther inland in south-shore areas of the city and in Indiana suburbs, where the angle between wind-flow and shoreline is greatest. The effect of Lake Michigan, both on winter temperatures and lake-produced snowfall, is enhanced by non-freezing of much of the lake during the winter, even though areas and harbors are often ice-choked.

Summer thunderstorms are often locally heavy and variable, parts of the city may receive substantial rainfall and other parts none. Longer periods of continuous precipitation are mostly in autumn, winter, and spring. About one-half the precipitation in winter, and about 10 percent of the yearly total precipitation, falls as snow. Snowfall from month to month and year to year is greatly variable. There is a 50 percent likelihood that the first and last 1-inch snowfall of a season will occur by December 5 and March 20, respectively.

Channeling of winds between tall buildings often causes locally stronger gusts in ·the central business area. However, the nickname, windy city, is a misnomer as the average wind speed is not greater than in many other parts of the U.S.

## TABLE 1    NORMALS, MEANS AND EXTREMES

CHICAGO, OHARE INTERNATIONAL AIRPORT, ILLINOIS

LATITUDE: 41°59'N    LONGITUDE: 87°54'W    ELEVATION: FT. GRND 658 BARO 692    TIME ZONE: CENTRAL    WBAN: 94846

| | (a) | JAN | FEB | MAR | APR | MAY | JUNE | JULY | AUG | SEP | OCT | NOV | DEC | YEAR |
|---|---|---|---|---|---|---|---|---|---|---|---|---|---|---|
| **TEMPERATURE °F:** | | | | | | | | | | | | | | |
| Normals | | | | | | | | | | | | | | |
| -Daily Maximum | | 29.2 | 33.9 | 44.3 | 58.8 | 70.0 | 79.4 | 83.3 | 82.1 | 75.5 | 64.1 | 48.2 | 35.0 | 58.7 |
| -Daily Minimum | | 13.6 | 18.1 | 27.6 | 38.8 | 48.1 | 57.7 | 62.7 | 61.7 | 53.9 | 42.9 | 31.4 | 20.3 | 39.7 |
| -Monthly | | 21.4 | 26.0 | 36.0 | 48.8 | 59.1 | 68.6 | 73.0 | 71.9 | 64.7 | 53.5 | 39.8 | 27.7 | 49.2 |
| Extremes | | | | | | | | | | | | | | |
| -Record Highest | 31 | 65 | 71 | 88 | 91 | 93 | 104 | 102 | 100 | 99 | 91 | 78 | 71 | 104 |
| -Year | | 1989 | 1976 | 1986 | 1980 | 1977 | 1988 | 1988 | 1988 | 1985 | 1963 | 1978 | 1982 | JUN 1988 |
| -Record Lowest | 31 | -27 | -17 | -8 | 7 | 24 | 36 | 40 | 41 | 28 | 17 | 1 | -25 | -27 |
| -Year | | 1985 | 1967 | 1962 | 1982 | 1966 | 1972 | 1965 | 1965 | 1974 | 1981 | 1976 | 1983 | JAN 1985 |
| **NORMAL DEGREE DAYS:** | | | | | | | | | | | | | | |
| Heating (base 65°F) | | 1352 | 1092 | 899 | 486 | 224 | 38 | 0 | 9 | 75 | 368 | 756 | 1156 | 6455 |
| Cooling (base 65°F) | | 0 | 0 | 0 | 0 | 41 | 146 | 252 | 223 | 66 | 12 | 0 | 0 | 740 |
| **% OF POSSIBLE SUNSHINE** | 9 | 48 | 46 | 52 | 52 | 60 | 70 | 68 | 66 | 59 | 53 | 38 | 44 | 55 |
| **MEAN SKY COVER (tenths)** | | | | | | | | | | | | | | |
| Sunrise - Sunset | 31 | 6.8 | 6.9 | 7.2 | 6.8 | 6.2 | 5.9 | 5.6 | 5.7 | 5.8 | 6.0 | 7.2 | 7.2 | 6.5 |
| **MEAN NUMBER OF DAYS:** | | | | | | | | | | | | | | |
| Sunrise to Sunset | | | | | | | | | | | | | | |
| -Clear | 31 | 7.0 | 6.0 | 4.8 | 6.3 | 7.2 | 7.3 | 8.7 | 8.9 | 8.7 | 8.5 | 5.6 | 5.9 | 84.9 |
| -Partly Cloudy | 31 | 6.1 | 6.4 | 8.5 | 7.7 | 9.9 | 11.5 | 12.5 | 11.4 | 9.7 | 9.0 | 6.4 | 6.3 | 105.5 |
| -Cloudy | 31 | 17.9 | 15.9 | 17.6 | 16.1 | 13.9 | 11.2 | 9.7 | 10.7 | 11.6 | 13.5 | 18.0 | 18.8 | 174.8 |
| Precipitation | | | | | | | | | | | | | | |
| .01 inches or more | 31 | 11.1 | 9.6 | 12.4 | 12.4 | 11.0 | 9.9 | 9.7 | 9.4 | 9.5 | 9.3 | 10.6 | 11.5 | 126.4 |
| Snow,Ice pellets | | | | | | | | | | | | | | |
| 1.0 inches or more | 31 | 3.4 | 2.6 | 2.0 | 0.4 | 0.0 | 0.0 | 0.0 | 0.0 | 0.0 | 0.2 | 0.7 | 2.6 | 11.9 |
| Thunderstorms | 31 | 0.3 | 0.4 | 2.0 | 4.1 | 5.0 | 6.2 | 6.1 | 5.8 | 4.7 | 1.7 | 1.1 | 0.6 | 38.1 |
| Heavy Fog Visibility | | | | | | | | | | | | | | |
| 1/4 mile or less | 31 | 1.4 | 1.8 | 2.1 | 0.9 | 1.3 | 0.6 | 0.5 | 0.7 | 0.5 | 0.9 | 1.4 | 2.0 | 14.2 |
| Temperature °F | | | | | | | | | | | | | | |
| -Maximum | | | | | | | | | | | | | | |
| 90° and above | 31 | 0.0 | 0.0 | 0.0 | 0.* | 0.8 | 3.8 | 6.7 | 4.5 | 1.7 | 0.1 | 0.0 | 0.0 | 17.5 |
| 32° and below | 31 | 18.3 | 13.3 | 4.4 | 0.1 | 0.0 | 0.0 | 0.0 | 0.0 | 0.0 | 0.0 | 2.0 | 11.9 | 49.9 |
| -Minimum | | | | | | | | | | | | | | |
| 32° and below | 31 | 28.9 | 25.3 | 21.4 | 7.6 | 0.9 | 0.0 | 0.0 | 0.0 | 0.0 | 0.2 | 5.0 | 16.7 | 26.6 | 132.8 |
| 0° and below | 31 | 7.1 | 3.3 | 0.3 | 0.0 | 0.0 | 0.0 | 0.0 | 0.0 | 0.0 | 0.0 | 0.0 | 2.8 | 13.5 |
| **AVG. STATION PRESS.(mb)** | 17 | 993.5 | 993.8 | 991.0 | 990.2 | 990.0 | 990.2 | 991.7 | 992.6 | 993.2 | 993.6 | 992.4 | 993.3 | 992.1 |
| **RELATIVE HUMIDITY (%)** | | | | | | | | | | | | | | |
| Hour 00 | 31 | 75 | 76 | 76 | 72 | 74 | 75 | 79 | 81 | 81 | 76 | 77 | 78 | 77 |
| Hour 06 (Local Time) | 31 | 76 | 77 | 79 | 77 | 77 | 78 | 82 | 85 | 85 | 82 | 81 | 80 | 80 |
| Hour 12 | 31 | 67 | 65 | 61 | 55 | 53 | 55 | 57 | 57 | 57 | 56 | 64 | 70 | 60 |
| Hour 18 | 31 | 71 | 69 | 65 | 57 | 54 | 55 | 57 | 61 | 63 | 64 | 70 | 71 | 63 |
| **PRECIPITATION (inches):** | | | | | | | | | | | | | | |
| Water Equivalent | | | | | | | | | | | | | | |
| -Normal | | 1.60 | 1.31 | 2.59 | 3.66 | 3.15 | 4.08 | 3.63 | 3.53 | 3.35 | 2.28 | 2.06 | 2.10 | 33.34 |
| -Maximum Monthly | 31 | 4.11 | 3.46 | 5.91 | 7.69 | 7.14 | 7.94 | 8.33 | 17.10 | 11.44 | 6.55 | 8.22 | 8.56 | 17.10 |
| -Year | | 1965 | 1985 | 1976 | 1983 | 1970 | 1967 | 1982 | 1987 | 1961 | 1969 | 1985 | 1982 | AUG 1987 |
| -Minimum Monthly | 31 | 0.10 | 0.12 | 0.63 | 0.97 | 1.19 | 1.05 | 1.18 | 0.51 | 0.02 | 0.16 | 0.65 | 0.23 | 0.02 |
| -Year | | 1981 | 1969 | 1981 | 1971 | 1988 | 1988 | 1977 | 1969 | 1979 | 1964 | 1976 | 1962 | SEP 1979 |
| -Maximum in 24 hrs | 31 | 2.00 | 1.90 | 2.39 | 2.78 | 3.45 | 3.09 | 2.89 | 9.35 | 3.00 | 4.62 | 2.80 | 4.53 | 9.35 |
| -Year | | 1960 | 1985 | 1985 | 1983 | 1981 | 1967 | 1962 | 1987 | 1978 | 1969 | 1985 | 1982 | AUG 1987 |
| Snow,Ice pellets | | | | | | | | | | | | | | |
| -Maximum Monthly | 31 | 34.3 | 21.5 | 24.7 | 11.1 | 1.6 | 0.0 | 0.0 | T | T | 6.6 | 10.4 | 35.3 | 35.3 |
| -Year | | 1979 | 1967 | 1965 | 1975 | 1966 | | | 1989 | 1967 | 1967 | 1959 | 1978 | DEC 1978 |
| -Maximum in 24 hrs | 31 | 18.1 | 9.7 | 10.6 | 10.9 | 1.6 | 0.0 | 0.0 | T | T | 6.6 | 5.8 | 11.0 | 18.1 |
| -Year | | 1967 | 1981 | 1970 | 1975 | 1966 | | | 1989 | 1967 | 1967 | 1975 | 1969 | JAN 1967 |
| **WIND:** | | | | | | | | | | | | | | |
| Mean Speed (mph) | 31 | 11.6 | 11.4 | 11.9 | 11.9 | 10.5 | 9.2 | 8.1 | 8.1 | 8.8 | 9.9 | 11.0 | 11.0 | 10.3 |
| Prevailing Direction | | | | | | | | | | | | | | |
| Fastest Obs. 1 Min. | | | | | | | | | | | | | | |
| -Direction (!!!) | 31 | 28 | 25 | 01 | 24 | 34 | 24 | 36 | 32 | 23 | 20 | 23 | 26 | 23 |
| -Speed (MPH) | 31 | 47 | 45 | 54 | 54 | 52 | 41 | 55 | 46 | 58 | 48 | 51 | 46 | 58 |
| -Year | | 1971 | 1967 | 1964 | 1965 | 1962 | 1970 | 1980 | 1960 | 1959 | 1971 | 1958 | 1970 | SEP 1959 |
| Peak Gust | | | | | | | | | | | | | | |
| -Direction (!!!) | 5 | W | N | SW | S | S | W | NE | W | N | S | NW | W | S |
| -Speed (mph) | 5 | 58 | 52 | 53 | 69 | 55 | 46 | 54 | 64 | 58 | 46 | 46 | 52 | 69 |
| -Date | | 1989 | 1987 | 1986 | 1984 | 1988 | 1985 | 1984 | 1987 | 1989 | 1985 | 1989 | 1984 | APR 1984 |

**See Reference Notes to this table on the following page.**

PRECIPITATION (inches)    CHICAGO, OHARE INTERNATIONAL AIRPORT, ILLINOIS

**TABLE 2**

| YEAR | JAN | FEB | MAR | APR | MAY | JUNE | JULY | AUG | SEP | OCT | NOV | DEC | ANNUAL |
|---|---|---|---|---|---|---|---|---|---|---|---|---|---|
| 1961 | 0.27 | 0.88 | 4.01 | 2.47 | 2.03 | 4.20 | 3.69 | 1.34 | 11.44 | 3.34 | 1.76 | 1.35 | 36.78 |
| 1962 | 2.39 | 1.18 | 1.33 | 1.14 | 3.38 | 2.13 | 5.27 | 1.62 | 1.50 | 0.89 | 0.71 | 0.23 | 21.77 |
| 1963 | 0.84 | 0.36 | 2.26 | 4.88 | 1.92 | 2.30 | 4.09 | 2.73 | 2.88 | 0.28 | 2.00 | 0.73 | 25.27 |
| 1964 | 0.72 | 0.52 | 3.45 | 5.22 | 2.26 | 2.86 | 4.23 | 1.95 | 3.96 | 0.16 | 2.90 | 1.51 | 29.74 |
| 1965 | 4.11 | 1.18 | 3.06 | 3.48 | 2.36 | 3.44 | 3.66 | 6.40 | 5.03 | 1.57 | 1.47 | 3.32 | 39.08 |
| 1966 | 1.09 | 1.75 | 2.64 | 6.28 | 4.77 | 2.95 | 2.19 | 1.00 | 0.55 | 2.16 | 4.74 | 1.88 | 32.00 |
| 1967 | 2.22 | 1.82 | 2.30 | 3.97 | 1.61 | 7.94 | 1.87 | 2.60 | 2.45 | 3.89 | 2.41 | 2.41 | 35.27 |
| 1968 | 1.77 | 0.87 | 0.90 | 2.31 | 2.99 | 4.15 | 2.03 | 5.32 | 3.88 | 1.04 | 3.70 | 2.77 | 31.73 |
| 1969 | 1.62 | 0.12 | 1.93 | 4.02 | 3.17 | 7.76 | 3.43 | 0.51 | 3.01 | 6.55 | 1.11 | 1.18 | 34.41 |
| 1970 | 0.82 | 0.59 | 2.12 | 4.29 | 7.14 | 7.14 | 4.08 | 1.50 | 8.69 | 2.48 | 2.78 | 1.77 | 43.40 |
| 1971 | 0.93 | 1.94 | 1.54 | 0.97 | 2.23 | 2.62 | 3.57 | 3.97 | 2.39 | 0.72 | 1.32 | 5.37 | 27.57 |
| 1972 | 1.01 | 0.73 | 3.45 | 4.77 | 3.02 | 3.55 | 4.97 | 6.97 | 8.14 | 2.92 | 3.05 | 2.89 | 45.47 |
| 1973 | 1.24 | 1.38 | 3.91 | 4.99 | 3.69 | 2.87 | 5.27 | 0.67 | 6.01 | 2.86 | 1.50 | 3.71 | 38.10 |
| 1974 | 3.29 | 2.11 | 2.40 | 4.27 | 5.09 | 4.69 | 2.96 | 2.60 | 1.47 | 1.88 | 2.47 | 2.12 | 35.35 |
| 1975 | 3.69 | 2.48 | 2.02 | 5.50 | 3.02 | 5.07 | 2.19 | 7.37 | 0.80 | 1.90 | 2.53 | 3.05 | 39.62 |
| 1976 | 0.85 | 1.87 | 4.05 | 4.03 | 2.93 | 1.44 | 1.29 | 1.49 | 1.41 | 0.65 | 1.96 | 0.64 | 26.56 |
| 1977 | 0.55 | 0.71 | 3.67 | 2.62 | 1.88 | 5.12 | 1.18 | 5.39 | 6.07 | 1.36 | 2.05 | 1.96 | 32.56 |
| 1978 | 1.48 | 0.43 | 1.16 | 3.94 | 2.80 | 6.36 | 4.61 | 1.96 | 6.88 | 1.08 | 2.24 | 4.41 | 37.35 |
| 1979 | 2.81 | 1.02 | 4.49 | 4.92 | 2.58 | 4.63 | 2.19 | 7.57 | 0.02 | 1.49 | 2.80 | 2.58 | 37.10 |
| 1980 | 1.04 | 1.24 | 1.96 | 3.41 | 3.22 | 3.42 | 3.56 | 8.54 | 5.65 | 2.09 | 1.10 | 3.43 | 38.66 |
| 1981 | 0.10 | 2.35 | 0.63 | 6.14 | 5.85 | 4.46 | 4.50 | 6.60 | 3.25 | 1.80 | 2.46 | 1.05 | 39.19 |
| 1982 | 2.90 | 0.41 | 4.15 | 2.78 | 2.08 | 1.56 | 8.33 | 3.93 | 1.15 | 1.88 | 6.95 | 8.56 | 44.68 |
| 1983 | 0.66 | 2.06 | 3.56 | 7.69 | 6.26 | 4.11 | 4.25 | 2.08 | 5.41 | 4.41 | 5.87 | 2.99 | 49.35 |
| 1984 | 1.15 | 1.39 | 3.00 | 4.11 | 4.49 | 2.02 | 3.19 | 2.10 | 3.84 | 3.15 | 2.64 | 2.92 | 34.00 |
| 1985 | 1.48 | 3.46 | 4.73 | 1.48 | 2.79 | 1.97 | 3.75 | 3.90 | 1.82 | 4.98 | 8.22 | 1.49 | 40.07 |
| 1986 | 0.39 | 2.58 | 1.49 | 1.85 | 3.11 | 3.49 | 4.30 | 1.15 | 7.12 | 3.75 | 1.41 | 1.09 | 31.73 |
| 1987 | 1.67 | 0.99 | 1.59 | 2.34 | 2.21 | 2.19 | 4.19 | 17.10 | 0.94 | 1.59 | 2.77 | 3.77 | 41.35 |
| 1988 | 1.88 | 1.29 | 2.15 | 2.08 | 1.19 | 1.05 | 2.74 | 3.29 | 3.79 | 5.05 | 6.45 | 2.40 | 33.36 |
| 1989 | 0.82 | 0.77 | 1.67 | 1.37 | 1.59 | 2.01 | 5.89 | 7.31 | 3.91 | 1.49 | 2.16 | 0.46 | 29.45 |
| 1990 | 1.97 | 2.25 | 3.09 | 1.79 | 6.85 | 4.50 | 2.25 | 7.75 | 1.03 | 4.10 | 5.60 | 1.94 | 43.12 |
| Record Mean | 1.59 | 1.41 | 2.66 | 3.58 | 3.30 | 3.73 | 3.73 | 4.13 | 3.68 | 2.43 | 2.81 | 2.34 | 35.37 |

**TABLE 3**    AVERAGE TEMPERATURE (deg. F)    CHICAGO, OHARE INTERNATIONAL AIRPORT, ILLINOIS

| YEAR | JAN | FEB | MAR | APR | MAY | JUNE | JULY | AUG | SEP | OCT | NOV | DEC | ANNUAL |
|---|---|---|---|---|---|---|---|---|---|---|---|---|---|
| 1961 | 20.3 | 31.4 | 38.0 | 43.3 | 54.8 | 67.4 | 71.1 | 70.9 | 65.6 | 53.6 | 39.9 | 25.3 | 48.5 |
| 1962 | 16.8 | 24.4 | 33.5 | 48.8 | 65.0 | 67.9 | 69.2 | 71.8 | 60.7 | 55.8 | 40.1 | 23.2 | 48.1 |
| 1963 | 11.5 | 16.9 | 39.8 | 50.9 | 56.3 | 69.0 | 72.1 | 68.5 | 64.8 | 60.5 | 41.9 | 13.3 | 47.1 |
| 1964 | 27.7 | 26.6 | 33.7 | 49.1 | 62.7 | 69.0 | 67.7 | 63.3 | 63.3 | 48.0 | 41.4 | 24.7 | 48.9 |
| 1965 | 21.4 | 24.3 | 26.6 | 46.6 | 61.7 | 64.9 | 69.4 | 68.0 | 63.8 | 53.2 | 40.3 | 35.3 | 47.9 |
| 1966 | 16.3 | 26.1 | 39.6 | 45.2 | 53.4 | 68.5 | 74.5 | 69.6 | 62.5 | 51.4 | 42.5 | 27.1 | 48.1 |
| 1967 | 27.7 | 19.8 | 36.5 | 48.4 | 53.8 | 69.8 | 68.4 | 66.2 | 61.7 | 52.9 | 37.3 | 30.3 | 47.7 |
| 1968 | 23.8 | 23.6 | 42.7 | 52.3 | 57.0 | 70.2 | 72.0 | 73.7 | 65.5 | 54.7 | 40.0 | 27.8 | 50.3 |
| 1969 | 21.1 | 29.9 | 34.4 | 50.8 | 60.4 | 64.3 | 73.0 | 73.9 | 65.3 | 51.8 | 38.3 | 28.0 | 49.3 |
| 1970 | 16.3 | 26.1 | 34.8 | 51.7 | 61.9 | 69.4 | 74.7 | 72.9 | 65.2 | 55.4 | 40.7 | 30.8 | 50.0 |
| 1971 | 18.9 | 28.2 | 35.0 | 48.6 | 57.2 | 73.5 | 71.5 | 72.0 | 69.7 | 61.7 | 41.7 | 34.2 | 51.0 |
| 1972 | 19.6 | 23.6 | 34.0 | 44.8 | 61.0 | 65.7 | 73.6 | 73.8 | 63.5 | 49.3 | 37.7 | 23.9 | 47.6 |
| 1973 | 28.2 | 28.7 | 44.0 | 48.1 | 54.8 | 71.1 | 74.7 | 74.6 | 66.0 | 57.9 | 41.9 | 28.1 | 51.5 |
| 1974 | 24.8 | 27.4 | 38.6 | 52.3 | 56.8 | 65.5 | 73.6 | 70.0 | 60.5 | 52.8 | 40.6 | 30.2 | 49.4 |
| 1975 | 27.3 | 26.2 | 34.1 | 43.3 | 62.3 | 70.5 | 75.5 | 76.3 | 61.4 | 55.8 | 47.2 | 31.5 | 50.9 |
| 1976 | 19.9 | 35.2 | 42.8 | 52.3 | 55.9 | 71.0 | 74.0 | 70.8 | 62.7 | 48.3 | 32.4 | 19.4 | 48.6 |
| 1977 | 10.7 | 26.9 | 44.9 | 55.0 | 67.2 | 69.3 | 77.5 | 71.9 | 66.0 | 51.5 | 40.0 | 24.2 | 50.4 |
| 1978 | 15.7 | 16.8 | 31.9 | 47.5 | 58.3 | 67.6 | 72.0 | 72.4 | 68.8 | 51.4 | 40.8 | 25.8 | 47.4 |
| 1979 | 12.5 | 16.2 | 36.4 | 45.5 | 59.3 | 69.2 | 72.0 | 71.0 | 66.1 | 53.3 | 40.6 | 33.7 | 48.0 |
| 1980 | 23.4 | 21.5 | 32.6 | 46.5 | 59.7 | 65.3 | 75.7 | 75.7 | 66.0 | 48.4 | 39.9 | 28.0 | 48.6 |
| 1981 | 22.6 | 28.0 | 37.6 | 51.8 | 55.3 | 69.8 | 72.5 | 71.2 | 61.7 | 49.1 | 40.8 | 24.9 | 48.8 |
| 1982 | 12.2 | 21.5 | 35.1 | 44.5 | 64.3 | 62.1 | 74.1 | 68.8 | 62.1 | 53.2 | 39.1 | 36.0 | 47.8 |
| 1983 | 26.3 | 30.5 | 37.4 | 43.4 | 53.2 | 69.7 | 76.7 | 77.3 | 64.6 | 52.8 | 41.1 | 14.3 | 49.0 |
| 1984 | 17.1 | 33.9 | 29.5 | 45.8 | 55.5 | 70.3 | 70.3 | 72.8 | 61.1 | 54.7 | 37.9 | 31.0 | 48.3 |
| 1985 | 14.4 | 20.4 | 39.4 | 52.6 | 60.2 | 63.6 | 71.4 | 69.2 | 65.4 | 52.5 | 37.8 | 17.0 | 47.0 |
| 1986 | 22.8 | 24.0 | 40.4 | 51.5 | 59.5 | 66.3 | 74.9 | 68.5 | 66.8 | 53.7 | 36.0 | 30.6 | 49.6 |
| 1987 | 25.9 | 33.9 | 40.8 | 50.6 | 63.4 | 72.4 | 76.7 | 71.9 | 65.1 | 47.3 | 43.9 | 32.2 | 52.0 |
| 1988 | 19.8 | 22.7 | 38.1 | 48.2 | 61.0 | 71.7 | 76.8 | 76.8 | 62.0 | 46.1 | 41.7 | 27.7 | 49.7 |
| 1989 | 32.4 | 19.6 | 36.6 | 46.8 | 57.8 | 67.5 | 73.9 | 71.4 | 62.0 | 54.0 | 37.7 | 17.4 | 48.1 |
| 1990 | 33.9 | 31.3 | 41.3 | 49.9 | 56.2 | 69.6 | 71.7 | 71.9 | 65.9 | 51.6 | 44.7 | 28.6 | 51.4 |
| Record Mean | 21.1 | 25.5 | 36.5 | 48.6 | 59.0 | 68.4 | 73.2 | 71.9 | 64.5 | 52.7 | 40.0 | 26.8 | 49.0 |
| Max | 29.0 | 33.4 | 45.1 | 58.7 | 70.0 | 79.5 | 83.6 | 82.1 | 75.0 | 63.1 | 48.3 | 34.2 | 58.5 |
| Min | 13.1 | 17.5 | 28.0 | 38.5 | 47.9 | 57.3 | 62.7 | 61.7 | 54.0 | 42.2 | 31.7 | 19.3 | 39.5 |

## REFERENCE NOTES FOR TABLES 1, 2, 3 and 6    (CHICAGO, IL)

### GENERAL

T - TRACE AMOUNT
BLANK ENTRIES DENOTE MISSING/UNREPORTED DATA.
# INDICATES A STATION OR INSTRUMENT RELOCATION.

### SPECIFIC

#### TABLE 1

(a) - LENGTH OF RECORD IN YEARS. ALTHOUGH INDIVIDUAL MONTHS MAY BE MISSING.

* LESS THAN .05

NORMALS — BASED ON THE 1951-1980 RECORD PERIOD.
EXTREMES — DATES ARE THE MOST RECENT OCCURRENCE.
WIND DIR. — NUMERALS SHOW TENS OF DEGREES CLOCKWISE FROM TRUE NORTH. "00" INDICATES CALM.
RESULTANT WIND DIRECTIONS ARE GIVEN TO WHOLE DEGREES.

#### TABLE 3

MAX AND MIN ARE LONG-TERM MEAN DAILY MAXIMUM AND MEAN DAILY MINIMUM TEMPERATURES.

### EXCEPTIONS

#### TABLES 2, 3, and 6

RECORD MEANS ARE THROUGH THE CURRENT YEAR, BEGINNING IN
1958 FOR TEMPERATURE
1958 FOR PRECIPITATION
1958 FOR SNOWFALL

**TABLE 4**  HEATING DEGREE DAYS Base 65 deg. F    CHICAGO, OHARE INTERNATIONAL AIRPORT, ILLINOIS

| SEASON | JULY | AUG | SEP | OCT | NOV | DEC | JAN | FEB | MAR | APR | MAY | JUNE | TOTAL |
|---|---|---|---|---|---|---|---|---|---|---|---|---|---|
| 1961-62 | 15 | 11 | 126 | 360 | 747 | 1223 | 1459 | 1128 | 970 | 504 | 147 | 50 | 6770 |
| 1962-63 | 6 | 1 | 179 | 310 | 740 | 1291 | 1655 | 1339 | 776 | 425 | 281 | 59 | 7062 |
| 1963-64 | 16 | 24 | 86 | 176 | 684 | 1598 | 1749 | 1106 | 963 | 479 | 139 | 63 | 6483 |
| 1964-65 | 10 | 52 | 148 | 521 | 699 | 1240 | 1345 | 1134 | 1185 | 545 | 157 | 77 | 7113 |
| 1965-66 | 12 | 53 | 110 | 370 | 733 | 915 | 1512 | 1079 | 782 | 587 | 371 | 53 | 6567 |
| 1966-67 | 1 | 12 | 127 | 420 | 669 | 1170 | 1148 | 1257 | 878 | 491 | 362 | 19 | 6554 |
| 1967-68 | 39 | 53 | 160 | 395 | 827 | 1068 | 1274 | 1192 | 682 | 376 | 257 | 28 | 6351 |
| 1968-69 | 14 | 12 | 59 | 355 | 740 | 1146 | 1355 | 976 | 941 | 419 | 204 | 124 | 6345 |
| 1969-70 | 4 | 0 | 75 | 423 | 794 | 1138 | 1506 | 1086 | 929 | 418 | 168 | 44 | 6585 |
| 1970-71 | 2 | 0 | 85 | 302 | 725 | 1055 | 1422 | 1026 | 923 | 484 | 262 | 14 | 6300 |
| 1971-72 | 7 | 3 | 64 | 154 | 693 | 948 | 1406 | 1197 | 954 | 602 | 178 | 80 | 6285 |
| 1972-73 | 15 | 10 | 109 | 481 | 811 | 1269 | 1135 | 1012 | 645 | 503 | 311 | 0 | 6301 |
| 1973-74 | 0 | 0 | 72 | 244 | 687 | 1139 | 1240 | 1046 | 812 | 383 | 266 | 63 | 5952 |
| 1974-75 | 0 | 1 | 176 | 384 | 724 | 1072 | 1160 | 1078 | 951 | 643 | 152 | 30 | 6371 |
| 1975-76 | 1 | 0 | 147 | 303 | 531 | 1033 | 1392 | 859 | 681 | 411 | 285 | 17 | 5660 |
| 1976-77 | 0 | 9 | 119 | 522 | 973 | 1408 | 1619 | 1060 | 616 | 332 | 115 | 41 | 6874 |
| 1977-78 | 0 | 8 | 42 | 413 | 741 | 1254 | 1521 | 1346 | 1020 | 518 | 264 | 46 | 7173 |
| 1978-79 | 1 | 4 | 59 | 418 | 718 | 1206 | 1622 | 1360 | 879 | 580 | 233 | 30 | 7110 |
| 1979-80 | 16 | 19 | 62 | 382 | 722 | 967 | 1291 | 1254 | 995 | 558 | 198 | 83 | 6537 |
| 1980-81 | 0 | 3 | 71 | 511 | 746 | 1140 | 1308 | 1031 | 846 | 397 | 313 | 6 | 6372 |
| 1981-82 | 8 | 6 | 135 | 489 | 719 | 1236 | 1632 | 1213 | 922 | 608 | 93 | 118 | 7179 |
| 1982-83 | 7 | 37 | 152 | 372 | 772 | 891 | 1194 | 961 | 847 | 643 | 364 | 38 | 6278 |
| 1983-84 | 16 | 0 | 125 | 383 | 714 | 1568 | 1479 | 894 | 1095 | 575 | 300 | 18 | 7167 |
| 1984-85 | 19 | 1 | 189 | 320 | 807 | 1046 | 1563 | 1245 | 787 | 418 | 183 | 103 | 6681 |
| 1985-86 | 0 | 6 | 141 | 380 | 813 | 1480 | 1302 | 1142 | 765 | 417 | 202 | 74 | 6722 |
| 1986-87 | 3 | 29 | 64 | 343 | 863 | 1060 | 1205 | 866 | 742 | 432 | 162 | 14 | 5783 |
| 1987-88 | 4 | 19 | 74 | 541 | 629 | 1011 | 1396 | 1221 | 828 | 503 | 176 | 40 | 6442 |
| 1988-89 | 0 | 9 | 63 | 583 | 693 | 1149 | 1003 | 1265 | 882 | 540 | 261 | 43 | 6491 |
| 1989-90 | 0 | 5 | 131 | 344 | 813 | 1471 | 956 | 938 | 733 | 491 | 271 | 33 | 6186 |
| 1990-91 | 10 | 5 | 103 | 425 | 605 | 1120 | | | | | | | |

**TABLE 5**  COOLING DEGREE DAYS Base 65 deg. F    CHICAGO, OHARE INTERNATIONAL AIRPORT, ILLINOIS

| YEAR | JAN | FEB | MAR | APR | MAY | JUNE | JULY | AUG | SEP | OCT | NOV | DEC | TOTAL |
|---|---|---|---|---|---|---|---|---|---|---|---|---|---|
| 1971 | 0 | 0 | 0 | 0 | 27 | 275 | 213 | 228 | 213 | 59 | 0 | 0 | 1015 |
| 1972 | 0 | 0 | 0 | 0 | 64 | 106 | 289 | 289 | 72 | 0 | 0 | 0 | 820 |
| 1973 | 0 | 0 | 0 | 0 | 3 | 189 | 308 | 301 | 108 | 32 | 0 | 0 | 946 |
| 1974 | 0 | 0 | 0 | 10 | 21 | 83 | 274 | 162 | 48 | 12 | 0 | 0 | 610 |
| 1975 | 0 | 0 | 0 | 0 | 76 | 203 | 332 | 358 | 46 | 24 | 1 | 0 | 1040 |
| 1976 | 0 | 0 | 0 | 36 | 6 | 178 | 286 | 196 | 56 | 8 | 0 | 0 | 766 |
| 1977 | 0 | 0 | 0 | 39 | 191 | 178 | 395 | 229 | 76 | 0 | 0 | 0 | 1108 |
| 1978 | 0 | 0 | 0 | 0 | 60 | 132 | 227 | 243 | 181 | 2 | 0 | 0 | 845 |
| 1979 | 0 | 0 | 0 | 2 | 61 | 164 | 241 | 213 | 99 | 26 | 0 | 0 | 806 |
| 1980 | 0 | 0 | 0 | 10 | 43 | 101 | 338 | 342 | 107 | 2 | 0 | 0 | 943 |
| 1981 | 0 | 0 | 0 | 9 | 20 | 157 | 248 | 204 | 44 | 0 | 0 | 0 | 682 |
| 1982 | 0 | 0 | 0 | 0 | 79 | 38 | 295 | 161 | 69 | 14 | 0 | 0 | 656 |
| 1983 | 0 | 0 | 1 | 0 | 4 | 189 | 385 | 388 | 122 | 10 | 0 | 0 | 1099 |
| 1984 | 0 | 0 | 0 | 5 | 11 | 184 | 190 | 254 | 77 | 8 | 0 | 0 | 729 |
| 1985 | 0 | 0 | 0 | 53 | 42 | 71 | 204 | 142 | 158 | 0 | 0 | 0 | 670 |
| 1986 | 0 | 0 | 7 | 17 | 37 | 118 | 318 | 145 | 123 | 3 | 0 | 0 | 768 |
| 1987 | 0 | 0 | 0 | 6 | 116 | 241 | 377 | 238 | 83 | 0 | 1 | 0 | 1062 |
| 1988 | 0 | 0 | 0 | 5 | 59 | 247 | 373 | 383 | 96 | 1 | 0 | 0 | 1164 |
| 1989 | 0 | 0 | 2 | 0 | 44 | 121 | 282 | 207 | 48 | 11 | 0 | 0 | 715 |
| 1990 | 0 | 0 | 7 | 43 | 8 | 179 | 226 | 224 | 137 | 11 | 1 | 0 | 836 |

**TABLE 6**  SNOWFALL (inches)    CHICAGO, OHARE INTERNATIONAL AIRPORT, ILLINOIS

| SEASON | JULY | AUG | SEP | OCT | NOV | DEC | JAN | FEB | MAR | APR | MAY | JUNE | TOTAL |
|---|---|---|---|---|---|---|---|---|---|---|---|---|---|
| 1961-62 | 0.0 | 0.0 | 0.0 | T | 2.0 | 10.7 | 18.6 | 10.0 | 5.7 | 0.7 | 0.0 | 0.0 | 47.7 |
| 1962-63 | 0.0 | 0.0 | 0.0 | T | 0.3 | 2.3 | 16.8 | 8.4 | 7.5 | T | 0.0 | 0.0 | 35.3 |
| 1963-64 | 0.0 | 0.0 | 0.0 | 0.0 | T | 8.9 | 1.6 | 5.9 | 19.8 | T | 0.0 | 0.0 | 36.2 |
| 1964-65 | 0.0 | 0.0 | 0.0 | 0.0 | 2.3 | 11.1 | 11.7 | 11.5 | 24.7 | T | 0.0 | 0.0 | 61.3 |
| 1965-66 | 0.0 | 0.0 | 0.0 | T | 0.2 | 6.6 | 15.5 | 4.3 | 0.7 | T | 1.6 | 0.0 | 28.9 |
| 1966-67 | 0.0 | 0.0 | 0.0 | T | 0.5 | 8.4 | 25.1 | 21.5 | 8.8 | 3.4 | T | 0.0 | 67.7 |
| 1967-68 | 0.0 | 0.0 | T | 6.6 | 2.4 | 2.9 | 10.4 | 3.8 | 1.5 | 0.1 | 0.0 | 0.0 | 27.7 |
| 1968-69 | 0.0 | 0.0 | 0.0 | 0.0 | 0.7 | 10.9 | 3.7 | 2.3 | 4.7 | 0.0 | T | 0.0 | 22.3 |
| 1969-70 | 0.0 | 0.0 | 0.0 | 0.0 | 2.0 | 19.3 | 9.5 | 6.3 | 11.8 | 7.2 | 0.0 | 0.0 | 56.1 |
| 1970-71 | 0.0 | 0.0 | 0.0 | 0.0 | 0.2 | 2.7 | 10.0 | 1.4 | 8.0 | 0.8 | T | 0.0 | 23.1 |
| 1971-72 | 0.0 | 0.0 | 0.0 | 0.0 | 1.3 | 7.6 | 7.7 | 16.8 | 3.3 | 0.0 | 0.0 | 0.0 | 36.9 |
| 1972-73 | 0.0 | 0.0 | 0.0 | 0.1 | 0.9 | 11.2 | 0.5 | 9.3 | 3.4 | 0.2 | T | 0.0 | 25.6 |
| 1973-74 | 0.0 | 0.0 | 0.0 | 0.0 | T | 18.8 | 7.4 | 9.6 | 1.4 | T | 0.0 | 0.0 | 37.2 |
| 1974-75 | 0.0 | 0.0 | 0.0 | 0.0 | 1.0 | 9.4 | 3.5 | 8.2 | 4.5 | 11.1 | 0.0 | 0.0 | 37.7 |
| 1975-76 | 0.0 | 0.0 | 0.0 | 0.0 | 6.4 | 6.8 | 10.0 | 1.6 | 1.9 | 0.8 | T | 0.0 | 27.5 |
| 1976-77 | 0.0 | 0.0 | 0.0 | 1.6 | 0.5 | 6.5 | 7.2 | 4.0 | 4.9 | T | 0.0 | 0.0 | 24.7 |
| 1977-78 | 0.0 | 0.0 | 0.0 | 0.0 | 5.2 | 12.7 | 21.9 | 7.9 | 4.5 | 0.2 | 0.0 | 0.0 | 52.4 |
| 1978-79 | 0.0 | 0.0 | 0.0 | 0.0 | 5.2 | 35.3 | 34.3 | 6.8 | 2.0 | 0.1 | 0.0 | 0.0 | 83.7 |
| 1979-80 | 0.0 | 0.0 | 0.0 | 0.0 | 4.0 | 0.9 | 6.2 | 14.7 | 11.6 | 4.2 | 0.0 | 0.0 | 41.6 |
| 1980-81 | 0.0 | 0.0 | 0.0 | T | 5.1 | 9.7 | 2.0 | 15.9 | 2.3 | 0.0 | 0.0 | 0.0 | 35.0 |
| 1981-82 | 0.0 | 0.0 | 0.0 | T | 3.6 | 4.9 | 21.1 | 4.8 | 14.3 | 10.6 | 0.0 | 0.0 | 59.3 |
| 1982-83 | 0.0 | 0.0 | 0.0 | 0.0 | 0.4 | 2.1 | 5.0 | 8.9 | 9.0 | 1.2 | 0.0 | 0.0 | 26.6 |
| 1983-84 | 0.0 | 0.0 | 0.0 | 0.0 | 1.0 | 16.5 | 17.2 | 1.9 | 9.7 | 2.7 | 0.0 | 0.0 | 49.0 |
| 1984-85 | 0.0 | 0.0 | 0.0 | 0.0 | T | 6.6 | 18.9 | 13.3 | 0.3 | T | 0.0 | 0.0 | 39.1 |
| 1985-86 | 0.0 | 0.0 | 0.0 | 0.0 | 1.1 | 5.2 | 6.9 | 10.9 | 4.1 | 0.8 | 0.0 | 0.0 | 29.0 |
| 1986-87 | 0.0 | 0.0 | 0.0 | 0.0 | 3.8 | 0.4 | 17.3 | T | 4.7 | T | 0.0 | 0.0 | 26.2 |
| 1987-88 | 0.0 | 0.0 | 0.0 | 0.1 | 1.0 | 18.7 | 5.4 | 15.5 | 1.9 | T | 0.0 | 0.0 | 42.6 |
| 1988-89 | 0.0 | 0.0 | 0.0 | T | 0.9 | 5.0 | 0.4 | 15.1 | 2.0 | 0.6 | 0.5 | 0.0 | 24.5 |
| 1989-90 | 0.0 | T | 0.0 | 6.3 | 3.9 | 5.4 | 3.2 | 13.6 | 1.3 | 0.1 | T | 0.0 | 33.8 |
| 1990-91 | 0.0 | 0.0 | 0.0 | T | T | 3.2 | | | | | | | |
| Record Mean | 0.0 | T | T | 0.5 | 2.0 | 8.6 | 10.7 | 8.5 | 6.6 | 1.7 | 0.1 | 0.0 | 38.7 |

**See Reference Notes, relative to all above tables, on preceding page.**

The airport station is situated on a rather level tableland surrounded by well-drained and gently rolling terrain. It is set back a mile from the rim of the Illinois River Valley and is almost 200 feet above the river bed. Exposures of all instruments are good. The climate of this area is typically continental as shown by its changeable weather and the wide range of temperature extremes.

June and September are usually the most pleasant months of the year. Then during October or the first of November, Indian Summer is often experienced with an extended period of warm, dry weather.

Precipitation is normally heaviest during the growing season and lowest during midwinter.

The earliest snowfalls have occurred in September and the latest in the spring have occurred as late as May. Heavy snowfalls have rarely exceeded 20 inches.

Based on the 1951-1980 period, the average first occurrence of 32 degrees Fahrenheit in the fall is October 20 and the average last occurrence in the spring is April 24.

# TABLE 1 NORMALS, MEANS AND EXTREMES

PEORIA, ILLINOIS

LATITUDE: 40°40'N   LONGITUDE: 89°41'W   ELEVATION: FT. GRND 652 BARO 683   TIME ZONE: CENTRAL   WBAN: 14842

| | (a) | JAN | FEB | MAR | APR | MAY | JUNE | JULY | AUG | SEP | OCT | NOV | DEC | YEAR |
|---|---|---|---|---|---|---|---|---|---|---|---|---|---|---|
| **TEMPERATURE °F:** | | | | | | | | | | | | | | |
| Normals | | | | | | | | | | | | | | |
| -Daily Maximum | | 29.7 | 35.2 | 46.5 | 61.9 | 72.5 | 82.1 | 85.5 | 83.4 | 76.7 | 64.8 | 48.5 | 35.4 | 60.2 |
| -Daily Minimum | | 13.3 | 18.4 | 28.1 | 40.6 | 50.6 | 60.2 | 64.6 | 62.7 | 54.5 | 42.9 | 30.9 | 20.2 | 40.6 |
| -Monthly | | 21.5 | 26.8 | 37.3 | 51.3 | 61.6 | 71.2 | 75.0 | 73.1 | 65.6 | 53.9 | 39.8 | 27.8 | 50.4 |
| Extremes | | | | | | | | | | | | | | |
| -Record Highest | 50 | 70 | 72 | 86 | 92 | 93 | 105 | 103 | 103 | 100 | 90 | 81 | 71 | 105 |
| -Year | | 1989 | 1976 | 1986 | 1986 | 1987 | 1988 | 1940 | 1988 | 1953 | 1963 | 1950 | 1982 | JUN 1988 |
| -Record Lowest | 50 | -25 | -18 | -10 | 14 | 25 | 39 | 47 | 41 | 26 | 19 | -2 | -23 | -25 |
| -Year | | 1977 | 1979 | 1960 | 1982 | 1966 | 1945 | 1972 | 1986 | 1942 | 1972 | 1977 | 1989 | JAN 1977 |
| **NORMAL DEGREE DAYS:** | | | | | | | | | | | | | | |
| Heating (base 65°F) | | 1349 | 1070 | 859 | 411 | 176 | 22 | 0 | 5 | 64 | 361 | 756 | 1153 | 6226 |
| Cooling (base 65°F) | | 0 | 0 | 0 | 0 | 71 | 208 | 314 | 256 | 82 | 17 | 0 | 0 | 948 |
| **% OF POSSIBLE SUNSHINE** | 46 | 47 | 50 | 51 | 55 | 60 | 67 | 69 | 67 | 65 | 61 | 44 | 41 | 56 |
| **MEAN SKY COVER (tenths)** | | | | | | | | | | | | | | |
| Sunrise - Sunset | 46 | 6.8 | 6.7 | 7.0 | 6.7 | 6.3 | 6.0 | 5.5 | 5.5 | 5.2 | 5.3 | 6.8 | 7.0 | 6.2 |
| **MEAN NUMBER OF DAYS:** | | | | | | | | | | | | | | |
| Sunrise to Sunset | | | | | | | | | | | | | | |
| -Clear | 46 | 7.4 | 6.9 | 6.0 | 6.4 | 7.2 | 7.3 | 9.3 | 10.1 | 11.1 | 11.2 | 7.0 | 6.6 | 96.4 |
| -Partly Cloudy | 46 | 6.0 | 5.8 | 7.3 | 8.0 | 9.6 | 10.5 | 12.0 | 10.3 | 8.5 | 7.7 | 6.1 | 6.0 | 97.8 |
| -Cloudy | 46 | 17.7 | 15.6 | 17.7 | 15.6 | 14.2 | 12.2 | 9.7 | 10.6 | 10.4 | 12.1 | 16.9 | 18.4 | 171.1 |
| Precipitation | | | | | | | | | | | | | | |
| .01 inches or more | 50 | 9.3 | 8.3 | 10.8 | 11.7 | 11.3 | 9.6 | 8.6 | 8.2 | 8.6 | 7.7 | 9.1 | 9.8 | 113.1 |
| Snow,Ice pellets | | | | | | | | | | | | | | |
| 1.0 inches or more | 46 | 2.2 | 1.7 | 1.4 | 0.3 | 0.0 | 0.0 | 0.0 | 0.0 | 0.0 | 0.* | 0.6 | 2.0 | 8.2 |
| Thunderstorms | 46 | 0.6 | 0.6 | 2.6 | 5.1 | 6.7 | 8.3 | 7.8 | 6.8 | 5.1 | 2.5 | 1.4 | 0.7 | 47.9 |
| Heavy Fog Visibility | | | | | | | | | | | | | | |
| 1/4 mile or less | 46 | 3.0 | 2.7 | 2.2 | 0.9 | 0.9 | 0.6 | 1.0 | 1.4 | 1.3 | 1.5 | 2.1 | 3.4 | 21.2 |
| Temperature °F | | | | | | | | | | | | | | |
| -Maximum | | | | | | | | | | | | | | |
| 90° and above | 30 | 0.0 | 0.0 | 0.0 | 0.1 | 0.5 | 4.7 | 8.3 | 5.1 | 1.7 | 0.* | 0.0 | 0.0 | 20.4 |
| 32° and below | 30 | 17.8 | 12.2 | 4.0 | 0.1 | 0.0 | 0.0 | 0.0 | 0.0 | 0.0 | 0.0 | 1.7 | 12.9 | 48.7 |
| -Minimum | | | | | | | | | | | | | | |
| 32° and below | 30 | 29.4 | 25.5 | 19.9 | 5.8 | 0.5 | 0.0 | 0.0 | 0.0 | 0.1 | 4.5 | 17.0 | 26.7 | 129.3 |
| 0° and below | 30 | 6.7 | 3.4 | 0.3 | 0.0 | 0.0 | 0.0 | 0.0 | 0.0 | 0.0 | 0.0 | 0.1 | 3.0 | 13.4 |
| **AVG. STATION PRESS.(mb)** | 17 | 995.4 | 995.0 | 991.6 | 990.8 | 990.4 | 991.0 | 992.4 | 993.2 | 993.8 | 994.6 | 993.6 | 994.9 | 993.1 |
| **RELATIVE HUMIDITY (%)** | | | | | | | | | | | | | | |
| Hour 00 | 30 | 77 | 78 | 76 | 71 | 74 | 76 | 82 | 83 | 82 | 78 | 79 | 81 | 78 |
| Hour 06 | 30 | 78 | 80 | 81 | 78 | 80 | 81 | 86 | 89 | 88 | 85 | 83 | 83 | 83 |
| Hour 12 (Local Time) | 30 | 68 | 67 | 62 | 55 | 56 | 56 | 59 | 60 | 59 | 58 | 66 | 71 | 61 |
| Hour 18 | 30 | 72 | 70 | 64 | 55 | 55 | 56 | 60 | 63 | 64 | 63 | 71 | 76 | 64 |
| **PRECIPITATION (inches):** | | | | | | | | | | | | | | |
| Water Equivalent | | | | | | | | | | | | | | |
| -Normal | | 1.60 | 1.41 | 2.86 | 3.81 | 3.84 | 3.88 | 3.99 | 3.39 | 3.63 | 2.51 | 1.96 | 2.01 | 34.89 |
| -Maximum Monthly | 50 | 8.11 | 5.18 | 6.95 | 8.66 | 7.96 | 11.69 | 8.42 | 8.61 | 13.09 | 10.80 | 7.62 | 6.34 | 13.09 |
| -Year | | 1965 | 1942 | 1973 | 1947 | 1957 | 1974 | 1958 | 1965 | 1961 | 1941 | 1985 | 1949 | SEP 1961 |
| -Minimum Monthly | 50 | 0.22 | 0.33 | 0.39 | 0.71 | 1.04 | 0.60 | 0.33 | 0.78 | 0.03 | 0.03 | 0.43 | 0.33 | 0.03 |
| -Year | | 1986 | 1947 | 1958 | 1971 | 1964 | 1988 | 1988 | 1984 | 1979 | 1964 | 1953 | 1962 | SEP 1979 |
| -Maximum in 24 hrs | 46 | 4.45 | 1.92 | 3.39 | 5.06 | 3.62 | 4.44 | 3.56 | 4.32 | 4.15 | 3.70 | 2.45 | 3.38 | 5.06 |
| -Year | | 1965 | 1954 | 1944 | 1950 | 1956 | 1974 | 1953 | 1955 | 1961 | 1969 | 1946 | 1949 | APR 1950 |
| Snow,Ice pellets | | | | | | | | | | | | | | |
| -Maximum Monthly | 46 | 24.7 | 15.2 | 16.9 | 13.4 | 0.1 | 0.0 | 0.0 | 0.0 | 0.0 | 1.8 | 9.1 | 21.7 | 24.7 |
| -Year | | 1979 | 1989 | 1960 | 1982 | 1966 | | | | | 1967 | 1974 | 1977 | JAN 1979 |
| -Maximum in 24 hrs | 46 | 12.2 | 7.6 | 9.0 | 6.1 | 0.1 | 0.0 | 0.0 | 0.0 | 0.0 | 1.8 | 7.2 | 10.2 | 12.2 |
| -Year | | 1979 | 1944 | 1946 | 1982 | 1966 | | | | | 1967 | 1951 | 1973 | JAN 1979 |
| **WIND:** | | | | | | | | | | | | | | |
| Mean Speed (mph) | 46 | 11.2 | 11.2 | 12.1 | 11.9 | 10.0 | 8.9 | 7.8 | 7.7 | 8.5 | 9.4 | 11.0 | 10.9 | 10.1 |
| Prevailing Direction | | | | | | | | | | | | | | |
| through 1963 | | S | WNW | WNW | S | S | S | S | S | S | S | S | S | S |
| Fastest Mile | | | | | | | | | | | | | | |
| -Direction (!!!) | 41 | S | W | W | SW | SW | NW | NW | W | W | SW | W | SW | NW |
| -Speed (MPH) | 41 | 54 | 52 | 56 | 66 | 61 | 66 | 75 | 65 | 73 | 60 | 56 | 58 | 75 |
| -Year | | 1950 | 1953 | 1959 | 1947 | 1950 | 1981 | 1953 | 1956 | 1965 | 1958 | 1964 | 1948 | JUL 1953 |
| Peak Gust | | | | | | | | | | | | | | |
| -Direction (!!!) | 6 | NW | NW | NW | N | W | NW | W | 22 | S | W | S | NE | N |
| -Speed (mph) | 6 | 53 | 48 | 51 | 69 | 55 | 63 | 48 | 52 | 49 | 48 | 62 | 59 | 69 |
| -Date | | 1985 | 1987 | 1988 | 1989 | 1988 | 1987 | 1984 | 1987 | 1986 | 1985 | 1988 | 1987 | APR 1989 |

**See Reference Notes to this table on the following page.**

## TABLE 2 — PRECIPITATION (inches) — PEORIA, ILLINOIS

| YEAR | JAN | FEB | MAR | APR | MAY | JUNE | JULY | AUG | SEP | OCT | NOV | DEC | ANNUAL |
|------|-----|-----|-----|-----|-----|------|------|-----|-----|-----|-----|-----|--------|
| 1961 | 0.32 | 1.07 | 3.26 | 2.38 | 2.19 | 3.39 | 5.56 | 1.94 | 13.09 | 1.77 | 2.79 | 1.69 | 39.45 |
| 1962 | 1.97 | 1.23 | 2.15 | 0.89 | 5.67 | 2.11 | 2.77 | 1.80 | 1.29 | 3.56 | 1.05 | 0.33 | 24.82 |
| 1963 | 0.56 | 0.48 | 5.32 | 4.08 | 1.24 | 1.53 | 3.56 | 2.99 | 3.63 | 0.03 | 3.01 | 0.78 | 25.66 |
| 1964 | 1.02 | 0.54 | 3.77 | 6.92 | 1.04 | 4.22 | 1.59 | 2.06 | 3.63 | 0.69 | 1.12 | 3.35 | 28.95 |
| 1965 | 8.11 | 0.93 | 3.40 | 5.58 | 3.85 | 1.04 | 3.31 | 8.61 | 8.17 | 0.69 | 1.22 | 3.35 | 48.26 |
| 1966 | 1.49 | 2.60 | 1.78 | 3.98 | 4.50 | 2.29 | 3.66 | 2.56 | 3.06 | 1.80 | 2.42 | 3.00 | 33.14 |
| 1967 | 1.08 | 1.07 | 2.33 | 5.47 | 2.80 | 2.03 | 5.74 | 2.34 | 5.56 | 2.18 | 2.63 | 2.80 | 35.95 |
| 1968 | 1.12 | 1.55 | 0.93 | 2.20 | 4.70 | 6.16 | 4.32 | 1.71 | 4.83 | 0.58 | 2.99 | 1.13 | 33.89 |
| 1969 | 2.43 | 0.56 | 1.20 | 2.94 | 2.37 | 4.93 | 5.55 | 2.82 | 3.31 | 5.67 | 0.79 | 1.13 | 33.70 |
| 1970 | 0.56 | 0.64 | 1.60 | 7.18 | 3.89 | 3.92 | 5.46 | 3.21 | 11.49 | 4.36 | 1.11 | 1.30 | 44.72 |
| 1971 | 0.59 | 1.64 | 1.09 | 0.71 | 2.80 | 0.98 | 5.21 | 2.19 | 3.07 | 1.71 | 1.43 | 4.96 | 26.38 |
| 1972 | 0.81 | 0.74 | 2.48 | 4.38 | 1.30 | 5.97 | 3.54 | 4.26 | 5.21 | 2.50 | 2.56 | 2.48 | 36.23 |
| 1973 | 1.76 | 0.99 | 6.95 | 4.26 | 4.51 | 6.46 | 6.04 | 0.90 | 7.58 | 5.18 | 1.48 | 4.11 | 50.22 |
| 1974 | 3.09 | 1.65 | 2.69 | 4.11 | 6.26 | 11.69 | 2.63 | 0.81 | 1.45 | 2.07 | 4.13 | 1.93 | 42.51 |
| 1975 | 2.59 | 2.85 | 1.73 | 3.92 | 5.19 | 3.90 | 4.26 | 5.62 | 2.74 | 3.63 | 2.75 | 2.04 | 41.22 |
| 1976 | 0.78 | 2.56 | 4.25 | 4.86 | 5.11 | 2.92 | 2.98 | 2.48 | 1.78 | 0.83 | 0.38 | 2.25 | 31.23 |
| 1977 | 1.22 | 0.95 | 4.41 | 1.24 | 3.54 | 2.06 | 3.43 | 7.28 | 6.26 | 4.00 | 1.77 | 2.25 | 38.41 |
| 1978 | 0.69 | 0.59 | 1.56 | 4.69 | 7.72 | 1.96 | 3.47 | 1.28 | 2.54 | 1.73 | 3.54 | 2.32 | 32.09 |
| 1979 | 2.48 | 1.37 | 4.42 | 4.48 | 1.96 | 1.77 | 4.81 | 0.87 | 0.03 | 1.70 | 2.76 | 2.33 | 28.98 |
| 1980 | 0.59 | 1.06 | 2.79 | 2.78 | 2.05 | 8.94 | 1.43 | 6.16 | 4.09 | 2.44 | 0.67 | 2.25 | 35.25 |
| 1981 | 0.48 | 2.41 | 0.92 | 5.71 | 5.77 | 6.22 | 7.08 | 5.61 | 1.31 | 1.37 | 1.64 | 1.24 | 39.76 |
| 1982 | 2.88 | 1.13 | 4.80 | 5.40 | 3.15 | 3.15 | 7.53 | 3.97 | 1.24 | 1.47 | 5.45 | 2.65 | 45.12 |
| 1983 | 0.53 | 1.01 | 2.84 | 7.06 | 6.66 | 4.48 | 1.99 | 1.09 | 5.08 | 3.01 | 5.58 | 2.65 | 41.98 |
| 1984 | 0.59 | 2.28 | 3.95 | 5.18 | 4.84 | 2.90 | 5.02 | 0.78 | 2.38 | 5.07 | 3.95 | 3.82 | 40.76 |
| 1985 | 0.99 | 2.62 | 5.77 | 1.14 | 3.14 | 5.11 | 3.43 | 3.70 | 3.43 | 4.61 | 7.62 | 2.24 | 43.80 |
| 1986 | 0.22 | 1.79 | 0.87 | 1.39 | 2.95 | 6.53 | 7.00 | 1.74 | 6.39 | 4.64 | 1.32 | 2.60 | 37.44 |
| 1987 | 1.49 | 0.84 | 1.98 | 1.84 | 1.69 | 3.27 | 2.90 | 4.02 | 2.82 | 1.62 | 2.88 | 4.15 | 27.41 |
| 1988 | 1.99 | 0.71 | 2.83 | 1.59 | 1.68 | 0.60 | 0.33 | 2.11 | 2.86 | 1.08 | 4.19 | 2.23 | 22.16 |
| 1989 | 1.00 | 1.17 | 1.14 | 4.39 | 2.23 | 1.28 | 2.22 | 2.86 | 2.87 | 1.57 | 0.93 | 0.87 | 22.53 |
| 1990 | 1.73 | 3.59 | 3.95 | 2.32 | 6.19 | 7.99 | 9.18 | 5.31 | 1.03 | 3.17 | 7.19 | 3.70 | 55.35 |
| Record Mean | 1.75 | 1.78 | 2.81 | 3.53 | 3.92 | 3.90 | 3.82 | 3.08 | 3.65 | 2.47 | 2.38 | 2.08 | 35.17 |

## TABLE 3 — AVERAGE TEMPERATURE (deg. F) — PEORIA, ILLINOIS

| YEAR | JAN | FEB | MAR | APR | MAY | JUNE | JULY | AUG | SEP | OCT | NOV | DEC | ANNUAL |
|------|-----|-----|-----|-----|-----|------|------|-----|-----|-----|-----|-----|--------|
| 1961 | 21.3 | 31.8 | 40.6 | 44.4 | 56.5 | 69.4 | 73.3 | 72.3 | 66.2 | 53.7 | 39.6 | 24.1 | 49.4 |
| 1962 | 16.5 | 25.9 | 33.7 | 50.2 | 59.0 | 71.0 | 72.0 | 73.6 | 62.6 | 54.9 | 40.8 | 23.6 | 49.4 |
| 1963 | 12.8 | 18.6 | 41.5 | 52.9 | 59.0 | 73.0 | 74.3 | 70.4 | 65.2 | 64.2 | 43.0 | 15.5 | 49.2 |
| 1964 | 28.7 | 28.1 | 36.0 | 52.2 | 66.3 | 72.7 | 76.2 | 72.4 | 65.4 | 50.8 | 43.5 | 25.7 | 51.5 |
| 1965 | 24.3 | 27.0 | 28.0 | 50.9 | 66.7 | 71.3 | 73.7 | 71.2 | 64.7 | 52.5 | 41.2 | 35.4 | 50.6 |
| 1966 | 19.5 | 27.8 | 40.7 | 48.1 | 57.1 | 70.4 | 78.4 | 70.0 | 63.8 | 51.3 | 42.6 | 29.2 | 49.9 |
| 1967 | 27.6 | 21.8 | 40.2 | 52.7 | 56.4 | 72.3 | 72.0 | 68.1 | 63.3 | 52.6 | 36.8 | 29.8 | 49.5 |
| 1968 | 22.1 | 23.7 | 43.0 | 52.4 | 57.7 | 72.4 | 73.2 | 73.8 | 64.3 | 53.9 | 40.4 | 27.6 | 50.4 |
| 1969 | 20.3 | 30.4 | 33.0 | 52.6 | 61.4 | 66.4 | 75.6 | 73.1 | 64.8 | 51.5 | 37.5 | 25.8 | 49.4 |
| 1970 | 15.1 | 25.9 | 35.3 | 52.2 | 64.2 | 69.8 | 74.9 | 72.3 | 65.8 | 53.6 | 39.1 | 29.9 | 49.8 |
| 1971 | 19.2 | 27.7 | 35.5 | 51.9 | 57.7 | 76.8 | 71.2 | 71.6 | 68.9 | 60.0 | 40.5 | 34.3 | 51.3 |
| 1972 | 19.7 | 24.5 | 36.9 | 48.9 | 63.2 | 68.0 | 73.2 | 72.4 | 66.2 | 50.0 | 36.2 | 23.8 | 48.6 |
| 1973 | 27.4 | 28.9 | 46.5 | 50.9 | 57.9 | 71.8 | 75.0 | 74.7 | 67.0 | 57.7 | 42.4 | 24.8 | 52.1 |
| 1974 | 23.1 | 29.4 | 41.1 | 53.6 | 59.3 | 66.7 | 76.9 | 72.2 | 61.1 | 63.6 | 39.6 | 29.9 | 50.5 |
| 1975 | 27.5 | 26.1 | 33.8 | 47.0 | 64.6 | 72.1 | 73.8 | 74.7 | 60.9 | 55.3 | 44.9 | 30.2 | 50.9 |
| 1976 | 19.5 | 34.9 | 43.9 | 54.1 | 58.2 | 70.5 | 75.3 | 70.3 | 63.3 | 47.3 | 32.0 | 21.0 | 49.2 |
| 1977 | 8.6 | 27.0 | 44.6 | 57.1 | 68.6 | 70.2 | 78.2 | 71.4 | 66.4 | 51.3 | 40.3 | 22.8 | 50.5 |
| 1978 | 13.3 | 15.4 | 32.4 | 51.2 | 60.3 | 71.3 | 75.0 | 73.2 | 70.5 | 52.1 | 41.3 | 26.8 | 48.6 |
| 1979 | 9.4 | 14.7 | 37.9 | 47.7 | 60.5 | 71.2 | 73.0 | 72.5 | 65.6 | 52.6 | 38.0 | 31.8 | 47.9 |
| 1980 | 23.6 | 19.9 | 35.6 | 49.2 | 63.0 | 69.3 | 78.5 | 76.9 | 67.9 | 49.6 | 40.7 | 28.9 | 50.2 |
| 1981 | 23.7 | 27.8 | 40.7 | 55.4 | 58.7 | 73.2 | 75.4 | 72.8 | 65.9 | 53.4 | 45.0 | 27.3 | 51.6 |
| 1982 | 15.8 | 24.8 | 37.7 | 46.5 | 58.4 | 67.2 | 75.7 | 71.3 | 64.9 | 55.0 | 41.5 | 37.4 | 50.5 |
| 1983 | 28.2 | 33.5 | 40.3 | 46.8 | 58.6 | 72.6 | 80.2 | 80.8 | 67.9 | 55.3 | 44.9 | 15.2 | 52.0 |
| 1984 | 20.6 | 35.5 | 31.3 | 49.6 | 58.8 | 74.3 | 73.0 | 74.0 | 64.0 | 56.7 | 40.3 | 33.9 | 51.2 |
| 1985 | 16.8 | 23.2 | 43.8 | 57.0 | 64.3 | 68.7 | 73.7 | 70.2 | 66.6 | 55.5 | 39.0 | 18.6 | 49.8 |
| 1986 | 26.6 | 23.5 | 43.2 | 55.4 | 64.0 | 72.3 | 77.4 | 68.9 | 68.9 | 55.2 | 36.2 | 30.9 | 51.9 |
| 1987 | 25.2 | 35.7 | 44.1 | 54.1 | 68.4 | 74.0 | 79.0 | 73.7 | 65.7 | 48.0 | 44.6 | 32.4 | 53.7 |
| 1988 | 22.7 | 23.5 | 39.9 | 51.1 | 65.4 | 78.6 | 78.5 | 78.6 | 68.2 | 48.2 | 41.5 | 29.7 | 51.7 |
| 1989 | 33.9 | 18.7 | 39.2 | 50.7 | 59.1 | 69.8 | 75.3 | 72.4 | 62.2 | 54.9 | 39.8 | 16.2 | 49.4 |
| 1990 | 34.8 | 33.7 | 43.4 | 50.0 | 57.8 | 71.0 | 72.6 | 72.1 | 66.1 | 51.9 | 45.2 | 27.7 | 52.2 |
| Record Mean | 23.9 | 27.6 | 38.7 | 51.0 | 61.7 | 71.3 | 75.7 | 73.7 | 66.2 | 54.3 | 40.4 | 28.3 | 51.1 |
| Max | 32.1 | 35.9 | 48.0 | 61.5 | 72.6 | 82.1 | 86.5 | 84.4 | 77.3 | 65.2 | 49.2 | 35.9 | 60.9 |
| Min | 15.8 | 19.3 | 29.4 | 40.6 | 50.7 | 60.5 | 64.8 | 62.9 | 55.1 | 43.4 | 31.6 | 20.6 | 41.2 |

## REFERENCE NOTES FOR TABLES 1, 2, 3 and 6 — (PEORIA, IL)

### GENERAL

T - TRACE AMOUNT
BLANK ENTRIES DENOTE MISSING/UNREPORTED DATA.
# INDICATES A STATION OR INSTRUMENT RELOCATION.

### SPECIFIC

#### TABLE 1

(a) - LENGTH OF RECORD IN YEARS. ALTHOUGH INDIVIDUAL MONTHS MAY BE MISSING.

* LESS THAN .05

NORMALS — BASED ON THE 1951-1980 RECORD PERIOD.
EXTREMES — DATES ARE THE MOST RECENT OCCURRENCE.
WIND DIR. — NUMERALS SHOW TENS OF DEGREES CLOCKWISE FROM TRUE NORTH. "00" INDICATES CALM.
RESULTANT WIND DIRECTIONS ARE GIVEN TO WHOLE DEGREES.

#### TABLE 3

MAX AND MIN ARE LONG-TERM MEAN DAILY MAXIMUM AND MEAN DAILY MINIMUM TEMPERATURES.

### EXCEPTIONS

#### TABLES 2, 3, and 6

RECORD MEANS ARE THROUGH THE CURRENT YEAR, BEGINNING IN

1905 FOR TEMPERATURE
1856 FOR PRECIPITATION
1944 FOR SNOWFALL

**TABLE 4**   HEATING DEGREE DAYS Base 65 deg. F     PEORIA, ILLINOIS

| SEASON | JULY | AUG | SEP | OCT | NOV | DEC | JAN | FEB | MAR | APR | MAY | JUNE | TOTAL |
|---|---|---|---|---|---|---|---|---|---|---|---|---|---|
| 1961-62 | 2 | 5 | 120 | 347 | 752 | 1262 | 1501 | 1088 | 960 | 455 | 63 | 14 | 6569 |
| 1962-63 | 4 | 0 | 137 | 341 | 717 | 1279 | 1613 | 1292 | 723 | 367 | 200 | 14 | 6687 |
| 1963-64 | 2 | 22 | 64 | 93 | 652 | 1534 | 1118 | 1066 | 891 | 384 | 66 | 17 | 5909 |
| 1964-65 | 2 | 8 | 108 | 435 | 637 | 1212 | 1254 | 1058 | 1139 | 416 | 72 | 1 | 6342 |
| 1965-66 | 0 | 18 | 100 | 391 | 707 | 914 | 1406 | 1037 | 746 | 502 | 260 | 22 | 6103 |
| 1966-67 | 0 | 10 | 106 | 419 | 666 | 1103 | 1151 | 1205 | 766 | 371 | 291 | 7 | 6095 |
| 1967-68 | 10 | 30 | 113 | 394 | 841 | 1083 | 1323 | 1192 | 673 | 371 | 229 | 13 | 6272 |
| 1968-69 | 5 | 7 | 68 | 377 | 732 | 1150 | 1377 | 962 | 984 | 367 | 172 | 73 | 6274 |
| 1969-70 | 0 | 0 | 77 | 443 | 818 | 1211 | 1545 | 1088 | 914 | 402 | 115 | 28 | 6641 |
| 1970-71 | 2 | 3 | 84 | 353 | 774 | 1080 | 1418 | 1035 | 906 | 402 | 241 | 0 | 6298 |
| 1971-72 | 17 | 5 | 85 | 186 | 728 | 945 | 1402 | 1167 | 866 | 475 | 150 | 42 | 6068 |
| 1972-73 | 9 | 19 | 87 | 461 | 855 | 1271 | 1161 | 1005 | 566 | 423 | 216 | 0 | 6073 |
| 1973-74 | 0 | 0 | 54 | 253 | 671 | 1237 | 1292 | 991 | 736 | 348 | 214 | 42 | 5838 |
| 1974-75 | 0 | 1 | 157 | 354 | 756 | 1081 | 1156 | 1085 | 959 | 534 | 92 | 17 | 6192 |
| 1975-76 | 13 | 1 | 171 | 306 | 596 | 1069 | 1404 | 868 | 648 | 351 | 221 | 5 | 5653 |
| 1976-77 | 0 | 9 | 106 | 556 | 981 | 1357 | 1747 | 1061 | 623 | 273 | 60 | 17 | 6790 |
| 1977-78 | 0 | 6 | 39 | 418 | 734 | 1301 | 1595 | 1383 | 1006 | 405 | 222 | 14 | 7123 |
| 1978-79 | 0 | 4 | 49 | 390 | 704 | 1174 | 1722 | 1403 | 833 | 510 | 194 | 10 | 6993 |
| 1979-80 | 3 | 19 | 70 | 401 | 804 | 1022 | 1279 | 1300 | 907 | 474 | 123 | 26 | 6428 |
| 1980-81 | 0 | 0 | 65 | 470 | 722 | 1112 | 1273 | 1037 | 748 | 295 | 221 | 1 | 5944 |
| 1981-82 | 1 | 0 | 60 | 360 | 594 | 1163 | 1520 | 1119 | 839 | 548 | 29 | 28 | 6261 |
| 1982-83 | 0 | 13 | 94 | 325 | 697 | 849 | 1133 | 875 | 758 | 537 | 206 | 17 | 5504 |
| 1983-84 | 2 | 0 | 92 | 311 | 595 | 1541 | 1371 | 849 | 1038 | 467 | 206 | 1 | 6473 |
| 1984-85 | 1 | 1 | 153 | 246 | 734 | 956 | 1489 | 1164 | 656 | 284 | 71 | 38 | 5793 |
| 1985-86 | 0 | 6 | 111 | 287 | 774 | 1432 | 1184 | 1156 | 683 | 314 | 92 | 7 | 6046 |
| 1986-87 | 0 | 26 | 37 | 305 | 858 | 1048 | 1228 | 814 | 640 | 340 | 53 | 2 | 5351 |
| 1987-88 | 0 | 16 | 68 | 520 | 609 | 1001 | 1306 | 1198 | 772 | 409 | 64 | 12 | 5975 |
| 1988-89 | 0 | 4 | 38 | 517 | 698 | 1090 | 958 | 1290 | 796 | 442 | 231 | 25 | 6089 |
| 1989-90 | 0 | 3 | 134 | 317 | 749 | 1509 | 929 | 871 | 672 | 475 | 226 | 16 | 5901 |
| 1990-91 | 8 | 3 | 99 | 409 | 589 | 1148 |  |  |  |  |  |  |  |

**TABLE 5**   COOLING DEGREE DAYS Base 65 deg. F     PEORIA, ILLINOIS

| YEAR | JAN | FEB | MAR | APR | MAY | JUNE | JULY | AUG | SEP | OCT | NOV | DEC | TOTAL |
|---|---|---|---|---|---|---|---|---|---|---|---|---|---|
| 1969 | 0 | 0 | 0 | 0 | 67 | 122 | 334 | 260 | 80 | 30 | 0 | 0 | 893 |
| 1970 | 0 | 0 | 0 | 24 | 99 | 178 | 317 | 239 | 109 | 6 | 0 | 0 | 972 |
| 1971 | 0 | 0 | 0 | 14 | 22 | 359 | 217 | 214 | 210 | 37 | 0 | 0 | 1073 |
| 1972 | 0 | 0 | 0 | 0 | 103 | 140 | 273 | 253 | 130 | 3 | 0 | 0 | 902 |
| 1973 | 0 | 0 | 0 | 7 | 3 | 211 | 315 | 306 | 121 | 35 | 0 | 0 | 998 |
| 1974 | 0 | 0 | 0 | 12 | 43 | 99 | 377 | 233 | 47 | 6 | 0 | 0 | 817 |
| 1975 | 0 | 0 | 0 | 0 | 83 | 237 | 292 | 307 | 55 | 14 | 0 | 0 | 988 |
| 1976 | 0 | 0 | 0 | 28 | 14 | 176 | 326 | 180 | 62 | 14 | 0 | 0 | 800 |
| 1977 | 0 | 0 | 0 | 42 | 176 | 179 | 416 | 209 | 88 | 0 | 0 | 0 | 1110 |
| 1978 | 0 | 0 | 0 | 0 | 81 | 208 | 316 | 267 | 221 | 0 | 0 | 0 | 1093 |
| 1979 | 0 | 0 | 0 | 0 | 62 | 206 | 259 | 258 | 95 | 23 | 0 | 0 | 903 |
| 1980 | 0 | 0 | 0 | 6 | 70 | 160 | 425 | 378 | 156 | 1 | 0 | 0 | 1196 |
| 1981 | 0 | 0 | 0 | 13 | 33 | 250 | 331 | 250 | 93 | 6 | 1 | 0 | 977 |
| 1982 | 0 | 0 | 0 | 0 | 141 | 101 | 338 | 215 | 96 | 26 | 0 | 0 | 917 |
| 1983 | 0 | 0 | 0 | 0 | 14 | 250 | 479 | 494 | 188 | 17 | 0 | 0 | 1442 |
| 1984 | 0 | 0 | 0 | 12 | 24 | 285 | 256 | 315 | 129 | 22 | 0 | 0 | 1043 |
| 1985 | 0 | 0 | 3 | 48 | 54 | 155 | 279 | 173 | 164 | 0 | 0 | 0 | 876 |
| 1986 | 0 | 0 | 15 | 30 | 68 | 234 | 392 | 157 | 161 | 6 | 0 | 0 | 1063 |
| 1987 | 0 | 0 | 0 | 19 | 166 | 278 | 440 | 293 | 92 | 0 | 3 | 0 | 1291 |
| 1988 | 0 | 0 | 0 | 2 | 84 | 266 | 431 | 428 | 140 | 5 | 0 | 0 | 1356 |
| 1989 | 0 | 0 | 2 | 20 | 56 | 177 | 324 | 240 | 57 | 11 | 0 | 0 | 887 |
| 1990 | 0 | 0 | 9 | 34 | 8 | 204 | 251 | 230 | 138 | 9 | 0 | 0 | 883 |

**TABLE 6**   SNOWFALL (inches)     PEORIA, ILLINOIS

| SEASON | JULY | AUG | SEP | OCT | NOV | DEC | JAN | FEB | MAR | APR | MAY | JUNE | TOTAL |
|---|---|---|---|---|---|---|---|---|---|---|---|---|---|
| 1961-62 | 0.0 | 0.0 | 0.0 | 0.0 | 0.7 | 10.5 | 10.5 | 7.5 | 2.0 | 1.1 | 0.0 | 0.0 | 32.3 |
| 1962-63 | 0.0 | 0.0 | 0.0 | T | T | 2.1 | 7.0 | 6.2 | T | 0.0 | 0.0 | 0.0 | 15.3 |
| 1963-64 | 0.0 | 0.0 | 0.0 | 0.0 | 0.4 | 6.1 | 4.8 | 6.2 | 7.9 | T | 0.0 | 0.0 | 25.4 |
| 1964-65 | 0.0 | 0.0 | 0.0 | 0.0 | 1.0 | 7.2 | 5.5 | 5.8 | 13.5 | 0.0 | 0.0 | 0.0 | 33.0 |
| 1965-66 | 0.0 | 0.0 | 0.0 | 0.0 | 0.1 | 4.2 | 0.6 | 2.0 | 0.8 | T | 0.1 | 0.0 | 7.8 |
| 1966-67 | 0.0 | 0.0 | 0.0 | 0.0 | T | 3.8 | 10.0 | 3.6 | 2.7 | 1.4 | 0.0 | 0.0 | 21.5 |
| 1967-68 | 0.0 | 0.0 | 0.0 | 1.8 | 2.5 | 2.2 | 8.4 | 1.6 | 1.1 | T | 0.0 | 0.0 | 17.6 |
| 1968-69 | 0.0 | 0.0 | 0.0 | 0.0 | 1.5 | 4.6 | 4.6 | 2.2 | 4.1 | 0.0 | 0.0 | 0.0 | 17.0 |
| 1969-70 | 0.0 | 0.0 | 0.0 | 0.0 | 0.6 | 11.0 | 7.3 | 5.9 | 8.3 | 4.6 | 0.0 | 0.0 | 37.7 |
| 1970-71 | 0.0 | 0.0 | 0.0 | 0.0 | T | 3.4 | 5.4 | 0.6 | 5.8 | 0.0 | 0.0 | 0.0 | 15.2 |
| 1971-72 | 0.0 | 0.0 | 0.0 | 0.0 | 4.0 | 10.2 | 6.2 | 8.0 | 0.9 | 0.0 | 0.0 | 0.0 | 29.3 |
| 1972-73 | 0.0 | 0.0 | 0.0 | 0.3 | 7.3 | 4.7 | 0.8 | 2.7 | 1.2 | 0.7 | 0.0 | 0.0 | 17.7 |
| 1973-74 | 0.0 | 0.0 | 0.0 | 0.0 | 0.1 | 18.9 | 6.7 | 1.9 | 1.2 | 0.9 | 0.0 | 0.0 | 29.7 |
| 1974-75 | 0.0 | 0.0 | 0.0 | 0.0 | 9.1 | 6.2 | 8.8 | 12.8 | 3.8 | 1.6 | 0.0 | 0.0 | 42.3 |
| 1975-76 | 0.0 | 0.0 | 0.0 | 0.0 | 8.1 | 1.4 | 8.6 | 2.5 | 2.0 | 0.0 | 0.0 | 0.0 | 22.6 |
| 1976-77 | 0.0 | 0.0 | 0.0 | T | 0.4 | 4.1 | 16.3 | 4.1 | 2.4 | 1.4 | 0.0 | 0.0 | 28.7 |
| 1977-78 | 0.0 | 0.0 | 0.0 | 0.0 | 6.4 | 21.7 | 7.0 | 5.0 | 5.0 | 0.0 | 0.0 | 0.0 | 47.1 |
| 1978-79 | 0.0 | 0.0 | 0.0 | 0.0 | 2.6 | 14.2 | 24.7 | 3.6 | 6.5 | T | 0.0 | 0.0 | 51.6 |
| 1979-80 | 0.0 | 0.0 | 0.0 | 0.0 | 0.8 | 3.3 | 3.7 | 11.3 | 5.3 | 6.3 | 0.0 | 0.0 | 27.5 |
| 1980-81 | 0.0 | 0.0 | 0.0 | T | 4.1 | 3.3 | 5.9 | 10.5 | T | 0.0 | 0.0 | 0.0 | 23.8 |
| 1981-82 | 0.0 | 0.0 | 0.0 | 0.0 | 0.1 | 9.8 | 11.0 | 6.1 | 6.5 | 13.4 | 0.0 | 0.0 | 46.9 |
| 1982-83 | 0.0 | 0.0 | 0.0 | 0.0 | 0.9 | 2.0 | 5.6 | 4.8 | 5.7 | 0.1 | 0.0 | 0.0 | 19.1 |
| 1983-84 | 0.0 | 0.0 | 0.0 | 0.0 | 3.3 | 15.9 | 6.9 | 4.1 | 6.0 | 0.0 | 0.0 | 0.0 | 36.2 |
| 1984-85 | 0.0 | 0.0 | 0.0 | 0.0 | T | 0.9 | 9.8 | 6.2 | T | T | 0.0 | 0.0 | 16.9 |
| 1985-86 | 0.0 | 0.0 | 0.0 | 0.0 | 1.0 | 6.2 | 1.3 | 13.9 | 0.4 | 0.1 | 0.0 | 0.0 | 22.9 |
| 1986-87 | 0.0 | 0.0 | 0.0 | 0.0 | 1.0 | 18.0 | 0.1 | T | 0.0 | 0.0 | 0.0 | 0.0 | 19.1 |
| 1987-88 | 0.0 | 0.0 | 0.0 | T | 0.3 | 9.8 | 1.9 | 9.7 | 1.9 | 0.0 | 0.0 | 0.0 | 23.6 |
| 1988-89 | 0.0 | 0.0 | 0.0 | 0.0 | 0.7 | 4.7 | 0.3 | 15.2 | T | 0.9 | T | 0.0 | 21.8 |
| 1989-90 | 0.0 | 0.0 | 0.0 | 0.6 | T | 10.5 | 4.8 | 6.2 | T | T | 0.0 | 0.0 | 22.1 |
| 1990-91 | T | 0.0 | 0.0 | T | T | 3.8 |  |  |  |  |  |  |  |
| Record Mean | T | 0.0 | 0.0 | 0.1 | 2.0 | 6.0 | 6.5 | 5.5 | 4.1 | 0.9 | T | 0.0 | 25.1 |

**See Reference Notes, relative to all above tables, on preceding page.**

The location of Springfield near the center of North America gives it a typical continental climate with warm summers and fairly cold winters. The surrounding country is nearly level. There are no large hills in the vicinity, but rolling terrain is found near the Sangamon River and Spring Creek.

Monthly temperatures range from the upper 20s for January to the upper 70s for July. Considerable variation may take place within the seasons. Temperatures of 70 degrees or higher may occur in winter and temperatures near 50 degrees are sometimes recorded during the summer months.

There are no wet and dry seasons. Monthly precipitation ranges from a little over 4 inches in May and June to about 2 inches in January. There is some variation in rainfall totals from year to year. Thunderstorms are common during hot weather, and these are sometimes locally severe with brief but heavy showers. The average year has about fifty thunderstorms of which two-thirds occur during the months of May through August. Damaging hail accompanies only a few of the thunderstorms and the areas affected are usually small.

Sunshine is particularly abundant during the summer months when days are long and not very cloudy. January is the cloudiest month, with only about a third as much sunshine as July or August. March is the windiest month, and August the month with the least wind. Velocities of more than 40 mph are not unusual for brief periods in most months of the year. The prevailing wind direction is southerly during most of the year with northwesterly winds during the late fall and early spring months.

An overall description of the climate of Springfield would be one indicating pleasant conditions with sharp seasonal changes, but no extended periods of severely cold weather. Summer weather is often uncomfortably warm and humid.

Based on the 1951-1980 period, the average first occurrence of 32 degrees Fahrenheit in the fall is October 19 and the average last occurrence in the spring is April 17.

## TABLE 1     NORMALS, MEANS AND EXTREMES

SPRINGFIELD, ILLINOIS

LATITUDE: 39°50'N    LONGITUDE: 89°40' W    ELEVATION: FT. GRND   588 BARO   597   TIME ZONE: CENTRAL    WBAN: 93822

| | (a) | JAN | FEB | MAR | APR | MAY | JUNE | JULY | AUG | SEP | OCT | NOV | DEC | YEAR |
|---|---|---|---|---|---|---|---|---|---|---|---|---|---|---|
| **TEMPERATURE °F:** | | | | | | | | | | | | | | |
| Normals | | | | | | | | | | | | | | |
| -Daily Maximum | | 32.8 | 38.0 | 48.9 | 64.0 | 74.6 | 84.1 | 87.1 | 84.7 | 79.3 | 67.5 | 51.2 | 38.4 | 62.6 |
| -Daily Minimum | | 16.3 | 20.9 | 30.3 | 42.6 | 52.5 | 62.0 | 65.9 | 63.7 | 55.8 | 44.4 | 32.9 | 23.0 | 42.5 |
| -Monthly | | 24.6 | 29.5 | 39.6 | 53.4 | 63.6 | 73.1 | 76.5 | 74.2 | 67.6 | 55.9 | 42.1 | 30.7 | 52.6 |
| Extremes | | | | | | | | | | | | | | |
| -Record Highest | 42 | 71 | 74 | 87 | 90 | 95 | 103 | 112 | 103 | 101 | 93 | 83 | 74 | 112 |
| -Year | | 1950 | 1972 | 1981 | 1986 | 1967 | 1954 | 1954 | 1964 | 1984 | 1954 | 1950 | 1984 | JUL 1954 |
| -Record Lowest | 42 | -21 | -22 | -12 | 19 | 28 | 40 | 48 | 43 | 32 | 17 | -3 | -21 | -22 |
| -Year | | 1985 | 1963 | 1960 | 1982 | 1966 | 1966 | 1975 | 1986 | 1984 | 1952 | 1964 | 1989 | FEB 1963 |
| **NORMAL DEGREE DAYS:** | | | | | | | | | | | | | | |
| Heating (base 65°F) | | 1252 | 994 | 787 | 354 | 149 | 13 | 0 | 0 | 48 | 307 | 687 | 1063 | 5654 |
| Cooling (base 65°F) | | 0 | 0 | 0 | 6 | 106 | 256 | 357 | 289 | 126 | 25 | 0 | 0 | 1165 |
| **% OF POSSIBLE SUNSHINE** | 41 | 48 | 51 | 51 | 57 | 64 | 69 | 72 | 71 | 69 | 63 | 48 | 43 | 59 |
| **MEAN SKY COVER (tenths)** | | | | | | | | | | | | | | |
| Sunrise - Sunset | 42 | 6.7 | 6.5 | 6.9 | 6.5 | 6.1 | 5.8 | 5.4 | 5.2 | 5.0 | 5.2 | 6.4 | 6.9 | 6.1 |
| **MEAN NUMBER OF DAYS:** | | | | | | | | | | | | | | |
| Sunrise to Sunset | | | | | | | | | | | | | | |
| -Clear | 42 | 7.4 | 7.6 | 6.4 | 7.3 | 8.2 | 8.7 | 10.4 | 11.2 | 12.1 | 12.1 | 8.1 | 7.0 | 106.3 |
| -Partly Cloudy | 42 | 6.4 | 5.6 | 7.0 | 7.9 | 9.5 | 9.4 | 10.5 | 9.6 | 7.8 | 7.3 | 6.2 | 6.3 | 93.4 |
| -Cloudy | 42 | 17.2 | 15.1 | 17.6 | 14.9 | 13.4 | 12.0 | 10.1 | 10.2 | 10.2 | 11.6 | 15.6 | 17.7 | 165.7 |
| Precipitation | | | | | | | | | | | | | | |
| .01 inches or more | 42 | 9.0 | 8.7 | 11.8 | 11.5 | 10.3 | 9.8 | 8.8 | 8.3 | 8.1 | 7.6 | 9.2 | 10.0 | 113.1 |
| Snow,Ice pellets | | | | | | | | | | | | | | |
| 1.0 inches or more | 42 | 1.9 | 1.9 | 1.4 | 0.3 | 0.0 | 0.0 | 0.0 | 0.0 | 0.0 | 0.0 | 0.5 | 1.6 | 7.6 |
| Thunderstorms | 42 | 0.5 | 0.7 | 2.6 | 5.5 | 6.8 | 8.0 | 8.6 | 6.9 | 4.6 | 2.2 | 1.5 | 0.6 | 48.4 |
| Heavy Fog Visibility 1/4 mile or less | 42 | 2.7 | 2.7 | 1.9 | 0.8 | 0.9 | 0.3 | 0.7 | 1.1 | 1.0 | 1.1 | 1.6 | 2.5 | 17.3 |
| Temperature °F | | | | | | | | | | | | | | |
| -Maximum | | | | | | | | | | | | | | |
| 90° and above | 30 | 0.0 | 0.0 | 0.0 | 0.* | 1.7 | 7.6 | 11.2 | 6.7 | 3.1 | 0.1 | 0.0 | 0.0 | 30.5 |
| 32° and below | 30 | 15.2 | 9.9 | 2.7 | 0.* | 0.0 | 0.0 | 0.0 | 0.0 | 0.0 | 0.0 | 1.1 | 9.9 | 38.8 |
| -Minimum | | | | | | | | | | | | | | |
| 32° and below | 30 | 28.2 | 23.8 | 17.3 | 4.2 | 0.2 | 0.0 | 0.0 | 0.0 | 0.* | 3.5 | 14.7 | 25.4 | 117.3 |
| 0° and below | 30 | 5.0 | 2.7 | 0.1 | 0.0 | 0.0 | 0.0 | 0.0 | 0.0 | 0.0 | 0.0 | 0.* | 2.1 | 9.9 |
| **AVG. STATION PRESS.(mb)** | 16 | 997.7 | 997.0 | 993.3 | 992.4 | 991.9 | 992.4 | 993.9 | 994.6 | 995.4 | 996.5 | 995.5 | 996.8 | 994.8 |
| **RELATIVE HUMIDITY (%)** | | | | | | | | | | | | | | |
| Hour 00 | 30 | 77 | 78 | 77 | 72 | 75 | 77 | 81 | 84 | 82 | 76 | 78 | 80 | 78 |
| Hour 06 | 30 | 78 | 80 | 81 | 79 | 80 | 82 | 85 | 89 | 88 | 83 | 82 | 82 | 82 |
| Hour 12 (Local Time) | 30 | 68 | 68 | 63 | 56 | 54 | 54 | 57 | 60 | 56 | 54 | 65 | 71 | 61 |
| Hour 18 | 30 | 72 | 71 | 65 | 56 | 54 | 55 | 59 | 64 | 62 | 61 | 70 | 76 | 64 |
| **PRECIPITATION (inches):** | | | | | | | | | | | | | | |
| Water Equivalent | | | | | | | | | | | | | | |
| -Normal | | 1.56 | 1.78 | 3.14 | 3.97 | 3.34 | 3.71 | 3.53 | 3.20 | 3.05 | 2.52 | 1.93 | 2.05 | 33.78 |
| -Maximum Monthly | 42 | 5.67 | 4.43 | 7.89 | 9.91 | 6.37 | 8.87 | 10.76 | 8.37 | 8.57 | 6.15 | 6.94 | 8.94 | 10.76 |
| -Year | | 1949 | 1951 | 1973 | 1964 | 1974 | 1960 | 1981 | 1981 | 1986 | 1955 | 1985 | 1982 | JUL 1981 |
| -Minimum Monthly | 42 | 0.04 | 0.51 | 0.63 | 0.73 | 0.56 | 0.23 | 0.91 | 0.63 | T | 0.16 | 0.43 | 0.15 | T |
| -Year | | 1986 | 1958 | 1956 | 1971 | 1987 | 1959 | 1974 | 1984 | 1979 | 1964 | 1949 | 1955 | SEP 1979 |
| -Maximum in 24 hrs | 42 | 2.78 | 1.89 | 2.84 | 4.45 | 2.48 | 4.73 | 4.43 | 4.79 | 5.12 | 3.51 | 2.46 | 6.12 | 6.12 |
| -Year | | 1975 | 1976 | 1972 | 1979 | 1975 | 1958 | 1981 | 1956 | 1959 | 1973 | 1964 | 1982 | DEC 1982 |
| Snow,Ice pellets | | | | | | | | | | | | | | |
| -Maximum Monthly | 42 | 21.1 | 15.1 | 20.3 | 7.3 | T | 0.0 | 0.0 | 0.0 | 0.0 | 0.3 | 9.2 | 22.7 | 22.7 |
| -Year | | 1977 | 1986 | 1960 | 1980 | 1989 | | | | | 1989 | 1951 | 1973 | DEC 1973 |
| -Maximum in 24 hrs | 42 | 8.8 | 10.3 | 8.2 | 6.1 | T | 0.0 | 0.0 | 0.0 | 0.0 | 0.3 | 8.0 | 10.9 | 10.9 |
| -Year | | 1964 | 1965 | 1978 | 1980 | 1989 | | | | | 1989 | 1951 | 1973 | DEC 1973 |
| **WIND:** | | | | | | | | | | | | | | |
| Mean Speed (mph) | 42 | 12.7 | 12.5 | 13.7 | 13.2 | 11.3 | 9.8 | 8.4 | 8.0 | 9.1 | 10.4 | 12.5 | 12.5 | 11.2 |
| Prevailing Direction through 1963 | | NW | NW | NW | S | SSW | SSW | SSW | SSW | SSW | S | S | S | SSW |
| Fastest Obs. 1 Min. | | | | | | | | | | | | | | |
| -Direction (!!!) | 10 | 25 | 17 | 19 | 24 | 23 | 35 | 02 | 29 | 18 | 24 | 24 | 25 | 24 |
| -Speed (MPH) | 10 | 35 | 33 | 38 | 46 | 39 | 35 | 32 | 41 | 39 | 38 | 46 | 35 | 46 |
| -Year | | 1982 | 1988 | 1982 | 1988 | 1987 | 1984 | 1981 | 1987 | 1988 | 1983 | 1988 | 1985 | APR 1988 |
| Peak Gust | | | | | | | | | | | | | | |
| -Direction (!!!) | 6 | W | NW | SW | SW | SW | N | NE | W | NE | SW | SW | S | W |
| -Speed (mph) | 6 | 48 | 46 | 56 | 63 | 52 | 46 | 60 | 69 | 54 | 53 | 58 | 60 | 69 |
| -Date | | 1986 | 1987 | 1988 | 1984 | 1987 | 1984 | 1986 | 1987 | 1989 | 1988 | 1988 | 1984 | AUG 1987 |

**See Reference Notes to this table on the following page.**

# SPRINGFIELD, ILLINOIS

PRECIPITATION (inches)    SPRINGFIELD, ILLINOIS

**TABLE 2**

| YEAR | JAN | FEB | MAR | APR | MAY | JUNE | JULY | AUG | SEP | OCT | NOV | DEC | ANNUAL |
|------|-----|-----|-----|-----|-----|------|------|-----|-----|-----|-----|-----|--------|
| 1961 | 0.35 | 1.79 | 3.47 | 3.95 | 4.22 | 2.43 | 6.38 | 3.08 | .35 | 2.01 | 2.60 | 1.28 | 37.91 |
| 1962 | 3.04 | 1.48 | 3.54 | 1.31 | 3.16 | 3.62 | 3.82 | 1.11 | .42 | 5.68 | 1.91 | 0.53 | 30.62 |
| 1963 | 0.41 | 0.89 | 5.05 | 2.25 | 2.65 | 1.30 | 6.97 | 5.46 | .74 | 1.07 | 1.51 | 0.59 | 28.89 |
| 1964 | 1.64 | 1.27 | 4.00 | 9.91 | 1.82 | 2.26 | 1.32 | 2.20 | .24 | 0.16 | 4.19 | 1.01 | 31.02 |
| 1965 | 3.17 | 1.88 | 2.62 | 4.59 | 1.67 | 6.54 | 2.05 | 5.90 | .43 | 0.85 | 0.89 | 2.49 | 39.08 |
| 1966 | 0.36 | 2.20 | 1.04 | 5.75 | 3.54 | 1.35 | 0.96 | 2.71 | .72 | 2.37 | 3.08 | 2.62 | 30.70 |
| 1967 | 2.41 | 0.91 | 2.61 | 2.11 | 4.42 | 2.54 | 3.39 | 2.51 | .03 | 4.20 | 1.18 | 6.00 | 36.31 |
| 1968 | 1.79 | 1.15 | 1.25 | 2.44 | 5.69 | 3.25 | 4.67 | 0.99 | 3.29 | 1.43 | 3.08 | 2.64 | 31.67 |
| 1969 | 2.50 | 1.96 | 2.00 | 5.35 | 0.96 | 2.68 | 4.60 | 2.34 | .37 | 5.80 | 1.13 | 1.39 | 34.68 |
| 1970 | 0.54 | 0.67 | 1.99 | 9.10 | 2.26 | 4.68 | 2.55 | 4.20 | .3 | 2.50 | 0.70 | 1.33 | 38.25 |
| 1971 | 1.24 | 2.36 | 1.18 | 0.73 | 3.59 | 0.96 | 5.96 | 1.06 | .76 | 0.99 | 1.41 | 4.38 | 27.62 |
| 1972 | 1.03 | 0.82 | 4.03 | 3.35 | 1.88 | 2.72 | 1.70 | 4.52 | .95 | 1.40 | 3.27 | 3.36 | 32.03 |
| 1973 | 1.31 | 0.84 | 7.89 | 5.29 | 2.62 | 7.29 | 3.36 | 1.66 | .28 | 5.46 | 1.43 | 3.86 | 44.29 |
| 1974 | 2.61 | 3.15 | 3.39 | 3.11 | 6.37 | 5.00 | 0.91 | 7.70 | .7 | 1.39 | 3.58 | 1.44 | 40.82 |
| 1975 | 4.28 | 3.63 | 1.91 | 2.89 | 5.90 | 4.38 | 2.71 | 3.34 | .94 | 1.37 | 2.50 | 1.91 | 37.66 |
| 1976 | 0.98 | 3.67 | 5.60 | 1.07 | 1.96 | 1.41 | 2.29 | 2.33 | .20 | 3.00 | 0.53 | 0.66 | 25.70 |
| 1977 | 1.51 | 1.21 | 5.09 | 2.78 | 5.78 | 4.26 | 1.16 | 5.95 | .34 | 5.16 | 1.63 | 2.24 | 42.71 |
| 1978 | 0.72 | 0.83 | 4.20 | 2.84 | 5.81 | 1.73 | 2.99 | 4.04 | .8 | 1.57 | 2.13 | 3.39 | 31.83 |
| 1979 | 1.90 | 1.09 | 3.75 | 7.17 | 1.32 | 0.94 | 4.63 | 2.85 | | 1.34 | 1.98 | 2.36 | 29.33 |
| 1980 | 0.72 | 1.42 | 4.29 | 2.22 | 2.22 | 3.23 | 2.08 | 3.91 | .35 | 1.47 | 0.57 | 1.99 | 29.07 |
| 1981 | 0.43 | 2.12 | 2.27 | 4.57 | 6.17 | 5.80 | 10.76 | 8.37 | .3 | 1.94 | 2.21 | 2.35 | 48.12 |
| 1982 | 4.48 | 1.81 | 3.04 | 3.40 | 4.12 | 2.54 | 2.53 | 3.68 | .75 | 2.69 | 4.50 | 8.94 | 44.48 |
| 1983 | 0.46 | 0.96 | 3.44 | 5.02 | 4.53 | 2.62 | 1.60 | 0.84 | .35 | 3.63 | 4.71 | 3.50 | 32.67 |
| 1984 | 0.70 | 1.97 | 4.00 | 5.45 | 6.32 | 2.26 | 3.46 | 0.63 | .30 | 4.74 | 4.36 | 3.91 | 42.60 |
| 1985 | 0.65 | 2.96 | 4.19 | 1.46 | 1.75 | 5.82 | 2.95 | 6.03 | .54 | 3.08 | 6.94 | 2.43 | 38.90 |
| 1986 | 0.04 | 1.80 | 1.45 | 1.57 | 2.56 | 6.23 | 5.39 | 1.13 | .57 | 3.63 | 1.95 | 1.40 | 35.72 |
| 1987 | 1.46 | 0.73 | 2.08 | 2.59 | 0.56 | 4.08 | 4.12 | 3.23 | .39 | 1.26 | 3.25 | 5.00 | 29.35 |
| 1988 | 2.17 | 1.39 | 2.69 | 1.27 | 1.76 | 0.62 | 1.74 | 1.56 | .4 | 1.68 | 4.37 | 3.22 | 25.31 |
| 1989 | 0.88 | 1.27 | 1.68 | 5.50 | 4.18 | 0.89 | 3.13 | 2.57 | .3 | 1.02 | 0.84 | 0.58 | 28.03 |
| 1990 | 1.49 | 4.89 | 3.41 | 1.28 | 8.84 | 9.22 | 5.48 | 2.68 | .1 | 5.03 | 3.47 | 4.97 | 52.67 |
| Record Mean | 1.91 | 2.04 | 3.09 | 3.53 | 4.06 | 3.97 | 3.20 | 3.02 | 3.36 | 2.65 | 2.46 | 2.21 | 35.51 |

**TABLE 3**    AVERAGE TEMPERATURE (deg. F)    SPRINGFIELD, ILLINOIS

| YEAR | JAN | FEB | MAR | APR | MAY | JUNE | JULY | AUG | SEP | OCT | NOV | DEC | ANNUAL |
|------|-----|-----|-----|-----|-----|------|------|-----|-----|-----|-----|-----|--------|
| 1961 | 24.5 | 33.5 | 43.8 | 47.7 | 58.4 | 71.0 | 75.8 | 73.6 | 65 | 56.8 | 42.5 | 27.8 | 52.1 |
| 1962 | 20.2 | 30.4 | 37.1 | 52.7 | 72.3 | 74.0 | 73.8 | 73.4 | 65 | 58.4 | 43.0 | 26.6 | 52.2 |
| 1963 | 16.9 | 22.0 | 44.6 | 55.7 | 62.2 | 75.3 | 74.6 | 70.6 | 66 | 66.4 | 45.2 | 18.9 | 51.6 |
| 1964 | 30.7 | 29.1 | 38.3 | 55.1 | 68.7 | 75.1 | 77.9 | 74.5 | 69 | 53.3 | 46.5 | 29.4 | 53.9 |
| 1965 | 27.3 | 30.0 | 31.1 | 54.6 | 70.3 | 73.2 | 74.2 | | 68.5 | 55.1 | 45.6 | 38.2 | 52.4 |
| 1966 | 21.9 | 29.5 | 43.1 | 49.5 | 57.7 | 71.5 | 80.8 | 72.0 | 64 | 52.3 | 44.1 | 30.5 | 51.4 |
| 1967 | 29.5 | 26.4 | 43.8 | 56.5 | 59.3 | 73.8 | 72.9 | 68.6 | 63 | 54.9 | 38.5 | 31.4 | 51.6 |
| 1968 | 23.8 | 25.6 | 42.8 | 52.9 | 59.0 | 74.5 | 75.8 | 75.2 | 66 | 54.8 | 41.3 | 29.1 | 51.8 |
| 1969 | 23.4 | 31.5 | 32.6 | 54.6 | 64.2 | 70.7 | 77.9 | 74.0 | 66 | 54.0 | 39.7 | 28.2 | 51.5 |
| 1970 | 17.9 | 28.7 | 37.9 | 54.7 | 66.5 | 71.5 | 76.4 | 74.0 | 69 | 56.2 | 41.7 | 34.0 | 52.4 |
| 1971 | 23.7 | 30.7 | 39.1 | 54.4 | 60.4 | 79.0 | 72.4 | 72.5 | 71 | 62.9 | 43.8 | 38.5 | 54.1 |
| 1972 | 24.4 | 29.0 | 40.8 | 52.5 | 64.7 | 70.5 | 75.9 | 73.8 | 68 | 52.9 | 38.3 | 26.7 | 51.5 |
| 1973 | 29.7 | 30.7 | 48.3 | 51.9 | 59.6 | 73.2 | 76.0 | 76.0 | 69 | 60.7 | 45.5 | 28.0 | 54.1 |
| 1974 | 26.1 | 32.6 | 44.2 | 54.8 | 61.6 | 68.3 | 78.8 | 72.9 | 61 | 55.8 | 42.2 | 32.7 | 52.7 |
| 1975 | 31.1 | 29.4 | 37.4 | 50.4 | 66.5 | 73.6 | 74.7 | 76.6 | 63 | 57.7 | 47.1 | 33.4 | 53.5 |
| 1976 | 23.5 | 39.6 | 45.4 | 55.0 | 59.7 | 72.4 | 77.4 | 71.6 | 65 | 49.4 | 34.6 | 24.1 | 51.5 |
| 1977 | 10.3 | 29.5 | 47.6 | 59.9 | 71.0 | 71.6 | 79.4 | 72.8 | 68 | 53.8 | 42.8 | 27.0 | 52.9 |
| 1978 | 15.6 | 16.7 | 33.6 | 53.9 | 62.3 | 74.2 | 76.3 | 73.1 | 70 | 53.7 | 45.2 | 31.4 | 50.6 |
| 1979 | 12.4 | 17.1 | 40.3 | 50.4 | 64.0 | 74.9 | 75.4 | 74.0 | 67 | 55.7 | 42.0 | 35.8 | 50.8 |
| 1980 | 27.8 | 21.8 | 37.1 | 51.1 | 64.6 | 72.0 | 81.4 | 79.3 | 68 | 52.8 | 42.3 | 31.7 | 52.6 |
| 1981 | 26.4 | 32.4 | 44.1 | 60.4 | 60.3 | 74.9 | 77.1 | 73.8 | 67 | 54.6 | 45.3 | 26.8 | 53.6 |
| 1982 | 17.0 | 24.2 | 40.3 | 48.1 | 70.0 | 68.3 | 77.1 | 72.5 | 66 | 55.4 | 43.0 | 38.8 | 51.7 |
| 1983 | 28.7 | 34.9 | 40.6 | 47.8 | 59.9 | 73.8 | 80.4 | 80.0 | 69 | 57.2 | 45.7 | 16.1 | 52.9 |
| 1984 | 22.3 | 35.9 | 31.8 | 50.4 | 60.3 | 75.2 | 74.5 | 76.9 | 65 | 55.9 | 41.7 | 35.9 | 52.5 |
| 1985 | 18.5 | 24.9 | 45.7 | 57.8 | 65.2 | 69.7 | 74.3 | 70.8 | 67 | 58.1 | 42.8 | 21.5 | 51.4 |
| 1986 | 29.1 | 26.9 | 45.3 | 57.4 | 65.9 | 74.7 | 78.8 | 70.0 | 70 | 56.1 | 37.9 | 32.6 | 53.8 |
| 1987 | 26.1 | 36.6 | 45.4 | 54.7 | 70.5 | 75.4 | 78.8 | 75.3 | 67 | 50.6 | 46.2 | 34.6 | 55.2 |
| 1988 | 25.6 | 25.6 | 41.5 | 52.8 | 65.8 | 73.8 | 78.7 | 78.7 | 68 | 49.7 | 43.0 | 31.6 | 53.0 |
| 1989 | 36.0 | 20.3 | 40.6 | 52.3 | 59.3 | 70.5 | 75.4 | 73.3 | 63 | 56.9 | 42.0 | 18.7 | 50.8 |
| 1990 | 37.1 | 36.1 | 45.5 | 50.8 | 59.9 | 73.1 | 75.2 | 74.0 | 68 | 53.5 | 47.8 | 30.0 | 54.3 |
| Record Mean | 26.9 | 30.1 | 40.8 | 53.3 | 63.6 | 73.2 | 77.3 | 74.9 | 67 | 56.4 | 42.5 | 31.2 | 53.2 |
| Max | 34.7 | 38.2 | 49.8 | 63.3 | 74.0 | 83.4 | 87.6 | 85.2 | 78 | 66.7 | 50.9 | 38.5 | 62.6 |
| Min | 19.0 | 22.0 | 31.9 | 43.2 | 53.2 | 62.9 | 66.9 | 64.7 | 57 | 46.1 | 34.0 | 23.9 | 43.8 |

## REFERENCE NOTES FOR TABLES 1, 2, 3 and 6    (SPRINGFIELD, IL)

### GENERAL

T - TRACE AMOUNT
BLANK ENTRIES DENOTE MISSING/UNREPORTED DATA.
# INDICATES A STATION OR INSTRUMENT RELOCATION.

### SPECIFIC

**TABLE 1**

(a) - LENGTH OF RECORD IN YEARS. ALTHOUGH
INDIVIDUAL MONTHS MAY BE MISSING.
* LESS THAN .05

NORMALS — BASED ON THE 1951-1980 RECORD PERIOD.
EXTREMES — DATES ARE THE MOST RECENT OCCURRENCE.
WIND DIR. — NUMERALS SHOW TENS OF DEGREES
CLOCKWISE FROM TRUE NORTH.
"00" INDICATES CALM.
RESULTANT WIND DIRECTIONS ARE GIVEN TO WHOLE DEGREES.

**TABLE 3**
MAX AND MIN ARE LONG-TERM MEAN DAILY MAXIMUM
AND MEAN DAILY MINIMUM TEMPERATURES.

### EXCEPTIONS

**TABLES 2, 3, and 6**

RECORD MEANS ARE THROUGH THE CURRENT YEAR,
BEGINNING IN     1897 FOR TEMPERATURE
                 1897 FOR PRECIPITATION
                 1948 FOR SNOWFALL

HEATING DEGREE DAYS Base 65 deg. F        SPRINGFIELD, ILLINOIS

**TABLE 4**

| SEASON | JULY | AUG | SEP | OCT | NOV | DEC | JAN | FEB | MAR | APR | MAY | JUNE | TOTAL |
|---|---|---|---|---|---|---|---|---|---|---|---|---|---|
| 1961-62 | 0 | 4 | 75 | 275 | 669 | 1150 | 1381 | 963 | 855 | 397 | 30 | 4 | 5803 |
| 1962-63 | 2 | 2 | 90 | 268 | 653 | 1186 | 1486 | 1198 | 630 | 291 | 126 | 6 | 5938 |
| 1963-64 | 2 | 18 | 45 | 80 | 589 | 1420 | 1055 | 1034 | 822 | 307 | 47 | 6 | 5425 |
| 1964-65 | 0 | 10 | 66 | 356 | 554 | 1100 | 1158 | 973 | 1041 | 320 | 36 | 0 | 5614 |
| 1965-66 | 0 | 13 | 54 | 321 | 575 | 822 | 1329 | 987 | 670 | 459 | 242 | 15 | 5487 |
| 1966-67 | 0 | 5 | 100 | 388 | 618 | 1065 | 1091 | 1074 | 662 | 289 | 230 | 10 | 5532 |
| 1967-68 | 9 | 34 | 104 | 337 | 789 | 1032 | 1271 | 1134 | 684 | 358 | 203 | 8 | 5963 |
| 1968-69 | 1 | 2 | 31 | 353 | 703 | 1107 | 1282 | 934 | 995 | 314 | 130 | 31 | 5883 |
| 1969-70 | 0 | 0 | 59 | 370 | 748 | 1135 | 1457 | 1013 | 830 | 332 | 83 | 26 | 6053 |
| 1970-71 | 0 | 1 | 41 | 281 | 690 | 952 | 1275 | 952 | 793 | 342 | 168 | 0 | 5495 |
| 1971-72 | 9 | 1 | 65 | 130 | 633 | 820 | 1253 | 1040 | 745 | 375 | 114 | 27 | 5212 |
| 1972-73 | 3 | 11 | 58 | 375 | 795 | 1181 | 1089 | 957 | 512 | 398 | 174 | 0 | 5553 |
| 1973-74 | 0 | 0 | 30 | 191 | 578 | 1140 | 1200 | 901 | 642 | 316 | 167 | 29 | 5194 |
| 1974-75 | 0 | 2 | 135 | 299 | 680 | 996 | 1044 | 992 | 848 | 435 | 63 | 7 | 5501 |
| 1975-76 | 10 | 0 | 125 | 253 | 528 | 973 | 1280 | 732 | 601 | 321 | 188 | 2 | 5013 |
| 1976-77 | 0 | 3 | 84 | 497 | 905 | 1260 | 1693 | 989 | 532 | 222 | 44 | 12 | 6241 |
| 1977-78 | 0 | 2 | 21 | 340 | 661 | 1172 | 1521 | 1348 | 968 | 334 | 186 | 4 | 6557 |
| 1978-79 | 0 | 0 | 36 | 349 | 591 | 1035 | 1627 | 1336 | 758 | 435 | 119 | 0 | 6286 |
| 1979-80 | 0 | 9 | 50 | 323 | 684 | 898 | 1146 | 1249 | 857 | 421 | 95 | 8 | 5740 |
| 1980-81 | 0 | 0 | 49 | 395 | 675 | 1028 | 1193 | 906 | 648 | 181 | 184 | 0 | 5259 |
| 1981-82 | 0 | 0 | 51 | 332 | 581 | 1175 | 1483 | 1139 | 760 | 502 | 9 | 20 | 6052 |
| 1982-83 | 0 | 5 | 86 | 325 | 656 | 806 | 1117 | 836 | 749 | 510 | 169 | 14 | 5273 |
| 1983-84 | 0 | 0 | 75 | 269 | 574 | 1512 | 1320 | 835 | 1023 | 446 | 170 | 1 | 6225 |
| 1984-85 | 0 | 0 | 127 | 194 | 691 | 899 | 1437 | 1116 | 601 | 262 | 67 | 32 | 5426 |
| 1985-86 | 0 | 11 | 99 | 223 | 658 | 1340 | 1105 | 1060 | 618 | 261 | 74 | 1 | 5450 |
| 1986-87 | 0 | 19 | 25 | 284 | 807 | 999 | 1199 | 788 | 599 | 325 | 34 | 0 | 5079 |
| 1987-88 | 0 | 3 | 44 | 440 | 565 | 934 | 1216 | 1139 | 720 | 360 | 59 | 11 | 5491 |
| 1988-89 | 0 | 5 | 33 | 475 | 654 | 1027 | 890 | 1242 | 749 | 405 | 224 | 19 | 5723 |
| 1989-90 | 0 | 4 | 106 | 269 | 683 | 1431 | 856 | 803 | 613 | 459 | 168 | 10 | 5402 |
| 1990-91 | 7 | 2 | 72 | 360 | 512 | 1080 | | | | | | | |

**TABLE 5**   COOLING DEGREE DAYS Base 65 deg. F        SPRINGFIELD, ILLINOIS

| YEAR | JAN | FEB | MAR | APR | MAY | JUNE | JULY | AUG | SEP | OCT | NOV | DEC | TOTAL |
|---|---|---|---|---|---|---|---|---|---|---|---|---|---|
| 1969 | 0 | 0 | 0 | 6 | 110 | 206 | 407 | 288 | 108 | 37 | 0 | 0 | 1162 |
| 1970 | 0 | 0 | 0 | 31 | 136 | 229 | 361 | 284 | 174 | 17 | 0 | 0 | 1232 |
| 1971 | 0 | 0 | 0 | 32 | 33 | 425 | 248 | 241 | 254 | 69 | 2 | 0 | 1304 |
| 1972 | 0 | 0 | 0 | 6 | 114 | 199 | 347 | 291 | 178 | 10 | 0 | 0 | 1145 |
| 1973 | 0 | 0 | 0 | 12 | 12 | 251 | 350 | 348 | 184 | 64 | 0 | 0 | 1221 |
| 1974 | 0 | 0 | 7 | 14 | 70 | 136 | 437 | 252 | 49 | 17 | 2 | 0 | 984 |
| 1975 | 0 | 0 | 0 | 2 | 115 | 271 | 315 | 367 | 94 | 36 | 0 | 0 | 1200 |
| 1976 | 0 | 0 | 3 | 28 | 34 | 228 | 393 | 214 | 98 | 23 | 0 | 0 | 1021 |
| 1977 | 0 | 0 | 0 | 76 | 238 | 217 | 452 | 251 | 134 | 0 | 1 | 0 | 1369 |
| 1978 | 0 | 0 | 1 | 8 | 107 | 289 | 358 | 258 | 222 | 5 | 5 | 0 | 1253 |
| 1979 | 0 | 0 | 0 | 2 | 93 | 305 | 327 | 295 | 138 | 41 | 0 | 0 | 1201 |
| 1980 | 0 | 0 | 0 | 10 | 88 | 228 | 515 | 452 | 169 | 20 | 0 | 0 | 1482 |
| 1981 | 0 | 0 | 8 | 50 | 43 | 303 | 380 | 280 | 121 | 13 | 0 | 0 | 1198 |
| 1982 | 0 | 0 | 0 | 1 | 173 | 131 | 379 | 244 | 126 | 32 | 1 | 1 | 1088 |
| 1983 | 0 | 0 | 1 | 1 | 17 | 289 | 483 | 471 | 205 | 34 | 0 | 0 | 1501 |
| 1984 | 0 | 0 | 0 | 16 | 30 | 312 | 303 | 375 | 155 | 44 | 0 | 1 | 1236 |
| 1985 | 0 | 0 | 7 | 52 | 80 | 178 | 293 | 202 | 191 | 17 | 0 | 0 | 1020 |
| 1986 | 0 | 0 | 14 | 38 | 109 | 299 | 434 | 182 | 193 | 14 | 0 | 0 | 1283 |
| 1987 | 0 | 0 | 0 | 21 | 212 | 318 | 436 | 329 | 130 | 0 | 8 | 0 | 1454 |
| 1988 | 0 | 0 | 0 | 3 | 93 | 281 | 430 | 437 | 150 | 6 | 0 | 0 | 1400 |
| 1989 | 0 | 0 | 2 | 30 | 57 | 190 | 332 | 268 | 77 | 24 | 0 | 0 | 980 |
| 1990 | 0 | 0 | 14 | 39 | 18 | 261 | 328 | 289 | 182 | 12 | 1 | 0 | 1144 |

**TABLE 6**   SNOWFALL (inches)        SPRINGFIELD, ILLINOIS

| SEASON | JULY | AUG | SEP | OCT | NOV | DEC | JAN | FEB | MAR | APR | MAY | JUNE | TOTAL |
|---|---|---|---|---|---|---|---|---|---|---|---|---|---|
| 1961-62 | 0.0 | 0.0 | 0.0 | 0.0 | 5.5 | 9.5 | 12.7 | 9.6 | 2.6 | 0.3 | 0.0 | 0.0 | 40.2 |
| 1962-63 | 0.0 | 0.0 | 0.0 | T | T | 4.7 | 5.2 | 11.9 | 0.2 | T | 0.0 | 0.0 | 22.0 |
| 1963-64 | 0.0 | 0.0 | 0.0 | 0.0 | T | 5.2 | 10.8 | 13.6 | 6.3 | T | 0.0 | 0.0 | 35.9 |
| 1964-65 | 0.0 | 0.0 | 0.0 | 0.0 | 4.4 | 1.6 | 9.1 | 14.2 | 11.1 | T | 0.0 | 0.0 | 40.4 |
| 1965-66 | 0.0 | 0.0 | 0.0 | 0.0 | T | 1.7 | 0.4 | 8.6 | 3.5 | T | T | 0.0 | 14.2 |
| 1966-67 | 0.0 | 0.0 | 0.0 | 0.0 | 0.3 | 2.0 | 6.4 | 3.7 | 2.4 | 0.1 | 0.0 | 0.0 | 14.9 |
| 1967-68 | 0.0 | 0.0 | 0.0 | 0.1 | 2.8 | 6.4 | 13.0 | 1.7 | 4.5 | T | 0.0 | 0.0 | 28.5 |
| 1968-69 | 0.0 | 0.0 | 0.0 | 0.0 | 0.7 | 4.7 | 5.0 | 6.8 | 7.0 | 0.0 | 0.0 | 0.0 | 24.2 |
| 1969-70 | 0.0 | 0.0 | 0.0 | 0.0 | 0.5 | 10.2 | 7.0 | 3.9 | 4.3 | 1.1 | 0.0 | 0.0 | 27.0 |
| 1970-71 | 0.0 | 0.0 | 0.0 | 0.0 | T | 0.9 | 4.2 | 3.4 | 0.7 | 3.8 | 0.0 | 0.0 | 13.0 |
| 1971-72 | 0.0 | 0.0 | 0.0 | 0.0 | 4.4 | T | 8.1 | 6.0 | 3.6 | T | 0.0 | 0.0 | 22.1 |
| 1972-73 | 0.0 | 0.0 | 0.0 | 0.0 | 5.4 | 3.1 | 0.6 | 3.1 | 0.3 | 0.9 | 0.0 | 0.0 | 13.4 |
| 1973-74 | 0.0 | 0.0 | 0.0 | 0.0 | 1.3 | 22.7 | 7.3 | 5.3 | 4.4 | 0.4 | 0.0 | 0.0 | 41.4 |
| 1974-75 | 0.0 | 0.0 | 0.0 | 0.0 | 6.8 | 2.5 | 4.5 | 14.2 | 4.5 | 0.4 | 0.0 | 0.0 | 32.9 |
| 1975-76 | 0.0 | 0.0 | 0.0 | 0.0 | 8.5 | 4.3 | 8.5 | 2.1 | 2.2 | 0.0 | 0.0 | 0.0 | 25.6 |
| 1976-77 | 0.0 | 0.0 | 0.0 | T | T | 6.9 | 21.1 | 8.9 | 0.6 | 1.1 | 0.0 | 0.0 | 38.6 |
| 1977-78 | 0.0 | 0.0 | 0.0 | 0.0 | 6.4 | 8.9 | 8.9 | 9.4 | 18.5 | T | 0.0 | 0.0 | 52.1 |
| 1978-79 | 0.0 | 0.0 | 0.0 | 0.0 | T | 3.2 | 15.9 | 4.6 | 8.1 | T | 0.0 | 0.0 | 31.8 |
| 1979-80 | 0.0 | 0.0 | 0.0 | 0.0 | 0.8 | 0.1 | 5.1 | 11.7 | 5.5 | 7.3 | 0.0 | 0.0 | 30.5 |
| 1980-81 | 0.0 | 0.0 | 0.0 | T | 3.5 | 2.1 | 2.7 | 8.6 | 0.6 | 0.0 | 0.0 | 0.0 | 17.5 |
| 1981-82 | 0.0 | 0.0 | 0.0 | 0.0 | 0.1 | 21.6 | 12.0 | 11.4 | 4.6 | 0.0 | 0.0 | 0.0 | 50.4 |
| 1982-83 | 0.0 | 0.0 | 0.0 | 0.0 | 0.0 | 0.2 | 0.9 | 2.4 | 1.3 | 5.4 | 0.2 | 0.0 | 10.4 |
| 1983-84 | 0.0 | 0.0 | 0.0 | T | 0.0 | 16.2 | 3.9 | 9.8 | 5.7 | 0.0 | 0.0 | 0.0 | 35.6 |
| 1984-85 | 0.0 | 0.0 | 0.0 | 0.0 | 1.8 | 0.7 | 9.3 | 2.5 | T | T | 0.0 | 0.0 | 14.3 |
| 1985-86 | 0.0 | 0.0 | 0.0 | 0.0 | T | 4.3 | 0.2 | 15.1 | 0.6 | 0.1 | 0.0 | 0.0 | 20.3 |
| 1986-87 | 0.0 | 0.0 | 0.0 | 0.0 | 0.5 | T | 20.3 | T | 0.0 | 0.0 | 0.0 | 0.0 | 20.8 |
| 1987-88 | 0.0 | 0.0 | 0.0 | 0.0 | 0.1 | 5.7 | 0.4 | 10.2 | 5.0 | 0.0 | 0.0 | 0.0 | 21.4 |
| 1988-89 | 0.0 | 0.0 | 0.0 | 0.0 | T | 5.5 | 0.3 | 13.7 | 5.2 | T | T | 0.0 | 24.7 |
| 1989-90 | 0.0 | 0.0 | 0.0 | 0.3 | T | 6.7 | 0.6 | 0.5 | 1.2 | T | 0.0 | 0.0 | 9.3 |
| 1990-91 | 0.0 | 0.0 | 0.0 | 0.0 | T | 9.4 | | | | | | | |
| Record Mean | 0.0 | 0.0 | 0.0 | T | 1.7 | 5.1 | 5.7 | 6.4 | 4.2 | 0.7 | T | 0.0 | 23.9 |

**See Reference Notes, relative to all above tables, on preceding page.**

Indianapolis is located in the central part of the state and is situated on level or slightly rolling terrain. The greater part of the city lies east of the White River which flows in a general north to south direction.

The National Weather Service Forecast Office is located approximately 7 miles southwest of the central part of the city at the Indianapolis International Airport. From a field elevation of 797 feet above sea level at the Indianapolis International Airport the terrain slopes gradually downward to a little below 645 feet at the White River, then upward to just over 910 feet in the northwest corner and eastern sections of the county. The street elevation at the former city office located in the Old Federal Building is 718 feet.

Indianapolis has a temperate climate, with very warm summers and without a dry season. Very cold temperatures may be produced by the invasion of continental polar air in the winter from northern latitudes. The polar air can be quite frigid with very low humidity. The arrival of maritime tropical air from the Gulf in the summer brings warm temperatures and moderate humidity. One of the longest and most severe heat waves brought temperatures of 100 degrees or more for nine consecutive days.

Precipitation is distributed fairly evenly throughout the year, and therefore there is no pronounced wet or dry season. Rainfall in the spring and summer is produced mostly by showers and thunderstorms. A rainfall of about 2 1/2 inches in a 24-hour period can be expected about once a year. Snowfalls of 3 inches or more occur on an average of two or three times in the winter.

Local levees and/or channel improvements now protect some formerly flood-prone areas.

Based on the 1951-1980 period, the average first occurrence of 32 degrees Fahrenheit in the fall is October 20 and the average last occurrence in the spring is April 22.

## TABLE 1 — NORMALS, MEANS AND EXTREMES

INDIANAPOLIS, INDIANA

LATITUDE: 39°44'N  LONGITUDE: 86°16'W  ELEVATION: FT. GRND  792  BARO  837  TIME ZONE: EASTERN  WBAN: 93819

| | (a) | JAN | FEB | MAR | APR | MAY | JUNE | JULY | AUG | SEP | OCT | NOV | DEC | YEAR |
|---|---|---|---|---|---|---|---|---|---|---|---|---|---|---|
| **TEMPERATURE °F:** | | | | | | | | | | | | | | |
| Normals | | | | | | | | | | | | | | |
| -Daily Maximum | | 34.2 | 38.5 | 49.3 | 63.1 | 73.4 | 82.3 | 85.2 | 83.7 | 77.9 | 66.1 | 50.8 | 39.2 | 62.0 |
| -Daily Minimum | | 17.8 | 21.1 | 30.7 | 41.7 | 51.5 | 60.9 | 64.9 | 62.7 | 55.3 | 43.4 | 32.8 | 23.7 | 42.2 |
| -Monthly | | 26.0 | 29.9 | 40.0 | 52.4 | 62.5 | 71.6 | 75.1 | 73.2 | 66.6 | 54.8 | 41.8 | 31.5 | 52.1 |
| Extremes | | | | | | | | | | | | | | |
| -Record Highest | 50 | 71 | 74 | 85 | 89 | 93 | 102 | 104 | 102 | 100 | 90 | 81 | 74 | 104 |
| -Year | | 1950 | 1972 | 1981 | 1970 | 1988 | 1988 | 1954 | 1988 | 1954 | 1954 | 1950 | 1982 | JUL 1954 |
| -Record Lowest | 50 | -22 | -21 | -7 | 16 | 28 | 39 | 44 | 41 | 28 | 17 | -2 | -23 | -23 |
| -Year | | 1985 | 1982 | 1980 | 1940 | 1966 | 1956 | 1942 | 1965 | 1942 | 1942 | 1958 | 1989 | DEC 1989 |
| **NORMAL DEGREE DAYS:** | | | | | | | | | | | | | | |
| Heating (base 65°F) | | 1209 | 983 | 775 | 382 | 158 | 15 | 0 | 0 | 63 | 330 | 696 | 1039 | 5650 |
| Cooling (base 65°F) | | 0 | 0 | 0 | 0 | 80 | 213 | 313 | 257 | 111 | 14 | 0 | 0 | 988 |
| **% OF POSSIBLE SUNSHINE** | 45 | 41 | 49 | 50 | 54 | 61 | 66 | 66 | 69 | 66 | 61 | 42 | 39 | 55 |
| **MEAN SKY COVER (tenths)** | | | | | | | | | | | | | | |
| Sunrise - Sunset | 47 | 7.2 | 7.0 | 7.2 | 6.9 | 6.5 | 6.1 | 5.8 | 5.6 | 5.4 | 5.5 | 7.0 | 7.4 | 6.5 |
| **MEAN NUMBER OF DAYS:** | | | | | | | | | | | | | | |
| Sunrise to Sunset | | | | | | | | | | | | | | |
| -Clear | 58 | 6.0 | 5.7 | 5.6 | 6.1 | 7.2 | 7.2 | 8.6 | 9.2 | 10.6 | 11.1 | 6.4 | 5.2 | 88.7 |
| -Partly Cloudy | 58 | 6.0 | 6.3 | 7.1 | 7.4 | 9.0 | 10.5 | 12.5 | 11.7 | 8.7 | 7.4 | 6.7 | 6.2 | 99.5 |
| -Cloudy | 58 | 19.0 | 16.3 | 18.4 | 16.5 | 14.8 | 12.3 | 9.9 | 10.1 | 10.7 | 12.5 | 16.9 | 19.7 | 177.1 |
| Precipitation | | | | | | | | | | | | | | |
| .01 inches or more | 50 | 11.7 | 10.1 | 13.0 | 12.2 | 12.1 | 9.8 | 9.4 | 8.7 | 7.7 | 8.1 | 10.3 | 11.9 | 125.1 |
| Snow,Ice pellets | | | | | | | | | | | | | | |
| 1.0 inches or more | 48 | 2.0 | 2.0 | 1.2 | 0.1 | 0.0 | 0.0 | 0.0 | 0.0 | 0.0 | 0.1 | 0.6 | 1.8 | 7.8 |
| Thunderstorms | 47 | 0.7 | 0.7 | 2.7 | 4.6 | 6.4 | 7.3 | 7.7 | 6.2 | 3.7 | 1.8 | 1.1 | 0.5 | 43.4 |
| Heavy Fog Visibility | | | | | | | | | | | | | | |
| 1/4 mile or less | 47 | 3.3 | 2.6 | 1.7 | 0.6 | 0.8 | 0.7 | 1.1 | 1.7 | 1.5 | 1.3 | 1.7 | 2.9 | 20.0 |
| Temperature °F | | | | | | | | | | | | | | |
| -Maximum | | | | | | | | | | | | | | |
| 90° and above | 30 | 0.0 | 0.0 | 0.0 | 0.0 | 0.6 | 3.9 | 7.1 | 4.1 | 1.8 | 0.0 | 0.0 | 0.0 | 17.5 |
| 32° and below | 30 | 14.2 | 9.4 | 2.5 | 0.* | 0.0 | 0.0 | 0.0 | 0.0 | 0.0 | 0.0 | 0.9 | 8.9 | 36.0 |
| -Minimum | | | | | | | | | | | | | | |
| 32° and below | 30 | 27.8 | 23.9 | 17.2 | 5.4 | 0.4 | 0.0 | 0.0 | 0.0 | 0.0 | 4.3 | 14.4 | 25.2 | 118.6 |
| 0° and below | 30 | 4.4 | 2.2 | 0.3 | 0.0 | 0.0 | 0.0 | 0.0 | 0.0 | 0.0 | 0.0 | 0.0 | 2.0 | 8.8 |
| **AVG. STATION PRESS.(mb)** | 17 | 989.9 | 989.5 | 986.9 | 986.1 | 985.9 | 986.6 | 987.9 | 988.7 | 989.3 | 990.1 | 989.0 | 989.8 | 988.3 |
| **RELATIVE HUMIDITY (%)** | | | | | | | | | | | | | | |
| Hour 01 | 30 | 78 | 77 | 75 | 72 | 77 | 79 | 84 | 86 | 85 | 80 | 80 | 80 | 79 |
| Hour 07 | 30 | 80 | 80 | 79 | 78 | 81 | 82 | 87 | 90 | 90 | 86 | 84 | 83 | 83 |
| Hour 13 (Local Time) | 30 | 70 | 67 | 62 | 55 | 55 | 56 | 60 | 61 | 58 | 57 | 66 | 72 | 62 |
| Hour 19 | 30 | 72 | 70 | 65 | 57 | 57 | 57 | 62 | 66 | 66 | 64 | 72 | 76 | 65 |
| **PRECIPITATION (inches):** | | | | | | | | | | | | | | |
| Water Equivalent | | | | | | | | | | | | | | |
| -Normal | | 2.65 | 2.46 | 3.61 | 3.68 | 3.66 | 3.99 | 4.32 | 3.46 | 2.74 | 2.51 | 3.04 | 3.00 | 39.12 |
| -Maximum Monthly | 50 | 12.69 | 5.35 | 10.74 | 8.09 | 10.10 | 9.74 | 11.06 | 8.34 | 8.06 | 8.36 | 8.50 | 6.70 | 12.69 |
| -Year | | 1950 | 1971 | 1963 | 1964 | 1943 | 1942 | 1979 | 1980 | 1989 | 1941 | 1985 | 1957 | JAN 1950 |
| -Minimum Monthly | 50 | 0.21 | 0.36 | 1.03 | 0.98 | 1.06 | 0.36 | 0.99 | 0.68 | 0.24 | 0.17 | 0.82 | 0.45 | 0.17 |
| -Year | | 1944 | 1978 | 1941 | 1976 | 1988 | 1988 | 1941 | 1964 | 1963 | 1963 | 1976 | 1976 | OCT 1963 |
| -Maximum in 24 hrs | 47 | 3.47 | 2.50 | 3.05 | 2.56 | 3.53 | 3.80 | 5.32 | 4.72 | 3.07 | 3.90 | 3.02 | 2.21 | 5.32 |
| -Year | | 1950 | 1977 | 1963 | 1961 | 1961 | 1963 | 1987 | 1976 | 1961 | 1959 | 1955 | 1971 | JUL 1987 |
| Snow,Ice pellets | | | | | | | | | | | | | | |
| -Maximum Monthly | 58 | 30.6 | 18.0 | 10.5 | 4.0 | 0.2 | 0.0 | 0.0 | T | 0.0 | 9.3 | 8.3 | 27.5 | 30.6 |
| -Year | | 1978 | 1979 | 1975 | 1940 | 1989 | | | 1989 | | 1989 | 1966 | 1973 | JAN 1978 |
| -Maximum in 24 hrs | 47 | 12.2 | 12.5 | 5.6 | 3.1 | 0.2 | 0.0 | 0.0 | T | 0.0 | 7.5 | 8.2 | 11.5 | 12.5 |
| -Year | | 1978 | 1965 | 1948 | 1953 | 1989 | | | 1989 | | 1989 | 1966 | 1973 | FEB 1965 |
| **WIND:** | | | | | | | | | | | | | | |
| Mean Speed (mph) | 41 | 10.9 | 10.8 | 11.7 | 11.2 | 9.5 | 8.5 | 7.4 | 7.2 | 7.9 | 8.8 | 10.4 | 10.5 | 9.6 |
| Prevailing Direction | | | | | | | | | | | | | | |
| through 1963 | | NW | WNW | WNW | SW | SW | SW | SW | SW | SW | SW | SW | SW | SW |
| Fastest Obs. 1 Min. | | | | | | | | | | | | | | |
| -Direction (!!!) | 10 | 29 | 33 | 24 | 33 | 32 | 29 | 36 | 32 | 30 | 23 | 25 | 22 | 33 |
| -Speed (MPH) | 10 | 39 | 38 | 35 | 46 | 37 | 46 | 40 | 40 | 28 | 35 | 31 | 40 | 46 |
| -Year | | 1980 | 1980 | 1985 | 1988 | 1986 | 1980 | 1987 | 1980 | 1986 | 1988 | 1987 | 1987 | APR 1988 |
| Peak Gust | | | | | | | | | | | | | | |
| -Direction (!!!) | 6 | NW | SW | SW | NW | NW | NW | SW | NW | NW | SW | SW | SW | NW |
| -Speed (mph) | 6 | 45 | 53 | 54 | 74 | 62 | 58 | 54 | 70 | 41 | 48 | 63 | 64 | 74 |
| -Date | 6 | 1988 | 1988 | 1985 | 1988 | 1986 | 1986 | 1989 | 1985 | 1986 | 1988 | 1988 | 1987 | APR 1988 |

**See Reference Notes to this table on the following page.**

## TABLE 2 — PRECIPITATION (inches)  INDIANAPOLIS, INDIANA

| YEAR | JAN | FEB | MAR | APR | MAY | JUNE | JULY | AUG | SEP | OCT | NOV | DEC | ANNUAL |
|------|-----|-----|-----|-----|-----|------|------|-----|-----|-----|-----|-----|--------|
| 1961 | 1.22 | 3.15 | 7.91 | 6.68 | 6.46 | 3.47 | 2.61 | 2.70 | 4.40 | 1.27 | 3.72 | 3.05 | 46.64 |
| 1962 | 4.58 | 2.27 | 4.01 | 1.69 | 5.14 | 1.45 | 6.87 | 5.78 | 4.13 | 2.83 | 1.42 | 1.09 | 41.26 |
| 1963 | 1.15 | 0.58 | 10.74 | 2.58 | 2.10 | 5.30 | 4.66 | 2.22 | 0.24 | 0.17 | 2.18 | 0.86 | 32.78 |
| 1964 | 2.04 | 2.01 | 7.20 | 8.09 | 1.42 | 2.73 | 4.09 | 0.68 | 1.27 | 0.64 | 3.13 | 3.05 | 36.35 |
| 1965 | 3.86 | 4.33 | 2.17 | 5.80 | 1.44 | 3.49 | 3.18 | 3.25 | 5.16 | 1.05 | 1.41 | 2.97 | 38.11 |
| 1966 | 1.13 | 2.91 | 1.31 | 3.32 | 1.47 | 1.28 | 2.71 | 1.31 | 5.73 | 1.60 | 4.72 | 5.23 | 32.72 |
| 1967 | 1.81 | 1.84 | 3.33 | 3.00 | 5.00 | 1.07 | 2.34 | 2.38 | 0.80 | 5.72 | 2.54 | 4.92 | 34.75 |
| 1968 | 2.96 | 1.51 | 3.73 | 2.86 | 9.25 | 2.51 | 2.19 | 4.45 | 1.54 | 1.13 | 4.74 | 4.18 | 41.05 |
| 1969 | 6.19 | 1.23 | 1.33 | 4.42 | 1.82 | 4.16 | 8.02 | 2.98 | 4.83 | 2.86 | 2.04 | 2.07 | 42.77 |
| 1970 | 1.17 | 1.86 | 2.51 | 6.53 | 2.43 | 1.97 | 4.43 | 1.82 | 2.41 | 3.66 | 2.12 | 0.78 | 32.98 |
| 1971 | 1.98 | 5.35 | 1.49 | 1.16 | 4.25 | 3.39 | 5.68 | 1.93 | 3.10 | 1.84 | 1.29 | 6.02 | 37.48 |
| 1972 | 1.57 | 1.15 | 2.48 | 5.81 | 1.89 | 6.04 | 2.01 | 2.94 | 5.65 | 2.25 | 5.65 | 2.83 | 40.27 |
| 1973 | 2.27 | 1.11 | 5.63 | 2.76 | 1.79 | 5.91 | 6.67 | 2.74 | 2.43 | 3.11 | 3.62 | 4.27 | 42.31 |
| 1974 | 3.39 | 2.58 | 3.60 | 3.45 | 6.27 | 5.15 | 1.20 | 5.63 | 3.25 | 0.99 | 2.99 | 2.81 | 41.31 |
| 1975 | 4.37 | 4.13 | 4.16 | 4.14 | 2.42 | 5.73 | 4.63 | 4.68 | 2.32 | 2.80 | 3.63 | 3.71 | 46.72 |
| 1976 | 2.29 | 2.90 | 3.46 | 0.98 | 3.10 | 3.97 | 3.09 | 7.95 | 2.02 | 2.79 | 0.82 | 0.45 | 33.82 |
| 1977 | 1.50 | 3.62 | 3.83 | 1.91 | 2.78 | 3.86 | 2.57 | 4.47 | 3.40 | 2.79 | 3.01 | 4.31 | 38.05 |
| 1978 | 3.80 | 0.36 | 3.54 | 3.59 | 4.21 | 4.43 | 5.04 | 6.89 | 0.85 | 2.38 | 4.03 | 2.57 | 42.94 |
| 1979 | 3.24 | 2.86 | 2.43 | 3.14 | 2.23 | 3.93 | 11.06 | 6.09 | 0.36 | 2.32 | 4.37 | 0.78 | 44.60 |
| 1980 | 1.67 | 1.84 | 4.26 | 2.10 | 2.26 | 4.15 | 2.87 | 8.34 | 3.31 | 1.87 | 1.41 | 0.78 | 34.86 |
| 1981 | 0.38 | 2.88 | 1.22 | 5.81 | 9.23 | 1.64 | 5.75 | 1.69 | 2.04 | 2.35 | 1.12 | 3.40 | 37.49 |
| 1982 | 5.64 | 1.62 | 4.73 | 2.40 | 5.94 | 5.16 | 3.44 | 1.00 | 1.20 | 0.91 | 4.16 | 5.78 | 41.98 |
| 1983 | 1.05 | 1.03 | 2.94 | 4.47 | 4.68 | 4.53 | 1.58 | 2.79 | 1.28 | 3.87 | 4.55 | 3.43 | 36.20 |
| 1984 | 0.97 | 3.16 | 3.14 | 3.90 | 4.35 | 1.51 | 4.83 | 3.27 | 4.69 | 5.38 | 4.33 | 4.33 | 42.13 |
| 1985 | 1.37 | 3.73 | 5.94 | 2.60 | 4.60 | 3.06 | 4.06 | 5.29 | 2.71 | 1.82 | 8.50 | 3.30 | 46.98 |
| 1986 | 0.73 | 2.84 | 3.93 | 4.34 | 7.37 | 3.58 | 4.88 | 1.18 | 5.68 | 7.84 | 2.32 | 1.71 | 46.40 |
| 1987 | 1.55 | 1.28 | 1.84 | 2.68 | 1.77 | 4.11 | 9.22 | 0.86 | 1.41 | 1.36 | 2.60 | 4.77 | 33.45 |
| 1988 | 2.35 | 3.04 | 3.22 | 4.02 | 1.06 | 0.36 | 4.71 | 1.46 | 1.14 | 3.07 | 4.39 | 2.50 | 31.32 |
| 1989 | 1.75 | 1.32 | 3.72 | 4.32 | 5.79 | 3.80 | 6.15 | 8.05 | 8.06 | 2.92 | 2.79 | 1.90 | 50.57 |
| 1990 | 1.79 | 5.17 | 3.93 | 2.44 | 7.59 | 3.11 | 3.68 | 4.46 | 2.68 | 4.64 | 3.23 | 7.72 | 50.44 |
| Record Mean | 2.86 | 2.54 | 3.77 | 3.66 | 3.96 | 4.02 | 3.92 | 3.32 | 3.14 | 2.70 | 3.21 | 2.98 | 40.08 |

## TABLE 3 — AVERAGE TEMPERATURE (deg. F)  INDIANAPOLIS, INDIANA

| YEAR | JAN | FEB | MAR | APR | MAY | JUNE | JULY | AUG | SEP | OCT | NOV | DEC | ANNUAL |
|------|-----|-----|-----|-----|-----|------|------|-----|-----|-----|-----|-----|--------|
| 1961 | 23.6 | 34.0 | 43.6 | 45.6 | 56.4 | 67.9 | 73.4 | 71.4 | 70.9 | 56.2 | 42.0 | 29.1 | 51.2 |
| 1962 | 23.7 | 30.7 | 37.7 | 51.1 | 69.2 | 73.2 | 73.3 | 72.4 | 62.6 | 55.7 | 42.4 | 25.5 | 51.5 |
| 1963 | 19.5 | 21.1 | 42.4 | 53.3 | 59.7 | 71.3 | 73.4 | 68.9 | 65.4 | 62.1 | 45.1 | 18.5 | 50.0 |
| 1964 | 30.7 | 29.0 | 40.6 | 54.7 | 65.6 | 73.4 | 74.6 | 72.5 | 67.2 | 51.7 | 45.3 | 32.2 | 53.1 |
| 1965 | 27.5 | 29.5 | 33.7 | 54.4 | 68.3 | 71.7 | 72.9 | 71.1 | 67.5 | 53.7 | 44.7 | 38.6 | 52.8 |
| 1966 | 22.4 | 30.4 | 43.3 | 51.3 | 58.4 | 72.4 | 79.2 | 73.2 | 65.2 | 51.9 | 43.8 | 33.7 | 52.0 |
| 1967 | 32.6 | 27.7 | 44.0 | 53.6 | 59.3 | 73.9 | 73.8 | 71.1 | 65.9 | 55.2 | 39.4 | 33.7 | 52.5 |
| 1968 | 25.1 | 26.4 | 42.8 | 53.7 | 58.6 | 72.3 | 75.3 | 74.5 | 65.8 | 54.4 | 42.9 | 30.6 | 51.9 |
| 1969 | 25.7 | 31.7 | 35.7 | 54.0 | 63.4 | 69.8 | 75.8 | 72.7 | 65.2 | 53.8 | 37.5 | 28.2 | 51.1 |
| 1970 | 17.9 | 28.6 | 38.1 | 55.1 | 65.6 | 71.5 | 75.2 | 74.2 | 69.1 | 55.2 | 40.9 | 34.7 | 52.2 |
| 1971 | 23.4 | 28.9 | 37.3 | 51.0 | 58.9 | 75.6 | 72.3 | 71.3 | 69.4 | 62.0 | 43.1 | 38.4 | 52.7 |
| 1972 | 26.5 | 28.4 | 39.8 | 52.1 | 65.0 | 68.8 | 74.6 | 73.1 | 68.3 | 51.5 | 39.9 | 31.9 | 51.7 |
| 1973 | 30.7 | 31.5 | 49.4 | 51.3 | 59.5 | 73.3 | 76.0 | 74.4 | 69.9 | 59.4 | 46.4 | 30.9 | 54.4 |
| 1974 | 31.6 | 32.4 | 45.3 | 55.0 | 62.1 | 68.6 | 76.0 | 71.8 | 60.6 | 52.5 | 42.5 | 32.9 | 52.6 |
| 1975 | 32.0 | 32.0 | 36.9 | 48.9 | 65.5 | 71.5 | 73.5 | 76.1 | 62.6 | 55.9 | 46.4 | 32.8 | 52.8 |
| 1976 | 23.9 | 38.8 | 46.6 | 53.4 | 58.8 | 71.3 | 73.9 | 71.3 | 63.6 | 48.7 | 34.7 | 24.6 | 50.8 |
| 1977 | 10.3 | 28.2 | 46.5 | 57.1 | 70.6 | 71.2 | 78.0 | 74.0 | 69.6 | 54.2 | 45.9 | 29.2 | 52.9 |
| 1978 | 18.2 | 17.8 | 36.7 | 55.2 | 63.5 | 74.0 | 77.2 | 75.0 | 70.4 | 52.7 | 45.7 | 34.4 | 51.7 |
| 1979 | 18.0 | 18.8 | 43.4 | 49.8 | 61.1 | 71.1 | 73.0 | 72.4 | 64.9 | 53.1 | 41.3 | 34.9 | 50.2 |
| 1980 | 28.5 | 22.5 | 36.0 | 49.1 | 64.0 | 69.1 | 78.5 | 76.6 | 67.9 | 50.9 | 40.3 | 31.8 | 51.3 |
| 1981 | 23.5 | 33.0 | 39.9 | 57.4 | 59.9 | 73.3 | 75.4 | 72.8 | 64.6 | 53.1 | 44.2 | 27.8 | 52.1 |
| 1982 | 20.1 | 26.4 | 42.5 | 48.6 | 68.6 | 67.8 | 76.2 | 71.7 | 64.4 | 55.7 | 44.2 | 40.2 | 52.2 |
| 1983 | 30.6 | 35.5 | 42.9 | 48.2 | 58.2 | 71.8 | 79.7 | 80.1 | 69.4 | 57.5 | 44.1 | 20.2 | 53.2 |
| 1984 | 22.8 | 37.3 | 33.0 | 50.0 | 58.8 | 75.3 | 72.4 | 74.3 | 64.2 | 61.3 | 43.0 | 38.9 | 52.6 |
| 1985 | 20.4 | 26.1 | 44.6 | 57.1 | 64.9 | 70.6 | 74.3 | 71.2 | 66.2 | 57.6 | 46.6 | 22.5 | 51.8 |
| 1986 | 28.5 | 31.4 | 43.9 | 53.8 | 63.5 | 72.8 | 77.5 | 75.8 | 70.1 | 55.6 | 39.8 | 32.3 | 53.3 |
| 1987 | 27.6 | 35.5 | 44.5 | 52.5 | 68.1 | 73.7 | 75.8 | 73.6 | 68.1 | 48.6 | 46.3 | 35.8 | 54.2 |
| 1988 | 25.9 | 27.2 | 41.4 | 51.9 | 64.4 | 73.4 | 78.3 | 77.5 | 67.3 | 48.2 | 44.2 | 18.8 | 52.6 |
| 1989 | 36.3 | 27.2 | 42.5 | 51.4 | 59.4 | 71.4 | 75.7 | 71.8 | 64.4 | 55.4 | 40.9 | 18.8 | 51.3 |
| 1990 | 37.3 | 37.6 | 46.2 | 51.4 | 60.1 | 71.3 | 73.9 | 72.5 | 66.9 | 53.9 | 47.5 | 34.6 | 54.4 |
| Record Mean | 28.0 | 30.6 | 40.4 | 52.0 | 62.5 | 71.8 | 75.7 | 73.6 | 66.8 | 55.3 | 42.2 | 31.7 | 52.5 |
| Max | 35.1 | 38.7 | 49.2 | 61.8 | 72.6 | 81.7 | 85.7 | 83.6 | 77.2 | 65.4 | 50.4 | 39.0 | 61.8 |
| Min | 20.2 | 22.5 | 31.5 | 42.2 | 52.4 | 61.8 | 65.7 | 63.6 | 56.5 | 45.1 | 33.9 | 24.4 | 43.3 |

## REFERENCE NOTES FOR TABLES 1, 2, 3 and 6  (INDIANAPOLIS, IN)

### GENERAL

T - TRACE AMOUNT
BLANK ENTRIES DENOTE MISSING/UNREPORTED DATA.
# INDICATES A STATION OR INSTRUMENT RELOCATION.

### SPECIFIC

#### TABLE 1

(a) - LENGTH OF RECORD IN YEARS. ALTHOUGH INDIVIDUAL MONTHS MAY BE MISSING.

*  LESS THAN .05

NORMALS — BASED ON THE 1951-1980 RECORD PERIOD.
EXTREMES — DATES ARE THE MOST RECENT OCCURRENCE.
WIND DIR. — NUMERALS SHOW TENS OF DEGREES CLOCKWISE FROM TRUE NORTH. "00" INDICATES CALM.
RESULTANT WIND DIRECTIONS ARE GIVEN TO WHOLE DEGREES.

#### TABLE 3

MAX AND MIN ARE LONG-TERM MEAN DAILY MAXIMUM AND MEAN DAILY MINIMUM TEMPERATURES.

### EXCEPTIONS

#### TABLES 2, 3, and 6

RECORD MEANS ARE THROUGH THE CURRENT YEAR, BEGINNING IN
1871 FOR TEMPERATURE
1871 FOR PRECIPITATION
1932 FOR SNOWFALL

## TABLE 4

HEATING DEGREE DAYS Base 65 deg. F  INDIANAPOLIS, INDIANA

| SEASON | JULY | AUG | SEP | OCT | NOV | DEC | JAN | FEB | MAR | APR | MAY | JUNE | TOTAL |
|---|---|---|---|---|---|---|---|---|---|---|---|---|---|
| 1961-62 | 0 | 3 | 60 | 276 | 684 | 1108 | 1272 | 957 | 839 | 441 | 41 | 2 | 5683 |
| 1962-63 | 3 | 2 | 142 | 286 | 673 | 1221 | 1406 | 1222 | 691 | 352 | 185 | 16 | 6199 |
| 1963-64 | 0 | 20 | 71 | 117 | 590 | 1437 | 1056 | 1037 | 750 | 308 | 64 | 11 | 5461 |
| 1964-65 | 2 | 16 | 73 | 405 | 581 | 1009 | 1155 | 989 | 964 | 323 | 39 | 0 | 5556 |
| 1965-66 | 0 | 18 | 66 | 355 | 603 | 811 | 1312 | 962 | 668 | 412 | 223 | 11 | 5441 |
| 1966-67 | 0 | 0 | 77 | 402 | 631 | 995 | 997 | 1040 | 652 | 353 | 219 | 2 | 5368 |
| 1967-68 | 3 | 9 | 83 | 327 | 761 | 964 | 1232 | 1112 | 680 | 333 | 205 | 11 | 5720 |
| 1968-69 | 4 | 13 | 49 | 354 | 656 | 1057 | 1211 | 925 | 904 | 329 | 121 | 38 | 5661 |
| 1969-70 | 0 | 0 | 85 | 358 | 816 | 1137 | 1458 | 1012 | 829 | 316 | 95 | 11 | 6117 |
| 1970-71 | 4 | 0 | 51 | 301 | 715 | 930 | 1281 | 1006 | 852 | 417 | 198 | 0 | 5755 |
| 1971-72 | 3 | 1 | 49 | 129 | 648 | 813 | 1186 | 1054 | 774 | 389 | 89 | 35 | 5170 |
| 1972-73 | 8 | 4 | 36 | 413 | 746 | 1018 | 1059 | 937 | 477 | 416 | 184 | 0 | 5298 |
| 1973-74 | 0 | 0 | 20 | 211 | 552 | 1052 | 1028 | 905 | 617 | 314 | 158 | 18 | 4875 |
| 1974-75 | 0 | 5 | 163 | 380 | 671 | 988 | 1016 | 918 | 866 | 481 | 78 | 22 | 5588 |
| 1975-76 | 8 | 0 | 137 | 288 | 551 | 992 | 1265 | 754 | 564 | 363 | 203 | 1 | 5126 |
| 1976-77 | 0 | 2 | 79 | 503 | 904 | 1249 | 1693 | 1025 | 567 | 276 | 45 | 19 | 6362 |
| 1977-78 | 0 | 0 | 30 | 326 | 575 | 1104 | 1443 | 1313 | 873 | 292 | 150 | 4 | 6110 |
| 1978-79 | 0 | 0 | 36 | 377 | 571 | 944 | 1453 | 1288 | 665 | 455 | 170 | 5 | 5964 |
| 1979-80 | 3 | 13 | 87 | 384 | 705 | 929 | 1123 | 1224 | 893 | 474 | 93 | 36 | 5964 |
| 1980-81 | 0 | 0 | 45 | 438 | 734 | 1022 | 1279 | 889 | 769 | 244 | 180 | 1 | 5601 |
| 1981-82 | 1 | 0 | 94 | 368 | 621 | 1146 | 1388 | 1075 | 690 | 486 | 26 | 18 | 5913 |
| 1982-83 | 0 | 2 | 110 | 325 | 621 | 764 | 1062 | 819 | 681 | 498 | 211 | 21 | 5114 |
| 1983-84 | 1 | 0 | 64 | 246 | 619 | 1386 | 1304 | 796 | 987 | 447 | 211 | 1 | 6062 |
| 1984-85 | 1 | 0 | 119 | 138 | 653 | 803 | 1375 | 1082 | 631 | 269 | 85 | 16 | 5172 |
| 1985-86 | 0 | 1 | 97 | 245 | 544 | 1311 | 1126 | 935 | 652 | 344 | 114 | 7 | 5376 |
| 1986-87 | 0 | 24 | 30 | 312 | 750 | 1009 | 1150 | 820 | 627 | 378 | 51 | 0 | 5151 |
| 1987-88 | 2 | 5 | 37 | 504 | 553 | 900 | 1205 | 1090 | 726 | 390 | 84 | 15 | 5511 |
| 1988-89 | 0 | 2 | 37 | 517 | 618 | 1024 | 882 | 1052 | 693 | 419 | 226 | 11 | 5481 |
| 1989-90 | 0 | 8 | 106 | 313 | 718 | 1426 | 851 | 760 | 588 | 432 | 153 | 19 | 5374 |
| 1990-91 | 4 | 1 | 86 | 348 | 518 | 932 | | | | | | | |

## TABLE 5

COOLING DEGREE DAYS Base 65 deg. F  INDIANAPOLIS, INDIANA

| YEAR | JAN | FEB | MAR | APR | MAY | JUNE | JULY | AUG | SEP | OCT | NOV | DEC | TOTAL |
|---|---|---|---|---|---|---|---|---|---|---|---|---|---|
| 1969 | 0 | 0 | 0 | 5 | 78 | 190 | 344 | 245 | 95 | 18 | 0 | 0 | 975 |
| 1970 | 0 | 0 | 0 | 26 | 122 | 213 | 327 | 292 | 182 | 5 | 0 | 0 | 1167 |
| 1971 | 0 | 0 | 0 | 2 | 17 | 324 | 237 | 202 | 189 | 40 | 0 | 0 | 1011 |
| 1972 | 0 | 0 | 0 | 8 | 95 | 156 | 313 | 266 | 141 | 0 | 0 | 0 | 979 |
| 1973 | 0 | 0 | 0 | 11 | 20 | 256 | 349 | 302 | 172 | 44 | 1 | 0 | 1155 |
| 1974 | 0 | 0 | 11 | 19 | 73 | 131 | 346 | 225 | 40 | 3 | 2 | 0 | 850 |
| 1975 | 0 | 0 | 0 | 3 | 100 | 222 | 281 | 355 | 71 | 14 | 0 | 0 | 1046 |
| 1976 | 0 | 0 | 0 | 21 | 15 | 198 | 284 | 205 | 43 | 4 | 0 | 0 | 770 |
| 1977 | 0 | 0 | 3 | 45 | 226 | 212 | 410 | 286 | 175 | 0 | 6 | 0 | 1363 |
| 1978 | 0 | 0 | 0 | 4 | 110 | 282 | 382 | 318 | 203 | 1 | 0 | 0 | 1300 |
| 1979 | 0 | 0 | 0 | 7 | 57 | 197 | 255 | 250 | 92 | 24 | 0 | 0 | 882 |
| 1980 | 0 | 0 | 0 | 3 | 68 | 168 | 425 | 368 | 139 | 6 | 0 | 0 | 1177 |
| 1981 | 0 | 0 | 1 | 23 | 29 | 256 | 332 | 249 | 88 | 5 | 0 | 0 | 983 |
| 1982 | 0 | 0 | 0 | 0 | 146 | 109 | 356 | 214 | 98 | 40 | 3 | 1 | 967 |
| 1983 | 0 | 0 | 1 | 3 | 9 | 231 | 464 | 474 | 202 | 18 | 0 | 0 | 1402 |
| 1984 | 0 | 0 | 0 | 6 | 25 | 318 | 237 | 291 | 103 | 28 | 0 | 0 | 1008 |
| 1985 | 0 | 0 | 0 | 5 | 36 | 90 | 296 | 199 | 143 | 21 | 0 | 0 | 980 |
| 1986 | 0 | 0 | 6 | 12 | 74 | 249 | 395 | 189 | 181 | 24 | 0 | 0 | 1130 |
| 1987 | 0 | 0 | 0 | 6 | 156 | 265 | 343 | 279 | 137 | 0 | 0 | 0 | 1186 |
| 1988 | 0 | 0 | 1 | 3 | 72 | 274 | 422 | 395 | 114 | 2 | 0 | 0 | 1283 |
| 1989 | 0 | 0 | 1 | 20 | 57 | 215 | 338 | 227 | 94 | 21 | 0 | 0 | 973 |
| 1990 | 0 | 0 | 13 | 30 | 10 | 215 | 289 | 241 | 147 | 10 | 1 | 0 | 956 |

## TABLE 6

SNOWFALL (inches)  INDIANAPOLIS, INDIANA

| SEASON | JULY | AUG | SEP | OCT | NOV | DEC | JAN | FEB | MAR | APR | MAY | JUNE | TOTAL |
|---|---|---|---|---|---|---|---|---|---|---|---|---|---|
| 1961-62 | 0.0 | 0.0 | 0.0 | 0.0 | 0.5 | 6.2 | 5.1 | 14.0 | 1.7 | T | 0.0 | 0.0 | 27.5 |
| 1962-63 | 0.0 | 0.0 | 0.0 | 1.2 | 0.2 | 6.1 | 9.0 | 6.8 | 6.1 | 0.0 | 0.0 | 0.0 | 29.4 |
| 1963-64 | 0.0 | 0.0 | 0.0 | 0.0 | 0.3 | 7.8 | 9.2 | 12.7 | 4.1 | 0.2 | 0.0 | 0.0 | 34.3 |
| 1964-65 | 0.0 | 0.0 | 0.0 | 0.0 | 2.6 | 1.1 | 12.2 | 15.3 | 5.3 | T | 0.0 | 0.0 | 36.5 |
| 1965-66 | 0.0 | 0.0 | 0.0 | 0.0 | T | 2.9 | 2.5 | 6.3 | 0.8 | T | T | 0.0 | 12.5 |
| 1966-67 | 0.0 | 0.0 | 0.0 | 0.0 | 8.3 | 3.3 | 2.4 | 8.1 | 3.0 | 0.0 | 0.0 | 0.0 | 25.1 |
| 1967-68 | 0.0 | 0.0 | 0.0 | T | 6.3 | 3.5 | 17.0 | 1.1 | 8.8 | T | 0.0 | 0.0 | 36.7 |
| 1968-69 | 0.0 | 0.0 | 0.0 | 0.0 | 0.6 | 1.6 | 9.3 | 0.8 | 6.4 | T | 0.0 | 0.0 | 18.7 |
| 1969-70 | 0.0 | 0.0 | 0.0 | 0.0 | 2.5 | 12.9 | 7.8 | 9.2 | 5.6 | 0.2 | 0.0 | 0.0 | 38.2 |
| 1970-71 | 0.0 | 0.0 | 0.0 | 0.0 | 0.2 | 0.4 | 1.5 | 8.2 | 2.8 | T | 0.0 | 0.0 | 13.1 |
| 1971-72 | 0.0 | 0.0 | 0.0 | 0.0 | 4.4 | 0.4 | 7.9 | 6.3 | 0.3 | 0.6 | 0.0 | 0.0 | 19.9 |
| 1972-73 | 0.0 | 0.0 | 0.0 | T | 1.9 | 1.1 | 0.4 | 1.4 | 2.0 | 1.1 | 0.0 | 0.0 | 7.9 |
| 1973-74 | 0.0 | 0.0 | 0.0 | 0.0 | 0.4 | 27.5 | 3.8 | 8.0 | 3.0 | 2.1 | 0.0 | 0.0 | 44.8 |
| 1974-75 | 0.0 | 0.0 | 0.0 | 0.0 | 3.8 | 5.8 | 6.8 | 4.8 | 10.5 | 0.1 | 0.0 | 0.0 | 31.8 |
| 1975-76 | 0.0 | 0.0 | 0.0 | 0.0 | 4.5 | 8.1 | 5.6 | 0.6 | 2.3 | 0.0 | 0.0 | 0.0 | 21.1 |
| 1976-77 | 0.0 | 0.0 | 0.0 | 0.0 | 0.4 | 3.1 | 20.9 | 3.6 | 1.6 | 0.4 | 0.0 | 0.0 | 30.0 |
| 1977-78 | 0.0 | 0.0 | 0.0 | 0.0 | 2.8 | 15.2 | 30.6 | 3.9 | 5.4 | 0.0 | 0.0 | 0.0 | 57.9 |
| 1978-79 | 0.0 | 0.0 | 0.0 | 0.0 | T | 0.7 | 19.1 | 18.0 | 0.2 | 0.4 | 0.0 | 0.0 | 38.4 |
| 1979-80 | 0.0 | 0.0 | 0.0 | T | 0.8 | 0.2 | 5.0 | 14.5 | 3.6 | 0.7 | 0.0 | 0.0 | 24.8 |
| 1980-81 | 0.0 | 0.0 | 0.0 | T | 3.4 | 2.1 | 3.9 | 7.2 | 0.7 | 0.0 | 0.0 | 0.0 | 17.3 |
| 1981-82 | 0.0 | 0.0 | 0.0 | T | 0.4 | 15.6 | 21.8 | 13.6 | 3.5 | 3.3 | 0.0 | 0.0 | 58.2 |
| 1982-83 | 0.0 | 0.0 | 0.0 | 0.0 | 0.1 | 0.4 | 2.8 | 2.5 | 1.3 | T | 0.0 | 0.0 | 7.1 |
| 1983-84 | 0.0 | 0.0 | 0.0 | 0.0 | 0.1 | 8.3 | 7.2 | 17.1 | 9.2 | T | 0.0 | 0.0 | 41.9 |
| 1984-85 | 0.0 | 0.0 | 0.0 | 2.5 | 3.6 | 10.6 | 11.0 | T | 0.1 | 0.0 | 0.0 | 0.0 | 27.8 |
| 1985-86 | 0.0 | 0.0 | 0.0 | 0.0 | T | 8.1 | 1.7 | 9.5 | 1.1 | T | 0.0 | 0.0 | 20.4 |
| 1986-87 | 0.0 | 0.0 | 0.0 | 0.0 | T | 1.6 | 11.6 | 5.3 | 1.4 | T | 0.0 | 0.0 | 19.9 |
| 1987-88 | 0.0 | 0.0 | 0.0 | 0.0 | T | 1.1 | 2.9 | 4.8 | 2.5 | T | 0.0 | 0.0 | 11.3 |
| 1988-89 | 0.0 | 0.0 | 0.0 | T | 0.4 | 6.8 | 0.1 | 2.4 | 1.9 | 1.7 | 0.2 | 0.0 | 13.5 |
| 1989-90 | 0.0 | T | 0.0 | 9.3 | 0.6 | 8.2 | 4.1 | 2.5 | 1.3 | T | 0.0 | 0.0 | 26.0 |
| 1990-91 | 0.0 | 0.0 | 0.0 | 0.0 | 0.0 | 9.6 | | | | | | | |
| Record Mean | 0.0 | T | 0.0 | 0.2 | 1.8 | 5.0 | 6.1 | 5.8 | 3.5 | 0.5 | T | 0.0 | 22.9 |

**See Reference Notes, relative to all above tables, on preceding page.**

South Bend is located on the Saint Joseph River in the northern portion of Saint Joseph County, situated on mostly level to gently rolling terrain and some former marshland. Drainage for the area is through the Saint Joseph River and Kankakee River.

South Bend is under the climatic influence of Lake Michigan with its nearest shore 20 miles to the northwest. The lake has a moderating effect on the temperature. Temperatures of 100 degrees or higher are rare and cold waves are less severe than at many locations at the same latitude. This results in favorable conditions for orchard and vegetable growth.

Based on the 1951-1980 period, the average first occurrence of 32 degrees Fahrenheit in the fall is October 18 and the average last occurrence in the spring is May 1.

Precipitation is fairly evenly distributed throughout the year with the greatest amounts during the growing season. The predominant snow season is from November through March, although there are also generally lighter amounts in October and April.

Winter is marked by considerable cloudiness and rather high humidity along with frequent periods of snow. Heavy snowfalls, resulting from a cold northwest wind passing over Lake Michigan are not uncommon.

## TABLE 1 — NORMALS, MEANS AND EXTREMES

SOUTH BEND, INDIANA

LATITUDE: 41°42'N    LONGITUDE: 86°19' W    ELEVATION: FT. GRND    773 BARO    782    TIME ZONE: EASTERN    WBAN: 14848

| | (a) | JAN | FEB | MAR | APR | MAY | JUNE | JULY | AUG | SEP | OCT | NOV | DEC | YEAR |
|---|---|---|---|---|---|---|---|---|---|---|---|---|---|---|
| **TEMPERATURE °F:** | | | | | | | | | | | | | | |
| Normals | | | | | | | | | | | | | | |
| -Daily Maximum | | 30.4 | 34.1 | 44.3 | 58.6 | 69.9 | 79.5 | 82.7 | 81.0 | 74.6 | 63.1 | 47.8 | 35.7 | 58.5 |
| -Daily Minimum | | 15.9 | 18.6 | 27.7 | 38.4 | 48.1 | 58.1 | 62.3 | 60.8 | 53.7 | 43.4 | 32.8 | 22.5 | 40.2 |
| -Monthly | | 23.2 | 26.4 | 36.0 | 48.5 | 59.1 | 68.8 | 72.5 | 70.9 | 64.2 | 53.2 | 40.3 | 29.1 | 49.4 |
| Extremes | | | | | | | | | | | | | | |
| -Record Highest | 50 | 68 | 69 | 85 | 91 | 95 | 104 | 101 | 103 | 99 | 92 | 82 | 70 | 104 |
| -Year | | 1950 | 1976 | 1981 | 1942 | 1942 | 1988 | 1941 | 1988 | 1953 | 1963 | 1950 | 1982 | JUN 1988 |
| -Record Lowest | 50 | -22 | -17 | -13 | 11 | 24 | 35 | 44 | 40 | 29 | 20 | -7 | -16 | -22 |
| -Year | | 1943 | 1951 | 1943 | 1972 | 1968 | 1972 | 1972 | 1965 | 1942 | 1988 | 1950 | 1960 | JAN 1943 |
| **NORMAL DEGREE DAYS:** | | | | | | | | | | | | | | |
| Heating (base 65°F) | | 1296 | 1081 | 899 | 495 | 230 | 35 | 6 | 17 | 88 | 376 | 741 | 1113 | 6377 |
| Cooling (base 65°F) | | 0 | 0 | 0 | 0 | 47 | 149 | 239 | 200 | 64 | 11 | 0 | 0 | 710 |
| **% OF POSSIBLE SUNSHINE** | | | | | | | | | | | | | | |
| **MEAN SKY COVER (tenths)** | | | | | | | | | | | | | | |
| Sunrise - Sunset | 44 | 8.0 | 7.7 | 7.5 | 6.8 | 6.3 | 6.1 | 5.6 | 5.7 | 5.8 | 6.2 | 7.8 | 8.2 | 6.8 |
| **MEAN NUMBER OF DAYS:** | | | | | | | | | | | | | | |
| Sunrise to Sunset | | | | | | | | | | | | | | |
| -Clear | 50 | 3.4 | 3.6 | 4.6 | 6.0 | 6.8 | 7.2 | 8.5 | 8.7 | 9.0 | 8.5 | 3.6 | 3.0 | 73.0 |
| -Partly Cloudy | 50 | 5.9 | 5.5 | 7.3 | 7.8 | 9.7 | 10.3 | 12.7 | 12.2 | 8.9 | 8.2 | 6.1 | 5.5 | 100.1 |
| -Cloudy | 50 | 21.7 | 19.1 | 19.1 | 16.2 | 14.5 | 12.5 | 9.8 | 10.1 | 12.2 | 14.3 | 20.3 | 22.6 | 192.2 |
| Precipitation | | | | | | | | | | | | | | |
| .01 inches or more | 50 | 15.5 | 12.5 | 14.1 | 13.1 | 11.3 | 10.6 | 9.4 | 9.3 | 9.1 | 10.1 | 12.8 | 15.4 | 143.3 |
| Snow,Ice pellets | | | | | | | | | | | | | | |
| 1.0 inches or more | 50 | 6.0 | 5.1 | 2.9 | 0.7 | 0.0 | 0.0 | 0.0 | 0.0 | 0.* | 0.3 | 2.5 | 5.6 | 23.1 |
| Thunderstorms | 50 | 0.4 | 0.4 | 2.4 | 4.5 | 5.2 | 8.1 | 7.4 | 6.4 | 4.3 | 1.8 | 1.1 | 0.5 | 42.5 |
| Heavy Fog Visibility | | | | | | | | | | | | | | |
| 1/4 mile or less | 50 | 2.5 | 2.2 | 1.9 | 1.2 | 1.5 | 1.1 | 1.2 | 2.1 | 2.0 | 2.2 | 1.9 | 3.1 | 23.0 |
| Temperature °F | | | | | | | | | | | | | | |
| -Maximum | | | | | | | | | | | | | | |
| 90° and above | 26 | 0.0 | 0.0 | 0.0 | 0.0 | 0.5 | 2.9 | 5.3 | 3.1 | 0.7 | 0.0 | 0.0 | 0.0 | 12.5 |
| 32° and below | 26 | 17.0 | 12.9 | 4.1 | 0.2 | 0.0 | 0.0 | 0.0 | 0.0 | 0.0 | 0.0 | 1.7 | 10.3 | 46.2 |
| -Minimum | | | | | | | | | | | | | | |
| 32° and below | 26 | 28.2 | 24.5 | 20.0 | 7.5 | 0.8 | 0.0 | 0.0 | 0.0 | 0.0 | 3.2 | 13.9 | 25.2 | 123.3 |
| 0° and below | 26 | 4.1 | 2.6 | 0.1 | 0.0 | 0.0 | 0.0 | 0.0 | 0.0 | 0.0 | 0.0 | 0.0 | 1.4 | 8.2 |
| **AVG. STATION PRESS.(mb)** | 17 | 989.3 | 989.8 | 987.3 | 986.6 | 986.5 | 986.9 | 988.3 | 989.2 | 989.7 | 990.2 | 988.7 | 989.3 | 988.5 |
| **RELATIVE HUMIDITY (%)** | | | | | | | | | | | | | | |
| Hour 01 | 26 | 79 | 78 | 76 | 73 | 75 | 77 | 81 | 84 | 84 | 79 | 79 | 81 | 79 |
| Hour 07 | 26 | 80 | 80 | 80 | 78 | 78 | 80 | 84 | 88 | 88 | 84 | 82 | 83 | 82 |
| Hour 13 (Local Time) | 26 | 72 | 69 | 62 | 57 | 54 | 55 | 57 | 59 | 60 | 60 | 69 | 76 | 63 |
| Hour 19 | 26 | 75 | 72 | 66 | 59 | 56 | 57 | 59 | 63 | 67 | 68 | 74 | 79 | 66 |
| **PRECIPITATION (inches):** | | | | | | | | | | | | | | |
| Water Equivalent | | | | | | | | | | | | | | |
| -Normal | | 2.48 | 1.99 | 3.05 | 4.06 | 2.81 | 3.94 | 3.67 | 3.94 | 3.22 | 3.22 | 2.83 | 2.95 | 38.16 |
| -Maximum Monthly | 50 | 5.28 | 5.23 | 7.96 | 9.20 | 6.79 | 9.09 | 7.47 | 8.30 | 9.01 | 9.75 | 6.72 | 5.50 | 9.75 |
| -Year | | 1959 | 1976 | 1976 | 1947 | 1981 | 1968 | 1982 | 1979 | 1977 | 1954 | 1985 | 1965 | OCT 1954 |
| -Minimum Monthly | 50 | 0.44 | 0.54 | 0.54 | 0.50 | 1.19 | 0.48 | 0.02 | 0.32 | 0.01 | 0.42 | 1.37 | 0.60 | 0.01 |
| -Year | | 1945 | 1969 | 1958 | 1971 | 1988 | 1988 | 1946 | 1950 | 1979 | 1950 | 1962 | 1943 | SEP 1979 |
| -Maximum in 24 hrs | 50 | 2.81 | 2.64 | 2.33 | 3.14 | 2.99 | 4.70 | 3.64 | 3.70 | 3.00 | 3.49 | 1.91 | 3.33 | 4.70 |
| -Year | | 1960 | 1954 | 1972 | 1947 | 1976 | 1968 | 1989 | 1966 | 1977 | 1988 | 1950 | 1965 | JUN 1968 |
| Snow,Ice pellets | | | | | | | | | | | | | | |
| -Maximum Monthly | 50 | 86.1 | 35.1 | 33.9 | 14.0 | 0.6 | T | T | T | 1.2 | 8.8 | 30.3 | 41.9 | 86.1 |
| -Year | | 1978 | 1958 | 1960 | 1982 | 1966 | 1989 | 1989 | 1989 | 1942 | 1989 | 1977 | 1962 | JAN 1978 |
| -Maximum in 24 hrs | 50 | 16.7 | 10.3 | 14.8 | 8.7 | 0.6 | T | T | T | 1.0 | 8.8 | 17.5 | 13.7 | 17.5 |
| -Year | | 1978 | 1967 | 1960 | 1982 | 1966 | 1989 | 1989 | 1989 | 1942 | 1989 | 1977 | 1981 | NOV 1977 |
| **WIND:** | | | | | | | | | | | | | | |
| Mean Speed (mph) | 41 | 12.0 | 11.4 | 12.1 | 11.8 | 10.3 | 9.2 | 8.2 | 7.8 | 8.6 | 9.6 | 11.2 | 11.4 | 10.3 |
| Prevailing Direction | | | | | | | | | | | | | | |
| through 1963 | | SW | SW | NNW | NNW | SSW | SSW | SSW | SSW | SSW | SSW | SSW | SW | SSW |
| Fastest Obs. 1 Min. | | | | | | | | | | | | | | |
| -Direction (!!!) | 40 | 22 | 20 | 20 | 27 | 27 | 27 | 34 | 32 | 30 | 25 | 22 | 23 | 27 |
| -Speed (MPH) | 40 | 52 | 47 | 51 | 55 | 68 | 50 | 45 | 63 | 35 | 38 | 58 | 43 | 68 |
| -Year | | 1975 | 1953 | 1961 | 1962 | 1989 | 1950 | 1951 | 1953 | 1986 | 1955 | 1988 | 1953 | MAY 1989 |
| Peak Gust | | | | | | | | | | | | | | |
| -Direction (!!!) | 6 | NW | NW | SW | SW | W | SW | NW | SW | W | W | SW | W | W |
| -Speed (mph) | 6 | 59 | 58 | 53 | 66 | 86 | 71 | 52 | 45 | 63 | 44 | 74 | 54 | 86 |
| -Date | | 1985 | 1987 | 1985 | 1984 | 1989 | 1987 | 1985 | 1988 | 1988 | 1988 | 1988 | 1987 | MAY 1989 |

**See Reference Notes to this table on the following page.**

PRECIPITATION (inches)  SOUTH BEND, INDIANA

**TABLE 2**

| YEAR | JAN | FEB | MAR | APR | MAY | JUNE | JULY | AUG | SEP | OCT | NOV | DEC | ANNUAL |
|------|-----|-----|-----|-----|-----|------|------|-----|-----|-----|-----|-----|--------|
| 1961 | 0.95 | 1.55 | 3.80 | 4.93 | 1.19 | 3.66 | 3.76 | 2.82 | 5.78 | 1.82 | 1.49 | 2.03 | 33.78 |
| 1962 | 3.36 | 1.74 | 1.82 | 2.34 | 2.19 | 5.02 | 4.87 | 3.49 | 1.28 | 4.39 | 1.37 | 2.64 | 34.51 |
| 1963 | 1.28 | 1.11 | 3.03 | 2.42 | 2.48 | 1.81 | 5.11 | 1.30 | 1.18 | 1.21 | 2.32 | 1.90 | 25.15 |
| 1964 | 1.57 | 1.03 | 5.01 | 5.37 | 1.32 | 4.45 | 4.80 | 3.42 | 3.39 | 0.89 | 2.33 | 2.54 | 36.12 |
| 1965 | 4.74 | 2.70 | 3.35 | 4.87 | 1.67 | 2.24 | 2.22 | 5.43 | 5.55 | 2.53 | 1.65 | 5.50 | 42.45 |
| 1966 | 1.54 | 1.73 | 2.58 | 5.72 | 3.89 | 1.90 | 4.40 | 5.48 | 1.10 | 1.32 | 4.89 | 4.73 | 39.28 |
| 1967 | 3.56 | 2.26 | 1.73 | 4.96 | 1.57 | 5.49 | 2.11 | 2.77 | 2.59 | 5.01 | 3.34 | 4.08 | 39.47 |
| 1968 | 2.06 | 3.21 | 1.24 | 2.40 | 2.44 | 9.09 | 2.06 | 3.17 | 4.38 | 1.43 | 4.42 | 3.42 | 39.32 |
| 1969 | 3.61 | 0.54 | 1.92 | 5.51 | 4.26 | 5.17 | 4.88 | 0.44 | 1.42 | 4.70 | 2.29 | 1.25 | 35.99 |
| 1970 | 1.34 | 0.76 | 2.81 | 5.43 | 3.35 | 3.92 | 4.14 | 3.37 | 5.37 | 3.68 | 3.57 | 1.78 | 39.52 |
| 1971 | 1.55 | 2.12 | 2.10 | 0.50 | 1.64 | 1.13 | 4.16 | 2.80 | 5.16 | 2.23 | 1.83 | 4.58 | 29.80 |
| 1972 | 1.82 | 1.39 | 3.63 | 3.23 | 3.01 | 2.72 | 4.52 | 3.85 | 7.67 | 3.76 | 2.90 | 4.78 | 43.28 |
| 1973 | 1.64 | 1.02 | 3.85 | 3.88 | 3.61 | 4.85 | 3.33 | 1.29 | 2.11 | 3.49 | 1.45 | 4.30 | 34.82 |
| 1974 | 3.24 | 2.20 | 2.81 | 4.17 | 4.82 | 4.08 | 1.17 | 1.70 | 4.65 | 2.46 | 3.21 | 3.00 | 37.51 |
| 1975 | 4.58 | 3.26 | 2.96 | 6.02 | 2.08 | 5.46 | 2.58 | 7.55 | 1.15 | 1.31 | 4.73 | 3.72 | 45.40 |
| 1976 | 2.21 | 5.23 | 7.96 | 5.20 | 6.67 | 6.60 | 5.96 | 2.44 | 3.34 | 3.23 | 3.23 | 2.21 | 54.28 |
| 1977 | 1.63 | 1.27 | 7.05 | 2.75 | 1.92 | 5.71 | 2.68 | 6.03 | 9.01 | 3.08 | 4.27 | 3.65 | 49.05 |
| 1978 | 4.03 | 0.86 | 2.37 | 4.35 | 3.35 | 3.79 | 5.21 | 3.80 | 3.07 | 3.99 | 2.79 | 4.43 | 42.04 |
| 1979 | 3.22 | 1.51 | 4.03 | 5.80 | 3.03 | 4.66 | 1.75 | 8.30 | 0.01 | 4.79 | 4.88 | 3.66 | 45.64 |
| 1980 | 1.52 | 1.51 | 3.74 | 3.44 | 1.65 | 5.97 | 3.29 | 7.84 | 5.64 | 3.35 | 1.47 | 3.91 | 43.33 |
| 1981 | 0.68 | 1.92 | 0.88 | 5.28 | 6.79 | 6.97 | 3.71 | 2.30 | 3.81 | 1.23 | 2.23 | 1.81 | 37.61 |
| 1982 | 2.95 | 1.17 | 4.54 | 1.46 | 5.51 | 3.12 | 7.47 | 2.84 | 2.51 | 0.91 | 4.52 | 3.40 | 40.40 |
| 1983 | 0.77 | 0.79 | 2.46 | 5.36 | 4.83 | 2.04 | 2.45 | 1.28 | 2.81 | 1.66 | 2.60 | 3.23 | 30.28 |
| 1984 | 0.86 | 1.45 | 2.10 | 4.22 | 4.02 | 3.43 | 1.76 | 1.47 | 4.02 | 4.38 | 2.73 | 4.42 | 34.86 |
| 1985 | 2.58 | 4.32 | 3.86 | 1.93 | 1.50 | 2.88 | 3.80 | 3.82 | 1.88 | 3.36 | 6.72 | 2.51 | 39.16 |
| 1986 | 1.24 | 2.46 | 2.09 | 1.87 | 3.42 | 5.06 | 6.15 | 1.90 | 4.27 | 3.81 | 2.90 | 1.67 | 36.84 |
| 1987 | 2.31 | 1.32 | 1.18 | 2.67 | 3.50 | 3.57 | 3.61 | 3.34 | 3.64 | 3.20 | 2.11 | 4.12 | 34.57 |
| 1988 | 2.21 | 1.98 | 3.03 | 2.91 | 1.40 | 0.48 | 1.28 | 5.63 | 4.42 | 6.68 | 5.72 | 2.91 | 38.65 |
| 1989 | 1.58 | 1.05 | 2.27 | 2.83 | 2.72 | 3.49 | 5.90 | 5.65 | 3.78 | 1.45 | 3.55 | 1.83 | 36.10 |
| 1990 | 2.36 | 3.66 | 2.79 | 2.91 | 6.86 | 4.40 | 5.45 | 4.60 | 3.76 | 7.09 | 6.69 | 5.04 | 55.61 |
| Record Mean | 2.27 | 1.83 | 2.88 | 3.41 | 3.57 | 3.65 | 3.38 | 3.46 | 3.34 | 3.02 | 2.87 | 2.65 | 36.34 |

**TABLE 3**  AVERAGE TEMPERATURE (deg. F)  SOUTH BEND, INDIANA

| YEAR | JAN | FEB | MAR | APR | MAY | JUNE | JULY | AUG | SEP | OCT | NOV | DEC | ANNUAL |
|------|-----|-----|-----|-----|-----|------|------|-----|-----|-----|-----|-----|--------|
| 1961 | 21.8 | 30.5 | 38.8 | 42.5 | 54.2 | 67.7 | 71.7 | 71.2 | 68.2 | 54.1 | 40.1 | 26.7 | 49.0 |
| 1962 | 19.1 | 24.1 | 34.0 | 47.6 | 64.9 | 69.0 | 69.3 | 71.3 | 61.0 | 54.4 | 40.1 | 24.0 | 48.2 |
| #1963 | 13.3 | 18.0 | 38.5 | 49.2 | 56.6 | 69.5 | 71.7 | 67.6 | 64.6 | 61.8 | 45.1 | 19.4 | 47.9 |
| 1964 | 29.3 | 27.3 | 35.8 | 50.4 | 63.5 | 71.1 | 74.0 | 69.0 | 63.0 | 48.9 | 43.2 | 27.5 | 50.2 |
| 1965 | 24.7 | 27.0 | 28.7 | 46.9 | 64.2 | 67.5 | 69.9 | 68.1 | 63.7 | 51.6 | 40.6 | 36.4 | 49.1 |
| 1966 | 20.3 | 28.1 | 39.1 | 45.3 | 52.2 | 68.8 | 72.9 | 67.2 | 62.3 | 51.7 | 42.8 | 29.9 | 48.4 |
| 1967 | 29.0 | 21.1 | 36.5 | 48.9 | 54.3 | 70.6 | 69.8 | 67.9 | 62.5 | 51.7 | 36.0 | 30.5 | 48.2 |
| 1968 | 22.3 | 22.3 | 39.7 | 50.0 | 55.2 | 68.9 | 71.0 | 71.6 | 64.6 | 53.7 | 40.7 | 27.0 | 48.9 |
| 1969 | 22.3 | 27.8 | 32.9 | 50.3 | 59.5 | 64.9 | 73.1 | 73.0 | 63.6 | 51.4 | 37.2 | 27.5 | 48.6 |
| 1970 | 16.8 | 25.7 | 32.3 | 48.8 | 61.0 | 67.8 | 72.0 | 70.4 | 64.4 | 54.4 | 39.4 | 30.4 | 48.6 |
| 1971 | 20.0 | 28.6 | 33.9 | 46.2 | 56.3 | 73.9 | 69.5 | 68.1 | 67.1 | 60.4 | 40.9 | 36.0 | 50.1 |
| 1972 | 23.9 | 26.5 | 33.4 | 45.4 | 60.0 | 63.6 | 71.4 | 69.4 | 62.9 | 49.7 | 38.1 | 28.8 | 47.8 |
| 1973 | 29.9 | 30.0 | 46.7 | 50.1 | 56.1 | 72.3 | 74.4 | 74.1 | 67.0 | 58.3 | 44.4 | 29.2 | 52.7 |
| 1974 | 27.9 | 28.1 | 39.6 | 51.7 | 57.3 | 66.8 | 75.0 | 71.9 | 62.0 | 53.0 | 42.4 | 32.9 | 50.7 |
| 1975 | 30.0 | 27.8 | 34.4 | 43.6 | 63.2 | 70.3 | 71.8 | 73.6 | 60.1 | 55.9 | 48.1 | 32.7 | 51.0 |
| 1976 | 21.6 | 35.3 | 43.6 | 52.5 | 57.0 | 70.9 | 72.8 | 69.0 | 61.3 | 47.9 | 33.2 | 22.8 | 49.0 |
| 1977 | 12.3 | 26.8 | 44.1 | 55.4 | 68.7 | 67.1 | 76.2 | 69.8 | 65.3 | 50.5 | 42.6 | 25.9 | 50.4 |
| 1978 | 18.5 | 14.8 | 31.2 | 48.7 | 59.5 | 69.2 | 71.7 | 71.9 | 68.9 | 51.9 | 42.9 | 29.5 | 48.2 |
| 1979 | 17.9 | 16.3 | 39.2 | 46.2 | 58.5 | 70.1 | 72.3 | 71.3 | 65.4 | 54.2 | 42.3 | 34.8 | 49.0 |
| 1980 | 27.1 | 23.6 | 35.5 | 49.0 | 62.1 | 67.8 | 76.6 | 75.0 | 66.3 | 50.4 | 41.6 | 31.1 | 50.5 |
| 1981 | 23.4 | 32.1 | 40.7 | 52.5 | 56.6 | 69.2 | 71.4 | 70.6 | 62.8 | 50.0 | 41.5 | 27.6 | 49.9 |
| 1982 | 15.6 | 22.7 | 35.1 | 44.7 | 66.0 | 64.5 | 73.3 | 68.9 | 63.3 | 54.0 | 42.5 | 39.0 | 49.1 |
| 1983 | 29.3 | 33.2 | 40.2 | 45.5 | 55.3 | 72.0 | 78.7 | 78.3 | 66.5 | 53.8 | 43.8 | 18.4 | 51.3 |
| 1984 | 18.5 | 35.9 | 30.0 | 48.2 | 56.1 | 72.3 | 71.7 | 74.4 | 63.8 | 57.1 | 41.0 | 34.4 | 50.3 |
| 1985 | 19.6 | 23.7 | 41.3 | 55.2 | 63.1 | 66.8 | 73.1 | 69.8 | 65.6 | 54.6 | 41.6 | 20.1 | 49.5 |
| 1986 | 25.8 | 24.8 | 40.4 | 51.3 | 59.9 | 67.7 | 74.8 | 67.6 | 65.9 | 53.0 | 36.1 | 31.2 | 49.9 |
| 1987 | 25.3 | 30.8 | 40.0 | 50.4 | 64.7 | 72.8 | 75.8 | 71.7 | 64.6 | 46.8 | 43.7 | 32.8 | 51.6 |
| 1988 | 21.3 | 22.7 | 37.3 | 48.4 | 62.2 | 72.0 | 76.4 | 75.9 | 64.5 | 45.9 | 42.5 | 28.8 | 49.8 |
| 1989 | 33.4 | 22.2 | 37.0 | 47.3 | 57.2 | 68.0 | 73.9 | 70.6 | 61.8 | 52.9 | 38.8 | 17.7 | 48.4 |
| 1990 | 34.0 | 31.3 | 40.9 | 48.7 | 56.7 | 68.8 | 71.2 | 69.9 | 65.0 | 52.3 | 45.9 | 31.8 | 51.4 |
| Record Mean | 24.4 | 26.0 | 36.4 | 48.2 | 59.2 | 68.9 | 73.3 | 71.5 | 64.7 | 53.3 | 40.2 | 28.5 | 49.5 |
| Max | 31.8 | 33.9 | 45.2 | 58.5 | 70.3 | 79.8 | 84.1 | 82.3 | 75.3 | 63.3 | 48.0 | 35.3 | 59.0 |
| Min | 16.9 | 18.0 | 27.6 | 37.8 | 48.1 | 57.9 | 62.4 | 60.6 | 54.0 | 43.3 | 32.4 | 21.6 | 40.1 |

**REFERENCE NOTES FOR TABLES 1, 2, 3 and 6     (SOUTH BEND, IN)**

**GENERAL**

T - TRACE AMOUNT
BLANK ENTRIES DENOTE MISSING/UNREPORTED DATA.
# INDICATES A STATION OR INSTRUMENT RELOCATION.

**SPECIFIC**

**TABLE 1**

(a) -  LENGTH OF RECORD IN YEARS. ALTHOUGH
       INDIVIDUAL MONTHS MAY BE MISSING.
 *  LESS THAN .05

NORMALS — BASED ON THE 1951-1980 RECORD PERIOD.
EXTREMES — DATES ARE THE MOST RECENT OCCURRENCE.
WIND DIR. — NUMERALS SHOW TENS OF DEGREES
            CLOCKWISE FROM TRUE NORTH.
            "00" INDICATES CALM.
RESULTANT WIND DIRECTIONS ARE GIVEN TO WHOLE DEGREES.

**TABLE 3**
MAX AND MIN ARE LONG-TERM MEAN DAILY MAXIMUM
AND MEAN DAILY MINIMUM TEMPERATURES.

**EXCEPTIONS**

**TABLES 2, 3, and 6**

RECORD MEANS ARE THROUGH THE CURRENT YEAR,
BEGINNING IN    1894 FOR TEMPERATURE
                1894 FOR PRECIPITATION
                1940 FOR SNOWFALL

HEATING DEGREE DAYS Base 65 deg. F          SOUTH BEND, INDIANA

**TABLE 4**

| SEASON | JULY | AUG | SEP | OCT | NOV | DEC | JAN | FEB | MAR | APR | MAY | JUNE | TOTAL |
|---|---|---|---|---|---|---|---|---|---|---|---|---|---|
| 1961-62 | 7 | 5 | 79 | 342 | 740 | 1178 | 1413 | 1140 | 955 | 539 | 133 | 29 | 6560 |
| 1962-63 | 10 | 8 | 181 | 340 | 741 | 1264 | 1598 | 1312 | 813 | 475 | 278 | 59 | 7079 |
| #1963-64 | 9 | 38 | 79 | 144 | 592 | 1407 | 1100 | 1085 | 898 | 437 | 119 | 38 | 5946 |
| 1964-65 | 5 | 40 | 155 | 493 | 648 | 1157 | 1244 | 1058 | 1120 | 535 | 99 | 36 | 6590 |
| 1965-66 | 3 | 56 | 121 | 411 | 727 | 879 | 1377 | 1028 | 796 | 584 | 402 | 47 | 6431 |
| 1966-67 | 4 | 31 | 128 | 412 | 658 | 1079 | 1109 | 1220 | 880 | 474 | 337 | 8 | 6340 |
| 1967-68 | 31 | 30 | 137 | 429 | 861 | 1064 | 1317 | 1233 | 779 | 444 | 311 | 35 | 6671 |
| 1968-69 | 11 | 27 | 69 | 372 | 724 | 1171 | 1316 | 1034 | 988 | 433 | 226 | 105 | 6476 |
| 1969-70 | 0 | 0 | 110 | 421 | 826 | 1158 | 1485 | 1094 | 1007 | 497 | 181 | 68 | 6847 |
| 1970-71 | 18 | 11 | 93 | 327 | 766 | 1066 | 1387 | 1012 | 959 | 562 | 280 | 7 | 6488 |
| 1971-72 | 16 | 13 | 86 | 171 | 716 | 892 | 1269 | 1110 | 972 | 582 | 197 | 109 | 6133 |
| 1972-73 | 24 | 35 | 112 | 468 | 801 | 1115 | 1080 | 977 | 561 | 446 | 268 | 0 | 5887 |
| 1973-74 | 0 | 4 | 60 | 229 | 611 | 1102 | 1142 | 1028 | 780 | 403 | 250 | 51 | 5660 |
| 1974-75 | 0 | 3 | 144 | 378 | 672 | 985 | 1077 | 1035 | 944 | 634 | 136 | 37 | 6045 |
| 1975-76 | 13 | 1 | 175 | 300 | 503 | 992 | 1338 | 856 | 658 | 407 | 253 | 9 | 5505 |
| 1976-77 | 0 | 19 | 139 | 525 | 949 | 1302 | 1628 | 1063 | 640 | 327 | 85 | 68 | 6745 |
| 1977-78 | 2 | 18 | 58 | 443 | 669 | 1206 | 1436 | 1041 | 795 | 480 | 233 | 41 | 7028 |
| 1978-79 | 5 | 4 | 57 | 399 | 656 | 1095 | 1453 | 1356 | 795 | 560 | 241 | 22 | 6643 |
| 1979-80 | 3 | 17 | 73 | 353 | 672 | 928 | 1172 | 1195 | 908 | 482 | 147 | 58 | 6008 |
| 1980-81 | 0 | 1 | 62 | 449 | 694 | 1047 | 1282 | 915 | 749 | 374 | 271 | 6 | 5850 |
| 1981-82 | 4 | 8 | 132 | 460 | 700 | 1154 | 1523 | 1178 | 922 | 604 | 64 | 72 | 6821 |
| 1982-83 | 2 | 30 | 114 | 353 | 668 | 798 | 1100 | 886 | 760 | 581 | 298 | 30 | 5620 |
| 1983-84 | 6 | 0 | 94 | 352 | 628 | 1440 | 1431 | 838 | 1080 | 503 | 290 | 4 | 6666 |
| 1984-85 | 7 | 0 | 128 | 244 | 714 | 940 | 1401 | 1153 | 727 | 339 | 116 | 47 | 5816 |
| 1985-86 | 0 | 4 | 121 | 319 | 694 | 1381 | 1208 | 1117 | 760 | 425 | 192 | 46 | 6267 |
| 1986-87 | 3 | 48 | 81 | 369 | 858 | 1038 | 1224 | 950 | 766 | 436 | 139 | 16 | 5928 |
| 1987-88 | 5 | 25 | 78 | 558 | 638 | 993 | 1347 | 1220 | 851 | 498 | 158 | 37 | 6408 |
| 1988-89 | 1 | 11 | 72 | 581 | 670 | 1116 | 972 | 1190 | 865 | 528 | 271 | 40 | 6317 |
| 1989-90 | 0 | 12 | 147 | 381 | 779 | 1462 | 954 | 936 | 751 | 521 | 257 | 40 | 6246 |
| 1990-91 | 6 | 14 | 110 | 408 | 565 | 1021 | | | | | | | |

**TABLE 5**          COOLING DEGREE DAYS Base 65 deg. F          SOUTH BEND, INDIANA

| YEAR | JAN | FEB | MAR | APR | MAY | JUNE | JULY | AUG | SEP | OCT | NOV | DEC | TOTAL |
|---|---|---|---|---|---|---|---|---|---|---|---|---|---|
| 1969 | 0 | 0 | 0 | 0 | 59 | 109 | 257 | 256 | 73 | 3 | 0 | 0 | 757 |
| 1970 | 0 | 0 | 0 | 19 | 63 | 158 | 240 | 185 | 82 | 5 | 0 | 0 | 752 |
| 1971 | 0 | 0 | 0 | 3 | 17 | 283 | 163 | 114 | 155 | 34 | 0 | 0 | 769 |
| 1972 | 0 | 0 | 0 | 0 | 47 | 74 | 226 | 180 | 55 | 0 | 0 | 0 | 582 |
| 1973 | 0 | 0 | 0 | 7 | 1 | 226 | 297 | 292 | 126 | 29 | 0 | 0 | 978 |
| 1974 | 0 | 0 | 0 | 10 | 17 | 114 | 321 | 222 | 60 | 11 | 0 | 0 | 755 |
| 1975 | 0 | 0 | 0 | 0 | 86 | 203 | 232 | 274 | 32 | 25 | 1 | 0 | 853 |
| 1976 | 0 | 0 | 1 | 37 | 13 | 192 | 249 | 150 | 36 | 4 | 0 | 0 | 682 |
| 1977 | 0 | 0 | 0 | 47 | 206 | 137 | 355 | 173 | 74 | 0 | 2 | 0 | 994 |
| 1978 | 0 | 0 | 0 | 0 | 70 | 173 | 218 | 227 | 179 | 0 | 1 | 0 | 868 |
| 1979 | 0 | 0 | 0 | 2 | 48 | 181 | 236 | 220 | 93 | 21 | 0 | 0 | 801 |
| 1980 | 0 | 0 | 0 | 9 | 65 | 145 | 367 | 319 | 107 | 6 | 0 | 0 | 1018 |
| 1981 | 0 | 0 | 2 | 6 | 15 | 137 | 211 | 191 | 72 | 0 | 0 | 0 | 634 |
| 1982 | 0 | 0 | 0 | 3 | 105 | 65 | 266 | 159 | 71 | 17 | 0 | 0 | 686 |
| 1983 | 0 | 0 | 0 | 1 | 3 | 247 | 440 | 417 | 146 | 13 | 0 | 0 | 1267 |
| 1984 | 0 | 0 | 0 | 5 | 19 | 228 | 226 | 298 | 98 | 7 | 0 | 0 | 881 |
| 1985 | 0 | 0 | 0 | 52 | 64 | 109 | 260 | 159 | 147 | 3 | 0 | 0 | 794 |
| 1986 | 0 | 0 | 4 | 22 | 41 | 135 | 312 | 136 | 113 | 2 | 0 | 0 | 765 |
| 1987 | 0 | 0 | 0 | 3 | 136 | 256 | 345 | 240 | 71 | 0 | 3 | 0 | 1054 |
| 1988 | 0 | 0 | 0 | 3 | 77 | 254 | 362 | 357 | 65 | 0 | 0 | 0 | 1118 |
| 1989 | 0 | 0 | 1 | 6 | 37 | 137 | 283 | 194 | 55 | 11 | 0 | 0 | 724 |
| 1990 | 0 | 0 | 9 | 37 | 8 | 167 | 203 | 171 | 117 | 21 | 0 | 0 | 733 |

**TABLE 6**          SNOWFALL (inches)          SOUTH BEND, INDIANA

| SEASON | JULY | AUG | SEP | OCT | NOV | DEC | JAN | FEB | MAR | APR | MAY | JUNE | TOTAL |
|---|---|---|---|---|---|---|---|---|---|---|---|---|---|
| 1961-62 | 0.0 | 0.0 | 0.0 | T | 0.7 | 9.5 | 18.7 | 17.4 | 9.2 | 1.8 | 0.0 | 0.0 | 57.3 |
| 1962-63 | 0.0 | 0.0 | 0.0 | 8.6 | 3.0 | 41.9 | 16.4 | 21.7 | 10.4 | 0.5 | 0.0 | 0.0 | 102.5 |
| 1963-64 | 0.0 | 0.0 | 0.0 | 0.0 | 7.2 | 25.0 | 10.0 | 14.4 | 22.7 | 0.3 | 0.0 | 0.0 | 79.6 |
| 1964-65 | 0.0 | 0.0 | 0.0 | T | 13.5 | 18.5 | 14.7 | 20.1 | 20.5 | 0.4 | 0.0 | 0.0 | 87.7 |
| 1965-66 | 0.0 | 0.0 | 0.0 | 2.4 | 7.3 | 8.6 | 26.9 | 10.7 | 11.4 | 5.4 | 0.6 | 0.0 | 73.3 |
| 1966-67 | 0.0 | 0.0 | T | T | 16.2 | 18.2 | 30.4 | 31.6 | 11.3 | 2.9 | 0.0 | 0.0 | 110.6 |
| 1967-68 | 0.0 | 0.0 | T | 5.0 | 7.0 | 12.5 | 12.6 | 20.1 | 8.7 | 5.1 | T | 0.0 | 67.4 |
| 1968-69 | 0.0 | 0.0 | 0.0 | T | 8.8 | 27.9 | 24.1 | 10.0 | 6.8 | T | 0.0 | 0.0 | 77.6 |
| 1969-70 | 0.0 | 0.0 | 0.0 | T | 10.5 | 17.1 | 24.8 | 11.2 | 16.7 | 7.9 | 0.0 | 0.0 | 88.2 |
| 1970-71 | 0.0 | 0.0 | 0.0 | 0.0 | 11.0 | 20.0 | 22.5 | 7.5 | 19.1 | 2.6 | 0.0 | 0.0 | 82.7 |
| 1971-72 | 0.0 | 0.0 | 0.0 | 0.0 | 16.3 | 4.4 | 19.2 | 21.2 | 16.1 | 7.1 | 0.0 | 0.0 | 84.3 |
| 1972-73 | 0.0 | 0.0 | 0.0 | 1.5 | 12.6 | 19.7 | 5.5 | 10.6 | 4.7 | 1.7 | 0.0 | 0.0 | 56.3 |
| 1973-74 | 0.0 | 0.0 | 0.0 | 0.0 | 1.0 | 22.6 | 14.4 | 11.9 | 9.4 | 1.2 | 0.0 | 0.0 | 60.5 |
| 1974-75 | 0.0 | 0.0 | 0.0 | 0.6 | 7.9 | 19.9 | 9.2 | 13.9 | 17.8 | 5.4 | 0.0 | 0.0 | 74.7 |
| 1975-76 | 0.0 | 0.0 | 0.0 | 0.0 | 10.7 | 14.0 | 31.2 | 13.9 | 3.8 | 0.6 | 0.1 | 0.0 | 74.3 |
| 1976-77 | 0.0 | 0.0 | 0.0 | 0.8 | 21.6 | 37.6 | 37.2 | 13.9 | 15.8 | 2.3 | 0.0 | 0.0 | 129.2 |
| 1977-78 | 0.0 | 0.0 | 0.0 | 0.3 | 30.3 | 33.6 | 86.1 | 16.6 | 5.1 | T | 0.0 | 0.0 | 172.0 |
| 1978-79 | 0.0 | 0.0 | 0.0 | 0.0 | 7.5 | 26.4 | 45.1 | 15.9 | 6.3 | 0.1 | 0.0 | 0.0 | 101.3 |
| 1979-80 | 0.0 | 0.0 | 0.0 | T | 7.5 | 13.6 | 11.5 | 22.3 | 9.8 | 1.7 | 0.0 | 0.0 | 66.4 |
| 1980-81 | 0.0 | 0.0 | 0.0 | 1.1 | 8.8 | 24.3 | 23.8 | 20.7 | 6.3 | T | 0.0 | 0.0 | 85.0 |
| 1981-82 | 0.0 | 0.0 | 0.0 | 0.1 | 9.1 | 41.3 | 41.3 | 19.2 | 10.2 | 14.0 | 0.0 | 0.0 | 135.2 |
| 1982-83 | 0.0 | 0.0 | 0.0 | 0.0 | 2.1 | 2.5 | 8.0 | 9.6 | 12.0 | 1.1 | 0.0 | 0.0 | 35.3 |
| 1983-84 | 0.0 | 0.0 | 0.0 | 0.0 | 1.4 | 35.6 | 16.7 | 15.9 | 11.1 | 0.4 | 0.0 | 0.0 | 81.1 |
| 1984-85 | 0.0 | 0.0 | 0.0 | 0.0 | 0.6 | 14.1 | 40.0 | 28.9 | 1.6 | 3.1 | 0.0 | 0.0 | 88.3 |
| 1985-86 | 0.0 | 0.0 | 0.0 | 0.0 | 2.2 | 40.4 | 26.3 | 11.3 | 3.6 | 0.2 | 0.0 | 0.0 | 84.0 |
| 1986-87 | 0.0 | 0.0 | 0.0 | 0.0 | 9.7 | 4.8 | 31.4 | 5.9 | 2.0 | 1.5 | 0.0 | 0.0 | 55.3 |
| 1987-88 | 0.0 | 0.0 | T | T | 1.6 | 13.1 | 11.4 | 22.9 | 12.1 | T | 0.0 | 0.0 | 61.1 |
| 1988-89 | 0.0 | 0.0 | 0.0 | 0.3 | 7.8 | 14.8 | 3.1 | 16.3 | 2.5 | 1.7 | T | 0.0 | 46.5 |
| 1989-90 | T | T | 0.0 | 8.8 | 15.2 | 29.4 | 3.1 | 1.2 | 3.4 | 1.1 | T | T | 73.0 |
| 1990-91 | 0.0 | 0.0 | 0.0 | T | T | 17.5 | | | | | | | |
| Record Mean | T | T | T | 0.7 | 8.1 | 18.1 | 19.1 | 14.4 | 8.9 | 2.1 | T | T | 71.5 |

**See Reference Notes, relative to all above tables, on preceding page.**

Located in the heart of North America, Des Moines has a climate which is continental in character. This results in a marked seasonal contrast in both temperature and precipitation. There is a gently rolling terrain in and around the Des Moines metropolitan area. Drainage of the area is generally to the southeast to the Des Moines River and its tributaries.

Since agriculture and services for it are the mainstay of the area, it is convenient to separate the year into arbitrary seasons corresponding to the growing seasons of the principal crops of the section. The winter season, when most plant life is dormant, is from mid-November to late March. The summer season, when corn and soybeans can be grown, lasts from early May to early October. The spring growing season, including part of the growing season of oats and forage crops, and the fall harvest season, each runs about 6 weeks. There is a large variation in annual precipitation from a minimum of about 17 inches to a maximum of about 56 inches. The average annual snowfall is 32 inches. Annual variation of snowfall is also large, ranging from a minimum of about 8 inches to as much as 72 inches.

The winter is a season of cold dry air, interrupted by occasional storms of short duration. At the beginning and the end of the season, the precipitation may occur as rain, but during the major portion of the season it falls as snow. Drifting snow may be extensive and impede transportation. The average precipitation for this season is approximately 20 percent of the annual amount. Although occasional cold waves follow the storms, bitterly cold days on which the temperatures fail to rise above zero occur on an average of only 3 days in 4 years.

The average growing season with temperatures above 32 degrees normally spans 160 to 165 days between late April and mid-October. The growing season is characterized by prevailing southerly winds and precipitation falling primarily as showers and thunderstorms, occasionally with damaging wind, erosive downpours or hail. Some 60 percent of the annual precipitation falls during the crop season with the maximum rate normally in late May and June. The autumn is characteristically sunny with diminishing precipitation, a condition favorable for drying and harvesting crops.

## TABLE 1  NORMALS, MEANS AND EXTREMES

DES MOINES, IOWA

LATITUDE: 41°32'N   LONGITUDE: 93°39'W   ELEVATION: FT. GRND  938 BARO  966   TIME ZONE: CENTRAL   WBAN: 14933

| | (a) | JAN | FEB | MAR | APR | MAY | JUNE | JULY | AUG | SEP | OCT | NOV | DEC | YEAR |
|---|---|---|---|---|---|---|---|---|---|---|---|---|---|---|
| **TEMPERATURE °F:** | | | | | | | | | | | | | | |
| Normals | | | | | | | | | | | | | | |
| -Daily Maximum | | 27.0 | 33.2 | 44.2 | 61.0 | 72.6 | 81.8 | 86.2 | 84.0 | 75.7 | 65.0 | 47.6 | 33.7 | 59.3 |
| -Daily Minimum | | 10.1 | 15.8 | 26.0 | 39.9 | 51.6 | 61.4 | 66.3 | 63.7 | 54.4 | 43.3 | 29.5 | 17.6 | 40.0 |
| -Monthly | | 18.6 | 24.5 | 35.1 | 50.5 | 62.1 | 71.6 | 76.3 | 73.9 | 65.1 | 54.2 | 38.6 | 25.7 | 49.7 |
| Extremes | | | | | | | | | | | | | | |
| -Record Highest | 50 | 65 | 73 | 91 | 93 | 98 | 103 | 105 | 108 | 101 | 95 | 76 | 69 | 108 |
| -Year | | 1989 | 1972 | 1986 | 1980 | 1967 | 1988 | 1955 | 1983 | 1939 | 1963 | 1980 | 1984 | AUG 1983 |
| -Record Lowest | 50 | -24 | -20 | -22 | 9 | 30 | 38 | 47 | 40 | 26 | 14 | -3 | -22 | -24 |
| -Year | | 1970 | 1958 | 1962 | 1975 | 1967 | 1945 | 1971 | 1950 | 1942 | 1972 | 1964 | 1989 | JAN 1970 |
| **NORMAL DEGREE DAYS:** | | | | | | | | | | | | | | |
| Heating (base 65°F) | | 1438 | 1134 | 927 | 435 | 156 | 17 | 0 | 0 | 80 | 357 | 792 | 1218 | 6554 |
| Cooling (base 65°F) | | 0 | 0 | 0 | 0 | 66 | 215 | 354 | 279 | 83 | 22 | 0 | 0 | 1019 |
| **% OF POSSIBLE SUNSHINE** | 39 | 51 | 54 | 55 | 56 | 61 | 68 | 73 | 70 | 66 | 62 | 49 | 46 | 59 |
| **MEAN SKY COVER (tenths)** | | | | | | | | | | | | | | |
| Sunrise - Sunset | 40 | 6.5 | 6.4 | 6.8 | 6.5 | 6.4 | 5.8 | 5.1 | 5.2 | 5.1 | 5.3 | 6.5 | 6.8 | 6.0 |
| **MEAN NUMBER OF DAYS:** | | | | | | | | | | | | | | |
| Sunrise to Sunset | | | | | | | | | | | | | | |
| -Clear | 40 | 7.9 | 7.6 | 6.6 | 7.3 | 7.7 | 8.2 | 10.8 | 10.8 | 11.8 | 11.6 | 7.6 | 7.0 | 105.0 |
| -Partly Cloudy | 40 | 7.2 | 5.7 | 7.4 | 7.8 | 8.6 | 10.5 | 11.1 | 10.4 | 7.3 | 7.2 | 6.9 | 6.6 | 96.7 |
| -Cloudy | 40 | 15.9 | 14.9 | 17.0 | 14.9 | 14.8 | 11.3 | 9.1 | 9.8 | 10.9 | 12.2 | 15.5 | 17.4 | 163.6 |
| Precipitation | | | | | | | | | | | | | | |
| .01 inches or more | 50 | 7.4 | 7.3 | 10.0 | 10.5 | 11.2 | 10.6 | 9.1 | 9.2 | 8.7 | 7.6 | 7.0 | 7.9 | 106.5 |
| Snow, Ice pellets | | | | | | | | | | | | | | |
| 1.0 inches or more | 50 | 2.4 | 2.3 | 2.0 | 0.6 | 0.0 | 0.0 | 0.0 | 0.0 | 0.0 | 0.1 | 0.8 | 2.3 | 10.3 |
| Thunderstorms | 50 | 0.3 | 0.4 | 2.0 | 4.3 | 7.3 | 9.3 | 8.3 | 7.4 | 5.2 | 2.8 | 1.1 | 0.4 | 48.7 |
| Heavy Fog Visibility | | | | | | | | | | | | | | |
| 1/4 mile or less | 40 | 2.0 | 2.3 | 2.0 | 0.9 | 0.7 | 0.6 | 0.6 | 1.1 | 1.3 | 1.3 | 1.9 | 2.7 | 17.3 |
| Temperature °F | | | | | | | | | | | | | | |
| -Maximum | | | | | | | | | | | | | | |
| 90° and above | 28 | 0.0 | 0.0 | 0.* | 0.2 | 0.5 | 4.5 | 10.4 | 7.2 | 1.8 | 0.1 | 0.0 | 0.0 | 24.8 |
| 32° and below | 28 | 17.9 | 13.4 | 4.9 | 0.3 | 0.0 | 0.0 | 0.0 | 0.0 | 0.0 | 0.0 | 3.2 | 14.2 | 53.8 |
| -Minimum | | | | | | | | | | | | | | |
| 32° and below | 28 | 30.0 | 25.7 | 20.8 | 6.3 | 0.2 | 0.0 | 0.0 | 0.0 | 0.3 | 4.8 | 18.4 | 28.8 | 135.1 |
| 0° and below | 28 | 8.6 | 4.3 | 0.3 | 0.0 | 0.0 | 0.0 | 0.0 | 0.0 | 0.0 | 0.0 | 0.2 | 3.8 | 17.1 |
| **AVG. STATION PRESS. (mb)** | 17 | 984.9 | 984.0 | 980.1 | 979.3 | 978.8 | 979.4 | 981.0 | 981.5 | 982.3 | 983.0 | 982.0 | 983.6 | 981.7 |
| **RELATIVE HUMIDITY (%)** | | | | | | | | | | | | | | |
| Hour 00 | 28 | 74 | 76 | 73 | 69 | 69 | 72 | 75 | 78 | 78 | 73 | 75 | 78 | 74 |
| Hour 06 | 28 | 75 | 78 | 78 | 77 | 77 | 79 | 82 | 84 | 85 | 79 | 79 | 79 | 79 |
| Hour 12 (Local Time) | 28 | 67 | 65 | 60 | 55 | 54 | 55 | 57 | 58 | 59 | 56 | 63 | 69 | 60 |
| Hour 18 | 28 | 68 | 66 | 59 | 52 | 52 | 53 | 56 | 58 | 60 | 58 | 66 | 71 | 60 |
| **PRECIPITATION (inches):** | | | | | | | | | | | | | | |
| Water Equivalent | | | | | | | | | | | | | | |
| -Normal | | 1.01 | 1.12 | 2.20 | 3.21 | 3.96 | 4.18 | 3.22 | 4.11 | 3.09 | 2.16 | 1.52 | 1.05 | 30.83 |
| -Maximum Monthly | 50 | 4.38 | 2.99 | 5.37 | 7.76 | 7.53 | 14.19 | 10.51 | 13.68 | 10.19 | 7.29 | 6.52 | 3.43 | 14.19 |
| -Year | | 1960 | 1951 | 1961 | 1976 | 1960 | 1947 | 1958 | 1977 | 1961 | 1941 | 1983 | 1982 | JUN 1947 |
| -Minimum Monthly | 50 | 0.07 | 0.13 | 0.37 | 0.23 | 1.23 | 1.13 | 0.04 | 0.25 | 0.41 | 0.03 | 0.03 | 0.12 | 0.03 |
| -Year | | 1954 | 1968 | 1989 | 1985 | 1949 | 1963 | 1975 | 1984 | 1950 | 1952 | 1969 | 1976 | NOV 1969 |
| -Maximum in 24 hrs | 50 | 2.97 | 1.77 | 2.42 | 3.80 | 2.79 | 5.50 | 5.14 | 6.18 | 4.47 | 2.81 | 3.35 | 1.69 | 6.18 |
| -Year | | 1960 | 1961 | 1945 | 1974 | 1954 | 1947 | 1958 | 1975 | 1961 | 1947 | 1952 | 1982 | AUG 1975 |
| Snow, Ice pellets | | | | | | | | | | | | | | |
| -Maximum Monthly | 50 | 19.8 | 21.3 | 18.8 | 15.6 | 0.2 | 0.0 | 0.0 | 0.0 | T | 7.4 | 13.5 | 23.9 | 23.9 |
| -Year | | 1942 | 1962 | 1948 | 1982 | 1944 | | | | 1985 | 1980 | 1968 | 1961 | DEC 1961 |
| -Maximum in 24 hrs | 50 | 19.8 | 12.1 | 8.5 | 10.4 | 0.2 | 0.0 | 0.0 | 0.0 | T | 7.4 | 11.8 | 11.0 | 19.8 |
| -Year | | 1942 | 1950 | 1957 | 1973 | 1944 | | | | 1985 | 1980 | 1968 | 1961 | JAN 1942 |
| **WIND:** | | | | | | | | | | | | | | |
| Mean Speed (mph) | 40 | 11.8 | 11.6 | 12.9 | 12.9 | 11.2 | 10.3 | 9.0 | 8.7 | 9.5 | 10.4 | 11.5 | 11.4 | 10.9 |
| Prevailing Direction | | | | | | | | | | | | | | |
| through 1963 | | NW | NW | NW | NW | SE | S | S | S | S | S | NW | NW | NW |
| Fastest Mile | | | | | | | | | | | | | | |
| -Direction (!!!) | 36 | NW | W | S | W | W | NW | W | SSE | NW | W | W | SW | W |
| -Speed (MPH) | 36 | 66 | 56 | 66 | 76 | 70 | 76 | 73 | 60 | 55 | 56 | 72 | 61 | 76 |
| -Year | | 1953 | 1952 | 1953 | 1965 | 1955 | 1953 | 1968 | 1960 | 1953 | 1952 | 1952 | 1951 | APR 1965 |
| Peak Gust | | | | | | | | | | | | | | |
| -Direction (!!!) | 6 | NW | NW | W | SW | E | NW | NW | NW | W | NW | SW | NW | NW |
| -Speed (mph) | 6 | 54 | 62 | 58 | 66 | 54 | 56 | 67 | 63 | 54 | 60 | 62 | 55 | 67 |
| -Date | | 1986 | 1984 | 1985 | 1989 | 1988 | 1989 | 1986 | 1989 | 1985 | 1985 | 1986 | 1985 | JUL 1986 |

**See reference Notes to this table on the following page.**

541

PRECIPITATION (inches)          DES MOINES, IOWA

**TABLE 2**

| YEAR | JAN | FEB | MAR | APR | MAY | JUNE | JULY | AUG | SEP | OCT | NOV | DEC | ANNUAL |
|------|-----|-----|-----|-----|-----|------|------|-----|-----|-----|-----|-----|--------|
| 1961 | 0.33 | 2.68 | 5.37 | 2.39 | 1.58 | 2.92 | ?.?5 | 2.77 | 10.19 | 3.00 | 2.78 | 1.82 | 42.88 |
| 1962 | 0.54 | 1.60 | 1.42 | 2.51 | 6.02 | 3.96 | 2.94 | 1.60 | 1.93 | 3.22 | 0.80 | 0.50 | 27.04 |
| 1963 | 0.83 | 0.72 | 2.39 | 4.18 | 3.94 | 1.13 | 4.0? | 4.83 | 1.83 | 2.56 | 1.36 | 0.54 | 28.32 |
| 1964 | 0.51 | 0.28 | 1.25 | 3.29 | 2.90 | 6.49 | 3.37 | 3.94 | 4.28 | 0.29 | 0.95 | 0.87 | 28.42 |
| 1965 | 1.62 | 1.14 | 3.02 | 4.18 | 3.89 | 4.80 | .93 | 1.93 | 7.23 | 0.79 | 1.79 | 1.64 | 33.96 |
| 1966 | 0.96 | 0.25 | 1.56 | 1.74 | 5.37 | 5.22 | 2.43 | 2.09 | 0.75 | 0.29 | 0.70 | 0.49 | 21.85 |
| 1967 | 0.77 | 0.28 | 1.64 | 2.25 | 2.22 | 7.39 | 5.8? | 2.54 | 1.93 | 0.47 | 0.73 | | 21.82 |
| 1968 | 0.78 | 0.13 | 0.93 | 4.19 | 2.62 | 3.42 | 4.48 | 4.05 | 2.63 | 1.47 | 1.90 | 1.71 | 28.31 |
| 1969 | 1.01 | 0.97 | 1.41 | 4.46 | 4.75 | 7.32 | 4.3? | 1.83 | 2.87 | 0.03 | 1.01 | | 32.43 |
| 1970 | 0.26 | 0.24 | 3.28 | 2.28 | 4.21 | 2.45 | .96 | 4.95 | 6.51 | 5.20 | 1.46 | 0.83 | 33.63 |
| 1971 | 1.75 | 2.34 | 0.41 | 1.54 | 3.87 | 4.31 | 2.1? | 1.83 | 2.19 | 3.51 | 3.29 | 1.12 | 28.32 |
| 1972 | 0.44 | 0.63 | 1.05 | 3.56 | 3.05 | 2.58 | 5.86 | 6.65 | 5.45 | 2.36 | 2.43 | 1.96 | 36.02 |
| 1973 | 2.09 | 2.21 | 4.15 | 4.67 | 5.01 | 2.04 | 3.1? | 1.37 | 7.07 | 3.26 | 1.49 | 2.65 | 45.18 |
| 1974 | 1.51 | 0.84 | 1.99 | 6.31 | 7.19 | 4.62 | .33 | 2.81 | 2.08 | 3.96 | 1.20 | 1.83 | 35.67 |
| 1975 | 1.41 | 1.48 | 1.90 | 2.65 | 3.41 | 5.98 | 3.0? | 9.73 | 1.70 | 0.63 | 2.20 | 0.48 | 31.61 |
| 1976 | 0.23 | 2.43 | 3.04 | 7.76 | 2.84 | 7.25 | .8? | 2.26 | 1.00 | 1.11 | 0.10 | 0.12 | 30.01 |
| 1977 | 0.50 | 0.36 | 3.57 | 2.45 | 2.29 | 1.25 | 2.63 | 13.68 | 2.82 | 5.10 | 0.69 | 1.81 | 37.15 |
| 1978 | 0.28 | 1.27 | 0.90 | 4.57 | 3.49 | 2.74 | 2.95 | 3.10 | 6.39 | 1.14 | 3.16 | 1.37 | 31.36 |
| 1979 | 1.72 | 0.52 | 4.23 | 3.23 | 2.50 | 5.78 | 2.96 | 5.07 | 0.97 | 3.23 | 1.43 | 0.20 | 31.84 |
| 1980 | 1.80 | 0.64 | 1.15 | 0.86 | 1.94 | 5.56 | .52 | 7.24 | 1.03 | 1.90 | 0.45 | 1.00 | 25.09 |
| 1981 | 0.25 | 0.97 | 0.39 | 2.00 | 2.46 | 5.02 | 5.?5 | 6.32 | 2.30 | 2.06 | 2.63 | 1.14 | 31.30 |
| 1982 | 2.63 | 0.78 | 3.30 | 5.03 | 5.79 | 2.59 | 2.?? | 5.25 | 2.94 | 3.44 | 2.62 | 3.43 | 44.80 |
| 1983 | 1.17 | 1.95 | 3.72 | 3.80 | 3.93 | 3.65 | 2.4? | 3.01 | 3.87 | 5.54 | 6.52 | 1.57 | 41.17 |
| 1984 | 0.99 | 0.82 | 1.65 | 5.85 | 5.58 | 7.81 | 5.22 | 0.25 | 2.76 | 6.28 | 1.16 | 2.41 | 41.78 |
| 1985 | 0.64 | 1.98 | 3.37 | 0.23 | 1.56 | 3.72 | 2.0? | 2.83 | 5.42 | 3.75 | 1.65 | 1.31 | 28.50 |
| 1986 | 0.12 | 1.76 | 2.92 | 5.66 | 4.35 | 7.08 | 3.9? | 4.52 | 6.41 | 3.89 | 0.99 | 0.98 | 42.58 |
| 1987 | 0.42 | 1.38 | 2.99 | 2.92 | 3.75 | 2.10 | 5.0? | 10.04 | 1.40 | 1.03 | 3.27 | 2.59 | 36.97 |
| 1988 | 0.37 | 0.59 | 0.66 | 0.75 | 1.46 | 2.75 | 4.7? | 3.05 | 2.89 | 0.59 | 3.38 | 0.84 | 22.11 |
| 1989 | 1.30 | 1.05 | 0.37 | 1.95 | 3.62 | 2.22 | 3.65 | 6.53 | 5.41 | 2.28 | 0.19 | 0.57 | 29.14 |
| 1990 | 1.43 | 0.89 | 5.82 | 3.43 | 4.36 | 9.52 | 3.75 | 1.83 | 1.40 | 1.80 | 2.52 | 2.18 | 43.93 |
| Record Mean | 1.11 | 1.13 | 2.00 | 2.92 | 4.15 | 4.66 | 3.46 | 3.77 | 3.38 | 2.44 | 1.64 | 1.22 | 31.88 |

**TABLE 3**    AVERAGE TEMPERATURE (deg. F)          DES MOINES, IOWA

| YEAR | JAN | FEB | MAR | APR | MAY | JUNE | JULY | AUG | SEP | OCT | NOV | DEC | ANNUAL |
|------|-----|-----|-----|-----|-----|------|------|-----|-----|-----|-----|-----|--------|
| #1961 | 22.0 | 30.1 | 37.5 | 44.7 | 58.7 | 70.6 | 74.? | 73.2 | 62.4 | 55.0 | 36.7 | 18.5 | 48.6 |
| 1962 | 13.0 | 20.5 | 29.8 | 49.3 | 69.2 | 71.3 | 74.3 | 74.2 | 63.3 | 40.5 | 24.0 | | 48.9 |
| 1963 | 8.5 | 18.9 | 39.4 | 51.7 | 59.7 | 74.0 | 75.9 | 71.4 | 65.9 | 64.5 | 43.2 | 15.2 | 49.0 |
| 1964 | 27.8 | 26.3 | 30.4 | 48.0 | 64.3 | 69.9 | 77.2 | 70.4 | 63.6 | 50.8 | 41.2 | 23.3 | 49.4 |
| 1965 | 17.6 | 20.2 | 22.7 | 48.1 | 66.2 | 70.3 | 74.8 | 72.9 | 61.0 | 55.3 | 41.0 | 35.3 | 48.8 |
| 1966 | 14.2 | 24.7 | 41.0 | 46.0 | 57.7 | 70.4 | 78.6 | 70.8 | 62.4 | 52.9 | 38.4 | 24.8 | 48.5 |
| 1967 | 23.7 | 22.2 | 40.3 | 51.1 | 57.1 | 69.0 | 72.? | 70.3 | 62.3 | 51.5 | 36.5 | 28.9 | 48.8 |
| 1968 | 22.3 | 23.9 | 42.6 | 51.1 | 57.0 | 72.4 | 74.2 | 73.0 | 63.3 | 53.8 | 34.8 | 21.3 | 49.2 |
| 1969 | 16.2 | 25.9 | 28.2 | 52.5 | 62.9 | 67.3 | 76.0 | 74.7 | 66.1 | 50.0 | 39.0 | 23.8 | 48.5 |
| 1970 | 12.7 | 27.1 | 32.9 | 51.7 | 65.8 | 72.4 | 76.6 | 73.9 | 65.5 | 54.1 | 39.8 | 28.8 | 50.1 |
| 1971 | 15.7 | 23.1 | 35.2 | 52.1 | 58.7 | 76.8 | 72.? | 73.2 | 68.1 | 60.5 | 39.6 | 28.2 | 50.3 |
| 1972 | 16.6 | 19.9 | 37.1 | 48.9 | 62.5 | 70.2 | 73.9 | 72.4 | 64.6 | 40.0 | 33.9 | 18.4 | 47.2 |
| 1973 | 22.0 | 27.7 | 45.6 | 49.2 | 59.8 | 73.6 | 76.4 | 76.9 | 65.7 | 59.0 | 40.7 | 22.1 | 51.6 |
| 1974 | 19.5 | 28.0 | 39.8 | 53.0 | 60.3 | 69.1 | 80.9 | 71.1 | 60.9 | 55.0 | 39.6 | 28.2 | 50.4 |
| 1975 | 22.7 | 22.4 | 29.7 | 46.9 | 65.9 | 72.3 | 77.9 | 77.1 | 61.8 | 57.2 | 43.5 | 29.9 | 50.6 |
| 1976 | 22.9 | 34.1 | 39.7 | 55.4 | 60.7 | 71.4 | 77.2 | 73.8 | 65.7 | 48.5 | 32.6 | 21.8 | 50.3 |
| 1977 | 10.1 | 29.8 | 44.7 | 58.5 | 69.5 | 74.7 | 81.0 | 72.1 | 66.5 | 52.3 | 39.1 | 23.2 | 51.8 |
| 1978 | 11.0 | 13.3 | 33.2 | 50.5 | 61.6 | 72.8 | 75.8 | 75.1 | 70.5 | 52.4 | 39.0 | 23.0 | 48.2 |
| 1979 | 7.5 | 13.8 | 35.2 | 47.0 | 61.1 | 70.9 | 74.5 | 74.3 | 66.8 | 54.3 | 38.0 | 31.6 | 47.9 |
| 1980 | 23.4 | 21.3 | 34.7 | 52.0 | 63.5 | 71.2 | 79.9 | 76.2 | 66.8 | 49.6 | 41.6 | 26.6 | 50.6 |
| 1981 | 25.7 | 29.8 | 42.7 | 57.6 | 60.4 | 72.9 | 76.? | 72.4 | 66.0 | 51.7 | 42.8 | 25.5 | 51.9 |
| 1982 | 9.6 | 22.9 | 35.4 | 46.9 | 64.7 | 67.1 | 76.9 | 73.2 | 64.9 | 56.4 | 38.4 | 31.6 | 48.8 |
| 1983 | 27.3 | 32.3 | 39.4 | 45.4 | 58.4 | 73.2 | 80.9 | 83.3 | 67.7 | 52.6 | 40.7 | 9.8 | 50.9 |
| 1984 | 19.7 | 35.5 | 31.1 | 48.8 | 58.7 | 73.2 | 75.9 | 77.5 | 62.4 | 52.8 | 39.5 | 27.6 | 50.2 |
| 1985 | 15.8 | 22.2 | 42.0 | 55.2 | 65.1 | 68.4 | 76.5 | 71.9 | 64.8 | 52.6 | 30.0 | 13.4 | 48.2 |
| 1986 | 26.9 | 21.7 | 42.5 | 53.9 | 62.6 | 73.3 | 77.2 | 69.3 | 67.4 | 52.6 | 33.3 | 28.8 | 50.8 |
| 1987 | 26.6 | 35.7 | 42.7 | 54.6 | 66.8 | 74.7 | 78.5 | 72.1 | 65.2 | 48.2 | 43.1 | 30.0 | 53.2 |
| 1988 | 19.6 | 21.6 | 40.2 | 51.4 | 67.4 | 75.6 | 78.8 | 78.8 | 66.9 | 47.7 | 39.8 | 28.8 | 51.4 |
| 1989 | 32.5 | 15.4 | 37.1 | 52.3 | 61.0 | 68.9 | 77.? | 73.3 | 62.2 | 54.1 | 36.0 | 16.9 | 48.9 |
| 1990 | 31.7 | 31.1 | 42.0 | 50.0 | 57.9 | 71.6 | 73.8 | 74.4 | 68.1 | 52.4 | 43.7 | 22.9 | 51.6 |
| Record Mean | 20.7 | 24.8 | 36.6 | 50.6 | 61.6 | 71.2 | 76.2 | 73.8 | 65.4 | 53.9 | 38.5 | 25.9 | 50.0 |
| Max | 29.5 | 33.7 | 45.8 | 60.9 | 71.9 | 81.2 | 86.6 | 84.1 | 76.0 | 64.5 | 47.6 | 34.0 | 59.7 |
| Min | 11.9 | 15.8 | 27.4 | 40.3 | 51.3 | 61.2 | 65.8 | 63.5 | 54.8 | 43.3 | 29.3 | 17.7 | 40.2 |

## REFERENCE NOTES FOR TABLES 1, 2, 3 and 6          (DES MOINES, IA)

### GENERAL

T - TRACE AMOUNT
BLANK ENTRIES DENOTE MISSING/UNREPORTED DATA.
# INDICATES A STATION OR INSTRUMENT RELOCATION.

### SPECIFIC

**TABLE 1**

(a) - LENGTH OF RECORD IN YEARS. ALTHOUGH
      INDIVIDUAL MONTHS MAY BE MISSING.
* LESS THAN .05

NORMALS — BASED ON THE 1951-1980 RECORD PERIOD.
EXTREMES — DATES ARE THE MOST RECENT OCCURRENCE.
WIND DIR. — NUMERALS SHOW TENS OF DEGREES
            CLOCKWISE FROM TRUE NORTH.
            "00" INDICATES CALM.
RESULTANT WIND DIRECTIONS ARE GIVEN TO WHOLE DEGREES.

**TABLE 3**
MAX AND MIN ARE LONG-TERM MEAN DAILY MAXIMUM
AND MEAN DAILY MINIMUM TEMPERATURES.

### EXCEPTIONS

**TABLES 2, 3, and 6**

RECORD MEANS ARE THROUGH THE CURRENT YEAR,
BEGINNING IN      1878 FOR TEMPERATURE
                  1877 FOR PRECIPITATION
                  1940 FOR SNOWFALL

HEATING DEGREE DAYS Base 65 deg. F          DES MOINES, IOWA

**TABLE 4**

| SEASON | JULY | AUG | SEP | OCT | NOV | DEC | JAN | FEB | MAR | APR | MAY | JUNE | TOTAL |
|---|---|---|---|---|---|---|---|---|---|---|---|---|---|
| 1961-62 | 0 | 0 | 167 | 311 | 841 | 1434 | 1609 | 1239 | 1086 | 474 | 32 | 17 | 7210 |
| 1962-63 | 0 | 0 | 110 | 289 | 728 | 1266 | 1751 | 1285 | 787 | 400 | 195 | 3 | 6814 |
| 1963-64 | 0 | 18 | 54 | 95 | 649 | 1542 | 1145 | 1116 | 1069 | 504 | 91 | 25 | 6308 |
| 1964-65 | 0 | 28 | 124 | 433 | 707 | 1286 | 1465 | 1247 | 1305 | 509 | 86 | 1 | 7191 |
| 1965-66 | 0 | 14 | 154 | 310 | 715 | 915 | 1568 | 1122 | 737 | 565 | 256 | 16 | 6372 |
| 1966-67 | 0 | 13 | 136 | 375 | 789 | 1239 | 1276 | 1192 | 767 | 421 | 308 | 22 | 6538 |
| 1967-68 | 14 | 18 | 109 | 440 | 850 | 1112 | 1317 | 1184 | 685 | 411 | 260 | 24 | 6424 |
| 1968-69 | 2 | 11 | 92 | 378 | 898 | 1351 | 1508 | 1086 | 1135 | 368 | 159 | 50 | 7038 |
| 1969-70 | 0 | 0 | 45 | 478 | 773 | 1270 | 1617 | 1055 | 987 | 422 | 99 | 9 | 6755 |
| 1970-71 | 0 | 0 | 100 | 352 | 748 | 1114 | 1521 | 1167 | 915 | 393 | 211 | 0 | 6521 |
| 1971-72 | 8 | 4 | 96 | 184 | 756 | 1132 | 1303 | 1303 | 857 | 478 | 149 | 23 | 6485 |
| 1972-73 | 7 | 10 | 112 | 523 | 925 | 1442 | 1326 | 1039 | 594 | 470 | 173 | 0 | 6621 |
| 1973-74 | 0 | 0 | 68 | 209 | 719 | 1325 | 1406 | 1033 | 775 | 363 | 189 | 20 | 6107 |
| 1974-75 | 0 | 12 | 168 | 307 | 755 | 1131 | 1308 | 1185 | 1090 | 539 | 81 | 11 | 6587 |
| 1975-76 | 0 | 0 | 148 | 267 | 637 | 1085 | 1297 | 890 | 780 | 302 | 160 | 4 | 5570 |
| 1976-77 | 0 | 1 | 76 | 527 | 964 | 1333 | 1700 | 981 | 624 | 234 | 25 | 2 | 6467 |
| 1977-78 | 0 | 3 | 35 | 388 | 769 | 1289 | 1667 | 1442 | 988 | 427 | 181 | 9 | 7198 |
| 1978-79 | 0 | 0 | 48 | 385 | 776 | 1293 | 1779 | 1433 | 912 | 532 | 163 | 13 | 7334 |
| 1979-80 | 1 | 10 | 57 | 339 | 801 | 1031 | 1281 | 1263 | 932 | 408 | 124 | 9 | 6256 |
| 1980-81 | 0 | 0 | 77 | 473 | 695 | 1182 | 1214 | 979 | 684 | 241 | 177 | 0 | 5722 |
| 1981-82 | 6 | 2 | 57 | 406 | 660 | 1218 | 1713 | 1175 | 911 | 536 | 73 | 30 | 6787 |
| 1982-83 | 0 | 6 | 113 | 326 | 791 | 1026 | 1162 | 908 | 787 | 587 | 219 | 17 | 5942 |
| 1983-84 | 0 | 0 | 96 | 394 | 720 | 1709 | 1401 | 851 | 1043 | 488 | 217 | 1 | 6920 |
| 1984-85 | 0 | 0 | 172 | 376 | 759 | 1154 | 1520 | 1192 | 707 | 335 | 59 | 27 | 6301 |
| 1985-86 | 0 | 0 | 172 | 378 | 1046 | 1596 | 1181 | 1208 | 702 | 344 | 116 | 2 | 6745 |
| 1986-87 | 0 | 25 | 51 | 378 | 941 | 1114 |  | 813 | 687 | 336 | 58 | 6 | 5593 |
| 1987-88 | 0 | 24 | 54 | 513 | 648 | 1083 | 1399 | 1254 | 764 | 400 | 33 | 3 | 6175 |
| 1988-89 | 0 | 6 | 35 | 524 | 749 | 1114 | 1002 | 1384 | 866 | 417 | 170 | 31 | 6298 |
| 1989-90 | 0 | 6 | 140 | 345 | 865 | 1489 | 1025 | 943 | 703 | 469 | 221 | 21 | 6227 |
| 1990-91 | 3 | 0 | 85 | 394 | 633 | 1301 |  |  |  |  |  |  |  |

**TABLE 5**     COOLING DEGREE DAYS Base 65 deg. F     DES MOINES, IOWA

| YEAR | JAN | FEB | MAR | APR | MAY | JUNE | JULY | AUG | SEP | OCT | NOV | DEC | TOTAL |
|---|---|---|---|---|---|---|---|---|---|---|---|---|---|
| 1969 | 0 | 0 | 0 | 0 | 99 | 129 | 349 | 308 | 84 | 20 | 0 | 0 | 989 |
| 1970 | 0 | 0 | 0 | 31 | 131 | 238 | 368 | 280 | 123 | 20 | 0 | 0 | 1191 |
| 1971 | 0 | 0 | 0 | 13 | 26 | 362 | 234 | 263 | 194 | 52 | 0 | 0 | 1144 |
| 1972 | 0 | 0 | 0 | 3 | 77 | 184 | 289 | 247 | 109 | 0 | 0 | 0 | 909 |
| 1973 | 0 | 0 | 0 | 2 | 19 | 267 | 358 | 378 | 98 | 30 | 0 | 0 | 1152 |
| 1974 | 0 | 0 | 0 | 9 | 52 | 149 | 499 | 209 | 52 | 4 | 0 | 0 | 974 |
| 1975 | 0 | 0 | 0 | 3 | 116 | 237 | 408 | 383 | 58 | 32 | 0 | 0 | 1237 |
| 1976 | 0 | 0 | 0 | 19 | 36 | 203 | 385 | 283 | 104 | 20 | 0 | 0 | 1050 |
| 1977 | 0 | 0 | 0 | 48 | 172 | 298 | 505 | 232 | 86 | 1 | 0 | 0 | 1342 |
| 1978 | 0 | 0 | 6 | 0 | 83 | 251 | 341 | 321 | 221 | 3 | 0 | 0 | 1226 |
| 1979 | 0 | 0 | 0 | 0 | 48 | 194 | 304 | 305 | 118 | 15 | 0 | 0 | 984 |
| 1980 | 0 | 0 | 0 | 22 | 83 | 200 | 469 | 353 | 138 | 2 | 0 | 0 | 1267 |
| 1981 | 0 | 0 | 1 | 27 | 42 | 243 | 358 | 239 | 95 | 2 | 0 | 0 | 1007 |
| 1982 | 0 | 0 | 0 | 0 | 71 | 101 | 374 | 269 | 120 | 11 | 0 | 0 | 946 |
| 1983 | 0 | 0 | 0 | 4 | 20 | 272 | 502 | 574 | 183 | 19 | 0 | 0 | 1574 |
| 1984 | 0 | 0 | 0 | 8 | 27 | 254 | 345 | 397 | 101 | 2 | 0 | 0 | 1134 |
| 1985 | 0 | 0 | 0 | 46 | 69 | 134 | 361 | 221 | 174 | 0 | 0 | 0 | 1005 |
| 1986 | 0 | 0 | 11 | 17 | 46 | 258 | 386 | 162 | 130 | 0 | 0 | 0 | 1010 |
| 1987 | 0 | 0 | 0 | 31 | 121 | 304 | 426 | 250 | 65 | 0 | 0 | 0 | 1197 |
| 1988 | 0 | 0 | 0 | 1 | 112 | 329 | 425 | 444 | 101 | 3 | 0 | 0 | 1415 |
| 1989 | 0 | 0 | 6 | 44 | 53 | 156 | 379 | 269 | 61 | 15 | 0 | 0 | 983 |
| 1990 | 0 | 0 | 1 | 26 | 5 | 226 | 283 | 297 | 184 | 11 | 2 | 0 | 1035 |

**TABLE 6**     SNOWFALL (inches)          DES MOINES, IOWA

| SEASON | JULY | AUG | SEP | OCT | NOV | DEC | JAN | FEB | MAR | APR | MAY | JUNE | TOTAL |
|---|---|---|---|---|---|---|---|---|---|---|---|---|---|
| 1961-62 | 0.0 | 0.0 | 0.0 | 0.0 | 2.7 | 23.9 | 4.2 | 21.3 | 11.1 | 0.9 | 0.0 | 0.0 | 64.1 |
| 1962-63 | 0.0 | 0.0 | 0.0 | 1.4 | 1.5 | 3.1 | 15.9 | 6.5 | 6.2 | 0.0 | 0.0 | 0.0 | 34.6 |
| 1963-64 | 0.0 | 0.0 | 0.0 | 0.0 | T | 7.6 | 6.4 | 4.1 | 10.1 | T | 0.0 | 0.0 | 28.2 |
| 1964-65 | 0.0 | 0.0 | 0.0 | T | 0.5 | 2.6 | 7.4 | 7.6 | 17.3 | 0.0 | 0.0 | 0.0 | 35.4 |
| 1965-66 | 0.0 | 0.0 | 0.0 | 0.0 | T | 2.4 | 3.6 | 0.5 | 1.8 | T | T | 0.0 | 8.3 |
| 1966-67 | 0.0 | 0.0 | 0.0 | T | T | 7.1 | 4.0 | 2.3 | 0.5 | 0.9 | T | 0.0 | 14.8 |
| 1967-68 | 0.0 | 0.0 | 0.0 | 2.4 | 0.7 | 2.6 | 8.5 | 2.1 | T | 0.1 | T | 0.0 | 16.4 |
| 1968-69 | 0.0 | 0.0 | 0.0 | T | 13.5 | 5.2 | 6.8 | 12.3 | 2.8 | 0.0 | 0.0 | 0.0 | 40.6 |
| 1969-70 | 0.0 | 0.0 | 0.0 | T | T | 12.0 | 3.2 | 1.2 | 9.8 | 3.9 | 0.0 | 0.0 | 30.1 |
| 1970-71 | 0.0 | 0.0 | 0.0 | 0.0 | 0.2 | 1.4 | 15.9 | 13.7 | 5.3 | 0.4 | 0.0 | 0.0 | 36.9 |
| 1971-72 | 0.0 | 0.0 | 0.0 | 0.0 | 10.3 | 2.9 | 5.8 | 9.0 | 1.6 | 0.6 | 0.0 | 0.0 | 30.2 |
| 1972-73 | 0.0 | 0.0 | 0.0 | T | 10.2 | 9.5 | 15.3 | 4.6 | T | 15.1 | 0.0 | 0.0 | 54.7 |
| 1973-74 | 0.0 | 0.0 | 0.0 | 0.0 | T | 9.6 | 10.6 | 1.9 | 1.2 | 0.0 | 0.0 | 0.0 | 29.4 |
| 1974-75 | 0.0 | 0.0 | 0.0 | 0.0 | 9.3 | 9.1 | 13.3 | 17.9 | 5.6 | 4.5 | 0.0 | 0.0 | 59.7 |
| 1975-76 | 0.0 | 0.0 | 0.0 | 0.0 | 7.0 | 0.5 | 2.4 | 11.8 | 0.9 | 0.0 | T | 0.0 | 22.6 |
| 1976-77 | 0.0 | 0.0 | 0.0 | T | 1.1 | 2.8 | 7.6 | 0.9 | 4.8 | 1.9 | 0.0 | 0.0 | 19.1 |
| 1977-78 | 0.0 | 0.0 | 0.0 | 0.0 | 2.2 | 22.0 | 2.7 | 18.6 | 9.9 | 0.3 | 0.0 | 0.0 | 55.7 |
| 1978-79 | 0.0 | 0.0 | 0.0 | 0.0 | 5.8 | 11.0 | 16.6 | 8.2 | 4.1 | 8.0 | 0.0 | 0.0 | 53.7 |
| 1979-80 | 0.0 | 0.0 | 0.0 | T | 0.7 | 0.4 | 7.9 | 5.7 | 5.8 | 2.8 | 0.0 | 0.0 | 23.3 |
| 1980-81 | 0.0 | 0.0 | 0.0 | 7.4 | T | 3.7 | 3.7 | 6.6 | T | 0.0 | 0.0 | 0.0 | 20.4 |
| 1981-82 | 0.0 | 0.0 | 0.0 | 0.4 | 3.2 | 10.7 | 18.5 | 2.6 | 11.9 | 15.6 | 0.0 | 0.0 | 62.9 |
| 1982-83 | 0.0 | 0.0 | 0.0 | 0.8 | 0.3 | 3.6 | 4.2 | 16.8 | 13.2 | 12.6 | 0.0 | 0.0 | 51.5 |
| 1983-84 | 0.0 | 0.0 | 0.0 | T | 9.8 | 19.6 | 12.5 | 1.3 | 13.7 | 0.1 | 0.0 | 0.0 | 57.0 |
| 1984-85 | 0.0 | 0.0 | 0.0 | T | 2.7 | 7.7 | 7.7 | 6.9 | 6.7 | T | 0.0 | 0.0 | 31.6 |
| 1985-86 | 0.0 | 0.0 | T | 0.0 | 8.1 | 15.9 | 1.3 | 6.7 | 0.2 | 0.1 | 0.0 | 0.0 | 32.3 |
| 1986-87 | 0.0 | 0.0 | 0.0 | T | 3.1 | 5.1 |  | 2.8 | 5.5 | 0.0 | 0.0 | 0.0 | 19.4 |
| 1987-88 | 0.0 | 0.0 | 0.0 | T | 0.1 | 13.0 | 1.2 | 7.6 | 0.8 | 0.0 | 0.0 | 0.0 | 22.7 |
| 1988-89 | 0.0 | 0.0 | 0.0 | 0.0 | 1.1 | 1.0 | 0.1 | 16.3 | 1.2 | 0.6 | T | 0.0 | 20.3 |
| 1989-90 | 0.0 | 0.0 | 0.0 | T | 1.7 | 6.6 | 11.3 | 7.4 | 0.1 | T | 0.0 | 0.0 | 27.1 |
| 1990-91 | 0.0 | 0.0 | 0.0 | T | 1.3 | 12.1 |  |  |  |  |  |  |  |
| Record Mean | 0.0 | 0.0 | T | 0.2 | 2.7 | 6.9 | 8.1 | 7.3 | 6.5 | 2.0 | T | 0.0 | 33.7 |

See Reference Notes, relative to all above tables, on preceding page.

Topeka, is located near the geographical center of the United States, and the middle of the temperate zone. The city straddles the Kansas River about 60 miles above its junction with the Missouri River. The Kansas River flows in an easterly direction through northeastern Kansas. Near Topeka, the river valley ranges from 2 to 4 miles wide, and is bordered on both sides by rolling prairie uplands of some 200 to 300 feet. The city is built on both banks of the Kansas River and along two tributaries, Soldier Creek in north Topeka and Shunganunga Creek in the south and east part of town. Flooding is always a threat following periods of heavy rains but protective construction has reduced the problem.

Seventy percent of the annual precipitation normally falls during the six crop-growing months, April through September. The rains of this period are usually of short duration, predominantly of the thunderstorm type. They occur more frequently during the nighttime and early morning hours than at other times of the day. Excessive precipitation rates may occur with warm-season thunderstorms. Rainfall accumulations over 8 inches in 24 hours have occurred in Topeka. Tornadoes have occurred in the area on several occasions and caused severe damage and numerous injuries.

Individual summers show wide departures from average conditions. Hottest summers may produce temperatures of 100 degrees or higher on more than 50 days. On the other hand, 25 percent of the summers pass with two or fewer 100 degree days. Similarly, precipitation has shown a wide range for June, July, and August, varying from under 3 inches to more than 27 inches during the 3 months. Summers are hot with low relative humidity and persistent southerly winds. Oppressively warm periods with high relative humidity are usually of short duration.

Winter temperatures average about 45 degrees cooler than summer. Cold spells are seldom prolonged. Only on rare occasions do daytime temperatures fail to rise above freezing. Winter precipitation is often in the form of snow, sleet, or glaze, but storms of such severity to prevent normal movement of traffic or to interfere with scheduled activity are not common.

In the transitional spring and fall seasons, the numerous days of fair weather are interspersed with short intervals of stormy weather. Strong, blustery winds are quite common in late winter and spring. Autumn is characteristically a season of warm days, cool nights, and infrequent precipitation, with cold air invasions gradually increasing in intensity as the season progresses.

Nearly all crops of the temperate zone can be produced in the vicinity of Topeka. Wheat and other small grains, clover, soybeans, fruit, and berries do well, and the area supports an extensive dairy industry.

Based on the 1951-1980 period, the average first occurrence of 32 degrees Fahrenheit in the fall is October 14 and the average last occurrence in the spring is April 21.

## TABLE 1 — NORMALS, MEANS AND EXTREMES

TOPEKA, KANSAS

LATITUDE: 39°04'N   LONGITUDE: 95°38'W   ELEVATION: FT. GRND 877 BARO 884   TIME ZONE: CENTRAL   WBAN: 13996

| | (a) | JAN | FEB | MAR | APR | MAY | JUNE | JULY | AUG | SEP | OCT | NOV | DEC | YEAR |
|---|---|---|---|---|---|---|---|---|---|---|---|---|---|---|
| **TEMPERATURE °F:** | | | | | | | | | | | | | | |
| Normals -Daily Maximum | | 36.3 | 43.0 | 53.2 | 66.5 | 76.0 | 84.6 | 89.6 | 88.5 | 80.7 | 69.9 | 53.8 | 41.8 | 65.3 |
| -Daily Minimum | | 15.7 | 21.9 | 30.4 | 42.7 | 53.2 | 63.1 | 67.5 | 65.6 | 56.2 | 44.1 | 31.5 | 21.8 | 42.8 |
| -Monthly | | 26.1 | 32.5 | 41.8 | 54.6 | 64.6 | 73.9 | 78.6 | 77.0 | 68.5 | 57.0 | 42.7 | 31.8 | 54.1 |
| Extremes -Record Highest | 43 | 73 | 84 | 89 | 95 | 97 | 107 | 110 | 110 | 109 | 96 | 85 | 73 | 110 |
| -Year | | 1967 | 1972 | 1986 | 1987 | 1975 | 1953 | 1980 | 1984 | 1947 | 1963 | 1980 | 1984 | AUG 1984 |
| -Record Lowest | 43 | -20 | -23 | -7 | 10 | 26 | 43 | 43 | 41 | 29 | 19 | 2 | -26 | -26 |
| -Year | | 1974 | 1979 | 1978 | 1975 | 1963 | 1988 | 1972 | 1988 | 1984 | 1976 | 1976 | 1989 | DEC 1989 |
| **NORMAL DEGREE DAYS:** | | | | | | | | | | | | | | |
| Heating (base 65°F) | | 1206 | 910 | 719 | 321 | 117 | 14 | 5 | 0 | 53 | 276 | 669 | 1029 | 5319 |
| Cooling (base 65°F) | | 0 | 0 | 0 | 9 | 105 | 281 | 427 | 372 | 158 | 28 | 0 | 0 | 1380 |
| **% OF POSSIBLE SUNSHINE** | 40 | 56 | 54 | 56 | 57 | 60 | 65 | 70 | 69 | 65 | 62 | 54 | 51 | 60 |
| **MEAN SKY COVER (tenths)** Sunrise - Sunset | 43 | 6.1 | 6.4 | 6.6 | 6.3 | 6.3 | 5.9 | 5.1 | 5.0 | 5.0 | 5.1 | 5.8 | 6.1 | 5.8 |
| **MEAN NUMBER OF DAYS:** | | | | | | | | | | | | | | |
| Sunrise to Sunset -Clear | 43 | 9.4 | 7.9 | 7.4 | 7.9 | 7.2 | 8.1 | 11.1 | 11.8 | 12.1 | 12.6 | 9.8 | 9.0 | 114.3 |
| -Partly Cloudy | 43 | 6.5 | 6.2 | 7.3 | 8.0 | 9.8 | 10.4 | 10.6 | 10.3 | 7.6 | 7.0 | 6.9 | 6.6 | 97.3 |
| -Cloudy | 43 | 15.1 | 14.1 | 16.2 | 14.2 | 14.0 | 11.5 | 9.3 | 8.8 | 10.3 | 11.4 | 13.3 | 15.3 | 153.5 |
| Precipitation .01 inches or more | 43 | 6.1 | 6.2 | 8.7 | 9.7 | 11.4 | 10.4 | 8.6 | 8.3 | 7.5 | 6.7 | 6.1 | 6.2 | 95.9 |
| Snow,Ice pellets 1.0 inches or more | 43 | 1.9 | 1.4 | 1.3 | 0.2 | 0.0 | 0.0 | 0.0 | 0.0 | 0.0 | 0.0 | 0.4 | 1.6 | 6.8 |
| Thunderstorms | 43 | 0.4 | 0.7 | 2.4 | 5.5 | 9.2 | 10.2 | 8.7 | 8.0 | 6.2 | 3.4 | 1.2 | 0.4 | 56.2 |
| Heavy Fog Visibility 1/4 mile or less | 43 | 1.9 | 1.8 | 1.1 | 0.8 | 0.9 | 0.6 | 0.6 | 1.1 | 1.1 | 1.6 | 1.1 | 1.9 | 14.3 |
| Temperature °F -Maximum 90° and above | 25 | 0.0 | 0.0 | 0.0 | 0.4 | 0.9 | 6.8 | 15.5 | 12.9 | 4.7 | 0.4 | 0.0 | 0.0 | 41.7 |
| 32° and below | 25 | 11.3 | 7.4 | 1.6 | 0.* | 0.0 | 0.0 | 0.0 | 0.0 | 0.0 | 0.0 | 1.2 | 7.3 | 28.9 |
| -Minimum 32° and below | 25 | 28.8 | 23.0 | 16.6 | 4.0 | 0.2 | 0.0 | 0.0 | 0.0 | 0.2 | 4.1 | 16.4 | 26.9 | 120.3 |
| 0° and below | 25 | 3.9 | 2.4 | 0.1 | 0.0 | 0.0 | 0.0 | 0.0 | 0.0 | 0.0 | 0.0 | 0.0 | 1.6 | 7.9 |
| **AVG. STATION PRESS.(mb)** | 17 | 988.7 | 987.5 | 982.9 | 982.1 | 981.4 | 982.1 | 983.4 | 983.9 | 984.9 | 986.1 | 985.6 | 987.6 | 984.7 |
| **RELATIVE HUMIDITY (%)** | | | | | | | | | | | | | | |
| Hour 00 | 25 | 75 | 75 | 72 | 72 | 78 | 80 | 78 | 79 | 82 | 77 | 77 | 77 | 77 |
| Hour 06 | 25 | 77 | 78 | 78 | 80 | 84 | 86 | 86 | 87 | 88 | 83 | 81 | 80 | 82 |
| Hour 12 (Local Time) | 25 | 63 | 62 | 57 | 54 | 57 | 60 | 59 | 59 | 58 | 55 | 60 | 65 | 59 |
| Hour 18 | 25 | 64 | 61 | 53 | 51 | 55 | 57 | 56 | 58 | 59 | 58 | 63 | 67 | 59 |
| **PRECIPITATION (inches):** | | | | | | | | | | | | | | |
| Water Equivalent -Normal | | 0.88 | 1.05 | 2.18 | 3.08 | 3.99 | 5.14 | 4.04 | 3.69 | 3.45 | 2.82 | 1.75 | 1.31 | 33.38 |
| -Maximum Monthly | 43 | 5.24 | 3.49 | 8.44 | 8.12 | 9.39 | 15.20 | 12.02 | 11.18 | 12.71 | 7.24 | 6.27 | 4.30 | 15.20 |
| -Year | | 1949 | 1971 | 1973 | 1967 | 1982 | 1967 | 1950 | 1977 | 1973 | 1980 | 1964 | 1973 | JUN 1967 |
| -Minimum Monthly | 43 | T | 0.14 | 0.10 | 0.62 | 0.41 | 0.56 | 0.59 | 0.26 | 0.66 | 0.04 | T | 0.05 | T |
| -Year | | 1986 | 1963 | 1966 | 1989 | 1966 | 1980 | 1983 | 1971 | 1952 | 1952 | 1989 | 1979 | NOV 1989 |
| -Maximum in 24 hrs | 43 | 1.55 | 2.33 | 3.76 | 3.59 | 3.62 | 5.52 | 4.19 | 4.48 | 4.80 | 4.10 | 4.66 | 2.65 | 5.52 |
| -Year | | 1988 | 1971 | 1987 | 1967 | 1978 | 1967 | 1951 | 1962 | 1989 | 1985 | 1964 | 1980 | JUN 1967 |
| Snow,Ice pellets -Maximum Monthly | 43 | 20.1 | 22.4 | 22.1 | 6.8 | T | T | 0.0 | 0.0 | 0.0 | 0.8 | 9.4 | 18.8 | 22.4 |
| -Year | | 1979 | 1971 | 1960 | 1970 | 1989 | 1989 | | | | 1970 | 1972 | 1983 | FEB 1971 |
| -Maximum in 24 hrs | 43 | 11.3 | 15.2 | 8.4 | 7.6 | T | T | 0.0 | 0.0 | 0.0 | 0.8 | 7.4 | 9.0 | 15.2 |
| -Year | | 1985 | 1971 | 1960 | 1970 | 1989 | 1989 | | | | 1970 | 1975 | 1973 | FEB 1971 |
| **WIND:** | | | | | | | | | | | | | | |
| Mean Speed (mph) | 40 | 10.1 | 10.4 | 12.2 | 12.1 | 10.6 | 9.8 | 8.6 | 8.5 | 8.8 | 9.2 | 10.0 | 9.9 | 10.0 |
| Prevailing Direction through 1963 | | N | N | E | S | S | S | S | S | S | S | S | S | S |
| Fastest Mile -Direction (!!) | 34 | S | NW | SW | SE | N | SW | N | N | N | NE | SW | NW | N |
| -Speed (MPH) | 34 | 52 | 47 | 66 | 63 | 72 | 72 | 81 | 57 | 57 | 63 | 56 | 61 | 81 |
| -Year | | 1962 | 1967 | 195- | 1957 | 1963 | 1966 | 1958 | 1959 | 1952 | 1954 | 1963 | 1963 | JUL 1958 |
| Peak Gust -Direction (!!) | 6 | NW | NW | S | S | SE | N | S | E | NE | S | S | SW | N |
| -Speed (mph) | 6 | 53 | 53 | 62 | 62 | 48 | 82 | 56 | 53 | 61 | 49 | 58 | 44 | 82 |
| -Date | | 1984 | 1984 | 1985 | 1984 | 1985 | 1984 | 1989 | 1987 | 1989 | 1984 | 1988 | 1987 | JUN 1984 |

**See Reference Notes to this table on the following page.**

## TABLE 2 — PRECIPITATION (inches)   TOPEKA, KANSAS

| YEAR | JAN | FEB | MAR | APR | MAY | JUNE | JULY | AUG | SEP | OCT | NOV | DEC | ANNUAL |
|---|---|---|---|---|---|---|---|---|---|---|---|---|---|
| 1961 | 0.07 | 1.59 | 6.32 | 2.65 | 5.29 | 2.43 | 7.25 | 1.92 | 5.69 | 4.88 | 2.50 | .07 | 41.66 |
| 1962 | 1.99 | 1.28 | 1.43 | 1.23 | 4.23 | 4.46 | 3.68 | 6.64 | 4.50 | 1.36 | 1.04 | .42 | 32.26 |
| 1963 | 0.56 | 0.14 | 2.53 | 0.65 | 4.91 | 2.71 | 3.13 | 1.30 | 1.00 | 0.96 | 0.96 | .22 | 19.07 |
| 1964 | 0.54 | 0.29 | 1.73 | 4.70 | 2.09 | 8.10 | 1.81 | 8.24 | 1.13 | 0.14 | 6.27 | .34 | 35.98 |
| 1965 | 1.60 | 1.27 | 1.58 | 2.31 | 3.41 | 10.14 | 3.33 | 3.53 | 7.22 | 0.92 | 0.20 | 2.46 | 37.97 |
| 1966 | 0.16 | 0.54 | 0.10 | 1.98 | 0.41 | 8.83 | 0.75 | 3.62 | 1.46 | 0.42 | 0.24 | .79 | 19.30 |
| 1967 | 1.06 | 0.21 | 1.91 | 8.12 | 5.07 | 15.20 | 3.06 | 1.84 | 4.64 | 6.01 | 0.41 | 3.11 | 50.64 |
| 1968 | 0.89 | 0.56 | 0.46 | 4.20 | 3.37 | 3.18 | 10.17 | 7.40 | 2.50 | 4.19 | 1.56 | 2.10 | 40.58 |
| 1969 | 0.84 | 0.42 | 1.37 | 7.14 | 3.77 | 8.46 | 3.26 | 0.87 | 2.03 | 3.98 | 0.10 | .24 | 33.48 |
| 1970 | 0.19 | 0.34 | 1.03 | 3.49 | 5.46 | 5.82 | 1.39 | 0.83 | 7.70 | 2.49 | 1.23 | .65 | 31.62 |
| 1971 | 1.20 | 3.49 | 0.64 | 1.08 | 4.83 | 3.10 | 4.07 | 0.26 | 1.35 | 3.87 | 3.03 | .83 | 28.75 |
| 1972 | 0.47 | 0.56 | 1.37 | 3.93 | 2.90 | 1.14 | 4.81 | 3.26 | 4.89 | 2.11 | 3.99 | .78 | 31.21 |
| 1973 | 2.67 | 1.71 | 8.44 | 4.03 | 4.37 | 2.96 | 10.16 | 2.83 | 12.71 | 4.57 | 2.14 | 4.30 | 60.89 |
| 1974 | 0.99 | 1.20 | 1.22 | 2.78 | 3.59 | 3.72 | 2.90 | 4.89 | 1.40 | 5.16 | 2.19 | .18 | 31.22 |
| 1975 | 1.50 | 1.67 | 1.66 | 3.26 | 3.88 | 4.85 | 0.68 | 1.69 | 4.35 | 0.05 | 4.44 | .12 | 29.15 |
| 1976 | 0.41 | 0.51 | 1.38 | 4.85 | 4.63 | 1.69 | 2.04 | 0.86 | 1.12 | 3.01 | 0.04 | .21 | 20.75 |
| 1977 | 0.90 | 0.22 | 2.06 | 2.46 | 7.83 | 10.91 | 1.37 | 11.18 | 3.22 | 4.92 | 3.38 | .26 | 48.71 |
| 1978 | 0.19 | 0.84 | 1.63 | 2.35 | 5.75 | 4.57 | 2.26 | 2.89 | 6.65 | 0.36 | 3.22 | .55 | 31.26 |
| 1979 | 1.81 | 0.63 | 3.95 | 2.37 | 2.25 | 5.63 | 5.84 | 4.05 | 2.17 | 1.80 | .05 | 3.86 | 34.70 |
| 1980 | 1.34 | 0.91 | 4.15 | 1.03 | 4.85 | 0.56 | 0.87 | 5.86 | 1.19 | 7.24 | 0.25 | 3.86 | 32.11 |
| 1981 | 0.32 | 0.21 | 1.61 | 1.98 | 5.93 | 9.40 | 7.63 | 3.92 | 2.03 | 3.72 | 3.63 | .22 | 40.60 |
| 1982 | 1.67 | 0.59 | 1.14 | 1.58 | 9.39 | 5.99 | 5.08 | 4.53 | 1.17 | 1.25 | 2.26 | 3.61 | 38.26 |
| 1983 | 0.69 | 0.63 | 4.39 |  | 4.93 | 6.29 | 0.59 | 0.62 | 2.25 | 5.19 | 3.61 | .34 | 36.61 |
| 1984 | 0.11 | 1.35 | 4.57 | 4.26 | 3.45 | 10.17 | 1.66 | 1.04 | 4.24 | 4.10 | 0.72 | 2.36 | 38.03 |
| 1985 | 0.70 | 2.02 | 2.38 | 3.60 | 3.79 | 5.15 | 2.90 | 7.97 | 8.16 | 5.20 | 2.02 | .71 | 44.60 |
| 1986 | T | 1.55 | 1.35 | 3.15 | 7.53 | 2.51 | 4.21 | 5.50 | 6.21 | 3.30 | 0.87 | .20 | 37.38 |
| 1987 | 1.09 | 2.71 | 5.92 | 2.33 | 3.89 | 4.86 | 2.78 | 5.90 | 1.81 | 1.86 | 1.94 | .87 | 36.96 |
| 1988 | 2.04 | 0.48 | 0.73 | 2.93 | 3.08 | 3.13 | 1.74 | 1.34 | 1.94 | 0.26 | 0.86 | 2.86 | 19.39 |
| 1989 | 1.24 | 0.86 | 3.11 | 0.62 | 4.05 | 4.76 | 5.21 | 6.22 | 8.65 | 3.44 | T | 3.61 | 38.77 |
| 1990 | 1.22 | 2.31 | 3.75 | 1.01 | 4.45 | 5.57 | 3.01 | 5.69 | 0.83 | 2.71 | 2.91 | 2.97 | 34.43 |
| Record Mean | 0.97 | 1.26 | 2.14 | 3.03 | 4.43 | 4.84 | 3.85 | 4.07 | 3.58 | 2.62 | 1.67 | .20 | 33.66 |

## TABLE 3 — AVERAGE TEMPERATURE (deg. F)   TOPEKA, KANSAS

| YEAR | JAN | FEB | MAR | APR | MAY | JUNE | JULY | AUG | SEP | OCT | NOV | DEC | ANNUAL |
|---|---|---|---|---|---|---|---|---|---|---|---|---|---|
| 1961 | 28.8 | 35.6 | 43.3 | 50.2 | 59.8 | 72.0 | 76.7 | 74.4 | 65.0 | 57.0 | 41.0 | 25.0 | 52.4 |
| 1962 | 21.2 | 32.8 | 38.9 | 52.2 | 72.7 | 72.5 | 76.2 | 76.7 | 65.4 | 60.0 | 44.0 | 31.9 | 53.7 |
| 1963 | 18.0 | 32.5 | 47.3 | 57.4 | 65.3 | 77.3 | 80.3 | 78.4 | 71.9 | 67.6 | 47.4 | 23.4 | 55.6 |
| #1964 | 34.2 | 34.3 | 40.0 | 56.4 | 68.9 | 72.1 | 81.2 | 74.5 | 68.1 | 54.6 | 46.2 | 29.8 | 55.0 |
| 1965 | 31.0 | 30.8 | 33.0 | 57.2 | 68.6 | 73.1 | 77.0 | 74.0 | 66.9 | 57.3 | 45.7 | 39.9 | 54.6 |
| 1966 | 26.0 | 31.9 | 47.0 | 50.8 | 63.8 | 72.7 | 83.1 | 74.8 | 65.8 | 55.4 | 44.1 | 30.7 | 53.8 |
| 1967 | 31.5 | 33.4 | 47.0 | 57.4 | 60.8 | 72.1 | 75.0 | 72.1 | 63.6 | 54.7 | 41.7 | 33.0 | 53.5 |
| 1968 | 26.6 | 31.6 | 46.4 | 53.5 | 59.1 | 74.1 | 76.4 | 75.5 | 66.6 | 57.3 | 40.0 | 29.0 | 53.0 |
| 1969 | 25.8 | 33.9 | 37.1 | 55.5 | 65.3 | 68.7 | 79.4 | 75.5 | 69.0 | 52.7 | 42.5 | 29.9 | 52.9 |
| 1970 | 23.3 | 35.9 | 39.5 | 53.5 | 68.1 | 71.8 | 77.8 | 80.6 | 69.1 | 54.2 | 41.2 | 34.3 | 54.1 |
| 1971 | 24.1 | 26.8 | 41.1 | 56.3 | 61.4 | 77.5 | 74.5 | 71.6 | 61.6 | 45.4 | 34.8 | 34.2 | 54.2 |
| 1972 | 25.6 | 31.8 | 46.7 | 54.7 | 63.6 | 74.3 | 74.4 | 74.7 | 68.5 | 54.6 | 39.4 | 27.7 | 53.0 |
| 1973 | 27.5 | 33.9 | 47.5 | 52.6 | 61.3 | 74.9 | 77.4 | 77.1 | 66.6 | 60.4 | 44.8 | 29.9 | 54.5 |
| 1974 | 22.3 | 35.9 | 46.9 | 56.8 | 67.2 | 70.0 | 80.6 | 74.1 | 61.9 | 58.4 | 43.1 | 32.7 | 54.2 |
| 1975 | 30.7 | 28.8 | 37.8 | 54.4 | 67.3 | 74.2 | 77.3 | 79.3 | 64.0 | 59.3 | 45.5 | 34.5 | 54.4 |
| 1976 | 27.8 | 42.7 | 45.4 | 57.0 | 60.4 | 72.7 | 78.0 | 76.9 | 69.0 | 50.3 | 35.4 | 28.5 | 53.7 |
| 1977 | 15.2 | 37.4 | 49.6 | 60.2 | 70.1 | 75.2 | 79.4 | 76.4 | 71.6 | 56.7 | 42.7 | 30.1 | 55.4 |
| 1978 | 17.3 | 20.4 | 38.4 | 55.9 | 63.0 | 74.6 | 77.3 | 75.7 | 72.9 | 54.6 | 43.0 | 30.0 | 51.9 |
| 1979 | 11.8 | 19.2 | 42.6 | 51.6 | 63.1 | 72.4 | 77.8 | 76.9 | 68.0 | 57.0 | 40.0 | 35.5 | 51.3 |
| 1980 | 28.6 | 26.0 | 40.8 | 53.7 | 62.8 | 76.5 | 86.4 | 80.7 | 70.0 | 53.9 | 45.0 | 32.6 | 54.7 |
| 1981 | 31.4 | 35.5 | 46.1 | 60.6 | 60.9 | 75.5 | 79.5 | 73.1 | 68.0 | 56.1 | 47.2 | 30.1 | 55.4 |
| 1982 | 21.9 | 28.5 | 43.2 | 50.2 | 63.7 | 69.0 | 78.7 | 75.5 | 66.5 | 55.9 | 42.0 | 35.8 | 52.6 |
| 1983 | 32.5 | 36.1 | 44.9 | 49.4 | 62.5 | 73.5 | 81.1 | 83.0 | 72.2 | 58.7 | 45.8 | 14.4 | 54.5 |
| 1984 | 26.0 | 40.2 | 38.1 | 51.7 | 62.4 | 73.9 | 77.0 | 78.0 | 66.5 | 56.6 | 45.5 | 36.8 | 54.4 |
| 1985 | 19.9 | 25.6 | 48.6 | 58.7 | 66.5 | 72.8 | 79.7 | 72.8 | 66.8 | 56.7 | 36.7 | 25.1 | 52.4 |
| 1986 | 35.8 | 32.5 | 49.8 | 57.7 | 65.9 | 77.0 | 80.4 | 72.3 | 71.6 | 56.6 | 38.3 | 34.6 | 56.0 |
| 1987 | 29.7 | 40.3 | 46.7 | 57.1 | 70.4 | 76.2 | 78.1 | 75.5 | 68.2 | 52.6 | 47.4 | 35.9 | 56.5 |
| 1988 | 28.1 | 30.8 | 43.4 | 53.9 | 68.8 | 75.1 | 76.7 | 79.5 | 70.3 | 52.8 | 45.2 | 35.3 | 55.0 |
| 1989 | 38.0 | 36.2 | 44.4 | 57.9 | 64.2 | 71.4 | 77.6 | 74.8 | 62.3 | 57.1 | 42.3 | 21.0 | 52.8 |
| 1990 | 37.3 | 36.2 | 45.5 | 51.9 | 60.3 | 77.2 | 77.2 | 76.5 | 71.6 | 57.0 | 49.1 | 29.6 | 55.8 |
| Record Mean | 28.3 | 32.3 | 42.9 | 55.0 | 64.5 | 74.0 | 78.9 | 77.3 | 69.1 | 57.6 | 43.5 | 32.3 | 54.6 |
| Max | 38.0 | 42.6 | 54.0 | 66.3 | 75.3 | 84.6 | 89.9 | 88.4 | 80.7 | 69.5 | 54.1 | 41.7 | 65.4 |
| Min | 18.5 | 22.1 | 31.8 | 43.6 | 53.6 | 63.4 | 67.9 | 66.2 | 57.5 | 45.7 | 32.8 | 22.9 | 43.8 |

## REFERENCE NOTES FOR TABLES 1, 2, 3 and 6          (TOPEKA, KS)

### GENERAL

T - TRACE AMOUNT
BLANK ENTRIES DENOTE MISSING/UNREPORTED DATA.
# INDICATES A STATION OR INSTRUMENT RELOCATION.

### SPECIFIC

**TABLE 1**

(a) - LENGTH OF RECORD IN YEARS. ALTHOUGH INDIVIDUAL MONTHS MAY BE MISSING.
* LESS THAN .05

NORMALS — BASED ON THE 1951-1980 RECORD PERIOD.
EXTREMES — DATES ARE THE MOST RECENT OCCURRENCE.
WIND DIR. — NUMERALS SHOW TENS OF DEGREES CLOCKWISE FROM TRUE NORTH.
"00" INDICATES CALM.
RESULTANT WIND DIRECTIONS ARE GIVEN TO WHOLE DEGREES.

**TABLE 3**
MAX AND MIN ARE LONG-TERM MEAN DAILY MAXIMUM AND MEAN DAILY MINIMUM TEMPERATURES.

### EXCEPTIONS

**TABLE 1**

1. FASTEST MILE OF 81/N ON JULY 11, 1958 WAS ESTIMATED FROM 5-MINUTE PERIOD RECORD.

**TABLES 2, 3, and 6**

RECORD MEANS ARE THROUGH THE CURRENT YEAR, BEGINNING IN     1887 FOR TEMPERATURE
1878 FOR PRECIPITATION
1947 FOR SNOWFALL

TABLE 4    HEATING DEGREE DAYS Base 65 deg. F          TOPEKA, KANSAS

| SEASON | JULY | AUG | SEP | OCT | NOV | DEC | JAN | FEB | MAR | APR | MAY | JUNE | TOTAL |
|---|---|---|---|---|---|---|---|---|---|---|---|---|---|
| 1961-62 | 0 | .5 | 116 | 257 | 714 | 1234 | 1352 | 896 | 803 | 393 | 10 | 4 | 5784 |
| 1962-63 | 0 | 0 | 92 | 225 | 620 | 1018 | 1452 | 903 | 544 | 244 | 91 | 0 | 5189 |
| 1963-64 | 0 | 2 | 16 | 64 | 521 | 1286 | 945 | 882 | 765 | 264 | 51 | 25 | 4821 |
| #1964-65 | 0 | 9 | 67 | 316 | 572 | 1087 | 1044 | 955 | 984 | 263 | 30 | 0 | 5327 |
| 1965-66 | 0 | 0 | 74 | 253 | 572 | 770 | 1202 | 922 | 552 | 423 | 107 | 6 | 4881 |
| 1966-67 | 0 | 2 | 64 | 316 | 620 | 1053 | 1032 | 875 | 570 | 247 | 205 | 15 | 4999 |
| 1967-68 | 1 | 7 | 87 | 356 | 690 | 985 | 1184 | 965 | 572 | 338 | 202 | 5 | 5392 |
| 1968-69 | 0 | 1 | 35 | 282 | 745 | 1108 | 1210 | 866 | 857 | 282 | 94 | 42 | 5522 |
| 1969-70 | 0 | 0 | 17 | 408 | 666 | 1083 | 1284 | 811 | 785 | 376 | 45 | 29 | 5504 |
| 1970-71 | 0 | 0 | 57 | 344 | 706 | 945 | 1262 | 1065 | 735 | 274 | 144 | 0 | 5532 |
| 1971-72 | 4 | 0 | 69 | 143 | 580 | 927 | 1216 | 958 | 567 | 324 | 109 | 10 | 4907 |
| 1972-73 | 10 | 0 | 59 | 337 | 764 | 1152 | 1158 | 864 | 537 | 378 | 129 | 0 | 5388 |
| 1973-74 | 0 | 0 | 58 | 191 | 603 | 1082 | 1317 | 807 | 558 | 258 | 64 | 7 | 4945 |
| 1974-75 | 0 | 3 | 134 | 213 | 649 | 991 | 1056 | 1008 | 839 | 352 | 46 | 7 | 5298 |
| 1975-76 | 2 | 0 | 137 | 230 | 581 | 941 | 1148 | 639 | 599 | 269 | 178 | 5 | 4729 |
| 1976-77 | 0 | 0 | 45 | 471 | 881 | 1126 | 1537 | 767 | 469 | 180 | 11 | 0 | 5487 |
| 1977-78 | 0 | 0 | 6 | 263 | 662 | 1075 | 1473 | 1240 | 824 | 280 | 156 | 6 | 5985 |
| 1978-79 | 0 | 0 | 34 | 319 | 655 | 1078 | 1643 | 1277 | 693 | 401 | 129 | 9 | 6238 |
| 1979-80 | 0 | 0 | 45 | 267 | 741 | 908 | 1123 | 1123 | 744 | 344 | 129 | 3 | 5431 |
| 1980-81 | 0 | 0 | 65 | 344 | 591 | 1001 | 1035 | 822 | 579 | 175 | 176 | 0 | 4788 |
| 1981-82 | 0 | 2 | 46 | 283 | 529 | 1076 | 1329 | 1014 | 664 | 449 | 76 | 32 | 5500 |
| 1982-83 | 0 | 0 | 93 | 303 | 683 | 896 | 1002 | 804 | 615 | 466 | 120 | 13 | 4995 |
| 1983-84 | 0 | 0 | 56 | 223 | 570 | 1565 | 1204 | 713 | 830 | 405 | 137 | 0 | 5703 |
| 1984-85 | 0 | 0 | 145 | 276 | 578 | 871 | 1389 | 1098 | 501 | 228 | 35 | 8 | 5129 |
| 1985-86 | 0 | 0 | 127 | 259 | 844 | 1228 | 899 | 906 | 491 | 252 | 49 | 0 | 5055 |
| 1986-87 | 0 | 9 | 27 | 263 | 792 | 934 | 1084 | 688 | 560 | 292 | 16 | 0 | 4665 |
| 1987-88 | 0 | 3 | 24 | 376 | 531 | 893 | 1136 | 988 | 662 | 331 | 16 | 5 | 4965 |
| 1988-89 | 2 | 4 | 24 | 383 | 587 | 912 | 832 | 1174 | 641 | 296 | 125 | 5 | 4985 |
| 1989-90 | 0 | 2 | 155 | 276 | 672 | 1360 | 851 | 801 | 600 | 413 | 176 | 4 | 5310 |
| 1990-91 | 1 | 1 | 39 | 276 | 477 | 1093 | | | | | | | |

TABLE 5    COOLING DEGREE DAYS Base 65 deg. F          TOPEKA, KANSAS

| YEAR | JAN | FEB | MAR | APR | MAY | JUNE | JULY | AUG | SEP | OCT | NOV | DEC | TOTAL |
|---|---|---|---|---|---|---|---|---|---|---|---|---|---|
| 1969 | 0 | 0 | 0 | 4 | 107 | 158 | 456 | 330 | 146 | 32 | 0 | 0 | 1233 |
| 1970 | 0 | 0 | 0 | 35 | 149 | 239 | 407 | 490 | 188 | 16 | 0 | 0 | 1524 |
| 1971 | 0 | 0 | 3 | 21 | 42 | 381 | 309 | 345 | 273 | 42 | 0 | 0 | 1416 |
| 1972 | 0 | 0 | 5 | 22 | 74 | 297 | 308 | 309 | 169 | 20 | 0 | 0 | 1204 |
| 1973 | 0 | 0 | 0 | 13 | 21 | 304 | 394 | 384 | 115 | 52 | 0 | 0 | 1283 |
| 1974 | 0 | 0 | 6 | 21 | 140 | 165 | 490 | 292 | 47 | 12 | 0 | 0 | 1173 |
| 1975 | 0 | 0 | 0 | 38 | 129 | 289 | 390 | 448 | 116 | 61 | 3 | 0 | 1474 |
| 1976 | 0 | 0 | 1 | 34 | 40 | 242 | 410 | 376 | 171 | 20 | 0 | 0 | 1294 |
| 1977 | 0 | 0 | 0 | 40 | 176 | 311 | 453 | 360 | 209 | 14 | 0 | 0 | 1563 |
| 1978 | 0 | 0 | 6 | 15 | 101 | 298 | 390 | 339 | 277 | 5 | 3 | 0 | 1434 |
| 1979 | 0 | 0 | 4 | 7 | 76 | 237 | 401 | 379 | 144 | 27 | 0 | 0 | 1275 |
| 1980 | 0 | 0 | 0 | 9 | 69 | 356 | 670 | 496 | 220 | 9 | 0 | 0 | 1829 |
| 1981 | 0 | 0 | 0 | 53 | 58 | 321 | 457 | 260 | 143 | 17 | 0 | 0 | 1309 |
| 1982 | 0 | 0 | 0 | 11 | 43 | 157 | 432 | 334 | 147 | 28 | 0 | 0 | 1152 |
| 1983 | 0 | 0 | 0 | 7 | 50 | 274 | 509 | 564 | 278 | 33 | 2 | 0 | 1717 |
| 1984 | 0 | 0 | 0 | 14 | 67 | 274 | 379 | 407 | 196 | 20 | 0 | 3 | 1360 |
| 1985 | 0 | 0 | 0 | 46 | 88 | 225 | 461 | 249 | 188 | 6 | 0 | 0 | 1263 |
| 1986 | 0 | 0 | 26 | 42 | 85 | 363 | 488 | 243 | 233 | 9 | 0 | 0 | 1489 |
| 1987 | 0 | 0 | 0 | 61 | 192 | 344 | 410 | 335 | 126 | 0 | 9 | 0 | 1477 |
| 1988 | 0 | 0 | 0 | 4 | 140 | 314 | 375 | 458 | 191 | 11 | 0 | 0 | 1493 |
| 1989 | 0 | 0 | 11 | 90 | 107 | 206 | 399 | 311 | 81 | 41 | 0 | 0 | 1246 |
| 1990 | 0 | 0 | 1 | 26 | 39 | 377 | 403 | 366 | 241 | 37 | 7 | 0 | 1497 |

TABLE 6    SNOWFALL (inches)          TOPEKA, KANSAS

| SEASON | JULY | AUG | SEP | OCT | NOV | DEC | JAN | FEB | MAR | APR | MAY | JUNE | TOTAL |
|---|---|---|---|---|---|---|---|---|---|---|---|---|---|
| 1961-62 | 0.0 | 0.0 | 0.0 | 0.0 | 1.2 | 11.2 | 18.0 | 2.4 | 0.1 | T | 0.0 | 0.0 | 32.9 |
| 1962-63 | 0.0 | 0.0 | 0.0 | T | T | 2.3 | 5.5 | 2.2 | 0.2 | 0.0 | 0.0 | 0.0 | 10.2 |
| 1963-64 | 0.0 | 0.0 | 0.0 | 0.0 | T | 3.6 | 2.3 | 2.0 | 2.9 | 0.0 | 0.0 | 0.0 | 10.8 |
| 1964-65 | 0.0 | 0.0 | 0.0 | 0.0 | 1.3 | 4.3 | 2.9 | 7.3 | 5.0 | 0.0 | 0.0 | 0.0 | 20.8 |
| 1965-66 | 0.0 | 0.0 | 0.0 | 0.0 | T | 3.6 | 0.5 | 0.6 | T | T | 0.0 | 0.0 | 4.7 |
| 1966-67 | 0.0 | 0.0 | 0.0 | 0.0 | T | 8.3 | 3.4 | 1.9 | 0.8 | 0.0 | 0.0 | 0.0 | 14.4 |
| 1967-68 | 0.0 | 0.0 | 0.0 | 0.0 | T | 11.1 | 4.7 | 5.7 | T | T | 0.0 | 0.0 | 21.5 |
| 1968-69 | 0.0 | 0.0 | 0.0 | 0.0 | T | 0.8 | 6.2 | 3.4 | 2.0 | 0.0 | 0.0 | 0.0 | 12.4 |
| 1969-70 | 0.0 | 0.0 | 0.0 | 0.0 | 0.8 | 9.4 | 2.1 | T | 4.9 | 6.8 | 0.0 | 0.0 | 24.0 |
| 1970-71 | 0.0 | 0.0 | 0.0 | 0.8 | T | 7.9 | 2.1 | 22.4 | 7.5 | T | 0.0 | 0.0 | 40.7 |
| 1971-72 | 0.0 | 0.0 | 0.0 | 0.0 | 2.4 | T | 3.0 | 6.7 | 3.0 | T | 0.0 | 0.0 | 16.3 |
| 1972-73 | 0.0 | 0.0 | 0.0 | 0.0 | 9.4 | 4.0 | 13.5 | 1.7 | 0.0 | 0.1 | 0.0 | 0.0 | 28.7 |
| 1973-74 | 0.0 | 0.0 | 0.0 | 0.0 | T | 15.2 | 7.8 | 2.1 | 1.5 | 1.3 | 0.0 | 0.0 | 27.9 |
| 1974-75 | 0.0 | 0.0 | 0.0 | 0.0 | 1.3 | 1.4 | 5.0 | 6.7 | 7.8 | 3.6 | 0.0 | 0.0 | 25.8 |
| 1975-76 | 0.0 | 0.0 | 0.0 | 0.0 | 8.3 | 2.7 | 6.4 | 0.7 | 2.9 | 0.0 | 0.0 | 0.0 | 21.0 |
| 1976-77 | 0.0 | 0.0 | 0.0 | T | 0.3 | T | 13.6 | 0.1 | T | 0.2 | 0.0 | 0.0 | 14.2 |
| 1977-78 | 0.0 | 0.0 | 0.0 | 0.0 | 0.1 | 0.2 | 3.9 | 12.4 | 6.2 | 0.0 | 0.0 | 0.0 | 22.8 |
| 1978-79 | 0.0 | 0.0 | 0.0 | 0.0 | T | 11.1 | 20.1 | 3.1 | 7.5 | 1.1 | 0.0 | 0.0 | 42.9 |
| 1979-80 | 0.0 | 0.0 | 0.0 | 0.0 | T | T | 3.5 | 11.4 | 3.4 | 0.0 | 0.0 | 0.0 | 18.3 |
| 1980-81 | 0.0 | 0.0 | 0.0 | T | 0.0 | 3.8 | 2.6 | 2.5 | 0.0 | 0.0 | 0.0 | 0.0 | 8.9 |
| 1981-82 | 0.0 | 0.0 | 0.0 | 0.0 | T | 1.4 | 3.2 | 8.0 | 0.3 | 0.5 | 0.0 | 0.0 | 13.4 |
| 1982-83 | 0.0 | 0.0 | 0.0 | 0.0 | 1.1 | 5.0 | 6.1 | 10.1 | 0.6 | 4.5 | 0.0 | 0.0 | 27.4 |
| 1983-84 | 0.0 | 0.0 | 0.0 | 0.0 | 4.1 | 18.8 | 2.6 | T | 4.2 | 0.0 | 0.0 | 0.0 | 29.7 |
| 1984-85 | 0.0 | 0.0 | 0.0 | 0.0 | T | 9.8 | 18.2 | 7.9 | 0.5 | 0.0 | 0.0 | 0.0 | 36.4 |
| 1985-86 | 0.0 | 0.0 | 0.0 | 0.0 | 3.3 | 5.8 | T | 1.5 | T | 0.0 | 0.0 | 0.0 | 10.6 |
| 1986-87 | 0.0 | 0.0 | 0.0 | T | 0.7 | 1.7 | 15.1 | 2.3 | 0.5 | 0.0 | 0.0 | 0.0 | 20.3 |
| 1987-88 | 0.0 | 0.0 | 0.0 | 0.0 | 0.9 | 9.6 | 0.6 | 6.0 | 4.7 | 0.0 | 0.0 | 0.0 | 21.8 |
| 1988-89 | 0.0 | 0.0 | 0.0 | 0.0 | 0.7 | 0.8 | T | 9.0 | 1.6 | 0.0 | 0.0 | 0.0 | 12.1 |
| 1989-90 | 0.0 | 0.0 | 0.0 | 0.0 | T | 9.5 | 1.0 | 0.1 | 7.6 | T | T | T | 18.2 |
| 1990-91 | 0.0 | 0.0 | 0.0 | 0.0 | T | 2.9 | | | | | | | |
| Record Mean | 0.0 | 0.0 | 0.0 | T | 1.2 | 5.1 | 5.8 | 4.7 | 3.9 | 0.6 | T | T | 21.2 |

**See Reference Notes, relative to all above tables, on preceding page.**

Wichita is in the Central Great Plains where masses of warm, moist air from the Gulf of Mexico collide with cold, dry air from the Arctic region to create a wide range of weather the year around. Summers are usually warm and humid, and can be very hot and dry. The winters are usually mild, with brief periods of very cold weather.

The elevation is just over 1,300 feet above sea level. The terrain is basically flat with natural tree areas mainly along the Arkansas River and its tributaries.

The temperature extremes for the period of weather records at Wichita range from more than 110 degrees to less than −20 degrees. Temperatures above 90 degrees occur an average of 63 days per year, while very cold temperatures below zero occur about 2 days per year.

Precipitation averages about 30 inches per year, with 70 percent of that falling from April through September during the growing season. The wettest years have recorded over 50 inches. The driest years less than 15 inches.

Thunderstorms occur mainly during the spring and early summer. They can be severe and cause damage from heavy rain, large hail, strong winds and tornadoes.

The city of Wichita is protected against floods from the Arkansas River and its local tributaries by the Wichita—Vally Center Flood Control Project, which is designed to protect against floods up to the 75 to 100 year frequency class.

Snowfall normally is 15 inches per year, falling from December through March. Monthly snowfalls in excess of 20 inches and 24-hour snowfalls of more than 13 inches have occurred.

The prevailing wind direction is south with the windiest months March and April. July has the least wind. Strong north winds often occur with the passage of cold fronts from late fall through early spring. Extremely low wind chill factors are experienced with very cold outbreaks during the mid winter. On rare occasions during the summer, strong, hot, dry southwest winds can do considerable damage to crops.

## TABLE 1 NORMALS, MEANS AND EXTREMES

WICHITA, KANSAS

LATITUDE: 37°39'N   LONGITUDE: 97°25'W   ELEVATION: FT. GRND 1321 BARO 1342   TIME ZONE: CENTRAL   WBAN: 03928

| | (a) | JAN | FEB | MAR | APR | MAY | JUNE | JULY | AUG | SEP | OCT | NOV | DEC | YEAR |
|---|---|---|---|---|---|---|---|---|---|---|---|---|---|---|
| **TEMPERATURE °F:** | | | | | | | | | | | | | | |
| Normals | | | | | | | | | | | | | | |
| -Daily Maximum | | 39.8 | 46.1 | 55.8 | 68.1 | 77.1 | 87.4 | 92.9 | 91.5 | 82.0 | 71.2 | 55.1 | 44.6 | 67.6 |
| -Daily Minimum | | 19.4 | 24.1 | 32.4 | 44.5 | 54.6 | 64.7 | 69.8 | 67.9 | 59.2 | 46.9 | 33.5 | 24.2 | 45.1 |
| -Monthly | | 29.6 | 35.1 | 44.1 | 56.3 | 65.9 | 76.1 | 81.4 | 79.7 | 70.6 | 59.1 | 44.3 | 34.4 | 56.4 |
| Extremes | | | | | | | | | | | | | | |
| -Record Highest | 37 | 75 | 84 | 89 | 96 | 100 | 110 | 113 | 110 | 105 | 95 | 85 | 83 | 113 |
| -Year | | 1967 | 1976 | 1989 | 1972 | 1967 | 1980 | 1954 | 1984 | 1985 | 1979 | 1980 | 1955 | JUL 1954 |
| -Record Lowest | 37 | -12 | -21 | -2 | 15 | 31 | 43 | 51 | 48 | 31 | 21 | 1 | -16 | -21 |
| -Year | | 1962 | 1982 | 1960 | 1975 | 1976 | 1969 | 1975 | 1967 | 1984 | 1976 | 1975 | 1989 | FEB 1982 |
| **NORMAL DEGREE DAYS:** | | | | | | | | | | | | | | |
| Heating (base 65°F) | | 1097 | 837 | 656 | 275 | 89 | 7 | 0 | 0 | 37 | 219 | 621 | 949 | 4787 |
| Cooling (base 65°F) | | 0 | 0 | 8 | 14 | 117 | 340 | 508 | 456 | 205 | 36 | 0 | 0 | 1684 |
| **% OF POSSIBLE SUNSHINE** | 36 | 61 | 60 | 62 | 64 | 65 | 69 | 76 | 74 | 68 | 65 | 59 | 58 | 65 |
| **MEAN SKY COVER (tenths)** | | | | | | | | | | | | | | |
| Sunrise - Sunset | 36 | 5.9 | 6.1 | 6.2 | 5.9 | 6.0 | 5.4 | 4.6 | 4.5 | 4.8 | 4.9 | 5.5 | 5.9 | 5.5 |
| **MEAN NUMBER OF DAYS:** | | | | | | | | | | | | | | |
| Sunrise to Sunset | | | | | | | | | | | | | | |
| -Clear | 36 | 10.6 | 8.2 | 9.1 | 8.9 | 8.4 | 9.4 | 13.0 | 13.5 | 13.2 | 13.1 | 10.8 | 10.1 | 128.4 |
| -Partly Cloudy | 36 | 6.2 | 6.9 | 7.2 | 8.2 | 9.6 | 10.6 | 10.5 | 10.0 | 6.8 | 7.0 | 6.5 | 7.0 | 96.5 |
| -Cloudy | 36 | 14.3 | 13.1 | 14.7 | 12.9 | 12.9 | 10.0 | 7.5 | 7.5 | 10.0 | 10.8 | 12.6 | 13.9 | 140.4 |
| Precipitation | | | | | | | | | | | | | | |
| .01 inches or more | 36 | 5.4 | 5.3 | 7.6 | 7.9 | 10.6 | 9.3 | 7.4 | 7.6 | 7.7 | 6.3 | 4.9 | 5.6 | 85.6 |
| Snow,Ice pellets | | | | | | | | | | | | | | |
| 1.0 inches or more | 36 | 1.4 | 1.3 | 0.6 | 0.1 | 0.0 | 0.0 | 0.0 | 0.0 | 0.0 | 0.0 | 0.4 | 1.1 | 4.9 |
| Thunderstorms | 36 | 0.3 | 0.7 | 2.8 | 5.4 | 9.1 | 9.9 | 7.8 | 7.5 | 6.1 | 3.3 | 1.1 | 0.3 | 54.2 |
| Heavy Fog Visibility | | | | | | | | | | | | | | |
| 1/4 mile or less | 36 | 2.8 | 2.8 | 1.4 | 0.7 | 0.8 | 0.3 | 0.2 | 0.2 | 1.1 | 1.4 | 2.0 | 3.1 | 16.6 |
| Temperature °F | | | | | | | | | | | | | | |
| -Maximum | | | | | | | | | | | | | | |
| 90° and above | 36 | 0.0 | 0.0 | 0.0 | 0.4 | 2.1 | 11.8 | 21.7 | 19.6 | 7.4 | 0.9 | 0.0 | 0.0 | 63.9 |
| 32° and below | 36 | 9.6 | 5.8 | 1.3 | 0.1 | 0.0 | 0.0 | 0.0 | 0.0 | 0.0 | 0.* | 0.8 | 5.3 | 22.9 |
| -Minimum | | | | | | | | | | | | | | |
| 32° and below | 36 | 28.6 | 22.8 | 15.3 | 2.7 | 0.1 | 0.0 | 0.0 | 0.0 | 0.0 | 1.3 | 14.5 | 26.6 | 111.9 |
| 0° and below | 36 | 1.9 | 0.9 | 0.1 | 0.0 | 0.0 | 0.0 | 0.0 | 0.0 | 0.0 | 0.0 | 0.0 | 0.7 | 3.6 |
| **AVG. STATION PRESS.(mb)** | 17 | 971.8 | 970.5 | 966.1 | 965.9 | 965.2 | 966.1 | 967.6 | 967.8 | 968.7 | 969.8 | 969.2 | 971.0 | 968.3 |
| **RELATIVE HUMIDITY (%)** | | | | | | | | | | | | | | |
| Hour 00 | 36 | 76 | 75 | 70 | 70 | 76 | 75 | 67 | 68 | 73 | 73 | 75 | 76 | 73 |
| Hour 06 | 36 | 79 | 79 | 77 | 78 | 83 | 83 | 78 | 79 | 82 | 80 | 79 | 80 | 80 |
| Hour 12 (Local Time) | 36 | 63 | 60 | 54 | 52 | 56 | 53 | 48 | 50 | 54 | 53 | 57 | 62 | 55 |
| Hour 18 | 36 | 65 | 60 | 52 | 50 | 54 | 49 | 44 | 45 | 52 | 55 | 62 | 66 | 55 |
| **PRECIPITATION (inches):** | | | | | | | | | | | | | | |
| Water Equivalent | | | | | | | | | | | | | | |
| -Normal | | 0.68 | 0.85 | 2.01 | 2.30 | 3.91 | 4.06 | 3.62 | 2.80 | 3.45 | 2.47 | 1.47 | 0.99 | 28.61 |
| -Maximum Monthly | 36 | 2.73 | 3.33 | 9.17 | 5.57 | 8.85 | 10.46 | 9.22 | 7.91 | 9.46 | 6.13 | 5.88 | 4.71 | 10.46 |
| -Year | | 1973 | 1987 | 1973 | 1976 | 1977 | 1957 | 1962 | 1960 | 1973 | 1959 | 1964 | 1984 | JUN 1957 |
| -Minimum Monthly | 36 | T | 0.02 | 0.01 | 0.22 | 0.52 | 0.94 | 0.05 | 0.31 | 0.03 | T | T | 0.03 | T |
| -Year | | 1986 | 1963 | 1971 | 1963 | 1973 | 1954 | 1975 | 1976 | 1956 | 1958 | 1989 | 1955 | NOV 1989 |
| -Maximum in 24 hrs | 36 | 1.72 | 1.53 | 2.65 | 2.51 | 4.70 | 4.98 | 3.86 | 3.76 | 3.29 | 5.03 | 4.33 | 2.60 | 5.03 |
| -Year | | 1980 | 1973 | 1961 | 1988 | 1963 | 1965 | 1983 | 1987 | 1989 | 1985 | 1964 | 1984 | OCT 1985 |
| Snow,Ice pellets | | | | | | | | | | | | | | |
| -Maximum Monthly | 36 | 19.7 | 16.7 | 16.5 | 4.6 | T | T | 0.0 | 0.0 | 0.0 | 0.1 | 7.1 | 13.8 | 19.7 |
| -Year | | 1987 | 1971 | 1970 | 1979 | 1989 | 1989 | | | | 1960 | 1972 | 1983 | JAN 1987 |
| -Maximum in 24 hrs | 36 | 13.0 | 11.9 | 13.5 | 4.6 | T | T | 0.0 | 0.0 | 0.0 | 0.1 | 6.8 | 9.0 | 13.5 |
| -Year | | 1962 | 1971 | 1970 | 1979 | 1989 | 1989 | | | | 1960 | 1984 | 1983 | MAR 1970 |
| **WIND:** | | | | | | | | | | | | | | |
| Mean Speed (mph) | 36 | 12.2 | 12.7 | 14.2 | 14.1 | 12.5 | 12.1 | 11.2 | 11.1 | 11.6 | 11.9 | 12.2 | 12.1 | 12.3 |
| Prevailing Direction | | | | | | | | | | | | | | |
| through 1963 | | S | N | S | S | S | S | S | S | S | S | S | S | S |
| Fastest Obs. 1 Min. | | | | | | | | | | | | | | |
| -Direction (!!!) | 8 | 35 | 36 | 19 | 31 | 30 | 33 | 30 | 30 | 19 | 19 | 35 | 24 | 31 |
| -Speed (MPH) | 8 | 35 | 37 | 40 | 48 | 46 | 44 | 43 | 43 | 44 | 38 | 36 | 35 | 48 |
| -Year | | 1988 | 1987 | 1986 | 1982 | 1989 | 1987 | 1987 | 1982 | 1984 | 1985 | 1988 | 1988 | APR 1982 |
| Peak Gust | | | | | | | | | | | | | | |
| -Direction (!!!) | 6 | NW | N | S | N | S | NW | NW | NW | N | S | SW | SW | S |
| -Speed (mph) | 6 | 47 | 53 | 54 | 61 | 75 | 63 | 62 | 62 | 59 | 52 | 63 | 52 | 75 |
| -Date | 6 | 1986 | 1987 | 1986 | 1984 | 1988 | 1987 | 1987 | 1985 | 1989 | 1985 | 1988 | 1988 | MAY 1988 |

**See Reference Notes to this table on the following page.**

PRECIPITATION (inches)     WICHITA, KANSAS

**TABLE 2**

| YEAR | JAN | FEB | MAR | APR | MAY | JUNE | JULY | AUG | SEP | OCT | NOV | DEC | ANNUAL |
|---|---|---|---|---|---|---|---|---|---|---|---|---|---|
| 1961 | 0.02 | 1.51 | 4.83 | 2.00 | 4.02 | 2.61 | 6.56 | 3.80 | 5.24 | 4.87 | 2.80 | 1.01 | 39.27 |
| 1962 | 1.07 | 0.47 | 0.26 | 1.02 | 0.99 | 4.80 | 9.22 | 2.95 | 8.23 | 1.32 | 1.62 | 0.60 | 32.55 |
| 1963 | 1.22 | 0.02 | 1.67 | 0.22 | 6.15 | 4.51 | 2.70 | 2.86 | 4.90 | 2.47 | 1.04 | 0.34 | 28.10 |
| 1964 | 0.71 | 0.53 | 0.89 | 2.97 | 5.84 | 3.73 | 2.23 | 6.10 | 2.66 | 1.64 | 5.88 | 1.03 | 34.21 |
| 1965 | 0.56 | 1.39 | 0.48 | 2.63 | 6.26 | 8.00 | 3.62 | 4.91 | 8.44 | 0.32 | 0.11 | 2.25 | 38.97 |
| 1966 | 0.23 | 1.44 | 0.26 | 2.21 | 0.76 | 2.67 | 1.78 | 1.09 | 0.72 | 0.47 | 0.09 | 0.43 | 12.15 |
| 1967 | 0.28 | 0.09 | 0.57 | 1.30 | 1.42 | 5.62 | 4.28 | 1.91 | 3.19 | 2.98 | 0.39 | 1.41 | 23.44 |
| 1968 | 0.14 | 0.20 | 1.36 | 2.16 | 4.37 | 2.38 | 3.65 | 6.41 | 5.91 | 3.06 | 2.47 | 1.31 | 33.42 |
| 1969 | 0.45 | 1.35 | 1.73 | 4.30 | 3.28 | 6.82 | 6.23 | 1.07 | 4.77 | 2.80 | 0.01 | 1.36 | 34.17 |
| 1970 | 0.28 | 0.21 | 2.70 | 4.49 | 1.58 | 6.72 | 0.47 | 2.37 | 4.04 | 1.88 | 0.05 | 0.49 | 25.28 |
| 1971 | 0.98 | 1.70 | 0.01 | 2.35 | 3.02 | 2.70 | 6.65 | 1.49 | 1.73 | 5.54 | 2.49 | 0.95 | 29.61 |
| 1972 | 0.15 | 0.28 | 0.56 | 3.32 | 2.47 | 2.02 | 3.86 | 3.31 | 1.31 | 2.00 | 3.06 | 0.97 | 23.31 |
| 1973 | 2.73 | 1.20 | 9.17 | 3.78 | 0.52 | 1.21 | 6.07 | 0.68 | 9.46 | 3.43 | 0.91 | 2.80 | 41.96 |
| 1974 | 0.56 | 0.25 | 2.36 | 4.29 | 4.65 | 2.79 | 0.09 | 4.11 | 1.08 | 3.43 | 2.69 | 2.22 | 28.53 |
| 1975 | 1.28 | 2.12 | 1.72 | 1.57 | 8.60 | 6.88 | 0.05 | 2.77 | 1.19 | 0.08 | 2.89 | 0.48 | 29.63 |
| 1976 | 0.04 | 0.25 | 1.50 | 5.57 | 2.69 | 3.12 | 6.13 | 0.31 | 2.02 | 1.82 | 0.06 | 0.07 | 23.58 |
| 1977 | 0.54 | 0.08 | 1.42 | 3.32 | 8.85 | 3.15 | 3.98 | 6.31 | 4.35 | 1.19 | 2.38 | 0.19 | 35.76 |
| 1978 | 0.49 | 1.71 | 2.10 | 2.71 | 2.24 | 3.19 | 1.49 | 1.90 | 3.58 | 0.05 | 2.21 | 0.59 | 22.26 |
| 1979 | 1.57 | 0.23 | 4.47 | 1.46 | 3.05 | 6.54 | 2.18 | 0.67 | 1.54 | 2.96 | 2.05 | 1.99 | 28.71 |
| 1980 | 1.82 | 0.81 | 3.99 | 1.07 | 2.66 | 1.34 | 0.47 | 3.76 | 0.67 | 1.25 | 0.54 | 2.11 | 20.49 |
| 1981 | 0.25 | 0.22 | 2.15 | 0.38 | 6.33 | 4.25 | 1.27 | 2.65 | 2.25 | 4.69 | 2.93 | 0.29 | 27.66 |
| 1982 | 1.68 | 0.77 | 2.05 | 0.73 | 7.82 | 8.28 | 0.56 | 1.51 | 1.08 | 0.41 | 0.73 | 1.51 | 27.13 |
| 1983 | 1.66 | 1.23 | 4.26 | 3.80 | 4.08 | 7.38 | 3.86 | 1.39 | 2.53 | 2.97 | 2.39 | 1.13 | 36.68 |
| 1984 | 0.20 | 1.23 | 7.57 | 3.71 | 1.15 | 2.30 | 0.30 | 0.75 | 2.18 | 2.78 | 1.44 | 4.71 | 28.32 |
| 1985 | 0.26 | 2.07 | 1.64 | 2.28 | 2.01 | 4.79 | 3.97 | 2.86 | 5.97 | 5.58 | 1.60 | 0.61 | 33.64 |
| 1986 | T | 1.26 | 1.22 | 1.80 | 2.98 | 5.39 | 3.42 | 6.00 | 3.81 | 3.61 | 0.58 | 1.22 | 31.29 |
| 1987 | 1.40 | 3.33 | 4.13 | 0.61 | 8.01 | 4.50 | 2.14 | 7.69 | 2.10 | 0.90 | 1.50 | 2.25 | 38.56 |
| 1988 | 0.51 | 0.18 | 2.91 | 4.46 | 2.40 | 1.86 | 0.91 | 1.10 | 0.53 | 0.94 | 0.77 | 0.50 | 17.07 |
| 1989 | 0.79 | 0.39 | 2.38 | 0.23 | 4.96 | 7.96 | 4.07 | 5.72 | 7.38 | 0.37 | T | 0.44 | 34.69 |
| 1990 | 1.73 | 2.19 | 2.68 | 0.80 | 1.29 | 1.91 | 1.72 | 2.01 | 1.95 | 0.64 | 2.01 | 0.78 | 19.71 |
| Record Mean | 0.82 | 1.12 | 1.98 | 2.77 | 4.18 | 4.44 | 3.30 | 3.02 | 3.23 | 2.35 | 1.51 | 1.09 | 29.80 |

**TABLE 3**     AVERAGE TEMPERATURE (deg. F)     WICHITA, KANSAS

| YEAR | JAN | FEB | MAR | APR | MAY | JUNE | JULY | AUG | SEP | OCT | NOV | DEC | ANNUAL |
|---|---|---|---|---|---|---|---|---|---|---|---|---|---|
| 1961 | 31.4 | 37.2 | 46.6 | 53.8 | 63.3 | 74.2 | 78.8 | 76.8 | 66.8 | 59.6 | 41.8 | 29.4 | 55.0 |
| 1962 | 25.6 | 37.1 | 43.4 | 55.1 | 75.4 | 75.1 | 80.0 | 80.6 | 68.6 | 62.3 | 45.4 | 34.9 | 56.9 |
| 1963 | 22.2 | 36.9 | 50.0 | 60.5 | 68.3 | 78.8 | 82.6 | 81.2 | 72.5 | 67.7 | 47.3 | 26.6 | 57.9 |
| 1964 | 36.8 | 36.1 | 42.1 | 59.2 | 70.2 | 76.9 | 85.0 | 76.8 | 70.8 | 58.7 | 47.2 | 31.2 | 57.6 |
| 1965 | 35.2 | 34.4 | 36.8 | 60.4 | 68.8 | 76.3 | 81.9 | 78.2 | 68.5 | 60.4 | 50.5 | 41.2 | 57.7 |
| 1966 | 28.3 | 33.6 | 49.1 | 53.5 | 65.7 | 76.2 | 84.9 | 76.1 | 68.6 | 58.0 | 48.3 | 32.7 | 56.2 |
| 1967 | 34.3 | 36.3 | 50.5 | 61.5 | 64.0 | 74.5 | 76.2 | 74.7 | 65.9 | 57.7 | 43.2 | 34.6 | 56.1 |
| 1968 | 32.5 | 33.8 | 48.0 | 55.5 | 61.0 | 76.1 | 80.3 | 77.9 | 67.9 | 59.3 | 41.7 | 30.7 | 55.4 |
| 1969 | 30.1 | 36.1 | 36.1 | 56.4 | 65.2 | 71.0 | 82.9 | 78.9 | 71.9 | 54.6 | 44.5 | 34.6 | 55.2 |
| 1970 | 27.3 | 38.5 | 39.7 | 55.1 | 69.3 | 74.5 | 81.3 | 83.2 | 69.7 | 53.9 | 41.5 | 36.9 | 55.9 |
| 1971 | 28.8 | 28.8 | 44.0 | 57.0 | 63.9 | 79.9 | 78.0 | 76.8 | 70.8 | 60.6 | 43.9 | 35.8 | 55.6 |
| 1972 | 27.0 | 34.8 | 47.9 | 55.3 | 64.1 | 76.7 | 77.1 | 78.4 | 71.0 | 55.6 | 39.8 | 28.5 | 54.7 |
| 1973 | 27.4 | 35.6 | 48.4 | 52.2 | 61.9 | 76.8 | 80.3 | 79.8 | 67.8 | 61.1 | 46.7 | 31.9 | 55.8 |
| 1974 | 24.9 | 38.7 | 47.9 | 56.4 | 68.3 | 72.5 | 84.4 | 76.7 | 64.1 | 60.5 | 44.9 | 35.1 | 56.2 |
| 1975 | 33.4 | 28.5 | 40.4 | 54.7 | 64.0 | 73.6 | 79.2 | 81.4 | 65.8 | 60.3 | 44.8 | 36.0 | 55.2 |
| 1976 | 32.0 | 45.5 | 46.3 | 57.5 | 60.2 | 73.7 | 78.4 | 79.7 | 69.8 | 52.4 | 38.3 | 33.7 | 55.6 |
| 1977 | 24.5 | 41.7 | 50.2 | 59.8 | 69.2 | 78.3 | 83.6 | 77.9 | 73.2 | 56.8 | 46.1 | 35.0 | 58.3 |
| 1978 | 20.5 | 23.8 | 43.6 | 59.0 | 65.0 | 76.8 | 85.1 | 81.2 | 76.3 | 58.6 | 45.0 | 32.0 | 55.6 |
| 1979 | 16.7 | 24.0 | 46.9 | 54.1 | 64.1 | 74.5 | 80.4 | 79.8 | 72.7 | 61.9 | 41.8 | 37.7 | 54.6 |
| 1980 | 31.4 | 28.2 | 41.5 | 54.3 | 63.5 | 79.9 | 90.5 | 85.3 | 75.2 | 58.8 | 46.9 | 36.9 | 57.7 |
| 1981 | 34.1 | 40.1 | 47.6 | 63.7 | 62.6 | 77.9 | 83.6 | 78.1 | 72.0 | 58.5 | 47.0 | 32.9 | 58.0 |
| 1982 | 25.5 | 28.0 | 46.0 | 53.5 | 65.3 | 70.4 | 81.5 | 82.0 | 71.9 | 58.0 | 43.0 | 36.1 | 55.1 |
| 1983 | 31.7 | 35.5 | 43.3 | 48.0 | 60.5 | 71.5 | 81.6 | 85.0 | 72.7 | 58.5 | 45.5 | 16.4 | 54.2 |
| 1984 | 26.7 | 41.4 | 40.7 | 51.8 | 63.6 | 77.7 | 81.6 | 82.8 | 70.3 | 58.3 | 45.5 | 37.2 | 56.5 |
| 1985 | 25.2 | 31.2 | 49.1 | 59.9 | 67.7 | 74.0 | 81.7 | 77.5 | 69.8 | 57.4 | 39.4 | 24.8 | 55.1 |
| 1986 | 38.1 | 37.8 | 51.9 | 58.7 | 66.7 | 78.7 | 83.0 | 75.9 | 73.6 | 57.6 | 39.9 | 35.8 | 58.1 |
| 1987 | 29.3 | 42.3 | 47.0 | 57.4 | 69.7 | 76.4 | 80.1 | 78.7 | 70.4 | 55.7 | 47.7 | 34.9 | 57.5 |
| 1988 | 27.0 | 34.1 | 44.2 | 53.9 | 68.3 | 78.6 | 80.9 | 83.0 | 72.0 | 56.7 | 47.5 | 38.5 | 57.1 |
| 1989 | 38.5 | 27.5 | 47.0 | 59.6 | 66.0 | 72.0 | 79.0 | 77.0 | 65.7 | 60.7 | 45.5 | 25.2 | 55.3 |
| 1990 | 39.5 | 38.8 | 46.9 | 54.3 | 63.7 | 81.7 | 81.7 | 80.8 | 74.3 | 58.4 | 50.4 | 30.2 | 58.4 |
| Record Mean | 31.3 | 35.1 | 44.9 | 56.3 | 65.4 | 75.4 | 80.5 | 79.5 | 71.1 | 59.3 | 45.0 | 34.6 | 56.5 |
| Max | 40.9 | 45.5 | 56.1 | 67.4 | 75.8 | 86.1 | 91.5 | 90.6 | 82.1 | 70.4 | 55.3 | 44.0 | 67.1 |
| Min | 21.6 | 24.7 | 33.7 | 45.2 | 54.9 | 64.7 | 69.5 | 68.3 | 60.0 | 48.2 | 34.8 | 25.2 | 45.9 |

## REFERENCE NOTES FOR TABLES 1, 2, 3 and 6          (WICHITA, KS)

### GENERAL

T - TRACE AMOUNT
BLANK ENTRIES DENOTE MISSING/UNREPORTED DATA.
# INDICATES A STATION OR INSTRUMENT RELOCATION.

### SPECIFIC

#### TABLE 1

(a) - LENGTH OF RECORD IN YEARS. ALTHOUGH INDIVIDUAL MONTHS MAY BE MISSING.
* LESS THAN .05

NORMALS — BASED ON THE 1951-1980 RECORD PERIOD.
EXTREMES — DATES ARE THE MOST RECENT OCCURRENCE.
WIND DIR. — NUMERALS SHOW TENS OF DEGREES CLOCKWISE FROM TRUE NORTH.
"00" INDICATES CALM.
RESULTANT WIND DIRECTIONS ARE GIVEN TO WHOLE DEGREES.

#### TABLE 3

MAX AND MIN ARE LONG-TERM MEAN DAILY MAXIMUM AND MEAN DAILY MINIMUM TEMPERATURES.

### EXCEPTIONS

#### TABLE 1

1. FASTEST MILE WINDS ARE THROUGH 1981.

#### TABLES 2, 3, and 6

RECORD MEANS ARE THROUGH THE CURRENT YEAR, BEGINNING IN     1889 FOR TEMPERATURE
1889 FOR PRECIPITATION
1954 FOR SNOWFALL

## TABLE 4

HEATING DEGREE DAYS Base 65 deg. F    WICHITA, KANSAS

| SEASON | JULY | AUG | SEP | OCT | NOV | DEC | JAN | FEB | MAR | APR | MAY | JUNE | TOTAL |
|---|---|---|---|---|---|---|---|---|---|---|---|---|---|
| 1961-62 | 0 | 2 | 86 | 184 | 688 | 1097 | 1213 | 776 | 665 | 315 | 8 | 4 | 5038 |
| 1962-63 | 0 | 0 | 40 | 172 | 581 | 927 | 1323 | 780 | 463 | 170 | 72 | 0 | 4528 |
| 1963-64 | 0 | 0 | 9 | 50 | 523 | 1184 | 867 | 831 | 702 | 200 | 41 | 10 | 4417 |
| 1964-65 | 0 | 1 | 34 | 200 | 531 | 1038 | 918 | 851 | 868 | 176 | 23 | 0 | 4640 |
| 1965-66 | 0 | 1 | 73 | 179 | 428 | 733 | 1131 | 871 | 490 | 342 | 100 | 2 | 4350 |
| 1966-67 | 2 | 0 | 33 | 247 | 499 | 996 | 945 | 798 | 463 | 160 | 143 | 5 | 4291 |
| 1967-68 | 2 | 1 | 63 | 280 | 645 | 936 | 998 | 899 | 525 | 285 | 153 | 1 | 4788 |
| 1968-69 | 0 | 5 | 22 | 224 | 691 | 1054 | 1076 | 804 | 887 | 254 | 77 | 20 | 5114 |
| 1969-70 | 0 | 0 | 2 | 361 | 610 | 939 | 1163 | 738 | 778 | 312 | 43 | 26 | 4972 |
| 1970-71 | 1 | 0 | 64 | 358 | 696 | 866 | 1118 | 1005 | 643 | 253 | 95 | 0 | 5099 |
| 1971-72 | 4 | 0 | 77 | 165 | 628 | 897 | 1171 | 871 | 524 | 310 | 109 | 0 | 4756 |
| 1972-73 | 2 | 0 | 46 | 319 | 750 | 1123 | 1159 | 816 | 506 | 386 | 125 | 0 | 5232 |
| 1973-74 | 0 | 0 | 58 | 159 | 541 | 1021 | 1237 | 732 | 529 | 263 | 42 | 1 | 4583 |
| 1974-75 | 0 | 0 | 92 | 156 | 596 | 920 | 974 | 1016 | 757 | 333 | 72 | 9 | 4925 |
| 1975-76 | 0 | 0 | 98 | 201 | 596 | 892 | 1015 | 562 | 575 | 238 | 173 | 2 | 4352 |
| 1976-77 | 0 | 0 | 38 | 409 | 794 | 966 | 1253 | 646 | 456 | 170 | 12 | 0 | 4744 |
| 1977-78 | 0 | 0 | 1 | 176 | 558 | 926 | 1375 | 1149 | 663 | 194 | 112 | 6 | 5160 |
| 1978-79 | 0 | 0 | 18 | 210 | 598 | 1016 | 1491 | 1143 | 560 | 333 | 104 | 3 | 5476 |
| 1979-80 | 0 | 0 | 10 | 156 | 690 | 838 | 1038 | 1063 | 723 | 318 | 116 | 0 | 4952 |
| 1980-81 | 0 | 0 | 28 | 239 | 535 | 864 | 954 | 692 | 533 | 104 | 126 | 0 | 4075 |
| 1981-82 | 0 | 0 | 24 | 292 | 537 | 990 | 1214 | 1033 | 583 | 356 | 54 | 17 | 5100 |
| 1982-83 | 0 | 0 | 37 | 239 | 653 | 889 | 1022 | 818 | 664 | 507 | 168 | 20 | 5017 |
| 1983-84 | 0 | 0 | 47 | 221 | 582 | 1504 | 1180 | 680 | 747 | 394 | 95 | 0 | 5450 |
| 1984-85 | 0 | 0 | 103 | 237 | 576 | 856 | 1224 | 938 | 487 | 184 | 33 | 8 | 4646 |
| 1985-86 | 0 | 0 | 111 | 230 | 762 | 1116 | 826 | 755 | 416 | 220 | 41 | 0 | 4477 |
| 1986-87 | 0 | 3 | 11 | 233 | 747 | 899 | 1099 | 631 | 551 | 263 | 14 | 0 | 4451 |
| 1987-88 | 0 | 2 | 7 | 282 | 523 | 924 | 1170 | 891 | 637 | 330 | 33 | 0 | 4799 |
| 1988-89 | 0 | 0 | 16 | 265 | 519 | 813 | 817 | 1044 | 556 | 238 | 90 | 8 | 4366 |
| 1989-90 | 0 | 0 | 105 | 193 | 578 | 1228 | 783 | 728 | 555 | 332 | 112 | 0 | 4614 |
| 1990-91 | 0 | 0 | 18 | 238 | 445 | 1074 | | | | | | | |

## TABLE 5

COOLING DEGREE DAYS Base 65 deg. F    WICHITA, KANSAS

| YEAR | JAN | FEB | MAR | APR | MAY | JUNE | JULY | AUG | SEP | OCT | NOV | DEC | TOTAL |
|---|---|---|---|---|---|---|---|---|---|---|---|---|---|
| 1969 | 0 | 0 | 0 | 1 | 90 | 208 | 563 | 437 | 214 | 45 | 0 | 0 | 1558 |
| 1970 | 0 | 0 | 2 | 24 | 187 | 315 | 513 | 573 | 212 | 22 | 0 | 0 | 1848 |
| 1971 | 0 | 0 | 0 | 19 | 65 | 425 | 414 | 372 | 259 | 34 | 0 | 0 | 1588 |
| 1972 | 0 | 0 | 2 | 26 | 88 | 358 | 385 | 421 | 234 | 34 | 0 | 0 | 1548 |
| 1973 | 0 | 0 | 0 | 7 | 39 | 360 | 482 | 468 | 149 | 47 | 0 | 0 | 1552 |
| 1974 | 0 | 0 | 4 | 12 | 149 | 233 | 608 | 368 | 69 | 23 | 0 | 0 | 1466 |
| 1975 | 0 | 0 | 0 | 32 | 49 | 275 | 450 | 515 | 128 | 63 | 0 | 0 | 1512 |
| 1976 | 0 | 0 | 2 | 19 | 32 | 270 | 420 | 464 | 187 | 23 | 0 | 0 | 1417 |
| 1977 | 0 | 0 | 3 | 19 | 152 | 404 | 581 | 404 | 254 | 24 | 0 | 0 | 1841 |
| 1978 | 0 | 0 | 6 | 20 | 122 | 366 | 631 | 510 | 364 | 23 | 0 | 0 | 2042 |
| 1979 | 0 | 0 | 5 | 14 | 81 | 294 | 488 | 465 | 249 | 67 | 0 | 0 | 1663 |
| 1980 | 0 | 0 | 0 | 3 | 75 | 456 | 796 | 635 | 340 | 52 | 0 | 1 | 2358 |
| 1981 | 0 | 0 | 0 | 72 | 56 | 393 | 412 | 240 | 17 | 0 | 0 | 0 | 1772 |
| 1982 | 0 | 0 | 1 | 16 | 70 | 186 | 516 | 534 | 253 | 29 | 0 | 0 | 1605 |
| 1983 | 0 | 0 | 0 | 2 | 34 | 220 | 521 | 628 | 286 | 28 | 5 | 0 | 1724 |
| 1984 | 0 | 0 | 0 | 6 | 61 | 388 | 520 | 558 | 272 | 35 | 0 | 0 | 1940 |
| 1985 | 0 | 0 | 0 | 36 | 122 | 285 | 523 | 394 | 262 | 1 | 0 | 0 | 1623 |
| 1986 | 0 | 0 | 17 | 40 | 102 | 419 | 563 | 349 | 275 | 10 | 0 | 0 | 1775 |
| 1987 | 0 | 0 | 0 | 42 | 166 | 350 | 473 | 434 | 177 | 3 | 10 | 0 | 1655 |
| 1988 | 0 | 0 | 0 | 3 | 140 | 415 | 497 | 566 | 235 | 15 | 0 | 0 | 1871 |
| 1989 | 0 | 0 | 5 | 81 | 129 | 225 | 442 | 379 | 132 | 70 | 0 | 0 | 1463 |
| 1990 | 0 | 0 | 0 | 17 | 79 | 508 | 525 | 497 | 306 | 41 | 11 | 0 | 1984 |

## TABLE 6

SNOWFALL (inches)    WICHITA, KANSAS

| SEASON | JULY | AUG | SEP | OCT | NOV | DEC | JAN | FEB | MAR | APR | MAY | JUNE | TOTAL |
|---|---|---|---|---|---|---|---|---|---|---|---|---|---|
| 1961-62 | 0.0 | 0.0 | 0.0 | 0.0 | 0.1 | 4.9 | 18.5 | T | T | 0.0 | 0.0 | 0.0 | 23.5 |
| 1962-63 | 0.0 | 0.0 | 0.0 | 0.0 | T | 4.2 | 3.7 | 0.2 | T | 0.0 | 0.0 | 0.0 | 8.1 |
| 1963-64 | 0.0 | 0.0 | 0.0 | 0.0 | 0.0 | 4.7 | 0.2 | 1.5 | T | 0.0 | 0.0 | 0.0 | 6.4 |
| 1964-65 | 0.0 | 0.0 | 0.0 | 0.0 | 0.1 | 5.4 | 3.3 | 2.7 | T | 0.0 | 0.0 | 0.0 | 11.5 |
| 1965-66 | 0.0 | 0.0 | 0.0 | 0.0 | 0.0 | 0.9 | 4.7 | 0.8 | T | 0.0 | 0.0 | 0.0 | 6.4 |
| 1966-67 | 0.0 | 0.0 | 0.0 | 0.0 | T | 5.0 | 2.1 | T | 0.7 | 0.0 | 0.0 | 0.0 | 7.8 |
| 1967-68 | 0.0 | 0.0 | 0.0 | 0.0 | 2.2 | 9.7 | 0.6 | 1.0 | T | 0.0 | 0.0 | 0.0 | 13.5 |
| 1968-69 | 0.0 | 0.0 | 0.0 | 0.0 | 0.3 | 2.8 | T | 8.3 | 5.1 | 0.0 | 0.0 | 0.0 | 16.5 |
| 1969-70 | 0.0 | 0.0 | 0.0 | 0.0 | T | 3.5 | 2.8 | T | 16.5 | 0.1 | 0.0 | 0.0 | 22.9 |
| 1970-71 | 0.0 | 0.0 | 0.0 | T | T | T | T | 16.7 | T | 0.0 | 0.0 | 0.0 | 16.7 |
| 1971-72 | 0.0 | 0.0 | 0.0 | 0.0 | 2.3 | 1.7 | 4.4 | 0.8 | T | 0.0 | 0.0 | 0.0 | 11.6 |
| 1972-73 | 0.0 | 0.0 | 0.0 | 0.0 | 7.1 | 2.7 | 17.7 | 0.2 | T | 2.3 | 0.0 | 0.0 | 30.0 |
| 1973-74 | 0.0 | 0.0 | 0.0 | 0.0 | T | 8.7 | 4.1 | 0.7 | 2.0 | 0.3 | 0.0 | 0.0 | 15.8 |
| 1974-75 | 0.0 | 0.0 | 0.0 | 0.0 | 1.8 | 2.2 | 7.6 | 15.2 | 7.6 | T | 0.0 | 0.0 | 34.4 |
| 1975-76 | 0.0 | 0.0 | 0.0 | 0.0 | 5.5 | 0.6 | 0.6 | 0.9 | T | 0.0 | 0.0 | 0.0 | 7.0 |
| 1976-77 | 0.0 | 0.0 | 0.0 | T | 0.3 | T | 3.6 | T | T | T | 0.0 | 0.0 | 3.9 |
| 1977-78 | 0.0 | 0.0 | 0.0 | 0.0 | T | T | 7.4 | 7.8 | 0.3 | 0.0 | 0.0 | 0.0 | 15.5 |
| 1978-79 | 0.0 | 0.0 | 0.0 | 0.0 | T | 6.7 | 13.9 | 1.9 | 1.6 | 4.6 | 0.0 | 0.0 | 28.7 |
| 1979-80 | 0.0 | 0.0 | 0.0 | 0.0 | T | T | T | 12.3 | 0.4 | 0.0 | 0.0 | 0.0 | 12.7 |
| 1980-81 | 0.0 | 0.0 | 0.0 | T | T | 0.4 | T | 2.5 | 0.2 | 0.0 | 0.0 | 0.0 | 3.1 |
| 1981-82 | 0.0 | 0.0 | 0.0 | 0.0 | T | 1.2 | T | 12.7 | T | 0.0 | 0.0 | 0.0 | 13.9 |
| 1982-83 | 0.0 | 0.0 | 0.0 | 0.0 | 0.0 | 1.4 | 13.0 | 8.9 | 1.5 | 0.7 | 0.0 | 0.0 | 25.5 |
| 1983-84 | 0.0 | 0.0 | 0.0 | 0.0 | 4.1 | 13.8 | 4.3 | T | 6.9 | 0.0 | 0.0 | 0.0 | 29.1 |
| 1984-85 | 0.0 | 0.0 | 0.0 | 0.0 | 6.8 | 7.6 | 3.5 | 3.6 | 0.2 | 0.0 | 0.0 | 0.0 | 21.7 |
| 1985-86 | 0.0 | 0.0 | 0.0 | 0.0 | 1.0 | 3.0 | 0.0 | 7.5 | 0.0 | 0.0 | 0.0 | 0.0 | 11.5 |
| 1986-87 | 0.0 | 0.0 | 0.0 | 0.0 | T | 0.4 | 19.7 | 6.0 | T | 0.0 | 0.0 | 0.0 | 26.1 |
| 1987-88 | 0.0 | 0.0 | 0.0 | 0.0 | 6.2 | 12.6 | 8.5 | 1.1 | 11.0 | 0.0 | 0.0 | 0.0 | 39.4 |
| 1988-89 | 0.0 | 0.0 | 0.0 | 0.0 | 3.0 | 0.7 | 0.3 | 0.8 | T | T | T | T | 4.8 |
| 1989-90 | 0.0 | 0.0 | 0.0 | 0.0 | T | 4.4 | 0.3 | 7.0 | 0.7 | 0.1 | T | T | 12.5 |
| 1990-91 | 0.0 | 0.0 | 0.0 | 0.0 | T | 4.8 | | | | | | | |
| Record Mean | 0.0 | 0.0 | 0.0 | T | 1.2 | 3.4 | 4.7 | 4.4 | 2.6 | 0.3 | T | T | 16.6 |

**See Reference Notes, relative to all above tables, on preceding page.**

Lexington, County Seat of Fayette County, is located in the heart of the famed Kentucky Blue Grass Region. Fayette County is a gently rolling plateau with the elevation varying between 900 and 1,050 feet above sea level. It is noted for its beauty, the fertility of its soil, excellent grass, stock farms, and burley tobacco. The soil has a high phosphorus content and this is very valuable in growing pasture grasses for the grazing of cattle and horses. Lexington has a decided continental climate with a rather large diurnal temperature range. The climate is temperate and well suited to a varied plant and animal life. There are no bodies of water close enough to have any effect on the climate. The closest river is the Kentucky which makes an arc about 15 to 20 miles to the southeast, south, and southwest on its course to the Ohio River. There are numerous small creeks that rise in the county and flow into the river. The reservoirs of the Lexington Water Company are about 5 miles southeast of the city and are the largest bodies of water in the area.

Lexington is subject to rather sudden and large changes in temperature with the spells generally of rather short duration. Temperatures above 100 degrees and below zero degrees are relatively rare. The average temperature for the winter is 35 degrees, spring 62 degrees, fall 50 degrees, and summer 74 degrees.

Precipitation is evenly distributed throughout the winter, spring, and summer, with about 12 inches recorded on the average for each of these seasons. The fall season averages nearly 8 1/2 inches. Snowfall amounts are variable and the ground does not retain snow cover more than a few days at a time.

The months of September and October are the most pleasant of the year. They have the least amount of precipitation, the greatest number of clear days, and generally comfortable temperatures are the rule during these months.

Based on the 1951–1980 period, the average first occurrence of 32 degrees Fahrenheit in the fall is October 25 and the average last occurrence in the spring is April 17.

## TABLE 1    NORMALS, MEANS AND EXTREMES

LEXINGTON, KENTUCKY

LATITUDE: 38°02'N    LONGITUDE: 84°36'W    ELEVATION: FT. GRND 966 BARO 990    TIME ZONE: EASTERN    WBAN: 93820

| | (a) | JAN | FEB | MAR | APR | MAY | JUNE | JULY | AUG | SEP | OCT | NOV | DEC | YEAR |
|---|---|---|---|---|---|---|---|---|---|---|---|---|---|---|
| **TEMPERATURE °F:** | | | | | | | | | | | | | | |
| Normals | | | | | | | | | | | | | | |
| -Daily Maximum | | 39.8 | 43.7 | 53.7 | 65.8 | 74.9 | 82.6 | 85.9 | 85.0 | 79.3 | 67.6 | 54.1 | 44.4 | 64.7 |
| -Daily Minimum | | 23.1 | 25.4 | 34.1 | 44.3 | 53.6 | 61.8 | 65.9 | 64.8 | 58.1 | 45.9 | 35.7 | 27.8 | 45.0 |
| -Monthly | | 31.5 | 34.6 | 43.9 | 55.1 | 64.2 | 72.2 | 76.0 | 74.9 | 68.7 | 56.8 | 44.9 | 36.1 | 54.9 |
| Extremes | | | | | | | | | | | | | | |
| -Record Highest | 45 | 76 | 76 | 83 | 88 | 92 | 101 | 103 | 103 | 103 | 91 | 83 | 75 | 103 |
| -Year | | 1950 | 1945 | 1945 | 1962 | 1987 | 1988 | 1988 | 1988 | 1983 | 1954 | 1959 | 1982 | JUL 1988 |
| -Record Lowest | 45 | -21 | -15 | -2 | 18 | 26 | 39 | 47 | 42 | 35 | 20 | -3 | -19 | -21 |
| -Year | | 1963 | 1951 | 1960 | 1982 | 1966 | 1966 | 1972 | 1965 | 1965 | 1976 | 1950 | 1989 | JAN 1963 |
| **NORMAL DEGREE DAYS:** | | | | | | | | | | | | | | |
| Heating (base 65°F) | | 1039 | 851 | 661 | 306 | 121 | 10 | 0 | 0 | 47 | 280 | 603 | 896 | 4814 |
| Cooling (base 65°F) | | 0 | 0 | 7 | 9 | 96 | 226 | 341 | 307 | 158 | 26 | 0 | 0 | 1170 |
| **% OF POSSIBLE SUNSHINE** | | | | | | | | | | | | | | |
| **MEAN SKY COVER (tenths)** | | | | | | | | | | | | | | |
| Sunrise - Sunset | 45 | 7.3 | 7.1 | 7.1 | 6.6 | 6.3 | 6.0 | 5.8 | 5.5 | 5.4 | 5.3 | 6.7 | 7.2 | 6.3 |
| **MEAN NUMBER OF DAYS:** | | | | | | | | | | | | | | |
| Sunrise to Sunset | | | | | | | | | | | | | | |
| -Clear | 45 | 5.8 | 5.9 | 5.6 | 6.4 | 7.3 | 7.3 | 7.9 | 9.5 | 10.5 | 11.8 | 7.0 | 5.9 | 90.9 |
| -Partly Cloudy | 45 | 5.8 | 5.6 | 7.6 | 8.5 | 10.0 | 11.2 | 12.3 | 12.0 | 8.5 | 7.2 | 6.5 | 5.9 | 101.1 |
| -Cloudy | 45 | 19.4 | 16.7 | 17.8 | 15.2 | 13.7 | 11.4 | 10.8 | 9.6 | 11.0 | 12.0 | 16.5 | 19.2 | 173.3 |
| Precipitation | | | | | | | | | | | | | | |
| .01 inches or more | 45 | 12.3 | 11.2 | 12.8 | 12.2 | 11.7 | 10.5 | 11.2 | 9.1 | 8.0 | 8.1 | 10.8 | 11.5 | 129.5 |
| Snow,Ice pellets | | | | | | | | | | | | | | |
| 1.0 inches or more | 45 | 1.8 | 1.5 | 0.7 | 0.1 | 0.0 | 0.0 | 0.0 | 0.0 | 0.0 | 0.0 | 0.4 | 0.8 | 5.3 |
| Thunderstorms | 45 | 0.8 | 0.9 | 3.0 | 4.0 | 6.4 | 8.0 | 9.4 | 6.7 | 3.2 | 1.4 | 1.0 | 0.4 | 45.3 |
| Heavy Fog Visibility | | | | | | | | | | | | | | |
| 1/4 mile or less | 45 | 2.5 | 2.0 | 1.4 | 0.7 | 1.0 | 1.0 | 1.4 | 1.9 | 2.2 | 1.8 | 1.4 | 2.0 | 19.3 |
| Temperature °F | | | | | | | | | | | | | | |
| -Maximum | | | | | | | | | | | | | | |
| 90° and above | 26 | 0.0 | 0.0 | 0.0 | 0.0 | 0.3 | 3.6 | 7.2 | 6.1 | 1.7 | 0.0 | 0.0 | 0.0 | 18.9 |
| 32° and below | 26 | 10.1 | 6.2 | 0.9 | 0.0 | 0.0 | 0.0 | 0.0 | 0.0 | 0.0 | 0.0 | 0.5 | 4.8 | 22.6 |
| -Minimum | | | | | | | | | | | | | | |
| 32° and below | 26 | 24.5 | 20.7 | 13.7 | 3.4 | 0.1 | 0.0 | 0.0 | 0.0 | 0.0 | 2.5 | 10.9 | 20.4 | 96.2 |
| 0° and below | 26 | 1.8 | 0.8 | 0.1 | 0.0 | 0.0 | 0.0 | 0.0 | 0.0 | 0.0 | 0.0 | 0.0 | 0.5 | 3.2 |
| **AVG. STATION PRESS.(mb)** | 17 | 983.7 | 982.9 | 980.7 | 980.0 | 979.9 | 980.8 | 981.9 | 982.5 | 983.1 | 984.0 | 983.2 | 983.7 | 982.2 |
| **RELATIVE HUMIDITY (%)** | | | | | | | | | | | | | | |
| Hour 01 | 25 | 76 | 75 | 71 | 69 | 76 | 80 | 82 | 83 | 82 | 77 | 76 | 77 | 77 |
| Hour 07 | 26 | 79 | 79 | 76 | 75 | 80 | 82 | 85 | 87 | 88 | 84 | 81 | 80 | 81 |
| Hour 13 (Local Time) | 26 | 68 | 64 | 58 | 54 | 56 | 56 | 58 | 58 | 58 | 56 | 63 | 68 | 60 |
| Hour 19 | 26 | 70 | 66 | 58 | 55 | 59 | 60 | 63 | 64 | 66 | 64 | 68 | 71 | 64 |
| **PRECIPITATION (inches):** | | | | | | | | | | | | | | |
| Water Equivalent | | | | | | | | | | | | | | |
| -Normal | | 3.57 | 3.26 | 4.83 | 4.01 | 4.23 | 4.25 | 4.95 | 3.96 | 3.28 | 2.26 | 3.30 | 3.78 | 45.68 |
| -Maximum Monthly | 45 | 16.65 | 10.12 | 10.38 | 9.30 | 10.84 | 11.69 | 10.64 | 11.18 | 9.69 | 6.13 | 6.87 | 9.97 | 16.65 |
| -Year | | 1950 | 1989 | 1975 | 1970 | 1983 | 1960 | 1958 | 1974 | 1979 | 1983 | 1951 | 1978 | JAN 1950 |
| -Minimum Monthly | 45 | 0.37 | 0.67 | 0.99 | 0.79 | 1.20 | 0.61 | 1.83 | 0.56 | 0.24 | 0.33 | 0.45 | 0.61 | 0.24 |
| -Year | | 1981 | 1978 | 1966 | 1946 | 1965 | 1988 | 1951 | 1984 | 1959 | 1963 | 1976 | 1965 | SEP 1959 |
| -Maximum in 24 hrs | 45 | 2.98 | 3.79 | 3.85 | 4.39 | 3.24 | 5.88 | 4.73 | 3.56 | 4.35 | 3.21 | 2.71 | 3.77 | 5.88 |
| -Year | | 1951 | 1989 | 1952 | 1948 | 1983 | 1960 | 1978 | 1968 | 1979 | 1962 | 1988 | 1978 | JUN 1960 |
| Snow,Ice pellets | | | | | | | | | | | | | | |
| -Maximum Monthly | 45 | 21.9 | 16.4 | 17.7 | 5.9 | T | 0.0 | T | T | 0.0 | 0.2 | 9.7 | 10.7 | 21.9 |
| -Year | | 1978 | 1960 | 1960 | 1987 | 1989 | | 1989 | 1989 | | 1972 | 1950 | 1967 | JAN 1978 |
| -Maximum in 24 hrs | 45 | 9.4 | 7.3 | 9.5 | 4.9 | T | 0.0 | T | T | 0.0 | 0.2 | 7.5 | 7.8 | 9.5 |
| -Year | | 1966 | 1971 | 1947 | 1987 | 1989 | | 1989 | 1989 | | 1972 | 1966 | 1967 | MAR 1947 |
| **WIND:** | | | | | | | | | | | | | | |
| Mean Speed (mph) | 42 | 10.9 | 10.9 | 11.3 | 10.7 | 8.8 | 8.0 | 7.3 | 6.9 | 7.6 | 8.3 | 10.1 | 10.7 | 9.3 |
| Prevailing Direction | | | | | | | | | | | | | | |
| through 1963 | | S | SSW | SSW | SSW | S | S | SSW | S | S | S | S | S | S |
| Fastest Obs. 1 Min. | | | | | | | | | | | | | | |
| -Direction (!!!) | 28 | 27 | 32 | 27 | 32 | 22 | 22 | 29 | 22 | 32 | 26 | 15 | 19 | 32 |
| -Speed (MPH) | 28 | 41 | 46 | 36 | 46 | 35 | 35 | 37 | 39 | 32 | 32 | 39 | 37 | 46 |
| -Year | | 1978 | 1962 | 1962 | 1963 | 1965 | 1968 | 1966 | 1964 | 1980 | 1965 | 1983 | 1971 | APR 1963 |
| Peak Gust | | | | | | | | | | | | | | |
| -Direction (!!!) | 6 | SW | W | E | S | W | N | W | NW | NW | SW | W | SW | W |
| -Speed (mph) | 6 | 53 | 49 | 47 | 54 | 41 | 45 | 56 | 51 | 40 | 40 | 43 | 54 | 56 |
| -Date | | 1985 | 1984 | 1986 | 1986 | 1985 | 1985 | 1987 | 1988 | 1989 | 1984 | 1988 | 1985 | JUL 1987 |

**See Reference Notes to this table on the following page.**

PRECIPITATION (inches)    LEXINGTON, KENTUCKY

**TABLE 2**

| YEAR | JAN | FEB | MAR | APR | MAY | JUNE | JULY | AUG | SEP | OCT | NOV | DEC | ANNUAL |
|------|------|------|------|------|------|------|------|------|------|------|------|------|--------|
| 1961 | 1.71 | 3.89 | 6.18 | 6.04 | 6.14 | 5.12 | 5.98 | 2.62 | 1.50 | 0.88 | 3.04 | 3.89 | 46.99 |
| 1962 | 4.29 | 7.24 | 5.16 | 2.61 | 5.68 | 4.68 | 4.24 | 2.71 | 2.66 | 4.46 | 3.92 | 2.36 | 50.01 |
| 1963 | 1.47 | 1.81 | 6.82 | 1.61 | 3.48 | 3.27 | 7.18 | 4.14 | 0.37 | 0.33 | 1.81 | 0.81 | 33.10 |
| 1964 | 2.83 | 2.52 | 10.06 | 2.86 | 1.68 | 3.55 | 3.99 | 1.96 | 4.91 | 0.57 | 2.37 | 6.18 | 43.48 |
| 1965 | 2.83 | 2.92 | 5.45 | 3.24 | 1.20 | 3.28 | 3.64 | 1.92 | 3.55 | 2.44 | 1.02 | 0.61 | 32.10 |
| 1966 | 3.99 | 3.64 | 0.99 | 7.16 | 4.85 | 1.36 | 5.74 | 4.55 | 4.03 | 1.44 | 4.01 | 4.60 | 46.36 |
| 1967 | 1.35 | 2.29 | 6.03 | 3.61 | 6.94 | 2.65 | 5.87 | 3.63 | 2.97 | 2.11 | 4.15 | 3.99 | 45.59 |
| 1968 | 1.44 | 0.71 | 6.76 | 3.23 | 6.87 | 2.83 | 4.54 | 5.27 | 2.98 | 2.57 | 3.23 | 2.89 | 43.32 |
| 1969 | 4.26 | 1.60 | 1.50 | 3.83 | 3.78 | 4.61 | 4.37 | 5.96 | 0.49 | 1.53 | 3.42 | 4.15 | 39.50 |
| 1970 | 0.95 | 3.60 | 4.72 | 9.30 | 3.18 | 3.81 | 3.39 | 2.61 | 5.71 | 2.37 | 2.35 | 5.51 | 47.50 |
| 1971 | 3.29 | 4.72 | 2.02 | 2.10 | 6.14 | 7.84 | 7.64 | 0.88 | 3.51 | 0.52 | 1.71 | 4.30 | 44.67 |
| 1972 | 4.10 | 5.60 | 4.04 | 8.75 | 3.84 | 3.61 | 5.58 | 3.95 | 4.30 | 2.71 | 4.21 | 6.92 | 57.61 |
| 1973 | 1.53 | 1.58 | 5.08 | 5.67 | 8.22 | 6.06 | 5.15 | 3.58 | 1.40 | 2.65 | 6.58 | 3.42 | 50.92 |
| 1974 | 6.39 | 2.24 | 5.89 | 3.33 | 5.52 | 7.21 | 4.82 | 11.18 | 4.18 | 1.53 | 4.08 | 3.72 | 60.09 |
| 1975 | 3.66 | 5.70 | 10.38 | 6.17 | 2.69 | 2.23 | 5.60 | 3.96 | 6.46 | 5.09 | 2.93 | 4.24 | 59.11 |
| 1976 | 3.59 | 4.67 | 3.72 | 1.24 | 3.16 | 3.34 | 6.74 | 1.26 | 4.23 | 3.86 | 0.45 | 1.22 | 37.48 |
| 1977 | 2.30 | 1.03 | 4.21 | 3.42 | 1.51 | 4.80 | 4.59 | 4.83 | 2.71 | 3.77 | 3.95 | 3.04 | 40.16 |
| 1978 | 6.38 | 0.67 | 2.87 | 3.15 | 5.74 | 1.94 | 7.60 | 10.00 | 3.10 | 3.20 | 3.11 | 9.97 | 57.73 |
| 1979 | 4.07 | 2.92 | 3.22 | 4.92 | 4.17 | 2.80 | 4.72 | 6.20 | 9.69 | 2.96 | 4.52 | 3.81 | 54.00 |
| 1980 | 1.63 | 1.17 | 6.04 | 2.82 | 2.27 | 1.88 | 5.55 | 5.10 | 2.47 | 2.07 | 2.02 | 1.67 | 34.69 |
| 1981 | 0.37 | 4.76 | 1.76 | 4.88 | 5.10 | 2.29 | 3.25 | 2.72 | 1.97 | 2.44 | 1.99 | 3.10 | 36.65 |
| 1982 | 5.48 | 2.16 | 3.89 | 2.19 | 2.51 | 3.95 | 3.82 | 4.01 | 1.21 | 1.56 | 3.45 | 4.53 | 38.76 |
| 1983 | 1.29 | 1.61 | 1.48 | 5.18 | 10.84 | 2.18 | 2.41 | 1.26 | 1.33 | 6.13 | 3.59 | 3.46 | 40.76 |
| 1984 | 1.64 | 3.31 | 4.09 | 5.02 | 5.34 | 2.20 | 4.80 | 0.56 | 1.36 | 3.87 | 5.19 | 4.89 | 42.27 |
| 1985 | 1.91 | 1.11 | 3.69 | 2.34 | 4.34 | 4.98 | 3.37 | 3.76 | 1.93 | 4.23 | 4.96 | 1.13 | 37.75 |
| 1986 | 0.53 | 2.48 | 2.43 | 1.65 | 3.24 | 1.29 | 5.64 | 2.67 | 3.08 | 2.06 | 6.49 | 3.30 | 34.86 |
| 1987 | 1.30 | 3.62 | 3.13 | 2.23 | 1.80 | 6.59 | 3.48 | 4.18 | 0.91 | 0.55 | 2.72 | 6.17 | 36.68 |
| 1988 | 2.94 | 3.06 | 2.34 | 2.93 | 3.02 | 0.61 | 3.51 | 4.18 | 5.96 | 1.34 | 5.39 | 3.62 | 38.90 |
| 1989 | 3.99 | 10.12 | 6.08 | 2.60 | 5.39 | 4.26 | 4.20 | 3.98 | 4.98 | 3.38 | 2.38 | 1.80 | 53.16 |
| 1990 | 4.17 | 3.43 | 1.89 | 2.37 | 5.41 | 4.59 | 6.45 | 4.36 | 2.12 | 4.49 | 2.69 | 10.17 | 52.14 |
| Record Mean | 3.97 | 3.24 | 4.43 | 3.65 | 3.91 | 4.06 | 4.49 | 3.52 | 2.89 | 2.44 | 3.26 | 3.71 | 43.57 |

**TABLE 3**   AVERAGE TEMPERATURE (deg. F)    LEXINGTON, KENTUCKY

| YEAR | JAN | FEB | MAR | APR | MAY | JUNE | JULY | AUG | SEP | OCT | NOV | DEC | ANNUAL |
|------|------|------|------|------|------|------|------|------|------|------|------|------|--------|
| 1961 | 27.8 | 40.7 | 47.0 | 48.7 | 59.3 | 70.1 | 74.1 | 71.9 | 58.1 | 45.3 | 35.5 | 54.5 |  |
| 1962 | 29.9 | 38.8 | 41.7 | 52.3 | 71.6 | 72.9 | 75.4 | 75.6 | 65.0 | 58.8 | 44.1 | 30.8 | 54.4 |
| #1963 | 26.6 | 28.6 | 48.9 | 57.3 | 62.8 | 72.0 | 73.6 | 72.5 | 66.6 | 63.9 | 46.8 | 25.5 | 53.8 |
| 1964 | 35.0 | 32.0 | 45.3 | 58.3 | 66.9 | 74.3 | 75.2 | 75.0 | 68.2 | 52.7 | 48.0 | 37.4 | 55.7 |
| 1965 | 32.2 | 34.3 | 37.9 | 55.9 | 66.8 | 71.3 | 73.7 | 74.5 | 58.8 | 53.9 | 46.2 | 39.6 | 54.8 |
| 1966 | 25.3 | 33.3 | 44.6 | 52.6 | 60.5 | 71.6 | 77.4 | 72.6 | 65.3 | 54.2 | 45.7 | 35.5 | 53.2 |
| 1967 | 37.3 | 30.2 | 50.0 | 58.8 | 62.0 | 72.1 | 72.5 | 70.6 | 64.9 | 56.1 | 40.7 | 39.0 | 54.5 |
| 1968 | 29.6 | 28.0 | 46.0 | 55.1 | 62.1 | 72.0 | 75.9 | 75.5 | 67.8 | 56.6 | 46.4 | 34.6 | 54.1 |
| 1969 | 32.1 | 36.2 | 38.9 | 56.3 | 65.5 | 72.8 | 77.8 | 74.7 | 67.8 | 57.9 | 42.8 | 32.7 | 54.6 |
| 1970 | 25.8 | 32.4 | 40.5 | 57.2 | 66.5 | 71.3 | 74.1 | 74.6 | 72.7 | 57.7 | 43.6 | 38.3 | 54.5 |
| 1971 | 29.7 | 34.8 | 40.3 | 52.0 | 59.2 | 73.7 | 73.9 | 73.9 | 72.5 | 64.7 | 47.2 | 45.7 | 55.6 |
| 1972 | 35.4 | 33.2 | 42.2 | 53.7 | 63.2 | 67.6 | 73.8 | 72.9 | 69.8 | 53.0 | 44.5 | 40.9 | 54.2 |
| 1973 | 35.1 | 35.2 | 53.8 | 52.9 | 60.1 | 73.6 | 75.8 | 74.9 | 72.2 | 60.9 | 48.5 | 36.4 | 56.6 |
| 1974 | 40.7 | 37.4 | 48.5 | 55.8 | 63.6 | 67.2 | 74.4 | 73.3 | 62.6 | 54.3 | 45.7 | 37.8 | 55.1 |
| 1975 | 37.3 | 39.5 | 41.4 | 52.2 | 67.4 | 73.5 | 76.4 | 77.5 | 63.4 | 57.7 | 45.8 | 35.8 | 55.9 |
| 1976 | 28.4 | 43.9 | 50.0 | 54.5 | 60.6 | 71.1 | 73.0 | 71.2 | 64.1 | 49.7 | 37.1 | 30.9 | 52.9 |
| 1977 | 17.8 | 34.9 | 50.8 | 59.6 | 69.8 | 72.3 | 78.4 | 75.7 | 72.2 | 56.1 | 49.0 | 33.4 | 55.8 |
| 1978 | 21.6 | 21.3 | 40.4 | 57.0 | 61.1 | 73.1 | 76.0 | 74.1 | 70.9 | 53.7 | 48.4 | 37.9 | 53.0 |
| 1979 | 23.6 | 26.9 | 48.0 | 53.8 | 63.1 | 70.9 | 74.0 | 74.0 | 66.9 | 55.6 | 45.7 | 37.9 | 53.4 |
| 1980 | 32.4 | 28.3 | 41.5 | 52.5 | 64.8 | 71.2 | 78.8 | 78.2 | 70.6 | 53.7 | 43.6 | 36.0 | 54.3 |
| 1981 | 27.5 | 37.0 | 42.6 | 59.6 | 60.4 | 73.8 | 75.8 | 73.4 | 65.8 | 55.6 | 45.9 | 33.0 | 54.2 |
| 1982 | 28.2 | 34.9 | 47.1 | 50.6 | 69.8 | 68.5 | 77.1 | 72.9 | 65.6 | 58.3 | 48.4 | 44.2 | 55.5 |
| 1983 | 33.8 | 37.2 | 46.3 | 50.8 | 60.7 | 72.8 | 79.8 | 80.5 | 70.2 | 59.0 | 46.5 | 28.4 | 55.5 |
| 1984 | 27.6 | 41.2 | 39.7 | 53.1 | 60.6 | 76.0 | 72.9 | 74.9 | 66.5 | 63.5 | 41.8 | 45.4 | 55.3 |
| 1985 | 23.8 | 30.5 | 48.5 | 58.5 | 64.7 | 70.3 | 75.1 | 72.8 | 67.6 | 60.5 | 53.0 | 29.6 | 54.6 |
| 1986 | 33.2 | 38.6 | 46.8 | 57.3 | 65.5 | 74.2 | 78.6 | 72.9 | 71.0 | 58.0 | 44.9 | 35.7 | 56.4 |
| 1987 | 31.9 | 38.0 | 46.8 | 53.7 | 70.3 | 75.0 | 77.1 | 77.5 | 70.0 | 52.0 | 50.0 | 38.9 | 56.8 |
| 1988 | 29.8 | 33.7 | 44.8 | 54.2 | 64.5 | 74.3 | 79.1 | 77.9 | 67.8 | 49.6 | 46.1 | 36.5 | 54.9 |
| 1989 | 40.5 | 33.1 | 47.3 | 54.2 | 61.6 | 71.6 | 76.5 | 77.1 | 67.6 | 57.0 | 45.0 | 23.0 | 54.2 |
| 1990 | 41.6 | 43.1 | 48.9 | 53.2 | 61.6 | 72.2 | 75.3 | 73.8 | 68.5 | 56.4 | 49.9 | 40.4 | 57.1 |
| Record Mean | 33.0 | 35.0 | 44.2 | 54.3 | 64.1 | 72.7 | 76.2 | 74.8 | 68.9 | 57.3 | 45.0 | 36.0 | 55.1 |
| Max | 41.1 | 43.7 | 53.7 | 64.4 | 74.2 | 82.6 | 85.9 | 84.7 | 79.2 | 67.5 | 53.8 | 43.8 | 64.5 |
| Min | 25.0 | 26.4 | 34.6 | 44.1 | 53.9 | 62.7 | 66.4 | 65.0 | 58.7 | 47.0 | 36.2 | 28.1 | 45.7 |

## REFERENCE NOTES FOR TABLES 1, 2, 3 and 6     (LEXINGTON, KY)

### GENERAL

T - TRACE AMOUNT
BLANK ENTRIES DENOTE MISSING/UNREPORTED DATA.
# INDICATES A STATION OR INSTRUMENT RELOCATION.

### SPECIFIC

#### TABLE 1

(a) - LENGTH OF RECORD IN YEARS. ALTHOUGH INDIVIDUAL MONTHS MAY BE MISSING.

* LESS THAN .05

NORMALS — BASED ON THE 1951-1980 RECORD PERIOD.
EXTREMES — DATES ARE THE MOST RECENT OCCURRENCE.
WIND DIR. — NUMERALS SHOW TENS OF DEGREES
CLOCKWISE FROM TRUE NORTH.
"00" INDICATES CALM.
RESULTANT WIND DIRECTIONS ARE GIVEN TO WHOLE DEGREES.

#### TABLE 3

MAX AND MIN ARE LONG-TERM MEAN DAILY MAXIMUM AND MEAN DAILY MINIMUM TEMPERATURES.

### EXCEPTIONS

#### TABLES 2, 3, and 6

RECORD MEANS ARE THROUGH THE CURRENT YEAR, BEGINNING IN      1871 FOR TEMPERATURE
1871 FOR PRECIPITATION
1945 FOR SNOWFALL

HEATING DEGREE DAYS Base 65 deg. F LEXINGTON, KENTUCKY

**TABLE 4**

| SEASON | JULY | AUG | SEP | OCT | NOV | DEC | JAN | FEB | MAR | APR | MAY | JUNE | TOTAL |
|---|---|---|---|---|---|---|---|---|---|---|---|---|---|
| 1961-62 | 0 | 0 | 32 | 226 | 588 | 907 | 1081 | 726 | 718 | 411 | 21 | 3 | 4713 |
| 1962-63 | 0 | 0 | 94 | 243 | 621 | 1054 | 1183 | 1014 | 495 | 268 | 126 | 2 | 5100 |
| #1963-64 | 0 | 1 | 55 | 84 | 540 | 1217 | 924 | 952 | 606 | 222 | 55 | 16 | 4672 |
| 1964-65 | 0 | 11 | 61 | 375 | 502 | 850 | 1010 | 851 | 834 | 277 | 26 | 8 | 4805 |
| 1965-66 | 0 | 9 | 52 | 346 | 558 | 777 | 1225 | 883 | 631 | 373 | 167 | 21 | 5042 |
| 1966-67 | 0 | 3 | 62 | 340 | 570 | 908 | 851 | 967 | 468 | 223 | 138 | 23 | 4553 |
| 1967-68 | 1 | 4 | 83 | 289 | 722 | 800 | 1090 | 1065 | 581 | 298 | 124 | 8 | 5065 |
| 1968-69 | 0 | 5 | 20 | 296 | 552 | 938 | 1011 | 799 | 800 | 261 | 77 | 17 | 4776 |
| 1969-70 | 0 | 0 | 44 | 274 | 657 | 996 | 1209 | 908 | 750 | 251 | 84 | 1 | 5174 |
| 1970-71 | 6 | 0 | 31 | 229 | 637 | 821 | 1087 | 838 | 759 | 382 | 198 | 0 | 4988 |
| 1971-72 | 0 | 0 | 8 | 69 | 536 | 591 | 909 | 917 | 700 | 343 | 96 | 47 | 4216 |
| 1972-73 | 10 | 1 | 20 | 366 | 612 | 739 | 920 | 827 | 353 | 371 | 167 | 0 | 4386 |
| 1973-74 | 0 | 1 | 21 | 172 | 490 | 880 | 744 | 767 | 514 | 289 | 128 | 37 | 4043 |
| 1974-75 | 0 | 0 | 125 | 338 | 578 | 836 | 852 | 705 | 726 | 387 | 51 | 4 | 4602 |
| 1975-76 | 0 | 0 | 128 | 249 | 488 | 895 | 1130 | 606 | 608 | 339 | 158 | 2 | 4463 |
| 1976-77 | 1 | 4 | 64 | 474 | 829 | 1050 | 1457 | 836 | 444 | 208 | 52 | 19 | 5438 |
| 1977-78 | 0 | 0 | 6 | 277 | 498 | 972 | 1338 | 1219 | 755 | 254 | 179 | 6 | 5504 |
| 1978-79 | 0 | 0 | 20 | 348 | 492 | 834 | 1277 | 1061 | 522 | 337 | 110 | 15 | 5016 |
| 1979-80 | 0 | 5 | 40 | 307 | 574 | 833 | 1005 | 1057 | 721 | 371 | 88 | 17 | 5018 |
| 1980-81 | 0 | 0 | 23 | 358 | 633 | 892 | 1156 | 777 | 687 | 182 | 180 | 0 | 4888 |
| 1981-82 | 0 | 0 | 77 | 286 | 568 | 985 | 1134 | 840 | 549 | 429 | 14 | 9 | 4891 |
| 1982-83 | 0 | 1 | 75 | 259 | 500 | 646 | 961 | 772 | 580 | 422 | 151 | 7 | 4374 |
| 1983-84 | 0 | 0 | 59 | 201 | 550 | 1128 | 1152 | 685 | 778 | 370 | 178 | 3 | 5104 |
| 1984-85 | 2 | 0 | 89 | 84 | 689 | 601 | 1275 | 959 | 510 | 228 | 66 | 23 | 4526 |
| 1985-86 | 0 | 0 | 72 | 179 | 360 | 1092 | 978 | 735 | 561 | 259 | 94 | 2 | 4332 |
| 1986-87 | 0 | 15 | 14 | 250 | 595 | 903 | 1016 | 749 | 559 | 342 | 39 | 0 | 4482 |
| 1987-88 | 0 | 0 | 17 | 399 | 447 | 804 | 1085 | 901 | 620 | 328 | 90 | 18 | 4709 |
| 1988-89 | 0 | 3 | 30 | 474 | 560 | 877 | 750 | 887 | 548 | 351 | 196 | 8 | 4684 |
| 1989-90 | 0 | 6 | 61 | 267 | 592 | 1297 | 720 | 608 | 505 | 378 | 128 | 17 | 4579 |
| 1990-91 | 0 | 3 | 57 | 288 | 453 | 757 | | | | | | | |

**TABLE 5** COOLING DEGREE DAYS Base 65 deg. F LEXINGTON, KENTUCKY

| YEAR | JAN | FEB | MAR | APR | MAY | JUNE | JULY | AUG | SEP | OCT | NOV | DEC | TOTAL |
|---|---|---|---|---|---|---|---|---|---|---|---|---|---|
| 1969 | 0 | 0 | 0 | 7 | 97 | 260 | 404 | 309 | 134 | 57 | 0 | 0 | 1268 |
| 1970 | 0 | 0 | 0 | 26 | 137 | 199 | 295 | 306 | 266 | 11 | 0 | 0 | 1240 |
| 1971 | 0 | 0 | 0 | 0 | 25 | 266 | 281 | 285 | 239 | 65 | 10 | 0 | 1171 |
| 1972 | 0 | 0 | 0 | 11 | 47 | 130 | 287 | 250 | 171 | 0 | 4 | 0 | 900 |
| 1973 | 0 | 0 | 12 | 18 | 21 | 266 | 342 | 314 | 245 | 51 | 0 | 0 | 1269 |
| 1974 | 0 | 0 | 10 | 21 | 94 | 108 | 296 | 264 | 60 | 11 | 4 | 0 | 868 |
| 1975 | 0 | 0 | 0 | 11 | 130 | 267 | 357 | 394 | 86 | 18 | 0 | 0 | 1263 |
| 1976 | 0 | 0 | 9 | 30 | 26 | 193 | 257 | 205 | 46 | 4 | 0 | 0 | 770 |
| 1977 | 0 | 0 | 11 | 52 | 206 | 241 | 422 | 337 | 232 | 8 | 23 | 0 | 1532 |
| 1978 | 0 | 0 | 0 | 19 | 69 | 257 | 349 | 290 | 202 | 4 | 0 | 0 | 1190 |
| 1979 | 0 | 0 | 2 | 8 | 57 | 199 | 287 | 292 | 102 | 21 | 0 | 0 | 968 |
| 1980 | 0 | 0 | 0 | 4 | 87 | 210 | 438 | 415 | 199 | 17 | 0 | 0 | 1370 |
| 1981 | 0 | 0 | 1 | 29 | 43 | 270 | 341 | 267 | 109 | 2 | 0 | 0 | 1062 |
| 1982 | 0 | 0 | 0 | 4 | 171 | 121 | 383 | 252 | 101 | 62 | 9 | 7 | 1110 |
| 1983 | 0 | 0 | 4 | 3 | 27 | 248 | 465 | 487 | 219 | 21 | 0 | 0 | 1474 |
| 1984 | 0 | 0 | 0 | 17 | 50 | 340 | 254 | 312 | 141 | 44 | 1 | 0 | 1159 |
| 1985 | 0 | 0 | 5 | 40 | 67 | 189 | 317 | 245 | 155 | 49 | 4 | 0 | 1071 |
| 1986 | 0 | 0 | 4 | 34 | 115 | 285 | 427 | 269 | 197 | 42 | 0 | 0 | 1373 |
| 1987 | 0 | 0 | 0 | 10 | 212 | 304 | 383 | 395 | 173 | 2 | 5 | 0 | 1484 |
| 1988 | 0 | 0 | 1 | 8 | 81 | 306 | 442 | 407 | 120 | 5 | 0 | 0 | 1370 |
| 1989 | 0 | 0 | 8 | 34 | 66 | 214 | 362 | 296 | 146 | 27 | 0 | 0 | 1153 |
| 1990 | 0 | 0 | 13 | 29 | 32 | 239 | 326 | 285 | 168 | 26 | 5 | 0 | 1123 |

**TABLE 6** SNOWFALL (inches) LEXINGTON, KENTUCKY

| SEASON | JULY | AUG | SEP | OCT | NOV | DEC | JAN | FEB | MAR | APR | MAY | JUNE | TOTAL |
|---|---|---|---|---|---|---|---|---|---|---|---|---|---|
| 1961-62 | 0.0 | 0.0 | 0.0 | 0.0 | 1.2 | 5.1 | 6.1 | 0.8 | 2.4 | 0.8 | 0.0 | 0.0 | 16.4 |
| 1962-63 | 0.0 | 0.0 | 0.0 | T | T | 2.4 | 6.8 | 8.2 | T | 0.0 | 0.0 | 0.0 | 17.4 |
| 1963-64 | 0.0 | 0.0 | 0.0 | 0.0 | 1.0 | 8.2 | 10.8 | 12.0 | 0.3 | 0.0 | 0.0 | 0.0 | 32.3 |
| 1964-65 | 0.0 | 0.0 | 0.0 | 0.0 | 0.7 | 0.7 | 9.9 | 1.8 | 2.8 | 0.0 | 0.0 | 0.0 | 15.9 |
| 1965-66 | 0.0 | 0.0 | 0.0 | 0.0 | T | 1.3 | 12.4 | 6.5 | 1.2 | T | 0.0 | 0.0 | 21.4 |
| 1966-67 | 0.0 | 0.0 | 0.0 | 0.0 | 8.4 | 0.3 | 1.5 | 11.1 | 4.3 | 0.0 | 0.0 | 0.0 | 25.6 |
| 1967-68 | 0.0 | 0.0 | 0.0 | 0.0 | T | 10.7 | 12.1 | 3.1 | 8.6 | 0.0 | 0.0 | 0.0 | 34.5 |
| 1968-69 | 0.0 | 0.0 | 0.0 | 0.0 | 1.0 | 1.5 | 1.9 | 6.1 | 1.7 | 0.0 | 0.0 | 0.0 | 12.2 |
| 1969-70 | 0.0 | 0.0 | 0.0 | 0.0 | 1.4 | 5.2 | 8.4 | 9.9 | 6.2 | T | 0.0 | 0.0 | 31.1 |
| 1970-71 | 0.0 | 0.0 | 0.0 | 0.0 | T | 1.2 | 4.0 | 9.1 | 5.3 | 0.0 | 0.0 | 0.0 | 19.6 |
| 1971-72 | 0.0 | 0.0 | 0.0 | 0.0 | 0.7 | T | 1.4 | 6.3 | 2.4 | T | 0.0 | 0.0 | 10.8 |
| 1972-73 | 0.0 | 0.0 | 0.0 | 0.2 | 1.7 | 0.4 | 1.0 | 1.4 | 0.4 | 0.2 | 0.0 | 0.0 | 5.3 |
| 1973-74 | 0.0 | 0.0 | 0.0 | 0.0 | 0.0 | 4.3 | T | 3.6 | 0.7 | T | 0.0 | 0.0 | 8.6 |
| 1974-75 | 0.0 | 0.0 | 0.0 | T | 1.4 | 2.8 | 4.6 | 1.5 | 5.6 | T | 0.0 | 0.0 | 15.9 |
| 1975-76 | 0.0 | 0.0 | 0.0 | 0.0 | T | 0.9 | 6.5 | 0.4 | 2.2 | 0.0 | 0.0 | 0.0 | 10.0 |
| 1976-77 | 0.0 | 0.0 | 0.0 | 0.0 | 2.9 | 1.6 | 18.5 | 3.5 | 0.1 | 0.8 | 0.0 | 0.0 | 27.4 |
| 1977-78 | 0.0 | 0.0 | 0.0 | 0.0 | 1.7 | 3.0 | 21.9 | 7.1 | 8.4 | 0.0 | 0.0 | 0.0 | 42.1 |
| 1978-79 | 0.0 | 0.0 | 0.0 | 0.0 | 0.0 | 0.7 | 11.4 | 11.6 | 0.1 | T | 0.0 | 0.0 | 23.8 |
| 1979-80 | 0.0 | 0.0 | 0.0 | 0.0 | 0.1 | T | 11.9 | 4.0 | 4.2 | 0.3 | 0.0 | 0.0 | 20.5 |
| 1980-81 | 0.0 | 0.0 | 0.0 | 0.0 | 0.1 | 0.5 | 2.2 | 0.4 | 0.5 | 0.0 | 0.0 | 0.0 | 3.7 |
| 1981-82 | 0.0 | 0.0 | 0.0 | 0.0 | 0.4 | 1.7 | 5.6 | 3.9 | 0.3 | 0.7 | 0.0 | 0.0 | 12.6 |
| 1982-83 | 0.0 | 0.0 | 0.0 | 0.0 | 0.0 | 0.2 | 7.5 | 0.3 | T | 0.0 | 0.0 | 0.0 | 8.0 |
| 1983-84 | 0.0 | 0.0 | 0.0 | 0.0 | T | 1.7 | 8.4 | 4.6 | 0.3 | 0.0 | 0.0 | 0.0 | 15.0 |
| 1984-85 | 0.0 | 0.0 | 0.0 | 0.0 | 0.0 | 4.9 | 10.2 | 10.7 | T | 0.5 | 0.0 | 0.0 | 26.3 |
| 1985-86 | 0.0 | 0.0 | 0.0 | 0.0 | 0.0 | 0.0 | 3.5 | 1.2 | 8.9 | 0.7 | T | 0.0 | 14.3 |
| 1986-87 | 0.0 | 0.0 | 0.0 | 0.0 | 0.2 | T | 3.6 | 3.5 | 2.1 | 5.9 | 0.0 | 0.0 | 15.3 |
| 1987-88 | 0.0 | 0.0 | 0.0 | 0.0 | 1.0 | 1.8 | 3.3 | 3.4 | 0.7 | 0.0 | 0.0 | 0.0 | 10.2 |
| 1988-89 | 0.0 | 0.0 | 0.0 | 0.0 | 0.7 | T | 1.5 | T | T | T | 0.0 | 0.0 | 2.2 |
| 1989-90 | T | T | 0.0 | T | 1.1 | 9.3 | 0.2 | T | 3.7 | T | 0.0 | 0.0 | 14.3 |
| 1990-91 | 0.0 | 0.0 | 0.0 | 0.0 | 0.0 | 0.8 | | | | | | | |
| Record Mean | T | T | 0.0 | T | 0.6 | 1.8 | 5.8 | 4.8 | 2.6 | 0.3 | T | 0.0 | 15.9 |

**See Reference Notes, relative to all above tables, on preceding page.**

Louisville is located on the south bank of the Ohio River, 604 miles below Pittsburgh, Pennsylvania, and 377 miles above the mouth of the river at Cairo, Illinois. The city is divided by Beargrass Creek and its south fork into two portions with entirely different types of topography. The eastern portion is rolling, containing several creeks, and consists of plateaus and rolling hillsides. The highest elevation in this area is 565 feet. The western portion is mostly flat with an average elevation about 100 feet lower than the eastern area. Much of the western section lies in the flood plain of the Ohio River. Nearly all of the industries in the city are located in the western portion, while the eastern portion is almost entirely residential. A range of low hills about five miles northwest of Louisville, on the Indiana side of the Ohio River, present a partial barrier to arctic blasts in the winter months. During colder months, snow is frequently observed on the summits of these hills when there is no snow in the city of Louisville or in riverside communities on the Indiana side of the Ohio River.

The climate of Louisville, while continental in type, is of a variable nature because of its position with respect to the paths of high and low pressure systems and the occasional influx of warm moist air from the Gulf of Mexico. In winter and summer there are occasional cold and hot spells of short duration. As a whole, winters are moderately cold and summers are quite warm. Temperatures of 100 degrees or more in summer and zero degrees or less in winter are rare.

Thunderstorms with high rainfall intensities are common during the spring and summer months. The precipitation in Louisville is nonseasonal and varies from year to year. The fall months are usually the driest. Generally, March has the most rainfall and October the least. Snowfall usually occurs from November through March. As with rainfall, amounts vary from year to year and month to month. Some snow has also been recorded in the months of October and April. Mean total amounts for the months of January, February, and March are about the same with January showing a slight edge in total amount. Relative humidity remains rather high throughout the summer months. Cloud cover is about equally distributed throughout the year with the winter months showing somewhat of an increase in amount. The percentage of possible sunshine at Louisville varies from month to month with the greatest amount during the summer months as a result of the decreasing sky cover during that season. Heavy fog is unusual and there is only an average of 10 days during the year with heavy fog and these occur generally in the months of September through March.

The average date for the last occurrence in the spring of temperatures as low as 32 degrees is mid-April, and the first occurrence in the fall is generally in late October.

The prevailing direction of the wind has a southerly component and the velocity averages under 10 mph. The strongest winds are usually associated with thunderstorms.

## TABLE 1     NORMALS, MEANS AND EXTREMES

LOUISVILLE, KENTUCKY

LATITUDE: 38°11'N   LONGITUDE: 85°44'W   ELEVATION: FT. GRND  477 BARO  485  TIME ZONE: EASTERN   WBAN: 93821

| | (a) | JAN | FEB | MAR | APR | MAY | JUNE | JULY | AUG | SEP | OCT | NOV | DEC | YEAR |
|---|---|---|---|---|---|---|---|---|---|---|---|---|---|---|
| **TEMPERATURE °F:** | | | | | | | | | | | | | | |
| Normals | | | | | | | | | | | | | | |
| -Daily Maximum | | 40.8 | 45.0 | 54.9 | 67.5 | 76.2 | 84.0 | 87.6 | 86.7 | 80.6 | 69.2 | 55.5 | 45.4 | 66.1 |
| -Daily Minimum | | 24.1 | 26.8 | 35.2 | 45.6 | 54.6 | 63.3 | 67.5 | 66.1 | 59.1 | 46.2 | 36.6 | 28.9 | 46.2 |
| -Monthly | | 32.5 | 35.9 | 45.1 | 56.6 | 65.4 | 73.7 | 77.6 | 76.4 | 69.9 | 57.7 | 46.1 | 37.2 | 56.2 |
| Extremes | | | | | | | | | | | | | | |
| -Record Highest | 42 | 77 | 77 | 86 | 91 | 95 | 102 | 105 | 101 | 104 | 92 | 84 | 76 | 105 |
| -Year | | 1950 | 1972 | 1981 | 1960 | 1959 | 1952 | 1954 | 1988 | 1954 | 1959 | 1958 | 1982 | JUL 1954 |
| -Record Lowest | 42 | -20 | -19 | -1 | 22 | 31 | 42 | 50 | 46 | 33 | 23 | -1 | -15 | -20 |
| -Year | | 1963 | 1951 | 1960 | 1982 | 1966 | 1966 | 1972 | 1986 | 1949 | 1952 | 1950 | 1989 | JAN 1963 |
| **NORMAL DEGREE DAYS:** | | | | | | | | | | | | | | |
| Heating (base 65°F) | | 1008 | 815 | 624 | 264 | 98 | 5 | 0 | 0 | 32 | 250 | 567 | 862 | 4525 |
| Cooling (base 65°F) | | 0 | 0 | 7 | 12 | 110 | 266 | 391 | 353 | 179 | 24 | 0 | 0 | 1342 |
| **% OF POSSIBLE SUNSHINE** | 42 | 42 | 48 | 51 | 56 | 61 | 66 | 66 | 66 | 65 | 61 | 46 | 41 | 56 |
| **MEAN SKY COVER (tenths)** | | | | | | | | | | | | | | |
| Sunrise - Sunset | 42 | 7.3 | 7.0 | 7.0 | 6.6 | 6.2 | 5.9 | 5.8 | 5.3 | 5.3 | 5.3 | 6.6 | 7.2 | 6.3 |
| **MEAN NUMBER OF DAYS:** | | | | | | | | | | | | | | |
| Sunrise to Sunset | | | | | | | | | | | | | | |
| -Clear | 42 | 5.8 | 5.8 | 5.9 | 6.4 | 7.9 | 7.8 | 7.7 | 10.2 | 10.4 | 11.6 | 7.5 | 6.2 | 93.2 |
| -Partly Cloudy | 42 | 5.7 | 6.4 | 7.5 | 8.9 | 9.4 | 11.2 | 12.8 | 11.5 | 9.0 | 7.6 | 6.0 | 6.1 | 102.1 |
| -Cloudy | 42 | 19.5 | 16.0 | 17.6 | 14.7 | 13.7 | 11.0 | 10.5 | 9.3 | 10.5 | 11.8 | 16.3 | 18.7 | 169.7 |
| Precipitation | | | | | | | | | | | | | | |
| .01 inches or more | 42 | 11.2 | 10.6 | 13.0 | 11.8 | 11.5 | 9.9 | 10.5 | 8.4 | 7.9 | 7.6 | 10.4 | 11.3 | 124.0 |
| Snow,Ice pellets | | | | | | | | | | | | | | |
| 1.0 inches or more | 42 | 1.7 | 1.3 | 0.7 | 0.1 | 0.0 | 0.0 | 0.0 | 0.0 | 0.0 | 0.* | 0.3 | 0.7 | 4.8 |
| Thunderstorms | 42 | 0.9 | 1.0 | 3.1 | 4.4 | 6.5 | 7.3 | 8.3 | 6.8 | 3.3 | 1.6 | 1.4 | 0.6 | 45.2 |
| Heavy Fog Visibility | | | | | | | | | | | | | | |
| 1/4 mile or less | 42 | 0.9 | 0.9 | 0.5 | 0.2 | 0.2 | 0.4 | 0.6 | 0.9 | 1.0 | 1.5 | 0.7 | 0.7 | 8.5 |
| Temperature °F | | | | | | | | | | | | | | |
| -Maximum | | | | | | | | | | | | | | |
| 90° and above | 29 | 0.0 | 0.0 | 0.0 | 0.* | 0.4 | 5.7 | 10.8 | 9.1 | 2.9 | 0.0 | 0.0 | 0.0 | 29.0 |
| 32° and below | 29 | 9.5 | 5.3 | 0.6 | 0.0 | 0.0 | 0.0 | 0.0 | 0.0 | 0.0 | 0.0 | 0.3 | 4.5 | 20.2 |
| -Minimum | | | | | | | | | | | | | | |
| 32° and below | 29 | 24.8 | 20.3 | 11.8 | 2.2 | 0.1 | 0.0 | 0.0 | 0.0 | 0.0 | 1.6 | 9.0 | 20.5 | 90.5 |
| 0° and below | 29 | 1.4 | 0.2 | 0.0 | 0.0 | 0.0 | 0.0 | 0.0 | 0.0 | 0.0 | 0.0 | 0.0 | 0.4 | 2.0 |
| **AVG. STATION PRESS.(mb)** | 17 | 1002.6 | 1001.6 | 998.7 | 997.8 | 997.2 | 997.9 | 998.8 | 999.5 | 1000.4 | 1001.6 | 1001.2 | 1002.2 | 1000.0 |
| **RELATIVE HUMIDITY (%)** | | | | | | | | | | | | | | |
| Hour 01 | 29 | 72 | 72 | 69 | 68 | 76 | 79 | 81 | 82 | 83 | 79 | 75 | 73 | 76 |
| Hour 07 | 29 | 76 | 77 | 75 | 75 | 82 | 83 | 85 | 88 | 89 | 85 | 79 | 77 | 81 |
| Hour 13 (Local Time) | 29 | 64 | 62 | 57 | 52 | 55 | 57 | 58 | 58 | 59 | 55 | 61 | 64 | 59 |
| Hour 19 | 29 | 64 | 62 | 57 | 52 | 56 | 58 | 60 | 61 | 63 | 61 | 65 | 67 | 61 |
| **PRECIPITATION (inches):** | | | | | | | | | | | | | | |
| Water Equivalent | | | | | | | | | | | | | | |
| -Normal | | 3.38 | 3.23 | 4.73 | 4.11 | 4.15 | 3.60 | 4.10 | 3.31 | 3.35 | 2.63 | 3.49 | 3.48 | 43.56 |
| -Maximum Monthly | 42 | 11.38 | 9.02 | 14.91 | 11.10 | 10.58 | 10.11 | 10.05 | 8.79 | 10.49 | 6.47 | 9.12 | 7.64 | 14.91 |
| -Year | | 1950 | 1989 | 1964 | 1970 | 1983 | 1960 | 1979 | 1974 | 1979 | 1983 | 1957 | 1978 | MAR 1964 |
| -Minimum Monthly | 42 | 0.45 | 0.76 | 1.02 | 0.76 | 1.37 | 0.49 | 0.99 | 0.23 | 0.27 | 0.39 | 0.72 | 0.65 | 0.23 |
| -Year | | 1981 | 1978 | 1966 | 1977 | 1977 | 1984 | 1983 | 1953 | 1987 | 1976 | 1976 | 1976 | AUG 1953 |
| -Maximum in 24 hrs | 42 | 3.00 | 2.98 | 6.97 | 4.85 | 4.60 | 5.14 | 5.46 | 3.05 | 4.97 | 3.25 | 3.58 | 2.79 | 6.97 |
| -Year | | 1988 | 1989 | 1964 | 1970 | 1961 | 1960 | 1979 | 1970 | 1979 | 1977 | 1948 | 1978 | MAR 1964 |
| Snow,Ice pellets | | | | | | | | | | | | | | |
| -Maximum Monthly | 42 | 28.4 | 13.1 | 22.9 | 1.6 | T | 0.0 | 0.0 | 0.0 | 0.0 | 1.4 | 13.2 | 9.3 | 28.4 |
| -Year | | 1978 | 1948 | 1960 | 1973 | 1989 | | | | | 1989 | 1966 | 1961 | JAN 1978 |
| -Maximum in 24 hrs | 42 | 14.1 | 11.0 | 12.1 | 1.6 | T | 0.0 | 0.0 | 0.0 | 0.0 | 1.4 | 13.0 | 5.0 | 14.1 |
| -Year | | 1978 | 1966 | 1968 | 1973 | 1989 | | | | | 1989 | 1966 | 1961 | JAN 1978 |
| **WIND:** | | | | | | | | | | | | | | |
| Mean Speed (mph) | 42 | 9.7 | 9.6 | 10.3 | 9.8 | 8.0 | 7.4 | 6.7 | 6.4 | 6.8 | 7.2 | 8.9 | 9.3 | 8.3 |
| Prevailing Direction | | | | | | | | | | | | | | |
| through 1963 | | S | NW | NW | SW | SE | S | S | N | SE | SE | S | S | S |
| Fastest Mile | | | | | | | | | | | | | | |
| -Direction (!!!) | 36 | S | NW | W | W | W | W | NW | NW | NW | SE | SE | SW | NW |
| -Speed (MPH) | 36 | 50 | 61 | 56 | 57 | 57 | 58 | 60 | 52 | 57 | 38 | 60 | 61 | 61 |
| -Year | | 1950 | 1967 | 1952 | 1953 | 1957 | 1957 | 1966 | 1956 | 1954 | 1955 | 1952 | 1953 | FEB 1967 |
| Peak Gust | | | | | | | | | | | | | | |
| -Direction (!!!) | 6 | NW | SW | NW | S | S | W | NW | S | NW | SE | W | S | NW |
| -Speed (mph) | 6 | 46 | 51 | 60 | 49 | 60 | 56 | 78 | 53 | 48 | 44 | 45 | 52 | 78 |
| -Date | | 1987 | 1988 | 1986 | 1985 | 1985 | 1985 | 1987 | 1984 | 1984 | 1984 | 1988 | 1987 | JUL 1987 |

**See Reference Notes to this table on the following page.**

## TABLE 2 — PRECIPITATION (inches)  LOUISVILLE, KENTUCKY

| YEAR | JAN | FEB | MAR | APR | MAY | JUNE | JULY | AUG | SEP | OCT | NOV | DEC | ANNUAL |
|------|-----|-----|-----|-----|-----|------|------|-----|-----|-----|-----|-----|--------|
| 1961 | 1.57 | 5.24 | 7.63 | 4.83 | 9.00 | 3.59 | 5.16 | 1.56 | 1.48 | 2.00 | 4.23 | 3.75 | 50.04 |
| 1962 | 4.03 | 6.58 | 3.58 | 1.01 | 3.33 | 4.75 | 1.84 | 2.20 | 3.56 | 4.70 | 1.59 | 2.74 | 39.91 |
| 1963 | 1.18 | 1.11 | 9.04 | 1.87 | 4.56 | 4.18 | 7.33 | 2.13 | 3.48 | 0.81 | 1.69 | 1.06 | 38.44 |
| 1964 | 2.45 | 2.45 | 14.91 | 3.06 | 1.85 | 2.24 | 3.03 | 2.63 | 4.16 | 0.62 | 3.32 | 5.86 | 46.58 |
| 1965 | 2.76 | 4.67 | 4.82 | 3.28 | 1.60 | 2.27 | 4.86 | 2.12 | 8.41 | 2.54 | 1.33 | 1.14 | 39.80 |
| 1966 | 5.73 | 5.01 | 1.02 | 9.56 | 3.91 | 0.75 | 2.13 | 5.18 | 2.59 | 1.04 | 3.67 | 4.33 | 44.92 |
| 1967 | 1.11 | 2.01 | 4.37 | 4.39 | 4.62 | 4.41 | 7.33 | 4.30 | 1.73 | 3.06 | 3.08 | 3.51 | 43.92 |
| 1968 | 2.13 | 0.80 | 6.23 | 3.94 | 5.16 | 1.70 | 3.07 | 3.68 | 2.61 | 1.00 | 3.34 | 3.62 | 37.28 |
| 1969 | 5.31 | 1.65 | 1.94 | 3.77 | 3.91 | 2.97 | 4.05 | 3.65 | 1.08 | 1.69 | 3.08 | 3.69 | 36.79 |
| 1970 | 1.40 | 2.87 | 4.52 | 11.10 | 1.85 | 5.20 | 3.33 | 7.65 | 3.57 | 4.79 | 1.75 | 4.18 | 52.21 |
| 1971 | 2.64 | 6.28 | 2.12 | 2.16 | 6.15 | 2.64 | 6.74 | 1.83 | 4.72 | 1.96 | 2.06 | 2.98 | 42.28 |
| 1972 | 2.87 | 3.94 | 4.07 | 8.48 | 4.46 | 1.08 | 3.64 | 2.45 | 4.24 | 2.55 | 6.31 | 5.29 | 49.38 |
| 1973 | 1.96 | 1.60 | 6.26 | 5.77 | 7.04 | 6.20 | 9.38 | 0.91 | 2.34 | 2.28 | 7.59 | 2.64 | 53.97 |
| 1974 | 4.38 | 1.64 | 5.41 | 2.74 | 3.86 | 2.58 | 2.04 | 8.79 | 3.52 | 2.09 | 3.03 | 4.89 | 42.93 |
| 1975 | 4.87 | 4.53 | 9.65 | 6.47 | 4.50 | 3.15 | 1.91 | 3.89 | 2.64 | 6.12 | 3.69 | | 56.31 |
| 1976 | 3.85 | 3.13 | 2.87 | 0.76 | 5.09 | 4.71 | 2.10 | 3.18 | 3.10 | 3.99 | 0.72 | 0.65 | 34.15 |
| 1977 | 2.33 | 1.45 | 4.69 | 3.40 | 1.37 | 7.59 | 3.29 | 6.12 | 3.67 | 4.76 | 6.11 | 4.32 | 49.10 |
| 1978 | 5.90 | 0.76 | 3.76 | 3.33 | 4.76 | 2.67 | 3.77 | 5.50 | 0.96 | 2.26 | 5.14 | 7.64 | 46.45 |
| 1979 | 3.81 | 4.49 | 2.71 | 7.32 | 3.59 | 3.03 | 10.05 | 2.37 | 10.49 | 2.27 | 5.85 | 3.82 | 59.80 |
| 1980 | 1.71 | 1.09 | 4.80 | 2.63 | 4.58 | 3.70 | 5.41 | 3.76 | 3.17 | 3.37 | 2.42 | 1.25 | 37.89 |
| 1981 | 0.45 | 3.23 | 1.54 | 4.44 | 4.63 | 3.23 | 3.98 | 3.21 | 3.22 | 1.60 | 2.40 | 2.02 | 33.95 |
| 1982 | 5.28 | 1.55 | 5.89 | 3.05 | 2.96 | 3.86 | 3.72 | 3.74 | 2.39 | 1.26 | 5.50 | 5.11 | 45.38 |
| 1983 | 1.63 | 1.52 | 2.16 | 7.10 | 10.58 | 4.42 | 0.99 | 2.39 | 1.13 | 6.47 | 5.03 | 3.96 | 47.38 |
| 1984 | 0.92 | 1.68 | 4.41 | 5.53 | 6.78 | 0.49 | 6.94 | 5.08 | 3.70 | 2.12 | 5.87 | 5.86 | 49.38 |
| 1985 | 2.20 | 2.08 | 4.43 | 1.69 | 3.93 | 4.37 | 3.45 | 4.49 | 1.48 | 4.24 | 4.43 | 0.96 | 37.75 |
| 1986 | 0.91 | 3.90 | 2.69 | 1.04 | 4.28 | 2.32 | 7.04 | 2.19 | 2.75 | 3.08 | 4.62 | 2.69 | 37.51 |
| 1987 | 0.81 | 4.42 | 3.05 | 2.35 | 1.61 | 3.58 | 5.31 | 2.66 | 1.15 | 0.39 | 2.62 | 4.70 | 32.65 |
| 1988 | 4.00 | 3.58 | 2.97 | 3.52 | 2.68 | 0.87 | 4.68 | 3.00 | 1.48 | 1.54 | 5.76 | 1.45 | 37.53 |
| 1989 | 3.68 | 9.02 | 5.50 | 4.93 | 4.39 | 5.26 | 6.90 | 2.20 | 2.42 | 2.65 | 2.57 | 1.45 | 50.97 |
| 1990 | 3.90 | 6.72 | 2.78 | 3.46 | 11.57 | 6.13 | 1.96 | 3.21 | 2.57 | 3.97 | 2.34 | 8.86 | 57.47 |
| Record Mean | 3.76 | 3.39 | 4.48 | 3.94 | 4.00 | 3.84 | 3.83 | 3.28 | 2.79 | 2.61 | 3.53 | 3.59 | 43.03 |

## TABLE 3 — AVERAGE TEMPERATURE (deg. F)  LOUISVILLE, KENTUCKY

| YEAR | JAN | FEB | MAR | APR | MAY | JUNE | JULY | AUG | SEP | OCT | NOV | DEC | ANNUAL |
|------|-----|-----|-----|-----|-----|------|------|-----|-----|-----|-----|-----|--------|
| 1961 | 28.8 | 39.1 | 47.6 | 49.2 | 59.0 | 68.9 | 76.5 | 75.1 | 73.0 | 57.9 | 45.2 | 36.4 | 54.7 |
| 1962 | 30.5 | 39.1 | 42.3 | 53.1 | 71.4 | 73.4 | 76.2 | 76.4 | 65.0 | 59.3 | 44.2 | 30.3 | 55.1 |
| 1963 | 26.1 | 30.2 | 49.5 | 59.0 | 63.3 | 73.0 | 74.8 | 73.4 | 66.8 | 63.5 | 48.4 | 26.7 | 54.6 |
| 1964 | 35.9 | 33.4 | 45.3 | 58.4 | 66.8 | 75.1 | 76.4 | 76.2 | 69.1 | 53.4 | 48.0 | 38.0 | 56.3 |
| 1965 | 34.3 | 35.9 | 38.9 | 58.3 | 70.0 | 73.4 | 76.3 | 75.2 | 70.5 | 55.7 | 47.3 | 42.3 | 56.5 |
| 1966 | 27.1 | 34.1 | 46.1 | 53.4 | 62.3 | 73.1 | 81.1 | 75.6 | 67.4 | 54.6 | 47.2 | 35.6 | 54.8 |
| 1967 | 36.3 | 30.9 | 50.6 | 59.7 | 62.4 | 73.4 | 74.5 | 72.2 | 65.7 | 57.2 | 42.7 | 39.4 | 55.4 |
| 1968 | 30.3 | 30.1 | 45.7 | 56.8 | 63.4 | 74.0 | 77.7 | 77.9 | 69.0 | 57.4 | 48.0 | 35.7 | 55.5 |
| 1969 | 33.1 | 36.9 | 39.9 | 58.0 | 66.2 | 73.5 | 78.7 | 74.7 | 67.5 | 57.3 | 43.3 | 33.5 | 55.2 |
| 1970 | 27.9 | 33.6 | 42.3 | 59.3 | 67.2 | 72.9 | 75.8 | 76.0 | 73.4 | 58.1 | 45.3 | 39.6 | 56.0 |
| 1971 | 30.9 | 35.0 | 42.0 | 54.7 | 61.5 | 76.5 | 74.8 | 74.1 | 72.2 | 64.4 | 47.0 | 45.1 | 56.5 |
| 1972 | 35.2 | 34.9 | 44.8 | 56.2 | 65.5 | 70.6 | 77.1 | 76.1 | 72.3 | 55.3 | 44.0 | 39.1 | 55.9 |
| 1973 | 35.0 | 36.4 | 53.7 | 54.4 | 61.5 | 75.6 | 78.4 | 77.0 | 73.6 | 62.3 | 49.8 | 37.1 | 57.9 |
| 1974 | 39.8 | 39.3 | 49.8 | 57.2 | 65.1 | 68.7 | 75.9 | 75.0 | 63.2 | 54.9 | 47.0 | 39.1 | 56.3 |
| 1975 | 38.1 | 40.2 | 43.3 | 54.4 | 69.0 | 75.4 | 77.7 | 79.3 | 66.2 | 59.4 | 50.6 | 38.9 | 57.7 |
| 1976 | 31.3 | 45.4 | 52.4 | 57.5 | 62.9 | 72.9 | 76.8 | 74.2 | 66.8 | 52.5 | 39.5 | 33.1 | 55.4 |
| 1977 | 18.6 | 36.9 | 51.7 | 60.3 | 71.2 | 73.9 | 80.2 | 77.5 | 72.5 | 55.5 | 49.6 | 34.6 | 56.9 |
| 1978 | 22.9 | 23.8 | 41.7 | 58.0 | 63.8 | 75.7 | 78.5 | 77.1 | 73.7 | 55.5 | 50.0 | 40.0 | 55.1 |
| 1979 | 24.6 | 28.0 | 48.3 | 55.0 | 64.2 | 73.9 | 75.3 | 76.1 | 69.4 | 58.2 | 46.9 | 39.2 | 54.9 |
| 1980 | 33.5 | 29.6 | 41.8 | 53.6 | 66.8 | 73.4 | 81.5 | 81.0 | 73.5 | 55.8 | 46.3 | 38.3 | 56.3 |
| 1981 | 30.4 | 38.8 | 45.7 | 62.4 | 62.9 | 76.2 | 78.8 | 76.1 | 67.7 | 56.5 | 47.4 | 33.8 | 56.4 |
| 1982 | 28.6 | 34.9 | 47.1 | 51.3 | 70.3 | 69.3 | 78.0 | 73.5 | 66.8 | 59.0 | 48.7 | 44.9 | 56.0 |
| 1983 | 34.7 | 37.5 | 46.7 | 51.7 | 62.1 | 73.4 | 81.1 | 81.7 | 71.0 | 59.1 | 47.8 | 28.4 | 56.3 |
| 1984 | 28.9 | 41.5 | 40.4 | 55.0 | 62.6 | 77.7 | 75.5 | 76.0 | 67.2 | 63.9 | 44.0 | 45.9 | 56.6 |
| 1985 | 25.4 | 32.8 | 50.2 | 60.3 | 66.5 | 72.1 | 77.2 | 74.8 | 69.2 | 61.4 | 53.7 | 30.4 | 56.2 |
| 1986 | 34.5 | 39.9 | 48.3 | 58.5 | 67.0 | 75.7 | 80.3 | 74.3 | 73.1 | 59.5 | 45.9 | 36.7 | 57.8 |
| 1987 | 33.7 | 39.5 | 47.9 | 55.4 | 71.5 | 76.2 | 78.9 | 78.2 | 71.2 | 52.6 | 50.8 | 40.2 | 58.0 |
| 1988 | 31.0 | 34.7 | 46.1 | 57.0 | 67.1 | 75.6 | 80.3 | 80.0 | 70.1 | 52.3 | 47.8 | 38.0 | 56.7 |
| 1989 | 41.6 | 34.0 | 48.4 | 56.7 | 62.6 | 73.5 | 78.1 | 76.6 | 69.4 | 58.4 | 46.7 | 25.3 | 55.9 |
| 1990 | 43.1 | 44.3 | 51.2 | 55.5 | 64.2 | 75.1 | 78.5 | 77.5 | 71.8 | 58.7 | 52.0 | 40.8 | 59.4 |
| Record Mean | 34.2 | 36.7 | 45.8 | 56.4 | 65.9 | 74.6 | 78.3 | 76.8 | 70.3 | 58.7 | 46.6 | 37.1 | 56.2 |
| Max | 42.1 | 45.2 | 55.1 | 66.4 | 76.1 | 84.4 | 88.1 | 86.6 | 80.5 | 69.1 | 55.2 | 45.0 | 66.2 |
| Min | 26.2 | 28.1 | 36.4 | 46.3 | 55.8 | 64.7 | 68.6 | 66.9 | 60.1 | 48.3 | 37.9 | 29.2 | 47.4 |

## REFERENCE NOTES FOR TABLES 1, 2, 3 and 6    (LOUISVILLE, KY)

### GENERAL

T - TRACE AMOUNT
BLANK ENTRIES DENOTE MISSING/UNREPORTED DATA.
# INDICATES A STATION OR INSTRUMENT RELOCATION.

### SPECIFIC

#### TABLE 1

(a) - LENGTH OF RECORD IN YEARS. ALTHOUGH INDIVIDUAL MONTHS MAY BE MISSING.
* LESS THAN .05

NORMALS — BASED ON THE 1951-1980 RECORD PERIOD.
EXTREMES — DATES ARE THE MOST RECENT OCCURRENCE.
WIND DIR. — NUMERALS SHOW TENS OF DEGREES CLOCKWISE FROM TRUE NORTH.
"00" INDICATES CALM.
RESULTANT WIND DIRECTIONS ARE GIVEN TO WHOLE DEGREES.

#### TABLE 3

MAX AND MIN ARE LONG-TERM MEAN DAILY MAXIMUM AND MEAN DAILY MINIMUM TEMPERATURES.

### EXCEPTIONS

#### TABLES 2, 3, and 6

RECORD MEANS ARE THROUGH THE CURRENT YEAR, BEGINNING IN
1873 FOR TEMPERATURE
1873 FOR PRECIPITATION
1948 FOR SNOWFALL

## TABLE 4 — HEATING DEGREE DAYS Base 65 deg. F — LOUISVILLE, KENTUCKY

| SEASON | JULY | AUG | SEP | OCT | NOV | DEC | JAN | FEB | MAR | APR | MAY | JUNE | TOTAL |
|---|---|---|---|---|---|---|---|---|---|---|---|---|---|
| 1961-62 | 0 | 0 | 30 | 232 | 593 | 877 | 1065 | 720 | 694 | 385 | 16 | 0 | 4612 |
| 1962-63 | 0 | 0 | 95 | 224 | 617 | 1071 | 1200 | 968 | 476 | 231 | 109 | 1 | 4992 |
| 1963-64 | 0 | 1 | 71 | 86 | 493 | 1178 | 895 | 910 | 603 | 215 | 55 | 7 | 4514 |
| 1964-65 | 0 | 5 | 44 | 349 | 502 | 829 | 943 | 808 | 802 | 223 | 20 | 0 | 4525 |
| 1965-66 | 0 | 2 | 45 | 304 | 526 | 697 | 1170 | 857 | 580 | 353 | 127 | 8 | 4669 |
| 1966-67 | 0 | 0 | 35 | 324 | 531 | 907 | 882 | 949 | 453 | 209 | 139 | 13 | 4442 |
| 1967-68 | 0 | 0 | 68 | 259 | 660 | 788 | 1069 | 1007 | 590 | 247 | 98 | 4 | 4790 |
| 1968-69 | 0 | 1 | 10 | 276 | 511 | 903 | 987 | 778 | 771 | 213 | 61 | 14 | 4525 |
| 1969-70 | 0 | 0 | 42 | 282 | 645 | 971 | 1141 | 875 | 697 | 200 | 70 | 0 | 4923 |
| 1970-71 | 0 | 0 | 23 | 220 | 582 | 781 | 1052 | 833 | 707 | 303 | 137 | 0 | 4638 |
| 1971-72 | 0 | 0 | 13 | 65 | 537 | 610 | 914 | 866 | 623 | 282 | 61 | 19 | 3990 |
| 1972-73 | 0 | 0 | 16 | 298 | 628 | 793 | 927 | 796 | 349 | 343 | 129 | 0 | 4279 |
| 1973-74 | 0 | 0 | 13 | 144 | 450 | 860 | 772 | 714 | 487 | 257 | 99 | 19 | 3815 |
| 1974-75 | 0 | 0 | 122 | 314 | 543 | 794 | 830 | 688 | 665 | 333 | 22 | 0 | 4311 |
| 1975-76 | 0 | 0 | 73 | 205 | 431 | 801 | 1040 | 562 | 405 | 266 | 111 | 1 | 3895 |
| 1976-77 | 0 | 0 | 29 | 393 | 757 | 982 | 1435 | 780 | 421 | 183 | 36 | 7 | 5023 |
| 1977-78 | 0 | 0 | 6 | 295 | 472 | 935 | 1294 | 1145 | 720 | 221 | 142 | 1 | 5231 |
| 1978-79 | 0 | 0 | 4 | 293 | 442 | 765 | 1246 | 1030 | 514 | 301 | 94 | 5 | 4694 |
| 1979-80 | 0 | 0 | 19 | 244 | 534 | 792 | 969 | 1021 | 713 | 342 | 68 | 8 | 4710 |
| 1980-81 | 0 | 0 | 12 | 309 | 555 | 821 | 1065 | 728 | 595 | 142 | 122 | 0 | 4349 |
| 1981-82 | 0 | 0 | 61 | 268 | 523 | 960 | 1124 | 837 | 549 | 408 | 13 | 3 | 4746 |
| 1982-83 | 0 | 1 | 56 | 246 | 495 | 624 | 933 | 763 | 571 | 399 | 121 | 5 | 4214 |
| 1983-84 | 0 | 0 | 54 | 196 | 509 | 1128 | 1115 | 673 | 757 | 315 | 141 | 0 | 4888 |
| 1984-85 | 0 | 0 | 73 | 84 | 623 | 584 | 1222 | 896 | 458 | 180 | 52 | 16 | 4188 |
| 1985-86 | 0 | 0 | 53 | 160 | 347 | 1067 | 941 | 696 | 516 | 224 | 69 | 0 | 4073 |
| 1986-87 | 0 | 12 | 5 | 210 | 570 | 869 | 962 | 706 | 526 | 294 | 21 | 0 | 4175 |
| 1987-88 | 0 | 0 | 9 | 377 | 423 | 762 | 1048 | 872 | 580 | 244 | 38 | 7 | 4360 |
| 1988-89 | 0 | 0 | 13 | 398 | 510 | 833 | 720 | 860 | 513 | 291 | 156 | 4 | 4298 |
| 1989-90 | 0 | 0 | 49 | 230 | 539 | 1222 | 672 | 574 | 445 | 320 | 82 | 13 | 4146 |
| 1990-91 | 0 | 0 | 34 | 229 | 387 | 745 | | | | | | | |

## TABLE 5 — COOLING DEGREE DAYS Base 65 deg. F — LOUISVILLE, KENTUCKY

| YEAR | JAN | FEB | MAR | APR | MAY | JUNE | JULY | AUG | SEP | OCT | NOV | DEC | TOTAL |
|---|---|---|---|---|---|---|---|---|---|---|---|---|---|
| 1969 | 0 | 0 | 0 | 9 | 106 | 277 | 431 | 308 | 127 | 49 | 0 | 0 | 1307 |
| 1970 | 0 | 0 | 0 | 36 | 147 | 244 | 343 | 346 | 283 | 15 | 0 | 0 | 1414 |
| 1971 | 0 | 0 | 0 | 2 | 35 | 351 | 310 | 291 | 237 | 58 | 3 | 0 | 1287 |
| 1972 | 0 | 0 | 3 | 25 | 81 | 193 | 386 | 351 | 242 | 2 | 4 | 0 | 1287 |
| 1973 | 0 | 0 | 7 | 29 | 28 | 325 | 422 | 380 | 280 | 71 | 2 | 0 | 1544 |
| 1974 | 0 | 0 | 22 | 31 | 109 | 136 | 345 | 319 | 75 | 8 | 10 | 0 | 1055 |
| 1975 | 0 | 0 | 0 | 24 | 152 | 320 | 402 | 451 | 116 | 36 | 5 | 0 | 1506 |
| 1976 | 0 | 0 | 21 | 47 | 51 | 243 | 372 | 294 | 92 | 10 | 0 | 0 | 1130 |
| 1977 | 0 | 0 | 14 | 50 | 234 | 281 | 479 | 396 | 238 | 5 | 20 | 0 | 1717 |
| 1978 | 0 | 0 | 0 | 20 | 110 | 323 | 425 | 383 | 270 | 6 | 2 | 0 | 1539 |
| 1979 | 0 | 0 | 5 | 10 | 73 | 279 | 326 | 350 | 154 | 39 | 0 | 0 | 1236 |
| 1980 | 0 | 0 | 0 | 8 | 134 | 266 | 519 | 504 | 276 | 31 | 1 | 0 | 1739 |
| 1981 | 0 | 0 | 5 | 68 | 63 | 343 | 435 | 348 | 150 | 10 | 0 | 0 | 1422 |
| 1982 | 0 | 0 | 1 | 2 | 183 | 139 | 408 | 274 | 118 | 10 | 0 | 0 | 1214 |
| 1983 | 0 | 0 | 7 | 8 | 39 | 264 | 504 | 524 | 240 | 68 | 13 | 8 | 1605 |
| 1984 | 0 | 0 | 0 | 20 | 69 | 386 | 333 | 349 | 183 | 19 | 0 | 0 | 1359 |
| 1985 | 0 | 2 | 8 | 48 | 106 | 233 | 387 | 311 | 145 | 56 | 0 | 1 | 1349 |
| 1986 | 0 | 0 | 5 | 37 | 138 | 330 | 481 | 306 | 255 | 46 | 0 | 0 | 1598 |
| 1987 | 0 | 0 | 0 | 14 | 232 | 342 | 439 | 416 | 203 | 1 | 4 | 0 | 1651 |
| 1988 | 0 | 0 | 4 | 10 | 111 | 333 | 481 | 472 | 173 | 10 | 0 | 0 | 1594 |
| 1989 | 0 | 0 | 6 | 48 | 88 | 264 | 412 | 364 | 188 | 30 | 0 | 0 | 1400 |
| 1990 | 0 | 0 | 22 | 44 | 65 | 323 | 427 | 392 | 244 | 42 | 7 | 0 | 1566 |

## TABLE 6 — SNOWFALL (inches) — LOUISVILLE, KENTUCKY

| SEASON | JULY | AUG | SEP | OCT | NOV | DEC | JAN | FEB | MAR | APR | MAY | JUNE | TOTAL |
|---|---|---|---|---|---|---|---|---|---|---|---|---|---|
| 1961-62 | 0.0 | 0.0 | 0.0 | 0.0 | 0.9 | 9.3 | 4.8 | 2.5 | 1.6 | 1.0 | 0.0 | 0.0 | 20.1 |
| 1962-63 | 0.0 | 0.0 | 0.0 | T | T | 1.8 | 6.0 | 3.4 | 0.3 | 0.0 | 0.0 | 0.0 | 11.5 |
| 1963-64 | 0.0 | 0.0 | 0.0 | 0.0 | T | 7.1 | 15.1 | 7.7 | 0.2 | 0.0 | 0.0 | 0.0 | 30.1 |
| 1964-65 | 0.0 | 0.0 | 0.0 | 0.0 | 0.9 | 0.2 | 11.8 | 3.9 | 4.6 | 0.0 | 0.0 | 0.0 | 21.4 |
| 1965-66 | 0.0 | 0.0 | 0.0 | 0.0 | 0.0 | T | 7.0 | 11.4 | 1.3 | 0.4 | 0.0 | 0.0 | 20.1 |
| 1966-67 | 0.0 | 0.0 | 0.0 | 0.0 | 13.2 | 0.5 | 0.4 | 7.8 | 9.3 | 0.0 | 0.0 | 0.0 | 31.2 |
| 1967-68 | 0.0 | 0.0 | 0.0 | 0.0 | T | 2.7 | 13.8 | 1.8 | 12.7 | 0.0 | 0.0 | 0.0 | 31.0 |
| 1968-69 | 0.0 | 0.0 | 0.0 | 0.0 | 0.3 | 1.1 | 3.2 | 6.3 | 2.2 | 0.0 | 0.0 | 0.0 | 13.1 |
| 1969-70 | 0.0 | 0.0 | 0.0 | 0.0 | 0.7 | 7.7 | 7.9 | 7.4 | 10.7 | T | 0.0 | 0.0 | 34.4 |
| 1970-71 | 0.0 | 0.0 | 0.0 | 0.0 | 0.3 | 0.8 | 3.2 | 11.9 | 5.2 | 0.1 | 0.0 | 0.0 | 21.5 |
| 1971-72 | 0.0 | 0.0 | 0.0 | 0.0 | 5.4 | T | 1.6 | 3.4 | 1.2 | T | 0.0 | 0.0 | 11.6 |
| 1972-73 | 0.0 | 0.0 | 0.0 | 0.0 | 2.0 | 2.2 | 1.1 | 1.1 | 0.5 | 1.6 | 0.0 | 0.0 | 8.5 |
| 1973-74 | 0.0 | 0.0 | 0.0 | 0.0 | T | 4.5 | 1.0 | 0.9 | 2.8 | 1.6 | 0.0 | 0.0 | 9.2 |
| 1974-75 | 0.0 | 0.0 | 0.0 | 0.0 | 1.0 | 1.2 | 3.0 | 1.3 | 10.0 | T | 0.0 | 0.0 | 16.5 |
| 1975-76 | 0.0 | 0.0 | 0.0 | 0.0 | 0.1 | 0.7 | 2.5 | 0.1 | 0.7 | 0.0 | 0.0 | 0.0 | 4.1 |
| 1976-77 | 0.0 | 0.0 | 0.0 | 0.0 | 1.6 | 1.1 | 19.6 | 0.8 | 0.1 | 0.8 | 0.0 | 0.0 | 24.0 |
| 1977-78 | 0.0 | 0.0 | 0.0 | 0.0 | 4.8 | 2.2 | 28.4 | 5.3 | 9.4 | T | 0.0 | 0.0 | 50.1 |
| 1978-79 | 0.0 | 0.0 | 0.0 | 0.0 | T | T | 8.5 | 10.9 | 0.9 | T | 0.0 | 0.0 | 20.3 |
| 1979-80 | 0.0 | 0.0 | 0.0 | 0.0 | 0.1 | T | 10.7 | 3.6 | 3.9 | T | 0.0 | 0.0 | 18.3 |
| 1980-81 | 0.0 | 0.0 | 0.0 | T | T | T | 2.5 | 0.3 | 0.1 | 0.0 | 0.0 | 0.0 | 2.9 |
| 1981-82 | 0.0 | 0.0 | 0.0 | 0.0 | 0.1 | 3.6 | 2.7 | 2.9 | 0.3 | 1.4 | 0.0 | 0.0 | 11.0 |
| 1982-83 | 0.0 | 0.0 | 0.0 | 0.0 | 0.0 | 0.0 | 0.6 | 4.5 | 0.1 | T | 0.0 | 0.0 | 5.2 |
| 1983-84 | 0.0 | 0.0 | 0.0 | 0.0 | 0.0 | 0.6 | 3.1 | 8.8 | 1.0 | 0.0 | 0.0 | 0.0 | 13.5 |
| 1984-85 | 0.0 | 0.0 | 0.0 | 0.0 | 0.0 | 4.8 | 7.4 | 6.7 | T | T | 0.0 | 0.0 | 18.9 |
| 1985-86 | 0.0 | 0.0 | 0.0 | 0.0 | 0.0 | 1.6 | 1.1 | 8.8 | 0.1 | 0.0 | 0.0 | 0.0 | 11.6 |
| 1986-87 | 0.0 | 0.0 | 0.0 | 0.0 | T | T | 2.2 | 6.7 | 9.3 | T | 0.0 | 0.0 | 18.2 |
| 1987-88 | 0.0 | 0.0 | 0.0 | 0.0 | T | T | 3.0 | 5.0 | 0.5 | 0.0 | 0.0 | 0.0 | 8.5 |
| 1988-89 | 0.0 | 0.0 | 0.0 | 0.0 | T | T | 0.3 | T | 0.6 | T | 0.0 | 0.0 | 0.9 |
| 1989-90 | 0.0 | 0.0 | 0.0 | 1.4 | T | 6.5 | 1.9 | 0.8 | 4.1 | T | 0.0 | 0.0 | 14.7 |
| 1990-91 | 0.0 | 0.0 | 0.0 | 0.0 | 0.0 | 4.1 | | | | | | | |
| Record Mean | 0.0 | 0.0 | 0.0 | T | 1.1 | 2.2 | 5.4 | 4.4 | 3.3 | 0.1 | T | 0.0 | 16.6 |

**See Reference Notes, relative to all above tables, on preceding page.**

The New Orleans metropolitan area is virtually surrounded by water. Lake Pontchartrain, some 610 square miles in area, borders the city on the north and is connected to the Gulf of Mexico through Lake Borgne on the east. In other directions there are bayous, lakes, and marshy delta land. The proximity of the Gulf of Mexico also has a great influence on the climate. Elevations in the city vary from a few feet below to a few feet above mean sea level. A massive levee system surrounding the city and along the Mississippi River offers protection against flooding from the river and tidal surges. The New Orleans International Airport is located 12 miles west of downtown New Orleans, between the Mississippi River and Lake Pontchartrain.

The climate of the city can best be described as humid with the surrounding water modifying the temperature and decreasing the range between the extremes. Almost daily sporadic afternoon thunderstorms from mid–June through September keep the temperature from rising much above 90 degrees. From about mid–November to mid–March, the area is subjected alternately to the southerly flow of warm tropical air and to the northerly flow of cold continental air in periods of varying lengths. The usual track of winter storms is to the north of New Orleans, but occasionally one moves this far south, bringing large and rather sudden drops in temperature. However, the cold spells seldom last over three or four days. The lowest temperatures observed are below 10 degrees. In about two–thirds of the years, the lowest temperature is about 24 degrees or warmer. The lowest temperatures in some years are entirely above freezing.

During the winter and spring, the cold Mississippi River water enhances the formation of river fogs, particularly when light southerly winds bring warm, moist air into the area from the Gulf of Mexico. The nearby lakes and marshes also contribute to fog formation. Even so, the fog usually does not seriously affect automobile traffic except for brief periods. However, air travel will be suspended for several hours and river traffic, at times, will be unable to move between New Orleans and the Gulf for several days.

Rather frequent and sometimes very heavy rains are typical for this area. There are an average of 120 days of measurable rain per year and an annual average accumulation of over 60 inches. A fairly definite rainy period occurs from mid–December to mid–March. Precipitation during this period is most likely to be steady rain for two to three day periods. April, May, October, and November are generally dry, but there have been some extremely heavy showers in those months. The greatest 24–hour amounts have exceeded 14 inches. Snowfall is rather infrequent and light. However, on rare occasions, snowstorms have produced accumulations over 8 inches.

While thunder occurs with most of the showers in the area, thunderstorms with damaging winds are infrequent. Hail of a damaging nature seldom occurs, and tornadoes are extremely rare. However, waterspouts are observed quite often on nearby lakes. Hurricanes have effected the area.

The lower Mississippi River floods result from runoff upstream. If the water level in the river becomes dangerously high, the spillways upriver can be opened to divert the floodwaters. Rainfall in the New Orleans area is pumped into the surrounding lakes and bayous. Local street and minor urban flooding of short duration result from occasional downpours.

Air pollution is not a serious problem. The area is not highly industrialized, and long periods of air stagnation are rare.

Based on the 1951–1980 period, the average first occurrence of 32 degrees Fahrenheit in the fall is December 5 and the average last occurrence in the spring is February 20.

## TABLE 1     NORMALS, MEANS AND EXTREMES

NEW ORLEANS, LOUISIANA

LATITUDE: 29°59'N    LONGITUDE: 90°15'W    ELEVATION: FT. GRND   4 BARO   20   TIME ZONE: CENTRAL    WBAN: 12916

| | (a) | JAN | FEB | MAR | APR | MAY | JUNE | JULY | AUG | SEP | OCT | NOV | DEC | YEAR |
|---|---|---|---|---|---|---|---|---|---|---|---|---|---|---|
| **TEMPERATURE °F:** | | | | | | | | | | | | | | |
| Normals | | | | | | | | | | | | | | |
| -Daily Maximum | | 61.8 | 64.6 | 71.2 | 78.6 | 84.5 | 89.5 | 90.7 | 90.2 | 86.8 | 79.4 | 70.1 | 64.4 | 77.7 |
| -Daily Minimum | | 43.0 | 44.8 | 51.6 | 58.8 | 65.3 | 70.9 | 73.5 | 73.1 | 70.1 | 59.0 | 49.9 | 44.8 | 58.7 |
| -Monthly | | 52.4 | 54.7 | 61.4 | 68.7 | 74.9 | 80.3 | 82.1 | 81.7 | 78.5 | 69.2 | 60.0 | 54.6 | 68.2 |
| Extremes | | | | | | | | | | | | | | |
| -Record Highest | 43 | 83 | 85 | 89 | 92 | 96 | 100 | 101 | 102 | 101 | 92 | 87 | 84 | 102 |
| -Year | | 1982 | 1972 | 1982 | 1987 | 1953 | 1954 | 1981 | 1980 | 1980 | 1986 | 1986 | 1978 | AUG 1980 |
| -Record Lowest | 43 | 14 | 19 | 25 | 32 | 41 | 50 | 60 | 60 | 42 | 35 | 24 | 11 | 11 |
| -Year | | 1985 | 1970 | 1980 | 1971 | 1960 | 1984 | 1967 | 1968 | 1967 | 1989 | 1970 | 1989 | DEC 1989 |
| **NORMAL DEGREE DAYS:** | | | | | | | | | | | | | | |
| Heating (base 65°F) | | 423 | 318 | 171 | 25 | 0 | 0 | 0 | 0 | 0 | 31 | 186 | 336 | 1490 |
| Cooling (base 65°F) | | 32 | 30 | 59 | 136 | 307 | 459 | 530 | 518 | 405 | 161 | 36 | 13 | 2686 |
| **% OF POSSIBLE SUNSHINE** | 16 | 49 | 52 | 60 | 67 | 66 | 67 | 63 | 63 | 64 | 67 | 54 | 52 | 60 |
| **MEAN SKY COVER (tenths)** | | | | | | | | | | | | | | |
| Sunrise - Sunset | 41 | 6.7 | 6.3 | 6.3 | 5.7 | 5.5 | 5.5 | 6.4 | 5.8 | 5.4 | 4.4 | 5.4 | 6.3 | 5.8 |
| **MEAN NUMBER OF DAYS:** | | | | | | | | | | | | | | |
| Sunrise to Sunset | | | | | | | | | | | | | | |
| -Clear | 41 | 6.9 | 7.7 | 7.9 | 8.1 | 9.3 | 8.5 | 4.6 | 7.3 | 9.6 | 14.7 | 10.3 | 8.0 | 103.0 |
| -Partly Cloudy | 41 | 7.3 | 6.6 | 8.2 | 10.7 | 11.3 | 12.4 | 14.6 | 13.7 | 10.5 | 7.8 | 8.0 | 7.6 | 118.7 |
| -Cloudy | 41 | 16.8 | 14.0 | 14.9 | 11.2 | 10.4 | 9.0 | 11.8 | 10.0 | 9.9 | 8.5 | 11.7 | 15.4 | 143.6 |
| Precipitation | | | | | | | | | | | | | | |
| .01 inches or more | 41 | 10.0 | 9.1 | 8.9 | 7.0 | 7.6 | 10.7 | 14.6 | 13.2 | 9.8 | 5.6 | 7.4 | 10.0 | 114.1 |
| Snow,Ice pellets | | | | | | | | | | | | | | |
| 1.0 inches or more | 41 | 0.0 | 0.* | 0.0 | 0.0 | 0.0 | 0.0 | 0.0 | 0.0 | 0.0 | 0.0 | 0.0 | 0.* | * |
| Thunderstorms | 41 | 1.7 | 2.8 | 4.0 | 4.2 | 5.9 | 9.4 | 15.0 | 12.9 | 6.8 | 1.9 | 1.9 | 2.2 | 68.6 |
| Heavy Fog Visibility 1/4 mile or less | 41 | 6.2 | 4.2 | 3.9 | 1.8 | 0.9 | 0.2 | 0.1 | 0.1 | 0.2 | 1.7 | 3.7 | 4.9 | 27.8 |
| Temperature °F | | | | | | | | | | | | | | |
| -Maximum | | | | | | | | | | | | | | |
| 90° and above | 43 | 0.0 | 0.0 | 0.0 | 0.2 | 3.4 | 15.8 | 20.4 | 19.7 | 8.8 | 0.9 | 0.0 | 0.0 | 69.3 |
| 32° and below | 43 | 0.1 | 0.0 | 0.0 | 0.0 | 0.0 | 0.0 | 0.0 | 0.0 | 0.0 | 0.0 | 0.0 | 0.1 | 0.3 |
| -Minimum | | | | | | | | | | | | | | |
| 32° and below | 43 | 5.3 | 3.0 | 0.5 | 0.* | 0.0 | 0.0 | 0.0 | 0.0 | 0.0 | 0.0 | 0.7 | 3.8 | 13.4 |
| 0° and below | 43 | 0.0 | 0.0 | 0.0 | 0.0 | 0.0 | 0.0 | 0.0 | 0.0 | 0.0 | 0.0 | 0.0 | 0.0 | 0.0 |
| **AVG. STATION PRESS.(mb)** | 17 | 1020.1 | 1018.8 | 1015.8 | 1015.3 | 1013.8 | 1014.6 | 1015.9 | 1015.4 | 1014.8 | 1017.4 | 1018.2 | 1019.9 | 1016.7 |
| **RELATIVE HUMIDITY (%)** | | | | | | | | | | | | | | |
| Hour 00 | 41 | 82 | 81 | 81 | 84 | 86 | 87 | 89 | 89 | 86 | 84 | 84 | 83 | 85 |
| Hour 06 | 41 | 85 | 84 | 84 | 88 | 89 | 89 | 91 | 91 | 89 | 87 | 86 | 86 | 87 |
| Hour 12 (Local Time) | 41 | 66 | 63 | 60 | 59 | 60 | 63 | 66 | 66 | 65 | 59 | 62 | 66 | 63 |
| Hour 18 | 41 | 72 | 67 | 64 | 65 | 65 | 68 | 73 | 73 | 74 | 72 | 75 | 74 | 70 |
| **PRECIPITATION (inches):** | | | | | | | | | | | | | | |
| Water Equivalent | | | | | | | | | | | | | | |
| -Normal | | 4.97 | 5.23 | 4.73 | 4.50 | 5.07 | 4.63 | 6.73 | 6.02 | 5.87 | 2.66 | 4.06 | 5.27 | 59.74 |
| -Maximum Monthly | 43 | 13.63 | 12.59 | 19.09 | 16.12 | 14.33 | 15.01 | 13.07 | 16.12 | 16.74 | 13.20 | 19.81 | 10.77 | 19.81 |
| -Year | | 1978 | 1983 | 1948 | 1980 | 1959 | 1987 | 1982 | 1977 | 1971 | 1985 | 1989 | 1967 | NOV 1989 |
| -Minimum Monthly | 43 | 0.54 | 0.15 | 0.24 | 0.28 | 0.99 | 0.23 | 1.92 | 1.68 | 0.24 | 0.00 | 0.21 | 1.46 | 0.00 |
| -Year | | 1968 | 1989 | 1955 | 1976 | 1949 | 1979 | 1981 | 1980 | 1953 | 1978 | 1949 | 1958 | OCT 1978 |
| -Maximum in 24 hrs | 43 | 6.08 | 5.60 | 7.87 | 8.08 | 9.86 | 7.40 | 4.30 | 4.82 | 6.50 | 4.51 | 12.66 | 5.71 | 12.66 |
| -Year | | 1978 | 1961 | 1948 | 1988 | 1959 | 1988 | 1966 | 1975 | 1971 | 1985 | 1989 | 1982 | NOV 1989 |
| Snow,Ice pellets | | | | | | | | | | | | | | |
| -Maximum Monthly | 43 | 0.4 | 2.0 | T | 0.0 | T | 0.0 | 0.0 | 0.0 | 0.0 | 0.0 | T | 2.7 | 2.7 |
| -Year | | 1985 | 1958 | 1989 | | 1989 | | | | | | 1950 | 1963 | DEC 1963 |
| -Maximum in 24 hrs | 43 | 0.4 | 2.0 | T | 0.0 | T | 0.0 | 0.0 | 0.0 | 0.0 | 0.0 | T | 2.7 | 2.7 |
| -Year | | 1985 | 1958 | 1989 | | 1989 | | | | | | 1950 | 1963 | DEC 1963 |
| **WIND:** | | | | | | | | | | | | | | |
| Mean Speed (mph) | 41 | 9.4 | 9.8 | 9.9 | 9.4 | 8.1 | 6.9 | 6.1 | 6.0 | 7.3 | 7.5 | 8.7 | 9.0 | 8.2 |
| Prevailing Direction | | | | | | | | | | | | | | |
| Fastest Obs. 1 Min. | | | | | | | | | | | | | | |
| -Direction (!!) | 30 | 21 | 26 | 16 | 20 | 36 | 05 | 13 | 33 | 09 | 17 | 21 | 28 | 09 |
| -Speed (MPH) | 30 | 46 | 43 | 38 | 35 | 55 | 48 | 44 | 42 | 69 | 40 | 32 | 46 | 69 |
| -Year | | 1975 | 1970 | 1987 | 1980 | 1973 | 1971 | 1979 | 1969 | 1965 | 1964 | 1983 | 1973 | SEP 1965 |
| Peak Gust | | | | | | | | | | | | | | |
| -Direction (!!) | 6 | S | S | S | SW | W | W | SE | SW | N | NE | NW | NE | SW |
| -Speed (mph) | 6 | 41 | 49 | 47 | 41 | 60 | 52 | 41 | 61 | 53 | 49 | 41 | 39 | 61 |
| -Date | | 1988 | 1984 | 1987 | 1985 | 1989 | 1985 | 1989 | 1985 | 1988 | 1985 | 1989 | 1986 | AUG 1985 |

**See Reference Notes to this table on the following page.**

PRECIPITATION (inches)   NEW ORLEANS, LOUISIANA

**TABLE 2**

| YEAR | JAN | FEB | MAR | APR | MAY | JUNE | JULY | AUG | SEP | OCT | NOV | DEC | ANNUAL |
|---|---|---|---|---|---|---|---|---|---|---|---|---|---|
| 1961 | 6.94 | 9.00 | 8.53 | 2.88 | 6.46 | 8.01 | 10.38 | 7.26 | 8.90 | 0.51 | 8.66 | 6.01 | 83.53 |
| 1962 | 4.19 | 1.02 | 1.60 | 2.66 | 1.31 | 8.87 | 4.70 | 2.41 | 2.52 | 3.29 | 1.96 | 4.47 | 39.00 |
| 1963 | 5.21 | 5.90 | 1.00 | 1.84 | 3.17 | 4.16 | 6.40 | 2.12 | 7.35 | T | 7.85 | 5.25 | 50.25 |
| 1964 | 9.60 | 5.35 | 5.45 | 5.66 | 1.69 | 5.52 | 5.90 | 3.88 | 4.93 | 3.50 | 3.51 | 3.10 | 58.09 |
| 1965 | 4.48 | 5.25 | 1.95 | 0.33 | 3.62 | 2.21 | 5.26 | 6.34 | 10.03 | 1.03 | 1.49 | 7.35 | 49.34 |
| 1966 | 12.62 | 10.11 | 1.60 | 1.90 | 4.92 | 2.10 | 9.42 | 2.84 | 5.55 | 3.15 | 0.72 | 5.44 | 68.08 |
| 1967 | 4.22 | 6.80 | 1.60 | 2.18 | 3.56 | 2.40 | 6.42 | 7.51 | 3.73 | 3.79 | 0.45 | 10.77 | 53.43 |
| 1968 | 0.54 | 3.02 | 3.49 | 3.59 | 4.13 | 3.69 | 4.96 | 4.78 | 2.44 | 1.40 | 4.97 | 6.14 | 43.15 |
| 1969 | 3.12 | 4.80 | 7.08 | 6.04 | 5.51 | 2.47 | 6.64 | 7.80 | 1.08 | 0.51 | 1.73 | 5.26 | 52.04 |
| 1970 | 2.53 | 2.28 | 7.22 | 0.43 | 4.68 | 4.97 | 3.70 | 10.21 | 4.25 | 4.94 | 0.85 | 4.28 | 50.34 |
| 1971 | 1.13 | 4.87 | 3.61 | 1.53 | 1.38 | 8.02 | 4.55 | 5.75 | 16.74 | 0.58 | 2.63 | 6.64 | 57.43 |
| 1972 | 6.98 | 6.03 | 6.07 | 1.64 | 6.31 | 3.10 | 3.90 | 4.92 | 3.29 | 4.64 | 8.45 | 8.65 | 63.98 |
| 1973 | 2.68 | 5.40 | 12.17 | 10.47 | 4.68 | 6.08 | 5.94 | 3.37 | 11.07 | 5.07 | 4.04 | 8.31 | 79.28 |
| 1974 | 8.46 | 5.53 | 6.64 | 5.52 | 9.84 | 3.83 | 5.66 | 6.70 | 7.58 | 2.26 | 5.88 | 4.89 | 72.79 |
| 1975 | 2.95 | 3.64 | 5.32 | 6.69 | 8.03 | 12.28 | 8.35 | 10.11 | 3.97 | 4.00 | 11.35 | 3.81 | 80.50 |
| 1976 | 2.61 | 3.85 | 3.08 | 0.28 | 5.58 | 3.36 | 5.67 | 1.69 | 1.57 | 5.08 | 5.80 | 8.81 | 47.38 |
| 1977 | 5.62 | 2.75 | 3.96 | 6.38 | 2.59 | 1.74 | 2.91 | 16.12 | 13.48 | 4.33 | 8.77 | 4.15 | 72.80 |
| 1978 | 13.63 | 2.53 | 2.67 | 3.44 | 9.72 | 7.82 | 10.34 | 14.68 | 2.98 | 0.00 | 4.67 | 4.42 | 76.90 |
| 1979 | 5.55 | 12.49 | 3.31 | 4.90 | 4.38 | 0.23 | 11.43 | 4.57 | 4.55 | 1.49 | 4.27 | 3.07 | 60.24 |
| 1980 | 6.37 | 3.09 | 10.08 | 16.12 | 9.65 | 3.69 | 4.84 | 1.68 | 6.31 | 5.87 | 3.85 | 1.54 | 73.09 |
| 1981 | 0.94 | 8.34 | 2.70 | 2.28 | 5.35 | 8.47 | 1.92 | 11.10 | 4.78 | 2.03 | 1.10 | 5.50 | 54.51 |
| 1982 | 2.76 | 7.88 | 2.56 | 5.86 | 1.19 | 5.43 | 13.07 | 1.92 | 5.40 | 3.84 | 5.45 | 9.15 | 65.30 |
| 1983 | 3.31 | 12.59 | 4.88 | 14.86 | 3.71 | 10.64 | 2.95 | 6.29 | 3.79 | 2.84 | 2.80 | 2.53 | 52.07 |
| 1984 | 4.10 | 5.27 | 4.90 | 1.72 | 3.54 | 7.21 | 3.86 | 9.51 | 3.79 | 13.20 | 0.96 | 4.78 | 66.98 |
| 1985 | 4.83 | 9.28 | 7.07 | 2.11 | 1.16 | 4.56 | 6.92 | 6.37 | 5.74 | 4.94 | 3.94 | 1.54 | 57.86 |
| 1986 | 3.49 | 2.93 | 1.88 | 1.50 | 1.61 | 8.87 | 3.60 | 6.74 | 1.42 | 2.87 | 7.90 | 5.05 | 47.86 |
| 1987 | 8.88 | 7.38 | 4.39 | 2.27 | 3.46 | 15.01 | 6.38 | 5.05 | 1.29 | 0.72 | 2.92 | 2.88 | 60.63 |
| 1988 | 3.74 | 11.31 | 8.90 | 9.25 | 1.68 | 11.28 | 6.78 | 7.53 | 5.86 | 2.87 | 1.26 | 3.94 | 74.40 |
| 1989 | 2.47 | 0.15 | 7.14 | 3.20 | 3.50 | 8.22 | 8.34 | 3.31 | 4.53 | 0.51 | 19.81 | 6.28 | 67.46 |
| 1990 | 7.59 | 11.45 | 5.98 | 4.59 | 5.87 | 1.01 | 2.30 | 2.45 | 4.55 | 2.38 | 3.21 | 9.67 | 61.05 |
| Record Mean | 4.70 | 5.15 | 5.26 | 4.71 | 4.65 | 5.18 | 6.63 | 5.99 | 5.39 | 3.12 | 4.34 | 5.16 | 60.28 |

**TABLE 3**   AVERAGE TEMPERATURE (deg. F)   NEW ORLEANS, LOUISIANA

| YEAR | JAN | FEB | MAR | APR | MAY | JUNE | JULY | AUG | SEP | OCT | NOV | DEC | ANNUAL |
|---|---|---|---|---|---|---|---|---|---|---|---|---|---|
| 1961 | 47.4 | 58.1 | 64.6 | 64.7 | 72.7 | 77.3 | 79.7 | 79.7 | 78.1 | 68.0 | 61.1 | 56.2 | 67.3 |
| 1962 | 50.5 | 63.9 | 57.9 | 65.8 | 76.1 | 79.3 | 83.7 | 82.3 | 78.5 | 71.6 | 60.3 | 46.1 | 68.2 |
| 1963 | 47.5 | 48.2 | 65.6 | 72.6 | 75.2 | 79.5 | 81.2 | 81.6 | 77.0 | 70.0 | 61.8 | 56.4 | 67.2 |
| 1964 | 50.0 | 49.8 | 60.5 | 70.6 | 74.6 | 78.9 | 80.6 | 81.7 | 76.2 | 66.7 | 64.5 | 54.0 | 67.8 |
| 1965 | 54.9 | 54.4 | 58.9 | 70.9 | 75.5 | 78.5 | 81.0 | 77.7 | 77.0 | 61.6 | 63.3 | 53.3 | 66.9 |
| 1966 | 46.9 | 52.0 | 59.0 | 68.7 | 75.0 | 77.1 | 82.2 | 80.4 | 77.0 | 68.9 | 61.6 | 58.2 | 68.0 |
| 1967 | 52.5 | 52.5 | 63.2 | 72.2 | 73.8 | 81.6 | 80.5 | 80.0 | 75.1 | 65.6 | 60.3 | 58.2 | 68.0 |
| 1968 | 51.6 | 47.2 | 55.9 | 68.1 | 74.1 | 80.4 | 82.4 | 82.1 | 76.7 | 71.1 | 58.5 | 54.5 | 67.3 |
| 1969 | 54.2 | 54.6 | 53.8 | 68.8 | 73.3 | 80.3 | 82.1 | 80.1 | 80.1 | 68.7 | 55.4 | 57.9 | 67.4 |
| 1970 | 47.3 | 51.7 | 60.1 | 70.7 | 74.2 | 79.6 | 81.6 | 81.5 | 78.9 | 71.7 | 59.2 | 63.4 | 68.6 |
| 1971 | 55.1 | 53.9 | 59.2 | 66.9 | 72.9 | 80.0 | 81.4 | 81.1 | 79.6 | 70.4 | 56.6 | 55.3 | 68.6 |
| 1972 | 58.6 | 56.1 | 61.9 | 69.8 | 73.9 | 80.8 | 79.4 | 81.1 | 79.7 | 73.4 | 66.6 | 54.1 | 68.9 |
| 1973 | 50.3 | 52.6 | 65.5 | 64.2 | 72.5 | 81.7 | 84.4 | 80.4 | 77.0 | 66.9 | 59.8 | 55.3 | 69.1 |
| 1974 | 63.3 | 55.9 | 67.3 | 69.0 | 75.8 | 78.1 | 80.3 | 80.4 | 75.1 | 69.9 | 61.2 | 51.9 | 68.2 |
| 1975 | 57.2 | 58.9 | 61.4 | 66.8 | 75.1 | 79.4 | 80.2 | 80.5 | 77.8 | 64.0 | 52.7 | 50.6 | 66.7 |
| 1976 | 50.6 | 58.2 | 64.8 | 68.5 | 72.3 | 78.3 | 81.2 | 81.5 | 77.8 | 62.9 | 54.3 | 54.3 | 68.4 |
| 1977 | 43.4 | 53.8 | 65.0 | 69.0 | 75.9 | 82.4 | 83.9 | 81.9 | 80.2 | 68.2 | 67.1 | 55.9 | 68.2 |
| 1978 | 44.1 | 45.0 | 59.9 | 71.4 | 76.9 | 81.2 | 82.6 | 83.2 | 79.3 | 71.0 | 58.0 | 52.5 | 68.0 |
| 1979 | 45.9 | 52.9 | 62.6 | 71.1 | 74.6 | 81.1 | 83.6 | 82.9 | 83.5 | 68.8 | 60.0 | 53.6 | 69.6 |
| 1980 | 56.1 | 52.0 | 62.0 | 66.2 | 77.9 | 83.3 | 85.0 | 85.5 | 83.5 | 68.8 | 64.9 | 54.5 | 69.4 |
| 1981 | 48.5 | 55.3 | 61.9 | 71.4 | 74.8 | 83.8 | 85.0 | 83.1 | 77.9 | 71.1 | 64.9 | 54.5 | 69.6 |
| 1982 | 54.5 | 55.0 | 65.9 | 69.8 | 76.5 | 81.5 | 81.4 | 82.2 | 76.8 | 70.4 | 62.5 | 59.4 | 69.6 |
| 1983 | 50.2 | 53.8 | 58.3 | 64.3 | 77.6 | 81.5 | 82.4 | 75.3 | 73.5 | 69.1 | 60.0 | 49.5 | 66.3 |
| 1984 | 46.6 | 53.9 | 59.3 | 67.5 | 73.7 | 77.4 | 78.8 | 79.2 | 76.3 | 73.5 | 62.4 | 51.0 | 68.0 |
| 1985 | 45.2 | 52.3 | 65.3 | 69.0 | 74.7 | 79.3 | 80.2 | 81.6 | 77.0 | 72.6 | 67.3 | 53.6 | 69.3 |
| 1986 | 51.2 | 59.2 | 60.6 | 67.2 | 76.7 | 81.0 | 83.2 | 81.6 | 81.0 | 70.4 | 66.3 | 53.2 | 69.3 |
| 1987 | 50.0 | 56.3 | 60.3 | 66.2 | 76.8 | 79.9 | 82.9 | 83.5 | 78.2 | 64.4 | 61.6 | 59.0 | 68.3 |
| 1988 | 49.4 | 53.2 | 60.9 | 68.4 | 73.3 | 78.5 | 81.6 | 81.4 | 79.8 | 68.0 | 65.6 | 56.0 | 68.2 |
| 1989 | 60.2 | 55.9 | 62.8 | 67.0 | 76.4 | 79.4 | 81.4 | 81.7 | 76.9 | 67.5 | 62.4 | 46.9 | 68.2 |
| 1990 | 57.2 | 61.3 | 63.3 | 67.6 | 76.2 | 82.6 | 82.3 | 83.0 | 79.6 | 68.1 | 62.3 | 59.0 | 70.2 |
| Record Mean | 53.3 | 56.0 | 61.8 | 68.7 | 75.4 | 80.7 | 82.3 | 82.1 | 78.8 | 70.3 | 61.1 | 55.3 | 68.8 |
| Max | 62.1 | 65.1 | 71.1 | 78.0 | 84.4 | 89.4 | 90.6 | 90.3 | 86.7 | 79.7 | 70.4 | 64.3 | 77.7 |
| Min | 44.4 | 46.8 | 52.5 | 59.4 | 66.3 | 71.9 | 73.9 | 73.9 | 70.8 | 61.0 | 51.7 | 46.2 | 59.9 |

## REFERENCE NOTES FOR TABLES 1, 2, 3 and 6   (NEW ORLEANS, LA)

### GENERAL

T - TRACE AMOUNT
BLANK ENTRIES DENOTE MISSING/UNREPORTED DATA.
# INDICATES A STATION OR INSTRUMENT RELOCATION.

### SPECIFIC

#### TABLE 1

(a) - LENGTH OF RECORD IN YEARS. ALTHOUGH INDIVIDUAL MONTHS MAY BE MISSING.

\* LESS THAN .05

NORMALS — BASED ON THE 1951-1980 RECORD PERIOD.
EXTREMES — DATES ARE THE MOST RECENT OCCURRENCE.
WIND DIR. — NUMERALS SHOW TENS OF DEGREES
CLOCKWISE FROM TRUE NORTH.
"00" INDICATES CALM.
RESULTANT WIND DIRECTIONS ARE GIVEN TO WHOLE DEGREES.

#### TABLE 3
MAX AND MIN ARE LONG-TERM MEAN DAILY MAXIMUM AND MEAN DAILY MINIMUM TEMPERATURES.

### EXCEPTIONS

**TABLES 2, 3, and 6**

RECORD MEANS ARE THROUGH THE CURRENT YEAR, BEGINNING IN   1947 FOR TEMPERATURE
1947 FOR PRECIPITATION
1947 FOR SNOWFALL

HEATING DEGREE DAYS Base 65 deg. F          NEW ORLEANS, LOUISIANA

**TABLE 4**

| SEASON | JULY | AUG | SEP | OCT | NOV | DEC | JAN | FEB | MAR | APR | MAY | JUNE | TOTAL |
|---|---|---|---|---|---|---|---|---|---|---|---|---|---|
| 1961-62 | 0 | 0 | 0 | 26 | 173 | 306 | 467 | 98 | 250 | 87 | 0 | 0 | 1407 |
| 1962-63 | 0 | 0 | 0 | 24 | 211 | 427 | 540 | 469 | 91 | 6 | 0 | 0 | 1768 |
| 1963-64 | 0 | 0 | 0 | 9 | 170 | 583 | 459 | 432 | 180 | 29 | 0 | 0 | 1862 |
| 1964-65 | 0 | 0 | 0 | 73 | 163 | 297 | 315 | 316 | 231 | 11 | 1 | 0 | 1407 |
| 1965-66 | 0 | 0 | 0 | 54 | 84 | 339 | 560 | 361 | 201 | 31 | 0 | 0 | 1630 |
| 1966-67 | 0 | 0 | 0 | 33 | 150 | 376 | 390 | 353 | 129 | 2 | 3 | 0 | 1436 |
| 1967-68 | 0 | 0 | 20 | 56 | 187 | 265 | 407 | 511 | 303 | 29 | 2 | 0 | 1780 |
| 1968-69 | 0 | 0 | 0 | 55 | 303 | 435 | 353 | 304 | 339 | 12 | 0 | 0 | 1801 |
| 1969-70 | 0 | 0 | 0 | 19 | 224 | 330 | 561 | 367 | 171 | 24 | 5 | 0 | 1701 |
| 1970-71 | 0 | 0 | 0 | 24 | 284 | 248 | 329 | 328 | 216 | 88 | 2 | 0 | 1519 |
| 1971-72 | 0 | 0 | 0 | 10 | 208 | 137 | 245 | 278 | 126 | 25 | 0 | 0 | 1029 |
| 1972-73 | 0 | 0 | 0 | 28 | 293 | 314 | 447 | 351 | 72 | 114 | 9 | 0 | 1628 |
| 1973-74 | 0 | 0 | 0 | 18 | 80 | 355 | 117 | 274 | 71 | 16 | 0 | 0 | 931 |
| 1974-75 | 0 | 0 | 0 | 24 | 194 | 341 | 270 | 210 | 183 | 73 | 0 | 0 | 1295 |
| 1975-76 | 0 | 0 | 6 | 16 | 222 | 417 | 445 | 205 | 98 | 21 | 0 | 0 | 1430 |
| 1976-77 | 0 | 0 | 0 | 93 | 375 | 438 | 664 | 318 | 117 | 18 | 0 | 0 | 2023 |
| 1977-78 | 0 | 0 | 0 | 43 | 113 | 342 | 646 | 556 | 191 | 2 | 0 | 0 | 1893 |
| 1978-79 | 0 | 0 | 0 | 16 | 39 | 324 | 586 | 347 | 128 | 8 | 0 | 0 | 1450 |
| 1979-80 | 0 | 0 | 0 | 13 | 230 | 396 | 278 | 385 | 154 | 38 | 2 | 0 | 1494 |
| 1980-81 | 0 | 0 | 0 | 35 | 195 | 363 | 504 | 275 | 123 | 12 | 0 | 0 | 1507 |
| 1981-82 | 0 | 0 | 0 | 36 | 100 | 333 | 365 | 278 | 127 | 29 | 0 | 0 | 1268 |
| 1982-83 | 0 | 0 | 0 | 31 | 146 | 234 | 453 | 309 | 217 | 81 | 1 | 0 | 1472 |
| 1983-84 | 0 | 0 | 1 | 37 | 183 | 483 | 564 | 321 | 197 | 48 | 2 | 0 | 1836 |
| 1984-85 | 0 | 0 | 2 | 14 | 214 | 146 | 605 | 359 | 62 | 28 | 0 | 0 | 1430 |
| 1985-86 | 0 | 0 | 0 | 12 | 49 | 443 | 421 | 195 | 160 | 28 | 0 | 0 | 1308 |
| 1986-87 | 0 | 0 | 0 | 28 | 85 | 370 | 464 | 242 | 168 | 75 | 0 | 0 | 1432 |
| 1987-88 | 0 | 0 | 0 | 58 | 149 | 222 | 490 | 351 | 166 | 23 | 0 | 0 | 1459 |
| 1988-89 | 0 | 0 | 0 | 12 | 92 | 301 | 186 | 292 | 155 | 60 | 0 | 0 | 1098 |
| 1989-90 | 0 | 0 | 0 | 53 | 142 | 559 | 253 | 136 | 101 | 41 | 0 | 0 | 1285 |
| 1990-91 | 0 | 0 | 0 | 62 | 122 | 244 | | | | | | | |

**TABLE 5**   COOLING DEGREE DAYS Base 65 deg. F          NEW ORLEANS, LOUISIANA

| YEAR | JAN | FEB | MAR | APR | MAY | JUNE | JULY | AUG | SEP | OCT | NOV | DEC | TOTAL |
|---|---|---|---|---|---|---|---|---|---|---|---|---|---|
| 1969 | 28 | 17 | 1 | 133 | 266 | 462 | 537 | 474 | 360 | 213 | 34 | 9 | 2534 |
| 1970 | 20 | 0 | 25 | 200 | 297 | 442 | 520 | 520 | 460 | 148 | 2 | 32 | 2666 |
| 1971 | 29 | 25 | 44 | 151 | 252 | 456 | 514 | 508 | 424 | 221 | 40 | 92 | 2756 |
| 1972 | 50 | 26 | 38 | 175 | 281 | 479 | 453 | 507 | 446 | 200 | 48 | 19 | 2722 |
| 1973 | 0 | 9 | 96 | 99 | 247 | 507 | 607 | 524 | 448 | 289 | 136 | 24 | 2986 |
| 1974 | 71 | 27 | 147 | 144 | 345 | 402 | 484 | 484 | 368 | 93 | 45 | 16 | 2655 |
| 1975 | 34 | 45 | 80 | 132 | 321 | 440 | 479 | 491 | 314 | 171 | 114 | 16 | 2637 |
| 1976 | 4 | 18 | 100 | 132 | 234 | 404 | 509 | 518 | 390 | 68 | 13 | 0 | 2390 |
| 1977 | 0 | 10 | 123 | 145 | 345 | 528 | 593 | 532 | 463 | 151 | 56 | 16 | 2962 |
| 1978 | 5 | 0 | 39 | 203 | 380 | 493 | 553 | 569 | 489 | 169 | 110 | 49 | 3059 |
| 1979 | 0 | 14 | 63 | 198 | 307 | 491 | 581 | 559 | 435 | 206 | 25 | 16 | 2895 |
| 1980 | 10 | 13 | 70 | 85 | 409 | 554 | 653 | 640 | 561 | 160 | 51 | 17 | 3223 |
| 1981 | 0 | 12 | 35 | 210 | 311 | 570 | 627 | 565 | 396 | 231 | 102 | 12 | 3071 |
| 1982 | 49 | 6 | 160 | 182 | 366 | 504 | 517 | 541 | 363 | 208 | 78 | 66 | 3040 |
| 1983 | 0 | 0 | 16 | 67 | 286 | 385 | 518 | 545 | 317 | 171 | 42 | 10 | 2357 |
| 1984 | 0 | 6 | 31 | 130 | 281 | 379 | 436 | 448 | 351 | 286 | 33 | 71 | 2452 |
| 1985 | 0 | 10 | 78 | 154 | 308 | 437 | 480 | 521 | 366 | 251 | 124 | 13 | 2742 |
| 1986 | 0 | 40 | 32 | 99 | 370 | 487 | 573 | 524 | 488 | 203 | 127 | 9 | 2952 |
| 1987 | 3 | 4 | 30 | 120 | 373 | 456 | 562 | 580 | 402 | 48 | 53 | 42 | 2673 |
| 1988 | 14 | 15 | 49 | 131 | 263 | 411 | 523 | 513 | 448 | 113 | 118 | 30 | 2628 |
| 1989 | 46 | 43 | 95 | 124 | 363 | 439 | 515 | 525 | 365 | 137 | 70 | 6 | 2728 |
| 1990 | 17 | 40 | 56 | 127 | 353 | 538 | 545 | 567 | 448 | 166 | 50 | 62 | 2969 |

**TABLE 6**   SNOWFALL (inches)          NEW ORLEANS, LOUISIANA

| SEASON | JULY | AUG | SEP | OCT | NOV | DEC | JAN | FEB | MAR | APR | MAY | JUNE | TOTAL |
|---|---|---|---|---|---|---|---|---|---|---|---|---|---|
| 1970-71 | 0.0 | 0.0 | 0.0 | 0.0 | 0.0 | 0.0 | 0.0 | 0.0 | 0.0 | 0.0 | 0.0 | 0.0 | 0.0 |
| 1971-72 | 0.0 | 0.0 | 0.0 | 0.0 | 0.0 | 0.0 | 0.0 | 0.0 | 0.0 | 0.0 | 0.0 | 0.0 | 0.0 |
| 1972-73 | 0.0 | 0.0 | 0.0 | 0.0 | 0.0 | 0.0 | 0.1 | 0.6 | 0.0 | 0.0 | 0.0 | 0.0 | 0.7 |
| 1973-74 | 0.0 | 0.0 | 0.0 | 0.0 | 0.0 | T | 0.0 | 0.0 | 0.0 | 0.0 | 0.0 | 0.0 | T |
| 1974-75 | 0.0 | 0.0 | 0.0 | 0.0 | 0.0 | 0.0 | 0.0 | 0.0 | 0.0 | 0.0 | 0.0 | 0.0 | 0.0 |
| 1975-76 | 0.0 | 0.0 | 0.0 | 0.0 | 0.0 | 0.0 | 0.0 | 0.0 | 0.0 | 0.0 | 0.0 | 0.0 | 0.0 |
| 1976-77 | 0.0 | 0.0 | 0.0 | 0.0 | 0.0 | 0.0 | 0.0 | 0.0 | 0.0 | 0.0 | 0.0 | 0.0 | 0.0 |
| 1977-78 | 0.0 | 0.0 | 0.0 | 0.0 | 0.0 | 0.0 | T | 0.0 | 0.0 | 0.0 | 0.0 | 0.0 | T |
| 1978-79 | 0.0 | 0.0 | 0.0 | 0.0 | 0.0 | 0.0 | T | 0.0 | 0.0 | 0.0 | 0.0 | 0.0 | T |
| 1979-80 | 0.0 | 0.0 | 0.0 | 0.0 | 0.0 | 0.0 | T | 0.0 | 0.0 | 0.0 | 0.0 | 0.0 | T |
| 1980-81 | 0.0 | 0.0 | 0.0 | 0.0 | 0.0 | 0.0 | 0.0 | 0.0 | T | 0.0 | 0.0 | 0.0 | T |
| 1981-82 | 0.0 | 0.0 | 0.0 | 0.0 | 0.0 | 0.0 | 0.0 | 0.0 | 0.0 | 0.0 | 0.0 | 0.0 | 0.0 |
| 1982-83 | 0.0 | 0.0 | 0.0 | 0.0 | 0.0 | 0.0 | T | 0.0 | 0.0 | 0.0 | 0.0 | 0.0 | T |
| 1983-84 | 0.0 | 0.0 | 0.0 | 0.0 | 0.0 | 0.0 | 0.0 | 0.0 | 0.0 | 0.0 | 0.0 | 0.0 | 0.0 |
| 1984-85 | 0.0 | 0.0 | 0.0 | 0.0 | 0.0 | 0.0 | 0.4 | 0.0 | 0.0 | 0.0 | 0.0 | 0.0 | 0.4 |
| 1985-86 | 0.0 | 0.0 | 0.0 | 0.0 | 0.0 | 0.0 | 0.0 | 0.0 | 0.0 | 0.0 | 0.0 | 0.0 | 0.0 |
| 1986-87 | 0.0 | 0.0 | 0.0 | 0.0 | 0.0 | 0.0 | 0.0 | 0.0 | 0.0 | 0.0 | 0.0 | 0.0 | 0.0 |
| 1987-88 | 0.0 | 0.0 | 0.0 | 0.0 | 0.0 | 0.0 | 0.0 | T | 0.0 | 0.0 | 0.0 | 0.0 | T |
| 1988-89 | 0.0 | 0.0 | 0.0 | 0.0 | 0.0 | 0.0 | 0.0 | 0.0 | T | 0.0 | T | 0.0 | T |
| 1989-90 | 0.0 | 0.0 | 0.0 | 0.0 | 0.0 | 0.5 | 0.0 | 0.0 | 0.0 | T | 0.0 | 0.0 | 0.5 |
| 1990-91 | 0.0 | 0.0 | 0.0 | 0.0 | 0.0 | 0.0 | | | | | | | |
| Record Mean | 0.0 | 0.0 | 0.0 | 0.0 | T | 0.1 | T | 0.1 | T | T | T | 0.0 | 0.1 |

**See Reference Notes, relative to all above tables, on preceding page.**

Shreveport is located in the northwestern section of Louisiana, some 30 miles south of Arkansas and 15 miles east of Texas. A portion of the city is situated in the Red River bottom lands and the remainder in gently rolling hills that begin about 1 mile west of the river. The NOAA National Weather Service Office is at the Shreveport Regional Airport, about 7 miles southwest of the downtown area. Elevations in the Shreveport area range from about 170 to 280 feet above sea level. The climate of Shreveport is transitional between the subtropical humid type prevalent to the south and the continental climates of the Great Plains and Middle West to the north. During winter, masses of moderate to severely cold air move periodically through the area. Rainfall is abundant with the normal annual total near 45 inches. Amounts are substantial from late autumn to spring and there is a summer—early autumn low amount with monthly averages less than 3 inches in August, September, and October.

The winter months are normally mild with cold spells generally of short duration. Freezing temperatures are recorded on an average of 34 days during the year. The average first occurrence of 32 degrees in the autumn is mid—November, and the last occurrence in the spring is early March Although temperatures have fallen below zero degrees, they normally drop below about 15 degrees in about one—half the years. Temperatures recorded at the NWS Office at the airport on clear, calm nights are normally 2 to 5 degrees warmer than those experienced in the river bottom lands. The summer months are consistently quite warm and humid with temperatures exceeding 100 degrees on about 10 days a year and exceeding 95 degrees about 45 days per year. Late afternoon humidity rarely drops below 55 percent.

Measurable snow occurs only once every other year on average. Many consecutive years may pass with no measurable snow. The heaviest snowstorms in the Shreveport area have produced more than 10 inches. More troublesome than the infrequent heavy snowfall are ice and sleet storms which may cause considerable damage to trees and utility lines, as well as make travel very difficult.

Thunderstorms occur each month, but are most frequent in spring and summer months. Severe local storms, including hailstorms, tornadoes, and local windstorms have occurred over small areas in all seasons, but are most frequent during the spring months, with a secondary peak from late November through early January. Large hail of a damaging nature is infrequent, although hail as large as grapefruit has fallen on a few occasions.

Tropical cyclones are in the dissipating stages by the time they reach this portion of the state and winds from them are usually not a destructive factor. Associated heavy rainfall can contribute to local flooding.

## TABLE 1     NORMALS, MEANS AND EXTREMES

SHREVEPORT, LOUISIANA

LATITUDE: 32°28'N    LONGITUDE: 93°49'W    ELEVATION: FT. GRND · 254 BARO   268   TIME ZONE: CENTRAL    WBAN: 13957

| | (a) | JAN | FEB | MAR | APR | MAY | JUNE | JULY | AUG | SEP | OCT | NOV | DEC | YEAR |
|---|---|---|---|---|---|---|---|---|---|---|---|---|---|---|
| **TEMPERATURE °F:** | | | | | | | | | | | | | | |
| Normals | | | | | | | | | | | | | | |
| -Daily Maximum | | 55.8 | 60.6 | 68.1 | 76.7 | 83.5 | 90.1 | 93.3 | 93.2 | 87.7 | 78.9 | 66.8 | 59.2 | 76.2 |
| -Daily Minimum | | 36.2 | 39.0 | 45.8 | 54.6 | 62.4 | 69.4 | 72.5 | 71.5 | 66.5 | 54.5 | 44.5 | 38.2 | 54.6 |
| -Monthly | | 46.0 | 49.8 | 57.0 | 65.7 | 73.0 | 79.8 | 82.9 | 82.4 | 77.1 | 66.7 | 55.7 | 48.7 | 65.4 |
| Extremes | | | | | | | | | | | | | | |
| -Record Highest | 37 | 84 | 89 | 92 | 94 | 95 | 101 | 106 | 107 | 103 | 97 | 88 | 84 | 107 |
| -Year | | 1972 | 1986 | 1974 | 1987 | 1977 | 1988 | 1980 | 1962 | 1980 | 1954 | 1984 | 1955 | AUG 1962 |
| -Record Lowest | 37 | 3 | 12 | 20 | 31 | 42 | 52 | 58 | 54 | 42 | 29 | 16 | 5 | 3 |
| -Year | | 1962 | 1978 | 1980 | 1989 | 1960 | 1977 | 1972 | 1986 | 1984 | 1989 | 1976 | 1989 | JAN 1962 |
| **NORMAL DEGREE DAYS:** | | | | | | | | | | | | | | |
| Heating (base 65°F) | | 597 | 438 | 282 | 69 | 9 | 0 | 0 | 0 | 0 | 76 | 293 | 505 | 2269 |
| Cooling (base 65°F) | | 8 | 12 | 34 | 90 | 257 | 444 | 555 | 539 | 363 | 128 | 14 | 0 | 2444 |
| **% OF POSSIBLE SUNSHINE** | 37 | 50 | 55 | 58 | 59 | 64 | 71 | 74 | 73 | 69 | 69 | 58 | 53 | 63 |
| **MEAN SKY COVER (tenths)** | | | | | | | | | | | | | | |
| Sunrise - Sunset | 37 | 6.7 | 6.3 | 6.3 | 6.2 | 6.0 | 5.4 | 5.3 | 5.1 | 5.1 | 4.8 | 5.5 | 6.1 | 5.7 |
| **MEAN NUMBER OF DAYS:** | | | | | | | | | | | | | | |
| Sunrise to Sunset | | | | | | | | | | | | | | |
| -Clear | 37 | 7.9 | 8.1 | 8.6 | 8.0 | 8.0 | 8.9 | 10.2 | 10.7 | 11.4 | 13.2 | 10.9 | 9.4 | 115.4 |
| -Partly Cloudy | 37 | 5.4 | 5.3 | 6.2 | 7.7 | 10.3 | 12.2 | 11.8 | 12.3 | 8.9 | 7.5 | 6.0 | 6.4 | 100.1 |
| -Cloudy | 37 | 17.7 | 14.9 | 16.2 | 14.3 | 12.7 | 8.8 | 9.0 | 8.0 | 9.6 | 10.3 | 13.1 | 15.2 | 149.8 |
| Precipitation | | | | | | | | | | | | | | |
| .01 inches or more | 37 | 9.2 | 8.1 | 9.2 | 8.6 | 8.8 | 7.9 | 7.9 | 6.8 | 6.7 | 6.6 | 8.2 | 9.1 | 97.1 |
| Snow, Ice pellets | | | | | | | | | | | | | | |
| 1.0 inches or more | 37 | 0.3 | 0.2 | 0.1 | 0.0 | 0.0 | 0.0 | 0.0 | 0.0 | 0.0 | 0.0 | 0.* | 0.1 | 0.6 |
| Thunderstorms | 37 | 1.8 | 2.7 | 4.9 | 5.6 | 7.1 | 7.2 | 8.0 | 6.6 | 4.0 | 2.7 | 3.0 | 2.2 | 55.9 |
| Heavy Fog Visibility | | | | | | | | | | | | | | |
| 1/4 mile or less | 37 | 3.5 | 2.2 | 1.4 | 1.2 | 0.8 | 0.5 | 0.3 | 0.5 | 1.1 | 2.3 | 2.7 | 2.9 | 19.4 |
| Temperature °F | | | | | | | | | | | | | | |
| -Maximum | | | | | | | | | | | | | | |
| 90° and above | 37 | 0.0 | 0.0 | 0.* | 0.3 | 4.4 | 17.6 | 25.4 | 25.0 | 13.9 | 2.5 | 0.0 | 0.0 | 89.1 |
| 32° and below | 37 | 1.1 | 0.3 | 0.* | 0.0 | 0.0 | 0.0 | 0.0 | 0.0 | 0.0 | 0.0 | 0.0 | 0.4 | 1.8 |
| -Minimum | | | | | | | | | | | | | | |
| 32° and below | 37 | 13.2 | 8.1 | 2.7 | 0.1 | 0.0 | 0.0 | 0.0 | 0.0 | 0.0 | 0.2 | 3.1 | 10.2 | 37.6 |
| 0° and below | 37 | 0.0 | 0.0 | 0.0 | 0.0 | 0.0 | 0.0 | 0.0 | 0.0 | 0.0 | 0.0 | 0.0 | 0.0 | 0.0 |
| **AVG. STATION PRESS. (mb)** | 17 | 1011.8 | 1010.2 | 1006.4 | 1005.9 | 1004.5 | 1005.6 | 1006.9 | 1006.7 | 1007.0 | 1009.3 | 1009.4 | 1011.2 | 1007.9 |
| **RELATIVE HUMIDITY (%)** | | | | | | | | | | | | | | |
| Hour 00 | 37 | 77 | 76 | 75 | 79 | 83 | 84 | 83 | 82 | 82 | 81 | 80 | 79 | 80 |
| Hour 06 | 37 | 83 | 83 | 83 | 87 | 90 | 90 | 90 | 91 | 91 | 89 | 86 | 85 | 87 |
| Hour 12 (Local Time) | 37 | 63 | 59 | 56 | 56 | 59 | 58 | 57 | 55 | 57 | 54 | 58 | 62 | 58 |
| Hour 18 | 37 | 65 | 58 | 54 | 56 | 60 | 59 | 58 | 57 | 61 | 62 | 66 | 67 | 60 |
| **PRECIPITATION (inches):** | | | | | | | | | | | | | | |
| Water Equivalent | | | | | | | | | | | | | | |
| -Normal | | 4.02 | 3.46 | 3.77 | 4.71 | 4.70 | 3.54 | 3.56 | 2.52 | 3.29 | 2.63 | 3.77 | 3.87 | 43.84 |
| -Maximum Monthly | 37 | 10.09 | 8.57 | 7.23 | 11.19 | 11.78 | 17.11 | 9.46 | 6.83 | 9.59 | 12.05 | 10.81 | 10.00 | 17.11 |
| -Year | | 1974 | 1983 | 1969 | 1957 | 1967 | 1989 | 1972 | 1955 | 1968 | 1984 | 1987 | 1982 | JUN 1989 |
| -Minimum Monthly | 37 | 0.27 | 0.90 | 0.56 | 0.43 | 0.42 | 0.13 | 0.15 | 0.35 | 0.17 | 0.00 | 0.71 | 0.59 | 0.00 |
| -Year | | 1971 | 1954 | 1966 | 1987 | 1988 | 1988 | 1964 | 1985 | 1956 | 1963 | 1967 | 1981 | OCT 1963 |
| -Maximum in 24 hrs | 37 | 3.18 | 3.53 | 3.63 | 7.17 | 5.27 | 7.06 | 4.30 | 4.64 | 5.39 | 3.88 | 6.51 | 3.35 | 7.17 |
| -Year | | 1979 | 1965 | 1979 | 1953 | 1978 | 1986 | 1972 | 1955 | 1961 | 1957 | 1987 | 1965 | APR 1953 |
| Snow, Ice pellets | | | | | | | | | | | | | | |
| -Maximum Monthly | 37 | 5.9 | 4.4 | 4.0 | 0.3 | T | 0.0 | 0.0 | 0.0 | 0.0 | 0.0 | 1.3 | 5.4 | 5.9 |
| -Year | | 1978 | 1985 | 1965 | 1987 | 1989 | | | | | | 1980 | 1983 | JAN 1978 |
| -Maximum in 24 hrs | 37 | 5.6 | 4.4 | 4.0 | 0.3 | T | 0.0 | 0.0 | 0.0 | 0.0 | 0.0 | 1.3 | 5.4 | 5.6 |
| -Year | | 1982 | 1985 | 1965 | 1987 | 1989 | | | | | | 1980 | 1983 | JAN 1982 |
| **WIND:** | | | | | | | | | | | | | | |
| Mean Speed (mph) | 37 | 9.3 | 9.7 | 10.2 | 9.8 | 8.4 | 7.5 | 7.1 | 6.9 | 7.3 | 7.4 | 8.6 | 9.0 | 8.4 |
| Prevailing Direction | | | | | | | | | | | | | | |
| through 1963 | | S | S | S | S | S | S | S | S | ENE | SSE | S | S | S |
| Fastest Obs. 1 Min. | | | | | | | | | | | | | | |
| -Direction (!!!) | 27 | 22 | 27 | 29 | 28 | 28 | 16 | 29 | 25 | 19 | 31 | 29 | 14 | 28 |
| -Speed (MPH) | 27 | 37 | 40 | 41 | 52 | 39 | 37 | 46 | 37 | 44 | 35 | 38 | 37 | 52 |
| -Year | | 1967 | 1965 | 1964 | 1975 | 1981 | 1963 | 1982 | 1963 | 1965 | 1966 | 1975 | 1965 | APR 1975 |
| Peak Gust | | | | | | | | | | | | | | |
| -Direction (!!!) | 6 | N | W | NW | NW | NE | NW | NW | N | NE | NW | NW | W | NW |
| -Speed (mph) | 6 | 41 | 49 | 58 | 63 | 52 | 55 | 66 | 49 | 38 | 41 | 47 | 64 | 66 |
| -Date | | 1984 | 1987 | 1986 | 1984 | 1989 | 1985 | 1989 | 1984 | 1987 | 1985 | 1988 | 1987 | JUL 1989 |

**See reference Notes to this table on the following page.**

## TABLE 2 — PRECIPITATION (inches)    SHREVEPORT, LOUISIANA

| YEAR | JAN | FEB | MAR | APR | MAY | JUNE | JULY | AUG | SEP | OCT | NOV | DEC | ANNUAL |
|---|---|---|---|---|---|---|---|---|---|---|---|---|---|
| 1961 | 3.79 | 3.88 | 6.15 | 1.70 | 1.46 | 12.39 | 3.95 | 2.26 | 5.75 | 3.51 | 5.16 | 7.50 | 57.50 |
| 1962 | 4.26 | 2.12 | 3.28 | 5.78 | 1.22 | 4.70 | 0.60 | 3.96 | 2.57 | 1.26 | 3.52 | 2.35 | 35.62 |
| 1963 | 1.46 | 2.42 | 0.91 | 3.53 | 2.25 | 2.65 | 1.00 | 3.74 | 2.36 | 0.00 | 6.72 | 2.99 | 30.03 |
| 1964 | 2.57 | 2.74 | 4.24 | 7.27 | 1.41 | 1.87 | 0.15 | 4.71 | 2.51 | 0.64 | 1.65 | 2.55 | 32.31 |
| 1965 | 3.77 | 6.51 | 3.39 | 1.16 | 5.40 | 3.18 | 1.49 | 1.82 | 6.55 | 0.36 | 1.20 | 6.29 | 41.12 |
| 1966 | 4.22 | 3.45 | 0.56 | 8.02 | 3.78 | 2.05 | 0.58 | 1.71 | 3.27 | 1.62 | 0.97 | 3.63 | 33.86 |
| 1967 | 1.36 | 2.91 | 1.02 | 2.11 | 11.78 | 0.89 | 6.15 | 4.67 | 1.27 | 1.34 | 0.71 | 3.92 | 38.13 |
| 1968 | 8.33 | 2.22 | 1.89 | 9.38 | 6.05 | 2.78 | 4.68 | 1.89 | 9.59 | 1.90 | 5.85 | 3.27 | 57.83 |
| 1969 | 1.14 | 4.32 | 7.23 | 6.63 | 5.18 | 1.16 | 1.06 | 0.50 | 0.97 | 3.16 | 7.50 | 3.95 | 42.80 |
| 1970 | 1.23 | 4.70 | 4.30 | 5.12 | 4.36 | 1.14 | 3.94 | 2.04 | 1.64 | 7.44 | 2.09 | 3.80 | 41.80 |
| 1971 | 0.27 | 4.13 | 2.11 | 1.06 | 5.26 | 0.97 | 6.15 | 2.99 | 1.30 | 3.86 | 3.75 | 3.65 | 35.50 |
| 1972 | 5.97 | 0.94 | 2.45 | 2.06 | 2.76 | 9.46 | 1.27 | 2.10 | 6.32 | 5.32 | 4.18 | 4.13 | 46.96 |
| 1973 | 5.65 | 1.52 | 5.01 | 6.44 | 2.00 | 5.84 | 7.63 | 0.77 | 6.39 | 5.38 | 5.16 | 6.37 | 58.16 |
| 1974 | 10.09 | 3.67 | 3.60 | 3.09 | 4.58 | 6.29 | 7.73 | 3.84 | 6.64 | 3.79 | 5.80 | 2.34 | 61.46 |
| 1975 | 4.55 | 4.51 | 5.84 | 3.91 | 5.31 | 3.48 | 3.45 | 1.65 | 0.98 | 3.87 | 4.44 | 1.88 | 43.87 |
| 1976 | 2.07 | 2.45 | 6.67 | 1.75 | 5.95 | 4.42 | 3.47 | 2.96 | 6.28 | 2.08 | 1.63 | 3.77 | 43.50 |
| 1977 | 3.00 | 3.68 | 4.94 | 2.05 | 2.40 | 2.41 | 3.89 | 4.28 | 0.53 | 0.31 | 2.11 | 2.58 | 32.18 |
| 1978 | 4.89 | 1.90 | 2.66 | 2.79 | 7.92 | 1.21 | 1.74 | 3.90 | 2.40 | 2.74 | 4.18 | 5.13 | 41.46 |
| 1979 | 9.22 | 4.98 | 5.74 | 7.42 | 7.99 | 3.04 | 7.50 | 1.86 | 4.33 | 3.96 | 4.76 | 3.12 | 63.92 |
| 1980 | 4.67 | 3.10 | 3.75 | 5.34 | 4.42 | 2.60 | 1.83 | 0.42 | 1.63 | 2.48 | 3.59 | 0.74 | 34.57 |
| 1981 | 1.43 | 3.83 | 3.33 | 1.97 | 9.96 | 6.45 | 2.36 | 0.94 | 3.32 | 5.63 | 1.49 | 0.59 | 41.30 |
| 1982 | 3.59 | 3.19 | 2.59 | 2.72 | 2.32 | 1.84 | 4.25 | 2.20 | 1.11 | 5.19 | 5.72 | 10.00 | 44.72 |
| 1983 | 2.45 | 8.57 | 3.68 | 1.47 | 8.22 | 6.60 | 1.18 | 1.67 | 3.12 | 0.79 | 4.90 | 7.18 | 49.83 |
| 1984 | 2.10 | 5.66 | 3.58 | 2.52 | 5.86 | 3.56 | 2.20 | 0.87 | 2.61 | 12.05 | 4.46 | 2.88 | 48.35 |
| 1985 | 2.38 | 4.42 | 4.28 | 3.05 | 1.96 | 4.57 | 8.40 | 0.35 | 4.40 | 9.87 | 4.25 | 3.37 | 51.30 |
| 1986 | 0.49 | 3.48 | 0.75 | 3.50 | 6.60 | 14.67 | 2.92 | 1.68 | 3.51 | 6.63 | 9.19 | 4.69 | 58.11 |
| 1987 | 2.26 | 7.80 | 1.48 | 0.43 | 6.67 | 5.43 | 1.21 | 3.50 | 0.94 | 5.49 | 10.81 | 8.12 | 54.14 |
| 1988 | 2.06 | 3.59 | 3.89 | 3.45 | 0.42 | 0.13 | 3.12 | 3.52 | 1.61 | 4.44 | 5.44 | 4.71 | 36.38 |
| 1989 | 7.20 | 4.06 | 3.41 | 2.41 | 10.07 | 17.11 | 4.46 | 3.94 | 1.08 | 1.50 | 2.32 | 3.34 | 60.90 |
| 1990 | 10.02 | 6.92 | 4.90 | 4.29 | 10.48 | 2.56 | 3.53 | 2.88 | 2.93 | 4.33 | 8.81 | 3.99 | 65.64 |
| Record Mean | 4.13 | 3.69 | 4.13 | 4.51 | 4.62 | 3.52 | 3.53 | 2.55 | 2.88 | 3.14 | 3.97 | 4.45 | 45.13 |

## TABLE 3 — AVERAGE TEMPERATURE (deg. F)    SHREVEPORT, LOUISIANA

| YEAR | JAN | FEB | MAR | APR | MAY | JUNE | JULY | AUG | SEP | OCT | NOV | DEC | ANNUAL |
|---|---|---|---|---|---|---|---|---|---|---|---|---|---|
| 1961 | 43.4 | 52.7 | 61.2 | 62.7 | 71.7 | 75.5 | 79.5 | 79.0 | 76.5 | 66.7 | 54.7 | 48.1 | 64.3 |
| 1962 | 42.4 | 57.2 | 53.3 | 64.0 | 75.4 | 78.6 | 84.0 | 84.8 | 78.4 | 70.7 | 55.2 | 39.9 | 66.0 |
| 1963 | 39.6 | 46.4 | 62.2 | 68.7 | 75.1 | 81.0 | 84.2 | 84.0 | 78.5 | 64.2 | 59.3 | 50.1 | 66.2 |
| 1964 | 46.5 | 45.6 | 56.8 | 68.7 | 75.1 | 81.0 | 84.0 | 82.1 | 77.2 | 64.2 | 53.0 | 52.0 | 66.3 |
| 1965 | 50.8 | 49.4 | 49.6 | 70.1 | 73.7 | 78.4 | 83.0 | 82.1 | 77.2 | 66.1 | 63.2 | 52.0 | 66.3 |
| 1966 | 42.3 | 47.5 | 58.1 | 66.2 | 72.7 | 79.0 | 85.0 | 81.0 | 75.3 | 64.0 | 60.4 | 46.9 | 64.9 |
| 1967 | 47.6 | 46.5 | 63.5 | 71.0 | 71.1 | 80.9 | 79.8 | 80.0 | 73.2 | 66.5 | 57.1 | 48.9 | 65.5 |
| 1968 | 45.4 | 43.6 | 55.9 | 66.5 | 72.7 | 80.1 | 80.1 | 82.0 | 73.6 | 66.6 | 53.7 | 46.6 | 64.0 |
| 1969 | 49.3 | 49.2 | 50.1 | 65.1 | 72.4 | 80.5 | 86.6 | 84.3 | 78.2 | 67.8 | 54.7 | 48.3 | 65.5 |
| 1970 | 42.0 | 49.4 | 53.8 | 67.4 | 72.7 | 78.8 | 81.7 | 84.3 | 81.1 | 65.1 | 54.7 | 54.3 | 65.5 |
| 1971 | 50.6 | 50.6 | 55.4 | 64.3 | 70.8 | 81.7 | 83.3 | 80.6 | 78.1 | 70.7 | 55.4 | 45.5 | 66.5 |
| 1972 | 49.4 | 51.9 | 59.8 | 66.9 | 72.3 | 80.8 | 81.0 | 82.6 | 80.2 | 67.2 | 50.9 | 45.8 | 65.7 |
| 1973 | 44.7 | 49.5 | 60.9 | 62.0 | 71.7 | 78.5 | 81.1 | 78.2 | 74.9 | 68.2 | 61.5 | 47.3 | 64.8 |
| 1974 | 47.8 | 51.2 | 63.6 | 64.3 | 74.0 | 76.6 | 82.1 | 80.1 | 71.0 | 66.2 | 55.6 | 49.3 | 65.0 |
| 1975 | 50.2 | 48.4 | 55.6 | 63.7 | 72.4 | 78.2 | 80.9 | 80.7 | 73.7 | 68.0 | 56.3 | 49.3 | 64.8 |
| 1976 | 47.1 | 59.2 | 60.2 | 67.3 | 67.9 | 75.7 | 78.6 | 78.7 | 74.3 | 59.9 | 49.3 | 46.3 | 63.7 |
| 1977 | 37.3 | 50.8 | 59.6 | 65.5 | 74.1 | 79.5 | 83.5 | 80.3 | 78.7 | 66.3 | 56.5 | 47.3 | 64.9 |
| 1978 | 34.9 | 38.1 | 52.8 | 65.5 | 73.6 | 80.5 | 85.4 | 83.3 | 77.8 | 66.0 | 48.0 | 48.9 | 63.8 |
| 1979 | 37.4 | 46.6 | 59.1 | 66.0 | 70.2 | 78.0 | 81.2 | 80.3 | 74.2 | 67.0 | 52.8 | 49.1 | 63.5 |
| 1980 | 48.3 | 47.9 | 54.9 | 63.0 | 74.3 | 83.4 | 86.9 | 85.5 | 82.1 | 63.5 | 54.2 | 49.1 | 66.1 |
| 1981 | 44.7 | 49.8 | 56.0 | 70.0 | 69.2 | 80.2 | 82.8 | 81.3 | 73.9 | 65.0 | 56.8 | 46.9 | 64.7 |
| 1982 | 46.1 | 45.6 | 61.5 | 63.3 | 74.4 | 78.6 | 83.3 | 83.2 | 75.6 | 64.6 | 55.4 | 51.2 | 65.2 |
| 1983 | 44.6 | 48.8 | 55.0 | 59.7 | 70.0 | 77.4 | 82.3 | 84.0 | 75.7 | 66.7 | 55.9 | 37.5 | 63.1 |
| 1984 | 40.6 | 50.4 | 58.0 | 64.9 | 72.1 | 79.3 | 81.1 | 82.1 | 75.0 | 70.6 | 56.4 | 60.0 | 65.9 |
| 1985 | 40.0 | 46.2 | 61.4 | 67.0 | 72.8 | 79.3 | 83.1 | 84.8 | 76.3 | 68.5 | 61.5 | 44.2 | 65.4 |
| 1986 | 49.0 | 54.4 | 59.7 | 66.5 | 72.3 | 79.9 | 83.7 | 80.8 | 79.4 | 65.2 | 55.6 | 46.1 | 66.1 |
| 1987 | 44.8 | 51.7 | 55.7 | 64.2 | 75.3 | 79.1 | 82.3 | 85.3 | 76.7 | 64.1 | 56.1 | 50.2 | 65.5 |
| 1988 | 42.2 | 49.3 | 56.3 | 65.2 | 71.8 | 79.8 | 83.3 | 83.7 | 77.8 | 64.1 | 58.6 | 49.2 | 65.1 |
| 1989 | 51.5 | 45.8 | 56.7 | 65.6 | 73.8 | 76.7 | 81.2 | 81.0 | 73.7 | 66.5 | 58.6 | 40.8 | 64.3 |
| 1990 | 52.5 | 56.4 | 59.4 | 65.6 | 72.6 | 82.7 | 82.2 | 83.3 | 79.7 | 65.0 | 58.9 | 48.5 | 67.2 |
| Record Mean | 47.1 | 50.5 | 58.0 | 66.0 | 73.2 | 80.3 | 83.0 | 82.7 | 77.1 | 67.0 | 56.2 | 49.0 | 65.8 |
| Max | 56.2 | 60.2 | 68.3 | 76.4 | 83.1 | 90.3 | 92.9 | 92.9 | 87.4 | 78.1 | 66.6 | 58.3 | 75.9 |
| Min | 37.9 | 40.7 | 47.6 | 55.6 | 63.2 | 70.3 | 73.1 | 72.4 | 66.8 | 55.9 | 45.8 | 39.7 | 55.8 |

## REFERENCE NOTES FOR TABLES 1, 2, 3 and 6    (SHREVEPORT, LA)

### GENERAL

T - TRACE AMOUNT
BLANK ENTRIES DENOTE MISSING/UNREPORTED DATA.
# INDICATES A STATION OR INSTRUMENT RELOCATION.

### SPECIFIC

#### TABLE 1

(a) - LENGTH OF RECORD IN YEARS. ALTHOUGH INDIVIDUAL MONTHS MAY BE MISSING.

* LESS THAN .05

NORMALS — BASED ON THE 1951-1980 RECORD PERIOD.
EXTREMES — DATES ARE THE MOST RECENT OCCURRENCE.
WIND DIR. — NUMERALS SHOW TENS OF DEGREES CLOCKWISE FROM TRUE NORTH.
"00" INDICATES CALM.
RESULTANT WIND DIRECTIONS ARE GIVEN TO WHOLE DEGREES.

#### TABLE 3

MAX AND MIN ARE LONG-TERM MEAN DAILY MAXIMUM AND MEAN DAILY MINIMUM TEMPERATURES.

### EXCEPTIONS

#### TABLES 2, 3, and 6

RECORD MEANS ARE THROUGH THE CURRENT YEAR, BEGINNING IN
1875 FOR TEMPERATURE
1872 FOR PRECIPITATION
1953 FOR SNOWFALL

**TABLE 4**

HEATING DEGREE DAYS Base 65 deg. F          SHREVEPORT, LOUISIANA

| SEASON | JULY | AUG | SEP | OCT | NOV | DEC | JAN | FEB | MAR | APR | MAY | JUNE | TOTAL |
|---|---|---|---|---|---|---|---|---|---|---|---|---|---|
| 1961-62 | 0 | 0 | 1 | 71 | 320 | 518 | 690 | 227 | 356 | 104 | 1 | 0 | 2288 |
| 1962-63 | 0 | 0 | 0 | 47 | 294 | 502 | 785 | 512 | 162 | 30 | 11 | 0 | 2343 |
| 1963-64 | 0 | 0 | 0 | 12 | 234 | 772 | 568 | 556 | 254 | 35 | 0 | 0 | 2431 |
| 1964-65 | 0 | 0 | 6 | 93 | 216 | 479 | 446 | 432 | 473 | 28 | 0 | 0 | 2173 |
| 1965-66 | 0 | 0 | 3 | 78 | 103 | 400 | 703 | 485 | 238 | 62 | 8 | 0 | 2080 |
| 1966-67 | 0 | 0 | 0 | 99 | 181 | 570 | 553 | 511 | 140 | 13 | 13 | 0 | 2080 |
| 1967-68 | 0 | 0 | 15 | 72 | 244 | 500 | 604 | 614 | 308 | 49 | 0 | 0 | 2406 |
| 1968-69 | 0 | 0 | 0 | 57 | 346 | 560 | 495 | 438 | 455 | 44 | 2 | 0 | 2397 |
| 1969-70 | 0 | 0 | 0 | 86 | 314 | 510 | 713 | 429 | 344 | 58 | 14 | 0 | 2468 |
| 1970-71 | 0 | 0 | 0 | 97 | 324 | 351 | 459 | 398 | 316 | 94 | 15 | 0 | 2054 |
| 1971-72 | 0 | 0 | 4 | 7 | 282 | 304 | 499 | 382 | 185 | 62 | 0 | 0 | 1725 |
| 1972-73 | 0 | 0 | 6 | 92 | 419 | 597 | 621 | 429 | 135 | 145 | 9 | 0 | 2453 |
| 1973-74 | 0 | 0 | 0 | 40 | 164 | 557 | 533 | 386 | 152 | 78 | 2 | 0 | 1912 |
| 1974-75 | 0 | 0 | 14 | 32 | 312 | 541 | 473 | 457 | 305 | 124 | 0 | 0 | 2258 |
| 1975-76 | 0 | 0 | 4 | 39 | 286 | 492 | 551 | 186 | 202 | 38 | 17 | 0 | 1815 |
| 1976-77 | 0 | 0 | 0 | 199 | 471 | 574 | 851 | 399 | 188 | 46 | 0 | 0 | 2728 |
| 1977-78 | 0 | 0 | 0 | 72 | 260 | 549 | 933 | 746 | 374 | 61 | 30 | 0 | 3025 |
| 1978-79 | 0 | 0 | 0 | 57 | 181 | 528 | 849 | 517 | 216 | 50 | 11 | 0 | 2409 |
| 1979-80 | 0 | 0 | 0 | 52 | 366 | 498 | 508 | 494 | 312 | 96 | 4 | 0 | 2330 |
| 1980-81 | 0 | 0 | 3 | 128 | 340 | 488 | 620 | 425 | 279 | 14 | 20 | 0 | 2317 |
| 1981-82 | 0 | 0 | 8 | 129 | 246 | 554 | 588 | 537 | 202 | 125 | 4 | 0 | 2393 |
| 1982-83 | 0 | 0 | 9 | 120 | 309 | 457 | 624 | 449 | 308 | 186 | 12 | 0 | 2474 |
| 1983-84 | 0 | 0 | 15 | 69 | 305 | 848 | 747 | 421 | 247 | 81 | 11 | 0 | 2744 |
| 1984-85 | 0 | 0 | 19 | 36 | 286 | 208 | 770 | 528 | 151 | 42 | 1 | 0 | 2041 |
| 1985-86 | 0 | 0 | 11 | 49 | 174 | 638 | 490 | 331 | 176 | 44 | 1 | 0 | 1914 |
| 1986-87 | 0 | 0 | 0 | 86 | 299 | 579 | 618 | 366 | 286 | 117 | 0 | 0 | 2351 |
| 1987-88 | 0 | 0 | 0 | 79 | 279 | 456 | 701 | 453 | 278 | 54 | 1 | 0 | 2301 |
| 1988-89 | 0 | 0 | 0 | 76 | 218 | 482 | 418 | 535 | 295 | 93 | 2 | 0 | 2119 |
| 1989-90 | 0 | 0 | 17 | 85 | 244 | 743 | 382 | 243 | 216 | 92 | 3 | 0 | 2025 |
| 1990-91 | 0 | 0 | 6 | 126 | 208 | 509 | | | | | | | |

**TABLE 5**

COOLING DEGREE DAYS Base 65 deg. F          SHREVEPORT, LOUISIANA

| YEAR | JAN | FEB | MAR | APR | MAY | JUNE | JULY | AUG | SEP | OCT | NOV | DEC | TOTAL |
|---|---|---|---|---|---|---|---|---|---|---|---|---|---|
| 1969 | 15 | 0 | 0 | 57 | 241 | 470 | 675 | 604 | 402 | 177 | 11 | 0 | 2652 |
| 1970 | 9 | 0 | 5 | 138 | 259 | 420 | 528 | 606 | 492 | 106 | 23 | 28 | 2614 |
| 1971 | 22 | 1 | 24 | 82 | 203 | 510 | 576 | 488 | 403 | 191 | 28 | 9 | 2537 |
| 1972 | 22 | 10 | 31 | 128 | 235 | 480 | 501 | 553 | 467 | 167 | 1 | 0 | 2595 |
| 1973 | 0 | 2 | 16 | 64 | 223 | 412 | 504 | 417 | 305 | 145 | 66 | 0 | 2154 |
| 1974 | 7 | 6 | 115 | 63 | 288 | 355 | 541 | 477 | 200 | 77 | 35 | 0 | 2164 |
| 1975 | 23 | 0 | 21 | 91 | 238 | 403 | 501 | 493 | 271 | 141 | 34 | 12 | 2228 |
| 1976 | 2 | 26 | 58 | 116 | 112 | 326 | 428 | 432 | 288 | 48 | 7 | 0 | 1843 |
| 1977 | 0 | 7 | 28 | 69 | 289 | 443 | 580 | 479 | 419 | 119 | 12 | 9 | 2454 |
| 1978 | 5 | 0 | 3 | 84 | 303 | 472 | 637 | 570 | 391 | 96 | 39 | 8 | 2608 |
| 1979 | 0 | 8 | 39 | 86 | 178 | 395 | 509 | 483 | 284 | 124 | 8 | 2 | 2116 |
| 1980 | 1 | 6 | 6 | 43 | 298 | 560 | 686 | 643 | 522 | 86 | 22 | 1 | 2874 |
| 1981 | 0 | 5 | 10 | 171 | 157 | 463 | 558 | 511 | 284 | 135 | 6 | 0 | 2300 |
| 1982 | 14 | 0 | 99 | 81 | 300 | 413 | 573 | 573 | 333 | 115 | 24 | 32 | 2557 |
| 1983 | 0 | 0 | 7 | 34 | 176 | 381 | 540 | 595 | 343 | 126 | 39 | 0 | 2241 |
| 1984 | 0 | 5 | 38 | 83 | 235 | 436 | 511 | 540 | 329 | 219 | 35 | 61 | 2492 |
| 1985 | 0 | 8 | 49 | 109 | 252 | 436 | 568 | 620 | 356 | 163 | 78 | 0 | 2639 |
| 1986 | 2 | 41 | 17 | 95 | 236 | 454 | 586 | 494 | 438 | 101 | 24 | 0 | 2488 |
| 1987 | 1 | 0 | 7 | 99 | 327 | 431 | 544 | 634 | 357 | 57 | 19 | 5 | 2481 |
| 1988 | 3 | 3 | 14 | 67 | 220 | 449 | 575 | 587 | 390 | 53 | 37 | 1 | 2399 |
| 1989 | 8 | 7 | 43 | 121 | 283 | 358 | 508 | 503 | 286 | 140 | 57 | 0 | 2314 |
| 1990 | 2 | 9 | 50 | 115 | 244 | 538 | 536 | 572 | 453 | 132 | 30 | 3 | 2684 |

**TABLE 6**

SNOWFALL (inches)          SHREVEPORT, LOUISIANA

| SEASON | JULY | AUG | SEP | OCT | NOV | DEC | JAN | FEB | MAR | APR | MAY | JUNE | TOTAL |
|---|---|---|---|---|---|---|---|---|---|---|---|---|---|
| 1970-71 | 0.0 | 0.0 | 0.0 | 0.0 | 0.0 | 0.0 | 0.8 | 0.6 | 0.3 | 0.0 | 0.0 | 0.0 | 1.7 |
| 1971-72 | 0.0 | 0.0 | 0.0 | 0.0 | T | 0.0 | T | 0.0 | 0.0 | 0.0 | 0.0 | 0.0 | T |
| 1972-73 | 0.0 | 0.0 | 0.0 | 0.0 | 0.0 | 0.0 | 0.6 | T | 0.0 | 0.0 | 0.0 | 0.0 | 0.6 |
| 1973-74 | 0.0 | 0.0 | 0.0 | 0.0 | 0.0 | T | 0.0 | 0.0 | 0.0 | 0.0 | 0.0 | 0.0 | T |
| 1974-75 | 0.0 | 0.0 | 0.0 | 0.0 | 0.0 | 0.0 | 3.4 | T | T | 0.0 | 0.0 | 0.0 | 3.4 |
| 1975-76 | 0.0 | 0.0 | 0.0 | 0.0 | T | 0.0 | 0.0 | 0.0 | 0.0 | 0.0 | 0.0 | 0.0 | T |
| 1976-77 | 0.0 | 0.0 | 0.0 | 0.0 | T | 0.0 | 5.4 | 0.0 | 0.0 | 0.0 | 0.0 | 0.0 | 5.4 |
| 1977-78 | 0.0 | 0.0 | 0.0 | 0.0 | 0.0 | 0.0 | 5.9 | 2.0 | 0.3 | 0.0 | 0.0 | 0.0 | 8.2 |
| 1978-79 | 0.0 | 0.0 | 0.0 | 0.0 | 0.0 | 0.0 | T | 1.5 | 0.0 | 0.0 | 0.0 | 0.0 | 1.5 |
| 1979-80 | 0.0 | 0.0 | 0.0 | 0.0 | T | 0.0 | 0.0 | 1.4 | T | 0.0 | 0.0 | 0.0 | 1.4 |
| 1980-81 | 0.0 | 0.0 | 0.0 | 0.0 | 1.3 | 0.0 | 0.7 | 0.1 | 0.0 | 0.0 | 0.0 | 0.0 | 2.1 |
| 1981-82 | 0.0 | 0.0 | 0.0 | 0.0 | 0.0 | T | 5.6 | T | T | 0.0 | 0.0 | 0.0 | 5.6 |
| 1982-83 | 0.0 | 0.0 | 0.0 | 0.0 | 0.0 | 0.0 | T | T | T | 0.0 | 0.0 | 0.0 | T |
| 1983-84 | 0.0 | 0.0 | 0.0 | 0.0 | 0.0 | 5.4 | T | T | 0.0 | 0.0 | 0.0 | 0.0 | 5.4 |
| 1984-85 | 0.0 | 0.0 | 0.0 | 0.0 | 0.0 | 0.0 | 0.4 | 4.4 | 0.0 | 0.0 | 0.0 | 0.0 | 4.8 |
| 1985-86 | 0.0 | 0.0 | 0.0 | 0.0 | 0.0 | 0.0 | T | T | 0.0 | 0.0 | 0.0 | 0.0 | T |
| 1986-87 | 0.0 | 0.0 | 0.0 | 0.0 | 0.0 | T | 0.0 | T | T | 0.3 | 0.0 | 0.0 | 0.3 |
| 1987-88 | 0.0 | 0.0 | 0.0 | 0.0 | 0.0 | 0.0 | 1.2 | 0.8 | 0.0 | 0.0 | 0.0 | 0.0 | 2.0 |
| 1988-89 | 0.0 | 0.0 | 0.0 | 0.0 | 0.0 | 0.0 | T | T | T | 0.0 | T | 0.0 | T |
| 1989-90 | 0.0 | 0.0 | 0.0 | 0.0 | 0.0 | T | 0.0 | T | T | 0.0 | 0.0 | 0.0 | T |
| 1990-91 | 0.0 | 0.0 | 0.0 | 0.0 | 0.0 | T | 0.0 | | | | | | |
| Record Mean | 0.0 | 0.0 | 0.0 | 0.0 | T | 0.2 | 0.8 | 0.5 | 0.2 | T | T | 0.0 | 1.8 |

**See Reference Notes, relative to all above tables, on preceding page.**

The Caribou Municipal Airport is located in Aroostook County, the largest and northernmost county in the state. The airport lies on top of high land which is about on the same level as most of the surrounding gently rolling hills. The Aroostook River, which runs about 1 mile to the east and southeast of the station, has little effect on the local weather. Even though Caribou is located only 150 miles from the Atlantic coast, its climate can be justly classed as a severe typical continental type. Winters are particularly long and windy, and seasonal snowfalls averaging over 100 inches are not unusual. While the extreme low temperatures may be less severe than one might expect, temperatures of zero or lower normally occur over 40 times per year. A study of heating degree day data will show the outstanding part that cold weather plays here.

Summers are cool and generally favored with abundant rainfall, which is one of the most important factors in the high yield of the potato and grain crops throughout the county. Our location high up in the St. Lawrence Valley allows Aroostook County to come under the influence of the Summer Polar Front, resulting in practically no dry periods of more than 3 or 4 days in the growing season. The growing season at Caribou averages more than 120 days, with the average last freeze in the spring in mid-May and the average first freeze in autumn in late September.

Autumn climate is nearly ideal, with mostly sunny warm days and crisp cool nights predominating. Aroostook County, even with its relatively short growing season, provides profitable farming. The principal crops are potatoes, peas, a variety of grains, and some hardy vegetables.

Probably unknown to many victims of hay fever and similar afflictions, the immediate Caribou area offers sparkling visibility and relatively pollen-free air in the late summer months. This latter condition is principally due to the extremely high degree of cultivation of all available land.

**TABLE 1**     # NORMALS, MEANS AND EXTREMES

CARIBOU, MAINE

LATITUDE: 46°52'N    LONGITUDE: 68°01'W    ELEVATION: FT. GRND 624 BARO 630    TIME ZONE: EASTERN    WBAN: 14607

| | (a) | JAN | FEB | MAR | APR | MAY | JUNE | JULY | AUG | SEP | OCT | NOV | DEC | YEAR |
|---|---|---|---|---|---|---|---|---|---|---|---|---|---|---|
| **TEMPERATURE °F:** | | | | | | | | | | | | | | |
| Normals | | | | | | | | | | | | | | |
| -Daily Maximum | | 19.9 | 22.9 | 33.5 | 45.8 | 60.7 | 71.0 | 75.7 | 73.1 | 63.9 | 51.7 | 38.0 | 23.9 | 48.3 |
| -Daily Minimum | | 1.4 | 3.0 | 15.1 | 28.8 | 39.7 | 49.6 | 54.5 | 51.8 | 43.2 | 34.5 | 24.2 | 7.5 | 29.4 |
| -Monthly | | 10.6 | 13.0 | 24.3 | 37.3 | 50.2 | 60.4 | 65.2 | 62.5 | 53.6 | 43.1 | 31.1 | 15.7 | 38.9 |
| Extremes | | | | | | | | | | | | | | |
| -Record Highest | 50 | 52 | 52 | 73 | 82 | 96 | 96 | 95 | 95 | 91 | 79 | 68 | 58 | 96 |
| -Year | | 1986 | 1981 | 1962 | 1987 | 1977 | 1944 | 1989 | 1975 | 1945 | 1968 | 1956 | 1950 | MAY 1977 |
| -Record Lowest | 50 | -32 | -41 | -20 | -2 | 18 | 30 | 36 | 34 | 23 | 14 | -5 | -31 | -41 |
| -Year | | 1976 | 1955 | 1967 | 1964 | 1974 | 1958 | 1969 | 1982 | 1980 | 1972 | 1989 | 1989 | FEB 1955 |
| **NORMAL DEGREE DAYS:** | | | | | | | | | | | | | | |
| Heating (base 65°F) | | 1686 | 1456 | 1262 | 831 | 459 | 150 | 86 | 120 | 342 | 679 | 1017 | 1528 | 9616 |
| Cooling (base 65°F) | | 0 | 0 | 0 | 0 | 0 | 12 | 92 | 43 | 0 | 0 | 0 | 0 | 147 |
| **% OF POSSIBLE SUNSHINE** | | | | | | | | | | | | | | |
| **MEAN SKY COVER (tenths)** | | | | | | | | | | | | | | |
| Sunrise - Sunset | 44 | 6.9 | 6.8 | 6.9 | 7.3 | 7.3 | 7.3 | 7.0 | 6.8 | 6.8 | 7.2 | 8.0 | 7.3 | 7.1 |
| **MEAN NUMBER OF DAYS:** | | | | | | | | | | | | | | |
| Sunrise to Sunset | | | | | | | | | | | | | | |
| -Clear | 48 | 6.7 | 6.1 | 6.7 | 5.1 | 4.1 | 3.3 | 3.1 | 4.4 | 5.4 | 4.8 | 2.8 | 5.5 | 58.1 |
| -Partly Cloudy | 48 | 7.1 | 6.3 | 6.9 | 6.9 | 9.0 | 9.8 | 12.9 | 11.5 | 9.2 | 7.9 | 6.2 | 6.6 | 100.2 |
| -Cloudy | 48 | 17.2 | 15.8 | 17.4 | 18.1 | 17.9 | 16.9 | 15.0 | 15.1 | 15.4 | 18.3 | 21.0 | 18.9 | 207.0 |
| Precipitation | | | | | | | | | | | | | | |
| .01 inches or more | 50 | 14.4 | 12.3 | 12.8 | 13.0 | 13.3 | 13.6 | 13.9 | 13.2 | 12.4 | 12.3 | 14.5 | 14.5 | 160.1 |
| Snow,Ice pellets | | | | | | | | | | | | | | |
| 1.0 inches or more | 48 | 6.0 | 5.6 | 4.9 | 2.7 | 0.3 | 0.0 | 0.0 | 0.0 | 0.0 | 0.5 | 3.2 | 6.4 | 29.6 |
| Thunderstorms | 25 | 0.* | 0.0 | 0.1 | 0.5 | 1.9 | 4.3 | 6.7 | 4.1 | 1.3 | 1.0 | 0.* | 0.0 | 20.1 |
| Heavy Fog Visibility | | | | | | | | | | | | | | |
| 1/4 mile or less | 25 | 2.0 | 1.6 | 1.7 | 2.2 | 1.0 | 1.6 | 2.6 | 2.3 | 3.2 | 2.3 | 3.7 | 2.7 | 26.9 |
| Temperature °F | | | | | | | | | | | | | | |
| -Maximum | | | | | | | | | | | | | | |
| 90° and above | 50 | 0.0 | 0.0 | 0.0 | 0.0 | 0.1 | 0.5 | 1.0 | 0.5 | 0.* | 0.0 | 0.0 | 0.0 | 2.2 |
| 32° and below | 50 | 26.3 | 22.9 | 13.2 | 1.8 | 0.* | 0.0 | 0.0 | 0.0 | 0.0 | 0.3 | 9.2 | 23.8 | 97.5 |
| -Minimum | | | | | | | | | | | | | | |
| 32° and below | 50 | 30.7 | 27.9 | 29.0 | 21.8 | 5.5 | 0.1 | 0.0 | 0.0 | 3.0 | 14.2 | 24.9 | 30.3 | 187.4 |
| 0° and below | 50 | 16.2 | 12.5 | 4.3 | 0.* | 0.0 | 0.0 | 0.0 | 0.0 | 0.0 | 0.0 | 0.3 | 10.3 | 43.6 |
| **AVG. STATION PRESS.(mb)** | 10 | 987.8 | 989.3 | 988.7 | 988.0 | 990.0 | 989.6 | 989.2 | 991.8 | 992.1 | 991.7 | 990.2 | 989.9 | 989.9 |
| **RELATIVE HUMIDITY (%)** | | | | | | | | | | | | | | |
| Hour 01 | 19 | 74 | 75 | 76 | 79 | 79 | 84 | 84 | 89 | 89 | 86 | 85 | 79 | 82 |
| Hour 07 | 45 | 74 | 74 | 76 | 76 | 74 | 78 | 83 | 86 | 87 | 86 | 85 | 79 | 80 |
| Hour 13 (Local Time) | 45 | 66 | 63 | 61 | 57 | 53 | 56 | 58 | 59 | 60 | 62 | 72 | 71 | 62 |
| Hour 19 | 44 | 72 | 70 | 67 | 65 | 61 | 65 | 70 | 73 | 75 | 75 | 79 | 79 | 71 |
| **PRECIPITATION (inches):** | | | | | | | | | | | | | | |
| Water Equivalent | | | | | | | | | | | | | | |
| -Normal | | 2.36 | 2.14 | 2.44 | 2.59 | 2.88 | 3.18 | 4.03 | 3.97 | 3.52 | 3.11 | 3.22 | 3.15 | 36.59 |
| -Maximum Monthly | 50 | 5.10 | 4.13 | 5.13 | 5.26 | 6.27 | 7.11 | 6.83 | 12.09 | 8.14 | 6.35 | 8.15 | 7.97 | 12.09 |
| -Year | | 1978 | 1955 | 1953 | 1973 | 1947 | 1940 | 1957 | 1981 | 1954 | 1970 | 1983 | 1973 | AUG 1981 |
| -Minimum Monthly | 50 | 0.12 | 0.26 | 0.66 | 0.54 | 0.47 | 0.88 | 1.75 | 0.93 | 0.86 | 0.63 | 0.45 | 0.74 | 0.12 |
| -Year | | 1944 | 1978 | 1965 | 1967 | 1982 | 1983 | 1977 | 1957 | 1968 | 1955 | 1939 | 1963 | JAN 1944 |
| -Maximum in 24 hrs | 50 | 1.48 | 1.38 | 1.70 | 2.11 | 2.25 | 2.37 | 2.92 | 6.89 | 6.23 | 4.07 | 2.27 | 2.80 | 6.89 |
| -Year | | 1986 | 1988 | 1984 | 1958 | 1948 | 1957 | 1957 | 1981 | 1954 | 1970 | 1983 | 1973 | AUG 1981 |
| Snow,Ice pellets | | | | | | | | | | | | | | |
| -Maximum Monthly | 50 | 41.4 | 41.0 | 47.1 | 36.4 | 10.9 | T | 0.0 | 0.0 | T | 12.1 | 34.9 | 59.9 | 59.9 |
| -Year | | 1978 | 1960 | 1955 | 1982 | 1967 | 1980 | | | 1989 | 1963 | 1974 | 1972 | DEC 1972 |
| -Maximum in 24 hrs | 50 | 15.9 | 18.2 | 28.6 | 21.1 | 5.8 | T | 0.0 | 0.0 | T | 9.4 | 21.0 | 19.7 | 28.6 |
| -Year | | 1986 | 1952 | 1984 | 1982 | 1967 | 1980 | | | 1989 | 1963 | 1986 | 1989 | MAR 1984 |
| **WIND:** | | | | | | | | | | | | | | |
| Mean Speed (mph) | 15 | 12.4 | 12.0 | 12.9 | 11.7 | 11.4 | 10.4 | 9.8 | 9.3 | 10.4 | 10.9 | 11.1 | 11.5 | 11.2 |
| Prevailing Direction | | | | | | | | | | | | | | |
| through 1962 | | NW | NW | NW | NW | NW | WSW | WSW | WSW | WSW | NNW | WSW | WSW | WSW |
| Fastest Obs. 1 Min. | | | | | | | | | | | | | | |
| -Direction (!!!) | | | | | | | | | | | | | | |
| -Speed (MPH) | | | | | | | | | | | | | | |
| -Year | | | | | | | | | | | | | | |
| Peak Gust | | | | | | | | | | | | | | |
| -Direction (!!!) | | | | | | | | | | | | | | |
| -Speed (mph) | | | | | | | | | | | | | | |
| -Date | | | | | | | | | | | | | | |

**See Reference Notes to this table on the following page.**

## TABLE 2 — PRECIPITATION (inches)  CARIBOU, MAINE

| YEAR | JAN | FEB | MAR | APR | MAY | JUNE | JULY | AUG | SEP | OCT | NOV | DEC | ANNUAL |
|------|------|------|------|------|------|------|------|------|------|------|------|------|--------|
| 1961 | 1.08 | 2.48 | 2.64 | 2.93 | 4.71 | 3.02 | 3.74 | 4.95 | 6.19 | 1.64 | 2.39 | 3.18 | 38.16 |
| 1962 | 1.84 | 1.16 | 0.70 | 2.94 | 2.91 | 2.36 | 6.72 | 3.05 | 3.84 | 3.33 | 4.35 | 0.74 | 36.38 |
| 1963 | 2.40 | 2.28 | 2.22 | 3.16 | 2.34 | 1.68 | 3.66 | 6.35 | 3.40 | 4.19 | 2.28 | 2.98 | 39.35 |
| 1964 | 2.64 | 0.56 | 3.12 | 2.17 | 2.81 | 1.80 | 3.58 | 3.38 | 3.07 | 4.14 | 4.75 | 1.56 | 30.74 |
| 1965 | 1.21 | 2.33 | 0.66 | 1.10 | 2.35 | 1.25 | 3.71 | 3.60 |      | 3.47 | 3.60 | 2.17 | 29.73 |
| 1966 | 2.06 | 1.49 | 2.61 | 1.73 | 1.73 | 2.06 | 3.27 | 1.54 | 3.19 | 2.81 | 2.79 | 4.58 | 27.92 |
| 1967 | 2.23 | 1.75 | 1.07 | 1.54 | 3.95 | 1.69 | 4.18 | 4.81 | 6.61 | 3.51 | 4.16 | 37.01 |
| 1968 | 2.31 | 1.46 | 4.01 | 1.15 | 1.33 | 1.65 | 4.24 | 2.01 | 0.86 | 3.51 | 3.98 | 3.59 | 31.67 |
| 1969 | 3.00 | 2.25 | 1.49 | 2.60 | 2.88 | 3.47 | 3.73 | 4.02 | 6.80 | 1.55 | 4.36 | 3.59 | 39.74 |
| 1970 | 0.31 | 2.09 | 2.25 | 3.56 | 4.26 | 3.25 | 2.54 | 3.18 | 5.46 | 6.35 | 1.85 | 2.58 | 37.68 |
| 1971 | 1.71 | 2.16 | 3.20 | 2.09 | 2.06 | 2.62 | 2.79 | 3.39 | 2.62 | 3.43 | 2.76 | 2.46 | 31.84 |
| 1972 | 1.32 | 2.38 | 4.72 | 1.29 | 3.69 | 4.97 | 4.21 | 5.07 | 3.88 | 4.03 | 2.63 | 7.97 | 43.40 |
| 1973 | 2.60 | 2.89 | 2.48 | 3.26 | 5.03 | 2.13 | 4.62 | 2.95 | 2.62 | 1.47 | 4.16 | 2.05 | 42.65 |
| 1974 | 1.89 | 1.37 | 3.56 | 3.51 | 3.61 | 2.82 | 3.39 | 3.98 | 3.40 | 1.15 | 3.40 | 4.05 | 35.19 |
| 1975 | 2.71 | 1.66 | 1.94 | 1.95 | 3.04 | 2.40 | 4.28 | 1.39 | 2.98 | 1.51 | 3.40 |      | 31.31 |
| 1976 | 3.51 | 3.43 | 2.57 | 3.31 | 5.11 | 2.85 | 6.74 | 6.17 | 2.52 | 5.46 | 2.33 | 4.63 | 48.63 |
| 1977 | 3.42 | 2.99 | 2.36 | 1.93 | 0.74 | 6.44 | 1.75 | 7.86 | 3.54 | 5.30 | 1.63 | 3.59 | 41.45 |
| 1978 | 5.10 | 0.26 | 2.69 | 2.33 | 1.98 | 3.70 | 5.56 | 1.95 | 2.74 | 1.94 | 1.84 | 3.04 | 33.13 |
| 1979 | 4.49 | 2.22 | 3.70 | 3.08 | 4.27 | 3.39 | 3.36 | 4.98 | 4.68 | 1.68 | 2.90 | 3.05 | 41.80 |
| 1980 | 1.55 | 0.82 | 3.15 | 2.57 | 2.05 | 2.19 | 5.42 | 2.28 | 4.06 | 2.51 | 3.21 | 2.74 | 32.55 |
| 1981 | 1.68 | 2.39 | 3.43 | 2.17 | 3.18 | 4.15 | 2.62 | 12.09 | 2.38 | 6.28 | 2.51 | 3.81 | 46.69 |
| 1982 | 2.46 | 2.17 | 2.72 | 4.11 | 0.47 | 3.08 | 4.25 | 4.78 | 3.70 | 1.61 | 5.50 | 2.51 | 37.26 |
| 1983 | 2.95 | 1.77 | 3.84 | 4.22 | 5.28 | 0.88 | 5.92 | 3.86 | 2.70 | 1.81 | 8.15 | 5.01 | 46.37 |
| 1984 | 2.10 | 3.06 | 2.55 | 1.72 | 5.72 | 5.90 | 4.52 | 1.65 | 1.54 | 1.81 | 2.01 | 3.00 | 35.60 |
| 1985 | 0.99 | 2.77 | 1.87 | 1.90 | 2.64 | 2.89 | 5.05 | 1.74 | 2.30 | 1.42 | 3.50 | 2.24 | 29.21 |
| 1986 | 4.86 | 1.13 | 2.32 | 2.29 | 2.13 | 1.96 | 4.21 | 4.97 | 3.58 | 1.47 | 3.96 | 1.66 | 34.54 |
| 1987 | 2.29 | 0.33 | 1.24 | 1.75 | 2.46 | 3.59 | 3.16 | 1.82 | 4.37 | 2.18 | 2.33 | 2.56 | 28.08 |
| 1988 | 2.79 | 2.65 | 1.23 | 1.39 | 1.84 | 2.37 | 2.28 | 5.65 | 1.82 | 3.09 | 4.10 | 1.00 | 30.81 |
| 1989 | 1.88 | 1.43 | 1.40 | 2.24 | 4.13 | 2.29 | 2.63 | 5.41 | 3.52 | 1.62 | 3.88 | 2.35 | 32.78 |
| 1990 | 3.36 | 1.84 | 1.16 | 2.23 | 3.53 | 4.56 | 4.15 | 3.23 | 3.78 | 8.73 | 4.22 | 5.60 | 46.44 |
| Record Mean | 2.30 | 2.06 | 2.39 | 2.53 | 3.01 | 3.41 | 4.01 | 3.94 | 3.36 | 3.16 | 3.43 | 2.96 | 36.53 |

## TABLE 3 — AVERAGE TEMPERATURE (deg. F)  CARIBOU, MAINE

| YEAR | JAN | FEB | MAR | APR | MAY | JUNE | JULY | AUG | SEP | OCT | NOV | DEC | ANNUAL |
|------|------|------|------|------|------|------|------|------|------|------|------|------|--------|
| 1961 | 3.8 | 12.6 | 21.0 | 35.1 | 47.3 | 60.2 | 64.7 | 63.2 | 59.5 | 46.0 | 34.5 | 21.4 | 39.2 |
| 1962 | 9.7 | 7.4 | 30.7 | 36.2 | 49.1 | 60.6 | 60.3 | 62.2 | 51.6 | 42.3 | 29.4 | 16.6 | 38.0 |
| 1963 | 13.4 | 6.0 | 19.9 | 35.3 | 49.8 | 61.9 | 67.5 | 59.0 | 50.9 | 47.6 | 34.5 | 8.7 | 37.9 |
| 1964 | 13.4 | 15.9 | 24.1 | 37.1 | 51.8 | 58.8 | 65.8 | 58.6 | 50.8 | 41.0 | 29.3 | 16.9 | 38.6 |
| 1965 | 8.7 | 11.5 | 25.6 | 37.0 | 49.1 | 61.5 | 61.5 | 60.9 | 53.9 | 41.0 | 25.1 | 15.9 | 37.6 |
| 1966 | 16.7 | 15.3 | 28.2 | 37.6 | 49.0 | 60.4 | 64.1 | 62.0 | 51.7 | 42.7 | 34.8 | 21.1 | 40.3 |
| 1967 | 14.3 | 6.7 | 17.4 | 34.4 | 42.7 | 62.1 | 68.4 | 64.2 | 55.8 | 44.2 | 31.4 | 17.3 | 38.2 |
| 1968 | 6.1 | 9.9 | 25.7 | 41.0 | 49.7 | 59.1 | 66.3 | 59.1 | 58.5 | 48.4 | 28.2 | 18.0 | 39.2 |
| 1969 | 15.3 | 17.8 | 25.4 | 35.9 | 48.2 | 60.7 | 62.9 | 64.0 | 52.8 | 41.1 | 34.9 | 21.9 | 40.0 |
| 1970 | 4.9 | 13.1 | 25.3 | 38.2 | 50.6 | 61.7 | 69.7 | 66.0 | 53.9 | 47.4 | 34.6 | 10.1 | 39.6 |
| 1971 | 5.8 | 14.3 | 25.4 | 36.1 | 51.6 | 59.3 | 64.0 | 61.3 | 56.2 | 46.4 | 27.9 | 11.7 | 38.3 |
| 1972 | 8.2 | 6.4 | 18.3 | 34.1 | 52.4 | 61.5 | 64.7 | 60.5 | 54.2 | 38.3 | 27.1 | 7.6 | 36.2 |
| 1973 | 9.7 | 12.6 | 29.6 | 37.9 | 48.9 | 63.0 | 68.6 | 66.4 | 52.9 | 43.9 | 27.5 | 23.9 | 40.4 |
| 1974 | 6.7 | 10.8 | 21.0 | 36.8 | 45.2 | 62.7 | 64.7 | 64.3 | 52.7 | 39.3 | 31.4 | 18.5 | 37.9 |
| 1975 | 9.6 | 11.5 | 23.1 | 35.1 | 53.7 | 61.4 | 68.6 | 64.4 | 54.5 | 42.3 | 32.8 | 10.9 | 39.0 |
| 1976 | 5.3 | 13.5 | 22.7 | 38.4 | 51.2 | 64.0 | 63.7 | 62.6 | 51.5 | 39.2 | 25.6 | 7.9 | 37.1 |
| 1977 | 6.0 | 12.9 | 32.3 | 36.4 | 53.3 | 58.8 | 65.2 | 64.2 | 51.2 | 43.5 | 33.3 | 16.9 | 39.5 |
| 1978 | 9.9 | 12.5 | 20.8 | 34.9 | 55.3 | 60.8 | 66.2 | 64.9 | 50.4 | 41.6 | 27.7 | 16.3 | 38.4 |
| 1979 | 15.4 | 10.4 | 31.8 | 41.2 | 54.6 | 63.0 | 68.6 | 61.9 | 54.4 | 45.2 | 35.8 | 19.2 | 41.8 |
| 1980 | 13.3 | 11.9 | 24.0 | 42.5 | 51.2 | 59.4 | 64.8 | 66.0 | 50.8 | 40.9 | 30.1 | 9.0 | 38.7 |
| 1981 | 5.6 | 27.6 | 28.0 | 39.5 | 54.2 | 62.6 | 66.3 | 64.5 | 53.1 | 40.4 | 23.1 | 43.1 |
| 1982 | 4.0 | 11.3 | 24.5 | 35.1 | 53.6 | 60.3 | 66.4 | 58.7 | 54.9 | 44.4 | 32.7 | 22.1 | 39.0 |
| 1983 | 14.9 | 15.3 | 27.0 | 41.1 | 48.9 | 61.9 | 64.5 | 64.3 | 57.2 | 43.6 | 32.2 | 14.5 | 40.7 |
| 1984 | 6.7 | 22.4 | 19.3 | 39.8 | 49.2 | 59.2 | 65.8 | 65.5 | 51.7 | 44.5 | 33.4 | 18.4 | 39.7 |
| 1985 | 6.0 | 16.2 | 23.5 | 35.3 | 49.5 | 58.2 | 66.0 | 62.2 | 56.1 | 43.8 | 28.3 | 12.1 | 38.1 |
| 1986 | 11.8 | 12.2 | 24.4 | 42.8 | 52.2 | 56.9 | 62.6 | 60.7 | 50.5 | 41.2 | 25.9 | 16.2 | 38.1 |
| 1987 | 9.9 | 12.5 | 28.0 | 43.9 | 50.6 | 60.3 | 65.8 | 61.1 | 54.5 | 44.2 | 29.0 | 18.7 | 39.9 |
| 1988 | 12.1 | 13.6 | 23.1 | 39.1 | 54.6 | 58.5 | 67.4 | 64.4 | 52.4 | 40.5 | 33.5 | 13.8 | 39.4 |
| 1989 | 12.3 | 10.4 | 19.5 | 36.7 | 56.7 | 60.1 | 64.7 | 63.5 | 55.6 | 45.0 | 27.6 | 3.5 | 38.0 |
| 1990 | 17.3 | 11.7 | 24.7 | 39.6 | 49.0 | 62.9 | 66.2 | 66.6 | 53.5 | 44.7 | 31.0 | 20.5 | 40.6 |
| Record Mean | 10.2 | 13.1 | 23.8 | 37.3 | 50.5 | 59.9 | 65.3 | 62.8 | 53.8 | 43.2 | 30.9 | 15.6 | 38.9 |
| Max | 19.6 | 23.1 | 33.2 | 46.0 | 61.2 | 70.6 | 76.0 | 73.5 | 64.2 | 52.0 | 37.7 | 23.9 | 48.4 |
| Min | 0.8 | 3.0 | 14.4 | 28.5 | 39.7 | 49.2 | 54.5 | 52.0 | 43.3 | 34.3 | 24.0 | 7.4 | 29.3 |

## REFERENCE NOTES FOR TABLES 1, 2, 3 and 6   (CARIBOU, ME)

### GENERAL

T - TRACE AMOUNT
BLANK ENTRIES DENOTE MISSING/UNREPORTED DATA.
# INDICATES A STATION OR INSTRUMENT RELOCATION.

### SPECIFIC

#### TABLE 1

(a) - LENGTH OF RECORD IN YEARS. ALTHOUGH INDIVIDUAL MONTHS MAY BE MISSING.
* LESS THAN .05

NORMALS — BASED ON THE 1951-1980 RECORD PERIOD.
EXTREMES — DATES ARE THE MOST RECENT OCCURRENCE.
WIND DIR. — NUMERALS SHOW TENS OF DEGREES CLOCKWISE FROM TRUE NORTH. "00" INDICATES CALM.
RESULTANT WIND DIRECTIONS ARE GIVEN TO WHOLE DEGREES.

#### TABLE 3 .
MAX AND MIN ARE LONG-TERM MEAN DAILY MAXIMUM AND MEAN DAILY MINIMUM TEMPERATURES.

### EXCEPTIONS

#### TABLE 1

1. RELATIVE HUMIDITY HOUR 01, AND MEAN WIND SPEED ARE THROUGH 1962.
2. THUNDERSTORMS AND HEAVY FOG ARE THROUGH 1964 AND MAY BE INCOMPLETE, DUE TO PART-TIME OPERATIONS.

#### TABLES 2, 3, and 6

RECORD MEANS ARE THROUGH THE CURRENT YEAR, BEGINNING IN
1939 FOR TEMPERATURE
1939 FOR PRECIPITATION
1939 FOR SNOWFALL

HEATING DEGREE DAYS Base 65 deg. F          CARIBOU, MAINE

**TABLE 4**

| SEASON | JULY | AUG | SEP | OCT | NOV | DEC | JAN | FEB | MAR | APR | MAY | JUNE | TOTAL |
|---|---|---|---|---|---|---|---|---|---|---|---|---|---|
| 1961-62 | 61 | 104 | 188 | 580 | 905 | 1343 | 1713 | 1613 | 1054 | 858 | 492 | 161 | 9072 |
| 1962-63 | 151 | 115 | 400 | 695 | 1062 | 1497 | 1597 | 1649 | 1390 | 884 | 461 | 134 | 10035 |
| 1963-64 | 42 | 189 | 417 | 535 | 905 | 1484 | 1595 | 1417 | 1259 | 830 | 407 | 198 | 9535 |
| 1964-65 | 46 | 199 | 419 | 737 | 1063 | 1484 | 1743 | 1493 | 1213 | 831 | 485 | 164 | 9877 |
| 1965-66 | 115 | 161 | 351 | 737 | 1191 | 1514 | 1489 | 1388 | 1135 | 813 | 499 | 160 | 9553 |
| 1966-67 | 64 | 106 | 393 | 683 | 899 | 1354 | 1567 | 1629 | 1468 | 912 | 682 | 121 | 9878 |
| 1967-68 | 14 | 55 | 276 | 636 | 1000 | 1471 | 1823 | 1594 | 1211 | 715 | 468 | 171 | 9434 |
| 1968-69 | 48 | 191 | 199 | 515 | 1097 | 1452 | 1534 | 1316 | 1219 | 876 | 512 | 167 | 9126 |
| 1969-70 | 109 | 86 | 364 | 732 | 895 | 1331 | 1861 | 1449 | 1221 | 800 | 440 | 142 | 9430 |
| 1970-71 | 17 | 80 | 328 | 540 | 905 | 1697 | 1833 | 1415 | 1224 | 860 | 411 | 199 | 9509 |
| 1971-72 | 59 | 141 | 274 | 569 | 1106 | 1648 | 1759 | 1698 | 1440 | 903 | 405 | 134 | 10136 |
| 1972-73 | 55 | 145 | 326 | 818 | 1130 | 1775 | 1711 | 1464 | 1092 | 807 | 491 | 122 | 9936 |
| 1973-74 | 9 | 44 | 373 | 649 | 1117 | 1270 | 1810 | 1512 | 1359 | 837 | 609 | 81 | 9670 |
| 1974-75 | 40 | 66 | 369 | 789 | 998 | 1433 | 1717 | 1498 | 1295 | 890 | 343 | 158 | 9596 |
| 1975-76 | 19 | 93 | 310 | 700 | 960 | 1674 | 1849 | 1489 | 1302 | 793 | 426 | 123 | 9738 |
| 1976-77 | 84 | 132 | 405 | 793 | 1175 | 1765 | 1828 | 1453 | 1002 | 850 | 406 | 203 | 10096 |
| 1977-78 | 56 | 93 | 408 | 657 | 944 | 1489 | 1702 | 1467 | 1364 | 894 | 333 | 156 | 9563 |
| 1978-79 | 53 | 86 | 434 | 717 | 1114 | 1503 | 1534 | 1527 | 1018 | 708 | 326 | 104 | 9124 |
| 1979-80 | 34 | 146 | 327 | 612 | 870 | 1413 | 1593 | 1534 | 1265 | 664 | 420 | 200 | 9078 |
| 1980-81 | 71 | 41 | 425 | 740 | 1042 | 1733 | 1839 | 1040 | 1141 | 757 | 333 | 125 | 9287 |
| 1981-82 | 37 | 77 | 355 | 757 | 984 | 1292 | 1891 | 1499 | 1251 | 890 | 355 | 145 | 9533 |
| 1982-83 | 60 | 199 | 314 | 632 | 961 | 1325 | 1325 | 1387 | 1171 | 712 | 493 | 148 | 8942 |
| 1983-84 | 75 | 78 | 257 | 656 | 978 | 1562 | 1804 | 1229 | 1412 | 748 | 493 | 199 | 9491 |
| 1984-85 | 38 | 57 | 396 | 630 | 940 | 1441 | 1822 | 1363 | 1281 | 884 | 472 | 198 | 9522 |
| 1985-86 | 43 | 118 | 272 | 650 | 1094 | 1636 | 1646 | 1473 | 1255 | 660 | 394 | 246 | 9487 |
| 1986-87 | 105 | 147 | 427 | 733 | 1167 | 1505 | 1704 | 1465 | 1140 | 629 | 442 | 142 | 9606 |
| 1987-88 | 79 | 152 | 314 | 641 | 1071 | 1430 | 1636 | 1485 | 1289 | 760 | 321 | 232 | 9410 |
| 1988-89 | 47 | 114 | 373 | 752 | 939 | 1583 | 1627 | 1524 | 1402 | 841 | 257 | 181 | 9640 |
| 1989-90 | 66 | 101 | 303 | 613 | 1116 | 1905 | 1471 | 1490 | 1241 | 759 | 490 | 107 | 9662 |
| 1990-91 | 57 | 47 | 337 | 623 | 1014 | 1370 | | | | | | | |

**TABLE 5**

COOLING DEGREE DAYS Base 65 deg. F          CARIBOU, MAINE

| YEAR | JAN | FEB | MAR | APR | MAY | JUNE | JULY | AUG | SEP | OCT | NOV | DEC | TOTAL |
|---|---|---|---|---|---|---|---|---|---|---|---|---|---|
| 1969 | 0 | 0 | 0 | 0 | 0 | 45 | 48 | 62 | 4 | 0 | 0 | 0 | 159 |
| 1970 | 0 | 0 | 0 | 0 | 2 | 47 | 164 | 117 | 1 | 0 | 0 | 0 | 331 |
| 1971 | 0 | 0 | 0 | 0 | 2 | 36 | 38 | 33 | 16 | 0 | 0 | 0 | 125 |
| 1972 | 0 | 0 | 0 | 0 | 21 | 35 | 51 | 11 | 9 | 0 | 0 | 0 | 127 |
| 1973 | 0 | 0 | 0 | 0 | 0 | 67 | 126 | 97 | 17 | 0 | 0 | 0 | 307 |
| 1974 | 0 | 0 | 0 | 0 | 2 | 21 | 38 | 50 | 5 | 0 | 0 | 0 | 116 |
| 1975 | 0 | 0 | 0 | 0 | 0 | 54 | 137 | 80 | 0 | 0 | 0 | 0 | 271 |
| 1976 | 0 | 0 | 0 | 0 | 6 | 104 | 52 | 65 | 4 | 0 | 0 | 0 | 231 |
| 1977 | 0 | 0 | 0 | 0 | 52 | 24 | 69 | 77 | 1 | 0 | 0 | 0 | 223 |
| 1978 | 0 | 0 | 0 | 0 | 38 | 35 | 97 | 93 | 1 | 0 | 0 | 0 | 264 |
| 1979 | 0 | 0 | 0 | 0 | 8 | 50 | 153 | 57 | 16 | 6 | 0 | 0 | 290 |
| 1980 | 0 | 0 | 0 | 0 | 0 | 37 | 71 | 78 | 8 | 0 | 0 | 0 | 194 |
| 1981 | 0 | 0 | 0 | 0 | 3 | 17 | 83 | 68 | 4 | 0 | 0 | 0 | 175 |
| 1982 | 0 | 0 | 0 | 0 | 11 | 10 | 110 | 9 | 12 | 0 | 0 | 0 | 152 |
| 1983 | 0 | 0 | 0 | 0 | 0 | 62 | 65 | 66 | 32 | 1 | 0 | 0 | 226 |
| 1984 | 0 | 0 | 0 | 0 | 9 | 33 | 72 | 79 | 1 | 0 | 0 | 0 | 193 |
| 1985 | 0 | 0 | 0 | 0 | 0 | 0 | 82 | 40 | 10 | 0 | 0 | 0 | 132 |
| 1986 | 0 | 0 | 0 | 0 | 5 | 10 | 39 | 20 | 1 | 0 | 0 | 0 | 75 |
| 1987 | 0 | 0 | 0 | 0 | 2 | 10 | 111 | 38 | 8 | 0 | 0 | 0 | 169 |
| 1988 | 0 | 0 | 0 | 0 | 6 | 45 | 131 | 103 | 1 | 0 | 0 | 0 | 286 |
| 1989 | 0 | 0 | 0 | 0 | 9 | 37 | 64 | 63 | 19 | 0 | 0 | 0 | 192 |
| 1990 | 0 | 0 | 0 | 2 | 0 | 51 | 102 | 106 | 0 | 0 | 0 | 0 | 261 |

**TABLE 6**

SNOWFALL (inches)          CARIBOU, MAINE

| SEASON | JULY | AUG | SEP | OCT | NOV | DEC | JAN | FEB | MAR | APR | MAY | JUNE | TOTAL |
|---|---|---|---|---|---|---|---|---|---|---|---|---|---|
| 1961-62 | 0.0 | 0.0 | 0.0 | 4.1 | 7.1 | 8.9 | 12.7 | 16.3 | 7.7 | 11.7 | T | 0.0 | 68.5 |
| 1962-63 | 0.0 | 0.0 | 0.0 | 11.0 | 3.9 | 37.4 | 30.7 | 30.6 | 23.0 | 10.9 | T | 0.0 | 147.5 |
| 1963-64 | 0.0 | 0.0 | T | 12.1 | 16.8 | 6.5 | 20.2 | 10.1 | 24.7 | 11.5 | 0.0 | T | 101.9 |
| 1964-65 | 0.0 | 0.0 | 0.0 | 0.9 | 37.2 | 18.7 | 18.7 | 14.8 | 6.1 | 4.0 | 0.0 | 0.0 | 94.6 |
| 1965-66 | 0.0 | 0.0 | 0.0 | 1.2 | 27.0 | 17.8 | 30.3 | 20.9 | 10.7 | 2.8 | 8.2 | 0.0 | 118.9 |
| 1966-67 | 0.0 | 0.0 | 0.0 | 0.4 | 7.1 | 24.2 | 27.8 | 26.0 | 10.5 | 2.2 | 10.9 | 0.0 | 109.1 |
| 1967-68 | 0.0 | 0.0 | 0.0 | T | 9.3 | 31.3 | 33.5 | 5.3 | 26.3 | T | 0.0 | 0.0 | 105.7 |
| 1968-69 | 0.0 | 0.0 | 0.0 | T | 28.0 | 31.2 | 29.5 | 29.7 | 19.5 | 14.1 | 0.0 | 0.0 | 152.0 |
| 1969-70 | 0.0 | 0.0 | 0.0 | 2.3 | 4.6 | 28.6 | 6.0 | 15.0 | 19.8 | 11.7 | 0.0 | 0.0 | 88.0 |
| 1970-71 | 0.0 | 0.0 | 0.0 | 7.6 | 11.0 | 32.4 | 16.6 | 16.3 | 38.6 | 12.2 | 0.0 | T | 134.7 |
| 1971-72 | 0.0 | 0.0 | 0.0 | T | 18.9 | 26.3 | 15.7 | 25.1 | 41.4 | 9.4 | T | 0.0 | 136.8 |
| 1972-73 | 0.0 | 0.0 | 0.0 | 1.7 | 13.3 | 59.9 | 20.3 | 27.8 | 7.8 | 22.2 | 0.0 | 0.0 | 153.0 |
| 1973-74 | 0.0 | 0.0 | T | T | 14.5 | 23.4 | 20.7 | 11.9 | 21.6 | 13.1 | 4.2 | 0.0 | 109.4 |
| 1974-75 | 0.0 | 0.0 | 0.0 | 0.4 | 34.9 | 12.6 | 31.2 | 9.8 | 18.2 | 15.1 | 0.0 | 0.0 | 122.2 |
| 1975-76 | 0.0 | 0.0 | 0.0 | T | 10.4 | 36.4 | 30.1 | 30.2 | 23.3 | 1.5 | 0.5 | 0.0 | 132.4 |
| 1976-77 | 0.0 | 0.0 | 0.0 | 3.7 | 10.2 | 31.9 | 39.1 | 34.4 | 16.0 | 10.6 | T | 0.0 | 145.9 |
| 1977-78 | 0.0 | 0.0 | 0.0 | 0.0 | 5.5 | 37.7 | 41.4 | 4.4 | 13.7 | 15.3 | 0.8 | 0.0 | 118.8 |
| 1978-79 | 0.0 | 0.0 | T | T | 9.2 | 40.3 | 32.1 | 18.1 | 8.6 | 14.9 | T | 0.0 | 123.2 |
| 1979-80 | 0.0 | 0.0 | 0.0 | 0.7 | 3.0 | 18.0 | 7.9 | 12.6 | 27.6 | 0.8 | 0.0 | T | 70.6 |
| 1980-81 | 0.0 | 0.0 | T | 0.2 | 12.0 | 28.9 | 35.2 | 8.6 | 36.4 | 1.4 | 0.2 | 0.0 | 122.9 |
| 1981-82 | 0.0 | 0.0 | T | 2.6 | 4.8 | 34.3 | 30.9 | 25.1 | 23.7 | 36.4 | 1.0 | 0.0 | 158.8 |
| 1982-83 | 0.0 | 0.0 | 0.0 | T | 14.6 | 4.0 | 22.8 | 22.8 | 13.9 | 4.8 | T | 0.0 | 82.9 |
| 1983-84 | 0.0 | 0.0 | 0.0 | T | 21.0 | 26.6 | 27.3 | 20.1 | 35.4 | 3.9 | 0.2 | 0.0 | 134.5 |
| 1984-85 | 0.0 | 0.0 | 0.0 | 0.8 | 3.8 | 30.7 | 10.5 | 26.8 | 11.9 | 5.0 | 1.3 | 0.0 | 90.8 |
| 1985-86 | 0.0 | 0.0 | 0.0 | T | 14.8 | 18.3 | 30.0 | 11.9 | 18.6 | 11.3 | T | 0.0 | 104.9 |
| 1986-87 | 0.0 | 0.0 | T | 0.4 | 28.1 | 26.4 | 4.1 | 12.3 | 5.2 | T | 0.0 | | 85.0 |
| 1987-88 | 0.0 | 0.0 | T | T | 5.2 | 22.6 | 32.1 | 28.2 | 3.9 | T | 0.0 | | 98.4 |
| 1988-89 | 0.0 | 0.0 | 0.0 | 1.2 | 13.8 | 11.5 | 18.4 | 16.6 | 11.9 | 9.4 | 0.0 | 0.0 | 82.8 |
| 1989-90 | 0.0 | 0.0 | T | 0.1 | 14.3 | 38.0 | 28.5 | 18.3 | 7.6 | 10.7 | 0.6 | T | 118.1 |
| 1990-91 | 0.0 | 0.0 | 0.0 | T | 12.0 | 22.6 | | | | | | | |
| Record Mean | 0.0 | 0.0 | T | 1.8 | 12.3 | 23.4 | 23.9 | 21.4 | 19.3 | 8.5 | 0.7 | T | 111.3 |

**See Reference Notes, relative to all above tables, on preceding page.**

The Portland City Airport is located 2 3/4 miles west of the site of the former city office. The surrounding country is mostly open, rolling and sloping generally toward the Fore River, a body of brackish water about 1,000 feet wide at a distance of about 1/2 mile from the station and forming one boundary (north through east) of the field. The airport is about 5 1/2 miles west–northwest of the open ocean. A slight rise reaching an elevation of 100 feet, lying northwest of the field, cuts down the wind slightly from that direction. The older portion of the city is situated on a hill rising abruptly from sea level to 170 feet, 1 1/2 miles east of the airport and on the opposite side of the Fore River. A line of low hills southeast of the airport, near the ocean, which reach a maximum height of 160 feet, shuts off sight of the ocean from the airport. Sebago Lake with an area of 44 square miles is situated about 15 miles to the northwest and 45 miles farther are the White Mountains, averaging 3,000 to 5,000 feet in height.

As a rule, Portland has very pleasant summers and falls, cold winters with frequent thaws, and disagreeable springs. Very few summer nights are too warm and humid for comfortable sleeping. Autumn has the greatest number of sunny days and the least cloudiness. Winters are quite severe, but begin late and then extend deeply into the normal springtime.

Heavy seasonal snowfalls, over 100 inches, normally occur about each 10 years. True blizzards are very rare. The White Mountains, to the northwest, keep considerable snow from reaching the Portland area and also moderate the temperature. Normal monthly precipitation is remarkably uniform throughout the year.

Winds are generally quite light with the highest velocities being confined mostly to March and November. Even in these months the occasional northeasterly gales have usually lost much of their severity before reaching the coast of Maine.

Temperatures well below zero are recorded frequently each winter. Cold waves sometimes come in on strong winds, but extremely low temperatures are generally accompanied by light winds.

The average freeze–free season at the airport station is 139 days. Mid–May is the average occurrence of the last freeze in spring, and the average occurrence of the first freeze in fall is late September. The freeze–free period is longer in the city proper, but may be even shorter at susceptible places further inland.

Daily maximum temperatures at the present airport site agree closely with those near the former intown office, but minimum temperatures on clear, quiet mornings range as much as 15 degrees lower at the airport.

# TABLE 1    NORMALS, MEANS AND EXTREMES

PORTLAND, MAINE

LATITUDE: 43°39'N    LONGITUDE: 70°19'W    ELEVATION: FT. GRND  43  BARO  78    TIME ZONE: EASTERN    WBAN: 14764

| | (a) | JAN | FEB | MAR | APR | MAY | JUNE | JULY | AUG | SEP | OCT | NOV | DEC | YEAR |
|---|---|---|---|---|---|---|---|---|---|---|---|---|---|---|
| **TEMPERATURE °F:** | | | | | | | | | | | | | | |
| Normals | | | | | | | | | | | | | | |
| -Daily Maximum | | 31.0 | 33.1 | 40.5 | 52.5 | 63.4 | 72.8 | 78.9 | 77.5 | 69.6 | 59.0 | 47.1 | 34.9 | 55.0 |
| -Daily Minimum | | 11.9 | 12.9 | 23.7 | 33.0 | 42.1 | 51.4 | 57.3 | 55.8 | 47.7 | 37.9 | 29.6 | 16.7 | 35.0 |
| -Monthly | | 21.5 | 23.0 | 32.1 | 42.8 | 52.8 | 62.2 | 68.1 | 66.6 | 58.6 | 48.4 | 38.4 | 25.8 | 45.0 |
| Extremes | | | | | | | | | | | | | | |
| -Record Highest | 49 | 64 | 64 | 86 | 85 | 94 | 97 | 99 | 103 | 95 | 88 | 74 | 69 | 103 |
| -Year | | 1950 | 1957 | 1946 | 1957 | 1987 | 1988 | 1977 | 1975 | 1983 | 1963 | 1987 | 1982 | AUG 1975 |
| -Record Lowest | 49 | -26 | -39 | -21 | 8 | 23 | 33 | 40 | 33 | 23 | 15 | 3 | -21 | -39 |
| -Year | | 1971 | 1943 | 1950 | 1954 | 1956 | 1944 | 1965 | 1965 | 1941 | 1976 | 1989 | 1963 | FEB 1943 |
| **NORMAL DEGREE DAYS:** | | | | | | | | | | | | | | |
| Heating (base 65°F) | | 1349 | 1176 | 1020 | 666 | 378 | 107 | 22 | 54 | 201 | 515 | 798 | 1215 | 7501 |
| Cooling (base 65°F) | | 0 | 0 | 0 | 0 | 0 | 23 | 118 | 104 | 9 | 0 | 0 | 0 | 254 |
| **% OF POSSIBLE SUNSHINE** | 49 | 56 | 59 | 56 | 55 | 55 | 59 | 63 | 64 | 62 | 58 | 48 | 53 | 57 |
| **MEAN SKY COVER (tenths)** | | | | | | | | | | | | | | |
| Sunrise - Sunset | 46 | 6.1 | 6.0 | 6.3 | 6.6 | 6.7 | 6.4 | 6.2 | 5.9 | 5.7 | 5.7 | 6.6 | 6.2 | 6.2 |
| **MEAN NUMBER OF DAYS:** | | | | | | | | | | | | | | |
| Sunrise to Sunset | | | | | | | | | | | | | | |
| -Clear | 49 | 10.2 | 8.8 | 8.7 | 7.5 | 6.4 | 7.0 | 7.3 | 9.1 | 10.5 | 10.6 | 7.6 | 9.3 | 102.9 |
| -Partly Cloudy | 49 | 6.4 | 7.1 | 7.1 | 7.2 | 9.4 | 9.8 | 11.2 | 10.7 | 7.8 | 7.7 | 7.0 | 7.3 | 98.8 |
| -Cloudy | 49 | 14.4 | 12.3 | 15.2 | 15.2 | 15.2 | 13.1 | 12.5 | 11.2 | 11.8 | 12.7 | 15.4 | 14.4 | 163.6 |
| Precipitation | | | | | | | | | | | | | | |
| .01 inches or more | 49 | 11.0 | 10.0 | 11.3 | 12.0 | 12.5 | 11.4 | 9.7 | 9.5 | 8.4 | 9.2 | 11.6 | 11.4 | 128.0 |
| Snow,Ice pellets | | | | | | | | | | | | | | |
| 1.0 inches or more | 49 | 4.6 | 3.8 | 3.3 | 0.8 | 0.1 | 0.0 | 0.0 | 0.0 | 0.0 | 0.1 | 1.0 | 3.7 | 17.5 |
| Thunderstorms | 49 | 0.* | 0.1 | 0.4 | 0.5 | 2.0 | 4.1 | 4.5 | 3.5 | 1.5 | 0.6 | 0.4 | 0.1 | 17.7 |
| Heavy Fog Visibility 1/4 mile or less | 49 | 1.9 | 2.0 | 3.3 | 3.1 | 5.4 | 5.2 | 6.4 | 5.6 | 5.4 | 4.8 | 3.7 | 1.9 | 48.8 |
| Temperature °F | | | | | | | | | | | | | | |
| -Maximum | | | | | | | | | | | | | | |
| 90° and above | 49 | 0.0 | 0.0 | 0.0 | 0.0 | 0.1 | 1.1 | 2.0 | 1.6 | 0.3 | 0.0 | 0.0 | 0.0 | 5.1 |
| 32° and below | 49 | 17.0 | 12.2 | 4.4 | 0.1 | 0.0 | 0.0 | 0.0 | 0.0 | 0.0 | 0.0 | 0.9 | 12.1 | 46.7 |
| -Minimum | | | | | | | | | | | | | | |
| 32° and below | 49 | 29.8 | 26.8 | 25.9 | 14.0 | 2.4 | 0.0 | 0.0 | 0.0 | 1.1 | 9.1 | 19.5 | 28.8 | 157.6 |
| 0° and below | 49 | 6.3 | 4.2 | 0.7 | 0.0 | 0.0 | 0.0 | 0.0 | 0.0 | 0.0 | 0.0 | 0.0 | 2.9 | 14.1 |
| **AVG. STATION PRESS.(mb)** | 17 | 1012.6 | 1013.6 | 1012.7 | 1011.0 | 1012.3 | 1011.6 | 1011.9 | 1013.8 | 1015.2 | 1015.8 | 1014.0 | 1013.9 | 1013.2 |
| **RELATIVE HUMIDITY (%)** | | | | | | | | | | | | | | |
| Hour 01 | 49 | 75 | 73 | 75 | 79 | 84 | 88 | 89 | 89 | 89 | 85 | 81 | 77 | 82 |
| Hour 07 | 49 | 76 | 76 | 75 | 73 | 75 | 78 | 80 | 83 | 85 | 84 | 83 | 79 | 79 |
| Hour 13 (Local Time) | 49 | 61 | 58 | 58 | 55 | 58 | 60 | 59 | 59 | 60 | 59 | 63 | 61 | 59 |
| Hour 19 | 49 | 69 | 67 | 69 | 69 | 71 | 73 | 74 | 77 | 79 | 77 | 75 | 72 | 73 |
| **PRECIPITATION (inches):** | | | | | | | | | | | | | | |
| Water Equivalent | | | | | | | | | | | | | | |
| -Normal | | 3.78 | 3.57 | 3.98 | 3.90 | 3.27 | 3.06 | 2.83 | 2.82 | 3.27 | 3.83 | 4.70 | 4.51 | 43.52 |
| -Maximum Monthly | 49 | 11.92 | 7.10 | 9.97 | 9.90 | 9.64 | 6.75 | 7.48 | 8.30 | 9.81 | 12.27 | 13.50 | 9.69 | 13.50 |
| -Year | | 1979 | 1981 | 1953 | 1973 | 1984 | 1982 | 1976 | 1946 | 1954 | 1962 | 1983 | 1969 | NOV 1983 |
| -Minimum Monthly | 49 | 0.76 | 0.04 | 0.81 | 0.71 | 0.49 | 0.70 | 0.61 | 0.27 | 0.30 | 0.26 | 0.90 | 0.98 | 0.04 |
| -Year | | 1970 | 1987 | 1965 | 1941 | 1965 | 1941 | 1965 | 1947 | 1948 | 1947 | 1976 | 1955 | FEB 1987 |
| -Maximum in 24 hrs | 49 | 3.56 | 3.41 | 3.47 | 5.26 | 4.66 | 5.58 | 2.68 | 4.18 | 7.49 | 7.71 | 4.56 | 3.82 | 7.71 |
| -Year | | 1977 | 1981 | 1951 | 1973 | 1989 | 1967 | 1979 | 1946 | 1954 | 1962 | 1988 | 1969 | OCT 1962 |
| Snow,Ice pellets | | | | | | | | | | | | | | |
| -Maximum Monthly | 49 | 62.4 | 61.2 | 46.6 | 15.9 | 7.0 | 0.0 | 0.0 | 0.0 | T | 3.8 | 15.6 | 54.8 | 62.4 |
| -Year | | 1979 | 1969 | 1956 | 1982 | 1945 | | | | 1987 | 1969 | 1972 | 1970 | JAN 1979 |
| -Maximum in 24 hrs | 49 | 27.1 | 21.5 | 15.5 | 15.9 | 7.0 | 0.0 | 0.0 | 0.0 | T | 3.6 | 11.1 | 22.8 | 27.1 |
| -Year | | 1979 | 1969 | 1984 | 1982 | 1945 | | | | 1987 | 1969 | 1972 | 1970 | JAN 1979 |
| **WIND:** | | | | | | | | | | | | | | |
| Mean Speed (mph) | 49 | 9.2 | 9.4 | 10.0 | 10.0 | 9.1 | 8.2 | 7.6 | 7.5 | 7.8 | 8.4 | 8.8 | 9.0 | 8.8 |
| Prevailing Direction through 1963 | | N | N | W | S | S | S | S | S | S | N | W | N | S |
| Fastest Mile | | | | | | | | | | | | | | |
| -Direction (!!!) | 45 | SE | N | NE | S | NW | SW | W | E | SE | N | NE | SE | NE |
| -Speed (MPH) | 45 | 50 | 58 | 76 | 57 | 49 | 45 | 44 | 69 | 62 | 45 | 76 | 62 | 76 |
| -Year | | 1951 | 1952 | 1947 | 1946 | 1950 | 1969 | 1941 | 1954 | 1960 | 1963 | 1945 | 1957 | MAR 1947 |
| Peak Gust | | | | | | | | | | | | | | |
| -Direction (!!!) | 6 | NW | E | NE | E | SE | S | NW | NW | SE | NE | W | SE | SE |
| -Speed (mph) | 6 | 49 | 45 | 48 | 44 | 45 | 48 | 45 | 48 | 70 | 47 | 47 | 56 | 70 |
| -Date | | 1989 | 1985 | 1984 | 1988 | 1989 | 1988 | 1987 | 1987 | 1985 | 1988 | 1984 | 1986 | SEP 1985 |

**See Reference Notes to this table on the following page.**

PRECIPITATION (inches)                PORTLAND, MAINE

**TABLE 2**

| YEAR | JAN | FEB | MAR | APR | MAY | JUNE | JULY | AUG | SEP | OCT | NOV | DEC | ANNUAL |
|---|---|---|---|---|---|---|---|---|---|---|---|---|---|
| 1961 | 1.46 | 3.58 | 2.48 | 6.48 | 2.97 | 3.11 | 2.87 | 2.25 | 4.21 | 1.69 | 4.69 | 2.96 | 38.75 |
| 1962 | 2.68 | 2.25 | 2.15 | 4.51 | 1.84 | 2.65 | 2.89 | 2.87 | 2.53 | 12.27 | 4.25 | 5.47 | 46.36 |
| 1963 | 2.73 | 2.95 | 3.38 | 2.19 | 3.52 | 1.95 | 2.51 | 3.25 | 2.29 | 1.85 | 9.81 | 2.16 | 38.59 |
| 1964 | 4.74 | 2.66 | 3.64 | 3.27 | 1.55 | 2.01 | 3.47 | 1.77 | 1.02 | 3.45 | 3.25 | 3.75 | 34.59 |
| 1965 | 1.68 | 6.36 | 0.81 | 2.93 | 0.45 | 2.27 | 0.61 | 1.84 | 2.31 | 2.49 | 3.96 | 2.40 | 28.15 |
| 1966 | 4.97 | 3.43 | 3.77 | 1.00 | 1.95 | 3.04 | 0.96 | 4.99 | 3.84 | 3.61 | 5.01 | 3.46 | 40.04 |
| 1967 | 2.52 | 4.63 | 2.16 | 4.74 | 5.34 | 6.23 | 3.46 | 2.57 | 2.68 | 1.31 | 2.52 | 6.00 | 44.16 |
| 1968 | 3.00 | 1.26 | 4.16 | 3.37 | 3.81 | 4.04 | 0.65 | 2.00 | 1.40 | 2.00 | 7.74 | 9.69 | 55.00 |
| 1969 | 3.63 | 6.28 | 3.36 | 2.86 | 1.67 | 3.53 | 5.45 | 2.20 | 5.28 | 2.51 | 8.54 | 5.14 | 41.44 |
| 1970 | 0.76 | 4.31 | 4.22 | 4.14 | 3.15 | 2.91 | 0.95 | 5.12 | 4.49 | 3.87 | 2.38 | 5.14 | 41.44 |
| 1971 | 2.25 | 6.76 | 4.74 | 1.86 | 4.09 | 1.09 | 3.14 | 3.24 | 3.55 | 3.95 | 4.13 | 2.85 | 41.65 |
| 1972 | 2.09 | 5.14 | 6.01 | 2.53 | 3.17 | 4.24 | 2.05 | 0.80 | 4.31 | 3.92 | 7.87 | 6.49 | 48.62 |
| 1973 | 2.58 | 2.57 | 3.33 | 9.90 | 6.28 | 4.87 | 1.70 | 3.48 | 2.23 | 3.38 | 2.40 | 9.57 | 52.29 |
| 1974 | 3.41 | 2.07 | 3.82 | 3.82 | 4.20 | 4.69 | 3.66 | 1.45 | 1.74 | 4.85 | 4.41 | 4.41 | 43.55 |
| 1975 | 4.40 | 2.51 | 3.20 | 3.71 | 1.09 | 4.87 | 2.06 | 3.89 | 4.34 | 4.50 | 6.01 | 8.14 | 48.72 |
| 1976 | 4.44 | 2.84 | 2.47 | 2.42 | 3.99 | 1.53 | 7.48 | 4.87 | 1.86 | 5.37 | 0.90 | 3.22 | 41.39 |
| 1977 | 6.46 | 3.75 | 6.92 | 3.46 | 2.04 | 3.38 | 2.83 | 2.79 | 4.63 | 8.30 | 6.46 | 6.61 | 57.63 |
| 1978 | 6.91 | 0.87 | 4.19 | 4.46 | 4.36 | 2.42 | 1.67 | 2.36 | 0.59 | 3.23 | 2.26 | 3.15 | 36.47 |
| 1979 | 11.92 | 3.50 | 4.17 | 6.48 | 5.15 | 1.97 | 5.90 | 5.53 | 3.28 | 6.71 | 3.95 | 2.59 | 61.15 |
| 1980 | 0.98 | 1.36 | 4.54 | 5.78 | 1.83 | 3.34 | 1.99 | 2.14 | 3.00 | 2.99 | 4.75 | 1.18 | 33.88 |
| 1981 | 0.93 | 7.10 | 1.44 | 3.46 | 2.27 | 4.59 | 5.44 | 2.31 | 6.14 | 4.71 | 2.80 | 4.51 | 45.70 |
| 1982 | 5.17 | 2.53 | 3.20 | 4.54 | 2.91 | 6.75 | 2.61 | 3.35 | 1.90 | 1.93 | 3.61 | 1.18 | 39.68 |
| 1983 | 4.59 | 3.94 | 9.75 | 6.82 | 5.98 | 1.35 | 4.31 | 2.58 | 1.35 | 3.38 | 13.50 | 8.78 | 66.33 |
| 1984 | 2.56 | 4.99 | 5.12 | 4.81 | 9.64 | 3.87 | 3.86 | 2.09 | 0.84 | 3.26 | 3.69 | 3.44 | 48.17 |
| 1985 | 1.03 | 1.54 | 3.15 | 1.25 | 2.03 | 2.74 | 3.30 | 3.18 | 2.97 | 4.07 | 6.36 | 2.39 | 34.01 |
| 1986 | 6.58 | 2.61 | 4.21 | 3.49 | 2.51 | 3.91 | 3.44 | 1.87 | 2.64 | 2.09 | 5.18 | 5.91 | 44.44 |
| 1987 | 5.21 | 0.04 | 4.29 | 6.33 | 2.62 | 5.01 | 1.79 | 2.48 | 4.64 | 2.54 | 3.82 | 2.01 | 40.78 |
| 1988 | 1.97 | 3.34 | 1.85 | 3.68 | 4.27 | 2.36 | 5.89 | 5.24 | 1.50 | 3.47 | 8.84 | 1.21 | 43.62 |
| 1989 | 1.15 | 2.37 | 2.14 | 2.94 | 8.74 | 4.49 | 2.50 | 1.73 | 4.48 | 4.81 | 3.97 | 2.23 | 41.55 |
| 1990 | 3.19 | 2.49 | 1.42 | 5.16 | 5.23 | 4.12 | 3.21 | 1.89 | 3.12 | 7.46 | 7.50 | 7.90 | 52.69 |
| Record Mean | 3.87 | 3.67 | 3.91 | 3.62 | 3.47 | 3.28 | 3.12 | 2.99 | 3.19 | 3.40 | 4.12 | 3.96 | 42.60 |

**TABLE 3**

AVERAGE TEMPERATURE (deg. F)                PORTLAND, MAINE

| YEAR | JAN | FEB | MAR | APR | MAY | JUNE | JULY | AUG | SEP | OCT | NOV | DEC | ANNUAL |
|---|---|---|---|---|---|---|---|---|---|---|---|---|---|
| 1961 | 15.3 | 24.2 | 30.1 | 41.9 | 51.1 | 62.6 | 65.8 | 66.3 | 64.1 | 50.8 | 39.7 | 26.1 | 44.8 |
| 1962 | 20.6 | 18.1 | 33.4 | 42.0 | 51.1 | 62.3 | 64.0 | 64.8 | 56.1 | 47.6 | 36.1 | 23.8 | 43.3 |
| 1963 | 23.6 | 17.4 | 31.9 | 42.4 | 52.5 | 63.1 | 68.9 | 62.9 | 54.8 | 52.3 | 41.7 | 16.6 | 44.0 |
| 1964 | 24.4 | 23.0 | 31.9 | 40.9 | 54.8 | 62.6 | 67.6 | 61.1 | 55.6 | 47.1 | 36.2 | 25.3 | 44.2 |
| 1965 | 19.8 | 21.6 | 33.3 | 41.1 | 54.8 | 63.1 | 66.3 | 66.5 | 58.0 | 47.6 | 36.6 | 27.9 | 44.7 |
| 1966 | 22.3 | 22.6 | 32.7 | 39.9 | 50.4 | 63.1 | 67.7 | 66.2 | 56.2 | 47.1 | 41.1 | 26.7 | 44.7 |
| 1967 | 24.4 | 17.2 | 26.5 | 41.5 | 47.3 | 63.3 | 67.5 | 66.8 | 59.9 | 49.7 | 34.8 | 27.8 | 43.9 |
| 1968 | 16.6 | 19.2 | 33.2 | 45.1 | 51.0 | 60.0 | 70.0 | 66.4 | 61.7 | 52.8 | 36.7 | 25.2 | 44.8 |
| 1969 | 24.2 | 25.0 | 31.1 | 43.0 | 52.8 | 62.6 | 67.6 | 71.3 | 60.9 | 48.9 | 41.1 | 28.7 | 46.5 |
| 1970 | 16.7 | 25.4 | 32.4 | 43.6 | 55.7 | 63.5 | 70.1 | 68.8 | 61.0 | 51.7 | 41.3 | 19.6 | 45.8 |
| 1971 | 12.2 | 21.9 | 31.6 | 41.6 | 52.7 | 64.3 | 69.0 | 68.9 | 61.3 | 52.5 | 35.4 | 27.3 | 44.9 |
| 1972 | 22.2 | 21.1 | 28.9 | 40.6 | 52.6 | 59.6 | 67.5 | 65.3 | 58.7 | 45.2 | 35.0 | 24.0 | 43.4 |
| 1973 | 23.1 | 23.4 | 37.7 | 45.5 | 51.3 | 63.8 | 70.8 | 70.9 | 58.4 | 49.2 | 37.7 | 33.5 | 47.1 |
| 1974 | 23.2 | 24.5 | 33.9 | 45.1 | 50.6 | 61.3 | 68.2 | 67.9 | 58.8 | 44.7 | 39.3 | 30.2 | 45.6 |
| 1975 | 26.7 | 25.0 | 29.8 | 40.0 | 55.6 | 61.5 | 70.1 | 66.8 | 57.2 | 49.3 | 43.0 | 24.3 | 45.8 |
| 1976 | 15.7 | 28.2 | 31.5 | 45.0 | 52.3 | 65.9 | 65.9 | 65.4 | 57.3 | 43.6 | 36.1 | 19.4 | 43.9 |
| 1977 | 14.6 | 21.9 | 36.2 | 42.4 | 54.4 | 59.0 | 68.2 | 66.6 | 57.6 | 48.1 | 39.4 | 25.4 | 44.5 |
| 1978 | 21.1 | 19.2 | 30.2 | 40.6 | 52.7 | 61.0 | 68.0 | 68.4 | 57.8 | 48.2 | 36.4 | 26.1 | 44.2 |
| 1979 | 23.7 | 15.6 | 35.6 | 42.2 | 55.3 | 62.7 | 69.3 | 64.8 | 57.4 | 47.5 | 42.4 | 29.8 | 45.5 |
| 1980 | 22.7 | 20.5 | 32.0 | 44.3 | 53.7 | 61.0 | 69.6 | 71.2 | 61.5 | 45.9 | 36.2 | 21.3 | 45.0 |
| 1981 | 13.8 | 32.3 | 35.7 | 45.2 | 55.3 | 63.9 | 68.8 | 66.0 | 58.6 | 46.6 | 38.9 | 29.2 | 46.2 |
| 1982 | 15.0 | 23.3 | 32.1 | 42.0 | 54.6 | 58.3 | 69.2 | 64.4 | 59.2 | 48.1 | 41.3 | 32.0 | 45.0 |
| 1983 | 25.2 | 26.2 | 35.8 | 44.4 | 52.0 | 63.8 | 69.7 | 67.6 | 63.0 | 47.9 | 40.2 | 26.1 | 46.8 |
| 1984 | 19.8 | 32.0 | 28.2 | 43.3 | 53.0 | 63.9 | 69.6 | 69.1 | 57.8 | 49.6 | 39.2 | 31.2 | 46.4 |
| 1985 | 16.2 | 26.4 | 34.8 | 44.1 | 53.7 | 61.7 | 69.6 | 66.6 | 60.7 | 50.8 | 39.9 | 24.6 | 45.8 |
| 1986 | 25.0 | 23.4 | 34.6 | 46.5 | 53.6 | 60.0 | 66.3 | 66.2 | 57.4 | 47.9 | 36.3 | 29.6 | 45.6 |
| 1987 | 21.6 | 23.0 | 34.0 | 44.9 | 54.6 | 63.8 | 68.0 | 66.2 | 59.6 | 47.1 | 38.1 | 30.2 | 45.9 |
| 1988 | 21.6 | 25.7 | 34.2 | 43.5 | 54.7 | 63.8 | 71.1 | 71.1 | 59.4 | 46.5 | 41.0 | 26.0 | 46.6 |
| 1989 | 26.8 | 24.0 | 31.6 | 41.1 | 55.6 | 63.9 | 69.4 | 68.0 | 60.5 | 49.8 | 37.3 | 14.1 | 45.2 |
| 1990 | 30.2 | 25.7 | 34.7 | 44.6 | 51.8 | 62.4 | 70.3 | 69.8 | 59.8 | 52.4 | 41.8 | 33.7 | 48.1 |
| Record Mean | 22.3 | 23.5 | 32.4 | 42.9 | 53.3 | 62.3 | 68.3 | 66.7 | 59.5 | 49.4 | 38.7 | 26.9 | 45.5 |
| Max | 30.8 | 32.3 | 40.3 | 51.3 | 62.2 | 71.6 | 77.5 | 75.6 | 68.5 | 58.2 | 46.3 | 34.7 | 54.1 |
| Min | 13.7 | 14.8 | 24.5 | 34.5 | 44.3 | 53.1 | 59.1 | 57.8 | 50.4 | 40.5 | 31.0 | 19.0 | 36.9 |

## REFERENCE NOTES FOR TABLES 1, 2, 3 and 6          (PORTLAND, ME)

### GENERAL

T - TRACE AMOUNT
BLANK ENTRIES DENOTE MISSING/UNREPORTED DATA.
# INDICATES A STATION OR INSTRUMENT RELOCATION.

### SPECIFIC

#### TABLE 1

(a) - LENGTH OF RECORD IN YEARS, ALTHOUGH INDIVIDUAL MONTHS MAY BE MISSING.

* LESS THAN .05

NORMALS — BASED ON THE 1951-1980 RECORD PERIOD.
EXTREMES — DATES ARE THE MOST RECENT OCCURRENCE.
WIND DIR. — NUMERALS SHOW TENS OF DEGREES
             CLOCKWISE FROM TRUE NORTH.
             "00" INDICATES CALM.
RESULTANT WIND DIRECTIONS ARE GIVEN TO WHOLE DEGREES.

#### TABLE 3

MAX AND MIN ARE LONG-TERM MEAN DAILY MAXIMUM AND MEAN DAILY MINIMUM TEMPERATURES.

### EXCEPTIONS

**TABLES 2, 3, and 6**

RECORD MEANS ARE THROUGH THE CURRENT YEAR,
BEGINNING IN      1874 FOR TEMPERATURE
                  1871 FOR PRECIPITATION
                  1941 FOR SNOWFALL

HEATING DEGREE DAYS Base 65 deg. F          PORTLAND, MAINE

**TABLE 4**

| SEASON | JULY | AUG | SEP | OCT | NOV | DEC | JAN | FEB | MAR | APR | MAY | JUNE | TOTAL |
|---|---|---|---|---|---|---|---|---|---|---|---|---|---|
| 1961-62 | 66 | 47 | 104 | 433 | 751 | 1196 | 1369 | 1307 | 976 | 686 | 438 | 107 | 7480 |
| 1962-63 | 68 | 52 | 272 | 529 | 859 | 1266 | 1277 | 1327 | 1019 | 673 | 379 | 108 | 7829 |
| 1963-64 | 31 | 94 | 299 | 395 | 691 | 1497 | 1251 | 1214 | 1020 | 718 | 324 | 111 | 7645 |
| 1964-65 | 28 | 134 | 293 | 549 | 857 | 1222 | 1396 | 1212 | 975 | 710 | 320 | 125 | 7821 |
| 1965-66 | 41 | 61 | 242 | 532 | 845 | 1145 | 1315 | 1183 | 994 | 745 | 449 | 108 | 7660 |
| 1966-67 | 19 | 29 | 264 | 549 | 710 | 1181 | 1254 | 1330 | 1187 | 699 | 544 | 92 | 7858 |
| 1967-68 | 15 | 27 | 155 | 467 | 900 | 1147 | 1496 | 1320 | 981 | 590 | 424 | 164 | 7686 |
| 1968-69 | 8 | 46 | 110 | 375 | 841 | 1228 | 1259 | 1112 | 1043 | 652 | 377 | 118 | 7169 |
| 1969-70 | 30 | 7 | 179 | 494 | 710 | 1120 | 1491 | 1104 | 1005 | 637 | 283 | 93 | 7153 |
| 1970-71 | 7 | 14 | 159 | 408 | 704 | 1400 | 1634 | 1202 | 1028 | 695 | 373 | 81 | 7705 |
| 1971-72 | 3 | 20 | 147 | 381 | 878 | 1164 | 1322 | 1265 | 1112 | 725 | 379 | 155 | 7551 |
| 1972-73 | 27 | 53 | 190 | 607 | 893 | 1264 | 1292 | 1157 | 842 | 575 | 419 | 99 | 7418 |
| 1973-74 | 0 | 9 | 231 | 480 | 813 | 970 | 1290 | 1126 | 958 | 595 | 444 | 131 | 7047 |
| 1974-75 | 15 | 17 | 206 | 624 | 762 | 1071 | 1177 | 1112 | 1086 | 746 | 286 | 146 | 7248 |
| 1975-76 | 13 | 59 | 230 | 480 | 653 | 1258 | 1522 | 1061 | 1030 | 594 | 389 | 94 | 7383 |
| 1976-77 | 45 | 73 | 229 | 660 | 858 | 1404 | 1559 | 1199 | 888 | 674 | 354 | 184 | 8127 |
| 1977-78 | 29 | 54 | 233 | 518 | 761 | 1219 | 1353 | 1276 | 1071 | 724 | 377 | 134 | 7749 |
| 1978-79 | 39 | 32 | 230 | 513 | 852 | 1201 | 1272 | 1380 | 905 | 677 | 311 | 97 | 7509 |
| 1979-80 | 21 | 82 | 240 | 539 | 672 | 1083 | 1305 | 1284 | 1018 | 613 | 346 | 163 | 7366 |
| 1980-81 | 16 | 6 | 163 | 584 | 855 | 1349 | 1578 | 910 | 901 | 588 | 312 | 54 | 7316 |
| 1981-82 | 16 | 45 | 189 | 566 | 778 | 1102 | 1543 | 1161 | 1014 | 684 | 320 | 198 | 7616 |
| 1982-83 | 20 | 78 | 185 | 519 | 704 | 1015 | 1225 | 1080 | 895 | 612 | 393 | 101 | 6827 |
| 1983-84 | 8 | 38 | 139 | 527 | 738 | 1198 | 1397 | 949 | 1132 | 642 | 368 | 110 | 7246 |
| 1984-85 | 11 | 13 | 223 | 469 | 767 | 1043 | 1506 | 1076 | 930 | 620 | 347 | 115 | 7120 |
| 1985-86 | 4 | 32 | 157 | 433 | 747 | 1245 | 1236 | 1161 | 935 | 548 | 354 | 138 | 6990 |
| 1986-87 | 47 | 52 | 242 | 523 | 855 | 1092 | 1336 | 1172 | 955 | 597 | 343 | 77 | 7291 |
| 1987-88 | 20 | 58 | 171 | 548 | 798 | 1070 | 1339 | 1130 | 950 | 641 | 323 | 112 | 7160 |
| 1988-89 | 13 | 32 | 180 | 569 | 713 | 1201 | 1174 | 1141 | 1028 | 708 | 286 | 91 | 7136 |
| 1989-90 | 6 | 25 | 167 | 464 | 824 | 1573 | 1071 | 1093 | 935 | 607 | 402 | 107 | 7274 |
| 1990-91 | 12 | 24 | 170 | 388 | 690 | 964 | | | | | | | |

**TABLE 5**     COOLING DEGREE DAYS Base 65 deg. F          PORTLAND, MAINE

| YEAR | JAN | FEB | MAR | APR | MAY | JUNE | JULY | AUG | SEP | OCT | NOV | DEC | TOTAL |
|---|---|---|---|---|---|---|---|---|---|---|---|---|---|
| 1969 | 0 | 0 | 0 | 0 | 3 | 56 | 118 | 211 | 59 | 0 | 0 | 0 | 447 |
| 1970 | 0 | 0 | 0 | 0 | 4 | 55 | 172 | 136 | 41 | 0 | 0 | 0 | 408 |
| 1971 | 0 | 0 | 0 | 0 | 0 | 66 | 135 | 149 | 43 | 1 | 0 | 0 | 394 |
| 1972 | 0 | 0 | 0 | 0 | 0 | 3 | 114 | 71 | 8 | 0 | 0 | 0 | 196 |
| 1973 | 0 | 0 | 0 | 0 | 1 | 71 | 189 | 201 | 40 | 0 | 0 | 0 | 502 |
| 1974 | 0 | 0 | 0 | 2 | 4 | 26 | 121 | 115 | 28 | 0 | 0 | 0 | 296 |
| 1975 | 0 | 0 | 0 | 0 | 1 | 49 | 179 | 120 | 2 | 0 | 0 | 0 | 351 |
| 1976 | 0 | 0 | 0 | 0 | 2 | 128 | 80 | 93 | 5 | 0 | 0 | 0 | 308 |
| 1977 | 0 | 0 | 0 | 1 | 32 | 12 | 135 | 109 | 19 | 0 | 0 | 0 | 308 |
| 1978 | 0 | 0 | 0 | 0 | 6 | 22 | 138 | 150 | 20 | 0 | 0 | 0 | 336 |
| 1979 | 0 | 0 | 0 | 0 | 15 | 34 | 162 | 83 | 19 | 3 | 0 | 0 | 316 |
| 1980 | 0 | 0 | 0 | 0 | 1 | 50 | 163 | 205 | 67 | 0 | 0 | 0 | 486 |
| 1981 | 0 | 0 | 0 | 0 | 20 | 30 | 138 | 84 | 5 | 0 | 0 | 0 | 277 |
| 1982 | 0 | 0 | 0 | 0 | 6 | 4 | 158 | 66 | 17 | 0 | 0 | 0 | 251 |
| 1983 | 0 | 0 | 0 | 0 | 0 | 73 | 161 | 125 | 84 | 3 | 0 | 0 | 446 |
| 1984 | 0 | 0 | 0 | 0 | 0 | 84 | 162 | 147 | 12 | 0 | 0 | 0 | 405 |
| 1985 | 0 | 0 | 0 | 0 | 5 | 25 | 161 | 92 | 35 | 1 | 0 | 0 | 319 |
| 1986 | 0 | 0 | 0 | 0 | 8 | 23 | 93 | 96 | 19 | 0 | 0 | 0 | 239 |
| 1987 | 0 | 0 | 0 | 0 | 28 | 47 | 121 | 103 | 17 | 0 | 0 | 0 | 316 |
| 1988 | 0 | 0 | 0 | 0 | 11 | 85 | 209 | 227 | 17 | 2 | 0 | 0 | 551 |
| 1989 | 0 | 0 | 0 | 0 | 2 | 67 | 151 | 126 | 38 | 0 | 0 | 0 | 384 |
| 1990 | 0 | 0 | 0 | 0 | 0 | 34 | 181 | 179 | 19 | 7 | 0 | 0 | 420 |

**TABLE 6**     SNOWFALL (inches)          PORTLAND, MAINE

| SEASON | JULY | AUG | SEP | OCT | NOV | DEC | JAN | FEB | MAR | APR | MAY | JUNE | TOTAL |
|---|---|---|---|---|---|---|---|---|---|---|---|---|---|
| 1961-62 | 0.0 | 0.0 | 0.0 | 0.8 | 9.7 | 19.1 | 9.9 | 32.3 | 12.1 | 7.7 | 0.0 | 0.0 | 91.6 |
| 1962-63 | 0.0 | 0.0 | 0.0 | 3.6 | 1.3 | 14.3 | 18.4 | 22.6 | 19.1 | 0.8 | T | 0.0 | 80.1 |
| 1963-64 | 0.0 | 0.0 | 0.0 | 1.7 | T | 19.8 | 17.4 | 17.8 | 21.2 | 1.7 | 0.0 | 0.0 | 79.6 |
| 1964-65 | 0.0 | 0.0 | 0.0 | 0.0 | T | 20.5 | 15.8 | 13.2 | 3.4 | 2.6 | 0.0 | 0.0 | 55.5 |
| 1965-66 | 0.0 | 0.0 | 0.0 | T | 0.6 | 9.1 | 38.2 | 21.3 | 2.8 | 0.7 | 2.0 | 0.0 | 74.7 |
| 1966-67 | 0.0 | 0.0 | 0.0 | 0.0 | 0.0 | 14.7 | 12.4 | 45.8 | 17.5 | 15.7 | 0.1 | 0.0 | 106.2 |
| 1967-68 | 0.0 | 0.0 | 0.0 | 0.0 | 3.6 | 18.9 | 20.0 | 4.5 | 11.9 | 0.0 | 0.0 | 0.0 | 58.9 |
| 1968-69 | 0.0 | 0.0 | T | | 15.3 | 18.8 | 5.4 | 61.2 | 9.3 | T | 0.0 | 0.0 | 110.0 |
| 1969-70 | 0.0 | 0.0 | 0.0 | 3.8 | T | 24.7 | 6.2 | 9.8 | 20.7 | 2.9 | 0.0 | 0.0 | 68.1 |
| 1970-71 | 0.0 | 0.0 | 0.0 | T | 0.0 | 54.8 | 17.2 | 35.6 | 24.7 | 9.2 | 0.0 | 0.0 | 141.5 |
| 1971-72 | 0.0 | 0.0 | 0.0 | 0.0 | 6.2 | 12.5 | 7.0 | 38.0 | 21.7 | 6.3 | 0.0 | 0.0 | 91.7 |
| 1972-73 | 0.0 | 0.0 | 0.0 | T | 15.6 | 35.1 | 9.6 | 6.6 | 0.5 | 2.3 | 0.0 | 0.0 | 69.7 |
| 1973-74 | 0.0 | 0.0 | 0.0 | 0.0 | 0.0 | 7.2 | 15.0 | 4.3 | 6.2 | 8.3 | 0.0 | 0.0 | 41.0 |
| 1974-75 | 0.0 | 0.0 | 0.0 | T | 3.2 | 8.2 | 15.4 | 11.6 | 6.3 | 1.7 | 0.0 | 0.0 | 46.4 |
| 1975-76 | 0.0 | 0.0 | 0.0 | T | 3.6 | 25.3 | 18.1 | 4.9 | 22.2 | T | 0.0 | 0.0 | 74.1 |
| 1976-77 | 0.0 | 0.0 | 0.0 | 0.0 | 1.5 | 23.3 | 35.2 | 7.9 | 19.3 | 1.4 | T | 0.0 | 88.6 |
| 1977-78 | 0.0 | 0.0 | 0.0 | 0.0 | 1.9 | 23.1 | 30.7 | 8.2 | 12.5 | 0.8 | 0.0 | 0.0 | 77.2 |
| 1978-79 | 0.0 | 0.0 | 0.0 | 0.0 | 3.6 | 18.9 | 62.4 | 4.5 | T | 2.9 | 0.0 | 0.0 | 92.3 |
| 1979-80 | 0.0 | 0.0 | 0.0 | 1.7 | T | 1.8 | 6.0 | 11.2 | 6.8 | 0.0 | 0.0 | 0.0 | 27.5 |
| 1980-81 | 0.0 | 0.0 | 0.0 | 0.0 | 8.9 | 13.0 | 9.2 | 4.6 | 3.1 | T | 0.0 | 0.0 | 38.8 |
| 1981-82 | 0.0 | 0.0 | 0.0 | 0.0 | T | 24.0 | 25.9 | 11.0 | 8.5 | 15.9 | 0.0 | 0.0 | 85.3 |
| 1982-83 | 0.0 | 0.0 | 0.0 | 0.0 | 0.6 | 5.7 | 12.4 | 24.5 | 2.1 | T | 0.0 | 0.0 | 45.3 |
| 1983-84 | 0.0 | 0.0 | 0.0 | 0.0 | T | 12.6 | 28.3 | 3.3 | 26.4 | T | 0.0 | 0.0 | 70.6 |
| 1984-85 | 0.0 | 0.0 | 0.0 | 0.0 | T | 17.0 | 7.2 | 7.2 | 13.1 | 2.4 | 0.0 | 0.0 | 51.8 |
| 1985-86 | 0.0 | 0.0 | 0.0 | 0.0 | 3.1 | 11.2 | 18.6 | 12.0 | 6.4 | T | 0.0 | 0.0 | 51.3 |
| 1986-87 | 0.0 | 0.0 | 0.0 | 0.0 | 5.2 | 4.0 | 50.7 | 0.8 | 14.3 | 3.4 | 0.0 | 0.0 | 78.4 |
| 1987-88 | 0.0 | 0.0 | T | 0.0 | 5.4 | 9.1 | 19.8 | 20.8 | 3.0 | 4.2 | 0.0 | 0.0 | 62.3 |
| 1988-89 | 0.0 | 0.0 | 0.0 | T | T | 3.5 | 4.0 | 13.8 | 8.9 | 0.7 | 0.0 | 0.0 | 30.9 |
| 1989-90 | 0.0 | 0.0 | 0.0 | 0.0 | 5.0 | 15.6 | 20.4 | 25.6 | 3.2 | T | 0.0 | 0.0 | 69.8 |
| 1990-91 | 0.0 | 0.0 | T | 0.0 | 0.2 | 6.8 | | | | | | | |
| Record Mean | 0.0 | 0.0 | T | 0.2 | 3.1 | 14.7 | 19.4 | 17.5 | 12.4 | 2.9 | 0.2 | 0.0 | 70.4 |

**See Reference Notes, relative to all above tables, on preceding page.**

# BALTIMORE, MARYLAND

Baltimore–Washington International Airport lies in a region about midway between the rigorous climates of the North and the mild climates of the South, and adjacent to the modifying influences of the Chesapeake Bay and Atlantic Ocean to the east and the Appalachian Mountains to the west. Since this region is near the average path of the low pressure systems which move across the country, changes in wind direction are frequent and contribute to the changeable character of the weather. The net effect of the mountains to the west and the bay and ocean to the east is to produce a more equable climate compared with other continental locations farther inland at the same latitude.

Rainfall distribution throughout the year is rather uniform, however, the greatest intensities are confined to the summer and early fall months, the season for hurricanes and severe thunderstorms. Moisture deficiencies for crops occur occasionally during the growing season, but severe droughts are rare. Rainfall during the growing season occurs principally in the form of thunderstorms, and rainfall totals during these months vary appreciably.

The average date for the last occurrence in spring of temperatures as low as 32 degrees is mid–April. The average date for the first occurrence in fall of temperatures as low as 32 degrees is late October. The freeze–free period is approximately 194 days.

In summer, the area is under the influence of the large semi–permanent high pressure system commonly known as the Bermuda High and centered over the Atlantic Ocean near 30 degrees N Latitude. This pressure system brings warm humid air to the area. The proximity of large water areas and the inflow of southerly winds contribute to high relative humidities during much of the year.

January is the coldest month, and July, the warmest. Snowfall occurs on about eleven days per year on the average, however, an average of only about six days annually produces snowfalls of 1 inch or greater. Snow is frequently mixed with rain and sleet, and snow seldom remains on the ground more than a few days.

Glaze or freezing rain which is hazardous to highway traffic occurs on an average of two to three times per year, generally in January or February. Some years pass without the occurrence of freezing rain, while in others it occurs on as many as eight to ten days. Sleet is observed on about five days annually with the greatest frequency of occurrence in January.

The annual prevailing wind direction is from the west. Winter and spring months have the highest average wind speed. Destructive velocities are rare and occur mostly during summer thunderstorms. Only rarely have hurricanes in the vicinity caused widespread damage, then primarily through flooding.

**TABLE 1**     # NORMALS, MEANS AND EXTREMES

BALTIMORE, MARYLAND

LATITUDE: 39°11'N   LONGITUDE: 76°40'W   ELEVATION: FT. GRND 148 BARO 197   TIME ZONE: EASTERN   WBAN: 93721

| | (a) | JAN | FEB | MAR | APR | MAY | JUNE | JULY | AUG | SEP | OCT | NOV | DEC | YEAR |
|---|---|---|---|---|---|---|---|---|---|---|---|---|---|---|
| **TEMPERATURE °F:** | | | | | | | | | | | | | | |
| Normals | | | | | | | | | | | | | | |
| -Daily Maximum | | 41.0 | 43.7 | 53.1 | 65.1 | 74.2 | 82.9 | 87.1 | 85.5 | 79.1 | 67.7 | 55.9 | 45.1 | 65.0 |
| -Daily Minimum | | 24.3 | 25.7 | 33.4 | 42.9 | 52.5 | 61.5 | 66.5 | 65.7 | 58.6 | 46.1 | 36.6 | 27.9 | 45.1 |
| -Monthly | | 32.7 | 34.7 | 43.3 | 54.0 | 63.4 | 72.2 | 76.8 | 75.6 | 68.9 | 56.9 | 46.3 | 36.5 | 55.1 |
| Extremes | | | | | | | | | | | | | | |
| -Record Highest | 39 | 75 | 79 | 87 | 94 | 98 | 100 | 104 | 105 | 100 | 92 | 83 | 77 | 105 |
| -Year | | 1975 | 1985 | 1979 | 1960 | 1962 | 1988 | 1988 | 1983 | 1983 | 1954 | 1974 | 1984 | AUG 1983 |
| -Record Lowest | 39 | -7 | -3 | 6 | 20 | 32 | 40 | 50 | 45 | 35 | 25 | 13 | 0 | -7 |
| -Year | | 1984 | 1979 | 1960 | 1965 | 1966 | 1972 | 1988 | 1986 | 1963 | 1969 | 1955 | 1983 | JAN 1984 |
| **NORMAL DEGREE DAYS:** | | | | | | | | | | | | | | |
| Heating (base 65°F) | | 1001 | 848 | 673 | 334 | 115 | 0 | 0 | 0 | 29 | 261 | 561 | 884 | 4706 |
| Cooling (base 65°F) | | 0 | 0 | 0 | 0 | 66 | 221 | 366 | 329 | 146 | 10 | 0 | 0 | 1138 |
| **% OF POSSIBLE SUNSHINE** | 39 | 51 | 55 | 56 | 56 | 56 | 62 | 64 | 62 | 60 | 58 | 51 | 49 | 57 |
| **MEAN SKY COVER (tenths)** | | | | | | | | | | | | | | |
| Sunrise - Sunset | 39 | 6.3 | 6.3 | 6.2 | 6.1 | 6.2 | 5.7 | 5.6 | 5.6 | 5.4 | 5.2 | 6.1 | 6.3 | 5.9 |
| **MEAN NUMBER OF DAYS:** | | | | | | | | | | | | | | |
| Sunrise to Sunset | | | | | | | | | | | | | | |
| -Clear | 39 | 8.4 | 7.8 | 8.0 | 7.8 | 7.8 | 8.6 | 9.3 | 9.5 | 10.7 | 11.9 | 8.4 | 8.5 | 106.7 |
| -Partly Cloudy | 39 | 7.6 | 6.8 | 8.9 | 9.1 | 10.2 | 11.2 | 12.0 | 10.6 | 8.6 | 7.9 | 8.2 | 7.2 | 108.1 |
| -Cloudy | 39 | 15.1 | 13.6 | 14.1 | 13.1 | 13.1 | 10.2 | 9.7 | 10.8 | 10.7 | 11.3 | 13.4 | 15.4 | 150.5 |
| Precipitation | | | | | | | | | | | | | | |
| .01 inches or more | 39 | 10.5 | 9.2 | 10.6 | 10.6 | 11.0 | 9.3 | 9.0 | 9.6 | 7.5 | 7.4 | 9.1 | 9.1 | 112.8 |
| Snow, Ice pellets | | | | | | | | | | | | | | |
| 1.0 inches or more | 39 | 2.1 | 1.9 | 1.2 | 0.* | 0.0 | 0.0 | 0.0 | 0.0 | 0.0 | 0.0 | 0.4 | 1.0 | 6.6 |
| Thunderstorms | 39 | 0.3 | 0.2 | 0.9 | 2.3 | 4.0 | 5.5 | 5.9 | 5.1 | 1.9 | 0.9 | 0.4 | 0.1 | 27.5 |
| Heavy Fog Visibility | | | | | | | | | | | | | | |
| 1/4 mile or less | 39 | 3.2 | 3.4 | 2.6 | 1.7 | 1.7 | 1.0 | 0.9 | 1.1 | 1.4 | 2.8 | 2.5 | 3.5 | 25.8 |
| Temperature °F | | | | | | | | | | | | | | |
| -Maximum | | | | | | | | | | | | | | |
| 90° and above | 39 | 0.0 | 0.0 | 0.0 | 0.4 | 1.4 | 6.2 | 11.2 | 8.0 | 3.3 | 0.1 | 0.0 | 0.0 | 30.5 |
| 32° and below | 39 | 6.6 | 3.9 | 0.6 | 0.0 | 0.0 | 0.0 | 0.0 | 0.0 | 0.0 | 0.0 | 0.1 | 3.8 | 15.0 |
| -Minimum | | | | | | | | | | | | | | |
| 32° and below | 39 | 25.3 | 21.3 | 14.5 | 3.0 | 0.* | 0.0 | 0.0 | 0.0 | 0.0 | 1.7 | 10.9 | 21.3 | 97.8 |
| 0° and below | 39 | 0.4 | 0.1 | 0.0 | 0.0 | 0.0 | 0.0 | 0.0 | 0.0 | 0.0 | 0.0 | 0.0 | 0.1 | 0.6 |
| **AVG. STATION PRESS.(mb)** | 17 | 1013.1 | 1013.1 | 1011.3 | 1009.4 | 1009.6 | 1009.9 | 1010.6 | 1011.8 | 1013.0 | 1014.0 | 1013.4 | 1013.8 | 1011.9 |
| **RELATIVE HUMIDITY (%)** | | | | | | | | | | | | | | |
| Hour 01 | 36 | 68 | 67 | 66 | 68 | 77 | 81 | 81 | 83 | 83 | 80 | 74 | 71 | 75 |
| Hour 07 | 36 | 71 | 71 | 71 | 71 | 77 | 79 | 81 | 84 | 85 | 83 | 78 | 74 | 77 |
| Hour 13 (Local Time) | 36 | 57 | 54 | 50 | 49 | 53 | 53 | 53 | 55 | 55 | 54 | 55 | 57 | 54 |
| Hour 19 | 36 | 62 | 59 | 54 | 53 | 60 | 62 | 64 | 67 | 69 | 68 | 64 | 64 | 62 |
| **PRECIPITATION (inches):** | | | | | | | | | | | | | | |
| Water Equivalent | | | | | | | | | | | | | | |
| -Normal | | 3.00 | 2.98 | 3.72 | 3.35 | 3.44 | 3.76 | 3.89 | 4.62 | 3.46 | 3.11 | 3.11 | 3.40 | 41.84 |
| -Maximum Monthly | 39 | 7.84 | 7.16 | 6.80 | 8.15 | 8.71 | 9.95 | 8.18 | 18.35 | 8.62 | 8.09 | 7.68 | 7.44 | 18.35 |
| -Year | | 1979 | 1979 | 1983 | 1952 | 1989 | 1972 | 1960 | 1955 | 1975 | 1976 | 1952 | 1969 | AUG 1955 |
| -Minimum Monthly | 39 | 0.29 | 0.56 | 0.93 | 0.39 | 0.37 | 0.15 | 0.30 | 0.77 | 0.21 | T | 0.31 | 0.20 | T |
| -Year | | 1955 | 1978 | 1966 | 1985 | 1986 | 1954 | 1955 | 1951 | 1967 | 1963 | 1981 | 1955 | OCT 1963 |
| -Maximum in 24 hrs | 39 | 3.11 | 3.26 | 3.18 | 2.80 | 3.64 | 5.23 | 5.86 | 8.35 | 6.04 | 3.49 | 3.43 | 3.39 | 8.35 |
| -Year | | 1976 | 1983 | 1958 | 1952 | 1960 | 1972 | 1952 | 1955 | 1985 | 1955 | 1952 | 1977 | AUG 1955 |
| Snow, Ice pellets | | | | | | | | | | | | | | |
| -Maximum Monthly | 39 | 25.1 | 33.1 | 21.6 | 0.7 | T | 0.0 | 0.0 | 0.0 | 0.0 | 0.3 | 8.4 | 20.4 | 33.1 |
| -Year | | 1987 | 1979 | 1960 | 1985 | 1963 | | | | | 1979 | 1967 | 1966 | FEB 1979 |
| -Maximum in 24 hrs | 39 | 12.3 | 22.8 | 13.0 | 0.7 | T | 0.0 | 0.0 | 0.0 | 0.0 | 0.3 | 8.4 | 14.1 | 22.8 |
| -Year | | 1987 | 1983 | 1962 | 1985 | 1963 | | | | | 1979 | 1967 | 1960 | FEB 1983 |
| **WIND:** | | | | | | | | | | | | | | |
| Mean Speed (mph) | 39 | 9.8 | 10.3 | 10.9 | 10.6 | 9.2 | 8.5 | 7.9 | 7.9 | 8.1 | 8.7 | 9.3 | 9.3 | 9.2 |
| Prevailing Direction through 1963 | | WNW | NW | WNW | WNW | W | WNW | W | W | S | NW | WNW | WNW | WNW |
| Fastest Mile | | | | | | | | | | | | | | |
| -Direction (!!) | 39 | NE | W | SE | W | SW | SW | NW | NE | W | SE | E | W | SE |
| -Speed (MPH) | 39 | 63 | 68 | 80 | 70 | 65 | 80 | 57 | 54 | 56 | 73 | 58 | 57 | 80 |
| -Year | | 1958 | 1956 | 1952 | 1954 | 1961 | 1952 | 1962 | 1955 | 1952 | 1954 | 1952 | 1953 | MAR 1952 |
| Peak Gust | | | | | | | | | | | | | | |
| -Direction (!!) | 6 | NW | NW | W | W | NW | NW | NW | SW | NW | NW | NW | NW | NW |
| -Speed (mph) | 6 | 51 | 51 | 58 | 48 | 49 | 45 | 68 | 55 | 45 | 39 | 64 | 77 | 77 |
| -Date | | 1985 | 1987 | 1985 | 1985 | 1984 | 1985 | 1987 | 1987 | 1985 | 1986 | 1989 | 1988 | DEC 1988 |

**See Reference Notes to this table on the following page.**

## TABLE 2 — PRECIPITATION (inches)   BALTIMORE, MARYLAND

| YEAR | JAN | FEB | MAR | APR | MAY | JUNE | JULY | AUG | SEP | OCT | NOV | DEC | ANNUAL |
|---|---|---|---|---|---|---|---|---|---|---|---|---|---|
| 1961 | 2.91 | 4.63 | 3.87 | 4.45 | 2.72 | 5.19 | 4.57 | 4.31 | 1.57 | 3.70 | 1.98 | 2.85 | 42.75 |
| 1962 | 2.02 | 4.41 | 4.85 | 4.25 | 2.43 | 3.16 | 2.09 | 2.26 | 2.39 | 2.96 | 2.92 | 2.92 | 40.24 |
| 1963 | 1.84 | 2.07 | 4.68 | 2.15 | 1.70 | 9.16 | 0.69 | 4.21 | 4.12 | T | 6.85 | 2.08 | 39.55 |
| 1964 | 5.27 | 4.36 | 2.98 | 4.37 | 0.43 | 2.40 | 2.66 | 1.96 | 2.61 | 1.19 | 2.51 | 3.94 | 34.68 |
| 1965 | 3.09 | 2.89 | 4.31 | 1.72 | 1.79 | 1.94 | 2.61 | 4.72 | 1.94 | 1.90 | 0.68 | 0.63 | 28.22 |
| 1966 | 4.15 | 4.24 | 0.93 | 4.39 | 4.53 | 1.18 | 1.48 | 1.87 | 8.50 | 4.80 | 2.78 | 3.53 | 42.38 |
| 1967 | 0.99 | 2.25 | 4.39 | 1.73 | 3.79 | 1.89 | 3.56 | 8.87 | 0.21 | 1.34 | 2.60 | 5.31 | 36.93 |
| 1968 | 3.42 | 0.72 | 4.41 | 1.61 | 5.41 | 3.35 | 2.75 | 4.16 | 4.39 | 3.13 | 3.85 | 2.60 | 39.80 |
| 1969 | 1.38 | 1.75 | 1.63 | 1.80 | 1.46 | 3.65 | 5.22 | 3.81 | 2.60 | 1.10 | 1.74 | 7.44 | 33.58 |
| 1970 | 0.94 | 3.34 | 3.07 | 4.53 | 1.69 | 4.10 | 4.32 | 1.33 | 0.46 | 3.04 | 5.11 | 3.50 | 35.43 |
| 1971 | 2.02 | 6.21 | 1.90 | 1.75 | 6.12 | 2.92 | 4.03 | 10.91 | 5.55 | 6.88 | 1.29 | 3.75 | 53.33 |
| 1972 | 2.82 | 6.01 | 2.38 | 5.30 | 4.11 | 9.95 | 2.81 | 2.22 | 1.15 | 3.51 | 7.05 | 5.02 | 52.33 |
| 1973 | 2.81 | 2.82 | 2.82 | 6.41 | 3.73 | 3.16 | 4.22 | 3.35 | 4.87 | 2.86 | 1.28 | 6.36 | 45.83 |
| 1974 | 2.92 | 0.94 | 4.12 | 2.59 | 3.58 | 2.84 | 0.85 | 5.85 | 5.45 | 1.53 | 1.39 | 5.70 | 37.76 |
| 1975 | 3.47 | 2.47 | 5.17 | 2.73 | 4.63 | 3.82 | 7.15 | 4.23 | 8.62 | 2.89 | 2.03 | 4.61 | 51.82 |
| 1976 | 4.10 | 2.16 | 2.23 | 1.27 | 5.03 | 2.49 | 5.56 | 2.98 | 6.93 | 8.09 | 0.56 | 2.04 | 43.44 |
| 1977 | 1.36 | 0.63 | 3.93 | 3.05 | 1.49 | 3.44 | 2.62 | 3.31 | 0.62 | 5.17 | 5.01 | 5.76 | 36.39 |
| 1978 | 7.34 | 0.56 | 4.74 | 1.26 | 5.49 | 2.81 | 6.83 | 3.39 | 1.03 | 0.71 | 2.70 | 4.63 | 41.49 |
| 1979 | 7.84 | 7.16 | 2.05 | 3.37 | 4.15 | 5.74 | 3.71 | 9.38 | 6.73 | 5.53 | 2.45 | 0.87 | 58.98 |
| 1980 | 2.58 | 1.06 | 5.46 | 4.24 | 3.58 | 3.04 | 3.25 | 4.00 | 1.00 | 3.08 | 2.72 | 0.70 | 34.71 |
| 1981 | 0.49 | 2.93 | 1.14 | 2.04 | 3.63 | 5.40 | 4.59 | 1.93 | 2.89 | 2.57 | 0.31 | 3.30 | 31.22 |
| 1982 | 3.37 | 4.04 | 3.03 | 3.61 | 1.85 | 5.70 | 2.16 | 0.95 | 3.63 | 2.31 | 3.13 | 2.39 | 36.17 |
| 1983 | 2.21 | 4.81 | 6.80 | 6.55 | 5.47 | 5.23 | 1.31 | 1.57 | 1.76 | 3.58 | 5.02 | 6.72 | 51.03 |
| 1984 | 1.96 | 3.90 | 5.79 | 2.95 | 4.29 | 1.65 | 3.27 | 4.11 | 2.38 | 1.94 | 3.01 | 1.77 | 36.96 |
| 1985 | 2.03 | 3.03 | 2.37 | 0.39 | 6.01 | 2.44 | 2.53 | 3.72 | 6.22 | 2.48 | 4.71 | 0.84 | 36.77 |
| 1986 | 2.16 | 3.78 | 0.96 | 2.64 | 0.37 | 1.46 | 4.12 | 4.26 | 0.58 | 1.86 | 5.96 | 5.52 | 33.67 |
| 1987 | 5.85 | 2.22 | 0.99 | 1.86 | 4.16 | 2.63 | 5.05 | 1.61 | 7.34 | 2.25 | 5.05 | 2.07 | 41.08 |
| 1988 | 3.24 | 3.25 | 2.35 | 2.44 | 4.37 | 0.84 | 3.78 | 2.64 | 2.05 | 1.59 | 4.78 | 0.97 | 32.30 |
| 1989 | 3.07 | 3.36 | 4.24 | 3.16 | 8.71 | 5.98 | 7.35 | 3.38 | 3.64 | 4.90 | 1.97 | 2.12 | 51.88 |
| 1990 | 3.71 | 1.48 | 2.54 | 4.23 | 4.92 | 2.55 | 5.68 | 6.17 | 1.07 | 2.57 | 2.10 | 4.86 | 41.88 |
| Record Mean | 2.95 | 3.06 | 3.55 | 3.26 | 3.67 | 3.67 | 3.91 | 4.22 | 3.38 | 2.98 | 3.24 | 3.32 | 41.22 |

## TABLE 3 — AVERAGE TEMPERATURE (deg. F)   BALTIMORE, MARYLAND

| YEAR | JAN | FEB | MAR | APR | MAY | JUNE | JULY | AUG | SEP | OCT | NOV | DEC | ANNUAL |
|---|---|---|---|---|---|---|---|---|---|---|---|---|---|
| 1961 | 27.6 | 37.0 | 45.0 | 50.0 | 60.3 | 71.4 | 76.5 | 74.6 | 73.2 | 57.7 | 47.6 | 33.4 | 54.5 |
| 1962 | 32.4 | 32.3 | 42.2 | 53.9 | 66.2 | 72.3 | 73.6 | 74.6 | 64.8 | 57.7 | 41.5 | 30.9 | 53.5 |
| 1963 | 28.8 | 27.8 | 45.9 | 54.0 | 61.4 | 73.1 | 76.3 | 72.9 | 64.0 | 58.6 | 47.3 | 28.8 | 53.3 |
| 1964 | 33.8 | 33.2 | 44.4 | 50.9 | 65.3 | 72.7 | 77.0 | 73.5 | 68.1 | 53.3 | 49.8 | 39.1 | 55.1 |
| 1965 | 30.8 | 34.9 | 39.2 | 50.3 | 66.9 | 70.1 | 76.8 | 75.5 | 70.8 | 53.9 | 45.6 | 38.3 | 54.4 |
| 1966 | 29.8 | 30.5 | 43.3 | 49.5 | 61.7 | 72.9 | 78.9 | 76.5 | 66.7 | 53.4 | 46.4 | 35.6 | 53.8 |
| 1967 | 37.4 | 30.7 | 41.8 | 54.0 | 57.0 | 72.7 | 75.2 | 73.4 | 65.3 | 55.3 | 42.0 | 37.3 | 53.5 |
| 1968 | 29.2 | 32.2 | 46.6 | 54.0 | 59.7 | 72.6 | 78.2 | 78.7 | 70.3 | 59.7 | 48.2 | 34.6 | 55.3 |
| 1969 | 31.7 | 34.9 | 40.7 | 56.2 | 65.5 | 74.9 | 77.4 | 76.5 | 69.5 | 57.7 | 46.1 | 35.2 | 55.5 |
| 1970 | 27.8 | 35.4 | 40.4 | 53.3 | 66.6 | 73.0 | 77.2 | 77.4 | 73.7 | 61.5 | 48.6 | 38.2 | 56.1 |
| 1971 | 30.0 | 37.4 | 41.8 | 52.7 | 61.2 | 74.0 | 76.5 | 74.2 | 70.9 | 62.9 | 46.4 | 43.7 | 56.0 |
| 1972 | 37.6 | 34.3 | 43.6 | 51.6 | 62.7 | 68.1 | 76.9 | 75.4 | 69.8 | 53.5 | 43.2 | 40.4 | 54.8 |
| 1973 | 34.6 | 34.3 | 48.3 | 53.1 | 59.6 | 73.5 | 75.9 | 76.9 | 69.8 | 58.2 | 47.3 | 37.3 | 55.7 |
| 1974 | 37.9 | 33.8 | 45.2 | 55.3 | 61.9 | 68.5 | 76.5 | 75.0 | 67.5 | 55.3 | 48.2 | 40.3 | 55.4 |
| 1975 | 38.5 | 39.1 | 42.1 | 50.4 | 66.3 | 73.0 | 76.1 | 77.9 | 66.0 | 60.7 | 51.9 | 37.2 | 56.6 |
| 1976 | 30.8 | 44.1 | 48.1 | 56.9 | 62.1 | 74.8 | 76.9 | 73.9 | 67.5 | 52.9 | 40.9 | 32.6 | 55.0 |
| 1977 | 22.9 | 36.5 | 50.0 | 57.9 | 66.7 | 71.4 | 79.0 | 77.7 | 72.1 | 56.0 | 49.2 | 35.6 | 56.3 |
| 1978 | 29.2 | 27.3 | 41.7 | 54.2 | 62.4 | 73.1 | 76.9 | 78.1 | 69.7 | 56.1 | 48.7 | 40.2 | 54.7 |
| 1979 | 33.1 | 25.6 | 48.5 | 53.1 | 64.7 | 70.7 | 75.9 | 75.7 | 68.8 | 55.7 | 50.6 | 40.3 | 55.2 |
| 1980 | 33.8 | 31.5 | 41.5 | 55.7 | 65.5 | 71.3 | 78.2 | 78.7 | 72.2 | 55.3 | 44.2 | 35.5 | 55.3 |
| 1981 | 27.9 | 38.8 | 41.9 | 57.0 | 62.2 | 74.3 | 77.3 | 74.4 | 67.7 | 53.2 | 46.2 | 34.5 | 54.6 |
| 1982 | 25.5 | 35.8 | 42.9 | 50.7 | 66.1 | 69.4 | 77.1 | 73.0 | 67.3 | 56.3 | 48.4 | 42.0 | 54.6 |
| 1983 | 34.6 | 34.7 | 45.4 | 51.8 | 61.5 | 72.1 | 78.7 | 78.0 | 69.5 | 57.3 | 47.1 | 33.2 | 55.3 |
| 1984 | 28.5 | 41.7 | 38.2 | 51.5 | 61.3 | 73.4 | 73.9 | 75.0 | 64.8 | 62.2 | 43.9 | 44.1 | 54.9 |
| 1985 | 29.3 | 38.7 | 46.0 | 57.9 | 65.1 | 70.4 | 76.4 | 74.5 | 69.4 | 58.8 | 52.4 | 33.8 | 56.1 |
| 1986 | 33.2 | 32.9 | 45.0 | 53.5 | 66.7 | 74.4 | 79.4 | 73.1 | 68.9 | 58.9 | 44.8 | 38.2 | 55.8 |
| 1987 | 32.5 | 34.3 | 46.2 | 53.1 | 65.0 | 74.5 | 80.0 | 76.1 | 69.3 | 51.5 | 47.8 | 39.8 | 55.8 |
| 1988 | 28.7 | 35.9 | 45.1 | 52.0 | 64.0 | 73.0 | 80.3 | 78.5 | 66.8 | 51.3 | 48.1 | 36.3 | 55.0 |
| 1989 | 37.9 | 36.5 | 43.8 | 52.5 | 62.0 | 73.9 | 76.0 | 74.4 | 69.0 | 58.3 | 44.8 | 25.4 | 54.5 |
| 1990 | 42.0 | 42.3 | 47.6 | 54.8 | 62.3 | 73.3 | 78.4 | 74.6 | 67.3 | 60.7 | 49.6 | 42.2 | 57.9 |
| Record Mean | 32.5 | 35.3 | 43.4 | 53.9 | 63.3 | 72.3 | 77.0 | 75.4 | 68.6 | 56.9 | 44.6 | 36.5 | 55.1 |
| Max | 40.9 | 44.2 | 53.3 | 64.8 | 74.1 | 82.9 | 87.2 | 85.2 | 78.7 | 67.5 | 56.1 | 45.1 | 65.0 |
| Min | 24.1 | 26.4 | 33.5 | 42.9 | 52.6 | 61.7 | 66.8 | 65.6 | 58.4 | 46.2 | 36.7 | 28.0 | 45.2 |

### REFERENCE NOTES FOR TABLES 1, 2, 3 and 6        (BALTIMORE, MD)

**GENERAL**

T - TRACE AMOUNT
BLANK ENTRIES DENOTE MISSING/UNREPORTED DATA.
# INDICATES A STATION OR INSTRUMENT RELOCATION.

**SPECIFIC**

**TABLE 1**

(a) - LENGTH OF RECORD IN YEARS. ALTHOUGH INDIVIDUAL MONTHS MAY BE MISSING.
* LESS THAN .05

NORMALS — BASED ON THE 1951-1980 RECORD PERIOD.
EXTREMES — DATES ARE THE MOST RECENT OCCURRENCE.
WIND DIR. — NUMERALS SHOW TENS OF DEGREES CLOCKWISE FROM TRUE NORTH. "00" INDICATES CALM. RESULTANT WIND DIRECTIONS ARE GIVEN TO WHOLE DEGREES.

**TABLE 3**
MAX AND MIN ARE LONG-TERM MEAN DAILY MAXIMUM AND MEAN DAILY MINIMUM TEMPERATURES.

**EXCEPTIONS**

**TABLES 2, 3, and 6**

RECORD MEANS ARE THROUGH THE CURRENT YEAR, BEGINNING IN
1951 FOR TEMPERATURE
1951 FOR PRECIPITATION
1951 FOR SNOWFALL

**TABLE 4** HEATING DEGREE DAYS Base 65 deg. F  BALTIMORE, MARYLAND

| SEASON | JULY | AUG | SEP | OCT | NOV | DEC | JAN | FEB | MAR | APR | MAY | JUNE | TOTAL |
|---|---|---|---|---|---|---|---|---|---|---|---|---|---|
| 1961-62 | 0 | 0 | 30 | 230 | 533 | 975 | 1004 | 909 | 704 | 360 | 100 | 0 | 4845 |
| 1962-63 | 0 | 0 | 102 | 242 | 667 | 1048 | 1114 | 1037 | 583 | 341 | 153 | 1 | 5288 |
| 1963-64 | 0 | 2 | 95 | 197 | 524 | 1116 | 959 | 916 | 631 | 425 | 87 | 14 | 4966 |
| 1964-65 | 0 | 0 | 41 | 358 | 448 | 797 | 1052 | 838 | 792 | 433 | 55 | 44 | 4858 |
| 1965-66 | 0 | 5 | 34 | 336 | 576 | 819 | 1085 | 961 | 665 | 460 | 157 | 23 | 5121 |
| 1966-67 | 0 | 0 | 68 | 353 | 555 | 905 | 846 | 955 | 715 | 338 | 254 | 6 | 4995 |
| 1967-68 | 0 | 0 | 75 | 318 | 684 | 851 | 1100 | 943 | 566 | 324 | 173 | 1 | 5035 |
| 1968-69 | 0 | 1 | 4 | 197 | 500 | 934 | 1028 | 835 | 748 | 273 | 69 | 0 | 4589 |
| 1969-70 | 0 | 0 | 26 | 251 | 561 | 916 | 1148 | 822 | 752 | 346 | 77 | 0 | 4899 |
| 1970-71 | 0 | 0 | 20 | 149 | 484 | 824 | 1080 | 766 | 712 | 364 | 134 | 2 | 4535 |
| 1971-72 | 0 | 0 | 24 | 96 | 571 | 652 | 841 | 884 | 663 | 396 | 94 | 42 | 4263 |
| 1972-73 | 2 | 0 | 16 | 357 | 649 | 759 | 935 | 854 | 511 | 365 | 191 | 1 | 4640 |
| 1973-74 | 0 | 0 | 24 | 221 | 524 | 852 | 830 | 868 | 613 | 309 | 148 | 14 | 4403 |
| 1974-75 | 0 | 0 | 49 | 303 | 509 | 759 | 818 | 720 | 702 | 436 | 66 | 2 | 4364 |
| 1975-76 | 0 | 0 | 50 | 156 | 397 | 853 | 1050 | 603 | 518 | 293 | 133 | 11 | 4064 |
| 1976-77 | 0 | 0 | 34 | 377 | 716 | 1001 | 1296 | 790 | 469 | 245 | 62 | 18 | 5008 |
| 1977-78 | 0 | 0 | 9 | 278 | 476 | 904 | 1101 | 1048 | 715 | 318 | 141 | 9 | 4999 |
| 1978-79 | 0 | 0 | 33 | 280 | 483 | 763 | 984 | 1100 | 520 | 354 | 75 | 6 | 4598 |
| 1979-80 | 2 | 3 | 22 | 311 | 425 | 757 | 962 | 967 | 723 | 273 | 74 | 6 | 4525 |
| 1980-81 | 0 | 0 | 20 | 311 | 620 | 908 | 1145 | 727 | 706 | 252 | 148 | 1 | 4838 |
| 1981-82 | 0 | 0 | 51 | 363 | 557 | 940 | 1218 | 808 | 677 | 422 | 58 | 20 | 5114 |
| 1982-83 | 0 | 5 | 42 | 289 | 495 | 707 | 936 | 842 | 602 | 410 | 152 | 6 | 4486 |
| 1983-84 | 0 | 0 | 70 | 257 | 530 | 979 | 1123 | 671 | 825 | 397 | 169 | 9 | 5030 |
| 1984-85 | 0 | 1 | 96 | 123 | 625 | 643 | 1101 | 731 | 589 | 252 | 79 | 10 | 4250 |
| 1985-86 | 0 | 0 | 41 | 201 | 378 | 962 | 980 | 892 | 613 | 342 | 86 | 6 | 4501 |
| 1986-87 | 0 | 23 | 34 | 236 | 598 | 822 | 1002 | 853 | 576 | 357 | 106 | 1 | 4608 |
| 1987-88 | 0 | 1 | 15 | 412 | 511 | 774 | 1120 | 838 | 613 | 389 | 96 | 27 | 4796 |
| 1988-89 | 2 | 0 | 39 | 424 | 504 | 882 | 834 | 792 | 663 | 374 | 145 | 0 | 4659 |
| 1989-90 | 0 | 0 | 51 | 229 | 600 | 1221 | 707 | 631 | 552 | 341 | 102 | 5 | 4439 |
| 1990-91 | 1 | 0 | 63 | 195 | 454 | 701 | | | | | | | |

**TABLE 5** COOLING DEGREE DAYS Base 65 deg. F  BALTIMORE, MARYLAND

| YEAR | JAN | FEB | MAR | APR | MAY | JUNE | JULY | AUG | SEP | OCT | NOV | DEC | TOTAL |
|---|---|---|---|---|---|---|---|---|---|---|---|---|---|
| 1969 | 0 | 0 | 0 | 16 | 93 | 304 | 392 | 364 | 169 | 33 | 0 | 0 | 1371 |
| 1970 | 0 | 0 | 0 | 4 | 134 | 246 | 389 | 390 | 291 | 45 | 0 | 0 | 1499 |
| 1971 | 0 | 0 | 0 | 0 | 24 | 278 | 363 | 293 | 208 | 36 | 20 | 0 | 1222 |
| 1972 | 0 | 0 | 5 | 1 | 29 | 140 | 379 | 331 | 166 | 7 | 0 | 0 | 1058 |
| 1973 | 0 | 0 | 0 | 15 | 29 | 263 | 344 | 376 | 173 | 19 | 0 | 0 | 1219 |
| 1974 | 0 | 0 | 4 | 24 | 57 | 126 | 361 | 317 | 130 | 8 | 11 | 0 | 1038 |
| 1975 | 0 | 0 | 4 | 4 | 112 | 252 | 351 | 404 | 85 | 27 | 10 | 0 | 1245 |
| 1976 | 0 | 1 | 0 | 58 | 51 | 315 | 317 | 284 | 114 | 9 | 0 | 0 | 1149 |
| 1977 | 0 | 0 | 10 | 37 | 124 | 217 | 439 | 401 | 229 | 7 | 10 | 0 | 1474 |
| 1978 | 0 | 0 | 0 | 0 | 63 | 260 | 344 | 413 | 182 | 12 | 0 | 0 | 1274 |
| 1979 | 0 | 0 | 15 | 4 | 72 | 183 | 348 | 341 | 145 | 28 | 1 | 0 | 1137 |
| 1980 | 0 | 0 | 0 | 0 | 97 | 203 | 415 | 431 | 245 | 17 | 0 | 0 | 1408 |
| 1981 | 0 | 0 | 0 | 19 | 69 | 287 | 389 | 296 | 141 | 5 | 0 | 0 | 1206 |
| 1982 | 0 | 0 | 0 | 4 | 99 | 160 | 381 | 259 | 119 | 26 | 4 | 1 | 1053 |
| 1983 | 0 | 0 | 0 | 18 | 51 | 228 | 430 | 410 | 214 | 24 | 0 | 0 | 1375 |
| 1984 | 0 | 0 | 0 | 0 | 59 | 268 | 281 | 316 | 98 | 41 | 0 | 2 | 1065 |
| 1985 | 0 | 2 | 7 | 43 | 89 | 179 | 363 | 298 | 178 | 17 | 0 | 5 | 1181 |
| 1986 | 0 | 0 | 0 | 1 | 143 | 295 | 452 | 281 | 158 | 54 | 0 | 0 | 1384 |
| 1987 | 0 | 0 | 0 | 7 | 115 | 292 | 473 | 352 | 152 | 0 | 0 | 0 | 1391 |
| 1988 | 0 | 0 | 2 | 4 | 71 | 274 | 485 | 427 | 100 | 8 | 0 | 0 | 1371 |
| 1989 | 0 | 0 | 14 | 5 | 58 | 276 | 351 | 298 | 178 | 25 | 1 | 0 | 1206 |
| 1990 | 0 | 0 | 19 | 38 | 26 | 261 | 422 | 303 | 137 | 68 | 0 | 0 | 1274 |

**TABLE 6** SNOWFALL (inches)  BALTIMORE, MARYLAND

| SEASON | JULY | AUG | SEP | OCT | NOV | DEC | JAN | FEB | MAR | APR | MAY | JUNE | TOTAL |
|---|---|---|---|---|---|---|---|---|---|---|---|---|---|
| 1961-62 | 0.0 | 0.0 | 0.0 | 0.0 | 3.2 | 7.2 | 2.0 | 9.2 | 13.6 | 0.0 | 0.0 | 0.0 | 35.2 |
| 1962-63 | 0.0 | 0.0 | 0.0 | 0.0 | 0.3 | 11.7 | 3.7 | 2.1 | 1.8 | 0.0 | T | 0.0 | 19.6 |
| 1963-64 | 0.0 | 0.0 | 0.0 | 0.0 | T | 9.7 | 10.3 | 18.2 | 13.2 | 0.0 | 0.0 | 0.0 | 51.8 |
| 1964-65 | 0.0 | 0.0 | 0.0 | 0.0 | T | 0.8 | 8.3 | 1.1 | 8.4 | 0.0 | 0.0 | 0.0 | 18.6 |
| 1965-66 | 0.0 | 0.0 | 0.0 | 0.0 | 0.0 | T | 21.4 | 11.4 | 0.0 | 0.0 | T | 0.0 | 32.8 |
| 1966-67 | 0.0 | 0.0 | 0.0 | 0.0 | T | 20.4 | 0.4 | 20.1 | 2.5 | 0.0 | 0.0 | 0.0 | 43.4 |
| 1967-68 | 0.0 | 0.0 | 0.0 | 0.0 | 8.4 | 4.6 | 2.5 | 2.6 | 5.3 | 0.0 | 0.0 | 0.0 | 23.4 |
| 1968-69 | 0.0 | 0.0 | 0.0 | 0.0 | 4.3 | T | 0.1 | 6.4 | 7.8 | 0.0 | 0.0 | 0.0 | 18.6 |
| 1969-70 | 0.0 | 0.0 | 0.0 | 0.0 | T | 9.0 | 6.1 | 4.0 | 1.9 | T | 0.0 | 0.0 | 21.0 |
| 1970-71 | 0.0 | 0.0 | 0.0 | 0.0 | 0.0 | 6.3 | 4.1 | 0.6 | 2.0 | T | 0.0 | 0.0 | 13.0 |
| 1971-72 | 0.0 | 0.0 | 0.0 | 0.0 | 1.0 | T | 1.1 | 11.4 | 0.2 | 0.3 | 0.0 | 0.0 | 14.0 |
| 1972-73 | 0.0 | 0.0 | 0.0 | T | T | T | T | 1.2 | T | T | 0.0 | 0.0 | 1.2 |
| 1973-74 | 0.0 | 0.0 | 0.0 | 0.0 | 0.0 | 8.3 | 1.2 | 7.6 | T | T | 0.0 | 0.0 | 17.1 |
| 1974-75 | 0.0 | 0.0 | 0.0 | 0.0 | T | 0.4 | 5.1 | 5.5 | 1.2 | T | 0.0 | 0.0 | 12.2 |
| 1975-76 | 0.0 | 0.0 | 0.0 | 0.0 | 0.0 | 0.7 | 1.7 | 1.3 | 7.8 | 0.0 | 0.0 | 0.0 | 11.5 |
| 1976-77 | 0.0 | 0.0 | 0.0 | 0.0 | 1.1 | 1.5 | 8.5 | T | T | T | 0.0 | 0.0 | 11.1 |
| 1977-78 | 0.0 | 0.0 | 0.0 | T | 0.6 | 0.5 | 12.4 | 12.3 | 8.5 | T | 0.0 | 0.0 | 34.3 |
| 1978-79 | 0.0 | 0.0 | 0.0 | 0.0 | 3.7 | T | 5.7 | 33.1 | T | 0.0 | 0.0 | 0.0 | 42.5 |
| 1979-80 | 0.0 | 0.0 | 0.0 | 0.3 | T | 0.1 | 4.7 | 3.8 | 5.7 | 0.0 | 0.0 | 0.0 | 14.6 |
| 1980-81 | 0.0 | 0.0 | 0.0 | 0.0 | T | 0.2 | 4.1 | T | 0.3 | 0.0 | 0.0 | 0.0 | 4.6 |
| 1981-82 | 0.0 | 0.0 | 0.0 | 0.0 | T | 2.4 | 14.8 | 7.6 | 0.7 | T | 0.0 | 0.0 | 25.5 |
| 1982-83 | 0.0 | 0.0 | 0.0 | 0.0 | 0.0 | 7.2 | 1.2 | 27.2 | T | T | 0.0 | 0.0 | 35.6 |
| 1983-84 | 0.0 | 0.0 | 0.0 | 0.0 | T | T | 8.4 | T | 6.1 | T | 0.0 | 0.0 | 14.5 |
| 1984-85 | 0.0 | 0.0 | 0.0 | 0.0 | T | 0.1 | 9.1 | 0.4 | T | 0.7 | 0.0 | 0.0 | 10.3 |
| 1985-86 | 0.0 | 0.0 | 0.0 | 0.0 | 0.0 | 0.7 | 1.9 | 13.0 | T | T | 0.0 | 0.0 | 15.6 |
| 1986-87 | 0.0 | 0.0 | 0.0 | 0.0 | 0.0 | T | 25.1 | 10.1 | T | T | 0.0 | 0.0 | 35.2 |
| 1987-88 | 0.0 | 0.0 | 0.0 | 0.0 | 6.0 | 0.5 | 13.7 | 0.2 | T | T | 0.0 | 0.0 | 20.4 |
| 1988-89 | 0.0 | 0.0 | 0.0 | 0.0 | 0.0 | 0.9 | 6.0 | 1.1 | 0.3 | 0.0 | 0.0 | 0.0 | 8.3 |
| 1989-90 | 0.0 | 0.0 | 0.0 | 0.0 | 3.8 | 10.2 | 0.5 | T | 2.7 | 0.1 | 0.0 | 0.0 | 17.3 |
| 1990-91 | 0.0 | 0.0 | 0.0 | 0.0 | 0.0 | 4.8 | | | | | | | |
| Record Mean | 0.0 | 0.0 | 0.0 | T | 1.1 | 3.6 | 6.1 | 6.7 | 3.7 | 0.1 | T | 0.0 | 21.3 |

**See Reference Notes, relative to all above tables, on preceding page.**

Climate is the composite of numerous weather elements. Three important influences are responsible for the main features of the Boston climate. First, the latitude places the city in the zone of prevailing west to east atmospheric flow. Both polar and tropical air masses influence the region. Secondly, Boston is situated on or near several tracks frequently followed by low pressure storm systems. The weather fluctuates regularly from fair to cloudy to stormy conditions and assures an adequate amount of precipitation. The third factor is the east-coast location of Boston. The ocean has a moderating influence on temperature extremes of winter and summer.

Hot summer afternoons are frequently relieved by the locally celebrated sea breeze, as air flows inland from the cool water surface to displace the warm air over the land. This refreshing east wind is more commonly experienced along the shore than in the interior of the city or the western suburbs. In winter, under appropriate conditions, the severity of cold waves is reduced by the nearness of the relatively warm ocean. The average last occurrence of freezing temperature in spring is early April and the first occurrence of freezing temperature in autumn is early November. In suburban areas, especially away from the coast, these dates are later in spring and earlier in autumn by up to one month in the more susceptible localities.

Boston has no dry season. Most growing seasons have several shorter dry spells during which irrigation for high-value crops may be useful. Much of the rainfall from June to September comes from showers and thunderstorms. During the rest of the year, low pressure systems pass more or less regularly and produce precipitation on an average of roughly one day in three. Coastal storms, or northeasters, are prolific producers of rain and snow. The main snow season extends from December through March. Periods when the ground is bare or nearly bare of snow may occur at any time in the winter.

Relative humidity has been known to fall as low as 5 percent but such desert dryness is very rare. Heavy fog occurs on an average of about two days per month with its prevalence increasing eastward from the interior of Boston Bay to the open waters beyond.

Although winds of 30 mph or higher may be expected on at least one day in every month of the year, gales are both more common and more severe in winter.

## TABLE 1  NORMALS, MEANS AND EXTREMES

BOSTON, MASSACHUSETTS

LATITUDE: 42°22'N  LONGITUDE: 71°02' W  ELEVATION: FT. GRND  15 BARO  30  TIME ZONE: EASTERN  WBAN: 14739

| | (a) | JAN | FEB | MAR | APR | MAY | JUNE | JULY | AUG | SEP | OCT | NOV | DEC | YEAR |
|---|---|---|---|---|---|---|---|---|---|---|---|---|---|---|
| **TEMPERATURE °F:** | | | | | | | | | | | | | | |
| Normals | | | | | | | | | | | | | | |
| -Daily Maximum | | 36.4 | 37.7 | 45.0 | 56.6 | 67.0 | 76.6 | 81.8 | 79.8 | 72.3 | 62.5 | 51.6 | 40.3 | 59.0 |
| -Daily Minimum | | 22.8 | 23.7 | 31.8 | 40.8 | 50.0 | 59.3 | 65.1 | 63.9 | 56.9 | 47.1 | 38.7 | 27.1 | 43.9 |
| -Monthly | | 29.6 | 30.7 | 38.4 | 48.7 | 58.5 | 68.0 | 73.5 | 71.9 | 64.6 | 54.8 | 45.2 | 33.7 | 51.5 |
| Extremes | | | | | | | | | | | | | | |
| -Record Highest | 38 | 63 | 70 | 81 | 94 | 95 | 100 | 102 | 102 | 100 | 90 | 78 | 73 | 102 |
| -Year | | 1974 | 1985 | 1989 | 1976 | 1979 | 1952 | 1977 | 1975 | 1953 | 1963 | 1987 | 1984 | JUL 1977 |
| -Record Lowest | 38 | -12 | -4 | 6 | 16 | 34 | 45 | 50 | 47 | 38 | 28 | 15 | -7 | -12 |
| -Year | | 1957 | 1961 | 1984 | 1982 | 1956 | 1986 | 1988 | 1986 | 1965 | 1976 | 1989 | 1980 | JAN 1957 |
| **NORMAL DEGREE DAYS:** | | | | | | | | | | | | | | |
| Heating (base 65°F) | | 1097 | 960 | 825 | 489 | 218 | 25 | 0 | 6 | 80 | 329 | 594 | 970 | 5593 |
| Cooling (base 65°F) | | 0 | 0 | 0 | 0 | 17 | 115 | 266 | 220 | 68 | 13 | 0 | 0 | 699 |
| **% OF POSSIBLE SUNSHINE** | 54 | 53 | 56 | 57 | 56 | 58 | 63 | 66 | 65 | 63 | 60 | 50 | 52 | 58 |
| **MEAN SKY COVER (tenths)** | | | | | | | | | | | | | | |
| Sunrise - Sunset | 54 | 6.2 | 6.1 | 6.4 | 6.5 | 6.6 | 6.3 | 6.2 | 5.7 | 5.5 | 5.6 | 6.4 | 6.2 | 6.1 |
| **MEAN NUMBER OF DAYS:** | | | | | | | | | | | | | | |
| Sunrise to Sunset | | | | | | | | | | | | | | |
| -Clear | 54 | 9.3 | 8.3 | 7.8 | 7.0 | 6.3 | 6.7 | 6.7 | 9.1 | 10.4 | 10.9 | 8.0 | 8.7 | 99.2 |
| -Partly Cloudy | 54 | 6.6 | 6.8 | 8.1 | 8.2 | 9.9 | 10.4 | 12.3 | 10.8 | 8.1 | 7.9 | 7.2 | 7.5 | 103.8 |
| -Cloudy | 54 | 15.1 | 13.2 | 15.1 | 14.8 | 14.9 | 12.9 | 12.0 | 11.1 | 11.6 | 12.3 | 14.8 | 14.7 | 162.3 |
| Precipitation | | | | | | | | | | | | | | |
| .01 inches or more | 38 | 11.4 | 10.4 | 11.7 | 11.4 | 11.6 | 10.6 | 9.2 | 10.0 | 8.6 | 8.8 | 10.9 | 11.5 | 126.3 |
| Snow,Ice pellets | | | | | | | | | | | | | | |
| 1.0 inches or more | 54 | 3.1 | 2.6 | 2.1 | 0.3 | 0.0 | 0.0 | 0.0 | 0.0 | 0.0 | 0.0 | 0.5 | 2.1 | 10.7 |
| Thunderstorms | 54 | 0.1 | 0.1 | 0.6 | 1.0 | 2.3 | 3.7 | 4.4 | 3.7 | 1.6 | 0.6 | 0.4 | 0.2 | 18.7 |
| Heavy Fog Visibility | | | | | | | | | | | | | | |
| 1/4 mile or less | 54 | 1.7 | 1.7 | 2.0 | 1.7 | 2.9 | 1.9 | 2.2 | 1.8 | 1.9 | 2.1 | 1.9 | 1.4 | 23.2 |
| Temperature °F | | | | | | | | | | | | | | |
| -Maximum | | | | | | | | | | | | | | |
| 90° and above | 25 | 0.0 | 0.0 | 0.0 | 0.* | 0.4 | 2.6 | 5.4 | 3.3 | 0.8 | 0.0 | 0.0 | 0.0 | 12.6 |
| 32° and below | 25 | 11.7 | 7.9 | 2.0 | 0.* | 0.0 | 0.0 | 0.0 | 0.0 | 0.0 | 0.0 | 0.3 | 6.0 | 28.0 |
| -Minimum | | | | | | | | | | | | | | |
| 32° and below | 25 | 26.3 | 23.5 | 16.6 | 2.6 | 0.0 | 0.0 | 0.0 | 0.0 | 0.0 | 0.6 | 7.2 | 22.0 | 98.9 |
| 0° and below | 25 | 0.6 | 0.4 | 0.0 | 0.0 | 0.0 | 0.0 | 0.0 | 0.0 | 0.0 | 0.0 | 0.0 | 0.2 | 1.2 |
| **AVG. STATION PRESS.(mb)** | 17 | 1014.5 | 1015.3 | 1014.3 | 1012.6 | 1013.8 | 1013.3 | 1013.7 | 1015.5 | 1016.9 | 1017.4 | 1015.9 | 1015.8 | 1014.9 |
| **RELATIVE HUMIDITY (%)** | | | | | | | | | | | | | | |
| Hour 01 | 25 | 65 | 64 | 67 | 69 | 74 | 77 | 77 | 79 | 80 | 76 | 72 | 68 | 72 |
| Hour 07 | 25 | 66 | 67 | 68 | 68 | 72 | 73 | 74 | 76 | 79 | 77 | 74 | 70 | 72 |
| Hour 13 (Local Time) | 25 | 57 | 56 | 56 | 55 | 59 | 59 | 56 | 59 | 60 | 58 | 60 | 59 | 58 |
| Hour 19 | 25 | 60 | 59 | 62 | 61 | 65 | 67 | 66 | 69 | 71 | 67 | 66 | 63 | 65 |
| **PRECIPITATION (inches):** | | | | | | | | | | | | | | |
| Water Equivalent | | | | | | | | | | | | | | |
| -Normal | | 3.99 | 3.70 | 4.13 | 3.73 | 3.52 | 2.92 | 2.68 | 3.68 | 3.41 | 3.36 | 4.21 | 4.48 | 43.81 |
| -Maximum Monthly | 38 | 10.55 | 7.81 | 11.00 | 9.46 | 13.38 | 13.20 | 8.12 | 17.09 | 8.31 | 8.68 | 8.89 | 9.74 | 17.09 |
| -Year | | 1979 | 1984 | 1953 | 1987 | 1954 | 1982 | 1959 | 1955 | 1954 | 1962 | 1983 | 1969 | AUG 1955 |
| -Minimum Monthly | 38 | 0.61 | 0.72 | 0.62 | 1.24 | 0.53 | 0.48 | 0.52 | 0.83 | 0.35 | 0.96 | 0.64 | 0.81 | 0.35 |
| -Year | | 1989 | 1987 | 1981 | 1966 | 1964 | 1953 | 1952 | 1972 | 1957 | 1967 | 1976 | 1989 | SEP 1957 |
| -Maximum in 24 hrs | 38 | 2.72 | 2.68 | 4.13 | 2.99 | 5.74 | 4.17 | 2.43 | 8.40 | 5.64 | 4.26 | 3.33 | 4.17 | 8.40 |
| -Year | | 1979 | 1969 | 1968 | 1987 | 1954 | 1984 | 1988 | 1955 | 1954 | 1962 | 1955 | 1969 | AUG 1955 |
| Snow,Ice pellets | | | | | | | | | | | | | | |
| -Maximum Monthly | 54 | 35.9 | 41.3 | 31.2 | 13.3 | 0.5 | 0.0 | 0.0 | 0.0 | 0.0 | 0.2 | 10.0 | 27.9 | 41.3 |
| -Year | | 1978 | 1969 | 1956 | 1982 | 1977 | | | | | 1979 | 1938 | 1970 | FEB 1969 |
| -Maximum in 24 hrs | 54 | 21.0 | 23.6 | 17.7 | 13.2 | 0.5 | 0.0 | 0.0 | 0.0 | 0.0 | 0.2 | 8.0 | 13.0 | 23.6 |
| -Year | | 1978 | 1978 | 1960 | 1982 | 1977 | | | | | 1979 | 1987 | 1960 | FEB 1978 |
| **WIND:** | | | | | | | | | | | | | | |
| Mean Speed (mph) | 32 | 13.9 | 13.8 | 13.7 | 13.2 | 12.2 | 11.5 | 11.0 | 10.8 | 11.2 | 12.0 | 12.9 | 13.6 | 12.5 |
| Prevailing Direction | | | | | | | | | | | | | | |
| through 1963 | | NW | WNW | NW | WNW | SW | SW | SW | SW | SW | SW | SW | WNW | SW |
| Fastest Mile | | | | | | | | | | | | | | |
| -Direction (!!!) | 27 | NW | NE | NE | NW | NE | NW | N | SW | S | SE | NE | NW | S |
| -Speed (MPH) | 27 | 61 | 61 | 60 | 52 | 50 | 47 | 46 | 45 | 61 | 48 | 54 | 49 | 61 |
| -Year | | 1974 | 1978 | 1977 | 1963 | 1967 | 1981 | 1977 | 1971 | 1985 | 1980 | 1968 | 1962 | SEP 1985 |
| Peak Gust | | | | | | | | | | | | | | |
| -Direction (!!!) | 6 | NW | SW | NE | NE | S | W | NW | SE | S | E | NW | NE | S |
| -Speed (mph) | 6 | 51 | 54 | 63 | 48 | 52 | 68 | 54 | 60 | 76 | 54 | 55 | 63 | 76 |
| -Date | | 1989 | 1989 | 1984 | 1987 | 1989 | 1988 | 1989 | 1989 | 1985 | 1988 | 1989 | 1986 | SEP 1985 |

**See Reference Notes to this table on the following page.**

PRECIPITATION (inches)          BOSTON, MASSACHUSETTS

**TABLE 2**

| YEAR | JAN | FEB | MAR | APR | MAY | JUNE | JULY | AUG | SEP | OCT | NOV | DEC | ANNUAL |
|------|------|------|------|------|------|------|------|------|------|------|------|------|--------|
| 1961 | 2.92 | 4.94 | 4.71 | 6.59 | 4.51 | 1.67 | 3.29 | 3.17 | 7.04 | 2.46 | 3.18 | 3.36 | 47.84 |
| 1962 | 3.11 | 4.16 | 1.48 | 3.85 | 1.86 | 2.33 | 1.61 | 3.72 | 4.10 | 8.68 | 3.80 | 4.53 | 43.23 |
| 1963 | 3.13 | 2.60 | 4.39 | 1.48 | 2.86 | 1.92 | 1.72 | 1.67 | 3.05 | 1.25 | 7.74 | 3.03 | 34.84 |
| 1964 | 4.56 | 4.67 | 3.48 | 3.69 | 0.53 | 1.91 | 3.12 | 1.78 | 2.65 | 2.82 | 2.18 | 5.08 | 36.47 |
| 1965 | 2.64 | 3.17 | 2.22 | 2.32 | 0.93 | 2.99 | 0.55 | 1.48 | 2.01 | 1.59 | 2.08 | 1.73 | 23.71 |
| 1966 | 5.29 | 3.48 | 1.98 | 1.24 | 2.66 | 3.40 | 3.21 | 1.25 | 3.42 | 2.62 | 4.43 | 3.03 | 36.01 |
| 1967 | 2.28 | 4.05 | 4.67 | 4.83 | 7.32 | 3.48 | 2.47 | 5.74 | 2.00 | 0.96 | 3.38 | 6.42 | 47.60 |
| 1968 | 3.85 | 1.15 | 7.86 | 1.72 | 3.26 | 5.65 | 0.55 | 1.63 | 1.79 | 1.85 | 6.74 | 6.23 | 42.28 |
| 1969 | 2.26 | 7.08 | 2.63 | 4.37 | 1.96 | 0.63 | 2.98 | 1.89 | 4.42 | 1.64 | 8.18 | 9.74 | 47.78 |
| 1970 | 0.89 | 4.65 | 4.32 | 2.79 | 3.01 | 4.62 | 1.27 | 4.12 | 2.60 | 2.63 | 4.09 | 6.92 | 41.91 |
| 1971 | 1.88 | 5.05 | 3.08 | 2.92 | 3.72 | 1.74 | 2.84 | 1.59 | 1.55 | 2.16 | 6.74 | 2.40 | 35.67 |
| 1972 | 2.05 | 5.29 | 5.37 | 3.34 | 5.26 | 6.76 | 2.19 | 0.83 | 5.94 | 2.98 | 7.02 | 6.08 | 53.11 |
| 1973 | 3.12 | 2.13 | 2.20 | 5.65 | 3.76 | 4.68 | 4.83 | 2.78 | 1.95 | 2.71 | 1.74 | 7.20 | 42.75 |
| 1974 | 3.22 | 3.24 | 4.01 | 3.86 | 2.87 | 2.29 | 1.54 | 3.41 | 7.03 | 3.12 | 1.73 | 3.92 | 40.24 |
| 1975 | 5.70 | 3.37 | 2.74 | 2.40 | 1.78 | 2.10 | 2.35 | 5.52 | 5.49 | 4.41 | 5.13 | 4.80 | 45.79 |
| 1976 | 5.29 | 2.45 | 2.42 | 2.00 | 1.98 | 0.58 | 4.30 | 7.99 | 1.56 | 4.16 | 0.64 | 3.35 | 36.72 |
| 1977 | 4.41 | 2.40 | 4.76 | 4.07 | 3.52 | 2.49 | 2.21 | 2.91 | 4.03 | 4.63 | 2.54 | 6.20 | 44.17 |
| 1978 | 8.12 | 2.97 | 2.46 | 1.79 | 4.50 | 1.53 | 1.48 | 4.62 | 1.30 | 3.13 | 2.21 | 3.63 | 37.64 |
| 1979 | 10.55 | 3.46 | 3.03 | 3.19 | 4.24 | 0.86 | 2.36 | 5.02 | 3.61 | 3.14 | 3.29 | 1.42 | 44.17 |
| 1980 | 0.74 | 0.88 | 5.37 | 4.36 | 2.30 | 3.05 | 2.20 | 1.55 | 0.82 | 4.14 | 3.01 | 0.97 | 29.39 |
| 1981 | 0.95 | 6.65 | 0.62 | 3.14 | 1.17 | 1.65 | 3.47 | 1.04 | 2.54 | 3.43 | 4.78 | 6.27 | 35.71 |
| 1982 | 4.69 | 2.66 | 2.17 | 3.42 | 2.58 | 13.20 | 4.22 | 2.22 | 1.57 | 3.19 | 3.42 | 1.27 | 44.61 |
| 1983 | 5.03 | 5.00 | 9.72 | 6.86 | 2.94 | 1.07 | 1.07 | 3.28 | 1.06 | 3.74 | 8.89 | 4.94 | 53.60 |
| 1984 | 2.31 | 7.81 | 6.82 | 4.43 | 8.77 | 3.06 | 4.43 | 1.60 | 1.22 | 5.18 | 1.68 | 2.93 | 50.24 |
| 1985 | 1.12 | 1.83 | 2.29 | 1.62 | 3.36 | 3.94 | 3.51 | 6.67 | 3.00 | 1.65 | 6.39 | 1.21 | 36.59 |
| 1986 | 3.42 | 2.83 | 3.42 | 1.59 | 1.31 | 7.74 | 3.96 | 3.32 | 1.08 | 3.27 | 6.01 | 6.38 | 44.33 |
| 1987 | 7.28 | 0.72 | 4.27 | 9.46 | 1.75 | 2.62 | 0.82 | 2.93 | 7.29 | 2.73 | 3.49 | 2.12 | 45.48 |
| 1988 | 2.50 | 3.93 | 3.52 | 1.47 | 2.86 | 1.29 | 7.62 | 1.11 | 1.29 | 1.60 | 6.57 | 1.02 | 34.78 |
| 1989 | 0.61 | 2.51 | 3.07 | 3.58 | 3.54 | 2.84 | 5.09 | 5.92 | 4.61 | 5.71 | 4.13 | 0.81 | 42.42 |
| 1990 | 3.78 | 3.60 | 1.71 | 5.94 | 6.53 | 0.69 | 4.08 | 6.57 | 1.67 | 7.36 | 1.39 | 3.18 | 46.50 |
| Record Mean | 3.64 | 3.39 | 3.82 | 3.60 | 3.27 | 3.16 | 3.18 | 3.60 | 3.15 | 3.29 | 3.89 | 3.59 | 41.58 |

**TABLE 3**  AVERAGE TEMPERATURE (deg. F)          BOSTON, MASSACHUSETTS

| YEAR | JAN | FEB | MAR | APR | MAY | JUNE | JULY | AUG | SEP | OCT | NOV | DEC | ANNUAL |
|------|------|------|------|------|------|------|------|------|------|------|------|------|--------|
| 1961 | 25.0 | 31.6 | 36.8 | 45.3 | 56.3 | 68.9 | 72.1 | 72.5 | 69.0 | 57.3 | 44.6 | 32.8 | 51.0 |
| 1962 | 28.7 | 26.7 | 38.5 | 49.4 | 57.2 | 68.4 | 70.4 | 70.0 | 62.9 | 54.1 | 41.7 | 30.0 | 49.8 |
| #1963 | 29.5 | 25.9 | 39.1 | 48.9 | 59.4 | 69.5 | 74.7 | 70.4 | 60.8 | 60.0 | 48.3 | 25.9 | 51.0 |
| #1964 | 31.7 | 29.1 | 38.7 | 46.1 | 60.3 | 67.1 | 71.5 | 66.4 | 62.0 | 52.5 | 44.1 | 32.4 | 50.2 |
| 1965 | 25.4 | 28.0 | 35.8 | 44.2 | 59.5 | 67.4 | 71.0 | 70.5 | 62.5 | 52.8 | 42.1 | 36.1 | 49.6 |
| 1966 | 28.8 | 31.3 | 39.8 | 45.9 | 57.3 | 69.4 | 74.9 | 71.3 | 63.5 | 54.6 | 46.9 | 34.2 | 51.5 |
| 1967 | 35.1 | 26.4 | 33.2 | 44.9 | 51.7 | 67.2 | 73.0 | 70.9 | 62.7 | 53.8 | 40.1 | 35.0 | 49.5 |
| 1968 | 25.6 | 26.1 | 39.1 | 49.6 | 56.1 | 64.9 | 75.2 | 74.0 | 65.0 | 57.9 | 43.8 | 30.0 | 50.4 |
| 1969 | 29.3 | 29.5 | 35.4 | 50.6 | 58.5 | 69.3 | 71.0 | 74.3 | 63.7 | 54.3 | 44.9 | 33.4 | 51.2 |
| 1970 | 23.0 | 30.2 | 37.4 | 49.0 | 59.6 | 67.0 | 74.3 | 73.6 | 65.6 | 54.9 | 44.8 | 28.9 | 50.9 |
| 1971 | 23.8 | 30.5 | 36.7 | 45.1 | 55.7 | 69.1 | 73.4 | 73.4 | 68.0 | 59.8 | 43.1 | 36.3 | 51.2 |
| 1972 | 33.0 | 29.6 | 36.3 | 44.9 | 57.6 | 65.4 | 73.8 | 71.5 | 65.7 | 51.8 | 42.3 | 33.0 | 50.4 |
| 1973 | 31.4 | 30.1 | 43.3 | 49.9 | 57.0 | 70.0 | 74.3 | 74.8 | 64.4 | 55.6 | 45.8 | 39.6 | 53.0 |
| 1974 | 31.7 | 29.1 | 38.7 | 50.9 | 54.7 | 64.8 | 72.4 | 72.0 | 63.7 | 50.1 | 45.3 | 37.8 | 50.9 |
| 1975 | 34.9 | 32.1 | 36.9 | 45.1 | 61.5 | 67.5 | 75.9 | 72.9 | 63.9 | 57.3 | 51.8 | 34.4 | 52.8 |
| 1976 | 26.1 | 37.3 | 41.2 | 55.1 | 60.2 | 73.4 | 72.9 | 72.0 | 64.9 | 52.3 | 41.9 | 29.0 | 52.2 |
| 1977 | 23.3 | 30.7 | 44.7 | 51.3 | 62.6 | 67.4 | 74.9 | 73.4 | 64.4 | 55.3 | 48.1 | 34.2 | 52.5 |
| 1978 | 28.5 | 27.1 | 36.2 | 48.8 | 59.3 | 68.3 | 72.1 | 71.6 | 61.4 | 52.5 | 43.6 | 35.3 | 50.4 |
| 1979 | 32.5 | 33.1 | 42.5 | 48.7 | 61.1 | 68.2 | 74.7 | 71.7 | 64.9 | 52.7 | 48.6 | 36.7 | 52.1 |
| 1980 | 29.4 | 27.9 | 36.9 | 48.7 | 59.4 | 66.3 | 75.8 | 74.2 | 67.0 | 52.4 | 41.2 | 28.6 | 50.6 |
| 1981 | 21.4 | 36.4 | 39.1 | 51.7 | 60.4 | 70.7 | 74.6 | 72.1 | 63.7 | 51.2 | 43.9 | 33.2 | 51.5 |
| 1982 | 22.9 | 30.8 | 38.7 | 48.2 | 57.8 | 63.3 | 74.9 | 70.3 | 64.1 | 54.2 | 47.6 | 39.6 | 51.0 |
| 1983 | 31.2 | 32.8 | 40.6 | 49.1 | 58.2 | 70.7 | 78.0 | 73.6 | 70.6 | 55.2 | 46.1 | 32.1 | 53.2 |
| 1984 | 26.7 | 37.6 | 31.9 | 46.1 | 58.0 | 70.5 | 74.7 | 74.6 | 62.1 | 53.3 | 44.6 | 39.5 | 51.6 |
| 1985 | 24.4 | 32.8 | 40.4 | 49.3 | 59.3 | 64.8 | 73.5 | 70.4 | 65.4 | 55.4 | 45.4 | 31.3 | 51.0 |
| 1986 | 31.4 | 28.9 | 40.7 | 48.4 | 58.4 | 66.1 | 71.0 | 70.5 | 63.2 | 54.0 | 42.3 | 35.5 | 50.9 |
| 1987 | 28.9 | 29.1 | 38.5 | 45.1 | 57.2 | 65.1 | 71.7 | 70.3 | 65.4 | 54.3 | 43.9 | 36.1 | 50.5 |
| 1988 | 27.8 | 32.2 | 39.2 | 46.8 | 57.6 | 68.5 | 73.7 | 75.5 | 64.6 | 50.8 | 46.7 | 32.8 | 51.4 |
| 1989 | 34.5 | 30.5 | 37.3 | 45.9 | 59.4 | 67.8 | 72.8 | 71.6 | 64.7 | 55.3 | 42.8 | 21.7 | 50.4 |
| 1990 | 36.4 | 34.1 | 40.1 | 47.6 | 54.9 | 66.6 | 73.1 | 73.3 | 64.6 | 58.3 | 48.5 | 40.7 | 53.2 |
| Record Mean | 28.8 | 29.4 | 37.1 | 47.1 | 57.8 | 67.1 | 72.7 | 70.9 | 64.1 | 54.1 | 43.7 | 32.8 | 50.5 |
| Max | 36.3 | 37.0 | 44.6 | 55.1 | 66.4 | 75.8 | 81.1 | 78.9 | 72.1 | 62.0 | 50.8 | 39.8 | 58.3 |
| Min | 21.3 | 21.7 | 29.6 | 39.1 | 49.2 | 58.3 | 64.3 | 62.9 | 56.1 | 46.2 | 36.5 | 25.7 | 42.6 |

## REFERENCE NOTES FOR TABLES 1, 2, 3 and 6          (BOSTON, MA)

### GENERAL

T - TRACE AMOUNT
BLANK ENTRIES DENOTE MISSING/UNREPORTED DATA.
# INDICATES A STATION OR INSTRUMENT RELOCATION.

### SPECIFIC

#### TABLE 1

(a) - LENGTH OF RECORD IN YEARS. ALTHOUGH
INDIVIDUAL MONTHS MAY BE MISSING.

* LESS THAN .05

NORMALS — BASED ON THE 1951-1980 RECORD PERIOD.
EXTREMES — DATES ARE THE MOST RECENT OCCURRENCE.
WIND DIR. — NUMERALS SHOW TENS OF DEGREES
CLOCKWISE FROM TRUE NORTH.
"00" INDICATES CALM.
RESULTANT WIND DIRECTIONS ARE GIVEN TO WHOLE DEGREES.

#### TABLE 3
MAX AND MIN ARE LONG-TERM MEAN DAILY MAXIMUM
AND MEAN DAILY MINIMUM TEMPERATURES.

### EXCEPTIONS

#### TABLES 2, 3, and 6

RECORD MEANS ARE THROUGH THE CURRENT YEAR,
BEGINNING IN      1872 FOR TEMPERATURE
                  1871 FOR PRECIPITATION
                  1936 FOR SNOWFALL

## TABLE 4 — HEATING DEGREE DAYS Base 65 deg. F — BOSTON, MASSACHUSETTS

| SEASON | JULY | AUG | SEP | OCT | NOV | DEC | JAN | FEB | MAR | APR | MAY | JUNE | TOTAL |
|---|---|---|---|---|---|---|---|---|---|---|---|---|---|
| 1961-62 | 6 | 3 | 51 | 246 | 604 | 991 | 1118 | 1066 | 814 | 467 | 271 | 35 | 5672 |
| 1962-63 | 6 | 13 | 105 | 330 | 691 | 1078 | 1094 | 1087 | 798 | 477 | 196 | 38 | 5913 |
| #1963-64 | 1 | 3 | 160 | 198 | 495 | 1207 | 1026 | 1033 | 808 | 559 | 187 | 57 | 5734 |
| 1964-65 | 14 | 26 | 140 | 380 | 620 | 1004 | 1220 | 1032 | 900 | 617 | 195 | 80 | 6228 |
| 1965-66 | 2 | 37 | 136 | 371 | 680 | 888 | 1115 | 936 | 776 | 566 | 258 | 46 | 5811 |
| 1966-67 | 0 | 1 | 88 | 322 | 535 | 950 | 921 | 1075 | 977 | 596 | 403 | 58 | 5926 |
| 1967-68 | 0 | 4 | 110 | 347 | 739 | 923 | 1214 | 1122 | 797 | 454 | 270 | 76 | 6056 |
| 1968-69 | 1 | 9 | 46 | 247 | 630 | 1050 | 1099 | 987 | 911 | 430 | 208 | 21 | 5639 |
| 1969-70 | 2 | 3 | 107 | 326 | 595 | 973 | 1295 | 909 | 846 | 473 | 184 | 52 | 5765 |
| 1970-71 | 0 | 0 | 68 | 314 | 598 | 1113 | 1269 | 962 | 868 | 586 | 287 | 25 | 6090 |
| 1971-72 | 0 | 2 | 37 | 169 | 651 | 882 | 985 | 1021 | 883 | 598 | 250 | 54 | 5532 |
| 1972-73 | 3 | 4 | 51 | 405 | 673 | 985 | 1033 | 971 | 666 | 450 | 258 | 24 | 5523 |
| 1973-74 | 0 | 2 | 94 | 289 | 570 | 782 | 1023 | 1000 | 809 | 429 | 335 | 77 | 5410 |
| 1974-75 | 0 | 2 | 102 | 458 | 587 | 836 | 925 | 918 | 866 | 590 | 162 | 59 | 5505 |
| 1975-76 | 0 | 8 | 70 | 239 | 395 | 941 | 1198 | 800 | 733 | 331 | 166 | 16 | 4897 |
| 1976-77 | 1 | 10 | 55 | 393 | 688 | 1108 | 1290 | 956 | 623 | 414 | 158 | 43 | 5739 |
| 1977-78 | 0 | 4 | 85 | 304 | 498 | 948 | 1127 | 1057 | 885 | 480 | 209 | 18 | 5615 |
| 1978-79 | 11 | 11 | 150 | 381 | 635 | 916 | 1002 | 1169 | 691 | 481 | 149 | 19 | 5615 |
| 1979-80 | 2 | 15 | 80 | 390 | 484 | 873 | 1096 | 1071 | 866 | 481 | 185 | 66 | 5609 |
| 1980-81 | 2 | 5 | 72 | 387 | 706 | 1120 | 1344 | 794 | 796 | 393 | 200 | 7 | 5826 |
| 1981-82 | 2 | 6 | 91 | 419 | 628 | 979 | 1300 | 948 | 811 | 496 | 231 | 113 | 6024 |
| 1982-83 | 2 | 19 | 71 | 338 | 515 | 783 | 1040 | 896 | 749 | 478 | 223 | 22 | 5136 |
| 1983-84 | 0 | 8 | 42 | 327 | 561 | 1012 | 1182 | 790 | 1020 | 563 | 239 | 36 | 5780 |
| 1984-85 | 3 | 0 | 142 | 359 | 605 | 781 | 1255 | 897 | 758 | 471 | 204 | 71 | 5546 |
| 1985-86 | 3 | 11 | 65 | 298 | 580 | 1035 | 1035 | 1008 | 746 | 490 | 258 | 66 | 5595 |
| 1986-87 | 21 | 16 | 98 | 344 | 674 | 904 | 1112 | 997 | 814 | 588 | 285 | 76 | 5929 |
| 1987-88 | 8 | 18 | 57 | 326 | 626 | 888 | 1145 | 945 | 792 | 541 | 253 | 61 | 5660 |
| 1988-89 | 9 | 10 | 64 | 443 | 541 | 992 | 938 | 959 | 853 | 565 | 196 | 51 | 5621 |
| 1989-90 | 2 | 4 | 88 | 294 | 660 | 1336 | 880 | 857 | 762 | 524 | 307 | 60 | 5774 |
| 1990-91 | 4 | 5 | 84 | 236 | 496 | 744 | | | | | | | |

## TABLE 5 — COOLING DEGREE DAYS Base 65 deg. F — BOSTON, MASSACHUSETTS

| YEAR | JAN | FEB | MAR | APR | MAY | JUNE | JULY | AUG | SEP | OCT | NOV | DEC | TOTAL |
|---|---|---|---|---|---|---|---|---|---|---|---|---|---|
| 1969 | 0 | 0 | 0 | 9 | 13 | 156 | 196 | 297 | 74 | 1 | 0 | 0 | 746 |
| 1970 | 0 | 0 | 0 | 0 | 25 | 118 | 294 | 273 | 91 | 9 | 0 | 0 | 810 |
| 1971 | 0 | 0 | 0 | 0 | 6 | 155 | 269 | 271 | 132 | 15 | 1 | 0 | 849 |
| 1972 | 0 | 0 | 0 | 0 | 26 | 74 | 279 | 213 | 79 | 0 | 0 | 0 | 671 |
| 1973 | 0 | 0 | 0 | 7 | 18 | 180 | 296 | 316 | 84 | 3 | 0 | 0 | 904 |
| 1974 | 0 | 0 | 0 | 10 | 22 | 81 | 235 | 226 | 68 | 1 | 3 | 0 | 646 |
| 1975 | 0 | 0 | 0 | 0 | 60 | 139 | 345 | 261 | 44 | 9 | 4 | 0 | 862 |
| 1976 | 0 | 0 | 0 | 43 | 25 | 276 | 251 | 231 | 61 | 8 | 0 | 0 | 895 |
| 1977 | 0 | 0 | 1 | 13 | 92 | 124 | 314 | 272 | 75 | 6 | 0 | 0 | 897 |
| 1978 | 0 | 0 | 0 | 0 | 40 | 122 | 237 | 221 | 48 | 0 | 0 | 0 | 668 |
| 1979 | 0 | 0 | 0 | 0 | 35 | 122 | 304 | 226 | 85 | 17 | 0 | 0 | 789 |
| 1980 | 0 | 0 | 0 | 0 | 18 | 114 | 347 | 299 | 137 | 1 | 0 | 0 | 916 |
| 1981 | 0 | 0 | 0 | 0 | 67 | 185 | 306 | 232 | 60 | 0 | 0 | 0 | 850 |
| 1982 | 0 | 0 | 0 | 0 | 15 | 67 | 314 | 192 | 49 | 10 | 2 | 0 | 649 |
| 1983 | 0 | 0 | 0 | 7 | 18 | 200 | 410 | 283 | 217 | 27 | 0 | 0 | 1162 |
| 1984 | 0 | 0 | 0 | 3 | 31 | 207 | 312 | 306 | 62 | 3 | 0 | 0 | 924 |
| 1985 | 0 | 0 | 0 | 5 | 30 | 72 | 271 | 183 | 83 | 8 | 0 | 0 | 652 |
| 1986 | 0 | 0 | 0 | 0 | 60 | 105 | 211 | 190 | 55 | 10 | 0 | 0 | 631 |
| 1987 | 0 | 0 | 0 | 0 | 48 | 87 | 221 | 189 | 76 | 0 | 2 | 0 | 623 |
| 1988 | 0 | 0 | 0 | 0 | 31 | 173 | 287 | 342 | 59 | 11 | 0 | 0 | 903 |
| 1989 | 0 | 0 | 1 | 0 | 29 | 142 | 248 | 214 | 89 | 0 | 0 | 0 | 723 |
| 1990 | 0 | 0 | 0 | 10 | 2 | 116 | 261 | 268 | 77 | 34 | 8 | 0 | 776 |

## TABLE 6 — SNOWFALL (inches) — BOSTON, MASSACHUSETTS

| SEASON | JULY | AUG | SEP | OCT | NOV | DEC | JAN | FEB | MAR | APR | MAY | JUNE | TOTAL |
|---|---|---|---|---|---|---|---|---|---|---|---|---|---|
| 1961-62 | 0.0 | 0.0 | 0.0 | T | 0.9 | 11.4 | 2.5 | 28.7 | 1.1 | 0.1 | 0.0 | 0.0 | 44.7 |
| 1962-63 | 0.0 | 0.0 | 0.0 | T | 0.9 | 5.3 | 6.5 | 4.6 | 13.6 | T | 0.0 | 0.0 | 30.9 |
| 1963-64 | 0.0 | 0.0 | 0.0 | T | 0.0 | 17.7 | 14.4 | 23.2 | 7.7 | T | 0.0 | 0.0 | 63.0 |
| 1964-65 | 0.0 | 0.0 | 0.0 | T | T | 12.2 | 22.2 | 4.7 | 9.7 | 1.6 | 0.0 | 0.0 | 50.4 |
| 1965-66 | 0.0 | 0.0 | 0.0 | 0.0 | T | 2.3 | 26.4 | 12.1 | 3.3 | T | T | 0.0 | 44.1 |
| 1966-67 | 0.0 | 0.0 | 0.0 | 0.0 | 0.0 | 9.9 | 0.5 | 23.5 | 22.9 | 3.3 | T | 0.0 | 60.1 |
| 1967-68 | 0.0 | 0.0 | 0.0 | 0.0 | 2.2 | 14.7 | 17.7 | 3.4 | 6.8 | 0.0 | 0.0 | 0.0 | 44.8 |
| 1968-69 | 0.0 | 0.0 | 0.0 | 0.0 | 0.4 | 5.1 | 0.9 | 41.3 | 6.1 | T | 0.0 | 0.0 | 53.8 |
| 1969-70 | 0.0 | 0.0 | 0.0 | T | T | 12.6 | 7.4 | 10.5 | 18.2 | 0.1 | 0.0 | 0.0 | 48.8 |
| 1970-71 | 0.0 | 0.0 | 0.0 | T | T | 27.9 | 12.0 | 8.1 | 7.4 | 1.9 | 0.0 | 0.0 | 57.3 |
| 1971-72 | 0.0 | 0.0 | 0.0 | 0.0 | 2.8 | 7.9 | 7.8 | 16.5 | 12.1 | 0.4 | 0.0 | 0.0 | 47.5 |
| 1972-73 | 0.0 | 0.0 | 0.0 | T | 0.6 | 3.3 | 3.6 | 2.5 | 0.3 | T | 0.0 | 0.0 | 10.3 |
| 1973-74 | 0.0 | 0.0 | 0.0 | 0.0 | 0.0 | T | 16.0 | 17.8 | 0.1 | 3.0 | 0.0 | 0.0 | 36.9 |
| 1974-75 | 0.0 | 0.0 | 0.0 | 0.0 | 2.0 | 3.6 | 2.2 | 17.0 | 1.8 | 1.0 | 0.0 | 0.0 | 27.6 |
| 1975-76 | 0.0 | 0.0 | 0.0 | T | 0.1 | 19.3 | 15.0 | 1.4 | 10.8 | 0.0 | 0.0 | 0.0 | 46.6 |
| 1976-77 | 0.0 | 0.0 | 0.0 | 0.0 | 1.0 | 17.2 | 23.2 | 5.9 | 10.7 | T | 0.5 | 0.0 | 58.5 |
| 1977-78 | 0.0 | 0.0 | 0.0 | 0.0 | 0.7 | 5.2 | 35.9 | 27.2 | 16.1 | T | 0.0 | 0.0 | 85.1 |
| 1978-79 | 0.0 | 0.0 | 0.0 | 0.0 | 4.2 | 5.8 | 10.5 | 6.6 | 0.4 | 0.0 | 0.0 | 0.0 | 27.5 |
| 1979-80 | 0.0 | 0.0 | 0.0 | 0.2 | T | 2.0 | 0.4 | 6.5 | 3.6 | T | 0.0 | 0.0 | 12.7 |
| 1980-81 | 0.0 | 0.0 | 0.0 | 0.0 | 2.4 | 5.6 | 11.9 | 1.9 | 0.5 | 0.0 | 0.0 | 0.0 | 22.3 |
| 1981-82 | 0.0 | 0.0 | 0.0 | 0.0 | T | 17.6 | 18.0 | 7.6 | 5.3 | 13.3 | 0.0 | 0.0 | 61.8 |
| 1982-83 | 0.0 | 0.0 | 0.0 | 0.0 | T | 5.5 | 4.7 | 22.3 | 0.2 | T | 0.0 | 0.0 | 32.7 |
| 1983-84 | 0.0 | 0.0 | 0.0 | 0.0 | T | 2.6 | 21.1 | 0.3 | 19.0 | T | 0.0 | 0.0 | 43.0 |
| 1984-85 | 0.0 | 0.0 | 0.0 | 0.0 | T | 3.7 | 7.0 | 10.2 | 3.7 | 2.0 | 0.0 | 0.0 | 26.6 |
| 1985-86 | 0.0 | 0.0 | 0.0 | T | 3.0 | 1.3 | 0.8 | 10.4 | 2.6 | T | 0.0 | 0.0 | 18.1 |
| 1986-87 | 0.0 | 0.0 | 0.0 | 0.0 | 3.5 | 3.4 | 24.3 | 3.7 | 3.5 | 4.1 | 0.0 | 0.0 | 42.5 |
| 1987-88 | 0.0 | 0.0 | 0.0 | 0.0 | 9.0 | 7.5 | 17.0 | 14.1 | 5.0 | T | 0.0 | 0.0 | 52.6 |
| 1988-89 | 0.0 | 0.0 | T | 0.0 | 0.0 | 3.7 | 1.5 | 6.7 | 3.2 | 0.4 | 0.0 | 0.0 | 15.5 |
| 1989-90 | 0.0 | 0.0 | 0.0 | 0.0 | 4.5 | 6.2 | 7.0 | 16.9 | 4.1 | 0.5 | 0.0 | 0.0 | 39.2 |
| 1990-91 | 0.0 | 0.0 | 0.0 | 0.0 | T | 1.2 | | | | | | | |
| Record Mean | 0.0 | 0.0 | 0.0 | T | 1.4 | 7.4 | 12.2 | 11.4 | 7.4 | 0.9 | T | 0.0 | 40.8 |

**See Reference Notes, relative to all above tables, on preceding page.**

Worcester Municipal Airport is located on the crest of a hill, 1,000 feet above sea level. It is about 500 feet above and 3 1/2 miles northwest of the city proper. The airport is surrounded by ridges and valleys with many of the valleys containing reservoirs. Only two of the ridges extend above the airport elevation. One is 400 feet higher and 2 1/2 miles to the northwest, and the other is 1,000 feet higher and 15 miles to the north.

The proximity to the Atlantic Ocean, Long Island Sound, and the Berkshire Hills plays an important part in determining the weather and, hence, the climate of Worcester. Rapid weather changes occur when storms move up the east coast after developing off the Carolina Coast. In the majority of these cases, they pass to the south and east, resulting in northeast and easterly winds with rain or snow and fog. Storms developing in the Texas–Oklahoma area normally travel up the St. Lawrence River Valley and, depending on the movement and intensity, usually deposit little precipitation over the area. However, they do bring an influx of warm air into the region. Wintertime cold snaps are quite frequent, but temperatures are usually modified by the passage of the air over land and mountains before reaching the county. Summertime thunderstorms develop over the hills to the west, with a majority moving toward the northeast. From the use of radar, we find many break up just before reaching Worcester, or pass either north or south of the city proper.

Airport site temperatures are moderate. The normal mean for the warmest month, July, is around 70 degrees. Though winters are reasonably cold, prolonged periods of severe cold weather are extremely rare. The three coldest months, December through February, have an average temperature of over 25 degrees. A review of Worcester Cooperative records since 1901 shows maximum temperatures above 100 degrees and minimum temperatures below −24 degrees.

Precipitation is usually plentiful and well distributed throughout the year. The annual snowfall for all Worcester sites since 1901, averages slightly less than 60 inches. The airport location averages slightly higher.

Based on the 1951–1980 period, the average first occurrence of 32 degrees Fahrenheit in the fall is October 17 and the average last occurrence in the spring is April 27.

## TABLE 1

# NORMALS, MEANS AND EXTREMES

WORCESTER, MASSACHUSETTS

LATITUDE: 42°16'N    LONGITUDE: 71°52'W    ELEVATION: FT. GRND    986 BARO    1001    TIME ZONE: EASTERN    WBAN: 94746

| | (a) | JAN | FEB | MAR | APR | MAY | JUNE | JULY | AUG | SEP | OCT | NOV | DEC | YEAR |
|---|---|---|---|---|---|---|---|---|---|---|---|---|---|---|
| **TEMPERATURE °F:** | | | | | | | | | | | | | | |
| Normals | | | | | | | | | | | | | | |
| -Daily Maximum | | 30.9 | 32.9 | 41.1 | 54.5 | 65.9 | 74.4 | 79.0 | 77.0 | 69.4 | 59.3 | 46.9 | 34.7 | 55.5 |
| -Daily Minimum | | 15.6 | 16.6 | 25.2 | 35.4 | 45.5 | 54.8 | 60.7 | 59.0 | 51.3 | 41.3 | 32.0 | 20.1 | 38.1 |
| -Monthly | | 23.3 | 24.8 | 33.1 | 45.0 | 55.7 | 64.6 | 69.9 | 68.0 | 60.3 | 50.3 | 39.5 | 27.4 | 46.8 |
| Extremes | | | | | | | | | | | | | | |
| -Record Highest | 34 | 60 | 67 | 80 | 91 | 92 | 94 | 96 | 96 | 91 | 85 | 78 | 70 | 96 |
| -Year | | 1974 | 1985 | 1977 | 1976 | 1962 | 1988 | 1988 | 1975 | 1983 | 1963 | 1982 | 1984 | JUL 1988 |
| -Record Lowest | 34 | -19 | -12 | -4 | 11 | 28 | 36 | 43 | 38 | 30 | 20 | 6 | -13 | -19 |
| -Year | | 1957 | 1967 | 1986 | 1982 | 1970 | 1986 | 1988 | 1965 | 1957 | 1969 | 1989 | 1962 | JAN 1957 |
| **NORMAL DEGREE DAYS:** | | | | | | | | | | | | | | |
| Heating (base 65°F) | | 1293 | 1126 | 989 | 600 | 296 | 68 | 10 | 22 | 159 | 456 | 765 | 1166 | 6950 |
| Cooling (base 65°F) | | 0 | 0 | 0 | 0 | 8 | 56 | 162 | 115 | 18 | 0 | 0 | 0 | 359 |
| **% OF POSSIBLE SUNSHINE** | | | | | | | | | | | | | | |
| **MEAN SKY COVER (tenths)** | | | | | | | | | | | | | | |
| Sunrise - Sunset | 33 | 6.1 | 6.2 | 6.5 | 6.5 | 6.7 | 6.5 | 6.3 | 6.0 | 5.8 | 5.7 | 6.7 | 6.4 | 6.3 |
| **MEAN NUMBER OF DAYS:** | | | | | | | | | | | | | | |
| Sunrise to Sunset | | | | | | | | | | | | | | |
| -Clear | 34 | 9.0 | 7.7 | 7.7 | 6.7 | 6.0 | 5.9 | 6.0 | 7.8 | 9.1 | 10.2 | 7.1 | 7.7 | 90.9 |
| -Partly Cloudy | 34 | 7.7 | 7.0 | 7.9 | 8.6 | 9.7 | 10.8 | 12.0 | 11.3 | 8.5 | 8.1 | 7.6 | 7.7 | 106.8 |
| -Cloudy | 34 | 14.3 | 13.6 | 15.4 | 14.6 | 15.3 | 13.4 | 13.0 | 11.9 | 12.4 | 12.6 | 15.4 | 15.6 | 167.5 |
| Precipitation | | | | | | | | | | | | | | |
| .01 inches or more | 34 | 11.4 | 10.8 | 12.1 | 11.4 | 12.2 | 11.4 | 9.9 | 10.1 | 9.2 | 8.7 | 11.8 | 12.5 | 131.6 |
| Snow,Ice pellets | | | | | | | | | | | | | | |
| 1.0 inches or more | 34 | 4.3 | 3.7 | 3.1 | 1.0 | 0.1 | 0.0 | 0.0 | 0.0 | 0.0 | 0.1 | 0.9 | 3.7 | 16.9 |
| Thunderstorms | 23 | 0.* | 0.1 | 0.7 | 1.2 | 3.0 | 4.2 | 5.3 | 4.1 | 1.5 | 1.0 | 0.5 | 0.1 | 21.6 |
| Heavy Fog Visibility | | | | | | | | | | | | | | |
| 1/4 mile or less | 23 | 5.7 | 5.6 | 7.6 | 7.0 | 7.1 | 8.0 | 6.3 | 6.2 | 8.2 | 7.2 | 7.9 | 7.0 | 83.8 |
| Temperature °F | | | | | | | | | | | | | | |
| -Maximum | | | | | | | | | | | | | | |
| 90° and above | 34 | 0.0 | 0.0 | 0.0 | 0.* | 0.1 | 0.8 | 1.4 | 0.7 | 0.* | 0.0 | 0.0 | 0.0 | 3.1 |
| 32° and below | 34 | 18.0 | 13.8 | 5.4 | 0.2 | 0.0 | 0.0 | 0.0 | 0.0 | 0.0 | 0.0 | 1.8 | 13.7 | 52.9 |
| -Minimum | | | | | | | | | | | | | | |
| 32° and below | 34 | 29.6 | 26.8 | 25.5 | 11.1 | 0.6 | 0.0 | 0.0 | 0.0 | 0.1 | 5.0 | 16.6 | 28.1 | 143.4 |
| 0° and below | 34 | 3.2 | 1.9 | 0.1 | 0.0 | 0.0 | 0.0 | 0.0 | 0.0 | 0.0 | 0.0 | 0.0 | 1.0 | 6.2 |
| **AVG. STATION PRESS. (mb)** | 17 | 976.7 | 977.8 | 977.4 | 976.4 | 977.9 | 978.2 | 979.0 | 980.4 | 981.3 | 981.0 | 979.1 | 978.5 | 978.6 |
| **RELATIVE HUMIDITY (%)** | | | | | | | | | | | | | | |
| Hour 01 | 32 | 69 | 69 | 68 | 68 | 73 | 78 | 79 | 81 | 83 | 78 | 76 | 73 | 75 |
| Hour 07 | 34 | 71 | 71 | 70 | 67 | 69 | 73 | 76 | 79 | 81 | 78 | 77 | 75 | 74 |
| Hour 13 (Local Time) | 34 | 58 | 57 | 54 | 50 | 51 | 56 | 57 | 59 | 61 | 56 | 61 | 62 | 57 |
| Hour 19 | 34 | 64 | 62 | 60 | 57 | 60 | 66 | 68 | 72 | 75 | 69 | 69 | 69 | 66 |
| **PRECIPITATION (inches):** | | | | | | | | | | | | | | |
| Water Equivalent | | | | | | | | | | | | | | |
| -Normal | | 3.82 | 3.29 | 4.16 | 3.90 | 3.86 | 3.46 | 3.58 | 4.42 | 4.25 | 4.21 | 4.43 | 4.22 | 47.60 |
| -Maximum Monthly | 34 | 11.16 | 8.37 | 7.96 | 8.79 | 9.94 | 12.17 | 8.11 | 7.39 | 13.13 | 8.56 | 10.40 | 9.83 | 13.13 |
| -Year | | 1979 | 1981 | 1972 | 1987 | 1984 | 1982 | 1959 | 1979 | 1974 | 1962 | 1972 | 1973 | SEP 1974 |
| -Minimum Monthly | 34 | 0.89 | 0.25 | 0.74 | 1.26 | 0.86 | 0.79 | 0.74 | 1.03 | 0.69 | 1.46 | 0.67 | 0.74 | 0.25 |
| -Year | | 1970 | 1987 | 1981 | 1985 | 1959 | 1979 | 1987 | 1981 | 1986 | 1953 | 1976 | 1989 | FEB 1987 |
| -Maximum in 24 hrs | 34 | 2.97 | 2.46 | 4.56 | 3.15 | 3.03 | 3.98 | 3.87 | 3.90 | 4.79 | 3.77 | 2.98 | 3.00 | 4.79 |
| -Year | | 1978 | 1973 | 1987 | 1987 | 1967 | 1986 | 1985 | 1985 | 1960 | 1959 | 1972 | 1986 | SEP 1960 |
| Snow,Ice pellets | | | | | | | | | | | | | | |
| -Maximum Monthly | 34 | 46.8 | 45.2 | 36.5 | 21.0 | 12.7 | 0.0 | 0.0 | 0.0 | 0.0 | 7.5 | 20.7 | 32.1 | 46.8 |
| -Year | | 1987 | 1962 | 1958 | 1987 | 1977 | | | | | 1979 | 1971 | 1969 | JAN 1987 |
| -Maximum in 24 hrs | 34 | 18.7 | 24.0 | 16.6 | 17.0 | 12.7 | 0.0 | 0.0 | 0.0 | 0.0 | 7.5 | 14.8 | 15.6 | 24.0 |
| -Year | | 1961 | 1962 | 1960 | 1987 | 1977 | | | | | 1979 | 1971 | 1961 | FEB 1962 |
| **WIND:** | | | | | | | | | | | | | | |
| Mean Speed (mph) | 29 | 11.9 | 11.6 | 11.4 | 11.0 | 10.0 | 8.9 | 8.4 | 8.3 | 8.6 | 9.4 | 10.2 | 10.9 | 10.0 |
| Prevailing Direction | | | | | | | | | | | | | | |
| through 1963 | | WSW | WNW | W | W | SW | SW | SW | SW | SW | WSW | WSW | WSW | SW |
| Fastest Obs. 1 Min. | | | | | | | | | | | | | | |
| -Direction (!!!) | 33 | 25 | 32 | 29 | 05 | 27 | 25 | 32 | 30 | 14 | 25 | 20 | 23 | 32 |
| -Speed (MPH) | 33 | 60 | 76 | 76 | 54 | 48 | 39 | 43 | 37 | 36 | 43 | 54 | 51 | 76 |
| -Year | | 1959 | 1956 | 1956 | 1956 | 1956 | 1958 | 1957 | 1982 | 1985 | 1958 | 1956 | 1957 | FEB 1956 |
| Peak Gust | | | | | | | | | | | | | | |
| -Direction (!!!) | 6 | NW | NW | NE | SW | S | NW | NW | N | SE | NW | S | NW | SE |
| -Speed (mph) | 6 | 58 | 58 | 60 | 52 | 61 | 54 | 48 | 44 | 71 | 56 | 62 | 60 | 71 |
| Date | | 1989 | 1985 | 1984 | 1985 | 1989 | 1988 | 1984 | 1989 | 1985 | 1986 | 1989 | 1988 | SEP 1985 |

**See Reference Notes to this table on the following page.**

PRECIPITATION (inches)  WORCESTER, MASSACHUSETTS

**TABLE 2**

| YEAR | JAN | FEB | MAR | APR | MAY | JUNE | JULY | AUG | SEP | OCT | NOV | DEC | ANNUAL |
|---|---|---|---|---|---|---|---|---|---|---|---|---|---|
| 1961 | 3.02 | 3.28 | 4.05 | 5.72 | 3.40 | 2.29 | 4.42 | 4.90 | 5.66 | 2.68 | 3.41 | 3.35 | 46.18 |
| 1962 | 4.15 | 4.82 | 2.03 | 3.44 | 3.99 | 3.16 | 1.97 | 5.42 | 4.38 | 8.56 | 3.85 | 2.38 | 49.48 |
| 1963 | 3.10 | 3.03 | 4.63 | 1.89 | 3.00 | 2.48 | 1.88 | 2.65 | 1.46 | 8.20 | 3.17 | 4.92 | 39.08 |
| 1964 | 5.42 | 3.54 | 3.65 | 4.01 | 1.18 | 1.77 | 3.02 | 2.93 | 1.78 | 2.83 | 3.02 | 2.90 | 37.65 |
| 1965 | 1.71 | 4.30 | 2.31 | 3.56 | 1.51 | 3.14 | 1.03 | 3.40 | 2.83 | 6.06 | 2.90 | 3.05 | 31.98 |
| 1966 | 4.22 | 4.05 | 2.52 | 1.62 | 3.21 | 1.91 | 3.76 | 1.95 | 5.59 | 4.13 | 4.93 | 3.05 | 40.94 |
| 1967 | 2.38 | 3.15 | 3.73 | 5.10 | 7.01 | 3.72 | 5.91 | 3.47 | 5.06 | 1.83 | 3.65 | 5.72 | 50.73 |
| 1968 | 3.00 | 1.26 | 7.67 | 2.24 | 6.83 | 7.78 | 1.06 | 1.25 | 1.94 | 1.88 | 5.75 | 6.16 | 46.82 |
| 1969 | 1.29 | 3.04 | 2.53 | 5.30 | 3.09 | 1.26 | 3.81 | 3.34 | 6.16 | 1.78 | 6.81 | 7.69 | 46.10 |
| 1970 | 0.89 | 5.47 | 3.51 | 3.44 | 4.18 | 3.88 | 1.08 | 5.86 | 2.17 | 3.47 | 3.75 | 3.09 | 40.79 |
| 1971 | 1.97 | 5.60 | 1.93 | 1.71 | 5.22 | 1.88 | 5.27 | 4.67 | 2.38 | 3.66 | 5.01 | 2.68 | 43.83 |
| 1972 | 2.34 | 4.91 | 7.96 | 4.29 | 7.83 | 9.25 | 6.39 | 2.89 | 4.98 | 4.93 | 10.40 | 5.49 | 71.66 |
| 1973 | 4.04 | 3.30 | 3.50 | 6.33 | 4.73 | 6.98 | 3.82 | 4.29 | 3.80 | 4.63 | 2.00 | 9.83 | 57.25 |
| 1974 | 3.54 | 2.75 | 5.05 | 3.24 | 5.15 | 4.35 | 3.22 | 3.50 | 13.13 | 3.45 | 3.06 | 6.04 | 56.48 |
| 1975 | 5.35 | 3.52 | 3.37 | 2.66 | 2.07 | 4.59 | 3.92 | 4.59 | 7.21 | 6.06 | 5.28 | 4.61 | 51.96 |
| 1976 | 6.03 | 2.57 | 2.74 | 2.45 | 3.46 | 2.95 | 3.28 | 5.72 | 2.38 | 4.99 | 0.67 | 3.20 | 40.44 |
| 1977 | 2.76 | 2.46 | 5.75 | 3.69 | 2.20 | 4.00 | 3.84 | 2.73 | 6.54 | 6.33 | 4.99 | 3.56 | 48.98 |
| 1978 | 9.90 | 2.08 | 3.22 | 2.24 | 3.69 | 1.57 | 3.57 | 5.00 | 1.02 | 3.85 | 1.89 | 2.07 | 41.77 |
| 1979 | 11.16 | 2.64 | 3.71 | 4.49 | 4.14 | 0.79 | 5.74 | 7.39 | 3.80 | 4.36 | 3.58 | 1.06 | 53.69 |
| 1980 | 0.95 | 0.73 | 6.86 | 4.77 | 2.23 | 4.55 | 3.59 | 1.95 | 1.82 | 6.16 | 4.58 | 1.06 | 39.25 |
| 1981 | 0.93 | 8.37 | 0.74 | 3.85 | 4.48 | 2.45 | 7.90 | 1.03 | 4.66 | 2.67 | 1.70 | 5.94 | 48.97 |
| 1982 | 5.00 | 3.22 | 3.67 | 4.30 | 2.96 | 12.17 | 3.61 | 3.36 | 2.69 | 4.32 | 6.37 | 1.85 | 49.67 |
| 1983 | 4.85 | 4.67 | 7.84 | 8.59 | 5.97 | 2.56 | 1.32 | 6.26 | 1.38 | 5.77 | 8.75 | 2.84 | 64.33 |
| 1984 | 2.44 | 5.78 | 5.47 | 4.23 | 9.94 | 2.85 | 5.69 | 1.17 | 1.68 | 3.99 | 2.71 | 1.93 | 48.79 |
| 1985 | 1.16 | 2.72 | 2.89 | 1.26 | 5.46 | 5.24 | 6.35 | 3.74 | 3.77 | 3.12 | 6.41 | 7.25 | 44.05 |
| 1986 | 5.56 | 3.14 | 2.93 | 1.59 | 3.14 | 7.21 | 4.83 | 3.20 | 0.69 | 5.63 | 2.77 | 2.77 | 47.89 |
| 1987 | 5.52 | 0.25 | 6.57 | 8.79 | 1.55 | 4.55 | 0.74 | 4.61 | 6.37 | 4.18 | 1.85 | 1.42 | 47.75 |
| 1988 | 2.71 | 2.78 | 3.46 | 3.45 | 4.47 | 1.25 | 6.27 | 2.19 | 2.70 | 3.66 | 7.91 | 0.74 | 42.27 |
| 1989 | 1.18 | 2.47 | 2.66 | 4.25 | 6.17 | 5.27 | 5.67 | 5.65 | 4.71 | 8.21 | 4.00 | 0.74 | 50.98 |
| 1990 | 3.75 | 3.88 | 1.52 | 4.78 | 7.65 | 1.74 | 2.44 | 6.84 | 1.73 | 10.19 | 2.41 | 5.46 | 52.39 |
| Record Mean | 3.71 | 3.38 | 4.00 | 4.05 | 4.08 | 3.65 | 3.73 | 4.25 | 3.83 | 4.30 | 4.54 | 4.01 | 47.52 |

**TABLE 3** AVERAGE TEMPERATURE (deg. F)  WORCESTER, MASSACHUSETTS

| YEAR | JAN | FEB | MAR | APR | MAY | JUNE | JULY | AUG | SEP | OCT | NOV | DEC | ANNUAL |
|---|---|---|---|---|---|---|---|---|---|---|---|---|---|
| 1961 | 18.7 | 27.7 | 33.0 | 41.8 | 53.7 | 66.0 | 69.4 | 67.7 | 66.0 | 52.4 | 39.5 | 26.9 | 46.9 |
| 1962 | 23.5 | 22.1 | 34.3 | 45.0 | 55.0 | 65.0 | 66.0 | 66.1 | 58.2 | 49.2 | 37.3 | 24.2 | 45.5 |
| 1963 | 22.5 | 19.9 | 34.0 | 44.9 | 55.8 | 65.5 | 70.0 | 65.8 | 56.5 | 49.6 | 41.2 | 20.2 | 46.2 |
| 1964 | 27.2 | 23.9 | 35.2 | 43.7 | 58.9 | 64.3 | 68.6 | 63.4 | 59.3 | 49.6 | 36.7 | 28.4 | 47.0 |
| 1965 | 20.9 | 24.3 | 31.3 | 42.9 | 52.9 | 63.7 | 68.2 | 67.4 | 58.2 | 49.0 | 43.1 | 30.1 | 46.2 |
| 1966 | 22.2 | 25.8 | 34.2 | 42.0 | 52.9 | 66.1 | 70.7 | 67.8 | 60.6 | 51.5 | 34.4 | 29.8 | 46.7 |
| 1967 | 29.4 | 20.5 | 28.8 | 41.7 | 48.8 | 62.2 | 71.2 | 68.0 | 63.5 | 53.0 | 37.1 | 24.0 | 45.9 |
| 1968 | 19.2 | 20.0 | 35.6 | 48.5 | 53.8 | 66.3 | 68.4 | 70.4 | 60.8 | 49.7 | 39.1 | 25.3 | 46.3 |
| 1969 | 23.2 | 25.1 | 30.8 | 48.8 | 56.3 | 63.7 | 71.1 | 70.1 | 60.6 | 51.7 | 40.2 | 22.2 | 45.9 |
| 1970 | 14.9 | 24.2 | 30.4 | 44.6 | 56.9 | 63.7 | 70.6 | 68.2 | 63.4 | 56.5 | 36.6 | 30.5 | 46.8 |
| 1971 | 17.7 | 25.9 | 29.9 | 42.5 | 54.2 | 65.6 | 70.6 | 68.2 | 63.4 | 56.5 | 36.6 | 30.5 | 46.8 |
| 1972 | 26.4 | 23.3 | 30.4 | 40.4 | 55.7 | 62.2 | 71.1 | 66.9 | 59.7 | 44.7 | 34.9 | 27.6 | 45.3 |
| 1973 | 26.1 | 24.7 | 40.9 | 46.3 | 54.2 | 67.4 | 71.1 | 71.7 | 60.1 | 51.3 | 39.8 | 30.4 | 48.8 |
| 1974 | 26.4 | 23.9 | 33.5 | 47.5 | 52.4 | 64.0 | 69.7 | 69.7 | 59.7 | 45.8 | 39.4 | 30.4 | 46.9 |
| 1975 | 27.5 | 25.2 | 31.3 | 40.8 | 60.1 | 63.6 | 71.8 | 67.5 | 57.3 | 46.4 | 35.2 | 27.3 | 47.4 |
| 1976 | 19.2 | 31.2 | 35.1 | 49.1 | 55.0 | 68.0 | 67.8 | 67.2 | 58.9 | 46.4 | 34.6 | 21.9 | 46.2 |
| 1977 | 16.2 | 24.9 | 39.1 | 45.9 | 58.1 | 62.4 | 69.3 | 68.6 | 59.6 | 49.3 | 41.1 | 26.0 | 46.7 |
| 1978 | 20.9 | 20.0 | 30.8 | 42.4 | 56.6 | 64.3 | 68.2 | 68.1 | 57.6 | 48.4 | 39.2 | 28.8 | 45.4 |
| 1979 | 25.3 | 16.5 | 38.2 | 44.7 | 57.7 | 63.6 | 71.2 | 67.7 | 60.0 | 49.0 | 44.3 | 31.9 | 47.5 |
| 1980 | 25.0 | 22.2 | 33.1 | 46.0 | 57.0 | 61.5 | 71.3 | 69.9 | 61.1 | 47.3 | 36.4 | 24.2 | 46.3 |
| 1981 | 15.9 | 32.8 | 34.7 | 47.4 | 57.9 | 66.0 | 70.7 | 67.4 | 58.2 | 46.7 | 39.1 | 27.8 | 47.1 |
| 1982 | 17.1 | 25.7 | 33.8 | 43.6 | 58.3 | 61.5 | 71.5 | 65.9 | 61.3 | 50.8 | 43.8 | 34.8 | 47.3 |
| 1983 | 26.1 | 29.1 | 36.6 | 46.6 | 54.7 | 67.9 | 72.3 | 70.2 | 64.9 | 55.0 | 42.0 | 27.3 | 49.0 |
| 1984 | 22.7 | 34.0 | 29.2 | 45.6 | 55.4 | 68.1 | 70.0 | 71.4 | 59.6 | 53.9 | 41.1 | 34.9 | 48.8 |
| 1985 | 20.1 | 28.6 | 37.2 | 47.4 | 57.8 | 61.4 | 70.4 | 70.4 | 59.4 | 49.6 | 37.1 | 25.3 | 47.6 |
| 1986 | 25.9 | 23.1 | 36.4 | 48.1 | 57.9 | 62.6 | 68.2 | 66.8 | 59.4 | 49.6 | 37.1 | 30.3 | 47.1 |
| 1987 | 24.0 | 24.5 | 36.8 | 45.7 | 57.6 | 65.8 | 70.7 | 66.6 | 60.6 | 48.8 | 39.4 | 30.8 | 47.6 |
| 1988 | 23.0 | 26.6 | 35.0 | 43.8 | 57.3 | 64.6 | 72.6 | 72.3 | 60.2 | 45.5 | 41.7 | 27.2 | 47.5 |
| 1989 | 28.5 | 24.4 | 33.0 | 42.4 | 57.0 | 64.0 | 68.7 | 67.3 | 60.6 | 50.7 | 36.5 | 15.1 | 45.7 |
| 1990 | 31.3 | 28.8 | 36.2 | 43.9 | 51.5 | 64.6 | 69.2 | 68.8 | 59.3 | 53.0 | 42.1 | 34.0 | 48.6 |
| Record Mean | 23.6 | 25.5 | 33.5 | 45.1 | 55.8 | 64.8 | 70.1 | 68.2 | 60.3 | 50.4 | 39.7 | 27.9 | 47.0 |
| Max | 31.4 | 33.6 | 41.7 | 54.6 | 66.1 | 74.6 | 79.4 | 77.2 | 69.3 | 59.4 | 47.3 | 35.2 | 55.8 |
| Min | 15.9 | 17.4 | 25.2 | 35.6 | 45.6 | 54.9 | 60.8 | 59.2 | 51.3 | 41.4 | 32.1 | 20.5 | 38.3 |

**REFERENCE NOTES FOR TABLES 1, 2, 3 and 6**      **(WORCESTER, MA)**

**GENERAL**

T - TRACE AMOUNT
BLANK ENTRIES DENOTE MISSING/UNREPORTED DATA.
# INDICATES A STATION OR INSTRUMENT RELOCATION.

**SPECIFIC**

TABLE 1

(a) - LENGTH OF RECORD IN YEARS. ALTHOUGH INDIVIDUAL MONTHS MAY BE MISSING.

\* LESS THAN .05

* NORMALS — BASED ON THE 1951-1980 RECORD PERIOD.
EXTREMES — DATES ARE THE MOST RECENT OCCURRENCE.
WIND DIR. — NUMERALS SHOW TENS OF DEGREES CLOCKWISE FROM TRUE NORTH. "00" INDICATES CALM.
RESULTANT WIND DIRECTIONS ARE GIVEN TO WHOLE DEGREES.

TABLE 3
MAX AND MIN ARE LONG-TERM MEAN DAILY MAXIMUM AND MEAN DAILY MINIMUM TEMPERATURES.

**EXCEPTIONS**

TABLE 1

1. THUNDERSTORMS, AND HEAVY FOG ARE THROUGH 1977.

TABLES 2, 3, and 6

RECORD MEANS ARE THROUGH THE CURRENT YEAR, BEGINNING IN
1948 FOR TEMPERATURE
1948 FOR PRECIPITATION
1956 FOR SNOWFALL

**TABLE 4**  HEATING DEGREE DAYS Base 65 deg. F  WORCESTER, MASSACHUSETTS

| SEASON | JULY | AUG | SEP | OCT | NOV | DEC | JAN | FEB | MAR | APR | MAY | JUNE | TOTAL |
|---|---|---|---|---|---|---|---|---|---|---|---|---|---|
| 1961-62 | 24 | 29 | 88 | 382 | 758 | 1175 | 1280 | 1195 | 943 | 596 | 329 | 70 | 6869 |
| 1962-63 | 35 | 49 | 217 | 483 | 825 | 1258 | 1310 | 1267 | 953 | 599 | 290 | 85 | 7360 |
| 1963-64 | 28 | 46 | 256 | 277 | 655 | 1383 | 1167 | 1187 | 921 | 632 | 290 | 92 | 6868 |
| 1964-65 | 36 | 80 | 189 | 472 | 704 | 1122 | 1362 | 1136 | 1040 | 658 | 224 | 118 | 7123 |
| 1965-66 | 14 | 61 | 163 | 486 | 843 | 1076 | 1320 | 1093 | 948 | 685 | 206 | 80 | 7145 |
| 1966-67 | 4 | 19 | 218 | 489 | 649 | 1141 | 1097 | 1242 | 1115 | 691 | 493 | 73 | 7231 |
| 1967-68 | 4 | 28 | 151 | 422 | 912 | 1087 | 1414 | 1300 | 904 | 490 | 343 | 126 | 7181 |
| 1968-69 | 8 | 35 | 79 | 375 | 830 | 1264 | 1286 | 1111 | 1056 | 487 | 282 | 49 | 6858 |
| 1969-70 | 19 | 15 | 163 | 468 | 773 | 1224 | 1547 | 1137 | 1068 | 604 | 261 | 99 | 7378 |
| 1970-71 | 2 | 12 | 174 | 410 | 738 | 1319 | 1461 | 1087 | 1083 | 667 | 327 | 61 | 7341 |
| 1971-72 | 3 | 35 | 98 | 258 | 844 | 1061 | 1189 | 1203 | 1065 | 733 | 290 | 116 | 6895 |
| 1972-73 | 16 | 41 | 171 | 622 | 897 | 1152 | 1200 | 1120 | 738 | 555 | 338 | 37 | 6887 |
| 1973-74 | 6 | 9 | 202 | 420 | 750 | 1017 | 1191 | 1145 | 969 | 520 | 391 | 82 | 6701 |
| 1974-75 | 6 | 9 | 190 | 592 | 760 | 1063 | 1158 | 1110 | 1037 | 721 | 180 | 104 | 6930 |
| 1975-76 | 2 | 47 | 223 | 413 | 586 | 1161 | 1412 | 972 | 920 | 511 | 310 | 60 | 6617 |
| 1976-77 | 17 | 46 | 192 | 571 | 905 | 1331 | 1508 | 1115 | 798 | 571 | 244 | 115 | 7413 |
| 1977-78 | 16 | 32 | 189 | 481 | 711 | 1202 | 1359 | 1255 | 1054 | 674 | 288 | 69 | 7330 |
| 1978-79 | 33 | 38 | 229 | 511 | 767 | 1116 | 1225 | 1354 | 824 | 601 | 243 | 80 | 7021 |
| 1979-80 | 25 | 53 | 180 | 500 | 614 | 1019 | 1235 | 1233 | 983 | 562 | 246 | 148 | 6798 |
| 1980-81 | 2 | 19 | 165 | 540 | 853 | 1259 | 1516 | 894 | 934 | 521 | 241 | 42 | 6986 |
| 1981-82 | 1 | 29 | 204 | 562 | 772 | 1145 | 1478 | 1094 | 961 | 639 | 212 | 127 | 7224 |
| 1982-83 | 7 | 55 | 140 | 436 | 632 | 929 | 1199 | 996 | 871 | 548 | 318 | 44 | 6175 |
| 1983-84 | 5 | 20 | 115 | 459 | 682 | 1163 | 1303 | 892 | 1099 | 577 | 300 | 54 | 6669 |
| 1984-85 | 9 | | 184 | 338 | 713 | 928 | 1382 | 1011 | 855 | 518 | 230 | 121 | 6290 |
| 1985-86 | 2 | 25 | 128 | 406 | 713 | 1223 | 1206 | 1166 | 879 | 501 | 262 | 119 | 6630 |
| 1986-87 | 48 | 49 | 182 | 471 | 830 | 1069 | 1266 | 1130 | 867 | 571 | 273 | 58 | 6814 |
| 1987-88 | 9 | 56 | 152 | 495 | 761 | 1052 | 1298 | 1107 | 922 | 629 | 253 | 115 | 6849 |
| 1988-89 | 19 | 32 | 155 | 597 | 693 | 1166 | 1123 | 1129 | 984 | 674 | 257 | 90 | 6919 |
| 1989-90 | 7 | 38 | 172 | 436 | 846 | 1540 | 1035 | 1006 | 884 | 632 | 413 | 58 | 7067 |
| 1990-91 | 22 | 30 | 192 | 379 | 683 | 957 | | | | | | | |

**TABLE 5**  COOLING DEGREE DAYS Base 65 deg. F  WORCESTER, MASSACHUSETTS

| YEAR | JAN | FEB | MAR | APR | MAY | JUNE | JULY | AUG | SEP | OCT | NOV | DEC | TOTAL |
|---|---|---|---|---|---|---|---|---|---|---|---|---|---|
| 1969 | 0 | 0 | 0 | 5 | 17 | 98 | 131 | 192 | 44 | 1 | 0 | 0 | 488 |
| 1970 | 0 | 0 | 0 | 0 | 16 | 70 | 197 | 177 | 50 | 6 | 0 | 0 | 516 |
| 1971 | 0 | 0 | 0 | 0 | 0 | 87 | 184 | 141 | 57 | 2 | 0 | 0 | 471 |
| 1972 | 0 | 0 | 0 | 0 | 9 | 41 | 215 | 109 | 20 | 0 | 0 | 0 | 394 |
| 1973 | 0 | 0 | 0 | 1 | 11 | 118 | 201 | 224 | 62 | 0 | 0 | 0 | 617 |
| 1974 | 0 | 0 | 0 | 4 | 8 | 59 | 159 | 164 | 36 | 0 | 0 | 0 | 430 |
| 1975 | 0 | 0 | 0 | 0 | 33 | 69 | 218 | 132 | 0 | 1 | 0 | 0 | 453 |
| 1976 | 0 | 0 | 0 | 37 | 7 | 154 | 110 | 119 | 16 | 0 | 0 | 0 | 443 |
| 1977 | 0 | 0 | 2 | 4 | 37 | 44 | 156 | 150 | 32 | 0 | 0 | 0 | 425 |
| 1978 | 0 | 0 | 0 | 0 | 32 | 57 | 138 | 137 | 14 | 0 | 0 | 0 | 378 |
| 1979 | 0 | 0 | 0 | 0 | 24 | 44 | 225 | 142 | 38 | 10 | 0 | 0 | 483 |
| 1980 | 0 | 0 | 0 | 0 | 8 | 48 | 206 | 178 | 57 | 0 | 0 | 0 | 497 |
| 1981 | 0 | 0 | 0 | 0 | 29 | 78 | 184 | 110 | 10 | 0 | 0 | 0 | 411 |
| 1982 | 0 | 0 | 0 | 0 | 8 | 29 | 216 | 92 | 34 | 0 | 0 | 0 | 379 |
| 1983 | 0 | 0 | 0 | 4 | 4 | 138 | 238 | 188 | 118 | 11 | 0 | 0 | 701 |
| 1984 | 0 | 0 | 0 | 2 | 10 | 156 | 171 | 209 | 30 | 0 | 0 | 0 | 578 |
| 1985 | 0 | 0 | 0 | 0 | 15 | 22 | 177 | 120 | 47 | 0 | 0 | 0 | 381 |
| 1986 | 0 | 0 | 0 | 0 | 50 | 54 | 151 | 111 | 21 | 2 | 0 | 0 | 389 |
| 1987 | 0 | 0 | 0 | 0 | 49 | 90 | 193 | 110 | 25 | 0 | 0 | 0 | 467 |
| 1988 | 0 | 0 | 0 | 0 | 24 | 112 | 260 | 266 | 17 | 1 | 0 | 0 | 680 |
| 1989 | 0 | 0 | 0 | 0 | 16 | 70 | 131 | 116 | 47 | 0 | 0 | 0 | 380 |
| 1990 | 0 | 0 | 0 | 6 | 0 | 52 | 159 | 153 | 25 | 10 | 0 | 0 | 405 |

**TABLE 6**  SNOWFALL (inches)  WORCESTER, MASSACHUSETTS

| SEASON | JULY | AUG | SEP | OCT | NOV | DEC | JAN | FEB | MAR | APR | MAY | JUNE | TOTAL |
|---|---|---|---|---|---|---|---|---|---|---|---|---|---|
| 1961-62 | 0.0 | 0.0 | 0.0 | 0.9 | 8.3 | 20.3 | 2.0 | 45.2 | 4.5 | 1.8 | T | 0.0 | 83.0 |
| 1962-63 | 0.0 | 0.0 | 0.0 | 4.7 | 3.6 | 18.1 | 11.7 | 22.2 | 15.3 | 0.1 | T | 0.0 | 75.7 |
| 1963-64 | 0.0 | 0.0 | 0.0 | 0.5 | T | 16.7 | 14.9 | 27.3 | 6.0 | 1.2 | 0.0 | 0.0 | 66.6 |
| 1964-65 | 0.0 | 0.0 | 0.0 | 2.1 | T | 11.7 | 18.7 | 5.9 | 17.7 | 6.7 | 0.0 | 0.0 | 62.8 |
| 1965-66 | 0.0 | 0.0 | 0.0 | T | 0.6 | 2.3 | 44.0 | 19.7 | 5.8 | 0.8 | T | 0.0 | 73.2 |
| 1966-67 | 0.0 | 0.0 | 0.0 | 0.0 | 0.7 | 13.6 | 2.5 | 35.5 | 34.6 | 7.3 | T | 0.0 | 94.2 |
| 1967-68 | 0.0 | 0.0 | 0.0 | 0.0 | 9.8 | 22.2 | 18.6 | 6.4 | 9.2 | T | 0.0 | 0.0 | 66.2 |
| 1968-69 | 0.0 | 0.0 | 0.0 | 0.0 | 15.3 | 12.2 | 1.8 | 39.5 | 6.9 | T | 0.0 | 0.0 | 75.7 |
| 1969-70 | 0.0 | 0.0 | 0.0 | T | 0.3 | 29.5 | 7.7 | 11.4 | 19.9 | 3.3 | T | 0.0 | 72.1 |
| 1970-71 | 0.0 | 0.0 | 0.0 | T | T | 32.1 | 16.6 | 11.4 | 12.1 | 7.8 | 0.0 | 0.0 | 80.0 |
| 1971-72 | 0.0 | 0.0 | 0.0 | 0.0 | 20.7 | 9.6 | 6.7 | 35.0 | 20.1 | 7.2 | 0.0 | 0.0 | 99.3 |
| 1972-73 | 0.0 | 0.0 | 0.0 | T | 6.1 | 13.8 | 17.9 | 5.8 | 0.4 | 0.0 | 0.0 | 0.0 | 44.4 |
| 1973-74 | 0.0 | 0.0 | 0.0 | 0.0 | T | 0.9 | 12.5 | 15.0 | 1.7 | 3.7 | 0.0 | 0.0 | 33.8 |
| 1974-75 | 0.0 | 0.0 | 0.0 | T | 1.2 | 13.1 | 22.6 | 21.9 | 4.9 | 1.4 | 0.0 | 0.0 | 65.1 |
| 1975-76 | 0.0 | 0.0 | 0.0 | T | 1.5 | 18.1 | 21.6 | 4.7 | 16.4 | T | T | 0.0 | 62.3 |
| 1976-77 | 0.0 | 0.0 | 0.0 | T | 3.0 | 13.5 | 21.7 | 13.8 | 21.5 | 1.0 | 12.7 | 0.0 | 87.2 |
| 1977-78 | 0.0 | 0.0 | 0.0 | 0.0 | 2.2 | 13.7 | 34.2 | 20.8 | 15.0 | T | T | 0.0 | 85.9 |
| 1978-79 | 0.0 | 0.0 | 0.0 | 0.0 | 5.4 | 13.1 | 16.0 | 6.5 | 1.3 | 5.4 | 0.0 | 0.0 | 47.7 |
| 1979-80 | 0.0 | 0.0 | 0.0 | 7.5 | 0.0 | 2.1 | 0.8 | 6.5 | 9.7 | T | 0.0 | 0.0 | 26.6 |
| 1980-81 | 0.0 | 0.0 | 0.0 | 0.0 | 9.0 | 6.8 | 12.5 | 11.4 | 3.3 | T | T | 0.0 | 43.0 |
| 1981-82 | 0.0 | 0.0 | 0.0 | T | T | 24.6 | 16.7 | 6.5 | 11.0 | 15.1 | 0.0 | 0.0 | 73.9 |
| 1982-83 | 0.0 | 0.0 | 0.0 | 0.0 | 0.5 | 6.4 | 18.6 | 32.1 | 3.5 | 2.3 | T | 0.0 | 63.4 |
| 1983-84 | 0.0 | 0.0 | 0.0 | T | 1.1 | 17.2 | 24.1 | 3.3 | 30.9 | T | T | 0.0 | 76.6 |
| 1984-85 | 0.0 | 0.0 | 0.0 | T | T | 7.0 | 9.7 | 11.0 | 7.2 | 4.9 | 0.0 | 0.0 | 39.8 |
| 1985-86 | 0.0 | 0.0 | 0.0 | 0.0 | 6.9 | 9.1 | 5.8 | 14.5 | 2.3 | 0.1 | 0.3 | 0.0 | 39.0 |
| 1986-87 | 0.0 | 0.0 | 0.0 | 0.0 | 11.5 | 4.9 | 46.8 | 3.0 | 6.4 | 21.0 | 0.0 | 0.0 | 93.6 |
| 1987-88 | 0.0 | 0.0 | 0.0 | 0.0 | 10.2 | 12.9 | 25.2 | 15.8 | 6.4 | 0.6 | 0.0 | 0.0 | 71.1 |
| 1988-89 | 0.0 | 0.0 | 0.0 | 0.4 | T | 5.0 | 2.8 | 7.7 | 8.5 | 3.7 | 0.0 | 0.0 | 28.1 |
| 1989-90 | 0.0 | 0.0 | 0.0 | 0.0 | 7.9 | 10.2 | 11.3 | 15.2 | 6.4 | 2.1 | 0.0 | T | 53.1 |
| 1990-91 | 0.0 | 0.0 | 0.0 | 0.0 | 0.7 | 5.0 | | | | | | | |
| Record Mean | 0.0 | 0.0 | 0.0 | 0.6 | 3.7 | 12.7 | 16.7 | 16.2 | 13.4 | 3.9 | 0.4 | T | 67.6 |

**See Reference Notes, relative to all above tables, on preceding page.**

Detroit and the immediate suburbs, including nearby urban areas in Canada, occupy an area approximately 25 miles in radius. The waterway, consisting of the Detroit and St. Clair Rivers, Lake St. Clair, and the west end of Lake Erie, lies at an elevation of 568 to 580 feet above sea level. Nearly flat land slopes up gently from the waters edge northwestward for about 10 miles and then gives way to increasingly rolling terrain. The Irish Hills, parallel to and about 40 miles northwest of the waterway, have tops 1,000 to 1,250 feet above sea level. On the Canadian side of the waterway the land is relatively level.

Northwest winds in winter bring snow flurry accumulations to all of Michigan except in the Detroit Metropolitan area while summer showers moving from the northwest weaken and sometimes dissipate as they approach Detroit. On the other hand, much of the heaviest precipitation in winter comes from southeast winds, especially to the northwest suburbs of the city.

The climate of Detroit is influenced by its location with respect to major storm tracks and the influence of the Great Lakes. The normal wintertime storm track is south of the city, which brings on the average, about 3 inch snowfalls. Winter storms can bring combinations of rain, snow, freezing rain, and sleet with heavy snowfall accumulations possible at times. In summer, most storms pass to the north allowing for intervals of warm, humid, sunny skies with occasional thunderstorms followed by days of mild, dry, and fair weather. Temperatures of 90 degrees or higher are reached during each summer.

The most pronounced lake effect occurs in the winter when arctic air moving across the lakes is warmed and moistened. This produces an excess of cloudiness but a moderation of cold wave temperatures.

Local climatic variations are due largely to the immediate effect of Lake St. Clair and the urban heat island. On warm days in late spring or early summer, lake breezes often lower temperatures by 10 to 15 degrees in the eastern part of the city and the northeastern suburbs. The urban heat island effect shows up mainly at night where minimum temperatures at the Metropolitan Airport average 4 degrees lower than downtown Detroit. On humid summer nights or on very cold winter nights, this difference can exceed 10 degrees.

The growing season averages 180 days and has ranged from 145 days to 205 days. On average, the last freezing temperature occurs in late April while the average first freezing temperature occurs in late October. A freeze has occurred as late as mid-May and as early as late September.

Air pollution comes primarily from heavy industry spread along both shores of the waterway from Port Huron to Toledo. However, wind dispersion is usually sufficient to keep it from becoming a major hazard.

## TABLE 1
# NORMALS. MEANS AND EXTREMES
### DETROIT, METROPOLITAN AIRPORT MICHIGAN

LATITUDE: 42°14'N  LONGITUDE: 83°20'W  ELEVATION: FT. GRND  633 BARO  647  TIME ZONE: EASTERN  WBAN: 94847

| | (a) | JAN | FEB | MAR | APR | MAY | JUNE | JULY | AUG | SEP | OCT | NOV | DEC | YEAR |
|---|---|---|---|---|---|---|---|---|---|---|---|---|---|---|
| **TEMPERATURE °F:** | | | | | | | | | | | | | | |
| Normals | | | | | | | | | | | | | | |
| -Daily Maximum | | 30.6 | 33.5 | 43.4 | 57.7 | 69.4 | 79.0 | 83.1 | 81.5 | 74.4 | 62.5 | 47.6 | 35.4 | 58.2 |
| -Daily Minimum | | 16.1 | 18.0 | 26.5 | 36.9 | 46.7 | 56.3 | 60.7 | 59.4 | 52.2 | 41.2 | 31.4 | 21.6 | 38.9 |
| -Monthly | | 23.4 | 25.8 | 35.0 | 47.4 | 58.1 | 67.7 | 71.9 | 70.5 | 63.3 | 51.9 | 39.5 | 28.5 | 48.6 |
| Extremes | | | | | | | | | | | | | | |
| -Record Highest | 31 | 62 | 65 | 81 | 89 | 93 | 104 | 102 | 100 | 98 | 91 | 77 | 68 | 104 |
| -Year | | 1965 | 1976 | 1986 | 1977 | 1988 | 1988 | 1988 | 1988 | 1976 | 1963 | 1968 | 1982 | JUN 1988 |
| -Record Lowest | 31 | -21 | -15 | -4 | 10 | 25 | 36 | 41 | 38 | 29 | 17 | 9 | -10 | -21 |
| -Year | | 1984 | 1985 | 1978 | 1982 | 1966 | 1972 | 1965 | 1982 | 1974 | 1974 | 1969 | 1983 | JAN 1984 |
| **NORMAL DEGREE DAYS:** | | | | | | | | | | | | | | |
| Heating (base 65°F) | | 1290 | 1098 | 930 | 528 | 247 | 36 | 5 | 12 | 106 | 414 | 765 | 1132 | 6563 |
| Cooling (base 65°F) | | 0 | 0 | 0 | 0 | 33 | 117 | 219 | 183 | 55 | 8 | 0 | 0 | 615 |
| **% OF POSSIBLE SUNSHINE** | 24 | 41 | 47 | 52 | 55 | 61 | 66 | 69 | 68 | 61 | 50 | 35 | 30 | 53 |
| **MEAN SKY COVER (tenths)** | | | | | | | | | | | | | | |
| Sunrise - Sunset | 31 | 7.5 | 7.2 | 7.1 | 6.7 | 6.3 | 5.8 | 5.5 | 5.7 | 6.1 | 6.4 | 7.6 | 7.9 | 6.7 |
| **MEAN NUMBER OF DAYS:** | | | | | | | | | | | | | | |
| Sunrise to Sunset | | | | | | | | | | | | | | |
| -Clear | 31 | 4.3 | 4.7 | 5.6 | 6.3 | 6.7 | 7.9 | 9.2 | 9.0 | 8.2 | 7.4 | 4.0 | 3.4 | 76.7 |
| -Partly Cloudy | 31 | 6.9 | 6.9 | 7.3 | 7.7 | 10.3 | 11.1 | 12.3 | 11.2 | 9.5 | 8.8 | 6.7 | 6.2 | 104.9 |
| -Cloudy | 31 | 19.8 | 16.6 | 18.0 | 16.0 | 14.0 | 11.0 | 9.5 | 10.9 | 12.3 | 14.8 | 19.3 | 21.4 | 183.6 |
| Precipitation | | | | | | | | | | | | | | |
| .01 inches or more | 31 | 13.1 | 11.2 | 13.2 | 12.5 | 11.2 | 10.4 | 9.2 | 9.4 | 9.7 | 9.6 | 11.7 | 13.9 | 135.0 |
| Snow,Ice pellets | | | | | | | | | | | | | | |
| 1.0 inches or more | 31 | 3.2 | 3.0 | 2.2 | 0.6 | 0.0 | 0.0 | 0.0 | 0.0 | 0.0 | 0.1 | 1.2 | 3.3 | 13.5 |
| Thunderstorms | 31 | 0.1 | 0.5 | 1.7 | 3.4 | 4.0 | 6.0 | 5.8 | 5.5 | 4.2 | 1.2 | 0.7 | 0.4 | 33.4 |
| Heavy Fog Visibility 1/4 mile or less | 31 | 2.2 | 2.3 | 2.2 | 0.9 | 0.6 | 0.7 | 0.6 | 1.4 | 1.7 | 2.4 | 2.0 | 3.0 | 20.0 |
| Temperature °F | | | | | | | | | | | | | | |
| -Maximum | | | | | | | | | | | | | | |
| 90° and above | 31 | 0.0 | 0.0 | 0.0 | 0.0 | 0.4 | 2.7 | 5.1 | 2.9 | 0.9 | 0.1 | 0.0 | 0.0 | 12.1 |
| 32° and below | 31 | 17.5 | 13.4 | 4.5 | 0.2 | 0.0 | 0.0 | 0.0 | 0.0 | 0.0 | 0.0 | 1.4 | 11.9 | 48.9 |
| -Minimum | | | | | | | | | | | | | | |
| 32° and below | 31 | 29.3 | 25.7 | 23.1 | 9.7 | 0.9 | 0.0 | 0.0 | 0.0 | 0.1 | 5.0 | 16.7 | 26.5 | 137.0 |
| 0° and below | 31 | 3.8 | 2.2 | 0.1 | 0.0 | 0.0 | 0.0 | 0.0 | 0.0 | 0.0 | 0.0 | 0.0 | 1.5 | 7.6 |
| **AVG. STATION PRESS.(mb)** | 17 | 992.7 | 993.7 | 991.5 | 990.5 | 990.3 | 990.6 | 991.8 | 992.9 | 993.6 | 994.1 | 992.6 | 993.0 | 992.3 |
| **RELATIVE HUMIDITY (%)** | | | | | | | | | | | | | | |
| Hour 01 | 31 | 78 | 77 | 76 | 74 | 76 | 79 | 81 | 83 | 84 | 80 | 79 | 79 | 79 |
| Hour 07 | 31 | 79 | 79 | 79 | 78 | 78 | 79 | 82 | 86 | 87 | 84 | 82 | 81 | 81 |
| Hour 13 (Local Time) | 31 | 69 | 65 | 61 | 54 | 53 | 54 | 53 | 56 | 57 | 57 | 66 | 71 | 60 |
| Hour 19 | 31 | 73 | 70 | 65 | 59 | 56 | 58 | 58 | 63 | 67 | 68 | 73 | 76 | 66 |
| **PRECIPITATION (inches):** | | | | | | | | | | | | | | |
| Water Equivalent | | | | | | | | | | | | | | |
| -Normal | | 1.86 | 1.69 | 2.54 | 3.15 | 2.77 | 3.43 | 3.10 | 3.21 | 2.25 | 2.12 | 2.33 | 2.52 | 30.97 |
| -Maximum Monthly | 31 | 3.63 | 3.83 | 4.48 | 5.40 | 5.88 | 7.04 | 6.02 | 7.83 | 7.52 | 4.87 | 5.68 | 6.00 | 7.83 |
| -Year | | 1965 | 1985 | 1973 | 1961 | 1968 | 1987 | 1969 | 1975 | 1986 | 1967 | 1982 | 1965 | AUG 1975 |
| -Minimum Monthly | 31 | 0.27 | 0.15 | 0.82 | 0.92 | 0.87 | 0.97 | 0.59 | 0.72 | 0.43 | 0.35 | 0.79 | 0.46 | 0.15 |
| -Year | | 1961 | 1969 | 1981 | 1971 | 1988 | 1988 | 1974 | 1982 | 1960 | 1964 | 1976 | 1965 | FEB 1969 |
| -Maximum in 24 hrs | 31 | 1.72 | 1.49 | 1.69 | 1.97 | 2.87 | 2.84 | 3.19 | 3.21 | 2.16 | 2.57 | 2.20 | 3.71 | 3.71 |
| -Year | | 1967 | 1981 | 1985 | 1965 | 1968 | 1983 | 1966 | 1964 | 1981 | 1985 | 1982 | 1965 | DEC 1965 |
| Snow,Ice pellets | | | | | | | | | | | | | | |
| -Maximum Monthly | 31 | 29.6 | 20.8 | 16.1 | 9.0 | T | 0.0 | 0.0 | 0.0 | 0.0 | 2.9 | 11.8 | 34.9 | 34.9 |
| -Year | | 1978 | 1986 | 1965 | 1982 | 1989 | | | | | 1980 | 1966 | 1974 | DEC 1974 |
| -Maximum in 24 hrs | 31 | 10.0 | 10.3 | 9.2 | 7.4 | T | 0.0 | 0.0 | 0.0 | 0.0 | 2.9 | 5.6 | 19.2 | 19.2 |
| -Year | | 1982 | 1965 | 1973 | 1982 | 1989 | | | | | 1980 | 1977 | 1974 | DEC 1974 |
| **WIND:** | | | | | | | | | | | | | | |
| Mean Speed (mph) | 31 | 11.9 | 11.5 | 11.8 | 11.6 | 10.2 | 9.2 | 8.4 | 8.3 | 8.7 | 9.8 | 11.2 | 11.5 | 10.3 |
| Prevailing Direction through 1963 | | WSW | WSW | WSW | WSW | WSW | SW | SW | SW | SW | WSW | SW | SW | SW |
| Fastest Obs. 1 Min. | | | | | | | | | | | | | | |
| -Direction (!!!) | 10 | 24 | 22 | 25 | 28 | 31 | 28 | 33 | 25 | 26 | 28 | 17 | 22 | 22 |
| -Speed (MPH) | 10 | 40 | 33 | 44 | 44 | 39 | 30 | 40 | 32 | 30 | 35 | 37 | 48 | 48 |
| -Year | | 1982 | 1988 | 1989 | 1982 | 1988 | 1988 | 1980 | 1984 | 1988 | 1981 | 1988 | 1987 | DEC 1987 |
| Peak Gust | | | | | | | | | | | | | | |
| -Direction (!!!) | 6 | W | NW | W | SW | S | E | NW | SW | NW | W | W | SW | SW |
| -Speed (mph) | 6 | 51 | 51 | 60 | 63 | 58 | 51 | 48 | 46 | 54 | 52 | 52 | 59 | 63 |
| -Date | | 1989 | 1987 | 1989 | 1984 | 1984 | 1987 | 1987 | 1987 | 1987 | 1985 | 1988 | 1987 | APR 1984 |

**See reference Notes to this table on the following page.**

# DETROIT, MICHIGAN

PRECIPITATION (inches)  DETROIT, METROPOLITAN AIRPORT MICHIGAN

**TABLE 2**

| YEAR | JAN | FEB | MAR | APR | MAY | JUNE | JULY | AUG | SEP | OCT | NOV | DEC | ANNUAL |
|---|---|---|---|---|---|---|---|---|---|---|---|---|---|
| 1961 | 0.27 | 2.06 | 2.34 | 5.40 | 2.21 | 3.17 | 3.57 | 7.30 | 5.83 | 1.13 | 2.80 | 1.20 | 37.28 |
| 1962 | 1.98 | 2.39 | 1.08 | 2.93 | 1.63 | 2.94 | 5.08 | 3.10 | 3.41 | 2.30 | 1.34 | 1.13 | 29.31 |
| 1963 | 0.85 | 0.67 | 2.77 | 2.30 | 4.09 | 2.59 | 1.92 | 1.44 | 1.42 | 0.57 | 1.27 | 1.12 | 21.01 |
| 1964 | 2.20 | 0.68 | 2.98 | 4.13 | 1.72 | 3.84 | 1.11 | 7.70 | 1.31 | 0.35 | 0.80 | 1.92 | 28.74 |
| 1965 | 3.63 | 2.54 | 3.59 | 3.30 | 1.15 | 2.28 | 2.38 | 6.94 | 1.91 | 3.89 | 1.49 | 6.00 | 39.10 |
| 1966 | 0.61 | 1.64 | 2.62 | 2.65 | 2.18 | 4.16 | 5.24 | 5.03 | 1.51 | 1.15 | 3.13 | 4.53 | 34.45 |
| 1967 | 2.34 | 1.28 | 1.03 | 3.67 | 1.63 | 4.23 | 2.85 | 2.01 | 1.96 | 4.87 | 2.77 | 5.19 | 33.83 |
| 1968 | 2.30 | 1.48 | 2.04 | 1.71 | 5.88 | 4.99 | 5.14 | 1.83 | 1.87 | 1.09 | 3.31 | 3.59 | 35.23 |
| 1969 | 2.83 | 0.15 | 1.62 | 3.77 | 3.74 | 4.26 | 5.02 | 1.06 | 0.68 | 1.41 | 2.46 | 1.33 | 29.33 |
| 1970 | 1.11 | 0.86 | 2.62 | 3.32 | 3.01 | 3.90 | 3.30 | 2.75 | 1.63 | 1.91 | 2.73 | 1.61 | 28.75 |
| 1971 | 1.03 | 2.68 | 1.59 | 0.92 | 1.97 | 2.17 | 1.95 | 1.62 | 2.72 | 1.01 | 1.34 | 3.79 | 22.79 |
| 1972 | 1.28 | 1.00 | 2.55 | 3.63 | 2.68 | 3.30 | 2.21 | 3.07 | 3.40 | 2.24 | 3.19 | 3.11 | 31.66 |
| 1973 | 1.65 | 1.08 | 4.48 | 1.42 | 3.72 | 4.86 | 1.66 | 1.67 | 1.82 | 2.01 | 3.21 | 3.51 | 34.09 |
| 1974 | 3.26 | 2.37 | 4.20 | 2.75 | 3.49 | 2.38 | 2.59 | 2.95 | 2.22 | 0.81 | 2.86 | 4.00 | 31.88 |
| 1975 | 2.90 | 2.65 | 1.66 | 2.50 | 2.82 | 2.39 | 1.98 | 7.83 | 3.18 | 1.29 | 2.39 | 3.00 | 34.59 |
| 1976 | 1.91 | 2.87 | 4.24 | 3.15 | 3.26 | 3.16 | 1.47 | 1.68 | 3.66 | 2.01 | 0.79 | 0.79 | 29.09 |
| 1977 | 0.98 | 1.64 | 3.57 | 4.17 | 2.40 | 3.16 | 3.28 | 2.23 | 4.23 | 1.37 | 2.88 | 2.97 | 32.88 |
| 1978 | 3.16 | 0.45 | 2.05 | 2.49 | 3.58 | 2.69 | 1.97 | 1.73 | 1.82 | 2.49 | 2.41 | 2.81 | 27.65 |
| 1979 | 1.52 | 0.57 | 2.44 | 4.97 | 2.82 | 4.04 | 4.96 | 2.99 | 0.94 | 1.24 | 4.19 | 2.36 | 33.04 |
| 1980 | 0.69 | 1.00 | 3.88 | 4.23 | 3.22 | 6.42 | 4.33 | 6.09 | 2.94 | 1.26 | 0.98 | 2.30 | 37.24 |
| 1981 | 0.57 | 3.13 | 0.82 | 3.44 | 2.60 | 3.33 | 4.29 | 2.32 | 5.47 | 3.92 | 1.26 | 2.38 | 33.53 |
| 1982 | 3.43 | 1.10 | 3.14 | 1.60 | 2.83 | 4.11 | 4.78 | 0.72 | 2.55 | 1.01 | 5.68 | 3.29 | 34.24 |
| 1983 | 0.84 | 0.89 | 1.87 | 4.20 | 5.47 | 4.88 | 4.53 | 1.57 | 2.49 | 2.85 | 4.28 | 3.78 | 37.65 |
| 1984 | 0.78 | 1.31 | 3.12 | 2.48 | 3.62 | 1.04 | 3.95 | 3.00 | 2.30 | 2.59 | 2.49 | 2.90 | 26.27 |
| 1985 | 2.63 | 3.83 | 4.42 | 2.11 | 3.11 | 1.62 | 3.96 | 4.88 | 2.59 | 3.91 | 5.51 | 1.51 | 40.08 |
| 1986 | 1.30 | 3.46 | 2.29 | 2.73 | 1.36 | 5.75 | 3.47 | 3.52 | 7.52 | 3.05 | 1.88 | 2.28 | 37.61 |
| 1987 | 2.35 | 0.53 | 2.19 | 2.14 | 2.50 | 7.04 | 2.20 | 6.87 | 2.69 | 2.00 | 3.17 | 4.60 | 38.28 |
| 1988 | 1.30 | 2.02 | 1.16 | 1.50 | 0.87 | 0.97 | 2.43 | 3.13 | 3.65 | 3.57 | 4.29 | 1.97 | 26.86 |
| 1989 | 1.28 | 0.77 | 2.16 | 2.22 | 4.16 | 3.79 | 4.21 | 2.14 | 3.03 | 1.73 | 2.53 | 1.24 | 29.26 |
| 1990 | 1.80 | 5.02 | 1.91 | 2.72 | 3.74 | 4.92 | 1.47 | 3.85 | 6.06 | 4.14 | 2.64 | 4.37 | 42.64 |
| Record Mean | 1.82 | 1.76 | 2.49 | 2.96 | 2.92 | 3.65 | 3.11 | 3.44 | 2.83 | 2.17 | 2.63 | 2.74 | 32.52 |

**TABLE 3**  AVERAGE TEMPERATURE (deg. F)  DETROIT, METROPOLITAN AIRPORT MICHIGAN

| YEAR | JAN | FEB | MAR | APR | MAY | JUNE | JULY | AUG | SEP | OCT | NOV | DEC | ANNUAL |
|---|---|---|---|---|---|---|---|---|---|---|---|---|---|
| 1961 | 21.7 | 30.9 | 39.0 | 42.6 | 54.7 | 66.5 | 72.1 | 71.1 | 67.9 | 54.6 | 40.1 | 28.5 | 49.1 |
| 1962 | 21.5 | 22.3 | 33.3 | 46.4 | 63.0 | 68.5 | 69.4 | 68.6 | 60.5 | 53.7 | 39.0 | 24.2 | 47.5 |
| 1963 | 15.8 | 17.6 | 36.8 | 47.4 | 56.0 | 68.2 | 71.5 | 66.8 | 60.2 | 58.2 | 42.5 | 20.9 | 46.8 |
| 1964 | 28.1 | 25.9 | 34.3 | 47.6 | 60.9 | 66.2 | 72.9 | 65.3 | 60.7 | 46.5 | 41.2 | 28.1 | 48.1 |
| 1965 | 24.7 | 25.9 | 30.1 | 45.1 | 62.4 | 66.2 | 69.2 | 68.0 | 63.3 | 48.2 | 40.5 | 35.0 | 48.3 |
| 1966 | 20.4 | 27.4 | 37.1 | 44.4 | 51.9 | 68.4 | 73.5 | 69.1 | 62.2 | 51.0 | 41.8 | 28.7 | 48.0 |
| 1967 | 29.3 | 23.8 | 35.9 | 48.0 | 51.9 | 70.4 | 69.0 | 67.3 | 60.4 | 50.7 | 35.2 | 30.9 | 47.7 |
| 1968 | 20.9 | 24.3 | 38.2 | 50.9 | 56.1 | 68.4 | 71.7 | 72.5 | 65.5 | 53.5 | 41.0 | 28.1 | 49.3 |
| 1969 | 23.1 | 28.2 | 33.5 | 49.4 | 57.4 | 64.7 | 73.2 | 73.1 | 64.8 | 51.4 | 37.9 | 26.4 | 48.6 |
| 1970 | 16.6 | 24.4 | 32.9 | 49.3 | 60.9 | 68.4 | 72.6 | 72.1 | 64.5 | 54.2 | 40.0 | 29.0 | 48.8 |
| 1971 | 20.7 | 27.4 | 32.0 | 45.2 | 56.4 | 70.8 | 69.6 | 70.3 | 66.6 | 58.5 | 37.4 | 33.3 | 49.1 |
| 1972 | 23.8 | 24.6 | 32.6 | 44.6 | 60.3 | 64.2 | 71.2 | 69.1 | 63.0 | 47.3 | 37.4 | 29.4 | 47.3 |
| 1973 | 28.8 | 25.3 | 43.3 | 48.8 | 55.5 | 69.3 | 72.6 | 72.9 | 64.9 | 56.2 | 41.4 | 28.7 | 50.7 |
| 1974 | 26.5 | 23.6 | 35.7 | 49.2 | 55.2 | 65.9 | 72.5 | 72.3 | 59.7 | 48.8 | 40.6 | 28.6 | 48.2 |
| 1975 | 28.3 | 27.5 | 32.5 | 40.9 | 62.8 | 69.0 | 72.2 | 72.3 | 59.1 | 52.4 | 46.8 | 29.1 | 49.5 |
| 1976 | 19.2 | 33.3 | 40.4 | 50.0 | 56.4 | 70.6 | 72.7 | 70.2 | 62.1 | 47.4 | 33.5 | 21.5 | 48.1 |
| 1977 | 12.8 | 25.2 | 41.5 | 52.4 | 64.4 | 65.5 | 75.8 | 70.6 | 65.1 | 47.9 | 40.5 | 25.5 | 48.9 |
| 1978 | 19.6 | 16.3 | 30.0 | 45.5 | 59.3 | 66.8 | 70.6 | 71.9 | 67.5 | 50.2 | 40.5 | 28.9 | 47.3 |
| 1979 | 18.6 | 16.5 | 37.7 | 44.6 | 56.5 | 66.6 | 70.4 | 67.9 | 62.6 | 50.1 | 39.5 | 31.9 | 46.9 |
| 1980 | 24.5 | 22.2 | 31.3 | 45.9 | 59.8 | 63.7 | 72.7 | 72.7 | 63.8 | 46.3 | 37.4 | 26.0 | 47.2 |
| 1981 | 19.0 | 28.8 | 36.5 | 49.8 | 55.9 | 68.4 | 72.4 | 70.0 | 60.9 | 47.6 | 41.1 | 27.8 | 48.2 |
| 1982 | 17.1 | 20.7 | 33.0 | 43.2 | 64.3 | 64.2 | 72.4 | 67.7 | 61.8 | 52.6 | 41.6 | 37.3 | 48.0 |
| 1983 | 28.7 | 31.6 | 38.4 | 44.2 | 54.4 | 68.2 | 74.5 | 73.6 | 64.0 | 51.6 | 41.2 | 20.8 | 49.3 |
| 1984 | 18.0 | 33.3 | 28.9 | 47.8 | 54.5 | 70.8 | 70.8 | 72.7 | 61.2 | 54.9 | 38.6 | 34.0 | 48.8 |
| 1985 | 20.4 | 23.5 | 38.4 | 51.0 | 60.1 | 62.8 | 71.3 | 69.2 | 64.3 | 53.0 | 42.4 | 22.2 | 48.2 |
| 1986 | 23.9 | 24.6 | 37.6 | 50.6 | 61.3 | 67.3 | 75.0 | 68.9 | 65.9 | 52.6 | 37.3 | 31.7 | 49.7 |
| 1987 | 26.1 | 29.6 | 39.8 | 50.8 | 63.3 | 71.3 | 76.1 | 71.6 | 64.6 | 43.5 | 33.6 | 34.8 | 51.4 |
| 1988 | 23.8 | 23.4 | 36.9 | 48.5 | 62.0 | 70.4 | 77.1 | 75.1 | 63.3 | 46.0 | 42.2 | 28.7 | 49.8 |
| 1989 | 32.8 | 24.1 | 35.2 | 45.1 | 57.5 | 67.5 | 73.0 | 67.5 | 61.9 | 52.1 | 38.2 | 18.0 | 47.9 |
| 1990 | 33.6 | 30.7 | 39.5 | 49.0 | 56.6 | 68.5 | 72.2 | 71.2 | 64.5 | 52.8 | 44.2 | 32.8 | 51.3 |
| Record Mean | 23.0 | 25.5 | 35.3 | 47.4 | 58.5 | 67.6 | 72.3 | 70.6 | 63.4 | 51.3 | 40.0 | 28.3 | 48.6 |
| Max | 30.3 | 33.2 | 44.0 | 57.8 | 69.7 | 78.8 | 83.3 | 81.4 | 74.0 | 61.5 | 48.0 | 35.2 | 58.1 |
| Min | 15.6 | 17.7 | 26.6 | 36.9 | 47.2 | 56.3 | 61.2 | 59.8 | 52.7 | 41.0 | 32.1 | 21.4 | 39.1 |

## REFERENCE NOTES FOR TABLES 1, 2, 3 and 6  (DETROIT, MI)

### GENERAL

T - TRACE AMOUNT
BLANK ENTRIES DENOTE MISSING/UNREPORTED DATA.
# INDICATES A STATION OR INSTRUMENT RELOCATION.

### SPECIFIC

#### TABLE 1

(a) - LENGTH OF RECORD IN YEARS. ALTHOUGH INDIVIDUAL MONTHS MAY BE MISSING.
* LESS THAN .05

NORMALS — BASED ON THE 1951-1980 RECORD PERIOD.
EXTREMES — DATES ARE THE MOST RECENT OCCURRENCE.
WIND DIR. — NUMERALS SHOW TENS OF DEGREES CLOCKWISE FROM TRUE NORTH. "00" INDICATES CALM.
RESULTANT WIND DIRECTIONS ARE GIVEN TO WHOLE DEGREES.

#### TABLE 3
MAX AND MIN ARE LONG-TERM MEAN DAILY MAXIMUM AND MEAN DAILY MINIMUM TEMPERATURES.

### EXCEPTIONS

#### TABLES 2, 3, and 6

RECORD MEANS ARE THROUGH THE CURRENT YEAR, BEGINNING IN  1959 FOR TEMPERATURE
1959 FOR PRECIPITATION
1959 FOR SNOWFALL

## TABLE 4 — HEATING DEGREE DAYS Base 65 deg. F — DETROIT. METROPOLITAN AIRPORT MICHIGAN

| SEASON | JULY | AUG | SEP | OCT | NOV | DEC | JAN | FEB | MAR | APR | MAY | JUNE | TOTAL |
|---|---|---|---|---|---|---|---|---|---|---|---|---|---|
| 1961-62 | 4 | 5 | 74 | 323 | 742 | 1124 | 1342 | 1190 | 978 | 558 | 170 | 26 | 6536 |
| 1962-63 | 8 | 10 | 177 | 358 | 776 | 1259 | 1520 | 1320 | 866 | 524 | 295 | 49 | 7162 |
| 1963-64 | 11 | 34 | 158 | 221 | 670 | 1365 | 1139 | 1128 | 943 | 519 | 172 | 88 | 6448 |
| 1964-65 | 4 | 82 | 175 | 566 | 710 | 1137 | 1239 | 1088 | 1074 | 591 | 131 | 45 | 6842 |
| 1965-66 | 18 | 48 | 128 | 510 | 729 | 927 | 1377 | 1046 | 860 | 612 | 406 | 53 | 6714 |
| 1966-67 | 0 | 13 | 136 | 427 | 688 | 1119 | 1148 | 894 | 505 | 406 | | 9 | 6442 |
| 1967-68 | 32 | 29 | 158 | 452 | 886 | 1050 | 1360 | 1173 | 823 | 416 | 275 | 29 | 6683 |
| 1968-69 | 3 | 17 | 71 | 384 | 714 | 1137 | 1289 | 1024 | 972 | 464 | 259 | 102 | 6436 |
| 1969-70 | 0 | 0 | 93 | 418 | 804 | 1189 | 1491 | 1130 | 993 | 479 | 168 | 49 | 6814 |
| 1970-71 | 8 | 8 | 108 | 339 | 742 | 1105 | 1368 | 1047 | 1015 | 588 | 278 | 22 | 6628 |
| 1971-72 | 13 | 6 | 72 | 213 | 788 | 977 | 1272 | 1165 | 997 | 608 | 174 | 91 | 6376 |
| 1972-73 | 24 | 28 | 113 | 539 | 822 | 1096 | 1115 | 1103 | 667 | 480 | 289 | 3 | 6279 |
| 1973-74 | 0 | 10 | 98 | 276 | 702 | 1119 | 1189 | 1152 | 901 | 476 | 308 | 54 | 6285 |
| 1974-75 | 0 | 2 | 189 | 495 | 726 | 1123 | 1129 | 1043 | 996 | 714 | 142 | 41 | 6600 |
| 1975-76 | 4 | 0 | 178 | 375 | 537 | 1107 | 1413 | 914 | 757 | 473 | 269 | 6 | 6033 |
| 1976-77 | 1 | 15 | 133 | 540 | 938 | 1341 | 1609 | 1106 | 721 | 395 | 122 | 85 | 7006 |
| 1977-78 | 1 | 17 | 85 | 524 | 729 | 1218 | 1400 | 1357 | 1077 | 580 | 235 | 65 | 7288 |
| 1978-79 | 17 | 0 | 73 | 452 | 728 | 1112 | 1432 | 1355 | 843 | 604 | 291 | 55 | 6962 |
| 1979-80 | 12 | 29 | 126 | 471 | 758 | 1019 | 1249 | 1233 | 1036 | 568 | 191 | 104 | 6796 |
| 1980-81 | 0 | 0 | 110 | 578 | 822 | 1201 | 1418 | 1008 | 878 | 452 | 293 | 19 | 6779 |
| 1981-82 | 3 | 9 | 167 | 534 | 710 | 1144 | 1477 | 1237 | 985 | 647 | 75 | 70 | 7058 |
| 1982-83 | 2 | 39 | 145 | 383 | 696 | 852 | 1119 | 928 | 816 | 618 | 323 | 59 | 5980 |
| 1983-84 | 6 | 0 | 125 | 418 | 708 | 1367 | 1450 | 912 | 1112 | 507 | 334 | 9 | 6948 |
| 1984-85 | 11 | 4 | 164 | 310 | 785 | 955 | 1377 | 1154 | 818 | 435 | 177 | 93 | 6283 |
| 1985-86 | 2 | 8 | 129 | 366 | 672 | 1317 | 1271 | 1125 | 842 | 435 | 166 | 48 | 6381 |
| 1986-87 | 1 | 33 | 76 | 380 | 824 | 1028 | 1198 | 984 | 776 | 423 | 158 | 11 | 5892 |
| 1987-88 | 4 | 30 | 69 | 566 | 639 | 969 | 1273 | 1201 | 864 | 486 | 138 | 46 | 6285 |
| 1988-89 | 2 | 3 | 90 | 590 | 679 | 1118 | 991 | 1138 | 916 | 591 | 254 | 33 | 6405 |
| 1989-90 | 0 | 11 | 151 | 400 | 797 | 1451 | 966 | 955 | 785 | 506 | 258 | 27 | 6307 |
| 1990-91 | 1 | 1 | 112 | 380 | 618 | 994 | | | | | | | |

## TABLE 5 — COOLING DEGREE DAYS Base 65 deg. F — DETROIT. METROPOLITAN AIRPORT MICHIGAN

| YEAR | JAN | FEB | MAR | APR | MAY | JUNE | JULY | AUG | SEP | OCT | NOV | DEC | TOTAL |
|---|---|---|---|---|---|---|---|---|---|---|---|---|---|
| 1969 | 0 | 0 | 0 | 1 | 28 | 98 | 260 | 259 | 91 | 4 | 0 | 0 | 741 |
| 1970 | 0 | 0 | 0 | 17 | 50 | 161 | 249 | 236 | 100 | 12 | 0 | 0 | 825 |
| 1971 | 0 | 0 | 0 | 0 | 14 | 205 | 161 | 177 | 128 | 17 | 0 | 0 | 702 |
| 1972 | 0 | 0 | 0 | 0 | 36 | 73 | 222 | 160 | 59 | 0 | 0 | 0 | 550 |
| 1973 | 0 | 0 | 0 | 3 | 2 | 156 | 241 | 261 | 104 | 11 | 0 | 0 | 778 |
| 1974 | 0 | 0 | 0 | 8 | 10 | 91 | 237 | 237 | 36 | 1 | 0 | 0 | 620 |
| 1975 | 0 | 0 | 0 | 0 | 82 | 171 | 233 | 232 | 7 | 6 | 0 | 0 | 731 |
| 1976 | 0 | 0 | 0 | 30 | 10 | 182 | 246 | 182 | 53 | 3 | 0 | 0 | 706 |
| 1977 | 0 | 0 | 0 | 25 | 108 | 107 | 341 | 198 | 94 | 0 | 0 | 0 | 873 |
| 1978 | 0 | 0 | 0 | 0 | 63 | 122 | 200 | 221 | 154 | 0 | 0 | 0 | 760 |
| 1979 | 0 | 0 | 0 | 0 | 32 | 109 | 184 | 124 | 57 | 16 | 0 | 0 | 522 |
| 1980 | 0 | 0 | 0 | 3 | 38 | 69 | 246 | 248 | 79 | 3 | 0 | 0 | 686 |
| 1981 | 0 | 0 | 0 | 1 | 17 | 118 | 241 | 168 | 51 | 0 | 0 | 0 | 596 |
| 1982 | 0 | 0 | 0 | 0 | 58 | 55 | 237 | 129 | 57 | 5 | 0 | 0 | 541 |
| 1983 | 0 | 0 | 0 | 2 | 0 | 160 | 306 | 272 | 104 | 6 | 0 | 0 | 850 |
| 1984 | 0 | 0 | 0 | 0 | 15 | 189 | 197 | 252 | 55 | 2 | 0 | 0 | 710 |
| 1985 | 0 | 0 | 0 | 25 | 32 | 32 | 201 | 146 | 116 | 0 | 0 | 0 | 552 |
| 1986 | 0 | 0 | 0 | 10 | 55 | 120 | 319 | 160 | 110 | 3 | 0 | 0 | 777 |
| 1987 | 0 | 0 | 0 | 4 | 111 | 207 | 355 | 245 | 64 | 0 | 1 | 0 | 987 |
| 1988 | 0 | 0 | 0 | 0 | 52 | 214 | 385 | 322 | 46 | 8 | 0 | 0 | 1027 |
| 1989 | 0 | 0 | 0 | 0 | 29 | 114 | 256 | 171 | 64 | 5 | 0 | 0 | 639 |
| 1990 | 0 | 0 | 1 | 32 | 8 | 139 | 234 | 200 | 101 | 11 | 0 | 0 | 726 |

## TABLE 6 — SNOWFALL (inches) — DETROIT. METROPOLITAN AIRPORT MICHIGAN

| SEASON | JULY | AUG | SEP | OCT | NOV | DEC | JAN | FEB | MAR | APR | MAY | JUNE | TOTAL |
|---|---|---|---|---|---|---|---|---|---|---|---|---|---|
| 1961-62 | 0.0 | 0.0 | 0.0 | T | T | 4.5 | 5.1 | 17.4 | 2.6 | 0.5 | 0.0 | 0.0 | 30.1 |
| 1962-63 | 0.0 | 0.0 | 0.0 | T | T | 17.3 | 9.2 | 8.3 | 2.8 | T | 0.0 | 0.0 | 37.6 |
| 1963-64 | 0.0 | 0.0 | 0.0 | 0.0 | T | 8.9 | 5.3 | 7.7 | 11.5 | 0.8 | 0.0 | 0.0 | 34.2 |
| 1964-65 | 0.0 | 0.0 | 0.0 | T | 4.3 | 7.2 | 11.7 | 17.3 | 16.1 | 2.5 | 0.0 | 0.0 | 59.1 |
| 1965-66 | 0.0 | 0.0 | 0.0 | T | 0.4 | 1.6 | 8.4 | 3.9 | 2.5 | 1.8 | 0.0 | 0.0 | 18.6 |
| 1966-67 | 0.0 | 0.0 | 0.0 | 0.0 | 11.8 | 14.9 | 5.4 | 11.0 | 5.8 | 1.7 | 0.0 | 0.0 | 50.6 |
| 1967-68 | 0.0 | 0.0 | 0.0 | T | 1.4 | 4.5 | 11.8 | 2.8 | 10.0 | 0.1 | 0.0 | 0.0 | 30.6 |
| 1968-69 | 0.0 | 0.0 | 0.0 | T | T | 5.9 | 6.3 | 2.3 | 2.3 | 0.3 | 0.0 | 0.0 | 17.1 |
| 1969-70 | 0.0 | 0.0 | 0.0 | T | 3.9 | 10.0 | 10.9 | 9.4 | 6.7 | 4.2 | T | 0.0 | 45.1 |
| 1970-71 | 0.0 | 0.0 | 0.0 | 0.0 | 1.7 | 9.8 | 8.7 | 5.9 | 8.7 | 0.6 | 0.0 | 0.0 | 35.4 |
| 1971-72 | 0.0 | 0.0 | 0.0 | 0.0 | 4.2 | 2.6 | 7.9 | 9.3 | 2.5 | 2.5 | 0.0 | 0.0 | 29.0 |
| 1972-73 | 0.0 | 0.0 | 0.0 | T | 7.1 | 12.5 | 2.4 | 12.8 | 10.1 | 0.1 | T | 0.0 | 45.0 |
| 1973-74 | 0.0 | 0.0 | 0.0 | 0.0 | 0.1 | 16.4 | 14.1 | 11.2 | 5.7 | 1.7 | T | 0.0 | 49.2 |
| 1974-75 | 0.0 | 0.0 | 0.0 | T | 7.7 | 34.9 | 4.9 | 7.5 | 4.5 | 3.6 | 0.0 | 0.0 | 63.1 |
| 1975-76 | 0.0 | 0.0 | 0.0 | 0.0 | 6.5 | 19.8 | 15.1 | 4.9 | 7.5 | 2.1 | T | 0.0 | 55.9 |
| 1976-77 | 0.0 | 0.0 | 0.0 | T | 1.4 | 9.8 | 14.7 | 5.0 | 12.3 | 0.7 | 0.0 | 0.0 | 43.9 |
| 1977-78 | 0.0 | 0.0 | 0.0 | 0.0 | 7.4 | 16.6 | 29.6 | 5.3 | 2.5 | 0.3 | 0.0 | 0.0 | 61.7 |
| 1978-79 | 0.0 | 0.0 | 0.0 | 0.0 | 6.1 | 6.6 | 13.3 | 3.9 | 2.7 | 3.0 | 0.0 | 0.0 | 35.6 |
| 1979-80 | 0.0 | 0.0 | 0.0 | T | 3.2 | 2.3 | 2.8 | 5.5 | 11.7 | 1.4 | 0.0 | 0.0 | 26.9 |
| 1980-81 | 0.0 | 0.0 | 0.0 | 2.9 | 3.4 | 10.5 | 7.6 | 13.4 | 0.6 | 0.0 | 0.0 | | 38.4 |
| 1981-82 | 0.0 | 0.0 | 0.0 | 0.1 | 0.7 | 17.3 | 20.0 | 13.3 | 13.6 | 9.0 | 0.0 | 0.0 | 74.0 |
| 1982-83 | 0.0 | 0.0 | 0.0 | T | 1.8 | 1.4 | 1.5 | 4.3 | 7.6 | 3.4 | 0.0 | 0.0 | 20.0 |
| 1983-84 | 0.0 | 0.0 | 0.0 | 3.5 | 19.9 | 9.9 | 8.7 | 9.7 | 0.1 | 0.0 | 0.0 | | 51.8 |
| 1984-85 | 0.0 | 0.0 | 0.0 | 0.0 | 4.1 | 6.2 | 20.9 | 16.9 | 6.1 | 0.9 | 0.0 | 0.0 | 55.1 |
| 1985-86 | 0.0 | 0.0 | 0.0 | 0.0 | 2.0 | 14.1 | 8.6 | 20.8 | 7.4 | 1.3 | 0.0 | 0.0 | 54.2 |
| 1986-87 | 0.0 | 0.0 | 0.0 | T | 3.3 | 6.0 | 24.0 | 2.0 | 13.3 | 1.1 | 0.0 | 0.0 | 49.7 |
| 1987-88 | 0.0 | 0.0 | 0.0 | T | 0.7 | 15.3 | 7.0 | 19.2 | 2.7 | 0.2 | 0.0 | 0.0 | 45.1 |
| 1988-89 | 0.0 | 0.0 | 0.0 | T | 1.0 | 6.3 | 5.3 | 9.6 | 2.4 | 0.5 | T | 0.0 | 25.1 |
| 1989-90 | 0.0 | 0.0 | 0.0 | 2.7 | 2.4 | 11.8 | 4.0 | 11.1 | 7.8 | 2.0 | 0.0 | 0.0 | 41.8 |
| 1990-91 | 0.0 | 0.0 | T | 0.0 | T | 13.2 | | | | | | | |
| Record Mean | 0.0 | 0.0 | T | 0.2 | 3.1 | 10.6 | 10.0 | 9.1 | 6.8 | 1.7 | T | 0.0 | 41.5 |

**See Reference Notes, relative to all above tables, on preceding page.**

Grand Rapids, Michigan, is located in the west-central part of Kent County, in the picturesque Grand River valley about 30 air miles east of Lake Michigan. The Grand River, the longest stream in Michigan, flows through the city and bisects it into east and west sections. High hills rise on either side of the valley. Elevations range from 602 feet on the valley floor to 1,020 feet in the extreme southern part of Kent County, southwest of the airport.

Grand Rapids is under the natural climatic influence of Lake Michigan. In spring the cooling effect of Lake Michigan helps retard the growth of vegetation until the danger of frost has passed. The warming effect in the fall retards frost until most of the crops have matured. Fall is a colorful time of year in western Michigan, compensating for the late spring. During the winter, excessive cloudiness and numerous snow flurries occur with strong westerly winds. The tempering effect of Lake Michigan on cold waves coming in from the west and northwest is quite evident.

The tempering effect of the lake promotes the growth of a great variety of fruit trees and berries, especially apples, peaches, cherries, and blueberries. The intense cold of winter is modified, thus reducing winter kill of fruit trees. Summer days are pleasantly warm and most summer nights are quite comfortable, although there are about three weeks of hot, humid weather during most summers. Prolonged severe cold waves with below-zero temperatures are infrequent. The temperature usually rises to above zero during the daytime hours regardless of early morning readings.

July is the sunniest month and December is the month with the least sunshine. November through January is usually a period of excessive cloudiness and minimal sunshine.

Precipitation is usually ample for the growth and development of all vegetation. About one-half of the annual precipitation falls during the growing season, May through September. Droughts occur occasionally, but are seldom of protracted length. The snowfall season extends from mid-November to mid-March. Some winters have had continuous snow cover throughout this period, although there is usually a mid-winter thaw. The Grand River flows through the city and reaches critical heights a couple of times each year, generally once in January-February and again in March-April. Overflow is generally limited to the lowlands of the flood plain.

November is one of the windiest months and although violent windstorms are infrequent, gusts have on occasion exceeded 65 mph. Summer thunderstorms occasionally produce gusty winds over 60 mph.

## TABLE 1 — NORMALS, MEANS AND EXTREMES

GRAND RAPIDS, MICHIGAN

LATITUDE: 42°53'N    LONGITUDE: 85°31'W    ELEVATION: FT. GRND  784 BARO  819    TIME ZONE: EASTERN    WBAN: 94860

| | (a) | JAN | FEB | MAR | APR | MAY | JUNE | JULY | AUG | SEP | OCT | NOV | DEC | YEAR |
|---|---|---|---|---|---|---|---|---|---|---|---|---|---|---|
| **TEMPERATURE °F:** | | | | | | | | | | | | | | |
| Normals | | | | | | | | | | | | | | |
| -Daily Maximum | | 29.0 | 31.7 | 41.6 | 56.9 | 69.4 | 78.9 | 83.0 | 81.1 | 73.4 | 61.4 | 46.0 | 33.8 | 57.2 |
| -Daily Minimum | | 14.9 | 15.6 | 24.5 | 35.6 | 45.5 | 55.3 | 59.8 | 58.1 | 50.8 | 40.4 | 30.9 | 20.7 | 37.7 |
| -Monthly | | 22.0 | 23.7 | 33.1 | 46.3 | 57.5 | 67.1 | 71.4 | 69.6 | 62.1 | 50.9 | 38.5 | 27.3 | 47.5 |
| Extremes | | | | | | | | | | | | | | |
| -Record Highest | 26 | 62 | 67 | 78 | 88 | 92 | 98 | 100 | 100 | 93 | 87 | 77 | 67 | 100 |
| -Year | | 1967 | 1976 | 1986 | 1970 | 1978 | 1988 | 1988 | 1964 | 1973 | 1975 | 1975 | 1982 | JUL 1988 |
| -Record Lowest | 26 | -21 | -19 | -8 | 3 | 22 | 33 | 41 | 39 | 28 | 18 | 5 | -18 | -21 |
| -Year | | 1979 | 1973 | 1978 | 1982 | 1966 | 1972 | 1983 | 1976 | 1974 | 1988 | 1977 | 1983 | JAN 1979 |
| **NORMAL DEGREE DAYS:** | | | | | | | | | | | | | | |
| Heating (base 65°F) | | 1333 | 1156 | 989 | 561 | 262 | 54 | 12 | 23 | 130 | 443 | 795 | 1169 | 6927 |
| Cooling (base 65°F) | | 0 | 0 | 0 | 0 | 29 | 117 | 210 | 165 | 43 | 6 | 0 | 0 | 570 |
| **% OF POSSIBLE SUNSHINE** | 26 | 30 | 39 | 45 | 52 | 55 | 61 | 64 | 61 | 54 | 44 | 27 | 22 | 46 |
| **MEAN SKY COVER (tenths)** | | | | | | | | | | | | | | |
| Sunrise - Sunset | 26 | 8.3 | 7.7 | 7.4 | 6.8 | 6.4 | 6.1 | 5.7 | 5.9 | 6.3 | 7.0 | 8.2 | 8.6 | 7.1 |
| **MEAN NUMBER OF DAYS:** | | | | | | | | | | | | | | |
| Sunrise to Sunset | | | | | | | | | | | | | | |
| -Clear | 26 | 2.6 | 3.4 | 4.7 | 6.4 | 6.8 | 6.7 | 8.3 | 8.2 | 7.3 | 5.5 | 2.8 | 2.0 | 64.7 |
| -Partly Cloudy | 26 | 5.0 | 6.1 | 7.1 | 7.1 | 9.3 | 11.3 | 12.3 | 11.5 | 9.0 | 8.3 | 5.2 | 3.8 | 96.0 |
| -Cloudy | 26 | 23.4 | 18.8 | 19.2 | 16.5 | 14.9 | 12.0 | 10.4 | 11.3 | 13.8 | 17.2 | 22.0 | 25.1 | 204.7 |
| Precipitation | | | | | | | | | | | | | | |
| .01 inches or more | 26 | 16.2 | 11.9 | 12.6 | 13.0 | 10.4 | 10.0 | 9.1 | 9.5 | 10.3 | 11.3 | 13.3 | 16.5 | 144.1 |
| Snow,Ice pellets | | | | | | | | | | | | | | |
| 1.0 inches or more | 26 | 7.0 | 4.1 | 3.0 | 0.9 | 0.0 | 0.0 | 0.0 | 0.0 | 0.0 | 0.2 | 2.6 | 6.0 | 23.8 |
| Thunderstorms | 26 | 0.3 | 0.3 | 1.7 | 3.5 | 3.8 | 5.7 | 6.1 | 5.7 | 4.3 | 1.5 | 1.4 | 0.5 | 34.7 |
| Heavy Fog Visibility | | | | | | | | | | | | | | |
| 1/4 mile or less | 26 | 2.0 | 2.2 | 2.3 | 1.8 | 1.6 | 1.5 | 1.3 | 2.1 | 2.3 | 2.2 | 2.3 | 3.5 | 25.0 |
| Temperature °F | | | | | | | | | | | | | | |
| -Maximum | | | | | | | | | | | | | | |
| 90° and above | 26 | 0.0 | 0.0 | 0.0 | 0.0 | 0.5 | 2.2 | 5.2 | 2.7 | 0.4 | 0.0 | 0.0 | 0.0 | 11.0 |
| 32° and below | 26 | 19.6 | 15.4 | 5.8 | 0.5 | 0.0 | 0.0 | 0.0 | 0.0 | 0.0 | 0.0 | 2.5 | 14.2 | 58.0 |
| -Minimum | | | | | | | | | | | | | | |
| 32° and below | 26 | 29.5 | 26.3 | 24.1 | 11.8 | 2.3 | 0.0 | 0.0 | 0.0 | 0.3 | 6.3 | 17.6 | 27.8 | 145.9 |
| 0° and below | 26 | 4.1 | 3.0 | 0.5 | 0.0 | 0.0 | 0.0 | 0.0 | 0.0 | 0.0 | 0.0 | 0.0 | 1.5 | 9.0 |
| **AVG. STATION PRESS.(mb)** | 17 | 987.2 | 988.3 | 986.2 | 985.3 | 985.4 | 985.6 | 987.1 | 988.0 | 988.6 | 988.8 | 987.1 | 987.4 | 987.1 |
| **RELATIVE HUMIDITY (%)** | | | | | | | | | | | | | | |
| Hour 01 | 26 | 80 | 79 | 76 | 74 | 76 | 80 | 82 | 85 | 86 | 82 | 81 | 81 | 80 |
| Hour 07 | 26 | 81 | 80 | 80 | 79 | 79 | 81 | 84 | 88 | 89 | 85 | 83 | 83 | 83 |
| Hour 13 (Local Time) | 26 | 72 | 68 | 63 | 57 | 53 | 55 | 55 | 58 | 61 | 62 | 69 | 75 | 62 |
| Hour 19 | 26 | 76 | 72 | 66 | 59 | 55 | 57 | 57 | 62 | 71 | 72 | 76 | 79 | 67 |
| **PRECIPITATION (inches):** | | | | | | | | | | | | | | |
| Water Equivalent | | | | | | | | | | | | | | |
| -Normal | | 1.91 | 1.53 | 2.48 | 3.56 | 3.03 | 3.86 | 3.02 | 3.45 | 3.14 | 2.89 | 2.93 | 2.55 | 34.35 |
| -Maximum Monthly | 26 | 4.36 | 3.34 | 5.12 | 6.11 | 8.29 | 8.21 | 6.42 | 8.46 | 11.85 | 6.30 | 7.81 | 6.63 | 11.85 |
| -Year | | 1975 | 1986 | 1974 | 1981 | 1981 | 1967 | 1969 | 1987 | 1986 | 1969 | 1966 | 1971 | SEP 1986 |
| -Minimum Monthly | 26 | 0.47 | 0.33 | 1.08 | 1.79 | 0.94 | 0.25 | 0.81 | 0.14 | T | 0.60 | 0.95 | 0.66 | T |
| -Year | | 1981 | 1969 | 1968 | 1989 | 1987 | 1988 | 1976 | 1969 | 1979 | 1964 | 1986 | 1969 | SEP 1979 |
| -Maximum in 24 hrs | 26 | 1.81 | 1.52 | 1.78 | 2.07 | 5.48 | 3.28 | 2.53 | 3.68 | 4.55 | 2.01 | 2.66 | 2.79 | 5.48 |
| -Year | | 1975 | 1985 | 1985 | 1976 | 1981 | 1972 | 1969 | 1987 | 1986 | 1969 | 1966 | 1982 | MAY 1981 |
| Snow,Ice pellets | | | | | | | | | | | | | | |
| -Maximum Monthly | 26 | 45.5 | 25.1 | 36.0 | 12.4 | 0.1 | 0.0 | 0.0 | 0.0 | T | 8.4 | 19.4 | 34.8 | 45.5 |
| -Year | | 1979 | 1989 | 1965 | 1982 | 1976 | | | | 1967 | 1967 | 1989 | 1983 | JAN 1979 |
| -Maximum in 24 hrs | 26 | 16.1 | 9.1 | 13.2 | 9.8 | 0.1 | 0.0 | 0.0 | 0.0 | T | 8.4 | 8.3 | 15.1 | 16.1 |
| -Year | | 1978 | 1985 | 1970 | 1975 | 1976 | | | | 1967 | 1967 | 1965 | 1970 | JAN 1978 |
| **WIND:** | | | | | | | | | | | | | | |
| Mean Speed (mph) | 26 | 11.4 | 10.6 | 11.1 | 11.0 | 9.6 | 8.9 | 8.1 | 7.9 | 8.3 | 9.3 | 10.4 | 10.8 | 9.8 |
| Prevailing Direction | | | | | | | | | | | | | | |
| Fastest Obs. 1 Min. | | | | | | | | | | | | | | |
| -Direction (!!!) | 10 | 26 | 33 | 25 | 24 | 24 | 30 | 29 | 20 | 36 | 23 | 23 | 24 | 24 |
| -Speed (MPH) | 10 | 39 | 37 | 41 | 41 | 37 | 35 | 35 | 31 | 31 | 29 | 40 | 39 | 41 |
| -Year | | 1980 | 1987 | 1982 | 1984 | 1985 | 1989 | 1980 | 1989 | 1989 | 1987 | 1985 | 1982 | APR 1984 |
| Peak Gust | | | | | | | | | | | | | | |
| -Direction (!!!) | 6 | W | NW | SW | SW | SW | NW | SW | N | N | SW | SW | E | SW |
| -Speed (mph) | 6 | 51 | 55 | 52 | 63 | 68 | 54 | 48 | 61 | 52 | 45 | 52 | 51 | 68 |
| -Date | | 1989 | 1987 | 1985 | 1984 | 1987 | 1989 | 1988 | 1984 | 1989 | 1988 | 1988 | 1987 | MAY 1987 |

**See Reference Notes to this table on the following page.**

## TABLE 2 — PRECIPITATION (inches)  GRAND RAPIDS, MICHIGAN

| YEAR | JAN | FEB | MAR | APR | MAY | JUNE | JULY | AUG | SEP | OCT | NOV | DEC | ANNUAL |
|------|-----|-----|-----|-----|-----|------|------|-----|-----|-----|-----|-----|--------|
| 1961 | 1.35 | 0.90 | 3.26 | 3.98 | 1.03 | 1.29 | 1.90 | 2.06 | 9.15 | 1.62 | 1.55 | 1.54 | 29.63 |
| 1962 | 3.02 | 1.68 | 1.74 | 2.66 | 2.41 | 1.11 | 2.14 | 1.08 | 2.82 | 1.64 | 0.63 | 1.84 | 22.77 |
| #1963 | 2.26 | 0.46 | 3.45 | 3.84 | 2.74 | 2.71 | 3.41 | 3.31 | 2.97 | 1.04 | 2.50 | 1.54 | 30.23 |
| 1964 | 1.42 | 0.73 | 3.54 | 5.28 | 3.96 | 4.12 | 2.14 | 5.36 | 3.16 | 0.60 | 2.13 | 2.01 | 32.28 |
| 1965 | 3.99 | 1.58 | 3.11 | 2.49 | 1.53 | 2.89 |  | 1.96 | 6.62 | 2.10 | 2.35 | 4.23 | 38.21 |
| 1966 | 1.22 | 2.28 | 2.65 | 4.62 | 2.16 | 2.36 | 1.95 | 3.82 | 1.92 | 2.33 | 4.35 | 3.60 | 40.75 |
| 1967 | 1.94 | 1.13 | 2.49 | 4.27 | 1.86 | 8.21 | 2.77 | 3.34 | 2.37 | 4.42 | 4.28 | 3.16 | 36.14 |
| 1968 | 1.55 | 2.12 | 1.08 | 2.40 | 2.67 | 5.02 | 2.74 | 2.86 | 4.21 | 4.05 | 3.00 | 0.66 | 34.76 |
| 1969 | 2.39 | 0.33 | 1.29 | 5.16 | 3.40 | 4.74 | 6.42 | 0.93 | 2.89 | 6.30 | 3.65 | 1.89 | 43.51 |
| 1970 | 1.18 | 0.51 | 2.43 | 3.27 | 4.24 | 6.53 | 6.32 | 2.89 | 1.39 | 2.84 | 6.63 | 0.95 | 31.16 |
| 1971 | 1.04 | 2.48 | 1.77 | 2.27 | 1.05 | 2.01 | 2.46 | 0.92 | 6.30 | 2.92 | 2.06 | 4.96 | 37.38 |
| 1972 | 1.26 | 0.90 | 2.11 | 3.85 | 1.99 | 4.64 | 3.72 | 5.01 | 3.96 | 4.12 | 3.54 | 3.28 | 34.43 |
| 1973 | 1.66 | 1.15 | 3.34 | 3.47 | 4.31 | 3.58 | 2.06 | 1.45 | 2.47 | 2.44 | 3.11 | 1.83 | 36.82 |
| 1974 | 3.23 | 2.09 | 5.12 | 2.93 | 4.01 | 0.97 | 4.61 | 4.43 | 2.05 | 2.44 | 3.82 | 4.02 | 41.25 |
| 1975 | 4.36 | 1.92 | 2.28 | 4.07 | 2.08 | 5.97 | 2.31 | 7.38 | 2.00 | 1.04 | 3.82 | 4.02 | 30.57 |
| 1976 | 1.67 | 2.13 | 4.99 | 4.75 | 6.63 | 2.79 | 0.81 | 1.03 | 1.21 | 2.00 | 1.51 | 1.05 | 37.78 |
| 1977 | 1.59 | 1.35 | 3.81 | 4.04 | 1.33 | 3.50 | 5.16 | 4.77 | 4.26 | 2.28 | 2.34 | 3.35 | 36.53 |
| 1978 | 2.22 | 0.54 | 2.01 | 2.55 | 2.91 | 4.65 | 2.83 | 5.00 | 5.62 | 3.05 | 1.83 | 3.32 | 32.64 |
| 1979 | 2.09 | 0.61 | 3.72 | 3.56 | 1.37 | 4.16 | 2.27 | 4.33 | T | 2.10 | 5.46 | 2.97 | 36.90 |
| 1980 | 1.76 | 1.76 | 1.74 | 3.64 | 3.19 | 4.00 | 3.74 | 3.18 | 4.57 | 1.99 | 1.57 | 3.60 |  |
| 1981 | 0.47 | 2.03 | 1.29 | 6.11 | 8.29 | 4.22 | 3.74 | 2.95 | 9.52 | 1.42 | 2.54 | 2.58 | 44.84 |
| 1982 | 2.98 | 0.36 | 3.36 | 2.11 | 3.63 | 2.45 | 3.81 | 3.07 | 1.92 | 5.36 | 6.49 | 1.10 | 36.96 |
| 1983 | 1.33 | 1.12 | 3.30 | 5.06 | 4.64 | 2.09 | 4.76 | 1.49 | 4.87 | 2.66 | 2.79 | 4.37 | 37.11 |
| 1984 | 0.94 | 1.15 | 2.77 | 2.10 | 4.77 | 0.62 | 2.12 | 1.49 | 2.16 | 3.34 | 2.85 | 2.00 | 28.68 |
| 1985 | 1.94 | 3.26 | 4.20 | 2.54 | 1.36 | 1.68 | 3.09 | 6.48 | 4.26 | 4.64 | 5.45 | 1.04 | 40.90 |
| 1986 | 1.07 | 3.34 | 2.35 | 2.58 | 3.88 | 7.14 | 5.27 | 5.30 | 11.85 | 2.76 | 2.49 | 3.29 | 47.53 |
| 1987 | 0.67 | 0.37 | 1.15 | 2.40 | 0.94 | 3.56 | 2.93 | 8.46 | 4.47 | 2.33 | 4.82 | 1.88 | 33.06 |
| 1988 | 2.39 | 1.14 | 2.12 | 3.11 | 1.07 | 0.25 | 3.69 | 3.04 | 7.49 | 5.37 | 1.53 | 0.97 | 36.37 |
| 1989 | 0.95 | 1.01 | 2.47 | 1.79 | 4.33 | 5.02 | 1.29 | 4.78 | 4.90 | 1.53 | 4.86 | 2.97 | 33.90 |
| 1990 | 2.39 | 2.08 | 1.96 | 2.23 | 4.39 | 3.00 | 3.73 | 3.40 | 4.22 | 5.05 | 7.14 | 2.97 | 42.56 |
| Record Mean | 2.18 | 1.84 | 2.50 | 2.96 | 3.31 | 3.55 | 2.92 | 2.83 | 3.55 | 2.77 | 2.80 | 2.48 | 33.67 |

## TABLE 3 — AVERAGE TEMPERATURE (deg. F)  GRAND RAPIDS, MICHIGAN

| YEAR | JAN | FEB | MAR | APR | MAY | JUNE | JULY | AUG | SEP | OCT | NOV | DEC | ANNUAL |
|------|-----|-----|-----|-----|-----|------|------|-----|-----|-----|-----|-----|--------|
| 1961 | 20.9 | 29.2 | 37.7 | 42.3 | 54.3 | 65.9 | 71.4 | 70.0 | 67.0 | 52.9 | 40.1 | 27.4 | 48.3 |
| 1962 | 19.3 | 21.6 | 32.6 | 45.9 | 55.4 | 68.2 | 69.7 | 70.7 | 60.4 | 53.3 | 24.5 | 24.5 | 47.3 |
| #1963 | 15.9 | 16.9 | 35.4 | 47.6 | 55.4 | 69.1 | 72.1 | 67.3 | 61.2 | 47.2 | 41.8 | 26.0 | 48.6 |
| 1964 | 27.5 | 25.0 | 34.5 | 48.2 | 62.0 | 68.9 | 73.1 | 67.9 | 62.3 | 50.0 | 40.0 | 33.5 | 47.3 |
| 1965 | 22.5 | 23.8 | 26.2 | 42.8 | 62.3 | 65.9 | 70.0 | 67.9 | 62.3 | 50.0 | 40.0 | 29.2 | 47.7 |
| 1966 | 19.1 | 25.5 | 37.1 | 43.8 | 52.0 | 69.2 | 73.6 | 68.5 | 61.4 | 51.2 | 42.1 | 29.2 | 47.7 |
| 1967 | 28.6 | 20.4 | 34.1 | 46.4 | 51.9 | 69.3 | 69.3 | 68.6 | 60.3 | 49.9 | 34.5 | 29.9 | 46.7 |
| 1968 | 21.0 | 21.4 | 38.0 | 48.8 | 54.0 | 66.7 | 69.8 | 70.6 | 63.7 | 51.8 | 33.5 | 25.0 | 47.3 |
| 1969 | 20.8 | 24.4 | 29.3 | 46.4 | 55.7 | 61.8 | 71.3 | 72.1 | 62.4 | 47.9 | 33.5 | 25.7 | 45.9 |
| 1970 | 17.0 | 22.4 | 28.8 | 46.8 | 59.4 | 66.8 | 69.2 | 70.1 | 65.6 | 58.3 | 38.0 | 32.0 | 46.8 |
| 1971 | 18.3 | 24.1 | 29.0 | 43.9 | 54.0 | 63.5 | 70.9 | 68.7 | 62.0 | 46.1 | 39.6 | 26.6 | 47.6 |
| 1972 | 20.8 | 21.9 | 29.7 | 42.3 | 59.3 | 63.5 | 63.5 | 72.7 | 63.4 | 55.0 | 39.9 | 26.2 | 49.3 |
| 1973 | 27.4 | 22.8 | 41.9 | 46.8 | 53.7 | 63.9 | 69.0 | 72.4 | 67.3 | 56.4 | 28.4 | 28.4 | 47.5 |
| 1974 | 25.7 | 21.1 | 33.6 | 47.2 | 53.2 | 63.0 | 71.1 | 70.6 | 57.0 | 53.0 | 44.7 | 27.3 | 47.5 |
| 1975 | 25.2 | 24.3 | 28.8 | 39.8 | 60.7 | 67.6 | 70.5 | 67.6 | 60.2 | 45.7 | 31.5 | 19.1 | 47.0 |
| 1976 | 18.9 | 31.0 | 37.9 | 48.2 | 53.9 | 69.5 | 72.5 | 68.9 | 60.2 | 48.6 | 39.5 | 25.9 | 46.4 |
| 1977 | 12.7 | 22.8 | 40.0 | 52.1 | 65.8 | 64.5 | 74.0 | 67.9 | 62.9 | 47.2 | 37.6 | 26.6 | 48.1 |
| 1978 | 19.3 | 14.4 | 27.9 | 45.3 | 59.9 | 66.8 | 70.4 | 68.1 | 63.4 | 51.5 | 40.5 | 33.0 | 45.6 |
| 1979 | 17.1 | 15.0 | 36.9 | 44.5 | 57.7 | 67.6 | 71.1 | 68.5 | 62.7 | 45.8 | 35.7 | 25.1 | 47.2 |
| 1980 | 25.1 | 22.7 | 32.5 | 47.0 | 59.9 | 64.4 | 72.7 | 72.6 | 62.7 | 48.2 | 39.8 | 28.7 | 47.3 |
| 1981 | 20.8 | 30.2 | 35.1 | 47.3 | 55.5 | 68.6 | 72.1 | 70.7 | 60.9 | 53.6 | 40.8 | 36.2 | 48.2 |
| 1982 | 17.2 | 22.1 | 32.5 | 41.8 | 65.0 | 62.8 | 73.1 | 68.6 | 61.9 | 50.7 | 40.7 | 19.2 | 48.0 |
| 1983 | 27.6 | 30.9 | 36.9 | 42.6 | 52.8 | 67.7 | 74.7 | 72.2 | 62.4 | 60.5 | 54.2 | 32.2 | 48.2 |
| 1984 | 17.1 | 34.0 | 28.9 | 47.3 | 53.5 | 70.1 | 70.1 | 73.0 | 60.5 | 54.2 | 40.3 | 22.3 | 47.1 |
| 1985 | 18.6 | 21.3 | 36.2 | 51.7 | 60.4 | 63.8 | 70.7 | 67.4 | 63.6 | 50.6 | 38.4 | 22.3 | 47.6 |
| 1986 | 22.7 | 22.5 | 36.7 | 49.7 | 58.8 | 64.4 | 72.5 | 66.0 | 62.8 | 50.2 | 35.0 | 29.8 | 47.6 |
| 1987 | 25.4 | 29.9 | 37.3 | 50.1 | 62.6 | 71.2 | 74.1 | 69.3 | 62.2 | 45.0 | 41.1 | 31.5 | 50.0 |
| 1988 | 20.8 | 20.7 | 34.1 | 47.1 | 60.9 | 68.5 | 74.7 | 73.4 | 61.3 | 44.2 | 40.7 | 27.3 | 47.8 |
| 1989 | 30.5 | 19.7 | 31.8 | 43.9 | 55.8 | 65.9 | 70.3 | 68.4 | 59.4 | 51.1 | 35.7 | 17.2 | 45.9 |
| 1990 | 32.1 | 28.1 | 37.1 | 47.7 | 55.0 | 67.1 | 70.3 | 69.0 | 62.8 | 49.9 | 43.3 | 30.0 | 49.4 |
| Record Mean | 24.0 | 24.4 | 34.0 | 46.7 | 58.0 | 67.8 | 72.6 | 70.4 | 63.0 | 51.6 | 39.2 | 28.2 | 48.4 |
| Max | 30.5 | 31.6 | 42.2 | 56.6 | 68.8 | 78.8 | 83.4 | 81.1 | 73.2 | 60.9 | 47.1 | 34.1 | 57.3 |
| Min | 17.4 | 17.1 | 25.8 | 36.7 | 47.1 | 56.8 | 61.8 | 59.8 | 52.8 | 42.3 | 32.3 | 22.3 | 39.4 |

## REFERENCE NOTES FOR TABLES 1, 2, 3 and 6    (GRAND RAPIDS, MI)

### GENERAL

T - TRACE AMOUNT
BLANK ENTRIES DENOTE MISSING/UNREPORTED DATA.
# INDICATES A STATION OR INSTRUMENT RELOCATION.

### SPECIFIC

#### TABLE 1

(a) - LENGTH OF RECORD IN YEARS. ALTHOUGH INDIVIDUAL MONTHS MAY BE MISSING.

\* LESS THAN .05

NORMALS — BASED ON THE 1951-1980 RECORD PERIOD.
EXTREMES — DATES ARE THE MOST RECENT OCCURRENCE.
WIND DIR. — NUMERALS SHOW TENS OF DEGREES CLOCKWISE FROM TRUE NORTH.
"00" INDICATES CALM.
RESULTANT WIND DIRECTIONS ARE GIVEN TO WHOLE DEGREES.

#### TABLE 3

MAX AND MIN ARE LONG-TERM MEAN DAILY MAXIMUM AND MEAN DAILY MINIMUM TEMPERATURES.

### EXCEPTIONS

#### TABLES 2, 3, and 6

RECORD MEANS ARE THROUGH THE CURRENT YEAR, BEGINNING IN  1894 FOR TEMPERATURE
1870 FOR PRECIPITATION
1964 FOR SNOWFALL

**TABLE 4**

HEATING DEGREE DAYS Base 65 deg. F — GRAND RAPIDS, MICHIGAN

| SEASON | JULY | AUG | SEP | OCT | NOV | DEC | JAN | FEB | MAR | APR | MAY | JUNE | TOTAL |
|---|---|---|---|---|---|---|---|---|---|---|---|---|---|
| 1961-62 | 4 | 14 | 89 | 374 | 741 | 1158 | 1409 | 1209 | 997 | 581 | 167 | 35 | 6778 |
| 1962-63 | 10 | 7 | 184 | 372 | 763 | 1253 | 1513 | 1342 | 911 | 514 | 307 | 62 | 7238 |
| #1963-64 | 8 | 36 | 135 | 203 | 620 | 1345 | 1157 | 1154 | 940 | 501 | 149 | 73 | 6321 |
| 1964-65 | 12 | 54 | 179 | 545 | 690 | 1202 | 1310 | 1145 | 1197 | 657 | 142 | 57 | 7190 |
| 1965-66 | 5 | 50 | 145 | 462 | 743 | 968 | 1414 | 1102 | 860 | 632 | 400 | 47 | 6828 |
| 1966-67 | 0 | 12 | 146 | 426 | 680 | 1102 | 1120 | 1242 | 950 | 554 | 410 | 9 | 6651 |
| 1967-68 | 38 | 47 | 179 | 477 | 909 | 1080 | 1356 | 1255 | 827 | 482 | 342 | 70 | 7062 |
| 1968-69 | 30 | 36 | 90 | 434 | 805 | 1254 | 1360 | 1132 | 1102 | 550 | 300 | 151 | 7244 |
| 1969-70 | 3 | 2 | 145 | 524 | 938 | 1232 | 1481 | 1186 | 1117 | 559 | 216 | 61 | 7464 |
| 1970-71 | 13 | 17 | 150 | 397 | 798 | 1210 | 1441 | 1140 | 1110 | 626 | 342 | 35 | 7279 |
| 1971-72 | 15 | 11 | 107 | 233 | 800 | 1016 | 1365 | 1240 | 1089 | 675 | 204 | 102 | 6857 |
| 1972-73 | 28 | 41 | 126 | 577 | 867 | 1185 | 1162 | 1178 | 708 | 552 | 341 | 4 | 6769 |
| 1973-74 | 1 | 7 | 136 | 314 | 748 | 1196 | 1212 | 1225 | 967 | 532 | 364 | 113 | 6815 |
| 1974-75 | 5 | 22 | 275 | 555 | 816 | 1127 | 1227 | 1133 | 1113 | 750 | 191 | 61 | 7275 |
| 1975-76 | 16 | 5 | 242 | 382 | 602 | 1161 | 1420 | 980 | 835 | 526 | 342 | 18 | 6529 |
| 1976-77 | 0 | 32 | 185 | 591 | 999 | 1415 | 1616 | 1177 | 765 | 401 | 106 | 91 | 7378 |
| 1977-78 | 3 | 48 | 99 | 501 | 759 | 1204 | 1407 | 1413 | 863 | 584 | 213 | 62 | 7433 |
| 1978-79 | 15 | 22 | 124 | 545 | 816 | 1182 | 1477 | 1393 | 863 | 607 | 264 | 42 | 7350 |
| 1979-80 | 7 | 31 | 109 | 431 | 731 | 984 | 1230 | 1221 | 1000 | 541 | 189 | 106 | 6580 |
| 1980-81 | 0 | 4 | 115 | 588 | 821 | 1227 | 1363 | 969 | 919 | 525 | 298 | 8 | 6837 |
| 1981-82 | 7 | 5 | 173 | 513 | 749 | 1196 | 1475 | 1196 | 998 | 689 | 91 | 98 | 7110 |
| 1982-83 | 6 | 34 | 140 | 361 | 717 | 884 | 1151 | 949 | 866 | 663 | 373 | 61 | 6205 |
| 1983-84 | 16 | 2 | 149 | 440 | 721 | 1413 | 1480 | 892 | 1107 | 532 | 353 | 13 | 7118 |
| 1984-85 | 16 | 4 | 189 | 333 | 735 | 1014 | 1431 | 1216 | 886 | 428 | 173 | 81 | 6506 |
| 1985-86 | 9 | 17 | 157 | 436 | 790 | 1316 | 1302 | 1186 | 871 | 466 | 214 | 75 | 6839 |
| 1986-87 | 11 | 56 | 118 | 452 | 894 | 1084 | 1220 | 978 | 849 | 440 | 178 | 20 | 6300 |
| 1987-88 | 18 | 36 | 118 | 610 | 712 | 1032 | 1364 | 1277 | 950 | 531 | 169 | 60 | 6877 |
| 1988-89 | 3 | 21 | 135 | 639 | 722 | 1162 | 1062 | 1263 | 1023 | 625 | 297 | 51 | 7003 |
| 1989-90 | 2 | 23 | 203 | 424 | 874 | 1477 | 1014 | 1026 | 865 | 549 | 306 | 45 | 6808 |
| 1990-91 | 11 | 15 | 139 | 475 | 645 | 1077 | | | | | | | |

**TABLE 5**

COOLING DEGREE DAYS Base 65 deg. F — GRAND RAPIDS, MICHIGAN

| YEAR | JAN | FEB | MAR | APR | MAY | JUNE | JULY | AUG | SEP | OCT | NOV | DEC | TOTAL |
|---|---|---|---|---|---|---|---|---|---|---|---|---|---|
| 1969 | 0 | 0 | 0 | 0 | 21 | 61 | 202 | 229 | 76 | 1 | 0 | 0 | 590 |
| 1970 | 0 | 0 | 0 | 19 | 49 | 122 | 242 | 180 | 55 | 6 | 0 | 0 | 673 |
| 1971 | 0 | 0 | 0 | 0 | 8 | 218 | 154 | 129 | 132 | 31 | 0 | 0 | 672 |
| 1972 | 0 | 0 | 0 | 10 | 37 | 61 | 200 | 163 | 42 | 0 | 0 | 0 | 503 |
| 1973 | 0 | 0 | 0 | 4 | 0 | 157 | 238 | 255 | 96 | 12 | 0 | 0 | 768 |
| 1974 | 0 | 0 | 0 | 0 | 6 | 60 | 201 | 103 | 23 | 3 | 0 | 0 | 400 |
| 1975 | 0 | 0 | 0 | 0 | 65 | 148 | 199 | 184 | 8 | 15 | 0 | 0 | 619 |
| 1976 | 0 | 0 | 0 | 27 | 4 | 158 | 239 | 161 | 49 | 0 | 0 | 0 | 638 |
| 1977 | 0 | 0 | 0 | 19 | 137 | 85 | 286 | 143 | 44 | 0 | 0 | 0 | 714 |
| 1978 | 0 | 0 | 0 | 0 | 62 | 123 | 188 | 125 | 90 | 0 | 0 | 0 | 588 |
| 1979 | 0 | 0 | 0 | 0 | 46 | 129 | 204 | 147 | 69 | 19 | 0 | 0 | 614 |
| 1980 | 0 | 0 | 0 | 6 | 34 | 96 | 247 | 245 | 53 | 0 | 0 | 0 | 681 |
| 1981 | 0 | 0 | 0 | 0 | 13 | 124 | 236 | 190 | 55 | 0 | 0 | 0 | 618 |
| 1982 | 0 | 0 | 0 | 0 | 99 | 40 | 263 | 153 | 55 | 12 | 0 | 0 | 622 |
| 1983 | 0 | 0 | 0 | 0 | 2 | 146 | 325 | 234 | 76 | 5 | 0 | 0 | 788 |
| 1984 | 0 | 0 | 0 | 7 | 5 | 174 | 179 | 259 | 60 | 6 | 0 | 0 | 690 |
| 1985 | 0 | 0 | 0 | 36 | 39 | 52 | 193 | 99 | 119 | 0 | 0 | 0 | 538 |
| 1986 | 0 | 0 | 0 | 14 | 26 | 64 | 252 | 94 | 61 | 0 | 0 | 0 | 511 |
| 1987 | 0 | 0 | 0 | 2 | 110 | 213 | 306 | 174 | 38 | 0 | 0 | 0 | 843 |
| 1988 | 0 | 0 | 0 | 0 | 50 | 170 | 310 | 289 | 29 | 2 | 0 | 0 | 850 |
| 1989 | 0 | 0 | 0 | 0 | 19 | 84 | 223 | 135 | 40 | 0 | 0 | 0 | 501 |
| 1990 | 0 | 0 | 6 | 37 | 6 | 115 | 185 | 144 | 83 | 13 | 0 | 0 | 589 |

**TABLE 6**

SNOWFALL (inches) — GRAND RAPIDS, MICHIGAN

| SEASON | JULY | AUG | SEP | OCT | NOV | DEC | JAN | FEB | MAR | APR | MAY | JUNE | TOTAL |
|---|---|---|---|---|---|---|---|---|---|---|---|---|---|
| 1961-62 | 0.0 | 0.0 | 0.0 | 0.0 | 0.6 | 18.7 | 36.1 | 21.4 | 8.0 | 3.1 | 0.0 | 0.0 | 87.9 |
| 1962-63 | 0.0 | 0.0 | 0.0 | 2.6 | 0.8 | 26.2 | 42.6 | 8.4 | 5.0 | 4.1 | 0.0 | 0.0 | 89.7 |
| #1963-64 | 0.0 | 0.0 | 0.0 | 0.0 | 0.9 | 21.6 | 18.6 | 11.6 | 16.5 | 1.2 | 0.0 | 0.0 | 70.4 |
| 1964-65 | 0.0 | 0.0 | 0.0 | T | 5.8 | 13.4 | 24.1 | 16.7 | 36.0 | 5.4 | 0.0 | 0.0 | 101.4 |
| 1965-66 | 0.0 | 0.0 | T | 0.0 | 9.1 | | 25.9 | 15.0 | 4.6 | 2.8 | T | 0.0 | 67.0 |
| 1966-67 | 0.0 | 0.0 | 0.0 | 0.0 | 16.6 | 17.6 | 29.8 | 17.5 | 10.3 | T | T | 0.0 | 91.8 |
| 1967-68 | 0.0 | 0.0 | T | 8.4 | 11.0 | 9.6 | 11.8 | 8.5 | 4.2 | 1.6 | 0.0 | 0.0 | 55.1 |
| 1968-69 | 0.0 | 0.0 | 0.0 | 0.0 | 4.2 | 26.2 | 27.7 | 6.3 | 7.9 | 0.0 | 0.0 | 0.0 | 72.3 |
| 1969-70 | 0.0 | 0.0 | 0.0 | T | 14.3 | 11.8 | 23.2 | 8.2 | 19.3 | 7.8 | 0.0 | 0.0 | 84.6 |
| 1970-71 | 0.0 | 0.0 | 0.0 | 0.0 | 6.1 | 33.3 | 27.2 | 4.4 | 25.9 | 4.1 | 0.0 | 0.0 | 101.0 |
| 1971-72 | 0.0 | 0.0 | 0.0 | 0.0 | 14.9 | 3.7 | 22.6 | 16.9 | 14.2 | 7.5 | 0.0 | 0.0 | 79.8 |
| 1972-73 | 0.0 | 0.0 | 0.0 | 0.9 | 11.0 | 19.8 | 7.0 | 13.2 | 8.5 | 5.0 | 0.1 | 0.0 | 65.5 |
| 1973-74 | 0.0 | 0.0 | 0.0 | 0.0 | 0.4 | 20.0 | 13.3 | 18.4 | 11.3 | 1.0 | T | 0.0 | 64.4 |
| 1974-75 | 0.0 | 0.0 | 0.0 | 0.4 | 8.9 | 16.5 | 10.7 | 10.6 | 11.8 | 10.0 | 0.0 | 0.0 | 68.9 |
| 1975-76 | 0.0 | 0.0 | 0.0 | 0.0 | 6.6 | 23.3 | 25.0 | 6.5 | 3.5 | 4.2 | 0.1 | 0.0 | 69.2 |
| 1976-77 | 0.0 | 0.0 | 0.0 | 2.0 | 8.5 | 17.7 | 26.1 | 5.0 | 9.5 | 2.0 | 0.0 | 0.0 | 70.8 |
| 1977-78 | 0.0 | 0.0 | 0.0 | 0.0 | 10.6 | 23.2 | 35.8 | 8.8 | 6.2 | T | 0.0 | 0.0 | 84.6 |
| 1978-79 | 0.0 | 0.0 | 0.0 | T | 6.2 | 30.0 | 45.5 | 5.3 | 7.2 | 1.8 | 0.0 | 0.0 | 96.0 |
| 1979-80 | 0.0 | 0.0 | 0.0 | T | 9.4 | 2.6 | 13.3 | 12.6 | 6.6 | 4.0 | T | 0.0 | 48.5 |
| 1980-81 | 0.0 | 0.0 | 0.0 | 0.4 | 5.5 | 17.3 | 8.1 | 18.8 | 1.4 | T | 0.0 | 0.0 | 51.5 |
| 1981-82 | 0.0 | 0.0 | 0.0 | T | 4.4 | 8.9 | 30.3 | 6.7 | 11.8 | 12.4 | 0.0 | 0.0 | 74.5 |
| 1982-83 | 0.0 | 0.0 | 0.0 | 0.0 | 5.2 | 8.2 | 5.7 | 2.9 | 13.2 | 0.7 | 0.0 | 0.0 | 35.9 |
| 1983-84 | 0.0 | 0.0 | 0.0 | T | 4.7 | 34.8 | 19.6 | 1.6 | 10.6 | 0.1 | T | 0.0 | 71.4 |
| 1984-85 | 0.0 | 0.0 | 0.0 | T | 15.7 | 22.6 | 21.3 | 6.7 | 3.3 | 0.2 | 0.0 | 0.0 | 69.6 |
| 1985-86 | 0.0 | 0.0 | 0.0 | 0.0 | 3.5 | 30.7 | 18.4 | 20.2 | 6.1 | 0.2 | 0.0 | 0.0 | 79.1 |
| 1986-87 | 0.0 | 0.0 | 0.0 | 0.0 | 5.3 | 12.7 | 19.2 | 0.9 | 5.7 | 3.8 | 0.0 | 0.0 | 47.6 |
| 1987-88 | 0.0 | 0.0 | 0.0 | 1.6 | 0.7 | 18.2 | 21.9 | 18.1 | 3.4 | 0.3 | 0.0 | 0.0 | 64.2 |
| 1988-89 | 0.0 | 0.0 | 0.0 | 0.2 | 5.5 | 14.4 | 8.7 | 25.1 | 6.3 | 2.2 | T | 0.0 | 62.4 |
| 1989-90 | 0.0 | 0.0 | 0.0 | 5.8 | 19.4 | 25.2 | 10.6 | 23.8 | 2.7 | 2.1 | 0.2 | 0.0 | 89.8 |
| 1990-91 | T | 0.0 | 0.0 | T | 2.0 | 18.6 | | | | | | | |
| Record Mean | T | 0.0 | T | 0.7 | 7.4 | 17.9 | 20.5 | 12.0 | 10.1 | 3.1 | T | 0.0 | 71.7 |

**See Reference Notes, relative to all above tables, on preceding page.**

Houghton Lake is located in north-central lower Michigan. The present station is on the northeast shore of Houghton Lake, the largest inland lake in Michigan, with a circumference of about 32 miles. The Muskegon River source is Higgins Lake, 8 miles to the north. It flows through Houghton Lake, then southwestward to Lake Michigan. The station lies within an elongated bowl shaped 1,000-foot plateau, which extends roughly 50 miles north, 75 miles southwest, and about 20 miles southeast of Houghton Lake. In the immediate area, the land is level to rolling, but there are hills and ridges from 100 to 300 feet higher in elevation surrounding the station. Soils are generally sand, or sandy loam supporting little agricultural production, but the area is rich in natural resources of forests, lakes, and streams.

The interior location diminishes the influence of the larger Great Lakes, which lie 70 to 80 miles east and west of Houghton Lake. Hence, the daily temperature range is larger, especially in summer, and temperature extremes are greater than are found nearer the shores of either Lake Michigan or Lake Huron. Temperatures reach the 100 degree mark about one summer out of ten, and at the other extreme, fall below zero an average of twenty-two times during the winter season.

Precipitation is normally a little heavier during the summer season. About 60 percent of the annual total falls in the six-month period from April through September. The heaviest precipitation occurs with summertime thunderstorms.

Snowfall averages above 80 inches per year at Houghton Lake, with considerable variation from year to year. Much heavier snows, averaging over 100 inches a season, fall within a 30- to 60-mile radius to the north and west of Houghton Lake. Seasonal totals have ranged from 24 inches to over 124 inches. Measurable amounts of snow have occurred in nine of the twelve months, and the average number of months with measurable snowfall is six.

Cloudiness is greatest in the late fall and early winter, while sunshine percentage is highest in the spring and summer. Cloudiness is increased in the late fall due to the moisture and warmth picked up by the westerly and northwesterly winds while crossing Lake Michigan.

The growing season is normally quite short, averaging about 90 days between spring and fall freezes.

**TABLE 1**     # NORMALS, MEANS AND EXTREMES

HOUGHTON LAKE, MICHIGAN

LATITUDE: 44°22'N    LONGITUDE: 84°41'W    ELEVATION: FT. GRND 1149 BARO 1157    TIME ZONE: EASTERN    WBAN: 94814

| | (a) | JAN | FEB | MAR | APR | MAY | JUNE | JULY | AUG | SEP | OCT | NOV | DEC | YEAR |
|---|---|---|---|---|---|---|---|---|---|---|---|---|---|---|
| **TEMPERATURE °F:** | | | | | | | | | | | | | | |
| Normals | | | | | | | | | | | | | | |
| -Daily Maximum | | 25.2 | 28.0 | 37.3 | 52.6 | 65.8 | 74.8 | 78.9 | 76.5 | 68.0 | 56.7 | 41.8 | 29.9 | 53.0 |
| -Daily Minimum | | 8.7 | 8.0 | 17.5 | 31.2 | 41.5 | 50.8 | 55.0 | 53.8 | 46.5 | 37.5 | 27.9 | 15.8 | 32.8 |
| -Monthly | | 17.0 | 18.0 | 27.4 | 41.9 | 53.7 | 62.8 | 67.0 | 65.2 | 57.3 | 47.1 | 34.9 | 22.9 | 42.9 |
| Extremes | | | | | | | | | | | | | | |
| -Record Highest | 25 | 53 | 59 | 71 | 86 | 90 | 95 | 98 | 94 | 92 | 85 | 70 | 63 | 98 |
| -Year | | 1973 | 1984 | 1986 | 1980 | 1988 | 1987 | 1987 | 1988 | 1985 | 1971 | 1978 | 1982 | JUL 1987 |
| -Record Lowest | 25 | -26 | -34 | -23 | 3 | 21 | 29 | 33 | 29 | 21 | 16 | -2 | -21 | -34 |
| -Year | | 1981 | 1979 | 1967 | 1982 | 1966 | 1972 | 1965 | 1982 | 1989 | 1969 | 1989 | 1976 | FEB 1979 |
| **NORMAL DEGREE DAYS:** | | | | | | | | | | | | | | |
| Heating (base 65°F) | | 1488 | 1316 | 1166 | 693 | 364 | 129 | 42 | 89 | 242 | 561 | 903 | 1305 | 8298 |
| Cooling (base 65°F) | | 0 | 0 | 0 | 0 | 14 | 63 | 104 | 95 | 11 | 6 | 0 | 0 | 293 |
| **% OF POSSIBLE SUNSHINE** | | | | | | | | | | | | | | |
| **MEAN SKY COVER (tenths)** | | | | | | | | | | | | | | |
| Sunrise - Sunset | 24 | 8.0 | 7.4 | 7.1 | 6.7 | 6.4 | 6.1 | 5.7 | 5.9 | 6.5 | 7.2 | 8.4 | 8.4 | 7.0 |
| **MEAN NUMBER OF DAYS:** | | | | | | | | | | | | | | |
| Sunrise to Sunset | | | | | | | | | | | | | | |
| -Clear | 24 | 3.0 | 4.4 | 5.9 | 6.5 | 7.2 | 6.6 | 7.8 | 8.4 | 6.4 | 5.2 | 2.4 | 2.3 | 66.1 |
| -Partly Cloudy | 24 | 6.5 | 6.3 | 6.8 | 7.3 | 9.7 | 11.5 | 13.2 | 10.7 | 9.2 | 7.8 | 5.0 | 5.5 | 99.5 |
| -Cloudy | 24 | 21.5 | 17.5 | 18.3 | 16.1 | 14.1 | 11.9 | 10.0 | 11.9 | 14.4 | 18.0 | 22.6 | 23.1 | 199.6 |
| Precipitation | | | | | | | | | | | | | | |
| .01 inches or more | 25 | 14.9 | 11.6 | 12.2 | 11.8 | 10.3 | 10.6 | 9.0 | 10.0 | 11.6 | 11.8 | 13.3 | 15.6 | 142.9 |
| Snow,Ice pellets | | | | | | | | | | | | | | |
| 1.0 inches or more | 25 | 6.3 | 4.8 | 3.6 | 1.5 | 0.1 | 0.0 | 0.0 | 0.0 | 0.0 | 0.3 | 3.1 | 5.6 | 25.2 |
| Thunderstorms | 25 | 0.1 | 0.1 | 0.8 | 2.1 | 4.1 | 5.6 | 6.0 | 6.3 | 4.2 | 1.5 | 0.6 | 0.2 | 31.8 |
| Heavy Fog Visibility | | | | | | | | | | | | | | |
| 1/4 mile or less | 25 | 1.9 | 1.7 | 2.5 | 1.5 | 1.4 | 1.3 | 2.2 | 3.6 | 3.9 | 3.2 | 2.8 | 3.0 | 29.0 |
| Temperature °F | | | | | | | | | | | | | | |
| -Maximum | | | | | | | | | | | | | | |
| 90° and above | 25 | 0.0 | 0.0 | 0.0 | 0.0 | 0.* | 0.9 | 2.0 | 0.5 | 0.* | 0.0 | 0.0 | 0.0 | 3.4 |
| 32° and below | 25 | 24.1 | 18.8 | 9.3 | 1.0 | 0.0 | 0.0 | 0.0 | 0.0 | 0.0 | 0.0 | 5.4 | 19.7 | 78.2 |
| -Minimum | | | | | | | | | | | | | | |
| 32° and below | 25 | 30.8 | 27.8 | 27.7 | 17.3 | 5.1 | 0.3 | 0.0 | 0.* | 1.6 | 9.4 | 22.1 | 29.7 | 171.7 |
| 0° and below | 25 | 9.2 | 8.3 | 3.2 | 0.0 | 0.0 | 0.0 | 0.0 | 0.0 | 0.0 | 0.0 | 0.1 | 3.2 | 24.0 |
| **AVG. STATION PRESS.(mb)** | 7 | 972.5 | 972.5 | 972.2 | 973.1 | 971.9 | 972.4 | 973.9 | 975.7 | 975.5 | 975.6 | 973.1 | 971.9 | 973.4 |
| **RELATIVE HUMIDITY (%)** | | | | | | | | | | | | | | |
| Hour 01 | 14 | 83 | 81 | 80 | 77 | 78 | 84 | 84 | 88 | 88 | 85 | 86 | 86 | 83 |
| Hour 07 | 25 | 82 | 82 | 83 | 80 | 78 | 81 | 85 | 91 | 91 | 88 | 87 | 85 | 84 |
| Hour 13 (Local Time) | 25 | 72 | 69 | 64 | 55 | 50 | 55 | 54 | 60 | 63 | 65 | 74 | 77 | 63 |
| Hour 19 | 25 | 77 | 73 | 67 | 58 | 53 | 57 | 58 | 66 | 73 | 74 | 80 | 81 | 68 |
| **PRECIPITATION (inches):** | | | | | | | | | | | | | | |
| Water Equivalent | | | | | | | | | | | | | | |
| -Normal | | 1.49 | 1.30 | 1.88 | 2.58 | 2.59 | 3.10 | 2.89 | 2.96 | 2.77 | 2.28 | 2.26 | 1.89 | 27.99 |
| -Maximum Monthly | 25 | 3.13 | 3.36 | 5.67 | 4.56 | 5.99 | 6.67 | 4.96 | 7.18 | 9.49 | 5.45 | 5.10 | 4.48 | 9.49 |
| -Year | | 1974 | 1971 | 1976 | 1967 | 1983 | 1969 | 1975 | 1975 | 1986 | 1969 | 1988 | 1971 | SEP 1986 |
| -Minimum Monthly | 25 | 0.60 | 0.29 | 0.78 | 0.97 | 0.40 | 0.85 | 0.55 | 0.85 | 0.01 | 0.47 | 0.45 | 0.65 | 0.01 |
| -Year | | 1977 | 1982 | 1987 | 1987 | 1966 | 1988 | 1989 | 1969 | 1979 | 1971 | 1986 | 1976 | SEP 1979 |
| -Maximum in 24 hrs | 25 | 1.39 | 1.43 | 2.18 | 1.32 | 1.94 | 2.59 | 3.83 | 3.12 | 2.55 | 1.57 | 1.82 | 1.70 | 3.83 |
| -Year | | 1974 | 1971 | 1976 | 1971 | 1973 | 1969 | 1984 | 1981 | 1985 | 1970 | 1988 | 1971 | JUL 1984 |
| Snow,Ice pellets | | | | | | | | | | | | | | |
| -Maximum Monthly | 25 | 38.0 | 23.6 | 28.7 | 11.6 | 2.3 | 0.0 | T | 0.0 | 0.1 | 4.4 | 18.9 | 30.4 | 38.0 |
| -Year | | 1982 | 1971 | 1971 | 1979 | 1979 | | 1970 | | 1967 | 1980 | 1968 | 1968 | JAN 1982 |
| -Maximum in 24 hrs | 25 | 15.4 | 8.5 | 11.7 | 7.6 | 2.3 | 0.0 | T | 0.0 | 0.1 | 3.5 | 14.4 | 13.2 | 15.4 |
| -Year | | 1978 | 1974 | 1970 | 1979 | 1979 | | 1970 | | 1967 | 1980 | 1981 | 1980 | JAN 1978 |
| **WIND:** | | | | | | | | | | | | | | |
| Mean Speed (mph) | 14 | 10.1 | 9.2 | 9.3 | 9.8 | 9.0 | 8.0 | 7.6 | 7.2 | 8.0 | 9.1 | 9.9 | 9.6 | 8.9 |
| Prevailing Direction | | | | | | | | | | | | | | |
| Fastest Obs. 1 Min. | | | | | | | | | | | | | | |
| -Direction (!!!) | 14 | 26 | 27 | 22 | 30 | 27 | 27 | 32 | 26 | 23 | 23 | 27 | 27 | 26 |
| -Speed (MPH) | 14 | 40 | 35 | 31 | 36 | 35 | 40 | 32 | 26 | 32 | 32 | 40 | 32 | 40 |
| -Year | | 1972 | 1979 | 1977 | 1979 | 1971 | 1969 | 1966 | 1977 | 1970 | 1968 | 1970 | 1970 | JAN 1972 |
| Peak Gust | | | | | | | | | | | | | | |
| -Direction (!!!) | 6 | SW | NW | E | SW | S | SW | NW | SW | NW | W | NW | SW | S |
| -Speed (mph) | 6 | 46 | 48 | 44 | 53 | 60 | 45 | 58 | 59 | 46 | 40 | 59 | 48 | 60 |
| -Date | | 1989 | 1987 | 1985 | 1984 | 1988 | 1984 | 1987 | 1988 | 1985 | 1988 | 1989 | 1984 | MAY 1988 |

**See Reference Notes to this table on the following page.**

## TABLE 2 — PRECIPITATION (inches)   HOUGHTON LAKE, MICHIGAN

| YEAR | JAN | FEB | MAR | APR | MAY | JUNE | JULY | AUG | SEP | OCT | NOV | DEC | ANNUAL |
|---|---|---|---|---|---|---|---|---|---|---|---|---|---|
| 1961 | 0.44 | 1.47 | 1.59 | 2.31 | 1.49 | 2.44 | 4.25 | 3.05 | 6.34 | 1.89 | 2.29 | 1.12 | 28.68 |
| 1962 | 1.86 | 1.77 | 0.87 | 1.17 | 2.56 | 2.82 | 2.86 | 4.56 | 2.61 | 2.62 | 0.96 | 1.07 | 25.73 |
| 1963 | 0.70 | 0.55 | 2.89 | 1.34 | 3.58 | 2.88 | 2.60 | 3.15 | 1.97 | 0.85 | 2.78 | 1.11 | 24.08 |
| #1964 | 1.10 | 0.39 | 1.55 | 2.64 | 2.56 | 1.25 | 3.03 | 2.77 | 3.61 | 1.29 | 2.41 | 2.73 | 32.97 |
| 1965 | 2.47 | 1.40 | 1.83 | 2.85 | 2.81 | 2.43 | 1.26 | 5.05 | 5.76 | 1.97 |  |  |  |
| 1966 | 1.02 | 1.02 | 2.30 | 2.08 | 0.40 | 0.95 | 1.74 | 1.92 | 2.25 | 1.79 | 4.81 | 3.46 | 23.74 |
| 1967 | 2.02 | 0.88 | 1.32 | 4.56 | 2.41 | 5.65 | 1.28 | 1.66 | 1.73 | 2.73 | 2.82 | 2.41 | 29.47 |
| 1968 | 1.03 | 1.57 | 0.85 | 1.28 | 2.62 | 5.54 | 1.84 | 1.32 | 1.63 | 3.09 | 2.47 | 2.50 | 28.28 |
| 1969 | 1.87 | 0.32 | 0.86 | 2.59 | 3.57 | 6.67 | 3.57 | 0.85 | 5.45 | 2.19 | 0.94 |  | 30.51 |
| 1970 | 1.16 | 0.70 | 1.86 | 1.50 | 2.67 | 4.15 | 3.93 | 1.26 | 5.85 | 2.75 | 3.79 | 2.00 | 31.62 |
| 1971 | 1.30 | 3.36 | 1.79 | 2.19 | 1.52 | 2.84 | 3.14 | 1.76 | 1.20 | 0.47 | 1.96 | 4.48 | 26.01 |
| 1972 | 0.82 | 0.99 | 2.36 | 1.40 | 1.79 | 2.00 | 2.52 | 4.63 | 2.67 | 2.50 | 0.99 | 3.48 | 26.15 |
| 1973 | 1.22 | 1.33 | 1.95 | 1.66 | 4.88 | 2.84 | 2.34 | 2.29 | 1.95 | 3.11 | 1.34 | 1.81 | 26.72 |
| 1974 | 3.13 | 1.14 | 1.44 | 3.47 | 2.92 | 4.60 | 4.70 | 2.78 | 2.53 | 1.40 | 1.41 | 1.43 | 30.95 |
| 1975 | 1.97 | 1.14 | 1.50 | 2.63 | 2.79 | 3.79 | 4.96 | 7.18 | 1.52 | 0.85 | 2.20 | 1.33 | 31.86 |
| 1976 | 1.77 | 2.49 | 5.67 | 1.86 | 2.86 | 2.77 | 1.22 | 1.07 | 0.99 | 1.31 | 0.75 | 0.65 | 23.41 |
| 1977 | 0.60 | 1.46 | 2.40 | 2.29 | 1.39 | 0.94 | 1.72 | 5.70 | 4.19 | 1.89 | 2.14 | 2.20 | 26.92 |
| 1978 | 1.93 | 0.55 | 1.20 | 1.35 | 2.42 | 2.38 | 0.91 | 4.10 | 6.70 | 1.43 | 1.28 | 2.08 | 26.33 |
| 1979 | 1.51 | 0.63 | 3.05 | 3.18 | 1.85 | 4.46 | 0.87 | 3.90 | 0.01 | 2.43 | 2.47 | 1.71 | 26.07 |
| 1980 | 1.61 | 0.69 | 1.10 | 3.30 | 1.55 | 3.44 | 2.29 | 2.01 | 3.75 | 1.91 | 1.55 | 1.95 | 25.15 |
| 1981 | 0.79 | 2.10 | 0.88 | 3.88 | 1.73 | 4.02 | 1.89 | 7.06 | 1.89 | 2.61 | 2.07 | 1.08 | 30.00 |
| 1982 | 2.43 | 0.29 | 2.41 | 2.46 | 2.98 | 3.21 | 3.31 | 3.25 | 3.58 | 1.86 | 2.52 | 3.47 | 31.77 |
| 1983 | 1.20 | 0.79 | 3.11 | 1.86 | 5.99 | 0.95 | 1.40 | 3.89 | 4.63 | 3.66 | 1.60 | 1.69 | 30.77 |
| 1984 | 1.06 | 0.88 | 2.28 | 1.96 | 2.60 | 3.01 | 4.30 | 2.95 | 2.74 | 2.17 | 1.99 | 2.93 | 28.87 |
| 1985 | 1.64 | 1.99 | 3.55 | 2.42 | 1.87 | 1.71 | 2.28 | 4.76 | 6.14 | 1.63 | 3.56 | 2.14 | 33.69 |
| 1986 | 1.06 | 1.73 | 2.20 | 1.73 | 3.20 | 5.43 | 4.38 | 9.49 | 1.75 | 0.45 | 0.85 |  | 34.03 |
| 1987 | 1.06 | 0.61 | 0.78 | 0.97 | 1.56 | 1.04 | 1.62 | 6.69 | 4.35 | 2.21 | 2.63 | 2.45 | 25.97 |
| 1988 | 2.09 | 0.75 | 2.39 | 2.37 | 0.56 | 0.85 | 2.49 | 4.50 | 3.63 | 3.38 | 5.10 | 1.86 | 29.97 |
| 1989 | 0.97 | 0.70 | 2.99 | 0.98 | 3.19 | 2.90 | 0.55 | 2.62 | 1.03 | 1.30 | 2.08 | 0.92 | 20.23 |
| 1990 | 2.43 | 1.09 | 1.47 | 1.77 | 4.15 | 2.57 | 3.82 | 3.28 | 3.00 | 2.94 | 2.90 | 1.55 | 30.97 |
| Record Mean | 1.45 | 1.24 | 1.93 | 2.37 | 2.78 | 3.05 | 2.69 | 2.93 | 3.18 | 2.53 | 2.35 | 1.78 | 28.27 |

## TABLE 3 — AVERAGE TEMPERATURE (deg. F)   HOUGHTON LAKE, MICHIGAN

| YEAR | JAN | FEB | MAR | APR | MAY | JUNE | JULY | AUG | SEP | OCT | NOV | DEC | ANNUAL |
|---|---|---|---|---|---|---|---|---|---|---|---|---|---|
| 1961 | 17.1 | 25.0 | 32.9 | 40.9 | 53.1 | 63.5 | 68.3 | 66.7 | 63.9 | 50.7 | 36.7 | 25.1 | 45.3 |
| 1962 | 16.7 | 16.0 | 29.9 | 43.3 | 60.5 | 64.0 | 65.4 | 66.3 | 56.9 | 50.4 | 36.1 | 22.8 | 44.0 |
| 1963 | 12.1 | 12.0 | 30.6 | 46.3 | 52.8 | 66.9 | 69.0 | 64.2 | 58.0 | 57.6 | 41.5 | 19.6 | 44.2 |
| #1964 | 23.7 | 23.9 | 30.0 | 45.3 | 59.6 | 65.0 | 68.2 | 62.3 | 56.3 | 43.5 | 38.5 | 21.8 | 44.8 |
| 1965 | 15.5 | 18.3 | 22.5 | 37.9 | 57.9 | 61.4 | 63.0 | 63.0 | 56.7 | 45.7 | 35.4 | 28.9 | 42.1 |
| 1966 | 12.9 | 21.7 | 31.9 | 39.3 | 47.6 | 64.7 | 64.7 | 64.7 | 55.8 | 45.6 | 34.4 | 23.0 | 42.6 |
| 1967 | 21.7 | 11.9 | 27.0 | 42.1 | 48.4 | 66.4 | 65.2 | 62.1 | 55.4 | 46.2 | 30.7 | 24.2 | 41.8 |
| 1968 | 17.6 | 14.8 | 32.3 | 45.3 | 50.7 | 62.6 | 65.7 | 65.6 | 60.2 | 48.9 | 34.7 | 21.0 | 43.3 |
| 1969 | 18.3 | 19.4 | 23.2 | 43.1 | 52.9 | 56.9 | 67.5 | 68.4 | 57.2 | 45.4 | 33.4 | 21.6 | 42.3 |
| 1970 | 12.5 | 15.8 | 23.9 | 42.2 | 53.9 | 63.2 | 69.2 | 66.1 | 58.1 | 49.5 | 35.5 | 21.9 | 42.6 |
| 1971 | 14.7 | 18.7 | 23.4 | 38.8 | 51.6 | 67.0 | 64.7 | 63.4 | 60.8 | 54.7 | 34.4 | 26.2 | 43.2 |
| 1972 | 16.3 | 16.4 | 22.3 | 36.6 | 56.9 | 59.1 | 64.6 | 56.8 | 56.4 | 41.7 | 33.6 | 22.0 | 41.1 |
| 1973 | 22.1 | 18.1 | 38.1 | 43.1 | 50.6 | 64.9 | 67.7 | 68.9 | 57.4 | 51.3 | 35.8 | 22.9 | 45.1 |
| 1974 | 20.3 | 14.4 | 27.0 | 43.2 | 50.0 | 61.6 | 67.8 | 65.0 | 53.9 | 44.3 | 36.3 | 26.1 | 42.5 |
| 1975 | 22.0 | 20.7 | 24.3 | 37.0 | 59.7 | 64.1 | 68.1 | 65.0 | 53.7 | 49.6 | 40.8 | 23.8 | 44.1 |
| 1976 | 14.0 | 24.1 | 34.8 | 45.5 | 50.8 | 66.1 | 67.0 | 64.6 | 55.6 | 42.3 | 28.3 | 13.8 | 41.9 |
| 1977 | 8.7 | 17.8 | 34.8 | 46.6 | 60.3 | 61.0 | 70.1 | 61.2 | 58.3 | 45.1 | 35.8 | 21.4 | 43.5 |
| 1978 | 14.5 | 10.8 | 23.6 | 39.1 | 56.9 | 61.6 | 61.6 | 66.4 | 58.6 | 44.3 | 35.9 | 21.8 | 41.6 |
| 1979 | 11.5 | 10.4 | 30.9 | 40.0 | 52.6 | 62.3 | 66.9 | 62.7 | 59.2 | 45.7 | 35.0 | 27.6 | 42.0 |
| 1980 | 19.1 | 15.7 | 25.0 | 41.9 | 56.0 | 59.2 | 67.4 | 68.0 | 56.7 | 41.6 | 33.9 | 18.9 | 41.9 |
| 1981 | 14.8 | 24.0 | 32.5 | 44.3 | 53.0 | 63.6 | 66.8 | 65.6 | 55.9 | 42.9 | 35.6 | 25.3 | 43.7 |
| 1982 | 11.4 | 17.9 | 25.8 | 37.3 | 60.9 | 57.4 | 66.3 | 61.9 | 57.2 | 48.9 | 36.2 | 31.2 | 42.9 |
| 1983 | 21.8 | 25.9 | 32.4 | 40.3 | 48.5 | 63.3 | 71.5 | 68.6 | 59.7 | 46.4 | 36.6 | 16.8 | 44.3 |
| 1984 | 12.4 | 28.2 | 24.1 | 44.8 | 50.1 | 65.2 | 66.4 | 68.8 | 56.1 | 49.2 | 35.4 | 27.0 | 44.0 |
| 1985 | 14.9 | 17.9 | 30.3 | 46.5 | 57.0 | 59.5 | 66.1 | 63.9 | 59.8 | 47.5 | 34.5 | 18.0 | 43.0 |
| 1986 | 17.3 | 18.4 | 30.9 | 47.3 | 56.9 | 60.5 | 69.7 | 62.8 | 58.1 | 46.8 | 32.3 | 26.8 | 44.0 |
| 1987 | 21.6 | 23.4 | 33.6 | 47.3 | 58.1 | 67.1 | 71.4 | 65.6 | 59.5 | 43.9 | 37.7 | 28.7 | 46.5 |
| 1988 | 17.3 | 16.3 | 28.0 | 43.7 | 58.6 | 64.8 | 71.4 | 68.8 | 57.9 | 42.4 | 36.6 | 23.7 | 44.1 |
| 1989 | 24.9 | 15.5 | 25.0 | 41.1 | 54.5 | 62.2 | 69.5 | 64.8 | 56.2 | 47.9 | 30.7 | 12.9 | 42.1 |
| 1990 | 26.2 | 21.3 | 32.1 | 44.9 | 51.9 | 63.4 | 66.8 | 65.0 | 57.9 | 45.3 | 38.9 | 25.8 | 45.0 |
| Record Mean | 18.7 | 19.4 | 28.5 | 42.3 | 54.3 | 63.5 | 67.7 | 65.6 | 58.1 | 47.7 | 35.3 | 23.7 | 43.7 |
| Max | 27.2 | 29.5 | 39.0 | 54.0 | 67.8 | 77.0 | 81.4 | 78.6 | 69.9 | 58.4 | 42.7 | 30.7 | 54.7 |
| Min | 10.1 | 9.3 | 17.9 | 30.5 | 41.0 | 50.1 | 53.9 | 52.5 | 46.3 | 36.9 | 27.8 | 16.6 | 32.7 |

## REFERENCE NOTES FOR TABLES 1, 2, 3 and 6   (HOUGHTON LAKE, MI)

### GENERAL

T - TRACE AMOUNT
BLANK ENTRIES DENOTE MISSING/UNREPORTED DATA.
# INDICATES A STATION OR INSTRUMENT RELOCATION.

### SPECIFIC

#### TABLE 1

(a) - LENGTH OF RECORD IN YEARS. ALTHOUGH INDIVIDUAL MONTHS MAY BE MISSING.

* LESS THAN .05

NORMALS — BASED ON THE 1951-1980 RECORD PERIOD.
EXTREMES — DATES ARE THE MOST RECENT OCCURRENCE.
WIND DIR. — NUMERALS SHOW TENS OF DEGREES CLOCKWISE FROM TRUE NORTH. "00" INDICATES CALM.
RESULTANT WIND DIRECTIONS ARE GIVEN TO WHOLE DEGREES.

#### TABLE 3
MAX AND MIN ARE LONG-TERM MEAN DAILY MAXIMUM AND MEAN DAILY MINIMUM TEMPERATURES.

### EXCEPTIONS

#### TABLE 1

1. MEAN WIND SPEED IS THROUGH 1978
2. FASTEST OBSERVED WIND IS THROUGH JUNE 1979
3. THUNDERSTORMS AND HEAVY FOG MAY BE INCOMPLETE, DUE TO PART-TIME OPERATIONS.

#### TABLES 2, 3, and 6

RECORD MEANS ARE THROUGH THE CURRENT YEAR, BEGINNING IN   1918 FOR TEMPERATURE
1918 FOR PRECIPITATION
1965 FOR SNOWFALL

## TABLE 4

HEATING DEGREE DAYS Base 65 deg. F    HOUGHTON LAKE. MICHIGAN

| SEASON | JULY | AUG | SEP | OCT | NOV | DEC | JAN | FEB | MAR | APR | MAY | JUNE | TOTAL |
|---|---|---|---|---|---|---|---|---|---|---|---|---|---|
| 1961-62 | 28 | 42 | 126 | 437 | 846 | 1233 | 1492 | 1368 | 1082 | 655 | 220 | 71 | 7600 |
| 1962-63 | 50 | 54 | 254 | 452 | 859 | 1302 | 1640 | 1481 | 1061 | 558 | 374 | 75 | 8160 |
| #1963-64 | 37 | 63 | 211 | 238 | 699 | 1274 | 1187 | 1533 | 1078 | 586 | 208 | 122 | 7104 |
| 1964-65 | 38 | 136 | 283 | 659 | 789 | 1331 | 1533 | 1303 | 1314 | 807 | 237 | 144 | 8574 |
| 1965-66 | 109 | 123 | 266 | 593 | 883 | 1114 | 1607 | 1205 | 1020 | 763 | 535 | 91 | 8309 |
| 1966-67 | 19 | 65 | 280 | 592 | 911 | 1295 | 1335 | 1484 | 1168 | 678 | 510 | 33 | 8370 |
| 1967-68 | 69 | 116 | 288 | 579 | 1022 | 1260 | 1468 | 1453 | 1005 | 582 | 438 | 137 | 8417 |
| 1968-69 | 71 | 100 | 159 | 510 | 903 | 1353 | 1444 | 1272 | 1290 | 651 | 378 | 254 | 8385 |
| 1969-70 | 38 | 28 | 250 | 601 | 939 | 1342 | 1621 | 1373 | 1296 | 682 | 346 | 122 | 8640 |
| 1970-71 | 30 | 54 | 225 | 478 | 878 | 1330 | 1556 | 1289 | 1282 | 781 | 415 | 65 | 8383 |
| 1971-72 | 70 | 95 | 183 | 327 | 912 | 1197 | 1502 | 1401 | 1320 | 847 | 254 | 191 | 8299 |
| 1972-73 | 77 | 92 | 242 | 716 | 933 | 1326 | 1324 | 1307 | 829 | 653 | 442 | 54 | 7995 |
| 1973-74 | 26 | 25 | 280 | 420 | 871 | 1298 | 1380 | 1411 | 1171 | 649 | 463 | 135 | 8129 |
| 1974-75 | 27 | 56 | 337 | 633 | 856 | 1197 | 1327 | 1234 | 1254 | 836 | 215 | 101 | 8073 |
| 1975-76 | 44 | 68 | 333 | 472 | 720 | 1272 | 1575 | 1180 | 1054 | 590 | 434 | 53 | 7795 |
| 1976-77 | 24 | 92 | 296 | 698 | 1094 | 1582 | 1743 | 1315 | 932 | 544 | 199 | 159 | 8678 |
| 1977-78 | 29 | 134 | 200 | 610 | 869 | 1347 | 1556 | 1513 | 1276 | 769 | 289 | 144 | 8736 |
| 1978-79 | 79 | 46 | 220 | 636 | 869 | 1333 | 1655 | 1530 | 1053 | 742 | 396 | 135 | 8694 |
| 1979-80 | 48 | 109 | 196 | 597 | 893 | 1153 | 1416 | 1424 | 1233 | 690 | 286 | 209 | 8254 |
| 1980-81 | 18 | 27 | 258 | 716 | 928 | 1423 | 1553 | 1143 | 1001 | 613 | 368 | 80 | 8128 |
| 1981-82 | 50 | 44 | 280 | 676 | 872 | 1222 | 1658 | 1315 | 1209 | 824 | 148 | 224 | 8522 |
| 1982-83 | 12 | 139 | 255 | 494 | 855 | 1040 | 1331 | 1087 | 1003 | 733 | 505 | 116 | 7570 |
| 1983-84 | 25 | 29 | 209 | 569 | 846 | 1487 | 1628 | 1062 | 1262 | 599 | 458 | 53 | 8227 |
| 1984-85 | 42 | 28 | 270 | 481 | 881 | 1168 | 1547 | 1313 | 1071 | 571 | 248 | 172 | 7792 |
| 1985-86 | 46 | 88 | 209 | 535 | 908 | 1451 | 1474 | 1297 | 1048 | 532 | 274 | 148 | 8010 |
| 1986-87 | 23 | 109 | 212 | 557 | 975 | 1179 | 1335 | 1159 | 963 | 523 | 271 | 57 | 7363 |
| 1987-88 | 41 | 60 | 169 | 649 | 813 | 1117 | 1473 | 1406 | 1140 | 636 | 225 | 106 | 7835 |
| 1988-89 | 7 | 75 | 218 | 692 | 847 | 1276 | 1236 | 1381 | 1234 | 711 | 333 | 126 | 8136 |
| 1989-90 | 19 | 79 | 277 | 520 | 1025 | 1607 | 1196 | 1217 | 1009 | 627 | 398 | 97 | 8071 |
| 1990-91 | 32 | 51 | 248 | 604 | 773 | 1208 | | | | | | | |

## TABLE 5

COOLING DEGREE DAYS Base 65 deg. F    HOUGHTON LAKE. MICHIGAN

| YEAR | JAN | FEB | MAR | APR | MAY | JUNE | JULY | AUG | SEP | OCT | NOV | DEC | TOTAL |
|---|---|---|---|---|---|---|---|---|---|---|---|---|---|
| 1969 | 0 | 0 | 0 | 0 | 10 | 18 | 120 | 138 | 24 | 0 | 0 | 0 | 310 |
| 1970 | 0 | 0 | 0 | 6 | 15 | 74 | 167 | 95 | 24 | 1 | 0 | 0 | 382 |
| 1971 | 0 | 0 | 0 | 0 | 5 | 131 | 68 | 50 | 62 | 17 | 0 | 0 | 333 |
| 1972 | 0 | 0 | 0 | 0 | 11 | 19 | 131 | 78 | 4 | 0 | 0 | 0 | 243 |
| 1973 | 0 | 0 | 0 | 1 | 0 | 58 | 119 | 155 | 60 | 2 | 0 | 0 | 395 |
| 1974 | 0 | 0 | 0 | 1 | 6 | 41 | 120 | 62 | 11 | 0 | 0 | 0 | 241 |
| 1975 | 0 | 0 | 0 | 0 | 58 | 83 | 146 | 78 | 2 | 2 | 0 | 0 | 369 |
| 1976 | 0 | 0 | 0 | 13 | 0 | 92 | 93 | 86 | 24 | 0 | 0 | 0 | 308 |
| 1977 | 0 | 0 | 0 | 0 | 61 | 46 | 192 | 50 | 5 | 0 | 0 | 0 | 354 |
| 1978 | 0 | 0 | 0 | 0 | 44 | 49 | 85 | 96 | 34 | 0 | 0 | 0 | 308 |
| 1979 | 0 | 0 | 0 | 0 | 18 | 58 | 112 | 45 | 31 | 7 | 0 | 0 | 271 |
| 1980 | 0 | 0 | 0 | 2 | 17 | 43 | 98 | 124 | 16 | 0 | 0 | 0 | 300 |
| 1981 | 0 | 0 | 0 | 0 | 3 | 47 | 114 | 70 | 13 | 0 | 0 | 0 | 247 |
| 1982 | 0 | 0 | 0 | 0 | 27 | 3 | 132 | 52 | 29 | 3 | 0 | 0 | 246 |
| 1983 | 0 | 0 | 0 | 0 | 0 | 73 | 235 | 148 | 56 | 0 | 0 | 0 | 512 |
| 1984 | 0 | 0 | 0 | 1 | 2 | 65 | 90 | 151 | 11 | 0 | 0 | 0 | 320 |
| 1985 | 0 | 0 | 0 | 22 | 8 | 11 | 86 | 61 | 60 | 0 | 0 | 0 | 248 |
| 1986 | 0 | 0 | 0 | 8 | 29 | 22 | 175 | 46 | 15 | 0 | 0 | 0 | 295 |
| 1987 | 0 | 0 | 0 | 1 | 64 | 125 | 250 | 86 | 12 | 0 | 0 | 0 | 538 |
| 1988 | 0 | 0 | 0 | 0 | 35 | 108 | 213 | 199 | 11 | 0 | 0 | 0 | 566 |
| 1989 | 0 | 0 | 0 | 0 | 10 | 49 | 164 | 83 | 19 | 0 | 0 | 0 | 325 |
| 1990 | 0 | 0 | 0 | 29 | 0 | 55 | 94 | 56 | 41 | 0 | 0 | 0 | 275 |

## TABLE 6

SNOWFALL (inches)    HOUGHTON LAKE. MICHIGAN

| SEASON | JULY | AUG | SEP | OCT | NOV | DEC | JAN | FEB | MAR | APR | MAY | JUNE | TOTAL |
|---|---|---|---|---|---|---|---|---|---|---|---|---|---|
| 1961-62 | 0.0 | 0.0 | 0.0 | 0.0 | 5.0 | 7.0 | 25.1 | 20.6 | 7.4 | | T | 0.0 | 65.1 |
| 1962-63 | 0.0 | 0.0 | 0.0 | 9.5 | 4.0 | 19.0 | 13.3 | 9.4 | 11.8 | 9.0 | T | 0.0 | 76.0 |
| #1963-64 | 0.0 | 0.0 | 0.0 | 0.0 | 6.5 | 9.3 | 6.3 | 12.0 | 1.0 | 1.0 | T | 0.0 | 41.0 |
| 1964-65 | 0.0 | 0.0 | 0.0 | 4.1 | 3.8 | 12.5 | 26.5 | 12.9 | 17.9 | 10.8 | 0.1 | 0.0 | 88.5 |
| 1965-66 | 0.0 | 0.0 | T | 0.3 | 6.5 | 11.8 | 19.5 | 7.3 | 9.2 | 7.1 | 0.1 | 0.0 | 61.8 |
| 1966-67 | 0.0 | 0.0 | 0.0 | T | 15.1 | 15.4 | 22.6 | 14.3 | 9.4 | 4.5 | T | 0.0 | 81.3 |
| 1967-68 | 0.0 | 0.0 | 0.1 | 3.0 | 12.6 | 10.6 | 9.0 | 15.6 | 4.9 | 0.7 | 0.0 | 0.0 | 56.5 |
| 1968-69 | 0.0 | 0.0 | 0.0 | 1.0 | 18.9 | 30.4 | 25.8 | 8.7 | 9.5 | 0.4 | 0.3 | 0.0 | 95.0 |
| 1969-70 | 0.0 | 0.0 | 0.0 | 2.0 | 17.6 | 20.0 | 22.7 | 12.8 | 24.5 | 3.8 | T | 0.0 | 103.4 |
| 1970-71 | T | 0.0 | 0.0 | T | 17.7 | 23.1 | 27.5 | 23.6 | 28.7 | 3.5 | T | 0.0 | 124.1 |
| 1971-72 | 0.0 | 0.0 | 0.0 | T | 16.7 | 16.7 | 15.0 | 18.7 | 26.8 | 2.9 | 0.0 | 0.0 | 96.8 |
| 1972-73 | 0.0 | 0.0 | 0.0 | 0.6 | 4.1 | 29.2 | 8.3 | 15.2 | 5.3 | 7.9 | 0.8 | 0.0 | 71.4 |
| 1973-74 | 0.0 | 0.0 | 0.0 | T | 4.8 | 13.0 | 11.2 | 17.5 | 12.3 | 3.1 | 1.0 | 0.0 | 62.9 |
| 1974-75 | 0.0 | 0.0 | T | T | 6.0 | 18.0 | 11.8 | 12.4 | 14.0 | 4.5 | 0.0 | 0.0 | 66.7 |
| 1975-76 | 0.0 | 0.0 | T | T | 5.9 | 14.6 | 29.6 | 20.8 | 17.6 | 6.0 | 0.6 | 0.0 | 95.1 |
| 1976-77 | 0.0 | 0.0 | 0.0 | 0.7 | 13.6 | 18.6 | 16.3 | 11.4 | 3.9 | 2.7 | 0.0 | 0.0 | 67.2 |
| 1977-78 | 0.0 | 0.0 | 0.0 | T | 16.0 | 14.0 | 33.3 | 13.1 | 12.5 | 0.3 | 0.0 | 0.0 | 89.2 |
| 1978-79 | 0.0 | 0.0 | 0.0 | T | 10.5 | 29.0 | 21.8 | 8.3 | 5.7 | 11.6 | 2.3 | 0.0 | 89.2 |
| 1979-80 | 0.0 | 0.0 | 0.0 | 0.7 | 5.0 | 7.1 | 14.4 | 12.3 | 12.1 | 7.7 | 0.0 | 0.0 | 59.3 |
| 1980-81 | 0.0 | 0.0 | 0.0 | 4.4 | 3.2 | 25.6 | 19.3 | 16.3 | 5.4 | 0.2 | 0.0 | 0.0 | 74.4 |
| 1981-82 | 0.0 | 0.0 | 0.0 | 3.0 | 16.1 | 15.7 | 38.0 | 6.1 | 14.3 | 5.5 | 0.0 | 0.0 | 98.7 |
| 1982-83 | 0.0 | 0.0 | 0.0 | 0.2 | 7.7 | 4.8 | 9.0 | 15.4 | 13.3 | 2.7 | 1.0 | 0.0 | 51.5 |
| 1983-84 | 0.0 | 0.0 | 0.0 | 0.0 | 5.0 | 19.8 | 17.0 | 6.3 | 6.5 | 5.1 | 0.4 | 0.0 | 60.1 |
| 1984-85 | 0.0 | 0.0 | 0.0 | 0.0 | 0.6 | 11.7 | 11.7 | 18.7 | 14.1 | 10.0 | 0.0 | 0.0 | 80.4 |
| 1985-86 | 0.0 | 0.0 | 0.0 | 0.0 | 12.6 | 23.1 | 12.7 | 14.0 | 8.9 | 0.3 | 0.0 | 0.0 | 71.6 |
| 1986-87 | 0.0 | 0.0 | 0.0 | T | 3.4 | 10.3 | 14.1 | 6.4 | 2.3 | 2.0 | 0.0 | 0.0 | 38.5 |
| 1987-88 | 0.0 | 0.0 | 0.0 | 2.4 | 8.7 | 18.6 | 13.4 | 12.9 | 10.3 | 1.4 | 0.0 | 0.0 | 67.7 |
| 1988-89 | 0.0 | 0.0 | 0.0 | 0.0 | 7.8 | 12.3 | 9.3 | 13.5 | 18.7 | 3.1 | T | 0.0 | |
| 1989-90 | 0.0 | 0.0 | T | 0.6 | 12.2 | 15.0 | 21.7 | 11.0 | 2.4 | 2.1 | 0.9 | 0.0 | 65.9 |
| 1990-91 | 0.0 | 0.0 | 0.0 | T | 9.1 | 15.3 | | | | | | | |
| Record Mean | T | 0.0 | T | 0.8 | 9.9 | 17.1 | 19.3 | 12.9 | 11.9 | 4.2 | 0.3 | 0.0 | 76.4 |

**See Reference Notes, relative to all above tables, on preceding page.**

The Marquette County Airport lies about 7.5 miles southwest of the nearest shoreline of Lake Superior and about 8 miles west of the city of Marquette. Lake Superior is the largest body of fresh water in the world and the deepest and coldest of the Great Lakes. An irregular northwest-southeast ridge line lies just to the east of the airport. There are several water storage basins in the vicinity of the station. One basin, about 20 miles long, is 3 miles northwest and another, about 8 miles in diameter, is 3 miles west.

The climate is influenced considerably by the proximity of Lake Superior. As a consequence of the cool expanse of water in the summer, there is rarely a long period of sweltering hot weather. Periods of drought are extremely rare. In the winter, cold outbreaks are tempered considerably by the waters of Lake Superior if the lake is unfrozen. However, winds blowing across these relatively warmer waters pick up moisture and cause cloudy weather throughout the winter, as well as frequent periods of light snow. Lake-formed snow showers and snow squalls are intensified near the station by upslope winds, especially from the northwest through northeast. With a northeast through east wind, especially in autumn, the upslope condition will cause light snow at the airport, while along the lakeshore, only drizzle or no precipitation may occur.

The growing season averages 117 days. Precipitation is rather evenly distributed throughout the year, with an average precipitation of 4 inches or more in June and September and less than 2 inch averages only in January and February. One hundred inches or more of snow occur in nine of ten winter seasons.

## TABLE 1     NORMALS, MEANS AND EXTREMES

MARQUETTE COUNTY AIRPORT, MICHIGAN

LATITUDE: 46°32'N   LONGITUDE: 87°33'W   ELEVATION: FT. GRND 1415 BARO 1415   TIME ZONE: EASTERN   WBAN: 94850

| | (a) | JAN | FEB | MAR | APR | MAY | JUNE | JULY | AUG | SEP | OCT | NOV | DEC | YEAR |
|---|---|---|---|---|---|---|---|---|---|---|---|---|---|---|
| **TEMPERATURE °F:** | | | | | | | | | | | | | | |
| Normals | | | | | | | | | | | | | | |
| -Daily Maximum | | 20.1 | 23.8 | 33.2 | 47.4 | 61.5 | 70.4 | 75.3 | 73.3 | 63.9 | 53.4 | 36.5 | 24.6 | 48.6 |
| -Daily Minimum | | 4.1 | 4.8 | 13.2 | 27.4 | 38.9 | 48.8 | 53.8 | 51.8 | 44.1 | 35.2 | 23.6 | 11.2 | 29.7 |
| -Monthly | | 12.1 | 14.3 | 23.2 | 37.4 | 50.2 | 59.6 | 64.6 | 62.6 | 54.0 | 44.3 | 30.1 | 17.9 | 39.2 |
| Extremes | | | | | | | | | | | | | | |
| -Record Highest | 11 | 46 | 61 | 68 | 92 | 93 | 95 | 99 | 95 | 92 | 78 | 67 | 59 | 99 |
| -Year | | 1981 | 1981 | 1989 | 1980 | 1986 | 1988 | 1988 | 1988 | 1983 | 1989 | 1981 | 1982 | JUL 1988 |
| -Record Lowest | 11 | -25 | -34 | -23 | -5 | 17 | 28 | 36 | 34 | 25 | 14 | -5 | -28 | -34 |
| -Year | | 1982 | 1979 | 1982 | 1979 | 1983 | 1986 | 1989 | 1984 | 1989 | 1984 | 1989 | 1983 | FEB 1979 |
| **NORMAL DEGREE DAYS:** | | | | | | | | | | | | | | |
| Heating (base 65°F) | | 1640 | 1420 | 1296 | 828 | 469 | 179 | 86 | 123 | 330 | 642 | 1047 | 1460 | 9520 |
| Cooling (base 65°F) | | 0 | 0 | 0 | 0 | 10 | 17 | 73 | 48 | 0 | 0 | 0 | 0 | 148 |
| **% OF POSSIBLE SUNSHINE** | 9 | 31 | 36 | 42 | 51 | 57 | 58 | 64 | 55 | 47 | 40 | 27 | 26 | 45 |
| **MEAN SKY COVER (tenths)** | | | | | | | | | | | | | | |
| Sunrise - Sunset | | | | | | | | | | | | | | |
| **MEAN NUMBER OF DAYS:** | | | | | | | | | | | | | | |
| Sunrise to Sunset | | | | | | | | | | | | | | |
| -Clear | | | | | | | | | | | | | | |
| -Partly Cloudy | | | | | | | | | | | | | | |
| -Cloudy | | | | | | | | | | | | | | |
| Precipitation | | | | | | | | | | | | | | |
| .01 inches or more | 11 | 18.0 | 13.4 | 14.7 | 12.2 | 10.5 | 12.3 | 9.6 | 13.1 | 14.5 | 15.8 | 15.9 | 18.5 | 168.5 |
| Snow,Ice pellets | | | | | | | | | | | | | | |
| 1.0 inches or more | 11 | 11.4 | 7.1 | 7.4 | 3.5 | 0.1 | 0.0 | 0.0 | 0.0 | 0.0 | 2.6 | 6.5 | 9.2 | 47.7 |
| Thunderstorms | 11 | 0.0 | 0.1 | 0.5 | 1.3 | 3.1 | 5.9 | 6.4 | 5.8 | 3.8 | 1.7 | 0.0 | 0.0 | 28.6 |
| Heavy Fog Visibility | | | | | | | | | | | | | | |
| 1/4 mile or less | 11 | 0.6 | 1.7 | 2.4 | 2.3 | 2.8 | 1.2 | 2.2 | 4.1 | 4.2 | 2.9 | 1.4 | 1.8 | 27.5 |
| Temperature °F | | | | | | | | | | | | | | |
| -Maximum | | | | | | | | | | | | | | |
| 90° and above | 11 | 0.0 | 0.0 | 0.0 | 0.1 | 0.2 | 0.5 | 2.3 | 0.5 | 0.2 | 0.0 | 0.0 | 0.0 | 3.7 |
| 32° and below | 11 | 26.8 | 20.4 | 14.0 | 2.4 | 0.1 | 0.0 | 0.0 | 0.0 | 0.0 | 0.5 | 9.5 | 24.2 | 97.9 |
| -Minimum | | | | | | | | | | | | | | |
| 32° and below | 11 | 31.0 | 28.0 | 29.0 | 21.5 | 8.5 | 0.5 | 0.0 | 0.0 | 2.3 | 17.1 | 27.1 | 30.6 | 195.7 |
| 0° and below | 11 | 12.1 | 12.2 | 5.1 | 0.2 | 0.0 | 0.0 | 0.0 | 0.0 | 0.0 | 0.0 | 0.9 | 7.8 | 38.3 |
| **AVG. STATION PRESS.(mb)** | | | | | | | | | | | | | | |
| **RELATIVE HUMIDITY (%)** | | | | | | | | | | | | | | |
| Hour 01 | | | | | | | | | | | | | | |
| Hour 07 (Local Time) | | | | | | | | | | | | | | |
| Hour 13 | | | | | | | | | | | | | | |
| Hour 19 | | | | | | | | | | | | | | |
| **PRECIPITATION (inches):** | | | | | | | | | | | | | | |
| Water Equivalent | | | | | | | | | | | | | | |
| -Normal | | 2.00 | 1.87 | 2.83 | 3.63 | 3.96 | 3.85 | 3.21 | 3.25 | 3.92 | 3.25 | 2.92 | 2.44 | 37.13 |
| -Maximum Monthly | 11 | 4.02 | 3.68 | 6.08 | 6.56 | 6.49 | 6.61 | 4.88 | 8.59 | 6.94 | 7.59 | 8.25 | 4.33 | 8.59 |
| -Year | | 1988 | 1984 | 1979 | 1985 | 1983 | 1981 | 1987 | 1988 | 1980 | 1979 | 1988 | 1981 | AUG 1988 |
| -Minimum Monthly | 11 | 1.27 | 0.59 | 0.56 | 1.48 | 0.06 | 0.71 | 0.57 | 1.41 | 1.21 | 2.03 | 1.04 | 0.52 | 0.06 |
| -Year | | 1984 | 1982 | 1980 | 1989 | 1986 | 1988 | 1981 | 1979 | 1989 | 1984 | 1986 | 1986 | MAY 1986 |
| -Maximum in 24 hrs | 10 | 2.23 | 2.05 | 2.40 | 3.09 | 3.44 | 2.80 | 2.64 | 2.34 | 2.01 | 3.66 | 2.97 | 2.48 | 3.66 |
| -Year | | 1988 | 1983 | 1986 | 1985 | 1983 | 1989 | 1985 | 1988 | 1983 | 1985 | 1988 | 1985 | OCT 1985 |
| Snow,Ice pellets | | | | | | | | | | | | | | |
| -Maximum Monthly | 11 | 68.8 | 51.4 | 59.1 | 29.2 | 1.4 | 0.0 | 0.0 | T | 0.5 | 18.6 | 41.7 | 82.6 | 82.6 |
| -Year | | 1982 | 1985 | 1985 | 1982 | 1980 | | | 1989 | 1989 | 1979 | 1989 | 1981 | DEC 1981 |
| -Maximum in 24 hrs | 10 | 23.3 | 20.6 | 25.4 | 20.0 | 1.2 | 0.0 | 0.0 | T | 0.5 | 12.7 | 17.3 | 25.8 | 25.8 |
| -Year | | 1988 | 1983 | 1986 | 1985 | 1980 | | | 1989 | 1989 | 1989 | 1988 | 1985 | DEC 1985 |
| **WIND:** | | | | | | | | | | | | | | |
| Mean Speed (mph) | | | | | | | | | | | | | | |
| Prevailing Direction | | | | | | | | | | | | | | |
| Fastest Mile | | | | | | | | | | | | | | |
| -Direction (!!!) | 6 | NW | NW | NW | NW | N | NW | NW | NW | W | SE | NW | SW | NW |
| -Speed (MPH) | 6 | 44 | 31 | 40 | 44 | 34 | 38 | 35 | 37 | 35 | 38 | 31 | 35 | 44 |
| -Year | | 1980 | 1985 | 1982 | 1982 | 1981 | 1984 | 1982 | 1984 | 1983 | 1984 | 1979 | 1982 | APR 1982 |
| Peak Gust | | | | | | | | | | | | | | |
| -Direction (!!!) | | | | | | | | | | | | | | |
| -Speed (mph) | | | | | | | | | | | | | | |
| -Date | | | | | | | | | | | | | | |

**See Reference Notes to this table on the following page.**

PRECIPITATION (inches)  —  MARQUETTE COUNTY AIRPORT, MICHIGAN

**TABLE 2**

| YEAR | JAN | FEB | MAR | APR | MAY | JUNE | JULY | AUG | SEP | OCT | NOV | DEC | ANNUAL |
|---|---|---|---|---|---|---|---|---|---|---|---|---|---|
| 1961 | 0.97 | 1.90 | 2.94 | 2.96 | 2.37 | 3.08 | 1.32 | 0.98 | 4.84 | 1.80 | 2.33 | 2.13 | 27.61 |
| 1962 | 1.38 | 2.47 | 1.33 | 1.38 | 2.17 | 2.16 | 1.43 | 3.37 | 4.66 | 1.91 | 1.16 | 2.57 | 25.99 |
| 1963 | 1.25 | 0.89 | 1.49 | 2.39 | 1.73 | 3.99 | 2.53 | 1.73 | 3.91 | 0.90 | 2.68 | 2.13 | 24.16 |
| 1964 | 1.31 | 1.42 | 1.74 | 2.91 | 3.13 | 2.50 | 2.95 | 5.04 | 3.91 | 1.79 | 2.65 | 2.13 | 31.48 |
| 1965 | 1.16 | 1.61 | 1.72 | 1.43 | 3.61 | 1.51 | 2.10 | 3.02 | 4.25 | 2.23 | 3.51 | 2.02 | 28.17 |
| 1966 | 1.33 | 0.72 | 4.46 | 1.58 | 1.10 | 2.46 | 1.80 | 3.90 | 3.10 | 3.18 | 3.62 | 2.79 | 30.04 |
| 1967 | 2.71 | 1.35 | 1.33 | 3.06 | 1.63 | 3.67 | 1.44 | 2.80 | 1.20 | 5.50 | 1.71 | 0.73 | 27.13 |
| 1968 | 1.24 | 3.08 | 0.76 | 3.11 | 2.86 | 7.07 | 1.81 | 2.44 | 7.22 | 2.47 | 1.68 | 3.96 | 37.70 |
| 1969 | 2.39 | 0.79 | 1.82 | 2.49 | 2.22 | 2.76 | 0.53 | 1.48 | 3.23 | 5.20 | 1.86 | 2.11 | 26.88 |
| 1970 | 1.90 | 1.20 | 1.17 | 1.55 | 4.86 | 1.46 | 5.36 | 0.94 | 5.47 | 2.29 | 2.68 | 1.75 | 30.63 |
| 1971 | 3.57 | 2.54 | 2.06 | 1.41 | 2.53 | 4.12 | 2.22 | 1.45 | 3.80 | 4.71 | 2.33 | 2.89 | 33.63 |
| 1972 | 1.53 | 1.43 | 3.25 | 2.62 | 2.50 | 1.70 | 2.85 | 4.12 | 5.32 | 1.96 | 3.39 | 3.03 | 33.70 |
| 1973 | 1.47 | 0.99 | 2.37 | 3.01 | 7.16 | 3.42 | 2.16 | 1.80 | 3.87 | 4.01 | 2.87 | 0.81 | 31.66 |
| 1974 | 1.31 | 1.42 | 0.61 | 3.28 | 2.49 | 3.57 | 1.01 | 2.97 | 2.80 | 1.34 | 3.16 | 1.87 | 29.09 |
| 1975 | 2.85 | 2.10 | 2.11 | 2.41 | 3.53 | 4.59 | 1.06 | 2.97 | 2.80 | 2.24 | 1.68 | 1.79 | 30.79 |
| 1976 | 2.65 | 2.22 | 3.95 | 1.83 | 2.95 | 1.63 | 1.52 | 0.50 | 1.32 | 2.24 | 1.68 | 3.24 | 24.28 |
| 1977 | 1.01 | 1.57 | 4.09 | 3.19 | 2.04 | 3.10 | 3.89 | 3.55 | 5.17 | 2.65 | 2.52 | 2.18 | 36.02 |
| 1978 | 3.03 | 0.89 | 0.56 | 1.49 | 3.34 | 2.68 | 4.10 | 4.47 | 4.54 | 1.72 | 2.72 | 1.56 | 31.72 |
| #1979 | 2.43 | 1.99 | 6.08 | 1.84 | 2.70 | 6.13 | 4.63 | 1.41 | 2.09 | 7.59 | 2.47 | 1.92 | 40.92 |
| 1980 | 2.95 | 1.47 | 0.56 | 4.11 | 1.87 | 3.18 | 2.51 | 3.49 | 6.94 | 2.71 | 1.92 | 2.21 | 33.92 |
| 1981 | 1.96 | 2.18 | 2.30 | 3.10 | 2.43 | 6.61 | 0.57 | 2.28 | 2.11 | 4.63 | 2.00 | 4.33 | 34.50 |
| 1982 | 3.80 | 0.59 | 1.89 | 4.45 | 2.76 | 1.24 | 4.65 | 3.45 | 5.00 | 3.87 | 2.53 | 2.83 | 37.06 |
| 1983 | 2.67 | 3.14 | 4.85 | 3.17 | 6.49 | 1.62 | 1.45 | 3.21 | 4.98 | 5.75 | 5.68 | 3.35 | 46.36 |
| 1984 | 1.27 | 3.68 | 3.99 | 2.46 | 0.79 | 2.81 | 1.92 | 4.29 | 6.32 | 2.03 | 2.35 | 2.60 | 32.48 |
| 1985 | 2.96 | 2.91 | 4.63 | 6.56 | 3.59 | 1.49 | 3.76 | 4.78 | 6.32 | 4.88 | 5.74 | 3.97 | 51.59 |
| 1986 | 2.94 | 1.21 | 4.77 | 2.36 | 0.06 | 2.45 | 3.07 | 4.62 | 2.85 | 4.50 | 1.04 | 0.52 | 30.39 |
| 1987 | 1.42 | 1.53 | 2.07 | 2.30 | 3.93 | 2.01 | 0.71 | 4.88 | 3.58 | 4.31 | 8.25 | 2.36 | 36.30 |
| 1988 | 4.02 | 0.95 | 3.66 | 1.48 | 1.34 | 2.15 | 1.46 | 8.59 | 3.97 | 5.01 | 3.43 | 2.58 | 41.80 |
| 1989 | 1.82 | 1.60 | 2.89 | 1.48 | 2.15 | 5.36 | 0.91 | 2.61 | 1.21 | 3.49 | 5.01 | 1.00 | 29.53 |
| 1990 | 1.74 | 1.96 | 1.88 | 2.32 | 4.25 | 3.13 | 2.01 | 2.70 | 4.76 | 5.27 | 1.00 | 1.71 | 32.73 |
| Record Mean | 2.08 | 1.71 | 2.17 | 2.47 | 2.91 | 3.36 | 3.00 | 2.88 | 3.52 | 2.88 | 2.91 | 2.30 | 32.20 |

**TABLE 3**  AVERAGE TEMPERATURE (deg. F)  —  MARQUETTE COUNTY AIRPORT, MICHIGAN

| YEAR | JAN | FEB | MAR | APR | MAY | JUNE | JULY | AUG | SEP | OCT | NOV | DEC | ANNUAL |
|---|---|---|---|---|---|---|---|---|---|---|---|---|---|
| 1961 | 16.0 | 24.8 | 30.6 | 37.6 | 48.0 | 59.9 | 65.1 | 67.4 | 59.8 | 49.0 | 35.6 | 22.4 | 43.0 |
| 1962 | 14.2 | 14.6 | 28.4 | 38.1 | 54.0 | 62.9 | 64.1 | 64.6 | 57.2 | 48.8 | 36.3 | 21.7 | 41.3 |
| 1963 | 9.2 | 11.7 | 27.7 | 41.2 | 50.5 | 61.3 | 68.6 | 63.9 | 57.2 | 58.8 | 39.3 | 18.9 | 42.4 |
| 1964 | 25.3 | 23.5 | 25.4 | 40.9 | 56.5 | 62.2 | 67.6 | 63.9 | 56.0 | 47.4 | 36.5 | 21.0 | 43.4 |
| 1965 | 15.8 | 15.8 | 23.3 | 38.2 | 54.2 | 60.1 | 63.1 | 62.6 | 53.1 | 47.4 | 33.9 | 28.9 | 41.4 |
| 1966 | 15.4 | 21.1 | 31.6 | 37.8 | 47.1 | 60.9 | 69.9 | 64.0 | 58.5 | 46.6 | 32.9 | 23.9 | 42.7 |
| 1967 | 20.4 | 13.1 | 28.3 | 39.2 | 45.8 | 60.5 | 64.6 | 63.6 | 59.0 | 45.5 | 31.0 | 24.7 | 41.3 |
| 1968 | 17.8 | 16.2 | 33.6 | 42.3 | 48.6 | 56.4 | 66.1 | 64.3 | 60.3 | 50.5 | 35.0 | 24.1 | 42.9 |
| 1969 | 21.3 | 22.6 | 25.6 | 41.7 | 51.9 | 55.4 | 65.3 | 70.8 | 59.3 | 44.5 | 34.6 | 25.6 | 43.2 |
| 1970 | 14.9 | 17.5 | 25.1 | 40.2 | 47.0 | 60.8 | 68.8 | 67.8 | 58.8 | 50.7 | 35.2 | 24.2 | 42.6 |
| 1971 | 14.4 | 19.2 | 26.3 | 39.7 | 48.4 | 61.3 | 64.2 | 63.4 | 61.1 | 53.6 | 34.9 | 25.4 | 42.7 |
| 1972 | 13.6 | 14.9 | 22.8 | 34.9 | 52.3 | 57.0 | 63.9 | 63.3 | 54.6 | 43.6 | 33.3 | 18.9 | 39.4 |
| 1973 | 22.1 | 20.5 | 35.2 | 39.8 | 45.4 | 60.3 | 67.0 | 69.1 | 58.6 | 53.4 | 35.1 | 23.0 | 44.1 |
| 1974 | 17.1 | 16.4 | 27.4 | 39.9 | 47.7 | 59.7 | 69.1 | 64.5 | 52.9 | 46.7 | 36.6 | 29.4 | 42.2 |
| 1975 | 20.4 | 23.2 | 26.5 | 35.4 | 54.7 | 61.1 | 70.3 | 67.1 | 54.2 | 50.1 | 39.4 | 23.1 | 43.8 |
| 1976 | 15.6 | 26.1 | 28.4 | 43.1 | 48.5 | 64.1 | 66.5 | 61.8 | 56.8 | 43.4 | 29.1 | 14.6 | 42.0 |
| 1977 | 10.1 | 19.9 | 34.3 | 43.8 | 58.4 | 59.2 | 67.3 | 61.8 | 56.6 | 48.4 | 35.0 | 22.0 | 43.1 |
| 1978 | 17.9 | 18.6 | 27.4 | 37.3 | 53.3 | 60.5 | 65.1 | 66.4 | 58.7 | 47.0 | 34.2 | 20.1 | 42.2 |
| #1979 | 5.6 | 6.9 | 24.4 | 34.4 | 46.2 | 58.1 | 64.7 | 60.8 | 55.6 | 39.5 | 28.8 | 23.5 | 37.4 |
| 1980 | 13.1 | 12.8 | 21.3 | 39.1 | 54.5 | 56.9 | 65.7 | 64.5 | 52.9 | 38.6 | 29.8 | 15.4 | 38.7 |
| 1981 | 13.9 | 18.4 | 27.3 | 39.0 | 48.1 | 59.6 | 65.7 | 63.8 | 52.0 | 40.1 | 34.5 | 18.7 | 40.1 |
| 1982 | 4.8 | 12.1 | 23.1 | 32.8 | 54.9 | 54.0 | 66.0 | 59.8 | 53.8 | 45.4 | 29.1 | 23.3 | 38.2 |
| 1983 | 18.0 | 21.9 | 26.0 | 33.8 | 44.1 | 60.5 | 70.1 | 67.9 | 57.5 | 43.2 | 31.9 | 8.7 | 40.3 |
| 1984 | 9.0 | 25.3 | 17.5 | 40.3 | 48.2 | 62.0 | 64.4 | 65.4 | 52.4 | 46.7 | 30.5 | 18.7 | 40.0 |
| 1985 | 11.3 | 11.8 | 26.7 | 40.9 | 52.1 | 56.8 | 62.6 | 61.4 | 54.7 | 44.0 | 26.2 | 9.7 | 38.2 |
| 1986 | 14.4 | 14.8 | 26.4 | 42.0 | 54.8 | 57.1 | 66.3 | 60.0 | 53.2 | 42.7 | 25.2 | 21.3 | 39.9 |
| 1987 | 18.0 | 22.9 | 30.1 | 44.6 | 53.7 | 63.8 | 67.8 | 62.7 | 56.9 | 39.0 | 32.6 | 23.5 | 43.0 |
| 1988 | 11.6 | 10.8 | 23.1 | 38.5 | 54.7 | 62.3 | 68.6 | 65.0 | 54.9 | 38.0 | 31.8 | 16.3 | 39.6 |
| 1989 | 19.1 | 8.4 | 19.4 | 34.7 | 50.8 | 57.5 | 66.7 | 63.2 | 55.7 | 45.3 | 24.8 | 9.2 | 37.9 |
| 1990 | 22.0 | 18.1 | 28.5 | 42.3 | 46.9 | 59.9 | 63.7 | 63.2 | 53.7 | 41.3 | 34.0 | 18.0 | 41.0 |
| Record Mean | 16.9 | 17.7 | 25.9 | 38.7 | 49.4 | 59.3 | 65.8 | 64.4 | 57.1 | 46.8 | 33.3 | 22.5 | 41.5 |
| Max | 23.9 | 25.3 | 33.4 | 46.5 | 58.3 | 69.0 | 75.1 | 72.8 | 65.3 | 54.1 | 39.1 | 28.4 | 49.3 |
| Min | 9.9 | 10.1 | 18.3 | 30.9 | 40.5 | 49.6 | 56.6 | 55.9 | 48.9 | 39.4 | 27.4 | 16.6 | 33.7 |

## REFERENCE NOTES FOR TABLES 1, 2, 3 and 6  (MARQUETTE, MI)

### GENERAL

T - TRACE AMOUNT
BLANK ENTRIES DENOTE MISSING/UNREPORTED DATA.
# INDICATES A STATION OR INSTRUMENT RELOCATION.

### SPECIFIC

**TABLE 1**

(a) - LENGTH OF RECORD IN YEARS. ALTHOUGH INDIVIDUAL MONTHS MAY BE MISSING.

* LESS THAN .05

NORMALS — BASED ON THE 1951-1980 RECORD PERIOD.
EXTREMES — DATES ARE THE MOST RECENT OCCURRENCE.
WIND DIR. — NUMERALS SHOW TENS OF DEGREES CLOCKWISE FROM TRUE NORTH. "00" INDICATES CALM.
RESULTANT WIND DIRECTIONS ARE GIVEN TO WHOLE DEGREES.

**TABLE 3**
MAX AND MIN ARE LONG-TERM <u>MEAN DAILY MAXIMUM</u> AND <u>MEAN DAILY MINIMUM</u> TEMPERATURES.

### EXCEPTIONS

**TABLES 2, 3, and 6**

RECORD MEANS ARE THROUGH THE CURRENT YEAR, BEGINNING IN
1875 FOR TEMPERATURE
1872 FOR PRECIPITATION
1938 FOR SNOWFALL

HEATING DEGREE DAYS Base 65 deg. F — MARQUETTE COUNTY AIRPORT, MICHIGAN

**TABLE 4**

| SEASON | JULY | AUG | SEP | OCT | NOV | DEC | JAN | FEB | MAR | APR | MAY | JUNE | TOTAL |
|---|---|---|---|---|---|---|---|---|---|---|---|---|---|
| 1961-62 | 55 | 41 | 224 | 494 | 873 | 1313 | 1568 | 1406 | 1128 | 801 | 372 | 259 | 8534 |
| 1962-63 | 96 | 96 | 318 | 504 | 852 | 1338 | 1728 | 1487 | 1150 | 708 | 453 | 198 | 8928 |
| 1963-64 | 51 | 112 | 242 | 222 | 763 | 1422 | 1225 | 1195 | 1221 | 717 | 286 | 230 | 7686 |
| 1964-65 | 43 | 137 | 268 | 540 | 850 | 1355 | 1520 | 1370 | 1287 | 795 | 344 | 187 | 8696 |
| 1965-66 | 105 | 131 | 355 | 547 | 929 | 1113 | 1533 | 1223 | 1026 | 809 | 559 | 149 | 8479 |
| 1966-67 | 24 | 84 | 225 | 565 | 956 | 1267 | 1375 | 1448 | 1131 | 767 | 587 | 172 | 8601 |
| 1967-68 | 85 | 118 | 203 | 598 | 1010 | 1243 | 1459 | 1411 | 963 | 676 | 501 | 263 | 8530 |
| 1968-69 | 81 | 106 | 166 | 465 | 890 | 1262 | 1349 | 1182 | 1214 | 692 | 436 | 297 | 8140 |
| 1969-70 | 93 | 21 | 209 | 628 | 905 | 1215 | 1548 | 1323 | 1234 | 739 | 557 | 186 | 8658 |
| 1970-71 | 49 | 44 | 224 | 443 | 887 | 1257 | 1563 | 1279 | 1189 | 754 | 513 | 162 | 8364 |
| 1971-72 | 90 | 123 | 182 | 350 | 897 | 1218 | 1586 | 1447 | 1304 | 897 | 403 | 257 | 8754 |
| 1972-73 | 103 | 121 | 305 | 653 | 950 | 1423 | 1323 | 1239 | 916 | 752 | 598 | 159 | 8542 |
| 1973-74 | 59 | 37 | 244 | 360 | 889 | 1296 | 1482 | 1354 | 1180 | 747 | 535 | 192 | 8375 |
| 1974-75 | 27 | 77 | 360 | 563 | 843 | 1097 | 1376 | 1165 | 1188 | 880 | 320 | 176 | 8072 |
| 1975-76 | 49 | 45 | 317 | 455 | 762 | 1290 | 1525 | 1120 | 1128 | 653 | 506 | 94 | 7944 |
| 1976-77 | 36 | 79 | 293 | 668 | 1069 | 1556 | 1695 | 1253 | 946 | 630 | 239 | 193 | 8657 |
| 1977-78 | 50 | 126 | 244 | 504 | 894 | 1329 | 1455 | 1295 | 1156 | 826 | 381 | 183 | 8443 |
| #1978-79 | 64 | 57 | 220 | 554 | 918 | 1385 | 1840 | 1626 | 1254 | 914 | 577 | 214 | 9623 |
| 1979-80 | 93 | 153 | 295 | 785 | 1080 | 1282 | 1604 | 1508 | 1350 | 772 | 340 | 271 | 9533 |
| 1980-81 | 53 | 68 | 361 | 813 | 1050 | 1532 | 1581 | 1303 | 1160 | 776 | 519 | 168 | 9384 |
| 1981-82 | 73 | 78 | 384 | 766 | 907 | 1425 | 1864 | 1480 | 1292 | 960 | 313 | 326 | 9868 |
| 1982-83 | 37 | 190 | 350 | 598 | 1069 | 1289 | 1446 | 1201 | 1205 | 929 | 638 | 207 | 9159 |
| 1983-84 | 35 | 38 | 264 | 672 | 989 | 1740 | 1737 | 1145 | 1469 | 733 | 517 | 124 | 9463 |
| 1984-85 | 71 | 72 | 369 | 560 | 1028 | 1431 | 1658 | 1486 | 1178 | 724 | 400 | 249 | 9226 |
| 1985-86 | 111 | 146 | 323 | 645 | 1156 | 1709 | 1564 | 1400 | 1191 | 684 | 334 | 250 | 9513 |
| 1986-87 | 71 | 169 | 349 | 684 | 1185 | 1348 | 1450 | 1171 | 1075 | 606 | 387 | 106 | 8601 |
| 1987-88 | 58 | 130 | 247 | 800 | 964 | 1278 | 1650 | 1569 | 1295 | 787 | 347 | 166 | 9291 |
| 1988-89 | 37 | 101 | 305 | 833 | 988 | 1504 | 1416 | 1584 | 1412 | 902 | 432 | 245 | 9759 |
| 1989-90 | 65 | 117 | 283 | 610 | 1199 | 1727 | 1324 | 1308 | 1123 | 702 | 556 | 176 | 9190 |
| 1990-91 | 104 | 111 | 347 | 726 | 921 | 1454 | | | | | | | |

**TABLE 5**  COOLING DEGREE DAYS Base 65 deg. F — MARQUETTE COUNTY AIRPORT, MICHIGAN

| YEAR | JAN | FEB | MAR | APR | MAY | JUNE | JULY | AUG | SEP | OCT | NOV | DEC | TOTAL |
|---|---|---|---|---|---|---|---|---|---|---|---|---|---|
| 1969 | 0 | 0 | 0 | 0 | 35 | 14 | 109 | 210 | 44 | 0 | 0 | 0 | 412 |
| 1970 | 0 | 0 | 0 | 0 | 6 | 66 | 176 | 139 | 46 | 7 | 0 | 0 | 440 |
| 1971 | 0 | 0 | 0 | 0 | 6 | 57 | 73 | 81 | 73 | 4 | 0 | 0 | 294 |
| 1972 | 0 | 0 | 0 | 0 | 14 | 26 | 76 | 73 | 0 | 0 | 0 | 0 | 189 |
| 1973 | 0 | 0 | 0 | 0 | 0 | 25 | 127 | 172 | 59 | 0 | 0 | 0 | 389 |
| 1974 | 0 | 0 | 0 | 0 | 5 | 40 | 162 | 70 | 3 | 0 | 0 | 0 | 280 |
| 1975 | 0 | 0 | 0 | 0 | 9 | 67 | 218 | 118 | 1 | 0 | 0 | 0 | 413 |
| 1976 | 0 | 0 | 0 | 3 | 0 | 75 | 92 | 166 | 53 | 4 | 0 | 0 | 393 |
| 1977 | 0 | 0 | 0 | 0 | 44 | 24 | 126 | 35 | 0 | 0 | 0 | 0 | 229 |
| 1978 | 0 | 0 | 0 | 0 | 25 | 53 | 76 | 108 | 38 | 2 | 0 | 0 | 302 |
| #1979 | 0 | 0 | 0 | 0 | 0 | 15 | 92 | 29 | 19 | 0 | 0 | 0 | 155 |
| 1980 | 0 | 0 | 0 | 2 | 21 | 36 | 83 | 61 | 5 | 0 | 0 | 0 | 208 |
| 1981 | 0 | 0 | 0 | 0 | 1 | 13 | 103 | 50 | 2 | 0 | 0 | 0 | 169 |
| 1982 | 0 | 0 | 0 | 0 | 7 | 2 | 75 | 35 | 23 | 0 | 0 | 0 | 142 |
| 1983 | 0 | 0 | 0 | 0 | 0 | 78 | 200 | 135 | 47 | 1 | 0 | 0 | 461 |
| 1984 | 0 | 0 | 0 | 0 | 3 | 42 | 59 | 89 | 0 | 0 | 0 | 0 | 193 |
| 1985 | 0 | 0 | 0 | 7 | 7 | 10 | 44 | 41 | 21 | 0 | 0 | 0 | 130 |
| 1986 | 0 | 0 | 0 | 1 | 21 | 17 | 119 | 21 | 0 | 0 | 0 | 0 | 179 |
| 1987 | 0 | 0 | 0 | 3 | 41 | 77 | 150 | 65 | 13 | 0 | 0 | 0 | 349 |
| 1988 | 0 | 0 | 0 | 0 | 32 | 89 | 157 | 106 | 8 | 0 | 0 | 0 | 392 |
| 1989 | 0 | 0 | 0 | 0 | 1 | 27 | 123 | 70 | 13 | 1 | 0 | 0 | 235 |
| 1990 | 0 | 0 | 0 | 24 | 0 | 29 | 70 | 63 | 14 | 0 | 0 | 0 | 200 |

**TABLE 6**  SNOWFALL (inches) — MARQUETTE COUNTY AIRPORT, MICHIGAN

| SEASON | JULY | AUG | SEP | OCT | NOV | DEC | JAN | FEB | MAR | APR | MAY | JUNE | TOTAL |
|---|---|---|---|---|---|---|---|---|---|---|---|---|---|
| 1961-62 | 0.0 | 0.0 | T | T | 8.2 | 33.5 | 24.1 | 35.9 | 12.0 | 2.0 | 1.1 | 0.0 | 116.8 |
| 1962-63 | 0.0 | 0.0 | 0.0 | 4.5 | 4.5 | 23.2 | 16.5 | 12.2 | 15.0 | 0.7 | 0.7 | 0.0 | 77.3 |
| 1963-64 | 0.0 | 0.0 | 0.0 | T | 8.6 | 27.8 | 11.6 | 21.7 | 18.2 | 3.6 | 0.0 | 0.0 | 91.5 |
| 1964-65 | 0.0 | 0.0 | 0.0 | 1.7 | 14.9 | 27.9 | 17.0 | 20.1 | 22.4 | 2.9 | T | 0.0 | 106.9 |
| 1965-66 | 0.0 | 0.0 | T | 0.1 | 12.6 | 7.6 | 20.6 | 13.0 | 31.5 | 12.4 | 0.3 | 0.0 | 98.1 |
| 1966-67 | 0.0 | 0.0 | 0.0 | 1.1 | 28.0 | 32.6 | 29.8 | 23.5 | 10.4 | 2.4 | 4.5 | 0.0 | 132.3 |
| 1967-68 | 0.0 | 0.0 | 0.0 | 5.4 | 17.4 | 6.2 | 11.6 | 44.4 | 4.1 | 5.5 | T | 0.0 | 94.6 |
| 1968-69 | 0.0 | 0.0 | 0.0 | 2.0 | 15.6 | 41.1 | 29.5 | 12.2 | 17.7 | 1.0 | 0.1 | 0.0 | 119.2 |
| 1969-70 | 0.0 | 0.0 | 0.0 | 4.3 | 7.5 | 30.9 | 30.8 | 18.3 | 11.1 | 0.9 | 1.6 | 0.0 | 105.4 |
| 1970-71 | 0.0 | 0.0 | T | 0.1 | 11.0 | 26.6 | 52.6 | 22.7 | 15.9 | 2.7 | 3.9 | 0.0 | 135.5 |
| 1971-72 | 0.0 | 0.0 | 0.0 | T | 11.2 | 25.3 | 22.6 | 23.2 | 34.3 | 14.4 | 0.0 | 0.0 | 131.0 |
| 1972-73 | 0.0 | 0.0 | 0.0 | 2.2 | 6.5 | 37.7 | 14.8 | 12.8 | 0.4 | 2.5 | 3.1 | 0.0 | 80.0 |
| 1973-74 | 0.0 | 0.0 | 0.0 | T | 7.4 | 27.9 | 15.5 | 18.2 | 5.2 | 13.2 | 2.3 | 0.0 | 89.7 |
| 1974-75 | 0.0 | 0.0 | 5.1 | 5.8 | 10.3 | 10.6 | 34.7 | 28.7 | 29.0 | 0.2 | 0.0 | 0.0 | 124.4 |
| 1975-76 | 0.0 | 0.0 | T | 0.1 | 16.9 | 15.3 | 45.6 | 25.9 | 44.3 | 1.4 | 4.3 | 0.0 | 153.8 |
| 1976-77 | 0.0 | 0.0 | T | 17.5 | 17.6 | 33.3 | 16.7 | 17.5 | 16.7 | 13.5 | T | 0.0 | 132.8 |
| 1977-78 | 0.0 | 0.0 | 0.0 | T | 12.2 | 38.3 | 43.3 | 16.3 | 6.1 | 1.0 | 0.0 | 0.0 | 117.2 |
| #1978-79 | 0.0 | 0.0 | 0.0 | 0.4 | 13.0 | 24.2 | 39.6 | 23.1 | 43.9 | 11.8 | T | 0.0 | 156.0 |
| 1979-80 | 0.0 | 0.0 | 0.0 | 18.6 | 24.8 | 18.9 | 33.9 | 30.2 | 7.0 | 11.3 | 1.4 | 0.0 | 146.1 |
| 1980-81 | 0.0 | 0.0 | 0.1 | 11.9 | 13.1 | 41.5 | 41.9 | 29.5 | 34.0 | 4.1 | T | 0.0 | 176.1 |
| 1981-82 | 0.0 | 0.0 | 0.0 | 14.2 | 15.3 | 82.6 | 68.8 | 9.6 | 24.1 | 29.2 | 0.0 | 0.0 | 243.8 |
| 1982-83 | 0.0 | 0.0 | 0.0 | 7.2 | 15.1 | 17.4 | 42.4 | 42.9 | 54.1 | 20.2 | T | 0.0 | 199.3 |
| 1983-84 | 0.0 | 0.0 | T | 2.5 | 31.6 | 54.3 | 30.2 | 38.1 | 46.3 | 1.1 | 0.0 | 0.0 | 204.1 |
| 1984-85 | 0.0 | 0.0 | T | T | 13.6 | 30.6 | 56.2 | 51.4 | 59.1 | 18.1 | 0.0 | 0.0 | 229.0 |
| 1985-86 | 0.0 | 0.0 | 0.0 | T | 28.1 | 56.4 | 49.8 | 17.4 | 49.1 | 6.8 | 0.1 | 0.0 | 207.7 |
| 1986-87 | 0.0 | T | 0.0 | 2.3 | 15.7 | 10.5 | 21.9 | 27.7 | 27.7 | 11.3 | 0.1 | 0.0 | 108.8 |
| 1987-88 | 0.0 | 0.0 | T | 8.3 | 21.4 | 36.1 | 62.8 | 28.0 | 49.0 | 5.8 | 0.0 | 0.0 | 211.4 |
| 1988-89 | 0.0 | 0.0 | 0.0 | 10.9 | 4.2 | 41.7 | 43.1 | 33.7 | 44.3 | 7.8 | 0.2 | 0.0 | 185.9 |
| 1989-90 | 0.0 | T | 0.0 | 0.5 | 16.6 | 41.7 | 58.4 | 26.4 | 35.8 | 16.3 | 22.6 | T | 235.4 |
| 1990-91 | 0.0 | 0.0 | T | 9.6 | 2.5 | 27.8 | | | | | | | |
| Record Mean | 0.0 | T | 0.2 | 3.8 | 15.7 | 26.7 | 26.7 | 22.3 | 21.2 | 8.5 | 1.5 | T | 126.6 |

**See Reference Notes, relative to all above tables, on preceding page.**

Duluth, Minnesota is located at the western tip of Lake Superior. The city, about 20 miles long, lies at the base of a range of hills that rise abruptly to 600 – 800 feet above the level of Lake Superior. The range runs in a northeast and southwest direction. Two or 3 miles from the lake the land becomes a slightly rolling plateau.

Duluth in the summer is known as the Air Conditioned City. Being situated below high terrain and along the lake, any easterly component winds automatically cool the city. However, with westerly flow in the summer, the wind generally abates at night, thus, allowing cool lake air to move back into the city area near the lake.

An important influence on the climate is the passage of a succession of high and low pressure systems west and east. The proximity of Lake Superior, which is the largest and coldest of the Great Lakes, modifies the local weather. Summer temperatures are cooler and winter temperatures are warmer. The lake effect at Duluth is most prevalent when low pressure systems pass to the south creating easterly winds. In the summer, warm, moist air flowing over the cold lake surface has a stabilizing effect that results in cool, cloudy weather over Duluth. However, during the winter cold air flowing over the warm open lake surface absorbs moisture that is later precipitated over Duluth as snow. The lake effect is further reflected from the low frequency of severe storms such as wind, hail, tornadoes, freezing rain (glaze), and blizzards when compared to other areas that are a further distance from the lake.

Easterly component winds at Duluth occur 40 to 50 percent of the time from March through August and 20 to 25 percent of the time from November through February. During the winter 60 to 70 percent of the winds are from a westerly component.

The climate of Duluth is predominantly continental with significant local Lake Superior effects. Duluth averages 143 days between the last occurrence of 32 degrees in mid–May and the first in early October. At the Duluth Airport about six miles away from the lake, the average first and last occurrences of 32 degrees are late May and late September, giving a freeze–free period of 123 days.

Fall colors throughout this area are outstanding. Reds, yellows, browns, and combinations of these are an experience to see. Recreation is superb from December through March for cross–country and down–hill skiing and snowmobiling. The snow is dry.

Ice in the harbor forms about mid–November and generally is gone by mid–April. The shipping season can vary from year to year depending on temperatures and the winds that move the ice around. In most years there is little or no shipping during February and March on Lake Superior.

## TABLE 1    NORMALS, MEANS AND EXTREMES

DULUTH, MINNESOTA

LATITUDE: 46°50'N    LONGITUDE: 92°11'W    ELEVATION: FT. GRND 1428 BARO 1430    TIME ZONE: CENTRAL    WBAN: 14913

| | (a) | JAN | FEB | MAR | APR | MAY | JUNE | JULY | AUG | SEP | OCT | NOV | DEC | YEAR |
|---|---|---|---|---|---|---|---|---|---|---|---|---|---|---|
| **TEMPERATURE °F:** | | | | | | | | | | | | | | |
| Normals | | | | | | | | | | | | | | |
| -Daily Maximum | | 15.5 | 21.7 | 31.9 | 47.6 | 61.3 | 70.5 | 76.4 | 73.6 | 63.6 | 53.0 | 35.2 | 21.8 | 47.7 |
| -Daily Minimum | | -2.9 | 2.2 | 13.9 | 28.9 | 39.3 | 48.2 | 54.3 | 52.8 | 44.3 | 35.4 | 21.2 | 5.8 | 28.6 |
| -Monthly | | 6.3 | 12.0 | 22.9 | 38.3 | 50.3 | 59.4 | 65.3 | 63.2 | 54.0 | 44.2 | 28.2 | 13.8 | 38.2 |
| Extremes | | | | | | | | | | | | | | |
| -Record Highest | 48 | 52 | 55 | 78 | 88 | 90 | 93 | 97 | 97 | 95 | 86 | 70 | 55 | 97 |
| -Year | | 1942 | 1976 | 1946 | 1952 | 1986 | 1980 | 1988 | 1947 | 1976 | 1953 | 1978 | 1962 | JUL 1988 |
| -Record Lowest | 48 | -39 | -33 | -29 | -5 | 17 | 27 | 35 | 32 | 22 | 8 | -23 | -34 | -39 |
| -Year | | 1972 | 1988 | 1989 | 1975 | 1967 | 1972 | 1988 | 1986 | 1942 | 1976 | 1964 | 1983 | JAN 1972 |
| **NORMAL DEGREE DAYS:** | | | | | | | | | | | | | | |
| Heating (base 65°F) | | 1820 | 1484 | 1305 | 801 | 456 | 179 | 71 | 115 | 334 | 645 | 1104 | 1587 | 9901 |
| Cooling (base 65°F) | | 0 | 0 | 0 | 0 | 0 | 11 | 80 | 59 | 0 | 0 | 0 | 0 | 150 |
| **% OF POSSIBLE SUNSHINE** | 39 | 49 | 52 | 54 | 56 | 57 | 59 | 65 | 60 | 52 | 46 | 35 | 40 | 52 |
| **MEAN SKY COVER (tenths)** | | | | | | | | | | | | | | |
| Sunrise - Sunset | 41 | 6.7 | 6.6 | 6.8 | 6.8 | 6.6 | 6.6 | 6.0 | 6.1 | 6.6 | 6.8 | 7.6 | 7.2 | 6.7 |
| **MEAN NUMBER OF DAYS:** | | | | | | | | | | | | | | |
| Sunrise to Sunset | | | | | | | | | | | | | | |
| -Clear | 41 | 7.3 | 7.4 | 6.9 | 6.3 | 6.3 | 5.2 | 7.1 | 7.1 | 6.3 | 6.5 | 4.4 | 6.0 | 76.7 |
| -Partly Cloudy | 41 | 6.9 | 6.0 | 7.1 | 7.8 | 9.4 | 11.1 | 13.1 | 12.3 | 8.6 | 7.9 | 5.8 | 6.0 | 101.9 |
| -Cloudy | 41 | 16.8 | 14.9 | 17.0 | 16.0 | 15.3 | 13.7 | 10.9 | 11.6 | 15.1 | 16.7 | 19.7 | 19.0 | 186.6 |
| Precipitation | | | | | | | | | | | | | | |
| .01 inches or more | 48 | 11.7 | 9.7 | 10.8 | 10.4 | 12.2 | 12.5 | 11.2 | 11.5 | 11.7 | 9.5 | 10.9 | 11.6 | 133.8 |
| Snow,Ice pellets | | | | | | | | | | | | | | |
| 1.0 inches or more | 46 | 4.6 | 3.5 | 4.0 | 1.8 | 0.3 | 0.0 | 0.0 | 0.0 | 0.0 | 0.4 | 2.9 | 4.2 | 21.7 |
| Thunderstorms | 47 | 0.1 | 0.* | 0.7 | 1.6 | 3.6 | 6.9 | 8.2 | 7.3 | 3.9 | 1.3 | 0.4 | 0.1 | 34.0 |
| Heavy Fog Visibility | | | | | | | | | | | | | | |
| 1/4 mile or less | 41 | 2.2 | 2.3 | 3.3 | 3.5 | 5.5 | 6.6 | 5.3 | 6.7 | 5.8 | 4.7 | 3.6 | 3.1 | 52.5 |
| Temperature °F | | | | | | | | | | | | | | |
| -Maximum | | | | | | | | | | | | | | |
| 90° and above | 28 | 0.0 | 0.0 | 0.0 | 0.0 | 0.1 | 0.1 | 1.1 | 0.7 | 0.1 | 0.0 | 0.0 | 0.0 | 2.3 |
| 32° and below | 28 | 28.2 | 22.8 | 15.5 | 1.9 | 0.0 | 0.0 | 0.0 | 0.0 | 0.0 | 0.6 | 12.1 | 26.6 | 107.8 |
| -Minimum | | | | | | | | | | | | | | |
| 32° and below | 28 | 31.0 | 28.1 | 29.0 | 20.0 | 5.4 | 0.4 | 0.0 | 0.* | 2.6 | 12.1 | 25.5 | 30.8 | 184.9 |
| 0° and below | 28 | 17.8 | 13.3 | 4.9 | 0.1 | 0.0 | 0.0 | 0.0 | 0.0 | 0.0 | 0.0 | 1.6 | 12.5 | 50.1 |
| **AVG. STATION PRESS.(mb)** | 17 | 963.7 | 965.1 | 963.3 | 963.5 | 962.9 | 962.4 | 964.2 | 964.8 | 964.8 | 964.5 | 963.4 | 963.7 | 963.9 |
| **RELATIVE HUMIDITY (%)** | | | | | | | | | | | | | | |
| Hour 00 | 28 | 74 | 72 | 73 | 70 | 71 | 79 | 81 | 84 | 84 | 77 | 78 | 78 | 77 |
| Hour 06 (Local Time) | 28 | 76 | 76 | 78 | 76 | 76 | 81 | 84 | 88 | 87 | 82 | 81 | 79 | 80 |
| Hour 12 | 28 | 70 | 65 | 63 | 56 | 53 | 59 | 59 | 63 | 64 | 62 | 70 | 74 | 63 |
| Hour 18 | 28 | 69 | 64 | 62 | 54 | 52 | 58 | 59 | 64 | 68 | 66 | 72 | 74 | 64 |
| **PRECIPITATION (inches):** | | | | | | | | | | | | | | |
| Water Equivalent | | | | | | | | | | | | | | |
| -Normal | | 1.20 | 0.90 | 1.78 | 2.16 | 3.15 | 3.96 | 3.96 | 4.12 | 3.26 | 2.21 | 1.69 | 1.29 | 29.68 |
| -Maximum Monthly | 48 | 4.70 | 2.37 | 5.12 | 5.84 | 7.67 | 8.04 | 8.48 | 10.31 | 6.61 | 7.53 | 5.01 | 3.70 | 10.31 |
| -Year | | 1969 | 1971 | 1965 | 1948 | 1962 | 1986 | 1949 | 1972 | 1980 | 1949 | 1983 | 1968 | AUG 1972 |
| -Minimum Monthly | 48 | 0.14 | 0.13 | 0.22 | 0.24 | 0.15 | 0.83 | 0.97 | 0.71 | 0.19 | 0.13 | 0.19 | 0.16 | 0.13 |
| -Year | | 1961 | 1988 | 1959 | 1987 | 1976 | 1947 | 1987 | 1970 | 1952 | 1944 | 1976 | 1979 | FEB 1988 |
| -Maximum in 24 hrs | 40 | 1.74 | 1.38 | 2.38 | 2.27 | 3.25 | 4.05 | 3.68 | 5.79 | 3.77 | 2.90 | 2.64 | 2.12 | 5.79 |
| -Year | | 1975 | 1965 | 1977 | 1954 | 1979 | 1958 | 1987 | 1978 | 1972 | 1973 | 1968 | 1950 | AUG 1978 |
| Snow,Ice pellets | | | | | | | | | | | | | | |
| -Maximum Monthly | 46 | 46.8 | 31.5 | 45.5 | 31.5 | 8.1 | 0.2 | 0.0 | T | 0.7 | 8.1 | 37.7 | 44.3 | 46.8 |
| -Year | | 1969 | 1955 | 1965 | 1950 | 1954 | 1945 | | 1989 | 1985 | 1966 | 1983 | 1950 | JAN 1969 |
| -Maximum in 24 hrs | 46 | 14.7 | 17.0 | 19.4 | 11.6 | 4.3 | 0.2 | 0.0 | T | 0.7 | 7.9 | 16.6 | 25.4 | 25.4 |
| -Year | | 1982 | 1948 | 1965 | 1983 | 1954 | 1945 | | 1989 | 1985 | 1966 | 1983 | 1950 | DEC 1950 |
| **WIND:** | | | | | | | | | | | | | | |
| Mean Speed (mph) | 40 | 11.7 | 11.3 | 11.9 | 12.6 | 11.7 | 10.5 | 9.5 | 9.5 | 10.5 | 11.2 | 11.7 | 11.3 | 11.1 |
| Prevailing Direction | | | | | | | | | | | | | | |
| through 1963 | | NW | NW | WNW | NW | E | E | WNW | E | WNW | WNW | WNW | NW | WNW |
| Fastest Mile | | | | | | | | | | | | | | |
| -Direction (!!!) | 34 | W | E | NE | NE | W | W | W | W | NW | S | E | NW | NE |
| -Speed (MPH) | 34 | 63 | 67 | 57 | 75 | 61 | 47 | 72 | 56 | 53 | 61 | 68 | 65 | 75 |
| -Year | | 1958 | 1958 | 1966 | 1958 | 1959 | 1952 | 1952 | 1952 | 1960 | 1956 | 1960 | 1957 | APR 1958 |
| Peak Gust | | | | | | | | | | | | | | |
| -Direction (!!!) | 6 | NW | NW | E | E | E | W | W | SW | SW | NW | E | NW | E |
| -Speed (mph) | 6 | 56 | 47 | 71 | 60 | 59 | 69 | 46 | 41 | 52 | 70 | 53 | 49 | 71 |
| -Date | | 1986 | 1987 | 1985 | 1986 | 1989 | 1986 | 1984 | 1988 | 1985 | 1987 | 1985 | 1989 | MAR 1985 |

**See Reference Notes to this table on the following page.**

PRECIPITATION (inches)  DULUTH, MINNESOTA

**TABLE 2**

| YEAR | JAN | FEB | MAR | APR | MAY | JUNE | JULY | AUG | SEP | OCT | NOV | DEC | ANNUAL |
|---|---|---|---|---|---|---|---|---|---|---|---|---|---|
| 1961 | 0.14 | 0.65 | 2.53 | 4.72 | 3.26 | 1.33 | 2.47 | 0.71 | 3.01 | 1.79 | 1.61 | 1.26 | 23.48 |
| 1962 | 0.88 | 1.82 | 1.08 | 2.67 | 7.67 | 3.01 | 2.97 | 4.40 | 3.03 | 0.86 | 0.28 | 0.90 | 29.57 |
| 1963 | 0.32 | 0.87 | 1.50 | 2.21 | 2.28 | 4.04 | 1.82 | 2.96 | 2.80 | 1.01 | 1.51 | 1.08 | 22.40 |
| 1964 | 1.10 | 0.57 | 1.10 | 4.10 | 5.74 | 3.50 | 1.47 | 6.57 | 6.58 | 0.59 | 1.84 | 1.79 | 34.95 |
| 1965 | 0.89 | 1.73 | 5.12 | 1.64 | 2.96 | 4.51 | 3.57 | 3.76 | 5.56 | 3.30 | 3.33 | 1.67 | 38.04 |
| 1966 | 0.98 | 1.31 | 3.84 | 1.99 | 1.53 | 4.14 | 6.13 | 6.42 | 1.52 | 3.56 | 1.17 | 0.91 | 34.15 |
| 1967 | 3.12 | 0.24 | 0.66 | 1.99 | 0.80 | 5.21 | 2.91 | 2.31 | 1.34 | 1.44 | 0.50 | 0.91 | 21.43 |
| 1968 | 0.77 | 0.22 | 1.89 | 4.83 | 4.02 | 5.39 | 3.60 | 2.07 | 3.42 | 5.28 | 3.10 | 3.70 | 38.29 |
| 1969 | 4.70 | 0.26 | 0.39 | 1.46 | 2.82 | 2.18 | 3.03 | 2.18 | 4.13 | 2.42 | 1.25 | 2.67 | 27.49 |
| 1970 | 0.51 | 0.43 | 1.15 | 3.16 | 2.81 | 1.68 | 3.58 | 0.71 | 2.01 | 6.07 | 3.39 | 1.97 | 27.47 |
| 1971 | 1.56 | 2.37 | 2.02 | 1.29 | 3.45 | 3.25 | 3.91 | 4.50 | 2.67 | 6.09 | 2.07 | 1.22 | 34.40 |
| 1972 | 2.28 | 1.47 | 2.17 | 2.17 | 2.00 | 3.70 | 6.71 | 10.31 | 5.30 | 0.83 | 1.37 | 2.02 | 39.61 |
| 1973 | 0.67 | 0.29 | 1.54 | 1.35 | 3.81 | 2.43 | 2.36 | 8.46 | 4.28 | 4.56 | 1.61 | 0.69 | 32.05 |
| 1974 | 0.97 | 0.82 | 0.78 | 2.07 | 3.09 | 4.07 | 4.85 | 3.79 | 0.98 | 1.57 | 1.36 | 1.15 | 25.50 |
| 1975 | 3.69 | 0.76 | 2.59 | 2.21 | 1.44 | 5.59 | 2.26 | 2.52 | 2.32 | 1.20 | 4.19 | 0.64 | 29.41 |
| 1976 | 1.57 | 1.05 | 3.67 | 0.73 | 0.15 | 6.16 | 2.60 | 1.84 | 1.84 | 0.48 | 0.19 | 0.39 | 20.67 |
| 1977 | 0.36 | 0.47 | 4.43 | 1.27 | 3.50 | 3.97 | 3.91 | 3.26 | 5.97 | 3.20 | 2.37 | 1.31 | 34.02 |
| 1978 | 0.52 | 0.35 | 0.47 | 1.96 | 3.49 | 2.96 | 7.67 | 7.49 | 1.52 | 0.77 | 1.27 | 1.19 | 29.66 |
| 1979 | 0.76 | 1.89 | 3.58 | 1.15 | 6.01 | 4.33 | 5.45 | 2.10 | 2.01 | 3.01 | 0.47 | 0.16 | 30.92 |
| 1980 | 1.55 | 0.56 | 1.02 | 0.41 | 0.82 | 2.35 | 3.94 | 5.34 | 6.61 | 1.64 | 0.70 | 0.63 | 25.57 |
| 1981 | 0.32 | 1.50 | 1.05 | 4.48 | 1.15 | 5.83 | 3.26 | 2.84 | 2.42 | 3.59 | 0.96 | 0.97 | 28.37 |
| 1982 | 2.02 | 0.48 | 2.06 | 2.06 | 4.30 | 1.97 | 6.21 | 1.60 | 4.19 | 5.07 | 3.08 | 1.19 | 34.23 |
| 1983 | 1.34 | 0.49 | 2.05 | 2.28 | 2.12 | 2.00 | 3.51 | 3.37 | 5.57 | 2.32 | 5.01 | 1.97 | 32.03 |
| 1984 | 0.78 | 0.61 | 0.54 | 2.34 | 1.83 | 5.70 | 1.33 | 1.96 | 3.82 | 5.19 | 0.82 | 1.91 | 26.83 |
| 1985 | 0.39 | 0.66 | 1.85 | 2.35 | 4.44 | 3.18 | 4.16 | 3.91 | 6.02 | 1.76 | 2.33 | 0.78 | 31.83 |
| 1986 | 0.66 | 0.74 | 0.88 | 4.11 | 2.59 | 8.04 | 4.58 | 5.29 | 6.26 | 0.66 | 2.01 | 0.45 | 36.27 |
| 1987 | 0.69 | 0.31 | 0.60 | 0.24 | 4.02 | 0.83 | 5.46 | 1.87 | 2.93 | 0.96 | 1.26 | 0.67 | 19.84 |
| 1988 | 0.78 | 0.13 | 2.55 | 0.44 | 3.96 | 4.56 | 1.14 | 6.82 | 6.18 | 1.05 | 3.44 | 1.12 | 32.17 |
| 1989 | 1.87 | 0.34 | 1.49 | 2.11 | 3.50 | 3.81 | 1.09 | 5.02 | 4.40 | 1.02 | 1.01 | 0.63 | 26.29 |
| 1990 | 0.51 | 0.51 | 3.35 | 3.76 | 1.48 | 4.83 | 2.42 | 5.39 | 6.49 | 3.51 | 0.65 | 0.49 | 33.39 |
| Record Mean | 1.11 | 0.91 | 1.67 | 2.17 | 3.08 | 3.96 | 3.69 | 3.55 | 3.39 | 2.23 | 1.68 | 1.12 | 28.56 |

**TABLE 3**  AVERAGE TEMPERATURE (deg. F)  DULUTH, MINNESOTA

| YEAR | JAN | FEB | MAR | APR | MAY | JUNE | JULY | AUG | SEP | OCT | NOV | DEC | ANNUAL |
|---|---|---|---|---|---|---|---|---|---|---|---|---|---|
| #1961 | 7.9 | 19.7 | 29.4 | 35.3 | 49.8 | 61.3 | 65.1 | 67.6 | 54.7 | 45.6 | 29.1 | 12.9 | 39.9 |
| 1962 | 3.4 | 7.5 | 24.3 | 34.2 | 50.0 | 56.8 | 60.8 | 61.9 | 51.9 | 33.8 | 35.7 | 9.6 | 37.0 |
| 1963 | 0.9 | 7.1 | 27.5 | 41.0 | 49.6 | 61.3 | 66.3 | 59.1 | 52.4 | 44.4 | 30.2 | 8.4 | 38.8 |
| 1964 | 16.9 | 16.4 | 19.8 | 38.7 | 54.3 | 58.0 | 61.9 | 61.1 | 48.0 | 44.8 | 27.8 | 21.1 | 36.6 |
| 1965 | 5.2 | 6.0 | 15.8 | 38.0 | 52.0 | | | | | | | | |
| 1966 | -1.3 | 12.3 | 27.1 | 34.7 | 47.3 | 61.1 | 68.0 | 61.5 | 54.8 | 43.2 | 25.2 | 13.5 | 37.3 |
| 1967 | 11.2 | 3.7 | 24.8 | 37.0 | 45.6 | 58.2 | 64.1 | 61.7 | 56.0 | 42.4 | 26.6 | 16.3 | 37.3 |
| 1968 | 9.1 | 9.3 | 32.0 | 40.5 | 48.4 | 57.4 | 64.2 | 61.7 | 56.6 | 46.2 | 28.9 | 11.9 | 38.8 |
| 1969 | 7.5 | 14.4 | 21.4 | 40.6 | 50.6 | 53.8 | 64.0 | 65.5 | 56.7 | 40.7 | 28.9 | 17.5 | 38.7 |
| 1970 | 2.4 | 8.4 | 21.1 | 38.7 | 46.6 | 60.8 | 68.8 | 66.0 | 55.5 | 44.4 | 28.1 | 14.7 | 37.8 |
| 1971 | 0.6 | 12.6 | 21.8 | 38.3 | 48.1 | 61.7 | 62.0 | 62.4 | 57.3 | 47.7 | 25.9 | 14.7 | 37.9 |
| 1972 | 0.2 | 6.4 | 17.9 | 33.3 | 53.5 | 58.4 | 61.2 | 61.9 | 50.0 | 38.9 | 27.9 | 11.7 | 34.6 |
| 1973 | 11.6 | 13.7 | 31.8 | 38.3 | 47.8 | 59.1 | 64.8 | 65.5 | 53.6 | 48.2 | 29.2 | 19.5 | 39.5 |
| 1974 | 5.6 | 11.0 | 20.6 | 37.9 | 46.6 | 58.6 | 67.1 | 60.1 | 47.9 | 42.8 | 29.2 | 11.8 | 37.2 |
| 1975 | 9.6 | 12.0 | 18.2 | 31.0 | 53.3 | 57.9 | 68.7 | 62.0 | 50.9 | 46.7 | 31.3 | 11.8 | 37.8 |
| 1976 | 4.7 | 20.7 | 22.0 | 42.6 | 50.6 | 63.2 | 66.1 | 64.9 | 55.3 | 37.1 | 22.1 | 4.5 | 37.8 |
| 1977 | -0.2 | 17.2 | 31.4 | 44.4 | 57.4 | 60.0 | 65.9 | 58.6 | 53.2 | 44.3 | 28.0 | 11.3 | 39.3 |
| 1978 | 5.1 | 10.5 | 25.6 | 38.3 | 54.8 | 60.2 | 64.7 | 63.6 | 57.3 | 44.9 | 26.2 | 10.1 | 38.5 |
| 1979 | 0.6 | 5.0 | 23.0 | 34.5 | 47.2 | 59.8 | 66.1 | 62.0 | 56.9 | 43.0 | 29.4 | 22.2 | 37.5 |
| 1980 | 8.7 | 10.7 | 19.7 | 41.4 | 54.9 | 59.5 | 67.6 | 63.6 | 52.9 | 38.9 | 30.1 | 11.6 | 38.3 |
| 1981 | 11.9 | 16.3 | 28.3 | 39.2 | 50.2 | 58.7 | 65.5 | 64.3 | 52.9 | 40.5 | 34.7 | 14.8 | 39.8 |
| 1982 | -3.2 | 10.6 | 20.8 | 35.7 | 52.8 | 54.8 | 64.5 | 60.8 | 54.3 | 45.1 | 24.4 | 19.6 | 36.7 |
| 1983 | 13.2 | 21.1 | 25.6 | 35.1 | 46.7 | 59.9 | 69.7 | 66.6 | 56.6 | 44.9 | 31.6 | 1.8 | 39.6 |
| 1984 | 7.1 | 23.0 | 18.7 | 42.4 | 50.5 | 61.4 | 66.6 | 67.7 | 51.9 | 45.7 | 28.4 | 13.2 | 39.7 |
| 1985 | 6.5 | 11.6 | 30.3 | 42.1 | 54.9 | 56.5 | 64.6 | 59.7 | 52.1 | 42.7 | 19.9 | 3.0 | 37.1 |
| 1986 | 11.7 | 11.5 | 28.5 | 42.1 | 51.8 | 58.9 | 64.7 | 60.8 | 52.7 | 43.4 | 24.0 | 18.8 | 39.1 |
| 1987 | 15.3 | 23.7 | 31.6 | 46.1 | 53.1 | 63.1 | 67.6 | 63.5 | 57.2 | 39.4 | 32.2 | 20.4 | 42.8 |
| 1988 | 4.8 | 6.2 | 24.4 | 40.1 | 56.0 | 62.8 | 70.0 | 64.5 | 55.4 | 38.6 | 28.9 | 13.5 | 38.8 |
| 1989 | 3.4 | 3.4 | 18.9 | 36.8 | 51.7 | 58.4 | 68.6 | 64.8 | 55.9 | 44.4 | 23.2 | 4.1 | 37.0 |
| 1990 | 18.7 | 14.9 | 27.1 | 40.2 | 48.3 | 61.5 | 64.6 | 64.1 | 56.2 | 42.1 | 31.4 | 12.6 | 40.1 |
| Record Mean | 8.4 | 12.4 | 24.1 | 38.3 | 49.4 | 58.6 | 65.3 | 63.7 | 55.0 | 44.2 | 28.7 | 14.4 | 38.5 |
| Max | 17.2 | 21.5 | 32.5 | 47.2 | 59.5 | 69.1 | 75.7 | 73.3 | 64.1 | 52.5 | 35.6 | 22.1 | 47.5 |
| Min | -0.4 | 3.3 | 15.7 | 29.3 | 39.2 | 48.1 | 54.9 | 54.0 | 46.0 | 35.9 | 21.8 | 6.7 | 29.6 |

**REFERENCE NOTES FOR TABLES 1, 2, 3 and 6       (DULUTH, MN)**

**GENERAL**

T - TRACE AMOUNT
BLANK ENTRIES DENOTE MISSING/UNREPORTED DATA.
# INDICATES A STATION OR INSTRUMENT RELOCATION.

**SPECIFIC**

TABLE 1

(a) - LENGTH OF RECORD IN YEARS. ALTHOUGH INDIVIDUAL MONTHS MAY BE MISSING.

* LESS THAN .05

NORMALS — BASED ON THE 1951-1980 RECORD PERIOD.
EXTREMES — DATES ARE THE MOST RECENT OCCURRENCE.
WIND DIR. — NUMERALS SHOW TENS OF DEGREES
      CLOCKWISE FROM TRUE NORTH.
      "00" INDICATES CALM.
RESULTANT WIND DIRECTIONS ARE GIVEN TO WHOLE DEGREES.

TABLE 3
MAX AND MIN ARE LONG-TERM MEAN DAILY MAXIMUM
AND MEAN DAILY MINIMUM TEMPERATURES.

**EXCEPTIONS**

TABLES 2, 3, and 6

RECORD MEANS ARE THROUGH THE CURRENT YEAR,
BEGINNING IN      1904 FOR TEMPERATURE
                  1904 FOR PRECIPITATION
                  1944 FOR SNOWFALL

HEATING DEGREE DAYS Base 65 deg. F          DULUTH, MINNESOTA

**TABLE 4**

| SEASON | JULY | AUG | SEP | OCT | NOV | DEC | JAN | FEB | MAR | APR | MAY | JUNE | TOTAL |
|---|---|---|---|---|---|---|---|---|---|---|---|---|---|
| 1961-62 | 58 | 32 | 343 | 597 | 1070 | 1612 | 1912 | 1609 | 1255 | 917 | 468 | 263 | 10136 |
| 1962-63 | 132 | 121 | 388 | 611 | 930 | 1560 | 1989 | 1620 | 1159 | 711 | 471 | 160 | 9852 |
| 1963-64 | 50 | 107 | 216 | 280 | 874 | 1715 | 1487 | 1407 | 1396 | 783 | 338 | 238 | 8891 |
| 1964-65 | 50 | 215 | 377 | 631 | 1037 | 1751 | 1854 | 1650 | 1519 | 802 | 397 | 209 | 10492 |
| 1965-66 | 127 | 158 | 506 | 617 | 1109 | 1355 | 2053 | 1473 | 1166 | 903 | 546 | 165 | 10178 |
| 1966-67 | 36 | 145 | 304 | 670 | 1187 | 1589 | 1662 | 1714 | 1243 | 832 | 592 | 210 | 10184 |
| 1967-68 | 80 | 144 | 269 | 694 | 1147 | 1504 | 1730 | 1611 | 1017 | 729 | 507 | 227 | 9659 |
| 1968-69 | 90 | 140 | 254 | 576 | 1073 | 1644 | 1780 | 1411 | 1346 | 725 | 449 | 332 | 9820 |
| 1969-70 | 99 | 20 | 258 | 746 | 1075 | 1466 | 1939 | 1581 | 1355 | 781 | 573 | 162 | 10055 |
| 1970-71 | 38 | 67 | 311 | 630 | 1107 | 1616 | 1996 | 1464 | 1332 | 794 | 518 | 124 | 9997 |
| 1971-72 | 111 | 133 | 273 | 531 | 1099 | 1553 | 2012 | 1698 | 1458 | 946 | 357 | 211 | 10382 |
| 1972-73 | 134 | 146 | 440 | 802 | 1167 | 1792 | 1654 | 1429 | 1022 | 793 | 526 | 171 | 10076 |
| 1973-74 | 72 | 66 | 354 | 513 | 1106 | 1651 | 1843 | 1508 | 1373 | 806 | 565 | 206 | 10063 |
| 1974-75 | 45 | 160 | 507 | 684 | 1069 | 1404 | 1713 | 1479 | 1447 | 1013 | 358 | 226 | 10105 |
| 1975-76 | 46 | 129 | 418 | 561 | 1003 | 1642 | 1867 | 1279 | 1325 | 667 | 440 | 101 | 9478 |
| 1976-77 | 35 | 112 | 310 | 860 | 1280 | 1871 | 2017 | 1334 | 1033 | 612 | 242 | 170 | 9876 |
| 1977-78 | 46 | 196 | 347 | 636 | 1101 | 1662 | 1852 | 1520 | 1212 | 794 | 324 | 176 | 9866 |
| 1978-79 | 71 | 99 | 262 | 615 | 1159 | | 1999 | 1679 | 1293 | 910 | 549 | 172 | 10507 |
| 1979-80 | 52 | 115 | 252 | 674 | 1059 | 1317 | 1745 | 1573 | 1398 | 702 | 326 | 201 | 9414 |
| 1980-81 | 39 | 76 | 357 | 800 | 1043 | 1644 | | 1358 | 1133 | 769 | 455 | 185 | 9509 |
| 1981-82 | 74 | 62 | 363 | 752 | 903 | 1549 | 2117 | 1523 | 1363 | 875 | 370 | 303 | 10254 |
| 1982-83 | 66 | 161 | 332 | 609 | 1212 | 1398 | 1598 | 1226 | 1214 | 887 | 562 | 185 | 9450 |
| 1983-84 | 30 | 9 | 285 | 615 | 996 | 1959 | 1792 | 1210 | 1429 | 671 | 446 | 116 | 9558 |
| 1984-85 | 40 | 40 | 391 | 588 | 1093 | 1601 | 1809 | 1494 | 1067 | 679 | 314 | 252 | 9368 |
| 1985-86 | 57 | 178 | 394 | 686 | 1349 | 1925 | 1646 | 1492 | 1127 | 680 | 416 | 196 | 10146 |
| 1986-87 | 76 | 151 | 361 | 663 | 1224 | 1426 | 1537 | 1153 | 1027 | 561 | 376 | 112 | 8667 |
| 1987-88 | 34 | 100 | 234 | 782 | 977 | 1377 | 1862 | 1704 | 1253 | 741 | 300 | 146 | 9510 |
| 1988-89 | 22 | 97 | 287 | 812 | 1081 | 1590 | 1567 | 1721 | 1424 | 839 | 405 | 206 | 10051 |
| 1989-90 | 27 | 78 | 272 | 633 | 1249 | 1887 | 1428 | 1398 | 1166 | 745 | 506 | 130 | 9519 |
| 1990-91 | 76 | 94 | 273 | 700 | 1003 | 1623 | | | | | | | |

**TABLE 5**  COOLING DEGREE DAYS Base 65 deg. F          DULUTH, MINNESOTA

| YEAR | JAN | FEB | MAR | APR | MAY | JUNE | JULY | AUG | SEP | OCT | NOV | DEC | TOTAL |
|---|---|---|---|---|---|---|---|---|---|---|---|---|---|
| 1969 | 0 | 0 | 0 | 0 | 11 | 4 | 76 | 135 | 16 | 0 | 0 | 0 | 242 |
| 1970 | 0 | 0 | 0 | 0 | 8 | 42 | 162 | 102 | 30 | 0 | 0 | 0 | 344 |
| 1971 | 0 | 0 | 0 | 0 | 0 | 32 | 24 | 60 | 47 | 1 | 0 | 0 | 164 |
| 1972 | 0 | 0 | 0 | 0 | 8 | 22 | 24 | 59 | 0 | 0 | 0 | 0 | 113 |
| 1973 | 0 | 0 | 0 | 0 | 0 | 1 | 72 | 84 | 18 | 0 | 0 | 0 | 175 |
| 1974 | 0 | 0 | 0 | 0 | 0 | 19 | 115 | 15 | 0 | 0 | 0 | 0 | 149 |
| 1975 | 0 | 0 | 0 | 0 | 2 | 18 | 168 | 41 | 0 | 0 | 0 | 0 | 229 |
| 1976 | 0 | 0 | 0 | 0 | 0 | 53 | 75 | 117 | 26 | 0 | 0 | 0 | 271 |
| 1977 | 0 | 0 | 0 | 0 | 12 | 24 | 80 | 6 | 0 | 0 | 0 | 0 | 122 |
| 1978 | 0 | 0 | 0 | 0 | 17 | 34 | 70 | 64 | 39 | 0 | 0 | 0 | 224 |
| 1979 | 0 | 0 | 0 | 0 | 4 | 25 | 95 | 30 | 15 | 0 | 0 | 0 | 169 |
| 1980 | 0 | 0 | 0 | 0 | 25 | 46 | 126 | 40 | 3 | 0 | 0 | 0 | 240 |
| 1981 | 0 | 0 | 0 | 0 | 2 | 2 | 97 | 48 | 6 | 0 | 0 | 0 | 155 |
| 1982 | 0 | 0 | 0 | 0 | 0 | 0 | 58 | 36 | 18 | 0 | 0 | 0 | 112 |
| 1983 | 0 | 0 | 0 | 0 | 0 | 42 | 179 | 165 | 42 | 0 | 0 | 0 | 428 |
| 1984 | 0 | 0 | 0 | 0 | 4 | 13 | 96 | 133 | 4 | 0 | 0 | 0 | 250 |
| 1985 | 0 | 0 | 0 | 0 | 9 | 4 | 54 | 20 | 15 | 0 | 0 | 0 | 102 |
| 1986 | 0 | 0 | 0 | 0 | 13 | 18 | 74 | 26 | 0 | 0 | 0 | 0 | 131 |
| 1987 | 0 | 0 | 0 | 0 | 13 | 13 | 62 | 121 | 60 | 7 | 0 | 0 | 263 |
| 1988 | 0 | 0 | 0 | 0 | 27 | 83 | 183 | 89 | 4 | 0 | 0 | 0 | 386 |
| 1989 | 0 | 0 | 0 | 0 | 0 | 17 | 147 | 80 | 7 | 0 | 0 | 0 | 251 |
| 1990 | 0 | 0 | 0 | 7 | 0 | 32 | 70 | 73 | 16 | 0 | 0 | 0 | 198 |

**TABLE 6**  SNOWFALL (inches)          DULUTH, MINNESOTA

| SEASON | JULY | AUG | SEP | OCT | NOV | DEC | JAN | FEB | MAR | APR | MAY | JUNE | TOTAL |
|---|---|---|---|---|---|---|---|---|---|---|---|---|---|
| 1961-62 | 0.0 | 0.0 | T | T | 2.8 | 14.4 | 14.2 | 18.3 | 7.7 | 5.7 | 0.2 | 0.0 | 63.3 |
| 1962-63 | 0.0 | 0.0 | 0.0 | 0.7 | 1.8 | 8.4 | 3.6 | 14.4 | 19.1 | 0.2 | 0.2 | 0.0 | 48.4 |
| 1963-64 | 0.0 | 0.0 | 0.0 | 0.0 | 1.6 | 15.9 | 10.8 | 6.8 | 13.5 | 5.6 | 0.0 | 0.0 | 54.2 |
| 1964-65 | 0.0 | 0.0 | T | T | 8.6 | 24.3 | 10.6 | 19.3 | 45.5 | 1.6 | 1.0 | 0.0 | 110.9 |
| 1965-66 | 0.0 | 0.0 | T | T | 25.9 | 8.6 | 11.8 | 4.3 | 24.5 | 10.2 | 1.7 | 0.0 | 87.0 |
| 1966-67 | 0.0 | 0.0 | T | 8.1 | 7.6 | 15.4 | 36.7 | 2.7 | 6.9 | 1.6 | 1.3 | 0.0 | 80.3 |
| 1967-68 | 0.0 | 0.0 | 0.0 | 0.8 | 4.2 | 4.3 | 10.8 | 2.7 | 8.7 | 3.7 | 0.0 | 0.0 | 39.3 |
| 1968-69 | 0.0 | 0.0 | 0.0 | T | 21.8 | 37.7 | 46.8 | 3.0 | 3.0 | 8.7 | T | 0.0 | 121.0 |
| 1969-70 | 0.0 | 0.0 | 0.0 | 4.3 | 9.1 | 38.8 | 7.5 | 8.9 | 9.9 | 14.8 | 1.6 | 0.0 | 94.9 |
| 1970-71 | 0.0 | 0.0 | 0.0 | 0.2 | 16.8 | 20.9 | 31.8 | 27.4 | 12.7 | 6.5 | 0.6 | 0.0 | 116.9 |
| 1971-72 | 0.0 | 0.0 | 0.0 | 0.2 | 6.4 | 17.5 | 30.9 | 20.7 | 11.0 | 20.4 | T | 0.0 | 107.1 |
| 1972-73 | 0.0 | 0.0 | T | 0.5 | 6.7 | 20.0 | 9.2 | 3.0 | 2.1 | 2.8 | 1.5 | 0.0 | 45.8 |
| 1973-74 | 0.0 | 0.0 | 0.0 | T | 7.6 | 15.7 | 13.4 | 15.3 | 15.1 | 5.2 | 1.0 | 0.0 | 73.3 |
| 1974-75 | 0.0 | 0.0 | 0.3 | 0.8 | 4.5 | 19.1 | 32.7 | 12.3 | 30.3 | 0.4 | T | 0.0 | 100.4 |
| 1975-76 | 0.0 | 0.0 | 0.0 | 0.1 | 25.7 | 7.8 | 20.6 | 8.8 | 26.4 | 0.0 | T | 0.0 | 89.4 |
| 1976-77 | 0.0 | 0.0 | 0.0 | 0.8 | 2.7 | 7.8 | 8.8 | 5.1 | 5.3 | 0.1 | 0.0 | 0.0 | 40.6 |
| 1977-78 | 0.0 | 0.0 | 0.0 | 1.7 | 16.0 | 12.0 | 13.5 | 11.4 | 8.3 | 6.8 | 0.0 | 0.0 | 69.7 |
| 1978-79 | 0.0 | 0.0 | 0.0 | T | 10.1 | 20.8 | 11.9 | 23.3 | 17.0 | 4.2 | 1.4 | 0.0 | 88.7 |
| 1979-80 | 0.0 | 0.0 | 0.0 | 0.8 | 6.0 | 2.0 | 21.9 | 10.3 | 12.6 | 1.5 | T | 0.0 | 55.1 |
| 1980-81 | 0.0 | 0.0 | 0.0 | 1.3 | 1.6 | 7.1 | 4.7 | 13.3 | 4.3 | T | 0.0 | 0.0 | 36.5 |
| 1981-82 | 0.0 | 0.0 | T | 1.4 | 12.5 | 15.5 | 34.2 | 8.0 | 17.8 | 6.3 | 0.0 | 0.0 | 95.7 |
| 1982-83 | 0.0 | 0.0 | 0.0 | 0.8 | 16.0 | 21.4 | 15.7 | 9.0 | 9.9 | 23.7 | T | 0.0 | 96.5 |
| 1983-84 | 0.0 | 0.0 | T | T | 37.7 | 32.1 | 20.0 | 4.0 | 9.9 | 3.3 | 0.3 | 0.0 | 107.3 |
| 1984-85 | 0.0 | 0.0 | T | 3.5 | 2.4 | 8.2 | 15.3 | 12.0 | 26.7 | 3.3 | 0.0 | 0.0 | 68.2 |
| 1985-86 | 0.0 | 0.0 | 0.7 | 2.3 | 34.1 | 18.8 | 11.5 | 10.3 | 11.4 | 0.2 | T | 0.0 | 89.3 |
| 1986-87 | 0.0 | 0.0 | 0.0 | 1.8 | 8.2 | 7.3 | 11.2 | 5.1 | 6.7 | 0.3 | T | 0.0 | 40.6 |
| 1987-88 | 0.0 | 0.0 | 0.0 | 3.9 | 5.8 | 11.3 | 16.7 | 2.3 | 13.7 | 0.1 | 0.0 | 0.0 | 53.8 |
| 1988-89 | 0.0 | 0.0 | 0.0 | 0.3 | 24.3 | 20.7 | 31.2 | 5.3 | 17.6 | 19.0 | 0.7 | 0.0 | 119.1 |
| 1989-90 | 0.0 | T | 0.0 | 0.6 | 8.4 | 14.2 | 5.5 | 15.0 | 11.6 | 2.4 | 0.6 | T | 58.3 |
| 1990-91 | 0.0 | 0.0 | 0.0 | 3.2 | 5.1 | 13.5 | | | | | | | |
| Record Mean | 0.0 | T | T | 1.3 | 11.0 | 15.5 | 16.9 | 11.3 | 13.8 | 6.4 | 0.7 | T | 76.9 |

**See Reference Notes, relative to all above tables, on preceding page.**

# MINNEAPOLIS-ST. PAUL, MINNESOTA

The Twin Cities of Minneapolis and St. Paul are located at the confluence of the Mississippi and Minnesota Rivers over the heart of an artesian water basin. Its flat or gently rolling terrain varies little in elevation from that of the official observation station at International Airport. Numerous lakes dot the surrounding area. Minneapolis alone boasts of 22 lakes within the city park system. The largest body of water, nearly 15,000 acres, is Lake Minnetonka, located about 15 miles west of the airport. Most bodies of water are relatively small and shallow and are ice covered during winter.

The climate of the Minneapolis–St. Paul area is predominantly continental. Seasonal temperature variations are quite large. Temperatures range from less than −30 degrees to over 100 degrees. The growing season is 166 days. Because of this favorable growing season, all crops generally mature before the autumn freeze occurs.

The Twin Cities lie near the northern edge of the influx of moisture from the Gulf of Mexico. Severe storms such as blizzards, freezing rain (glaze), tornadoes, wind and hail storms do occur. The total annual precipitation is important. Even more significant is its proper distribution during the growing season. During the five month growing season, May through September, the major crops produced are corn, soybeans, small grains, and hay. During this period, the normal rainfall is over 16 inches, approximately 65 percent of the annual precipitation. Winter snowfall is nearly 48 inches. Winter recreational weather is excellent because of the dry snow. These conditions exist from about Christmas into early March. Snow depths average 6 to 8 inches in the city and 8 to 10 inches in the suburbs during this period.

Floods occur along the Mississippi River due to spring snow melt, excessive rainfall, or both. Occasionally an ice jam forms and creates a local flood condition. The flood problem at St. Paul is complicated because the Minnesota River empties into the Mississippi River between the two cities. Consequently, high water or flooding on the Minnesota River creates a greater flood potential at St. Paul. Flood stage at St. Paul can be expected on the average once in every eight years.

# TABLE 1 NORMALS, MEANS AND EXTREMES

MINNEAPOLIS – ST. PAUL, MINNESOTA

LATITUDE: 44°53'N  LONGITUDE: 93°13'W  ELEVATION: FT. GRND 834 BARO 860  TIME ZONE: CENTRAL  WBAN: 14922

| | (a) | JAN | FEB | MAR | APR | MAY | JUNE | JULY | AUG | SEP | OCT | NOV | DEC | YEAR |
|---|---|---|---|---|---|---|---|---|---|---|---|---|---|---|
| **TEMPERATURE °F:** | | | | | | | | | | | | | | |
| Normals | | | | | | | | | | | | | | |
| -Daily Maximum | | 19.9 | 26.4 | 37.5 | 56.0 | 69.4 | 78.5 | 83.4 | 80.9 | 71.0 | 59.7 | 41.1 | 26.7 | 54.2 |
| -Daily Minimum | | 2.4 | 8.5 | 20.8 | 36.0 | 47.6 | 57.7 | 62.7 | 60.3 | 50.2 | 39.4 | 25.3 | 11.7 | 35.2 |
| -Monthly | | 11.2 | 17.5 | 29.2 | 46.0 | 58.5 | 68.1 | 73.1 | 70.6 | 60.6 | 49.6 | 33.2 | 19.2 | 44.7 |
| Extremes | | | | | | | | | | | | | | |
| -Record Highest | 51 | 58 | 60 | 83 | 95 | 96 | 102 | 105 | 102 | 98 | 89 | 75 | 63 | 105 |
| -Year | | 1944 | 1981 | 1986 | 1980 | 1978 | 1985 | 1988 | 1947 | 1976 | 1953 | 1944 | 1982 | JUL 1988 |
| -Record Lowest | 51 | -34 | -28 | -32 | 2 | 18 | 34 | 43 | 39 | 26 | 15 | -17 | -29 | -34 |
| -Year | | 1970 | 1965 | 1962 | 1962 | 1967 | 1945 | 1972 | 1967 | 1974 | 1972 | 1964 | 1983 | JAN 1970 |
| **NORMAL DEGREE DAYS:** | | | | | | | | | | | | | | |
| Heating (base 65°F) | | 1668 | 1330 | 1110 | 570 | 238 | 41 | 12 | 16 | 160 | 488 | 954 | 1420 | 8007 |
| Cooling (base 65°F) | | 0 | 0 | 0 | 0 | 36 | 134 | 263 | 190 | 28 | 11 | 0 | 0 | 662 |
| **% OF POSSIBLE SUNSHINE** | 51 | 53 | 59 | 57 | 58 | 61 | 65 | 72 | 68 | 62 | 55 | 39 | 42 | 58 |
| **MEAN SKY COVER (tenths)** | | | | | | | | | | | | | | |
| Sunrise - Sunset | 51 | 6.3 | 6.2 | 6.7 | 6.5 | 6.4 | 6.0 | 5.2 | 5.3 | 5.6 | 5.8 | 7.1 | 7.0 | 6.2 |
| **MEAN NUMBER OF DAYS:** | | | | | | | | | | | | | | |
| Sunrise to Sunset | | | | | | | | | | | | | | |
| -Clear | 51 | 8.4 | 7.8 | 6.8 | 7.0 | 7.2 | 7.5 | 10.3 | 10.2 | 9.9 | 10.0 | 5.5 | 6.3 | 97.1 |
| -Partly Cloudy | 51 | 7.3 | 6.9 | 7.5 | 7.8 | 9.1 | 10.3 | 11.8 | 11.1 | 8.5 | 7.5 | 6.7 | 6.5 | 101.0 |
| -Cloudy | 51 | 15.3 | 13.6 | 16.6 | 15.2 | 14.7 | 12.2 | 8.9 | 9.6 | 11.5 | 13.5 | 17.8 | 18.2 | 167.2 |
| Precipitation | | | | | | | | | | | | | | |
| .01 inches or more | 51 | 8.7 | 7.4 | 10.3 | 10.1 | 11.3 | 11.7 | 9.6 | 10.0 | 9.5 | 8.0 | 8.4 | 9.2 | 114.1 |
| Snow,Ice pellets | | | | | | | | | | | | | | |
| 1.0 inches or more | 51 | 3.3 | 2.7 | 3.0 | 0.8 | 0.1 | 0.0 | 0.0 | 0.0 | 0.* | 0.1 | 2.1 | 3.1 | 15.1 |
| Thunderstorms | 51 | 0.* | 0.2 | 1.0 | 2.7 | 5.2 | 7.4 | 7.6 | 6.5 | 4.1 | 1.8 | 0.6 | 0.2 | 37.4 |
| Heavy Fog Visibility | | | | | | | | | | | | | | |
| 1/4 mile or less | 51 | 1.2 | 1.3 | 1.2 | 0.5 | 0.6 | 0.5 | 0.4 | 0.6 | 0.9 | 1.0 | 1.2 | 1.4 | 10.7 |
| Temperature °F | | | | | | | | | | | | | | |
| -Maximum | | | | | | | | | | | | | | |
| 90° and above | 30 | 0.0 | 0.0 | 0.0 | 0.1 | 0.8 | 2.9 | 6.8 | 3.9 | 0.9 | 0.0 | 0.0 | 0.0 | 15.4 |
| 32° and below | 30 | 24.1 | 18.3 | 9.2 | 0.4 | 0.0 | 0.0 | 0.0 | 0.0 | 0.0 | 0.0 | 6.8 | 21.7 | 80.5 |
| -Minimum | | | | | | | | | | | | | | |
| 32° and below | 30 | 30.8 | 27.3 | 25.3 | 10.9 | 1.2 | 0.0 | 0.0 | 0.0 | 0.5 | 7.5 | 22.7 | 29.8 | 155.9 |
| 0° and below | 30 | 14.2 | 8.7 | 2.0 | 0.0 | 0.0 | 0.0 | 0.0 | 0.0 | 0.0 | 0.0 | 0.6 | 8.0 | 33.6 |
| **AVG. STATION PRESS.(mb)** | 17 | 987.7 | 988.3 | 985.0 | 984.2 | 983.3 | 983.0 | 984.7 | 985.3 | 986.0 | 986.5 | 985.9 | 987.3 | 985.6 |
| **RELATIVE HUMIDITY (%)** | | | | | | | | | | | | | | |
| Hour 00 | 30 | 72 | 73 | 72 | 67 | 67 | 72 | 74 | 77 | 79 | 74 | 77 | 76 | 73 |
| Hour 06 | 30 | 73 | 75 | 76 | 74 | 75 | 78 | 80 | 83 | 85 | 81 | 80 | 78 | 78 |
| Hour 12 (Local Time) | 30 | 67 | 65 | 62 | 52 | 51 | 54 | 53 | 56 | 59 | 58 | 66 | 70 | 59 |
| Hour 18 | 30 | 68 | 66 | 61 | 51 | 49 | 52 | 52 | 56 | 61 | 61 | 69 | 72 | 60 |
| **PRECIPITATION (inches):** | | | | | | | | | | | | | | |
| Water Equivalent | | | | | | | | | | | | | | |
| -Normal | | 0.82 | 0.85 | 1.71 | 2.05 | 3.20 | 4.07 | 3.51 | 3.64 | 2.50 | 1.85 | 1.29 | 0.87 | 26.36 |
| -Maximum Monthly | 51 | 3.63 | 2.14 | 4.75 | 5.88 | 8.03 | 7.99 | 17.90 | 9.31 | 7.53 | 5.68 | 5.15 | 4.27 | 17.90 |
| -Year | | 1967 | 1981 | 1965 | 1986 | 1962 | 1975 | 1987 | 1977 | 1942 | 1971 | 1940 | 1982 | JUL 1987 |
| -Minimum Monthly | 51 | 0.11 | 0.06 | 0.32 | 0.16 | 0.61 | 0.22 | 0.58 | 0.43 | 0.41 | 0.01 | 0.02 | T | T |
| -Year | | 1959 | 1964 | 1958 | 1987 | 1967 | 1988 | 1975 | 1946 | 1940 | 1952 | 1939 | 1943 | DEC 1943 |
| -Maximum in 24 hrs | 51 | 1.21 | 1.10 | 1.66 | 2.23 | 3.03 | 3.00 | 10.00 | 7.36 | 3.55 | 2.95 | 2.91 | 2.47 | 10.00 |
| -Year | | 1967 | 1966 | 1965 | 1975 | 1965 | 1986 | 1987 | 1977 | 1942 | 1966 | 1940 | 1982 | JUL 1987 |
| Snow,Ice pellets | | | | | | | | | | | | | | |
| -Maximum Monthly | 51 | 46.4 | 26.5 | 40.0 | 21.8 | 3.0 | T | 0.0 | 0.0 | 1.7 | 3.7 | 30.4 | 33.2 | 46.4 |
| -Year | | 1982 | 1962 | 1951 | 1983 | 1946 | 1989 | | | 1942 | 1959 | 1983 | 1969 | JAN 1982 |
| -Maximum in 24 hrs | 51 | 18.5 | 9.3 | 14.7 | 13.6 | 3.0 | T | 0.0 | 0.0 | 1.7 | 3.0 | 16.2 | 16.5 | 18.5 |
| -Year | | 1982 | 1939 | 1985 | 1983 | 1946 | 1989 | | | 1942 | 1977 | 1940 | 1982 | JAN 1982 |
| **WIND:** | | | | | | | | | | | | | | |
| Mean Speed (mph) | 51 | 10.5 | 10.5 | 11.4 | 12.3 | 11.2 | 10.5 | 9.4 | 9.2 | 9.9 | 10.5 | 11.0 | 10.4 | 10.6 |
| Prevailing Direction | | | | | | | | | | | | | | |
| through 1963 | | NW | NW | NW | NW | SE | SE | S | SE | S | SE | NW | NW | NW |
| Fastest Obs. 1 Min. | | | | | | | | | | | | | | |
| -Direction (!!!) | 10 | 32 | 34 | 08 | 19 | 23 | 01 | 35 | 20 | 18 | 33 | 25 | 34 | 32 |
| -Speed (MPH) | 10 | 51 | 37 | 33 | 41 | 35 | 46 | 43 | 44 | 36 | 33 | 41 | 35 | 51 |
| -Year | | 1986 | 1987 | 1985 | 1984 | 1986 | 1980 | 1980 | 1983 | 1988 | 1981 | 1986 | 1989 | JAN 1986 |
| Peak Gust | | | | | | | | | | | | | | |
| -Direction (!!!) | 6 | NW | NW | W | SW | N | SW | NW | W | N | NW | W | NW | W |
| -Speed (mph) | 6 | 67 | 55 | 60 | 61 | 67 | 49 | 51 | 71 | 52 | 53 | 66 | 48 | 71 |
| -Date | | 1986 | 1987 | 1988 | 1984 | 1985 | 1989 | 1984 | 1988 | 1989 | 1987 | 1986 | 1989 | AUG 1988 |

**See Reference Notes to this table on the following page.**

PRECIPITATION (inches)     MINNEAPOLIS – ST. PAUL, MINNESOTA

**TABLE 2**

| YEAR | JAN | FEB | MAR | APR | MAY | JUNE | JULY | AUG | SEP | OCT | NOV | DEC | ANNUAL |
|------|-----|-----|-----|-----|-----|------|------|-----|-----|-----|-----|-----|--------|
| 1961 | 0.28 | 0.89 | 2.81 | 2.39 | 3.48 | 1.87 | 2.94 | 2.38 | 3.01 | 3.03 | 1.06 | 1.60 | 25.74 |
| 1962 | 0.55 | 2.07 | 1.87 | 1.31 | 8.03 | 1.48 | 5.12 | 3.47 | 2.46 | 1.69 | 0.52 | 0.26 | 28.83 |
| 1963 | 0.46 | 0.41 | 1.18 | 2.07 | 5.06 | 1.91 | 1.53 | 1.55 | 3.47 | 0.81 | 0.52 | 0.60 | 19.57 |
| 1964 | 0.47 | 0.06 | 1.35 | 2.98 | 3.44 | 2.18 | 2.02 | 5.42 | 5.21 | 0.57 | 1.19 | 1.08 | 25.97 |
| 1965 | 0.47 | 1.59 | 4.75 | 3.52 | 7.86 | 4.01 | 4.69 | 4.04 | 4.90 | 0.90 | 1.98 | 1.23 | 39.94 |
| 1966 | 0.95 | 1.55 | 2.48 | 0.89 | 1.46 | 3.51 | 2.47 | 4.40 | 1.69 | 3.53 | 0.39 | 1.02 | 24.34 |
| 1967 | 3.63 | 1.59 | 0.96 | 4.07 | 0.61 | 7.53 | 1.36 | 2.79 | 0.63 | 1.73 | 0.09 | 0.45 | 25.44 |
| 1968 | 0.71 | 0.13 | 1.89 | 2.94 | 3.74 | 6.78 | 6.46 | 0.75 | 6.16 | 5.62 | 0.54 | 2.21 | 37.93 |
| 1969 | 2.05 | 0.31 | 0.90 | 1.55 | 1.98 | 2.93 | 2.95 | 0.99 | 0.49 | 2.53 | 0.65 | 2.06 | 19.39 |
| 1970 | 0.47 | 0.16 | 2.05 | 3.55 | 4.77 | 1.27 | 3.66 | 2.19 | 3.19 | 4.97 | 3.82 | 0.43 | 30.53 |
| 1971 | 1.22 | 1.74 | 1.21 | 1.11 | 3.14 | 3.52 | 3.94 | 1.78 | 2.73 | 5.68 | 2.67 | 0.70 | 29.44 |
| 1972 | 0.84 | 0.49 | 1.25 | 1.69 | 2.18 | 3.31 | 5.12 | 2.48 | 1.96 | 1.77 | 1.11 | 1.57 | 23.77 |
| 1973 | 0.92 | 0.84 | 1.12 | 2.32 | 2.48 | 1.06 | 2.90 | 3.05 | 2.08 | 1.29 | 1.97 | 1.10 | 21.13 |
| 1974 | 0.17 | 1.06 | 1.00 | 2.42 | 2.08 | 5.21 | 1.14 | 2.75 | 0.58 | 1.69 | 0.66 | 0.35 | 19.11 |
| 1975 | 2.82 | 0.79 | 1.67 | 5.40 | 3.81 | 7.99 | 0.58 | 4.92 | 1.31 | 0.27 | 4.80 | 0.79 | 35.15 |
| 1976 | 0.87 | 0.59 | 2.83 | 0.80 | 1.13 | 3.86 | 2.45 | 1.39 | 1.42 | 0.49 | 0.16 | 0.51 | 16.50 |
| 1977 | 0.65 | 0.93 | 2.66 | 1.84 | 2.86 | 3.57 | 3.72 | 9.31 | 4.43 | 2.34 | 1.42 | 1.15 | 34.88 |
| 1978 | 0.38 | 0.24 | 0.79 | 3.63 | 3.79 | 7.09 | 3.19 | 5.77 | 2.47 | 0.19 | 1.84 | 0.88 | 30.26 |
| 1979 | 1.09 | 1.39 | 2.55 | 0.66 | 4.55 | 4.78 | 2.34 | 7.04 | 2.20 | 3.16 | 0.98 | 0.33 | 31.07 |
| 1980 | 0.94 | 0.67 | 1.12 | 0.83 | 2.29 | 5.52 | 2.30 | 3.26 | 3.68 | 0.66 | 0.26 | 0.24 | 21.77 |
| 1981 | 0.30 | 2.14 | 0.71 | 2.17 | 2.18 | 4.42 | 4.09 | 4.73 | 1.46 | 2.69 | 2.16 | 0.92 | 27.97 |
| 1982 | 2.45 | 0.43 | 2.09 | 1.62 | 4.99 | 1.44 | 0.92 | 3.80 | 1.50 | 3.45 | 3.27 | 4.27 | 30.23 |
| 1983 | 0.67 | 1.19 | 3.22 | 3.97 | 6.20 | 5.22 | 3.07 | 3.12 | 3.34 | 2.61 | 4.93 | 1.53 | 39.07 |
| 1984 | 0.88 | 1.64 | 1.47 | 3.86 | 2.29 | 7.95 | 3.03 | 5.15 | 2.65 | 5.48 | 0.31 | 2.24 | 36.95 |
| 1985 | 0.87 | 0.50 | 4.48 | 1.81 | 3.65 | 2.18 | 2.20 | 5.02 | 4.37 | 3.66 | 1.72 | 1.20 | 31.66 |
| 1986 | 0.90 | 0.84 | 2.03 | 5.88 | 3.48 | 5.34 | 4.11 | 4.44 | 6.90 | 1.77 | 0.62 | 0.31 | 36.62 |
| 1987 | 0.63 | 0.13 | 0.64 | 0.16 | 1.88 | 1.95 | 17.90 | 3.67 | 1.28 | 0.60 | 2.07 | 1.25 | 32.16 |
| 1988 | 1.37 | 0.30 | 1.33 | 1.58 | 1.70 | 0.22 | 1.17 | 4.29 | 2.79 | 0.80 | 2.86 | 0.67 | 19.08 |
| 1989 | 0.52 | 1.04 | 2.19 | 2.66 | 3.38 | 3.50 | 3.50 | 2.92 | 1.28 | 0.53 | 1.38 | 0.42 | 23.32 |
| 1990 | 0.10 | 0.77 | 3.66 | 3.80 | 3.36 | 9.82 | 5.06 | 1.71 | 1.88 | 1.23 | 0.65 | 1.01 | 33.05 |
| Record Mean | 0.83 | 0.86 | 1.60 | 2.16 | 3.37 | 4.16 | 3.52 | 3.36 | 2.85 | 2.01 | 1.41 | 0.95 | 27.09 |

**TABLE 3**  AVERAGE TEMPERATURE (deg. F)     MINNEAPOLIS – ST. PAUL, MINNESOTA

| YEAR | JAN | FEB | MAR | APR | MAY | JUNE | JULY | AUG | SEP | OCT | NOV | DEC | ANNUAL |
|------|-----|-----|-----|-----|-----|------|------|-----|-----|-----|-----|-----|--------|
| 1961 | 12.0 | 22.5 | 32.0 | 38.5 | 54.7 | 68.1 | 70.8 | 71.3 | 59.1 | 52.2 | 33.5 | 15.3 | 44.2 |
| 1962 | 7.1 | 11.7 | 24.5 | 42.2 | 60.6 | 66.2 | 67.5 | 68.3 | 56.4 | 50.2 | 35.0 | 19.0 | 42.4 |
| 1963 | 2.9 | 12.1 | 34.2 | 47.3 | 55.4 | 69.8 | 73.5 | 68.9 | 62.2 | 58.1 | 38.3 | 10.0 | 44.4 |
| 1964 | 20.0 | 23.9 | 25.8 | 46.8 | 61.5 | 68.7 | 76.0 | 68.5 | 58.9 | 48.2 | 35.0 | 14.8 | 45.7 |
| 1965 | 10.0 | 11.8 | 19.5 | 41.8 | 58.7 | 66.5 | 70.5 | 68.6 | 52.8 | 50.7 | 33.1 | 28.0 | 42.7 |
| 1966 | 3.3 | 16.3 | 35.8 | 42.2 | 53.6 | 68.4 | 76.8 | 68.2 | 60.3 | 47.5 | 30.1 | 18.1 | 43.4 |
| 1967 | 14.6 | 8.7 | 29.8 | 44.7 | 52.3 | 66.9 | 68.8 | 66.2 | 60.3 | 46.3 | 30.7 | 21.8 | 42.6 |
| 1968 | 14.3 | 15.2 | 38.8 | 48.5 | 53.4 | 67.2 | 71.1 | 70.7 | 61.1 | 50.7 | 33.6 | 16.9 | 45.2 |
| 1969 | 9.4 | 19.3 | 24.1 | 49.3 | 60.6 | 61.8 | 73.6 | 74.4 | 63.0 | 46.5 | 33.6 | 20.3 | 44.7 |
| 1970 | 5.6 | 15.4 | 26.0 | 46.1 | 58.5 | 71.2 | 75.2 | 71.9 | 61.2 | 49.6 | 32.7 | 18.2 | 44.3 |
| 1971 | 6.5 | 17.0 | 28.0 | 47.0 | 55.4 | 71.5 | 68.8 | 69.6 | 62.8 | 51.4 | 32.7 | 18.4 | 44.1 |
| 1972 | 5.5 | 10.5 | 26.5 | 41.9 | 61.3 | 66.0 | 68.5 | 69.8 | 57.9 | 43.7 | 32.2 | 11.3 | 41.3 |
| 1973 | 17.4 | 21.6 | 40.2 | 44.4 | 55.2 | 69.5 | 73.8 | 73.4 | 60.1 | 53.8 | 34.3 | 16.7 | 46.7 |
| 1974 | 11.9 | 16.9 | 29.5 | 47.1 | 54.4 | 65.5 | 76.6 | 67.3 | 55.3 | 49.8 | 33.7 | 24.4 | 44.4 |
| 1975 | 14.5 | 15.5 | 22.1 | 38.9 | 60.9 | 68.8 | 76.3 | 71.7 | 57.7 | 52.8 | 37.5 | 21.3 | 44.8 |
| 1976 | 11.6 | 27.8 | 31.4 | 51.8 | 58.9 | 71.7 | 76.1 | 73.3 | 61.8 | 44.6 | 28.3 | 13.6 | 45.9 |
| 1977 | 0.3 | 22.7 | 37.5 | 53.0 | 66.9 | 68.4 | 74.8 | 66.1 | 60.5 | 47.1 | 30.8 | 14.4 | 45.2 |
| 1978 | 5.5 | 11.6 | 30.0 | 45.2 | 61.8 | 67.8 | 71.1 | 72.2 | 67.3 | 49.8 | 32.5 | 15.2 | 44.2 |
| 1979 | 3.2 | 10.0 | 28.9 | 44.0 | 55.5 | 67.3 | 73.6 | 69.9 | 63.4 | 46.6 | 31.7 | 26.0 | 43.3 |
| 1980 | 15.3 | 15.3 | 27.3 | 49.2 | 61.5 | 67.6 | 75.2 | 70.7 | 59.5 | 45.1 | 36.6 | 19.8 | 45.2 |
| 1981 | 18.0 | 23.4 | 37.7 | 49.1 | 57.1 | 67.0 | 70.9 | 69.3 | 60.0 | 46.7 | 38.0 | 17.5 | 46.2 |
| 1982 | 2.3 | 15.8 | 29.0 | 43.8 | 62.5 | 63.7 | 75.6 | 71.8 | 60.9 | 50.3 | 31.5 | 25.7 | 44.4 |
| 1983 | 19.6 | 26.9 | 34.2 | 42.3 | 54.6 | 68.0 | 77.2 | 76.8 | 62.6 | 48.4 | 34.0 | 3.7 | 45.7 |
| 1984 | 12.0 | 27.5 | 24.8 | 47.1 | 56.0 | 69.7 | 72.2 | 73.5 | 57.2 | 50.7 | 33.3 | 17.9 | 45.2 |
| 1985 | 10.1 | 16.5 | 35.6 | 52.1 | 62.2 | 63.9 | 73.9 | 67.6 | 59.9 | 47.5 | 24.8 | 7.7 | 43.5 |
| 1986 | 17.5 | 15.7 | 33.9 | 49.6 | 59.4 | 68.6 | 73.9 | 67.1 | 59.8 | 49.2 | 28.2 | 24.7 | 45.6 |
| 1987 | 21.2 | 31.6 | 38.7 | 53.5 | 63.5 | 72.8 | 76.0 | 69.0 | 62.5 | 44.6 | 37.9 | 25.0 | 49.7 |
| 1988 | 10.4 | 13.9 | 33.8 | 47.4 | 65.4 | 74.4 | 78.1 | 73.9 | 62.4 | 44.0 | 32.7 | 20.5 | 46.4 |
| 1989 | 21.2 | 8.6 | 26.6 | 45.3 | 57.5 | 68.4 | 70.8 | 70.6 | 60.7 | 49.9 | 28.0 | 10.6 | 43.7 |
| 1990 | 26.3 | 23.7 | 35.7 | 46.8 | 56.3 | 69.5 | 71.3 | 70.6 | 64.4 | 48.1 | 37.4 | 16.9 | 47.3 |
| Record Mean | 13.1 | 17.1 | 30.0 | 46.0 | 58.2 | 67.9 | 73.3 | 70.7 | 61.5 | 49.6 | 32.9 | 19.2 | 45.0 |
| Max | 21.7 | 25.7 | 38.3 | 55.8 | 68.4 | 77.8 | 83.3 | 80.6 | 71.4 | 59.0 | 40.5 | 26.7 | 54.1 |
| Min | 4.5 | 8.4 | 21.7 | 36.3 | 47.9 | 58.0 | 63.2 | 60.7 | 51.6 | 40.2 | 25.3 | 11.6 | 35.8 |

## REFERENCE NOTES FOR TABLES 1, 2, 3 and 6     (MINNEAPOLIS, MN)

**GENERAL**

T - TRACE AMOUNT
BLANK ENTRIES DENOTE MISSING/UNREPORTED DATA.
# INDICATES A STATION OR INSTRUMENT RELOCATION.

**SPECIFIC**

TABLE 1

(a) - LENGTH OF RECORD IN YEARS. ALTHOUGH
      INDIVIDUAL MONTHS MAY BE MISSING.

* LESS THAN .05

NORMALS — BASED ON THE 1951-1980 RECORD PERIOD.
EXTREMES — DATES ARE THE MOST RECENT OCCURRENCE.
WIND DIR. — NUMERALS SHOW TENS OF DEGREES
            CLOCKWISE FROM TRUE NORTH.
            ''00'' INDICATES CALM.
RESULTANT WIND DIRECTIONS ARE GIVEN TO WHOLE DEGREES.

TABLE 3
MAX AND MIN ARE LONG-TERM MEAN DAILY MAXIMUM
AND MEAN DAILY MINIMUM TEMPERATURES.

**EXCEPTIONS**

TABLES 2, 3, and 6

RECORD MEANS ARE THROUGH THE CURRENT YEAR,
BEGINNING IN     1891 FOR TEMPERATURE
                 1891 FOR PRECIPITATION
                 1939 FOR SNOWFALL

HEATING DEGREE DAYS Base 65 deg. F  MINNEAPOLIS – ST. PAUL, MINNESOTA

**TABLE 4**

| SEASON | JULY | AUG | SEP | OCT | NOV | DEC | JAN | FEB | MAR | APR | MAY | JUNE | TOTAL |
|---|---|---|---|---|---|---|---|---|---|---|---|---|---|
| 1961-62 | 0 | 10 | 239 | 396 | 938 | 1536 | 1794 | 1488 | 1248 | 691 | 198 | 68 | 8606 |
| 1962-63 | 27 | 15 | 262 | 461 | 891 | 1422 | 1927 | 1478 | 946 | 526 | 319 | 46 | 8320 |
| 1963-64 | 1 | 32 | 129 | 216 | 793 | 1703 | 1390 | 1186 | 1209 | 543 | 154 | 49 | 7405 |
| 1964-65 | 0 | 63 | 224 | 515 | 894 | 1551 | 1702 | 1486 | 1405 | 690 | 211 | 19 | 8760 |
| 1965-66 | 7 | 40 | 368 | 447 | 950 | 1140 | 1909 | 1358 | 899 | 678 | 357 | 41 | 8194 |
| 1966-67 | 0 | 40 | 185 | 536 | 1042 | 1446 | 1556 | 1572 | 1086 | 600 | 404 | 30 | 8497 |
| 1967-68 | 36 | 65 | 166 | 577 | 1024 | 1335 | 1567 | 1440 | 808 | 491 | 358 | 62 | 7929 |
| 1968-69 | 10 | 28 | 143 | 451 | 922 | 1486 | 1723 | 1274 | 1261 | 461 | 204 | 136 | 8099 |
| 1969-70 | 5 | 0 | 131 | 580 | 933 | 1379 | 1842 | 1382 | 1204 | 577 | 249 | 20 | 8302 |
| 1970-71 | 3 | 5 | 190 | 476 | 959 | 1443 | 1811 | 1341 | 1139 | 537 | 297 | 18 | 8219 |
| 1971-72 | 16 | 22 | 164 | 413 | 962 | 1438 | 1844 | 1576 | 1188 | 687 | 204 | 73 | 8587 |
| 1972-73 | 34 | 52 | 218 | 651 | 974 | 1664 | 1474 | 1208 | 761 | 611 | 299 | 13 | 7959 |
| 1973-74 | 1 | 3 | 185 | 350 | 915 | 1493 | 1642 | 1344 | 1092 | 535 | 338 | 72 | 7970 |
| 1974-75 | 0 | 48 | 289 | 467 | 933 | 1252 | 1561 | 1379 | 1324 | 775 | 188 | 39 | 8255 |
| 1975-76 | 15 | 7 | 231 | 387 | 818 | 1346 | 1650 | 1074 | 1031 | 405 | 195 | 11 | 7170 |
| 1976-77 | 0 | 4 | 162 | 632 | 1092 | 1590 | 2005 | 1180 | 844 | 365 | 75 | 17 | 7966 |
| 1977-78 | 0 | 35 | 145 | 548 | 1016 | 1565 | 1842 | 1488 | 1080 | 584 | 162 | 46 | 8511 |
| 1978-79 | 5 | 7 | 89 | 464 | 968 | 1538 | 1914 | 1537 | 1112 | 623 | 307 | 38 | 8602 |
| 1979-80 | 0 | 24 | 105 | 566 | 992 | 1203 | 1536 | 1436 | 1165 | 484 | 184 | 34 | 7729 |
| 1980-81 | 0 | 12 | 194 | 611 | 845 | 1396 | 1453 | 1160 | 838 | 472 | 249 | 28 | 7258 |
| 1981-82 | 11 | 11 | 172 | 564 | 803 | 1466 | 1945 | 1374 | 1111 | 629 | 117 | 71 | 8274 |
| 1982-83 | 0 | 14 | 168 | 448 | 997 | 1212 | 1400 | 1061 | 947 | 673 | 313 | 49 | 7282 |
| 1983-84 | 2 | 0 | 161 | 514 | 923 | 1901 | 1641 | 1082 | 1240 | 531 | 284 | 7 | 8286 |
| 1984-85 | 5 | 12 | 251 | 435 | 943 | 1453 | 1694 | 1355 | 904 | 403 | 123 | 104 | 7682 |
| 1985-86 | 0 | 28 | 240 | 537 | 1201 | 1774 | 1466 | 1377 | 957 | 454 | 212 | 30 | 8276 |
| 1986-87 | 0 | 43 | 177 | 480 | 1096 | 1243 | 1352 | 929 | 809 | 347 | 134 | 13 | 6623 |
| 1987-88 | 2 | 29 | 106 | 623 | 804 | 1236 | 1688 | 1479 | 962 | 523 | 76 | 4 | 7532 |
| 1988-89 | 1 | 16 | 116 | 646 | 963 | 1373 | 1353 | 1576 | 1184 | 583 | 251 | 44 | 8106 |
| 1989-90 | 0 | 6 | 159 | 470 | 1105 | 1683 | 1194 | 1151 | 899 | 569 | 274 | 37 | 7547 |
| 1990-91 | 2 | 5 | 136 | 516 | 820 | 1484 | | | | | | | |

**TABLE 5**  COOLING DEGREE DAYS Base 65 deg. F  MINNEAPOLIS – ST. PAUL, MINNESOTA

| YEAR | JAN | FEB | MAR | APR | MAY | JUNE | JULY | AUG | SEP | OCT | NOV | DEC | TOTAL |
|---|---|---|---|---|---|---|---|---|---|---|---|---|---|
| 1969 | 0 | 0 | 0 | 0 | 76 | 49 | 276 | 298 | 77 | 12 | 0 | 0 | 788 |
| 1970 | 0 | 0 | 0 | 17 | 54 | 213 | 323 | 225 | 83 | 5 | 0 | 0 | 920 |
| 1971 | 0 | 0 | 0 | 2 | 5 | 218 | 141 | 168 | 106 | 3 | 0 | 0 | 643 |
| 1972 | 0 | 0 | 0 | 0 | 94 | 109 | 148 | 208 | 13 | 0 | 0 | 0 | 572 |
| 1973 | 0 | 0 | 0 | 1 | 4 | 158 | 280 | 271 | 47 | 8 | 0 | 0 | 769 |
| 1974 | 0 | 0 | 0 | 5 | 18 | 93 | 369 | 127 | 6 | 1 | 0 | 0 | 619 |
| 1975 | 0 | 0 | 0 | 0 | 66 | 159 | 371 | 220 | 18 | 16 | 0 | 0 | 850 |
| 1976 | 0 | 0 | 0 | 14 | 14 | 223 | 351 | 269 | 72 | 7 | 0 | 0 | 950 |
| 1977 | 0 | 0 | 0 | 12 | 145 | 129 | 310 | 76 | 19 | 0 | 0 | 0 | 691 |
| 1978 | 0 | 0 | 0 | 0 | 72 | 138 | 201 | 236 | 164 | 0 | 0 | 0 | 811 |
| 1979 | 0 | 0 | 0 | 0 | 17 | 113 | 275 | 181 | 65 | 0 | 0 | 0 | 651 |
| 1980 | 0 | 0 | 0 | 16 | 82 | 121 | 322 | 194 | 38 | 1 | 0 | 0 | 774 |
| 1981 | 0 | 0 | 0 | 0 | 10 | 96 | 200 | 151 | 28 | 0 | 0 | 0 | 485 |
| 1982 | 0 | 0 | 0 | 0 | 46 | 40 | 338 | 232 | 53 | 0 | 0 | 0 | 709 |
| 1983 | 0 | 0 | 0 | 0 | 0 | 145 | 389 | 368 | 98 | 8 | 0 | 0 | 1008 |
| 1984 | 0 | 0 | 0 | 0 | 13 | 155 | 237 | 280 | 24 | 0 | 0 | 0 | 709 |
| 1985 | 0 | 0 | 0 | 22 | 43 | 77 | 284 | 118 | 93 | 0 | 0 | 0 | 637 |
| 1986 | 0 | 0 | 0 | 1 | 45 | 148 | 286 | 115 | 32 | 0 | 0 | 0 | 627 |
| 1987 | 0 | 0 | 0 | 11 | 95 | 253 | 348 | 159 | 37 | 0 | 0 | 0 | 903 |
| 1988 | 0 | 0 | 0 | 1 | 96 | 296 | 412 | 302 | 45 | 0 | 0 | 0 | 1152 |
| 1989 | 0 | 0 | 0 | 0 | 26 | 153 | 359 | 192 | 41 | 8 | 0 | 0 | 779 |
| 1990 | 0 | 0 | 0 | 28 | 11 | 178 | 206 | 191 | 125 | 1 | 0 | 0 | 740 |

**TABLE 6**  SNOWFALL (inches)  MINNEAPOLIS – ST. PAUL, MINNESOTA

| SEASON | JULY | AUG | SEP | OCT | NOV | DEC | JAN | FEB | MAR | APR | MAY | JUNE | TOTAL |
|---|---|---|---|---|---|---|---|---|---|---|---|---|---|
| 1961-62 | 0.0 | 0.0 | 0.1 | 0.0 | 2.5 | 18.1 | 5.9 | 26.5 | 21.8 | 6.4 | 0.0 | 0.0 | 81.3 |
| 1962-63 | 0.0 | 0.0 | 0.0 | T | 5.6 | 3.2 | 5.0 | 5.4 | 9.8 | 5.5 | T | 0.0 | 34.5 |
| 1963-64 | 0.0 | 0.0 | 0.0 | 0.0 | T | 7.6 | 5.0 | 1.0 | 9.7 | 5.6 | 0.0 | 0.0 | 28.9 |
| 1964-65 | 0.0 | 0.0 | 0.0 | T | 4.3 | 8.1 | 10.5 | 11.7 | 37.1 | 2.0 | T | 0.0 | 73.7 |
| 1965-66 | 0.0 | 0.0 | 0.0 | 0.0 | 1.6 | 1.2 | 11.9 | 6.8 | 14.2 | 0.4 | T | 0.0 | 36.1 |
| 1966-67 | 0.0 | 0.0 | 0.0 | 0.0 | 3.4 | 12.7 | 35.3 | 23.7 | 2.6 | 0.2 | 0.3 | 0.0 | 78.4 |
| 1967-68 | 0.0 | 0.0 | 0.0 | 0.3 | 0.8 | 2.4 | 10.6 | 2.2 | 0.8 | 0.4 | 0.0 | 0.0 | 17.5 |
| 1968-69 | 0.0 | 0.0 | 0.0 | T | 4.9 | 28.7 | 21.6 | 5.3 | 7.3 | 0.3 | 0.0 | 0.0 | 68.1 |
| 1969-70 | 0.0 | 0.0 | 0.0 | 2.4 | 3.8 | 33.2 | 9.8 | 4.3 | 8.6 | 1.3 | T | 0.0 | 63.4 |
| 1970-71 | 0.0 | 0.0 | 0.0 | T | 6.3 | 5.5 | 19.9 | 13.9 | 7.0 | 1.9 | 0.2 | 0.0 | 54.7 |
| 1971-72 | 0.0 | 0.0 | 0.0 | 0.0 | 13.2 | 12.8 | 12.2 | 7.6 | 10.4 | 8.0 | 0.0 | 0.0 | 64.2 |
| 1972-73 | 0.0 | 0.0 | T | T | 1.1 | 15.3 | 11.6 | 11.3 | 0.4 | 2.0 | 0.0 | 0.0 | 41.7 |
| 1973-74 | 0.0 | 0.0 | 0.0 | 0.0 | 0.1 | 17.9 | 2.5 | 15.7 | 7.7 | 7.3 | 0.0 | 0.0 | 51.2 |
| 1974-75 | 0.0 | 0.0 | 0.0 | 0.0 | 1.2 | 6.1 | 27.4 | 9.0 | 18.3 | 2.2 | 0.0 | 0.0 | 64.2 |
| 1975-76 | 0.0 | 0.0 | 0.0 | 0.0 | 16.2 | 5.6 | 12.8 | 5.1 | 13.6 | 0.0 | 1.2 | 0.0 | 54.5 |
| 1976-77 | 0.0 | 0.0 | 0.0 | 2.3 | 1.4 | 8.3 | 13.4 | 1.8 | 14.6 | 1.8 | 0.0 | 0.0 | 43.6 |
| 1977-78 | 0.0 | 0.0 | 0.0 | 3.0 | 11.7 | 14.2 | 6.8 | 4.6 | 8.5 | 1.9 | 0.0 | 0.0 | 50.7 |
| 1978-79 | 0.0 | 0.0 | 0.0 | 0.0 | 16.5 | 15.1 | 14.2 | 13.5 | 8.4 | 0.7 | 0.0 | 0.0 | 68.4 |
| 1979-80 | 0.0 | 0.0 | 0.0 | T | 7.7 | 1.7 | 12.9 | 8.8 | 13.7 | 8.5 | 0.0 | 0.0 | 53.3 |
| 1980-81 | 0.0 | 0.0 | 0.0 | T | 0.9 | 2.8 | 4.6 | 11.0 | 0.1 | 1.7 | 0.0 | 0.0 | 21.1 |
| 1981-82 | 0.0 | 0.0 | 0.0 | 0.9 | 14.0 | 10.6 | 46.4 | 7.4 | 10.9 | 4.8 | 0.0 | 0.0 | 95.0 |
| 1982-83 | 0.0 | 0.0 | 0.0 | 1.4 | 3.6 | 19.3 | 3.2 | 10.8 | 14.3 | 21.8 | 0.0 | 0.0 | 74.4 |
| 1983-84 | 0.0 | 0.0 | 0.0 | T | 30.4 | 21.0 | 10.6 | 9.3 | 17.3 | 9.8 | 0.0 | 0.0 | 98.4 |
| 1984-85 | 0.0 | 0.0 | 0.0 | 0.3 | 2.0 | 16.3 | 13.1 | 4.2 | 36.8 | T | 0.0 | 0.0 | 72.7 |
| 1985-86 | 0.0 | 0.0 | 0.4 | T | 23.9 | 13.5 | 10.3 | 12.3 | 8.7 | 0.4 | 0.0 | 0.0 | 69.5 |
| 1986-87 | 0.0 | 0.0 | 0.0 | T | 4.4 | 4.2 | 5.5 | 1.2 | 2.1 | T | 0.0 | 0.0 | 17.4 |
| 1987-88 | 0.0 | 0.0 | 0.0 | 0.3 | 4.5 | 7.5 | 19.5 | 4.5 | 3.7 | 2.4 | 0.0 | 0.0 | 42.4 |
| 1988-89 | 0.0 | 0.0 | 0.0 | 0.2 | 15.8 | 7.2 | 6.0 | 17.3 | 22.7 | 0.8 | 0.1 | T | 70.1 |
| 1989-90 | 0.0 | 0.0 | 0.0 | 0.0 | 11.3 | 7.0 | 1.1 | 10.7 | 3.2 | 2.2 | 0.0 | 0.0 | 35.5 |
| 1990-91 | 0.0 | 0.0 | 0.0 | T | 5.0 | 11.7 | | | | | | | |
| Record Mean | 0.0 | 0.0 | T | 0.4 | 7.1 | 9.4 | 9.9 | 8.4 | 10.9 | 3.0 | 0.1 | T | 49.2 |

**See Reference Notes, relative to all above tables, on preceding page.**

Jackson is located on the west bank of the Pearl River, about 45 miles east of the Mississippi River and 150 miles north of the Gulf of Mexico. The nearby terrain is gently rolling with no topographic features that appreciably influence the weather. The National Weather Service Office is nearly 7 miles east-northeast of the Jackson Post Office and over 5 miles southwest of the Ross Barnett Reservoir. Alluvial plains up to 3 miles wide extend along the river near Jackson, where some levees have been built on both sides of the river.

The climate is significantly humid during most of the year, with relatively short mild winters and long warm summers. The Gulf of Mexico has a moderating effect on the climate. Cold spells are fairly frequent in winter, but are usually of short duration. Sub-zero temperatures rarely occur. Temperatures occasionally exceed 80 degrees in mid-winter. In summer, temperatures reach 90 degrees or higher on about two-thirds of the days, 100 degree readings are infrequent. Extended periods of very hot weather are rare. On unusual occasions, temperatures at night may drop into the 50s, even in July or August.

Snowfall averages less than two inches per season, with nearly two-thirds of the seasons having only a trace of snow or none at all. Ice storms occasionally cause major damage to trees and power lines during the winter or early spring season. Rainfall is abundant and fairly well-distributed throughout the year. The area does not have a true dry season. However, the six-month period, June through November, is relatively dry in comparison with the December through May period when 60 percent of the annual precipitation can be expected.

Excessive rainfall may occur in any season. In spite of the normally abundant rainfall, fairly serious droughts occasionally occur during the summer or fall season. Tropical disturbances, including hurricanes and their remnants, are infrequent. However, those that pass near or visit the Mississippi Coast in the summer or early fall may bring several days of heavy rain to the Jackson area.

Thunderstorms can be expected on an average of 65 days a year, usually occurring in each month. They are most frequent in summer when they occur on about one-third of the days. At other times of the year, thunderstorms are usually associated with passing weather systems and are likely to be attended by higher winds than in summer. Severe thunderstorms normally affect portions of the metropolitan area a few times each year.

# TABLE 1 NORMALS, MEANS AND EXTREMES

JACKSON, MISSISSIPPI

LATITUDE: 32°19'N  LONGITUDE: 90°05' W  ELEVATION: FT. GRND 291 BARO 297  TIME ZONE: CENTRAL  WBAN: 03940

| | (a) | JAN | FEB | MAR | APR | MAY | JUNE | JULY | AUG | SEP | OCT | NOV | DEC | YEAR |
|---|---|---|---|---|---|---|---|---|---|---|---|---|---|---|
| **TEMPERATURE °F:** | | | | | | | | | | | | | | |
| Normals | | | | | | | | | | | | | | |
| -Daily Maximum | | 56.5 | 60.9 | 68.4 | 77.3 | 84.1 | 90.5 | 92.5 | 92.1 | 87.6 | 78.6 | 67.5 | 60.0 | 76.3 |
| -Daily Minimum | | 34.9 | 37.2 | 44.2 | 52.9 | 60.8 | 67.9 | 71.3 | 70.2 | 65.1 | 51.4 | 42.3 | 37.1 | 52.9 |
| -Monthly | | 45.7 | 49.1 | 56.3 | 65.1 | 72.5 | 79.2 | 81.9 | 81.2 | 76.4 | 65.0 | 54.9 | 48.6 | 64.6 |
| Extremes | | | | | | | | | | | | | | |
| -Record Highest | 26 | 82 | 85 | 89 | 94 | 99 | 105 | 106 | 102 | 104 | 95 | 88 | 84 | 106 |
| -Year | | 1972 | 1989 | 1982 | 1987 | 1964 | 1988 | 1980 | 1981 | 1980 | 1986 | 1971 | 1978 | JUL 1980 |
| -Record Lowest | 26 | 2 | 11 | 15 | 27 | 38 | 47 | 51 | 55 | 35 | 29 | 17 | 4 | 2 |
| -Year | | 1985 | 1970 | 1980 | 1987 | 1971 | 1984 | 1967 | 1989 | 1967 | 1989 | 1976 | 1989 | JAN 1985 |
| **NORMAL DEGREE DAYS:** | | | | | | | | | | | | | | |
| Heating (base 65°F) | | 611 | 462 | 303 | 77 | 9 | 0 | 0 | 0 | 0 | 98 | 316 | 513 | 2389 |
| Cooling (base 65°F) | | 13 | 17 | 34 | 80 | 241 | 426 | 524 | 502 | 342 | 98 | 13 | 0 | 2290 |
| **% OF POSSIBLE SUNSHINE** | 25 | 49 | 54 | 60 | 65 | 64 | 70 | 65 | 65 | 61 | 66 | 55 | 49 | 60 |
| **MEAN SKY COVER (tenths)** | | | | | | | | | | | | | | |
| Sunrise - Sunset | 26 | 6.6 | 6.2 | 6.1 | 5.7 | 5.8 | 5.4 | 5.8 | 5.5 | 5.4 | 4.5 | 5.7 | 6.2 | 5.7 |
| **MEAN NUMBER OF DAYS:** | | | | | | | | | | | | | | |
| Sunrise to Sunset | | | | | | | | | | | | | | |
| -Clear | 26 | 8.1 | 8.2 | 9.1 | 9.7 | 8.6 | 9.3 | 7.6 | 9.0 | 10.3 | 14.7 | 9.8 | 9.0 | 113.5 |
| -Partly Cloudy | 26 | 5.8 | 5.9 | 7.0 | 7.2 | 10.5 | 11.6 | 12.9 | 12.7 | 9.1 | 6.5 | 7.2 | 6.3 | 102.7 |
| -Cloudy | 26 | 17.1 | 14.2 | 14.9 | 13.0 | 11.9 | 9.1 | 10.5 | 9.3 | 10.6 | 9.8 | 13.0 | 15.6 | 149.0 |
| Precipitation | | | | | | | | | | | | | | |
| .01 inches or more | 26 | 10.7 | 9.2 | 10.2 | 8.3 | 9.3 | 8.3 | 10.4 | 9.7 | 8.4 | 6.2 | 8.3 | 10.0 | 109.0 |
| Snow,Ice pellets | | | | | | | | | | | | | | |
| 1.0 inches or more | 26 | 0.2 | 0.1 | 0.* | 0.0 | 0.0 | 0.0 | 0.0 | 0.0 | 0.0 | 0.0 | 0.0 | 0.0 | 0.3 |
| Thunderstorms | 26 | 1.8 | 2.6 | 5.8 | 5.5 | 7.3 | 8.3 | 12.5 | 10.7 | 5.0 | 2.1 | 2.5 | 2.7 | 66.7 |
| Heavy Fog Visibility | | | | | | | | | | | | | | |
| 1/4 mile or less | 26 | 3.5 | 2.2 | 1.7 | 1.5 | 1.0 | 0.7 | 1.2 | 1.5 | 1.7 | 2.1 | 2.4 | 3.0 | 22.5 |
| Temperature °F | | | | | | | | | | | | | | |
| -Maximum | | | | | | | | | | | | | | |
| 90° and above | 26 | 0.0 | 0.0 | 0.0 | 0.3 | 4.8 | 18.4 | 23.8 | 22.5 | 11.6 | 1.0 | 0.0 | 0.0 | 82.4 |
| 32° and below | 26 | 0.9 | 0.3 | 0.0 | 0.0 | 0.0 | 0.0 | 0.0 | 0.0 | 0.0 | 0.0 | 0.* | 0.3 | 1.6 |
| -Minimum | | | | | | | | | | | | | | |
| 32° and below | 26 | 15.6 | 11.8 | 4.2 | 0.4 | 0.0 | 0.0 | 0.0 | 0.0 | 0.0 | 0.5 | 5.9 | 12.3 | 50.7 |
| 0° and below | 26 | 0.0 | 0.0 | 0.0 | 0.0 | 0.0 | 0.0 | 0.0 | 0.0 | 0.0 | 0.0 | 0.0 | 0.0 | 0.0 |
| **AVG. STATION PRESS.(mb)** | 17 | 1009.4 | 1007.9 | 1004.8 | 1004.3 | 1003.1 | 1004.0 | 1005.1 | 1004.8 | 1004.9 | 1007.2 | 1007.5 | 1009.1 | 1006.0 |
| **RELATIVE HUMIDITY (%)** | | | | | | | | | | | | | | |
| Hour 00 | 26 | 84 | 82 | 82 | 84 | 87 | 87 | 90 | 90 | 90 | 89 | 87 | 84 | 86 |
| Hour 06 | 26 | 87 | 87 | 87 | 90 | 92 | 91 | 93 | 94 | 94 | 93 | 90 | 88 | 91 |
| Hour 12 (Local Time) | 26 | 64 | 60 | 57 | 54 | 56 | 56 | 59 | 59 | 59 | 53 | 58 | 63 | 58 |
| Hour 18 | 26 | 70 | 63 | 58 | 57 | 60 | 60 | 66 | 67 | 70 | 72 | 74 | 74 | 66 |
| **PRECIPITATION (inches):** | | | | | | | | | | | | | | |
| Water Equivalent | | | | | | | | | | | | | | |
| -Normal | | 5.00 | 4.48 | 5.86 | 5.85 | 4.83 | 2.94 | 4.40 | 3.71 | 3.55 | 2.62 | 4.18 | 5.40 | 52.82 |
| -Maximum Monthly | 26 | 14.10 | 10.28 | 15.13 | 15.53 | 10.82 | 8.17 | 13.25 | 7.44 | 9.61 | 9.13 | 9.98 | 17.70 | 17.70 |
| -Year | | 1979 | 1987 | 1976 | 1983 | 1967 | 1989 | 1979 | 1979 | 1965 | 1970 | 1977 | 1982 | DEC 1982 |
| -Minimum Monthly | 26 | 0.75 | 1.43 | 2.05 | 1.21 | 0.29 | 0.10 | 1.04 | 1.45 | 0.56 | 0.00 | 0.51 | 0.91 | 0.00 |
| -Year | | 1986 | 1976 | 1966 | 1987 | 1988 | 1988 | 1987 | 1980 | 1969 | 1963 | 1985 | 1980 | OCT 1963 |
| -Maximum in 24 hrs | 26 | 5.63 | 3.46 | 3.87 | 8.42 | 3.43 | 3.38 | 5.37 | 4.45 | 5.86 | 6.99 | 4.34 | 6.71 | 8.42 |
| -Year | | 1979 | 1974 | 1964 | 1979 | 1989 | 1989 | 1981 | 1985 | 1965 | 1975 | 1983 | 1982 | APR 1979 |
| Snow,Ice pellets | | | | | | | | | | | | | | |
| -Maximum Monthly | 26 | 6.3 | 3.6 | 5.3 | 1.1 | 0.0 | 0.0 | 0.0 | 0.0 | 0.0 | 0.0 | 0.2 | 3.1 | 6.3 |
| -Year | | 1982 | 1968 | 1968 | 1987 | | | | | | | 1976 | 1963 | JAN 1982 |
| -Maximum in 24 hrs | 26 | 6.0 | 3.6 | 5.3 | 1.1 | 0.0 | 0.0 | 0.0 | 0.0 | 0.0 | 0.0 | 0.2 | 1.8 | 6.0 |
| -Year | | 1982 | 1968 | 1968 | 1987 | | | | | | | 1976 | 1963 | JAN 1982 |
| **WIND:** | | | | | | | | | | | | | | |
| Mean Speed (mph) | 26 | 8.6 | 8.7 | 9.2 | 8.4 | 7.3 | 6.4 | 6.0 | 5.7 | 6.5 | 6.5 | 7.6 | 8.4 | 7.4 |
| Prevailing Direction | | | | | | | | | | | | | | |
| Fastest Obs. 1 Min. | | | | | | | | | | | | | | |
| -Direction (!!!) | 13 | 16 | 19 | 16 | 15 | 22 | 35 | 33 | 17 | 21 | 14 | 14 | 35 | 16 |
| -Speed (MPH) | 13 | 29 | 36 | 44 | 33 | 35 | 40 | 44 | 37 | 25 | 25 | 41 | 35 | 44 |
| -Year | | 1987 | 1986 | 1986 | 1986 | 1987 | 1984 | 1982 | 1981 | 1986 | 1987 | 1987 | 1976 | MAR 1986 |
| Peak Gust | | | | | | | | | | | | | | |
| -Direction (!!!) | 6 | SW | N | SE | SW | SW | NE | N | E | W | NE | SW | W | SW |
| -Speed (mph) | 6 | 43 | 51 | 51 | 63 | 43 | 55 | 49 | 49 | 52 | 40 | 69 | 48 | 69 |
| -Date | 6 | 1987 | 1984 | 1987 | 1985 | 1984 | 1986 | 1988 | 1987 | 1984 | 1985 | 1987 | 1987 | NOV 1987 |

**See reference Notes to this table on the following page.**

PRECIPITATION (inches)          JACKSON, MISSISSIPPI

**TABLE 2**

| YEAR | JAN | FEB | MAR | APR | MAY | JUNE | JULY | AUG | SEP | OCT | NOV | DEC | ANNUAL |
|---|---|---|---|---|---|---|---|---|---|---|---|---|---|
| 1961 | 3.07 | 6.59 | 8.90 | 2.00 | 2.96 | 7.49 | 8.55 | 3.96 | 1.22 | 0.84 | 8.33 | 11.16 | 65.07 |
| 1962 | 7.06 | 2.75 | 3.61 | 8.55 | 2.59 | 1.36 | 1.49 | 2.91 | 2.34 | 1.70 | 2.88 | 3.25 | 40.49 |
| #1963 | 5.33 | 2.82 | 1.93 | 2.44 | 1.47 | 3.29 | 6.28 | 1.65 | 0.88 | 0.00 | 4.55 | 4.39 | 35.03 |
| 1964 | 5.21 | 2.32 | 2.32 | 10.92 | 11.88 | 2.45 | 5.17 | 6.43 | 3.67 | 7.83 | 6.44 | 6.95 | 71.46 |
| 1965 | 2.86 | 7.90 | 6.86 | 1.25 | 1.36 | 2.54 | 1.92 | 3.61 | 9.61 | 0.84 | 1.79 | 3.65 | 43.99 |
| 1966 | 8.23 | 7.84 | 2.05 | 5.76 | 7.96 | 1.45 | 3.14 | 6.65 | 4.87 | 1.63 | 3.66 | 4.83 | 58.07 |
| 1967 | 1.86 | 3.56 | 2.32 | 1.66 | 10.82 | 3.76 | 4.05 | 3.49 | 1.80 | 2.78 | 0.93 | 8.68 | 45.71 |
| 1968 | 4.56 | 2.54 | 2.83 | 7.20 | 7.54 | 1.02 | 2.24 | 3.90 | 1.95 | 0.28 | 5.55 | 5.58 | 45.19 |
| 1969 | 0.86 | 3.02 | 4.90 | 6.59 | 1.52 | 1.29 | 5.46 | 3.35 | 0.56 | 2.26 | 1.87 | 7.22 | 38.90 |
| 1970 | 2.09 | 2.63 | 5.40 | 2.75 | 2.43 | 2.54 | 2.34 | 5.64 | 6.48 | 9.13 | 2.70 | 4.23 | 48.36 |
| 1971 | 3.02 | 5.68 | 7.68 | 6.86 | 8.05 | 3.40 | 6.28 | 2.64 | 6.00 | 0.09 | 2.54 | 9.82 | 62.06 |
| 1972 | 5.94 | 3.09 | 5.57 | 2.44 | 4.52 | 2.01 | 3.31 | 2.84 | 5.04 | 2.08 | 3.52 | 9.67 | 50.03 |
| 1973 | 4.59 | 4.23 | 6.12 | 9.44 | 5.96 | 0.32 | 1.99 | 2.38 | 4.44 | 2.72 | 6.15 | 6.71 | 55.05 |
| 1974 | 11.00 | 6.72 | 3.50 | 6.74 | 3.01 | 3.39 | 1.54 | 6.17 | 5.06 | 1.74 | 4.12 | 7.22 | 60.21 |
| 1975 | 4.57 | 6.18 | 4.86 | 5.07 | 6.53 | 7.44 | 9.81 | 6.21 | 2.68 | 8.25 | 4.34 | 4.29 | 70.23 |
| 1976 | 3.64 | 1.43 | 15.13 | 2.08 | 8.01 | 2.80 | 4.96 | 5.26 | 3.78 | 3.52 | 3.34 | 3.44 | 57.39 |
| 1977 | 6.18 | 2.26 | 6.41 | 7.98 | 0.74 | 2.17 | 6.22 | 1.45 | 3.93 | 2.79 | 9.98 | 3.47 | 53.58 |
| 1978 | 5.32 | 2.36 | 3.37 | 3.54 | 10.48 | 1.03 | 3.65 | 1.80 | 2.90 | 1.21 | 3.30 | 8.37 | 47.33 |
| 1979 | 14.10 | 8.35 | 4.67 | 14.38 | 5.52 | 4.38 | 13.25 | 7.44 | 5.93 | 1.76 | 8.79 | 4.18 | 92.75 |
| 1980 | 7.53 | 3.19 | 13.57 | 14.33 | 6.60 | 1.74 | 2.91 | 1.45 | 3.25 | 3.47 | 4.11 | 0.91 | 63.06 |
| 1981 | 1.41 | 2.63 | 6.19 | 1.26 | 6.64 | 3.66 | 6.51 | 2.81 | 3.51 | 5.12 | 1.97 | 4.90 | 46.61 |
| 1982 | 4.48 | 5.22 | 5.13 | 6.59 | 0.77 | 6.27 | 9.29 | 4.97 | 1.05 | 6.73 | 7.43 | 17.70 | 75.63 |
| 1983 | 8.17 | 6.55 | 6.00 | 15.53 | 9.41 | 2.93 | 1.70 | 3.70 | 2.70 | 1.52 | 8.11 | 6.95 | 73.27 |
| 1984 | 2.64 | 4.64 | 4.84 | 3.96 | 5.61 | 3.18 | 3.07 | 4.56 | 0.93 | 7.68 | 6.48 | 2.17 | 49.76 |
| 1985 | 4.05 | 7.55 | 3.13 | 3.31 | 0.86 | 1.74 | 4.43 | 7.06 | 3.94 | 7.17 | 0.51 | 3.61 | 47.36 |
| 1986 | 0.75 | 1.53 | 3.34 | 1.75 | 10.00 | 3.72 | 4.78 | 2.03 | 2.63 | 5.10 | 9.40 | 4.98 | 50.01 |
| 1987 | 4.66 | 10.28 | 5.47 | 1.21 | 4.98 | 6.17 | 1.04 | 4.03 | 1.50 | 0.27 | 4.20 | 3.50 | 47.31 |
| 1988 | 2.25 | 3.89 | 7.46 | 5.37 | 0.29 | 0.10 | 2.73 | 3.02 | 2.28 | 6.14 | 5.66 | 4.80 | 43.99 |
| 1989 | 4.38 | 2.52 | 4.53 | 2.13 | 7.92 | 8.17 | 4.47 | 1.74 | 5.40 | 0.23 | 6.86 | 4.20 | 52.55 |
| 1990 | 12.17 | 8.30 | 3.55 | 3.66 | 6.34 | 1.46 | 2.84 | 0.61 | 4.83 | 1.24 | 3.33 | 5.71 | 54.04 |
| Record Mean | 4.96 | 4.79 | 5.58 | 5.33 | 4.65 | 3.74 | 4.50 | 3.59 | 2.86 | 2.51 | 4.02 | 5.52 | 52.05 |

**TABLE 3**  AVERAGE TEMPERATURE (deg. F)          JACKSON, MISSISSIPPI

| YEAR | JAN | FEB | MAR | APR | MAY | JUNE | JULY | AUG | SEP | OCT | NOV | DEC | ANNUAL |
|---|---|---|---|---|---|---|---|---|---|---|---|---|---|
| 1961 | 40.6 | 52.9 | 60.5 | 61.0 | 70.4 | 75.5 | 79.1 | 79.1 | 75.9 | 64.1 | 55.5 | 48.2 | 68.6 |
| 1962 | 42.7 | 57.2 | 52.5 | 62.6 | 75.3 | 78.5 | 84.3 | 83.2 | 77.2 | 68.3 | 53.6 | 46.5 | 65.1 |
| #1963 | 40.5 | 43.5 | 61.5 | 68.1 | 74.4 | 80.7 | 81.1 | 81.9 | 75.0 | 70.0 | 56.4 | 38.6 | 64.3 |
| #1964 | 45.3 | 44.4 | 56.3 | 68.1 | 74.7 | 80.7 | 81.3 | 81.7 | 77.1 | 62.5 | 59.4 | 50.5 | 65.2 |
| 1965 | 48.5 | 47.2 | 50.2 | 67.8 | 74.0 | 77.7 | 81.5 | 79.5 | 76.3 | 62.6 | 60.1 | 49.4 | 64.6 |
| 1966 | 40.8 | 46.3 | 54.7 | 64.8 | 70.9 | 76.1 | 82.4 | 78.3 | 74.4 | 61.1 | 56.2 | 46.5 | 62.7 |
| 1967 | 46.4 | 44.2 | 60.5 | 69.3 | 69.6 | 78.3 | 77.3 | 77.0 | 69.8 | 61.4 | 52.7 | 50.1 | 63.1 |
| 1968 | 43.4 | 39.9 | 53.9 | 65.9 | 71.2 | 79.6 | 80.7 | 80.9 | 73.3 | 66.2 | 52.7 | 45.7 | 62.8 |
| 1969 | 48.0 | 48.1 | 49.3 | 65.1 | 72.3 | 80.3 | 83.5 | 79.6 | 75.2 | 66.2 | 52.4 | 47.1 | 63.9 |
| 1970 | 41.2 | 46.3 | 54.0 | 68.1 | 72.9 | 79.1 | 80.8 | 81.6 | 80.1 | 64.7 | 52.8 | 52.7 | 64.5 |
| 1971 | 48.7 | 49.1 | 52.4 | 62.2 | 67.9 | 79.9 | 81.0 | 80.5 | 78.3 | 70.1 | 54.7 | 57.9 | 65.2 |
| 1972 | 51.5 | 51.2 | 58.8 | 66.4 | 71.9 | 79.6 | 80.4 | 82.8 | 81.5 | 68.0 | 52.0 | 50.1 | 66.2 |
| 1973 | 44.3 | 46.9 | 62.1 | 62.5 | 70.9 | 81.3 | 83.7 | 80.1 | 77.6 | 68.6 | 61.7 | 49.3 | 65.7 |
| 1974 | 55.1 | 50.1 | 62.4 | 63.1 | 73.8 | 74.8 | 80.4 | 79.3 | 72.0 | 64.1 | 55.6 | 50.4 | 65.1 |
| 1975 | 51.8 | 52.9 | 56.8 | 63.5 | 74.1 | 78.3 | 81.2 | 80.6 | 72.3 | 66.2 | 56.6 | 47.4 | 65.1 |
| 1976 | 44.3 | 56.7 | 60.0 | 65.4 | 67.9 | 76.7 | 80.8 | 80.2 | 74.8 | 59.9 | 47.2 | 45.0 | 63.2 |
| 1977 | 35.3 | 49.3 | 59.7 | 66.3 | 75.5 | 81.7 | 82.7 | 82.0 | 78.4 | 62.0 | 57.1 | 47.5 | 64.8 |
| 1978 | 36.5 | 39.6 | 52.5 | 65.4 | 71.9 | 80.0 | 83.4 | 82.0 | 78.4 | 63.6 | 60.3 | 48.8 | 63.6 |
| 1979 | 38.3 | 46.0 | 57.4 | 64.8 | 70.3 | 76.7 | 80.2 | 79.7 | 73.8 | 64.1 | 50.9 | 46.2 | 62.4 |
| 1980 | 47.4 | 45.5 | 54.3 | 61.6 | 72.8 | 80.7 | 85.8 | 84.7 | 82.4 | 61.4 | 53.2 | 46.2 | 64.7 |
| 1981 | 41.8 | 48.7 | 55.1 | 71.0 | 69.9 | 81.8 | 83.6 | 82.6 | 73.2 | 65.4 | 58.6 | 46.6 | 64.9 |
| 1982 | 47.2 | 48.8 | 62.1 | 63.8 | 74.7 | 79.5 | 82.4 | 81.8 | 74.1 | 65.1 | 56.4 | 52.9 | 65.7 |
| 1983 | 43.7 | 47.4 | 53.9 | 60.1 | 70.7 | 76.6 | 82.9 | 82.7 | 74.1 | 65.8 | 55.1 | 41.8 | 62.9 |
| 1984 | 39.9 | 49.7 | 56.5 | 63.9 | 71.0 | 78.9 | 80.6 | 79.9 | 74.6 | 71.2 | 53.6 | 58.3 | 64.8 |
| 1985 | 38.0 | 44.8 | 61.3 | 65.2 | 72.2 | 78.8 | 80.5 | 80.3 | 74.0 | 68.0 | 62.5 | 42.7 | 64.0 |
| 1986 | 45.3 | 52.6 | 57.0 | 64.1 | 72.9 | 80.4 | 83.2 | 80.5 | 79.8 | 66.1 | 60.1 | 46.6 | 65.7 |
| 1987 | 44.4 | 51.3 | 55.5 | 62.2 | 75.9 | 79.0 | 82.0 | 82.9 | 75.2 | 59.9 | 56.6 | 52.1 | 64.8 |
| 1988 | 41.7 | 47.5 | 55.8 | 64.6 | 70.8 | 79.8 | 82.5 | 82.6 | 77.9 | 61.6 | 59.3 | 49.3 | 64.5 |
| 1989 | 52.5 | 48.2 | 58.8 | 63.2 | 72.0 | 78.4 | 80.6 | 80.8 | 74.1 | 63.9 | 57.1 | 40.4 | 64.2 |
| 1990 | 51.0 | 56.2 | 60.0 | 63.7 | 71.8 | 81.3 | 81.5 | 82.3 | 78.4 | 63.7 | 58.0 | 51.8 | 66.6 |
| Record Mean | 47.4 | 50.5 | 57.3 | 65.2 | 72.5 | 79.6 | 81.9 | 81.5 | 76.8 | 66.1 | 55.8 | 49.2 | 65.3 |
| Max | 57.9 | 61.5 | 68.9 | 77.0 | 84.0 | 90.8 | 92.6 | 92.5 | 88.4 | 79.4 | 68.3 | 59.9 | 76.8 |
| Min | 36.8 | 39.4 | 45.7 | 53.3 | 61.0 | 68.3 | 71.2 | 70.5 | 65.1 | 52.8 | 43.3 | 38.4 | 53.8 |

## REFERENCE NOTES FOR TABLES 1, 2, 3 and 6          (JACKSON, MS)

### GENERAL

T - TRACE AMOUNT
BLANK ENTRIES DENOTE MISSING/UNREPORTED DATA.
# INDICATES A STATION OR INSTRUMENT RELOCATION.

### SPECIFIC

#### TABLE 1

(a) - LENGTH OF RECORD IN YEARS. ALTHOUGH
INDIVIDUAL MONTHS MAY BE MISSING.

\* LESS THAN .05

NORMALS — BASED ON THE 1951-1980 RECORD PERIOD.
EXTREMES — DATES ARE THE MOST RECENT OCCURRENCE.
WIND DIR. — NUMERALS SHOW TENS OF DEGREES
CLOCKWISE FROM TRUE NORTH.
"00" INDICATES CALM.
RESULTANT WIND DIRECTIONS ARE GIVEN TO WHOLE DEGREES.

#### TABLE 3

MAX AND MIN ARE LONG-TERM MEAN DAILY MAXIMUM
AND MEAN DAILY MINIMUM TEMPERATURES.

### EXCEPTIONS

#### TABLES 2, 3, and 6

RECORD MEANS ARE THROUGH THE CURRENT YEAR,
BEGINNING IN          1909 FOR TEMPERATURE
1909 FOR PRECIPITATION
1964 FOR SNOWFALL

HEATING DEGREE DAYS Base 65 deg. F    JACKSON, MISSISSIPPI

**TABLE 4**

| SEASON | JULY | AUG | SEP | OCT | NOV | DEC | JAN | FEB | MAR | APR | MAY | JUNE | TOTAL |
|---|---|---|---|---|---|---|---|---|---|---|---|---|---|
| 1961-62 | 0 | 0 | 5 | 109 | 308 | 516 | 690 | 236 | 387 | 151 | 2 | 0 | 2464 |
| #1962-63 | 0 | 0 | 0 | 73 | 340 | 567 | 752 | 597 | 179 | 45 | 8 | 0 | 2561 |
| #1963-64 | 0 | 0 | 3 | 27 | 265 | 810 | 602 | 592 | 280 | 44 | 0 | 0 | 2623 |
| 1964-65 | 0 | 0 | 0 | 124 | 219 | 465 | 512 | 500 | 459 | 48 | 2 | 0 | 2329 |
| 1965-66 | 0 | 0 | 9 | 129 | 173 | 481 | 747 | 520 | 326 | 98 | 13 | 0 | 2496 |
| 1966-67 | 0 | 0 | 0 | 155 | 270 | 581 | 570 | 574 | 192 | 20 | 26 | 0 | 2388 |
| 1967-68 | 0 | 0 | 35 | 141 | 368 | 461 | 662 | 721 | 362 | 64 | 12 | 0 | 2826 |
| 1968-69 | 0 | 0 | 0 | 93 | 369 | 592 | 523 | 470 | 476 | 65 | 3 | 0 | 2591 |
| 1969-70 | 0 | 0 | 0 | 95 | 372 | 550 | 741 | 516 | 340 | 72 | 23 | 0 | 2709 |
| 1970-71 | 0 | 0 | 0 | 85 | 367 | 388 | 507 | 444 | 394 | 147 | 40 | 0 | 2372 |
| 1971-72 | 0 | 0 | 0 | 19 | 328 | 235 | 431 | 410 | 216 | 76 | 1 | 0 | 1716 |
| 1972-73 | 0 | 0 | 4 | 71 | 400 | 466 | 634 | 503 | 135 | 146 | 19 | 0 | 2378 |
| 1973-74 | 0 | 0 | 0 | 61 | 173 | 486 | 327 | 419 | 165 | 115 | 1 | 0 | 1747 |
| 1974-75 | 0 | 0 | 6 | 79 | 308 | 465 | 429 | 348 | 293 | 138 | 0 | 0 | 2066 |
| 1975-76 | 0 | 0 | 26 | 59 | 304 | 543 | 635 | 252 | 201 | 59 | 18 | 0 | 2097 |
| 1976-77 | 0 | 0 | 0 | 197 | 528 | 614 | 913 | 435 | 196 | 43 | 1 | 0 | 2927 |
| 1977-78 | 0 | 0 | 0 | 136 | 246 | 538 | 881 | 706 | 377 | 73 | 14 | 0 | 2971 |
| 1978-79 | 0 | 0 | 0 | 98 | 164 | 519 | 821 | 531 | 262 | 69 | 20 | 0 | 2484 |
| 1979-80 | 0 | 0 | 0 | 98 | 421 | 580 | 540 | 570 | 337 | 124 | 3 | 0 | 2673 |
| 1980-81 | 0 | 0 | 0 | 158 | 363 | 575 | 711 | 454 | 312 | 20 | 18 | 0 | 2611 |
| 1981-82 | 0 | 0 | 16 | 104 | 217 | 568 | 569 | 451 | 199 | 123 | 4 | 0 | 2251 |
| 1982-83 | 0 | 0 | 19 | 120 | 286 | 421 | 653 | 487 | 347 | 176 | 12 | 0 | 2521 |
| 1983-84 | 0 | 0 | 21 | 83 | 315 | 716 | 770 | 440 | 289 | 113 | 29 | 0 | 2776 |
| 1984-85 | 0 | 0 | 12 | 27 | 350 | 249 | 832 | 562 | 158 | 92 | 2 | 0 | 2284 |
| 1985-86 | 0 | 0 | 14 | 54 | 148 | 685 | 606 | 360 | 261 | 90 | 8 | 0 | 2226 |
| 1986-87 | 0 | 0 | 0 | 79 | 183 | 566 | 632 | 378 | 297 | 150 | 0 | 0 | 2285 |
| 1987-88 | 0 | 0 | 0 | 161 | 271 | 408 | 716 | 502 | 292 | 74 | 4 | 0 | 2428 |
| 1988-89 | 0 | 0 | 0 | 134 | 208 | 484 | 392 | 495 | 239 | 135 | 20 | 0 | 2107 |
| 1989-90 | 0 | 0 | 11 | 109 | 265 | 754 | 429 | 261 | 209 | 125 | 9 | 0 | 2172 |
| 1990-91 | 0 | 0 | 5 | 145 | 227 | 427 | | | | | | | |

**TABLE 5**   COOLING DEGREE DAYS Base 65 deg. F    JACKSON, MISSISSIPPI

| YEAR | JAN | FEB | MAR | APR | MAY | JUNE | JULY | AUG | SEP | OCT | NOV | DEC | TOTAL |
|---|---|---|---|---|---|---|---|---|---|---|---|---|---|
| 1969 | 3 | 0 | 0 | 75 | 235 | 465 | 577 | 460 | 312 | 137 | 3 | 0 | 2267 |
| 1970 | 7 | 0 | 5 | 173 | 274 | 431 | 496 | 522 | 460 | 81 | 7 | 18 | 2474 |
| 1971 | 9 | 7 | 10 | 69 | 138 | 453 | 503 | 487 | 406 | 181 | 29 | 20 | 2312 |
| 1972 | 20 | 17 | 30 | 126 | 221 | 445 | 487 | 561 | 506 | 169 | 15 | 16 | 2613 |
| 1973 | 1 | 0 | 51 | 77 | 210 | 498 | 583 | 477 | 382 | 181 | 81 | 5 | 2546 |
| 1974 | 25 | 8 | 91 | 64 | 279 | 298 | 487 | 451 | 223 | 57 | 34 | 19 | 2036 |
| 1975 | 26 | 17 | 46 | 96 | 290 | 407 | 509 | 487 | 255 | 101 | 59 | 7 | 2300 |
| 1976 | 0 | 17 | 52 | 76 | 116 | 357 | 497 | 481 | 300 | 47 | 0 | 0 | 1943 |
| 1977 | 0 | 3 | 39 | 89 | 331 | 508 | 555 | 534 | 409 | 47 | 16 | 4 | 2535 |
| 1978 | 2 | 0 | 0 | 92 | 235 | 456 | 576 | 536 | 409 | 60 | 31 | 24 | 2421 |
| 1979 | 0 | 2 | 35 | 69 | 190 | 357 | 482 | 461 | 269 | 76 | 4 | 2 | 1947 |
| 1980 | 0 | 11 | 11 | 28 | 253 | 476 | 652 | 619 | 527 | 52 | 14 | 1 | 2644 |
| 1981 | 0 | 3 | 12 | 207 | 174 | 514 | 582 | 555 | 267 | 127 | 30 | 2 | 2473 |
| 1982 | 25 | 3 | 116 | 93 | 310 | 443 | 544 | 530 | 297 | 130 | 35 | 51 | 2577 |
| 1983 | 0 | 0 | 13 | 35 | 194 | 354 | 564 | 555 | 300 | 115 | 24 | 6 | 2160 |
| 1984 | 0 | 5 | 35 | 87 | 221 | 422 | 489 | 470 | 310 | 227 | 19 | 49 | 2334 |
| 1985 | 0 | 3 | 54 | 105 | 233 | 424 | 486 | 480 | 290 | 153 | 79 | 0 | 2307 |
| 1986 | 0 | 21 | 18 | 70 | 259 | 469 | 572 | 487 | 446 | 122 | 44 | 2 | 2510 |
| 1987 | 0 | 0 | 9 | 72 | 344 | 429 | 533 | 560 | 311 | 14 | 22 | 15 | 2309 |
| 1988 | 0 | 1 | 14 | 67 | 193 | 452 | 552 | 552 | 395 | 34 | 45 | 3 | 2308 |
| 1989 | 8 | 30 | 54 | 87 | 245 | 406 | 489 | 498 | 293 | 84 | 36 | 0 | 2230 |
| 1990 | 3 | 25 | 60 | 92 | 226 | 494 | 515 | 544 | 412 | 113 | 24 | 24 | 2532 |

**TABLE 6**   SNOWFALL (inches)    JACKSON, MISSISSIPPI

| SEASON | JULY | AUG | SEP | OCT | NOV | DEC | JAN | FEB | MAR | APR | MAY | JUNE | TOTAL |
|---|---|---|---|---|---|---|---|---|---|---|---|---|---|
| 1961-62 | 0.0 | 0.0 | 0.0 | 0.0 | 0.0 | 0.0 | 4.0 | 0.0 | 0.0 | 0.0 | 0.0 | 0.0 | 4.0 |
| #1962-63 | 0.0 | 0.0 | 0.0 | 0.0 | 0.0 | 0.0 | 0.0 | 1.0 | 0.0 | 0.0 | 0.0 | 0.0 | 1.0 |
| 1963-64 | 0.0 | 0.0 | 0.0 | 0.0 | 0.0 | 3.1 | 1.5 | T | T | 0.0 | 0.0 | 0.0 | 4.6 |
| 1964-65 | 0.0 | 0.0 | 0.0 | 0.0 | T | T | T | T | T | 0.0 | 0.0 | 0.0 | T |
| 1965-66 | 0.0 | 0.0 | 0.0 | 0.0 | 0.0 | 0.0 | T | 0.0 | 0.0 | 0.0 | 0.0 | 0.0 | T |
| 1966-67 | 0.0 | 0.0 | 0.0 | 0.0 | T | T | 0.0 | T | 0.0 | 0.0 | 0.0 | 0.0 | T |
| 1967-68 | 0.0 | 0.0 | 0.0 | 0.0 | 0.0 | T | T | 3.6 | 5.3 | 0.0 | 0.0 | 0.0 | 8.9 |
| 1968-69 | 0.0 | 0.0 | 0.0 | 0.0 | 0.0 | 0.0 | 0.0 | T | 0.0 | 0.0 | 0.0 | 0.0 | 0.0 |
| 1969-70 | 0.0 | 0.0 | 0.0 | 0.0 | 0.0 | 0.0 | T | 0.0 | T | 0.0 | 0.0 | 0.0 | T |
| 1970-71 | 0.0 | 0.0 | 0.0 | 0.0 | 0.0 | 0.0 | T | T | T | 0.0 | 0.0 | 0.0 | T |
| 1971-72 | 0.0 | 0.0 | 0.0 | 0.0 | T | 0.0 | 0.0 | T | 0.0 | 0.0 | 0.0 | 0.0 | T |
| 1972-73 | 0.0 | 0.0 | 0.0 | 0.0 | 0.0 | 0.0 | T | T | 0.0 | 0.0 | 0.0 | 0.0 | T |
| 1973-74 | 0.0 | 0.0 | 0.0 | 0.0 | 0.0 | 0.3 | 0.0 | 0.0 | 0.0 | 0.0 | 0.0 | 0.0 | 0.3 |
| 1974-75 | 0.0 | 0.0 | 0.0 | 0.0 | T | 0.0 | T | 0.0 | T | 0.0 | 0.0 | 0.0 | T |
| 1975-76 | 0.0 | 0.0 | 0.0 | 0.0 | T | T | T | 0.0 | 0.0 | 0.0 | 0.0 | 0.0 | T |
| 1976-77 | 0.0 | 0.0 | 0.0 | 0.0 | 0.2 | 0.0 | 5.8 | 0.0 | 0.0 | 0.0 | 0.0 | 0.0 | 6.0 |
| 1977-78 | 0.0 | 0.0 | 0.0 | 0.0 | 0.0 | 0.0 | 1.1 | T | 0.1 | 0.0 | 0.0 | 0.0 | 1.2 |
| 1978-79 | 0.0 | 0.0 | 0.0 | 0.0 | 0.0 | T | T | T | 0.0 | 0.0 | 0.0 | 0.0 | T |
| 1979-80 | 0.0 | 0.0 | 0.0 | 0.0 | 0.0 | 0.0 | T | T | T | T | 0.0 | 0.0 | T |
| 1980-81 | 0.0 | 0.0 | 0.0 | 0.0 | 0.0 | T | T | T | 0.0 | 0.0 | 0.0 | 0.0 | T |
| 1981-82 | 0.0 | 0.0 | 0.0 | 0.0 | 0.0 | T | 6.3 | T | T | 0.0 | 0.0 | 0.0 | 6.3 |
| 1982-83 | 0.0 | 0.0 | 0.0 | 0.0 | 0.0 | 0.0 | T | T | T | T | 0.0 | 0.0 | T |
| 1983-84 | 0.0 | 0.0 | 0.0 | 0.0 | 0.0 | T | T | T | 0.0 | 0.0 | 0.0 | 0.0 | T |
| 1984-85 | 0.0 | 0.0 | 0.0 | 0.0 | 0.0 | T | 0.3 | 1.4 | 0.0 | 0.0 | 0.0 | 0.0 | 1.7 |
| 1985-86 | 0.0 | 0.0 | 0.0 | 0.0 | 0.0 | T | T | 0.0 | 0.0 | 0.0 | 0.0 | 0.0 | T |
| 1986-87 | 0.0 | 0.0 | 0.0 | 0.0 | 0.0 | 0.0 | T | 0.0 | T | 1.1 | 0.0 | 0.0 | 1.1 |
| 1987-88 | 0.0 | 0.0 | 0.0 | 0.0 | 0.0 | 0.0 | T | T | 0.0 | 0.0 | 0.0 | 0.0 | T |
| 1988-89 | 0.0 | 0.0 | 0.0 | 0.0 | 0.0 | T | 0.0 | T | T | T | 0.0 | 0.0 | T |
| 1989-90 | 0.0 | 0.0 | 0.0 | 0.0 | T | 0.1 | 0.0 | 0.0 | 0.0 | 0.0 | 0.0 | 0.0 | 0.1 |
| 1990-91 | 0.0 | 0.0 | 0.0 | 0.0 | 0.0 | T | | | | | | | |
| Record Mean | 0.0 | 0.0 | 0.0 | 0.0 | T | T | 0.6 | 0.2 | 0.2 | T | 0.0 | 0.0 | 1.0 |

**See Reference Notes, relative to all above tables, on preceding page.**

The National Weather Service Office at Kansas City is very near the geographical center of the United States. The surrounding terrain is gently rolling. It has a modified continental climate. There are no natural topographic obstructions to prevent the free sweep of air from all directions. The influx of moist air from the Gulf of Mexico, or dry air from the semi-arid regions of the southwest, determine whether wet or dry conditions will prevail. There is often conflict between the warm moist gulf air and the cold polar continental air from the north in this area.

Early spring brings a period of frequent and rapid fluctuations in weather, with the fluctuations generally less frequent as spring progresses. The summer season is characterized by warm days and mild nights, with moderate humidities. July is the warmest month. The fall season is normally mild and usually includes a period near the middle of the season characterized by mild, sunny days, and cool nights. Winters are not severely cold. January is the coldest month. Falls of snow to a depth of 10 inches or more are comparatively rare. The distribution of measurable snow normally extends from November to April.

Nearly 60 percent of the annual precipitation occurs during the six months from April through September. More than 75 percent of the annual moisture normally falls during the growing season. The frequency and distribution of precipitation over a normal day is also important. The maximum frequency of precipitation, from April through October, occurs during the six hours following midnight and the minimum frequency occurs during the six hours following noon.

## TABLE 1    NORMALS, MEANS AND EXTREMES

KANSAS CITY, MISSOURI INTERNATIONAL AIRPORT.

LATITUDE: 39°17'N    LONGITUDE: 94°43'W    ELEVATION: FT. GRND 973 BARO 975    TIME ZONE: CENTRAL    WBAN: 03947

| | (a) | JAN | FEB | MAR | APR | MAY | JUNE | JULY | AUG | SEP | OCT | NOV | DEC | YEAR |
|---|---|---|---|---|---|---|---|---|---|---|---|---|---|---|
| **TEMPERATURE °F:** | | | | | | | | | | | | | | |
| Normals | | | | | | | | | | | | | | |
| -Daily Maximum | | 34.5 | 41.1 | 51.3 | 65.1 | 74.6 | 83.3 | 88.5 | 86.8 | 78.6 | 67.9 | 52.1 | 40.1 | 63.7 |
| -Daily Minimum | | 17.2 | 23.0 | 31.7 | 44.4 | 54.6 | 63.8 | 68.5 | 66.5 | 58.1 | 47.0 | 34.0 | 23.7 | 44.4 |
| -Monthly | | 25.9 | 32.1 | 41.5 | 54.8 | 64.6 | 73.6 | 78.5 | 76.7 | 68.4 | 57.5 | 43.1 | 31.9 | 54.1 |
| Extremes | | | | | | | | | | | | | | |
| -Record Highest | 17 | 69 | 76 | 86 | 93 | 92 | 105 | 107 | 109 | 98 | 92 | 82 | 70 | 109 |
| -Year | | 1989 | 1981 | 1986 | 1987 | 1985 | 1980 | 1974 | 1984 | 1984 | 1976 | 1980 | 1980 | AUG 1984 |
| -Record Lowest | 17 | -17 | -19 | -10 | 12 | 30 | 43 | 52 | 43 | 33 | 21 | 1 | -23 | -23 |
| -Year | | 1982 | 1982 | 1978 | 1975 | 1976 | 1983 | 1973 | 1986 | 1984 | 1972 | 1976 | 1989 | DEC 1989 |
| **NORMAL DEGREE DAYS:** | | | | | | | | | | | | | | |
| Heating (base 65°F) | | 1212 | 921 | 729 | 314 | 112 | 12 | 0 | 0 | 42 | 258 | 657 | 1026 | 5283 |
| Cooling (base 65°F) | | 0 | 0 | 0 | 8 | 99 | 270 | 423 | 363 | 144 | 26 | 0 | 0 | 1333 |
| **% OF POSSIBLE SUNSHINE** | 17 | 60 | 56 | 59 | 65 | 64 | 69 | 74 | 67 | 65 | 60 | 50 | 51 | 62 |
| **MEAN SKY COVER (tenths)** | | | | | | | | | | | | | | |
| Sunrise - Sunset | 17 | 5.9 | 6.3 | 6.5 | 6.0 | 6.2 | 5.4 | 4.4 | 4.9 | 5.0 | 5.1 | 6.0 | 6.0 | 5.6 |
| **MEAN NUMBER OF DAYS:** | | | | | | | | | | | | | | |
| Sunrise to Sunset | | | | | | | | | | | | | | |
| -Clear | 17 | 9.9 | 7.8 | 7.4 | 9.2 | 7.9 | 9.9 | 14.1 | 12.4 | 12.3 | 12.4 | 8.8 | 9.8 | 121.8 |
| -Partly Cloudy | 17 | 6.7 | 6.2 | 7.5 | 6.7 | 9.6 | 9.7 | 9.6 | 10.4 | 7.6 | 7.4 | 7.2 | 6.2 | 94.9 |
| -Cloudy | 17 | 14.4 | 14.2 | 16.1 | 14.1 | 13.5 | 10.4 | 7.3 | 8.2 | 10.1 | 11.2 | 14.1 | 15.0 | 148.5 |
| Precipitation | | | | | | | | | | | | | | |
| .01 inches or more | 17 | 7.1 | 7.2 | 10.0 | 10.5 | 11.2 | 10.2 | 7.3 | 9.1 | 8.2 | 7.7 | 7.6 | 7.5 | 103.6 |
| Snow,Ice pellets | | | | | | | | | | | | | | |
| 1.0 inches or more | 17 | 2.1 | 1.9 | 0.9 | 0.4 | 0.0 | 0.0 | 0.0 | 0.0 | 0.0 | 0.0 | 0.4 | 1.3 | 6.9 |
| Thunderstorms | 17 | 0.3 | 0.5 | 2.4 | 4.8 | 8.6 | 9.2 | 7.2 | 7.8 | 5.6 | 3.4 | 1.2 | 0.5 | 51.6 |
| Heavy Fog Visibility | | | | | | | | | | | | | | |
| 1/4 mile or less | 17 | 1.9 | 2.7 | 2.2 | 0.9 | 1.2 | 0.6 | 0.5 | 1.4 | 1.5 | 1.7 | 2.0 | 3.1 | 19.6 |
| Temperature °F | | | | | | | | | | | | | | |
| -Maximum | | | | | | | | | | | | | | |
| 90° and above | 17 | 0.0 | 0.0 | 0.0 | 0.5 | 0.3 | 5.6 | 16.8 | 11.8 | 3.5 | 0.2 | 0.0 | 0.0 | 38.6 |
| 32° and below | 17 | 12.9 | 9.1 | 1.9 | 0.1 | 0.0 | 0.0 | 0.0 | 0.0 | 0.0 | 0.0 | 2.2 | 8.4 | 34.5 |
| -Minimum | | | | | | | | | | | | | | |
| 32° and below | 17 | 28.1 | 22.0 | 14.4 | 3.5 | 0.1 | 0.0 | 0.0 | 0.0 | 0.0 | 2.2 | 13.7 | 26.5 | 110.5 |
| 0° and below | 17 | 4.3 | 2.7 | 0.2 | 0.0 | 0.0 | 0.0 | 0.0 | 0.0 | 0.0 | 0.0 | 0.0 | 2.1 | 9.2 |
| **AVG. STATION PRESS.(mb)** | 17 | 983.0 | 982.0 | 977.7 | 977.2 | 976.6 | 977.5 | 978.9 | 979.4 | 980.3 | 981.2 | 980.3 | 982.1 | 979.7 |
| **RELATIVE HUMIDITY (%)** | | | | | | | | | | | | | | |
| Hour 00 | 17 | 72 | 74 | 71 | 68 | 75 | 78 | 75 | 78 | 79 | 73 | 74 | 74 | 74 |
| Hour 06 | 17 | 75 | 77 | 78 | 77 | 82 | 84 | 84 | 86 | 86 | 80 | 79 | 78 | 81 |
| Hour 12 (Local Time) | 17 | 63 | 64 | 59 | 55 | 58 | 58 | 56 | 59 | 59 | 56 | 62 | 65 | 60 |
| Hour 18 | 17 | 64 | 63 | 57 | 52 | 56 | 56 | 54 | 58 | 60 | 59 | 65 | 67 | 59 |
| **PRECIPITATION (inches):** | | | | | | | | | | | | | | |
| Water Equivalent | | | | | | | | | | | | | | |
| -Normal | | 1.08 | 1.19 | 2.41 | 3.23 | 4.42 | 4.66 | 4.35 | 3.57 | 4.14 | 3.10 | 1.63 | 1.38 | 35.16 |
| -Maximum Monthly | 17 | 2.66 | 2.69 | 9.08 | 6.82 | 10.07 | 7.44 | 8.71 | 9.58 | 11.34 | 7.67 | 3.95 | 5.42 | 11.34 |
| -Year | | 1982 | 1985 | 1973 | 1984 | 1974 | 1981 | 1973 | 1982 | 1977 | 1977 | 1985 | 1980 | SEP 1977 |
| -Minimum Monthly | 17 | 0.02 | 0.31 | 1.18 | 1.02 | 2.14 | 1.80 | 0.25 | 0.75 | 1.13 | 0.21 | T | 0.05 | T |
| -Year | | 1986 | 1981 | 1974 | 1980 | 1988 | 1988 | 1988 | 1975 | 1984 | 1974 | 1988 | 1979 | NOV 1989 |
| -Maximum in 24 hrs | 17 | 1.83 | 1.39 | 1.78 | 4.69 | 4.26 | 2.67 | 5.08 | 6.19 | 8.82 | 4.92 | 2.03 | 3.67 | 8.82 |
| -Year | | 1982 | 1987 | 1973 | 1975 | 1974 | 1976 | 1986 | 1982 | 1977 | 1973 | 1973 | 1980 | SEP 1977 |
| Snow,Ice pellets | | | | | | | | | | | | | | |
| -Maximum Monthly | 17 | 14.2 | 12.7 | 11.4 | 7.2 | T | T | 0.0 | 0.0 | 0.0 | T | 7.1 | 13.2 | 14.2 |
| -Year | | 1977 | 1982 | 1978 | 1983 | 1989 | 1989 | | | | 1987 | 1975 | 1983 | JAN 1977 |
| -Maximum in 24 hrs | 17 | 7.6 | 9.3 | 7.2 | 4.0 | T | T | 0.0 | 0.0 | 0.0 | T | 6.1 | 10.8 | 10.8 |
| -Year | | 1985 | 1978 | 1978 | 1983 | 1989 | 1989 | | | | 1987 | 1975 | 1987 | DEC 1987 |
| **WIND:** | | | | | | | | | | | | | | |
| Mean Speed (mph) | 17 | 11.4 | 11.4 | 12.6 | 12.4 | 10.3 | 9.8 | 9.3 | 9.2 | 9.6 | 10.3 | 11.3 | 11.3 | 10.7 |
| Prevailing Direction | | | | | | | | | | | | | | |
| Fastest Obs. 1 Min. | | | | | | | | | | | | | | |
| -Direction (!!!) | 5 | 19 | 31 | 26 | 32 | 33 | 36 | 18 | 31 | 29 | 16 | 32 | 20 | 36 |
| -Speed (MPH) | 5 | 35 | 31 | 38 | 32 | 45 | 46 | 41 | 40 | 40 | 32 | 35 | 39 | 46 |
| -Year | | 1988 | 1988 | 1989 | 1988 | 1987 | 1987 | 1987 | 1987 | 1988 | 1985 | 1988 | 1988 | JUN 1987 |
| Peak Gust | | | | | | | | | | | | | | |
| -Direction (!!!) | 6 | NW | NW | S | SW | NW | N | NW | NW | N | S | S | S | N |
| -Speed (mph) | 6 | 58 | 56 | 53 | 62 | 52 | 63 | 55 | 54 | 63 | 46 | 49 | 51 | 63 |
| -Date | | 1984 | 1984 | 1986 | 1984 | 1987 | 1987 | 1986 | 1987 | 1987 | 1985 | 1984 | 1984 | JUN 1987 |

**See Reference Notes to this table on the following page.**

PRECIPITATION (inches)  KANSAS CITY, MISSOURI INTERNATIONAL AIRPORT.

**TABLE 2**

| YEAR | JAN | FEB | MAR | APR | MAY | JUNE | JULY | AUG | SEP | OCT | NOV | DEC | ANNUAL |
|---|---|---|---|---|---|---|---|---|---|---|---|---|---|
| 1961 | 0.05 | 2.44 | 6.66 | 4.20 | 5.20 | 6.55 | 9.02 | 3.81 | 11.58 | 3.24 | 5.54 | 1.96 | 60.25 |
| 1962 | 2.95 | 2.02 | 1.94 | 1.10 | 5.29 | 2.93 | 6.17 | 3.10 | 7.32 | 1.89 | 1.24 | 1.04 | 36.99 |
| 1963 | 0.59 | 0.41 | 1.94 | 0.80 | 4.17 | 3.21 | 4.40 | 4.08 | 1.44 | 0.94 | 2.30 | 0.37 | 24.65 |
| 1964 | 1.20 | 1.50 | 3.20 | 5.40 | 5.50 | 5.40 | 2.94 | 3.79 | 7.75 | 1.83 | 0.24 | 2.25 | 38.82 |
| 1965 | 2.35 | 1.81 | 3.51 | 2.21 | 2.19 | 7.50 | 9.83 | 6.27 | 2.67 | 0.45 | 1.05 | 0.91 | 47.74 |
| 1966 | 0.21 | 0.76 | 1.88 | 3.04 | 2.48 | 8.63 | 0.89 | 4.24 | 2.67 | 0.45 | 1.05 | 0.91 | 27.21 |
| 1967 | 2.09 | 0.35 | 2.85 | 6.86 | 6.04 | 9.71 | 1.81 | 0.31 | 7.87 | 8.63 | 0.45 | 1.72 | 48.69 |
| 1968 | 0.27 | 1.20 | 0.73 | 3.91 | 5.19 | 2.33 | 5.13 | 4.32 | 1.04 | 3.52 | 3.03 | 0.72 | 31.96 |
| 1969 | 1.31 | 0.49 | 1.36 | 4.77 | 3.89 | 10.57 | 10.29 | 8.70 | 3.67 | 6.50 | 0.08 | 1.74 | 52.35 |
| 1970 | 0.21 | 0.46 | 1.02 | 3.95 | 4.75 | 5.32 | 0.62 | 4.02 | 10.79 | 2.30 | 0.94 | 1.74 | 36.12 |
| 1971 | 1.48 | 0.89 | 0.87 | 1.29 | 3.02 | 3.20 | 3.13 | 1.04 | 2.70 | 3.47 | 1.68 | 3.82 | 26.59 |
| #1972 | 0.56 | 0.41 | 2.13 | 3.98 | 2.18 | 2.71 | 3.43 | 2.90 | 2.69 | 2.29 | 3.00 | 1.47 | 27.75 |
| 1973 | 2.05 | 1.35 | 9.08 | 2.91 | 5.65 | 2.84 | 8.71 | 1.60 | 10.32 | 5.80 | 2.36 | 2.59 | 55.26 |
| 1974 | 1.05 | 1.12 | 1.18 | 10.07 | 2.16 | 4.98 | 1.13 | 4.85 | 6.10 | 0.35 | 1.62 | 2.03 | 36.12 |
| 1975 | 2.14 | 1.59 | 1.49 | 6.61 | 3.45 | 2.46 | 0.25 | 4.89 | 1.63 | 4.13 | 2.75 | 2.03 | 34.07 |
| 1976 | 0.53 | 0.66 | 2.53 | 3.30 | 5.49 | 5.08 | 0.77 | 0.76 | 1.41 | 2.84 | 0.21 | 0.10 | 23.68 |
| 1977 | 1.15 | 0.57 | 2.59 | 2.35 | 5.43 | 6.18 | 2.74 | 7.99 | 11.34 | 7.67 | 1.36 | 0.37 | 49.74 |
| 1978 | 0.39 | 1.32 | 1.77 | 5.36 | 4.98 | 2.64 | 5.49 | 2.66 | 4.04 | 0.33 | 3.93 | 1.05 | 33.96 |
| #1979 | 2.35 | 0.78 | 2.96 | 2.35 | 3.00 | 5.37 | 1.99 | 4.89 | 1.63 | 4.13 | 0.45 | 5.42 | 31.75 |
| 1980 | 1.60 | 1.44 | 3.64 | 1.02 | 3.06 | 2.52 | 1.99 | 4.89 | 1.63 | 4.13 | 2.84 | 0.45 | 31.79 |
| 1981 | 0.49 | 0.31 | 1.43 | 1.94 | 9.46 | 7.44 | 8.43 | 2.43 | 2.71 | 4.14 | 2.84 | 0.45 | 42.07 |
| 1982 | 2.66 | 1.13 | 2.94 | 1.55 | 9.81 | 6.04 | 2.73 | 9.58 | 1.58 | 3.04 | 3.94 | 1.42 | 47.21 |
| 1983 | 0.58 | 0.57 | 2.93 | 5.52 | 6.03 | 5.03 | 0.26 | 0.86 | 1.89 | 3.85 | 1.24 | 3.57 | 32.88 |
| 1984 | 0.14 | 1.96 | 4.52 | 6.82 | 2.26 | 4.14 | 3.91 | 0.75 | 3.42 | 6.04 | 3.95 | 1.24 | 38.77 |
| 1985 | 0.94 | 2.69 | 2.05 | 1.75 | 7.00 | 3.56 | 5.82 | 6.98 | 9.23 | 7.51 | 3.95 | 1.24 | 52.72 |
| 1986 | 0.02 | 1.25 | 1.34 | 2.12 | 4.76 | 2.48 | 8.36 | 3.16 | 10.40 | 3.17 | 1.18 | 1.20 | 39.44 |
| 1987 | 0.77 | 2.26 | 2.85 | 2.24 | 4.74 | 4.74 | 3.00 | 4.58 | 3.66 | 1.32 | 1.88 | 2.05 | 33.99 |
| 1988 | 1.40 | 0.72 | 1.43 | 2.15 | 2.14 | 1.80 | 1.21 | 1.87 | 8.48 | 0.21 | 1.96 | 0.85 | 24.22 |
| 1989 | 0.98 | 0.59 | 2.13 | 1.50 | 4.56 | 3.44 | 4.76 | 7.38 | 8.87 | 2.88 | T | 0.55 | 37.64 |
| 1990 | 1.20 | 2.11 | 3.90 | 2.47 | 7.36 | 6.27 | 4.40 | 5.04 | 1.28 | 2.46 | 3.01 | 1.11 | 40.61 |
| Record Mean | 1.30 | 1.43 | 2.59 | 3.31 | 4.80 | 4.76 | 3.86 | 3.98 | 4.37 | 3.01 | 1.89 | 1.48 | 36.77 |

**TABLE 3**  AVERAGE TEMPERATURE (deg. F)  KANSAS CITY, MISSOURI INTERNATIONAL AIRPORT.

| YEAR | JAN | FEB | MAR | APR | MAY | JUNE | JULY | AUG | SEP | OCT | NOV | DEC | ANNUAL |
|---|---|---|---|---|---|---|---|---|---|---|---|---|---|
| 1961 | 31.7 | 38.6 | 43.8 | 50.1 | 60.6 | 72.3 | 77.3 | 75.4 | 66.0 | 59.0 | 43.8 | 28.5 | 54.0 |
| 1962 | 23.5 | 34.9 | 40.1 | 54.5 | 74.7 | 74.7 | 78.0 | 79.3 | 66.8 | 61.8 | 46.5 | 32.8 | 55.7 |
| 1963 | 19.8 | 32.3 | 49.2 | 59.2 | 67.5 | 79.3 | 81.7 | 79.0 | 74.1 | 72.0 | 49.8 | 25.2 | 57.4 |
| 1964 | 37.2 | 36.2 | 41.8 | 57.4 | 70.1 | 73.7 | 82.5 | 76.0 | 69.4 | 57.6 | 49.9 | 32.3 | 57.0 |
| 1965 | 31.4 | 32.3 | 34.0 | 58.5 | 71.6 | 74.6 | 78.5 | 77.1 | 69.9 | 60.5 | 48.2 | 44.0 | 56.7 |
| 1966 | 28.0 | 33.7 | 49.1 | 52.8 | 65.6 | 73.3 | 83.4 | 74.9 | 68.8 | 59.7 | 49.1 | 34.8 | 56.1 |
| 1967 | 33.9 | 33.6 | 47.8 | 58.9 | 61.7 | 72.9 | 76.5 | 75.1 | 67.9 | 58.6 | 44.4 | 35.4 | 55.6 |
| 1968 | 28.4 | 32.3 | 48.1 | 57.0 | 62.2 | 77.6 | 79.4 | 77.8 | 69.5 | 59.6 | 41.2 | 29.7 | 55.3 |
| 1969 | 26.5 | 34.2 | 37.6 | 56.3 | 66.1 | 70.2 | 81.4 | 78.9 | 71.8 | 55.7 | 46.1 | 33.1 | 54.8 |
| 1970 | 26.1 | 36.7 | 42.0 | 57.4 | 72.1 | 74.5 | 80.8 | 82.4 | 71.6 | 58.6 | 44.4 | 38.9 | 57.1 |
| 1971 | 27.7 | 31.5 | 43.7 | 59.7 | 64.4 | 79.4 | 76.4 | 78.3 | 72.6 | 64.0 | 46.9 | 37.0 | 56.8 |
| #1972 | 27.3 | 33.2 | 47.1 | 57.4 | 67.1 | 76.9 | 77.2 | 77.3 | 70.9 | 53.9 | 39.6 | 27.5 | 54.6 |
| 1973 | 27.3 | 33.8 | 47.7 | 51.8 | 61.5 | 76.6 | 76.6 | 77.1 | 66.7 | 60.7 | 45.5 | 30.1 | 54.5 |
| 1974 | 23.8 | 35.3 | 46.9 | 56.2 | 65.6 | 70.5 | 82.1 | 73.0 | 61.6 | 57.7 | 42.8 | 32.2 | 54.0 |
| 1975 | 29.9 | 27.8 | 36.5 | 52.8 | 67.1 | 74.2 | 80.9 | 79.8 | 63.5 | 58.9 | 45.9 | 34.1 | 54.3 |
| 1976 | 27.5 | 42.7 | 45.0 | 56.3 | 60.0 | 71.3 | 79.0 | 77.7 | 69.0 | 50.8 | 35.9 | 29.0 | 53.7 |
| 1977 | 15.6 | 35.1 | 48.0 | 59.7 | 69.0 | 74.5 | 79.7 | 74.4 | 69.0 | 55.7 | 42.3 | 29.5 | 54.4 |
| 1978 | 16.8 | 19.5 | 37.6 | 55.5 | 62.1 | 74.6 | 79.3 | 76.5 | 73.6 | 56.4 | 44.4 | 31.0 | 52.3 |
| #1979 | 12.5 | 20.9 | 42.2 | 51.6 | 63.5 | 72.2 | 75.9 | 75.7 | 68.6 | 57.7 | 40.7 | 35.2 | 51.4 |
| 1980 | 28.7 | 25.2 | 38.7 | 54.6 | 63.9 | 75.3 | 85.2 | 80.3 | 69.6 | 54.1 | 44.5 | 32.1 | 54.4 |
| 1981 | 30.3 | 33.4 | 45.2 | 61.1 | 60.5 | 74.1 | 78.3 | 72.9 | 68.4 | 55.3 | 45.6 | 29.0 | 54.5 |
| 1982 | 18.6 | 27.8 | 42.5 | 51.1 | 65.5 | 68.8 | 79.4 | 75.0 | 67.5 | 55.6 | 41.9 | 35.5 | 52.4 |
| 1983 | 30.1 | 35.9 | 43.1 | 46.3 | 59.6 | 70.8 | 81.5 | 83.5 | 71.2 | 57.2 | 44.3 | 13.2 | 53.1 |
| 1984 | 25.0 | 38.9 | 36.0 | 50.3 | 60.4 | 74.3 | 76.1 | 79.0 | 66.1 | 56.8 | 43.9 | 35.5 | 53.5 |
| 1985 | 18.7 | 25.3 | 47.4 | 57.9 | 66.0 | 68.8 | 77.0 | 72.1 | 66.7 | 56.5 | 36.8 | 22.9 | 51.3 |
| 1986 | 34.5 | 30.5 | 48.5 | 57.1 | 65.2 | 76.5 | 79.7 | 79.9 | 71.8 | 56.9 | 37.9 | 34.5 | 55.4 |
| 1987 | 29.7 | 39.4 | 47.1 | 56.8 | 70.6 | 76.0 | 79.9 | 76.4 | 67.8 | 52.0 | 46.7 | 35.1 | 56.5 |
| 1988 | 26.7 | 27.9 | 43.2 | 54.5 | 69.1 | 78.1 | 79.6 | 81.3 | 70.5 | 52.2 | 44.8 | 35.2 | 55.3 |
| 1989 | 37.7 | 22.8 | 43.8 | 56.9 | 63.2 | 71.1 | 77.8 | 75.5 | 63.2 | 57.9 | 42.3 | 21.1 | 52.8 |
| 1990 | 37.9 | 36.2 | 45.7 | 52.7 | 60.4 | 75.5 | 77.3 | 77.1 | 72.1 | 57.1 | 50.1 | 29.3 | 56.0 |
| Record Mean | 29.1 | 32.7 | 43.3 | 55.4 | 65.1 | 74.5 | 79.4 | 77.8 | 69.8 | 58.6 | 44.5 | 33.0 | 55.3 |
| Max | 37.7 | 41.7 | 53.0 | 65.3 | 74.6 | 83.9 | 89.0 | 87.4 | 79.7 | 68.7 | 53.5 | 41.1 | 64.6 |
| Min | 20.5 | 23.7 | 33.5 | 45.5 | 55.5 | 65.0 | 69.8 | 68.1 | 59.9 | 48.5 | 35.4 | 25.0 | 45.9 |

## REFERENCE NOTES FOR TABLES 1, 2, 3 and 6   (KANSAS CITY, MO [INT. AIRP.])

### GENERAL

T - TRACE AMOUNT
BLANK ENTRIES DENOTE MISSING/UNREPORTED DATA.
# INDICATES A STATION OR INSTRUMENT RELOCATION.

### SPECIFIC

**TABLE 1**

(a) - LENGTH OF RECORD IN YEARS. ALTHOUGH INDIVIDUAL MONTHS MAY BE MISSING.

* LESS THAN .05

NORMALS — BASED ON THE 1951-1980 RECORD PERIOD.
EXTREMES — DATES ARE THE MOST RECENT OCCURRENCE.
WIND DIR. — NUMERALS SHOW TENS OF DEGREES CLOCKWISE FROM TRUE NORTH.
        "00" INDICATES CALM.
RESULTANT WIND DIRECTIONS ARE GIVEN TO WHOLE DEGREES.

**TABLE 3**
MAX AND MIN ARE LONG-TERM MEAN DAILY MAXIMUM AND MEAN DAILY MINIMUM TEMPERATURES.

### EXCEPTIONS

**TABLES 2, 3, and 6**

RECORD MEANS ARE THROUGH THE CURRENT YEAR,
BEGINNING IN  1889 FOR TEMPERATURE
        1889 FOR PRECIPITATION
        1936 FOR SNOWFALL

HEATING DEGREE DAYS Base 65 deg. F          KANSAS CITY, MISSOURI INTERNATIONAL AIRPORT.

**TABLE 4**

| SEASON | JULY | AUG | SEP | OCT | NOV | DEC | JAN | FEB | MAR | APR | MAY | JUNE | TOTAL |
|---|---|---|---|---|---|---|---|---|---|---|---|---|---|
| 1961-62 | 0 | 1 | 100 | 196 | 626 | 1124 | 1280 | 835 | 766 | 339 | 5 | 3 | 5275 |
| 1962-63 | 0 | 0 | 62 | 184 | 550 | 995 | 1394 | 908 | 490 | 204 | 71 | 0 | 4858 |
| 1963-64 | 0 | 1 | 10 | 35 | 448 | 1225 | 857 | 830 | 714 | 239 | 41 | 12 | 4412 |
| 1964-65 | 0 | 2 | 49 | 235 | 473 | 1004 | 1033 | 911 | 955 | 237 | 15 | 0 | 4914 |
| 1965-66 | 0 | 0 | 44 | 175 | 497 | 646 | 1141 | 869 | 492 | 365 | 95 | 9 | 4333 |
| 1966-67 | 0 | 2 | 29 | 203 | 478 | 931 | 956 | 874 | 546 | 213 | 193 | 11 | 4438 |
| 1967-68 | 0 | 3 | 48 | 255 | 609 | 909 | 1125 | 941 | 529 | 245 | 131 | 3 | 4797 |
| 1968-69 | 0 | 1 | 13 | 224 | 706 | 1090 | 1186 | 857 | 845 | 258 | 86 | 24 | 5290 |
| 1969-70 | 0 | 0 | 3 | 330 | 562 | 984 | 1198 | 785 | 707 | 280 | 86 | 24 | 4897 |
| 1970-71 | 0 | 0 | 25 | 231 | 610 | 801 | 1151 | 931 | 659 | 208 | 92 | 0 | 4708 |
| 1971-72 | 4 | 0 | 57 | 87 | 538 | 863 | 1163 | 920 | 557 | 263 | 71 | 0 | 4523 |
| #1972-73 | 1 | 0 | 37 | 355 | 751 | 1155 | 1160 | 868 | 529 | 394 | 127 | 0 | 5377 |
| 1973-74 | 0 | 0 | 53 | 173 | 578 | 1077 | 1272 | 823 | 559 | 270 | 84 | 6 | 4895 |
| 1974-75 | 0 | 6 | 141 | 227 | 660 | 1009 | 1084 | 1036 | 878 | 381 | 42 | 5 | 5469 |
| 1975-76 | 0 | 0 | 142 | 226 | 567 | 954 | 1155 | 640 | 616 | 277 | 178 | 6 | 4761 |
| 1976-77 | 0 | 0 | 45 | 469 | 865 | 1108 | 1527 | 832 | 521 | 192 | 22 | 0 | 5581 |
| 1977-78 | 0 | 0 | 21 | 293 | 673 | 1094 | 1487 | 1266 | 848 | 291 | 172 | 6 | 6151 |
| #1978-79 | 0 | 0 | 28 | 272 | 618 | 1050 | 1624 | 1230 | 698 | 400 | 115 | 5 | 6040 |
| 1979-80 | 5 | 5 | 35 | 247 | 720 | 918 | 1118 | 1148 | 809 | 327 | 98 | 3 | 5433 |
| 1980-81 | 0 | 0 | 63 | 347 | 609 | 1011 | 1069 | 880 | 607 | 169 | 179 | 2 | 4936 |
| 1981-82 | 0 | 2 | 40 | 309 | 573 | 1112 | 1432 | 1037 | 690 | 416 | 51 | 32 | 5694 |
| 1982-83 | 0 | 2 | 78 | 307 | 688 | 911 | 1074 | 810 | 675 | 557 | 180 | 29 | 5311 |
| 1983-84 | 0 | 0 | 57 | 271 | 617 | 1602 | 1234 | 750 | 891 | 443 | 175 | 1 | 6041 |
| 1984-85 | 0 | 0 | 143 | 269 | 624 | 907 | 1431 | 1102 | 538 | 256 | 41 | 19 | 5330 |
| 1985-86 | 0 | 3 | 131 | 260 | 841 | 1297 | 940 | 960 | 528 | 267 | 60 | 0 | 5287 |
| 1986-87 | 0 | 12 | 23 | 251 | 805 | 938 | 1088 | 712 | 549 | 298 | 15 | 0 | 4691 |
| 1987-88 | 0 | 3 | 30 | 398 | 552 | 922 | 1180 | 1069 | 668 | 311 | 19 | 0 | 5152 |
| 1988-89 | 2 | 1 | 18 | 394 | 599 | 915 | 836 | 1176 | 658 | 319 | 135 | 7 | 5060 |
| 1989-90 | 0 | 1 | 138 | 267 | 675 | 1360 | 836 | 800 | 607 | 398 | 167 | 10 | 5253 |
| 1990-91 | 1 | 0 | 44 | 278 | 452 | 1104 | | | | | | | |

**TABLE 5**   COOLING DEGREE DAYS Base 65 deg. F          KANSAS CITY, MISSOURI INTERNATIONAL AIRPORT.

| YEAR | JAN | FEB | MAR | APR | MAY | JUNE | JULY | AUG | SEP | OCT | NOV | DEC | TOTAL |
|---|---|---|---|---|---|---|---|---|---|---|---|---|---|
| #1969 | 0 | 0 | 0 | 4 | 126 | 188 | 513 | 435 | 216 | 52 | 0 | 0 | 1534 |
| 1970 | 0 | 0 | 0 | 58 | 250 | 317 | 493 | 546 | 232 | 39 | 0 | 0 | 1935 |
| 1971 | 0 | 0 | 5 | 54 | 81 | 437 | 366 | 421 | 295 | 64 | 3 | 0 | 1726 |
| 1972 | 0 | 3 | 7 | 41 | 146 | 368 | 386 | 389 | 219 | 16 | 0 | 0 | 1575 |
| 1973 | 0 | 0 | 0 | 4 | 30 | 291 | 368 | 382 | 110 | 46 | 0 | 0 | 1231 |
| 1974 | 0 | 0 | 4 | 13 | 109 | 176 | 538 | 264 | 47 | 8 | 0 | 0 | 1159 |
| 1975 | 0 | 0 | 0 | 22 | 117 | 284 | 498 | 464 | 105 | 43 | 1 | 0 | 1534 |
| 1976 | 0 | 0 | 0 | 22 | 29 | 199 | 444 | 399 | 169 | 34 | 0 | 0 | 1296 |
| 1977 | 0 | 0 | 0 | 39 | 154 | 291 | 463 | 298 | 147 | 11 | 0 | 0 | 1403 |
| 1978 | 0 | 0 | 5 | 14 | 86 | 300 | 452 | 364 | 295 | 11 | 8 | 0 | 1535 |
| #1979 | 0 | 0 | 1 | 3 | 77 | 229 | 348 | 340 | 147 | 29 | 0 | 0 | 1174 |
| 1980 | 0 | 0 | 0 | 21 | 69 | 316 | 632 | 483 | 210 | 15 | 0 | 0 | 1746 |
| 1981 | 0 | 0 | 0 | 58 | 44 | 279 | 418 | 253 | 149 | 14 | 0 | 0 | 1215 |
| 1982 | 0 | 0 | 0 | 8 | 75 | 154 | 452 | 320 | 156 | 26 | 0 | 0 | 1193 |
| 1983 | 0 | 0 | 3 | 5 | 19 | 210 | 517 | 582 | 251 | 31 | 1 | 0 | 1619 |
| 1984 | 0 | 0 | 0 | 9 | 41 | 287 | 353 | 445 | 184 | 23 | 0 | 0 | 1342 |
| 1985 | 0 | 0 | 0 | 49 | 77 | 137 | 379 | 230 | 191 | 5 | 0 | 0 | 1068 |
| 1986 | 0 | 0 | 24 | 35 | 73 | 352 | 466 | 237 | 232 | 7 | 0 | 0 | 1426 |
| 1987 | 0 | 0 | 0 | 58 | 196 | 336 | 474 | 364 | 118 | 1 | 9 | 0 | 1556 |
| 1988 | 0 | 0 | 2 | 5 | 151 | 400 | 459 | 514 | 188 | 5 | 0 | 0 | 1724 |
| 1989 | 0 | 0 | 9 | 85 | 88 | 196 | 402 | 334 | 87 | 56 | 0 | 0 | 1257 |
| 1990 | 0 | 0 | 8 | 33 | 33 | 331 | 394 | 384 | 263 | 40 | 11 | 0 | 1497 |

**TABLE 6**   SNOWFALL (inches)          KANSAS CITY, MISSOURI INTERNATIONAL AIRPORT.

| SEASON | JULY | AUG | SEP | OCT | NOV | DEC | JAN | FEB | MAR | APR | MAY | JUNE | TOTAL |
|---|---|---|---|---|---|---|---|---|---|---|---|---|---|
| 1961-62 | 0.0 | 0.0 | 0.0 | 0.0 | 0.2 | 16.6 | 30.5 | 6.2 | 0.4 | 1.1 | 0.0 | 0.0 | 55.0 |
| 1962-63 | 0.0 | 0.0 | 0.0 | 0.0 | T | 5.1 | 5.9 | 3.3 | 0.3 | 0.0 | 0.0 | 0.0 | 14.6 |
| 1963-64 | 0.0 | 0.0 | 0.0 | 0.0 | 0.0 | 4.3 | 7.5 | 8.5 | 5.3 | 0.0 | 0.0 | 0.0 | 25.6 |
| 1964-65 | 0.0 | 0.0 | 0.0 | 0.0 | 2.1 | 6.2 | 4.2 | 7.7 | 9.6 | 0.0 | 0.0 | 0.0 | 29.8 |
| 1965-66 | 0.0 | 0.0 | 0.0 | 0.0 | T | 2.5 | T | 3.7 | 3.5 | T | T | 0.0 | 9.7 |
| 1966-67 | 0.0 | 0.0 | 0.0 | 0.0 | T | 7.2 | 7.6 | 0.9 | 1.1 | T | 0.0 | 0.0 | 16.8 |
| 1967-68 | 0.0 | 0.0 | 0.0 | T | 0.2 | 7.0 | 2.8 | 2.7 | T | T | 0.0 | 0.0 | 12.7 |
| 1968-69 | 0.0 | 0.0 | 0.0 | 0.0 | 3.2 | 0.8 | 6.0 | 1.6 | 2.8 | 0.0 | 0.0 | 0.0 | 14.4 |
| 1969-70 | 0.0 | 0.0 | 0.0 | 0.0 | 0.6 | 3.8 | 2.5 | 2.2 | 1.0 | 4.6 | 0.0 | 0.0 | 14.7 |
| 1970-71 | 0.0 | 0.0 | 0.0 | T | T | 3.6 | 1.3 | 8.2 | 7.4 | 0.0 | 0.0 | 0.0 | 20.5 |
| 1971-72 | 0.0 | 0.0 | 0.0 | 0.0 | 0.2 | 1.0 | 3.0 | 2.9 | 3.3 | T | 0.0 | 0.0 | 10.4 |
| #1972-73 | 0.0 | 0.0 | 0.0 | 0.0 | 3.6 | 3.1 | 10.9 | 0.3 | 0.0 | 1.3 | 0.0 | 0.0 | 19.2 |
| 1973-74 | 0.0 | 0.0 | 0.0 | 0.0 | T | 8.0 | 4.8 | 0.3 | 0.5 | 0.3 | 0.0 | 0.0 | 13.9 |
| 1974-75 | 0.0 | 0.0 | 0.0 | 0.0 | 1.4 | 1.2 | 5.4 | 4.6 | 5.9 | 2.3 | 0.0 | 0.0 | 20.8 |
| 1975-76 | 0.0 | 0.0 | 0.0 | 0.0 | 7.1 | 2.8 | 5.2 | 5.2 | 1.5 | 0.0 | 0.0 | 0.0 | 21.8 |
| 1976-77 | 0.0 | 0.0 | 0.0 | T | 0.8 | 0.2 | 14.2 | 0.3 | T | 0.6 | 0.0 | 0.0 | 16.1 |
| 1977-78 | 0.0 | 0.0 | 0.0 | 0.0 | T | 1.2 | 3.9 | 12.7 | 11.4 | 0.0 | 0.0 | 0.0 | 29.2 |
| #1978-79 | 0.0 | 0.0 | 0.0 | 0.0 | 0.2 | 11.7 | 13.3 | 1.5 | 4.7 | 2.0 | 0.0 | 0.0 | 33.4 |
| 1979-80 | 0.0 | 0.0 | 0.0 | 0.0 | T | T | 5.4 | 12.7 | 5.4 | 0.0 | 0.0 | 0.0 | 23.5 |
| 1980-81 | 0.0 | 0.0 | 0.0 | T | T | 3.2 | 4.2 | 2.9 | 0.1 | 0.0 | 0.0 | 0.0 | 10.2 |
| 1981-82 | 0.0 | 0.0 | 0.0 | 0.0 | 0.1 | 5.3 | 6.0 | 12.7 | 4.0 | 1.3 | 0.0 | 0.0 | 29.4 |
| 1982-83 | 0.0 | 0.0 | 0.0 | 0.0 | 0.5 | 6.3 | 7.4 | 1.3 | 7.2 | 0.0 | 0.0 | 0.0 | 23.4 |
| 1983-84 | 0.0 | 0.0 | 0.0 | 0.0 | 0.7 | 13.2 | 1.3 | 0.5 | 8.7 | 0.0 | 0.0 | 0.0 | 24.4 |
| 1984-85 | 0.0 | 0.0 | 0.0 | 0.0 | 0.4 | 7.0 | 11.8 | 6.9 | 0.3 | 0.0 | 0.0 | 0.0 | 26.4 |
| 1985-86 | 0.0 | 0.0 | 0.0 | 0.0 | 3.5 | 5.4 | T | 4.5 | T | T | 0.0 | 0.0 | 13.4 |
| 1986-87 | 0.0 | 0.0 | 0.0 | T | 0.6 | 1.2 | 10.5 | 5.0 | T | 0.0 | 0.0 | 0.0 | 17.3 |
| 1987-88 | 0.0 | 0.0 | 0.0 | T | 2.0 | 11.9 | 0.9 | 9.3 | 2.2 | 0.0 | 0.0 | 0.0 | 26.3 |
| 1988-89 | 0.0 | 0.0 | 0.0 | 0.0 | 0.1 | 0.1 | 0.2 | 6.5 | T | 0.0 | T | T | 6.9 |
| 1989-90 | 0.0 | 0.0 | 0.0 | 0.0 | T | 6.8 | 1.0 | 2.1 | 9.6 | 0.0 | T | 0.0 | 19.5 |
| 1990-91 | 0.0 | 0.0 | 0.0 | 0.0 | 1.7 | 1.6 | | | | | | | |
| Record Mean | 0.0 | 0.0 | 0.0 | T | 1.0 | 4.5 | 5.7 | 4.4 | 3.7 | 0.7 | T | T | 20.1 |

**See Reference Notes, relative to all above tables, on preceding page.**

Saint Louis is located at the confluence of the Missouri and Mississippi Rivers and near the geographical center of the United States. Thus, with a somewhat modified continental climate, it is in the enviable position of being able to enjoy the changes of a four-season climate without the undue hardship of prolonged periods of extreme heat or high humidity. To the south is the warm, moist air of the Gulf of Mexico, and to the north, in Canada, is a favored region of cold air masses. The alternate invasion of Saint Louis by air masses from these sources, and the conflict along the frontal zones where they come together, produce a variety of weather conditions, none of which are likely to persist to the point of monotony.

Winters are brisk and stimulating, seldom severe. Records since 1870 show that temperatures drop to zero or below an average of two or three days per year. Temperatures remain as cold as 32 degrees or lower less than 25 days in most years. Snowfall has averaged a little over 18 inches per winter season. Snowfall of an inch or more is received on five to ten days in most years.

The long-term record for Saint Louis (since 1870) indicates that temperatures of 90 degrees or higher occur on about 35-40 days a year. Extremely hot days of 100 degrees or more are expected on no more than five days per year.

Normal annual precipitation for the Saint Louis area, is a little less than 34 inches. The three winter months are the driest, with an average total of about 6 inches of precipitation. The spring months of March through May are normally the wettest with normal total precipitation of just under 10 1/2 inches. It is not unusual to have extended dry periods of one to two weeks during the growing season.

Thunderstorms occur normally on between 40 and 50 days per year. During any year, there are usually a few of these that can be classified as severe storms with hail and damaging winds. Tornadoes have produced extensive damage and loss of life in the Saint Louis area.

# TABLE 1    NORMALS, MEANS AND EXTREMES

ST. LOUIS, MISSOURI

LATITUDE: 38 °45'N    LONGITUDE: 90 °22' W    ELEVATION: FT. GRND  535 BARO  565  TIME ZONE: CENTRAL    WBAN: 13994

| | (a) | JAN | FEB | MAR | APR | MAY | JUNE | JULY | AUG | SEP | OCT | NOV | DEC | YEAR |
|---|---|---|---|---|---|---|---|---|---|---|---|---|---|---|
| **TEMPERATURE °F:** | | | | | | | | | | | | | | |
| Normals | | | | | | | | | | | | | | |
| -Daily Maximum | | 37.6 | 43.1 | 53.4 | 67.1 | 76.4 | 85.2 | 89.0 | 87.4 | 80.7 | 69.1 | 54.0 | 42.6 | 65.5 |
| -Daily Minimum | | 19.9 | 24.5 | 33.0 | 45.1 | 54.7 | 64.3 | 68.8 | 66.6 | 58.6 | 46.7 | 35.1 | 25.7 | 45.3 |
| -Monthly | | 28.8 | 33.8 | 43.2 | 56.1 | 65.6 | 74.8 | 78.9 | 77.0 | 69.7 | 57.9 | 44.6 | 34.2 | 55.4 |
| Extremes | | | | | | | | | | | | | | |
| -Record Highest | 32 | 76 | 85 | 89 | 93 | 93 | 102 | 107 | 107 | 104 | 94 | 85 | 76 | 107 |
| -Year | | 1970 | 1972 | 1985 | 1989 | 1989 | 1988 | 1980 | 1984 | 1984 | 1963 | 1989 | 1970 | AUG 1984 |
| -Record Lowest | 32 | -18 | -10 | -5 | 22 | 31 | 43 | 51 | 47 | 36 | 23 | 1 | -16 | -18 |
| -Year | | 1985 | 1979 | 1960 | 1975 | 1976 | 1969 | 1972 | 1986 | 1974 | 1976 | 1964 | 1989 | JAN 1985 |
| **NORMAL DEGREE DAYS:** | | | | | | | | | | | | | | |
| Heating (base 65°F) | | 1122 | 874 | 676 | 279 | 110 | 12 | 0 | 0 | 40 | 258 | 612 | 955 | 4938 |
| Cooling (base 65°F) | | 0 | 0 | 0 | 12 | 128 | 306 | 431 | 372 | 181 | 38 | 0 | 0 | 1468 |
| **% OF POSSIBLE SUNSHINE** | 30 | 52 | 52 | 54 | 57 | 60 | 66 | 69 | 64 | 63 | 59 | 47 | 43 | 57 |
| **MEAN SKY COVER (tenths)** | | | | | | | | | | | | | | |
| Sunrise - Sunset | 41 | 6.7 | 6.6 | 6.8 | 6.4 | 6.2 | 5.9 | 5.5 | 5.3 | 5.1 | 5.1 | 6.2 | 6.8 | 6.1 |
| **MEAN NUMBER OF DAYS:** | | | | | | | | | | | | | | |
| Sunrise to Sunset | | | | | | | | | | | | | | |
| -Clear | 41 | 7.6 | 6.9 | 6.6 | 7.2 | 7.5 | 7.5 | 9.5 | 10.4 | 11.6 | 12.2 | 8.8 | 7.2 | 102.9 |
| -Partly Cloudy | 41 | 6.5 | 6.5 | 8.1 | 8.3 | 9.9 | 10.9 | 11.4 | 10.9 | 8.2 | 7.7 | 6.7 | 6.6 | 101.6 |
| -Cloudy | 41 | 16.9 | 14.9 | 16.3 | 14.5 | 13.6 | 11.6 | 10.1 | 9.7 | 10.3 | 11.1 | 14.6 | 17.1 | 160.8 |
| Precipitation | | | | | | | | | | | | | | |
| .01 inches or more | 32 | 8.3 | 8.2 | 11.3 | 11.0 | 10.5 | 9.4 | 8.5 | 8.0 | 8.0 | 8.4 | 9.4 | 9.4 | 110.4 |
| Snow,Ice pellets | | | | | | | | | | | | | | |
| 1.0 inches or more | 32 | 1.9 | 1.5 | 0.9 | 0.2 | 0.0 | 0.0 | 0.0 | 0.0 | 0.0 | 0.0 | 0.5 | 1.3 | 6.3 |
| Thunderstorms | 32 | 0.7 | 0.8 | 3.3 | 5.6 | 6.4 | 7.1 | 7.1 | 6.5 | 3.8 | 2.5 | 1.7 | 0.7 | 46.2 |
| Heavy Fog Visibility | | | | | | | | | | | | | | |
| 1/4 mile or less | 32 | 2.1 | 1.6 | 1.5 | 0.5 | 0.5 | 0.3 | 0.3 | 0.4 | 0.6 | 0.8 | 1.2 | 1.9 | 11.5 |
| Temperature °F | | | | | | | | | | | | | | |
| -Maximum | | | | | | | | | | | | | | |
| 90° and above | 29 | 0.0 | 0.0 | 0.0 | 0.3 | 1.4 | 7.9 | 15.0 | 11.7 | 4.3 | 0.2 | 0.0 | 0.0 | 40.9 |
| 32° and below | 29 | 11.8 | 7.3 | 1.3 | 0.0 | 0.0 | 0.0 | 0.0 | 0.0 | 0.0 | 0.0 | 0.7 | 7.0 | 28.1 |
| -Minimum | | | | | | | | | | | | | | |
| 32° and below | 29 | 27.0 | 21.8 | 13.6 | 2.8 | 0.1 | 0.0 | 0.0 | 0.0 | 0.0 | 1.7 | 11.3 | 23.4 | 101.7 |
| 0° and below | 29 | 2.3 | 0.6 | 0.* | 0.0 | 0.0 | 0.0 | 0.0 | 0.0 | 0.0 | 0.0 | 0.0 | 1.1 | 4.0 |
| **AVG. STATION PRESS.(mb)** | 17 | 1000.1 | 999.1 | 995.4 | 994.5 | 994.0 | 994.7 | 996.0 | 996.7 | 997.5 | 998.6 | 997.9 | 999.4 | 997.0 |
| **RELATIVE HUMIDITY (%)** | | | | | | | | | | | | | | |
| Hour 00 | 29 | 77 | 77 | 74 | 70 | 75 | 77 | 77 | 80 | 81 | 76 | 77 | 80 | 77 |
| Hour 06 | 29 | 82 | 82 | 81 | 78 | 82 | 83 | 85 | 88 | 89 | 85 | 83 | 83 | 83 |
| Hour 12 (Local Time) | 29 | 66 | 64 | 59 | 54 | 55 | 55 | 56 | 56 | 58 | 56 | 63 | 68 | 59 |
| Hour 18 | 29 | 69 | 66 | 60 | 53 | 55 | 55 | 56 | 58 | 60 | 60 | 68 | 73 | 61 |
| **PRECIPITATION (inches):** | | | | | | | | | | | | | | |
| Water Equivalent | | | | | | | | | | | | | | |
| -Normal | | 1.72 | 2.14 | 3.28 | 3.55 | 3.54 | 3.73 | 3.63 | 2.55 | 2.70 | 2.32 | 2.53 | 2.22 | 33.91 |
| -Maximum Monthly | 32 | 5.38 | 4.68 | 6.67 | 9.09 | 7.25 | 9.43 | 10.71 | 6.44 | 8.88 | 7.12 | 9.95 | 7.82 | 10.71 |
| -Year | | 1975 | 1986 | 1978 | 1970 | 1961 | 1985 | 1981 | 1970 | 1984 | 1984 | 1985 | 1982 | JUL 1981 |
| -Minimum Monthly | 32 | 0.10 | 0.25 | 1.09 | 0.99 | 1.02 | 0.47 | 0.60 | 0.08 | T | 0.21 | 0.44 | 0.32 | T |
| -Year | | 1986 | 1963 | 1966 | 1971 | 1972 | 1959 | 1970 | 1971 | 1979 | 1975 | 1969 | 1958 | SEP 1979 |
| -Maximum in 24 hrs | 32 | 2.43 | 2.56 | 2.95 | 4.91 | 2.94 | 3.29 | 3.47 | 2.66 | 3.50 | 2.70 | 3.71 | 4.03 | 4.91 |
| -Year | | 1975 | 1959 | 1977 | 1979 | 1974 | 1960 | 1982 | 1974 | 1986 | 1986 | 1985 | 1982 | APR 1979 |
| Snow,Ice pellets | | | | | | | | | | | | | | |
| -Maximum Monthly | 53 | 23.9 | 12.9 | 22.3 | 6.5 | T | 0.0 | 0.0 | 0.0 | 0.0 | T | 11.3 | 26.3 | 26.3 |
| -Year | | 1977 | 1961 | 1960 | 1971 | 1944 | | | | | 1989 | 1951 | 1973 | DEC 1973 |
| -Maximum in 24 hrs | 53 | 13.9 | 8.3 | 10.7 | 6.1 | T | 0.0 | 0.0 | 0.0 | 0.0 | T | 10.3 | 12.0 | 13.9 |
| -Year | | 1982 | 1966 | 1989 | 1971 | 1944 | | | | | 1989 | 1951 | 1973 | JAN 1982 |
| **WIND:** | | | | | | | | | | | | | | |
| Mean Speed (mph) | 40 | 10.6 | 10.8 | 11.8 | 11.4 | 9.5 | 8.8 | 7.9 | 7.6 | 8.1 | 8.8 | 10.1 | 10.4 | 9.7 |
| Prevailing Direction | | | | | | | | | | | | | | |
| through 1963 | | NW | NW | WNW | WNW | S | S | S | S | S | S | S | WNW | S |
| Fastest Obs. 1 Min. | | | | | | | | | | | | | | |
| -Direction (!!!) | 10 | 29 | 30 | 27 | 27 | 17 | 27 | 36 | 31 | 25 | 28 | 11 | 29 | 28 |
| -Speed (MPH) | 10 | 40 | 45 | 48 | 49 | 35 | 48 | 46 | 40 | 41 | 52 | 41 | 39 | 52 |
| -Year | | 1984 | 1980 | 1984 | 1982 | 1986 | 1982 | 1987 | 1987 | 1986 | 1981 | 1987 | 1985 | OCT 1981 |
| Peak Gust | | | | | | | | | | | | | | |
| -Direction (!!!) | 6 | NW | W | W | SW | W | N | N | S | W | NW | W | SW | W |
| -Speed (mph) | 6 | 51 | 49 | 66 | 58 | 49 | 48 | 62 | 53 | 49 | 58 | 64 | 55 | 66 |
| -Date | | 1985 | 1988 | 1984 | 1984 | 1988 | 1984 | 1987 | 1985 | 1986 | 1988 | 1984 | 1984 | MAR 1984 |

**See reference Notes to this table on the following page.**

# ST. LOUIS, MISSOURI

PRECIPITATION (inches)　　　　ST. LOUIS, MISSOURI

**TABLE 2**

| YEAR | JAN | FEB | MAR | APR | MAY | JUNE | JULY | AUG | SEP | OCT | NOV | DEC | ANNUAL |
|---|---|---|---|---|---|---|---|---|---|---|---|---|---|
| 1961 | 0.39 | 2.06 | 4.75 | 3.47 | 7.25 | 3.67 | 6.20 | 1.88 | 4.01 | 2.67 | 2.90 | 1.95 | 41.20 |
| 1962 | 3.56 | 2.53 | 3.00 | 2.52 | 2.44 | 4.75 | 5.49 | 2.29 | 2.63 | 2.70 | 0.71 | 1.99 | 34.61 |
| 1963 | 0.74 | 0.25 | 5.54 | 1.98 | 4.77 | 3.87 | 1.37 | 2.55 | 1.13 | 2.85 | 2.90 | 0.67 | 28.62 |
| 1964 | 1.70 | 2.30 | 3.84 | 4.99 | 2.68 | 2.73 | 4.25 | 2.39 | 1.47 | 0.73 | 3.84 | 1.24 | 32.16 |
| 1965 | 2.51 | 1.16 | 2.34 | 3.67 | 1.38 | 3.03 | 3.17 | 3.59 | 3.00 | 0.46 | 0.78 | 3.17 | 28.26 |
| 1966 | 0.65 | 4.12 | 1.09 | 6.03 | 4.59 | 1.59 | 1.26 | 3.72 | 2.15 | 2.18 | 2.47 | 2.49 | 32.34 |
| 1967 | 2.89 | 1.72 | 2.77 | 3.40 | 4.73 | 4.46 | 3.84 | 1.36 | 4.33 | 3.45 | 2.15 | 6.20 | 41.30 |
| 1968 | 1.86 | 1.09 | 2.06 | 1.48 | 6.78 | 0.90 | 3.92 | 1.60 | 3.74 | 0.69 | 2.63 | 2.49 | 32.49 |
| 1969 | 3.61 | 2.04 | 2.47 | 4.01 | 2.11 | 8.65 | 7.08 | 0.52 | 5.03 | 5.77 | 0.44 | 1.99 | 43.72 |
| 1970 | 0.22 | 0.64 | 2.17 | 9.09 | 2.04 | 5.08 | 0.60 | 6.44 | 5.54 | 2.21 | 0.77 | 1.40 | 36.20 |
| 1971 | 0.66 | 3.08 | 1.81 | 1.65 | 5.66 | 2.43 | 4.70 | 0.08 | 3.98 | 1.51 | 1.67 | 6.50 | 33.73 |
| 1972 | 0.77 | 0.74 | 2.93 | 4.49 | 1.02 | 1.47 | 3.10 | 2.69 | 6.21 | 1.47 | 5.59 | 3.54 | 33.74 |
| 1973 | 1.40 | 1.04 | 5.81 | 4.25 | 3.92 | 4.23 | 2.85 | 2.46 | 3.52 | 2.33 | 3.65 | 4.36 | 39.82 |
| 1974 | 3.51 | 4.17 | 2.58 | 2.40 | 5.90 | 3.45 | 0.90 | 5.05 | 2.50 | 1.51 | 3.15 | 1.71 | 36.83 |
| 1975 | 5.38 | 3.59 | 4.08 | 4.56 | 3.23 | 3.78 | 2.56 | 5.44 | 2.48 | 0.21 | 2.62 | 2.28 | 40.21 |
| 1976 | 0.83 | 1.08 | 4.28 | 1.37 | 3.90 | 2.32 | 2.28 | 1.27 | 0.90 | 3.37 | 0.73 | 1.13 | 23.46 |
| 1977 | 2.38 | 2.47 | 6.28 | 0.99 | 2.13 | 5.47 | 4.28 | 5.34 | 3.64 | 3.76 | 4.33 | 2.34 | 43.41 |
| 1978 | 1.70 | 1.60 | 6.67 | 3.21 | 3.69 | 2.39 | 6.03 | 0.76 | 3.10 | 2.28 | 4.47 | 1.81 | 37.71 |
| 1979 | 1.95 | 1.48 | 3.63 | 7.47 | 1.62 | 1.67 | 3.67 | 2.26 | T | 1.81 | 2.07 | 1.85 | 29.48 |
| 1980 | 0.63 | 1.96 | 3.98 | 1.54 | 3.40 | 2.19 | 3.56 | 2.72 | 3.12 | 2.89 | 1.25 | 0.66 | 27.48 |
| 1981 | 0.64 | 2.18 | 2.97 | 3.40 | 6.79 | 5.82 | 10.71 | 3.31 | 1.17 | 3.81 | 2.71 | 2.01 | 45.52 |
| 1982 | 4.90 | 1.37 | 2.88 | 2.55 | 4.85 | 5.96 | 7.91 | 5.27 | 5.27 | 2.30 | 3.89 | 7.82 | 54.97 |
| 1983 | 0.72 | 0.95 | 3.54 | 7.30 | 6.32 | 4.32 | 1.23 | 2.24 | 1.24 | 5.40 | 7.79 | 3.75 | 44.80 |
| 1984 | 0.84 | 3.43 | 5.37 | 6.29 | 5.19 | 2.74 | 0.76 | 0.64 | 8.88 | 7.12 | 5.50 | 4.89 | 51.65 |
| 1985 | 0.53 | 3.77 | 5.18 | 3.60 | 3.30 | 9.43 | 5.23 | 3.66 | 0.43 | 1.96 | 9.95 | 3.69 | 50.73 |
| 1986 | 0.10 | 4.68 | 1.22 | 1.23 | 2.42 | 4.43 | 2.61 | 2.22 | 7.99 | 5.34 | 1.58 | 1.06 | 34.88 |
| 1987 | 1.98 | 1.40 | 2.16 | 1.74 | 2.00 | 3.59 | 5.04 | 5.56 | 1.62 | 1.74 | 4.09 | 7.46 | 38.38 |
| 1988 | 3.30 | 2.27 | 4.73 | 1.15 | 1.44 | 1.97 | 3.02 | 2.31 | 1.99 | 1.86 | 6.65 | 3.24 | 33.93 |
| 1989 | 2.58 | 1.43 | 4.53 | 2.10 | 4.11 | 2.34 | 4.59 | 3.00 | 1.01 | 0.95 | 0.59 | 0.69 | 28.60 |
| 1990 | 1.42 | 3.53 | 2.66 | 3.07 | 9.59 | 3.02 | 3.34 | 2.84 | 0.78 | 0.78 | 3.36 | 6.52 | 45.09 |
| Record Mean | 2.14 | 2.29 | 3.35 | 3.67 | 4.11 | 4.06 | 3.41 | 2.95 | 3.14 | 2.72 | 2.80 | 2.36 | 37.02 |

**TABLE 3**　　AVERAGE TEMPERATURE (deg. F)　　　ST. LOUIS, MISSOURI

| YEAR | JAN | FEB | MAR | APR | MAY | JUNE | JULY | AUG | SEP | OCT | NOV | DEC | ANNUAL |
|---|---|---|---|---|---|---|---|---|---|---|---|---|---|
| 1961 | 28.3 | 35.9 | 45.5 | 50.0 | 58.3 | 70.1 | 76.2 | 75.4 | 71.1 | 59.2 | 44.1 | 32.0 | 53.8 |
| 1962 | 36.6 | 36.6 | 39.6 | 53.1 | 72.1 | 74.0 | 75.8 | 75.6 | 66.4 | 61.0 | 31.2 | 34.6 | 54.6 |
| 1963 | 21.3 | 28.5 | 48.8 | 58.2 | 63.9 | 75.4 | 77.3 | 74.9 | 68.5 | 66.9 | 45.7 | 22.2 | 54.3 |
| 1964 | 34.7 | 34.3 | 42.3 | 58.7 | 69.6 | 74.8 | 78.5 | 76.5 | 69.3 | 54.0 | 47.3 | 31.9 | 56.0 |
| 1965 | 31.9 | 33.8 | 34.5 | 58.4 | 70.5 | 75.1 | 76.8 | 75.8 | 69.1 | 56.4 | 48.5 | 41.7 | 56.1 |
| 1966 | 25.0 | 32.1 | 46.7 | 51.7 | 61.7 | 73.7 | 82.9 | 65.6 | 65.6 | 54.2 | 47.1 | 34.8 | 54.1 |
| 1967 | 34.7 | 31.3 | 48.3 | 58.5 | 60.8 | 74.0 | 74.9 | 72.4 | 66.5 | 57.5 | 42.0 | 34.8 | 54.7 |
| 1968 | 28.6 | 29.3 | 46.1 | 55.6 | 61.9 | 77.0 | 77.6 | 77.5 | 68.0 | 56.9 | 43.5 | 32.3 | 54.5 |
| 1969 | 29.2 | 35.3 | 37.8 | 56.9 | 65.7 | 72.5 | 80.5 | 77.0 | 69.3 | 56.1 | 43.4 | 32.1 | 54.7 |
| 1970 | 24.8 | 33.0 | 40.6 | 58.0 | 69.3 | 72.3 | 77.9 | 76.3 | 71.8 | 56.1 | 43.6 | 37.0 | 55.1 |
| 1971 | 27.4 | 33.9 | 41.7 | 55.9 | 62.3 | 78.9 | 75.4 | 75.7 | 72.5 | 63.7 | 46.0 | 40.6 | 56.2 |
| 1972 | 29.9 | 34.3 | 45.0 | 56.1 | 66.4 | 73.4 | 77.5 | 76.3 | 71.1 | 54.8 | 39.8 | 30.4 | 54.6 |
| 1973 | 32.6 | 34.5 | 50.9 | 53.7 | 61.7 | 74.6 | 78.7 | 76.9 | 70.0 | 60.7 | 47.0 | 30.0 | 55.9 |
| 1974 | 29.8 | 36.1 | 48.1 | 57.5 | 65.0 | 69.5 | 79.8 | 74.5 | 62.3 | 57.8 | 44.0 | 34.0 | 54.9 |
| 1975 | 33.2 | 32.0 | 39.0 | 53.4 | 67.6 | 74.9 | 77.8 | 77.9 | 64.7 | 59.0 | 48.3 | 35.5 | 55.3 |
| 1976 | 28.1 | 43.5 | 48.8 | 56.5 | 60.8 | 72.7 | 79.5 | 74.3 | 68.2 | 50.9 | 37.0 | 28.5 | 54.1 |
| 1977 | 15.1 | 34.8 | 49.6 | 60.8 | 71.1 | 74.7 | 81.2 | 76.4 | 70.7 | 55.5 | 44.7 | 30.6 | 55.4 |
| 1978 | 19.6 | 21.1 | 37.9 | 56.2 | 63.6 | 74.4 | 78.5 | 76.4 | 73.1 | 55.6 | 45.7 | 35.0 | 53.2 |
| 1979 | 16.6 | 23.1 | 44.1 | 52.9 | 65.5 | 76.5 | 79.2 | 78.4 | 70.8 | 59.2 | 44.5 | 38.7 | 54.1 |
| 1980 | 31.4 | 27.9 | 41.0 | 54.5 | 66.9 | 75.5 | 85.0 | 83.5 | 72.5 | 55.9 | 46.4 | 36.6 | 56.4 |
| 1981 | 31.2 | 36.8 | 46.7 | 63.1 | 60.7 | 75.7 | 78.7 | 76.1 | 69.2 | 55.7 | 48.7 | 31.1 | 56.1 |
| 1982 | 22.5 | 28.6 | 45.3 | 51.5 | 70.7 | 70.6 | 79.3 | 75.2 | 68.0 | 58.3 | 46.3 | 41.6 | 54.9 |
| 1983 | 32.3 | 38.1 | 44.5 | 50.3 | 62.3 | 75.3 | 83.5 | 84.2 | 72.0 | 59.7 | 48.2 | 20.5 | 55.9 |
| 1984 | 28.3 | 40.4 | 37.1 | 54.1 | 63.2 | 79.5 | 78.3 | 80.7 | 68.2 | 61.8 | 44.3 | 40.7 | 56.4 |
| 1985 | 22.6 | 30.5 | 49.5 | 60.4 | 67.6 | 71.6 | 79.3 | 74.7 | 70.9 | 61.4 | 46.5 | 27.3 | 55.2 |
| 1986 | 34.9 | 34.5 | 49.2 | 60.8 | 68.2 | 78.3 | 82.8 | 74.0 | 73.3 | 58.3 | 41.5 | 35.4 | 57.6 |
| 1987 | 30.6 | 40.1 | 48.6 | 56.9 | 72.6 | 77.9 | 81.0 | 78.9 | 70.5 | 53.8 | 49.1 | 38.0 | 58.2 |
| 1988 | 29.2 | 30.5 | 45.2 | 57.1 | 69.0 | 77.7 | 81.6 | 82.7 | 72.5 | 53.9 | 47.2 | 37.2 | 57.0 |
| 1989 | 41.2 | 28.2 | 45.0 | 57.7 | 64.3 | 74.8 | 79.3 | 77.8 | 67.4 | 61.3 | 47.1 | 24.1 | 55.7 |
| 1990 | 42.9 | 41.3 | 49.8 | 55.7 | 63.6 | 77.2 | 80.2 | 77.9 | 74.1 | 58.1 | 52.7 | 34.7 | 59.0 |
| Record Mean | 31.2 | 34.6 | 44.4 | 56.1 | 65.9 | 75.2 | 79.5 | 77.6 | 70.2 | 58.8 | 45.4 | 35.0 | 56.2 |
| Max | 39.5 | 43.2 | 53.7 | 65.8 | 75.5 | 84.5 | 88.8 | 87.0 | 79.9 | 68.6 | 54.0 | 42.8 | 65.3 |
| Min | 22.9 | 26.0 | 35.1 | 46.4 | 56.3 | 65.8 | 70.1 | 68.1 | 60.4 | 48.9 | 36.8 | 27.3 | 47.0 |

## REFERENCE NOTES FOR TABLES 1, 2, 3 and 6　　　(ST. LOUIS, MO)

### GENERAL

T - TRACE AMOUNT
BLANK ENTRIES DENOTE MISSING/UNREPORTED DATA.
# INDICATES A STATION OR INSTRUMENT RELOCATION.

### SPECIFIC

#### TABLE 1

(a) - LENGTH OF RECORD IN YEARS. ALTHOUGH
INDIVIDUAL MONTHS MAY BE MISSING.
* LESS THAN .05

NORMALS — BASED ON THE 1951-1980 RECORD PERIOD.
EXTREMES — DATES ARE THE MOST RECENT OCCURRENCE.
WIND DIR. — NUMERALS SHOW TENS OF DEGREES
CLOCKWISE FROM TRUE NORTH.
"00" INDICATES CALM.
RESULTANT WIND DIRECTIONS ARE GIVEN TO WHOLE DEGREES.

#### TABLE 3
MAX AND MIN ARE LONG-TERM MEAN DAILY MAXIMUM
AND MEAN DAILY MINIMUM TEMPERATURES.

### EXCEPTIONS

#### TABLES 2, 3, and 6

RECORD MEANS ARE THROUGH THE CURRENT YEAR,
BEGINNING IN　　1873 FOR TEMPERATURE
1871 FOR PRECIPITATION
1937 FOR SNOWFALL

622

## TABLE 4 — HEATING DEGREE DAYS Base 65 deg. F — ST. LOUIS, MISSOURI

| SEASON | JULY | AUG | SEP | OCT | NOV | DEC | JAN | FEB | MAR | APR | MAY | JUNE | TOTAL |
|---|---|---|---|---|---|---|---|---|---|---|---|---|---|
| 1961-62 | 0 | 0 | 52 | 211 | 623 | 1015 | 1242 | 792 | 783 | 370 | 25 | 1 | 5114 |
| 1962-63 | 0 | 0 | 62 | 194 | 595 | 1041 | 1347 | 1016 | 507 | 247 | 103 | 3 | 5115 |
| 1963-64 | 0 | 11 | 33 | 74 | 574 | 1320 | 932 | 884 | 696 | 216 | 41 | 6 | 4787 |
| 1964-65 | 0 | 2 | 55 | 333 | 526 | 1019 | 1016 | 869 | 938 | 250 | 19 | 0 | 5027 |
| 1965-66 | 0 | 7 | 49 | 286 | 489 | 717 | 1233 | 915 | 570 | 397 | 156 | 4 | 4823 |
| 1966-67 | 0 | 0 | 78 | 336 | 534 | 931 | 932 | 940 | 530 | 257 | 188 | 12 | 4738 |
| 1967-68 | 3 | 7 | 67 | 268 | 682 | 928 | 1121 | 1031 | 587 | 290 | 137 | 2 | 5123 |
| 1968-69 | 0 | 2 | 14 | 293 | 640 | 1008 | 1106 | 826 | 834 | 247 | 85 | 15 | 5070 |
| 1969-70 | 0 | 0 | 27 | 313 | 644 | 1013 | 1241 | 893 | 751 | 257 | 55 | 20 | 5214 |
| 1970-71 | 0 | 0 | 24 | 287 | 635 | 863 | 1159 | 866 | 718 | 303 | 122 | 0 | 4977 |
| 1971-72 | 2 | 0 | 47 | 97 | 574 | 751 | 1081 | 884 | 619 | 295 | 80 | 10 | 4438 |
| 1972-73 | 2 | 0 | 29 | 317 | 751 | 1069 | 997 | 849 | 430 | 348 | 121 | 0 | 4913 |
| 1973-74 | 0 | 0 | 31 | 182 | 538 | 1077 | 1083 | 804 | 539 | 253 | 101 | 21 | 4629 |
| 1974-75 | 0 | 0 | 127 | 242 | 625 | 954 | 979 | 919 | 803 | 353 | 48 | 1 | 5051 |
| 1975-76 | 2 | 0 | 110 | 228 | 498 | 910 | 1137 | 619 | 505 | 288 | 158 | 0 | 4455 |
| 1976-77 | 0 | 0 | 24 | 456 | 832 | 1125 | 1541 | 839 | 471 | 190 | 36 | 3 | 5517 |
| 1977-78 | 0 | 0 | 11 | 291 | 601 | 1059 | 1401 | 1223 | 840 | 275 | 158 | 5 | 5864 |
| 1978-79 | 0 | 0 | 24 | 292 | 528 | 923 | 1496 | 1167 | 644 | 364 | 80 | 0 | 5518 |
| 1979-80 | 0 | 0 | 16 | 223 | 610 | 810 | 1035 | 1071 | 740 | 331 | 54 | 0 | 4890 |
| 1980-81 | 0 | 0 | 30 | 305 | 553 | 877 | 1039 | 784 | 569 | 127 | 168 | 0 | 4452 |
| 1981-82 | 0 | 0 | 35 | 298 | 483 | 1048 | 1308 | 1015 | 603 | 407 | 9 | 11 | 5217 |
| 1982-83 | 0 | 0 | 49 | 261 | 569 | 721 | 1008 | 745 | 632 | 437 | 117 | 7 | 4546 |
| 1983-84 | 0 | 0 | 58 | 192 | 498 | 1376 | 1133 | 705 | 860 | 342 | 115 | 0 | 5279 |
| 1984-85 | 0 | 0 | 103 | 151 | 616 | 746 | 1308 | 960 | 487 | 200 | 42 | 10 | 4623 |
| 1985-86 | 0 | 0 | 64 | 145 | 550 | 1159 | 929 | 850 | 506 | 194 | 44 | 0 | 4441 |
| 1986-87 | 0 | 11 | 12 | 221 | 699 | 910 | 1062 | 691 | 501 | 267 | 10 | 0 | 4384 |
| 1987-88 | 0 | 12 | 12 | 346 | 490 | 830 | 1102 | 995 | 610 | 241 | 17 | 3 | 4646 |
| 1988-89 | 0 | 0 | 5 | 354 | 528 | 854 | 730 | 1029 | 625 | 293 | 128 | 4 | 4550 |
| 1989-90 | 0 | 0 | 73 | 183 | 536 | 1261 | 679 | 657 | 496 | 327 | 85 | 9 | 4306 |
| 1990-91 | 3 | 0 | 24 | 250 | 375 | 934 | | | | | | | |

## TABLE 5 — COOLING DEGREE DAYS Base 65 deg. F — ST. LOUIS, MISSOURI

| YEAR | JAN | FEB | MAR | APR | MAY | JUNE | JULY | AUG | SEP | OCT | NOV | DEC | TOTAL |
|---|---|---|---|---|---|---|---|---|---|---|---|---|---|
| 1969 | 0 | 0 | 0 | 9 | 113 | 246 | 486 | 381 | 162 | 43 | 0 | 0 | 1440 |
| 1970 | 0 | 0 | 0 | 54 | 195 | 247 | 410 | 360 | 236 | 17 | 0 | 0 | 1519 |
| 1971 | 0 | 0 | 2 | 35 | 45 | 427 | 326 | 340 | 279 | 62 | 10 | 0 | 1526 |
| 1972 | 0 | 0 | 5 | 35 | 129 | 268 | 394 | 358 | 219 | 9 | 0 | 0 | 1417 |
| 1973 | 0 | 0 | 1 | 17 | 25 | 294 | 435 | 375 | 187 | 57 | 4 | 0 | 1395 |
| 1974 | 0 | 0 | 24 | 36 | 109 | 164 | 463 | 300 | 52 | 25 | 2 | 0 | 1175 |
| 1975 | 0 | 0 | 2 | 12 | 133 | 308 | 405 | 406 | 110 | 51 | 4 | 0 | 1431 |
| 1976 | 0 | 0 | 8 | 38 | 34 | 239 | 458 | 298 | 129 | 25 | 0 | 0 | 1229 |
| 1977 | 0 | 0 | 2 | 69 | 231 | 302 | 509 | 360 | 190 | 4 | 0 | 0 | 1667 |
| 1978 | 0 | 0 | 7 | 17 | 120 | 295 | 426 | 360 | 276 | 10 | 8 | 0 | 1519 |
| 1979 | 0 | 0 | 2 | 9 | 102 | 354 | 446 | 420 | 195 | 50 | 0 | 0 | 1578 |
| 1980 | 0 | 0 | 0 | 23 | 120 | 320 | 626 | 580 | 262 | 31 | 2 | 0 | 1964 |
| 1981 | 0 | 0 | 7 | 77 | 42 | 327 | 431 | 353 | 166 | 13 | 1 | 0 | 1417 |
| 1982 | 0 | 0 | 0 | 7 | 191 | 186 | 453 | 322 | 146 | 63 | 15 | 4 | 1387 |
| 1983 | 0 | 0 | 3 | 3 | 41 | 322 | 578 | 603 | 274 | 36 | 2 | 0 | 1862 |
| 1984 | 0 | 0 | 0 | 24 | 67 | 442 | 423 | 493 | 202 | 57 | 2 | 1 | 1711 |
| 1985 | 0 | 0 | 14 | 70 | 128 | 214 | 451 | 310 | 245 | 43 | 2 | 0 | 1477 |
| 1986 | 0 | 0 | 25 | 75 | 150 | 407 | 561 | 298 | 267 | 21 | 0 | 0 | 1804 |
| 1987 | 0 | 0 | 0 | 32 | 251 | 393 | 501 | 439 | 183 | 5 | 20 | 0 | 1824 |
| 1988 | 0 | 0 | 4 | 10 | 144 | 389 | 521 | 556 | 238 | 16 | 0 | 0 | 1878 |
| 1989 | 0 | 0 | 11 | 80 | 111 | 305 | 450 | 403 | 151 | 75 | 6 | 0 | 1592 |
| 1990 | 0 | 0 | 30 | 55 | 47 | 382 | 480 | 408 | 304 | 41 | 12 | 0 | 1759 |

## TABLE 6 — SNOWFALL (inches) — ST. LOUIS, MISSOURI

| SEASON | JULY | AUG | SEP | OCT | NOV | DEC | JAN | FEB | MAR | APR | MAY | JUNE | TOTAL |
|---|---|---|---|---|---|---|---|---|---|---|---|---|---|
| 1961-62 | 0.0 | 0.0 | 0.0 | 0.0 | 4.7 | 3.7 | 13.2 | 3.6 | 0.6 | T | 0.0 | 0.0 | 25.8 |
| 1962-63 | 0.0 | 0.0 | 0.0 | 0.0 | 0.0 | 0.8 | 3.5 | 1.8 | 1.2 | T | 0.0 | 0.0 | 7.3 |
| 1963-64 | 0.0 | 0.0 | 0.0 | 0.0 | T | 6.4 | 8.1 | 8.8 | 8.2 | T | 0.0 | 0.0 | 31.5 |
| 1964-65 | 0.0 | 0.0 | 0.0 | 0.0 | 3.1 | 0.3 | 7.3 | 5.7 | 8.7 | 0.0 | 0.0 | 0.0 | 25.1 |
| 1965-66 | 0.0 | 0.0 | 0.0 | 0.0 | T | 0.1 | 2.5 | 7.1 | 0.9 | T | 0.0 | 0.0 | 10.6 |
| 1966-67 | 0.0 | 0.0 | 0.0 | 0.0 | T | 0.1 | 1.4 | 0.9 | 1.2 | T | 0.0 | 0.0 | 3.6 |
| 1967-68 | 0.0 | 0.0 | 0.0 | T | 1.6 | 4.2 | 6.9 | 0.4 | 7.7 | 0.0 | 0.0 | 0.0 | 20.8 |
| 1968-69 | 0.0 | 0.0 | 0.0 | 0.0 | T | 1.3 | 2.3 | 5.8 | 2.7 | 0.0 | 0.0 | 0.0 | 12.1 |
| 1969-70 | 0.0 | 0.0 | 0.0 | 0.0 | T | 10.2 | 2.1 | 3.7 | 5.0 | 1.0 | 0.0 | 0.0 | 22.0 |
| 1970-71 | 0.0 | 0.0 | 0.0 | 0.0 | T | 0.9 | 0.4 | 1.4 | 0.2 | 6.5 | 0.0 | 0.0 | 9.4 |
| 1971-72 | 0.0 | 0.0 | 0.0 | 0.0 | 1.3 | T | 4.1 | 1.9 | 0.3 | T | 0.0 | 0.0 | 7.6 |
| 1972-73 | 0.0 | 0.0 | 0.0 | 0.0 | 5.2 | 1.0 | 2.2 | 3.0 | 0.2 | 0.2 | 0.0 | 0.0 | 11.8 |
| 1973-74 | 0.0 | 0.0 | 0.0 | 0.0 | 0.0 | 26.3 | 4.2 | 4.5 | 7.4 | 0.0 | 0.0 | 0.0 | 42.4 |
| 1974-75 | 0.0 | 0.0 | 0.0 | 0.0 | 1.2 | 1.5 | 4.1 | 12.1 | 6.3 | T | 0.0 | 0.0 | 25.2 |
| 1975-76 | 0.0 | 0.0 | 0.0 | 0.0 | 7.6 | 3.9 | 4.5 | 4.5 | 4.8 | 0.0 | 0.0 | 0.0 | 25.3 |
| 1976-77 | 0.0 | 0.0 | 0.0 | 0.0 | 0.3 | 5.2 | 23.9 | 6.7 | 0.1 | 0.1 | 0.0 | 0.0 | 36.3 |
| 1977-78 | 0.0 | 0.0 | 0.0 | 0.0 | 6.7 | 11.7 | 22.9 | 9.3 | 15.4 | 0.0 | 0.0 | 0.0 | 66.0 |
| 1978-79 | 0.0 | 0.0 | 0.0 | 0.0 | 0.0 | 1.4 | 18.4 | 4.8 | 2.0 | 0.0 | 0.0 | 0.0 | 26.6 |
| 1979-80 | 0.0 | 0.0 | 0.0 | 0.0 | 0.3 | T | 4.2 | 7.4 | 8.7 | 5.0 | 0.0 | 0.0 | 25.6 |
| 1980-81 | 0.0 | 0.0 | 0.0 | 0.0 | 8.0 | 1.1 | 0.6 | 8.2 | 0.2 | 0.0 | 0.0 | 0.0 | 18.1 |
| 1981-82 | 0.0 | 0.0 | 0.0 | 0.0 | T | 7.9 | 16.6 | 9.0 | 0.4 | 2.7 | 0.0 | 0.0 | 36.6 |
| 1982-83 | 0.0 | 0.0 | 0.0 | 0.0 | T | T | 3.3 | 0.3 | 1.4 | 2.4 | 0.0 | 0.0 | 7.4 |
| 1983-84 | 0.0 | 0.0 | 0.0 | 0.0 | T | 6.5 | 2.3 | 9.9 | 5.2 | 0.0 | 0.0 | 0.0 | 23.9 |
| 1984-85 | 0.0 | 0.0 | 0.0 | 0.0 | 1.7 | 1.8 | 5.1 | 1.3 | T | 0.0 | 0.0 | 0.0 | 9.9 |
| 1985-86 | 0.0 | 0.0 | 0.0 | 0.0 | T | 5.7 | 1.0 | 6.1 | 0.2 | T | 0.0 | 0.0 | 13.0 |
| 1986-87 | 0.0 | 0.0 | 0.0 | 0.0 | T | T | 23.6 | 0.6 | T | 0.0 | 0.0 | 0.0 | 24.2 |
| 1987-88 | 0.0 | 0.0 | 0.0 | 0.0 | T | 7.3 | 1.4 | 6.7 | 2.8 | 0.0 | 0.0 | 0.0 | 18.2 |
| 1988-89 | 0.0 | 0.0 | 0.0 | 0.0 | 2.9 | 5.9 | 0.1 | 3.9 | 11.0 | 0.0 | 0.0 | 0.0 | 23.8 |
| 1989-90 | 0.0 | 0.0 | 0.0 | T | T | 9.1 | 0.2 | 6.9 | 8.4 | T | T | T | 24.6 |
| 1990-91 | 0.0 | 0.0 | 0.0 | 0.0 | T | 13.2 | | | | | | | |
| Record Mean | 0.0 | 0.0 | 0.0 | T | 1.4 | 4.0 | 5.3 | 4.5 | 4.3 | 0.4 | T | T | 19.9 |

**See Reference Notes, relative to all above tables, on preceding page.**

Helena is located on the south side of an intermountain valley bounded on the west and south by the main chain of the Continental Divide. The valley is approximately 25 miles in width from north to south and 35 miles long from east to west. The average height of the mountains above the valley floor is about 3,000 feet.

The climate of Helena may be described as modified continental. Several factors enter into modifying the continental climate characteristics. Some of these are invasion by Pacific Ocean air masses, drainage of cool air into the valley from the surrounding mountains, and the protecting mountain shield in all directions.

The mountains to the north and east sometimes deflect shallow masses of invading cold Arctic air to the east. Following periods of extreme cold, when the return circulation of maritime air has brought warming to most of the eastern part of the state, cold air may remain trapped in the valley for several days before being replaced by warmer air. During these periods of transition from cold-to-warm temperatures, inversions are often quite pronounced.

As may be expected in a northern latitude, cold waves may occur from November through February, with temperatures occasionally dropping to zero or lower.

Summertime temperatures are moderate, with maximum readings generally under 90 degrees and very seldom reaching 100 degrees. Like all mountain stations, there is usually a marked change in temperature from day to night. During the summer this tends to produce an agreeable combination of fairly warm days and cool nights.

Most of the precipitation falls from April through July from frequent showers or thunderstorms, but usually with some steady rains in June, the wettest month of the year. Like summer, fall and winter months are relatively dry. During the April to September growing season, precipitation varies considerably.

Thunderstorms are rather frequent from May through August. Snow can be expected from September through May, but amounts during the spring and fall are usually light, and snow on the ground ordinarily lasts only a day or two. During the winter months snow may remain on the ground for several weeks at a time. There is little drifting of snow in the valley, and blizzard conditions are very infrequent.

Severe ice, sleet, and hailstorms are very seldom observed. Since 1880, only a few hailstorms have caused extensive damage in the city of Helena.

In winter, hours of sunshine are more than would be expected at a mountain location.

Due to the sheltering influence of the mountains, Foehn (Chinook) winds are not as pronounced as might be expected for a location on the eastern slopes of the Rocky Mountains. Strong winds can occur at any time throughout the year, but generally do not last more than a few hours at a time.

Based on the 1951-1980 period, the average first occurrence of 32 degrees Fahrenheit in the fall is September 18 and the average last occurrence in the spring is May 18.

## TABLE 1    NORMALS, MEANS AND EXTREMES

HELENA, MONTANA

LATITUDE: 46°36'N   LONGITUDE: 112°00'W   ELEVATION: FT. GRND 3828 BARO 3898   TIME ZONE: MOUNTAIN   WBAN: 24144

| | (a) | JAN | FEB | MAR | APR | MAY | JUNE | JULY | AUG | SEP | OCT | NOV | DEC | YEAR |
|---|---|---|---|---|---|---|---|---|---|---|---|---|---|---|
| **TEMPERATURE °F:** | | | | | | | | | | | | | | |
| Normals | | | | | | | | | | | | | | |
| -Daily Maximum | | 28.1 | 36.2 | 42.5 | 54.7 | 64.9 | 73.1 | 83.6 | 81.3 | 70.3 | 58.6 | 42.3 | 33.3 | 55.7 |
| -Daily Minimum | | 8.1 | 15.7 | 20.6 | 29.8 | 39.5 | 47.0 | 52.2 | 50.3 | 40.8 | 31.5 | 20.4 | 13.5 | 30.8 |
| -Monthly | | 18.1 | 26.0 | 31.6 | 42.3 | 52.2 | 60.1 | 67.9 | 65.9 | 55.6 | 45.1 | 31.4 | 23.5 | 43.3 |
| Extremes | | | | | | | | | | | | | | |
| -Record Highest | 49 | 62 | 68 | 77 | 85 | 92 | 100 | 102 | 105 | 99 | 85 | 70 | 64 | 105 |
| -Year | | 1953 | 1950 | 1978 | 1980 | 1986 | 1988 | 1981 | 1969 | 1967 | 1963 | 1953 | 1980 | AUG 1969 |
| -Record Lowest | 49 | -42 | -33 | -30 | 1 | 17 | 30 | 36 | 32 | 18 | -3 | -39 | -38 | -42 |
| -Year | | 1957 | 1989 | 1955 | 1954 | 1954 | 1969 | 1971 | 1956 | 1970 | 1972 | 1959 | 1964 | JAN 1957 |
| **NORMAL DEGREE DAYS:** | | | | | | | | | | | | | | |
| Heating (base 65°F) | | 1454 | 1092 | 1035 | 681 | 397 | 179 | 41 | 77 | 308 | 617 | 1008 | 1287 | 8176 |
| Cooling (base 65°F) | | 0 | 0 | 0 | 0 | 0 | 32 | 131 | 105 | 26 | 0 | 0 | 0 | 294 |
| **% OF POSSIBLE SUNSHINE** | 49 | 46 | 53 | 60 | 59 | 61 | 63 | 78 | 75 | 67 | 60 | 44 | 41 | 59 |
| **MEAN SKY COVER (tenths)** | | | | | | | | | | | | | | |
| Sunrise - Sunset | 49 | 7.5 | 7.4 | 7.4 | 7.2 | 6.8 | 6.3 | 4.1 | 4.5 | 5.4 | 6.1 | 7.2 | 7.5 | 6.5 |
| **MEAN NUMBER OF DAYS:** | | | | | | | | | | | | | | |
| Sunrise to Sunset | | | | | | | | | | | | | | |
| -Clear | 49 | 4.8 | 4.1 | 3.7 | 3.9 | 5.0 | 5.7 | 14.5 | 13.1 | 10.2 | 8.4 | 4.6 | 4.0 | 82.0 |
| -Partly Cloudy | 49 | 6.0 | 6.4 | 8.2 | 8.7 | 9.8 | 11.1 | 10.8 | 10.8 | 8.7 | 8.5 | 7.4 | 7.0 | 103.5 |
| -Cloudy | 49 | 20.2 | 17.7 | 19.2 | 17.4 | 16.2 | 13.1 | 5.6 | 7.1 | 11.1 | 14.1 | 18.0 | 20.0 | 179.7 |
| Precipitation | | | | | | | | | | | | | | |
| .01 inches or more | 49 | 7.9 | 6.7 | 8.6 | 8.1 | 11.1 | 11.3 | 7.4 | 7.6 | 6.8 | 5.6 | 7.0 | 7.9 | 95.8 |
| Snow,Ice pellets | | | | | | | | | | | | | | |
| 1.0 inches or more | 49 | 2.7 | 2.0 | 2.4 | 1.4 | 0.4 | 0.* | 0.0 | 0.0 | 0.5 | 0.7 | 1.8 | 2.4 | 14.3 |
| Thunderstorms | 49 | 0.1 | 0.1 | 0.1 | 0.9 | 4.1 | 7.5 | 9.0 | 7.9 | 1.8 | 0.3 | 0.1 | 0.* | 32.0 |
| Heavy Fog Visibility | | | | | | | | | | | | | | |
| 1/4 mile or less | 49 | 1.5 | 1.3 | 0.8 | 0.2 | 0.2 | 0.1 | 0.* | 0.1 | 0.2 | 0.5 | 1.2 | 1.9 | 8.0 |
| Temperature °F | | | | | | | | | | | | | | |
| -Maximum | | | | | | | | | | | | | | |
| 90° and above | 26 | 0.0 | 0.0 | 0.0 | 0.0 | 0.2 | 2.2 | 7.7 | 6.5 | 1.2 | 0.0 | 0.0 | 0.0 | 17.8 |
| 32° and below | 26 | 14.7 | 8.5 | 4.2 | 0.5 | 0.0 | 0.0 | 0.0 | 0.0 | 0.0 | 0.5 | 5.6 | 14.8 | 48.8 |
| -Minimum | | | | | | | | | | | | | | |
| 32° and below | 26 | 29.4 | 26.7 | 27.3 | 18.3 | 3.8 | 0.1 | 0.0 | 0.0 | 3.6 | 17.1 | 26.9 | 29.5 | 182.9 |
| 0° and below | 26 | 8.8 | 4.5 | 1.6 | 0.0 | 0.0 | 0.0 | 0.0 | 0.0 | 0.0 | 0.1 | 1.7 | 6.2 | 23.0 |
| **AVG. STATION PRESS.(mb)** | 17 | 881.7 | 881.0 | 878.1 | 879.5 | 879.2 | 880.4 | 881.9 | 881.9 | 882.6 | 882.8 | 880.9 | 881.6 | 881.0 |
| **RELATIVE HUMIDITY (%)** | | | | | | | | | | | | | | |
| Hour 05 | 24 | 70 | 72 | 72 | 70 | 71 | 72 | 66 | 67 | 72 | 73 | 74 | 72 | 71 |
| Hour 11 | 26 | 66 | 63 | 55 | 46 | 44 | 44 | 39 | 41 | 48 | 53 | 62 | 68 | 52 |
| Hour 17 (Local Time) | 26 | 63 | 55 | 46 | 38 | 38 | 37 | 29 | 30 | 36 | 42 | 58 | 66 | 45 |
| Hour 23 | 26 | 69 | 69 | 66 | 59 | 59 | 59 | 51 | 52 | 60 | 64 | 70 | 71 | 62 |
| **PRECIPITATION (inches):** | | | | | | | | | | | | | | |
| Water Equivalent | | | | | | | | | | | | | | |
| -Normal | | 0.66 | 0.44 | 0.69 | 1.01 | 1.72 | 2.01 | 1.04 | 1.18 | 0.83 | 0.65 | 0.54 | 0.60 | 11.37 |
| -Maximum Monthly | 49 | 2.78 | 1.20 | 1.62 | 3.00 | 6.09 | 4.74 | 3.89 | 4.23 | 3.37 | 2.68 | 1.50 | 1.48 | 6.09 |
| -Year | | 1969 | 1986 | 1982 | 1975 | 1981 | 1944 | 1975 | 1974 | 1965 | 1975 | 1950 | 1977 | MAY 1981 |
| -Minimum Monthly | 49 | T | 0.03 | 0.02 | 0.10 | 0.29 | 0.08 | 0.08 | 0.02 | 0.08 | 0.02 | 0.04 | 0.04 | T |
| -Year | | 1987 | 1987 | 1959 | 1977 | 1979 | 1985 | 1973 | 1988 | 1972 | 1978 | 1969 | 1976 | JAN 1987 |
| -Maximum in 24 hrs | 49 | 0.77 | 0.58 | 1.01 | 1.25 | 2.31 | 1.78 | 2.26 | 1.86 | 1.61 | 0.85 | 0.82 | 0.51 | 2.31 |
| -Year | | 1969 | 1953 | 1957 | 1951 | 1981 | 1979 | 1983 | 1974 | 1980 | 1954 | 1959 | 1982 | MAY 1981 |
| Snow,Ice pellets | | | | | | | | | | | | | | |
| -Maximum Monthly | 49 | 35.6 | 19.7 | 21.6 | 20.6 | 12.7 | 2.7 | T | T | 13.7 | 11.0 | 32.9 | 22.8 | 35.6 |
| -Year | | 1969 | 1959 | 1955 | 1967 | 1967 | 1969 | 1972 | 1989 | 1965 | 1969 | 1959 | 1967 | JAN 1969 |
| -Maximum in 24 hrs | 49 | 11.5 | 8.6 | 8.7 | 12.9 | 12.5 | 2.7 | T | T | 13.3 | 7.4 | 21.5 | 10.7 | 21.5 |
| -Year | | 1969 | 1959 | 1955 | 1960 | 1967 | 1969 | 1972 | 1989 | 1957 | 1969 | 1959 | 1941 | NOV 1959 |
| **WIND:** | | | | | | | | | | | | | | |
| Mean Speed (mph) | 49 | 6.8 | 7.4 | 8.4 | 9.2 | 8.9 | 8.6 | 7.8 | 7.5 | 7.4 | 7.1 | 7.0 | 6.8 | 7.7 |
| Prevailing Direction | | | | | | | | | | | | | | |
| through 1963 | | W | W | W | W | W | W | W | W | W | W | W | W | W |
| Fastest Mile | | | | | | | | | | | | | | |
| -Direction (!!!) | 49 | SW | W | SW | W | SW | W | SW | S | NW | W | SW | NW | W |
| -Speed (MPH) | 49 | 73 | 73 | 61 | 52 | 56 | 56 | 65 | 65 | 54 | 62 | 56 | 59 | 73 |
| -Year | | 1944 | 1949 | 1955 | 1950 | 1975 | 1970 | 1975 | 1947 | 1943 | 1948 | 1962 | 1946 | FEB 1949 |
| Peak Gust | | | | | | | | | | | | | | |
| -Direction (!!!) | 6 | W | W | W | W | W | S | W | SW | W | W | NW | W | W |
| -Speed (mph) | 6 | 59 | 63 | 52 | 55 | 58 | 58 | 62 | 56 | 51 | 54 | 54 | 58 | 63 |
| -Date | | 1984 | 1988 | 1987 | 1989 | 1989 | 1988 | 1989 | 1988 | 1984 | 1988 | 1986 | 1988 | FEB 1988 |

**See Reference Notes to this table on the following page.**

# HELENA, MONTANA

PRECIPITATION (inches)  HELENA, MONTANA

## TABLE 2

| YEAR | JAN | FEB | MAR | APR | MAY | JUNE | JULY | AUG | SEP | OCT | NOV | DEC | ANNUAL |
|---|---|---|---|---|---|---|---|---|---|---|---|---|---|
| 1961 | 0.12 | 0.06 | 1.03 | 0.90 | 1.36 | 0.78 | 1.05 | 0.62 | 1.16 | 0.16 | 0.37 | 0.55 | 8.16 |
| 1962 | 0.67 | 0.51 | 0.69 | 0.90 | 3.77 | 2.50 | 1.27 | 1.80 | 0.31 | 0.95 | 0.57 | 0.14 | 14.08 |
| 1963 | 0.50 | 0.25 | 0.44 | 0.81 | 1.34 | 2.59 | 0.80 | 0.80 | 1.10 | 1.39 | 0.29 | 1.27 | 11.58 |
| 1964 | 0.31 | 0.27 | 0.51 | 1.56 | 3.52 | 2.98 | 0.83 | 1.91 | 0.16 | 0.04 | 0.53 | 0.99 | 13.61 |
| 1965 | 0.36 | 0.49 | 0.85 | 0.98 | 2.20 | 3.85 | 0.60 | 1.92 | 3.37 | 0.13 | 0.62 | 0.15 | 15.52 |
| 1966 | 0.46 | 0.33 | 0.28 | 0.51 | 0.43 | 0.96 | 0.32 | 0.42 | 0.34 | 0.75 | 1.04 | 0.62 | 6.46 |
| 1967 | 0.61 | 0.62 | 1.43 | 2.38 | 2.08 | 2.36 | 0.46 | 0.58 | 0.68 | 1.50 | 0.31 | 1.39 | 14.40 |
| 1968 | 0.59 | 0.16 | 0.53 | 1.21 | 1.62 | 2.68 | 0.26 | 2.00 | 2.22 | 0.23 | 0.92 | 0.75 | 13.17 |
| 1969 | 2.78 | 0.22 | 0.57 | 0.60 | 1.13 | 3.50 | 1.77 | 0.38 | 0.33 | 1.06 | 0.04 | 0.31 | 12.69 |
| 1970 | 0.51 | 0.67 | 0.96 | 0.81 | 1.20 | 2.11 | 0.93 | 0.63 | 0.36 | 0.58 | 0.44 | 0.54 | 9.74 |
| 1971 | 1.38 | 0.63 | 0.41 | 0.58 | 1.77 | 0.93 | 0.56 | 1.22 | 0.89 | 0.39 | 0.34 | 1.02 | 10.12 |
| 1972 | 1.12 | 0.54 | 0.63 | 0.41 | 0.77 | 1.12 | 0.56 | 1.63 | 0.08 | 0.57 | 0.33 | 0.46 | 8.22 |
| 1973 | 0.22 | 0.13 | 0.05 | 0.66 | 1.08 | 0.73 | 0.08 | 0.56 | 0.43 | 0.66 | 1.03 | 0.63 | 6.26 |
| 1974 | 0.66 | 0.23 | 0.38 | 0.76 | 2.07 | 0.34 | 0.49 | 4.23 | 0.22 | 0.51 | 0.30 | 0.26 | 10.45 |
| 1975 | 1.26 | 0.72 | 0.88 | 3.00 | 1.95 | 2.83 | 3.89 | 2.47 | 0.47 | 2.68 | 0.48 | 0.31 | 20.94 |
| 1976 | 0.26 | 0.38 | 0.41 | 1.34 | 0.87 | 2.74 | 0.29 | 1.58 | 1.82 | 0.04 | 0.30 | 0.04 | 10.07 |
| 1977 | 0.65 | 0.13 | 1.11 | 0.10 | 1.82 | 1.37 | 1.37 | 0.72 | 1.93 | 0.17 | 0.48 | 1.48 | 11.33 |
| 1978 | 0.96 | 0.61 | 0.31 | 0.94 | 1.20 | 0.44 | 2.83 | 0.59 | 1.11 | 0.02 | 1.19 | 0.76 | 10.96 |
| 1979 | 0.77 | 0.72 | 1.34 | 2.26 | 0.29 | 2.75 | 0.32 | 0.79 | 0.12 | 0.38 | 0.06 | 0.59 | 10.39 |
| 1980 | 0.62 | 0.74 | 0.88 | 0.63 | 4.32 | 3.16 | 1.92 | 0.28 | 2.57 | 1.21 | 0.32 | 0.40 | 17.05 |
| 1981 | 0.15 | 0.10 | 1.10 | 0.75 | 6.09 | 1.15 | 1.78 | 0.10 | 0.90 | 0.82 | 0.54 | 0.33 | 13.81 |
| 1982 | 0.80 | 0.58 | 1.62 | 0.54 | 1.77 | 2.99 | 0.49 | 0.74 | 2.74 | 0.35 | 0.31 | 1.05 | 13.98 |
| 1983 | 0.24 | 0.07 | 0.36 | 0.29 | 1.79 | 2.20 | 3.48 | 2.67 | 1.56 | 0.35 | 0.26 | 0.76 | 14.03 |
| 1984 | 0.17 | 0.15 | 0.49 | 1.45 | 1.03 | 2.14 | 0.11 | 1.11 | 0.73 | 0.74 | 0.47 | 0.41 | 9.00 |
| 1985 | 0.16 | 0.38 | 0.32 | 0.46 | 0.75 | 2.64 | 0.10 | 2.64 | 2.11 | 0.76 | 0.84 | 0.35 | 8.95 |
| 1986 | 0.32 | 1.20 | 0.49 | 1.08 | 0.83 | 1.56 | 1.37 | 1.84 | 2.45 | 0.03 | 0.54 | 0.38 | 12.09 |
| 1987 | T | 0.03 | 1.19 | 0.76 | 1.90 | 1.50 | 2.88 | 0.38 | 0.80 | 0.05 | 0.12 | 0.42 | 10.03 |
| 1988 | 0.27 | 0.50 | 0.45 | 1.32 | 1.82 | 1.50 | 0.36 | 0.02 | 2.09 | 0.69 | 0.69 | 0.32 | 10.03 |
| 1989 | 1.42 | 0.82 | 1.35 | 0.72 | 1.00 | 1.43 | 1.55 | 1.61 | 1.31 | 0.54 | 0.26 | 0.48 | 12.49 |
| 1990 | 0.47 | 0.14 | 0.91 | 0.43 | 1.54 | 0.92 | 0.40 | 2.57 | 0.11 | 0.11 | 0.36 | 0.47 | 8.43 |
| Record Mean | 0.71 | 0.52 | 0.74 | 0.97 | 1.88 | 2.16 | 1.10 | 0.95 | 1.15 | 0.74 | 0.61 | 0.63 | 12.16 |

## TABLE 3

AVERAGE TEMPERATURE (deg. F)  HELENA, MONTANA

| YEAR | JAN | FEB | MAR | APR | MAY | JUNE | JULY | AUG | SEP | OCT | NOV | DEC | ANNUAL |
|---|---|---|---|---|---|---|---|---|---|---|---|---|---|
| 1961 | 27.4 | 36.6 | 37.0 | 40.6 | 53.7 | 68.5 | 70.9 | 71.3 | 48.9 | 43.7 | 27.8 | 22.6 | 45.8 |
| 1962 | 15.7 | 24.5 | 29.1 | 47.2 | 51.7 | 60.9 | 65.2 | 64.9 | 55.0 | 48.1 | 36.9 | 29.2 | 44.0 |
| #1963 | 10.5 | 34.8 | 37.6 | 42.6 | 53.4 | 60.0 | 68.2 | 68.0 | 61.2 | 50.9 | 34.8 | 16.9 | 44.9 |
| 1964 | 22.0 | 27.2 | 29.9 | 41.8 | 51.7 | 59.0 | 70.2 | 63.4 | 53.8 | 47.4 | 30.5 | 19.1 | 43.0 |
| 1965 | 29.6 | 26.6 | 24.6 | 44.4 | 50.1 | 59.5 | 67.7 | 65.8 | 45.6 | 49.3 | 34.7 | 27.5 | 43.8 |
| 1966 | 20.6 | 27.0 | 36.5 | 42.5 | 56.5 | 59.3 | 71.5 | 66.7 | 62.7 | 46.4 | 33.8 | 27.4 | 45.9 |
| 1967 | 28.7 | 32.7 | 29.0 | 37.8 | 52.1 | 59.9 | 70.5 | 71.4 | 61.9 | 47.4 | 33.0 | 19.0 | 45.3 |
| 1968 | 15.7 | 28.9 | 39.6 | 39.7 | 49.6 | 58.3 | 68.2 | 63.2 | 55.0 | 44.4 | 33.5 | 16.7 | 42.8 |
| 1969 | 7.2 | 14.5 | 21.3 | 46.7 | 55.2 | 57.8 | 67.9 | 70.1 | 58.0 | 38.1 | 33.5 | 25.9 | 41.4 |
| 1970 | 18.8 | 32.5 | 28.2 | 36.5 | 51.5 | 62.3 | 68.2 | 67.9 | 51.1 | 40.2 | 29.3 | 20.6 | 42.2 |
| 1971 | 19.0 | 28.5 | 31.9 | 41.5 | 51.4 | 57.0 | 63.2 | 69.0 | 49.7 | 42.0 | 33.6 | 15.6 | 41.9 |
| 1972 | 12.4 | 26.8 | 39.1 | 39.8 | 50.9 | 61.8 | 61.7 | 66.0 | 50.9 | 39.0 | 31.1 | 13.6 | 41.1 |
| 1973 | 17.7 | 22.8 | 36.0 | 40.3 | 52.9 | 61.2 | 68.9 | 66.8 | 54.4 | 45.8 | 24.5 | 28.2 | 43.3 |
| 1974 | 18.1 | 32.8 | 33.9 | 46.0 | 48.6 | 64.9 | 70.4 | 61.5 | 53.5 | 45.8 | 34.7 | 27.7 | 44.8 |
| 1975 | 21.1 | 13.7 | 28.8 | 32.9 | 48.6 | 56.9 | 69.2 | 61.2 | 54.1 | 43.3 | 29.9 | 26.0 | 40.5 |
| 1976 | 24.9 | 29.5 | 30.4 | 43.2 | 54.1 | 56.6 | 67.6 | 64.8 | 57.9 | 44.9 | 33.8 | 28.7 | 44.7 |
| 1977 | 18.0 | 34.1 | 32.4 | 46.9 | 50.4 | 63.6 | 66.3 | 63.6 | 56.3 | 45.6 | 31.2 | 20.7 | 44.1 |
| 1978 | 16.9 | 22.8 | 38.8 | 47.7 | 53.2 | 63.2 | 67.2 | 65.5 | 57.9 | 46.5 | 22.7 | 15.2 | 43.2 |
| 1979 | 1.1 | 20.1 | 34.7 | 42.7 | 53.2 | 62.0 | 69.2 | 67.7 | 61.3 | 47.8 | 29.0 | 28.2 | 43.1 |
| 1980 | 14.3 | 25.3 | 31.3 | 49.0 | 55.4 | 59.8 | 67.3 | 62.9 | 56.8 | 45.4 | 34.9 | 26.9 | 44.1 |
| 1981 | 28.4 | 29.7 | 38.0 | 46.4 | 52.8 | 58.9 | 67.7 | 69.5 | 58.8 | 43.8 | 36.4 | 25.3 | 46.3 |
| 1982 | 16.5 | 23.7 | 33.9 | 40.5 | 50.9 | 61.2 | 68.6 | 69.1 | 55.5 | 44.9 | 27.4 | 22.7 | 42.9 |
| 1983 | 30.6 | 35.3 | 38.3 | 43.1 | 51.5 | 60.2 | 66.0 | 70.8 | 53.5 | 46.0 | 34.7 | 5.5 | 44.6 |
| 1984 | 27.3 | 32.4 | 37.2 | 43.5 | 52.8 | 60.0 | 70.0 | 69.8 | 52.3 | 41.7 | 33.1 | 11.6 | 44.3 |
| 1985 | 12.3 | 18.8 | 33.4 | 46.9 | 56.2 | 63.3 | 75.0 | 63.1 | 49.6 | 42.3 | 12.6 | 15.0 | 40.7 |
| 1986 | 25.5 | 21.8 | 42.9 | 43.3 | 53.6 | 66.4 | 64.2 | 68.0 | 51.2 | 45.3 | 29.0 | 18.6 | 44.2 |
| 1987 | 23.3 | 31.9 | 37.0 | 50.2 | 55.9 | 64.4 | 66.2 | 62.8 | 59.9 | 46.8 | 34.7 | 24.7 | 46.5 |
| 1988 | 18.8 | 29.1 | 36.1 | 47.1 | 55.5 | 68.4 | 71.3 | 68.6 | 56.4 | 50.3 | 33.8 | 23.1 | 46.5 |
| 1989 | 24.5 | 6.1 | 27.6 | 44.5 | 51.7 | 62.2 | 72.0 | 64.3 | 55.6 | 45.1 | 36.8 | 23.8 | 42.9 |
| 1990 | 28.8 | 26.9 | 34.9 | 45.8 | 51.0 | 61.5 | 69.4 | 68.4 | 63.6 | 45.3 | 37.4 | 14.0 | 45.6 |
| Record Mean | 19.8 | 24.5 | 32.5 | 43.5 | 52.2 | 60.0 | 67.8 | 66.3 | 55.7 | 45.4 | 32.4 | 23.9 | 43.7 |
| Max | 28.8 | 33.9 | 42.6 | 54.9 | 63.9 | 72.2 | 82.1 | 80.5 | 68.6 | 56.9 | 41.9 | 32.5 | 54.9 |
| Min | 10.8 | 15.0 | 22.5 | 32.1 | 40.5 | 47.9 | 53.6 | 52.1 | 42.8 | 33.8 | 22.9 | 15.2 | 32.4 |

## REFERENCE NOTES FOR TABLES 1, 2, 3 and 6    (HELENA, MT)

### GENERAL

T - TRACE AMOUNT
BLANK ENTRIES DENOTE MISSING/UNREPORTED DATA.
# INDICATES A STATION OR INSTRUMENT RELOCATION.

### SPECIFIC

TABLE 1

(a) - LENGTH OF RECORD IN YEARS. ALTHOUGH INDIVIDUAL MONTHS MAY BE MISSING.

* LESS THAN .05

NORMALS — BASED ON THE 1951-1980 RECORD PERIOD.
EXTREMES — DATES ARE THE MOST RECENT OCCURRENCE.
WIND DIR. — NUMERALS SHOW TENS OF DEGREES CLOCKWISE FROM TRUE NORTH. "00" INDICATES CALM.
RESULTANT WIND DIRECTIONS ARE GIVEN TO WHOLE DEGREES.

TABLE 3
MAX AND MIN ARE LONG-TERM MEAN DAILY MAXIMUM AND MEAN DAILY MINIMUM TEMPERATURES.

### EXCEPTIONS

TABLES 2, 3, and 6

RECORD MEANS ARE THROUGH THE CURRENT YEAR, BEGINNING IN 1881 FOR TEMPERATURE
1881 FOR PRECIPITATION
1940 FOR SNOWFALL

626

HEATING DEGREE DAYS Base 65 deg. F     HELENA, MONTANA

**TABLE 4**

| SEASON | JULY | AUG | SEP | OCT | NOV | DEC | JAN | FEB | MAR | APR | MAY | JUNE | TOTAL |
|---|---|---|---|---|---|---|---|---|---|---|---|---|---|
| 1961-62 | 1 | 7 | 476 | 652 | 1109 | 1311 | 1528 | 1133 | 1104 | 527 | 404 | 147 | 8399 |
| 1962-63 | 58 | 77 | 295 | 515 | 837 | 1106 | 1687 | 842 | 842 | 665 | 358 | 172 | 7454 |
| #1963-64 | 32 | 32 | 131 | 427 | 897 | 1328 | 1328 | 1089 | 1080 | 690 | 411 | 192 | 7793 |
| 1964-65 | 1 | 101 | 332 | 542 | 1028 | 1420 | 1090 | 1070 | 1250 | 612 | 454 | 169 | 8069 |
| 1965-66 | 14 | 69 | 578 | 478 | 903 | 1153 | 1370 | 1058 | 874 | 670 | 267 | 188 | 7622 |
| 1966-67 | 8 | 51 | 117 | 570 | 930 | 1157 | 1120 | 898 | 1107 | 807 | 396 | 171 | 7332 |
| 1967-68 | 0 | 1 | 130 | 539 | 954 | 1422 | 1525 | 1042 | 780 | 751 | 472 | 206 | 7822 |
| 1968-69 | 23 | 102 | 294 | 633 | 937 | 1493 | 1788 | 1407 | 1348 | 543 | 301 | 226 | 9095 |
| 1969-70 | 35 | 14 | 219 | 826 | 938 | 1207 | 1427 | 904 | 1132 | 849 | 409 | 153 | 8113 |
| 1970-71 | 22 | 12 | 413 | 763 | 1063 | 1372 | 1422 | 1013 | 1020 | 699 | 414 | 251 | 8464 |
| 1971-72 | 91 | 22 | 454 | 707 | 936 | 1524 | 1628 | 1102 | 796 | 747 | 430 | 120 | 8557 |
| 1972-73 | 136 | 49 | 418 | 798 | 1010 | 1588 | 1465 | 1174 | 892 | 732 | 155 | 155 | 8791 |
| 1973-74 | 23 | 47 | 317 | 588 | 1208 | 1136 | 1452 | 897 | 956 | 564 | 500 | 99 | 7787 |
| 1974-75 | 16 | 130 | 338 | 588 | 905 | 1355 | 1429 | 1114 | 954 | 501 | 235 | 88 | 8714 |
| 1975-76 | 14 | 119 | 322 | 666 | 1045 | 1199 | 1236 | 1023 | 1064 | 649 | 331 | 257 | 7925 |
| 1976-77 | 15 | 45 | 219 | 615 | 928 | 1120 | 1449 | 862 | 1005 | 535 | 443 | 90 | 7326 |
| 1977-78 | 52 | 92 | 270 | 593 | 1008 | 1367 | 1485 | 1175 | 806 | 512 | 361 | 87 | 7808 |
| 1978-79 | 32 | 60 | 244 | 564 | 1263 | 1540 | 1979 | 1250 | 930 | 665 | 359 | 128 | 9014 |
| 1979-80 | 11 | 15 | 127 | 528 | 1072 | 1138 | 1566 | 1148 | 1039 | 473 | 304 | 164 | 7585 |
| 1980-81 | 25 | 81 | 242 | 602 | 899 | 1175 | 1127 | 986 | 832 | 552 | 371 | 191 | 7083 |
| 1981-82 | 21 | 16 | 195 | 650 | 853 | 1227 | 1497 | 1153 | 959 | 726 | 428 | 136 | 7861 |
| 1982-83 | 30 | 16 | 304 | 618 | 1120 | 1306 | 1059 | 828 | 823 | 649 | 417 | 152 | 7322 |
| 1983-84 | 76 | 0 | 351 | 584 | 901 | 1842 | 1164 | 941 | 856 | 640 | 380 | 174 | 7909 |
| 1984-85 | 2 | 7 | 377 | 716 | 954 | 1654 | 1625 | 1291 | 973 | 538 | 266 | 97 | 8500 |
| 1985-86 | 3 | 105 | 455 | 696 | 1571 | 1545 | 1218 | 1202 | 677 | 645 | 380 | 42 | 8539 |
| 1986-87 | 66 | 23 | 409 | 602 | 1077 | 1432 | 1288 | 923 | 862 | 437 | 276 | 77 | 7472 |
| 1987-88 | 75 | 104 | 163 | 556 | 901 | 1241 | 1426 | 1034 | 889 | 529 | 297 | 63 | 7278 |
| 1988-89 | 10 | 13 | 282 | 449 | 934 | 1292 | 1251 | 1650 | 1156 | 610 | 407 | 107 | 8161 |
| 1989-90 | 0 | 92 | 274 | 611 | 839 | 1268 | 1116 | 1058 | 925 | 573 | 426 | 177 | 7359 |
| 1990-91 | 15 | 31 | 78 | 604 | 823 | 1579 | | | | | | | |

**TABLE 5**    COOLING DEGREE DAYS Base 65 deg. F     HELENA, MONTANA

| YEAR | JAN | FEB | MAR | APR | MAY | JUNE | JULY | AUG | SEP | OCT | NOV | DEC | TOTAL |
|---|---|---|---|---|---|---|---|---|---|---|---|---|---|
| 1969 | 0 | 0 | 0 | 0 | 1 | 18 | 128 | 178 | 20 | 0 | 0 | 0 | 345 |
| 1970 | 0 | 0 | 0 | 0 | 0 | 76 | 130 | 109 | 5 | 0 | 0 | 0 | 320 |
| 1971 | 0 | 0 | 0 | 0 | 0 | 14 | 42 | 154 | 0 | 0 | 0 | 0 | 210 |
| 1972 | 0 | 0 | 0 | 0 | 2 | 30 | 42 | 89 | 0 | 0 | 0 | 0 | 163 |
| 1973 | 0 | 0 | 0 | 0 | 4 | 45 | 151 | 108 | 3 | 0 | 0 | 0 | 311 |
| 1974 | 0 | 0 | 0 | 0 | 0 | 102 | 190 | 31 | 0 | 0 | 0 | 0 | 323 |
| 1975 | 0 | 0 | 0 | 0 | 0 | 1 | 154 | 12 | 0 | 0 | 0 | 0 | 167 |
| 1976 | 0 | 0 | 0 | 0 | 0 | 14 | 102 | 45 | 10 | 0 | 0 | 0 | 171 |
| 1977 | 0 | 0 | 0 | 0 | 0 | 57 | 101 | 54 | 13 | 0 | 0 | 0 | 225 |
| 1978 | 0 | 0 | 0 | 0 | 3 | 37 | 109 | 85 | 37 | 0 | 0 | 0 | 271 |
| 1979 | 0 | 0 | 0 | 0 | 1 | 45 | 152 | 103 | 21 | 0 | 0 | 0 | 322 |
| 1980 | 0 | 0 | 0 | 0 | 14 | 14 | 104 | 25 | 4 | 0 | 0 | 0 | 161 |
| 1981 | 0 | 0 | 0 | 0 | 0 | 15 | 109 | 165 | 16 | 0 | 0 | 0 | 305 |
| 1982 | 0 | 0 | 0 | 0 | 0 | 30 | 147 | 151 | 25 | 0 | 0 | 0 | 353 |
| 1983 | 0 | 0 | 0 | 0 | 4 | 16 | 115 | 186 | 12 | 0 | 0 | 0 | 333 |
| 1984 | 0 | 0 | 0 | 0 | 10 | 31 | 165 | 163 | 4 | 0 | 0 | 0 | 373 |
| 1985 | 0 | 0 | 0 | 0 | 2 | 55 | 318 | 54 | 0 | 0 | 0 | 0 | 429 |
| 1986 | 0 | 0 | 0 | 0 | 35 | 91 | 45 | 123 | 1 | 0 | 0 | 0 | 295 |
| 1987 | 0 | 0 | 0 | 0 | 3 | 66 | 122 | 41 | 15 | 0 | 0 | 0 | 247 |
| 1988 | 0 | 0 | 0 | 0 | 8 | 170 | 211 | 132 | 30 | 0 | 0 | 0 | 551 |
| 1989 | 0 | 0 | 0 | 0 | 0 | 30 | 222 | 82 | 0 | 0 | 0 | 0 | 334 |
| 1990 | 0 | 0 | 0 | 0 | 0 | 77 | 159 | 142 | 42 | 0 | 0 | 0 | 420 |

**TABLE 6**    SNOWFALL (inches)     HELENA, MONTANA

| SEASON | JULY | AUG | SEP | OCT | NOV | DEC | JAN | FEB | MAR | APR | MAY | JUNE | TOTAL |
|---|---|---|---|---|---|---|---|---|---|---|---|---|---|
| 1961-62 | 0.0 | 0.0 | T | 1.3 | 6.4 | 4.2 | 10.1 | 7.3 | 7.3 | 8.7 | 0.0 | 0.0 | 45.3 |
| 1962-63 | 0.0 | 0.0 | 0.4 | 0.0 | 1.2 | 1.5 | 9.8 | 2.0 | 5.9 | 2.3 | 0.0 | 0.0 | 23.1 |
| 1963-64 | 0.0 | 0.0 | 0.0 | T | 2.7 | 21.2 | 6.2 | 6.3 | 7.4 | 6.6 | 10.1 | 0.0 | 60.5 |
| 1964-65 | 0.0 | 0.0 | 0.0 | 0.0 | 6.3 | 13.2 | 2.3 | 9.4 | 12.9 | 6.3 | 5.0 | 0.0 | 55.4 |
| 1965-66 | 0.0 | 0.0 | 13.7 | 0.0 | 2.1 | 1.4 | 6.3 | 5.1 | 2.3 | 1.9 | T | 0.0 | 32.8 |
| 1966-67 | 0.0 | 0.0 | 0.0 | T | 9.5 | 5.7 | 7.3 | 10.5 | 14.9 | 20.6 | 12.7 | 0.0 | 81.2 |
| 1967-68 | 0.0 | 0.0 | 0.0 | T | 2.7 | 22.8 | 8.7 | 0.9 | 0.8 | 10.0 | T | 0.0 | 45.9 |
| 1968-69 | 0.0 | 0.0 | 3.0 | 0.4 | 7.4 | 11.0 | 35.6 | 3.6 | 7.0 | 2.6 | 0.7 | 2.7 | 74.0 |
| 1969-70 | 0.0 | 0.0 | 0.0 | 11.0 | 0.1 | 6.1 | 7.0 | 9.5 | 9.0 | 7.9 | 1.4 | 0.0 | 52.0 |
| 1970-71 | 0.0 | 0.0 | T | 1.4 | 5.4 | 7.5 | 16.2 | 3.5 | 2.5 | 0.7 | T | 0.0 | 37.2 |
| 1971-72 | 0.0 | 0.0 | T | 0.8 | 4.6 | 14.5 | 14.9 | 3.3 | 4.5 | 3.8 | T | 0.0 | 46.4 |
| 1972-73 | T | 0.0 | 0.3 | 4.7 | 0.7 | 7.8 | 3.2 | 1.8 | 0.1 | 6.5 | T | 0.0 | 25.1 |
| 1973-74 | 0.0 | 0.0 | 1.3 | 7.2 | 12.5 | 7.2 | 9.9 | 5.9 | 2.2 | 1.5 | 0.2 | 0.0 | 47.9 |
| 1974-75 | 0.0 | 0.0 | T | 1.5 | 0.8 | 2.7 | 15.2 | 10.7 | 12.3 | 15.4 | 0.2 | 0.0 | 58.8 |
| 1975-76 | 0.0 | 0.0 | 0.0 | 6.3 | 4.9 | 3.9 | 3.3 | 4.4 | 6.7 | 10.9 | 0.0 | 0.0 | 40.4 |
| 1976-77 | 0.0 | 0.0 | 0.0 | T | 2.9 | 0.9 | 13.8 | 0.8 | 14.1 | 0.5 | 1.0 | 0.0 | 34.0 |
| 1977-78 | 0.0 | 0.0 | 0.0 | 0.4 | 6.8 | 19.5 | 15.7 | 13.3 | 2.6 | 0.9 | T | 0.0 | 59.2 |
| 1978-79 | 0.0 | 0.0 | T | T | 22.1 | 13.8 | 11.7 | 7.2 | 12.4 | 9.3 | T | T | 76.5 |
| 1979-80 | 0.0 | 0.0 | 0.0 | 0.2 | 0.6 | 6.5 | 9.3 | 10.5 | 10.1 | 3.1 | 0.0 | 0.0 | 40.3 |
| 1980-81 | 0.0 | 0.0 | 0.0 | 3.7 | 1.2 | 3.8 | 2.7 | 2.1 | 3.3 | 0.1 | T | 0.0 | 16.9 |
| 1981-82 | 0.0 | 0.0 | 0.0 | 5.2 | 3.4 | 6.1 | 18.4 | 4.8 | 13.9 | 4.1 | 0.8 | 0.0 | 56.7 |
| 1982-83 | 0.0 | 0.0 | 6.5 | 0.5 | 4.1 | 11.3 | 3.2 | 0.2 | 2.2 | 1.1 | 9.9 | 0.0 | 39.0 |
| 1983-84 | 0.0 | 0.0 | 6.4 | 0.0 | 1.3 | 13.0 | 1.3 | 1.5 | 5.7 | 2.3 | 0.8 | 0.0 | 32.3 |
| 1984-85 | 0.0 | 0.0 | 6.3 | 9.0 | 5.7 | 7.5 | 3.9 | 6.2 | 4.0 | 0.8 | 0.0 | 0.0 | 43.4 |
| 1985-86 | 0.0 | 0.0 | 2.9 | 8.8 | 10.4 | 8.5 | 4.2 | 15.6 | 1.2 | 11.6 | 0.0 | 0.0 | 63.4 |
| 1986-87 | 0.0 | 0.0 | 0.0 | T | 7.6 | 5.0 | 0.2 | 0.2 | 9.1 | 4.3 | 3.8 | 0.0 | 30.2 |
| 1987-88 | 0.0 | 0.0 | 0.0 | 0.3 | 0.9 | 1.2 | 4.4 | 8.0 | 5.2 | 2.9 | 0.0 | 0.0 | 22.9 |
| 1988-89 | 0.0 | 0.0 | 5.9 | 1.5 | 6.0 | 5.0 | 23.0 | 13.0 | 20.7 | 7.9 | 3.5 | T | 86.5 |
| 1989-90 | 0.0 | T | T | 2.6 | 1.8 | 9.4 | 4.3 | 1.8 | 14.0 | 0.8 | 0.1 | 0.0 | 34.8 |
| 1990-91 | 0.0 | 0.5 | 0.0 | 0.5 | 8.6 | 11.6 | | | | | | | |
| Record Mean | T | T | 1.6 | 2.1 | 6.4 | 8.4 | 8.8 | 6.1 | 7.6 | 4.9 | 1.5 | 0.1 | 47.6 |

**See Reference Notes, relative to all above tables, on preceding page.**

The climate of North Platte is characterized throughout the year by frequent rapid changes in the weather. During the winter, most North Pacific lows cross the country north of North Platte. The passage usually brings little or no snowfall, and only a moderate drop in temperature. Only when there is a major outbreak of cold air from Canada does the temperature fall to zero or below. The duration of below—zero temperature is hardly more than two mornings, and by the third or fourth day the temperature is ordinarily rising to the 40s or higher. Snowfall at the onset of a cold outbreak is usually less than 2 inches.

Only when a low moves from the middle Rockies through Nebraska, allowing easterly winds to draw moist air into the low circulation, does snowfall of appreciable amounts occur. Few of these storms move slowly enough, or are intense enough, to deposit much precipitation in the North Platte area. However, during some winters the cold outbreak and intense low from the mid—Rockies combine to produce severe cold and snow several inches in depth, with blizzard conditions following. During and after these snowfalls and blizzards, rail and highway traffic may be stalled until the snow is cleared. Widespread loss of unsheltered livestock and wild life results from such conditions.

The sudden and frequent weather changes of the winter continue through spring with decreasing intensity of temperature changes but increasing precipitation. The summer and fall months bring frequent changes from hot to cool weather. Most summer and fall precipitation is associated with thunderstorms, so the amounts are extremely variable. The surrounding area is occasionally damaged by locally severe winds and hailstorms.

Temperatures may reach into the upper 90s and lower 100s frequently during the summer months, but the elevation and clear skies bring rapid cooling after sunset to lows in the 60s or below by daybreak. Since the humidity is generally low, the extremely hot days of summer are not uncomfortable.

Based on the 1951—1980 period, the average first occurrence of 32 degrees Fahrenheit in the fall is September 24 and the average last occurrence in the spring is May 11.

## TABLE 1  NORMALS, MEANS AND EXTREMES

NORTH PLATTE, NEBRASKA

LATITUDE: 41°08'N  LONGITUDE: 100°41'W  ELEVATION: FT. GRND 2775 BARO 2782  TIME ZONE: CENTRAL  WBAN: 24023

| | (a) | JAN | FEB | MAR | APR | MAY | JUNE | JULY | AUG | SEP | OCT | NOV | DEC | YEAR |
|---|---|---|---|---|---|---|---|---|---|---|---|---|---|---|
| **TEMPERATURE °F:** | | | | | | | | | | | | | | |
| Normals | | | | | | | | | | | | | | |
| -Daily Maximum | | 34.2 | 40.5 | 47.8 | 61.5 | 71.5 | 81.6 | 87.8 | 86.4 | 77.3 | 66.7 | 49.4 | 39.3 | 62.0 |
| -Daily Minimum | | 8.3 | 14.1 | 21.5 | 33.6 | 44.8 | 55.0 | 60.6 | 58.3 | 46.5 | 33.7 | 20.5 | 12.5 | 34.1 |
| -Monthly | | 21.3 | 27.3 | 34.7 | 47.6 | 58.2 | 68.3 | 74.2 | 72.4 | 61.9 | 50.2 | 35.0 | 25.9 | 48.1 |
| Extremes | | | | | | | | | | | | | | |
| -Record Highest | 38 | 70 | 79 | 86 | 94 | 97 | 107 | 112 | 105 | 102 | 91 | 82 | 75 | 112 |
| -Year | | 1981 | 1962 | 1986 | 1980 | 1953 | 1952 | 1954 | 1954 | 1979 | 1989 | 1980 | 1980 | JUL 1954 |
| -Record Lowest | 38 | -23 | -22 | -22 | 7 | 19 | 29 | 40 | 35 | 17 | 11 | -13 | -34 | -34 |
| -Year | | 1979 | 1981 | 1962 | 1975 | 1989 | 1969 | 1952 | 1976 | 1984 | 1989 | 1976 | 1989 | DEC 1989 |
| **NORMAL DEGREE DAYS:** | | | | | | | | | | | | | | |
| Heating (base 65°F) | | 1355 | 1056 | 939 | 522 | 235 | 59 | 8 | 9 | 151 | 463 | 900 | 1212 | 6909 |
| Cooling (base 65°F) | | 0 | 0 | 0 | 0 | 24 | 158 | 294 | 239 | 58 | 0 | 0 | 0 | 773 |
| **% OF POSSIBLE SUNSHINE** | 37 | 60 | 59 | 60 | 64 | 64 | 70 | 76 | 74 | 70 | 69 | 59 | 60 | 65 |
| **MEAN SKY COVER (tenths)** | | | | | | | | | | | | | | |
| Sunrise - Sunset | 37 | 6.2 | 6.4 | 6.6 | 6.2 | 6.4 | 5.3 | 4.6 | 4.8 | 4.7 | 4.9 | 5.9 | 5.9 | 5.7 |
| **MEAN NUMBER OF DAYS:** | | | | | | | | | | | | | | |
| Sunrise to Sunset | | | | | | | | | | | | | | |
| -Clear | 37 | 8.5 | 6.9 | 7.2 | 7.3 | 6.8 | 10.3 | 12.3 | 11.8 | 12.9 | 12.7 | 8.9 | 9.4 | 115.0 |
| -Partly Cloudy | 37 | 8.6 | 7.6 | 7.6 | 9.2 | 10.3 | 10.8 | 12.1 | 11.5 | 8.3 | 8.4 | 8.3 | 8.1 | 110.9 |
| -Cloudy | 37 | 14.0 | 13.8 | 16.2 | 13.4 | 13.9 | 8.9 | 6.6 | 7.7 | 8.8 | 9.9 | 12.7 | 13.4 | 139.3 |
| Precipitation | | | | | | | | | | | | | | |
| .01 inches or more | 37 | 5.0 | 5.5 | 6.9 | 7.9 | 10.9 | 9.3 | 9.6 | 7.7 | 6.7 | 4.9 | 4.7 | 4.4 | 83.4 |
| Snow, Ice pellets | | | | | | | | | | | | | | |
| 1.0 inches or more | 37 | 1.6 | 1.7 | 1.9 | 0.8 | 0.1 | 0.0 | 0.0 | 0.0 | 0.* | 0.4 | 1.1 | 1.4 | 9.1 |
| Thunderstorms | 37 | 0.1 | 0.1 | 0.7 | 2.7 | 6.5 | 9.9 | 10.2 | 8.3 | 4.2 | 1.1 | 0.2 | 0.0 | 44.0 |
| Heavy Fog Visibility | | | | | | | | | | | | | | |
| 1/4 mile or less | 37 | 1.2 | 2.1 | 2.0 | 0.8 | 0.8 | 0.8 | 1.0 | 1.7 | 2.0 | 2.1 | 2.3 | 1.5 | 18.4 |
| Temperature °F | | | | | | | | | | | | | | |
| -Maximum | | | | | | | | | | | | | | |
| 90° and above | 25 | 0.0 | 0.0 | 0.0 | 0.4 | 0.9 | 5.8 | 13.6 | 11.1 | 3.4 | 0.2 | 0.0 | 0.0 | 35.4 |
| 32° and below | 25 | 13.0 | 8.6 | 4.1 | 0.2 | 0.* | 0.0 | 0.0 | 0.0 | 0.0 | 0.1 | 3.8 | 10.7 | 40.6 |
| -Minimum | | | | | | | | | | | | | | |
| 32° and below | 25 | 31.0 | 27.9 | 27.0 | 12.8 | 2.4 | 0.* | 0.0 | 0.0 | 2.4 | 14.5 | 27.8 | 30.8 | 176.6 |
| 0° and below | 25 | 8.7 | 3.9 | 0.7 | 0.0 | 0.0 | 0.0 | 0.0 | 0.0 | 0.0 | 0.0 | 0.8 | 4.8 | 18.8 |
| **AVG. STATION PRESS.(mb)** | 17 | 919.0 | 918.5 | 915.1 | 915.4 | 915.3 | 916.4 | 918.1 | 918.3 | 918.7 | 919.2 | 918.0 | 918.7 | 917.6 |
| **RELATIVE HUMIDITY (%)** | | | | | | | | | | | | | | |
| Hour 00 | 25 | 76 | 76 | 73 | 71 | 73 | 74 | 73 | 75 | 74 | 72 | 76 | 77 | 74 |
| Hour 06 (Local Time) | 25 | 78 | 78 | 79 | 79 | 82 | 83 | 82 | 84 | 82 | 80 | 80 | 79 | 81 |
| Hour 12 | 25 | 63 | 59 | 52 | 46 | 50 | 51 | 50 | 50 | 48 | 46 | 55 | 61 | 53 |
| Hour 18 | 25 | 64 | 57 | 48 | 42 | 47 | 47 | 47 | 47 | 46 | 47 | 57 | 63 | 51 |
| **PRECIPITATION (inches):** | | | | | | | | | | | | | | |
| Water Equivalent | | | | | | | | | | | | | | |
| -Normal | | 0.40 | 0.55 | 1.12 | 1.85 | 3.36 | 3.72 | 2.98 | 1.92 | 1.67 | 0.91 | 0.56 | 0.43 | 19.47 |
| -Maximum Monthly | 38 | 1.12 | 1.98 | 2.89 | 5.01 | 8.01 | 6.81 | 7.05 | 5.36 | 6.03 | 2.91 | 2.89 | 1.22 | 8.01 |
| -Year | | 1960 | 1978 | 1977 | 1984 | 1962 | 1965 | 1979 | 1957 | 1963 | 1969 | 1979 | 1977 | MAY 1962 |
| -Minimum Monthly | 38 | T | 0.01 | 0.09 | 0.10 | 0.77 | 0.33 | 0.42 | 0.06 | T | 0.05 | 0.02 | T | T |
| -Year | | 1964 | 1954 | 1967 | 1989 | 1966 | 1952 | 1955 | 1967 | 1953 | 1988 | 1989 | 1988 | DEC 1988 |
| -Maximum in 24 hrs | 38 | 0.69 | 1.15 | 2.26 | 2.42 | 2.95 | 3.80 | 3.15 | 2.93 | 2.53 | 1.37 | 1.48 | 0.79 | 3.80 |
| -Year | | 1960 | 1971 | 1959 | 1971 | 1962 | 1965 | 1964 | 1957 | 1963 | 1982 | 1979 | 1978 | JUN 1965 |
| Snow, Ice pellets | | | | | | | | | | | | | | |
| -Maximum Monthly | 38 | 17.1 | 20.6 | 21.9 | 14.5 | 3.6 | 0.0 | T | 0.0 | 3.1 | 15.7 | 17.5 | 14.1 | 21.9 |
| -Year | | 1976 | 1978 | 1980 | 1984 | 1967 | | 1989 | | 1985 | 1969 | 1979 | 1973 | MAR 1980 |
| -Maximum in 24 hrs | 38 | 11.9 | 9.7 | 15.1 | 8.5 | 2.3 | 0.0 | T | 0.0 | 3.1 | 8.8 | 8.8 | 8.6 | 15.1 |
| -Year | | 1976 | 1955 | 1980 | 1984 | 1967 | | 1989 | | 1985 | 1969 | 1979 | 1968 | MAR 1980 |
| **WIND:** | | | | | | | | | | | | | | |
| Mean Speed (mph) | 37 | 9.3 | 9.9 | 11.8 | 12.7 | 11.7 | 10.4 | 9.6 | 9.4 | 9.7 | 9.6 | 9.6 | 9.1 | 10.2 |
| Prevailing Direction | | | | | | | | | | | | | | |
| through 1963 | | NW | NW | N | N | SE | SE | SE | SSE | SSE | SSE | NW | NW | NW |
| Fastest Obs. 1 Min. | | | | | | | | | | | | | | |
| -Direction (!!!) | 10 | 30 | 35 | 17 | 32 | 31 | 32 | 31 | 18 | 18 | 29 | 03 | 02 | 02 |
| -Speed (MPH) | 10 | 40 | 39 | 44 | 45 | 44 | 52 | 46 | 41 | 38 | 37 | 41 | 52 | 52 |
| -Year | | 1986 | 1981 | 1982 | 1986 | 1980 | 1981 | 1981 | 1985 | 1986 | 1989 | 1983 | 1982 | DEC 1982 |
| Peak Gust | | | | | | | | | | | | | | |
| -Direction (!!!) | 6 | NW | NW | N | S | NE | NW | N | S | S | W | N | NW | S |
| -Speed (mph) | 6 | 60 | 55 | 60 | 76 | 72 | 62 | 56 | 72 | 58 | 55 | 52 | 56 | 76 |
| -Date | 6 | 1987 | 1988 | 1987 | 1985 | 1985 | 1986 | 1989 | 1985 | 1986 | 1985 | 1989 | 1988 | APR 1985 |

See Reference Notes to this table on the following page.

## TABLE 2 — PRECIPITATION (inches)  NORTH PLATTE, NEBRASKA

| YEAR | JAN | FEB | MAR | APR | MAY | JUNE | JULY | AUG | SEP | OCT | NOV | DEC | ANNUAL |
|------|-----|-----|-----|-----|-----|------|------|-----|-----|-----|-----|-----|--------|
| 1961 | T | 0.07 | 2.24 | 2.49 | 5.15 | 2.58 | 1.23 | 1.08 | 2.78 | 0.15 | 0.50 | 0.44 | 18.71 |
| 1962 | 0.07 | 0.72 | 1.15 | 0.51 | 8.01 | 5.30 | 5.33 | 0.10 | 2.38 | 0.43 | 0.09 | 0.66 | 24.75 |
| 1963 | 0.48 | 0.15 | 0.71 | 1.09 | 3.98 | 1.82 | 1.60 | 2.18 | 6.03 | 0.67 | 0.39 | 0.24 | 19.34 |
| 1964 | T | 0.62 | 1.26 | 3.76 | 2.06 | 4.78 | 4.52 | 2.63 | 5.69 | 0.73 | 0.05 | 1.02 | 29.61 |
| 1965 | 0.61 | 0.35 | 0.25 | 1.42 | 4.18 | 6.81 | 6.68 | 1.82 | 2.09 | 0.31 | 0.04 | 0.51 | 17.57 |
| 1966 | 0.30 | 0.15 | 1.12 | 1.05 | 0.77 | 5.14 | 3.35 | 2.74 | 1.12 | 0.58 | 0.19 | 0.15 | 17.45 |
| 1967 | 0.47 | 0.03 | 0.09 | 1.03 | 3.94 | 6.05 | 3.74 | 0.06 | 1.50 | 0.82 | 0.46 | 0.87 | 17.04 |
| 1968 | 0.12 | 0.36 | 0.11 | 3.04 | 1.72 | 2.25 | 1.82 | 3.97 | 0.80 | 2.91 | 0.18 | 0.10 | 15.19 |
| 1969 | 0.94 | 0.26 | 0.17 | 0.15 | 1.35 | 4.20 | 2.52 | 1.61 | 0.80 | 1.27 | 0.91 | 0.22 | 16.21 |
| 1970 | 0.23 | 0.28 | 0.97 | 2.46 | 1.31 | 4.33 | 1.68 | 0.28 | 2.27 | | | | |
| 1971 | 0.47 | 1.28 | 0.97 | 3.94 | 2.54 | 5.84 | 3.48 | 0.91 | 2.01 | 1.75 | 0.90 | 0.16 | 24.25 |
| 1972 | 0.16 | 0.08 | 0.65 | 1.19 | 3.18 | 2.96 | 3.58 | 1.46 | 0.62 | 1.12 | 0.42 | 16.37 | |
| 1973 | 0.40 | 0.10 | 2.45 | 1.45 | 3.85 | 0.88 | 2.87 | 2.82 | 3.98 | 1.26 | 0.54 | 1.13 | 21.73 |
| 1974 | 0.27 | 0.08 | 0.42 | 1.17 | 1.64 | 3.86 | 2.27 | 1.15 | 0.24 | 0.61 | 0.04 | 0.42 | 12.17 |
| 1975 | 0.26 | 0.17 | 0.92 | 1.77 | 2.12 | 6.12 | 2.51 | 0.25 | 0.56 | 0.14 | 1.15 | 0.22 | 16.19 |
| 1976 | 0.99 | 0.14 | 2.03 | 2.80 | 2.88 | 2.43 | 0.92 | 2.87 | 2.03 | 1.18 | 0.08 | 0.01 | 18.36 |
| 1977 | 0.18 | 0.27 | 2.89 | 4.85 | 5.90 | 1.31 | 4.41 | 1.79 | 1.48 | 0.18 | 0.39 | 1.22 | 24.87 |
| 1978 | 0.52 | 1.98 | 0.40 | 1.96 | 4.84 | 1.75 | 3.70 | 1.92 | 0.33 | 0.43 | 1.03 | 0.99 | 19.85 |
| 1979 | 0.86 | 0.09 | 2.78 | 1.46 | 2.96 | 3.37 | 7.05 | 1.49 | 0.45 | 1.32 | 2.89 | 0.28 | 25.00 |
| 1980 | 0.52 | 0.82 | 2.56 | 0.77 | 2.59 | 1.89 | 0.64 | 3.04 | 0.34 | 1.00 | 0.13 | 0.02 | 14.32 |
| 1981 | 0.07 | 0.05 | 2.72 | 2.47 | 5.37 | 2.32 | 5.09 | 2.48 | 0.25 | 0.60 | 1.94 | 0.43 | 23.79 |
| 1982 | 0.20 | 0.15 | 0.99 | 1.42 | 6.32 | 2.35 | 1.78 | 1.18 | 1.26 | 2.44 | 0.73 | 1.08 | 19.90 |
| 1983 | 0.33 | 0.25 | 1.54 | 2.12 | 3.20 | 3.32 | 3.74 | 1.98 | 0.14 | 0.56 | 1.56 | 0.46 | 19.20 |
| 1984 | 0.36 | 0.87 | 1.20 | 5.01 | 2.82 | 4.37 | 0.94 | 1.38 | 0.39 | 2.41 | 0.69 | 0.72 | 21.16 |
| 1985 | 0.55 | 0.14 | 0.44 | 1.84 | 4.01 | 0.87 | 3.98 | 1.16 | 3.23 | 1.24 | 1.09 | 0.79 | 19.34 |
| 1986 | 0.02 | 1.10 | 0.70 | 3.77 | 2.80 | 1.70 | 2.57 | 1.22 | 1.02 | 1.58 | 0.19 | 0.27 | 16.94 |
| 1987 | 0.16 | 1.55 | 1.65 | 1.01 | 3.19 | 3.95 | 2.81 | 1.19 | 1.16 | 1.67 | 1.26 | 0.81 | 20.41 |
| 1988 | 0.72 | 0.03 | 0.37 | 2.02 | 3.59 | 3.12 | 3.03 | 3.93 | 1.59 | 0.05 | 0.40 | T | 18.85 |
| 1989 | 0.55 | 0.73 | 0.73 | 0.10 | 3.02 | 3.51 | 1.86 | 2.37 | 1.11 | 0.08 | 0.02 | 0.28 | 14.01 |
| 1990 | 0.27 | 0.18 | 1.75 | 1.52 | 3.65 | 1.90 | 1.99 | 1.79 | 0.31 | 1.48 | 0.87 | 0.09 | 15.80 |
| Record Mean | 0.40 | 0.49 | 0.97 | 2.06 | 3.01 | 3.22 | 2.73 | 2.17 | 1.53 | 1.04 | 0.54 | 0.50 | 18.66 |

## TABLE 3 — AVERAGE TEMPERATURE (deg. F)  NORTH PLATTE, NEBRASKA

| YEAR | JAN | FEB | MAR | APR | MAY | JUNE | JULY | AUG | SEP | OCT | NOV | DEC | ANNUAL |
|------|-----|-----|-----|-----|-----|------|------|-----|-----|-----|-----|-----|--------|
| 1961 | 26.6 | 32.2 | 37.9 | 42.8 | 55.2 | 69.0 | 73.4 | 74.8 | 57.5 | 49.3 | 33.9 | 22.5 | 47.9 |
| 1962 | 21.9 | 26.9 | 32.0 | 49.6 | 63.9 | 66.8 | 72.0 | 72.7 | 60.2 | 53.2 | 39.7 | 27.6 | 48.9 |
| 1963 | 13.1 | 32.3 | 40.8 | 50.8 | 60.5 | 72.9 | 77.5 | 73.4 | 65.9 | 58.1 | 38.8 | 21.9 | 50.5 |
| #1964 | 28.1 | 24.9 | 32.3 | 47.0 | 60.9 | 67.2 | 77.5 | 69.8 | 63.1 | 50.3 | 35.8 | 25.2 | 48.5 |
| 1965 | 26.3 | 23.4 | 25.5 | 51.4 | 60.1 | 67.1 | 73.1 | 70.5 | 53.8 | 54.0 | 40.9 | 28.9 | 47.9 |
| 1966 | 15.6 | 21.4 | 38.5 | 43.8 | 60.0 | 68.8 | 77.6 | 67.8 | 62.1 | 50.5 | 36.0 | 24.5 | 47.2 |
| 1967 | 24.9 | 30.8 | 39.9 | 49.3 | 51.9 | 64.6 | 70.3 | 68.8 | 61.2 | 49.8 | 33.9 | 22.8 | 47.3 |
| 1968 | 22.2 | 27.1 | 39.9 | 46.2 | 53.3 | 69.5 | 72.6 | 71.6 | 61.1 | 51.1 | 34.4 | 19.0 | 47.4 |
| 1969 | 16.2 | 24.2 | 29.0 | 51.4 | 61.0 | 69.0 | 73.0 | 73.6 | 65.8 | 41.7 | 38.3 | 28.4 | 47.1 |
| 1970 | 22.3 | 31.8 | 31.3 | 45.6 | 61.8 | 68.1 | 74.3 | 75.6 | 60.8 | 45.4 | 34.8 | 26.8 | 48.2 |
| 1971 | 22.1 | 24.5 | 33.4 | 48.0 | 54.7 | 70.2 | 69.8 | 72.2 | 59.7 | 49.5 | 37.1 | 27.6 | 47.4 |
| 1972 | 20.7 | 29.9 | 40.7 | 46.6 | 58.1 | 68.4 | 70.4 | 70.8 | 61.2 | 46.4 | 29.8 | 17.2 | 46.7 |
| 1973 | 21.5 | 30.3 | 40.4 | 45.8 | 56.0 | 67.7 | 72.8 | 73.7 | 58.4 | 51.7 | 35.0 | 23.2 | 48.0 |
| 1974 | 16.0 | 33.0 | 40.1 | 50.0 | 59.5 | 66.5 | 77.5 | 67.1 | 57.5 | 52.9 | 34.8 | 24.2 | 48.3 |
| 1975 | 25.7 | 23.4 | 31.5 | 46.6 | 57.1 | 65.7 | 74.6 | 73.2 | 58.5 | 50.9 | 30.2 | 26.4 | 47.0 |
| 1976 | 17.8 | 32.7 | 34.0 | 47.4 | 53.1 | 64.6 | 72.8 | 70.6 | 59.8 | 45.2 | 30.5 | 28.2 | 46.4 |
| 1977 | 16.6 | 32.0 | 37.0 | 51.7 | 63.1 | 70.5 | 74.5 | 68.5 | 63.8 | 50.0 | 35.8 | 24.9 | 49.0 |
| 1978 | 11.2 | 14.7 | 35.1 | 48.4 | 56.6 | 68.2 | 74.5 | 71.0 | 65.4 | 49.2 | 32.1 | 14.6 | 45.1 |
| 1979 | 6.0 | 17.2 | 37.0 | 48.4 | 57.4 | 68.1 | 74.1 | 72.9 | 67.1 | 53.8 | 32.2 | 34.0 | 47.3 |
| 1980 | 25.1 | 26.8 | 35.5 | 50.5 | 60.2 | 72.5 | 78.0 | 74.0 | 63.7 | 48.9 | 38.5 | 32.0 | 50.5 |
| 1981 | 29.7 | 29.1 | 40.2 | 55.8 | 54.8 | 68.6 | 73.8 | 70.1 | 63.0 | 49.0 | 39.9 | 26.7 | 50.1 |
| 1982 | 17.1 | 28.1 | 36.3 | 44.8 | 57.3 | 63.4 | 75.0 | 73.1 | 61.7 | 49.2 | 33.3 | 28.1 | 47.3 |
| 1983 | 27.1 | 35.1 | 37.2 | 42.3 | 54.0 | 65.2 | 75.3 | 78.0 | 64.8 | 51.3 | 36.7 | 7.5 | 47.9 |
| 1984 | 20.4 | 33.2 | 34.1 | 43.3 | 58.1 | 68.0 | 73.7 | 75.5 | 58.4 | 48.0 | 37.2 | 22.5 | 47.7 |
| 1985 | 18.3 | 23.1 | 40.5 | 52.2 | 60.8 | 65.4 | 75.3 | 70.1 | 59.8 | 48.6 | 24.6 | 19.2 | 46.5 |
| 1986 | 31.6 | 27.0 | 44.3 | 48.9 | 58.0 | 71.4 | 75.6 | 71.3 | 63.0 | 50.4 | 35.5 | 30.2 | 50.6 |
| 1987 | 29.5 | 35.8 | 36.7 | 51.3 | 63.1 | 70.2 | 75.7 | 70.3 | 61.3 | 47.0 | 38.2 | 27.7 | 50.6 |
| 1988 | 16.4 | 26.5 | 37.8 | 48.5 | 60.7 | 74.6 | 74.5 | 73.4 | 62.0 | 48.7 | 38.0 | 30.3 | 49.3 |
| 1989 | 30.2 | 17.8 | 35.7 | 51.1 | 59.0 | 65.8 | 74.3 | 71.7 | 61.0 | 50.7 | 37.6 | 20.6 | 48.0 |
| 1990 | 30.6 | 30.9 | 40.0 | 48.5 | 56.7 | 71.1 | 73.7 | 74.0 | 67.6 | 50.2 | 38.1 | 21.9 | 50.3 |
| Record Mean | 23.3 | 27.7 | 36.4 | 48.7 | 58.7 | 68.6 | 74.8 | 72.9 | 63.3 | 51.0 | 36.7 | 26.9 | 49.1 |
| Max | 35.7 | 40.2 | 49.3 | 61.8 | 71.1 | 81.1 | 87.7 | 86.2 | 77.6 | 66.0 | 50.2 | 39.2 | 62.2 |
| Min | 10.9 | 15.2 | 23.5 | 35.5 | 46.2 | 56.0 | 61.8 | 59.7 | 49.0 | 36.1 | 23.1 | 14.6 | 36.0 |

## REFERENCE NOTES FOR TABLES 1, 2, 3 and 6  (NORTH PLATTE, NE)

### GENERAL

T - TRACE AMOUNT
BLANK ENTRIES DENOTE MISSING/UNREPORTED DATA.
# INDICATES A STATION OR INSTRUMENT RELOCATION.

### SPECIFIC

#### TABLE 1

(a) - LENGTH OF RECORD IN YEARS. ALTHOUGH INDIVIDUAL MONTHS MAY BE MISSING.

* LESS THAN .05

NORMALS — BASED ON THE 1951-1980 RECORD PERIOD.
EXTREMES — DATES ARE THE MOST RECENT OCCURRENCE.
WIND DIR. — NUMERALS SHOW TENS OF DEGREES CLOCKWISE FROM TRUE NORTH.
"00" INDICATES CALM.
RESULTANT WIND DIRECTIONS ARE GIVEN TO WHOLE DEGREES.

#### TABLE 3
MAX AND MIN ARE LONG-TERM MEAN DAILY MAXIMUM AND MEAN DAILY MINIMUM TEMPERATURES.

### EXCEPTIONS

#### TABLES 2, 3, and 6

RECORD MEANS ARE THROUGH THE CURRENT YEAR, BEGINNING IN
1875 FOR TEMPERATURE
1875 FOR PRECIPITATION
1953 FOR SNOWFALL

**TABLE 4**  HEATING DEGREE DAYS Base 65 deg. F  NORTH PLATTE. NEBRASKA

| SEASON | JULY | AUG | SEP | OCT | NOV | DEC | JAN | FEB | MAR | APR | MAY | JUNE | TOTAL |
|---|---|---|---|---|---|---|---|---|---|---|---|---|---|
| 1961-62 | 0 | 0 | 278 | 479 | 926 | 1312 | 1333 | 1062 | 1017 | 463 | 90 | 57 | 7017 |
| 1962-63 | 3 | 4 | 171 | 363 | 755 | 1152 | 1607 | 911 | 745 | 423 | 165 | 10 | 6309 |
| 1963-64 | 0 | 1 | 65 | 219 | 780 | 1329 | 1140 | 1157 | 1006 | 534 | 190 | 63 | 6484 |
| #1964-65 | 0 | 43 | 143 | 450 | 870 | 1229 | 1189 | 1158 | 1217 | 405 | 173 | 26 | 6903 |
| 1965-66 | 0 | 11 | 345 | 335 | 718 | 1113 | 1530 | 1213 | 815 | 628 | 199 | 48 | 6955 |
| 1966-67 | 0 | 34 | 136 | 442 | 863 | 1250 | 1240 | 950 | 771 | 465 | 427 | 70 | 6648 |
| 1967-68 | 19 | 29 | 132 | 479 | 926 | 1305 | 1321 | 1096 | 770 | 558 | 363 | 26 | 7024 |
| 1968-69 | 17 | 18 | 150 | 428 | 911 | 1421 | 1509 | 1133 | 1106 | 399 | 178 | 122 | 7392 |
| 1969-70 | 1 | 0 | 45 | 716 | 795 | 1315 | 1315 | 923 | 1041 | 582 | 136 | 55 | 6738 |
| 1970-71 | 2 | 1 | 214 | 600 | 899 | 1177 | 1320 | 1127 | 974 | 501 | 311 | 13 | 7139 |
| 1971-72 | 12 | 0 | 210 | 472 | 829 | 1013 | 1368 | 1013 | 745 | 549 | 250 | 32 | 6637 |
| 1972-73 | 24 | 15 | 169 | 567 | 1047 | 1479 | 1343 | 967 | 756 | 567 | 283 | 34 | 7251 |
| 1973-74 | 10 | 0 | 219 | 407 | 892 | 1290 | 1518 | 889 | 765 | 445 | 190 | 62 | 6687 |
| 1974-75 | 0 | 40 | 256 | 373 | 900 | 1262 | 1216 | 1160 | 1032 | 558 | 247 | 62 | 7106 |
| 1975-76 | 6 | 0 | 228 | 437 | 1035 | 1191 | 1460 | 929 | 956 | 521 | 363 | 70 | 7196 |
| 1976-77 | 0 | 13 | 178 | 608 | 1028 | 1133 | 1493 | 920 | 858 | 395 | 81 | 2 | 6709 |
| 1977-78 | 2 | 34 | 96 | 458 | 869 | 1236 | 1662 | 1400 | 924 | 491 | 275 | 71 | 7518 |
| 1978-79 | 5 | 24 | 99 | 488 | 982 | 1560 | 1828 | 1335 | 862 | 491 | 259 | 56 | 7989 |
| 1979-80 | 4 | 11 | 52 | 341 | 975 | 957 | 1233 | 1102 | 909 | 439 | 166 | 10 | 6199 |
| 1980-81 | 0 | 6 | 107 | 491 | 790 | 1019 | 1089 | 1000 | 762 | 283 | 318 | 26 | 5891 |
| 1981-82 | 9 | 4 | 101 | 492 | 749 | 1179 | 1479 | 1030 | 885 | 601 | 239 | 111 | 6879 |
| 1982-83 | 0 | 18 | 160 | 484 | 946 | 1138 | 1167 | 833 | 854 | 672 | 343 | 90 | 6705 |
| 1983-84 | 2 | 0 | 128 | 419 | 840 | 1780 | 1379 | 915 | 953 | 647 | 236 | 33 | 7332 |
| 1984-85 | 0 | 0 | 247 | 519 | 829 | 1312 | 1440 | 1168 | 752 | 393 | 156 | 83 | 6899 |
| 1985-86 | 0 | 23 | 252 | 502 | 1205 | 1416 | 1029 | 1060 | 634 | 479 | 219 | 2 | 6821 |
| 1986-87 | 0 | 14 | 98 | 446 | 878 | 1074 | 1093 | 810 | 868 | 420 | 102 | 15 | 5818 |
| 1987-88 | 13 | 36 | 139 | 551 | 796 | 1152 | 1501 | 1109 | 839 | 490 | 170 | 3 | 6799 |
| 1988-89 | 0 | 13 | 128 | 498 | 803 | 1067 | 1072 | 1316 | 902 | 430 | 211 | 67 | 6507 |
| 1989-90 | 2 | 7 | 180 | 437 | 815 | 1374 | 1061 | 948 | 771 | 502 | 259 | 15 | 6371 |
| 1990-91 | 15 | 1 | 84 | 457 | 797 | 1331 | | | | | | | |

**TABLE 5**  COOLING DEGREE DAYS Base 65 deg. F  NORTH PLATTE. NEBRASKA

| YEAR | JAN | FEB | MAR | APR | MAY | JUNE | JULY | AUG | SEP | OCT | NOV | DEC | TOTAL |
|---|---|---|---|---|---|---|---|---|---|---|---|---|---|
| 1969 | 0 | 0 | 0 | 0 | 58 | 63 | 257 | 276 | 76 | 0 | 0 | 0 | 730 |
| 1970 | 0 | 0 | 0 | 4 | 48 | 155 | 300 | 341 | 96 | 0 | 0 | 0 | 944 |
| 1971 | 0 | 0 | 0 | 0 | 1 | 177 | 167 | 229 | 59 | 1 | 0 | 0 | 634 |
| 1972 | 0 | 0 | 0 | 0 | 43 | 137 | 199 | 202 | 64 | 0 | 0 | 0 | 645 |
| 1973 | 0 | 0 | 0 | 0 | 11 | 121 | 260 | 278 | 29 | 3 | 0 | 0 | 702 |
| 1974 | 0 | 0 | 0 | 5 | 24 | 117 | 394 | 115 | 40 | 3 | 0 | 0 | 698 |
| 1975 | 0 | 0 | 0 | 10 | 11 | 89 | 311 | 260 | 39 | 7 | 0 | 0 | 727 |
| 1976 | 0 | 0 | 0 | 0 | 5 | 62 | 247 | 192 | 27 | 0 | 0 | 0 | 533 |
| 1977 | 0 | 0 | 0 | 2 | 26 | 174 | 305 | 149 | 64 | 0 | 0 | 0 | 720 |
| 1978 | 0 | 0 | 0 | 0 | 1 | 21 | 174 | 307 | 218 | .5 | 0 | 0 | 843 |
| 1979 | 0 | 0 | 0 | 0 | 27 | 156 | 294 | 262 | 123 | 0 | 0 | 0 | 862 |
| 1980 | 0 | 0 | 0 | 10 | 27 | 243 | 411 | 289 | 74 | 0 | 0 | 0 | 1054 |
| 1981 | 0 | 0 | 0 | 10 | 9 | 141 | 288 | 168 | 47 | 1 | 0 | 0 | 664 |
| 1982 | 0 | 0 | 0 | 0 | 0 | 70 | 314 | 276 | 68 | 0 | 0 | 0 | 736 |
| 1983 | 0 | 0 | 0 | 0 | 8 | 103 | 331 | 412 | 128 | 1 | 0 | 0 | 983 |
| 1984 | 0 | 0 | 0 | 0 | 27 | 129 | 281 | 331 | 55 | 2 | 0 | 0 | 825 |
| 1985 | 0 | 0 | 0 | 14 | 32 | 100 | 326 | 189 | 100 | 0 | 0 | 0 | 761 |
| 1986 | 0 | 0 | 0 | 3 | 11 | 201 | 334 | 217 | 43 | 0 | 0 | 0 | 809 |
| 1987 | 0 | 0 | 0 | 16 | 48 | 176 | 352 | 208 | 35 | 0 | 0 | 0 | 835 |
| 1988 | 0 | 0 | 0 | 1 | 41 | 293 | 301 | 282 | 46 | 0 | 0 | 0 | 964 |
| 1989 | 0 | 0 | 0 | 21 | 35 | 99 | 295 | 220 | 67 | 2 | 0 | 0 | 739 |
| 1990 | 0 | 0 | 0 | 15 | 10 | 205 | 291 | 289 | 165 | 5 | 0 | 0 | 980 |

**TABLE 6**  SNOWFALL (inches)  NORTH PLATTE. NEBRASKA

| SEASON | JULY | AUG | SEP | OCT | NOV | DEC | JAN | FEB | MAR | APR | MAY | JUNE | TOTAL |
|---|---|---|---|---|---|---|---|---|---|---|---|---|---|
| 1961-62 | 0.0 | 0.0 | T | 0.0 | 4.0 | 7.3 | 1.7 | 10.7 | 7.1 | T | 0.0 | 0.0 | 30.8 |
| 1962-63 | 0.0 | 0.0 | 0.0 | 0.0 | 1.5 | 6.1 | 8.7 | 0.9 | 9.5 | 0.2 | 0.0 | 0.0 | 26.9 |
| 1963-64 | 0.0 | 0.0 | 0.0 | 0.0 | T | 5.3 | T | 8.6 | 5.4 | 5.6 | 0.0 | 0.0 | 24.9 |
| 1964-65 | 0.0 | 0.0 | 0.0 | 0.0 | T | 1.8 | 9.2 | 7.2 | 5.0 | T | 0.0 | 0.0 | 23.2 |
| 1965-66 | 0.0 | 0.0 | T | 0.0 | 0.5 | 6.3 | 10.5 | 1.7 | 9.6 | 5.0 | 0.2 | 0.0 | 33.8 |
| 1966-67 | 0.0 | 0.0 | 0.0 | 1.4 | 0.5 | 8.5 | 9.3 | 0.8 | 0.7 | 4.5 | 3.6 | 0.0 | 29.3 |
| 1967-68 | 0.0 | 0.0 | 0.0 | T | 2.9 | 3.4 | 1.6 | 3.0 | 0.8 | 2.2 | 0.0 | 0.0 | 13.9 |
| 1968-69 | 0.0 | 0.0 | 0.0 | 0.0 | 0.3 | 10.3 | 12.4 | 3.2 | 1.8 | T | T | 0.0 | 28.0 |
| 1969-70 | 0.0 | 0.0 | 0.0 | 15.7 | 0.8 | 1.8 | 3.6 | 4.0 | 18.4 | 0.4 | 0.0 | 0.0 | 44.7 |
| 1970-71 | 0.0 | 0.0 | 0.0 | 9.0 | 3.6 | 1.8 | 5.6 | 2.7 | 19.0 | 0.8 | T | 0.0 | 42.5 |
| 1971-72 | 0.0 | 0.0 | 0.0 | 2.0 | 2.5 | 2.1 | 2.6 | 1.9 | 0.1 | 0.1 | 0.0 | 0.0 | 11.3 |
| 1972-73 | 0.0 | 0.0 | 0.0 | 0.8 | 8.0 | 8.7 | 3.8 | 0.4 | 1.6 | 1.7 | 0.0 | 0.0 | 25.0 |
| 1973-74 | 0.0 | 0.0 | 0.0 | T | 4.3 | 14.1 | 4.2 | 1.0 | 2.3 | 0.7 | 0.0 | 0.0 | 26.6 |
| 1974-75 | 0.0 | 0.0 | 0.0 | 0.0 | T | 4.5 | 2.2 | 2.6 | 3.9 | 3.0 | 0.0 | 0.0 | 16.2 |
| 1975-76 | 0.0 | 0.0 | 0.0 | 0.8 | 10.9 | 1.2 | 17.1 | 1.6 | 5.2 | T | 0.0 | 0.0 | 36.8 |
| 1976-77 | 0.0 | 0.0 | 0.0 | 1.0 | 0.6 | T | 2.5 | 2.2 | 9.9 | 8.1 | 0.0 | 0.0 | 24.3 |
| 1977-78 | 0.0 | 0.0 | 0.0 | T | 0.3 | 6.4 | 6.2 | 20.6 | 2.0 | T | T | 0.0 | 35.5 |
| 1978-79 | 0.0 | 0.0 | 0.0 | T | 7.6 | 10.3 | 6.3 | 0.3 | 5.9 | 2.3 | T | 0.0 | 32.7 |
| 1979-80 | 0.0 | 0.0 | 0.0 | 2.9 | 17.5 | 2.3 | 5.2 | 9.1 | 21.9 | 7.4 | 0.0 | 0.0 | 66.3 |
| 1980-81 | 0.0 | 0.0 | 0.0 | 0.6 | 1.2 | T | 0.7 | 0.5 | 0.4 | 0.0 | 0.0 | 0.0 | 3.9 |
| 1981-82 | 0.0 | 0.0 | 0.0 | T | 5.3 | 6.4 | 4.4 | 1.7 | 6.4 | 0.9 | 0.0 | 0.0 | 25.1 |
| 1982-83 | 0.0 | 0.0 | 0.0 | 1.0 | 2.0 | 9.7 | 1.6 | 0.1 | 5.4 | 0.0 | 0.0 | 0.0 | 25.7 |
| 1983-84 | 0.0 | 0.0 | T | 0.0 | 12.1 | 7.3 | 5.3 | 9.6 | 8.8 | 14.5 | 0.2 | 0.0 | 57.8 |
| 1984-85 | 0.0 | 0.0 | 0.0 | 0.3 | 0.9 | 8.7 | 8.5 | 0.8 | 2.1 | 0.0 | 0.0 | 0.0 | 21.3 |
| 1985-86 | 0.0 | 0.0 | 3.1 | T | 13.0 | 8.1 | 0.2 | 8.7 | 3.8 | T | 0.0 | 0.0 | 36.9 |
| 1986-87 | 0.0 | 0.0 | 0.0 | 2.0 | 1.0 | 2.6 | 1.6 | 9.2 | 7.2 | 0.1 | 0.0 | 0.0 | 23.7 |
| 1987-88 | 0.0 | 0.0 | 0.0 | 1.3 | 8.2 | 7.2 | 12.6 | 0.6 | 3.8 | 2.1 | 0.0 | 0.0 | 35.8 |
| 1988-89 | 0.0 | 0.0 | 0.0 | T | 2.5 | T | 6.1 | 10.6 | 4.3 | 0.3 | 0.0 | 0.0 | 23.8 |
| 1989-90 | T. | 0.0 | T | T | T | 2.2 | 5.9 | 1.9 | 5.3 | 0.3 | T | T | 15.6 |
| 1990-91 | 0.0 | 0.0 | 0.0 | 2.0 | 9.7 | 0.8 | | | | | | | |
| Record Mean | T | 0.0 | 0.1 | 1.3 | 4.1 | 4.8 | 5.3 | 5.0 | 7.0 | 2.8 | 0.2 | T | 30.6 |

See Reference Notes, relative to all above tables, on preceding page.

Omaha, Nebraska, is situated on the west bank of the Missouri River. The river level at Omaha is normally about 965 feet above sea level and the rolling hills in and around Omaha rise to about 1,300 feet above sea level. The climate is typically continental with relatively warm summers and cold, dry winters. It is situated midway between two distinctive climatic zones, the humid east and the dry west. Fluctuations between these two zones produce weather conditions for periods that are characteristic of either zone, or combinations of both. Omaha is also affected by most low pressure systems that cross the country. This causes periodic and rapid changes in weather, especially during the winter months.

Most of the precipitation in Omaha falls during sharp showers or thunderstorms, and these occur mostly during the growing season from April to September. Of the total precipitation, about 75 percent falls during this six-month period. The rain occurs mostly as evening or nighttime showers and thunderstorms. Although winters are relatively cold, precipitation is light, with only 10 percent of the total annual precipitation falling during the winter months.

Sunshine is fairly abundant, ranging around 50 percent of the possible in the winter to 75 percent of the possible in the summer.

## TABLE 1     NORMALS, MEANS AND EXTREMES

OMAHA (EPPLEY AIRFIELD), NEBRASKA

LATITUDE: 41°18'N    LONGITUDE: 95°54'W    ELEVATION: FT. GRND 997 BARO 985    TIME ZONE: CENTRAL    WBAN: 14942

| | (a) | JAN | FEB | MAR | APR | MAY | JUNE | JULY | AUG | SEP | OCT | NOV | DEC | YEAR |
|---|---|---|---|---|---|---|---|---|---|---|---|---|---|---|
| **TEMPERATURE °F:** | | | | | | | | | | | | | | |
| Normals | | | | | | | | | | | | | | |
|  -Daily Maximum | | 30.2 | 37.3 | 47.7 | 64.0 | 74.7 | 84.2 | 88.5 | 86.2 | 77.5 | 67.0 | 50.3 | 36.9 | 62.0 |
|  -Daily Minimum | | 10.2 | 17.1 | 26.9 | 40.3 | 51.8 | 61.7 | 66.8 | 64.2 | 54.0 | 42.0 | 28.6 | 17.4 | 40.1 |
|  -Monthly | | 20.2 | 27.2 | 37.3 | 52.2 | 63.3 | 73.0 | 77.7 | 75.2 | 65.8 | 54.5 | 39.5 | 27.2 | 51.1 |
| Extremes | | | | | | | | | | | | | | |
|  -Record Highest | 53 | 69 | 78 | 89 | 97 | 99 | 105 | 114 | 110 | 104 | 96 | 80 | 72 | 114 |
|  -Year | | 1944 | 1972 | 1986 | 1989 | 1939 | 1953 | 1936 | 1936 | 1939 | 1938 | 1980 | 1939 | JUL 1936 |
|  -Record Lowest | 53 | -23 | -21 | -16 | 5 | 27 | 38 | 44 | 43 | 25 | 13 | -9 | -23 | -23 |
|  -Year | | 1982 | 1981 | 1948 | 1975 | 1980 | 1983 | 1972 | 1967 | 1984 | 1972 | 1964 | 1989 | DEC 1989 |
| **NORMAL DEGREE DAYS:** | | | | | | | | | | | | | | |
| Heating (base 65°F) | | 1389 | 1058 | 859 | 390 | 130 | 16 | 0 | 0 | 73 | 342 | 765 | 1172 | 6194 |
| Cooling (base 65°F) | | 0 | 0 | 0 | 6 | 77 | 256 | 394 | 320 | 97 | 16 | 0 | 0 | 1166 |
| **% OF POSSIBLE SUNSHINE** | | | | | | | | | | | | | | |
| **MEAN SKY COVER (tenths)** | | | | | | | | | | | | | | |
| Sunrise - Sunset | 44 | 6.1 | 6.3 | 6.6 | 6.3 | 6.2 | 5.6 | 4.8 | 4.8 | 4.9 | 4.8 | 6.0 | 6.4 | 5.7 |
| **MEAN NUMBER OF DAYS:** | | | | | | | | | | | | | | |
| Sunrise to Sunset | | | | | | | | | | | | | | |
|  -Clear | 44 | 9.0 | 7.5 | 7.0 | 7.5 | 7.4 | 8.4 | 11.7 | 12.5 | 12.4 | 13.0 | 8.8 | 8.0 | 113.3 |
|  -Partly Cloudy | 44 | 7.9 | 7.4 | 8.1 | 8.6 | 9.9 | 11.2 | 12.2 | 10.1 | 7.4 | 8.1 | 7.4 | 7.5 | 105.9 |
|  -Cloudy | 44 | 14.1 | 13.3 | 15.9 | 13.9 | 13.7 | 10.4 | 7.1 | 8.4 | 10.2 | 9.9 | 13.7 | 15.4 | 146.1 |
| Precipitation | | | | | | | | | | | | | | |
|  .01 inches or more | 53 | 6.3 | 6.6 | 8.5 | 9.5 | 11.6 | 10.5 | 8.9 | 9.1 | 8.5 | 6.5 | 5.5 | 6.3 | 97.9 |
| Snow, Ice pellets | | | | | | | | | | | | | | |
|  1.0 inches or more | 54 | 2.3 | 1.9 | 2.1 | 0.4 | 0.* | 0.0 | 0.0 | 0.0 | 0.0 | 0.1 | 0.8 | 1.8 | 9.4 |
| Thunderstorms | 54 | 0.1 | 0.4 | 1.5 | 3.9 | 7.3 | 9.3 | 8.1 | 7.9 | 5.3 | 2.4 | 0.8 | 0.2 | 47.2 |
| Heavy Fog Visibility | | | | | | | | | | | | | | |
|  1/4 mile or less | 54 | 1.8 | 2.0 | 1.4 | 0.5 | 0.8 | 0.4 | 0.5 | 1.5 | 1.4 | 1.5 | 1.6 | 2.1 | 15.4 |
| Temperature °F | | | | | | | | | | | | | | |
|  -Maximum | | | | | | | | | | | | | | |
|   90° and above | 25 | 0.0 | 0.0 | 0.0 | 0.6 | 1.5 | 7.2 | 13.8 | 9.0 | 2.6 | 0.2 | 0.0 | 0.0 | 35.0 |
|   32° and below | 25 | 14.7 | 10.4 | 3.7 | 0.1 | 0.0 | 0.0 | 0.0 | 0.0 | 0.0 | 0.0 | 2.4 | 11.9 | 43.3 |
|  -Minimum | | | | | | | | | | | | | | |
|   32° and below | 25 | 30.1 | 26.2 | 21.4 | 6.6 | 0.4 | 0.0 | 0.0 | 0.0 | 0.5 | 6.0 | 20.2 | 29.3 | 140.8 |
|   0° and below | 25 | 7.4 | 3.8 | 0.4 | 0.0 | 0.0 | 0.0 | 0.0 | 0.0 | 0.0 | 0.0 | 0.3 | 3.4 | 15.3 |
| **AVG. STATION PRESS.(mb)** | 7 | 982.5 | 983.8 | 978.8 | 978.4 | 977.5 | 977.9 | 979.6 | 980.2 | 981.2 | 983.0 | 981.3 | 983.1 | 980.6 |
| **RELATIVE HUMIDITY (%)** | | | | | | | | | | | | | | |
| Hour 00 | 25 | 75 | 76 | 72 | 68 | 72 | 75 | 78 | 80 | 82 | 76 | 76 | 78 | 76 |
| Hour 06 (Local Time) | 25 | 77 | 79 | 78 | 76 | 79 | 82 | 84 | 86 | 87 | 82 | 81 | 80 | 81 |
| Hour 12 | 25 | 65 | 63 | 57 | 52 | 54 | 55 | 57 | 59 | 60 | 55 | 62 | 68 | 59 |
| Hour 18 | 25 | 67 | 63 | 54 | 48 | 50 | 52 | 55 | 58 | 60 | 57 | 65 | 71 | 58 |
| **PRECIPITATION (inches):** | | | | | | | | | | | | | | |
| Water Equivalent | | | | | | | | | | | | | | |
|  -Normal | | 0.77 | 0.91 | 1.91 | 2.94 | 4.33 | 4.08 | 3.62 | 4.10 | 3.50 | 2.09 | 1.32 | 0.77 | 30.34 |
|  -Maximum Monthly | 53 | 3.70 | 2.97 | 5.96 | 6.45 | 10.33 | 10.81 | 9.60 | 10.16 | 13.75 | 4.99 | 4.70 | 5.42 | 13.75 |
|  -Year | | 1949 | 1965 | 1973 | 1951 | 1959 | 1947 | 1958 | 1987 | 1965 | 1961 | 1983 | 1984 | SEP 1965 |
|  -Minimum Monthly | 53 | T | 0.09 | 0.12 | 0.23 | 0.56 | 1.03 | 0.39 | 0.61 | 0.41 | T | 0.03 | T | T |
|  -Year | | 1986 | 1981 | 1956 | 1936 | 1948 | 1972 | 1983 | 1953 | 1952 | 1976 | 1943 | 1986 | JAN 1986 |
|  -Maximum in 24 hrs | 47 | 1.52 | 2.24 | 1.45 | 2.56 | 4.16 | 3.48 | 3.37 | 5.27 | 6.47 | 3.13 | 2.53 | 3.03 | 6.47 |
|  -Year | | 1967 | 1954 | 1959 | 1938 | 1987 | 1942 | 1958 | 1987 | 1965 | 1968 | 1948 | 1984 | SEP 1965 |
| Snow, Ice pellets | | | | | | | | | | | | | | |
|  -Maximum Monthly | 54 | 25.7 | 25.4 | 27.2 | 8.6 | 2.0 | 0.0 | 0.0 | 0.0 | T | 7.2 | 12.0 | 19.9 | 27.2 |
|  -Year | | 1936 | 1965 | 1948 | 1945 | 1945 | | | | 1985 | 1941 | 1957 | 1969 | MAR 1948 |
|  -Maximum in 24 hrs | 47 | 13.1 | 18.3 | 13.0 | 8.6 | 2.0 | T | 0.0 | 0.0 | T | 7.2 | 8.7 | 10.2 | 18.3 |
|  -Year | | 1949 | 1965 | 1948 | 1945 | 1945 | 1985 | | | 1985 | 1941 | 1957 | 1969 | FEB 1965 |
| **WIND:** | | | | | | | | | | | | | | |
| Mean Speed (mph) | 53 | 10.9 | 11.1 | 12.3 | 12.7 | 10.9 | 10.1 | 8.9 | 8.9 | 9.5 | 9.8 | 10.9 | 10.7 | 10.6 |
| Prevailing Direction | | | | | | | | | | | | | | |
|  through 1963 | | NNW | NNW | NNW | NNW | SSE | SSE | SSE | SSE | SSE | SSE | SSE | SSE | SSE |
| Fastest Mile | | | | | | | | | | | | | | |
|  -Direction (!!!) | 41 | NW | NW | NW | NW | NW | N | N | N | E | NW | NW | NW | N |
|  -Speed (MPH) | 41 | 57 | 57 | 73 | 65 | 73 | 72 | 109 | 66 | 47 | 62 | 56 | 52 | 109 |
|  -Year | | 1938 | 1947 | 1950 | 1937 | 1936 | 1942 | 1936 | 1944 | 1948 | 1966 | 1951 | 1938 | JUL 1936 |
| Peak Gust | | | | | | | | | | | | | | |
|  -Direction (!!!) | | | | | | | | | | | | | | |
|  -Speed (mph) | | | | | | | | | | | | | | |
|  -Date | | | | | | | | | | | | | | |

**See Reference Notes to this table on the following page.**

## TABLE 2 — PRECIPITATION (inches)    OMAHA (NORTH), NEBRASKA

| YEAR | JAN | FEB | MAR | APR | MAY | JUNE | JULY | AUG | SEP | OCT | NOV | DEC | ANNUAL |
|---|---|---|---|---|---|---|---|---|---|---|---|---|---|
| 1961 | 0.19 | 0.87 | 3.21 | 1.81 | 4.15 | 3.70 | 2.75 | 2.60 | 4.74 | 3.95 | .38 | 1.18 | 31.53 |
| 1962 | 0.36 | 1.89 | 1.39 | 0.51 | 3.98 | 3.02 | 7.10 | 5.59 | 4.08 | 1.77 | .71 | 0.64 | 31.04 |
| 1963 | 0.92 | 0.38 | 3.77 | 2.43 | 1.52 | 6.97 | 1.32 | 3.62 | 2.23 | 1.12 | .31 | 0.47 | 25.06 |
| 1964 | 0.30 | 0.34 | 1.50 | 5.42 | 5.43 | 6.30 | 3.90 | 3.71 | 3.25 | 0.36 | .84 | 0.79 | 32.14 |
| 1965 | 0.51 | 2.86 | 2.40 | 3.27 | 6.89 | 3.72 | 4.42 | 2.17 | 14.10 | 0.88 | .33 | 0.83 | 43.38 |
| 1966 | 0.78 | 0.42 | 0.87 | 0.89 | 5.04 | 6.12 | 3.41 | 3.94 | 1.82 | 0.79 | .13 | 0.53 | 24.74 |
| 1967 | 0.91 | 0.18 | 0.71 | 2.41 | 2.74 | 7.85 | 2.00 | 1.99 | 3.94 | 1.80 | .29 | 0.87 | 25.69 |
| 1968 | 0.42 | 0.09 | 0.82 | 4.43 | 4.64 | 3.55 | 3.19 | 3.62 | 4.33 | 4.40 | .35 | 1.78 | 32.62 |
| 1969 | 1.06 | 1.47 | 1.04 | 2.89 | 3.64 | 3.01 | 6.00 | 4.60 | 1.32 | 2.45 | .10 | 1.80 | 29.38 |
| 1970 | 0.25 | 0.15 | 0.89 | 2.43 | 3.31 | 2.41 | 4.25 | 3.43 | 3.52 | 4.09 | .03 | 0.13 | 25.89 |
| 1971 | 1.04 | 2.42 | 0.82 | 0.67 | 7.03 | 2.29 | 1.71 | 0.63 | 1.26 | 4.87 | .28 | 0.72 | 25.74 |
| 1972 | 0.40 | 0.29 | 1.28 | 4.65 | 5.37 | 0.95 | 5.63 | 2.78 | 4.54 | 3.61 | .22 | 1.63 | 34.35 |
| 1973 | 1.61 | 0.82 | 5.17 | 2.44 | 6.68 | 1.86 | 5.66 | 0.74 | 6.97 | 2.88 | .53 | 1.67 | 38.03 |
| 1974 | 0.64 | 0.20 | 0.70 |  | 2.57 | 5.68 | 0.10 | 4.98 | 1.89 | 3.17 |  |  | 23.58 |
| 1975 | 1.85 | 1.06 | 1.88 | 3.15 | 3.98 | 3.36 | 0.29 | 1.96 | 2.30 | 0.08 | .73 | 0.94 |  |
| 1976 | 0.15 | 1.67 | 2.04 | 2.60 | 4.07 | 2.96 | 0.86 | 0.73 | 2.40 | 0.88 | .04 | 0.21 | 18.61 |
| 1977 | 0.75 | 0.17 | 3.84 | 2.26 | 5.59 | 2.19 | 7.28 | 7.13 | 5.33 | 4.66 | .70 | 0.62 | 41.52 |
| 1978 | 0.20 | 1.35 | 1.21 | 4.33 | 3.39 | 1.84 | 3.35 | 2.46 | 4.64 | 0.63 | .12 | 0.71 | 25.23 |
| 1979 | 1.22 | 0.38 | 4.13 | 2.70 | 2.99 | 3.55 | 2.22 | 2.54 | 2.31 | 4.46 | .58 | 0.22 | 28.30 |
| 1980 | 0.61 | 0.75 | 1.55 | 1.32 | 1.87 | 7.54 | 2.48 | 7.72 | 1.40 | 3.43 | .12 | 0.33 | 29.12 |
| 1981 | 0.30 | 0.17 | 0.93 | 1.69 | 3.90 | 1.99 | 4.45 | 7.92 | 1.49 | 1.74 | 3.61 | 0.60 | 28.79 |
| 1982 | 1.33 | 0.24 | 3.22 | 1.79 | 9.00 | 3.97 | 2.15 | 3.03 | 3.96 | 1.84 | 2.05 | 1.68 | 34.26 |
| 1983 | 1.14 | 1.03 | 5.27 | 2.02 | 4.82 | 4.93 | 1.15 | 1.03 | 2.84 | 1.91 | .11 | 0.69 | 31.94 |
| 1984 | 0.32 | 0.82 | 2.74 | 7.12 | 3.96 | 8.16 | 1.18 | 0.88 | 3.42 | 4.50 | .83 | 4.45 | 38.38 |
| 1985 | 0.35 | 0.73 | 1.62 | 2.44 | 4.16 | 2.52 | 2.71 | 1.55 | 2.84 | 1.94 | .65 | 0.34 | 21.85 |
| 1986 | T | 0.97 | 3.00 | 6.89 | 3.98 | 3.18 | 2.64 | 3.41 | 6.46 | 5.34 | .59 | 0.68 | 37.14 |
| 1987 | 0.03 | 0.60 | 4.16 | 2.43 | 6.08 | 1.90 | 4.68 | 7.44 | 1.58 | 1.65 | .95 | 0.75 | 32.25 |
| 1988 | 0.43 | 0.18 | 0.07 | 1.87 | 5.49 | 2.89 | 2.59 | 1.46 | 2.22 | 3.58 | .89 | 0.78 | 21.34 |
| 1989 | 0.89 | 0.64 | 0.31 | 2.27 | 0.55 | 4.38 | 3.18 | 2.22 | 6.14 | 0.11 | .03 | 0.50 | 22.35 |
| 1990 | 0.63 | 0.41 | 3.22 | 0.34 | 4.04 | 4.19 | 5.59 | 0.84 | 0.96 | 1.86 | .10 | 0.75 | 23.93 |
| Record Mean | 0.68 | 0.79 | 2.07 | 2.60 | 4.36 | 4.04 | 3.48 | 3.62 | 3.56 | 2.23 | .27 | 0.84 | 29.56 |

## TABLE 3 — AVERAGE TEMPERATURE (deg. F)    OMAHA (NORTH), NEBRASKA

| YEAR | JAN | FEB | MAR | APR | MAY | JUNE | JULY | AUG | SEP | OCT | NOV | DEC | ANNUAL |
|---|---|---|---|---|---|---|---|---|---|---|---|---|---|
| 1961 | 22.2 | 29.6 | 37.7 | 45.8 | 58.5 | 69.8 | 74.6 | 73.4 | 60.8 | 54.6 | 35.5 | 18.3 | 48.5 |
| 1962 | 16.2 | 22.9 | 29.7 | 49.6 | 68.5 | 70.1 | 73.4 | 73.1 | 61.6 | 55.7 | 40.8 | 26.3 | 49.0 |
| 1963 | 11.8 | 25.4 | 41.3 | 52.9 | 61.4 | 74.4 | 76.4 | 73.3 | 66.6 | 64.1 | 43.3 | 17.0 | 50.7 |
| 1964 | 28.0 | 29.2 | 32.3 | 51.1 | 66.1 | 69.8 | 77.7 | 68.9 | 63.4 | 52.7 | 39.7 | 22.3 | 50.1 |
| 1965 | 20.5 | 20.1 | 24.1 | 50.7 | 64.7 | 69.6 | 73.9 | 72.1 | 58.0 | 56.5 | 40.4 | 34.4 | 48.8 |
| 1966 | 15.5 | 25.8 | 41.4 | 45.4 | 59.8 | 70.3 | 74.6 | 70.1 | 61.8 | 53.2 | 37.7 | 25.6 | 48.7 |
| 1967 | 22.8 | 24.0 | 41.6 | 52.0 | 57.6 | 69.1 | 72.8 | 71.0 | 62.5 | 51.4 | 37.4 | 27.1 | 49.1 |
| 1968 | 21.3 | 25.4 | 43.8 | 51.2 | 56.9 | 72.5 | 74.8 | 73.5 | 63.7 | 54.4 | 38.1 | 21.7 | 49.6 |
| 1969 | 16.1 | 25.5 | 28.8 | 51.8 | 62.4 | 66.9 | 76.2 | 74.0 | 66.2 | 48.3 | 37.7 | 23.2 | 48.3 |
| 1970 | 13.7 | 29.8 | 33.2 | 51.1 | 66.1 | 72.2 | 74.9 | 74.6 | 64.5 | 50.4 | 38.2 | 27.0 | 49.5 |
| 1971 | 15.7 | 23.0 | 34.4 | 52.7 | 58.4 | 75.8 | 71.7 | 73.4 | 66.4 | 56.6 | 39.0 | 27.3 | 49.5 |
| 1972 | 18.7 | 23.8 | 39.1 | 49.6 | 61.6 | 71.4 | 73.0 | 72.2 | 64.4 | 49.1 | 35.7 | 20.2 | 48.2 |
| 1973 | 22.6 | 27.0 | 42.8 | 49.2 | 59.5 | 72.7 | 73.9 | 76.3 | 62.9 | 56.8 | 39.2 | 22.4 | 50.4 |
| 1974 | 18.4 | 29.7 | 41.2 |  |  | 69.6 | 81.8 | 69.5 | 59.9 | 53.9 |  |  |  |
| 1975 | 21.7 | 20.5 | 29.8 | 46.9 | 64.9 | 70.7 | 77.4 | 77.5 | 61.3 | 57.7 | 40.0 | 28.3 | 49.7 |
| 1976 | 23.6 | 35.7 | 38.6 | 54.6 | 59.6 | 71.5 | 77.5 | 75.9 | 66.0 | 48.2 | 32.7 | 23.5 | 50.6 |
| 1977 | 11.7 | 31.4 | 43.3 | 57.2 | 68.0 | 72.9 | 78.7 | 70.7 | 65.9 | 52.0 | 37.9 | 23.9 | 51.1 |
| 1978 | 10.0 | 13.5 | 33.9 | 50.5 | 67.0 | 72.4 | 75.0 | 74.0 | 69.7 | 52.5 | 37.0 | 21.0 | 47.5 |
| 1979 | 7.9 | 13.6 | 35.0 | 47.6 | 59.8 | 70.8 | 74.3 | 74.1 | 67.9 | 53.3 | 36.9 | 31.9 | 47.8 |
| 1980 | 23.9 | 22.0 | 34.3 | 52.5 | 63.5 | 72.4 | 79.3 | 76.4 | 67.1 | 50.8 | 42.4 | 27.5 | 51.0 |
| 1981 | 27.3 | 30.5 | 42.9 | 58.4 | 60.0 | 73.7 | 76.9 | 71.5 | 65.7 | 50.9 | 42.2 | 24.5 | 52.1 |
| 1982 | 10.2 | 24.1 | 36.0 | 47.9 | 63.1 | 66.6 | 76.8 | 72.5 | 64.0 | 54.4 | 36.8 | 29.7 | 48.5 |
| 1983 | 25.8 | 31.0 | 37.6 | 43.9 | 57.5 | 70.6 | 79.5 | 81.8 | 68.0 | 53.2 | 38.7 | 7.8 | 49.6 |
| 1984 | 21.5 | 33.9 | 30.8 | 47.0 | 58.8 | 72.3 | 75.9 | 77.3 | 62.8 | 53.2 | 40.5 | 26.8 | 50.1 |
| 1985 | 18.6 | 24.1 | 43.6 | 55.6 | 65.2 | 68.4 | 75.8 | 70.8 | 62.9 | 53.8 | 28.9 | 17.5 | 48.8 |
| 1986 | 31.0 | 24.5 | 44.1 | 53.1 | 62.0 | 74.5 | 77.6 | 69.8 | 67.2 | 53.4 | 34.3 | 29.3 | 51.8 |
| 1987 | 29.2 | 37.5 | 42.4 | 55.8 | 66.9 | 74.8 | 78.6 | 71.4 | 65.1 | 49.1 | 43.4 | 30.9 | 53.8 |
| 1988 | 20.9 | 24.4 | 41.2 | 51.6 | 68.0 | 77.4 | 76.7 | 77.9 | 67.8 | 50.4 | 40.3 | 21.0 | 52.3 |
| 1989 | 33.1 | 16.7 | 37.3 | 54.6 | 62.9 | 69.8 | 77.7 | 74.7 | 63.7 | 54.6 | 36.9 | 17.5 | 50.0 |
| 1990 | 34.3 | 31.3 | 42.3 | 50.7 | 59.0 | 73.7 | 74.7 | 75.6 | 70.0 | 54.4 | 43.8 | 21.6 | 52.6 |
| Record Mean | 20.2 | 25.1 | 36.7 | 49.4 | 60.3 | 71.3 | 76.0 | 73.8 | 64.6 | 53.4 | 38.1 | 25.1 | 49.5 |
| Max | 29.3 | 34.3 | 46.4 | 60.2 | 70.6 | 81.6 | 85.9 | 83.8 | 74.9 | 64.0 | 47.4 | 33.8 | 59.3 |
| Min | 11.1 | 16.0 | 26.9 | 38.6 | 50.0 | 60.9 | 66.0 | 63.8 | 54.3 | 42.7 | 29.7 | 16.4 | 39.6 |

## REFERENCE NOTES FOR TABLES 1, 2, 3 and 6    (OMAHA, NE)

### GENERAL

T - TRACE AMOUNT
BLANK ENTRIES DENOTE MISSING/UNREPORTED DATA.
\# INDICATES A STATION OR INSTRUMENT RELOCATION.

### SPECIFIC

#### TABLE 1

(a) - LENGTH OF RECORD IN YEARS. ALTHOUGH INDIVIDUAL MONTHS MAY BE MISSING.

∗ LESS THAN .05

NORMALS — BASED ON THE 1951-1980 RECORD PERIOD.
EXTREMES — DATES ARE THE MOST RECENT OCCURRENCE.
WIND DIR. — NUMERALS SHOW TENS OF DEGREES CLOCKWISE FROM TRUE NORTH. "00" INDICATES CALM.
RESULTANT WIND DIRECTIONS ARE GIVEN TO WHOLE DEGREES.

#### TABLE 3

MAX AND MIN ARE LONG-TERM MEAN DAILY MAXIMUM AND MEAN DAILY MINIMUM TEMPERATURES.

### EXCEPTIONS

TABLES 2, 3, and 6

RECORD MEANS ARE THROUGH THE CURRENT YEAR, BEGINNING IN 1954 FOR TEMPERATURE, 1954 FOR PRECIPITATION 1954 FOR SNOWFALL

PERCENT OF POSSIBLE SUNSHINE IS FROM OMAHA'S EPPLEY FIELD STATION THROUGH MAY 1977

**TABLE 4**  HEATING DEGREE DAYS Base 65 deg. F   OMAHA (NORTH), NEBRASKA

| SEASON | JULY | AUG | SEP | OCT | NOV | DEC | JAN | FEB | MAR | APR | MAY | JUNE | TOTAL |
|---|---|---|---|---|---|---|---|---|---|---|---|---|---|
| 1961-62 | 0 | 6 | 204 | 322 | 848 | 1442 | 1507 | 1173 | 1087 | 467 | 34 | 26 | 7116 |
| 1962-63 | 0 | 0 | 149 | 317 | 718 | 1194 | 1643 | 1103 | 726 | 364 | 158 | 4 | 6376 |
| 1963-64 | 0 | 11 | 54 | 98 | 644 | 1487 | 1145 | 1032 | 1010 | 416 | 84 | 28 | 6009 |
| 1964-65 | 0 | 31 | 132 | 379 | 753 | 1319 | 1373 | 1254 | 1262 | 433 | 95 | 5 | 7036 |
| 1965-66 | 0 | 9 | 230 | 270 | 731 | 944 | 1531 | 1092 | 723 | 582 | 222 | 25 | 6359 |
| 1966-67 | 0 | 18 | 141 | 375 | 813 | 1212 | 1303 | 1141 | 727 | 387 | 300 | 23 | 6440 |
| 1967-68 | 12 | 18 | 105 | 435 | 823 | 1170 | 1351 | 1144 | 657 | 414 | 264 | 24 | 6417 |
| 1968-69 | 2 | 3 | 90 | 345 | 858 | 1338 | 1514 | 1098 | 1114 | 388 | 162 | 63 | 6975 |
| 1969-70 | 0 | 3 | 38 | 532 | 750 | 1290 | 1585 | 982 | 979 | 440 | 92 | 13 | 6704 |
| 1970-71 | 4 | 0 | 131 | 464 | 860 | 1169 | 1519 | 1168 | 941 | 368 | 215 | 2 | 6841 |
| 1971-72 | 9 | 3 | 111 | 276 | 776 | 1162 | 1431 | 1188 | 795 | 461 | 171 | 21 | 6404 |
| 1972-73 | 7 | 12 | 116 | 491 | 871 | 1383 | 1308 | 1057 | 681 | 468 | 199 | 3 | 6596 |
| 1973-74 | 2 | 0 | 112 | 263 | 770 | 1315 | 1439 | 734 | | | | | |
| 1974-75 | 0 | 10 | 188 | 340 | | | 1338 | 1242 | 1084 | 541 | 90 | 19 | |
| 1975-76 | 1 | 0 | 167 | 261 | 744 | 1131 | 1275 | 841 | 811 | 314 | 190 | 12 | 5747 |
| 1976-77 | 0 | 0 | 87 | 538 | 962 | 1279 | 1646 | 935 | 664 | 262 | 16 | 1 | 6390 |
| 1977-78 | 0 | 3 | 41 | 394 | 803 | 1268 | 1702 | 1437 | 963 | 432 | 185 | 23 | 7251 |
| 1978-79 | 0 | 3 | 52 | 385 | 837 | 1358 | 1767 | 1435 | 921 | 514 | 199 | 24 | 7495 |
| 1979-80 | 4 | 15 | 48 | 354 | 837 | 1016 | 1267 | 1241 | 945 | 396 | 129 | 9 | 6261 |
| 1980-81 | 0 | 3 | 67 | 444 | 671 | 1157 | 1161 | 961 | 677 | 226 | 189 | 1 | 5557 |
| 1981-82 | 8 | 4 | 73 | 430 | 677 | 1251 | 1695 | 1143 | 894 | 512 | 94 | 50 | 6831 |
| 1982-83 | 0 | 12 | 123 | 333 | 844 | 1206 | 1091 | 946 | 625 | 244 | 26 | | 6294 |
| 1983-84 | 0 | 0 | 94 | 376 | 782 | 1768 | 1344 | 896 | 1054 | 538 | 212 | 3 | 7067 |
| 1984-85 | 0 | 1 | 165 | 363 | 726 | 1177 | 1436 | 1139 | 656 | 315 | 65 | 35 | 6078 |
| 1985-86 | 0 | 7 | 209 | 342 | 1077 | 1467 | 1048 | 1130 | 662 | 357 | 99 | 1 | 6399 |
| 1986-87 | 0 | 17 | 45 | 352 | 917 | 1102 | 1103 | 765 | 692 | 316 | 72 | 2 | 5383 |
| 1987-88 | 2 | 33 | 65 | 486 | 640 | 1053 | 1362 | 1172 | 734 | 401 | 33 | 5 | 5986 |
| 1988-89 | 2 | 4 | 38 | 448 | 733 | 1061 | 984 | 1348 | 861 | 380 | 127 | 25 | 6011 |
| 1989-90 | 2 | 5 | 131 | 343 | 834 | 1470 | 945 | 938 | 696 | 460 | 189 | 19 | 6032 |
| 1990-91 | 5 | 0 | 70 | 334 | 635 | 1341 | | | | | | | |

**TABLE 5**  COOLING DEGREE DAYS Base 65 deg. F   OMAHA (NORTH), NEBRASKA

| YEAR | JAN | FEB | MAR | APR | MAY | JUNE | JULY | AUG | SEP | OCT | NOV | DEC | TOTAL |
|---|---|---|---|---|---|---|---|---|---|---|---|---|---|
| 1977 | 0 | 0 | 0 | 35 | 115 | 246 | 436 | 186 | 76 | 0 | 0 | 0 | 1094 |
| 1978 | 0 | 0 | 5 | 2 | 58 | 252 | 317 | 290 | 202 | 2 | 0 | 0 | 1128 |
| 1979 | 0 | 0 | 0 | 1 | 47 | 206 | 301 | 303 | 142 | 2 | 0 | 0 | 1002 |
| 1980 | 0 | 0 | 0 | 25 | 87 | 237 | 451 | 362 | 137 | 11 | 0 | 0 | 1310 |
| 1981 | 0 | 0 | 0 | 34 | 38 | 269 | 384 | 209 | 101 | 0 | 0 | 0 | 1035 |
| 1982 | 0 | 0 | 0 | 4 | 43 | 104 | 375 | 250 | 99 | 12 | 0 | 0 | 887 |
| 1983 | 0 | 0 | 0 | 0 | 21 | 200 | 454 | 526 | 193 | 17 | 0 | 0 | 1411 |
| 1984 | 0 | 0 | 0 | 5 | 27 | 225 | 346 | 389 | 105 | 4 | 0 | 0 | 1101 |
| 1985 | 0 | 0 | 0 | 39 | 79 | 142 | 344 | 196 | 153 | 1 | 0 | 0 | 954 |
| 1986 | 0 | 0 | 16 | 8 | 45 | 294 | 399 | 172 | 119 | 0 | 0 | 0 | 1053 |
| 1987 | 0 | 0 | 0 | 47 | 138 | 302 | 430 | 235 | 73 | 3 | 1 | 0 | 1229 |
| 1988 | 0 | 0 | 0 | 4 | 128 | 384 | 374 | 410 | 129 | 4 | 0 | 0 | 1433 |
| 1989 | 0 | 0 | 10 | 77 | 67 | 172 | 400 | 315 | 98 | 30 | 0 | 0 | 1169 |
| 1990 | 0 | 0 | 0 | 38 | 11 | 289 | 311 | 333 | 228 | 15 | 3 | 0 | 1228 |

**TABLE 6**  SNOWFALL (inches)   OMAHA (NORTH), NEBRASKA

| SEASON | JULY | AUG | SEP | OCT | NOV | DEC | JAN | FEB | MAR | APR | MAY | JUNE | TOTAL |
|---|---|---|---|---|---|---|---|---|---|---|---|---|---|
| 1961-62 | 0.0 | 0.0 | T | 0.0 | 4.2 | 15.6 | 4.5 | 12.6 | 8.0 | 0.6 | 0.0 | 0.0 | 45.5 |
| 1962-63 | 0.0 | 0.0 | 0.0 | T | 0.5 | 5.9 | 11.2 | 3.1 | 14.6 | 0.0 | 0.0 | 0.0 | 35.3 |
| 1963-64 | 0.0 | 0.0 | 0.0 | 0.0 | 0.0 | 5.9 | 4.7 | 2.4 | 9.0 | T | 0.0 | 0.0 | 22.0 |
| 1964-65 | 0.0 | 0.0 | 0.0 | 0.0 | 2.8 | 5.6 | 6.5 | 23.2 | 15.9 | 0.0 | 0.0 | 0.0 | 54.0 |
| 1965-66 | 0.0 | 0.0 | 0.0 | 0.0 | 0.2 | 1.2 | 3.5 | 0.4 | 8.4 | T | T | 0.0 | 13.7 |
| 1966-67 | 0.0 | 0.0 | 0.0 | 0.0 | T | 6.2 | 7.8 | 1.1 | 0.4 | 0.8 | 0.7 | 0.0 | 17.0 |
| 1967-68 | 0.0 | 0.0 | 0.0 | 0.0 | 0.0 | 6.2 | 4.9 | 0.7 | T | T | T | 0.0 | 11.8 |
| 1968-69 | 0.0 | 0.0 | 0.0 | T | 5.1 | 8.5 | 7.6 | 14.1 | 2.1 | 0.0 | 0.0 | 0.0 | 37.4 |
| 1969-70 | 0.0 | 0.0 | 0.0 | T | 0.2 | 19.3 | 2.9 | 1.6 | 5.1 | T | T | 0.0 | 29.1 |
| 1970-71 | 0.0 | 0.0 | 0.0 | 4.1 | T | 0.3 | 12.8 | 17.6 | 6.3 | 0.4 | 0.0 | 0.0 | 41.5 |
| 1971-72 | 0.0 | 0.0 | 0.0 | T | 7.8 | 3.3 | 3.6 | 4.3 | 3.0 | 1.2 | 0.0 | 0.0 | 23.2 |
| 1972-73 | 0.0 | 0.0 | 0.0 | T | 8.8 | 7.2 | 16.5 | 6.3 | 0.0 | 2.9 | 0.0 | 0.0 | 41.7 |
| 1973-74 | 0.0 | 0.0 | 0.0 | 0.0 | 3.6 | 9.0 | 10.6 | 2.9 | 4.6 | 0.0 | 0.0 | 0.0 | |
| 1974-75 | 0.0 | 0.0 | 0.0 | 0.0 | | | 21.5 | 12.2 | 5.0 | 3.7 | 0.0 | 0.0 | |
| 1975-76 | 0.0 | 0.0 | 0.0 | 8.0 | 0.6 | 2.6 | 7.6 | 5.0 | 0.0 | 0.0 | 0.0 | | 23.8 |
| 1976-77 | 0.0 | 0.0 | 0.0 | 1.4 | 0.7 | 2.8 | 13.7 | T | 3.3 | 3.0 | 0.0 | 0.0 | 24.9 |
| 1977-78 | 0.0 | 0.0 | 0.0 | 0.0 | 3.0 | 7.4 | 4.0 | 22.0 | 8.6 | T | 0.0 | 0.0 | 45.0 |
| 1978-79 | 0.0 | 0.0 | 0.0 | 0.0 | 5.3 | 8.8 | 13.6 | 3.9 | 6.6 | 4.8 | 0.0 | 0.0 | 43.0 |
| 1979-80 | 0.0 | 0.0 | 0.0 | 1.9 | 0.2 | 1.5 | 7.2 | 9.8 | 8.0 | 0.2 | 0.0 | 0.0 | 28.8 |
| 1980-81 | 0.0 | 0.0 | 0.0 | 5.2 | 0.2 | 0.8 | 4.3 | 3.6 | 0.6 | 0.0 | 0.0 | 0.0 | 14.7 |
| 1981-82 | 0.0 | 0.0 | 0.0 | 0.9 | 4.7 | 7.8 | 5.9 | 3.5 | 5.2 | 3.9 | 0.0 | 0.0 | 31.9 |
| 1982-83 | 0.0 | 0.0 | 0.0 | 0.8 | 0.4 | 5.1 | 8.9 | 11.4 | 14.1 | 10.3 | 0.0 | 0.0 | 51.0 |
| 1983-84 | 0.0 | 0.0 | 0.0 | 0.0 | 13.6 | 15.9 | 3.1 | 3.4 | 18.3 | 1.5 | 0.0 | 0.0 | 55.8 |
| 1984-85 | 0.0 | 0.0 | 0.0 | T | 1.6 | 9.7 | 4.6 | 3.3 | 8.7 | T | 0.0 | 0.0 | 27.9 |
| 1985-86 | 0.0 | 0.0 | 0.3 | 0.0 | 6.9 | 5.5 | T | 7.0 | 0.5 | 1.1 | 0.0 | 0.0 | 21.3 |
| 1986-87 | 0.0 | 0.0 | 0.0 | 0.0 | 0.8 | 5.1 | 1.4 | 14.1 | 0.1 | 0.0 | 0.0 | | 22.2 |
| 1987-88 | 0.0 | 0.0 | 0.0 | 0.4 | 6.8 | 2.0 | 3.3 | 2.8 | 0.9 | 0.0 | 0.0 | 0.0 | 16.2 |
| 1988-89 | 0.0 | 0.0 | 0.0 | 0.0 | 4.4 | 3.3 | 1.3 | 10.2 | 2.2 | T | 0.0 | 0.0 | 21.4 |
| 1989-90 | 0.0 | 0.0 | 0.0 | T | 0.4 | 6.2 | 5.1 | 5.8 | 5.4 | T | 0.0 | 0.0 | 22.9 |
| 1990-91 | 0.0 | 0.0 | 0.0 | T | 4.0 | 8.2 | | | | | | | |
| Record Mean | 0.0 | 0.0 | T | 0.4 | 3.2 | 5.5 | 7.0 | 6.7 | 7.2 | 1.2 | T | 0.0 | 31.3 |

**See Reference Notes, relative to all above tables, on preceding page.**

Las Vegas is situated near the center of a broad desert valley, which is almost surrounded by mountains ranging from 2,000 to 10,000 feet higher than the floor of the valley. This Vegas Valley, comprising about 600 square miles, runs from northwest to southeast, and slopes gradually upward on each side toward the surrounding mountains. Weather observations are taken at McCarran Airport, 7 miles south of downtown Las Vegas, and about 5 miles southwest and 300 feet higher than the lower portions of the valley. Since mountains encircle the valley, drainage winds are usually downslope toward the center, or lowest portion of the valley. This condition also affects minimum temperatures, which in lower portions of the valley can be from 15 to 25 degrees colder than recorded at the airport on clear, calm nights.

The four seasons are well defined. Summers display desert conditions, with maximum temperatures usually in the 100 degree range. The proximity of the mountains contributes to the relatively cool summer nights, with the majority of minimum temperatures in the mid 70s. During about 2 weeks almost every summer warm, moist air predominates in this area, and causes scattered thunderstorms, occasionally quite severe, together with higher than average humidity. Soil erosion, especially near the mountains and foothills surrounding the valley, is evidence of the intensity of some of the thunderstorm activity. Winters, on the whole, are mild and pleasant. Daytime temperatures average near 60 degrees with mostly clear skies. The spring and fall seasons are generally considered most ideal, although rather sharp temperature changes can occur during these months. There are very few days during the spring and fall months when outdoor activities are affected in any degree by the weather.

The Sierra Nevada Mountains of California and the Spring Mountains immediately west of the Vegas Valley, the latter rising to elevations over 10,000 feet above the valley floor, act as effective barriers to moisture moving eastward from the Pacific Ocean. It is mainly these barriers that result in a minimum of dark overcast and rainy days. Rainy days average less than one in June to three per month in the winter months. Snow rarely falls in this valley and it usually melts as it falls, or shortly thereafter. Notable exceptions have occurred.

Strong winds, associated with major storms, usually reach this valley from the southwest or through the pass from the northwest. Winds over 50 mph are infrequent but, when they do occur, are probably the most provoking of the elements experienced in the Vegas Valley, because of the blowing dust and sand associated with them.

Based on the 1951–1980 period, the average first occurrence of 32 degrees Fahrenheit in the fall is November 21 and the average last occurrence in the spring is March 7.

# TABLE 1    NORMALS, MEANS AND EXTREMES

LAS VEGAS, NEVADA

LATITUDE: 36°05'N    LONGITUDE: 115°10'W    ELEVATION: FT. GRND 2162 BARO 2179    TIME ZONE: PACIFIC    WBAN: 23169

| | (a) | JAN | FEB | MAR | APR | MAY | JUNE | JULY | AUG | SEP | OCT | NOV | DEC | YEAR |
|---|---|---|---|---|---|---|---|---|---|---|---|---|---|---|
| **TEMPERATURE °F:** | | | | | | | | | | | | | | |
| Normals | | | | | | | | | | | | | | |
| -Daily Maximum | | 56.0 | 62.4 | 68.3 | 77.2 | 87.4 | 98.6 | 104.5 | 101.9 | 94.7 | 81.5 | 66.0 | 57.1 | 79.6 |
| -Daily Minimum | | 33.0 | 37.7 | 42.3 | 49.8 | 59.0 | 68.6 | 75.9 | 73.9 | 65.6 | 53.5 | 41.2 | 33.6 | 52.8 |
| -Monthly | | 44.6 | 50.1 | 55.3 | 63.5 | 73.3 | 83.6 | 90.3 | 88.0 | 80.1 | 67.6 | 53.6 | 45.4 | 66.3 |
| Extremes | | | | | | | | | | | | | | |
| -Record Highest | 41 | 77 | 87 | 91 | 99 | 109 | 115 | 116 | 116 | 113 | 103 | 87 | 77 | 116 |
| -Year | | 1975 | 1986 | 1966 | 1981 | 1951 | 1970 | 1985 | 1979 | 1950 | 1978 | 1988 | 1980 | JUL 1985 |
| -Record Lowest | 41 | 8 | 16 | 23 | 31 | 40 | 49 | 60 | 56 | 46 | 26 | 21 | 15 | 8 |
| -Year | | 1963 | 1989 | 1971 | 1975 | 1964 | 1955 | 1987 | 1968 | 1965 | 1971 | 1952 | 1968 | JAN 1963 |
| **NORMAL DEGREE DAYS:** | | | | | | | | | | | | | | |
| Heating (base 65°F) | | 632 | 417 | 313 | 131 | 22 | 0 | 0 | 0 | 0 | 63 | 346 | 608 | 2532 |
| Cooling (base 65°F) | | 0 | 0 | 12 | 86 | 279 | 558 | 784 | 713 | 453 | 144 | 0 | 0 | 3029 |
| **% OF POSSIBLE SUNSHINE** | 40 | 77 | 81 | 84 | 87 | 88 | 92 | 87 | 88 | 91 | 86 | 80 | 78 | 85 |
| **MEAN SKY COVER (tenths)** | | | | | | | | | | | | | | |
| Sunrise - Sunset | 41 | 4.8 | 4.7 | 4.5 | 3.7 | 3.4 | 2.1 | 2.8 | 2.5 | 2.0 | 2.8 | 3.9 | 4.4 | 3.5 |
| **MEAN NUMBER OF DAYS:** | | | | | | | | | | | | | | |
| Sunrise to Sunset | | | | | | | | | | | | | | |
| -Clear | 41 | 13.9 | 12.5 | 13.8 | 16.1 | 18.2 | 22.2 | 19.8 | 21.5 | 22.5 | 20.4 | 15.7 | 14.8 | 211.4 |
| -Partly Cloudy | 41 | 6.3 | 7.0 | 8.8 | 7.6 | 8.0 | 5.3 | 7.8 | 6.7 | 5.0 | 6.4 | 7.4 | 6.7 | 82.8 |
| -Cloudy | 41 | 10.8 | 8.7 | 8.4 | 6.3 | 4.9 | 2.5 | 3.5 | 2.8 | 2.5 | 4.2 | 6.9 | 9.5 | 71.1 |
| Precipitation | | | | | | | | | | | | | | |
| .01 inches or more | 41 | 3.0 | 2.6 | 3.0 | 1.9 | 1.4 | 0.7 | 2.6 | 3.0 | 1.6 | 1.7 | 2.0 | 2.5 | 25.9 |
| Snow,Ice pellets | | | | | | | | | | | | | | |
| 1.0 inches or more | 41 | 0.3 | 0.0 | 0.0 | 0.0 | 0.0 | 0.0 | 0.0 | 0.0 | 0.0 | 0.0 | 0.1 | 0.* | 0.4 |
| Thunderstorms | 41 | 0.* | 0.2 | 0.3 | 0.5 | 1.0 | 1.0 | 4.2 | 4.1 | 1.6 | 0.5 | 0.2 | 0.* | 13.8 |
| Heavy Fog Visibility | | | | | | | | | | | | | | |
| 1/4 mile or less | 41 | 0.3 | 0.1 | 0.1 | 0.0 | 0.0 | 0.0 | 0.0 | 0.0 | 0.* | 0.* | 0.1 | 0.1 | 0.7 |
| Temperature °F | | | | | | | | | | | | | | |
| -Maximum | | | | | | | | | | | | | | |
| 90° and above | 29 | 0.0 | 0.0 | 0.* | 3.1 | 15.5 | 25.8 | 30.4 | 29.9 | 21.8 | 5.8 | 0.0 | 0.0 | 132.3 |
| 32° and below | 29 | 0.1 | 0.0 | 0.0 | 0.0 | 0.0 | 0.0 | 0.0 | 0.0 | 0.0 | 0.0 | 0.0 | 0.* | 0.2 |
| -Minimum | | | | | | | | | | | | | | |
| 32° and below | 29 | 12.9 | 4.6 | 1.3 | 0.1 | 0.0 | 0.0 | 0.0 | 0.0 | 0.0 | 0.1 | 2.2 | 11.2 | 32.4 |
| 0° and below | 29 | 0.0 | 0.0 | 0.0 | 0.0 | 0.0 | 0.0 | 0.0 | 0.0 | 0.0 | 0.0 | 0.0 | 0.0 | 0.0 |
| **AVG. STATION PRESS.(mb)** | 17 | 942.4 | 940.8 | 937.2 | 936.0 | 934.0 | 933.7 | 935.0 | 935.4 | 935.8 | 938.8 | 940.5 | 942.5 | 937.7 |
| **RELATIVE HUMIDITY (%)** | | | | | | | | | | | | | | |
| Hour 04 | 29 | 55 | 50 | 44 | 35 | 32 | 24 | 29 | 35 | 34 | 38 | 46 | 55 | 40 |
| Hour 10 (Local Time) | 29 | 41 | 36 | 29 | 22 | 19 | 15 | 19 | 24 | 22 | 25 | 33 | 41 | 27 |
| Hour 16 | 29 | 30 | 26 | 21 | 16 | 13 | 10 | 15 | 17 | 17 | 19 | 27 | 32 | 20 |
| Hour 22 | 29 | 49 | 42 | 36 | 26 | 22 | 17 | 22 | 26 | 26 | 31 | 40 | 49 | 32 |
| **PRECIPITATION (inches):** | | | | | | | | | | | | | | |
| Water Equivalent | | | | | | | | | | | | | | |
| -Normal | | 0.50 | 0.46 | 0.41 | 0.22 | 0.20 | 0.09 | 0.45 | 0.54 | 0.32 | 0.25 | 0.43 | 0.32 | 4.19 |
| -Maximum Monthly | 41 | 2.41 | 2.49 | 1.83 | 2.44 | 0.96 | 0.82 | 2.48 | 2.59 | 1.58 | 1.12 | 2.22 | 1.68 | 2.59 |
| -Year | | 1949 | 1976 | 1973 | 1965 | 1969 | 1967 | 1984 | 1957 | 1963 | 1972 | 1965 | 1984 | AUG 1957 |
| -Minimum Monthly | 41 | T | 0.00 | 0.00 | 0.00 | 0.00 | 0.00 | 0.00 | 0.00 | 0.00 | 0.00 | 0.00 | 0.00 | 0.00 |
| -Year | | 1984 | 1977 | 1972 | 1962 | 1970 | 1982 | 1981 | 1980 | 1971 | 1979 | 1980 | 1981 | JUN 1982 |
| -Maximum in 24 hrs | 41 | 1.01 | 1.19 | 1.14 | 0.97 | 0.83 | 0.75 | 1.36 | 2.59 | 1.07 | 0.70 | 1.78 | 0.95 | 2.59 |
| -Year | | 1952 | 1976 | 1952 | 1965 | 1987 | 1967 | 1984 | 1957 | 1963 | 1976 | 1960 | 1977 | AUG 1957 |
| Snow,Ice pellets | | | | | | | | | | | | | | |
| -Maximum Monthly | 41 | 16.7 | 0.6 | 0.1 | T | 0.0 | 0.0 | 0.0 | T | 0.0 | T | 4.0 | 2.0 | 16.7 |
| -Year | | 1949 | 1987 | 1976 | 1970 | | | | 1989 | | 1956 | 1964 | 1967 | JAN 1949 |
| -Maximum in 24 hrs | 41 | 9.0 | 6.9 | 0.1 | T | 0.0 | 0.0 | 0.0 | T | 0.0 | T | 4.0 | 2.0 | 9.0 |
| -Year | | 1974 | 1979 | 1976 | 1970 | | | | 1989 | | 1956 | 1964 | 1967 | JAN 1974 |
| **WIND:** | | | | | | | | | | | | | | |
| Mean Speed (mph) | 41 | 7.5 | 8.6 | 10.3 | 11.0 | 11.1 | 11.0 | 10.3 | 9.6 | 9.0 | 8.1 | 7.7 | 7.3 | 9.3 |
| Prevailing Direction | | | | | | | | | | | | | | |
| through 1963 | | W | SW | SW | SW | SW | SW | SW | SW | SW | WSW | W | W | SW |
| Fastest Mile | | | | | | | | | | | | | | |
| -Direction (!!!) | 21 | SW | NW | NW | SW | SW | SW | NE | NE | NW | NW | S | SW | NE |
| -Speed (MPH) | 21 | 52 | 60 | 52 | 52 | 54 | 52 | 64 | 62 | 54 | 52 | 63 | 54 | 64 |
| -Year | | 1965 | 1976 | 1977 | 1976 | 1977 | 1977 | 1976 | 1981 | 1971 | 1970 | 1983 | 1964 | JUL 1976 |
| Peak Gust | | | | | | | | | | | | | | |
| -Direction (!!!) | 6 | SW | NW | NW | W | SE | NE | SW | SE | SW | SW | SW | NW | SE |
| -Speed (mph) | 6 | 54 | 67 | 82 | 69 | 62 | 59 | 53 | 90 | 49 | 52 | 68 | 52 | 90 |
| -Date | | 1987 | 1984 | 1984 | 1988 | 1984 | 1984 | 1984 | 1989 | 1989 | 1984 | 1987 | 1984 | AUG 1989 |

**See Reference Notes to this table on the following page.**

# LAS VEGAS, NEVADA

## TABLE 2 — PRECIPITATION (inches)     LAS VEGAS, NEVADA

| YEAR | JAN | FEB | MAR | APR | MAY | JUNE | JULY | AUG | SEP | OCT | NOV | DEC | ANNUAL |
|---|---|---|---|---|---|---|---|---|---|---|---|---|---|
| 1961 | 0.22 | 0.01 | 0.51 | 0.02 | T | | 0.53 | 0.80 | 0.26 | 0.26 | 0.10 | 0.46 | 3.17 |
| 1962 | 0.10 | 0.39 | 0.17 | 0.00 | 0.06 | 0.01 | T | T | 0.03 | 0.45 | T | 0.24 | 1.45 |
| 1963 | 0.12 | 0.33 | 0.23 | 0.10 | | 0.15 | 0.00 | 0.42 | 1.58 | 0.61 | 0.33 | 0.00 | 3.87 |
| 1964 | 0.05 | 0.02 | 0.02 | 0.03 | 0.05 | 0.03 | 0.24 | 0.05 | T | T | 0.63 | T | 1.12 |
| 1965 | 0.05 | 0.45 | 0.74 | 2.44 | 0.40 | T | 0.28 | 0.38 | T | T | 2.22 | 1.00 | 7.96 |
| 1966 | T | 0.07 | 0.04 | 0.01 | T | 0.15 | 0.30 | 0.09 | 0.35 | 0.09 | 0.33 | 0.48 | 1.91 |
| 1967 | 0.47 | 0.00 | T | 0.09 | 0.21 | 0.82 | 0.20 | 0.38 | 1.03 | 0.00 | 1.52 | 0.82 | 5.54 |
| 1968 | 0.01 | 0.22 | 0.22 | 0.10 | T | 0.31 | 0.11 | 0.04 | 0.01 | T | 0.02 | 0.07 | 1.11 |
| 1969 | 1.57 | 0.96 | 0.57 | T | 0.96 | 0.23 | 0.06 | 0.33 | 0.08 | 0.27 | 0.06 | T | 5.09 |
| 1970 | 0.01 | 0.86 | 0.28 | 0.04 | 0.00 | 0.18 | 0.58 | 1.79 | 0.00 | 0.02 | 0.38 | 0.15 | 4.29 |
| 1971 | T | 0.03 | T | 0.07 | 0.84 | T | 0.08 | 0.90 | 0.00 | 0.06 | 0.12 | 0.51 | 2.54 |
| 1972 | 0.00 | T | 0.00 | 0.07 | 0.46 | 0.32 | 0.13 | 0.84 | 0.63 | 1.12 | 1.09 | 0.19 | 4.85 |
| 1973 | 0.49 | 1.64 | 1.83 | 0.35 | 0.09 | 0.03 | T | 0.08 | T | 0.02 | 0.14 | 0.01 | 4.68 |
| 1974 | 2.00 | 0.11 | 0.16 | T | T | 0.00 | 0.58 | 0.08 | 0.16 | 0.61 | 0.23 | 0.59 | 4.52 |
| 1975 | 0.01 | 0.05 | 1.07 | 0.42 | 0.35 | T | 0.26 | 0.06 | 1.17 | 0.03 | T | 0.05 | 3.47 |
| 1976 | 0.00 | 2.49 | 0.02 | 0.13 | 0.34 | 0.00 | 1.95 | | 1.09 | 0.70 | 0.02 | 0.03 | 6.77 |
| 1977 | 0.21 | 0.00 | 0.28 | 0.01 | 0.72 | 0.05 | T | 1.38 | 0.19 | 0.06 | 0.01 | 1.06 | 3.97 |
| 1978 | 1.00 | 1.51 | 1.13 | 0.36 | 0.54 | 0.00 | 0.19 | 0.53 | 0.03 | 0.62 | 0.59 | 1.15 | 7.65 |
| 1979 | 2.18 | 0.07 | 0.96 | 0.06 | 0.35 | 0.00 | 0.78 | 2.12 | T | 0.00 | 0.03 | 0.24 | 6.79 |
| 1980 | 1.45 | 2.25 | 0.94 | 0.18 | 0.15 | T | 0.43 | 0.00 | 0.18 | 0.04 | 0.00 | 0.01 | 5.63 |
| 1981 | 0.09 | 0.20 | 1.44 | 0.02 | 0.50 | T | 0.00 | 0.20 | 0.25 | 0.15 | 0.29 | 0.00 | 3.14 |
| 1982 | 0.09 | 1.10 | 0.29 | 0.01 | 0.31 | 0.00 | 0.05 | 0.71 | 0.07 | 0.04 | 0.60 | 0.72 | 3.99 |
| 1983 | 0.43 | 0.32 | 0.90 | 0.45 | 0.16 | T | 0.06 | 1.25 | 0.50 | 0.26 | 0.10 | 0.43 | 4.86 |
| 1984 | T | 0.03 | T | 0.04 | 0.00 | 0.22 | 2.48 | 0.99 | 0.47 | T | 0.94 | 1.68 | 6.85 |
| 1985 | 0.19 | 0.02 | 0.06 | 0.31 | T | 0.02 | 0.13 | 0.00 | 0.08 | 0.07 | 0.37 | 0.02 | 1.27 |
| 1986 | 0.23 | 0.15 | 0.32 | 0.10 | 0.28 | T | 0.13 | 0.04 | 0.05 | 0.07 | 0.81 | 0.47 | 2.65 |
| 1987 | 1.13 | 0.45 | 0.49 | 0.17 | 0.90 | 0.13 | 0.13 | 0.01 | T | 0.49 | 1.80 | 0.89 | 6.59 |
| 1988 | 0.65 | 0.26 | 0.00 | 0.76 | T | 0.04 | 0.04 | 0.46 | T | T | 0.00 | T | 2.29 |
| 1989 | 0.51 | 0.06 | 0.05 | T | 0.64 | T | 0.05 | 0.80 | T | 0.19 | T | T | 2.11 |
| 1990 | 1.18 | 0.37 | T | 0.18 | T | 0.97 | 0.59 | T | 0.19 | 0.17 | 0.10 | T | 3.75 |
| Record Mean | 0.51 | 0.43 | 0.43 | 0.23 | 0.19 | 0.08 | 0.43 | 0.48 | 0.32 | 0.23 | 0.38 | 0.38 | 4.09 |

## TABLE 3 — AVERAGE TEMPERATURE (deg. F)     LAS VEGAS, NEVADA

| YEAR | JAN | FEB | MAR | APR | MAY | JUNE | JULY | AUG | SEP | OCT | NOV | DEC | ANNUAL |
|---|---|---|---|---|---|---|---|---|---|---|---|---|---|
| 1961 | 45.1 | 51.0 | 56.2 | 65.1 | 72.9 | 87.0 | 91.0 | 87.7 | 75.6 | 64.1 | 50.3 | 42.5 | 65.7 |
| 1962 | 44.3 | 49.9 | 51.3 | 70.3 | 70.6 | 82.3 | 88.3 | 89.8 | 81.4 | 68.7 | 57.3 | 45.9 | 66.7 |
| 1963 | 41.1 | 55.8 | 54.0 | 58.5 | 75.9 | 78.6 | 90.4 | 87.9 | 80.5 | 70.1 | 55.0 | 44.6 | 66.0 |
| 1964 | 42.0 | 45.6 | 52.3 | 61.8 | 70.9 | 80.9 | 90.7 | 87.6 | 78.4 | 72.0 | 50.0 | 45.3 | 64.8 |
| 1965 | 47.1 | 49.5 | 53.2 | 61.2 | 69.6 | 78.0 | 88.7 | 87.9 | 74.8 | 69.8 | 55.9 | 45.0 | 65.1 |
| 1966 | 42.7 | 45.8 | 57.9 | 66.4 | 77.5 | 83.9 | 89.3 | 89.6 | 80.1 | 66.5 | 55.4 | 46.1 | 66.8 |
| 1967 | 45.3 | 50.6 | 59.3 | 56.2 | 72.5 | 79.6 | 91.7 | 90.3 | 80.0 | 69.1 | 56.7 | 41.6 | 66.1 |
| 1968 | 44.2 | 55.7 | 57.5 | 62.0 | 73.5 | 84.0 | 89.0 | 83.5 | 79.7 | 67.0 | 54.5 | 40.8 | 66.0 |
| 1969 | 47.5 | 46.3 | 53.0 | 64.4 | 76.8 | 81.4 | 89.7 | 92.2 | 82.5 | 62.8 | 53.5 | 45.8 | 66.3 |
| 1970 | 44.0 | 52.5 | 54.9 | 58.6 | 75.3 | 83.4 | 91.1 | 88.8 | 77.2 | 63.8 | 55.0 | 44.5 | 65.8 |
| 1971 | 44.4 | 49.7 | 55.8 | 63.0 | 68.0 | 83.3 | 92.8 | 89.0 | 77.6 | 61.7 | 50.9 | 41.4 | 64.8 |
| 1972 | 42.3 | 52.0 | 63.7 | 65.1 | 74.5 | 84.7 | 93.1 | 86.5 | 78.0 | 63.5 | 49.7 | 41.3 | 66.2 |
| 1973 | 40.9 | 49.6 | 50.7 | 62.2 | 76.7 | 85.2 | 91.7 | 87.6 | 78.9 | 67.7 | 53.4 | 46.2 | 65.9 |
| 1974 | 41.0 | 48.9 | 59.5 | 63.4 | 77.0 | 89.1 | 88.8 | 87.7 | 83.4 | 69.3 | 54.8 | 44.4 | 67.3 |
| 1975 | 45.3 | 48.8 | 53.9 | 56.6 | 72.5 | 83.8 | 90.3 | 87.5 | 81.7 | 66.1 | 53.0 | 48.2 | 65.6 |
| 1976 | 46.9 | 53.2 | 53.4 | 62.6 | 77.8 | 81.5 | 86.9 | 85.5 | 78.7 | 58.0 | | 46.4 | 66.5 |
| 1977 | 45.7 | 54.2 | 52.6 | 68.6 | 67.7 | 88.0 | 92.4 | 90.1 | 80.6 | 71.4 | 57.2 | 51.9 | 66.3 |
| 1978 | 47.9 | 52.1 | 59.9 | 63.1 | 73.1 | 87.1 | 91.9 | 89.0 | 79.0 | 73.5 | 54.2 | 42.9 | 67.8 |
| 1979 | 41.1 | 48.4 | 56.0 | 66.1 | 75.4 | 85.5 | 91.1 | 85.9 | 85.3 | 70.7 | 51.6 | 47.2 | 67.1 |
| 1980 | 49.5 | 53.2 | 54.2 | 63.5 | 69.0 | 83.9 | 92.0 | 90.2 | 81.4 | 68.9 | 56.8 | 52.7 | 67.9 |
| 1981 | 51.1 | 52.5 | 56.4 | 70.6 | 74.3 | 88.8 | 92.7 | 90.0 | 82.5 | 64.4 | 58.0 | 48.8 | 69.2 |
| 1982 | 45.6 | 50.5 | 55.1 | 63.8 | 73.6 | 81.5 | 88.1 | 87.3 | 77.9 | 63.0 | 50.5 | 44.5 | 65.1 |
| 1983 | 46.6 | 51.7 | 56.4 | 58.5 | 72.8 | 82.8 | 88.5 | 83.8 | 82.5 | 67.8 | 55.3 | 47.9 | 66.2 |
| 1984 | 47.1 | 50.1 | 57.9 | 63.1 | 80.7 | 83.5 | 88.2 | 85.4 | 81.7 | 63.0 | 52.7 | 44.0 | 66.5 |
| 1985 | 44.4 | 47.4 | 54.9 | 68.2 | 76.9 | 87.4 | 92.0 | 89.9 | 75.4 | 67.3 | 51.7 | 48.3 | 67.0 |
| 1986 | 51.7 | 55.8 | 63.0 | 66.2 | 76.6 | 87.8 | 87.6 | 91.2 | 75.4 | 65.0 | 55.8 | 46.0 | 68.5 |
| 1987 | 44.7 | 51.4 | 54.6 | 68.4 | 74.5 | 86.3 | 86.9 | 88.2 | 81.2 | 71.0 | 53.4 | 42.5 | 66.9 |
| 1988 | 45.1 | 52.4 | 58.1 | 64.2 | 73.4 | 85.3 | 92.6 | 86.9 | 79.1 | 74.9 | 56.0 | 46.0 | 67.8 |
| 1989 | 43.9 | 50.0 | 63.4 | 72.7 | 75.7 | 85.3 | 93.4 | 86.9 | 80.0 | 67.2 | 57.3 | 48.0 | 68.7 |
| 1990 | 45.2 | 48.8 | 60.5 | 68.8 | 74.5 | 85.9 | 90.8 | 87.8 | 82.0 | 69.2 | 55.1 | 40.2 | 67.4 |
| Record Mean | 44.5 | 49.7 | 55.8 | 64.3 | 73.8 | 83.4 | 89.8 | 87.6 | 79.9 | 67.2 | 53.5 | 45.7 | 66.3 |
| Max | 56.5 | 62.3 | 69.0 | 78.4 | 88.3 | 98.7 | 104.7 | 102.2 | 94.8 | 81.6 | 66.7 | 57.8 | 80.1 |
| Min | 32.5 | 37.1 | 42.5 | 50.3 | 59.2 | 68.2 | 74.9 | 73.0 | 64.9 | 52.7 | 40.3 | 33.5 | 52.4 |

## REFERENCE NOTES FOR TABLES 1, 2, 3 and 6     (LAS VEGAS, NV)

### GENERAL

T - TRACE AMOUNT
BLANK ENTRIES DENOTE MISSING/UNREPORTED DATA.
# INDICATES A STATION OR INSTRUMENT RELOCATION.

### SPECIFIC

#### TABLE 1

(a) - LENGTH OF RECORD IN YEARS. ALTHOUGH
INDIVIDUAL MONTHS MAY BE MISSING.

* LESS THAN .05

NORMALS — BASED ON THE 1951-1980 RECORD PERIOD.
EXTREMES — DATES ARE THE MOST RECENT OCCURRENCE.
WIND DIR. — NUMERALS SHOW TENS OF DEGREES
CLOCKWISE FROM TRUE NORTH.
"00" INDICATES CALM.
RESULTANT WIND DIRECTIONS ARE GIVEN TO WHOLE DEGREES.

#### TABLE 3
MAX AND MIN ARE LONG-TERM MEAN DAILY MAXIMUM
AND MEAN DAILY MINIMUM TEMPERATURES.

### EXCEPTIONS

#### TABLES 2, 3, and 6

RECORD MEANS ARE THROUGH THE CURRENT YEAR,
BEGINNING IN     1937 FOR TEMPERATURE
1937 FOR PRECIPITATION
1949 FOR SNOWFALL

## TABLE 4 — HEATING DEGREE DAYS Base 65 deg. F — LAS VEGAS, NEVADA

| SEASON | JULY | AUG | SEP | OCT | NOV | DEC | JAN | FEB | MAR | APR | MAY | JUNE | TOTAL |
|---|---|---|---|---|---|---|---|---|---|---|---|---|---|
| 1961-62 | 0 | 0 | 0 | 136 | 438 | 593 | 635 | 418 | 420 | 13 | 30 | 0 | 2783 |
| 1962-63 | 0 | 0 | 0 | 28 | 229 | 588 | 733 | 254 | 337 | 109 | 7 | 0 | 2285 |
| 1963-64 | 0 | 0 | 0 | 17 | 295 | 526 | 703 | 557 | 394 | 141 | 72 | 0 | 2805 |
| 1964-65 | 0 | 0 | 0 | 12 | 444 | 506 | 551 | 427 | 358 | 220 | 49 | 0 | 2667 |
| 1965-66 | 0 | 0 | 15 | 17 | 266 | 515 | 685 | 529 | 235 | 54 | 0 | 0 | 2416 |
| 1966-67 | 0 | 0 | 0 | 47 | 286 | 578 | 606 | 397 | 189 | 261 | 25 | 0 | 2389 |
| 1967-68 | 0 | 0 | 0 | 18 | 244 | 716 | 638 | 265 | 231 | 110 | 8 | 0 | 2230 |
| 1968-69 | 0 | 0 | 1 | 28 | 304 | 743 | 536 | 518 | 381 | 74 | 16 | 0 | 2601 |
| 1969-70 | 0 | 0 | 0 | 112 | 341 | 589 | 643 | 344 | 304 | 208 | 8 | 0 | 2549 |
| 1970-71 | 0 | 0 | 0 | 111 | 295 | 631 | 630 | 421 | 306 | 105 | 47 | 0 | 2546 |
| 1971-72 | 0 | 0 | 4 | 207 | 417 | 724 | 697 | 373 | 99 | 69 | 6 | 0 | 2596 |
| 1972-73 | 0 | 0 | 0 | 108 | 453 | 727 | 744 | 428 | 437 | 132 | 12 | 0 | 3041 |
| 1973-74 | 0 | 0 | 0 | 42 | 349 | 576 | 738 | 443 | 188 | 82 | 13 | 0 | 2431 |
| 1974-75 | 0 | 0 | 0 | 55 | 300 | 634 | 607 | 446 | 340 | 249 | 37 | 0 | 2668 |
| 1975-76 | 0 | 0 | 0 | 73 | 354 | 516 | 553 | 339 | 357 | 124 | 1 | 0 | 2317 |
| 1976-77 | 0 | 0 | 0 | 39 | 212 | 569 | 593 | 297 | 374 | 45 | 56 | 0 | 2185 |
| 1977-78 | 0 | 0 | 0 | 3 | 226 | 399 | 522 | 356 | 168 | 91 | 16 | 0 | 1781 |
| 1978-79 | 0 | 0 | 1 | 2 | 324 | 676 | 737 | 458 | 270 | 66 | 18 | 0 | 2552 |
| 1979-80 | 0 | 0 | 0 | 44 | 395 | 546 | 474 | 335 | 328 | 108 | 32 | 0 | 2262 |
| 1980-81 | 0 | 0 | 0 | 82 | 255 | 374 | 426 | 344 | 263 | 29 | 2 | 0 | 1775 |
| 1981-82 | 0 | 0 | 0 | 74 | 214 | 497 | 594 | 398 | 301 | 98 | 9 | 0 | 2185 |
| 1982-83 | 0 | 0 | 10 | 84 | 429 | 531 | 564 | 364 | 263 | 198 | 21 | 0 | 2564 |
| 1983-84 | 0 | 0 | 0 | 3 | 297 | 524 | 548 | 424 | 216 | 111 | 0 | 0 | 2123 |
| 1984-85 | 0 | 0 | 0 | 127 | 363 | 641 | 629 | 487 | 188 | 41 | 0 | 0 | 2596 |
| 1985-86 | 0 | 0 | 1 | 31 | 393 | 512 | 404 | 270 | 125 | 57 | 11 | 0 | 1804 |
| 1986-87 | 0 | 0 | 14 | 53 | 268 | 586 | 622 | 375 | 316 | 40 | 1 | 0 | 2275 |
| 1987-88 | 0 | 0 | 0 | 18 | 342 | 589 | 612 | 357 | 225 | 83 | 33 | 0 | 2359 |
| 1988-89 | 0 | 0 | 0 | 0 | 291 | 588 | 647 | 425 | 118 | 23 | 16 | 0 | 2101 |
| 1989-90 | 0 | 0 | 0 | 70 | 224 | 519 | 606 | 449 | 172 | 12 | 0 | 0 | 2052 |
| 1990-91 | 0 | 0 | 0 | 23 | 290 | 561 | | | | | | | |

## TABLE 5 — COOLING DEGREE DAYS Base 65 deg. F — LAS VEGAS, NEVADA

| YEAR | JAN | FEB | MAR | APR | MAY | JUNE | JULY | AUG | SEP | OCT | NOV | DEC | TOTAL |
|---|---|---|---|---|---|---|---|---|---|---|---|---|---|
| 1969 | 0 | 0 | 13 | 62 | 390 | 500 | 772 | 852 | 532 | 54 | 0 | 0 | 3175 |
| 1970 | 0 | 0 | 0 | 21 | 334 | 560 | 818 | 748 | 371 | 81 | 1 | 0 | 2934 |
| 1971 | 0 | 0 | 24 | 53 | 148 | 556 | 871 | 752 | 390 | 112 | 0 | 0 | 2906 |
| 1972 | 0 | 2 | 66 | 80 | 308 | 597 | 876 | 675 | 398 | 69 | 0 | 0 | 3071 |
| 1973 | 0 | 0 | 0 | 54 | 382 | 612 | 833 | 708 | 424 | 134 | 8 | 0 | 3155 |
| 1974 | 0 | 0 | 24 | 43 | 394 | 731 | 744 | 713 | 559 | 195 | 0 | 0 | 3403 |
| 1975 | 0 | 0 | 0 | 2 | 276 | 570 | 792 | 704 | 508 | 117 | 2 | 0 | 2973 |
| 1976 | 0 | 0 | 2 | 57 | 404 | 500 | 687 | 641 | 419 | 93 | 6 | 0 | 2809 |
| 1977 | 0 | 0 | 0 | 161 | 149 | 594 | 858 | 781 | 476 | 210 | 3 | 0 | 3332 |
| 1978 | 0 | 0 | 17 | 40 | 277 | 672 | 841 | 752 | 425 | 268 | 8 | 0 | 3300 |
| 1979 | 0 | 0 | 0 | 104 | 346 | 625 | 813 | 656 | 614 | 229 | 0 | 0 | 3387 |
| 1980 | 0 | 0 | 0 | 68 | 160 | 575 | 842 | 788 | 498 | 211 | 15 | 0 | 3157 |
| 1981 | 0 | 0 | 5 | 205 | 296 | 721 | 866 | 781 | 531 | 64 | 12 | 0 | 3481 |
| 1982 | 0 | 0 | 2 | 70 | 281 | 601 | 721 | 699 | 404 | 30 | 0 | 0 | 2708 |
| 1983 | 0 | 0 | 2 | 9 | 269 | 541 | 735 | 589 | 534 | 94 | 10 | 0 | 2783 |
| 1984 | 0 | 0 | 3 | 61 | 496 | 563 | 724 | 641 | 508 | 74 | 1 | 0 | 3071 |
| 1985 | 0 | 0 | 0 | 143 | 377 | 678 | 844 | 778 | 319 | 110 | 2 | 0 | 3251 |
| 1986 | 0 | 20 | 69 | 98 | 379 | 593 | 707 | 821 | 332 | 59 | 0 | 0 | 3178 |
| 1987 | 0 | 0 | 0 | 148 | 302 | 645 | 685 | 729 | 495 | 211 | 0 | 0 | 3215 |
| 1988 | 0 | 0 | 16 | 64 | 300 | 615 | 864 | 685 | 434 | 312 | 31 | 0 | 3321 |
| 1989 | 0 | 11 | 74 | 259 | 351 | 614 | 887 | 687 | 456 | 143 | 0 | 0 | 3482 |
| 1990 | 0 | 0 | 42 | 134 | 302 | 634 | 810 | 713 | 516 | 163 | 0 | 0 | 3314 |

## TABLE 6 — SNOWFALL (inches) — LAS VEGAS, NEVADA

| SEASON | JULY | AUG | SEP | OCT | NOV | DEC | JAN | FEB | MAR | APR | MAY | JUNE | TOTAL |
|---|---|---|---|---|---|---|---|---|---|---|---|---|---|
| 1970-71 | 0.0 | 0.0 | 0.0 | 0.0 | 0.0 | T | T | 0.0 | 0.0 | 0.0 | 0.0 | 0.0 | T |
| 1971-72 | 0.0 | 0.0 | 0.0 | 0.0 | 0.0 | T | 0.0 | 0.0 | 0.0 | 0.0 | 0.0 | 0.0 | T |
| 1972-73 | 0.0 | 0.0 | 0.0 | 0.0 | 0.0 | 0.0 | 0.3 | 0.0 | T | 0.0 | 0.0 | 0.0 | 0.3 |
| 1973-74 | 0.0 | 0.0 | 0.0 | 0.0 | 0.0 | 0.0 | 13.4 | 0.0 | 0.0 | 0.0 | 0.0 | 0.0 | 13.4 |
| 1974-75 | 0.0 | 0.0 | 0.0 | 0.0 | 0.0 | 0.0 | T | 0.0 | T | T | 0.0 | 0.0 | T |
| 1975-76 | 0.0 | 0.0 | 0.0 | 0.0 | 0.0 | T | 0.0 | 0.0 | 0.1 | 0.0 | 0.0 | 0.0 | 0.1 |
| 1976-77 | 0.0 | 0.0 | 0.0 | 0.0 | 0.0 | 0.0 | 0.0 | 0.0 | 0.0 | 0.0 | 0.0 | 0.0 | 0.0 |
| 1977-78 | 0.0 | 0.0 | 0.0 | 0.0 | 0.0 | 0.0 | 0.0 | 0.0 | 0.0 | 0.0 | 0.0 | 0.0 | 0.0 |
| 1978-79 | 0.0 | 0.0 | 0.0 | 0.0 | 0.0 | T | 9.9 | 0.3 | 0.0 | 0.0 | 0.0 | 0.0 | 10.2 |
| 1979-80 | 0.0 | 0.0 | 0.0 | 0.0 | 0.0 | 0.0 | 0.0 | 0.0 | 0.0 | 0.0 | 0.0 | 0.0 | 0.0 |
| 1980-81 | 0.0 | 0.0 | 0.0 | 0.0 | 0.0 | 0.0 | 0.0 | 0.0 | 0.0 | 0.0 | 0.0 | 0.0 | 0.0 |
| 1981-82 | 0.0 | 0.0 | 0.0 | 0.0 | 0.0 | 0.0 | 0.0 | 0.0 | 0.0 | 0.0 | 0.0 | 0.0 | 0.0 |
| 1982-83 | 0.0 | 0.0 | 0.0 | 0.0 | 0.0 | 0.0 | 0.0 | 0.0 | 0.0 | 0.0 | 0.0 | 0.0 | 0.0 |
| 1983-84 | 0.0 | 0.0 | 0.0 | 0.0 | 0.0 | 0.0 | 0.0 | 0.0 | 0.0 | 0.0 | 0.0 | 0.0 | 0.0 |
| 1984-85 | 0.0 | 0.0 | 0.0 | 0.0 | 0.0 | T | 0.0 | 0.0 | 0.0 | 0.0 | 0.0 | 0.0 | T |
| 1985-86 | 0.0 | 0.0 | 0.0 | 0.0 | 0.0 | T | 0.0 | 0.0 | 0.0 | 0.0 | 0.0 | 0.0 | T |
| 1986-87 | 0.0 | 0.0 | 0.0 | 0.0 | 0.0 | 0.0 | T | 0.6 | 0.0 | 0.0 | 0.0 | 0.0 | 0.6 |
| 1987-88 | 0.0 | 0.0 | 0.0 | 0.0 | 0.0 | 0.0 | 0.0 | T | 0.0 | 0.0 | 0.0 | 0.0 | T |
| 1988-89 | 0.0 | 0.0 | 0.0 | 0.0 | 0.0 | T | 0.0 | 0.3 | 0.0 | 0.0 | 0.0 | 0.0 | 0.3 |
| 1989-90 | 0.0 | T | 0.0 | 0.0 | 0.0 | 0.0 | T | 1.4 | 0.0 | 0.0 | 0.0 | 0.0 | 1.4 |
| 1990-91 | 0.0 | 0.0 | 0.0 | 0.0 | 0.0 | 0.0 | | | | | | | |
| Record Mean | 0.0 | T | 0.0 | T | 0.1 | 0.1 | 1.0 | 0.1 | T | T | 0.0 | 0.0 | 1.3 |

**See Reference Notes, relative to all above tables, on preceding page.**

Concord, the Capital of New Hampshire, is situated near the geographical center of New England at an altitude of approximately 300 feet above sea level on the Merrimack River. Its surroundings are hilly with many lakes and ponds. The countryside is generously wooded, mostly on land reclaimed from fields which were formerly cleared for farming. From the coast about 50 miles to the southeast, the terrain slopes gently upward to the city. West of the city, the land rises some 2,000 feet higher in only half that distance. Mount Washington, at an elevation of 6,288 feet is in the White Mountains 75 miles north of town.

Northwesterly winds are prevalent. They bring cold, dry air during the winter and pleasantly cool, dry air in the summer. Stronger southerly winds occur during July and August, and easterly winds usually accompany summer and winter storms. Winter breezes are somewhat lighter, and winds are frequently calm during the night and early morning hours. Low temperatures, as a rule, do not interrupt normal out-of-doors activity because winds are calm or light, producing a low wind chill factor.

Very hot summer weather is infrequent. During any month, temperatures considerably above the average maxima and much below the normal minima are observed.

The average amount of precipitation for the warmer half of the year differs little from that for the colder half. Precipitation occurrences average approximately one day of three for the year, with a somewhat higher frequency for the April-May period, offsetting the lower frequency of August-October. The more significant rains and heavier snowfalls are associated with easterly winds, especially northeasterly winds. The first snowfall of an inch or more is likely to come between the middle of November and the middle of December. The snow cover normally lasts from mid-December until the last week of March, but bare ground is not rare in the winter, nor is a snowscape rare earlier or later in the season. Rain, sleet, or freezing rain may also occur.

Agriculture is neither intensive nor large-scale in the vicinity of the station. Potatoes and other frost-resistant vegetables, hardy fruits such as apples, forage for the dairy industry, and maple sugar are the principal crops.

Based on the 1951-1980 period, the average first occurrence of 32 degrees Fahrenheit in the fall is September 22 and the average last occurrence in the spring is May 23. Freezing temperatures have occurred as late as June and as early as August.

## TABLE 1     NORMALS, MEANS AND EXTREMES

CONCORD, NEW HAMPSHIRE

LATITUDE: 43°12'N    LONGITUDE: 71°30' W    ELEVATION: FT. GRND 342 BARO 343    TIME ZONE: EASTERN    WBAN: 14745

| | (a) | JAN | FEB | MAR | APR | MAY | JUNE | JULY | AUG | SEP | OCT | NOV | DEC | YEAR |
|---|---|---|---|---|---|---|---|---|---|---|---|---|---|---|
| **TEMPERATURE °F:** | | | | | | | | | | | | | | |
| Normals | | | | | | | | | | | | | | |
|  -Daily Maximum | | 30.8 | 33.2 | 41.9 | 56.5 | 68.9 | 77.7 | 82.6 | 80.1 | 71.9 | 61.0 | 47.2 | 34.4 | 57.2 |
|  -Daily Minimum | | 9.0 | 11.0 | 22.2 | 31.6 | 41.4 | 51.6 | 56.4 | 54.5 | 46.2 | 35.5 | 27.3 | 14.5 | 33.4 |
|  -Monthly | | 19.9 | 22.2 | 32.1 | 44.1 | 55.2 | 64.7 | 69.5 | 67.3 | 59.1 | 48.2 | 37.3 | 24.5 | 45.3 |
| Extremes | | | | | | | | | | | | | | |
|  -Record Highest | 48 | 68 | 66 | 85 | 95 | 97 | 98 | 102 | 101 | 98 | 90 | 80 | 68 | 102 |
|  -Year | | 1950 | 1957 | 1977 | 1976 | 1962 | 1980 | 1966 | 1975 | 1953 | 1963 | 1950 | 1982 | JUL 1966 |
|  -Record Lowest | 48 | -33 | -37 | -16 | 8 | 21 | 30 | 35 | 29 | 21 | 10 | -5 | -22 | -37 |
|  -Year | | 1984 | 1943 | 1967 | 1969 | 1966 | 1972 | 1965 | 1965 | 1947 | 1972 | 1989 | 1951 | FEB 1943 |
| **NORMAL DEGREE DAYS:** | | | | | | | | | | | | | | |
| Heating (base 65°F) | | 1398 | 1198 | 1020 | 627 | 314 | 67 | 20 | 39 | 191 | 521 | 831 | 1256 | 7482 |
| Cooling (base 65°F) | | 0 | 0 | 0 | 0 | 10 | 58 | 160 | 111 | 14 | 0 | 0 | 0 | 353 |
| **% OF POSSIBLE SUNSHINE** | 48 | 53 | 55 | 53 | 53 | 54 | 59 | 63 | 60 | 56 | 53 | 42 | 48 | 54 |
| **MEAN SKY COVER (tenths)** | | | | | | | | | | | | | | |
| Sunrise - Sunset | 48 | 6.1 | 6.1 | 6.3 | 6.5 | 6.7 | 6.3 | 6.1 | 5.9 | 5.9 | 5.9 | 6.8 | 6.4 | 6.3 |
| **MEAN NUMBER OF DAYS:** | | | | | | | | | | | | | | |
| Sunrise to Sunset | | | | | | | | | | | | | | |
|  -Clear | 48 | 9.3 | 7.6 | 7.9 | 7.0 | 6.2 | 6.1 | 6.7 | 8.0 | 8.9 | 9.3 | 6.3 | 7.9 | 91.3 |
|  -Partly Cloudy | 48 | 7.0 | 7.7 | 8.1 | 8.2 | 9.7 | 11.8 | 12.6 | 11.6 | 8.9 | 8.9 | 7.6 | 7.9 | 109.9 |
|  -Cloudy | 48 | 14.7 | 12.9 | 15.1 | 14.7 | 15.1 | 12.1 | 11.7 | 11.4 | 12.3 | 12.8 | 16.1 | 15.2 | 164.0 |
| Precipitation | | | | | | | | | | | | | | |
| .01 inches or more | 48 | 10.7 | 9.6 | 10.9 | 11.6 | 12.0 | 10.9 | 10.0 | 9.9 | 8.8 | 8.7 | 11.5 | 10.7 | 125.3 |
| Snow,Ice pellets | | | | | | | | | | | | | | |
| 1.0 inches or more | 48 | 4.5 | 3.9 | 3.1 | 0.6 | 0.* | 0.0 | 0.0 | 0.0 | 0.0 | 0.* | 1.4 | 4.0 | 17.6 |
| Thunderstorms | 48 | 0.* | 0.1 | 0.3 | 0.8 | 2.4 | 4.4 | 5.4 | 3.8 | 1.8 | 0.5 | 0.1 | 0.* | 19.7 |
| Heavy Fog Visibility | | | | | | | | | | | | | | |
| 1/4 mile or less | 48 | 2.1 | 1.8 | 2.8 | 2.0 | 3.2 | 3.7 | 5.4 | 7.0 | 9.2 | 6.5 | 3.6 | 2.6 | 49.7 |
| Temperature °F | | | | | | | | | | | | | | |
|  -Maximum | | | | | | | | | | | | | | |
|   90° and above | 24 | 0.0 | 0.0 | 0.0 | 0.1 | 0.9 | 2.3 | 4.8 | 2.8 | 0.5 | 0.0 | 0.0 | 0.0 | 11.4 |
|   32° and below | 24 | 18.4 | 13.5 | 4.4 | 0.2 | 0.0 | 0.0 | 0.0 | 0.0 | 0.0 | 0.* | 1.9 | 13.8 | 52.1 |
|  -Minimum | | | | | | | | | | | | | | |
|   32° and below | 24 | 30.5 | 27.2 | 25.8 | 17.2 | 5.6 | 0.3 | 0.0 | 0.1 | 2.3 | 14.2 | 21.6 | 29.2 | 173.9 |
|   0° and below | 24 | 10.2 | 6.9 | 1.3 | 0.0 | 0.0 | 0.0 | 0.0 | 0.0 | 0.0 | 0.0 | 0.2 | 5.6 | 24.2 |
| **AVG. STATION PRESS.(mb)** | 17 | 1002.5 | 1003.4 | 1002.5 | 1001.0 | 1002.1 | 1001.8 | 1002.3 | 1004.1 | 1005.4 | 1005.8 | 1004.0 | 1003.7 | 1003.2 |
| **RELATIVE HUMIDITY (%)** | | | | | | | | | | | | | | |
| Hour 01 | 23 | 74 | 72 | 73 | 76 | 83 | 88 | 90 | 91 | 91 | 86 | 81 | 77 | 82 |
| Hour 07 | 24 | 75 | 76 | 76 | 75 | 77 | 82 | 84 | 88 | 90 | 87 | 83 | 80 | 81 |
| Hour 13 (Local Time) | 24 | 58 | 55 | 53 | 46 | 48 | 53 | 52 | 53 | 55 | 53 | 60 | 62 | 54 |
| Hour 19 | 24 | 66 | 62 | 59 | 55 | 58 | 64 | 65 | 70 | 76 | 73 | 73 | 70 | 66 |
| **PRECIPITATION (inches):** | | | | | | | | | | | | | | |
| Water Equivalent | | | | | | | | | | | | | | |
|  -Normal | | 2.78 | 2.47 | 2.93 | 3.01 | 2.93 | 2.91 | 2.93 | 3.26 | 3.12 | 3.10 | 3.66 | 3.43 | 36.53 |
|  -Maximum Monthly | 48 | 8.09 | 7.77 | 7.81 | 5.88 | 9.52 | 10.10 | 6.53 | 6.88 | 7.78 | 8.78 | 7.36 | 7.52 | 10.10 |
|  -Year | | 1979 | 1981 | 1953 | 1983 | 1984 | 1944 | 1988 | 1973 | 1960 | 1962 | 1983 | 1973 | JUN 1944 |
|  -Minimum Monthly | 48 | 0.40 | 0.03 | 0.86 | 1.02 | 0.60 | 0.64 | 0.96 | 0.95 | 0.41 | 0.59 | 0.75 | 0.58 | 0.03 |
|  -Year | | 1970 | 1987 | 1981 | 1985 | 1965 | 1979 | 1955 | 1944 | 1948 | 1947 | 1976 | 1943 | FEB 1987 |
|  -Maximum in 24 hrs | 48 | 2.12 | 2.26 | 2.27 | 2.27 | 2.59 | 4.47 | 2.54 | 3.71 | 4.12 | 4.24 | 2.89 | 3.31 | 4.47 |
|  -Year | | 1979 | 1981 | 1974 | 1987 | 1984 | 1944 | 1971 | 1973 | 1960 | 1962 | 1947 | 1969 | JUN 1944 |
| Snow,Ice pellets | | | | | | | | | | | | | | |
|  -Maximum Monthly | 48 | 45.4 | 49.8 | 38.3 | 15.3 | 5.0 | 0.0 | 0.0 | 0.0 | 0.0 | 2.1 | 18.4 | 38.1 | 49.8 |
|  -Year | | 1987 | 1969 | 1956 | 1982 | 1945 | | | | | 1969 | 1971 | 1956 | FEB 1969 |
|  -Maximum in 24 hrs | 48 | 19.0 | 14.2 | 14.4 | 13.9 | 5.0 | 0.0 | 0.0 | 0.0 | 0.0 | 2.1 | 9.5 | 14.6 | 19.0 |
|  -Year | | 1944 | 1972 | 1984 | 1982 | 1945 | | | | | 1969 | 1961 | 1946 | JAN 1944 |
| **WIND:** | | | | | | | | | | | | | | |
| Mean Speed (mph) | 47 | 7.3 | 7.8 | 8.2 | 7.9 | 7.0 | 6.4 | 5.7 | 5.3 | 5.5 | 5.9 | 6.6 | 7.0 | 6.7 |
| Prevailing Direction | | | | | | | | | | | | | | |
|  through 1963 | | NW | NW | NW | NW | NW | NW | NW | NW | NW | NW | NW | NW | NW |
| Fastest Mile | | | | | | | | | | | | | | |
|  -Direction (!!!) | 46 | NW | N | NE | NW | NW | SW | SW | E | E | NW | NE | NW | NE |
|  -Speed (MPH) | 46 | 44 | 42 | 71 | 52 | 48 | 44 | 45 | 56 | 42 | 39 | 72 | 52 | 72 |
|  -Year | | 1972 | 1950 | 1950 | 1945 | 1945 | 1986 | 1971 | 1934 | 1960 | 1944 | 1950 | 1962 | NOV 1950 |
| Peak Gust | | | | | | | | | | | | | | |
|  -Direction (!!!) | 6 | NW | E | NW | NW | SE | SW | N | NW | SE | NW | NW | NW | E |
|  -Speed (mph) | 6 | 46 | 60 | 43 | 48 | 39 | 59 | 53 | 45 | 44 | 41 | 53 | 45 | 60 |
|  -Date | | 1989 | 1988 | 1988 | 1985 | 1988 | 1986 | 1987 | 1987 | 1985 | 1986 | 1989 | 1985 | FEB 1988 |

**See reference Notes to this table on the following page.**

PRECIPITATION (inches)  CONCORD, NEW HAMPSHIRE

**TABLE 2**

| YEAR | JAN | FEB | MAR | APR | MAY | JUNE | JULY | AUG | SEP | OCT | NOV | DEC | ANNUAL |
|------|-----|-----|-----|-----|-----|------|------|-----|-----|-----|-----|-----|--------|
| 1961 | 1.07 | 2.33 | 1.48 | 3.35 | 2.85 | 2.15 | 3.13 | 3.55 | 3.44 | 2.06 | 3.70 | 2.88 | 31.99 |
| 1962 | 2.66 | 2.59 | 1.64 | 2.13 | 2.58 | 3.30 | 2.99 | 2.59 | 1.76 | 8.78 | 2.65 | 3.15 | 36.82 |
| 1963 | 2.05 | 2.37 | 2.12 | 1.23 | 2.17 | 1.22 | 2.94 | 2.74 | 2.12 | 1.22 | 6.78 | 1.57 | 28.53 |
| 1964 | 3.64 | 1.93 | 3.01 | 2.05 | 1.15 | 0.81 | 3.37 | 2.74 | 2.42 | 2.24 | 3.47 | 3.07 | 27.90 |
| 1965 | 0.97 | 3.06 | 0.93 | 2.49 | 0.60 | 2.72 | 1.73 | 3.12 | .87 | 2.71 | 2.45 | 1.52 | 24.17 |
| 1966 | 2.69 | 2.13 | 2.19 | 1.16 | 2.16 | 1.78 | 2.30 | 4.05 | 5.40 | 3.31 | 3.01 | 2.42 | 32.60 |
| 1967 | 1.23 | 2.36 | 2.36 | 3.52 | 3.92 | 3.82 | 5.91 | 1.97 | 2.04 | 0.99 | 2.86 | 3.82 | 34.19 |
| 1968 | 1.79 | 0.93 | 3.80 | 2.85 | 5.20 | 5.90 | 1.62 | 3.60 | 2.34 | 2.23 | 5.24 | 5.82 | 41.32 |
| 1969 | 1.34 | 3.69 | 2.36 | 2.75 | 1.26 | 4.70 | 4.40 | 2.84 | 4.43 | 1.56 | 5.87 | 7.10 | 42.30 |
| 1970 | 0.40 | 4.27 | 2.78 | 3.38 | 3.04 | 2.26 | 2.33 | 3.06 | 3.40 | 3.64 | 3.03 | 3.08 | 34.67 |
| 1971 | 1.63 | 3.87 | 2.28 | 2.19 | 3.36 | 1.67 | 5.14 | 2.79 | .91 | 2.69 | 2.91 | 2.36 | 32.80 |
| 1972 | 1.44 | 2.60 | 4.16 | 2.71 | 4.20 | 3.54 | 5.40 | 2.12 | 2.55 | 2.23 | 6.57 | 4.55 | 42.07 |
| 1973 | 2.44 | 1.91 | 2.58 | 4.55 | 4.20 | 4.86 | 1.05 | 6.88 | .77 | 2.46 | 1.82 | 7.52 | 42.04 |
| 1974 | 2.80 | 2.32 | 3.98 | 2.58 | 3.74 | 1.82 | 1.41 | 2.20 | 4.74 | 1.64 | 3.20 | 4.02 | 34.45 |
| 1975 | 4.12 | 2.36 | 2.37 | 2.47 | 1.22 | 3.87 | 3.71 | 3.94 | 5.15 | 4.29 | 4.91 | 3.12 | 42.28 |
| 1976 | 3.40 | 2.36 | 2.02 | 2.43 | 3.90 | 2.74 | 3.20 | 2.66 | 2.73 | 4.05 | 0.75 | 2.27 | 32.51 |
| 1977 | 2.16 | 2.02 | 4.51 | 4.04 | 2.44 | 3.47 | 1.26 | 3.51 | 5.64 | 5.52 | 3.07 | 4.00 | 41.64 |
| 1978 | 6.32 | 0.67 | 2.16 | 2.06 | 2.67 | 3.18 | 1.08 | 2.87 | 2.46 | 2.72 | 1.77 | 2.91 | 28.87 |
| 1979 | 8.09 | 2.29 | 2.85 | 3.10 | 4.86 | 0.64 | 3.45 | 4.20 | 2.15 | 3.79 | 2.92 | 1.93 | 41.27 |
| 1980 | 0.43 | 0.78 | 3.37 | 3.72 | 0.86 | 2.83 | 2.35 | 3.99 | 2.19 | 2.63 | 3.12 | 0.79 | 27.06 |
| 1981 | 0.48 | 7.77 | 0.86 | 3.12 | 3.21 | 2.81 | 5.54 | 3.25 | 4.61 | 6.51 | 3.51 | 4.17 | 45.84 |
| 1982 | 3.98 | 2.88 | 2.47 | 3.08 | 1.91 | 7.84 | 2.83 | 2.54 | .85 | 1.52 | 2.93 | 0.91 | 34.74 |
| 1983 | 3.92 | 2.17 | 7.07 | 5.88 | 5.19 | 2.52 | 2.07 | 2.07 | .21 | 3.28 | 7.36 | 5.35 | 48.09 |
| 1984 | 1.89 | 5.06 | 2.92 | 3.74 | 9.52 | 2.83 | 4.44 | 0.97 | .08 | 4.42 | 2.67 | 2.70 | 42.24 |
| 1985 | 0.95 | 1.99 | 2.86 | 1.02 | 2.05 | 3.05 | 2.83 | 2.51 | 3.78 | 3.62 | 4.58 | 1.65 | 30.89 |
| 1986 | 4.78 | 2.23 | 3.58 | 1.85 | 4.95 | 4.77 | 3.72 | 2.27 | 1.71 | 4.48 | 4.50 | 40.28 |
| 1987 | 3.00 | 0.03 | 3.47 | 4.71 | 1.08 | 5.77 | 3.77 | 2.84 | 3.94 | 4.14 | 2.50 | 1.55 | 36.80 |
| 1988 | 1.97 | 2.24 | 1.32 | 2.75 | 3.35 | 0.80 | 6.53 | 5.44 | .56 | 1.23 | 5.06 | 1.05 | 33.30 |
| 1989 | 0.74 | 2.05 | 2.18 | 3.40 | 5.11 | 4.25 | 3.62 | 3.55 | 4.22 | 4.86 | 3.34 | 0.91 | 38.23 |
| 1990 | 2.82 | 2.63 | 1.64 | 3.00 | 5.09 | 2.51 | 1.79 | 7.19 | 2.31 | 4.93 | 3.25 | 4.12 | 41.28 |
| Record Mean | 2.90 | 2.61 | 3.06 | 3.01 | 3.17 | 3.31 | 3.55 | 3.42 | 3.36 | 3.19 | 3.46 | 3.04 | 38.07 |

**TABLE 3**  AVERAGE TEMPERATURE (deg. F)  CONCORD, NEW HAMPSHIRE

| YEAR | JAN | FEB | MAR | APR | MAY | JUNE | JULY | AUG | SEP | OCT | NOV | DEC | ANNUAL |
|------|-----|-----|-----|-----|-----|------|------|-----|-----|-----|-----|-----|--------|
| 1961 | 14.5 | 24.8 | 32.4 | 42.6 | 53.2 | 65.4 | 69.5 | 68.5 | 57.1 | 52.4 | 39.5 | 27.0 | 46.4 |
| 1962 | 20.6 | 17.8 | 34.0 | 45.3 | 54.6 | 66.3 | 66.6 | 67.8 | 57.7 | 48.1 | 36.1 | 22.6 | 44.8 |
| 1963 | 20.8 | 18.8 | 33.5 | 43.4 | 55.5 | 66.4 | 72.1 | 65.6 | 56.5 | 53.8 | 42.3 | 17.3 | 45.5 |
| 1964 | 22.9 | 22.4 | 33.6 | 43.6 | 58.8 | 65.6 | 70.8 | 62.7 | 57.4 | 47.4 | 37.1 | 25.1 | 45.6 |
| #1965 | 18.9 | 22.2 | 31.9 | 41.3 | 57.1 | 62.5 | 65.9 | 66.6 | 58.8 | 46.8 | 34.8 | 27.3 | 44.5 |
| 1966 | 20.4 | 22.5 | 34.6 | 42.2 | 53.4 | 66.8 | 72.2 | 69.6 | 57.0 | 48.0 | 41.5 | 26.2 | 46.2 |
| 1967 | 24.8 | 17.5 | 27.1 | 42.0 | 48.8 | 66.1 | 70.2 | 67.2 | 58.4 | 49.3 | 32.7 | 27.8 | 44.3 |
| 1968 | 15.8 | 18.0 | 34.8 | 44.8 | 51.1 | 62.0 | 69.3 | 64.6 | 61.0 | 51.2 | 34.8 | 22.5 | 44.2 |
| 1969 | 21.9 | 23.2 | 28.3 | 44.3 | 52.3 | 63.0 | 65.4 | 68.9 | 59.7 | 47.5 | 38.9 | 23.7 | 44.8 |
| 1970 | 11.0 | 22.6 | 30.7 | 45.8 | 57.3 | 63.1 | 70.9 | 68.7 | 60.6 | 51.0 | 39.3 | 20.3 | 45.1 |
| 1971 | 12.5 | 23.3 | 30.4 | 42.1 | 54.1 | 65.5 | 68.3 | 67.0 | 61.1 | 51.9 | 32.4 | 26.6 | 44.6 |
| 1972 | 22.0 | 21.2 | 27.9 | 40.2 | 56.8 | 62.8 | 69.3 | 64.1 | 57.5 | 42.3 | 31.2 | 23.4 | 43.2 |
| 1973 | 21.0 | 20.2 | 35.5 | 45.0 | 52.9 | 66.9 | 70.3 | 72.3 | 58.8 | 48.2 | 36.1 | 28.9 | 46.3 |
| 1974 | 21.4 | 21.1 | 31.8 | 45.8 | 51.1 | 62.8 | 67.5 | 67.0 | 58.9 | 42.5 | 35.9 | 26.7 | 44.4 |
| 1975 | 21.6 | 21.5 | 30.1 | 40.4 | 61.3 | 65.0 | 72.9 | 66.5 | 56.1 | 47.6 | 39.9 | 21.9 | 45.4 |
| 1976 | 10.9 | 24.7 | 31.9 | 46.7 | 53.6 | 66.8 | 66.8 | 65.3 | 57.2 | 45.0 | 31.7 | 16.1 | 43.3 |
| 1977 | 10.6 | 20.5 | 36.7 | 45.1 | 58.3 | 62.9 | 69.0 | 68.0 | 58.5 | 47.0 | 39.4 | 21.0 | 44.8 |
| 1978 | 17.5 | 13.5 | 28.0 | 40.6 | 57.5 | 65.2 | 69.7 | 65.9 | 55.9 | 46.7 | 35.3 | 22.7 | 43.5 |
| 1979 | 23.3 | 15.1 | 37.6 | 44.2 | 56.3 | 63.8 | 71.2 | 67.5 | 59.8 | 47.4 | 42.2 | 29.4 | 46.5 |
| 1980 | 22.4 | 19.1 | 31.8 | 44.4 | 55.6 | 62.8 | 70.6 | 68.4 | 58.2 | 45.1 | 34.8 | 19.2 | 44.4 |
| 1981 | 12.5 | 30.8 | 34.2 | 47.1 | 57.5 | 66.1 | 69.9 | 66.6 | 58.7 | 45.2 | 37.8 | 25.4 | 46.0 |
| 1982 | 10.9 | 20.8 | 30.2 | 41.6 | 57.3 | 60.9 | 69.5 | 65.4 | 60.2 | 47.6 | 41.7 | 32.4 | 44.9 |
| 1983 | 23.1 | 26.1 | 35.9 | 45.2 | 53.1 | 65.1 | 70.1 | 69.3 | 62.3 | 48.2 | 39.4 | 23.4 | 46.8 |
| 1984 | 16.0 | 30.5 | 28.2 | 44.6 | 52.9 | 65.9 | 68.7 | 69.3 | 57.8 | 50.4 | 38.3 | 30.3 | 46.1 |
| 1985 | 15.9 | 25.8 | 35.7 | 45.2 | 56.1 | 62.2 | 70.3 | 66.7 | 60.5 | 49.2 | 38.5 | 22.0 | 45.7 |
| 1986 | 23.0 | 21.3 | 35.5 | 48.2 | 57.5 | 61.3 | 67.3 | 66.1 | 57.3 | 47.4 | 34.1 | 29.0 | 45.7 |
| 1987 | 20.0 | 22.0 | 34.5 | 46.8 | 56.7 | 64.4 | 70.6 | 65.1 | 58.7 | 45.8 | 36.9 | 28.1 | 45.8 |
| 1988 | 18.5 | 23.5 | 33.4 | 43.9 | 57.3 | 62.9 | 72.6 | 70.5 | 57.8 | 44.9 | 39.1 | 23.2 | 45.6 |
| 1989 | 25.7 | 22.6 | 31.8 | 41.4 | 58.3 | 65.0 | 69.5 | 67.7 | 60.8 | 49.1 | 35.8 | 11.9 | 45.0 |
| 1990 | 28.6 | 24.6 | 34.7 | 45.6 | 52.8 | 65.3 | 70.8 | 69.8 | 59.7 | 51.8 | 40.1 | 30.9 | 47.9 |
| Record Mean | 21.0 | 22.8 | 32.1 | 44.4 | 56.2 | 65.2 | 70.0 | 67.3 | 59.7 | 47.8 | 37.5 | 25.4 | 45.8 |
| Max | 31.3 | 33.5 | 41.8 | 56.0 | 68.8 | 77.1 | 82.1 | 79.0 | 71.4 | 60.5 | 46.9 | 34.7 | 56.9 |
| Min | 10.6 | 12.0 | 22.4 | 32.8 | 43.5 | 52.5 | 57.9 | 55.6 | 47.9 | 37.2 | 28.1 | 16.1 | 34.7 |

## REFERENCE NOTES FOR TABLES 1, 2, 3 and 6    (CONCORD, NH)

### GENERAL

T - TRACE AMOUNT
BLANK ENTRIES DENOTE MISSING/UNREPORTED DATA.
# INDICATES A STATION OR INSTRUMENT RELOCATION.

### SPECIFIC

#### TABLE 1

(a) -  LENGTH OF RECORD IN YEARS. ALTHOUGH
INDIVIDUAL MONTHS MAY BE MISSING.
*  LESS THAN .05

NORMALS — BASED ON THE 1951-1980 RECORD PERIOD.
EXTREMES — DATES ARE THE MOST RECENT OCCURRENCE.
WIND DIR. — NUMERALS SHOW TENS OF DEGREES
CLOCKWISE FROM TRUE NORTH.
"00" INDICATES CALM.
RESULTANT WIND DIRECTIONS ARE GIVEN TO WHOLE DEGREES.

#### TABLE 3

MAX AND MIN ARE LONG-TERM MEAN DAILY MAXIMUM
AND MEAN DAILY MINIMUM TEMPERATURES.

### EXCEPTIONS

**TABLES 2, 3, and 6**

RECORD MEANS ARE THROUGH THE CURRENT YEAR,
BEGINNING IN     1871 FOR TEMPERATURE
1855 FOR PRECIPITATION
1942 FOR SNOWFALL

## TABLE 4

HEATING DEGREE DAYS Base 65 deg. F    CONCORD, NEW HAMPSHIRE

| SEASON | JULY | AUG | SEP | OCT | NOV | DEC | JAN | FEB | MAR | APR | MAY | JUNE | TOTAL |
|---|---|---|---|---|---|---|---|---|---|---|---|---|---|
| 1961-62 | 21 | 25 | 86 | 389 | 756 | 1172 | 1369 | 1316 | 956 | 585 | 341 | 33 | 7049 |
| 1962-63 | 31 | 30 | 234 | 519 | 860 | 1312 | 1363 | 1287 | 966 | 639 | 291 | 70 | 7602 |
| 1963-64 | 20 | 57 | 267 | 342 | 675 | 1472 | 1295 | 1231 | 964 | 636 | 221 | 70 | 7250 |
| #1964-65 | 8 | 106 | 246 | 539 | 831 | 1230 | 1418 | 1191 | 1015 | 704 | 257 | 133 | 7678 |
| 1965-66 | 50 | 78 | 227 | 556 | 899 | 1163 | 1376 | 1184 | 935 | 681 | 362 | 73 | 7584 |
| 1966-67 | 6 | 5 | 244 | 520 | 697 | 1196 | 1241 | 1323 | 1164 | 683 | 496 | 57 | 7632 |
| 1967-68 | 8 | 34 | 208 | 482 | 965 | 1144 | 1520 | 1358 | 928 | 598 | 424 | 118 | 7787 |
| 1968-69 | 18 | 92 | 133 | 424 | 899 | 1311 | 1330 | 1165 | 1128 | 613 | 389 | 119 | 7621 |
| 1969-70 | 64 | 40 | 193 | 534 | 777 | 1275 | 1668 | 1179 | 1055 | 572 | 256 | 108 | 7721 |
| 1970-71 | 4 | 25 | 181 | 431 | 760 | 1379 | 1622 | 1165 | 1064 | 682 | 332 | 73 | 7718 |
| 1971-72 | 26 | 49 | 165 | 396 | 970 | 1327 | 1267 | 1142 | 736 | 262 | 112 | | 7637 |
| 1972-73 | 27 | 82 | 223 | 695 | 1007 | 1284 | 1357 | 1250 | 905 | 596 | 370 | 78 | 7874 |
| 1973-74 | 15 | 9 | 244 | 518 | 860 | 1112 | 1345 | 1223 | 1025 | 573 | 432 | 99 | 7455 |
| 1974-75 | 34 | 26 | 213 | 694 | 865 | 1182 | 1339 | 1218 | 1075 | 730 | 152 | 98 | 7626 |
| 1975-76 | 10 | 78 | 260 | 532 | 747 | 1330 | 1672 | 1162 | 1019 | 565 | 356 | 60 | 7791 |
| 1976-77 | 37 | 84 | 234 | 615 | 992 | 1506 | 1683 | 1242 | 870 | 594 | 259 | 119 | 8235 |
| 1977-78 | 37 | 58 | 222 | 551 | 760 | 1360 | 1466 | 1435 | 1138 | 725 | 270 | 72 | 8094 |
| 1978-79 | 45 | 34 | 275 | 563 | 882 | 1304 | 1284 | 1392 | 841 | 617 | 280 | 99 | 7616 |
| 1979-80 | 33 | 64 | 199 | 546 | 675 | 1098 | 1317 | 1324 | 1022 | 610 | 290 | 123 | 7301 |
| 1980-81 | 13 | 33 | 245 | 611 | 899 | 1417 | 1626 | 953 | 951 | 530 | 267 | 40 | 7585 |
| 1981-82 | 12 | 43 | 192 | 608 | 810 | 1222 | 1674 | 1233 | 1072 | 695 | 246 | 136 | 7943 |
| 1982-83 | 25 | 66 | 169 | 535 | 692 | 1007 | 1291 | 1086 | 895 | 588 | 364 | 82 | 6800 |
| 1983-84 | 14 | 33 | 167 | 521 | 760 | 1283 | 1516 | 993 | 1135 | 607 | 382 | 85 | 7496 |
| 1984-85 | 19 | 27 | 238 | 446 | 792 | 1072 | 1514 | 1092 | 901 | 588 | 286 | 106 | 7081 |
| 1985-86 | 9 | 38 | 166 | 485 | 785 | 1326 | 1295 | 1216 | 907 | 499 | 267 | 140 | 7133 |
| 1986-87 | 41 | 67 | 251 | 538 | 919 | 1109 | 1390 | 1199 | 939 | 542 | 296 | 77 | 7368 |
| 1987-88 | 18 | 89 | 201 | 589 | 837 | 1138 | 1436 | 1194 | 971 | 626 | 254 | 137 | 7490 |
| 1988-89 | 19 | 60 | 219 | 622 | 769 | 1289 | 1211 | 1182 | 1022 | 703 | 219 | 80 | 7395 |
| 1989-90 | 6 | 53 | 169 | 484 | 865 | 1639 | 1121 | 1121 | 933 | 585 | 369 | 67 | 7412 |
| 1990-91 | 22 | 15 | 183 | 409 | 737 | 1049 | | | | | | | |

## TABLE 5

COOLING DEGREE DAYS Base 65 deg. F    CONCORD, NEW HAMPSHIRE

| YEAR | JAN | FEB | MAR | APR | MAY | JUNE | JULY | AUG | SEP | OCT | NOV | DEC | TOTAL |
|---|---|---|---|---|---|---|---|---|---|---|---|---|---|
| 1969 | 0 | 0 | 0 | 0 | 4 | 65 | 82 | 168 | 44 | 0 | 0 | 0 | 363 |
| 1970 | 0 | 0 | 0 | 1 | 27 | 58 | 196 | 145 | 56 | 6 | 0 | 0 | 489 |
| 1971 | 0 | 0 | 0 | 0 | 0 | 95 | 135 | 118 | 55 | 0 | 0 | 0 | 403 |
| 1972 | 0 | 0 | 0 | 0 | 17 | 52 | 167 | 60 | 5 | 0 | 0 | 0 | 301 |
| 1973 | 0 | 0 | 0 | 3 | 2 | 145 | 184 | 242 | 67 | 2 | 0 | 0 | 645 |
| 1974 | 0 | 0 | 0 | 3 | 9 | 40 | 118 | 92 | 40 | 0 | 0 | 0 | 302 |
| 1975 | 0 | 0 | 0 | 0 | 48 | 108 | 263 | 134 | 0 | 0 | 0 | 0 | 553 |
| 1976 | 0 | 0 | 0 | 18 | 9 | 184 | 100 | 99 | 8 | 1 | 0 | 0 | 419 |
| 1977 | 0 | 0 | 0 | 5 | 57 | 64 | 168 | 156 | 38 | 0 | 0 | 0 | 488 |
| 1978 | 0 | 0 | 0 | 0 | 46 | 83 | 198 | 186 | 8 | 0 | 0 | 0 | 521 |
| 1979 | 0 | 0 | 0 | 1 | 15 | 69 | 232 | 150 | 46 | 6 | 0 | 0 | 519 |
| 1980 | 0 | 0 | 0 | 0 | 0 | 5 | 64 | 193 | 145 | 51 | 0 | 0 | 458 |
| 1981 | 0 | 0 | 0 | 0 | 38 | 80 | 172 | 101 | 11 | 0 | 0 | 0 | 402 |
| 1982 | 0 | 0 | 0 | 0 | 11 | 17 | 171 | 87 | 31 | 0 | 0 | 0 | 317 |
| 1983 | 0 | 0 | 0 | 0 | 2 | 93 | 179 | 172 | 93 | 5 | 0 | 0 | 544 |
| 1984 | 0 | 0 | 0 | 15 | 117 | 139 | 165 | 28 | 0 | 0 | 0 | 0 | 464 |
| 1985 | 0 | 0 | 0 | 0 | 16 | 27 | 184 | 93 | 36 | 1 | 0 | 0 | 357 |
| 1986 | 0 | 0 | 0 | 0 | 44 | 37 | 118 | 109 | 23 | 0 | 0 | 0 | 331 |
| 1987 | 0 | 0 | 0 | 0 | 1 | 45 | 64 | 198 | 96 | 21 | 0 | 0 | 425 |
| 1988 | 0 | 0 | 0 | 0 | 19 | 81 | 262 | 238 | 7 | 4 | 0 | 0 | 611 |
| 1989 | 0 | 0 | 0 | 0 | 17 | 87 | 153 | 141 | 50 | 0 | 0 | 0 | 448 |
| 1990 | 0 | 0 | 0 | 10 | 0 | 80 | 210 | 170 | 30 | 8 | 0 | 0 | 508 |

## TABLE 6

SNOWFALL (inches)    CONCORD, NEW HAMPSHIRE

| SEASON | JULY | AUG | SEP | OCT | NOV | DEC | JAN | FEB | MAR | APR | MAY | JUNE | TOTAL |
|---|---|---|---|---|---|---|---|---|---|---|---|---|---|
| 1961-62 | 0.0 | 0.0 | 0.0 | T | 10.0 | 19.7 | 6.7 | 29.8 | 4.5 | 0.4 | 0.0 | 0.0 | 71.1 |
| 1962-63 | 0.0 | 0.0 | 0.0 | T | 0.4 | 12.7 | 15.3 | 14.8 | 13.9 | 0.5 | T | 0.0 | 57.6 |
| 1963-64 | 0.0 | 0.0 | 0.0 | T | T | 16.9 | 24.3 | 19.1 | 15.8 | 1 | 0.0 | 0.0 | 76.1 |
| 1964-65 | 0.0 | 0.0 | 0.0 | T | T | 12.4 | 13.2 | 6.5 | 5.2 | 1.3 | 0.0 | 0.0 | 38.6 |
| 1965-66 | 0.0 | 0.0 | 0.0 | T | 1.0 | 4.6 | 32.9 | 17.7 | 3.7 | T | 1.1 | 0.0 | 61.0 |
| 1966-67 | 0.0 | 0.0 | 0.0 | 0.0 | T | 14.3 | 8.3 | 32.6 | 19.6 | 6.0 | T | 0.0 | 80.8 |
| 1967-68 | 0.0 | 0.0 | 0.0 | 0.0 | 15.0 | 15.0 | 15.8 | 6.7 | 7.4 | 0.0 | 0.0 | 0.0 | 59.9 |
| 1968-69 | 0.0 | 0.0 | 0.0 | 0.0 | 11.6 | 13.4 | 4.7 | 49.8 | 5.7 | T | 0.0 | 0.0 | 85.2 |
| 1969-70 | 0.0 | 0.0 | 0.0 | 2.1 | T | 20.7 | 5.0 | 13.8 | 14.2 | 2.8 | 0.0 | 0.0 | 58.6 |
| 1970-71 | 0.0 | 0.0 | 0.0 | 0.0 | T | 30.1 | 15.6 | 19.8 | 24.0 | 6.3 | 0.0 | 0.0 | 95.8 |
| 1971-72 | 0.0 | 0.0 | 0.0 | 0.0 | 18.4 | 17.4 | 10.8 | 29.8 | 13.6 | 10.0 | 0.0 | 0.0 | 100.0 |
| 1972-73 | 0.0 | 0.0 | 0.0 | 0.0 | 12.9 | 23.2 | 13.1 | 5.6 | 0.1 | 3.4 | 0.0 | 0.0 | 58.3 |
| 1973-74 | 0.0 | 0.0 | 0.0 | 0.0 | T | 6.6 | 15.4 | 7.0 | 6.5 | 3.9 | 0.0 | 0.0 | 39.4 |
| 1974-75 | 0.0 | 0.0 | 0.0 | 0.0 | 2.9 | 18.3 | 19.5 | 17.1 | 4.7 | 5.5 | 0.0 | 0.0 | 68.0 |
| 1975-76 | 0.0 | 0.0 | 0.0 | 0.0 | 2.2 | 25.1 | 14.7 | 8.4 | 24.3 | T | 0.0 | 0.0 | 74.7 |
| 1976-77 | 0.0 | 0.0 | 0.0 | T | 3.1 | 11.6 | 37.1 | 11.7 | 22.3 | 0.5 | T | 0.0 | 86.3 |
| 1977-78 | 0.0 | 0.0 | 0.0 | 0.0 | 1.5 | 20.2 | 37.1 | 13.5 | 11.5 | 0.4 | T | 0.0 | 84.2 |
| 1978-79 | 0.0 | 0.0 | 0.0 | 0.0 | 10.5 | 16.2 | 42.3 | 4.5 | 0.2 | 5.1 | 0.0 | 0.0 | 78.8 |
| 1979-80 | 0.0 | 0.0 | 0.0 | 1.3 | T | 2.1 | 3.1 | 11.9 | 8.6 | T | 0.0 | 0.0 | 27.0 |
| 1980-81 | 0.0 | 0.0 | 0.0 | T | 9.4 | 9.2 | 20.9 | 5.4 | T | 0.0 | 0.0 | | 54.7 |
| 1981-82 | 0.0 | 0.0 | 0.0 | 0.0 | T | 33.0 | 26.2 | 9.0 | 6.5 | 15.3 | 0.0 | 0.0 | 90.0 |
| 1982-83 | 0.0 | 0.0 | 0.0 | 0.0 | 1.3 | 3.6 | 9.0 | 20.8 | 4.0 | T | T | 0.0 | 38.7 |
| 1983-84 | 0.0 | 0.0 | 0.0 | 0.0 | T | 17.5 | 20.4 | 12.7 | 25.0 | T | T | 0.0 | 75.6 |
| 1984-85 | 0.0 | 0.0 | 0.0 | 0.0 | T | 16.5 | 11.6 | 11.0 | 12.4 | 1.0 | 0.0 | 0.0 | 52.5 |
| 1985-86 | 0.0 | 0.0 | 0.0 | 0.0 | 8.3 | 11.2 | 15.1 | 11.5 | 4.4 | T | T | 0.0 | 50.5 |
| 1986-87 | 0.0 | 0.0 | 0.0 | 0.0 | 14.4 | 7.7 | 45.4 | 0.6 | 7.0 | 9.4 | 0.0 | 0.0 | 84.5 |
| 1987-88 | 0.0 | 0.0 | 0.0 | 0.0 | 5.8 | 12.0 | 19.3 | 23.7 | 4.6 | 0.1 | 0.0 | 0.0 | 65.5 |
| 1988-89 | 0.0 | 0.0 | T | 0.0 | 0.5 | 5.0 | 5.6 | 7.0 | 10.2 | 0.8 | T | 0.0 | 29.1 |
| 1989-90 | 0.0 | 0.0 | 0.0 | 4.7 | 12.0 | 23.1 | 22.0 | 1.3 | T | 0.0 | | | 63.1 |
| 1990-91 | 0.0 | 0.0 | 0.0 | 0.0 | 0.6 | 8.8 | | | | | | | |
| Record Mean | 0.0 | 0.0 | 0.0 | 0.1 | 4.0 | 13.7 | 18.1 | 14.7 | 10.6 | 2.3 | 0.1 | 0.0 | 63.6 |

See Reference Notes, relative to all above tables, on preceding page.

The Atlantic City National Weather Service Office is located at the National Aviation Facilities Experimental Center, Pomona, which is about 10 miles west-northwest of Atlantic City and the Atlantic Ocean. The surrounding terrain is fairly flat at an elevation of 50 to 60 feet above sea level. Vegetation in the area consists of scrub pine and low underbrush, but clearing for the air facility has been quite extensive. Bays and salt marshes are as near as 6 miles east of the airport. Atlantic City is located on Abescon Island on the southeast coast of New Jersey. Surrounding terrain, composed of tidal marshes and beach sand, is flat and lies slightly above sea level. The climate is principally continental in character. However, the moderating influence of the Atlantic Ocean is apparent throughout the year, being more marked in the city than at the airport. As a result, summers are relatively cooler and winters milder than elsewhere at the same latitude.

Land and sea breezes, local circulations resulting from the differential heating and cooling of the land and sea, often prevail. These winds occur when moderate or intense storms are not present in the area, thus enabling the local circulation to overcome the general wind pattern. During the warm season sea breezes in the late morning and afternoon hours prevent excessive heating. Frequently, the temperature at Atlantic City during the afternoon hours in the summer averages several degrees lower than at the airport and the airport averages several degrees lower than localities farther inland. On occasions, sea breezes have lowered the temperature as much as 15 to 20 degrees within a half hour. However, the major effect of the sea breeze at the airport is preventing the temperature from rising above the 80s. Because the change in ocean temperature lags behind the air temperature from season to season, the weather tends to remain comparatively mild late into the fall, but on the other hand, warming is retarded in the spring. Normal ocean temperatures range from an average near 37 degrees in January to near 72 degrees in August.

Precipitation is moderate and well distributed throughout the year, with June the driest month and August the wettest. Tropical storms or hurricanes occasionally bring excessive rainfall to the area. The bulk of winter precipitation results from storms which move northeastward along or near the east coast of the United States. Snowfall is considerably less than elsewhere at the same latitude and does not remain long on the ground. Precipitation, often beginning as snow, will frequently become mixed with or change to rain while continuing as snow over more interior sections. In addition, ice storms and resultant glaze are relatively infrequent.

**TABLE 1**     # NORMALS, MEANS AND EXTREMES

ATLANTIC CITY, NEW JERSEY N.A.F.E.C.

LATITUDE: 39°27'N   LONGITUDE: 74°34' W   ELEVATION: FT. GRND   64 BARO   118   TIME ZONE: EASTERN   WBAN: 93730

| | (a) | JAN | FEB | MAR | APR | MAY | JUNE | JULY | AUG | SEP | OCT | NOV | DEC | YEAR |
|---|---|---|---|---|---|---|---|---|---|---|---|---|---|---|
| **TEMPERATURE °F:** | | | | | | | | | | | | | | |
| Normals | | | | | | | | | | | | | | |
| -Daily Maximum | | 40.6 | 42.4 | 50.3 | 61.6 | 71.0 | 79.6 | 84.0 | 82.5 | 76.7 | 66.1 | 55.4 | 45.0 | 62.9 |
| -Daily Minimum | | 22.9 | 23.9 | 31.6 | 40.4 | 49.9 | 58.8 | 64.8 | 63.5 | 56.4 | 44.8 | 35.8 | 26.6 | 43.3 |
| -Monthly | | 31.8 | 33.2 | 41.0 | 51.0 | 60.5 | 69.2 | 74.4 | 73.0 | 66.6 | 55.5 | 45.6 | 35.8 | 53.1 |
| Extremes | | | | | | | | | | | | | | |
| -Record Highest | 46 | 78 | 75 | 87 | 94 | 99 | 106 | 104 | 102 | 99 | 90 | 84 | 75 | 106 |
| -Year | | 1967 | 1985 | 1945 | 1969 | 1969 | 1969 | 1966 | 1948 | 1983 | 1959 | 1950 | 1984 | JUN 1969 |
| -Record Lowest | 46 | -10 | -11 | 5 | 12 | 25 | 37 | 42 | 40 | 32 | 20 | 10 | -7 | -11 |
| -Year | | 1977 | 1979 | 1984 | 1969 | 1966 | 1980 | 1988 | 1976 | 1969 | 1988 | 1989 | 1950 | FEB 1979 |
| **NORMAL DEGREE DAYS:** | | | | | | | | | | | | | | |
| Heating (base 65°F) | | 1029 | 890 | 744 | 420 | 165 | 26 | 0 | 0 | 27 | 298 | 582 | 905 | 5086 |
| Cooling (base 65°F) | | 0 | 0 | 0 | 0 | 26 | 152 | 291 | 248 | 75 | 0 | 0 | 0 | 792 |
| **% OF POSSIBLE SUNSHINE** | 29 | 49 | 52 | 55 | 55 | 55 | 59 | 60 | 64 | 61 | 58 | 49 | 46 | 55 |
| **MEAN SKY COVER (tenths)** | | | | | | | | | | | | | | |
| Sunrise - Sunset | 31 | 6.3 | 6.3 | 6.2 | 6.2 | 6.4 | 6.1 | 6.1 | 6.0 | 5.7 | 5.4 | 6.2 | 6.3 | 6.1 |
| **MEAN NUMBER OF DAYS:** | | | | | | | | | | | | | | |
| Sunrise to Sunset | | | | | | | | | | | | | | |
| -Clear | 31 | 8.4 | 7.5 | 8.0 | 7.2 | 6.4 | 7.1 | 7.1 | 7.3 | 9.8 | 10.5 | 7.5 | 8.2 | 95.0 |
| -Partly Cloudy | 31 | 7.9 | 6.9 | 8.3 | 9.4 | 10.4 | 10.9 | 11.2 | 11.6 | 8.3 | 8.7 | 9.0 | 7.7 | 110.4 |
| -Cloudy | 31 | 14.7 | 13.8 | 14.7 | 13.4 | 14.2 | 12.0 | 12.7 | 12.1 | 12.0 | 11.7 | 13.5 | 15.1 | 159.9 |
| Precipitation | | | | | | | | | | | | | | |
| .01 inches or more | 46 | 10.6 | 9.8 | 10.6 | 10.9 | 10.2 | 8.9 | 8.6 | 8.6 | 7.5 | 7.3 | 9.4 | 9.6 | 112.1 |
| Snow,Ice pellets | | | | | | | | | | | | | | |
| 1.0 inches or more | 45 | 1.7 | 1.5 | 0.6 | 0.1 | 0.0 | 0.0 | 0.0 | 0.0 | 0.0 | 0.0 | 0.2 | 0.6 | 4.6 |
| Thunderstorms | 31 | 0.2 | 0.5 | 1.0 | 2.3 | 3.4 | 4.7 | 6.2 | 5.2 | 2.0 | 0.7 | 0.5 | 0.2 | 26.9 |
| Heavy Fog Visibility | | | | | | | | | | | | | | |
| 1/4 mile or less | 31 | 3.1 | 3.3 | 3.4 | 3.6 | 4.5 | 4.3 | 4.1 | 3.6 | 3.2 | 4.7 | 3.3 | 2.7 | 43.9 |
| Temperature °F | | | | | | | | | | | | | | |
| -Maximum | | | | | | | | | | | | | | |
| 90° and above | 25 | 0.0 | 0.0 | 0.0 | 0.2 | 0.8 | 3.4 | 6.8 | 5.0 | 1.4 | 0.0 | 0.0 | 0.0 | 17.6 |
| 32° and below | 25 | 8.1 | 5.4 | 0.7 | 0.0 | 0.0 | 0.0 | 0.0 | 0.0 | 0.0 | 0.0 | 0.2 | 3.4 | 17.7 |
| -Minimum | | | | | | | | | | | | | | |
| 32° and below | 25 | 26.0 | 22.1 | 17.2 | 6.3 | 0.4 | 0.0 | 0.0 | 0.0 | 0.1 | 3.6 | 12.6 | 22.1 | 110.3 |
| 0° and below | 25 | 1.0 | 0.5 | 0.0 | 0.0 | 0.0 | 0.0 | 0.0 | 0.0 | 0.0 | 0.0 | 0.0 | 0.2 | 1.7 |
| **AVG. STATION PRESS.(mb)** | 17 | 1015.3 | 1015.4 | 1013.9 | 1012.0 | 1012.6 | 1012.7 | 1013.3 | 1014.5 | 1015.8 | 1016.6 | 1016.0 | 1016.1 | 1014.5 |
| **RELATIVE HUMIDITY (%)** | | | | | | | | | | | | | | |
| Hour 01 | 25 | 75 | 76 | 76 | 78 | 84 | 87 | 87 | 88 | 88 | 86 | 81 | 76 | 82 |
| Hour 07 (Local Time) | 25 | 77 | 78 | 77 | 76 | 79 | 81 | 83 | 86 | 87 | 87 | 84 | 78 | 81 |
| Hour 13 | 25 | 58 | 56 | 54 | 52 | 56 | 56 | 57 | 58 | 58 | 56 | 58 | 58 | 56 |
| Hour 19 | 25 | 70 | 68 | 66 | 65 | 69 | 70 | 71 | 75 | 79 | 78 | 75 | 71 | 71 |
| **PRECIPITATION (inches):** | | | | | | | | | | | | | | |
| Water Equivalent | | | | | | | | | | | | | | |
| -Normal | | 3.47 | 3.34 | 4.04 | 3.20 | 3.07 | 2.78 | 4.02 | 4.72 | 2.89 | 3.06 | 3.73 | 3.61 | 41.93 |
| -Maximum Monthly | 46 | 7.71 | 5.98 | 6.80 | 7.95 | 11.51 | 6.36 | 13.09 | 11.98 | 6.27 | 7.50 | 9.65 | 7.33 | 13.09 |
| -Year | | 1948 | 1958 | 1953 | 1952 | 1948 | 1970 | 1959 | 1967 | 1966 | 1943 | 1972 | 1969 | JUL 1959 |
| -Minimum Monthly | 46 | 0.26 | 0.82 | 0.62 | 0.84 | 0.40 | 0.10 | 0.51 | 0.34 | 0.41 | 0.15 | 0.68 | 0.62 | 0.10 |
| -Year | | 1955 | 1980 | 1945 | 1976 | 1957 | 1954 | 1983 | 1943 | 1970 | 1963 | 1976 | 1955 | JUN 1954 |
| -Maximum in 24 hrs | 46 | 2.86 | 2.59 | 2.66 | 3.37 | 4.15 | 2.91 | 6.46 | 6.40 | 3.98 | 2.95 | 3.93 | 2.75 | 6.46 |
| -Year | | 1944 | 1966 | 1979 | 1952 | 1959 | 1952 | 1959 | 1966 | 1954 | 1958 | 1953 | 1951 | JUL 1959 |
| Snow,Ice pellets | | | | | | | | | | | | | | |
| -Maximum Monthly | 45 | 20.3 | 35.2 | 17.6 | 3.2 | T | 0.0 | 0.0 | 0.0 | 0.0 | T | 7.8 | 9.3 | 35.2 |
| -Year | | 1987 | 1967 | 1969 | 1965 | 1989 | | | | | 1980 | 1967 | 1989 | FEB 1967 |
| -Maximum in 24 hrs | 45 | 16.3 | 17.1 | 11.5 | 3.2 | T | 0.0 | 0.0 | 0.0 | 0.0 | T | 7.8 | 7.5 | 17.1 |
| -Year | | 1987 | 1979 | 1969 | 1965 | 1989 | | | | | 1980 | 1967 | 1960 | FEB 1979 |
| **WIND:** | | | | | | | | | | | | | | |
| Mean Speed (mph) | 31 | 11.1 | 11.3 | 12.0 | 11.8 | 10.2 | 9.2 | 8.5 | 8.1 | 8.4 | 9.0 | 10.5 | 10.6 | 10.1 |
| Prevailing Direction | | | | | | | | | | | | | | |
| through 1963 | | WNW | W | WNW | S | S | S | S | S | ENE | W | W | WNW | S |
| Fastest Obs. 1 Min. | | | | | | | | | | | | | | |
| -Direction (!!!) | 30 | 29 | 27 | 24 | 07 | 18 | 29 | 26 | 12 | 32 | 29 | 27 | 36 | 32 |
| -Speed (MPH) | 30 | 47 | 43 | 46 | 46 | 35 | 37 | 37 | 35 | 60 | 41 | 40 | 55 | 60 |
| -Year | | 1971 | 1960 | 1973 | 1961 | 1989 | 1964 | 1970 | 1971 | 1960 | 1961 | 1960 | 1960 | SEP 1960 |
| Peak Gust | | | | | | | | | | | | | | |
| -Direction (!!!) | 6 | NW | S | S | W | S | NW | W | S | NW | SW | NW | W | NW |
| -Speed (mph) | 6 | 44 | 53 | 56 | 47 | 55 | 51 | 45 | 46 | 69 | 43 | 61 | 55 | 69 |
| -Date | | 1988 | 1989 | 1987 | 1985 | 1989 | 1988 | 1985 | 1988 | 1985 | 1989 | 1989 | 1988 | SEP 1985 |

PRECIPITATION (inches)  ATLANTIC CITY, NEW JERSEY N.A.F.E.C.

**TABLE 2**

| YEAR | JAN | FEB | MAR | APR | MAY | JUNE | JULY | AUG | SEP | OCT | NOV | DEC | ANNUAL |
|------|-----|-----|-----|-----|-----|------|------|-----|-----|-----|-----|-----|--------|
| 1961 | 4.06 | 4.51 | 6.36 | 3.12 | 3.17 | 3.00 | 3.40 | 1.73 | 3.36 | 4.73 | 2.83 | 3.38 | 43.65 |
| 1962 | 4.21 | 3.47 | 5.42 | 3.50 | 1.77 | 4.20 | 1.72 | 5.29 | 3.09 | 2.04 | 4.88 | 3.84 | 43.43 |
| 1963 | 2.94 | 2.50 | 5.21 | 1.39 | 2.95 | 3.07 | 2.60 | 2.93 | 4.35 | 0.15 | 6.46 | 2.35 | 36.90 |
| 1964 | 6.35 | 4.32 | 2.80 | 7.59 | 1.46 | 0.84 | 2.79 | 1.63 | 5.91 | 2.67 | 1.18 | 3.47 | 41.01 |
| 1965 | 3.58 | 2.44 | 3.75 | 2.00 | 2.59 | 1.24 | 2.61 | 2.40 | 1.60 | 1.18 | 0.79 | 1.09 | 25.27 |
| 1966 | 3.45 | 5.17 | 0.70 | 2.58 | 3.17 | 1.87 | 2.59 | 9.04 | 6.27 | 3.73 | 1.91 | 4.81 | 45.29 |
| 1967 | 1.16 | 3.24 | 3.78 | 2.76 | 3.68 | 1.37 | 4.19 | 11.98 | 1.50 | 2.86 | 1.72 | 5.57 | 43.81 |
| 1968 | 2.77 | 1.69 | 4.99 | 1.50 | 5.55 | 2.86 | 1.75 | 2.20 | 0.43 | 2.73 | 3.10 | 3.89 | 33.46 |
| 1969 | 1.68 | 2.38 | 3.19 | 3.55 | 1.68 | 1.42 | 12.64 | 2.56 | 1.65 | 4.28 | 7.33 | 44.45 | 44.45 |
| 1970 | 1.50 | 3.08 | 3.11 | 4.66 | 1.81 | 6.36 | 2.83 | 2.70 | 0.41 | 3.73 | 5.73 | 3.04 | 38.96 |
| 1971 | 2.67 | 5.26 | 1.64 | 1.29 | 1.88 | 0.69 | 3.65 | 10.40 | 4.39 | 4.20 | 5.02 | 2.08 | 43.17 |
| 1972 | 2.93 | 4.31 | 3.59 | 4.62 | 3.51 | 4.82 | 2.81 | 0.44 | 3.66 | 5.11 | 9.65 | 3.63 | 49.08 |
| 1973 | 3.26 | 3.63 | 3.08 | 4.39 | 3.08 | 4.32 | 3.28 | 2.05 | 4.73 | 2.74 | 1.43 | 5.48 | 41.47 |
| 1974 | 3.47 | 2.40 | 4.62 | 2.66 | 2.61 | 2.52 | 1.99 | 5.50 | 2.95 | 1.90 | 1.08 | 4.76 | 36.46 |
| 1975 | 5.94 | 3.08 | 3.84 | 3.90 | 5.44 | 3.86 | 6.02 | 5.01 | 5.16 | 1.76 | 3.76 | 2.53 | 50.30 |
| 1976 | 4.52 | 2.70 | 1.39 | 0.84 | 3.61 | 0.97 | 2.23 | 2.79 | 3.06 | 6.60 | 0.68 | 2.52 | 33.82 |
| 1977 | 3.45 | 1.41 | 3.42 | 2.13 | 0.64 | 1.53 | 1.53 | 6.49 | 2.97 | 4.19 | 4.75 | 4.69 | 38.46 |
| 1978 | 5.70 | 1.11 | 5.17 | 1.53 | 6.71 | 3.00 | 5.77 | 6.82 | 1.51 | 1.21 | 2.96 | 3.52 | 45.01 |
| 1979 | 7.13 | 5.76 | 3.62 | 2.98 | 2.80 | 3.15 | 7.63 | 4.11 | 3.32 | 2.19 | 3.23 | 2.19 | 48.11 |
| 1980 | 2.63 | 0.82 | 6.38 | 5.40 | 1.61 | 3.58 | 2.47 | 2.63 | 1.74 | 3.20 | 3.63 | 0.75 | 34.84 |
| 1981 | 0.56 | 3.72 | 1.41 | 6.20 | 3.18 | 4.91 | 1.28 | 3.25 | 1.96 | 2.96 | 1.12 | 3.94 | 34.49 |
| 1982 | 4.11 | 2.06 | 2.70 | 3.85 | 2.42 | 3.03 | 3.62 | 1.63 | 1.34 | 1.14 | 4.17 | 2.85 | 32.92 |
| 1983 | 2.46 | 3.32 | 5.85 | 7.45 | 5.21 | 3.01 | 0.51 | 2.90 | 2.22 | 3.48 | 6.70 | 5.06 | 48.17 |
| 1984 | 2.41 | 3.70 | 5.92 | 4.84 | 6.58 | 1.62 | 4.35 | 2.44 | 1.31 | 1.46 | 3.02 | 1.79 | 39.44 |
| 1985 | 2.07 | 1.71 | 2.38 | 1.02 | 5.04 | 1.55 | 4.36 | 3.94 | 2.26 | 0.90 | 3.81 | 0.93 | 29.97 |
| 1986 | 3.73 | 3.42 | 1.88 | 4.57 | 0.54 | 2.41 | 4.50 | 3.35 | 2.39 | 3.90 | 5.04 | 4.85 | 40.58 |
| 1987 | 6.23 | 1.54 | 3.36 | 5.83 | 2.96 | 2.10 | 6.12 | 2.64 | 3.51 | 2.56 | 2.27 | 2.19 | 41.31 |
| 1988 | 2.99 | 3.80 | 2.21 | 1.77 | 3.20 | 1.03 | 4.58 | 2.78 | 3.07 | 5.92 | 4.45 | 0.64 | 33.48 |
| 1989 | 2.41 | 3.47 | 4.67 | 4.55 | 4.64 | 3.74 | 6.40 | 5.68 | 5.92 | 1.46 | 2.87 | 1.61 | 50.41 |
| 1990 | 2.70 | 1.00 | 2.60 | 3.46 | 5.71 | 1.52 | 3.64 | 5.96 | 1.91 | 2.63 | 2.01 | 3.57 | 36.71 |
| Record Mean | 3.35 | 3.08 | 3.64 | 3.49 | 3.33 | 2.55 | 4.36 | 4.26 | 2.94 | 2.99 | 3.46 | 3.26 | 40.72 |

**TABLE 3**  AVERAGE TEMPERATURE (deg. F)  ATLANTIC CITY, NEW JERSEY N.A.F.E.C.

| YEAR | JAN | FEB | MAR | APR | MAY | JUNE | JULY | AUG | SEP | OCT | NOV | DEC | ANNUAL |
|------|-----|-----|-----|-----|-----|------|------|-----|-----|-----|-----|-----|--------|
| 1961 | 26.9 | 36.1 | 43.0 | 49.1 | 59.2 | 69.4 | 76.6 | 74.9 | 73.4 | 58.1 | 47.7 | 35.1 | 54.6 |
| 1962 | 33.2 | 34.1 | 40.8 | 52.2 | 63.2 | 70.6 | 72.9 | 73.0 | 64.6 | 57.1 | 43.7 | 32.3 | 53.1 |
| 1963 | 31.3 | 29.5 | 45.5 | 52.5 | 60.3 | 70.5 | 76.1 | 72.4 | 63.9 | 59.9 | 50.2 | 30.5 | 53.5 |
| #1964 | 35.3 | 33.2 | 43.1 | 49.7 | 64.0 | 70.9 | 76.3 | 72.2 | 67.6 | 53.5 | 47.0 | 36.8 | 54.1 |
| 1965 | 27.6 | 33.0 | 37.8 | 48.7 | 64.1 | 67.6 | 72.8 | 72.1 | 68.0 | 53.1 | 44.9 | 36.4 | 52.2 |
| 1966 | 28.5 | 30.1 | 41.4 | 47.2 | 56.6 | 70.2 | 75.2 | 73.4 | 65.2 | 52.7 | 47.7 | 36.2 | 52.0 |
| 1967 | 38.9 | 29.2 | 38.6 | 51.4 | 54.1 | 69.0 | 73.4 | 71.5 | 61.2 | 52.4 | 39.5 | 35.1 | 51.2 |
| 1968 | 26.1 | 27.1 | 43.0 | 51.0 | 58.9 | 70.1 | 74.2 | 73.9 | 66.5 | 55.0 | 43.8 | 31.5 | 51.8 |
| 1969 | 30.3 | 31.8 | 37.4 | 53.6 | 62.0 | 69.5 | 73.2 | 73.3 | 65.5 | 53.9 | 43.9 | 34.5 | 52.4 |
| 1970 | 26.9 | 33.8 | 38.2 | 49.6 | 61.5 | 68.9 | 73.7 | 73.9 | 69.4 | 58.2 | 47.6 | 36.5 | 53.2 |
| 1971 | 28.8 | 35.7 | 39.0 | 47.6 | 57.6 | 69.7 | 72.0 | 70.4 | 67.5 | 60.7 | 44.5 | 41.1 | 52.9 |
| 1972 | 33.9 | 32.5 | 38.4 | 46.5 | 59.1 | 74.1 | 75.6 | 73.5 | 68.2 | 51.6 | 44.3 | 42.5 | 52.7 |
| 1973 | 36.2 | 34.7 | 48.0 | 51.3 | 58.8 | 72.5 | 75.1 | 75.9 | 66.4 | 57.4 | 47.4 | 39.9 | 55.3 |
| 1974 | 39.3 | 33.2 | 44.4 | 54.5 | 60.3 | 68.0 | 75.0 | 74.2 | 65.9 | 52.2 | 46.3 | 39.0 | 54.3 |
| 1975 | 37.2 | 36.5 | 40.1 | 45.9 | 63.3 | 69.6 | 74.5 | 73.8 | 62.8 | 57.0 | 47.9 | 35.5 | 53.7 |
| 1976 | 28.4 | 39.5 | 43.2 | 51.5 | 57.4 | 69.6 | 72.5 | 75.3 | 64.9 | 51.2 | 39.6 | 30.1 | 51.6 |
| 1977 | 19.7 | 32.8 | 45.8 | 52.5 | 61.7 | 67.5 | 75.3 | 75.3 | 69.5 | 49.6 | 35.4 | 34.4 | 53.4 |
| 1978 | 30.4 | 23.8 | 38.1 | 49.3 | 57.2 | 68.7 | 72.1 | 76.5 | 63.4 | 53.1 | 47.8 | 37.9 | 51.5 |
| 1979 | 31.5 | 21.7 | 44.8 | 51.2 | 62.9 | 66.9 | 74.6 | 72.7 | 65.6 | 54.4 | 48.7 | 38.0 | 52.7 |
| 1980 | 30.8 | 28.6 | 38.7 | 51.6 | 61.6 | 64.3 | 72.4 | 73.1 | 67.9 | 52.3 | 41.3 | 31.2 | 51.2 |
| 1981 | 22.8 | 34.2 | 36.7 | 50.4 | 57.8 | 70.2 | 76.5 | 73.8 | 67.6 | 53.4 | 44.8 | 34.4 | 51.9 |
| 1982 | 26.4 | 36.8 | 43.1 | 49.8 | 64.1 | 69.9 | 76.9 | 71.8 | 64.8 | 55.2 | 48.5 | 41.0 | 54.0 |
| 1983 | 33.4 | 35.5 | 44.9 | 51.7 | 60.3 | 70.7 | 78.7 | 75.9 | 67.9 | 56.5 | 45.5 | 33.9 | 54.7 |
| 1984 | 28.0 | 40.1 | 36.6 | 49.7 | 60.7 | 73.6 | 75.3 | 77.1 | 62.3 | 44.6 | 44.4 | 33.1 | 54.8 |
| 1985 | 26.8 | 35.4 | 44.8 | 55.1 | 64.5 | 70.0 | 76.9 | 73.7 | 68.4 | 58.1 | 53.4 | 33.1 | 55.0 |
| 1986 | 32.6 | 32.1 | 43.0 | 50.0 | 63.1 | 70.5 | 75.9 | 71.9 | 66.3 | 56.6 | 44.7 | 37.9 | 53.7 |
| 1987 | 31.7 | 31.0 | 42.0 | 49.4 | 61.3 | 71.9 | 76.6 | 72.0 | 66.8 | 50.7 | 47.4 | 38.4 | 53.3 |
| 1988 | 27.9 | 34.3 | 42.2 | 48.7 | 59.5 | 69.1 | 77.1 | 76.1 | 64.3 | 49.7 | 45.9 | 34.2 | 52.4 |
| 1989 | 36.3 | 33.8 | 40.6 | 49.4 | 59.9 | 72.2 | 74.0 | 73.3 | 67.3 | 57.2 | 44.2 | 24.7 | 52.7 |
| 1990 | 40.6 | 40.5 | 44.5 | 51.3 | 59.2 | 70.2 | 75.1 | 73.4 | 64.5 | 59.2 | 48.0 | 41.4 | 55.7 |
| Record Mean | 31.1 | 33.2 | 41.3 | 50.6 | 60.5 | 69.7 | 74.9 | 73.7 | 66.4 | 55.4 | 46.1 | 35.6 | 53.2 |
| Max | 40.2 | 42.5 | 51.1 | 61.2 | 71.1 | 80.2 | 84.5 | 83.2 | 76.7 | 66.2 | 56.0 | 45.0 | 63.2 |
| Min | 21.9 | 23.8 | 31.4 | 40.0 | 50.0 | 59.1 | 65.3 | 64.1 | 56.2 | 44.6 | 36.2 | 26.2 | 43.2 |

## REFERENCE NOTES FOR TABLES 1, 2, 3 and 6      (ATLANTIC CITY [N.A.F.E.C.], NJ)

**GENERAL**

T - TRACE AMOUNT
BLANK ENTRIES DENOTE MISSING/UNREPORTED DATA.
# INDICATES A STATION OR INSTRUMENT RELOCATION.

**SPECIFIC**

**TABLE 1**

(a) - LENGTH OF RECORD IN YEARS. ALTHOUGH
INDIVIDUAL MONTHS MAY BE MISSING.
* LESS THAN .05

NORMALS — BASED ON THE 1951-1980 RECORD PERIOD.
EXTREMES — DATES ARE THE MOST RECENT OCCURRENCE.
WIND DIR. — NUMERALS SHOW TENS OF DEGREES
CLOCKWISE FROM TRUE NORTH.
"00" INDICATES CALM.
RESULTANT WIND DIRECTIONS ARE GIVEN TO WHOLE DEGREES.

**TABLE 3**
MAX AND MIN ARE LONG-TERM MEAN DAILY MAXIMUM
AND MEAN DAILY MINIMUM TEMPERATURES.

**EXCEPTIONS**

**TABLE 1**

1. TEMPERATURE AND PRECIPITATION INCLUDE
DATA FROM U.S. NAVAL AIR STATION RECORDS.

**TABLES 2, 3, and 6**

RECORD MEANS ARE THROUGH THE CURRENT YEAR,
BEGINNING IN     1958 FOR TEMPERATURE
1958 FOR PRECIPITATION
1945 FOR SNOWFALL

**TABLE 4**  HEATING DEGREE DAYS Base 65 deg. F  ATLANTIC CITY, NEW JERSEY N.A.F.E.C.

| SEASON | JULY | AUG | SEP | OCT | NOV | DEC | JAN | FEB | MAR | APR | MAY | JUNE | TOTAL |
|---|---|---|---|---|---|---|---|---|---|---|---|---|---|
| 1961-62 | 0 | 0 | 29 | 226 | 525 | 920 | 977 | 860 | 743 | 392 | 134 | 12 | 4818 |
| 1962-63 | 0 | 2 | 83 | 250 | 630 | 1007 | 1040 | 986 | 596 | 375 | 178 | 13 | 5160 |
| 1963-64 | 0 | 1 | 102 | 170 | 438 | 1059 | 916 | 913 | 674 | 461 | 121 | 33 | 4888 |
| #1964-65 | 0 | 1 | 42 | 351 | 532 | 869 | 1152 | 890 | 838 | 485 | 109 | 77 | 5346 |
| 1965-66 | 3 | 24 | 70 | 368 | 596 | 879 | 1125 | 971 | 726 | 529 | 275 | 43 | 5609 |
| 1966-67 | 0 | 0 | 85 | 373 | 513 | 888 | 801 | 996 | 813 | 411 | 341 | 23 | 5244 |
| 1967-68 | 0 | 1 | 149 | 399 | 757 | 922 | 1195 | 1094 | 674 | 417 | 196 | 13 | 5817 |
| 1968-69 | 0 | 18 | 45 | 314 | 629 | 1031 | 1068 | 926 | 847 | 354 | 150 | 29 | 5411 |
| 1969-70 | 4 | 16 | 108 | 356 | 626 | 939 | 1174 | 867 | 820 | 453 | 166 | 13 | 5542 |
| 1970-71 | 0 | 0 | 49 | 224 | 515 | 876 | 1117 | 814 | 798 | 514 | 228 | 29 | 5164 |
| 1971-72 | 4 | 15 | 47 | 143 | 620 | 736 | 958 | 936 | 816 | 550 | 187 | 44 | 5056 |
| 1972-73 | 5 | 8 | 28 | 410 | 612 | 691 | 885 | 842 | 523 | 414 | 207 | 3 | 4628 |
| 1973-74 | 0 | 0 | 64 | 245 | 519 | 773 | 788 | 885 | 632 | 329 | 184 | 27 | 4446 |
| 1974-75 | 0 | 0 | 68 | 393 | 557 | 800 | 857 | 790 | 763 | 566 | 121 | 17 | 4932 |
| 1975-76 | 0 | 2 | 108 | 251 | 505 | 904 | 1128 | 733 | 668 | 409 | 242 | 55 | 5005 |
| 1976-77 | 0 | 17 | 71 | 424 | 757 | 1075 | 1398 | 895 | 587 | 380 | 145 | 42 | 5791 |
| 1977-78 | 2 | 0 | 28 | 311 | 457 | 910 | 1069 | 1146 | 826 | 463 | 256 | 24 | 5492 |
| 1978-79 | 6 | 0 | 116 | 365 | 512 | 831 | 1032 | 1208 | 623 | 406 | 110 | 39 | 5248 |
| 1979-80 | 6 | 19 | 80 | 341 | 483 | 830 | 1053 | 1050 | 808 | 394 | 145 | 102 | 5311 |
| 1980-81 | 3 | 5 | 38 | 392 | 705 | 1042 | 1299 | 855 | 871 | 436 | 251 | 14 | 5911 |
| 1981-82 | 0 | 0 | 47 | 356 | 600 | 940 | 1187 | 787 | 670 | 448 | 79 | 13 | 5127 |
| 1982-83 | 0 | 14 | 64 | 318 | 498 | 740 | 973 | 820 | 617 | 405 | 166 | 16 | 4631 |
| 1983-84 | 0 | 6 | 94 | 288 | 547 | 958 | 1137 | 714 | 874 | 451 | 171 | 8 | 5248 |
| 1984-85 | 0 | 0 | 80 | 129 | 604 | 646 | 1179 | 821 | 621 | 319 | 106 | 14 | 4519 |
| 1985-86 | 0 | 0 | 53 | 225 | 346 | 981 | 997 | 915 | 674 | 444 | 157 | 25 | 4817 |
| 1986-87 | 0 | 30 | 56 | 289 | 600 | 834 | 1023 | 947 | 705 | 459 | 194 | 6 | 5143 |
| 1987-88 | 0 | 10 | 46 | 436 | 520 | 814 | 1145 | 885 | 698 | 481 | 200 | 68 | 5303 |
| 1988-89 | 5 | 9 | 79 | 476 | 565 | 949 | 883 | 867 | 751 | 464 | 184 | 3 | 5235 |
| 1989-90 | 0 | 1 | 67 | 260 | 617 | 1239 | 747 | 680 | 630 | 421 | 188 | 19 | 4869 |
| 1990-91 | 1 | 1 | 90 | 240 | 504 | 722 | | | | | | | |

**TABLE 5**  COOLING DEGREE DAYS Base 65 deg. F  ATLANTIC CITY, NEW JERSEY N.A.F.E.C.

| YEAR | JAN | FEB | MAR | APR | MAY | JUNE | JULY | AUG | SEP | OCT | NOV | DEC | TOTAL |
|---|---|---|---|---|---|---|---|---|---|---|---|---|---|
| 1969 | 0 | 0 | 0 | 17 | 65 | 170 | 264 | 282 | 129 | 18 | 0 | 0 | 945 |
| 1970 | 0 | 0 | 0 | 0 | 63 | 136 | 279 | 285 | 187 | 20 | 0 | 0 | 970 |
| 1971 | 0 | 0 | 0 | 0 | 6 | 178 | 228 | 191 | 129 | 17 | 12 | 0 | 761 |
| 1972 | 0 | 0 | 0 | 0 | 11 | 83 | 341 | 282 | 132 | 4 | 0 | 0 | 853 |
| 1973 | 0 | 0 | 0 | 10 | 21 | 233 | 321 | 345 | 113 | 20 | 0 | 0 | 1063 |
| 1974 | 0 | 0 | 0 | 19 | 44 | 121 | 319 | 292 | 103 | 2 | 6 | 0 | 906 |
| 1975 | 0 | 0 | 0 | 0 | 74 | 164 | 305 | 282 | 48 | 10 | 0 | 0 | 883 |
| 1976 | 0 | 0 | 0 | 13 | 15 | 201 | 238 | 221 | 74 | 3 | 0 | 0 | 765 |
| 1977 | 0 | 0 | 2 | 15 | 51 | 120 | 328 | 325 | 168 | 7 | 2 | 0 | 1018 |
| 1978 | 0 | 0 | 0 | 0 | 19 | 143 | 233 | 364 | 74 | 4 | 0 | 0 | 837 |
| 1979 | 0 | 0 | 5 | 0 | 50 | 103 | 308 | 266 | 103 | 15 | 0 | 0 | 850 |
| 1980 | 0 | 0 | 0 | 0 | 47 | 88 | 238 | 262 | 132 | 6 | 0 | 0 | 773 |
| 1981 | 0 | 0 | 0 | 6 | 31 | 177 | 364 | 279 | 132 | 1 | 0 | 0 | 990 |
| 1982 | 0 | 0 | 0 | 0 | 56 | 165 | 375 | 231 | 64 | 23 | 9 | 0 | 923 |
| 1983 | 0 | 0 | 0 | 15 | 30 | 196 | 431 | 350 | 190 | 33 | 0 | 0 | 1245 |
| 1984 | 0 | 0 | 0 | 0 | 43 | 273 | 326 | 382 | 115 | 53 | 0 | 1 | 1193 |
| 1985 | 0 | 0 | 0 | 3 | 99 | 170 | 376 | 278 | 163 | 18 | 3 | 0 | 1140 |
| 1986 | 0 | 0 | 0 | 0 | 104 | 198 | 343 | 250 | 99 | 38 | 0 | 0 | 1032 |
| 1987 | 0 | 0 | 0 | 0 | 87 | 217 | 366 | 231 | 106 | 0 | 0 | 0 | 1007 |
| 1988 | 0 | 0 | 0 | 0 | 38 | 197 | 388 | 360 | 63 | 5 | 0 | 0 | 1051 |
| 1989 | 0 | 0 | 3 | 1 | 35 | 225 | 289 | 267 | 145 | 23 | 2 | 0 | 990 |
| 1990 | 0 | 0 | 4 | 15 | 16 | 180 | 319 | 270 | 84 | 67 | 0 | 0 | 955 |

**TABLE 6**  SNOWFALL (inches)  ATLANTIC CITY, NEW JERSEY N.A.F.E.C.

| SEASON | JULY | AUG | SEP | OCT | NOV | DEC | JAN | FEB | MAR | APR | MAY | JUNE | TOTAL |
|---|---|---|---|---|---|---|---|---|---|---|---|---|---|
| 1961-62 | 0.0 | 0.0 | 0.0 | 0.0 | 0.0 | 1.0 | 7.1 | 4.6 | 3.9 | T | 0.0 | 0.0 | 16.6 |
| 1962-63 | 0.0 | 0.0 | 0.0 | T | T | 5.1 | 4.4 | 0.3 | T | 0.0 | 0.0 | 0.0 | 9.8 |
| 1963-64 | 0.0 | 0.0 | 0.0 | 0.0 | 0.0 | 7.6 | 15.1 | 12.0 | 3.4 | T | 0.0 | 0.0 | 38.1 |
| 1964-65 | 0.0 | 0.0 | 0.0 | 0.0 | T | 1.0 | 8.2 | 3.3 | 2.8 | 3.2 | 0.0 | 0.0 | 18.5 |
| 1965-66 | 0.0 | 0.0 | 0.0 | 0.0 | 0.0 | 0.0 | 15.1 | 8.0 | T | 0.0 | 0.0 | 0.0 | 23.1 |
| 1966-67 | 0.0 | 0.0 | 0.0 | 0.0 | 0.0 | 8.5 | 1.1 | 35.2 | 2.1 | T | 0.0 | 0.0 | 46.9 |
| 1967-68 | 0.0 | 0.0 | 0.0 | 0.0 | 7.8 | 3.9 | 0.8 | 4.2 | 1.8 | 0.0 | 0.0 | 0.0 | 18.5 |
| 1968-69 | 0.0 | 0.0 | 0.0 | 0.0 | T | 4.3 | 0.5 | 7.0 | 17.6 | 0.0 | 0.0 | 0.0 | 29.4 |
| 1969-70 | 0.0 | 0.0 | 0.0 | 0.0 | T | 0.6 | 10.3 | 5.9 | T | 0.0 | 0.0 | 0.0 | 16.8 |
| 1970-71 | 0.0 | 0.0 | 0.0 | 0.0 | 0.0 | 1.4 | 7.2 | 1.9 | 0.9 | T | 0.0 | 0.0 | 11.4 |
| 1971-72 | 0.0 | 0.0 | 0.0 | 0.0 | 0.0 | 0.1 | 2.9 | 5.9 | T | T | 0.0 | 0.0 | 8.9 |
| 1972-73 | 0.0 | 0.0 | 0.0 | T | T | T | 0.0 | 0.4 | T | T | 0.0 | 0.0 | 0.4 |
| 1973-74 | 0.0 | 0.0 | 0.0 | 0.0 | 0.1 | T | 0.4 | 9.9 | T | T | 0.0 | 0.0 | 10.4 |
| 1974-75 | 0.0 | 0.0 | 0.0 | 0.0 | 0.2 | T | 3.3 | 1.6 | 2.0 | T | 0.0 | 0.0 | 7.1 |
| 1975-76 | 0.0 | 0.0 | 0.0 | 0.0 | 0.0 | 0.8 | 4.9 | 1.0 | 3.3 | 0.0 | 0.0 | 0.0 | 10.0 |
| 1976-77 | 0.0 | 0.0 | 0.0 | 0.0 | T | 4.0 | 7.8 | 0.5 | 0.0 | 0.0 | T | 0.0 | 12.3 |
| 1977-78 | 0.0 | 0.0 | 0.0 | 0.0 | T | T | 2.4 | 14.6 | 8.1 | T | 0.0 | 0.0 | 25.1 |
| 1978-79 | 0.0 | 0.0 | 0.0 | 0.0 | 1.2 | T | 14.2 | 27.7 | T | 0.0 | 0.0 | 0.0 | 43.1 |
| 1979-80 | 0.0 | 0.0 | 0.0 | T | 0.0 | 4.8 | 6.3 | 0.8 | 2.6 | T | 0.0 | 0.0 | 14.5 |
| 1980-81 | 0.0 | 0.0 | 0.0 | T | T | 0.1 | 3.2 | 0.0 | T | 0.0 | 0.0 | 0.0 | 3.3 |
| 1981-82 | 0.0 | 0.0 | 0.0 | 0.0 | 0.0 | 0.6 | 7.8 | 4.4 | T | 2.0 | 0.0 | 0.0 | 14.8 |
| 1982-83 | 0.0 | 0.0 | 0.0 | 0.0 | 0.0 | 6.7 | T | 14.9 | T | 0.7 | 0.0 | 0.0 | 22.3 |
| 1983-84 | 0.0 | 0.0 | 0.0 | 0.0 | 0.1 | 0.4 | 3.8 | T | 4.0 | T | 0.0 | 0.0 | 8.3 |
| 1984-85 | 0.0 | 0.0 | 0.0 | 0.0 | T | T | 15.1 | 0.0 | T | 1.3 | 0.0 | 0.0 | 16.4 |
| 1985-86 | 0.0 | 0.0 | 0.0 | 0.0 | 0.0 | 4.2 | 3.9 | 9.6 | T | T | 0.0 | 0.0 | 17.7 |
| 1986-87 | 0.0 | 0.0 | 0.0 | 0.0 | 0.0 | T | 20.3 | 10.7 | 1.6 | 0.7 | 0.0 | 0.0 | 33.3 |
| 1987-88 | 0.0 | 0.0 | 0.0 | 0.0 | T | T | 7.1 | 0.2 | T | T | 0.0 | 0.0 | 7.3 |
| 1988-89 | 0.0 | 0.0 | 0.0 | 0.0 | 0.0 | 0.4 | 0.9 | 12.8 | 3.4 | T | T | 0.0 | 17.5 |
| 1989-90 | 0.0 | 0.0 | 0.0 | 0.0 | 6.0 | 9.3 | T | T | 3.8 | 3.9 | 0.0 | 0.0 | 23.0 |
| 1990-91 | 0.0 | 0.0 | 0.0 | T | 0.0 | 3.1 | | | | | | | |
| Record Mean | 0.0 | 0.0 | 0.0 | T | 0.4 | 2.3 | 5.3 | 5.5 | 2.7 | 0.4 | T | 0.0 | 16.7 |

**See Reference Notes, relative to all above tables, on preceding page.**

Terrain in vicinity of the station is flat and rather marshy. To the northwest are ridges oriented roughly in a south-southwest to north-northeast direction. They rise to an elevation of about 200 feet at 4.5 to 5 miles and to 500 to 600 feet at 7 to 8 miles. All winds between west-northwest and north-northwest are downslope and therefore are subject to some adiabatic temperature increase. This effect is evident in the rapid improvement which normally occurs with shift of wind to westerly, following a coastal storm or frontal passage. The drying effect of the downslope winds accounts for the relatively few local thunderstorms occurring at the station, compared to areas to the west. Easterly winds, particularly southeasterly, moderate the temperature because of the influence of the Atlantic Ocean.

Temperature falls of 5 to 15 degrees, depending on the season, are not uncommon when the wind backs from southwesterly to southeasterly. Periods of very hot weather, lasting as long as a week, are associated with a west-southwest air flow which has a long trajectory over land. Extremes of cold are related to rapidly moving outbreaks of cold air traveling southeastward from the Hudson Bay region. Temperatures of zero or below occur in one winter out of four, but are much more common several miles to the west of the station. Average dates of the last occurrence in spring and the first occurrence in autumn of temperatures as low as 32 degrees are in mid-April and the end of October or early November. Areas to the west of the station experience a growing season at least a month shorter than that at the airport.

A considerable amount of precipitation is realized from the Northeasters of the Atlantic coast. These storms, more typical of the fall and winter, generally last for a period of two days and commonly produce between 1 and 2 inches of precipitation. Storms producing 4 inches or more of snow occur from two to five times a winter. Snowstorms producing 8 inches or more have occurred in about one-half the winters. As many as three such storms have been experienced in one winter. The frequency and intensity of snow storms and the duration of snow cover increase dramatically within a few miles to the west of the station.

## TABLE 1    NORMALS, MEANS AND EXTREMES

NEWARK, NEW JERSEY

LATITUDE: 40°42'N    LONGITUDE: 74°10'W    ELEVATION: FT. GRND  7  BARO  29  TIME ZONE: EASTERN    WBAN: 14734

| | (a) | JAN | FEB | MAR | APR | MAY | JUNE | JULY | AUG | SEP | OCT | NOV | DEC | YEAR |
|---|---|---|---|---|---|---|---|---|---|---|---|---|---|---|
| **TEMPERATURE °F:** | | | | | | | | | | | | | | |
| Normals | | | | | | | | | | | | | | |
| -Daily Maximum | | 38.2 | 40.3 | 49.1 | 61.3 | 71.6 | 80.6 | 85.6 | 84.0 | 76.9 | 66.0 | 54.0 | 42.3 | 62.5 |
| -Daily Minimum | | 24.2 | 25.3 | 33.3 | 42.9 | 53.0 | 62.4 | 67.9 | 67.0 | 59.4 | 48.3 | 39.0 | 28.6 | 45.9 |
| -Monthly | | 31.3 | 32.8 | 41.2 | 52.1 | 62.3 | 71.5 | 76.8 | 75.5 | 68.2 | 57.2 | 46.5 | 35.5 | 54.2 |
| Extremes | | | | | | | | | | | | | | |
| -Record Highest | 48 | 74 | 76 | 89 | 93 | 98 | 102 | 105 | 103 | 105 | 92 | 85 | 72 | 105 |
| -Year | | 1950 | 1949 | 1945 | 1976 | 1987 | 1952 | 1966 | 1948 | 1953 | 1949 | 1950 | 1982 | JUL 1966 |
| -Record Lowest | 48 | -8 | -7 | 6 | 16 | 33 | 43 | 52 | 45 | 35 | 28 | 15 | -1 | -8 |
| -Year | | 1985 | 1943 | 1943 | 1982 | 1947 | 1945 | 1945 | 1982 | 1947 | 1969 | 1955 | 1980 | JAN 1985 |
| **NORMAL DEGREE DAYS:** | | | | | | | | | | | | | | |
| Heating (base 65°F) | | 1045 | 902 | 738 | 387 | 140 | 0 | 0 | 0 | 36 | 254 | 555 | 915 | 4972 |
| Cooling (base 65°F) | | 0 | 0 | 0 | 0 | 56 | 199 | 366 | 326 | 132 | 12 | 0 | 0 | 1091 |
| **% OF POSSIBLE SUNSHINE** | | | | | | | | | | | | | | |
| **MEAN SKY COVER (tenths)** | | | | | | | | | | | | | | |
| Sunrise - Sunset | 43 | 6.5 | 6.4 | 6.3 | 6.4 | 6.5 | 6.2 | 6.2 | 6.0 | 5.7 | 5.5 | 6.4 | 6.4 | 6.2 |
| **MEAN NUMBER OF DAYS:** | | | | | | | | | | | | | | |
| Sunrise to Sunset | | | | | | | | | | | | | | |
| -Clear | 47 | 7.9 | 7.3 | 8.0 | 7.3 | 6.4 | 6.9 | 6.6 | 7.7 | 9.7 | 10.8 | 7.5 | 8.1 | 94.1 |
| -Partly Cloudy | 47 | 7.7 | 7.5 | 8.7 | 8.9 | 10.6 | 10.6 | 12.3 | 11.6 | 8.8 | 8.6 | 8.3 | 7.9 | 111.6 |
| -Cloudy | 47 | 15.4 | 13.4 | 14.4 | 13.8 | 14.0 | 12.4 | 12.1 | 11.7 | 11.5 | 11.6 | 14.2 | 15.0 | 159.5 |
| Precipitation | | | | | | | | | | | | | | |
| .01 inches or more | 48 | 11.0 | 9.6 | 11.1 | 10.9 | 12.0 | 10.2 | 10.0 | 9.3 | 8.3 | 7.9 | 10.3 | 10.8 | 121.3 |
| Snow,Ice pellets | | | | | | | | | | | | | | |
| 1.0 inches or more | 48 | 2.2 | 1.9 | 1.2 | 0.2 | 0.0 | 0.0 | 0.0 | 0.0 | 0.0 | 0.0 | 0.2 | 1.4 | 7.2 |
| Thunderstorms | 48 | 0.2 | 0.2 | 1.0 | 1.6 | 3.6 | 4.8 | 6.0 | 4.6 | 2.2 | 1.0 | 0.5 | 0.2 | 25.9 |
| Heavy Fog Visibility | | | | | | | | | | | | | | |
| 1/4 mile or less | 48 | 2.2 | 1.7 | 1.5 | 1.0 | 1.8 | 1.2 | 0.5 | 0.5 | 0.9 | 1.9 | 1.9 | 1.8 | 16.8 |
| Temperature °F | | | | | | | | | | | | | | |
| -Maximum | | | | | | | | | | | | | | |
| 90° and above | 24 | 0.0 | 0.0 | 0.0 | 0.2 | 1.2 | 4.5 | 8.7 | 6.7 | 1.4 | 0.0 | 0.0 | 0.0 | 22.6 |
| 32° and below | 24 | 10.4 | 5.8 | 1.0 | 0.* | 0.0 | 0.0 | 0.0 | 0.0 | 0.0 | 0.0 | 0.1 | 4.2 | 21.4 |
| -Minimum | | | | | | | | | | | | | | |
| 32° and below | 24 | 24.4 | 21.3 | 12.6 | 1.7 | 0.0 | 0.0 | 0.0 | 0.0 | 0.0 | 0.6 | 6.0 | 19.5 | 86.0 |
| 0° and below | 24 | 0.5 | 0.2 | 0.0 | 0.0 | 0.0 | 0.0 | 0.0 | 0.0 | 0.0 | 0.0 | 0.0 | 0.1 | 0.8 |
| **AVG. STATION PRESS.(mb)** | 16 | 1016.7 | 1016.8 | 1015.9 | 1013.3 | 1014.0 | 1014.0 | 1014.5 | 1015.9 | 1017.5 | 1018.2 | 1017.6 | 1017.9 | 1016.0 |
| **RELATIVE HUMIDITY (%)** | | | | | | | | | | | | | | |
| Hour 01 | 24 | 70 | 69 | 66 | 65 | 72 | 72 | 73 | 76 | 77 | 76 | 73 | 71 | 72 |
| Hour 07 | 24 | 74 | 72 | 69 | 65 | 70 | 71 | 72 | 75 | 78 | 79 | 77 | 74 | 73 |
| Hour 13 (Local Time) | 24 | 58 | 55 | 50 | 47 | 51 | 52 | 51 | 53 | 55 | 53 | 57 | 58 | 53 |
| Hour 19 | 24 | 64 | 60 | 57 | 54 | 58 | 58 | 59 | 62 | 64 | 64 | 65 | 64 | 61 |
| **PRECIPITATION (inches):** | | | | | | | | | | | | | | |
| Water Equivalent | | | | | | | | | | | | | | |
| -Normal | | 3.13 | 3.05 | 4.15 | 3.57 | 3.59 | 2.94 | 3.85 | 4.30 | 3.66 | 3.09 | 3.59 | 3.42 | 42.34 |
| -Maximum Monthly | 48 | 10.10 | 4.94 | 11.14 | 11.14 | 10.22 | 6.40 | 9.98 | 11.84 | 10.28 | 8.20 | 11.53 | 9.47 | 11.84 |
| -Year | | 1979 | 1979 | 1983 | 1983 | 1984 | 1975 | 1988 | 1955 | 1944 | 1943 | 1977 | 1983 | AUG 1955 |
| -Minimum Monthly | 48 | 0.45 | 1.22 | 1.10 | 0.90 | 0.52 | 0.07 | 0.89 | 0.50 | 0.95 | 0.21 | 0.51 | 0.27 | 0.07 |
| -Year | | 1981 | 1968 | 1981 | 1963 | 1964 | 1949 | 1966 | 1964 | 1951 | 1963 | 1976 | 1955 | JUN 1949 |
| -Maximum in 24 hrs | 36 | 3.59 | 2.45 | 2.66 | 3.73 | 4.22 | 2.31 | 3.63 | 7.84 | 5.27 | 3.04 | 7.22 | 2.77 | 7.84 |
| -Year | | 1979 | 1961 | 1978 | 1984 | 1979 | 1973 | 1988 | 1971 | 1971 | 1973 | 1977 | 1983 | AUG 1971 |
| Snow,Ice pellets | | | | | | | | | | | | | | |
| -Maximum Monthly | 48 | 27.4 | 26.1 | 26.0 | 13.8 | T | 0.0 | 0.0 | 0.0 | 0.0 | 0.3 | 5.7 | 29.1 | 29.1 |
| -Year | | 1978 | 1979 | 1956 | 1982 | 1977 | | | | | 1952 | 1989 | 1947 | DEC 1947 |
| -Maximum in 24 hrs | 48 | 17.8 | 20.0 | 17.6 | 12.8 | T | 0.0 | 0.0 | 0.0 | 0.3 | 5.7 | 26.0 | 26.0 |
| -Year | | 1978 | 1961 | 1956 | 1982 | 1977 | | | | | 1952 | 1989 | 1947 | DEC 1947 |
| **WIND:** | | | | | | | | | | | | | | |
| Mean Speed (mph) | 45 | 11.2 | 11.5 | 12.0 | 11.3 | 10.1 | 9.5 | 8.9 | 8.7 | 9.0 | 9.4 | 10.2 | 10.8 | 10.2 |
| Prevailing Direction through 1963 | | NE | NW | NW | WNW | SW | SW | SW | SW | SW | SW | SW | SW | SW |
| Fastest Obs. 1 Min. | | | | | | | | | | | | | | |
| -Direction (!!!) | 41 | 30 | 23 | 27 | 27 | 32 | 26 | 35 | 09 | 05 | 11 | 09 | 32 | 09 |
| -Speed (MPH) | 41 | 52 | 46 | 43 | 50 | 50 | 58 | 52 | 46 | 51 | 48 | 82 | 55 | 82 |
| -Year | | 1964 | 1965 | 1950 | 1951 | 1963 | 1984 | 1988 | 1955 | 1960 | 1954 | 1950 | 1962 | NOV 1950 |
| Peak Gust | | | | | | | | | | | | | | |
| -Direction (!!!) | 6 | W | NW | W | E | NW | W | NW | N | W | NW | NW | NW | W |
| -Speed (mph) | 6 | 53 | 58 | 56 | 55 | 58 | 83 | 69 | 68 | 67 | 46 | 63 | 60 | 83 |
| -Date | | 1987 | 1984 | 1986 | 1987 | 1988 | 1984 | 1988 | 1985 | 1985 | 1986 | 1989 | 1988 | JUN 1984 |

**See Reference Notes to this table on the following page.**

PRECIPITATION (inches)　　　　NEWARK, NEW JERSEY

## TABLE 2

| YEAR | JAN | FEB | MAR | APR | MAY | JUNE | JULY | AUG | SEP | OCT | NOV | DEC | ANNUAL |
|---|---|---|---|---|---|---|---|---|---|---|---|---|---|
| 1961 | 3.34 | 3.97 | 4.96 | 5.28 | 3.35 | 2.46 | 7.95 | 4.22 | 1.49 | 2.06 | 2.64 | 3.65 | 45.37 |
| 1962 | 2.56 | 4.25 | 3.35 | 3.44 | 1.46 | 3.89 | 2.34 | 5.73 | 3.33 | 3.72 | 4.39 | 2.39 | 40.85 |
| 1963 | 2.19 | 2.16 | 3.92 | 0.90 | 2.37 | 2.01 | 2.24 | 1.93 | 3.94 | 0.21 | 5.68 | 1.97 | 29.52 |
| 1964 | 5.12 | 2.59 | 2.27 | 5.56 | 0.52 | 3.09 | 4.74 | 0.50 | 1.30 | 1.55 | 2.08 | 4.10 | 33.42 |
| 1965 | 2.86 | 2.91 | 2.81 | 2.60 | 1.23 | 1.23 | 1.73 | 2.87 | 2.20 | 2.31 | 1.48 | 1.86 | 26.09 |
| 1966 | 2.29 | 4.41 | 1.12 | 3.01 | 4.86 | 0.49 | 0.89 | 3.08 | 7.86 | 3.78 | 3.06 | 3.01 | 37.86 |
| 1967 | 1.15 | 3.00 | 5.86 | 2.84 | 3.57 | 3.31 | 7.53 | 5.53 | 1.35 | 2.87 | 2.35 | 4.65 | 44.01 |
| 1968 | 1.71 | 1.22 | 3.59 | 2.24 | 6.28 | 4.37 | 1.87 | 2.41 | 2.48 | 2.02 | 4.38 | 4.32 | 36.89 |
| 1969 | 1.47 | 2.68 | 3.53 | 3.51 | 2.73 | 2.53 | 7.11 | 2.24 | 6.63 | 1.75 | 2.80 | 4.97 | 41.95 |
| 1970 | 0.87 | 3.29 | 3.42 | 3.52 | 2.64 | 2.41 | 3.68 | 3.91 | 1.83 | 2.36 | 4.41 | 2.05 | 34.39 |
| 1971 | 2.74 | 4.44 | 3.29 | 1.35 | 3.65 | 1.48 | 6.98 | 10.63 | 7.88 | 2.96 | 3.86 | 1.51 | 50.77 |
| 1972 | 2.26 | 4.01 | 3.09 | 3.08 | 6.02 | 6.02 | 4.70 | 2.30 | 1.03 | 4.83 | 8.42 | 4.10 | 49.86 |
| 1973 | 3.65 | 3.39 | 3.63 | 5.77 | 3.56 | 4.03 | 3.63 | 3.36 | 3.39 | 3.35 | 1.29 | 7.24 | 46.29 |
| 1974 | 2.84 | 1.44 | 4.11 | 2.37 | 3.49 | 3.60 | 1.31 | 7.17 | 5.76 | 1.85 | 0.80 | 4.02 | 38.76 |
| 1975 | 3.99 | 2.56 | 2.94 | 2.29 | 3.27 | 6.40 | 8.02 | 4.36 | 9.00 | 3.24 | 3.67 | 2.91 | 52.65 |
| 1976 | 5.04 | 2.52 | 2.33 | 2.50 | 4.12 | 1.54 | 3.91 | 2.98 | 2.50 | 5.07 | 0.51 | 2.17 | 35.19 |
| 1977 | 1.55 | 2.77 | 5.67 | 3.16 | 1.31 | 3.89 | 1.51 | 4.29 | 3.99 | 3.53 | 11.53 | 4.77 | 47.97 |
| 1978 | 7.76 | 2.26 | 4.58 | 2.60 | 7.97 | 2.05 | 4.99 | 7.30 | 4.23 | 1.64 | 2.66 | 5.37 | 53.41 |
| 1979 | 10.10 | 4.94 | 3.65 | 3.66 | 7.78 | 2.73 | 3.39 | 4.38 | 5.72 | 4.58 | 3.09 | 2.08 | 56.10 |
| 1980 | 1.66 | 1.28 | 9.13 | 7.28 | 2.61 | 3.27 | 2.78 | 0.92 | 1.87 | 3.37 | 3.71 | 0.63 | 38.51 |
| 1981 | 0.45 | 4.81 | 1.10 | 3.15 | 3.88 | 2.61 | 4.51 | 0.57 | 3.42 | 3.47 | 1.75 | 5.32 | 35.04 |
| 1982 | 6.77 | 2.36 | 2.82 | 6.20 | 2.96 | 5.28 | 2.86 | 2.78 | 2.39 | 1.68 | 3.16 | 1.32 | 40.58 |
| 1983 | 4.37 | 3.03 | 11.14 | 11.14 | 4.22 | 2.81 | 1.59 | 3.46 | 2.93 | 5.80 | 5.54 | 9.47 | 65.50 |
| 1984 | 2.78 | 4.57 | 6.96 | 6.36 | 10.22 | 4.77 | 8.65 | 1.74 | 2.46 | 3.93 | 2.88 | 3.69 | 59.01 |
| 1985 | 1.22 | 2.58 | 1.59 | 1.17 | 4.23 | 4.29 | 4.52 | 2.58 | 4.19 | 1.29 | 8.32 | 1.31 | 37.29 |
| 1986 | 4.44 | 3.88 | 1.95 | 5.88 | 1.41 | 1.71 | 6.62 | 4.16 | 1.96 | 1.93 | 6.78 | 5.23 | 45.95 |
| 1987 | 6.21 | 1.30 | 3.81 | 5.06 | 2.55 | 4.13 | 4.66 | 5.26 | 3.87 | 3.37 | 2.94 | 2.37 | 45.53 |
| 1988 | 3.74 | 4.15 | 2.13 | 1.97 | 5.86 | 1.06 | 9.98 | 1.82 | 1.66 | 2.45 | 7.71 | 0.98 | 43.51 |
| 1989 | 1.98 | 2.70 | 4.42 | 3.25 | 8.80 | 5.41 | 5.23 | 7.03 | 6.45 | 5.40 | 2.57 | 0.75 | 53.99 |
| 1990 | 4.72 | 1.71 | 2.81 | 3.98 | 6.87 | 3.68 | 4.98 | 7.71 | 2.72 | 5.11 | 2.82 | 5.19 | 52.30 |
| Record Mean | 3.37 | 2.92 | 3.98 | 3.68 | 3.89 | 3.33 | 4.09 | 4.17 | 3.71 | 3.08 | 3.64 | 3.33 | 43.18 |

## TABLE 3

AVERAGE TEMPERATURE (deg. F)　　　　NEWARK, NEW JERSEY

| YEAR | JAN | FEB | MAR | APR | MAY | JUNE | JULY | AUG | SEP | OCT | NOV | DEC | ANNUAL |
|---|---|---|---|---|---|---|---|---|---|---|---|---|---|
| 1961 | 26.6 | 35.8 | 41.2 | 48.6 | 59.7 | 71.9 | 77.3 | 75.8 | 74.5 | 59.5 | 47.4 | 33.8 | 54.4 |
| 1962 | 30.8 | 30.3 | 42.0 | 52.5 | 64.3 | 72.5 | 73.9 | 72.9 | 64.7 | 57.3 | 43.5 | 31.1 | 53.0 |
| 1963 | 29.6 | 27.5 | 42.5 | 52.6 | 61.1 | 72.0 | 77.0 | 74.0 | 64.0 | 61.2 | 49.7 | 29.3 | 53.4 |
| 1964 | 34.3 | 31.9 | 42.6 | 49.1 | 65.4 | 71.2 | 76.0 | 73.9 | 68.9 | 55.9 | 49.4 | 35.9 | 54.6 |
| #1965 | 28.3 | 32.4 | 39.0 | 50.0 | 67.3 | 71.6 | 75.7 | 74.5 | 68.4 | 54.0 | 44.4 | 38.8 | 53.7 |
| 1966 | 30.4 | 33.2 | 41.7 | 48.2 | 59.3 | 73.8 | 79.6 | 76.5 | 66.6 | 55.5 | 48.9 | 36.5 | 54.2 |
| 1967 | 36.9 | 29.4 | 37.6 | 50.9 | 54.3 | 72.0 | 74.2 | 73.5 | 66.6 | 56.4 | 42.2 | 38.3 | 52.7 |
| 1968 | 27.8 | 29.9 | 43.1 | 54.0 | 59.6 | 69.7 | 78.2 | 76.9 | 70.7 | 59.7 | 45.7 | 32.5 | 54.0 |
| 1969 | 31.3 | 31.3 | 38.8 | 54.6 | 64.1 | 72.8 | 74.2 | 77.3 | 67.5 | 56.2 | 45.5 | 33.1 | 53.9 |
| 1970 | 24.2 | 33.0 | 39.0 | 51.9 | 64.6 | 70.9 | 77.2 | 77.3 | 70.6 | 59.5 | 49.1 | 35.3 | 54.4 |
| 1971 | 27.3 | 35.2 | 41.2 | 51.4 | 60.6 | 74.8 | 78.4 | 76.0 | 71.8 | 63.2 | 46.2 | 41.4 | 55.6 |
| 1972 | 35.4 | 31.3 | 40.5 | 50.0 | 63.0 | 68.8 | 77.9 | 75.9 | 69.8 | 53.3 | 44.8 | 39.7 | 54.2 |
| 1973 | 35.5 | 33.3 | 48.6 | 54.2 | 60.4 | 74.6 | 78.7 | 79.6 | 71.0 | 60.3 | 48.8 | 39.4 | 57.0 |
| 1974 | 35.4 | 31.9 | 43.4 | 56.5 | 62.7 | 70.1 | 77.1 | 76.5 | 66.6 | 53.9 | 47.5 | 38.9 | 55.0 |
| 1975 | 36.9 | 35.1 | 39.7 | 47.3 | 65.8 | 71.6 | 76.9 | 75.1 | 64.3 | 59.1 | 51.7 | 35.4 | 54.9 |
| 1976 | 26.8 | 39.3 | 44.0 | 55.2 | 61.1 | 73.6 | 74.9 | 74.4 | 66.5 | 52.6 | 39.9 | 29.1 | 53.1 |
| 1977 | 20.9 | 32.3 | 46.8 | 53.7 | 65.4 | 70.3 | 78.2 | 75.1 | 68.0 | 54.3 | 47.1 | 33.3 | 53.9 |
| 1978 | 27.2 | 25.5 | 38.5 | 51.0 | 60.5 | 71.6 | 75.1 | 76.7 | 66.1 | 57.5 | 48.8 | 38.1 | 53.1 |
| 1979 | 32.5 | 30.8 | 46.2 | 52.0 | 64.5 | 69.4 | 77.0 | 76.6 | 69.1 | 56.5 | 51.8 | 40.2 | 54.9 |
| 1980 | 34.0 | 30.8 | 38.9 | 52.6 | 65.9 | 70.2 | 78.9 | 78.6 | 70.8 | 55.0 | 42.9 | 30.4 | 54.1 |
| 1981 | 24.1 | 37.6 | 40.2 | 55.3 | 64.0 | 74.6 | 79.3 | 75.1 | 67.2 | 53.1 | 46.0 | 34.6 | 54.3 |
| 1982 | 24.2 | 36.2 | 41.8 | 50.6 | 63.2 | 67.9 | 78.4 | 72.5 | 66.7 | 56.9 | 48.8 | 42.8 | 54.2 |
| 1983 | 35.0 | 35.9 | 44.7 | 52.2 | 60.8 | 73.5 | 79.6 | 77.6 | 70.6 | 57.8 | 47.8 | 34.2 | 55.8 |
| 1984 | 27.8 | 40.8 | 36.5 | 52.7 | 62.2 | 75.0 | 76.6 | 77.3 | 65.4 | 62.3 | 45.3 | 40.8 | 55.2 |
| 1985 | 24.9 | 33.5 | 44.5 | 57.0 | 67.1 | 69.4 | 76.3 | 75.6 | 70.2 | 58.5 | 49.5 | 33.3 | 55.0 |
| 1986 | 33.0 | 31.1 | 44.2 | 53.4 | 66.7 | 72.7 | 76.9 | 74.2 | 68.6 | 58.0 | 45.0 | 38.1 | 55.2 |
| 1987 | 31.5 | 33.0 | 45.0 | 53.9 | 63.9 | 74.5 | 79.4 | 75.3 | 68.7 | 53.7 | 47.6 | 38.4 | 55.4 |
| 1988 | 28.7 | 34.4 | 43.9 | 51.1 | 63.4 | 73.0 | 80.5 | 79.8 | 68.0 | 52.6 | 48.9 | 35.5 | 55.0 |
| 1989 | 37.0 | 34.2 | 42.4 | 52.5 | 63.2 | 74.3 | 77.2 | 76.3 | 69.9 | 59.1 | 45.0 | 25.6 | 54.7 |
| 1990 | 40.4 | 39.8 | 44.9 | 53.3 | 61.1 | 73.4 | 77.8 | 76.6 | 68.6 | 62.4 | 50.0 | 42.3 | 57.6 |
| Record Mean | 31.4 | 32.8 | 41.1 | 51.6 | 62.3 | 71.4 | 76.6 | 75.0 | 67.7 | 56.9 | 46.2 | 35.2 | 54.0 |
| Max | 38.5 | 40.4 | 49.4 | 60.9 | 71.9 | 80.8 | 85.7 | 83.8 | 76.7 | 66.1 | 54.1 | 42.3 | 62.5 |
| Min | 24.3 | 25.1 | 32.8 | 42.3 | 52.7 | 62.0 | 67.5 | 66.2 | 58.7 | 47.7 | 38.3 | 28.1 | 45.5 |

## REFERENCE NOTES FOR TABLES 1, 2, 3 and 6　　　(NEWARK, NJ)

### GENERAL

T - TRACE AMOUNT
BLANK ENTRIES DENOTE MISSING/UNREPORTED DATA.
# INDICATES A STATION OR INSTRUMENT RELOCATION.

### SPECIFIC

#### TABLE 1

(a) - LENGTH OF RECORD IN YEARS. ALTHOUGH
INDIVIDUAL MONTHS MAY BE MISSING.
* LESS THAN .05

NORMALS — BASED ON THE 1951-1980 RECORD PERIOD.
EXTREMES — DATES ARE THE MOST RECENT OCCURRENCE.
WIND DIR. — NUMERALS SHOW TENS OF DEGREES
CLOCKWISE FROM TRUE NORTH.
"00" INDICATES CALM.
RESULTANT WIND DIRECTIONS ARE GIVEN TO WHOLE DEGREES.

#### TABLE 3

MAX AND MIN ARE LONG-TERM MEAN DAILY MAXIMUM
AND MEAN DAILY MINIMUM TEMPERATURES.

### EXCEPTIONS

#### TABLES 2, 3, and 6

RECORD MEANS ARE THROUGH THE CURRENT YEAR,
BEGINNING IN 　　1931 FOR TEMPERATURE
　　　　　　　　　1931 FOR PRECIPITATION
　　　　　　　　　1942 FOR SNOWFALL

HEATING DEGREE DAYS Base 65 deg. F    NEWARK, NEW JERSEY

**TABLE 4**

| SEASON | JULY | AUG | SEP | OCT | NOV | DEC | JAN | FEB | MAR | APR | MAY | JUNE | TOTAL |
|---|---|---|---|---|---|---|---|---|---|---|---|---|---|
| 1961-62 | 0 | 0 | 21 | 200 | 526 | 960 | 1052 | 963 | 705 | 393 | 2 | 7 | 4947 |
| 1962-63 | 0 | 7 | 81 | 250 | 640 | 1046 | 1091 | 1041 | 691 | 368 | 6 | 4 | 5383 |
| 1963-64 | 0 | 0 | 108 | 139 | 454 | 1100 | 946 | 955 | 687 | 473 | 88 | 21 | 4971 |
| #1964-65 | 1 | 0 | 40 | 278 | 461 | 895 | 1133 | 905 | 799 | 442 | 55 | 17 | 5026 |
| 1965-66 | 0 | 11 | 50 | 339 | 610 | 807 | 1066 | 882 | 717 | 500 | 212 | 14 | 5208 |
| 1966-67 | 0 | 0 | 63 | 286 | 480 | 876 | 864 | 991 | 842 | 425 | 33 | 5 | 5163 |
| 1967-68 | 0 | 1 | 58 | 285 | 677 | 823 | 1148 | 1012 | 676 | 325 | 16 | 12 | 5184 |
| 1968-69 | 0 | 0 | 6 | 193 | 573 | 1003 | 1039 | 938 | 804 | 317 | 0 | 2 | 4976 |
| 1969-70 | 0 | 0 | 49 | 284 | 575 | 984 | 1255 | 892 | 796 | 390 | 9 | 5 | 5327 |
| 1970-71 | 0 | 0 | 24 | 199 | 472 | 914 | 1160 | 827 | 732 | 402 | 55 | 7 | 4892 |
| 1971-72 | 0 | 1 | 12 | 95 | 569 | 724 | 909 | 969 | 757 | 444 | 93 | 19 | 4592 |
| 1972-73 | 0 | 0 | 22 | 356 | 599 | 776 | 906 | 882 | 504 | 339 | 63 | 1 | 4548 |
| 1973-74 | 0 | 0 | 18 | 166 | 479 | 787 | 909 | 921 | 661 | 273 | 2 | 12 | 4353 |
| 1974-75 | 0 | 0 | 62 | 341 | 521 | 802 | 864 | 832 | 775 | 524 | 81 | 6 | 4811 |
| 1975-76 | 0 | 1 | 59 | 195 | 400 | 913 | 1177 | 738 | 645 | 338 | 4 | 17 | 4624 |
| 1976-77 | 0 | 4 | 56 | 381 | 745 | 1107 | 1361 | 895 | 563 | 352 | 89 | 24 | 5577 |
| 1977-78 | 0 | 0 | 50 | 319 | 527 | 975 | 1168 | 1099 | 814 | 411 | 90 | 13 | 5566 |
| 1978-79 | 6 | 0 | 66 | 239 | 481 | 830 | 1001 | 1155 | 577 | 386 | 58 | 11 | 4820 |
| 1979-80 | 2 | 4 | 28 | 289 | 393 | 763 | 953 | 987 | 802 | 366 | 62 | 24 | 4673 |
| 1980-81 | 0 | 0 | 28 | 314 | 654 | 1066 | 1261 | 762 | 764 | 290 | 96 | 0 | 5235 |
| 1981-82 | 0 | 0 | 52 | 360 | 563 | 934 | 1258 | 802 | 712 | 433 | 85 | 42 | 5241 |
| 1982-83 | 0 | 13 | 36 | 267 | 493 | 679 | 923 | 810 | 622 | 395 | 62 | 5 | 4405 |
| 1983-84 | 0 | 0 | 52 | 249 | 510 | 949 | 1144 | 696 | 874 | 366 | 22 | 9 | 4977 |
| 1984-85 | 0 | 0 | 83 | 114 | 584 | 745 | 1235 | 877 | 641 | 268 | 56 | 15 | 4624 |
| 1985-86 | 0 | 0 | 21 | 212 | 462 | 971 | 985 | 942 | 642 | 341 | 8 | 7 | 4672 |
| 1986-87 | 0 | 11 | 22 | 240 | 594 | 826 | 1030 | 893 | 616 | 331 | 140 | 3 | 4706 |
| 1987-88 | 0 | 1 | 25 | 342 | 518 | 818 | 1117 | 880 | 647 | 410 | 20 | 28 | 4906 |
| 1988-89 | 1 | 0 | 18 | 386 | 476 | 906 | 859 | 853 | 698 | 366 | 32 | 6 | 4701 |
| 1989-90 | 0 | 0 | 37 | 190 | 594 | 1215 | 756 | 699 | 622 | 369 | 22 | 2 | 4606 |
| 1990-91 | 1 | 1 | 50 | 163 | 446 | 697 | | | | | | | |

**TABLE 5**    COOLING DEGREE DAYS Base 65 deg. F    NEWARK, NEW JERSEY

| YEAR | JAN | FEB | MAR | APR | MAY | JUNE | JULY | AUG | SEP | OCT | NOV | DEC | TOTAL |
|---|---|---|---|---|---|---|---|---|---|---|---|---|---|
| 1969 | 0 | 0 | 0 | 15 | 80 | 243 | 293 | 390 | 131 | 17 | 0 | 0 | 1169 |
| 1970 | 0 | 0 | 0 | 4 | 94 | 187 | 384 | 387 | 201 | 33 | 0 | 0 | 1290 |
| 1971 | 0 | 0 | 0 | 0 | 25 | 307 | 403 | 350 | 222 | 46 | 12 | 0 | 1365 |
| 1972 | 0 | 0 | 3 | 4 | 41 | 142 | 406 | 347 | 175 | 3 | 0 | 0 | 1121 |
| 1973 | 0 | 0 | 0 | 20 | 26 | 296 | 432 | 459 | 205 | 28 | 0 | 0 | 1466 |
| 1974 | 0 | 0 | 0 | 28 | 64 | 172 | 381 | 361 | 115 | 1 | 3 | 0 | 1125 |
| 1975 | 0 | 0 | 0 | 0 | 117 | 211 | 375 | 321 | 46 | 20 | 10 | 0 | 1100 |
| 1976 | 0 | 0 | 0 | 50 | 30 | 281 | 317 | 305 | 110 | 6 | 0 | 0 | 1099 |
| 1977 | 0 | 0 | 6 | 18 | 111 | 191 | 414 | 321 | 146 | 1 | 0 | 0 | 1208 |
| 1978 | 0 | 0 | 0 | 0 | 59 | 217 | 325 | 367 | 105 | 15 | 0 | 0 | 1088 |
| 1979 | 0 | 0 | 0 | 2 | 59 | 147 | 381 | 372 | 158 | 34 | 0 | 0 | 1156 |
| 1980 | 0 | 0 | 0 | 0 | 0 | 97 | 187 | 435 | 427 | 209 | 10 | 3 | 1365 |
| 1981 | 0 | 0 | 0 | 6 | 75 | 293 | 446 | 319 | 124 | 0 | 0 | 0 | 1263 |
| 1982 | 0 | 0 | 0 | 6 | 39 | 136 | 421 | 249 | 95 | 24 | 12 | 0 | 982 |
| 1983 | 0 | 0 | 0 | 19 | 39 | 268 | 458 | 396 | 226 | 36 | 0 | 0 | 1442 |
| 1984 | 0 | 0 | 0 | 2 | 47 | 316 | 365 | 388 | 102 | 36 | 0 | 0 | 1256 |
| 1985 | 0 | 0 | 11 | 36 | 134 | 152 | 357 | 335 | 183 | 19 | 3 | 0 | 1230 |
| 1986 | 0 | 0 | 2 | 2 | 149 | 243 | 380 | 303 | 136 | 30 | 0 | 0 | 1245 |
| 1987 | 0 | 0 | 0 | 6 | 116 | 293 | 453 | 327 | 143 | 0 | 0 | 0 | 1339 |
| 1988 | 0 | 0 | 0 | 0 | 75 | 274 | 488 | 465 | 115 | 10 | 0 | 0 | 1427 |
| 1989 | 0 | 0 | 3 | 1 | 81 | 294 | 385 | 360 | 194 | 16 | 0 | 0 | 1334 |
| 1990 | 0 | 0 | 7 | 23 | 11 | 262 | 403 | 365 | 165 | 89 | 2 | 0 | 1327 |

**TABLE 6**    SNOWFALL (inches)    NEWARK, NEW JERSEY

| SEASON | JULY | AUG | SEP | OCT | NOV | DEC | JAN | FEB | MAR | APR | MAY | JUNE | TOTAL |
|---|---|---|---|---|---|---|---|---|---|---|---|---|---|
| 1961-62 | 0.0 | 0.0 | 0.0 | 0.0 | 0.8 | 13.2 | 1.0 | 13.1 | 1.5 | T | 0.0 | 0.0 | 29.6 |
| 1962-63 | 0.0 | 0.0 | 0.0 | T | 0.3 | 7.8 | 7.5 | 3.6 | 2.5 | T | 0.0 | 0.0 | 21.7 |
| 1963-64 | 0.0 | 0.0 | 0.0 | 0.0 | T | 10.7 | 13.5 | 15.0 | 4.0 | T | 0.0 | 0.0 | 43.2 |
| 1964-65 | 0.0 | 0.0 | 0.0 | 0.0 | 0.0 | 3.9 | 16.1 | 1.8 | 4.6 | 0.7 | 0.0 | 0.0 | 27.1 |
| 1965-66 | 0.0 | 0.0 | 0.0 | T | 0.0 | T | 10.2 | 8.6 | T | 0.0 | 0.0 | 0.0 | 18.8 |
| 1966-67 | 0.0 | 0.0 | 0.0 | 0.0 | 0.0 | 12.6 | 1.3 | 25.4 | 18.0 | T | 0.0 | 0.0 | 57.3 |
| 1967-68 | 0.0 | 0.0 | 0.0 | 0.0 | 3.1 | 3.9 | 4.6 | 0.6 | 1.7 | 0.0 | 0.0 | 0.0 | 13.9 |
| 1968-69 | 0.0 | 0.0 | 0.0 | 0.0 | 0.4 | 4.7 | 1.1 | 16.5 | 5.9 | 0.0 | 0.0 | 0.0 | 28.6 |
| 1969-70 | 0.0 | 0.0 | 0.0 | 0.0 | T | 8.5 | 9.1 | 5.5 | 4.3 | T | 0.0 | 0.0 | 27.4 |
| 1970-71 | 0.0 | 0.0 | 0.0 | 0.0 | 0.0 | 2.9 | 13.2 | 1.1 | 4.2 | 2.2 | 0.0 | 0.0 | 23.6 |
| 1971-72 | 0.0 | 0.0 | 0.0 | 0.0 | T | 0.4 | 3.1 | 12.3 | 1.0 | T | 0.0 | 0.0 | 16.8 |
| 1972-73 | 0.0 | 0.0 | 0.0 | T | T | T | 0.7 | 0.6 | 0.6 | T | 0.0 | 0.0 | 1.9 |
| 1973-74 | 0.0 | 0.0 | 0.0 | 0.0 | 0.0 | 2.1 | 6.8 | 8.1 | 3.1 | 0.3 | 0.0 | 0.0 | 20.4 |
| 1974-75 | 0.0 | 0.0 | 0.0 | 0.0 | T | 1.2 | 1.4 | 12.7 | 1.1 | T | 0.0 | 0.0 | 16.4 |
| 1975-76 | 0.0 | 0.0 | 0.0 | 0.0 | T | 2.4 | 7.2 | 6.1 | 4.2 | T | 0.0 | 0.0 | 19.9 |
| 1976-77 | 0.0 | 0.0 | 0.0 | 0.0 | 6.7 | 10.8 | 5.8 | 1.7 | T | T | 0.0 | 0.0 | 25.0 |
| 1977-78 | 0.0 | 0.0 | 0.0 | 0.0 | 1.5 | 0.2 | 27.4 | 25.3 | 10.5 | T | T | 0.0 | 64.9 |
| 1978-79 | 0.0 | 0.0 | 0.0 | 0.0 | 2.6 | T | 9.4 | 26.1 | T | T | 0.0 | 0.0 | 38.1 |
| 1979-80 | 0.0 | 0.0 | 0.0 | T | 0.0 | 3.7 | 2.5 | 1.8 | 6.3 | T | 0.0 | 0.0 | 14.3 |
| 1980-81 | 0.0 | 0.0 | 0.0 | 0.0 | 0.4 | 3.1 | 6.9 | T | 9.1 | 0.0 | 0.0 | 0.0 | 19.5 |
| 1981-82 | 0.0 | 0.0 | 0.0 | 0.0 | T | 3.4 | 12.3 | 0.5 | 0.8 | 13.8 | 0.0 | 0.0 | 30.8 |
| 1982-83 | 0.0 | 0.0 | 0.0 | 0.0 | T | 2.9 | 2.3 | 21.5 | 0.2 | 4.1 | 0.0 | 0.0 | 31.0 |
| 1983-84 | 0.0 | 0.0 | 0.0 | 0.0 | 1.2 | 2.4 | 13.7 | 0.3 | 11.3 | T | 0.0 | 0.0 | 28.9 |
| 1984-85 | 0.0 | 0.0 | 0.0 | 0.0 | T | 0.6 | 8.9 | 7.4 | 0.1 | T | 0.0 | 0.0 | 23.2 |
| 1985-86 | 0.0 | 0.0 | 0.0 | 0.0 | 0.6 | 4.6 | 2.8 | 13.9 | T | 0.1 | 0.0 | 0.0 | 22.0 |
| 1986-87 | 0.0 | 0.0 | 0.0 | 0.0 | T | 2.3 | 21.4 | 6.5 | 2.4 | 0.0 | 0.0 | 0.0 | 32.6 |
| 1987-88 | 0.0 | 0.0 | 0.0 | 0.0 | 1.5 | 2.3 | 15.4 | 2.7 | 0.9 | T | 0.0 | | |
| 1988-89 | 0.0 | 0.0 | 0.0 | 0.0 | 0.0 | 0.1 | 4.1 | 0.6 | 2.7 | 0.0 | 0.0 | 0.0 | 7.5 |
| 1989-90 | 0.0 | 0.0 | 0.0 | 0.0 | 5.7 | 0.5 | 2.4 | 2.8 | 2.5 | 0.6 | 0.0 | 0.0 | 14.5 |
| 1990-91 | 0.0 | 0.0 | 0.0 | 0.0 | T | 7.6 | | | | | | | |
| Record Mean | 0.0 | 0.0 | 0.0 | T | 0.6 | 5.7 | 7.7 | 8.0 | 4.6 | 0.7 | T | 0.0 | 27.3 |

**See Reference Notes, relative to all above tables, on preceding page.**

The Albuquerque metropolitan area is largely situated in the Rio Grande Valley and on the mesas and piedmont slopes which rise either side of the valley floor. The Rio Grande flows from north to south through the area. The Sandia and Manzano Mountains rise abruptly at the eastern edge of the city with Tijeras Canyon separating the two ranges. West of the city the land gradually rises to the Continental Divide, some 90 miles away.

The climate of Albuquerque is best described as arid continental with abundant sunshine, low humidity, scant precipitation, and a wide yet tolerable seasonal range of temperatures. Sunny days and low humidity are renowned features of the climate. More than three-fourths of the daylight hours have sunshine, even in the winter months. The air is normally dry and muggy days are rare. The combination of dry air and plentiful solar radiation allows widespread use of energy-efficient devices such as evaporative coolers and solar collectors.

Precipitation within the valley area is adequate only for native desert vegetation and deep-rooted imports. However, irrigation supports successful farming and fruit growing in the Rio Grande Valley. On the east slopes of the Sandias and Manzanos, precipitation is sufficient for thick stands of timber and good grass cover.

Meager amounts of precipitation fall in the winter, much of it as snow. Snowfalls of an inch or more occur about four times a year in the Rio Grande Valley, while the mountains receive substantial snowfall on occasion. Snow seldom remains on the ground more than 24 hours in the city proper. However, snow cover on the east slopes of the Sandias is sufficient for skiing during most winters.

Nearly half of the annual precipitation in Albuquerque results from afternoon and evening thunderstorms during the summer. Thunderstorm frequency increases rapidly around July 1st, peaks during August, then tapers off by the end of September. Thunderstorms are usually brief, sometimes produce heavy rainfall, and often lower afternoon temperatures noticeably. Hailstorms are infrequent and tornadoes rare.

Temperatures in Albuquerque are those characteristic of a dry, high altitude, continental climate. The average daily range of temperature is relatively high, but extreme temperatures are rare. High temperatures during the winter are near 50 degrees with only a few days on which the temperature fails to rise above the freezing mark. In the summer, daytime maxima are about 90 degrees, but with the large daily range, the nights usually are comfortably cool.

The average number of days between the last freezing temperature in spring and the first freeze in fall varies widely across the Albuquerque metropolitan area. The growing season in Albuquerque and adjacent suburbs ranges from around 170 days in the Rio Grande Valley to about 200 days in parts of the northeast section of the city.

Sustained winds of 12 mph or less occur approximately 80 percent of the time at the Albuquerque International Airport, while sustained winds greater than 25 mph have a frequency less than 3 percent. Late winter and spring storms along with occasional east winds out of Tijeras Canyon are the main sources of strong wind conditions. Blowing dust, the least attractive feature of the climate, often accompanies the occasional strong winds of winter and spring.

# TABLE 1     NORMALS, MEANS AND EXTREMES

ALBUQUERQUE, NEW MEXICO

LATITUDE: 35°03'N    LONGITUDE: 106°37'W    ELEVATION: FT. GRND 5311 BARO 5313    TIME ZONE: MOUNTAIN    WBAN: 23050

| | (a) | JAN | FEB | MAR | APR | MAY | JUNE | JULY | AUG | SEP | OCT | NOV | DEC | YEAR |
|---|---|---|---|---|---|---|---|---|---|---|---|---|---|---|
| **TEMPERATURE °F:** | | | | | | | | | | | | | | |
| Normals | | | | | | | | | | | | | | |
| -Daily Maximum | | 47.2 | 52.9 | 60.7 | 70.6 | 79.9 | 90.6 | 92.8 | 89.4 | 83.0 | 71.7 | 57.2 | 48.0 | 70.3 |
| -Daily Minimum | | 22.3 | 25.9 | 31.7 | 39.5 | 48.6 | 58.4 | 64.7 | 62.8 | 54.9 | 43.1 | 30.7 | 23.2 | 42.1 |
| -Monthly | | 34.8 | 39.4 | 46.2 | 55.1 | 64.3 | 74.5 | 78.8 | 76.1 | 69.0 | 57.4 | 44.0 | 35.6 | 56.2 |
| Extremes | | | | | | | | | | | | | | |
| -Record Highest | 50 | 69 | 76 | 85 | 89 | 98 | 105 | 105 | 101 | 100 | 91 | 77 | 72 | 105 |
| -Year | | 1971 | 1986 | 1971 | 1989 | 1951 | 1980 | 1980 | 1979 | 1979 | 1979 | 1975 | 1958 | JUN 1980 |
| -Record Lowest | 50 | -17 | -5 | 8 | 19 | 28 | 40 | 52 | 52 | 37 | 25 | -7 | 3 | -17 |
| -Year | | 1971 | 1951 | 1948 | 1980 | 1975 | 1980 | 1985 | 1968 | 1971 | 1980 | 1976 | 1974 | JAN 1971 |
| **NORMAL DEGREE DAYS:** | | | | | | | | | | | | | | |
| Heating (base 65°F) | | 936 | 717 | 583 | 302 | 81 | 0 | 0 | 0 | 12 | 242 | 630 | 911 | 4414 |
| Cooling (base 65°F) | | 0 | 0 | 0 | 0 | 59 | 285 | 428 | 344 | 132 | 6 | 0 | 0 | 1254 |
| **% OF POSSIBLE SUNSHINE** | 50 | 72 | 73 | 73 | 77 | 79 | 83 | 76 | 76 | 79 | 79 | 77 | 72 | 76 |
| **MEAN SKY COVER (tenths)** | | | | | | | | | | | | | | |
| Sunrise - Sunset | 50 | 4.8 | 5.0 | 5.0 | 4.5 | 4.2 | 3.4 | 4.5 | 4.3 | 3.6 | 3.5 | 4.0 | 4.6 | 4.3 |
| **MEAN NUMBER OF DAYS:** | | | | | | | | | | | | | | |
| Sunrise to Sunset | | | | | | | | | | | | | | |
| -Clear | 50 | 13.0 | 11.2 | 11.5 | 12.8 | 14.5 | 17.6 | 12.0 | 13.5 | 16.8 | 17.2 | 15.2 | 13.9 | 169.1 |
| -Partly Cloudy | 50 | 7.7 | 7.7 | 9.8 | 9.4 | 10.2 | 8.6 | 14.3 | 12.5 | 7.7 | 7.8 | 7.7 | 7.5 | 111.0 |
| -Cloudy | 50 | 10.3 | 9.4 | 9.6 | 7.8 | 6.3 | 3.8 | 4.7 | 5.0 | 5.5 | 6.0 | 7.1 | 9.6 | 85.2 |
| Precipitation | | | | | | | | | | | | | | |
| .01 inches or more | 50 | 4.0 | 4.0 | 4.5 | 3.3 | 4.4 | 3.9 | 8.8 | 9.4 | 5.7 | 4.9 | 3.4 | 4.1 | 60.3 |
| Snow,Ice pellets | | | | | | | | | | | | | | |
| 1.0 inches or more | 50 | 1.0 | 0.9 | 0.7 | 0.2 | 0.* | 0.0 | 0.0 | 0.0 | 0.0 | 0.* | 0.4 | 0.9 | 4.2 |
| Thunderstorms | 50 | 0.1 | 0.3 | 0.9 | 1.5 | 3.9 | 5.0 | 10.9 | 10.9 | 4.6 | 2.4 | 0.6 | 0.2 | 41.4 |
| Heavy Fog Visibility 1/4 mile or less | 50 | 1.1 | 0.9 | 0.6 | 0.2 | 0.* | 0.* | 0.1 | 0.* | 0.1 | 0.4 | 0.6 | 1.4 | 5.5 |
| Temperature °F | | | | | | | | | | | | | | |
| -Maximum | | | | | | | | | | | | | | |
| 90° and above | 29 | 0.0 | 0.0 | 0.0 | 0.0 | 2.7 | 16.9 | 23.5 | 16.1 | 3.8 | 0.1 | 0.0 | 0.0 | 63.1 |
| 32° and below | 29 | 2.4 | 0.8 | 0.1 | 0.0 | 0.0 | 0.0 | 0.0 | 0.0 | 0.0 | 0.0 | 0.2 | 1.7 | 5.2 |
| -Minimum | | | | | | | | | | | | | | |
| 32° and below | 29 | 28.9 | 22.7 | 16.1 | 4.6 | 0.2 | 0.0 | 0.0 | 0.0 | 0.0 | 2.1 | 16.2 | 28.6 | 119.4 |
| 0° and below | 29 | 0.4 | 0.0 | 0.0 | 0.0 | 0.0 | 0.0 | 0.0 | 0.0 | 0.0 | 0.0 | 0.1 | 0.0 | 0.5 |
| **AVG. STATION PRESS.(mb)** | 17 | 838.9 | 837.9 | 835.0 | 835.8 | 836.0 | 838.1 | 840.4 | 840.6 | 840.1 | 840.0 | 838.8 | 839.2 | 838.4 |
| **RELATIVE HUMIDITY (%)** | | | | | | | | | | | | | | |
| Hour 05 | 29 | 70 | 65 | 56 | 49 | 48 | 46 | 60 | 66 | 62 | 62 | 65 | 70 | 60 |
| Hour 11 (Local Time) | 29 | 51 | 44 | 33 | 26 | 25 | 24 | 34 | 39 | 40 | 38 | 42 | 50 | 37 |
| Hour 17 | 29 | 40 | 32 | 24 | 18 | 18 | 18 | 27 | 30 | 31 | 30 | 35 | 43 | 29 |
| Hour 23 | 29 | 61 | 53 | 43 | 35 | 34 | 33 | 47 | 53 | 52 | 50 | 54 | 61 | 48 |
| **PRECIPITATION (inches):** | | | | | | | | | | | | | | |
| Water Equivalent | | | | | | | | | | | | | | |
| -Normal | | 0.41 | 0.40 | 0.52 | 0.40 | 0.46 | 0.51 | 1.30 | 1.51 | 0.85 | 0.86 | 0.38 | 0.52 | 8.12 |
| -Maximum Monthly | 50 | 1.32 | 1.42 | 2.18 | 1.97 | 3.07 | 2.57 | 3.33 | 3.30 | 2.63 | 3.08 | 1.45 | 1.85 | 3.33 |
| -Year | | 1978 | 1948 | 1973 | 1942 | 1941 | 1986 | 1968 | 1967 | 1988 | 1972 | 1940 | 1959 | JUL 1968 |
| -Minimum Monthly | 50 | T | T | T | T | T | T | 0.08 | T | T | 0.00 | 0.00 | 0.00 | 0.00 |
| -Year | | 1970 | 1984 | 1966 | 1989 | 1945 | 1975 | 1980 | 1962 | 1957 | 1952 | 1949 | 1981 | DEC 1981 |
| -Maximum in 24 hrs | 50 | 0.87 | 0.51 | 1.11 | 1.66 | 1.14 | 1.64 | 1.77 | 1.75 | 1.92 | 1.80 | 0.76 | 1.35 | 1.92 |
| -Year | | 1962 | 1981 | 1973 | 1969 | 1969 | 1952 | 1961 | 1980 | 1955 | 1969 | 1940 | 1958 | SEP 1955 |
| Snow,Ice pellets | | | | | | | | | | | | | | |
| -Maximum Monthly | 50 | 9.5 | 10.3 | 13.9 | 8.1 | 1.0 | 0.0 | 0.0 | 0.0 | T | 3.2 | 9.3 | 14.7 | 14.7 |
| -Year | | 1973 | 1986 | 1973 | 1973 | 1979 | | | | 1971 | 1986 | 1940 | 1959 | DEC 1959 |
| -Maximum in 24 hrs | 50 | 5.1 | 6.0 | 10.7 | 10.9 | 1.0 | 0.0 | 0.0 | 0.0 | T | 3.2 | 5.5 | 14.2 | 14.2 |
| -Year | | 1973 | 1986 | 1973 | 1988 | 1979 | | | | 1971 | 1986 | 1946 | 1958 | DEC 1958 |
| **WIND:** | | | | | | | | | | | | | | |
| Mean Speed (mph) | 50 | 8.1 | 8.9 | 10.1 | 11.0 | 10.6 | 10.0 | 9.1 | 8.2 | 8.6 | 8.3 | 7.9 | 7.7 | 9.0 |
| Prevailing Direction through 1963 | | N | N | SE | S | S | S | SE | SE | SE | SE | N | N | SE |
| Fastest Obs. 1 Min. | | | | | | | | | | | | | | |
| -Direction (!!!) | 5 | 09 | 09 | 28 | 17 | 28 | 09 | 36 | 36 | 25 | 09 | 27 | 09 | 09 |
| -Speed (MPH) | 5 | 52 | 40 | 41 | 46 | 46 | 39 | 48 | 40 | 40 | 32 | 48 | 47 | 52 |
| -Year | | 1987 | 1989 | 1986 | 1985 | 1986 | 1988 | 1988 | 1986 | 1985 | 1986 | 1988 | 1987 | JAN 1987 |
| Peak Gust | | | | | | | | | | | | | | |
| -Direction (!!!) | 6 | E | W | NW | SW | S | E | N | E | W | NW | W | E | E |
| -Speed (mph) | 6 | 67 | 63 | 66 | 64 | 61 | 67 | 66 | 63 | 61 | 51 | 63 | 71 | 71 |
| -Date | | 1987 | 1984 | 1986 | 1984 | 1987 | 1986 | 1988 | 1989 | 1985 | 1986 | 1988 | 1987 | DEC 1987 |

**See Reference Notes to this table on the following page.**

PRECIPITATION (inches)    ALBUQUERQUE, NEW MEXICO

**TABLE 2**

| YEAR | JAN | FEB | MAR | APR | MAY | JUNE | JULY | AUG | SEP | OCT | NOV | DEC | ANNUAL |
|------|-----|-----|-----|-----|-----|------|------|-----|-----|-----|-----|-----|--------|
| 1961 | 0.23 | 0.10 | 0.61 | 0.73 | 0.01 | 0.11 | 2.70 | 1.69 | 1.09 | 0.47 | 0.49 | 0.65 | 8.87 |
| 1962 | 1.01 | 0.11 | 0.18 | 0.07 | 0.01 | 0.19 | 1.24 | T | 0.71 | 0.75 | 0.61 | 0.51 | 5.39 |
| 1963 | 0.29 | 0.24 | 0.55 | 0.14 | 0.03 | 0.11 | 1.43 | 3.00 | 0.63 | 0.76 | 0.29 | T | 7.47 |
| 1964 | 0.07 | 1.12 | 0.13 | 0.61 | 0.35 | T | 1.87 | 0.98 | 1.57 | 0.04 | 0.21 | 0.49 | 7.44 |
| 1965 | 0.47 | 0.60 | 0.49 | 0.49 | 0.19 | 0.99 | 1.65 | 0.61 | 1.18 | 0.89 | 0.33 | 1.42 | 9.31 |
| 1966 | 0.42 | 0.30 | T | 0.04 | 0.02 | 1.66 | 1.63 | 1.06 | 1.04 | 0.54 | 0.09 | 0.01 | 6.81 |
| 1967 | 0.01 | 0.44 | 0.25 | T | 0.04 | 1.71 | 0.61 | 3.30 | 0.79 | 0.18 | 0.15 | 0.56 | 8.04 |
| 1968 | 0.01 | 0.98 | 1.48 | 0.51 | 0.99 | 0.05 | 3.33 | 1.49 | 0.30 | 0.12 | 0.53 | 0.82 | 10.67 |
| 1969 | 0.08 | 0.34 | 0.41 | 1.76 | 1.31 | 0.59 | 0.94 | 0.95 | 1.08 | 2.37 | 0.01 | 0.72 | 10.56 |
| 1970 | T | 0.27 | 0.42 | 0.05 | 0.33 | 0.40 | 1.22 | 2.24 | 0.79 | 0.25 | 0.03 | 0.23 | 6.28 |
| 1971 | 0.27 | 0.21 | 0.03 | 0.78 | 0.16 | 0.02 | 1.05 | 0.87 | 1.44 | 1.15 | 0.67 | 1.40 | 8.05 |
| 1972 | 0.12 | 0.12 | 0.08 | T | 0.18 | 0.55 | 1.00 | 2.93 | 1.00 | 3.08 | 0.63 | 0.36 | 10.11 |
| 1973 | 0.85 | 0.33 | 2.18 | 0.91 | 0.66 | 1.37 | 1.80 | 1.19 | 1.13 | 0.35 | 0.08 | 0.03 | 10.88 |
| 1974 | 0.88 | 0.11 | 0.85 | 0.14 | 0.01 | 0.22 | 2.40 | 0.79 | 1.58 | 1.96 | 0.38 | 0.51 | 9.83 |
| 1975 | 0.26 | 0.99 | 0.95 | 0.10 | 0.66 | T | 1.43 | 1.40 | 1.66 | T | 0.28 | 0.28 | 8.01 |
| 1976 | 0.00 | 0.40 | 0.09 | 0.31 | 0.82 | 0.60 | 1.32 | 0.73 | 0.45 | 0.03 | 0.24 | 0.20 | 5.19 |
| 1977 | 0.88 | 0.13 | 0.63 | 1.07 | 0.10 | 0.04 | 0.69 | 2.28 | 0.78 | 0.76 | 0.42 | 0.13 | 7.91 |
| 1978 | 1.32 | 1.02 | 0.54 | 0.05 | 0.69 | 1.05 | 0.24 | 2.49 | 0.59 | 1.22 | 1.05 | 0.76 | 10.97 |
| 1979 | 1.07 | 0.62 | 0.14 | 0.24 | 2.48 | 1.02 | 0.80 | 1.53 | 0.40 | 0.27 | 0.91 | 0.87 | 10.35 |
| 1980 | 0.87 | 0.58 | 0.60 | 0.60 | 0.56 | 0.01 | 0.08 | 2.61 | 1.83 | 0.09 | 0.30 | 0.74 | 8.87 |
| 1981 | 0.05 | 0.67 | 0.80 | 0.30 | 0.53 | 0.35 | 1.07 | 1.68 | 0.41 | 1.43 | 0.37 | 0.00 | 7.66 |
| 1982 | 0.32 | 0.20 | 0.84 | 0.05 | 0.52 | 0.09 | 1.32 | 1.09 | 1.34 | 0.26 | 0.60 | 0.78 | 7.41 |
| 1983 | 1.10 | 0.71 | 0.61 | 0.02 | 0.32 | 1.21 | 0.55 | 0.27 | 0.91 | 1.20 | 0.44 | 0.42 | 7.76 |
| 1984 | 0.33 | T | 0.62 | 0.50 | 0.16 | 0.48 | 1.13 | 2.70 | 1.13 | 3.04 | 0.63 | 1.36 | 12.08 |
| 1985 | 0.49 | 0.54 | 0.70 | 1.69 | 1.12 | 0.56 | 1.16 | 0.49 | 1.53 | 2.15 | 0.19 | 0.16 | 10.75 |
| 1986 | 0.22 | 1.01 | 0.17 | 0.33 | 1.11 | 2.57 | 1.51 | 2.26 | 0.53 | 1.54 | 1.29 | 0.44 | 12.98 |
| 1987 | 0.66 | 0.61 | 0.07 | 1.00 | 0.58 | 0.13 | 0.91 | 2.98 | 0.20 | 0.44 | 0.42 | 0.34 | 8.34 |
| 1988 | 0.15 | 0.07 | 0.85 | 1.42 | 0.62 | 1.25 | 2.26 | 3.29 | 2.63 | 0.32 | 0.22 | 0.03 | 13.11 |
| 1989 | 0.57 | 0.35 | 0.48 | T | 0.02 | 0.02 | 1.51 | 0.48 | 0.31 | 0.97 | T | 0.28 | 4.99 |
| 1990 | 0.21 | 0.49 | 0.41 | 1.71 | 0.45 | 0.27 | 2.36 | 1.79 | 0.96 | 0.15 | 0.86 | 0.59 | 10.25 |
| Record Mean | 0.39 | 0.38 | 0.45 | 0.56 | 0.62 | 0.60 | 1.40 | 1.40 | 0.93 | 0.84 | 0.43 | 0.45 | 8.45 |

**TABLE 3**    AVERAGE TEMPERATURE (deg. F)    ALBUQUERQUE, NEW MEXICO

| YEAR | JAN | FEB | MAR | APR | MAY | JUNE | JULY | AUG | SEP | OCT | NOV | DEC | ANNUAL |
|------|-----|-----|-----|-----|-----|------|------|-----|-----|-----|-----|-----|--------|
| 1961 | 33.9 | 40.6 | 47.0 | 54.5 | 65.9 | 75.8 | 76.7 | 75.2 | 65.6 | 56.8 | 40.3 | 34.1 | 55.5 |
| 1962 | 31.6 | 42.3 | 41.2 | 58.1 | 64.1 | 72.7 | 76.3 | 77.6 | 69.4 | 58.1 | 46.3 | 36.9 | 56.3 |
| 1963 | 29.4 | 40.5 | 45.2 | 57.7 | 68.0 | 74.6 | 81.4 | 75.9 | 72.5 | 61.5 | 45.7 | 34.8 | 57.3 |
| 1964 | 30.0 | 29.1 | 41.5 | 51.7 | 65.8 | 73.6 | 78.2 | 76.8 | 69.3 | 59.4 | 43.7 | 35.5 | 54.5 |
| 1965 | 38.8 | 39.4 | 44.8 | 54.8 | 61.7 | 69.4 | 77.9 | 75.4 | 66.6 | 58.0 | 48.1 | 35.8 | 55.9 |
| 1966 | 30.1 | 33.2 | 45.6 | 54.6 | 67.2 | 72.8 | 79.8 | 75.7 | 68.4 | 56.8 | 46.7 | 34.3 | 55.4 |
| 1967 | 33.2 | 40.5 | 52.0 | 57.8 | 63.8 | 71.5 | 79.2 | 74.5 | 68.4 | 58.2 | 46.1 | 32.4 | 56.5 |
| 1968 | 36.8 | 43.3 | 46.7 | 53.4 | 62.7 | 75.2 | 76.1 | 72.4 | 68.0 | 58.3 | 42.8 | 30.0 | 55.5 |
| 1969 | 38.0 | 38.5 | 41.1 | 57.4 | 66.2 | 73.6 | 80.2 | 79.0 | 70.0 | 53.8 | 41.1 | 39.1 | 56.6 |
| 1970 | 34.5 | 42.8 | 44.1 | 52.5 | 66.2 | 72.7 | 79.6 | 77.8 | 67.5 | 52.6 | 44.5 | 36.4 | 56.0 |
| 1971 | 33.6 | 38.9 | 44.7 | 53.3 | 61.7 | 73.8 | 78.1 | 73.9 | 66.4 | 53.8 | 45.2 | 31.9 | 54.8 |
| 1972 | 36.1 | 42.5 | 53.6 | 56.9 | 64.0 | 73.7 | 78.6 | 74.1 | 68.1 | 57.6 | 40.7 | 35.0 | 56.7 |
| 1973 | 31.8 | 35.9 | 45.1 | 50.2 | 62.7 | 73.5 | 78.4 | 78.0 | 67.5 | 56.4 | 44.6 | 34.0 | 54.8 |
| 1974 | 33.6 | 37.9 | 52.8 | 56.4 | 68.5 | 80.1 | 77.0 | 72.7 | 66.1 | 58.1 | 45.2 | 32.0 | 56.7 |
| 1975 | 30.8 | 38.0 | 41.4 | 49.9 | 61.0 | 73.0 | 76.8 | 76.1 | 66.3 | 56.5 | 42.6 | 35.6 | 54.3 |
| 1976 | 33.2 | 43.3 | 44.3 | 54.6 | 62.8 | 73.4 | 77.0 | 75.0 | 68.0 | 53.1 | 40.6 | 33.0 | 54.9 |
| 1977 | 29.8 | 40.7 | 43.2 | 56.5 | 64.2 | 75.5 | 78.6 | 77.4 | 69.4 | 58.9 | 46.1 | 40.4 | 56.8 |
| 1978 | 36.8 | 39.3 | 50.2 | 57.7 | 60.5 | 75.5 | 81.6 | 75.5 | 69.1 | 60.3 | 47.5 | 34.3 | 57.4 |
| 1979 | 32.9 | 41.1 | 48.4 | 56.9 | 63.7 | 73.3 | 80.6 | 77.1 | 72.3 | 61.5 | 41.0 | 37.7 | 57.2 |
| 1980 | 40.2 | 44.2 | 46.1 | 52.1 | 61.1 | 77.2 | 82.7 | 77.4 | 69.9 | 54.5 | 43.5 | 40.5 | 57.4 |
| 1981 | 38.0 | 42.9 | 46.2 | 59.0 | 64.5 | 77.0 | 79.8 | 76.4 | 69.4 | 55.7 | 47.0 | 40.5 | 58.0 |
| 1982 | 35.9 | 39.4 | 47.4 | 56.1 | 63.0 | 74.8 | 79.1 | 77.4 | 69.5 | 54.8 | 42.9 | 34.4 | 56.2 |
| 1983 | 35.0 | 39.7 | 46.9 | 50.2 | 63.0 | 73.4 | 80.4 | 79.4 | 73.4 | 58.3 | 45.1 | 36.7 | 56.8 |
| 1984 | 34.1 | 40.1 | 46.8 | 52.8 | 69.9 | 73.6 | 78.9 | 75.7 | 68.8 | 51.6 | 43.7 | 35.6 | 56.0 |
| 1985 | 33.8 | 38.3 | 47.5 | 57.4 | 64.0 | 74.1 | 77.1 | 76.6 | 65.9 | 57.5 | 45.4 | 37.6 | 56.3 |
| 1986 | 41.3 | 43.0 | 50.9 | 56.5 | 63.7 | 72.7 | 74.7 | 76.0 | 66.5 | 54.6 | 42.0 | 36.3 | 56.5 |
| 1987 | 32.3 | 39.2 | 43.7 | 54.8 | 62.8 | 73.0 | 77.3 | 74.7 | 68.8 | 61.3 | 45.1 | 35.3 | 55.7 |
| 1988 | 34.6 | 43.9 | 47.0 | 55.1 | 64.3 | 74.4 | 78.1 | 75.0 | 66.3 | 61.1 | 45.4 | 33.9 | 56.6 |
| 1989 | 35.5 | 41.9 | 52.8 | 61.4 | 68.8 | 75.6 | 78.6 | 74.3 | 69.4 | 56.7 | 46.4 | 35.1 | 58.0 |
| 1990 | 34.6 | 38.5 | 48.6 | 57.3 | 63.6 | 79.0 | 76.8 | 73.8 | 70.9 | 58.3 | 45.0 | 32.1 | 56.5 |
| Record Mean | 34.6 | 39.7 | 46.5 | 54.9 | 63.8 | 73.6 | 77.3 | 75.3 | 68.4 | 56.8 | 44.0 | 35.3 | 55.9 |
| Max | 47.1 | 53.0 | 60.9 | 70.0 | 79.0 | 89.1 | 91.2 | 88.7 | 82.2 | 71.1 | 57.5 | 47.5 | 69.8 |
| Min | 22.1 | 26.4 | 32.1 | 39.8 | 48.6 | 58.0 | 63.5 | 61.8 | 54.7 | 42.6 | 30.4 | 23.0 | 41.9 |

## REFERENCE NOTES FOR TABLES 1, 2, 3 and 6    (ALBUQUERQUE, NM)

### GENERAL

T - TRACE AMOUNT
BLANK ENTRIES DENOTE MISSING/UNREPORTED DATA.
# INDICATES A STATION OR INSTRUMENT RELOCATION.

### SPECIFIC

#### TABLE 1

(a) - LENGTH OF RECORD IN YEARS. ALTHOUGH INDIVIDUAL MONTHS MAY BE MISSING.

* LESS THAN .05

NORMALS — BASED ON THE 1951-1980 RECORD PERIOD.
EXTREMES — DATES ARE THE MOST RECENT OCCURRENCE.
WIND DIR. — NUMERALS SHOW TENS OF DEGREES CLOCKWISE FROM TRUE NORTH.
            "00" INDICATES CALM.
RESULTANT WIND DIRECTIONS ARE GIVEN TO WHOLE DEGREES.

#### TABLE 3
MAX AND MIN ARE LONG-TERM MEAN DAILY MAXIMUM AND MEAN DAILY MINIMUM TEMPERATURES.

### EXCEPTIONS

#### TABLES 2, 3, and 6

RECORD MEANS ARE THROUGH THE CURRENT YEAR, BEGINNING IN
1893 FOR TEMPERATURE
1893 FOR PRECIPITATION
1940 FOR SNOWFALL

HEATING DEGREE DAYS Base 65 deg. F          ALBUQUERQUE, NEW MEXICO

**TABLE 4**

| SEASON | JULY | AUG | SEP | OCT | NOV | DEC | JAN | FEB | MAR | APR | MAY | JUNE | TOTAL |
|---|---|---|---|---|---|---|---|---|---|---|---|---|---|
| 1961-62 | 0 | 0 | 43 | 248 | 731 | 951 | 1030 | 629 | 730 | 214 | 78 | 2 | 4656 |
| 1962-63 | 0 | 0 | 22 | 208 | 534 | 863 | 1098 | 680 | 605 | 219 | 7 | 2 | 4238 |
| 1963-64 | 0 | 0 | 0 | 124 | 573 | 931 | 1076 | 1036 | 722 | 391 | 85 | 3 | 4941 |
| 1964-65 | 2 | 0 | 20 | 173 | 632 | 909 | 805 | 709 | 624 | 300 | 128 | 24 | 4326 |
| 1965-66 | 0 | 0 | 56 | 217 | 492 | 895 | 1074 | 882 | 595 | 305 | 53 | 0 | 4569 |
| 1966-67 | 0 | 0 | 15 | 247 | 541 | 942 | 980 | 682 | 396 | 211 | 109 | 0 | 4123 |
| 1967-68 | 0 | 0 | 13 | 220 | 557 | 1003 | 870 | 623 | 559 | 343 | 107 | 8 | 4303 |
| 1968-69 | 2 | 0 | 12 | 208 | 660 | 1080 | 831 | 735 | 735 | 228 | 84 | 0 | 4575 |
| 1969-70 | 0 | 0 | 1 | 348 | 701 | 795 | 938 | 612 | 644 | 367 | 63 | 11 | 4480 |
| 1970-71 | 0 | 0 | 58 | 380 | 605 | 878 | 968 | 725 | 533 | 343 | 122 | 5 | 4617 |
| 1971-72 | 0 | 0 | 101 | 341 | 587 | 1022 | 889 | 648 | 346 | 244 | 76 | 0 | 4254 |
| 1972-73 | 0 | 3 | 14 | 244 | 740 | 925 | 1020 | 811 | 607 | 440 | 113 | 3 | 4920 |
| 1973-74 | 0 | 0 | 43 | 257 | 606 | 955 | 963 | 754 | 373 | 255 | 29 | 4 | 4239 |
| 1974-75 | 0 | 2 | 68 | 212 | 593 | 1020 | 1051 | 748 | 614 | 449 | 143 | 6 | 4906 |
| 1975-76 | 0 | 0 | 47 | 256 | 664 | 905 | 979 | 622 | 634 | 304 | 99 | 1 | 4511 |
| 1976-77 | 0 | 0 | 35 | 367 | 726 | 985 | 1084 | 675 | 669 | 250 | 61 | 0 | 4852 |
| 1977-78 | 0 | 0 | 1 | 192 | 551 | 757 | 870 | 713 | 454 | 215 | 175 | 2 | 3930 |
| 1978-79 | 0 | 0 | 20 | 167 | 521 | 945 | 988 | 665 | 509 | 241 | 100 | 12 | 4168 |
| 1979-80 | 0 | 0 | 23 | 148 | 715 | 840 | 763 | 595 | 577 | 379 | 139 | 2 | 4181 |
| 1980-81 | 0 | 0 | 6 | 335 | 640 | 752 | 827 | 611 | 575 | 197 | 62 | 2 | 4007 |
| 1981-82 | 0 | 0 | 3 | 280 | 534 | 754 | 895 | 709 | 538 | 268 | 94 | 0 | 4075 |
| 1982-83 | 0 | 0 | 23 | 314 | 658 | 941 | 922 | 703 | 556 | 439 | 127 | 0 | 4683 |
| 1983-84 | 0 | 0 | 11 | 198 | 592 | 875 | 948 | 714 | 559 | 362 | 22 | 3 | 4284 |
| 1984-85 | 0 | 0 | 51 | 411 | 631 | 903 | 960 | 744 | 536 | 220 | 74 | 7 | 4537 |
| 1985-86 | 0 | 0 | 61 | 228 | 581 | 842 | 727 | 610 | 431 | 249 | 80 | 8 | 3817 |
| 1986-87 | 0 | 0 | 51 | 313 | 680 | 882 | 1004 | 717 | 653 | 300 | 81 | 2 | 4683 |
| 1987-88 | 0 | 0 | 2 | 133 | 589 | 914 | 937 | 605 | 551 | 290 | 103 | 2 | 4126 |
| 1988-89 | 0 | 5 | 39 | 118 | 579 | 959 | 909 | 640 | 373 | 133 | 31 | 0 | 3786 |
| 1989-90 | 0 | 0 | 10 | 260 | 551 | 918 | 934 | 735 | 501 | 233 | 103 | 0 | 4245 |
| 1990-91 | 0 | 0 | 14 | 202 | 595 | 1013 | | | | | | | |

**TABLE 5**  COOLING DEGREE DAYS Base 65 deg. F          ALBUQUERQUE, NEW MEXICO

| YEAR | JAN | FEB | MAR | APR | MAY | JUNE | JULY | AUG | SEP | OCT | NOV | DEC | TOTAL |
|---|---|---|---|---|---|---|---|---|---|---|---|---|---|
| 1969 | 0 | 0 | 0 | 6 | 127 | 263 | 478 | 442 | 158 | 7 | 0 | 0 | 1481 |
| 1970 | 0 | 0 | 0 | 0 | 105 | 246 | 461 | 405 | 141 | 4 | 0 | 0 | 1362 |
| 1971 | 0 | 0 | 5 | 0 | 26 | 277 | 414 | 282 | 149 | 0 | 0 | 0 | 1153 |
| 1972 | 0 | 0 | 0 | 5 | 52 | 267 | 428 | 294 | 113 | 23 | 0 | 0 | 1182 |
| 1973 | 0 | 0 | 0 | 0 | 48 | 267 | 422 | 409 | 124 | 0 | 0 | 0 | 1270 |
| 1974 | 0 | 0 | 0 | 5 | 144 | 464 | 380 | 247 | 107 | 6 | 0 | 0 | 1353 |
| 1975 | 0 | 0 | 0 | 0 | 25 | 256 | 372 | 351 | 96 | 0 | 0 | 0 | 1100 |
| 1976 | 0 | 0 | 0 | 0 | 38 | 260 | 382 | 319 | 137 | 5 | 0 | 0 | 1141 |
| 1977 | 0 | 0 | 0 | 0 | 44 | 324 | 427 | 392 | 141 | 7 | 0 | 0 | 1335 |
| 1978 | 0 | 0 | 0 | 4 | 41 | 324 | 521 | 330 | 151 | 27 | 0 | 0 | 1398 |
| 1979 | 0 | 0 | 0 | 5 | 67 | 269 | 491 | 382 | 249 | 45 | 0 | 0 | 1508 |
| 1980 | 0 | 0 | 0 | 0 | 27 | 375 | 557 | 392 | 160 | 15 | 0 | 0 | 1526 |
| 1981 | 0 | 0 | 0 | 28 | 51 | 368 | 470 | 360 | 152 | 1 | 0 | 0 | 1430 |
| 1982 | 0 | 0 | 0 | 6 | 38 | 301 | 441 | 394 | 163 | 4 | 0 | 0 | 1347 |
| 1983 | 0 | 0 | 0 | 1 | 72 | 260 | 484 | 450 | 267 | 1 | 0 | 0 | 1535 |
| 1984 | 0 | 0 | 0 | 4 | 179 | 266 | 441 | 340 | 169 | 1 | 0 | 0 | 1400 |
| 1985 | 0 | 0 | 0 | 0 | 51 | 289 | 383 | 368 | 97 | 0 | 0 | 0 | 1188 |
| 1986 | 0 | 0 | 0 | 1 | 50 | 245 | 310 | 349 | 103 | 0 | 0 | 0 | 1058 |
| 1987 | 0 | 0 | 0 | 0 | 17 | 251 | 404 | 308 | 120 | 25 | 0 | 0 | 1125 |
| 1988 | 0 | 0 | 0 | 1 | 85 | 288 | 411 | 322 | 86 | 3 | 0 | 0 | 1196 |
| 1989 | 0 | 0 | 0 | 31 | 154 | 323 | 426 | 295 | 150 | 10 | 0 | 0 | 1389 |
| 1990 | 0 | 0 | 0 | 10 | 66 | 426 | 374 | 281 | 200 | 2 | 0 | 0 | 1359 |

**TABLE 6**  SNOWFALL (inches)          ALBUQUERQUE, NEW MEXICO

| SEASON | JULY | AUG | SEP | OCT | NOV | DEC | JAN | FEB | MAR | APR | MAY | JUNE | TOTAL |
|---|---|---|---|---|---|---|---|---|---|---|---|---|---|
| 1961-62 | 0.0 | 0.0 | 0.0 | T | 3.4 | 2.4 | 4.0 | T | 0.2 | 0.0 | 0.0 | 0.0 | 10.0 |
| 1962-63 | 0.0 | 0.0 | 0.0 | 0.0 | T | 1.0 | 2.5 | 0.8 | 2.5 | 0.0 | 0.0 | 0.0 | 6.8 |
| 1963-64 | 0.0 | 0.0 | 0.0 | 0.0 | T | T | 0.5 | 8.2 | 1.3 | T | 0.0 | 0.0 | 10.0 |
| 1964-65 | 0.0 | 0.0 | 0.0 | 0.0 | T | 0.3 | 1.4 | 3.6 | T | T | 0.0 | 0.0 | 5.3 |
| 1965-66 | 0.0 | 0.0 | 0.0 | 0.0 | T | 3.0 | 5.4 | 1.0 | 0.0 | T | 0.0 | 0.0 | 9.4 |
| 1966-67 | 0.0 | 0.0 | 0.0 | 0.0 | T | T | T | 1.0 | 1.1 | T | 0.0 | 0.0 | 2.1 |
| 1967-68 | 0.0 | 0.0 | 0.0 | 0.2 | 1.0 | 2.8 | T | 2.0 | 1.4 | T | 0.0 | 0.0 | 7.4 |
| 1968-69 | 0.0 | 0.0 | 0.0 | 0.0 | T | 7.4 | T | 1.8 | 5.5 | T | 0.0 | 0.0 | 14.7 |
| 1969-70 | 0.0 | 0.0 | 0.0 | 0.0 | T | 1.1 | T | 2.7 | 3.3 | 0.0 | 0.0 | 0.0 | 7.1 |
| 1970-71 | 0.0 | 0.0 | 0.0 | 0.5 | T | T | 3.0 | 2.3 | 0.5 | T | 0.0 | 0.0 | 6.8 |
| 1971-72 | 0.0 | 0.0 | T | T | T | 6.8 | 1.2 | 1.1 | 0.0 | T | 0.0 | 0.0 | 9.1 |
| 1972-73 | 0.0 | 0.0 | 0.0 | T | 2.9 | 1.2 | 9.5 | 13.9 | 8.1 | 0.0 | 0.0 | 0.0 | 37.4 |
| 1973-74 | 0.0 | 0.0 | 0.0 | 0.3 | 0.6 | 0.1 | 9.3 | 0.6 | 2.0 | 0.0 | 0.0 | 0.0 | 12.9 |
| 1974-75 | 0.0 | 0.0 | 0.0 | 0.0 | T | 4.9 | 0.9 | 6.7 | 3.8 | 0.2 | 0.0 | 0.0 | 16.5 |
| 1975-76 | 0.0 | 0.0 | 0.0 | 0.0 | 0.2 | 2.9 | 0.0 | T | 0.5 | 0.2 | 0.0 | 0.0 | 3.8 |
| 1976-77 | 0.0 | 0.0 | 0.0 | T | 2.4 | 1.2 | 8.4 | 1.4 | 2.3 | 2.6 | 0.0 | 0.0 | 18.3 |
| 1977-78 | 0.0 | 0.0 | 0.0 | 0.0 | 0.0 | T | 6.0 | 3.4 | 2.0 | 0.0 | 0.1 | 0.0 | 11.5 |
| 1978-79 | 0.0 | 0.0 | 0.0 | 0.0 | T | 1.0 | 2.6 | 6.0 | T | 0.5 | 1.0 | 0.0 | 11.1 |
| 1979-80 | 0.0 | 0.0 | 0.0 | 0.9 | 0.8 | 2.7 | T | 0.9 | 3.1 | T | T | 0.0 | 8.4 |
| 1980-81 | 0.0 | 0.0 | 0.0 | T | 2.8 | 7.4 | 0.5 | 2.6 | 0.9 | T | 0.0 | 0.0 | 14.2 |
| 1981-82 | 0.0 | 0.0 | 0.0 | 0.0 | 0.0 | 0.0 | 3.6 | 1.2 | 0.7 | T | 0.0 | 0.0 | 5.5 |
| 1982-83 | 0.0 | 0.0 | 0.0 | 0.0 | 0.9 | 3.3 | 7.3 | 4.2 | 1.0 | T | T | 0.0 | 16.7 |
| 1983-84 | 0.0 | 0.0 | 0.0 | 0.0 | 0.8 | 0.8 | 4.1 | T | 0.1 | 3.0 | 0.0 | 0.0 | 8.8 |
| 1984-85 | 0.0 | 0.0 | 0.0 | T | T | 3.4 | 2.0 | 2.9 | 0.6 | 0.0 | 0.0 | 0.0 | 8.9 |
| 1985-86 | 0.0 | 0.0 | 0.0 | 0.0 | 0.7 | 0.9 | 2.9 | 10.3 | 0.3 | 0.0 | T | 0.0 | 15.1 |
| 1986-87 | 0.0 | 0.0 | 0.0 | 3.2 | 0.6 | 0.2 | 4.9 | 4.9 | 0.2 | 2.2 | 0.0 | 0.0 | 16.2 |
| 1987-88 | 0.0 | 0.0 | 0.0 | 0.0 | 1.1 | 1.7 | 1.2 | T | 7.9 | 4.2 | 0.0 | 0.0 | 16.1 |
| 1988-89 | 0.0 | 0.0 | 0.0 | 0.0 | 1.7 | 0.3 | 3.4 | 3.2 | 3.1 | 0.0 | 0.0 | 0.0 | 11.7 |
| 1989-90 | 0.0 | 0.0 | 0.0 | 0.0 | T | 6.3 | 1.8 | 4.8 | T | 0.3 | T | T | 9.4 |
| 1990-91 | T | 0.0 | 0.0 | 0.0 | 2.2 | 6.3 | | | | | | | |
| Record Mean | T | 0.0 | T | 0.1 | 1.1 | 2.6 | 2.5 | 2.2 | 1.9 | 0.6 | T | T | 11.1 |

**See Reference Notes, relative to all above tables, on preceding page.**

Albany is located on the west bank of the Hudson River some 150 miles north of New York City, and 8 miles south of the confluence of the Mohawk and Hudson Rivers. The river-front portion of the city is only a few feet above sea level, and there is a tidal effect upstream to Troy. Eleven miles west of Albany the Helderberg escarpment rises to 1,800 feet. Between it and the Hudson River the valley floor is gently rolling, ranging some 200 to 500 feet above sea level. East of the city there is more rugged terrain 5 or 6 miles wide with elevations of 300 to 600 feet. Farther to the east the terrain rises more sharply. It reaches a north-south range of hills 12 miles east of Albany with elevations ranging to 2,000 feet.

The climate at Albany is primarily continental in character, but is subjected to some modification by the Atlantic Ocean. The moderating effect on temperatures is more pronounced during the warmer months than in winter when outbursts of cold air sweep down from Canada. In the warmer seasons, temperatures rise rapidly in the daytime. However, temperatures also fall rapidly after sunset so that the nights are relatively cool. Occasionally there are extended periods of oppressive heat up to a week or more in duration.

Winters are usually cold and sometimes fairly severe. Maximum temperatures during the colder winters are often below freezing and nighttime lows are frequently below 10 degrees. Sub-zero readings occur about twelve times a year. Snowfall throughout the area is quite variable and snow flurries are quite frequent during the winter. Precipitation is sufficient to serve the economy of the region in most years, and only occasionally do periods of drought exist. Most of the rainfall in the summer is from thunderstorms. Tornadoes are quite rare and hail is not usually of any consequence.

Wind velocities are moderate. The north-south Hudson River Valley has a marked effect on the lighter winds and in the warm months, average wind direction is usually southerly. Destructive winds rarely occur.

The area enjoys one of the highest percentages of sunshine in the entire state. Seldom does the area experience long periods of cloudy days and long periods of smog are rare.

Based on the 1951-1980 period, the average first occurrence of 32 degrees Fahrenheit in the fall is September 29 and the average last occurrence in the spring is May 7.

# TABLE 1 NORMALS, MEANS AND EXTREMES

ALBANY, NEW YORK

LATITUDE: 42°45'N  LONGITUDE: 73°48' W  ELEVATION: FT. GRND  275 BARO  296  TIME ZONE: EASTERN  WBAN: 14735

| | (a) | JAN | FEB | MAR | APR | MAY | JUNE | JULY | AUG | SEP | OCT | NOV | DEC | YEAR |
|---|---|---|---|---|---|---|---|---|---|---|---|---|---|---|
| **TEMPERATURE °F:** | | | | | | | | | | | | | | |
| Normals | | | | | | | | | | | | | | |
| -Daily Maximum | | 30.2 | 32.7 | 42.5 | 57.6 | 69.5 | 78.3 | 83.2 | 80.7 | 72.8 | 61.5 | 47.8 | 34.6 | 57.6 |
| -Daily Minimum | | 11.9 | 14.0 | 24.6 | 35.5 | 45.4 | 55.0 | 59.6 | 57.6 | 49.6 | 39.4 | 30.8 | 18.2 | 36.8 |
| -Monthly | | 21.1 | 23.4 | 33.6 | 46.6 | 57.5 | 66.7 | 71.4 | 69.2 | 61.2 | 50.5 | 39.3 | 26.5 | 47.3 |
| Extremes | | | | | | | | | | | | | | |
| -Record Highest | 43 | 62 | 67 | 86 | 92 | 94 | 99 | 100 | 99 | 100 | 89 | 82 | 71 | 100 |
| -Year | | 1974 | 1976 | 1986 | 1976 | 1981 | 1952 | 1953 | 1955 | 1953 | 1963 | 1950 | 1984 | JUL 1953 |
| -Record Lowest | 43 | -28 | -21 | -21 | 10 | 26 | 36 | 40 | 34 | 24 | 16 | 5 | -22 | -28 |
| -Year | | 1971 | 1973 | 1948 | 1965 | 1968 | 1986 | 1978 | 1982 | 1947 | 1969 | 1972 | 1969 | JAN 1971 |
| **NORMAL DEGREE DAYS:** | | | | | | | | | | | | | | |
| Heating (base 65°F) | | 1361 | 1165 | 973 | 552 | 252 | 38 | 7 | 15 | 149 | 450 | '771 | 1194 | 6927 |
| Cooling (base 65°F) | | 0 | 0 | 0 | 0 | 19 | 89 | 206 | 145 | 35 | 0 | 0 | 0 | 494 |
| **% OF POSSIBLE SUNSHINE** | 51 | 46 | 52 | 54 | 54 | 55 | 59 | 63 | 60 | 57 | 52 | 36 | 39 | 52 |
| **MEAN SKY COVER (tenths)** | | | | | | | | | | | | | | |
| Sunrise - Sunset | 51 | 7.0 | 6.9 | 6.9 | 6.9 | 6.9 | 6.5 | 6.3 | 6.2 | 6.1 | 6.3 | 7.5 | 7.3 | 6.7 |
| **MEAN NUMBER OF DAYS:** | | | | | | | | | | | | | | |
| Sunrise to Sunset | | | | | | | | | | | | | | |
| -Clear | 51 | 5.5 | 5.5 | 6.1 | 5.6 | 5.1 | 5.2 | 5.9 | 6.7 | 7.8 | 7.5 | 3.6 | 5.0 | 69.6 |
| -Partly Cloudy | 51 | 8.0 | 7.3 | 7.9 | 8.2 | 9.2 | 11.3 | 13.0 | 11.7 | 9.8 | 9.3 | 8.0 | 6.7 | 110.5 |
| -Cloudy | 51 | 17.4 | 15.4 | 16.9 | 16.2 | 16.6 | 13.5 | 12.1 | 12.6 | 12.4 | 14.1 | 18.5 | 19.3 | 185.1 |
| Precipitation | | | | | | | | | | | | | | |
| .01 inches or more | 43 | 12.1 | 10.5 | 11.9 | 12.1 | 13.2 | 11.3 | 10.3 | 10.3 | 9.6 | 9.0 | 12.0 | 12.3 | 134.4 |
| Snow, Ice pellets | | | | | | | | | | | | | | |
| 1.0 inches or more | 43 | 4.0 | 3.3 | 2.5 | 0.7 | 0.* | 0.0 | 0.0 | 0.0 | 0.0 | 0.* | 1.1 | 4.0 | 15.7 |
| Thunderstorms | 51 | 0.1 | 0.2 | 0.5 | 1.2 | 3.5 | 5.5 | 6.5 | 4.7 | 2.4 | 0.9 | 0.4 | 0.1 | 25.8 |
| Heavy Fog Visibility | | | | | | | | | | | | | | |
| 1/4 mile or less | 51 | 1.1 | 0.9 | 1.2 | 0.8 | 1.4 | 1.2 | 1.5 | 2.6 | 3.7 | 4.4 | 1.6 | 1.6 | 22.0 |
| Temperature °F | | | | | | | | | | | | | | |
| -Maximum | | | | | | | | | | | | | | |
| 90° and above | 24 | 0.0 | 0.0 | 0.0 | 0.1 | 0.4 | 1.6 | 4.1 | 2.0 | 0.5 | 0.0 | 0.0 | 0.0 | 8.7 |
| 32° and below | 24 | 17.8 | 13.3 | 4.0 | 0.2 | 0.0 | 0.0 | 0.0 | 0.0 | 0.0 | 0.0 | 1.3 | 11.8 | 48.3 |
| -Minimum | | | | | | | | | | | | | | |
| 32° and below | 24 | 29.7 | 26.1 | 24.2 | 12.6 | 1.9 | 0.0 | 0.0 | 0.0 | 0.5 | 8.9 | 18.3 | 27.7 | 149.9 |
| 0° and below | 24 | 7.3 | 4.3 | 0.5 | 0.0 | 0.0 | 0.0 | 0.0 | 0.0 | 0.0 | 0.0 | 0.0 | 2.5 | 14.5 |
| **AVG. STATION PRESS.(mb)** | 17 | 1006.4 | 1007.3 | 1005.8 | 1003.8 | 1004.2 | 1004.2 | 1004.8 | 1006.4 | 1007.7 | 1008.4 | 1007.1 | 1007.4 | 1006.1 |
| **RELATIVE HUMIDITY (%)** | | | | | | | | | | | | | | |
| Hour 01 | 24 | 76 | 74 | 72 | 70 | 78 | 83 | 84 | 87 | 88 | 83 | 79 | 78 | 79 |
| Hour 07 | 24 | 77 | 76 | 75 | 71 | 76 | 79 | 81 | 86 | 89 | 86 | 81 | 80 | 80 |
| Hour 13 (Local Time) | 24 | 63 | 59 | 53 | 49 | 53 | 56 | 55 | 57 | 59 | 57 | 62 | 65 | 57 |
| Hour 19 | 24 | 71 | 66 | 61 | 55 | 60 | 64 | 64 | 70 | 75 | 72 | 73 | 73 | 67 |
| **PRECIPITATION (inches):** | | | | | | | | | | | | | | |
| Water Equivalent | | | | | | | | | | | | | | |
| -Normal | | 2.39 | 2.26 | 3.01 | 2.94 | 3.31 | 3.29 | 3.00 | 3.34 | 3.23 | 2.93 | 3.04 | 3.00 | 35.74 |
| -Maximum Monthly | 43 | 6.44 | 5.02 | 5.90 | 7.95 | 8.96 | 7.36 | 6.96 | 7.33 | 7.89 | 8.83 | 8.07 | 6.73 | 8.96 |
| -Year | | 1978 | 1981 | 1977 | 1983 | 1953 | 1973 | 1975 | 1950 | 1960 | 1955 | 1972 | 1973 | MAY 1953 |
| -Minimum Monthly | 43 | 0.42 | 0.24 | 0.26 | 1.14 | 1.05 | 0.65 | 0.49 | 0.73 | 0.40 | 0.20 | 0.91 | 0.64 | 0.20 |
| -Year | | 1980 | 1987 | 1981 | 1963 | 1980 | 1964 | 1968 | 1947 | 1964 | 1963 | 1978 | 1958 | OCT 1963 |
| -Maximum in 24 hrs | 43 | 1.91 | 1.50 | 2.38 | 2.20 | 2.17 | 3.48 | 2.70 | 4.52 | 3.66 | 3.31 | 2.01 | 4.02 | 4.52 |
| -Year | | 1978 | 1975 | 1986 | 1968 | 1968 | 1952 | 1960 | 1971 | 1960 | 1987 | 1959 | 1948 | AUG 1971 |
| Snow, Ice pellets | | | | | | | | | | | | | | |
| -Maximum Monthly | 43 | 47.8 | 34.5 | 34.7 | 17.7 | 1.6 | 0.0 | T | 0.0 | T | 6.5 | 24.6 | 57.5 | 57.5 |
| -Year | | 1987 | 1962 | 1956 | 1982 | 1977 | | 1989 | | 1989 | 1987 | 1972 | 1969 | DEC 1969 |
| -Maximum in 24 hrs | 43 | 21.2 | 17.9 | 17.0 | 17.5 | 1.6 | 0.0 | T | 0.0 | T | 6.5 | 21.9 | 18.3 | 21.9 |
| -Year | | 1983 | 1958 | 1984 | 1982 | 1977 | | 1989 | | 1989 | 1987 | 1971 | 1966 | NOV 1971 |
| **WIND:** | | | | | | | | | | | | | | |
| Mean Speed (mph) | 51 | 9.8 | 10.3 | 10.6 | 10.5 | 9.0 | 8.2 | 7.4 | 7.0 | 7.4 | 8.0 | 9.1 | 9.3 | 8.9 |
| Prevailing Direction | | | | | | | | | | | | | | |
| through 1963 | | WNW | WNW | WNW | WNW | S | S | S | S | S | S | S | S | S |
| Fastest Obs. 1 Min. | | | | | | | | | | | | | | |
| -Direction (!!!) | 6 | 28 | 27 | 28 | 30 | 33 | 33 | 23 | 30 | 18 | 32 | 36 | 28 | 28 |
| -Speed (MPH) | 6 | 36 | 33 | 38 | 33 | 30 | 29 | 25 | 36 | 30 | 29 | 35 | 32 | 38 |
| -Year | | 1985 | 1985 | 1984 | 1989 | 1986 | 1986 | 1986 | 1988 | 1989 | 1986 | 1989 | 1989 | MAR 1984 |
| Peak Gust | | | | | | | | | | | | | | |
| -Direction (!!!) | 6 | W | W | NW | NW | NE | NW | N | NW | S | S | W | NW | W |
| -Speed (mph) | 6 | 55 | 56 | 51 | 44 | 44 | 46 | 48 | 48 | 47 | 45 | 58 | 56 | 58 |
| -Date | | 1989 | 1985 | 1986 | 1987 | 1986 | 1988 | 1987 | 1988 | 1989 | 1988 | 1988 | 1985 | NOV 1988 |

**See Reference Notes to this table on the following page.**

PRECIPITATION (inches) — ALBANY, NEW YORK

**TABLE 2**

| YEAR | JAN | FEB | MAR | APR | MAY | JUNE | JULY | AUG | SEP | OCT | NOV | DEC | ANNUAL |
|------|-----|-----|-----|-----|-----|------|------|-----|-----|-----|-----|-----|--------|
| 1961 | 1.47 | 2.47 | 3.11 | 3.09 | 4.44 | 2.97 | 4.78 | 4.76 | 2.47 | 1.22 | 2.98 | 1.96 | 35.72 |
| 1962 | 2.05 | 3.65 | 1.70 | 3.25 | 1.40 | 1.15 | 2.12 | 2.60 | 3.45 | 3.58 | 2.11 | 2.24 | 29.30 |
| 1963 | 2.38 | 1.84 | 3.45 | 1.14 | 1.90 | 2.94 | 1.20 | 2.49 | 2.69 | 0.20 | 4.15 | 1.86 | 26.24 |
| 1964 | 3.35 | 1.63 | 2.93 | 2.17 | 1.31 | 0.65 | 1.29 | 2.55 | 0.40 | 0.54 | 1.45 | 3.28 | 21.55 |
| 1965 | 1.95 | 1.92 | 1.73 | 2.38 | 1.22 | 1.91 | 3.52 | 4.32 | 3.76 | 2.37 | 1.89 | 0.97 | 27.94 |
| 1966 | 2.29 | 2.71 | 3.63 | 1.46 | 2.35 | 2.95 | 1.44 | 3.88 | 5.61 | 2.22 | 1.79 | 3.04 | 33.37 |
| 1967 | 1.22 | 1.76 | 2.56 | 3.69 | 3.36 | 2.85 | 3.38 | 2.17 | 2.23 | 3.48 | 2.68 | 3.90 | 33.28 |
| 1968 | 1.48 | 0.36 | 2.62 | 2.64 | 4.79 | 4.38 | 0.49 | 1.77 | 1.49 | 2.18 | 5.48 | 4.60 | 32.28 |
| 1969 | 2.13 | 1.66 | 1.32 | 3.51 | 2.64 | 5.30 | 5.08 | 2.18 | 2.06 | 1.55 | 5.56 | 6.51 | 39.50 |
| 1970 | 0.81 | 1.98 | 2.87 | 3.01 | 1.78 | 3.14 | 3.35 | 1.93 | 3.79 | 2.49 | 1.48 | 3.89 | 30.52 |
| 1971 | 1.78 | 4.10 | 3.11 | 2.00 | 3.48 | 2.81 | 3.89 | 7.04 | 2.40 | 2.09 | 3.78 | 3.09 | 39.57 |
| 1972 | 1.21 | 3.04 | 4.05 | 3.63 | 5.98 | 6.84 | 3.10 | 1.48 | 1.99 | 3.60 | 8.07 | 4.19 | 47.18 |
| 1973 | 2.16 | 1.34 | 1.99 | 4.47 | 5.45 | 7.36 | 1.68 | 2.89 | 1.33 | 2.07 | 1.27 | 6.73 | 38.74 |
| 1974 | 2.04 | 2.12 | 3.10 | 2.80 | 3.31 | 3.31 | 4.84 | 3.53 | 5.37 | 1.49 | 3.83 | 2.57 | 38.47 |
| 1975 | 2.75 | 3.58 | 2.72 | 2.18 | 2.96 | 3.80 | 6.96 | 5.98 | 4.57 | 5.88 | 2.89 | 2.78 | 47.05 |
| 1976 | 3.78 | 2.60 | 3.57 | 3.63 | 4.89 | 5.37 | 2.60 | 5.04 | 2.61 | 5.65 | 1.41 | 1.39 | 42.54 |
| 1977 | 1.51 | 2.63 | 3.41 | 2.29 | 2.87 | 2.31 | 3.66 | 6.66 | 4.00 | 4.85 | 0.91 | 4.21 | 44.30 |
| 1978 | 6.44 | 0.88 | 1.99 | 1.68 | 1.96 | 4.60 | 4.04 | 3.06 | 1.87 | 2.95 | 3.08 | 0.94 | 33.46 |
| 1979 | 6.37 | 1.71 | 1.83 | 3.89 | 4.13 | 1.94 | 2.78 | 2.67 | 4.05 | 3.42 | 3.41 | 0.94 | 37.14 |
| 1980 | 0.42 | 0.89 | 4.44 | 3.02 | 1.05 | 4.90 | 2.69 | 6.45 | 2.24 | 2.27 | 2.99 | 1.23 | 32.59 |
| 1981 | 0.59 | 5.02 | 0.26 | 1.99 | 2.44 | 2.78 | 3.50 | 1.76 | 3.45 | 3.55 | 1.56 | 3.54 | 30.44 |
| 1982 | 3.18 | 2.14 | 3.23 | 2.46 | 2.60 | 6.48 | 2.43 | 2.01 | 1.42 | 0.99 | 3.80 | 1.33 | 32.07 |
| 1983 | 3.73 | 2.03 | 5.33 | 7.95 | 6.26 | 1.95 | 1.34 | 3.41 | 2.28 | 4.73 | 5.10 | 46.29 |
| 1984 | 1.28 | 2.98 | 3.04 | 4.29 | 7.92 | 1.74 | 3.97 | 3.25 | 1.53 | 2.50 | 2.15 | 2.48 | 37.13 |
| 1985 | 0.81 | 1.18 | 1.57 | 1.44 | 2.71 | 4.12 | 1.86 | 2.23 | 3.07 | 1.81 | 5.00 | 2.05 | 29.95 |
| 1986 | 3.17 | 3.00 | 3.72 | 1.49 | 3.11 | 5.43 | 6.68 | 4.09 | 2.61 | 2.12 | 4.62 | 3.92 | 43.96 |
| 1987 | 4.23 | 0.24 | 1.99 | 4.25 | 1.57 | 3.54 | 2.50 | 3.67 | 6.98 | 6.90 | 1.78 | 1.64 | 39.29 |
| 1988 | 1.95 | 3.00 | 1.62 | 2.22 | 2.95 | 1.42 | 3.12 | 4.77 | 1.50 | 1.40 | 4.58 | 1.02 | 29.55 |
| 1989 | 0.46 | 1.60 | 2.69 | 2.68 | 5.92 | 6.52 | 5.91 | 2.90 | 2.81 | 5.53 | 1.90 | 0.75 | 39.67 |
| 1990 | 3.84 | 3.94 | 3.66 | 3.87 | 6.12 | 2.66 | 1.68 | 6.66 | 1.81 | 4.60 | 3.67 | 3.50 | 46.01 |
| Record Mean | 2.48 | 2.36 | 2.76 | 2.78 | 3.35 | 3.70 | 3.68 | 3.54 | 3.27 | 3.07 | 2.94 | 2.64 | 36.58 |

**TABLE 3**

AVERAGE TEMPERATURE (deg. F) — ALBANY, NEW YORK

| YEAR | JAN | FEB | MAR | APR | MAY | JUNE | JULY | AUG | SEP | OCT | NOV | DEC | ANNUAL |
|------|-----|-----|-----|-----|-----|------|------|-----|-----|-----|-----|-----|--------|
| 1961 | 15.3 | 25.5 | 33.0 | 43.9 | 55.4 | 67.0 | 71.6 | 69.7 | 68.7 | 53.9 | 39.4 | 27.7 | 47.6 |
| 1962 | 21.9 | 20.5 | 34.7 | 47.0 | 59.8 | 68.1 | 69.0 | 69.0 | 58.7 | 50.2 | 35.0 | 23.0 | 46.4 |
| 1963 | 20.3 | 17.2 | 33.6 | 45.8 | 56.6 | 67.3 | 72.0 | 66.4 | 56.8 | 55.5 | 44.4 | 18.1 | 46.2 |
| #1964 | 23.9 | 22.3 | 34.9 | 45.7 | 61.7 | 66.5 | 74.4 | 66.2 | 61.0 | 49.2 | 41.4 | 27.9 | 47.9 |
| 1965 | 18.1 | 22.3 | 31.2 | 42.2 | 59.6 | 66.9 | 68.9 | 69.4 | 63.6 | 51.2 | 37.6 | 30.8 | 46.8 |
| 1966 | 21.5 | 23.3 | 34.3 | 44.0 | 53.9 | 67.4 | 72.2 | 69.2 | 58.0 | 48.5 | 42.3 | 27.3 | 46.8 |
| 1967 | 27.0 | 18.0 | 29.0 | 43.5 | 50.4 | 69.9 | 71.6 | 69.3 | 61.3 | 51.0 | 34.8 | 28.9 | 46.2 |
| 1968 | 14.7 | 21.1 | 37.1 | 51.1 | 54.9 | 66.7 | 72.7 | 68.6 | 63.7 | 53.3 | 38.5 | 23.5 | 47.2 |
| 1969 | 20.9 | 24.7 | 31.1 | 47.6 | 56.3 | 66.0 | 72.0 | 70.6 | 62.4 | 49.0 | 39.7 | 21.6 | 46.6 |
| 1970 | 9.7 | 23.1 | 32.0 | 48.7 | 60.5 | 65.9 | 72.0 | 69.6 | 63.3 | 52.9 | 41.9 | 21.6 | 46.8 |
| 1971 | 13.9 | 25.4 | 30.6 | 42.3 | 54.9 | 66.3 | 68.4 | 66.8 | 64.8 | 54.7 | 36.9 | 30.0 | 46.3 |
| 1972 | 22.9 | 21.1 | 30.5 | 41.2 | 59.5 | 63.6 | 70.9 | 67.2 | 60.7 | 45.7 | 35.1 | 28.9 | 45.6 |
| 1973 | 27.0 | 22.0 | 41.9 | 48.8 | 55.3 | 68.7 | 72.8 | 72.9 | 60.5 | 51.0 | 39.9 | 28.2 | 49.1 |
| 1974 | 23.3 | 21.3 | 32.4 | 48.1 | 54.1 | 65.0 | 69.3 | 67.9 | 58.3 | 44.4 | 38.6 | 28.9 | 46.0 |
| 1975 | 25.7 | 24.9 | 30.8 | 40.7 | 61.9 | 65.1 | 72.8 | 70.0 | 59.4 | 53.3 | 45.5 | 26.1 | 48.0 |
| 1976 | 16.0 | 31.5 | 36.7 | 49.7 | 55.0 | 69.4 | 68.5 | 67.4 | 59.0 | 46.5 | 34.9 | 21.4 | 46.3 |
| 1977 | 15.5 | 24.5 | 40.0 | 46.8 | 60.2 | 64.6 | 71.7 | 67.8 | 61.4 | 49.7 | 42.6 | 26.7 | 47.6 |
| 1978 | 21.5 | 18.2 | 30.8 | 43.4 | 58.4 | 64.4 | 68.9 | 69.2 | 56.8 | 48.6 | 38.6 | 24.4 | 45.6 |
| 1979 | 22.1 | 14.4 | 38.9 | 45.4 | 60.0 | 66.0 | 72.5 | 69.0 | 61.2 | 50.2 | 44.1 | 31.4 | 47.9 |
| 1980 | 24.1 | 19.8 | 33.3 | 48.0 | 59.5 | 63.3 | 72.2 | 70.7 | 62.6 | 47.4 | 34.8 | 19.9 | 46.3 |
| 1981 | 14.0 | 33.1 | 34.7 | 48.1 | 58.9 | 66.7 | 69.3 | 68.5 | 58.8 | 44.8 | 37.7 | 25.7 | 46.7 |
| 1982 | 14.3 | 23.4 | 32.8 | 44.3 | 59.5 | 62.9 | 70.1 | 65.5 | 60.5 | 50.6 | 43.0 | 33.7 | 46.7 |
| 1983 | 24.3 | 26.8 | 37.4 | 46.7 | 54.9 | 67.2 | 72.2 | 69.8 | 62.6 | 49.6 | 39.2 | 24.0 | 47.9 |
| 1984 | 18.1 | 32.4 | 29.0 | 47.6 | 53.2 | 66.4 | 68.9 | 71.8 | 60.2 | 53.8 | 40.3 | 33.8 | 48.0 |
| 1985 | 19.9 | 26.8 | 37.3 | 49.7 | 60.0 | 62.2 | 70.7 | 68.7 | 63.3 | 50.2 | 40.1 | 24.5 | 47.8 |
| 1986 | 23.0 | 22.8 | 37.2 | 50.5 | 61.3 | 64.6 | 71.3 | 67.8 | 60.1 | 48.9 | 35.7 | 30.8 | 47.8 |
| 1987 | 21.7 | 21.7 | 37.7 | 50.4 | 60.0 | 68.3 | 73.5 | 67.2 | 60.6 | 46.6 | 40.1 | 30.7 | 48.2 |
| 1988 | 20.6 | 24.1 | 34.2 | 46.6 | 59.5 | 65.1 | 75.0 | 72.3 | 60.0 | 46.0 | 41.0 | 26.6 | 47.6 |
| 1989 | 27.8 | 24.2 | 33.5 | 44.6 | 59.5 | 68.0 | 71.6 | 69.8 | 62.5 | 51.5 | 39.3 | 13.7 | 47.2 |
| 1990 | 32.8 | 28.2 | 37.8 | 48.9 | 55.3 | 67.3 | 73.0 | 70.9 | 61.7 | 53.1 | 41.8 | 33.6 | 50.4 |
| Record Mean | 22.8 | 23.9 | 33.7 | 46.6 | 58.5 | 67.3 | 72.3 | 70.1 | 62.5 | 51.1 | 39.6 | 27.6 | 48.0 |
| Max | 31.1 | 32.5 | 42.3 | 56.4 | 69.2 | 77.9 | 82.8 | 80.4 | 72.7 | 60.9 | 47.3 | 35.0 | 57.4 |
| Min | 14.4 | 15.2 | 25.1 | 36.7 | 47.7 | 56.8 | 61.7 | 59.7 | 52.2 | 41.3 | 31.9 | 20.1 | 38.6 |

## REFERENCE NOTES FOR TABLES 1, 2, 3 and 6    (ALBANY, NY)

### GENERAL

T - TRACE AMOUNT
BLANK ENTRIES DENOTE MISSING/UNREPORTED DATA.
# INDICATES A STATION OR INSTRUMENT RELOCATION.

### SPECIFIC

#### TABLE 1

(a) - LENGTH OF RECORD IN YEARS. ALTHOUGH
INDIVIDUAL MONTHS MAY BE MISSING.

* LESS THAN .05

NORMALS — BASED ON THE 1951-1980 RECORD PERIOD.
EXTREMES — DATES ARE THE MOST RECENT OCCURRENCE.
WIND DIR. — NUMERALS SHOW TENS OF DEGREES
CLOCKWISE FROM TRUE NORTH.
"00" INDICATES CALM.
RESULTANT WIND DIRECTIONS ARE GIVEN TO WHOLE DEGREES.

#### TABLE 3
MAX AND MIN ARE LONG-TERM MEAN DAILY MAXIMUM
AND MEAN DAILY MINIMUM TEMPERATURES.

### EXCEPTIONS

#### TABLES 2, 3, and 6

RECORD MEANS ARE THROUGH THE CURRENT YEAR,
BEGINNING IN    1874 FOR TEMPERATURE
1826 FOR PRECIPITATION
1947 FOR SNOWFALL

**TABLE 4**  HEATING DEGREE DAYS Base 65 deg. F       ALBANY, NEW YORK

| SEASON | JULY | AUG | SEP | OCT | NOV | DEC | JAN | FEB | MAR | APR | MAY | JUNE | TOTAL |
|--------|------|-----|-----|-----|-----|-----|-----|-----|-----|-----|-----|------|-------|
| 1961-62 | 11 | 18 | 79 | 335 | 761 | 1152 | 1327 | 1240 | 933 | 552 | 211 | 27 | 6646 |
| 1962-63 | 6 | 23 | 207 | 451 | 894 | 1297 | 1381 | 1331 | 968 | 571 | 261 | 62 | 7452 |
| 1963-64 | 18 | 29 | 251 | 296 | 612 | 1446 | 1266 | 1233 | 927 | 571 | 145 | 78 | 6872 |
| #1964-65 | 1 | 48 | 169 | 484 | 702 | 1141 | 1449 | 1193 | 1041 | 679 | 197 | 68 | 7172 |
| 1965-66 | 11 | 49 | 120 | 421 | 817 | 1051 | 1342 | 1162 | 948 | 623 | 347 | 57 | 6948 |
| 1966-67 | 3 | 5 | 216 | 502 | 673 | 1163 | 1169 | 1312 | 1111 | 639 | 447 | 11 | 7251 |
| 1967-68 | 0 | 19 | 153 | 429 | 899 | 1112 | 1557 | 1269 | 857 | 412 | 304 | 46 | 7057 |
| 1968-69 | 7 | 45 | 76 | 359 | 787 | 1281 | 1360 | 1122 | 1043 | 518 | 284 | 55 | 6937 |
| 1969-70 | 13 | 22 | 137 | 491 | 749 | 1339 | 1708 | 1168 | 1016 | 495 | 165 | 75 | 7378 |
| 1970-71 | 3 | 7 | 127 | 377 | 686 | 1336 | 1580 | 1104 | 1059 | 672 | 315 | 50 | 7316 |
| 1971-72 | 20 | 45 | 109 | 311 | 838 | 1080 | 1298 | 1269 | 1060 | 707 | 175 | 97 | 7009 |
| 1972-73 | 16 | 38 | 154 | 590 | 890 | 1113 | 1168 | 1198 | 709 | 486 | 299 | 47 | 6708 |
| 1973-74 | 2 | 3 | 200 | 431 | 750 | 1136 | 1285 | 1216 | 1005 | 511 | 343 | 54 | 6936 |
| 1974-75 | 17 | 14 | 227 | 631 | 786 | 1113 | 1212 | 1115 | 1053 | 722 | 145 | 88 | 7123 |
| 1975-76 | 0 | 19 | 173 | 357 | 580 | 1511 | 964 | 871 | 472 | 315 | 43 | 6504 |
| 1976-77 | 7 | 40 | 196 | 564 | 895 | 1345 | 1526 | 1127 | 764 | 545 | 205 | 85 | 7299 |
| 1977-78 | 7 | 51 | 156 | 471 | 666 | 1179 | 1340 | 1306 | 1051 | 642 | 245 | 84 | 7198 |
| 1978-79 | 43 | 19 | 256 | 503 | 784 | 1119 | 1324 | 1414 | 803 | 579 | 188 | 63 | 7095 |
| 1979-80 | 19 | 37 | 163 | 468 | 619 | 1036 | 1259 | 1303 | 974 | 503 | 190 | 106 | 6677 |
| 1980-81 | 0 | 7 | 140 | 539 | 900 | 1393 | 1575 | 885 | 930 | 502 | 235 | 30 | 7136 |
| 1981-82 | 8 | 22 | 204 | 622 | 816 | 1209 | 1564 | 1160 | 992 | 617 | 182 | 87 | 7483 |
| 1982-83 | 20 | 65 | 156 | 436 | 657 | 969 | 1255 | 1062 | 843 | 539 | 312 | 58 | 6372 |
| 1983-84 | 5 | 24 | 150 | 479 | 766 | 1265 | 1448 | 939 | 1109 | 517 | 363 | 60 | 7125 |
| 1984-85 | 12 | 8 | 170 | 344 | 737 | 1389 | 1295 | 1177 | 859 | 432 | 154 | 75 | 6576 |
| 1985-86 | 7 | 16 | 123 | 452 | 740 | 1246 | 1295 | 1177 | 859 | 432 | 154 | 75 | 6576 |
| 1986-87 | 17 | 46 | 173 | 495 | 872 | 1053 | 1332 | 1207 | 842 | 433 | 210 | 29 | 6709 |
| 1987-88 | 2 | 56 | 154 | 567 | 741 | 1056 | 1370 | 1181 | 946 | 546 | 198 | 99 | 6916 |
| 1988-89 | 8 | 30 | 160 | 584 | 714 | 1185 | 1146 | 1133 | 968 | 607 | 194 | 35 | 6764 |
| 1989-90 | 0 | 22 | 134 | 413 | 766 | 1584 | 990 | 1026 | 839 | 500 | 298 | 44 | 6616 |
| 1990-91 | 5 | 6 | 148 | 388 | 689 | 964 | | | | | | | |

**TABLE 5**  COOLING DEGREE DAYS Base 65 deg. F       ALBANY, NEW YORK

| YEAR | JAN | FEB | MAR | APR | MAY | JUNE | JULY | AUG | SEP | OCT | NOV | DEC | TOTAL |
|------|-----|-----|-----|-----|-----|------|------|-----|-----|-----|-----|-----|-------|
| 1969 | 0 | 0 | 0 | 2 | 23 | 95 | 165 | 203 | 68 | 0 | 0 | 0 | 556 |
| 1970 | 0 | 0 | 0 | 12 | 36 | 107 | 225 | 160 | 83 | 7 | 0 | 0 | 630 |
| 1971 | 0 | 0 | 0 | 0 | 9 | 98 | 132 | 107 | 109 | 1 | 0 | 0 | 456 |
| 1972 | 0 | 0 | 0 | 0 | 12 | 58 | 208 | 112 | 31 | 0 | 0 | 0 | 421 |
| 1973 | 0 | 0 | 0 | 7 | 6 | 164 | 248 | 255 | 71 | 2 | 0 | 0 | 753 |
| 1974 | 0 | 0 | 0 | 11 | 12 | 59 | 157 | 111 | 35 | 0 | 1 | 0 | 386 |
| 1975 | 0 | 0 | 0 | 0 | 58 | 97 | 248 | 180 | 12 | 0 | 2 | 0 | 597 |
| 1976 | 0 | 0 | 0 | 19 | 11 | 184 | 120 | 120 | 22 | 0 | 0 | 0 | 476 |
| 1977 | 0 | 0 | 0 | 8 | 66 | 79 | 222 | 146 | 53 | 0 | 0 | 0 | 574 |
| 1978 | 0 | 0 | 0 | 0 | 47 | 70 | 169 | 154 | 16 | 0 | 0 | 0 | 456 |
| 1979 | 0 | 0 | 0 | 0 | 39 | 99 | 258 | 168 | 55 | 17 | 0 | 0 | 636 |
| 1980 | 0 | 0 | 0 | 0 | 28 | 63 | 230 | 189 | 73 | 0 | 0 | 0 | 583 |
| 1981 | 0 | 0 | 0 | 2 | 53 | 87 | 149 | 137 | 25 | 0 | 0 | 0 | 453 |
| 1982 | 0 | 0 | 0 | 0 | 0 | 19 | 31 | 184 | 88 | 29 | 4 | 0 | 355 |
| 1983 | 0 | 0 | 0 | 0 | 8 | 134 | 236 | 179 | 86 | 6 | 0 | 0 | 649 |
| 1984 | 0 | 0 | 0 | 0 | 3 | 107 | 140 | 226 | 35 | 3 | 0 | 0 | 514 |
| 1985 | 0 | 0 | 0 | 5 | 37 | 27 | 191 | 140 | 80 | 2 | 0 | 0 | 482 |
| 1986 | 0 | 0 | 6 | 4 | 46 | 69 | 220 | 140 | 33 | 1 | 0 | 0 | 519 |
| 1987 | 0 | 0 | 0 | 4 | 62 | 136 | 271 | 133 | 29 | 0 | 0 | 0 | 635 |
| 1988 | 0 | 0 | 0 | 0 | 36 | 110 | 326 | 263 | 16 | 4 | 0 | 0 | 755 |
| 1989 | 0 | 0 | 1 | 0 | 31 | 132 | 213 | 178 | 63 | 0 | 0 | 0 | 618 |
| 1990 | 0 | 0 | 2 | 22 | 1 | 119 | 261 | 197 | 55 | 24 | 0 | 0 | 681 |

**TABLE 6**  SNOWFALL (inches)       ALBANY, NEW YORK

| SEASON | JULY | AUG | SEP | OCT | NOV | DEC | JAN | FEB | MAR | APR | MAY | JUNE | TOTAL |
|--------|------|-----|-----|-----|-----|-----|-----|-----|-----|-----|-----|------|-------|
| 1961-62 | 0.0 | 0.0 | 0.0 | 0.0 | 3.6 | 14.4 | 2.3 | 34.5 | 3.2 | 4.6 | 0.0 | 0.0 | 62.6 |
| 1962-63 | 0.0 | 0.0 | 0.0 | T | 1.6 | 11.3 | 24.5 | 15.5 | 18.4 | T | 0.0 | 0.0 | 71.3 |
| 1963-64 | 0.0 | 0.0 | 0.0 | 0.0 | T | 21.0 | 27.3 | 21.4 | 7.3 | T | 0.0 | 0.0 | 77.0 |
| 1964-65 | 0.0 | 0.0 | 0.0 | T | T | 11.2 | 20.4 | 3.7 | 8.4 | 2.1 | 0.0 | 0.0 | 45.8 |
| 1965-66 | 0.0 | 0.0 | 0.0 | T | 0.5 | 2.7 | 28.8 | 24.5 | 9.2 | T | 1.4 | 0.0 | 67.1 |
| 1966-67 | 0.0 | 0.0 | 0.0 | 0.0 | T | 29.4 | 5.7 | 16.3 | 26.2 | 3.1 | 0.2 | 0.0 | 80.9 |
| 1967-68 | 0.0 | 0.0 | 0.0 | T | 9.0 | 17.8 | 8.0 | 1.8 | 5.6 | 0.0 | 0.0 | 0.0 | 42.2 |
| 1968-69 | 0.0 | 0.0 | 0.0 | 0.0 | 13.5 | 18.1 | 6.3 | 20.7 | 4.5 | 0.2 | 0.0 | 0.0 | 63.3 |
| 1969-70 | 0.0 | 0.0 | 0.0 | T | 3.2 | 57.5 | 7.4 | 11.2 | 1.2 | T | 0.0 | 0.0 | 87.7 |
| 1970-71 | 0.0 | 0.0 | 0.0 | T | T | 43.8 | 15.2 | 17.6 | 32.0 | 3.9 | 0.0 | 0.0 | 112.5 |
| 1971-72 | 0.0 | 0.0 | 0.0 | 0.0 | 24.0 | 10.1 | 8.5 | 24.8 | 15.9 | 6.0 | 0.0 | 0.0 | 89.3 |
| 1972-73 | 0.0 | 0.0 | 0.0 | T | 24.6 | 22.5 | 11.2 | 12.5 | T | 0.1 | 0.0 | 0.0 | 70.9 |
| 1973-74 | 0.0 | 0.0 | 0.0 | 0.0 | 0.1 | 18.9 | 10.0 | 12.4 | 5.6 | 11.3 | 0.0 | 0.0 | 58.3 |
| 1974-75 | 0.0 | 0.0 | 0.0 | T | 2.2 | 12.5 | 14.0 | 21.2 | 2.9 | 1.8 | 0.0 | 0.0 | 54.6 |
| 1975-76 | 0.0 | 0.0 | 0.0 | 0.0 | 3.6 | 16.4 | 15.0 | 4.4 | 14.8 | T | T | 0.0 | 54.2 |
| 1976-77 | 0.0 | 0.0 | 0.0 | T | 5.7 | 22.1 | 17.9 | 15.2 | 0.3 | 1.6 | 0.0 | 0.0 | 70.6 |
| 1977-78 | 0.0 | 0.0 | 0.0 | 0.0 | 8.4 | 19.8 | 40.8 | 15.8 | 7.4 | 0.2 | T | 0.0 | 92.4 |
| 1978-79 | 0.0 | 0.0 | 0.0 | 0.0 | 3.4 | 19.9 | 26.5 | 4.6 | 0.9 | 8.2 | 0.0 | 0.0 | 63.5 |
| 1979-80 | 0.0 | 0.0 | 0.0 | T | 0.0 | 5.8 | 0.6 | 10.2 | 10.8 | 0.0 | 0.0 | 0.0 | 27.4 |
| 1980-81 | 0.0 | 0.0 | 0.0 | 0.0 | 11.8 | 12.8 | 11.9 | 6.9 | 1.5 | T | 0.0 | 0.0 | 44.9 |
| 1981-82 | 0.0 | 0.0 | 0.0 | 0.0 | 1.1 | 31.4 | 18.2 | 9.6 | 19.1 | 17.7 | 0.0 | 0.0 | 97.1 |
| 1982-83 | 0.0 | 0.0 | 0.0 | 0.0 | 0.6 | 5.5 | 27.5 | 17.4 | 9.2 | 14.7 | 0.1 | 0.0 | 75.0 |
| 1983-84 | 0.0 | 0.0 | 0.0 | 0.0 | 1.7 | 11.6 | 16.5 | 7.2 | 28.2 | T | 0.0 | 0.0 | 65.2 |
| 1984-85 | 0.0 | 0.0 | 0.0 | 0.0 | 2.2 | 11.7 | 8.4 | 10.1 | 8.7 | 0.2 | 0.0 | 0.0 | 41.3 |
| 1985-86 | 0.0 | 0.0 | 0.0 | 0.0 | 11.8 | 11.5 | 18.0 | 16.1 | 3.4 | 1.7 | T | 0.0 | 62.5 |
| 1986-87 | 0.0 | 0.0 | 0.0 | 0.0 | 8.3 | 20.3 | 47.8 | 2.8 | 0.8 | 0.6 | 0.0 | 0.0 | 80.6 |
| 1987-88 | 0.0 | 0.0 | 0.0 | 6.5 | 6.2 | 11.4 | 21.7 | 26.0 | 4.8 | 0.1 | 0.0 | 0.0 | 76.7 |
| 1988-89 | 0.0 | 0.0 | 0.0 | T | T | 7.8 | 1.3 | 5.1 | 4.7 | 0.1 | 0.0 | 0.0 | 19.0 |
| 1989-90 | T | 0.0 | T | 0.0 | 1.9 | 8.0 | 20.3 | 22.8 | 4.9 | T | 0.0 | 0.0 | 57.9 |
| 1990-91 | 0.0 | 0.0 | 0.0 | T | 0.4 | 8.5 | | | | | | | |
| Record Mean | T | 0.0 | T | 0.2 | 4.3 | 15.2 | 16.5 | 14.3 | 10.9 | 2.8 | 0.1 | 0.0 | 64.1 |

**See Reference Notes, relative to all above tables, on preceding page.**

The country surrounding Buffalo is comparatively low and level to the west. To the east and south the land is gently rolling, rising to pronounced hills within 12 to 18 miles, and to 1,000 feet above the level of Lake Erie about 35 miles south-southeast of the city. An escarpment of 50 to 100 feet lies east-west 1-1/2 miles to the north. The eastern end of Lake Erie is 9 miles to the west-southwest, while Lake Ontario lies 25 miles to the north, the two being connected by the Niagara River, which flows north-northwestward from the end of Lake Erie.

Buffalo is located near the mean position of the polar front. Its weather is varied and changeable, characteristic of the latitude. Wide seasonal swings of temperature from hot to cold are tempered appreciably by the proximity of Lakes Erie and Ontario. Lake Erie lies to the southwest, the direction of the prevailing wind. Wind flow throughout the year is somewhat higher due to this exposure. The vigorous interplay of warm and cold air masses during the winter and early spring months causes one or more windstorms. Precipitation is moderate and fairly evenly divided throughout the twelve months.

The spring season is more cloudy and cooler than points not affected by the cold lake. Spring growth of vegetation is retarded, protecting it from late spring frosts. With heavy winter ice accumulations in the lake, typical spring conditions are delayed until late May or early June.

Summer comes suddenly in mid-June. Lake breezes temper the extreme heat of the summer season. Temperatures of 90 degrees and above are infrequent. There is more summer sunshine here than in any other section of the state. Due to the stabilizing effects of Lake Erie, thunderstorms are relatively infrequent. Most of them are caused by frontal action. To the north and south of the city thunderstorms occur more often.

Autumn has long, dry periods and is frost free usually until mid-October. Cloudiness increases in November, continuing mostly cloudy throughout the winter and early spring. Snow flurries off the lake begin in mid-November or early December. Outbreaks of Arctic air in December and throughout the winter months produce locally heavy snowfalls from the lake. At the same time, temperatures of well below zero over Canada and the midwest are raised 10 to 30 degrees in crossing the lakes. Only on rare occasions do polar air masses drop southward from eastern Hudson Bay across Lake Ontario without appreciable warming.

## TABLE 1    NORMALS, MEANS AND EXTREMES

BUFFALO, NEW YORK

LATITUDE: 42°56'N    LONGITUDE: 78°44'W    ELEVATION: FT. GRND    705 BARO    715    TIME ZONE: EASTERN    WBAN: 14733

| | (a) | JAN | FEB | MAR | APR | MAY | JUNE | JULY | AUG | SEP | OCT | NOV | DEC | YEAR |
|---|---|---|---|---|---|---|---|---|---|---|---|---|---|---|
| **TEMPERATURE °F:** | | | | | | | | | | | | | | |
| Normals | | | | | | | | | | | | | | |
| –Daily Maximum | | 30.0 | 31.4 | 40.4 | 54.4 | 65.9 | 75.6 | 80.2 | 78.2 | 71.4 | 60.2 | 47.0 | 35.0 | 55.8 |
| –Daily Minimum | | 17.0 | 17.5 | 25.6 | 36.3 | 46.3 | 56.4 | 61.2 | 59.6 | 52.7 | 42.7 | 33.6 | 22.5 | 39.3 |
| –Monthly | | 23.5 | 24.5 | 33.0 | 45.4 | 56.1 | 66.0 | 70.7 | 68.9 | 62.1 | 51.5 | 40.3 | 28.8 | 47.6 |
| Extremes | | | | | | | | | | | | | | |
| –Record Highest | 46 | 72 | 65 | 81 | 88 | 90 | 96 | 97 | 99 | 98 | 87 | 80 | 74 | 99 |
| –Year | | 1950 | 1981 | 1945 | 1986 | 1987 | 1988 | 1988 | 1948 | 1953 | 1951 | 1961 | 1982 | AUG 1948 |
| –Record Lowest | 46 | -16 | -20 | -7 | 12 | 26 | 35 | 43 | 38 | 32 | 20 | 9 | -10 | -20 |
| –Year | | 1982 | 1961 | 1984 | 1982 | 1947 | 1945 | 1945 | 1982 | 1963 | 1965 | 1971 | 1980 | FEB 1961 |
| **NORMAL DEGREE DAYS:** | | | | | | | | | | | | | | |
| Heating (base 65°F) | | 1287 | 1134 | 992 | 588 | 294 | 53 | 9 | 25 | 130 | 423 | 741 | 1122 | 6798 |
| Cooling (base 65°F) | | 0 | 0 | 0 | 0 | 18 | 83 | 186 | 146 | 43 | 0 | 0 | 0 | 476 |
| **% OF POSSIBLE SUNSHINE** | 46 | 32 | 38 | 46 | 51 | 58 | 65 | 68 | 64 | 58 | 50 | 29 | 27 | 49 |
| **MEAN SKY COVER (tenths)** | | | | | | | | | | | | | | |
| Sunrise - Sunset | 46 | 8.4 | 8.2 | 7.6 | 7.1 | 6.8 | 6.3 | 6.0 | 6.2 | 6.4 | 6.7 | 8.4 | 8.5 | 7.2 |
| **MEAN NUMBER OF DAYS:** | | | | | | | | | | | | | | |
| Sunrise to Sunset | | | | | | | | | | | | | | |
| –Clear | 46 | 1.4 | 2.0 | 3.8 | 5.0 | 5.6 | 6.2 | 6.9 | 6.8 | 6.4 | 6.3 | 2.0 | 1.2 | 53.7 |
| –Partly Cloudy | 46 | 6.2 | 5.5 | 7.6 | 8.0 | 9.7 | 11.5 | 13.0 | 11.8 | 9.9 | 8.3 | 5.5 | 6.0 | 102.9 |
| –Cloudy | 46 | 23.4 | 20.8 | 19.6 | 17.0 | 15.7 | 12.3 | 11.1 | 12.4 | 13.7 | 16.3 | 22.6 | 23.7 | 208.7 |
| Precipitation | | | | | | | | | | | | | | |
| .01 inches or more | 46 | 19.9 | 17.1 | 16.1 | 14.2 | 12.3 | 10.5 | 9.9 | 10.6 | 10.9 | 11.7 | 16.0 | 19.6 | 168.7 |
| Snow,Ice pellets | | | | | | | | | | | | | | |
| 1.0 inches or more | 46 | 7.3 | 5.6 | 3.6 | 1.0 | 0.1 | 0.0 | 0.0 | 0.0 | 0.0 | 0.1 | 3.0 | 6.1 | 26.7 |
| Thunderstorms | 46 | 0.2 | 0.2 | 1.3 | 2.3 | 2.9 | 5.2 | 5.6 | 6.0 | 3.7 | 1.6 | 1.1 | 0.5 | 30.6 |
| Heavy Fog Visibility | | | | | | | | | | | | | | |
| 1/4 mile or less | 46 | 1.5 | 1.7 | 2.5 | 2.3 | 2.3 | 1.3 | 0.9 | 0.9 | 1.1 | 1.3 | 1.3 | 1.2 | 18.3 |
| Temperature °F | | | | | | | | | | | | | | |
| –Maximum | | | | | | | | | | | | | | |
| 90° and above | 29 | 0.0 | 0.0 | 0.0 | 0.0 | 0.1 | 0.6 | 1.5 | 0.7 | 0.* | 0.0 | 0.0 | 0.0 | 2.8 |
| 32° and below | 29 | 18.0 | 15.8 | 7.3 | 0.6 | 0.0 | 0.0 | 0.0 | 0.0 | 0.0 | 0.0 | 2.1 | 12.6 | 56.2 |
| –Minimum | | | | | | | | | | | | | | |
| 32° and below | 29 | 28.7 | 25.9 | 24.1 | 10.7 | 0.7 | 0.0 | 0.0 | 0.0 | 0.* | 3.1 | 13.8 | 25.9 | 132.9 |
| 0° and below | 29 | 2.3 | 1.5 | 0.2 | 0.0 | 0.0 | 0.0 | 0.0 | 0.0 | 0.0 | 0.0 | 0.0 | 0.7 | 4.7 |
| **AVG. STATION PRESS.(mb)** | 17 | 990.3 | 991.6 | 990.1 | 988.8 | 989.1 | 989.4 | 990.4 | 991.6 | 992.3 | 992.5 | 990.9 | 990.9 | 990.7 |
| **RELATIVE HUMIDITY (%)** | | | | | | | | | | | | | | |
| Hour 01 | 29 | 77 | 79 | 78 | 75 | 76 | 79 | 79 | 83 | 83 | 80 | 79 | 80 | 79 |
| Hour 07 | 29 | 79 | 80 | 80 | 77 | 75 | 77 | 78 | 83 | 84 | 82 | 81 | 81 | 80 |
| Hour 13 (Local Time) | 29 | 72 | 70 | 65 | 57 | 56 | 56 | 55 | 58 | 60 | 60 | 69 | 73 | 63 |
| Hour 19 | 29 | 76 | 75 | 73 | 64 | 62 | 61 | 60 | 66 | 72 | 73 | 76 | 78 | 70 |
| **PRECIPITATION (inches):** | | | | | | | | | | | | | | |
| Water Equivalent | | | | | | | | | | | | | | |
| –Normal | | 3.02 | 2.40 | 2.97 | 3.06 | 2.89 | 2.72 | 2.96 | 4.16 | 3.37 | 2.93 | 3.62 | 3.42 | 37.52 |
| –Maximum Monthly | 46 | 6.88 | 5.80 | 5.59 | 5.90 | 7.22 | 8.36 | 6.43 | 10.67 | 8.99 | 9.13 | 9.75 | 8.02 | 10.67 |
| –Year | | 1982 | 1960 | 1976 | 1961 | 1989 | 1987 | 1963 | 1977 | 1977 | 1954 | 1985 | 1977 | AUG 1977 |
| –Minimum Monthly | 46 | 1.03 | 0.81 | 1.20 | 1.27 | 1.21 | 0.11 | 0.93 | 1.10 | 0.77 | 0.30 | 1.44 | 0.69 | 0.11 |
| –Year | | 1946 | 1968 | 1967 | 1946 | 1965 | 1955 | 1989 | 1948 | 1964 | 1963 | 1944 | 1943 | JUN 1955 |
| –Maximum in 24 hrs | 46 | 2.57 | 2.31 | 2.14 | 1.71 | 3.52 | 5.01 | 3.38 | 3.88 | 4.94 | 3.49 | 2.51 | 2.16 | 5.01 |
| –Year | | 1982 | 1954 | 1954 | 1977 | 1986 | 1987 | 1963 | 1963 | 1979 | 1945 | 1949 | 1945 | JUN 1987 |
| Snow,Ice pellets | | | | | | | | | | | | | | |
| –Maximum Monthly | 46 | 68.3 | 54.2 | 29.2 | 15.0 | 7.9 | T | 0.0 | 0.0 | T | 3.1 | 31.3 | 68.4 | 68.4 |
| –Year | | 1977 | 1958 | 1959 | 1975 | 1989 | 1980 | | | 1956 | 1972 | 1976 | 1985 | DEC 1985 |
| –Maximum in 24 hrs | 46 | 25.3 | 19.4 | 15.8 | 6.8 | 7.9 | T | 0.0 | 0.0 | T | 2.5 | 19.9 | 24.3 | 25.3 |
| –Year | | 1982 | 1984 | 1954 | 1975 | 1989 | 1980 | | | 1956 | 1972 | 1955 | 1945 | JAN 1982 |
| **WIND:** | | | | | | | | | | | | | | |
| Mean Speed (mph) | 50 | 14.3 | 13.6 | 13.3 | 12.7 | 11.5 | 11.0 | 10.3 | 9.8 | 10.3 | 11.1 | 12.7 | 13.4 | 12.0 |
| Prevailing Direction | | | | | | | | | | | | | | |
| through 1963 | | WSW | SW | SW | SW | SW | SW | SW | SW | S | S | S | WSW | SW |
| Fastest Mile | | | | | | | | | | | | | | |
| –Direction (!!!) | 43 | SW | SW | W | W | SW | NW | NW | SW | SW | SW | SW | S | SW |
| –Speed (MPH) | 43 | 91 | 70 | 68 | 67 | 63 | 56 | 59 | 56 | 59 | 63 | 66 | 60 | 91 |
| –Year | | 1950 | 1946 | 1959 | 1957 | 1950 | 1954 | 1953 | 1944 | 1954 | 1954 | 1948 | 1945 | JAN 1950 |
| Peak Gust | | | | | | | | | | | | | | |
| –Direction (!!!) | 6 | SW | S | W | W | SW | SW | W | W | S | S | W | SW | W |
| –Speed (mph) | 6 | 71 | 55 | 72 | 74 | 55 | 52 | 47 | 71 | 62 | 53 | 68 | 66 | 74 |
| –Date | | 1985 | 1988 | 1986 | 1985 | 1984 | 1988 | 1989 | 1988 | 1987 | 1988 | 1988 | 1985 | APR 1985 |

**See Reference Notes to this table on the following page.**

PRECIPITATION (inches)  BUFFALO, NEW YORK

**TABLE 2**

| YEAR | JAN | FEB | MAR | APR | MAY | JUNE | JULY | AUG | SEP | OCT | NOV | DEC | ANNUAL |
|---|---|---|---|---|---|---|---|---|---|---|---|---|---|
| 1961 | 1.41 | 2.63 | 2.59 | 5.90 | 3.01 | 3.66 | 3.02 | 4.03 | 2.53 | 2.41 | 3.30 | 2.62 | 37.11 |
| 1962 | 2.78 | 2.65 | 1.23 | 2.25 | 2.36 | 2.80 | 1.89 | 3.00 | 3.14 | 1.90 | 1.78 | 2.77 | 28.55 |
| 1963 | 1.51 | 1.03 | 2.19 | 2.77 | 2.22 | 0.61 | 6.43 | 8.04 | 1.20 | 0.30 | 5.07 | 1.83 | 33.20 |
| 1964 | 2.12 | 1.09 | 3.72 | 3.36 | 2.91 | 1.55 | 2.57 | 5.02 | 0.77 | 1.89 | 2.09 | 2.58 | 29.67 |
| 1965 | 3.27 | 2.99 | 1.97 | 1.99 | 1.21 | 1.50 | 3.69 | 4.12 | 2.37 | 5.07 | 4.69 | 2.60 | 35.47 |
| 1966 | 3.74 | 2.11 | 2.78 | 2.06 | 1.36 | 1.97 | 4.92 | 3.60 | 2.65 | 0.93 | 4.50 | 2.25 | 32.87 |
| 1967 | 1.18 | 1.39 | 1.20 | 2.60 | 3.69 | 2.50 | 1.57 | 4.04 | 6.36 | 4.78 | 3.13 | 2.16 | 34.60 |
| 1968 | 2.18 | 0.81 | 2.67 | 1.78 | 3.30 | 4.45 | 1.19 | 5.33 | 5.63 | 3.03 | 4.47 | 3.42 | 38.26 |
| 1969 | 3.85 | 0.97 | 1.62 | 4.16 | 3.75 | 3.51 | 3.83 | 2.48 | 2.04 | 2.77 | 4.09 | 3.09 | 36.16 |
| 1970 | 2.06 | 1.74 | 1.72 | 2.54 | 2.87 | 2.55 | 4.02 | 2.01 | 4.55 | 4.20 | 3.20 | 3.25 | 34.71 |
| 1971 | 1.46 | 3.03 | 2.07 | 1.48 | 1.56 | 4.25 | 4.50 | 4.43 | 1.88 | 1.57 | 3.07 | 3.61 | 32.91 |
| 1972 | 2.17 | 3.44 | 3.99 | 2.99 | 3.64 | 6.06 | 0.99 | 4.19 | 3.06 | 2.96 | 4.28 | 3.86 | 41.63 |
| 1973 | 2.03 | 1.98 | 3.27 | 3.56 | 2.99 | 1.68 | 3.68 | 2.98 | 1.44 | 4.27 | 4.07 | 4.89 | 36.84 |
| 1974 | 2.44 | 2.19 | 3.19 | 3.15 | 3.36 | 3.86 | 1.80 | 3.64 | 2.42 | 1.75 | 5.38 | 3.13 | 36.31 |
| 1975 | 2.11 | 2.93 | 2.92 | 1.86 | 3.31 | 3.65 | 2.34 | 8.49 | 2.44 | 1.13 | 2.77 | 4.58 | 38.53 |
| 1976 | 3.19 | 3.43 | 5.59 | 4.01 | 4.70 | 3.36 | 5.65 | 1.65 | 5.39 | 3.61 | 2.11 | 3.83 | 46.52 |
| 1977 | 3.38 | 1.59 | 2.42 | 3.60 | 1.39 | 2.79 | 3.64 | 10.67 | 8.99 | 2.61 | 4.45 | 8.02 | 53.55 |
| 1978 | 6.29 | 1.36 | 1.72 | 1.84 | 3.95 | 2.42 | 1.48 | 3.51 | 4.40 | 3.72 | 1.55 | 3.50 | 35.74 |
| 1979 | 5.43 | 2.03 | 2.48 | 3.16 | 1.63 | 2.18 | 3.51 | 6.26 | 5.61 | 3.88 | 4.14 | 3.43 | 43.74 |
| 1980 | 1.97 | 1.08 | 4.05 | 2.43 | 1.60 | 5.82 | 3.55 | 3.58 | 4.53 | 4.69 | 2.36 | 2.65 | 38.31 |
| 1981 | 1.11 | 3.50 | 1.70 | 3.09 | 2.56 | 3.68 | 5.05 | 3.13 | 4.24 | 3.31 | 2.22 | 2.87 | 36.46 |
| 1982 | 6.88 | 1.28 | 2.64 | 2.33 | 3.66 | 3.14 | 1.50 | 4.62 | 3.37 | 2.06 | 6.31 | 3.32 | 41.11 |
| 1983 | 1.44 | 1.30 | 3.20 | 2.55 | 3.28 | 2.99 | 2.01 | 3.51 | 2.11 | 4.62 | 5.19 | 7.30 | 39.50 |
| 1984 | 1.54 | 3.59 | 1.77 | 2.53 | 4.67 | 6.86 | 1.37 | 4.16 | 3.73 | 0.87 | 2.66 | 3.67 | 37.42 |
| 1985 | 4.27 | 3.34 | 4.42 | 1.33 | 3.46 | 3.21 | 1.81 | 4.63 | 1.20 | 3.73 | 9.75 | 4.85 | 46.00 |
| 1986 | 2.31 | 2.60 | 1.95 | 3.33 | 4.42 | 4.15 | 2.82 | 2.73 | 3.88 | 4.34 | 3.11 | 4.02 | 39.66 |
| 1987 | 2.90 | 0.85 | 3.66 | 3.40 | 1.35 | 8.36 | 3.39 | 5.32 | 2.62 | | 4.44 | 2.78 | 42.15 |
| 1988 | 1.58 | 4.07 | 2.99 | 2.96 | 2.74 | 1.56 | 6.35 | 2.69 | 2.07 | 6.08 | 3.37 | 2.15 | 38.61 |
| 1989 | 1.77 | 2.54 | 3.15 | 1.88 | 7.22 | 7.83 | 0.93 | 1.84 | 3.85 | 2.98 | 4.83 | 2.34 | 41.16 |
| 1990 | 2.69 | 5.90 | 1.50 | 5.22 | 6.08 | 3.55 | 3.14 | 3.25 | 3.65 | 4.59 | 2.61 | 8.71 | 50.89 |
| Record Mean | 3.07 | 2.70 | 2.76 | 2.71 | 2.95 | 2.93 | 2.91 | 3.22 | 3.08 | 3.09 | 3.32 | 3.31 | 36.06 |

**TABLE 3**  AVERAGE TEMPERATURE (deg. F)  BUFFALO, NEW YORK

| YEAR | JAN | FEB | MAR | APR | MAY | JUNE | JULY | AUG | SEP | OCT | NOV | DEC | ANNUAL |
|---|---|---|---|---|---|---|---|---|---|---|---|---|---|
| 1961 | 18.5 | 26.5 | 34.2 | 39.8 | 53.1 | 63.4 | 69.7 | 69.6 | 68.6 | 54.5 | 40.8 | 29.7 | 47.4 |
| 1962 | 22.6 | 21.3 | 32.5 | 44.9 | 60.9 | 64.9 | 64.9 | 68.1 | 57.8 | 51.5 | 37.1 | 25.1 | 46.3 |
| 1963 | 18.9 | 18.8 | 35.4 | 44.2 | 52.9 | 66.7 | 70.2 | 64.3 | 57.1 | 57.1 | 43.6 | 23.4 | 46.1 |
| 1964 | 29.3 | 23.5 | 34.0 | 46.9 | 59.2 | 65.7 | 71.3 | 64.9 | 60.0 | 48.1 | 42.1 | 29.5 | 48.1 |
| 1965 | 23.6 | 25.8 | 30.0 | 41.2 | 59.6 | 64.3 | 67.6 | 67.8 | 63.5 | 47.8 | 40.0 | 34.3 | 47.1 |
| 1966 | 20.4 | 24.9 | 34.7 | 43.3 | 52.2 | 67.4 | 71.4 | 68.5 | 58.7 | 48.8 | 41.5 | 28.6 | 46.7 |
| 1967 | 29.8 | 20.6 | 30.9 | 46.1 | 50.1 | 72.5 | 71.2 | 68.1 | 60.7 | 51.9 | 36.3 | 33.0 | 47.6 |
| 1968 | 19.9 | 20.7 | 35.7 | 49.2 | 53.4 | 64.8 | 71.2 | 69.4 | 66.1 | 53.5 | 40.7 | 26.8 | 47.6 |
| 1969 | 25.0 | 24.6 | 30.9 | 46.8 | 54.4 | 64.4 | 70.5 | 71.2 | 62.2 | 51.0 | 39.1 | 24.8 | 47.1 |
| 1970 | 17.6 | 24.8 | 30.1 | 46.9 | 57.3 | 66.0 | 71.0 | 70.2 | 64.0 | 54.5 | 41.6 | 27.4 | 47.6 |
| 1971 | 20.9 | 27.0 | 29.8 | 41.8 | 54.5 | 67.6 | 68.7 | 67.8 | 65.4 | 58.7 | 39.1 | 33.5 | 47.9 |
| 1972 | 25.5 | 22.0 | 30.1 | 41.1 | 59.1 | 62.6 | 71.0 | 67.7 | 62.8 | 46.2 | 36.0 | 30.8 | 46.3 |
| 1973 | 27.6 | 22.9 | 42.4 | 46.9 | 54.5 | 68.2 | 72.3 | 71.8 | 61.7 | 54.3 | 40.8 | 29.0 | 49.4 |
| 1974 | 27.1 | 22.3 | 33.0 | 46.2 | 53.1 | 65.6 | 69.9 | 69.9 | 59.6 | 49.2 | 40.2 | 31.7 | 47.3 |
| 1975 | 30.1 | 29.1 | 30.8 | 39.3 | 62.1 | 68.0 | 72.3 | 69.7 | 58.3 | 53.1 | 46.9 | 28.3 | 49.0 |
| 1976 | 19.7 | 31.8 | 37.2 | 46.5 | 53.4 | 68.4 | 67.8 | 67.5 | 60.1 | 46.3 | 34.1 | 22.0 | 46.3 |
| 1977 | 13.8 | 24.6 | 39.8 | 47.0 | 60.3 | 64.4 | 72.0 | 68.1 | 62.6 | 49.6 | 43.3 | 27.9 | 47.8 |
| 1978 | 20.4 | 15.5 | 28.2 | 42.5 | 57.4 | 65.1 | 70.4 | 70.3 | 60.8 | 49.5 | 40.4 | 30.4 | 45.9 |
| 1979 | 20.5 | 14.9 | 38.2 | 44.3 | 56.9 | 66.5 | 71.3 | 67.5 | 61.9 | 50.7 | 43.5 | 33.4 | 47.5 |
| 1980 | 25.8 | 21.2 | 31.8 | 46.1 | 58.1 | 61.9 | 71.7 | 72.6 | 62.4 | 48.7 | 39.4 | 25.3 | 47.1 |
| 1981 | 19.3 | 32.9 | 33.9 | 47.2 | 56.4 | 66.2 | 71.8 | 70.0 | 60.0 | 48.2 | 40.4 | 29.0 | 48.0 |
| 1982 | 17.2 | 23.2 | 32.5 | 41.6 | 61.0 | 62.2 | 71.8 | 65.0 | 61.6 | 52.6 | 43.0 | 37.5 | 47.5 |
| 1983 | 27.0 | 29.6 | 36.7 | 43.6 | 53.9 | 67.6 | 74.2 | 71.2 | 63.7 | 51.7 | 40.8 | 22.7 | 48.6 |
| 1984 | 20.4 | 33.8 | 27.1 | 47.7 | 52.9 | 67.8 | 70.3 | 70.3 | 58.5 | 53.2 | 39.0 | 35.6 | 48.1 |
| 1985 | 21.1 | 24.8 | 35.6 | 49.5 | 59.5 | 62.7 | 69.7 | 69.2 | 64.2 | 52.5 | 42.0 | 25.6 | 48.0 |
| 1986 | 25.5 | 24.5 | 36.2 | 47.8 | 59.7 | 64.1 | 71.1 | 67.9 | 61.8 | 50.9 | 37.7 | 32.4 | 48.3 |
| 1987 | 26.1 | 25.0 | 37.7 | 50.0 | 60.5 | 68.9 | 74.2 | 68.9 | 63.4 | 47.9 | 42.5 | 34.3 | 50.0 |
| 1988 | 26.6 | 24.3 | 35.2 | 46.1 | 59.7 | 64.0 | 74.8 | 72.4 | 62.1 | 46.9 | 43.0 | 30.0 | 48.8 |
| 1989 | 31.3 | 22.7 | 33.0 | 41.9 | 55.1 | 65.9 | 71.5 | 68.5 | 60.8 | 51.5 | 37.9 | 17.4 | 46.5 |
| 1990 | 33.4 | 29.3 | 36.9 | 48.5 | 54.9 | 66.7 | 71.4 | 70.4 | 61.7 | 52.5 | 43.4 | 34.4 | 50.3 |
| Record Mean | 24.9 | 24.6 | 32.6 | 43.7 | 55.0 | 64.8 | 70.5 | 69.0 | 62.5 | 51.5 | 40.0 | 29.5 | 47.4 |
| Max | 31.3 | 31.5 | 39.9 | 51.9 | 63.5 | 72.6 | 78.3 | 77.0 | 70.5 | 59.1 | 46.3 | 35.3 | 54.8 |
| Min | 18.4 | 17.7 | 25.3 | 35.4 | 46.4 | 56.9 | 62.6 | 60.9 | 54.4 | 44.0 | 33.8 | 23.6 | 40.0 |

## REFERENCE NOTES FOR TABLES 1, 2, 3 and 6    (BUFFALO, NY)

### GENERAL

T - TRACE AMOUNT
BLANK ENTRIES DENOTE MISSING/UNREPORTED DATA.
# INDICATES A STATION OR INSTRUMENT RELOCATION.

### SPECIFIC

**TABLE 1**

(a) - LENGTH OF RECORD IN YEARS. ALTHOUGH
INDIVIDUAL MONTHS MAY BE MISSING.

* LESS THAN .05

NORMALS — BASED ON THE 1951-1980 RECORD PERIOD.
EXTREMES — DATES ARE THE MOST RECENT OCCURRENCE.
WIND DIR. — NUMERALS SHOW TENS OF DEGREES
CLOCKWISE FROM TRUE NORTH.
"00" INDICATES CALM.
RESULTANT WIND DIRECTIONS ARE GIVEN TO WHOLE DEGREES.

**TABLE 3**
MAX AND MIN ARE LONG-TERM <u>MEAN DAILY MAXIMUM</u>
AND <u>MEAN DAILY MINIMUM</u> TEMPERATURES.

### EXCEPTIONS

**TABLES 2, 3, and 6**

RECORD MEANS ARE THROUGH THE CURRENT YEAR,
BEGINNING IN     1874 FOR TEMPERATURE
1871 FOR PRECIPITATION
1944 FOR SNOWFALL

**TABLE 4**  HEATING DEGREE DAYS Base 65 deg. F    BUFFALO, NEW YORK

| SEASON | JULY | AUG | SEP | OCT | NOV | DEC | JAN | FEB | MAR | APR | MAY | JUNE | TOTAL |
|---|---|---|---|---|---|---|---|---|---|---|---|---|---|
| 1961-62 | 30 | 17 | 76 | 323 | 722 | 1089 | 1310 | 1216 | 1002 | 609 | 195 | 66 | 6655 |
| 1962-63 | 9 | 26 | 213 | 415 | 832 | 1231 | 1420 | 1288 | 907 | 618 | 370 | 57 | 7386 |
| 1963-64 | 20 | 72 | 240 | 241 | 635 | 1282 | 1099 | 1198 | 955 | 535 | 204 | 98 | 6679 |
| 1964-65 | 5 | 68 | 176 | 518 | 680 | 1097 | 1277 | 1092 | 1080 | 706 | 186 | 100 | 6985 |
| 1965-66 | 23 | 46 | 122 | 525 | 742 | 942 | 1374 | 1114 | 931 | 648 | 401 | 68 | 6936 |
| 1966-67 | 7 | 19 | 199 | 495 | 700 | 1124 | 1086 | 1239 | 1047 | 560 | 457 | 4 | 6937 |
| 1967-68 | 12 | 26 | 162 | 403 | 853 | 985 | 1393 | 1281 | 901 | 469 | 352 | 84 | 6921 |
| 1968-69 | 11 | 29 | 58 | 374 | 722 | 1180 | 1233 | 1125 | 1052 | 540 | 325 | 102 | 6751 |
| 1969-70 | 13 | 16 | 147 | 433 | 769 | 1240 | 1459 | 1121 | 1076 | 552 | 255 | 66 | 7147 |
| 1970-71 | 6 | 6 | 93 | 328 | 695 | 1161 | 1361 | 1057 | 1085 | 691 | 327 | 36 | 6846 |
| 1971-72 | 11 | 29 | 87 | 202 | 771 | 971 | 1218 | 1237 | 1070 | 707 | 187 | 112 | 6602 |
| 1972-73 | 16 | 33 | 113 | 574 | 860 | 1054 | 1152 | 1173 | 696 | 542 | 318 | 24 | 6555 |
| 1973-74 | 2 | 14 | 171 | 326 | 720 | 1107 | 1167 | 1187 | 989 | 553 | 365 | 51 | 6652 |
| 1974-75 | 2 | 0 | 187 | 483 | 738 | 1024 | 1077 | 1001 | 1053 | 764 | 175 | 32 | 6536 |
| 1975-76 | 3 | 15 | 197 | 368 | 535 | 1134 | 1400 | 958 | 853 | 557 | 358 | 40 | 6418 |
| 1976-77 | 15 | 35 | 180 | 573 | 921 | 1328 | 1580 | 1123 | 775 | 544 | 207 | 90 | 7371 |
| 1977-78 | 5 | 40 | 110 | 473 | 646 | 1146 | 1376 | 1378 | 1130 | 670 | 282 | 81 | 7337 |
| 1978-79 | 14 | 3 | 154 | 472 | 732 | 1067 | 1371 | 1400 | 823 | 619 | 285 | 65 | 7005 |
| 1979-80 | 16 | 35 | 134 | 455 | 636 | 973 | 1208 | 1265 | 1022 | 559 | 240 | 142 | 6685 |
| 1980-81 | 2 | 0 | 128 | 498 | 759 | 1224 | 1411 | 895 | 956 | 527 | 269 | 33 | 6702 |
| 1981-82 | 6 | 11 | 170 | 514 | 732 | 1108 | 1476 | 1163 | 1002 | 698 | 147 | 95 | 7122 |
| 1982-83 | 4 | 65 | 140 | 382 | 656 | 848 | 1172 | 987 | 868 | 636 | 342 | 71 | 6171 |
| 1983-84 | 5 | 10 | 125 | 418 | 722 | 1304 | 1378 | 899 | 1167 | 519 | 385 | 35 | 6967 |
| 1984-85 | 11 | 22 | 210 | 360 | 774 | 1067 | 1354 | 1120 | 902 | 476 | 196 | 95 | 6425 |
| 1985-86 | 8 | 12 | 114 | 378 | 685 | 1215 | 1215 | 1128 | 885 | 519 | 197 | 80 | 6436 |
| 1986-87 | 4 | 42 | 137 | 430 | 811 | 1003 | 1199 | 1115 | 837 | 447 | 213 | 28 | 6266 |
| 1987-88 | 3 | 25 | 91 | 527 | 665 | 948 | 1184 | 1174 | 916 | 560 | 186 | 113 | 6392 |
| 1988-89 | 5 | 17 | 122 | 560 | 654 | 1078 | 1038 | 1177 | 985 | 687 | 321 | 60 | 6704 |
| 1989-90 | 1 | 28 | 170 | 411 | 806 | 1466 | 970 | 995 | 866 | 518 | 311 | 46 | 6588 |
| 1990-91 | 5 | 2 | 141 | 395 | 640 | 941 | | | | | | | |

**TABLE 5**  COOLING DEGREE DAYS Base 65 deg. F    BUFFALO, NEW YORK

| YEAR | JAN | FEB | MAR | APR | MAY | JUNE | JULY | AUG | SEP | OCT | NOV | DEC | TOTAL |
|---|---|---|---|---|---|---|---|---|---|---|---|---|---|
| 1969 | 0 | 0 | 0 | 0 | 1 | 88 | 192 | 212 | 69 | 6 | 0 | 0 | 568 |
| 1970 | 0 | 0 | 0 | 16 | 21 | 108 | 197 | 173 | 72 | 12 | 0 | 0 | 599 |
| 1971 | 0 | 0 | 0 | 0 | 9 | 119 | 136 | 122 | 107 | 15 | 0 | 0 | 508 |
| 1972 | 0 | 0 | 0 | 0 | 12 | 48 | 210 | 123 | 57 | 0 | 0 | 0 | 450 |
| 1973 | 0 | 0 | 0 | 6 | 2 | 126 | 233 | 230 | 78 | 3 | 0 | 0 | 678 |
| 1974 | 0 | 0 | 0 | 0 | 7 | 71 | 163 | 158 | 29 | 0 | 0 | 0 | 428 |
| 1975 | 0 | 0 | 0 | 0 | 90 | 129 | 238 | 171 | 3 | 3 | 0 | 0 | 634 |
| 1976 | 0 | 0 | 0 | 8 | 7 | 149 | 109 | 119 | 40 | 0 | 0 | 0 | 432 |
| 1977 | 0 | 0 | 0 | 12 | 68 | 78 | 228 | 142 | 45 | 0 | 1 | 0 | 574 |
| 1978 | 0 | 0 | 0 | 0 | 52 | 91 | 189 | 173 | 35 | 0 | 0 | 0 | 540 |
| 1979 | 0 | 0 | 0 | 6 | 40 | 118 | 217 | 120 | 49 | 20 | 0 | 0 | 570 |
| 1980 | 0 | 0 | 0 | 0 | 32 | 56 | 217 | 242 | 58 | 2 | 0 | 0 | 607 |
| 1981 | 0 | 0 | 0 | 2 | 13 | 78 | 225 | 173 | 55 | 0 | 0 | 0 | 546 |
| 1982 | 0 | 0 | 0 | 3 | 31 | 18 | 221 | 74 | 45 | 2 | 0 | 2 | 396 |
| 1983 | 0 | 0 | 0 | 0 | 5 | 157 | 300 | 214 | 90 | 15 | 0 | 0 | 781 |
| 1984 | 0 | 0 | 0 | 5 | 16 | 123 | 183 | 193 | 23 | 1 | 0 | 0 | 544 |
| 1985 | 0 | 0 | 0 | 18 | 32 | 32 | 161 | 151 | 96 | 0 | 1 | 0 | 491 |
| 1986 | 0 | 0 | 0 | 7 | 38 | 60 | 200 | 137 | 46 | 0 | 0 | 0 | 488 |
| 1987 | 0 | 0 | 0 | 4 | 79 | 151 | 298 | 152 | 49 | 0 | 0 | 0 | 733 |
| 1988 | 0 | 0 | 0 | 0 | 29 | 88 | 315 | 255 | 41 | 8 | 0 | 0 | 736 |
| 1989 | 0 | 0 | 0 | 0 | 21 | 97 | 207 | 143 | 50 | 0 | 0 | 0 | 518 |
| 1990 | 0 | 0 | 3 | 29 | 4 | 104 | 208 | 176 | 47 | 14 | 0 | 0 | 585 |

**TABLE 6**  SNOWFALL (inches)    BUFFALO, NEW YORK

| SEASON | JULY | AUG | SEP | OCT | NOV | DEC | JAN | FEB | MAR | APR | MAY | JUNE | TOTAL |
|---|---|---|---|---|---|---|---|---|---|---|---|---|---|
| 1961-62 | 0.0 | 0.0 | 0.0 | T | 5.6 | 30.2 | 26.2 | 28.2 | 6.7 | 4.5 | 0.0 | 0.0 | 101.4 |
| 1962-63 | 0.0 | 0.0 | 0.0 | 2.0 | 2.5 | 30.2 | 31.5 | 15.5 | 12.8 | 0.3 | 0.1 | 0.0 | 89.8 |
| 1963-64 | 0.0 | 0.0 | 0.0 | 0.0 | 3.1 | 24.0 | 13.7 | 14.6 | 12.8 | 3.3 | 0.0 | 0.0 | 71.5 |
| 1964-65 | 0.0 | 0.0 | 0.0 | T | 5.4 | 15.2 | 19.2 | 9.4 | 11.4 | 4.2 | 0.0 | 0.0 | 70.9 |
| 1965-66 | 0.0 | 0.0 | 0.0 | 1.2 | 12.2 | 7.0 | 48.0 | 15.2 | 11.4 | 3.2 | 0.1 | 0.0 | 98.3 |
| 1966-67 | 0.0 | 0.0 | 0.0 | 0.0 | 10.0 | 12.1 | 11.6 | 19.8 | 10.8 | 0.6 | 1.2 | 0.0 | 66.1 |
| 1967-68 | 0.0 | 0.0 | 0.0 | T | 19.7 | 10.4 | 19.1 | 11.7 | 10.6 | 0.1 | 0.0 | 0.0 | 71.6 |
| 1968-69 | 0.0 | 0.0 | 0.0 | T | 11.6 | 11.7 | 31.2 | 12.8 | 8.0 | 3.1 | 0.0 | 0.0 | 78.4 |
| 1969-70 | 0.0 | 0.0 | 0.0 | 1.0 | 22.1 | 23.4 | 38.0 | 21.9 | 12.6 | 1.5 | T | 0.0 | 120.5 |
| 1970-71 | 0.0 | 0.0 | 0.0 | 0.0 | 2.6 | 32.3 | 17.2 | 19.4 | 22.6 | 2.9 | 0.0 | 0.0 | 97.0 |
| 1971-72 | 0.0 | 0.0 | 0.0 | 0.0 | 18.7 | 12.9 | 27.6 | 31.4 | 5.2 | 0.0 | 0.0 | 0.0 | 109.9 |
| 1972-73 | 0.0 | 0.0 | 0.0 | 3.1 | 18.9 | 19.8 | 9.9 | 16.1 | 8.5 | 2.4 | 0.1 | 0.0 | 78.8 |
| 1973-74 | 0.0 | 0.0 | 0.0 | 0.0 | 3.0 | 23.1 | 19.7 | 22.8 | 12.9 | 7.1 | 0.1 | 0.0 | 88.7 |
| 1974-75 | 0.0 | 0.0 | 0.0 | T | 22.1 | 23.6 | 11.0 | 16.3 | 7.6 | 15.0 | 0.0 | 0.0 | 95.6 |
| 1975-76 | 0.0 | 0.0 | 0.0 | T | 5.5 | 27.3 | 21.6 | 8.3 | 17.3 | 2.5 | T | 0.0 | 82.5 |
| 1976-77 | 0.0 | 0.0 | 0.0 | 0.2 | 31.3 | 60.7 | 68.3 | 22.7 | 13.5 | 2.2 | 0.5 | 0.0 | 199.4 |
| 1977-78 | 0.0 | 0.0 | 0.0 | T | 15.0 | 53.4 | 56.5 | 21.7 | 5.8 | 1.8 | 0.1 | 0.0 | 154.3 |
| 1978-79 | 0.0 | 0.0 | 0.0 | T | 3.0 | 10.1 | 42.6 | 28.3 | 4.6 | 8.7 | 0.0 | 0.0 | 97.3 |
| 1979-80 | 0.0 | 0.0 | 0.0 | T | 12.6 | 19.7 | 10.2 | 11.7 | 13.9 | 0.3 | T | T | 68.4 |
| 1980-81 | 0.0 | 0.0 | 0.0 | T | 6.7 | 21.6 | 14.4 | 5.0 | 13.2 | T | 0.0 | 0.0 | 60.9 |
| 1981-82 | 0.0 | 0.0 | 0.0 | T | 1.8 | 24.8 | 53.2 | 12.7 | 9.0 | 10.9 | 0.0 | 0.0 | 112.4 |
| 1982-83 | 0.0 | 0.0 | 0.0 | 0.0 | 15.8 | 12.9 | 9.0 | 5.5 | 2.3 | T | T | 0.0 | 52.4 |
| 1983-84 | 0.0 | 0.0 | 0.0 | T | 17.7 | 52.0 | 13.4 | 32.5 | 16.0 | 0.9 | T | 0.0 | 132.5 |
| 1984-85 | 0.0 | 0.0 | 0.0 | 0.0 | 1.4 | 11.2 | 65.9 | 20.9 | 6.3 | 1.5 | 0.0 | 0.0 | 107.2 |
| 1985-86 | 0.0 | 0.0 | 0.0 | 0.0 | 5.2 | 68.4 | 17.3 | 17.3 | 4.8 | 1.7 | T | 0.0 | 114.7 |
| 1986-87 | 0.0 | 0.0 | 0.0 | 0.0 | 13.7 | 4.8 | 28.5 | 7.7 | 10.8 | 2.0 | 0.0 | 0.0 | 67.5 |
| 1987-88 | 0.0 | 0.0 | 0.0 | T | 0.9 | 9.8 | 6.9 | 31.9 | 6.1 | 0.8 | 0.0 | 0.0 | 56.4 |
| 1988-89 | 0.0 | 0.0 | 0.0 | 0.5 | 0.6 | 5.4 | 29.6 | 10.1 | 2.5 | 7.9 | 0.0 | 0.0 | 67.4 |
| 1989-90 | 0.0 | 0.0 | 0.0 | 0.0 | 7.8 | 34.8 | 11.8 | 28.0 | 1.4 | 9.9 | T | 0.0 | 93.7 |
| 1990-91 | 0.0 | 0.0 | 0.0 | T | 0.7 | 15.4 | | | | | | | |
| Record Mean | 0.0 | 0.0 | T | 0.2 | 11.4 | 22.8 | 23.8 | 18.5 | 11.1 | 3.2 | 0.3 | T | 91.3 |

**See Reference Notes, relative to all above tables, on preceding page.**

New York City, in area exceeding 300 square miles, is located on the Atlantic coastal plain at the mouth of the Hudson River. The terrain is laced with numerous waterways, all but one of the five boroughs in the city are situated on islands. Elevations range from less than 50 feet over most of Manhattan, Brooklyn, and Queens to almost 300 feet in northern Manhattan and the Bronx, and over 400 feet in Staten Island. Extensive suburban areas on Long Island, and in Connecticut, New York State and New Jersey border the city on the east, north, and west. About 30 miles to the west and northwest, hills rise to about 1,500 feet and to the north in upper Westchester County to 800 feet. To the southwest and to the east are the low-lying land areas of the New Jersey coastal plain and of Long Island, bordering on the Atlantic.

The New York Metropolitan area is close to the path of most storm and frontal systems which move across the North American continent. Therefore, weather conditions affecting the city most often approach from a westerly direction. New York City can thus experience higher temperatures in summer and lower ones in winter than would otherwise be expected in a coastal area. However, the frequent passage of weather systems often helps reduce the length of both warm and cold spells, and is also a major factor in keeping periods of prolonged air stagnation to a minimum.

Although continental influence predominates, oceanic influence is by no means absent. During the summer local sea breezes, winds blowing onshore from the cool water surface, often moderate the afternoon heat. The effect of the sea breeze diminishes inland. On winter mornings, ocean temperatures which are warm relative to the land reinforce the effect of the city heat island and low temperatures are often 10-20 degrees lower in the inland suburbs than in the central city. The relatively warm water temperatures also delay the advent of winter snows. Conversely, the lag in warming of water temperatures keeps spring temperatures relatively cool. One year-round measure of the ocean influence is the small average daily variation in temperature.

Precipitation is moderate and distributed fairly evenly throughout the year. Most of the rainfall from May through October comes from thunderstorms, usually of brief duration and sometimes intense. Heavy rains of long duration associated with tropical storms occur infrequently in late summer or fall. For the other months of the year precipitation is more likely to be associated with widespread storm areas, so that day-long rain, snow or a mixture of both is more common. Coastal storms, occurring most often in the fall and winter months, produce on occasion considerable amounts of precipitation and have been responsible for record rains, snows, and high winds.

The average annual precipitation is reasonably uniform within the city but is higher in the northern and western suburbs and less on eastern Long Island. Annual snowfall totals also show a consistent increase to the north and west of the city with lesser amounts along the south shores and the eastern end of Long Island, reflecting the influence of the ocean waters.

Local Climatological Data is published for three locations in New York City, Central Park, La Guardia Airport, and John F. Kennedy International Airport. Other nearby locations for which it is published are Newark, New Jersey, and Bridgeport, Connecticut.

Based on the 1951-1980 period, the average first occurrence of 32 degrees Fahrenheit in the fall is November 11 and the average last occurrence in the spring is April 1.

## TABLE 1 — NORMALS, MEANS AND EXTREMES

NEW YORK, CENTRAL PARK, NEW YORK

LATITUDE: 40°47'N  LONGITUDE: 73°58'W  ELEVATION: FT. GRND 132 BARO 87  TIME ZONE: EASTERN  WBAN: 94728

| | (a) | JAN | FEB | MAR | APR | MAY | JUNE | JULY | AUG | SEP | OCT | NOV | DEC | YEAR |
|---|---|---|---|---|---|---|---|---|---|---|---|---|---|---|
| **TEMPERATURE °F:** | | | | | | | | | | | | | | |
| Normals | | | | | | | | | | | | | | |
| -Daily Maximum | | 38.0 | 40.1 | 48.6 | 61.1 | 71.5 | 80.1 | 85.3 | 83.7 | 76.4 | 65.6 | 53.6 | 42.1 | 62.2 |
| -Daily Minimum | | 25.6 | 26.6 | 34.1 | 43.8 | 53.3 | 62.7 | 68.2 | 67.1 | 60.1 | 49.9 | 40.8 | 30.3 | 46.9 |
| -Monthly | | 31.8 | 33.4 | 41.4 | 52.4 | 62.5 | 71.4 | 76.7 | 75.4 | 68.3 | 57.7 | 47.2 | 36.2 | 54.5 |
| Extremes | | | | | | | | | | | | | | |
| -Record Highest | 121 | 72 | 75 | 86 | 96 | 99 | 101 | 106 | 104 | 102 | 94 | 84 | 72 | 106 |
| -Year | | 1950 | 1985 | 1945 | 1976 | 1962 | 1966 | 1936 | 1918 | 1953 | 1941 | 1950 | 1982 | JUL 1936 |
| -Record Lowest | 121 | -6 | -15 | 3 | 12 | 32 | 44 | 52 | 50 | 39 | 28 | 5 | -13 | -15 |
| -Year | | 1882 | 1934 | 1872 | 1923 | 1891 | 1945 | 1943 | 1986 | 1912 | 1936 | 1875 | 1917 | FEB 1934 |
| **NORMAL DEGREE DAYS:** | | | | | | | | | | | | | | |
| Heating (base 65°F) | | 1029 | 885 | 732 | 378 | 134 | 7 | 0 | 0 | 36 | 240 | 534 | 893 | 4868 |
| Cooling (base 65°F) | | 0 | 0 | 0 | 0 | 56 | 199 | 363 | 322 | 135 | 14 | 0 | 0 | 1089 |
| **% OF POSSIBLE SUNSHINE** | 103 | 51 | 55 | 57 | 59 | 61 | 64 | 65 | 64 | 62 | 61 | 52 | 50 | 58 |
| **MEAN SKY COVER (tenths)** | | | | | | | | | | | | | | |
| Sunrise - Sunset | 42 | 6.0 | 5.8 | 5.7 | 6.0 | 5.7 | 5.6 | 5.5 | 5.5 | 5.2 | 4.9 | 5.8 | 5.9 | 5.6 |
| **MEAN NUMBER OF DAYS:** | | | | | | | | | | | | | | |
| Sunrise to Sunset | | | | | | | | | | | | | | |
| -Clear | 42 | 8.1 | 8.3 | 8.8 | 7.6 | 8.0 | 8.0 | 8.5 | 9.2 | 10.6 | 11.8 | 9.0 | 8.9 | 106.7 |
| -Partly Cloudy | 42 | 9.2 | 8.7 | 10.1 | 10.5 | 12.4 | 12.4 | 13.0 | 12.1 | 10.0 | 9.7 | 9.5 | 9.1 | 126.7 |
| -Cloudy | 42 | 13.7 | 11.2 | 12.1 | 11.9 | 10.7 | 9.6 | 9.5 | 9.7 | 9.4 | 9.5 | 11.5 | 13.0 | 131.8 |
| Precipitation | | | | | | | | | | | | | | |
| .01 inches or more | 120 | 11.1 | 9.8 | 11.4 | 10.7 | 11.1 | 10.2 | 10.5 | 9.8 | 8.3 | 8.2 | 9.3 | 10.3 | 120.6 |
| Snow,Ice pellets | | | | | | | | | | | | | | |
| 1.0 inches or more | 119 | 2.2 | 2.2 | 1.5 | 0.2 | 0.0 | 0.0 | 0.0 | 0.0 | 0.0 | 0.0 | 0.3 | 1.5 | 8.0 |
| Thunderstorms | 26 | 0.1 | 0.3 | 0.9 | 1.0 | 2.5 | 3.8 | 4.1 | 3.6 | 1.2 | 0.8 | 0.3 | 0.1 | 18.7 |
| Heavy Fog Visibility 1/4 mile or less | 2 | 0.0 | 0.0 | 0.0 | 0.0 | 0.0 | 0.0 | 0.0 | 0.0 | 0.0 | 0.0 | 0.0 | 0.0 | 0.0 |
| Temperature °F | | | | | | | | | | | | | | |
| -Maximum | | | | | | | | | | | | | | |
| 90° and above | 76 | 0.0 | 0.0 | 0.0 | 0.1 | 1.0 | 3.2 | 6.6 | 4.5 | 1.4 | 0.1 | 0.0 | 0.0 | 16.9 |
| 32° and below | 76 | 8.8 | 5.7 | 1.3 | 0.* | 0.0 | 0.0 | 0.0 | 0.0 | 0.0 | 0.0 | 0.2 | 5.0 | 21.0 |
| -Minimum | | | | | | | | | | | | | | |
| 32° and below | 76 | 22.7 | 20.3 | 12.5 | 1.5 | 0.* | 0.0 | 0.0 | 0.0 | 0.0 | 0.3 | 4.7 | 18.1 | 80.0 |
| 0° and below | 76 | 0.2 | 0.2 | 0.0 | 0.0 | 0.0 | 0.0 | 0.0 | 0.0 | 0.0 | 0.0 | 0.0 | 0.1 | 0.5 |
| **AVG. STATION PRESS.(mb)** | 10 | 1013.9 | 1013.7 | 1012.3 | 1011.5 | 1011.3 | 1012.3 | 1012.5 | 1014.2 | 1014.7 | 1015.1 | 1014.5 | 1014.5 | 1013.4 |
| **RELATIVE HUMIDITY (%)** | | | | | | | | | | | | | | |
| Hour 01 | 49 | 65 | 64 | 64 | 64 | 70 | 73 | 74 | 76 | 76 | 72 | 69 | 67 | 70 |
| Hour 07 (Local Time) | 61 | 68 | 68 | 67 | 67 | 71 | 74 | 75 | 78 | 79 | 76 | 73 | 69 | 72 |
| Hour 13 | 61 | 60 | 58 | 55 | 51 | 53 | 55 | 55 | 57 | 57 | 55 | 59 | 60 | 56 |
| Hour 19 | 61 | 60 | 59 | 57 | 56 | 60 | 61 | 63 | 66 | 66 | 63 | 63 | 62 | 61 |
| **PRECIPITATION (inches):** | | | | | | | | | | | | | | |
| Water Equivalent | | | | | | | | | | | | | | |
| -Normal | | 3.21 | 3.13 | 4.22 | 3.75 | 3.76 | 3.23 | 3.77 | 4.03 | 3.66 | 3.41 | 4.14 | 3.81 | 44.12 |
| -Maximum Monthly | 120 | 10.52 | 6.87 | 10.41 | 8.77 | 10.24 | 9.78 | 11.89 | 10.86 | 16.85 | 13.31 | 12.41 | 9.98 | 16.85 |
| -Year | | 1979 | 1869 | 1980 | 1874 | 1989 | 1903 | 1889 | 1955 | 1882 | 1903 | 1972 | 1973 | SEP 1882 |
| -Minimum Monthly | 120 | 0.58 | 0.46 | 0.90 | 0.95 | 0.30 | 0.02 | 0.49 | 0.24 | 0.21 | 0.14 | 0.34 | 0.25 | 0.02 |
| -Year | | 1981 | 1895 | 1885 | 1881 | 1903 | 1949 | 1910 | 1964 | 1884 | 1963 | 1976 | 1955 | JUN 1949 |
| -Maximum in 24 hrs | 77 | 3.91 | 3.04 | 4.25 | 4.22 | 4.88 | 4.74 | 3.60 | 5.78 | 8.30 | 11.17 | 8.09 | 3.21 | 11.17 |
| -Year | | 1979 | 1973 | 1876 | 1984 | 1968 | 1884 | 1971 | 1971 | 1882 | 1903 | 1977 | 1909 | OCT 1903 |
| Snow,Ice pellets | | | | | | | | | | | | | | |
| -Maximum Monthly | 121 | 27.4 | 27.9 | 30.5 | 13.5 | T | 0.0 | 0.0 | 0.0 | 0.0 | 0.8 | 19.0 | 29.6 | 30.5 |
| -Year | | 1925 | 1934 | 1896 | 1875 | 1977 | | | | | 1925 | 1898 | 1947 | MAR 1896 |
| -Maximum in 24 hrs | 121 | 13.6 | 17.6 | 18.1 | 10.2 | T | 0.0 | 0.0 | 0.0 | 0.0 | 0.8 | 10.0 | 26.4 | 26.4 |
| -Year | | 1978 | 1983 | 1941 | 1915 | 1977 | | | | | 1925 | 1898 | 1947 | DEC 1947 |
| **WIND:** | | | | | | | | | | | | | | |
| Mean Speed (mph) | 58 | 10.7 | 10.8 | 11.0 | 10.5 | 8.8 | 8.1 | 7.6 | 7.6 | 8.1 | 8.9 | 9.9 | 10.4 | 9.4 |
| Prevailing Direction through 1963 | | NW | NW | NW | NW | SW | SW | SW | SW | SW | SW | NW | NW | SW |
| Fastest Obs. 1 Min. | | | | | | | | | | | | | | |
| -Direction (!!!) | 6 | 31 | 05 | 04 | 05 | 18 | 29 | 35 | 30 | 27 | 05 | 31 | 30 | 04 |
| -Speed (MPH) | 6 | 25 | 28 | 35 | 26 | 24 | 25 | 29 | 21 | 23 | 25 | 29 | 29 | 35 |
| -Year | | 1989 | 1988 | 1984 | 1986 | 1989 | 1985 | 1986 | 1986 | 1985 | 1988 | 1989 | 1988 | MAR 1984 |
| Peak Gust | | | | | | | | | | | | | | |
| -Direction (!!!) | 6 | NW | NE | NE | SE | ENE | WSW | WSW | S | W | NE | NW | W | NE |
| -Speed (mph) | 6 | 43 | 51 | 63 | 46 | 44 | 40 | 37 | 43 | 52 | 46 | 58 | 51 | 63 |
| -Date | 6 | 1989 | 1984 | 1984 | 1984 | 1989 | 1987 | 1988 | 1986 | 1985 | 1988 | 1989 | 1988 | MAR 1984 |

**See reference Notes to this table on the following page.**

PRECIPITATION (inches)  NEW YORK, CENTRAL PARK, NEW YORK

**TABLE 2**

| YEAR | JAN | FEB | MAR | APR | MAY | JUNE | JULY | AUG | SEP | OCT | NOV | DEC | ANNUAL |
|------|-----|-----|-----|-----|-----|------|------|-----|-----|-----|-----|-----|--------|
| 1961 | 1.88 | 3.96 | 4.23 | 5.08 | 3.60 | 2.86 | 4.92 | 3.13 | 1.70 | 2.21 | 2.71 | 3.04 | 39.32 |
| 1962 | 2.62 | 3.74 | 2.97 | 3.00 | 1.26 | 3.73 | 1.67 | 5.71 | 3.10 | 3.15 | 3.94 | 2.26 | 37.15 |
| 1963 | 1.93 | 2.55 | 3.61 | 1.27 | 2.15 | 2.72 | 2.19 | 3.21 | 3.95 | 0.14 | 8.24 | 2.31 | 34.28 |
| 1964 | 4.62 | 2.93 | 2.57 | 5.09 | 0.57 | 2.6 | 4.17 | 2.73 | 1.69 | 1.73 | 2.16 | 1.72 | 32.99 |
| 1965 | 3.09 | 3.66 | 2.49 | 2.90 | 1.58 | 1.27 | 1.33 | 1.70 | 1.46 | 2.55 | 4.16 | 26.09 |
| 1966 | 2.63 | 4.96 | 0.94 | 2.69 | 4.26 | 1.17 | 1.25 | 1.89 | 8.82 | 4.64 | 3.47 | 3.18 | 39.90 |
| 1967 | 1.39 | 2.68 | 5.97 | 3.45 | 4.08 | 4.64 | 6.99 | 5.94 | 1.84 | 3.47 | 2.59 | 6.08 | 49.12 |
| 1968 | 2.04 | 1.13 | 4.79 | 2.82 | 7.06 | 6.15 | 2.63 | 2.88 | 1.97 | 2.20 | 5.75 | 4.15 | 43.57 |
| 1969 | 1.10 | 3.05 | 3.73 | 3.99 | 2.67 | 3.16 | 7.37 | 2.53 | 8.32 | 1.97 | 3.58 | 7.07 | 48.54 |
| 1970 | 0.66 | 4.52 | 4.18 | 3.48 | 3.34 | 2.27 | 2.19 | 2.47 | 1.74 | 2.48 | 5.14 | 2.82 | 35.29 |
| 1971 | 2.67 | 5.33 | 3.80 | 2.95 | 4.24 | 2.31 | 7.20 | 9.37 | 7.36 | 4.14 | 5.64 | 1.76 | 56.77 |
| 1972 | 2.41 | 5.90 | 4.55 | 3.92 | 8.39 | 9.30 | 4.54 | 1.92 | 1.33 | 6.27 | 12.41 | 6.09 | 67.03 |
| 1973 | 4.53 | 4.55 | 3.60 | 8.05 | 4.51 | 4.55 | 5.89 | 3.08 | 2.75 | 3.92 | 1.82 | 9.98 | 57.23 |
| 1974 | 3.80 | 1.49 | 5.76 | 3.83 | 4.29 | 3.29 | 1.33 | 5.99 | 8.05 | 2.59 | 0.94 | 6.33 | 47.69 |
| 1975 | 4.76 | 3.33 | 3.32 | 3.04 | 3.39 | 7.58 | 11.77 | 3.05 | 9.32 | 3.70 | 4.33 | 3.63 | 61.21 |
| 1976 | 5.78 | 3.13 | 2.99 | 2.80 | 4.77 | 2.78 | 1.42 | 6.52 | 3.15 | 5.31 | 0.34 | 2.29 | 41.28 |
| 1977 | 2.25 | 2.51 | 7.41 | 3.75 | 1.71 | 3.83 | 1.60 | 4.57 | 4.75 | 5.03 | 12.26 | 5.06 | 54.73 |
| 1978 | 8.27 | 1.59 | 2.73 | 2.38 | 9.15 | 1.69 | 4.48 | 5.50 | 4.06 | 1.50 | 2.85 | 5.61 | 49.81 |
| 1979 | 10.52 | 4.58 | 4.40 | 4.04 | 6.23 | 1.56 | 1.76 | 4.27 | 4.83 | 3.87 | 3.38 | 2.69 | 52.13 |
| 1980 | 1.72 | 1.04 | 10.41 | 8.26 | 2.33 | 3.84 | 5.26 | 1.16 | 1.98 | 3.86 | 4.11 | 0.58 | 44.55 |
| 1981 | 0.58 | 6.04 | 1.19 | 3.42 | 3.56 | 2.71 | 6.21 | 0.59 | 3.45 | 3.49 | 1.69 | 5.18 | 38.11 |
| 1982 | 6.46 | 2.37 | 2.56 | 5.67 | 2.43 | 5.12 | 3.14 | 4.66 | 1.77 | 2.31 | 3.44 | 1.47 | 41.40 |
| 1983 | | | | | | | | | | 3.63 | 4.07 | 3.26 | 57.03 |
| 1984 | 1.87 | 4.86 | 6.30 | 6.62 | 9.74 | 5.76 | 7.03 | 1.38 | 2.51 | 4.75 | 1.30 | 0.83 | 38.82 |
| 1985 | 1.00 | 2.41 | 1.91 | 1.41 | 5.72 | 4.41 | 4.41 | 2.58 | 6.85 | 6.16 | 8.09 | 42.95 |
| 1986 | 4.23 | 2.86 | 1.46 | 3.93 | 1.68 | 1.86 | 5.56 | 4.24 | 2.20 | 1.92 | 2.17 | 2.21 | 42.31 |
| 1987 | 5.81 | 1.01 | 4.93 | 5.90 | 1.15 | 3.94 | 4.43 | 4.89 | 5.25 | 3.89 | 8.90 | 1.13 | 46.44 |
| 1988 | 3.64 | 3.91 | 2.10 | 2.20 | 5.27 | 1.29 | 8.14 | 2.19 | 2.34 | 3.56 | 6.90 | 0.83 | 44.67 |
| 1989 | 2.29 | 3.03 | 4.93 | 4.26 | 10.24 | 8.79 | 5.13 | 8.44 | 6.90 | 7.48 | 2.79 | 5.58 | 65.11 |
| 1990 | 5.34 | 2.33 | 3.64 | 5.12 | 9.10 | 2.50 | 3.51 | 12.36 | 2.24 | 6.38 | 2.82 | | 60.92 |
| Record Mean | 3.44 | 3.37 | 3.84 | 3.54 | 3.66 | 3.46 | 4.29 | 4.33 | 3.70 | 3.52 | 3.53 | 3.44 | 44.14 |

**TABLE 3**  AVERAGE TEMPERATURE (deg. F)  NEW YORK, CENTRAL PARK, NEW YORK

| YEAR | JAN | FEB | MAR | APR | MAY | JUNE | JULY | AUG | SEP | OCT | NOV | DEC | ANNUAL |
|------|-----|-----|-----|-----|-----|------|------|-----|-----|-----|-----|-----|--------|
| 1961 | 27.7 | 36.7 | 41.5 | 49.0 | 59.9 | 72.3 | 78.1 | 76.4 | 73.6 | 61.1 | 48.8 | 35.5 | 55.1 |
| 1962 | 32.6 | 31.8 | 43.1 | 53.3 | 64.5 | 72.5 | 74.0 | 72.4 | 64.9 | 57.4 | 43.2 | 31.5 | 53.4 |
| 1963 | 30.1 | 28.3 | 43.7 | 53.7 | 61.1 | 70.9 | 76.4 | 72.1 | 63.1 | 61.8 | 50.4 | 31.2 | 53.6 |
| 1964 | 35.7 | 32.9 | 43.1 | 49.7 | 65.4 | 71.6 | 75.4 | 72.9 | 67.2 | 55.0 | 49.4 | 36.4 | 54.6 |
| 1965 | 29.7 | 33.9 | 40.0 | 50.6 | 66.4 | 70.1 | 74.3 | 73.2 | 67.5 | 57.3 | 46.8 | 40.5 | 54.2 |
| 1966 | 32.2 | 35.1 | 42.7 | 49.7 | 61.6 | 75.4 | 79.7 | 76.9 | 66.5 | 56.2 | 48.9 | 35.7 | 55.1 |
| 1967 | 37.4 | 29.2 | 37.6 | 49.6 | 55.2 | 72.8 | 75.3 | 73.9 | 66.7 | 57.2 | 42.5 | 38.2 | 53.0 |
| 1968 | 26.7 | 28.9 | 43.3 | 55.0 | 59.6 | 69.7 | 77.3 | 76.0 | 70.6 | 60.5 | 46.9 | 34.3 | 54.1 |
| 1969 | 31.8 | 32.6 | 40.1 | 55.9 | 65.3 | 73.1 | 74.8 | 77.4 | 69.0 | 57.7 | 46.4 | 33.4 | 54.8 |
| 1970 | 25.1 | 33.0 | 38.7 | 52.1 | 64.0 | 70.9 | 77.1 | 77.6 | 70.8 | 58.9 | 48.5 | 34.4 | 54.3 |
| 1971 | 27.0 | 35.1 | 40.1 | 50.8 | 61.4 | 74.2 | 77.8 | 75.9 | 71.6 | 62.7 | 45.1 | 40.8 | 55.2 |
| 1972 | 35.1 | 31.4 | 39.8 | 50.1 | 63.3 | 67.9 | 77.2 | 75.6 | 69.5 | 53.5 | 44.4 | 38.5 | 53.8 |
| 1973 | 35.5 | 32.5 | 46.4 | 53.4 | 59.5 | 73.4 | 77.4 | 77.6 | 69.5 | 60.2 | 48.3 | 39.0 | 56.1 |
| 1974 | 35.3 | 31.7 | 42.1 | 55.2 | 61.0 | 69.0 | 77.2 | 76.4 | 66.7 | 54.1 | 48.2 | 39.4 | 54.7 |
| 1975 | 37.3 | 35.8 | 40.2 | 47.9 | 65.9 | 70.5 | 75.8 | 74.4 | 64.2 | 59.2 | 52.3 | 35.9 | 54.9 |
| 1976 | 27.4 | 39.9 | 44.4 | 55.0 | 60.2 | 73.2 | 74.8 | 74.3 | 66.6 | 52.9 | 41.7 | 29.9 | 53.4 |
| 1977 | 22.1 | 33.5 | 46.8 | 53.7 | 65.0 | 70.2 | 79.0 | 75.7 | 68.2 | 54.9 | 47.3 | 35.7 | 54.3 |
| 1978 | 28.0 | 27.2 | 39.0 | 51.6 | 61.5 | 71.3 | 74.4 | 76.3 | 65.0 | 54.9 | 47.8 | 38.9 | 53.0 |
| 1979 | 33.6 | 25.5 | 46.9 | 52.6 | 65.3 | 69.2 | 76.9 | 76.8 | 70.5 | 57.3 | 52.5 | 41.1 | 55.7 |
| 1980 | 33.7 | 31.4 | 41.2 | 54.5 | 65.6 | 70.3 | 79.3 | 80.3 | 70.8 | 55.2 | 44.6 | 32.5 | 55.0 |
| 1981 | 26.3 | 39.3 | 42.3 | 56.2 | 64.8 | 73.0 | 78.5 | 76.0 | 67.6 | 54.4 | 47.7 | 36.5 | 55.2 |
| 1982 | 26.1 | 35.3 | 42.0 | 51.2 | 64.1 | 68.6 | 77.9 | 73.2 | 68.3 | 58.5 | 50.4 | 42.8 | 54.9 |
| 1983 | 34.5 | 36.4 | 44.0 | 52.3 | 60.2 | 73.4 | 79.5 | 77.7 | 71.8 | 57.9 | 49.9 | 35.2 | 56.0 |
| 1984 | 29.9 | 40.6 | 36.7 | 51.9 | 61.6 | 74.5 | 74.7 | 76.7 | 65.9 | 61.8 | 47.3 | 43.8 | 55.5 |
| 1985 | 28.8 | 36.6 | 45.8 | 55.5 | 65.3 | 68.6 | 76.2 | 75.4 | 70.5 | 59.5 | 50.0 | 34.2 | 55.5 |
| 1986 | 34.1 | 32.0 | 45.1 | 54.5 | 66.0 | 71.6 | 76.0 | 73.1 | 67.9 | 58.0 | 45.7 | 39.0 | 55.3 |
| 1987 | 32.3 | 33.2 | 45.2 | 53.4 | 63.6 | 72.8 | 78.0 | 74.2 | 67.7 | 53.8 | 47.7 | 39.5 | 55.1 |
| 1988 | 29.5 | 35.0 | 43.6 | 51.2 | 62.7 | 71.8 | 79.3 | 78.8 | 67.4 | 52.8 | 49.4 | 35.9 | 54.8 |
| 1989 | 37.4 | 34.5 | 42.4 | 52.2 | 62.1 | 72.0 | 75.0 | 74.0 | 68.1 | 58.2 | 45.7 | 25.9 | 54.0 |
| 1990 | 41.4 | 39.8 | 45.1 | 53.5 | 60.2 | 72.1 | 76.8 | 75.3 | 67.5 | 61.9 | 50.4 | 42.6 | 57.2 |
| Record Mean | 32.1 | 33.1 | 41.2 | 51.5 | 62.1 | 71.0 | 76.3 | 74.8 | 68.1 | 57.7 | 46.9 | 35.9 | 54.2 |
| Max | 38.4 | 39.9 | 48.7 | 59.9 | 71.1 | 79.7 | 84.8 | 83.0 | 76.3 | 65.6 | 53.4 | 41.9 | 61.9 |
| Min | 25.7 | 26.2 | 33.6 | 43.1 | 53.1 | 62.3 | 67.8 | 66.6 | 59.8 | 49.8 | 40.4 | 29.8 | 46.5 |

## REFERENCE NOTES FOR TABLES 1, 2, 3 and 6      (NEW YORK, NY)

### GENERAL

T - TRACE AMOUNT
BLANK ENTRIES DENOTE MISSING/UNREPORTED DATA.
# INDICATES A STATION OR INSTRUMENT RELOCATION.

### SPECIFIC

#### TABLE 1

(a) - LENGTH OF RECORD IN YEARS. ALTHOUGH
       INDIVIDUAL MONTHS MAY BE MISSING.
 *  LESS THAN .05

NORMALS — BASED ON THE 1951-1980 RECORD PERIOD.
EXTREMES — DATES ARE THE MOST RECENT OCCURRENCE.
WIND DIR. — NUMERALS SHOW TENS OF DEGREES
              CLOCKWISE FROM TRUE NORTH.
              "00" INDICATES CALM.
RESULTANT WIND DIRECTIONS ARE GIVEN TO WHOLE DEGREES.

#### TABLE 3
MAX AND MIN ARE LONG-TERM MEAN DAILY MAXIMUM
AND MEAN DAILY MINIMUM TEMPERATURES.

### EXCEPTIONS

#### TABLE 1

1. MEAN SKY COVER, AND DAYS CLEAR - PARTLY CLOUDY
   -CLOUDY ARE THROUGH 1966.
2. PERCENT OF POSSIBLE SUNSHINE, AND MEAN WIND
   SPEED ARE THROUGH 1976.
3. FASTEST MILE WINDS ARE THROUGH MARCH 1977 AND
   FEBRUARY 1980 THROUGH OCTOBER 1981.
4. RELATIVE HUMIDITY IS THROUGH 1980.
5. LIQUID PRECIPITATION FOR 1983 IS NOT CONSIDERED IN
   DETERMINING EXTREMES.

#### TABLES 2, 3, and 6

RECORD MEANS ARE THROUGH THE CURRENT YEAR,
BEGINNING IN     1912 FOR TEMPERATURE
                 1869 FOR PRECIPITATION
                 1869 FOR SNOWFALL

**TABLE 4**

HEATING DEGREE DAYS Base 65 deg. F    NEW YORK, CENTRAL PARK, NEW YORK

| SEASON | JULY | AUG | SEP | OCT | NOV | DEC | JAN | FEB | MAR | APR | MAY | JUNE | TOTAL |
|---|---|---|---|---|---|---|---|---|---|---|---|---|---|
| 1961-62 | 0 | 0 | 20 | 168 | 490 | 907 | 997 | 921 | 675 | 370 | 123 | 12 | 4683 |
| 1962-63 | 1 | 10 | 78 | 243 | 646 | 1032 | 1074 | 1021 | 653 | 337 | 161 | 9 | 5265 |
| 1963-64 | 0 | 0 | 125 | 134 | 431 | 1040 | 902 | 927 | 669 | 454 | 90 | 23 | 4795 |
| 1964-65 | 3 | 0 | 63 | 308 | 461 | 879 | 1088 | 867 | 765 | 426 | 64 | 30 | 4954 |
| 1965-66 | 0 | 13 | 54 | 239 | 538 | 755 | 1007 | 830 | 685 | 451 | 166 | 9 | 4747 |
| 1966-67 | 0 | 0 | 63 | 270 | 475 | 901 | 849 | 999 | 843 | 462 | 305 | 5 | 5172 |
| 1967-68 | 0 | 4 | 55 | 264 | 671 | 825 | 1179 | 1042 | 668 | 292 | 170 | 15 | 5185 |
| 1968-69 | 0 | 0 | 3 | 183 | 538 | 944 | 1023 | 902 | 768 | 285 | 74 | 0 | 4720 |
| 1969-70 | 0 | 0 | 28 | 240 | 551 | 974 | 1227 | 890 | 809 | 387 | 109 | 6 | 5221 |
| 1970-71 | 0 | 0 | 27 | 210 | 490 | 940 | 1173 | 830 | 764 | 419 | 135 | 9 | 4997 |
| 1971-72 | 0 | 0 | 14 | 106 | 596 | 743 | 920 | 965 | 775 | 445 | 94 | 26 | 4684 |
| 1972-73 | 2 | 0 | 25 | 355 | 611 | 812 | 907 | 903 | 572 | 362 | 188 | 2 | 4739 |
| 1973-74 | 0 | 0 | 29 | 162 | 493 | 800 | 913 | 925 | 704 | 309 | 165 | 27 | 4527 |
| 1974-75 | 1 | 0 | 59 | 333 | 502 | 789 | 852 | 812 | 764 | 507 | 86 | 11 | 4716 |
| 1975-76 | 0 | 3 | 62 | 193 | 387 | 898 | 1163 | 723 | 630 | 360 | 167 | 18 | 4604 |
| 1976-77 | 0 | 4 | 44 | 373 | 692 | 1082 | 1322 | 877 | 560 | 354 | 100 | 27 | 5435 |
| 1977-78 | 0 | 0 | 56 | 307 | 524 | 903 | 1140 | 1051 | 797 | 394 | 179 | 13 | 5364 |
| 1978-79 | 5 | 0 | 75 | 311 | 510 | 802 | 969 | 1100 | 554 | 369 | 55 | 14 | 4764 |
| 1979-80 | 4 | 4 | 20 | 271 | 373 | 734 | 963 | 969 | 731 | 310 | 67 | 22 | 4468 |
| 1980-81 | 0 | 0 | 31 | 305 | 602 | 1000 | 1194 | 715 | 698 | 264 | 78 | 3 | 4890 |
| 1981-82 | 0 | 0 | 48 | 320 | 513 | 876 | 1198 | 825 | 707 | 413 | 74 | 36 | 5010 |
| 1982-83 | 0 | 5 | 24 | 229 | 446 | 679 | 936 | 793 | 644 | 393 | 161 | 3 | 4313 |
| 1983-84 | 0 | 0 | 34 | 249 | 480 | 914 | 1082 | 698 | 870 | 389 | 137 | 9 | 4862 |
| 1984-85 | 0 | 0 | 69 | 114 | 525 | 654 | 1113 | 789 | 596 | 305 | 79 | 24 | 4268 |
| 1985-86 | 0 | 0 | 17 | 188 | 448 | 947 | 950 | 917 | 615 | 312 | 89 | 11 | 4494 |
| 1986-87 | 0 | 10 | 27 | 236 | 572 | 797 | 1008 | 883 | 608 | 348 | 146 | 8 | 4643 |
| 1987-88 | 0 | 2 | 29 | 343 | 512 | 780 | 1093 | 867 | 656 | 409 | 133 | 31 | 4855 |
| 1988-89 | 3 | 0 | 23 | 385 | 459 | 896 | 844 | 849 | 696 | 376 | 143 | 14 | 4688 |
| 1989-90 | 0 | 1 | 54 | 217 | 572 | 1205 | 724 | 702 | 612 | 366 | 150 | 4 | 4607 |
| 1990-91 | 3 | 2 | 57 | 166 | 436 | 686 | | | | | | | |

**TABLE 5**

COOLING DEGREE DAYS Base 65 deg. F    NEW YORK, CENTRAL PARK, NEW YORK

| YEAR | JAN | FEB | MAR | APR | MAY | JUNE | JULY | AUG | SEP | OCT | NOV | DEC | TOTAL |
|---|---|---|---|---|---|---|---|---|---|---|---|---|---|
| 1969 | 0 | 0 | 0 | 20 | 88 | 250 | 310 | 392 | 154 | 20 | 0 | 0 | 1234 |
| 1970 | 0 | 0 | 0 | 8 | 86 | 190 | 385 | 398 | 207 | 30 | 0 | 0 | 1304 |
| 1971 | 0 | 0 | 0 | 0 | 29 | 290 | 404 | 347 | 218 | 40 | 7 | 0 | 1335 |
| 1972 | 0 | 0 | 0 | 5 | 47 | 118 | 384 | 338 | 169 | 3 | 0 | 0 | 1064 |
| 1973 | 0 | 0 | 0 | 20 | 23 | 260 | 390 | 401 | 171 | 22 | 2 | 0 | 1289 |
| 1974 | 0 | 0 | 0 | 19 | 47 | 155 | 385 | 360 | 115 | 1 | 6 | 0 | 1088 |
| 1975 | 0 | 0 | 0 | 0 | 120 | 185 | 341 | 299 | 43 | 22 | 15 | 0 | 1025 |
| 1976 | 0 | 0 | 0 | 65 | 24 | 270 | 310 | 299 | 103 | 5 | 0 | 0 | 1076 |
| 1977 | 0 | 0 | 3 | 22 | 110 | 189 | 442 | 338 | 159 | 0 | 0 | 0 | 1263 |
| 1978 | 0 | 0 | 0 | 0 | 77 | 209 | 301 | 348 | 81 | 4 | 0 | 0 | 1020 |
| 1979 | 0 | 0 | 0 | 4 | 71 | 149 | 378 | 376 | 192 | 43 | 5 | 0 | 1218 |
| 1980 | 0 | 0 | 0 | 1 | 94 | 448 | 448 | 480 | 213 | 11 | 0 | 0 | 1435 |
| 1981 | 0 | 0 | 0 | 4 | 78 | 252 | 425 | 347 | 129 | 0 | 0 | 0 | 1235 |
| 1982 | 0 | 0 | 0 | 7 | 55 | 152 | 405 | 266 | 129 | 36 | 16 | 0 | 1066 |
| 1983 | 0 | 0 | 0 | 19 | 16 | 259 | 460 | 404 | 244 | 35 | 0 | 0 | 1437 |
| 1984 | 0 | 0 | 0 | 3 | 39 | 301 | 306 | 367 | 106 | 26 | 0 | 0 | 1148 |
| 1985 | 0 | 0 | 8 | 28 | 95 | 139 | 353 | 329 | 189 | 21 | 5 | 0 | 1167 |
| 1986 | 0 | 0 | 5 | 4 | 127 | 214 | 348 | 269 | 120 | 27 | 0 | 0 | 1114 |
| 1987 | 0 | 0 | 0 | 5 | 110 | 251 | 406 | 295 | 118 | 0 | 2 | 0 | 1187 |
| 1988 | 0 | 0 | 0 | 0 | 66 | 243 | 455 | 435 | 104 | 12 | 0 | 0 | 1315 |
| 1989 | 0 | 0 | 4 | 0 | 61 | 231 | 313 | 287 | 151 | 10 | 0 | 0 | 1057 |
| 1990 | 0 | 0 | 4 | 25 | 8 | 225 | 375 | 328 | 140 | 77 | 4 | 0 | 1186 |

**TABLE 6**

HEATING DEGREE DAYS Base 65 deg. F    NEW YORK, CENTRAL PARK, NEW YORK

| SEASON | JULY | AUG | SEP | OCT | NOV | DEC | JAN | FEB | MAR | APR | MAY | JUNE | TOTAL |
|---|---|---|---|---|---|---|---|---|---|---|---|---|---|
| 1961-62 | 0 | 0 | 20 | 168 | 490 | 907 | 997 | 921 | 675 | 370 | 123 | 12 | 4683 |
| 1962-63 | 1 | 10 | 78 | 243 | 646 | 1032 | 1074 | 1021 | 653 | 337 | 161 | 9 | 5265 |
| 1963-64 | 0 | 0 | 125 | 134 | 431 | 1040 | 902 | 927 | 669 | 454 | 90 | 23 | 4795 |
| 1964-65 | 3 | 0 | 63 | 308 | 461 | 879 | 1088 | 867 | 765 | 426 | 64 | 30 | 4954 |
| 1965-66 | 0 | 13 | 54 | 239 | 538 | 755 | 1007 | 830 | 685 | 451 | 166 | 9 | 4747 |
| 1966-67 | 0 | 0 | 63 | 270 | 475 | 901 | 849 | 999 | 843 | 462 | 305 | 5 | 5172 |
| 1967-68 | 0 | 4 | 55 | 264 | 671 | 825 | 1179 | 1042 | 668 | 292 | 170 | 15 | 5185 |
| 1968-69 | 0 | 0 | 3 | 183 | 538 | 944 | 1023 | 902 | 768 | 285 | 74 | 0 | 4720 |
| 1969-70 | 0 | 0 | 28 | 240 | 551 | 974 | 1227 | 890 | 809 | 387 | 109 | 6 | 5221 |
| 1970-71 | 0 | 0 | 27 | 210 | 490 | 940 | 1173 | 830 | 764 | 419 | 135 | 9 | 4997 |
| 1971-72 | 0 | 0 | 14 | 106 | 596 | 743 | 920 | 965 | 775 | 445 | 94 | 26 | 4684 |
| 1972-73 | 2 | 0 | 25 | 355 | 611 | 812 | 907 | 903 | 572 | 362 | 188 | 2 | 4739 |
| 1973-74 | 0 | 0 | 29 | 162 | 493 | 800 | 913 | 925 | 704 | 309 | 165 | 27 | 4527 |
| 1974-75 | 1 | 0 | 59 | 333 | 502 | 789 | 852 | 812 | 764 | 507 | 86 | 11 | 4716 |
| 1975-76 | 0 | 3 | 62 | 193 | 387 | 898 | 1163 | 723 | 630 | 360 | 167 | 18 | 4604 |
| 1976-77 | 0 | 4 | 44 | 373 | 692 | 1082 | 1322 | 877 | 560 | 354 | 100 | 27 | 5435 |
| 1977-78 | 0 | 0 | 56 | 307 | 524 | 903 | 1140 | 1051 | 797 | 394 | 179 | 13 | 5364 |
| 1978-79 | 5 | 0 | 75 | 311 | 510 | 802 | 969 | 1100 | 554 | 369 | 55 | 14 | 4764 |
| 1979-80 | 4 | 4 | 20 | 271 | 373 | 734 | 963 | 969 | 731 | 310 | 55 | 22 | 4468 |
| 1980-81 | 0 | 0 | 31 | 305 | 602 | 1000 | 1194 | 715 | 698 | 264 | 67 | 3 | 4890 |
| 1981-82 | 0 | 0 | 48 | 320 | 513 | 876 | 1198 | 825 | 707 | 413 | 74 | 36 | 5010 |
| 1982-83 | 0 | 5 | 24 | 229 | 446 | 679 | 936 | 793 | 644 | 393 | 161 | 3 | 4313 |
| 1983-84 | 0 | 0 | 34 | 249 | 480 | 914 | 1082 | 698 | 870 | 389 | 137 | 9 | 4862 |
| 1984-85 | 0 | 0 | 69 | 114 | 525 | 654 | 1113 | 789 | 596 | 305 | 79 | 24 | 4268 |
| 1985-86 | 0 | 0 | 17 | 188 | 448 | 947 | 950 | 917 | 615 | 312 | 89 | 11 | 4494 |
| 1986-87 | 0 | 10 | 27 | 236 | 572 | 797 | 1008 | 883 | 608 | 348 | 146 | 8 | 4643 |
| 1987-88 | 0 | 2 | 29 | 343 | 512 | 780 | 1093 | 867 | 656 | 409 | 133 | 31 | 4855 |
| 1988-89 | 3 | 0 | 23 | 385 | 459 | 896 | 844 | 849 | 696 | 376 | 143 | 14 | 4688 |
| 1989-90 | 0 | 1 | 54 | 217 | 572 | 1205 | 724 | 702 | 612 | 366 | 150 | 4 | 4607 |
| 1990-91 | 3 | 2 | 57 | 166 | 436 | 686 | | | | | | | |

**See Reference Notes, relative to all above tables, on preceding page.**

# ROCHESTER, NEW YORK

Rochester is located at the mouth of the Genesee River at about the mid point of the south shore of Lake Ontario. The river flows northward from northwest Pennsylvania and empties into Lake Ontario. The land slopes from a lakeshore elevation of 246 feet to over 1,000 feet some 20 miles south. The airport is located just south of the city.

Lake Ontario plays a major role in the Rochester weather. In the summer its cooling effect inhibits the temperature from rising much above the low to mid 90s. In the winter the modifying temperature effect prevents temperatures from falling below −15 degrees most of the time, although temperatures at locations more than 15 miles inland do drop below −30 degrees.

The lake plays a major role in winter snowfall distribution. Well inland from the lake and toward the airport, the seasonal snowfall is usually less than in the area north of the airport and toward the lakeshore where wide variations occur. This is due to what is called the lake effect. Snowfalls of one to two feet or more in 24 hours are common near the lake in winter due the lake effect alone. The lake rarely freezes over because of its depth. The area is also prone to other heavy snowstorms and blizzards because of its proximity to the paths of low pressure systems coming up the east coast, out of the Ohio Valley, or, to a lesser extent, from the Alberta area. The climate is favorable for winter sports activities with a continuous snow cover likely from December through March.

Moisture in the air from the lake enhances the climatic conditions for fruit growing. Apples, peaches, pears, cantaloupes, plums, cherries, and grapes are grown abundantly in Greater Rochester and the Western Finger Lakes Region.

Precipitation is rather evenly distributed throughout the year. Excessive rains occur infrequently but may be caused by slowly moving thunderstorms, slowly moving or stalled major low pressure systems, or by hurricanes and tropical storms that move inland. Hail occurs occasionally and heavy fog is rare.

The growing season averages 150 to 180 days. The years first frost usually occurs in late September and the last frost typically occurs in mid−May.

668

# TABLE 1  NORMALS, MEANS AND EXTREMES

ROCHESTER, NEW YORK

LATITUDE: 43°07'N  LONGITUDE: 77°40'W  ELEVATION: FT. GRND 547 BARO 547  TIME ZONE: EASTERN  WBAN: 14768

| | (a) | JAN | FEB | MAR | APR | MAY | JUNE | JULY | AUG | SEP | OCT | NOV | DEC | YEAR |
|---|---|---|---|---|---|---|---|---|---|---|---|---|---|---|
| **TEMPERATURE °F:** | | | | | | | | | | | | | | |
| Normals | | | | | | | | | | | | | | |
| -Daily Maximum | | 30.8 | 32.2 | 41.2 | 56.0 | 67.7 | 77.7 | 82.3 | 80.1 | 72.8 | 61.5 | 48.0 | 35.5 | 57.2 |
| -Daily Minimum | | 16.3 | 16.7 | 25.3 | 36.1 | 46.0 | 55.7 | 60.3 | 58.7 | 51.6 | 41.8 | 33.2 | 22.3 | 38.7 |
| -Monthly | | 23.6 | 24.4 | 33.3 | 46.0 | 56.9 | 66.7 | 71.3 | 69.5 | 62.2 | 51.7 | 40.6 | 29.0 | 47.9 |
| Extremes | | | | | | | | | | | | | | |
| -Record Highest | 49 | 74 | 67 | 84 | 93 | 94 | 100 | 98 | 99 | 99 | 91 | 81 | 72 | 100 |
| -Year | | 1950 | 1947 | 1945 | 1970 | 1987 | 1953 | 1988 | 1948 | 1953 | 1951 | 1950 | 1982 | JUN 1953 |
| -Record Lowest | 49 | -16 | -19 | -6 | 13 | 26 | 35 | 42 | 36 | 28 | 20 | 5 | -16 | -19 |
| -Year | | 1957 | 1979 | 1980 | 1982 | 1979 | 1949 | 1963 | 1965 | 1947 | 1972 | 1971 | 1942 | FEB 1979 |
| **NORMAL DEGREE DAYS:** | | | | | | | | | | | | | | |
| Heating (base 65°F) | | 1283 | 1137 | 983 | 570 | 274 | 41 | 10 | 23 | 132 | 412 | 732 | 1116 | 6713 |
| Cooling (base 65°F) | | 0 | 0 | 0 | 0 | 23 | 92 | 205 | 163 | 48 | 0 | 0 | 0 | 531 |
| **% OF POSSIBLE SUNSHINE** | 49 | 36 | 41 | 49 | 54 | 59 | 66 | 69 | 66 | 59 | 48 | 30 | 30 | 51 |
| **MEAN SKY COVER (tenths)** | | | | | | | | | | | | | | |
| Sunrise - Sunset | 49 | 8.2 | 7.9 | 7.3 | 6.7 | 6.6 | 6.0 | 5.7 | 6.0 | 6.1 | 6.7 | 8.2 | 8.4 | 7.0 |
| **MEAN NUMBER OF DAYS:** | | | | | | | | | | | | | | |
| Sunrise to Sunset | | | | | | | | | | | | | | |
| -Clear | 49 | 2.0 | 2.3 | 4.4 | 6.3 | 6.0 | 7.2 | 8.1 | 7.7 | 7.1 | 6.5 | 2.1 | 1.9 | 61.8 |
| -Partly Cloudy | 49 | 6.9 | 6.7 | 8.3 | 7.9 | 9.7 | 10.9 | 12.6 | 11.7 | 10.6 | 8.3 | 6.2 | 5.6 | 105.5 |
| -Cloudy | 49 | 22.1 | 19.2 | 18.2 | 15.8 | 15.3 | 11.9 | 10.4 | 11.6 | 12.3 | 16.1 | 21.6 | 23.4 | 198.0 |
| Precipitation | | | | | | | | | | | | | | |
| .01 inches or more | 49 | 17.4 | 15.8 | 14.6 | 13.3 | 11.9 | 10.7 | 9.5 | 10.0 | 10.6 | 11.7 | 15.0 | 17.6 | 158.1 |
| Snow,Ice pellets | | | | | | | | | | | | | | |
| 1.0 inches or more | 49 | 7.3 | 7.0 | 4.0 | 1.0 | 0.1 | 0.0 | 0.0 | 0.0 | 0.0 | 0.* | 1.9 | 6.2 | 27.6 |
| Thunderstorms | 49 | 0.1 | 0.1 | 0.9 | 2.0 | 3.6 | 5.3 | 6.2 | 5.7 | 3.1 | 1.0 | 0.4 | 0.2 | 28.7 |
| Heavy Fog Visibility 1/4 mile or less | 49 | 0.9 | 0.6 | 1.4 | 1.0 | 1.2 | 1.1 | 0.6 | 0.8 | 1.3 | 1.7 | 0.7 | 1.0 | 12.4 |
| Temperature °F | | | | | | | | | | | | | | |
| -Maximum | | | | | | | | | | | | | | |
| 90° and above | 26 | 0.0 | 0.0 | 0.0 | 0.* | 0.3 | 1.7 | 4.5 | 2.2 | 0.6 | 0.0 | 0.0 | 0.0 | 9.4 |
| 32° and below | 26 | 17.2 | 14.7 | 6.4 | 0.5 | 0.0 | 0.0 | 0.0 | 0.0 | 0.0 | 0.0 | 1.7 | 10.9 | 51.5 |
| -Minimum | | | | | | | | | | | | | | |
| 32° and below | 26 | 28.7 | 25.5 | 23.1 | 11.1 | 1.1 | 0.0 | 0.0 | 0.0 | 0.* | 4.3 | 14.9 | 25.7 | 134.4 |
| 0° and below | 26 | 3.2 | 2.1 | 0.2 | 0.0 | 0.0 | 0.0 | 0.0 | 0.0 | 0.0 | 0.0 | 0.0 | 0.8 | 6.3 |
| **AVG. STATION PRESS.(mb)** | 17 | 996.1 | 997.5 | 995.9 | 994.5 | 994.6 | 994.7 | 995.7 | 997.0 | 997.8 | 998.3 | 996.8 | 996.9 | 996.3 |
| **RELATIVE HUMIDITY (%)** | | | | | | | | | | | | | | |
| Hour 01 | 26 | 76 | 77 | 76 | 76 | 78 | 82 | 83 | 86 | 87 | 82 | 80 | 80 | 80 |
| Hour 07 | 26 | 77 | 79 | 78 | 77 | 77 | 80 | 82 | 87 | 89 | 85 | 82 | 81 | 81 |
| Hour 13 (Local Time) | 26 | 69 | 67 | 62 | 55 | 54 | 56 | 54 | 57 | 61 | 61 | 68 | 73 | 61 |
| Hour 19 | 26 | 74 | 73 | 69 | 61 | 60 | 61 | 60 | 67 | 75 | 75 | 77 | 78 | 69 |
| **PRECIPITATION (inches):** | | | | | | | | | | | | | | |
| Water Equivalent | | | | | | | | | | | | | | |
| -Normal | | 2.30 | 2.32 | 2.53 | 2.64 | 2.58 | 2.78 | 2.48 | 3.20 | 2.66 | 2.54 | 2.65 | 2.59 | 31.27 |
| -Maximum Monthly | 49 | 5.79 | 5.07 | 5.42 | 4.90 | 6.62 | 6.77 | 9.70 | 6.00 | 6.30 | 7.85 | 6.99 | 5.05 | 9.70 |
| -Year | | 1978 | 1950 | 1942 | 1944 | 1974 | 1980 | 1947 | 1984 | 1977 | 1955 | 1985 | 1944 | JUL 1947 |
| -Minimum Monthly | 49 | 0.72 | 0.66 | 0.47 | 1.28 | 0.36 | 0.22 | 0.98 | 0.76 | 0.28 | 0.23 | 0.44 | 0.62 | 0.22 |
| -Year | | 1988 | 1987 | 1958 | 1971 | 1977 | 1963 | 1989 | 1951 | 1960 | 1963 | 1976 | 1958 | JUN 1963 |
| -Maximum in 24 hrs | 49 | 1.64 | 2.43 | 2.21 | 1.99 | 3.85 | 2.86 | 3.25 | 2.39 | 3.54 | 2.98 | 3.13 | 1.60 | 3.85 |
| -Year | | 1966 | 1950 | 1942 | 1943 | 1974 | 1950 | 1987 | 1968 | 1979 | 1980 | 1945 | 1978 | MAY 1974 |
| Snow,Ice pellets | | | | | | | | | | | | | | |
| -Maximum Monthly | 49 | 60.4 | 64.8 | 40.3 | 20.2 | 10.9 | 0.0 | 0.0 | T | T | 1.4 | 17.6 | 46.1 | 64.8 |
| -Year | | 1978 | 1958 | 1959 | 1979 | 1989 | | | 1965 | 1956 | 1960 | 1983 | 1981 | FEB 1958 |
| -Maximum in 24 hrs | 49 | 18.2 | 22.8 | 17.6 | 8.3 | 10.8 | 0.0 | 0.0 | T | T | 1.4 | 11.2 | 19.1 | 22.8 |
| -Year | | 1966 | 1978 | 1959 | 1979 | 1989 | | | 1965 | 1956 | 1960 | 1953 | 1978 | FEB 1978 |
| **WIND:** | | | | | | | | | | | | | | |
| Mean Speed (mph) | 49 | 11.7 | 11.3 | 11.1 | 10.8 | 9.3 | 8.5 | 7.9 | 7.6 | 8.0 | 8.7 | 10.2 | 10.8 | 9.7 |
| Prevailing Direction through 1963 | | WSW | WSW | WSW | WSW | WSW | SW | SW | SW | SW | SW | WSW | WSW | WSW |
| Fastest Mile | | | | | | | | | | | | | | |
| -Direction (!!!) | 45 | W | W | W | SW | SW | SW | W | NE | SW | NW | E | W | W |
| -Speed (MPH) | 45 | 73 | 66 | 65 | 60 | 63 | 61 | 56 | 59 | 59 | 50 | 59 | 56 | 73 |
| -Year | | 1950 | 1956 | 1956 | 1979 | 1950 | 1949 | 1956 | 1955 | 1949 | 1941 | 1950 | 1949 | JAN 1950 |
| Peak Gust | | | | | | | | | | | | | | |
| -Direction (!!!) | 6 | W | SW | W | SW | NW | N | NW | W | W | N | SW | SW | W |
| -Speed (mph) | 6 | 63 | 52 | 67 | 67 | 43 | 52 | 45 | 62 | 44 | 51 | 66 | 51 | 67 |
| -Date | | 1988 | 1988 | 1986 | 1984 | 1987 | 1988 | 1988 | 1986 | 1984 | 1989 | 1988 | 1985 | MAR 1986 |

**See Reference Notes to this table on the following page.**

PRECIPITATION (inches)   ROCHESTER, NEW YORK

**TABLE 2**

| YEAR | JAN | FEB | MAR | APR | MAY | JUNE | JULY | AUG | SEP | OCT | NOV | DEC | ANNUAL |
|---|---|---|---|---|---|---|---|---|---|---|---|---|---|
| 1961 | 1.10 | 3.21 | 2.70 | 4.07 | 2.96 | 3.78 | 2.41 | 3.09 | 0.39 | 1.58 | 3.99 | 1.23 | 30.51 |
| 1962 | 1.84 | 2.87 | 1.25 | 2.62 | 2.70 | 3.02 | 1.89 | 3.53 | 4.01 | 1.99 | 1.95 | 1.58 | 29.25 |
| 1963 | 1.24 | 1.43 | 2.53 | 2.74 | 2.33 | 0.22 | 2.72 | 3.26 | 1.17 | 0.23 | 4.32 | 1.90 | 24.09 |
| 1964 | 1.99 | 0.89 | 2.89 | 3.54 | 2.77 | 1.13 | 1.52 | 2.74 | 0.58 | 0.76 | 1.60 | 2.04 | 22.45 |
| 1965 | 3.05 | 2.24 | 2.07 | 1.85 | 0.50 | 0.64 | 1.46 | 2.94 | 1.98 | 2.82 | 3.40 | 2.21 | 25.16 |
| 1966 | 4.10 | 2.51 | 1.42 | 2.04 | 1.26 | 1.85 | 2.77 | 2.14 | 2.47 | 0.68 | 3.12 | 1.75 | 26.11 |
| 1967 | 0.94 | 1.67 | 1.31 | 1.69 | 2.74 | 1.57 | 2.68 | 4.64 | 3.84 | 4.35 | 2.89 | 1.52 | 29.84 |
| 1968 | 1.91 | 0.74 | 1.33 | 2.84 | 2.84 | 1.42 | 5.95 | 1.86 | 2.89 | 4.28 | 3.31 |  | 31.75 |
| 1969 | 2.46 | 0.91 | 1.16 | 3.48 | 2.25 | 4.69 | 1.83 | 1.82 | 1.77 | 1.69 | 3.42 | 3.66 | 29.14 |
| 1970 | 1.80 | 2.28 | 1.49 | 2.58 | 3.03 | 3.74 | 4.91 | 3.88 | 2.49 | 3.96 | 3.50 | 4.12 | 37.78 |
| 1971 | 2.66 | 4.21 | 3.43 | 1.28 | 1.71 | 3.52 | 5.59 | 3.18 | 1.79 | 1.34 | 1.96 | 3.49 | 34.16 |
| 1972 | 1.50 | 3.96 | 2.19 | 2.68 | 3.32 | 6.56 | 1.43 | 3.14 | 3.84 | 2.25 | 4.83 | 2.58 | 38.28 |
| 1973 | 1.28 | 1.70 | 2.92 | 3.21 | 2.68 | 2.84 | 1.14 | 1.94 | 1.41 | 2.67 | 3.82 | 3.62 | 29.23 |
| 1974 | 1.75 | 2.06 | 3.61 | 2.60 | 6.62 | 2.59 | 2.82 | 3.64 | 3.48 | 1.34 | 3.23 | 2.86 | 36.60 |
| 1975 | 1.83 | 2.82 | 2.74 | 1.43 | 2.85 | 5.35 | 1.18 | 2.31 | 3.15 | 1.83 | 1.35 | 3.76 | 30.60 |
| 1976 | 2.33 | 1.67 | 3.54 | 3.81 | 2.63 | 3.37 | 5.15 | 3.04 | 2.13 | 4.73 | 0.44 | 1.48 | 34.32 |
| 1977 | 1.49 | 0.97 | 2.18 | 2.49 | 0.36 | 1.33 | 3.26 | 5.65 | 6.30 | 2.64 | 3.78 | 4.65 | 35.10 |
| 1978 | 5.79 | 2.40 | 1.48 | 2.25 | 2.03 | 1.30 | 2.17 | 2.66 | 3.63 | 2.56 | 1.14 | 4.35 | 31.76 |
| 1979 | 4.18 | 2.40 | 1.76 | 3.78 | 3.14 | 1.85 | 3.16 | 2.05 | 5.32 | 2.60 | 1.80 | 2.86 | 34.90 |
| 1980 | 1.11 | 1.16 | 3.83 | 2.35 | 1.49 | 6.77 | 1.90 | 3.44 | 3.57 | 3.73 | 2.52 | 2.45 | 34.32 |
| 1981 | 1.24 | 3.13 | 1.04 | 1.95 | 2.27 | 2.70 | 4.60 | 4.44 | 5.37 | 3.29 | 2.18 | 2.78 | 34.99 |
| 1982 | 4.16 | 1.01 | 1.73 | 1.63 | 1.77 | 3.92 | 3.13 | 3.00 | 3.57 | 1.79 | 3.95 | 2.17 | 31.83 |
| 1983 | 1.43 | 1.23 | 2.45 | 3.50 | 3.44 | 2.40 | 1.13 | 5.43 | 1.56 | 4.91 | 4.47 |  | 35.21 |
| 1984 | 1.62 | 2.97 | 2.08 | 3.05 | 5.47 | 1.67 | 1.90 | 6.00 | 3.34 | 0.76 | 1.47 | 3.31 | 33.64 |
| 1985 | 2.49 | 1.78 | 3.47 | 1.30 | 2.08 | 2.63 | 1.86 | 1.11 | 2.49 | 2.34 | 6.99 | 1.46 | 30.00 |
| 1986 | 1.63 | 2.46 | 1.90 | 3.80 | 1.64 | 4.27 | 3.13 | 3.29 | 5.11 | 3.56 | 1.93 | 3.56 | 36.28 |
| 1987 | 1.89 | 0.66 | 1.98 | 3.68 | 1.19 | 3.94 | 5.85 | 3.92 | 4.60 | 1.65 | 2.74 | 1.98 | 34.08 |
| 1988 | 0.72 | 2.18 | 1.62 | 2.32 | 1.73 | 1.10 | 4.30 | 3.81 | 1.69 | 2.34 | 1.68 | 1.11 | 24.60 |
| 1989 | 1.18 | 1.55 | 3.69 | 1.62 | 5.99 | 5.65 | 0.98 | 2.46 | 2.82 | 3.13 | 2.01 | 1.58 | 32.66 |
| 1990 | 1.61 | 3.93 | 1.56 | 3.58 | 5.76 | 2.88 | 3.05 | 3.59 | 3.36 | 4.37 | 2.27 | 4.18 | 40.14 |
| Record Mean | 2.45 | 2.37 | 2.60 | 2.59 | 2.91 | 3.00 | 3.07 | 2.90 | 2.77 | 2.75 | 2.69 | 2.59 | 32.69 |

**TABLE 3**   AVERAGE TEMPERATURE (deg. F)   ROCHESTER, NEW YORK

| YEAR | JAN | FEB | MAR | APR | MAY | JUNE | JULY | AUG | SEP | OCT | NOV | DEC | ANNUAL |
|---|---|---|---|---|---|---|---|---|---|---|---|---|---|
| 1961 | 19.4 | 27.5 | 34.3 | 41.7 | 53.9 | 65.4 | 70.8 | 69.9 | 68.5 | 55.5 | 40.6 | 29.6 | 48.1 |
| 1962 | 22.9 | 21.4 | 33.5 | 45.7 | 62.4 | 66.0 | 67.6 | 68.9 | 58.9 | 51.8 | 36.9 | 26.0 | 46.8 |
| #1963 | 19.3 | 17.9 | 35.7 | 46.2 | 54.3 | 67.1 | 70.9 | 65.5 | 56.7 | 57.3 | 44.3 | 21.7 | 46.4 |
| 1964 | 28.3 | 24.0 | 34.4 | 47.2 | 60.3 | 65.8 | 73.8 | 66.2 | 61.2 | 48.7 | 42.3 | 29.6 | 48.5 |
| 1965 | 21.6 | 25.7 | 29.5 | 41.3 | 60.1 | 64.4 | 67.5 | 68.4 | 63.8 | 48.8 | 39.8 | 34.6 | 47.1 |
| 1966 | 22.6 | 25.5 | 36.6 | 44.4 | 53.0 | 67.8 | 73.0 | 68.9 | 59.2 | 50.1 | 43.5 | 30.8 | 48.0 |
| 1967 | 31.1 | 21.4 | 32.5 | 46.4 | 49.1 | 70.4 | 69.4 | 67.6 | 60.4 | 52.1 | 36.3 | 32.3 | 47.4 |
| 1968 | 19.8 | 20.8 | 36.0 | 49.5 | 53.2 | 64.7 | 70.7 | 69.4 | 64.8 | 53.8 | 41.2 | 27.7 | 47.6 |
| 1969 | 25.2 | 26.0 | 32.0 | 47.6 | 55.6 | 65.0 | 70.7 | 72.0 | 63.6 | 50.9 | 40.1 | 25.1 | 47.8 |
| 1970 | 18.0 | 23.7 | 30.8 | 48.4 | 59.5 | 68.1 | 72.2 | 70.1 | 63.0 | 53.9 | 41.4 | 25.5 | 47.9 |
| 1971 | 19.5 | 26.9 | 28.5 | 41.1 | 54.0 | 65.4 | 68.8 | 68.8 | 67.4 | 59.0 | 38.4 | 30.9 | 47.6 |
| 1972 | 26.0 | 23.4 | 30.3 | 42.2 | 60.4 | 65.2 | 73.0 | 69.8 | 64.3 | 47.6 | 37.0 | 33.1 | 47.7 |
| 1973 | 28.7 | 22.2 | 42.5 | 48.0 | 56.1 | 70.7 | 73.4 | 73.0 | 62.5 | 55.0 | 43.0 | 31.2 | 50.5 |
| 1974 | 27.1 | 22.5 | 33.0 | 49.4 | 53.9 | 65.7 | 71.3 | 70.6 | 59.2 | 47.6 | 39.5 | 31.4 | 47.6 |
| 1975 | 29.5 | 28.4 | 31.6 | 39.3 | 63.2 | 67.1 | 73.0 | 70.0 | 58.4 | 53.1 | 47.2 | 27.8 | 49.0 |
| 1976 | 19.8 | 33.3 | 37.2 | 48.6 | 55.4 | 69.8 | 69.2 | 68.4 | 60.9 | 47.5 | 35.4 | 23.6 | 47.4 |
| 1977 | 15.5 | 25.4 | 39.8 | 47.9 | 60.7 | 64.8 | 72.9 | 68.7 | 62.7 | 49.4 | 43.6 | 28.4 | 48.3 |
| 1978 | 22.9 | 16.2 | 29.7 | 43.6 | 60.2 | 67.4 | 72.6 | 71.6 | 62.4 | 51.0 | 41.0 | 30.0 | 47.4 |
| 1979 | 21.5 | 13.7 | 38.6 | 44.0 | 56.4 | 66.2 | 72.3 | 67.1 | 61.3 | 50.3 | 43.0 | 32.3 | 47.2 |
| 1980 | 24.0 | 19.7 | 32.4 | 47.8 | 60.0 | 63.1 | 72.9 | 74.3 | 63.7 | 48.8 | 38.8 | 24.7 | 47.5 |
| 1981 | 15.7 | 32.3 | 34.5 | 48.0 | 57.2 | 67.3 | 71.9 | 69.4 | 59.8 | 47.3 | 39.9 | 28.7 | 47.7 |
| 1982 | 16.1 | 23.0 | 33.5 | 43.2 | 60.9 | 63.6 | 72.0 | 66.1 | 62.8 | 52.7 | 43.4 | 37.4 | 47.9 |
| 1983 | 27.4 | 29.1 | 37.2 | 43.9 | 53.8 | 66.7 | 73.8 | 70.7 | 63.9 | 52.0 | 40.7 | 25.1 | 48.8 |
| 1984 | 20.4 | 33.2 | 26.5 | 47.5 | 52.6 | 66.8 | 69.2 | 72.0 | 60.6 | 54.9 | 40.7 | 35.9 | 48.4 |
| 1985 | 21.9 | 25.6 | 36.7 | 49.6 | 58.6 | 61.7 | 68.8 | 68.7 | 63.8 | 51.0 | 41.4 | 25.0 | 47.7 |
| 1986 | 25.0 | 24.5 | 37.0 | 47.9 | 59.8 | 63.3 | 69.8 | 65.7 | 59.8 | 49.9 | 36.9 | 31.7 | 47.6 |
| 1987 | 25.3 | 23.6 | 37.1 | 49.7 | 59.9 | 67.9 | 72.7 | 67.3 | 61.6 | 47.1 | 40.6 | 32.6 | 48.8 |
| 1988 | 25.0 | 23.7 | 34.7 | 45.0 | 58.7 | 64.2 | 73.7 | 71.1 | 60.1 | 45.8 | 42.6 | 29.4 | 47.8 |
| 1989 | 30.3 | 22.5 | 32.3 | 42.1 | 56.3 | 67.4 | 72.8 | 68.5 | 61.7 | 52.6 | 38.1 | 17.1 | 46.8 |
| 1990 | 33.6 | 29.3 | 37.3 | 48.8 | 54.4 | 67.2 | 70.7 | 69.9 | 60.7 | 52.1 | 42.4 | 33.8 | 50.0 |
| Record Mean | 24.7 | 24.6 | 32.9 | 45.1 | 56.8 | 66.4 | 71.4 | 69.3 | 62.5 | 51.4 | 39.9 | 29.0 | 47.8 |
| Max | 31.6 | 31.9 | 40.6 | 54.1 | 66.7 | 76.6 | 81.3 | 78.9 | 72.1 | 60.2 | 46.7 | 35.2 | 56.3 |
| Min | 17.7 | 17.2 | 25.2 | 36.1 | 46.8 | 56.3 | 61.4 | 59.7 | 52.9 | 42.5 | 33.0 | 22.7 | 39.3 |

## REFERENCE NOTES FOR TABLES 1, 2, 3 and 6   (ROCHESTER, NY)

### GENERAL

T - TRACE AMOUNT
BLANK ENTRIES DENOTE MISSING/UNREPORTED DATA.
# INDICATES A STATION OR INSTRUMENT RELOCATION.

### SPECIFIC

#### TABLE 1

(a) - LENGTH OF RECORD IN YEARS. ALTHOUGH INDIVIDUAL MONTHS MAY BE MISSING.

* LESS THAN .05

NORMALS — BASED ON THE 1951-1980 RECORD PERIOD.
EXTREMES — DATES ARE THE MOST RECENT OCCURRENCE.
WIND DIR. — NUMERALS SHOW TENS OF DEGREES CLOCKWISE FROM TRUE NORTH. "00" INDICATES CALM.
RESULTANT WIND DIRECTIONS ARE GIVEN TO WHOLE DEGREES.

#### TABLE 3

MAX AND MIN ARE LONG-TERM MEAN DAILY MAXIMUM AND MEAN DAILY MINIMUM TEMPERATURES.

### EXCEPTIONS

#### TABLES 2, 3, and 6

RECORD MEANS ARE THROUGH THE CURRENT YEAR, BEGINNING IN  1872 FOR TEMPERATURE
1829 FOR PRECIPITATION
1941 FOR SNOWFALL

**TABLE 4**  HEATING DEGREE DAYS Base 65 deg. F    ROCHESTER, NEW YORK

| SEASON | JULY | AUG | SEP | OCT | NOV | DEC | JAN | FEB | MAR | APR | MAY | JUNE | TOTAL |
|---|---|---|---|---|---|---|---|---|---|---|---|---|---|
| 1961-62 | 28 | 21 | 82 | 302 | 728 | 1092 | 1296 | 1215 | 969 | 589 | 181 | 52 | 6555 |
| #1962-63 | 10 | 21 | 209 | 409 | 836 | 1202 | 1412 | 1309 | 902 | 556 | 332 | 51 | 7249 |
| 1963-64 | 24 | 52 | 253 | 247 | 615 | 1335 | 1132 | 1181 | 939 | 526 | 187 | 98 | 6589 |
| 1964-65 | 3 | 48 | 169 | 500 | 674 | 1090 | 1337 | 1096 | 1095 | 706 | 192 | 114 | 7024 |
| 1965-66 | 24 | 53 | 122 | 496 | 748 | 937 | 1307 | 1098 | 871 | 612 | 382 | 57 | 6707 |
| 1966-67 | 0 | 16 | 190 | 458 | 639 | 1053 | 1046 | 1216 | 998 | 551 | 486 | 8 | 6661 |
| 1967-68 | 25 | 28 | 164 | 401 | 856 | 1005 | 1399 | 1275 | 894 | 463 | 357 | 78 | 6945 |
| 1968-69 | 15 | 36 | 67 | 369 | 710 | 1150 | 1229 | 1087 | 1013 | 517 | 302 | 86 | 6581 |
| 1969-70 | 18 | 10 | 126 | 437 | 737 | 1231 | 1448 | 1149 | 1053 | 506 | 209 | 49 | 6973 |
| 1970-71 | 3 | 11 | 126 | 349 | 699 | 1218 | 1405 | 1059 | 1122 | 707 | 342 | 49 | 7090 |
| 1971-72 | 17 | 33 | 74 | 194 | 792 | 1048 | 1200 | 1199 | 1071 | 677 | 161 | 78 | 6544 |
| 1972-73 | 7 | 24 | 92 | 534 | 833 | 982 | 1118 | 1189 | 690 | 519 | 279 | 17 | 6284 |
| 1973-74 | 2 | 14 | 162 | 305 | 653 | 1040 | 1167 | 1187 | 983 | 475 | 352 | 59 | 6399 |
| 1974-75 | 1 | 1 | 209 | 535 | 755 | 1034 | 1096 | 1017 | 1031 | 764 | 139 | 52 | 6634 |
| 1975-76 | 4 | 14 | 194 | 365 | 525 | 1146 | 1395 | 914 | 858 | 507 | 300 | 35 | 6257 |
| 1976-77 | 11 | 27 | 173 | 538 | 879 | 1279 | 1524 | 1103 | 777 | 523 | 204 | 89 | 7127 |
| 1977-78 | 9 | 44 | 113 | 477 | 634 | 1127 | 1298 | 1360 | 1087 | 634 | 220 | 63 | 7066 |
| 1978-79 | 5 | 1 | 136 | 428 | 711 | 1077 | 1342 | 1432 | 813 | 626 | 310 | 79 | 6960 |
| 1979-80 | 13 | 37 | 155 | 468 | 655 | 1006 | 1264 | 1306 | 1003 | 510 | 195 | 125 | 6737 |
| 1980-81 | 1 | 0 | 108 | 498 | 782 | 1243 | 1522 | 908 | 938 | 507 | 260 | 26 | 6793 |
| 1981-82 | 6 | 12 | 201 | 546 | 748 | 1119 | 1510 | 1171 | 972 | 648 | 162 | 67 | 7162 |
| 1982-83 | 10 | 54 | 113 | 377 | 643 | 847 | 1161 | 998 | 854 | 627 | 347 | 78 | 6109 |
| 1983-84 | 2 | 8 | 121 | 387 | 723 | 1228 | 1376 | 917 | 1187 | 520 | 395 | 50 | 6921 |
| 1984-85 | 14 | 7 | 162 | 307 | 724 | 897 | 1330 | 1097 | 869 | 471 | 217 | 119 | 6214 |
| 1985-86 | 15 | 23 | 121 | 429 | 700 | 1231 | 1235 | 1129 | 864 | 506 | 206 | 100 | 6559 |
| 1986-87 | 16 | 62 | 175 | 462 | 840 | 1026 | 1223 | 1153 | 858 | 454 | 234 | 39 | 6542 |
| 1987-88 | 7 | 50 | 139 | 547 | 722 | 997 | 1232 | 1192 | 933 | 594 | 220 | 126 | 6759 |
| 1988-89 | 6 | 40 | 164 | 596 | 664 | 1095 | 1070 | 1184 | 1009 | 682 | 288 | 33 | 6831 |
| 1989-90 | 0 | 33 | 149 | 383 | 801 | 1478 | 967 | 993 | 853 | 520 | 327 | 46 | 6550 |
| 1990-91 | 7 | 6 | 171 | 406 | 669 | 959 | | | | | | | |

**TABLE 5**  COOLING DEGREE DAYS Base 65 deg. F    ROCHESTER, NEW YORK

| YEAR | JAN | FEB | MAR | APR | MAY | JUNE | JULY | AUG | SEP | OCT | NOV | DEC | TOTAL |
|---|---|---|---|---|---|---|---|---|---|---|---|---|---|
| 1969 | 0 | 0 | 0 | 0 | 18 | 94 | 202 | 233 | 92 | 7 | 0 | 0 | 646 |
| 1970 | 0 | 0 | 0 | 16 | 47 | 148 | 235 | 176 | 69 | 13 | 0 | 0 | 704 |
| 1971 | 0 | 0 | 0 | 0 | 10 | 133 | 143 | 159 | 155 | 15 | 0 | 0 | 615 |
| 1972 | 0 | 0 | 0 | 0 | 24 | 94 | 261 | 179 | 79 | 0 | 0 | 0 | 637 |
| 1973 | 0 | 0 | 0 | 15 | 6 | 194 | 267 | 269 | 96 | 4 | 0 | 0 | 851 |
| 1974 | 0 | 0 | 0 | 13 | 14 | 88 | 204 | 181 | 40 | 0 | 0 | 0 | 540 |
| 1975 | 0 | 0 | 0 | 0 | 89 | 121 | 257 | 178 | 5 | 6 | 0 | 0 | 656 |
| 1976 | 0 | 0 | 0 | 24 | 9 | 189 | 150 | 138 | 55 | 1 | 0 | 0 | 566 |
| 1977 | 0 | 0 | 3 | 16 | 80 | 88 | 260 | 164 | 50 | 0 | 1 | 0 | 662 |
| 1978 | 0 | 0 | 0 | 0 | 77 | 141 | 245 | 212 | 66 | 3 | 0 | 0 | 744 |
| 1979 | 0 | 0 | 0 | 1 | 52 | 121 | 244 | 112 | 49 | 18 | 0 | 0 | 597 |
| 1980 | 0 | 0 | 0 | 0 | 46 | 73 | 253 | 294 | 76 | 2 | 0 | 0 | 744 |
| 1981 | 0 | 0 | 0 | 5 | 23 | 102 | 228 | 156 | 50 | 0 | 0 | 0 | 564 |
| 1982 | 0 | 0 | 0 | 3 | 40 | 30 | 232 | 95 | 52 | 3 | 1 | 0 | 456 |
| 1983 | 0 | 0 | 0 | 0 | 7 | 136 | 289 | 192 | 96 | 20 | 0 | 0 | 740 |
| 1984 | 0 | 0 | 0 | 1 | 14 | 113 | 152 | 233 | 35 | 1 | 0 | 0 | 549 |
| 1985 | 0 | 0 | 0 | 15 | 23 | 27 | 139 | 145 | 90 | 0 | 0 | 0 | 439 |
| 1986 | 0 | 0 | 1 | 0 | 50 | 53 | 168 | 94 | 28 | 0 | 0 | 0 | 394 |
| 1987 | 0 | 0 | 0 | 1 | 82 | 131 | 254 | 127 | 42 | 0 | 0 | 0 | 637 |
| 1988 | 0 | 0 | 0 | 0 | 34 | 107 | 284 | 232 | 29 | 7 | 0 | 0 | 693 |
| 1989 | 0 | 0 | 0 | 0 | 26 | 111 | 248 | 153 | 60 | 3 | 0 | 0 | 601 |
| 1990 | 0 | 0 | 3 | 41 | 5 | 122 | 192 | 164 | 45 | 14 | 0 | 0 | 586 |

**TABLE 6**  SNOWFALL (inches)    ROCHESTER, NEW YORK

| SEASON | JULY | AUG | SEP | OCT | NOV | DEC | JAN | FEB | MAR | APR | MAY | JUNE | TOTAL |
|---|---|---|---|---|---|---|---|---|---|---|---|---|---|
| 1961-62 | 0.0 | 0.0 | 0.0 | 0.0 | 7.5 | 6.0 | 11.7 | 28.2 | 4.6 | 7.6 | T | 0.0 | 65.6 |
| 1962-63 | 0.0 | 0.0 | 0.0 | 0.8 | 6.0 | 14.2 | 23.7 | 22.9 | 6.7 | 1.1 | 1.0 | 0.0 | 76.4 |
| 1963-64 | 0.0 | 0.0 | 0.0 | 0.0 | 4.4 | 34.6 | 20.2 | 13.1 | 16.1 | 3.6 | 0.0 | 0.0 | 92.0 |
| 1964-65 | 0.0 | 0.0 | 0.0 | T | 5.1 | 11.6 | 26.6 | 10.3 | 15.6 | 1.9 | 0.0 | 0.0 | 71.1 |
| 1965-66 | 0.0 | T | 0.0 | 0.9 | 8.0 | 6.0 | 60.2 | 21.0 | 6.2 | 0.9 | T | 0.0 | 103.2 |
| 1966-67 | 0.0 | 0.0 | 0.0 | 0.0 | 3.0 | 14.4 | 12.7 | 27.6 | 16.0 | T | 0.3 | 0.0 | 74.0 |
| 1967-68 | 0.0 | 0.0 | 0.0 | T | 10.0 | 6.9 | 24.2 | 20.4 | 15.2 | T | 0.0 | 0.0 | 76.7 |
| 1968-69 | 0.0 | 0.0 | 0.0 | T | 8.6 | 22.2 | 25.6 | 17.8 | 4.6 | 1.0 | 0.0 | 0.0 | 79.8 |
| 1969-70 | 0.0 | 0.0 | 0.0 | T | 5.8 | 42.0 | 37.9 | 27.7 | 4.9 | 1.3 | T | 0.0 | 119.6 |
| 1970-71 | 0.0 | 0.0 | 0.0 | 0.2 | 3.6 | 44.2 | 34.1 | 29.7 | 29.7 | 1.2 | 0.0 | 0.0 | 142.7 |
| 1971-72 | 0.0 | 0.0 | 0.0 | 0.0 | 11.2 | 13.8 | 18.1 | 35.7 | 19.0 | 7.3 | 0.0 | 0.0 | 105.1 |
| 1972-73 | 0.0 | 0.0 | 0.0 | 0.2 | 16.9 | 22.7 | 8.9 | 18.4 | 4.4 | 1.5 | T | 0.0 | 73.0 |
| 1973-74 | 0.0 | 0.0 | 0.0 | 0.0 | 4.2 | 23.4 | 14.4 | 26.6 | 22.3 | 8.2 | T | 0.0 | 99.1 |
| 1974-75 | 0.0 | 0.0 | 0.0 | 0.3 | 4.6 | 26.5 | 10.8 | 23.2 | 10.9 | 14.9 | 0.0 | 0.0 | 91.2 |
| 1975-76 | 0.0 | 0.0 | 0.0 | T | 1.8 | 28.3 | 29.9 | 8.8 | 15.2 | 1.8 | 0.4 | 0.0 | 86.2 |
| 1976-77 | 0.0 | 0.0 | 0.0 | 0.5 | 6.5 | 24.5 | 30.2 | 15.0 | 13.0 | 1.8 | 0.6 | 0.0 | 92.1 |
| 1977-78 | 0.0 | 0.0 | 0.0 | T | 12.7 | 35.2 | 60.4 | 40.7 | 7.5 | 4.2 | 0.2 | 0.0 | 160.9 |
| 1978-79 | 0.0 | 0.0 | 0.0 | T | 3.3 | 30.9 | 36.8 | 39.1 | 8.2 | 20.2 | 0.0 | 0.0 | 138.5 |
| 1979-80 | 0.0 | 0.0 | 0.0 | 0.2 | 1.2 | 12.2 | 13.1 | 24.0 | 21.2 | 0.3 | 0.0 | 0.0 | 72.2 |
| 1980-81 | 0.0 | 0.0 | 0.0 | T | 8.4 | 31.8 | 31.5 | 9.3 | 12.0 | 1.4 | 0.0 | 0.0 | 94.4 |
| 1981-82 | 0.0 | 0.0 | 0.0 | 0.1 | 2.4 | 46.1 | 43.6 | 14.9 | 8.9 | 12.4 | 0.0 | 0.0 | 128.4 |
| 1982-83 | 0.0 | 0.0 | 0.0 | T | 3.0 | 11.6 | 10.2 | 13.6 | 9.3 | 12.2 | T | 0.0 | 59.9 |
| 1983-84 | 0.0 | 0.0 | 0.0 | 0.0 | 17.6 | 19.6 | 23.4 | 27.8 | 29.1 | 0.5 | T | 0.0 | 118.0 |
| 1984-85 | 0.0 | 0.0 | 0.0 | 0.0 | 1.6 | 11.6 | 36.8 | 26.1 | 8.4 | 2.6 | 0.0 | 0.0 | 87.1 |
| 1985-86 | 0.0 | 0.0 | 0.0 | 0.0 | 7.6 | 18.3 | 15.5 | 17.9 | 9.3 | 2.1 | T | 0.0 | 70.7 |
| 1986-87 | 0.0 | 0.0 | 0.0 | 0.0 | 7.4 | 9.3 | 29.6 | 13.0 | 5.3 | 2.5 | 0.0 | 0.0 | 67.1 |
| 1987-88 | 0.0 | 0.0 | 0.0 | T | 4.6 | 19.3 | 9.8 | 29.4 | 5.6 | 1.1 | 0.0 | 0.0 | 69.8 |
| 1988-89 | 0.0 | 0.0 | 0.0 | 0.1 | 0.2 | 10.3 | 15.0 | 30.6 | 15.6 | 3.9 | 10.9 | 0.0 | 86.6 |
| 1989-90 | 0.0 | 0.0 | 0.0 | 0.1 | 6.5 | 32.8 | 14.0 | 31.3 | 5.4 | 15.8 | T | 0.0 | 105.8 |
| 1990-91 | T | 0.0 | 0.0 | T | 4.4 | 18.2 | | | | | | | |
| Record Mean | T | T | T | 0.1 | 6.5 | 19.4 | 22.7 | 22.6 | 13.7 | 3.7 | 0.3 | 0.0 | 88.9 |

**See Reference Notes, relative to all above tables, on preceding page.**

Syracuse is located approximately at the geographical center of the state. Gently rolling terrain stretches northward for about 30 miles to the eastern end of Lake Ontario. Oneida Lake is about 8 miles northeast of Syracuse. Approximately 5 miles south of the city, hills rise to 1,500 feet. Immediately to the west, the terrain is gently rolling with elevations 500 to 800 feet above sea level.

The climate of Syracuse is primarily continental in character and comparatively humid. Nearly all cyclonic systems moving from the interior of the country through the St. Lawrence Valley will affect the Syracuse area. Seasonal and diurnal changes are marked and produce an invigorating climate.

In the summer and in portions of the transitional seasons, temperatures usually rise rapidly during the daytime to moderate levels and as a rule fall rapidly after sunset. The nights are relatively cool and comfortable. There are only a few days in a year when atmospheric humidity causes great personal discomfort.

Winters are usually cold and are sometimes severe in part. Daytime temperatures average in the low 30s with nighttime lows in the teens. Low winter temperatures below −25 degrees have been recorded. The autumn, winter, and spring seasons display marked variability.

Based on the 1951–1980 period, the average first occurrence of 32 degrees Fahrenheit in the fall is October 16 and the average last occurrence in the spring is April 28.

Precipitation in the Syracuse area is derived principally from cyclonic storms which pass from the interior of the country through the St. Lawrence Valley. Lake Ontario provides the source of significant winter precipitation. The lake is quite deep and never freezes so cold air flowing over the lake is quickly saturated and produces the cloudiness and snow squalls which are a well-known feature of winter weather in the Syracuse area.

The area enjoys sufficient precipitation in most years to meet the needs of agriculture and water supplies. The precipitation is uncommonly well distributed, averaging about 3 inches per month throughout the year. Snowfall is moderately heavy with an average just over 100 inches. There are about 30 days per year with thunderstorms, mostly during the warmer months.

Wind velocities are moderate, but during the winter months there are numerous days with sufficient winds to cause blowing and drifting snow.

During December, January, and February there is much cloudiness. Syracuse receives only about one-third of possible sunshine during winter months. Approximately two-thirds of possible sunshine is received during the warm months.

## TABLE 1 — NORMALS, MEANS AND EXTREMES

SYRACUSE, NEW YORK

LATITUDE: 43°07'N  LONGITUDE: 76°07'W  ELEVATION: FT. GRND 410 BARO 420  TIME ZONE: EASTERN  WBAN: 14771

| | (a) | JAN | FEB | MAR | APR | MAY | JUNE | JULY | AUG | SEP | OCT | NOV | DEC | YEAR |
|---|---|---|---|---|---|---|---|---|---|---|---|---|---|---|
| **TEMPERATURE °F:** | | | | | | | | | | | | | | |
| Normals | | | | | | | | | | | | | | |
| -Daily Maximum | | 30.6 | 32.2 | 41.4 | 56.2 | 67.9 | 77.2 | 81.6 | 79.6 | 72.3 | 60.9 | 47.9 | 35.3 | 56.9 |
| -Daily Minimum | | 15.0 | 15.8 | 25.2 | 36.0 | 46.0 | 55.4 | 60.3 | 58.9 | 51.8 | 41.7 | 33.3 | 21.3 | 38.4 |
| -Monthly | | 22.8 | 24.0 | 33.3 | 46.1 | 57.0 | 66.3 | 70.9 | 69.3 | 62.1 | 51.3 | 40.6 | 28.3 | 47.7 |
| Extremes | | | | | | | | | | | | | | |
| -Record Highest | 40 | 70 | 69 | 87 | 89 | 96 | 98 | 97 | 97 | 97 | 87 | 81 | 70 | 98 |
| -Year | | 1967 | 1981 | 1986 | 1962 | 1977 | 1953 | 1988 | 1987 | 1953 | 1963 | 1950 | 1966 | JUN 1953 |
| -Record Lowest | 40 | -26 | -26 | -16 | 9 | 25 | 35 | 45 | 40 | 28 | 19 | 5 | -22 | -26 |
| -Year | | 1966 | 1979 | 1950 | 1972 | 1966 | 1966 | 1976 | 1965 | 1965 | 1976 | 1976 | 1980 | FEB 1979 |
| **NORMAL DEGREE DAYS:** | | | | | | | | | | | | | | |
| Heating (base 65°F) | | 1308 | 1148 | 983 | 567 | 269 | 47 | 12 | 25 | 133 | 425 | 732 | 1138 | 6787 |
| Cooling (base 65°F) | | 0 | 0 | 0 | 0 | 21 | 86 | 195 | 158 | 46 | 0 | 0 | 0 | 506 |
| **% OF POSSIBLE SUNSHINE** | 40 | 34 | 39 | 46 | 50 | 54 | 59 | 64 | 59 | 53 | 44 | 26 | 25 | 46 |
| **MEAN SKY COVER (tenths)** | | | | | | | | | | | | | | |
| Sunrise - Sunset | 40 | 8.1 | 7.9 | 7.4 | 6.8 | 6.6 | 6.2 | 5.9 | 6.2 | 6.3 | 6.8 | 8.3 | 8.4 | 7.1 |
| **MEAN NUMBER OF DAYS:** | | | | | | | | | | | | | | |
| Sunrise to Sunset | | | | | | | | | | | | | | |
| -Clear | 40 | 2.7 | 3.0 | 4.7 | 6.4 | 6.0 | 7.2 | 7.8 | 6.9 | 6.8 | 6.5 | 2.2 | 2.3 | 62.5 |
| -Partly Cloudy | 40 | 6.7 | 5.9 | 6.9 | 6.7 | 9.8 | 10.4 | 12.3 | 11.4 | 10.2 | 7.8 | 5.4 | 4.8 | 98.4 |
| -Cloudy | 40 | 21.7 | 19.3 | 19.4 | 17.0 | 15.1 | 12.4 | 10.8 | 12.7 | 12.9 | 16.7 | 22.4 | 23.9 | 204.4 |
| Precipitation | | | | | | | | | | | | | | |
| .01 inches or more | 40 | 18.8 | 15.9 | 16.7 | 14.1 | 12.9 | 11.3 | 10.8 | 11.0 | 11.1 | 12.2 | 16.3 | 19.2 | 170.3 |
| Snow, Ice pellets | | | | | | | | | | | | | | |
| 1.0 inches or more | 40 | 8.6 | 7.6 | 4.9 | 1.3 | 0.1 | 0.0 | 0.0 | 0.0 | 0.0 | 0.3 | 2.8 | 7.8 | 33.3 |
| Thunderstorms | 40 | 0.2 | 0.2 | 0.8 | 1.8 | 3.2 | 5.4 | 6.2 | 5.5 | 2.5 | 1.0 | 0.6 | 0.1 | 27.4 |
| Heavy Fog Visibility | | | | | | | | | | | | | | |
| 1/4 mile or less | 40 | 0.6 | 0.6 | 0.8 | 0.6 | 0.7 | 0.6 | 0.5 | 0.7 | 0.9 | 1.2 | 0.6 | 0.7 | 8.5 |
| Temperature °F | | | | | | | | | | | | | | |
| -Maximum | | | | | | | | | | | | | | |
| 90° and above | 26 | 0.0 | 0.0 | 0.0 | 0.0 | 0.4 | 1.3 | 3.8 | 1.8 | 0.3 | 0.0 | 0.0 | 0.0 | 7.5 |
| 32° and below | 26 | 17.4 | 14.7 | 5.8 | 0.3 | 0.0 | 0.0 | 0.0 | 0.0 | 0.0 | 0.0 | 1.6 | 11.6 | 51.5 |
| -Minimum | | | | | | | | | | | | | | |
| 32° and below | 26 | 28.8 | 25.4 | 23.7 | 12.0 | 1.0 | 0.0 | 0.0 | 0.0 | 0.1 | 5.2 | 14.6 | 26.2 | 136.9 |
| 0° and below | 26 | 4.8 | 2.8 | 0.7 | 0.0 | 0.0 | 0.0 | 0.0 | 0.0 | 0.0 | 0.0 | 0.0 | 1.6 | 10.0 |
| **AVG. STATION PRESS. (mb)** | 17 | 1001.6 | 1002.8 | 1001.2 | 999.5 | 999.7 | 999.7 | 1000.5 | 1002.0 | 1003.0 | 1003.6 | 1002.2 | 1002.4 | 1001.5 |
| **RELATIVE HUMIDITY (%)** | | | | | | | | | | | | | | |
| Hour 01 | 26 | 76 | 76 | 76 | 75 | 78 | 83 | 84 | 87 | 86 | 83 | 80 | 79 | 80 |
| Hour 07 | 26 | 77 | 78 | 78 | 76 | 77 | 79 | 81 | 87 | 88 | 85 | 81 | 80 | 81 |
| Hour 13 (Local Time) | 26 | 68 | 65 | 60 | 53 | 55 | 57 | 56 | 59 | 62 | 61 | 68 | 71 | 61 |
| Hour 19 | 26 | 74 | 72 | 67 | 59 | 60 | 63 | 63 | 70 | 76 | 75 | 76 | 78 | 69 |
| **PRECIPITATION (inches):** | | | | | | | | | | | | | | |
| Water Equivalent | | | | | | | | | | | | | | |
| -Normal | | 2.61 | 2.65 | 3.11 | 3.34 | 3.16 | 3.63 | 3.76 | 3.77 | 3.29 | 3.14 | 3.45 | 3.20 | 39.11 |
| -Maximum Monthly | 40 | 5.77 | 5.38 | 6.84 | 8.12 | 7.41 | 12.30 | 9.52 | 8.41 | 8.81 | 8.29 | 6.79 | 5.50 | 12.30 |
| -Year | | 1978 | 1951 | 1955 | 1976 | 1976 | 1972 | 1974 | 1956 | 1975 | 1955 | 1972 | 1983 | JUN 1972 |
| -Minimum Monthly | 40 | 1.02 | 0.63 | 1.01 | 1.22 | 0.75 | 1.10 | 0.90 | 1.33 | 0.75 | 0.21 | 1.25 | 1.73 | 0.21 |
| -Year | | 1970 | 1987 | 1981 | 1985 | 1977 | 1962 | 1969 | 1980 | 1964 | 1963 | 1978 | 1958 | OCT 1963 |
| -Maximum in 24 hrs | 40 | 1.47 | 1.99 | 1.34 | 2.85 | 3.13 | 3.88 | 4.07 | 4.27 | 4.14 | 3.60 | 2.09 | 2.18 | 4.27 |
| -Year | | 1958 | 1961 | 1974 | 1976 | 1969 | 1972 | 1974 | 1954 | 1975 | 1955 | 1967 | 1952 | AUG 1954 |
| Snow, Ice pellets | | | | | | | | | | | | | | |
| -Maximum Monthly | 40 | 72.2 | 72.6 | 40.3 | 16.4 | 1.2 | 0.0 | 0.0 | 0.0 | T | 5.7 | 25.9 | 64.6 | 72.6 |
| -Year | | 1978 | 1958 | 1984 | 1983 | 1973 | | | | 1989 | 1988 | 1976 | 1989 | FEB 1958 |
| -Maximum in 24 hrs | 40 | 24.5 | 21.4 | 14.7 | 7.1 | 1.2 | 0.0 | 0.0 | 0.0 | T | 2.9 | 12.1 | 16.7 | 24.5 |
| -Year | | 1966 | 1961 | 1971 | 1975 | 1973 | | | | 1989 | 1988 | 1973 | 1989 | JAN 1966 |
| **WIND:** | | | | | | | | | | | | | | |
| Mean Speed (mph) | 40 | 10.9 | 10.8 | 10.9 | 10.6 | 9.1 | 8.4 | 8.0 | 7.8 | 8.3 | 8.8 | 10.2 | 10.4 | 9.5 |
| Prevailing Direction through 1963 | | WSW | WNW | WNW | WNW | WNW | WNW | WNW | WSW | S | WSW | WSW | WSW | WNW |
| Fastest Mile | | | | | | | | | | | | | | |
| -Direction (!!!) | 40 | W | W | SE | NW | NW | NW | NW | NW | W | SE | E | W | SE |
| -Speed (MPH) | 40 | 60 | 62 | 56 | 52 | 50 | 49 | 47 | 43 | 52 | 63 | 59 | 52 | 63 |
| -Year | | 1974 | 1967 | 1956 | 1957 | 1964 | 1961 | 1982 | 1958 | 1962 | 1954 | 1950 | 1962 | OCT 1954 |
| Peak Gust | | | | | | | | | | | | | | |
| -Direction (!!!) | 6 | W | SW | SW | W | W | SE | NW | W | W | W | W | W | SE |
| -Speed (mph) | 6 | 51 | 56 | 54 | 61 | 49 | 67 | 53 | 46 | 48 | 43 | 54 | 52 | 67 |
| -Date | | 1985 | 1985 | 1986 | 1985 | 1985 | 1989 | 1985 | 1987 | 1989 | 1986 | 1989 | 1985 | JUN 1989 |

**See Reference Notes to this table on the following page.**

PRECIPITATION (inches)    SYRACUSE, NEW YORK

**TABLE 2**

| YEAR | JAN | FEB | MAR | APR | MAY | JUNE | JULY | AUG | SEP | OCT | NOV | DEC | ANNUAL |
|---|---|---|---|---|---|---|---|---|---|---|---|---|---|
| 1961 | 2.30 | 4.14 | 4.22 | 3.74 | 2.40 | 3.68 | 5.08 | 1.78 | 1.21 | 3.59 | 2.99 | 2.45 | 37.58 |
| 1962 | 2.87 | 2.96 | 1.96 | 3.57 | 1.05 | 1.10 | 2.74 | 4.63 | 1.99 | 3.30 | 2.22 | 2.25 | 30.64 |
| 1963 | 1.85 | 2.05 | 2.79 | 2.22 | 2.84 | 2.49 | 1.21 | 3.59 | 0.85 | 0.21 | 5.65 | 2.06 | 27.81 |
| 1964 | 2.18 | 1.13 | 3.83 | 3.66 | 2.31 | 1.41 | 2.15 | 3.09 | 0.75 | 1.52 | 2.20 | 2.87 | 27.10 |
| 1965 | 2.28 | 2.82 | 1.63 | 3.53 | 1.61 | 2.04 | 1.34 | 1.95 | 3.60 | 2.70 | 2.97 | 1.92 | 28.39 |
| 1966 | 3.98 | 2.96 | 2.27 | 3.05 | 1.79 | 2.73 | 2.09 | 2.64 | 4.75 | 0.90 | 2.05 | 3.93 | 33.14 |
| 1967 | 1.47 | 1.49 | 1.34 | 2.11 | 3.33 | 1.56 | 6.33 | 5.00 | 2.73 | 3.52 | 4.48 | 2.66 | 36.02 |
| 1968 | 2.08 | 1.10 | 3.13 | 2.40 | 3.46 | 6.14 | 3.77 | 4.17 | 3.43 | 5.81 | 4.07 | 4.67 | 44.23 |
| 1969 | 3.37 | 1.49 | 1.08 | 3.95 | 4.34 | 3.74 | 0.90 | 1.77 | 1.13 | 2.30 | 4.56 | 3.42 | 32.05 |
| 1970 | 1.02 | 1.84 | 2.45 | 3.68 | 2.79 | 2.93 | 4.42 | 4.07 | 4.33 | 3.84 | 3.53 | 3.33 | 38.23 |
| 1971 | 1.90 | 4.07 | 2.90 | 2.19 | 3.40 | 3.26 | 6.49 | 4.01 | 2.56 | 1.62 | 3.52 | 3.95 | 39.18 |
| 1972 | 1.10 | 2.87 | 2.49 | 4.03 | 6.19 | 12.30 | 3.45 | 3.76 | 4.12 | 4.36 | 6.79 | 4.38 | 55.41 |
| 1973 | 1.85 | 1.71 | 3.45 | 6.91 | 5.58 | 7.07 | 3.62 | 2.97 | 4.57 | 3.81 | 6.73 | 3.47 | 52.65 |
| 1974 | 2.08 | 1.70 | 4.34 | 5.78 | 4.67 | 9.52 | 4.60 | 4.45 | 1.58 | 4.95 | 3.47 |  | 50.23 |
| 1975 | 2.54 | 3.05 | 2.67 | 2.01 | 2.74 | 4.08 | 9.32 | 5.35 | 8.81 | 3.69 | 3.54 | 4.10 | 51.90 |
| 1976 | 2.79 | 2.71 | 4.62 | 8.12 | 7.41 | 7.42 | 5.24 | 6.73 | 3.27 | 6.53 | 1.53 | 1.80 | 58.17 |
| 1977 | 1.84 | 1.62 | 3.47 | 3.04 | 0.75 | 3.30 | 4.76 | 4.93 | 6.54 | 4.75 | 5.31 | 4.33 | 44.64 |
| 1978 | 5.77 | 0.80 | 3.08 | 1.87 | 1.90 | 3.58 | 2.78 | 3.31 | 3.93 | 2.68 | 1.25 | 4.12 | 35.07 |
| 1979 | 4.70 | 2.54 | 2.73 | 3.89 | 3.07 | 2.33 | 2.33 | 3.69 | 5.25 | 2.91 | 3.25 | 1.84 | 38.53 |
| 1980 | 1.47 | 1.38 | 4.34 | 3.33 | 1.34 | 4.45 | 2.57 | 1.40 | 3.40 | 2.56 | 2.64 | 3.27 | 32.08 |
| 1981 | 1.34 | 2.72 | 1.01 | 2.04 | 2.61 | 1.89 | 2.68 | 2.63 | 5.58 | 6.66 | 3.09 | 2.96 | 35.21 |
| 1982 | 3.59 | 1.26 | 2.63 | 1.71 | 2.87 | 4.64 | 3.83 | 2.60 | 4.22 | 0.72 | 4.52 | 2.55 | 35.14 |
| 1983 | 1.92 | 1.07 | 2.30 | 6.34 | 3.33 | 1.50 | 2.31 | 2.80 | 2.98 | 1.98 | 4.30 | 5.50 | 36.33 |
| 1984 | 1.30 | 2.88 | 2.39 | 3.16 | 4.97 | 2.02 | 3.66 | 5.17 | 2.61 | 1.95 | 3.48 | 4.38 | 37.97 |
| 1985 | 2.49 | 1.55 | 2.61 | 1.22 | 3.39 | 2.80 | 2.75 | 1.44 | 3.88 | 3.39 | 5.18 | 1.80 | 32.50 |
| 1986 | 2.41 | 2.27 | 2.82 | 3.42 | 2.67 | 4.89 | 5.23 | 3.36 | 5.47 | 3.32 | 3.74 | 3.33 | 42.93 |
| 1987 | 3.03 | 0.63 | 1.86 | 3.31 | 1.41 | 5.04 | 2.16 | 2.12 | 5.99 | 3.13 | 3.02 | 1.99 | 33.69 |
| 1988 | 1.50 | 2.13 | 1.79 | 2.70 | 3.05 | 2.46 | 5.72 | 3.77 | 1.88 | 3.57 | 3.95 | 1.92 | 34.44 |
| 1989 | 1.06 | 1.71 | 3.13 | 1.52 | 4.27 | 5.41 | 2.20 | 2.68 | 5.96 | 4.08 | 2.78 | 2.13 | 36.93 |
| 1990 | 2.13 | 3.95 | 3.70 | 4.09 | 5.62 | 2.92 | 3.72 | 5.33 | 3.45 | 6.09 | 3.23 | 5.24 | 49.47 |
| Record Mean | 2.66 | 2.49 | 3.05 | 3.08 | 3.04 | 3.59 | 3.47 | 3.33 | 3.16 | 3.09 | 3.02 | 2.96 | 36.94 |

**TABLE 3**  AVERAGE TEMPERATURE (deg. F)    SYRACUSE, NEW YORK

| YEAR | JAN | FEB | MAR | APR | MAY | JUNE | JULY | AUG | SEP | OCT | NOV | DEC | ANNUAL |
|---|---|---|---|---|---|---|---|---|---|---|---|---|---|
| 1961 | 18.8 | 25.9 | 33.2 | 42.9 | 55.5 | 66.6 | 71.8 | 70.4 | 69.5 | 55.8 | 40.7 | 29.1 | 48.3 |
| 1962 | 24.1 | 21.5 | 34.6 | 47.3 | 62.3 | 68.3 | 69.2 | 69.1 | 59.7 | 51.2 | 35.5 | 24.5 | 47.3 |
| #1963 | 20.8 | 18.4 | 34.2 | 45.6 | 54.7 | 66.6 | 71.7 | 66.1 | 57.2 | 56.3 | 44.9 | 20.8 | 46.4 |
| 1964 | 25.9 | 23.7 | 35.1 | 46.5 | 61.6 | 66.0 | 73.2 | 67.5 | 61.6 | 49.5 | 43.6 | 29.6 | 48.6 |
| 1965 | 20.5 | 24.6 | 30.3 | 42.3 | 59.4 | 63.7 | 67.5 | 69.1 | 62.8 | 47.9 | 38.7 | 32.1 | 46.6 |
| 1966 | 19.0 | 23.1 | 34.4 | 42.6 | 51.2 | 65.5 | 71.1 | 70.4 | 59.5 | 42.9 | 29.2 |  | 46.6 |
| 1967 | 30.6 | 19.2 | 31.6 | 44.9 | 50.2 | 69.5 | 67.7 | 66.6 | 60.7 | 51.8 | 37.6 | 32.7 | 46.9 |
| 1968 | 18.5 | 21.1 | 33.2 | 48.1 | 53.6 | 64.9 | 69.9 | 68.8 | 64.8 | 52.5 | 40.0 | 27.2 | 46.9 |
| 1969 | 24.3 | 23.6 | 30.4 | 46.9 | 55.7 | 64.5 | 69.9 | 71.3 | 63.8 | 51.1 | 40.4 | 23.8 | 47.1 |
| 1970 | 16.1 | 24.1 | 31.7 | 47.2 | 57.5 | 63.5 | 69.7 | 68.0 | 61.4 | 52.3 | 41.7 | 25.4 | 46.5 |
| 1971 | 18.5 | 26.5 | 31.2 | 42.8 | 55.8 | 67.9 | 69.0 | 67.1 | 65.6 | 56.6 | 36.9 | 33.2 | 47.6 |
| 1972 | 26.4 | 22.9 | 29.4 | 40.5 | 58.5 | 64.5 | 72.9 | 69.2 | 63.5 | 46.5 | 37.0 | 30.8 | 46.9 |
| 1973 | 28.4 | 21.4 | 42.6 | 46.8 | 54.3 | 69.6 | 72.7 | 73.5 | 62.0 | 53.7 | 40.7 | 29.5 | 49.6 |
| 1974 | 26.0 | 21.6 | 32.3 | 48.8 | 54.1 | 65.6 | 69.1 | 68.9 | 59.1 | 46.5 | 40.6 | 30.4 | 46.9 |
| 1975 | 29.4 | 28.1 | 31.7 | 39.9 | 62.9 | 67.1 | 71.7 | 68.2 | 57.1 | 53.2 | 46.6 | 27.6 | 48.6 |
| 1976 | 18.1 | 32.5 | 36.6 | 48.4 | 54.2 | 67.9 | 66.7 | 66.0 | 59.8 | 46.9 | 35.8 | 22.6 | 46.3 |
| 1977 | 15.7 | 26.0 | 40.1 | 48.2 | 60.3 | 62.7 | 70.8 | 67.3 | 62.5 | 50.6 | 44.0 | 27.3 | 48.0 |
| 1978 | 21.3 | 17.6 | 29.4 | 42.2 | 58.3 | 64.8 | 71.9 | 71.7 | 59.9 | 49.9 | 40.3 | 30.6 | 46.4 |
| 1979 | 22.4 | 12.9 | 39.1 | 45.1 | 58.6 | 66.0 | 71.7 | 67.9 | 61.4 | 50.9 | 44.5 | 33.4 | 47.8 |
| 1980 | 25.6 | 19.8 | 32.4 | 47.8 | 59.8 | 63.0 | 72.5 | 73.8 | 63.4 | 48.8 | 37.6 | 22.6 | 47.3 |
| 1981 | 15.0 | 33.7 | 36.4 | 50.0 | 59.2 | 68.0 | 73.3 | 70.4 | 61.6 | 47.9 | 39.0 | 29.0 | 48.6 |
| 1982 | 14.8 | 25.1 | 33.2 | 43.9 | 59.4 | 63.1 | 70.4 | 65.3 | 60.6 | 50.4 | 43.9 | 34.1 | 47.0 |
| 1983 | 23.4 | 26.4 | 35.7 | 44.3 | 53.7 | 66.7 | 72.0 | 69.0 | 62.5 | 50.3 | 39.0 | 22.5 | 47.1 |
| 1984 | 18.7 | 32.0 | 24.5 | 46.0 | 52.4 | 65.4 | 68.0 | 68.8 | 57.7 | 52.2 | 38.3 | 33.5 | 46.5 |
| 1985 | 22.0 | 27.3 | 36.3 | 47.8 | 59.5 | 62.0 | 69.8 | 68.9 | 63.5 | 51.4 | 41.2 | 26.0 | 48.0 |
| 1986 | 23.9 | 23.4 | 37.4 | 49.2 | 61.0 | 64.3 | 71.0 | 66.8 | 60.5 | 49.7 | 36.8 | 31.6 | 48.0 |
| 1987 | 23.8 | 21.7 | 38.0 | 51.9 | 60.3 | 68.3 | 73.6 | 68.5 | 61.1 | 47.7 | 40.9 | 32.3 | 49.0 |
| 1988 | 23.1 | 24.6 | 34.4 | 45.7 | 59.7 | 64.7 | 74.0 | 71.8 | 60.8 | 46.6 | 43.0 | 27.8 | 48.0 |
| 1989 | 28.6 | 22.7 | 32.9 | 43.5 | 58.2 | 67.3 | 71.1 | 68.2 | 61.8 | 51.7 | 38.8 | 14.7 | 46.6 |
| 1990 | 33.2 | 29.0 | 37.5 | 49.3 | 54.5 | 67.3 | 71.8 | 70.3 | 61.2 | 52.8 | 42.2 | 33.5 | 50.2 |
| Record Mean | 23.8 | 24.2 | 33.5 | 45.6 | 57.1 | 66.1 | 71.2 | 69.1 | 62.1 | 51.3 | 40.2 | 28.1 | 47.7 |
| Max | 31.6 | 32.2 | 41.7 | 54.9 | 67.3 | 76.3 | 81.2 | 78.9 | 71.8 | 60.3 | 47.3 | 35.0 | 56.5 |
| Min | 16.0 | 16.1 | 25.4 | 36.2 | 46.8 | 55.9 | 61.1 | 59.3 | 52.4 | 42.2 | 33.1 | 21.3 | 38.8 |

## REFERENCE NOTES FOR TABLES 1, 2, 3 and 6    (SYRACUSE, NY)

### GENERAL

T - TRACE AMOUNT
BLANK ENTRIES DENOTE MISSING/UNREPORTED DATA.
# INDICATES A STATION OR INSTRUMENT RELOCATION.

### SPECIFIC

#### TABLE 1

(a) - LENGTH OF RECORD IN YEARS. ALTHOUGH INDIVIDUAL MONTHS MAY BE MISSING.

* LESS THAN .05

NORMALS — BASED ON THE 1951-1980 RECORD PERIOD.
EXTREMES — DATES ARE THE MOST RECENT OCCURRENCE.
WIND DIR. — NUMERALS SHOW TENS OF DEGREES CLOCKWISE FROM TRUE NORTH.
"00" INDICATES CALM.
RESULTANT WIND DIRECTIONS ARE GIVEN TO WHOLE DEGREES.

#### TABLE 3

MAX AND MIN ARE LONG-TERM MEAN DAILY MAXIMUM AND MEAN DAILY MINIMUM TEMPERATURES.

### EXCEPTIONS

#### TABLES 2, 3, and 6

RECORD MEANS ARE THROUGH THE CURRENT YEAR, BEGINNING IN   1902 FOR TEMPERATURE
1902 FOR PRECIPITATION
1950 FOR SNOWFALL

HEATING DEGREE DAYS Base 65 deg. F    SYRACUSE, NEW YORK

**TABLE 4**

| SEASON | JULY | AUG | SEP | OCT | NOV | DEC | JAN | FEB | MAR | APR | MAY | JUNE | TOTAL |
|---|---|---|---|---|---|---|---|---|---|---|---|---|---|
| 1961-62 | 14 | 13 | 70 | 292 | 724 | 1107 | 1262 | 1211 | 937 | 552 | 172 | 25 | 6379 |
| #1962-63 | 6 | 16 | 185 | 422 | 875 | 1250 | 1364 | 1300 | 948 | 575 | 319 | 70 | 7330 |
| 1963-64 | 14 | 43 | 240 | 276 | 597 | 1365 | 1205 | 1190 | 922 | 546 | 160 | 89 | 6647 |
| 1964-65 | 2 | 30 | 154 | 475 | 636 | 1087 | 1370 | 1125 | 1069 | 676 | 215 | 132 | 6971 |
| 1965-66 | 27 | 50 | 144 | 521 | 782 | 1011 | 1422 | 1168 | 945 | 665 | 429 | 80 | 7244 |
| 1966-67 | 6 | 7 | 186 | 473 | 652 | 1104 | 1059 | 1275 | 1030 | 595 | 453 | 13 | 6853 |
| 1967-68 | 24 | 35 | 154 | 407 | 812 | 995 | 1438 | 1266 | 979 | 501 | 345 | 83 | 7039 |
| 1968-69 | 27 | 41 | 54 | 391 | 745 | 1163 | 1256 | 1152 | 1063 | 536 | 306 | 103 | 6837 |
| 1969-70 | 22 | 20 | 134 | 425 | 730 | 1269 | 1508 | 1139 | 1027 | 536 | 244 | 115 | 7169 |
| 1970-71 | 7 | 27 | 150 | 388 | 692 | 1222 | 1437 | 1069 | 1040 | 658 | 295 | 50 | 7035 |
| 1971-72 | 13 | 51 | 96 | 256 | 840 | 980 | 1189 | 1216 | 1098 | 731 | 204 | 84 | 6758 |
| 1972-73 | 9 | 23 | 98 | 567 | 833 | 1053 | 1128 | 1217 | 687 | 547 | 325 | 31 | 6518 |
| 1973-74 | 2 | 12 | 164 | 344 | 723 | 1094 | 1200 | 1206 | 1004 | 493 | 339 | 52 | 6633 |
| 1974-75 | 16 | 3 | 202 | 565 | 726 | 1069 | 1100 | 1026 | 1026 | 749 | 138 | 46 | 6666 |
| 1975-76 | 3 | 32 | 230 | 357 | 545 | 1154 | 1449 | 936 | 872 | 509 | 329 | 47 | 6463 |
| 1976-77 | 24 | 45 | 179 | 556 | 869 | 1303 | 1520 | 1086 | 767 | 511 | 209 | 111 | 7180 |
| 1977-78 | 14 | 60 | 121 | 444 | 624 | 1162 | 1348 | 1322 | 1097 | 677 | 252 | 92 | 7213 |
| 1978-79 | 10 | 1 | 184 | 470 | 735 | 1062 | 1315 | 1457 | 796 | 591 | 242 | 74 | 6937 |
| 1979-80 | 19 | 39 | 146 | 454 | 607 | 971 | 1215 | 1302 | 1007 | 511 | 194 | 115 | 6580 |
| 1980-81 | 3 | 0 | 120 | 496 | 814 | 1307 | 1544 | 869 | 882 | 446 | 221 | 27 | 6729 |
| 1981-82 | 2 | 4 | 145 | 523 | 775 | 1110 | 1552 | 1114 | 978 | 626 | 183 | 79 | 7091 |
| 1982-83 | 13 | 57 | 152 | 449 | 628 | 951 | 1280 | 1073 | 902 | 615 | 351 | 67 | 6538 |
| 1983-84 | 11 | 25 | 140 | 457 | 769 | 1312 | 1432 | 949 | 1246 | 563 | 386 | 68 | 7358 |
| 1984-85 | 16 | 33 | 227 | 390 | 797 | 971 | 1329 | 1048 | 882 | 514 | 193 | 109 | 6509 |
| 1985-86 | 10 | 18 | 121 | 415 | 702 | 1200 | 1266 | 1156 | 856 | 471 | 172 | 76 | 6463 |
| 1986-87 | 12 | 50 | 155 | 468 | 838 | 1027 | 1270 | 1208 | 831 | 395 | 211 | 35 | 6500 |
| 1987-88 | 7 | 27 | 138 | 529 | 717 | 1007 | 1290 | 1167 | 942 | 571 | 187 | 131 | 6713 |
| 1988-89 | 9 | 33 | 150 | 574 | 653 | 1148 | 1120 | 1175 | 989 | 639 | 242 | 38 | 6770 |
| 1989-90 | 3 | 36 | 151 | 406 | 779 | 1554 | 976 | 1001 | 849 | 496 | 319 | 43 | 6613 |
| 1990-91 | 4 | 4 | 160 | 386 | 675 | 967 | | | | | | | |

**TABLE 5**    COOLING DEGREE DAYS Base 65 deg. F    SYRACUSE, NEW YORK

| YEAR | JAN | FEB | MAR | APR | MAY | JUNE | JULY | AUG | SEP | OCT | NOV | DEC | TOTAL |
|---|---|---|---|---|---|---|---|---|---|---|---|---|---|
| 1969 | 0 | 0 | 0 | 0 | 22 | 94 | 183 | 222 | 102 | 1 | 0 | 0 | 624 |
| 1970 | 0 | 0 | 0 | 8 | 22 | 74 | 160 | 127 | 51 | 3 | 0 | 0 | 445 |
| 1971 | 0 | 0 | 0 | 0 | 17 | 145 | 145 | 124 | 117 | 4 | 0 | 0 | 552 |
| 1972 | 0 | 0 | 0 | 0 | 9 | 78 | 262 | 160 | 61 | 0 | 0 | 0 | 570 |
| 1973 | 0 | 0 | 0 | 7 | 0 | 177 | 249 | 281 | 79 | 2 | 0 | 0 | 795 |
| 1974 | 0 | 0 | 0 | 14 | 6 | 77 | 148 | 128 | 31 | 1 | 0 | 0 | 405 |
| 1975 | 0 | 0 | 0 | 0 | 80 | 114 | 221 | 138 | 1 | 1 | 0 | 0 | 555 |
| 1976 | 0 | 0 | 0 | 16 | 2 | 141 | 84 | 83 | 31 | 0 | 0 | 0 | 357 |
| 1977 | 0 | 0 | 1 | 12 | 71 | 47 | 202 | 138 | 49 | 0 | 0 | 0 | 520 |
| 1978 | 0 | 0 | 0 | 0 | 49 | 92 | 231 | 215 | 36 | 0 | 0 | 0 | 623 |
| 1979 | 0 | 0 | 0 | 2 | 50 | 109 | 232 | 134 | 46 | 22 | 0 | 0 | 595 |
| 1980 | 0 | 0 | 0 | 0 | 41 | 62 | 243 | 279 | 80 | 1 | 0 | 0 | 706 |
| 1981 | 0 | 0 | 3 | 4 | 47 | 125 | 264 | 180 | 49 | 0 | 0 | 0 | 672 |
| 1982 | 0 | 0 | 0 | 0 | 18 | 25 | 186 | 72 | 25 | 0 | 3 | 0 | 329 |
| 1983 | 0 | 0 | 0 | 0 | 2 | 125 | 236 | 155 | 70 | 7 | 0 | 0 | 595 |
| 1984 | 0 | 0 | 0 | 0 | 4 | 88 | 119 | 154 | 14 | 1 | 0 | 0 | 380 |
| 1985 | 0 | 0 | 0 | 7 | 30 | 26 | 165 | 144 | 87 | 0 | 0 | 0 | 459 |
| 1986 | 0 | 0 | 5 | 1 | 52 | 62 | 201 | 112 | 28 | 0 | 0 | 0 | 461 |
| 1987 | 0 | 0 | 0 | 7 | 73 | 142 | 280 | 143 | 29 | 0 | 0 | 0 | 674 |
| 1988 | 0 | 0 | 0 | 0 | 33 | 112 | 296 | 251 | 32 | 9 | 0 | 0 | 733 |
| 1989 | 0 | 0 | 0 | 0 | 37 | 112 | 198 | 144 | 59 | 0 | 0 | 0 | 550 |
| 1990 | 0 | 0 | 5 | 33 | 2 | 118 | 222 | 177 | 51 | 16 | 0 | 0 | 624 |

**TABLE 6**    SNOWFALL (inches)    SYRACUSE, NEW YORK

| SEASON | JULY | AUG | SEP | OCT | NOV | DEC | JAN | FEB | MAR | APR | MAY | JUNE | TOTAL |
|---|---|---|---|---|---|---|---|---|---|---|---|---|---|
| 1961-62 | 0.0 | 0.0 | 0.0 | T | 9.5 | 22.3 | 13.6 | 25.0 | 1.2 | 5.7 | 0.0 | 0.0 | 77.3 |
| 1962-63 | 0.0 | 0.0 | 0.0 | 2.8 | 11.0 | 33.8 | 22.2 | 28.3 | 15.8 | 1.8 | 0.8 | 0.0 | 116.5 |
| 1963-64 | 0.0 | 0.0 | 0.0 | T | 4.0 | 28.4 | 18.8 | 16.1 | 15.2 | 1.3 | 0.0 | 0.0 | 83.8 |
| 1964-65 | 0.0 | 0.0 | 0.0 | 0.3 | 4.0 | 18.3 | 31.8 | 24.9 | 13.3 | 4.7 | 0.0 | 0.0 | 97.3 |
| 1965-66 | 0.0 | 0.0 | 0.0 | 1.8 | 2.7 | 7.1 | 71.0 | 27.0 | 7.8 | 0.5 | 0.9 | 0.0 | 118.8 |
| 1966-67 | 0.0 | 0.0 | 0.0 | 0.0 | T | 33.0 | 18.3 | 21.0 | 10.4 | 0.3 | T | 0.0 | 83.0 |
| 1967-68 | 0.0 | 0.0 | 0.0 | T | 14.4 | 14.4 | 18.5 | 23.2 | 10.7 | T | 0.0 | 0.0 | 81.2 |
| 1968-69 | 0.0 | 0.0 | 0.0 | 0.8 | 16.5 | 25.4 | 24.5 | 21.3 | 9.4 | T | 0.0 | 0.0 | 97.9 |
| 1969-70 | 0.0 | 0.0 | 0.0 | 1.7 | 9.7 | 52.5 | 21.7 | 25.8 | 12.7 | 1.2 | 0.2 | 0.0 | 125.5 |
| 1970-71 | 0.0 | 0.0 | 0.0 | 0.8 | 7.0 | 51.9 | 30.3 | 25.2 | 37.2 | 4.8 | 0.0 | 0.0 | 157.2 |
| 1971-72 | 0.0 | 0.0 | 0.0 | 0.0 | 16.7 | 18.3 | 18.2 | 50.0 | 22.7 | 7.8 | 0.0 | 0.0 | 133.7 |
| 1972-73 | 0.0 | 0.0 | 0.0 | 0.3 | 15.8 | 29.8 | 11.9 | 13.3 | 3.6 | 5.3 | 1.2 | 0.0 | 81.2 |
| 1973-74 | 0.0 | 0.0 | 0.0 | T | 20.6 | 24.4 | 15.5 | 23.7 | 31.2 | 7.8 | 0.0 | 0.0 | 123.2 |
| 1974-75 | 0.0 | 0.0 | 0.0 | 2.8 | 4.8 | 26.2 | 11.8 | 27.3 | 20.6 | 12.0 | 0.0 | 0.0 | 105.5 |
| 1975-76 | 0.0 | 0.0 | 0.0 | T | 2.8 | 27.0 | 35.8 | 12.7 | 16.6 | 0.9 | T | 0.0 | 95.8 |
| 1976-77 | 0.0 | 0.0 | 0.0 | 0.3 | 25.9 | 25.7 | 52.3 | 24.4 | 13.5 | 1.9 | 1.0 | 0.0 | 145.0 |
| 1977-78 | 0.0 | 0.0 | 0.0 | 0.0 | 11.3 | 40.1 | 72.2 | 26.1 | 11.1 | 0.4 | T | 0.0 | 161.2 |
| 1978-79 | 0.0 | 0.0 | 0.0 | T | 3.9 | 40.9 | 27.9 | 20.7 | 14.9 | 10.2 | 0.0 | 0.0 | 118.5 |
| 1979-80 | 0.0 | 0.0 | 0.0 | 0.1 | 1.5 | 13.8 | 24.5 | 32.8 | 20.5 | 0.2 | 0.0 | 0.0 | 93.4 |
| 1980-81 | 0.0 | 0.0 | 0.0 | T | 7.3 | 28.8 | 23.4 | 8.5 | 10.6 | 0.4 | 0.0 | 0.0 | 79.0 |
| 1981-82 | 0.0 | 0.0 | 0.0 | 0.5 | 12.1 | 37.3 | 48.2 | 11.6 | 14.4 | 13.0 | 0.0 | 0.0 | 137.1 |
| 1982-83 | 0.0 | 0.0 | 0.0 | T | 1.9 | 10.9 | 20.3 | 8.2 | 8.3 | 16.4 | T | 0.0 | 66.0 |
| 1983-84 | 0.0 | 0.0 | 0.0 | 0.0 | 7.6 | 24.2 | 21.8 | 19.7 | 40.3 | T | 0.0 | 0.0 | 113.6 |
| 1984-85 | 0.0 | 0.0 | 0.0 | 0.0 | 5.0 | 23.4 | 57.3 | 21.6 | 7.1 | 2.0 | 0.0 | 0.0 | 116.4 |
| 1985-86 | 0.0 | 0.0 | 0.0 | 0.0 | 8.0 | 28.2 | 29.9 | 26.1 | 11.0 | 1.7 | T | 0.0 | 104.9 |
| 1986-87 | 0.0 | 0.0 | 0.0 | 0.0 | 16.1 | 8.8 | 49.2 | 15.1 | 3.0 | 1.3 | 0.0 | 0.0 | 93.5 |
| 1987-88 | 0.0 | 0.0 | 0.0 | T | 10.8 | 20.7 | 18.0 | 46.1 | 10.2 | 5.6 | 0.0 | 0.0 | 111.4 |
| 1988-89 | 0.0 | 0.0 | 0.0 | 5.7 | 0.2 | 34.4 | 19.4 | 21.7 | 9.9 | 6.5 | 0.0 | 0.0 | 97.8 |
| 1989-90 | 0.0 | 0.0 | T | T | 12.9 | 64.6 | 27.4 | 33.3 | 15.2 | 8.6 | 0.0 | 0.0 | 162.0 |
| 1990-91 | 0.0 | 0.0 | 0.0 | 0.2 | 7.8 | 24.5 | | | | | | | |
| Record Mean | 0.0 | 0.0 | T | 0.6 | 9.1 | 26.5 | 28.7 | 25.5 | 16.3 | 3.8 | 0.1 | 0.0 | 110.7 |

**See Reference Notes, relative to all above tables, on preceding page.**

The city of Asheville is located on both banks of the French Broad River, near the center of the French Broad Basin. Upstream from Asheville, the valley runs south for 18 miles and then curves toward the south-southwest. Downstream from the city, the valley is oriented toward the north-northwest. Two miles upstream from the principal section of Asheville, the Swannanoa River joins the French Broad from the east. The entire valley is known as the Asheville Plateau, having an average elevation near 2,200 feet above sea level, and is flanked by mountain ridges to the east and west, whose peaks range from 2,000 to 4,400 feet above the valley floor. At the Carolina-Tennessee border, about 25 miles north-northwest of Asheville, a relatively high ridge of mountains blocks the northern end of the valley. Thirty miles south, the Blue Ridge Mountains form an escarpment, having a general elevation of about 2,700 feet above sea level. The tallest peaks near Asheville are Mt. Mitchell, 6,684 feet above sea level, 20 miles northeast of the city, and Big Pisgah Mountain, 5,721 feet above sea level, 16 miles to the southwest.

Asheville has a temperate, but invigorating, climate. Considerable variation in temperature often occurs from day to day in summer, as well as during the other seasons.

While the office was located in the city, the combination of roof exposure conditions and a smoke blanket, caused by inversions in temperature in the valley on quiet nights, resulted in higher early morning temperatures at City Office sites than were experienced nearer ground level in nearby rural areas. The growing season in this area is of sufficient length for commercial crops, the average length of freeze-free period being about 195 days. The average last occurrence in spring of a temperature 32 degrees or lower is mid-April and the average first occurrence in fall of 32 degrees is late October.

The orientation of the French Broad Valley appears to have a pronounced influence on the wind direction. Prevailing winds are from the northwest during all months of the year. Also, the shielding effect of the nearby mountain barriers apparently has a direct bearing on the annual amount of precipitation received in this vicinity. In an area northwest of Asheville, the average annual precipitation is the lowest in North Carolina. Precipitation increases sharply in all other directions, especially to the south and southwest.

Destructive events caused directly by meteorological conditions are infrequent. The most frequent, occurring at approximately 12-year intervals, are floods on the French Broad River. These floods are usually associated with heavy rains caused by storms moving out of the Gulf of Mexico. Snowstorms which have seriously disrupted normal life in this community are infrequent. Hailstorms that cause property damage are extremely rare.

## TABLE 1 — NORMALS, MEANS AND EXTREMES

ASHEVILLE, NORTH CAROLINA

LATITUDE: 35°26'N   LONGITUDE: 82°33'W   ELEVATION: FT. GRND 2140 BARO 2161   TIME ZONE: EASTERN   WBAN: 03812

| | (a) | JAN | FEB | MAR | APR | MAY | JUNE | JULY | AUG | SEP | OCT | NOV | DEC | YEAR |
|---|---|---|---|---|---|---|---|---|---|---|---|---|---|---|
| **TEMPERATURE °F:** | | | | | | | | | | | | | | |
| Normals | | | | | | | | | | | | | | |
| -Daily Maximum | | 47.5 | 50.6 | 58.4 | 68.6 | 75.6 | 81.4 | 84.0 | 83.5 | 77.9 | 68.7 | 58.6 | 50.3 | 67.1 |
| -Daily Minimum | | 26.0 | 27.6 | 34.4 | 42.7 | 51.0 | 58.2 | 62.4 | 61.6 | 55.8 | 43.3 | 34.2 | 28.2 | 43.8 |
| -Monthly | | 36.8 | 39.1 | 46.4 | 55.7 | 63.3 | 69.8 | 73.2 | 72.6 | 66.9 | 56.0 | 46.4 | 39.3 | 55.5 |
| Extremes | | | | | | | | | | | | | | |
| -Record Highest | 25 | 78 | 77 | 83 | 89 | 91 | 96 | 96 | 100 | 92 | 86 | 81 | 78 | 100 |
| -Year | | 1975 | 1989 | 1985 | 1972 | 1969 | 1969 | 1988 | 1983 | 1975 | 1986 | 1974 | 1971 | AUG 1983 |
| -Record Lowest | 25 | -16 | -2 | 9 | 22 | 28 | 35 | 44 | 42 | 30 | 21 | 8 | -7 | -16 |
| -Year | | 1985 | 1967 | 1980 | 1987 | 1989 | 1966 | 1988 | 1986 | 1967 | 1976 | 1970 | 1983 | JAN 1985 |
| **NORMAL DEGREE DAYS:** | | | | | | | | | | | | | | |
| Heating (base 65°F) | | 874 | 725 | 577 | 283 | 114 | 23 | 0 | 0 | 57 | 286 | 558 | 797 | 4294 |
| Cooling (base 65°F) | | 0 | 0 | 0 | 0 | 61 | 167 | 254 | 239 | 114 | 7 | 0 | 0 | 842 |
| **% OF POSSIBLE SUNSHINE** | 25 | 56 | 60 | 62 | 66 | 61 | 63 | 58 | 54 | 54 | 61 | 57 | 56 | 59 |
| **MEAN SKY COVER (tenths)** | | | | | | | | | | | | | | |
| Sunrise - Sunset | 25 | 6.0 | 5.9 | 5.9 | 5.5 | 6.1 | 6.0 | 6.4 | 6.3 | 6.2 | 5.1 | 5.5 | 5.9 | 5.9 |
| **MEAN NUMBER OF DAYS:** | | | | | | | | | | | | | | |
| Sunrise to Sunset | | | | | | | | | | | | | | |
| -Clear | 25 | 9.8 | 9.2 | 9.2 | 10.2 | 7.7 | 6.7 | 5.1 | 5.2 | 6.7 | 12.3 | 10.6 | 10.2 | 102.8 |
| -Partly Cloudy | 25 | 7.3 | 6.1 | 8.3 | 8.5 | 10.0 | 12.1 | 13.7 | 13.8 | 10.5 | 7.8 | 7.2 | 7.3 | 112.6 |
| -Cloudy | 25 | 13.9 | 13.0 | 13.4 | 11.3 | 13.4 | 11.2 | 12.2 | 12.0 | 12.8 | 10.9 | 12.2 | 13.5 | 149.9 |
| Precipitation | | | | | | | | | | | | | | |
| .01 inches or more | 25 | 10.1 | 9.4 | 11.2 | 9.4 | 11.8 | 11.2 | 12.0 | 12.3 | 9.5 | 8.0 | 9.5 | 9.6 | 124.0 |
| Snow,Ice pellets | | | | | | | | | | | | | | |
| 1.0 inches or more | 25 | 1.5 | 1.4 | 0.7 | 0.2 | 0.0 | 0.0 | 0.0 | 0.0 | 0.0 | 0.0 | 0.2 | 0.5 | 4.5 |
| Thunderstorms | 25 | 0.4 | 0.7 | 2.3 | 3.2 | 7.2 | 8.1 | 9.4 | 8.9 | 3.3 | 0.9 | 0.8 | 0.4 | 45.4 |
| Heavy Fog Visibility | | | | | | | | | | | | | | |
| 1/4 mile or less | 25 | 3.9 | 3.0 | 2.4 | 2.4 | 5.6 | 8.2 | 9.8 | 14.2 | 11.9 | 8.1 | 4.6 | 4.6 | 78.6 |
| Temperature °F | | | | | | | | | | | | | | |
| -Maximum | | | | | | | | | | | | | | |
| 90° and above | 25 | 0.0 | 0.0 | 0.0 | 0.0 | 0.* | 1.9 | 4.4 | 2.6 | 0.2 | 0.0 | 0.0 | 0.0 | 9.1 |
| 32° and below | 25 | 3.5 | 1.6 | 0.2 | 0.0 | 0.0 | 0.0 | 0.0 | 0.0 | 0.0 | 0.0 | 0.1 | 1.1 | 6.5 |
| -Minimum | | | | | | | | | | | | | | |
| 32° and below | 25 | 24.2 | 20.9 | 13.6 | 4.3 | 0.3 | 0.0 | 0.0 | 0.0 | 0.* | 4.2 | 13.3 | 21.1 | 101.9 |
| 0° and below | 25 | 0.6 | 0.* | 0.0 | 0.0 | 0.0 | 0.0 | 0.0 | 0.0 | 0.0 | 0.0 | 0.0 | 0.1 | 0.7 |
| **AVG. STATION PRESS. (mb)** | 17 | 941.4 | 941.0 | 940.3 | 940.0 | 940.7 | 942.2 | 943.5 | 943.9 | 943.8 | 944.1 | 943.0 | 942.5 | 942.2 |
| **RELATIVE HUMIDITY (%)** | | | | | | | | | | | | | | |
| Hour 01 | 25 | 81 | 78 | 79 | 77 | 89 | 93 | 95 | 96 | 96 | 91 | 86 | 82 | 87 |
| Hour 07 | 25 | 85 | 84 | 85 | 85 | 92 | 94 | 96 | 97 | 97 | 94 | 88 | 86 | 90 |
| Hour 13 (Local Time) | 25 | 59 | 56 | 53 | 50 | 57 | 60 | 63 | 64 | 64 | 57 | 57 | 59 | 58 |
| Hour 19 | 25 | 68 | 63 | 60 | 55 | 67 | 70 | 74 | 78 | 81 | 74 | 70 | 69 | 69 |
| **PRECIPITATION (inches):** | | | | | | | | | | | | | | |
| Water Equivalent | | | | | | | | | | | | | | |
| -Normal | | 3.48 | 3.60 | 5.13 | 3.84 | 4.19 | 4.20 | 4.43 | 4.79 | 3.96 | 3.29 | 3.29 | 3.51 | 47.71 |
| -Maximum Monthly | 25 | 7.47 | 7.02 | 9.86 | 7.26 | 8.83 | 10.73 | 9.92 | 11.28 | 9.12 | 7.05 | 7.76 | 8.48 | 11.28 |
| -Year | | 1978 | 1982 | 1975 | 1979 | 1973 | 1989 | 1982 | 1967 | 1977 | 1971 | 1979 | 1973 | AUG 1967 |
| -Minimum Monthly | 25 | 0.45 | 0.44 | 0.77 | 0.25 | 1.06 | 0.94 | 0.46 | 0.52 | 0.16 | 0.30 | 1.19 | 0.16 | 0.16 |
| -Year | | 1981 | 1978 | 1985 | 1976 | 1988 | 1988 | 1986 | 1981 | 1984 | 1978 | 1981 | 1965 | SEP 1984 |
| -Maximum in 24 hrs | 25 | 2.95 | 3.47 | 5.13 | 3.06 | 4.95 | 3.93 | 4.02 | 4.12 | 3.41 | 2.95 | 4.03 | 2.66 | 5.13 |
| -Year | | 1978 | 1982 | 1968 | 1973 | 1973 | 1987 | 1969 | 1967 | 1975 | 1977 | 1977 | 1973 | MAR 1968 |
| Snow,Ice pellets | | | | | | | | | | | | | | |
| -Maximum Monthly | 25 | 17.6 | 25.5 | 13.0 | 11.5 | T | 0.0 | 0.0 | 0.0 | 0.0 | T | 9.6 | 16.3 | 25.5 |
| -Year | | 1966 | 1969 | 1969 | 1987 | 1979 | | | | | 1989 | 1968 | 1971 | FEB 1969 |
| -Maximum in 24 hrs | 25 | 14.0 | 11.7 | 10.9 | 11.5 | T | 0.0 | 0.0 | 0.0 | 0.0 | T | 5.7 | 16.3 | 16.3 |
| -Year | | 1988 | 1969 | 1969 | 1987 | 1979 | | | | | 1989 | 1968 | 1971 | DEC 1971 |
| **WIND:** | | | | | | | | | | | | | | |
| Mean Speed (mph) | 25 | 9.7 | 9.6 | 9.4 | 8.9 | 7.1 | 6.1 | 5.9 | 5.4 | 5.6 | 6.7 | 8.2 | 8.9 | 7.6 |
| Prevailing Direction | | | | | | | | | | | | | | |
| Fastest Obs. 1 Min. | | | | | | | | | | | | | | |
| -Direction (!!!) | 25 | 34 | 34 | 35 | 22 | 34 | 36 | 35 | 34 | 32 | 33 | 32 | 34 | 34 |
| -Speed (MPH) | 25 | 40 | 60 | 46 | 44 | 40 | 40 | 43 | 40 | 35 | 35 | 40 | 44 | 60 |
| -Year | | 1975 | 1972 | 1969 | 1970 | 1971 | 1977 | 1966 | 1973 | 1980 | 1972 | 1974 | 1965 | FEB 1972 |
| Peak Gust | | | | | | | | | | | | | | |
| -Direction (!!!) | 6 | NW | NW | SW | N | N | N | NE | NW | N | N | N | N | NW |
| -Speed (mph) | 6 | 49 | 54 | 45 | 51 | 44 | 52 | 38 | 36 | 37 | 38 | 49 | 46 | 54 |
| -Date | | 1984 | 1987 | 1984 | 1988 | 1989 | 1987 | 1989 | 1985 | 1989 | 1987 | 1989 | 1987 | FEB 1987 |

**See Reference Notes to this table on the following page.**

PRECIPITATION (inches)  ASHEVILLE, NORTH CAROLINA

**TABLE 2**

| YEAR | JAN | FEB | MAR | APR | MAY | JUNE | JULY | AUG | SEP | OCT | NOV | DEC | ANNUAL |
|------|-----|-----|-----|-----|-----|------|------|-----|-----|-----|-----|-----|--------|
| 1961 | 1.45 | 5.18 | 3.19 | 2.98 | 3.04 | 4.44 | 2.54 | 8.13 | 1.07 | 2.36 | 4.85 | 6.09 | 45.32 |
| 1962 | 4.46 | 3.58 | 4.13 | 3.25 | 2.83 | 6.20 | 3.24 | 3.47 | 2.40 | 2.40 | 2.40 | 1.66 | 40.02 |
| 1963 | 1.73 | 1.76 | 7.66 | 3.02 | 2.53 | 2.71 | 2.93 | 3.83 | 3.64 | T | 4.42 | 2.44 | 36.67 |
| #1964 | 2.83 | 3.58 | 5.13 | 5.21 | 0.94 | 0.80 | 3.29 | 8.88 | 5.37 | 8.46 | 2.51 | 2.88 | 49.88 |
| 1965 | 2.16 | 4.60 | 5.10 | 2.62 | 3.33 | 4.12 | 4.47 | 4.03 | 4.69 | 2.92 | 1.30 | 0.16 | 39.50 |
| 1966 | 3.37 | 6.56 | 2.59 | 5.47 | 4.73 | 2.46 | 3.24 | 7.73 | 4.55 | 5.37 | 3.32 | 2.36 | 51.75 |
| 1967 | 2.02 | 2.20 | 2.86 | 1.11 | 6.79 | 4.45 | 6.90 | 11.28 | 2.53 | 3.30 | 2.54 | 6.13 | 52.11 |
| 1968 | 2.93 | 0.62 | 6.65 | 2.37 | 2.92 | 5.06 | 7.18 | 3.31 | 2.64 | 5.02 | 2.98 | 3.10 | 44.78 |
| 1969 | 2.64 | 5.08 | 4.01 | 3.53 | 3.32 | 3.82 | 7.53 | 6.47 | 3.04 | 2.63 | 1.91 | 4.63 | 48.61 |
| 1970 | 1.75 | 2.42 | 2.62 | 2.96 | 1.72 | 2.72 | 5.02 | 2.46 | 1.17 | 5.55 | 1.83 | 2.72 | 32.94 |
| 1971 | 2.53 | 4.93 | 3.48 | 2.06 | 3.54 | 5.00 | 5.47 | 3.03 | 3.80 | 7.05 | 2.84 | 4.32 | 48.05 |
| 1972 | 3.57 | 2.02 | 3.19 | 1.49 | 6.63 | 6.54 | 4.66 | 1.88 | 5.29 | 4.44 | 4.42 | 3.89 | 48.02 |
| 1973 | 4.26 | 4.23 | 8.91 | 5.71 | 8.83 | 3.87 | 6.95 | 4.57 | 3.12 | 2.41 | 3.57 | 8.48 | 64.91 |
| 1974 | 3.44 | 4.44 | 3.18 | 4.99 | 5.58 | 3.73 | 3.93 | 1.24 | 4.13 | 1.28 | 4.22 | 2.38 | 48.44 |
| 1975 | 3.86 | 4.56 | 9.86 | 0.61 | 8.17 | 2.12 | 3.31 | 3.63 | 7.53 | 3.94 | 4.89 | 4.44 | 56.92 |
| 1976 | 3.51 | 2.20 | 4.96 | 0.25 | 8.67 | 5.51 | 3.18 | 4.23 | 3.50 | 5.59 | 1.58 | 4.05 | 47.23 |
| 1977 | 2.09 | 1.02 | 7.29 | 4.05 | 3.96 | 5.11 | 1.03 | 3.68 | 9.12 | 3.79 | 6.88 | 2.43 | 50.45 |
| 1978 | 7.47 | 0.44 | 5.22 | 2.97 | 4.65 | 2.29 | 0.63 | 6.91 | 2.57 | 0.30 | 2.49 | 4.32 | 40.26 |
| 1979 | 6.81 | 5.14 | 5.72 | 7.26 | 5.35 | 2.20 | 5.52 | 3.63 | 5.60 | 1.40 | 7.76 | 1.05 | 57.44 |
| 1980 | 2.85 | 0.53 | 8.26 | 4.77 | 4.54 | 4.68 | 2.21 | 2.38 | 4.36 | 2.62 | 3.04 | 0.59 | 40.83 |
| 1981 | 0.45 | 4.80 | 3.24 | 2.07 | 7.50 | 4.41 | 2.06 | 0.52 | 1.36 | 2.19 | 1.19 | 4.79 | 34.58 |
| 1982 | 5.41 | 7.02 | 1.92 | 3.62 | 3.78 | 3.98 | 9.92 | 1.73 | 5.66 | 4.43 | 4.77 | 8.30 | 52.92 |
| 1983 | 3.39 | 5.63 | 6.27 | 5.27 | 3.48 | 3.71 | 1.06 | 0.95 | 5.66 | 4.43 | 2.61 | 1.34 | 45.71 |
| 1984 | 2.36 | 6.43 | 4.82 | 4.05 | 6.62 | 3.69 | 5.88 | 5.02 | 0.16 | 2.73 | 3.41 | 0.70 | 35.94 |
| 1985 | 2.95 | 4.74 | 0.77 | 2.74 | 1.59 | 1.47 | 4.37 | 7.04 | 1.25 | 3.41 | 4.91 | 0.70 | 35.94 |
| 1986 | 1.11 | 1.85 | 2.75 | 0.57 | 3.55 | 1.28 | 0.46 | 6.10 | 3.15 | 4.19 | 5.28 | 4.28 | 34.57 |
| 1987 | 3.49 | 6.17 | 2.85 | 3.67 | 1.87 | 8.94 | 1.86 | 1.79 | 6.79 | 0.36 | 3.09 | 2.33 | 43.21 |
| 1988 | 3.71 | 0.88 | 1.31 | 3.46 | 1.06 | 0.94 | 2.65 | 1.78 | 2.79 | 3.12 | 3.47 | 1.41 | 26.58 |
| 1989 | 1.65 | 4.61 | 2.91 | 3.17 | 5.54 | 10.73 | 8.33 | 4.98 | 8.17 | 2.98 | 4.27 | 3.29 | 60.63 |
| 1990 | 3.27 | 8.07 | 5.95 | 1.96 | 5.09 | 0.90 | 6.55 | 7.78 | 1.43 | 8.82 | 1.55 | 4.50 | 55.87 |
| Record Mean | 3.19 | 3.88 | 4.49 | 3.18 | 4.72 | 3.99 | 4.40 | 4.39 | 3.84 | 3.59 | 3.51 | 3.46 | 46.66 |

**TABLE 3**  AVERAGE TEMPERATURE (deg. F)  ASHEVILLE, NORTH CAROLINA

| YEAR | JAN | FEB | MAR | APR | MAY | JUNE | JULY | AUG | SEP | OCT | NOV | DEC | ANNUAL |
|------|-----|-----|-----|-----|-----|------|------|-----|-----|-----|-----|-----|--------|
| 1961 | 33.5 | 44.1 | 50.1 | 50.4 | 60.0 | 68.6 | 72.5 | 72.0 | 68.4 | 55.3 | 50.4 | 39.7 | 55.5 |
| 1962 | 37.4 | 45.8 | 43.4 | 52.9 | 69.4 | 70.2 | 73.7 | 72.3 | 65.4 | 58.3 | 47.8 | 31.4 | 54.8 |
| 1963 | 34.4 | 34.2 | 51.0 | 57.6 | 63.6 | 69.2 | 72.9 | 72.0 | 66.0 | 59.6 | 51.4 | 42.9 | 56.1 |
| #1964 | 38.1 | 34.7 | 46.3 | 57.3 | 65.3 | 72.8 | 72.9 | 71.1 | 66.0 | 53.8 | 46.4 | 40.3 | 54.8 |
| 1965 | 37.0 | 37.9 | 42.4 | 57.4 | 65.8 | 66.8 | 72.2 | 71.1 | 66.8 | 53.8 | 45.0 | 41.4 | 54.8 |
| 1966 | 30.1 | 36.2 | 43.5 | 52.0 | 60.1 | 66.1 | 71.1 | 69.9 | 62.9 | 51.7 | 45.0 | 37.6 | 52.2 |
| 1967 | 38.7 | 35.0 | 49.8 | 57.6 | 59.7 | 66.8 | 68.7 | 68.5 | 60.2 | 53.5 | 42.7 | 41.8 | 53.6 |
| 1968 | 34.3 | 32.4 | 46.6 | 54.8 | 61.0 | 69.5 | 73.1 | 74.1 | 64.1 | 56.7 | 46.0 | 36.2 | 54.0 |
| 1969 | 36.7 | 37.8 | 41.3 | 56.7 | 65.2 | 73.1 | 75.9 | 70.7 | 65.8 | 56.2 | 44.0 | 36.5 | 55.0 |
| 1970 | 30.9 | 39.1 | 46.8 | 57.6 | 63.7 | 70.1 | 74.4 | 73.1 | 70.7 | 59.0 | 46.0 | 42.7 | 56.2 |
| 1971 | 36.5 | 39.5 | 43.1 | 55.2 | 61.1 | 72.4 | 72.5 | 72.2 | 69.5 | 61.8 | 45.8 | 47.7 | 56.5 |
| 1972 | 42.1 | 37.6 | 46.5 | 55.8 | 61.2 | 66.5 | 72.3 | 72.5 | 69.0 | 55.0 | 45.5 | 45.2 | 55.7 |
| 1973 | 37.5 | 38.5 | 52.7 | 52.8 | 60.3 | 71.0 | 74.1 | 74.2 | 70.0 | 58.8 | 49.1 | 39.8 | 56.5 |
| 1974 | 48.2 | 40.5 | 51.1 | 54.9 | 64.2 | 66.7 | 72.9 | 72.3 | 65.7 | 54.6 | 47.4 | 40.3 | 56.6 |
| 1975 | 41.7 | 42.5 | 44.8 | 54.1 | 66.0 | 68.8 | 72.4 | 72.9 | 65.2 | 57.3 | 48.2 | 38.6 | 56.1 |
| 1976 | 33.6 | 45.3 | 50.6 | 54.9 | 59.5 | 68.1 | 71.2 | 70.2 | 63.1 | 51.5 | 41.2 | 36.2 | 53.8 |
| 1977 | 24.8 | 37.4 | 50.7 | 58.2 | 64.6 | 69.7 | 75.7 | 73.8 | 69.1 | 54.3 | 49.3 | 36.8 | 55.3 |
| 1978 | 29.3 | 33.4 | 45.9 | 56.8 | 62.0 | 71.1 | 73.4 | 74.1 | 70.0 | 55.7 | 51.8 | 41.0 | 55.4 |
| 1979 | 34.2 | 35.8 | 50.0 | 55.9 | 64.3 | 68.8 | 72.2 | 73.2 | 66.5 | 55.3 | 49.2 | 42.0 | 55.6 |
| 1980 | 40.5 | 35.1 | 46.2 | 56.5 | 64.8 | 71.7 | 77.5 | 74.8 | 70.2 | 54.7 | 47.1 | 39.6 | 56.5 |
| 1981 | 33.3 | 39.9 | 44.9 | 60.1 | 60.7 | 74.3 | 75.0 | 71.7 | 66.1 | 54.5 | 48.2 | 35.8 | 55.4 |
| 1982 | 32.3 | 41.2 | 50.0 | 53.6 | 67.3 | 71.5 | 74.6 | 71.7 | 64.5 | 56.3 | 47.1 | 44.9 | 56.3 |
| 1983 | 36.7 | 38.8 | 46.7 | 51.1 | 61.6 | 69.0 | 75.7 | 76.5 | 66.6 | 57.5 | 47.3 | 36.4 | 55.3 |
| 1984 | 34.0 | 40.5 | 44.8 | 51.7 | 59.9 | 70.0 | 70.6 | 71.6 | 62.8 | 62.7 | 43.1 | 46.3 | 54.8 |
| 1985 | 30.5 | 38.3 | 48.1 | 56.6 | 62.6 | 69.8 | 72.2 | 70.9 | 64.2 | 60.5 | 56.0 | 34.7 | 55.4 |
| 1986 | 35.0 | 42.2 | 46.0 | 56.0 | 63.3 | 71.7 | 76.1 | 70.9 | 68.0 | 57.4 | 50.7 | 39.8 | 56.4 |
| 1987 | 35.3 | 38.9 | 46.5 | 52.6 | 66.7 | 71.2 | 74.7 | 74.7 | 66.5 | 50.1 | 47.0 | 42.2 | 55.5 |
| 1988 | 32.1 | 37.1 | 47.1 | 54.6 | 61.1 | 69.3 | 73.8 | 74.6 | 66.3 | 50.2 | 46.7 | 38.7 | 54.3 |
| 1989 | 42.1 | 39.8 | 50.3 | 54.5 | 59.4 | 70.0 | 73.3 | 71.9 | 65.8 | 56.1 | 46.2 | 31.6 | 55.1 |
| 1990 | 42.8 | 45.6 | 50.4 | 54.2 | 63.3 | 70.9 | 73.8 | 73.9 | 67.6 | 57.8 | 49.9 | 45.5 | 58.0 |
| Record Mean | 35.8 | 38.7 | 47.2 | 55.2 | 62.7 | 69.8 | 73.4 | 72.6 | 66.4 | 55.9 | 47.2 | 39.9 | 55.4 |
| Max | 46.6 | 50.1 | 59.3 | 68.1 | 74.8 | 81.3 | 83.9 | 83.0 | 77.1 | 68.2 | 59.0 | 50.8 | 66.9 |
| Min | 24.9 | 27.3 | 35.0 | 42.3 | 50.5 | 58.2 | 62.9 | 62.1 | 55.7 | 43.6 | 35.3 | 29.0 | 43.9 |

## REFERENCE NOTES FOR TABLES 1, 2, 3 and 6 (ASHEVILLE, NC)

### GENERAL

T - TRACE AMOUNT
BLANK ENTRIES DENOTE MISSING/UNREPORTED DATA.
# INDICATES A STATION OR INSTRUMENT RELOCATION.

### SPECIFIC

#### TABLE 1

(a) - LENGTH OF RECORD IN YEARS. ALTHOUGH INDIVIDUAL MONTHS MAY BE MISSING.

x  LESS THAN .05

NORMALS — BASED ON THE 1951-1980 RECORD PERIOD.
EXTREMES — DATES ARE THE MOST RECENT OCCURRENCE.
WIND DIR. — NUMERALS SHOW TENS OF DEGREES CLOCKWISE FROM TRUE NORTH.
"00" INDICATES CALM.
RESULTANT WIND DIRECTIONS ARE GIVEN TO WHOLE DEGREES.

#### TABLE 3
MAX AND MIN ARE LONG-TERM MEAN DAILY MAXIMUM AND MEAN DAILY MINIMUM TEMPERATURES.

### EXCEPTIONS

#### TABLES 2, 3, and 6

RECORD MEANS ARE THROUGH THE CURRENT YEAR,
BEGINNING IN    1965 FOR TEMPERATURE
1965 FOR PRECIPITATION
1965 FOR SNOWFALL

**TABLE 4**  HEATING DEGREE DAYS Base 65 deg. F    ASHEVILLE, NORTH CAROLINA

| SEASON | JULY | AUG | SEP | OCT | NOV | DEC | JAN | FEB | MAR | APR | MAY | JUNE | TOTAL |
|---|---|---|---|---|---|---|---|---|---|---|---|---|---|
| 1961-62 | 2 | 0 | 49 | 295 | 433 | 778 | 85 | 531 | 664 | 371 | 27 | 1 | 4002 |
| 1962-63 | 0 | 0 | 91 | 224 | 565 | 941 | 943 | 857 | 426 | 241 | 98 | 6 | 4392 |
| 1963-64 | 4 | 0 | 51 | 164 | 513 | 1038 | 821 | 873 | 572 | 251 | 59 | 8 | 4359 |
| #1964-65 | 0 | 20 | 46 | 372 | 399 | 679 | 862 | 751 | 691 | 232 | 23 | 27 | 4103 |
| 1965-66 | 0 | 7 | 39 | 344 | 550 | 759 | 1075 | 800 | 660 | 383 | 149 | 42 | 4808 |
| 1966-67 | 1 | 1 | 87 | 405 | 593 | 838 | 811 | 834 | 465 | 226 | 185 | 51 | 4496 |
| 1967-68 | 7 | 2 | 158 | 351 | 660 | 713 | 947 | 939 | 566 | 306 | 150 | 7 | 4806 |
| 1968-69 | 0 | 20 | 42 | 258 | 563 | 884 | 873 | 755 | 729 | 246 | 70 | 9 | 4449 |
| 1969-70 | 0 | 8 | 59 | 280 | 623 | 875 | 1051 | 720 | 557 | 236 | 86 | 3 | 4497 |
| 1970-71 | 0 | 0 | 29 | 194 | 565 | 682 | 875 | 707 | 672 | 290 | 137 | 0 | 4151 |
| 1971-72 | 0 | 0 | 6 | 129 | 576 | 530 | 744 | 790 | 569 | 294 | 116 | 35 | 3749 |
| 1972-73 | 3 | 0 | 8 | 304 | 578 | 605 | 847 | 737 | 374 | 362 | 158 | 0 | 3975 |
| 1973-74 | 0 | 0 | 7 | 205 | 473 | 772 | 513 | 680 | 423 | 299 | 83 | 24 | 3482 |
| 1974-75 | 0 | 0 | 65 | 316 | 519 | 760 | 713 | 624 | 619 | 331 | 46 | 7 | 4002 |
| 1975-76 | 0 | 0 | 77 | 232 | 498 | 812 | 963 | 566 | 439 | 296 | 168 | 33 | 4087 |
| 1976-77 | 2 | 3 | 83 | 411 | 706 | 884 | 1233 | 768 | 437 | 198 | 66 | 25 | 4822 |
| 1977-78 | 0 | 0 | 14 | 331 | 466 | 868 | 1100 | 878 | 586 | 241 | 139 | 0 | 4624 |
| 1978-79 | 0 | 0 | 12 | 283 | 390 | 741 | 953 | 810 | 457 | 268 | 71 | 18 | 4001 |
| 1979-80 | 5 | 0 | 44 | 299 | 468 | 707 | 753 | 861 | 573 | 258 | 65 | 2 | 4035 |
| 1980-81 | 0 | 0 | 37 | 315 | 533 | 778 | 973 | 696 | 615 | 152 | 152 | 0 | 4256 |
| 1981-82 | 0 | 1 | 57 | 326 | 499 | 897 | 1005 | 659 | 458 | 333 | 38 | 0 | 4274 |
| 1982-83 | 0 | 0 | 74 | 274 | 531 | 616 | 871 | 725 | 562 | 410 | 127 | 13 | 4204 |
| 1983-84 | 0 | 0 | 84 | 229 | 527 | 882 | 955 | 706 | 618 | 391 | 176 | 9 | 4577 |
| 1984-85 | 1 | 0 | 107 | 91 | 648 | 576 | 1061 | 737 | 520 | 249 | 109 | 19 | 4121 |
| 1985-86 | 0 | 6 | 111 | 156 | 266 | 932 | 923 | 633 | 581 | 273 | 91 | 2 | 3974 |
| 1986-87 | 0 | 32 | 16 | 268 | 419 | 774 | 913 | 725 | 567 | 369 | 40 | 1 | 4124 |
| 1987-88 | 0 | 0 | 47 | 452 | 532 | 702 | 1013 | 802 | 545 | 308 | 132 | 31 | 4564 |
| 1988-89 | 5 | 0 | 33 | 453 | 544 | 808 | 701 | 698 | 454 | 331 | 200 | 4 | 4232 |
| 1989-90 | 1 | 8 | 74 | 279 | 558 | 1028 | 653 | 535 | 446 | 321 | 91 | 3 | 4023 |
| 1990-91 | 0 | 0 | 55 | 229 | 445 | 601 |  |  |  |  |  |  |  |

**TABLE 5**  COOLING DEGREE DAYS Base 65 deg. F    ASHEVILLE, NORTH CAROLINA

| YEAR | JAN | FEB | MAR | APR | MAY | JUNE | JULY | AUG | SEP | OCT | NOV | DEC | TOTAL |
|---|---|---|---|---|---|---|---|---|---|---|---|---|---|
| 1969 | 0 | 0 | 0 | 4 | 85 | 262 | 343 | 196 | 92 | 15 | 0 | 0 | 997 |
| 1970 | 0 | 0 | 0 | 22 | 52 | 159 | 299 | 259 | 206 | 17 | 0 | 0 | 1011 |
| 1971 | 0 | 0 | 0 | 3 | 25 | 232 | 239 | 231 | 149 | 37 | 8 | 0 | 923 |
| 1972 | 0 | 0 | 0 | 24 | 6 | 84 | 236 | 237 | 134 | 0 | 1 | 0 | 722 |
| 1973 | 0 | 0 | 0 | 1 | 16 | 190 | 288 | 292 | 163 | 19 | 0 | 0 | 969 |
| 1974 | 0 | 0 | 0 | 3 | 65 | 82 | 254 | 234 | 92 | 1 | 0 | 0 | 731 |
| 1975 | 0 | 0 | 0 | 11 | 82 | 124 | 237 | 252 | 89 | 0 | 0 | 0 | 795 |
| 1976 | 0 | 0 | 0 | 0 | 5 | 135 | 198 | 170 | 35 | 2 | 0 | 0 | 545 |
| 1977 | 0 | 0 | 0 | 2 | 59 | 173 | 341 | 279 | 146 | 7 | 1 | 0 | 1007 |
| 1978 | 0 | 0 | 0 | 2 | 53 | 188 | 266 | 292 | 168 | 4 | 0 | 0 | 973 |
| 1979 | 0 | 0 | 0 | 1 | 55 | 141 | 234 | 261 | 96 | 4 | 0 | 0 | 792 |
| 1980 | 0 | 0 | 0 | 8 | 64 | 210 | 395 | 311 | 198 | 4 | 0 | 0 | 1191 |
| 1981 | 0 | 0 | 0 | 10 | 25 | 286 | 316 | 213 | 98 | 7 | 0 | 0 | 955 |
| 1982 | 0 | 0 | 0 | 0 | 0 | 117 | 206 | 305 | 215 | 64 | 16 | 0 | 923 |
| 1983 | 0 | 0 | 0 | 0 | 25 | 139 | 335 | 362 | 141 | 5 | 0 | 0 | 1007 |
| 1984 | 0 | 0 | 0 | 0 | 25 | 165 | 185 | 211 | 49 | 27 | 0 | 0 | 657 |
| 1985 | 0 | 0 | 5 | 2 | 43 | 170 | 225 | 194 | 90 | 25 | 4 | 0 | 762 |
| 1986 | 0 | 0 | 0 | 8 | 43 | 209 | 353 | 222 | 112 | 38 | 0 | 0 | 985 |
| 1987 | 0 | 0 | 0 | 7 | 97 | 192 | 372 | 309 | 97 | 0 | 0 | 0 | 1012 |
| 1988 | 0 | 0 | 0 | 0 | 18 | 168 | 282 | 304 | 79 | 3 | 0 | 0 | 854 |
| 1989 | 0 | 0 | 5 | 23 | 34 | 159 | 266 | 229 | 107 | 11 | 0 | 0 | 832 |
| 1990 | 0 | 0 | 0 | 3 | 48 | 187 | 278 | 283 | 141 | 11 | 0 | 0 | 952 |

**TABLE 6**  SNOWFALL (inches)    ASHEVILLE, NORTH CAROLINA

| SEASON | JULY | AUG | SEP | OCT | NOV | DEC | JAN | FEB | MAR | APR | MAY | JUNE | TOTAL |
|---|---|---|---|---|---|---|---|---|---|---|---|---|---|
| 1961-62 | 0.0 | 0.0 | 0.0 | T | T | 1.2 | 13.3 | T | 8.3 | T | 0.0 | 0.0 | 22.8 |
| 1962-63 | 0.0 | 0.0 | 0.0 | 0.0 | 0.3 | 4.2 | T | 4.5 | T | 0.0 | 0.0 | 0.0 | 9.0 |
| 1963-64 | 0.0 | 0.0 | 0.0 | 0.0 | 1.2 | 8.9 | 1.7 | 13.9 | 0.1 | 0.0 | 0.0 | 0.0 | 25.8 |
| #1964-65 | 0.0 | 0.0 | 0.0 | 0.0 | T | T | 5.5 | 4.3 | 5.0 | 0.0 | 0.0 | 0.0 | 14.8 |
| 1965-66 | 0.0 | 0.0 | 0.0 | 0.0 | T | T | 17.6 | 6.2 | 0.2 | T | 0.0 | 0.0 | 24.0 |
| 1966-67 | 0.0 | 0.0 | 0.0 | 0.0 | 1.3 | 0.8 | 1.5 | 4.2 | T | 0.0 | 0.0 | 0.0 | 7.8 |
| 1967-68 | 0.0 | 0.0 | 0.0 | 0.0 | 0.0 | 1.9 | 7.2 | 6.0 | 0.1 | 0.0 | 0.0 | 0.0 | 15.2 |
| 1968-69 | 0.0 | 0.0 | 0.0 | 0.0 | 9.6 | T | 0.1 | 25.5 | 13.0 | 0.0 | 0.0 | 0.0 | 48.2 |
| 1969-70 | 0.0 | 0.0 | 0.0 | 0.0 | T | 10.9 | 4.8 | 1.1 | 0.5 | 0.0 | 0.0 | 0.0 | 17.3 |
| 1970-71 | 0.0 | 0.0 | 0.0 | 0.0 | T | 6.1 | 0.1 | 0.1 | 8.9 | 0.2 | 0.0 | 0.0 | 15.4 |
| 1971-72 | 0.0 | 0.0 | 0.0 | 0.0 | 0.6 | 16.3 | T | 7.4 | 7.4 | 0.0 | 0.0 | 0.0 | 31.7 |
| 1972-73 | 0.0 | 0.0 | 0.0 | 0.0 | 0.6 | T | 7.1 | 0.5 | 1.0 | T | 0.0 | 0.0 | 9.2 |
| 1973-74 | 0.0 | 0.0 | 0.0 | 0.0 | 0.0 | 0.0 | T | 0.3 | 1.1 | T | 0.0 | 0.0 | 4.4 |
| 1974-75 | 0.0 | 0.0 | 0.0 | 0.0 | 3.1 | 3.0 | 0.4 | 4.3 | 3.7 | T | 0.0 | 0.0 | 14.5 |
| 1975-76 | 0.0 | 0.0 | 0.0 | 0.0 | 5.0 | 0.4 | 1.6 | 3.5 | T | 0.0 | 0.0 | 0.0 | 10.5 |
| 1976-77 | 0.0 | 0.0 | 0.0 | 0.0 | 0.1 | 0.3 | 11.9 | 0.7 | 0.0 | 0.0 | 0.0 | 0.0 | 13.0 |
| 1977-78 | 0.0 | 0.0 | 0.0 | T | T | 1.5 | 9.7 | 5.3 | 5.3 | T | 0.0 | 0.0 | 21.8 |
| 1978-79 | 0.0 | 0.0 | 0.0 | 0.0 | 0.0 | T | 5.2 | 17.8 | T | 0.0 | 0.0 | 0.0 | 23.0 |
| 1979-80 | 0.0 | 0.0 | 0.0 | 0.0 | T | T | 2.1 | 6.3 | 5.4 | T | 0.0 | 0.0 | 13.8 |
| 1980-81 | 0.0 | 0.0 | 0.0 | 0.0 | T | T | 4.7 | T | 9.9 | 0.0 | 0.0 | 0.0 | 14.6 |
| 1981-82 | 0.0 | 0.0 | 0.0 | 0.0 | T | 2.0 | 8.6 | 8.1 | 0.1 | 3.0 | 0.0 | 0.0 | 21.8 |
| 1982-83 | 0.0 | 0.0 | 0.0 | 0.0 | 0.0 | 0.4 | 10.5 | 9.3 | 4.5 | 2.0 | 0.0 | 0.0 | 26.7 |
| 1983-84 | 0.0 | 0.0 | 0.0 | 0.0 | T | T | 0.2 | 2.9 | T | 0.0 | 0.0 | 0.0 | 3.1 |
| 1984-85 | 0.0 | 0.0 | 0.0 | 0.0 | 0.0 | T | 4.5 | 3.1 | 0.1 | 0.4 | 0.0 | 0.0 | 8.1 |
| 1985-86 | 0.0 | 0.0 | 0.0 | 0.0 | 0.0 | 0.4 | 0.8 | 3.7 | 0.1 | T | 0.0 | 0.0 | 5.0 |
| 1986-87 | 0.0 | 0.0 | 0.0 | 0.0 | T | T | 15.0 | 2.7 | 0.3 | 11.5 | 0.0 | 0.0 | 29.5 |
| 1987-88 | 0.0 | 0.0 | 0.0 | 0.0 | 0.3 | 0.5 | 14.2 | T | T | 1.2 | 0.0 | 0.0 | 16.2 |
| 1988-89 | 0.0 | 0.0 | 0.0 | 0.0 | 0.0 | T | 1.2 | 6.0 | T | 1.0 | 0.0 | 0.0 | 8.2 |
| 1989-90 | 0.0 | 0.0 | 0.0 | T | T | 3.0 | T | T | T | 0.0 | 0.0 | 0.0 | 3.0 |
| 1990-91 | 0.0 | T | 0.0 | 0.0 | 0.0 | T |  |  |  |  |  |  |  |
| Record Mean | 0.0 | T | 0.0 | T | 0.8 | 1.9 | 5.2 | 5.0 | 2.6 | 0.7 | T | 0.0 | 16.2 |

**See Reference Notes, relative to all above tables, on preceding page.**

The Raleigh-Durham Airport is located in the zone of transition between the Coastal Plain and the Piedmont Plateau. The surrounding terrain is rolling, with an average elevation of around 400 feet, the range over a 10-mile radius is roughly between 200 and 550 feet. Being centrally located between the mountains on the west and the coast on the south and east, the Raleigh-Durham area enjoys a favorable climate. The mountains form a partial barrier to cold air masses moving eastward from the interior of the nation. As a result, there are few days in the heart of the winter season when the temperature falls below 20 degrees. Tropical air is present over the eastern and central sections of North Carolina during much of the summer season, bringing warm temperatures and rather high humidities to the Raleigh-Durham area. Afternoon temperatures reach 90 degrees or higher on about one-fourth of the days in the middle of summer, but reach 100 degrees less than once per year. Even in the hottest weather, early morning temperatures almost always drop into the lower 70s.

Rainfall is well distributed throughout the year as a whole. July and August have the greatest amount of rainfall, and October and November the least. There are times in spring and summer when soil moisture is scanty. This usually results from too many days between rains rather than from a shortage of total rainfall, but occasionally the accumulated total during the growing season falls short of plant needs. Most summer rain is produced by thunderstorms, which may occasionally be accompanied by strong winds, intense rains, and hail. The Raleigh-Durham area is far enough from the coast so that the bad weather effects of coastal storms are reduced. While snow and sleet usually occur each year, excessive accumulations of snow are rare.

From September 1887 to December 1950, the office was located in the downtown areas of Raleigh. The various buildings occupied were within an area of three blocks. All thermometers were exposed on the roof, and this, plus the smoke over the city, had an effect on the temperature record of that period. Lowest temperatures at the city office were frequently from 2 to 5 degrees higher than those recorded in surrounding rural areas. Maximum temperatures in the city were generally a degree or two lower. These observations are supported by a period of simultaneous record from the Municipal Airport and the city office location between 1937 and 1940.

From September 1946 to May 1954, simultaneous records were kept at a surface location on the North Carolina State College campus in Raleigh, and at the Raleigh-Durham Airport 10 1/2 air miles to the northwest.

Based on the 1951-1980 period, the average first occurrence of 32 degrees Fahrenheit in the fall is October 27 and the average last occurrence in the spring is April 11.

## TABLE 1    NORMALS, MEANS AND EXTREMES

RALEIGH, NORTH CAROLINA

LATITUDE: 35°52'N    LONGITUDE: 78°47'W    ELEVATION: FT. GRND 416 BARO 415    TIME ZONE: EASTERN    WBAN: 13722

| | (a) | JAN | FEB | MAR | APR | MAY | JUNE | JULY | AUG | SEP | OCT | NOV | DEC | YEAR |
|---|---|---|---|---|---|---|---|---|---|---|---|---|---|---|
| **TEMPERATURE °F:** | | | | | | | | | | | | | | |
| Normals | | | | | | | | | | | | | | |
|   -Daily Maximum | | 50.1 | 52.8 | 61.0 | 72.3 | 79.0 | 85.2 | 88.2 | 87.1 | 81.6 | 71.6 | 61.8 | 52.7 | 70.3 |
|   -Daily Minimum | | 29.1 | 30.3 | 37.7 | 46.5 | 55.3 | 62.6 | 67.1 | 66.8 | 60.4 | 47.7 | 38.1 | 31.2 | 47.7 |
|   -Monthly | | 39.6 | 41.6 | 49.3 | 59.5 | 67.2 | 73.9 | 77.7 | 77.0 | 71.0 | 59.7 | 50.0 | 42.0 | 59.0 |
| Extremes | | | | | | | | | | | | | | |
|   -Record Highest | 45 | 79 | 84 | 92 | 95 | 97 | 104 | 105 | 105 | 104 | 98 | 88 | 79 | 105 |
|   -Year | | 1952 | 1977 | 1945 | 1980 | 1953 | 1954 | 1952 | 1988 | 1954 | 1954 | 1950 | 1978 | AUG 1988 |
|   -Record Lowest | 45 | -9 | 5 | 11 | 23 | 31 | 38 | 48 | 46 | 37 | 19 | 11 | 4 | -9 |
|   -Year | | 1985 | 1971 | 1980 | 1985 | 1977 | 1977 | 1975 | 1965 | 1983 | 1962 | 1970 | 1983 | JAN 1985 |
| **NORMAL DEGREE DAYS:** | | | | | | | | | | | | | | |
| Heating (base 65°F) | | 787 | 655 | 496 | 181 | 53 | 0 | 0 | 0 | 9 | 187 | 450 | 713 | 3531 |
| Cooling (base 65°F) | | 0 | 0 | 9 | 16 | 121 | 270 | 394 | 372 | 189 | 23 | 0 | 0 | 1394 |
| **% OF POSSIBLE SUNSHINE** | 35 | 54 | 57 | 62 | 64 | 59 | 61 | 60 | 59 | 59 | 61 | 57 | 55 | 59 |
| **MEAN SKY COVER (tenths)** | | | | | | | | | | | | | | |
| Sunrise - Sunset | 40 | 6.1 | 6.0 | 5.9 | 5.6 | 6.0 | 5.8 | 6.0 | 6.0 | 5.7 | 5.0 | 5.4 | 5.8 | 5.8 |
| **MEAN NUMBER OF DAYS:** | | | | | | | | | | | | | | |
| Sunrise to Sunset | | | | | | | | | | | | | | |
|   -Clear | 41 | 9.2 | 8.7 | 9.5 | 9.8 | 8.3 | 7.8 | 7.2 | 7.5 | 9.6 | 12.8 | 11.4 | 10.2 | 111.9 |
|   -Partly Cloudy | 41 | 6.9 | 6.1 | 7.6 | 8.9 | 10.0 | 11.7 | 11.9 | 12.2 | 8.9 | 7.0 | 7.2 | 7.0 | 105.4 |
|   -Cloudy | 41 | 14.9 | 13.4 | 13.9 | 11.4 | 12.7 | 10.6 | 11.9 | 11.3 | 11.5 | 11.2 | 11.4 | 13.9 | 147.9 |
| Precipitation | | | | | | | | | | | | | | |
| .01 inches or more | 45 | 10.0 | 9.8 | 10.3 | 8.9 | 10.2 | 9.3 | 11.2 | 10.0 | 7.7 | 6.9 | 8.3 | 8.9 | 111.6 |
| Snow,Ice pellets | | | | | | | | | | | | | | |
| 1.0 inches or more | 45 | 0.9 | 0.7 | 0.3 | 0.* | 0.0 | 0.0 | 0.0 | 0.0 | 0.0 | 0.0 | 0.1 | 0.3 | 2.4 |
| Thunderstorms | 45 | 0.4 | 0.8 | 1.9 | 3.4 | 6.2 | 7.2 | 10.5 | 7.9 | 3.5 | 1.4 | 0.8 | 0.3 | 44.3 |
| Heavy Fog Visibility | | | | | | | | | | | | | | |
| 1/4 mile or less | 40 | 3.5 | 3.0 | 2.3 | 1.5 | 2.4 | 2.0 | 2.8 | 3.3 | 3.5 | 3.6 | 3.3 | 3.5 | 34.6 |
| Temperature °F | | | | | | | | | | | | | | |
|   -Maximum | | | | | | | | | | | | | | |
|    90° and above | 25 | 0.0 | 0.0 | 0.0 | 0.5 | 1.3 | 6.8 | 12.0 | 10.2 | 2.9 | 0.2 | 0.0 | 0.0 | 33.8 |
|    32° and below | 25 | 2.4 | 0.6 | 0.1 | 0.0 | 0.0 | 0.0 | 0.0 | 0.0 | 0.0 | 0.0 | 0.* | 0.9 | 4.0 |
|   -Minimum | | | | | | | | | | | | | | |
|    32° and below | 25 | 21.1 | 17.9 | 10.0 | 2.3 | 0.* | 0.0 | 0.0 | 0.0 | 0.0 | 1.6 | 9.3 | 17.5 | 79.7 |
|    0° and below | 25 | 0.2 | 0.0 | 0.0 | 0.0 | 0.0 | 0.0 | 0.0 | 0.0 | 0.0 | 0.0 | 0.0 | 0.0 | 0.2 |
| **AVG. STATION PRESS.(mb)** | 17 | 1003.4 | 1002.9 | 1001.3 | 999.8 | 1000.0 | 1000.6 | 1001.4 | 1002.1 | 1002.8 | 1004.0 | 1003.9 | 1004.2 | 1002.2 |
| **RELATIVE HUMIDITY (%)** | | | | | | | | | | | | | | |
| Hour 01 | 25 | 73 | 70 | 71 | 73 | 84 | 86 | 88 | 89 | 88 | 85 | 78 | 74 | 80 |
| Hour 07 | 25 | 78 | 77 | 80 | 80 | 86 | 87 | 89 | 92 | 92 | 89 | 84 | 80 | 85 |
| Hour 13 (Local Time) | 25 | 55 | 52 | 49 | 45 | 54 | 56 | 58 | 60 | 59 | 53 | 52 | 54 | 54 |
| Hour 19 | 25 | 63 | 58 | 56 | 53 | 66 | 67 | 71 | 75 | 77 | 76 | 67 | 66 | 66 |
| **PRECIPITATION (inches):** | | | | | | | | | | | | | | |
| Water Equivalent | | | | | | | | | | | | | | |
|   -Normal | | 3.55 | 3.43 | 3.69 | 2.91 | 3.67 | 3.66 | 4.38 | 4.44 | 3.29 | 2.73 | 2.87 | 3.14 | 41.76 |
|   -Maximum Monthly | 45 | 7.52 | 6.42 | 7.78 | 6.10 | 7.67 | 9.38 | 10.05 | 12.18 | 12.94 | 7.53 | 8.22 | 6.65 | 12.94 |
|   -Year | | 1954 | 1989 | 1983 | 1978 | 1974 | 1973 | 1945 | 1986 | 1945 | 1971 | 1948 | 1983 | SEP 1945 |
|   -Minimum Monthly | 45 | 0.87 | 1.00 | 1.03 | 0.23 | 0.92 | 0.55 | 0.80 | 0.81 | 0.23 | 0.44 | 0.61 | 0.25 | 0.23 |
|   -Year | | 1981 | 1968 | 1985 | 1976 | 1964 | 1981 | 1953 | 1950 | 1985 | 1963 | 1973 | 1965 | SEP 1985 |
|   -Maximum in 24 hrs | 45 | 3.11 | 3.22 | 3.70 | 4.04 | 4.40 | 3.44 | 3.89 | 5.20 | 5.16 | 4.10 | 4.70 | 3.18 | 5.20 |
|   -Year | | 1984 | 1973 | 1983 | 1978 | 1957 | 1967 | 1952 | 1955 | 1944 | 1954 | 1963 | 1958 | AUG 1955 |
| Snow,Ice pellets | | | | | | | | | | | | | | |
|   -Maximum Monthly | 45 | 14.4 | 17.2 | 14.0 | 1.8 | 0.0 | 0.0 | 0.0 | 0.0 | 0.0 | 0.0 | 2.6 | 10.6 | 17.2 |
|   -Year | | 1955 | 1979 | 1960 | 1983 | | | | | | | 1975 | 1958 | FEB 1979 |
|   -Maximum in 24 hrs | 45 | 9.0 | 10.4 | 9.3 | 1.8 | 0.0 | 0.0 | 0.0 | 0.0 | 0.0 | 0.0 | 2.6 | 9.1 | 10.4 |
|   -Year | | 1966 | 1979 | 1969 | 1983 | | | | | | | 1975 | 1958 | FEB 1979 |
| **WIND:** | | | | | | | | | | | | | | |
| Mean Speed (mph) | 40 | 8.5 | 8.9 | 9.3 | 9.0 | 7.7 | 7.0 | 6.6 | 6.4 | 6.8 | 7.1 | 7.7 | 8.0 | 7.8 |
| Prevailing Direction | | | | | | | | | | | | | | |
| through 1963 | | SW | SW | SW | SW | SW | SW | SW | NE | NE | NNE | SW | SW | SW |
| Fastest Obs. 1 Min. | | | | | | | | | | | | | | |
|   -Direction (!!!) | 36 | 27 | 12 | 32 | 14 | 20 | 33 | 23 | 33 | 23 | 29 | 32 | 21 | 29 |
|   -Speed (MPH) | 36 | 41 | 44 | 44 | 40 | 54 | 39 | 69 | 46 | 35 | 73 | 35 | 35 | 73 |
|   -Year | | 1971 | 1984 | 1967 | 1961 | 1972 | 1977 | 1962 | 1969 | 1972 | 1954 | 1969 | 1968 | OCT 1954 |
| Peak Gust | | | | | | | | | | | | | | |
|   -Direction (!!!) | 6 | NW | SE | W | NW | W | NW | W | SW | S | NE | S | NW | SE |
|   -Speed (mph) | 6 | 48 | 62 | 52 | 56 | 55 | 41 | 44 | 61 | 46 | 35 | 41 | 45 | 62 |
|   -Date | | 1989 | 1984 | 1989 | 1987 | 1984 | 1988 | 1986 | 1986 | 1989 | 1987 | 1989 | 1987 | FEB 1984 |

**See Reference Notes to this table on the following page.**

PRECIPITATION (inches)  RALEIGH, NORTH CAROLINA

**TABLE 2**

| YEAR | JAN | FEB | MAR | APR | MAY | JUNE | JULY | AUG | SEP | OCT | NOV | DEC | ANNUAL |
|---|---|---|---|---|---|---|---|---|---|---|---|---|---|
| 1961 | 2.88 | 5.75 | 4.37 | 2.23 | 2.94 | 4.05 | 3.10 | 6.52 | 1.25 | 1.16 | 2.10 | 4.76 | 41.11 |
| 1962 | 6.56 | 2.74 | 4.85 | 3.22 | 1.37 | 6.37 | 7.07 | 1.98 | 3.72 | 0.99 | 7.19 | 2.21 | 48.27 |
| 1963 | 2.96 | 3.45 | 3.80 | 1.77 | 4.05 | 1.72 | 3.51 | 2.10 | 2.77 | 0.44 | 7.06 | 3.28 | 36.91 |
| 1964 | 3.66 | 4.11 | 2.93 | 3.39 | 0.92 | 3.41 | 4.06 | 5.68 | 5.29 | 3.95 | 1.38 | 4.13 | 42.91 |
| 1965 | 1.47 | 2.40 | 4.08 | 1.51 | 2.20 | 8.32 | 5.54 | 3.00 | 2.65 | 1.77 | 1.23 | 0.25 | 34.42 |
| 1966 | 5.42 | 4.76 | 1.81 | 2.02 | 4.95 | 3.68 | 0.91 | 5.79 | 3.58 | 2.01 | 2.06 | 2.61 | 39.60 |
| 1967 | 1.64 | 3.80 | 1.62 | 3.02 | 4.15 | 4.57 | 3.49 | 6.22 | 1.74 | 2.26 | 2.14 | 4.93 | 39.58 |
| 1968 | 2.88 | 1.00 | 2.22 | 3.03 | 3.82 | 1.74 | 2.50 | 1.77 | 5.15 | 3.59 | 2.75 |  | 35.60 |
| 1969 | 1.55 | 3.60 | 3.95 | 1.43 | 2.85 | 4.81 | 4.40 | 6.31 | 6.21 | 2.09 | 1.01 | 3.31 | 41.52 |
| 1970 | 2.26 | 3.47 | 4.04 | 2.07 | 3.36 | 0.87 | 5.64 | 4.47 | 1.20 | 4.47 | 1.59 | 2.57 | 36.01 |
| 1971 | 3.28 | 3.85 | 3.69 | 2.59 | 4.68 | 2.79 | 4.56 | 6.26 | 2.91 | 7.53 | 1.81 | 1.69 | 45.64 |
| 1972 | 1.97 | 4.13 | 2.50 | 1.92 | 5.34 | 4.16 | 6.80 | 4.17 | 5.80 | 3.96 | 5.98 | 5.01 | 51.74 |
| 1973 | 2.67 | 5.50 | 4.06 | 4.40 | 3.99 | 9.38 | 3.12 | 4.60 | 1.13 | 0.60 | 0.61 | 6.38 | 46.44 |
| 1974 | 4.39 | 2.87 | 3.34 | 1.32 | 7.67 | 4.02 | 1.56 | 4.82 | 3.71 | 1.23 | 1.79 | 4.02 | 40.74 |
| 1975 | 6.09 | 2.85 | 6.26 | 1.64 | 3.84 | 1.66 | 6.74 | 2.11 | 5.77 | 1.23 | 4.60 | 4.04 | 46.83 |
| 1976 | 3.07 | 1.54 | 3.17 | 0.23 | 4.74 | 2.55 | 1.00 | 1.52 | 5.99 | 3.97 | 1.89 | 4.04 | 33.71 |
| 1977 | 2.82 | 2.13 | 5.63 | 1.89 | 3.94 | 0.84 | 0.89 | 4.12 | 3.86 | 5.06 | 2.22 | 3.70 | 37.10 |
| 1978 | 7.03 | 1.43 | 4.40 | 6.10 | 4.20 | 4.06 | 3.63 | 1.86 | 1.37 | 1.46 | 4.17 | 3.26 | 42.97 |
| #1979 | 5.71 | 5.55 | 2.69 | 2.63 | 4.71 | 3.27 | 4.84 | 1.66 | 6.76 | 1.88 | 4.73 | 0.94 | 45.37 |
| 1980 | 4.39 | 1.91 | 5.87 | 1.97 | 2.33 | 4.89 | 2.11 | 1.87 | 3.76 | 2.25 | 2.87 | 1.42 | 35.64 |
| 1981 | 0.87 | 3.02 | 2.35 | 1.03 | 4.28 | 0.55 | 5.69 | 5.34 | 2.70 | 4.64 | 0.95 | 4.96 | 36.38 |
| 1982 | 3.43 | 4.97 | 3.02 | 3.33 | 4.20 | 8.39 | 3.34 | 1.83 | 1.55 | 3.93 | 2.34 | 4.02 | 44.35 |
| 1983 | 1.79 | 6.00 | 7.78 | 3.54 | 5.89 | 3.09 | 1.10 | 1.81 | 2.13 | 3.59 | 3.86 | 6.65 | 47.23 |
| 1984 | 4.93 | 5.65 | 5.40 | 4.45 | 5.43 | 3.08 | 9.20 | 1.13 | 2.31 | 0.73 | 1.64 | 2.32 | 46.27 |
| 1985 | 4.83 | 4.44 | 1.03 | 0.64 | 3.95 | 2.87 | 6.28 | 3.73 | 0.23 | 1.75 | 7.61 | 0.81 | 38.17 |
| 1986 | 1.88 | 1.65 | 3.06 | 1.01 | 2.98 | 1.92 | 4.32 | 12.18 | 0.95 | 1.28 | 2.77 | 2.95 | 36.95 |
| 1987 | 6.53 | 5.52 | 2.88 | 4.68 | 1.19 | 2.11 | 1.78 | 5.80 | 5.48 | 1.71 | 1.39 | 3.02 | 42.09 |
| 1988 | 3.15 | 2.42 | 1.76 | 3.56 | 2.85 | 2.88 | 2.69 | 3.40 | 4.90 | 5.67 | 3.34 | 1.04 | 37.66 |
| 1989 | 1.35 | 6.42 | 5.40 | 4.91 | 3.88 | 7.30 | 5.46 | 5.08 | 3.96 | 3.44 | 3.94 | 3.01 | 54.15 |
| 1990 | 3.07 | 3.82 | 5.02 | 2.19 | 6.97 | 1.03 | 2.22 | 2.65 | 0.30 | 5.69 | 1.51 | 3.08 | 37.55 |
| Record Mean | 3.41 | 3.72 | 3.73 | 3.22 | 3.91 | 4.10 | 5.14 | 5.02 | 3.63 | 2.91 | 2.63 | 3.25 | 44.68 |

**TABLE 3**  AVERAGE TEMPERATURE (deg. F)  RALEIGH, NORTH CAROLINA

| YEAR | JAN | FEB | MAR | APR | MAY | JUNE | JULY | AUG | SEP | OCT | NOV | DEC | ANNUAL |
|---|---|---|---|---|---|---|---|---|---|---|---|---|---|
| 1961 | 36.5 | 44.9 | 52.7 | 53.6 | 64.2 | 72.8 | 77.6 | 76.6 | 73.2 | 59.1 | 52.4 | 41.3 | 58.7 |
| 1962 | 38.8 | 43.9 | 45.5 | 57.4 | 72.0 | 73.5 | 75.7 | 75.8 | 68.2 | 61.8 | 47.7 | 38.0 | 58.2 |
| 1963 | 36.7 | 36.1 | 53.4 | 60.5 | 65.4 | 72.7 | 76.0 | 76.3 | 67.1 | 60.5 | 51.0 | 34.7 | 57.5 |
| #1964 | 41.2 | 39.4 | 50.6 | 59.6 | 68.1 | 75.6 | 76.4 | 74.9 | 69.3 | 55.2 | 52.7 | 43.3 | 58.9 |
| 1965 | 40.5 | 42.9 | 44.6 | 58.3 | 71.9 | 71.9 | 76.2 | 77.2 | 72.7 | 58.8 | 50.9 | 43.8 | 59.1 |
| 1966 | 35.8 | 42.3 | 49.7 | 57.0 | 66.5 | 73.4 | 79.1 | 77.7 | 71.0 | 58.6 | 50.8 | 41.9 | 58.7 |
| 1967 | 44.8 | 38.9 | 53.7 | 62.5 | 63.9 | 72.0 | 76.3 | 76.3 | 67.5 | 59.4 | 46.8 | 46.3 | 59.1 |
| 1968 | 37.1 | 36.4 | 52.6 | 58.1 | 63.9 | 73.6 | 76.9 | 79.2 | 70.9 | 62.0 | 51.7 | 38.8 | 58.4 |
| 1969 | 37.4 | 40.9 | 43.4 | 58.7 | 66.2 | 74.7 | 78.0 | 73.8 | 67.5 | 58.6 | 46.1 | 37.7 | 56.9 |
| 1970 | 32.9 | 38.9 | 46.2 | 59.4 | 66.0 | 72.7 | 76.1 | 75.3 | 73.3 | 61.0 | 49.4 | 42.7 | 57.8 |
| 1971 | 37.0 | 42.1 | 45.1 | 56.4 | 64.4 | 75.4 | 76.6 | 75.3 | 72.0 | 64.8 | 48.1 | 50.3 | 59.0 |
| 1972 | 44.7 | 40.0 | 49.5 | 58.0 | 64.3 | 69.9 | 77.1 | 75.6 | 70.4 | 57.4 | 48.1 | 46.2 | 58.5 |
| 1973 | 39.3 | 40.0 | 54.8 | 57.9 | 64.5 | 75.1 | 76.6 | 76.3 | 73.2 | 62.2 | 54.6 | 42.5 | 59.8 |
| 1974 | 49.3 | 42.9 | 54.4 | 60.2 | 67.4 | 71.8 | 76.5 | 76.0 | 69.0 | 56.5 | 48.7 | 43.2 | 59.7 |
| 1975 | 43.8 | 43.7 | 47.1 | 55.8 | 68.2 | 73.7 | 75.6 | 78.3 | 71.1 | 62.2 | 53.5 | 42.0 | 59.6 |
| 1976 | 37.6 | 50.1 | 56.2 | 60.7 | 66.8 | 74.7 | 78.6 | 75.4 | 69.7 | 55.7 | 42.5 | 37.1 | 58.7 |
| 1977 | 26.6 | 39.3 | 53.3 | 62.6 | 68.4 | 73.3 | 80.6 | 78.1 | 72.8 | 56.4 | 51.8 | 39.9 | 58.6 |
| 1978 | 35.3 | 33.1 | 48.2 | 59.2 | 66.0 | 75.8 | 78.0 | 79.9 | 73.7 | 59.5 | 55.1 | 44.9 | 59.1 |
| 1979 | 39.1 | 36.5 | 52.2 | 59.7 | 66.8 | 69.8 | 75.4 | 77.2 | 71.2 | 59.9 | 52.0 | 43.4 | 58.6 |
| 1980 | 40.6 | 36.5 | 46.5 | 62.0 | 69.8 | 75.0 | 78.9 | 79.6 | 74.9 | 58.7 | 49.1 | 40.7 | 59.3 |
| 1981 | 33.4 | 43.9 | 46.2 | 61.7 | 64.0 | 78.9 | 80.8 | 74.6 | 68.3 | 57.2 | 50.7 | 39.7 | 58.3 |
| 1982 | 35.5 | 45.5 | 51.7 | 57.4 | 71.0 | 74.7 | 79.1 | 76.5 | 70.5 | 60.6 | 51.9 | 47.5 | 60.2 |
| 1983 | 38.1 | 40.7 | 50.7 | 55.1 | 65.4 | 72.5 | 79.1 | 79.1 | 70.7 | 60.4 | 50.9 | 39.5 | 58.5 |
| 1984 | 36.3 | 45.7 | 47.2 | 55.9 | 65.5 | 75.5 | 74.9 | 76.6 | 67.5 | 66.3 | 47.1 | 49.7 | 59.0 |
| 1985 | 34.0 | 41.9 | 52.7 | 62.0 | 67.3 | 73.9 | 76.8 | 75.2 | 69.7 | 63.7 | 58.4 | 39.4 | 59.6 |
| 1986 | 38.5 | 44.5 | 51.7 | 61.2 | 67.4 | 78.4 | 81.7 | 75.6 | 72.3 | 63.0 | 52.9 | 42.6 | 60.8 |
| 1987 | 38.3 | 40.4 | 49.2 | 56.9 | 69.3 | 76.3 | 81.2 | 79.2 | 73.0 | 54.6 | 52.8 | 44.5 | 59.6 |
| 1988 | 34.7 | 41.9 | 50.6 | 57.8 | 66.0 | 72.4 | 79.0 | 80.3 | 70.3 | 54.4 | 52.0 | 42.4 | 58.5 |
| 1999 | 44.8 | 42.9 | 50.7 | 58.0 | 65.7 | 77.0 | 78.1 | 76.2 | 71.7 | 61.3 | 51.7 | 34.6 | 59.3 |
| 1990 | 48.0 | 51.0 | 54.9 | 60.3 | 67.4 | 75.2 | 80.0 | 78.0 | 72.2 | 64.1 | 54.2 | 48.1 | 62.8 |
| Record Mean | 41.1 | 42.9 | 50.5 | 59.3 | 67.9 | 75.2 | 78.3 | 77.2 | 71.6 | 60.8 | 50.8 | 42.8 | 59.8 |
| Max | 50.6 | 52.9 | 61.4 | 70.9 | 79.0 | 85.7 | 88.1 | 86.7 | 81.4 | 71.5 | 61.3 | 52.3 | 70.2 |
| Min | 31.6 | 32.8 | 39.5 | 47.6 | 56.8 | 64.7 | 68.5 | 67.6 | 61.7 | 50.0 | 40.3 | 33.2 | 49.5 |

## REFERENCE NOTES FOR TABLES 1, 2, 3 and 6   (RALEIGH, NC)

### GENERAL

T - TRACE AMOUNT
BLANK ENTRIES DENOTE MISSING/UNREPORTED DATA.
# INDICATES A STATION OR INSTRUMENT RELOCATION.

### SPECIFIC

#### TABLE 1

(a) - LENGTH OF RECORD IN YEARS. ALTHOUGH INDIVIDUAL MONTHS MAY BE MISSING.

* LESS THAN .05

NORMALS — BASED ON THE 1951-1980 RECORD PERIOD.
EXTREMES — DATES ARE THE MOST RECENT OCCURRENCE.
WIND DIR. — NUMERALS SHOW TENS OF DEGREES CLOCKWISE FROM TRUE NORTH. "00" INDICATES CALM.
RESULTANT WIND DIRECTIONS ARE GIVEN TO WHOLE DEGREES.

#### TABLE 3

MAX AND MIN ARE LONG-TERM MEAN DAILY MAXIMUM AND MEAN DAILY MINIMUM TEMPERATURES.

### EXCEPTIONS

#### TABLES 2, 3, and 6

RECORD MEANS ARE THROUGH THE CURRENT YEAR, BEGINNING IN     1887 FOR TEMPERATURE
1887 FOR PRECIPITATION
1945 FOR SNOWFALL

**TABLE 4**  HEATING DEGREE DAYS Base 65 deg. F    RALEIGH, NORTH CAROLINA

| SEASON | JULY | AUG | SEP | OCT | NOV | DEC | JAN | FEB | MAR | APR | MAY | JUNE | TOTAL |
|---|---|---|---|---|---|---|---|---|---|---|---|---|---|
| 1961-62 | 0 | 0 | 19 | 197 | 403 | 730 | 810 | 584 | 598 | 261 | 11 | 0 | 3613 |
| 1962-63 | 0 | 0 | 61 | 166 | 510 | 832 | 870 | 803 | 354 | 193 | 86 | 0 | 3879 |
| 1963-64 | 0 | 0 | 57 | 149 | 413 | 933 | 731 | 735 | 445 | 205 | 54 | 0 | 3722 |
| #1964-65 | 0 | 1 | 25 | 305 | 365 | 665 | 754 | 616 | 628 | 232 | 0 | 15 | 3606 |
| 1965-66 | 0 | 5 | 7 | 208 | 416 | 650 | 898 | 629 | 473 | 263 | 72 | 12 | 3633 |
| 1966-67 | 0 | 0 | 11 | 216 | 425 | 709 | 623 | 723 | 361 | 151 | 105 | 13 | 3337 |
| 1967-68 | 0 | 0 | 35 | 199 | 539 | 574 | 855 | 824 | 391 | 213 | 87 | 0 | 3717 |
| 1968-69 | 0 | 0 | 0 | 151 | 396 | 805 | 848 | 667 | 667 | 195 | 61 | 0 | 3790 |
| 1969-70 | 0 | 0 | 45 | 222 | 561 | 841 | 989 | 725 | 576 | 200 | 74 | 0 | 4233 |
| 1970-71 | 0 | 0 | 22 | 154 | 460 | 684 | 863 | 636 | 611 | 258 | 87 | 0 | 3775 |
| 1971-72 | 0 | 0 | 3 | 61 | 496 | 456 | 623 | 718 | 478 | 237 | 51 | 16 | 3139 |
| 1972-73 | 0 | 0 | 9 | 238 | 504 | 576 | 790 | 692 | 334 | 231 | 88 | 0 | 3462 |
| 1973-74 | 0 | 0 | 2 | 126 | 312 | 690 | 481 | 614 | 346 | 187 | 48 | 0 | 2806 |
| 1974-75 | 0 | 0 | 44 | 268 | 501 | 668 | 651 | 589 | 553 | 293 | 34 | 0 | 3601 |
| 1975-76 | 0 | 0 | 17 | 117 | 351 | 705 | 843 | 426 | 300 | 194 | 52 | 6 | 3011 |
| 1976-77 | 0 | 0 | 7 | 302 | 668 | 857 | 1183 | 715 | 358 | 132 | 49 | 14 | 4285 |
| 1977-78 | 0 | 0 | 4 | 283 | 411 | 768 | 914 | 883 | 514 | 196 | 83 | 0 | 4056 |
| 1978-79 | 0 | 0 | 7 | 184 | 292 | 627 | 793 | 792 | 398 | 183 | 43 | 8 | 3327 |
| 1979-80 | 0 | 0 | 13 | 196 | 394 | 661 | 753 | 820 | 564 | 130 | 33 | 0 | 3564 |
| 1980-81 | 0 | 0 | 16 | 225 | 477 | 747 | 973 | 583 | 579 | 149 | 99 | 0 | 3848 |
| 1981-82 | 0 | 4 | 31 | 253 | 425 | 776 | 907 | 538 | 411 | 244 | 15 | 0 | 3604 |
| 1982-83 | 0 | 0 | 14 | 182 | 392 | 542 | 828 | 675 | 438 | 305 | 79 | 7 | 3462 |
| 1983-84 | 0 | 0 | 59 | 180 | 417 | 784 | 882 | 553 | 545 | 283 | 83 | 5 | 3791 |
| 1984-85 | 0 | 0 | 63 | 42 | 530 | 468 | 954 | 644 | 395 | 146 | 42 | 4 | 3288 |
| 1985-86 | 0 | 0 | 36 | 96 | 207 | 789 | 812 | 569 | 415 | 157 | 59 | 0 | 3140 |
| 1986-87 | 0 | 11 | 12 | 149 | 370 | 687 | 820 | 681 | 484 | 248 | 29 | 0 | 3491 |
| 1987-88 | 0 | 0 | 1 | 319 | 362 | 631 | 932 | 665 | 444 | 228 | 62 | 22 | 3666 |
| 1988-89 | 0 | 0 | 8 | 336 | 386 | 695 | 619 | 623 | 459 | 257 | 102 | 0 | 3485 |
| 1989-90 | 0 | 3 | 30 | 167 | 404 | 934 | 518 | 390 | 357 | 186 | 37 | 0 | 3026 |
| 1990-91 | 0 | 0 | 18 | 124 | 323 | 520 | | | | | | | |

**TABLE 5**  COOLING DEGREE DAYS Base 65 deg. F    RALEIGH, NORTH CAROLINA

| YEAR | JAN | FEB | MAR | APR | MAY | JUNE | JULY | AUG | SEP | OCT | NOV | DEC | TOTAL |
|---|---|---|---|---|---|---|---|---|---|---|---|---|---|
| 1969 | 0 | 0 | 0 | 12 | 105 | 295 | 413 | 283 | 128 | 28 | 0 | 0 | 1264 |
| 1970 | 0 | 0 | 0 | 41 | 113 | 236 | 350 | 327 | 278 | 38 | 0 | 0 | 1383 |
| 1971 | 0 | 0 | 0 | 6 | 78 | 320 | 364 | 329 | 222 | 61 | 17 | 5 | 1402 |
| 1972 | 0 | 0 | 5 | 37 | 36 | 170 | 382 | 336 | 177 | 6 | 6 | 2 | 1157 |
| 1973 | 0 | 0 | 24 | 26 | 81 | 310 | 363 | 365 | 254 | 48 | 7 | 0 | 1478 |
| 1974 | 0 | 0 | 25 | 51 | 130 | 210 | 363 | 347 | 169 | 9 | 21 | 0 | 1325 |
| 1975 | 0 | 0 | 3 | 22 | 141 | 269 | 337 | 421 | 209 | 38 | 12 | 0 | 1452 |
| 1976 | 0 | 3 | 31 | 71 | 116 | 304 | 428 | 330 | 157 | 19 | 0 | 0 | 1459 |
| 1977 | 0 | 2 | 4 | 68 | 162 | 272 | 490 | 414 | 245 | 25 | 19 | 0 | 1701 |
| 1978 | 0 | 0 | 2 | 30 | 120 | 330 | 412 | 468 | 275 | 21 | 3 | 10 | 1671 |
| 1979 | 0 | 0 | 6 | 28 | 105 | 159 | 332 | 384 | 205 | 46 | 10 | 0 | 1275 |
| 1980 | 0 | 0 | 0 | 45 | 190 | 306 | 441 | 460 | 321 | 38 | 6 | 0 | 1807 |
| 1981 | 0 | 0 | 2 | 56 | 75 | 425 | 497 | 309 | 139 | 19 | 0 | 0 | 1522 |
| 1982 | 0 | 0 | 3 | 24 | 208 | 299 | 443 | 363 | 183 | 53 | 5 | 7 | 1588 |
| 1983 | 0 | 0 | 0 | 16 | 97 | 238 | 441 | 447 | 239 | 42 | 0 | 0 | 1520 |
| 1984 | 0 | 0 | 0 | 16 | 108 | 324 | 311 | 366 | 143 | 90 | 0 | 0 | 1358 |
| 1985 | 0 | 3 | 20 | 65 | 121 | 277 | 373 | 323 | 181 | 64 | 14 | 0 | 1441 |
| 1986 | 0 | 0 | 7 | 51 | 142 | 408 | 526 | 349 | 237 | 96 | 15 | 0 | 1831 |
| 1987 | 0 | 0 | 0 | 11 | 170 | 347 | 508 | 447 | 250 | 0 | 2 | 0 | 1735 |
| 1988 | 0 | 3 | 5 | 17 | 98 | 249 | 438 | 482 | 172 | 14 | 0 | 0 | 1481 |
| 1989 | 0 | 11 | 23 | 54 | 110 | 367 | 412 | 359 | 237 | 59 | 3 | 0 | 1636 |
| 1990 | 0 | 3 | 49 | 51 | 117 | 312 | 472 | 410 | 239 | 102 | 4 | 5 | 1764 |

**TABLE 6**  SNOWFALL (inches)    RALEIGH, NORTH CAROLINA

| SEASON | JULY | AUG | SEP | OCT | NOV | DEC | JAN | FEB | MAR | APR | MAY | JUNE | TOTAL |
|---|---|---|---|---|---|---|---|---|---|---|---|---|---|
| 1961-62 | 0.0 | 0.0 | 0.0 | 0.0 | 0.0 | 0.0 | 10.1 | 0.4 | 4.3 | 0.0 | 0.0 | 0.0 | 14.8 |
| 1962-63 | 0.0 | 0.0 | 0.0 | 0.0 | 1.3 | T | 0.1 | 6.9 | 0.0 | 0.0 | 0.0 | 0.0 | 8.3 |
| 1963-64 | 0.0 | 0.0 | 0.0 | 0.0 | 0.0 | T | 0.4 | 3.1 | T | 0.0 | 0.0 | 0.0 | 3.5 |
| 1964-65 | 0.0 | 0.0 | 0.0 | 0.0 | 0.4 | 0.0 | 9.7 | 3.4 | T | 0.0 | 0.0 | 0.0 | 13.5 |
| 1965-66 | 0.0 | 0.0 | 0.0 | 0.0 | 0.0 | 0.0 | 12.3 | T | 0.0 | 0.0 | 0.0 | 0.0 | 12.3 |
| 1966-67 | 0.0 | 0.0 | 0.0 | 0.0 | T | 1.0 | 0.5 | 9.1 | 0.0 | 0.0 | 0.0 | 0.0 | 10.6 |
| 1967-68 | 0.0 | 0.0 | 0.0 | 0.0 | T | 1.4 | 3.0 | 1.3 | T | 0.0 | 0.0 | 0.0 | 5.7 |
| 1968-69 | 0.0 | 0.0 | 0.0 | 0.0 | 1.2 | 0.7 | T | 0.8 | 9.3 | 0.0 | 0.0 | 0.0 | 12.0 |
| 1969-70 | 0.0 | 0.0 | 0.0 | 0.0 | 0.0 | 0.0 | 2.0 | T | T | 0.0 | 0.0 | 0.0 | 2.0 |
| 1970-71 | 0.0 | 0.0 | 0.0 | 0.0 | 0.0 | 0.6 | T | T | 5.3 | 0.0 | 0.0 | 0.0 | 5.9 |
| 1971-72 | 0.0 | 0.0 | 0.0 | 0.0 | T | 3.7 | 0.0 | 1.4 | 2.6 | 0.0 | 0.0 | 0.0 | 7.7 |
| 1972-73 | 0.0 | 0.0 | 0.0 | 0.0 | T | 0.0 | 6.4 | 4.5 | 0.4 | 0.0 | 0.0 | 0.0 | 11.3 |
| 1973-74 | 0.0 | 0.0 | 0.0 | 0.0 | 0.0 | 2.8 | 0.0 | T | 2.9 | 0.0 | 0.0 | 0.0 | 5.7 |
| 1974-75 | 0.0 | 0.0 | 0.0 | 0.0 | T | 0.0 | T | T | 0.6 | 0.0 | 0.0 | 0.0 | 0.6 |
| 1975-76 | 0.0 | 0.0 | 0.0 | 0.0 | 2.6 | T | 0.4 | T | 0.0 | 0.0 | 0.0 | 0.0 | 3.0 |
| 1976-77 | 0.0 | 0.0 | 0.0 | 0.0 | 0.0 | 0.0 | 2.1 | 1.5 | T | 0.0 | 0.0 | 0.0 | 3.6 |
| 1977-78 | 0.0 | 0.0 | 0.0 | 0.0 | T | T | T | 9.0 | 1.6 | 0.0 | 0.0 | 0.0 | 10.6 |
| 1978-79 | 0.0 | 0.0 | 0.0 | 0.0 | 0.0 | 0.0 | 0.4 | 17.2 | T | 0.0 | 0.0 | 0.0 | 17.6 |
| #1979-80 | 0.0 | 0.0 | 0.0 | 0.0 | 0.0 | 0.0 | 2.2 | 5.0 | 11.1 | 0.0 | 0.0 | 0.0 | 18.3 |
| 1980-81 | 0.0 | 0.0 | 0.0 | 0.0 | 0.0 | 3.1 | 2.6 | 0.0 | T | 0.0 | 0.0 | 0.0 | 5.7 |
| 1981-82 | 0.0 | 0.0 | 0.0 | 0.0 | 0.0 | T | 6.0 | 0.6 | 0.0 | 0.0 | 0.0 | 0.0 | 6.6 |
| 1982-83 | 0.0 | 0.0 | 0.0 | 0.0 | 0.0 | T | T | 2.7 | 7.3 | 1.8 | 0.0 | 0.0 | 11.8 |
| 1983-84 | 0.0 | 0.0 | 0.0 | 0.0 | 0.0 | 0.0 | T | 6.9 | T | 0.0 | 0.0 | 0.0 | 6.9 |
| 1984-85 | 0.0 | 0.0 | 0.0 | 0.0 | 0.0 | 0.0 | 4.1 | T | 0.0 | 0.0 | 0.0 | 0.0 | 4.1 |
| 1985-86 | 0.0 | 0.0 | 0.0 | 0.0 | 0.0 | T | T | 0.9 | 0.0 | 0.0 | 0.0 | 0.0 | 0.9 |
| 1986-87 | 0.0 | 0.0 | 0.0 | 0.0 | T | 0.0 | 0.6 | 10.2 | T | T | 0.0 | 0.0 | 10.8 |
| 1987-88 | 0.0 | 0.0 | 0.0 | 0.0 | 0.6 | 0.0 | 7.3 | T | T | 0.0 | 0.0 | 0.0 | 7.9 |
| 1988-89 | 0.0 | 0.0 | 0.0 | 0.0 | 0.0 | 0.1 | 0.0 | 0.0 | 11.1 | 0.5 | 0.3 | 0.0 | 12.0 |
| 1989-90 | 0.0 | 0.0 | 0.0 | 0.0 | 0.0 | 2.7 | 0.0 | T | 0.0 | 0.0 | 0.0 | 0.0 | 2.7 |
| 1990-91 | 0.0 | 0.0 | 0.0 | 0.0 | 0.0 | T | | | | | | | |
| Record Mean | 0.0 | 0.0 | 0.0 | 0.0 | 0.1 | 0.8 | 2.4 | 2.7 | 1.4 | T | 0.0 | 0.0 | 7.5 |

**See Reference Notes, relative to all above tables, on preceding page.**

Moorhead, Minnesota, and Fargo are twin cities in the Red River Valley of the north. The Red River of the north flows northward between the two cities and is a part of the Hudson Bay drainage area. The Red River is approximately 2 miles east of the airport at its nearest point and has no significant effect on the weather. In recent years, spring floods due to melting snow have been common. Summer floods caused by heavy rains are infrequent.

The surrounding terrain is flat and open. Northerly winds blowing up the valley occasionally causing low cloudiness and fog. However, this upslope cloudiness is very infrequent. Aside from this, there are no pronounced climatic differences due to geographical features in the immediate area.

The summers are generally comfortable with very few days of hot and humid weather. Nights, with few exceptions, are comfortably cool. The winter months are cold and dry with temperatures rising above freezing only on an average of six days each month, and nighttime lows dropping below zero approximately half of the time.

Precipitation is the most important climatic factor in the area. The Red River Valley lies in an area where lighter amounts fall to the west and heavier amounts to the east. Seventy-five percent of the precipitation occurs during the growing season (April to September) and is often accompanied by electrical storms and heavy falls in a short time. Winter precipitation is light, indicating that heavy snowfall is the exception rather than the rule. The first light snow in the fall occasionally falls in September, but usually very little, if any, occurs until October or November. The latest fall is generally in April.

With the flat terrain, surface friction has little effect on the wind in the area and this fact has led to the legendary Dakota blizzards. Strong winds with even light snowfall cause much drifting and blowing snow, reducing visibility to near zero. Fortunately, these conditions occur only several times during the winter months.

# TABLE 1   NORMALS, MEANS AND EXTREMES

FARGO, NORTH DAKOTA

LATITUDE: 46°54'N   LONGITUDE: 96°48'W   ELEVATION: FT. GRND 896 BARO 911   TIME ZONE: CENTRAL   WBAN: 14914

| | (a) | JAN | FEB | MAR | APR | MAY | JUNE | JULY | AUG | SEP | OCT | NOV | DEC | YEAR |
|---|---|---|---|---|---|---|---|---|---|---|---|---|---|---|
| **TEMPERATURE °F:** | | | | | | | | | | | | | | |
| Normals | | | | | | | | | | | | | | |
| -Daily Maximum | | 13.7 | 20.5 | 33.2 | 52.5 | 68.1 | 76.9 | 82.7 | 81.1 | 69.8 | 57.7 | 37.0 | 21.3 | 51.2 |
| -Daily Minimum | | -5.1 | 1.5 | 14.8 | 31.6 | 43.0 | 53.5 | 58.4 | 56.4 | 45.7 | 34.9 | 19.4 | 4.0 | 29.8 |
| -Monthly | | 4.3 | 11.0 | 24.0 | 42.1 | 55.6 | 65.2 | 70.6 | 68.8 | 57.8 | 46.3 | 28.2 | 12.7 | 40.5 |
| Extremes | | | | | | | | | | | | | | |
| -Record Highest | 37 | 52 | 66 | 78 | 100 | 98 | 99 | 106 | 106 | 102 | 93 | 73 | 57 | 106 |
| -Year | | 1981 | 1958 | 1967 | 1980 | 1964 | 1959 | 1988 | 1976 | 1959 | 1963 | 1978 | 1962 | JUL 1988 |
| -Record Lowest | 37 | -35 | -34 | -23 | -7 | 20 | 30 | 36 | 33 | 19 | 7 | -24 | -32 | -35 |
| -Year | | 1977 | 1962 | 1980 | 1975 | 1966 | 1969 | 1967 | 1982 | 1965 | 1976 | 1985 | 1967 | JAN 1977 |
| **NORMAL DEGREE DAYS:** | | | | | | | | | | | | | | |
| Heating (base 65°F) | | 1882 | 1512 | 1271 | 687 | 311 | 86 | 17 | 36 | 236 | 580 | 1104 | 1621 | 9343 |
| Cooling (base 65°F) | | 0 | 0 | 0 | 0 | 19 | 92 | 191 | 154 | 20 | 0 | 0 | 0 | 476 |
| **% OF POSSIBLE SUNSHINE** | 47 | 50 | 56 | 57 | 59 | 60 | 61 | 72 | 69 | 59 | 54 | 40 | 43 | 57 |
| **MEAN SKY COVER (tenths)** | | | | | | | | | | | | | | |
| Sunrise - Sunset | 44 | 6.7 | 6.7 | 7.0 | 6.6 | 6.4 | 6.1 | 5.0 | 5.2 | 5.8 | 6.1 | 7.1 | 7.0 | 6.3 |
| **MEAN NUMBER OF DAYS:** | | | | | | | | | | | | | | |
| Sunrise to Sunset | | | | | | | | | | | | | | |
| -Clear | 47 | 6.7 | 6.3 | 5.4 | 6.6 | 7.0 | 6.8 | 10.5 | 10.5 | 8.8 | 8.8 | 5.6 | 6.1 | 89.0 |
| -Partly Cloudy | 47 | 7.5 | 7.3 | 8.9 | 8.7 | 9.7 | 10.9 | 13.4 | 11.9 | 9.0 | 8.3 | 6.5 | 7.4 | 109.4 |
| -Cloudy | 47 | 16.8 | 14.7 | 16.8 | 14.7 | 14.3 | 12.3 | 7.1 | 8.6 | 12.2 | 13.9 | 18.0 | 17.5 | 166.9 |
| Precipitation | | | | | | | | | | | | | | |
| .01 inches or more | 47 | 8.6 | 7.0 | 7.9 | 8.1 | 10.0 | 10.4 | 9.6 | 9.1 | 8.0 | 6.5 | 6.1 | 8.0 | 99.4 |
| Snow,Ice pellets | | | | | | | | | | | | | | |
| 1.0 inches or more | 47 | 2.5 | 1.7 | 2.1 | 1.0 | 0.* | 0.0 | 0.0 | 0.0 | 0.0 | 0.3 | 1.8 | 2.2 | 11.6 |
| Thunderstorms | 47 | 0.0 | 0.* | 0.3 | 1.3 | 3.9 | 7.3 | 8.6 | 7.0 | 3.0 | 1.0 | 0.1 | 0.* | 32.3 |
| Heavy Fog Visibility | | | | | | | | | | | | | | |
| 1/4 mile or less | 47 | 0.7 | 1.7 | 1.8 | 0.6 | 0.4 | 0.6 | 0.7 | 1.1 | 0.9 | 0.9 | 1.4 | 1.8 | 12.5 |
| Temperature °F | | | | | | | | | | | | | | |
| -Maximum | | | | | | | | | | | | | | |
| 90° and above | 30 | 0.0 | 0.0 | 0.0 | 0.1 | 0.7 | 2.3 | 5.7 | 5.3 | 1.1 | 0.* | 0.0 | 0.0 | 15.2 |
| 32° and below | 30 | 27.6 | 21.7 | 13.1 | 1.2 | 0.* | 0.0 | 0.0 | 0.0 | 0.0 | 0.5 | 10.5 | 25.3 | 99.9 |
| -Minimum | | | | | | | | | | | | | | |
| 32° and below | 30 | 31.0 | 28.2 | 27.7 | 16.3 | 4.1 | 0.* | 0.0 | 0.0 | 1.8 | 12.6 | 26.8 | 30.9 | 179.4 |
| 0° and below | 30 | 19.0 | 13.1 | 4.7 | 0.1 | 0.0 | 0.0 | 0.0 | 0.0 | 0.0 | 0.0 | 2.2 | 13.5 | 52.7 |
| **AVG. STATION PRESS.(mb)** | 17 | 985.4 | 986.1 | 982.8 | 982.1 | 980.2 | 979.5 | 981.1 | 981.6 | 982.5 | 983.1 | 983.5 | 984.8 | 982.7 |
| **RELATIVE HUMIDITY (%)** | | | | | | | | | | | | | | |
| Hour 00 | 30 | 74 | 77 | 80 | 73 | 67 | 75 | 77 | 77 | 78 | 76 | 80 | 78 | 76 |
| Hour 06 (Local Time) | 30 | 74 | 77 | 82 | 79 | 77 | 82 | 85 | 86 | 85 | 81 | 82 | 78 | 81 |
| Hour 12 | 30 | 71 | 72 | 71 | 57 | 50 | 56 | 54 | 55 | 58 | 60 | 71 | 74 | 62 |
| Hour 18 | 30 | 73 | 74 | 71 | 54 | 46 | 51 | 51 | 50 | 55 | 61 | 73 | 76 | 61 |
| **PRECIPITATION (inches):** | | | | | | | | | | | | | | |
| Water Equivalent | | | | | | | | | | | | | | |
| -Normal | | 0.55 | 0.42 | 0.83 | 1.90 | 2.24 | 3.06 | 3.34 | 2.67 | 1.87 | 1.29 | 0.79 | 0.63 | 19.59 |
| -Maximum Monthly | 48 | 1.85 | 1.74 | 2.27 | 5.28 | 7.30 | 9.40 | 8.42 | 8.52 | 6.13 | 7.03 | 4.58 | 2.19 | 9.40 |
| -Year | | 1989 | 1979 | 1983 | 1986 | 1977 | 1975 | 1952 | 1944 | 1957 | 1982 | 1977 | 1951 | JUN 1975 |
| -Minimum Monthly | 48 | 0.09 | 0.03 | 0.03 | 0.01 | 0.46 | 0.58 | 0.42 | 0.18 | 0.13 | 0.05 | 0.04 | 0.04 | 0.01 |
| -Year | | 1961 | 1954 | 1958 | 1988 | 1976 | 1972 | 1950 | 1984 | 1974 | 1986 | 1967 | 1958 | APR 1988 |
| -Maximum in 24 hrs | 48 | 1.00 | 1.22 | 1.16 | 1.91 | 4.10 | 4.02 | 3.93 | 4.72 | 3.97 | 3.22 | 1.99 | 0.87 | 4.72 |
| -Year | | 1989 | 1946 | 1950 | 1963 | 1977 | 1975 | 1952 | 1943 | 1957 | 1982 | 1977 | 1960 | AUG 1943 |
| Snow,Ice pellets | | | | | | | | | | | | | | |
| -Maximum Monthly | 48 | 31.5 | 19.5 | 18.7 | 12.8 | 1.0 | 0.0 | 0.0 | T | 0.6 | 8.1 | 24.3 | 20.3 | 31.5 |
| -Year | | 1989 | 1979 | 1975 | 1970 | 1950 | | | 1989 | 1942 | 1951 | 1985 | 1951 | JAN 1989 |
| -Maximum in 24 hrs | 48 | 19.4 | 11.2 | 10.4 | 8.6 | 1.0 | 0.0 | 0.0 | T | 0.6 | 7.8 | 12.6 | 9.3 | 19.4 |
| -Year | | 1989 | 1951 | 1975 | 1970 | 1950 | | | 1989 | 1942 | 1951 | 1977 | 1988 | JAN 1989 |
| **WIND:** | | | | | | | | | | | | | | |
| Mean Speed (mph) | 47 | 12.7 | 12.5 | 13.1 | 14.0 | 13.0 | 11.7 | 10.6 | 11.0 | 11.9 | 12.6 | 12.8 | 12.3 | 12.4 |
| Prevailing Direction | | | | | | | | | | | | | | |
| through 1963 | | SSE | N | N | N | N | SSE | S | SSE | SSE | SSE | S | S | SSE |
| Fastest Mile | | | | | | | | | | | | | | |
| -Direction (!!!) | 43 | SE | W | N | NW | NW | NW | S | NW | N | NW | N | N | NW |
| -Speed (MPH) | 43 | 62 | 56 | 56 | 68 | 72 | 115 | 60 | 71 | 88 | 57 | 66 | 58 | 115 |
| -Year | | 1968 | 1957 | 1960 | 1964 | 1960 | 1959 | 1965 | 1955 | 1960 | 1960 | 1956 | 1957 | JUN 1959 |
| Peak Gust | | | | | | | | | | | | | | |
| -Direction (!!!) | 6 | NW | N | SE | SW | NW | SE | NW | NW | NW | SE | SE | N | NW |
| -Speed (mph) | 6 | 59 | 59 | 53 | 45 | 62 | 52 | 69 | 60 | 62 | 51 | 48 | 55 | 69 |
| -Date | | 1985 | 1984 | 1985 | 1988 | 1988 | 1984 | 1987 | 1988 | 1988 | 1989 | 1985 | 1985 | JUL 1987 |

**See Reference Notes to this table on the following page.**

# FARGO, NORTH DAKOTA

## PRECIPITATION (inches) — FARGO, NORTH DAKOTA

**TABLE 2**

| YEAR | JAN | FEB | MAR | APR | MAY | JUNE | JULY | AUG | SEP | OCT | NOV | DEC | ANNUAL |
|------|-----|-----|-----|-----|-----|------|------|-----|-----|-----|-----|-----|--------|
| 1961 | 0.09 | 0.18 | 0.38 | 2.27 | 2.71 | 1.36 | 3.00 | 1.02 | 4.44 | 1.70 | 0.06 | 0.57 | 17.78 |
| 1962 | 1.07 | 0.97 | 1.08 | 1.51 | 5.95 | 2.78 | 5.92 | 3.25 | 2.42 | 0.86 | 0.54 | 0.30 | 26.65 |
| 1963 | 0.13 | 0.33 | 0.51 | 2.67 | 2.61 | 1.69 | 0.66 | 4.41 | 1.19 | 0.23 | 0.12 | 0.39 | 14.94 |
| 1964 | 0.54 | 0.27 | 0.92 | 3.76 | 0.87 | 4.85 | 0.77 | 2.85 | 1.70 | 0.10 | 0.72 | 0.91 | 18.26 |
| 1965 | 0.10 | 0.14 | 1.36 | 3.04 | 3.06 | 3.10 | 4.81 | 2.55 | 3.50 | 0.55 | 0.79 | 1.01 | 24.01 |
| 1966 | 0.40 | 0.26 | 1.92 | 1.78 | 1.27 | 2.91 | 4.01 | 3.80 | 0.54 | 1.40 | 0.18 | 0.50 | 18.97 |
| 1967 | 1.03 | 0.21 | 0.34 | 4.14 | 1.00 | 2.54 | 0.60 | 0.41 | 0.31 | 1.06 | 0.04 | 1.36 | 13.04 |
| 1968 | 0.37 | 0.27 | 1.29 | 4.09 | 2.08 | 3.94 | 1.49 | 1.61 | 2.23 | 1.75 | 0.37 | 1.11 | 20.60 |
| 1969 | 1.27 | 0.46 | 0.54 | 1.55 | 2.36 | 2.03 | 5.92 | 0.38 | 1.55 | 1.51 | 0.14 | 0.81 | 18.52 |
| 1970 | 0.10 | 0.20 | 1.52 | 2.30 | 2.83 | 2.63 | 0.43 | 1.24 | 3.61 | 1.61 | 0.96 | 0.47 | 17.90 |
| 1971 | 0.81 | 0.34 | 0.56 | 1.10 | 2.68 | 3.51 | 2.80 | 0.92 | 4.30 | 4.42 | 0.83 | 0.59 | 22.86 |
| 1972 | 0.94 | 0.61 | 0.74 | 0.96 | 3.52 | 0.58 | 2.78 | 3.45 | 1.22 | 1.25 | 0.22 | 1.51 | 17.78 |
| 1973 | 0.12 | 0.13 | 1.25 | 0.70 | 1.65 | 1.78 | 3.60 | 3.85 | 4.98 | 1.54 | 0.90 | 1.02 | 21.52 |
| 1974 | 0.35 | 0.36 | 0.71 | 3.40 | 4.03 | 0.90 | 4.75 | 6.46 | 0.13 | 3.10 | 0.48 | 0.32 | 24.99 |
| 1975 | 1.32 | 0.27 | 1.48 | 3.24 | 1.45 | 9.40 | 2.42 | 2.90 | 1.24 | 1.76 | 0.64 | 0.18 | 26.30 |
| 1976 | 1.25 | 0.35 | 1.00 | 1.19 | 0.46 | 2.34 | 0.43 | 0.41 | 0.55 | 0.16 | 0.26 | 0.24 | 8.84 |
| 1977 | 0.65 | 1.24 | 1.72 | 0.84 | 7.30 | 1.64 | 5.36 | 2.53 | 3.21 | 2.46 | 4.58 | 0.75 | 32.28 |
| 1978 | 0.16 | 0.18 | 0.43 | 1.15 | 1.78 | 4.40 | 2.92 | 3.79 | 0.92 | 0.13 | 1.11 | 0.47 | 17.44 |
| 1979 | 0.44 | 1.74 | 2.00 | 3.04 | 2.02 | 2.92 | 3.38 | 0.90 | 0.31 | 2.60 | 0.48 | 0.14 | 19.97 |
| 1980 | 1.23 | 0.57 | 0.62 | 0.02 | 0.64 | 2.68 | 0.76 | 4.24 | 2.52 | 1.06 | 0.47 | 0.30 | 15.11 |
| 1981 | 0.11 | 0.49 | 0.67 | 0.61 | 3.46 | 2.56 | 3.21 | 1.76 | 1.11 | 2.36 | 0.40 | 0.85 | 17.59 |
| 1982 | 1.32 | 0.54 | 1.25 | 0.45 | 1.82 | 1.61 | 2.64 | 1.12 | 1.12 | 7.03 | 1.13 | 0.17 | 20.20 |
| 1983 | 0.46 | 0.21 | 2.27 | 0.42 | 2.00 | 2.34 | 4.16 | 2.56 | 1.63 | 1.62 | 1.04 | 0.96 | 19.67 |
| 1984 | 0.79 | 0.90 | 1.12 | 1.68 | 0.61 | 5.38 | 0.64 | 0.18 | 1.23 | 6.76 | 0.18 | 0.90 | 20.37 |
| 1985 | 0.20 | 0.18 | 1.35 | 0.60 | 5.03 | 1.44 | 3.91 | 2.30 | 1.39 | 1.12 | 1.06 | 0.59 | 19.17 |
| 1986 | 0.85 | 0.27 | 0.19 | 5.28 | 1.00 | 3.98 | 4.78 | 1.72 | 3.67 | 0.05 | 1.43 | 0.29 | 23.51 |
| 1987 | 0.27 | 0.86 | 0.49 | 0.12 | 3.46 | 0.66 | 2.86 | 3.23 | 1.70 | 0.18 | 0.48 | 0.69 | 15.00 |
| 1988 | 1.62 | 0.22 | 1.02 | 0.01 | 1.82 | 1.24 | 0.46 | 2.14 | 3.22 | 0.49 | 1.18 | 1.11 | 14.53 |
| 1989 | 1.85 | 0.21 | 1.49 | 1.03 | 2.60 | 1.51 | 0.62 | 6.07 | 2.10 | 0.31 | 1.18 | 0.24 | 19.21 |
| 1990 | 0.13 | 0.58 | 1.54 | 1.78 | 1.52 | 6.05 | 0.78 | 0.99 | 1.75 | 1.22 | 0.02 | 0.77 | 17.13 |
| Record Mean | 0.64 | 0.59 | 0.92 | 1.93 | 2.45 | 3.36 | 3.08 | 2.76 | 1.95 | 1.53 | 0.86 | 0.66 | 20.73 |

## AVERAGE TEMPERATURE (deg. F) — FARGO, NORTH DAKOTA

**TABLE 3**

| YEAR | JAN | FEB | MAR | APR | MAY | JUNE | JULY | AUG | SEP | OCT | NOV | DEC | ANNUAL |
|------|-----|-----|-----|-----|-----|------|------|-----|-----|-----|-----|-----|--------|
| 1961 | 6.8 | 18.7 | 34.5 | 37.8 | 53.2 | 68.7 | 70.5 | 73.5 | 56.0 | 47.9 | 30.1 | 10.7 | 42.4 |
| 1962 | 4.4 | 5.6 | 22.7 | 39.9 | 56.6 | 66.2 | 71.6 | 71.6 | 62.2 | 51.1 | 35.0 | 16.6 | 41.3 |
| 1963 | 2.0 | 10.1 | 29.0 | 43.5 | 54.3 | 68.8 | 73.6 | 70.3 | 62.2 | 57.3 | 34.7 | 8.6 | 42.9 |
| 1964 | 15.6 | 18.9 | 20.8 | 46.4 | 61.1 | 67.2 | 74.0 | 64.9 | 55.4 | 45.2 | 29.2 | 3.8 | 41.9 |
| 1965 | -1.2 | 7.1 | 13.7 | 41.6 | 54.4 | 63.9 | 68.5 | 66.5 | 48.9 | 47.3 | 26.0 | 19.2 | 38.0 |
| 1966 | -6.4 | 6.2 | 29.7 | 37.2 | 51.4 | 66.1 | 73.8 | 65.5 | 58.2 | 44.0 | 23.1 | 11.9 | 38.4 |
| 1967 | 9.3 | 3.8 | 26.8 | 38.3 | 49.7 | 62.6 | 67.9 | 66.7 | 60.8 | 44.0 | 29.0 | 15.1 | 39.5 |
| 1968 | 7.7 | 9.9 | 34.1 | 43.9 | 52.9 | 64.1 | 69.6 | 68.1 | 59.3 | 46.7 | 31.0 | 8.9 | 41.4 |
| 1969 | -1.6 | 12.8 | 15.3 | 45.4 | 54.8 | 57.3 | 68.4 | 72.4 | 59.0 | 40.3 | 30.5 | 15.6 | 39.2 |
| 1970 | 0.6 | 10.9 | 18.6 | 39.1 | 54.2 | 67.9 | 71.7 | 69.7 | 56.7 | 46.8 | 27.8 | 9.3 | 39.5 |
| 1971 | -0.7 | 12.7 | 27.6 | 44.5 | 54.2 | 67.5 | 65.1 | 68.3 | 58.5 | 47.4 | 29.6 | 12.2 | 40.6 |
| 1972 | 2.7 | 4.1 | 23.9 | 41.0 | 59.8 | 66.9 | 68.4 | 70.5 | 56.9 | 42.4 | 28.6 | 3.8 | 39.1 |
| 1973 | 10.3 | 16.3 | 36.0 | 41.4 | 54.2 | 64.7 | 68.3 | 71.7 | 54.8 | 50.2 | 25.1 | 10.1 | 41.9 |
| 1974 | 1.7 | 9.6 | 22.9 | 42.2 | 51.1 | 64.4 | 73.7 | 64.3 | 57.5 | 47.5 | 29.2 | 20.9 | 40.1 |
| 1975 | 12.3 | 10.1 | 18.4 | 35.9 | 56.6 | 65.2 | 74.3 | 68.1 | 55.4 | 49.4 | 31.1 | 14.8 | 41.0 |
| 1976 | 7.7 | 21.4 | 23.0 | 47.0 | 55.8 | 68.5 | 71.8 | 73.6 | 60.0 | 39.5 | 23.2 | 6.9 | 41.5 |
| 1977 | -3.3 | 17.5 | 32.0 | 49.5 | 66.5 | 66.6 | 72.2 | 62.5 | 57.9 | 47.1 | 25.6 | 6.5 | 41.7 |
| 1978 | -1.4 | 3.4 | 23.5 | 42.5 | 59.1 | 64.7 | 69.5 | 69.1 | 63.6 | 46.4 | 22.8 | 7.3 | 39.2 |
| 1979 | -4.2 | -1.5 | 20.4 | 36.0 | 50.4 | 65.4 | 71.9 | 67.3 | 62.0 | 42.6 | 24.5 | 20.7 | 38.0 |
| 1980 | 6.6 | 8.3 | 20.7 | 49.0 | 61.4 | 65.7 | 71.9 | 67.5 | 56.9 | 42.4 | 33.1 | 12.7 | 41.6 |
| 1981 | 11.8 | 19.6 | 33.5 | 45.6 | 55.5 | 62.8 | 71.1 | 69.6 | 57.4 | 44.5 | 35.4 | 8.7 | 43.0 |
| 1982 | -7.0 | 8.9 | 22.9 | 40.7 | 58.1 | 59.1 | 70.9 | 68.5 | 57.5 | 45.7 | 24.1 | 20.9 | 39.2 |
| 1983 | 16.1 | 21.8 | 29.9 | 40.2 | 52.1 | 66.1 | 73.5 | 72.9 | 56.7 | 44.4 | 31.3 | -0.3 | 42.1 |
| 1984 | 9.7 | 24.9 | 23.4 | 45.6 | 54.2 | 65.8 | 70.6 | 73.3 | 54.4 | 47.4 | 29.7 | 9.6 | 42.4 |
| 1985 | 5.1 | 10.9 | 32.9 | 46.6 | 60.2 | 60.0 | 69.0 | 64.5 | 53.9 | 44.6 | 15.4 | 3.9 | 38.9 |
| 1986 | 13.8 | 10.5 | 31.6 | 43.9 | 57.5 | 67.5 | 71.5 | 65.6 | 56.1 | 45.3 | 23.1 | 20.3 | 42.3 |
| 1987 | 18.2 | 27.5 | 31.4 | 51.5 | 61.7 | 69.1 | 74.0 | 66.8 | 59.6 | 42.6 | 33.4 | 20.6 | 46.4 |
| 1988 | 5.9 | 9.3 | 29.5 | 44.5 | 63.9 | 73.8 | 75.8 | 72.2 | 58.5 | 42.9 | 27.5 | 15.2 | 43.3 |
| 1989 | 11.4 | 1.7 | 20.1 | 42.2 | 58.2 | 64.1 | 75.9 | 70.8 | 58.5 | 45.8 | 24.0 | 4.3 | 39.8 |
| 1990 | 21.8 | 17.6 | 31.4 | 43.6 | 55.0 | 67.0 | 70.0 | 71.1 | 62.3 | 45.6 | 32.1 | 12.2 | 44.1 |
| Record Mean | 5.4 | 9.9 | 24.4 | 42.5 | 55.1 | 64.8 | 70.3 | 68.1 | 58.0 | 45.6 | 27.4 | 12.6 | 40.4 |
| Max | 14.9 | 19.5 | 33.6 | 53.1 | 67.2 | 76.1 | 82.1 | 80.2 | 69.7 | 56.4 | 36.1 | 21.4 | 50.9 |
| Min | -4.1 | 0.4 | 15.3 | 31.8 | 43.0 | 53.4 | 58.4 | 55.9 | 46.2 | 34.7 | 18.7 | 3.9 | 29.8 |

## REFERENCE NOTES FOR TABLES 1, 2, 3 and 6 (FARGO, ND)

### GENERAL

T - TRACE AMOUNT
BLANK ENTRIES DENOTE MISSING/UNREPORTED DATA.
# INDICATES A STATION OR INSTRUMENT RELOCATION.

### SPECIFIC

#### TABLE 1

(a) - LENGTH OF RECORD IN YEARS. ALTHOUGH INDIVIDUAL MONTHS MAY BE MISSING.

\* LESS THAN .05

NORMALS — BASED ON THE 1951-1980 RECORD PERIOD.
EXTREMES — DATES ARE THE MOST RECENT OCCURRENCE.
WIND DIR. — NUMERALS SHOW TENS OF DEGREES CLOCKWISE FROM TRUE NORTH.
"00" INDICATES CALM.
RESULTANT WIND DIRECTIONS ARE GIVEN TO WHOLE DEGREES.

#### TABLE 3

MAX AND MIN ARE LONG-TERM MEAN DAILY MAXIMUM AND MEAN DAILY MINIMUM TEMPERATURES.

### EXCEPTIONS

#### TABLES 2, 3, and 6

RECORD MEANS ARE THROUGH THE CURRENT YEAR, BEGINNING IN
1881 FOR TEMPERATURE
1881 FOR PRECIPITATION
1943 FOR SNOWFALL

**TABLE 4**

HEATING DEGREE DAYS Base 65 deg. F     FARGO, NORTH DAKOTA

| SEASON | JULY | AUG | SEP | OCT | NOV | DEC | JAN | FEB | MAR | APR | MAY | JUNE | TOTAL |
|---|---|---|---|---|---|---|---|---|---|---|---|---|---|
| 1961-62 | 2 | 9 | 301 | 527 | 1039 | 1681 | 1880 | 1660 | 1304 | 749 | 258 | 61 | 9471 |
| 1962-63 | 11 | 5 | 232 | 439 | 892 | 1492 | 1957 | 1535 | 1112 | 640 | 339 | 45 | 8699 |
| 1963-64 | 5 | 14 | 127 | 262 | 901 | 1748 | 1528 | 1331 | 1364 | 553 | 177 | 68 | 8078 |
| 1964-65 | 5 | 94 | 304 | 604 | 1065 | 1902 | 2051 | 1618 | 1582 | 695 | 324 | 66 | 10310 |
| 1965-66 | 19 | 59 | 477 | 544 | 1161 | 1415 | 2216 | 1649 | 1089 | 829 | 430 | 86 | 9974 |
| 1966-67 | 0 | 84 | 230 | 644 | 1253 | 1642 | 1723 | 1716 | 1178 | 795 | 480 | 96 | 9841 |
| 1967-68 | 65 | 49 | 158 | 645 | 1073 | 1544 | 1773 | 1592 | 952 | 628 | 375 | 79 | 8933 |
| 1968-69 | 31 | 66 | 201 | 565 | 1015 | 1736 | 2066 | 1460 | 1536 | 582 | 348 | 230 | 9836 |
| 1969-70 | 20 | 10 | 229 | 757 | 1028 | 1522 | 1996 | 1511 | 1431 | 773 | 407 | 55 | 9739 |
| 1970-71 | 16 | 26 | 251 | 560 | 1109 | 1723 | 2035 | 1461 | 1153 | 609 | 333 | 30 | 9306 |
| 1971-72 | 57 | 36 | 241 | 535 | 1052 | 1630 | 1931 | 1763 | 1269 | 718 | 231 | 60 | 9523 |
| 1972-73 | 25 | 41 | 261 | 695 | 1089 | 1897 | 1688 | 1361 | 893 | 701 | 328 | 79 | 9058 |
| 1973-74 | 32 | 3 | 309 | 451 | 1187 | 1698 | 1963 | 1550 | 1298 | 676 | 431 | 86 | 9684 |
| 1974-75 | 3 | 91 | 345 | 537 | 1066 | 1362 | 1630 | 1535 | 1438 | 867 | 265 | 79 | 9218 |
| 1975-76 | 14 | 22 | 284 | 492 | 1012 | 1550 | 1774 | 1257 | 1296 | 533 | 285 | 55 | 8574 |
| 1976-77 | 13 | 9 | 227 | 788 | 1247 | 1797 | 2119 | 1327 | 1015 | 466 | 74 | 30 | 9112 |
| 1977-78 | 7 | 95 | 211 | 549 | 1178 | 1817 | 2061 | 1721 | 1284 | 668 | 209 | 90 | 9890 |
| 1978-79 | 15 | 39 | 179 | 571 | 1262 | 1788 | 2147 | 1863 | 1377 | 861 | 457 | 64 | 10623 |
| 1979-80 | 3 | 45 | 139 | 689 | 1209 | 1367 | 1808 | 1644 | 1363 | 493 | 206 | 61 | 9027 |
| 1980-81 | 3 | 35 | 267 | 696 | 951 | 1616 | 1645 | 1266 | 971 | 574 | 298 | 84 | 8406 |
| 1981-82 | 14 | 10 | 250 | 627 | 881 | 1742 | 2236 | 1570 | 1298 | 725 | 222 | 187 | 9762 |
| 1982-83 | 0 | 66 | 257 | 589 | 1219 | 1359 | 1513 | 1206 | 1082 | 738 | 390 | 74 | 8493 |
| 1983-84 | 16 | 2 | 301 | 631 | 1004 | 2023 | 1714 | 1154 | 1280 | 576 | 344 | 52 | 9097 |
| 1984-85 | 15 | 13 | 339 | 541 | 1053 | 1715 | 1853 | 1514 | 988 | 550 | 179 | 172 | 8932 |
| 1985-86 | 13 | 72 | 329 | 625 | 1487 | 1895 | 1585 | 1527 | 1027 | 627 | 266 | 45 | 9498 |
| 1986-87 | 0 | 69 | 268 | 602 | 1251 | 1360 | 1447 | 1047 | 1036 | 415 | 163 | 39 | 7697 |
| 1987-88 | 15 | 59 | 177 | 688 | 940 | 1369 | 1832 | 1614 | 1092 | 609 | 131 | 8 | 8534 |
| 1988-89 | 3 | 25 | 207 | 677 | 1118 | 1537 | 1658 | 1771 | 1386 | 677 | 224 | 96 | 9379 |
| 1989-90 | 0 | 17 | 224 | 599 | 1224 | 1881 | 1332 | 1324 | 1034 | 666 | 314 | 58 | 8673 |
| 1990-91 | 8 | 18 | 173 | 594 | 982 | 1637 | | | | | | | |

**TABLE 5**    COOLING DEGREE DAYS Base 65 deg. F     FARGO, NORTH DAKOTA

| YEAR | JAN | FEB | MAR | APR | MAY | JUNE | JULY | AUG | SEP | OCT | NOV | DEC | TOTAL |
|---|---|---|---|---|---|---|---|---|---|---|---|---|---|
| 1969 | 0 | 0 | 0 | 0 | 39 | 5 | 131 | 249 | 59 | 0 | 0 | 0 | 483 |
| 1970 | 0 | 0 | 0 | 0 | 2 | 146 | 233 | 180 | 95 | 3 | 0 | 0 | 659 |
| 1971 | 0 | 0 | 0 | 0 | 3 | 109 | 65 | 142 | 56 | 0 | 0 | 0 | 375 |
| 1972 | 0 | 0 | 0 | 0 | 74 | 125 | 135 | 217 | 23 | 0 | 0 | 0 | 574 |
| 1973 | 0 | 0 | 0 | 0 | 0 | 76 | 140 | 219 | 13 | 0 | 0 | 0 | 448 |
| 1974 | 0 | 0 | 0 | 0 | 9 | 75 | 281 | 75 | 3 | 1 | 0 | 0 | 444 |
| 1975 | 0 | 0 | 0 | 0 | 11 | 92 | 308 | 126 | 1 | 15 | 0 | 0 | 553 |
| 1976 | 0 | 0 | 0 | 0 | 4 | 164 | 228 | 283 | 83 | 4 | 0 | 0 | 766 |
| 1977 | 0 | 0 | 0 | 6 | 129 | 86 | 235 | 23 | 8 | 0 | 0 | 0 | 487 |
| 1978 | 0 | 0 | 0 | 0 | 31 | 86 | 165 | 176 | 146 | 0 | 0 | 0 | 604 |
| 1979 | 0 | 0 | 0 | 0 | 12 | 85 | 225 | 124 | 58 | 0 | 0 | 0 | 504 |
| 1980 | 0 | 0 | 0 | 18 | 102 | 89 | 222 | 119 | 31 | 1 | 0 | 0 | 582 |
| 1981 | 0 | 0 | 0 | 0 | 9 | 25 | 212 | 159 | 26 | 0 | 0 | 0 | 431 |
| 1982 | 0 | 0 | 0 | 2 | 11 | 20 | 189 | 179 | 39 | 0 | 0 | 0 | 440 |
| 1983 | 0 | 0 | 0 | 0 | 2 | 113 | 288 | 252 | 55 | 0 | 0 | 0 | 710 |
| 1984 | 0 | 0 | 0 | 0 | 18 | 81 | 196 | 279 | 24 | 4 | 0 | 0 | 602 |
| 1985 | 0 | 0 | 0 | 6 | 31 | 35 | 143 | 63 | 4 | 0 | 0 | 0 | 282 |
| 1986 | 0 | 0 | 0 | 0 | 41 | 126 | 208 | 92 | 10 | 0 | 0 | 0 | 477 |
| 1987 | 0 | 0 | 0 | 17 | 66 | 169 | 303 | 121 | 25 | 0 | 0 | 0 | 701 |
| 1988 | 0 | 0 | 0 | 0 | 102 | 280 | 346 | 252 | 22 | 0 | 0 | 0 | 1002 |
| 1989 | 0 | 0 | 0 | 0 | 19 | 76 | 345 | 201 | 34 | 11 | 0 | 0 | 686 |
| 1990 | 0 | 0 | 0 | 29 | 10 | 123 | 172 | 214 | 98 | 1 | 0 | 0 | 647 |

**TABLE 6**    SNOWFALL (inches)     FARGO, NORTH DAKOTA

| SEASON | JULY | AUG | SEP | OCT | NOV | DEC | JAN | FEB | MAR | APR | MAY | JUNE | TOTAL |
|---|---|---|---|---|---|---|---|---|---|---|---|---|---|
| 1961-62 | 0.0 | 0.0 | 0.0 | T | 0.5 | 6.5 | 10.9 | 10.1 | 10.7 | 2.0 | 0.0 | 0.0 | 40.7 |
| 1962-63 | 0.0 | 0.0 | 0.0 | 0.2 | 3.1 | 2.5 | 1.3 | 3.9 | 5.3 | 6.0 | 0.1 | 0.0 | 22.4 |
| 1963-64 | 0.0 | 0.0 | 0.0 | 0.0 | 0.4 | 4.3 | 8.4 | 6.2 | 8.4 | 9.2 | 0.0 | 0.0 | 36.9 |
| 1964-65 | 0.0 | 0.0 | 0.0 | T | 2.7 | 11.9 | 1.2 | 1.7 | 13.1 | 2.5 | T | 0.0 | 33.1 |
| 1965-66 | 0.0 | 0.0 | T | 0.0 | 6.1 | 6.1 | 5.0 | 1.1 | 15.4 | 5.0 | 0.0 | 0.0 | 38.7 |
| 1966-67 | 0.0 | 0.0 | 0.0 | 1.2 | 1.3 | 3.4 | 15.1 | 2.6 | 4.9 | 5.0 | T | 0.0 | 33.5 |
| 1967-68 | 0.0 | 0.0 | 0.0 | 0.7 | 0.7 | 10.3 | 4.0 | 2.4 | 2.0 | 11.6 | 0.4 | 0.0 | 32.1 |
| 1968-69 | 0.0 | 0.0 | 0.0 | 0.8 | 3.9 | 11.4 | 14.5 | 7.8 | 3.0 | T | T | 0.0 | 41.4 |
| 1969-70 | 0.0 | 0.0 | 0.0 | 2.0 | 1.9 | 9.5 | 2.3 | 3.6 | 9.1 | 12.8 | T | 0.0 | 41.2 |
| 1970-71 | 0.0 | 0.0 | 0.0 | 0.9 | 6.4 | 8.3 | 15.1 | 4.8 | 1.8 | 1.0 | T | 0.0 | 38.3 |
| 1971-72 | 0.0 | 0.0 | 0.0 | 3.8 | 2.3 | 10.0 | 16.5 | 10.9 | 7.1 | 3.1 | 0.0 | 0.0 | 53.7 |
| 1972-73 | 0.0 | 0.0 | T | 3.8 | 1.7 | 18.5 | 1.7 | 1.4 | 1.4 | 2.4 | 0.0 | 0.0 | 30.9 |
| 1973-74 | 0.0 | 0.0 | 0.0 | T | 3.9 | 12.3 | 6.1 | 7.1 | 10.5 | 2.7 | 0.0 | 0.0 | 42.6 |
| 1974-75 | 0.0 | 0.0 | 0.0 | 0.4 | 1.0 | 5.1 | 18.3 | 5.9 | 18.7 | 3.7 | T | 0.0 | 53.1 |
| 1975-76 | 0.0 | 0.0 | 0.0 | 0.4 | 3.8 | 1.9 | 14.0 | 6.2 | 14.0 | T | 0.1 | 0.0 | 40.4 |
| 1976-77 | 0.0 | 0.0 | 0.0 | 0.1 | 2.7 | 5.5 | 12.6 | 10.7 | 4.6 | 2.1 | 0.0 | 0.0 | 38.3 |
| 1977-78 | 0.0 | 0.0 | 0.0 | T | 24.2 | 7.2 | 4.6 | 3.9 | 7.1 | 2.8 | 0.0 | 0.0 | 49.8 |
| 1978-79 | 0.0 | 0.0 | 0.0 | T | 8.5 | 11.7 | 7.8 | 19.5 | 4.3 | 2.7 | 0.8 | 0.0 | 55.3 |
| 1979-80 | 0.0 | 0.0 | 0.0 | 1.4 | 6.0 | 1.5 | 17.3 | 7.2 | 6.5 | T | 0.0 | 0.0 | 39.9 |
| 1980-81 | 0.0 | 0.0 | 0.0 | 0.5 | 1.1 | 4.6 | 2.1 | 4.5 | 0.3 | T | 0.0 | 0.0 | 13.1 |
| 1981-82 | 0.0 | 0.0 | T | 2.3 | 2.2 | 9.9 | 30.0 | 10.9 | 14.0 | 0.2 | 0.0 | 0.0 | 69.5 |
| 1982-83 | 0.0 | 0.0 | 0.0 | 0.0 | 6.8 | 0.3 | 3.8 | 2.0 | 7.4 | 2.9 | T | 0.0 | 23.2 |
| 1983-84 | 0.0 | 0.0 | T | T | 5.3 | 11.8 | 11.5 | 3.1 | 3.1 | 0.5 | 0.0 | 0.0 | 39.9 |
| 1984-85 | 0.0 | 0.0 | T | T | 1.4 | 7.4 | 3.7 | 3.1 | 12.6 | T | 0.0 | 0.0 | 28.2 |
| 1985-86 | 0.0 | 0.0 | 0.0 | T | 24.3 | 10.4 | 11.2 | 6.7 | 0.7 | 3.7 | T | 0.0 | 57.0 |
| 1986-87 | 0.0 | 0.0 | 0.0 | T | 5.3 | 3.8 | 2.8 | 10.4 | 1.2 | T | 0.0 | 0.0 | 23.5 |
| 1987-88 | 0.0 | 0.0 | 0.0 | T | 3.0 | 6.6 | 24.3 | 4.4 | 6.2 | T | 0.0 | 0.0 | 44.5 |
| 1988-89 | 0.0 | 0.0 | 0.0 | T | 11.6 | 14.9 | 31.5 | 2.3 | 12.4 | 0.9 | T | 0.0 | 73.6 |
| 1989-90 | 0.0 | T | T | T | 16.3 | 2.6 | 0.8 | 7.9 | 11.5 | 7.2 | T | 0.0 | 46.3 |
| 1990-91 | 0.0 | 0.0 | 0.0 | 1.3 | 0.2 | 12.4 | | | | | | | |
| Record Mean | 0.0 | T | T | 0.6 | 5.3 | 7.0 | 8.5 | 5.8 | 6.8 | 3.1 | 0.1 | 0.0 | 37.2 |

**See Reference Notes, relative to all above tables, on preceding page.**

Greater Cincinnati Airport is located on a gently rolling plateau about 12 miles southwest of downtown Cincinnati and 2 miles south of the Ohio River at its nearest point. The river valley is rather narrow and steep-sided varying from 1 to 3 miles in width and the river bed is 500 feet below the level of the airport.

The climate is continental with a rather wide range of temperatures from winter to summer. A precipitation maximum occurs during winter and spring with a late summer and fall minimum. On the average, the maximum snowfall occurs during January, although the heaviest 24-hour amounts have been recorded during late November and February.

The heaviest precipitation, as well as the precipitation of the longest duration, is normally associated with low pressure disturbances moving in a general southwest to northeast direction through the Ohio valley and south of the Cincinnati area.

Summers are warm and rather humid. The temperature will reach 100 degrees or more in 1 year out of 3. However, the temperature will reach 90 degrees or higher on about 19 days each year. Winters are moderately cold with frequent periods of extensive cloudiness.

The freeze free period lasts on the average 187 days from mid-April to the latter part of October.

# TABLE 1 — NORMALS, MEANS AND EXTREMES

CINCINNATI, (GREATER CINCINNATI AIRPORT) OHIO

LATITUDE: 39°03'N  LONGITUDE: 84°40'W  ELEVATION: FT. GRND 869 BARO 888  TIME ZONE: EASTERN  WBAN: 93814

| | (a) | JAN | FEB | MAR | APR | MAY | JUNE | JULY | AUG | SEP | OCT | NOV | DEC | YEAR |
|---|---|---|---|---|---|---|---|---|---|---|---|---|---|---|
| **TEMPERATURE °F:** | | | | | | | | | | | | | | |
| Normals | | | | | | | | | | | | | | |
| -Daily Maximum | | 37.3 | 41.2 | 51.5 | 64.5 | 74.2 | 82.3 | 85.8 | 84.8 | 78.7 | 66.7 | 52.6 | 41.9 | 63.5 |
| -Daily Minimum | | 20.4 | 23.0 | 32.0 | 42.4 | 51.7 | 60.5 | 64.9 | 63.3 | 56.3 | 43.9 | 34.1 | 25.7 | 43.2 |
| -Monthly | | 28.9 | 32.1 | 41.8 | 53.5 | 63.0 | 71.4 | 75.4 | 74.1 | 67.5 | 55.3 | 43.4 | 33.8 | 53.4 |
| Extremes | | | | | | | | | | | | | | |
| -Record Highest | 28 | 69 | 73 | 84 | 89 | 93 | 102 | 103 | 102 | 98 | 88 | 81 | 75 | 103 |
| -Year | | 1967 | 1972 | 1986 | 1976 | 1962 | 1988 | 1988 | 1962 | 1964 | 1963 | 1987 | 1982 | JUL 1988 |
| -Record Lowest | 28 | -25 | -11 | -11 | 17 | 27 | 39 | 47 | 43 | 33 | 16 | 1 | -20 | -25 |
| -Year | | 1977 | 1982 | 1980 | 1964 | 1963 | 1972 | 1963 | 1986 | 1983 | 1962 | 1976 | 1989 | JAN 1977 |
| **NORMAL DEGREE DAYS:** | | | | | | | | | | | | | | |
| Heating (base 65°F) | | 1119 | 921 | 719 | 350 | 143 | 12 | 0 | 0 | 52 | 316 | 648 | 967 | 5247 |
| Cooling (base 65°F) | | 0 | 0 | 0 | 5 | 81 | 204 | 322 | 282 | 127 | 16 | 0 | 0 | 1037 |
| **% OF POSSIBLE SUNSHINE** | 6 | 42 | 43 | 51 | 59 | 59 | 66 | 64 | 63 | 63 | 53 | 39 | 36 | 53 |
| **MEAN SKY COVER (tenths)** | | | | | | | | | | | | | | |
| Sunrise - Sunset | 38 | 7.4 | 7.3 | 7.3 | 6.9 | 6.6 | 6.1 | 6.0 | 5.7 | 5.6 | 5.6 | 7.1 | 7.5 | 6.6 |
| **MEAN NUMBER OF DAYS:** | | | | | | | | | | | | | | |
| Sunrise to Sunset | | | | | | | | | | | | | | |
| -Clear | 38 | 5.2 | 5.2 | 5.2 | 5.9 | 6.1 | 7.2 | 7.7 | 8.3 | 9.6 | 10.5 | 6.1 | 5.2 | 82.3 |
| -Partly Cloudy | 38 | 6.1 | 5.7 | 6.9 | 7.6 | 9.8 | 10.3 | 11.6 | 11.8 | 9.0 | 7.4 | 5.8 | 5.8 | 97.7 |
| -Cloudy | 38 | 19.7 | 17.3 | 18.9 | 16.6 | 15.1 | 12.5 | 11.7 | 10.9 | 11.4 | 13.1 | 18.1 | 19.9 | 185.2 |
| Precipitation | | | | | | | | | | | | | | |
| .01 inches or more | 42 | 11.9 | 11.1 | 13.2 | 12.4 | 11.3 | 10.5 | 10.0 | 9.0 | 7.8 | 8.3 | 11.0 | 12.1 | 128.7 |
| Snow,Ice pellets | | | | | | | | | | | | | | |
| 1.0 inches or more | 42 | 2.2 | 1.8 | 1.2 | 0.2 | 0.0 | 0.0 | 0.0 | 0.0 | 0.0 | 0.* | 0.5 | 1.2 | 7.2 |
| Thunderstorms | 42 | 0.7 | 0.8 | 2.4 | 4.2 | 5.7 | 7.0 | 8.1 | 7.4 | 3.2 | 1.4 | 1.2 | 0.5 | 42.6 |
| Heavy Fog Visibility 1/4 mile or less | 26 | 2.4 | 1.9 | 1.6 | 0.8 | 1.3 | 1.2 | 1.8 | 2.8 | 3.7 | 2.7 | 1.6 | 2.5 | 24.5 |
| Temperature °F | | | | | | | | | | | | | | |
| -Maximum | | | | | | | | | | | | | | |
| 90° and above | 27 | 0.0 | 0.0 | 0.0 | 0.0 | 0.5 | 4.4 | 8.0 | 5.3 | 1.9 | 0.0 | 0.0 | 0.0 | 20.0 |
| 32° and below | 27 | 12.4 | 8.2 | 1.4 | 0.0 | 0.0 | 0.0 | 0.0 | 0.0 | 0.0 | 0.0 | 0.6 | 6.6 | 29.1 |
| -Minimum | | | | | | | | | | | | | | |
| 32° and below | 27 | 26.7 | 22.9 | 16.1 | 4.4 | 0.3 | 0.0 | 0.0 | 0.0 | 0.0 | 3.5 | 12.7 | 22.4 | 109.0 |
| 0° and below | 27 | 3.3 | 1.7 | 0.1 | 0.0 | 0.0 | 0.0 | 0.0 | 0.0 | 0.0 | 0.0 | 0.0 | 1.3 | 6.4 |
| **AVG. STATION PRESS.(mb)** | 17 | 987.5 | 987.0 | 984.6 | 983.9 | 983.7 | 984.5 | 985.7 | 986.4 | 987.0 | 988.0 | 987.0 | 987.6 | 986.1 |
| **RELATIVE HUMIDITY (%)** | | | | | | | | | | | | | | |
| Hour 01 | 27 | 75 | 74 | 73 | 70 | 77 | 80 | 83 | 83 | 82 | 77 | 75 | 76 | 77 |
| Hour 07 (Local Time) | 27 | 78 | 78 | 77 | 76 | 80 | 82 | 85 | 88 | 88 | 83 | 80 | 79 | 81 |
| Hour 13 | 27 | 67 | 64 | 59 | 53 | 54 | 56 | 57 | 57 | 57 | 55 | 63 | 69 | 59 |
| Hour 19 | 27 | 69 | 65 | 60 | 55 | 57 | 59 | 61 | 63 | 66 | 65 | 68 | 72 | 63 |
| **PRECIPITATION (inches):** | | | | | | | | | | | | | | |
| Water Equivalent | | | | | | | | | | | | | | |
| -Normal | | 3.13 | 2.73 | 3.95 | 3.58 | 3.84 | 4.09 | 4.28 | 2.97 | 2.91 | 2.54 | 3.12 | 3.00 | 40.14 |
| -Maximum Monthly | 42 | 9.43 | 6.72 | 12.18 | 7.19 | 9.48 | 7.36 | 8.36 | 7.71 | 8.61 | 8.60 | 7.51 | 6.46 | 12.18 |
| -Year | | 1950 | 1955 | 1964 | 1970 | 1968 | 1977 | 1962 | 1982 | 1979 | 1983 | 1985 | 1978 | MAR 1964 |
| -Minimum Monthly | 42 | 0.57 | 0.25 | 1.14 | 1.04 | 1.13 | 0.95 | 1.18 | 0.31 | 0.18 | 0.25 | 0.43 | 0.51 | 0.18 |
| -Year | | 1981 | 1978 | 1960 | 1971 | 1964 | 1965 | 1951 | 1953 | 1963 | 1963 | 1949 | 1976 | SEP 1963 |
| -Maximum in 24 hrs | 42 | 4.33 | 2.60 | 5.21 | 2.72 | 3.71 | 3.45 | 4.28 | 3.12 | 4.54 | 4.47 | 3.36 | 2.96 | 5.21 |
| -Year | | 1959 | 1988 | 1964 | 1950 | 1956 | 1974 | 1988 | 1957 | 1979 | 1985 | 1948 | 1948 | MAR 1964 |
| Snow,Ice pellets | | | | | | | | | | | | | | |
| -Maximum Monthly | 42 | 31.5 | 13.3 | 13.0 | 3.7 | 0.2 | 0.0 | 0.0 | 0.0 | 0.0 | 5.9 | 12.1 | 12.5 | 31.5 |
| -Year | | 1978 | 1971 | 1968 | 1977 | 1989 | | | | | 1989 | 1966 | 1989 | JAN 1978 |
| -Maximum in 24 hrs | 42 | 8.1 | 9.3 | 9.8 | 3.6 | 0.2 | 0.0 | 0.0 | 0.0 | 0.0 | 5.0 | 9.0 | 7.3 | 9.8 |
| -Year | | 1978 | 1966 | 1968 | 1977 | 1989 | | | | | 1989 | 1966 | 1984 | MAR 1968 |
| **WIND:** | | | | | | | | | | | | | | |
| Mean Speed (mph) | 42 | 10.7 | 10.4 | 11.1 | 10.7 | 8.7 | 7.9 | 7.1 | 6.7 | 7.4 | 8.2 | 9.7 | 10.3 | 9.1 |
| Prevailing Direction through 1963 | | SSW | SSW | SSW | SSW | SSW | SSW | SSW | SSW | SSW | SSW | SSW | SSW | SSW |
| Fastest Obs. 1 Min. | | | | | | | | | | | | | | |
| -Direction (!!) | 26 | 28 | 29 | 25 | 25 | 31 | 24 | 34 | 31 | 24 | 27 | 21 | 21 | 25 |
| -Speed (MPH) | 26 | 46 | 40 | 44 | 46 | 37 | 40 | 35 | 37 | 32 | 35 | 35 | 40 | 46 |
| -Year | | 1976 | 1967 | 1977 | 1982 | 1986 | 1971 | 1980 | 1983 | 1975 | 1967 | 1988 | 1973 | APR 1982 |
| Peak Gust | | | | | | | | | | | | | | |
| -Direction (!!) | 6 | W | SW | SW | S | W | W | W | N | N | SW | W | SW | SW |
| -Speed (mph) | 6 | 48 | 55 | 64 | 61 | 53 | 52 | 48 | 40 | 40 | 43 | 56 | 59 | 64 |
| -Date | | 1985 | 1988 | 1986 | 1985 | 1987 | 1987 | 1987 | 1989 | 1989 | 1986 | 1988 | 1987 | MAR 1986 |

**See reference Notes to this table on the following page.**

PRECIPITATION (inches)    CINCINNATI. (GREATER CINCINNATI AIRPORT) OHIO

**TABLE 2**

| YEAR | JAN | FEB | MAR | APR | MAY | JUNE | JULY | AUG | SEP | OCT | NOV | DEC | ANNUAL |
|---|---|---|---|---|---|---|---|---|---|---|---|---|---|
| 1961 | 1.87 | 3.56 | 4.76 | 2.81 | 7.31 | 2.28 | 5.11 | 1.07 | 0.97 | 1.88 | 3.36 | 3.39 | 38.37 |
| 1962 | 3.98 | 5.58 | 4.25 | 1.26 | 3.64 | 4.40 | 8.36 | 2.14 | 2.67 | 2.87 | 2.37 | 1.36 | 42.88 |
| 1963 | 2.04 | 1.09 | 9.91 | 2.01 | 2.73 | 1.59 | 4.34 | 1.83 | 0.18 | 0.25 | 0.94 | 1.08 | 27.99 |
| 1964 | 2.88 | 1.98 | 12.18 | 6.73 | 1.13 | 4.32 | 2.56 | 2.25 | 1.65 | 0.59 | 2.69 | 4.92 | 43.88 |
| 1965 | 3.11 | 5.07 | 2.86 | 4.90 | 1.46 | 0.95 | 4.42 | 3.24 | 6.06 | 3.81 | 1.26 | 1.19 | 38.33 |
| 1966 | 3.84 | 3.73 | 1.22 | 5.38 | 2.42 | 2.52 | 4.06 | 4.31 | 3.13 | 0.57 | 4.18 | 3.31 | 38.67 |
| 1967 | 0.75 | 1.86 | 3.63 | 3.66 | 5.64 | 1.72 | 4.99 | 0.77 | 1.79 | 2.65 | 3.84 | 3.94 | 35.24 |
| 1968 | 1.79 | 0.64 | 4.24 | 3.47 | 9.48 | 2.43 | 7.50 | 2.26 | 2.16 | 1.35 | 3.21 | 4.01 | 42.54 |
| 1969 | 4.64 | 1.27 | 1.42 | 3.59 | 2.05 | 4.91 | 3.28 | 2.15 | 2.87 | 1.53 | 3.67 | 2.59 | 33.97 |
| 1970 | 1.27 | 1.68 | 4.71 | 7.19 | 1.88 | 5.73 | 3.47 | 2.96 | 3.87 | 2.44 | 2.29 | 3.32 | 40.81 |
| 1971 | 2.47 | 5.89 | 2.55 | 1.04 | 3.31 | 5.18 | 3.70 | 3.45 | 6.56 | 1.44 | 1.68 | 3.39 | 40.66 |
| 1972 | 1.96 | 2.20 | 3.68 | 5.89 | 6.02 | 2.41 | 1.50 | 2.64 | 5.96 | 2.55 | 6.26 | 4.23 | 45.30 |
| 1973 | 1.79 | 1.58 | 6.11 | 5.81 | 3.46 | 6.27 | 7.16 | 2.62 | 2.63 | 4.39 | 4.95 | 2.66 | 49.43 |
| 1974 | 3.65 | 1.63 | 4.39 | 5.08 | 5.53 | 4.38 | 3.82 | 5.75 | 4.44 | 1.07 | 4.19 | 2.83 | 46.76 |
| 1975 | 4.05 | 3.38 | 6.76 | 4.16 | 3.11 | 5.09 | 1.62 | 1.97 | 3.64 | 4.59 | 2.50 | 3.36 | 44.23 |
| 1976 | 3.00 | 2.37 | 2.14 | 1.21 | 1.80 | 5.94 | 2.33 | 4.36 | 1.95 | 3.85 | 0.83 | 0.51 | 30.29 |
| 1977 | 1.90 | 1.29 | 4.52 | 4.16 | 1.53 | 7.36 | 1.90 | 5.45 | 1.80 | 3.74 | 3.90 | 4.00 | 41.55 |
| 1978 | 4.52 | 0.25 | 1.99 | 2.28 | 5.30 | 6.63 | 6.86 | 4.41 | 0.43 | 5.03 | 2.67 | 6.46 | 46.83 |
| 1979 | 3.68 | 3.77 | 2.05 | 4.90 | 4.00 | 5.92 | 5.49 | 4.80 | 8.61 | 1.77 | 4.86 | 2.91 | 52.76 |
| 1980 | 2.26 | 1.04 | 4.50 | 1.96 | 4.59 | 4.13 | 5.51 | 4.19 | 1.83 | 3.28 | 2.58 | 1.26 | 37.13 |
| 1981 | 0.57 | 3.86 | 1.72 | 5.05 | 5.07 | 3.34 | 3.66 | 2.15 | 1.47 | 2.33 | 2.94 | 2.39 | 34.55 |
| 1982 | 7.17 | 1.17 | 4.67 | 2.18 | 4.60 | 3.61 | 2.44 | 7.71 | 1.27 | 0.99 | 5.08 | 4.25 | 45.14 |
| 1983 | 1.56 | 1.14 | 2.02 | 4.84 | 8.89 | 2.22 | 1.96 | 3.23 | 1.22 | 8.60 | 4.20 | 2.84 | 42.72 |
| 1984 | 0.75 | 2.40 | 3.61 | 4.88 | 4.82 | 2.11 | 2.57 | 3.30 | 3.50 | 3.85 | 6.00 | 4.21 | 42.00 |
| 1985 | 1.68 | 2.25 | 6.90 | 1.34 | 6.18 | 4.55 | 5.59 | 2.02 | 0.76 | 5.83 | 7.51 | 1.52 | 44.13 |
| 1986 | 1.01 | 2.85 | 3.07 | 1.57 | 3.59 | 1.46 | 3.33 | 3.78 | 3.53 | 3.08 | 3.79 | 2.58 | 33.64 |
| 1987 | 0.92 | 1.62 | 4.65 | 2.88 | 2.73 | 4.62 | 5.07 | 2.27 | 1.17 | 1.42 | 1.82 | 3.43 | 32.60 |
| 1988 | 2.75 | 4.94 | 3.42 | 3.92 | 1.99 | 1.19 | 6.85 | 2.44 | 3.05 | 1.86 | 4.78 | 2.78 | 39.97 |
| 1989 | 3.21 | 4.67 | 6.40 | 5.19 | 4.64 | 3.04 | 5.97 | 5.33 | 2.97 | 3.18 | 3.05 | 1.96 | 49.61 |
| 1990 | 2.59 | 5.82 | 2.75 | 3.22 | 9.41 | 5.01 | 3.68 | 5.67 | 4.13 | 5.09 | 2.31 | 7.90 | 57.58 |
| Record Mean | 3.19 | 2.91 | 3.93 | 3.54 | 4.05 | 3.91 | 4.20 | 3.14 | 2.82 | 2.76 | 3.42 | 3.11 | 40.96 |

**TABLE 3**    AVERAGE TEMPERATURE (deg. F)    CINCINNATI. (GREATER CINCINNATI AIRPORT) OHIO

| YEAR | JAN | FEB | MAR | APR | MAY | JUNE | JULY | AUG | SEP | OCT | NOV | DEC | ANNUAL |
|---|---|---|---|---|---|---|---|---|---|---|---|---|---|
| 1961 | 27.8 | 38.7 | 46.5 | 48.4 | 59.3 | 70.1 | 75.4 | 74.4 | 71.8 | 58.1 | 44.2 | 33.5 | 54.0 |
| #1962 | 28.2 | 34.9 | 40.7 | 52.3 | 68.4 | 72.4 | 74.3 | 75.1 | 63.5 | 56.2 | 42.8 | 28.5 | 53.1 |
| 1963 | 22.2 | 24.4 | 44.8 | 53.8 | 58.9 | 69.2 | 70.5 | 70.5 | 61.8 | 45.2 | 22.9 | | 51.0 |
| 1964 | 32.1 | 30.2 | 43.1 | 56.1 | 65.8 | 71.9 | 74.2 | 73.7 | 67.1 | 52.7 | 47.1 | 35.5 | 54.1 |
| 1965 | 30.6 | 32.9 | 36.6 | 53.3 | 67.1 | 71.9 | 72.5 | | 67.1 | 53.4 | 44.2 | 38.8 | 53.5 |
| 1966 | 23.8 | 31.5 | 42.9 | 50.1 | 60.4 | 73.1 | 78.8 | 74.5 | 66.5 | 51.0 | 44.7 | 33.6 | 52.6 |
| 1967 | 35.4 | 27.5 | 44.8 | 55.4 | 60.5 | 73.0 | 72.9 | 71.1 | 65.3 | 55.5 | 40.3 | 36.8 | 53.2 |
| 1968 | 26.8 | 28.1 | 45.2 | 55.5 | 60.7 | 72.9 | 75.7 | 75.3 | 67.4 | 55.9 | 45.6 | 33.7 | 53.6 |
| 1969 | 30.2 | 33.7 | 37.3 | 55.2 | 65.0 | 71.9 | 77.3 | 74.0 | 66.5 | 55.7 | 40.3 | 30.6 | 53.1 |
| 1970 | 24.0 | 30.6 | 39.0 | 56.8 | 66.8 | 72.2 | 75.5 | 75.1 | 73.7 | 58.6 | 45.0 | 38.0 | 54.6 |
| 1971 | 28.3 | 33.3 | 40.2 | 53.1 | 60.8 | 75.8 | 74.8 | 72.4 | 70.3 | 61.4 | 43.2 | 41.2 | 54.6 |
| 1972 | 30.2 | 29.5 | 40.6 | 52.5 | 63.1 | 65.3 | 75.5 | 73.4 | 68.7 | 51.7 | 40.3 | 36.1 | 52.3 |
| 1973 | 31.7 | 33.0 | 50.6 | 51.1 | 58.4 | 72.3 | 74.8 | 73.7 | 69.6 | 59.0 | 44.8 | 33.6 | 54.4 |
| 1974 | 35.7 | 33.9 | 45.9 | 54.3 | 61.9 | 67.7 | 75.2 | 74.3 | 61.6 | 53.2 | 44.4 | 34.4 | 53.5 |
| 1975 | 34.0 | 37.1 | 39.8 | 50.6 | 67.6 | 72.3 | 74.6 | 76.9 | 62.4 | 57.5 | 49.1 | 37.4 | 54.9 |
| 1976 | 27.1 | 41.7 | 47.0 | 56.1 | 60.0 | 71.5 | 73.6 | 71.2 | 63.6 | 48.8 | 34.9 | 27.6 | 52.0 |
| 1977 | 12.0 | 29.8 | 46.5 | 56.3 | 68.2 | 68.7 | 77.9 | 73.9 | 69.8 | 52.3 | 45.4 | 28.7 | 52.5 |
| 1978 | 18.4 | 18.2 | 36.4 | 53.4 | 60.1 | 72.2 | 75.0 | 73.0 | 70.8 | 52.6 | 46.4 | 36.0 | 51.0 |
| 1979 | 21.3 | 21.4 | 46.6 | 53.4 | 60.2 | 69.4 | 72.3 | 72.3 | 66.1 | 54.3 | 44.2 | 36.2 | 51.4 |
| 1980 | 29.9 | 24.0 | 38.5 | 50.3 | 64.9 | 70.1 | 76.6 | 76.5 | 68.6 | 50.6 | 41.5 | 32.9 | 52.0 |
| 1981 | 24.1 | 34.2 | 40.1 | 58.1 | 59.8 | 72.3 | 75.9 | 73.6 | 65.2 | 53.9 | 44.7 | 29.0 | 52.5 |
| 1982 | 23.9 | 30.6 | 44.3 | 49.6 | 68.1 | 67.4 | 77.0 | 71.3 | 66.9 | 59.3 | 48.4 | 42.9 | 54.1 |
| 1983 | 31.6 | 35.3 | 44.7 | 49.4 | 59.0 | 71.6 | 79.2 | 78.3 | 67.2 | 55.7 | 44.7 | 24.6 | 53.4 |
| 1984 | 23.7 | 38.2 | 34.4 | 51.1 | 58.9 | 74.1 | 72.2 | 74.3 | 65.7 | 61.5 | 42.0 | 42.4 | 53.2 |
| 1985 | 22.7 | 29.4 | 47.5 | 57.9 | 65.4 | 69.9 | 75.1 | 72.5 | 67.5 | 59.3 | 49.4 | 26.2 | 53.6 |
| 1986 | 30.9 | 35.2 | 45.2 | 55.3 | 64.5 | 72.9 | 77.6 | 72.0 | 70.1 | 56.4 | 42.7 | 34.0 | 54.7 |
| 1987 | 30.7 | 37.3 | 45.0 | 53.0 | 69.3 | 73.6 | 76.1 | 75.2 | 68.3 | 49.3 | 48.0 | 36.8 | 55.2 |
| 1988 | 27.5 | 30.5 | 42.2 | 52.4 | 64.4 | 72.4 | 78.5 | 77.5 | 67.2 | 48.5 | 45.0 | 34.1 | 53.4 |
| 1989 | 38.6 | 30.8 | 45.4 | 52.9 | 60.1 | 71.3 | 76.1 | 73.5 | 66.4 | 55.7 | 43.9 | 21.6 | 53.1 |
| 1990 | 40.0 | 40.8 | 48.2 | 52.8 | 61.6 | 71.8 | 74.7 | 73.7 | 67.7 | 55.9 | 48.9 | 38.3 | 56.2 |
| Record Mean | 29.4 | 32.9 | 42.3 | 53.4 | 63.1 | 71.7 | 75.6 | 74.1 | 67.4 | 55.6 | 43.9 | 33.8 | 53.7 |
| Max | 37.7 | 41.8 | 52.0 | 64.2 | 74.1 | 82.5 | 86.0 | 84.8 | 78.3 | 66.4 | 52.9 | 41.8 | 63.6 |
| Min | 21.1 | 24.0 | 32.6 | 42.6 | 52.1 | 60.9 | 65.2 | 63.4 | 56.4 | 44.7 | 34.9 | 25.9 | 43.7 |

## REFERENCE NOTES FOR TABLES 1, 2, 3 and 6    (CINCINNATI, OH)

**GENERAL**

T - TRACE AMOUNT
BLANK ENTRIES DENOTE MISSING/UNREPORTED DATA.
# INDICATES A STATION OR INSTRUMENT RELOCATION.

**SPECIFIC**

**TABLE 1**

(a) - LENGTH OF RECORD IN YEARS. ALTHOUGH
INDIVIDUAL MONTHS MAY BE MISSING.
* LESS THAN .05

NORMALS — BASED ON THE 1951-1980 RECORD PERIOD.
EXTREMES — DATES ARE THE MOST RECENT OCCURRENCE.
WIND DIR. — NUMERALS SHOW TENS OF DEGREES
CLOCKWISE FROM TRUE NORTH.
"00" INDICATES CALM.
RESULTANT WIND DIRECTIONS ARE GIVEN TO WHOLE DEGREES.

**TABLE 3**
MAX AND MIN ARE LONG-TERM MEAN DAILY MAXIMUM
AND MEAN DAILY MINIMUM TEMPERATURES.

**EXCEPTIONS**

**TABLES 2, 3, and 6**

RECORD MEANS ARE THROUGH THE CURRENT YEAR,
BEGINNING IN    1948 FOR TEMPERATURE
1948 FOR PRECIPITATION
1948 FOR SNOWFALL

**TABLE 4**  HEATING DEGREE DAYS Base 65 deg. F    CINCINNATI. (GREATER CINCINNATI AIRPORT) OHIO

| SEASON | JULY | AUG | SEP | OCT | NOV | DEC | JAN | FEB | MAR | APR | MAY | JUNE | TOTAL |
|---|---|---|---|---|---|---|---|---|---|---|---|---|---|
| #1961-62 | 0 | 0 | 47 | 226 | 622 | 970 | 1132 | 838 | 747 | 402 | 51 | 4 | 5039 |
| 1962-63 | 2 | 2 | 129 | 311 | 660 | 1126 | 1321 | 1132 | 619 | 359 | 202 | 25 | 5888 |
| 1963-64 | 1 | 6 | 75 | 119 | 586 | 1296 | 1011 | 1005 | 671 | 273 | 64 | 26 | 5133 |
| 1964-65 | 0 | 14 | 68 | 376 | 529 | 907 | 1058 | 894 | 872 | 350 | 43 | 0 | 5111 |
| 1965-66 | 2 | 15 | 64 | 362 | 614 | 803 | 1270 | 931 | 681 | 442 | 181 | 15 | 5380 |
| 1966-67 | 0 | 0 | 70 | 428 | 602 | 969 | 910 | 1043 | 622 | 305 | 175 | 9 | 5133 |
| 1967-68 | 0 | 2 | 82 | 313 | 736 | 867 | 1178 | 1063 | 609 | 284 | 151 | 6 | 5291 |
| 1968-69 | 0 | 4 | 32 | 316 | 576 | 965 | 1072 | 872 | 852 | 298 | 84 | 29 | 5100 |
| 1969-70 | 0 | 0 | 66 | 309 | 737 | 1058 | 1265 | 954 | 797 | 264 | 91 | 2 | 5543 |
| 1970-71 | 4 | 0 | 28 | 212 | 591 | 829 | 1133 | 881 | 758 | 351 | 157 | 0 | 4944 |
| 1971-72 | 0 | 0 | 31 | 128 | 649 | 731 | 1073 | 1024 | 751 | 374 | 116 | 79 | 4956 |
| 1972-73 | 2 | 3 | 24 | 404 | 733 | 891 | 1025 | 888 | 445 | 425 | 206 | 3 | 5049 |
| 1973-74 | 0 | 1 | 27 | 217 | 583 | 964 | 901 | 863 | 591 | 332 | 161 | 31 | 4671 |
| 1974-75 | 0 | 0 | 147 | 371 | 614 | 942 | 953 | 774 | 778 | 435 | 50 | 10 | 5074 |
| 1975-76 | 5 | 0 | 142 | 244 | 474 | 848 | 1168 | 670 | 558 | 321 | 176 | 5 | 4611 |
| 1976-77 | 0 | 4 | 72 | 498 | 893 | 1157 | 1640 | 980 | 571 | 276 | 67 | 36 | 6194 |
| 1977-78 | 0 | 2 | 32 | 391 | 586 | 1118 | 1440 | 1303 | 880 | 346 | 207 | 10 | 6315 |
| 1978-79 | 0 | 0 | 21 | 381 | 552 | 891 | 1348 | 1216 | 563 | 425 | 179 | 15 | 5591 |
| 1979-80 | 1 | 14 | 60 | 346 | 616 | 887 | 1080 | 1182 | 814 | 434 | 92 | 24 | 5550 |
| 1980-81 | 0 | 0 | 48 | 446 | 697 | 988 | 1261 | 858 | 768 | 230 | 191 | 6 | 5493 |
| 1981-82 | 0 | 0 | 87 | 344 | 634 | 1107 | 1268 | 956 | 635 | 460 | 28 | 19 | 5538 |
| 1982-83 | 0 | 1 | 56 | 244 | 505 | 682 | 1029 | 825 | 627 | 466 | 199 | 21 | 4655 |
| 1983-84 | 1 | 0 | 89 | 288 | 600 | 1247 | 1274 | 773 | 939 | 425 | 219 | 4 | 5859 |
| 1984-85 | 0 | 0 | 101 | 128 | 684 | 692 | 1306 | 992 | 543 | 256 | 72 | 22 | 4796 |
| 1985-86 | 0 | 0 | 78 | 212 | 450 | 1195 | 1056 | 828 | 613 | 305 | 105 | 3 | 4845 |
| 1986-87 | 0 | 21 | 25 | 292 | 664 | 955 | 1058 | 766 | 612 | 365 | 52 | 2 | 4812 |
| 1987-88 | 0 | 1 | 39 | 477 | 505 | 868 | 1156 | 991 | 699 | 374 | 84 | 22 | 5216 |
| 1988-89 | 1 | 0 | 38 | 509 | 595 | 949 | 811 | 949 | 608 | 380 | 211 | 14 | 5065 |
| 1989-90 | 0 | 4 | 77 | 297 | 630 | 1335 | 770 | 671 | 531 | 390 | 127 | 21 | 4853 |
| 1990-91 | 0 | 1 | 66 | 296 | 477 | 821 | | | | | | | |

**TABLE 5**  COOLING DEGREE DAYS Base 65 deg. F    CINCINNATI. (GREATER CINCINNATI AIRPORT) OHIO

| YEAR | JAN | FEB | MAR | APR | MAY | JUNE | JULY | AUG | SEP | OCT | NOV | DEC | TOTAL |
|---|---|---|---|---|---|---|---|---|---|---|---|---|---|
| 1969 | 0 | 0 | 0 | 9 | 92 | 240 | 389 | 285 | 116 | 31 | 0 | 0 | 1162 |
| 1970 | 0 | 0 | 0 | 28 | 151 | 225 | 336 | 320 | 292 | 21 | 0 | 0 | 1373 |
| 1971 | 0 | 0 | 0 | 0 | 33 | 335 | 313 | 236 | 195 | 25 | 0 | 0 | 1137 |
| 1972 | 0 | 0 | 0 | 7 | 65 | 96 | 334 | 268 | 142 | 0 | 0 | 0 | 912 |
| 1973 | 0 | 0 | 4 | 13 | 7 | 228 | 310 | 278 | 170 | 36 | 0 | 0 | 1046 |
| 1974 | 0 | 0 | 8 | 17 | 70 | 121 | 323 | 297 | 50 | 12 | 2 | 0 | 900 |
| 1975 | 0 | 0 | 0 | 8 | 138 | 236 | 309 | 376 | 72 | 19 | 3 | 0 | 1161 |
| 1976 | 0 | 0 | 6 | 59 | 28 | 207 | 276 | 202 | 39 | 5 | 5 | 0 | 822 |
| 1977 | 0 | 0 | 7 | 22 | 171 | 152 | 407 | 285 | 181 | 4 | 5 | 0 | 1234 |
| 1978 | 0 | 0 | 0 | 4 | 63 | 231 | 315 | 255 | 200 | 2 | 0 | 0 | 1070 |
| 1979 | 0 | 0 | 2 | 8 | 38 | 154 | 271 | 248 | 102 | 22 | 0 | 0 | 845 |
| 1980 | 0 | 0 | 0 | 0 | 98 | 187 | 364 | 363 | 166 | 5 | 0 | 0 | 1183 |
| 1981 | 0 | 0 | 1 | 31 | 34 | 234 | 343 | 275 | 99 | 9 | 0 | 0 | 1026 |
| 1982 | 0 | 0 | 4 | 5 | 129 | 99 | 381 | 203 | 120 | 73 | 13 | 8 | 1031 |
| 1983 | 0 | 0 | 4 | 4 | 18 | 225 | 448 | 417 | 161 | 8 | 0 | 0 | 1285 |
| 1984 | 0 | 0 | 0 | 13 | 38 | 289 | 233 | 295 | 130 | 29 | 0 | 0 | 1027 |
| 1985 | 0 | 0 | 6 | 47 | 93 | 174 | 318 | 241 | 162 | 41 | 5 | 0 | 1087 |
| 1986 | 0 | 0 | 4 | 22 | 97 | 247 | 399 | 243 | 183 | 30 | 0 | 0 | 1225 |
| 1987 | 0 | 0 | 0 | 12 | 193 | 266 | 353 | 325 | 147 | 0 | 4 | 0 | 1300 |
| 1988 | 0 | 0 | 2 | 3 | 70 | 251 | 425 | 392 | 111 | 6 | 0 | 0 | 1260 |
| 1989 | 0 | 0 | 7 | 26 | 67 | 210 | 369 | 275 | 125 | 17 | 0 | 0 | 1096 |
| 1990 | 0 | 0 | 17 | 32 | 27 | 230 | 309 | 276 | 155 | 21 | 3 | 0 | 1070 |

**TABLE 6**  SNOWFALL (inches)    CINCINNATI. (GREATER CINCINNATI AIRPORT) OHIO

| SEASON | JULY | AUG | SEP | OCT | NOV | DEC | JAN | FEB | MAR | APR | MAY | JUNE | TOTAL |
|---|---|---|---|---|---|---|---|---|---|---|---|---|---|
| 1961-62 | 0.0 | 0.0 | 0.0 | 0.0 | 0.9 | 8.1 | 3.9 | 9.0 | 5.2 | 1.7 | 0.0 | 0.0 | 28.8 |
| 1962-63 | 0.0 | 0.0 | 0.0 | 1.7 | 0.8 | 4.7 | 9.6 | 6.4 | 0.1 | 0.0 | 0.0 | 0.0 | 23.3 |
| 1963-64 | 0.0 | 0.0 | 0.0 | 0.0 | 2.3 | 7.6 | 15.3 | 6.7 | 1.3 | T | 0.0 | 0.0 | 33.2 |
| 1964-65 | 0.0 | 0.0 | 0.0 | 0.0 | 1.7 | 0.9 | 9.3 | 5.9 | 6.2 | T | 0.0 | 0.0 | 24.0 |
| 1965-66 | 0.0 | 0.0 | 0.0 | T | 2.5 | 6.8 | 9.5 | 1.2 | 0.1 | T | 0.0 | 0.0 | 20.1 |
| 1966-67 | 0.0 | 0.0 | 0.0 | 0.0 | 12.1 | 1.6 | 2.5 | 7.3 | 8.1 | 0.0 | 0.0 | 0.0 | 31.6 |
| 1967-68 | 0.0 | 0.0 | 0.0 | T | 3.1 | 3.1 | 8.7 | 3.6 | 13.0 | 0.0 | 0.0 | 0.0 | 31.5 |
| 1968-69 | 0.0 | 0.0 | 0.0 | 0.0 | 0.4 | 2.0 | 1.0 | 0.3 | 2.8 | 0.0 | 0.0 | 0.0 | 6.5 |
| 1969-70 | 0.0 | 0.0 | 0.0 | 0.0 | 1.1 | 6.0 | 6.7 | 4.3 | 12.0 | T | 0.0 | 0.0 | 30.1 |
| 1970-71 | 0.0 | 0.0 | 0.0 | 0.0 | 0.4 | 0.4 | 3.2 | 13.3 | 9.7 | T | 0.0 | 0.0 | 27.0 |
| 1971-72 | 0.0 | 0.0 | 0.0 | 0.0 | 3.0 | T | 1.6 | 10.8 | 0.1 | 0.5 | 0.0 | 0.0 | 16.0 |
| 1972-73 | 0.0 | 0.0 | 0.0 | T | 6.5 | 1.9 | 0.5 | 3.1 | 1.8 | 0.0 | 0.0 | 0.0 | 17.7 |
| 1973-74 | 0.0 | 0.0 | 0.0 | 0.0 | 0.4 | 2.0 | 1.7 | 3.2 | 3.4 | 0.5 | 0.0 | 0.0 | 11.2 |
| 1974-75 | 0.0 | 0.0 | 0.0 | T | 5.0 | 5.6 | 2.0 | 2.2 | 6.8 | 0.2 | 0.0 | 0.0 | 21.8 |
| 1975-76 | 0.0 | 0.0 | 0.0 | 0.0 | 3.7 | 1.7 | 8.0 | 0.1 | 0.6 | 0.0 | 0.0 | 0.0 | 14.1 |
| 1976-77 | 0.0 | 0.0 | 0.0 | 0.0 | 2.7 | 30.3 | 4.2 | 5.4 | 3.7 | 3.7 | 0.0 | 0.0 | 47.3 |
| 1977-78 | 0.0 | 0.0 | 0.0 | 0.0 | 4.0 | 6.3 | 31.5 | 4.6 | 7.5 | 0.0 | 0.0 | 0.0 | 53.9 |
| 1978-79 | 0.0 | 0.0 | 0.0 | 0.0 | T | 0.7 | 17.5 | 11.7 | 0.6 | 0.1 | 0.0 | 0.0 | 30.6 |
| 1979-80 | 0.0 | 0.0 | 0.0 | 0.0 | 1.0 | 1.0 | 8.3 | 11.9 | 7.9 | T | 0.0 | 0.0 | 30.1 |
| 1980-81 | 0.0 | 0.0 | 0.0 | T | 1.2 | 3.7 | 4.0 | 2.6 | 2.5 | 0.0 | 0.0 | 0.0 | 14.0 |
| 1981-82 | 0.0 | 0.0 | 0.0 | T | 0.3 | 10.9 | 7.1 | 3.9 | 0.5 | 1.5 | 0.0 | 0.0 | 24.2 |
| 1982-83 | 0.0 | 0.0 | 0.0 | 0.0 | T | T | 0.8 | 5.5 | 0.3 | T | 0.0 | 0.0 | 6.6 |
| 1983-84 | 0.0 | 0.0 | 0.0 | 0.0 | T | 1.7 | 4.1 | 6.7 | 4.1 | 0.0 | 0.0 | 0.0 | 16.6 |
| 1984-85 | 0.0 | 0.0 | 0.0 | 0.0 | 1.4 | 7.3 | 12.2 | 9.5 | 0.4 | 1.7 | 0.0 | 0.0 | 32.5 |
| 1985-86 | 0.0 | 0.0 | 0.0 | 0.0 | 0.0 | 5.0 | 2.8 | 11.3 | 0.8 | T | 0.0 | 0.0 | 19.9 |
| 1986-87 | 0.0 | 0.0 | 0.0 | 0.0 | T | 0.8 | 1.6 | 2.4 | 8.8 | 2.3 | 0.0 | 0.0 | 15.9 |
| 1987-88 | 0.0 | 0.0 | 0.0 | 0.0 | 0.1 | 0.2 | 4.3 | 4.7 | 2.3 | T | 0.0 | 0.0 | 11.6 |
| 1988-89 | 0.0 | 0.0 | 0.0 | 0.0 | 0.7 | 2.9 | T | 3.0 | 1.2 | 0.3 | 0.2 | 0.0 | 8.3 |
| 1989-90 | 0.0 | 0.0 | 0.0 | 5.9 | 0.2 | 12.5 | 1.3 | 3.6 | 5.6 | T | 0.0 | 0.0 | 29.1 |
| 1990-91 | 0.0 | 0.0 | 0.0 | 0.0 | 0.0 | 8.6 | | | | | | | |
| Record Mean | 0.0 | 0.0 | 0.0 | 0.2 | 2.1 | 4.0 | 7.0 | 5.4 | 4.3 | 0.5 | T | 0.0 | 23.4 |

**See Reference Notes, relative to all above tables, on preceding page.**

Cleveland is on the south shore of Lake Erie in northeast Ohio. The metropolitan area has a lake frontage of 31 miles. The surrounding terrain is generally level except for an abrupt ridge on the eastern edge of the city which rises some 500 feet above the shore terrain. The Cuyahoga River, which flows through a rather deep but narrow north–south valley, bisects the city.

Local climate is continental in character but with strong modifying influences by Lake Erie. West to northerly winds blowing off Lake Erie tend to lower daily high temperatures in summer and raise temperatures in winter. Temperatures at Hopkins Airport which is 5 miles south of the lakeshore average from 2–4 degrees higher than the lakeshore in summer, while overnight low temperatures average from 2–4 degrees lower than the lakefront during all seasons.

In this area, summers are moderately warm and humid with occasional days when temperatures exceed 90 degrees. Winters are relatively cold and cloudy with an average of 5 days with sub-zero temperatures. Weather changes occur every few days from the passing of cold fronts.

The daily range in temperature is usually greatest in late summer and least in winter. Annual extremes in temperature normally occur soon after late June and December. Maximum temperatures below freezing occur most often in December, January, and February. Temperatures of 100 degrees or higher are rare. On the average, freezing temperatures in fall are first recorded in October while the last freezing temperature in spring normally occurs in April.

As is characteristic of continental climates, precipitation varies widely from year to year. However, it is normally abundant and well distributed throughout the year with spring being the wettest season. Showers and thunderstorms account for most of the rainfall during the growing season. Thunderstorms are most frequent from April through August. Snowfall may fluctuate widely. Mean annual snowfall increases from west to east in Cuyahoga County ranging from about 45 inches in the west to more than 90 inches in the extreme east.

Damaging winds of 50 mph or greater are usually associated with thunderstorms. Tornadoes, one of the most destructive of all atmospheric storms, occasionally occur in Cuyahoga County.

## TABLE 1   NORMALS, MEANS AND EXTREMES

CLEVELAND, OHIO

LATITUDE: 41°25'N   LONGITUDE: 81°52'W   ELEVATION: FT. GRND   777 BARO   779   TIME ZONE: EASTERN   WBAN: 14820

| | (a) | JAN | FEB | MAR | APR | MAY | JUNE | JULY | AUG | SEP | OCT | NOV | DEC | YEAR |
|---|---|---|---|---|---|---|---|---|---|---|---|---|---|---|
| **TEMPERATURE °F:** | | | | | | | | | | | | | | |
| Normals | | | | | | | | | | | | | | |
| -Daily Maximum | | 32.5 | 34.8 | 44.8 | 57.9 | 68.5 | 78.0 | 81.7 | 80.3 | 74.2 | 62.7 | 49.3 | 37.5 | 58.5 |
| -Daily Minimum | | 18.5 | 19.9 | 28.4 | 38.3 | 47.9 | 57.2 | 61.4 | 60.5 | 54.0 | 43.6 | 34.3 | 24.6 | 40.7 |
| -Monthly | | 25.5 | 27.4 | 36.6 | 48.1 | 58.2 | 67.6 | 71.6 | 70.4 | 64.1 | 53.2 | 41.8 | 31.1 | 49.6 |
| Extremes | | | | | | | | | | | | | | |
| -Record Highest | 48 | 73 | 69 | 83 | 88 | 92 | 104 | 103 | 102 | 101 | 90 | 82 | 77 | 104 |
| -Year | | 1950 | 1961 | 1945 | 1986 | 1959 | 1988 | 1941 | 1948 | 1953 | 1946 | 1950 | 1982 | JUN 1988 |
| -Record Lowest | 48 | -19 | -15 | -5 | 10 | 25 | 31 | 41 | 38 | 32 | 19 | 3 | -15 | -19 |
| -Year | | 1963 | 1963 | 1984 | 1964 | 1966 | 1972 | 1968 | 1982 | 1942 | 1988 | 1976 | 1989 | JAN 1963 |
| **NORMAL DEGREE DAYS:** | | | | | | | | | | | | | | |
| Heating (base 65°F) | | 1225 | 1053 | 880 | 507 | 244 | 33 | 8 | 11 | 99 | 371 | 696 | 1051 | 6178 |
| Cooling (base 65°F) | | 0 | 0 | 0 | 0 | 33 | 111 | 213 | 178 | 72 | 5 | 0 | 0 | 612 |
| **% OF POSSIBLE SUNSHINE** | 46 | 31 | 37 | 45 | 53 | 58 | 65 | 67 | 63 | 60 | 52 | 31 | 26 | 49 |
| **MEAN SKY COVER (tenths)** | | | | | | | | | | | | | | |
| Sunrise - Sunset | 48 | 8.3 | 7.9 | 7.5 | 7.0 | 6.6 | 6.1 | 5.6 | 5.7 | 5.9 | 6.3 | 8.0 | 8.4 | 7.0 |
| **MEAN NUMBER OF DAYS:** | | | | | | | | | | | | | | |
| Sunrise to Sunset | | | | | | | | | | | | | | |
| -Clear | 48 | 2.8 | 3.0 | 4.4 | 5.2 | 6.0 | 6.7 | 8.5 | 8.6 | 8.2 | 8.0 | 3.0 | 2.5 | 67.1 |
| -Partly Cloudy | 48 | 4.8 | 5.5 | 6.6 | 8.0 | 9.9 | 11.3 | 11.9 | 11.1 | 9.5 | 7.9 | 5.8 | 4.7 | 97.0 |
| -Cloudy | 48 | 23.4 | 19.8 | 20.0 | 16.9 | 15.0 | 12.0 | 10.6 | 11.2 | 12.3 | 15.0 | 21.1 | 23.8 | 201.2 |
| Precipitation | | | | | | | | | | | | | | |
| .01 inches or more | 48 | 16.3 | 14.3 | 15.4 | 14.3 | 13.1 | 11.0 | 10.1 | 9.7 | 9.8 | 11.2 | 14.5 | 16.4 | 156.0 |
| Snow, Ice pellets | | | | | | | | | | | | | | |
| 1.0 inches or more | 48 | 4.2 | 3.9 | 3.2 | 0.8 | 0.* | 0.0 | 0.0 | 0.0 | 0.0 | 0.2 | 1.8 | 4.2 | 18.3 |
| Thunderstorms | 48 | 0.1 | 0.5 | 1.8 | 3.5 | 5.0 | 6.7 | 6.4 | 5.2 | 3.4 | 1.5 | 1.0 | 0.3 | 35.3 |
| Heavy Fog Visibility | | | | | | | | | | | | | | |
| 1/4 mile or less | 48 | 1.4 | 1.7 | 1.8 | 1.2 | 1.3 | 0.7 | 0.5 | 0.9 | 0.6 | 0.9 | 0.6 | 1.1 | 12.5 |
| Temperature °F | | | | | | | | | | | | | | |
| -Maximum | | | | | | | | | | | | | | |
| 90° and above | 29 | 0.0 | 0.0 | 0.0 | 0.0 | 0.2 | 1.8 | 4.0 | 2.0 | 0.6 | 0.0 | 0.0 | 0.0 | 8.6 |
| 32° and below | 29 | 16.0 | 13.1 | 5.0 | 0.2 | 0.0 | 0.0 | 0.0 | 0.0 | 0.0 | 0.0 | 1.2 | 10.5 | 46.0 |
| -Minimum | | | | | | | | | | | | | | |
| 32° and below | 29 | 28.1 | 24.6 | 21.2 | 9.3 | 1.0 | 0.* | 0.0 | 0.0 | 0.0 | 2.9 | 12.6 | 24.8 | 124.5 |
| 0° and below | 29 | 3.3 | 2.1 | 0.1 | 0.0 | 0.0 | 0.0 | 0.0 | 0.0 | 0.0 | 0.0 | 0.0 | 0.9 | 6.4 |
| **AVG. STATION PRESS.(mb)** | 17 | 988.6 | 989.2 | 987.2 | 986.3 | 986.4 | 986.9 | 988.0 | 989.0 | 989.6 | 990.2 | 988.8 | 989.1 | 988.3 |
| **RELATIVE HUMIDITY (%)** | | | | | | | | | | | | | | |
| Hour 01 | 29 | 75 | 76 | 74 | 73 | 76 | 79 | 81 | 83 | 82 | 77 | 75 | 76 | 77 |
| Hour 07 (Local Time) | 29 | 77 | 78 | 78 | 76 | 77 | 78 | 81 | 85 | 84 | 80 | 77 | 77 | 79 |
| Hour 13 | 29 | 69 | 68 | 63 | 57 | 57 | 57 | 57 | 60 | 60 | 59 | 65 | 70 | 62 |
| Hour 19 | 29 | 72 | 72 | 68 | 61 | 59 | 61 | 61 | 66 | 70 | 69 | 71 | 74 | 67 |
| **PRECIPITATION (inches):** | | | | | | | | | | | | | | |
| Water Equivalent | | | | | | | | | | | | | | |
| -Normal | | 2.47 | 2.20 | 2.99 | 3.32 | 3.30 | 3.49 | 3.37 | 3.38 | 2.92 | 2.45 | 2.76 | 2.75 | 35.40 |
| -Maximum Monthly | 48 | 7.01 | 4.64 | 6.07 | 6.61 | 9.14 | 9.06 | 6.47 | 8.96 | 6.75 | 9.50 | 8.80 | 5.60 | 9.50 |
| -Year | | 1950 | 1950 | 1954 | 1961 | 1989 | 1972 | 1969 | 1975 | 1981 | 1954 | 1985 | 1951 | OCT 1954 |
| -Minimum Monthly | 48 | 0.36 | 0.48 | 0.78 | 1.18 | 1.00 | 0.65 | 1.21 | 0.53 | 0.74 | 0.61 | 0.80 | 0.71 | 0.36 |
| -Year | | 1961 | 1978 | 1958 | 1946 | 1963 | 1988 | 1982 | 1969 | 1964 | 1952 | 1976 | 1958 | JAN 1961 |
| -Maximum in 24 hrs | 48 | 2.33 | 2.33 | 2.76 | 2.24 | 3.73 | 4.00 | 2.87 | 3.07 | 2.38 | 3.44 | 2.73 | 2.06 | 4.00 |
| -Year | | 1959 | 1959 | 1948 | 1961 | 1955 | 1972 | 1969 | 1947 | 1979 | 1954 | 1985 | 1974 | JUN 1972 |
| Snow, Ice pellets | | | | | | | | | | | | | | |
| -Maximum Monthly | 48 | 42.8 | 27.1 | 26.3 | 14.5 | 2.1 | 0.0 | 0.0 | 0.0 | T | 8.0 | 22.3 | 30.3 | 42.8 |
| -Year | | 1978 | 1984 | 1954 | 1943 | 1974 | | | | 1976 | 1962 | 1950 | 1962 | JAN 1978 |
| -Maximum in 24 hrs | 48 | 10.5 | 11.5 | 16.0 | 11.6 | 2.1 | 0.0 | 0.0 | 0.0 | T | 6.7 | 15.0 | 12.2 | 16.0 |
| -Year | | 1978 | 1984 | 1987 | 1982 | 1974 | | | | 1976 | 1962 | 1950 | 1974 | MAR 1987 |
| **WIND:** | | | | | | | | | | | | | | |
| Mean Speed (mph) | 48 | 12.3 | 12.0 | 12.3 | 11.7 | 10.1 | 9.3 | 8.6 | 8.3 | 9.0 | 10.0 | 11.9 | 12.2 | 10.6 |
| Prevailing Direction | | | | | | | | | | | | | | |
| through 1963 | | SW | S | W | S | S | S | S | S | S | S | S | S | S |
| Fastest Obs. 1 Min. | | | | | | | | | | | | | | |
| -Direction (!!!) | 12 | 22 | 23 | 27 | 23 | 20 | 23 | 23 | 31 | 34 | 23 | 21 | 21 | 22 |
| -Speed (MPH) | 12 | 53 | 39 | 41 | 44 | 42 | 37 | 36 | 36 | 31 | 37 | 39 | 43 | 53 |
| -Year | | 1978 | 1988 | 1986 | 1982 | 1983 | 1982 | 1983 | 1988 | 1986 | 1983 | 1988 | 1982 | JAN 1978 |
| Peak Gust | | | | | | | | | | | | | | |
| -Direction (!!!) | 6 | SW | SW | SW | SW | NW | W | SW | NW | W | W | S | SW | SW |
| -Speed (mph) | 6 | 55 | 58 | 63 | 69 | 54 | 56 | 51 | 49 | 45 | 52 | 59 | 63 | 69 |
| -Date | | 1985 | 1988 | 1986 | 1984 | 1988 | 1988 | 1988 | 1988 | 1986 | 1988 | 1988 | 1987 | APR 1984 |

**See Reference Notes to this table on the following page.**

## PRECIPITATION (inches)     CLEVELAND. OHIO

**TABLE 2**

| YEAR | JAN | FEB | MAR | APR | MAY | JUNE | JULY | AUG | SEP | OCT | NOV | DEC | ANNUAL |
|------|-----|-----|-----|-----|-----|------|------|-----|-----|-----|-----|-----|--------|
| 1961 | 0.36 | 3.23 | 3.20 | 6.61 | 1.31 | 2.95 | 4.30 | 4.28 | 1.35 | 2.15 | 2.78 | 1.84 | 35.36 |
| 1962 | 2.83 | 1.85 | 1.73 | 1.78 | 1.91 | 2.95 | 3.42 | 1.30 | 1.39 | 3.60 | 2.77 | 3.05 | 31.58 |
| 1963 | 1.06 | 0.73 | 2.83 | 2.41 | 1.00 | 1.93 | 1.88 | 1.70 | 1.00 | 0.71 | 1.33 | 1.05 | 18.63 |
| 1964 | 1.45 | 1.49 | 5.21 | 4.87 | 3.02 | 2.06 | 3.37 | 3.82 | 1.74 | 1.78 | 0.92 | 2.67 | 31.40 |
| 1965 | 4.45 | 3.00 | 1.66 | 1.83 | 2.29 | 3.05 | 3.01 | 3.58 | 1.53 | 2.55 | 1.89 | 2.07 | 31.91 |
| 1966 | 1.53 | 2.31 | 2.26 | 3.61 | 2.21 | 1.83 | 3.89 | 3.48 | 1.66 | 1.18 | 5.16 | 2.84 | 31.96 |
| 1967 | 0.97 | 2.35 | 2.08 | 3.12 | 3.82 | 1.17 | 1.90 | 1.85 | 2.08 | 2.11 | 2.88 | 2.46 | 26.79 |
| 1968 | 3.27 | 0.79 | 2.07 | 2.25 | 4.08 | 2.32 | 3.58 | 1.82 | 3.36 | 2.90 | 4.35 | 3.94 | 34.73 |
| 1969 | 2.84 | 0.75 | 1.82 | 4.49 | 5.73 | 4.61 | 6.47 | 0.53 | 4.92 | 1.90 | 2.86 | 2.46 | 39.38 |
| 1970 | 1.28 | 1.35 | 2.32 | 2.64 | 2.95 | 4.98 | 4.14 | 0.92 | 3.16 | 3.98 | 3.69 | 2.25 | 33.66 |
| 1971 | 1.35 | 3.69 | 2.01 | 1.24 | 3.29 | 3.79 | 3.72 | 0.91 | 4.27 | 1.61 | 2.02 | 3.90 | 31.80 |
| 1972 | 1.95 | 2.01 | 2.97 | 3.40 | 3.74 | 9.06 | 4.44 | 6.38 | 4.91 | 1.64 | 4.58 | 3.26 | 48.34 |
| 1973 | 1.62 | 2.40 | 3.48 | 3.40 | 4.79 | 6.72 | 2.94 | 3.11 | 2.69 | 3.95 | 2.62 | 3.53 | 41.25 |
| 1974 | 2.56 | 2.43 | 3.88 | 3.64 | 4.78 | 3.57 | 1.90 | 3.29 | 3.06 | 1.19 | 4.72 | 4.86 | 39.88 |
| 1975 | 3.06 | 3.20 | 3.47 | 1.31 | 3.23 | 4.10 | 2.54 | 8.36 | 3.35 | 1.73 | 2.09 | 3.77 | 40.81 |
| 1976 | 3.38 | 3.97 | 3.11 | 2.17 | 2.94 | 3.64 | 3.48 | 3.50 | 3.71 | 2.54 | 0.80 | 1.57 | 34.81 |
| 1977 | 1.29 | 1.38 | 4.49 | 3.56 | 1.02 | 4.91 | 3.94 | 3.92 | 2.52 | 1.93 | 3.62 | 3.51 | 36.09 |
| 1978 | 3.67 | 0.48 | 2.17 | 3.02 | 3.01 | 3.30 | 2.40 | 3.58 | 3.68 | 3.23 | 1.19 | 2.96 | 32.69 |
| 1979 | 2.61 | 2.74 | 2.33 | 3.09 | 4.77 | 3.47 | 3.76 | 4.46 | 3.66 | 1.79 | 3.16 | 4.00 | 39.84 |
| 1980 | 1.18 | 1.27 | 3.66 | 2.65 | 3.13 | 2.69 | 4.77 | 4.38 | 3.11 | 2.38 | 1.29 | 2.10 | 32.61 |
| 1981 | 0.76 | 2.72 | 1.61 | 4.62 | 2.19 | 4.68 | 5.31 | 2.61 | 5.75 | 2.33 | 1.99 | 3.44 | 39.01 |
| 1982 | 4.00 | 1.41 | 3.77 | 1.62 | 2.65 | 5.01 | 1.21 | 2.66 | 1.82 | 0.93 | 5.17 | 3.68 | 36.93 |
| 1983 | 1.08 | 0.77 | 3.54 | 4.48 | 4.17 | 3.45 | 4.16 | 3.15 | 2.87 | 4.14 | 5.89 | 2.92 | 40.62 |
| 1984 | 1.25 | 3.82 | 3.82 | 2.29 | 5.95 | 3.40 | 3.35 | 5.51 | 2.43 | 2.20 | 3.38 | 4.41 | 41.33 |
| 1985 | 1.78 | 2.60 | 4.97 | 1.38 | 3.45 | 2.93 | 3.23 | 4.01 | 2.05 | 3.45 | 8.80 | 2.63 | 41.28 |
| 1986 | 2.23 | 3.08 | 2.44 | 3.90 | 4.34 | 2.97 | 3.10 | 3.58 | 4.41 | 2.83 | 3.01 | 2.82 | 40.71 |
| 1987 | 1.98 | 0.49 | 3.84 | 2.97 | 2.40 | 7.94 | 3.36 | 5.51 | 3.07 | 3.41 | 1.02 | 2.96 | 37.95 |
| 1988 | 1.03 | 2.84 | 2.20 | 3.47 | 1.33 | 0.65 | 3.42 | 3.35 | 0.77 | 2.51 | 4.63 | 2.49 | 29.69 |
| 1989 | 2.07 | 1.73 | 3.46 | 3.73 | 9.14 | 5.22 | 3.02 | 1.09 | 4.61 | 4.50 | 3.61 | 1.72 | 43.90 |
| 1990 | 2.35 | 4.70 | 0.86 | 4.57 | 6.10 | 1.72 | 5.62 | 4.79 | 7.33 | 4.92 | 2.28 | 8.59 | 53.83 |
| Record Mean | 2.47 | 2.34 | 2.89 | 2.84 | 3.23 | 3.38 | 3.42 | 3.07 | 3.19 | 2.62 | 2.73 | 2.55 | 34.73 |

**TABLE 3**    AVERAGE TEMPERATURE (deg. F)     CLEVELAND. OHIO

| YEAR | JAN | FEB | MAR | APR | MAY | JUNE | JULY | AUG | SEP | OCT | NOV | DEC | ANNUAL |
|------|-----|-----|-----|-----|-----|------|------|-----|-----|-----|-----|-----|--------|
| 1961 | 21.6 | 31.6 | 40.0 | 43.4 | 54.3 | 65.0 | 71.3 | 70.9 | 58.5 | 56.8 | 42.5 | 29.7 | 49.7 |
| 1962 | 23.9 | 26.0 | 33.8 | 47.4 | 65.0 | 67.9 | 70.2 | 70.2 | 62.0 | 54.6 | 42.4 | 25.9 | 49.0 |
| 1963 | 18.0 | 17.5 | 39.1 | 48.4 | 54.7 | 67.8 | 71.3 | 66.7 | 60.3 | 59.4 | 43.9 | 21.9 | 47.4 |
| 1964 | 29.8 | 25.5 | 37.1 | 48.8 | 60.7 | 67.5 | 72.2 | 67.5 | 63.5 | 49.2 | 44.2 | 32.2 | 49.8 |
| 1965 | 27.2 | 28.0 | 31.7 | 45.6 | 63.2 | 66.9 | 69.0 | 68.7 | 57.4 | 51.3 | 42.5 | 37.4 | 49.9 |
| 1966 | 21.9 | 26.7 | 37.2 | 46.2 | 54.2 | 68.9 | 72.7 | 68.8 | 60.9 | 50.3 | 42.8 | 30.5 | 48.5 |
| 1967 | 32.4 | 25.9 | 37.2 | 49.7 | 52.3 | 71.7 | 69.7 | 68.8 | 61.7 | 54.0 | 38.6 | 34.7 | 49.7 |
| 1968 | 23.0 | 22.6 | 37.6 | 49.4 | 54.4 | 66.5 | 70.0 | 71.7 | 63.9 | 52.1 | 42.4 | 30.0 | 48.6 |
| 1969 | 25.4 | 27.9 | 34.3 | 49.4 | 58.6 | 65.5 | 72.4 | 71.8 | 63.6 | 51.9 | 40.2 | 27.2 | 49.0 |
| 1970 | 18.9 | 27.2 | 33.8 | 50.2 | 62.7 | 69.8 | 71.9 | 69.9 | 66.0 | 54.4 | 41.6 | 32.2 | 49.9 |
| 1971 | 21.4 | 27.9 | 31.6 | 43.2 | 56.5 | 71.0 | 69.5 | 68.9 | 57.7 | 59.9 | 41.4 | 38.1 | 49.8 |
| 1972 | 27.3 | 25.7 | 34.8 | 46.0 | 58.6 | 62.7 | 71.4 | 68.9 | 53.8 | 49.1 | 39.6 | 34.5 | 48.5 |
| 1973 | 30.4 | 27.9 | 46.5 | 50.2 | 56.7 | 70.4 | 72.6 | 73.2 | 66.3 | 57.7 | 44.6 | 34.3 | 52.6 |
| 1974 | 32.0 | 27.8 | 39.6 | 51.3 | 56.4 | 66.2 | 72.2 | 70.4 | 59.9 | 51.2 | 42.9 | 31.7 | 50.1 |
| 1975 | 31.9 | 30.4 | 34.6 | 41.8 | 62.3 | 69.8 | 71.3 | 72.3 | 58.6 | 53.8 | 47.0 | 32.0 | 50.5 |
| 1976 | 21.6 | 36.0 | 45.0 | 49.1 | 55.3 | 69.5 | 71.6 | 68.4 | 61.1 | 48.1 | 33.7 | 23.3 | 48.6 |
| 1977 | 11.0 | 25.0 | 42.7 | 51.4 | 61.8 | 63.3 | 73.1 | 69.6 | 55.6 | 52.6 | 45.4 | 29.2 | 49.3 |
| 1978 | 20.1 | 16.8 | 32.4 | 47.0 | 59.4 | 69.0 | 72.3 | 73.0 | 69.2 | 53.2 | 44.2 | 33.7 | 49.2 |
| 1979 | 22.0 | 19.1 | 42.9 | 46.6 | 56.9 | 66.9 | 71.1 | 71.5 | 65.0 | 52.4 | 42.3 | 33.7 | 49.2 |
| 1980 | 25.5 | 21.9 | 33.6 | 46.1 | 58.5 | 64.0 | 72.3 | 73.2 | 64.7 | 47.9 | 39.4 | 28.5 | 48.0 |
| 1981 | 20.1 | 31.5 | 36.0 | 50.6 | 55.7 | 68.2 | 71.3 | 70.0 | 62.4 | 50.0 | 42.6 | 30.6 | 49.1 |
| 1982 | 19.8 | 25.2 | 37.1 | 44.6 | 64.9 | 64.1 | 73.6 | 67.9 | 62.7 | 55.3 | 45.4 | 40.5 | 50.1 |
| 1983 | 30.7 | 33.9 | 40.8 | 47.1 | 55.7 | 69.0 | 75.2 | 73.7 | 65.1 | 53.4 | 43.9 | 23.2 | 51.0 |
| 1984 | 20.7 | 34.5 | 28.4 | 46.8 | 54.0 | 69.5 | 68.7 | 70.6 | 61.1 | 56.3 | 40.9 | 36.5 | 49.0 |
| 1985 | 20.8 | 25.2 | 40.3 | 53.6 | 60.4 | 62.7 | 71.1 | 68.9 | 64.9 | 54.0 | 46.0 | 24.3 | 49.4 |
| 1986 | 26.7 | 28.8 | 39.5 | 49.8 | 60.8 | 67.2 | 73.1 | 69.0 | 67.0 | 54.3 | 40.3 | 32.6 | 50.8 |
| 1987 | 27.4 | 30.5 | 39.0 | 49.1 | 63.0 | 70.2 | 75.2 | 70.8 | 63.5 | 47.5 | 46.1 | 34.8 | 51.4 |
| 1988 | 25.6 | 25.8 | 37.5 | 47.9 | 59.7 | 68.9 | 75.9 | 74.2 | 64.0 | 47.1 | 43.8 | 31.3 | 50.1 |
| 1989 | 35.0 | 26.1 | 38.1 | 45.3 | 57.6 | 68.3 | 73.4 | 71.0 | 64.0 | 54.0 | 41.0 | 19.2 | 49.4 |
| 1990 | 35.8 | 34.1 | 42.0 | 49.4 | 56.3 | 67.6 | 71.2 | 69.8 | 63.4 | 53.7 | 45.3 | 35.6 | 52.0 |
| Record Mean | 27.0 | 27.7 | 36.2 | 47.2 | 58.3 | 67.8 | 72.3 | 70.6 | 64.6 | 53.5 | 41.7 | 31.2 | 49.9 |
| Max | 33.9 | 35.0 | 44.0 | 55.9 | 67.2 | 76.7 | 80.8 | 79.0 | 73.2 | 61.8 | 48.6 | 37.4 | 57.8 |
| Min | 20.1 | 20.4 | 28.3 | 38.5 | 49.3 | 59.0 | 63.7 | 62.2 | 55.9 | 45.3 | 34.8 | 24.9 | 41.9 |

## REFERENCE NOTES FOR TABLES 1, 2, 3 and 6     (CLEVELAND, OH)

**GENERAL**

T - TRACE AMOUNT
BLANK ENTRIES DENOTE MISSING/UNREPORTED DATA.
# INDICATES A STATION OR INSTRUMENT RELOCATION.

**SPECIFIC**

TABLE 1

(a) - LENGTH OF RECORD IN YEARS. ALTHOUGH
     INDIVIDUAL MONTHS MAY BE MISSING.
*   LESS THAN .05

NORMALS — BASED ON THE 1951-1980 RECORD PERIOD.
EXTREMES — DATES ARE THE MOST RECENT OCCURRENCE.
WIND DIR. — NUMERALS SHOW TENS OF DEGREES
           CLOCKWISE FROM TRUE NORTH.
           "00" INDICATES CALM.
RESULTANT WIND DIRECTIONS ARE GIVEN TO WHOLE DEGREES.

TABLE 3
MAX AND MIN ARE LONG-TERM MEAN DAILY MAXIMUM
AND MEAN DAILY MINIMUM TEMPERATURES.

**EXCEPTIONS**

TABLES 2, 3, and 6

RECORD MEANS ARE THROUGH THE CURRENT YEAR,
BEGINNING IN    1871 FOR TEMPERATURE
                 1871 FOR PRECIPITATION
                 1942 FOR SNOWFALL

HEATING DEGREE DAYS Base 65 deg. F    CLEVELAND, OHIO

**TABLE 4**

| SEASON | JULY | AUG | SEP | OCT | NOV | DEC | JAN | FEB | MAR | APR | MAY | JUNE | TOTAL |
|---|---|---|---|---|---|---|---|---|---|---|---|---|---|
| 1961-62 | 19 | 3 | 74 | 258 | 668 | 1085 | 1264 | 1085 | 958 | 547 | 124 | 43 | 6128 |
| 1962-63 | 10 | 17 | 151 | 331 | 674 | 1206 | 1452 | 1327 | 793 | 500 | 328 | 52 | 6841 |
| 1963-64 | 30 | 32 | 152 | 191 | 627 | 1326 | 1084 | 1139 | 859 | 481 | 179 | 80 | 6180 |
| 1964-65 | 3 | 46 | 117 | 483 | 617 | 1009 | 1165 | 1032 | 1025 | 576 | 130 | 64 | 6267 |
| 1965-66 | 24 | 49 | 67 | 418 | 671 | 852 | 1328 | 1067 | 837 | 562 | 346 | 53 | 6274 |
| 1966-67 | 6 | 15 | 162 | 452 | 655 | 1063 | 1000 | 1087 | 858 | 461 | 393 | 17 | 6169 |
| 1967-68 | 21 | 19 | 137 | 351 | 784 | 934 | 1295 | 1224 | 845 | 459 | 328 | 59 | 6456 |
| 1968-69 | 26 | 34 | 93 | 414 | 672 | 1080 | 1220 | 1032 | 946 | 471 | 234 | 100 | 6322 |
| 1969-70 | 1 | 7 | 121 | 406 | 736 | 1166 | 1425 | 1052 | 960 | 462 | 154 | 39 | 6529 |
| 1970-71 | 9 | 12 | 86 | 332 | 696 | 1009 | 1344 | 1032 | 1031 | 650 | 277 | 16 | 6494 |
| 1971-72 | 9 | 13 | 63 | 168 | 704 | 828 | 1160 | 1133 | 930 | 564 | 196 | 124 | 5892 |
| 1972-73 | 32 | 27 | 95 | 485 | 752 | 937 | 1067 | 1033 | 569 | 450 | 254 | 3 | 5704 |
| 1973-74 | 3 | 9 | 73 | 234 | 605 | 946 | 1015 | 1035 | 777 | 419 | 280 | 49 | 5445 |
| 1974-75 | 2 | 5 | 176 | 423 | 660 | 1026 | 1021 | 962 | 934 | 691 | 154 | 38 | 6092 |
| 1975-76 | 5 | 4 | 187 | 345 | 532 | 1015 | 1336 | 836 | 614 | 493 | 309 | 25 | 5701 |
| 1976-77 | 0 | 25 | 150 | 519 | 932 | 1286 | 1672 | 1113 | 689 | 423 | 166 | 115 | 7090 |
| 1977-78 | 4 | 26 | 60 | 378 | 592 | 1103 | 1387 | 1343 | 1005 | 534 | 218 | 43 | 6693 |
| 1978-79 | 7 | 2 | 43 | 362 | 620 | 965 | 1328 | 1281 | 680 | 552 | 290 | 60 | 6190 |
| 1979-80 | 20 | 11 | 87 | 403 | 670 | 967 | 1218 | 1244 | 967 | 561 | 223 | 103 | 6474 |
| 1980-81 | 3 | 2 | 97 | 521 | 763 | 1125 | 1385 | 935 | 894 | 430 | 298 | 30 | 6483 |
| 1981-82 | 11 | 11 | 145 | 458 | 664 | 1059 | 1393 | 1109 | 860 | 608 | 78 | 75 | 6471 |
| 1982-83 | 5 | 42 | 136 | 310 | 586 | 760 | 1056 | 864 | 742 | 533 | 294 | 56 | 5384 |
| 1983-84 | 7 | 0 | 116 | 362 | 628 | 1291 | 1366 | 878 | 1126 | 544 | 347 | 19 | 6684 |
| 1984-85 | 16 | 17 | 174 | 270 | 716 | 877 | 1364 | 1110 | 757 | 370 | 187 | 99 | 5957 |
| 1985-86 | 2 | 7 | 118 | 338 | 565 | 1255 | 1180 | 1009 | 785 | 459 | 172 | 52 | 5942 |
| 1986-87 | 3 | 40 | 63 | 332 | 736 | 999 | 1158 | 958 | 795 | 473 | 170 | 23 | 5750 |
| 1987-88 | 3 | 22 | 90 | 535 | 562 | 929 | 1213 | 1129 | 848 | 506 | 208 | 60 | 6105 |
| 1988-89 | 8 | 5 | 83 | 557 | 629 | 1040 | 922 | 1084 | 831 | 585 | 272 | 33 | 6049 |
| 1989-90 | 0 | 6 | 108 | 350 | 716 | 1416 | 898 | 858 | 718 | 492 | 270 | 56 | 5888 |
| 1990-91 | 7 | 3 | 121 | 350 | 585 | 906 | | | | | | | |

**TABLE 5**

COOLING DEGREE DAYS Base 65 deg. F    CLEVELAND, OHIO

| YEAR | JAN | FEB | MAR | APR | MAY | JUNE | JULY | AUG | SEP | OCT | NOV | DEC | TOTAL |
|---|---|---|---|---|---|---|---|---|---|---|---|---|---|
| 1969 | 0 | 0 | 0 | 10 | 41 | 120 | 237 | 223 | 84 | 10 | 0 | 0 | 725 |
| 1970 | 0 | 0 | 0 | 22 | 89 | 189 | 230 | 171 | 121 | 10 | 0 | 0 | 832 |
| 1971 | 0 | 0 | 0 | 0 | 22 | 198 | 158 | 143 | 152 | 19 | 0 | 0 | 692 |
| 1972 | 0 | 0 | 0 | 1 | 5 | 63 | 239 | 157 | 64 | 0 | 0 | 0 | 529 |
| 1973 | 0 | 0 | 0 | 13 | 7 | 168 | 244 | 273 | 119 | 17 | 0 | 0 | 841 |
| 1974 | 0 | 0 | 0 | 14 | 18 | 91 | 231 | 180 | 30 | 3 | 2 | 0 | 569 |
| 1975 | 0 | 0 | 0 | 0 | 75 | 187 | 206 | 241 | 6 | 5 | 0 | 0 | 720 |
| 1976 | 0 | 0 | 3 | 23 | 14 | 167 | 214 | 138 | 39 | 2 | 0 | 0 | 600 |
| 1977 | 0 | 0 | 4 | 22 | 74 | 73 | 262 | 175 | 84 | 0 | 9 | 0 | 703 |
| 1978 | 0 | 0 | 0 | 0 | 53 | 170 | 237 | 256 | 177 | 3 | 0 | 0 | 896 |
| 1979 | 0 | 0 | 0 | 6 | 42 | 122 | 213 | 218 | 93 | 21 | 0 | 0 | 715 |
| 1980 | 0 | 0 | 0 | 0 | 27 | 83 | 235 | 263 | 97 | 0 | 0 | 0 | 705 |
| 1981 | 0 | 0 | 0 | 4 | 16 | 132 | 214 | 175 | 73 | 0 | 0 | 0 | 614 |
| 1982 | 0 | 0 | 0 | 3 | 84 | 54 | 278 | 140 | 73 | 17 | 6 | 6 | 661 |
| 1983 | 0 | 0 | 0 | 5 | 12 | 185 | 327 | 277 | 127 | 12 | 0 | 0 | 945 |
| 1984 | 0 | 0 | 0 | 3 | 13 | 159 | 139 | 197 | 60 | 5 | 0 | 0 | 576 |
| 1985 | 0 | 0 | 0 | 38 | 52 | 34 | 201 | 131 | 122 | 4 | 2 | 0 | 584 |
| 1986 | 0 | 0 | 1 | 9 | 48 | 128 | 259 | 168 | 131 | 8 | 0 | 0 | 752 |
| 1987 | 0 | 0 | 0 | 0 | 114 | 183 | 322 | 209 | 53 | 0 | 3 | 0 | 884 |
| 1988 | 0 | 0 | 0 | 0 | 47 | 185 | 348 | 297 | 58 | 9 | 0 | 0 | 944 |
| 1989 | 0 | 0 | 4 | 0 | 46 | 138 | 268 | 199 | 83 | 14 | 0 | 0 | 752 |
| 1990 | 0 | 0 | 10 | 31 | 8 | 141 | 208 | 158 | 80 | 8 | 1 | 0 | 645 |

**TABLE 6**

SNOWFALL (inches)    CLEVELAND, OHIO

| SEASON | JULY | AUG | SEP | OCT | NOV | DEC | JAN | FEB | MAR | APR | MAY | JUNE | TOTAL |
|---|---|---|---|---|---|---|---|---|---|---|---|---|---|
| 1961-62 | 0.0 | 0.0 | 0.0 | T | 0.9 | 4.3 | 6.0 | 16.2 | 8.9 | 1.0 | 0.0 | 0.0 | 37.3 |
| 1962-63 | 0.0 | 0.0 | 0.0 | 8.0 | T | 30.3 | 12.4 | 13.4 | 10.4 | 0.3 | 0.1 | 0.0 | 74.9 |
| 1963-64 | 0.0 | 0.0 | 0.0 | 0.0 | 0.1 | 14.1 | 16.9 | 15.7 | 8.5 | 0.5 | 0.0 | 0.0 | 55.8 |
| 1964-65 | 0.0 | 0.0 | 0.0 | T | 1.0 | 8.7 | 13.6 | 15.6 | 12.9 | 0.4 | 0.0 | 0.0 | 52.2 |
| 1965-66 | 0.0 | 0.0 | 0.0 | T | 1.2 | 1.2 | 15.3 | 10.1 | 7.0 | 2.5 | T | 0.0 | 37.3 |
| 1966-67 | 0.0 | 0.0 | 0.0 | 0.0 | 8.8 | 10.9 | 2.0 | 18.5 | 7.3 | 0.1 | 0.0 | 0.0 | 47.6 |
| 1967-68 | 0.0 | 0.0 | 0.0 | 0.1 | 9.1 | 2.8 | 14.5 | 8.9 | 7.7 | 0.2 | T | 0.0 | 43.3 |
| 1968-69 | 0.0 | 0.0 | 0.0 | T | 6.8 | 8.3 | 5.8 | 5.6 | 9.0 | 1.5 | T | 0.0 | 37.0 |
| 1969-70 | 0.0 | 0.0 | 0.0 | 0.6 | 6.6 | 17.4 | 10.5 | 6.6 | 11.5 | 0.2 | T | 0.0 | 53.4 |
| 1970-71 | 0.0 | 0.0 | T | T | 5.2 | 6.0 | 8.6 | 14.3 | 16.6 | 0.7 | 0.0 | 0.0 | 51.4 |
| 1971-72 | 0.0 | 0.0 | 0.0 | 0.0 | 5.3 | 1.9 | 15.0 | 14.8 | 6.3 | 2.3 | 0.0 | 0.0 | 45.6 |
| 1972-73 | 0.0 | 0.0 | 0.0 | 5.5 | 7.8 | 15.2 | 9.8 | 20.4 | 8.3 | 0.9 | 0.6 | 0.0 | 68.5 |
| 1973-74 | 0.0 | 0.0 | 0.0 | T | 3.3 | 13.8 | 8.9 | 16.9 | 7.1 | 6.4 | 2.1 | 0.0 | 58.5 |
| 1974-75 | 0.0 | 0.0 | 0.0 | 1.6 | 5.3 | 24.1 | 9.7 | 9.9 | 15.2 | 1.2 | 0.0 | 0.0 | 67.0 |
| 1975-76 | 0.0 | 0.0 | 0.0 | 0.0 | 5.6 | 13.1 | 21.5 | 6.8 | 5.8 | 1.6 | T | 0.0 | 54.4 |
| 1976-77 | 0.0 | 0.0 | T | 1.6 | 8.9 | 16.3 | 21.1 | 9.6 | 4.2 | 1.7 | 0.0 | 0.0 | 63.4 |
| 1977-78 | 0.0 | 0.0 | 0.0 | T | 9.7 | 23.1 | 42.8 | 10.8 | 3.5 | 0.2 | 0.0 | 0.0 | 90.1 |
| 1978-79 | 0.0 | 0.0 | 0.0 | 0.0 | 1.9 | 2.5 | 15.1 | 16.0 | 2.4 | 0.4 | 0.0 | 0.0 | 38.3 |
| 1979-80 | 0.0 | 0.0 | 0.0 | 0.2 | 0.5 | 4.0 | 11.3 | 19.2 | 3.5 | T | T | 0.0 | 38.7 |
| 1980-81 | 0.0 | 0.0 | 0.0 | T | 5.4 | 13.5 | 15.0 | 9.7 | 16.9 | T | 0.0 | 0.0 | 60.5 |
| 1981-82 | 0.0 | 0.0 | 0.0 | 4.0 | 2.9 | 27.1 | 28.1 | 7.6 | 17.6 | 13.2 | 0.0 | 0.0 | 100.5 |
| 1982-83 | 0.0 | 0.0 | 0.0 | T | 2.2 | 6.3 | 6.5 | 8.3 | 11.3 | 3.4 | 0.0 | 0.0 | 38.0 |
| 1983-84 | 0.0 | 0.0 | 0.0 | 0.0 | 7.1 | 13.0 | 12.9 | 27.1 | 19.3 | T | 0.0 | 0.0 | 79.4 |
| 1984-85 | 0.0 | 0.0 | 0.0 | 4.0 | 8.9 | 25.5 | 18.2 | 1.2 | 5.9 | 0.0 | 0.0 | 0.0 | 63.7 |
| 1985-86 | 0.0 | 0.0 | 0.0 | 0.0 | T | 23.4 | 17.2 | 10.8 | 6.7 | 0.2 | 0.0 | 0.0 | 58.3 |
| 1986-87 | 0.0 | 0.0 | 0.0 | 0.0 | 3.1 | 1.1 | 16.4 | 5.0 | 26.2 | 4.0 | 0.0 | 0.0 | 55.8 |
| 1987-88 | 0.0 | 0.0 | 0.0 | T | 1.0 | 16.4 | 8.7 | 22.9 | 20.4 | 1.9 | 0.0 | 0.0 | 71.3 |
| 1988-89 | 0.0 | 0.0 | 0.0 | T | 1.7 | 17.9 | 6.6 | 13.8 | 9.9 | 4.9 | T | 0.0 | 54.8 |
| 1989-90 | 0.0 | 0.0 | 0.0 | T | 9.1 | 24.0 | 10.5 | 9.9 | 4.4 | 4.7 | 0.0 | 0.0 | 62.6 |
| 1990-91 | 0.0 | 0.0 | 0.0 | T | T | 7.4 | | | | | | | |
| Record Mean | 0.0 | 0.0 | T | 0.6 | 5.0 | 11.9 | 12.3 | 11.7 | 10.3 | 2.4 | 0.1 | 0.0 | 54.4 |

**See Reference Notes, relative to all above tables, on preceding page.**

Columbus is located in the center of the state and in the drainage area of the Ohio River. The airport is located at the eastern boundary of the city approximately 7 miles from the center of the business district.

Four nearly parallel streams run through or adjacent to the city. The Scioto River is the principal stream and flows from the northwest into the center of the city and then flows straight south toward the Ohio River. The Olentangy River runs almost due south and empties into the Scioto just west of the business district. Two minor streams run through portions of Columbus or skirt the eastern and southern fringes of the area. They are Alum Creek and Big Walnut Creek. Alum Creek empties into the Big Walnut southeast of the city and the Big Walnut empties into the Scioto a few miles downstream. The Scioto and Olentangy are gorge-like in character with very little flood plain and the two creeks have only a little more flood plain or bottomland.

The narrow valleys associated with the streams flowing through the city supply the only variation in the micro-climate of the area. The city proper shows the typical metropolitan effect with shrubs and flowers blossoming earlier than in the immediate surroundings and in retarding light frost on clear quiet nights. Many small areas to the southeast and to the north and northeast show marked effects of air drainage as evidenced by the frequent formation of shallow ground fog at daybreak during the summer and fall months and the higher frequency of frost in the spring and fall.

The average occurrence of the last freezing temperature in the spring within the city proper is mid-April, and the first freeze in the fall is very late October, but in the immediate surroundings there is much variation. For example, at Valley Crossing located at the southeastern outskirts of the city, the average occurrence of the last 32 degree temperature in the spring is very early May, while the first 32 degree temperature in the fall is mid-October.

The records show a high frequency of calm or very low wind speeds during the late evening and early morning hours, from June through September. The rolling landscape is conducive to air drainage and from the Weather Service location at the airport the air drainage is toward the northwest with the wind direction indicated as southeast. Air drainage takes place at speeds generally 4 mph or less and frequently provides the only perceptible breeze during the night.

Columbus is located in the area of changeable weather. Air masses from central and northwest Canada frequently invade this region. Air from the Gulf of Mexico often reachs central Ohio during the summer and to a much lesser extent in the fall and winter. There are also occasional weather changes brought about by cool outbreaks from the Hudson Bay region of Canada, especially during the spring months. At infrequent intervals the general circulation will bring showers or snow to Columbus from the Atlantic. Although Columbus does not have a wet or dry season as such, the month of October usually has the least amount of precipitation.

## TABLE 1 — NORMALS, MEANS AND EXTREMES

COLUMBUS, OHIO

LATITUDE: 40°00'N   LONGITUDE: 82°53'W   ELEVATION: FT. GRND   813 BARO   816   TIME ZONE: EASTERN   WBAN: 14821

| | (a) | JAN | FEB | MAR | APR | MAY | JUNE | JULY | AUG | SEP | OCT | NOV | DEC | YEAR |
|---|---|---|---|---|---|---|---|---|---|---|---|---|---|---|
| **TEMPERATURE °F:** | | | | | | | | | | | | | | |
| Normals | | | | | | | | | | | | | | |
| -Daily Maximum | | 34.7 | 38.1 | 49.3 | 62.3 | 72.6 | 81.3 | 84.4 | 83.0 | 76.9 | 65.0 | 50.7 | 39.4 | 61.5 |
| -Daily Minimum | | 19.4 | 21.5 | 30.6 | 40.5 | 50.2 | 59.0 | 63.2 | 61.7 | 54.6 | 42.8 | 33.5 | 24.7 | 41.8 |
| -Monthly | | 27.1 | 29.8 | 40.0 | 51.4 | 61.4 | 70.2 | 73.8 | 72.4 | 65.8 | 53.9 | 42.1 | 32.1 | 51.7 |
| Extremes | | | | | | | | | | | | | | |
| -Record Highest | 50 | 74 | 73 | 85 | 89 | 94 | 102 | 100 | 101 | 100 | 90 | 80 | 76 | 102 |
| -Year | | 1950 | 1957 | 1945 | 1948 | 1941 | 1944 | 1988 | 1983 | 1951 | 1951 | 1987 | 1982 | JUN 1944 |
| -Record Lowest | 50 | -19 | -13 | -6 | 14 | 25 | 35 | 43 | 39 | 31 | 20 | 5 | -17 | -19 |
| -Year | | 1985 | 1977 | 1984 | 1982 | 1966 | 1972 | 1972 | 1965 | 1963 | 1962 | 1976 | 1989 | JAN 1985 |
| **NORMAL DEGREE DAYS:** | | | | | | | | | | | | | | |
| Heating (base 65°F) | | 1175 | 986 | 775 | 408 | 178 | 19 | 0 | 5 | 78 | 355 | 687 | 1020 | 5686 |
| Cooling (base 65°F) | | 0 | 0 | 0 | 0 | 66 | 175 | 273 | 235 | 102 | 11 | 0 | 0 | 862 |
| **% OF POSSIBLE SUNSHINE** | 38 | 37 | 42 | 44 | 51 | 56 | 60 | 61 | 60 | 61 | 55 | 37 | 30 | 50 |
| **MEAN SKY COVER (tenths)** | | | | | | | | | | | | | | |
| Sunrise - Sunset | 40 | 7.7 | 7.5 | 7.4 | 6.9 | 6.6 | 6.2 | 6.0 | 5.9 | 5.7 | 5.7 | 7.4 | 7.8 | 6.7 |
| **MEAN NUMBER OF DAYS:** | | | | | | | | | | | | | | |
| Sunrise to Sunset | | | | | | | | | | | | | | |
| -Clear | 40 | 4.4 | 4.1 | 4.9 | 5.5 | 6.2 | 6.3 | 6.7 | 7.2 | 9.3 | 10.2 | 4.9 | 4.1 | 73.8 |
| -Partly Cloudy | 40 | 6.4 | 6.1 | 6.8 | 8.0 | 10.2 | 11.3 | 13.3 | 12.8 | 9.1 | 7.4 | 6.7 | 5.8 | 104.0 |
| -Cloudy | 40 | 20.2 | 18.1 | 19.2 | 16.5 | 14.6 | 12.3 | 10.9 | 11.0 | 11.6 | 13.4 | 18.5 | 21.0 | 187.4 |
| Precipitation | | | | | | | | | | | | | | |
| .01 inches or more | 50 | 13.3 | 11.5 | 13.8 | 12.9 | 12.7 | 11.0 | 10.7 | 9.4 | 8.3 | 8.9 | 11.6 | 12.8 | 136.8 |
| Snow, Ice pellets | | | | | | | | | | | | | | |
| 1.0 inches or more | 41 | 2.8 | 2.1 | 1.4 | 0.2 | 0.0 | 0.0 | 0.0 | 0.0 | 0.0 | 0.* | 0.7 | 1.9 | 9.2 |
| Thunderstorms | 50 | 0.4 | 0.5 | 2.1 | 4.0 | 6.4 | 7.9 | 8.1 | 6.3 | 2.9 | 1.2 | 1.0 | 0.3 | 41.2 |
| Heavy Fog Visibility | | | | | | | | | | | | | | |
| 1/4 mile or less | 40 | 1.9 | 1.5 | 1.0 | 0.6 | 1.0 | 1.0 | 1.1 | 1.7 | 1.9 | 1.5 | 1.2 | 1.6 | 16.0 |
| Temperature °F | | | | | | | | | | | | | | |
| -Maximum | | | | | | | | | | | | | | |
| 90° and above | 30 | 0.0 | 0.0 | 0.0 | 0.0 | 0.5 | 3.4 | 5.9 | 3.5 | 1.2 | 0.0 | 0.0 | 0.0 | 14.5 |
| 32° and below | 30 | 13.9 | 9.8 | 2.9 | 0.1 | 0.0 | 0.0 | 0.0 | 0.0 | 0.0 | 0.0 | 1.2 | 9.2 | 37.0 |
| -Minimum | | | | | | | | | | | | | | |
| 32° and below | 30 | 27.3 | 23.8 | 18.7 | 6.8 | 0.7 | 0.0 | 0.0 | 0.0 | 0.1 | 4.1 | 13.7 | 24.2 | 119.3 |
| 0° and below | 30 | 3.0 | 1.6 | 0.1 | 0.0 | 0.0 | 0.0 | 0.0 | 0.0 | 0.0 | 0.0 | 0.0 | 1.0 | 5.7 |
| **AVG. STATION PRESS.(mb)** | 17 | 988.8 | 988.6 | 986.4 | 985.5 | 985.4 | 986.1 | 987.3 | 988.2 | 988.9 | 989.5 | 988.6 | 989.0 | 987.7 |
| **RELATIVE HUMIDITY (%)** | | | | | | | | | | | | | | |
| Hour 01 | 30 | 74 | 73 | 69 | 70 | 77 | 80 | 82 | 84 | 83 | 78 | 77 | 76 | 77 |
| Hour 07 | 30 | 76 | 76 | 74 | 75 | 79 | 81 | 84 | 87 | 87 | 82 | 80 | 78 | 80 |
| Hour 13 (Local Time) | 30 | 67 | 64 | 57 | 52 | 54 | 55 | 56 | 58 | 58 | 55 | 63 | 69 | 59 |
| Hour 19 | 30 | 69 | 67 | 60 | 54 | 57 | 58 | 60 | 63 | 65 | 64 | 69 | 72 | 63 |
| **PRECIPITATION (inches):** | | | | | | | | | | | | | | |
| Water Equivalent | | | | | | | | | | | | | | |
| -Normal | | 2.75 | 2.18 | 3.23 | 3.41 | 3.76 | 4.01 | 4.01 | 3.70 | 2.76 | 1.91 | 2.64 | 2.61 | 36.97 |
| -Maximum Monthly | 50 | 8.29 | 4.60 | 9.59 | 6.36 | 9.11 | 9.75 | 9.46 | 8.63 | 6.76 | 5.24 | 10.67 | 5.07 | 10.67 |
| -Year | | 1950 | 1981 | 1964 | 1964 | 1968 | 1958 | 1958 | 1979 | 1979 | 1954 | 1985 | 1951 | NOV 1985 |
| -Minimum Monthly | 50 | 0.53 | 0.29 | 0.61 | 0.67 | 0.95 | 0.71 | 0.48 | 0.58 | 0.51 | 0.11 | 0.60 | 0.46 | 0.11 |
| -Year | | 1944 | 1978 | 1941 | 1971 | 1977 | 1984 | 1940 | 1951 | 1963 | 1963 | 1976 | 1955 | OCT 1963 |
| -Maximum in 24 hrs | 42 | 4.81 | 2.15 | 3.40 | 2.37 | 2.72 | 2.93 | 3.82 | 3.79 | 4.86 | 2.21 | 2.47 | 1.74 | 4.86 |
| -Year | | 1959 | 1975 | 1964 | 1957 | 1968 | 1958 | 1969 | 1972 | 1979 | 1986 | 1985 | 1978 | SEP 1979 |
| Snow, Ice pellets | | | | | | | | | | | | | | |
| -Maximum Monthly | 42 | 34.4 | 16.4 | 13.5 | 12.6 | 0.8 | 0.0 | 0.0 | 0.0 | T | 1.3 | 15.2 | 17.3 | 34.4 |
| -Year | | 1978 | 1979 | 1962 | 1987 | 1989 | | | | 1967 | 1962 | 1950 | 1960 | JAN 1978 |
| -Maximum in 24 hrs | 42 | 7.5 | 8.9 | 8.6 | 12.3 | 0.8 | 0.0 | 0.0 | 0.0 | T | 1.3 | 8.2 | 8.7 | 12.3 |
| -Year | | 1978 | 1971 | 1962 | 1987 | 1989 | | | | 1967 | 1962 | 1950 | 1960 | APR 1987 |
| **WIND:** | | | | | | | | | | | | | | |
| Mean Speed (mph) | 40 | 10.1 | 9.9 | 10.5 | 9.9 | 8.3 | 7.4 | 6.7 | 6.3 | 6.6 | 7.5 | 9.3 | 9.7 | 8.5 |
| Prevailing Direction | | | | | | | | | | | | | | |
| through 1963 | | SSW | NW | SSW | WNW | S | SSW | SSW | NNW | S | S | S | W | S |
| Fastest Obs. 1 Min. | | | | | | | | | | | | | | |
| -Direction (!!!) | 8 | 23 | 18 | 28 | 22 | 25 | 26 | 23 | 27 | 20 | 25 | 25 | 23 | 25 |
| -Speed (MPH) | 8 | 37 | 30 | 35 | 40 | 52 | 31 | 35 | 38 | 27 | 35 | 35 | 35 | 52 |
| -Year | | 1985 | 1988 | 1985 | 1982 | 1982 | 1983 | 1981 | 1984 | 1983 | 1981 | 1988 | 1987 | MAY 1982 |
| Peak Gust | | | | | | | | | | | | | | |
| -Direction (!!!) | 6 | W | SW | W | S | W | SW | N | W | S | NW | W | SW | W |
| -Speed (mph) | 6 | 51 | 51 | 53 | 52 | 52 | 40 | 47 | 56 | 38 | 37 | 53 | 55 | 56 |
| -Date | | 1985 | 1988 | 1985 | 1985 | 1985 | 1989 | 1985 | 1984 | 1985 | 1985 | 1988 | 1987 | AUG 1984 |

**See Reference Notes to this table on the following page.**

PRECIPITATION (inches)  COLUMBUS, OHIO

**TABLE 2**

| YEAR | JAN | FEB | MAR | APR | MAY | JUNE | JULY | AUG | SEP | OCT | NOV | DEC | ANNUAL |
|---|---|---|---|---|---|---|---|---|---|---|---|---|---|
| 1961 | 0.65 | 2.90 | 4.83 | 4.58 | 2.90 | 3.49 | 4.61 | 2.73 | 1.05 | 1.18 | 3.49 | 2.42 | 34.83 |
| 1962 | 3.17 | 3.46 | 2.43 | 1.33 | 2.31 | 2.26 | 3.59 | 2.31 | 3.62 | 2.06 | 2.94 | 1.76 | 31.24 |
| 1963 | 1.39 | 1.01 | 7.14 | 3.27 | 1.61 | 1.25 | 2.90 | 3.67 | 0.51 | 0.11 | 0.80 | 0.85 | 24.51 |
| 1964 | 1.82 | 1.68 | 9.59 | 6.36 | 1.95 | 5.71 | 2.97 | 3.19 | 1.66 | 0.38 | 1.81 | 4.09 | 41.21 |
| 1965 | 2.70 | 3.76 | 2.90 | 5.90 | 4.00 | 2.42 | 3.76 | 4.62 | 6.18 | 3.98 | 1.19 | 1.24 | 42.65 |
| 1966 | 2.87 | 2.59 | 1.04 | 4.89 | 3.13 | 1.28 | 5.91 | 4.90 | 3.56 | 0.79 | 4.05 | 3.33 | 38.34 |
| 1967 | 0.78 | 2.46 | 4.40 | 3.29 | 4.59 | 2.92 | 4.22 | 1.51 | 2.63 | 1.39 | 3.22 | 2.55 | 33.96 |
| 1968 | 2.22 | 0.38 | 3.01 | 2.20 | 9.11 | 2.96 | 2.80 | 3.08 | 1.77 | 2.59 | 4.26 | 3.40 | 37.78 |
| 1969 | 3.40 | 1.17 | 1.32 | 3.10 | 3.04 | 8.19 | 7.65 | 3.25 | 1.40 | 1.52 | 3.87 | 2.30 | 40.21 |
| 1970 | 1.60 | 1.68 | 3.04 | 5.52 | 5.37 | 5.65 | 3.73 | 3.94 | 3.95 | 2.07 | 2.88 | 2.50 | 41.93 |
| 1971 | 1.57 | 3.16 | 2.70 | 0.67 | 3.66 | 4.16 | 4.22 | 2.81 | 3.08 | 1.32 | 1.73 | 4.61 | 33.69 |
| 1972 | 1.40 | 1.74 | 2.86 | 3.74 | 6.56 | 3.98 | 2.50 | 7.96 | 5.13 | 1.74 | 4.40 | 3.49 | 45.60 |
| 1973 | 2.46 | 1.29 | 3.43 | 3.72 | 3.36 | 8.77 | 4.07 | 4.97 | 2.82 | 3.29 | 5.37 | 2.70 | 46.25 |
| 1974 | 2.40 | 2.30 | 4.38 | 2.66 | 3.29 | 5.04 | 1.14 | 4.88 | 3.32 | 1.51 | 3.39 | 2.68 | 36.99 |
| 1975 | 3.21 | 3.47 | 4.10 | 2.71 | 3.17 | 3.53 | 2.04 | 4.51 | 5.46 | 2.29 | 1.54 | 3.01 | 39.04 |
| 1976 | 3.15 | 2.03 | 2.17 | 1.44 | 1.41 | 4.52 | 5.12 | 5.08 | 2.54 | 2.86 | 0.60 | 0.93 | 31.85 |
| 1977 | 1.57 | 1.02 | 3.88 | 4.04 | 0.95 | 4.02 | 2.52 | 4.76 | 3.48 | 2.57 | 3.77 | 3.54 | 36.12 |
| 1978 | 5.89 | 0.29 | 2.98 | 3.02 | 4.15 | 3.65 | 1.14 | 5.23 | 1.16 | 2.39 | 1.56 | 5.01 | 37.14 |
| 1979 | 3.32 | 2.88 | 1.01 | 4.01 | 3.27 | 4.23 | 8.06 | 8.63 | 6.76 | 1.26 | 3.91 | 1.83 | 49.17 |
| 1980 | 1.69 | 1.38 | 3.77 | 1.59 | 4.56 | 5.17 | 4.58 | 6.26 | 1.86 | 2.53 | 2.07 | 1.96 | 37.42 |
| 1981 | 0.70 | 4.60 | 1.11 | 5.38 | 6.50 | 5.73 | 4.14 | 1.41 | 2.28 | 1.40 | 1.65 | 2.88 | 37.78 |
| 1982 | 4.77 | 1.49 | 3.99 | 1.90 | 4.68 | 3.37 | 3.90 | 1.02 | 4.25 | 0.92 | 5.19 | 3.84 | 39.32 |
| 1983 | 1.20 | 0.74 | 1.69 | 5.58 | 5.06 | 4.59 | 2.80 | 2.23 | 1.91 | 4.45 | 5.00 | 3.16 | 38.41 |
| 1984 | 1.07 | 1.97 | 3.89 | 3.10 | 4.93 | 0.71 | 3.15 | 2.96 | 1.48 | 2.91 | 4.41 | 2.84 | 33.42 |
| 1985 | 1.31 | 1.67 | 3.78 | 0.73 | 4.96 | 1.41 | 6.88 | 2.34 | 1.18 | 1.93 | 10.67 | 1.81 | 38.67 |
| 1986 | 1.54 | 2.96 | 2.61 | 1.31 | 2.47 | 5.53 | 3.60 | 1.61 | 3.44 | 4.16 | 3.00 | 2.81 | 35.04 |
| 1987 | 1.14 | 0.59 | 2.04 | 2.02 | 2.85 | 3.60 | 3.60 | 2.96 | 1.53 | 1.57 | 1.63 | 2.88 | 26.70 |
| 1988 | 2.14 | 4.26 | 2.54 | 2.24 | 2.27 | 1.34 | 7.80 | 2.68 | 3.52 | 1.70 | 3.59 | 2.49 | 36.57 |
| 1989 | 1.97 | 3.10 | 4.16 | 3.30 | 4.69 | 6.36 | 6.79 | 4.30 | 2.16 | 2.49 | 2.65 | 1.79 | 43.76 |
| 1990 | 2.43 | 5.15 | 1.32 | 2.82 | 7.01 | 5.25 | 8.00 | 1.86 | 5.26 | 5.05 | 2.03 | 6.98 | 53.16 |
| Record Mean | 2.84 | 2.47 | 3.91 | 3.13 | 3.72 | 3.73 | 3.83 | 3.23 | 2.63 | 2.26 | 2.79 | 2.63 | 37.17 |

**TABLE 3**  AVERAGE TEMPERATURE (deg. F)  COLUMBUS, OHIO

| YEAR | JAN | FEB | MAR | APR | MAY | JUNE | JULY | AUG | SEP | OCT | NOV | DEC | ANNUAL |
|---|---|---|---|---|---|---|---|---|---|---|---|---|---|
| 1961 | 23.5 | 36.9 | 45.3 | 47.1 | 56.5 | 67.2 | 73.7 | 73.1 | 71.0 | 55.3 | 41.8 | 29.7 | 51.8 |
| 1962 | 24.6 | 28.8 | 36.9 | 48.7 | | 67.2 | 72.3 | 71.3 | 61.5 | 54.4 | 44.6 | 24.9 | 50.2 |
| 1963 | 21.7 | 22.4 | 42.8 | 51.1 | 58.8 | 70.8 | 73.9 | 69.9 | 63.7 | 59.9 | 44.6 | 21.6 | 50.1 |
| 1964 | 30.1 | 27.7 | 41.1 | 53.6 | 63.4 | 70.3 | 74.1 | 71.2 | 65.0 | 51.1 | 45.1 | 33.9 | 52.3 |
| 1965 | 28.3 | 29.1 | 34.8 | 51.4 | 68.1 | 69.4 | 72.0 | 71.0 | 68.3 | 54.4 | 43.3 | 36.6 | 52.2 |
| 1966 | 22.2 | 29.4 | 41.8 | 49.4 | 56.1 | 71.4 | 75.6 | 71.3 | 63.2 | 50.7 | 42.6 | 32.6 | 50.5 |
| 1967 | 34.8 | 25.8 | 40.4 | 52.6 | 55.4 | 71.8 | 71.7 | 68.3 | 60.4 | 51.9 | 36.7 | 34.3 | 50.3 |
| 1968 | 23.6 | 25.7 | 43.3 | 53.1 | 58.5 | 71.5 | 74.1 | 73.0 | 64.1 | 54.1 | 44.0 | 31.1 | 51.5 |
| 1969 | 27.0 | 31.4 | 35.3 | 51.5 | 61.7 | 68.5 | 74.1 | 71.2 | 63.8 | 53.9 | 39.3 | 26.8 | 50.4 |
| 1970 | 20.6 | 28.5 | 36.9 | 53.4 | 64.9 | 69.8 | 73.5 | 72.4 | 65.6 | 55.6 | 42.4 | 34.3 | 51.8 |
| 1971 | 24.3 | 30.8 | 36.6 | 49.0 | 58.0 | 73.5 | 70.5 | 68.9 | 67.8 | 59.8 | 40.4 | 38.4 | 51.5 |
| 1972 | 28.2 | 27.7 | 37.0 | 48.8 | 60.8 | 63.6 | 71.0 | 70.1 | 64.6 | 49.6 | 40.5 | 36.1 | 49.9 |
| 1973 | 31.2 | 31.4 | 50.4 | 51.1 | 59.5 | 72.6 | 74.3 | 74.2 | 68.9 | 58.6 | 45.1 | 33.7 | 54.3 |
| 1974 | 33.2 | 31.2 | 44.6 | 54.3 | 60.8 | 67.7 | 74.0 | 74.0 | 62.2 | 52.8 | 44.5 | 34.0 | 52.8 |
| 1975 | 32.5 | 33.4 | 37.3 | 46.7 | 66.6 | 72.4 | 75.1 | 77.3 | 62.7 | 54.7 | 47.5 | 33.5 | 53.3 |
| 1976 | 24.0 | 37.4 | 46.5 | 50.9 | 58.1 | 70.5 | 72.0 | 68.3 | 61.7 | 47.5 | 33.9 | 24.8 | 49.6 |
| 1977 | 11.4 | 26.5 | 45.6 | 54.8 | 66.8 | 67.5 | 76.2 | 72.0 | 62.2 | 52.0 | 45.1 | 29.5 | 51.3 |
| 1978 | 19.0 | 16.5 | 34.5 | 50.6 | 59.6 | 70.4 | 73.5 | 73.2 | 69.8 | 51.5 | 44.4 | 34.4 | 49.8 |
| 1979 | 21.4 | 19.3 | 44.3 | 50.1 | 60.5 | 69.6 | 71.8 | 71.9 | 65.1 | 53.3 | 43.6 | 35.1 | 50.5 |
| 1980 | 29.3 | 25.2 | 37.2 | 49.5 | 62.4 | 67.4 | 75.9 | 75.9 | 68.3 | 50.8 | 40.8 | 32.5 | 51.3 |
| 1981 | 23.3 | 34.0 | 40.2 | 55.8 | 59.5 | 70.9 | 71.9 | 70.4 | 62.3 | 51.1 | 40.9 | 30.6 | 50.9 |
| 1982 | 21.2 | 29.2 | 40.4 | 46.4 | 66.8 | 65.8 | 74.4 | 69.2 | 63.5 | 56.2 | 45.4 | 40.4 | 51.6 |
| 1983 | 29.9 | 34.0 | 43.3 | 48.4 | 57.6 | 69.4 | 76.7 | 76.2 | 67.1 | 54.5 | 44.0 | 24.8 | 52.2 |
| 1984 | 23.3 | 37.4 | 32.3 | 50.0 | 57.6 | 73.1 | 71.2 | 72.9 | 63.1 | 59.4 | 40.6 | 39.5 | 51.7 |
| 1985 | 21.7 | 26.0 | 43.7 | 56.3 | 62.6 | 66.9 | 72.7 | 71.2 | 66.6 | 57.3 | 48.7 | 26.0 | 51.7 |
| 1986 | 30.1 | 32.7 | 42.5 | 54.5 | 64.3 | 70.6 | 75.7 | 71.0 | 69.2 | 56.3 | 41.3 | 33.3 | 53.5 |
| 1987 | 29.9 | 34.9 | 44.3 | 52.1 | 66.0 | 72.7 | 76.6 | 74.3 | 66.0 | 49.1 | 47.6 | 35.7 | 54.2 |
| 1988 | 26.5 | 29.3 | 40.2 | 50.3 | 62.6 | 69.6 | 77.5 | 75.3 | 65.2 | 47.4 | 43.9 | 31.6 | 51.6 |
| 1989 | 36.6 | 28.7 | 42.0 | 48.2 | 57.2 | 68.3 | 73.9 | 71.2 | 65.2 | 54.2 | 42.1 | 19.8 | 50.7 |
| 1990 | 37.7 | 37.5 | 45.3 | 50.7 | 59.1 | 70.3 | 73.6 | 72.5 | 66.4 | 55.1 | 46.2 | 37.2 | 54.3 |
| Record Mean | 28.9 | 30.7 | 40.2 | 51.1 | 61.8 | 70.7 | 74.7 | 72.8 | 66.4 | 54.8 | 42.4 | 32.4 | 52.3 |
| Max | 36.4 | 38.7 | 49.2 | 61.4 | 72.4 | 81.2 | 85.1 | 83.2 | 77.1 | 65.1 | 50.6 | 39.5 | 61.7 |
| Min | 21.3 | 22.6 | 31.1 | 40.8 | 51.2 | 60.2 | 64.2 | 62.4 | 55.8 | 44.5 | 34.2 | 25.2 | 42.8 |

## REFERENCE NOTES FOR TABLES 1, 2, 3 and 6   (COLUMBUS, OH)

### GENERAL

T - TRACE AMOUNT
BLANK ENTRIES DENOTE MISSING/UNREPORTED DATA.
# INDICATES A STATION OR INSTRUMENT RELOCATION.

### SPECIFIC

**TABLE 1**

(a) - LENGTH OF RECORD IN YEARS. ALTHOUGH INDIVIDUAL MONTHS MAY BE MISSING.

* LESS THAN .05

NORMALS — BASED ON THE 1951-1980 RECORD PERIOD.
EXTREMES — DATES ARE THE MOST RECENT OCCURRENCE.
WIND DIR. — NUMERALS SHOW TENS OF DEGREES
CLOCKWISE FROM TRUE NORTH.
"00" INDICATES CALM.
RESULTANT WIND DIRECTIONS ARE GIVEN TO WHOLE DEGREES.

**TABLE 3**
MAX AND MIN ARE LONG-TERM MEAN DAILY MAXIMUM AND MEAN DAILY MINIMUM TEMPERATURES.

### EXCEPTIONS

**TABLES 2, 3, and 6**

RECORD MEANS ARE THROUGH THE CURRENT YEAR,
BEGINNING IN      1879 FOR TEMPERATURE
1879 FOR PRECIPITATION
1948 FOR SNOWFALL

**TABLE 4**

HEATING DEGREE DAYS Base 65 deg. F        COLUMBUS, OHIO

| SEASON | JULY | AUG | SEP | OCT | NOV | DEC | JAN | FEB | MAR | APR | MAY | JUNE | TOTAL |
|---|---|---|---|---|---|---|---|---|---|---|---|---|---|
| 1961-62 | 2 | 2 | 60 | 297 | 689 | 1087 | 1249 | 1005 | 366 | 496 | 76 | 2 | 5831 |
| 1962-63 | 8 | 3 | 165 | 342 | 721 | 1238 | 1334 | 1186 | 683 | 424 | 208 | 18 | 6330 |
| 1963-64 | 6 | 14 | 93 | 174 | 603 | 1336 | 1076 | 1075 | 735 | 340 | 113 | 40 | 5605 |
| 1964-65 | 0 | 28 | 90 | 424 | 589 | 957 | 1132 | 999 | 832 | 403 | 39 | 26 | 5619 |
| 1965-66 | 4 | 28 | 53 | 330 | 645 | 873 | 1325 | 989 | 710 | 465 | 286 | 29 | 5737 |
| 1966-67 | 1 | 5 | 106 | 440 | 671 | 999 | 929 | 1093 | 756 | 374 | 300 | 9 | 5683 |
| 1967-68 | 7 | 23 | 164 | 406 | 843 | 942 | 1276 | 1133 | 667 | 351 | 205 | 6 | 6023 |
| 1968-69 | 6 | 20 | 57 | 362 | 624 | 1043 | 1173 | 933 | 816 | 402 | 143 | 54 | 5733 |
| 1969-70 | 0 | 2 | 107 | 359 | 763 | 1175 | 1369 | 1017 | 861 | 365 | 119 | 13 | 6150 |
| 1970-71 | 10 | 0 | 58 | 297 | 674 | 944 | 1256 | 950 | 871 | 475 | 230 | 4 | 5769 |
| 1971-72 | 3 | 5 | 52 | 181 | 733 | 815 | 1133 | 1077 | 860 | 482 | 146 | 101 | 5588 |
| 1972-73 | 22 | 18 | 77 | 473 | 727 | 889 | 1041 | 934 | 444 | 427 | 184 | 0 | 5236 |
| 1973-74 | 0 | 3 | 35 | 219 | 589 | 963 | 977 | 940 | 628 | 332 | 178 | 31 | 4895 |
| 1974-75 | 0 | 0 | 130 | 374 | 609 | 954 | 999 | 878 | 650 | 542 | 73 | 18 | 5427 |
| 1975-76 | 0 | 0 | 110 | 321 | 520 | 1263 | 973 | 791 | 570 | 440 | 229 | 4 | 5221 |
| 1976-77 | 1 | 25 | 118 | 537 | 925 | 1241 | 1659 | 1071 | 601 | 324 | 91 | 64 | 6657 |
| 1977-78 | 1 | 17 | 36 | 394 | 594 | 1091 | 1420 | 1346 | 938 | 424 | 223 | 23 | 6507 |
| 1978-79 | 0 | 0 | 38 | 411 | 610 | 943 | 1346 | 1270 | 637 | 449 | 185 | 18 | 5907 |
| 1979-80 | 11 | 16 | 83 | 376 | 632 | 920 | 1099 | 1148 | 855 | 458 | 133 | 53 | 5784 |
| 1980-81 | 0 | 0 | 46 | 435 | 717 | 1000 | 1286 | 864 | 761 | 287 | 195 | 14 | 5605 |
| 1981-82 | 8 | 5 | 141 | 429 | 713 | 1061 | 1351 | 997 | 758 | 556 | 45 | 33 | 6097 |
| 1982-83 | 3 | 19 | 107 | 304 | 585 | 759 | 1081 | 863 | 669 | 493 | 239 | 30 | 5152 |
| 1983-84 | 6 | 0 | 83 | 325 | 626 | 1236 | 1284 | 796 | 507 | 447 | 254 | 3 | 6067 |
| 1984-85 | 6 | 3 | 143 | 182 | 727 | 782 | 1339 | 1086 | 654 | 286 | 134 | 35 | 5377 |
| 1985-86 | 0 | 2 | 96 | 249 | 500 | 1202 | 1076 | 901 | 694 | 328 | 113 | 19 | 5180 |
| 1986-87 | 0 | 26 | 41 | 287 | 702 | 974 | 1083 | 838 | 637 | 393 | 103 | 9 | 5093 |
| 1987-88 | 0 | 4 | 53 | 489 | 521 | 900 | 1187 | 1029 | 762 | 433 | 119 | 49 | 5546 |
| 1988-89 | 3 | 7 | 57 | 547 | 624 | 1032 | 873 | 1009 | 711 | 499 | 274 | 28 | 5664 |
| 1989-90 | 0 | 11 | 90 | 345 | 680 | 1394 | 840 | 766 | 613 | 444 | 190 | 26 | 5399 |
| 1990-91 | 0 | 3 | 83 | 310 | 558 | 857 | | | | | | | |

**TABLE 5**

COOLING DEGREE DAYS Base 65 deg. F        COLUMBUS, OHIO

| YEAR | JAN | FEB | MAR | APR | MAY | JUNE | JULY | AUG | SEP | OCT | NOV | DEC | TOTAL |
|---|---|---|---|---|---|---|---|---|---|---|---|---|---|
| 1969 | 0 | 0 | 0 | 3 | 45 | 165 | 290 | 203 | 76 | 18 | 0 | 0 | 800 |
| 1970 | 0 | 0 | 0 | 22 | 125 | 166 | 281 | 237 | 79 | 13 | 0 | 0 | 1023 |
| 1971 | 0 | 0 | 0 | 0 | 21 | 266 | 181 | 135 | 44 | 24 | 0 | 0 | 771 |
| 1972 | 0 | 0 | 0 | 1 | 24 | 67 | 245 | 183 | 71 | 0 | 0 | 0 | 591 |
| 1973 | 0 | 0 | 3 | 14 | 17 | 236 | 295 | 292 | 60 | 25 | 0 | 0 | 1042 |
| 1974 | 0 | 0 | 4 | 20 | 58 | 117 | 296 | 286 | 52 | 3 | 0 | 0 | 836 |
| 1975 | 0 | 0 | 0 | 1 | 130 | 248 | 320 | 389 | 48 | 10 | 1 | 0 | 1147 |
| 1976 | 0 | 0 | 3 | 23 | 23 | 174 | 223 | 135 | 25 | 2 | 0 | 0 | 608 |
| 1977 | 0 | 0 | 8 | 24 | 151 | 148 | 354 | 242 | 39 | 0 | 7 | 0 | 1073 |
| 1978 | 0 | 0 | 0 | 0 | 59 | 190 | 270 | 261 | 88 | 0 | 0 | 0 | 968 |
| 1979 | 0 | 0 | 0 | 7 | 54 | 163 | 230 | 239 | 93 | 22 | 0 | 0 | 808 |
| 1980 | 0 | 0 | 0 | 0 | 61 | 132 | 343 | 344 | 51 | 3 | 0 | 0 | 1034 |
| 1981 | 0 | 0 | 0 | 16 | 32 | 198 | 231 | 181 | 64 | 4 | 0 | 0 | 726 |
| 1982 | 0 | 0 | 0 | 4 | 111 | 66 | 301 | 154 | 67 | 39 | 7 | 4 | 753 |
| 1983 | 0 | 0 | 1 | 2 | 17 | 167 | 377 | 355 | 52 | 9 | 0 | 0 | 1080 |
| 1984 | 0 | 0 | 0 | 8 | 30 | 253 | 205 | 254 | 94 | 14 | 0 | 0 | 858 |
| 1985 | 0 | 0 | 2 | 32 | 64 | 97 | 245 | 201 | 52 | 19 | 2 | 0 | 814 |
| 1986 | 0 | 0 | 2 | 19 | 95 | 194 | 339 | 221 | 71 | 25 | 0 | 0 | 1066 |
| 1987 | 0 | 0 | 0 | 0 | 11 | 142 | 246 | 366 | 16 | 0 | 5 | 0 | 1185 |
| 1988 | 0 | 0 | 0 | 0 | 54 | 194 | 396 | 333 | 70 | 5 | 0 | 0 | 1052 |
| 1989 | 0 | 0 | 5 | 2 | 40 | 149 | 282 | 211 | 106 | 12 | 0 | 0 | 807 |
| 1990 | 0 | 0 | 11 | 21 | 13 | 191 | 273 | 244 | 133 | 9 | 3 | 0 | 898 |

**TABLE 6**

SNOWFALL (inches)        COLUMBUS, OHIO

| SEASON | JULY | AUG | SEP | OCT | NOV | DEC | JAN | FEB | MAR | APR | MAY | JUNE | TOTAL |
|---|---|---|---|---|---|---|---|---|---|---|---|---|---|
| 1961-62 | 0.0 | 0.0 | 0.0 | 0.0 | 1.3 | 8.8 | 3.9 | 8.8 | 13.5 | 1.1 | 0.0 | 0.0 | 37.4 |
| 1962-63 | 0.0 | 0.0 | 0.0 | 1.3 | T | 9.5 | 10.1 | 8.7 | 2.4 | T | 0.0 | 0.0 | 32.0 |
| 1963-64 | 0.0 | 0.0 | 0.0 | 0.0 | 1.2 | 7.3 | 12.3 | 11.3 | 2.4 | T | 0.0 | 0.0 | 35.0 |
| 1964-65 | 0.0 | 0.0 | 0.0 | 0.0 | 1.0 | 3.2 | 10.2 | 7.6 | 8.6 | T | 0.0 | 0.0 | 30.6 |
| 1965-66 | 0.0 | 0.0 | 0.0 | 0.0 | 0.2 | 1.1 | 7.6 | 6.7 | 1.2 | 0.7 | T | 0.0 | 17.5 |
| 1966-67 | 0.0 | 0.0 | 0.0 | T | 10.4 | 6.4 | 2.8 | 15.6 | 11.4 | 0.0 | 0.0 | 0.0 | 46.6 |
| 1967-68 | 0.0 | 0.0 | T | 0.0 | 6.5 | 5.2 | 11.6 | 2.8 | 6.1 | T | 0.0 | 0.0 | 32.2 |
| 1968-69 | 0.0 | 0.0 | 0.0 | 0.0 | 1.0 | 6.8 | 2.5 | 2.5 | 1.9 | 0.5 | 0.0 | 0.0 | 15.2 |
| 1969-70 | 0.0 | 0.0 | 0.0 | 0.0 | 1.8 | 9.7 | 18.4 | 3.2 | 10.3 | 0.9 | 0.0 | 0.0 | 44.3 |
| 1970-71 | 0.0 | 0.0 | 0.0 | 0.0 | 0.9 | 1.4 | 6.5 | 12.3 | 12.3 | T | 0.0 | 0.0 | 33.4 |
| 1971-72 | 0.0 | 0.0 | 0.0 | 0.0 | 5.0 | 0.6 | 5.8 | 6.6 | 5.0 | 0.6 | 0.0 | 0.0 | 23.6 |
| 1972-73 | 0.0 | 0.0 | 0.0 | T | 6.3 | 2.8 | 4.4 | 1.8 | 2.1 | 7.1 | 0.0 | 0.0 | 24.5 |
| 1973-74 | 0.0 | 0.0 | 0.0 | 0.0 | T | 6.4 | 2.3 | 5.0 | 4.5 | 0.3 | 0.0 | 0.0 | 18.5 |
| 1974-75 | 0.0 | 0.0 | 0.0 | T | 0.3 | 7.4 | 8.1 | 3.7 | 2.6 | T | 0.0 | 0.0 | 22.1 |
| 1975-76 | 0.0 | 0.0 | 0.0 | 0.0 | 1.1 | 2.9 | 12.4 | 1.8 | 1.0 | T | 0.0 | 0.0 | 19.2 |
| 1976-77 | 0.0 | 0.0 | 0.0 | 0.0 | 3.1 | 4.6 | 18.1 | 6.7 | 0.3 | 0.1 | 0.0 | 0.0 | 32.9 |
| 1977-78 | 0.0 | 0.0 | 0.0 | 0.0 | 2.2 | 7.5 | 34.4 | 4.5 | 5.5 | T | 0.0 | 0.0 | 54.1 |
| 1978-79 | 0.0 | 0.0 | 0.0 | T | 1.3 | 1.8 | 17.3 | 16.4 | 0.8 | 0.3 | 0.0 | 0.0 | 37.9 |
| 1979-80 | 0.0 | 0.0 | 0.0 | 0.0 | 0.1 | 0.2 | 7.0 | 8.1 | 1.2 | T | 0.0 | 0.0 | 16.6 |
| 1980-81 | 0.0 | 0.0 | 0.0 | T | | 7.3 | 7.8 | 3.7 | 3.3 | 0.0 | 0.0 | 0.0 | 30.1 |
| 1981-82 | 0.0 | 0.0 | 0.0 | 0.0 | 1.9 | 9.8 | 11.8 | 3.7 | 3.2 | 4.7 | 0.0 | 0.0 | 35.1 |
| 1982-83 | 0.0 | 0.0 | 0.0 | 0.0 | T | 1.5 | 2.6 | 4.5 | 2.8 | 0.1 | 0.0 | 0.0 | 11.5 |
| 1983-84 | 0.0 | 0.0 | 0.0 | 0.0 | 0.5 | 5.7 | 9.0 | 10.8 | 9.8 | 0.3 | 0.0 | 0.0 | 36.1 |
| 1984-85 | 0.0 | 0.0 | 0.0 | 0.0 | 0.9 | 7.3 | 21.9 | 12.5 | T | 0.8 | 0.0 | 0.0 | 43.4 |
| 1985-86 | 0.0 | 0.0 | 0.0 | 0.0 | 0.0 | 8.6 | 4.8 | 9.8 | 1.8 | T | 0.0 | 0.0 | 25.0 |
| 1986-87 | 0.0 | 0.0 | 0.0 | 0.0 | 0.4 | 0.4 | 2.7 | 1.2 | 5.9 | 12.6 | 0.0 | 0.0 | 23.2 |
| 1987-88 | 0.0 | 0.0 | 0.0 | 0.0 | 0.6 | 4.6 | 8.4 | 6.5 | 3.8 | T | 0.0 | 0.0 | 23.9 |
| 1988-89 | 0.0 | 0.0 | 0.0 | T | 0.8 | 5.9 | 0.6 | 3.9 | 6.6 | 0.1 | 0.8 | 0.0 | 18.7 |
| 1989-90 | 0.0 | 0.0 | 0.0 | 0.4 | 0.3 | 9.4 | 3.3 | 6.0 | 1.4 | 0.4 | 0.0 | T | 21.2 |
| 1990-91 | 0.0 | 0.0 | 0.0 | 0.0 | 0.0 | 3.7 | | | | | | | |
| Record Mean | 0.0 | 0.0 | T | T | 2.3 | 5.7 | 8.3 | 6.2 | 4.5 | 1.0 | T | T | 28.0 |

**See Reference Notes, relative to all above tables, on preceding page.**

Toledo is located on the western end of Lake Erie at the mouth of the Maumee River. Except for a bank up from the river about 30 feet, the terrain is generally level with only a slight slope toward the river and Lake Erie. The city has quite a diversified industrial section and excellent harbor facilities, making it a large transportation center for rail, water, and motor freight. Generally rich agricultural land is found in the surrounding area, especially up the Maumee Valley toward the Indiana state line.

Rainfall is usually sufficient for general agriculture. The terrain is level and drainage rather poor, therefore, a little less than the normal precipitation during the growing season is better than excessive amounts. Snowfall is generally light in this area, distributed throughout the winter from November to March with frequent thaws.

The nearness of Lake Erie and the other Great Lakes has a moderating effect on the temperature, and extremes are seldom recorded. On average, only fifteen days a year experience temperatures of 90 degrees or higher, and only eight days when it drops to zero or lower. The growing season averages 160 days, but has ranged from over 220 to less than 125 days.

Humidity is rather high throughout the year in this area, and there is an excessive amount of cloudiness. In the winter months the sun shines during only about 30 percent of the daylight hours. December and January, the cloudiest months, sometimes have as little as 16 percent of the possible hours of sunshine.

Severe windstorms, causing more than minor damage, occur infrequently. There are on the average twenty-three days per year having a sustained wind velocity of 32 mph or more.

Flooding in the Toledo area is produced by several factors. Heavy rains of 1 inch or more will cause a sudden rise in creeks and drainage ditches to the point of overflow. The western shores of Lake Erie are subject to flooding when the lake level is high and prolonged periods of east to northeast winds prevail.

# TABLE 1 NORMALS, MEANS AND EXTREMES

TOLEDO, OHIO

LATITUDE: 41°36'N  LONGITUDE: 83°48'W  ELEVATION: FT. GRND  669 BARO  694  TIME ZONE: EASTERN  WBAN: 94830

| | (a) | JAN | FEB | MAR | APR | MAY | JUNE | JULY | AUG | SEP | OCT | NOV | DEC | YEAR |
|---|---|---|---|---|---|---|---|---|---|---|---|---|---|---|
| **TEMPERATURE °F:** | | | | | | | | | | | | | | |
| Normals | | | | | | | | | | | | | | |
| -Daily Maximum | | 30.7 | 34.0 | 44.6 | 59.1 | 70.5 | 79.9 | 83.4 | 81.8 | 75.1 | 63.3 | 47.9 | 35.5 | 58.8 |
| -Daily Minimum | | 15.5 | 17.5 | 26.1 | 36.5 | 46.6 | 56.0 | 60.2 | 58.4 | 51.2 | 40.1 | 30.6 | 20.6 | 38.3 |
| -Monthly | | 23.1 | 25.8 | 35.4 | 47.8 | 58.6 | 68.0 | 71.8 | 70.1 | 63.2 | 51.7 | 39.3 | 28.1 | 48.6 |
| Extremes | | | | | | | | | | | | | | |
| -Record Highest | 34 | 62 | 68 | 80 | 88 | 95 | 104 | 103 | 98 | 98 | 91 | 78 | 68 | 104 |
| -Year | | 1989 | 1957 | 1986 | 1977 | 1962 | 1988 | 1988 | 1987 | 1978 | 1963 | 1987 | 1982 | JUN 1988 |
| -Record Lowest | 34 | -20 | -14 | -6 | 8 | 25 | 32 | 40 | 34 | 26 | 15 | 2 | -19 | -20 |
| -Year | | 1984 | 1982 | 1984 | 1982 | 1974 | 1972 | 1988 | 1988 | 1982 | 1974 | 1976 | 1958 | 1989 | JAN 1984 |
| **NORMAL DEGREE DAYS:** | | | | | | | | | | | | | | |
| Heating (base 65°F) | | 1299 | 1098 | 918 | 516 | 237 | 39 | 0 | 16 | 113 | 419 | 771 | 1144 | 6570 |
| Cooling (base 65°F) | | 0 | 0 | 0 | 0 | 38 | 129 | 215 | 174 | 59 | 7 | 0 | 0 | 622 |
| **% OF POSSIBLE SUNSHINE** | 34 | 42 | 47 | 50 | 54 | 60 | 64 | 66 | 63 | 60 | 54 | 37 | 33 | 53 |
| **MEAN SKY COVER (tenths)** | | | | | | | | | | | | | | |
| Sunrise - Sunset | 34 | 7.4 | 7.3 | 7.3 | 6.8 | 6.4 | 6.0 | 5.7 | 5.7 | 5.9 | 6.2 | 7.6 | 7.9 | 6.7 |
| **MEAN NUMBER OF DAYS:** | | | | | | | | | | | | | | |
| Sunrise to Sunset | | | | | | | | | | | | | | |
| -Clear | 34 | 4.8 | 4.4 | 5.0 | 6.1 | 6.5 | 6.9 | 7.7 | 8.2 | 8.4 | 8.0 | 3.7 | 3.1 | 72.8 |
| -Partly Cloudy | 34 | 6.8 | 7.1 | 7.4 | 7.9 | 10.7 | 11.9 | 13.4 | 12.3 | 9.6 | 8.9 | 7.1 | 6.5 | 109.5 |
| -Cloudy | 34 | 19.4 | 16.8 | 18.6 | 16.0 | 13.8 | 11.2 | 9.8 | 10.5 | 12.0 | 14.1 | 19.2 | 21.4 | 182.9 |
| Precipitation | | | | | | | | | | | | | | |
| .01 inches or more | 34 | 13.3 | 10.9 | 13.1 | 12.6 | 12.0 | 10.2 | 9.5 | 9.1 | 10.1 | 9.2 | 11.8 | 14.4 | 136.4 |
| Snow, Ice pellets | | | | | | | | | | | | | | |
| 1.0 inches or more | 34 | 2.9 | 2.4 | 2.0 | 0.5 | 0.0 | 0.0 | 0.0 | 0.0 | 0.0 | 0.* | 1.1 | 2.8 | 11.9 |
| Thunderstorms | 34 | 0.1 | 0.5 | 2.0 | 3.8 | 4.9 | 7.2 | 7.0 | 6.3 | 3.9 | 1.1 | 0.8 | 0.2 | 37.9 |
| Heavy Fog Visibility | | | | | | | | | | | | | | |
| 1/4 mile or less | 34 | 1.4 | 1.9 | 1.5 | 0.8 | 0.7 | 0.9 | 0.8 | 1.8 | 1.9 | 2.0 | 1.7 | 2.1 | 17.5 |
| Temperature °F | | | | | | | | | | | | | | |
| -Maximum | | | | | | | | | | | | | | |
| 90° and above | 34 | 0.0 | 0.0 | 0.0 | 0.0 | 0.8 | 3.5 | 5.1 | 3.2 | 1.2 | 0.* | 0.0 | 0.0 | 13.8 |
| 32° and below | 34 | 17.8 | 13.2 | 4.6 | 0.2 | 0.0 | 0.0 | 0.0 | 0.0 | 0.0 | 0.0 | 2.1 | 12.1 | 50.0 |
| -Minimum | | | | | | | | | | | | | | |
| 32° and below | 34 | 29.3 | 26.0 | 23.2 | 10.9 | 1.6 | 0.* | 0.0 | 0.0 | 0.4 | 6.9 | 17.6 | 26.7 | 142.6 |
| 0° and below | 34 | 4.6 | 3.0 | 0.2 | 0.0 | 0.0 | 0.0 | 0.0 | 0.0 | 0.0 | 0.0 | 0.0 | 1.9 | 9.7 |
| **AVG. STATION PRESS. (mb)** | 17 | 992.5 | 993.2 | 990.9 | 989.9 | 989.8 | 990.2 | 991.4 | 992.4 | 993.0 | 993.6 | 992.3 | 992.8 | 991.8 |
| **RELATIVE HUMIDITY (%)** | | | | | | | | | | | | | | |
| Hour 01 | 34 | 75 | 75 | 75 | 76 | 78 | 82 | 84 | 88 | 87 | 82 | 81 | 82 | 80 |
| Hour 07 | 34 | 79 | 80 | 81 | 80 | 80 | 82 | 86 | 91 | 91 | 86 | 83 | 83 | 84 |
| Hour 13 (Local Time) | 34 | 69 | 66 | 61 | 55 | 52 | 54 | 55 | 59 | 58 | 57 | 66 | 73 | 60 |
| Hour 19 | 34 | 74 | 71 | 66 | 59 | 56 | 58 | 61 | 67 | 72 | 70 | 74 | 78 | 67 |
| **PRECIPITATION (inches):** | | | | | | | | | | | | | | |
| Water Equivalent | | | | | | | | | | | | | | |
| -Normal | | 1.99 | 1.80 | 2.64 | 3.04 | 2.90 | 3.49 | 3.26 | 3.19 | 2.53 | 1.94 | 2.41 | 2.59 | 31.78 |
| -Maximum Monthly | 34 | 4.61 | 4.43 | 5.70 | 6.10 | 5.13 | 8.48 | 6.75 | 8.47 | 8.10 | 4.78 | 6.86 | 6.81 | 8.48 |
| -Year | | 1965 | 1976 | 1985 | 1977 | 1968 | 1981 | 1969 | 1965 | 1972 | 1986 | 1982 | 1967 | JUN 1981 |
| -Minimum Monthly | 34 | 0.27 | 0.27 | 0.58 | 0.88 | 0.96 | 0.27 | 0.68 | 0.40 | 0.58 | 0.28 | 0.55 | 0.54 | 0.27 |
| -Year | | 1961 | 1969 | 1958 | 1962 | 1964 | 1988 | 1974 | 1976 | 1963 | 1964 | 1976 | 1958 | JUN 1988 |
| -Maximum in 24 hrs | 34 | 1.78 | 1.61 | 2.60 | 3.43 | 1.96 | 3.21 | 4.39 | 2.42 | 3.97 | 3.21 | 3.17 | 3.53 | 4.39 |
| -Year | | 1959 | 1981 | 1985 | 1977 | 1970 | 1978 | 1969 | 1972 | 1972 | 1988 | 1982 | 1967 | JUL 1969 |
| Snow, Ice pellets | | | | | | | | | | | | | | |
| -Maximum Monthly | 34 | 30.8 | 14.4 | 15.0 | 12.0 | 1.3 | 0.0 | 0.0 | 0.0 | T | 2.0 | 17.9 | 24.2 | 30.8 |
| -Year | | 1978 | 1967 | 1977 | 1957 | 1989 | | | | 1967 | 1989 | 1966 | 1977 | JAN 1978 |
| -Maximum in 24 hrs | 34 | 10.4 | 7.7 | 7.8 | 9.8 | 1.3 | 0.0 | 0.0 | 0.0 | T | 1.8 | 8.3 | 13.9 | 13.9 |
| -Year | | 1978 | 1981 | 1977 | 1957 | 1989 | | | | 1967 | 1989 | 1966 | 1974 | DEC 1974 |
| **WIND:** | | | | | | | | | | | | | | |
| Mean Speed (mph) | 34 | 10.9 | 10.6 | 11.1 | 10.9 | 9.5 | 8.4 | 7.3 | 7.1 | 7.6 | 8.7 | 10.2 | 10.4 | 9.4 |
| Prevailing Direction | | | | | | | | | | | | | | |
| through 1963 | | WSW | WSW | WSW | E | WSW | SW | WSW | SW | SSW | WSW | WSW | SW | WSW |
| Fastest Mile | | | | | | | | | | | | | | |
| -Direction (!!!) | 34 | W | SW | W | SW | W | W | NW | W | NW | SW | SW | SW | SW |
| -Speed (MPH) | 34 | 47 | 56 | 56 | 72 | 45 | 50 | 54 | 47 | 47 | 40 | 65 | 45 | 72 |
| -Year | | 1972 | 1967 | 1957 | 1956 | 1957 | 1969 | 1970 | 1965 | 1969 | 1956 | 1957 | 1971 | APR 1956 |
| Peak Gust | | | | | | | | | | | | | | |
| -Direction (!!!) | 6 | W | NE | W | W | W | NW | W | SE | NW | W | NW | SW | SE |
| -Speed (mph) | 6 | 45 | 49 | 54 | 58 | 58 | 45 | 51 | 75 | 54 | 46 | 51 | 56 | 75 |
| -Date | | 1988 | 1986 | 1985 | 1984 | 1989 | 1986 | 1987 | 1988 | 1986 | 1988 | 1989 | 1987 | AUG 1988 |

**See Reference Notes to this table on the following page.**

## TABLE 2 — PRECIPITATION (inches)     TOLEDO, OHIO

| YEAR | JAN | FEB | MAR | APR | MAY | JUNE | JULY | AUG | SEP | OCT | NOV | DEC | ANNUAL |
|---|---|---|---|---|---|---|---|---|---|---|---|---|---|
| 1961 | 0.2? | 2.64 | 3.09 | 4.94 | 2.15 | 2.70 | 2.78 | 2.02 | 2.86 | 0.86 | 2.04 | 1.29 | 27.64 |
| 1962 | 2.46 | 2.17 | 1.74 | 0.88 | 2.83 | 2.22 | 4.28 | 1.38 | 3.39 | 2.08 | 1.70 | 1.23 | 26.36 |
| 1963 | 0.93 | 3.81 | 3.14 | 2.17 | 2.63 | 4.31 | 1.98 | 2.22 | 0.58 | 0.67 | 0.77 | 2.20 | 22.05 |
| 1964 | 1.8? | 0.95 | 4.88 | 3.49 | 0.96 | 1.89 | 1.58 | 3.80 | 1.61 | 0.28 | 0.77 | 2.20 | 24.28 |
| 1965 | 4.6? | 1.96 | 1.77 | 2.07 | 3.80 | 2.57 | 2.03 | 8.47 | 4.93 | 3.28 | 1.75 | 3.61 | 40.85 |
| 1966 | 0.46 | 1.46 | 1.82 | 2.81 | 1.88 | 3.42 | 3.73 | 4.60 | 1.17 | 0.97 | 4.63 | 5.12 | 32.07 |
| 1967 | 1.29 | 2.12 | 1.72 | 2.77 | 2.28 | 1.92 | 3.95 | 0.81 | 2.14 | 2.85 | 6.81 | | 31.73 |
| 1968 | 1.91 | 1.29 | 2.26 | 3.01 | 5.13 | 3.40 | 4.50 | 1.45 | 1.52 | 1.11 | 3.52 | 3.97 | 33.07 |
| 1969 | 3.7C | 0.27 | 1.54 | 3.64 | 3.74 | 4.82 | 6.75 | 1.15 | 2.70 | 1.58 | 3.81 | 2.10 | 35.80 |
| 1970 | 1.09 | 0.89 | 2.61 | 4.26 | 4.05 | 4.59 | 5.99 | 3.00 | 5.78 | 2.00 | 2.09 | 1.49 | 37.84 |
| 1971 | 0.82 | 2.59 | 1.34 | 1.08 | 2.33 | 2.64 | 2.77 | 1.10 | 1.84 | 1.77 | 1.17 | 3.73 | 23.18 |
| 1972 | 1.4? | 0.77 | 2.33 | 3.74 | 2.63 | 4.09 | 2.77 | 4.47 | 8.10 | 1.46 | 3.55 | 3.08 | 38.41 |
| 1973 | 1.63 | 1.05 | 4.20 | 1.79 | 2.85 | 6.51 | 3.17 | 1.18 | 1.09 | 2.76 | 3.27 | 3.17 | 32.67 |
| 1974 | 2.2? | 2.00 | 2.93 | 2.55 | 4.18 | 3.31 | 0.68 | 1.61 | 1.41 | 0.70 | 3.57 | 3.41 | 28.62 |
| 1975 | 2.5? | 2.57 | 1.90 | 2.34 | 3.83 | 4.21 | 4.99 | 5.52 | 2.70 | 2.42 | 2.17 | 3.35 | 38.57 |
| 1976 | 2.8C | 4.43 | 3.56 | 2.79 | 1.72 | 3.70 | 2.08 | 0.40 | 3.68 | 2.14 | 0.55 | 0.93 | 28.78 |
| 1977 | 1.29 | 1.99 | 4.43 | 6.10 | 1.53 | 3.48 | 1.83 | 5.79 | 3.19 | 1.77 | 2.72 | 3.56 | 38.76 |
| 1978 | 3.14 | 0.54 | 2.34 | 3.74 | 2.48 | 5.34 | 1.86 | 1.67 | 2.90 | 1.65 | 2.48 | 3.31 | 31.74 |
| 1979 | 1.24 | 0.70 | 2.55 | 4.03 | 3.15 | 4.23 | 3.96 | 4.71 | 1.63 | 2.02 | 4.25 | 2.46 | 36.20 |
| 1980 | 0.7? | 0.96 | 3.65 | 3.13 | 2.93 | 3.26 | 4.49 | 5.89 | 1.63 | 1.79 | 0.97 | 2.48 | 31.92 |
| 1981 | 0.48 | 3.27 | 0.63 | 3.54 | 2.38 | 8.48 | 3.72 | 2.28 | 6.05 | 3.79 | 0.84 | 2.93 | 38.39 |
| 1982 | 3.6? | 1.15 | 3.74 | 1.53 | 2.61 | 2.01 | 1.97 | 1.38 | 2.03 | 1.14 | 6.86 | 3.48 | 31.51 |
| 1983 | 0.88 | 0.59 | 1.86 | 4.28 | 3.98 | 4.06 | 3.39 | 2.15 | 1.42 | 3.59 | 5.56 | 3.91 | 35.67 |
| 1984 | 0.99 | 1.18 | 2.95 | 5.15 | 3.48 | 1.49 | 2.30 | 3.87 | 2.02 | 1.75 | 2.74 | 3.22 | 31.14 |
| 1985 | 2.02 | 3.23 | 5.70 | 1.40 | 1.85 | 2.90 | 3.86 | 4.30 | 2.53 | 3.05 | 5.89 | 1.62 | 38.35 |
| 1986 | 0.99 | 2.46 | 2.16 | 2.81 | 2.72 | 5.32 | 3.37 | 5.93 | 4.75 | 4.78 | 1.66 | 1.87 | 38.82 |
| 1987 | 1.8? | 0.53 | 1.78 | 1.72 | 2.32 | 5.62 | 1.51 | 4.45 | 2.31 | 2.21 | 2.59 | 3.80 | 30.71 |
| 1988 | 1.17 | 1.33 | 1.69 | 1.45 | 1.37 | 0.27 | 3.76 | 5.11 | 1.80 | 4.37 | 4.27 | 1.96 | 28.55 |
| 1989 | 1.8C | 0.74 | 2.03 | 3.50 | 4.87 | 6.74 | 6.31 | 3.59 | 3.30 | 1.36 | 1.89 | 1.29 | 37.42 |
| 1990 | 2.18 | 5.39 | 3.46 | 2.09 | 4.63 | 3.14 | 1.89 | 3.32 | 1.72 | 2.63 | 2.27 | 5.69 | 38.41 |
| Record Mean | 2.12 | 1.91 | 2.59 | 2.84 | 3.15 | 3.50 | 3.00 | 2.95 | 2.66 | 2.31 | 2.44 | 2.42 | 31.91 |

## TABLE 3 — AVERAGE TEMPERATURE (deg. F)     TOLEDO, OHIO

| YEAR | JAN | FEB | MAR | APR | MAY | JUNE | JULY | AUG | SEP | OCT | NOV | DEC | ANNUAL |
|---|---|---|---|---|---|---|---|---|---|---|---|---|---|
| 1961 | 22.4 | 31.2 | 39.1 | 41.6 | 54.6 | 65.2 | 70.1 | 69.8 | 67.6 | 53.9 | 38.9 | 26.5 | 48.4 |
| 1962 | 21.8 | 24.8 | 35.0 | 48.3 | 65.6 | 69.6 | 69.6 | 70.6 | 61.2 | 54.2 | 38.3 | 22.7 | 48.5 |
| 1963 | 14.9 | 18.1 | 37.0 | 47.5 | 55.3 | 67.9 | 72.7 | 67.4 | 61.7 | 59.1 | 43.1 | 19.6 | 47.0 |
| 1964 | 28.5 | 25.9 | 35.0 | 48.6 | 62.6 | 68.8 | 73.8 | 67.8 | 62.5 | 47.5 | 42.3 | 27.8 | 49.2 |
| 1965 | 24.? | 25.8 | 29.8 | 46.8 | 63.5 | 66.9 | 68.5 | 67.2 | 63.7 | 49.1 | 39.5 | 34.1 | 48.3 |
| 1966 | 20.2 | 27.0 | 38.1 | 45.6 | 53.8 | 70.8 | 74.1 | 69.1 | 61.7 | 50.4 | 40.4 | 27.7 | 48.2 |
| 1967 | 29.? | 23.0 | 34.8 | 49.0 | 52.4 | 71.1 | 70.1 | 65.4 | 58.4 | 51.2 | 34.8 | 31.6 | 47.5 |
| 1968 | 22.? | 24.5 | 38.6 | 49.5 | 55.9 | 69.6 | 71.9 | 74.0 | 65.2 | 52.0 | 40.6 | 26.6 | 49.2 |
| 1969 | 21.6 | 27.4 | 33.2 | 49.3 | 58.4 | 64.6 | 71.4 | 69.6 | 64.4 | 50.5 | 37.7 | 25.7 | 47.9 |
| 1970 | 16.2 | 24.3 | 31.8 | 48.9 | 61.1 | 67.2 | 71.1 | 69.6 | 64.4 | 54.0 | 39.8 | 28.9 | 48.1 |
| 1971 | 20.3 | 27.9 | 32.9 | 46.1 | 56.4 | 71.3 | 69.0 | 69.0 | 66.8 | 59.0 | 37.6 | 33.6 | 49.1 |
| 1972 | 23.? | 24.4 | 34.1 | 46.1 | 60.4 | 63.9 | 71.4 | 68.4 | 62.2 | 47.2 | 37.7 | 30.3 | 47.5 |
| 1973 | 28.2 | 25.2 | 44.1 | 48.3 | 55.7 | 70.1 | 72.3 | 71.3 | 64.4 | 55.7 | 41.9 | 27.5 | 50.4 |
| 1974 | 26.? | 23.2 | 36.2 | 48.8 | 56.0 | 65.4 | 72.5 | 71.5 | 59.6 | 49.5 | 40.4 | 28.9 | 48.2 |
| 1975 | 29.2 | 28.3 | 33.3 | 42.7 | 62.5 | 69.0 | 70.8 | 72.0 | 60.5 | 51.9 | 45.3 | 28.9 | 47.3 |
| 1976 | 19.8 | 32.8 | 41.6 | 49.3 | 56.0 | 69.3 | 72.2 | 68.2 | 60.5 | 45.6 | 32.3 | 19.9 | 47.3 |
| 1977 | 9.6 | 24.3 | 41.6 | 53.3 | 63.6 | 65.0 | 74.6 | 69.3 | 65.0 | 49.3 | 41.0 | 24.7 | 48.4 |
| 1978 | 16.7 | 11.8 | 28.7 | 45.8 | 58.9 | 67.6 | 70.9 | 70.4 | 68.0 | 49.8 | 40.3 | 30.1 | 46.6 |
| 1979 | 17.6 | 15.1 | 38.7 | 45.5 | 57.9 | 67.7 | 70.1 | 68.8 | 63.0 | 51.3 | 40.6 | 32.1 | 47.4 |
| 1980 | 24.3 | 21.4 | 32.4 | 46.8 | 59.5 | 65.5 | 73.6 | 73.3 | 63.8 | 46.8 | 37.4 | 26.0 | 47.6 |
| 1981 | 17.6 | 28.5 | 36.5 | 49.9 | 55.4 | 68.4 | 71.7 | 69.8 | 61.3 | 47.7 | 39.6 | 27.4 | 47.8 |
| 1982 | 15.3 | 20.2 | 33.4 | 42.7 | 64.4 | 64.3 | 72.6 | 67.5 | 61.9 | 52.7 | 41.8 | 36.6 | 47.8 |
| 1983 | 27.6 | 30.5 | 37.9 | 44.2 | 54.8 | 67.9 | 74.7 | 73.8 | 64.2 | 51.9 | 41.3 | 20.0 | 49.1 |
| 1984 | 16.6 | 33.0 | 27.6 | 46.8 | 54.4 | 71.2 | 69.8 | 71.2 | 60.8 | 55.2 | 38.7 | 34.0 | 48.3 |
| 1985 | 19.5 | 22.6 | 39.3 | 53.5 | 61.6 | 64.8 | 73.2 | 69.1 | 64.0 | 53.3 | 43.9 | 22.3 | 48.9 |
| 1986 | 25.6 | 25.0 | 39.2 | 50.0 | 60.3 | 66.8 | 73.8 | 67.0 | 65.3 | 53.2 | 37.2 | 31.6 | 49.6 |
| 1987 | 25.8 | 30.0 | 39.7 | 50.3 | 62.5 | 70.8 | 74.9 | 71.0 | 63.8 | 45.4 | 44.4 | 33.0 | 51.0 |
| 1988 | 23.8 | 23.3 | 37.5 | 48.1 | 61.0 | 69.3 | 75.9 | 73.9 | 62.5 | 45.2 | 41.8 | 28.0 | 49.2 |
| 1989 | 33.? | 24.5 | 36.7 | 45.5 | 57.2 | 68.2 | 73.2 | 69.8 | 61.8 | 52.2 | 38.5 | 16.8 | 48.1 |
| 1990 | 34.3 | 32.4 | 41.1 | 49.4 | 56.6 | 69.1 | 71.8 | 70.0 | 63.7 | 51.8 | 44.3 | 33.1 | 51.5 |
| Record Mean | 25.4 | 26.8 | 35.9 | 47.5 | 59.0 | 68.7 | 73.2 | 71.0 | 64.3 | 52.7 | 40.5 | 29.4 | 49.6 |
| Max | 32.6 | 34.3 | 44.3 | 57.1 | 69.0 | 78.7 | 83.2 | 80.9 | 74.2 | 62.2 | 48.0 | 36.1 | 58.4 |
| Min | 18.3 | 19.2 | 27.5 | 38.0 | 48.9 | 58.7 | 63.1 | 61.1 | 54.3 | 43.2 | 32.9 | 22.7 | 40.7 |

## REFERENCE NOTES FOR TABLES 1, 2, 3 and 6     (TOLEDO, OH)

### GENERAL

T - TRACE AMOUNT
BLANK ENTRIES DENOTE MISSING/UNREPORTED DATA.
# INDICATES A STATION OR INSTRUMENT RELOCATION.

### SPECIFIC

#### TABLE 1

(a) - LENGTH OF RECORD IN YEARS. ALTHOUGH INDIVIDUAL MONTHS MAY BE MISSING.

* LESS THAN .05

NORMALS — BASED ON THE 1951-1980 RECORD PERIOD.
EXTREMES — DATES ARE THE MOST RECENT OCCURRENCE.
WIND DIR. — NUMERALS SHOW TENS OF DEGREES
CLOCKWISE FROM TRUE NORTH.
"00" INDICATES CALM.
RESULTANT WIND DIRECTIONS ARE GIVEN TO WHOLE DEGREES.

#### TABLE 3

MAX AND MIN ARE LONG-TERM MEAN DAILY MAXIMUM AND MEAN DAILY MINIMUM TEMPERATURES.

### EXCEPTIONS

#### TABLES 2, 3, and 6

RECORD MEANS ARE THROUGH THE CURRENT YEAR, BEGINNING IN

| | |
|---|---|
| 1874 | FOR TEMPERATURE |
| 1871 | FOR PRECIPITATION |
| 1956 | FOR SNOWFALL |

## TABLE 4

HEATING DEGREE DAYS Base 65 deg. F — TOLEDO, OHIO

| SEASON | JULY | AUG | SEP | OCT | NOV | DEC | JAN | FEB | MAR | APR | MAY | JUNE | TOTAL |
|---|---|---|---|---|---|---|---|---|---|---|---|---|---|
| 1961-62 | 27 | 12 | 87 | 344 | 775 | 1188 | 1333 | 1120 | 924 | 510 | 125 | 17 | 6462 |
| 1962-63 | 1 | 2 | 169 | 348 | 795 | 1305 | 1549 | 1310 | 859 | 520 | 317 | 55 | 7230 |
| 1963-64 | 9 | 33 | 120 | 199 | 646 | 1399 | 1121 | 1128 | 920 | 493 | 146 | 58 | 6272 |
| 1964-65 | 1 | 55 | 150 | 536 | 676 | 1149 | 1242 | 1088 | 1084 | 538 | 123 | 51 | 6693 |
| 1965-66 | 27 | 57 | 129 | 486 | 759 | 953 | 1381 | 1058 | 828 | 579 | 348 | 30 | 6635 |
| 1966-67 | 1 | 15 | 147 | 451 | 729 | 1150 | 1105 | 1170 | 929 | 479 | 390 | 16 | 6582 |
| 1967-68 | 27 | 57 | 206 | 437 | 900 | 1031 | 1324 | 1168 | 814 | 458 | 284 | 27 | 6733 |
| 1968-69 | 8 | 17 | 71 | 424 | 726 | 1184 | 1340 | 1047 | 976 | 470 | 239 | 107 | 6609 |
| 1969-70 | 3 | 7 | 126 | 446 | 818 | 1213 | 1507 | 1130 | 1022 | 495 | 176 | 70 | 7013 |
| 1970-71 | 14 | 11 | 118 | 345 | 749 | 1111 | 1379 | 1035 | 987 | 561 | 272 | 22 | 6604 |
| 1971-72 | 18 | 12 | 78 | 197 | 813 | 966 | 1283 | 1169 | 952 | 560 | 158 | 95 | 6301 |
| 1972-73 | 28 | 36 | 134 | 543 | 810 | 1073 | 1135 | 1106 | 639 | 499 | 285 | 3 | 6291 |
| 1973-74 | 3 | 16 | 114 | 289 | 686 | 1157 | 1197 | 1166 | 885 | 483 | 295 | 71 | 6362 |
| 1974-75 | 2 | 0 | 190 | 478 | 730 | 1108 | 1104 | 1021 | 974 | 664 | 148 | 45 | 6464 |
| 1975-76 | 7 | 6 | 227 | 406 | 585 | 1110 | 927 | 717 | 497 | 277 | 16 | | 6168 |
| 1976-77 | 1 | 33 | 162 | 596 | 976 | 1393 | 1708 | 1135 | 718 | 381 | 135 | 91 | 7329 |
| 1977-78 | 3 | 29 | 71 | 481 | 713 | 1241 | 1490 | 1484 | 1121 | 573 | 243 | 43 | 7492 |
| 1978-79 | 11 | 11 | 74 | 466 | 732 | 1076 | 1461 | 1390 | 808 | 577 | 259 | 42 | 6907 |
| 1979-80 | 16 | 33 | 121 | 440 | 724 | 1009 | 1258 | 1256 | 1005 | 542 | 199 | 83 | 6686 |
| 1980-81 | 0 | 3 | 113 | 560 | 822 | 1206 | 1464 | 1015 | 879 | 450 | 309 | 24 | 6845 |
| 1981-82 | 7 | 15 | 169 | 529 | 754 | 1160 | 1522 | 1250 | 972 | 665 | 81 | 76 | 7200 |
| 1982-83 | 3 | 47 | 148 | 386 | 690 | 871 | 1154 | 958 | 833 | 624 | 311 | 55 | 6080 |
| 1983-84 | 8 | 0 | 127 | 407 | 705 | 1389 | 1494 | 920 | 1151 | 545 | 341 | 9 | 7096 |
| 1984-85 | 11 | 15 | 173 | 297 | 782 | 951 | 1404 | 1182 | 791 | 368 | 158 | 58 | 6190 |
| 1985-86 | 0 | 16 | 138 | 356 | 626 | 1316 | 1216 | 1113 | 793 | 449 | 185 | 54 | 6262 |
| 1986-87 | 2 | 54 | 87 | 365 | 828 | 1027 | 1209 | 972 | 778 | 439 | 173 | 20 | 5954 |
| 1987-88 | 5 | 34 | 89 | 601 | 611 | 986 | 1269 | 1202 | 845 | 498 | 159 | 53 | 6352 |
| 1988-89 | 4 | 5 | 104 | 613 | 691 | 1141 | 979 | 1127 | 869 | 578 | 270 | 29 | 6410 |
| 1989-90 | 0 | 14 | 159 | 396 | 789 | 1488 | 947 | 907 | 742 | 492 | 262 | 31 | 6227 |
| 1990-91 | 4 | 3 | 125 | 415 | 612 | 981 | | | | | | | |

## TABLE 5

COOLING DEGREE DAYS Base 65 deg. F — TOLEDO, OHIO

| YEAR | JAN | FEB | MAR | APR | MAY | JUNE | JULY | AUG | SEP | OCT | NOV | DEC | TOTAL |
|---|---|---|---|---|---|---|---|---|---|---|---|---|---|
| 1969 | 0 | 0 | 0 | 7 | 43 | 101 | 220 | 215 | 69 | 1 | 0 | 0 | 656 |
| 1970 | 0 | 0 | 0 | 19 | 62 | 142 | 210 | 159 | 107 | 10 | 0 | 0 | 709 |
| 1971 | 0 | 0 | 0 | 1 | 13 | 219 | 148 | 143 | 138 | 18 | 0 | 0 | 680 |
| 1972 | 0 | 0 | 0 | 0 | 22 | 67 | 236 | 148 | 55 | 0 | 0 | 0 | 528 |
| 1973 | 0 | 0 | 0 | 5 | 3 | 163 | 237 | 222 | 103 | 9 | 0 | 0 | 742 |
| 1974 | 0 | 0 | 0 | 4 | 25 | 91 | 243 | 206 | 34 | 5 | 0 | 0 | 608 |
| 1975 | 0 | 0 | 0 | 0 | 79 | 172 | 197 | 230 | 7 | 7 | 0 | 0 | 692 |
| 1976 | 0 | 0 | 0 | 31 | 10 | 155 | 230 | 137 | 34 | 2 | 0 | 0 | 599 |
| 1977 | 0 | 0 | 0 | 37 | 95 | 99 | 309 | 167 | 77 | 0 | 0 | 0 | 784 |
| 1978 | 0 | 0 | 0 | 0 | 58 | 128 | 200 | 184 | 170 | 1 | 0 | 0 | 741 |
| 1979 | 0 | 0 | 0 | 0 | 46 | 127 | 182 | 158 | 67 | 22 | 0 | 0 | 602 |
| 1980 | 0 | 0 | 0 | 3 | 35 | 106 | 275 | 265 | 84 | 4 | 0 | 0 | 772 |
| 1981 | 0 | 0 | 1 | 2 | 17 | 132 | 220 | 170 | 64 | 0 | 0 | 0 | 606 |
| 1982 | 0 | 0 | 0 | 0 | 68 | 61 | 245 | 132 | 62 | 11 | 0 | 0 | 579 |
| 1983 | 0 | 0 | 0 | 4 | 2 | 148 | 311 | 279 | 109 | 11 | 0 | 0 | 864 |
| 1984 | 0 | 0 | 0 | 5 | 17 | 203 | 168 | 214 | 51 | 1 | 0 | 0 | 659 |
| 1985 | 0 | 0 | 0 | 29 | 60 | 58 | 263 | 147 | 116 | 0 | 0 | 0 | 673 |
| 1986 | 0 | 0 | 1 | 4 | 48 | 113 | 282 | 125 | 103 | 4 | 0 | 0 | 680 |
| 1987 | 0 | 0 | 0 | 5 | 105 | 202 | 318 | 225 | 59 | 0 | 4 | 0 | 918 |
| 1988 | 0 | 0 | 0 | 0 | 43 | 190 | 350 | 286 | 39 | 5 | 0 | 0 | 913 |
| 1989 | 0 | 0 | 2 | 0 | 34 | 132 | 259 | 168 | 69 | 5 | 0 | 0 | 669 |
| 1990 | 0 | 0 | 7 | 32 | 11 | 164 | 222 | 164 | 91 | 14 | 0 | 0 | 705 |

## TABLE 6

SNOWFALL (inches) — TOLEDO, OHIO

| SEASON | JULY | AUG | SEP | OCT | NOV | DEC | JAN | FEB | MAR | APR | MAY | JUNE | TOTAL |
|---|---|---|---|---|---|---|---|---|---|---|---|---|---|
| 1961-62 | 0.0 | 0.0 | 0.0 | 0.0 | 0.9 | 8.9 | 6.9 | 14.2 | 9.6 | T | 0.0 | 0.0 | 40.5 |
| 1962-63 | 0.0 | 0.0 | 0.0 | 0.2 | T | 13.2 | 12.4 | 9.4 | 5.6 | 0.3 | 0.0 | 0.0 | 41.1 |
| 1963-64 | 0.0 | 0.0 | 0.0 | 0.0 | T | 8.1 | 8.6 | 12.4 | 11.6 | 0.1 | 0.0 | 0.0 | 40.8 |
| 1964-65 | 0.0 | 0.0 | 0.0 | 0.0 | 3.6 | 7.4 | 9.0 | 12.6 | 10.2 | 1.4 | 0.0 | 0.0 | 44.2 |
| 1965-66 | 0.0 | 0.0 | 0.0 | 0.0 | 0.1 | 0.9 | 5.3 | 4.5 | 7.9 | 1.1 | T | 0.0 | 19.8 |
| 1966-67 | 0.0 | 0.0 | 0.0 | 0.0 | 17.9 | 13.6 | 4.1 | 14.4 | 9.8 | 0.8 | 0.0 | 0.0 | 60.6 |
| 1967-68 | 0.0 | 0.0 | T | T | 1.9 | 5.1 | 10.4 | 5.6 | 11.2 | 0.2 | 0.0 | 0.0 | 34.4 |
| 1968-69 | 0.0 | 0.0 | 0.0 | 0.0 | 1.8 | 8.2 | 9.2 | 2.5 | 4.9 | 1.5 | 0.0 | 0.0 | 28.1 |
| 1969-70 | 0.0 | 0.0 | 0.0 | T | 5.7 | 19.0 | 14.2 | 7.7 | 8.3 | 4.5 | 0.0 | 0.0 | 59.4 |
| 1970-71 | 0.0 | 0.0 | 0.0 | 0.0 | 3.6 | 8.1 | 8.5 | 8.0 | 5.2 | T | 0.0 | 0.0 | 33.4 |
| 1971-72 | 0.0 | 0.0 | 0.0 | 0.0 | 5.7 | 1.4 | 10.1 | 7.6 | 3.3 | 1.8 | 0.0 | 0.0 | 29.9 |
| 1972-73 | 0.0 | 0.0 | 0.0 | 0.2 | 5.0 | 7.7 | 3.0 | 11.6 | 4.0 | T | 0.0 | 0.0 | 31.5 |
| 1973-74 | 0.0 | 0.0 | 0.0 | 0.0 | 0.2 | 13.8 | 7.5 | 11.6 | 2.9 | 1.1 | T | 0.0 | 37.1 |
| 1974-75 | 0.0 | 0.0 | 0.0 | T | 2.8 | 23.9 | 5.4 | 5.5 | 5.3 | 1.8 | 0.0 | 0.0 | 44.7 |
| 1975-76 | 0.0 | 0.0 | 0.0 | 0.0 | 5.7 | 12.2 | 14.5 | 8.4 | 4.0 | 1.3 | 0.0 | 0.0 | 46.1 |
| 1976-77 | 0.0 | 0.0 | 0.0 | T | 1.3 | 11.1 | 17.2 | 8.7 | 15.0 | 0.6 | 0.0 | 0.0 | 53.9 |
| 1977-78 | 0.0 | 0.0 | 0.0 | 0.0 | 6.6 | 24.2 | 30.8 | 9.0 | 2.5 | T | 0.0 | 0.0 | 73.1 |
| 1978-79 | 0.0 | 0.0 | 0.0 | 0.0 | 2.8 | 2.3 | 7.6 | 5.1 | 1.2 | 4.0 | 0.0 | 0.0 | 23.0 |
| 1979-80 | 0.0 | 0.0 | 0.0 | T | 1.6 | 1.5 | 4.1 | 6.4 | 3.4 | 0.5 | T | 0.0 | 17.5 |
| 1980-81 | 0.0 | 0.0 | 0.0 | 0.9 | 3.5 | 11.6 | 6.9 | 11.2 | 3.6 | 0.0 | 0.0 | 0.0 | 37.7 |
| 1981-82 | 0.0 | 0.0 | 0.0 | T | 0.8 | 14.9 | 18.4 | 14.3 | 10.7 | 9.1 | 0.0 | 0.0 | 68.2 |
| 1982-83 | 0.0 | 0.0 | 0.0 | T | 2.2 | 1.2 | 0.7 | 4.1 | 3.6 | 0.7 | 0.0 | 0.0 | 12.5 |
| 1983-84 | 0.0 | 0.0 | 0.0 | 0.0 | 3.4 | 13.4 | 12.2 | 6.3 | 9.8 | T | T | 0.0 | 45.1 |
| 1984-85 | 0.0 | 0.0 | 0.0 | 0.0 | 2.4 | 5.1 | 14.0 | 12.4 | 2.6 | 2.0 | 0.0 | 0.0 | 38.5 |
| 1985-86 | 0.0 | 0.0 | 0.0 | 0.0 | 2.5 | 8.7 | 6.6 | 10.2 | 2.2 | 0.2 | 0.0 | 0.0 | 30.4 |
| 1986-87 | 0.0 | 0.0 | 0.0 | T | 4.5 | 1.3 | 20.5 | 0.5 | 10.0 | 2.4 | 0.0 | 0.0 | 39.2 |
| 1987-88 | 0.0 | 0.0 | 0.0 | T | 0.1 | 11.1 | 8.3 | 14.3 | 4.2 | T | 0.0 | 0.0 | 38.0 |
| 1988-89 | 0.0 | 0.0 | 0.0 | T | 2.3 | 6.6 | 2.4 | 4.8 | 2.6 | 0.7 | 1.3 | 0.0 | 20.7 |
| 1989-90 | 0.0 | 0.0 | 0.0 | 2.0 | 2.3 | 6.5 | 2.5 | 10.4 | 3.5 | 0.3 | 0.0 | 0.0 | 27.5 |
| 1990-91 | 0.0 | 0.0 | 0.0 | 0.0 | T | 8.2 | | | | | | | |
| Record Mean | 0.0 | 0.0 | T | 0.1 | 3.0 | 8.8 | 9.5 | 8.2 | 5.9 | 1.6 | T | 0.0 | 37.3 |

**See Reference Notes, relative to all above tables, on preceding page.**

Oklahoma City is located along the North Canadian River, a frequently nearly-dry stream, at the geographic center of the state. It is not quite 1,000 miles south of the Canadian Border and a little less than 500 miles north of the Gulf of Mexico. The surrounding country is gently rolling with the nearest hills or low mountains, the Arbuckles, 80 miles south. The elevation ranges around 1,250 feet above sea level.

Although some influence is exerted at times by warm, moist air currents from the Gulf of Mexico, the climate of Oklahoma City falls mainly under continental controls characteristic of the Great Plains Region. The continental effect produces pronounced daily and seasonal temperature changes and considerable variation in seasonal and annual precipitation. Summers are long and usually hot. Winters are comparatively mild and short.

During the year, temperatures of 100 degrees or more occur on an average of 10 days, but have occurred on as many as 50 days or more. While summers are usually hot, the discomforting effect of extreme heat is considerably mitigated by low humidity and the prevalence of a moderate southerly breeze. Approximately one winter in three has temperatures of zero or lower.

The length of the growing season varies from 180 to 251 days. Average date of last freeze is early April and average date of first freeze is early November. Freezes have occurred in early October.

During an average year, skies are clear approximately 40 percent of the time, partly cloudy 25 percent, and cloudy 35 percent of the time. The city is almost smoke-free as a result of favorable atmospheric conditions and the almost exclusive use of natural gas for heating. Flying conditions are generally very good with flight by visual flight rules possible about 96 percent of the time.

Summer rainfall comes mainly from showers and thunderstorms. Winter precipitation is generally associated with frontal passages. Measurable precipitation has occurred on as many as 122 days and as few as 55 days during the year. The seasonal distribution of precipitation is normally 12 percent in winter, 34 percent in spring, 30 percent in summer, and 24 percent in fall. The The period with the least number of days with precipitation is November through January, and the month with the most rainy days is May. Thunderstorms occur most often in late spring and early summer. Large hail and/or destructive winds on occasion accompany these thunderstorms.

Snowfall averages less than 10 inches per year and seldom remains on the ground very long. Occasional brief periods of freezing rain and sleet storms occur.

Heavy fogs are infrequent. Prevailing winds are southerly except in January and February when northerly breezes predominate.

## TABLE 1     NORMALS, MEANS AND EXTREMES

OKLAHOMA CITY, OKLAHOMA

LATITUDE: 35°24'N    LONGITUDE: 97°36'W    ELEVATION: FT. GRND 1285 BARO 1283    TIME ZONE: CENTRAL    WBAN: 13967

| | (a) | JAN | FEB | MAR | APR | MAY | JUNE | JULY | AUG | SEP | OCT | NOV | DEC | YEAR |
|---|---|---|---|---|---|---|---|---|---|---|---|---|---|---|
| **TEMPERATURE °F:** | | | | | | | | | | | | | | |
| Normals | | | | | | | | | | | | | | |
| -Daily Maximum | | 46.6 | 52.2 | 61.0 | 71.7 | 79.0 | 87.6 | 93.5 | 92.8 | 84.7 | 74.3 | 59.9 | 50.7 | 71.2 |
| -Daily Minimum | | 25.2 | 29.4 | 37.1 | 48.6 | 57.7 | 66.3 | 70.6 | 69.4 | 61.9 | 50.2 | 37.6 | 29.1 | 48.6 |
| -Monthly | | 35.9 | 40.8 | 49.1 | 60.2 | 68.4 | 77.0 | 82.1 | 81.1 | 73.3 | 62.3 | 48.8 | 39.9 | 59.9 |
| Extremes | | | | | | | | | | | | | | |
| -Record Highest | 36 | 80 | 84 | 93 | 100 | 104 | 105 | 109 | 110 | 102 | 96 | 87 | 86 | 110 |
| -Year | | 1986 | 1981 | 1967 | 1972 | 1985 | 1980 | 1986 | 1980 | 1985 | 1972 | 1980 | 1955 | AUG 1980 |
| -Record Lowest | 36 | -4 | -3 | 3 | 20 | 37 | 47 | 53 | 51 | 36 | 22 | 11 | -8 | -8 |
| -Year | | 1988 | 1979 | 1960 | 1957 | 1981 | 1954 | 1971 | 1956 | 1989 | 1957 | 1959 | 1989 | DEC 1989 |
| **NORMAL DEGREE DAYS:** | | | | | | | | | | | | | | |
| Heating (base 65°F) | | 902 | 678 | 506 | 184 | 41 | 0 | 0 | 0 | 15 | 145 | 486 | 778 | 3735 |
| Cooling (base 65°F) | | 0 | 0 | 13 | 40 | 147 | 360 | 530 | 499 | 264 | 61 | 0 | 0 | 1914 |
| **% OF POSSIBLE SUNSHINE** | 35 | 61 | 60 | 65 | 68 | 68 | 75 | 80 | 80 | 73 | 70 | 62 | 59 | 68 |
| **MEAN SKY COVER (tenths)** | | | | | | | | | | | | | | |
| Sunrise - Sunset | 41 | 5.8 | 5.9 | 5.8 | 5.7 | 5.8 | 5.1 | 4.4 | 4.3 | 4.6 | 4.6 | 5.1 | 5.5 | 5.2 |
| **MEAN NUMBER OF DAYS:** | | | | | | | | | | | | | | |
| Sunrise to Sunset | | | | | | | | | | | | | | |
| -Clear | 41 | 10.6 | 8.9 | 9.8 | 9.5 | 8.7 | 10.7 | 14.5 | 14.6 | 13.5 | 14.3 | 12.1 | 11.8 | 139.0 |
| -Partly Cloudy | 41 | 6.3 | 6.9 | 8.0 | 7.9 | 10.1 | 10.6 | 9.5 | 9.8 | 7.9 | 6.8 | 6.7 | 5.9 | 96.4 |
| -Cloudy | 41 | 14.1 | 12.5 | 13.2 | 12.6 | 12.2 | 8.7 | 7.0 | 7.0 | 8.6 | 9.9 | 11.1 | 13.3 | 129.8 |
| Precipitation | | | | | | | | | | | | | | |
| .01 inches or more | 50 | 5.4 | 6.4 | 7.1 | 7.6 | 10.0 | 8.6 | 6.4 | 6.5 | 7.0 | 6.4 | 5.2 | 5.4 | 81.9 |
| Snow,Ice pellets | | | | | | | | | | | | | | |
| 1.0 inches or more | 50 | 1.0 | 1.0 | 0.4 | 0.0 | 0.0 | 0.0 | 0.0 | 0.0 | 0.0 | 0.0 | 0.2 | 0.6 | 3.1 |
| Thunderstorms | 50 | 0.5 | 1.4 | 3.0 | 5.3 | 9.0 | 8.6 | 6.1 | 6.2 | 4.8 | 3.1 | 1.3 | 0.6 | 50.1 |
| Heavy Fog Visibility 1/4 mile or less | 41 | 3.8 | 3.2 | 1.8 | 0.9 | 0.7 | 0.4 | 0.3 | 0.3 | 0.8 | 1.6 | 2.2 | 3.3 | 19.4 |
| Temperature °F | | | | | | | | | | | | | | |
| -Maximum | | | | | | | | | | | | | | |
| 90° and above | 24 | 0.0 | 0.0 | 0.2 | 0.4 | 1.8 | 11.3 | 22.3 | 22.7 | 8.7 | 0.8 | 0.0 | 0.0 | 68.3 |
| 32° and below | 24 | 5.6 | 2.8 | 0.2 | 0.0 | 0.0 | 0.0 | 0.0 | 0.0 | 0.0 | 0.0 | 0.1 | 2.5 | 11.1 |
| -Minimum | | | | | | | | | | | | | | |
| 32° and below | 24 | 23.1 | 17.1 | 7.9 | 1.0 | 0.0 | 0.0 | 0.0 | 0.0 | 0.0 | 0.5 | 8.4 | 20.3 | 78.4 |
| 0° and below | 24 | 0.4 | 0.2 | 0.0 | 0.0 | 0.0 | 0.0 | 0.0 | 0.0 | 0.0 | 0.0 | 0.0 | 0.3 | 0.9 |
| **AVG. STATION PRESS.(mb)** | 17 | 973.6 | 972.0 | 967.9 | 967.7 | 966.7 | 968.0 | 969.5 | 969.6 | 970.3 | 971.6 | 971.1 | 972.8 | 970.1 |
| **RELATIVE HUMIDITY (%)** | | | | | | | | | | | | | | |
| Hour 00 | 24 | 73 | 72 | 68 | 69 | 76 | 76 | 70 | 70 | 75 | 72 | 73 | 73 | 72 |
| Hour 06 | 24 | 78 | 78 | 75 | 76 | 83 | 83 | 80 | 80 | 83 | 79 | 79 | 77 | 79 |
| Hour 12 (Local Time) | 24 | 59 | 58 | 52 | 51 | 57 | 56 | 49 | 50 | 55 | 52 | 55 | 58 | 54 |
| Hour 18 | 24 | 59 | 55 | 48 | 48 | 54 | 53 | 46 | 46 | 53 | 55 | 59 | 61 | 53 |
| **PRECIPITATION (inches):** | | | | | | | | | | | | | | |
| Water Equivalent | | | | | | | | | | | | | | |
| -Normal | | 0.96 | 1.29 | 2.07 | 2.91 | 5.50 | 3.87 | 3.04 | 2.40 | 3.41 | 2.71 | 1.53 | 1.20 | 30.89 |
| -Maximum Monthly | 50 | 5.68 | 4.05 | 7.85 | 10.78 | 12.07 | 14.66 | 8.44 | 6.77 | 9.64 | 13.18 | 5.46 | 8.14 | 14.66 |
| -Year | | 1949 | 1987 | 1988 | 1947 | 1982 | 1989 | 1959 | 1966 | 1970 | 1983 | 1964 | 1984 | JUN 1989 |
| -Minimum Monthly | 50 | 0.00 | T | T | 0.17 | 0.33 | 0.63 | T | 0.25 | T | T | T | 0.03 | 0.00 |
| -Year | | 1985 | 1947 | 1940 | 1989 | 1942 | 1952 | 1983 | 1978 | 1948 | 1958 | 1949 | 1955 | JAN 1985 |
| -Maximum in 24 hrs | 50 | 3.10 | 2.21 | 3.44 | 3.80 | 5.63 | 4.56 | 5.75 | 3.56 | 7.68 | 8.95 | 2.21 | 2.55 | 8.95 |
| -Year | | 1982 | 1978 | 1944 | 1970 | 1970 | 1989 | 1981 | 1989 | 1970 | 1983 | 1986 | 1984 | OCT 1983 |
| Snow,Ice pellets | | | | | | | | | | | | | | |
| -Maximum Monthly | 50 | 17.3 | 12.0 | 13.9 | 0.7 | T | 0.0 | 0.0 | 0.0 | 0.0 | T | 7.5 | 8.3 | 17.3 |
| -Year | | 1949 | 1978 | 1968 | 1957 | 1989 | | | | | 1967 | 1972 | 1987 | JAN 1949 |
| -Maximum in 24 hrs | 50 | 8.9 | 6.5 | 8.4 | 0.7 | T | 0.0 | 0.0 | 0.0 | 0.0 | T | 5.5 | 8.3 | 8.9 |
| -Year | | 1988 | 1986 | 1948 | 1957 | 1989 | | | | | 1967 | 1972 | 1987 | JAN 1988 |
| **WIND:** | | | | | | | | | | | | | | |
| Mean Speed (mph) | 41 | 12.8 | 13.2 | 14.6 | 14.4 | 12.7 | 12.0 | 10.9 | 10.5 | 11.1 | 11.9 | 12.4 | 12.5 | 12.4 |
| Prevailing Direction through 1963 | | N | N | SSE | SSE | SSE | SSE | SSE | SSE | SSE | SSE | S | S | SSE |
| Fastest Obs. 1 Min. | | | | | | | | | | | | | | |
| -Direction (!!!) | 8 | 36 | 35 | 36 | 31 | 33 | 35 | 03 | 27 | 21 | 36 | 26 | 36 | 21 |
| -Speed (MPH) | 8 | 43 | 36 | 39 | 46 | 46 | 48 | 43 | 35 | 52 | 37 | 46 | 33 | 52 |
| -Year | | 1985 | 1988 | 1989 | 1985 | 1986 | 1989 | 1989 | 1988 | 1986 | 1985 | 1988 | 1989 | SEP 1986 |
| Peak Gust | | | | | | | | | | | | | | |
| -Direction (!!!) | 6 | SW | N | SW | NW | NW | N | NE | W | W | W | N | N | W |
| -Speed (mph) | 6 | 51 | 51 | 62 | 66 | 60 | 66 | 62 | 51 | 69 | 52 | 63 | 46 | 69 |
| -Date | | 1989 | 1988 | 1985 | 1985 | 1986 | 1989 | 1989 | 1988 | 1987 | 1984 | 1988 | 1989 | SEP 1987 |

**See Reference Notes to this table on the following page.**

PRECIPITATION (inches)     OKLAHOMA CITY, OKLAHOMA

**TABLE 2**

| YEAR | JAN | FEB | MAR | APR | MAY | JUNE | JULY | AUG | SEP | OCT | NOV | DEC | ANNUAL |
|---|---|---|---|---|---|---|---|---|---|---|---|---|---|
| 1961 | 0.15 | 1.98 | 3.35 | 0.73 | 1.92 | 3.86 | 4.82 | 2.91 | 7.37 | 2.86 | 3.81 | 1.04 | 34.80 |
| 1962 | 1.45 | 1.02 | 0.80 | 2.16 | 2.64 | 7.84 | 1.71 | 2.26 | 3.08 | 2.43 | 1.34 | 0.76 | 27.49 |
| 1963 | 0.21 | 0.22 | 3.21 | 2.77 | 1.91 | 2.35 | 6.19 | 1.61 | 1.91 | 2.05 | 2.45 | 0.89 | 25.77 |
| 1964 | 0.83 | 2.17 | 1.30 | 2.06 | 5.21 | 0.77 | 2.01 | 4.91 | 2.96 | 0.84 | 5.46 | 0.62 | 29.14 |
| 1965 | 0.98 | 0.85 | 0.86 | 3.24 | 2.14 | 3.65 | 1.57 | 3.37 | 3.94 | 1.00 | 0.06 | 2.51 | 24.17 |
| 1966 | 1.05 | 2.39 | 1.30 | 3.68 | 0.88 | 2.63 | 2.38 | 6.77 | 2.82 | 0.37 | 0.84 | 0.45 | 25.56 |
| 1967 | 0.77 | 0.20 | 2.49 | 5.71 | 4.25 | 2.27 | 1.21 | 1.40 | 3.15 | 2.92 | 0.40 | 1.04 | 25.81 |
| 1968 | 2.19 | 1.02 | 2.84 | 3.03 | 8.40 | 2.39 | 1.41 | 3.75 | 2.64 | 4.11 | 1.33 |  | 35.51 |
| 1969 | 0.20 | 1.93 | 3.01 | 1.66 | 3.99 | 4.92 | 1.42 | 2.38 | 6.51 | 1.58 | 0.06 | 1.44 | 29.10 |
| 1970 | 0.32 | 0.29 | 2.09 | 5.33 | 6.53 | 2.45 | 1.30 | 0.80 | 9.64 | 3.29 | 1.03 | 0.26 | 33.33 |
| 1971 | 0.75 | 1.95 | 0.07 | 0.62 | 2.68 | 5.15 | 4.13 | 2.13 | 4.25 | 2.62 | 0.29 | 2.79 | 27.43 |
| 1972 | 0.21 | 0.43 | 1.13 | 3.10 | 4.03 | 1.36 | 3.22 | 1.82 | 2.04 | 2.28 | 0.84 | 0.47 | 27.63 |
| 1973 | 3.39 | 0.31 | 6.76 | 2.32 | 3.61 | 6.31 | 3.38 | 1.36 | 8.00 | 3.05 | 2.81 | 0.47 | 41.77 |
| 1974 | 0.10 | 2.68 | 3.12 | 4.66 | 5.01 | 3.36 | 0.48 | 4.42 | 6.24 | 5.57 | 2.34 | 1.47 | 39.45 |
| 1975 | 1.99 | 1.90 | 1.72 | 1.92 | 8.76 | 4.82 | 7.71 | 0.60 | 1.92 | 0.84 | 1.77 | 1.30 | 35.25 |
| 1976 | T | 0.33 | 3.09 | 2.94 | 4.36 | 0.88 | 1.38 | 1.46 | 1.53 | 1.78 | 0.12 | 0.19 | 18.06 |
| 1977 | 0.32 | 1.40 | 1.30 | 2.88 | 7.97 | 2.00 | 4.10 | 3.08 | 1.20 | 2.41 | 1.59 | 0.34 | 28.59 |
| 1978 | 1.26 | 3.23 | 1.32 | 1.65 | 10.12 | 4.04 | 3.75 | 0.25 | 0.96 | 1.02 | 2.88 | 0.70 | 31.18 |
| 1979 | 1.55 | 0.63 | 2.73 | 2.78 | 7.29 | 9.94 | 5.62 | 3.78 | 0.72 | 1.58 | 1.93 | 2.57 | 41.12 |
| 1980 | 1.69 | 1.29 | 1.38 | 2.16 | 9.00 | 2.52 | 0.42 | 0.60 | 2.21 | 0.99 | 0.51 | 1.58 | 24.35 |
| 1981 | 0.19 | 1.15 | 2.87 | 2.97 | 2.73 | 7.49 | 6.45 | 3.61 | 1.48 | 7.70 | 2.11 | 0.20 | 38.95 |
| 1982 | 3.68 | 0.98 | 1.63 | 1.92 | 12.07 | 4.06 | 2.11 | 1.13 | 2.86 | 1.03 | 2.78 | 1.94 | 36.19 |
| 1983 | 2.62 | 1.71 | 2.51 | 2.34 | 6.88 | 3.18 | T | 3.18 | 0.90 | 13.18 | 1.90 | 0.70 | 39.10 |
| 1984 | 0.35 | 1.16 | 4.70 | 1.79 | 1.62 | 3.48 | 0.30 | 2.35 | 1.01 | 6.64 | 2.05 | 8.14 | 33.59 |
| 1985 | 0.92 | 3.71 | 6.60 | 5.35 | 1.49 | 8.34 | 1.33 | 2.63 | 4.59 | 5.23 | 3.73 | 0.26 | 44.18 |
| 1986 | 0.00 | 0.68 | 1.75 | 4.42 | 8.21 | 3.11 | 0.38 | 3.29 | 9.54 | 8.00 | 4.63 | 1.16 | 45.17 |
| 1987 | 2.45 | 4.05 | 2.33 | 0.41 | 11.86 | 6.50 | 2.99 | 1.83 | 4.58 | 1.82 | 1.92 | 3.75 | 44.49 |
| 1988 | 1.24 | 0.41 | 7.85 | 3.19 | 1.07 | 3.59 | 1.92 | 1.60 | 5.19 | 2.04 | 2.45 | 1.39 | 31.94 |
| 1989 | 1.17 | 2.20 | 2.72 | 0.17 | 4.33 | 14.66 | 1.91 | 5.55 | 4.51 | 3.26 | 0.09 | 0.32 | 40.89 |
| 1990 | 1.85 | 4.63 | 4.43 | 5.11 | 5.79 | 3.16 | 2.65 | 3.16 | 7.35 | 1.27 | 1.59 | 1.46 | 40.54 |
| Record Mean | 1.26 | 1.31 | 2.28 | 3.17 | 5.20 | 4.08 | 2.70 | 2.68 | 3.28 | 2.97 | 1.91 | 1.48 | 32.32 |

**TABLE 3**     AVERAGE TEMPERATURE (deg. F)     OKLAHOMA CITY, OKLAHOMA

| YEAR | JAN | FEB | MAR | APR | MAY | JUNE | JULY | AUG | SEP | OCT | NOV | DEC | ANNUAL |
|---|---|---|---|---|---|---|---|---|---|---|---|---|---|
| 1961 | 36.3 | 42.7 | 52.2 | 59.2 | 67.7 | 74.1 | 79.1 | 78.4 | 70.6 | 63.0 | 46.5 | 36.7 | 58.9 |
| 1962 | 32.3 | 45.1 | 48.1 | 58.3 | 74.3 | 75.3 | 82.2 | 82.5 | 71.4 | 64.7 | 49.4 | 40.6 | 60.4 |
| 1963 | 28.3 | 40.0 | 53.8 | 64.8 | 70.3 | 78.7 | 83.1 | 82.0 | 75.1 | 71.1 | 52.3 | 33.0 | 61.1 |
| 1964 | 40.1 | 38.5 | 47.1 | 64.1 | 70.0 | 77.4 | 85.3 | 80.8 | 72.3 | 60.3 | 49.9 | 37.9 | 60.3 |
| #1965 | 38.8 | 39.5 | 40.7 | 65.5 | 71.3 | 78.0 | 84.6 | 80.6 | 73.9 | 62.8 | 56.3 | 48.8 | 61.8 |
| 1966 | 33.8 | 38.6 | 52.8 | 57.8 | 68.7 | 77.9 | 86.4 | 78.8 | 70.5 | 60.9 | 54.3 | 37.8 | 59.9 |
| 1967 | 41.8 | 41.7 | 56.4 | 65.4 | 66.9 | 77.4 | 79.7 | 79.3 | 70.9 | 62.6 | 49.4 | 39.8 | 60.9 |
| 1968 | 36.6 | 36.4 | 50.7 | 58.1 | 64.7 | 74.8 | 79.8 | 80.0 | 70.5 | 62.6 | 46.2 | 38.1 | 58.1 |
| 1969 | 38.8 | 42.3 | 42.0 | 60.4 | 67.7 | 75.0 | 83.9 | 80.2 | 73.3 | 57.6 | 48.7 | 40.4 | 59.2 |
| 1970 | 31.8 | 42.7 | 45.0 | 60.2 | 69.2 | 76.3 | 82.1 | 83.6 | 75.1 | 57.9 | 46.0 | 43.9 | 59.5 |
| 1971 | 36.9 | 39.1 | 49.1 | 60.4 | 67.3 | 78.6 | 80.7 | 77.2 | 73.3 | 63.4 | 49.0 | 42.2 | 58.8 |
| 1972 | 34.9 | 42.1 | 53.4 | 63.2 | 67.6 | 79.0 | 79.8 | 80.4 | 75.8 | 61.1 | 43.4 | 34.4 | 59.6 |
| 1973 | 33.3 | 39.8 | 52.5 | 56.0 | 66.8 | 75.2 | 79.7 | 79.6 | 70.6 | 64.3 | 53.1 | 39.3 | 59.2 |
| 1974 | 35.0 | 44.4 | 54.8 | 60.0 | 71.5 | 74.1 | 82.7 | 78.5 | 65.5 | 63.5 | 49.3 | 39.6 | 59.9 |
| 1975 | 40.3 | 36.5 | 46.1 | 58.7 | 67.4 | 75.1 | 78.0 | 80.1 | 68.3 | 63.4 | 50.7 | 41.8 | 58.8 |
| 1976 | 39.0 | 52.2 | 52.4 | 61.6 | 63.6 | 74.8 | 79.8 | 81.3 | 72.6 | 56.5 | 43.9 | 38.8 | 59.7 |
| 1977 | 29.2 | 45.9 | 54.1 | 62.5 | 70.0 | 79.6 | 83.0 | 80.7 | 78.0 | 62.7 | 50.9 | 40.0 | 61.4 |
| 1978 | 26.3 | 29.4 | 49.1 | 64.5 | 68.1 | 77.3 | 87.0 | 82.6 | 79.7 | 64.7 | 50.4 | 36.9 | 59.7 |
| 1979 | 25.4 | 31.5 | 51.2 | 58.1 | 65.8 | 75.2 | 81.0 | 80.0 | 73.1 | 65.7 | 46.5 | 43.3 | 58.1 |
| 1980 | 38.2 | 38.2 | 46.3 | 56.7 | 69.0 | 81.4 | 88.0 | 88.0 | 76.3 | 61.1 | 50.3 | 41.9 | 61.3 |
| 1981 | 37.7 | 43.9 | 51.9 | 65.6 | 65.7 | 78.4 | 84.2 | 78.8 | 74.1 | 60.1 | 50.3 | 39.1 | 60.8 |
| 1982 | 35.3 | 37.7 | 52.7 | 57.5 | 68.2 | 72.2 | 81.0 | 84.1 | 74.5 | 62.7 | 48.6 | 43.2 | 59.8 |
| 1983 | 38.6 | 42.6 | 48.8 | 54.0 | 64.6 | 73.4 | 81.6 | 84.0 | 74.9 | 62.7 | 50.4 | 25.8 | 58.5 |
| 1984 | 34.0 | 45.4 | 46.4 | 56.5 | 68.4 | 78.6 | 81.6 | 82.6 | 71.5 | 61.6 | 49.7 | 43.0 | 59.9 |
| 1985 | 30.6 | 37.2 | 53.0 | 62.7 | 70.0 | 76.0 | 80.9 | 81.3 | 73.1 | 61.2 | 46.1 | 35.1 | 58.9 |
| 1986 | 43.6 | 44.8 | 55.5 | 62.8 | 69.0 | 79.0 | 85.9 | 80.0 | 74.8 | 61.6 | 44.8 | 40.8 | 61.9 |
| 1987 | 35.1 | 45.9 | 50.3 | 61.8 | 72.6 | 77.1 | 80.1 | 82.2 | 72.4 | 60.5 | 50.5 | 40.6 | 60.7 |
| 1988 | 34.2 | 40.3 | 49.5 | 58.9 | 70.3 | 78.4 | 81.6 | 82.8 | 73.5 | 59.3 | 51.2 | 43.9 | 60.3 |
| 1989 | 42.8 | 33.1 | 51.1 | 63.4 | 69.4 | 74.3 | 79.6 | 78.3 | 67.8 | 63.1 | 52.2 | 32.7 | 59.0 |
| 1990 | 45.9 | 46.0 | 52.6 | 59.2 | 68.6 | 82.0 | 80.7 | 81.6 | 77.0 | 60.9 | 54.9 | 37.1 | 62.2 |
| Record Mean | 37.0 | 40.8 | 50.0 | 60.3 | 68.2 | 77.0 | 81.6 | 81.2 | 73.8 | 62.5 | 49.4 | 39.7 | 60.1 |
| Max | 47.0 | 51.5 | 61.4 | 71.3 | 78.3 | 87.2 | 92.3 | 92.3 | 84.7 | 73.6 | 60.1 | 49.5 | 70.8 |
| Min | 26.9 | 30.0 | 38.5 | 49.2 | 58.0 | 66.8 | 70.8 | 70.1 | 62.8 | 51.3 | 38.7 | 29.8 | 49.4 |

## REFERENCE NOTES FOR TABLES 1, 2, 3 and 6     (OKLAHOMA CITY, OK)

### GENERAL

T - TRACE AMOUNT
BLANK ENTRIES DENOTE MISSING/UNREPORTED DATA.
# INDICATES A STATION OR INSTRUMENT RELOCATION.

### SPECIFIC

#### TABLE 1

(a) - LENGTH OF RECORD IN YEARS. ALTHOUGH
INDIVIDUAL MONTHS MAY BE MISSING.
* LESS THAN .05

NORMALS — BASED ON THE 1951-1980 RECORD PERIOD.
EXTREMES — DATES ARE THE MOST RECENT OCCURRENCE.
WIND DIR. — NUMERALS SHOW TENS OF DEGREES
CLOCKWISE FROM TRUE NORTH.
''00'' INDICATES CALM.
RESULTANT WIND DIRECTIONS ARE GIVEN TO WHOLE DEGREES.

#### TABLE 3
MAX AND MIN ARE LONG-TERM MEAN DAILY MAXIMUM
AND MEAN DAILY MINIMUM TEMPERATURES.

### EXCEPTIONS

#### TABLE 1

1. FASTEST MILE WIND IS THOROUGH OCTOBER 1981.

#### TABLES 2, 3, and 6

RECORD MEANS ARE THROUGH THE CURRENT YEAR,
BEGINNING IN     1891 FOR TEMPERATURE
1891 FOR PRECIPITATION
1940 FOR SNOWFALL

**TABLE 4**

HEATING DEGREE DAYS Base 65 deg. F    OKLAHOMA CITY, OKLAHOMA

| SEASON | JULY | AUG | SEP | OCT | NOV | DEC | JAN | FEB | MAR | APR | MAY | JUNE | TOTAL |
|---|---|---|---|---|---|---|---|---|---|---|---|---|---|
| 1961-62 | 0 | 0 | 40 | 106 | 547 | 868 | 1006 | 560 | 524 | 230 | 5 | 0 | 3886 |
| 1962-63 | 0 | 0 | 19 | 129 | 458 | 750 | 1131 | 692 | 372 | 101 | 50 | 0 | 3702 |
| 1963-64 | 0 | 0 | 7 | 23 | 381 | 988 | 761 | 762 | 547 | 116 | 27 | 6 | 3618 |
| 1964-65 | 0 | 0 | 24 | 150 | 454 | 831 | 808 | 706 | 745 | 71 | 2 | 0 | 3791 |
| #1965-66 | 0 | 0 | 28 | 129 | 262 | 496 | 961 | 734 | 388 | 223 | 62 | 0 | 3283 |
| 1966-67 | 0 | 0 | 6 | 166 | 338 | 837 | 713 | 647 | 307 | 71 | 77 | 0 | 3162 |
| 1967-68 | 0 | 0 | 27 | 155 | 464 | 773 | 872 | 826 | 444 | 215 | 71 | 0 | 3847 |
| 1968-69 | 0 | 0 | 0 | 152 | 561 | 829 | 808 | 629 | 708 | 158 | 38 | 2 | 3885 |
| 1969-70 | 0 | 0 | 0 | 274 | 481 | 752 | 1022 | 620 | 615 | 187 | 31 | 12 | 3994 |
| 1970-71 | 0 | 0 | 18 | 254 | 559 | 651 | 866 | 718 | 492 | 163 | 36 | 0 | 3757 |
| 1971-72 | 0 | 0 | 59 | 88 | 475 | 702 | 923 | 660 | 365 | 144 | 46 | 0 | 3462 |
| 1972-73 | 0 | 0 | 23 | 225 | 640 | 940 | 975 | 701 | 380 | 283 | 55 | 0 | 4222 |
| 1973-74 | 0 | 0 | 37 | 99 | 362 | 787 | 922 | 573 | 330 | 168 | 8 | 0 | 3286 |
| 1974-75 | 0 | 0 | 56 | 88 | 463 | 784 | 763 | 792 | 583 | 235 | 8 | 0 | 3793 |
| 1975-76 | 0 | 0 | 64 | 126 | 430 | 713 | 801 | 367 | 406 | 128 | 100 | 0 | 3135 |
| 1976-77 | 0 | 0 | 19 | 306 | 629 | 805 | 1103 | 529 | 338 | 107 | 7 | 0 | 3843 |
| 1977-78 | 0 | 0 | 0 | 115 | 420 | 766 | 1192 | 990 | 493 | 90 | 64 | 0 | 4130 |
| 1978-79 | 0 | 0 | 2 | 89 | 437 | 866 | 1221 | 932 | 434 | 217 | 81 | 0 | 4279 |
| 1979-80 | 0 | 0 | 2 | 92 | 551 | 669 | 823 | 771 | 572 | 249 | 24 | 0 | 3753 |
| 1980-81 | 0 | 0 | 23 | 180 | 444 | 710 | 839 | 587 | 400 | 69 | 69 | 0 | 3321 |
| 1981-82 | 0 | 0 | 22 | 189 | 434 | 797 | 913 | 759 | 382 | 248 | 25 | 13 | 3782 |
| 1982-83 | 0 | 0 | 14 | 156 | 490 | 671 | 809 | 622 | 496 | 345 | 96 | 9 | 3708 |
| 1983-84 | 0 | 0 | 25 | 117 | 439 | 1207 | 955 | 561 | 572 | 263 | 45 | 0 | 4184 |
| 1984-85 | 0 | 0 | 75 | 162 | 462 | 676 | 1059 | 773 | 377 | 108 | 10 | 0 | 3702 |
| 1985-86 | 0 | 0 | 63 | 146 | 562 | 921 | 656 | 562 | 308 | 122 | 17 | 0 | 3357 |
| 1986-87 | 0 | 0 | 2 | 137 | 599 | 742 | 918 | 528 | 450 | 177 | 3 | 0 | 3556 |
| 1987-88 | 0 | 0 | 1 | 165 | 442 | 748 | 948 | 712 | 473 | 204 | 14 | 0 | 3707 |
| 1988-89 | 0 | 0 | 8 | 196 | 408 | 644 | 679 | 887 | 441 | 140 | 38 | 0 | 3441 |
| 1989-90 | 0 | 0 | 78 | 135 | 386 | 993 | 583 | 525 | 387 | 202 | 52 | 0 | 3341 |
| 1990-91 | 0 | 0 | 9 | 169 | 307 | 860 | | | | | | | |

**TABLE 5**

COOLING DEGREE DAYS Base 65 deg. F    OKLAHOMA CITY, OKLAHOMA

| YEAR | JAN | FEB | MAR | APR | MAY | JUNE | JULY | AUG | SEP | OCT | NOV | DEC | TOTAL |
|---|---|---|---|---|---|---|---|---|---|---|---|---|---|
| 1969 | 0 | 0 | 0 | 29 | 128 | 310 | 593 | 477 | 255 | 52 | 0 | 0 | 1844 |
| 1970 | 0 | 0 | 1 | 47 | 169 | 357 | 536 | 582 | 328 | 38 | 0 | 0 | 2058 |
| 1971 | 0 | 0 | 4 | 31 | 117 | 416 | 493 | 388 | 313 | 45 | 3 | 0 | 1810 |
| 1972 | 0 | 2 | 11 | 97 | 133 | 429 | 470 | 483 | 351 | 109 | 0 | 0 | 2085 |
| 1973 | 0 | 0 | 0 | 19 | 119 | 312 | 465 | 462 | 216 | 83 | 11 | 0 | 1687 |
| 1974 | 0 | 0 | 22 | 26 | 217 | 280 | 553 | 426 | 80 | 47 | 0 | 0 | 1651 |
| 1975 | 0 | 0 | 1 | 53 | 108 | 310 | 410 | 476 | 170 | 83 | 4 | 0 | 1615 |
| 1976 | 0 | 1 | 23 | 33 | 62 | 300 | 468 | 512 | 253 | 50 | 0 | 0 | 1702 |
| 1977 | 0 | 1 | 8 | 37 | 170 | 445 | 565 | 491 | 395 | 49 | 2 | 0 | 2163 |
| 1978 | 0 | 0 | 8 | 80 | 165 | 378 | 690 | 553 | 450 | 87 | 7 | 0 | 2418 |
| 1979 | 0 | 0 | 10 | 18 | 112 | 314 | 505 | 471 | 252 | 121 | 2 | 0 | 1805 |
| 1980 | 0 | 0 | 0 | 7 | 155 | 498 | 729 | 721 | 366 | 65 | 11 | 2 | 2554 |
| 1981 | 0 | 4 | 0 | 94 | 98 | 409 | 603 | 435 | 304 | 47 | 0 | 0 | 1994 |
| 1982 | 0 | 0 | 9 | 28 | 130 | 234 | 503 | 598 | 305 | 90 | 3 | 1 | 1901 |
| 1983 | 0 | 0 | 0 | 20 | 91 | 266 | 523 | 599 | 329 | 54 | 8 | 0 | 1890 |
| 1984 | 0 | 0 | 0 | 16 | 159 | 414 | 521 | 551 | 279 | 64 | 5 | 0 | 2009 |
| 1985 | 0 | 0 | 12 | 43 | 172 | 336 | 501 | 512 | 313 | 38 | 0 | 0 | 1927 |
| 1986 | 0 | 2 | 21 | 63 | 147 | 425 | 653 | 473 | 301 | 40 | 0 | 0 | 2125 |
| 1987 | 0 | 0 | 0 | 88 | 242 | 371 | 475 | 543 | 230 | 18 | 12 | 0 | 1979 |
| 1988 | 0 | 0 | 1 | 29 | 186 | 410 | 525 | 558 | 270 | 25 | 1 | 0 | 2005 |
| 1989 | 0 | 0 | 16 | 100 | 179 | 285 | 459 | 419 | 170 | 83 | 8 | 0 | 1719 |
| 1990 | 0 | 0 | 12 | 33 | 169 | 517 | 495 | 522 | 378 | 48 | 13 | 0 | 2187 |

**TABLE 6**

SNOWFALL (inches)    OKLAHOMA CITY, OKLAHOMA

| SEASON | JULY | AUG | SEP | OCT | NOV | DEC | JAN | FEB | MAR | APR | MAY | JUNE | TOTAL |
|---|---|---|---|---|---|---|---|---|---|---|---|---|---|
| 1961-62 | 0.0 | 0.0 | 0.0 | 0.0 | 0.0 | 0.8 | 8.5 | 0.8 | 0.0 | 0.0 | 0.0 | 0.0 | 10.1 |
| 1962-63 | 0.0 | 0.0 | 0.0 | 0.0 | T | 1.2 | 0.5 | 1.6 | 0.0 | 0.0 | 0.0 | 0.0 | 3.3 |
| 1963-64 | 0.0 | 0.0 | 0.0 | 0.0 | 0.0 | 2.5 | T | 0.6 | 1.5 | 0.0 | 0.0 | 0.0 | 4.6 |
| 1964-65 | 0.0 | 0.0 | 0.0 | 0.0 | 0.0 | T | 2.0 | 0.9 | 0.1 | 0.0 | 0.0 | 0.0 | 3.0 |
| 1965-66 | 0.0 | 0.0 | 0.0 | 0.0 | 0.0 | T | 5.8 | 2.3 | 0.0 | 0.0 | 0.0 | 0.0 | 8.1 |
| 1966-67 | 0.0 | 0.0 | 0.0 | 0.0 | T | 0.6 | T | 0.1 | 0.4 | 0.0 | 0.0 | 0.0 | 1.1 |
| 1967-68 | 0.0 | 0.0 | 0.0 | T | 1.2 | 1.2 | 0.4 | 7.7 | 13.9 | 0.0 | 0.0 | 0.0 | 24.4 |
| 1968-69 | 0.0 | 0.0 | 0.0 | 0.0 | 1.4 | 1.3 | T | 1.3 | 8.2 | 0.0 | 0.0 | 0.0 | 12.2 |
| 1969-70 | 0.0 | 0.0 | 0.0 | 0.0 | 0.0 | 4.2 | 0.4 | T | 2.3 | T | 0.0 | 0.0 | 6.9 |
| 1970-71 | 0.0 | 0.0 | 0.0 | 0.0 | T | T | T | 5.1 | 0.7 | 0.0 | 0.0 | 0.0 | 5.8 |
| 1971-72 | 0.0 | 0.0 | 0.0 | 0.0 | 0.5 | 5.2 | 0.8 | 4.9 | 0.0 | 0.0 | 0.0 | 0.0 | 11.4 |
| 1972-73 | 0.0 | 0.0 | 0.0 | 0.0 | 7.5 | 1.4 | 8.3 | 0.2 | T | 0.0 | 0.0 | 0.0 | 17.4 |
| 1973-74 | 0.0 | 0.0 | 0.0 | 0.0 | 0.0 | 0.6 | 0.7 | 1.0 | 0.5 | 0.0 | 0.0 | 0.0 | 2.8 |
| 1974-75 | 0.0 | 0.0 | 0.0 | 0.0 | 1.0 | 2.0 | 0.6 | 0.9 | 0.1 | 0.0 | 0.0 | 0.0 | 4.6 |
| 1975-76 | 0.0 | 0.0 | 0.0 | 0.0 | 0.7 | 3.9 | T | 0.3 | 0.0 | 0.0 | 0.0 | 0.0 | 4.9 |
| 1976-77 | 0.0 | 0.0 | 0.0 | 0.0 | 0.3 | T | 2.8 | 0.4 | 0.0 | 0.0 | 0.0 | 0.0 | 3.5 |
| 1977-78 | 0.0 | 0.0 | 0.0 | 0.0 | T | 0.0 | 8.4 | 12.0 | 0.0 | 0.0 | 0.0 | 0.0 | 20.4 |
| 1978-79 | 0.0 | 0.0 | 0.0 | 0.0 | 0.0 | 3.3 | 4.0 | 6.1 | 0.0 | 0.0 | 0.0 | 0.0 | 13.4 |
| 1979-80 | 0.0 | 0.0 | 0.0 | 0.0 | T | T | T | 1.8 | T | 0.0 | 0.0 | 0.0 | 1.8 |
| 1980-81 | 0.0 | 0.0 | 0.0 | 0.0 | 4.0 | 0.0 | T | T | 0.0 | 0.0 | 0.0 | 0.0 | 4.0 |
| 1981-82 | 0.0 | 0.0 | 0.0 | 0.0 | 0.0 | T | 1.0 | 3.9 | 2.5 | 0.0 | 0.0 | 0.0 | 7.4 |
| 1982-83 | 0.0 | 0.0 | 0.0 | 0.0 | T | T | 5.1 | 4.3 | T | 0.0 | 0.0 | 0.0 | 9.4 |
| 1983-84 | 0.0 | 0.0 | 0.0 | 0.0 | T | 1.9 | 5.6 | 2.0 | 0.0 | 0.0 | 0.0 | 0.0 | 9.5 |
| 1984-85 | 0.0 | 0.0 | 0.0 | 0.0 | T | 6.1 | 1.5 | 2.3 | 0.0 | 0.0 | 0.0 | 0.0 | 9.9 |
| 1985-86 | 0.0 | 0.0 | 0.0 | 0.0 | T | 2.9 | 0.0 | 10.9 | 0.0 | 0.0 | 0.0 | 0.0 | 13.8 |
| 1986-87 | 0.0 | 0.0 | 0.0 | 0.0 | 0.0 | T | 10.0 | 1.0 | T | 0.0 | 0.0 | 0.0 | 11.0 |
| 1987-88 | 0.0 | 0.0 | 0.0 | 0.0 | 2.0 | 8.3 | 12.1 | 0.2 | 0.9 | 0.0 | 0.0 | 0.0 | 23.5 |
| 1988-89 | 0.0 | 0.0 | 0.0 | 0.0 | 0.6 | 2.0 | 4.8 | T | 4.0 | 0.6 | 0.0 | 0.0 | 12.0 |
| 1989-90 | 0.0 | 0.0 | 0.0 | 0.0 | T | 1.7 | T | 1.7 | 0.1 | 0.0 | T | 0.0 | 3.5 |
| 1990-91 | 0.0 | 0.0 | 0.0 | 0.0 | T | 4.2 | | | | | | | |
| Record Mean | 0.0 | 0.0 | 0.0 | T | 0.5 | 1.8 | 3.1 | 2.6 | 1.4 | T | T | 0.0 | 9.4 |

**See Reference Notes, relative to all above tables, on preceding page.**

The city of Tulsa lies along the Arkansas River at an elevation of 700 feet above sea level. The surrounding terrain is gently rolling.

At latitude 36 degrees, Tulsa is far enough north to escape the long periods of heat in summer, yet far enough south to miss the extreme cold of winter. The influence of warm moist air from the Gulf of Mexico is often noted, due to the high humidity, but the climate is essentially continental characterized by rapid changes in temperature. Generally the winter months are mild. Temperatures occasionally fall below zero but only last a very short time. Temperatures of 100 degrees or higher are often experienced from late July to early September, but are usually accompanied by low relative humidity and a good southerly breeze. The fall season is long with a great number of pleasant, sunny days and cool, bracing nights.

Rainfall is ample for most agricultural pursuits and is distributed favorably throughout the year. Spring is the wettest season, having an abundance of rain in the form of showers and thunderstorms.

The steady rains of fall are a contrast to the spring and summer showers and provide a good supply of moisture and more ideal conditions for the growth of winter grains and pastures. The greatest amounts of snow are received in January and early March. The snow is usually light and only remains on the ground for brief periods.

The average date of the last 32 degree temperature occurrence is late March and the average date of the first 32 degree occurrence is early November. The average growing season is 216 days.

The Tulsa area is occasionally subjected to large hail and violent windstorms which occur mostly during spring and early summer, although occurrences have been noted throughout the year.

Prevailing surface winds are southerly during most of the year. Heavy fogs are infrequent. Sunshine is abundant. The prevalence of good flying weather throughout the year has contributed to the development of Tulsa as an aviation center.

## TABLE 1     NORMALS, MEANS AND EXTREMES

TULSA, OKLAHOMA

LATITUDE: 36 °12'N    LONGITUDE: 95 °54' W    ELEVATION: FT. GRND   650 BARO   669   TIME ZONE: CENTRAL    WBAN: 13968

| | (a) | JAN | FEB | MAR | APR | MAY | JUNE | JULY | AUG | SEP | OCT | NOV | DEC | YEAR |
|---|---|---|---|---|---|---|---|---|---|---|---|---|---|---|
| **TEMPERATURE °F:** | | | | | | | | | | | | | | |
| Normals | | | | | | | | | | | | | | |
| -Daily Maximum | | 45.6 | 51.9 | 60.8 | 72.4 | 79.7 | 87.9 | 93.9 | 93.0 | 85.0 | 74.9 | 60.2 | 50.3 | 71.3 |
| -Daily Minimum | | 24.8 | 29.5 | 37.7 | 49.5 | 58.5 | 67.5 | 72.4 | 70.3 | 62.5 | 50.3 | 38.1 | 29.3 | 49.2 |
| -Monthly | | 35.2 | 40.7 | 49.3 | 60.9 | 69.1 | 77.7 | 83.2 | 81.7 | 73.8 | 62.6 | 49.2 | 39.8 | 60.3 |
| Extremes | | | | | | | | | | | | | | |
| -Record Highest | 51 | 79 | 86 | 96 | 102 | 96 | 103 | 112 | 110 | 109 | 98 | 87 | 80 | 112 |
| -Year | | 1950 | 1962 | 1974 | 1972 | 1985 | 1953 | 1954 | 1970 | 1939 | 1979 | 1945 | 1966 | JUL 1954 |
| -Record Lowest | 51 | -8 | -7 | -3 | 22 | 35 | 49 | 51 | 52 | 35 | 26 | 10 | -8 | -8 |
| -Year | | 1947 | 1979 | 1948 | 1957 | 1961 | 1954 | 1971 | 1988 | 1984 | 1952 | 1976 | 1989 | DEC 1989 |
| **NORMAL DEGREE DAYS:** | | | | | | | | | | | | | | |
| Heating (base 65°F) | | 924 | 680 | 500 | 168 | 40 | 0 | 0 | 0 | 18 | 146 | 474 | 781 | 3731 |
| Cooling (base 65°F) | | 0 | 0 | 14 | 45 | 167 | 381 | 564 | 518 | 282 | 72 | 0 | 0 | 2043 |
| **% OF POSSIBLE SUNSHINE** | 47 | 53 | 55 | 57 | 59 | 59 | 66 | 73 | 73 | 66 | 63 | 56 | 54 | 61 |
| **MEAN SKY COVER (tenths)** | | | | | | | | | | | | | | |
| Sunrise - Sunset | 47 | 5.9 | 5.9 | 5.9 | 5.9 | 6.0 | 5.4 | 4.6 | 4.4 | 4.8 | 4.7 | 5.3 | 5.8 | 5.4 |
| **MEAN NUMBER OF DAYS:** | | | | | | | | | | | | | | |
| Sunrise to Sunset | | | | | | | | | | | | | | |
| -Clear | 51 | 9.4 | 8.7 | 9.3 | 8.4 | 8.1 | 9.1 | 12.9 | 13.5 | 12.6 | 13.5 | 11.4 | 10.3 | 127.1 |
| -Partly Cloudy | 51 | 7.1 | 6.5 | 8.1 | 8.9 | 10.1 | 11.3 | 10.7 | 10.7 | 7.9 | 7.4 | 6.8 | 7.4 | 103.0 |
| -Cloudy | 51 | 14.5 | 13.1 | 13.7 | 12.8 | 12.8 | 9.5 | 7.3 | 6.8 | 9.5 | 10.1 | 11.8 | 13.3 | 135.2 |
| Precipitation | | | | | | | | | | | | | | |
| .01 inches or more | 51 | 6.2 | 7.1 | 8.1 | 8.7 | 10.5 | 8.9 | 6.4 | 6.9 | 7.3 | 6.6 | 6.1 | 6.5 | 89.4 |
| Snow, Ice pellets | | | | | | | | | | | | | | |
| 1.0 inches or more | 51 | 1.4 | 1.0 | 0.4 | 0.* | 0.0 | 0.0 | 0.0 | 0.0 | 0.0 | 0.0 | 0.2 | 0.6 | 3.5 |
| Thunderstorms | 51 | 0.7 | 1.3 | 3.4 | 5.9 | 9.1 | 8.3 | 5.8 | 6.2 | 5.1 | 3.1 | 1.5 | 0.8 | 50.9 |
| Heavy Fog Visibility | | | | | | | | | | | | | | |
| 1/4 mile or less | 51 | 2.0 | 1.6 | 0.9 | 0.2 | 0.4 | 0.3 | 0.2 | 0.1 | 0.6 | 1.1 | 1.2 | 1.6 | 10.3 |
| Temperature °F | | | | | | | | | | | | | | |
| -Maximum | | | | | | | | | | | | | | |
| 90° and above | 29 | 0.0 | 0.0 | 0.3 | 0.8 | 2.1 | 13.0 | 24.0 | 22.0 | 9.2 | 1.6 | 0.0 | 0.0 | 73.0 |
| 32° and below | 29 | 6.0 | 2.7 | 0.3 | 0.0 | 0.0 | 0.0 | 0.0 | 0.0 | 0.0 | 0.0 | 0.2 | 3.1 | 12.2 |
| -Minimum | | | | | | | | | | | | | | |
| 32° and below | 29 | 24.2 | 17.5 | 8.5 | 0.6 | 0.0 | 0.0 | 0.0 | 0.0 | 0.0 | 0.3 | 7.8 | 20.3 | 79.1 |
| 0° and below | 29 | 0.7 | 0.1 | 0.0 | 0.0 | 0.0 | 0.0 | 0.0 | 0.0 | 0.0 | 0.0 | 0.0 | 0.4 | 1.1 |
| **AVG. STATION PRESS.(mb)** | 17 | 996.8 | 995.0 | 990.4 | 989.8 | 988.7 | 989.7 | 991.0 | 991.2 | 992.2 | 993.8 | 993.6 | 995.8 | 992.3 |
| **RELATIVE HUMIDITY (%)** | | | | | | | | | | | | | | |
| Hour 00 | 29 | 72 | 71 | 68 | 68 | 78 | 78 | 72 | 73 | 79 | 76 | 74 | 73 | 74 |
| Hour 06 | 29 | 78 | 77 | 75 | 78 | 85 | 86 | 82 | 84 | 87 | 82 | 80 | 79 | 81 |
| Hour 12 (Local Time) | 29 | 60 | 57 | 53 | 51 | 58 | 59 | 53 | 53 | 59 | 53 | 57 | 60 | 56 |
| Hour 18 | 29 | 58 | 55 | 49 | 48 | 56 | 56 | 49 | 50 | 57 | 55 | 59 | 61 | 54 |
| **PRECIPITATION (inches):** | | | | | | | | | | | | | | |
| Water Equivalent | | | | | | | | | | | | | | |
| -Normal | | 1.35 | 1.74 | 3.14 | 4.15 | 5.14 | 4.57 | 3.51 | 3.01 | 4.37 | 3.41 | 2.56 | 1.82 | 38.77 |
| -Maximum Monthly | 51 | 6.65 | 5.73 | 11.94 | 9.23 | 18.00 | 11.17 | 10.88 | 7.47 | 18.81 | 16.51 | 7.57 | 8.70 | 18.81 |
| -Year | | 1949 | 1985 | 1973 | 1947 | 1943 | 1948 | 1961 | 1942 | 1971 | 1941 | 1946 | 1984 | SEP 1971 |
| -Minimum Monthly | 51 | 0.00 | 0.40 | 0.08 | 0.34 | 1.17 | 0.53 | 0.03 | 0.21 | T | T | 0.01 | 0.16 | 0.00 |
| -Year | | 1986 | 1947 | 1971 | 1989 | 1988 | 1963 | 1954 | 1945 | 1948 | 1952 | 1949 | 1950 | JAN 1986 |
| -Maximum in 24 hrs | 51 | 2.25 | 4.34 | 2.67 | 4.58 | 9.27 | 5.01 | 7.54 | 5.37 | 6.39 | 5.80 | 5.14 | 3.27 | 9.27 |
| -Year | | 1946 | 1985 | 1969 | 1964 | 1984 | 1941 | 1963 | 1989 | 1940 | 1983 | 1974 | 1984 | MAY 1984 |
| Snow, Ice pellets | | | | | | | | | | | | | | |
| -Maximum Monthly | 51 | 12.7 | 10.1 | 11.8 | 1.7 | 0.0 | 0.0 | 0.0 | 0.0 | 0.0 | T | 5.6 | 9.9 | 12.7 |
| -Year | | 1979 | 1960 | 1968 | 1957 | | | | | | 1967 | 1972 | 1958 | JAN 1979 |
| -Maximum in 24 hrs | 51 | 9.0 | 6.3 | 9.8 | 1.7 | 0.0 | 0.0 | 0.0 | 0.0 | 0.0 | T | 4.0 | 8.8 | 9.8 |
| -Year | | 1944 | 1944 | 1968 | 1957 | | | | | | 1967 | 1972 | 1954 | MAR 1968 |
| **WIND:** | | | | | | | | | | | | | | |
| Mean Speed (mph) | 41 | 10.5 | 10.9 | 12.2 | 12.0 | 10.7 | 10.0 | 9.3 | 9.0 | 9.2 | 9.8 | 10.4 | 10.3 | 10.3 |
| Prevailing Direction | | | | | | | | | | | | | | |
| through 1963 | | N | N | SSE | S | S | S | S | SSE | SSE | SSE | S | S | S |
| Fastest Obs. 1 Min. | | | | | | | | | | | | | | |
| -Direction (!!!) | 12 | 02 | 23 | 16 | 29 | 31 | 29 | 23 | 36 | 21 | 18 | 23 | 18 | 29 |
| -Speed (MPH) | 12 | 35 | 30 | 37 | 52 | 37 | 40 | 36 | 32 | 31 | 35 | 38 | 35 | 52 |
| -Year | | 1985 | 1984 | 1989 | 1982 | 1989 | 1989 | 1986 | 1979 | 1986 | 1985 | 1988 | 1988 | APR 1982 |
| Peak Gust | | | | | | | | | | | | | | |
| -Direction (!!!) | 6 | SW | SW | SW | SW | NW | NW | SW | NW | S | S | NW | S | NW |
| -Speed (mph) | 6 | 46 | 46 | 61 | 52 | 61 | 62 | 46 | 45 | 51 | 47 | 52 | 49 | 62 |
| -Date | | 1989 | 1984 | 1986 | 1984 | 1986 | 1989 | 1986 | 1989 | 1986 | 1985 | 1985 | 1988 | JUN 1989 |

**See Reference Notes to this table on the following page.**

PRECIPITATION (inches)  TULSA, OKLAHOMA

**TABLE 2**

| YEAR | JAN | FEB | MAR | APR | MAY | JUNE | JULY | AUG | SEP | OCT | NOV | DEC | ANNUAL |
|------|-----|-----|-----|-----|-----|------|------|-----|-----|-----|-----|-----|--------|
| 1961 | 0.66 | 2.86 | 3.30 | 1.49 | 9.09 | 6.36 | 10.88 | 3.16 | 7.37 | 0.86 | 3.18 | 2.18 | 51.39 |
| 1962 | 1.33 | 1.44 | 3.24 | 3.40 | 1.69 | 5.52 | 4.83 | 3.10 | 10.50 | 3.92 | 2.13 | 0.36 | 41.46 |
| 1963 | 0.98 | 0.42 | 2.84 | 2.21 | 2.49 | 0.53 | 10.60 | 3.28 | 2.01 | 1.24 | 2.28 | 0.98 | 28.80 |
| 1964 | 0.63 | 2.17 | 3.96 | 5.87 | 4.77 | 5.79 | 1.80 | 6.14 | 3.33 | 0.26 | 6.90 | 4.29 | 44.27 |
| 1965 | 1.56 | 1.45 | 0.73 | 3.00 | 3.91 | 3.76 | 3.39 | 3.72 | 4.59 | 0.26 | 0.03 | 4.29 | 30.69 |
| 1966 | 0.69 | 2.35 | 0.86 | 4.84 | 1.86 | 2.56 | 2.00 | 4.59 | 2.68 | 1.39 | 0.51 | 2.53 | 26.86 |
| 1967 | 1.51 | 0.65 | 1.42 | 5.09 | 5.34 | 4.60 | 6.88 | 0.57 | 4.89 | 3.75 | 1.09 | 1.12 | 36.91 |
| 1968 | 3.26 | 1.08 | 3.49 | 4.40 | 3.56 | 4.08 | 1.37 | 1.90 | 2.80 | 2.64 | 5.19 | 2.01 | 35.78 |
| 1969 | 1.63 | 1.34 | 3.25 | 1.56 | 1.98 | 6.40 | 1.08 | 3.24 | 1.67 | 5.86 | 0.32 | 1.62 | 29.95 |
| 1970 | 0.41 | 0.57 | 2.05 | 5.66 | 4.20 | 4.60 | 0.13 | 1.85 | 6.73 | 5.83 | 0.84 | 1.15 | 34.02 |
| 1971 | 1.37 | 4.18 | 0.08 | 1.37 | 6.59 | 3.27 | 3.34 | 1.86 | 18.81 | 7.99 | 1.21 | 6.34 | 56.41 |
| 1972 | 0.17 | 0.49 | 0.91 | 4.45 | 2.43 | 2.69 | 2.68 | 5.16 | 2.95 | 7.58 | 5.00 | 1.03 | 35.54 |
| 1973 | 3.39 | 0.74 | 11.94 | 7.22 | 5.30 | 7.69 | 6.47 | 4.70 | 6.56 | 6.16 | 6.32 | 3.39 | 69.88 |
| 1974 | 0.79 | 3.17 | 2.62 | 3.65 | 6.94 | 7.88 | 0.55 | 5.30 | 11.78 | 6.40 | 7.30 | 2.88 | 59.26 |
| 1975 | 2.61 | 3.44 | 5.45 | 2.20 | 7.22 | 6.75 | 2.14 | 3.52 | 3.34 | 1.47 | 3.53 | 3.04 | 44.71 |
| 1976 | 0.21 | 0.84 | 3.95 | 8.27 | 6.75 | 1.87 | 4.37 | 1.17 | 2.60 | 2.65 | 0.68 | 0.55 | 33.91 |
| 1977 | 1.43 | 1.57 | 5.58 | 2.05 | 5.72 | 6.69 | 2.00 | 4.86 | 5.57 | 2.75 | 2.31 | 0.93 | 41.46 |
| 1978 | 0.81 | 2.84 | 2.99 | 7.14 | 9.28 | 6.06 | 0.36 | 1.37 | 0.13 | 0.95 | 5.48 | 0.78 | 38.19 |
| 1979 | 2.07 | 0.81 | 3.97 | 4.47 | 6.15 | 8.90 | 2.68 | 4.77 | 0.28 | 2.20 | 5.60 | 0.45 | 42.35 |
| 1980 | 2.07 | 1.32 | 3.59 | 3.44 | 7.23 | 5.57 | 0.09 | 2.34 | 3.47 | 2.05 | 0.79 | 1.37 | 33.33 |
| 1981 | 0.69 | 1.63 | 1.67 | 1.90 | 6.70 | 3.31 | 6.22 | 2.47 | 3.11 | 6.73 | 2.25 | 0.20 | 36.88 |
| 1982 | 3.58 | 0.67 | 1.04 | 1.28 | 9.30 | 4.13 | 1.65 | 1.42 | 2.95 | 1.22 | 4.61 | 3.39 | 35.24 |
| 1983 | 2.95 | 1.98 | 2.19 | 3.88 | 6.85 | 1.47 | 0.58 | 0.65 | 2.11 | 9.33 | 2.14 | 0.61 | 34.74 |
| 1984 | 1.00 | 1.95 | 6.72 | 2.44 | 11.25 | 1.72 | 0.48 | 1.96 | 2.77 | 6.98 | 2.80 | 8.70 | 48.77 |
| 1985 | 1.24 | 5.74 | 5.39 | 5.62 | 4.19 | 7.63 | 2.38 | 1.91 | 3.29 | 6.26 | 6.27 | 1.39 | 51.30 |
| 1986 | 0.00 | 1.22 | 2.28 | 5.10 | 6.97 | 4.23 | 1.15 | 3.96 | 8.36 | 5.53 | 2.99 | 0.97 | 42.76 |
| 1987 | 2.21 | 4.72 | 0.70 | 10.02 | 2.31 | 4.20 | 3.72 | 3.52 | 1.27 | 5.17 | 5.87 | 2.20 | 45.91 |
| 1988 | 1.11 | 1.03 | 6.52 | 3.18 | 1.17 | 0.58 | 4.20 | 2.43 | 5.37 | 1.43 | 4.38 | 1.82 | 33.22 |
| 1989 | 2.94 | 2.26 | 3.14 | 0.34 | 3.95 | 5.16 | 4.09 | 6.69 | 3.32 | 2.80 | 0.15 | 0.26 | 35.10 |
| 1990 | 2.93 | 4.14 | 6.51 | 5.31 | 5.21 | 1.08 | 0.24 | 1.83 | 4.19 | 2.15 | 2.41 | 2.94 | 38.94 |
| Record Mean | 1.67 | 1.70 | 2.96 | 4.02 | 5.37 | 4.57 | 3.07 | 3.16 | 3.81 | 3.45 | 2.53 | 1.93 | 38.25 |

**TABLE 3** AVERAGE TEMPERATURE (deg. F)  TULSA, OKLAHOMA

| YEAR | JAN | FEB | MAR | APR | MAY | JUNE | JULY | AUG | SEP | OCT | NOV | DEC | ANNUAL |
|------|-----|-----|-----|-----|-----|------|------|-----|-----|-----|-----|-----|--------|
| 1961 | 34.3 | 42.7 | 52.0 | 57.6 | 65.9 | 73.8 | 78.6 | 77.3 | 70.7 | 62.6 | 46.2 | 35.1 | 58.1 |
| 1962 | 30.2 | 42.5 | 46.1 | 57.6 | 75.3 | 75.2 | 81.5 | 81.4 | 70.7 | 64.9 | 49.8 | 39.9 | 59.6 |
| 1963 | 28.6 | 38.5 | 54.8 | 65.6 | 70.9 | 81.7 | 85.0 | 82.7 | 76.0 | 72.2 | 52.3 | 31.3 | 61.6 |
| 1964 | 40.9 | 39.4 | 46.9 | 65.7 | 71.7 | 78.2 | 84.9 | 80.7 | 73.0 | 60.1 | 57.2 | 39.1 | 61.1 |
| 1965 | 39.8 | 39.4 | 40.5 | 66.2 | 72.6 | 78.1 | 83.2 | 81.7 | 75.3 | 63.3 | 55.7 | 46.8 | 61.9 |
| 1966 | 32.8 | 39.0 | 52.7 | 57.9 | 67.6 | 77.3 | 87.3 | 78.5 | 70.3 | 59.5 | 53.4 | 37.2 | 59.5 |
| 1967 | 39.6 | 38.9 | 55.1 | 64.3 | 65.2 | 76.5 | 77.5 | 76.0 | 69.2 | 61.2 | 48.2 | 39.7 | 59.3 |
| 1968 | 36.0 | 37.0 | 49.8 | 59.3 | 65.5 | 76.8 | 80.6 | 80.9 | 71.9 | 62.2 | 46.7 | 36.8 | 58.6 |
| 1969 | 36.9 | 41.4 | 42.7 | 61.6 | 69.9 | 75.0 | 82.8 | 84.8 | 74.9 | 59.5 | 48.1 | 39.3 | 59.7 |
| 1970 | 29.7 | 41.9 | 44.6 | 60.7 | 70.7 | 76.9 | 79.0 | 84.8 | 74.5 | 58.9 | 45.6 | 42.5 | 59.4 |
| 1971 | 36.5 | 39.0 | 49.9 | 60.2 | 66.7 | 79.4 | 80.0 | 79.0 | 73.0 | 65.0 | 50.1 | 43.7 | 60.2 |
| 1972 | 34.8 | 41.8 | 53.0 | 62.8 | 68.0 | 79.5 | 80.4 | 81.7 | 75.5 | 60.9 | 43.6 | 33.7 | 59.6 |
| 1973 | 34.0 | 39.8 | 54.3 | 58.2 | 67.5 | 76.7 | 81.2 | 79.3 | 72.3 | 65.0 | 53.4 | 38.1 | 60.0 |
| 1974 | 34.1 | 43.7 | 55.2 | 61.8 | 72.1 | 73.8 | 85.4 | 78.3 | 64.7 | 63.0 | 49.1 | 40.1 | 60.1 |
| 1975 | 39.9 | 36.9 | 45.3 | 60.4 | 69.1 | 76.0 | 81.2 | 82.2 | 69.2 | 63.2 | 50.8 | 37.1 | 59.5 |
| 1976 | 37.2 | 51.1 | 51.9 | 61.5 | 63.0 | 75.0 | 81.4 | 79.7 | 72.8 | 56.1 | 43.1 | 37.1 | 59.2 |
| 1977 | 26.9 | 46.6 | 55.0 | 64.4 | 72.6 | 81.0 | 84.8 | 81.7 | 75.6 | 62.2 | 51.1 | 39.0 | 61.7 |
| 1978 | 24.9 | 29.4 | 47.5 | 63.5 | 68.3 | 77.6 | 87.8 | 84.3 | 80.6 | 63.5 | 51.6 | 38.0 | 59.7 |
| 1979 | 23.1 | 30.2 | 52.4 | 61.0 | 68.7 | 77.8 | 83.4 | 81.8 | 74.7 | 66.2 | 47.5 | 44.4 | 59.3 |
| 1980 | 38.6 | 37.1 | 48.3 | 61.1 | 70.6 | 82.5 | 85.9 | 91.7 | 78.3 | 61.5 | 50.5 | 42.3 | 62.7 |
| 1981 | 37.6 | 43.6 | 53.3 | 68.0 | 65.9 | 80.0 | 85.9 | 79.4 | 73.9 | 60.9 | 51.4 | 38.5 | 61.5 |
| 1982 | 33.6 | 38.2 | 55.3 | 59.3 | 72.9 | 74.7 | 84.2 | 85.3 | 74.6 | 63.4 | 50.6 | 44.4 | 61.4 |
| 1983 | 39.1 | 42.9 | 49.0 | 55.4 | 67.0 | 76.6 | 84.7 | 88.1 | 77.4 | 64.5 | 52.9 | 26.7 | 60.4 |
| 1984 | 34.4 | 46.4 | 48.3 | 58.0 | 67.5 | 80.1 | 82.0 | 82.7 | 71.5 | 63.8 | 50.4 | 44.7 | 60.8 |
| 1985 | 30.2 | 35.9 | 54.7 | 63.3 | 70.6 | 75.8 | 82.9 | 81.7 | 74.6 | 63.1 | 47.8 | 34.5 | 59.6 |
| 1986 | 42.8 | 43.2 | 55.0 | 62.6 | 69.4 | 79.7 | 86.6 | 78.2 | 74.7 | 61.0 | 51.6 | 40.0 | 61.4 |
| 1987 | 36.0 | 45.4 | 51.5 | 63.2 | 74.1 | 78.9 | 81.9 | 83.1 | 72.4 | 59.3 | 51.6 | 41.4 | 61.6 |
| 1988 | 34.8 | 39.3 | 49.3 | 59.5 | 71.0 | 79.9 | 82.6 | 83.0 | 73.2 | 58.5 | 51.7 | 43.4 | 60.5 |
| 1989 | 43.4 | 31.9 | 49.3 | 63.3 | 69.2 | 74.8 | 80.2 | 80.4 | 68.7 | 64.0 | 52.7 | 31.6 | 59.1 |
| 1990 | 46.1 | 46.1 | 53.2 | 59.6 | 67.4 | 82.1 | 83.2 | 83.5 | 78.3 | 61.2 | 56.4 | 38.5 | 63.0 |
| Record Mean | 36.8 | 41.3 | 50.3 | 60.8 | 68.8 | 77.8 | 82.8 | 81.9 | 74.1 | 62.8 | 49.9 | 40.0 | 60.6 |
| Max | 47.1 | 52.3 | 61.9 | 72.2 | 79.4 | 88.2 | 93.9 | 93.6 | 85.7 | 74.8 | 61.0 | 50.1 | 71.7 |
| Min | 26.6 | 30.3 | 38.7 | 49.5 | 58.2 | 67.3 | 71.6 | 70.2 | 62.5 | 50.7 | 38.7 | 29.9 | 49.5 |

## REFERENCE NOTES FOR TABLES 1, 2, 3 and 6 (TULSA, OK)

### GENERAL

T - TRACE AMOUNT
BLANK ENTRIES DENOTE MISSING/UNREPORTED DATA.
# INDICATES A STATION OR INSTRUMENT RELOCATION.

### SPECIFIC

**TABLE 1**

(a) - LENGTH OF RECORD IN YEARS. ALTHOUGH INDIVIDUAL MONTHS MAY BE MISSING.

* LESS THAN .05

NORMALS — BASED ON THE 1951-1980 RECORD PERIOD.
EXTREMES — DATES ARE THE MOST RECENT OCCURRENCE.
WIND DIR. — NUMERALS SHOW TENS OF DEGREES CLOCKWISE FROM TRUE NORTH. "00" INDICATES CALM.
RESULTANT WIND DIRECTIONS ARE GIVEN TO WHOLE DEGREES.

**TABLE 3**
MAX AND MIN ARE LONG-TERM MEAN DAILY MAXIMUM AND MEAN DAILY MINIMUM TEMPERATURES.

### EXCEPTIONS

**TABLES 2, 3, and 6**

RECORD MEANS ARE THROUGH THE CURRENT YEAR, BEGINNING IN 1906 FOR TEMPERATURE
1888 FOR PRECIPITATION
1939 FOR SNOWFALL

HEATING DEGREE DAYS Base 65 deg. F    TULSA, OKLAHOMA

**TABLE 4**

| SEASON | JULY | AUG | SEP | OCT | NOV | DEC | JAN | FEB | MAR | APR | MAY | JUNE | TOTAL |
|---|---|---|---|---|---|---|---|---|---|---|---|---|---|
| 1961-62 | 0 | 0 | 37 | 129 | 563 | 918 | 1072 | 628 | 586 | 250 | 3 | 0 | 4186 |
| 1962-63 | 0 | 0 | 21 | 117 | 450 | 771 | 1119 | 736 | 343 | 90 | 46 | 0 | 3693 |
| 1963-64 | 0 | 0 | 5 | 20 | 376 | 1038 | 739 | 734 | 553 | 87 | 19 | 1 | 3572 |
| 1964-65 | 0 | 0 | 18 | 162 | 385 | 797 | 775 | 711 | 752 | 73 | 1 | 0 | 3674 |
| 1965-66 | 0 | 0 | 15 | 122 | 283 | 556 | 992 | 722 | 395 | 227 | 67 | 0 | 3379 |
| 1966-67 | 0 | 0 | 13 | 202 | 376 | 859 | 776 | 724 | 362 | 100 | 101 | 0 | 3513 |
| 1967-68 | 0 | 0 | 37 | 184 | 498 | 781 | 892 | 803 | 479 | 184 | 67 | 0 | 3925 |
| 1968-69 | 0 | 0 | 1 | 160 | 543 | 864 | 863 | 652 | 680 | 127 | 24 | 2 | 3916 |
| 1969-70 | 0 | 0 | 0 | 241 | 498 | 789 | 1088 | 642 | 625 | 174 | 26 | 18 | 4101 |
| 1970-71 | 0 | 0 | 18 | 217 | 577 | 692 | 878 | 721 | 463 | 176 | 37 | 0 | 3779 |
| 1971-72 | 0 | 0 | 53 | 60 | 446 | 653 | 932 | 670 | 373 | 161 | 47 | 0 | 3395 |
| 1972-73 | 0 | 0 | 19 | 183 | 634 | 964 | 954 | 700 | 321 | 233 | 42 | 0 | 4050 |
| 1973-74 | 0 | 0 | 24 | 95 | 343 | 824 | 951 | 591 | 341 | 137 | 5 | 0 | 3311 |
| 1974-75 | 0 | 0 | 74 | 94 | 473 | 777 | 773 | 780 | 610 | 205 | 19 | 0 | 3805 |
| 1975-76 | 0 | 0 | 57 | 146 | 429 | 762 | 855 | 402 | 407 | 126 | 109 | 0 | 3293 |
| 1976-77 | 0 | 0 | 16 | 317 | 648 | 858 | 1173 | 511 | 309 | 99 | 1 | 0 | 3932 |
| 1977-78 | 0 | 0 | 1 | 118 | 412 | 801 | 1236 | 989 | 541 | 110 | 67 | 0 | 4275 |
| 1978-79 | 0 | 0 | 0 | 121 | 406 | 834 | 1293 | 972 | 391 | 164 | 47 | 0 | 4228 |
| 1979-80 | 0 | 0 | 0 | 90 | 525 | 632 | 812 | 801 | 513 | 154 | 22 | 0 | 3549 |
| 1980-81 | 0 | 0 | 13 | 172 | 438 | 703 | 843 | 598 | 360 | 48 | 58 | 0 | 3233 |
| 1981-82 | 0 | 0 | 23 | 178 | 402 | 817 | 967 | 747 | 322 | 208 | 11 | 5 | 3680 |
| 1982-83 | 0 | 0 | 23 | 146 | 437 | 635 | 794 | 611 | 492 | 321 | 50 | 0 | 3509 |
| 1983-84 | 0 | 0 | 19 | 89 | 378 | 1179 | 941 | 533 | 509 | 229 | 47 | 0 | 3924 |
| 1984-85 | 0 | 0 | 73 | 130 | 438 | 628 | 1073 | 809 | 330 | 103 | 7 | 0 | 3591 |
| 1985-86 | 0 | 0 | 46 | 111 | 510 | 936 | 680 | 602 | 322 | 127 | 13 | 0 | 3347 |
| 1986-87 | 0 | 0 | 5 | 148 | 632 | 771 | 893 | 544 | 413 | 149 | 0 | 0 | 3555 |
| 1987-88 | 0 | 0 | 1 | 189 | 416 | 727 | 928 | 739 | 483 | 187 | 9 | 0 | 3679 |
| 1988-89 | 0 | 0 | 8 | 218 | 393 | 662 | 663 | 921 | 487 | 155 | 53 | 0 | 3560 |
| 1989-90 | 0 | 0 | 67 | 126 | 375 | 1029 | 580 | 527 | 376 | 194 | 54 | 0 | 3328 |
| 1990-91 | 0 | 0 | 8 | 172 | 271 | 813 |  |  |  |  |  |  |  |

**TABLE 5**    COOLING DEGREE DAYS Base 65 deg. F    TULSA, OKLAHOMA

| YEAR | JAN | FEB | MAR | APR | MAY | JUNE | JULY | AUG | SEP | OCT | NOV | DEC | TOTAL |
|---|---|---|---|---|---|---|---|---|---|---|---|---|---|
| 1969 | 0 | 0 | 0 | 29 | 185 | 312 | 656 | 496 | 307 | 77 | 0 | 0 | 2062 |
| 1970 | 0 | 0 | 0 | 50 | 209 | 382 | 555 | 619 | 307 | 39 | 0 | 0 | 2161 |
| 1971 | 0 | 0 | 3 | 40 | 97 | 442 | 471 | 444 | 298 | 65 | 7 | 0 | 1867 |
| 1972 | 0 | 6 | 11 | 99 | 144 | 446 | 487 | 524 | 339 | 64 | 0 | 0 | 2120 |
| 1973 | 0 | 0 | 0 | 35 | 124 | 357 | 508 | 452 | 249 | 101 | 5 | 0 | 1831 |
| 1974 | 0 | 0 | 47 | 48 | 232 | 270 | 641 | 419 | 71 | 40 | 2 | 0 | 1770 |
| 1975 | 0 | 0 | 9 | 77 | 156 | 335 | 509 | 542 | 192 | 97 | 12 | 0 | 1929 |
| 1976 | 0 | 6 | 7 | 28 | 52 | 307 | 520 | 461 | 256 | 48 | 0 | 0 | 1685 |
| 1977 | 0 | 1 | 6 | 84 | 248 | 486 | 619 | 525 | 327 | 38 | 0 | 0 | 2334 |
| 1978 | 0 | 0 | 7 | 73 | 180 | 388 | 713 | 605 | 476 | 79 | 14 | 0 | 2535 |
| 1979 | 0 | 0 | 9 | 48 | 167 | 388 | 577 | 527 | 298 | 137 | 6 | 0 | 2157 |
| 1980 | 0 | 0 | 0 | 43 | 200 | 533 | 833 | 774 | 419 | 69 | 6 | 4 | 2881 |
| 1981 | 0 | 5 | 4 | 145 | 96 | 456 | 658 | 452 | 296 | 57 | 1 | 0 | 2170 |
| 1982 | 0 | 0 | 28 | 44 | 266 | 300 | 601 | 637 | 319 | 106 | 10 | 5 | 2316 |
| 1983 | 0 | 0 | 3 | 40 | 120 | 353 | 615 | 725 | 396 | 80 | 20 | 0 | 2352 |
| 1984 | 0 | 0 | 0 | 25 | 132 | 464 | 534 | 556 | 272 | 100 | 9 | 2 | 2094 |
| 1985 | 0 | 0 | 19 | 59 | 185 | 333 | 564 | 523 | 340 | 57 | 0 | 0 | 2080 |
| 1986 | 0 | 0 | 20 | 60 | 157 | 448 | 676 | 415 | 303 | 31 | 0 | 0 | 2110 |
| 1987 | 0 | 0 | 2 | 102 | 290 | 421 | 532 | 567 | 230 | 18 | 19 | 0 | 2181 |
| 1988 | 0 | 0 | 2 | 30 | 200 | 454 | 555 | 564 | 262 | 23 | 1 | 0 | 2091 |
| 1989 | 0 | 0 | 6 | 107 | 191 | 300 | 475 | 483 | 183 | 105 | 14 | 0 | 1864 |
| 1990 | 0 | 0 | 17 | 38 | 137 | 521 | 571 | 581 | 416 | 63 | 21 | 0 | 2365 |

**TABLE 6**    SNOWFALL (inches)    TULSA, OKLAHOMA

| SEASON | JULY | AUG | SEP | OCT | NOV | DEC | JAN | FEB | MAR | APR | MAY | JUNE | TOTAL |
|---|---|---|---|---|---|---|---|---|---|---|---|---|---|
| 1961-62 | 0.0 | 0.0 | 0.0 | 0.0 | T | 2.7 | 1.8 |  | 0.0 | 0.0 | 0.0 | 0.0 | 6.5 |
| 1962-63 | 0.0 | 0.0 | 0.0 | 0.0 |  | 1.0 | 0.6 | 1.5 | 0.0 | 0.0 | 0.0 | 0.0 | 3.1 |
| 1963-64 | 0.0 | 0.0 | 0.0 | 0.0 | 0.0 | 4.0 | 1.1 | T | 8.8 | 0.0 | 0.0 | 0.0 | 13.9 |
| 1964-65 | 0.0 | 0.0 | 0.0 | 0.0 | 0.0 | T | 0.3 | 1.5 | 0.6 | 0.0 | 0.0 | 0.0 | 2.4 |
| 1965-66 | 0.0 | 0.0 | 0.0 | 0.0 | 0.0 | 4.3 | 5.1 | T |  | 0.0 | 0.0 | 0.0 | 9.4 |
| 1966-67 | 0.0 | 0.0 | 0.0 | 0.0 | T | 3.1 | 0.7 | 0.9 | 1.1 | 0.0 | 0.0 | 0.0 | 5.8 |
| 1967-68 | 0.0 | 0.0 | 0.0 | T | 0.9 | 1.6 | 0.6 | 2.1 | 11.8 | 0.0 | 0.0 | 0.0 | 17.0 |
| 1968-69 | 0.0 | 0.0 | 0.0 | 0.0 | T | 1.4 | T | 5.3 | 1.3 | 0.0 | 0.0 | 0.0 | 8.0 |
| 1969-70 | 0.0 | 0.0 | 0.0 | 0.0 | 0.0 | 5.8 | 4.7 | T | 9.9 | T | 0.0 | 0.0 | 20.4 |
| 1970-71 | 0.0 | 0.0 | 0.0 | 0.0 | T | 0.0 | T | 6.5 | T | 0.0 | 0.0 | 0.0 | 6.5 |
| 1971-72 | 0.0 | 0.0 | 0.0 | 0.0 | 2.0 | 1.0 | 0.8 | 4.9 | T | 0.0 | 0.0 | 0.0 | 8.7 |
| 1972-73 | 0.0 | 0.0 | 0.0 | 0.0 | 5.6 | 1.7 | 4.3 | 2.2 | 0.0 | 0.3 | 0.0 | 0.0 | 14.1 |
| 1973-74 | 0.0 | 0.0 | 0.0 | 0.0 | T | 1.8 | T | T | T | T | 0.0 | 0.0 | 1.8 |
| 1974-75 | 0.0 | 0.0 | 0.0 | 0.0 | 1.7 | T | T | 3.0 | 1.8 | T | 0.0 | 0.0 | 6.5 |
| 1975-76 | 0.0 | 0.0 | 0.0 | 0.0 | 0.8 | 1.3 | T | T | T | 0.0 | 0.0 | 0.0 | 2.1 |
| 1976-77 | 0.0 | 0.0 | 0.0 | 0.0 | 0.5 | T | 10.5 | 0.3 | 0.0 | 0.0 | 0.0 | 0.0 | 11.3 |
| 1977-78 | 0.0 | 0.0 | 0.0 | 0.0 | T | 0.0 | 5.4 | 6.3 | T | 0.0 | 0.0 | 0.0 | 11.7 |
| 1978-79 | 0.0 | 0.0 | 0.0 | 0.0 | 0.0 | 2.8 | 12.7 | 3.4 | 0.0 | T | 0.0 | 0.0 | 18.9 |
| 1979-80 | 0.0 | 0.0 | 0.0 | 0.0 | T | 0.0 | 0.4 | 3.8 | T | 0.0 | 0.0 | 0.0 | 4.2 |
| 1980-81 | 0.0 | 0.0 | 0.0 | 0.0 | T | 0.0 | T | 0.9 | T | 0.0 | 0.0 | 0.0 | 0.9 |
| 1981-82 | 0.0 | 0.0 | 0.0 | 0.0 |  | 0.0 | T | 0.3 | 5.6 | T | 0.0 | 0.0 | 5.9 |
| 1982-83 | 0.0 | 0.0 | 0.0 | 0.0 |  | T | T | 3.8 | 1.4 | T | 0.0 | 0.0 | 5.2 |
| 1983-84 | 0.0 | 0.0 | 0.0 | 0.0 |  | T | 3.0 | 4.6 | 0.2 | T | 0.0 | 0.0 | 7.8 |
| 1984-85 | 0.0 | 0.0 | 0.0 | 0.0 |  | 0.0 | 6.6 | 3.3 | 4.3 | 0.0 | 0.0 | 0.0 | 14.2 |
| 1985-86 | 0.0 | 0.0 | 0.0 | 0.0 |  | T | 2.5 | 0.0 | 4.9 | 0.0 | 0.0 | 0.0 | 7.4 |
| 1986-87 | 0.0 | 0.0 | 0.0 | 0.0 | 0.0 | 0.0 | 8.7 | 4.6 | 0.0 | 0.0 | 0.0 | 0.0 | 13.3 |
| 1987-88 | 0.0 | 0.0 | 0.0 | 0.0 | T | 6.7 | 11.0 | T | 0.5 | T | 0.0 | 0.0 | 18.2 |
| 1988-89 | 0.0 | 0.0 | 0.0 | 0.0 | 0.4 | 2.7 | 3.4 | 0.3 | 9.7 | 0.0 | 0.0 | 0.0 | 16.5 |
| 1989-90 | 0.0 | 0.0 | T | 0.0 | 0.0 | 2.0 | T | T | 0.2 | 0.0 | 0.0 |  | 2.2 |
| 1990-91 | 0.0 | 0.0 | T | 0.0 | 0.0 | 4.6 |  |  |  |  |  |  |  |
| Record Mean | 0.0 | 0.0 | T | T | 0.4 | 1.7 | 3.4 | 2.4 | 1.5 | T | 0.0 | 0.0 | 9.4 |

**See Reference Notes, relative to all above tables, on preceding page.**

Pendleton is located in the southeastern part of the Columbia Basin, that low country of northern Oregon and central and eastern Washington which is almost entirely surrounded by mountains. This Basin is bounded on the south by the high country of central Oregon, on the north by the mountains of western Canada, on the west by the Cascade Range and on the east by the Blue Mountains and the north Idaho plateau. The gorge in the Cascades through which the Columbia River reaches the Pacific is the most important break in the barriers surrounding this basin. These physical features have important influences on the general climate of Pendleton and the surrounding territory.

The Weather Service Office at Pendleton Airport is located in rolling country which slopes generally upward toward the Blue Mountains about 15 miles to the east and southeast. The Columbia River approaches the area from the northwest to its junction with the Walla Walla River at an elevation of 351 feet and some 25 miles north of Pendleton, then turns southwestward to be joined a few miles below by the Umatilla River. Both the Walla Walla and Umatilla Rivers have their sources in the Blue Mountains and flow westward to the Columbia. The observation station is at an elevation of nearly 1,500 feet, about 3 miles northwest of downtown Pendleton. The city of Pendleton lies in the shallow east–west valley of the Umatilla River, approximately 400 feet lower than the airport.

Precipitation in the Pendleton area is definitely seasonal in occurrence with an average of only 10 percent of the annual total occurring in the three–month period, July–September. Most precipitation reaching this area accompanies cyclonic storms moving in from the Pacific Ocean. These storms reach their greatest intensity and frequency from October through April. The Cascade Range west of the Columbia Basin reduces the amount of precipitation received from the Pacific cyclonic storms. This influence is felt, particularly, in the desert area of the central part of the Basin. A gradual rise in elevation from the Columbia River to the foothills of the Blue Mountains again results in increased precipitation. This increase supplies sufficient moisture for productive wheat, pea, and stock raising activity in the area surrounding Pendleton.

The lighter summertime precipitation usually accompanies thunderstorms which often move into the area from the south or southwest. On occasion, these storms are quite intense, causing flash flooding with resultant heavy property damage and even loss of life.

Seasonal temperature extremes are usually quite moderate for the latitude. The last occurrence in spring of temperatures as low as 32 degrees is mid–April, and the average last occurrence in the fall of 32 degrees is late October. At the city station, where cool air settles in the valley on still nights, temperatures of 32 degrees have been recorded later in the spring and earlier in the fall. Under usual atmospheric conditions, air from the Pacific, with moderate temperature characteristics, moves across the Cascades or through the Columbia Gorge resulting in mild temperatures in the Pendleton area. When this flow of air from the west is impeded by slow–moving high pressure systems over the interior of the continent, temperature conditions sometimes become rather severe, hot in summer and cold in winter. During the summer or early fall, if a stagnant high predominates to the north or east of Pendleton, the hot, dry conditions may prove detrimental to crops during late May and June, and cause fire danger in the forest and grassland areas during late summer and early fall. During winter, coldest temperatures occur when air from a cold high pressure system in central Canada moves southwestward across the Rockies and flows down into the Columbia Basin. Under this condition the heavy cold air sometimes remains at low levels in the Basin for several days while warmer air from the Pacific flows above it, causing comparatively mild temperatures at higher elevations. Extreme winter temperatures are not particularly common in the Pendleton area. Below zero readings are recorded in approximately 60 percent of winters. Maximum temperatures usually reach 100 degrees or slightly higher on a few days during the summer.

## TABLE 1   NORMALS, MEANS AND EXTREMES

PENDLETON, OREGON

LATITUDE: 45°41'N   LONGITUDE: 118°51'W   ELEVATION: FT. GRND 1482 BARO 1507   TIME ZONE: PACIFIC   WBAN: 24155

| | (a) | JAN | FEB | MAR | APR | MAY | JUNE | JULY | AUG | SEP | OCT | NOV | DEC | YEAR |
|---|---|---|---|---|---|---|---|---|---|---|---|---|---|---|
| **TEMPERATURE °F:** | | | | | | | | | | | | | | |
| Normals | | | | | | | | | | | | | | |
| -Daily Maximum | | 39.4 | 46.9 | 53.4 | 61.4 | 70.6 | 79.6 | 88.9 | 85.9 | 77.1 | 63.7 | 48.7 | 42.5 | 63.2 |
| -Daily Minimum | | 26.3 | 31.8 | 34.4 | 39.2 | 46.1 | 52.9 | 58.6 | 57.5 | 50.5 | 41.3 | 33.4 | 29.5 | 41.8 |
| -Monthly | | 32.8 | 39.4 | 43.9 | 50.3 | 58.4 | 66.2 | 73.8 | 71.7 | 63.8 | 52.5 | 41.1 | 36.0 | 52.5 |
| Extremes | | | | | | | | | | | | | | |
| -Record Highest | 54 | 68 | 72 | 79 | 91 | 100 | 108 | 110 | 113 | 102 | 92 | 77 | 67 | 113 |
| -Year | | 1974 | 1986 | 1964 | 1977 | 1986 | 1961 | 1939 | 1961 | 1955 | 1980 | 1975 | 1980 | AUG 1961 |
| -Record Lowest | 54 | -22 | -18 | 10 | 18 | 25 | 36 | 42 | 40 | 30 | 11 | -12 | -19 | -22 |
| -Year | | 1957 | 1950 | 1955 | 1936 | 1954 | 1966 | 1971 | 1980 | 1970 | 1935 | 1985 | 1983 | JAN 1957 |
| **NORMAL DEGREE DAYS:** | | | | | | | | | | | | | | |
| Heating (base 65°F) | | 998 | 717 | 654 | 441 | 220 | 75 | 7 | 27 | 120 | 388 | 717 | 899 | 5263 |
| Cooling (base 65°F) | | 0 | 0 | 0 | 0 | 16 | 111 | 280 | 235 | 84 | 0 | 0 | 0 | 726 |
| **% OF POSSIBLE SUNSHINE** | | | | | | | | | | | | | | |
| **MEAN SKY COVER (tenths)** | | | | | | | | | | | | | | |
| Sunrise - Sunset | 44 | 8.4 | 8.1 | 7.3 | 6.8 | 6.1 | 5.4 | 3.0 | 3.4 | 4.2 | 5.7 | 7.9 | 8.4 | 6.2 |
| **MEAN NUMBER OF DAYS:** | | | | | | | | | | | | | | |
| Sunrise to Sunset | | | | | | | | | | | | | | |
| -Clear | 54 | 2.4 | 2.7 | 4.8 | 5.4 | 7.5 | 9.8 | 19.5 | 18.1 | 14.8 | 10.2 | 3.5 | 2.6 | 101.3 |
| -Partly Cloudy | 54 | 5.3 | 5.6 | 7.5 | 9.4 | 10.7 | 10.1 | 7.6 | 7.8 | 7.9 | 7.9 | 6.5 | 4.6 | 90.8 |
| -Cloudy | 54 | 23.4 | 20.0 | 18.7 | 15.2 | 12.8 | 10.2 | 3.9 | 5.1 | 7.3 | 13.0 | 20.0 | 23.8 | 173.2 |
| Precipitation | | | | | | | | | | | | | | |
| .01 inches or more | 54 | 12.3 | 10.8 | 10.9 | 8.9 | 7.8 | 6.6 | 2.6 | 3.2 | 4.4 | 7.2 | 11.4 | 12.6 | 98.7 |
| Snow, Ice pellets | | | | | | | | | | | | | | |
| 1.0 inches or more | 54 | 2.7 | 1.1 | 0.4 | 0.1 | 0.0 | 0.0 | 0.0 | 0.0 | 0.0 | 0.* | 0.5 | 1.4 | 6.2 |
| Thunderstorms | 52 | 0.0 | 0.* | 0.2 | 0.8 | 1.8 | 1.9 | 1.8 | 2.1 | 1.1 | 0.3 | 0.1 | 0.* | 10.0 |
| Heavy Fog Visibility | | | | | | | | | | | | | | |
| 1/4 mile or less | 52 | 7.3 | 4.7 | 1.8 | 0.3 | 0.2 | 0.1 | 0.0 | 0.* | 0.3 | 1.0 | 6.0 | 8.6 | 30.4 |
| Temperature °F | | | | | | | | | | | | | | |
| -Maximum | | | | | | | | | | | | | | |
| 90° and above | 54 | 0.0 | 0.0 | 0.0 | 0.* | 0.9 | 4.6 | 14.3 | 10.5 | 2.7 | 0.* | 0.0 | 0.0 | 33.0 |
| 32° and below | 54 | 9.4 | 2.9 | 0.2 | 0.0 | 0.0 | 0.0 | 0.0 | 0.0 | 0.0 | 0.0 | 2.0 | 7.3 | 21.9 |
| -Minimum | | | | | | | | | | | | | | |
| 32° and below | 54 | 21.4 | 15.8 | 9.5 | 2.5 | 0.1 | 0.0 | 0.0 | 0.0 | 0.1 | 2.5 | 12.5 | 19.2 | 83.6 |
| 0° and below | 54 | 1.7 | 0.7 | 0.0 | 0.0 | 0.0 | 0.0 | 0.0 | 0.0 | 0.0 | 0.0 | 0.1 | 0.5 | 3.0 |
| **AVG. STATION PRESS. (mb)** | 16 | 966.5 | 964.7 | 961.5 | 962.6 | 962.0 | 961.7 | 961.8 | 961.3 | 962.9 | 964.9 | 964.1 | 966.6 | 963.4 |
| **RELATIVE HUMIDITY (%)** | | | | | | | | | | | | | | |
| Hour 04 | 48 | 81 | 79 | 73 | 71 | 69 | 65 | 54 | 54 | 62 | 72 | 79 | 82 | 70 |
| Hour 10 (Local Time) | 50 | 78 | 71 | 59 | 51 | 47 | 42 | 34 | 37 | 43 | 55 | 73 | 78 | 56 |
| Hour 16 | 50 | 75 | 65 | 49 | 42 | 37 | 32 | 23 | 26 | 32 | 47 | 69 | 78 | 48 |
| Hour 22 | 47 | 80 | 77 | 69 | 63 | 58 | 52 | 38 | 41 | 51 | 66 | 78 | 81 | 63 |
| **PRECIPITATION (inches):** | | | | | | | | | | | | | | |
| Water Equivalent | | | | | | | | | | | | | | |
| -Normal | | 1.73 | 1.11 | 1.06 | 0.99 | 1.09 | 0.70 | 0.30 | 0.55 | 0.58 | 0.95 | 1.48 | 1.66 | 12.20 |
| -Maximum Monthly | 54 | 3.92 | 3.03 | 2.82 | 2.78 | 3.02 | 2.70 | 1.26 | 2.58 | 2.34 | 2.79 | 3.76 | 4.68 | 4.68 |
| -Year | | 1970 | 1940 | 1983 | 1978 | 1962 | 1947 | 1948 | 1977 | 1941 | 1947 | 1973 | 1973 | DEC 1973 |
| -Minimum Monthly | 54 | 0.21 | 0.07 | 0.24 | 0.01 | 0.03 | 0.03 | T | 0.00 | T | T | 0.04 | 0.21 | 0.00 |
| -Year | | 1949 | 1964 | 1941 | 1956 | 1964 | 1986 | 1967 | 1969 | 1974 | 1987 | 1939 | 1989 | AUG 1969 |
| -Maximum in 24 hrs | 54 | 1.29 | 1.09 | 1.33 | 1.23 | 1.52 | 1.49 | 1.19 | 1.48 | 1.23 | 1.88 | 1.35 | 1.25 | 1.88 |
| -Year | | 1956 | 1959 | 1983 | 1988 | 1972 | 1947 | 1948 | 1977 | 1981 | 1982 | 1971 | 1978 | OCT 1982 |
| Snow, Ice pellets | | | | | | | | | | | | | | |
| -Maximum Monthly | 54 | 41.6 | 15.8 | 4.9 | 2.2 | T | 0.0 | 0.0 | 0.0 | 0.0 | 3.2 | 14.9 | 26.6 | 41.6 |
| -Year | | 1950 | 1936 | 1971 | 1975 | 1989 | | | | | 1973 | 1985 | 1983 | JAN 1950 |
| -Maximum in 24 hrs | 54 | 13.3 | 9.7 | 4.0 | 2.2 | T | 0.0 | 0.0 | 0.0 | 0.0 | 3.2 | 8.0 | 9.9 | 13.3 |
| -Year | | 1950 | 1949 | 1970 | 1975 | 1989 | | | | | 1973 | 1977 | 1948 | JAN 1950 |
| **WIND:** | | | | | | | | | | | | | | |
| Mean Speed (mph) | 36 | 7.9 | 8.4 | 9.5 | 10.0 | 9.6 | 9.7 | 9.0 | 8.7 | 8.5 | 7.7 | 7.7 | 7.8 | 8.7 |
| Prevailing Direction | | | | | | | | | | | | | | |
| through 1963 | | SE | SE | W | W | W | W | WNW | SE | SE | SE | SE | SE | SE |
| Fastest Obs. 1 Min. | | | | | | | | | | | | | | |
| -Direction (!!!) | 34 | 27 | 25 | 29 | 27 | 27 | 29 | 28 | 27 | 27 | 25 | 27 | 29 | 27 |
| -Speed (MPH) | 34 | 49 | 54 | 63 | 77 | 48 | 62 | 46 | 40 | 47 | 49 | 62 | 63 | 77 |
| -Year | | 1962 | 1955 | 1956 | 1960 | 1959 | 1956 | 1968 | 1961 | 1954 | 1959 | 1959 | 1959 | APR 1960 |
| Peak Gust | | | | | | | | | | | | | | |
| -Direction (!!!) | 6 | W | SW | W | SW | W | W | SW | W | W | W | W | W | W |
| -Speed (mph) | 6 | 46 | 52 | 63 | 61 | 60 | 49 | 44 | 46 | 56 | 47 | 58 | 51 | 63 |
| -Date | | 1986 | 1988 | 1984 | 1987 | 1988 | 1986 | 1985 | 1984 | 1984 | 1985 | 1989 | 1987 | MAR 1984 |

**See reference Notes to this table on the following page.**

PRECIPITATION (inches)    PENDLETON, OREGON

**TABLE 2**

| YEAR | JAN | FEB | MAR | APR | MAY | JUNE | JULY | AUG | SEP | OCT | NOV | DEC | ANNUAL |
|---|---|---|---|---|---|---|---|---|---|---|---|---|---|
| 1961 | 0.47 | 2.46 | 2.25 | 1.30 | 0.94 | 0.28 | 0.08 | 0.09 | 0.17 | 0.70 | 1.46 | 1.27 | 11.47 |
| 1962 | 0.70 | 0.72 | 1.14 | 0.76 | 3.02 | 0.15 | T | 0.43 | 0.79 | 1.62 | 1.38 | 1.46 | 12.17 |
| 1963 | 1.40 | 1.67 | 0.37 | 1.86 | 0.65 | 0.21 | 0.32 | 0.30 | 0.70 | 0.44 | 2.03 | 1.29 | 11.24 |
| 1964 | 1.07 | 0.07 | 0.66 | 0.34 | 0.03 | 1.01 | 0.64 | 0.21 | 0.15 | 0.80 | 1.93 | 3.23 | 10.14 |
| 1965 | 3.08 | 0.37 | 0.29 | 0.65 | 0.57 | 1.10 | 0.51 | 1.21 | 0.23 | 0.19 | 1.95 | 0.27 | 10.42 |
| 1966 | 2.19 | 0.83 | 0.96 | 0.08 | 0.07 | 0.55 | 0.79 | 0.17 | 0.43 | 0.75 | 2.09 | 2.65 | 11.56 |
| 1967 | 1.59 | 0.15 | 0.89 | 1.05 | 0.56 | 0.41 | T | T | 0.40 | 0.64 | 0.63 | 0.45 | 6.77 |
| 1968 | 0.59 | 1.82 | 0.47 | 0.17 | 0.66 | 0.89 | 0.17 | 0.61 | 0.57 | 1.03 | 2.06 | 2.19 | 11.23 |
| 1969 | 2.88 | 0.88 | 0.57 | 2.05 | 1.40 | 0.86 | 0.02 | 0.00 | 0.42 | 1.13 | 0.36 | 1.88 | 12.45 |
| 1970 | 3.92 | 1.48 | 0.99 | 0.63 | 0.32 | 0.57 | 0.08 | 0.03 | 0.78 | 0.81 | 1.78 | 0.80 | 12.19 |
| 1971 | 0.84 | 0.69 | 1.11 | 1.15 | 1.41 | 1.73 | 0.32 | 0.14 | 1.03 | 0.70 | 2.73 | 2.59 | 14.44 |
| 1972 | 0.96 | 1.08 | 1.47 | 0.68 | 1.97 | 0.80 | 0.58 | 0.36 | 0.16 | 0.58 | 0.70 | 2.31 | 11.65 |
| 1973 | 0.50 | 1.09 | 0.43 | 0.27 | 0.67 | 0.15 | 0.01 | 0.08 | 1.34 | 1.71 | 3.76 | 4.68 | 14.69 |
| 1974 | 0.79 | 1.57 | 0.81 | 2.13 | 0.26 | 0.19 | 0.90 | T | 0.29 | 1.00 | 1.59 |  | 9.53 |
| 1975 | 3.53 | 1.30 | 0.65 | 0.97 | 0.30 | 0.28 | 0.73 | 0.67 | 0.00 | 1.80 | 0.84 | 1.98 | 13.05 |
| 1976 | 1.77 | 1.00 | 1.65 | 1.09 | 0.92 | 0.33 | 0.16 | 1.77 | 0.18 | 0.54 | 0.19 | 0.44 | 10.04 |
| 1977 | 0.48 | 0.64 | 1.51 | 0.18 | 1.87 | 0.37 | 0.06 | 2.58 | 1.17 | 0.51 | 2.00 | 2.42 | 13.79 |
| 1978 | 2.82 | 1.60 | 1.03 | 2.78 | 0.63 | 0.76 | 0.77 | 2.21 | 0.92 | T | 2.37 | 1.86 | 17.75 |
| 1979 | 1.43 | 1.72 | 1.18 | 1.17 | 0.39 | 0.21 | 0.09 | 1.40 | 0.30 | 1.68 | 1.83 | 0.62 | 12.02 |
| 1980 | 2.48 | 1.39 | 1.60 | 0.59 | 2.14 | 1.12 | 0.77 | 0.03 | 0.59 | 1.22 | 0.84 | 1.20 | 13.97 |
| 1981 | 0.89 | 1.35 | 1.43 | 1.20 | 1.59 | 1.53 | 0.94 | 0.03 | 1.31 | 0.86 | 1.91 | 2.31 | 15.35 |
| 1982 | 1.54 | 0.77 | 1.22 | 0.84 | 0.31 | 0.63 | 0.51 | 0.24 | 1.47 | 2.67 | 0.34 | 2.20 | 12.74 |
| 1983 | 0.86 | 1.57 | 2.82 | 0.70 | 0.73 | 1.44 | 0.52 | 0.56 | 0.46 | 0.84 | 1.67 | 3.42 | 15.59 |
| 1984 | 0.53 | 1.74 | 1.83 | 1.70 | 1.02 | 1.13 | 0.06 | 0.44 | 0.39 | 1.02 | 2.14 | 0.92 | 12.92 |
| 1985 | 0.44 | 1.33 | 1.13 | 0.37 | 0.44 | 0.69 | 0.34 | 0.26 | 2.10 | 0.89 | 2.11 | 1.27 | 11.37 |
| 1986 | 1.66 | 2.58 | 1.13 | 0.43 | 1.18 | 0.03 | 0.48 | 0.02 | 1.28 | 0.80 | 2.12 | 0.82 | 12.53 |
| 1987 | 1.48 | 0.64 | 0.85 | 0.47 | 0.85 | 0.38 | 0.34 | 0.05 | 0.03 | T | 0.76 | 1.23 | 7.62 |
| 1988 | 1.86 | 0.12 | 0.95 | 2.47 | 1.56 | 0.31 | 0.01 | T | 0.31 | 0.10 | 2.16 | 0.37 | 10.22 |
| 1989 | 1.86 | 1.36 | 1.72 | 1.57 | 1.47 | 0.57 | 0.09 | 1.25 | 0.12 | 0.84 | 1.27 | 0.21 | 12.33 |
| 1990 | 0.77 | 0.28 | 1.14 | 1.54 | 1.83 | 0.58 | 0.18 | 0.62 | T | 0.78 | 0.87 | 0.84 | 9.43 |
| Record Mean | 1.57 | 1.30 | 1.23 | 1.05 | 1.12 | 0.93 | 0.32 | 0.44 | 0.71 | 1.07 | 1.53 | 1.59 | 12.86 |

**TABLE 3**    AVERAGE TEMPERATURE (deg. F)    PENDLETON, OREGON

| YEAR | JAN | FEB | MAR | APR | MAY | JUNE | JULY | AUG | SEP | OCT | NOV | DEC | ANNUAL |
|---|---|---|---|---|---|---|---|---|---|---|---|---|---|
| 1961 | 37.1 | 45.5 | 46.3 | 50.2 | 57.4 | 71.6 | 75.8 | 76.9 | 59.5 | 50.0 | 36.3 | 36.9 | 53.7 |
| 1962 | 32.3 | 39.8 | 43.5 | 53.8 | 54.0 | 65.1 | 72.9 | 69.8 | 65.0 | 52.7 | 45.2 | 39.3 | 52.8 |
| 1963 | 27.0 | 42.8 | 45.4 | 48.0 | 58.9 | 65.8 | 68.6 | 71.7 | 67.6 | 55.5 | 44.4 | 32.7 | 52.4 |
| 1964 | 40.3 | 41.1 | 43.5 | 48.5 | 56.8 | 64.9 | 72.2 | 68.4 | 62.7 | 51.9 | 40.1 | 32.9 | 51.9 |
| 1965 | 35.4 | 41.1 | 40.6 | 52.9 | 58.0 | 66.0 | 73.8 | 71.5 | 60.1 | 57.5 | 44.7 | 36.9 | 53.2 |
| 1966 | 38.3 | 39.7 | 45.4 | 52.0 | 59.9 | 64.6 | 71.0 | 72.4 | 66.6 | 54.0 | 45.1 | 41.1 | 54.2 |
| 1967 | 42.4 | 42.5 | 43.5 | 45.8 | 58.5 | 69.7 | 76.4 | 79.7 | 69.9 | 54.9 | 41.1 | 36.8 | 55.1 |
| 1968 | 37.3 | 42.8 | 48.5 | 49.6 | 59.7 | 67.5 | 77.2 | 70.9 | 65.9 | 50.8 | 42.6 | 33.3 | 53.8 |
| 1969 | 22.0 | 35.5 | 44.6 | 49.8 | 61.7 | 69.8 | 72.5 | 70.1 | 64.7 | 49.3 | 43.2 | 34.9 | 51.5 |
| 1970 | 32.3 | 39.5 | 43.5 | 45.8 | 57.8 | 68.7 | 74.8 | 72.5 | 56.3 | 47.4 | 40.4 | 35.7 | 51.2 |
| 1971 | 40.0 | 39.8 | 40.5 | 49.4 | 60.5 | 63.3 | 76.1 | 76.8 | 59.1 | 51.4 | 43.7 | 36.9 | 53.1 |
| 1972 | 34.0 | 37.4 | 47.8 | 47.6 | 60.9 | 68.3 | 74.7 | 76.2 | 61.1 | 51.1 | 42.6 | 27.1 | 52.4 |
| 1973 | 31.3 | 38.4 | 45.8 | 50.3 | 61.3 | 66.9 | 75.3 | 71.7 | 64.0 | 52.8 | 42.6 | 41.5 | 53.5 |
| 1974 | 30.4 | 43.8 | 46.4 | 51.7 | 57.3 | 71.1 | 73.3 | 75.5 | 67.5 | 54.8 | 44.8 | 40.6 | 54.8 |
| 1975 | 37.1 | 39.0 | 45.2 | 47.5 | 59.3 | 65.8 | 78.4 | 70.1 | 67.0 | 54.3 | 42.3 | 40.5 | 53.9 |
| 1976 | 39.2 | 37.9 | 42.8 | 50.2 | 58.8 | 63.9 | 73.4 | 67.7 | 67.3 | 53.1 | 42.7 | 35.9 | 52.7 |
| 1977 | 26.3 | 41.5 | 44.2 | 55.3 | 55.1 | 69.1 | 70.3 | 74.9 | 58.5 | 50.0 | 38.3 | 34.8 | 51.5 |
| 1978 | 32.2 | 39.3 | 45.7 | 48.0 | 54.4 | 66.3 | 72.2 | 69.4 | 60.5 | 51.7 | 33.5 | 29.5 | 50.2 |
| 1979 | 15.3 | 37.7 | 46.0 | 50.4 | 59.5 | 66.6 | 72.8 | 70.6 | 65.5 | 54.3 | 34.7 | 38.2 | 51.0 |
| 1980 | 25.6 | 36.1 | 41.3 | 51.9 | 56.4 | 60.4 | 72.1 | 66.9 | 63.3 | 51.3 | 42.0 | 39.2 | 50.6 |
| 1981 | 36.2 | 38.9 | 45.7 | 50.4 | 56.0 | 61.6 | 69.2 | 74.3 | 63.8 | 50.6 | 44.2 | 37.2 | 52.3 |
| 1982 | 35.0 | 38.1 | 43.5 | 47.6 | 56.8 | 67.6 | 71.1 | 71.5 | 60.7 | 50.7 | 37.3 | 35.7 | 51.3 |
| 1983 | 40.8 | 43.8 | 47.8 | 49.0 | 58.9 | 62.7 | 68.4 | 72.7 | 58.9 | 52.5 | 45.9 | 23.2 | 52.1 |
| 1984 | 34.6 | 39.7 | 46.8 | 48.2 | 54.7 | 62.1 | 72.9 | 72.2 | 60.4 | 49.1 | 41.8 | 30.4 | 51.1 |
| 1985 | 26.3 | 33.5 | 43.2 | 53.1 | 58.5 | 65.6 | 77.4 | 68.1 | 57.0 | 50.3 | 26.5 | 19.5 | 48.3 |
| 1986 | 35.9 | 39.0 | 48.8 | 50.0 | 58.6 | 70.0 | 67.6 | 75.8 | 58.9 | 54.0 | 42.2 | 31.5 | 52.7 |
| 1987 | 30.4 | 39.1 | 46.4 | 53.9 | 59.7 | 67.2 | 68.9 | 70.6 | 66.2 | 54.1 | 42.6 | 32.7 | 52.7 |
| 1988 | 32.4 | 41.1 | 44.1 | 51.9 | 56.8 | 63.9 | 72.0 | 70.0 | 63.4 | 58.4 | 44.3 | 33.9 | 52.7 |
| 1989 | 38.3 | 25.1 | 42.5 | 52.9 | 55.9 | 65.9 | 70.3 | 68.8 | 63.6 | 51.8 | 44.6 | 33.2 | 51.1 |
| 1990 | 39.6 | 37.9 | 45.7 | 54.8 | 56.4 | 64.7 | 75.2 | 72.2 | 68.2 | 51.3 | 45.4 | 25.8 | 53.1 |
| Record Mean | 32.5 | 37.9 | 45.0 | 51.4 | 58.4 | 65.6 | 73.1 | 71.4 | 63.0 | 51.3 | 41.3 | 35.1 | 52.3 |
| Max | 39.5 | 46.0 | 55.1 | 63.5 | 71.5 | 79.6 | 89.5 | 87.3 | 77.4 | 64.7 | 49.6 | 41.7 | 63.8 |
| Min | 25.6 | 29.8 | 34.8 | 39.2 | 45.2 | 51.6 | 56.7 | 55.5 | 48.6 | 40.3 | 33.0 | 28.5 | 40.7 |

## REFERENCE NOTES FOR TABLES 1, 2, 3 and 6    (PENDLETON, OR)

### GENERAL

T - TRACE AMOUNT
BLANK ENTRIES DENOTE MISSING/UNREPORTED DATA.
# INDICATES A STATION OR INSTRUMENT RELOCATION.

### SPECIFIC

**TABLE 1**

(a) - LENGTH OF RECORD IN YEARS. ALTHOUGH INDIVIDUAL MONTHS MAY BE MISSING.

* LESS THAN .05

NORMALS — BASED ON THE 1951-1980 RECORD PERIOD.
EXTREMES — DATES ARE THE MOST RECENT OCCURRENCE.
WIND DIR. — NUMERALS SHOW TENS OF DEGREES CLOCKWISE FROM TRUE NORTH. "00" INDICATES CALM.
RESULTANT WIND DIRECTIONS ARE GIVEN TO WHOLE DEGREES.

**TABLE 3**
MAX AND MIN ARE LONG-TERM <u>MEAN DAILY MAXIMUM</u> AND <u>MEAN DAILY MINIMUM</u> TEMPERATURES.

### EXCEPTIONS

**TABLES 2, 3, and 6**

RECORD MEANS ARE THROUGH THE CURRENT YEAR, BEGINNING IN
1900 FOR TEMPERATURE
1900 FOR PRECIPITATION
1936 FOR SNOWFALL

**TABLE 4**

HEATING DEGREE DAYS Base 65 deg. F          PENDLETON, OREGON

| SEASON | JULY | AUG | SEP | OCT | NOV | DEC | JAN | FEB | MAR | APR | MAY | JUNE | TOTAL |
|---|---|---|---|---|---|---|---|---|---|---|---|---|---|
| 1961-62 | 0 | 0 | 167 | 458 | 855 | 863 | 1006 | 699 | 660 | 333 | 334 | 86 | 5461 |
| 1962-63 | 15 | 16 | 67 | 375 | 585 | 789 | 1170 | 613 | 598 | 504 | 205 | 61 | 4998 |
| 1963-64 | 8 | 9 | 57 | 308 | 611 | 993 | 760 | 688 | 662 | 487 | 257 | 70 | 4910 |
| 1964-65 | 6 | 30 | 92 | 397 | 742 | 990 | 912 | 664 | 750 | 357 | 223 | 44 | 5207 |
| 1965-66 | 15 | 19 | 153 | 226 | 602 | 865 | 820 | 702 | 597 | 382 | 194 | 75 | 4650 |
| 1966-67 | 19 | 10 | 48 | 333 | 590 | 736 | 691 | 621 | 659 | 571 | 218 | 21 | 4517 |
| 1967-68 | 0 | 0 | 24 | 306 | 711 | 866 | 850 | 638 | 505 | 462 | 174 | 46 | 4582 |
| 1968-69 | 0 | 15 | 73 | 434 | 664 | 977 | 1327 | 820 | 623 | 450 | 140 | 32 | 5555 |
| 1969-70 | 0 | 11 | 79 | 480 | 646 | 926 | 1007 | 707 | 660 | 568 | 228 | 83 | 5395 |
| 1970-71 | 0 | 1 | 260 | 540 | 731 | 903 | 767 | 698 | 755 | 460 | 169 | 95 | 5379 |
| 1971-72 | 11 | 9 | 182 | 428 | 633 | 868 | 955 | 793 | 528 | 515 | 171 | 29 | 5122 |
| 1972-73 | 5 | 4 | 165 | 422 | 663 | 1170 | 1036 | 738 | 588 | 434 | 169 | 73 | 5467 |
| 1973-74 | 1 | 16 | 97 | 372 | 666 | 721 | 1064 | 589 | 573 | 391 | 241 | 29 | 4760 |
| 1974-75 | 8 | 0 | 39 | 313 | 600 | 750 | 857 | 721 | 609 | 517 | 194 | 57 | 4665 |
| 1975-76 | 0 | 12 | 43 | 332 | 673 | 751 | 791 | 782 | 679 | 436 | 206 | 89 | 4794 |
| 1976-77 | 4 | 42 | 31 | 363 | 660 | 896 | 1192 | 653 | 639 | 299 | 301 | 26 | 5106 |
| 1977-78 | 20 | 35 | 200 | 461 | 792 | 927 | 1011 | 714 | 593 | 504 | 322 | 46 | 5625 |
| 1978-79 | 7 | 41 | 146 | 403 | 936 | 1094 | 1533 | 757 | 582 | 432 | 184 | 62 | 6177 |
| 1979-80 | 12 | 0 | 43 | 326 | 902 | 823 | 1210 | 829 | 728 | 388 | 267 | 141 | 5669 |
| 1980-81 | 4 | 33 | 88 | 438 | 681 | 794 | 886 | 724 | 593 | 435 | 275 | 126 | 5077 |
| 1981-82 | 20 | 1 | 128 | 440 | 617 | 855 | 919 | 747 | 662 | 515 | 256 | 72 | 5232 |
| 1982-83 | 22 | 7 | 171 | 435 | 825 | 901 | 741 | 588 | 528 | 470 | 242 | 95 | 5025 |
| 1983-84 | 42 | 1 | 180 | 381 | 569 | 1292 | 935 | 729 | 558 | 496 | 316 | 134 | 5633 |
| 1984-85 | 4 | 0 | 182 | 490 | 692 | 1065 | 1196 | 876 | 665 | 351 | 224 | 65 | 5810 |
| 1985-86 | 4 | 22 | 242 | 452 | 1149 | 1402 | 898 | 722 | 497 | 446 | 277 | 25 | 6136 |
| 1986-87 | 33 | 0 | 213 | 335 | 675 | 1031 | 1065 | 717 | 571 | 332 | 201 | 71 | 5244 |
| 1987-88 | 25 | 12 | 65 | 334 | 668 | 995 | 1004 | 689 | 637 | 387 | 264 | 126 | 5206 |
| 1988-89 | 22 | 4 | 120 | 208 | 616 | 957 | 821 | 1113 | 691 | 354 | 279 | 42 | 5227 |
| 1989-90 | 11 | 17 | 76 | 403 | 607 | 978 | 781 | 752 | 591 | 299 | 262 | 89 | 4866 |
| 1990-91 | 9 | 13 | 11 | 419 | 583 | 1211 | | | | | | | |

**TABLE 5**

COOLING DEGREE DAYS Base 65 deg. F          PENDLETON, OREGON

| YEAR | JAN | FEB | MAR | APR | MAY | JUNE | JULY | AUG | SEP | OCT | NOV | DEC | TOTAL |
|---|---|---|---|---|---|---|---|---|---|---|---|---|---|
| 1969 | 0 | 0 | 0 | 0 | 45 | 183 | 238 | 177 | 76 | 0 | 0 | 0 | 719 |
| 1970 | 0 | 0 | 0 | 0 | 11 | 201 | 313 | 243 | 4 | 0 | 0 | 0 | 772 |
| 1971 | 0 | 0 | 0 | 0 | 36 | 50 | 363 | 379 | 12 | 13 | 0 | 0 | 853 |
| 1972 | 0 | 0 | 0 | 0 | 50 | 134 | 314 | 358 | 55 | 0 | 0 | 0 | 911 |
| 1973 | 0 | 0 | 0 | 0 | 63 | 137 | 327 | 232 | 72 | 0 | 0 | 0 | 831 |
| 1974 | 0 | 0 | 0 | 0 | 9 | 219 | 272 | 332 | 122 | 4 | 0 | 0 | 958 |
| 1975 | 0 | 0 | 0 | 0 | 27 | 88 | 423 | 179 | 109 | 8 | 0 | 0 | 834 |
| 1976 | 0 | 0 | 0 | 0 | 20 | 53 | 270 | 129 | 103 | 3 | 0 | 0 | 578 |
| 1977 | 0 | 0 | 0 | 16 | 3 | 152 | 190 | 348 | 16 | 0 | 0 | 0 | 725 |
| 1978 | 0 | 0 | 0 | 0 | 1 | 93 | 236 | 182 | 16 | 0 | 0 | 0 | 528 |
| 1979 | 0 | 0 | 0 | 0 | 21 | 114 | 261 | 186 | 65 | 3 | 0 | 0 | 650 |
| 1980 | 0 | 0 | 0 | 2 | 5 | 13 | 232 | 101 | 44 | 20 | 0 | 0 | 417 |
| 1981 | 0 | 0 | 0 | 4 | 2 | 28 | 155 | 297 | 101 | 0 | 0 | 0 | 587 |
| 1982 | 0 | 0 | 0 | 0 | 7 | 158 | 219 | 215 | 47 | 0 | 0 | 0 | 646 |
| 1983 | 0 | 0 | 0 | 0 | 60 | 32 | 155 | 246 | 6 | 0 | 0 | 0 | 499 |
| 1984 | 0 | 0 | 0 | 0 | 7 | 55 | 256 | 231 | 51 | 3 | 0 | 0 | 603 |
| 1985 | 0 | 0 | 0 | 0 | 28 | 91 | 394 | 127 | 7 | 0 | 0 | 0 | 647 |
| 1986 | 0 | 0 | 0 | 2 | 88 | 184 | 121 | 341 | 35 | 1 | 0 | 0 | 772 |
| 1987 | 0 | 0 | 0 | 8 | 41 | 145 | 152 | 194 | 108 | 4 | 0 | 0 | 652 |
| 1988 | 0 | 0 | 0 | 0 | 16 | 98 | 246 | 164 | 78 | 9 | 0 | 0 | 611 |
| 1989 | 0 | 0 | 0 | 0 | 5 | 76 | 182 | 143 | 41 | 0 | 0 | 0 | 447 |
| 1990 | 0 | 0 | 0 | 0 | 4 | 92 | 330 | 245 | 114 | 3 | 0 | 0 | 788 |

**TABLE 6**

SNOWFALL (inches)          PENDLETON, OREGON

| SEASON | JULY | AUG | SEP | OCT | NOV | DEC | JAN | FEB | MAR | APR | MAY | JUNE | TOTAL |
|---|---|---|---|---|---|---|---|---|---|---|---|---|---|
| 1961-62 | 0.0 | 0.0 | 0.0 | T | 9.2 | 5.6 | 8.2 | 1.3 | 0.7 | T | 0.0 | 0.0 | 25.0 |
| 1962-63 | 0.0 | 0.0 | 0.0 | 0.0 | T | 12.1 | 0.3 | 0.3 | 1.0 | | 0.0 | 0.0 | 13.4 |
| 1963-64 | 0.0 | 0.0 | 0.0 | 0.0 | T | 2.0 | T | 0.3 | 0.5 | 1.0 | 0.0 | 0.0 | 2.8 |
| 1964-65 | 0.0 | 0.0 | 0.0 | 0.0 | 0.2 | 4.9 | 7.0 | 0.5 | 2.5 | 0.0 | 0.0 | 0.0 | 15.1 |
| 1965-66 | 0.0 | 0.0 | 0.0 | 0.0 | T | 0.1 | 11.5 | 1.6 | 0.2 | T | 0.0 | 0.0 | 13.4 |
| 1966-67 | 0.0 | 0.0 | 0.0 | T | 0.4 | 2.9 | 2.3 | 0.4 | 3.3 | T | 0.0 | 0.0 | 9.3 |
| 1967-68 | 0.0 | 0.0 | 0.0 | 0.0 | 0.8 | 2.5 | 1.3 | T | T | T | 0.0 | 0.0 | 4.6 |
| 1968-69 | 0.0 | 0.0 | 0.0 | 0.0 | T | 11.9 | 27.4 | 2.7 | T | 0.0 | 0.0 | 0.0 | 42.0 |
| 1969-70 | 0.0 | 0.0 | 0.0 | 0.0 | T | 3.5 | 9.9 | 3.8 | 1.3 | T | T | 0.0 | 18.5 |
| 1970-71 | 0.0 | 0.0 | 0.0 | 0.0 | 1.6 | 2.3 | 4.0 | 0.6 | 4.9 | T | T | 0.0 | 13.4 |
| 1971-72 | 0.0 | 0.0 | 0.0 | 1.9 | T | 11.8 | 3.6 | 6.2 | 0.1 | 1.1 | 0.0 | 0.0 | 24.7 |
| 1972-73 | 0.0 | 0.0 | 0.0 | T | T | 12.6 | 2.2 | 5.9 | T | 0.1 | 0.0 | 0.0 | 20.8 |
| 1973-74 | 0.0 | 0.0 | 0.0 | 3.2 | 9.1 | 5.3 | 2.6 | 0.5 | T | T | 0.0 | 0.0 | 20.7 |
| 1974-75 | 0.0 | 0.0 | 0.0 | 0.0 | T | T | 16.6 | 3.3 | T | 2.2 | T | 0.0 | 22.1 |
| 1975-76 | 0.0 | 0.0 | 0.0 | 0.0 | 5.2 | 3.0 | 0.3 | 0.3 | 0.1 | 0.0 | 0.0 | 0.0 | 8.9 |
| 1976-77 | 0.0 | 0.0 | 0.0 | 0.0 | 0.0 | 1.0 | 3.1 | 0.5 | 0.4 | 0.0 | 0.0 | 0.0 | 5.0 |
| 1977-78 | 0.0 | 0.0 | 0.0 | 0.0 | 8.5 | 11.5 | 6.1 | T | 3.9 | 0.0 | 0.0 | 0.0 | 30.0 |
| 1978-79 | 0.0 | 0.0 | 0.0 | 0.0 | 9.0 | 7.4 | 14.7 | 2.2 | T | 0.0 | 0.0 | 0.0 | 33.3 |
| 1979-80 | 0.0 | 0.0 | 0.0 | 0.0 | 4.3 | T | 16.6 | 0.9 | 3.9 | 0.0 | 0.0 | 0.0 | 25.7 |
| 1980-81 | 0.0 | 0.0 | 0.0 | 0.0 | 2.0 | 2.7 | 3.6 | 1.2 | 0.0 | 0.0 | 0.0 | 0.0 | 9.5 |
| 1981-82 | 0.0 | 0.0 | 0.0 | 0.0 | 0.6 | 5.1 | 5.7 | 1.5 | 1.9 | T | 0.0 | 0.0 | 14.8 |
| 1982-83 | 0.0 | 0.0 | 0.0 | 0.0 | T | 1.6 | 0.2 | 0.9 | 0.0 | 0.0 | 0.0 | 0.0 | 2.7 |
| 1983-84 | 0.0 | 0.0 | 0.0 | 0.0 | T | 26.6 | 1.0 | 1.2 | T | T | 0.0 | 0.0 | 28.8 |
| 1984-85 | 0.0 | 0.0 | 0.0 | 0.0 | T | 6.2 | 0.8 | 12.7 | 0.6 | T | 0.0 | 0.0 | 20.3 |
| 1985-86 | 0.0 | 0.0 | 0.0 | 0.0 | 14.9 | 9.1 | T | 7.6 | 0.0 | 0.0 | T | 0.0 | 31.6 |
| 1986-87 | 0.0 | 0.0 | 0.0 | 0.0 | 1.2 | 6.8 | 5.8 | 0.0 | T | 0.0 | 0.0 | 0.0 | 13.8 |
| 1987-88 | 0.0 | 0.0 | 0.0 | 0.0 | 0.3 | 2.3 | 10.6 | 0.0 | 1.5 | 0.0 | 0.0 | 0.0 | 14.7 |
| 1988-89 | 0.0 | 0.0 | 0.0 | 0.0 | T | T | 4.3 | 4.9 | 4.0 | 0.0 | T | 0.0 | 13.2 |
| 1989-90 | 0.0 | 0.0 | 0.0 | 0.0 | 0.0 | 1.0 | T | 2.0 | 1.3 | 0.0 | 0.0 | 0.0 | 4.3 |
| 1990-91 | 0.0 | 0.0 | 0.0 | 0.0 | T | 6.4 | | | | | | | |
| Record Mean | 0.0 | 0.0 | 0.0 | 0.1 | 1.8 | 4.1 | 7.2 | 3.4 | 1.0 | 0.1 | T | 0.0 | 17.6 |

**See Reference Notes, relative to all above tables, on preceding page.**

The Portland Weather Service Office is located 6 miles north-northeast of downtown Portland. Portland is situated about 65 miles inland from the Pacific Coast and midway between the northerly oriented low coast range on the west and the higher Cascade range on the east, each about 30 miles distant. The airport lies on the south bank of the Columbia River. The coast range provides limited shielding from the Pacific Ocean. The Cascade range provides a steep slope for orographic lift of moisture-laden westerly winds and consequent moderate rainfall, and also forms a barrier from continental air masses originating over the interior Columbia Basin. Airflow is usually northwesterly in Portland in spring and summer and southeasterly in fall and winter. The Portland Airport location is drier than most surrounding localities.

Portland has a very definite winter rainfall climate. Approximately 88 percent of the annual total occurs in the months of October through May, 9 percent in June and September, while only 3 percent comes in July and August. Precipitation is mostly rain, as on the average there are only five days each year with measurable snow. Snowfalls are seldom more than a couple of inches, and generally last only a few days.

The winter season is marked by relatively mild temperatures, cloudy skies and rain with southeasterly surface winds predominating. Summer produces pleasantly mild temperatures, northwesterly winds and very little precipitation. Fall and spring are transitional in nature. Fall and early winter are times with most frequent fog.

At all times, incursions of marine air are a frequent moderating influence. Outbreaks of continental high pressure from east of the Cascade Mountains produce strong easterly flow through the Columbia Gorge into the Portland area. In winter this brings the coldest weather with the extremes of low temperature registered in the cold air mass. Freezing rain and ice glaze are sometimes transitional effects. Temperatures below zero are very infrequent. In summer, hot, dry continental air brings the highest temperatures. Temperatures above 100 degrees are infrequent, but 90 degrees or higher are reached every year, but seldom persist for more than two or three days.

Destructive storms are infrequent in the Portland area. Surface winds seldom exceed gale force and rarely in the period of record have winds reached higher than 75 mph. Thunderstorms occur about once a month through the spring and summer months. Heavy downpours are infrequent but gentle rains occur almost daily during winter months.

Most rural areas around Portland are farmed for berries, green beans, and vegetables for fresh market and processing. The long growing season with mild temperatures and ample moisture favors local nursery and seed industries.

Based on the 1951–1980 period, the average first occurrence of 32 degrees Fahrenheit in the fall is November 7 and the average last occurrence in the spring is April 3.

## TABLE 1    NORMALS, MEANS AND EXTREMES

PORTLAND, OREGON

LATITUDE: 45°36'N    LONGITUDE: 122°36'W    ELEVATION: FT. GRND    21 BARO    27    TIME ZONE: PACIFIC    WBAN: 24229

| | (a) | JAN | FEB | MAR | APR | MAY | JUNE | JULY | AUG | SEP | OCT | NOV | DEC | YEAR |
|---|---|---|---|---|---|---|---|---|---|---|---|---|---|---|
| **TEMPERATURE °F:** | | | | | | | | | | | | | | |
| Normals | | | | | | | | | | | | | | |
| -Daily Maximum | | 44.3 | 50.4 | 54.5 | 60.2 | 66.9 | 72.7 | 79.5 | 78.6 | 74.2 | 63.9 | 52.3 | 46.4 | 62.0 |
| -Daily Minimum | | 33.5 | 36.0 | 37.4 | 40.6 | 46.4 | 52.2 | 55.8 | 55.8 | 51.1 | 44.6 | 38.6 | 35.4 | 44.0 |
| -Monthly | | 38.9 | 43.2 | 45.9 | 50.4 | 56.7 | 62.5 | 67.7 | 67.3 | 62.7 | 54.3 | 45.5 | 40.9 | 53.0 |
| Extremes | | | | | | | | | | | | | | |
| -Record Highest | 49 | 63 | 71 | 80 | 87 | 100 | 100 | 107 | 107 | 105 | 92 | 73 | 64 | 107 |
| -Year | | 1986 | 1988 | 1947 | 1957 | 1983 | 1982 | 1965 | 1981 | 1988 | 1987 | 1975 | 1980 | AUG 1981 |
| -Record Lowest | 49 | -2 | -3 | 19 | 29 | 29 | 39 | 43 | 44 | 34 | 26 | 13 | 6 | -3 |
| -Year | | 1950 | 1950 | 1989 | 1955 | 1954 | 1966 | 1955 | 1980 | 1965 | 1971 | 1985 | 1964 | FEB 1950 |
| **NORMAL DEGREE DAYS:** | | | | | | | | | | | | | | |
| Heating (base 65°F) | | 809 | 610 | 592 | 438 | 263 | 118 | 35 | 51 | 111 | 332 | 585 | 747 | 4691 |
| Cooling (base 65°F) | | 0 | 0 | 0 | 0 | 6 | 43 | 119 | 122 | 42 | 0 | 0 | 0 | 332 |
| **% OF POSSIBLE SUNSHINE** | 40 | 28 | 38 | 47 | 53 | 58 | 57 | 70 | 66 | 61 | 43 | 29 | 23 | 48 |
| **MEAN SKY COVER (tenths)** | | | | | | | | | | | | | | |
| Sunrise - Sunset | 41 | 8.5 | 8.3 | 8.1 | 7.7 | 7.2 | 6.7 | 4.8 | 5.2 | 5.5 | 7.1 | 8.2 | 8.7 | 7.2 |
| **MEAN NUMBER OF DAYS:** | | | | | | | | | | | | | | |
| Sunrise to Sunset | | | | | | | | | | | | | | |
| -Clear | 41 | 2.8 | 2.6 | 3.0 | 3.7 | 4.7 | 6.4 | 12.7 | 11.2 | 10.2 | 5.4 | 2.9 | 2.1 | 67.7 |
| -Partly Cloudy | 41 | 3.5 | 3.7 | 4.7 | 5.8 | 7.3 | 7.5 | 8.7 | 9.6 | 8.0 | 7.4 | 4.1 | 3.2 | 73.6 |
| -Cloudy | 41 | 24.7 | 22.0 | 23.4 | 20.5 | 19.0 | 16.0 | 9.6 | 10.2 | 11.8 | 18.2 | 23.0 | 25.7 | 224.0 |
| Precipitation | | | | | | | | | | | | | | |
| .01 inches or more | 49 | 18.2 | 16.1 | 17.2 | 14.0 | 11.7 | 9.1 | 3.8 | 4.9 | 7.9 | 12.4 | 17.9 | 18.7 | 151.9 |
| Snow,Ice pellets | | | | | | | | | | | | | | |
| 1.0 inches or more | 49 | 1.1 | 0.3 | 0.1 | 0.0 | 0.* | 0.0 | 0.0 | 0.0 | 0.0 | 0.0 | 0.1 | 0.5 | 2.2 |
| Thunderstorms | 49 | 0.* | 0.1 | 0.5 | 0.9 | 1.5 | 0.9 | 0.7 | 1.0 | 0.7 | 0.4 | 0.3 | 0.* | 7.0 |
| Heavy Fog Visibility | | | | | | | | | | | | | | |
| 1/4 mile or less | 47 | 4.2 | 3.8 | 2.3 | 1.1 | 0.1 | 0.1 | 0.1 | 0.2 | 2.8 | 7.7 | 6.1 | 4.9 | 33.5 |
| Temperature °F | | | | | | | | | | | | | | |
| -Maximum | | | | | | | | | | | | | | |
| 90° and above | 49 | 0.0 | 0.0 | 0.0 | 0.0 | 0.3 | 1.2 | 3.5 | 3.7 | 1.7 | 0.1 | 0.0 | 0.0 | 10.4 |
| 32° and below | 49 | 2.3 | 0.3 | 0.* | 0.0 | 0.0 | 0.0 | 0.0 | 0.0 | 0.0 | 0.0 | 0.3 | 0.8 | 3.7 |
| -Minimum | | | | | | | | | | | | | | |
| 32° and below | 49 | 13.3 | 8.3 | 4.9 | 1.1 | 0.1 | 0.0 | 0.0 | 0.0 | 0.0 | 0.6 | 5.2 | 9.5 | 42.9 |
| 0° and below | 49 | 0.* | 0.* | 0.0 | 0.0 | 0.0 | 0.0 | 0.0 | 0.0 | 0.0 | 0.0 | 0.0 | 0.0 | * |
| **AVG. STATION PRESS.(mb)** | 17 | 1018.6 | 1016.7 | 1015.3 | 1016.9 | 1016.6 | 1016.3 | 1016.3 | 1015.1 | 1015.3 | 1017.1 | 1016.5 | 1018.7 | 1016.6 |
| **RELATIVE HUMIDITY (%)** | | | | | | | | | | | | | | |
| Hour 04 | 49 | 86 | 86 | 86 | 86 | 85 | 84 | 82 | 84 | 87 | 90 | 88 | 87 | 86 |
| Hour 10 (Local Time) | 49 | 82 | 80 | 73 | 68 | 66 | 65 | 62 | 64 | 67 | 79 | 82 | 84 | 73 |
| Hour 16 | 49 | 75 | 67 | 60 | 55 | 53 | 49 | 45 | 46 | 49 | 63 | 74 | 79 | 60 |
| Hour 22 | 49 | 83 | 81 | 78 | 75 | 74 | 71 | 68 | 70 | 75 | 84 | 84 | 85 | 77 |
| **PRECIPITATION (inches):** | | | | | | | | | | | | | | |
| Water Equivalent | | | | | | | | | | | | | | |
| -Normal | | 6.16 | 3.93 | 3.61 | 2.31 | 2.08 | 1.47 | 0.46 | 1.13 | 1.61 | 3.05 | 5.17 | 6.41 | 37.39 |
| -Maximum Monthly | 49 | 12.83 | 9.46 | 7.52 | 4.72 | 4.57 | 4.06 | 2.68 | 4.53 | 4.30 | 8.04 | 11.57 | 11.12 | 12.83 |
| -Year | | 1953 | 1949 | 1957 | 1955 | 1945 | 1984 | 1983 | 1968 | 1986 | 1947 | 1942 | 1968 | JAN 1953 |
| -Minimum Monthly | 49 | 0.06 | 0.78 | 1.10 | 0.53 | 0.46 | 0.03 | 0.00 | T | T | 0.19 | 0.77 | 1.38 | 0.00 |
| -Year | | 1985 | 1964 | 1965 | 1956 | 1982 | 1951 | 1967 | 1970 | 1975 | 1988 | 1976 | 1976 | JUL 1967 |
| -Maximum in 24 hrs | 49 | 2.61 | 2.36 | 1.83 | 1.47 | 1.47 | 1.82 | 1.09 | 1.54 | 2.38 | 2.18 | 2.62 | 2.59 | 2.62 |
| -Year | | 1974 | 1987 | 1943 | 1962 | 1968 | 1958 | 1978 | 1977 | 1982 | 1941 | 1973 | 1977 | NOV 1973 |
| Snow,Ice pellets | | | | | | | | | | | | | | |
| -Maximum Monthly | 49 | 41.4 | 13.2 | 12.9 | T | 0.6 | T | 0.0 | T | T | 0.2 | 8.2 | 15.7 | 41.4 |
| -Year | | 1950 | 1949 | 1951 | 1989 | 1953 | 1981 | | 1989 | 1949 | 1950 | 1955 | 1968 | JAN 1950 |
| -Maximum in 24 hrs | 49 | 10.6 | 3.2 | 7.7 | T | 0.5 | T | 0.0 | T | T | 0.2 | 7.4 | 8.0 | 10.6 |
| -Year | | 1950 | 1962 | 1951 | 1989 | 1953 | 1981 | | 1989 | 1949 | 1950 | 1977 | 1964 | JAN 1950 |
| **WIND:** | | | | | | | | | | | | | | |
| Mean Speed (mph) | 41 | 9.9 | 9.1 | 8.3 | 7.3 | 7.1 | 7.1 | 7.6 | 7.1 | 6.5 | 6.5 | 8.6 | 9.5 | 7.9 |
| Prevailing Direction | | | | | | | | | | | | | | |
| through 1963 | | ESE | ESE | ESE | NW | NW | NW | NW | NW | NW | ESE | ESE | ESE | ESE |
| Fastest Mile | | | | | | | | | | | | | | |
| -Direction (!!!) | 39 | S | SW | S | S | SW | SW | SW | SW | S | S | SW | S | S |
| -Speed (MPH) | 39 | 54 | 61 | 57 | 60 | 42 | 40 | 33 | 29 | 61 | 88 | 56 | 57 | 88 |
| -Year | | 1951 | 1958 | 1963 | 1957 | 1960 | 1958 | 1983 | 1961 | 1963 | 1962 | 1961 | 1951 | OCT 1962 |
| Peak Gust | | | | | | | | | | | | | | |
| -Direction (!!!) | 6 | S | SE | SW | SE | SW | W | W | NW | E | E | SW | E | SE |
| -Speed (mph) | 6 | 53 | 61 | 43 | 43 | 41 | 32 | 31 | 28 | 39 | 37 | 52 | 53 | 61 |
| -Date | | 1988 | 1989 | 1985 | 1989 | 1985 | 1989 | 1987 | 1986 | 1985 | 1987 | 1984 | 1985 | FEB 1989 |

**See Reference Notes to this table on the following page.**

# PORTLAND, OREGON

## TABLE 2 — PRECIPITATION (inches)   PORTLAND, OREGON

| YEAR | JAN | FEB | MAR | APR | MAY | JUNE | JULY | AUG | SEP | OCT | NOV | DEC | ANNUAL |
|---|---|---|---|---|---|---|---|---|---|---|---|---|---|
| 1961 | 4.50 | 8.92 | 6.04 | 3.59 | 2.80 | 0.47 | 0.42 | 1.07 | 0.64 | 2.89 | 4.67 | 5.94 | 41.95 |
| 1962 | 1.58 | 3.43 | 4.25 | 3.15 | 2.56 | 0.78 | 0.06 | 1.49 | 1.66 | 3.31 | 9.32 | 2.59 | 34.18 |
| 1963 | 2.27 | 3.48 | 4.69 | 3.78 | 2.74 | 1.71 | 1.17 | 0.87 | 0.75 | 3.04 | 5.64 | 3.60 | 33.74 |
| 1964 | 9.51 | 0.78 | 2.30 | 1.56 | 1.04 | 1.96 | 0.68 | 0.90 | 1.61 | 0.84 | 6.78 | 9.92 | 37.88 |
| 1965 | 7.44 | 2.22 | 1.10 | 2.20 | 1.31 | 0.83 | 0.44 | 0.73 | 0.01 | 2.03 | 5.64 | 7.34 | 31.29 |
| 1966 | 5.74 | 1.70 | 4.71 | 0.85 | 0.91 | 1.02 | 1.19 | 0.59 | 1.70 | 3.06 | 5.50 | 6.89 | 33.86 |
| 1967 | 6.21 | 2.02 | 4.31 | 2.17 | 1.02 | 1.01 | 0.00 | T | 0.76 | 4.72 | 2.27 | 4.75 | 29.24 |
| 1968 | 4.58 | 6.64 | 2.68 | 1.91 | 3.63 | 2.20 | 0.14 | 4.53 | 2.20 | 5.03 | 6.23 | 11.12 | 50.89 |
| 1969 | 7.60 | 3.14 | 1.13 | 2.28 | 1.61 | 2.99 | 0.14 | 0.04 | 3.86 | 3.02 | 3.18 | 8.12 | 37.11 |
| 1970 | 11.81 | 4.77 | 2.58 | 2.94 | 1.55 | 0.49 | 0.05 | T | 1.10 | 2.85 | 5.72 | 7.49 | 41.35 |
| 1971 | 7.09 | 3.36 | 4.87 | 2.72 | 1.00 | 1.76 | 0.26 | 0.95 | 3.53 | 2.37 | 5.76 | 8.05 | 41.72 |
| 1972 | 5.71 | 4.08 | 5.41 | 2.98 | 2.23 | 0.68 | 0.56 | 0.67 | 3.06 | 0.87 | 3.78 | 8.79 | 38.82 |
| 1973 | 3.69 | 1.94 | 2.45 | 1.33 | 1.43 | 1.45 | 0.06 | 1.41 | 3.29 | 3.14 | 11.55 | 9.93 | 41.67 |
| 1974 | 8.51 | 4.61 | 5.65 | 1.76 | 1.74 | 0.80 | 2.01 | 0.07 | 0.21 | 2.14 | 6.73 | 6.05 | 40.28 |
| 1975 | 8.43 | 4.75 | 3.45 | 1.88 | 1.35 | 1.13 | 0.43 | 2.10 | T | 4.76 | 4.10 | 6.68 | 39.06 |
| 1976 | 5.14 | 4.92 | 2.93 | 2.34 | 2.29 | 0.78 | 0.66 | 3.29 | 0.73 | 1.48 | 0.77 | 1.38 | 26.71 |
| 1977 | 1.07 | 2.49 | 3.50 | 1.04 | 4.30 | 0.83 | 0.39 | 3.26 | 3.33 | 2.28 | 5.56 | 8.98 | 37.03 |
| 1978 | 4.85 | 3.28 | 1.49 | 3.96 | 3.17 | 1.69 | 1.36 | 2.05 | 2.07 | 0.36 | 3.83 | 2.51 | 30.62 |
| 1979 | 2.55 | 6.53 | 2.51 | 2.47 | 2.41 | 0.64 | 0.25 | 1.18 | 1.75 | 4.85 | 3.38 | 7.23 | 35.75 |
| 1980 | 8.51 | 4.01 | 3.11 | 2.58 | 2.19 | 2.50 | 0.19 | 0.39 | 1.56 | 1.18 | 6.47 | 9.72 | 42.41 |
| 1981 | 1.47 | 3.86 | 2.33 | 1.79 | 2.25 | 3.23 | 0.24 | 0.15 | 1.86 | 4.12 | 4.62 | 8.37 | 34.29 |
| 1982 | 6.31 | 5.98 | 2.38 | 3.56 | 0.46 | 1.66 | 0.94 | 1.66 | 3.98 | 4.44 | 8.16 | 3.51 | 43.04 |
| 1983 | 6.23 | 7.78 | 6.80 | 1.87 | 1.30 | 1.95 | 2.68 | 2.29 | 0.39 | 1.95 | 8.65 | 5.30 | 47.19 |
| 1984 | 2.01 | 3.93 | 3.19 | 3.20 | 3.41 | 4.06 | T | 0.09 | 1.46 | 3.85 | 9.74 | 2.56 | 37.50 |
| 1985 | 0.06 | 1.79 | 3.08 | 1.07 | 1.52 | 2.34 | 0.55 | 0.48 | 2.76 | 2.75 | 3.89 | 2.19 | 22.48 |
| 1986 | 4.65 | 5.31 | 2.60 | 1.91 | 2.19 | 0.23 | 1.20 | 0.10 | 4.30 | 1.99 | 6.26 | 4.30 | 35.04 |
| 1987 | 6.93 | 2.45 | 4.91 | 1.94 | 1.63 | 0.14 | 1.03 | 0.35 | 0.30 | 0.27 | 1.96 | 8.00 | 29.91 |
| 1988 | 4.95 | 1.17 | 3.13 | 4.57 | 2.53 | 2.34 | 0.69 | 0.10 | 1.76 | 0.19 | 7.92 | 2.37 | 31.72 |
| 1989 | 3.30 | 2.84 | 6.73 | 2.08 | 2.87 | 0.78 | 0.91 | 1.07 | 1.48 | 1.73 | 3.18 | 3.08 | 30.05 |
| 1990 | 7.95 | 3.43 | 2.52 | 2.31 | 2.37 | 1.94 | 0.32 | 0.95 | 0.34 | 4.65 | 3.68 | 2.40 | 32.86 |
| Record Mean | 5.52 | 4.01 | 3.64 | 2.28 | 2.11 | 1.58 | 0.57 | 0.94 | 1.72 | 3.14 | 5.47 | 5.94 | 36.92 |

## TABLE 3 — AVERAGE TEMPERATURE (deg. F)   PORTLAND, OREGON

| YEAR | JAN | FEB | MAR | APR | MAY | JUNE | JULY | AUG | SEP | OCT | NOV | DEC | ANNUAL |
|---|---|---|---|---|---|---|---|---|---|---|---|---|---|
| 1961 | 43.6 | 47.2 | 47.7 | 50.1 | 56.6 | 65.3 | 69.4 | 70.3 | 59.5 | 53.3 | 42.9 | 40.9 | 53.9 |
| 1962 | 38.6 | 43.0 | 45.3 | 52.6 | 53.9 | 61.6 | 66.4 | 66.0 | 63.3 | 55.1 | 47.6 | 42.6 | 53.0 |
| 1963 | 35.0 | 47.8 | 45.2 | 48.6 | 56.6 | 60.0 | 63.1 | 66.1 | 65.1 | 54.2 | 46.0 | 38.0 | 52.1 |
| 1964 | 40.9 | 40.1 | 43.8 | 46.7 | 52.6 | 58.7 | 64.5 | 63.7 | 58.4 | 53.2 | 41.0 | 37.0 | 50.1 |
| 1965 | 40.2 | 43.4 | 47.6 | 51.8 | 54.3 | 61.8 | 69.7 | 68.6 | 60.4 | 57.5 | 49.7 | 39.5 | 53.7 |
| 1966 | 40.3 | 42.8 | 47.2 | 50.6 | 57.0 | 62.4 | 66.4 | 67.5 | 64.4 | 53.7 | 47.1 | 44.2 | 53.7 |
| 1967 | 43.6 | 43.7 | 44.0 | 46.9 | 57.1 | 65.9 | 69.3 | 72.9 | 66.4 | 54.8 | 46.2 | 40.4 | 54.3 |
| 1968 | 39.3 | 48.2 | 48.2 | 48.0 | 56.3 | 62.2 | 66.8 | 65.8 | 61.5 | 52.1 | 46.5 | 37.3 | 52.8 |
| 1969 | 31.9 | 39.7 | 46.5 | 50.1 | 59.5 | 66.5 | 66.6 | 66.1 | 63.4 | 53.3 | 47.2 | 42.9 | 52.8 |
| 1970 | 40.6 | 46.0 | 46.9 | 48.4 | 57.0 | 65.9 | 69.2 | 68.2 | 60.7 | 53.0 | 47.1 | 40.0 | 53.6 |
| 1971 | 40.4 | 42.8 | 43.7 | 49.6 | 56.8 | 60.2 | 69.2 | 71.6 | 60.8 | 52.4 | 45.5 | 40.4 | 52.8 |
| 1972 | 39.2 | 43.8 | 49.8 | 48.0 | 60.2 | 64.0 | 70.9 | 71.7 | 61.2 | 53.0 | 48.2 | 37.4 | 53.9 |
| 1973 | 39.0 | 44.9 | 47.9 | 52.3 | 59.4 | 63.9 | 70.3 | 65.9 | 64.4 | 54.3 | 44.2 | 44.7 | 54.2 |
| 1974 | 38.0 | 43.0 | 47.2 | 51.3 | 55.7 | 64.4 | 67.1 | 68.9 | 67.3 | 55.2 | 48.1 | 44.1 | 54.2 |
| 1975 | 41.5 | 41.2 | 45.0 | 47.3 | 57.5 | 61.9 | 69.0 | 65.3 | 65.7 | 53.5 | 46.0 | 42.7 | 53.1 |
| 1976 | 42.2 | 42.1 | 44.4 | 50.3 | 56.6 | 60.4 | 67.2 | 65.5 | 64.2 | 54.7 | 47.0 | 39.5 | 52.8 |
| 1977 | 35.7 | 44.6 | 45.5 | 52.9 | 53.8 | 63.9 | 66.3 | 71.7 | 60.8 | 53.8 | 43.3 | 42.0 | 52.9 |
| 1978 | 40.1 | 44.7 | 49.1 | 50.5 | 54.7 | 65.1 | 68.4 | 67.6 | 60.9 | 54.7 | 39.1 | 35.3 | 52.5 |
| 1979 | 30.7 | 42.9 | 50.8 | 53.1 | 60.1 | 65.1 | 70.5 | 68.6 | 66.3 | 58.1 | 45.0 | 44.4 | 54.6 |
| 1980 | 35.1 | 42.5 | 46.3 | 53.8 | 57.3 | 60.7 | 68.9 | 66.4 | 63.6 | 56.0 | 48.5 | 44.0 | 53.6 |
| 1981 | 43.9 | 44.0 | 48.8 | 52.5 | 57.5 | 61.8 | 67.5 | 72.2 | 64.9 | 53.3 | 48.8 | 42.7 | 54.8 |
| 1982 | 39.7 | 43.6 | 48.5 | 49.0 | 57.6 | 66.0 | 67.5 | 68.6 | 63.2 | 54.9 | 44.4 | 41.7 | 53.7 |
| 1983 | 44.4 | 47.3 | 50.7 | 52.7 | 60.4 | 62.8 | 66.5 | 69.1 | 61.5 | 54.2 | 49.3 | 36.4 | 54.6 |
| 1984 | 42.2 | 45.9 | 51.1 | 50.4 | 56.4 | 62.2 | 69.4 | 69.4 | 63.7 | 52.9 | 46.7 | 38.3 | 54.0 |
| 1985 | 36.1 | 41.1 | 45.8 | 53.9 | 58.3 | 64.4 | 74.1 | 69.3 | 60.8 | 52.7 | 37.3 | 33.0 | 52.2 |
| 1986 | 42.5 | 43.7 | 51.3 | 50.2 | 57.6 | 66.3 | 65.3 | 72.3 | 61.5 | 57.0 | 47.7 | 40.6 | 54.7 |
| 1987 | 39.6 | 45.2 | 48.7 | 54.2 | 60.4 | 66.5 | 67.2 | 70.5 | 65.5 | 58.2 | 47.8 | 39.1 | 55.3 |
| 1988 | 39.0 | 44.7 | 47.2 | 52.2 | 56.4 | 62.4 | 68.4 | 68.0 | 64.0 | 58.3 | 47.5 | 42.0 | 54.2 |
| 1989 | 42.2 | 36.0 | 45.6 | 56.0 | 58.0 | 64.3 | 65.5 | 66.1 | 65.3 | 54.9 | 48.6 | 40.3 | 53.6 |
| 1990 | 43.4 | 41.9 | 49.4 | 54.5 | 56.7 | 63.6 | 71.2 | 70.9 | 67.0 | 53.9 | 48.4 | 34.7 | 54.6 |
| Record Mean | 38.9 | 43.1 | 46.6 | 51.1 | 57.1 | 61.3 | 66.5 | 66.4 | 63.0 | 54.3 | 45.8 | 40.6 | 52.9 |
| Max | 44.6 | 50.3 | 55.1 | 60.8 | 67.2 | 71.3 | 77.9 | 77.7 | 74.4 | 63.6 | 52.4 | 46.0 | 61.8 |
| Min | 33.2 | 35.9 | 38.1 | 41.4 | 47.0 | 51.2 | 55.0 | 55.1 | 51.5 | 45.0 | 39.2 | 35.2 | 44.0 |

## REFERENCE NOTES FOR TABLES 1, 2, 3 and 6          (PORTLAND, OR)

### GENERAL

T - TRACE AMOUNT
BLANK ENTRIES DENOTE MISSING/UNREPORTED DATA.
# INDICATES A STATION OR INSTRUMENT RELOCATION.

### SPECIFIC

#### TABLE 1

(a) - LENGTH OF RECORD IN YEARS. ALTHOUGH
    INDIVIDUAL MONTHS MAY BE MISSING.

* LESS THAN .05

NORMALS — BASED ON THE 1951-1980 RECORD PERIOD.
EXTREMES — DATES ARE THE MOST RECENT OCCURRENCE.
WIND DIR. — NUMERALS SHOW TENS OF DEGREES
    CLOCKWISE FROM TRUE NORTH.
    "00" INDICATES CALM.
RESULTANT WIND DIRECTIONS ARE GIVEN TO WHOLE DEGREES.

#### TABLE 3

MAX AND MIN ARE LONG-TERM MEAN DAILY MAXIMUM
AND MEAN DAILY MINIMUM TEMPERATURES.

### EXCEPTIONS

**TABLES 2, 3, and 6**

RECORD MEANS ARE THROUGH THE CURRENT YEAR,
BEGINNING IN   1941 FOR TEMPERATURE
              1941 FOR PRECIPITATION
              1941 FOR SNOWFALL

HEATING DEGREE DAYS Base 65 deg. F    PORTLAND, OREGON

**TABLE 4**

| SEASON | JULY | AUG | SEP | OCT | NOV | DEC | JAN | FEB | MAR | APR | MAY | JUNE | TOTAL |
|---|---|---|---|---|---|---|---|---|---|---|---|---|---|
| 1961-62 | 11 | 4 | 169 | 359 | 656 | 740 | 811 | 613 | 605 | 364 | 339 | 118 | 4789 |
| 1962-63 | 49 | 19 | 71 | 299 | 515 | 687 | 925 | 477 | 606 | 486 | 272 | 168 | 4574 |
| 1963-64 | 72 | 24 | 41 | 329 | 561 | 830 | 739 | 718 | 650 | 539 | 380 | 182 | 5065 |
| 1964-65 | 67 | 81 | 191 | 358 | 711 | 860 | 761 | 599 | 533 | 388 | 325 | 113 | 4987 |
| 1965-66 | 22 | 16 | 139 | 227 | 451 | 786 | 759 | 620 | 545 | 425 | 249 | 99 | 4338 |
| 1966-67 | 27 | 16 | 56 | 345 | 531 | 635 | 655 | 591 | 647 | 535 | 246 | 50 | 4334 |
| 1967-68 | 3 | 0 | 29 | 306 | 558 | 758 | 789 | 482 | 515 | 500 | 261 | 110 | 4311 |
| 1968-69 | 17 | 43 | 123 | 395 | 544 | 852 | 1022 | 703 | 570 | 442 | 178 | 51 | 4940 |
| 1969-70 | 17 | 22 | 85 | 357 | 526 | 678 | 751 | 526 | 553 | 493 | 246 | 71 | 4325 |
| 1970-71 | 14 | 14 | 130 | 369 | 530 | 771 | 757 | 615 | 653 | 454 | 253 | 149 | 4709 |
| 1971-72 | 33 | 5 | 123 | 388 | 578 | 756 | 793 | 607 | 466 | 501 | 174 | 61 | 4485 |
| 1972-73 | 10 | 6 | 153 | 363 | 497 | 848 | 799 | 560 | 525 | 378 | 202 | 89 | 4430 |
| 1973-74 | 6 | 47 | 59 | 326 | 618 | 624 | 832 | 610 | 545 | 403 | 282 | 72 | 4424 |
| 1974-75 | 32 | 16 | 29 | 301 | 500 | 640 | 722 | 660 | 615 | 523 | 240 | 127 | 4405 |
| 1975-76 | 24 | 41 | 48 | 354 | 565 | 686 | 698 | 658 | 632 | 437 | 258 | 155 | 4556 |
| 1976-77 | 15 | 41 | 47 | 319 | 536 | 783 | 901 | 564 | 596 | 358 | 340 | 68 | 4568 |
| 1977-78 | 40 | 19 | 131 | 339 | 644 | 707 | 764 | 561 | 485 | 430 | 317 | 58 | 4495 |
| 1978-79 | 29 | 26 | 134 | 312 | 772 | 915 | 1058 | 615 | 434 | 351 | 162 | 57 | 4865 |
| 1979-80 | 8 | 2 | 19 | 214 | 592 | 631 | 920 | 647 | 575 | 329 | 232 | 125 | 4294 |
| 1980-81 | 15 | 25 | 64 | 284 | 485 | 644 | 650 | 583 | 494 | 372 | 229 | 108 | 3953 |
| 1981-82 | 23 | 5 | 76 | 355 | 478 | 687 | 780 | 596 | 502 | 472 | 229 | 71 | 4274 |
| 1982-83 | 22 | 10 | 99 | 307 | 614 | 715 | 635 | 492 | 435 | 363 | 184 | 81 | 3957 |
| 1983-84 | 27 | 2 | 109 | 325 | 463 | 880 | 701 | 546 | 425 | 430 | 269 | 115 | 4292 |
| 1984-85 | 9 | 2 | 80 | 377 | 539 | 820 | 893 | 664 | 588 | 327 | 213 | 62 | 4574 |
| 1985-86 | 0 | 7 | 124 | 373 | 826 | 982 | 691 | 591 | 417 | 437 | 265 | 43 | 4756 |
| 1986-87 | 37 | 0 | 148 | 242 | 510 | 750 | 780 | 550 | 495 | 321 | 173 | 51 | 4057 |
| 1987-88 | 22 | 2 | 54 | 214 | 479 | 798 | 801 | 581 | 544 | 380 | 272 | 109 | 4256 |
| 1988-89 | 33 | 15 | 91 | 208 | 518 | 705 | 699 | 805 | 594 | 263 | 219 | 77 | 4227 |
| 1989-90 | 32 | 27 | 44 | 306 | 486 | 759 | 664 | 641 | 476 | 308 | 251 | 78 | 4072 |
| 1990-91 | 10 | 5 | 14 | 336 | 492 | 933 | | | | | | | |

**TABLE 5**    COOLING DEGREE DAYS Base 65 deg. F    PORTLAND, OREGON

| YEAR | JAN | FEB | MAR | APR | MAY | JUNE | JULY | AUG | SEP | OCT | NOV | DEC | TOTAL |
|---|---|---|---|---|---|---|---|---|---|---|---|---|---|
| 1969 | 0 | 0 | 0 | 0 | 13 | 102 | 74 | 65 | 43 | 0 | 0 | 0 | 297 |
| 1970 | 0 | 0 | 0 | 0 | 8 | 106 | 150 | 120 | 8 | 2 | 0 | 0 | 394 |
| 1971 | 0 | 0 | 0 | 0 | 5 | 14 | 170 | 217 | 7 | 3 | 0 | 0 | 416 |
| 1972 | 0 | 0 | 0 | 0 | 27 | 39 | 200 | 221 | 44 | 0 | 0 | 0 | 531 |
| 1973 | 0 | 0 | 0 | 0 | 34 | 65 | 178 | 81 | 45 | 0 | 0 | 0 | 403 |
| 1974 | 0 | 0 | 0 | 0 | 1 | 60 | 102 | 144 | 102 | 0 | 0 | 0 | 409 |
| 1975 | 0 | 0 | 0 | 0 | 12 | 39 | 157 | 57 | 75 | 2 | 0 | 0 | 342 |
| 1976 | 0 | 0 | 0 | 0 | 4 | 23 | 89 | 66 | 30 | 4 | 0 | 0 | 216 |
| 1977 | 0 | 0 | 0 | 0 | 0 | 42 | 90 | 233 | 10 | 0 | 0 | 0 | 375 |
| 1978 | 0 | 0 | 0 | 0 | 3 | 69 | 141 | 112 | 18 | 0 | 0 | 0 | 343 |
| 1979 | 0 | 0 | 0 | 0 | 18 | 65 | 183 | 124 | 65 | 7 | 0 | 0 | 462 |
| 1980 | 0 | 0 | 0 | 1 | 0 | 2 | 141 | 75 | 35 | 12 | 0 | 0 | 266 |
| 1981 | 0 | 0 | 0 | 3 | 4 | 16 | 109 | 232 | 82 | 0 | 0 | 0 | 446 |
| 1982 | 0 | 0 | 0 | 0 | 4 | 107 | 103 | 127 | 50 | 0 | 0 | 0 | 391 |
| 1983 | 0 | 0 | 0 | 0 | 48 | 23 | 80 | 137 | 12 | 0 | 0 | 0 | 300 |
| 1984 | 0 | 0 | 0 | 0 | 10 | 34 | 140 | 144 | 47 | 6 | 0 | 0 | 381 |
| 1985 | 0 | 0 | 0 | 0 | 11 | 53 | 291 | 145 | 5 | 0 | 0 | 0 | 505 |
| 1986 | 0 | 0 | 0 | 0 | 40 | 87 | 52 | 235 | 50 | 0 | 0 | 0 | 464 |
| 1987 | 0 | 0 | 0 | 4 | 37 | 102 | 95 | 177 | 77 | 12 | 0 | 0 | 504 |
| 1988 | 0 | 0 | 0 | 0 | 10 | 39 | 147 | 115 | 67 | 8 | 0 | 0 | 386 |
| 1989 | 0 | 0 | 0 | 0 | 9 | 62 | 53 | 66 | 60 | 0 | 0 | 0 | 250 |
| 1990 | 0 | 0 | 0 | 2 | 3 | 45 | 206 | 193 | 83 | 0 | 0 | 0 | 532 |

**TABLE 6**    SNOWFALL (inches)    PORTLAND, OREGON

| SEASON | JULY | AUG | SEP | OCT | NOV | DEC | JAN | FEB | MAR | APR | MAY | JUNE | TOTAL |
|---|---|---|---|---|---|---|---|---|---|---|---|---|---|
| 1961-62 | 0.0 | 0.0 | 0.0 | 0.0 | 0.0 | 1.0 | 0.7 | 3.8 | 0.1 | 0.0 | 0.0 | 0.0 | 5.6 |
| 1962-63 | 0.0 | 0.0 | 0.0 | 0.0 | 0.0 | 0.0 | 5.0 | 0.0 | 0.0 | T | 0.0 | 0.0 | 5.0 |
| 1963-64 | 0.0 | 0.0 | 0.0 | 0.0 | T | 0.0 | T | 0.0 | T | 0.0 | 0.0 | 0.0 | T |
| 1964-65 | 0.0 | 0.0 | 0.0 | 0.0 | T | 11.0 | T | 0.0 | 0.3 | 0.0 | T | 0.0 | 11.3 |
| 1965-66 | 0.0 | 0.0 | 0.0 | 0.0 | 0.0 | T | T | T | 0.6 | 0.0 | 0.0 | 0.0 | 0.6 |
| 1966-67 | 0.0 | 0.0 | 0.0 | 0.0 | 0.0 | 0.0 | 0.0 | T | T | T | 0.0 | 0.0 | T |
| 1967-68 | 0.0 | 0.0 | 0.0 | 0.0 | 0.0 | 5.7 | 5.2 | 0.0 | 0.0 | T | 0.0 | 0.0 | 10.9 |
| 1968-69 | 0.0 | 0.0 | 0.0 | 0.0 | 15.7 | 18.3 | T | 0.0 | 0.0 | 0.0 | 0.0 | 0.0 | 34.0 |
| 1969-70 | 0.0 | 0.0 | 0.0 | 0.0 | 0.0 | 0.0 | T | T | T | T | 0.0 | 0.0 | T |
| 1970-71 | 0.0 | 0.0 | 0.0 | 0.0 | T | 1.4 | 6.9 | 1.7 | T | T | 0.0 | 0.0 | 10.0 |
| 1971-72 | 0.0 | 0.0 | 0.0 | T | 0.0 | 4.6 | 0.4 | T | T | T | 0.0 | 0.0 | 5.0 |
| 1972-73 | 0.0 | 0.0 | 0.0 | 0.0 | 0.0 | 6.1 | 0.4 | T | T | T | 0.0 | 0.0 | 6.5 |
| 1973-74 | 0.0 | 0.0 | 0.0 | 0.0 | T | 0.0 | T | T | T | 0.0 | T | 0.0 | T |
| 1974-75 | 0.0 | 0.0 | 0.0 | 0.0 | 0.0 | T | T | 0.1 | T | T | T | 0.0 | 0.1 |
| 1975-76 | 0.0 | 0.0 | 0.0 | 0.0 | T | T | T | T | T | T | T | 0.0 | T |
| 1976-77 | 0.0 | 0.0 | 0.0 | 0.0 | 0.0 | 0.0 | T | 0.0 | T | 0.0 | T | 0.0 | T |
| 1977-78 | 0.0 | 0.0 | 0.0 | 0.0 | 0.0 | 7.6 | T | 0.0 | 0.1 | T | T | 0.0 | 7.7 |
| 1978-79 | 0.0 | 0.0 | 0.0 | 0.0 | 3.0 | 2.4 | 1.9 | 1.1 | T | T | T | 0.0 | 8.4 |
| 1979-80 | 0.0 | 0.0 | 0.0 | 0.0 | 0.0 | T | 12.4 | T | T | T | T | 0.0 | 12.4 |
| 1980-81 | 0.0 | 0.0 | 0.0 | 0.0 | 0.0 | T | T | 0.0 | T | T | T | T | T |
| 1981-82 | 0.0 | 0.0 | 0.0 | 0.0 | 0.0 | 2.0 | 2.1 | T | T | T | 0.0 | 0.0 | 4.1 |
| 1982-83 | 0.0 | 0.0 | 0.0 | T | T | 0.0 | 0.0 | 0.0 | T | T | T | 0.0 | T |
| 1983-84 | 0.0 | 0.0 | 0.0 | 0.0 | 0.0 | 2.3 | 0.1 | T | T | 0.0 | T | 0.0 | 2.4 |
| 1984-85 | 0.0 | 0.0 | 0.0 | T | 0.0 | 2.8 | T | 4.8 | T | T | 0.0 | 0.0 | 7.6 |
| 1985-86 | 0.0 | 0.0 | 0.0 | 0.0 | 3.4 | 1.6 | T | 5.8 | T | T | T | 0.0 | 10.8 |
| 1986-87 | 0.0 | 0.0 | 0.0 | 0.0 | T | 0.1 | 0.0 | T | T | T | 0.0 | 0.0 | 0.1 |
| 1987-88 | 0.0 | 0.0 | 0.0 | 0.0 | 0.0 | 2.9 | 0.6 | 0.0 | 0.0 | T | T | 0.0 | 3.5 |
| 1988-89 | 0.0 | 0.0 | 0.0 | 0.0 | T | T | 0.9 | 0.3 | 2.0 | T | 0.0 | 0.0 | 3.2 |
| 1989-90 | 0.0 | T | 0.0 | T | 0.0 | 0.0 | T | 8.3 | T | 0.0 | 0.0 | 0.0 | 8.3 |
| 1990-91 | 0.0 | 0.0 | 0.0 | 0.0 | 0.0 | 1.3 | | | | | | | |
| Record Mean | 0.0 | T | T | T | 0.5 | 1.4 | 3.4 | 0.9 | 0.5 | T | T | T | 6.7 |

**See Reference Notes, relative to all above tables, on preceding page.**

Harrisburg, the capital of Pennsylvania, is situated on the east bank of the Susquehanna River. It is in the Great Valley formed by the eastern foothills of the Appalachian Chain, and about 60 miles southeast of the Commonwealths geographic center. It is nestled in a saucer-like bowl, 10 miles south of Blue Mountain, which serves as a barrier to the severe winter climate experienced 50 to 100 miles to the north and west. Although the severity of the winter climate is lessened, the city lies a little too far inland to derive the full benefits of the coastal climate.

Air masses change with some regularity, and any one condition does not persist for many days in succession. The mountain barrier occasionally prevents cold waves from reaching the Great Valley. The city is favorably located to receive precipitation produced when warm, maritime air from the Atlantic Ocean is forced upslope to cross the Blue Ridge Mountains.

The growing season in the Harrisburg area is about 192 days. Prolonged dry spells occur on occasion. Flood stage on the Susquehanna River occurs on the average of about every three years in Harrisburg, but serious flooding is much less frequent. About one-third of all floods have occurred during the month of March. Tropical hurricanes rarely reach Harrisburg with destructive winds, but have produced rainfalls in excess of 15 inches.

## TABLE 1    NORMALS, MEANS AND EXTREMES

HARRISBURG, PENNSYLVANIA

LATITUDE: 40°13'N    LONGITUDE: 76°51'W    ELEVATION: FT. GRND  338 BARO  339  TIME ZONE: EASTERN    WBAN: 14751

| | (a) | JAN | FEB | MAR | APR | MAY | JUNE | JULY | AUG | SEP | OCT | NOV | DEC | YEAR |
|---|---|---|---|---|---|---|---|---|---|---|---|---|---|---|
| **TEMPERATURE °F:** | | | | | | | | | | | | | | |
| Normals | | | | | | | | | | | | | | |
| -Daily Maximum | | 36.7 | 39.5 | 49.6 | 62.9 | 73.0 | 81.8 | 86.2 | 84.4 | 77.2 | 65.4 | 52.4 | 40.6 | 62.5 |
| -Daily Minimum | | 22.1 | 23.5 | 31.5 | 41.5 | 51.0 | 60.5 | 65.3 | 64.2 | 56.6 | 44.6 | 35.4 | 26.2 | 43.5 |
| -Monthly | | 29.4 | 31.5 | 40.6 | 52.2 | 62.0 | 71.2 | 75.8 | 74.3 | 66.9 | 55.0 | 43.9 | 33.4 | 53.0 |
| Extremes | | | | | | | | | | | | | | |
| -Record Highest | 51 | 73 | 75 | 86 | 93 | 97 | 100 | 107 | 101 | 102 | 97 | 84 | 75 | 107 |
| -Year | | 1950 | 1985 | 1945 | 1985 | 1942 | 1966 | 1966 | 1944 | 1953 | 1941 | 1950 | 1984 | JUL 1966 |
| -Record Lowest | 51 | -9 | -5 | 5 | 19 | 31 | 40 | 49 | 45 | 30 | 23 | 13 | -8 | -9 |
| -Year | | 1985 | 1979 | 1984 | 1982 | 1966 | 1980 | 1945 | 1976 | 1963 | 1969 | 1955 | 1960 | JAN 1985 |
| **NORMAL DEGREE DAYS:** | | | | | | | | | | | | | | |
| Heating (base 65°F) | | 1104 | 938 | 756 | 384 | 150 | 12 | 0 | 0 | 58 | 320 | 633 | 980 | 5335 |
| Cooling (base 65°F) | | 0 | 0 | 0 | 0 | 57 | 198 | 335 | 291 | 115 | 10 | 0 | 0 | 1006 |
| **% OF POSSIBLE SUNSHINE** | 51 | 49 | 55 | 58 | 59 | 60 | 65 | 69 | 67 | 62 | 57 | 47 | 45 | 58 |
| **MEAN SKY COVER (tenths)** | | | | | | | | | | | | | | |
| Sunrise - Sunset | 39 | 6.7 | 6.6 | 6.5 | 6.5 | 6.5 | 6.0 | 6.0 | 5.9 | 5.8 | 5.7 | 6.8 | 6.9 | 6.3 |
| **MEAN NUMBER OF DAYS:** | | | | | | | | | | | | | | |
| Sunrise to Sunset | | | | | | | | | | | | | | |
| -Clear | 51 | 6.9 | 6.6 | 7.3 | 6.5 | 6.2 | 6.7 | 7.3 | 8.2 | 8.9 | 9.9 | 6.2 | 6.2 | 86.9 |
| -Partly Cloudy | 51 | 7.3 | 7.3 | 8.2 | 8.7 | 10.2 | 11.4 | 11.5 | 10.8 | 9.4 | 8.1 | 8.2 | 7.5 | 108.5 |
| -Cloudy | 51 | 16.7 | 14.4 | 15.5 | 14.9 | 14.6 | 11.9 | 12.2 | 12.0 | 11.7 | 13.0 | 15.6 | 17.2 | 169.8 |
| Precipitation | | | | | | | | | | | | | | |
| .01 inches or more | 11 | 10.5 | 10.6 | 10.8 | 12.5 | 13.2 | 11.6 | 9.5 | 9.5 | 8.5 | 9.0 | 10.5 | 9.5 | 125.5 |
| Snow, Ice pellets | | | | | | | | | | | | | | |
| 1.0 inches or more | 11 | 3.1 | 2.5 | 1.2 | 0.4 | 0.0 | 0.0 | 0.0 | 0.0 | 0.0 | 0.0 | 0.5 | 1.7 | 9.4 |
| Thunderstorms | 48 | 0.2 | 0.2 | 1.1 | 2.2 | 5.2 | 6.3 | 7.0 | 5.3 | 2.9 | 0.8 | 0.5 | 0.2 | 31.8 |
| Heavy Fog Visibility | | | | | | | | | | | | | | |
| 1/4 mile or less | 48 | 2.3 | 2.3 | 1.7 | 0.9 | 0.9 | 0.6 | 0.6 | 0.8 | 1.6 | 2.7 | 1.8 | 2.4 | 18.7 |
| Temperature °F | | | | | | | | | | | | | | |
| -Maximum | | | | | | | | | | | | | | |
| 90° and above | 51 | 0.0 | 0.0 | 0.0 | 0.3 | 1.0 | 4.6 | 8.9 | 6.1 | 1.9 | 0.1 | 0.0 | 0.0 | 22.8 |
| 32° and below | 51 | 9.8 | 6.1 | 1.4 | 0.0 | 0.0 | 0.0 | 0.0 | 0.0 | 0.0 | 0.0 | 0.3 | 5.6 | 23.1 |
| -Minimum | | | | | | | | | | | | | | |
| 32° and below | 51 | 26.4 | 23.1 | 17.1 | 3.6 | 0.1 | 0.0 | 0.0 | 0.0 | 0.1 | 2.0 | 11.0 | 23.0 | 106.4 |
| 0° and below | 51 | 0.6 | 0.2 | 0.0 | 0.0 | 0.0 | 0.0 | 0.0 | 0.0 | 0.0 | 0.0 | 0.0 | 0.2 | 1.0 |
| **AVG. STATION PRESS.(mb)** | 17 | 1006.1 | 1006.3 | 1004.6 | 1002.7 | 1002.9 | 1003.2 | 1004.0 | 1005.3 | 1006.6 | 1007.4 | 1006.5 | 1006.9 | 1005.2 |
| **RELATIVE HUMIDITY (%)** | | | | | | | | | | | | | | |
| Hour 01 | 47 | 69 | 68 | 67 | 67 | 74 | 79 | 79 | 82 | 80 | 79 | 74 | 70 | 74 |
| Hour 07 | 47 | 71 | 71 | 71 | 70 | 74 | 77 | 79 | 83 | 85 | 82 | 77 | 73 | 76 |
| Hour 13 (Local Time) | 46 | 58 | 55 | 52 | 49 | 52 | 53 | 52 | 55 | 56 | 54 | 57 | 58 | 54 |
| Hour 19 | 47 | 63 | 61 | 57 | 54 | 57 | 60 | 60 | 65 | 68 | 67 | 66 | 64 | 62 |
| **PRECIPITATION (inches):** | | | | | | | | | | | | | | |
| Water Equivalent | | | | | | | | | | | | | | |
| -Normal | | 2.96 | 2.73 | 3.50 | 3.19 | 3.67 | 3.63 | 3.32 | 3.29 | 3.60 | 2.73 | 3.24 | 3.23 | 39.09 |
| -Maximum Monthly | 11 | 8.01 | 5.93 | 5.47 | 7.96 | 9.71 | 8.12 | 7.20 | 6.26 | 8.41 | 5.59 | 6.23 | 7.57 | 9.71 |
| -Year | | 1979 | 1981 | 1980 | 1983 | 1989 | 1982 | 1989 | 1986 | 1987 | 1989 | 1985 | 1983 | MAY 1989 |
| -Minimum Monthly | 11 | 0.43 | 0.82 | 1.02 | 0.45 | 1.86 | 1.00 | 0.97 | 1.51 | 0.65 | 1.34 | 0.96 | 0.77 | 0.43 |
| -Year | | 1981 | 1980 | 1981 | 1985 | 1981 | 1988 | 1983 | 1980 | 1986 | 1985 | 1981 | 1980 | JAN 1981 |
| -Maximum in 24 hrs | 9 | 2.09 | 1.84 | 1.80 | 1.46 | 2.91 | 2.32 | 2.58 | 2.70 | 3.03 | 2.19 | 2.33 | 1.55 | 3.03 |
| -Year | | 1979 | 1985 | 1980 | 1986 | 1984 | 1987 | 1989 | 1989 | 1979 | 1980 | 1987 | 1986 | SEP 1979 |
| Snow, Ice pellets | | | | | | | | | | | | | | |
| -Maximum Monthly | 11 | 31.5 | 28.8 | 14.9 | 10.2 | 0.0 | 0.0 | 0.0 | 0.0 | 0.0 | T | 9.7 | 12.5 | 31.5 |
| -Year | | 1987 | 1983 | 1984 | 1982 | | | | | | 1982 | 1987 | 1981 | JAN 1987 |
| -Maximum in 24 hrs | 9 | 11.2 | 14.2 | 9.6 | 2.6 | 0.0 | 0.0 | 0.0 | 0.0 | 0.0 | T | 7.9 | 5.6 | 14.2 |
| -Year | | 1987 | 1979 | 1989 | 1985 | | | | | | 1979 | 1987 | 1981 | FEB 1979 |
| **WIND:** | | | | | | | | | | | | | | |
| Mean Speed (mph) | 47 | 8.3 | 9.0 | 9.6 | 9.2 | 7.6 | 6.8 | 6.2 | 5.9 | 6.1 | 6.6 | 7.8 | 8.0 | 7.6 |
| Prevailing Direction | | | | | | | | | | | | | | |
| through 1963 | | WNW | WNW | WNW | WNW | W | W | W | W | WNW | W | WNW | WNW | WNW |
| Fastest Obs. 1 Min. | | | | | | | | | | | | | | |
| -Direction (!!!) | 7 | 27 | 28 | 28 | 29 | 29 | 33 | 29 | 35 | 28 | 25 | 31 | 31 | 33 |
| -Speed (MPH) | 7 | 44 | 31 | 37 | 35 | 47 | 58 | 35 | 46 | 31 | 30 | 40 | 46 | 58 |
| -Year | | 1978 | 1988 | 1985 | 1979 | 1980 | 1980 | 1987 | 1979 | 1987 | 1981 | 1989 | 1978 | JUN 1980 |
| Peak Gust | | | | | | | | | | | | | | |
| -Direction (!!!) | | | | | | | | | | | | | | |
| -Speed (mph) | | | | | | | | | | | | | | |
| -Date | | | | | | | | | | | | | | |

**See Reference Notes to this table on the following pages.**

**PRECIPITATION (inches)**  HARRISBURG, PENNSYLVANIA

**TABLE 2**

| YEAR | JAN | FEB | MAR | APR | MAY | JUNE | JULY | AUG | SEP | OCT | NOV | DEC | ANNUAL |
|------|-----|-----|-----|-----|-----|------|------|-----|-----|-----|-----|-----|--------|
| 1961 | 3.46 | 3.07 | 4.19 | 4.56 | 2.03 | 1.93 | 6.60 | 5.49 | 1.24 | 0.92 | 3.56 | 3.42 | 40.47 |
| 1962 | 2.15 | 4.33 | 2.70 | 2.81 | 2.96 | 4.03 | 1.20 | 4.18 | 3.59 | 4.21 | 4.10 | 3.32 | 39.58 |
| 1963 | 2.19 | 1.83 | 3.86 | 1.52 | 2.66 | 2.36 | 1.97 | 2.55 | 2.82 | 0.04 | 5.93 | 2.36 | 30.09 |
| 1964 | 4.78 | 3.12 | 2.94 | 4.91 | 0.51 | 4.20 | 2.25 | 3.07 | 1.77 | 1.92 | 1.87 | 3.11 | 34.45 |
| 1965 | 2.70 | 3.29 | 3.61 | 1.25 | 2.38 | 2.60 | 3.10 | 3.99 | 2.12 | 3.65 | 1.63 | 0.87 | 31.19 |
| 1966 | 3.57 | 4.44 | 1.88 | 3.44 | 0.98 | 0.07 | 0.81 | 1.53 | 6.12 | 2.12 | 3.56 | 3.08 | 31.60 |
| 1967 | 1.81 | 1.54 | 5.26 | 2.58 | 4.32 | 1.90 | 5.96 | 5.61 | 1.80 | 3.15 | 2.89 | 4.27 | 41.09 |
| 1968 | 1.32 | 0.53 | 3.40 | 2.43 | 6.55 | 2.25 | 1.94 | 1.77 | 5.18 | 2.34 | 3.38 | 2.12 | 33.21 |
| 1969 | 1.06 | 1.70 | 2.20 | 2.13 | 1.56 | 2.54 | 9.72 | 2.07 | 2.32 | 1.63 | 3.29 | 6.46 | 36.68 |
| 1970 | 0.88 | 3.25 | 3.64 | 5.03 | 2.39 | 5.80 | 6.34 | 2.97 | 2.12 | 3.20 | 4.59 | 3.50 | 43.71 |
| 1971 | 2.70 | 5.62 | 2.67 | 1.04 | 5.30 | 1.80 | 2.84 | 7.77 | 1.94 | 2.85 | 4.96 | 1.93 | 41.42 |
| 1972 | 2.65 | 5.00 | 2.68 | 4.10 | 5.56 | 18.55 | 2.26 | 2.52 | 1.41 | 2.03 | 7.20 | 5.31 | 59.27 |
| 1973 | 3.24 | 2.50 | 2.00 | 6.23 | 6.37 | 3.34 | 2.18 | 2.19 | 5.73 | 2.47 | 1.04 | 6.52 | 43.81 |
| 1974 | 3.82 | 1.36 | 4.64 | 3.21 | 4.38 | 3.69 | 2.79 | 4.13 | 6.79 | 1.25 | 2.30 | 4.59 | 42.95 |
| 1975 | 4.12 | 3.10 | 3.78 | 2.80 | 5.25 | 6.51 | 3.13 | 1.83 | 14.97 | 2.62 | 2.92 | 3.19 | 54.22 |
| 1976 | 4.34 | 1.88 | 3.43 | 1.63 | 5.42 | 2.42 | 5.50 | 3.28 | 4.79 | 9.87 | 0.79 | 1.96 | 45.31 |
| 1977 | 1.44 | 1.75 | 6.10 | 4.48 | 1.00 | 3.17 | 3.01 | 0.93 | 3.73 | 3.66 | 5.61 | 4.82 | 39.70 |
| 1978 | 7.44 | 1.35 | 3.94 | 1.97 | 5.67 | 5.16 | 1.64 | 3.60 | 1.64 | 2.51 | 2.13 | 3.95 | 43.71 |
| #1979 | 8.01 | 4.74 | 1.93 | 3.60 | 4.66 | 2.62 | 3.14 | 3.24 | 6.62 | 3.91 | 2.67 | 1.46 | 46.60 |
| 1980 | 0.90 | 0.82 | 5.47 | 4.27 | 4.58 | 2.50 | 1.51 | 1.59 | 1.06 | 2.94 | 3.65 | 0.77 | 30.06 |
| 1981 | 0.43 | 5.93 | 1.02 | 2.77 | 1.86 | 4.66 | 4.67 | 4.11 | 2.20 | 3.76 | 0.96 | 2.41 | 34.78 |
| 1982 | 3.63 | 1.92 | 2.20 | 4.17 | 4.89 | 8.12 | 2.90 | 2.47 | 2.87 | 1.82 | 3.37 | 1.56 | 39.92 |
| 1983 | 2.26 | 3.38 | 4.86 | 7.96 | 5.36 | 2.81 | 0.97 | 2.50 | 1.40 | 4.21 | 5.29 | 7.57 | 48.57 |
| 1984 | 1.12 | 4.51 | 5.36 | 4.46 | 6.20 | 6.36 | 3.76 | 2.75 | 1.49 | 1.98 | 3.78 | 2.28 | 44.05 |
| 1985 | 1.06 | 2.91 | 2.78 | 0.45 | 6.29 | 3.07 | 2.50 | 2.14 | 3.76 | 1.34 | 6.23 | 1.28 | 33.81 |
| 1986 | 2.24 | 4.50 | 3.16 | 4.10 | 2.29 | 1.48 | 5.17 | 6.26 | 0.65 | 2.59 | 4.58 | 4.90 | 41.92 |
| 1987 | 3.69 | 1.59 | 1.43 | 2.93 | 3.73 | 3.46 | 1.96 | 2.89 | 8.41 | 2.63 | 4.96 | 1.84 | 39.52 |
| 1988 | 2.18 | 3.28 | 1.98 | 2.65 | 5.79 | 1.00 | 4.40 | 2.67 | 2.42 | 1.81 | 3.67 | 0.90 | 32.75 |
| 1989 | 2.29 | 1.90 | 3.60 | 1.10 | 9.71 | 6.02 | 7.20 | 3.03 | 2.63 | 5.59 | 2.17 | 1.27 | 46.51 |
| 1990 | 3.77 | 2.73 | 1.76 | 2.60 | 7.20 | 1.10 | 3.62 | 6.14 | 1.65 | 4.92 | 2.58 | 6.05 | 44.12 |
| Record Mean | 2.80 | 2.70 | 3.21 | 3.05 | 3.80 | 3.62 | 3.62 | 3.68 | 3.15 | 2.92 | 2.78 | 2.94 | 38.29 |

**TABLE 3**  AVERAGE TEMPERATURE (deg. F)  HARRISBURG, PENNSYLVANIA

| YEAR | JAN | FEB | MAR | APR | MAY | JUNE | JULY | AUG | SEP | OCT | NOV | DEC | ANNUAL |
|------|-----|-----|-----|-----|-----|------|------|-----|-----|-----|-----|-----|--------|
| 1961 | 25.1 | 33.6 | 41.5 | 48.1 | 59.1 | 69.9 | 75.1 | 73.5 | 72.3 | 57.2 | 46.0 | 31.1 | 52.7 |
| 1962 | 28.0 | 28.2 | 39.3 | 52.0 | 64.9 | 72.1 | 74.9 | 73.0 | 62.8 | 55.7 | 41.1 | 28.2 | 51.7 |
| 1963 | 26.2 | 25.2 | 43.2 | 54.4 | 61.6 | 72.3 | 76.4 | 70.1 | 61.5 | 57.1 | 45.8 | 26.9 | 51.7 |
| 1964 | 30.2 | 28.9 | 40.5 | 49.6 | 64.3 | 71.4 | 76.1 | 71.5 | 66.2 | 52.0 | 45.7 | 33.9 | 52.5 |
| 1965 | 26.4 | 32.5 | 37.5 | 50.1 | 66.5 | 71.7 | 75.6 | 74.6 | 69.8 | 53.4 | 42.2 | 35.7 | 53.0 |
| 1966 | 26.3 | 31.5 | 38.8 | 49.0 | 61.4 | 74.6 | 79.5 | 78.3 | 66.7 | 54.7 | 45.1 | 31.7 | 53.6 |
| 1967 | 33.6 | 26.9 | 38.8 | 53.0 | 55.2 | 73.9 | 74.2 | 71.8 | 65.3 | 53.3 | 39.8 | 34.8 | 51.7 |
| 1968 | 24.0 | 29.2 | 43.7 | 53.7 | 58.0 | 70.3 | 77.3 | 76.7 | 67.6 | 56.1 | 44.9 | 31.3 | 52.7 |
| 1969 | 29.9 | 33.3 | 38.6 | 53.4 | 63.2 | 72.4 | 75.3 | 73.4 | 65.6 | 53.8 | 42.7 | 31.4 | 52.8 |
| 1970 | 22.9 | 30.4 | 36.7 | 51.4 | 65.1 | 70.7 | 76.2 | 75.6 | 71.6 | 58.7 | 46.0 | 30.4 | 53.4 |
| 1971 | 26.4 | 33.2 | 38.6 | 50.4 | 60.0 | 72.5 | 75.5 | 72.2 | 69.9 | 60.6 | 43.5 | 40.3 | 53.6 |
| 1972 | 34.5 | 30.2 | 40.0 | 49.6 | 62.3 | 67.7 | 76.2 | 74.0 | 68.4 | 52.1 | 41.8 | 36.8 | 52.8 |
| 1973 | 33.7 | 31.7 | 45.2 | 50.9 | 57.8 | 73.4 | 75.5 | 76.1 | 68.6 | 57.4 | 46.9 | 36.2 | 54.5 |
| 1974 | 34.8 | 32.3 | 42.8 | 56.2 | 63.0 | 70.5 | 77.6 | 77.1 | 64.5 | 51.6 | 44.9 | 35.4 | 54.2 |
| 1975 | 33.3 | 32.4 | 38.3 | 47.4 | 64.8 | 70.7 | 75.3 | 76.2 | 63.3 | 57.7 | 50.0 | 34.2 | 53.7 |
| 1976 | 27.6 | 39.6 | 44.2 | 54.5 | 59.4 | 73.4 | 72.3 | 72.4 | 44.8 | 51.5 | 39.6 | 30.0 | 52.4 |
| 1977 | 20.1 | 30.4 | 46.0 | 54.1 | 64.5 | 68.6 | 75.9 | 74.3 | 68.3 | 52.7 | 46.1 | 31.6 | 52.7 |
| 1978 | 26.2 | 22.8 | 38.6 | 51.0 | 61.5 | 69.5 | 73.1 | 76.9 | 67.6 | 54.4 | 46.7 | 36.5 | 52.1 |
| 1979 | 29.2 | 22.6 | 45.1 | 50.4 | 62.2 | 68.5 | 73.4 | 72.9 | 65.5 | 52.3 | 46.8 | 37.6 | 52.2 |
| 1980 | 30.3 | 29.1 | 38.9 | 52.8 | 63.3 | 67.8 | 76.3 | 76.1 | 67.7 | 51.5 | 39.4 | 29.6 | 51.9 |
| 1981 | 23.7 | 34.6 | 38.7 | 53.7 | 61.9 | 71.7 | 75.7 | 72.2 | 63.9 | 50.7 | 44.7 | 31.9 | 51.9 |
| 1982 | 22.8 | 30.9 | 38.6 | 47.6 | 62.2 | 65.1 | 74.0 | 70.5 | 65.3 | 55.1 | 47.6 | 41.4 | 51.8 |
| 1983 | 33.0 | 33.4 | 42.7 | 49.3 | 58.4 | 69.1 | 75.9 | 74.9 | 66.2 | 53.6 | 43.9 | 28.7 | 52.4 |
| 1984 | 24.8 | 36.6 | 33.7 | 48.0 | 58.2 | 72.9 | 74.3 | 75.8 | 64.4 | 61.5 | 43.9 | 41.5 | 53.0 |
| 1985 | 27.9 | 34.4 | 44.5 | 56.9 | 65.2 | 69.4 | 75.9 | 74.1 | 69.2 | 57.2 | 47.9 | 31.0 | 54.5 |
| 1986 | 31.4 | 30.0 | 43.5 | 53.5 | 65.6 | 71.4 | 76.3 | 72.0 | 66.2 | 56.0 | 41.2 | 36.1 | 53.6 |
| 1987 | 30.0 | 32.3 | 44.1 | 52.3 | 63.2 | 72.6 | 78.2 | 73.1 | 65.7 | 49.4 | 43.9 | 36.6 | 53.5 |
| 1988 | 24.4 | 31.8 | 42.4 | 50.0 | 62.3 | 70.8 | 78.8 | 76.2 | 63.5 | 49.5 | 43.7 | 33.3 | 52.2 |
| 1989 | 34.8 | 32.4 | 40.4 | 50.4 | 60.0 | 70.6 | 73.7 | 72.6 | 66.0 | 55.6 | 42.7 | 22.6 | 51.8 |
| 1990 | 38.2 | 38.2 | 44.9 | 53.1 | 59.4 | 71.2 | 75.2 | 72.7 | 65.0 | 58.2 | 46.9 | 38.4 | 55.1 |
| Record Mean | 30.1 | 31.1 | 40.4 | 50.7 | 62.1 | 70.8 | 75.3 | 73.3 | 66.5 | 55.1 | 43.6 | 33.2 | 52.7 |
| Max | 37.0 | 38.5 | 48.8 | 59.6 | 72.1 | 80.6 | 84.9 | 82.7 | 75.9 | 64.4 | 51.5 | 40.0 | 61.3 |
| Min | 23.3 | 23.8 | 32.0 | 41.7 | 52.1 | 60.9 | 65.6 | 63.9 | 57.0 | 45.7 | 35.7 | 26.3 | 44.0 |

## REFERENCE NOTES FOR TABLES 1, 2, 3 and 6    (HARRISBURG, PA)

### GENERAL

T - TRACE AMOUNT
BLANK ENTRIES DENOTE MISSING/UNREPORTED DATA.
# INDICATES A STATION OR INSTRUMENT RELOCATION.

### SPECIFIC

**TABLE 1**

(a) - LENGTH OF RECORD IN YEARS. ALTHOUGH
     INDIVIDUAL MONTHS MAY BE MISSING.
 * LESS THAN .05

NORMALS — BASED ON THE 1951-1980 RECORD PERIOD.
EXTREMES — DATES ARE THE MOST RECENT OCCURRENCE.
WIND DIR. — NUMERALS SHOW TENS OF DEGREES
           CLOCKWISE FROM TRUE NORTH.
           "00" INDICATES CALM.
RESULTANT WIND DIRECTIONS ARE GIVEN TO WHOLE DEGREES.

**TABLE 3**
MAX AND MIN ARE LONG-TERM MEAN DAILY MAXIMUM
AND MEAN DAILY MINIMUM TEMPERATURES.

### EXCEPTIONS

**TABLE 1**

1. MAXIMUM 24-HOUR PRECIPITATION AND SNOW ARE
   FOR FEDERAL OFFICE BLDG., 1979 — CURRENT YEAR.

2. PERCENT OF POSSIBLE SUNSHINE IS FROM THE FEDERAL
   OFFICE BUILDING COMMENCING DECEMBER 1983.

**TABLES 1, 2, and 3**

COMMENCING JANUARY 12, 1979 FOR PRECIPITATION AND
JUNE 13, 1984 FOR TEMPERATURE, DATA ARE FROM THE
FEDERAL OFFICE BUILDING, 3.5 MILES NORTHWEST OF THE
AIRPORT.

**TABLES 2, 3, and 6**

RECORD MEANS ARE THROUGH THE CURRENT YEAR,
BEGINNING IN      1889 FOR TEMPERATURE
                  1889 FOR PRECIPITATION
                  1939 FOR SNOWFALL

HEATING DEGREE DAYS Base 65 deg. F     HARRISBURG, PENNSYLVANIA

## TABLE 4

| SEASON | JULY | AUG | SEP | OCT | NOV | DEC | JAN | FEB | MAR | APR | MAY | JUNE | TOTAL |
|---|---|---|---|---|---|---|---|---|---|---|---|---|---|
| 1961-62 | 0 | 2 | 41 | 244 | 569 | 1042 | 1139 | 1025 | 791 | 415 | 120 | 2 | 5390 |
| 1962-63 | 0 | 3 | 126 | 297 | 712 | 1132 | 1198 | 1107 | 666 | 325 | 146 | 4 | 5716 |
| 1963-64 | 1 | 7 | 149 | 242 | 570 | 1173 | 1072 | 1041 | 753 | 460 | 93 | 34 | 5595 |
| 1964-65 | 0 | 4 | 71 | 399 | 570 | 958 | 1192 | 902 | 847 | 441 | 66 | 27 | 5477 |
| 1965-66 | 0 | 7 | 44 | 357 | 677 | 900 | 1191 | 932 | 648 | 472 | 166 | 12 | 5406 |
| 1966-67 | 0 | 0 | 69 | 312 | 592 | 1024 | 966 | 1061 | 806 | 364 | 306 | 3 | 5503 |
| 1967-68 | 0 | 5 | 85 | 369 | 750 | 931 | 1266 | 1032 | 654 | 331 | 216 | 12 | 5651 |
| 1968-69 | 0 | 3 | 18 | 277 | 593 | 1038 | 1083 | 882 | 809 | 345 | 123 | 8 | 5179 |
| 1969-70 | 0 | 0 | 89 | 352 | 662 | 1036 | 1299 | 962 | 872 | 407 | 93 | 13 | 5785 |
| 1970-71 | 0 | 0 | 39 | 213 | 564 | 931 | 1192 | 884 | 812 | 432 | 165 | 12 | 5244 |
| 1971-72 | 0 | 3 | 40 | 146 | 643 | 759 | 940 | 1001 | 766 | 457 | 108 | 44 | 4907 |
| 1972-73 | 0 | 1 | 25 | 395 | 686 | 865 | 964 | 926 | 607 | 422 | 227 | 7 | 5125 |
| 1973-74 | 0 | 1 | 34 | 238 | 534 | 887 | 931 | 910 | 683 | 289 | 133 | 2 | 4642 |
| 1974-75 | 0 | 0 | 94 | 414 | 600 | 911 | 977 | 903 | 818 | 520 | 97 | 13 | 5347 |
| 1975-76 | 0 | 0 | 87 | 232 | 445 | 951 | 1150 | 730 | 639 | 354 | 193 | 23 | 4804 |
| 1976-77 | 0 | 5 | 75 | 418 | 756 | 1075 | 1387 | 966 | 588 | 340 | 106 | 32 | 5748 |
| 1977-78 | 0 | 5 | 35 | 377 | 562 | 1029 | 1196 | 1175 | 810 | 414 | 173 | 17 | 5793 |
| 1978-79 | 14 | 0 | 48 | 321 | 544 | 876 | 1104 | 1182 | 611 | 435 | 123 | 26 | 5284 |
| 1979-80 | 12 | 14 | 71 | 393 | 536 | 844 | 1070 | 1033 | 799 | 361 | 103 | 48 | 5284 |
| 1980-81 | 0 | 0 | 57 | 411 | 761 | 1091 | 1277 | 844 | 809 | 339 | 147 | 6 | 5742 |
| 1981-82 | 0 | 1 | 94 | 437 | 599 | 1021 | 1304 | 948 | 812 | 518 | 128 | 61 | 5923 |
| 1982-83 | 7 | 12 | 67 | 318 | 520 | 725 | 985 | 876 | 686 | 468 | 221 | 25 | 4910 |
| 1983-84 | 0 | 2 | 103 | 362 | 628 | 1117 | 1238 | 817 | 962 | 502 | 240 | 11 | 5982 |
| 1984-85 | 0 | 0 | 105 | 131 | 627 | 724 | 1143 | 849 | 627 | 292 | 87 | 16 | 4601 |
| 1985-86 | 0 | 0 | 41 | 237 | 508 | 1049 | 1038 | 974 | 664 | 349 | 89 | 9 | 4958 |
| 1986-87 | 2 | 17 | 46 | 300 | 705 | 890 | 1080 | 907 | 643 | 380 | 142 | 2 | 5114 |
| 1987-88 | 0 | 8 | 51 | 477 | 627 | 873 | 1252 | 961 | 693 | 445 | 131 | 41 | 5559 |
| 1988-89 | 4 | 5 | 88 | 475 | 633 | 975 | 931 | 912 | 760 | 433 | 196 | 9 | 5421 |
| 1989-90 | 1 | 6 | 81 | 292 | 663 | 1306 | 824 | 744 | 629 | 385 | 175 | 13 | 5119 |
| 1990-91 | 5 | 8 | 96 | 248 | 535 | 816 |  |  |  |  |  |  |  |

## TABLE 5   COOLING DEGREE DAYS Base 65 deg. F    HARRISBURG, PENNSYLVANIA

| YEAR | JAN | FEB | MAR | APR | MAY | JUNE | JULY | AUG | SEP | OCT | NOV | DEC | TOTAL |
|---|---|---|---|---|---|---|---|---|---|---|---|---|---|
| 1969 | 0 | 0 | 0 | 3 | 71 | 235 | 327 | 267 | 113 | 11 | 0 | 0 | 1027 |
| 1970 | 0 | 0 | 0 | 7 | 102 | 191 | 353 | 333 | 246 | 24 | 0 | 0 | 1256 |
| 1971 | 0 | 0 | 0 | 0 | 17 | 241 | 331 | 236 | 195 | 17 | 6 | 0 | 1043 |
| 1972 | 0 | 0 | 0 | 0 | 33 | 133 | 357 | 287 | 137 | 3 | 0 | 0 | 950 |
| 1973 | 0 | 0 | 0 | 8 | 13 | 266 | 334 | 352 | 148 | 9 | 0 | 0 | 1130 |
| 1974 | 0 | 0 | 0 | 34 | 79 | 176 | 401 | 381 | 88 | 1 | 3 | 0 | 1163 |
| 1975 | 0 | 0 | 0 | 0 | 97 | 192 | 325 | 354 | 44 | 12 | 2 | 0 | 1026 |
| 1976 | 0 | 0 | 0 | 47 | 22 | 283 | 233 | 240 | 73 | 3 | 0 | 0 | 901 |
| 1977 | 0 | 0 | 4 | 19 | 95 | 147 | 347 | 297 | 140 | 1 | 3 | 0 | 1053 |
| 1978 | 0 | 0 | 0 | 0 | 69 | 162 | 273 | 377 | 133 | 1 | 0 | 0 | 1015 |
| 1979 | 0 | 0 | 0 | 5 | 43 | 138 | 279 | 264 | 92 | 7 | 0 | 0 | 828 |
| 1980 | 0 | 0 | 0 | 0 | 57 | 138 | 355 | 350 | 145 | 0 | 0 | 0 | 1045 |
| 1981 | 0 | 0 | 0 | 6 | 60 | 213 | 339 | 232 | 66 | 0 | 0 | 0 | 916 |
| 1982 | 0 | 0 | 0 | 2 | 48 | 70 | 307 | 191 | 83 | 19 | 4 | 0 | 724 |
| 1983 | 0 | 0 | 0 | 6 | 22 | 154 | 343 | 315 | 146 | 13 | 0 | 0 | 999 |
| 1984 | 0 | 0 | 0 | 0 | 34 | 256 | 292 | 342 | 95 | 35 | 0 | 1 | 1055 |
| 1985 | 0 | 0 | 0 | 55 | 99 | 157 | 345 | 290 | 173 | 4 | 0 | 0 | 1123 |
| 1986 | 0 | 0 | 5 | 12 | 116 | 205 | 360 | 238 | 88 | 27 | 0 | 0 | 1051 |
| 1987 | 0 | 0 | 0 | 9 | 94 | 237 | 418 | 266 | 76 | 0 | 0 | 0 | 1100 |
| 1988 | 0 | 0 | 0 | 0 | 53 | 219 | 439 | 355 | 52 | 4 | 0 | 0 | 1122 |
| 1989 | 0 | 0 | 5 | 0 | 49 | 182 | 279 | 249 | 114 | 9 | 1 | 0 | 888 |
| 1990 | 0 | 0 | 14 | 34 | 12 | 205 | 330 | 254 | 102 | 43 | 0 | 0 | 994 |

## TABLE 6   SNOWFALL (inches)    HARRISBURG, PENNSYLVANIA

| SEASON | JULY | AUG | SEP | OCT | NOV | DEC | JAN | FEB | MAR | APR | MAY | JUNE | TOTAL |
|---|---|---|---|---|---|---|---|---|---|---|---|---|---|
| 1961-62 | 0.0 | 0.0 | 0.0 | 0.0 | 3.7 | 18.8 | 2.3 | 15.9 | 10.9 | T | 0.0 | 0.0 | 51.6 |
| 1962-63 | 0.0 | 0.0 | 0.0 | T | 4.5 | 16.6 | 9.1 | 14.2 | 6.1 | T | T | 0.0 | 50.5 |
| 1963-64 | 0.0 | 0.0 | 0.0 | T | T | 15.8 | 19.4 | 30.2 | 9.0 | 0.3 | 0.0 | 0.0 | 74.7 |
| 1964-65 | 0.0 | 0.0 | 0.0 | 0.0 | T | 1.4 | 13.4 | 1.7 | 15.1 | 0.2 | 0.0 | 0.0 | 31.8 |
| 1965-66 | 0.0 | 0.0 | 0.0 | T | T | 24.8 | 16.8 | 1.0 | T | T | 0.0 | 0.0 | 42.6 |
| 1966-67 | 0.0 | 0.0 | 0.0 | 0.0 | 0.2 | 19.9 | 1.6 | 16.5 | 10.2 | T | 0.0 | 0.0 | 48.4 |
| 1967-68 | 0.0 | 0.0 | 0.0 | 0.0 | 9.7 | 13.0 | 3.0 | 1.8 | 3.5 | 0.0 | 0.0 | 0.0 | 31.0 |
| 1968-69 | 0.0 | 0.0 | 0.0 | 0.0 | 3.0 | 0.2 | 1.2 | 16.8 | 3.8 | 0.0 | 0.0 | 0.0 | 25.0 |
| 1969-70 | 0.0 | 0.0 | 0.0 | T | 2.1 | 28.3 | 9.8 | 7.5 | 12.9 | T | 0.0 | 0.0 | 60.6 |
| 1970-71 | 0.0 | 0.0 | 0.0 | 0.0 | 0.0 | 10.9 | 11.6 | 5.1 | 5.3 | T | 0.0 | 0.0 | 32.9 |
| 1971-72 | 0.0 | 0.0 | 0.0 | 0.0 | 8.8 | T | 2.6 | 21.6 | 0.5 | 1.1 | 0.0 | 0.0 | 34.6 |
| 1972-73 | 0.0 | 0.0 | 0.0 | 1.2 | 5.9 | 0.5 | T | 5.7 | T | T | 0.0 | 0.0 | 13.3 |
| 1973-74 | 0.0 | 0.0 | 0.0 | 0.0 | T | 15.3 | 7.0 | 5.5 | T | T | 0.0 | 0.0 | 27.8 |
| 1974-75 | 0.0 | 0.0 | 0.0 | 0.0 | T | 0.5 | 11.3 | 13.1 | 6.1 | T | 0.0 | 0.0 | 31.0 |
| 1975-76 | 0.0 | 0.0 | 0.0 | 0.0 | T | 2.2 | 3.6 | 2.5 | 10.0 | 0.0 | 0.0 | 0.0 | 18.3 |
| 1976-77 | 0.0 | 0.0 | 0.0 | 0.0 | 1.4 | 5.1 | 12.2 | 4.5 | 0.2 | T | T | 0.0 | 23.4 |
| 1977-78 | 0.0 | 0.0 | 0.0 | T | 1.5 | 5.5 | 33.5 | 21.1 | 9.0 | 0.0 | 0.0 | 0.0 | 70.6 |
| #1978-79 | 0.0 | 0.0 | 0.0 | 0.0 | 4.0 | 0.3 | 9.2 | 26.0 | T | T | 0.0 | 0.0 | 39.5 |
| 1979-80 | 0.0 | 0.0 | 0.0 | T | T | 0.2 | 3.8 | 2.7 | 7.9 | 0.0 | 0.0 | 0.0 | 14.6 |
| 1980-81 | 0.0 | 0.0 | 0.0 | 0.0 | 4.0 | 4.3 | 5.5 | 4.4 | 6.7 | 0.0 | 0.0 | 0.0 | 24.9 |
| 1981-82 | 0.0 | 0.0 | 0.0 | 0.0 | 0.8 | 12.5 | 18.8 | 8.4 | 7.8 | 10.2 | 0.0 | 0.0 | 58.5 |
| 1982-83 | 0.0 | 0.0 | 0.0 | T | T | 1.1 | 1.1 | 28.8 | 0.4 | 1.3 | 0.0 | 0.0 | 36.0 |
| 1983-84 | 0.0 | 0.0 | 0.0 | 0.0 | T | 4.6 | 9.7 | 2.3 | 14.9 | T | 0.0 | 0.0 | 31.5 |
| 1984-85 | 0.0 | 0.0 | 0.0 | 0.0 | 1.9 | 2.6 | 10.6 | 11.4 | T | 3.6 | 0.0 | 0.0 | 30.1 |
| 1985-86 | 0.0 | 0.0 | 0.0 | 0.0 | T | 5.6 | 7.8 | 23.1 | T | T | 0.0 | 0.0 | 36.5 |
| 1986-87 | 0.0 | 0.0 | 0.0 | 0.0 | T | 1.9 | 31.5 | 10.1 | 1.4 | 1.0 | 0.0 | 0.0 | 45.9 |
| 1987-88 | 0.0 | 0.0 | 0.0 | 0.0 | 9.7 | 3.6 | 9.6 | 2.8 | 1.0 | T | 0.0 | 0.0 | 26.7 |
| 1988-89 | 0.0 | 0.0 | 0.0 | 0.0 | T | T | 6.4 | 2.2 | 11.3 | 0.0 | 0.0 | 0.0 | 19.9 |
| 1989-90 | 0.0 | 0.0 | 0.0 | 0.0 | 1.8 | 6.7 | 4.9 | 1.3 | 3.5 | 1.1 | 0.0 | 0.0 | 19.3 |
| 1990-91 | 0.0 | 0.0 | 0.0 | 0.0 | 0.0 | 9.3 |  |  |  |  |  |  |  |
| Record Mean | 0.0 | 0.0 | 0.0 | T | 2.0 | 6.8 | 9.8 | 9.4 | 6.1 | 0.5 | T | 0.0 | 34.7 |

**See Reference Notes, relative to all above tables, on preceding page.**

The Appalachian Mountains to the west and the Atlantic Ocean to the east have a moderating effect on climate. Periods of very high or very low temperatures seldom last for more than three or four days. Temperatures below zero or above 100 degrees are a rarity. On occasion, the area becomes engulfed with maritime air during the summer months, and high humidity adds to the discomfort of seasonably warm temperatures.

Precipitation is fairly evenly distributed throughout the year with maximum amounts during the late summer months. Much of the summer rainfall is from local thunderstorms and amounts vary in different areas of the city. This is due, in part, to the higher elevations to the west and north. Snowfall amounts are often considerably larger in the northern suburbs than in the central and southern parts of the city. In many cases, the precipitation will change from snow to rain within the city. Single storms of 10 inches or more occur about every five years.

The prevailing wind direction for the summer months is from the southwest, while northwesterly winds prevail during the winter. The annual prevailing direction is from the west-southwest. Destructive velocities are comparatively rare and occur mostly in gustiness during summer thunderstorms. High winds occurring in the winter months, as a rule, come with the advance of cold air after the passage of a deep low pressure system. Only rarely have hurricanes in the vicinity caused widespread damage, primarily because of flooding.

Flood stages in the Schuylkill River normally occur about twice a year. Flood stages seldom last over 12 hours and usually occur after excessive thunderstorms. Flooding rarely occurs on the Delaware River.

## TABLE 1 — NORMALS, MEANS AND EXTREMES

PHILADELPHIA, PENNSYLVANIA

LATITUDE: 39°53'N   LONGITUDE: 75°15'W   ELEVATION: FT. GRND   5 BARO   63   TIME ZONE: EASTERN   WBAN: 13739

| | (a) | JAN | FEB | MAR | APR | MAY | JUNE | JULY | AUG | SEP | OCT | NOV | DEC | YEAR |
|---|---|---|---|---|---|---|---|---|---|---|---|---|---|---|
| **TEMPERATURE °F:** | | | | | | | | | | | | | | |
| Normals | | | | | | | | | | | | | | |
| -Daily Maximum | | 38.6 | 41.1 | 50.5 | 63.2 | 73.0 | 81.7 | 86.1 | 84.6 | 77.8 | 66.5 | 54.5 | 43.0 | 63.4 |
| -Daily Minimum | | 23.8 | 25.0 | 33.1 | 42.6 | 52.5 | 61.5 | 66.8 | 66.0 | 58.6 | 46.5 | 37.1 | 28.0 | 45.1 |
| -Monthly | | 31.2 | 33.1 | 41.8 | 52.9 | 62.8 | 71.6 | 76.5 | 75.3 | 68.2 | 56.5 | 45.8 | 35.5 | 54.3 |
| Extremes | | | | | | | | | | | | | | |
| -Record Highest | 48 | 74 | 74 | 87 | 94 | 96 | 100 | 104 | 101 | 100 | 96 | 81 | 72 | 104 |
| -Year | | 1950 | 1985 | 1945 | 1976 | 1962 | 1988 | 1966 | 1955 | 1953 | 1941 | 1974 | 1984 | JUL 1966 |
| -Record Lowest | 48 | -7 | -4 | 7 | 19 | 28 | 44 | 51 | 44 | 35 | 25 | 15 | 1 | -7 |
| -Year | | 1984 | 1961 | 1984 | 1982 | 1966 | 1984 | 1966 | 1986 | 1963 | 1969 | 1976 | 1983 | JAN 1984 |
| **NORMAL DEGREE DAYS:** | | | | | | | | | | | | | | |
| Heating (base 65°F) | | 1048 | 893 | 719 | 363 | 127 | 0 | 0 | 0 | 33 | 273 | 576 | 915 | 4947 |
| Cooling (base 65°F) | | 0 | 0 | 0 | 0 | 59 | 202 | 357 | 319 | 129 | 9 | 0 | 0 | 1075 |
| **% OF POSSIBLE SUNSHINE** | 47 | 50 | 53 | 56 | 56 | 56 | 62 | 62 | 61 | 59 | 59 | 52 | 49 | 56 |
| **MEAN SKY COVER (tenths)** | | | | | | | | | | | | | | |
| Sunrise - Sunset | 49 | 6.6 | 6.4 | 6.3 | 6.4 | 6.5 | 6.1 | 6.0 | 5.9 | 5.7 | 5.6 | 6.3 | 6.5 | 6.2 |
| **MEAN NUMBER OF DAYS:** | | | | | | | | | | | | | | |
| Sunrise to Sunset | | | | | | | | | | | | | | |
| -Clear | 49 | 7.4 | 7.1 | 7.8 | 7.1 | 6.3 | 7.2 | 7.3 | 8.3 | 9.7 | 10.5 | 7.1 | 7.6 | 93.3 |
| -Partly Cloudy | 49 | 7.7 | 7.4 | 8.2 | 8.9 | 10.3 | 11.1 | 11.6 | 11.2 | 9.0 | 8.7 | 9.1 | 8.4 | 111.6 |
| -Cloudy | 49 | 15.9 | 13.8 | 15.0 | 14.0 | 14.4 | 11.7 | 12.1 | 11.5 | 11.3 | 11.9 | 13.8 | 15.0 | 160.3 |
| Precipitation | | | | | | | | | | | | | | |
| .01 inches or more | 49 | 10.9 | 9.4 | 10.8 | 10.7 | 11.3 | 10.1 | 9.3 | 9.0 | 8.0 | 7.6 | 9.5 | 10.0 | 116.7 |
| Snow, Ice pellets | | | | | | | | | | | | | | |
| 1.0 inches or more | 49 | 2.1 | 1.6 | 1.1 | 0.1 | 0.0 | 0.0 | 0.0 | 0.0 | 0.0 | 0.* | 0.2 | 0.9 | 6.0 |
| Thunderstorms | 49 | 0.2 | 0.3 | 1.0 | 1.9 | 4.3 | 5.4 | 5.7 | 5.0 | 2.3 | 0.8 | 0.6 | 0.2 | 27.7 |
| Heavy Fog Visibility 1/4 mile or less | 49 | 2.8 | 2.3 | 1.7 | 1.2 | 1.3 | 1.1 | 0.9 | 1.1 | 1.5 | 3.3 | 2.4 | 2.6 | 22.2 |
| Temperature °F | | | | | | | | | | | | | | |
| -Maximum | | | | | | | | | | | | | | |
| 90° and above | 30 | 0.0 | 0.0 | 0.0 | 0.3 | 0.8 | 4.0 | 8.5 | 6.1 | 1.8 | 0.0 | 0.0 | 0.0 | 21.4 |
| 32° and below | 30 | 9.4 | 5.7 | 1.0 | 0.0 | 0.0 | 0.0 | 0.0 | 0.0 | 0.0 | 0.0 | 0.1 | 4.5 | 20.6 |
| -Minimum | | | | | | | | | | | | | | |
| 32° and below | 30 | 26.4 | 22.8 | 14.5 | 2.5 | 0.* | 0.0 | 0.0 | 0.0 | 0.0 | 1.5 | 8.8 | 21.7 | 98.2 |
| 0° and below | 30 | 0.5 | 0.1 | 0.0 | 0.0 | 0.0 | 0.0 | 0.0 | 0.0 | 0.0 | 0.0 | 0.0 | 0.0 | 0.6 |
| **AVG. STATION PRESS. (mb)** | 17 | 1017.5 | 1017.6 | 1015.9 | 1013.9 | 1014.2 | 1014.3 | 1014.9 | 1016.2 | 1017.5 | 1018.6 | 1017.9 | 1018.2 | 1016.4 |
| **RELATIVE HUMIDITY (%)** | | | | | | | | | | | | | | |
| Hour 01 | 30 | 70 | 68 | 68 | 69 | 77 | 80 | 82 | 82 | 82 | 80 | 75 | 72 | 75 |
| Hour 07 (Local Time) | 30 | 73 | 71 | 71 | 70 | 75 | 77 | 79 | 81 | 83 | 83 | 78 | 74 | 76 |
| Hour 13 | 30 | 59 | 55 | 52 | 49 | 53 | 54 | 54 | 55 | 56 | 54 | 56 | 58 | 55 |
| Hour 19 | 30 | 65 | 61 | 57 | 54 | 59 | 61 | 63 | 65 | 69 | 69 | 67 | 66 | 63 |
| **PRECIPITATION (inches):** | | | | | | | | | | | | | | |
| Water Equivalent | | | | | | | | | | | | | | |
| -Normal | | 3.18 | 2.81 | 3.86 | 3.47 | 3.18 | 3.92 | 3.88 | 4.10 | 3.42 | 2.83 | 3.32 | 3.45 | 41.42 |
| -Maximum Monthly | 47 | 8.86 | 6.44 | 7.01 | 8.12 | 7.41 | 7.88 | 9.44 | 9.70 | 8.78 | 5.21 | 9.06 | 7.37 | 9.70 |
| -Year | | 1978 | 1979 | 1980 | 1983 | 1948 | 1973 | 1989 | 1955 | 1960 | 1943 | 1972 | 1983 | AUG 1955 |
| -Minimum Monthly | 47 | 0.45 | 0.96 | 0.68 | 0.52 | 0.47 | 0.11 | 0.64 | 0.49 | 0.44 | 0.09 | 0.32 | 0.25 | 0.09 |
| -Year | | 1955 | 1980 | 1966 | 1985 | 1964 | 1949 | 1957 | 1964 | 1968 | 1963 | 1976 | 1955 | OCT 1963 |
| -Maximum in 24 hrs | 43 | 2.70 | 1.96 | 2.39 | 2.76 | 3.18 | 4.62 | 4.49 | 5.68 | 5.45 | 3.85 | 3.99 | 2.04 | 5.68 |
| -Year | | 1979 | 1966 | 1968 | 1970 | 1984 | 1973 | 1989 | 1971 | 1960 | 1980 | 1977 | 1978 | AUG 1971 |
| Snow, Ice pellets | | | | | | | | | | | | | | |
| -Maximum Monthly | 47 | 23.4 | 27.6 | 13.4 | 4.3 | T | 0.0 | 0.0 | 0.0 | 0.0 | 2.1 | 8.8 | 18.8 | 27.6 |
| -Year | | 1978 | 1979 | 1958 | 1971 | 1963 | | | | | 1979 | 1953 | 1966 | FEB 1979 |
| -Maximum in 24 hrs | 47 | 13.2 | 21.3 | 10.0 | 4.3 | T | 0.0 | 0.0 | 0.0 | 0.0 | 2.1 | 8.7 | 14.6 | 21.3 |
| -Year | | 1961 | 1983 | 1958 | 1971 | 1963 | | | | | 1979 | 1953 | 1960 | FEB 1983 |
| **WIND:** | | | | | | | | | | | | | | |
| Mean Speed (mph) | 49 | 10.3 | 10.9 | 11.4 | 10.9 | 9.6 | 8.7 | 8.0 | 7.9 | 8.2 | 8.8 | 9.6 | 10.0 | 9.5 |
| Prevailing Direction through 1963 | | WNW | NW | N | SW | WSW | WSW | WSW | SW | SW | WSW | WSW | WNW | WSW |
| Fastest Mile | | | | | | | | | | | | | | |
| -Direction (!!!) | 49 | NE | NW | NW | SW | SW | NW | SW | E | NE | SW | SW | NW | NW |
| -Speed (MPH) | 49 | 61 | 59 | 56 | 59 | 56 | 73 | 49 | 67 | 49 | 66 | 60 | 48 | 73 |
| -Year | | 1958 | 1956 | 1989 | 1958 | 1957 | 1958 | 1980 | 1955 | 1960 | 1954 | 1958 | 1988 | JUN 1958 |
| Peak Gust | | | | | | | | | | | | | | |
| -Direction (!!!) | 6 | NW | NW | NW | NW | NW | NW | W | N | W | NW | NW | NW | NW |
| -Speed (mph) | 6 | 47 | 44 | 69 | 40 | 67 | 46 | 51 | 47 | 53 | 40 | 61 | 58 | 69 |
| -Date | | 1989 | 1987 | 1989 | 1988 | 1984 | 1985 | 1985 | 1988 | 1985 | 1988 | 1989 | 1988 | MAR 1989 |

See Reference Notes to this table on the following page.

PRECIPITATION (inches)   PHILADELPHIA, PENNSYLVANIA

**TABLE 2**

| YEAR | JAN | FEB | MAR | APR | MAY | JUNE | JULY | AUG | SEP | OCT | NOV | DEC | ANNUAL |
|------|-----|-----|-----|-----|-----|------|------|-----|-----|-----|-----|-----|--------|
| 1961 | 3.16 | 3.13 | 5.17 | 4.82 | 3.38 | 2.95 | 5.96 | 3.42 | 2.41 | 1.83 | 2.04 | 2.78 | 41.05 |
| 1962 | 2.95 | 3.51 | 3.91 | 3.69 | 1.85 | 7.40 | 2.30 | 6.58 | 2.77 | 0.95 | 4.60 | 2.11 | 42.62 |
| 1963 | 2.31 | 2.19 | 3.52 | 3.94 | 1.13 | 1.06 | 2.88 | 3.35 | 6.44 | 0.09 | 6.67 | 1.76 | 34.95 |
| 1964 | 3.92 | 2.83 | 1.94 | 5.27 | 0.47 | 0.21 | 3.83 | 0.49 | 2.42 | 1.73 | 1.64 | 5.13 | 29.88 |
| 1965 | 2.35 | 2.18 | 3.19 | 2.33 | 1.23 | 2.85 | 3.22 | 4.05 | 3.02 | 2.02 | 1.05 | 1.85 | 29.34 |
| 1966 | 2.82 | 4.30 | 0.68 | 4.35 | 2.95 | 0.41 | 2.35 | 1.63 | 8.70 | 5.12 | 2.36 | 4.33 | 40.00 |
| 1967 | 1.67 | 1.82 | 4.53 | 2.17 | 3.49 | 4.12 | 7.11 | 7.08 | 2.96 | 2.00 | 1.99 | 5.88 | 44.82 |
| 1968 | 2.90 | 1.40 | 4.98 | 1.57 | 5.17 | 5.89 | 2.00 | 1.24 | 0.44 | 3.15 | 4.17 | 2.54 | 35.45 |
| 1969 | 1.57 | 1.88 | 1.92 | 1.68 | 3.30 | 7.31 | 8.33 | 2.66 | 4.38 | 1.13 | 1.97 | 7.23 | 43.36 |
| 1970 | 0.74 | 2.08 | 3.83 | 6.12 | 2.57 | 4.60 | 2.75 | 3.99 | 0.82 | 3.66 | 4.71 | 3.27 | 39.14 |
| 1971 | 2.13 | 5.43 | 2.58 | 1.84 | 4.10 | 1.01 | 4.84 | 9.61 | 5.83 | 3.84 | 5.37 | 1.21 | 47.79 |
| 1972 | 2.34 | 5.09 | 2.69 | 4.08 | 4.11 | 5.79 | 2.62 | 3.76 | 1.12 | 3.77 | 9.06 | 5.20 | 49.63 |
| 1973 | 3.93 | 2.96 | 3.52 | 6.68 | 4.14 | 7.88 | 2.39 | 2.03 | 3.39 | 2.16 | 0.64 | 6.34 | 46.06 |
| 1974 | 2.95 | 2.14 | 4.91 | 2.77 | 3.21 | 4.43 | 2.08 | 3.83 | 4.68 | 1.93 | 0.81 | 4.04 | 37.78 |
| 1975 | 4.00 | 2.91 | 4.68 | 2.97 | 4.99 | 7.57 | 6.32 | 2.21 | 7.21 | 3.24 | 3.14 | 2.89 | 52.13 |
| 1976 | 4.50 | 1.66 | 2.38 | 2.06 | 4.35 | 3.42 | 4.04 | 2.17 | 2.44 | 4.30 | 0.32 | 1.63 | 33.27 |
| 1977 | 2.61 | 1.33 | 4.19 | 5.59 | 0.70 | 5.33 | 1.47 | 8.70 | 3.44 | 3.11 | 7.76 | 5.19 | 49.42 |
| 1978 | 8.86 | 1.35 | 4.31 | 1.76 | 6.01 | 1.75 | 5.27 | 6.04 | 1.59 | 1.20 | 2.20 | 5.61 | 45.95 |
| 1979 | 8.74 | 6.44 | 2.43 | 4.08 | 3.98 | 4.34 | 3.95 | 5.95 | 4.89 | 3.84 | 2.48 | 1.67 | 52.79 |
| 1980 | 2.27 | 0.96 | 7.01 | 4.79 | 3.22 | 1.73 | 6.58 | 0.80 | 2.79 | 5.03 | 2.85 | 0.77 | 38.80 |
| 1981 | 0.50 | 2.94 | 1.61 | 3.60 | 4.53 | 4.40 | 4.54 | 5.11 | 2.83 | 2.68 | 0.95 | 4.14 | 37.83 |
| 1982 | 4.45 | 3.16 | 2.66 | 6.06 | 4.47 | 5.76 | 1.94 | 2.20 | 2.32 | 1.94 | 3.67 | 1.80 | 40.43 |
| 1983 | 2.81 | 3.53 | 6.70 | 8.12 | 7.03 | 2.75 | 0.68 | 2.57 | 3.45 | 3.69 | 5.71 | 7.37 | 54.41 |
| 1984 | 2.22 | 2.81 | 6.14 | 4.25 | 6.87 | 2.85 | 6.99 | 3.28 | 1.96 | 2.56 | 1.56 | 2.17 | 43.66 |
| 1985 | 1.55 | 2.44 | 1.95 | 0.52 | 4.99 | 1.88 | 4.66 | 2.82 | 5.78 | 1.54 | 6.09 | 0.98 | 35.20 |
| 1986 | 4.13 | 3.38 | 1.25 | 4.46 | 0.70 | 1.99 | 4.10 | 3.70 | 2.33 | 2.22 | 6.27 | 5.89 | 40.42 |
| 1987 | 4.58 | 1.17 | 1.16 | 3.63 | 3.15 | 2.01 | 4.82 | 3.72 | 2.78 | 2.62 | 2.08 | 1.68 | 33.40 |
| 1988 | 2.72 | 4.11 | 2.24 | 2.92 | 3.67 | 0.57 | 8.07 | 3.16 | 2.62 | 2.16 | 5.17 | 1.00 | 38.41 |
| 1989 | 2.41 | 3.25 | 4.41 | 2.27 | 6.76 | 4.73 | 9.44 | 3.92 | 5.03 | 3.44 | 1.79 | 1.21 | 48.66 |
| 1990 | 4.09 | 1.44 | 2.59 | 3.16 | 6.08 | 3.39 | 2.62 | 4.07 | 1.71 | 1.68 | 1.17 | 3.79 | 35.79 |
| Record Mean | 3.24 | 3.06 | 3.50 | 3.36 | 3.47 | 3.59 | 4.16 | 4.42 | 3.37 | 2.79 | 3.13 | 3.18 | 41.26 |

**TABLE 3**   AVERAGE TEMPERATURE (deg. F)   PHILADELPHIA, PENNSYLVANIA

| YEAR | JAN | FEB | MAR | APR | MAY | JUNE | JULY | AUG | SEP | OCT | NOV | DEC | ANNUAL |
|------|-----|-----|-----|-----|-----|------|------|-----|-----|-----|-----|-----|--------|
| 1961 | 25.0 | 34.0 | 43.1 | 49.8 | 58.6 | 69.9 | 75.6 | 73.5 | 71.5 | 55.7 | 45.2 | 31.0 | 52.7 |
| 1962 | 30.0 | 30.4 | 40.5 | 52.0 | 64.1 | 71.7 | 72.0 | 72.0 | 63.1 | 56.3 | 42.1 | 31.0 | 52.1 |
| 1963 | 27.5 | 26.5 | 42.9 | 52.5 | 60.2 | 70.4 | 70.4 | 71.2 | 62.8 | 57.1 | 27.9 | 37.5 | 51.9 |
| 1964 | 33.0 | 31.8 | 42.7 | 50.8 | 65.1 | 72.4 | 76.6 | 72.2 | 67.2 | 52.6 | 47.1 | 37.5 | 54.1 |
| 1965 | 29.2 | 33.3 | 37.6 | 49.0 | 65.5 | 70.0 | 74.1 | 73.1 | 69.2 | 53.7 | 44.2 | 37.0 | 53.0 |
| 1966 | 29.1 | 31.5 | 42.5 | 47.8 | 59.5 | 72.1 | 77.9 | 74.8 | 65.2 | 53.1 | 46.8 | 35.5 | 53.0 |
| 1967 | 36.0 | 29.0 | 38.5 | 51.7 | 55.9 | 72.1 | 76.6 | 75.1 | 67.0 | 56.8 | 42.8 | 38.5 | 53.3 |
| 1968 | 28.9 | 30.4 | 44.4 | 54.6 | 59.7 | 71.2 | 77.1 | 77.8 | 69.4 | 58.1 | 45.6 | 32.3 | 54.1 |
| 1969 | 29.8 | 32.0 | 39.7 | 55.3 | 64.6 | 73.4 | 75.1 | 75.2 | 67.2 | 55.0 | 44.4 | 33.5 | 53.8 |
| 1970 | 24.5 | 33.1 | 38.3 | 51.5 | 64.9 | 71.6 | 76.9 | 76.7 | 72.0 | 60.1 | 48.2 | 35.8 | 54.5 |
| 1971 | 27.8 | 36.1 | 40.7 | 51.6 | 60.9 | 74.3 | 77.4 | 75.3 | 71.6 | 63.5 | 46.1 | 41.6 | 55.6 |
| 1972 | 35.1 | 32.4 | 40.7 | 49.7 | 63.6 | 68.7 | 77.1 | 76.0 | 69.2 | 52.7 | 43.6 | 39.9 | 54.1 |
| 1973 | 34.4 | 33.6 | 47.2 | 53.4 | 60.3 | 74.6 | 77.9 | 78.8 | 70.7 | 59.2 | 48.0 | 38.6 | 56.4 |
| 1974 | 35.9 | 31.7 | 43.3 | 55.8 | 62.4 | 70.3 | 76.9 | 76.8 | 68.1 | 54.8 | 48.5 | 39.4 | 55.3 |
| 1975 | 37.3 | 35.8 | 41.2 | 48.7 | 66.6 | 72.2 | 76.6 | 77.1 | 66.6 | 61.2 | 52.7 | 36.9 | 56.1 |
| 1976 | 28.7 | 40.9 | 46.3 | 56.6 | 62.7 | 75.2 | 75.3 | 74.8 | 67.3 | 52.5 | 39.9 | 30.3 | 54.2 |
| 1977 | 20.0 | 33.6 | 48.8 | 57.2 | 65.8 | 68.6 | 77.8 | 76.2 | 69.9 | 54.3 | 46.4 | 32.6 | 54.3 |
| 1978 | 28.0 | 24.7 | 39.0 | 50.6 | 61.4 | 72.6 | 75.6 | 79.2 | 68.5 | 55.5 | 47.9 | 38.6 | 53.5 |
| 1979 | 32.5 | 23.0 | 47.0 | 52.3 | 64.6 | 69.1 | 76.2 | 75.5 | 68.5 | 54.9 | 50.1 | 38.2 | 54.5 |
| 1980 | 31.8 | 29.7 | 40.2 | 54.7 | 65.4 | 70.6 | 78.5 | 80.0 | 72.2 | 54.9 | 43.2 | 32.5 | 54.5 |
| 1981 | 25.3 | 37.9 | 40.0 | 54.7 | 62.6 | 72.0 | 76.9 | 74.9 | 66.8 | 53.1 | 45.6 | 34.6 | 53.7 |
| 1982 | 24.7 | 34.4 | 41.7 | 50.2 | 65.9 | 68.7 | 76.9 | 73.5 | 67.6 | 56.9 | 48.4 | 41.3 | 54.2 |
| 1983 | 34.1 | 34.0 | 43.7 | 51.0 | 62.1 | 72.0 | 77.9 | 77.1 | 69.0 | 56.6 | 46.7 | 33.2 | 54.8 |
| 1984 | 26.2 | 38.7 | 35.5 | 50.2 | 60.2 | 73.0 | 73.9 | 75.2 | 64.7 | 61.2 | 44.4 | 41.9 | 53.8 |
| 1985 | 27.3 | 35.3 | 44.6 | 55.5 | 64.5 | 68.8 | 75.4 | 74.1 | 69.1 | 59.3 | 51.3 | 33.3 | 54.9 |
| 1986 | 32.8 | 32.1 | 44.5 | 53.3 | 66.8 | 73.8 | 78.1 | 74.0 | 68.3 | 57.8 | 44.5 | 37.9 | 55.3 |
| 1987 | 31.9 | 32.5 | 45.7 | 53.1 | 63.9 | 74.6 | 79.5 | 75.4 | 68.8 | 52.5 | 48.0 | 39.2 | 55.4 |
| 1988 | 27.3 | 34.6 | 44.7 | 51.3 | 63.6 | 72.3 | 80.7 | 78.3 | 66.7 | 51.8 | 47.7 | 35.4 | 54.5 |
| 1989 | 36.5 | 34.8 | 42.3 | 52.4 | 62.4 | 74.7 | 76.3 | 75.6 | 69.7 | 58.3 | 44.9 | 25.5 | 54.5 |
| 1990 | 40.3 | 41.2 | 46.1 | 53.3 | 61.3 | 72.2 | 78.0 | 75.8 | 68.0 | 61.9 | 49.7 | 42.1 | 57.5 |
| Record Mean | 32.6 | 33.8 | 41.8 | 52.3 | 63.0 | 71.8 | 76.7 | 74.9 | 68.4 | 57.3 | 46.3 | 36.1 | 54.6 |
| Max | 39.7 | 41.3 | 50.2 | 61.7 | 72.7 | 81.1 | 85.5 | 83.3 | 77.0 | 66.0 | 54.0 | 43.1 | 63.0 |
| Min | 25.5 | 26.2 | 33.4 | 42.9 | 53.4 | 62.5 | 67.9 | 66.4 | 59.8 | 48.5 | 38.5 | 29.1 | 46.2 |

## REFERENCE NOTES FOR TABLES 1, 2, 3 and 6   (PHILADELPHIA, PA)

### GENERAL

T - TRACE AMOUNT
BLANK ENTRIES DENOTE MISSING/UNREPORTED DATA.
# INDICATES A STATION OR INSTRUMENT RELOCATION.

### SPECIFIC

#### TABLE 1

(a) - LENGTH OF RECORD IN YEARS. ALTHOUGH
      INDIVIDUAL MONTHS MAY BE MISSING.
  * LESS THAN .05

NORMALS — BASED ON THE 1951-1980 RECORD PERIOD.
EXTREMES — DATES ARE THE MOST RECENT OCCURRENCE.
WIND DIR. — NUMERALS SHOW TENS OF DEGREES
            CLOCKWISE FROM TRUE NORTH.
            "00" INDICATES CALM.
RESULTANT WIND DIRECTIONS ARE GIVEN TO WHOLE DEGREES.

#### TABLE 3
MAX AND MIN ARE LONG-TERM MEAN DAILY MAXIMUM
AND MEAN DAILY MINIMUM TEMPERATURES.

### EXCEPTIONS

**TABLES 2, 3, and 6**

RECORD MEANS ARE THROUGH THE CURRENT YEAR,
BEGINNING IN    1874 FOR TEMPERATURE
                1872 FOR PRECIPITATION
                1943 FOR SNOWFALL

HEATING DEGREE DAYS Base 65 deg. F          PHILADELPHIA, PENNSYLVANIA

**TABLE 4**

| SEASON | JULY | AUG | SEP | OCT | NOV | DEC | JAN | FEB | MAR | APR | MAY | JUNE | TOTAL |
|---|---|---|---|---|---|---|---|---|---|---|---|---|---|
| 1961-62 | 0 | 0 | 45 | 283 | 593 | 1049 | 1078 | 963 | 748 | 408 | 133 | 7 | 5307 |
| 1962-63 | 0 | 4 | 109 | 272 | 681 | 1048 | 1159 | 1072 | 680 | 375 | 175 | 12 | 5587 |
| 1963-64 | 0 | 7 | 118 | 242 | 502 | 1144 | 985 | 955 | 685 | 424 | 76 | 13 | 5151 |
| 1964-65 | 0 | 2 | 51 | 377 | 532 | 847 | 1107 | 883 | 839 | 475 | 66 | 26 | 5205 |
| 1965-66 | 0 | 18 | 41 | 342 | 614 | 862 | 1110 | 931 | 693 | 509 | 207 | 21 | 5348 |
| 1966-67 | 0 | 0 | 83 | 362 | 538 | 908 | 893 | 1001 | 817 | 396 | 280 | 6 | 5284 |
| 1967-68 | 0 | 0 | 55 | 271 | 660 | 814 | 1112 | 995 | 633 | 305 | 170 | 7 | 5022 |
| 1968-69 | 0 | 0 | 14 | 234 | 576 | 1008 | 1084 | 918 | 782 | 290 | 84 | 2 | 4992 |
| 1969-70 | 0 | 0 | 54 | 316 | 611 | 970 | 1247 | 890 | 821 | 399 | 92 | 0 | 5400 |
| 1970-71 | 0 | 0 | 29 | 191 | 499 | 899 | 1145 | 802 | 746 | 394 | 140 | 3 | 4848 |
| 1971-72 | 0 | 0 | 17 | 79 | 576 | 719 | 920 | 941 | 748 | 450 | 86 | 26 | 4562 |
| 1972-73 | 0 | 0 | 22 | 378 | 635 | 775 | 940 | 874 | 547 | 359 | 176 | 1 | 4707 |
| 1973-74 | 0 | 0 | 18 | 196 | 507 | 810 | 897 | 926 | 667 | 292 | 128 | 11 | 4452 |
| 1974-75 | 0 | 0 | 46 | 313 | 500 | 786 | 852 | 812 | 732 | 483 | 66 | 4 | 4594 |
| 1975-76 | 0 | 0 | 45 | 152 | 372 | 866 | 1120 | 692 | 572 | 307 | 119 | 13 | 4258 |
| 1976-77 | 0 | 2 | 42 | 387 | 743 | 1069 | 1390 | 873 | 505 | 258 | 73 | 36 | 5378 |
| 1977-78 | 0 | 0 | 24 | 328 | 558 | 998 | 1139 | 1121 | 797 | 423 | 161 | 10 | 5559 |
| 1978-79 | 5 | 0 | 41 | 296 | 507 | 811 | 999 | 1170 | 556 | 378 | 38 | 17 | 4818 |
| 1979-80 | 4 | 7 | 28 | 324 | 439 | 823 | 1021 | 1016 | 763 | 301 | 72 | 17 | 4815 |
| 1980-81 | 0 | 0 | 22 | 320 | 646 | 999 | 1222 | 752 | 768 | 309 | 129 | 4 | 5171 |
| 1981-82 | 0 | 0 | 58 | 364 | 576 | 936 | 1243 | 850 | 714 | 440 | 50 | 25 | 5256 |
| 1982-83 | 0 | 8 | 31 | 277 | 497 | 730 | 951 | 861 | 653 | 423 | 128 | 2 | 4561 |
| 1983-84 | 0 | 0 | 70 | 283 | 540 | 981 | 1196 | 756 | 911 | 438 | 181 | 13 | 5369 |
| 1984-85 | 0 | 0 | 92 | 138 | 613 | 709 | 1161 | 824 | 627 | 306 | 89 | 9 | 4568 |
| 1985-86 | 0 | 0 | 38 | 187 | 407 | 975 | 990 | 914 | 628 | 345 | 77 | 6 | 4567 |
| 1986-87 | 0 | 21 | 23 | 255 | 609 | 838 | 1017 | 904 | 591 | 359 | 129 | 1 | 4747 |
| 1987-88 | 0 | 0 | 20 | 379 | 504 | 796 | 1162 | 876 | 624 | 404 | 105 | 32 | 4902 |
| 1988-89 | 0 | 0 | 35 | 408 | 513 | 908 | 876 | 840 | 700 | 371 | 138 | 0 | 4789 |
| 1989-90 | 0 | 0 | 43 | 220 | 594 | 1219 | 757 | 662 | 588 | 375 | 127 | 6 | 4591 |
| 1990-91 | 2 | 1 | 55 | 171 | 453 | 701 | | | | | | | |

**TABLE 5**  COOLING DEGREE DAYS Base 65 deg. F          PHILADELPHIA, PENNSYLVANIA

| YEAR | JAN | FEB | MAR | APR | MAY | JUNE | JULY | AUG | SEP | OCT | NOV | DEC | TOTAL |
|---|---|---|---|---|---|---|---|---|---|---|---|---|---|
| 1969 | 0 | 0 | 0 | 9 | 77 | 259 | 319 | 323 | 126 | 15 | 0 | 0 | 1128 |
| 1970 | 0 | 0 | 0 | 3 | 100 | 204 | 376 | 367 | 247 | 46 | 0 | 0 | 1343 |
| 1971 | 0 | 0 | 0 | 0 | 19 | 292 | 394 | 326 | 223 | 37 | 14 | 0 | 1305 |
| 1972 | 0 | 0 | 3 | 0 | 47 | 143 | 381 | 344 | 153 | 3 | 0 | 0 | 1074 |
| 1973 | 0 | 0 | 0 | 16 | 35 | 294 | 404 | 435 | 193 | 23 | 0 | 0 | 1400 |
| 1974 | 0 | 0 | 0 | 24 | 55 | 179 | 373 | 372 | 145 | 5 | 12 | 0 | 1165 |
| 1975 | 0 | 0 | 0 | 0 | 121 | 224 | 366 | 380 | 98 | 42 | 12 | 0 | 1243 |
| 1976 | 0 | 0 | 0 | 64 | 58 | 326 | 326 | 315 | 115 | 7 | 0 | 0 | 1211 |
| 1977 | 0 | 0 | 10 | 32 | 104 | 150 | 402 | 355 | 175 | 3 | 6 | 0 | 1237 |
| 1978 | 0 | 0 | 0 | 0 | 57 | 244 | 338 | 447 | 153 | 8 | 0 | 0 | 1247 |
| 1979 | 0 | 0 | 6 | 5 | 90 | 146 | 357 | 339 | 137 | 16 | 1 | 0 | 1097 |
| 1980 | 0 | 0 | 0 | 0 | 89 | 194 | 428 | 470 | 244 | 10 | 0 | 0 | 1435 |
| 1981 | 0 | 0 | 0 | 9 | 62 | 224 | 373 | 315 | 119 | 1 | 0 | 0 | 1103 |
| 1982 | 0 | 0 | 0 | 3 | 85 | 142 | 376 | 280 | 115 | 31 | 5 | 0 | 1037 |
| 1983 | 0 | 0 | 0 | 11 | 43 | 217 | 409 | 380 | 199 | 27 | 0 | 0 | 1286 |
| 1984 | 0 | 0 | 0 | 0 | 39 | 260 | 283 | 324 | 90 | 30 | 0 | 0 | 1026 |
| 1985 | 0 | 0 | 0 | 27 | 81 | 133 | 330 | 291 | 166 | 19 | 0 | 0 | 1047 |
| 1986 | 0 | 0 | 0 | 0 | 139 | 278 | 413 | 307 | 129 | 40 | 0 | 0 | 1306 |
| 1987 | 0 | 0 | 0 | 7 | 101 | 295 | 456 | 332 | 142 | 0 | 0 | 0 | 1333 |
| 1988 | 0 | 0 | 0 | 1 | 70 | 259 | 495 | 418 | 93 | 7 | 0 | 0 | 1343 |
| 1989 | 0 | 0 | 1 | 1 | 62 | 298 | 357 | 332 | 192 | 18 | 1 | 0 | 1262 |
| 1990 | 0 | 0 | 9 | 29 | 20 | 226 | 413 | 341 | 152 | 83 | 1 | 0 | 1274 |

**TABLE 6**  SNOWFALL (inches)          PHILADELPHIA, PENNSYLVANIA

| SEASON | JULY | AUG | SEP | OCT | NOV | DEC | JAN | FEB | MAR | APR | MAY | JUNE | TOTAL |
|---|---|---|---|---|---|---|---|---|---|---|---|---|---|
| 1961-62 | 0.0 | 0.0 | 0.0 | 0.0 | 3.2 | 5.2 | 1.1 | 12.5 | 7.2 | T | 0.0 | 0.0 | 29.2 |
| 1962-63 | 0.0 | 0.0 | 0.0 | T | T | 9.5 | 6.1 | 4.7 | 0.2 | 0.0 | T | 0.0 | 20.5 |
| 1963-64 | 0.0 | 0.0 | 0.0 | 0.0 | T | 8.0 | 7.4 | 12.4 | 5.1 | T | 0.0 | 0.0 | 32.9 |
| 1964-65 | 0.0 | 0.0 | 0.0 | 0.0 | T | 2.6 | 11.9 | 2.2 | 6.5 | 3.0 | 0.0 | 0.0 | 26.2 |
| 1965-66 | 0.0 | 0.0 | 0.0 | T | 0.0 | T | 16.0 | 11.4 | T | T | 0.0 | 0.0 | 27.4 |
| 1966-67 | 0.0 | 0.0 | 0.0 | 0.0 | T | 18.8 | 0.6 | 18.4 | 6.4 | 0.1 | 0.0 | 0.0 | 44.3 |
| 1967-68 | 0.0 | 0.0 | 0.0 | 0.0 | 4.9 | 5.6 | 1.5 | 1.7 | 2.2 | 0.0 | 0.0 | 0.0 | 15.9 |
| 1968-69 | 0.0 | 0.0 | 0.0 | 0.0 | 0.4 | 3.1 | 1.9 | 9.5 | 8.8 | 0.0 | 0.0 | 0.0 | 23.7 |
| 1969-70 | 0.0 | 0.0 | 0.0 | 0.0 | 0.2 | 7.5 | 7.5 | 2.7 | 2.4 | T | 0.0 | 0.0 | 20.3 |
| 1970-71 | 0.0 | 0.0 | 0.0 | T | 0.0 | 1.1 | 7.7 | 0.8 | 4.4 | 4.3 | 0.0 | 0.0 | 18.3 |
| 1971-72 | 0.0 | 0.0 | 0.0 | 0.0 | T | 0.1 | 3.2 | 8.2 | 0.3 | 0.4 | 0.0 | 0.0 | 12.2 |
| 1972-73 | 0.0 | 0.0 | 0.0 | T | T | T | T | T | T | T | 0.0 | 0.0 | T |
| 1973-74 | 0.0 | 0.0 | 0.0 | 0.0 | T | 4.6 | 4.1 | 12.1 | T | T | 0.0 | 0.0 | 20.8 |
| 1974-75 | 0.0 | 0.0 | 0.0 | 0.0 | T | 0.8 | 3.9 | 6.6 | 2.3 | T | 0.0 | 0.0 | 13.6 |
| 1975-76 | 0.0 | 0.0 | 0.0 | 0.0 | 0.0 | 1.1 | 6.4 | 3.1 | 6.9 | 0.0 | 0.0 | 0.0 | 17.5 |
| 1976-77 | 0.0 | 0.0 | 0.0 | 0.0 | T | 2.8 | 15.7 | 0.2 | T | 0.0 | 0.0 | 0.0 | 18.7 |
| 1977-78 | 0.0 | 0.0 | 0.0 | 0.0 | 0.2 | 0.2 | 23.4 | 19.0 | 12.1 | T | 0.0 | 0.0 | 54.9 |
| 1978-79 | 0.0 | 0.0 | 0.0 | 0.0 | 2.5 | 10.1 | 27.6 | T | T | 0.0 | 0.0 | 0.0 | 40.2 |
| 1979-80 | 0.0 | 0.0 | 0.0 | 2.1 | T | 4.9 | 6.1 | 0.4 | 7.4 | T | 0.0 | 0.0 | 20.9 |
| 1980-81 | 0.0 | 0.0 | 0.0 | 0.0 | 0.2 | 1.4 | 5.0 | T | 8.8 | 0.0 | 0.0 | 0.0 | 15.4 |
| 1981-82 | 0.0 | 0.0 | 0.0 | 0.0 | T | 2.8 | 14.0 | 3.5 | 1.1 | 4.0 | 0.0 | 0.0 | 25.4 |
| 1982-83 | 0.0 | 0.0 | 0.0 | 0.0 | 0.0 | 6.8 | 0.2 | 26.1 | 0.9 | 1.9 | 0.0 | 0.0 | 35.9 |
| 1983-84 | 0.0 | 0.0 | 0.0 | 0.0 | 0.8 | T | 10.5 | T | 10.3 | T | 0.0 | 0.0 | 21.6 |
| 1984-85 | 0.0 | 0.0 | 0.0 | 0.0 | T | 0.2 | 11.9 | 4.4 | T | T | 0.0 | 0.0 | 16.5 |
| 1985-86 | 0.0 | 0.0 | 0.0 | 0.0 | 0.0 | 1.5 | 3.4 | 11.5 | T | T | 0.0 | 0.0 | 16.4 |
| 1986-87 | 0.0 | 0.0 | 0.0 | 0.0 | T | 0.4 | 15.2 | 10.1 | T | T | 0.0 | 0.0 | 25.7 |
| 1987-88 | 0.0 | 0.0 | 0.0 | 0.0 | 1.4 | 1.5 | 10.6 | 1.5 | T | 0.0 | 0.0 | 0.0 | 15.0 |
| 1988-89 | 0.0 | 0.0 | 0.0 | 0.0 | 0.0 | 0.4 | 6.0 | 2.4 | 2.4 | 0.0 | 0.0 | 0.0 | 11.2 |
| 1989-90 | 0.0 | 0.0 | 0.0 | 0.0 | 4.6 | 5.3 | 1.4 | 0.9 | 2.4 | 2.4 | 0.0 | 0.0 | 17.0 |
| 1990-91 | 0.0 | 0.0 | 0.0 | 0.0 | 0.0 | 6.4 | | | | | | | |
| Record Mean | 0.0 | 0.0 | 0.0 | T | 0.7 | 3.6 | 6.6 | 6.5 | 3.6 | 0.3 | T | 0.0 | 21.4 |

**See Reference Notes, relative to all above tables, on preceding page.**

Pittsburgh lies at the foothills of the Allegheny Mountains at the confluence of the Allegheny and Monongahela Rivers which form the Ohio. The city is a little over 100 miles southeast of Lake Erie. It has a humid continental type of climate modified only slightly by its nearness to the Atlantic Seaboard and the Great Lakes.

The predominant winter air masses influencing the climate of Pittsburgh have a polar continental source in Canada and move in from the Hudson Bay region or the Canadian Rockies. During the summer, frequent invasions of air from the Gulf of Mexico bring warm humid weather. Occasionally, Gulf air reaches as far north as Pittsburgh during the winter and produces intermittent periods of thawing. The last spring temperature of 32 degrees usually occurs in late April and the first in late October. The average growing season is about 180 days. There is a wide variation in the time of the first and last frosts over a radius of 25 miles from the center of Pittsburgh due to terrain differences.

Precipitation is distributed well throughout the year. During the winter months about a fourth of the precipitation occurs as snow and there is about a 50 percent chance of measurable precipitation on any day. Thunderstorms occur normally during all months, except midwinter, and have a maximum frequency in midsummer. The first appreciable snowfall generally occurs in late November and usually the last occurs early in April. Snow lies on the ground in the suburbs on an average of about 33 days during the year.

Seven months of the year, April through October, have sunshine more than 50 percent of the possible time. During the remaining five months cloudiness is heavier because the track of migratory storms from west to east is closer to the area and because of the frequent periods of cloudy, showery weather associated with northwest winds from across the Great Lakes. Cold air drainage induced by the many hills leads to the frequent formation of early morning fog which may be quite persistent in the river valleys during the colder months.

Rising of the tributary streams cause occasional flooding at Pittsburgh. Serious inconvenience is occasioned by the Ohio River reaching the flood stage of 25 feet about once each year. Significant flooding, or a 30-foot stage, occurs about once each three years.

## TABLE 1   NORMALS, MEANS AND EXTREMES

### PITTSBURGH, GRTR. PITT. AIRPORT PENNSYLVANIA

LATITUDE: 40°30'N   LONGITUDE: 80°13'W   ELEVATION: FT. GRND 1137 BARO 1213   TIME ZONE: EASTERN   WBAN: 94823

| | (a) | JAN | FEB | MAR | APR | MAY | JUNE | JULY | AUG | SEP | OCT | NOV | DEC | YEAR |
|---|---|---|---|---|---|---|---|---|---|---|---|---|---|---|
| **TEMPERATURE °F:** | | | | | | | | | | | | | | |
| Normals | | | | | | | | | | | | | | |
| -Daily Maximum | | 34.1 | 36.8 | 47.6 | 60.7 | 70.8 | 79.1 | 82.7 | 81.1 | 74.8 | 62.9 | 49.8 | 38.4 | 59.9 |
| -Daily Minimum | | 19.2 | 20.7 | 29.4 | 39.4 | 48.5 | 57.1 | 61.3 | 60.1 | 53.3 | 42.1 | 33.3 | 24.3 | 40.7 |
| -Monthly | | 26.7 | 28.8 | 38.5 | 50.1 | 59.7 | 68.1 | 72.0 | 70.6 | 64.1 | 52.5 | 41.6 | 31.4 | 50.3 |
| Extremes | | | | | | | | | | | | | | |
| -Record Highest | 37 | 69 | 69 | 82 | 88 | 91 | 98 | 103 | 100 | 97 | 87 | 82 | 74 | 103 |
| -Year | | 1985 | 1954 | 1986 | 1986 | 1987 | 1988 | 1988 | 1988 | 1954 | 1959 | 1961 | 1982 | JUL 1988 |
| -Record Lowest | 37 | -18 | -12 | -1 | 14 | 26 | 34 | 42 | 39 | 31 | 16 | -1 | -12 | -18 |
| -Year | | 1985 | 1979 | 1980 | 1982 | 1970 | 1972 | 1963 | 1982 | 1959 | 1965 | 1958 | 1989 | JAN 1985 |
| **NORMAL DEGREE DAYS:** | | | | | | | | | | | | | | |
| Heating (base 65°F) | | 1187 | 1014 | 822 | 447 | 201 | 28 | 0 | 13 | 101 | 393 | 702 | 1042 | 5950 |
| Cooling (base 65°F) | | 0 | 0 | 0 | 0 | 37 | 121 | 222 | 186 | 74 | 5 | 0 | 0 | 645 |
| **% OF POSSIBLE SUNSHINE** | 37 | 33 | 37 | 44 | 47 | 51 | 57 | 58 | 56 | 56 | 51 | 37 | 29 | 46 |
| **MEAN SKY COVER (tenths)** | | | | | | | | | | | | | | |
| Sunrise - Sunset | 37 | 8.0 | 7.9 | 7.5 | 7.1 | 6.9 | 6.4 | 6.3 | 6.3 | 6.1 | 6.3 | 7.7 | 8.2 | 7.1 |
| **MEAN NUMBER OF DAYS:** | | | | | | | | | | | | | | |
| Sunrise to Sunset | | | | | | | | | | | | | | |
| -Clear | 37 | 2.9 | 3.3 | 4.3 | 4.6 | 5.2 | 5.1 | 5.3 | 6.4 | 7.5 | 7.8 | 3.8 | 2.6 | 58.8 |
| -Partly Cloudy | 37 | 6.1 | 5.9 | 6.9 | 8.1 | 9.2 | 11.7 | 13.1 | 11.6 | 10.1 | 8.6 | 6.3 | 5.7 | 103.3 |
| -Cloudy | 37 | 21.9 | 19.1 | 19.8 | 17.2 | 16.6 | 13.2 | 12.6 | 13.0 | 12.4 | 14.6 | 19.9 | 22.7 | 203.1 |
| Precipitation | | | | | | | | | | | | | | |
| .01 inches or more | 37 | 16.3 | 14.1 | 15.7 | 13.6 | 12.6 | 11.6 | 10.5 | 9.7 | 9.3 | 10.7 | 13.2 | 16.4 | 153.6 |
| Snow,Ice pellets | | | | | | | | | | | | | | |
| 1.0 inches or more | 37 | 3.7 | 2.9 | 2.3 | 0.5 | 0.1 | 0.0 | 0.0 | 0.0 | 0.0 | 0.1 | 1.0 | 2.6 | 13.1 |
| Thunderstorms | 37 | 0.1 | 0.4 | 1.8 | 3.2 | 5.2 | 6.8 | 6.8 | 5.5 | 3.0 | 1.3 | 0.6 | 0.3 | 35.0 |
| Heavy Fog Visibility | | | | | | | | | | | | | | |
| 1/4 mile or less | 37 | 1.3 | 1.2 | 1.0 | 0.8 | 1.2 | 1.1 | 1.6 | 2.1 | 2.5 | 1.8 | 1.5 | 1.7 | 17.9 |
| Temperature °F | | | | | | | | | | | | | | |
| -Maximum | | | | | | | | | | | | | | |
| 90° and above | 30 | 0.0 | 0.0 | 0.0 | 0.0 | 0.3 | 1.6 | 3.4 | 1.7 | 0.6 | 0.0 | 0.0 | 0.0 | 7.5 |
| 32° and below | 30 | 14.8 | 10.8 | 3.8 | 0.1 | 0.0 | 0.0 | 0.0 | 0.0 | 0.0 | 0.0 | 1.3 | 10.4 | 41.3 |
| -Minimum | | | | | | | | | | | | | | |
| 32° and below | 30 | 27.4 | 24.2 | 19.8 | 8.4 | 0.9 | 0.0 | 0.0 | 0.0 | 0.0 | 4.2 | 14.2 | 24.9 | 124.1 |
| 0° and below | 30 | 2.6 | 1.5 | 0.1 | 0.0 | 0.0 | 0.0 | 0.0 | 0.0 | 0.0 | 0.0 | 0.* | 0.9 | 5.2 |
| **AVG. STATION PRESS.(mb)** | 17 | 973.2 | 973.4 | 971.8 | 971.0 | 971.4 | 972.3 | 973.6 | 974.5 | 975.0 | 975.3 | 974.0 | 973.9 | 973.3 |
| **RELATIVE HUMIDITY (%)** | | | | | | | | | | | | | | |
| Hour 01 | 29 | 72 | 70 | 69 | 66 | 73 | 77 | 80 | 82 | 82 | 77 | 75 | 75 | 75 |
| Hour 07 | 29 | 75 | 74 | 74 | 72 | 76 | 79 | 82 | 85 | 86 | 81 | 78 | 77 | 78 |
| Hour 13 (Local Time) | 29 | 65 | 62 | 57 | 50 | 52 | 52 | 53 | 56 | 56 | 54 | 62 | 67 | 57 |
| Hour 19 | 29 | 66 | 63 | 58 | 52 | 55 | 57 | 59 | 62 | 66 | 62 | 68 | 70 | 62 |
| **PRECIPITATION (inches):** | | | | | | | | | | | | | | |
| Water Equivalent | | | | | | | | | | | | | | |
| -Normal | | 2.86 | 2.40 | 3.58 | 3.28 | 3.54 | 3.30 | 3.83 | 3.31 | 2.80 | 2.49 | 2.34 | 2.57 | 36.30 |
| -Maximum Monthly | 37 | 6.25 | 5.98 | 6.10 | 7.61 | 6.56 | 10.29 | 7.43 | 7.86 | 5.42 | 8.20 | 11.05 | 5.24 | 11.05 |
| -Year | | 1978 | 1956 | 1967 | 1964 | 1989 | 1989 | 1958 | 1987 | 1972 | 1954 | 1985 | 1978 | NOV 1985 |
| -Minimum Monthly | 37 | 0.77 | 0.51 | 1.14 | 0.48 | 1.21 | 0.90 | 1.62 | 0.78 | 0.28 | 0.16 | 0.90 | 0.40 | 0.16 |
| -Year | | 1981 | 1969 | 1969 | 1971 | 1965 | 1967 | 1989 | 1957 | 1985 | 1963 | 1976 | 1955 | OCT 1963 |
| -Maximum in 24 hrs | 37 | 1.69 | 2.30 | 2.00 | 2.15 | 2.44 | 2.96 | 2.97 | 3.06 | 2.25 | 3.56 | 1.97 | 1.76 | 3.56 |
| -Year | | 1986 | 1975 | 1964 | 1964 | 1971 | 1987 | 1971 | 1956 | 1975 | 1954 | 1985 | 1978 | OCT 1954 |
| Snow,Ice pellets | | | | | | | | | | | | | | |
| -Maximum Monthly | 37 | 40.2 | 24.2 | 21.3 | 8.1 | 3.1 | 0.0 | 0.0 | 0.0 | T | 1.3 | 11.0 | 21.2 | 40.2 |
| -Year | | 1978 | 1972 | 1960 | 1987 | 1966 | | | | 1989 | 1972 | 1958 | 1974 | JAN 1978 |
| -Maximum in 24 hrs | 37 | 14.0 | 12.3 | 14.7 | 7.7 | 3.1 | 0.0 | 0.0 | 0.0 | T | 1.8 | 10.5 | 12.5 | 14.7 |
| -Year | | 1966 | 1960 | 1962 | 1987 | 1966 | | | | 1989 | 1972 | 1958 | 1974 | MAR 1962 |
| **WIND:** | | | | | | | | | | | | | | |
| Mean Speed (mph) | 37 | 10.6 | 10.5 | 10.7 | 10.3 | 8.8 | 8.0 | 7.2 | 6.9 | 7.3 | 8.3 | 9.8 | 10.4 | 9.1 |
| Prevailing Direction | | | | | | | | | | | | | | |
| through 1963 | | WSW | WSW | WSW | WSW | WSW | WSW | WSW | WSW | WSW | WSW | WSW | WSW | WSW |
| Fastest Obs. 1 Min. | | | | | | | | | | | | | | |
| -Direction (!!!) | 37 | 23 | 26 | 25 | 27 | 23 | 27 | 25 | 29 | 02 | 25 | 29 | 25 | 26 |
| -Speed (MPH) | 37 | 52 | 58 | 48 | 46 | 44 | 40 | 51 | 46 | 32 | 35 | 45 | 48 | 58 |
| -Year | | 1978 | 1967 | 1954 | 1974 | 1988 | 1957 | 1956 | 1963 | 1960 | 1986 | 1969 | 1968 | FEB 1967 |
| Peak Gust | | | | | | | | | | | | | | |
| -Direction (!!!) | 6 | W | W | W | SW | SW | NW | W | W | W | W | W | SW | SW |
| -Speed (mph) | 6 | 46 | 49 | 60 | 58 | 61 | 47 | 56 | 56 | 47 | 46 | 58 | 54 | 61 |
| -Date | | 1989 | 1985 | 1985 | 1985 | 1988 | 1984 | 1984 | 1986 | 1987 | 1986 | 1989 | 1987 | MAY 1988 |

**See Reference Notes to this table on the following page.**

PRECIPITATION (inches)                    PITTSBURGH. GRTR. PITT. AIRPORT PENNSYLVANIA

**TABLE 2**

| YEAR | JAN | FEB | MAR | APR | MAY | JUNE | JULY | AUG | SEP | OCT | NOV | DEC | ANNUAL |
|---|---|---|---|---|---|---|---|---|---|---|---|---|---|
| 1961 | 1.95 | 3.13 | 3.48 | 5.21 | 2.80 | 4.21 | 5.53 | 2.11 | 1.98 | 2.58 | 3.41 | 1.71 | 38.10 |
| 1962 | 2.33 | 3.55 | 3.85 | 3.03 | 1.87 | 2.40 | 2.44 | 2.57 | 4.69 | 2.11 | 1.53 | 1.83 | 31.62 |
| 1963 | 1.96 | 2.09 | 5.28 | 2.39 | 1.57 | 2.40 | 3.45 | 2.31 | 1.40 | 0.16 | 2.54 | 1.24 | 26.79 |
| 1964 | 2.55 | 1.73 | 4.96 | 7.61 | 1.77 | 3.84 | 4.48 | 1.79 | 0.74 | 1.42 | 2.74 | 4.26 | 37.89 |
| 1965 | 3.84 | 2.98 | 3.16 | 1.79 | 1.21 | 2.31 | 1.82 | 3.26 | 4.07 | 2.82 | 2.35 | 0.63 | 30.24 |
| 1966 | 4.52 | 3.23 | 1.88 | 3.73 | 2.76 | 1.72 | 5.13 | 2.70 | 1.92 | 1.38 | 3.39 | 1.70 | 34.06 |
| 1967 | 1.06 | 2.54 | 0.79 | 4.41 | 5.21 | 0.90 | 4.54 | 2.67 | 1.61 | 2.05 | 3.07 | 2.22 | 36.38 |
| 1968 | 2.83 | 0.79 | 4.53 | 2.33 | 6.36 | 2.38 | 2.36 | 3.97 | 3.08 | 2.13 | 2.07 | 3.24 | 36.07 |
| 1969 | 2.02 | 0.51 | 1.14 | 2.91 | 1.89 | 3.74 | 4.52 | 2.96 | 0.91 | 2.59 | 2.44 | 3.95 | 29.58 |
| 1970 | 1.61 | 1.92 | 3.35 | 3.09 | 4.36 | 4.61 | 3.89 | 1.55 | 2.77 | 4.80 | 2.64 | 3.29 | 37.88 |
| 1971 | 2.29 | 4.04 | 3.20 | 0.48 | 3.87 | 1.41 | 6.82 | 1.23 | 3.86 | 0.84 | 1.94 | 3.24 | 33.22 |
| 1972 | 1.84 | 3.64 | 3.68 | 4.37 | 1.38 | 5.08 | 2.98 | 1.79 | 5.42 | 2.15 | 4.70 | 3.04 | 40.07 |
| 1973 | 2.03 | 1.80 | 3.86 | 4.69 | 5.87 | 3.12 | 2.16 | 3.40 | 3.56 | 4.45 | 2.65 | 2.15 | 39.74 |
| 1974 | 3.47 | 2.10 | 3.72 | 3.26 | 5.35 | 5.08 | 3.30 | 2.93 | 4.42 | 1.12 | 3.06 | 4.02 | 41.83 |
| 1975 | 3.34 | 4.64 | 4.62 | 2.27 | 1.84 | 4.58 | 4.38 | 7.56 | 5.06 | 3.46 | 1.77 | 2.90 | 46.42 |
| 1976 | 3.25 | 1.74 | 4.45 | 1.24 | 1.99 | 3.37 | 4.72 | 1.25 | 3.30 | 3.76 | 0.90 | 1.81 | 31.78 |
| 1977 | 2.06 | 0.87 | 4.12 | 3.26 | 2.57 | 2.85 | 3.38 | 2.66 | 3.13 | 2.44 | 2.59 | 3.27 | 33.20 |
| 1978 | 6.25 | 0.54 | 1.65 | 2.25 | 4.26 | 4.11 | 2.15 | 3.65 | 2.64 | 3.42 | 1.62 | 5.24 | 37.78 |
| 1979 | 4.80 | 3.12 | 1.32 | 3.17 | 4.49 | 1.73 | 4.31 | 6.84 | 3.60 | 2.46 | 2.43 | 2.29 | 40.56 |
| 1980 | 1.56 | 1.32 | 5.65 | 2.94 | 4.32 | 4.34 | 6.76 | 5.10 | 1.29 | 2.42 | 2.38 | 1.38 | 39.46 |
| 1981 | 0.77 | 4.20 | 2.12 | 4.92 | 2.04 | 8.20 | 3.82 | 0.98 | 4.13 | 1.82 | 1.50 | 3.00 | 37.50 |
| 1982 | 4.44 | 1.93 | 3.52 | 1.44 | 3.98 | 3.05 | 2.36 | 1.97 | 2.80 | 0.40 | 3.33 | 2.79 | 32.01 |
| 1983 | 1.19 | 1.58 | 3.50 | 4.33 | 5.24 | 4.82 | 3.32 | 3.13 | 2.42 | 3.67 | 3.94 | 4.27 | 41.41 |
| 1984 | 1.40 | 2.05 | 2.32 | 3.72 | 5.22 | 1.98 | 3.01 | 5.15 | 0.84 | 3.45 | 3.14 | 3.04 | 35.32 |
| 1985 | 1.43 | 1.45 | 3.37 | 1.64 | 5.80 | 2.26 | 4.06 | 2.64 | 0.28 | 2.27 | 11.05 | 2.26 | 38.51 |
| 1986 | 2.49 | 3.43 | 1.38 | 1.94 | 1.67 | 5.24 | 5.66 | 3.04 | 2.33 | 2.83 | 3.92 | 3.47 | 37.40 |
| 1987 | 2.23 | 0.71 | 2.65 | 5.30 | 2.41 | 6.30 | 2.42 | 7.86 | 3.97 | 0.92 | 2.02 | 2.41 | 39.20 |
| 1988 | 1.49 | 3.46 | 2.56 | 1.97 | 2.78 | 1.26 | 2.82 | 2.04 | 2.34 | 1.40 | 2.80 | 2.17 | 27.09 |
| 1989 | 1.99 | 3.42 | 5.52 | 1.43 | 6.56 | 10.29 | 1.62 | 1.12 | 4.57 | 2.04 | 1.56 | 2.39 | 42.51 |
| 1990 | 3.30 | 3.31 | 1.47 | 3.48 | 6.19 | 4.24 | 6.59 | 3.59 | 6.00 | 3.51 | 2.05 | 8.51 | 52.24 |
| Record Mean | 2.85 | 2.47 | 3.26 | 3.08 | 3.40 | 3.78 | 3.97 | 3.22 | 2.67 | 2.48 | 2.46 | 2.78 | 36.40 |

**TABLE 3**   AVERAGE TEMPERATURE (deg. F)       PITTSBURGH. GRTR. PITT. AIRPORT PENNSYLVANIA

| YEAR | JAN | FEB | MAR | APR | MAY | JUNE | JULY | AUG | SEP | OCT | NOV | DEC | ANNUAL |
|---|---|---|---|---|---|---|---|---|---|---|---|---|---|
| 1961 | 22.2 | 32.3 | 41.3 | 44.0 | 55.2 | 65.1 | 70.5 | 71.2 | 68.5 | 55.3 | 42.8 | 31.3 | 50.0 |
| 1962 | 26.2 | 28.3 | 36.5 | 48.4 | 65.3 | 69.3 | 70.1 | 70.8 | 58.6 | 53.3 | 41.1 | 24.1 | 49.4 |
| 1963 | 21.1 | 19.3 | 40.7 | 49.0 | 56.5 | 67.2 | 70.8 | 67.7 | 61.3 | 50.4 | 43.7 | 22.4 | 48.2 |
| 1964 | 31.4 | 27.0 | 40.0 | 51.7 | 62.7 | 67.9 | 72.3 | 67.1 | 63.7 | 50.4 | 45.5 | 34.0 | 51.1 |
| 1965 | 28.2 | 28.4 | 35.2 | 49.0 | 65.9 | 66.9 | 69.9 | 69.1 | 64.7 | 48.1 | 41.3 | 37.5 | 50.4 |
| 1966 | 23.1 | 30.3 | 40.9 | 47.9 | 56.1 | 70.4 | 75.6 | 71.1 | 61.3 | 50.8 | 42.8 | 31.4 | 50.1 |
| 1967 | 32.3 | 25.6 | 40.2 | 52.2 | 54.3 | 73.0 | 71.5 | 68.8 | 61.1 | 52.5 | 36.8 | 34.8 | 50.3 |
| 1968 | 23.4 | 22.2 | 40.4 | 51.2 | 54.7 | 66.9 | 72.4 | 71.8 | 64.8 | 52.2 | 41.3 | 27.6 | 49.1 |
| 1969 | 26.7 | 29.5 | 34.3 | 51.7 | 60.2 | 69.3 | 72.7 | 69.7 | 63.0 | 52.9 | 39.2 | 26.7 | 49.7 |
| 1970 | 20.7 | 27.7 | 35.5 | 52.5 | 63.9 | 68.2 | 71.6 | 71.6 | 67.8 | 54.9 | 42.2 | 32.1 | 50.7 |
| 1971 | 23.7 | 30.4 | 34.3 | 46.0 | 56.6 | 71.4 | 70.2 | 69.6 | 68.5 | 59.5 | 40.4 | 38.8 | 50.8 |
| 1972 | 29.6 | 26.5 | 36.4 | 48.5 | 61.8 | 63.8 | 71.2 | 70.6 | 65.3 | 48.4 | 39.3 | 37.2 | 49.9 |
| 1973 | 29.7 | 28.8 | 48.3 | 49.3 | 56.4 | 70.9 | 73.2 | 73.2 | 66.5 | 56.1 | 44.1 | 33.3 | 52.5 |
| 1974 | 34.0 | 29.9 | 41.2 | 51.8 | 58.3 | 65.2 | 73.1 | 72.8 | 62.2 | 52.4 | 43.9 | 32.5 | 51.4 |
| 1975 | 32.6 | 32.1 | 36.3 | 44.3 | 63.0 | 67.8 | 72.8 | 73.0 | 58.8 | 53.3 | 46.3 | 32.9 | 51.1 |
| 1976 | 23.5 | 37.2 | 45.2 | 50.6 | 55.6 | 68.4 | 67.4 | 65.3 | 59.9 | 45.9 | 33.1 | 23.9 | 48.0 |
| 1977 | 11.4 | 26.9 | 43.7 | 50.8 | 63.0 | 63.8 | 71.8 | 68.1 | 64.7 | 50.5 | 45.6 | 31.1 | 49.3 |
| 1978 | 22.6 | 20.9 | 36.9 | 51.0 | 60.2 | 69.4 | 73.0 | 71.4 | 66.2 | 49.1 | 43.0 | 32.7 | 49.7 |
| 1979 | 21.4 | 18.0 | 43.1 | 49.7 | 59.1 | 67.7 | 70.3 | 69.6 | 63.4 | 50.9 | 44.7 | 34.6 | 49.4 |
| 1980 | 26.9 | 24.2 | 35.6 | 48.1 | 60.3 | 66.2 | 75.0 | 74.5 | 67.1 | 49.5 | 38.6 | 28.6 | 49.5 |
| 1981 | 20.5 | 31.4 | 35.6 | 51.9 | 58.4 | 68.8 | 72.1 | 69.7 | 61.9 | 49.4 | 40.3 | 29.4 | 49.1 |
| 1982 | 20.9 | 28.4 | 38.4 | 45.3 | 64.7 | 63.7 | 72.4 | 68.2 | 63.4 | 54.4 | 44.7 | 39.9 | 50.4 |
| 1983 | 30.0 | 32.6 | 40.7 | 47.1 | 55.8 | 67.8 | 73.0 | 72.8 | 64.4 | 53.0 | 43.5 | 25.4 | 50.5 |
| 1984 | 23.2 | 36.4 | 32.2 | 49.2 | 55.3 | 69.7 | 68.5 | 70.8 | 61.4 | 58.3 | 40.2 | 39.3 | 50.4 |
| 1985 | 22.1 | 27.7 | 42.1 | 55.0 | 60.6 | 64.2 | 70.5 | 70.6 | 65.3 | 55.2 | 47.1 | 27.4 | 50.6 |
| 1986 | 28.3 | 31.3 | 41.1 | 53.1 | 62.0 | 68.3 | 73.3 | 68.6 | 66.6 | 54.2 | 40.4 | 33.1 | 51.7 |
| 1987 | 28.0 | 32.6 | 41.9 | 50.0 | 63.0 | 70.9 | 75.7 | 71.8 | 65.1 | 47.8 | 46.2 | 35.1 | 52.3 |
| 1988 | 26.6 | 29.0 | 39.3 | 49.4 | 61.4 | 68.5 | 76.9 | 75.1 | 63.5 | 46.6 | 44.2 | 31.9 | 51.0 |
| 1989 | 35.5 | 34.7 | 41.1 | 47.0 | 58.0 | 69.2 | 74.1 | 71.6 | 64.8 | 53.3 | 40.6 | 19.2 | 50.2 |
| 1990 | 36.8 | 36.9 | 44.0 | 51.3 | 57.7 | 68.3 | 71.7 | 70.5 | 63.7 | 55.0 | 45.5 | 38.0 | 53.3 |
| Record Mean | 29.9 | 31.1 | 39.9 | 51.0 | 61.6 | 70.2 | 74.3 | 72.5 | 66.3 | 54.7 | 43.1 | 33.3 | 52.3 |
| Max | 37.5 | 39.3 | 49.0 | 61.1 | 72.2 | 80.5 | 84.3 | 82.4 | 76.3 | 64.4 | 50.9 | 40.3 | 61.5 |
| Min | 22.3 | 22.9 | 30.8 | 40.8 | 51.1 | 59.9 | 64.2 | 62.6 | 56.2 | 45.0 | 35.3 | 26.3 | 43.1 |

## REFERENCE NOTES FOR TABLES 1, 2, 3 and 6        (PITTSBURGH, PA)

**GENERAL**

T - TRACE AMOUNT
BLANK ENTRIES DENOTE MISSING/UNREPORTED DATA.
# INDICATES A STATION OR INSTRUMENT RELOCATION.

**SPECIFIC**

TABLE 1

(a) - LENGTH OF RECORD IN YEARS. ALTHOUGH
      INDIVIDUAL MONTHS MAY BE MISSING.
*   LESS THAN .05

NORMALS — BASED ON THE 1951-1980 RECORD PERIOD.
EXTREMES — DATES ARE THE MOST RECENT OCCURRENCE.
WIND DIR. — NUMERALS SHOW TENS OF DEGREES
             CLOCKWISE FROM TRUE NORTH.
             "00" INDICATES CALM.
RESULTANT WIND DIRECTIONS ARE GIVEN TO WHOLE DEGREES.

TABLE 3
MAX AND MIN ARE LONG-TERM MEAN DAILY MAXIMUM
AND MEAN DAILY MINIMUM TEMPERATURES.

**EXCEPTIONS**

TABLE 1

1.  TEMPERATURE DATA MAY BE SUSPECT NOVEMBER 1977
    THROUGH JULY 1978 DUE TO INTERMITTENT INSTRUMENT
    MALFUNCTION.

TABLES 2, 3, and 6

RECORD MEANS ARE THROUGH THE CURRENT YEAR,
BEGINNING IN    1875 FOR TEMPERATURE
                1872 FOR PRECIPITATION
                1953 FOR SNOWFALL

**TABLE 4**

HEATING DEGREE DAYS Base 65 deg. F  PITTSBURGH, GRTR. PITT. AIRPORT PENNSYLVANIA

| SEASON | JULY | AUG | SEP | OCT | NOV | DEC | JAN | FEB | MAR | APR | MAY | JUNE | TOTAL |
|---|---|---|---|---|---|---|---|---|---|---|---|---|---|
| 1961–62 | 17 | 2 | 71 | 302 | 666 | 1039 | 1197 | 1020 | 873 | 513 | 100 | 18 | 5818 |
| 1962–63 | 11 | 12 | 216 | 365 | 707 | 1263 | 1354 | 1273 | 747 | 479 | 271 | 45 | 6743 |
| 1963–64 | 21 | 22 | 139 | 196 | 634 | 1315 | 1095 | 1035 | 769 | 395 | 116 | 63 | 5800 |
| 1964–65 | 1 | 51 | 99 | 447 | 577 | 954 | 1134 | 1018 | 920 | 476 | 63 | 53 | 5793 |
| 1965–66 | 9 | 40 | 99 | 518 | 702 | 848 | 1293 | 963 | 741 | 510 | 289 | 34 | 6046 |
| 1966–67 | 2 | 6 | 156 | 435 | 659 | 1035 | 1007 | 1097 | 765 | 387 | 332 | 4 | 5885 |
| 1967–68 | 10 | 13 | 146 | 391 | 840 | 931 | 1232 | 1284 | 758 | 406 | 313 | 60 | 6384 |
| 1968–69 | 8 | 31 | 54 | 400 | 703 | 1152 | 1181 | 988 | 944 | 394 | 182 | 35 | 6072 |
| 1969–70 | 0 | 8 | 127 | 383 | 770 | 1183 | 1370 | 1039 | 908 | 390 | 127 | 31 | 6336 |
| 1970–71 | 5 | 1 | 69 | 318 | 678 | 1013 | 1277 | 961 | 949 | 562 | 264 | 6 | 6103 |
| 1971–72 | 1 | 6 | 41 | 184 | 729 | 807 | 1093 | 1112 | 881 | 489 | 128 | 96 | 5567 |
| 1972–73 | 20 | 11 | 63 | 508 | 767 | 853 | 1087 | 1006 | 508 | 474 | 264 | 2 | 5563 |
| 1973–74 | 2 | 8 | 55 | 274 | 621 | 978 | 957 | 978 | 729 | 403 | 223 | 54 | 5282 |
| 1974–75 | 0 | 0 | 124 | 384 | 630 | 1001 | 997 | 916 | 881 | 617 | 116 | 48 | 5714 |
| 1975–76 | 0 | 0 | 192 | 362 | 554 | 989 | 1278 | 801 | 605 | 453 | 301 | 24 | 5559 |
| 1976–77 | 15 | 59 | 159 | 587 | 953 | 1268 | 1655 | 1060 | 658 | 436 | 138 | 102 | 7090 |
| 1977–78 | 11 | 41 | 78 | 442 | 583 | 1043 | 1307 | 1229 | 860 | 412 | 209 | 38 | 6253 |
| 1978–79 | 4 | 3 | 80 | 485 | 656 | 993 | 1346 | 1311 | 671 | 458 | 219 | 38 | 6264 |
| 1979–80 | 23 | 26 | 111 | 438 | 601 | 935 | 1175 | 1177 | 906 | 500 | 172 | 71 | 6135 |
| 1980–81 | 0 | 5 | 48 | 476 | 787 | 1117 | 1372 | 936 | 904 | 391 | 223 | 18 | 6277 |
| 1981–82 | 3 | 10 | 159 | 475 | 736 | 1098 | 1361 | 1017 | 819 | 586 | 82 | 67 | 6413 |
| 1982–83 | 9 | 23 | 119 | 336 | 605 | 770 | 1080 | 904 | 746 | 535 | 280 | 44 | 5451 |
| 1983–84 | 10 | 2 | 126 | 365 | 639 | 1223 | 1293 | 823 | 1008 | 471 | 305 | 16 | 6281 |
| 1984–85 | 12 | 7 | 165 | 214 | 734 | 790 | 1322 | 1038 | 701 | 334 | 163 | 65 | 5545 |
| 1985–86 | 3 | 9 | 116 | 300 | 531 | 1160 | 1131 | 936 | 737 | 368 | 148 | 37 | 5476 |
| 1986–87 | 1 | 40 | 65 | 346 | 733 | 983 | 1139 | 904 | 710 | 451 | 145 | 22 | 5539 |
| 1987–88 | 4 | 20 | 61 | 529 | 560 | 920 | 1040 | 1181 | 792 | 461 | 149 | 64 | 5781 |
| 1988–89 | 5 | 3 | 83 | 570 | 619 | 1018 | 905 | 1033 | 739 | 532 | 260 | 25 | 5792 |
| 1989–90 | 1 | 14 | 102 | 364 | 723 | 1414 | 869 | 781 | 657 | 439 | 229 | 49 | 5642 |
| 1990–91 | 4 | 1 | 116 | 314 | 577 | 829 |  |  |  |  |  |  |  |

**TABLE 5**

COOLING DEGREE DAYS Base 65 deg. F  PITTSBURGH, GRTR. PITT. AIRPORT PENNSYLVANIA

| YEAR | JAN | FEB | MAR | APR | MAY | JUNE | JULY | AUG | SEP | OCT | NOV | DEC | TOTAL |
|---|---|---|---|---|---|---|---|---|---|---|---|---|---|
| 1969 | 0 | 0 | 0 | 2 | 42 | 170 | 245 | 162 | 72 | 14 | 0 | 0 | 707 |
| 1970 | 0 | 0 | 0 | 21 | 100 | 133 | 215 | 213 | 162 | 11 | 0 | 0 | 855 |
| 1971 | 0 | 0 | 0 | 0 | 13 | 204 | 171 | 158 | 153 | 17 | 0 | 0 | 716 |
| 1972 | 0 | 0 | 0 | 0 | 34 | 68 | 219 | 192 | 76 | 0 | 0 | 0 | 589 |
| 1973 | 0 | 0 | 0 | 10 | 5 | 185 | 264 | 269 | 108 | 5 | 0 | 0 | 846 |
| 1974 | 0 | 0 | 0 | 13 | 19 | 66 | 258 | 247 | 45 | 5 | 4 | 0 | 657 |
| 1975 | 0 | 0 | 0 | 0 | 60 | 137 | 248 | 257 | 12 | 7 | 0 | 0 | 721 |
| 1976 | 0 | 0 | 1 | 25 | 14 | 134 | 99 | 73 | 12 | 0 | 0 | 0 | 358 |
| 1977 | 0 | 0 | 0 | 3 | 83 | 75 | 231 | 141 | 72 | 14 | 4 | 0 | 623 |
| 1978 | 0 | 0 | 0 | 0 | 69 | 178 | 260 | 207 | 122 | 0 | 0 | 0 | 836 |
| 1979 | 0 | 0 | 0 | 9 | 41 | 125 | 193 | 175 | 70 | 7 | 0 | 0 | 620 |
| 1980 | 0 | 0 | 0 | 0 | 34 | 115 | 317 | 306 | 118 | 0 | 0 | 0 | 890 |
| 1981 | 0 | 0 | 0 | 5 | 25 | 139 | 230 | 160 | 72 | 0 | 0 | 0 | 631 |
| 1982 | 0 | 0 | 0 | 0 | 79 | 33 | 246 | 127 | 77 | 15 | 3 | 0 | 580 |
| 1983 | 0 | 0 | 0 | 3 | 3 | 135 | 263 | 251 | 115 | 0 | 0 | 0 | 770 |
| 1984 | 0 | 0 | 0 | 3 | 12 | 165 | 127 | 194 | 63 | 13 | 0 | 0 | 577 |
| 1985 | 0 | 0 | 0 | 41 | 33 | 49 | 181 | 160 | 130 | 4 | 0 | 0 | 598 |
| 1986 | 0 | 0 | 3 | 20 | 65 | 144 | 265 | 157 | 121 | 20 | 0 | 0 | 795 |
| 1987 | 0 | 0 | 0 | 6 | 93 | 204 | 342 | 240 | 72 | 0 | 1 | 0 | 958 |
| 1988 | 0 | 0 | 0 | 0 | 44 | 174 | 381 | 322 | 47 | 7 | 0 | 0 | 975 |
| 1989 | 0 | 0 | 5 | 0 | 49 | 154 | 291 | 225 | 100 | 9 | 0 | 0 | 833 |
| 1990 | 0 | 0 | 14 | 37 | 9 | 153 | 218 | 179 | 83 | 13 | 0 | 0 | 706 |

**TABLE 6**

SNOWFALL (inches)  PITTSBURGH, GRTR. PITT. AIRPORT PENNSYLVANIA

| SEASON | JULY | AUG | SEP | OCT | NOV | DEC | JAN | FEB | MAR | APR | MAY | JUNE | TOTAL |
|---|---|---|---|---|---|---|---|---|---|---|---|---|---|
| 1961–62 | 0.0 | 0.0 | 0.0 | T | 2.2 | 5.6 | 4.0 | 8.6 | 19.1 | 3.6 | 0.0 | 0.0 | 43.1 |
| 1962–63 | 0.0 | 0.0 | 0.0 | 1.8 | T | 11.9 | 12.7 | 20.4 | 4.5 | 0.3 | 1.8 | 0.0 | 53.4 |
| 1963–64 | 0.0 | 0.0 | 0.0 | T | 5.8 | 16.4 | 20.3 | 13.7 | 6.1 | 0.3 | 0.0 | 0.0 | 62.6 |
| 1964–65 | 0.0 | 0.0 | 0.0 | T | 1.6 | 6.1 | 10.6 | 10.4 | 13.3 | 0.2 | 0.0 | 0.0 | 42.2 |
| 1965–66 | 0.0 | 0.0 | 0.0 | 0.2 | 1.8 | 6.9 | 24.6 | 0.2 | 8.5 | 2.7 | 3.1 | 0.0 | 48.0 |
| 1966–67 | 0.0 | 0.0 | 0.0 | 0.0 | 5.1 | 7.8 | 4.5 | 21.7 | 20.0 | 0.5 | 0.0 | 0.0 | 59.6 |
| 1967–68 | 0.0 | 0.0 | 0.0 | 0.0 | T | 10.1 | 7.9 | 15.4 | 6.1 | 11.0 | T | 0.0 | 50.5 |
| 1968–69 | 0.0 | 0.0 | 0.0 | 0.0 | T | 2.7 | 13.3 | 6.5 | 4.0 | 3.9 | 0.0 | T | 30.4 |
| 1969–70 | 0.0 | 0.0 | 0.0 | 0.4 | 7.9 | 20.6 | 12.6 | 13.0 | 16.1 | 0.1 | 0.0 | 0.0 | 70.7 |
| 1970–71 | 0.0 | 0.0 | 0.0 | T | 0.1 | 10.1 | 12.1 | 20.6 | 16.8 | 0.2 | 0.0 | 0.0 | 59.9 |
| 1971–72 | 0.0 | 0.0 | 0.0 | 0.0 | 10.5 | 0.7 | 4.9 | 24.2 | 9.8 | 1.8 | 0.0 | 0.0 | 51.9 |
| 1972–73 | 0.0 | 0.0 | 0.0 | 1.8 | 6.1 | 2.9 | 3.4 | 6.1 | 4.6 | 1.4 | T | 0.0 | 26.3 |
| 1973–74 | 0.0 | 0.0 | 0.0 | 0.0 | 0.8 | 4.8 | 4.9 | 2.2 | 2.3 | 1.6 | T | 0.0 | 16.6 |
| 1974–75 | 0.0 | 0.0 | 0.0 | T | 2.6 | 21.2 | 10.1 | 13.9 | 9.8 | 1.1 | 0.0 | 0.0 | 58.7 |
| 1975–76 | 0.0 | 0.0 | 0.0 | 0.0 | 1.9 | 3.8 | 21.8 | 3.3 | 4.3 | 0.5 | 0.0 | 0.0 | 35.6 |
| 1976–77 | 0.0 | 0.0 | 0.0 | T | 6.6 | 7.9 | 26.5 | 6.4 | 0.9 | 1.3 | T | 0.0 | 49.6 |
| 1977–78 | 0.0 | 0.0 | 0.0 | 0.0 | 3.3 | 9.1 | 40.2 | 5.4 | 4.0 | 0.2 | 0.0 | 0.0 | 62.2 |
| 1978–79 | 0.0 | 0.0 | 0.0 | 0.0 | 2.3 | 3.2 | 18.2 | 13.7 | 2.0 | 1.4 | 0.0 | 0.0 | 40.8 |
| 1979–80 | 0.0 | 0.0 | 0.0 | 0.0 | 1.1 | 1.1 | 7.8 | 6.2 | 7.9 | T | 0.0 | 0.0 | 24.1 |
| 1980–81 | 0.0 | 0.0 | 0.0 | T | 9.7 | 6.3 | 12.5 | 11.9 | 7.6 | T | 0.0 | 0.0 | 48.0 |
| 1981–82 | 0.0 | 0.0 | 0.0 | T | 0.6 | 11.5 | 13.4 | 3.6 | 12.2 | 3.8 | 0.0 | 0.0 | 45.1 |
| 1982–83 | 0.0 | 0.0 | 0.0 | T | 0.1 | 8.8 | 3.9 | 12.0 | 4.3 | 1.0 | 0.0 | 0.0 | 30.1 |
| 1983–84 | 0.0 | 0.0 | 0.0 | 0.0 | 6.1 | 10.5 | 10.8 | 11.4 | 10.4 | T | 0.0 | 0.0 | 49.2 |
| 1984–85 | 0.0 | 0.0 | 0.0 | 0.0 | 1.5 | 14.6 | 11.1 | 1.8 | 0.2 | 7.2 | 0.0 | 0.0 | 36.4 |
| 1985–86 | 0.0 | 0.0 | 0.0 | 0.0 | T | 15.3 | 11.1 | 12.4 | 4.8 | 2.7 | 0.0 | 0.0 | 46.3 |
| 1986–87 | 0.0 | 0.0 | 0.0 | 0.0 | 0.9 | 11.6 | 1.1 | 7.3 | 8.1 |  | 0.0 | 0.0 | 30.0 |
| 1987–88 | 0.0 | 0.0 | 0.0 | T | 4.1 | 7.9 | 5.5 | 6.9 | 9.8 | 0.9 | 0.0 | 0.0 | 35.1 |
| 1988–89 | 0.0 | 0.0 | 0.0 | 0.2 | 1.1 | 4.0 | 4.2 | 4.1 | 7.5 | 0.6 | T | 0.0 | 21.7 |
| 1989–90 | 0.0 | 0.0 | T | 0.2 | 1.6 | 12.5 | 7.7 | 2.5 | 0.6 | 3.3 | 0.0 | T | 28.4 |
| 1990–91 | 0.0 | 0.0 | 0.0 | 0.0 | T | 4.6 |  |  |  |  |  |  |  |
| Record Mean | 0.0 | 0.0 | T | 0.2 | 3.4 | 8.2 | 11.6 | 9.4 | 8.1 | 1.8 | 0.1 | T | 42.8 |

**See Reference Notes, relative to all above tables, on preceding page.**

The Wilkes-Barre Scranton National Weather Service Office is located about midway between the two cities, at the southwest end of the crescent-shaped Lackawanna River Valley. The river flows through this valley and empties into the Susquehanna River and the Wyoming Valley a few miles west of the airport. The surrounding mountains protect both cities and the airport from high winds. They influence the temperature and precipitation during both summer and winter, causing wide departures in both within a few miles of the station. Because of the proximity of the mountains, the climate is relatively cool in summer with frequent shower and thunderstorm activity, usually of brief duration. The winter temperatures in the valley are not severe. The occurrence of sub-zero temperatures and severe snowstorms is infrequent. A high percentage of the winter precipitation occurs as rain.

Although severe snowstorms are infrequent, when they do occur they approach blizzard conditions. High winds cause huge drifts and normal routines are disrupted for several days.

While the incidence of tornadoes is very low, Wilkes-Barre has occasionally been hit with these storms which caused loss of life and great property damage.

The area has felt the effects of tropical storms. Considerable wind damage has occasionally occurred, but the most devastating damage has come from flooding caused by the large amounts of precipitation deposited by the storms. The worst natural disaster to hit the region was the result of the flooding caused by a hurricane.

## TABLE 1  NORMALS, MEANS AND EXTREMES

AVOCA, WILKES-BARRE – SCRANTON PENNSYLVANIA

LATITUDE: 41°20'N   LONGITUDE: 75°44'W   ELEVATION: FT. GRND  930 BARO   959   TIME ZONE: EASTERN   WBAN: 14777

| | (a) | JAN | FEB | MAR | APR | MAY | JUNE | JULY | AUG | SEP | OCT | NOV | DEC | YEAR |
|---|---|---|---|---|---|---|---|---|---|---|---|---|---|---|
| **TEMPERATURE °F:** | | | | | | | | | | | | | | |
| Normals | | | | | | | | | | | | | | |
| -Daily Maximum | | 32.1 | 34.4 | 44.1 | 58.2 | 69.1 | 77.8 | 82.1 | 80.0 | 72.7 | 61.4 | 48.2 | 36.3 | 58.0 |
| -Daily Minimum | | 18.2 | 19.2 | 28.1 | 38.4 | 48.1 | 56.9 | 61.4 | 60.0 | 52.8 | 42.0 | 33.6 | 23.1 | 40.1 |
| -Monthly | | 25.2 | 26.8 | 36.1 | 48.3 | 58.6 | 67.4 | 71.8 | 70.0 | 62.8 | 51.7 | 40.9 | 29.7 | 49.1 |
| Extremes | | | | | | | | | | | | | | |
| -Record Highest | 34 | 67 | 71 | 83 | 92 | 93 | 97 | 101 | 94 | 95 | 84 | 80 | 67 | 101 |
| -Year | | 1967 | 1985 | 1977 | 1976 | 1962 | 1964 | 1988 | 1983 | 1983 | 1959 | 1982 | 1984 | JUL 1988 |
| -Record Lowest | 34 | -14 | -16 | -4 | 14 | 27 | 34 | 43 | 38 | 30 | 19 | 9 | -9 | -16 |
| -Year | | 1985 | 1979 | 1967 | 1982 | 1974 | 1972 | 1972 | 1979 | 1982 | 1974 | 1972 | 1976 | 1989 | FEB 1979 |
| **NORMAL DEGREE DAYS:** | | | | | | | | | | | | | | |
| Heating (base 65°F) | | 1234 | 1070 | 896 | 501 | 227 | 34 | 7 | 10 | 117 | 417 | 723 | 1094 | 6330 |
| Cooling (base 65°F) | | 0 | 0 | 0 | 0 | 29 | 106 | 218 | 165 | 51 | 0 | 0 | 0 | 569 |
| **% OF POSSIBLE SUNSHINE** | 34 | 43 | 47 | 50 | 53 | 55 | 60 | 62 | 60 | 54 | 51 | 36 | 34 | 50 |
| **MEAN SKY COVER (tenths)** | | | | | | | | | | | | | | |
| Sunrise - Sunset | 34 | 7.4 | 7.3 | 7.1 | 6.8 | 6.7 | 6.2 | 6.2 | 6.1 | 6.2 | 6.2 | 7.6 | 7.8 | 6.8 |
| **MEAN NUMBER OF DAYS:** | | | | | | | | | | | | | | |
| Sunrise to Sunset | | | | | | | | | | | | | | |
| -Clear | 34 | 4.4 | 4.4 | 5.4 | 6.3 | 5.8 | 6.9 | 6.2 | 7.0 | 7.1 | 8.1 | 3.8 | 3.8 | 69.4 |
| -Partly Cloudy | 34 | 7.3 | 6.9 | 7.7 | 7.4 | 9.6 | 10.9 | 12.8 | 11.7 | 9.5 | 8.5 | 6.9 | 6.6 | 105.8 |
| -Cloudy | 34 | 19.3 | 17.0 | 17.9 | 16.3 | 15.6 | 12.2 | 11.9 | 12.3 | 13.4 | 14.3 | 19.4 | 20.6 | 190.1 |
| Precipitation | | | | | | | | | | | | | | |
| .01 inches or more | 34 | 11.9 | 11.1 | 12.6 | 12.2 | 12.9 | 11.9 | 11.3 | 10.8 | 9.8 | 9.6 | 12.0 | 12.8 | 138.8 |
| Snow, Ice pellets | | | | | | | | | | | | | | |
| 1.0 inches or more | 34 | 3.2 | 2.9 | 2.6 | 0.7 | 0.* | 0.0 | 0.0 | 0.0 | 0.0 | 0.* | 1.0 | 2.4 | 12.9 |
| Thunderstorms | 34 | 0.1 | 0.2 | 0.9 | 1.9 | 3.6 | 5.9 | 7.0 | 5.1 | 2.6 | 0.9 | 0.4 | 0.2 | 28.9 |
| Heavy Fog Visibility | | | | | | | | | | | | | | |
| 1/4 mile or less | 34 | 1.9 | 2.1 | 1.9 | 1.4 | 1.3 | 1.3 | 1.6 | 1.9 | 2.9 | 2.2 | 1.9 | 2.2 | 22.6 |
| Temperature °F | | | | | | | | | | | | | | |
| -Maximum | | | | | | | | | | | | | | |
| 90° and above | 34 | 0.0 | 0.0 | 0.0 | 0.1 | 0.3 | 1.7 | 3.0 | 1.8 | 0.4 | 0.0 | 0.0 | 0.0 | 7.3 |
| 32° and below | 34 | 16.1 | 12.0 | 3.9 | 0.2 | 0.0 | 0.0 | 0.0 | 0.0 | 0.0 | 0.0 | 1.4 | 11.2 | 44.7 |
| -Minimum | | | | | | | | | | | | | | |
| 32° and below | 34 | 28.4 | 24.9 | 21.8 | 8.7 | 0.7 | 0.0 | 0.0 | 0.0 | 0.1 | 4.4 | 14.0 | 25.7 | 128.8 |
| 0° and below | 34 | 2.3 | 1.4 | 0.1 | 0.0 | 0.0 | 0.0 | 0.0 | 0.0 | 0.0 | 0.0 | 0.0 | 0.7 | 4.4 |
| **AVG. STATION PRESS.(mb)** | 17 | 982.3 | 983.0 | 981.8 | 980.3 | 981.1 | 981.7 | 982.5 | 984.0 | 984.8 | 985.1 | 983.7 | 983.4 | 982.8 |
| **RELATIVE HUMIDITY (%)** | | | | | | | | | | | | | | |
| Hour 01 | 34 | 72 | 71 | 68 | 67 | 72 | 80 | 81 | 83 | 83 | 79 | 75 | 75 | 76 |
| Hour 07 | 34 | 75 | 75 | 73 | 72 | 76 | 82 | 84 | 87 | 88 | 84 | 79 | 77 | 79 |
| Hour 13 (Local Time) | 34 | 66 | 63 | 58 | 52 | 52 | 56 | 56 | 58 | 61 | 59 | 64 | 67 | 59 |
| Hour 19 | 34 | 67 | 64 | 59 | 54 | 56 | 61 | 62 | 66 | 70 | 66 | 69 | 70 | 64 |
| **PRECIPITATION (inches):** | | | | | | | | | | | | | | |
| Water Equivalent | | | | | | | | | | | | | | |
| -Normal | | 2.27 | 2.05 | 2.63 | 3.01 | 3.16 | 3.42 | 3.39 | 3.47 | 3.36 | 2.78 | 2.98 | 2.54 | 35.06 |
| -Maximum Monthly | 34 | 6.48 | 8.06 | 4.83 | 9.56 | 8.02 | 7.22 | 7.25 | 5.23 | 8.15 | 8.12 | 7.69 | 6.58 | 9.56 |
| -Year | | 1979 | 1981 | 1977 | 1983 | 1989 | 1982 | 1986 | 1965 | 1987 | 1976 | 1972 | 1983 | APR 1983 |
| -Minimum Monthly | 34 | 0.39 | 0.30 | 0.49 | 0.97 | 0.77 | 0.27 | 1.23 | 1.23 | 0.82 | 0.03 | 0.80 | 0.35 | 0.03 |
| -Year | | 1980 | 1968 | 1981 | 1989 | 1959 | 1966 | 1972 | 1980 | 1964 | 1963 | 1976 | 1958 | OCT 1963 |
| -Maximum in 24 hrs | 34 | 1.89 | 3.11 | 3.02 | 3.80 | 2.58 | 3.61 | 2.33 | 3.18 | 6.52 | 3.27 | 2.91 | 2.86 | 6.52 |
| -Year | | 1978 | 1981 | 1986 | 1983 | 1972 | 1973 | 1969 | 1966 | 1985 | 1976 | 1972 | 1983 | SEP 1985 |
| Snow, Ice pellets | | | | | | | | | | | | | | |
| -Maximum Monthly | 34 | 29.6 | 22.0 | 29.7 | 26.7 | 2.4 | 0.0 | 0.0 | 0.0 | T | 4.4 | 22.5 | 33.9 | 33.9 |
| -Year | | 1987 | 1964 | 1967 | 1983 | 1977 | | | | 1956 | 1962 | 1971 | 1969 | DEC 1969 |
| -Maximum in 24 hrs | 34 | 20.1 | 13.3 | 15.5 | 12.2 | 2.4 | 0.0 | 0.0 | 0.0 | T | 4.4 | 20.5 | 12.4 | 20.5 |
| -Year | | 1964 | 1961 | 1960 | 1983 | 1977 | | | | 1956 | 1962 | 1971 | 1969 | NOV 1971 |
| **WIND:** | | | | | | | | | | | | | | |
| Mean Speed (mph) | 34 | 8.9 | 9.0 | 9.4 | 9.5 | 8.5 | 7.8 | 7.3 | 7.0 | 7.3 | 7.9 | 8.7 | 8.8 | 8.3 |
| Prevailing Direction | | | | | | | | | | | | | | |
| through 1963 | | SW | SW | NW | SW | WSW | SW | WSW | SW | SW | WSW | WSW | SW | SW |
| Fastest Mile | | | | | | | | | | | | | | |
| -Direction (!!!) | 34 | SE | W | S | NW | SW | W | NW | NE | SW | E | NW | SW | W |
| -Speed (MPH) | 34 | 47 | 60 | 49 | 47 | 46 | 43 | 43 | 50 | 47 | 40 | 49 | 47 | 60 |
| -Year | | 1977 | 1956 | 1970 | 1957 | 1980 | 1956 | 1988 | 1956 | 1989 | 1980 | 1989 | 1957 | FEB 1956 |
| Peak Gust | | | | | | | | | | | | | | |
| -Direction (!!!) | 6 | W | NW | W | SW | NW | NW | NW | W | SW | SW | NW | W | SW |
| -Speed (mph) | 6 | 44 | 48 | 55 | 64 | 44 | 49 | 58 | 48 | 52 | 39 | 60 | 51 | 64 |
| -Date | | 1988 | 1985 | 1986 | 1985 | 1984 | 1987 | 1988 | 1984 | 1989 | 1987 | 1989 | 1985 | APR 1985 |

**See Reference Notes to this table on the following page.**

PRECIPITATION (inches)  AVOCA, WILKES–BARRE – SCRANTON PENNSYLVANIA

**TABLE 2**

| YEAR | JAN | FEB | MAR | APR | MAY | JUNE | JULY | AUG | SEP | OCT | NOV | DEC | ANNUAL |
|------|-----|-----|-----|-----|-----|------|------|-----|-----|-----|-----|-----|--------|
| 1961 | 1.82 | 1.92 | 2.87 | 2.48 | 3.30 | 3.80 | 5.96 | 3.98 | 0.99 | 1.58 | 3.57 | 2.52 | 34.79 |
| 1962 | 2.67 | 3.04 | 1.98 | 2.59 | 0.84 | 1.71 | 1.48 | 4.05 | 3.14 | 2.80 | 2.20 | 1.94 | 31.96 |
| 1963 | 2.06 | 1.95 | 2.19 | 1.30 | 2.44 | 1.93 | 4.03 | 2.04 | 1.69 | 0.03 | 4.62 | 1.94 | 26.22 |
| 1964 | 3.40 | 2.03 | 3.54 | 3.82 | 0.98 | 5.00 | 1.23 | 2.85 | 0.82 | 1.13 | 1.86 | 3.67 | 30.33 |
| 1965 | 2.07 | 1.90 | 1.83 | 2.63 | 2.51 | 1.22 | 1.30 | 5.23 | 3.13 | 1.80 | 1.43 | 1.30 | 26.35 |
| 1966 | 1.66 | 2.31 | 1.60 | 2.91 | 3.32 | 0.27 | 1.89 | 4.76 | 2.70 | 2.04 | 2.97 | 2.00 | 28.43 |
| 1967 | 1.11 | 0.89 | 3.91 | 2.09 | 4.41 | 4.48 | 3.61 | 5.20 | 2.13 | 2.58 | 2.31 | 2.45 | 35.17 |
| 1968 | 2.03 | 0.30 | 2.73 | 2.37 | 4.64 | 4.82 | 1.23 | 4.20 | 1.65 | 3.40 | 1.95 |  | 30.75 |
| 1969 | 0.64 | 0.96 | 1.45 | 3.04 | 2.42 | 4.58 | 6.81 | 4.47 | 1.92 | 2.20 | 3.77 | 3.42 | 35.68 |
| 1970 | 0.52 | 2.41 | 2.33 | 3.07 | 2.75 | 2.44 | 5.19 | 2.72 | 3.03 | 2.24 | 2.87 | 1.85 | 31.54 |
| 1971 | 1.54 | 3.92 | 1.93 | 1.29 | 3.38 | 2.44 | 5.73 | 4.88 | 1.93 | 3.00 | 3.55 | 2.08 | 35.67 |
| 1972 | 2.05 | 2.42 | 4.00 | 3.31 | 7.33 | 7.04 | 1.23 | 1.64 | 1.57 | 3.30 | 7.69 | 3.61 | 45.19 |
| 1973 | 2.13 | 1.28 | 1.79 | 4.38 | 3.80 | 5.99 | 3.87 | 2.61 | 3.62 | 1.97 | 1.50 | 6.07 | 39.01 |
| 1974 | 2.66 | 1.48 | 4.75 | 2.71 | 1.89 | 3.85 | 2.80 | 3.50 | 6.85 | 1.07 | 2.26 | 3.40 | 37.22 |
| 1975 | 2.78 | 3.26 | 2.52 | 1.17 | 4.01 | 5.64 | 3.85 | 2.78 | 6.10 | 3.29 | 3.00 | 1.84 | 40.24 |
| 1976 | 3.25 | 2.14 | 2.18 | 2.27 | 3.24 | 5.43 | 3.20 | 2.57 | 3.81 | 8.12 | 0.80 | 1.50 | 38.51 |
| 1977 | 0.88 | 1.82 | 4.83 | 3.98 | 1.72 | 3.16 | 3.44 | 4.23 | 5.97 | 5.27 | 3.98 | 3.44 | 42.72 |
| 1978 | 5.33 | 0.93 | 2.30 | 1.67 | 4.30 | 2.48 | 2.16 | 3.28 | 3.06 | 3.35 | 1.02 | 3.09 | 32.97 |
| 1979 | 6.48 | 2.44 | 1.52 | 3.69 | 5.16 | 2.54 | 2.97 | 2.05 | 5.84 | 3.68 | 3.17 | 1.70 | 41.24 |
| 1980 | 0.39 | 0.69 | 3.72 | 2.35 | 2.37 | 4.36 | 3.76 | 1.23 | 1.43 | 2.17 | 2.83 | 1.24 | 26.54 |
| 1981 | 0.63 | 8.06 | 0.49 | 3.54 | 3.00 | 3.45 | 4.27 | 1.75 | 2.74 | 3.50 | 1.84 | 2.13 | 35.40 |
| 1982 | 2.71 | 2.28 | 2.55 | 3.48 | 3.52 | 7.22 | 3.32 | 3.42 | 1.10 | 0.84 | 3.44 | 1.52 | 35.40 |
| 1983 | 1.17 | 1.46 | 3.28 | 9.56 | 3.28 | 4.81 | 2.76 | 1.77 | 2.12 | 2.73 | 3.71 | 6.58 | 43.23 |
| 1984 | 1.11 | 2.92 | 2.42 | 4.09 | 6.70 | 4.75 | 5.12 | 2.81 | 1.36 | 2.30 | 2.63 | 2.36 | 38.57 |
| 1985 | 0.61 | 1.58 | 2.24 | 2.00 | 6.10 | 3.00 | 6.09 | 2.62 | 7.83 | 1.92 | 4.47 | 1.96 | 40.42 |
| 1986 | 2.59 | 2.58 | 4.25 | 2.98 | 2.24 | 6.77 | 7.25 | 3.94 | 3.07 | 2.61 | 3.94 | 2.04 | 44.26 |
| 1987 | 2.60 | 0.68 | 1.18 | 4.38 | 2.22 | 4.35 | 5.80 | 4.16 | 8.15 | 2.77 | 2.24 | 0.99 | 39.52 |
| 1988 | 1.41 | 2.32 | 1.97 | 2.65 | 4.24 | 0.82 | 6.26 | 5.03 | 1.89 | 1.93 | 3.33 | 1.08 | 32.93 |
| 1989 | 1.02 | 1.73 | 2.23 | 0.97 | 8.02 | 6.10 | 2.76 | 2.92 | 3.92 | 4.73 | 3.57 | 0.96 | 38.93 |
| 1990 | 3.81 | 2.70 | 1.88 | 2.48 | 5.27 | 4.78 | 4.36 | 5.69 | 3.16 | 4.33 | 3.33 | 4.30 | 46.09 |
| Record Mean | 2.33 | 2.28 | 2.80 | 3.09 | 3.34 | 3.82 | 4.09 | 3.60 | 3.21 | 2.91 | 2.79 | 2.60 | 36.86 |

**TABLE 3**  AVERAGE TEMPERATURE (deg. F)  AVOCA, WILKES–BARRE – SCRANTON PENNSYLVANIA

| YEAR | JAN | FEB | MAR | APR | MAY | JUNE | JULY | AUG | SEP | OCT | NOV | DEC | ANNUAL |
|------|-----|-----|-----|-----|-----|------|------|-----|-----|-----|-----|-----|--------|
| 1961 | 18.9 | 28.9 | 35.1 | 42.0 | 56.1 | 72.6 | 71.0 | 68.4 | 68.4 | 52.9 | 40.1 | 29.6 | 48.6 |
| 1962 | 24.9 | 24.6 | 36.6 | 49.0 | 62.6 | 68.5 | 70.3 | 70.4 | 59.5 | 51.6 | 36.6 | 24.0 | 48.2 |
| 1963 | 23.2 | 19.3 | 38.2 | 49.1 | 57.8 | 67.4 | 71.5 | 68.3 | 60.0 | 56.7 | 45.1 | 24.3 | 48.4 |
| 1964 | 27.9 | 23.5 | 36.9 | 46.6 | 62.0 | 67.4 | 74.1 | 68.2 | 63.8 | 49.4 | 44.1 | 31.6 | 49.6 |
| 1965 | 23.0 | 28.1 | 34.2 | 45.3 | 63.7 | 68.0 | 71.0 | 69.5 | 64.5 | 49.6 | 40.4 | 33.5 | 49.2 |
| 1966 | 23.8 | 27.2 | 39.0 | 46.0 | 55.7 | 70.1 | 75.0 | 72.4 | 60.2 | 50.2 | 43.4 | 30.5 | 49.4 |
| 1967 | 32.6 | 23.5 | 34.9 | 49.1 | 52.7 | 71.1 | 71.7 | 68.9 | 61.6 | 51.2 | 36.6 | 31.7 | 48.8 |
| 1968 | 20.0 | 24.1 | 40.4 | 52.9 | 56.3 | 67.5 | 73.7 | 71.0 | 64.4 | 53.4 | 40.7 | 27.2 | 49.3 |
| 1969 | 26.0 | 26.6 | 34.4 | 50.5 | 59.9 | 68.2 | 70.8 | 69.9 | 62.7 | 50.6 | 39.2 | 25.7 | 48.7 |
| 1970 | 17.7 | 25.7 | 31.8 | 48.4 | 60.4 | 64.9 | 70.8 | 69.6 | 64.2 | 52.8 | 41.5 | 27.3 | 47.9 |
| 1971 | 19.5 | 27.2 | 33.0 | 45.0 | 55.9 | 68.6 | 69.9 | 68.3 | 65.5 | 56.4 | 38.8 | 34.1 | 48.5 |
| 1972 | 27.6 | 24.3 | 32.8 | 43.5 | 60.0 | 62.9 | 71.5 | 69.6 | 61.9 | 45.3 | 36.0 | 32.9 | 47.4 |
| 1973 | 28.5 | 24.5 | 41.9 | 47.5 | 53.4 | 68.3 | 71.5 | 71.6 | 62.4 | 53.2 | 41.5 | 31.3 | 49.7 |
| 1974 | 27.8 | 24.2 | 34.7 | 49.1 | 56.2 | 64.4 | 70.8 | 68.5 | 61.2 | 48.5 | 43.0 | 34.4 | 48.6 |
| 1975 | 31.8 | 32.1 | 35.8 | 43.9 | 64.9 | 68.8 | 73.7 | 71.2 | 59.9 | 55.8 | 47.8 | 31.1 | 51.4 |
| 1976 | 22.1 | 35.0 | 41.0 | 51.3 | 56.7 | 70.4 | 69.2 | 69.1 | 60.9 | 48.0 | 37.0 | 22.9 | 48.6 |
| 1977 | 15.0 | 26.9 | 40.5 | 48.9 | 60.0 | 63.8 | 71.1 | 68.7 | 62.7 | 48.5 | 43.1 | 29.6 | 48.2 |
| 1978 | 24.4 | 19.2 | 33.1 | 46.0 | 58.7 | 65.2 | 69.4 | 71.0 | 60.5 | 50.7 | 40.5 | 29.1 | 47.3 |
| 1979 | 24.2 | 16.0 | 40.7 | 46.4 | 58.6 | 65.1 | 70.7 | 70.7 | 63.2 | 51.8 | 45.9 | 35.6 | 49.1 |
| 1980 | 27.8 | 24.2 | 35.9 | 51.0 | 61.8 | 65.3 | 73.2 | 75.2 | 66.1 | 49.8 | 37.6 | 25.7 | 49.5 |
| 1981 | 19.5 | 34.9 | 36.2 | 51.0 | 59.8 | 68.5 | 72.2 | 70.1 | 62.1 | 49.1 | 41.1 | 29.1 | 49.5 |
| 1982 | 18.7 | 27.8 | 36.0 | 46.3 | 61.2 | 64.3 | 71.0 | 66.2 | 62.4 | 52.3 | 44.3 | 36.7 | 48.9 |
| 1983 | 27.3 | 29.4 | 38.8 | 45.9 | 55.7 | 67.6 | 72.4 | 71.6 | 64.8 | 52.5 | 42.8 | 27.1 | 49.7 |
| 1984 | 23.0 | 35.9 | 30.9 | 48.3 | 57.5 | 69.3 | 71.6 | 72.6 | 61.7 | 58.0 | 40.8 | 37.3 | 50.6 |
| 1985 | 21.5 | 29.8 | 39.1 | 51.4 | 60.6 | 63.8 | 70.1 | 69.0 | 64.0 | 52.7 | 44.5 | 26.7 | 49.4 |
| 1986 | 27.2 | 26.1 | 39.8 | 49.3 | 62.7 | 66.2 | 71.0 | 67.4 | 61.6 | 51.2 | 37.3 | 32.8 | 49.4 |
| 1987 | 24.7 | 25.1 | 39.7 | 50.7 | 60.0 | 68.7 | 73.5 | 68.3 | 61.8 | 47.4 | 41.3 | 32.7 | 49.5 |
| 1988 | 22.0 | 27.4 | 38.1 | 46.6 | 60.1 | 65.5 | 75.8 | 72.9 | 60.4 | 46.3 | 43.3 | 29.8 | 49.0 |
| 1989 | 31.3 | 28.0 | 37.2 | 45.6 | 57.6 | 67.0 | 70.4 | 68.5 | 62.2 | 52.8 | 39.7 | 18.6 | 48.2 |
| 1990 | 35.3 | 33.3 | 40.6 | 50.2 | 56.1 | 67.6 | 71.7 | 69.5 | 61.6 | 55.3 | 44.2 | 36.0 | 51.8 |
| Record Mean | 26.7 | 27.4 | 36.9 | 48.0 | 59.1 | 67.3 | 72.1 | 69.9 | 63.0 | 52.2 | 41.2 | 30.2 | 49.5 |
| Max | 34.0 | 35.2 | 45.4 | 57.8 | 69.7 | 77.9 | 82.5 | 80.1 | 73.2 | 61.9 | 48.7 | 36.9 | 58.6 |
| Min | 19.4 | 19.5 | 28.3 | 38.1 | 48.5 | 56.8 | 61.6 | 59.8 | 52.9 | 42.4 | 33.6 | 23.5 | 40.4 |

## REFERENCE NOTES FOR TABLES 1, 2, 3 and 6  (WILKES-BARRE/SCRANTON, PA)

### GENERAL

T - TRACE AMOUNT
BLANK ENTRIES DENOTE MISSING/UNREPORTED DATA.
# INDICATES A STATION OR INSTRUMENT RELOCATION.

### SPECIFIC

#### TABLE 1

(a) - LENGTH OF RECORD IN YEARS. ALTHOUGH INDIVIDUAL MONTHS MAY BE MISSING.

* LESS THAN .05

NORMALS — BASED ON THE 1951-1980 RECORD PERIOD.
EXTREMES — DATES ARE THE MOST RECENT OCCURRENCE.
WIND DIR. — NUMERALS SHOW TENS OF DEGREES CLOCKWISE FROM TRUE NORTH.
''00'' INDICATES CALM.
RESULTANT WIND DIRECTIONS ARE GIVEN TO WHOLE DEGREES.

#### TABLE 3

MAX AND MIN ARE LONG-TERM MEAN DAILY MAXIMUM AND MEAN DAILY MINIMUM TEMPERATURES.

### EXCEPTIONS

#### TABLES 2, 3, and 6

RECORD MEANS ARE THROUGH THE CURRENT YEAR, BEGINNING IN     1901 FOR TEMPERATURE
1901 FOR PRECIPITATION
1956 FOR SNOWFALL

**TABLE 4**  HEATING DEGREE DAYS Base 65 deg. F   AVOCA, WILKES–BARRE – SCRANTON PENNSYLVANIA

| SEASON | JULY | AUG | SEP | OCT | NOV | DEC | JAN | FEB | MAR | APR | MAY | JUNE | TOTAL |
|---|---|---|---|---|---|---|---|---|---|---|---|---|---|
| 1961-62 | 3 | 7 | 80 | 370 | 743 | 1092 | 1236 | 1125 | 874 | 508 | 155 | 16 | 6209 |
| 1962-63 | 3 | 10 | 199 | 414 | 848 | 1260 | 1289 | 1272 | 820 | 475 | 236 | 45 | 6871 |
| 1963-64 | 11 | 20 | 175 | 253 | 588 | 1254 | 1140 | 1198 | 866 | 544 | 139 | 69 | 6257 |
| 1964-65 | 0 | 31 | 110 | 475 | 621 | 1028 | 1293 | 1027 | 951 | 582 | 100 | 55 | 6273 |
| 1965-66 | 7 | 35 | 99 | 471 | 731 | 971 | 1270 | 1053 | 799 | 565 | 300 | 41 | 6342 |
| 1966-67 | 1 | 0 | 170 | 451 | 642 | 1063 | 998 | 1154 | 923 | 475 | 379 | 12 | 6268 |
| 1967-68 | 5 | 17 | 139 | 427 | 844 | 1023 | 1388 | 1181 | 754 | 357 | 261 | 42 | 6438 |
| 1968-69 | 0 | 28 | 55 | 359 | 725 | 1165 | 1204 | 1068 | 943 | 434 | 188 | 38 | 6207 |
| 1969-70 | 6 | 15 | 134 | 440 | 765 | 1212 | 1459 | 1094 | 1022 | 500 | 176 | 76 | 6899 |
| 1970-71 | 2 | 5 | 109 | 371 | 695 | 1162 | 1404 | 1051 | 985 | 593 | 292 | 32 | 6701 |
| 1971-72 | 5 | 22 | 90 | 263 | 783 | 951 | 1152 | 1175 | 992 | 634 | 168 | 109 | 6344 |
| 1972-73 | 21 | 20 | 125 | 603 | 860 | 988 | 1124 | 1131 | 704 | 521 | 354 | 25 | 6476 |
| 1973-74 | 2 | 11 | 140 | 368 | 699 | 1036 | 1145 | 1135 | 934 | 480 | 291 | 65 | 6306 |
| 1974-75 | 5 | 2 | 155 | 503 | 655 | 941 | 1024 | 913 | 902 | 627 | 88 | 25 | 5840 |
| 1975-76 | 0 | 8 | 158 | 291 | 509 | 1043 | 1322 | 864 | 737 | 451 | 265 | 31 | 5679 |
| 1976-77 | 8 | 25 | 155 | 519 | 834 | 1297 | 1546 | 1058 | 756 | 487 | 206 | 90 | 6981 |
| 1977-78 | 14 | 37 | 119 | 505 | 653 | 1090 | 1252 | 1279 | 984 | 562 | 240 | 73 | 6808 |
| 1978-79 | 38 | 2 | 153 | 436 | 728 | 1103 | 1257 | 1370 | 747 | 552 | 221 | 66 | 6673 |
| 1979-80 | 34 | 31 | 120 | 420 | 568 | 900 | 1144 | 1175 | 895 | 414 | 137 | 94 | 5932 |
| 1980-81 | 1 | 0 | 82 | 466 | 813 | 1211 | 1407 | 835 | 886 | 416 | 195 | 19 | 6331 |
| 1981-82 | 2 | 5 | 132 | 485 | 706 | 1105 | 1426 | 1034 | 896 | 554 | 147 | 68 | 6560 |
| 1982-83 | 17 | 55 | 112 | 390 | 619 | 870 | 1158 | 992 | 805 | 569 | 292 | 41 | 5920 |
| 1983-84 | 7 | 11 | 119 | 392 | 659 | 1169 | 1297 | 837 | 1052 | 493 | 247 | 34 | 6317 |
| 1984-85 | 7 | 6 | 148 | 219 | 719 | 852 | 1342 | 981 | 799 | 421 | 162 | 78 | 5734 |
| 1985-86 | 4 | 11 | 127 | 376 | 610 | 1181 | 1163 | 1083 | 777 | 467 | 140 | 61 | 6000 |
| 1986-87 | 16 | 50 | 139 | 428 | 823 | 990 | 1243 | 1111 | 779 | 425 | 208 | 20 | 6232 |
| 1987-88 | 2 | 34 | 119 | 539 | 706 | 995 | 1326 | 1082 | 823 | 546 | 176 | 91 | 6439 |
| 1988-89 | 13 | 12 | 156 | 574 | 643 | 1083 | 1037 | 1031 | 853 | 575 | 251 | 39 | 6267 |
| 1989-90 | 6 | 31 | 133 | 377 | 750 | 1433 | 915 | 881 | 757 | 465 | 269 | 44 | 6061 |
| 1990-91 | 10 | 13 | 152 | 320 | 619 | 894 | | | | | | | |

**TABLE 5**  COOLING DEGREE DAYS Base 65 deg. F   AVOCA, WILKES–BARRE – SCRANTON PENNSYLVANIA

| YEAR | JAN | FEB | MAR | APR | MAY | JUNE | JULY | AUG | SEP | OCT | NOV | DEC | TOTAL |
|---|---|---|---|---|---|---|---|---|---|---|---|---|---|
| 1969 | 0 | 0 | 0 | 7 | 34 | 141 | 193 | 178 | 73 | 1 | 0 | 0 | 627 |
| 1970 | 0 | 0 | 0 | 10 | 40 | 81 | 189 | 159 | 92 | 2 | 0 | 0 | 573 |
| 1971 | 0 | 0 | 0 | 0 | 16 | 145 | 160 | 132 | 113 | 4 | 3 | 0 | 573 |
| 1972 | 0 | 0 | 0 | 0 | 20 | 53 | 232 | 167 | 42 | 0 | 0 | 0 | 514 |
| 1973 | 0 | 0 | 0 | 4 | 0 | 132 | 212 | 223 | 72 | 7 | 0 | 0 | 650 |
| 1974 | 0 | 0 | 0 | 10 | 28 | 52 | 194 | 117 | 46 | 0 | 0 | 0 | 447 |
| 1975 | 0 | 0 | 0 | 0 | 91 | 146 | 278 | 207 | 13 | 14 | 0 | 0 | 749 |
| 1976 | 0 | 0 | 0 | 46 | 16 | 198 | 145 | 159 | 37 | 0 | 0 | 0 | 601 |
| 1977 | 0 | 0 | 2 | 13 | 57 | 62 | 208 | 162 | 59 | 0 | 2 | 0 | 565 |
| 1978 | 0 | 0 | 0 | 0 | 52 | 84 | 181 | 194 | 26 | 0 | 0 | 0 | 537 |
| 1979 | 0 | 0 | 0 | 2 | 32 | 78 | 218 | 214 | 75 | 15 | 0 | 0 | 634 |
| 1980 | 0 | 0 | 0 | 0 | 42 | 107 | 263 | 322 | 122 | 3 | 0 | 0 | 859 |
| 1981 | 0 | 0 | 0 | 4 | 42 | 131 | 231 | 172 | 55 | 0 | 0 | 0 | 635 |
| 1982 | 0 | 0 | 0 | 1 | 34 | 55 | 208 | 98 | 41 | 3 | 5 | 0 | 445 |
| 1983 | 0 | 0 | 0 | 4 | 12 | 125 | 243 | 224 | 118 | 9 | 0 | 0 | 735 |
| 1984 | 0 | 0 | 0 | 0 | 20 | 165 | 218 | 248 | 58 | 12 | 0 | 0 | 721 |
| 1985 | 0 | 0 | 0 | 20 | 32 | 47 | 169 | 142 | 104 | 0 | 0 | 0 | 514 |
| 1986 | 0 | 0 | 2 | 0 | 76 | 104 | 205 | 131 | 44 | 8 | 0 | 0 | 570 |
| 1987 | 0 | 0 | 0 | 3 | 62 | 138 | 273 | 141 | 30 | 0 | 0 | 0 | 647 |
| 1988 | 0 | 0 | 0 | 0 | 34 | 111 | 356 | 266 | 23 | 3 | 0 | 0 | 793 |
| 1989 | 0 | 0 | 0 | 0 | 31 | 109 | 179 | 148 | 57 | 4 | 0 | 0 | 528 |
| 1990 | 0 | 0 | 8 | 29 | 2 | 127 | 225 | 160 | 56 | 24 | 0 | 0 | 631 |

**TABLE 6**  SNOWFALL (inches)   AVOCA, WILKES–BARRE – SCRANTON PENNSYLVANIA

| SEASON | JULY | AUG | SEP | OCT | NOV | DEC | JAN | FEB | MAR | APR | MAY | JUNE | TOTAL |
|---|---|---|---|---|---|---|---|---|---|---|---|---|---|
| 1961-62 | 0.0 | 0.0 | 0.0 | T | 2.4 | 12.8 | 2.7 | 11.2 | 2.8 | 3.0 | T | 0.0 | 34.9 |
| 1962-63 | 0.0 | 0.0 | 0.0 | 4.4 | 4.6 | 12.9 | 15.2 | 18.0 | 8.3 | 0.5 | 0.2 | 0.0 | 64.1 |
| 1963-64 | 0.0 | 0.0 | 0.0 | T | 1.4 | 13.1 | 27.9 | 22.0 | 9.7 | 0.6 | 0.0 | 0.0 | 74.7 |
| 1964-65 | 0.0 | 0.0 | 0.0 | 0.2 | 0.1 | 4.1 | 11.5 | 2.3 | 9.9 | 3.8 | 0.0 | 0.0 | 31.9 |
| 1965-66 | 0.0 | 0.0 | 0.0 | 0.6 | 0.5 | 1.3 | 20.7 | 17.5 | 3.8 | 0.7 | 0.6 | 0.0 | 45.7 |
| 1966-67 | 0.0 | 0.0 | 0.0 | T | T | 17.7 | 8.3 | 14.4 | 29.7 | 4.8 | 0.4 | 0.0 | 75.3 |
| 1967-68 | 0.0 | 0.0 | 0.0 | T | 7.2 | 13.8 | 6.0 | 2.9 | 2.7 | 0.0 | 0.0 | 0.0 | 32.6 |
| 1968-69 | 0.0 | 0.0 | 0.0 | T | 10.9 | 5.8 | 2.7 | 14.8 | 2.5 | 0.0 | 0.0 | 0.0 | 36.7 |
| 1969-70 | 0.0 | 0.0 | 0.0 | T | 2.7 | 33.9 | 9.5 | 9.5 | 20.6 | 0.6 | T | 0.0 | 76.8 |
| 1970-71 | 0.0 | 0.0 | 0.0 | 0.3 | T | 12.3 | 15.2 | 12.1 | 15.6 | 1.6 | 0.0 | 0.0 | 57.1 |
| 1971-72 | 0.0 | 0.0 | 0.0 | 0.0 | 22.5 | 4.1 | 5.9 | 19.7 | 6.6 | 3.8 | 0.0 | 0.0 | 62.6 |
| 1972-73 | 0.0 | 0.0 | 0.0 | 0.8 | 7.9 | 3.9 | 5.0 | 3.1 | 1.9 | 0.2 | 0.4 | 0.0 | 23.2 |
| 1973-74 | 0.0 | 0.0 | 0.0 | T | 0.4 | 16.0 | 12.8 | 4.5 | 15.7 | 2.8 | 0.0 | 0.0 | 52.2 |
| 1974-75 | 0.0 | 0.0 | 0.0 | 0.2 | 2.2 | 5.2 | 13.7 | 15.2 | 5.5 | 1.2 | 0.0 | 0.0 | 43.2 |
| 1975-76 | 0.0 | 0.0 | 0.0 | 0.0 | 1.3 | 3.7 | 13.0 | 7.5 | 10.2 | 0.5 | T | 0.0 | 36.2 |
| 1976-77 | 0.0 | 0.0 | 0.0 | 0.0 | 6.0 | 6.7 | 15.7 | 13.0 | 11.2 | 1.4 | 2.4 | 0.0 | 56.4 |
| 1977-78 | 0.0 | 0.0 | 0.0 | 0.6 | 8.7 | 9.8 | 28.8 | 18.2 | 6.5 | 0.9 | 0.0 | 0.0 | 73.5 |
| 1978-79 | 0.0 | 0.0 | 0.0 | T | 4.1 | 7.9 | 12.7 | 14.3 | 1.1 | 4.4 | 0.0 | 0.0 | 44.5 |
| 1979-80 | 0.0 | 0.0 | 0.0 | T | T | 5.5 | 1.4 | 8.1 | 10.5 | T | 0.0 | 0.0 | 25.5 |
| 1980-81 | 0.0 | 0.0 | 0.0 | T | 8.6 | 8.0 | 11.1 | 7.0 | 5.8 | T | 0.0 | 0.0 | 40.5 |
| 1981-82 | 0.0 | 0.0 | 0.0 | T | 1.0 | 14.2 | 14.1 | 13.5 | 8.7 | 8.1 | 0.0 | 0.0 | 59.6 |
| 1982-83 | 0.0 | 0.0 | 0.0 | 0.0 | 0.5 | 7.4 | 8.4 | 12.3 | 3.8 | 26.7 | 0.0 | 0.0 | 59.1 |
| 1983-84 | 0.0 | 0.0 | 0.0 | 0.0 | 3.1 | 2.7 | 11.2 | 4.0 | 18.4 | 0.0 | 0.0 | 0.0 | 39.4 |
| 1984-85 | 0.0 | 0.0 | 0.0 | 0.0 | 3.0 | 9.2 | 10.8 | 9.1 | 1.4 | 1.8 | 0.0 | 0.0 | 35.3 |
| 1985-86 | 0.0 | 0.0 | 0.0 | 0.0 | 1.7 | 13.4 | 12.9 | 11.6 | 1.1 | 8.6 | 0.0 | 0.0 | 49.3 |
| 1986-87 | 0.0 | 0.0 | 0.0 | 0.0 | 8.6 | 1.4 | 29.6 | 6.4 | 0.9 | 0.6 | 0.0 | 0.0 | 47.5 |
| 1987-88 | 0.0 | 0.0 | 0.0 | T | 6.4 | 6.4 | 13.0 | 14.9 | 4.3 | 0.7 | 0.0 | 0.0 | 45.7 |
| 1988-89 | 0.0 | 0.0 | 0.0 | T | T | 1.1 | 2.1 | 3.0 | 1.1 | T | 0.0 | 0.0 | 7.3 |
| 1989-90 | 0.0 | 0.0 | T | T | 2.6 | 8.3 | 10.8 | 7.3 | 6.2 | 2.1 | 0.0 | 0.0 | 37.3 |
| 1990-91 | 0.0 | 0.0 | T | T | 0.4 | 8.4 | | | | | | | |
| Record Mean | 0.0 | 0.0 | T | 0.2 | 3.6 | 9.0 | 11.7 | 11.0 | 8.8 | 3.2 | 0.1 | 0.0 | 47.7 |

**See Reference Notes, relative to all above tables, on preceding page.**

Block Island has an area of nearly 7,000 acres and is formed from glacial terminal moraine material. It is located in the Atlantic Ocean 12 miles east-northeast of Long Island and the same distance south of Charleston, RI. The climate is typically maritime, but conditions of extreme cold or heat on the mainland are also felt on the island. Temperatures have ranged from below zero in winter to above 90 degrees in summer but these are rare occurrences.

Summers are usually dry, but high monthly rainfall totals do occur. The island is too small to contribute to the development of thunderstorms. The greatest amounts of rainfall occur from storms moving in from the ocean. Fog occurs on one out of four days in the early summer, when the ocean is relatively cold.

Based on the 1951–1980 period, the average first occurrence of 32 degrees Fahrenheit in the fall is November 11 and the average last occurrence in the spring is April 10.

Winters are distinguished for their comparative mildness because of the ocean influence. Sea water temperatures are always somewhat above freezing. Since the surface winds are usually from the east when snow begins, it soon changes to rain or melts rapidly.

The ocean moderates the temperature of the air as it moves from the mainland over the island in summer as well as winter. Winds, unimpeded by mainland topography, can reach as high as 40 mph when anticyclonic conditions prevail on the mainland during the winter. The most pronounced winds come during frequent winter gales and summer or fall tropical storms moving up the coast.

## TABLE 1    NORMALS, MEANS AND EXTREMES

BLOCK ISLAND, RHODE ISLAND

LATITUDE: 41°10'N    LONGITUDE: 71°35'W    ELEVATION: FT. GRND  110 BARO  109   TIME ZONE: EASTERN    WBAN: 94793

| | (a) | JAN | FEB | MAR | APR | MAY | JUNE | JULY | AUG | SEP | OCT | NOV | DEC | YEAR |
|---|---|---|---|---|---|---|---|---|---|---|---|---|---|---|
| **TEMPERATURE °F:** | | | | | | | | | | | | | | |
| Normals | | | | | | | | | | | | | | |
| -Daily Maximum | | 37.2 | 36.9 | 42.8 | 51.8 | 60.7 | 69.8 | 76.0 | 75.8 | 69.7 | 60.8 | 51.5 | 41.9 | 56.2 |
| -Daily Minimum | | 25.0 | 25.1 | 31.4 | 38.9 | 47.6 | 56.9 | 63.6 | 63.8 | 57.9 | 48.9 | 40.2 | 29.6 | 44.1 |
| -Monthly | | 31.1 | 31.0 | 37.1 | 45.4 | 54.2 | 63.4 | 69.8 | 69.8 | 63.8 | 54.8 | 45.9 | 35.8 | 50.2 |
| Extremes | | | | | | | | | | | | | | |
| -Record Highest | 37 | 57 | 62 | 74 | 92 | 83 | 90 | 91 | 91 | 87 | 80 | 70 | 64 | 92 |
| -Year | | 1986 | 1976 | 1977 | 1976 | 1987 | 1952 | 1972 | 1973 | 1989 | 1986 | 1956 | 1953 | APR 1976 |
| -Record Lowest | 37 | -2 | -2 | 8 | 18 | 34 | 41 | 51 | 45 | 42 | 30 | 16 | -4 | -4 |
| -Year | | 1968 | 1961 | 1967 | 1982 | 1972 | 1967 | 1979 | 1982 | 1973 | 1976 | 1987 | 1962 | DEC 1962 |
| **NORMAL DEGREE DAYS:** | | | | | | | | | | | | | | |
| Heating (base 65°F) | | 1051 | 952 | 865 | 588 | 335 | 83 | 7 | 5 | 75 | 316 | 573 | 905 | 5755 |
| Cooling (base 65°F) | | 0 | 0 | 0 | 0 | 0 | 35 | 155 | 154 | 39 | 0 | 0 | 0 | 383 |
| **% OF POSSIBLE SUNSHINE** | | | | | | | | | | | | | | |
| **MEAN SKY COVER (tenths)** | | | | | | | | | | | | | | |
| Sunrise - Sunset | 19 | 6.5 | 6.0 | 5.8 | 6.3 | 6.2 | 6.3 | 6.8 | 6.6 | 5.9 | 5.4 | 6.6 | 6.2 | 6.2 |
| **MEAN NUMBER OF DAYS:** | | | | | | | | | | | | | | |
| Sunrise to Sunset | | | | | | | | | | | | | | |
| -Clear | 19 | 8.0 | 7.9 | 9.0 | 8.1 | 7.2 | 8.5 | 7.1 | 7.4 | 9.9 | 11.4 | 6.6 | 6.7 | 97.8 |
| -Partly Cloudy | 19 | 8.6 | 7.9 | 8.5 | 8.4 | 10.8 | 9.8 | 10.9 | 10.9 | 9.2 | 7.7 | 9.8 | 10.2 | 112.7 |
| -Cloudy | 19 | 14.4 | 12.5 | 13.5 | 13.5 | 13.1 | 11.7 | 13.0 | 12.6 | 10.9 | 11.9 | 13.6 | 14.1 | 154.8 |
| Precipitation | | | | | | | | | | | | | | |
| .01 inches or more | 34 | 10.0 | 9.2 | 10.6 | 10.2 | 10.0 | 8.7 | 7.3 | 7.9 | 7.4 | 7.8 | 10.2 | 11.1 | 110.3 |
| Snow,Ice pellets | | | | | | | | | | | | | | |
| 1.0 inches or more | 26 | 1.7 | 1.6 | 1.7 | 0.2 | 0.0 | 0.0 | 0.0 | 0.0 | 0.0 | 0.0 | 0.1 | 1.2 | 6.4 |
| Thunderstorms | 15 | 0.2 | 0.3 | 0.3 | 1.4 | 1.8 | 1.9 | 3.9 | 3.6 | 1.4 | 1.1 | 0.4 | 0.1 | 16.4 |
| Heavy Fog Visibility | | | | | | | | | | | | | | |
| 1/4 mile or less | 15 | 3.6 | 3.7 | 4.7 | 8.2 | 10.1 | 10.0 | 12.4 | 10.7 | 5.4 | 3.7 | 3.2 | 3.1 | 78.8 |
| Temperature °F | | | | | | | | | | | | | | |
| -Maximum | | | | | | | | | | | | | | |
| 90° and above | 37 | 0.0 | 0.0 | 0.0 | 0.* | 0.0 | 0.* | 0.1 | 0.1 | 0.0 | 0.0 | 0.0 | 0.0 | 0.2 |
| 32° and below | 37 | 9.1 | 6.8 | 1.4 | 0.* | 0.0 | 0.0 | 0.0 | 0.0 | 0.0 | 0.0 | 0.2 | 4.3 | 21.8 |
| -Minimum | | | | | | | | | | | | | | |
| 32° and below | 37 | 24.0 | 21.7 | 16.0 | 2.5 | 0.0 | 0.0 | 0.0 | 0.0 | 0.0 | 0.2 | 4.7 | 17.6 | 86.7 |
| 0° and below | 37 | 0.1 | 0.1 | 0.0 | 0.0 | 0.0 | 0.0 | 0.0 | 0.0 | 0.0 | 0.0 | 0.0 | 0.1 | 0.3 |
| **AVG. STATION PRESS.(mb)** | | | | | | | | | | | | | | |
| **RELATIVE HUMIDITY (%)** | | | | | | | | | | | | | | |
| Hour 01 | | | | | | | | | | | | | | |
| Hour 07 | 14 | 73 | 73 | 75 | 79 | 80 | 84 | 87 | 86 | 84 | 80 | 76 | 72 | 79 |
| Hour 13 (Local Time) | 14 | 65 | 65 | 65 | 65 | 67 | 69 | 72 | 71 | 70 | 66 | 65 | 65 | 67 |
| Hour 19 | | | | | | | | | | | | | | |
| **PRECIPITATION (inches):** | | | | | | | | | | | | | | |
| Water Equivalent | | | | | | | | | | | | | | |
| -Normal | | 3.53 | 3.38 | 3.98 | 3.55 | 3.37 | 2.28 | 2.71 | 4.06 | 3.51 | 3.21 | 3.99 | 4.34 | 41.91 |
| -Maximum Monthly | 35 | 6.74 | 6.88 | 8.52 | 9.21 | 6.09 | 8.66 | 7.09 | 9.73 | 11.51 | 8.74 | 9.11 | 8.12 | 11.51 |
| -Year | | 1958 | 1971 | 1959 | 1983 | 1984 | 1982 | 1989 | 1954 | 1961 | 1955 | 1988 | 1967 | SEP 1961 |
| -Minimum Monthly | 35 | 0.27 | 0.79 | 1.16 | 0.83 | 0.72 | T | 0.39 | 0.16 | 0.33 | 0.81 | 0.89 | 0.83 | T |
| -Year | | 1970 | 1987 | 1966 | 1985 | 1955 | 1957 | 1952 | 1984 | 1971 | 1952 | 1984 | 1955 | JUN 1957 |
| -Maximum in 24 hrs | 36 | 4.06 | 2.86 | 3.63 | 2.73 | 3.67 | 4.30 | 3.61 | 4.86 | 8.52 | 6.63 | 3.96 | 4.39 | 8.52 |
| -Year | | 1962 | 1972 | 1968 | 1983 | 1984 | 1981 | 1978 | 1953 | 1960 | 1955 | 1969 | 1967 | SEP 1960 |
| Snow,Ice pellets | | | | | | | | | | | | | | |
| -Maximum Monthly | 30 | 30.0 | 16.9 | 24.1 | 2.0 | 0.0 | 0.0 | 0.0 | 0.0 | 0.0 | T | 2.5 | 10.4 | 30.0 |
| -Year | | 1978 | 1961 | 1956 | 1973 | | | | | | 1970 | 1955 | 1963 | JAN 1978 |
| -Maximum in 24 hrs | 28 | 21.7 | 16.9 | 11.5 | 2.0 | 0.0 | 0.0 | 0.0 | 0.0 | 0.0 | T | 2.5 | 6.3 | 21.7 |
| -Year | | 1978 | 1961 | 1960 | 1973 | | | | | | 1970 | 1955 | 1960 | JAN 1978 |
| **WIND:** | | | | | | | | | | | | | | |
| Mean Speed (mph) | 4 | 13.0 | 12.0 | 11.7 | 10.8 | 10.2 | 10.0 | 9.7 | 8.0 | 8.0 | 9.3 | 12.6 | 11.8 | 10.6 |
| Prevailing Direction | | | | | | | | | | | | | | |
| Fastest Obs. 1 Min. | | | | | | | | | | | | | | |
| -Direction (!!!) | 10 | 27 | 36 | 05 | 13 | 05 | 21 | 30 | 04 | 16 | 08 | 27 | 25 | 16 |
| -Speed (MPH) | 10 | 36 | 46 | 45 | 28 | 29 | 25 | 28 | 29 | 53 | 37 | 36 | 40 | 53 |
| -Year | | 1980 | 1983 | 1984 | 1983 | 1989 | 1983 | 1983 | 1983 | 1985 | 1988 | 1983 | 1983 | SEP 1985 |
| Peak Gust | | | | | | | | | | | | | | |
| -Direction (!!!) | | | | | | | | | | | | | | |
| -Speed (mph) | | | | | | | | | | | | | | |
| -Date | | | | | | | | | | | | | | |

**See reference Notes to this table on the following page.**

PRECIPITATION (inches)　　　　　BLOCK ISLAND, RHODE ISLAND

**TABLE 2**

| YEAR | JAN | FEB | MAR | APR | MAY | JUNE | JULY | AUG | SEP | OCT | NOV | DEC | ANNUAL |
|------|-----|-----|-----|-----|-----|------|------|-----|-----|-----|-----|-----|--------|
| 1961 | 2.35 | 3.68 | 2.92 | 6.24 | 5.38 | 0.94 | 2.33 | 4.06 | 11.51 | 3.17 | 5.51 | 4.15 | 52.24 |
| 1962 | 5.07 | 6.44 | 2.52 | 6.11 | 1.59 | 6.81 | 1.97 | 6.74 | 4.24 | 7.31 | 7.49 | 3.30 | 59.59 |
| 1963 | 3.39 | 3.52 | 3.45 | 1.15 | 3.56 | 0.94 | 3.13 | 4.96 | 1.62 | 1.49 | 5.77 | 3.24 | 36.22 |
| 1964 | 3.37 | 3.54 | 2.99 | 5.82 | 1.41 | 1.32 | 1.89 | 0.26 | 3.73 | 2.73 | 1.29 | 6.61 | 34.96 |
| 1965 | 2.92 | 2.00 | 1.57 | 2.70 | 1.76 | 1.82 | 1.75 | 4.09 | 1.70 | 1.14 | 1.27 | 1.36 | 24.08 |
| 1966 | 3.23 | 2.29 | 1.16 | 1.32 | 5.62 | 1.55 | 1.18 | 1.41 | 4.74 | 2.40 | 2.89 | 2.49 | 30.28 |
| 1967 | 1.90 | 2.18 | 5.28 | 3.46 | 5.98 | 2.48 | 4.09 | 2.75 | 2.67 | 1.32 | 4.15 | 8.12 | 44.38 |
| 1968 | 2.37 | 1.20 | 6.69 | 1.26 | 2.78 | 4.50 | 0.78 | 1.28 | 0.65 | 2.74 | 5.41 | 5.38 | 35.04 |
| 1969 | 0.88 | 3.89 | 3.44 | 2.46 | 2.34 | 1.72 | 4.02 | 2.94 | 3.87 | 2.60 | 7.31 | 2.97 | 40.18 |
| 1970 | 0.27 | 3.63 | 4.74 | 2.99 | 1.69 | 3.09 | 2.63 | 5.35 | 2.79 | 3.83 | 6.20 |  |  |
| 1971 | 2.48 | 6.88 | 3.07 | 3.33 | 4.57 | 0.60 | 3.11 | 1.24 | 0.33 | 2.44 | 5.15 | 1.97 | 35.17 |
| 1972 | 2.18 | 5.85 | 4.95 | 3.98 | 4.73 | 6.20 | 1.87 | 0.99 | 6.53 | 2.16 | 7.88 | 5.86 | 53.18 |
| 1973 | 2.30 | 2.21 | 3.37 | 7.78 | 4.15 | 3.21 | 5.29 | 3.81 | 3.08 | 3.33 | 1.23 | 6.66 | 46.42 |
| 1974 | 3.85 | 2.12 | 3.58 | 3.17 | 3.17 | 2.88 | 2.10 | 2.90 | 2.73 | 1.91 | 1.36 | 4.71 | 34.48 |
| 1975 | 6.02 | 4.26 | 4.01 | 3.24 | 4.42 | 5.05 | 1.34 | 4.39 | 5.06 |  | 4.69 | 3.40 |  |
| 1976 | 5.59 | 2.49 | 3.63 | 1.26 | 1.93 | 0.78 | 1.78 | 8.98 | 1.92 | 4.75 | 1.04 | 3.03 | 37.18 |
| 1977 | 2.59 | 2.19 | 4.00 | 3.61 | 1.66 | 4.44 | 1.82 | 4.89 | 4.10 | 4.85 | 2.22 | 6.08 | 42.45 |
| 1978 | 8.05 | 1.25 | 2.46 | 1.31 | 5.75 | 0.75 |  | 3.04 | 3.70 | 2.28 | 1.78 | 5.51 |  |
| 1979 | 8.83 | 3.76 | 1.07 | 4.02 | 4.69 | 1.35 |  | 4.23 | 2.66 |  | 2.83 | 1.98 |  |
| 1980 | 0.80 | 0.80 | 8.05 | 3.95 | 1.70 | 1.69 | 1.62 | 2.37 | 0.82 | 3.18 | 3.20 | 2.29 | 30.47 |
| 1981 | 0.74 | 4.81 | 1.34 | 3.68 | 1.64 | 6.15 | 1.87 | 1.69 | 1.96 | 2.77 | 2.34 | 5.19 | 34.18 |
| 1982 | 4.13 | 1.82 | 3.20 | 4.05 | 2.57 | 8.66 | 1.36 | 2.74 | 3.19 | 1.47 | 3.44 | 2.27 | 38.90 |
| 1983 | 3.27 | 4.02 | 5.59 | 9.21 | 1.97 | 2.03 | 0.67 | 1.98 | 1.12 | 2.53 | 7.20 | 3.17 | 42.76 |
| 1984 | 2.68 | 4.87 | 5.11 | 3.36 | 6.09 | 4.25 | 5.64 | 0.16 | 1.86 | 2.69 | 0.89 | 2.23 | 39.83 |
| 1985 |  | 1.86 | 2.61 | 0.83 | 5.55 | 4.45 | 1.78 | 3.00 | 1.98 | 0.84 | 5.58 | 0.93 | 29.66 |
| 1986 | 4.58 | 2.40 | 2.62 | 1.61 | 2.20 | 4.17 | 6.43 | 7.02 | 0.71 | 4.44 | 6.10 | 5.83 | 48.11 |
| 1987 | 5.11 | 0.79 | 5.09 | 5.83 | 1.68 | 0.86 | 1.20 | 4.92 | 5.19 | 1.98 | 2.96 |  | 38.80 |
| 1988 | 2.69 | 5.46 | 3.48 | 2.15 | 2.71 | 0.56 | 3.31 | 1.06 | 2.79 | 2.58 | 9.11 | 1.23 | 37.13 |
| 1989 | 1.48 |  |  |  | 3.87 | 5.64 | 7.09 | 3.30 | 3.89 | 6.00 | 4.06 | 1.69 |  |
| 1990 | 6.17 | 2.39 | 1.33 | 5.82 | 5.70 | 1.00 | 2.37 | 0.35 | 1.65 | 2.59 | 1.33 | 3.25 | 33.95 |
| Record Mean | 3.56 | 3.45 | 3.85 | 3.59 | 3.28 | 2.71 | 2.82 | 3.49 | 3.02 | 3.24 | 3.79 | 3.72 | 40.52 |

**TABLE 3**　　AVERAGE TEMPERATURE (deg. F)　　　　　BLOCK ISLAND, RHODE ISLAND

| YEAR | JAN | FEB | MAR | APR | MAY | JUNE | JULY | AUG | SEP | OCT | NOV | DEC | ANNUAL |
|------|-----|-----|-----|-----|-----|------|------|-----|-----|-----|-----|-----|--------|
| 1961 | 26.6 | 31.9 | 36.4 | 43.6 | 51.4 | 61.6 | 69.1 | 69.3 | 67.7 | 56.6 | 45.6 | 34.6 | 49.6 |
| 1962 | 30.9 | 28.5 | 36.4 | 45.1 | 54.7 | 64.3 | 67.2 | 68.5 | 62.3 | 53.8 | 43.3 | 31.0 | 48.8 |
| 1963 | 30.1 | 26.6 | 37.0 | 45.3 | 52.3 | 63.5 | 69.4 | 67.9 | 59.7 | 56.2 | 48.8 | 30.0 | 48.9 |
| 1964 | 32.9 | 29.5 | 37.0 | 43.3 | 54.9 | 62.8 | 68.4 | 66.7 | 63.0 | 53.2 | 46.3 | 36.2 | 49.5 |
| 1965 | 28.1 | 29.7 | 35.0 | 42.5 | 54.6 | 61.0 | 68.5 | 69.6 | 62.9 | 51.7 | 42.9 | 36.4 | 48.6 |
| 1966 | 29.3 | 31.5 | 37.3 | 42.2 | 51.0 | 62.3 | 70.1 | 69.8 | 62.4 | 52.8 | 47.3 | 36.3 | 49.3 |
| 1967 | 35.8 | 28.7 | 33.2 | 42.2 | 48.5 | 61.6 | 69.9 | 68.8 | 61.5 | 55.5 | 41.6 | 36.8 | 48.7 |
| 1968 | 27.2 | 26.5 | 37.6 | 46.6 | 53.0 | 62.2 | 70.2 | 69.7 | 65.3 | 57.4 | 45.3 | 32.8 | 49.5 |
| 1969 | 30.7 | 30.6 | 34.7 | 45.7 | 54.8 | 64.9 | 69.0 | 71.4 | 64.3 | 54.6 | 45.8 | 34.4 | 50.1 |
| 1970 | 24.3 | 30.6 | 35.3 | 44.6 | 54.9 | 62.1 | 70.8 | 71.4 | 64.3 | 55.7 | 47.4 | 33.7 | 49.6 |
| 1971 | 26.8 | 31.8 | 36.3 | 42.9 | 53.3 | 63.6 | 70.8 | 70.1 | 67.4 | 59.7 | 44.1 | 38.8 | 50.4 |
| 1972 | 33.7 | 30.9 | 36.0 | 42.5 | 53.5 | 61.6 | 71.4 | 70.3 | 64.3 | 51.6 | 43.7 | 38.7 | 49.9 |
| 1973 | 33.0 | 31.6 | 41.6 | 46.7 | 54.4 | 65.2 | 72.0 | 72.0 | 63.9 | 56.1 | 45.6 | 39.6 | 51.7 |
| 1974 | 34.4 | 30.4 | 38.5 | 47.1 | 52.7 | 62.9 | 69.6 | 72.0 | 64.5 | 51.3 | 46.6 | 39.1 | 50.8 |
| 1975 | 36.5 | 33.1 | 36.7 | 42.9 | 55.9 | 64.0 | 71.7 | 71.3 | 62.9 | 50.5 | 34.3 |  |  |
| 1976 | 27.5 | 37.8 | 40.9 | 52.0 | 58.1 | 69.4 | 68.8 | 68.8 | 62.6 | 51.1 | 40.0 | 29.7 | 50.5 |
| 1977 | 22.6 | 28.6 | 40.1 | 46.4 | 56.0 | 63.5 | 71.1 | 70.9 | 64.1 | 55.1 | 47.9 | 35.8 | 50.2 |
| 1978 | 29.2 | 26.4 | 34.2 | 43.9 | 53.3 | 63.8 | 67.9 | 71.0 | 61.3 | 54.1 | 46.4 | 38.0 | 49.1 |
| 1979 | 33.1 | 22.1 | 40.0 | 45.3 | 57.2 | 63.2 | 71.0 | 70.6 | 65.2 | 54.7 | 40.8 | 32.1 | 51.2 |
| 1980 | 33.3 | 29.9 | 38.2 | 48.0 | 57.1 | 63.2 | 72.7 | 71.9 | 64.8 | 52.8 | 42.9 | 32.1 | 50.6 |
| 1981 | 23.9 | 35.1 | 35.8 | 46.2 | 55.0 | 65.0 | 70.8 | 68.3 | 62.4 | 51.9 | 44.9 | 35.8 | 49.6 |
| 1982 | 26.3 | 32.3 | 37.1 | 43.0 | 54.7 | 61.5 | 71.6 | 67.4 | 62.2 | 54.6 | 48.8 | 41.6 | 50.1 |
| 1983 | 34.2 | 34.7 | 40.7 | 47.5 | 54.2 | 65.5 | 71.5 | 69.9 | 67.1 | 56.3 | 49.2 | 35.2 | 52.2 |
| 1984 | 30.1 | 37.9 | 34.6 | 45.9 | 55.9 | 66.0 | 69.7 | 72.5 | 63.6 | 58.3 | 47.2 | 43.9 | 52.1 |
| 1985 |  | 32.8 | 39.3 | 47.8 | 56.3 | 62.6 | 70.5 | 70.8 | 65.9 | 57.2 | 50.3 | 36.9 | 51.7 |
| 1986 | 33.9 | 31.7 | 39.3 | 48.0 | 56.0 | 63.3 | 68.7 | 68.6 | 62.0 | 55.3 | 45.2 | 38.9 | 50.9 |
| 1987 | 32.6 | 30.6 | 39.3 | 46.4 | 54.6 | 64.2 | 70.2 | 68.8 | 64.4 | 53.2 | 45.2 | 38.1 | 50.5 |
| 1988 | 30.1 | 32.7 | 38.4 | 45.6 | 54.0 | 62.7 | 70.7 | 71.0 | 62.8 | 51.8 | 47.8 | 36.7 | 50.4 |
| 1989 | 36.3 |  |  |  | 56.0 | 66.1 | 69.9 | 66.6 | 64.8 | 54.8 | 44.0 | 26.6 |  |
| 1990 | 37.6 | 34.3 | 37.7 | 45.5 | 54.1 | 64.8 | 70.5 | 73.4 | 60.4 | 58.4 | 47.6 | 41.3 | 52.1 |
| Record Mean | 31.5 | 30.9 | 36.7 | 44.7 | 53.7 | 62.8 | 69.2 | 69.1 | 64.3 | 55.4 | 46.0 | 36.3 | 50.0 |
| Max | 37.6 | 36.8 | 42.3 | 50.6 | 59.8 | 68.8 | 75.0 | 74.7 | 69.9 | 60.9 | 51.5 | 42.2 | 55.8 |
| Min | 25.5 | 25.0 | 31.1 | 38.8 | 47.6 | 56.7 | 63.3 | 63.5 | 58.7 | 49.9 | 40.5 | 30.4 | 44.3 |

## REFERENCE NOTES FOR TABLES 1, 2, 3 and 6　　　(BLOCK ISLAND, RI)

### GENERAL

T - TRACE AMOUNT
BLANK ENTRIES DENOTE MISSING/UNREPORTED DATA.
# INDICATES A STATION OR INSTRUMENT RELOCATION.

### SPECIFIC

#### TABLE 1

(a) - LENGTH OF RECORD IN YEARS. ALTHOUGH INDIVIDUAL MONTHS MAY BE MISSING.

* LESS THAN .05

NORMALS — BASED ON THE 1951-1980 RECORD PERIOD.
EXTREMES — DATES ARE THE MOST RECENT OCCURRENCE.
WIND DIR. — NUMERALS SHOW TENS OF DEGREES CLOCKWISE FROM TRUE NORTH. "00" INDICATES CALM.
RESULTANT WIND DIRECTIONS ARE GIVEN TO WHOLE DEGREES.

#### TABLE 3

MAX AND MIN ARE LONG-TERM MEAN DAILY MAXIMUM AND MEAN DAILY MINIMUM TEMPERATURES.

### EXCEPTIONS

#### TABLE 1

1. THUNDERSTORMS AND HEAVY FOG MAY BE INCOMPLETE, DUE TO PART-TIME OPERATIONS.
2. THUNDERSTORMS, HEAVY FOG, AND RELATIVE HUMIDITY ARE THROUGH 1964.
3. MEAN SKY COVER, AND DAYS CLEAR - PARTLY CLOUDY - CLOUDY ARE THROUGH 1968 AND JANUARY-JULY 1974.
3. DAYS OF SNOW 1 INCH OR MORE ARE THROUGH 1977.
4. SNOW DATA IS THROUGH DECEMBER 1978.

#### TABLES 2, 3, and 6

RECORD MEANS ARE THROUGH THE CURRENT YEAR, BEGINNING IN　　1881 FOR TEMPERATURE
　　1881 FOR PRECIPITATION
　　1951 - 1978 FOR SNOWFALL

HEATING DEGREE DAYS Base 65 deg. F          BLOCK ISLAND, RHODE ISLAND

**TABLE 4**

| SEASON | JULY | AUG | SEP | OCT | NOV | DEC | JAN | FEB | MAR | APR | MAY | JUNE | TOTAL |
|---|---|---|---|---|---|---|---|---|---|---|---|---|---|
| 1961-62 | 7 | 4 | 39 | 257 | 577 | 932 | 1052 | 1015 | 881 | 591 | 313 | 65 | 5733 |
| 1962-63 | 11 | 11 | 106 | 344 | 645 | 1047 | 1073 | 1071 | 860 | 585 | 384 | 92 | 6229 |
| 1963-64 | 7 | 9 | 162 | 266 | 478 | 1076 | 988 | 1024 | 860 | 644 | 309 | 96 | 5919 |
| 1964-65 | 9 | 14 | 99 | 359 | 555 | 884 | 1136 | 982 | 923 | 669 | 320 | 132 | 6082 |
| 1965-66 | 1 | 20 | 96 | 405 | 657 | 877 | 1099 | 931 | 854 | 675 | 429 | 105 | 6149 |
| 1966-67 | 0 | 0 | 101 | 371 | 523 | 883 | 898 | 1012 | 977 | 676 | 507 | 105 | 6053 |
| 1967-68 | 2 | 9 | 115 | 294 | 695 | 865 | 1166 | 1109 | 846 | 543 | 365 | 103 | 6112 |
| 1968-69 | 7 | 10 | 40 | 239 | 583 | 992 | 1060 | 959 | 931 | 572 | 318 | 45 | 5756 |
| 1969-70 | 5 | 3 | 74 | 319 | 568 | 943 | 1255 | 957 | 915 | 601 | 307 | 95 | 6042 |
| 1970-71 | 0 | 0 | 70 | 288 | 524 | 963 | 1180 | 927 | 883 | 659 | 357 | 73 | 5924 |
| 1971-72 | 0 | 12 | 31 | 162 | 619 | 805 | 962 | 982 | 895 | 669 | 350 | 105 | 5592 |
| 1972-73 | 4 | 4 | 53 | 409 | 636 | 808 | 984 | 926 | 716 | 542 | 325 | 37 | 5444 |
| 1973-74 | 0 | 2 | 97 | 272 | 577 | 782 | 943 | 961 | 816 | 532 | 377 | 86 | 5445 |
| 1974-75 | 6 | 0 | 73 | 417 | 546 | 797 | 874 | 887 | 870 | 657 | 280 | 66 | 5473 |
| 1975-76 | 0 | 6 | 76 |  | 427 | 944 | 1154 | 783 | 740 | 402 | 217 | 29 |  |
| 1976-77 | 3 | 14 | 87 | 425 | 742 | 1088 | 1306 | 1014 | 764 | 549 | 278 | 70 | 6340 |
| 1977-78 | 0 | 3 | 84 | 301 | 508 | 899 | 1104 | 1073 | 946 | 624 | 358 | 72 | 5972 |
| 1978-79 | 16 | 5 | 125 | 331 | 550 | 827 | 985 | 1196 | 769 | 583 | 235 | 68 | 5690 |
| 1979-80 | 18 | 11 | 70 | 315 | 402 | 745 | 976 | 1011 | 823 | 505 | 242 | 74 | 5192 |
| 1980-81 | 0 | 1 | 68 | 372 | 656 | 1014 | 1268 | 831 | 897 | 559 | 305 | 30 | 6001 |
| 1981-82 | 0 | 13 | 93 | 400 | 597 | 899 | 1191 | 908 | 860 | 650 | 310 | 114 | 6035 |
| 1982-83 | 5 | 28 | 96 | 317 | 479 | 720 | 949 | 842 | 748 | 519 | 329 | 46 | 5078 |
| 1983-84 | 1 | 5 | 57 | 274 | 468 | 915 | 1073 | 779 | 934 | 565 | 276 | 40 | 5387 |
| 1984-85 | 0 | 0 | 81 | 201 | 525 | 645 |  | 897 | 790 | 509 | 263 | 82 |  |
| 1985-86 | 7 | 2 | 45 | 237 | 435 | 864 | 960 | 926 | 790 | 505 | 284 | 73 | 5128 |
| 1986-87 | 12 | 14 | 102 | 307 | 586 | 801 | 997 | 958 | 790 | 551 | 332 | 55 | 5505 |
| 1987-88 | 3 | 15 | 53 | 358 | 587 | 827 | 1072 | 931 | 821 | 574 | 340 | 99 | 5680 |
| 1988-89 | 6 | 11 | 85 | 404 | 509 | 872 | 880 |  |  |  | 276 | 33 |  |
| 1989-90 | 5 | 7 | 81 | 310 | 624 | 1188 | 843 | 853 | 841 | 575 | 331 | 61 | 5719 |
| 1990-91 | 8 | 0 | 149 | 220 | 515 | 727 |  |  |  |  |  |  |  |

**TABLE 5**  COOLING DEGREE DAYS Base 65 deg. F          BLOCK ISLAND, RHODE ISLAND

| YEAR | JAN | FEB | MAR | APR | MAY | JUNE | JULY | AUG | SEP | OCT | NOV | DEC | TOTAL |
|---|---|---|---|---|---|---|---|---|---|---|---|---|---|
| 1969 | 0 | 0 | 0 | 0 | 8 | 52 | 136 | 209 | 60 | 3 | 0 | 0 | 468 |
| 1970 | 0 | 0 | 0 | 0 | 0 | 12 | 186 | 208 | 55 | 5 | 0 | 0 | 466 |
| 1971 | 0 | 0 | 0 | 0 | 0 | 38 | 185 | 177 | 111 | 2 | 0 | 0 | 513 |
| 1972 | 0 | 0 | 0 | 0 | 0 | 8 | 208 | 174 | 38 | 0 | 0 | 0 | 428 |
| 1973 | 0 | 0 | 0 | 0 | 2 | 48 | 184 | 225 | 73 | 4 | 0 | 0 | 536 |
| 1974 | 0 | 0 | 0 | 0 | 0 | 32 | 157 | 227 | 64 | 0 | 0 | 0 | 480 |
| 1975 | 0 | 0 | 0 | 0 | 4 | 40 | 217 | 208 | 18 | 0 | 0 | 0 |  |
| 1976 | 0 | 0 | 0 | 18 | 10 | 166 | 128 | 138 | 21 | 0 | 0 | 0 | 481 |
| 1977 | 0 | 0 | 0 | 0 | 3 | 33 | 197 | 193 | 65 | 0 | 0 | 0 | 491 |
| 1978 | 0 | 0 | 0 | 0 | 0 | 42 | 113 | 198 | 25 | 0 | 0 | 0 | 378 |
| 1979 | 0 | 0 | 0 | 0 | 0 | 22 | 211 | 190 | 84 | 2 | 0 | 0 | 509 |
| 1980 | 0 | 0 | 0 | 0 | 0 | 27 | 245 | 222 | 70 | 0 | 0 | 0 | 564 |
| 1981 | 0 | 0 | 0 | 0 | 0 | 36 | 188 | 123 | 25 | 0 | 0 | 0 | 372 |
| 1982 | 0 | 0 | 0 | 0 | 0 | 16 | 215 | 109 | 18 | 1 | 0 | 0 | 359 |
| 1983 | 0 | 0 | 0 | 0 | 0 | 70 | 211 | 163 | 125 | 10 | 0 | 0 | 579 |
| 1984 | 0 | 0 | 0 | 0 | 0 | 78 | 153 | 239 | 45 | 0 | 0 | 0 | 515 |
| 1985 | 0 | 0 | 0 | 0 | 0 | 17 | 184 | 189 | 82 | 3 | 0 | 0 | 475 |
| 1986 | 0 | 0 | 0 | 0 | 9 | 28 | 135 | 133 | 15 | 13 | 0 | 0 | 333 |
| 1987 | 0 | 0 | 0 | 0 | 19 | 36 | 171 | 140 | 40 | 0 | 0 | 0 | 406 |
| 1988 | 0 | 0 | 0 | 0 | 5 | 39 | 191 | 203 | 27 | 0 | 0 | 0 | 465 |
| 1989 | 0 | 0 | 0 | 0 | 2 | 73 | 121 | 165 | 83 | 0 | 0 | 0 |  |
| 1990 | 0 | 0 | 0 | 0 | 0 | 63 | 184 | 265 | 21 | 23 | 0 | 0 | 556 |

**TABLE 6**  SNOWFALL (inches)          BLOCK ISLAND, RHODE ISLAND

| SEASON | JULY | AUG | SEP | OCT | NOV | DEC | JAN | FEB | MAR | APR | MAY | JUNE | TOTAL |
|---|---|---|---|---|---|---|---|---|---|---|---|---|---|
| 1961-62 | 0.0 | 0.0 | 0.0 | 0.0 | 0.0 | 4.2 | 3.8 | 12.0 | 0.8 | 0.0 | 0.0 | 0.0 | 20.8 |
| 1962-63 | 0.0 | 0.0 | 0.0 | T | 0.3 | 7.2 | 5.2 | 2.5 | 3.0 | 0.5 | 0.0 | 0.0 | 18.7 |
| 1963-64 | 0.0 | 0.0 | 0.0 | 0.0 | 0.1 | 10.4 | 5.9 | 12.1 | 1.9 | 0.0 | 0.0 | 0.0 | 30.4 |
| 1964-65 | 0.0 | 0.0 | 0.0 | 0.0 | 0.0 | 1.1 | 21.5 | 2.2 | 2.6 | 1.3 | 0.0 | 0.0 | 28.7 |
| 1965-66 | 0.0 | 0.0 | 0.0 | 0.0 | T | 8.5 | 4.6 | 2.0 | 0.0 | 0.0 | 0.0 | 0.0 | 15.1 |
| 1966-67 | 0.0 | 0.0 | 0.0 | 0.0 | 0.0 | 3.2 | 0.5 | 15.6 | 19.3 | T | 0.0 | 0.0 | 38.6 |
| 1967-68 | 0.0 | 0.0 | 0.0 | 0.0 | 0.4 | 3.7 | 8.8 | 2.8 | 4.4 | 0.0 | 0.0 | 0.0 | 20.1 |
| 1968-69 | 0.0 | 0.0 | 0.0 | 0.0 | 0.0 | 0.1 | T | 8.3 | 8.5 | 0.0 | 0.0 | 0.0 | 16.9 |
| 1969-70 | 0.0 | 0.0 | 0.0 | 0.0 | T | 1.5 | 1.4 | 2.2 | 11.7 | T | 0.0 | 0.0 | 16.8 |
| 1970-71 | 0.0 | 0.0 | 0.0 | T | 0.0 | 4.2 | 3.5 | 0.5 | T | 0.0 | 0.0 | 0.0 | 8.2 |
| 1971-72 | 0.0 | 0.0 | 0.0 | 0.0 | T | 1.0 | 2.2 | 5.0 | 0.2 | 0.5 | 0.0 | 0.0 | 8.9 |
| 1972-73 | 0.0 | 0.0 | 0.0 | 0.0 | T | 0.9 | 0.3 | 2.1 | 1.4 | 2.0 | 0.0 | 0.0 | 6.7 |
| 1973-74 | 0.0 | 0.0 | 0.0 | 0.0 | 0.0 | T | 8.8 | 8.5 | T | 0.6 | 0.0 | 0.0 | 17.9 |
| 1974-75 | 0.0 | 0.0 | 0.0 | 0.0 | T | 2.5 | 10.3 | 7.8 | T | 0.0 | 0.0 | 0.0 | 20.6 |
| 1975-76 | 0.0 | 0.0 | 0.0 | 0.0 | 0.0 | 1.8 | 9.3 | 2.8 | 7.6 | 0.0 | 0.0 | 0.0 | 21.5 |
| 1976-77 | 0.0 | 0.0 | 0.0 | 0.0 | 0.0 | 5.5 | 4.6 | 8.3 | 3.0 | 0.0 | 0.0 | 0.0 | 21.4 |
| 1977-78 | 0.0 | 0.0 | 0.0 | 0.0 | T | 0.8 | 30.0 | 11.1 | 9.8 | 0.0 | 0.0 | 0.0 | 51.7 |
| 1978-79 | 0.0 | 0.0 | 0.0 | 0.0 | T |  |  |  |  |  |  |  |  |
| 1979-80 |  |  |  |  |  |  |  |  |  |  |  |  |  |
| 1980-81 |  |  |  |  |  |  |  |  |  |  |  |  |  |
| 1981-82 |  |  |  |  |  |  |  |  |  |  |  |  |  |
| 1982-83 |  |  |  |  |  |  |  |  |  |  |  |  |  |
| 1983-84 |  |  |  |  |  |  |  |  |  |  |  |  |  |
| 1984-85 |  |  |  |  |  |  |  |  |  |  |  |  |  |
| 1985-86 |  |  |  |  |  |  |  |  |  |  |  |  |  |
| Record Mean | 0.0 | 0.0 | 0.0 | T | 0.2 | 2.9 | 5.1 | 6.3 | 5.7 | 0.3 | 0.0 | 0.0 | 20.4 |

**See Reference Notes, relative to all above tables, on preceding page.**

The proximity to Narragansett Bay and the Atlantic Ocean plays an important part in determining the climate for Providence and vicinity. In winter, the temperatures are modified considerably, and many major snowstorms change to rain before reaching the area. In summer, many days that could be uncomfortably warm are cooled by refreshing sea breezes. At other times of the year, sea fog may be advected in over land by onshore winds. In fact, most cases of dense fog are produced this way, but the number of such days is few, averaging two or three days per month. In early fall, severe coastal storms of tropical origin sometimes bring destructive winds to this area. Even at other times of the year, it is usually coastal storms which produce the severest weather.

The temperature for the entire year averages around 50 degrees with 70 degree temperatures common from near the end of May to the latter part of September. During this period, there may be several days reaching 90 degrees or more. Temperatures of 100 degrees and more are rare.

Freezing temperatures occur on the average about 125 days per year. They become a common daily occurrence in the latter part of November, and become less frequent near the end of March. The average date for the last freeze in spring is mid-April, while the average date for the first freeze in fall is late October, making the growing season about 195 days in length. Sub-zero weather in winter seldom occurs, averaging less than one day for December and one or two days each for January and February.

Measurable precipitation occurs on about one day out of every three, and is fairly evenly distributed throughout the year. There is usually no definite dry season, but occasionally droughts do occur.

Thunderstorms are responsible for much of the rainfall from May through August. They usually produce heavy, and sometimes even excessive amounts of rainfall. However, since their duration is relatively short, damage is ordinarily light. The thunderstorms of summer are frequently accompanied by extremely gusty winds, which may result in some damage to property.

The first measurable snowfall of winter usually comes toward the end of November, and the last in spring is about the middle of March. Winters with over 50 inches of snow are not common. The area normally receives less than 25 inches. The month of greatest snowfall is usually February, but January and March are close seconds. It is unusual for the ground to remain well covered with snow for any long period of time.

## TABLE 1 NORMALS, MEANS AND EXTREMES

PROVIDENCE, RHODE ISLAND

LATITUDE: 41°44'N    LONGITUDE: 71°26'W    ELEVATION: FT. GRND  51 BARO  58    TIME ZONE: EASTERN    WBAN: 14765

| | (a) | JAN | FEB | MAR | APR | MAY | JUNE | JULY | AUG | SEP | OCT | NOV | DEC | YEAR |
|---|---|---|---|---|---|---|---|---|---|---|---|---|---|---|
| **TEMPERATURE °F:** | | | | | | | | | | | | | | |
| Normals | | | | | | | | | | | | | | |
| -Daily Maximum | | 36.4 | 37.7 | 45.5 | 57.5 | 67.6 | 76.6 | 81.7 | 80.3 | 73.1 | 63.2 | 51.9 | 40.5 | 59.3 |
| -Daily Minimum | | 20.0 | 20.9 | 29.2 | 38.3 | 47.6 | 57.0 | 63.3 | 61.9 | 53.8 | 43.1 | 34.8 | 24.1 | 41.2 |
| -Monthly | | 28.2 | 29.3 | 37.4 | 47.9 | 57.6 | 66.8 | 72.5 | 71.1 | 63.5 | 53.2 | 43.4 | 32.3 | 50.3 |
| Extremes | | | | | | | | | | | | | | |
| -Record Highest | 36 | 66 | 72 | 80 | 98 | 94 | 97 | 100 | 104 | 100 | 86 | 78 | 70 | 104 |
| -Year | | 1974 | 1985 | 1989 | 1976 | 1987 | 1988 | 1980 | 1975 | 1983 | 1979 | 1974 | 1984 | AUG 1975 |
| -Record Lowest | 36 | -13 | -7 | 1 | 14 | 29 | 41 | 48 | 40 | 33 | 20 | 6 | -10 | -13 |
| -Year | | 1976 | 1979 | 1967 | 1954 | 1956 | 1980 | 1988 | 1965 | 1980 | 1976 | 1989 | 1980 | JAN 1976 |
| **NORMAL DEGREE DAYS:** | | | | | | | | | | | | | | |
| Heating (base 65°F) | | 1141 | 1000 | 856 | 513 | 239 | 31 | 0 | 6 | 94 | 366 | 648 | 1014 | 5908 |
| Cooling (base 65°F) | | 0 | 0 | 0 | 0 | 10 | 85 | 235 | 195 | 49 | 0 | 0 | 0 | 574 |
| **% OF POSSIBLE SUNSHINE** | 36 | 57 | 57 | 58 | 56 | 57 | 60 | 63 | 61 | 61 | 60 | 50 | 53 | 58 |
| **MEAN SKY COVER (tenths)** | | | | | | | | | | | | | | |
| Sunrise - Sunset | 36 | 6.2 | 6.3 | 6.5 | 6.6 | 6.7 | 6.4 | 6.3 | 6.2 | 5.8 | 5.5 | 6.3 | 6.2 | 6.3 |
| **MEAN NUMBER OF DAYS:** | | | | | | | | | | | | | | |
| Sunrise to Sunset | | | | | | | | | | | | | | |
| -Clear | 36 | 9.9 | 7.9 | 8.6 | 7.6 | 6.6 | 6.7 | 6.8 | 8.3 | 9.6 | 11.0 | 8.3 | 8.5 | 99.7 |
| -Partly Cloudy | 36 | 6.7 | 7.3 | 7.7 | 8.1 | 9.8 | 10.3 | 11.9 | 10.4 | 8.1 | 8.0 | 6.9 | 7.9 | 102.9 |
| -Cloudy | 36 | 14.4 | 13.1 | 14.7 | 14.3 | 14.6 | 13.0 | 12.3 | 12.4 | 12.3 | 12.0 | 14.8 | 14.6 | 162.5 |
| Precipitation | | | | | | | | | | | | | | |
| .01 inches or more | 36 | 10.9 | 9.9 | 11.6 | 11.1 | 11.3 | 10.9 | 9.0 | 9.5 | 8.3 | 8.5 | 11.0 | 12.0 | 124.0 |
| Snow, Ice pellets | | | | | | | | | | | | | | |
| 1.0 inches or more | 36 | 2.8 | 2.5 | 1.9 | 0.3 | 0.* | 0.0 | 0.0 | 0.0 | 0.0 | 0.1 | 0.3 | 2.1 | 9.9 |
| Thunderstorms | 36 | 0.2 | 0.2 | 0.7 | 1.2 | 2.6 | 3.8 | 4.6 | 3.7 | 1.7 | 1.0 | 0.8 | 0.2 | 20.6 |
| Heavy Fog Visibility | | | | | | | | | | | | | | |
| 1/4 mile or less | 36 | 2.0 | 2.0 | 2.1 | 2.1 | 2.3 | 2.3 | 1.9 | 1.4 | 1.8 | 3.0 | 2.1 | 1.9 | 25.1 |
| Temperature °F | | | | | | | | | | | | | | |
| -Maximum | | | | | | | | | | | | | | |
| 90° and above | 26 | 0.0 | 0.0 | 0.0 | 0.1 | 0.6 | 1.9 | 3.7 | 2.3 | 0.9 | 0.0 | 0.0 | 0.0 | 9.5 |
| 32° and below | 26 | 11.8 | 7.8 | 1.4 | 0.* | 0.0 | 0.0 | 0.0 | 0.0 | 0.0 | 0.0 | 0.3 | 6.4 | 27.8 |
| -Minimum | | | | | | | | | | | | | | |
| 32° and below | 26 | 28.0 | 24.5 | 19.6 | 5.6 | 0.2 | 0.0 | 0.0 | 0.0 | 0.0 | 3.8 | 12.8 | 24.9 | 119.5 |
| 0° and below | 26 | 1.5 | 0.7 | 0.0 | 0.0 | 0.0 | 0.0 | 0.0 | 0.0 | 0.0 | 0.0 | 0.0 | 0.3 | 2.5 |
| **AVG. STATION PRESS.(mb)** | 17 | 1013.9 | 1014.5 | 1013.5 | 1011.6 | 1012.8 | 1012.5 | 1013.0 | 1014.6 | 1016.0 | 1016.6 | 1015.2 | 1015.1 | 1014.1 |
| **RELATIVE HUMIDITY (%)** | | | | | | | | | | | | | | |
| Hour 01 | 26 | 69 | 67 | 69 | 70 | 77 | 82 | 82 | 84 | 84 | 80 | 75 | 72 | 76 |
| Hour 07 | 26 | 70 | 70 | 70 | 69 | 73 | 75 | 77 | 80 | 82 | 80 | 77 | 74 | 75 |
| Hour 13 (Local Time) | 26 | 56 | 54 | 52 | 48 | 53 | 56 | 56 | 56 | 55 | 53 | 57 | 57 | 54 |
| Hour 19 | 26 | 63 | 61 | 61 | 59 | 64 | 67 | 68 | 71 | 73 | 71 | 69 | 66 | 66 |
| **PRECIPITATION (inches):** | | | | | | | | | | | | | | |
| Water Equivalent | | | | | | | | | | | | | | |
| -Normal | | 4.06 | 3.72 | 4.29 | 3.95 | 3.48 | 2.79 | 3.01 | 4.04 | 3.54 | 3.75 | 4.22 | 4.47 | 45.32 |
| -Maximum Monthly | 36 | 11.66 | 7.20 | 8.84 | 12.74 | 8.38 | 11.08 | 8.08 | 11.12 | 7.92 | 11.89 | 11.01 | 10.75 | 12.74 |
| -Year | | 1979 | 1984 | 1983 | 1983 | 1984 | 1982 | 1976 | 1955 | 1961 | 1962 | 1983 | 1969 | APR 1983 |
| -Minimum Monthly | 36 | 0.50 | 0.39 | 0.56 | 1.48 | 0.71 | 0.39 | 1.00 | 0.71 | 0.77 | 1.62 | 0.81 | 0.58 | 0.39 |
| -Year | | 1970 | 1987 | 1981 | 1966 | 1964 | 1957 | 1970 | 1984 | 1959 | 1969 | 1976 | 1955 | FEB 1987 |
| -Maximum in 24 hrs | 36 | 3.34 | 3.14 | 4.53 | 4.45 | 5.17 | 5.03 | 4.83 | 6.71 | 4.89 | 6.63 | 4.18 | 3.85 | 6.71 |
| -Year | | 1962 | 1978 | 1968 | 1983 | 1984 | 1984 | 1976 | 1979 | 1961 | 1962 | 1983 | 1969 | AUG 1979 |
| Snow, Ice pellets | | | | | | | | | | | | | | |
| -Maximum Monthly | 36 | 28.7 | 30.9 | 31.6 | 7.6 | 7.0 | 0.0 | 0.0 | 0.0 | 0.0 | 2.5 | 8.0 | 19.8 | 31.6 |
| -Year | | 1965 | 1962 | 1956 | 1977 | 1977 | | | | | 1979 | 1989 | 1963 | MAR 1956 |
| -Maximum in 24 hrs | 36 | 10.8 | 27.6 | 16.9 | 7.6 | 7.0 | 0.0 | 0.0 | 0.0 | 0.0 | 2.5 | 8.0 | 11.9 | 27.6 |
| -Year | | 1978 | 1978 | 1960 | 1982 | 1977 | | | | | 1979 | 1989 | 1981 | FEB 1978 |
| **WIND:** | | | | | | | | | | | | | | |
| Mean Speed (mph) | 36 | 11.2 | 11.5 | 12.1 | 12.2 | 10.8 | 9.9 | 9.5 | 9.3 | 9.4 | 9.6 | 10.5 | 10.9 | 10.6 |
| Prevailing Direction | | | | | | | | | | | | | | |
| through 1963 | | NW | NNW | WNW | SW | S | SW | SW | SSW | SW | NW | SW | WNW | SW |
| Fastest Obs. 1 Min. | | | | | | | | | | | | | | |
| -Direction (!!!) | 36 | 20 | 16 | 18 | 20 | 20 | 20 | 34 | 11 | 18 | 14 | 18 | 14 | 11 |
| -Speed (MPH) | 36 | 46 | 46 | 60 | 51 | 42 | 40 | 35 | 90 | 58 | 41 | 52 | 48 | 90 |
| -Year | | 1978 | 1972 | 1959 | 1956 | 1956 | 1957 | 1964 | 1954 | 1960 | 1954 | 1957 | 1957 | AUG 1954 |
| Peak Gust | | | | | | | | | | | | | | |
| -Direction (!!!) | 6 | S | SW | SW | SE | N | SE | SW | S | S | SW | NW | NW | S |
| -Speed (mph) | 6 | 51 | 55 | 60 | 54 | 46 | 54 | 43 | 40 | 81 | 49 | 54 | 51 | 81 |
| -Date | | 1987 | 1989 | 1986 | 1984 | 1986 | 1989 | 1984 | 1988 | 1985 | 1985 | 1989 | 1988 | SEP 1985 |

**See Reference Notes to this table on the following page.**

## TABLE 2 — PRECIPITATION (inches)   PROVIDENCE. RHODE ISLAND

| YEAR | JAN | FEB | MAR | APR | MAY | JUNE | JULY | AUG | SEP | OCT | NOV | DEC | ANNUAL |
|------|-----|-----|-----|-----|-----|------|------|-----|-----|-----|-----|-----|--------|
| 1961 | 3.52 | 4.68 | 4.16 | 7.32 | 5.21 | 1.48 | 2.76 | 3.86 | 7.92 | 2.39 | 3.10 | 3.16 | 49.56 |
| 1962 | 4.70 | 5.16 | 1.93 | 3.85 | 2.14 | 5.52 | .62 | 2.73 | 3.67 | 11.89 | 4.49 | 2.63 | 50.33 |
| 1963 | 3.40 | 3.15 | 3.78 | 1.62 | 4.69 | 3.54 | 3.35 | 1.56 | 4.10 | 1.63 | 6.53 | 2.15 | 39.50 |
| 1964 | 5.65 | 3.15 | 2.26 | 5.34 | 0.71 | 2.34 | 2.63 | 2.38 | 3.95 | 2.11 | 2.43 | 5.46 | 38.41 |
| 1965 | 3.46 | 3.77 | 1.72 | 2.43 | 1.08 | 1.91 | .28 | 1.90 | 1.64 | 2.75 | 2.08 | 1.42 | 25.44 |
| 1966 | 3.40 | 4.30 | 2.40 | 1.48 | 3.85 | 2.31 | 2.77 | 3.37 | 5.23 | 2.60 | 3.93 | 3.04 | 38.68 |
| 1967 | 1.60 | 2.51 | 5.49 | 4.19 | 7.27 | 2.72 | 3.95 | 3.24 | 3.17 | 2.25 | 2.75 | 7.36 | 46.50 |
| 1968 | 3.50 | 1.31 | 7.83 | 1.49 | 3.54 | 4.74 | 1.49 | 1.61 | 1.14 | 1.79 | 6.22 | 6.70 | 41.36 |
| 1969 | 2.23 | 4.30 | 3.10 | 3.95 | 2.41 | 1.23 | 2.98 | 2.58 | 3.09 | 1.62 | 6.35 | 10.75 | 44.59 |
| 1970 | 0.50 | 5.34 | 4.75 | 3.91 | 3.03 | 4.25 | .00 | 6.59 | 1.79 | 4.41 | 5.31 | 4.54 | 45.42 |
| 1971 | 2.01 | 5.36 | 3.81 | 2.31 | 3.83 | 1.64 | 3.48 | 3.03 | 2.54 | 2.88 | 5.16 | 2.37 | 38.42 |
| 1972 | 1.85 | 5.19 | 6.70 | 3.71 | 5.73 | 6.83 | 4.25 | 2.98 | 7.31 | 4.36 | 8.45 | 7.70 | 65.06 |
| 1973 | 3.06 | 3.55 | 2.78 | 7.16 | 3.99 | 3.48 | 2.92 | 5.17 | 3.04 | 3.17 | 2.29 | 7.63 | 48.24 |
| 1974 | 4.45 | 3.04 | 4.51 | 2.86 | 2.74 | 3.10 | 1.64 | 3.10 | 6.15 | 2.79 | 1.56 | 4.54 | 40.66 |
| 1975 | 6.78 | 3.29 | 3.07 | 2.99 | 2.06 | 4.73 | 3.51 | 2.19 | 6.15 | 4.66 | 6.29 | 5.11 | 50.83 |
| 1976 | 6.38 | 2.91 | 3.44 | 2.00 | 2.53 | 1.60 | 9.08 | 7.01 | 1.57 | 6.52 | 0.81 | 3.47 | 46.32 |
| 1977 | 3.90 | 2.87 | 5.62 | 3.35 | 3.43 | 3.92 | 2.04 | 2.12 | 5.60 | 6.90 | 3.24 | 5.85 | 48.84 |
| 1978 | 9.01 | 3.20 | 3.10 | 2.53 | 5.27 | 1.97 | 2.63 | 6.46 | 1.82 | 3.22 | 2.61 | 5.19 | 47.01 |
| 1979 | 11.66 | 4.08 | 2.21 | 5.12 | 7.62 | 1.44 | .65 | 10.09 | 4.08 | 3.94 | 4.49 | 1.81 | 58.19 |
| 1980 | 1.40 | 1.16 | 8.11 | 6.18 | 1.78 | 3.85 | 2.03 | 1.99 | 0.90 | 3.41 | 3.73 | 1.57 | 36.11 |
| 1981 * | 0.77 | 4.79 | 0.56 | 4.10 | 1.92 | 2.31 | 3.75 | 2.65 | 2.58 | 3.38 | 3.20 | 6.36 | 36.37 |
| 1982 | 6.09 | 3.08 | 3.76 | 3.64 | 1.61 | 11.08 | 3.51 | 3.67 | 3.61 | 3.08 | 4.32 | 1.81 | 49.26 |
| 1983 | 4.32 | 4.81 | 8.84 | 12.74 | 4.67 | 1.91 | 2.14 | 2.71 | 2.16 | 4.50 | 11.01 | 7.71 | 67.52 |
| 1984 | 2.00 | 7.20 | 5.77 | 4.30 | 8.38 | 4.09 | 5.16 | 0.71 | 1.77 | 4.25 | 1.95 | 3.16 | 48.74 |
| 1985 | 1.18 | 1.57 | 3.08 | 1.65 | 4.76 | 4.70 | 2.88 | 8.57 | 1.78 | 7.14 |  | 1.42 | 40.42 |
| 1986 | 5.88 | 3.18 | 2.86 | 2.10 | 2.29 | 3.27 | 5.95 | 3.29 | 0.97 | 2.48 | 5.77 | 8.09 | 46.13 |
| 1987 | 4.73 | 0.39 | 5.62 | 6.91 | 1.80 | 2.00 | .20 | 2.58 | 7.47 | 2.28 | 3.40 | 2.29 | 40.67 |
| 1988 | 2.69 | 5.29 | 4.09 | 3.11 | 2.83 | 0.91 | 5.73 | 0.94 | 2.38 | 1.77 | 7.60 | 1.03 | 38.37 |
| 1989 | 1.17 | 2.69 | 4.13 | 5.30 | 6.07 | 5.84 | 5.59 | 6.14 | 4.75 | 8.37 | 4.35 | 1.66 | 56.06 |
| 1990 | 5.01 | 2.93 | 2.01 | 5.57 | 5.70 | 1.13 | 3.52 | 3.74 | 2.28 | 4.96 | 2.45 | 5.48 | 44.78 |
| Record Mean | 3.73 | 3.30 | 3.79 | 3.74 | 3.30 | 3.05 | 3.18 | 3.67 | 3.29 | 3.22 | 3.85 | 3.85 | 41.97 |

## TABLE 3 — AVERAGE TEMPERATURE (deg. F)   PROVIDENCE. RHODE ISLAND

| YEAR | JAN | FEB | MAR | APR | MAY | JUNE | JULY | AUG | SEP | OCT | NOV | DEC | ANNUAL |
|------|-----|-----|-----|-----|-----|------|------|-----|-----|-----|-----|-----|--------|
| 1961 | 23.7 | 30.6 | 37.0 | 45.4 | 55.2 | 67.5 | 72.2 | 71.0 | 69.0 | 55.8 | 43.6 | 32.1 | 50.3 |
| 1962 | 28.5 | 26.6 | 37.7 | 48.6 | 56.6 | 66.6 | 68.5 | 69.0 | 60.8 | 52.2 | 40.9 | 28.6 | 48.7 |
| #1963 | 28.9 | 26.3 | 38.9 | 48.3 | 57.1 | 67.5 | 72.8 | 69.4 | 56.8 | 46.9 |  | 24.7 | 49.8 |
| 1964 | 30.6 | 27.9 | 37.8 | 46.1 | 60.3 | 66.3 | 71.7 | 66.6 | 62.5 | 52.6 | 44.6 | 33.2 | 50.0 |
| 1965 | 25.0 | 28.4 | 36.1 | 45.4 | 60.0 | 67.0 | 71.6 | 71.6 | 64.1 | 52.1 | 41.1 | 35.4 | 49.8 |
| 1966 | 28.8 | 29.9 | 38.8 | 43.8 | 54.4 | 67.4 | 72.7 | 70.7 | 61.3 | 51.4 | 45.5 | 32.8 | 49.8 |
| 1967 | 33.7 | 25.7 | 33.3 | 44.8 | 51.2 | 66.8 | 72.8 | 70.6 | 62.7 | 53.7 | 39.5 | 34.5 | 49.1 |
| 1968 | 24.5 | 24.6 | 38.1 | 49.9 | 55.7 | 65.0 | 73.1 | 70.6 | 64.8 | 55.9 | 42.4 | 30.2 | 49.6 |
| 1969 | 28.8 | 28.7 | 35.0 | 49.7 | 57.7 | 68.2 | 71.5 | 74.3 | 64.0 | 53.3 | 42.4 | 30.5 | 50.4 |
| 1970 | 19.6 | 29.3 | 35.0 | 47.8 | 58.2 | 65.6 | 74.1 | 72.3 | 64.4 | 54.2 | 44.7 | 28.5 | 49.5 |
| 1971 | 22.9 | 30.9 | 36.7 | 45.9 | 58.1 | 69.0 | 72.6 | 73.0 | 68.7 | 59.2 | 40.9 | 35.0 | 51.2 |
| 1972 | 30.8 | 28.0 | 36.4 | 44.3 | 57.7 | 64.9 | 72.6 | 70.6 | 65.1 | 49.6 | 40.9 | 34.3 | 49.6 |
| 1973 | 31.1 | 29.6 | 43.7 | 50.0 | 56.7 | 70.3 | 73.6 | 75.0 | 65.4 | 54.2 | 43.8 | 38.3 | 52.5 |
| 1974 | 31.6 | 29.0 | 38.7 | 50.6 | 55.6 | 65.3 | 72.6 | 72.6 | 63.2 | 48.2 | 43.7 | 35.7 | 50.5 |
| 1975 | 34.1 | 30.4 | 35.5 | 44.5 | 61.4 | 66.0 | 74.3 | 71.4 | 61.0 | 55.3 | 48.0 | 32.1 | 51.2 |
| 1976 | 23.5 | 35.5 | 39.0 | 52.6 | 58.0 | 70.0 | 70.0 | 70.0 | 61.6 | 48.7 | 37.9 | 25.4 | 49.4 |
| 1977 | 20.9 | 29.8 | 43.6 | 50.6 | 61.2 | 66.7 | 74.3 | 73.0 | 64.1 | 52.9 | 45.9 | 31.6 | 51.2 |
| 1978 | 25.1 | 22.1 | 33.8 | 46.7 | 57.8 | 68.0 | 71.7 | 71.3 | 59.5 | 51.5 | 42.3 | 33.4 | 48.6 |
| 1979 | 30.0 | 19.7 | 40.4 | 46.8 | 60.3 | 65.1 | 75.3 | 70.2 | 64.0 | 53.0 | 48.3 | 37.3 | 50.7 |
| 1980 | 29.7 | 26.8 | 37.1 | 49.5 | 60.3 | 64.5 | 74.8 | 73.4 | 64.9 | 49.8 | 41.0 | 28.5 | 50.0 |
| 1981 | 20.3 | 37.4 | 38.7 | 51.4 | 58.5 | 69.4 | 75.6 | 70.0 | 62.4 | 49.1 | 43.0 | 31.1 | 50.6 |
| 1982 | 21.5 | 31.5 | 38.8 | 47.8 | 58.9 | 63.9 | 73.6 | 69.2 | 64.1 | 53.2 | 47.5 | 38.6 | 50.7 |
| 1983 | 31.4 | 32.9 | 40.4 | 49.9 | 56.9 | 70.2 | 76.9 | 74.3 | 69.6 | 55.3 | 46.0 | 32.5 | 53.0 |
| 1984 | 26.4 | 37.1 | 33.8 | 47.6 | 57.4 | 69.1 | 71.5 | 73.5 | 62.1 | 56.3 | 43.6 | 37.9 | 51.4 |
| 1985 | 22.5 | 32.1 | 42.1 | 51.0 | 60.2 | 64.8 | 73.0 | 71.1 | 65.2 | 54.6 | 45.9 | 30.4 | 51.0 |
| 1986 | 31.1 | 29.0 | 39.9 | 49.4 | 59.4 | 66.4 | 71.0 | 69.3 | 62.3 | 53.0 | 41.6 | 35.4 | 50.7 |
| 1987 | 29.0 | 28.6 | 39.8 | 48.4 | 59.3 | 68.4 | 72.2 | 69.6 | 64.3 | 51.4 | 43.0 | 35.1 | 50.8 |
| 1988 | 26.8 | 31.8 | 39.4 | 47.0 | 58.0 | 66.9 | 74.3 | 75.3 | 63.0 | 48.9 | 45.2 | 32.4 | 50.8 |
| 1989 | 33.8 | 29.9 | 37.5 | 46.2 | 59.3 | 68.7 | 72.3 | 72.1 | 65.3 | 54.1 | 42.1 | 21.8 | 50.3 |
| 1990 | 36.3 | 34.3 | 40.1 | 48.1 | 56.0 | 67.7 | 73.0 | 73.5 | 63.7 | 58.6 | 46.5 | 39.5 | 53.1 |
| Record Mean | 29.0 | 29.4 | 37.8 | 47.7 | 58.0 | 66.9 | 72.8 | 71.1 | 63.8 | 53.8 | 43.5 | 32.7 | 50.5 |
| Max | 36.9 | 37.6 | 46.1 | 56.9 | 67.7 | 76.6 | 81.9 | 80.1 | 73.2 | 63.2 | 51.6 | 40.3 | 59.3 |
| Min | 21.1 | 21.3 | 29.5 | 38.5 | 48.3 | 57.3 | 63.6 | 62.0 | 54.4 | 44.3 | 35.3 | 25.0 | 41.7 |

### REFERENCE NOTES FOR TABLES 1, 2, 3 and 6   (PROVIDENCE, RI)

**GENERAL**

T - TRACE AMOUNT
BLANK ENTRIES DENOTE MISSING/UNREPORTED DATA.
# INDICATES A STATION OR INSTRUMENT RELOCATION.

**SPECIFIC**

TABLE 1

(a) - LENGTH OF RECORD IN YEARS. ALTHOUGH
INDIVIDUAL MONTHS MAY BE MISSING.

* LESS THAN .05

NORMALS — BASED ON THE 1951-1980 RECORD PERIOD.
EXTREMES — DATES ARE THE MOST RECENT OCCURRENCE.
WIND DIR. — NUMERALS SHOW TENS OF DEGREES
CLOCKWISE FROM TRUE NORTH.
"00" INDICATES CALM.
RESULTANT WIND DIRECTIONS ARE GIVEN TO WHOLE DEGREES.

TABLE 3
MAX AND MIN ARE LONG-TERM MEAN DAILY MAXIMUM
AND MEAN DAILY MINIMUM TEMPERATURES.

**EXCEPTIONS**

TABLES 2, 3, and 6

RECORD MEANS ARE THROUGH THE CURRENT YEAR,
BEGINNING IN      1905 FOR TEMPERATURE
                  1905 FOR PRECIPITATION
                  1954 FOR SNOWFALL

HEATING DEGREE DAYS Base 65 deg. F          PROVIDENCE, RHODE ISLAND

**TABLE 4**

| SEASON | JULY | AUG | SEP | OCT | NOV | DEC | JAN | FEB | MAR | APR | MAY | JUNE | TOTAL |
|---|---|---|---|---|---|---|---|---|---|---|---|---|---|
| 1961-62 | 0 | 6 | 49 | 284 | 633 | 1013 | 1123 | 1068 | 840 | 489 | 274 | 40 | 5819 |
| 1962-63 | 12 | 14 | 152 | 389 | 717 | 1125 | 1115 | 1076 | 805 | 493 | 252 | 46 | 6196 |
| #1963-64 | 6 | 8 | 173 | 259 | 536 | 1242 | 1059 | 1066 | 835 | 560 | 188 | 52 | 5984 |
| 1964-65 | 9 | 24 | 125 | 377 | 605 | 981 | 1231 | 1018 | 891 | 581 | 182 | 67 | 6091 |
| 1965-66 | 3 | 29 | 99 | 395 | 711 | 907 | 1115 | 975 | 806 | 630 | 326 | 57 | 6053 |
| 1966-67 | 1 | 1 | 135 | 417 | 577 | 994 | 963 | 1093 | 976 | 598 | 424 | 48 | 6227 |
| 1967-68 | 0 | 7 | 103 | 356 | 761 | 937 | 1246 | 1166 | 827 | 447 | 281 | 74 | 6205 |
| 1968-69 | 2 | 16 | 59 | 295 | 672 | 1072 | 1117 | 1010 | 923 | 452 | 241 | 22 | 5881 |
| 1969-70 | 2 | 4 | 119 | 365 | 673 | 1065 | 1399 | 996 | 924 | 509 | 214 | 60 | 6330 |
| 1970-71 | 0 | 0 | 102 | 342 | 602 | 1124 | 1298 | 949 | 868 | 566 | 212 | 34 | 6097 |
| 1971-72 | 0 | 7 | 42 | 181 | 736 | 922 | 1054 | 1064 | 879 | 616 | 226 | 55 | 5782 |
| 1972-73 | 8 | 10 | 64 | 473 | 717 | 945 | 1044 | 984 | 653 | 451 | 268 | 16 | 5633 |
| 1973-74 | 2 | 3 | 125 | 331 | 632 | 819 | 1028 | 1003 | 808 | 433 | 313 | 62 | 5559 |
| 1974-75 | 0 | 0 | 114 | 512 | 634 | 899 | 951 | 962 | 907 | 606 | 160 | 64 | 5809 |
| 1975-76 | 0 | 13 | 132 | 298 | 506 | 1013 | 1283 | 850 | 798 | 403 | 223 | 39 | 5558 |
| 1976-77 | 2 | 23 | 124 | 501 | 806 | 1219 | 1361 | 983 | 653 | 434 | 176 | 51 | 6333 |
| 1977-78 | 0 | 6 | 103 | 368 | 568 | 1030 | 1231 | 1192 | 964 | 542 | 238 | 26 | 6268 |
| 1978-79 | 8 | 8 | 180 | 412 | 673 | 970 | 1075 | 1261 | 755 | 540 | 162 | 52 | 6096 |
| 1979-80 | 11 | 25 | 94 | 380 | 496 | 849 | 1088 | 1104 | 857 | 459 | 158 | 93 | 5614 |
| 1980-81 | 0 | 1 | 120 | 465 | 715 | 1125 | 1379 | 769 | 808 | 405 | 228 | 13 | 6028 |
| 1981-82 | 0 | 20 | 119 | 486 | 651 | 1044 | 1343 | 932 | 802 | 510 | 190 | 91 | 6188 |
| 1982-83 | 1 | 26 | 78 | 363 | 518 | 809 | 1038 | 892 | 755 | 449 | 254 | 13 | 5196 |
| 1983-84 | 0 | 4 | 62 | 323 | 563 | 1001 | 1190 | 802 | 961 | 513 | 236 | 36 | 5691 |
| 1984-85 | 1 | 0 | 125 | 270 | 637 | 832 | 1309 | 914 | 743 | 417 | 177 | 63 | 5488 |
| 1985-86 | 0 | 6 | 78 | 321 | 567 | 1065 | 1045 | 999 | 772 | 460 | 216 | 57 | 5586 |
| 1986-87 | 14 | 25 | 113 | 380 | 697 | 911 | 1111 | 1014 | 772 | 494 | 228 | 23 | 5782 |
| 1987-88 | 2 | 25 | 70 | 414 | 653 | 921 | 1177 | 954 | 787 | 532 | 238 | 67 | 5840 |
| 1988-89 | 8 | 10 | 89 | 491 | 587 | 1003 | 960 | 975 | 847 | 557 | 181 | 22 | 5730 |
| 1989-90 | 2 | 9 | 89 | 332 | 668 | 1329 | 882 | 854 | 761 | 511 | 275 | 24 | 5736 |
| 1990-91 | 6 | 0 | 107 | 242 | 549 | 781 |  |  |  |  |  |  |  |

**TABLE 5**   COOLING DEGREE DAYS Base 65 deg. F          PROVIDENCE, RHODE ISLAND

| YEAR | JAN | FEB | MAR | APR | MAY | JUNE | JULY | AUG | SEP | OCT | NOV | DEC | TOTAL |
|---|---|---|---|---|---|---|---|---|---|---|---|---|---|
| 1969 | 0 | 0 | 0 | 0 | 23 | 125 | 211 | 299 | 94 | 9 | 0 | 0 | 761 |
| 1970 | 0 | 0 | 0 | 0 | 13 | 86 | 289 | 237 | 91 | 14 | 0 | 0 | 730 |
| 1971 | 0 | 0 | 0 | 0 | 3 | 157 | 296 | 263 | 158 | 8 | 5 | 0 | 890 |
| 1972 | 0 | 0 | 0 | 1 | 7 | 60 | 248 | 190 | 76 | 1 | 0 | 0 | 583 |
| 1973 | 0 | 0 | 0 | 8 | 17 | 181 | 272 | 318 | 84 | 3 | 0 | 0 | 883 |
| 1974 | 0 | 0 | 0 | 7 | 27 | 79 | 242 | 244 | 66 | 0 | 1 | 0 | 666 |
| 1975 | 0 | 0 | 0 | 0 | 55 | 100 | 300 | 218 | 16 | 4 | 1 | 0 | 694 |
| 1976 | 0 | 0 | 0 | 40 | 13 | 196 | 163 | 183 | 33 | 3 | 0 | 0 | 631 |
| 1977 | 0 | 0 | 0 | 5 | 68 | 108 | 295 | 260 | 85 | 0 | 0 | 0 | 821 |
| 1978 | 0 | 0 | 0 | 0 | 25 | 126 | 224 | 211 | 24 | 0 | 0 | 0 | 610 |
| 1979 | 0 | 0 | 0 | 0 | 26 | 59 | 279 | 190 | 74 | 12 | 0 | 0 | 640 |
| 1980 | 0 | 0 | 0 | 0 | 21 | 84 | 312 | 272 | 122 | 0 | 0 | 0 | 811 |
| 1981 | 0 | 0 | 0 | 2 | 33 | 152 | 335 | 183 | 47 | 0 | 0 | 0 | 752 |
| 1982 | 0 | 0 | 0 | 0 | 11 | 64 | 276 | 165 | 59 | 3 | 2 | 0 | 580 |
| 1983 | 0 | 0 | 0 | 1 | 8 | 177 | 367 | 298 | 206 | 30 | 0 | 0 | 1087 |
| 1984 | 0 | 0 | 0 | 0 | 6 | 164 | 206 | 272 | 47 | 7 | 0 | 0 | 702 |
| 1985 | 0 | 0 | 0 | 5 | 34 | 65 | 256 | 203 | 90 | 5 | 0 | 0 | 658 |
| 1986 | 0 | 0 | 0 | 0 | 51 | 105 | 207 | 164 | 38 | 14 | 0 | 0 | 579 |
| 1987 | 0 | 0 | 0 | 0 | 57 | 130 | 231 | 177 | 53 | 0 | 0 | 0 | 648 |
| 1988 | 0 | 0 | 0 | 0 | 26 | 131 | 302 | 336 | 37 | 2 | 0 | 0 | 834 |
| 1989 | 0 | 0 | 0 | 0 | 10 | 141 | 237 | 237 | 103 | 0 | 0 | 0 | 728 |
| 1990 | 0 | 0 | 0 | 8 | 1 | 114 | 262 | 272 | 74 | 49 | 2 | 0 | 782 |

**TABLE 6**   SNOWFALL (inches)          PROVIDENCE, RHODE ISLAND

| SEASON | JULY | AUG | SEP | OCT | NOV | DEC | JAN | FEB | MAR | APR | MAY | JUNE | TOTAL |
|---|---|---|---|---|---|---|---|---|---|---|---|---|---|
| 1961-62 | 0.0 | 0.0 | 0.0 |  | T | 1.7 | 4.9 | 30.9 | T | 0.3 | 0.0 | 0.0 | 47.0 |
| 1962-63 | 0.0 | 0.0 | 0.0 | 1.6 | 1.7 | 6.6 | 5.3 | 5.2 | 9.4 | T | 0.0 | 0.0 | 29.8 |
| 1963-64 | 0.0 | 0.0 | 0.0 | T | T | 19.8 | 12.5 | 14.8 | 2.5 | T | 0.0 | 0.0 | 49.6 |
| 1964-65 | 0.0 | 0.0 | 0.0 | 0.0 | T | 6.9 | 28.7 | 2.7 | 6.6 | T | 0.0 | 0.0 | 44.9 |
| 1965-66 | 0.0 | 0.0 | 0.0 | 0.0 | T | 1.9 | 16.1 | 9.1 | 8.1 | T | 0.0 | 0.0 | 35.2 |
| 1966-67 | 0.0 | 0.0 | 0.0 | 0.0 | T | 7.2 | 1.3 | 23.1 | 24.9 | 1.6 | 0.0 | 0.0 | 58.1 |
| 1967-68 | 0.0 | 0.0 | 0.0 | 0.0 | 0.8 | 19.0 | 13.5 | 4.6 | 5.1 | 0.0 | 0.0 | 0.0 | 43.0 |
| 1968-69 | 0.0 | 0.0 | 0.0 | 0.0 | 0.1 | 2.7 | 0.5 | 26.7 | 6.0 | 0.0 | 0.0 | 0.0 | 36.0 |
| 1969-70 | 0.0 | 0.0 | 0.0 | 0.0 | T | 15.4 | 6.5 | 6.8 | 15.7 | 1.1 | 0.0 | 0.0 | 45.5 |
| 1970-71 | 0.0 | 0.0 | 0.0 | T | 0.0 | 17.8 | 11.0 | 5.0 | 6.1 | 1.9 | 0.0 | 0.0 | 41.8 |
| 1971-72 | 0.0 | 0.0 | 0.0 | 0.0 | T | 4.7 | 2.2 | 13.7 | 8.7 | 0.7 | 0.0 | 0.0 | 30.0 |
| 1972-73 | 0.0 | 0.0 | 0.0 | 0.7 | 0.3 | 4.1 | 2.0 | 3.2 | 0.6 | 0.4 | 0.0 | 0.0 | 11.3 |
| 1973-74 | 0.0 | 0.0 | 0.0 | 0.0 | T | T | 15.1 | 11.1 | 0.4 | 1.3 | 0.0 | 0.0 | 27.9 |
| 1974-75 | 0.0 | 0.0 | 0.0 | 0.0 | 0.3 | 2.1 | 2.0 | 18.2 | 2.2 | 0.2 | 0.0 | 0.0 | 25.0 |
| 1975-76 | 0.0 | 0.0 | 0.0 | T | 1.2 | 7.5 | 15.6 | 3.7 | 9.5 | 0.0 | 0.0 | 0.0 | 37.5 |
| 1976-77 | 0.0 | 0.0 | 0.0 | 0.0 | T | 9.8 | 14.0 | 11.4 | 4.4 | T | 7.0 | 0.0 | 46.6 |
| 1977-78 | 0.0 | 0.0 | 0.0 | 0.0 | 1.3 | 3.9 | 20.5 | 28.6 | 15.9 | T | 0.0 | 0.0 | 70.2 |
| 1978-79 | 0.0 | 0.0 | 0.0 | 0.0 | 2.3 | 2.4 | 6.0 | 5.5 | T | 1.1 | 0.0 | 0.0 | 17.3 |
| 1979-80 | 0.0 | 0.0 | 0.0 | 2.5 | 0.0 | T | 0.6 | 3.8 | 5.3 | 0.0 | 0.0 | 0.0 | 12.2 |
| 1980-81 | 0.0 | 0.0 | 0.0 | 0.0 | 4.1 | 3.6 | 12.9 | 0.6 | 0.3 | 0.0 | 0.0 | 0.0 | 21.5 |
| 1981-82 | 0.0 | 0.0 | 0.0 | T | T | 16.4 | 13.4 | 4.3 | 5.7 | 7.6 | 0.0 | 0.0 | 47.4 |
| 1982-83 | 0.0 | 0.0 | 0.0 | 0.0 | 0.0 | 7.3 | 3.8 | 21.3 | T | T | 0.0 | 0.0 | 32.4 |
| 1983-84 | 0.0 | 0.0 | 0.0 | 0.0 | T | 4.5 | 17.9 | T | 13.7 | T | 0.0 | 0.0 | 36.1 |
| 1984-85 | 0.0 | 0.0 | 0.0 | 0.0 | T | 2.0 | 9.8 | 10.0 | 0.6 | T | 0.0 | 0.0 | 22.4 |
| 1985-86 | 0.0 | 0.0 | 0.0 | 0.0 | 1.8 | 2.6 | 0.7 | 13.0 | 0.5 | T | T | 0.0 | 18.6 |
| 1986-87 | 0.0 | 0.0 | 0.0 | 0.0 | 4.4 | 8.0 | 21.5 | 4.7 | 1.6 | 1.1 | 0.0 | 0.0 | 41.3 |
| 1987-88 | 0.0 | 0.0 | 0.0 | 0.0 | 8.0 | 7.8 | 13.5 | 6.7 | 2.7 | T | 0.0 | 0.0 | 38.7 |
| 1988-89 | 0.0 | 0.0 | 0.0 | 0.0 | T | 1.2 | 0.2 | 7.3 | 1.9 | 0.3 | 0.0 | 0.0 | 10.9 |
| 1989-90 | 0.0 | 0.0 | 0.0 | 0.0 | 8.0 | 15.8 | 10.8 | 10.5 | 9.3 | 1.8 | 0.0 | 0.0 | 56.2 |
| 1990-91 | 0.0 | 0.0 | 0.0 | 0.0 | T | 6.9 |  |  |  |  |  |  |  |
| Record Mean | 0.0 | 0.0 | 0.0 | 0.1 | 1.1 | 7.1 | 9.8 | 9.8 | 7.4 | 0.7 | 0.2 | 0.0 | 36.2 |

**See Reference Notes, relative to all above tables, on preceding page.**

Charleston is a peninsula city bounded on the west and south by the Ashley River, on the east by the Cooper River, and on the southeast by a spacious harbor. Weather records for the airport are from a site some 10 miles inland. The terrain is generally level, ranging in elevation from sea level to 20 feet on the peninsula, with gradual increases in elevation toward inland areas. The soil is sandy to sandy loam with lesser amounts of loam. The drainage varies from good to poor. Because of the very low elevation, a considerable portion of this community and the nearby coastal islands are vulnerable to tidal flooding.

The climate is temperate, modified considerably by the nearness to the ocean. The marine influence is noticeable during winter when the low temperatures are sometimes 10–15 degrees higher on the peninsula than at the airport. By the same token, high temperatures are generally a few degrees lower on the peninsula. The prevailing winds are northerly in the fall and winter, southerly in the spring and summer.

Summer is warm and humid. Temperatures of 100 degrees or more are infrequent. High temperatures are generally several degrees lower along the coast than inland due to the cooling effect of the sea breeze. Summer is the rainiest season with 41 percent of the annual total. The rain, except during occasional tropical storms, generally occurs as showers or thunderstorms.

The fall season passes through the warm Indian Summer period to the pre–winter cold spells which begin late in November. From late September to early November the weather is mostly sunny and temperature extremes are rare. Late summer and early fall is the period of maximum threat to the South Carolina coast from hurricanes.

The winter months, December through February, are mild with periods of rain. However, the winter rainfall is generally of a more uniform type. There is some chance of a snow flurry, with the best probability of its occurrence in January, but a significant amount is rarely measured. An average winter would experience less than one cold wave and severe freeze. Temperatures of 20 degrees or less on the peninsula and along the coast are very unusual.

The most spectacular time of the year, weatherwise, is spring with its rapid changes from windy and cold in March to warm and pleasant in May. Severe local storms are more likely to occur in spring than in summer.

The average occurrence of the first freeze in the fall is early December, and the average last freeze is late February, giving an average growing season of about 294 days.

## TABLE 1     NORMALS, MEANS AND EXTREMES

CHARLESTON, SOUTH CAROLINA

LATITUDE: 32°54'N    LONGITUDE: 80°02'W    ELEVATION: FT. GRND   40 BARO   47   TIME ZONE: EASTERN    WBAN: 13880

| | (a) | JAN | FEB | MAR | APR | MAY | JUNE | JULY | AUG | SEP | OCT | NOV | DEC | YEAR |
|---|---|---|---|---|---|---|---|---|---|---|---|---|---|---|
| **TEMPERATURE °F:** | | | | | | | | | | | | | | |
| Normals | | | | | | | | | | | | | | |
|  -Daily Maximum | | 58.8 | 61.2 | 68.0 | 76.0 | 82.9 | 87.0 | 89.4 | 88.8 | 84.6 | 76.8 | 68.7 | 61.4 | 75.3 |
|  -Daily Minimum | | 36.9 | 38.4 | 45.3 | 52.5 | 61.4 | 68.0 | 71.6 | 71.2 | 66.7 | 54.7 | 44.6 | 38.5 | 54.2 |
|  -Monthly | | 47.9 | 49.8 | 56.7 | 64.3 | 72.2 | 77.6 | 80.5 | 80.0 | 75.7 | 65.8 | 56.7 | 50.0 | 64.8 |
| Extremes | | | | | | | | | | | | | | |
|  -Record Highest | 47 | 83 | 87 | 90 | 94 | 98 | 103 | 104 | 102 | 99 | 94 | 88 | 83 | 104 |
|  -Year | | 1950 | 1989 | 1974 | 1989 | 1989 | 1944 | 1986 | 1954 | 1944 | 1986 | 1961 | 1972 | JUL 1986 |
|  -Record Lowest | 47 | 6 | 12 | 15 | 29 | 36 | 50 | 58 | 56 | 42 | 27 | 15 | 8 | 6 |
|  -Year | | 1985 | 1973 | 1980 | 1944 | 1963 | 1972 | 1952 | 1979 | 1967 | 1976 | 1950 | 1962 | JAN 1985 |
| **NORMAL DEGREE DAYS:** | | | | | | | | | | | | | | |
| Heating (base 65°F) | | 543 | 434 | 286 | 69 | 6 | 0 | 0 | 0 | 0 | 76 | 262 | 471 | 2147 |
| Cooling (base 65°F) | | 13 | 9 | 29 | 48 | 229 | 378 | 481 | 465 | 321 | 101 | 13 | 6 | 2093 |
| **% OF POSSIBLE SUNSHINE** | 30 | 57 | 60 | 66 | 71 | 70 | 66 | 67 | 63 | 60 | 64 | 60 | 57 | 63 |
| **MEAN SKY COVER (tenths)** | | | | | | | | | | | | | | |
| Sunrise - Sunset | 40 | 6.2 | 6.0 | 5.9 | 5.3 | 5.9 | 6.3 | 6.6 | 6.3 | 6.3 | 5.2 | 5.2 | 5.9 | 5.9 |
| **MEAN NUMBER OF DAYS:** | | | | | | | | | | | | | | |
| Sunrise to Sunset | | | | | | | | | | | | | | |
|  -Clear | 41 | 9.0 | 8.9 | 9.2 | 11.4 | 8.1 | 6.2 | 5.0 | 5.7 | 6.7 | 11.6 | 12.0 | 9.7 | 103.5 |
|  -Partly Cloudy | 41 | 6.5 | 6.5 | 8.1 | 7.8 | 11.0 | 11.2 | 12.2 | 13.0 | 10.4 | 8.3 | 6.5 | 7.1 | 108.8 |
|  -Cloudy | 41 | 15.4 | 12.9 | 13.7 | 10.8 | 11.9 | 12.6 | 13.8 | 12.3 | 12.9 | 11.0 | 11.5 | 14.2 | 153.0 |
| Precipitation | | | | | | | | | | | | | | |
| .01 inches or more | 47 | 9.7 | 8.9 | 10.1 | 7.4 | 8.9 | 10.9 | 13.4 | 12.6 | 9.5 | 5.9 | 7.0 | 8.4 | 112.8 |
| Snow,Ice pellets | | | | | | | | | | | | | | |
| 1.0 inches or more | 47 | 0.0 | 0.1 | 0.* | 0.0 | 0.0 | 0.0 | 0.0 | 0.0 | 0.0 | 0.0 | 0.0 | 0.1 | 0.2 |
| Thunderstorms | 47 | 0.7 | 1.1 | 2.2 | 2.8 | 6.8 | 10.0 | 13.1 | 11.3 | 5.1 | 1.4 | 0.7 | 0.6 | 55.9 |
| Heavy Fog Visibility | | | | | | | | | | | | | | |
| 1/4 mile or less | 40 | 4.2 | 2.0 | 2.5 | 2.1 | 2.0 | 1.6 | 0.8 | 1.3 | 1.8 | 2.6 | 3.8 | 3.5 | 28.1 |
| Temperature °F | | | | | | | | | | | | | | |
|  -Maximum | | | | | | | | | | | | | | |
| 90° and above | 47 | 0.0 | 0.0 | 0.* | 0.8 | 4.0 | 11.2 | 16.0 | 14.4 | 5.1 | 0.4 | 0.0 | 0.0 | 51.8 |
| 32° and below | 47 | 0.2 | 0.1 | 0.* | 0.0 | 0.0 | 0.0 | 0.0 | 0.0 | 0.0 | 0.0 | 0.0 | 0.1 | 0.3 |
|  -Minimum | | | | | | | | | | | | | | |
| 32° and below | 47 | 11.2 | 8.0 | 2.9 | 0.2 | 0.0 | 0.0 | 0.0 | 0.0 | 0.0 | 0.1 | 3.3 | 9.4 | 35.1 |
| 0° and below | 47 | 0.0 | 0.0 | 0.0 | 0.0 | 0.0 | 0.0 | 0.0 | 0.0 | 0.0 | 0.0 | 0.0 | 0.0 | 0.0 |
| **AVG. STATION PRESS.(mb)** | 17 | 1018.6 | 1017.7 | 1016.1 | 1015.1 | 1014.5 | 1014.8 | 1015.9 | 1016.1 | 1015.9 | 1017.7 | 1018.2 | 1019.3 | 1016.6 |
| **RELATIVE HUMIDITY (%)** | | | | | | | | | | | | | | |
| Hour 01 | 47 | 80 | 79 | 81 | 83 | 88 | 89 | 90 | 91 | 90 | 87 | 85 | 81 | 85 |
| Hour 07 (Local Time) | 47 | 83 | 81 | 83 | 83 | 85 | 86 | 88 | 90 | 90 | 88 | 86 | 83 | 86 |
| Hour 13 | 47 | 55 | 52 | 51 | 49 | 53 | 59 | 62 | 63 | 62 | 55 | 53 | 55 | 56 |
| Hour 19 | 47 | 71 | 67 | 66 | 65 | 71 | 74 | 77 | 79 | 80 | 78 | 76 | 73 | 73 |
| **PRECIPITATION (inches):** | | | | | | | | | | | | | | |
| Water Equivalent | | | | | | | | | | | | | | |
|  -Normal | | 3.33 | 3.37 | 4.38 | 2.58 | 4.41 | 6.54 | 7.33 | 6.50 | 4.94 | 2.92 | 2.18 | 3.11 | 51.59 |
|  -Maximum Monthly | 47 | 7.17 | 6.35 | 11.11 | 9.50 | 9.28 | 27.24 | 18.46 | 16.99 | 17.31 | 9.12 | 7.35 | 7.09 | 27.24 |
|  -Year | | 1987 | 1983 | 1983 | 1958 | 1957 | 1973 | 1964 | 1974 | 1945 | 1959 | 1972 | 1953 | JUN 1973 |
|  -Minimum Monthly | 47 | 0.63 | 0.33 | 0.99 | 0.01 | 0.68 | 0.96 | 1.76 | 0.73 | 0.53 | 0.08 | 0.48 | 0.66 | 0.01 |
|  -Year | | 1950 | 1947 | 1963 | 1972 | 1944 | 1970 | 1972 | 1980 | 1971 | 1943 | 1966 | 1984 | APR 1972 |
|  -Maximum in 24 hrs | 47 | 2.49 | 3.28 | 6.63 | 4.10 | 6.23 | 10.10 | 5.81 | 5.77 | 8.84 | 5.77 | 5.24 | 3.40 | 10.10 |
|  -Year | | 1983 | 1944 | 1959 | 1958 | 1967 | 1973 | 1960 | 1964 | 1945 | 1944 | 1969 | 1978 | JUN 1973 |
| Snow,Ice pellets | | | | | | | | | | | | | | |
|  -Maximum Monthly | 47 | 1.0 | 7.1 | 2.0 | T | 0.0 | T | 0.0 | 0.0 | 0.0 | 0.0 | T | 8.0 | 8.0 |
|  -Year | | 1977 | 1973 | 1969 | 1985 | | 1989 | | | | | 1950 | 1989 | DEC 1989 |
|  -Maximum in 24 hrs | 47 | 0.8 | 5.9 | 2.0 | T | 0.0 | T | 0.0 | 0.0 | 0.0 | 0.0 | T | 6.6 | 6.6 |
|  -Year | | 1966 | 1973 | 1969 | 1985 | | 1989 | | | | | 1950 | 1989 | DEC 1989 |
| **WIND:** | | | | | | | | | | | | | | |
| Mean Speed (mph) | 40 | 9.1 | 9.9 | 10.0 | 9.7 | 8.6 | 8.4 | 7.9 | 7.5 | 7.8 | 8.1 | 8.1 | 8.6 | 8.6 |
| Prevailing Direction | | | | | | | | | | | | | | |
| through 1963 | | SW | NNE | SSW | SSW | S | S | SW | SW | NNE | NNE | N | NNE | NNE |
| Fastest Obs. 1 Min. | | | | | | | | | | | | | | |
|  -Direction (!!!) | 14 | 20 | 29 | 31 | 19 | 25 | 03 | 33 | 08 | 21 | 18 | 15 | 24 | 21 |
|  -Speed (MPH) | 14 | 40 | 37 | 37 | 36 | 32 | 40 | 37 | 35 | 52 | 30 | 37 | 39 | 52 |
|  -Year | | 1978 | 1976 | 1984 | 1983 | 1978 | 1981 | 1986 | 1988 | 1989 | 1976 | 1985 | 1975 | SEP 1989 |
| Peak Gust | | | | | | | | | | | | | | |
|  -Direction (!!!) | 6 | NW | W | NW | S | W | NW | NW | N | SW | NW | SE | NW | SW |
|  -Speed (mph) | 6 | 43 | 44 | 49 | 48 | 49 | 45 | 49 | 64 | 98 | 41 | 48 | 44 | 98 |
|  -Date | | 1987 | 1984 | 1984 | 1988 | 1984 | 1986 | 1986 | 1986 | 1989 | 1986 | 1985 | 1987 | SEP 1989 |

**See Reference Notes to this table on the following pages.**

PRECIPITATION (inches)  CHARLESTON, SOUTH CAROLINA

**TABLE 2**

| YEAR | JAN | FEB | MAR | APR | MAY | JUNE | JULY | AUG | SEP | OCT | NOV | DEC | ANNUAL |
|---|---|---|---|---|---|---|---|---|---|---|---|---|---|
| 1961 | 1.77 | 4.15 | 5.83 | 5.78 | 5.23 | 6.84 | 6.67 | 6.07 | 2.97 | 1.71 | 1.59 | 1.43 | 50.04 |
| 1962 | 3.59 | 1.28 | 7.88 | 2.52 | 1.81 | 16.07 | 5.93 | 11.54 | 3.81 | 3.25 | 2.01 | 1.46 | 61.15 |
| 1963 | 3.14 | 4.90 | 0.99 | 2.68 | 1.70 | 14.34 | 7.94 | 6.34 | 2.75 | 2.27 | 4.74 | 3.18 | 54.97 |
| 1964 | 6.53 | 6.32 | 4.40 | 2.72 | 4.77 | 6.95 | 18.46 | 7.67 | 4.11 | 7.53 | 0.52 | 3.01 | 72.99 |
| 1965 | 1.69 | 5.49 |  | 3.10 | 1.32 | 6.68 | 8.90 | 5.90 | 4.66 | 6.23 | 0.87 | 1.20 | 54.03 |
| 1966 | 6.68 | 4.61 | 2.65 | 2.83 | 7.71 | 6.03 | 11.48 | 3.45 | 2.20 | 1.70 | 0.48 | 3.76 | 53.58 |
| 1967 | 4.93 | 3.12 |  | 0.84 | 8.91 | 4.06 | 9.19 | 3.74 | 1.39 | 0.52 | 2.79 | 3.65 | 43.65 |
| 1968 | 2.25 | 1.27 | 1.35 | 1.99 | 2.54 | 9.41 | 7.77 | 4.42 | 1.66 | 6.86 | 2.67 | 3.65 | 45.84 |
| 1969 | 1.19 | 2.05 | 5.14 | 3.46 | 2.34 | 4.88 | 5.34 | 11.84 | 5.37 | 1.50 | 3.52 |  | 52.12 |
| 1970 | 2.51 | 2.86 | 7.72 | 1.34 | 3.78 | 0.96 | 5.93 | 10.64 | 2.53 | 4.08 | 0.67 | 2.90 | 45.92 |
| 1971 | 5.45 | 4.71 | 4.05 | 4.11 | 4.15 | 4.07 | 6.04 | 16.32 | 0.53 | 7.22 | 1.61 | 2.28 | 60.54 |
| 1972 | 4.13 | 5.18 | 2.52 | 0.01 | 5.67 | 5.29 | 1.76 | 4.52 | 1.82 | 0.25 | 7.35 | 4.36 | 42.86 |
| 1973 | 4.59 | 5.57 | 6.15 | 2.55 | 1.83 | 27.24 | 3.60 | 6.66 | 7.93 | 0.63 | 0.84 | 4.58 | 72.17 |
| 1974 | 1.42 | 2.96 | 3.04 | 0.86 | 4.82 | 9.45 | 3.09 | 16.99 | 4.80 | 0.40 | 3.78 | 3.00 | 54.61 |
| 1975 | 4.92 | 3.54 | 4.54 | 3.74 | 5.06 | 5.96 | 9.34 | 7.18 | 5.16 | 1.97 | 1.43 | 3.35 | 56.19 |
| 1976 | 1.62 | 0.95 | 2.33 | 0.62 | 8.87 | 5.59 | 4.48 | 5.22 | 6.03 | 4.10 | 3.57 | 5.12 | 48.50 |
| 1977 | 2.72 | 1.38 | 5.31 | 0.45 | 4.66 | 2.12 | 3.86 | 8.13 | 2.48 | 2.49 | 1.76 | 5.88 | 41.24 |
| 1978 | 4.31 | 1.82 | 3.25 | 1.97 | 4.68 | 3.42 | 6.19 | 4.01 | 5.06 | 0.18 | 1.87 | 4.13 | 40.89 |
| 1979 | 3.43 | 3.04 | 3.01 | 3.81 | 8.09 | 2.23 | 8.35 | 0.88 | 15.36 | 3.87 | 3.29 | 2.62 | 57.98 |
| 1980 | 3.99 | 1.25 | 7.99 | 3.43 | 5.85 | 3.15 | 6.97 | 0.73 | 2.60 | 1.52 | 2.19 | 1.25 | 40.92 |
| 1981 | 0.93 | 2.23 | 2.38 | 1.87 | 4.02 | 6.04 | 12.66 | 9.30 | 1.27 | 1.95 | 1.06 | 5.73 | 49.44 |
| 1982 | 2.18 | 3.64 | 1.26 | 6.51 | 3.04 | 9.16 | 5.40 | 4.10 | 3.92 | 2.42 | 1.19 | 4.20 | 47.02 |
| 1983 | 4.86 | 6.35 | 11.11 | 3.57 | 0.75 | 2.37 | 8.89 | 2.90 | 3.50 | 2.36 | 3.08 | 4.35 | 54.09 |
| 1984 | 5.12 | 3.51 | 5.63 | 6.30 | 6.89 | 2.96 | 4.87 | 1.96 | 5.27 | 1.67 | 0.66 | 1.21 | 46.23 |
| 1985 | 0.87 | 2.70 | 1.50 | 1.12 | 2.79 | 7.02 | 12.06 | 8.48 | 2.53 | 4.58 | 5.49 | 1.21 | 50.35 |
| 1986 | 2.05 | 4.17 | 2.67 | 0.83 | 0.93 | 2.51 | 5.07 | 13.41 | 4.60 | 2.95 | 4.03 | 5.21 | 48.43 |
| 1987 | 7.17 | 4.58 | 5.55 | 1.31 | 2.29 | 5.64 | 2.92 | 6.97 | 14.49 | 0.56 | 3.65 | 1.57 | 56.70 |
| 1988 | 2.76 | 2.38 | 1.78 | 3.21 | 1.86 | 2.32 | 4.13 | 11.88 | 9.72 | 0.73 | 1.08 | 0.72 | 42.57 |
| 1989 | 2.31 | 1.17 | 2.87 | 4.84 | 2.14 | 7.26 | 1.93 | 9.18 | 13.35 | 4.08 | 1.85 | 4.74 | 55.72 |
| 1990 | 3.96 | 1.68 | 6.63 | 1.65 | 1.91 | 3.12 | 5.95 | 6.32 | 0.18 | 7.29 | 3.75 | 2.69 | 45.13 |
| Record Mean | 3.03 | 3.26 | 3.72 | 2.76 | 3.52 | 5.18 | 7.12 | 6.73 | 5.13 | 3.11 | 2.30 | 2.90 | 48.76 |

**TABLE 3**  AVERAGE TEMPERATURE (deg. F)  CHARLESTON, SOUTH CAROLINA

| YEAR | JAN | FEB | MAR | APR | MAY | JUNE | JULY | AUG | SEP | OCT | NOV | DEC | ANNUAL |
|---|---|---|---|---|---|---|---|---|---|---|---|---|---|
| 1961 | 44.3 | 52.6 | 61.3 | 59.7 | 69.5 | 76.7 | 80.6 | 79.0 | 76.8 | 63.7 | 59.2 | 51.0 | 64.5 |
| 1962 | 47.1 | 56.2 | 53.2 | 62.1 | 75.9 | 76.3 | 80.8 | 73.9 | 73.8 | 66.5 | 45.6 | 46.2 | 64.2 |
| 1963 | 45.3 | 45.3 | 60.9 | 65.8 | 71.6 | 79.2 | 79.9 | 80.9 | 73.8 | 67.2 | 57.3 | 43.8 | 64.3 |
| 1964 | 48.5 | 47.5 | 57.6 | 66.0 | 73.1 | 80.0 | 78.0 | 79.6 | 75.4 | 62.5 | 60.5 | 52.9 | 65.1 |
| 1965 | 48.4 | 51.2 | 54.5 | 64.5 | 75.3 | 76.1 | 79.0 | 79.6 | 75.9 | 65.2 | 57.6 | 49.3 | 64.7 |
| 1966 | 43.9 | 49.6 | 53.9 | 63.2 | 70.6 | 73.7 | 79.6 | 80.0 | 75.8 | 56.3 | 48.9 | 53.4 | 63.6 |
| 1967 | 50.6 | 48.5 | 60.0 | 67.1 | 71.3 | 75.6 | 79.9 | 79.5 | 69.9 | 62.6 | 53.8 | 53.4 | 64.4 |
| 1968 | 43.5 | 41.8 | 55.7 | 65.7 | 71.7 | 77.8 | 81.5 | 81.5 | 75.1 | 67.1 | 53.7 | 46.5 | 63.5 |
| 1969 | 44.6 | 45.2 | 50.6 | 63.3 | 69.9 | 72.7 | 80.3 | 82.7 | 77.5 | 68.2 | 53.4 | 52.1 | 63.0 |
| 1970 | 41.0 | 48.5 | 57.1 | 66.3 | 72.7 | 78.4 | 82.5 | 80.6 | 77.3 | 67.3 | 54.1 | 52.1 | 64.8 |
| 1971 | 49.9 | 49.8 | 51.9 | 62.7 | 71.1 | 80.4 | 80.1 | 79.6 | 77.1 | 70.8 | 57.1 | 58.8 | 65.8 |
| 1972 | 54.8 | 48.9 | 56.9 | 64.0 | 69.8 | 74.0 | 80.1 | 80.4 | 76.4 | 67.3 | 56.8 | 55.7 | 65.5 |
| 1973 | 48.0 | 46.1 | 61.0 | 61.5 | 71.7 | 78.4 | 82.6 | 81.0 | 79.6 | 69.6 | 61.4 | 51.3 | 66.0 |
| 1974 | 61.8 | 51.5 | 62.0 | 63.6 | 74.0 | 75.4 | 78.2 | 79.3 | 75.0 | 61.8 | 55.5 | 51.0 | 65.8 |
| 1975 | 53.8 | 54.7 | 56.9 | 62.3 | 75.1 | 78.5 | 79.2 | 81.5 | 76.8 | 69.0 | 59.3 | 49.7 | 66.4 |
| 1976 | 44.8 | 55.9 | 62.3 | 64.0 | 70.3 | 75.8 | 81.0 | 77.2 | 73.9 | 61.4 | 50.9 | 48.8 | 63.9 |
| 1977 | 38.7 | 46.3 | 60.6 | 66.4 | 72.8 | 81.2 | 83.8 | 81.4 | 78.7 | 63.5 | 61.3 | 5.0 | 65.4 |
| 1978 | 43.5 | 42.7 | 55.2 | 66.5 | 72.0 | 78.6 | 81.1 | 81.3 | 76.5 | 66.0 | 59.4 | 48.7 | 64.7 |
| 1979 | 45.4 | 46.8 | 57.4 | 64.9 | 72.4 | 75.9 | 82.0 | 82.4 | 81.1 | 66.0 | 59.4 | 47.5 | 64.6 |
| 1980 | 48.7 | 45.9 | 54.6 | 64.3 | 71.4 | 78.4 | 82.4 | 82.1 | 79.8 | 65.0 | 55.4 | 47.5 | 64.6 |
| 1981 | 41.6 | 50.8 | 54.3 | 67.5 | 70.8 | 82.7 | 83.5 | 80.3 | 74.8 | 64.1 | 55.4 | 46.2 | 64.3 |
| 1982 | 45.1 | 51.5 | 59.2 | 61.8 | 72.2 | 78.8 | 81.2 | 80.0 | 74.5 | 65.1 | 60.9 | 57.0 | 65.6 |
| 1983 | 45.6 | 49.0 | 56.4 | 61.0 | 71.7 | 76.9 | 82.8 | 82.9 | 75.5 | 68.9 | 57.4 | 48.8 | 64.8 |
| 1984 | 46.1 | 52.8 | 57.6 | 64.0 | 71.7 | 78.8 | 79.9 | 81.1 | 73.0 | 71.3 | 54.2 | 57.2 | 65.6 |
| 1985 | 42.6 | 50.5 | 60.7 | 67.8 | 73.6 | 79.6 | 80.9 | 79.9 | 75.8 | 72.2 | 67.3 | 47.9 | 66.6 |
| 1986 | 45.8 | 55.5 | 58.0 | 66.1 | 74.3 | 81.4 | 86.1 | 79.9 | 78.6 | 68.8 | 63.1 | 52.8 | 67.5 |
| 1987 | 47.2 | 48.8 | 56.8 | 62.6 | 73.3 | 80.1 | 83.0 | 83.5 | 77.8 | 61.0 | 60.1 | 53.5 | 65.6 |
| 1988 | 43.2 | 49.2 | 57.4 | 64.4 | 71.9 | 76.7 | 81.8 | 82.0 | 76.3 | 62.7 | 60.6 | 43.2 | 64.8 |
| 1989 | 55.6 | 55.0 | 59.7 | 65.3 | 72.3 | 80.4 | 82.8 | 80.7 | 76.6 | 68.7 | 60.6 | 43.2 | 66.7 |
| 1990 | 55.4 | 59.2 | 62.5 | 66.0 | 74.4 | 81.0 | 83.6 | 82.5 | 79.2 | 70.5 | 60.4 | 56.4 | 69.3 |
| Record Mean | 49.7 | 51.5 | 57.5 | 64.6 | 72.6 | 78.7 | 81.3 | 80.5 | 76.5 | 67.2 | 58.0 | 51.0 | 65.8 |
| Max | 58.6 | 60.5 | 66.7 | 73.8 | 81.1 | 86.5 | 88.7 | 87.8 | 83.8 | 75.7 | 67.3 | 60.1 | 74.2 |
| Min | 40.7 | 42.4 | 48.4 | 55.4 | 64.0 | 70.9 | 73.8 | 73.2 | 69.2 | 58.6 | 48.6 | 42.0 | 57.3 |

## REFERENCE NOTES FOR TABLES 1, 2, 3 and 6  (CHARLESTON, SC)

### GENERAL

T - TRACE AMOUNT
BLANK ENTRIES DENOTE MISSING/UNREPORTED DATA.
# INDICATES A STATION OR INSTRUMENT RELOCATION.

### SPECIFIC

**TABLE 1**

(a) - LENGTH OF RECORD IN YEARS. ALTHOUGH INDIVIDUAL MONTHS MAY BE MISSING.

* LESS THAN .05

NORMALS — BASED ON THE 1951-1980 RECORD PERIOD.
EXTREMES — DATES ARE THE MOST RECENT OCCURRENCE.
WIND DIR. — NUMERALS SHOW TENS OF DEGREES
CLOCKWISE FROM TRUE NORTH.
"00" INDICATES CALM.
RESULTANT WIND DIRECTIONS ARE GIVEN TO WHOLE DEGREES.

**TABLE 3**
MAX AND MIN ARE LONG-TERM MEAN DAILY MAXIMUM AND MEAN DAILY MINIMUM TEMPERATURES.

### EXCEPTIONS

**TABLES 2, 3, and 6**

RECORD MEANS ARE THROUGH THE CURRENT YEAR, BEGINNING IN  1874 FOR TEMPERATURE
1871 FOR PRECIPITATION
1943 FOR SNOWFALL

## TABLE 4 — HEATING DEGREE DAYS Base 65 deg. F — CHARLESTON, SOUTH CAROLINA

| SEASON | JULY | AUG | SEP | OCT | NOV | DEC | JAN | FEB | MAR | APR | MAY | JUNE | TOTAL |
|---|---|---|---|---|---|---|---|---|---|---|---|---|---|
| 1961-62 | 0 | 0 | 3 | 92 | 251 | 443 | 553 | 263 | 363 | 160 | 0 | 0 | 2128 |
| 1962-63 | 0 | 0 | 8 | 95 | 339 | 597 | 604 | 545 | 172 | 69 | 29 | 0 | 2458 |
| 1963-64 | 0 | 0 | 2 | 33 | 233 | 650 | 504 | 500 | 240 | 61 | 4 | 0 | 2227 |
| 1964-65 | 0 | 0 | 0 | 135 | 153 | 385 | 507 | 392 | 340 | 95 | 0 | 0 | 2007 |
| 1965-66 | 0 | 0 | 0 | 95 | 225 | 481 | 644 | 427 | 338 | 119 | 15 | 2 | 2346 |
| 1966-67 | 0 | 0 | 0 | 51 | 280 | 498 | 443 | 460 | 194 | 50 | 29 | 4 | 2008 |
| 1967-68 | 0 | 0 | 15 | 112 | 334 | 367 | 655 | 667 | 307 | 67 | 4 | 0 | 2530 |
| 1968-69 | 0 | 0 | 0 | 80 | 334 | 564 | 624 | 551 | 444 | 90 | 6 | 0 | 2693 |
| 1969-70 | 0 | 0 | 1 | 50 | 349 | 567 | 735 | 454 | 249 | 82 | 9 | 0 | 2496 |
| 1970-71 | 0 | 0 | 11 | 42 | 324 | 392 | 465 | 424 | 404 | 127 | 16 | 0 | 2205 |
| 1971-72 | 0 | 0 | 0 | 13 | 261 | 220 | 317 | 463 | 249 | 113 | 8 | 0 | 1644 |
| 1972-73 | 0 | 0 | 0 | 33 | 268 | 302 | 521 | 524 | 167 | 141 | 18 | 0 | 1973 |
| 1973-74 | 0 | 0 | 0 | 34 | 158 | 428 | 135 | 378 | 150 | 114 | 2 | 0 | 1395 |
| 1974-75 | 0 | 0 | 5 | 136 | 299 | 432 | 353 | 294 | 273 | 152 | 0 | 0 | 1941 |
| 1975-76 | 0 | 0 | 0 | 40 | 221 | 466 | 621 | 265 | 146 | 94 | 15 | 3 | 1874 |
| 1976-77 | 0 | 0 | 0 | 159 | 418 | 501 | 805 | 516 | 186 | 58 | 17 | 0 | 2663 |
| 1977-78 | 0 | 0 | 0 | 112 | 175 | 459 | 663 | 616 | 309 | 52 | 18 | 0 | 2404 |
| 1978-79 | 0 | 0 | 0 | 57 | 83 | 399 | 602 | 505 | 241 | 70 | 2 | 0 | 1959 |
| 1979-80 | 0 | 0 | 0 | 68 | 203 | 500 | 495 | 555 | 321 | 82 | 17 | 0 | 2241 |
| 1980-81 | 0 | 0 | 0 | 80 | 287 | 537 | 715 | 393 | 333 | 55 | 16 | 0 | 2420 |
| 1981-82 | 0 | 0 | 3 | 88 | 291 | 577 | 617 | 372 | 214 | 132 | 3 | 0 | 2291 |
| 1982-83 | 0 | 0 | 0 | 102 | 154 | 276 | 593 | 440 | 264 | 146 | 2 | 0 | 1980 |
| 1983-84 | 0 | 0 | 4 | 24 | 230 | 500 | 577 | 347 | 240 | 92 | 16 | 0 | 2031 |
| 1984-85 | 0 | 0 | 9 | 13 | 337 | 249 | 692 | 418 | 183 | 47 | 4 | 0 | 1952 |
| 1985-86 | 0 | 0 | 2 | 16 | 54 | 526 | 588 | 261 | 244 | 74 | 4 | 0 | 1767 |
| 1986-87 | 0 | 0 | 0 | 56 | 128 | 376 | 545 | 446 | 272 | 131 | 7 | 0 | 1967 |
| 1987-88 | 0 | 6 | 0 | 135 | 188 | 358 | 665 | 458 | 239 | 85 | 7 | 2 | 2141 |
| 1988-89 | 0 | 0 | 0 | 107 | 145 | 442 | 285 | 312 | 220 | 121 | 14 | 0 | 1647 |
| 1989-90 | 0 | 0 | 1 | 50 | 169 | 669 | 294 | 189 | 137 | 67 | 0 | 0 | 1576 |
| 1990-91 | 0 | 0 | 0 | 65 | 152 | 280 |  |  |  |  |  |  |  |

## TABLE 5 — COOLING DEGREE DAYS Base 65 deg. F — CHARLESTON, SOUTH CAROLINA

| YEAR | JAN | FEB | MAR | APR | MAY | JUNE | JULY | AUG | SEP | OCT | NOV | DEC | TOTAL |
|---|---|---|---|---|---|---|---|---|---|---|---|---|---|
| 1969 | 0 | 0 | 1 | 46 | 165 | 465 | 555 | 394 | 268 | 158 | 6 | 0 | 2058 |
| 1970 | 0 | 0 | 9 | 126 | 253 | 410 | 552 | 487 | 384 | 130 | 3 | 1 | 2355 |
| 1971 | 2 | 5 | 5 | 65 | 215 | 469 | 480 | 457 | 369 | 199 | 31 | 32 | 2329 |
| 1972 | 7 | 3 | 5 | 93 | 163 | 275 | 475 | 488 | 351 | 110 | 30 | 22 | 2022 |
| 1973 | 1 | 0 | 50 | 42 | 233 | 412 | 554 | 501 | 445 | 184 | 56 | 10 | 2488 |
| 1974 | 41 | 7 | 63 | 80 | 288 | 319 | 417 | 450 | 312 | 46 | 18 | 3 | 2044 |
| 1975 | 8 | 13 | 26 | 74 | 318 | 414 | 449 | 516 | 361 | 171 | 58 | 0 | 2408 |
| 1976 | 2 | 9 | 73 | 70 | 187 | 329 | 502 | 384 | 274 | 52 | 2 | 1 | 1885 |
| 1977 | 0 | 1 | 54 | 107 | 263 | 493 | 586 | 518 | 417 | 71 | 71 | 1 | 2584 |
| 1978 | 0 | 0 | 13 | 106 | 242 | 414 | 505 | 514 | 378 | 86 | 40 | 21 | 2319 |
| 1979 | 0 | 2 | 9 | 71 | 241 | 335 | 533 | 514 | 354 | 105 | 40 | 0 | 2204 |
| 1980 | 0 | 9 | 7 | 69 | 221 | 407 | 549 | 539 | 451 | 87 | 5 | 1 | 2345 |
| 1981 | 0 | 0 | 9 | 138 | 199 | 539 | 582 | 481 | 307 | 66 | 9 | 0 | 2330 |
| 1982 | 0 | 2 | 42 | 42 | 232 | 420 | 510 | 475 | 293 | 111 | 36 | 0 | 2197 |
| 1983 | 0 | 0 | 6 | 32 | 217 | 362 | 559 | 567 | 322 | 149 | 10 | 34 | 2228 |
| 1984 | 0 | 1 | 19 | 67 | 228 | 420 | 470 | 509 | 254 | 212 | 21 | 4 | 2212 |
| 1985 | 7 | 17 | 57 | 136 | 276 | 445 | 501 | 470 | 332 | 245 | 129 | 10 | 2620 |
| 1986 | 0 | 0 | 36 | 114 | 300 | 499 | 662 | 474 | 414 | 182 | 78 | 5 | 2766 |
| 1987 | 0 | 0 | 26 | 62 | 269 | 459 | 560 | 580 | 389 | 18 | 48 | 9 | 2427 |
| 1988 | 0 | 2 | 12 | 74 | 229 | 359 | 529 | 534 | 349 | 43 | 30 | 4 | 2165 |
| 1989 | 5 | 37 | 64 | 136 | 246 | 470 | 561 | 493 | 358 | 173 | 44 | 0 | 2587 |
| 1990 | 4 | 34 | 65 | 105 | 302 | 487 | 583 | 548 | 430 | 238 | 24 | 21 | 2841 |

## TABLE 6 — SNOWFALL (inches) — CHARLESTON, SOUTH CAROLINA

| SEASON | JULY | AUG | SEP | OCT | NOV | DEC | JAN | FEB | MAR | APR | MAY | JUNE | TOTAL |
|---|---|---|---|---|---|---|---|---|---|---|---|---|---|
| 1970-71 | 0.0 | 0.0 | 0.0 | 0.0 | 0.0 | 0.0 | T | T | T | 0.0 | 0.0 | 0.0 | T |
| 1971-72 | 0.0 | 0.0 | 0.0 | 0.0 | 0.0 | 0.0 | 0.0 | 0.0 | 0.0 | 0.0 | 0.0 | 0.0 | 0.0 |
| 1972-73 | 0.0 | 0.0 | 0.0 | 0.0 | 0.0 | 0.0 | 0.0 | 0.0 | 0.0 | 0.0 | 0.0 | 0.0 | 0.0 |
| 1973-74 | 0.0 | 0.0 | 0.0 | 0.0 | 0.0 | 0.0 | T | 7.1 | 0.0 | 0.0 | 0.0 | 0.0 | 7.1 |
| 1974-75 | 0.0 | 0.0 | 0.0 | 0.0 | 0.0 | T | 0.0 | 0.0 | 0.0 | 0.0 | 0.0 | 0.0 | T |
| 1975-76 | 0.0 | 0.0 | 0.0 | 0.0 | 0.0 | 0.0 | 0.4 | 0.0 | 0.0 | 0.0 | 0.0 | 0.0 | 0.4 |
| 1976-77 | 0.0 | 0.0 | 0.0 | 0.0 | 0.0 | 0.0 | 1.0 | 0.3 | 0.0 | 0.0 | 0.0 | 0.0 | 1.3 |
| 1977-78 | 0.0 | 0.0 | 0.0 | 0.0 | 0.0 | 0.0 | T | 0.4 | T | 0.0 | 0.0 | 0.0 | 0.4 |
| 1978-79 | 0.0 | 0.0 | 0.0 | 0.0 | 0.0 | 0.0 | 0.0 | 1.8 | 0.0 | 0.0 | 0.0 | 0.0 | 1.8 |
| 1979-80 | 0.0 | 0.0 | 0.0 | 0.0 | 0.0 | 0.0 | 0.0 | T | 1.3 | 0.0 | 0.0 | 0.0 | 1.3 |
| 1980-81 | 0.0 | 0.0 | 0.0 | 0.0 | 0.0 | 3.8 | 0.0 | 0.0 | 0.0 | 0.0 | 0.0 | 0.0 | 3.8 |
| 1981-82 | 0.0 | 0.0 | 0.0 | 0.0 | 0.0 | 0.0 | T | 0.0 | 0.0 | 0.0 | 0.0 | 0.0 | T |
| 1982-83 | 0.0 | 0.0 | 0.0 | 0.0 | 0.0 | 0.0 | 0.0 | T | 0.0 | 0.0 | 0.0 | 0.0 | T |
| 1983-84 | 0.0 | 0.0 | 0.0 | 0.0 | 0.0 | 0.0 | T | 0.0 | 0.0 | 0.0 | 0.0 | 0.0 | T |
| 1984-85 | 0.0 | 0.0 | 0.0 | 0.0 | 0.0 | 0.0 | T | 0.0 | T | 0.0 | 0.0 | 0.0 | T |
| 1985-86 | 0.0 | 0.0 | 0.0 | 0.0 | 0.0 | 0.0 | 0.5 | 0.0 | 0.0 | 0.0 | 0.0 | 0.0 | 0.5 |
| 1986-87 | 0.0 | 0.0 | 0.0 | 0.0 | 0.0 | 0.0 | T | 0.0 | T | 0.0 | 0.0 | 0.0 | 0.5 |
| 1987-88 | 0.0 | 0.0 | 0.0 | 0.0 | 0.0 | 0.0 | T | 0.0 | T | 0.0 | 0.0 | 0.0 | T |
| 1988-89 | 0.0 | 0.0 | 0.0 | 0.0 | 0.0 | 0.0 | 0.4 | 0.0 | 0.0 | 0.0 | 0.0 | 0.0 | 0.4 |
| 1989-90 | 0.0 | 0.0 | 0.0 | 0.0 | 0.0 | T | 0.0 | 0.9 | T | 0.0 | 0.0 | 0.0 | 0.9 |
| 1990-91 | 0.0 | 0.0 | 0.0 | 0.0 | 0.0 | 8.0 | 0.0 | 0.0 | 0.0 | 0.0 | 0.0 | 0.0 | 8.0 |
| Record Mean | 0.0 | 0.0 | 0.0 | 0.0 | T | 0.3 | 0.1 | 0.3 | 0.1 | T | 0.0 | T | 0.7 |

See Reference Notes, relative to all above tables, on preceding page.

Rapid City, which is not far from the geographical center of North America, experiences the large temperature ranges, both daily and seasonal, that are typical of semi-arid continental climates.

The city is surrounded by contrasting landforms, with the forested Black Hills rising immediately west of the city, and rolling prairie extending out in the other directions. From 40 to 70 miles southeast lie the eroded Badlands. The Black Hills, many of which are more than 5,000 feet above sea level, with a number of peaks above 7,000 feet, exert a pronounced influence on the climate of this area. The rolling land to the east of the city is cut by the valleys of the Box Elder and Rapid Creeks, which flow generally east-southeastward. The station is located on the north slope of the irrigated Rapid Valley. An east-west ridge 200 to 300 feet higher than the airport separates the station from the Box Elder Creek Valley.

The principal agricultural products in the area are cattle and wheat, and ranchers and farmers are dependent on the current weather forecasts, which are at times of vital interest in the protection of livestock.

Although the annual precipitation is light at lower elevations, the distribution is beneficial to agriculture with the greatest amounts occurring during the growing season. The heaviest snows are expected in the spring, which helps to furnish moisture for the early maturing crops such as wheat, while heavy winter snows at the higher elevations provide irrigation water for the fertile valleys.

Summer days are normally warm with cool, comfortable nights. Nearly all of the summer precipitation occurs as thunderstorms. Hail is often associated with the more severe thunderstorms, with resultant damage to vegetation as well as other fragile material in the path of the storms. Autumn, which begins soon after the first of September, is characterized by mild, balmy days, and cool, invigorating mornings and evenings. Autumn weather usually extends into November and often into December.

Temperatures for the winter months of December, January, and February are among the warmest in South Dakota due to the protection of the Black Hills, the frequent occurrence of Chinook winds, and the fact that the winter tracks of arctic air masses usually pass east of Rapid City. Rapid City has become the retirement home for many farmers and ranchers from the western half of the state because of the cool summer nights and the relatively mild winters.

Snowfall is normally light with the greatest monthly average of about 8 inches occurring in March. Cold waves can be expected occasionally, and one or more blizzards may occur each winter.

Spring is characterized by unsettled conditions. Wide variations usually occur in temperatures, and snows may fall as late as May.

Based on the 1951-1980 period, the average first occurrence of 32 degrees Fahrenheit in the fall is September 29 and the average last occurrence in the spring is May 7.

## TABLE 1 — NORMALS, MEANS AND EXTREMES

RAPID CITY, SOUTH DAKOTA

LATITUDE: 44°03'N    LONGITUDE: 103°04' W    ELEVATION: FT. GRND  3162 BARO   3169   TIME ZONE: MOUNTAIN    WBAN: 24090

| | (a) | JAN | FEB | MAR | APR | MAY | JUNE | JULY | AUG | SEP | OCT | NOV | DEC | YEAR |
|---|---|---|---|---|---|---|---|---|---|---|---|---|---|---|
| **TEMPERATURE °F:** | | | | | | | | | | | | | | |
| Normals | | | | | | | | | | | | | | |
| –Daily Maximum | | 32.4 | 37.4 | 44.2 | 57.0 | 68.1 | 77.9 | 86.5 | 85.7 | 75.4 | 63.2 | 46.7 | 37.4 | 59.3 |
| –Daily Minimum | | 9.2 | 14.6 | 21.0 | 32.1 | 43.0 | 52.5 | 58.7 | 57.0 | 46.4 | 36.1 | 23.0 | 14.8 | 34.0 |
| –Monthly | | 20.8 | 26.0 | 32.6 | 44.6 | 55.6 | 65.2 | 72.6 | 71.4 | 60.9 | 49.7 | 34.9 | 26.1 | 46.7 |
| Extremes | | | | | | | | | | | | | | |
| –Record Highest | 47 | 76 | 75 | 82 | 93 | 98 | 106 | 110 | 106 | 104 | 94 | 77 | 75 | 110 |
| –Year | | 1987 | 1988 | 1946 | 1989 | 1969 | 1988 | 1989 | 1988 | 1978 | 1963 | 1965 | 1965 | JUL 1989 |
| –Record Lowest | 47 | -27 | -24 | -17 | 1 | 18 | 31 | 39 | 38 | 18 | 10 | -19 | -29 | -29 |
| –Year | | 1950 | 1989 | 1962 | 1975 | 1950 | 1951 | 1951 | 1987 | 1966 | 1985 | 1972 | 1959 | 1989 | DEC 1989 |
| **NORMAL DEGREE DAYS:** | | | | | | | | | | | | | | |
| Heating (base 65°F) | | 1370 | 1092 | 1004 | 612 | 298 | 101 | 21 | 24 | 188 | 482 | 903 | 1206 | 7301 |
| Cooling (base 65°F) | | 0 | 0 | 0 | 0 | 7 | 107 | 257 | 223 | 65 | 8 | 0 | 0 | 667 |
| **% OF POSSIBLE SUNSHINE** | 47 | 56 | 59 | 62 | 61 | 59 | 64 | 72 | 73 | 68 | 65 | 55 | 54 | 62 |
| **MEAN SKY COVER (tenths)** | | | | | | | | | | | | | | |
| Sunrise – Sunset | 47 | 6.4 | 6.5 | 6.7 | 6.5 | 6.3 | 5.5 | 4.4 | 4.3 | 4.5 | 5.0 | 6.2 | 6.2 | 5.7 |
| **MEAN NUMBER OF DAYS:** | | | | | | | | | | | | | | |
| Sunrise to Sunset | | | | | | | | | | | | | | |
| –Clear | 47 | 7.7 | 6.2 | 6.1 | 6.1 | 6.8 | 9.2 | 13.0 | 13.9 | 13.3 | 12.3 | 7.8 | 8.2 | 110.7 |
| –Partly Cloudy | 47 | 7.7 | 8.3 | 9.2 | 9.4 | 10.8 | 11.4 | 12.8 | 11.6 | 8.6 | 8.0 | 8.4 | 8.3 | 114.6 |
| –Cloudy | 47 | 15.6 | 13.7 | 15.7 | 14.5 | 13.4 | 9.5 | 5.2 | 5.4 | 8.1 | 10.6 | 13.8 | 14.5 | 140.0 |
| Precipitation | | | | | | | | | | | | | | |
| .01 inches or more | 47 | 6.6 | 7.2 | 8.7 | 9.2 | 11.7 | 12.3 | 9.0 | 7.9 | 6.5 | 4.9 | 5.7 | 6.1 | 95.9 |
| Snow, Ice pellets | | | | | | | | | | | | | | |
| 1.0 inches or more | 39 | 1.2 | 2.5 | 2.7 | 1.9 | 0.2 | 0.* | 0.0 | 0.0 | 0.1 | 0.4 | 1.7 | 1.7 | 12.5 |
| Thunderstorms | 47 | 0.0 | 0.0 | 0.1 | 1.2 | 5.8 | 10.7 | 11.7 | 8.9 | 3.3 | 0.4 | 0.* | 0.* | 42.1 |
| Heavy Fog Visibility | | | | | | | | | | | | | | |
| 1/4 mile or less | 47 | 1.6 | 2.0 | 2.6 | 1.6 | 0.9 | 1.1 | 0.5 | 0.5 | 0.6 | 0.6 | 1.9 | 2.0 | 15.9 |
| Temperature °F | | | | | | | | | | | | | | |
| –Maximum | | | | | | | | | | | | | | |
| 90° and above | 47 | 0.0 | 0.0 | 0.0 | 0.1 | 0.5 | 3.4 | 11.8 | 11.6 | 3.4 | 0.2 | 0.0 | 0.0 | 31.0 |
| 32° and below | 47 | 13.1 | 10.1 | 6.9 | 0.8 | 0.* | 0.0 | 0.0 | 0.0 | 0.0 | 0.3 | 5.1 | 10.8 | 47.1 |
| –Minimum | | | | | | | | | | | | | | |
| 32° and below | 47 | 30.1 | 26.9 | 27.3 | 14.9 | 2.6 | 0.1 | 0.0 | 0.0 | 1.6 | 10.1 | 24.5 | 29.9 | 168.0 |
| 0° and below | 47 | 8.1 | 4.5 | 2.1 | 0.0 | 0.0 | 0.0 | 0.0 | 0.0 | 0.0 | 0.0 | 1.1 | 4.3 | 20.1 |
| **AVG. STATION PRESS. (mb)** | 17 | 904.6 | 904.6 | 901.9 | 902.9 | 902.5 | 903.7 | 905.2 | 905.1 | 905.8 | 905.9 | 904.4 | 904.4 | 904.2 |
| **RELATIVE HUMIDITY (%)** | | | | | | | | | | | | | | |
| Hour 05 | 39 | 68 | 72 | 74 | 72 | 75 | 76 | 72 | 70 | 68 | 66 | 69 | 69 | 71 |
| Hour 11 | 39 | 59 | 59 | 56 | 48 | 49 | 51 | 45 | 42 | 41 | 42 | 52 | 59 | 50 |
| Hour 17 (Local Time) | 39 | 63 | 61 | 54 | 45 | 46 | 48 | 40 | 36 | 38 | 45 | 59 | 65 | 50 |
| Hour 23 | 39 | 68 | 71 | 72 | 67 | 70 | 72 | 64 | 61 | 60 | 62 | 67 | 68 | 67 |
| **PRECIPITATION (inches):** | | | | | | | | | | | | | | |
| Water Equivalent | | | | | | | | | | | | | | |
| –Normal | | 0.42 | 0.62 | 1.02 | 1.96 | 2.63 | 3.26 | 2.12 | 1.44 | 1.03 | 0.81 | 0.51 | 0.45 | 16.27 |
| –Maximum Monthly | 47 | 1.77 | 2.46 | 3.02 | 5.16 | 7.35 | 7.00 | 6.13 | 4.83 | 3.94 | 3.82 | 2.22 | 1.65 | 7.35 |
| –Year | | 1944 | 1953 | 1945 | 1967 | 1946 | 1968 | 1969 | 1982 | 1946 | 1982 | 1985 | 1975 | MAY 1946 |
| –Minimum Monthly | 47 | 0.01 | 0.06 | 0.12 | 0.02 | 0.33 | 0.64 | 0.38 | 0.10 | 0.03 | T | 0.03 | 0.01 | T |
| –Year | | 1952 | 1985 | 1981 | 1987 | 1966 | 1973 | 1988 | 1943 | 1975 | 1960 | 1945 | 1986 | OCT 1960 |
| –Maximum in 24 hrs | 47 | 1.26 | 1.00 | 2.19 | 3.01 | 3.40 | 4.01 | 2.51 | 2.60 | 2.13 | 2.49 | 1.09 | 1.04 | 4.01 |
| –Year | | 1944 | 1953 | 1945 | 1946 | 1965 | 1963 | 1944 | 1982 | 1966 | 1982 | 1944 | 1975 | JUN 1963 |
| Snow, Ice pellets | | | | | | | | | | | | | | |
| –Maximum Monthly | 47 | 24.0 | 23.7 | 30.7 | 30.6 | 11.6 | 3.6 | 0.0 | T | 2.0 | 10.2 | 33.6 | 17.9 | 33.6 |
| –Year | | 1949 | 1953 | 1950 | 1970 | 1950 | 1951 | | 1989 | 1970 | 1971 | 1985 | 1975 | NOV 1985 |
| –Maximum in 24 hrs | 47 | 16.3 | 10.0 | 14.9 | 16.0 | 13.4 | 3.6 | 0.0 | T | 2.0 | 7.6 | 9.4 | 9.8 | 16.3 |
| –Year | | 1944 | 1953 | 1973 | 1970 | 1967 | 1951 | | 1989 | 1970 | 1971 | 1977 | 1975 | JAN 1944 |
| **WIND:** | | | | | | | | | | | | | | |
| Mean Speed (mph) | 39 | 10.9 | 11.2 | 12.8 | 13.3 | 12.4 | 10.9 | 10.2 | 10.3 | 11.0 | 11.2 | 10.8 | 10.6 | 11.3 |
| Prevailing Direction | | | | | | | | | | | | | | |
| through 1963 | | NNW | NNW | NNW | NNW | NNW | NNW | NNW | NNW | NNW | NNW | NNW | NNW | NNW |
| Fastest Obs. 1 Min. | | | | | | | | | | | | | | |
| –Direction (!!!) | 6 | 33 | 32 | 34 | 33 | 34 | 33 | 35 | 23 | 33 | 33 | 34 | 33 | 34 |
| –Speed (MPH) | 6 | 52 | 45 | 53 | 48 | 46 | 49 | 40 | 41 | 44 | 44 | 44 | 46 | 53 |
| –Year | | 1987 | 1988 | 1988 | 1989 | 1988 | 1989 | 1986 | 1987 | 1988 | 1988 | 1988 | 1985 | MAR 1988 |
| Peak Gust | | | | | | | | | | | | | | |
| –Direction (!!!) | 6 | N | NW | N | NW | NW | NW | NW | NW | S | NW | NW | NW | NW |
| –Speed (mph) | 6 | 68 | 61 | 66 | 64 | 61 | 64 | 72 | 69 | 70 | 67 | 60 | 63 | 72 |
| –Date | | 1988 | 1984 | 1988 | 1989 | 1987 | 1989 | 1984 | 1985 | 1985 | 1988 | 1984 | 1985 | JUL 1984 |

See Reference Notes to this table on the following page.

PRECIPITATION (inches)    RAPID CITY, SOUTH DAKOTA

**TABLE 2**

| YEAR | JAN | FEB | MAR | APR | MAY | JUNE | JULY | AUG | SEP | OCT | NOV | DEC | ANNUAL |
|------|-----|-----|-----|-----|-----|------|------|-----|-----|-----|-----|-----|--------|
| 1961 | 0.10 | 0.22 | 0.75 | 1.53 | 1.29 | 0.76 | 2.11 | 0.43 | 0.98 | 0.94 | 0.36 | 0.51 | 9.98 |
| 1962 | 0.51 | 0.98 | 1.28 | 0.69 | 6.90 | 4.01 | 4.53 | 1.03 | 0.67 | 1.63 | 0.08 | 0.19 | 22.50 |
| 1963 | 1.03 | 0.92 | 1.60 | 3.80 | 1.18 | 5.47 | 2.03 | 1.32 | 0.77 | 1.21 | 0.12 | 0.32 | 19.77 |
| 1964 | 0.35 | 0.83 | 0.63 | 1.24 | 2.52 | 4.69 | 0.77 | 1.87 | 0.69 | 0.50 | 0.30 | 0.78 | 15.17 |
| 1965 | 0.61 | 0.22 | 0.46 | 1.50 | 6.97 | 3.56 | 0.60 | 1.46 | 1.46 | 0.57 | 0.15 | 0.12 | 17.68 |
| 1966 | 0.24 | 1.00 | 1.78 | 2.50 | 0.33 | 1.31 | 3.93 | 3.24 | 2.84 | 1.50 | 0.95 | 0.79 | 20.41 |
| 1967 | 0.47 | 0.59 | 0.82 | 5.16 | 3.20 | 6.78 | 1.07 | 0.95 | 2.10 | 0.28 | 0.28 | 0.89 | 22.59 |
| 1968 | 0.43 | 0.35 | 0.21 | 1.82 | 1.68 | 7.00 | 2.44 | 2.46 | 0.89 | 0.14 | 0.46 | 0.58 | 18.46 |
| 1969 | 0.11 | 0.73 | 0.66 | 1.60 | 2.20 | 2.04 | 6.13 | 0.31 | 0.35 | 0.85 | 0.35 | 0.57 | 15.90 |
| 1970 | 0.73 | 0.54 | 1.48 | 4.63 | 2.41 | 2.16 | 1.04 | 0.67 | 1.57 | 1.23 | 0.80 | 0.61 | 17.87 |
| 1971 | 1.18 | 1.00 | 1.25 | 2.86 | 3.70 | 1.92 | 1.46 | 0.52 | 2.32 | 2.02 | 0.79 | 0.15 | 19.17 |
| 1972 | 0.22 | 0.44 | 0.47 | 2.78 | 3.28 | 4.11 | 1.67 | 2.49 | 0.24 | 0.77 | 0.38 | 0.34 | 17.19 |
| 1973 | 0.11 | 0.31 | 2.71 | 2.69 | 2.37 | 0.64 | 1.46 | 0.74 | 1.44 | 1.38 | 0.73 | 0.54 | 15.12 |
| 1974 | 0.16 | 0.30 | 0.34 | 1.55 | 1.32 | 1.10 | 0.68 | 1.37 | 0.88 | 1.18 | 0.12 | 0.12 | 9.12 |
| 1975 | 1.05 | 0.35 | 2.45 | 1.37 | 1.23 | 5.63 | 1.57 | 0.87 | 0.03 | 0.69 | 0.57 | 1.65 | 17.46 |
| 1976 | 0.28 | 0.47 | 0.33 | 2.70 | 2.74 | 4.81 | 1.05 | 1.31 | 0.28 | 0.21 | 0.61 | 0.41 | 15.20 |
| 1977 | 0.83 | 0.25 | 2.63 | 1.57 | 2.49 | 1.76 | 2.98 | 1.79 | 2.86 | 1.06 | 0.82 | 0.36 | 19.40 |
| 1978 | 0.19 | 0.84 | 0.40 | 2.19 | 3.12 | 2.01 | 4.08 | 1.42 | 0.18 | 0.26 | 0.63 | 0.25 | 15.57 |
| 1979 | 0.49 | 0.33 | 0.47 | 0.31 | 1.17 | 3.60 | 4.11 | 2.32 | 0.07 | 0.90 | 0.15 | 0.07 | 13.99 |
| 1980 | 0.20 | 0.51 | 0.86 | 1.13 | 1.58 | 4.75 | 1.78 | 2.38 | 0.48 | 2.28 | 0.57 | 0.66 | 17.18 |
| 1981 | 0.14 | 0.09 | 0.12 | 0.32 | 2.81 | 1.89 | 4.47 | 1.74 | 0.16 | 1.81 | 0.23 | 0.35 | 14.13 |
| 1982 | 0.39 | 0.37 | 1.35 | 0.69 | 6.50 | 2.89 | 1.81 | 4.83 | 2.69 | 3.82 | 0.27 | 0.36 | 25.97 |
| 1983 | 0.34 | 0.18 | 0.84 | 1.00 | 2.18 | 3.01 | 1.94 | 2.39 | 0.33 | 1.74 | 1.07 | 0.47 | 15.49 |
| 1984 | 0.10 | 0.18 | 0.69 | 3.10 | 1.57 | 4.72 | 1.57 | 1.00 | 0.74 | 0.67 | 0.51 | 0.38 | 15.23 |
| 1985 | 0.46 | 0.06 | 1.55 | 0.32 | 1.24 | 1.58 | 1.03 | 1.86 | 1.57 | 0.98 | 2.22 | 0.77 | 13.64 |
| 1986 | 0.49 | 0.92 | 0.88 | 4.74 | 1.43 | 4.56 | 0.91 | 1.32 | 3.14 | 1.64 | 1.40 | 0.01 | 21.44 |
| 1987 | 0.04 | 1.71 | 1.14 | 0.02 | 3.39 | 1.37 | 0.83 | 2.37 | 0.68 | 0.26 | 0.30 | 0.31 | 12.42 |
| 1988 | 0.17 | 0.34 | 0.52 | 0.60 | 3.25 | 1.09 | 0.38 | 1.98 | 0.56 | 0.76 | 0.81 | 0.46 | 10.92 |
| 1989 | 0.02 | 0.34 | 0.96 | 1.46 | 1.40 | 1.04 | 0.82 | 1.70 | 3.09 | 1.49 | 0.43 | 0.82 | 13.57 |
| 1990 | 0.22 | 0.37 | 1.17 | 0.77 | 4.87 | 1.42 | 1.94 | 1.87 | 2.44 | 0.61 | 0.44 | 0.33 | 16.45 |
| Record Mean | 0.41 | 0.47 | 1.00 | 1.90 | 3.06 | 3.22 | 2.24 | 1.64 | 1.26 | 1.03 | 0.61 | 0.51 | 17.35 |

**TABLE 3**    AVERAGE TEMPERATURE (deg. F)    RAPID CITY, SOUTH DAKOTA

| YEAR | JAN | FEB | MAR | APR | MAY | JUNE | JULY | AUG | SEP | OCT | NOV | DEC | ANNUAL |
|------|-----|-----|-----|-----|-----|------|------|-----|-----|-----|-----|-----|--------|
| 1961 | 27.3 | 33.2 | 39.4 | 41.8 | 55.8 | 71.3 | 73.1 | 77.2 | 55.6 | 49.9 | 34.9 | 23.0 | 48.6 |
| 1962 | 19.3 | 24.2 | 28.6 | 49.1 | 58.3 | 65.3 | 69.2 | 71.2 | 60.3 | 52.9 | 40.6 | 30.1 | 47.4 |
| 1963 | 12.3 | 30.2 | 39.7 | 44.5 | 57.0 | 68.1 | 74.4 | 73.8 | 66.5 | 59.4 | 39.6 | 22.7 | 49.0 |
| 1964 | 28.4 | 28.1 | 29.9 | 46.3 | 58.5 | 64.9 | 76.7 | 69.5 | 59.0 | 51.7 | 33.7 | 18.9 | 47.1 |
| #1965 | 25.4 | 25.6 | 21.2 | 47.0 | 54.7 | 64.5 | 72.1 | 70.7 | 49.7 | 54.8 | 38.2 | 33.3 | 46.4 |
| 1966 | 14.2 | 14.0 | 35.0 | 38.7 | 56.0 | 65.3 | 76.6 | 70.6 | 61.3 | 48.6 | 34.6 | 26.7 | 45.2 |
| 1967 | 27.9 | 27.5 | 35.2 | 44.1 | 49.8 | 60.0 | 70.6 | 70.6 | 63.4 | 50.1 | 34.6 | 22.5 | 46.3 |
| 1968 | 23.4 | 27.4 | 40.4 | 42.6 | 50.8 | 60.8 | 69.2 | 67.0 | 59.8 | 51.0 | 35.5 | 18.5 | 45.7 |
| 1969 | 16.0 | 25.4 | 27.8 | 49.6 | 57.5 | 59.8 | 71.0 | 73.8 | 64.8 | 40.6 | 38.7 | 28.2 | 46.1 |
| 1970 | 17.8 | 30.8 | 27.5 | 39.2 | 55.6 | 65.6 | 72.7 | 73.8 | 59.1 | 44.1 | 34.2 | 21.9 | 45.2 |
| 1971 | 17.5 | 22.6 | 32.6 | 46.0 | 53.6 | 66.4 | 68.0 | 73.9 | 57.4 | 46.1 | 34.5 | 23.3 | 45.2 |
| 1972 | 17.3 | 24.0 | 36.5 | 43.6 | 55.2 | 64.7 | 65.6 | 69.1 | 59.4 | 43.8 | 31.0 | 18.6 | 44.1 |
| 1973 | 26.8 | 28.9 | 37.5 | 42.9 | 53.7 | 64.7 | 70.7 | 74.3 | 57.1 | 51.3 | 32.3 | 25.4 | 47.1 |
| 1974 | 21.9 | 32.5 | 37.6 | 47.2 | 53.8 | 66.6 | 77.3 | 67.7 | 57.6 | 51.7 | 36.4 | 28.9 | 48.3 |
| 1975 | 23.7 | 17.6 | 27.6 | 40.5 | 54.0 | 62.2 | 74.7 | 70.3 | 58.5 | 49.2 | 33.8 | 29.4 | 45.1 |
| 1976 | 23.9 | 34.6 | 34.4 | 46.9 | 55.4 | 64.3 | 72.8 | 72.6 | 63.3 | 45.4 | 31.7 | 26.8 | 47.7 |
| 1977 | 12.7 | 34.6 | 36.4 | 49.5 | 60.3 | 69.0 | 73.4 | 66.0 | 61.0 | 48.8 | 33.3 | 21.9 | 47.3 |
| 1978 | 11.0 | 15.3 | 35.4 | 45.2 | 55.1 | 65.1 | 71.1 | 69.7 | 66.2 | 50.5 | 29.2 | 17.1 | 44.2 |
| 1979 | 7.4 | 16.8 | 35.4 | 44.4 | 53.6 | 65.4 | 70.4 | 68.5 | 66.3 | 50.9 | 33.0 | 33.2 | 45.4 |
| 1980 | 21.0 | 27.1 | 31.5 | 48.9 | 57.4 | 67.1 | 74.9 | 68.6 | 61.6 | 48.9 | 39.3 | 30.3 | 48.0 |
| 1981 | 32.6 | 29.4 | 40.0 | 51.5 | 54.9 | 64.9 | 72.0 | 70.0 | 63.5 | 47.7 | 40.4 | 25.8 | 49.4 |
| 1982 | 11.9 | 23.9 | 33.0 | 42.1 | 53.3 | 59.7 | 70.7 | 70.2 | 58.7 | 47.2 | 32.7 | 28.6 | 44.3 |
| 1983 | 32.1 | 37.3 | 36.4 | 40.7 | 52.0 | 63.1 | 73.6 | 78.0 | 60.8 | 49.4 | 34.9 | 8.1 | 47.2 |
| 1984 | 28.0 | 36.1 | 34.3 | 43.8 | 53.6 | 62.8 | 72.2 | 74.8 | 57.2 | 47.2 | 37.5 | 21.4 | 47.4 |
| 1985 | 21.6 | 23.8 | 35.9 | 52.0 | 61.8 | 62.1 | 74.6 | 69.0 | 55.6 | 47.3 | 16.0 | 21.0 | 45.1 |
| 1986 | 29.8 | 21.5 | 43.0 | 44.2 | 54.9 | 67.6 | 70.9 | 69.6 | 55.0 | 48.7 | 30.6 | 30.5 | 47.2 |
| 1987 | 31.1 | 32.4 | 32.6 | 51.6 | 59.5 | 67.1 | 75.4 | 68.1 | 61.4 | 47.1 | 40.3 | 28.9 | 49.6 |
| 1988 | 21.7 | 26.9 | 35.6 | 47.1 | 60.0 | 75.6 | 76.1 | 72.5 | 60.4 | 49.7 | 36.4 | 28.4 | 49.2 |
| 1989 | 28.7 | 14.4 | 31.1 | 45.8 | 55.4 | 64.0 | 77.0 | 73.1 | 61.0 | 48.8 | 36.4 | 19.4 | 46.3 |
| 1990 | 32.4 | 28.9 | 36.4 | 45.0 | 53.2 | 66.6 | 71.7 | 73.8 | 65.9 | 48.2 | 40.5 | 17.8 | 48.4 |
| Record Mean | 22.9 | 25.4 | 33.3 | 45.0 | 55.1 | 64.7 | 72.4 | 70.8 | 60.7 | 49.3 | 35.8 | 26.3 | 46.8 |
| Max | 34.5 | 36.8 | 44.7 | 57.0 | 66.8 | 76.6 | 85.6 | 84.4 | 74.2 | 62.1 | 47.4 | 37.4 | 59.0 |
| Min | 11.3 | 14.0 | 21.8 | 33.1 | 43.3 | 52.7 | 59.2 | 57.3 | 47.2 | 36.4 | 24.2 | 15.1 | 34.6 |

## REFERENCE NOTES FOR TABLES 1, 2, 3 and 6    (RAPID CITY, SD)

### GENERAL

T - TRACE AMOUNT
BLANK ENTRIES DENOTE MISSING/UNREPORTED DATA.
# INDICATES A STATION OR INSTRUMENT RELOCATION.

### SPECIFIC

**TABLE 1**

(a) - LENGTH OF RECORD IN YEARS. ALTHOUGH
INDIVIDUAL MONTHS MAY BE MISSING.
* LESS THAN .05

NORMALS — BASED ON THE 1951-1980 RECORD PERIOD.
EXTREMES — DATES ARE THE MOST RECENT OCCURRENCE.
WIND DIR. — NUMERALS SHOW TENS OF DEGREES
CLOCKWISE FROM TRUE NORTH.
"00" INDICATES CALM.
RESULTANT WIND DIRECTIONS ARE GIVEN TO WHOLE DEGREES.

**TABLE 3**
MAX AND MIN ARE LONG-TERM MEAN DAILY MAXIMUM
AND MEAN DAILY MINIMUM TEMPERATURES.

### EXCEPTIONS

**TABLES 2, 3, and 6**

RECORD MEANS ARE THROUGH THE CURRENT YEAR,
BEGINNING IN    1900 FOR TEMPERATURE
1900 FOR PRECIPITATION
1943 FOR SNOWFALL

**TABLE 4**  HEATING DEGREE DAYS Base 65 deg. F    RAPID CITY, SOUTH DAKOTA

| SEASON | JULY | AUG | SEP | OCT | NOV | DEC | JAN | FEB | MAR | APR | MAY | JUNE | TOTAL |
|---|---|---|---|---|---|---|---|---|---|---|---|---|---|
| 1961-62 | 2 | 0 | 327 | 469 | 898 | 1295 | 1414 | 1139 | 1121 | 483 | 213 | 60 | 7421 |
| 1962-63 | 4 | 36 | 165 | 372 | 721 | 1073 | 1634 | 968 | 776 | 607 | 253 | 28 | 6637 |
| 1963-64 | 4 | 4 | 59 | 205 | 755 | 1305 | 1129 | 1064 | 1081 | 555 | 237 | 85 | 6483 |
| 1964-65 | 0 | 64 | 198 | 410 | 931 | 1419 | 1218 | 1098 | 1351 | 534 | 327 | 55 | 7605 |
| #1965-66 | 3 | 27 | 461 | 312 | 797 | 978 | 1573 | 1273 | 923 | 784 | 285 | 103 | 7519 |
| 1966-67 | 0 | 83 | 158 | 504 | 905 | 1180 | 1143 | 1042 | 917 | 622 | 473 | 162 | 7189 |
| 1967-68 | 31 | 19 | 129 | 464 | 902 | 1311 | 1285 | 1083 | 755 | 669 | 432 | 107 | 7187 |
| 1968-69 | 26 | 46 | 176 | 428 | 881 | 1438 | 1516 | 1102 | 1145 | 458 | 264 | 176 | 7656 |
| 1969-70 | 0 | 0 | 62 | 750 | 781 | 1135 | 1461 | 950 | 1157 | 767 | 293 | 74 | 7430 |
| 1970-71 | 2 | 0 | 245 | 644 | 918 | 1330 | 1463 | 1182 | 996 | 563 | 344 | 35 | 7722 |
| 1971-72 | 43 | 2 | 267 | 578 | 909 | 1284 | 1473 | 1182 | 877 | 634 | 322 | 74 | 7645 |
| 1972-73 | 74 | 43 | 193 | 649 | 1010 | 1436 | 1181 | 1008 | 847 | 659 | 350 | 83 | 7533 |
| 1973-74 | 16 | 0 | 246 | 416 | 972 | 1223 | 1329 | 905 | 840 | 530 | 343 | 87 | 6907 |
| 1974-75 | 1 | 42 | 242 | 407 | 849 | 1112 | 1274 | 1318 | 1151 | 728 | 343 | 119 | 7586 |
| 1975-76 | 3 | 16 | 206 | 493 | 929 | 1096 | 1269 | 878 | 940 | 535 | 295 | 98 | 6758 |
| 1976-77 | 3 | 6 | 132 | 606 | 991 | 1177 | 1616 | 846 | 877 | 459 | 165 | 17 | 6895 |
| 1977-78 | 1 | 48 | 163 | 494 | 944 | 1330 | 1669 | 1383 | 912 | 588 | 312 | 91 | 7935 |
| 1978-79 | 17 | 40 | 111 | 443 | 1068 | 1480 | 1781 | 1348 | 910 | 614 | 362 | 82 | 8256 |
| 1979-80 | 3 | 25 | 64 | 433 | 952 | 982 | 1359 | 1094 | 1032 | 483 | 251 | 54 | 6732 |
| 1980-81 | 1 | 18 | 144 | 510 | 763 | 1070 | 998 | 993 | 765 | 402 | 311 | 65 | 6040 |
| 1981-82 | 21 | 7 | 108 | 531 | 730 | 1209 | 1646 | 1146 | 985 | 682 | 358 | 170 | 7593 |
| 1982-83 | 7 | 21 | 226 | 545 | 962 | 1119 | 1012 | 772 | 880 | 723 | 407 | 113 | 6787 |
| 1983-84 | 8 | 0 | 208 | 474 | 896 | 1762 | 1139 | 832 | 948 | 626 | 366 | 101 | 7360 |
| 1984-85 | 0 | 0 | 268 | 546 | 820 | 1344 | 1341 | 1148 | 895 | 393 | 146 | 144 | 7045 |
| 1985-86 | 8 | 27 | 327 | 544 | 1466 | 1358 | 1083 | 1211 | 672 | 617 | 317 | 35 | 7665 |
| 1986-87 | 5 | 12 | 296 | 497 | 1025 | 1059 | 1045 | 907 | 997 | 408 | 199 | 46 | 6496 |
| 1987-88 | 10 | 49 | 147 | 545 | 736 | 1111 | 1340 | 1103 | 905 | 533 | 195 | 17 | 6691 |
| 1988-89 | 3 | 18 | 163 | 470 | 850 | 1127 | 1120 | 1414 | 1047 | 586 | 303 | 116 | 7217 |
| 1989-90 | 3 | 6 | 182 | 495 | 847 | 1410 | 1004 | 1004 | 880 | 597 | 363 | 68 | 6859 |
| 1990-91 | 10 | 5 | 112 | 514 | 730 | 1462 | | | | | | | |

**TABLE 5**  COOLING DEGREE DAYS Base 65 deg. F    RAPID CITY, SOUTH DAKOTA

| YEAR | JAN | FEB | MAR | APR | MAY | JUNE | JULY | AUG | SEP | OCT | NOV | DEC | TOTAL |
|---|---|---|---|---|---|---|---|---|---|---|---|---|---|
| 1969 | 0 | 0 | 0 | 0 | 35 | 29 | 193 | 280 | 63 | 0 | 0 | 0 | 600 |
| 1970 | 0 | 0 | 0 | 0 | 7 | 96 | 248 | 279 | 78 | 5 | 0 | 0 | 713 |
| 1971 | 0 | 0 | 0 | 0 | 0 | 81 | 142 | 284 | 43 | 0 | 0 | 0 | 550 |
| 1972 | 0 | 0 | 0 | 0 | 21 | 70 | 98 | 178 | 34 | 0 | 0 | 0 | 401 |
| 1973 | 0 | 0 | 0 | 0 | 7 | 80 | 202 | 295 | 15 | 0 | 0 | 0 | 599 |
| 1974 | 0 | 0 | 0 | 1 | 3 | 143 | 390 | 132 | 28 | 0 | 0 | 0 | 697 |
| 1975 | 0 | 0 | 0 | 0 | 9 | 41 | 314 | 188 | 19 | 12 | 0 | 0 | 583 |
| 1976 | 0 | 0 | 0 | 0 | 4 | 83 | 251 | 248 | 87 | 3 | 0 | 0 | 676 |
| 1977 | 0 | 0 | 0 | 0 | 25 | 143 | 270 | 85 | 51 | 0 | 0 | 0 | 574 |
| 1978 | 0 | 0 | 0 | 0 | 9 | 99 | 214 | 193 | 154 | 0 | 0 | 0 | 669 |
| 1979 | 0 | 0 | 0 | 4 | 15 | 99 | 179 | 141 | 110 | 2 | 0 | 0 | 550 |
| 1980 | 0 | 0 | 0 | 6 | 25 | 123 | 315 | 136 | 48 | 14 | 0 | 0 | 667 |
| 1981 | 0 | 0 | 0 | 3 | 5 | 67 | 243 | 170 | 74 | 0 | 0 | 0 | 562 |
| 1982 | 0 | 0 | 0 | 0 | 3 | 18 | 189 | 190 | 41 | 0 | 0 | 0 | 441 |
| 1983 | 0 | 0 | 0 | 0 | 9 | 62 | 282 | 407 | 88 | 0 | 0 | 0 | 848 |
| 1984 | 0 | 0 | 0 | 0 | 18 | 41 | 234 | 309 | 42 | 2 | 0 | 0 | 646 |
| 1985 | 0 | 0 | 0 | 10 | 53 | 64 | 312 | 158 | 51 | 0 | 0 | 0 | 648 |
| 1986 | 0 | 0 | 0 | 0 | 11 | 124 | 192 | 164 | 0 | 0 | 0 | 0 | 491 |
| 1987 | 0 | 0 | 0 | 13 | 33 | 118 | 341 | 152 | 45 | 0 | 0 | 0 | 702 |
| 1988 | 0 | 0 | 0 | 2 | 46 | 341 | 355 | 255 | 33 | 2 | 0 | 0 | 1034 |
| 1989 | 0 | 0 | 0 | 15 | 9 | 95 | 380 | 265 | 70 | 0 | 0 | 0 | 834 |
| 1990 | 0 | 0 | 0 | 2 | 4 | 120 | 226 | 282 | 147 | 3 | 0 | 0 | 784 |

**TABLE 6**  SNOWFALL (inches)    RAPID CITY, SOUTH DAKOTA

| SEASON | JULY | AUG | SEP | OCT | NOV | DEC | JAN | FEB | MAR | APR | MAY | JUNE | TOTAL |
|---|---|---|---|---|---|---|---|---|---|---|---|---|---|
| 1961-62 | 0.0 | 0.0 | 0.2 | 3.7 | 2.7 | 5.5 | 4.9 | 6.9 | 7.9 | 0.1 | 0.0 | 0.0 | 31.9 |
| 1962-63 | 0.0 | 0.0 | T | T | 0.4 | 1.6 | 10.8 | 12.0 | 17.3 | 7.4 | 0.0 | 0.0 | 49.5 |
| 1963-64 | 0.0 | 0.0 | 0.0 | T | 0.3 | 3.0 | 3.5 | 8.9 | 5.7 | 4.2 | 0.0 | 0.0 | 25.6 |
| 1964-65 | 0.0 | 0.0 | 0.0 | 2.6 | 7.8 | 4.3 | 1.9 | 4.6 | 5.5 | 8.8 | 0.0 | 0.0 | 35.5 |
| 1965-66 | 0.0 | 0.0 | 1.5 | 0.0 | 0.8 | 0.7 | 2.4 | 10.0 | 16.5 | 10.0 | 0.4 | 0.0 | 42.3 |
| 1966-67 | 0.0 | 0.0 | T | 2.1 | 6.4 | 8.5 | 4.0 | 7.4 | 7.6 | 14.0 | 3.1 | 0.0 | 53.1 |
| 1967-68 | 0.0 | 0.0 | 0.0 | 0.0 | 2.2 | 9.1 | 4.0 | 3.4 | 1.3 | 13.7 | T | 0.0 | 33.7 |
| 1968-69 | 0.0 | 0.0 | 0.0 | 0.0 | 2.7 | 7.5 | 1.2 | 7.9 | 6.3 | 5.2 | 0.5 | 0.0 | 31.3 |
| 1969-70 | 0.0 | 0.0 | 0.0 | 4.1 | 2.9 | 5.7 | 5.5 | 6.0 | 14.8 | 30.6 | T | 0.0 | 69.6 |
| 1970-71 | 0.0 | 0.0 | 2.0 | 5.7 | 4.5 | 7.8 | 13.2 | 15.7 | 13.8 | 5.3 | 0.0 | 0.0 | 68.0 |
| 1971-72 | 0.0 | 0.0 | 0.0 | 10.2 | 6.9 | 2.0 | 2.6 | 8.0 | 1.2 | 1.0 | T | 0.0 | 31.9 |
| 1972-73 | 0.0 | 0.0 | 0.0 | 0.7 | 3.6 | 6.0 | 2.0 | 3.1 | 16.9 | 1.9 | 0.0 | 0.0 | 34.2 |
| 1973-74 | 0.0 | 0.0 | 0.0 | 1.4 | 9.7 | 5.6 | 2.0 | 4.0 | 1.7 | 4.7 | 0.0 | 0.0 | 29.1 |
| 1974-75 | 0.0 | 0.0 | 0.0 | T | 1.5 | 1.4 | 13.7 | 6.1 | 27.4 | 1.3 | 0.0 | 0.0 | 51.4 |
| 1975-76 | 0.0 | 0.0 | 0.0 | 4.6 | 8.4 | 17.9 | 2.0 | 6.5 | 4.3 | 3.5 | 0.0 | 0.0 | 47.2 |
| 1976-77 | 0.0 | 0.0 | 0.0 | 0.5 | 7.0 | 6.1 | 11.1 | 2.6 | 26.0 | 3.4 | 0.0 | 0.0 | 56.7 |
| 1977-78 | 0.0 | 0.0 | 0.0 | 0.8 | 10.6 | 7.4 | 3.1 | 15.0 | 3.0 | 2.6 | T | 0.0 | 42.5 |
| 1978-79 | 0.0 | 0.0 | 0.0 | T | 9.8 | 4.0 | 6.1 | 4.4 | 2.6 | 1.8 | 2.8 | 0.0 | 31.5 |
| 1979-80 | 0.0 | 0.0 | 0.0 | T | 1.8 | 0.3 | 10.1 | 8.6 | 5.4 | 3.0 | 0.0 | 0.0 | 29.2 |
| 1980-81 | 0.0 | 0.0 | 0.0 | 1.4 | 6.9 | 6.1 | 1.2 | 1.3 | T | T | 0.0 | 0.0 | 16.9 |
| 1981-82 | 0.0 | 0.0 | 0.0 | 1.6 | 1.2 | 3.8 | 6.2 | 5.0 | 11.5 | 5.5 | 0.0 | 0.0 | 34.8 |
| 1982-83 | 0.0 | 0.0 | 0.0 | 1.4 | 1.2 | 4.0 | 2.9 | 0.3 | 6.5 | 4.3 | 4.3 | 0.0 | 24.9 |
| 1983-84 | 0.0 | 0.0 | 0.3 | 0.9 | 6.9 | 7.1 | 1.9 | 2.5 | 6.1 | 22.1 | 0.2 | 0.0 | 48.0 |
| 1984-85 | 0.0 | 0.0 | 1.3 | 0.7 | 2.0 | 4.9 | 3.8 | 0.7 | 16.2 | 0.4 | 0.0 | T | 30.0 |
| 1985-86 | 0.0 | 0.0 | 1.4 | 0.6 | 33.6 | 10.2 | 5.7 | 10.7 | 6.0 | 12.7 | 0.0 | 0.0 | 80.9 |
| 1986-87 | 0.0 | 0.0 | 0.0 | T | 12.6 | 0.1 | 0.5 | 21.5 | 10.9 | 0.3 | 0.0 | 0.0 | 45.9 |
| 1987-88 | 0.0 | 0.0 | 0.0 | 1.7 | T | 4.7 | 2.7 | 3.6 | 10.6 | 6.1 | 0.0 | 0.0 | 29.4 |
| 1988-89 | 0.0 | 0.0 | 0.0 | 0.0 | 2.2 | 9.0 | 0.4 | 7.3 | 10.7 | 6.4 | 0.0 | 0.0 | 36.0 |
| 1989-90 | 0.0 | T | 0.0 | 3.9 | 4.6 | 10.9 | 3.1 | 5.0 | 9.2 | 3.0 | 0.5 | T | 40.2 |
| 1990-91 | 0.0 | T | 0.0 | 0.0 | 1.5 | 1.0 | 6.2 | | | | | | |
| Record Mean | 0.0 | T | 0.1 | 1.5 | 4.9 | 5.0 | 4.8 | 6.4 | 9.1 | 6.0 | 0.8 | 0.1 | 38.7 |

**See Reference Notes, relative to all above tables, on preceding page.**

Sioux Falls is located in the Big Sioux River Valley in southeast South Dakota. The surrounding terrain is gently rolling. The land slopes upward for about 100 miles north and northwest to an elevation about 400 feet higher than the city. To the southeast, the land slopes downward 200 to 300 feet over the same distance. Little change in elevation occurs in the remaining directions.

The climate is of the continental type. There are frequent weather changes from day to day or week to week as the locality is visited by differing air masses. Cold air masses arrive from the interior of Canada, cool, dry air from the northern Pacific, warm, moist air from the Gulf of Mexico, or hot, dry air from the southwest.

Temperatures fluctuate frequently as cold air masses move in very rapidly. During the late fall and winter, cold fronts accompanied by strong, gusty winds drop temperatures by 20 to 30 degrees in a 24-hour period. Severe cold spells usually last only a few days. The winter months of December through February have experienced cold spells with average temperatures under 8 degrees and more than 60 consecutive days below 32 degrees.

Temperatures of 100 degrees and above occur about one in every three years, and will most likely happen in July. Summer nights are usually comfortable with temperatures below 70 degrees.

Rainfall is heavier during the spring and summer with lighter amounts in winter. Nearly 64 percent of the normal yearly precipitation falls during the growing season of April through August.

One or two very heavy snows usually fall each winter. Eight to 12 inches of snow may fall in 24 hours. There have been a few snows in excess of 15 inches and almost 30 inches have fallen during a severe winter storm. Strong winds often cause drifting snow, and blizzard conditions may block highways for a day or so.

Southerly winds prevail from late spring to early fall with northwest winds the remainder of the year. Strong winds of 70 mph with gusts to 90 mph have occurred.

Thunderstorms are frequent during the late spring and summer with June and July the most active months. The thunderstorms usually occur during the late afternoon and evening with a secondary peak of activity between 2 and 5 in the morning. Some of the most severe thunderstorms with damaging winds, hail and an occasional tornado, occur most frequently June.

There is occasional flooding in the lower areas of Sioux Falls along the Big Sioux River and Skunk Creek. Runoff from the melting snow in the spring often causes substantial rises in the rivers. A diversion canal around Sioux Falls has reduced the threat of damaging floods.

Based on the 1951–1980 period, the average first occurrence of 32 degrees Fahrenheit in the fall is October 1 and the average last occurrence in the spring is May 10.

## TABLE 1    NORMALS, MEANS AND EXTREMES

SIOUX FALLS, SOUTH DAKOTA

LATITUDE: 43°34'N    LONGITUDE: 96°44'W    ELEVATION: FT. GRND 1418 BARO 1429    TIME ZONE: CENTRAL    WBAN: 14944

| | (a) | JAN | FEB | MAR | APR | MAY | JUNE | JULY | AUG | SEP | OCT | NOV | DEC | YEAR |
|---|---|---|---|---|---|---|---|---|---|---|---|---|---|---|
| **TEMPERATURE °F:** | | | | | | | | | | | | | | |
| Normals | | | | | | | | | | | | | | |
| -Daily Maximum | | 22.9 | 29.3 | 40.1 | 58.1 | 70.5 | 80.3 | 86.2 | 83.9 | 73.5 | 62.1 | 43.7 | 29.3 | 56.7 |
| -Daily Minimum | | 1.9 | 8.9 | 20.6 | 34.6 | 45.7 | 56.3 | 61.8 | 59.7 | 48.5 | 36.7 | 22.3 | 10.1 | 33.9 |
| -Monthly | | 12.4 | 19.1 | 30.4 | 46.3 | 58.2 | 68.4 | 74.0 | 71.8 | 61.0 | 49.4 | 33.0 | 19.7 | 45.3 |
| Extremes | | | | | | | | | | | | | | |
| -Record Highest | 44 | 66 | 70 | 87 | 94 | 100 | 110 | 108 | 108 | 104 | 94 | 76 | 61 | 110 |
| -Year | | 1981 | 1982 | 1968 | 1962 | 1967 | 1988 | 1989 | 1973 | 1976 | 1963 | 1978 | 1984 | JUN 1988 |
| -Record Lowest | 44 | -36 | -31 | -23 | 5 | 17 | 33 | 38 | 34 | 22 | 9 | -17 | -26 | -36 |
| -Year | | 1970 | 1962 | 1948 | 1982 | 1967 | 1969 | 1971 | 1950 | 1974 | 1972 | 1964 | 1989 | JAN 1970 |
| **NORMAL DEGREE DAYS:** | | | | | | | | | | | | | | |
| Heating (base 65°F) | | 1631 | 1285 | 1073 | 561 | 240 | 52 | 14 | 15 | 161 | 489 | 960 | 1404 | 7885 |
| Cooling (base 65°F) | | 0 | 0 | 0 | 0 | 29 | 154 | 293 | 226 | 41 | 6 | 0 | 0 | 749 |
| **% OF POSSIBLE SUNSHINE** | | | | | | | | | | | | | | |
| **MEAN SKY COVER (tenths)** | | | | | | | | | | | | | | |
| Sunrise - Sunset | 44 | 6.4 | 6.6 | 6.9 | 6.5 | 6.3 | 5.6 | 4.8 | 4.9 | 5.1 | 5.5 | 6.6 | 6.6 | 6.0 |
| **MEAN NUMBER OF DAYS:** | | | | | | | | | | | | | | |
| Sunrise to Sunset | | | | | | | | | | | | | | |
| -Clear | 44 | 8.1 | 7.0 | 6.1 | 7.2 | 7.4 | 8.8 | 12.0 | 11.8 | 11.7 | 11.1 | 7.0 | 7.4 | 105.5 |
| -Partly Cloudy | 44 | 7.7 | 6.7 | 7.6 | 8.3 | 10.0 | 11.0 | 11.9 | 10.7 | 7.9 | 7.8 | 7.4 | 7.0 | 104.0 |
| -Cloudy | 44 | 15.2 | 14.6 | 17.2 | 14.5 | 13.7 | 10.2 | 7.2 | 8.6 | 10.5 | 12.1 | 15.5 | 16.5 | 155.8 |
| Precipitation | | | | | | | | | | | | | | |
| .01 inches or more | 44 | 6.1 | 6.5 | 8.7 | 9.2 | 10.5 | 10.7 | 9.4 | 8.9 | 8.2 | 6.1 | 6.2 | 6.1 | 96.8 |
| Snow,Ice pellets | | | | | | | | | | | | | | |
| 1.0 inches or more | 44 | 2.1 | 2.1 | 2.5 | 0.6 | 0.0 | 0.0 | 0.0 | 0.0 | 0.0 | 0.1 | 1.6 | 2.0 | 11.1 |
| Thunderstorms | 44 | 0.0 | 0.1 | 0.8 | 2.9 | 6.1 | 8.9 | 9.4 | 8.0 | 5.5 | 1.9 | 0.4 | 0.1 | 44.3 |
| Heavy Fog Visibility | | | | | | | | | | | | | | |
| 1/4 mile or less | 44 | 2.4 | 2.9 | 2.7 | 0.9 | 0.7 | 0.5 | 0.6 | 1.2 | 1.3 | 1.6 | 2.8 | 3.7 | 21.4 |
| Temperature °F | | | | | | | | | | | | | | |
| -Maximum | | | | | | | | | | | | | | |
| 90° and above | 26 | 0.0 | 0.0 | 0.0 | 0.2 | 0.8 | 4.2 | 11.1 | 7.5 | 1.5 | 0.0 | 0.0 | 0.0 | 25.3 |
| 32° and below | 26 | 21.4 | 15.7 | 7.7 | 0.3 | 0.0 | 0.0 | 0.0 | 0.0 | 0.0 | 0.* | 6.3 | 18.8 | 70.3 |
| -Minimum | | | | | | | | | | | | | | |
| 32° and below | 26 | 30.9 | 27.5 | 25.7 | 12.1 | 2.2 | 0.0 | 0.0 | 0.0 | 1.4 | 11.8 | 25.5 | 30.6 | 167.6 |
| 0° and below | 26 | 13.6 | 8.4 | 1.7 | 0.0 | 0.0 | 0.0 | 0.0 | 0.0 | 0.0 | 0.0 | 1.3 | 7.8 | 32.8 |
| **AVG. STATION PRESS.(mb)** | 17 | 966.7 | 966.8 | 963.2 | 962.7 | 962.1 | 962.4 | 964.0 | 964.4 | 965.0 | 965.6 | 964.9 | 966.0 | 964.5 |
| **RELATIVE HUMIDITY (%)** | | | | | | | | | | | | | | |
| Hour 00 | 26 | 75 | 78 | 78 | 73 | 71 | 74 | 75 | 78 | 79 | 75 | 79 | 79 | 76 |
| Hour 06 (Local Time) | 26 | 76 | 79 | 81 | 80 | 80 | 81 | 82 | 85 | 86 | 81 | 82 | 80 | 81 |
| Hour 12 (Local Time) | 26 | 67 | 68 | 64 | 54 | 53 | 55 | 53 | 55 | 57 | 55 | 65 | 71 | 60 |
| Hour 18 | 26 | 71 | 70 | 63 | 51 | 49 | 51 | 50 | 53 | 57 | 58 | 70 | 75 | 60 |
| **PRECIPITATION (inches):** | | | | | | | | | | | | | | |
| Water Equivalent | | | | | | | | | | | | | | |
| -Normal | | 0.50 | 0.93 | 1.58 | 2.36 | 3.21 | 3.70 | 2.71 | 3.13 | 2.79 | 1.57 | 0.92 | 0.72 | 24.12 |
| -Maximum Monthly | 44 | 1.71 | 4.05 | 3.60 | 5.79 | 7.29 | 8.43 | 7.79 | 9.09 | 9.26 | 5.73 | 2.95 | 2.62 | 9.26 |
| -Year | | 1969 | 1962 | 1977 | 1984 | 1965 | 1984 | 1948 | 1975 | 1986 | 1973 | 1983 | 1968 | SEP 1986 |
| -Minimum Monthly | 44 | 0.05 | 0.05 | 0.14 | 0.17 | 0.61 | 0.91 | 0.25 | 0.53 | 0.29 | T | 0.02 | T | T |
| -Year | | 1958 | 1986 | 1967 | 1969 | 1981 | 1988 | 1947 | 1980 | 1956 | 1952 | 1986 | 1986 | DEC 1986 |
| -Maximum in 24 hrs | 44 | 1.61 | 2.00 | 1.96 | 2.64 | 3.92 | 4.32 | 3.04 | 4.59 | 4.02 | 4.54 | 1.62 | 1.44 | 4.59 |
| -Year | | 1960 | 1962 | 1956 | 1953 | 1972 | 1957 | 1982 | 1975 | 1966 | 1973 | 1972 | 1955 | AUG 1975 |
| Snow,Ice pellets | | | | | | | | | | | | | | |
| -Maximum Monthly | 44 | 19.6 | 48.4 | 31.5 | 18.4 | 0.2 | 0.0 | 0.0 | 0.0 | 0.9 | 5.1 | 21.9 | 41.1 | 48.4 |
| -Year | | 1969 | 1962 | 1951 | 1983 | 1954 | | | | 1985 | 1970 | 1985 | 1968 | FEB 1962 |
| -Maximum in 24 hrs | 44 | 11.8 | 26.0 | 18.9 | 9.0 | 0.2 | 0.0 | 0.0 | 0.0 | 0.9 | 5.0 | 11.8 | 16.6 | 26.0 |
| -Year | | 1960 | 1962 | 1956 | 1957 | 1954 | | | | 1985 | 1970 | 1979 | 1968 | FEB 1962 |
| **WIND:** | | | | | | | | | | | | | | |
| Mean Speed (mph) | 41 | 11.1 | 11.1 | 12.5 | 13.2 | 11.9 | 10.6 | 9.8 | 9.8 | 10.2 | 10.7 | 11.5 | 10.7 | 11.1 |
| Prevailing Direction | | | | | | | | | | | | | | |
| through 1963 | | NW | NW | NW | NW | S | S | S | S | S | S | NW | NW | S |
| Fastest Obs. 1 Min. | | | | | | | | | | | | | | |
| -Direction (!!) | 41 | 31 | 30 | 02 | 25 | 11 | 23 | 36 | 29 | 16 | 27 | 36 | 36 | 23 |
| -Speed (MPH) | 41 | 45 | 44 | 60 | 48 | 46 | 70 | 69 | 52 | 50 | 60 | 52 | 46 | 70 |
| -Year | | 1975 | 1972 | 1950 | 1955 | 1950 | 1952 | 1982 | 1956 | 1953 | 1949 | 1975 | 1982 | JUN 1952 |
| Peak Gust | | | | | | | | | | | | | | |
| -Direction (!!) | 6 | W | NW | N | SW | NW | NW | NW | E | NW | NW | W | W | SW |
| -Speed (mph) | 6 | 48 | 55 | 52 | 64 | 53 | 52 | 64 | 47 | 46 | 53 | 58 | 52 | 64 |
| -Date | | 1989 | 1984 | 1989 | 1985 | 1985 | 1986 | 1984 | 1986 | 1988 | 1984 | 1986 | 1988 | APR 1985 |

**See Reference Notes to this table on the following page.**

PRECIPITATION (inches)    SIOUX FALLS, SOUTH DAKOTA

**TABLE 2**

| YEAR | JAN | FEB | MAR | APR | MAY | JUNE | JULY | AUG | SEP | OCT | NOV | DEC | ANNUAL |
|------|-----|-----|-----|-----|-----|------|------|-----|-----|-----|-----|-----|--------|
| 1961 | 0.25 | 0.92 | 1.14 | 1.04 | 4.67 | 3.86 | 2.16 | 1.79 | 2.36 | 2.66 | 1.40 | 0.80 | 23.05 |
| 1962 | 0.29 | 4.05 | 1.72 | 1.70 | 6.07 | 3.98 | 5.50 | 2.77 | 3.58 | 0.46 | 0.16 | 0.19 | 30.47 |
| 1963 | 0.90 | 0.53 | 1.16 | 1.25 | 2.00 | 2.51 | 6.45 | 0.94 | 2.40 | 1.65 | 0.36 | 0.85 | 21.00 |
| 1964 | 0.34 | 0.08 | 2.12 | 4.03 | 1.29 | 1.68 | 4.03 | 3.87 | 4.06 | 0.09 | 0.38 | 0.59 | 22.56 |
| 1965 | 0.24 | 1.46 | 1.09 | 3.35 | 7.29 | 4.91 | 1.49 | 1.29 | 4.91 | 1.05 | | 0.60 | 27.94 |
| 1966 | 0.54 | 0.99 | 0.70 | 1.71 | 1.94 | 2.68 | 1.54 | 2.12 | 6.34 | 1.43 | 0.20 | 0.65 | 20.84 |
| 1967 | 0.75 | 0.44 | 0.14 | 3.90 | 0.72 | 4.26 | 0.53 | 3.46 | 0.87 | 0.39 | 0.03 | 0.91 | 16.40 |
| 1968 | 0.33 | 0.09 | 4.34 | 2.69 | 4.10 | 4.10 | 2.37 | 1.70 | 4.01 | 4.57 | 0.39 | 2.62 | 27.82 |
| 1969 | 1.71 | 2.55 | 1.09 | 0.17 | 2.43 | 4.85 | 2.73 | 5.07 | 2.41 | 2.05 | 0.34 | 1.18 | 26.58 |
| 1970 | 0.37 | 0.10 | 2.03 | 3.75 | 4.83 | 3.81 | 2.98 | 0.53 | 3.14 | 3.13 | 2.17 | 0.54 | 27.38 |
| 1971 | 0.13 | 0.90 | 0.85 | 1.59 | 1.06 | 6.10 | 2.92 | 0.71 | 3.23 | 3.06 | 2.45 | 0.64 | 23.64 |
| 1972 | 0.18 | 0.40 | 0.97 | 2.73 | 7.25 | 2.09 | 3.49 | 2.65 | 1.75 | 1.78 | 1.89 | 1.25 | 26.43 |
| 1973 | 0.43 | 0.43 | 3.52 | 2.12 | 1.93 | 2.38 | 3.50 | 1.05 | 5.61 | 5.73 | 1.01 | 0.48 | 28.19 |
| 1974 | 0.13 | 0.30 | 1.65 | 1.33 | 3.11 | 2.79 | 1.27 | 5.16 | 0.58 | 0.34 | 0.27 | 0.10 | 17.03 |
| 1975 | 1.35 | 0.22 | 1.95 | 2.45 | 1.66 | 4.48 | 0.62 | 9.09 | 1.35 | 0.49 | 2.25 | 0.19 | 26.10 |
| 1976 | 0.41 | 0.48 | 1.60 | 2.15 | 1.02 | 1.02 | 1.53 | 1.31 | 0.76 | 0.71 | 0.07 | 0.36 | 11.42 |
| 1977 | 0.19 | 0.83 | 3.60 | 2.17 | 3.17 | 1.73 | 3.64 | 5.63 | 2.36 | 1.80 | 0.87 | 0.51 | 31.62 |
| 1978 | 0.47 | 0.33 | 0.56 | 3.98 | 3.47 | 2.91 | 4.79 | 3.08 | 2.45 | 0.14 | 0.48 | 0.04 | 23.17 |
| 1979 | 1.14 | 0.41 | 3.47 | 2.75 | 4.90 | 3.01 | 3.13 | 4.35 | 4.03 | 3.30 | 1.72 | 0.04 | 32.25 |
| 1980 | 0.18 | 0.47 | 0.70 | 0.77 | 2.52 | 2.17 | 1.63 | 2.92 | 0.79 | 1.36 | 0.02 | 0.29 | 13.82 |
| 1981 | 0.12 | 0.33 | 1.86 | 0.58 | 0.61 | 3.90 | 3.89 | 2.28 | 0.50 | 2.45 | 1.21 | 0.38 | 18.11 |
| 1982 | 0.76 | 0.13 | 1.17 | 1.87 | 4.72 | 1.18 | 4.60 | 5.23 | 3.49 | 5.18 | 2.94 | 1.99 | 33.26 |
| 1983 | 0.52 | 0.22 | 3.35 | 2.88 | 2.92 | 6.75 | 1.82 | 2.00 | 1.92 | 0.71 | 2.95 | 0.73 | 26.77 |
| 1984 | 0.37 | 1.10 | 1.83 | 5.79 | 2.95 | 8.43 | 1.63 | 0.76 | 1.62 | 4.11 | 0.03 | 1.02 | 29.64 |
| 1985 | 0.45 | 0.05 | 2.37 | 5.18 | 3.29 | 2.52 | 2.70 | 4.07 | 3.34 | 0.75 | 1.97 | 0.47 | 27.16 |
| 1986 | 0.72 | 0.05 | 1.50 | 5.15 | 2.42 | 3.93 | 2.59 | 2.77 | 9.26 | 1.22 | 0.89 | T | 30.50 |
| 1987 | 0.19 | 0.26 | 3.27 | 0.28 | 2.94 | 1.78 | 3.16 | 1.36 | 2.05 | 0.31 | 1.66 | 1.40 | 18.66 |
| 1988 | 1.54 | 0.25 | 0.63 | 3.00 | 1.54 | 0.91 | 0.49 | 4.02 | 4.39 | 0.02 | 1.98 | 0.37 | 19.14 |
| 1989 | 0.23 | 0.51 | 1.07 | 1.59 | 1.42 | 2.50 | 1.37 | 2.46 | 3.38 | 0.10 | 0.91 | 0.25 | 15.79 |
| 1990 | 0.08 | 0.31 | 1.57 | 1.86 | 4.07 | 4.86 | 1.77 | 1.17 | 0.47 | 1.82 | 0.61 | 0.61 | 19.20 |
| Record Mean | 0.60 | 0.75 | 1.44 | 2.50 | 3.47 | 4.10 | 2.94 | 3.08 | 2.73 | 1.57 | 1.05 | 0.72 | 24.97 |

**TABLE 3**   AVERAGE TEMPERATURE (deg. F)    SIOUX FALLS, SOUTH DAKOTA

| YEAR | JAN | FEB | MAR | APR | MAY | JUNE | JULY | AUG | SEP | OCT | NOV | DEC | ANNUAL |
|------|-----|-----|-----|-----|-----|------|------|-----|-----|-----|-----|-----|--------|
| 1961 | 14.2 | 23.6 | 35.6 | 41.9 | 55.0 | 68.8 | 72.2 | 74.0 | 59.3 | 51.3 | 33.4 | 16.0 | 45.5 |
| 1962 | 12.8 | 17.2 | 24.6 | 45.7 | 63.0 | 67.6 | 70.7 | 71.3 | 59.4 | 52.7 | 38.6 | 22.7 | 45.6 |
| #1963 | 6.7 | 19.8 | 38.9 | 49.4 | 59.4 | 73.5 | 70.8 | 64.3 | 58.1 | 39.2 | 13.2 | 15.5 | 47.4 |
| 1964 | 23.0 | 26.9 | 26.6 | 48.1 | 61.6 | 70.1 | 77.3 | 68.3 | 59.3 | 48.7 | 32.7 | 15.5 | 46.5 |
| 1965 | 12.0 | 13.0 | 21.7 | 45.9 | 59.0 | 65.5 | 70.8 | 69.4 | 51.5 | 51.7 | 32.8 | 28.4 | 43.5 |
| 1966 | 5.1 | 17.3 | 37.7 | 41.1 | 54.3 | 68.5 | 78.7 | 68.8 | 59.9 | 48.3 | 31.0 | 19.4 | 44.2 |
| 1967 | 17.6 | 15.3 | 37.1 | 46.0 | 53.1 | 66.3 | 71.7 | 69.9 | 61.3 | 47.2 | 32.7 | 21.9 | 45.0 |
| 1968 | 16.8 | 18.9 | 39.8 | 47.8 | 52.6 | 69.6 | 71.8 | 72.7 | 61.0 | 49.4 | 33.5 | 16.2 | 45.9 |
| 1969 | 8.8 | 19.0 | 20.5 | 48.4 | 59.6 | 61.4 | 73.5 | 73.3 | 62.3 | 43.4 | 19.5 | 19.5 | 43.6 |
| 1970 | 4.7 | 19.4 | 26.4 | 44.8 | 59.9 | 69.0 | 73.3 | 72.5 | 61.9 | 46.2 | 32.0 | 15.6 | 43.8 |
| 1971 | 8.3 | 18.8 | 31.2 | 47.8 | 55.3 | 71.3 | 69.3 | 73.0 | 61.5 | 51.7 | 17.4 | 17.4 | 44.9 |
| 1972 | 8.9 | 11.5 | 31.5 | 43.8 | 59.1 | 66.7 | 70.2 | 70.5 | 59.5 | 44.4 | 31.9 | 14.8 | 42.7 |
| 1973 | 18.5 | 23.1 | 39.7 | 46.4 | 56.9 | 68.9 | 74.4 | 76.7 | 60.1 | 52.9 | 34.7 | 17.1 | 47.5 |
| 1974 | 12.8 | 24.3 | 34.5 | 48.9 | 55.7 | 65.9 | 79.2 | 67.6 | 57.7 | 51.4 | 33.9 | 23.6 | 46.3 |
| 1975 | 17.1 | 16.5 | 25.5 | 41.4 | 61.1 | 67.6 | 78.5 | 72.7 | 57.0 | 52.1 | 33.5 | 20.4 | 45.3 |
| 1976 | 15.6 | 29.5 | 34.8 | 51.0 | 57.1 | 71.5 | 76.7 | 75.2 | 62.9 | 44.3 | 27.6 | 16.6 | 46.9 |
| 1977 | 4.7 | 25.6 | 36.0 | 53.8 | 66.8 | 71.1 | 77.0 | 68.1 | 61.9 | 47.7 | 31.3 | 16.3 | 46.7 |
| 1978 | 1.9 | 8.6 | 30.5 | 44.3 | 57.7 | 66.6 | 70.9 | 71.1 | 66.7 | 47.8 | 31.3 | 14.6 | 42.7 |
| 1979 | 1.8 | 7.5 | 28.2 | 44.1 | 55.2 | 67.8 | 74.0 | 69.9 | 64.3 | 48.2 | 30.2 | 27.1 | 43.2 |
| 1980 | 18.1 | 18.1 | 31.7 | 50.1 | 58.4 | 68.8 | 74.2 | 71.1 | 62.0 | 45.5 | 36.7 | 21.2 | 46.3 |
| 1981 | 22.3 | 26.0 | 38.4 | 53.5 | 58.3 | 70.4 | 75.5 | 71.1 | 63.0 | 48.7 | 39.5 | 18.0 | 48.8 |
| 1982 | 3.8 | 20.2 | 32.8 | 43.9 | 59.6 | 62.6 | 74.4 | 71.3 | 60.0 | 48.8 | 30.3 | 24.5 | 44.3 |
| 1983 | 20.1 | 26.2 | 33.1 | 41.5 | 55.1 | 66.7 | 77.1 | 78.3 | 63.5 | 49.6 | 34.9 | 2.1 | 45.7 |
| 1984 | 17.4 | 27.8 | 24.6 | 45.8 | 55.9 | 68.1 | 73.6 | 74.2 | 57.2 | 50.4 | 36.2 | 20.4 | 46.0 |
| 1985 | 13.4 | 19.9 | 37.8 | 52.8 | 62.7 | 64.2 | 71.5 | 66.3 | 58.2 | 46.6 | 20.7 | 9.5 | 43.6 |
| 1986 | 20.7 | 16.9 | 36.9 | 48.2 | 58.8 | 69.6 | 75.0 | 66.5 | 59.6 | 48.6 | 28.7 | 25.2 | 46.2 |
| 1987 | 24.0 | 32.8 | 37.8 | 52.6 | 64.9 | 71.4 | 77.0 | 68.8 | 62.6 | 43.9 | 38.1 | 24.4 | 49.9 |
| 1988 | 9.6 | 15.0 | 36.4 | 46.4 | 65.1 | 76.3 | 77.4 | 74.8 | 62.6 | 44.6 | 34.2 | 22.1 | 47.0 |
| 1989 | 25.5 | 9.2 | 29.8 | 47.8 | 58.0 | 66.9 | 77.3 | 72.0 | 60.2 | 49.5 | 29.5 | 11.5 | 44.8 |
| 1990 | 28.2 | 24.9 | 36.7 | 46.4 | 56.4 | 70.1 | 71.2 | 72.9 | 66.5 | 48.0 | 35.6 | 15.3 | 47.7 |
| Record Mean | 15.1 | 20.4 | 32.2 | 47.2 | 58.9 | 68.5 | 74.3 | 71.8 | 61.8 | 49.9 | 33.3 | 20.1 | 46.2 |
| Max | 25.1 | 30.4 | 42.1 | 59.0 | 71.1 | 80.4 | 86.4 | 83.6 | 73.7 | 61.8 | 43.1 | 29.5 | 57.2 |
| Min | 5.1 | 10.4 | 22.3 | 35.4 | 46.7 | 56.6 | 62.3 | 60.0 | 49.9 | 37.9 | 23.4 | 10.8 | 35.1 |

### REFERENCE NOTES FOR TABLES 1, 2, 3 and 6    (SIOUX FALLS, SD)

**GENERAL**

T - TRACE AMOUNT
BLANK ENTRIES DENOTE MISSING/UNREPORTED DATA.
# INDICATES A STATION OR INSTRUMENT RELOCATION.

**SPECIFIC**

TABLE 1

(a) - LENGTH OF RECORD IN YEARS. ALTHOUGH
INDIVIDUAL MONTHS MAY BE MISSING.
* LESS THAN .05

NORMALS — BASED ON THE 1951-1980 RECORD PERIOD.
EXTREMES — DATES ARE THE MOST RECENT OCCURRENCE.
WIND DIR. — NUMERALS SHOW TENS OF DEGREES
CLOCKWISE FROM TRUE NORTH.
"00" INDICATES CALM.
RESULTANT WIND DIRECTIONS ARE GIVEN TO WHOLE DEGREES.

TABLE 3
MAX AND MIN ARE LONG-TERM MEAN DAILY MAXIMUM
AND MEAN DAILY MINIMUM TEMPERATURES.

**EXCEPTIONS**

TABLES 2, 3, and 6

RECORD MEANS ARE THROUGH THE CURRENT YEAR,
BEGINNING IN    1921 FOR TEMPERATURE
1891 FOR PRECIPITATION
1946 FOR SNOWFALL

**TABLE 4**  HEATING DEGREE DAYS Base 65 deg. F   SIOUX FALLS, SOUTH DAKOTA

| SEASON | JULY | AUG | SEP | OCT | NOV | DEC | JAN | FEB | MAR | APR | MAY | JUNE | TOTAL |
|---|---|---|---|---|---|---|---|---|---|---|---|---|---|
| 1961-62 | 0 | 5 | 236 | 422 | 943 | 1512 | 1616 | 1333 | 1245 | 593 | 117 | 42 | 8064 |
| 1962-63 | 18 | 5 | 191 | 391 | 786 | 1305 | 1809 | 1261 | 803 | 467 | 203 | 7 | 7246 |
| #1963-64 | 0 | 24 | 92 | 222 | 767 | 1603 | 1299 | 1101 | 1181 | 509 | 174 | 47 | 7019 |
| 1964-65 | 0 | 55 | 210 | 499 | 965 | 1528 | 1639 | 1452 | 1340 | 568 | 195 | 41 | 8492 |
| 1965-66 | 2 | 37 | 405 | 408 | 964 | 1129 | 1856 | 1331 | 838 | 709 | 343 | 49 | 8071 |
| 1966-67 | 0 | 41 | 188 | 508 | 1016 | 1406 | 1462 | 1385 | 858 | 563 | 399 | 37 | 7863 |
| 1967-68 | 36 | 32 | 141 | 549 | 963 | 1328 | 1490 | 1331 | 776 | 511 | 380 | 53 | 7590 |
| 1968-69 | 14 | 14 | 152 | 489 | 938 | 1511 | 1742 | 1283 | 1373 | 493 | 217 | 143 | 8369 |
| 1969-70 | 2 | 2 | 117 | 668 | 941 | 1404 | 1867 | 1274 | 1192 | 603 | 206 | 46 | 8322 |
| 1970-71 | 16 | 3 | 195 | 577 | 986 | 1526 | 1754 | 1288 | 1041 | 511 | 297 | 17 | 8211 |
| 1971-72 | 29 | 12 | 177 | 409 | 945 | 1470 | 1737 | 1551 | 1031 | 628 | 236 | 50 | 8275 |
| 1972-73 | 29 | 43 | 194 | 631 | 984 | 1555 | 1440 | 1166 | 775 | 549 | 256 | 19 | 7641 |
| 1973-74 | 1 | 0 | 178 | 373 | 902 | 1481 | 1616 | 1133 | 939 | 477 | 303 | 85 | 7488 |
| 1974-75 | 2 | 39 | 240 | 419 | 927 | 1279 | 1476 | 1351 | 1217 | 701 | 157 | 51 | 7859 |
| 1975-76 | 3 | 5 | 271 | 407 |  |  | 1377 | 1023 | 929 | 418 | 261 | 23 |  |
| 1976-77 | 1 | 0 | 142 | 643 | 1114 | 1495 | 1867 | 1097 | 891 | 341 | 38 | 4 | 7633 |
| 1977-78 | 0 | 22 | 125 | 530 | 1000 | 1503 | 1957 | 1576 | 1063 | 613 | 252 | 78 | 8719 |
| 1978-79 | 11 | 18 | 104 | 525 | 1004 | 1554 | 1960 | 1607 | 1134 | 622 | 321 | 40 | 8900 |
| 1979-80 | 0 | 28 | 103 | 512 | 1038 | 1168 | 1448 | 1349 | 1027 | 464 | 243 | 32 | 7412 |
| 1980-81 | 1 | 14 | 157 | 602 | 841 | 1354 | 1318 | 1087 | 816 | 353 | 230 | 5 | 6778 |
| 1981-82 | 5 | 5 | 114 | 497 | 758 | 1452 | 1899 | 1247 | 991 | 632 | 174 | 105 | 7879 |
| 1982-83 | 0 | 28 | 188 | 494 | 1035 | 1249 | 1385 | 1082 | 982 | 699 | 317 | 67 | 7526 |
| 1983-84 | 1 | 0 | 160 | 476 | 894 | 1947 | 1468 | 1072 | 1247 | 569 | 285 | 23 | 8142 |
| 1984-85 | 2 | 12 | 265 | 451 | 857 | 1376 | 1594 | 1260 | 836 | 378 | 124 | 101 | 7256 |
| 1985-86 | 5 | 44 | 269 | 562 | 1327 | 1721 | 1363 | 1341 | 865 | 498 | 204 | 17 | 8216 |
| 1986-87 | 0 | 54 | 180 | 504 | 1082 | 1227 | 1265 | 896 | 835 | 387 | 96 | 23 | 6549 |
| 1987-88 | 5 | 54 | 110 | 649 | 801 | 1252 | 1715 | 1448 | 878 | 554 | 83 | 1 | 7550 |
| 1988-89 | 0 | 22 | 126 | 628 | 916 | 1321 | 1219 | 1559 | 1083 | 514 | 235 | 61 | 7684 |
| 1989-90 | 0 | 5 | 192 | 481 | 1056 | 1655 | 1131 | 1117 | 871 | 586 | 268 | 39 | 7401 |
| 1990-91 | 11 | 7 | 109 | 527 | 875 | 1538 |  |  |  |  |  |  |  |

**TABLE 5**  COOLING DEGREE DAYS Base 65 deg. F   SIOUX FALLS, SOUTH DAKOTA

| YEAR | JAN | FEB | MAR | APR | MAY | JUNE | JULY | AUG | SEP | OCT | NOV | DEC | TOTAL |
|---|---|---|---|---|---|---|---|---|---|---|---|---|---|
| 1969 | 0 | 0 | 0 | 0 | 58 | 43 | 270 | 265 | 41 | 4 | 0 | 0 | 681 |
| 1970 | 0 | 0 | 0 | 6 | 54 | 172 | 280 | 241 | 108 | 2 | 0 | 0 | 863 |
| 1971 | 0 | 0 | 0 | 4 | 1 | 211 | 167 | 268 | 79 | 2 | 0 | 0 | 732 |
| 1972 | 0 | 0 | 0 | 0 | 60 | 108 | 197 | 219 | 35 | 0 | 0 | 0 | 619 |
| 1973 | 0 | 0 | 0 | 0 | 13 | 143 | 300 | 370 | 38 | 8 | 0 | 0 | 872 |
| 1974 | 0 | 0 | 0 | 2 | 23 | 118 | 450 | 126 | 26 | 6 | 0 | 0 | 751 |
| 1975 | 0 | 0 | 0 | 0 | 44 | 134 | 428 | 252 | 36 | 16 | 0 | 0 | 910 |
| 1976 | 0 | 0 | 0 | 2 | 24 | 226 | 370 | 324 | 85 | 9 | 0 | 0 | 1040 |
| 1977 | 0 | 0 | 0 | 11 | 101 | 197 | 382 | 123 | 40 | 0 | 0 | 0 | 854 |
| 1978 | 0 | 0 | 0 | 0 | 32 | 133 | 202 | 213 | 163 | 0 | 0 | 0 | 743 |
| 1979 | 0 | 0 | 0 | 3 | 25 | 131 | 289 | 189 | 87 | 0 | 0 | 0 | 724 |
| 1980 | 0 | 0 | 0 | 23 | 46 | 153 | 290 | 207 | 74 | 6 | 0 | 0 | 799 |
| 1981 | 0 | 0 | 0 | 14 | 27 | 175 | 342 | 203 | 61 | 0 | 0 | 0 | 822 |
| 1982 | 0 | 0 | 0 | 4 | 12 | 42 | 298 | 230 | 45 | 0 | 0 | 0 | 631 |
| 1983 | 0 | 0 | 0 | 0 | 15 | 122 | 381 | 420 | 120 | 2 | 0 | 0 | 1060 |
| 1984 | 0 | 0 | 0 | 0 | 10 | 120 | 276 | 305 | 36 | 4 | 0 | 0 | 751 |
| 1985 | 0 | 0 | 0 | 19 | 59 | 85 | 212 | 93 | 72 | 0 | 0 | 0 | 540 |
| 1986 | 0 | 0 | 0 | 0 | 20 | 163 | 318 | 108 | 25 | 0 | 0 | 0 | 634 |
| 1987 | 0 | 0 | 0 | 20 | 100 | 219 | 381 | 178 | 53 | 0 | 0 | 0 | 951 |
| 1988 | 0 | 0 | 0 | 1 | 94 | 349 | 393 | 330 | 61 | 0 | 0 | 0 | 1228 |
| 1989 | 0 | 0 | 0 | 6 | 25 | 125 | 387 | 228 | 56 | 7 | 0 | 0 | 834 |
| 1990 | 0 | 0 | 0 | 31 | 11 | 198 | 209 | 258 | 160 | 7 | 0 | 0 | 874 |

**TABLE 6**  SNOWFALL (inches)   SIOUX FALLS, SOUTH DAKOTA

| SEASON | JULY | AUG | SEP | OCT | NOV | DEC | JAN | FEB | MAR | APR | MAY | JUNE | TOTAL |
|---|---|---|---|---|---|---|---|---|---|---|---|---|---|
| 1961-62 | 0.0 | 0.0 | T | 0.0 | 1.0 | 7.7 | 3.8 | 48.4 | 14.7 | 4.2 | 0.0 | 0.0 | 79.8 |
| 1962-63 | 0.0 | 0.0 | 0.0 | 0.7 | T | 1.7 | 11.0 | 6.8 | 2.8 | 2.3 | 0.0 | 0.0 | 25.3 |
| 1963-64 | 0.0 | 0.0 | 0.0 | 0.0 | 0.0 | 11.6 | 3.5 | 0.7 | 9.1 | T | 0.0 | 0.0 | 24.9 |
| 1964-65 | 0.0 | 0.0 | 0.0 | 0.0 | 3.9 | 6.5 | 3.3 | 21.1 | 13.3 | 0.4 | 0.0 | 0.0 | 48.5 |
| 1965-66 | 0.0 | 0.0 | 0.0 | 0.0 | 1.6 | 0.1 | 6.2 | 1.8 | 4.6 | 0.9 | T | 0.0 | 15.2 |
| 1966-67 | 0.0 | 0.0 | 0.0 | 0.4 | 2.3 | 9.3 | 6.0 | 11.8 | 1.0 | T | 0.1 | 0.0 | 30.9 |
| 1967-68 | 0.0 | 0.0 | 0.0 | 0.5 | 0.4 | 2.5 | 4.6 | 0.9 | T | 0.1 | 0.1 | 0.0 | 9.1 |
| 1968-69 | 0.0 | 0.0 | 0.0 | 0.7 | 1.9 | 41.1 | 19.6 | 28.5 | 2.9 | 0.0 | 0.0 | 0.0 | 94.7 |
| 1969-70 | 0.0 | 0.0 | 0.0 | T | 2.9 | 15.2 | 5.9 | 1.5 | 19.3 | 3.0 | T | 0.0 | 47.8 |
| 1970-71 | 0.0 | 0.0 | 0.0 | 5.1 | 0.5 | 8.5 | 1.9 | 1.7 | 4.7 | 0.3 | 0.0 | 0.0 | 22.7 |
| 1971-72 | 0.0 | 0.0 | 0.0 | T | 4.4 | 10.6 | 1.8 | 10.6 | 5.0 | 0.8 | 0.0 | 0.0 | 33.2 |
| 1972-73 | 0.0 | 0.0 | 0.0 | 0.2 | 2.5 | 6.2 | 5.5 | 7.4 | 0.3 | T | 0.0 | 0.0 | 22.1 |
| 1973-74 | 0.0 | 0.0 | 0.0 | T | 0.1 | 11.6 | 1.9 | 2.9 | 5.1 | 3.3 | 0.0 | 0.0 | 24.9 |
| 1974-75 | 0.0 | 0.0 | 0.0 | 0.0 | 2.5 | 1.1 | 18.3 | 3.1 | 17.9 | T | 0.0 | 0.0 | 42.9 |
| 1975-76 | 0.0 | 0.0 | 0.0 | T | 13.2 | 2.5 | 6.5 | 6.6 | 7.9 | T | 0.1 | 0.0 | 36.8 |
| 1976-77 | 0.0 | 0.0 | 0.0 | 3.4 | 0.7 | 6.7 | 2.7 | 1.9 | 13.5 | T | 0.0 | 0.0 | 28.9 |
| 1977-78 | 0.0 | 0.0 | 0.0 | 0.9 | 8.6 | 8.0 | 7.6 | 6.5 | 5.5 | 0.6 | 0.0 | 0.0 | 37.7 |
| 1978-79 | 0.0 | 0.0 | 0.0 | 0.0 | 2.9 | 9.5 | 19.0 | 7.3 | 13.2 | 1.5 | 0.0 | 0.0 | 53.4 |
| 1979-80 | 0.0 | 0.0 | 0.0 | T | 15.2 | 0.3 | 2.9 | 5.5 | 5.8 | T | 0.0 | 0.0 | 29.7 |
| 1980-81 | 0.0 | 0.0 | 0.0 | 0.8 | 0.4 | 4.6 | 1.4 | 3.1 | T | 0.5 | 0.0 | 0.0 | 10.8 |
| 1981-82 | 0.0 | 0.0 | 0.0 | 0.8 | 8.9 | 5.5 | 16.9 | 1.0 | 1.8 | 7.5 | 0.0 | 0.0 | 42.4 |
| 1982-83 | 0.0 | 0.0 | 0.0 | 3.3 | 4.1 | 17.6 | 4.7 | 3.6 | 18.8 | 18.4 | 0.0 | 0.0 | 70.5 |
| 1983-84 | 0.0 | 0.0 | T | T | 19.0 | 13.7 | 5.0 | 11.9 | 19.4 | 6.0 | 0.0 | 0.0 | 75.0 |
| 1984-85 | 0.0 | 0.0 | T | T | T | 4.7 | 7.4 | 0.7 | 16.1 | 2.5 | 0.0 | 0.0 | 31.4 |
| 1985-86 | 0.0 | 0.0 | 0.9 | 0.2 | 21.9 | 9.1 | 9.1 | 0.9 | 8.2 | 0.3 | 0.0 | 0.0 | 50.6 |
| 1986-87 | 0.0 | 0.0 | 0.0 | 0.0 | 5.4 | T | 2.4 | 0.3 | T | T | 0.0 | 0.0 | 8.1 |
| 1987-88 | 0.0 | 0.0 | 0.0 | 0.1 | 7.5 | 13.3 | 17.9 | 7.3 | 2.5 | 11.3 | 0.0 | 0.0 | 59.9 |
| 1988-89 | 0.0 | 0.0 | T | T | 10.9 | 2.2 | 2.0 | 10.0 | 16.0 | 0.7 | T | 0.0 | 41.8 |
| 1989-90 | 0.0 | 0.0 | 0.0 | 0.0 | 2.4 | 4.0 | 0.2 | 5.8 | 0.7 | T | T |  | 13.1 |
| 1990-91 | 0.0 | 0.0 | 0.0 | 1.2 | 8.4 | 8.8 |  |  |  |  |  |  |  |
| Record Mean | 0.0 | 0.0 | T | 0.5 | 5.2 | 7.4 | 6.5 | 8.0 | 9.7 | 2.3 | T | T | 39.5 |

**See Reference Notes, relative to all above tables, on preceding page.**

Knoxville is located in a broad valley between the Cumberland Mountains, which lie northwest of the city, and the Great Smoky Mountains, which lie southeast of the city. These two mountain ranges exercise a marked influence upon the climate of the valley. The Cumberland Mountains, to the northwest, serve to retard and weaken the force of the cold winter air which frequently penetrates far south of the latitude of Knoxville over the plains areas to the west of the mountains.

The mountains also serve to modify the hot summer winds which are common to the plains to the west. In addition, they serve as a fixed incline plane which lifts the warm, moist air flowing northward from the Gulf of Mexico and thereby increases the frequency of afternoon thunderstorms. Relief from extremely high temperatures which such thunderstorms produce serves to reduce the number of extremely warm days in the valley.

July is usually the warmest month of the year. The coldest weather usually occurs during the month of January. Sudden great temperature changes occur infrequently. This again is due mainly to the retarding effect of the mountains. Summer nights are nearly always comfortable.

Rainfall is ample for agricultural purposes and is favorably distributed during the year for most crops. Precipitation is greatest in the wintertime. Another peak period occurs during the late spring and summer months. The period of lowest rainfall occurs during the fall. A cumulative total of approximately 12 inches of snow falls annually. However, this usually comes in amounts of less than 4 inches at one time. It is unusual for snow to remain on the ground in measurable amounts longer than one week.

The topography also has a pronounced effect upon the prevailing wind direction. Daytime winds usually have a southwesterly component, while nighttime winds usually move from the northeast. The winds are relatively light and tornadoes are extremely rare.

## TABLE 1  NORMALS, MEANS AND EXTREMES

KNOXVILLE, TENNESSEE

LATITUDE: 35°49'N  LONGITUDE: 83°59'W  ELEVATION: FT. GRND  905 BARO  918  TIME ZONE: EASTERN  WBAN: 13891

| | (a) | JAN | FEB | MAR | APR | MAY | JUNE | JULY | AUG | SEP | OCT | NOV | DEC | YEAR |
|---|---|---|---|---|---|---|---|---|---|---|---|---|---|---|
| **TEMPERATURE °F:** | | | | | | | | | | | | | | |
| Normals | | | | | | | | | | | | | | |
| –Daily Maximum | | 46.9 | 51.2 | 60.1 | 71.0 | 78.3 | 84.6 | 87.2 | 86.9 | 81.7 | 70.9 | 59.1 | 50.3 | 69.0 |
| –Daily Minimum | | 29.5 | 31.7 | 39.3 | 48.2 | 56.5 | 64.0 | 68.0 | 67.1 | 61.2 | 48.1 | 38.4 | 31.9 | 48.7 |
| –Monthly | | 38.2 | 41.5 | 49.7 | 59.6 | 67.4 | 74.3 | 77.6 | 77.0 | 71.5 | 59.5 | 48.8 | 41.1 | 58.9 |
| Extremes | | | | | | | | | | | | | | |
| –Record Highest | 48 | 77 | 83 | 86 | 92 | 94 | 102 | 103 | 102 | 103 | 91 | 84 | 80 | 103 |
| –Year | | 1950 | 1977 | 1963 | 1942 | 1962 | 1988 | 1952 | 1944 | 1954 | 1953 | 1948 | 1982 | SEP 1954 |
| –Record Lowest | 48 | -24 | -2 | 1 | 22 | 32 | 43 | 49 | 49 | 36 | 25 | 5 | -6 | -24 |
| –Year | | 1985 | 1958 | 1980 | 1987 | 1986 | 1956 | 1988 | 1946 | 1967 | 1987 | 1950 | 1983 | JAN 1985 |
| **NORMAL DEGREE DAYS:** | | | | | | | | | | | | | | |
| Heating (base 65°F) | | 831 | 658 | 483 | 181 | 63 | 0 | 0 | 0 | 14 | 201 | 486 | 741 | 3658 |
| Cooling (base 65°F) | | 0 | 0 | 8 | 19 | 137 | 283 | 391 | 372 | 209 | 30 | 0 | 0 | 1449 |
| **% OF POSSIBLE SUNSHINE** | 47 | 41 | 46 | 53 | 62 | 64 | 64 | 63 | 63 | 60 | 60 | 49 | 40 | 55 |
| **MEAN SKY COVER (tenths)** | | | | | | | | | | | | | | |
| Sunrise – Sunset | 47 | 7.1 | 6.7 | 6.6 | 6.1 | 6.1 | 5.8 | 6.0 | 5.6 | 5.6 | 5.0 | 6.2 | 6.8 | 6.1 |
| **MEAN NUMBER OF DAYS:** | | | | | | | | | | | | | | |
| Sunrise to Sunset | | | | | | | | | | | | | | |
| –Clear | 47 | 6.3 | 6.6 | 7.3 | 8.3 | 8.1 | 7.7 | 6.9 | 8.5 | 9.4 | 12.4 | 8.6 | 7.1 | 97.1 |
| –Partly Cloudy | 47 | 6.6 | 6.0 | 7.4 | 8.5 | 9.8 | 12.3 | 12.9 | 12.2 | 9.6 | 7.8 | 6.8 | 6.8 | 106.7 |
| –Cloudy | 47 | 18.1 | 15.6 | 16.3 | 13.2 | 13.1 | 10.1 | 11.2 | 10.3 | 11.0 | 10.8 | 14.6 | 17.1 | 161.5 |
| Precipitation | | | | | | | | | | | | | | |
| .01 inches or more | 47 | 12.4 | 11.4 | 12.5 | 11.0 | 11.0 | 10.2 | 11.4 | 9.5 | 8.3 | 7.8 | 10.1 | 10.8 | 126.4 |
| Snow, Ice pellets | | | | | | | | | | | | | | |
| 1.0 inches or more | 47 | 1.4 | 1.1 | 0.5 | 0.1 | 0.0 | 0.0 | 0.0 | 0.0 | 0.0 | 0.0 | 0.1 | 0.6 | 3.7 |
| Thunderstorms | 47 | 0.8 | 1.4 | 3.3 | 4.3 | 6.7 | 8.2 | 9.7 | 6.9 | 3.0 | 1.4 | 1.0 | 0.5 | 47.2 |
| Heavy Fog Visibility | | | | | | | | | | | | | | |
| 1/4 mile or less | 47 | 3.0 | 1.8 | 1.5 | 1.1 | 2.2 | 2.1 | 2.2 | 3.3 | 4.0 | 4.7 | 3.2 | 2.6 | 31.5 |
| Temperature °F | | | | | | | | | | | | | | |
| –Maximum | | | | | | | | | | | | | | |
| 90° and above | 29 | 0.0 | 0.0 | 0.0 | 0.* | 0.8 | 5.1 | 10.4 | 8.5 | 2.5 | 0.0 | 0.0 | 0.0 | 27.3 |
| 32° and below | 29 | 3.7 | 1.4 | 0.1 | 0.0 | 0.0 | 0.0 | 0.0 | 0.0 | 0.0 | 0.0 | 0.1 | 1.4 | 6.6 |
| –Minimum | | | | | | | | | | | | | | |
| 32° and below | 29 | 21.1 | 16.9 | 8.7 | 1.8 | 0.* | 0.0 | 0.0 | 0.0 | 0.0 | 1.0 | 7.7 | 17.9 | 75.0 |
| 0° and below | 29 | 0.5 | 0.* | 0.0 | 0.0 | 0.0 | 0.0 | 0.0 | 0.0 | 0.0 | 0.0 | 0.0 | 0.1 | 0.7 |
| **AVG. STATION PRESS. (mb)** | 17 | 984.7 | 983.6 | 981.4 | 981.0 | 980.6 | 981.6 | 982.6 | 983.0 | 983.3 | 984.7 | 984.4 | 985.0 | 983.0 |
| **RELATIVE HUMIDITY (%)** | | | | | | | | | | | | | | |
| Hour 01 | 29 | 77 | 74 | 71 | 72 | 82 | 86 | 87 | 88 | 87 | 85 | 80 | 78 | 81 |
| Hour 07 | 29 | 81 | 79 | 80 | 81 | 86 | 88 | 90 | 92 | 92 | 89 | 84 | 82 | 85 |
| Hour 13 (Local Time) | 29 | 63 | 59 | 54 | 51 | 57 | 59 | 61 | 61 | 60 | 55 | 59 | 63 | 59 |
| Hour 19 | 29 | 66 | 60 | 55 | 52 | 60 | 62 | 65 | 66 | 68 | 64 | 67 | 68 | 63 |
| **PRECIPITATION (inches):** | | | | | | | | | | | | | | |
| Water Equivalent | | | | | | | | | | | | | | |
| –Normal | | 4.65 | 4.18 | 5.49 | 3.87 | 3.71 | 3.95 | 4.33 | 3.02 | 2.99 | 2.73 | 3.78 | 4.59 | 47.29 |
| –Maximum Monthly | 48 | 11.74 | 9.38 | 10.42 | 7.20 | 10.98 | 8.21 | 10.09 | 8.88 | 9.19 | 6.67 | 10.36 | 11.63 | 11.74 |
| –Year | | 1954 | 1944 | 1975 | 1970 | 1974 | 1989 | 1967 | 1942 | 1989 | 1949 | 1948 | 1961 | JAN 1954 |
| –Minimum Monthly | 48 | 0.95 | 0.74 | 1.69 | 0.39 | 0.74 | 0.20 | 0.70 | 0.77 | 0.42 | T | 0.97 | 0.45 | T |
| –Year | | 1986 | 1968 | 1986 | 1976 | 1970 | 1944 | 1957 | 1954 | 1985 | 1963 | 1942 | 1965 | OCT 1963 |
| –Maximum in 24 hrs | 48 | 3.89 | 2.89 | 4.85 | 3.65 | 3.40 | 3.57 | 4.69 | 3.25 | 5.08 | 2.44 | 4.06 | 4.89 | 5.08 |
| –Year | | 1946 | 1956 | 1973 | 1977 | 1984 | 1972 | 1942 | 1959 | 1944 | 1961 | 1948 | 1969 | SEP 1944 |
| Snow, Ice pellets | | | | | | | | | | | | | | |
| –Maximum Monthly | 48 | 15.1 | 23.3 | 20.2 | 10.7 | T | 0.0 | 0.0 | 0.0 | 0.0 | T | 18.2 | 12.2 | 23.3 |
| –Year | | 1962 | 1960 | 1960 | 1987 | 1945 | | | | | 1989 | 1952 | 1963 | FEB 1960 |
| –Maximum in 24 hrs | 48 | 12.0 | 17.5 | 12.1 | 10.7 | T | 0.0 | 0.0 | 0.0 | 0.0 | T | 18.2 | 8.9 | 18.2 |
| –Year | | 1962 | 1960 | 1942 | 1987 | 1945 | | | | | 1989 | 1952 | 1969 | NOV 1952 |
| **WIND:** | | | | | | | | | | | | | | |
| Mean Speed (mph) | 47 | 7.9 | 8.3 | 8.8 | 8.7 | 7.0 | 6.5 | 6.1 | 5.6 | 5.8 | 5.8 | 6.9 | 7.4 | 7.1 |
| Prevailing Direction through 1963 | | NE | NE | NE | WSW | SW | SW | WSW | NE | NE | NE | NE | NE | NE |
| Fastest Obs. 1 Min. | | | | | | | | | | | | | | |
| –Direction (!!!) | 15 | 27 | 26 | 22 | 29 | 30 | 07 | 36 | 32 | 36 | 27 | 23 | 20 | 23 |
| –Speed (MPH) | 15 | 35 | 32 | 36 | 39 | 31 | 35 | 35 | 29 | 26 | 28 | 40 | 39 | 40 |
| –Year | | 1978 | 1977 | 1977 | 1988 | 1989 | 1975 | 1985 | 1983 | 1989 | 1988 | 1988 | 1988 | NOV 1988 |
| Peak Gust | | | | | | | | | | | | | | |
| –Direction (!!!) | 5 | SW | SW | W | W | W | NW | NE | N | W | SW | W | SW | W |
| –Speed (mph) | 5 | 46 | 44 | 53 | 59 | 48 | 58 | 46 | 44 | 39 | 39 | 64 | 58 | 64 |
| –Date | 5 | 1989 | 1984 | 1989 | 1985 | 1989 | 1989 | 1985 | 1989 | 1989 | 1988 | 1988 | 1988 | NOV 1988 |

**See Reference Notes to this table on the following page.**

## PRECIPITATION (inches)  —  KNOXVILLE, TENNESSEE

**TABLE 2**

| YEAR | JAN | FEB | MAR | APR | MAY | JUNE | JULY | AUG | SEP | OCT | NOV | DEC | ANNUAL |
|---|---|---|---|---|---|---|---|---|---|---|---|---|---|
| 1961 | 2.55 | 7.82 | 7.80 | 2.50 | 4.18 | 4.54 | 3.49 | 3.04 | 0.50 | 3.41 | 3.04 | 11.64 | 54.51 |
| 1962 | 6.22 | 7.96 | 4.13 | 3.84 | 1.88 | 5.05 | 7.82 | 2.08 | 5.13 | 2.20 | 4.60 | 2.86 | 54.58 |
| 1963 | 4.20 | 3.54 | 9.92 | 3.63 | 3.32 | 4.92 | 3.64 | 5.75 | 2.37 | T | 5.23 | 4.02 | 48.14 |
| 1964 | 4.71 | 4.09 | 5.75 | 6.98 | 3.96 | 0.97 | 3.70 | 5.75 | 1.10 | 2.10 | 2.80 | 2.50 | 45.93 |
| 1965 | 3.94 | 3.25 | 9.31 | 4.16 | 3.13 | 4.84 | 3.49 | 2.18 | 2.48 | 1.08 | 2.50 | 0.45 | 40.81 |
| 1966 | 3.88 | 4.68 | 2.72 | 2.88 | 2.92 | 2.27 | 5.44 | 4.09 | 4.41 | 4.80 | 5.12 | 2.66 | 45.87 |
| 1967 | 2.67 | 4.58 | 4.08 | 2.00 | 4.10 | 6.53 | 10.09 | 4.06 | 2.70 | 2.33 | 5.57 | 6.95 | 55.66 |
| 1968 | 4.13 | 0.74 | 4.78 | 4.12 | 3.01 | 3.97 | 2.57 | 1.29 | 2.53 | 3.40 | 2.00 | 3.22 | 35.76 |
| 1969 | 4.11 | 5.54 | 2.89 | 2.41 | 1.33 | 7.58 | 3.51 | 6.72 | 3.03 | 1.56 | 2.56 | 7.74 | 48.98 |
| 1970 | 3.04 | 2.86 | 3.18 | 7.20 | 0.74 | 4.26 | 3.11 | 4.89 | 2.75 | 5.33 | 1.40 | 4.67 | 43.43 |
| 1971 | 5.03 | 4.93 | 4.21 | 3.87 | 3.78 | 3.73 | 8.76 | 3.05 | 3.41 | 1.98 | 2.21 | 5.48 | 50.44 |
| 1972 | 7.35 | 4.19 | 4.98 | 2.54 | 4.49 | 5.02 | 6.76 | 1.61 | 4.70 | 5.99 | 3.36 | 7.02 | 58.01 |
| 1973 | 3.24 | 2.59 | 10.24 | 5.15 | 5.71 | 5.26 | 4.38 | 2.31 | 3.28 | 3.48 | 5.01 | 7.38 | 58.03 |
| 1974 | 7.05 | 5.24 | 6.15 | 5.77 | 10.98 | 2.70 | 2.92 | 3.14 | 3.33 | 2.35 | 5.18 | 4.52 | 59.33 |
| 1975 | 4.66 | 4.68 | 10.42 | 2.43 | 2.98 | 2.43 | 2.25 | 1.61 | 3.28 | 4.02 | 2.92 | 3.59 | 45.27 |
| 1976 | 3.86 | 2.18 | 5.22 | 0.39 | 5.53 | 3.46 | 3.75 | 1.98 | 2.87 | 5.33 | 3.45 | 4.42 | 42.44 |
| 1977 | 2.55 | 1.52 | 6.08 | 6.96 | 1.16 | 6.49 | 1.08 | 5.78 | 6.91 | 4.04 | 3.62 | 3.30 | 50.93 |
| 1978 | 5.22 | 1.01 | 4.42 | 4.10 | 3.44 | 5.27 | 5.06 | 2.44 | 1.26 | 0.82 | 5.73 | 5.91 | 42.57 |
| 1979 | 6.18 | 4.17 | 4.21 | 4.30 | 7.21 | 3.80 | 9.47 | 2.29 | 2.64 | 1.97 | 1.92 | 1.78 | 53.89 |
| 1980 | 5.54 | 1.78 | 8.72 | 3.30 | 3.80 | 1.94 | 3.57 | 2.34 | 2.38 | 1.53 | 3.78 | 1.78 | 40.46 |
| 1981 | 1.05 | 3.62 | 2.83 | 4.84 | 3.02 | 5.53 | 2.03 | 3.48 | 6.09 | 4.15 | 3.01 | 4.14 | 43.79 |
| 1982 | 6.03 | 4.88 | 3.26 | 3.26 | 5.52 | 3.93 | 6.60 | 2.68 | 2.68 | 2.66 | 5.21 | 4.89 | 54.70 |
| 1983 | 1.58 | 2.90 | 1.99 | 5.88 | 5.42 | 3.26 | 3.18 | 3.89 | 0.95 | 3.34 | 4.40 | 5.69 | 42.48 |
| 1984 | 2.26 | 4.42 | 3.79 | 3.37 | 10.14 | 4.34 | 9.03 | 1.72 | 0.85 | 3.26 | 2.87 | 2.49 | 48.54 |
| 1985 | 3.17 | 4.11 | 1.98 | 2.86 | 1.60 | 4.77 | 2.63 | 4.07 | 0.42 | 3.04 | 5.39 | 2.36 | 36.40 |
| 1986 | 0.95 | 3.90 | 1.69 | 2.25 | 2.40 | 0.69 | 1.89 | 3.37 | 3.59 | 3.84 | 3.83 | 4.08 | 32.48 |
| 1987 | 4.68 | 4.63 | 2.91 | 2.18 | 4.62 | 2.66 | 4.67 | 1.08 | 1.93 | 0.60 | 1.21 | 3.49 | 34.66 |
| 1988 | 4.29 | 2.94 | 2.42 | 2.34 | 2.35 | 0.51 | 3.60 | 3.20 | 2.68 | 1.52 | 4.82 | 3.99 | 34.66 |
| 1989 | 4.96 | 6.26 | 3.82 | 3.50 | 5.31 | 8.21 | 2.68 | 3.16 | 9.19 | 1.47 | 4.92 | 2.74 | 56.22 |
| 1990 | 5.88 | 6.90 | 5.73 | 2.56 | 4.71 | 1.72 | 7.56 | 3.02 | 2.68 | 3.64 | 1.77 | 8.99 | 55.16 |
| Record Mean | 4.57 | 4.54 | 5.07 | 4.07 | 3.83 | 4.02 | 4.51 | 3.62 | 2.86 | 2.65 | 3.41 | 4.38 | 47.53 |

**TABLE 3**  —  AVERAGE TEMPERATURE (deg. F)  —  KNOXVILLE, TENNESSEE

| YEAR | JAN | FEB | MAR | APR | MAY | JUNE | JULY | AUG | SEP | OCT | NOV | DEC | ANNUAL |
|---|---|---|---|---|---|---|---|---|---|---|---|---|---|
| #1961 | 34.2 | 46.7 | 51.6 | 52.7 | 62.1 | 70.7 | 74.4 | 74.2 | 72.4 | 57.9 | 51.7 | 39.9 | 57.4 |
| 1962 | 37.0 | 47.2 | 46.8 | 54.7 | 74.0 | 74.4 | 78.3 | 78.2 | 70.9 | 62.5 | 46.4 | 37.0 | 59.0 |
| 1963 | 33.4 | 35.0 | 55.1 | 60.8 | 65.9 | 72.4 | 73.6 | 75.5 | 69.4 | 62.0 | 47.3 | 30.2 | 56.7 |
| 1964 | 36.3 | 36.1 | 47.7 | 60.5 | 66.9 | 75.1 | 73.7 | 70.0 | 70.0 | 55.5 | 52.3 | 43.5 | 57.8 |
| 1965 | 40.1 | 39.7 | 46.8 | 62.4 | 72.3 | 73.9 | 78.0 | 77.5 | 73.5 | 59.0 | 51.7 | 43.0 | 59.9 |
| 1966 | 34.0 | 41.6 | 50.4 | 58.9 | 66.1 | 74.3 | 75.0 | 75.0 | 68.9 | 57.5 | 49.1 | 40.0 | 57.9 |
| 1967 | 41.9 | 38.1 | 54.7 | 62.7 | 63.5 | 73.2 | 71.8 | 73.2 | 65.6 | 58.2 | 44.2 | 44.6 | 57.6 |
| 1968 | 37.1 | 33.3 | 49.9 | 59.0 | 65.3 | 73.6 | 77.2 | 78.4 | 69.1 | 58.8 | 48.1 | 37.0 | 57.3 |
| 1969 | 36.5 | 39.4 | 42.1 | 59.5 | 67.3 | 74.5 | 78.9 | 74.5 | 69.3 | 59.1 | 45.5 | 37.7 | 57.0 |
| 1970 | 30.6 | 39.3 | 48.7 | 61.2 | 68.6 | 73.4 | 78.5 | 77.1 | 75.3 | 62.8 | 48.1 | 44.1 | 59.0 |
| 1971 | 38.5 | 39.4 | 45.6 | 58.5 | 63.9 | 75.9 | 75.4 | 76.0 | 73.3 | 65.3 | 48.7 | 50.4 | 59.2 |
| 1972 | 42.5 | 39.4 | 48.2 | 59.5 | 64.9 | 70.8 | 75.9 | 75.9 | 71.9 | 56.8 | 47.5 | 44.8 | 58.1 |
| 1973 | 38.0 | 39.9 | 55.8 | 56.4 | 63.5 | 74.8 | 76.7 | 76.2 | 73.8 | 62.4 | 52.4 | 41.1 | 59.2 |
| 1974 | 49.3 | 43.1 | 51.2 | 59.8 | 68.1 | 70.5 | 77.7 | 76.5 | 69.8 | 58.6 | 50.8 | 41.9 | 60.1 |
| 1975 | 43.3 | 45.5 | 46.6 | 57.5 | 70.1 | 74.6 | 77.6 | 78.8 | 68.9 | 60.1 | 50.2 | 41.1 | 59.5 |
| 1976 | 34.3 | 48.2 | 52.6 | 58.9 | 63.4 | 73.9 | 76.2 | 74.9 | 67.7 | 54.5 | 43.2 | 37.5 | 57.1 |
| 1977 | 27.2 | 41.4 | 55.0 | 62.9 | 69.8 | 75.3 | 80.3 | 78.9 | 74.0 | 57.4 | 52.6 | 40.2 | 59.6 |
| 1978 | 29.4 | 34.6 | 49.0 | 61.1 | 66.6 | 75.4 | 78.7 | 77.1 | 74.8 | 58.2 | 54.4 | 42.8 | 58.5 |
| 1979 | 33.0 | 36.7 | 53.1 | 59.9 | 66.9 | 72.8 | 75.0 | 77.6 | 72.2 | 58.3 | 51.4 | 42.2 | 58.3 |
| 1980 | 41.6 | 36.6 | 47.6 | 59.1 | 68.1 | 75.2 | 82.1 | 81.7 | 73.7 | 56.0 | 47.3 | 40.1 | 59.1 |
| 1981 | 33.4 | 41.9 | 46.8 | 63.5 | 63.9 | 77.1 | 81.4 | 78.3 | 70.2 | 58.9 | 49.4 | 38.7 | 58.6 |
| 1982 | 33.8 | 43.1 | 53.0 | 55.2 | 69.3 | 72.6 | 76.7 | 77.0 | 70.0 | 59.5 | 50.9 | 46.4 | 59.0 |
| 1983 | 38.0 | 41.1 | 49.7 | 53.2 | 65.4 | 72.5 | 78.5 | 79.6 | 70.3 | 60.2 | 47.4 | 36.4 | 57.7 |
| 1984 | 35.3 | 43.4 | 47.7 | 57.3 | 62.8 | 74.8 | 73.3 | 74.1 | 67.1 | 67.6 | 46.3 | 47.5 | 58.1 |
| 1985 | 29.4 | 37.1 | 50.2 | 58.6 | 65.7 | 72.5 | 76.5 | 75.1 | 68.5 | 63.7 | 56.8 | 34.8 | 57.4 |
| 1986 | 35.0 | 43.9 | 48.7 | 58.6 | 68.1 | 77.2 | 81.4 | 76.7 | 72.8 | 60.2 | 52.4 | 39.1 | 59.5 |
| 1987 | 36.8 | 42.2 | 49.2 | 55.0 | 71.3 | 75.5 | 78.5 | 79.6 | 70.1 | 52.8 | 50.2 | 43.5 | 58.7 |
| 1988 | 33.9 | 39.4 | 50.1 | 57.2 | 65.0 | 74.4 | 78.7 | 79.6 | 71.3 | 52.7 | 49.7 | 40.4 | 57.7 |
| 1989 | 42.8 | 41.3 | 53.5 | 57.8 | 62.4 | 73.3 | 77.5 | 75.8 | 70.9 | 59.4 | 48.1 | 32.2 | 58.0 |
| 1990 | 44.7 | 48.9 | 53.6 | 57.9 | 65.9 | 75.4 | 78.0 | 77.9 | 72.1 | 59.9 | 52.1 | 45.1 | 61.0 |
| Record Mean | 38.9 | 41.8 | 49.5 | 58.7 | 67.2 | 74.8 | 77.8 | 76.8 | 71.4 | 59.7 | 48.5 | 40.6 | 58.8 |
| Max | 47.5 | 51.1 | 59.8 | 69.7 | 78.1 | 85.1 | 87.6 | 86.7 | 81.8 | 70.9 | 58.5 | 49.2 | 68.8 |
| Min | 30.3 | 32.4 | 39.1 | 47.7 | 56.3 | 64.4 | 67.9 | 66.9 | 60.9 | 48.5 | 38.4 | 32.0 | 48.7 |

## REFERENCE NOTES FOR TABLES 1, 2, 3 and 6      (KNOXVILLE, TN)

### GENERAL

T - TRACE AMOUNT
BLANK ENTRIES DENOTE MISSING/UNREPORTED DATA.
# INDICATES A STATION OR INSTRUMENT RELOCATION.

### SPECIFIC

#### TABLE 1

(a) - LENGTH OF RECORD IN YEARS. ALTHOUGH INDIVIDUAL MONTHS MAY BE MISSING.
* LESS THAN .05

NORMALS — BASED ON THE 1951-1980 RECORD PERIOD.
EXTREMES — DATES ARE THE MOST RECENT OCCURRENCE.
WIND DIR. — NUMERALS SHOW TENS OF DEGREES CLOCKWISE FROM TRUE NORTH.
"00" INDICATES CALM.
RESULTANT WIND DIRECTIONS ARE GIVEN TO WHOLE DEGREES.

#### TABLE 3

MAX AND MIN ARE LONG-TERM <u>MEAN DAILY MAXIMUM</u> AND <u>MEAN DAILY MINIMUM</u> TEMPERATURES.

### EXCEPTIONS

**TABLES 2, 3, and 6**

RECORD MEANS ARE THROUGH THE CURRENT YEAR, BEGINNING IN      1871 FOR TEMPERATURE
1871 FOR PRECIPITATION
1943 FOR SNOWFALL

**TABLE 4**  HEATING DEGREE DAYS Base 65 deg. F    KNOXVILLE, TENNESSEE

| SEASON | JULY | AUG | SEP | OCT | NOV | DEC | JAN | FEB | MAR | APR | MAY | JUNE | TOTAL |
|---|---|---|---|---|---|---|---|---|---|---|---|---|---|
| 1961-62 | 0 | 0 | 15 | 222 | 405 | 771 | 862 | 492 | 556 | 324 | 5 | 0 | 3652 |
| 1962-63 | 0 | 0 | 32 | 156 | 548 | 861 | 973 | 835 | 312 | 176 | 64 | 0 | 3957 |
| 1963-64 | 0 | 0 | 18 | 101 | 525 | 1072 | 884 | 834 | 532 | 160 | 44 | 1 | 4171 |
| 1964-65 | 0 | 8 | 9 | 308 | 374 | 657 | 765 | 701 | 559 | 125 | 0 | 0 | 3506 |
| 1965-66 | 0 | 0 | 13 | 200 | 393 | 674 | 956 | 650 | 452 | 217 | 59 | 9 | 3623 |
| 1966-67 | 0 | 0 | 9 | 232 | 472 | 767 | 709 | 748 | 330 | 112 | 110 | 8 | 3508 |
| 1967-68 | 1 | 0 | 63 | 229 | 617 | 626 | 860 | 912 | 467 | 191 | 66 | 0 | 4032 |
| 1968-69 | 0 | 0 | 5 | 215 | 501 | 859 | 879 | 710 | 704 | 175 | 50 | 4 | 4102 |
| 1969-70 | 0 | 0 | 11 | 200 | 579 | 840 | 1063 | 712 | 496 | 139 | 45 | 0 | 4085 |
| 1970-71 | 0 | 0 | 13 | 109 | 497 | 640 | 813 | 710 | 596 | 209 | 76 | 0 | 3663 |
| 1971-72 | 0 | 0 | 0 | 53 | 496 | 450 | 692 | 735 | 516 | 211 | 47 | 11 | 3211 |
| 1972-73 | 0 | 0 | 9 | 251 | 522 | 622 | 828 | 697 | 283 | 272 | 97 | 0 | 3581 |
| 1973-74 | 0 | 0 | 10 | 135 | 373 | 734 | 481 | 606 | 304 | 190 | 41 | 10 | 2884 |
| 1974-75 | 0 | 0 | 23 | 215 | 439 | 713 | 666 | 542 | 563 | 257 | 9 | 0 | 3427 |
| 1975-76 | 0 | 0 | 42 | 172 | 437 | 733 | 944 | 485 | 380 | 203 | 91 | 0 | 3487 |
| 1976-77 | 0 | 0 | 19 | 320 | 651 | 845 | 1166 | 658 | 319 | 110 | 33 | 2 | 4123 |
| 1977-78 | 0 | 0 | 3 | 242 | 374 | 764 | 1097 | 846 | 487 | 148 | 74 | 0 | 4035 |
| 1978-79 | 0 | 0 | 0 | 210 | 310 | 681 | 985 | 786 | 376 | 167 | 46 | 0 | 3561 |
| 1979-80 | 0 | 0 | 0 | 220 | 407 | 700 | 715 | 815 | 529 | 185 | 32 | 1 | 3604 |
| 1980-81 | 0 | 0 | 23 | 284 | 523 | 761 | 974 | 641 | 556 | 104 | 94 | 0 | 3960 |
| 1981-82 | 0 | 0 | 32 | 196 | 461 | 809 | 959 | 606 | 384 | 295 | 20 | 0 | 3762 |
| 1982-83 | 0 | 0 | 30 | 228 | 416 | 577 | 829 | 662 | 472 | 356 | 50 | 3 | 3623 |
| 1983-84 | 0 | 0 | 51 | 163 | 523 | 878 | 912 | 619 | 530 | 240 | 139 | 5 | 4060 |
| 1984-85 | 0 | 0 | 44 | 30 | 556 | 536 | 1095 | 776 | 459 | 208 | 51 | 13 | 3768 |
| 1985-86 | 0 | 0 | 44 | 86 | 250 | 927 | 922 | 582 | 499 | 206 | 51 | 0 | 3567 |
| 1986-87 | 0 | 2 | 0 | 197 | 377 | 797 | 863 | 631 | 483 | 313 | 13 | 0 | 3676 |
| 1987-88 | 0 | 0 | 15 | 370 | 437 | 660 | 956 | 734 | 458 | 247 | 66 | 9 | 3952 |
| 1988-89 | 0 | 0 | 3 | 384 | 454 | 755 | 681 | 660 | 360 | 258 | 148 | 0 | 3704 |
| 1989-90 | 0 | 1 | 36 | 204 | 499 | 1011 | 622 | 443 | 358 | 239 | 68 | 0 | 3481 |
| 1990-91 | 0 | 0 | 26 | 182 | 382 | 612 | | | | | | | |

**TABLE 5**  COOLING DEGREE DAYS Base 65 deg. F    KNOXVILLE, TENNESSEE

| YEAR | JAN | FEB | MAR | APR | MAY | JUNE | JULY | AUG | SEP | OCT | NOV | DEC | TOTAL |
|---|---|---|---|---|---|---|---|---|---|---|---|---|---|
| 1969 | 0 | 0 | 0 | 15 | 125 | 294 | 438 | 304 | 147 | 23 | 0 | 0 | 1346 |
| 1970 | 0 | 0 | 0 | 33 | 162 | 258 | 427 | 384 | 326 | 46 | 0 | 0 | 1636 |
| 1971 | 0 | 0 | 0 | 20 | 50 | 333 | 328 | 350 | 252 | 69 | 13 | 3 | 1418 |
| 1972 | 0 | 0 | 0 | 53 | 51 | 193 | 332 | 347 | 223 | 4 | 2 | 0 | 1205 |
| 1973 | 0 | 0 | 4 | 19 | 56 | 298 | 369 | 355 | 282 | 60 | 2 | 0 | 1445 |
| 1974 | 0 | 0 | 9 | 39 | 142 | 179 | 399 | 365 | 171 | 19 | 17 | 0 | 1340 |
| 1975 | 0 | 0 | 0 | 39 | 173 | 293 | 397 | 434 | 168 | 26 | 0 | 0 | 1530 |
| 1976 | 0 | 3 | 1 | 26 | 48 | 273 | 356 | 314 | 107 | 5 | 0 | 0 | 1133 |
| 1977 | 0 | 5 | 14 | 57 | 188 | 317 | 483 | 440 | 283 | 14 | 10 | 0 | 1811 |
| 1978 | 0 | 0 | 0 | 37 | 130 | 319 | 432 | 384 | 302 | 8 | 0 | 0 | 1612 |
| 1979 | 0 | 0 | 15 | 20 | 111 | 242 | 317 | 399 | 224 | 23 | 4 | 0 | 1355 |
| 1980 | 0 | 0 | 0 | 16 | 136 | 315 | 538 | 525 | 290 | 12 | 0 | 0 | 1832 |
| 1981 | 0 | 0 | 0 | 62 | 65 | 373 | 512 | 421 | 193 | 14 | 1 | 0 | 1641 |
| 1982 | 0 | 0 | 17 | 6 | 157 | 233 | 396 | 372 | 187 | 65 | 2 | 8 | 1443 |
| 1983 | 0 | 0 | 4 | 6 | 71 | 235 | 425 | 462 | 217 | 23 | 0 | 0 | 1443 |
| 1984 | 0 | 0 | 0 | 12 | 77 | 306 | 263 | 290 | 116 | 120 | 2 | 0 | 1186 |
| 1985 | 0 | 0 | 11 | 20 | 81 | 247 | 363 | 322 | 155 | 53 | 11 | 0 | 1263 |
| 1986 | 0 | 0 | 0 | 21 | 156 | 374 | 517 | 373 | 241 | 55 | 6 | 0 | 1743 |
| 1987 | 0 | 0 | 0 | 18 | 215 | 321 | 427 | 460 | 172 | 0 | 0 | 0 | 1613 |
| 1988 | 0 | 0 | 3 | 19 | 74 | 297 | 431 | 458 | 200 | 9 | 0 | 0 | 1491 |
| 1989 | 0 | 2 | 10 | 47 | 76 | 257 | 395 | 374 | 219 | 35 | 0 | 0 | 1415 |
| 1990 | 0 | 1 | 13 | 32 | 101 | 316 | 410 | 406 | 245 | 32 | 1 | 0 | 1557 |

**TABLE 6**  SNOWFALL (inches)    KNOXVILLE, TENNESSEE

| SEASON | JULY | AUG | SEP | OCT | NOV | DEC | JAN | FEB | MAR | APR | MAY | JUNE | TOTAL |
|---|---|---|---|---|---|---|---|---|---|---|---|---|---|
| 1961-62 | 0.0 | 0.0 | 0.0 | 0.0 | T | 4.5 | 15.1 | T | 1.9 | T | 0.0 | 0.0 | 21.5 |
| 1962-63 | 0.0 | 0.0 | 0.0 | T | T | 6.9 | 4.2 | 7.2 | T | 0.0 | 0.0 | 0.0 | 18.3 |
| 1963-64 | 0.0 | 0.0 | 0.0 | 0.0 | 5.9 | 12.2 | 8.5 | 5.2 | T | 0.0 | 0.0 | 0.0 | 31.8 |
| 1964-65 | 0.0 | 0.0 | 0.0 | 0.0 | T | T | 6.3 | 6.9 | 4.4 | 0.0 | 0.0 | 0.0 | 17.6 |
| 1965-66 | 0.0 | 0.0 | 0.0 | 0.0 | T | T | 14.2 | T | 0.5 | 0.0 | 0.0 | 0.0 | 14.7 |
| 1966-67 | 0.0 | 0.0 | 0.0 | 0.0 | T | 3.1 | 2.2 | 5.7 | 0.0 | 0.0 | 0.0 | 0.0 | 11.0 |
| 1967-68 | 0.0 | 0.0 | 0.0 | 0.0 | 0.0 | T | 5.9 | 4.7 | 1.9 | 0.0 | 0.0 | 0.0 | 12.5 |
| 1968-69 | 0.0 | 0.0 | 0.0 | 0.0 | 0.3 | 0.5 | 7.7 | 5.2 | 0.0 | 0.0 | 0.0 | 0.0 | 13.7 |
| 1969-70 | 0.0 | 0.0 | 0.0 | 0.0 | T | 8.9 | 12.9 | 4.6 | T | 0.0 | 0.0 | 0.0 | 26.4 |
| 1970-71 | 0.0 | 0.0 | 0.0 | 0.0 | T | 6.3 | 1.3 | 6.4 | 3.6 | 7.0 | 0.0 | 0.0 | 24.6 |
| 1971-72 | 0.0 | 0.0 | 0.0 | 0.0 | T | T | 0.4 | 4.2 | 6.7 | 0.0 | 0.0 | 0.0 | 11.3 |
| 1972-73 | 0.0 | 0.0 | 0.0 | 0.0 | T | T | 9.0 | 1.9 | T | 0.0 | 0.0 | 0.0 | 10.9 |
| 1973-74 | 0.0 | 0.0 | 0.0 | 0.0 | 0.0 | 2.0 | T | T | 1.8 | 0.0 | 0.0 | 0.0 | 3.8 |
| 1974-75 | 0.0 | 0.0 | 0.0 | 0.0 | T | 1.6 | 1.3 | T | 2.5 | 0.0 | 0.0 | 0.0 | 5.4 |
| 1975-76 | 0.0 | 0.0 | 0.0 | 0.0 | 0.0 | T | T | 0.3 | 2.8 | 0.0 | 0.0 | 0.0 | 3.1 |
| 1976-77 | 0.0 | 0.0 | 0.0 | 0.0 | 1.0 | 2.1 | 7.9 | 0.2 | 0.0 | 0.0 | 0.0 | 0.0 | 11.2 |
| 1977-78 | 0.0 | 0.0 | 0.0 | 0.0 | 0.1 | 0.6 | 11.3 | 5.5 | 1.8 | 0.0 | 0.0 | 0.0 | 19.3 |
| 1978-79 | 0.0 | 0.0 | 0.0 | 0.0 | 0.0 | T | 4.7 | 18.4 | T | 0.0 | 0.0 | 0.0 | 23.1 |
| 1979-80 | 0.0 | 0.0 | 0.0 | 0.0 | T | T | 0.5 | 11.0 | 3.5 | T | 0.0 | 0.0 | 15.0 |
| 1980-81 | 0.0 | 0.0 | 0.0 | 0.0 | T | T | 5.0 | 2.5 | T | 0.0 | 0.0 | 0.0 | 7.5 |
| 1981-82 | 0.0 | 0.0 | 0.0 | 0.0 | 0.0 | 0.1 | 4.4 | 0.1 | 1.1 | 0.0 | 0.0 | 0.0 | 5.7 |
| 1982-83 | 0.0 | 0.0 | 0.0 | 0.0 | 0.0 | 3.0 | 1.1 | 3.4 | 0.7 | 2.0 | 0.0 | 0.0 | 10.2 |
| 1983-84 | 0.0 | 0.0 | 0.0 | 0.0 | 0.0 | 0.7 | 2.8 | 3.5 | 0.0 | 0.0 | 0.0 | 0.0 | 7.0 |
| 1984-85 | 0.0 | 0.0 | 0.0 | 0.0 | 0.0 | T | 14.2 | 8.3 | 0.0 | 0.0 | 0.0 | 0.0 | 22.5 |
| 1985-86 | 0.0 | 0.0 | 0.0 | 0.0 | 0.0 | 0.4 | 3.6 | 5.0 | T | 0.0 | 0.0 | 0.0 | 9.0 |
| 1986-87 | 0.0 | 0.0 | 0.0 | 0.0 | T | T | 7.5 | T | 1.6 | 10.7 | 0.0 | 0.0 | 19.8 |
| 1987-88 | 0.0 | 0.0 | 0.0 | 0.0 | T | T | 9.2 | 0.9 | T | 0.0 | 0.0 | 0.0 | 10.1 |
| 1988-89 | 0.0 | 0.0 | 0.0 | 0.0 | T | 2.6 | 1.8 | 2.8 | T | 0.0 | 0.0 | 0.0 | 7.2 |
| 1989-90 | 0.0 | 0.0 | 0.0 | T | T | 1.1 | 1.1 | T | 0.0 | 0.0 | 0.0 | 0.0 | 7.2 |
| 1990-91 | 0.0 | 0.0 | 0.0 | 0.0 | 0.0 | T | | | | | | | 1.1 |
| Record Mean | 0.0 | 0.0 | 0.0 | T | 0.7 | 1.6 | 4.2 | 3.7 | 1.5 | 0.4 | T | 0.0 | 12.2 |

**See Reference Notes, relative to all above tables, on preceding page.**

Topography varies from the level alluvial area in east—central Arkansas to the slightly rolling area in northwestern Mississippi and southwestern Tennessee.

Agricultural interests are varied, with major crops being cotton, corn, hay, soybeans, peaches, apples, and a considerable number of vegetables. The climate is quite favorable for dairy interests, and for the raising of cattle and hogs.

The growing season is about 230 days in length. The average date for the last occurrence of temperatures as low as 32 degrees is late March. The average date of the first temperature of 32 degrees or below is early November.

Precipitation of nearly 50 inches per year is fairly well distributed. Crops and pastures receive, on the average, an adequate supply of moisture during the growing season, with lesser amounts during the fall harvesting period.

Sunshine averages slightly over 70 percent of the possible amount during the growing season. Relative humidity averages about 70 percent for the year.

Memphis, although not in the normal paths of storms coming from the Gulf or from western Canada, is affected by both, and thereby has comparatively frequent changes in weather. Extremely high or low temperatures, however, are relatively rare.

## TABLE 1    NORMALS, MEANS AND EXTREMES

MEMPHIS, TENNESSEE

LATITUDE: 35°03'N   LONGITUDE: 90°00' W   ELEVATION: FT. GRND 258 BARO 271   TIME ZONE: CENTRAL   WBAN: 13893

| | (a) | JAN | FEB | MAR | APR | MAY | JUNE | JULY | AUG | SEP | OCT | NOV | DEC | YEAR |
|---|---|---|---|---|---|---|---|---|---|---|---|---|---|---|
| **TEMPERATURE °F:** | | | | | | | | | | | | | | |
| Normals | | | | | | | | | | | | | | |
| -Daily Maximum | | 48.3 | 53.0 | 61.4 | 72.9 | 81.0 | 88.4 | 91.5 | 90.3 | 84.3 | 74.5 | 61.4 | 52.3 | 71.6 |
| -Daily Minimum | | 30.9 | 34.1 | 41.9 | 52.2 | 60.9 | 68.9 | 72.6 | 70.8 | 63.1 | 51.3 | 41.1 | 34.3 | 51.9 |
| -Monthly | | 39.6 | 43.5 | 51.7 | 62.6 | 71.0 | 78.7 | 82.1 | 80.6 | 74.2 | 62.9 | 51.3 | 43.3 | 61.8 |
| Extremes | | | | | | | | | | | | | | |
| -Record Highest | 48 | 78 | 81 | 85 | 94 | 99 | 104 | 108 | 105 | 103 | 95 | 85 | 81 | 108 |
| -Year | | 1972 | 1962 | 1986 | 1987 | 1977 | 1954 | 1980 | 1943 | 1954 | 1954 | 1955 | 1982 | JUL 1980 |
| -Record Lowest | 48 | -4 | -11 | 12 | 29 | 38 | 48 | 52 | 48 | 36 | 25 | 9 | -13 | -13 |
| -Year | | 1985 | 1951 | 1943 | 1987 | 1944 | 1966 | 1947 | 1946 | 1949 | 1952 | 1950 | 1963 | DEC 1963 |
| **NORMAL DEGREE DAYS:** | | | | | | | | | | | | | | |
| Heating (base 65°F) | | 787 | 602 | 433 | 126 | 25 | 0 | 0 | 0 | 9 | 137 | 415 | 673 | 3207 |
| Cooling (base 65°F) | | 0 | 0 | 20 | 54 | 211 | 411 | 530 | 484 | 285 | 72 | 0 | 0 | 2067 |
| **% OF POSSIBLE SUNSHINE** | 35 | 50 | 54 | 56 | 64 | 69 | 74 | 74 | 75 | 69 | 70 | 58 | 50 | 64 |
| **MEAN SKY COVER (tenths)** | | | | | | | | | | | | | | |
| Sunrise - Sunset | 39 | 6.8 | 6.4 | 6.5 | 6.0 | 5.8 | 5.3 | 5.4 | 4.9 | 5.1 | 4.6 | 5.6 | 6.3 | 5.7 |
| **MEAN NUMBER OF DAYS:** | | | | | | | | | | | | | | |
| Sunrise to Sunset | | | | | | | | | | | | | | |
| -Clear | 37 | 8.0 | 7.9 | 8.0 | 8.8 | 8.8 | 10.1 | 10.2 | 11.9 | 12.3 | 14.4 | 10.2 | 9.1 | 119.5 |
| -Partly Cloudy | 37 | 5.8 | 5.8 | 6.5 | 7.1 | 9.8 | 10.9 | 11.8 | 11.5 | 7.7 | 7.2 | 6.4 | 5.8 | 96.3 |
| -Cloudy | 37 | 17.2 | 14.6 | 16.5 | 14.1 | 12.5 | 9.0 | 9.0 | 7.6 | 9.9 | 9.5 | 13.4 | 16.1 | 149.4 |
| Precipitation | | | | | | | | | | | | | | |
| .01 inches or more | 39 | 10.0 | 9.5 | 10.8 | 10.2 | 9.2 | 8.5 | 8.7 | 7.7 | 7.2 | 6.2 | 8.8 | 9.6 | 106.1 |
| Snow, Ice pellets | | | | | | | | | | | | | | |
| 1.0 inches or more | 39 | 0.8 | 0.6 | 0.3 | 0.0 | 0.0 | 0.0 | 0.0 | 0.0 | 0.0 | 0.0 | 0.* | 0.2 | 1.8 |
| Thunderstorms | 39 | 1.9 | 2.3 | 4.5 | 6.4 | 6.8 | 7.3 | 8.3 | 6.1 | 3.4 | 1.9 | 2.3 | 1.6 | 52.9 |
| Heavy Fog Visibility | | | | | | | | | | | | | | |
| 1/4 mile or less | 39 | 2.1 | 1.3 | 0.8 | 0.3 | 0.2 | 0.2 | 0.3 | 0.4 | 0.6 | 1.1 | 1.4 | 1.7 | 10.4 |
| Temperature °F | | | | | | | | | | | | | | |
| -Maximum | | | | | | | | | | | | | | |
| 90° and above | 48 | 0.0 | 0.0 | 0.0 | 0.1 | 3.2 | 14.5 | 21.5 | 18.6 | 7.8 | 0.6 | 0.0 | 0.0 | 66.4 |
| 32° and below | 48 | 3.4 | 1.3 | 0.2 | 0.0 | 0.0 | 0.0 | 0.0 | 0.0 | 0.0 | 0.0 | 0.1 | 1.4 | 6.4 |
| -Minimum | | | | | | | | | | | | | | |
| 32° and below | 48 | 18.3 | 12.6 | 5.4 | 0.3 | 0.0 | 0.0 | 0.0 | 0.0 | 0.0 | 0.3 | 5.7 | 14.7 | 57.3 |
| 0° and below | 48 | 0.1 | 0.* | 0.0 | 0.0 | 0.0 | 0.0 | 0.0 | 0.0 | 0.0 | 0.0 | 0.0 | 0.1 | 0.3 |
| **AVG. STATION PRESS. (mb)** | 17 | 1011.6 | 1010.1 | 1006.5 | 1005.7 | 1004.6 | 1005.4 | 1006.4 | 1006.7 | 1007.4 | 1009.4 | 1009.3 | 1011.0 | 1007.9 |
| **RELATIVE HUMIDITY (%)** | | | | | | | | | | | | | | |
| Hour 00 | 50 | 75 | 73 | 70 | 71 | 76 | 78 | 79 | 80 | 80 | 77 | 74 | 74 | 76 |
| Hour 06 (Local Time) | 50 | 78 | 78 | 76 | 78 | 82 | 82 | 84 | 86 | 86 | 83 | 80 | 78 | 81 |
| Hour 12 | 50 | 63 | 60 | 56 | 53 | 55 | 56 | 57 | 57 | 56 | 51 | 56 | 61 | 57 |
| Hour 18 | 50 | 67 | 63 | 56 | 54 | 56 | 57 | 59 | 60 | 62 | 60 | 63 | 67 | 60 |
| **PRECIPITATION (inches):** | | | | | | | | | | | | | | |
| Water Equivalent | | | | | | | | | | | | | | |
| -Normal | | 4.61 | 4.33 | 5.44 | 5.77 | 5.06 | 3.58 | 4.03 | 3.74 | 3.62 | 2.37 | 4.17 | 4.85 | 51.57 |
| -Maximum Monthly | 39 | 12.21 | 10.51 | 12.08 | 12.29 | 11.58 | 7.20 | 8.84 | 9.65 | 7.61 | 7.75 | 10.52 | 13.81 | 13.81 |
| -Year | | 1951 | 1989 | 1975 | 1955 | 1953 | 1989 | 1959 | 1978 | 1958 | 1984 | 1988 | 1982 | DEC 1982 |
| -Minimum Monthly | 39 | 0.57 | 1.12 | 1.50 | 2.05 | 0.83 | 0.04 | 0.43 | 0.19 | T | 0.75 | 1.05 | T | OCT 1963 |
| -Year | | 1986 | 1980 | 1966 | 1965 | 1977 | 1953 | 1954 | 1953 | 1963 | 1965 | 1955 | | |
| -Maximum in 24 hrs | 39 | 3.89 | 4.24 | 5.95 | 4.35 | 4.94 | 4.76 | 4.71 | 4.04 | 4.63 | 3.40 | 5.65 | 5.42 | 5.95 |
| -Year | | 1974 | 1989 | 1975 | 1985 | 1958 | 1980 | 1980 | 1978 | 1957 | 1981 | 1988 | 1978 | MAR 1975 |
| Snow, Ice pellets | | | | | | | | | | | | | | |
| -Maximum Monthly | 39 | 12.4 | 8.3 | 17.3 | T | T | 0.0 | 0.0 | 0.0 | 0.0 | T | 1.5 | 14.3 | 17.3 |
| -Year | | 1985 | 1985 | 1968 | 1971 | 1989 | | | | | 1989 | 1976 | 1963 | MAR 1968 |
| -Maximum in 24 hrs | 39 | 8.1 | 5.8 | 16.1 | T | T | 0.0 | 0.0 | 0.0 | 0.0 | T | 1.2 | 14.3 | 16.1 |
| -Year | | 1985 | 1960 | 1968 | 1971 | 1989 | | | | | 1989 | 1976 | 1963 | MAR 1968 |
| **WIND:** | | | | | | | | | | | | | | |
| Mean Speed (mph) | 41 | 10.1 | 10.2 | 10.9 | 10.4 | 8.8 | 7.9 | 7.5 | 7.0 | 7.5 | 7.7 | 9.1 | 9.8 | 8.9 |
| Prevailing Direction | | | | | | | | | | | | | | |
| through 1963 | | S | S | S | S | S | S | S | E | S | S | S | S | S |
| Fastest Obs. 1 Min. | | | | | | | | | | | | | | |
| -Direction (!!!) | 13 | 34 | 32 | 16 | 24 | 34 | 02 | 34 | 20 | 36 | 28 | 23 | 30 | 24 |
| -Speed (MPH) | 13 | 35 | 35 | 40 | 46 | 40 | 40 | 40 | 35 | 35 | 39 | 40 | 36 | 46 |
| -Year | | 1976 | 1984 | 1973 | 1979 | 1979 | 1977 | 1982 | 1980 | 1972 | 1984 | 1979 | 1972 | APR 1979 |
| Peak Gust | | | | | | | | | | | | | | |
| -Direction (!!!) | | | | | | | | | | | | | | |
| -Speed (mph) | | | | | | | | | | | | | | |
| -Date | | | | | | | | | | | | | | |

**See reference Notes to this table on the following page.**

PRECIPITATION (inches)                    MEMPHIS, TENNESSEE

**TABLE 2**

| YEAR | JAN | FEB | MAR | APR | MAY | JUNE | JULY | AUG | SEP | OCT | NOV | DEC | ANNUAL |
|------|-----|-----|-----|-----|-----|------|------|-----|-----|-----|-----|-----|--------|
| 1961 | 0.84 | 6.89 | 7.13 | 4.65 | 4.40 | 1.49 | 3.97 | 1.71 | 0.66 | 1.28 | 8.06 | 8.56 | 49.64 |
| 1962 | 4.19 | 4.22 | 4.80 | 3.62 | 0.84 | 5.71 | 3.94 | 4.18 | 5.28 | 2.57 | 2.31 | 1.35 | 43.01 |
| 1963 | 1.28 | 2.91 | 6.17 | 5.60 | 3.77 | 4.33 | 4.38 | 2.15 | 2.06 | T | 2.72 | 3.31 | 38.68 |
| 1964 | 3.73 | 3.50 | 7.34 | 11.03 | 3.28 | 1.39 | 6.14 | 5.76 | 2.74 | 2.21 | 2.59 | 7.97 | 57.68 |
| 1965 | 4.79 | 6.78 | 5.35 | 2.05 | 7.42 | 0.98 | 1.60 | 3.98 | 7.38 | 0.54 | 0.75 | 1.17 | 42.79 |
| 1966 | 2.84 | 6.88 | 1.50 | 5.42 | 5.69 | 0.52 | 2.18 | 4.28 | 3.23 | 1.92 | 1.57 | 5.21 | 41.24 |
| 1967 | 2.23 | 2.33 | 4.65 | 4.46 | 6.38 | 1.70 | 6.01 | 5.17 | 1.86 | 2.38 | 1.90 | 7.37 | 46.44 |
| 1968 | 5.57 | 1.98 | 6.52 | 5.15 | 5.21 | 3.76 | 2.69 | 1.61 | 5.58 | 2.87 | 4.89 | 6.04 | 51.87 |
| 1969 | 3.14 | 3.20 | 2.63 | 8.29 | 1.34 | 1.60 | 1.92 | 6.62 | 0.90 | 1.24 | 4.19 | 7.05 | 42.12 |
| 1970 | 1.16 | 3.87 | 5.32 | 7.08 | 3.70 | 5.76 | 4.99 | 1.78 | 3.80 | 6.20 | 2.62 | 3.71 | 49.99 |
| 1971 | 2.15 | 7.21 | 3.64 | 2.89 | 3.90 | 3.82 | 2.90 | 6.00 | 3.42 | 0.06 | 1.49 | 6.71 | 44.19 |
| 1972 | 4.73 | 2.23 | 4.80 | 3.51 | 4.55 | 5.50 | 4.89 | 1.94 | 5.46 | 3.92 | 8.05 | 9.37 | 58.95 |
| 1973 | 4.62 | 3.62 | 7.63 | 9.44 | 6.23 | 1.00 | 4.49 | 4.88 | 5.06 | 3.37 | 8.49 | 5.35 | 64.18 |
| 1974 | 8.90 | 4.65 | 6.34 | 6.34 | 7.76 | 6.30 | 6.33 | 4.78 | 3.45 | 2.67 | 4.96 | 5.03 | 64.57 |
| 1975 | 4.65 | 5.53 | 12.08 | 4.98 | 8.72 | 2.42 | 2.26 | 2.03 | 2.62 | 2.69 | 7.77 | 2.93 | 58.68 |
| 1976 | 2.85 | 4.41 | 7.68 | 2.41 | 4.73 | 4.06 | 3.82 | 0.86 | 5.40 | 5.66 | 1.83 | 1.79 | 45.50 |
| 1977 | 2.57 | 1.99 | 4.13 | 5.42 | 0.83 | 3.38 | 3.41 | 1.62 | 6.43 | 2.02 | 6.01 | 3.39 | 41.20 |
| 1978 | 8.13 | 1.31 | 4.05 | 2.14 | 8.14 | 4.45 | 3.89 | 9.65 | 1.52 | 1.82 | 5.56 | 13.12 | 63.78 |
| 1979 | 5.98 | 5.66 | 6.60 | 11.47 | 7.78 | 4.93 | 3.12 | 5.92 | 4.49 | 2.60 | 7.42 | 4.92 | 70.89 |
| 1980 | 3.23 | 1.12 | 10.86 | 7.53 | 4.43 | 5.75 | 4.73 | 1.23 | 5.32 | 3.14 | 5.23 | 1.86 | 54.43 |
| 1981 | 1.38 | 3.66 | 4.98 | 3.67 | 7.06 | 2.93 | 1.71 | 4.21 | 0.61 | 5.83 | 2.12 | 1.84 | 40.00 |
| 1982 | 6.61 | 4.16 | 4.47 | 6.76 | 5.50 | 6.68 | 4.13 | 3.11 | 1.92 | 5.23 | 6.43 | 13.81 | 68.81 |
| 1983 | 2.32 | 2.61 | 3.66 | 8.84 | 9.58 | 3.50 | 3.83 | 0.61 | 1.52 | 2.94 | 9.56 | 8.68 | 57.65 |
| 1984 | 1.88 | 4.37 | 6.07 | 5.24 | 9.06 | 1.12 | 4.59 | 5.00 | 1.96 | 7.75 | 5.85 | 4.35 | 57.24 |
| 1985 | 3.78 | 4.10 | 4.96 | 6.51 | 2.23 | 4.55 | 3.50 | 3.50 | 4.03 | 3.36 | 3.87 | 3.27 | 47.66 |
| 1986 | 0.57 | 2.50 | 1.90 | 3.72 | 4.63 | 3.80 | 1.21 | 2.74 | 1.21 | 3.75 | 8.67 | 3.92 | 38.62 |
| 1987 | 1.76 | 5.81 | 3.38 | 3.78 | 2.96 | 3.66 | 2.06 | 4.12 | 2.01 | 1.96 | 10.45 | 11.39 | 53.34 |
| 1988 | 4.25 | 3.49 | 4.20 | 2.85 | 2.38 | 2.15 | 5.21 | 0.85 | 4.73 | 3.62 | 10.52 | 5.99 | 50.24 |
| 1989 | 7.91 | 10.51 | 5.50 | 2.13 | 2.36 | 7.20 | 7.55 | 1.43 | 6.08 | 2.37 | 3.65 | 2.20 | 58.89 |
| 1990 | 3.97 | 8.99 | 5.65 | 6.93 | 4.55 | 2.68 | 2.21 | 1.18 | 5.21 | 4.37 | 3.44 | 10.61 | 59.79 |
| Record Mean | 4.87 | 4.39 | 5.22 | 5.09 | 4.37 | 3.68 | 3.43 | 3.22 | 3.01 | 2.87 | 4.44 | 4.80 | 49.38 |

**TABLE 3**  AVERAGE TEMPERATURE (deg. F)          MEMPHIS, TENNESSEE

| YEAR | JAN | FEB | MAR | APR | MAY | JUNE | JULY | AUG | SEP | OCT | NOV | DEC | ANNUAL |
|------|-----|-----|-----|-----|-----|------|------|-----|-----|-----|-----|-----|--------|
| 1961 | 36.1 | 47.2 | 55.1 | 58.2 | 66.7 | 75.1 | 80.2 | 77.8 | 74.6 | 62.5 | 49.6 | 42.4 | 60.4 |
| 1962 | 36.2 | 50.3 | 47.3 | 58.8 | 76.8 | 77.1 | 81.3 | 80.8 | 73.4 | 65.9 | 50.2 | 39.9 | 61.5 |
| 1963 | 34.4 | 37.6 | 56.7 | 64.2 | 71.1 | 78.6 | 80.1 | 80.2 | 73.4 | 68.6 | 53.4 | 31.5 | 60.8 |
| 1964 | 41.1 | 40.2 | 51.7 | 64.0 | 71.9 | 79.3 | 80.6 | 78.6 | 72.9 | 58.9 | 54.4 | 44.3 | 61.5 |
| 1965 | 43.4 | 42.9 | 44.0 | 66.4 | 74.7 | 78.1 | 81.8 | 80.2 | 73.7 | 60.8 | 55.8 | 45.8 | 62.3 |
| 1966 | 34.2 | 42.2 | 52.8 | 60.6 | 67.9 | 76.6 | 84.7 | 76.9 | 70.8 | 58.1 | 53.7 | 41.4 | 60.0 |
| 1967 | 42.2 | 39.2 | 56.7 | 66.5 | 68.8 | 78.3 | 77.7 | 76.0 | 70.3 | 62.4 | 49.1 | 45.0 | 61.0 |
| 1968 | 38.9 | 37.3 | 50.9 | 62.7 | 69.7 | 79.5 | 80.8 | 82.0 | 71.3 | 62.2 | 50.9 | 41.7 | 60.7 |
| 1969 | 41.2 | 43.3 | 45.0 | 62.9 | 72.1 | 78.8 | 84.9 | 79.3 | 72.9 | 62.9 | 49.0 | 40.1 | 61.1 |
| 1970 | 35.3 | 41.7 | 48.7 | 65.0 | 72.3 | 77.3 | 79.7 | 81.2 | 77.9 | 61.7 | 49.8 | 46.4 | 61.4 |
| 1971 | 39.6 | 43.5 | 48.4 | 60.5 | 66.6 | 80.6 | 80.6 | 78.6 | 76.1 | 69.3 | 50.9 | 50.7 | 62.1 |
| 1972 | 42.3 | 44.7 | 52.2 | 63.1 | 69.7 | 77.5 | 79.4 | 75.9 | 75.4 | 61.4 | 45.5 | 40.0 | 60.9 |
| 1973 | 38.6 | 40.5 | 57.3 | 59.8 | 68.3 | 81.0 | 83.2 | 79.6 | 76.1 | 67.6 | 57.3 | 43.3 | 62.7 |
| 1974 | 45.7 | 45.6 | 58.7 | 61.8 | 72.1 | 74.7 | 82.5 | 79.2 | 68.5 | 62.4 | 53.3 | 45.2 | 62.5 |
| 1975 | 45.9 | 46.2 | 49.9 | 61.9 | 73.5 | 78.8 | 81.1 | 81.2 | 70.9 | 65.8 | 53.8 | 44.1 | 62.8 |
| 1976 | 39.5 | 53.8 | 58.5 | 63.6 | 65.6 | 76.4 | 81.5 | 78.9 | 73.0 | 58.1 | 45.5 | 41.9 | 61.5 |
| 1977 | 30.7 | 45.1 | 58.6 | 66.9 | 76.4 | 81.9 | 84.7 | 82.6 | 79.0 | 62.2 | 55.1 | 44.1 | 64.0 |
| 1978 | 32.7 | 35.0 | 50.3 | 66.3 | 70.9 | 79.8 | 83.8 | 80.9 | 77.7 | 62.5 | 57.7 | 44.0 | 61.8 |
| 1979 | 30.9 | 38.5 | 54.3 | 63.0 | 70.0 | 77.9 | 82.6 | 80.9 | 73.4 | 65.8 | 50.7 | 45.4 | 61.1 |
| 1980 | 43.2 | 39.5 | 49.4 | 60.9 | 72.5 | 80.9 | 88.8 | 87.2 | 80.5 | 62.7 | 53.3 | 45.9 | 63.8 |
| 1981 | 40.9 | 47.3 | 54.3 | 70.2 | 70.0 | 82.5 | 84.6 | 81.8 | 74.0 | 62.5 | 53.8 | 40.9 | 63.6 |
| 1982 | 36.6 | 40.5 | 55.5 | 58.5 | 74.5 | 78.0 | 85.0 | 82.9 | 73.3 | 63.7 | 53.4 | 49.5 | 62.6 |
| 1983 | 40.4 | 45.3 | 51.9 | 56.8 | 68.2 | 77.2 | 83.6 | 84.9 | 75.2 | 66.2 | 53.1 | 34.7 | 61.5 |
| 1984 | 35.9 | 47.6 | 51.1 | 61.0 | 69.5 | 80.9 | 80.9 | 79.8 | 71.9 | 68.4 | 50.9 | 53.8 | 62.6 |
| 1985 | 32.4 | 40.6 | 57.7 | 65.0 | 71.8 | 78.9 | 78.9 | 82.2 | 73.6 | 67.2 | 57.6 | 36.9 | 62.0 |
| 1986 | 41.9 | 48.0 | 55.2 | 64.4 | 72.5 | 81.0 | 86.5 | 79.2 | 79.1 | 64.2 | 51.1 | 42.6 | 63.8 |
| 1987 | 39.6 | 47.1 | 54.7 | 62.2 | 76.5 | 80.0 | 82.5 | 83.6 | 75.3 | 59.2 | 54.4 | 46.7 | 63.5 |
| 1988 | 36.8 | 42.2 | 52.3 | 62.8 | 71.8 | 80.3 | 81.6 | 83.7 | 76.3 | 59.1 | 54.6 | 44.9 | 62.2 |
| 1989 | 47.3 | 40.0 | 53.8 | 62.6 | 69.5 | 77.6 | 80.7 | 81.2 | 72.4 | 64.2 | 54.2 | 33.6 | 61.4 |
| 1990 | 48.5 | 52.0 | 55.3 | 61.4 | 68.3 | 80.7 | 82.5 | 82.0 | 77.9 | 61.3 | 57.1 | 45.8 | 64.4 |
| Record Mean | 40.9 | 44.0 | 52.5 | 62.3 | 70.5 | 78.4 | 81.4 | 80.2 | 74.2 | 63.5 | 51.9 | 43.5 | 62.0 |
| Max | 48.9 | 52.5 | 61.5 | 71.6 | 79.7 | 87.4 | 90.2 | 89.1 | 83.5 | 73.6 | 60.9 | 51.5 | 70.9 |
| Min | 32.9 | 35.6 | 43.5 | 52.9 | 61.3 | 69.3 | 72.7 | 71.3 | 64.9 | 53.3 | 42.8 | 35.5 | 53.0 |

## REFERENCE NOTES FOR TABLES 1, 2, 3 and 6          (MEMPHIS, TN)

### GENERAL

T - TRACE AMOUNT
BLANK ENTRIES DENOTE MISSING/UNREPORTED DATA.
# INDICATES A STATION OR INSTRUMENT RELOCATION.

### SPECIFIC

#### TABLE 1

(a) - LENGTH OF RECORD IN YEARS, ALTHOUGH
      INDIVIDUAL MONTHS MAY BE MISSING.
* LESS THAN .05

NORMALS — BASED ON THE 1951-1980 RECORD PERIOD.
EXTREMES — DATES ARE THE MOST RECENT OCCURRENCE.
WIND DIR. — NUMERALS SHOW TENS OF DEGREES
            CLOCKWISE FROM TRUE NORTH.
            "00" INDICATES CALM.
RESULTANT WIND DIRECTIONS ARE GIVEN TO WHOLE DEGREES.

#### TABLE 3
MAX AND MIN ARE LONG-TERM MEAN DAILY MAXIMUM
AND MEAN DAILY MINIMUM TEMPERATURES.

### EXCEPTIONS

#### TABLES 2, 3, and 6

RECORD MEANS ARE THROUGH THE CURRENT YEAR,
BEGINNING IN    1875 FOR TEMPERATURE
                1872 FOR PRECIPITATION
                1951 FOR SNOWFALL

**TABLE 4**  HEATING DEGREE DAYS Base 65 deg. F  MEMPHIS, TENNESSEE

| SEASON | JULY | AUG | SEP | OCT | NOV | DEC | JAN | FEB | MAR | APR | MAY | JUNE | TOTAL |
|---|---|---|---|---|---|---|---|---|---|---|---|---|---|
| 1961-62 | 0 | 0 | 8 | 148 | 467 | 690 | 887 | 410 | 543 | 229 | 5 | 0 | 3387 |
| 1962-63 | 0 | 0 | 14 | 107 | 436 | 772 | 944 | 760 | 291 | 119 | 34 | 0 | 3477 |
| 1963-64 | 0 | 0 | 10 | 33 | 352 | 1034 | 739 | 713 | 406 | 91 | 13 | 0 | 3391 |
| 1964-65 | 0 | 0 | 13 | 202 | 335 | 634 | 666 | 614 | 645 | 72 | 0 | 0 | 3181 |
| 1965-66 | 0 | 0 | 22 | 162 | 275 | 590 | 947 | 634 | 382 | 175 | 47 | 5 | 3239 |
| 1966-67 | 0 | 0 | 9 | 227 | 344 | 732 | 707 | 715 | 301 | 60 | 35 | 0 | 3130 |
| 1967-68 | 0 | 0 | 34 | 144 | 469 | 613 | 803 | 795 | 444 | 114 | 21 | 0 | 3437 |
| 1968-69 | 0 | 0 | 1 | 149 | 423 | 716 | 733 | 601 | 608 | 103 | 12 | 0 | 3346 |
| 1969-70 | 0 | 0 | 0 | 151 | 473 | 768 | 917 | 648 | 500 | 97 | 20 | 0 | 3574 |
| 1970-71 | 0 | 0 | 7 | 150 | 455 | 571 | 781 | 593 | 509 | 171 | 50 | 0 | 3287 |
| 1971-72 | 0 | 0 | 9 | 13 | 432 | 435 | 698 | 582 | 391 | 146 | 27 | 0 | 2733 |
| 1972-73 | 0 | 0 | 12 | 172 | 583 | 766 | 809 | 679 | 237 | 200 | 32 | 0 | 3490 |
| 1973-74 | 0 | 0 | 8 | 67 | 244 | 665 | 599 | 535 | 235 | 150 | 1 | 0 | 2504 |
| 1974-75 | 0 | 0 | 28 | 121 | 367 | 607 | 591 | 521 | 463 | 180 | 2 | 0 | 2880 |
| 1975-76 | 0 | 0 | 40 | 90 | 352 | 643 | 783 | 326 | 238 | 100 | 58 | 0 | 2630 |
| 1976-77 | 0 | 0 | 0 | 231 | 581 | 708 | 1056 | 547 | 212 | 61 | 4 | 0 | 3400 |
| 1977-78 | 0 | 0 | 0 | 123 | 313 | 640 | 995 | 835 | 454 | 74 | 47 | 0 | 3481 |
| 1978-79 | 0 | 0 | 0 | 116 | 230 | 643 | 1049 | 734 | 345 | 121 | 23 | 0 | 3261 |
| 1979-80 | 0 | 0 | 0 | 76 | 426 | 598 | 669 | 733 | 478 | 156 | 7 | 0 | 3143 |
| 1980-81 | 0 | 0 | 5 | 146 | 362 | 586 | 739 | 492 | 342 | 18 | 23 | 0 | 2713 |
| 1981-82 | 0 | 0 | 9 | 153 | 331 | 739 | 873 | 680 | 324 | 215 | 2 | 0 | 3326 |
| 1982-83 | 0 | 0 | 20 | 134 | 352 | 500 | 759 | 543 | 406 | 273 | 25 | 0 | 3012 |
| 1983-84 | 0 | 0 | 27 | 73 | 368 | 935 | 894 | 499 | 426 | 162 | 24 | 0 | 3408 |
| 1984-85 | 0 | 0 | 37 | 48 | 423 | 367 | 1004 | 683 | 254 | 100 | 6 | 0 | 2922 |
| 1985-86 | 0 | 0 | 17 | 54 | 257 | 864 | 708 | 475 | 307 | 102 | 8 | 0 | 2792 |
| 1986-87 | 0 | 0 | 0 | 102 | 413 | 687 | 782 | 492 | 322 | 154 | 0 | 0 | 2952 |
| 1987-88 | 0 | 0 | 0 | 186 | 324 | 559 | 867 | 657 | 393 | 108 | 0 | 0 | 3094 |
| 1988-89 | 0 | 0 | 1 | 202 | 314 | 619 | 544 | 694 | 369 | 174 | 41 | 0 | 2958 |
| 1989-90 | 0 | 0 | 24 | 102 | 337 | 966 | 503 | 363 | 321 | 181 | 38 | 0 | 2835 |
| 1990-91 | 0 | 0 | 11 | 182 | 249 | 593 | | | | | | | |

**TABLE 5**  COOLING DEGREE DAYS Base 65 deg. F  MEMPHIS, TENNESSEE

| YEAR | JAN | FEB | MAR | APR | MAY | JUNE | JULY | AUG | SEP | OCT | NOV | DEC | TOTAL |
|---|---|---|---|---|---|---|---|---|---|---|---|---|---|
| 1969 | 0 | 0 | 0 | 48 | 240 | 422 | 627 | 449 | 243 | 91 | 0 | 0 | 2120 |
| 1970 | 3 | 0 | 0 | 104 | 251 | 375 | 463 | 509 | 400 | 51 | 6 | 2 | 2164 |
| 1971 | 0 | 0 | 3 | 46 | 107 | 474 | 489 | 426 | 349 | 154 | 14 | 0 | 2062 |
| 1972 | 0 | 0 | 3 | 95 | 179 | 383 | 449 | 464 | 346 | 66 | 6 | 0 | 1991 |
| 1973 | 0 | 0 | 4 | 48 | 143 | 486 | 571 | 458 | 350 | 156 | 19 | 0 | 2235 |
| 1974 | 6 | 0 | 46 | 59 | 228 | 299 | 550 | 445 | 138 | 46 | 23 | 0 | 1840 |
| 1975 | 8 | 0 | 3 | 93 | 272 | 421 | 507 | 510 | 224 | 121 | 23 | 2 | 2184 |
| 1976 | 0 | 7 | 44 | 64 | 84 | 349 | 519 | 438 | 247 | 48 | 0 | 0 | 1800 |
| 1977 | 0 | 0 | 23 | 123 | 362 | 516 | 619 | 551 | 426 | 41 | 20 | 0 | 2681 |
| 1978 | 0 | 0 | 6 | 122 | 235 | 452 | 590 | 501 | 387 | 46 | 18 | 0 | 2357 |
| 1979 | 0 | 0 | 19 | 68 | 184 | 394 | 553 | 499 | 259 | 108 | 4 | 0 | 2088 |
| 1980 | 0 | 0 | 0 | 40 | 249 | 480 | 744 | 695 | 476 | 80 | 18 | 2 | 2784 |
| 1981 | 0 | 5 | 20 | 181 | 184 | 532 | 614 | 527 | 285 | 80 | 2 | 0 | 2430 |
| 1982 | 0 | 1 | 36 | 26 | 305 | 399 | 623 | 563 | 275 | 100 | 14 | 25 | 2367 |
| 1983 | 0 | 0 | 7 | 32 | 131 | 373 | 584 | 622 | 338 | 116 | 17 | 0 | 2220 |
| 1984 | 0 | 1 | 4 | 51 | 169 | 482 | 502 | 462 | 249 | 162 | 5 | 23 | 2110 |
| 1985 | 0 | 6 | 30 | 107 | 224 | 425 | 540 | 478 | 285 | 129 | 42 | 0 | 2266 |
| 1986 | 0 | 3 | 12 | 91 | 247 | 487 | 673 | 448 | 427 | 81 | 4 | 0 | 2473 |
| 1987 | 0 | 0 | 9 | 78 | 366 | 458 | 549 | 584 | 315 | 12 | 13 | 0 | 2384 |
| 1988 | 0 | 0 | 7 | 52 | 221 | 469 | 518 | 586 | 347 | 24 | 8 | 0 | 2232 |
| 1989 | 0 | 2 | 27 | 109 | 186 | 386 | 496 | 510 | 254 | 84 | 20 | 0 | 2074 |
| 1990 | 0 | 7 | 27 | 83 | 146 | 477 | 550 | 534 | 404 | 71 | 18 | 2 | 2319 |

**TABLE 6**  SNOWFALL (inches)  MEMPHIS, TENNESSEE

| SEASON | JULY | AUG | SEP | OCT | NOV | DEC | JAN | FEB | MAR | APR | MAY | JUNE | TOTAL |
|---|---|---|---|---|---|---|---|---|---|---|---|---|---|
| 1961-62 | 0.0 | 0.0 | 0.0 | 0.0 | T | T | 5.0 | T | T | 0.0 | 0.0 | 0.0 | 5.0 |
| 1962-63 | 0.0 | 0.0 | 0.0 | 0.0 | 0.0 | 3.0 | 1.2 | 0.8 | 0.0 | 0.0 | 0.0 | 0.0 | 5.0 |
| 1963-64 | 0.0 | 0.0 | 0.0 | 0.0 | 0.0 | 14.3 | 0.5 | T | T | 0.0 | 0.0 | 0.0 | 14.8 |
| 1964-65 | 0.0 | 0.0 | 0.0 | 0.0 | T | T | T | 3.3 | 4.6 | 0.0 | 0.0 | 0.0 | 7.9 |
| 1965-66 | 0.0 | 0.0 | 0.0 | 0.0 | 0.0 | 0.0 | 12.2 | T | T | 0.0 | 0.0 | 0.0 | 12.2 |
| 1966-67 | 0.0 | 0.0 | 0.0 | 0.0 | T | 0.7 | 0.6 | T | 0.3 | 0.0 | 0.0 | 0.0 | 1.6 |
| 1967-68 | 0.0 | 0.0 | 0.0 | 0.0 | 0.0 | T | 2.0 | 4.5 | 17.3 | 0.0 | 0.0 | 0.0 | 23.8 |
| 1968-69 | 0.0 | 0.0 | 0.0 | 0.0 | 0.0 | 0.0 | T | T | T | 0.0 | 0.0 | 0.0 | T |
| 1969-70 | 0.0 | 0.0 | 0.0 | 0.0 | T | 0.1 | 3.3 | 0.2 | T | 0.0 | 0.0 | 0.0 | 3.6 |
| 1970-71 | 0.0 | 0.0 | 0.0 | 0.0 | T | 1.0 | T | 6.7 | 1.6 | T | 0.0 | 0.0 | 9.3 |
| 1971-72 | 0.0 | 0.0 | 0.0 | 0.0 | 0.8 | 0.0 | 0.3 | 0.1 | T | 0.0 | 0.0 | 0.0 | 1.2 |
| 1972-73 | 0.0 | 0.0 | 0.0 | 0.0 | T | 1.4 | T | 0.0 | 0.0 | 0.0 | 0.0 | 0.0 | 1.4 |
| 1973-74 | 0.0 | 0.0 | 0.0 | 0.0 | 0.0 | 0.2 | 0.9 | 0.5 | T | 0.0 | 0.0 | 0.0 | 1.6 |
| 1974-75 | 0.0 | 0.0 | 0.0 | 0.0 | T | 0.2 | 3.9 | 0.5 | 1.4 | 0.0 | 0.0 | 0.0 | 6.0 |
| 1975-76 | 0.0 | 0.0 | 0.0 | 0.0 | 0.0 | 0.1 | 0.3 | T | 0.0 | 0.0 | 0.0 | 0.0 | 0.4 |
| 1976-77 | 0.0 | 0.0 | 0.0 | 0.0 | 1.5 | 0.3 | 3.5 | T | 0.0 | 0.0 | 0.0 | 0.0 | 5.3 |
| 1977-78 | 0.0 | 0.0 | 0.0 | 0.0 | 0.0 | T | 4.3 | 3.2 | T | 0.0 | 0.0 | 0.0 | 7.5 |
| 1978-79 | 0.0 | 0.0 | 0.0 | 0.0 | 0.0 | T | 3.0 | 7.4 | 0.0 | 0.0 | 0.0 | 0.0 | 10.4 |
| 1979-80 | 0.0 | 0.0 | 0.0 | 0.0 | T | 0.0 | 1.3 | 1.5 | 0.8 | 0.0 | 0.0 | 0.0 | 3.6 |
| 1980-81 | 0.0 | 0.0 | 0.0 | 0.0 | T | T | T | T | 0.0 | 0.0 | 0.0 | 0.0 | T |
| 1981-82 | 0.0 | 0.0 | 0.0 | 0.0 | 0.0 | T | 4.5 | 0.7 | 1.2 | 0.0 | 0.0 | 0.0 | 6.4 |
| 1982-83 | 0.0 | 0.0 | 0.0 | 0.0 | 0.0 | T | 7.3 | T | 0.2 | 0.0 | 0.0 | 0.0 | 7.5 |
| 1983-84 | 0.0 | 0.0 | 0.0 | 0.0 | 0.0 | 0.8 | T | T | 0.5 | 0.0 | 0.0 | 0.0 | 3.3 |
| 1984-85 | 0.0 | 0.0 | 0.0 | 0.0 | 0.0 | T | 12.4 | 8.3 | 0.0 | 0.0 | 0.0 | 0.0 | 20.7 |
| 1985-86 | 0.0 | 0.0 | 0.0 | 0.0 | 0.0 | T | T | 2.0 | 0.0 | 0.0 | 0.0 | 0.0 | 2.0 |
| 1986-87 | 0.0 | 0.0 | 0.0 | 0.0 | 0.0 | 0.0 | T | T | 0.4 | 0.0 | 0.0 | 0.0 | . |
| 1987-88 | 0.0 | 0.0 | 0.0 | 0.0 | 0.0 | 0.0 | 8.2 | 3.0 | T | 0.0 | 0.0 | 0.0 | 11.2 |
| 1988-89 | 0.0 | 0.0 | 0.0 | 0.0 | 0.0 | T | T | 0.3 | T | 0.0 | 0.0 | 0.0 | 0.3 |
| 1989-90 | 0.0 | 0.0 | 0.0 | T | T | 0.4 | 0.0 | 0.0 | 0.0 | T | 0.0 | 0.0 | 0.4 |
| 1990-91 | 0.0 | 0.0 | 0.0 | 0.0 | 0.0 | 0.4 | | | | | | | |
| Record Mean | 0.0 | 0.0 | 0.0 | T | 0.1 | 0.7 | 2.5 | 1.4 | 0.9 | T | T | 0.0 | 5.5 |

**See Reference Notes, relative to all above tables, on preceding page.**

The city of Nashville is located on the Cumberland River, in the northwestern corner of the Central Basin of middle Tennessee near the escarpment of the Highland Rim. The Rim, as it is called, rises to the height of 300 to 400 feet above the mean elevation of the basin, forming an amphitheater about the city from the southwest to the southeast, with the south being more or less open but undulating.

Temperatures are moderate, with great extremes of either heat or cold rarely occurring, yet there are changes of sufficient amplitude and frequency to give variety.

Based on the 1951–1980 period, the average first occurrence of 32 degrees Fahrenheit in the fall is October 29 and the average last occurrence in the spring is April 5.

Humidity is an important phase of climate in relation to bodily health and comfort. The Nashville records show that the average relative humidity is moderate as compared with the general conditions east of the Mississippi River and south of the Ohio.

Nashville is not in the most frequented path of general storms that cross the country, however, it is in the zone of moderate frequency of thunderstorms. The thunderstorm season usually begins in the latter part of March and continues through September.

## TABLE 1 — NORMALS, MEANS AND EXTREMES

NASHVILLE, TENNESSEE

LATITUDE: 36°07'N   LONGITUDE: 86°41'W   ELEVATION: FT. GRND  590 BARO  630   TIME ZONE: CENTRAL   WBAN: 13897

| | (a) | JAN | FEB | MAR | APR | MAY | JUNE | JULY | AUG | SEP | OCT | NOV | DEC | YEAR |
|---|---|---|---|---|---|---|---|---|---|---|---|---|---|---|
| **TEMPERATURE °F:** | | | | | | | | | | | | | | |
| Normals | | | | | | | | | | | | | | |
| -Daily Maximum | | 46.3 | 50.7 | 59.6 | 71.2 | 79.2 | 86.7 | 89.8 | 89.0 | 83.2 | 72.3 | 59.2 | 50.4 | 69.8 |
| -Daily Minimum | | 27.8 | 30.1 | 38.3 | 48.1 | 56.9 | 64.8 | 69.0 | 67.8 | 61.3 | 48.0 | 38.0 | 31.3 | 48.5 |
| -Monthly | | 37.1 | 40.4 | 49.0 | 59.6 | 68.1 | 75.8 | 79.4 | 78.4 | 72.3 | 60.2 | 48.6 | 40.9 | 59.2 |
| Extremes | | | | | | | | | | | | | | |
| -Record Highest | 50 | 78 | 84 | 86 | 91 | 97 | 106 | 107 | 104 | 105 | 94 | 84 | 79 | 107 |
| -Year | | 1972 | 1962 | 1982 | 1989 | 1941 | 1952 | 1952 | 1954 | 1954 | 1953 | 1971 | 1982 | JUL 1952 |
| -Record Lowest | 50 | -17 | -13 | 2 | 23 | 34 | 42 | 51 | 47 | 36 | 26 | -1 | -10 | -17 |
| -Year | | 1985 | 1951 | 1980 | 1982 | 1976 | 1966 | 1947 | 1946 | 1983 | 1987 | 1950 | 1989 | JAN 1985 |
| **NORMAL DEGREE DAYS:** | | | | | | | | | | | | | | |
| Heating (base 65°F) | | 865 | 689 | 510 | 186 | 55 | 0 | 0 | 0 | 19 | 193 | 492 | 747 | 3756 |
| Cooling (base 65°F) | | 0 | 0 | 14 | 24 | 151 | 328 | 446 | 415 | 238 | 45 | 0 | 0 | 1661 |
| **% OF POSSIBLE SUNSHINE** | 47 | 42 | 47 | 52 | 59 | 61 | 65 | 63 | 64 | 62 | 62 | 50 | 42 | 56 |
| **MEAN SKY COVER (tenths)** | | | | | | | | | | | | | | |
| Sunrise - Sunset | 49 | 7.0 | 6.7 | 6.6 | 6.0 | 5.9 | 5.6 | 5.6 | 5.2 | 5.2 | 4.9 | 6.1 | 6.7 | 6.0 |
| **MEAN NUMBER OF DAYS:** | | | | | | | | | | | | | | |
| Sunrise to Sunset | | | | | | | | | | | | | | |
| -Clear | 48 | 6.4 | 7.0 | 7.5 | 8.3 | 8.4 | 8.5 | 8.3 | 10.4 | 10.8 | 12.8 | 8.9 | 7.3 | 104.5 |
| -Partly Cloudy | 48 | 6.2 | 5.8 | 7.0 | 8.4 | 9.9 | 12.1 | 12.9 | 11.8 | 8.9 | 8.2 | 6.6 | 7.0 | 104.7 |
| -Cloudy | 48 | 18.4 | 15.5 | 16.5 | 13.3 | 12.7 | 9.4 | 9.9 | 8.9 | 10.4 | 10.1 | 14.5 | 16.8 | 156.1 |
| Precipitation | | | | | | | | | | | | | | |
| .01 inches or more | 48 | 11.0 | 10.7 | 11.9 | 10.8 | 10.7 | 9.4 | 10.3 | 8.8 | 7.9 | 7.0 | 9.5 | 10.9 | 118.8 |
| Snow, Ice pellets | | | | | | | | | | | | | | |
| 1.0 inches or more | 48 | 1.3 | 1.2 | 0.5 | 0.* | 0.0 | 0.0 | 0.0 | 0.0 | 0.0 | 0.0 | 0.1 | 0.5 | 3.6 |
| Thunderstorms | 48 | 1.3 | 1.7 | 4.2 | 5.3 | 7.4 | 8.3 | 9.6 | 7.8 | 3.6 | 1.5 | 1.7 | 1.1 | 53.5 |
| Heavy Fog Visibility | | | | | | | | | | | | | | |
| 1/4 mile or less | 48 | 2.4 | 1.3 | 1.1 | 0.5 | 0.9 | 0.9 | 1.1 | 1.6 | 1.8 | 2.1 | 1.8 | 1.8 | 17.4 |
| Temperature °F | | | | | | | | | | | | | | |
| -Maximum | | | | | | | | | | | | | | |
| 90° and above | 24 | 0.0 | 0.0 | 0.0 | 0.2 | 1.0 | 9.4 | 16.8 | 12.2 | 5.2 | 0.1 | 0.0 | 0.0 | 44.7 |
| 32° and below | 24 | 5.4 | 2.5 | 0.1 | 0.0 | 0.0 | 0.0 | 0.0 | 0.0 | 0.0 | 0.0 | 0.2 | 2.0 | 10.2 |
| -Minimum | | | | | | | | | | | | | | |
| 32° and below | 24 | 22.5 | 17.4 | 9.4 | 1.7 | 0.0 | 0.0 | 0.0 | 0.0 | 0.0 | 1.1 | 7.9 | 17.4 | 77.4 |
| 0° and below | 24 | 0.8 | 0.2 | 0.0 | 0.0 | 0.0 | 0.0 | 0.0 | 0.0 | 0.0 | 0.0 | 0.0 | 0.3 | 1.3 |
| **AVG. STATION PRESS.(mb)** | 17 | 999.2 | 997.9 | 995.1 | 994.4 | 993.7 | 994.5 | 995.4 | 995.9 | 996.6 | 998.2 | 997.9 | 999.0 | 996.5 |
| **RELATIVE HUMIDITY (%)** | | | | | | | | | | | | | | |
| Hour 00 | 24 | 75 | 74 | 71 | 72 | 82 | 84 | 85 | 85 | 86 | 81 | 77 | 76 | 79 |
| Hour 06 | 24 | 79 | 79 | 78 | 80 | 86 | 87 | 90 | 90 | 91 | 86 | 82 | 80 | 84 |
| Hour 12 (Local Time) | 24 | 63 | 60 | 53 | 51 | 55 | 55 | 57 | 58 | 59 | 54 | 59 | 63 | 57 |
| Hour 18 | 24 | 65 | 61 | 54 | 52 | 58 | 59 | 62 | 63 | 65 | 61 | 64 | 66 | 61 |
| **PRECIPITATION (inches):** | | | | | | | | | | | | | | |
| Water Equivalent | | | | | | | | | | | | | | |
| -Normal | | 4.49 | 4.03 | 5.58 | 4.47 | 4.56 | 3.70 | 3.82 | 3.40 | 3.71 | 2.58 | 3.52 | 4.63 | 48.49 |
| -Maximum Monthly | 50 | 13.92 | 10.31 | 12.35 | 8.41 | 11.04 | 9.37 | 7.75 | 8.31 | 11.44 | 6.13 | 9.04 | 13.63 | 13.92 |
| -Year | | 1950 | 1956 | 1975 | 1984 | 1983 | 1960 | 1950 | 1942 | 1979 | 1959 | 1945 | 1978 | JAN 1950 |
| -Minimum Monthly | 50 | 0.19 | 0.64 | 1.18 | 0.52 | 0.69 | 0.45 | 0.71 | 0.69 | 0.28 | T | 0.54 | 0.98 | T |
| -Year | | 1986 | 1968 | 1987 | 1986 | 1941 | 1988 | 1954 | 1968 | 1956 | 1963 | 1949 | 1985 | OCT 1963 |
| -Maximum in 24 hrs | 50 | 4.40 | 4.73 | 4.66 | 3.29 | 4.27 | 4.91 | 3.56 | 5.34 | 6.68 | 3.75 | 3.74 | 5.12 | 6.68 |
| -Year | | 1946 | 1989 | 1975 | 1979 | 1984 | 1960 | 1950 | 1963 | 1979 | 1975 | 1973 | 1978 | SEP 1979 |
| Snow, Ice pellets | | | | | | | | | | | | | | |
| -Maximum Monthly | 50 | 18.8 | 18.9 | 16.1 | 1.1 | 0.0 | 0.0 | 0.0 | T | 0.0 | T | 9.2 | 13.2 | 18.9 |
| -Year | | 1948 | 1979 | 1960 | 1971 | | | | 1989 | | 1989 | 1950 | 1963 | FEB 1979 |
| -Maximum in 24 hrs | 50 | 8.1 | 8.3 | 8.8 | 1.1 | 0.0 | 0.0 | 0.0 | T | 0.0 | T | 9.2 | 10.2 | 10.2 |
| -Year | | 1988 | 1979 | 1951 | 1971 | | | | 1989 | | 1989 | 1950 | 1963 | DEC 1963 |
| **WIND:** | | | | | | | | | | | | | | |
| Mean Speed (mph) | 48 | 9.2 | 9.4 | 10.0 | 9.4 | 7.7 | 7.1 | 6.5 | 6.1 | 6.4 | 6.8 | 8.4 | 9.0 | 8.0 |
| Prevailing Direction | | | | | | | | | | | | | | |
| through 1963 | | S | S | S | S | S | S | S | S | S | S | S | S | S |
| Fastest Obs. 1 Min. | | | | | | | | | | | | | | |
| -Direction (!!!) | 14 | 34 | 32 | 13 | 31 | 36 | 30 | 34 | 02 | 34 | 36 | 15 | 23 | 13 |
| -Speed (MPH) | 14 | 32 | 35 | 41 | 35 | 41 | 35 | 33 | 40 | 33 | 32 | 39 | 41 | 41 |
| -Year | | 1985 | 1980 | 1987 | 1982 | 1984 | 1981 | 1978 | 1983 | 1977 | 1986 | 1984 | 1987 | MAR 1987 |
| Peak Gust | | | | | | | | | | | | | | |
| -Direction (!!!) | 6 | W | SW | SE | W | NW | SW | N | W | N | N | W | SW | W |
| -Speed (mph) | 6 | 46 | 47 | 56 | 47 | 55 | 49 | 51 | 49 | 47 | 48 | 60 | 54 | 60 |
| -Date | | 1984 | 1988 | 1987 | 1989 | 1984 | 1988 | 1988 | 1989 | 1989 | 1986 | 1985 | 1987 | NOV 1985 |

**See Reference Notes to this table on the following page.**

**TABLE 2**  PRECIPITATION (inches)   NASHVILLE, TENNESSEE

| YEAR | JAN | FEB | MAR | APR | MAY | JUNE | JULY | AUG | SEP | OCT | NOV | DEC | ANNUAL |
|------|-----|-----|-----|-----|-----|------|------|-----|-----|-----|-----|-----|--------|
| 1961 | 1.44 | 5.33 | 6.52 | 4.50 | 4.36 | 2.96 | 5.34 | 2.62 | 0.35 | 1.12 | 3.87 | 6.44 | 44.85 |
| 1962 | 6.51 | 5.89 | 5.89 | 6.91 | 1.87 | 1.97 | 2.45 | 8.03 | 2.29 |  | 3.37 | 1.92 | 57.57 |
| 1963 | 1.60 | 2.83 | 10.03 | 3.37 | 2.47 | 3.09 | 5.33 | 7.63 | 3.43 | T | 2.43 | 2.15 | 44.36 |
| 1964 | 3.70 | 3.26 | 5.92 | 5.86 | 5.04 | 1.21 | 2.16 | 4.56 | 2.65 | 1.83 | 3.67 | 5.15 | 45.01 |
| 1965 | 2.98 | 4.71 | 6.13 | 5.72 | 3.12 | 2.74 | 3.32 | 2.53 | 5.02 | 0.57 | 1.82 | 1.01 | 39.67 |
| 1966 | 3.93 | 3.63 | 1.39 | 5.08 | 3.99 | 1.09 | 2.70 | 5.29 | 3.87 | 2.50 | 2.76 | 5.69 | 41.92 |
| 1967 | 1.62 | 1.78 | 4.44 | 3.40 | 6.98 | 4.23 | 7.46 | 2.06 | 1.93 | 1.57 | 3.87 | 5.88 | 45.22 |
| 1968 | 3.50 | 0.64 | 4.47 | 3.57 | 6.28 | 2.26 | 6.87 | 0.69 | 2.76 | 3.92 | 3.58 |  | 43.93 |
| 1969 | 4.96 | 4.48 | 2.12 | 6.03 | 4.81 | 3.34 | 5.33 | 2.27 | 2.06 | 2.01 | 1.83 | 8.03 | 47.27 |
| 1970 | 1.16 | 4.36 | 3.87 | 6.81 | 5.90 | 6.73 | 3.61 | 2.99 | 2.76 | 2.94 | 2.20 | 3.60 | 46.93 |
| 1971 | 2.66 | 4.70 | 2.95 | 3.34 | 2.93 | 3.47 | 5.00 | 5.87 | 2.11 | 1.27 | 1.18 | 5.17 | 40.65 |
| 1972 | 5.15 | 3.45 | 4.34 | 3.58 | 3.52 | 2.54 | 6.40 | 4.30 | 3.71 | 4.06 | 5.22 | 8.14 | 54.41 |
| 1973 | 3.40 | 3.63 | 9.88 | 7.00 | 5.72 | 4.80 | 7.67 | 1.79 | 1.56 | 3.32 | 7.78 | 3.23 | 59.78 |
| 1974 | 9.45 | 3.01 | 5.25 | 3.97 | 5.04 | 6.80 | 2.10 | 4.13 | 10.44 | 1.47 | 6.23 | 2.81 | 60.70 |
| 1975 | 4.67 | 5.22 | 12.35 | 3.55 | 6.52 | 2.22 | 2.96 | 4.69 | 5.42 | 5.86 | 3.00 | 4.12 | 60.58 |
| 1976 | 4.11 | 2.28 | 5.32 | 1.53 | 6.19 | 4.72 | 4.01 | 8.05 | 5.08 | 5.17 | 1.30 | 1.81 | 49.57 |
| 1977 | 2.53 | 3.27 | 5.83 | 7.87 | 1.65 | 4.29 | 1.15 | 4.65 | 5.04 | 4.22 | 5.96 | 4.25 | 50.71 |
| 1978 | 5.95 | 1.57 | 4.88 | 2.42 | 8.03 | 1.46 | 4.03 | 3.81 | 1.37 | 2.28 | 4.01 | 13.63 | 53.44 |
| 1979 | 7.13 | 4.01 | 4.92 | 7.80 | 8.18 | 2.79 | 4.27 | 4.59 | 11.44 | 3.97 | 5.98 | 5.04 | 70.12 |
| 1980 | 2.59 | 1.38 | 7.27 | 3.67 | 6.14 | 2.89 | 3.53 | 1.24 | 1.09 | 1.17 | 2.55 | 1.40 | 34.92 |
| 1981 | 1.60 | 3.83 | 3.38 | 4.78 | 3.05 | 8.05 | 3.49 | 3.10 | 1.37 | 2.82 | 3.83 | 2.38 | 41.68 |
| 1982 | 6.50 | 4.80 | 3.00 | 4.36 | 4.19 | 2.28 | 5.47 | 3.46 | 3.23 | 1.91 | 3.87 | 6.36 | 49.43 |
| 1983 | 2.56 | 2.93 | 3.44 | 6.80 | 11.04 | 3.93 | 1.71 | 1.36 | 0.45 | 2.77 | 6.98 | 7.75 | 51.72 |
| 1984 | 1.79 | 2.38 | 5.14 | 8.41 | 9.68 | 4.49 | 6.63 | 2.42 | 0.97 | 6.00 | 6.20 | 2.38 | 56.49 |
| 1985 | 3.02 | 3.30 | 2.70 | 2.91 | 2.65 | 1.53 | 2.00 | 3.91 | 2.52 | 1.59 | 3.81 | 0.98 | 30.92 |
| 1986 | 0.19 | 3.59 | 2.29 | 0.52 | 3.36 | 2.38 | 0.77 | 3.38 | 2.19 | 2.19 | 7.43 | 3.31 | 31.60 |
| 1987 | 1.61 | 4.87 | 1.18 | 1.03 | 4.41 | 2.82 | 2.56 | 0.73 | 1.95 | 0.21 | 3.40 | 5.46 | 30.23 |
| 1988 | 3.73 | 2.02 | 2.18 | 2.09 | 1.86 | 0.45 | 3.26 | 2.39 | 2.45 | 1.54 | 5.49 | 3.95 | 31.41 |
| 1989 | 4.52 | 9.36 | 5.31 | 2.68 | 4.61 | 7.87 | 3.18 | 3.67 | 6.30 | 3.62 | 3.94 | 1.97 | 57.03 |
| 1990 | 2.76 | 4.73 | 3.26 | 1.60 | 2.80 | 2.37 | 4.86 | 3.12 | 2.13 | 4.41 | 4.29 | 10.76 | 47.09 |
| Record Mean | 4.59 | 4.13 | 5.06 | 4.17 | 4.07 | 3.78 | 3.92 | 3.38 | 3.26 | 2.50 | 3.61 | 4.02 | 46.51 |

**TABLE 3**  AVERAGE TEMPERATURE (deg. F)   NASHVILLE, TENNESSEE

| YEAR | JAN | FEB | MAR | APR | MAY | JUNE | JULY | AUG | SEP | OCT | NOV | DEC | ANNUAL |
|------|-----|-----|-----|-----|-----|------|------|-----|-----|-----|-----|-----|--------|
| 1961 | 33.2 | 46.9 | 52.2 | 54.5 | 63.6 | 72.4 | 76.4 | 76.4 | 73.5 | 59.8 | 49.6 | 41.1 | 58.4 |
| 1962 | 35.3 | 46.2 | 45.3 | 56.0 | 75.2 | 75.0 | 79.1 | 79.7 | 69.3 | 62.9 | 47.9 | 35.0 | 58.9 |
| 1963 | 30.9 | 34.2 | 53.8 | 61.6 | 67.3 | 75.9 | 77.6 | 76.8 | 70.0 | 65.5 | 49.3 | 30.5 | 57.8 |
| 1964 | 38.9 | 37.2 | 49.0 | 62.6 | 69.7 | 77.7 | 78.7 | 77.2 | 71.3 | 56.7 | 51.7 | 42.7 | 59.4 |
| #1965 | 40.0 | 39.8 | 41.9 | 60.9 | 71.7 | 75.1 | 78.6 | 79.0 | 74.1 | 59.3 | 51.9 | 44.8 | 59.7 |
| 1966 | 32.3 | 41.3 | 50.5 | 58.8 | 65.3 | 75.1 | 82.3 | 76.5 | 69.5 | 57.0 | 50.7 | 40.2 | 58.3 |
| 1967 | 42.3 | 37.5 | 57.0 | 63.9 | 66.3 | 76.3 | 75.7 | 72.6 | 66.8 | 59.3 | 44.3 | 42.6 | 58.7 |
| 1968 | 34.0 | 32.4 | 47.8 | 58.7 | 66.3 | 74.9 | 77.8 | 79.5 | 69.9 | 59.5 | 48.7 | 38.1 | 57.3 |
| 1969 | 37.2 | 39.8 | 42.6 | 60.9 | 68.9 | 77.2 | 82.7 | 78.1 | 70.8 | 60.6 | 46.5 | 37.3 | 58.6 |
| 1970 | 32.4 | 38.4 | 46.8 | 61.3 | 68.4 | 73.6 | 77.2 | 79.2 | 76.9 | 61.0 | 47.5 | 43.2 | 58.8 |
| 1971 | 35.6 | 38.7 | 44.6 | 57.9 | 63.3 | 77.5 | 76.8 | 76.4 | 74.4 | 66.7 | 49.9 | 49.2 | 59.3 |
| 1972 | 41.8 | 41.8 | 50.2 | 60.5 | 67.4 | 73.0 | 77.3 | 77.2 | 75.7 | 60.2 | 47.3 | 42.8 | 59.6 |
| 1973 | 38.0 | 39.7 | 56.8 | 56.4 | 64.2 | 76.1 | 78.7 | 78.1 | 76.2 | 66.2 | 54.7 | 40.5 | 60.5 |
| 1974 | 45.4 | 41.8 | 54.9 | 58.6 | 70.0 | 71.4 | 78.0 | 77.6 | 67.5 | 59.4 | 50.0 | 42.6 | 59.8 |
| 1975 | 43.4 | 44.6 | 47.3 | 58.5 | 70.4 | 76.0 | 78.5 | 79.1 | 67.9 | 62.4 | 52.1 | 42.8 | 60.2 |
| 1976 | 36.7 | 50.5 | 55.9 | 59.9 | 64.0 | 73.3 | 76.4 | 74.4 | 66.8 | 53.9 | 40.9 | 36.6 | 57.5 |
| 1977 | 24.5 | 40.6 | 53.9 | 63.0 | 71.9 | 77.2 | 82.2 | 79.5 | 74.0 | 57.0 | 50.8 | 38.6 | 59.4 |
| 1978 | 27.6 | 29.2 | 46.9 | 61.0 | 66.7 | 76.2 | 80.5 | 78.7 | 75.5 | 57.4 | 53.6 | 42.4 | 58.0 |
| 1979 | 29.7 | 33.4 | 50.7 | 57.8 | 66.3 | 73.7 | 77.6 | 77.0 | 70.5 | 60.3 | 48.6 | 41.5 | 57.3 |
| 1980 | 39.7 | 35.7 | 46.3 | 57.3 | 67.8 | 75.5 | 82.8 | 81.7 | 76.0 | 57.8 | 48.5 | 41.0 | 59.2 |
| 1981 | 35.5 | 42.6 | 47.5 | 64.0 | 64.2 | 77.5 | 79.8 | 76.6 | 68.1 | 60.4 | 49.9 | 38.3 | 58.7 |
| 1982 | 34.0 | 39.5 | 52.5 | 54.6 | 71.0 | 73.3 | 79.8 | 76.1 | 69.6 | 61.1 | 51.4 | 48.2 | 59.3 |
| 1983 | 38.8 | 42.7 | 50.3 | 54.5 | 64.8 | 75.5 | 80.5 | 83.2 | 73.7 | 62.4 | 49.9 | 34.0 | 59.2 |
| 1984 | 32.2 | 43.4 | 46.1 | 58.2 | 64.2 | 77.4 | 76.1 | 76.5 | 68.6 | 66.7 | 46.0 | 49.6 | 58.8 |
| 1985 | 27.8 | 36.5 | 53.2 | 61.9 | 68.4 | 75.7 | 80.2 | 77.2 | 70.8 | 64.4 | 56.9 | 34.2 | 58.9 |
| 1986 | 37.2 | 44.7 | 50.8 | 60.8 | 68.6 | 76.5 | 82.4 | 76.7 | 74.9 | 61.0 | 49.9 | 39.9 | 60.3 |
| 1987 | 36.1 | 43.1 | 51.8 | 57.7 | 73.4 | 77.5 | 80.2 | 81.1 | 72.2 | 54.6 | 52.4 | 44.1 | 60.4 |
| 1988 | 34.4 | 38.7 | 49.3 | 57.1 | 67.3 | 77.3 | 81.4 | 81.9 | 72.8 | 54.2 | 51.1 | 42.4 | 59.0 |
| 1989 | 44.9 | 39.0 | 52.6 | 59.3 | 65.7 | 74.7 | 79.1 | 78.0 | 70.5 | 61.0 | 51.4 | 29.5 | 58.8 |
| 1990 | 45.8 | 49.9 | 53.6 | 58.4 | 66.4 | 78.2 | 80.4 | 79.6 | 74.7 | 60.1 | 54.3 | 43.7 | 62.1 |
| Record Mean | 38.5 | 41.0 | 49.7 | 59.4 | 68.1 | 76.2 | 79.4 | 78.3 | 72.2 | 60.9 | 49.1 | 41.0 | 59.5 |
| Max | 47.2 | 50.1 | 59.6 | 69.8 | 78.5 | 86.3 | 89.2 | 88.2 | 82.6 | 72.0 | 58.8 | 49.6 | 69.3 |
| Min | 29.9 | 31.8 | 39.7 | 48.9 | 57.7 | 66.1 | 69.6 | 68.4 | 61.7 | 49.7 | 39.4 | 32.4 | 49.6 |

## REFERENCE NOTES FOR TABLES 1, 2, 3 and 6   (NASHVILLE, TN)

**GENERAL**

T - TRACE AMOUNT
BLANK ENTRIES DENOTE MISSING/UNREPORTED DATA.
# INDICATES A STATION OR INSTRUMENT RELOCATION.

**SPECIFIC**

TABLE 1

(a) - LENGTH OF RECORD IN YEARS. ALTHOUGH INDIVIDUAL MONTHS MAY BE MISSING.

 * LESS THAN .05

NORMALS — BASED ON THE 1951-1980 RECORD PERIOD.
EXTREMES — DATES ARE THE MOST RECENT OCCURRENCE.
WIND DIR. — NUMERALS SHOW TENS OF DEGREES
    CLOCKWISE FROM TRUE NORTH.
    "00" INDICATES CALM.
RESULTANT WIND DIRECTIONS ARE GIVEN TO WHOLE DEGREES.

TABLE 3
MAX AND MIN ARE LONG-TERM MEAN DAILY MAXIMUM AND MEAN DAILY MINIMUM TEMPERATURES.

**EXCEPTIONS**

TABLES 2, 3, and 6

RECORD MEANS ARE THROUGH THE CURRENT YEAR,
BEGINNING IN   1871 FOR TEMPERATURE
    1871 FOR PRECIPITATION
    1942 FOR SNOWFALL

**TABLE 4**  HEATING DEGREE DAYS Base 65 deg. F    NASHVILLE, TENNESSEE

| SEASON | JULY | AUG | SEP | OCT | NOV | DEC | JAN | FEB | MAR | APR | MAY | JUNE | TOTAL |
|---|---|---|---|---|---|---|---|---|---|---|---|---|---|
| 1961-62 | 0 | 0 | 23 | 186 | 471 | 734 | 916 | 523 | 605 | 303 | 5 | 0 | 3766 |
| 1962-63 | 0 | 0 | 43 | 152 | 508 | 924 | 1050 | 855 | 358 | 170 | 63 | 0 | 4123 |
| 1963-64 | 0 | 0 | 28 | 48 | 465 | 1062 | 803 | 797 | 490 | 139 | 23 | 0 | 3855 |
| #1964-65 | 0 | 3 | 18 | 265 | 398 | 685 | 768 | 698 | 711 | 168 | 3 | 0 | 3717 |
| 1965-66 | 0 | 0 | 26 | 198 | 386 | 618 | 1007 | 657 | 452 | 234 | 78 | 7 | 3663 |
| 1966-67 | 0 | 0 | 13 | 255 | 423 | 763 | 697 | 763 | 300 | 106 | 69 | 1 | 3390 |
| 1967-68 | 0 | 3 | 58 | 216 | 615 | 688 | 952 | 941 | 531 | 205 | 64 | 1 | 4274 |
| 1968-69 | 0 | 0 | 4 | 220 | 484 | 825 | 855 | 700 | 692 | 149 | 38 | 3 | 3970 |
| 1969-70 | 0 | 0 | 10 | 201 | 551 | 854 | 1005 | 737 | 556 | 156 | 51 | 0 | 4121 |
| 1970-71 | 0 | 0 | 13 | 159 | 522 | 671 | 902 | 733 | 624 | 227 | 101 | 1 | 3952 |
| 1971-72 | 0 | 0 | 0 | 39 | 462 | 483 | 713 | 667 | 454 | 193 | 36 | 6 | 3053 |
| 1972-73 | 0 | 0 | 10 | 168 | 533 | 682 | 830 | 702 | 261 | 275 | 83 | 0 | 3544 |
| 1973-74 | 0 | 0 | 8 | 84 | 316 | 753 | 601 | 641 | 320 | 227 | 28 | 3 | 2981 |
| 1974-75 | 0 | 0 | 48 | 196 | 464 | 685 | 665 | 567 | 547 | 241 | 6 | 0 | 3419 |
| 1975-76 | 0 | 0 | 68 | 138 | 398 | 683 | 870 | 417 | 303 | 183 | 94 | 0 | 3154 |
| 1976-77 | 0 | 0 | 31 | 349 | 718 | 872 | 1250 | 679 | 350 | 129 | 28 | 1 | 4407 |
| 1977-78 | 0 | 0 | 3 | 255 | 425 | 813 | 1152 | 996 | 556 | 164 | 92 | 0 | 4456 |
| 1978-79 | 0 | 0 | 1 | 240 | 338 | 695 | 1088 | 877 | 449 | 213 | 57 | 0 | 3958 |
| 1979-80 | 0 | 0 | 5 | 180 | 487 | 723 | 777 | 848 | 571 | 240 | 38 | 0 | 3869 |
| 1980-81 | 0 | 0 | 9 | 259 | 487 | 739 | 909 | 621 | 537 | 97 | 96 | 0 | 3754 |
| 1981-82 | 0 | 0 | 42 | 175 | 445 | 820 | 956 | 707 | 416 | 309 | 8 | 0 | 3878 |
| 1982-83 | 0 | 0 | 30 | 194 | 413 | 537 | 806 | 620 | 458 | 322 | 71 | 0 | 3451 |
| 1983-84 | 0 | 0 | 45 | 121 | 447 | 956 | 1009 | 621 | 578 | 220 | 106 | 0 | 4103 |
| 1984-85 | 0 | 0 | 59 | 63 | 564 | 473 | 1146 | 794 | 383 | 145 | 25 | 6 | 3658 |
| 1985-86 | 0 | 0 | 30 | 91 | 264 | 948 | 854 | 561 | 432 | 171 | 55 | 0 | 3406 |
| 1986-87 | 0 | 3 | 0 | 175 | 447 | 773 | 889 | 608 | 401 | 242 | 6 | 0 | 3544 |
| 1987-88 | 0 | 0 | 7 | 317 | 376 | 640 | 941 | 756 | 485 | 242 | 43 | 2 | 3809 |
| 1988-89 | 0 | 0 | 5 | 343 | 408 | 693 | 618 | 721 | 397 | 258 | 90 | 0 | 3533 |
| 1989-90 | 0 | 0 | 36 | 158 | 408 | 1095 | 590 | 422 | 373 | 245 | 65 | 1 | 3393 |
| 1990-91 | 0 | 0 | 21 | 195 | 323 | 654 | | | | | | | |

**TABLE 5**  COOLING DEGREE DAYS Base 65 deg. F    NASHVILLE, TENNESSEE

| YEAR | JAN | FEB | MAR | APR | MAY | JUNE | JULY | AUG | SEP | OCT | NOV | DEC | TOTAL |
|---|---|---|---|---|---|---|---|---|---|---|---|---|---|
| 1969 | 0 | 0 | 0 | 33 | 165 | 378 | 554 | 416 | 191 | 74 | 0 | 0 | 1811 |
| 1970 | 0 | 0 | 0 | 56 | 163 | 265 | 386 | 446 | 374 | 40 | 1 | 1 | 1732 |
| 1971 | 0 | 0 | 0 | 23 | 55 | 380 | 374 | 360 | 293 | 101 | 16 | 1 | 1603 |
| 1972 | 0 | 0 | 1 | 62 | 117 | 250 | 385 | 387 | 341 | 24 | 6 | 0 | 1573 |
| 1973 | 0 | 0 | 14 | 25 | 61 | 339 | 432 | 412 | 351 | 128 | 8 | 0 | 1770 |
| 1974 | 0 | 0 | 16 | 39 | 191 | 203 | 410 | 399 | 130 | 30 | 22 | 0 | 1440 |
| 1975 | 3 | 0 | 3 | 55 | 183 | 341 | 424 | 444 | 164 | 62 | 19 | 0 | 1698 |
| 1976 | 0 | 1 | 28 | 36 | 68 | 257 | 363 | 299 | 92 | 10 | 0 | 0 | 1154 |
| 1977 | 0 | 0 | 11 | 74 | 253 | 371 | 543 | 458 | 281 | 13 | 4 | 0 | 2008 |
| 1978 | 0 | 0 | 1 | 50 | 152 | 344 | 489 | 432 | 324 | 13 | 2 | 0 | 1807 |
| 1979 | 0 | 0 | 11 | 5 | 103 | 264 | 393 | 381 | 175 | 44 | 0 | 0 | 1376 |
| 1980 | 0 | 0 | 0 | 17 | 131 | 322 | 562 | 527 | 344 | 44 | 1 | 0 | 1948 |
| 1981 | 0 | 0 | 1 | 71 | 81 | 383 | 464 | 366 | 145 | 42 | 0 | 0 | 1553 |
| 1982 | 0 | 0 | 37 | 4 | 199 | 256 | 470 | 352 | 177 | 84 | 12 | 21 | 1612 |
| 1983 | 0 | 0 | 9 | 12 | 69 | 320 | 488 | 568 | 315 | 49 | 2 | 0 | 1832 |
| 1984 | 0 | 0 | 0 | 21 | 87 | 382 | 352 | 364 | 173 | 121 | 0 | 1 | 1501 |
| 1985 | 0 | 2 | 24 | 59 | 137 | 335 | 479 | 386 | 206 | 79 | 29 | 0 | 1736 |
| 1986 | 0 | 0 | 1 | 52 | 174 | 352 | 551 | 371 | 304 | 59 | 0 | 0 | 1864 |
| 1987 | 0 | 0 | 0 | 31 | 272 | 381 | 479 | 507 | 227 | 3 | 7 | 0 | 1907 |
| 1988 | 0 | 0 | 5 | 17 | 120 | 380 | 515 | 531 | 246 | 17 | 0 | 0 | 1831 |
| 1989 | 0 | 0 | 21 | 93 | 120 | 298 | 446 | 408 | 208 | 39 | 8 | 0 | 1641 |
| 1990 | 0 | 4 | 26 | 51 | 115 | 401 | 485 | 458 | 315 | 52 | 10 | 0 | 1917 |

**TABLE 6**  SNOWFALL (inches)    NASHVILLE, TENNESSEE

| SEASON | JULY | AUG | SEP | OCT | NOV | DEC | JAN | FEB | MAR | APR | MAY | JUNE | TOTAL |
|---|---|---|---|---|---|---|---|---|---|---|---|---|---|
| 1961-62 | 0.0 | 0.0 | 0.0 | 0.0 | T | 2.0 | 2.2 | 1.1 | 1.4 | T | 0.0 | 0.0 | 6.7 |
| 1962-63 | 0.0 | 0.0 | 0.0 | 0.0 | T | 8.2 | 6.8 | 8.7 | 0.0 | 0.0 | 0.0 | 0.0 | 23.7 |
| 1963-64 | 0.0 | 0.0 | 0.0 | 0.0 | T | 13.2 | 5.0 | 4.2 | T | 0.0 | 0.0 | 0.0 | 22.4 |
| 1964-65 | 0.0 | 0.0 | 0.0 | 0.0 | T | 0.0 | 1.2 | 2.9 | 3.4 | 0.0 | 0.0 | 0.0 | 7.5 |
| 1965-66 | 0.0 | 0.0 | 0.0 | 0.0 | T | 0.0 | 11.4 | T | T | 0.0 | 0.0 | 0.0 | 11.4 |
| 1966-67 | 0.0 | 0.0 | 0.0 | 0.0 | 7.2 | 4.3 | 1.2 | T | T | 0.0 | 0.0 | 0.0 | 12.7 |
| 1967-68 | 0.0 | 0.0 | 0.0 | 0.0 | 0.0 | 8.4 | 7.2 | 2.9 | 8.5 | 0.0 | 0.0 | 0.0 | 27.0 |
| 1968-69 | 0.0 | 0.0 | 0.0 | 0.0 | T | T | 5.2 | 6.9 | 4.8 | 0.0 | 0.0 | 0.0 | 16.9 |
| 1969-70 | 0.0 | 0.0 | 0.0 | 0.0 | 0.3 | 3.8 | 5.6 | 3.0 | T | 0.0 | 0.0 | 0.0 | 12.7 |
| 1970-71 | 0.0 | 0.0 | 0.0 | 0.0 | T | 1.2 | 1.2 | 6.5 | 3.0 | 1.1 | 0.0 | 0.0 | 13.0 |
| 1971-72 | 0.0 | 0.0 | 0.0 | 0.0 | 0.1 | T | 0.4 | 0.5 | 0.9 | T | 0.0 | 0.0 | 1.9 |
| 1972-73 | 0.0 | 0.0 | 0.0 | 0.0 | 0.1 | 0.6 | 4.8 | T | 0.2 | 0.1 | 0.0 | 0.0 | 5.8 |
| 1973-74 | 0.0 | 0.0 | 0.0 | 0.0 | 0.0 | 2.4 | T | 0.3 | T | 0.0 | 0.0 | 0.0 | 2.7 |
| 1974-75 | 0.0 | 0.0 | 0.0 | 0.0 | T | 2.1 | 4.2 | T | T | T | 0.0 | 0.0 | 6.3 |
| 1975-76 | 0.0 | 0.0 | 0.0 | 0.0 | T | T | 1.1 | 2.3 | T | 0.0 | 0.0 | 0.0 | 3.4 |
| 1976-77 | 0.0 | 0.0 | 0.0 | 0.0 | 1.2 | 1.8 | 18.5 | T | 0.0 | T | 0.0 | 0.0 | 21.5 |
| 1977-78 | 0.0 | 0.0 | 0.0 | 0.0 | 0.0 | 0.1 | 12.9 | 9.8 | 2.4 | 0.0 | 0.0 | 0.0 | 25.2 |
| 1978-79 | 0.0 | 0.0 | 0.0 | 0.0 | 0.0 | T | 8.0 | 18.9 | 0.6 | 0.0 | 0.0 | 0.0 | 27.5 |
| 1979-80 | 0.0 | 0.0 | 0.0 | 0.0 | T | T | 0.3 | 6.6 | 3.1 | 0.0 | 0.0 | 0.0 | 10.0 |
| 1980-81 | 0.0 | 0.0 | 0.0 | 0.0 | T | T | 1.2 | 1.7 | T | 0.0 | 0.0 | 0.0 | 2.9 |
| 1981-82 | 0.0 | 0.0 | 0.0 | 0.0 | 0.0 | 0.2 | 4.8 | 3.7 | 1.0 | 0.0 | 0.0 | 0.0 | 9.7 |
| 1982-83 | 0.0 | 0.0 | 0.0 | 0.0 | 0.0 | 0.4 | 0.3 | 0.8 | T | 0.0 | 0.0 | 0.0 | 1.5 |
| 1983-84 | 0.0 | 0.0 | 0.0 | 0.0 | 0.0 | 0.7 | 5.3 | 3.7 | T | 0.0 | 0.0 | 0.0 | 9.7 |
| 1984-85 | 0.0 | 0.0 | 0.0 | 0.0 | 0.0 | 0.8 | 9.8 | 8.0 | 0.0 | 0.0 | 0.0 | 0.0 | 18.6 |
| 1985-86 | 0.0 | 0.0 | 0.0 | 0.0 | 0.0 | 0.5 | 0.4 | 2.1 | T | 0.0 | 0.0 | 0.0 | 3.0 |
| 1986-87 | 0.0 | 0.0 | 0.0 | 0.0 | 0.0 | T | 1.4 | 1.3 | 1.6 | T | 0.0 | 0.0 | 4.3 |
| 1987-88 | 0.0 | 0.0 | 0.0 | 0.0 | T | T | 8.6 | 1.4 | T | 0.0 | 0.0 | 0.0 | 10.0 |
| 1988-89 | 0.0 | 0.0 | 0.0 | 0.0 | 0.0 | 1.6 | T | 5.2 | 0.0 | 0.0 | 0.0 | 0.0 | 6.8 |
| 1989-90 | 0.0 | T | 0.0 | T | T | 0.4 | T | T | 0.4 | 0.0 | 0.0 | 0.0 | 0.8 |
| 1990-91 | 0.0 | 0.0 | 0.0 | 0.0 | 0.0 | 0.3 | | | | | | | |
| Record Mean | 0.0 | T | 0.0 | T | 0.5 | 1.6 | 4.0 | 3.1 | 1.4 | T | 0.0 | 0.0 | 10.7 |

**See Reference Notes, relative to all above tables, on preceding page.**

The station is located 7 statute miles east northeast of the downtown post office in a region of rather flat topography. The Canadian River flows eastward 18 miles north of the station, with its bed about 800 feet below the plains. The Prairie Dog Town Fork of the Red River flows southeastward about 15 miles south of the station where it enters the Palo Duro Canyon, which is about 1,000 feet deep. There are numerous shallow Playa lakes, often dry, over the area, and the nearly treeless grasslands slope downward to the east. The terrain gradually rises to the west and northwest.

Three-fourths of the total annual precipitation falls from April through September, occurring from thunderstorm activity. Snow usually melts within a few days after it falls. Heavier snowfalls of 10 inches or more, usually with near blizzard conditions, average once every 5 years and last 2 to 3 days.

The Amarillo area is subject to rapid and large temperature changes, especially during the winter months when cold fronts from the northern Rocky Mountain and Plains states sweep across the area. Temperature drops of 50 to 60 degrees within a 12-hour period are not uncommon. Temperature drops of 40 degrees have occurred within a few minutes.

Humidity averages are low, occasionally dropping below 20 percent in the spring. Low humidity moderates the effect of high summer afternoon temperatures, permits evaporative cooling systems to be very effective, and provides many pleasant evenings and nights.

Severe local storms are infrequent, although a few thunderstorms with damaging hail, lightning, and wind in a very localized area occur most years, usually in spring and summer. These storms are often accompanied by very heavy rain, which produces local flooding, particularly of roads and streets. Tornadoes are rare.

Based on the 1951-1980 period, the average first occurrence of 32 degrees Fahrenheit in the fall is October 29 and the average last occurrence in the spring is April 14.

## TABLE 1    NORMALS, MEANS AND EXTREMES

AMARILLO, TEXAS

LATITUDE: 35°14'N    LONGITUDE: 101°42'W    ELEVATION: FT. GRND 3604 BARO 3591    TIME ZONE: CENTRAL    WBAN: 23047

| | (a) | JAN | FEB | MAR | APR | MAY | JUNE | JULY | AUG | SEP | OCT | NOV | DEC | YEAR |
|---|---|---|---|---|---|---|---|---|---|---|---|---|---|---|
| **TEMPERATURE °F:** | | | | | | | | | | | | | | |
| Normals | | | | | | | | | | | | | | |
| -Daily Maximum | | 49.1 | 53.1 | 60.8 | 71.0 | 79.1 | 88.2 | 91.4 | 89.6 | 82.4 | 72.7 | 58.7 | 51.8 | 70.7 |
| -Daily Minimum | | 21.7 | 26.1 | 32.0 | 42.0 | 51.9 | 61.5 | 66.2 | 64.5 | 56.9 | 45.5 | 32.1 | 24.8 | 43.8 |
| -Monthly | | 35.4 | 39.6 | 46.4 | 56.5 | 65.5 | 74.9 | 78.8 | 77.0 | 69.7 | 59.2 | 45.4 | 38.3 | 57.2 |
| Extremes | | | | | | | | | | | | | | |
| -Record Highest | 49 | 81 | 88 | 94 | 98 | 102 | 108 | 105 | 106 | 102 | 95 | 87 | 81 | 108 |
| -Year | | 1950 | 1963 | 1971 | 1989 | 1953 | 1953 | 1981 | 1944 | 1983 | 1954 | 1980 | 1955 | JUN 1953 |
| -Record Lowest | 49 | -11 | -14 | -3 | 14 | 28 | 42 | 53 | 49 | 30 | 21 | 0 | -8 | -14 |
| -Year | | 1984 | 1951 | 1948 | 1945 | 1954 | 1955 | 1987 | 1956 | 1984 | 1980 | 1976 | 1989 | FEB 1951 |
| **NORMAL DEGREE DAYS:** | | | | | | | | | | | | | | |
| Heating (base 65°F) | | 918 | 711 | 577 | 271 | 92 | 6 | 0 | 0 | 25 | 215 | 588 | 828 | 4231 |
| Cooling (base 65°F) | | 0 | 0 | 0 | 16 | 108 | 303 | 428 | 372 | 166 | 35 | 0 | 0 | 1428 |
| **% OF POSSIBLE SUNSHINE** | 48 | 69 | 68 | 72 | 74 | 73 | 78 | 79 | 78 | 73 | 74 | 72 | 67 | 73 |
| **MEAN SKY COVER (tenths)** | | | | | | | | | | | | | | |
| Sunrise - Sunset | 48 | 5.1 | 5.3 | 5.2 | 5.0 | 5.2 | 4.4 | 4.4 | 4.3 | 4.1 | 3.9 | 4.4 | 4.8 | 4.7 |
| **MEAN NUMBER OF DAYS:** | | | | | | | | | | | | | | |
| Sunrise to Sunset | | | | | | | | | | | | | | |
| -Clear | 48 | 12.4 | 10.3 | 11.6 | 11.5 | 10.7 | 12.7 | 13.3 | 14.4 | 15.2 | 16.3 | 14.6 | 13.1 | 156.2 |
| -Partly Cloudy | 48 | 7.3 | 7.6 | 8.5 | 8.8 | 10.6 | 11.3 | 12.2 | 10.2 | 7.3 | 6.8 | 6.7 | 7.4 | 104.8 |
| -Cloudy | 48 | 11.3 | 10.3 | 10.8 | 9.6 | 9.7 | 6.0 | 5.5 | 6.5 | 7.5 | 7.8 | 8.7 | 10.5 | 104.3 |
| Precipitation | | | | | | | | | | | | | | |
| .01 inches or more | 48 | 4.0 | 4.4 | 4.6 | 5.1 | 8.4 | 8.3 | 8.1 | 8.5 | 5.9 | 4.8 | 3.3 | 4.0 | 69.4 |
| Snow,Ice pellets | | | | | | | | | | | | | | |
| 1.0 inches or more | 48 | 1.4 | 1.1 | 0.8 | 0.2 | 0.0 | 0.0 | 0.0 | 0.0 | 0.0 | 0.1 | 0.5 | 0.8 | 4.9 |
| Thunderstorms | 48 | 0.1 | 0.5 | 1.5 | 3.4 | 8.5 | 9.5 | 9.4 | 9.1 | 4.3 | 2.4 | 0.6 | 0.2 | 49.4 |
| Heavy Fog Visibility | | | | | | | | | | | | | | |
| 1/4 mile or less | 48 | 3.2 | 4.2 | 3.3 | 1.9 | 2.0 | 0.7 | 0.5 | 0.7 | 2.1 | 2.6 | 2.6 | 2.7 | 26.5 |
| Temperature °F | | | | | | | | | | | | | | |
| -Maximum | | | | | | | | | | | | | | |
| 90° and above | 28 | 0.0 | 0.0 | 0.1 | 1.0 | 4.7 | 12.4 | 21.4 | 16.6 | 6.4 | 1.1 | 0.0 | 0.0 | 63.6 |
| 32° and below | 28 | 4.8 | 2.8 | 0.9 | 0.* | 0.0 | 0.0 | 0.0 | 0.0 | 0.0 | 0.* | 0.7 | 3.6 | 12.9 |
| -Minimum | | | | | | | | | | | | | | |
| 32° and below | 28 | 27.4 | 21.8 | 14.9 | 3.5 | 0.1 | 0.0 | 0.0 | 0.0 | 0.0 | 0.2 | 1.8 | 14.5 | 110.9 |
| 0° and below | 28 | 1.1 | 0.5 | 0.0 | 0.0 | 0.0 | 0.0 | 0.0 | 0.0 | 0.0 | 0.0 | 0.0 | 0.* | 2.1 |
| **AVG. STATION PRESS.(mb)** | 17 | 892.3 | 891.3 | 888.2 | 889.0 | 888.9 | 890.7 | 892.9 | 893.0 | 892.9 | 893.1 | 891.6 | 892.2 | 891.4 |
| **RELATIVE HUMIDITY (%)** | | | | | | | | | | | | | | |
| Hour 00 | 28 | 65 | 65 | 58 | 55 | 64 | 65 | 61 | 67 | 70 | 65 | 65 | 66 | 64 |
| Hour 06 (Local Time) | 28 | 70 | 72 | 68 | 68 | 74 | 77 | 73 | 78 | 80 | 73 | 72 | 70 | 73 |
| Hour 12 | 28 | 50 | 50 | 42 | 38 | 43 | 45 | 42 | 46 | 49 | 44 | 47 | 49 | 45 |
| Hour 18 | 28 | 47 | 43 | 35 | 31 | 38 | 40 | 37 | 43 | 45 | 42 | 48 | 50 | 42 |
| **PRECIPITATION (inches):** | | | | | | | | | | | | | | |
| Water Equivalent | | | | | | | | | | | | | | |
| -Normal | | 0.46 | 0.57 | 0.87 | 1.08 | 2.79 | 3.50 | 2.70 | 2.95 | 1.72 | 1.39 | 0.58 | 0.49 | 19.10 |
| -Maximum Monthly | 49 | 2.33 | 1.83 | 3.99 | 3.74 | 9.81 | 10.73 | 7.59 | 7.55 | 5.02 | 7.64 | 2.26 | 4.52 | 10.73 |
| -Year | | 1968 | 1948 | 1973 | 1942 | 1951 | 1965 | 1960 | 1974 | 1950 | 1941 | 1961 | 1959 | JUN 1965 |
| -Minimum Monthly | 49 | 0.00 | T | T | T | 0.04 | 0.01 | 0.12 | 0.28 | 0.03 | 0.00 | 0.00 | T | 0.00 |
| -Year | | 1986 | 1943 | 1950 | 1964 | 1984 | 1983 | 1946 | 1983 | 1977 | 1952 | 1989 | 1976 | NOV 1989 |
| -Maximum in 24 hrs | 49 | 1.74 | 1.28 | 2.27 | 1.99 | 6.75 | 6.15 | 4.74 | 4.26 | 3.42 | 3.45 | 1.53 | 3.11 | 6.75 |
| -Year | | 1968 | 1971 | 1973 | 1985 | 1951 | 1960 | 1982 | 1945 | 1941 | 1948 | 1986 | 1943 | MAY 1951 |
| Snow,Ice pellets | | | | | | | | | | | | | | |
| -Maximum Monthly | 49 | 14.5 | 17.3 | 14.7 | 6.4 | 0.5 | T | 0.0 | 0.0 | 0.3 | 3.9 | 13.6 | 15.3 | 17.3 |
| -Year | | 1983 | 1971 | 1961 | 1947 | 1978 | 1989 | | | 1984 | 1976 | 1952 | 1987 | FEB 1971 |
| -Maximum in 24 hrs | 49 | 9.8 | 13.5 | 9.8 | 5.1 | 0.5 | T | 0.0 | 0.0 | 0.3 | 3.2 | 12.2 | 11.3 | 13.5 |
| -Year | | 1983 | 1971 | 1957 | 1947 | 1978 | 1989 | | | 1984 | 1976 | 1952 | 1987 | FEB 1971 |
| **WIND:** | | | | | | | | | | | | | | |
| Mean Speed (mph) | 48 | 13.0 | 14.0 | 15.5 | 15.4 | 14.6 | 14.2 | 12.6 | 12.0 | 12.9 | 12.9 | 13.1 | 12.9 | 13.6 |
| Prevailing Direction | | | | | | | | | | | | | | |
| through 1963 | | SW | SW | SW | SW | S | S | S | S | S | SW | SW | SW | SW |
| Fastest Obs. 1 Min. | | | | | | | | | | | | | | |
| -Direction (!!!) | 15 | 36 | 36 | 34 | 27 | 35 | 31 | 19 | 02 | 36 | 31 | 31 | 27 | 31 |
| -Speed (MPH) | 15 | 41 | 47 | 58 | 45 | 46 | 40 | 46 | 46 | 40 | 58 | 46 | 40 | 58 |
| -Year | | 1975 | 1984 | 1977 | 1981 | 1989 | 1981 | 1989 | 1989 | 1987 | 1979 | 1988 | 1988 | OCT 1979 |
| Peak Gust | | | | | | | | | | | | | | |
| -Direction (!!!) | 6 | N | NW | W | N | N | SE | S | N | SE | N | W | W | S |
| -Speed (mph) | 6 | 52 | 62 | 54 | 64 | 58 | 58 | 68 | 61 | 60 | 58 | 67 | 58 | 68 |
| -Date | | 1988 | 1984 | 1985 | 1989 | 1989 | 1989 | 1989 | 1989 | 1987 | 1985 | 1988 | 1988 | JUL 1989 |

**See Reference Notes to this table on the following page.**

**TABLE 2**

### PRECIPITATION (inches)　　　AMARILLO, TEXAS

| YEAR | JAN | FEB | MAR | APR | MAY | JUNE | JULY | AUG | SEP | OCT | NOV | DEC | ANNUAL |
|------|-----|-----|-----|-----|-----|------|------|-----|-----|-----|-----|-----|--------|
| 1961 | 0.12 | 0.27 | 2.55 | 0.24 | 3.40 | 3.42 | 4.10 | 3.14 | 1.87 | 0.91 | 2.26 | 0.16 | 22.44 |
| 1962 | 0.47 | 0.39 | 0.02 | 1.48 | 1.76 | 10.16 | 7.51 | 3.29 | 2.66 | 0.85 | 0.53 | 0.64 | 29.76 |
| 1963 | 0.06 | 0.67 | 0.28 | 0.47 | 3.66 | 3.60 | 2.04 | 3.93 | 0.43 | 1.54 | 0.33 | 0.29 | 17.30 |
| 1964 | T | 1.37 | 0.03 | T | 1.69 | 1.90 | 0.94 | 5.69 | 3.95 | 0.08 | 1.53 | 0.79 | 17.97 |
| 1965 | 0.55 | 0.47 | 0.72 | 0.23 | 1.88 | 10.73 | 1.54 | 1.71 | 0.79 | 1.02 | 0.07 | 0.38 | 20.09 |
| 1966 | 0.43 | 0.69 | 0.01 | 0.87 | 0.19 | 4.62 | 1.37 | 3.77 | 2.40 | 0.29 | 0.08 | 0.19 | 14.91 |
| 1967 | T | 0.15 | 0.42 | 1.95 | 1.40 | 2.55 | 3.70 | 1.81 | 2.47 | 1.61 | 0.28 | 0.51 | 16.85 |
| 1968 | 2.33 | 0.73 | 0.45 | 0.93 | 2.84 | 1.68 | 2.96 | 3.35 | 0.62 | 0.90 | 0.92 | 0.26 | 17.97 |
| 1969 | 0.02 | 0.50 | 1.15 | 0.30 | 2.93 | 4.09 | 2.55 | 4.51 | 2.77 | 2.56 | 0.34 | 0.83 | 22.55 |
| 1970 | 0.02 | 0.02 | 2.10 | 1.33 | 0.23 | 1.54 | 1.39 | 1.27 | 0.34 | 1.06 | 0.26 | T | 9.56 |
| 1971 | 0.10 | 1.65 | 0.10 | 0.77 | 0.91 | 4.17 | 1.75 | 3.33 | 4.70 | 2.59 | 2.08 | 0.89 | 23.04 |
| 1972 | 0.21 | 0.11 | 0.11 | 0.03 | 2.81 | 3.87 | 2.59 | 1.73 | 0.71 | 1.66 | 1.19 | 0.32 | 15.34 |
| 1973 | 0.56 | 0.42 | 3.99 | 1.88 | 1.43 | 0.84 | 4.08 | 2.31 | 1.22 | 1.05 | 0.10 | 0.17 | 18.05 |
| 1974 | 0.33 | 0.24 | 0.60 | 0.04 | 4.06 | 3.33 | 1.31 | 7.55 | 1.65 | 3.44 | 0.12 | 0.42 | 23.09 |
| 1975 | 0.28 | 1.33 | 0.51 | 1.02 | 2.47 | 4.15 | 5.19 | 3.97 | 0.76 | 0.33 | 0.92 | 0.15 | 21.08 |
| 1976 | T | 0.10 | 0.79 | 1.65 | 1.36 | 2.94 | 1.77 | 1.78 | 4.28 | 1.14 | 0.43 | T | 16.24 |
| 1977 | 0.64 | 0.53 | 0.24 | 2.74 | 4.01 | 2.06 | 3.14 | 4.94 | 0.03 | 0.26 | 0.32 | 0.27 | 19.18 |
| 1978 | 0.63 | 0.80 | 0.21 | 0.55 | 5.76 | 6.50 | 1.82 | 1.61 | 2.42 | 0.97 | 0.47 | 0.27 | 22.01 |
| 1979 | 0.92 | 0.28 | 1.46 | 1.29 | 3.94 | 3.19 | 2.03 | 5.08 | 0.52 | 1.28 | 0.40 | 0.07 | 20.46 |
| 1980 | 0.85 | 0.55 | 1.38 | 0.82 | 2.88 | 1.30 | 0.65 | 1.80 | 1.55 | 0.42 | 0.84 | 0.35 | 13.39 |
| 1981 | 0.11 | 0.23 | 1.87 | 0.90 | 2.11 | 1.04 | 2.73 | 5.22 | 3.47 | 1.79 | 1.50 | 0.03 | 21.00 |
| 1982 | 0.15 | 0.39 | 0.52 | 0.43 | 1.96 | 4.75 | 6.23 | 0.55 | 1.37 | 0.71 | 0.75 | 0.79 | 18.60 |
| 1983 | 1.78 | 1.19 | 0.98 | 0.83 | 2.85 | 1.76 | 0.74 | 0.28 | 0.37 | 3.23 | 0.33 | 0.64 | 14.98 |
| 1984 | 0.56 | 0.37 | 0.98 | 1.18 | 0.04 | 6.76 | 0.83 | 2.28 | 0.95 | 3.19 | 1.09 | 1.00 | 19.23 |
| 1985 | 0.99 | 0.77 | 1.49 | 2.79 | 0.86 | 3.08 | 2.07 | 1.67 | 4.96 | 3.07 | 0.39 | 0.26 | 22.40 |
| 1986 | 0.00 | 1.02 | 0.60 | 0.30 | 3.28 | 3.70 | 3.52 | 7.04 | 1.45 | 1.94 | 1.82 | 0.66 | 25.33 |
| 1987 | 1.26 | 0.84 | 0.92 | 0.57 | 4.28 | 3.29 | 0.83 | 3.28 | 3.40 | 1.17 | 0.43 | 1.75 | 22.02 |
| 1988 | 0.33 | 0.04 | 1.19 | 2.22 | 6.02 | 3.68 | 3.30 | 3.59 | 3.15 | 0.71 | 0.29 | 0.17 | 24.69 |
| 1989 | 0.16 | 0.55 | 0.52 | 0.75 | 2.51 | 6.07 | 2.74 | 3.22 | 1.80 | 0.74 | 0.00 | 0.49 | 19.55 |
| 1990 | 1.22 | 1.61 | 2.56 | 1.10 | 0.90 | 0.14 | 3.28 | 2.79 | 2.72 | 0.46 | 0.50 | 0.23 | 17.51 |
| Record Mean | 0.54 | 0.68 | 0.87 | 1.38 | 2.89 | 3.11 | 2.67 | 3.02 | 2.12 | 1.62 | 0.82 | 0.67 | 20.38 |

**TABLE 3**

### AVERAGE TEMPERATURE (deg. F)　　　AMARILLO, TEXAS

| YEAR | JAN | FEB | MAR | APR | MAY | JUNE | JULY | AUG | SEP | OCT | NOV | DEC | ANNUAL |
|------|-----|-----|-----|-----|-----|------|------|-----|-----|-----|-----|-----|--------|
| #1961 | 34.6 | 39.3 | 48.5 | 56.2 | 67.3 | 73.9 | 76.4 | 77.2 | 67.6 | 59.5 | 41.3 | 36.5 | 56.5 |
| 1962 | 31.7 | 45.5 | 46.7 | 57.2 | 71.7 | 72.4 | 78.0 | 78.3 | 70.4 | 61.5 | 47.8 | 40.9 | 58.5 |
| 1963 | 28.9 | 41.7 | 50.4 | 61.8 | 69.0 | 74.1 | 81.3 | 77.8 | 72.3 | 66.2 | 49.5 | 32.5 | 58.8 |
| 1964 | 37.2 | 32.1 | 44.8 | 57.9 | 68.9 | 76.5 | 81.9 | 78.1 | 69.6 | 60.6 | 47.5 | 39.1 | 57.9 |
| 1965 | 41.0 | 37.6 | 38.4 | 59.4 | 66.9 | 72.1 | 78.6 | 76.9 | 68.5 | 59.5 | 52.5 | 42.9 | 57.8 |
| 1966 | 27.8 | 34.1 | 50.0 | 54.5 | 66.0 | 74.2 | 82.9 | 73.5 | 68.5 | 57.7 | 51.6 | 35.5 | 56.3 |
| 1967 | 40.7 | 40.6 | 53.4 | 60.6 | 63.4 | 73.7 | 77.2 | 75.0 | 68.3 | 60.9 | 46.6 | 35.4 | 58.0 |
| 1968 | 38.3 | 38.0 | 48.7 | 55.3 | 63.4 | 74.9 | 77.0 | 77.0 | 69.1 | 62.1 | 45.4 | 36.9 | 57.2 |
| 1969 | 41.4 | 40.4 | 38.8 | 59.9 | 67.2 | 72.8 | 82.6 | 80.2 | 71.1 | 54.5 | 46.7 | 38.4 | 57.8 |
| 1970 | 33.2 | 43.2 | 41.7 | 56.0 | 68.8 | 74.5 | 80.7 | 79.1 | 70.9 | 54.0 | 46.4 | 43.4 | 57.7 |
| 1971 | 37.8 | 38.8 | 48.3 | 55.7 | 64.9 | 75.9 | 76.9 | 72.2 | 67.1 | 57.2 | 45.6 | 37.6 | 56.5 |
| 1972 | 35.7 | 40.9 | 51.7 | 59.5 | 63.2 | 73.6 | 74.5 | 73.9 | 69.2 | 57.9 | 36.9 | 32.9 | 55.8 |
| 1973 | 33.4 | 39.5 | 47.1 | 50.3 | 62.9 | 75.1 | 78.1 | 78.8 | 68.7 | 62.0 | 50.8 | 38.6 | 57.1 |
| 1974 | 35.0 | 42.2 | 53.1 | 60.2 | 71.5 | 75.0 | 79.3 | 73.6 | 62.9 | 59.0 | 45.7 | 36.1 | 57.8 |
| 1975 | 37.1 | 35.3 | 45.0 | 54.9 | 64.5 | 73.3 | 75.5 | 76.7 | 65.8 | 61.1 | 45.8 | 40.4 | 56.3 |
| 1976 | 36.9 | 47.8 | 46.5 | 56.8 | 60.2 | 72.2 | 74.8 | 75.1 | 66.5 | 49.9 | 38.5 | 37.5 | 55.2 |
| 1977 | 30.1 | 43.8 | 48.7 | 57.8 | 67.3 | 78.1 | 80.7 | 77.5 | 74.3 | 60.7 | 47.4 | 39.9 | 58.9 |
| 1978 | 29.0 | 30.1 | 47.2 | 61.4 | 63.7 | 75.4 | 80.7 | 76.1 | 70.7 | 59.4 | 45.6 | 32.7 | 56.0 |
| 1979 | 24.9 | 40.0 | 46.6 | 54.5 | 62.2 | 70.9 | 77.1 | 73.6 | 69.8 | 60.1 | 40.5 | 38.8 | 54.9 |
| 1980 | 34.9 | 37.7 | 43.9 | 52.4 | 61.9 | 78.3 | 82.9 | 78.5 | 70.7 | 56.6 | 42.7 | 41.4 | 56.8 |
| 1981 | 37.9 | 42.2 | 48.8 | 63.1 | 65.6 | 78.5 | 81.3 | 74.4 | 69.0 | 56.6 | 49.1 | 40.1 | 58.9 |
| 1982 | 37.1 | 35.9 | 47.3 | 53.8 | 63.3 | 72.2 | 78.8 | 78.7 | 71.1 | 57.3 | 45.6 | 36.1 | 56.4 |
| 1983 | 33.4 | 36.2 | 45.3 | 50.9 | 60.3 | 70.4 | 80.0 | 81.0 | 73.6 | 60.5 | 47.9 | 24.7 | 55.3 |
| 1984 | 31.6 | 40.3 | 44.0 | 51.8 | 66.9 | 74.6 | 75.6 | 75.3 | 65.7 | 56.9 | 47.0 | 40.5 | 55.9 |
| 1985 | 31.5 | 37.2 | 49.5 | 60.0 | 68.1 | 75.1 | 80.1 | 79.6 | 68.9 | 56.9 | 43.5 | 34.0 | 57.0 |
| 1986 | 42.5 | 40.4 | 52.7 | 59.4 | 65.1 | 73.3 | 80.6 | 74.4 | 68.8 | 55.7 | 42.7 | 37.1 | 57.7 |
| 1987 | 34.0 | 42.0 | 44.6 | 54.8 | 64.5 | 72.1 | 77.2 | 75.3 | 67.6 | 57.9 | 45.4 | 34.6 | 55.8 |
| 1988 | 32.2 | 38.3 | 44.3 | 54.1 | 63.6 | 73.3 | 75.8 | 76.4 | 67.7 | 59.0 | 47.6 | 38.5 | 55.9 |
| 1989 | 40.7 | 32.3 | 51.2 | 59.9 | 67.3 | 69.4 | 76.2 | 76.0 | 66.3 | 60.4 | 47.9 | 31.4 | 56.6 |
| 1990 | 39.2 | 40.8 | 47.0 | 55.9 | 63.6 | 81.3 | 76.4 | 76.3 | 72.0 | 57.7 | 49.7 | 33.2 | 57.8 |
| Record Mean | 36.2 | 39.2 | 47.0 | 56.3 | 64.8 | 74.1 | 78.0 | 76.8 | 69.7 | 58.8 | 46.3 | 37.7 | 57.0 |
| Max | 49.0 | 52.3 | 60.9 | 70.2 | 77.8 | 87.0 | 90.3 | 89.0 | 82.2 | 71.8 | 59.3 | 50.1 | 70.0 |
| Min | 23.4 | 26.0 | 33.0 | 42.3 | 51.7 | 61.2 | 65.6 | 64.5 | 57.2 | 45.8 | 33.3 | 25.3 | 44.1 |

## REFERENCE NOTES FOR TABLES 1, 2, 3 and 6　　　(AMARILLO, TX)

### GENERAL

T - TRACE AMOUNT
BLANK ENTRIES DENOTE MISSING/UNREPORTED DATA.
# INDICATES A STATION OR INSTRUMENT RELOCATION.

### SPECIFIC

#### TABLE 1

(a) - LENGTH OF RECORD IN YEARS. ALTHOUGH
　　　INDIVIDUAL MONTHS MAY BE MISSING.
　* LESS THAN .05

NORMALS — BASED ON THE 1951-1980 RECORD PERIOD.
EXTREMES — DATES ARE THE MOST RECENT OCCURRENCE.
WIND DIR. — NUMERALS SHOW TENS OF DEGREES
　　　　　　　CLOCKWISE FROM TRUE NORTH.
　　　　　　　"00" INDICATES CALM.
RESULTANT WIND DIRECTIONS ARE GIVEN TO WHOLE DEGREES.

#### TABLE 3

MAX AND MIN ARE LONG-TERM MEAN DAILY MAXIMUM
AND MEAN DAILY MINIMUM TEMPERATURES.

### EXCEPTIONS

#### TABLES 2, 3, and 6

RECORD MEANS ARE THROUGH THE CURRENT YEAR,
BEGINNING IN　　1892 FOR TEMPERATURE
　　　　　　　　1892 FOR PRECIPITATION
　　　　　　　　1942 FOR SNOWFALL

HEATING DEGREE DAYS Base 65 deg. F          AMARILLO, TEXAS

**TABLE 4**

| SEASON | JULY | AUG | SEP | OCT | NOV | DEC | JAN | FEB | MAR | APR | MAY | JUNE | TOTAL |
|---|---|---|---|---|---|---|---|---|---|---|---|---|---|
| 1961-62 | 0 | 0 | 63 | 189 | 702 | 879 | 1026 | 540 | 563 | 254 | 23 | 15 | 4254 |
| 1962-63 | 0 | 0 | 23 | 159 | 508 | 741 | 1114 | 648 | 450 | 139 | 61 | 7 | 3850 |
| 1963-64 | 0 | 0 | 11 | 42 | 458 | 1000 | 855 | 949 | 618 | 235 | 53 | 7 | 4228 |
| 1964-65 | 0 | 0 | 48 | 149 | 517 | 795 | 740 | 762 | 820 | 194 | 56 | 7 | 4088 |
| 1965-66 | 0 | 0 | 73 | 191 | 376 | 676 | 1145 | 857 | 456 | 312 | 99 | 1 | 4186 |
| 1966-67 | 0 | 23 | 22 | 250 | 395 | 908 | 743 | 675 | 356 | 159 | 135 | 9 | 3675 |
| 1967-68 | 0 | 1 | 23 | 185 | 544 | 911 | 820 | 777 | 504 | 290 | 109 | 0 | 4164 |
| 1968-69 | 0 | 0 | 6 | 159 | 583 | 865 | 726 | 681 | 808 | 176 | 69 | 24 | 4097 |
| 1969-70 | 0 | 0 | 1 | 374 | 543 | 817 | 981 | 602 | 713 | 280 | 50 | 33 | 4394 |
| 1970-71 | 0 | 0 | 47 | 359 | 544 | 661 | 837 | 726 | 524 | 290 | 89 | 0 | 4077 |
| 1971-72 | 1 | 0 | 120 | 245 | 575 | 843 | 900 | 692 | 409 | 203 | 106 | 0 | 4094 |
| 1972-73 | 13 | 2 | 48 | 274 | 833 | 987 | 972 | 706 | 548 | 438 | 113 | 0 | 4934 |
| 1973-74 | 0 | 0 | 56 | 154 | 420 | 813 | 922 | 633 | 368 | 190 | 17 | 0 | 3573 |
| 1974-75 | 0 | 0 | 119 | 199 | 571 | 890 | 853 | 826 | 612 | 323 | 67 | 16 | 4476 |
| 1975-76 | 0 | 0 | 104 | 158 | 569 | 757 | 861 | 492 | 567 | 253 | 171 | 0 | 3932 |
| 1976-77 | 0 | 0 | 59 | 464 | 790 | 846 | 1075 | 592 | 499 | 215 | 22 | 0 | 4562 |
| 1977-78 | 0 | 0 | 1 | 150 | 522 | 768 | 1107 | 972 | 551 | 136 | 139 | 6 | 4352 |
| 1978-79 | 0 | 0 | 33 | 197 | 574 | 992 | 1236 | 697 | 561 | 319 | 144 | 30 | 4783 |
| 1979-80 | 0 | 2 | 28 | 186 | 727 | 806 | 926 | 788 | 649 | 373 | 146 | 0 | 4631 |
| 1980-81 | 0 | 0 | 35 | 280 | 662 | 723 | 832 | 630 | 496 | 111 | 65 | 0 | 3834 |
| 1981-82 | 0 | 0 | 26 | 271 | 469 | 765 | 856 | 809 | 539 | 340 | 96 | 2 | 4173 |
| 1982-83 | 0 | 0 | 23 | 252 | 575 | 888 | 972 | 800 | 603 | 421 | 171 | 32 | 4737 |
| 1983-84 | 0 | 0 | 40 | 175 | 506 | 1241 | 1028 | 709 | 642 | 390 | 56 | 0 | 4787 |
| 1984-85 | 0 | 0 | 125 | 262 | 531 | 752 | 1034 | 769 | 474 | 169 | 37 | 5 | 4158 |
| 1985-86 | 0 | 0 | 111 | 249 | 640 | 957 | 691 | 681 | 379 | 203 | 72 | 0 | 3983 |
| 1986-87 | 0 | 2 | 26 | 290 | 665 | 858 | 954 | 634 | 624 | 315 | 70 | 9 | 4447 |
| 1987-88 | 0 | 8 | 18 | 226 | 584 | 936 | 1010 | 765 | 633 | 323 | 102 | 4 | 4609 |
| 1988-89 | 0 | 7 | 32 | 197 | 517 | 815 | 747 | 909 | 429 | 219 | 59 | 27 | 3958 |
| 1989-90 | 0 | 0 | 91 | 185 | 507 | 1037 | 795 | 672 | 551 | 276 | 140 | 0 | 4254 |
| 1990-91 | 0 | 0 | 11 | 234 | 454 | 981 |  |  |  |  |  |  |  |

**TABLE 5**  COOLING DEGREE DAYS Base 65 deg. F          AMARILLO, TEXAS

| YEAR | JAN | FEB | MAR | APR | MAY | JUNE | JULY | AUG | SEP | OCT | NOV | DEC | TOTAL |
|---|---|---|---|---|---|---|---|---|---|---|---|---|---|
| 1969 | 0 | 0 | 0 | 30 | 147 | 264 | 550 | 478 | 190 | 54 | 0 | 0 | 1713 |
| 1970 | 0 | 0 | 0 | 14 | 176 | 327 | 495 | 446 | 231 | 24 | 0 | 0 | 1713 |
| 1971 | 0 | 0 | 13 | 18 | 94 | 334 | 381 | 232 | 189 | 10 | 0 | 0 | 1271 |
| 1972 | 0 | 0 | 4 | 44 | 59 | 265 | 313 | 285 | 182 | 60 | 0 | 0 | 1212 |
| 1973 | 0 | 0 | 0 | 3 | 53 | 310 | 414 | 435 | 173 | 67 | 1 | 0 | 1456 |
| 1974 | 0 | 0 | 6 | 52 | 228 | 306 | 449 | 274 | 61 | 20 | 0 | 0 | 1396 |
| 1975 | 0 | 0 | 0 | 24 | 61 | 273 | 330 | 367 | 134 | 46 | 0 | 0 | 1235 |
| 1976 | 0 | 0 | 0 | 13 | 32 | 223 | 312 | 318 | 110 | 5 | 0 | 0 | 1013 |
| 1977 | 0 | 0 | 0 | 10 | 100 | 399 | 493 | 389 | 287 | 22 | 0 | 0 | 1700 |
| 1978 | 0 | 0 | 6 | 33 | 108 | 324 | 497 | 351 | 209 | 28 | 0 | 0 | 1556 |
| 1979 | 0 | 0 | 0 | 12 | 64 | 218 | 380 | 276 | 177 | 41 | 0 | 0 | 1168 |
| 1980 | 0 | 0 | 0 | 4 | 58 | 408 | 562 | 429 | 211 | 26 | 0 | 0 | 1698 |
| 1981 | 0 | 0 | 1 | 59 | 87 | 410 | 512 | 299 | 154 | 16 | 0 | 0 | 1538 |
| 1982 | 0 | 0 | 0 | 9 | 52 | 225 | 437 | 432 | 213 | 22 | 0 | 0 | 1390 |
| 1983 | 0 | 0 | 0 | 2 | 31 | 201 | 473 | 502 | 306 | 41 | 3 | 0 | 1559 |
| 1984 | 0 | 0 | 0 | 1 | 121 | 298 | 331 | 325 | 151 | 17 | 0 | 0 | 1244 |
| 1985 | 0 | 0 | 0 | 2 | 27 | 143 | 473 | 458 | 235 | 6 | 0 | 0 | 1659 |
| 1986 | 0 | 0 | 3 | 45 | 87 | 256 | 489 | 299 | 144 | 10 | 0 | 0 | 1333 |
| 1987 | 0 | 0 | 0 | 19 | 64 | 227 | 386 | 334 | 105 | 11 | 0 | 0 | 1146 |
| 1988 | 0 | 0 | 0 | 3 | 67 | 263 | 340 | 366 | 120 | 19 | 0 | 0 | 1178 |
| 1989 | 0 | 0 | 10 | 75 | 136 | 164 | 354 | 347 | 138 | 51 | 0 | 0 | 1275 |
| 1990 | 0 | 0 | 0 | 9 | 101 | 494 | 359 | 358 | 229 | 17 | 1 | 0 | 1568 |

**TABLE 6**  SNOWFALL (inches)          AMARILLO, TEXAS

| SEASON | JULY | AUG | SEP | OCT | NOV | DEC | JAN | FEB | MAR | APR | MAY | JUNE | TOTAL |
|---|---|---|---|---|---|---|---|---|---|---|---|---|---|
| 1961-62 | 0.0 | 0.0 | 0.0 | 0.0 | 4.9 | 0.5 | 2.3 | 0.1 | T | 0.0 | 0.0 | 0.0 | 7.8 |
| 1962-63 | 0.0 | 0.0 | 0.0 | 0.0 | 7.6 | 0.8 | 0.5 | 4.8 | T | 0.0 | 0.0 | 0.0 | 13.7 |
| 1963-64 | 0.0 | 0.0 | 0.0 | 0.0 | 0.0 | 3.6 | T | 17.3 | T | T | 0.0 | 0.0 | 20.9 |
| 1964-65 | 0.0 | 0.0 | 0.0 | 0.0 | T | 0.5 | 5.6 | 3.8 | 2.3 | 0.0 | 0.0 | 0.0 | 12.2 |
| 1965-66 | 0.0 | 0.0 | 0.0 | 0.0 | 0.0 | 1.4 | 7.2 | 0.4 | 0.1 | 0.0 | 0.0 | 0.0 | 9.1 |
| 1966-67 | 0.0 | 0.0 | 0.0 | T | T | 1.8 | T | 1.1 | 0.4 | 0.0 | 0.0 | 0.0 | 3.3 |
| 1967-68 | 0.0 | 0.0 | 0.0 | T | 2.1 | 6.1 | 0.6 | 8.0 | 2.9 | 0.0 | 0.0 | 0.0 | 19.7 |
| 1968-69 | 0.0 | 0.0 | 0.0 | 0.0 | 0.3 | 1.8 | 0.2 | 2.9 | 10.3 | 0.0 | 0.0 | 0.0 | 15.5 |
| 1969-70 | 0.0 | 0.0 | 0.0 | T | T | 7.1 | 0.1 | T | 14.1 | 1.8 | 0.0 | 0.0 | 23.1 |
| 1970-71 | 0.0 | 0.0 | 0.0 | 3.9 | 2.6 | T | 0.8 | 17.3 | 1.0 | T | 0.0 | 0.0 | 25.6 |
| 1971-72 | 0.0 | 0.0 | 0.0 | 0.0 | T | 2.0 | 1.6 | 2.0 | 0.6 | 0.0 | 0.0 | 0.0 | 12.1 |
| 1972-73 | 0.0 | 0.0 | 0.0 | 0.4 | 9.9 | 2.8 | 7.0 | 4.2 | 0.5 | 5.7 | 0.0 | 0.0 | 30.5 |
| 1973-74 | 0.0 | 0.0 | 0.0 | 0.0 | 0.4 | 1.5 | 3.6 | 1.2 | T | 0.0 | 0.0 | 0.0 | 6.7 |
| 1974-75 | 0.0 | 0.0 | 0.0 | 0.0 | T | 1.5 | 3.8 | 11.7 | 1.2 | T | 0.0 | 0.0 | 18.2 |
| 1975-76 | 0.0 | 0.0 | 0.0 | 0.0 | 0.0 | 0.4 | 1.8 | T | 4.2 | 0.0 | 0.0 | 0.0 | 6.4 |
| 1976-77 | 0.0 | 0.0 | 0.0 | 3.9 | 4.3 | T | 6.4 | 3.7 | T | T | 0.0 | 0.0 | 18.3 |
| 1977-78 | 0.0 | 0.0 | 0.0 | 0.0 | 1.3 | 0.2 | 8.2 | 9.4 | 1.5 | T | 0.5 | 0.0 | 21.1 |
| 1978-79 | 0.0 | 0.0 | 0.0 | 0.0 | 2.0 | 3.3 | 5.9 | 1.9 | T | 0.0 | 0.0 | 0.0 | 13.1 |
| 1979-80 | 0.0 | 0.0 | 0.0 | 1.6 | 2.2 | 0.3 | 1.4 | 5.2 | 1.0 | T | 0.0 | 0.0 | 11.7 |
| 1980-81 | 0.0 | 0.0 | 0.0 | 0.0 | 8.6 | T | 1.1 | 0.1 | 0.1 | 0.0 | 0.0 | 0.0 | 9.9 |
| 1981-82 | 0.0 | 0.0 | 0.0 | 0.0 | T | 0.3 | 1.1 | 4.7 | 1.7 | T | 0.0 | 0.0 | 7.8 |
| 1982-83 | 0.0 | 0.0 | 0.0 | 0.0 | 4.5 | 1.9 | 14.5 | 13.0 | 8.1 | 5.9 | 0.0 | 0.0 | 47.9 |
| 1983-84 | 0.0 | 0.0 | 0.0 | T | T | 5.2 | 7.0 | 3.5 | 2.5 | 0.2 | 0.0 | 0.0 | 18.2 |
| 1984-85 | 0.0 | 0.0 | 0.3 | 0.0 | 0.1 | 7.4 | 0.3 | 0.3 | 0.2 | 0.0 | 0.0 | 0.0 | 8.6 |
| 1985-86 | 0.0 | 0.0 | T | 0.0 | T | 2.8 | 0.0 | 10.9 | 1.0 | 0.0 | 0.0 | 0.0 | 14.7 |
| 1986-87 | 0.0 | 0.0 | 0.0 | T | 0.2 | 12.1 | 3.1 | 3.1 | 6.4 | 0.1 | 0.0 | 0.0 | 25.2 |
| 1987-88 | 0.0 | 0.0 | 0.0 | 0.0 | 0.7 | 15.3 | 4.3 | 0.5 | 8.5 | 4.2 | 0.0 | 0.0 | 33.5 |
| 1988-89 | 0.0 | 0.0 | 0.0 | 0.0 | 2.4 | 2.2 | T | 0.1 | 4.2 | 0.1 | T | T | 9.0 |
| 1989-90 | 0.0 | 0.0 | T | 0.0 | 0.0 | 5.4 | 8.5 | 3.0 | T | T | T | 0.0 | 16.9 |
| 1990-91 | 0.0 | 0.0 | 0.0 | 0.0 | 2.2 | 3.8 |  |  |  |  |  |  |  |
| Record Mean | 0.0 | 0.0 | T | 0.2 | 1.7 | 2.6 | 4.0 | 3.8 | 2.6 | 0.6 | T | T | 15.5 |

**See Reference Notes, relative to all above tables, on preceding page.**

The Dallas-Fort Worth Metroplex is located in North Central Texas, approximately 250 miles north of the Gulf of Mexico. It is near the headwaters of the Trinity River, which lie in the upper margins of the Coastal Plain. The rolling hills in the area range from 500 to 800 feet in elevation.

The Dallas-Fort Worth climate is humid subtropical with hot summers. It is also continental, characterized by a wide annual temperature range. Precipitation also varies considerably, ranging from less than 20 to more than 50 inches.

Winters are mild, but northers occur about three times each month, and often are accompanied by sudden drops in temperature. Periods of extreme cold that occasionally occur are short-lived, so that even in January mild weather occurs frequently.

The highest temperatures of summer are associated with fair skies, westerly winds and low humidities. Characteristically, hot spells in summer are broken into three-to-five day periods by thunderstorm activity. There are only a few nights each summer when the low temperature exceeds 80 degrees. Summer daytime temperatures frequently exceed 100 degrees. Air conditioners are recommended for maximum comfort indoors and while traveling via automobile.

Throughout the year, rainfall occurs more frequently during the night. Usually, periods of rainy weather last for only a day or two, and are followed by several days with fair skies. A large part of the annual precipitation results from thunderstorm activity, with occasional heavy rainfall over brief periods of time. Thunderstorms occur throughout the year, but are most frequent in the spring. Hail falls on about two or three days a year, ordinarily with only slight and scattered damage. Windstorms occurring during thunderstorm activity are sometimes destructive. Snowfall is rare.

The average length of the warm season (freeze-free period) in the Dallas-Fort Worth Metroplex is about 249 days. The average last occurrence of 32 degrees or below is mid March and the average first occurrence of 32 degrees or below is in late November.

**TABLE 1**     # NORMALS, MEANS AND EXTREMES

DALLAS – FORT WORTH, TEXAS

LATITUDE: 32°54'N    LONGITUDE: 97°02' W    ELEVATION: FT. GRND   551 BARO   575   TIME ZONE: CENTRAL    WBAN: 03927

| | (a) | JAN | FEB | MAR | APR | MAY | JUNE | JULY | AUG | SEP | OCT | NOV | DEC | YEAR |
|---|---|---|---|---|---|---|---|---|---|---|---|---|---|---|
| **TEMPERATURE °F:** | | | | | | | | | | | | | | |
| Normals | | | | | | | | | | | | | | |
| -Daily Maximum | | 54.0 | 59.1 | 67.2 | 76.8 | 84.4 | 93.2 | 97.8 | 97.3 | 89.7 | 79.5 | 66.2 | 58.1 | 76.9 |
| -Daily Minimum | | 33.9 | 37.8 | 44.9 | 55.0 | 62.9 | 70.8 | 74.7 | 73.7 | 67.5 | 56.3 | 44.9 | 37.4 | 55.0 |
| -Monthly | | 44.0 | 48.5 | 56.1 | 65.9 | 73.7 | 82.0 | 86.3 | 85.5 | 78.6 | 67.9 | 55.6 | 47.8 | 66.0 |
| Extremes | | | | | | | | | | | | | | |
| -Record Highest | 36 | 88 | 88 | 96 | 95 | 103 | 113 | 110 | 108 | 106 | 102 | 89 | 88 | 113 |
| -Year | | 1969 | 1986 | 1974 | 1989 | 1985 | 1980 | 1980 | 1964 | 1985 | 1979 | 1989 | 1955 | JUN 1980 |
| -Record Lowest | 36 | 4 | 7 | 15 | 29 | 41 | 51 | 59 | 56 | 43 | 29 | 20 | -1 | -1 |
| -Year | | 1964 | 1985 | 1980 | 1989 | 1978 | 1964 | 1972 | 1967 | 1984 | 1980 | 1959 | 1989 | DEC 1989 |
| **NORMAL DEGREE DAYS:** | | | | | | | | | | | | | | |
| Heating (base 65°F) | | 651 | 469 | 313 | 85 | 0 | 0 | 0 | 0 | 0 | 56 | 300 | 533 | 2407 |
| Cooling (base 65°F) | | 0 | 7 | 37 | 112 | 275 | 510 | 660 | 636 | 408 | 146 | 18 | 0 | 2809 |
| **% OF POSSIBLE SUNSHINE** | 11 | 57 | 55 | 62 | 66 | 63 | 69 | 78 | 75 | 72 | 61 | 59 | 56 | 64 |
| **MEAN SKY COVER (tenths)** | | | | | | | | | | | | | | |
| Sunrise - Sunset | 36 | 6.1 | 5.8 | 5.8 | 5.9 | 5.8 | 4.9 | 4.2 | 4.3 | 4.7 | 4.7 | 5.2 | 5.6 | 5.2 |
| **MEAN NUMBER OF DAYS:** | | | | | | | | | | | | | | |
| Sunrise to Sunset | | | | | | | | | | | | | | |
| -Clear | 36 | 9.9 | 9.7 | 9.9 | 8.9 | 8.3 | 10.9 | 15.0 | 14.8 | 12.9 | 13.6 | 12.0 | 11.4 | 137.4 |
| -Partly Cloudy | 36 | 6.0 | 5.7 | 7.7 | 8.1 | 10.7 | 11.5 | 9.6 | 10.2 | 8.9 | 7.4 | 6.0 | 6.2 | 97.9 |
| -Cloudy | 36 | 15.1 | 12.9 | 13.4 | 12.9 | 12.1 | 7.5 | 6.4 | 6.0 | 8.2 | 10.0 | 12.0 | 13.4 | 130.0 |
| Precipitation | | | | | | | | | | | | | | |
| .01 inches or more | 36 | 6.7 | 6.5 | 7.1 | 7.9 | 8.7 | 6.4 | 4.9 | 4.6 | 6.8 | 6.0 | 5.8 | 6.3 | 77.8 |
| Snow,Ice pellets | | | | | | | | | | | | | | |
| 1.0 inches or more | 36 | 0.6 | 0.4 | 0.1 | 0.0 | 0.0 | 0.0 | 0.0 | 0.0 | 0.0 | 0.0 | 0.* | 0.1 | 1.2 |
| Thunderstorms | 36 | 1.0 | 1.7 | 4.2 | 5.9 | 7.5 | 6.3 | 4.9 | 4.5 | 3.6 | 2.8 | 1.8 | 1.0 | 45.1 |
| Heavy Fog Visibility | | | | | | | | | | | | | | |
| 1/4 mile or less | 36 | 2.6 | 1.6 | 1.0 | 0.6 | 0.4 | 0.1 | 0.0 | 0.* | 0.1 | 0.9 | 1.6 | 2.4 | 11.2 |
| Temperature °F | | | | | | | | | | | | | | |
| -Maximum | | | | | | | | | | | | | | |
| 90° and above | 26 | 0.0 | 0.0 | 0.2 | 0.8 | 3.8 | 19.4 | 27.7 | 26.6 | 14.5 | 2.6 | 0.0 | 0.0 | 95.7 |
| 32° and below | 26 | 1.7 | 0.8 | 0.1 | 0.0 | 0.0 | 0.0 | 0.0 | 0.0 | 0.0 | 0.0 | 0.0 | 0.8 | 3.4 |
| -Minimum | | | | | | | | | | | | | | |
| 32° and below | 26 | 15.5 | 9.7 | 2.9 | 0.2 | 0.0 | 0.0 | 0.0 | 0.0 | 0.0 | 0.* | 2.6 | 10.2 | 41.2 |
| 0° and below | 26 | 0.0 | 0.0 | 0.0 | 0.0 | 0.0 | 0.0 | 0.0 | 0.0 | 0.0 | 0.0 | 0.0 | 0.* | * |
| **AVG. STATION PRESS.(mb)** | 17 | 999.7 | 997.9 | 993.8 | 993.2 | 991.7 | 992.8 | 994.2 | 993.9 | 994.6 | 996.7 | 997.0 | 998.8 | 995.4 |
| **RELATIVE HUMIDITY (%)** | | | | | | | | | | | | | | |
| Hour 00 | 26 | 73 | 72 | 70 | 72 | 79 | 74 | 67 | 66 | 74 | 73 | 73 | 72 | 72 |
| Hour 06 | 26 | 79 | 79 | 79 | 82 | 87 | 85 | 80 | 80 | 85 | 82 | 81 | 79 | 82 |
| Hour 12 (Local Time) | 26 | 60 | 59 | 56 | 56 | 60 | 55 | 48 | 49 | 56 | 55 | 57 | 59 | 56 |
| Hour 18 | 26 | 58 | 54 | 50 | 52 | 57 | 50 | 44 | 44 | 53 | 55 | 58 | 58 | 53 |
| **PRECIPITATION (inches):** | | | | | | | | | | | | | | |
| Water Equivalent | | | | | | | | | | | | | | |
| -Normal | | 1.65 | 1.93 | 2.42 | 3.63 | 4.27 | 2.59 | 2.00 | 1.76 | 3.31 | 2.47 | 1.76 | 1.67 | 29.46 |
| -Maximum Monthly | 36 | 3.60 | 6.20 | 6.39 | 12.19 | 13.66 | 8.75 | 11.13 | 6.85 | 9.52 | 14.18 | 6.23 | 6.99 | 14.18 |
| -Year | | 1968 | 1965 | 1968 | 1957 | 1982 | 1989 | 1973 | 1970 | 1964 | 1981 | 1964 | 1971 | OCT 1981 |
| -Minimum Monthly | 36 | T | 0.15 | 0.10 | 0.11 | 0.99 | 0.40 | 0.09 | T | 0.09 | T | 0.20 | 0.17 | T |
| -Year | | 1986 | 1963 | 1972 | 1987 | 1977 | 1964 | 1965 | 1980 | 1984 | 1975 | 1970 | 1981 | JAN 1986 |
| -Maximum in 24 hrs | 36 | 2.39 | 4.06 | 4.39 | 4.55 | 5.34 | 3.15 | 3.76 | 4.05 | 4.76 | 5.91 | 2.83 | 3.10 | 5.91 |
| -Year | | 1975 | 1965 | 1977 | 1957 | 1989 | 1989 | 1975 | 1976 | 1965 | 1959 | 1964 | 1971 | OCT 1959 |
| Snow,Ice pellets | | | | | | | | | | | | | | |
| -Maximum Monthly | 36 | 12.1 | 13.5 | 2.5 | 0.0 | T | 0.0 | 0.0 | 0.0 | 0.0 | 0.0 | 5.0 | 2.6 | 13.5 |
| -Year | | 1964 | 1978 | 1962 | | 1989 | | | | | | 1976 | 1963 | FEB 1978 |
| -Maximum in 24 hrs | 36 | 12.1 | 7.5 | 2.5 | 0.0 | T | 0.0 | 0.0 | 0.0 | 0.0 | 0.0 | 4.8 | 2.5 | 12.1 |
| -Year | | 1964 | 1978 | 1962 | | 1989 | | | | | | 1976 | 1963 | JAN 1964 |
| **WIND:** | | | | | | | | | | | | | | |
| Mean Speed (mph) | 36 | 11.2 | 11.9 | 12.9 | 12.6 | 11.2 | 10.6 | 9.6 | 9.1 | 9.5 | 9.8 | 10.8 | 11.0 | 10.9 |
| Prevailing Direction | | | | | | | | | | | | | | |
| through 1963 | | S | S | S | S | S | S | S | S | S | S | S | S | S |
| Fastest Obs. 1 Min. | | | | | | | | | | | | | | |
| -Direction (!!) | 36 | 36 | 36 | 29 | 32 | 14 | 32 | 36 | 36 | 11 | 27 | 34 | 32 | 36 |
| -Speed (MPH) | 36 | 55 | 51 | 55 | 55 | 55 | 52 | 65 | 73 | 53 | 44 | 50 | 53 | 73 |
| -Year | | 1985 | 1962 | 1954 | 1970 | 1955 | 1955 | 1961 | 1959 | 1961 | 1957 | 1957 | 1968 | AUG 1959 |
| Peak Gust | | | | | | | | | | | | | | |
| -Direction (!!) | 6 | N | S | S | N | S | NW | NE | NW | S | N | W | S | NW |
| -Speed (mph) | 6 | 66 | 54 | 53 | 49 | 54 | 58 | 54 | 81 | 51 | 41 | 56 | 55 | 81 |
| -Date | | 1985 | 1985 | 1985 | 1988 | 1987 | 1989 | 1989 | 1985 | 1986 | 1988 | 1988 | 1988 | AUG 1985 |

**See Reference Notes to this table on the following page.**

PRECIPITATION (inches)          DALLAS – FORT WORTH, TEXAS

**TABLE 2**

| YEAR | JAN | FEB | MAR | APR | MAY | JUNE | JULY | AUG | SEP | OCT | NOV | DEC | ANNUAL |
|---|---|---|---|---|---|---|---|---|---|---|---|---|---|
| 1961 | 3.29 | 2.20 | 2.95 | 2.23 | 1.06 | 5.93 | 2.32 | 0.02 | 2.92 | 2.82 | 2.72 | 2.12 | 30.58 |
| 1962 | 1.00 | 2.01 | 1.80 | 5.66 | 1.58 | 6.94 | 6.36 | 3.22 | 3.79 | 4.15 | 3.93 | 0.99 | 41.43 |
| 1963 | 0.86 | 0.15 | 0.48 | 6.20 | 2.52 | 0.57 | 2.28 | 2.73 | 1.70 | 0.23 | 1.29 | 1.45 | 20.46 |
| 1964 | 3.53 | 1.17 | 3.35 | 2.71 | 2.85 | 0.40 | 0.25 | 2.43 | 9.52 | 0.62 | 6.23 | 1.25 | 34.31 |
| 1965 | 2.77 | 6.20 | 1.45 | 2.15 | 8.97 | 1.50 | 0.09 | 2.26 | 5.04 | 1.97 | 2.43 | 1.73 | 36.56 |
| 1966 | 1.68 | 2.84 | 1.38 | 10.74 | 3.13 | 5.47 | 3.26 | 3.38 | 4.23 | 1.48 | 0.53 | 1.17 | 39.29 |
| 1967 | 0.28 | 0.32 | 2.09 | 3.84 | 4.02 | 0.72 | 2.20 | 0.48 | 5.94 | 4.19 | 2.30 | 0.92 | 27.30 |
| 1968 | 3.60 | 1.48 | 6.39 | 2.41 | 6.02 | 3.50 | 1.88 | 2.71 | 2.53 | 2.18 | 4.58 | 1.20 | 38.48 |
| 1969 | 1.26 | 1.99 | 3.62 | 3.40 | 7.12 | 0.63 | 0.77 | 2.56 | 4.55 | 5.82 | 1.22 | 2.75 | 35.69 |
| 1970 | 0.72 | 4.78 | 3.49 | 4.68 | 3.62 | 0.61 | 0.94 | 6.85 | 6.25 | 2.95 | 0.20 | 1.01 | 36.10 |
| 1971 | 0.19 | 1.32 | 0.34 | 2.76 | 1.88 | 0.83 | 3.60 | 5.70 | 3.24 | 7.64 | 1.77 | 6.99 | 36.26 |
| 1972 | 1.09 | 0.26 | 0.10 | 3.25 | 2.35 | 1.50 | 0.59 | 0.81 | 2.42 | 6.89 | 2.36 | 0.61 | 22.23 |
| 1973 | 3.26 | 1.92 | 2.28 | 6.06 | 3.18 | 5.88 | 11.13 | 0.01 | 7.16 | 6.85 | 2.06 | 0.83 | 50.62 |
| 1974 | 1.79 | 1.01 | 0.80 | 2.51 | 5.44 | 6.00 | 0.67 | 4.19 | 6.04 | 5.93 | 3.32 | 1.93 | 39.63 |
| 1975 | 3.34 | 3.72 | 1.67 | 3.40 | 6.88 | 1.95 | 5.06 | 0.30 | 0.87 | T | 0.42 | 1.49 | 29.10 |
| 1976 | 0.13 | 0.52 | 2.29 | 5.71 | 6.03 | 1.40 | 3.83 | 4.75 | 5.02 | 3.46 | 0.50 | 1.99 | 35.63 |
| 1977 | 2.39 | 1.68 | 5.88 | 4.31 | 0.99 | 0.69 | 2.20 | 2.33 | 1.72 | 2.96 | 1.79 | 0.25 | 27.19 |
| 1978 | 1.41 | 3.33 | 2.66 | 1.34 | 8.01 | 0.77 | 0.33 | 1.53 | 0.93 | 0.55 | 2.73 | 0.78 | 24.37 |
| 1979 | 3.35 | 1.52 | 6.33 | 2.03 | 5.90 | 1.36 | 1.94 | 2.47 | 0.99 | 3.38 | 0.43 | 2.72 | 32.42 |
| 1980 | 2.52 | 0.84 | 1.24 | 2.23 | 3.01 | 1.25 | 0.71 | T | 6.54 | 1.08 | 1.23 | 1.43 | 22.08 |
| 1981 | 0.58 | 1.44 | 3.39 | 2.69 | 6.24 | 7.85 | 1.81 | 2.32 | 2.40 | 14.18 | 1.53 | 0.17 | 44.60 |
| 1982 | 2.33 | 1.89 | 1.71 | 2.71 | 13.66 | 4.28 | 2.73 | 0.52 | 0.58 | 3.36 | 4.22 | 2.76 | 40.75 |
| 1983 | 2.55 | 1.25 | 4.36 | 0.59 | 5.83 | 2.07 | 1.56 | 5.55 | 0.22 | 4.04 | 2.22 | 0.83 | 31.07 |
| 1984 | 1.07 | 3.11 | 4.92 | 1.41 | 3.04 | 2.79 | 0.43 | 1.47 | 0.09 | 6.50 | 2.97 | 6.09 | 33.89 |
| 1985 | 0.81 | 2.62 | 3.70 | 3.75 | 2.13 | 3.78 | 2.40 | 0.53 | 3.35 | 3.91 | 3.11 | 0.61 | 30.70 |
| 1986 | T | 2.49 | 1.08 | 5.30 | 5.52 | 3.92 | 0.41 | 1.63 | 4.60 | 1.81 | 3.25 | 2.44 | 32.45 |
| 1987 | 1.22 | 3.67 | 1.70 | 0.11 | 5.95 | 3.45 | 1.77 | 0.81 | 1.38 | 0.12 | 4.17 | 2.90 | 27.25 |
| 1988 | 0.88 | 1.23 | 2.03 | 2.21 | 2.11 | 3.23 | 2.47 | 0.44 | 4.04 | 1.64 | 2.28 | 2.48 | 25.04 |
| 1989 | 2.56 | 3.70 | 3.72 | 1.86 | 9.62 | 8.75 | 2.61 | 1.89 | 2.40 | 2.02 | 0.49 | 0.33 | 39.95 |
| 1990 | 4.54 | 4.72 | 5.89 | 6.90 | 7.16 | 1.89 | 2.60 | 2.37 | 1.12 | 2.81 | 3.81 | 1.46 | 45.27 |
| Record Mean | 1.80 | 2.05 | 2.43 | 3.77 | 4.77 | 2.99 | 2.19 | 2.18 | 2.84 | 2.99 | 2.27 | 1.95 | 32.24 |

**TABLE 3**  AVERAGE TEMPERATURE (deg. F)          DALLAS – FORT WORTH, TEXAS

| YEAR | JAN | FEB | MAR | APR | MAY | JUNE | JULY | AUG | SEP | OCT | NOV | DEC | ANNUAL |
|---|---|---|---|---|---|---|---|---|---|---|---|---|---|
| 1961 | 40.9 | 50.3 | 59.3 | 64.0 | 73.1 | 77.9 | 82.3 | 82.7 | 76.9 | 67.3 | 52.7 | 45.8 | 64.5 |
| 1962 | 39.6 | 53.3 | 54.0 | 64.3 | 77.6 | 79.9 | 85.5 | 85.6 | 77.1 | 70.4 | 55.5 | 47.2 | 65.8 |
| #1963 | 37.8 | 46.4 | 61.2 | 70.4 | 75.0 | 83.1 | 87.4 | 87.3 | 79.2 | 73.5 | 58.4 | 40.3 | 66.7 |
| 1964 | 43.8 | 43.8 | 55.6 | 66.8 | 73.2 | 81.0 | 87.1 | 85.3 | 76.9 | 63.6 | 57.6 | 47.1 | 65.2 |
| 1965 | 47.1 | 45.8 | 47.0 | 68.4 | 72.9 | 79.9 | 86.3 | 84.1 | 79.4 | 66.6 | 62.9 | 52.8 | 66.1 |
| 1966 | 40.3 | 45.4 | 56.3 | 63.8 | 70.8 | 79.6 | 86.3 | 82.7 | 75.8 | 65.0 | 60.7 | 45.3 | 64.4 |
| 1967 | 48.3 | 46.8 | 63.3 | 71.1 | 71.4 | 81.4 | 82.9 | 83.1 | 74.1 | 65.4 | 55.6 | 47.0 | 65.9 |
| 1968 | 44.4 | 44.2 | 54.6 | 63.4 | 72.4 | 79.5 | 81.0 | 83.5 | 74.6 | 67.8 | 53.9 | 47.4 | 63.9 |
| 1969 | 49.0 | 50.0 | 49.8 | 65.4 | 71.9 | 79.8 | 87.9 | 84.2 | 77.1 | 65.3 | 55.1 | 49.9 | 65.5 |
| 1970 | 40.6 | 48.6 | 52.1 | 66.2 | 71.7 | 79.1 | 84.0 | 85.8 | 78.2 | 65.1 | 54.7 | 53.6 | 65.0 |
| 1971 | 46.7 | 49.2 | 55.6 | 64.0 | 70.5 | 82.9 | 84.4 | 79.5 | 77.1 | 70.1 | 57.0 | 52.2 | 65.8 |
| 1972 | 45.0 | 51.5 | 62.1 | 70.1 | 72.7 | 81.4 | 83.1 | 84.7 | 80.8 | 67.5 | 50.1 | 44.0 | 66.1 |
| 1973 | 42.5 | 47.9 | 60.0 | 60.7 | 71.7 | 79.3 | 83.9 | 82.9 | 76.1 | 68.3 | 59.8 | 48.4 | 65.1 |
| 1974 | 43.6 | 52.3 | 62.9 | 65.8 | 75.7 | 78.7 | 86.1 | 82.9 | 70.9 | 69.2 | 55.5 | 47.2 | 65.9 |
| 1975 | 49.0 | 46.6 | 53.8 | 64.7 | 72.4 | 80.9 | 83.6 | 84.8 | 75.6 | 69.8 | 57.3 | 49.0 | 65.6 |
| 1976 | 45.0 | 58.4 | 59.4 | 64.9 | 68.6 | 78.8 | 82.1 | 84.2 | 76.1 | 60.2 | 49.5 | 45.0 | 64.3 |
| 1977 | 34.7 | 49.4 | 57.2 | 66.8 | 77.4 | 84.1 | 87.1 | 84.9 | 81.6 | 66.7 | 56.4 | 47.6 | 66.2 |
| 1978 | 33.8 | 36.7 | 54.1 | 67.1 | 73.1 | 82.3 | 88.4 | 84.6 | 80.2 | 68.9 | 57.7 | 46.1 | 64.4 |
| 1979 | 35.4 | 42.2 | 56.7 | 64.4 | 69.7 | 81.0 | 84.5 | 82.5 | 77.0 | 70.8 | 52.9 | 49.4 | 63.9 |
| 1980 | 45.5 | 46.6 | 54.2 | 63.1 | 75.0 | 87.0 | 92.0 | 88.5 | 80.3 | 65.4 | 54.9 | 49.4 | 66.8 |
| 1981 | 44.6 | 48.9 | 55.7 | 69.2 | 70.5 | 80.3 | 85.9 | 83.4 | 76.2 | 66.1 | 57.5 | 47.3 | 65.4 |
| 1982 | 44.6 | 44.5 | 59.8 | 62.5 | 72.5 | 79.2 | 84.6 | 86.7 | 78.1 | 67.0 | 55.6 | 49.2 | 65.4 |
| 1983 | 43.4 | 48.5 | 54.5 | 60.6 | 69.5 | 77.3 | 83.6 | 84.9 | 77.1 | 67.8 | 57.3 | 34.8 | 63.3 |
| 1984 | 39.3 | 50.9 | 56.3 | 63.7 | 73.7 | 82.5 | 85.5 | 85.8 | 76.1 | 67.0 | 54.6 | 52.6 | 65.7 |
| 1985 | 37.8 | 45.0 | 60.8 | 67.2 | 74.0 | 80.2 | 84.4 | 87.6 | 77.7 | 67.6 | 56.3 | 42.3 | 65.1 |
| 1986 | 48.8 | 51.2 | 60.2 | 67.2 | 71.5 | 80.8 | 86.4 | 83.4 | 80.2 | 65.7 | 52.4 | 46.1 | 66.2 |
| 1987 | 44.5 | 50.8 | 53.9 | 65.0 | 75.1 | 79.6 | 83.4 | 86.5 | 77.1 | 66.5 | 55.7 | 47.3 | 65.5 |
| 1988 | 42.2 | 47.1 | 56.0 | 64.5 | 72.8 | 80.4 | 85.3 | 87.9 | 79.2 | 65.7 | 58.1 | 49.1 | 65.7 |
| 1989 | 50.0 | 42.2 | 56.7 | 66.4 | 74.3 | 77.9 | 82.8 | 82.3 | 74.7 | 69.0 | 58.2 | 39.0 | 64.5 |
| 1990 | 51.8 | 53.9 | 57.7 | 64.0 | 73.4 | 84.0 | 82.5 | 84.6 | 80.0 | 66.4 | 59.8 | 44.0 | 66.8 |
| Record Mean | 45.2 | 48.6 | 56.9 | 65.2 | 72.7 | 80.9 | 84.6 | 84.7 | 77.9 | 67.6 | 56.0 | 47.4 | 65.6 |
| Max | 55.5 | 59.3 | 68.0 | 75.9 | 82.7 | 91.1 | 95.0 | 95.3 | 88.3 | 78.5 | 66.6 | 57.5 | 76.1 |
| Min | 34.8 | 37.9 | 45.8 | 54.5 | 62.7 | 70.7 | 74.2 | 74.0 | 67.4 | 56.7 | 45.5 | 37.2 | 55.1 |

## REFERENCE NOTES FOR TABLES 1, 2, 3 and 6          (DALLAS/FT WORTH, TX)

### GENERAL

T - TRACE AMOUNT
BLANK ENTRIES DENOTE MISSING/UNREPORTED DATA.
# INDICATES A STATION OR INSTRUMENT RELOCATION.

### SPECIFIC

#### TABLE 1

(a) - LENGTH OF RECORD IN YEARS. ALTHOUGH
      INDIVIDUAL MONTHS MAY BE MISSING.
* LESS THAN .05

NORMALS — BASED ON THE 1951-1980 RECORD PERIOD.
EXTREMES — DATES ARE THE MOST RECENT OCCURRENCE.
WIND DIR. — NUMERALS SHOW TENS OF DEGREES
            CLOCKWISE FROM TRUE NORTH.
            "00" INDICATES CALM.
RESULTANT WIND DIRECTIONS ARE GIVEN TO WHOLE DEGREES.

#### TABLE 3

MAX AND MIN ARE LONG-TERM MEAN DAILY MAXIMUM
AND MEAN DAILY MINIMUM TEMPERATURES.

### EXCEPTIONS

**TABLES 2, 3, and 6**

RECORD MEANS ARE THROUGH THE CURRENT YEAR,
BEGINNING IN      1899 FOR TEMPERATURE
                  1899 FOR PRECIPITATION
                  1954 FOR SNOWFALL

HEATING DEGREE DAYS Base 65 deg. F    DALLAS - FORT WORTH, TEXAS

**TABLE 4**

| SEASON | JULY | AUG | SEP | OCT | NOV | DEC | JAN | FEB | MAR | APR | MAY | JUNE | TOTAL |
|---|---|---|---|---|---|---|---|---|---|---|---|---|---|
| 1961-62 | 0 | 0 | 0 | 50 | 381 | 590 | 781 | 328 | 345 | 107 | 2 | 0 | 2584 |
| #1962-63 | 0 | 0 | 0 | 46 | 280 | 545 | 839 | 517 | 185 | 34 | 13 | 0 | 2459 |
| 1963-64 | 0 | 0 | 0 | 4 | 227 | 760 | 651 | 608 | 285 | 65 | 1 | 0 | 2601 |
| 1964-65 | 0 | 0 | 6 | 81 | 260 | 550 | 550 | 530 | 551 | 36 | 0 | 0 | 2564 |
| 1965-66 | 0 | 0 | 2 | 60 | 103 | 376 | 760 | 542 | 274 | 84 | 26 | 0 | 2227 |
| 1966-67 | 0 | 0 | 0 | 79 | 182 | 627 | 514 | 503 | 146 | 15 | 21 | 0 | 2087 |
| 1967-68 | 0 | 0 | 13 | 80 | 282 | 548 | 631 | 598 | 330 | 100 | 2 | 0 | 2584 |
| 1968-69 | 0 | 0 | 0 | 47 | 348 | 540 | 492 | 416 | 468 | 49 | 6 | 4 | 2370 |
| 1969-70 | 0 | 0 | 0 | 116 | 306 | 463 | 756 | 455 | 404 | 63 | 21 | 1 | 2585 |
| 1970-71 | 0 | 0 | 7 | 105 | 316 | 369 | 564 | 440 | 307 | 97 | 19 | 0 | 2224 |
| 1971-72 | 0 | 0 | 12 | 7 | 270 | 389 | 615 | 398 | 143 | 26 | 1 | 0 | 1861 |
| 1972-73 | 0 | 0 | 3 | 96 | 446 | 644 | 690 | 475 | 155 | 182 | 12 | 0 | 2703 |
| 1973-74 | 0 | 0 | 1 | 36 | 182 | 509 | 656 | 352 | 173 | 70 | 1 | 0 | 1980 |
| 1974-75 | 0 | 0 | 20 | 16 | 296 | 546 | 489 | 508 | 355 | 112 | 0 | 0 | 2342 |
| 1975-76 | 0 | 0 | 4 | 33 | 266 | 500 | 616 | 217 | 222 | 48 | 20 | 0 | 1926 |
| 1976-77 | 0 | 0 | 0 | 214 | 459 | 614 | 931 | 431 | 241 | 37 | 0 | 0 | 2927 |
| 1977-78 | 0 | 0 | 0 | 55 | 257 | 536 | 962 | 786 | 346 | 54 | 41 | 0 | 3037 |
| 1978-79 | 0 | 0 | 0 | 27 | 247 | 578 | 911 | 635 | 261 | 78 | 29 | 0 | 2766 |
| 1979-80 | 0 | 0 | 0 | 34 | 370 | 478 | 597 | 530 | 339 | 102 | 6 | 0 | 2456 |
| 1980-81 | 0 | 0 | 18 | 99 | 330 | 486 | 625 | 448 | 284 | 26 | 23 | 0 | 2339 |
| 1981-82 | 0 | 0 | 10 | 116 | 228 | 541 | 625 | 569 | 232 | 140 | 9 | 0 | 2470 |
| 1982-83 | 0 | 0 | 1 | 94 | 316 | 495 | 663 | 454 | 324 | 186 | 21 | 2 | 2556 |
| 1983-84 | 0 | 0 | 12 | 52 | 269 | 933 | 789 | 401 | 281 | 89 | 11 | 0 | 2837 |
| 1984-85 | 0 | 0 | 38 | 66 | 322 | 389 | 837 | 558 | 171 | 37 | 0 | 0 | 2418 |
| 1985-86 | 0 | 0 | 19 | 53 | 285 | 696 | 495 | 400 | 164 | 41 | 5 | 0 | 2158 |
| 1986-87 | 0 | 0 | 0 | 61 | 376 | 580 | 632 | 387 | 342 | 109 | 0 | 0 | 2487 |
| 1987-88 | 0 | 0 | 0 | 55 | 297 | 540 | 703 | 512 | 301 | 70 | 0 | 0 | 2478 |
| 1988-89 | 0 | 0 | 0 | 51 | 240 | 487 | 460 | 630 | 294 | 102 | 4 | 0 | 2268 |
| 1989-90 | 0 | 0 | 14 | 80 | 251 | 799 | 401 | 306 | 251 | 102 | 19 | 0 | 2223 |
| 1990-91 | 0 | 0 | 0 | 100 | 190 | 646 | | | | | | | |

**TABLE 5**    COOLING DEGREE DAYS Base 65 deg. F    DALLAS - FORT WORTH, TEXAS

| YEAR | JAN | FEB | MAR | APR | MAY | JUNE | JULY | AUG | SEP | OCT | NOV | DEC | TOTAL |
|---|---|---|---|---|---|---|---|---|---|---|---|---|---|
| 1969 | 3 | 3 | 3 | 67 | 228 | 453 | 715 | 602 | 372 | 133 | 17 | 0 | 2596 |
| 1970 | 5 | 0 | 7 | 108 | 236 | 433 | 595 | 653 | 409 | 115 | 12 | 22 | 2595 |
| 1971 | 0 | 0 | 21 | 71 | 195 | 546 | 606 | 456 | 382 | 171 | 36 | 1 | 2491 |
| 1972 | 2 | 14 | 57 | 185 | 249 | 498 | 569 | 618 | 480 | 183 | 4 | 0 | 2859 |
| 1973 | 1 | 0 | 6 | 60 | 230 | 435 | 593 | 559 | 342 | 146 | 33 | 0 | 2405 |
| 1974 | 0 | 2 | 115 | 101 | 341 | 419 | 660 | 563 | 202 | 153 | 20 | 2 | 2578 |
| 1975 | 0 | 0 | 15 | 107 | 236 | 483 | 580 | 620 | 331 | 189 | 39 | 9 | 2609 |
| 1976 | 0 | 32 | 59 | 52 | 138 | 421 | 537 | 602 | 338 | 72 | 0 | 0 | 2251 |
| 1977 | 0 | 0 | 7 | 94 | 391 | 581 | 693 | 626 | 505 | 112 | 6 | 2 | 3017 |
| 1978 | 0 | 0 | 16 | 125 | 301 | 524 | 733 | 614 | 462 | 153 | 37 | 0 | 2965 |
| 1979 | 0 | 1 | 9 | 67 | 179 | 489 | 613 | 551 | 366 | 220 | 14 | 0 | 2509 |
| 1980 | 0 | 0 | 11 | 52 | 320 | 668 | 844 | 737 | 485 | 117 | 35 | 10 | 3279 |
| 1981 | 0 | 5 | 5 | 158 | 200 | 467 | 654 | 577 | 352 | 155 | 8 | 0 | 2581 |
| 1982 | 1 | 2 | 77 | 71 | 252 | 433 | 614 | 679 | 403 | 160 | 40 | 10 | 2742 |
| 1983 | 0 | 0 | 7 | 61 | 171 | 382 | 582 | 626 | 381 | 145 | 46 | 0 | 2401 |
| 1984 | 0 | 0 | 20 | 60 | 288 | 531 | 644 | 652 | 376 | 135 | 16 | 12 | 2734 |
| 1985 | 0 | 5 | 51 | 108 | 287 | 460 | 608 | 706 | 408 | 139 | 29 | 0 | 2801 |
| 1986 | 0 | 19 | 24 | 112 | 212 | 480 | 673 | 578 | 464 | 91 | 3 | 0 | 2656 |
| 1987 | 0 | 0 | 6 | 114 | 318 | 442 | 576 | 674 | 370 | 111 | 23 | 0 | 2634 |
| 1988 | 4 | 0 | 28 | 61 | 247 | 467 | 639 | 714 | 433 | 78 | 39 | 1 | 2711 |
| 1989 | 1 | 0 | 45 | 154 | 297 | 393 | 561 | 542 | 314 | 208 | 52 | 0 | 2567 |
| 1990 | 1 | 2 | 30 | 79 | 286 | 575 | 551 | 617 | 457 | 152 | 41 | 2 | 2793 |

**TABLE 6**    SNOWFALL (inches)    DALLAS - FORT WORTH, TEXAS

| SEASON | JULY | AUG | SEP | OCT | NOV | DEC | JAN | FEB | MAR | APR | MAY | JUNE | TOTAL |
|---|---|---|---|---|---|---|---|---|---|---|---|---|---|
| 1961-62 | 0.0 | 0.0 | 0.0 | 0.0 | 0.0 | 0.0 | 2.6 | T | 2.5 | 0.0 | 0.0 | 0.0 | 5.1 |
| 1962-63 | 0.0 | 0.0 | 0.0 | 0.0 | 0.0 | T | T | T | 0.1 | 0.0 | 0.0 | 0.0 | 0.1 |
| 1963-64 | 0.0 | 0.0 | 0.0 | 0.0 | 0.0 | 2.6 | 12.1 | 0.2 | 0.4 | 0.0 | 0.0 | 0.0 | 15.3 |
| 1964-65 | 0.0 | 0.0 | 0.0 | 0.0 | 0.0 | T | 0.0 | T | T | 0.0 | 0.0 | 0.0 | T |
| 1965-66 | 0.0 | 0.0 | 0.0 | 0.0 | 0.0 | 0.0 | 4.4 | 2.9 | 0.0 | 0.0 | 0.0 | 0.0 | 7.3 |
| 1966-67 | 0.0 | 0.0 | 0.0 | 0.0 | 0.0 | 0.0 | 0.0 | T | T | 0.0 | 0.0 | 0.0 | T |
| 1967-68 | 0.0 | 0.0 | 0.0 | 0.0 | 0.0 | 0.0 | 0.4 | 2.6 | T | 0.0 | 0.0 | 0.0 | 3.0 |
| 1968-69 | 0.0 | 0.0 | 0.0 | 0.0 | T | 0.0 | 0.0 | T | 0.0 | 0.0 | 0.0 | 0.0 | T |
| 1969-70 | 0.0 | 0.0 | 0.0 | 0.0 | 0.0 | T | T | 0.0 | 0.8 | 0.0 | 0.0 | 0.0 | 0.8 |
| 1970-71 | 0.0 | 0.0 | 0.0 | 0.0 | 0.0 | 0.0 | 0.0 | T | 1.6 | 0.0 | 0.0 | 0.0 | 1.6 |
| 1971-72 | 0.0 | 0.0 | 0.0 | 0.0 | T | 0.0 | T | T | 0.0 | 0.0 | 0.0 | 0.0 | T |
| 1972-73 | 0.0 | 0.0 | 0.0 | 0.0 | T | 1.4 | 2.3 | T | 0.0 | 0.0 | 0.0 | 0.0 | 3.7 |
| 1973-74 | 0.0 | 0.0 | 0.0 | 0.0 | 0.0 | 0.0 | T | 0.0 | 0.0 | 0.0 | 0.0 | 0.0 | T |
| 1974-75 | 0.0 | 0.0 | 0.0 | 0.0 | T | T | T | 3.7 | T | 0.0 | 0.0 | 0.0 | 3.7 |
| 1975-76 | 0.0 | 0.0 | 0.0 | 0.0 | 0.0 | 0.4 | 0.0 | 0.0 | T | 0.0 | 0.0 | 0.0 | 0.4 |
| 1976-77 | 0.0 | 0.0 | 0.0 | 0.0 | 5.0 | 0.0 | 5.4 | 0.0 | 0.0 | 0.0 | 0.0 | 0.0 | 10.4 |
| 1977-78 | 0.0 | 0.0 | 0.0 | 0.0 | 0.0 | 0.0 | 4.1 | 13.5 | T | 0.0 | 0.0 | 0.0 | 17.6 |
| 1978-79 | 0.0 | 0.0 | 0.0 | 0.0 | 0.0 | 0.8 | 1.8 | 0.7 | 0.0 | 0.0 | 0.0 | 0.0 | 3.3 |
| 1979-80 | 0.0 | 0.0 | 0.0 | 0.0 | 0.0 | T | 0.0 | 1.6 | 0.0 | 0.0 | 0.0 | 0.0 | 1.6 |
| 1980-81 | 0.0 | 0.0 | 0.0 | 0.0 | 0.0 | 0.0 | T | T | 0.0 | 0.0 | 0.0 | 0.0 | T |
| 1981-82 | 0.0 | 0.0 | 0.0 | 0.0 | 0.0 | 0.0 | 0.8 | T | 0.0 | 0.0 | 0.0 | 0.0 | 0.8 |
| 1982-83 | 0.0 | 0.0 | 0.0 | 0.0 | 0.0 | T | T | T | 0.0 | 0.0 | 0.0 | 0.0 | T |
| 1983-84 | 0.0 | 0.0 | 0.0 | 0.0 | 0.0 | 2.0 | 0.0 | 0.0 | 0.0 | 0.0 | 0.0 | 0.0 | 2.0 |
| 1984-85 | 0.0 | 0.0 | 0.0 | 0.0 | 0.0 | 0.0 | 3.4 | 1.7 | 0.0 | 0.0 | 0.0 | 0.0 | 5.1 |
| 1985-86 | 0.0 | 0.0 | 0.0 | 0.0 | 0.0 | T | 0.0 | 0.8 | 0.0 | 0.0 | 0.0 | 0.0 | 0.8 |
| 1986-87 | 0.0 | 0.0 | 0.0 | 0.0 | 0.0 | 1.7 | T | T | 0.5 | 0.0 | 0.0 | 0.0 | 2.2 |
| 1987-88 | 0.0 | 0.0 | 0.0 | 0.0 | 0.0 | 0.8 | 2.7 | 0.0 | 0.0 | 0.0 | 0.0 | 0.0 | 3.5 |
| 1988-89 | 0.0 | 0.0 | 0.0 | 0.0 | 0.0 | T | T | 0.7 | 1.1 | 0.0 | T | 0.0 | 1.8 |
| 1989-90 | 0.0 | 0.0 | 0.0 | 0.0 | 0.0 | 0.0 | 0.0 | 0.0 | 0.0 | T | T | 0.0 | T |
| 1990-91 | 0.0 | 0.0 | 0.0 | 0.0 | 0.0 | 0.3 | | | | | | | |
| Record Mean | 0.0 | 0.0 | 0.0 | 0.0 | 0.1 | 0.3 | 1.3 | 1.0 | 0.2 | T | T | 0.0 | 3.0 |

**See Reference Notes, relative to all above tables, on preceding page.**

The city of El Paso is located in the extreme west point of Texas at an elevation of about 3,700 feet . The National Weather Service station is located on a mesa about 200 feet higher than the city. The climate of the region is characterized by an abundance of sunshine throughout the year, high daytime summer temperatures, very low humidity, scanty rainfall, and a relatively mild winter season. The Franklin Mountains begin within the city limits and extend northward for about 16 miles. Peaks of these mountains range from 4,687 to 7,152 feet above sea level.

Rainfall throughout the year is light, insufficient for any growth except desert vegetation. Irrigation is necessary for crops, gardens, and lawns. Dry periods lasting several months are not unusual. Almost half of the precipitation occurs in the three-month period, July through September, from brief but often heavy thunderstorms. Small amounts of snow fall nearly every winter, but snow cover rarely amounts to more than an inch and seldom remains on the ground for more than a few hours.

Daytime summer temperatures are high, frequently above 90 degrees and occasionally above 100 degrees. Summer nights are usually comfortable, with temperatures in the 60s. It should be noted that when temperatures are high the relative humidity is generally quite low. A 20-year tabulation of observations with temperatures above 90 degrees shows that in April, May, and June the humidity averaged from 10 to 14 percent, while in July, August, and September it averaged 22 to 24 percent. This low humidity aids the efficiency of evaporative air coolers, which are widely used in homes and public buildings and are quite effective in cooling the air to comfortable temperatures.

Winter daytime temperatures are mild. At night they drop below freezing about half the time in December and January. The flat, irrigated land of the Rio Grande Valley in the vicinity of El Paso is noticeably cooler, particularly at night, than the airport or the city proper, both in summer and winter. This results in more comfortable temperatures in summer but increases the severity of freezes in winter. The cooler air in the Valley also causes marked short-period fluctuations of temperature and dewpoint at the airport with changes in wind direction, especially during the early morning hours.

Dust and sandstorms are the most unpleasant features of the weather in El Paso. While wind velocities are not excessively high, the soil surface is dry and loose and natural vegetation is sparse, so moderately strong winds raise considerable dust and sand. A tabulation of duststorms for a period of 20 years shows that they are most frequent in March and April, and comparatively rare in the period July through December. prevailing winds are from the north in winter and the south in summer.

## TABLE 1     NORMALS, MEANS AND EXTREMES

EL PASO, TEXAS

LATITUDE: 31°48'N   LONGITUDE: 106°24'W   ELEVATION: FT. GRND 3918 BARO 3932   TIME ZONE: MOUNTAIN   WBAN: 23044

| | (a) | JAN | FEB | MAR | APR | MAY | JUNE | JULY | AUG | SEP | OCT | NOV | DEC | YEAR |
|---|---|---|---|---|---|---|---|---|---|---|---|---|---|---|
| **TEMPERATURE °F:** | | | | | | | | | | | | | | |
| Normals | | | | | | | | | | | | | | |
| -Daily Maximum | | 57.9 | 62.7 | 69.6 | 78.7 | 87.1 | 95.9 | 95.3 | 93.0 | 87.5 | 78.5 | 65.7 | 58.2 | 77.5 |
| -Daily Minimum | | 30.4 | 34.1 | 40.5 | 48.5 | 56.6 | 65.7 | 69.6 | 67.5 | 60.6 | 48.7 | 37.0 | 30.6 | 49.2 |
| -Monthly | | 44.2 | 48.4 | 55.1 | 63.6 | 71.9 | 80.8 | 82.5 | 80.3 | 74.1 | 63.6 | 51.4 | 44.4 | 63.4 |
| Extremes | | | | | | | | | | | | | | |
| -Record Highest | 50 | 80 | 83 | 89 | 98 | 104 | 111 | 112 | 108 | 104 | 96 | 87 | 80 | 112 |
| -Year | | 1970 | 1986 | 1989 | 1989 | 1951 | 1978 | 1979 | 1980 | 1982 | 1979 | 1983 | 1973 | JUL 1979 |
| -Record Lowest | 50 | -8 | 8 | 14 | 23 | 31 | 46 | 57 | 56 | 41 | 25 | 1 | 5 | -8 |
| -Year | | 1962 | 1985 | 1971 | 1983 | 1967 | 1988 | 1988 | 1973 | 1945 | 1970 | 1976 | 1953 | JAN 1962 |
| **NORMAL DEGREE DAYS:** | | | | | | | | | | | | | | |
| Heating (base 65°F) | | 645 | 465 | 318 | 93 | 0 | 0 | 0 | 0 | 0 | 96 | 408 | 639 | 2664 |
| Cooling (base 65°F) | | 0 | 0 | 11 | 51 | 218 | 474 | 543 | 474 | 273 | 52 | 0 | 0 | 2096 |
| **% OF POSSIBLE SUNSHINE** | 47 | 78 | 82 | 85 | 88 | 89 | 89 | 81 | 81 | 82 | 84 | 83 | 78 | 83 |
| **MEAN SKY COVER (tenths)** | | | | | | | | | | | | | | |
| Sunrise - Sunset | 47 | 4.6 | 4.2 | 4.2 | 3.6 | 3.2 | 2.9 | 4.5 | 4.3 | 3.4 | 3.2 | 3.5 | 4.2 | 3.8 |
| **MEAN NUMBER OF DAYS:** | | | | | | | | | | | | | | |
| Sunrise to Sunset | | | | | | | | | | | | | | |
| -Clear | 47 | 14.1 | 13.9 | 15.1 | 16.4 | 18.7 | 19.6 | 12.2 | 13.7 | 17.7 | 18.8 | 17.4 | 15.3 | 193.1 |
| -Partly Cloudy | 47 | 7.3 | 7.4 | 8.1 | 8.1 | 8.0 | 7.5 | 13.2 | 12.2 | 7.2 | 6.8 | 6.3 | 7.3 | 99.7 |
| -Cloudy | 47 | 9.6 | 7.0 | 7.8 | 5.5 | 4.3 | 2.9 | 5.6 | 5.0 | 5.0 | 5.4 | 6.3 | 8.3 | 72.5 |
| Precipitation | | | | | | | | | | | | | | |
| .01 inches or more | 50 | 3.9 | 2.8 | 2.4 | 1.7 | 2.2 | 3.4 | 7.8 | 8.0 | 5.3 | 4.1 | 2.7 | 3.7 | 48.1 |
| Snow, Ice pellets | | | | | | | | | | | | | | |
| 1.0 inches or more | 50 | 0.5 | 0.3 | 0.* | 0.1 | 0.0 | 0.0 | 0.0 | 0.0 | 0.0 | 0.* | 0.3 | 0.5 | 1.8 |
| Thunderstorms | 50 | 0.2 | 0.4 | 0.5 | 1.0 | 2.7 | 4.6 | 10.2 | 10.2 | 4.1 | 1.9 | 0.3 | 0.2 | 36.3 |
| Heavy Fog Visibility | | | | | | | | | | | | | | |
| 1/4 mile or less | 50 | 0.7 | 0.2 | 0.1 | 0.* | 0.* | 0.0 | 0.0 | 0.0 | 0.1 | 0.1 | 0.3 | 0.6 | 2.1 |
| Temperature °F | | | | | | | | | | | | | | |
| -Maximum | | | | | | | | | | | | | | |
| 90° and above | 29 | 0.0 | 0.0 | 0.0 | 2.0 | 12.8 | 25.9 | 27.1 | 23.6 | 11.8 | 1.7 | 0.0 | 0.0 | 104.7 |
| 32° and below | 29 | 0.4 | 0.1 | 0.0 | 0.0 | 0.0 | 0.0 | 0.0 | 0.0 | 0.0 | 0.0 | 0.1 | 0.2 | 0.7 |
| -Minimum | | | | | | | | | | | | | | |
| 32° and below | 29 | 19.6 | 12.3 | 5.1 | 0.9 | 0.* | 0.0 | 0.0 | 0.0 | 0.0 | 0.3 | 7.8 | 18.9 | 65.0 |
| 0° and below | 29 | 0.1 | 0.0 | 0.0 | 0.0 | 0.0 | 0.0 | 0.0 | 0.0 | 0.0 | 0.0 | 0.0 | 0.0 | 0.1 |
| **AVG. STATION PRESS.(mb)** | 17 | 883.8 | 882.7 | 880.0 | 880.1 | 879.4 | 880.4 | 882.4 | 882.7 | 882.7 | 883.5 | 883.3 | 884.0 | 882.1 |
| **RELATIVE HUMIDITY (%)** | | | | | | | | | | | | | | |
| Hour 05 | 29 | 65 | 56 | 47 | 39 | 41 | 46 | 62 | 66 | 68 | 64 | 61 | 65 | 57 |
| Hour 11 | 29 | 44 | 37 | 29 | 23 | 23 | 25 | 37 | 41 | 43 | 38 | 38 | 45 | 35 |
| Hour 17 (Local Time) | 29 | 35 | 27 | 20 | 16 | 16 | 18 | 29 | 33 | 34 | 30 | 32 | 37 | 27 |
| Hour 23 | 29 | 55 | 45 | 34 | 28 | 29 | 32 | 46 | 52 | 54 | 53 | 51 | 56 | 45 |
| **PRECIPITATION (inches):** | | | | | | | | | | | | | | |
| Water Equivalent | | | | | | | | | | | | | | |
| -Normal | | 0.38 | 0.45 | 0.32 | 0.19 | 0.24 | 0.56 | 1.60 | 1.21 | 1.42 | 0.73 | 0.33 | 0.39 | 7.82 |
| -Maximum Monthly | 50 | 1.84 | 1.69 | 2.26 | 1.42 | 1.92 | 3.18 | 5.53 | 5.57 | 6.68 | 4.31 | 1.63 | 2.87 | 6.68 |
| -Year | | 1949 | 1973 | 1958 | 1983 | 1941 | 1984 | 1968 | 1984 | 1974 | 1945 | 1961 | 1987 | SEP 1974 |
| -Minimum Monthly | 50 | 0.00 | 0.00 | T | 0.00 | 0.00 | T | 0.04 | T | T | 0.00 | 0.00 | 0.00 | 0.00 |
| -Year | | 1967 | 1943 | 1982 | 1978 | 1962 | 1989 | 1978 | 1962 | 1959 | 1952 | 1964 | 1955 | APR 1978 |
| -Maximum in 24 hrs | 50 | 0.61 | 0.87 | 1.72 | 1.08 | 1.23 | 1.56 | 2.63 | 2.30 | 2.52 | 1.77 | 1.19 | 1.76 | 2.63 |
| -Year | | 1960 | 1956 | 1941 | 1966 | 1941 | 1986 | 1968 | 1984 | 1958 | 1945 | 1943 | 1987 | JUL 1968 |
| Snow, Ice pellets | | | | | | | | | | | | | | |
| -Maximum Monthly | 50 | 8.3 | 8.9 | 7.3 | 16.5 | T | 0.0 | 0.0 | 0.0 | 0.0 | 1.0 | 12.7 | 25.9 | 25.9 |
| -Year | | 1949 | 1956 | 1958 | 1983 | 1989 | | | | | 1980 | 1976 | 1987 | DEC 1987 |
| -Maximum in 24 hrs | 50 | 4.8 | 7.2 | 7.3 | 8.8 | T | 0.0 | 0.0 | 0.0 | 0.0 | 1.0 | 7.8 | 16.8 | 16.8 |
| -Year | | 1981 | 1956 | 1958 | 1983 | 1989 | | | | | 1980 | 1961 | 1987 | DEC 1987 |
| **WIND:** | | | | | | | | | | | | | | |
| Mean Speed (mph) | 47 | 8.4 | 9.2 | 11.1 | 11.1 | 10.3 | 9.3 | 8.3 | 7.8 | 7.6 | 7.5 | 8.0 | 7.9 | 8.9 |
| Prevailing Direction | | | | | | | | | | | | | | |
| through 1963 | | N | N | WSW | WSW | WSW | S | SSE | S | S | N | N | N | N |
| Fastest Obs. 1 Min. | | | | | | | | | | | | | | |
| -Direction (!!) | 14 | 28 | 26 | 30 | 30 | 13 | 22 | 13 | 13 | 08 | 27 | 24 | 24 | 26 |
| -Speed (MPH) | 14 | 40 | 48 | 48 | 42 | 35 | 40 | 37 | 35 | 29 | 35 | 40 | 42 | 48 |
| -Year | | 1976 | 1977 | 1977 | 1975 | 1987 | 1976 | 1988 | 1979 | 1979 | 1978 | 1975 | 1975 | FEB 1977 |
| Peak Gust | | | | | | | | | | | | | | |
| -Direction (!!) | 6 | W | W | W | W | SW | N | S | W | SW | W | W | W | W |
| -Speed (mph) | 6 | 47 | 60 | 55 | 55 | 48 | 48 | 55 | 41 | 46 | 45 | 49 | 40 | 60 |
| -Date | 6 | 1988 | 1987 | 1988 | 1984 | 1985 | 1985 | 1989 | 1988 | 1988 | 1984 | 1988 | 1987 | FEB 1987 |

**See Reference Notes to this table on the following page.**

PRECIPITATION (inches)　　　EL PASO, TEXAS

**TABLE 2**

| YEAR | JAN | FEB | MAR | APR | MAY | JUNE | JULY | AUG | SEP | OCT | NOV | DEC | ANNUAL |
|------|-----|-----|-----|-----|-----|------|------|-----|-----|-----|-----|-----|--------|
| 1961 | 0.41 | T | 0.29 | 0.01 | T | 0.27 | 2.18 | 1.40 | 0.69 | 0.18 | 1.63 | 0.63 | 7.69 |
| 1962 | 0.94 | 0.58 | 0.24 | 0.10 | 0.00 | T | 1.82 | T | 3.54 | 0.55 | 0.21 | 0.30 | 8.28 |
| 1963 | 0.13 | 0.53 | T | T | 0.71 | 0.05 | 0.52 | 1.03 | 0.64 | 0.55 | 0.76 | T | 4.92 |
| 1964 | T | T | 0.99 | 0.08 | 0.02 | T | 0.18 | 0.76 | 2.40 | 0.40 | 0.00 | 0.52 | 5.35 |
| 1965 | 0.19 | 0.59 | 0.03 | 0.01 | 0.11 | 0.66 | 0.17 | 0.49 | 2.12 | 0.18 | 0.12 | 0.74 | 5.41 |
| 1966 | 0.38 | 0.20 | T | 1.08 | 0.04 | 2.67 | 1.17 | 1.85 | 1.79 | 0.01 | 0.01 | 0.04 | 9.24 |
| 1967 | 0.00 | 0.04 | 0.17 | 0.03 | 0.05 | 1.41 | 0.84 | 0.54 | 1.54 | 0.09 | 0.23 | 0.78 | 5.72 |
| 1968 | 0.47 | 1.11 | 0.85 | 0.10 | T | 0.03 | 5.53 | 1.71 | 0.53 | 0.11 | 1.35 | 0.23 | 12.02 |
| 1969 | 0.05 | 0.08 | 0.17 | T | 0.28 | T | 1.14 | 0.28 | 0.43 | 0.59 | 0.63 | 0.69 | 4.34 |
| 1970 | 0.03 | 0.55 | 0.47 | T | 0.71 | 0.73 | 1.41 | 0.41 | 1.01 | 0.68 | T | 0.06 | 6.06 |
| 1971 | 0.17 | 0.04 | 0.00 | 0.42 | T | 0.01 | 2.34 | 1.59 | 0.96 | 1.07 | 0.14 | 0.50 | 7.24 |
| 1972 | 0.44 | T | T | 0.00 | 0.04 | 1.62 | 0.71 | 2.59 | 1.60 | 1.25 | 0.33 | 0.42 | 9.00 |
| 1973 | 1.23 | 1.69 | 0.60 | 0.00 | 0.29 | 0.71 | 2.12 | 0.73 | 0.01 | 0.07 | 0.08 | T | 7.53 |
| 1974 | 0.27 | T | 0.36 | 0.12 | 0.05 | 0.36 | 2.21 | 0.63 | 6.68 | 1.90 | 0.50 | 0.87 | 13.95 |
| 1975 | 0.70 | 0.59 | 0.19 | T | 0.03 | T | 1.11 | 0.45 | 2.18 | 0.25 | T | 0.71 | 6.21 |
| 1976 | 0.26 | 0.52 | T | 0.30 | 0.74 | 0.50 | 3.17 | 0.23 | 1.70 | 1.20 | 1.20 | 0.32 | 10.14 |
| 1977 | 0.57 | T | 0.17 | 0.09 | 0.06 | 0.04 | 1.09 | 1.36 | 0.16 | 1.65 | 0.05 | 0.26 | 5.50 |
| 1978 | 0.44 | 0.47 | 0.07 | 0.00 | 0.57 | 1.46 | 0.04 | 2.18 | 4.14 | 2.28 | 0.45 | 0.47 | 12.57 |
| 1979 | 0.77 | 0.68 | T | 0.28 | 0.24 | 0.03 | 0.98 | 2.16 | 0.41 | T | 0.04 | 0.25 | 5.84 |
| 1980 | 0.54 | 0.73 | 0.25 | 0.31 | 0.08 | T | 0.21 | 1.76 | 1.90 | 0.95 | 0.54 | 0.04 | 7.31 |
| 1981 | 1.10 | 0.36 | 0.39 | 0.65 | 0.72 | 0.64 | 2.08 | 5.26 | 0.52 | 0.53 | 0.30 | 0.08 | 12.63 |
| 1982 | 0.34 | 0.55 | T | 0.05 | 0.19 | 0.18 | 1.00 | 0.48 | 5.28 | T | 0.29 | 2.61 | 10.97 |
| 1983 | 0.35 | 0.60 | 0.45 | 1.42 | 0.05 | 0.23 | 0.43 | 0.97 | 1.51 | 1.48 | 0.34 | 0.16 | 7.99 |
| 1984 | 0.31 | 0.00 | 0.44 | 0.01 | 0.59 | 3.18 | 0.69 | 5.57 | 0.58 | 3.12 | 0.51 | 1.17 | 16.17 |
| 1985 | 0.95 | 0.19 | 0.59 | 0.07 | 0.01 | 0.10 | 1.32 | 1.46 | 1.47 | 1.82 | 0.13 | 0.05 | 8.16 |
| 1986 | 0.01 | 0.39 | 0.39 | T | 0.83 | 3.05 | 2.66 | 0.70 | 0.85 | 0.45 | 1.42 | 1.42 | 12.17 |
| 1987 | 0.29 | 0.30 | 0.49 | 0.32 | 0.24 | 2.24 | 0.64 | 2.22 | 0.89 | 0.15 | 0.29 | 2.87 | 10.94 |
| 1988 | 0.25 | 0.70 | 0.10 | 0.23 | 0.15 | 0.03 | 3.35 | 3.46 | 1.52 | 0.59 | 0.24 | 0.44 | 11.06 |
| 1989 | 0.11 | 0.72 | 0.62 | T | 0.65 | T | 1.23 | 3.06 | 0.48 | 0.23 | T | 0.16 | 7.26 |
| 1990 | 0.29 | 0.14 | 0.41 | 0.25 | 0.10 | T | 3.96 | 1.98 | 3.46 | 0.58 | 1.34 | 0.34 | 12.85 |
| Record Mean | 0.43 | 0.41 | 0.33 | 0.25 | 0.34 | 0.63 | 1.67 | 1.52 | 1.31 | 0.82 | 0.44 | 0.53 | 8.68 |

**TABLE 3**　　AVERAGE TEMPERATURE (deg. F)　　EL PASO, TEXAS

| YEAR | JAN | FEB | MAR | APR | MAY | JUNE | JULY | AUG | SEP | OCT | NOV | DEC | ANNUAL |
|------|-----|-----|-----|-----|-----|------|------|-----|-----|-----|-----|-----|--------|
| 1961 | 41.0 | 47.9 | 56.3 | 64.1 | 74.1 | 80.8 | 82.8 | 80.5 | 74.5 | 63.5 | 47.8 | 46.3 | 63.3 |
| 1962 | 40.5 | 53.5 | 50.9 | 67.3 | 74.1 | 80.0 | 81.3 | 84.0 | 73.9 | 64.9 | 53.7 | 45.2 | 64.1 |
| 1963 | 40.5 | 49.2 | 56.4 | 66.5 | 74.9 | 81.1 | 84.9 | 80.3 | 76.2 | 66.4 | 53.5 | 42.7 | 64.4 |
| 1964 | 39.3 | 40.8 | 53.6 | 63.2 | 73.9 | 81.5 | 84.5 | 82.6 | 75.2 | 63.4 | 51.8 | 44.0 | 62.8 |
| 1965 | 48.0 | 46.7 | 52.1 | 65.3 | 71.8 | 78.2 | 84.2 | 81.1 | 74.0 | 63.0 | 56.8 | 45.7 | 63.9 |
| 1966 | 40.1 | 42.9 | 56.4 | 65.1 | 74.5 | 79.5 | 83.6 | 78.7 | 73.4 | 62.1 | 54.5 | 42.4 | 62.8 |
| 1967 | 41.6 | 48.0 | 59.6 | 65.1 | 70.9 | 79.1 | 83.0 | 78.6 | 73.3 | 63.7 | 53.1 | 41.5 | 63.1 |
| 1968 | 42.4 | 50.4 | 53.0 | 61.4 | 73.0 | 81.0 | 79.1 | 76.5 | 72.4 | 65.0 | 51.0 | 41.3 | 62.2 |
| 1969 | 48.6 | 48.4 | 49.4 | 65.8 | 72.1 | 81.5 | 84.9 | 85.7 | 71.1 | 67.7 | 52.5 | 48.0 | 65.2 |
| 1970 | 46.9 | 52.3 | 55.6 | 63.5 | 72.2 | 79.7 | 82.8 | 81.4 | 74.2 | 59.5 | 51.9 | 46.0 | 64.0 |
| 1971 | 44.6 | 48.4 | 58.1 | 62.6 | 72.1 | 81.1 | 82.3 | 77.0 | 73.5 | 62.5 | 52.1 | 44.7 | 63.2 |
| 1972 | 45.2 | 52.3 | 61.2 | 65.2 | 69.8 | 78.3 | 82.2 | 77.7 | 72.9 | 65.7 | 48.8 | 46.6 | 63.8 |
| 1973 | 42.9 | 47.0 | 52.4 | 57.7 | 68.7 | 76.6 | 79.7 | 79.2 | 75.9 | 63.3 | 53.8 | 45.7 | 61.9 |
| 1974 | 44.3 | 44.8 | 59.6 | 65.0 | 75.6 | 82.8 | 79.6 | 77.0 | 69.4 | 63.0 | 49.9 | 41.3 | 62.7 |
| 1975 | 43.1 | 48.9 | 55.1 | 59.7 | 69.8 | 80.9 | 79.8 | 80.9 | 72.2 | 64.0 | 51.5 | 44.2 | 62.5 |
| 1976 | 42.3 | 52.6 | 55.9 | 64.1 | 69.5 | 79.4 | 78.2 | 78.7 | 70.5 | 58.5 | 44.8 | 41.9 | 61.4 |
| 1977 | 44.7 | 47.3 | 49.7 | 61.5 | 70.7 | 81.5 | 82.2 | 82.5 | 77.4 | 64.3 | 53.7 | 49.6 | 63.8 |
| #1978 | 45.4 | 48.8 | 58.6 | 66.1 | 73.6 | 83.4 | 84.5 | 80.0 | 72.3 | 63.6 | 55.8 | 44.6 | 64.7 |
| 1979 | 41.0 | 47.1 | 53.1 | 63.6 | 70.1 | 78.4 | 85.1 | 78.8 | 74.2 | 66.2 | 47.9 | 43.1 | 62.4 |
| 1980 | 46.8 | 50.6 | 54.1 | 60.6 | 70.5 | 86.3 | 87.2 | 82.4 | 75.6 | 60.3 | 49.2 | 48.5 | 64.3 |
| 1981 | 45.2 | 50.3 | 57.2 | 64.8 | 73.6 | 82.6 | 83.6 | 79.5 | 75.9 | 64.6 | 54.3 | 48.7 | 65.1 |
| 1982 | 42.3 | 48.7 | 57.7 | 64.4 | 69.6 | 80.9 | 84.2 | 83.5 | 77.1 | 64.6 | 53.2 | 43.3 | 64.1 |
| 1983 | 41.6 | 49.5 | 54.6 | 56.3 | 68.9 | 77.3 | 82.9 | 81.8 | 78.7 | 66.6 | 54.3 | 45.5 | 63.2 |
| 1984 | 44.4 | 47.0 | 55.7 | 62.0 | 75.0 | 79.5 | 81.1 | 80.4 | 72.9 | 61.4 | 51.6 | 45.7 | 63.1 |
| 1985 | 40.0 | 45.6 | 55.2 | 64.2 | 72.1 | 79.0 | 79.4 | 80.6 | 72.8 | 61.4 | 52.9 | 43.1 | 62.2 |
| 1986 | 44.7 | 52.1 | 55.7 | 67.3 | 71.5 | 77.7 | 80.0 | 80.4 | 74.1 | 62.4 | 49.4 | 42.6 | 63.2 |
| 1987 | 41.3 | 46.2 | 51.2 | 59.7 | 68.6 | 78.1 | 81.6 | 79.1 | 72.1 | 67.0 | 51.4 | 40.5 | 61.4 |
| 1988 | 42.6 | 48.4 | 53.4 | 61.1 | 70.3 | 79.0 | 80.3 | 77.6 | 72.4 | 66.7 | 54.0 | 42.6 | 62.4 |
| 1989 | 43.6 | 51.4 | 58.7 | 67.4 | 74.2 | 81.3 | 81.8 | 79.1 | 73.4 | 63.2 | 53.3 | 41.9 | 64.1 |
| 1990 | 44.1 | 49.1 | 56.1 | 66.4 | 73.1 | 87.1 | 80.2 | 76.8 | 73.9 | 63.4 | 52.9 | 44.8 | 64.0 |
| Record Mean | 44.5 | 49.2 | 55.6 | 63.6 | 72.1 | 80.7 | 82.0 | 80.2 | 74.7 | 64.5 | 52.4 | 45.0 | 63.7 |
| Max | 57.2 | 62.5 | 69.3 | 77.7 | 86.1 | 94.6 | 94.1 | 92.0 | 86.9 | 77.9 | 65.8 | 57.5 | 76.8 |
| Min | 31.8 | 35.9 | 41.8 | 49.6 | 58.1 | 66.8 | 69.8 | 68.4 | 62.5 | 51.1 | 39.0 | 32.6 | 50.6 |

## REFERENCE NOTES FOR TABLES 1, 2, 3 and 6　　(EL PASO, TX)

**GENERAL**

T - TRACE AMOUNT
BLANK ENTRIES DENOTE MISSING/UNREPORTED DATA.
# INDICATES A STATION OR INSTRUMENT RELOCATION.

**SPECIFIC**

**TABLE 1**

(a) - LENGTH OF RECORD IN YEARS. ALTHOUGH
INDIVIDUAL MONTHS MAY BE MISSING.

* LESS THAN ·05

NORMALS — BASED ON THE 1951-1980 RECORD PERIOD.
EXTREMES — DATES ARE THE MOST RECENT OCCURRENCE.
WIND DIR. — NUMERALS SHOW TENS OF DEGREES
CLOCKWISE FROM TRUE NORTH.
"00" INDICATES CALM.
RESULTANT WIND DIRECTIONS ARE GIVEN TO WHOLE DEGREES.

**TABLE 3**
MAX AND MIN ARE LONG-TERM MEAN DAILY MAXIMUM
AND MEAN DAILY MINIMUM TEMPERATURES.

**EXCEPTIONS**

**TABLES 2, 3, and 6**

RECORD MEANS ARE THROUGH THE CURRENT YEAR,
BEGINNING IN　　1887 FOR TEMPERATURE
1879 FOR PRECIPITATION
1940 FOR SNOWFALL

HEATING DEGREE DAYS Base 65 deg. F     EL PASO, TEXAS

**TABLE 4**

| SEASON | JULY | AUG | SEP | OCT | NOV | DEC | JAN | FEB | MAR | APR | MAY | JUNE | TOTAL |
|---|---|---|---|---|---|---|---|---|---|---|---|---|---|
| 1961-62 | 0 | 0 | 0 | 82 | 513 | 575 | 754 | 318 | 433 | 36 | 3 | 0 | 2714 |
| 1962-63 | 0 | 0 | 0 | 65 | 333 | 608 | 753 | 438 | 279 | 41 | 0 | 0 | 2517 |
| 1963-64 | 0 | 0 | 0 | 17 | 341 | 683 | 789 | 695 | 354 | 99 | 3 | 0 | 2981 |
| 1964-65 | 0 | 0 | 0 | 76 | 391 | 643 | 521 | 504 | 397 | 54 | 7 | 2 | 2595 |
| 1965-66 | 0 | 0 | 4 | 107 | 240 | 592 | 769 | 612 | 264 | 59 | 4 | 0 | 2651 |
| 1966-67 | 0 | 0 | 2 | 126 | 307 | 695 | 718 | 469 | 173 | 56 | 25 | 0 | 2571 |
| 1967-68 | 0 | 0 | 2 | 106 | 352 | 720 | 691 | 415 | 377 | 128 | 0 | 0 | 2791 |
| 1968-69 | 0 | 0 | 0 | 61 | 414 | 728 | 503 | 464 | 477 | 43 | 24 | 0 | 2714 |
| 1969-70 | 0 | 0 | 0 | 62 | 371 | 504 | 556 | 348 | 286 | 94 | 33 | 0 | 2254 |
| 1970-71 | 0 | 0 | 39 | 180 | 388 | 519 | 625 | 457 | 254 | 110 | 6 | 0 | 2578 |
| 1971-72 | 0 | 0 | 31 | 112 | 381 | 624 | 607 | 364 | 126 | 56 | 3 | 0 | 2304 |
| 1972-73 | 0 | 0 | 3 | 87 | 480 | 563 | 679 | 499 | 384 | 218 | 31 | 0 | 2944 |
| 1973-74 | 0 | 0 | 7 | 90 | 336 | 592 | 636 | 558 | 178 | 79 | 5 | 0 | 2481 |
| 1974-75 | 0 | 0 | 41 | 107 | 445 | 728 | 672 | 445 | 309 | 188 | 13 | 0 | 2948 |
| 1975-76 | 0 | 0 | 20 | 66 | 399 | 640 | 696 | 351 | 278 | 91 | 26 | 0 | 2567 |
| 1976-77 | 0 | 0 | 7 | 214 | 601 | 709 | 623 | 492 | 469 | 138 | 3 | 0 | 3256 |
| 1977-78 | 0 | 0 | 0 | 56 | 328 | 472 | 603 | 449 | 200 | 57 | 22 | 0 | 2187 |
| #1978-79 | 0 | 0 | 16 | 106 | 272 | 625 | 735 | 494 | 362 | 118 | 26 | 1 | 2755 |
| 1979-80 | 0 | 0 | 24 | 56 | 505 | 670 | 555 | 410 | 331 | 157 | 19 | 0 | 2727 |
| 1980-81 | 0 | 0 | 2 | 203 | 467 | 503 | 607 | 405 | 233 | 82 | 2 | 0 | 2504 |
| 1981-82 | 0 | 0 | 0 | 93 | 313 | 499 | 697 | 449 | 237 | 82 | 17 | 0 | 2387 |
| 1982-83 | 0 | 0 | 0 | 88 | 344 | 668 | 720 | 430 | 316 | 284 | 23 | 0 | 2873 |
| 1983-84 | 0 | 0 | 0 | 52 | 317 | 599 | 633 | 514 | 285 | 126 | 8 | 0 | 2534 |
| 1984-85 | 0 | 0 | 18 | 144 | 404 | 592 | 768 | 537 | 302 | 71 | 5 | 0 | 2841 |
| 1985-86 | 0 | 0 | 10 | 125 | 358 | 670 | 621 | 356 | 283 | 47 | 22 | 0 | 2492 |
| 1986-87 | 0 | 0 | 1 | 116 | 460 | 687 | 725 | 521 | 420 | 173 | 5 | 0 | 3108 |
| 1987-88 | 0 | 0 | 0 | 13 | 405 | 750 | 686 | 474 | 360 | 121 | 16 | 0 | 2825 |
| 1988-89 | 0 | 2 | 2 | 17 | 337 | 684 | 661 | 377 | 208 | 52 | 9 | 0 | 2349 |
| 1989-90 | 0 | 2 | 2 | 108 | 344 | 708 | 640 | 439 | 271 | 45 | 20 | 0 | 2577 |
| 1990-91 | 0 | 2 | 8 | 88 | 354 | 617 | | | | | | | |

**TABLE 5**    COOLING DEGREE DAYS Base 65 deg. F     EL PASO, TEXAS

| YEAR | JAN | FEB | MAR | APR | MAY | JUNE | JULY | AUG | SEP | OCT | NOV | DEC | TOTAL |
|---|---|---|---|---|---|---|---|---|---|---|---|---|---|
| 1969 | 0 | 0 | 1 | 71 | 250 | 501 | 627 | 647 | 372 | 155 | 2 | 0 | 2626 |
| 1970 | 0 | 0 | 2 | 57 | 263 | 448 | 559 | 514 | 321 | 19 | 0 | 0 | 2183 |
| 1971 | 0 | 0 | 45 | 45 | 235 | 492 | 543 | 375 | 293 | 43 | 0 | 0 | 2071 |
| 1972 | 0 | 4 | 15 | 70 | 159 | 404 | 543 | 401 | 247 | 120 | 0 | 0 | 1963 |
| 1973 | 0 | 0 | 0 | 7 | 152 | 355 | 459 | 448 | 340 | 44 | 7 | 0 | 1812 |
| 1974 | 0 | 0 | 19 | 84 | 338 | 540 | 459 | 378 | 181 | 54 | 0 | 0 | 2053 |
| 1975 | 0 | 0 | 9 | 35 | 170 | 482 | 469 | 502 | 241 | 41 | 1 | 0 | 1950 |
| 1976 | 0 | 0 | 4 | 71 | 170 | 441 | 418 | 434 | 179 | 18 | 0 | 0 | 1735 |
| 1977 | 0 | 0 | 0 | 39 | 186 | 500 | 540 | 552 | 380 | 43 | 0 | 0 | 2240 |
| #1978 | 0 | 0 | 0 | 8 | 98 | 295 | 559 | 612 | 474 | 238 | 70 | 2 | 2356 |
| 1979 | 0 | 0 | 0 | 84 | 190 | 414 | 630 | 432 | 308 | 99 | 0 | 0 | 2157 |
| 1980 | 0 | 0 | 0 | 0 | 34 | 198 | 646 | 693 | 546 | 329 | 63 | 0 | 2509 |
| 1981 | 0 | 2 | 2 | 84 | 275 | 534 | 586 | 455 | 333 | 89 | 0 | 2 | 2362 |
| 1982 | 0 | 0 | 14 | 70 | 167 | 484 | 602 | 583 | 371 | 82 | 0 | 0 | 2373 |
| 1983 | 0 | 0 | 0 | 32 | 151 | 374 | 564 | 527 | 417 | 108 | 6 | 0 | 2179 |
| 1984 | 0 | 0 | 2 | 44 | 324 | 441 | 507 | 482 | 260 | 38 | 8 | 0 | 2106 |
| 1985 | 0 | 0 | 9 | 55 | 233 | 428 | 457 | 488 | 252 | 18 | 0 | 0 | 1940 |
| 1986 | 0 | 3 | 0 | 122 | 228 | 391 | 474 | 485 | 281 | 41 | 0 | 0 | 2025 |
| 1987 | 0 | 0 | 0 | 22 | 121 | 399 | 521 | 446 | 222 | 83 | 2 | 0 | 1816 |
| 1988 | 0 | 0 | 9 | 15 | 186 | 429 | 478 | 399 | 226 | 76 | 16 | 0 | 1834 |
| 1989 | 0 | 2 | 20 | 130 | 300 | 494 | 530 | 442 | 261 | 60 | 0 | 0 | 2239 |
| 1990 | 0 | 1 | 0 | 96 | 278 | 667 | 480 | 374 | 282 | 43 | 0 | 0 | 2221 |

**TABLE 6**    SNOWFALL (inches)     EL PASO, TEXAS

| SEASON | JULY | AUG | SEP | OCT | NOV | DEC | JAN | FEB | MAR | APR | MAY | JUNE | TOTAL |
|---|---|---|---|---|---|---|---|---|---|---|---|---|---|
| 1961-62 | 0.0 | 0.0 | 0.0 | 0.0 | 7.8 | T | 1.6 | 0.0 | T | 0.0 | 0.0 | 0.0 | 9.4 |
| 1962-63 | 0.0 | 0.0 | 0.0 | 0.0 | 0.0 | 0.0 | 0.8 | 5.3 | 0.0 | 0.0 | 0.0 | 0.0 | 6.1 |
| 1963-64 | 0.0 | 0.0 | 0.0 | 0.0 | 0.0 | T | 0.0 | T | T | 0.0 | 0.0 | 0.0 | T |
| 1964-65 | 0.0 | 0.0 | 0.0 | 0.0 | 0.0 | T | 0.0 | 0.3 | T | 0.0 | 0.0 | 0.0 | 0.3 |
| 1965-66 | 0.0 | 0.0 | 0.0 | 0.0 | 0.0 | T | 0.4 | T | T | 0.0 | 0.0 | 0.0 | 0.4 |
| 1966-67 | 0.0 | 0.0 | 0.0 | 0.0 | 0.0 | T | 0.0 | T | 0.0 | T | 0.0 | 0.0 | T |
| 1967-68 | 0.0 | 0.0 | 0.0 | 0.0 | 0.0 | 5.6 | 2.1 | 2.3 | 0.8 | 0.0 | 0.0 | 0.0 | 10.8 |
| 1968-69 | 0.0 | 0.0 | 0.0 | 0.0 | 7.0 | T | 0.0 | 0.0 | T | 0.0 | 0.0 | 0.0 | 7.0 |
| 1969-70 | 0.0 | 0.0 | 0.0 | 0.0 | 6.0 | 1.9 | 0.3 | 1.7 | T | 0.0 | 0.0 | 0.0 | 9.9 |
| 1970-71 | 0.0 | 0.0 | 0.0 | 0.0 | 0.0 | 0.0 | 3.8 | T | 0.0 | T | 0.0 | 0.0 | 3.8 |
| 1971-72 | 0.0 | 0.0 | 0.0 | 0.0 | 0.0 | 1.0 | 2.5 | 0.0 | 0.0 | 0.0 | 0.0 | 0.0 | 3.5 |
| 1972-73 | 0.0 | 0.0 | 0.0 | 0.0 | 0.0 | 0.0 | 5.3 | 4.6 | T | 0.0 | 0.0 | 0.0 | 9.9 |
| 1973-74 | 0.0 | 0.0 | 0.0 | 0.0 | 0.0 | 0.0 | T | T | 0.0 | 0.0 | 0.0 | 0.0 | T |
| 1974-75 | 0.0 | 0.0 | 0.0 | 0.0 | 0.0 | 5.3 | 2.2 | 0.2 | 2.0 | T | 0.0 | 0.0 | 9.7 |
| 1975-76 | 0.0 | 0.0 | 0.0 | 0.0 | 0.0 | T | 1.0 | 0.0 | 0.0 | T | 0.0 | 0.0 | 1.0 |
| 1976-77 | 0.0 | 0.0 | 0.0 | T | 12.7 | 2.0 | T | T | 0.0 | 0.0 | 0.0 | 0.0 | 14.7 |
| 1977-78 | 0.0 | 0.0 | 0.0 | 0.0 | 0.0 | 0.0 | T | 0.0 | 0.0 | 0.0 | 0.0 | 0.0 | T |
| #1978-79 | 0.0 | 0.0 | 0.0 | 0.0 | T | T | T | 1.2 | 0.0 | 0.0 | 0.0 | 0.0 | 1.2 |
| 1979-80 | 0.0 | 0.0 | 0.0 | 0.0 | 0.0 | 0.0 | T | 3.6 | 0.0 | 2.0 | 0.0 | 0.0 | 5.6 |
| 1980-81 | 0.0 | 0.0 | 0.0 | 1.0 | 4.0 | 0.0 | 4.8 | 0.0 | 0.0 | 0.0 | 0.0 | 0.0 | 9.8 |
| 1981-82 | 0.0 | 0.0 | 0.0 | 0.0 | 0.0 | 0.0 | 0.0 | T | 0.0 | 0.0 | 0.0 | 0.0 | T |
| 1982-83 | 0.0 | 0.0 | 0.0 | 0.0 | 0.0 | 0.3 | 18.2 | T | 0.0 | 16.5 | 0.0 | 0.0 | 35.0 |
| 1983-84 | 0.0 | 0.0 | 0.0 | 0.0 | 0.0 | T | T | T | 6.1 | 0.0 | 0.0 | 0.0 | 6.1 |
| 1984-85 | 0.0 | 0.0 | 0.0 | 0.0 | 0.0 | 2.9 | 5.4 | 1.1 | 0.0 | 0.0 | 0.0 | 0.0 | 9.4 |
| 1985-86 | 0.0 | 0.0 | 0.0 | 0.0 | 0.0 | 0.9 | T | 0.9 | T | 0.0 | 0.0 | 0.0 | 1.8 |
| 1986-87 | 0.0 | 0.0 | 0.0 | 0.0 | 0.0 | 0.0 | 3.4 | 2.8 | 0.6 | 0.6 | 0.0 | 0.0 | 7.4 |
| 1987-88 | 0.0 | 0.0 | 0.0 | 0.0 | 0.0 | 25.9 | T | 6.6 | 0.0 | 0.0 | 0.0 | 0.0 | 32.5 |
| 1988-89 | 0.0 | 0.0 | 0.0 | T | 0.3 | 0.0 | 0.0 | 0.0 | T | 0.0 | 0.0 | | 0.3 |
| 1989-90 | 0.0 | 0.0 | 0.0 | 0.0 | 0.0 | 0.0 | T | T | 0.0 | T | T | 0.0 | T |
| 1990-91 | T | 0.0 | 0.0 | 0.0 | 4.3 | T | T | | | | | 0.0 | T |
| Record Mean | T | 0.0 | 0.0 | T | 1.0 | 1.7 | 1.3 | 0.9 | 0.4 | 0.4 | T | 0.0 | 5.7 |

**See Reference Notes, relative to all above tables, on preceding page.**

Houston, the largest city in Texas, is located in the flat Coastal Plains, about 50 miles from the Gulf of Mexico and about 25 miles from Galveston Bay. The climate is predominantly marine. The terrain includes numerous small streams and bayous which, together with the nearness to Galveston Bay, favor the development of both ground and advective fogs. Prevailing winds are from the southeast and south, except in January, when frequent passages of high pressure areas bring invasions of polar air and prevailing northerly winds.

Temperatures are moderated by the influence of winds from the Gulf, which result in mild winters. Another effect of the nearness of the Gulf is abundant rainfall, except for rare extended dry periods. Polar air penetrates the area frequently enough to provide variability in the weather.

Records of sky cover for daylight hours indicate about one-fourth of the days per year as clear, with a high number of clear days in October and November. Cloudy days are relatively frequent from December to May and partly cloudy days are the more frequent for June through September. Sunshine averages nearly 60 percent of the possible amount for the year ranging from 42 percent in January to 67 percent in June.

Heavy fog occurs on an average of 16 days a year and light fog occurs about 62 days a year in the city. The frequency of heavy fog is considerably higher at William P. Hobby Airport and at Intercontinental Airport.

Destructive windstorms are fairly infrequent, but both thundersqualls and tropical storms occasionally pass through the area.

## TABLE 1 — NORMALS, MEANS AND EXTREMES

HOUSTON, TEXAS

LATITUDE: 29°58'N  LONGITUDE: 95°21'W  ELEVATION: FT. GRND 96 BARO 122  TIME ZONE: CENTRAL  WBAN: 12960

| | (a) | JAN | FEB | MAR | APR | MAY | JUNE | JULY | AUG | SEP | OCT | NOV | DEC | YEAR |
|---|---|---|---|---|---|---|---|---|---|---|---|---|---|---|
| **TEMPERATURE °F:** | | | | | | | | | | | | | | |
| Normals | | | | | | | | | | | | | | |
| -Daily Maximum | | 61.9 | 65.7 | 72.1 | 79.0 | 85.1 | 90.9 | 93.6 | 93.1 | 88.7 | 81.9 | 71.6 | 65.2 | 79.1 |
| -Daily Minimum | | 40.8 | 43.2 | 49.8 | 58.3 | 64.7 | 70.2 | 72.5 | 72.1 | 68.1 | 57.5 | 48.6 | 42.7 | 57.4 |
| -Monthly | | 51.4 | 54.5 | 61.0 | 68.7 | 74.9 | 80.6 | 83.1 | 82.6 | 78.4 | 69.7 | 60.1 | 54.0 | 68.3 |
| Extremes | | | | | | | | | | | | | | |
| -Record Highest | 20 | 84 | 91 | 91 | 95 | 95 | 103 | 104 | 107 | 102 | 94 | 89 | 83 | 107 |
| -Year | | 1975 | 1986 | 1989 | 1987 | 1978 | 1980 | 1980 | 1980 | 1985 | 1981 | 1989 | 1978 | AUG 1980 |
| -Record Lowest | 20 | 12 | 20 | 22 | 31 | 44 | 52 | 62 | 62 | 48 | 32 | 19 | 7 | 7 |
| -Year | | 1982 | 1985 | 1980 | 1987 | 1978 | 1970 | 1972 | 1989 | 1975 | 1989 | 1976 | 1989 | DEC 1989 |
| **NORMAL DEGREE DAYS:** | | | | | | | | | | | | | | |
| Heating (base 65°F) | | 442 | 314 | 175 | 32 | 0 | 0 | 0 | 0 | 0 | 36 | 201 | 349 | 1549 |
| Cooling (base 65°F) | | 20 | 20 | 51 | 143 | 307 | 468 | 561 | 546 | 402 | 181 | 54 | 8 | 2761 |
| **% OF POSSIBLE SUNSHINE** | 20 | 43 | 48 | 50 | 53 | 57 | 64 | 66 | 64 | 62 | 60 | 49 | 52 | 56 |
| **MEAN SKY COVER (tenths)** | | | | | | | | | | | | | | |
| Sunrise - Sunset | 20 | 6.9 | 6.4 | 6.6 | 6.5 | 6.2 | 5.6 | 5.7 | 5.7 | 5.5 | 5.3 | 5.8 | 6.6 | 6.1 |
| **MEAN NUMBER OF DAYS:** | | | | | | | | | | | | | | |
| Sunrise to Sunset | | | | | | | | | | | | | | |
| -Clear | 20 | 7.7 | 7.6 | 7.1 | 7.6 | 6.6 | 8.1 | 7.1 | 6.1 | 8.9 | 10.9 | 9.3 | 8.1 | 94.9 |
| -Partly Cloudy | 20 | 5.3 | 5.7 | 6.7 | 7.1 | 11.1 | 12.8 | 15.6 | 16.8 | 10.9 | 9.1 | 7.2 | 5.8 | 113.8 |
| -Cloudy | 20 | 18.0 | 15.1 | 17.3 | 15.4 | 13.3 | 9.1 | 8.4 | 8.2 | 10.1 | 10.9 | 13.5 | 17.2 | 156.6 |
| Precipitation | | | | | | | | | | | | | | |
| .01 inches or more | 20 | 10.0 | 8.3 | 9.3 | 6.8 | 8.2 | 8.9 | 9.3 | 9.3 | 9.4 | 7.6 | 8.6 | 8.9 | 104.6 |
| Snow, Ice pellets | | | | | | | | | | | | | | |
| 1.0 inches or more | 20 | 0.1 | 0.2 | 0.0 | 0.0 | 0.0 | 0.0 | 0.0 | 0.0 | 0.0 | 0.0 | 0.0 | 0.1 | 0.3 |
| Thunderstorms | 20 | 1.6 | 1.6 | 3.8 | 3.3 | 6.8 | 7.5 | 10.6 | 10.1 | 7.2 | 3.6 | 2.8 | 1.8 | 60.7 |
| Heavy Fog Visibility | | | | | | | | | | | | | | |
| 1/4 mile or less | 20 | 5.6 | 3.8 | 3.2 | 3.0 | 1.9 | 0.6 | 0.3 | 0.4 | 1.4 | 3.0 | 3.8 | 4.4 | 31.6 |
| Temperature °F | | | | | | | | | | | | | | |
| -Maximum | | | | | | | | | | | | | | |
| 90° and above | 20 | 0.0 | 0.1 | 0.1 | 0.9 | 4.8 | 18.9 | 26.5 | 25.7 | 14.4 | 2.6 | 0.0 | 0.0 | 93.9 |
| 32° and below | 20 | 0.3 | 0.3 | 0.0 | 0.0 | 0.0 | 0.0 | 0.0 | 0.0 | 0.0 | 0.0 | 0.0 | 0.3 | 0.8 |
| -Minimum | | | | | | | | | | | | | | |
| 32° and below | 20 | 8.1 | 5.1 | 1.5 | 0.2 | 0.0 | 0.0 | 0.0 | 0.0 | 0.0 | 0.1 | 1.5 | 5.4 | 21.8 |
| 0° and below | 20 | 0.0 | 0.0 | 0.0 | 0.0 | 0.0 | 0.0 | 0.0 | 0.0 | 0.0 | 0.0 | 0.0 | 0.0 | 0.0 |
| **AVG. STATION PRESS.(mb)** | 17 | 1017.3 | 1015.9 | 1012.0 | 1011.3 | 1009.7 | 1010.6 | 1012.3 | 1011.7 | 1011.6 | 1014.2 | 1014.8 | 1016.7 | 1013.2 |
| **RELATIVE HUMIDITY (%)** | | | | | | | | | | | | | | |
| Hour 00 | 20 | 82 | 83 | 83 | 85 | 87 | 87 | 86 | 88 | 89 | 88 | 85 | 83 | 86 |
| Hour 06 | 20 | 85 | 86 | 87 | 89 | 92 | 92 | 93 | 93 | 93 | 91 | 89 | 86 | 90 |
| Hour 12 (Local Time) | 20 | 64 | 61 | 59 | 57 | 59 | 59 | 58 | 58 | 60 | 56 | 59 | 61 | 59 |
| Hour 18 | 20 | 67 | 61 | 60 | 60 | 63 | 62 | 62 | 63 | 67 | 69 | 72 | 70 | 65 |
| **PRECIPITATION (inches):** | | | | | | | | | | | | | | |
| Water Equivalent | | | | | | | | | | | | | | |
| -Normal | | 3.21 | 3.25 | 2.68 | 4.24 | 4.69 | 4.06 | 3.33 | 3.66 | 4.93 | 3.67 | 3.38 | 3.66 | 44.76 |
| -Maximum Monthly | 20 | 7.68 | 5.38 | 8.52 | 10.92 | 14.39 | 16.28 | 8.10 | 9.42 | 11.35 | 16.05 | 8.91 | 7.33 | 16.28 |
| -Year | | 1974 | 1985 | 1972 | 1976 | 1970 | 1989 | 1979 | 1983 | 1976 | 1984 | 1982 | 1971 | JUN 1989 |
| -Minimum Monthly | 20 | 0.36 | 0.38 | 0.88 | 0.43 | 0.79 | 0.26 | 0.61 | 1.14 | 0.80 | 0.05 | 0.41 | 0.64 | 0.05 |
| -Year | | 1971 | 1976 | 1987 | 1983 | 1977 | 1970 | 1986 | 1985 | 1975 | 1978 | 1988 | 1973 | OCT 1978 |
| -Maximum in 24 hrs | 20 | 2.56 | 2.22 | 7.47 | 8.16 | 10.36 | 10.35 | 3.99 | 6.83 | 7.98 | 9.31 | 4.19 | 3.43 | 10.36 |
| -Year | | 1984 | 1985 | 1972 | 1976 | 1989 | 1989 | 1973 | 1981 | 1976 | 1984 | 1986 | 1971 | MAY 1989 |
| Snow, Ice pellets | | | | | | | | | | | | | | |
| -Maximum Monthly | 20 | 2.0 | 2.8 | 0.0 | 0.0 | 0.0 | 0.0 | 0.0 | 0.0 | 0.0 | 0.0 | T | 1.7 | 2.8 |
| -Year | | 1973 | 1973 | | | | | | | | | 1979 | 1989 | FEB 1973 |
| -Maximum in 24 hrs | 20 | 2.0 | 1.4 | 0.0 | 0.0 | 0.0 | 0.0 | 0.0 | 0.0 | 0.0 | 0.0 | T | 1.7 | 2.0 |
| -Year | | 1973 | 1980 | | | | | | | | | 1979 | 1989 | JAN 1973 |
| **WIND:** | | | | | | | | | | | | | | |
| Mean Speed (mph) | 20 | 8.2 | 8.8 | 9.3 | 9.2 | 8.3 | 7.7 | 6.9 | 6.2 | 6.9 | 7.0 | 7.9 | 8.0 | 7.9 |
| Prevailing Direction through 1963 | | NNW | SSE | SSE | SSE | SSE | SSE | S | SSE | SSE | ESE | SSE | SSE | SSE |
| Fastest Obs. 1 Min. | | | | | | | | | | | | | | |
| -Direction (!!!) | 20 | 31 | 26 | 22 | 14 | 23 | 30 | 10 | 08 | 05 | 27 | 33 | 31 | 08 |
| -Speed (MPH) | 20 | 32 | 46 | 35 | 45 | 46 | 45 | 46 | 51 | 37 | 41 | 37 | 35 | 51 |
| -Year | | 1978 | 1984 | 1989 | 1978 | 1983 | 1973 | 1969 | 1983 | 1982 | 1988 | 1972 | 1973 | AUG 1983 |
| Peak Gust | | | | | | | | | | | | | | |
| -Direction (!!!) | 6 | N | W | SW | SE | NW | E | S | E | E | W | NW | SW | E |
| -Speed (mph) | 6 | 38 | 61 | 46 | 46 | 48 | 53 | 52 | 78 | 41 | 58 | 45 | 39 | 78 |
| -Date | | 1985 | 1984 | 1989 | 1984 | 1986 | 1989 | 1986 | 1983 | 1988 | 1988 | 1988 | 1984 | AUG 1983 |

**See Reference Notes to this table on the following page.**

PRECIPITATION (inches)  HOUSTON, TEXAS

**TABLE 2**

| YEAR | JAN | FEB | MAR | APR | MAY | JUNE | JULY | AUG | SEP | OCT | NOV | DEC | ANNUAL |
|---|---|---|---|---|---|---|---|---|---|---|---|---|---|
| 1961 | 4.44 | 3.88 | 1.84 | 2.42 | 3.59 | 11.11 | 10.07 | 4.17 | 7.89 | 0.05 | 10.20 | 3.31 | 62.97 |
| 1962 | 1.73 | 0.71 | 0.94 | 4.81 | 1.15 | 7.40 | 0.07 | 2.77 | 3.97 | 3.12 | 5.68 | 4.78 | 37.13 |
| 1963 | 3.09 | 2.60 | 0.55 | 0.92 | 0.62 | 7.79 | 2.08 | 1.85 | 1.94 | 0.30 | 5.72 | 4.83 | 32.29 |
| 1964 | 2.89 | 4.97 | 2.24 | 1.63 | 2.25 | 1.89 | 1.68 | 2.61 | 6.76 | 2.35 | 4.28 | 5.57 | 39.12 |
| 1965 | 1.87 | 3.27 | 0.81 | 0.95 | 6.53 | 3.0 | 1.57 | 2.29 | 3.56 | 3.09 | 4.82 | 6.15 | 37.97 |
| 1966 | 4.46 | 7.75 | 2.20 | 7.98 | 11.21 | 4.42 | 1.45 | 7.11 | 4.01 | 5.45 | 1.56 | 1.53 | 59.13 |
| 1967 | 2.41 | 2.17 | 1.83 | 4.42 | 2.54 | 0.17 | 7.77 | 1.60 | 4.84 | 3.18 | 0.50 | 5.02 | 36.45 |
| 1968 | 8.02 | 1.99 | 2.92 | 3.02 | 13.24 | 11.18 | 6.49 | 2.90 | 3.87 | 3.91 | 2.71 | 1.19 | 61.44 |
| #1969 | 2.74 | 5.31 | 3.18 | 3.34 | 4.73 | 1.51 | 3.89 | 2.67 | 6.08 | 3.30 | 2.13 | 4.38 | 43.26 |
| 1970 | 1.93 | 2.52 | 5.08 | 2.21 | 14.39 | 0.26 | 2.28 | 2.03 | 6.22 | 9.09 | 1.54 | 0.64 | 48.19 |
| 1971 | 0.36 | 2.11 | 1.21 | 2.14 | 3.41 | 2.42 | 1.42 | 6.95 | 5.17 | 3.49 | 1.82 | 7.33 | 37.83 |
| 1972 | 3.30 | 1.20 | 0.55 | 2.85 | 6.99 | 3.02 | 2.76 | 3.90 | 6.23 | 3.34 | 6.49 | 2.20 | 50.80 |
| 1973 | 5.00 | 3.40 | 3.68 | 7.15 | 4.22 | 13.46 | 6.77 | 3.73 | 9.38 | 9.31 | 1.59 | 2.47 | 70.16 |
| 1974 | 7.68 | 0.55 | 4.20 | 1.68 | 5.61 | 0.59 | 1.75 | 6.94 | 4.51 | 4.53 | 7.90 | 3.35 | 49.29 |
| 1975 | 1.97 | 2.63 | 3.19 | 4.80 | 7.57 | 7.50 | 5.48 | 5.72 | 0.80 | 5.62 | 2.08 | 3.61 | 50.97 |
| 1976 | 1.39 | 0.38 | 1.53 | 10.92 | 5.80 | 2.63 | 3.93 | 1.59 | 11.35 | 5.83 | 3.05 | 6.22 | 54.62 |
| 1977 | 2.67 | 1.70 | 1.95 | 4.34 | 0.79 | 3.55 | 2.69 | 4.45 | 3.92 | 0.82 | 5.17 | 2.89 | 34.94 |
| 1978 | 7.15 | 3.07 | 1.70 | 0.57 | 4.15 | 9.37 | 2.35 | 3.66 | 4.27 | 0.05 | 5.99 | 2.60 | 44.93 |
| 1979 | 6.30 | 5.23 | 2.88 | 7.79 | 3.78 | 1.88 | 8.10 | 4.57 | 9.83 | 2.80 | 1.78 | 4.03 | 58.97 |
| 1980 | 6.09 | 2.54 | 5.39 | 2.05 | 5.63 | 0.92 | 1.57 | 1.40 | 6.00 | 4.03 | 2.12 | 1.25 | 38.99 |
| 1981 | 2.32 | 2.21 | 1.74 | 2.69 | 8.75 | 9.65 | 4.43 | 7.01 | 2.91 | 6.96 | 5.26 | 2.05 | 55.98 |
| 1982 | 1.82 | 1.59 | 1.55 | 2.28 | 6.87 | 1.10 | 4.32 | 1.90 | 0.98 | 6.64 | 4.91 | 4.87 | 42.87 |
| 1983 | 2.00 | 3.97 | 3.85 | 0.43 | 7.29 | 5.37 | 5.23 | 9.42 | 7.23 | 1.56 | 3.17 | 3.69 | 53.21 |
| 1984 | 3.99 | 4.37 | 2.41 | 0.56 | 3.13 | 1.99 | 3.43 | 3.52 | 3.87 | 16.05 | 2.28 | 2.59 | 48.19 |
| 1985 | 2.10 | 5.38 | 4.52 | 4.31 | 1.57 | 5.29 | 4.93 | 1.14 | 4.67 | 6.54 | 4.84 | 3.85 | 49.14 |
| 1986 | 0.71 | 2.74 | 1.44 | 2.63 | 4.29 | 6.34 | 0.61 | 3.27 | 3.70 | 6.83 | 6.66 | 5.71 | 44.93 |
| 1987 | 2.42 | 4.26 | 0.88 | 0.47 | 5.39 | 9.31 | 4.79 | 1.48 | 3.46 | 0.17 | 3.41 | 4.56 | 40.60 |
| 1988 | 1.27 | 1.29 | 4.88 | 1.26 | 1.32 | 2.00 | 3.23 | 3.52 | 1.20 | 1.29 | 0.41 | 1.26 | 22.93 |
| 1989 | 4.80 | 0.90 | 3.96 | 1.48 | 13.56 | 16.28 | 1.92 | 2.74 | 2.69 | 1.76 | 1.84 | 0.80 | 52.73 |
| 1990 | 3.96 | 4.54 | 5.11 | 6.21 | 2.23 | 2.98 | 4.85 | 0.31 | 1.57 | 3.79 | 3.01 | 1.81 | 40.37 |
| Record Mean | 3.58 | 3.07 | 2.75 | 3.32 | 4.84 | 4.65 | 4.07 | 3.98 | 4.55 | 3.96 | 3.97 | 3.94 | 46.67 |

**TABLE 3**  AVERAGE TEMPERATURE (deg. F)  HOUSTON, TEXAS

| YEAR | JAN | FEB | MAR | APR | MAY | JUNE | JULY | AUG | SEP | OCT | NOV | DEC | ANNUAL |
|---|---|---|---|---|---|---|---|---|---|---|---|---|---|
| 1961 | 49.5 | 57.9 | 66.8 | 68.0 | 77.0 | 80.4 | 82.6 | 82.2 | 79.7 | 70.5 | 59.8 | 56.3 | 69.2 |
| 1962 | 49.3 | 63.9 | 58.9 | 68.1 | 75.7 | 79.8 | 84.1 | 85.9 | 81.3 | 74.6 | 60.1 | 54.8 | 69.7 |
| 1963 | 48.3 | 52.6 | 64.9 | 74.5 | 77.5 | 82.0 | 84.3 | 84.3 | 80.4 | 75.0 | 64.1 | 47.1 | 69.6 |
| 1964 | 51.6 | 49.4 | 60.4 | 70.2 | 75.8 | 80.4 | 83.7 | 84.4 | 79.3 | 67.8 | 65.0 | 55.9 | 68.7 |
| 1965 | 56.0 | 55.1 | 58.7 | 73.5 | 77.1 | 83.0 | 85.1 | 83.5 | 81.2 | 69.4 | 69.1 | 58.9 | 70.9 |
| 1966 | 48.4 | 52.8 | 61.5 | 70.6 | 75.9 | 80.0 | 84.3 | 82.4 | 79.6 | 69.7 | 64.7 | 54.2 | 68.7 |
| 1967 | 54.9 | 54.5 | 67.6 | 75.7 | 75.9 | 82.6 | 82.1 | 81.1 | 77.6 | 70.5 | 64.1 | 55.4 | 70.2 |
| 1968 | 52.7 | 50.4 | 59.0 | 71.1 | 76.3 | 80.5 | 82.5 | 84.0 | 78.6 | 73.5 | 59.7 | 55.7 | 68.7 |
| #1969 | 56.7 | 56.9 | 56.1 | 70.3 | 75.4 | 80.0 | 84.4 | 83.2 | 78.2 | 71.0 | 58.5 | 55.2 | 68.8 |
| 1970 | 46.7 | 53.9 | 56.9 | 69.3 | 72.1 | 78.4 | 81.4 | 83.1 | 78.3 | 66.7 | 56.9 | 60.5 | 67.1 |
| 1971 | 56.7 | 55.7 | 59.4 | 66.6 | 74.1 | 80.3 | 83.9 | 80.4 | 78.3 | 72.0 | 60.0 | 59.9 | 68.9 |
| 1972 | 56.5 | 55.2 | 64.3 | 71.2 | 73.7 | 80.8 | 80.3 | 80.3 | 79.6 | 69.8 | 54.7 | 52.0 | 68.2 |
| 1973 | 47.4 | 51.4 | 63.7 | 64.6 | 72.8 | 79.2 | 83.0 | 79.5 | 78.1 | 71.8 | 67.3 | 53.5 | 67.7 |
| 1974 | 55.0 | 56.2 | 66.8 | 67.2 | 76.9 | 79.9 | 82.8 | 81.6 | 74.6 | 70.6 | 60.2 | 54.6 | 68.9 |
| 1975 | 56.9 | 55.4 | 61.1 | 68.3 | 75.9 | 80.0 | 81.5 | 81.1 | 74.9 | 69.5 | 59.7 | 52.7 | 68.1 |
| 1976 | 50.6 | 60.1 | 62.2 | 67.7 | 70.5 | 78.4 | 80.5 | 81.4 | 76.2 | 60.6 | 51.8 | 49.2 | 65.8 |
| 1977 | 42.7 | 53.8 | 60.9 | 66.9 | 74.5 | 81.0 | 82.4 | 83.1 | 80.0 | 69.2 | 61.8 | 53.7 | 67.5 |
| 1978 | 40.8 | 45.1 | 57.3 | 67.6 | 76.0 | 80.4 | 83.7 | 83.1 | 79.3 | 68.9 | 64.7 | 52.9 | 66.7 |
| 1979 | 44.1 | 51.7 | 62.4 | 68.7 | 73.1 | 79.8 | 82.6 | 81.5 | 75.6 | 70.7 | 55.7 | 52.4 | 66.5 |
| 1980 | 55.0 | 53.7 | 60.9 | 66.2 | 77.3 | 85.1 | 87.5 | 86.6 | 83.2 | 67.8 | 58.0 | 55.2 | 69.7 |
| 1981 | 51.4 | 55.4 | 60.9 | 74.3 | 75.3 | 82.7 | 84.4 | 84.4 | 78.6 | 72.3 | 64.4 | 54.5 | 69.9 |
| 1982 | 52.9 | 52.1 | 64.9 | 67.8 | 75.3 | 83.0 | 85.4 | 84.1 | 79.3 | 69.5 | 60.9 | 55.4 | 69.2 |
| 1983 | 50.1 | 52.5 | 58.3 | 64.0 | 73.4 | 79.0 | 82.2 | 82.6 | 76.6 | 70.1 | 63.1 | 45.7 | 66.5 |
| 1984 | 47.0 | 54.0 | 61.9 | 67.8 | 74.9 | 78.6 | 81.8 | 82.9 | 77.4 | 74.2 | 60.0 | 63.4 | 68.7 |
| 1985 | 45.7 | 49.6 | 64.7 | 70.0 | 75.6 | 81.0 | 81.6 | 84.2 | 79.8 | 72.5 | 67.0 | 51.0 | 68.6 |
| 1986 | 54.4 | 59.9 | 63.3 | 71.7 | 75.8 | 82.0 | 85.9 | 82.6 | 81.8 | 68.9 | 62.0 | 51.7 | 70.0 |
| 1987 | 51.4 | 56.1 | 58.9 | 67.2 | 77.1 | 81.3 | 83.5 | 86.2 | 78.9 | 68.7 | 60.5 | 55.6 | 68.8 |
| 1988 | 54.1 | 54.1 | 61.3 | 67.6 | 73.6 | 80.5 | 84.4 | 85.3 | 80.8 | 72.0 | 65.7 | 55.4 | 69.1 |
| 1989 | 57.5 | 52.7 | 61.3 | 69.4 | 77.8 | 79.9 | 82.4 | 81.7 | 77.0 | 70.2 | 62.9 | 44.4 | 68.1 |
| 1990 | 57.0 | 59.1 | 62.9 | 69.4 | 78.1 | 84.8 | 82.1 | 85.1 | 80.1 | 68.7 | 63.4 | 53.6 | 70.4 |
| Record Mean | 50.8 | 54.2 | 61.6 | 68.3 | 74.9 | 80.7 | 83.1 | 82.9 | 78.5 | 69.8 | 60.9 | 53.8 | 68.3 |
| Max | 61.1 | 65.1 | 72.6 | 79.0 | 84.9 | 90.7 | 93.4 | 93.3 | 88.6 | 81.3 | 72.0 | 64.7 | 78.9 |
| Min | 40.5 | 43.2 | 50.6 | 57.5 | 64.9 | 70.7 | 72.7 | 72.5 | 68.4 | 58.3 | 49.7 | 42.8 | 57.7 |

## REFERENCE NOTES FOR TABLES 1, 2, 3 and 6  (HOUSTON, TX)

### GENERAL

T - TRACE AMOUNT
BLANK ENTRIES DENOTE MISSING/UNREPORTED DATA.
# INDICATES A STATION OR INSTRUMENT RELOCATION.

### SPECIFIC

#### TABLE 1

(a) - LENGTH OF RECORD IN YEARS. ALTHOUGH INDIVIDUAL MONTHS MAY BE MISSING.

* LESS THAN .05

NORMALS — BASED ON THE 1951-1980 RECORD PERIOD.
EXTREMES — DATES ARE THE MOST RECENT OCCURRENCE.
WIND DIR. — NUMERALS SHOW TENS OF DEGREES CLOCKWISE FROM TRUE NORTH.
 "00" INDICATES CALM.
RESULTANT WIND DIRECTIONS ARE GIVEN TO WHOLE DEGREES.

#### TABLE 3

MAX AND MIN ARE LONG-TERM MEAN DAILY MAXIMUM AND MEAN DAILY MINIMUM TEMPERATURES.

### EXCEPTIONS

#### TABLES 2, 3, and 6

RECORD MEANS ARE THROUGH THE CURRENT YEAR, BEGINNING IN    1969 FOR TEMPERATURE
 1933 FOR PRECIPITATION
 1935 FOR SNOWFALL

### HEATING DEGREE DAYS Base 65 deg. F — HOUSTON, TEXAS

**TABLE 4**

| SEASON | JULY | AUG | SEP | OCT | NOV | DEC | JAN | FEB | MAR | APR | MAY | JUNE | TOTAL |
|---|---|---|---|---|---|---|---|---|---|---|---|---|---|
| 1961-62 | 0 | 0 | 0 | 16 | 184 | 287 | 480 | 99 | 209 | 32 | 0 | 0 | 1307 |
| 1962-63 | 0 | 0 | 0 | 8 | 157 | 313 | 515 | 351 | 88 | 7 | 0 | 0 | 1439 |
| 1963-64 | 0 | 0 | 0 |  | 108 | 551 | 413 | 446 | 158 | 19 | 0 | 0 | 1695 |
| 1964-65 | 0 | 0 | 0 | 31 | 114 | 315 | 300 | 284 | 250 | 0 | 0 | 0 | 1294 |
| 1965-66 | 0 | 0 | 2 | 20 | 23 | 212 | 516 | 334 | 144 | 12 | 0 | 0 | 1263 |
| 1966-67 | 0 | 0 | 0 | 27 | 99 | 359 | 342 | 298 | 68 | 0 | 0 | 0 | 1193 |
| 1967-68 | 0 | 0 | 3 | 18 | 99 | 312 | 390 | 415 | 229 | 17 | 0 | 0 | 1483 |
| #1968-69 | 0 | 0 | 0 | 5 | 199 | 297 | 284 | 234 | 281 | 1 | 0 | 2 | 1303 |
| 1969-70 | 0 | 0 | 0 | 29 | 238 | 304 | 579 | 309 | 252 | 51 | 12 | 0 | 1774 |
| 1970-71 | 0 | 0 | 0 | 72 | 274 | 209 | 298 | 273 | 219 | 72 | 3 | 0 | 1420 |
| 1971-72 | 0 | 0 | 2 | 6 | 195 | 194 | 315 | 295 | 85 | 17 | 0 | 0 | 1109 |
| 1972-73 | 0 | 0 | 2 | 50 | 320 | 410 | 540 | 379 | 75 | 117 | 5 | 0 | 1898 |
| 1973-74 | 0 | 0 | 0 | 8 | 74 | 364 | 330 | 273 | 95 | 60 | 0 | 0 | 1204 |
| 1974-75 | 0 | 0 | 0 | 15 | 196 | 336 | 290 | 270 | 179 | 48 | 0 | 0 | 1334 |
| 1975-76 | 0 | 0 | 0 | 26 | 217 | 399 | 441 | 178 | 155 | 26 | 7 | 0 | 1449 |
| 1976-77 | 0 | 0 | 0 | 173 | 398 | 484 | 687 | 312 | 166 | 25 | 0 | 0 | 2245 |
| 1977-78 | 0 | 0 | 0 | 34 | 150 | 365 | 752 | 553 | 250 | 33 | 17 | 0 | 2154 |
| 1978-79 | 0 | 0 | 0 | 22 | 111 | 393 | 646 | 376 | 135 | 23 | 2 | 0 | 1708 |
| 1979-80 | 0 | 0 | 0 | 27 | 297 | 389 | 308 | 350 | 169 | 45 | 0 | 0 | 1585 |
| 1980-81 | 0 | 0 | 0 | 67 | 255 | 323 | 416 | 291 | 144 | 6 | 1 | 0 | 1503 |
| 1981-82 | 0 | 0 | 0 | 50 | 82 | 326 | 409 | 363 | 143 | 79 | 1 | 0 | 1453 |
| 1982-83 | 0 | 0 | 0 | 53 | 175 | 328 | 457 | 346 | 219 | 96 | 0 | 0 | 1674 |
| 1983-84 | 0 | 0 | 6 | 27 | 138 | 606 | 549 | 325 | 150 | 45 | 2 | 0 | 1848 |
| 1984-85 | 0 | 0 | 6 | 12 | 204 | 144 | 591 | 432 | 91 | 22 | 0 | 0 | 1502 |
| 1985-86 | 0 | 0 | 5 | 17 | 76 | 434 | 326 | 209 | 99 | 11 | 0 | 0 | 1177 |
| 1986-87 | 0 | 0 | 0 | 28 | 175 | 411 | 421 | 245 | 196 | 82 | 0 | 0 | 1558 |
| 1987-88 | 0 | 0 | 0 | 16 | 185 | 301 | 525 | 331 | 171 | 35 | 0 | 0 | 1564 |
| 1988-89 | 0 | 0 | 0 | 5 | 120 | 309 | 260 | 379 | 210 | 56 | 0 | 0 | 1339 |
| 1989-90 | 0 | 0 | 0 | 47 | 160 | 637 | 264 | 177 | 122 | 34 | 0 | 0 | 1441 |
| 1990-91 | 0 | 0 | 0 | 61 | 129 | 395 |  |  |  |  |  |  |  |

**TABLE 5**

### COOLING DEGREE DAYS Base 65 deg. F — HOUSTON, TEXAS

| YEAR | JAN | FEB | MAR | APR | MAY | JUNE | JULY | AUG | SEP | OCT | NOV | DEC | TOTAL |
|---|---|---|---|---|---|---|---|---|---|---|---|---|---|
| #1969 | 35 | 13 | 11 | 167 | 328 | 456 | 608 | 569 | 402 | 222 | 48 | 9 | 2868 |
| 1970 | 18 | 3 | 7 | 188 | 238 | 409 | 513 | 567 | 423 | 131 | 38 | 76 | 2611 |
| 1971 | 48 | 18 | 55 | 126 | 292 | 466 | 594 | 485 | 409 | 229 | 52 | 44 | 2818 |
| 1972 | 58 | 20 | 71 | 208 | 275 | 480 | 480 | 482 | 447 | 206 | 17 | 12 | 2756 |
| 1973 | 1 | 4 | 41 | 111 | 253 | 434 | 564 | 458 | 401 | 225 | 151 | 12 | 2655 |
| 1974 | 24 | 33 | 158 | 132 | 374 | 454 | 558 | 519 | 295 | 196 | 60 | 18 | 2821 |
| 1975 | 47 | 8 | 61 | 155 | 342 | 455 | 514 | 505 | 303 | 174 | 68 | 24 | 2656 |
| 1976 | 5 | 43 | 75 | 110 | 182 | 408 | 490 | 520 | 341 | 42 | 9 | 0 | 2225 |
| 1977 | 0 | 5 | 44 | 91 | 302 | 487 | 547 | 565 | 456 | 173 | 58 | 23 | 2751 |
| 1978 | 10 | 5 | 19 | 120 | 369 | 471 | 584 | 568 | 437 | 150 | 108 | 25 | 2866 |
| 1979 | 7 | 13 | 62 | 142 | 261 | 454 | 552 | 519 | 324 | 211 | 26 | 6 | 2577 |
| 1980 | 4 | 31 | 49 | 86 | 388 | 610 | 705 | 677 | 553 | 162 | 52 | 26 | 3343 |
| 1981 | 1 | 28 | 23 | 295 | 330 | 538 | 606 | 609 | 413 | 285 | 71 | 7 | 3206 |
| 1982 | 39 | 11 | 147 | 170 | 329 | 547 | 641 | 599 | 437 | 199 | 60 | 40 | 3219 |
| 1983 | 0 | 0 | 18 | 76 | 268 | 427 | 541 | 554 | 362 | 196 | 87 | 18 | 2547 |
| 1984 | 0 | 13 | 64 | 135 | 315 | 415 | 527 | 562 | 384 | 302 | 62 | 100 | 2879 |
| 1985 | 0 | 6 | 87 | 180 | 335 | 487 | 521 | 602 | 456 | 257 | 143 | 9 | 3083 |
| 1986 | 4 | 71 | 52 | 220 | 341 | 518 | 654 | 553 | 510 | 157 | 92 | 4 | 3172 |
| 1987 | 4 | 4 | 14 | 154 | 383 | 497 | 580 | 661 | 423 | 137 | 54 | 15 | 2926 |
| 1988 | 7 | 20 | 65 | 121 | 274 | 472 | 609 | 637 | 478 | 144 |  | 20 | 3076 |
| 1989 | 33 | 44 | 105 | 194 | 405 | 454 | 547 | 526 | 363 | 218 | 105 | 5 | 2999 |
| 1990 | 20 | 19 | 65 | 174 | 413 | 603 | 536 | 630 | 456 | 181 | 87 | 47 | 3231 |

**TABLE 6**

### SNOWFALL (inches) — HOUSTON, TEXAS

| SEASON | JULY | AUG | SEP | OCT | NOV | DEC | JAN | FEB | MAR | APR | MAY | JUNE | TOTAL |
|---|---|---|---|---|---|---|---|---|---|---|---|---|---|
| 1970-71 | 0.0 | 0.0 | 0.0 | 0.0 | 0.0 | 0.0 | T | 0.0 | 0.0 | 0.0 | 0.0 | 0.0 | T |
| 1971-72 | 0.0 | 0.0 | 0.0 | 0.0 | 0.0 | 0.0 | T | 0.0 | 0.0 | 0.0 | 0.0 | 0.0 | T |
| 1972-73 | 0.0 | 0.0 | 0.0 | 0.0 | 0.0 | 0.0 | 2.0 | 2.8 | 0.0 | 0.0 | 0.0 | 0.0 | 4.8 |
| 1973-74 | 0.0 | 0.0 | 0.0 | 0.0 | 0.0 | 0.0 | 0.0 | 0.0 | 0.0 | 0.0 | 0.0 | 0.0 | 0.0 |
| 1974-75 | 0.0 | 0.0 | 0.0 | 0.0 | 0.0 | 0.0 | T | 0.0 | 0.0 | 0.0 | 0.0 | 0.0 | T |
| 1975-76 | 0.0 | 0.0 | 0.0 | 0.0 | 0.0 | 0.0 | 0.0 | 0.0 | 0.0 | 0.0 | 0.0 | 0.0 | 0.0 |
| 1976-77 | 0.0 | 0.0 | 0.0 | 0.0 | T | 0.0 | 0.0 | 0.0 | 0.0 | 0.0 | 0.0 | 0.0 | T |
| 1977-78 | 0.0 | 0.0 | 0.0 | 0.0 |  | 0.0 | 0.4 | 0.0 | 0.0 | 0.0 | 0.0 | 0.0 | 0.4 |
| 1978-79 | 0.0 | 0.0 | 0.0 | 0.0 | 0.0 | 0.0 | T | 0.0 | 0.0 | 0.0 | 0.0 | 0.0 | T |
| 1979-80 | 0.0 | 0.0 | 0.0 | 0.0 | T | 0.0 | 0.0 | 1.4 | 0.0 | 0.0 | 0.0 | 0.0 | 1.4 |
| 1980-81 | 0.0 | 0.0 | 0.0 | 0.0 | 0.0 | 0.0 | T | T | 0.0 | 0.0 | 0.0 | 0.0 | T |
| 1981-82 | 0.0 | 0.0 | 0.0 | 0.0 | 0.0 | 0.0 | T | 0.0 | 0.0 | 0.0 | 0.0 | 0.0 | T |
| 1982-83 | 0.0 | 0.0 | 0.0 | 0.0 | 0.0 | 0.0 | 0.0 | 0.0 | 0.0 | 0.0 | 0.0 | 0.0 | 0.0 |
| 1983-84 | 0.0 | 0.0 | 0.0 | 0.0 | 0.0 | 0.0 | 0.0 | 0.0 | 0.0 | 0.0 | 0.0 | 0.0 | 0.0 |
| 1984-85 | 0.0 | 0.0 | 0.0 | 0.0 | 0.0 | 0.0 | 0.0 | 0.0 | 0.0 | 0.0 | 0.0 | 0.0 | 0.0 |
| 1985-86 | 0.0 | 0.0 | 0.0 | 0.0 | 0.0 | 0.0 | 1.4 | 0.3 | 0.0 | 0.0 | 0.0 | 0.0 | 1.7 |
| 1986-87 | 0.0 | 0.0 | 0.0 | 0.0 | 0.0 | 0.0 | 0.0 | 0.0 | 0.0 | 0.0 | 0.0 | 0.0 | 0.0 |
| 1987-88 | 0.0 | 0.0 | 0.0 | 0.0 | 0.0 | 0.0 | 0.0 | T | 0.0 | 0.0 | 0.0 | 0.0 | T |
| 1988-89 | 0.0 | 0.0 | 0.0 | 0.0 | 0.0 | 0.0 | 0.0 | T | 0.0 | 0.0 | 0.0 | 0.0 | T |
| 1989-90 | 0.0 | 0.0 | 0.0 | 0.0 | 0.0 | 1.7 | 0.0 | 0.0 | 0.0 | 0.0 | 0.0 | T | 1.7 |
| 1990-91 | 0.0 | 0.0 | 0.0 | 0.0 | 0.0 | 0.0 |  |  |  |  |  |  |  |
| Record Mean | 0.0 | 0.0 | 0.0 | 0.0 | T | T | 0.2 | 0.2 | T | 0.0 | 0.0 | T | 0.4 |

**See Reference Notes, relative to all above tables, on preceding page.**

The city of San Antonio is located in the south-central portion of Texas on the Balcones escarpment. Northwest of the city, the terrain slopes upward to the Edwards Plateau and to the southeast it slopes downward to the Gulf Coastal Plains. Soils are blackland clay and silty loam on the Plains and thin limestone soils on the Edwards Plateau.

The location of San Antonio on the edge of the Gulf Coastal Plains is influenced by a modified subtropical climate, predominantly continental during the winter months and marine during the summer months. Temperatures range from 50 degrees in January to the middle 80s in July and August. While the summer is hot, with daily temperatures above 90 degrees over 80 percent of the time, extremely high temperatures are rare. Mild weather prevails during much of the winter months, with below-freezing temperatures occurring on an average of about 20 days each year.

San Antonio is situated between a semi-arid area to the west and the coastal area of heavy precipitation to the east. The normal annual rainfall of nearly 28 inches is sufficient for the production of most crops. Precipitation is fairly well distributed throughout the year with the heaviest amounts occurring during May and September. The precipitation from April through September usually occurs from thunderstorms. Large amounts of precipitation may fall during short periods of time. Most of the winter precipitation occurs as light rain or drizzle. Thunderstorms and heavy rains have occurred in all months of the year. Hail of damaging intensity seldom occurs but light hail is frequent with the springtime thunderstorms. Measurable snow occurs only once in three or four years. Snowfall of 2 to 4 inches occurs about every ten years.

Northerly winds prevail during most of the winter, and strong northerly winds occasionally occur during storms called northers. Southeasterly winds from the Gulf of Mexico also occur frequently during winter and are predominant in summer.

Since San Antonio is located only 140 miles from the Gulf of Mexico, tropical storms occasionally affect the city with strong winds and heavy rains. One of the fastest winds recorded, 74 mph, occurred as a tropical storm moved inland east of the city in August 1942.

Relative humidity is above 80 percent during the early morning hours most of the year, dropping to near 50 percent in the late afternoon.

San Antonio has about 50 percent of the possible amount of sunshine during the winter months and more than 70 percent during the summer months. Skies are clear to partly cloudy more than 60 percent of the time and cloudy less than 40 percent. Air carried over San Antonio by southeasterly winds is lifted orographically, causing low stratus clouds to develop frequently during the later part of the night. These clouds usually dissipate around noon, and clear skies prevail a high percentage of the time during the afternoon.

The first occurrence of 32 degrees Fahrenheit is in late November and the average last occurrence is in early March.

## TABLE 1 — NORMALS, MEANS AND EXTREMES

SAN ANTONIO, TEXAS

LATITUDE: 29°32'N    LONGITUDE: 98°28'W    ELEVATION: FT. GRND  788 BARO  796   TIME ZONE: CENTRAL    WBAN: 12921

| | (a) | JAN | FEB | MAR | APR | MAY | JUNE | JULY | AUG | SEP | OCT | NOV | DEC | YEAR |
|---|---|---|---|---|---|---|---|---|---|---|---|---|---|---|
| **TEMPERATURE °F:** | | | | | | | | | | | | | | |
| Normals | | | | | | | | | | | | | | |
| -Daily Maximum | | 61.7 | 66.3 | 73.7 | 80.3 | 85.5 | 91.8 | 94.9 | 94.6 | 89.3 | 81.5 | 70.7 | 64.6 | 79.6 |
| -Daily Minimum | | 39.0 | 42.4 | 49.8 | 58.8 | 65.5 | 72.0 | 74.3 | 73.7 | 69.4 | 58.9 | 48.2 | 41.4 | 57.8 |
| -Monthly | | 50.4 | 54.3 | 61.8 | 69.6 | 75.5 | 81.9 | 84.6 | 84.2 | 79.4 | 70.2 | 59.5 | 53.0 | 68.7 |
| Extremes | | | | | | | | | | | | | | |
| -Record Highest | 48 | 89 | 97 | 100 | 100 | 103 | 105 | 106 | 108 | 103 | 98 | 94 | 90 | 108 |
| -Year | | 1971 | 1986 | 1971 | 1984 | 1989 | 1980 | 1989 | 1986 | 1985 | 1979 | 1988 | 1955 | AUG 1986 |
| -Record Lowest | 48 | 0 | 6 | 19 | 31 | 43 | 53 | 62 | 61 | 41 | 33 | 21 | 6 | 0 |
| -Year | | 1949 | 1951 | 1980 | 1987 | 1984 | 1964 | 1967 | 1966 | 1942 | 1980 | 1976 | 1989 | JAN 1949 |
| **NORMAL DEGREE DAYS:** | | | | | | | | | | | | | | |
| Heating (base 65°F) | | 463 | 319 | 178 | 28 | 0 | 0 | 0 | 0 | 0 | 41 | 199 | 378 | 1606 |
| Cooling (base 65°F) | | 10 | 19 | 78 | 166 | 326 | 507 | 608 | 595 | 432 | 202 | 34 | 6 | 2983 |
| **% OF POSSIBLE SUNSHINE** | 47 | 48 | 52 | 58 | 56 | 56 | 67 | 74 | 73 | 67 | 64 | 55 | 49 | 60 |
| **MEAN SKY COVER (tenths)** | | | | | | | | | | | | | | |
| Sunrise - Sunset | 47 | 6.2 | 6.1 | 6.1 | 6.3 | 6.4 | 5.5 | 5.0 | 4.9 | 5.2 | 5.0 | 5.5 | 6.0 | 5.7 |
| **MEAN NUMBER OF DAYS:** | | | | | | | | | | | | | | |
| Sunrise to Sunset | | | | | | | | | | | | | | |
| -Clear | 47 | 9.1 | 8.4 | 8.7 | 7.5 | 6.2 | 7.0 | 9.4 | 10.1 | 9.6 | 11.6 | 10.5 | 9.9 | 107.9 |
| -Partly Cloudy | 47 | 6.1 | 5.9 | 7.3 | 7.5 | 11.2 | 15.3 | 15.1 | 14.8 | 12.1 | 10.0 | 7.0 | 6.0 | 118.3 |
| -Cloudy | 47 | 15.8 | 14.0 | 15.0 | 15.0 | 13.7 | 7.7 | 6.6 | 6.1 | 8.3 | 9.4 | 12.6 | 15.1 | 139.0 |
| Precipitation | | | | | | | | | | | | | | |
| .01 inches or more | 47 | 7.8 | 7.7 | 7.0 | 7.2 | 8.4 | 6.2 | 4.3 | 5.1 | 7.1 | 6.5 | 6.5 | 7.3 | 81.0 |
| Snow,Ice pellets | | | | | | | | | | | | | | |
| 1.0 inches or more | 47 | 0.1 | 0.1 | 0.0 | 0.0 | 0.0 | 0.0 | 0.0 | 0.0 | 0.0 | 0.0 | 0.0 | 0.0 | 0.2 |
| Thunderstorms | 47 | 1.0 | 1.4 | 2.5 | 3.8 | 6.5 | 4.5 | 3.5 | 4.1 | 4.0 | 2.7 | 1.8 | 0.8 | 36.6 |
| Heavy Fog Visibility 1/4 mile or less | 47 | 5.2 | 3.0 | 2.4 | 1.4 | 0.7 | 0.1 | 0.1 | 0.* | 0.2 | 1.5 | 2.9 | 4.5 | 22.0 |
| Temperature °F | | | | | | | | | | | | | | |
| -Maximum | | | | | | | | | | | | | | |
| 90° and above | 47 | 0.0 | 0.1 | 0.9 | 2.4 | 8.4 | 21.6 | 28.3 | 28.1 | 17.3 | 4.1 | 0.1 | 0.* | 111.4 |
| 32° and below | 47 | 0.3 | 0.1 | 0.0 | 0.0 | 0.0 | 0.0 | 0.0 | 0.0 | 0.0 | 0.0 | 0.0 | 0.1 | 0.6 |
| -Minimum | | | | | | | | | | | | | | |
| 32° and below | 47 | 8.6 | 4.9 | 1.6 | 0.* | 0.0 | 0.0 | 0.0 | 0.0 | 0.0 | 0.0 | 1.8 | 6.0 | 22.9 |
| 0° and below | 47 | 0.* | 0.0 | 0.0 | 0.0 | 0.0 | 0.0 | 0.0 | 0.0 | 0.0 | 0.0 | 0.0 | 0.0 | * |
| **AVG. STATION PRESS.(mb)** | 17 | 991.9 | 990.4 | 986.5 | 985.9 | 984.4 | 985.7 | 987.5 | 987.1 | 987.1 | 989.3 | 989.7 | 991.4 | 988.1 |
| **RELATIVE HUMIDITY (%)** | | | | | | | | | | | | | | |
| Hour 00 | 47 | 75 | 75 | 72 | 75 | 81 | 80 | 75 | 74 | 77 | 77 | 76 | 76 | 76 |
| Hour 06 | 47 | 80 | 80 | 79 | 82 | 87 | 88 | 87 | 86 | 86 | 84 | 81 | 80 | 83 |
| Hour 12 (Local Time) | 47 | 59 | 57 | 53 | 56 | 59 | 56 | 51 | 51 | 55 | 54 | 55 | 57 | 55 |
| Hour 18 | 47 | 57 | 52 | 47 | 50 | 54 | 51 | 45 | 45 | 51 | 53 | 56 | 57 | 52 |
| **PRECIPITATION (inches):** | | | | | | | | | | | | | | |
| Water Equivalent | | | | | | | | | | | | | | |
| -Normal | | 1.55 | 1.86 | 1.33 | 2.73 | 3.67 | 3.03 | 1.92 | 2.69 | 3.75 | 2.88 | 2.34 | 1.38 | 29.13 |
| -Maximum Monthly | 47 | 8.52 | 6.43 | 4.19 | 9.32 | 12.85 | 11.95 | 8.19 | 11.14 | 15.78 | 9.56 | 6.01 | 7.11 | 15.78 |
| -Year | | 1968 | 1965 | 1957 | 1957 | 1987 | 1986 | 1942 | 1974 | 1946 | 1942 | 1977 | 1986 | SEP 1946 |
| -Minimum Monthly | 47 | 0.04 | 0.03 | 0.03 | 0.11 | 0.17 | 0.01 | T | 0.00 | 0.06 | T | T | 0.03 | 0.00 |
| -Year | | 1971 | 1954 | 1961 | 1984 | 1961 | 1967 | 1984 | 1952 | 1947 | 1952 | 1966 | 1950 | AUG 1952 |
| -Maximum in 24 hrs | 47 | 3.18 | 2.44 | 2.36 | 4.88 | 6.53 | 6.30 | 6.97 | 5.57 | 7.28 | 5.29 | 4.87 | 4.27 | 7.28 |
| -Year | | 1968 | 1986 | 1945 | 1977 | 1972 | 1986 | 1958 | 1950 | 1973 | 1942 | 1977 | 1986 | SEP 1973 |
| Snow,Ice pellets | | | | | | | | | | | | | | |
| -Maximum Monthly | 47 | 15.9 | 3.5 | T | 0.0 | 0.0 | T | 0.0 | 0.0 | 0.0 | 0.0 | 0.3 | 0.2 | 15.9 |
| -Year | | 1985 | 1966 | 1989 | | | 1989 | | | | | 1957 | 1964 | JAN 1985 |
| -Maximum in 24 hrs | 47 | 13.2 | 3.5 | T | 0.0 | 0.0 | T | 0.0 | 0.0 | 0.0 | 0.0 | 0.3 | 0.2 | 13.2 |
| -Year | | 1985 | 1966 | 1989 | | | 1989 | | | | | 1957 | 1964 | JAN 1985 |
| **WIND:** | | | | | | | | | | | | | | |
| Mean Speed (mph) | 47 | 9.0 | 9.7 | 10.4 | 10.4 | 10.0 | 10.0 | 9.2 | 8.6 | 8.5 | 8.5 | 8.8 | 8.6 | 9.3 |
| Prevailing Direction through 1963 | | N | NE | SE | SE | SE | SE | SSE | SE | SE | N | N | N | SE |
| Fastest Obs. 1 Min. | | | | | | | | | | | | | | |
| -Direction (!!!) | 13 | 31 | 31 | 36 | 35 | 02 | 34 | 09 | 20 | 18 | 02 | 33 | 32 | 09 |
| -Speed (MPH) | 13 | 35 | 42 | 35 | 39 | 43 | 35 | 48 | 37 | 42 | 31 | 37 | 30 | 48 |
| -Year | | 1979 | 1984 | 1980 | 1979 | 1983 | 1984 | 1979 | 1984 | 1977 | 1977 | 1983 | 1987 | JUL 1979 |
| Peak Gust | | | | | | | | | | | | | | |
| -Direction (!!!) | 6 | N | NW | NW | NW | NW | NW | SE | SW | N | N | NW | W | NW |
| -Speed (mph) | 6 | 51 | 56 | 46 | 47 | 55 | 51 | 41 | 49 | 51 | 43 | 41 | 48 | 56 |
| -Date | | 1985 | 1984 | 1984 | 1988 | 1987 | 1984 | 1989 | 1984 | 1987 | 1985 | 1987 | 1987 | FEB 1984 |

**See reference Notes to this table on the following page.**

PRECIPITATION (inches)    SAN ANTONIO, TEXAS

**TABLE 2**

| YEAR | JAN | FEB | MAR | APR | MAY | JUNE | JULY | AUG | SEP | OCT | NOV | DEC | ANNUAL |
|------|-----|-----|-----|-----|-----|------|------|-----|-----|-----|-----|-----|--------|
| 1961 | 0.68 | 1.79 | 0.03 | 0.32 | 0.17 | 7.87 | 7.04 | 0.15 | 2.24 | 3.39 | 2.09 | 0.70 | 26.47 |
| 1962 | 0.48 | 0.90 | 0.01 | 4.02 | 1.31 | 2.44 | 0.13 | 1.57 | 2.69 | 2.19 | 4.97 | 2.29 | 23.90 |
| 1963 | 0.27 | 3.59 | 0.21 | 1.88 | 3.03 | 2.28 | 0.03 | 0.63 | 1.11 | 1.64 | 4.81 | 0.94 | 18.65 |
| 1964 | 3.40 | 1.89 | 1.73 | 1.16 | 1.79 | 4.88 | 0.02 | 5.19 | 4.15 | 1.64 | 4.81 | 1.22 | 31.88 |
| 1965 | 2.40 | 6.43 | 2.30 | 1.97 | 8.18 | 2.42 | 0.08 | 1.65 | 3.13 | 2.69 | 0.89 | 4.51 | 36.65 |
| 1966 | 1.47 | 2.30 | 1.14 | 3.20 | 3.53 | 1.78 | 0.06 | 4.28 | 2.13 | 1.11 | T | 0.44 | 21.44 |
| 1967 | 0.18 | 0.48 | 2.18 | 0.94 | 2.22 | 0.01 | 2.12 | 3.17 | 11.16 | 2.00 | 3.42 | 1.38 | 29.26 |
| 1968 | 8.52 | 1.85 | 1.27 | 1.92 | 2.82 | 2.63 | 1.53 | 0.94 | 2.99 | 0.69 | 4.58 | 0.66 | 30.40 |
| 1969 | 1.76 | 2.90 | 2.35 | 2.46 | 4.61 | 2.32 | 0.36 | 4.19 | 1.32 | 5.85 | 1.02 | 2.28 | 31.42 |
| 1970 | 1.10 | 2.66 | 1.98 | 1.13 | 7.30 | 0.89 | 0.91 | 0.95 | 4.35 | 1.31 | 0.01 | 0.15 | 22.74 |
| 1971 | 0.04 | 0.81 | 0.04 | 1.39 | 1.52 | 2.74 | 1.05 | 9.42 | 4.57 | 4.62 | 2.74 | 2.86 | 31.80 |
| 1972 | 1.35 | 0.40 | 0.03 | 1.94 | 11.24 | 2.86 | 3.13 | 4.24 | 1.40 | 1.99 | 2.37 | 0.44 | 31.49 |
| 1973 | 2.77 | 2.76 | 1.58 | 5.41 | 2.73 | 10.44 | 0.91 | 1.29 | 13.09 | 4.85 | 0.29 | 0.16 | 52.28 |
| 1974 | 1.36 | 0.04 | 0.94 | 2.18 | 4.28 | 1.02 | 1.28 | 11.14 | 3.85 | 4.09 | 5.39 | 1.43 | 37.00 |
| 1975 | 1.04 | 3.30 | 0.52 | 2.69 | 6.91 | 4.60 | 1.06 | 1.28 | 0.51 | 2.25 | 0.03 | 1.48 | 25.67 |
| 1976 | 0.56 | 0.13 | 1.20 | 5.67 | 5.80 | 1.61 | 5.39 | 2.09 | 3.79 | 8.48 | 2.46 | 1.95 | 39.13 |
| 1977 | 3.10 | 0.91 | 0.88 | 8.80 | 1.62 | 2.26 | 0.10 | 0.06 | 2.11 | 3.47 | 6.01 | 0.32 | 29.64 |
| 1978 | 0.68 | 1.76 | 1.11 | 3.62 | 2.45 | 3.96 | 1.43 | 4.97 | 8.86 | 0.55 | 4.91 | 1.09 | 35.99 |
| 1979 | 4.07 | 1.38 | 3.55 | 5.34 | 1.98 | 5.59 | 7.38 | 2.09 | 0.86 | 0.11 | 1.43 | 2.86 | 36.64 |
| 1980 | 0.72 | 0.74 | 0.98 | 1.67 | 6.42 | 0.52 | 0.26 | 2.64 | 5.05 | 1.09 | 3.53 | 0.61 | 24.23 |
| 1981 | 2.06 | 0.96 | 1.96 | 2.21 | 6.43 | 8.71 | 0.25 | 2.41 | 1.36 | 8.61 | 0.72 | 0.69 | 36.37 |
| 1982 | 0.72 | 1.28 | 0.69 | 1.23 | 6.42 | 1.37 | 0.14 | 0.55 | 0.87 | 2.84 | 4.54 | 2.31 | 22.96 |
| 1983 | 1.48 | 1.54 | 3.89 | 0.18 | 4.37 | 1.27 | 2.43 | 2.00 | 3.86 | 1.64 | 3.06 | 0.39 | 26.11 |
| 1984 | 1.87 | 0.54 | 1.31 | 0.11 | 3.76 | 1.40 | T | 3.04 | 1.06 | 5.94 | 2.91 | 3.41 | 25.95 |
| 1985 | 2.68 | 1.91 | 2.35 | 3.27 | 2.47 | 8.20 | 5.80 | 0.45 | 4.80 | 3.91 | 5.00 | 0.09 | 41.43 |
| 1986 | 0.76 | 2.52 | 0.35 | 0.60 | 6.29 | 11.95 | 0.05 | 1.86 | 2.83 | 6.58 | 1.83 | 7.11 | 42.73 |
| 1987 | 1.13 | 4.78 | 1.10 | 1.48 | 12.85 | 7.69 | 1.21 | 0.33 | 2.24 | 0.44 | 2.53 | 2.18 | 37.96 |
| 1988 | 0.39 | 0.92 | 0.86 | 1.23 | 0.41 | 5.50 | 5.58 | 1.98 | 0.83 | 0.62 | 0.02 | 0.67 | 19.01 |
| 1989 | 2.96 | 0.29 | 1.24 | 2.55 | 0.33 | 3.96 | 0.69 | 0.48 | 1.54 | 5.81 | 1.93 | 0.36 | 22.14 |
| 1990 | 1.17 | 2.68 | 5.17 | 4.52 | 3.28 | 1.18 | 8.29 | 1.30 | 3.70 | 3.71 | 3.11 | 0.20 | 38.31 |
| Record Mean | 1.60 | 1.67 | 1.67 | 2.88 | 3.52 | 3.05 | 2.09 | 2.34 | 3.17 | 2.58 | 1.97 | 1.65 | 28.18 |

**TABLE 3**    AVERAGE TEMPERATURE (deg. F)    SAN ANTONIO, TEXAS

| YEAR | JAN | FEB | MAR | APR | MAY | JUNE | JULY | AUG | SEP | OCT | NOV | DEC | ANNUAL |
|------|-----|-----|-----|-----|-----|------|------|-----|-----|-----|-----|-----|--------|
| 1961 | 47.9 | 55.9 | 65.7 | 68.5 | 78.5 | 81.3 | 82.6 | 82.5 | 80.5 | 71.1 | 58.0 | 54.2 | 68.9 |
| 1962 | 45.9 | 62.8 | 59.1 | 69.7 | 77.9 | 82.3 | 86.9 | 87.5 | 80.9 | 60.4 | 52.2 | 52.2 | 70.1 |
| 1963 | 46.2 | 52.6 | 65.6 | 74.6 | 77.7 | 83.4 | 85.4 | 85.7 | 81.1 | 74.1 | 62.4 | 45.7 | 69.6 |
| 1964 | 51.0 | 49.8 | 61.5 | 70.5 | 77.6 | 82.4 | 86.3 | 86.2 | 80.0 | 62.6 | 62.6 | 52.3 | 68.9 |
| 1965 | 54.4 | 49.8 | 54.9 | 71.6 | 75.0 | 81.6 | 84.9 | 84.0 | 80.7 | 66.8 | 64.5 | 55.5 | 68.6 |
| 1966 | 45.4 | 49.8 | 60.0 | 68.6 | 73.5 | 78.8 | 84.2 | 81.9 | 77.5 | 67.0 | 63.0 | 50.7 | 66.7 |
| 1967 | 50.2 | 51.8 | 66.9 | 76.6 | 76.6 | 84.5 | 85.3 | 82.7 | 75.5 | 66.9 | 60.5 | 51.0 | 69.0 |
| 1968 | 49.8 | 48.3 | 58.0 | 68.1 | 75.3 | 80.5 | 82.7 | 84.2 | 76.0 | 72.2 | 56.4 | 50.7 | 66.8 |
| 1969 | 52.5 | 53.6 | 54.9 | 69.0 | 73.5 | 81.2 | 86.8 | 85.7 | 79.6 | 69.8 | 58.1 | 55.1 | 68.3 |
| 1970 | 45.6 | 54.8 | 56.8 | 70.2 | 72.9 | 80.7 | 84.0 | 85.7 | 81.1 | 67.7 | 58.0 | 60.1 | 68.1 |
| 1971 | 56.0 | 57.4 | 64.6 | 69.4 | 78.1 | 83.6 | 85.9 | 81.2 | 80.1 | 73.9 | 63.2 | 57.2 | 70.9 |
| 1972 | 52.8 | 56.7 | 66.3 | 73.7 | 72.8 | 80.3 | 82.2 | 82.1 | 82.0 | 71.9 | 54.0 | 50.3 | 68.8 |
| 1973 | 47.2 | 51.9 | 66.1 | 66.0 | 74.7 | 79.2 | 83.2 | 82.1 | 79.3 | 72.5 | 65.8 | 52.2 | 68.4 |
| 1974 | 51.0 | 56.5 | 67.9 | 69.7 | 77.3 | 79.4 | 83.0 | 81.2 | 72.3 | 68.2 | 57.3 | 50.9 | 67.9 |
| 1975 | 53.2 | 53.5 | 61.4 | 68.4 | 73.5 | 80.0 | 80.9 | 81.7 | 76.0 | 71.1 | 60.3 | 53.1 | 67.8 |
| 1976 | 49.6 | 61.2 | 63.8 | 68.9 | 71.3 | 79.8 | 79.8 | 81.6 | 77.5 | 61.1 | 52.1 | 49.9 | 66.4 |
| 1977 | 44.1 | 52.8 | 61.8 | 66.9 | 74.8 | 81.5 | 84.9 | 84.7 | 82.3 | 71.2 | 61.4 | 53.4 | 68.3 |
| 1978 | 43.4 | 46.4 | 59.6 | 68.9 | 77.1 | 82.7 | 86.1 | 83.1 | 78.5 | 69.3 | 62.4 | 51.7 | 67.5 |
| 1979 | 43.7 | 52.4 | 63.3 | 69.7 | 73.9 | 80.9 | 84.7 | 83.1 | 78.7 | 74.7 | 58.2 | 55.4 | 68.2 |
| 1980 | 52.6 | 53.7 | 61.5 | 67.6 | 76.1 | 85.1 | 88.1 | 85.3 | 83.7 | 70.7 | 58.3 | 55.0 | 69.8 |
| 1981 | 50.8 | 53.7 | 60.7 | 72.9 | 75.3 | 81.5 | 84.2 | 84.7 | 78.9 | 71.9 | 62.4 | 53.0 | 69.2 |
| 1982 | 50.8 | 49.7 | 63.1 | 66.9 | 74.5 | 81.6 | 85.5 | 86.0 | 80.1 | 69.3 | 59.4 | 52.4 | 68.3 |
| 1983 | 48.9 | 52.1 | 58.7 | 65.2 | 73.6 | 79.2 | 82.9 | 84.5 | 78.5 | 70.9 | 62.5 | 43.0 | 66.7 |
| 1984 | 46.7 | 54.1 | 64.2 | 69.7 | 77.1 | 82.8 | 85.0 | 84.7 | 77.6 | 71.2 | 58.8 | 59.6 | 69.3 |
| 1985 | 44.2 | 50.5 | 64.1 | 69.4 | 76.7 | 80.2 | 82.2 | 85.5 | 79.4 | 71.7 | 64.4 | 49.9 | 68.2 |
| 1986 | 53.4 | 58.0 | 62.9 | 72.6 | 74.6 | 81.5 | 85.8 | 85.7 | 83.7 | 69.7 | 59.4 | 51.6 | 69.9 |
| 1987 | 50.7 | 55.9 | 57.8 | 66.1 | 75.8 | 80.5 | 83.8 | 86.0 | 79.2 | 71.2 | 60.6 | 54.2 | 68.5 |
| 1988 | 47.6 | 54.3 | 61.3 | 69.1 | 76.1 | 81.2 | 84.6 | 86.4 | 80.7 | 73.2 | 65.1 | 56.0 | 69.6 |
| 1989 | 56.2 | 51.6 | 61.9 | 70.4 | 81.7 | 83.3 | 86.6 | 86.0 | 79.1 | 71.3 | 61.8 | 43.4 | 69.4 |
| 1990 | 56.4 | 58.9 | 61.5 | 69.7 | 79.3 | 87.5 | 83.4 | 85.3 | 80.0 | 69.3 | 63.0 | 51.9 | 70.5 |
| Record Mean | 51.7 | 55.2 | 62.2 | 69.3 | 75.5 | 81.6 | 84.0 | 84.2 | 79.3 | 70.9 | 60.5 | 53.5 | 69.0 |
| Max | 62.2 | 66.1 | 73.4 | 80.0 | 85.5 | 91.6 | 94.4 | 94.9 | 89.5 | 81.8 | 71.1 | 64.0 | 79.5 |
| Min | 41.2 | 44.2 | 50.9 | 58.6 | 65.5 | 71.6 | 73.6 | 73.5 | 69.2 | 59.9 | 49.9 | 43.0 | 58.4 |

**REFERENCE NOTES FOR TABLES 1, 2, 3 and 6      (SAN ANTONIO, TX)**

**GENERAL**

T - TRACE AMOUNT
BLANK ENTRIES DENOTE MISSING/UNREPORTED DATA.
# INDICATES A STATION OR INSTRUMENT RELOCATION.

**SPECIFIC**

**TABLE 1**

(a) - LENGTH OF RECORD IN YEARS. ALTHOUGH
      INDIVIDUAL MONTHS MAY BE MISSING.
  * LESS THAN .05

NORMALS — BASED ON THE 1951-1980 RECORD PERIOD.
EXTREMES — DATES ARE THE MOST RECENT OCCURRENCE.
WIND DIR. — NUMERALS SHOW TENS OF DEGREES
            CLOCKWISE FROM TRUE NORTH.
            "00" INDICATES CALM.
RESULTANT WIND DIRECTIONS ARE GIVEN TO WHOLE DEGREES.

**TABLE 3**
MAX AND MIN ARE LONG-TERM MEAN DAILY MAXIMUM
AND MEAN DAILY MINIMUM TEMPERATURES.

**EXCEPTIONS**

**TABLES 2, 3, and 6**

RECORD MEANS ARE THROUGH THE CURRENT YEAR,
BEGINNING IN      1885 FOR TEMPERATURE
                  1885 FOR PRECIPITATION
                  1943 FOR SNOWFALL

## TABLE 4 — HEATING DEGREE DAYS Base 65 deg. F    SAN ANTONIO, TEXAS

| SEASON | JULY | AUG | SEP | OCT | NOV | DEC | JAN | FEB | MAR | APR | MAY | JUNE | TOTAL |
|---|---|---|---|---|---|---|---|---|---|---|---|---|---|
| 1961-62 | 0 | 0 | 0 | 19 | 223 | 351 | 586 | 108 | 206 | 27 | C | 0 | 1520 |
| 1962-63 | 0 | 0 | 0 | 9 | 164 | 393 | 575 | 349 | 87 | 17 | 3 | 0 | 1597 |
| 1963-64 | 0 | 0 | 0 | 0 | 141 | 592 | 428 | 434 | 143 | 23 | C | 0 | 1761 |
| 1964-65 | 0 | 0 | 0 | 41 | 155 | 414 | 346 | 419 | 327 | 13 | C | 0 | 1715 |
| 1965-66 | 0 | 0 | 2 | 62 | 64 | 301 | 607 | 426 | 182 | 39 | 5 | 0 | 1688 |
| 1966-67 | 0 | 0 | 0 | 57 | 131 | 456 | 470 | 366 | 80 | 0 | C | 0 | 1560 |
| 1967-68 | 0 | 0 | 8 | 48 | 164 | 429 | 477 | 478 | 254 | 39 | C | 0 | 1897 |
| 1968-69 | 0 | 0 | 0 | 9 | 278 | 437 | 394 | 319 | 315 | 5 | 3 | 0 | 1760 |
| 1969-70 | 0 | 0 | 0 | 52 | 253 | 299 | 599 | 282 | 266 | 45 | 7 | 0 | 1803 |
| 1970-71 | 0 | 0 | 1 | 72 | 247 | 201 | 282 | 239 | 134 | 52 | 1 | 0 | 1229 |
| 1971-72 | 0 | 0 | 1 | 0 | 129 | 266 | 382 | 263 | 61 | 7 | C | 0 | 1109 |
| 1972-73 | 0 | 0 | 0 | 29 | 334 | 457 | 551 | 362 | 29 | 94 | 1 | 0 | 1857 |
| 1973-74 | 0 | 0 | 0 | 4 | 85 | 391 | 437 | 257 | 74 | 39 | C | 0 | 1287 |
| 1974-75 | 0 | 0 | 2 | 19 | 260 | 433 | 389 | 316 | 152 | 41 | C | 0 | 1612 |
| 1975-76 | 0 | 0 | 1 | 21 | 214 | 394 | 472 | 166 | 143 | 11 | 2 | 0 | 1424 |
| 1976-77 | 0 | 0 | 0 | 160 | 382 | 461 | 643 | 336 | 144 | 32 | C | 0 | 2158 |
| 1977-78 | 0 | 0 | 0 | 19 | 138 | 360 | 667 | 521 | 192 | 27 | 4 | 0 | 1928 |
| 1978-79 | 0 | 0 | 0 | 12 | 152 | 413 | 657 | 356 | 109 | 20 | 4 | 0 | 1723 |
| 1979-80 | 0 | 0 | 0 | 15 | 243 | 306 | 386 | 333 | 163 | 42 | C | 0 | 1488 |
| 1980-81 | 0 | 0 | 0 | 62 | 245 | 331 | 437 | 332 | 157 | 10 | C | 0 | 1574 |
| 1981-82 | 0 | 0 | 2 | 52 | 112 | 368 | 445 | 430 | 171 | 77 | 2 | 0 | 1659 |
| 1982-83 | 0 | 0 | 0 | 49 | 237 | 404 | 490 | 356 | 208 | 99 | 1 | 0 | 1844 |
| 1983-84 | 0 | 0 | 5 | 20 | 154 | 681 | 563 | 315 | 120 | 21 | 2 | 0 | 1881 |
| 1984-85 | 0 | 0 | 9 | 28 | 228 | 203 | 635 | 406 | 109 | 26 | C | 0 | 1644 |
| 1985-86 | 0 | 0 | 10 | 9 | 112 | 467 | 354 | 232 | 106 | 8 | 1 | 0 | 1299 |
| 1986-87 | 0 | 0 | 0 | 14 | 204 | 413 | 443 | 254 | 233 | 98 | C | 0 | 1659 |
| 1987-88 | 0 | 0 | 0 | 1 | 194 | 339 | 538 | 323 | 179 | 38 | C | 0 | 1612 |
| 1988-89 | 0 | 0 | 0 | 0 | 122 | 291 | 292 | 392 | 187 | 55 | C | 0 | 1339 |
| 1989-90 | 0 | 0 | 0 | 42 | 165 | 663 | 283 | 190 | 154 | 32 | C | 0 | 1529 |
| 1990-91 | 0 | 0 | 0 | 50 | 142 | 422 | | | | | | | |

## TABLE 5 — COOLING DEGREE DAYS Base 65 deg. F    SAN ANTONIO, TEXAS

| YEAR | JAN | FEB | MAR | APR | MAY | JUNE | JULY | AUG | SEP | OCT | NOV | DEC | TOTAL |
|---|---|---|---|---|---|---|---|---|---|---|---|---|---|
| 1969 | 11 | 5 | 8 | 133 | 273 | 494 | 683 | 652 | 448 | 207 | 53 | 2 | 2969 |
| 1970 | 3 | 3 | 20 | 208 | 259 | 592 | 592 | 651 | 493 | 163 | 40 | 57 | 2967 |
| 1971 | 14 | 36 | 130 | 189 | 414 | 564 | 658 | 509 | 459 | 281 | 81 | 31 | 3366 |
| 1972 | 11 | 31 | 105 | 276 | 252 | 465 | 542 | 539 | 515 | 249 | 12 | 6 | 3003 |
| 1973 | 8 | 0 | 69 | 129 | 310 | 431 | 570 | 536 | 437 | 242 | 114 | 0 | 2846 |
| 1974 | 11 | 22 | 171 | 188 | 387 | 439 | 568 | 506 | 229 | 124 | 34 | 5 | 2684 |
| 1975 | 29 | 1 | 51 | 151 | 273 | 457 | 502 | 524 | 337 | 217 | 8C | 30 | 2652 |
| 1976 | 3 | 62 | 113 | 136 | 202 | 451 | 467 | 521 | 383 | 45 | 0 | 0 | 2383 |
| 1977 | 0 | 3 | 52 | 98 | 311 | 502 | 620 | 618 | 525 | 218 | 38 | 5 | 2990 |
| 1978 | 3 | 7 | 30 | 152 | 384 | 537 | 660 | 567 | 410 | 154 | 79 | 11 | 2994 |
| 1979 | 3 | 13 | 65 | 166 | 285 | 482 | 619 | 570 | 418 | 322 | 42 | 13 | 2998 |
| 1980 | 11 | 14 | 61 | 127 | 355 | 614 | 725 | 635 | 567 | 245 | 51 | 26 | 3431 |
| 1981 | 3 | 24 | 30 | 255 | 324 | 502 | 603 | 619 | 459 | 273 | 41 | 3 | 3101 |
| 1982 | 11 | 5 | 117 | 142 | 304 | 504 | 645 | 659 | 459 | 191 | 72 | 19 | 3128 |
| 1983 | 0 | 0 | 21 | 111 | 276 | 435 | 560 | 611 | 417 | 207 | 84 | 8 | 2730 |
| 1984 | 0 | 8 | 101 | 169 | 383 | 541 | 625 | 618 | 394 | 230 | 46 | 44 | 3159 |
| 1985 | 0 | 8 | 85 | 165 | 368 | 462 | 539 | 641 | 450 | 223 | 101 | 5 | 3047 |
| 1986 | 2 | 45 | 49 | 244 | 304 | 500 | 652 | 646 | 568 | 166 | 40 | 4 | 3218 |
| 1987 | 4 | 5 | 17 | 135 | 340 | 471 | 589 | 658 | 434 | 199 | 67 | 12 | 2931 |
| 1988 | 6 | 19 | 71 | 166 | 352 | 492 | 617 | 671 | 480 | 264 | 131 | 20 | 3289 |
| 1989 | 24 | 23 | 99 | 222 | 524 | 557 | 678 | 656 | 429 | 244 | 75 | 0 | 3531 |
| 1990 | 22 | 26 | 53 | 177 | 450 | 681 | 578 | 635 | 459 | 192 | 91 | 23 | 3387 |

## TABLE 6 — SNOWFALL (inches)    SAN ANTONIO, TEXAS

| SEASON | JULY | AUG | SEP | OCT | NOV | DEC | JAN | FEB | MAR | APR | MAY | JUNE | TOTAL |
|---|---|---|---|---|---|---|---|---|---|---|---|---|---|
| 1961-62 | 0.0 | 0.0 | 0.0 | 0.0 | 0.0 | 0.0 | 0.0 | 0.0 | 0.0 | 0.0 | 0.0 | 0.0 | 0.0 |
| 1962-63 | 0.0 | 0.0 | 0.0 | 0.0 | 0.0 | 0.0 | 0.0 | 0.0 | 0.0 | 0.0 | 0.0 | 0.0 | T |
| 1963-64 | 0.0 | 0.0 | 0.0 | 0.0 | 0.0 | T | T | 2.0 | 0.0 | 0.0 | 0.0 | 0.0 | 2.0 |
| 1964-65 | 0.0 | 0.0 | 0.0 | 0.0 | 0.0 | 0.2 | 0.0 | T | 0.0 | 0.0 | 0.0 | 0.0 | 0.2 |
| 1965-66 | 0.0 | 0.0 | 0.0 | 0.0 | 0.0 | 0.0 | T | 3.5 | 0.0 | 0.0 | 0.0 | 0.0 | 3.5 |
| 1966-67 | 0.0 | 0.0 | 0.0 | 0.0 | 0.0 | 0.0 | T | T | 0.0 | 0.0 | 0.0 | 0.0 | T |
| 1967-68 | 0.0 | 0.0 | 0.0 | 0.0 | 0.0 | 0.0 | 0.0 | 0.0 | 0.0 | 0.0 | 0.0 | 0.0 | T |
| 1968-69 | 0.0 | 0.0 | 0.0 | 0.0 | 0.0 | 0.0 | 0.0 | 0.0 | 0.0 | 0.0 | 0.0 | 0.0 | 0.0 |
| 1969-70 | 0.0 | 0.0 | 0.0 | 0.0 | 0.0 | T | 0.0 | 0.0 | 0.0 | 0.0 | 0.0 | 0.0 | T |
| 1970-71 | 0.0 | 0.0 | 0.0 | 0.0 | 0.0 | T | T | 0.0 | 0.0 | 0.0 | 0.0 | 0.0 | 0.0 |
| 1971-72 | 0.0 | 0.0 | 0.0 | 0.0 | 0.0 | 0.0 | 0.0 | 0.0 | 0.0 | 0.0 | 0.0 | 0.0 | T |
| 1972-73 | 0.0 | 0.0 | 0.0 | 0.0 | 0.0 | T | 0.8 | 2.1 | 0.0 | 0.0 | 0.0 | 0.0 | 2.9 |
| 1973-74 | 0.0 | 0.0 | 0.0 | 0.0 | 0.0 | 0.0 | 0.0 | 0.0 | 0.0 | 0.0 | 0.0 | 0.0 | 0.0 |
| 1974-75 | 0.0 | 0.0 | 0.0 | 0.0 | 0.0 | T | T | 0.0 | 0.0 | 0.0 | 0.0 | 0.0 | T |
| 1975-76 | 0.0 | 0.0 | 0.0 | 0.0 | 0.0 | 0.0 | T | 0.0 | 0.0 | 0.0 | 0.0 | 0.0 | T |
| 1976-77 | 0.0 | 0.0 | 0.0 | 0.0 | T | T | 0.0 | 0.0 | 0.0 | 0.0 | 0.0 | 0.0 | T |
| 1977-78 | 0.0 | 0.0 | 0.0 | 0.0 | 0.0 | 0.0 | 0.0 | 0.0 | T | 0.0 | 0.0 | 0.0 | T |
| 1978-79 | 0.0 | 0.0 | 0.0 | 0.0 | 0.0 | 0.0 | T | 0.0 | 0.0 | 0.0 | 0.0 | 0.0 | T |
| 1979-80 | 0.0 | 0.0 | 0.0 | 0.0 | T | 0.0 | 0.0 | T | 0.0 | 0.0 | 0.0 | 0.0 | T |
| 1980-81 | 0.0 | 0.0 | 0.0 | 0.0 | T | 0.0 | T | 0.0 | 0.0 | 0.0 | 0.0 | 0.0 | T |
| 1981-82 | 0.0 | 0.0 | 0.0 | 0.0 | 0.0 | 0.0 | 0.5 | 0.0 | 0.0 | 0.0 | 0.0 | 0.0 | 0.5 |
| 1982-83 | 0.0 | 0.0 | 0.0 | 0.0 | 0.0 | 0.0 | 0.0 | 0.0 | 0.0 | 0.0 | 0.0 | 0.0 | 0.0 |
| 1983-84 | 0.0 | 0.0 | 0.0 | 0.0 | 0.0 | 0.0 | 0.0 | 0.0 | 0.0 | 0.0 | 0.0 | 0.0 | 0.0 |
| 1984-85 | 0.0 | 0.0 | 0.0 | 0.0 | 0.0 | 0.0 | 15.9 | T | 0.0 | 0.0 | 0.0 | 0.0 | 15.9 |
| 1985-86 | 0.0 | 0.0 | 0.0 | 0.0 | 0.0 | 0.0 | T | T | 0.0 | 0.0 | 0.0 | 0.0 | T |
| 1986-87 | 0.0 | 0.0 | 0.0 | 0.0 | 0.0 | 0.0 | 1.3 | 0.0 | 0.0 | 0.0 | 0.0 | 0.0 | 1.3 |
| 1987-88 | 0.0 | 0.0 | 0.0 | 0.0 | 0.0 | 0.0 | 0.0 | 0.1 | 0.0 | 0.0 | 0.0 | 0.0 | 0.1 |
| 1988-89 | 0.0 | 0.0 | 0.0 | 0.0 | 0.0 | 0.0 | 0.0 | 0.0 | 0.0 | 0.0 | T | 0.0 | T |
| 1989-90 | 0.0 | 0.0 | 0.0 | 0.0 | 0.0 | T | 0.0 | T | T | T | 0.0 | 0.0 | T |
| 1990-91 | 0.0 | 0.0 | 0.0 | 0.0 | 0.0 | T | 0.0 | | | | | | |
| Record Mean | 0.0 | 0.0 | 0.0 | 0.0 | T | T | 0.5 | 0.2 | T | T | 0.0 | T | 0.7 |

**See Reference Notes, relative to all above tables, on preceding page.**

Salt Lake City is located in a northern Utah valley surrounded by mountains on three sides and the Great Salt Lake to the northwest. The city varies in altitude from near 4,200 to 5,000 feet above sea level.

The Wasatch Mountains to the east have peaks to nearly 12,000 feet above sea level. Their orographic effects cause more precipitation in the eastern part of the city than over the western part.

The Oquirrh Mountains to the southwest of the city have several peaks to above 10,000 feet above sea level. The Traverse Mountain Range at the south end of the Salt Lake Valley rises to above 6,000 feet above sea level. These mountain ranges help to shelter the valleys from storms from the southwest in the winter, but are instrumental in developing thunderstorms which can drift over the valley in the summer.

Besides the mountain ranges, the most influential natural condition affecting the climate of Salt Lake City is the Great Salt Lake. This large inland body of water, which never freezes over due to its high salt content, can moderate the temperatures of cold winter winds blowing from the northwest and helps drive a lake/valley wind system. The warmer lake water during the winter and spring also contributes to increased precipitation in the valley downwind from the lake. The combination of the Great Salt Lake and the Wasatch Mountains often enhances storm precipitation in the valley.

Salt Lake City normally has a semi-arid continental climate with four well-defined seasons. Summers are characterized by hot, dry weather, but the high temperatures are usually not oppressive since the relative humidity is generally low and the nights usually cool. July is the hottest month with temperature readings in the 90s.

The mean diurnal temperature range is about 30 degrees in the summer and 18 degrees during the winter. Temperatures above 102 degrees in the summer or colder than -10 degrees in the winter are likely to occur one season out of four.

Winters are cold, but usually not severe. Mountains to the north and east act as a barrier to frequent invasions of cold continental air. The average annual snowfall is under 60 inches at the airport but much higher amounts fall in higher bench locations. Heavy fog can develop under temperature inversions in the winter and persist for several days.

Precipitation, generally light during the summer and early fall, is heavy in the spring when storms from the Pacific Ocean are moving through the area more frequently than at any other season of the year.

Winds are usually light, although occasional high winds have occurred in every month of the year, particularly in March.

The growing season is over five months in length. Yard and garden foilage generally are making good growth by mid-April. The last freezing temperature in the spring averages late April and the first freeze of the fall is mid-October.

## TABLE 1    NORMALS, MEANS AND EXTREMES

SALT LAKE CITY, UTAH

LATITUDE: 40°46'N    LONGITUDE: 111°58'W    ELEVATION: FT. GRND 4221 BARO 4224    TIME ZONE: MOUNTAIN    WBAN: 24127

| | (a) | JAN | FEB | MAR | APR | MAY | JUNE | JULY | AUG | SEP | OCT | NOV | DEC | YEAR |
|---|---|---|---|---|---|---|---|---|---|---|---|---|---|---|
| **TEMPERATURE °F:** | | | | | | | | | | | | | | |
| Normals | | | | | | | | | | | | | | |
| -Daily Maximum | | 37.4 | 43.7 | 51.5 | 61.1 | 72.4 | 83.3 | 93.2 | 90.0 | 80.0 | 66.7 | 50.2 | 38.9 | 64.0 |
| -Daily Minimum | | 19.7 | 24.4 | 29.9 | 37.2 | 45.2 | 53.3 | 61.8 | 59.7 | 50.0 | 39.3 | 29.2 | 21.6 | 39.3 |
| -Monthly | | 28.6 | 34.1 | 40.7 | 49.2 | 58.8 | 68.3 | 77.5 | 74.9 | 65.0 | 53.0 | 39.7 | 30.3 | 51.7 |
| Extremes | | | | | | | | | | | | | | |
| -Record Highest | 61 | 62 | 69 | 78 | 85 | 93 | 104 | 107 | 104 | 100 | 89 | 75 | 67 | 107 |
| -Year | | 1982 | 1972 | 1960 | 1989 | 1984 | 1979 | 1960 | 1979 | 1979 | 1963 | 1967 | 1969 | JUL 1960 |
| -Record Lowest | 61 | -22 | -30 | 2 | 14 | 25 | 35 | 40 | 37 | 27 | 16 | -14 | -21 | -30 |
| -Year | | 1949 | 1933 | 1966 | 1936 | 1965 | 1962 | 1968 | 1965 | 1965 | 1971 | 1955 | 1932 | FEB 1933 |
| **NORMAL DEGREE DAYS:** | | | | | | | | | | | | | | |
| Heating (base 65°F) | | 1128 | 865 | 753 | 474 | 220 | 53 | 0 | 0 | 97 | 377 | 759 | 1076 | 5802 |
| Cooling (base 65°F) | | 0 | 0 | 0 | 0 | 28 | 152 | 388 | 311 | 97 | 5 | 0 | 0 | 981 |
| **% OF POSSIBLE SUNSHINE** | 51 | 45 | 54 | 63 | 68 | 72 | 79 | 83 | 82 | 82 | 72 | 53 | 42 | 66 |
| **MEAN SKY COVER (tenths)** | | | | | | | | | | | | | | |
| Sunrise - Sunset | 54 | 7.3 | 7.1 | 6.7 | 6.4 | 5.7 | 4.3 | 3.6 | 3.6 | 3.6 | 4.6 | 6.3 | 7.2 | 5.5 |
| **MEAN NUMBER OF DAYS:** | | | | | | | | | | | | | | |
| Sunrise to Sunset | | | | | | | | | | | | | | |
| -Clear | 61 | 5.6 | 5.2 | 7.0 | 6.9 | 9.1 | 13.7 | 16.6 | 15.8 | 16.6 | 14.1 | 8.5 | 6.2 | 125.3 |
| -Partly Cloudy | 61 | 6.5 | 7.0 | 8.2 | 9.3 | 10.3 | 9.9 | 9.9 | 10.7 | 8.2 | 7.9 | 7.2 | 6.5 | 101.6 |
| -Cloudy | 61 | 18.9 | 16.0 | 15.8 | 13.8 | 11.6 | 6.4 | 4.5 | 4.5 | 5.2 | 9.0 | 14.3 | 18.3 | 138.4 |
| Precipitation | | | | | | | | | | | | | | |
| .01 inches or more | 61 | 9.9 | 8.8 | 9.9 | 9.4 | 8.1 | 5.4 | 4.5 | 5.6 | 5.3 | 6.3 | 7.8 | 9.1 | 90.3 |
| Snow,Ice pellets | | | | | | | | | | | | | | |
| 1.0 inches or more | 61 | 4.0 | 3.2 | 2.9 | 1.4 | 0.2 | 0.0 | 0.0 | 0.0 | 0.* | 0.3 | 2.0 | 3.8 | 17.9 |
| Thunderstorms | 61 | 0.3 | 0.7 | 1.3 | 2.2 | 5.2 | 5.5 | 6.9 | 7.8 | 4.2 | 2.0 | 0.5 | 0.3 | 36.9 |
| Heavy Fog Visibility | | | | | | | | | | | | | | |
| 1/4 mile or less | 61 | 4.3 | 2.3 | 0.3 | 0.1 | 0.* | 0.0 | 0.0 | 0.0 | 0.0 | 0.* | 0.9 | 3.7 | 11.6 |
| Temperature °F | | | | | | | | | | | | | | |
| -Maximum | | | | | | | | | | | | | | |
| 90° and above | 30 | 0.0 | 0.0 | 0.0 | 0.0 | 0.7 | 9.1 | 23.8 | 19.2 | 3.6 | 0.0 | 0.0 | 0.0 | 56.3 |
| 32° and below | 30 | 11.1 | 3.9 | 0.7 | 0.0 | 0.0 | 0.0 | 0.0 | 0.0 | 0.0 | 0.* | 0.5 | 8.6 | 24.8 |
| -Minimum | | | | | | | | | | | | | | |
| 32° and below | 30 | 27.5 | 22.8 | 16.5 | 6.7 | 0.8 | 0.0 | 0.0 | 0.0 | 0.4 | 5.0 | 17.8 | 27.4 | 124.8 |
| 0° and below | 30 | 1.8 | 0.4 | 0.0 | 0.0 | 0.0 | 0.0 | 0.0 | 0.0 | 0.0 | 0.0 | 0.0 | 0.6 | 2.8 |
| **AVG. STATION PRESS.(mb)** | 17 | 875.0 | 873.5 | 869.6 | 869.8 | 869.2 | 870.2 | 871.4 | 871.4 | 872.1 | 873.7 | 873.3 | 875.0 | 872.0 |
| **RELATIVE HUMIDITY (%)** | | | | | | | | | | | | | | |
| Hour 05 | 30 | 79 | 77 | 70 | 66 | 65 | 59 | 52 | 54 | 61 | 69 | 74 | 79 | 67 |
| Hour 11 | 30 | 71 | 64 | 52 | 44 | 38 | 31 | 27 | 30 | 35 | 43 | 58 | 70 | 47 |
| Hour 17 (Local Time) | 30 | 69 | 59 | 47 | 39 | 33 | 26 | 22 | 23 | 29 | 41 | 58 | 71 | 43 |
| Hour 23 | 30 | 78 | 76 | 68 | 61 | 57 | 50 | 42 | 45 | 54 | 66 | 73 | 78 | 62 |
| **PRECIPITATION (inches):** | | | | | | | | | | | | | | |
| Water Equivalent | | | | | | | | | | | | | | |
| -Normal | | 1.35 | 1.33 | 1.72 | 2.21 | 1.47 | 0.97 | 0.72 | 0.92 | 0.89 | 1.14 | 1.22 | 1.37 | 15.31 |
| -Maximum Monthly | 61 | 3.14 | 3.22 | 3.97 | 4.90 | 4.76 | 2.93 | 2.57 | 3.66 | 7.04 | 3.91 | 2.63 | 4.37 | 7.04 |
| -Year | | 1940 | 1936 | 1983 | 1944 | 1977 | 1947 | 1982 | 1968 | 1982 | 1981 | 1985 | 1983 | SEP 1982 |
| -Minimum Monthly | 61 | 0.09 | 0.12 | 0.10 | 0.45 | T | 0.01 | T | T | T | 0.00 | 0.01 | 0.08 | 0.00 |
| -Year | | 1961 | 1946 | 1956 | 1981 | 1934 | 1946 | 1963 | 1944 | 1951 | 1952 | 1939 | 1976 | OCT 1952 |
| -Maximum in 24 hrs | 61 | 1.36 | 1.05 | 1.83 | 2.41 | 2.03 | 1.88 | 2.35 | 1.96 | 2.30 | 1.76 | 1.13 | 1.82 | 2.41 |
| -Year | | 1953 | 1958 | 1944 | 1957 | 1942 | 1948 | 1962 | 1932 | 1982 | 1984 | 1954 | 1972 | APR 1957 |
| Snow,Ice pellets | | | | | | | | | | | | | | |
| -Maximum Monthly | 61 | 32.3 | 27.9 | 41.9 | 26.4 | 7.5 | T | 0.0 | 0.0 | 4.0 | 20.4 | 27.2 | 35.2 | 41.9 |
| -Year | | 1937 | 1969 | 1977 | 1974 | 1975 | 1984 | | | 1971 | 1984 | 1985 | 1972 | MAR 1977 |
| -Maximum in 24 hrs | 61 | 10.7 | 11.9 | 15.4 | 16.2 | 6.4 | T | 0.0 | 0.0 | 4.0 | 18.4 | 11.0 | 18.1 | 18.4 |
| -Year | | 1980 | 1989 | 1944 | 1974 | 1975 | 1984 | | | 1971 | 1984 | 1930 | 1972 | OCT 1984 |
| **WIND:** | | | | | | | | | | | | | | |
| Mean Speed (mph) | 60 | 7.6 | 8.2 | 9.4 | 9.6 | 9.5 | 9.4 | 9.5 | 9.7 | 9.2 | 8.5 | 8.0 | 7.5 | 8.8 |
| Prevailing Direction | | | | | | | | | | | | | | |
| through 1963 | | SSE | SE | SSE | SE | SE | SSE | SSE | SSE | SE | SE | SSE | SSE | SSE |
| Fastest Mile | | | | | | | | | | | | | | |
| -Direction (!!!) | 54 | NW | SE | NW | NW | NW | W | NW | SW | W | NW | NW | S | NW |
| -Speed (MPH) | 54 | 59 | 56 | 71 | 57 | 57 | 63 | 51 | 58 | 61 | 67 | 63 | 54 | 71 |
| -Year | | 1980 | 1954 | 1954 | 1964 | 1953 | 1963 | 1986 | 1946 | 1952 | 1950 | 1937 | 1955 | MAR 1954 |
| Peak Gust | | | | | | | | | | | | | | |
| -Direction (!!!) | 6 | N | S | NW | NW | SW | SW | NW | SW | S | NW | SE | S | SW |
| -Speed (mph) | 6 | 59 | 54 | 59 | 54 | 69 | 53 | 58 | 67 | 55 | 63 | 52 | 40 | 69 |
| -Date | | 1988 | 1989 | 1989 | 1984 | 1989 | 1989 | 1986 | 1989 | 1989 | 1985 | 1988 | 1988 | MAY 1989 |

**See Reference Notes to this table on the following page.**

PRECIPITATION (inches)  SALT LAKE CITY, UTAH

**TABLE 2**

| YEAR | JAN | FEB | MAR | APR | MAY | JUNE | JULY | AUG | SEP | OCT | NOV | DEC | ANNUAL |
|------|-----|-----|-----|-----|-----|------|------|-----|-----|-----|-----|-----|--------|
| 1961 | 0.09 | 2.06 | 1.85 | 0.95 | 0.24 | 0.09 | 0.54 | 1.20 | 1.10 | 1.60 | 1.15 | 0.88 | 11.75 |
| 1962 | 0.84 | 1.43 | 2.34 | 2.98 | 2.12 | 0.49 | 2.52 | 0.26 | 0.27 | 0.93 | 0.44 | 0.28 | 14.90 |
| 1963 | 0.53 | 0.67 | 2.11 | 3.86 | 0.23 | 1.67 | T | 0.54 | 1.08 | 1.05 | 1.56 | 0.79 | 14.09 |
| 1964 | 0.94 | 0.35 | 2.26 | 2.69 | 2.77 | 2.61 | 0.26 | 0.17 | 0.13 | 0.45 | 1.42 | 3.82 | 17.87 |
| 1965 | 2.13 | 1.13 | 0.14 | 2.30 | 2.02 | 1.87 | 1.50 | 2.08 | 1.93 | 0.39 | 1.13 | 1.81 | 18.43 |
| 1966 | 0.41 | 1.19 | 1.21 | 1.43 | 0.51 | 0.07 | 0.33 | 0.22 | 0.83 | 1.18 | 0.75 | 0.86 | 8.99 |
| 1967 | 2.05 | 0.67 | 1.94 | 2.08 | 2.15 | 2.73 | 1.14 | 0.07 | 0.73 | 0.66 | 0.66 | 1.64 | 16.52 |
| 1968 | 0.46 | 2.32 | 2.21 | 2.82 | 2.18 | 1.58 | 0.09 | 3.66 | 0.56 | 1.64 | 1.32 | 2.27 | 21.11 |
| 1969 | 1.69 | 2.84 | 0.57 | 1.38 | 0.18 | 2.83 | 1.51 | 0.34 | 0.18 | 1.96 | 0.92 | 1.69 | 16.09 |
| 1970 | 1.24 | 0.94 | 1.01 | 3.25 | 0.89 | 1.63 | 0.86 | 0.57 | 2.80 | 1.61 | 2.27 | 2.80 | 19.87 |
| 1971 | 1.06 | 2.13 | 1.01 | 2.16 | 1.34 | 0.64 | 0.94 | 2.15 | 1.75 | 3.23 | 1.03 | 1.35 | 18.79 |
| 1972 | 1.22 | 0.48 | 1.18 | 3.62 | 0.14 | 0.15 | 0.06 | 0.21 | 1.36 | 2.74 | 1.36 | 3.22 | 15.74 |
| 1973 | 1.49 | 0.91 | 2.67 | 1.64 | 1.74 | 0.19 | 1.07 | 1.16 | 4.07 | 0.67 | 2.52 | 2.26 | 20.39 |
| 1974 | 1.80 | 1.65 | 0.97 | 4.57 | 0.39 | 0.28 | 0.18 | 0.32 | 0.03 | 2.03 | 0.90 | 1.34 | 14.46 |
| 1975 | 1.28 | 1.24 | 3.44 | 2.46 | 2.58 | 1.81 | 0.28 | 0.10 | 0.08 | 1.91 | 1.71 | 1.03 | 17.92 |
| 1976 | 0.63 | 1.90 | 1.90 | 2.47 | 0.99 | 1.24 | 1.55 | 0.82 | 0.16 | 0.57 | 0.03 | 0.08 | 12.34 |
| 1977 | 0.76 | 0.64 | 3.10 | 0.59 | 4.76 | 0.06 | 0.61 | 1.85 | 1.85 | 0.83 | 1.20 | 1.42 | 17.67 |
| 1978 | 2.33 | 1.96 | 3.47 | 2.90 | 1.57 | 0.06 | 0.06 | 0.92 | 2.51 | T | 1.73 | 0.58 | 18.09 |
| 1979 | 0.72 | 1.05 | 0.80 | 1.04 | 0.84 | 0.35 | 0.40 | 0.63 | 0.05 | 1.29 | 0.98 | 0.55 | 8.70 |
| 1980 | 2.87 | 2.25 | 2.46 | 0.89 | 2.70 | 0.42 | 1.34 | 0.26 | 0.72 | 1.74 | 1.17 | 0.37 | 17.19 |
| 1981 | 0.64 | 0.81 | 2.11 | 0.45 | 3.68 | 1.03 | 0.33 | 0.23 | 0.48 | 3.91 | 1.03 | 1.89 | 16.59 |
| 1982 | 1.08 | 0.53 | 2.39 | 1.63 | 1.86 | 0.66 | 2.57 | 0.56 | 7.04 | 1.87 | 0.75 | 1.92 | 22.86 |
| 1983 | 1.19 | 1.36 | 3.97 | 1.63 | 2.58 | 0.62 | 1.02 | 2.64 | 1.03 | 1.62 | 2.23 | 4.37 | 24.26 |
| 1984 | 0.50 | 0.95 | 1.76 | 4.43 | 1.17 | 1.86 | 1.72 | 1.49 | 1.72 | 3.70 | 1.45 | 0.80 | 21.55 |
| 1985 | 0.91 | 0.85 | 1.80 | 0.64 | 2.95 | 1.30 | 0.85 | 0.03 | 1.98 | 1.61 | 2.63 | 1.42 | 16.97 |
| 1986 | 0.86 | 1.28 | 2.32 | 4.55 | 3.39 | 0.42 | 0.85 | 1.32 | 2.75 | 0.39 | 1.17 | 0.10 | 19.40 |
| 1987 | 1.53 | 1.41 | 1.52 | 0.79 | 2.41 | 0.19 | 0.79 | 0.36 | 0.05 | 1.18 | 1.17 | 1.10 | 12.50 |
| 1988 | 1.06 | 0.13 | 0.94 | 1.84 | 2.16 | 0.03 | 0.04 | 0.22 | 0.07 | 0.01 | 2.17 | 0.62 | 9.29 |
| 1989 | 0.56 | 1.57 | 1.77 | 0.46 | 1.83 | 0.22 | 0.39 | 0.90 | 0.49 | 1.82 | 0.73 | 0.13 | 10.87 |
| 1990 | 0.57 | 0.35 | 2.17 | 1.14 | 1.65 | 0.66 | 0.64 | 0.46 | 0.56 | 0.69 | 1.24 | 0.56 | 10.69 |
| Record Mean | 1.27 | 1.32 | 1.86 | 1.98 | 1.79 | 0.87 | 0.63 | 0.87 | 0.95 | 1.41 | 1.36 | 1.35 | 15.67 |

**TABLE 3**  AVERAGE TEMPERATURE (deg. F)  SALT LAKE CITY, UTAH

| YEAR | JAN | FEB | MAR | APR | MAY | JUNE | JULY | AUG | SEP | OCT | NOV | DEC | ANNUAL |
|------|-----|-----|-----|-----|-----|------|------|-----|-----|-----|-----|-----|--------|
| 1961 | 28.7 | 38.1 | 42.9 | 50.1 | 60.8 | 74.7 | 79.9 | 77.8 | 60.0 | 50.0 | 35.3 | 28.2 | 52.2 |
| 1962 | 20.5 | 31.4 | 35.1 | 52.8 | 58.7 | 68.2 | 75.9 | 73.1 | 65.8 | 55.3 | 41.6 | 28.4 | 50.6 |
| 1963 | 19.5 | 38.6 | 39.4 | 44.3 | 60.7 | 63.3 | 77.8 | 77.9 | 67.8 | 57.8 | 38.9 | 24.4 | 50.9 |
| 1964 | 21.9 | 25.8 | 32.0 | 45.6 | 55.8 | 63.2 | 77.5 | 71.9 | 61.5 | 53.0 | 37.8 | 33.3 | 48.3 |
| 1965 | 31.0 | 33.0 | 36.8 | 51.0 | 54.7 | 64.8 | 75.0 | 70.9 | 57.5 | 54.5 | 46.1 | 30.2 | 50.5 |
| 1966 | 30.6 | 29.4 | 41.6 | 49.6 | 62.7 | 69.2 | 80.1 | 74.1 | 67.5 | 49.9 | 43.1 | 29.2 | 52.3 |
| 1967 | 29.4 | 37.5 | 44.2 | 46.1 | 56.3 | 64.6 | 78.4 | 78.6 | 66.7 | 52.4 | 43.0 | 25.1 | 51.8 |
| 1968 | 24.5 | 38.2 | 44.7 | 45.4 | 56.4 | 67.5 | 78.3 | 69.4 | 61.4 | 51.7 | 38.5 | 26.8 | 50.2 |
| 1969 | 32.2 | 28.7 | 38.4 | 50.4 | 64.0 | 64.8 | 76.6 | 77.6 | 69.7 | 47.7 | 39.5 | 32.4 | 51.9 |
| 1970 | 34.6 | 40.4 | 40.6 | 44.2 | 58.8 | 67.6 | 76.6 | 77.7 | 59.0 | 47.1 | 42.6 | 29.2 | 51.5 |
| 1971 | 32.4 | 34.9 | 40.4 | 48.2 | 56.6 | 67.5 | 76.4 | 76.9 | 59.8 | 47.5 | 37.6 | 26.9 | 50.4 |
| 1972 | 29.8 | 37.8 | 46.9 | 48.1 | 60.5 | 71.9 | 77.2 | 75.8 | 63.9 | 53.6 | 39.4 | 22.7 | 52.3 |
| 1973 | 19.6 | 32.3 | 41.8 | 47.6 | 61.6 | 70.2 | 76.6 | 76.6 | 61.5 | 54.1 | 40.5 | 33.4 | 51.3 |
| 1974 | 26.7 | 31.4 | 45.2 | 48.1 | 58.8 | 73.4 | 79.2 | 74.2 | 66.5 | 54.7 | 43.4 | 31.7 | 52.8 |
| 1975 | 27.4 | 35.5 | 41.1 | 44.3 | 54.3 | 64.8 | 78.4 | 73.4 | 65.4 | 53.4 | 37.3 | 32.9 | 50.7 |
| 1976 | 27.9 | 34.1 | 38.1 | 49.3 | 62.2 | 67.6 | 78.7 | 72.3 | 66.4 | 51.0 | 41.8 | 29.4 | 51.6 |
| 1977 | 26.8 | 35.8 | 37.7 | 54.1 | 55.0 | 73.2 | 77.3 | 75.0 | 66.4 | 55.6 | 42.5 | 37.9 | 53.2 |
| 1978 | 36.3 | 39.8 | 48.0 | 50.2 | 56.0 | 69.2 | 78.0 | 74.0 | 64.0 | 55.5 | 41.0 | 26.8 | 53.3 |
| 1979 | 22.1 | 32.5 | 43.2 | 51.1 | 60.2 | 70.1 | 78.9 | 75.6 | 71.4 | 56.7 | 36.5 | 32.9 | 52.6 |
| 1980 | 33.7 | 36.0 | 41.5 | 52.7 | 57.0 | 67.5 | 77.6 | 74.1 | 66.3 | 52.6 | 41.3 | 33.6 | 52.8 |
| 1981 | 32.1 | 38.3 | 44.1 | 53.4 | 57.6 | 69.6 | 78.2 | 78.0 | 68.5 | 50.5 | 44.3 | 36.4 | 54.3 |
| 1982 | 29.8 | 32.3 | 43.3 | 46.5 | 56.7 | 68.0 | 75.5 | 78.4 | 64.0 | 48.8 | 38.1 | 29.9 | 51.0 |
| 1983 | 35.2 | 39.4 | 44.6 | 45.9 | 55.8 | 67.7 | 76.6 | 77.8 | 67.8 | 56.0 | 43.0 | 31.9 | 53.5 |
| 1984 | 23.8 | 25.8 | 40.1 | 48.5 | 61.6 | 67.3 | 78.5 | 77.2 | 66.5 | 49.5 | 42.7 | 29.9 | 51.0 |
| 1985 | 24.2 | 25.6 | 40.8 | 55.7 | 63.9 | 72.5 | 80.7 | 76.5 | 62.7 | 53.1 | 37.4 | 27.7 | 51.7 |
| 1986 | 29.0 | 41.4 | 47.7 | 48.8 | 57.2 | 73.5 | 74.2 | 77.9 | 60.2 | 51.3 | 40.9 | 29.8 | 52.7 |
| 1987 | 26.5 | 36.1 | 42.8 | 55.9 | 62.7 | 71.6 | 75.7 | 74.7 | 66.5 | 56.4 | 40.8 | 30.5 | 53.4 |
| 1988 | 25.0 | 34.8 | 41.4 | 52.0 | 59.6 | 75.7 | 80.9 | 76.5 | 63.8 | 60.0 | 41.1 | 28.1 | 53.2 |
| 1989 | 22.3 | 25.3 | 45.8 | 54.8 | 59.9 | 69.2 | 81.1 | 75.1 | 66.4 | 53.4 | 40.5 | 31.4 | 52.1 |
| 1990 | 33.4 | 32.8 | 45.0 | 54.9 | 57.8 | 72.0 | 78.9 | 76.2 | 72.0 | 54.0 | 41.4 | 21.0 | 53.3 |
| Record Mean | 28.1 | 33.3 | 41.0 | 49.3 | 58.4 | 68.4 | 77.4 | 75.5 | 65.2 | 53.2 | 40.5 | 31.3 | 51.8 |
| Max | 36.2 | 41.7 | 50.6 | 60.2 | 70.4 | 81.8 | 91.3 | 89.0 | 78.5 | 65.0 | 50.2 | 39.1 | 62.8 |
| Min | 20.0 | 24.9 | 31.3 | 38.4 | 46.3 | 54.9 | 63.4 | 61.9 | 51.9 | 41.3 | 30.9 | 23.4 | 40.7 |

## REFERENCE NOTES FOR TABLES 1, 2, 3 and 6    (SALT LAKE CITY, UT)

### GENERAL

T - TRACE AMOUNT
BLANK ENTRIES DENOTE MISSING/UNREPORTED DATA.
# INDICATES A STATION OR INSTRUMENT RELOCATION.

### SPECIFIC

#### TABLE 1

(a) - LENGTH OF RECORD IN YEARS. ALTHOUGH INDIVIDUAL MONTHS MAY BE MISSING.

* LESS THAN .05

NORMALS — BASED ON THE 1951-1980 RECORD PERIOD.
EXTREMES — DATES ARE THE MOST RECENT OCCURRENCE.
WIND DIR. — NUMERALS SHOW TENS OF DEGREES CLOCKWISE FROM TRUE NORTH. "00" INDICATES CALM.
RESULTANT WIND DIRECTIONS ARE GIVEN TO WHOLE DEGREES.

#### TABLE 3
MAX AND MIN ARE LONG-TERM MEAN DAILY MAXIMUM AND MEAN DAILY MINIMUM TEMPERATURES.

### EXCEPTIONS

#### TABLES 2, 3, and 6

RECORD MEANS ARE THROUGH THE CURRENT YEAR, BEGINNING IN    1874 FOR TEMPERATURE
1874 FOR PRECIPITATION
1929 FOR SNOWFALL

**TABLE 4**    HEATING DEGREE DAYS Base 65 deg. F    SALT LAKE CITY, UTAH

| SEASON | JULY | AUG | SEP | OCT | NOV | DEC | JAN | FEB | MAR | APR | MAY | JUNE | TOTAL |
|---|---|---|---|---|---|---|---|---|---|---|---|---|---|
| 1961-62 | 0 | 0 | 207 | 461 | 881 | 1132 | 1373 | 936 | 921 | 369 | 220 | 75 | 6575 |
| 1962-63 | 3 | 17 | 59 | 322 | 695 | 1128 | 1403 | 731 | 787 | 614 | 135 | 98 | 5992 |
| 1963-64 | 0 | 1 | 18 | 243 | 777 | 1252 | 1331 | 1130 | 1016 | 576 | 303 | 125 | 6772 |
| 1964-65 | 0 | 44 | 134 | 365 | 808 | 975 | 1046 | 889 | 869 | 414 | 316 | 61 | 5921 |
| 1965-66 | 0 | 20 | 239 | 317 | 564 | 1069 | 1058 | 989 | 717 | 456 | 140 | 40 | 5609 |
| 1966-67 | 0 | 4 | 57 | 460 | 649 | 1101 | 1097 | 763 | 638 | 564 | 287 | 76 | 5696 |
| 1967-68 | 0 | 0 | 57 | 387 | 653 | 1228 | 1246 | 772 | 622 | 583 | 276 | 57 | 5881 |
| 1968-69 | 3 | 49 | 166 | 407 | 786 | 1174 | 1009 | 1010 | 818 | 433 | 75 | 67 | 5997 |
| 1969-70 | 1 | 0 | 17 | 530 | 759 | 1003 | 935 | 681 | 754 | 619 | 218 | 69 | 5586 |
| 1970-71 | 0 | 0 | 218 | 550 | 667 | 1103 | 1002 | 836 | 754 | 499 | 258 | 55 | 5942 |
| 1971-72 | 0 | 0 | 201 | 535 | 817 | 1176 | 1085 | 783 | 556 | 499 | 168 | 2 | 5822 |
| 1972-73 | 0 | 0 | 110 | 347 | 761 | 1307 | 1400 | 909 | 711 | 515 | 135 | 67 | 6262 |
| 1973-74 | 1 | 0 | 140 | 333 | 732 | 975 | 1181 | 935 | 603 | 502 | 214 | 41 | 5657 |
| 1974-75 | 0 | 5 | 54 | 316 | 638 | 1025 | 1157 | 734 | 734 | 613 | 334 | 92 | 5787 |
| 1975-76 | 0 | 1 | 62 | 365 | 825 | 989 | 1144 | 890 | 826 | 464 | 112 | 67 | 5745 |
| 1976-77 | 0 | 7 | 37 | 432 | 689 | 1096 | 1175 | 813 | 838 | 333 | 304 | 0 | 5724 |
| 1977-78 | 0 | 11 | 73 | 282 | 670 | 835 | 880 | 697 | 522 | 433 | 293 | 36 | 4732 |
| 1978-79 | 0 | 12 | 144 | 284 | 714 | 1178 | 1327 | 902 | 666 | 414 | 196 | 57 | 5894 |
| 1979-80 | 0 | 0 | 7 | 270 | 846 | 987 | 964 | 835 | 723 | 371 | 250 | 77 | 5330 |
| 1980-81 | 0 | 10 | 57 | 379 | 704 | 965 | 1013 | 742 | 641 | 346 | 233 | 46 | 5136 |
| 1981-82 | 0 | 0 | 34 | 444 | 614 | 879 | 1087 | 909 | 668 | 548 | 259 | 62 | 5504 |
| 1982-83 | 7 | 0 | 134 | 495 | 800 | 1080 | 916 | 710 | 624 | 569 | 314 | 36 | 5685 |
| 1983-84 | 6 | 0 | 49 | 276 | 650 | 1018 | 1269 | 1130 | 763 | 493 | 157 | 76 | 5887 |
| 1984-85 | 0 | 0 | 98 | 480 | 662 | 1084 | 1260 | 1097 | 740 | 285 | 109 | 17 | 5832 |
| 1985-86 | 0 | 0 | 140 | 360 | 821 | 1151 | 1110 | 655 | 527 | 477 | 283 | 14 | 5538 |
| 1986-87 | 6 | 0 | 203 | 416 | 720 | 1085 | 1186 | 803 | 679 | 291 | 123 | 17 | 5529 |
| 1987-88 | 0 | 0 | 51 | 260 | 719 | 1060 | 1235 | 870 | 723 | 381 | 222 | 3 | 5524 |
| 1988-89 | 0 | 0 | 142 | 158 | 711 | 1138 | 1318 | 1105 | 587 | 313 | 193 | 35 | 5700 |
| 1989-90 | 0 | 15 | 44 | 355 | 729 | 1036 | 971 | 895 | 612 | 297 | 232 | 30 | 5216 |
| 1990-91 | 0 | 0 | 17 | 347 | 704 | 1359 | | | | | | | |

**TABLE 5**    COOLING DEGREE DAYS Base 65 deg. F    SALT LAKE CITY, UTAH

| YEAR | JAN | FEB | MAR | APR | MAY | JUNE | JULY | AUG | SEP | OCT | NOV | DEC | TOTAL |
|---|---|---|---|---|---|---|---|---|---|---|---|---|---|
| 1969 | 0 | 0 | 0 | 1 | 53 | 68 | 366 | 398 | 164 | 0 | 0 | 0 | 1050 |
| 1970 | 0 | 0 | 0 | 0 | 32 | 152 | 365 | 398 | 46 | 0 | 0 | 0 | 993 |
| 1971 | 0 | 0 | 0 | 0 | 5 | 136 | 361 | 374 | 50 | 0 | 0 | 0 | 926 |
| 1972 | 0 | 0 | 0 | 0 | 34 | 213 | 386 | 340 | 85 | 0 | 0 | 0 | 1058 |
| 1973 | 0 | 0 | 0 | 0 | 38 | 226 | 370 | 367 | 44 | 3 | 0 | 0 | 1048 |
| 1974 | 0 | 0 | 0 | 2 | 31 | 303 | 446 | 298 | 108 | 3 | 0 | 0 | 1191 |
| 1975 | 0 | 0 | 0 | 0 | 9 | 89 | 439 | 269 | 80 | 14 | 0 | 0 | 900 |
| 1976 | 0 | 0 | 0 | 0 | 34 | 151 | 431 | 237 | 87 | 3 | 0 | 0 | 943 |
| 1977 | 0 | 0 | 0 | 12 | 2 | 254 | 389 | 328 | 123 | 0 | 0 | 0 | 1108 |
| 1978 | 0 | 0 | 0 | 0 | 21 | 167 | 411 | 299 | 120 | 0 | 0 | 0 | 1018 |
| 1979 | 0 | 0 | 0 | 2 | 54 | 214 | 439 | 336 | 208 | 21 | 0 | 0 | 1274 |
| 1980 | 0 | 0 | 0 | 9 | 10 | 159 | 399 | 301 | 99 | 1 | 0 | 0 | 978 |
| 1981 | 0 | 0 | 0 | 3 | 12 | 190 | 412 | 409 | 145 | 2 | 0 | 0 | 1173 |
| 1982 | 0 | 0 | 0 | 0 | 11 | 158 | 338 | 423 | 109 | 0 | 0 | 0 | 1039 |
| 1983 | 0 | 0 | 0 | 0 | 37 | 123 | 370 | 405 | 138 | 4 | 0 | 0 | 1077 |
| 1984 | 0 | 0 | 0 | 3 | 58 | 153 | 426 | 383 | 147 | 4 | 0 | 0 | 1174 |
| 1985 | 0 | 0 | 0 | 11 | 78 | 249 | 493 | 364 | 79 | 0 | 0 | 0 | 1274 |
| 1986 | 0 | 0 | 0 | 0 | 47 | 277 | 296 | 407 | 66 | 0 | 0 | 0 | 1093 |
| 1987 | 0 | 0 | 0 | 25 | 60 | 222 | 338 | 309 | 103 | 0 | 0 | 0 | 1057 |
| 1988 | 0 | 0 | 0 | 0 | 61 | 334 | 501 | 363 | 112 | 9 | 0 | 0 | 1380 |
| 1989 | 0 | 0 | 0 | 13 | 43 | 171 | 506 | 337 | 92 | 0 | 0 | 0 | 1162 |
| 1990 | 0 | 0 | 0 | 2 | 19 | 247 | 438 | 351 | 235 | 11 | 0 | 0 | 1303 |

**TABLE 6**    SNOWFALL (inches)    SALT LAKE CITY, UTAH

| SEASON | JULY | AUG | SEP | OCT | NOV | DEC | JAN | FEB | MAR | APR | MAY | JUNE | TOTAL |
|---|---|---|---|---|---|---|---|---|---|---|---|---|---|
| 1961-62 | 0.0 | 0.0 | 0.0 | 8.3 | 11.1 | 8.5 | 15.6 | 10.1 | 25.3 | 1.6 | 0.0 | 0.0 | 80.5 |
| 1962-63 | 0.0 | 0.0 | 0.0 | T | 2.4 | 0.9 | 7.4 | 0.5 | 16.0 | 14.3 | 0.0 | 0.0 | 41.5 |
| 1963-64 | 0.0 | 0.0 | 0.0 | T | 7.6 | 12.9 | 8.2 | 8.0 | 33.5 | 1.9 | 5.3 | 0.0 | 87.4 |
| 1964-65 | 0.0 | 0.0 | 0.0 | 0.0 | 6.7 | 6.2 | 15.7 | 9.5 | 1.1 | 2.4 | 5.3 | 0.0 | 46.9 |
| 1965-66 | 0.0 | 0.0 | 2.2 | 0.0 | 2.6 | 12.8 | 5.9 | 18.1 | 17.4 | 2.8 | 0.0 | 0.0 | 61.8 |
| 1966-67 | 0.0 | 0.0 | 0.0 | 3.6 | 3.2 | 8.7 | 30.4 | 4.5 | 11.8 | 11.4 | 1.0 | 0.0 | 74.6 |
| 1967-68 | 0.0 | 0.0 | 0.0 | 0.0 | 4.2 | 27.1 | 6.8 | 13.6 | 8.4 | 14.2 | T | T | 74.3 |
| 1968-69 | 0.0 | 0.0 | 0.0 | T | 8.7 | 33.3 | 13.7 | 27.9 | 5.4 | 0.2 | 0.0 | 0.0 | 89.2 |
| 1969-70 | 0.0 | 0.0 | 0.0 | 0.1 | 5.6 | 16.0 | 2.8 | 3.9 | 5.2 | 23.6 | 0.0 | 0.0 | 57.2 |
| 1970-71 | 0.0 | 0.0 | 0.0 | 0.3 | 0.7 | 25.8 | 13.6 | 8.7 | 1.7 | 1.4 | 0.0 | 0.0 | 61.1 |
| 1971-72 | 0.0 | 0.0 | 4.0 | 16.6 | 5.4 | 17.7 | 10.5 | 7.6 | 1.4 | 15.0 | 0.0 | 0.0 | 78.2 |
| 1972-73 | 0.0 | 0.0 | 0.0 | 6.0 | 1.1 | 35.2 | 20.9 | 3.6 | 17.8 | 2.6 | 0.0 | 0.0 | 87.2 |
| 1973-74 | 0.0 | 0.0 | 0.0 | 1.3 | 19.5 | 19.6 | 20.1 | 17.2 | 6.7 | 26.4 | T | T | 110.8 |
| 1974-75 | 0.0 | 0.0 | 0.0 | T | T | 8.8 | 12.5 | 7.9 | 22.8 | 13.1 | 7.5 | 0.0 | 72.6 |
| 1975-76 | 0.0 | 0.0 | 0.0 | 0.1 | 18.0 | 11.8 | 8.6 | 15.8 | 18.7 | 3.5 | 0.0 | T | 76.5 |
| 1976-77 | 0.0 | 0.0 | 0.0 | 0.0 | T | 1.2 | 8.6 | 3.2 | 41.9 | 4.8 | 0.6 | 0.0 | 60.3 |
| 1977-78 | 0.0 | 0.0 | 0.0 | 0.2 | 8.5 | 8.2 | 15.6 | 15.5 | 6.2 | 2.5 | 4.6 | 0.0 | 61.3 |
| 1978-79 | 0.0 | 0.0 | 1.0 | 0.0 | 17.4 | 8.7 | 13.8 | 12.4 | 7.7 | T | 0.0 | 0.0 | 64.6 |
| 1979-80 | 0.0 | 0.0 | 0.0 | 0.0 | 4.6 | 8.5 | 24.5 | 2.9 | 19.9 | 1.2 | T | 0.0 | 61.6 |
| 1980-81 | 0.0 | 0.0 | 0.0 | T | 3.9 | 3.3 | 8.9 | 2.7 | 11.1 | 0.3 | T | T | 30.2 |
| 1981-82 | 0.0 | 0.0 | 0.0 | 4.4 | 2.4 | 11.5 | 15.3 | 4.5 | 10.2 | 9.5 | T | T | 57.8 |
| 1982-83 | 0.0 | 0.0 | 0.0 | 0.2 | 1.0 | 20.1 | 6.2 | 1.0 | 13.3 | 9.0 | 5.0 | 0.0 | 55.8 |
| 1983-84 | 0.0 | 0.0 | 0.0 | 0.0 | 5.9 | 34.2 | 7.6 | 18.5 | 6.7 | 25.1 | T | T | 98.0 |
| 1984-85 | 0.0 | 0.0 | T | 20.4 | 6.6 | 12.9 | 12.7 | 11.4 | 8.0 | 0.7 | 0.0 | 0.0 | 72.7 |
| 1985-86 | 0.0 | 0.0 | 0.0 | T | 27.2 | 14.7 | 14.7 | 3.9 | 1.7 | 5.5 | T | 0.0 | 54.0 |
| 1986-87 | 0.0 | 0.0 | T | 0.0 | 4.4 | 1.7 | 16.4 | 9.9 | 3.0 | 2.1 | 0.0 | 0.0 | 37.5 |
| 1987-88 | 0.0 | 0.0 | 0.0 | 0.0 | 0.6 | 11.0 | 16.3 | 0.4 | 6.1 | T | 0.9 | 0.0 | 35.3 |
| 1988-89 | 0.0 | 0.0 | T | 0.0 | 8.5 | 12.5 | 9.4 | 27.5 | 2.1 | T | 0.0 | 0.0 | 60.0 |
| 1989-90 | 0.0 | 0.0 | 0.0 | 2.7 | 2.4 | 1.7 | 8.2 | 8.5 | 11.8 | 0.7 | T | T | 36.0 |
| 1990-91 | 0.0 | 0.0 | T | 0.0 | 4.8 | 14.3 | | | | | | | |
| Record Mean | 0.0 | 0.0 | 0.1 | 1.3 | 6.4 | 12.0 | 13.0 | 9.5 | 9.9 | 5.0 | 0.6 | T | 57.8 |

**See Reference Notes, relative to all above tables, on preceding page.**

Burlington is located on the eastern shore of Lake Champlain at the widest part of the lake. About 35 miles to the west lie the highest peaks of the Adirondacks, while the foothills of the Green Mountains begin 10 miles to the east and southeast.

Its northerly latitude assures the variety and vigor of a true New England climate, while thanks to the modifying influence of the lake, the many rapid and marked weather changes are tempered in severity. Due to its location in the path of the St. Lawrence Valley storm track and the lake effects, the city is one of the cloudiest in the United States.

Lake Champlain exercises a tempering influence on the local temperature. During the winter months and prior to the lake freezing, temperatures along the lake shore are often 5-10 degrees warmer than at the airport 3 1/2 miles inland. At the airport the average occurrence of the last freeze in spring is around May 10th and that of the first in fall is early October, giving a growing season of 145 days. This location is justly proud of its delightful summer weather. On average, there are few days a year with maxima of 90 degrees or higher. This moderate summer heat gives way to a cooler, but none the less pleasant fall period, usually extending well into October. High pressure systems moving down rapidly from central Canada or Hudson Bay produce the coldest temperatures during the winter months, but extended periods of very cold weather are rare.

Precipitation, although generally plentiful and well distributed throughout the year, is less in the Champlain Valley than in other areas of Vermont due to the shielding effect of the mountain barriers to the east and west. The heaviest rainfall usually occurs during summer thunderstorms, but excessively heavy rainfall is quite uncommon. Droughts are infrequent.

Because of the trend of the Champlain Valley between the Adirondack and Green Mountain ranges, most winds have a northerly or southerly component. The prevailing direction most of the year is from the south. Winds of damaging force are very uncommon.

Smoke pollution is nearly non-existent since there is no concentration of heavy industry here, however, haze has been on the increase over the years due to the large increase in industry to the north and south. During the spring and fall months, fog occasionally forms along the Winooski River to the north and east and may drift over the airport with favorable winds. In spite of the high percentage of cloudiness, periods of low aircraft ceilings and visibilities are usually of short duration, allowing this area to have one of the highest percentages of flying weather in New England.

## TABLE 1    NORMALS, MEANS AND EXTREMES

BURLINGTON, VERMONT

LATITUDE: 44°28'N    LONGITUDE: 73°09'W    ELEVATION: FT. GRND    332 BARO    350    TIME ZONE: EASTERN    WBAN: 14742

| | (a) | JAN | FEB | MAR | APR | MAY | JUNE | JULY | AUG | SEP | OCT | NOV | DEC | YEAR |
|---|---|---|---|---|---|---|---|---|---|---|---|---|---|---|
| **TEMPERATURE °F:** | | | | | | | | | | | | | | |
| Normals | | | | | | | | | | | | | | |
| -Daily Maximum | | 25.4 | 27.3 | 37.7 | 52.6 | 66.4 | 75.9 | 80.5 | 77.6 | 68.8 | 57.0 | 43.6 | 30.3 | 53.6 |
| -Daily Minimum | | 7.7 | 8.8 | 20.8 | 32.7 | 44.0 | 54.0 | 58.6 | 56.6 | 48.7 | 38.7 | 29.6 | 14.9 | 34.6 |
| -Monthly | | 16.6 | 18.1 | 29.2 | 42.7 | 55.2 | 64.9 | 69.6 | 67.1 | 58.8 | 47.9 | 36.6 | 22.6 | 44.1 |
| Extremes | | | | | | | | | | | | | | |
| -Record Highest | 46 | 63 | 62 | 84 | 91 | 93 | 97 | 99 | 101 | 94 | 85 | 75 | 65 | 101 |
| -Year | | 1950 | 1981 | 1946 | 1976 | 1977 | 1988 | 1977 | 1944 | 1945 | 1949 | 1948 | 1982 | AUG 1944 |
| -Record Lowest | 46 | -30 | -30 | -20 | 2 | 24 | 33 | 39 | 35 | 25 | 15 | -2 | -26 | -30 |
| -Year | | 1957 | 1979 | 1948 | 1972 | 1966 | 1986 | 1962 | 1976 | 1963 | 1972 | 1958 | 1980 | FEB 1979 |
| **NORMAL DEGREE DAYS:** | | | | | | | | | | | | | | |
| Heating (base 65°F) | | 1500 | 1313 | 1110 | 669 | 326 | 64 | 23 | 50 | 202 | 530 | 852 | 1314 | 7953 |
| Cooling (base 65°F) | | 0 | 0 | 0 | 0 | 22 | 61 | 165 | 115 | 16 | 0 | 0 | 0 | 379 |
| **% OF POSSIBLE SUNSHINE** | 46 | 41 | 48 | 50 | 49 | 54 | 58 | 64 | 60 | 53 | 47 | 31 | 32 | 49 |
| **MEAN SKY COVER (tenths)** | | | | | | | | | | | | | | |
| Sunrise - Sunset | 46 | 7.5 | 7.3 | 7.1 | 7.1 | 7.0 | 6.8 | 6.4 | 6.4 | 6.5 | 6.9 | 8.2 | 8.1 | 7.1 |
| **MEAN NUMBER OF DAYS:** | | | | | | | | | | | | | | |
| Sunrise to Sunset | | | | | | | | | | | | | | |
| -Clear | 46 | 4.4 | 4.4 | 5.8 | 5.1 | 4.8 | 4.8 | 5.3 | 5.9 | 6.0 | 6.0 | 2.5 | 2.9 | 57.8 |
| -Partly Cloudy | 46 | 6.6 | 6.6 | 6.9 | 7.6 | 9.1 | 10.8 | 13.1 | 11.8 | 10.0 | 7.8 | 5.4 | 5.9 | 101.7 |
| -Cloudy | 46 | 20.0 | 17.2 | 18.3 | 17.3 | 17.0 | 14.4 | 12.7 | 13.3 | 14.0 | 17.2 | 22.1 | 22.2 | 205.7 |
| Precipitation | | | | | | | | | | | | | | |
| .01 inches or more | 46 | 14.1 | 11.5 | 13.2 | 12.3 | 13.6 | 12.5 | 11.8 | 12.5 | 11.6 | 11.7 | 14.2 | 14.7 | 153.7 |
| Snow,Ice pellets | | | | | | | | | | | | | | |
| 1.0 inches or more | 46 | 5.2 | 4.7 | 3.7 | 1.1 | 0.1 | 0.0 | 0.0 | 0.0 | 0.0 | 0.* | 2.0 | 5.3 | 22.1 |
| Thunderstorms | 46 | 0.* | 0.0 | 0.4 | 0.8 | 2.5 | 5.0 | 6.2 | 5.3 | 2.0 | 0.6 | 0.3 | 0.* | 23.2 |
| Heavy Fog Visibility | | | | | | | | | | | | | | |
| 1/4 mile or less | 46 | 0.8 | 1.0 | 1.2 | 1.2 | 0.9 | 1.1 | 0.8 | 1.4 | 2.5 | 2.0 | 1.2 | 1.2 | 15.1 |
| Temperature °F | | | | | | | | | | | | | | |
| -Maximum | | | | | | | | | | | | | | |
| 90° and above | 25 | 0.0 | 0.0 | 0.0 | 0.1 | 0.6 | 1.2 | 2.8 | 1.2 | 0.1 | 0.0 | 0.0 | 0.0 | 5.9 |
| 32° and below | 25 | 22.0 | 18.4 | 8.9 | 0.5 | 0.0 | 0.0 | 0.0 | 0.0 | 0.0 | 0.* | 4.6 | 17.2 | 71.6 |
| -Minimum | | | | | | | | | | | | | | |
| 32° and below | 25 | 29.9 | 26.5 | 25.8 | 15.2 | 2.8 | 0.0 | 0.0 | 0.0 | 0.6 | 8.6 | 18.8 | 27.8 | 156.1 |
| 0° and below | 25 | 10.5 | 8.4 | 2.0 | 0.0 | 0.0 | 0.0 | 0.0 | 0.0 | 0.0 | 0.0 | 0.0 | 5.0 | 25.9 |
| **AVG. STATION PRESS.(mb)** | 17 | 1003.5 | 1004.8 | 1003.4 | 1001.5 | 1001.9 | 1001.5 | 1002.3 | 1004.1 | 1005.3 | 1005.8 | 1004.3 | 1004.6 | 1003.6 |
| **RELATIVE HUMIDITY (%)** | | | | | | | | | | | | | | |
| Hour 01 | 24 | 70 | 71 | 72 | 73 | 77 | 81 | 82 | 84 | 85 | 79 | 76 | 74 | 77 |
| Hour 07 (Local Time) | 24 | 71 | 73 | 74 | 74 | 74 | 77 | 78 | 83 | 86 | 81 | 78 | 76 | 77 |
| Hour 13 | 24 | 63 | 62 | 58 | 53 | 51 | 55 | 53 | 57 | 61 | 61 | 66 | 68 | 59 |
| Hour 19 | 24 | 66 | 65 | 62 | 58 | 58 | 61 | 61 | 66 | 73 | 70 | 72 | 72 | 65 |
| **PRECIPITATION (inches):** | | | | | | | | | | | | | | |
| Water Equivalent | | | | | | | | | | | | | | |
| -Normal | | 1.85 | 1.73 | 2.20 | 2.77 | 2.96 | 3.64 | 3.43 | 3.87 | 3.20 | 2.81 | 2.80 | 2.43 | 33.69 |
| -Maximum Monthly | 46 | 4.69 | 5.38 | 3.58 | 6.55 | 6.31 | 7.69 | 6.12 | 11.54 | 8.18 | 6.22 | 6.85 | 5.95 | 11.54 |
| -Year | | 1978 | 1981 | 1972 | 1983 | 1983 | 1973 | 1972 | 1955 | 1945 | 1959 | 1983 | 1973 | AUG 1955 |
| -Minimum Monthly | 46 | 0.42 | 0.21 | 0.38 | 0.93 | 0.29 | 1.09 | 1.23 | 0.72 | 0.87 | 0.50 | 0.63 | 0.62 | 0.21 |
| -Year | | 1989 | 1978 | 1965 | 1966 | 1977 | 1949 | 1979 | 1957 | 1948 | 1963 | 1952 | 1960 | FEB 1978 |
| -Maximum in 24 hrs | 46 | 1.53 | 1.93 | 1.62 | 2.16 | 2.26 | 2.83 | 2.69 | 3.59 | 3.26 | 2.17 | 1.80 | 2.60 | 3.59 |
| -Year | | 1978 | 1981 | 1971 | 1968 | 1955 | 1972 | 1985 | 1955 | 1983 | 1983 | 1959 | 1950 | AUG 1955 |
| Snow,Ice pellets | | | | | | | | | | | | | | |
| -Maximum Monthly | 46 | 42.4 | 34.3 | 33.1 | 21.3 | 3.9 | 0.0 | T | 0.0 | T | 5.1 | 19.2 | 56.7 | 56.7 |
| -Year | | 1978 | 1958 | 1971 | 1983 | 1966 | | 1989 | | 1963 | 1969 | 1971 | 1970 | DEC 1970 |
| -Maximum in 24 hrs | 46 | 14.5 | 16.5 | 15.6 | 15.6 | 3.5 | 0.0 | T | 0.0 | T | 5.1 | 10.1 | 17.0 | 17.0 |
| -Year | | 1961 | 1966 | 1971 | 1983 | 1966 | | 1989 | | 1963 | 1969 | 1958 | 1978 | DEC 1978 |
| **WIND:** | | | | | | | | | | | | | | |
| Mean Speed (mph) | 46 | 9.7 | 9.3 | 9.4 | 9.4 | 8.9 | 8.4 | 7.9 | 7.5 | 8.2 | 8.7 | 9.7 | 9.8 | 8.9 |
| Prevailing Direction | | | | | | | | | | | | | | |
| through 1963 | | S | S | N | S | S | S | S | S | S | S | S | S | S |
| Fastest Obs. 1 Min. | | | | | | | | | | | | | | |
| -Direction (!!!) | 6 | 16 | 15 | 16 | 16 | 24 | 16 | 18 | 17 | 17 | 15 | 16 | 16 | 16 |
| -Speed (MPH) | 6 | 38 | 37 | 33 | 29 | 32 | 32 | 35 | 26 | 32 | 30 | 35 | 33 | 38 |
| -Year | | 1989 | 1988 | 1988 | 1989 | 1986 | 1989 | 1989 | 1987 | 1989 | 1987 | 1989 | 1985 | JAN 1989 |
| Peak Gust | | | | | | | | | | | | | | |
| -Direction (!!!) | 6 | SE | S | S | S | W | S | S | SE | S | S | SE | SE | SE |
| -Speed (mph) | 6 | 49 | 54 | 48 | 40 | 51 | 44 | 60 | 41 | 52 | 47 | 62 | 46 | 62 |
| -Date | | 1989 | 1988 | 1987 | 1989 | 1988 | 1989 | 1989 | 1986 | 1989 | 1988 | 1989 | 1985 | NOV 1989 |

**See Reference Notes to this table on the following page.**

PRECIPITATION (inches)  BURLINGTON, VERMONT

**TABLE 2**

| YEAR | JAN | FEB | MAR | APR | MAY | JUNE | JULY | AUG | SEP | OCT | NOV | DEC | ANNUAL |
|---|---|---|---|---|---|---|---|---|---|---|---|---|---|
| 1961 | 0.93 | 1.65 | .56 | 3.96 | 2.63 | 3.71 | 4.98 | 3.24 | 2.63 | 2.50 | 2.31 | 1.75 | 31.91 |
| 1962 | 1.07 | 1.36 | .86 | 2.59 | 2.24 | 2.66 | 5.93 | 3.46 | 3.56 | 3.28 | 2.75 | 1.73 | 32.49 |
| 1963 | 1.14 | 1.22 | 2.35 | 2.52 | 2.37 | 1.90 | 2.79 | 5.11 | 1.42 | 0.50 | 3.95 | 0.96 | 26.23 |
| 1964 | 2.27 | 0.63 | 2.64 | 2.11 | 4.67 | 3.00 | 2.87 | 4.10 | 1.49 | 2.20 | 2.10 | 1.63 | 29.71 |
| 1965 | 0.60 | 0.93 | 1.38 | 2.16 | 1.05 | 4.08 | 2.91 | 6.27 | 3.19 | 3.32 | 2.65 | 1.47 | 29.01 |
| 1966 | 2.02 | 2.49 | 2.63 | 0.93 | 2.49 | 2.63 | 1.92 | 4.46 | 3.33 | 1.41 | 1.41 | 2.82 | 28.54 |
| 1967 | 1.65 | 0.77 | .51 | 3.77 | 3.19 | 3.12 | 4.60 | 3.79 | 3.06 | 3.03 | 2.12 | 2.61 | 32.22 |
| 1968 | 1.26 | 1.23 | 3.23 | 3.54 | 2.43 | 3.66 | 2.70 | 2.36 | 2.06 | 2.73 | 4.37 | 3.12 | 32.74 |
| 1969 | 2.43 | 0.94 | .93 | 2.93 | 3.10 | 4.01 | 2.40 | 3.71 | 1.88 | 1.62 | 4.98 | 4.59 | 34.52 |
| 1970 | 0.65 | 1.95 | 2.01 | 2.78 | 3.14 | 4.38 | 1.92 | 3.44 | 3.93 | 2.66 | 2.35 | 3.77 | 32.98 |
| 1971 | 1.24 | 2.95 | 2.71 | 2.65 | 2.97 | 2.29 | 4.29 | 4.85 | 1.63 | 2.16 | 2.29 | 1.93 | 31.99 |
| 1972 | 0.93 | 1.69 | 3.58 | 2.26 | 2.83 | 6.52 | 6.12 | 2.35 | 1.69 | 2.60 | 4.10 | 3.43 | 38.10 |
| 1973 | 2.13 | 1.55 | 3.09 | 3.80 | 5.38 | 7.69 | 3.02 | 5.41 | 5.02 | 1.93 | 2.31 | 5.95 | 46.28 |
| 1974 | 1.90 | 1.63 | 2.73 | 3.47 | 4.61 | 4.45 | 3.70 | 2.60 | 3.23 | 0.78 | 3.60 | 2.08 | 34.69 |
| 1975 | 2.20 | 2.01 | 3.86 | 1.71 | 1.17 | 2.47 | 3.77 | 2.85 | 4.12 | 3.85 | 3.14 | 2.36 | 32.51 |
| 1976 | 2.99 | 2.85 | 2.35 | 2.54 | 5.86 | 4.04 | 3.05 | 4.69 | 3.77 | 4.34 | 1.63 | 1.97 | 40.08 |
| 1977 | 1.61 | 1.78 | 2.97 | 3.13 | 0.29 | 2.06 | 3.34 | 6.27 | 6.33 | 5.02 | 4.22 | 3.42 | 40.44 |
| 1978 | 4.69 | 0.21 | 2.98 | 2.51 | 2.16 | 4.36 | 3.50 | 1.82 | 2.07 | 3.72 | 0.95 | 2.11 | 31.08 |
| 1979 | 4.50 | 0.60 | 2.15 | 3.61 | 3.12 | 1.39 | 1.23 | 3.42 | 3.84 | 2.31 | 3.89 | 1.50 | 31.56 |
| 1980 | 0.61 | 0.57 | 2.44 | 2.39 | 1.61 | 1.92 | 6.11 | 3.83 | 4.41 | 2.48 | 2.92 | 1.50 | 30.89 |
| 1981 | 0.49 | 5.38 | 1.32 | 3.05 | 3.76 | 5.58 | 3.22 | 5.58 | 6.24 | 5.26 | 2.73 | 2.03 | 42.13 |
| 1982 | 2.74 | 1.43 | 2.31 | 2.63 | 1.95 | 4.95 | 3.07 | 3.55 | 2.12 | 2.31 | 3.59 | 1.69 | 32.34 |
| 1983 | 3.09 | 1.66 | 2.60 | 6.55 | 6.31 | 1.49 | 3.92 | 4.31 | 3.77 | 4.38 | 6.85 | 5.23 | 50.16 |
| 1984 | 0.81 | 2.73 | .72 | 4.25 | 5.27 | 1.70 | 5.11 | 3.30 | 2.81 | 1.89 | 3.08 | 3.14 | 35.81 |
| 1985 | 1.46 | 1.26 | 2.46 | 1.90 | 3.53 | 3.76 | 4.42 | 2.67 | 3.30 | 3.31 | 3.68 | 1.59 | 33.34 |
| 1986 | 3.69 | 1.58 | 3.17 | 0.95 | 4.11 | 4.40 | 4.53 | 5.82 | 4.86 | 2.50 | 2.99 | 1.32 | 40.02 |
| 1987 | 1.91 | 0.19 | .33 | 1.42 | 2.69 | 4.42 | 2.79 | 2.09 | 3.58 | 3.28 | 2.24 | 1.17 | 27.41 |
| 1988 | 0.69 | 1.69 | .55 | 1.91 | 1.80 | 3.26 | 2.55 | 4.27 | 1.50 | 2.05 | 4.51 | 0.90 | 26.68 |
| 1989 | 0.42 | 0.67 | 2.60 | 1.89 | 3.19 | 3.68 | 3.65 | 7.30 | 5.98 | 2.98 | 2.41 | 1.26 | 36.03 |
| 1990 | 2.36 | 2.92 | .81 | 2.97 | 3.66 | 3.08 | 5.12 | 4.85 | 2.03 | 5.99 | 3.91 | 3.58 | 42.18 |
| Record Mean | 1.82 | 1.67 | 2.16 | 2.51 | 3.04 | 3.49 | 3.62 | 3.54 | 3.36 | 2.94 | 2.80 | 2.10 | 33.04 |

**TABLE 3**  AVERAGE TEMPERATURE (deg. F)  BURLINGTON, VERMONT

| YEAR | JAN | FEB | MAR | APR | MAY | JUNE | JULY | AUG | SEP | OCT | NOV | DEC | ANNUAL |
|---|---|---|---|---|---|---|---|---|---|---|---|---|---|
| 1961 | 9.2 | 18.6 | 26.5 | 38.5 | 51.1 | 63.5 | 68.2 | 66.8 | 65.4 | 49.6 | 36.5 | 23.9 | 43.2 |
| 1962 | 15.5 | 13.7 | 29.0 | 41.9 | 55.7 | 64.6 | 64.0 | 65.5 | 55.7 | 46.3 | 31.6 | 20.1 | 42.0 |
| 1963 | 16.6 | 10.7 | 26.0 | 40.3 | 52.4 | 65.5 | 70.3 | 62.9 | 53.5 | 51.7 | 40.3 | 12.9 | 41.9 |
| #1964 | 21.9 | 17.2 | 31.1 | 43.3 | 58.6 | 63.0 | 69.6 | 62.9 | 55.8 | 45.3 | 35.7 | 24.8 | 44.1 |
| 1965 | 13.7 | 20.0 | 27.4 | 39.3 | 57.2 | 62.9 | 65.1 | 66.0 | 58.7 | 46.8 | 32.9 | 28.6 | 43.2 |
| 1966 | 15.5 | 17.9 | 30.3 | 41.3 | 51.2 | 65.3 | 69.6 | 67.4 | 55.7 | 47.0 | 40.6 | 23.4 | 43.7 |
| 1967 | 23.9 | 11.7 | 25.3 | 40.7 | 47.6 | 67.6 | 70.1 | 67.0 | 58.1 | 48.8 | 32.9 | 25.5 | 43.3 |
| 1968 | 8.4 | 11.0 | 29.6 | 46.2 | 51.7 | 60.8 | 68.7 | 63.7 | 61.0 | 49.8 | 32.2 | 17.9 | 41.8 |
| 1969 | 16.5 | 18.5 | 24.3 | 41.4 | 51.3 | 64.1 | 67.8 | 68.6 | 57.9 | 45.8 | 36.3 | 18.6 | 42.6 |
| 1970 | 3.6 | 16.9 | 25.8 | 42.6 | 54.1 | 63.7 | 70.6 | 68.4 | 60.1 | 50.5 | 39.0 | 14.3 | 42.5 |
| 1971 | 9.7 | 20.0 | 24.1 | 37.3 | 54.5 | 64.9 | 68.9 | 67.1 | 63.5 | 53.8 | 33.5 | 24.3 | 43.5 |
| 1972 | 21.1 | 17.0 | 24.8 | 35.6 | 56.2 | 63.1 | 69.5 | 65.3 | 58.7 | 42.4 | 32.1 | 22.5 | 42.4 |
| 1973 | 21.5 | 14.6 | 37.1 | 44.6 | 53.6 | 66.9 | 70.6 | 72.1 | 58.5 | 49.3 | 37.2 | 27.4 | 46.1 |
| 1974 | 18.7 | 15.6 | 29.2 | 44.4 | 51.3 | 66.5 | 70.2 | 69.1 | 58.2 | 43.4 | 36.2 | 28.5 | 44.3 |
| 1975 | 23.6 | 20.7 | 28.0 | 37.1 | 62.3 | 66.4 | 74.6 | 69.1 | 58.0 | 50.4 | 42.1 | 20.1 | 46.1 |
| 1976 | 11.1 | 24.6 | 33.4 | 47.4 | 54.7 | 69.2 | 68.5 | 65.7 | 57.0 | 43.7 | 33.0 | 16.3 | 43.7 |
| 1977 | 11.1 | 20.5 | 37.6 | 45.3 | 60.0 | 64.7 | 69.6 | 67.5 | 58.7 | 46.6 | 40.0 | 22.4 | 45.3 |
| 1978 | 15.1 | 9.5 | 26.0 | 38.7 | 60.1 | 63.9 | 69.4 | 68.3 | 55.2 | 46.4 | 34.8 | 25.2 | 42.7 |
| 1979 | 18.0 | 7.5 | 36.9 | 43.5 | 58.5 | 65.3 | 72.2 | 65.9 | 58.6 | 48.1 | 41.3 | 29.0 | 45.4 |
| 1980 | 21.2 | 17.6 | 31.1 | 46.5 | 58.9 | 64.4 | 70.6 | 70.7 | 57.9 | 45.0 | 32.3 | 15.0 | 44.2 |
| 1981 | 8.9 | 32.9 | 33.5 | 46.7 | 58.2 | 66.1 | 71.1 | 67.1 | 59.3 | 44.9 | 36.9 | 25.3 | 45.9 |
| 1982 | 9.6 | 19.1 | 30.3 | 43.4 | 57.3 | 60.7 | 69.5 | 65.9 | 62.3 | 50.1 | 42.3 | 31.9 | 45.2 |
| 1983 | 21.0 | 22.3 | 33.0 | 42.3 | 52.9 | 66.3 | 71.3 | 68.6 | 62.9 | 48.2 | 38.1 | 22.4 | 45.8 |
| 1984 | 16.5 | 28.7 | 21.9 | 44.7 | 52.3 | 66.0 | 70.3 | 71.1 | 57.2 | 50.0 | 38.4 | 30.3 | 45.6 |
| 1985 | 13.4 | 22.5 | 31.6 | 44.3 | 55.8 | 61.7 | 69.6 | 67.5 | 60.3 | 49.1 | 36.9 | 21.3 | 44.7 |
| 1986 | 18.5 | 16.2 | 33.7 | 48.5 | 58.3 | 62.3 | 68.5 | 66.1 | 58.1 | 46.9 | 34.5 | 27.8 | 45.0 |
| 1987 | 18.1 | 15.0 | 33.3 | 48.6 | 55.5 | 66.3 | 71.5 | 66.7 | 59.5 | 45.9 | 37.0 | 28.5 | 45.5 |
| 1988 | 19.9 | 21.4 | 29.7 | 44.3 | 57.9 | 63.4 | 73.2 | 70.7 | 58.2 | 44.4 | 39.6 | 22.9 | 45.5 |
| 1989 | 23.7 | 19.7 | 28.4 | 41.6 | 59.6 | 67.2 | 71.7 | 67.7 | 61.4 | 50.3 | 36.4 | 7.6 | 45.5 |
| 1990 | 29.8 | 23.5 | 33.8 | 46.2 | 52.9 | 65.9 | 70.2 | 69.8 | 59.4 | 49.4 | 39.5 | 30.1 | 47.5 |
| Record Mean | 17.9 | 18.6 | 29.6 | 42.9 | 55.5 | 64.8 | 69.8 | 67.4 | 59.5 | 48.5 | 36.7 | 23.3 | 44.5 |
| Max | 26.4 | 27.4 | 38.0 | 52.1 | 65.7 | 74.9 | 79.9 | 77.2 | 68.9 | 57.2 | 43.5 | 30.6 | 53.5 |
| Min | 9.3 | 9.8 | 21.2 | 33.7 | 45.2 | 54.7 | 59.8 | 57.7 | 50.1 | 39.8 | 29.9 | 16.0 | 35.6 |

## REFERENCE NOTES FOR TABLES 1, 2, 3 and 6  (BURLINGTON, VT)

### GENERAL

T - TRACE AMOUNT
BLANK ENTRIES DENOTE MISSING/UNREPORTED DATA.
# INDICATES A STATION OR INSTRUMENT RELOCATION.

### SPECIFIC

**TABLE 1**

(a) - LENGTH OF RECORD IN YEARS. ALTHOUGH
INDIVIDUAL MONTHS MAY BE MISSING.
* LESS THAN .05

NORMALS — BASED ON THE 1951-1980 RECORD PERIOD.
EXTREMES — DATES ARE THE MOST RECENT OCCURRENCE.
WIND DIR. — NUMERALS SHOW TENS OF DEGREES
CLOCKWISE FROM TRUE NORTH.
"00" INDICATES CALM.
RESULTANT WIND DIRECTIONS ARE GIVEN TO WHOLE DEGREES.

**TABLE 3**
MAX AND MIN ARE LONG-TERM MEAN DAILY MAXIMUM
AND MEAN DAILY MINIMUM TEMPERATURES.

### EXCEPTIONS

**TABLE 1**

1. FASTEST MILE WIND IS THROUGH NOVEMBER 1983.

**TABLES 2, 3, and 6**

RECORD MEANS ARE THROUGH THE CURRENT YEAR,
BEGINNING IN  1893 FOR TEMPERATURE
1884 FOR PRECIPITATION
1944 FOR SNOWFALL

HEATING DEGREE DAYS Base 65 deg. F        BURLINGTON, VERMONT

**TABLE 4**

| SEASON | JULY | AUG | SEP | OCT | NOV | DEC | JAN | FEB | MAR | APR | MAY | JUNE | TOTAL |
|---|---|---|---|---|---|---|---|---|---|---|---|---|---|
| 1961-62 | 34 | 47 | 104 | 468 | 849 | 1266 | 1529 | 1433 | 1109 | 690 | 324 | 73 | 7926 |
| 1962-63 | 71 | 54 | 296 | 571 | 997 | 1386 | 1491 | 1514 | 1204 | 731 | 385 | 84 | 8784 |
| 1963-64 | 30 | 118 | 343 | 411 | 735 | 1609 | 1327 | 1380 | 1046 | 677 | 229 | 124 | 8029 |
| #1964-65 | 12 | 102 | 280 | 601 | 872 | 1238 | 1585 | 1256 | 1159 | 766 | 257 | 136 | 8264 |
| 1965-66 | 43 | 80 | 236 | 558 | 956 | 1125 | 1531 | 1313 | 1069 | 707 | 432 | 91 | 8141 |
| 1966-67 | 17 | 26 | 280 | 551 | 725 | 1285 | 1269 | 1490 | 1225 | 722 | 533 | 29 | 8152 |
| 1967-68 | 11 | 35 | 223 | 495 | 957 | 1216 | 1751 | 1561 | 1089 | 562 | 407 | 140 | 8447 |
| 1968-69 | 32 | 104 | 127 | 472 | 979 | 1451 | 1496 | 1298 | 1256 | 700 | 422 | 107 | 8444 |
| 1969-70 | 41 | 41 | 244 | 589 | 856 | 1434 | 1906 | 1342 | 1208 | 663 | 341 | 105 | 8770 |
| 1970-71 | 10 | 36 | 174 | 444 | 773 | 1567 | 1710 | 1257 | 1263 | 821 | 336 | 83 | 8474 |
| 1971-72 | 12 | 49 | 131 | 344 | 938 | 1254 | 1357 | 1387 | 1239 | 872 | 281 | 113 | 7977 |
| 1972-73 | 26 | 69 | 212 | 694 | 982 | 1344 | 1344 | 1410 | 855 | 608 | 345 | 86 | 7941 |
| 1973-74 | 10 | 17 | 256 | 480 | 825 | 1160 | 1431 | 1378 | 1101 | 618 | 430 | 37 | 7743 |
| 1974-75 | 2 | 6 | 224 | 665 | 858 | 1128 | 1276 | 1236 | 1141 | 831 | 152 | 82 | 7601 |
| 1975-76 | 0 | 45 | 208 | 448 | 681 | 1385 | 1669 | 1168 | 973 | 545 | 331 | 50 | 7503 |
| 1976-77 | 20 | 68 | 254 | 654 | 954 | 1505 | 1667 | 1240 | 842 | 590 | 223 | 89 | 8106 |
| 1977-78 | 24 | 53 | 207 | 564 | 740 | 1314 | 1539 | 1547 | 1202 | 781 | 225 | 90 | 8286 |
| 1978-79 | 49 | 38 | 295 | 571 | 897 | 1227 | 1452 | 1610 | 866 | 641 | 224 | 90 | 7960 |
| 1979-80 | 23 | 65 | 213 | 528 | 703 | 1107 | 1350 | 1371 | 1043 | 550 | 204 | 91 | 7248 |
| 1980-81 | 10 | 3 | 240 | 611 | 976 | 1545 | 1738 | 894 | 969 | 544 | 239 | 43 | 7812 |
| 1981-82 | 13 | 36 | 204 | 617 | 837 | 1224 | 1716 | 1277 | 1069 | 643 | 255 | 133 | 8024 |
| 1982-83 | 30 | 54 | 124 | 455 | 676 | 1021 | 1356 | 1188 | 983 | 675 | 367 | 77 | 7006 |
| 1983-84 | 19 | 36 | 148 | 518 | 803 | 1317 | 1500 | 1044 | 1331 | 602 | 395 | 68 | 7781 |
| 1984-85 | 6 | 24 | 241 | 460 | 792 | 1068 | 1592 | 1185 | 1029 | 615 | 296 | 118 | 7426 |
| 1985-86 | 11 | 42 | 169 | 489 | 835 | 1344 | 1436 | 1361 | 966 | 492 | 219 | 113 | 7477 |
| 1986-87 | 40 | 60 | 215 | 553 | 906 | 1144 | 1446 | 1397 | 975 | 488 | 328 | 48 | 7600 |
| 1987-88 | 19 | 66 | 185 | 584 | 833 | 1125 | 1389 | 1260 | 1088 | 614 | 238 | 136 | 7535 |
| 1988-89 | 15 | 52 | 212 | 635 | 755 | 1298 | 1273 | 1265 | 1128 | 691 | 188 | 45 | 7557 |
| 1989-90 | 2 | 43 | 164 | 451 | 849 | 1776 | 1084 | 1156 | 961 | 577 | 370 | 63 | 7496 |
| 1990-91 | 19 | 10 | 180 | 480 | 758 | 1074 | | | | | | | |

**TABLE 5**  COOLING DEGREE DAYS Base 65 deg. F        BURLINGTON, VERMONT

| YEAR | JAN | FEB | MAR | APR | MAY | JUNE | JULY | AUG | SEP | OCT | NOV | DEC | TOTAL |
|---|---|---|---|---|---|---|---|---|---|---|---|---|---|
| 1969 | 0 | 0 | 0 | 0 | 2 | 86 | 134 | 160 | 38 | 0 | 0 | 0 | 420 |
| 1970 | 0 | 0 | 0 | 0 | 11 | 75 | 189 | 150 | 36 | 1 | 0 | 0 | 462 |
| 1971 | 0 | 0 | 0 | 0 | 17 | 87 | 138 | 118 | 90 | 4 | 0 | 0 | 454 |
| 1972 | 0 | 0 | 0 | 0 | 14 | 64 | 169 | 81 | 30 | 0 | 0 | 0 | 358 |
| 1973 | 0 | 0 | 0 | 3 | 0 | 149 | 187 | 243 | 68 | 0 | 0 | 0 | 650 |
| 1974 | 0 | 0 | 0 | 5 | 9 | 89 | 171 | 140 | 27 | 1 | 0 | 0 | 442 |
| 1975 | 0 | 0 | 0 | 0 | 75 | 131 | 306 | 181 | 5 | 1 | 0 | 0 | 699 |
| 1976 | 0 | 0 | 0 | 24 | 19 | 185 | 135 | 97 | 23 | 0 | 0 | 0 | 483 |
| 1977 | 0 | 0 | 0 | 7 | 75 | 86 | 174 | 138 | 27 | 0 | 0 | 0 | 507 |
| 1978 | 0 | 0 | 0 | 0 | 79 | 64 | 194 | 146 | 6 | 0 | 0 | 0 | 489 |
| 1979 | 0 | 0 | 0 | 2 | 29 | 106 | 253 | 101 | 27 | 13 | 0 | 0 | 531 |
| 1980 | 0 | 0 | 0 | 0 | 24 | 78 | 189 | 184 | 34 | 0 | 0 | 0 | 509 |
| 1981 | 0 | 0 | 0 | 2 | 35 | 85 | 211 | 110 | 39 | 0 | 0 | 0 | 482 |
| 1982 | 0 | 0 | 0 | 1 | 24 | 11 | 179 | 90 | 51 | 0 | 0 | 0 | 356 |
| 1983 | 0 | 0 | 0 | 0 | 0 | 121 | 223 | 155 | 92 | 6 | 0 | 0 | 597 |
| 1984 | 0 | 0 | 0 | 0 | 7 | 106 | 175 | 217 | 15 | 3 | 0 | 0 | 523 |
| 1985 | 0 | 0 | 0 | 0 | 15 | 25 | 160 | 123 | 34 | 0 | 0 | 0 | 357 |
| 1986 | 0 | 0 | 0 | 4 | 19 | 38 | 156 | 104 | 14 | 0 | 0 | 0 | 335 |
| 1987 | 0 | 0 | 0 | 3 | 42 | 92 | 228 | 126 | 30 | 0 | 0 | 0 | 521 |
| 1988 | 0 | 0 | 0 | 0 | 19 | 96 | 274 | 238 | 15 | 3 | 0 | 0 | 645 |
| 1989 | 0 | 0 | 0 | 0 | 28 | 117 | 216 | 134 | 63 | 0 | 0 | 0 | 558 |
| 1990 | 0 | 0 | 0 | 16 | 1 | 95 | 189 | 165 | 18 | 6 | 0 | 0 | 490 |

**TABLE 6**  SNOWFALL (inches)        BURLINGTON, VERMONT

| SEASON | JULY | AUG | SEP | OCT | NOV | DEC | JAN | FEB | MAR | APR | MAY | JUNE | TOTAL |
|---|---|---|---|---|---|---|---|---|---|---|---|---|---|
| 1961-62 | 0.0 | 0.0 | 0.0 | T | 5.9 | 21.1 | 6.9 | 24.3 | 15.0 | 3.6 | 0.0 | 0.0 | 76.8 |
| 1962-63 | 0.0 | 0.0 | 0.0 | 0.1 | 4.3 | 16.8 | 12.8 | 15.8 | 21.5 | 1.3 | T | 0.0 | 72.6 |
| 1963-64 | 0.0 | 0.0 | 0.0 | T | 4.4 | 14.8 | 7.5 | 8.8 | 14.4 | 6.5 | 0.0 | 0.0 | 56.4 |
| 1964-65 | 0.0 | 0.0 | 0.0 | 0.1 | 1.2 | 23.0 | 11.8 | 4.3 | 7.9 | 1.1 | 0.0 | 0.0 | 49.4 |
| 1965-66 | 0.0 | 0.0 | 0.0 | 0.4 | 12.4 | 11.9 | 41.3 | 28.5 | 8.3 | 4.9 | 3.9 | 0.0 | 111.6 |
| 1966-67 | 0.0 | 0.0 | 0.0 | T | 2.4 | 36.2 | 20.5 | 12.6 | 6.1 | 4.7 | 2.6 | 0.0 | 85.1 |
| 1967-68 | 0.0 | 0.0 | 0.0 | T | 10.3 | 17.1 | 18.4 | 24.8 | 14.5 | T | 0.0 | 0.0 | 85.1 |
| 1968-69 | 0.0 | 0.0 | 0.0 | T | 18.8 | 28.6 | 15.8 | 17.0 | 12.4 | 3.7 | 0.0 | 0.0 | 96.3 |
| 1969-70 | 0.0 | 0.0 | 0.0 | 5.1 | 10.5 | 50.8 | 17.1 | 13.8 | 10.5 | 2.4 | 0.4 | 0.0 | 104.6 |
| 1970-71 | 0.0 | 0.0 | 0.0 | 0.1 | 2.7 | 56.7 | 17.1 | 23.1 | 33.1 | 12.6 | 0.0 | 0.0 | 145.4 |
| 1971-72 | 0.0 | 0.0 | 0.0 | 0.0 | 19.2 | 19.3 | 14.3 | 25.1 | 21.8 | 9.2 | 0.0 | 0.0 | 108.9 |
| 1972-73 | 0.0 | 0.0 | 0.0 | T | 12.2 | 39.0 | 11.4 | 18.5 | 2.3 | 6.3 | 0.0 | 0.0 | 89.7 |
| 1973-74 | 0.0 | 0.0 | 0.0 | 0.1 | 2.6 | 24.1 | 21.5 | 9.9 | 20.9 | 16.8 | 0.0 | 0.0 | 95.9 |
| 1974-75 | 0.0 | 0.0 | 0.0 | 0.1 | 11.5 | 16.8 | 14.8 | 22.0 | 14.3 | 13.3 | 0.0 | 0.0 | 90.9 |
| 1975-76 | 0.0 | 0.0 | 0.0 | T | 5.3 | 16.0 | 28.3 | 20.4 | 18.8 | 0.9 | T | 0.0 | 89.7 |
| 1976-77 | 0.0 | 0.0 | 0.0 | 0.9 | 13.3 | 11.5 | 24.2 | 16.4 | 3.6 | 1.8 | T | 0.0 | 77.7 |
| 1977-78 | 0.0 | 0.0 | 0.0 | 0.0 | 16.0 | 22.6 | 42.4 | 4.0 | 12.5 | 1.9 | T | 0.0 | 99.4 |
| 1978-79 | 0.0 | 0.0 | 0.0 | T | 5.7 | 24.1 | 37.9 | 6.6 | 1.6 | 8.4 | 0.0 | 0.0 | 84.3 |
| 1979-80 | 0.0 | 0.0 | 0.0 | 1.5 | 0.4 | 6.0 | 3.0 | 11.6 | 16.8 | 0.3 | 0.0 | 0.0 | 39.6 |
| 1980-81 | 0.0 | 0.0 | 0.0 | T | 12.2 | 17.5 | 8.7 | 11.9 | 12.3 | 1.1 | 0.0 | 0.0 | 64.7 |
| 1981-82 | 0.0 | 0.0 | 0.0 | T | 3.9 | 32.8 | 19.4 | 8.3 | 13.0 | 4.1 | 0.0 | 0.0 | 81.5 |
| 1982-83 | 0.0 | 0.0 | 0.0 | T | 0.8 | 5.0 | 22.5 | 18.3 | 11.9 | 21.3 | 0.7 | 0.0 | 80.5 |
| 1983-84 | 0.0 | 0.0 | 0.0 | T | 4.7 | 14.4 | 15.2 | 13.7 | 16.1 | 0.4 | T | 0.0 | 64.5 |
| 1984-85 | 0.0 | 0.0 | 0.0 | 0.0 | 6.0 | 29.3 | 25.9 | 10.9 | 16.6 | 2.7 | 0.0 | 0.0 | 91.4 |
| 1985-86 | 0.0 | 0.0 | 0.0 | T | 4.6 | 21.3 | 33.6 | 18.3 | 8.4 | T | T | 0.0 | 86.2 |
| 1986-87 | 0.0 | 0.0 | 0.0 | T | 10.5 | 7.7 | 34.4 | 7.0 | 6.0 | 2.1 | 0.0 | 0.0 | 67.7 |
| 1987-88 | 0.0 | 0.0 | 0.0 | 0.6 | 6.5 | 12.4 | 9.2 | 26.9 | 6.4 | 2.4 | 0.0 | 0.0 | 64.4 |
| 1988-89 | 0.0 | 0.0 | 0.0 | 0.3 | 0.6 | 12.4 | 6.6 | 8.5 | 9.7 | 2.3 | 0.0 | 0.0 | 40.4 |
| 1989-90 | T | 0.0 | 0.0 | 0.0 | 5.6 | 17.6 | 20.5 | | 10.2 | 2.1 | 0.0 | 0.0 | 76.7 |
| 1990-91 | 0.0 | 0.0 | T | T | 7.3 | 10.3 | | | | | | | |
| Record Mean | T | 0.0 | T | 0.2 | 6.8 | 18.7 | 18.8 | 16.5 | 12.0 | 3.6 | 0.2 | 0.0 | 76.9 |

**See Reference Notes, relative to all above tables, on preceding page.**

The city of Norfolk, Virginia, is located near the coast and the southern border of the state. It is almost surrounded by water, with the Chesapeake Bay immediately to the north, Hampton Roads to the west, and the Atlantic Ocean only 18 miles to the east. It is traversed by numerous rivers and waterways and its average elevation above sea level is 13 feet. There are no nearby hilly areas and the land is low and level throughout the city. The climate is generally marine. The geographic location of the city with respect to the principal storm tracks, is especially favorable, being south of the average path of storms originating in the higher latitudes and north of the usual tracks of hurricanes and other tropical storms.

The winters are usually mild, while the autumn and spring seasons usually are delightful. Summers, though warm and long, frequently are tempered by cool periods, often associated with northeasterly winds off the Atlantic. Temperatures of 100 degrees or higher occur infrequently. Extreme cold waves seldom penetrate the area and temperatures of zero or below are almost nonexistent. Winters pass, on occasion, without a measurable amount of snowfall. Most of the snowfall in Norfolk is light and generally melts within 24 hours.

Based on the 1951–1980 period, the average first occurrence of 32 degrees Fahrenheit in the fall is November 17 and the average last occurrence in the spring is March 23.

## TABLE 1     NORMALS, MEANS AND EXTREMES

NORFOLK, VIRGINIA

LATITUDE: 36 °54'N    LONGITUDE: 76 °12' W    ELEVATION: FT. GRND   24 BARO   44   TIME ZONE: EASTERN    WBAN: 13737

| | (a) | JAN | FEB | MAR | APR | MAY | JUNE | JULY | AUG | SEP | OCT | NOV | DEC | YEAR |
|---|---|---|---|---|---|---|---|---|---|---|---|---|---|---|
| **TEMPERATURE °F:** | | | | | | | | | | | | | | |
| Normals | | | | | | | | | | | | | | |
|   -Daily Maximum | | 48.1 | 49.9 | 57.5 | 68.2 | 75.7 | 83.2 | 86.9 | 85.7 | 80.2 | 69.8 | 60.8 | 51.9 | 68.2 |
|   -Daily Minimum | | 31.7 | 32.3 | 39.4 | 48.1 | 57.2 | 65.3 | 69.9 | 69.6 | 64.2 | 52.8 | 43.0 | 35.0 | 50.7 |
|   -Monthly | | 39.9 | 41.1 | 48.5 | 58.2 | 66.4 | 74.3 | 78.4 | 77.7 | 72.2 | 61.3 | 51.9 | 43.5 | 59.5 |
| Extremes | | | | | | | | | | | | | | |
|   -Record Highest | 41 | 78 | 81 | 88 | 97 | 97 | 101 | 103 | 104 | 99 | 95 | 86 | 80 | 104 |
|   -Year | | 1970 | 1989 | 1985 | 1960 | 1956 | 1964 | 1952 | 1980 | 1983 | 1954 | 1974 | 1978 | AUG 1980 |
|   -Record Lowest | 41 | -3 | 8 | 18 | 28 | 36 | 45 | 54 | 49 | 45 | 27 | 20 | 7 | -3 |
|   -Year | | 1985 | 1965 | 1980 | 1982 | 1966 | 1967 | 1979 | 1982 | 1967 | 1976 | 1950 | 1983 | JAN 1985 |
| **NORMAL DEGREE DAYS:** | | | | | | | | | | | | | | |
| Heating (base 65°F) | | 778 | 669 | 512 | 219 | 53 | 0 | 0 | 0 | 9 | 146 | 393 | 667 | 3446 |
| Cooling (base 65°F) | | 0 | 0 | 0 | 15 | 96 | 282 | 415 | 394 | 225 | 31 | 0 | 0 | 1458 |
| **% OF POSSIBLE SUNSHINE** | 25 | 55 | 57 | 62 | 63 | 64 | 67 | 63 | 63 | 62 | 59 | 57 | 57 | 61 |
| **MEAN SKY COVER (tenths)** | | | | | | | | | | | | | | |
| Sunrise - Sunset | 41 | 6.2 | 6.2 | 6.1 | 5.8 | 6.1 | 5.8 | 6.0 | 5.8 | 5.7 | 5.4 | 5.5 | 6.0 | 5.9 |
| **MEAN NUMBER OF DAYS:** | | | | | | | | | | | | | | |
| Sunrise to Sunset | | | | | | | | | | | | | | |
|   -Clear | 41 | 9.1 | 8.2 | 9.0 | 8.9 | 7.9 | 7.7 | 7.6 | 7.9 | 9.0 | 11.6 | 10.4 | 9.4 | 106.8 |
|   -Partly Cloudy | 41 | 6.5 | 6.2 | 7.4 | 9.0 | 9.8 | 11.6 | 11.7 | 12.1 | 9.5 | 7.1 | 8.0 | 7.2 | 106.0 |
|   -Cloudy | 41 | 15.4 | 13.9 | 14.6 | 12.1 | 13.3 | 10.8 | 11.6 | 11.0 | 11.4 | 12.3 | 11.6 | 14.5 | 152.5 |
| Precipitation | | | | | | | | | | | | | | |
| .01 inches or more | 41 | 10.4 | 10.4 | 10.9 | 10.1 | 9.9 | 9.3 | 11.2 | 10.5 | 7.9 | 7.6 | 8.1 | 9.0 | 115.2 |
| Snow,Ice pellets | | | | | | | | | | | | | | |
| 1.0 inches or more | 41 | 0.9 | 0.7 | 0.2 | 0.* | 0.0 | 0.0 | 0.0 | 0.0 | 0.0 | 0.0 | 0.0 | 0.3 | 2.1 |
| Thunderstorms | 41 | 0.4 | 0.6 | 1.9 | 2.8 | 4.9 | 6.0 | 8.2 | 7.0 | 2.6 | 1.3 | 0.5 | 0.4 | 36.5 |
| Heavy Fog Visibility | | | | | | | | | | | | | | |
| 1/4 mile or less | 41 | 2.2 | 2.6 | 1.9 | 1.4 | 2.0 | 1.1 | 0.6 | 1.1 | 1.2 | 2.2 | 1.9 | 2.2 | 20.4 |
| Temperature °F | | | | | | | | | | | | | | |
|   -Maximum | | | | | | | | | | | | | | |
|     90° and above | 41 | 0.0 | 0.0 | 0.0 | 0.5 | 1.5 | 6.6 | 11.5 | 8.9 | 2.8 | 0.1 | 0.0 | 0.0 | 31.9 |
|     32° and below | 41 | 2.8 | 1.2 | 0.1 | 0.0 | 0.0 | 0.0 | 0.0 | 0.0 | 0.0 | 0.0 | 0.0 | 1.1 | 5.2 |
|   -Minimum | | | | | | | | | | | | | | |
|     32° and below | 41 | 17.0 | 14.5 | 6.2 | 0.3 | 0.0 | 0.0 | 0.0 | 0.0 | 0.0 | 0.1 | 3.1 | 13.7 | 55.0 |
|     0° and below | 41 | 0.* | 0.0 | 0.0 | 0.0 | 0.0 | 0.0 | 0.0 | 0.0 | 0.0 | 0.0 | 0.0 | 0.0 | * |
| **AVG. STATION PRESS.(mb)** | 17 | 1018.3 | 1018.0 | 1016.4 | 1014.7 | 1014.8 | 1015.1 | 1015.8 | 1016.7 | 1017.5 | 1018.8 | 1018.7 | 1019.1 | 1017.0 |
| **RELATIVE HUMIDITY (%)** | | | | | | | | | | | | | | |
| Hour 01 | 41 | 72 | 72 | 72 | 73 | 80 | 83 | 84 | 86 | 84 | 82 | 76 | 72 | 78 |
| Hour 07 | 41 | 74 | 74 | 74 | 73 | 77 | 79 | 82 | 84 | 83 | 82 | 79 | 75 | 78 |
| Hour 13 (Local Time) | 41 | 59 | 57 | 54 | 50 | 55 | 56 | 59 | 61 | 61 | 59 | 56 | 58 | 57 |
| Hour 19 | 41 | 67 | 66 | 62 | 61 | 66 | 67 | 70 | 74 | 75 | 74 | 69 | 68 | 68 |
| **PRECIPITATION (inches):** | | | | | | | | | | | | | | |
| Water Equivalent | | | | | | | | | | | | | | |
|   -Normal | | 3.72 | 3.28 | 3.86 | 2.87 | 3.75 | 3.45 | 5.15 | 5.33 | 4.35 | 3.41 | 2.88 | 3.17 | 45.22 |
|   -Maximum Monthly | 41 | 9.93 | 6.23 | 8.50 | 7.25 | 10.12 | 9.72 | 13.73 | 11.19 | 13.80 | 10.12 | 7.01 | 6.10 | 13.80 |
|   -Year | | 1987 | 1983 | 1989 | 1984 | 1979 | 1963 | 1975 | 1967 | 1979 | 1971 | 1951 | 1983 | SEP 1979 |
|   -Minimum Monthly | 41 | 1.05 | 0.86 | 0.75 | 0.43 | 1.41 | 0.37 | 0.77 | 0.74 | 0.26 | 0.57 | 0.49 | 0.67 | 0.26 |
|   -Year | | 1981 | 1950 | 1986 | 1985 | 1986 | 1954 | 1983 | 1975 | 1986 | 1984 | 1965 | 1988 | SEP 1986 |
|   -Maximum in 24 hrs | 41 | 3.80 | 2.71 | 3.18 | 2.93 | 3.41 | 6.85 | 5.64 | 11.40 | 6.79 | 4.38 | 3.35 | 2.76 | 11.40 |
|   -Year | | 1967 | 1983 | 1958 | 1984 | 1980 | 1963 | 1969 | 1964 | 1959 | 1971 | 1952 | 1983 | AUG 1964 |
| Snow,Ice pellets | | | | | | | | | | | | | | |
|   -Maximum Monthly | 41 | 14.2 | 24.4 | 13.7 | 1.2 | 0.0 | 0.0 | 0.0 | 0.0 | 0.0 | 0.0 | 0.6 | 14.7 | 24.4 |
|   -Year | | 1966 | 1989 | 1980 | 1964 | | | | | | | 1950 | 1958 | FEB 1989 |
|   -Maximum in 24 hrs | 41 | 9.1 | 14.2 | 9.9 | 1.2 | 0.0 | 0.0 | 0.0 | 0.0 | 0.0 | 0.0 | 0.6 | 11.4 | 14.2 |
|   -Year | | 1973 | 1989 | 1980 | 1964 | | | | | | | 1950 | 1958 | FEB 1989 |
| **WIND:** | | | | | | | | | | | | | | |
| Mean Speed (mph) | 41 | 11.6 | 12.0 | 12.5 | 11.8 | 10.4 | 9.8 | 8.9 | 8.9 | 9.7 | 10.4 | 10.7 | 11.1 | 10.6 |
| Prevailing Direction | | | | | | | | | | | | | | |
|   through 1963 | | SW | NNE | SW | SW | SW | SW | SW | SW | NE | NE | SW | SW | SW |
| Fastest Obs. 1 Min. | | | | | | | | | | | | | | |
|   -Direction (!!) | 17 | 23 | 36 | 22 | 06 | 28 | 30 | 34 | 35 | 30 | 04 | 21 | 01 | 04 |
|   -Speed (MPH) | 17 | 39 | 44 | 46 | 39 | 38 | 46 | 46 | 46 | 46 | 48 | 40 | 39 | 48 |
|   -Year | | 1978 | 1973 | 1973 | 1978 | 1989 | 1977 | 1973 | 1979 | 1985 | 1982 | 1989 | 1989 | OCT 1982 |
| Peak Gust | | | | | | | | | | | | | | |
|   -Direction (!!) | 6 | N | E | W | SW | NW | SW | N | E | NW | NE | E | N | SW |
|   -Speed (mph) | 6 | 58 | 56 | 62 | 56 | 66 | 69 | 63 | 63 | 67 | 46 | 55 | 53 | 69 |
|   -Date | | 1987 | 1984 | 1989 | 1985 | 1984 | 1987 | 1986 | 1986 | 1985 | 1986 | 1985 | 1989 | JUN 1987 |

**See Reference Notes to this table on the following page.**

PRECIPITATION (inches)   NORFOLK, VIRGINIA

**TABLE 2**

| YEAR | JAN | FEB | MAR | APR | MAY | JUNE | JULY | AUG | SEP | OCT | NOV | DEC | ANNUAL |
|---|---|---|---|---|---|---|---|---|---|---|---|---|---|
| 1961 | 3.52 | 4.56 | 3.59 | 2.74 | 7.77 | 6.70 | 1.69 | 7.42 | 1.62 | 4.12 | 1.20 | 3.74 | 48.67 |
| 1962 | 5.56 | 2.50 | 4.32 | 4.49 | 3.68 | 3.03 | 9.05 | 4.09 | 3.07 | 4.48 | 4.06 | 3.80 | 52.13 |
| 1963 | 3.36 | 3.75 | 2.98 | 1.29 | 1.55 | 9.72 | 2.01 | 2.40 | 6.84 | 1.21 | 5.31 | 2.85 | 43.27 |
| 1964 | 4.56 | 4.56 | 2.26 | 2.38 | 1.56 | 2.58 | 7.33 | 10.58 | 12.26 | 5.55 | 1.14 | 2.95 | 57.71 |
| 1965 | 2.73 | 2.53 | 2.83 | 2.24 | 1.48 | 4.69 | 3.46 | 3.08 | 0.77 | 1.29 | 0.49 | 1.08 | 26.67 |
| 1966 | 4.86 | 3.83 | 1.50 | 1.68 | 5.95 | 1.82 | 4.26 | 5.24 | 3.39 | 1.25 | 1.05 | 3.13 | 37.96 |
| 1967 | 5.44 | 3.56 | 1.34 | 1.31 | 3.25 | 1.37 | 7.21 | 11.19 | 3.02 | 0.93 | 1.75 | 4.84 | 45.21 |
| 1968 | 3.62 | 2.01 | 4.76 | 3.17 | 2.16 | 3.07 | 4.23 | 2.04 | 1.51 | 4.44 | 3.56 | 3.14 | 37.71 |
| 1969 | 2.26 | 2.16 | 4.88 | 2.07 | 2.05 | 4.13 | 12.70 | 5.28 | 2.72 | 3.18 | 2.97 | 3.93 | 48.33 |
| 1970 | 2.27 | 3.97 | 3.37 | 3.19 | 2.58 | 4.10 | 5.33 | 2.04 | 1.72 | 1.30 | 2.34 | 3.01 | 35.22 |
| 1971 | 4.03 | 3.59 | 3.88 | 2.18 | 4.46 | 2.16 | 4.81 | 4.63 | 5.46 | 10.12 | 0.97 | 1.44 | 47.73 |
| 1972 | 2.94 | 3.50 | 2.55 | 2.15 | 3.35 | 4.93 | 4.65 | 1.60 | 6.91 | 4.09 | 4.12 |  | 46.23 |
| 1973 | 2.54 | 3.21 | 4.69 | 3.44 | 3.62 | 5.93 | 4.19 | 7.92 | 0.86 | 1.37 | 1.90 | 5.83 | 45.50 |
| 1974 | 3.52 | 2.98 | 5.16 | 3.74 | 3.74 | 4.76 | 5.47 | 8.33 | 4.40 | 1.23 | 3.81 | 3.62 | 47.96 |
| 1975 | 4.18 | 4.18 | 5.72 | 4.19 | 3.37 | 1.56 | 13.73 | 0.74 | 4.82 | 3.19 | 1.63 | 3.62 | 50.53 |
| 1976 | 2.51 | 1.50 | 2.21 | 0.99 | 3.74 | 1.59 | 5.19 | 2.62 | 3.51 | 2.90 | 2.38 | 3.22 | 32.36 |
| 1977 | 3.33 | 2.23 | 4.05 | 2.20 | 3.86 | 2.41 | 2.70 | 4.57 | 3.00 | 6.09 | 5.41 | 3.92 | 43.77 |
| 1978 | 6.32 | 1.91 | 7.80 | 2.90 | 5.64 | 7.84 | 4.19 | 1.66 | 1.17 | 1.50 | 4.40 | 2.31 | 47.64 |
| 1979 | 6.47 | 5.01 | 5.13 | 7.00 | 10.12 | 2.97 | 4.69 | 1.79 | 13.80 | 1.74 | 5.26 | 0.98 | 64.96 |
| 1980 | 4.54 | 2.91 | 4.40 | 3.25 | 5.17 | 1.39 | 1.85 | 4.54 | 1.47 | 3.28 | 1.78 | 5.77 | 41.18 |
| 1981 | 1.05 | 2.26 | 1.88 | 2.26 | 2.75 | 5.00 | 5.10 | 6.87 | 3.18 | 4.25 | 3.43 | 4.30 | 49.15 |
| 1982 | 3.35 | 5.81 | 3.04 | 1.71 | 3.07 | 4.22 | 5.83 | 6.51 | 3.63 | 5.29 | 3.24 | 6.10 | 49.47 |
| 1983 | 2.21 | 6.23 | 4.55 | 6.13 | 3.52 | 3.84 | 0.77 | 3.07 | 4.52 | 0.57 | 2.68 | 2.22 | 44.82 |
| 1984 | 2.77 | 4.66 | 5.09 | 7.25 | 6.23 | 1.50 | 7.66 | 2.25 | 1.94 | 0.57 | 2.68 | 0.79 | 44.81 |
| 1985 | 3.98 | 3.53 | 2.02 | 0.43 | 3.23 | 6.81 | 6.14 | 1.89 | 6.36 | 3.92 | 5.71 | 0.79 | 44.81 |
| 1986 | 2.52 | 2.71 | 0.75 | 3.31 | 1.41 | 1.51 | 2.59 | 4.80 | 0.26 | 1.67 | 1.21 | 3.74 | 26.48 |
| 1987 | 9.93 | 3.11 | 2.30 | 3.83 | 2.65 | 2.98 | 3.20 | 2.04 | 7.00 | 1.81 | 3.51 | 2.33 | 44.69 |
| 1988 | 3.12 | 2.70 | 2.11 | 3.53 | 5.49 | 3.83 | 2.93 | 5.69 | 1.74 | 2.85 | 4.02 | 0.67 | 38.68 |
| 1989 | 2.70 | 5.80 | 8.50 | 3.62 | 2.97 | 5.10 | 4.86 | 7.49 | 5.10 | 2.94 | 3.69 | 3.86 | 56.63 |
| 1990 | 3.26 | 2.93 | 3.49 | 3.55 | 3.79 | 3.51 | 4.06 | 11.85 | 1.00 | 3.73 | 1.68 | 2.67 | 45.52 |
| Record Mean | 3.33 | 3.38 | 3.74 | 3.23 | 3.71 | 4.00 | 5.58 | 5.32 | 3.86 | 3.12 | 2.66 | 3.19 | 45.14 |

**TABLE 3**   AVERAGE TEMPERATURE (deg. F)   NORFOLK, VIRGINIA

| YEAR | JAN | FEB | MAR | APR | MAY | JUNE | JULY | AUG | SEP | OCT | NOV | DEC | ANNUAL |
|---|---|---|---|---|---|---|---|---|---|---|---|---|---|
| 1961 | 35.0 | 43.6 | 53.1 | 55.5 | 63.6 | 72.4 | 80.6 | 77.7 | 75.3 | 60.6 | 53.2 | 41.5 | 59.4 |
| 1962 | 38.9 | 41.0 | 56.4 | 60.3 | 64.6 | 73.4 | 75.2 | 76.0 | 69.1 | 66.7 | 60.1 | 52.0 | 37.2 | 57.6 |
| 1963 | 37.1 | 35.7 | 53.4 | 60.3 | 64.6 | 73.2 | 77.3 | 76.7 | 74.4 | 70.8 | 57.7 | 54.6 | 46.5 | 57.7 |
| 1964 | 42.3 | 39.9 | 49.5 | 55.2 | 66.4 | 74.5 | 72.8 | 77.3 | 77.1 | 73.6 | 59.0 | 51.6 | 43.5 | 59.1 |
| 1965 | 39.7 | 41.0 | 44.4 | 54.5 | 69.7 | 72.8 | 76.7 | 77.1 | 73.6 | 59.0 | 51.6 | 43.5 | 58.6 |
| 1966 | 35.8 | 38.6 | 47.9 | 54.5 | 63.6 | 71.6 | 78.0 | 74.9 | 69.9 | 59.3 | 50.5 | 41.4 | 57.1 |
| 1967 | 45.7 | 39.9 | 47.7 | 58.0 | 61.2 | 71.2 | 76.3 | 75.2 | 66.5 | 45.9 | 44.0 | 41.4 | 57.5 |
| 1968 | 34.8 | 34.0 | 50.0 | 55.1 | 64.6 | 74.9 | 78.0 | 80.5 | 71.5 | 52.9 | 41.4 | 40.9 | 58.4 |
| 1969 | 38.5 | 39.8 | 44.7 | 59.8 | 67.4 | 77.1 | 79.2 | 76.2 | 71.1 | 62.2 | 49.1 | 40.9 | 58.9 |
| 1970 | 33.9 | 39.3 | 44.7 | 56.7 | 67.5 | 74.9 | 76.9 | 74.9 | 74.7 | 66.7 | 51.7 | 47.0 | 59.1 |
| 1971 | 38.6 | 44.7 | 46.9 | 55.9 | 65.0 | 76.0 | 77.2 | 75.7 | 73.2 | 66.7 | 52.4 | 52.3 | 60.4 |
| 1972 | 46.4 | 43.2 | 49.0 | 56.4 | 63.5 | 70.9 | 77.6 | 78.3 | 75.0 | 64.2 | 53.5 | 46.2 | 60.5 |
| 1973 | 40.5 | 39.7 | 52.3 | 58.5 | 66.9 | 76.9 | 78.3 | 78.5 | 77.4 | 58.7 | 53.5 | 46.0 | 60.9 |
| 1974 | 48.6 | 43.4 | 53.1 | 60.8 | 66.8 | 72.8 | 78.3 | 79.6 | 72.3 | 63.4 | 55.7 | 43.2 | 60.8 |
| 1975 | 46.0 | 45.4 | 47.4 | 52.7 | 68.3 | 77.0 | 78.6 | 75.9 | 71.1 | 57.7 | 45.9 | 41.4 | 60.7 |
| 1976 | 38.9 | 49.9 | 53.4 | 61.9 | 66.3 | 75.9 | 78.2 | 75.9 | 71.1 | 57.7 | 45.9 | 41.4 | 59.7 |
| 1977 | 29.2 | 41.5 | 54.7 | 61.9 | 68.2 | 74.3 | 81.4 | 76.0 | 76.3 | 60.5 | 54.8 | 43.5 | 60.2 |
| 1978 | 37.0 | 32.6 | 49.1 | 57.2 | 65.6 | 70.4 | 74.1 | 78.5 | 73.2 | 60.4 | 56.0 | 45.3 | 58.7 |
| 1979 | 39.4 | 33.3 | 49.1 | 58.1 | 66.7 | 73.9 | 77.1 | 78.5 | 72.8 | 60.4 | 56.4 | 44.9 | 58.9 |
| 1980 | 40.3 | 34.7 | 46.5 | 58.6 | 67.8 | 73.9 | 80.9 | 76.1 | 70.7 | 59.6 | 50.7 | 42.3 | 59.4 |
| 1981 | 32.7 | 43.1 | 45.4 | 61.2 | 65.1 | 78.3 | 79.8 | 75.1 | 70.7 | 59.6 | 50.7 | 41.0 | 58.6 |
| 1982 | 35.4 | 42.0 | 48.8 | 55.0 | 69.4 | 73.4 | 78.6 | 75.3 | 72.6 | 62.7 | 54.4 | 48.8 | 59.3 |
| 1983 | 40.2 | 40.8 | 51.0 | 55.7 | 65.8 | 73.0 | 80.3 | 79.0 | 70.5 | 66.9 | 52.6 | 41.6 | 59.6 |
| 1984 | 35.5 | 46.7 | 45.4 | 55.6 | 67.8 | 76.2 | 76.7 | 78.4 | 70.5 | 65.9 | 49.9 | 50.9 | 60.0 |
| 1985 | 34.9 | 40.4 | 51.8 | 62.0 | 68.8 | 74.2 | 78.2 | 78.2 | 73.4 | 65.9 | 60.3 | 41.2 | 60.7 |
| 1986 | 39.3 | 42.1 | 49.9 | 57.3 | 67.6 | 76.1 | 82.1 | 76.6 | 72.4 | 65.4 | 54.9 | 44.8 | 60.7 |
| 1987 | 39.6 | 38.7 | 47.5 | 56.4 | 68.3 | 77.0 | 82.4 | 79.6 | 74.3 | 56.6 | 54.3 | 46.0 | 59.9 |
| 1988 | 37.3 | 42.5 | 49.5 | 56.5 | 65.8 | 73.6 | 80.1 | 80.8 | 70.5 | 56.9 | 54.2 | 42.4 | 59.2 |
| 1989 | 45.3 | 43.6 | 50.1 | 56.5 | 65.6 | 78.5 | 79.2 | 77.7 | 73.9 | 62.7 | 53.3 | 34.8 | 60.1 |
| 1990 | 47.3 | 50.2 | 53.2 | 58.7 | 66.6 | 75.5 | 80.6 | 78.0 | 71.6 | 65.9 | 55.0 | 50.5 | 62.8 |
| Record Mean | 41.2 | 42.2 | 48.9 | 57.5 | 66.7 | 74.7 | 78.7 | 77.6 | 72.4 | 62.2 | 52.3 | 43.7 | 59.8 |
| Max | 49.0 | 50.5 | 57.8 | 66.8 | 75.8 | 83.3 | 86.9 | 85.1 | 79.7 | 69.9 | 60.3 | 51.4 | 68.0 |
| Min | 33.3 | 33.8 | 40.0 | 48.1 | 57.6 | 66.1 | 70.5 | 70.0 | 65.1 | 54.4 | 44.2 | 35.9 | 51.6 |

---

## REFERENCE NOTES FOR TABLES 1, 2, 3 and 6   (NORFOLK, VA)

### GENERAL

T - TRACE AMOUNT
BLANK ENTRIES DENOTE MISSING/UNREPORTED DATA.
# INDICATES A STATION OR INSTRUMENT RELOCATION.

### SPECIFIC

**TABLE 1**

(a) - LENGTH OF RECORD IN YEARS. ALTHOUGH INDIVIDUAL MONTHS MAY BE MISSING.
* LESS THAN .05

NORMALS — BASED ON THE 1951-1980 RECORD PERIOD.
EXTREMES — DATES ARE THE MOST RECENT OCCURRENCE.
WIND DIR. — NUMERALS SHOW TENS OF DEGREES CLOCKWISE FROM TRUE NORTH.
   "00" INDICATES CALM.
RESULTANT WIND DIRECTIONS ARE GIVEN TO WHOLE DEGREES.

**TABLE 3**
MAX AND MIN ARE LONG-TERM <u>MEAN DAILY MAXIMUM</u> AND <u>MEAN DAILY MINIMUM</u> TEMPERATURES.

### EXCEPTIONS

**TABLE 1**

1. PERCENT OF POSSIBLE SUNSHINE IS THROUGH 1980.

**TABLES 2, 3, and 6**

RECORD MEANS ARE THROUGH THE CURRENT YEAR, BEGINNING IN 
   1875 FOR TEMPERATURE
   1871 FOR PRECIPITATION
   1949 FOR SNOWFALL

**TABLE 4**

HEATING DEGREE DAYS Base 65 deg. F          NORFOLK, VIRGINIA

| SEASON | JULY | AUG | SEP | OCT | NOV | DEC | JAN | FEB | MAR | APR | MAY | JUNE | TOTAL |
|---|---|---|---|---|---|---|---|---|---|---|---|---|---|
| 1961-62 | 0 | 0 | 7 | 155 | 368 | 722 | 800 | 668 | 655 | 288 | 50 | 0 | 3713 |
| 1962-63 | 0 | 0 | 37 | 148 | 449 | 854 | 859 | 815 | 357 | 202 | 108 | 0 | 3829 |
| 1963-64 | 0 | 0 | 44 | 156 | 384 | 920 | 697 | 719 | 482 | 303 | 108 | 4 | 3817 |
| 1964-65 | 0 | 0 | 4 | 232 | 312 | 575 | 780 | 667 | 635 | 320 | 29 | 15 | 3569 |
| 1965-66 | 0 | 6 | 1 | 195 | 398 | 657 | 897 | 734 | 527 | 330 | 121 | 21 | 3887 |
| 1966-67 | 0 | 0 | 22 | 191 | 437 | 725 | 588 | 699 | 533 | 244 | 157 | 21 | 3617 |
| 1967-68 | 0 | 0 | 36 | 211 | 566 | 644 | 928 | 895 | 471 | 294 | 88 | 0 | 4133 |
| 1968-69 | 0 | 0 | 0 | 124 | 361 | 726 | 814 | 697 | 624 | 192 | 44 | 0 | 3582 |
| 1969-70 | 0 | 0 | 8 | 131 | 469 | 741 | 960 | 714 | 622 | 263 | 57 | 0 | 3965 |
| 1970-71 | 0 | 0 | 16 | 93 | 393 | 552 | 812 | 567 | 555 | 269 | 69 | 0 | 3326 |
| 1971-72 | 0 | 0 | 3 | 27 | 391 | 390 | 572 | 628 | 494 | 272 | 81 | 11 | 2869 |
| 1972-73 | 0 | 0 | 4 | 197 | 406 | 486 | 752 | 703 | 403 | 217 | 47 | 0 | 3215 |
| 1973-74 | 0 | 0 | 0 | 83 | 353 | 575 | 504 | 599 | 377 | 183 | 63 | 0 | 2737 |
| 1974-75 | 0 | 0 | 16 | 213 | 371 | 584 | 584 | 547 | 541 | 382 | 47 | 0 | 3285 |
| 1975-76 | 0 | 0 | 6 | 98 | 290 | 671 | 804 | 443 | 362 | 186 | 62 | 6 | 2928 |
| 1976-77 | 0 | 0 | 0 | 245 | 566 | 726 | 1104 | 657 | 330 | 150 | 40 | 1 | 3819 |
| 1977-78 | 0 | 0 | 0 | 158 | 321 | 661 | 860 | 902 | 580 | 235 | 72 | 3 | 3792 |
| 1978-79 | 0 | 0 | 3 | 162 | 268 | 614 | 787 | 879 | 499 | 213 | 52 | 5 | 3482 |
| 1979-80 | 0 | 0 | 0 | 190 | 272 | 616 | 759 | 872 | 564 | 196 | 58 | 2 | 3529 |
| 1980-81 | 0 | 0 | 11 | 181 | 449 | 699 | 994 | 610 | 605 | 159 | 96 | 0 | 3804 |
| 1981-82 | 0 | 0 | 12 | 189 | 423 | 739 | 907 | 636 | 495 | 303 | 21 | 0 | 3725 |
| 1982-83 | 0 | 4 | 6 | 177 | 334 | 498 | 762 | 674 | 426 | 295 | 85 | 3 | 3264 |
| 1983-84 | 0 | 0 | 27 | 126 | 370 | 718 | 908 | 522 | 601 | 281 | 54 | 3 | 3610 |
| 1984-85 | 0 | 0 | 16 | 37 | 450 | 432 | 928 | 686 | 421 | 172 | 21 | 0 | 3163 |
| 1985-86 | 0 | 0 | 6 | 61 | 162 | 731 | 790 | 637 | 465 | 228 | 69 | 1 | 3150 |
| 1986-87 | 0 | 1 | 8 | 88 | 311 | 620 | 779 | 730 | 538 | 306 | 58 | 0 | 3439 |
| 1987-88 | 0 | 0 | 0 | 252 | 320 | 582 | 851 | 646 | 474 | 266 | 86 | 15 | 3492 |
| 1988-89 | 0 | 0 | 2 | 265 | 324 | 692 | 602 | 601 | 486 | 282 | 80 | 3 | 3334 |
| 1989-90 | 0 | 0 | 12 | 134 | 356 | 928 | 541 | 417 | 410 | 234 | 39 | 3 | 3074 |
| 1990-91 | 0 | 0 | 13 | 102 | 301 | 444 | | | | | | | |

**TABLE 5**

COOLING DEGREE DAYS Base 65 deg. F          NORFOLK, VIRGINIA

| YEAR | JAN | FEB | MAR | APR | MAY | JUNE | JULY | AUG | SEP | OCT | NOV | DEC | TOTAL |
|---|---|---|---|---|---|---|---|---|---|---|---|---|---|
| 1969 | 0 | 0 | 0 | 42 | 125 | 369 | 446 | 357 | 199 | 49 | 0 | 0 | 1587 |
| 1970 | 1 | 0 | 0 | 19 | 140 | 303 | 374 | 412 | 311 | 60 | 0 | 0 | 1620 |
| 1971 | 0 | 3 | 0 | 3 | 76 | 336 | 383 | 343 | 259 | 87 | 23 | 5 | 1518 |
| 1972 | 0 | 0 | 8 | 20 | 40 | 183 | 398 | 343 | 217 | 22 | 10 | 2 | 1243 |
| 1973 | 0 | 0 | 16 | 27 | 112 | 363 | 420 | 424 | 307 | 64 | 17 | 1 | 1751 |
| 1974 | 3 | 0 | 16 | 64 | 124 | 244 | 419 | 390 | 213 | 26 | 32 | 0 | 1531 |
| 1975 | 2 | 3 | 0 | 22 | 157 | 366 | 429 | 460 | 233 | 55 | 17 | 0 | 1744 |
| 1976 | 1 | 13 | 11 | 102 | 110 | 337 | 417 | 347 | 193 | 27 | 0 | 0 | 1558 |
| 1977 | 0 | 4 | 16 | 66 | 145 | 289 | 515 | 502 | 347 | 24 | 22 | 0 | 1930 |
| 1978 | 0 | 0 | 0 | 9 | 96 | 286 | 352 | 487 | 257 | 36 | 3 | 9 | 1535 |
| 1979 | 0 | 0 | 11 | 13 | 112 | 171 | 385 | 426 | 239 | 54 | 22 | 0 | 1433 |
| 1980 | 0 | 0 | 0 | 11 | 153 | 274 | 499 | 497 | 351 | 45 | 1 | 1 | 1832 |
| 1981 | 0 | 0 | 0 | 51 | 103 | 407 | 468 | 320 | 189 | 29 | 0 | 0 | 1567 |
| 1982 | 0 | 0 | 1 | 8 | 166 | 257 | 428 | 331 | 164 | 39 | 21 | 4 | 1419 |
| 1983 | 0 | 0 | 0 | 21 | 115 | 250 | 481 | 440 | 265 | 62 | 4 | 0 | 1638 |
| 1984 | 0 | 0 | 0 | 5 | 146 | 345 | 368 | 426 | 188 | 102 | 5 | 2 | 1587 |
| 1985 | 0 | 5 | 20 | 91 | 146 | 284 | 419 | 382 | 267 | 97 | 28 | 0 | 1739 |
| 1986 | 0 | 0 | 2 | 2 | 153 | 343 | 537 | 367 | 237 | 109 | 15 | 0 | 1765 |
| 1987 | 0 | 0 | 0 | 2 | 168 | 364 | 544 | 461 | 285 | 0 | 7 | 0 | 1831 |
| 1988 | 0 | 0 | 1 | 18 | 118 | 280 | 477 | 498 | 173 | 17 | 10 | 0 | 1592 |
| 1989 | 0 | 9 | 30 | 31 | 106 | 412 | 447 | 399 | 286 | 69 | 10 | 0 | 1799 |
| 1990 | 0 | 8 | 52 | 51 | 98 | 324 | 489 | 407 | 218 | 137 | 8 | 5 | 1797 |

**TABLE 6**

SNOWFALL (inches)          NORFOLK, VIRGINIA

| SEASON | JULY | AUG | SEP | OCT | NOV | DEC | JAN | FEB | MAR | APR | MAY | JUNE | TOTAL |
|---|---|---|---|---|---|---|---|---|---|---|---|---|---|
| 1961-62 | 0.0 | 0.0 | 0.0 | 0.0 | T | T | 11.9 | 0.8 | 1.2 | T | 0.0 | 0.0 | 13.9 |
| 1962-63 | 0.0 | 0.0 | 0.0 | 0.0 | 0.0 | 4.5 | 1.9 | 7.5 | T | 0.0 | 0.0 | 0.0 | 13.9 |
| 1963-64 | 0.0 | 0.0 | 0.0 | 0.0 | 0.0 | T | T | 5.8 | 1.0 | 1.2 | 0.0 | 0.0 | 8.0 |
| 1964-65 | 0.0 | 0.0 | 0.0 | 0.0 | T | 0.0 | 10.6 | 3.9 | T | 0.0 | 0.0 | 0.0 | 14.5 |
| 1965-66 | 0.0 | 0.0 | 0.0 | 0.0 | 0.0 | T | 14.2 | 0.5 | 0.0 | 0.0 | 0.0 | 0.0 | 14.7 |
| 1966-67 | 0.0 | 0.0 | 0.0 | 0.0 | T | 1.0 | 4.2 | 5.1 | T | 0.0 | 0.0 | 0.0 | 10.3 |
| 1967-68 | 0.0 | 0.0 | 0.0 | 0.0 | T | 2.0 | 1.5 | 2.9 | 0.9 | 0.0 | 0.0 | 0.0 | 7.3 |
| 1968-69 | 0.0 | 0.0 | 0.0 | 0.0 | T | 3.8 | T | 0.8 | 1.9 | 0.0 | 0.0 | 0.0 | 6.5 |
| 1969-70 | 0.0 | 0.0 | 0.0 | 0.0 | 0.0 | T | 3.0 | 2.8 | T | 0.0 | 0.0 | 0.0 | 5.8 |
| 1970-71 | 0.0 | 0.0 | 0.0 | 0.0 | T | T | T | 2.4 | 4.2 | T | 0.0 | 0.0 | 6.6 |
| 1971-72 | 0.0 | 0.0 | 0.0 | 0.0 | T | T | 0.0 | 1.8 | T | T | 0.0 | 0.0 | 1.8 |
| 1972-73 | 0.0 | 0.0 | 0.0 | 0.0 | T | 0.0 | 9.1 | 4.7 | T | 0.0 | 0.0 | 0.0 | 13.8 |
| 1973-74 | 0.0 | 0.0 | 0.0 | 0.0 | 0.0 | 1.4 | T | 0.9 | 7.5 | 0.0 | 0.0 | 0.0 | 9.8 |
| 1974-75 | 0.0 | 0.0 | 0.0 | 0.0 | 0.0 | T | 0.3 | T | 0.8 | T | 0.0 | 0.0 | 1.1 |
| 1975-76 | 0.0 | 0.0 | 0.0 | 0.0 | 0.0 | T | T | T | 0.0 | 0.0 | 0.0 | | T |
| 1976-77 | 0.0 | 0.0 | 0.0 | 0.0 | T | 1.0 | 4.7 | 1.4 | 0.0 | 0.0 | 0.0 | 0.0 | 7.1 |
| 1977-78 | 0.0 | 0.0 | 0.0 | 0.0 | 0.0 | T | 1.3 | 9.2 | 2.3 | 0.0 | 0.0 | 0.0 | 12.8 |
| 1978-79 | 0.0 | 0.0 | 0.0 | 0.0 | 0.0 | 0.0 | 1.0 | 12.7 | T | 0.0 | 0.0 | 0.0 | 13.7 |
| 1979-80 | 0.0 | 0.0 | 0.0 | 0.0 | 0.0 | 0.0 | 9.3 | 18.9 | 13.7 | 0.0 | 0.0 | 0.0 | 41.9 |
| 1980-81 | 0.0 | 0.0 | 0.0 | 0.0 | 0.0 | T | T | 0.3 | 0.0 | 0.0 | 0.0 | 0.0 | 0.3 |
| 1981-82 | 0.0 | 0.0 | 0.0 | 0.0 | 0.0 | 1.8 | 4.2 | 0.1 | T | T | 0.0 | 0.0 | 6.1 |
| 1982-83 | 0.0 | 0.0 | 0.0 | 0.0 | 0.0 | 0.4 | T | 3.0 | T | T | 0.0 | 0.0 | 3.4 |
| 1983-84 | 0.0 | 0.0 | 0.0 | 0.0 | 0.0 | T | T | 5.2 | T | 0.0 | 0.0 | 0.0 | 5.2 |
| 1984-85 | 0.0 | 0.0 | 0.0 | 0.0 | 0.0 | T | 4.3 | 0.0 | T | 0.0 | 0.0 | 0.0 | 4.3 |
| 1985-86 | 0.0 | 0.0 | 0.0 | 0.0 | 0.0 | T | 3.6 | 1.1 | T | 0.0 | 0.0 | 0.0 | 4.7 |
| 1986-87 | 0.0 | 0.0 | 0.0 | 0.0 | 0.0 | T | 1.6 | 1.0 | 1.2 | T | 0.0 | 0.0 | 3.8 |
| 1987-88 | 0.0 | 0.0 | 0.0 | 0.0 | 0.0 | 0.3 | T | 4.4 | T | 0.0 | 0.0 | 0.0 | 4.7 |
| 1988-89 | 0.0 | 0.0 | 0.0 | 0.0 | 0.0 | 0.0 | T | 24.4 | T | 0.5 | 0.0 | 0.0 | 24.9 |
| 1989-90 | 0.0 | 0.0 | 0.0 | 0.0 | 0.0 | 0.5 | 0.0 | 0.0 | T | 0.0 | 0.0 | T | 0.5 |
| 1990-91 | 0.0 | 0.0 | 0.0 | 0.0 | 0.0 | T | | | | | | | |
| Record Mean | 0.0 | 0.0 | 0.0 | 0.0 | T | 0.9 | 2.8 | 3.0 | 1.1 | T | 0.0 | T | 7.9 |

**See Reference Notes, relative to all above tables, on preceding page.**

Richmond is located in east-central Virginia at the head of navigation on the James River and along a line separating the Coastal Plains (Tidewater Virginia) from the Piedmont. The Blue Ridge Mountains lie about 90 miles to the west and the Chesapeake Bay 60 miles to the east. Elevations range from a few feet above sea level along the river to a little over 300 feet in parts of the western section of the city.

The climate might be classified as modified continental. Summers are warm and humid and winters generally mild. The mountains to the west act as a partial barrier to outbreaks of cold, continental air in winter. The cold winter air is delayed long enough to be modified, then further warmed as it subsides in its approach to Richmond. The open waters of the Chesapeake Bay and Atlantic Ocean contribute to the humid summers and mild winters. The coldest weather normally occurs in late December and January, when low temperatures usually average in the upper 20s, and the high temperatures in the upper 40s. Temperatures seldom lower to zero, but there have been several occurrences of below zero temperatures. Summertime high temperatures above 100 degrees are not uncommon, but do not occur every year.

Precipitation is rather uniformly distributed throughout the year. However, dry periods lasting several weeks do occur, especially in autumn when long periods of pleasant, mild weather are most common. There is considerable variability in total monthly amounts from year to year. Snow usually remains on the ground only one or two days at a time. Ice storms (freezing rain or glaze) are not uncommon, but they are seldom severe enough to do any considerable damage. A notable exception was the spectacular glaze storm of January 27-28, 1943, when nearly 1 inch of ice accumulation caused heavy damage to trees and overhead transmission lines.

The James River reaches tidewater at Richmond where flooding may occur in every month of the year, most frequently in March and least in July. Hurricanes and tropical storms have been responsible for most of the flooding during the summer and early fall months. Hurricanes passing near Richmond have produced record rainfalls. In 1955, three hurricanes brought record rainfall to Richmond within a six-week period. The most noteworthy of these were Hurricanes Connie and Diane that brought heavy rains five days apart.

Damaging storms occur mainly from snow and freezing rain in winter and from hurricanes, tornadoes, and severe thunderstorms in other seasons. Damage may be from wind, flooding, or rain, or from any combination of these. Tornadoes are infrequent but some notable occurrences have been observed within the Richmond area.

Based on the 1951-1980 period, the average first occurrence of 32 degrees Fahrenheit in the fall is October 26 and the average last occurrence in the spring is April 10.

## TABLE 1 — NORMALS, MEANS AND EXTREMES

RICHMOND, VIRGINIA

LATITUDE: 37°30'N   LONGITUDE: 77°20'W   ELEVATION: FT. GRND  164 BARO  178   TIME ZONE: EASTERN   WBAN: 13740

| | (a) | JAN | FEB | MAR | APR | MAY | JUNE | JULY | AUG | SEP | OCT | NOV | DEC | YEAR |
|---|---|---|---|---|---|---|---|---|---|---|---|---|---|---|
| **TEMPERATURE °F:** | | | | | | | | | | | | | | |
| Normals | | | | | | | | | | | | | | |
| -Daily Maximum | | 46.7 | 49.6 | 58.5 | 70.6 | 77.9 | 84.8 | 88.4 | 87.1 | 81.0 | 70.5 | 60.5 | 50.2 | 68.8 |
| -Daily Minimum | | 26.5 | 28.1 | 35.8 | 45.1 | 54.2 | 62.2 | 67.2 | 66.4 | 59.3 | 46.7 | 37.3 | 29.6 | 46.5 |
| -Monthly | | 36.6 | 38.9 | 47.2 | 57.9 | 66.1 | 73.5 | 77.8 | 76.8 | 70.2 | 58.6 | 48.9 | 39.9 | 57.7 |
| Extremes | | | | | | | | | | | | | | |
| -Record Highest | 60 | 80 | 83 | 93 | 96 | 100 | 104 | 105 | 102 | 103 | 99 | 86 | 80 | 105 |
| -Year | | 1950 | 1932 | 1938 | 1985 | 1941 | 1952 | 1977 | 1983 | 1954 | 1941 | 1974 | 1971 | JUL 1977 |
| -Record Lowest | 60 | -12 | -10 | 11 | 23 | 31 | 40 | 51 | 46 | 35 | 21 | 10 | -1 | -12 |
| -Year | | 1940 | 1936 | 1960 | 1985 | 1956 | 1967 | 1965 | 1934 | 1974 | 1962 | 1933 | 1942 | JAN 1940 |
| **NORMAL DEGREE DAYS:** | | | | | | | | | | | | | | |
| Heating (base 65°F) | | 880 | 731 | 552 | 226 | 65 | 0 | 0 | 0 | 24 | 221 | 483 | 778 | 3960 |
| Cooling (base 65°F) | | 0 | 0 | 0 | 13 | 99 | 258 | 397 | 366 | 180 | 23 | 0 | 0 | 1336 |
| **% OF POSSIBLE SUNSHINE** | 39 | 54 | 58 | 61 | 65 | 65 | 69 | 68 | 66 | 64 | 62 | 58 | 54 | 62 |
| **MEAN SKY COVER (tenths)** | | | | | | | | | | | | | | |
| Sunrise - Sunset | 44 | 6.4 | 6.2 | 6.2 | 6.1 | 6.3 | 6.0 | 6.1 | 6.0 | 5.8 | 5.4 | 5.8 | 6.1 | 6.0 |
| **MEAN NUMBER OF DAYS:** | | | | | | | | | | | | | | |
| Sunrise to Sunset | | | | | | | | | | | | | | |
| -Clear | 44 | 8.4 | 8.3 | 8.3 | 8.0 | 7.0 | 6.8 | 7.0 | 7.2 | 9.3 | 11.5 | 9.4 | 9.6 | 100.6 |
| -Partly Cloudy | 44 | 6.7 | 6.3 | 8.4 | 9.1 | 10.2 | 11.9 | 11.6 | 11.8 | 8.6 | 7.4 | 7.8 | 6.4 | 106.0 |
| -Cloudy | 44 | 15.9 | 13.7 | 14.4 | 12.9 | 13.8 | 11.3 | 12.5 | 12.0 | 12.1 | 12.2 | 12.9 | 15.0 | 158.6 |
| Precipitation | | | | | | | | | | | | | | |
| .01 inches or more | 52 | 10.3 | 9.3 | 10.7 | 9.3 | 10.7 | 9.6 | 11.0 | 9.8 | 7.9 | 7.3 | 8.4 | 8.8 | 112.9 |
| Snow,Ice pellets | | | | | | | | | | | | | | |
| 1.0 inches or more | 52 | 1.4 | 1.2 | 0.6 | 0.1 | 0.0 | 0.0 | 0.0 | 0.0 | 0.0 | 0.0 | 0.2 | 0.6 | 4.0 |
| Thunderstorms | 52 | 0.2 | 0.4 | 1.6 | 2.5 | 5.6 | 6.8 | 8.7 | 6.7 | 2.9 | 1.0 | 0.6 | 0.3 | 37.2 |
| Heavy Fog Visibility 1/4 mile or less | 60 | 2.7 | 2.1 | 1.7 | 1.7 | 1.9 | 1.5 | 2.1 | 2.5 | 3.0 | 3.3 | 2.3 | 2.8 | 27.7 |
| Temperature °F | | | | | | | | | | | | | | |
| -Maximum | | | | | | | | | | | | | | |
| 90° and above | 60 | 0.0 | 0.0 | 0.1 | 0.8 | 2.7 | 9.4 | 13.7 | 11.1 | 4.4 | 0.4 | 0.0 | 0.0 | 42.6 |
| 32° and below | 60 | 3.3 | 1.5 | 0.2 | 0.0 | 0.0 | 0.0 | 0.0 | 0.0 | 0.0 | 0.0 | 0.* | 1.7 | 6.8 |
| -Minimum | | | | | | | | | | | | | | |
| 32° and below | 60 | 21.6 | 19.0 | 10.4 | 2.2 | 0.1 | 0.0 | 0.0 | 0.0 | 0.0 | 1.8 | 10.1 | 20.2 | 85.3 |
| 0° and below | 60 | 0.4 | 0.1 | 0.0 | 0.0 | 0.0 | 0.0 | 0.0 | 0.0 | 0.0 | 0.0 | 0.0 | 0.* | 0.5 |
| **AVG. STATION PRESS.(mb)** | 17 | 1012.7 | 1012.4 | 1010.7 | 1008.9 | 1009.1 | 1009.5 | 1010.1 | 1011.1 | 1012.2 | 1013.4 | 1013.1 | 1013.5 | 1011.4 |
| **RELATIVE HUMIDITY (%)** | | | | | | | | | | | | | | |
| Hour 01 | 55 | 77 | 74 | 73 | 74 | 83 | 86 | 88 | 90 | 90 | 87 | 80 | 77 | 82 |
| Hour 07 | 55 | 80 | 79 | 78 | 76 | 80 | 82 | 85 | 89 | 90 | 89 | 84 | 81 | 83 |
| Hour 13 (Local Time) | 55 | 57 | 53 | 49 | 45 | 51 | 53 | 56 | 57 | 56 | 53 | 51 | 55 | 53 |
| Hour 19 | 55 | 68 | 63 | 58 | 55 | 64 | 67 | 71 | 75 | 78 | 76 | 70 | 70 | 68 |
| **PRECIPITATION (inches):** | | | | | | | | | | | | | | |
| Water Equivalent | | | | | | | | | | | | | | |
| -Normal | | 3.23 | 3.13 | 3.57 | 2.90 | 3.55 | 3.60 | 5.14 | 5.01 | 3.52 | 3.74 | 3.29 | 3.39 | 44.07 |
| -Maximum Monthly | 52 | 7.97 | 5.97 | 8.65 | 7.31 | 8.87 | 9.24 | 18.87 | 14.10 | 10.98 | 9.39 | 7.64 | 7.07 | 18.87 |
| -Year | | 1978 | 1979 | 1984 | 1987 | 1972 | 1938 | 1945 | 1955 | 1975 | 1971 | 1959 | 1973 | JUL 1945 |
| -Minimum Monthly | 52 | 0.64 | 0.48 | 0.94 | 0.64 | 0.87 | 0.38 | 0.51 | 0.52 | 0.26 | 0.30 | 0.36 | 0.40 | 0.26 |
| -Year | | 1981 | 1978 | 1966 | 1963 | 1965 | 1980 | 1983 | 1943 | 1978 | 1963 | 1965 | 1980 | SEP 1978 |
| -Maximum in 24 hrs | 52 | 3.31 | 2.67 | 2.54 | 2.97 | 3.08 | 4.61 | 5.73 | 8.79 | 4.02 | 6.50 | 4.07 | 3.16 | 8.79 |
| -Year | | 1962 | 1979 | 1984 | 1987 | 1981 | 1963 | 1969 | 1955 | 1985 | 1961 | 1956 | 1958 | AUG 1955 |
| Snow,Ice pellets | | | | | | | | | | | | | | |
| -Maximum Monthly | 52 | 28.5 | 21.4 | 19.7 | 2.0 | T | 0.0 | 0.0 | 0.0 | 0.0 | T | 7.3 | 12.5 | 28.5 |
| -Year | | 1940 | 1983 | 1960 | 1940 | 1989 | | | | | 1979 | 1953 | 1958 | JAN 1940 |
| -Maximum in 24 hrs | 52 | 21.6 | 16.8 | 12.1 | 2.0 | T | 0.0 | 0.0 | 0.0 | 0.0 | T | 7.3 | 7.5 | 21.6 |
| -Year | | 1940 | 1983 | 1962 | 1940 | 1989 | | | | | 1979 | 1953 | 1966 | JAN 1940 |
| **WIND:** | | | | | | | | | | | | | | |
| Mean Speed (mph) | 41 | 8.1 | 8.6 | 9.1 | 8.9 | 7.8 | 7.3 | 6.8 | 6.4 | 6.6 | 7.0 | 7.5 | 7.7 | 7.7 |
| Prevailing Direction through 1963 | | S | NNE | W | S | SSW | S | SSW | S | S | NNE | S | SW | S |
| Fastest Mile | | | | | | | | | | | | | | |
| -Direction (!!!) | 32 | NW | SW | SE | NW | N | NW | NW | W | SE | SE | NW | SW | SE |
| -Speed (MPH) | 32 | 43 | 45 | 42 | 40 | 45 | 52 | 56 | 54 | 45 | 68 | 38 | 40 | 68 |
| -Year | | 1971 | 1951 | 1952 | 1972 | 1962 | 1952 | 1955 | 1964 | 1952 | 1954 | 1977 | 1968 | OCT 1954 |
| Peak Gust | | | | | | | | | | | | | | |
| -Direction (!!!) | 5 | NW | NW | W | W | SW | NW | N | NW | N | SW | SW | SW | SW |
| -Speed (mph) | 5 | 48 | 48 | 67 | 48 | 79 | 53 | 61 | 44 | 49 | 40 | 54 | 49 | 79 |
| -Date | | 1985 | 1987 | 1989 | 1988 | 1989 | 1987 | 1986 | 1986 | 1989 | 1987 | 1988 | 1988 | MAY 1989 |

**See Reference Notes to this table on the following page.**

# RICHMOND, VIRGINIA

## PRECIPITATION (inches)     RICHMOND, VIRGINIA

**TABLE 2**

| YEAR | JAN | FEB | MAR | APR | MAY | JUNE | JULY | AUG | SEP | OCT | NOV | DEC | ANNUAL |
|------|-----|-----|-----|-----|-----|------|------|-----|-----|-----|-----|-----|--------|
| 1961 | 2.57 | 5.39 | 4.02 | 1.73 | 4.83 | 6.49 | 2.85 | 3.90 | 1.64 | 5.78 | 1.81 | 5.05 | 49.06 |
| 1962 | 5.95 | 3.00 | 4.87 | 3.80 | 4.08 | 5.57 | 5.65 | 2.37 | 3.46 | 2.50 | 6.73 | 2.64 | 48.62 |
| 1963 | 1.55 | 2.98 | 5.62 | 0.64 | 2.39 | 7.01 | 0.52 | 3.75 | 3.20 | 2.30 | 6.70 | 2.80 | 37.46 |
| 1964 | 4.16 | 4.46 | 2.61 | 2.71 | 1.14 | 2.40 | 6.46 | 9.88 | 2.56 | 2.52 | 1.98 | 3.05 | 45.03 |
| 1965 | 2.51 | 2.77 | 3.68 | 2.13 | 0.87 | 3.39 | 6.33 | 0.81 | 4.81 | 2.38 | 0.36 | 0.72 | 29.76 |
| 1966 | 4.58 | 3.80 | 0.94 | 2.18 | 2.58 | 2.54 | 4.07 | 1.31 | 5.06 | 4.31 | 1.31 | 3.07 | 36.25 |
| 1967 | 1.50 | 3.35 | 2.34 | 1.32 | 3.71 | 3.58 | 5.00 | 6.65 | 0.95 | 2.00 | 1.76 | 6.48 | 37.64 |
| 1968 | 2.53 | 0.98 | 4.00 | 2.93 | 3.13 | 2.89 | 3.41 | 3.71 | 1.78 | 2.59 | 3.87 | 2.28 | 33.10 |
| 1969 | 2.04 | 3.95 | 3.95 | 2.60 | 3.32 | 4.36 | 13.90 | 9.31 | 3.89 | 2.38 | 1.87 | 5.26 | 56.33 |
| 1970 | 1.32 | 2.37 | 3.70 | 2.84 | 1.84 | 1.12 | 4.74 | 1.69 | 1.02 | 2.55 | 3.10 | 3.00 | 28.29 |
| 1971 | 1.84 | 4.37 | 2.68 | 1.76 | 6.82 | 4.10 | 4.40 | 3.73 | 2.35 | 3.39 | 2.76 | 0.75 | 44.95 |
| 1972 | 1.43 | 5.15 | 2.11 | 3.35 | 8.87 | 8.82 | 5.80 | 3.84 | 3.35 | 2.89 | 5.82 | 2.91 | 59.34 |
| 1973 | 2.66 | 3.11 | 3.44 | 4.58 | 3.56 | 2.45 | 3.64 | 4.34 | 1.82 | 2.56 | 1.27 | 7.07 | 40.50 |
| 1974 | 3.21 | 2.54 | 3.79 | 1.58 | 3.02 | 1.80 | 2.25 | 6.84 | 4.83 | 2.39 | 1.23 | 4.22 | 35.70 |
| 1975 | 5.71 | 2.96 | 8.04 | 2.78 | 2.59 | 4.00 | 12.29 | 2.31 | 10.98 | 2.10 | 2.04 | 4.51 | 61.31 |
| 1976 | 3.39 | 1.35 | 2.14 | 1.08 | 3.76 | 2.85 | 2.63 | 1.35 | 4.78 | 6.99 | 1.88 | 2.56 | 34.76 |
| 1977 | 2.22 | 1.34 | 2.67 | 2.33 | 3.99 | 1.25 | 4.20 | 6.15 | 2.16 | 2.88 | 4.32 | 5.57 | 44.08 |
| 1978 | 7.97 | 0.48 | 5.67 | 4.31 | 3.92 | 5.26 | 4.24 | 5.93 | 0.26 | 3.21 | 4.57 | 3.80 | 47.62 |
| 1979 | 6.16 | 5.97 | 2.59 | 3.97 | 3.80 | 2.42 | 4.36 | 7.08 | 9.76 | 3.87 | 5.50 | 1.64 | 57.12 |
| 1980 | 6.05 | 1.01 | 5.49 | 4.28 | 4.68 | 0.38 | 5.18 | 2.15 | 2.37 | 2.96 | 2.18 | 0.40 | 41.13 |
| 1981 | 0.64 | 2.76 | 1.52 | 2.96 | 6.62 | 3.69 | 4.01 | 2.89 | 2.70 | 2.36 | 0.68 | 5.04 | 35.87 |
| 1982 | 2.76 | 4.44 | 3.74 | 2.97 | 3.48 | 3.97 | 9.21 | 4.39 | 2.55 | 2.90 | 2.70 | 3.37 | 46.48 |
| 1983 | 1.59 | 3.95 | 6.04 | 5.21 | 2.50 | 5.46 | 0.51 | 0.97 | 3.05 | 4.02 | 5.63 | 4.50 | 43.43 |
| 1984 | 3.98 | 3.97 | 8.65 | 5.92 | 4.52 | 2.01 | 3.55 | 4.58 | 1.86 | 2.14 | 3.34 | 1.52 | 46.04 |
| 1985 | 3.54 | 3.20 | 1.80 | 0.65 | 2.36 | 4.01 | 5.31 | 10.58 | 4.97 | 5.09 | 6.99 | 0.58 | 49.08 |
| 1986 | 2.69 | 2.67 | 1.16 | 1.16 | 3.15 | 1.30 | 7.01 | 6.75 | 0.63 | 2.43 | 2.46 | 5.15 | 36.56 |
| 1987 | 5.53 | 2.57 | 1.65 | 7.31 | 2.94 | 6.29 | 1.20 | 1.11 | 4.43 | 2.25 | 3.13 | 2.86 | 40.27 |
| 1988 | 2.53 | 3.08 | 1.98 | 2.55 | 4.81 | 2.25 | 7.50 | 2.95 | 1.74 | 2.74 | 4.34 | 0.79 | 37.26 |
| 1989 | 1.88 | 4.34 | 5.00 | 4.27 | 5.02 | 5.85 | 4.00 | 4.89 | 5.33 | 3.54 | 3.00 | 2.62 | 49.74 |
| 1990 | 2.84 | 2.38 | 2.54 | 2.81 | 6.85 | 0.97 | 6.74 | 5.76 | 1.92 | 3.90 | 1.70 | 3.52 | 41.93 |
| Record Mean | 3.12 | 3.03 | 3.50 | 3.01 | 3.78 | 3.65 | 5.45 | 4.89 | 3.53 | 3.35 | 3.23 | 3.13 | 43.67 |

**TABLE 3**

## AVERAGE TEMPERATURE (deg. F)     RICHMOND, VIRGINIA

| YEAR | JAN | FEB | MAR | APR | MAY | JUNE | JULY | AUG | SEP | OCT | NOV | DEC | ANNUAL |
|------|-----|-----|-----|-----|-----|------|------|-----|-----|-----|-----|-----|--------|
| 1961 | 33.5 | 42.2 | 50.8 | 53.0 | 63.6 | 72.8 | 78.5 | 77.1 | 73.5 | 59.1 | 50.1 | 37.1 | 57.5 |
| 1962 | 36.6 | 39.7 | 45.0 | 57.5 | 70.6 | 74.0 | 74.8 | 74.6 | 66.2 | 60.5 | 47.2 | 36.1 | 56.9 |
| 1963 | 35.9 | 33.3 | 50.8 | 59.2 | 64.0 | 72.0 | 76.1 | 75.7 | 65.5 | 58.6 | 50.1 | 32.4 | 56.1 |
| 1964 | 38.1 | 37.2 | 47.6 | 55.4 | 66.4 | 73.1 | 75.8 | 75.3 | 67.1 | 53.4 | 51.5 | 42.9 | 56.8 |
| 1965 | 35.6 | 38.8 | 43.0 | 53.9 | 69.6 | 70.7 | 74.9 | 75.9 | 70.7 | 56.1 | 48.2 | 41.3 | 56.6 |
| 1966 | 31.1 | 37.7 | 47.5 | 52.8 | 63.1 | 71.4 | 76.4 | 74.6 | 67.2 | 55.5 | 49.5 | 38.0 | 55.4 |
| 1967 | 40.9 | 34.8 | 46.6 | 58.8 | 60.7 | 72.1 | 76.6 | 75.5 | 65.7 | 57.2 | 44.0 | 41.9 | 56.2 |
| 1968 | 33.9 | 34.2 | 52.0 | 58.8 | 64.7 | 74.7 | 78.9 | 78.9 | 70.9 | 61.9 | 51.3 | 37.0 | 58.1 |
| 1969 | 33.9 | 36.8 | 42.3 | 57.6 | 65.5 | 75.7 | 78.3 | 75.1 | 68.1 | 59.5 | 46.8 | 35.5 | 56.2 |
| 1970 | 30.1 | 37.1 | 42.9 | 58.2 | 69.1 | 75.7 | 78.3 | 76.0 | 74.8 | 62.9 | 49.9 | 40.4 | 58.1 |
| 1971 | 33.8 | 39.5 | 44.5 | 55.0 | 63.3 | 74.7 | 76.6 | 75.3 | 71.4 | 64.6 | 48.5 | 48.0 | 57.9 |
| 1972 | 40.7 | 37.6 | 47.2 | 56.2 | 64.6 | 70.1 | 77.1 | 75.2 | 70.1 | 55.8 | 47.9 | 45.9 | 57.4 |
| 1973 | 37.6 | 38.5 | 52.6 | 57.9 | 65.1 | 76.0 | 77.4 | 77.5 | 72.3 | 60.6 | 51.3 | 40.8 | 59.0 |
| 1974 | 45.8 | 40.1 | 50.4 | 59.9 | 65.8 | 70.6 | 76.9 | 75.7 | 67.4 | 55.4 | 48.5 | 41.7 | 58.2 |
| 1975 | 40.7 | 41.4 | 45.3 | 52.9 | 67.7 | 73.6 | 76.0 | 78.8 | 69.3 | 62.5 | 53.6 | 40.0 | 58.5 |
| 1976 | 35.1 | 48.5 | 52.6 | 60.5 | 65.2 | 74.6 | 77.3 | 75.7 | 68.7 | 54.4 | 42.7 | 36.7 | 57.7 |
| 1977 | 25.3 | 40.5 | 53.7 | 61.1 | 68.2 | 73.0 | 81.4 | 79.8 | 74.2 | 57.3 | 52.3 | 39.5 | 58.9 |
| 1978 | 33.4 | 30.3 | 44.5 | 57.3 | 65.5 | 74.7 | 77.5 | 80.1 | 72.9 | 58.3 | 52.5 | 42.5 | 57.5 |
| 1979 | 36.4 | 28.6 | 51.1 | 58.4 | 67.1 | 70.8 | 76.9 | 77.8 | 71.0 | 58.3 | 53.3 | 42.3 | 57.7 |
| 1980 | 38.8 | 36.0 | 47.4 | 61.1 | 68.3 | 72.8 | 80.0 | 80.7 | 74.7 | 56.9 | 46.2 | 38.6 | 58.5 |
| 1981 | 31.2 | 42.2 | 44.6 | 60.6 | 64.1 | 77.9 | 79.6 | 75.1 | 69.4 | 56.4 | 49.1 | 38.0 | 57.3 |
| 1982 | 31.6 | 41.7 | 49.1 | 55.9 | 70.4 | 73.4 | 78.6 | 75.0 | 69.8 | 59.2 | 51.9 | 46.1 | 58.6 |
| 1983 | 37.8 | 39.1 | 50.4 | 56.1 | 66.1 | 75.6 | 79.4 | 77.7 | 68.8 | 58.1 | 49.0 | 36.2 | 57.9 |
| 1984 | 32.6 | 44.5 | 43.6 | 55.8 | 65.4 | 77.7 | 76.0 | 77.0 | 67.5 | 56.1 | 46.6 | 47.7 | 58.4 |
| 1985 | 32.6 | 40.2 | 49.7 | 62.0 | 68.0 | 74.3 | 79.0 | 77.5 | 70.8 | 62.6 | 56.6 | 37.8 | 59.3 |
| 1986 | 36.2 | 39.3 | 50.0 | 59.2 | 66.9 | 76.1 | 80.9 | 74.6 | 70.8 | 61.8 | 49.1 | 40.9 | 58.8 |
| 1987 | 34.7 | 37.0 | 47.1 | 54.3 | 67.3 | 75.8 | 81.3 | 78.5 | 72.3 | 52.9 | 51.3 | 43.0 | 58.0 |
| 1988 | 32.3 | 39.1 | 47.9 | 56.0 | 65.8 | 72.8 | 79.9 | 79.8 | 68.4 | 53.6 | 50.6 | 39.2 | 57.1 |
| 1989 | 42.3 | 39.6 | 47.9 | 55.8 | 64.1 | 76.1 | 77.7 | 75.3 | 70.8 | 60.2 | 49.3 | 31.3 | 57.5 |
| 1990 | 46.3 | 48.0 | 52.1 | 57.9 | 65.8 | 75.0 | 79.9 | 76.3 | 69.5 | 53.1 | 52.6 | 46.3 | 61.1 |
| Record Mean | 37.3 | 39.4 | 47.2 | 57.2 | 66.3 | 74.1 | 77.9 | 76.5 | 70.1 | 58.8 | 49.0 | 39.8 | 57.8 |
| Max | 47.1 | 50.0 | 58.7 | 69.6 | 78.1 | 85.3 | 88.3 | 86.6 | 80.9 | 70.7 | 60.5 | 49.9 | 68.8 |
| Min | 27.4 | 28.8 | 35.9 | 44.7 | 54.4 | 62.9 | 67.5 | 66.3 | 59.3 | 46.9 | 37.5 | 29.7 | 46.8 |

## REFERENCE NOTES FOR TABLES 1, 2, 3 and 6     (RICHMOND, VA)

### GENERAL

T - TRACE AMOUNT
BLANK ENTRIES DENOTE MISSING/UNREPORTED DATA.
# INDICATES A STATION OR INSTRUMENT RELOCATION.

### SPECIFIC

#### TABLE 1

(a) - LENGTH OF RECORD IN YEARS. ALTHOUGH
INDIVIDUAL MONTHS MAY BE MISSING.
* LESS THAN .05

NORMALS — BASED ON THE 1951-1980 RECORD PERIOD.
EXTREMES — DATES ARE THE MOST RECENT OCCURRENCE.
WIND DIR. — NUMERALS SHOW TENS OF DEGREES
CLOCKWISE FROM TRUE NORTH.
"00" INDICATES CALM.
RESULTANT WIND DIRECTIONS ARE GIVEN TO WHOLE DEGREES.

#### TABLE 3
MAX AND MIN ARE LONG-TERM MEAN DAILY MAXIMUM
AND MEAN DAILY MINIMUM TEMPERATURES.

### EXCEPTIONS

**TABLES 2, 3, and 6**

RECORD MEANS ARE THROUGH THE CURRENT YEAR,
BEGINNING IN     1930 FOR TEMPERATURE
1930 FOR PRECIPITATION
1938 FOR SNOWFALL

**TABLE 4**  HEATING DEGREE DAYS Base 65 deg. F    RICHMOND, VIRGINIA

| SEASON | JULY | AUG | SEP | OCT | NOV | DEC | JAN | FEB | MAR | APR | MAY | JUNE | TOTAL |
|---|---|---|---|---|---|---|---|---|---|---|---|---|---|
| 1961-62 | 0 | 0 | 27 | 218 | 459 | 860 | 875 | 702 | 623 | 276 | 32 | 0 | 4072 |
| 1962-63 | 0 | 0 | 73 | 175 | 526 | 891 | 897 | 882 | 434 | 218 | 102 | 1 | 4199 |
| 1963-64 | 0 | 0 | 71 | 197 | 439 | 1004 | 826 | 801 | 537 | 306 | 74 | 12 | 4267 |
| 1964-65 | 0 | 0 | 32 | 352 | 402 | 676 | 909 | 726 | 674 | 339 | 17 | 34 | 4161 |
| 1965-66 | 0 | 6 | 25 | 275 | 498 | 726 | 1043 | 759 | 538 | 371 | 133 | 27 | 4401 |
| 1966-67 | 0 | 0 | 47 | 293 | 466 | 833 | 738 | 841 | 560 | 230 | 171 | 17 | 4196 |
| 1967-68 | 0 | 0 | 64 | 256 | 623 | 708 | 956 | 887 | 416 | 191 | 86 | 0 | 4187 |
| 1968-69 | 0 | 0 | 0 | 161 | 403 | 864 | 957 | 783 | 695 | 237 | 66 | 0 | 4166 |
| 1969-70 | 0 | 0 | 45 | 221 | 541 | 907 | 1076 | 778 | 677 | 231 | 51 | 0 | 4527 |
| 1970-71 | 0 | 0 | 12 | 124 | 445 | 756 | 960 | 709 | 627 | 295 | 104 | 3 | 4035 |
| 1971-72 | 0 | 0 | 11 | 69 | 512 | 526 | 748 | 788 | 554 | 286 | 58 | 21 | 3573 |
| 1972-73 | 0 | 0 | 17 | 285 | 513 | 588 | 843 | 735 | 394 | 247 | 79 | 0 | 3701 |
| 1973-74 | 0 | 0 | 5 | 163 | 414 | 744 | 589 | 691 | 455 | 204 | 75 | 5 | 3345 |
| 1974-75 | 0 | 0 | 62 | 310 | 513 | 715 | 746 | 654 | 604 | 368 | 44 | 1 | 4017 |
| 1975-76 | 0 | 0 | 27 | 121 | 356 | 770 | 917 | 480 | 386 | 227 | 78 | 11 | 3373 |
| 1976-77 | 0 | 1 | 15 | 332 | 660 | 869 | 1227 | 680 | 366 | 176 | 42 | 7 | 4375 |
| 1977-78 | 0 | 0 | 4 | 259 | 401 | 784 | 974 | 964 | 627 | 235 | 88 | 5 | 4341 |
| 1978-79 | 0 | 0 | 16 | 214 | 366 | 694 | 876 | 1011 | 439 | 218 | 44 | 4 | 3882 |
| 1979-80 | 0 | 0 | 8 | 242 | 353 | 698 | 806 | 835 | 541 | 135 | 47 | 2 | 3667 |
| 1980-81 | 0 | 0 | 14 | 267 | 557 | 813 | 1042 | 633 | 626 | 171 | 107 | 0 | 4230 |
| 1981-82 | 0 | 1 | 29 | 273 | 473 | 834 | 1029 | 645 | 486 | 280 | 6 | 1 | 4057 |
| 1982-83 | 0 | 6 | 10 | 213 | 399 | 585 | 836 | 718 | 445 | 282 | 69 | 2 | 3565 |
| 1983-84 | 0 | 1 | 86 | 236 | 475 | 887 | 994 | 589 | 657 | 282 | 93 | 3 | 4303 |
| 1984-85 | 0 | 0 | 73 | 57 | 546 | 531 | 997 | 692 | 484 | 177 | 35 | 5 | 3597 |
| 1985-86 | 0 | 0 | 31 | 114 | 257 | 838 | 886 | 713 | 465 | 187 | 78 | 3 | 3572 |
| 1986-87 | 0 | 16 | 24 | 172 | 476 | 741 | 931 | 777 | 550 | 317 | 57 | 0 | 4061 |
| 1987-88 | 0 | 0 | 5 | 370 | 409 | 677 | 1008 | 746 | 527 | 279 | 79 | 32 | 4132 |
| 1988-89 | 0 | 0 | 27 | 361 | 425 | 794 | 696 | 709 | 546 | 293 | 108 | 0 | 3959 |
| 1989-90 | 0 | 3 | 38 | 181 | 468 | 1036 | 574 | 472 | 436 | 258 | 50 | 3 | 3519 |
| 1990-91 | 0 | 0 | 33 | 146 | 365 | 574 | | | | | | | |

**TABLE 5**  COOLING DEGREE DAYS Base 65 deg. F    RICHMOND, VIRGINIA

| YEAR | JAN | FEB | MAR | APR | MAY | JUNE | JULY | AUG | SEP | OCT | NOV | DEC | TOTAL |
|---|---|---|---|---|---|---|---|---|---|---|---|---|---|
| 1969 | 0 | 0 | 0 | 21 | 90 | 328 | 417 | 321 | 147 | 26 | 0 | 0 | 1350 |
| 1970 | 0 | 0 | 0 | 35 | 185 | 328 | 418 | 410 | 313 | 67 | 0 | 0 | 1756 |
| 1971 | 0 | 0 | 0 | 0 | 56 | 297 | 367 | 327 | 209 | 62 | 22 | 5 | 1345 |
| 1972 | 0 | 0 | 7 | 30 | 52 | 180 | 381 | 326 | 178 | 9 | 8 | 0 | 1171 |
| 1973 | 0 | 0 | 13 | 42 | 91 | 338 | 391 | 395 | 231 | 32 | 9 | 2 | 1544 |
| 1974 | 0 | 0 | 10 | 58 | 106 | 180 | 377 | 340 | 141 | 21 | 26 | 0 | 1259 |
| 1975 | 0 | 0 | 0 | 16 | 135 | 267 | 348 | 433 | 165 | 51 | 18 | 0 | 1433 |
| 1976 | 0 | 8 | 9 | 99 | 91 | 307 | 389 | 337 | 133 | 12 | 0 | 0 | 1385 |
| 1977 | 0 | 0 | 22 | 66 | 148 | 258 | 513 | 467 | 289 | 24 | 27 | 0 | 1814 |
| 1978 | 0 | 0 | 0 | 12 | 112 | 302 | 393 | 475 | 263 | 15 | 0 | 1 | 1573 |
| 1979 | 0 | 0 | 16 | 30 | 117 | 188 | 374 | 404 | 195 | 42 | 9 | 0 | 1375 |
| 1980 | 0 | 0 | 1 | 25 | 157 | 243 | 472 | 494 | 313 | 23 | 1 | 0 | 1729 |
| 1981 | 0 | 0 | 1 | 45 | 89 | 395 | 458 | 319 | 169 | 16 | 0 | 0 | 1492 |
| 1982 | 0 | 0 | 0 | 13 | 181 | 259 | 428 | 323 | 157 | 43 | 13 | 7 | 1424 |
| 1983 | 0 | 0 | 0 | 23 | 108 | 325 | 452 | 405 | 207 | 27 | 0 | 0 | 1547 |
| 1984 | 0 | 0 | 0 | 10 | 114 | 392 | 346 | 381 | 154 | 100 | 0 | 2 | 1499 |
| 1985 | 0 | 4 | 20 | 94 | 139 | 290 | 441 | 392 | 213 | 51 | 10 | 0 | 1654 |
| 1986 | 0 | 0 | 8 | 19 | 142 | 344 | 498 | 308 | 205 | 79 | 6 | 0 | 1609 |
| 1987 | 0 | 0 | 0 | 2 | 136 | 329 | 513 | 427 | 227 | 0 | 3 | 0 | 1637 |
| 1988 | 0 | 0 | 3 | 16 | 108 | 269 | 466 | 465 | 137 | 12 | 0 | 0 | 1476 |
| 1989 | 0 | 3 | 24 | 27 | 88 | 341 | 403 | 331 | 218 | 42 | 4 | 0 | 1481 |
| 1990 | 0 | 1 | 43 | 51 | 81 | 312 | 470 | 356 | 177 | 96 | 0 | 2 | 1589 |

**TABLE 6**  SNOWFALL (inches)    RICHMOND, VIRGINIA

| SEASON | JULY | AUG | SEP | OCT | NOV | DEC | JAN | FEB | MAR | APR | MAY | JUNE | TOTAL |
|---|---|---|---|---|---|---|---|---|---|---|---|---|---|
| 1961-62 | 0.0 | 0.0 | 0.0 | 0.0 | T | 0.9 | 20.6 | 1.2 | 16.2 | 0.0 | 0.0 | 0.0 | 38.9 |
| 1962-63 | 0.0 | 0.0 | 0.0 | 0.0 | 0.9 | 8.1 | 1.6 | 6.3 | T | 0.0 | 0.0 | 0.0 | 16.9 |
| 1963-64 | 0.0 | 0.0 | 0.0 | 0.0 | T | 0.4 | 5.7 | 10.2 | 7.0 | 1.2 | 0.0 | 0.0 | 24.5 |
| 1964-65 | 0.0 | 0.0 | 0.0 | 0.0 | 0.4 | 0.0 | 12.4 | 6.6 | 1.0 | 0.0 | 0.0 | 0.0 | 20.4 |
| 1965-66 | 0.0 | 0.0 | 0.0 | 0.0 | 0.0 | T | 26.2 | 3.0 | 0.0 | 0.0 | 0.0 | 0.0 | 29.2 |
| 1966-67 | 0.0 | 0.0 | 0.0 | 0.0 | 0.2 | 12.2 | 6.3 | 17.1 | T | 0.0 | 0.0 | 0.0 | 35.8 |
| 1967-68 | 0.0 | 0.0 | 0.0 | 0.0 | T | 5.6 | 2.3 | 2.4 | 2.8 | 0.0 | 0.0 | 0.0 | 13.1 |
| 1968-69 | 0.0 | 0.0 | 0.0 | 0.0 | 1.2 | 2.8 | T | T | 11.9 | 0.0 | 0.0 | 0.0 | 15.9 |
| 1969-70 | 0.0 | 0.0 | 0.0 | 0.0 | 0.0 | 1.8 | 5.4 | 0.4 | 0.0 | 0.0 | 0.0 | 0.0 | 7.6 |
| 1970-71 | 0.0 | 0.0 | 0.0 | 0.0 | 0.0 | 0.0 | 3.3 | 2.0 | 8.4 | 0.6 | 0.0 | 0.0 | 15.2 |
| 1971-72 | 0.0 | 0.0 | 0.0 | 0.0 | T | 0.0 | T | 13.7 | 0.0 | T | 0.0 | 0.0 | 13.7 |
| 1972-73 | 0.0 | 0.0 | 0.0 | 0.0 | T | 0.6 | 4.3 | 0.4 | 1.4 | 0.0 | 0.0 | 0.0 | 6.7 |
| 1973-74 | 0.0 | 0.0 | 0.0 | 0.0 | 0.0 | 9.9 | T | 5.0 | T | 0.0 | 0.0 | 0.0 | 14.9 |
| 1974-75 | 0.0 | 0.0 | 0.0 | 0.0 | 0.0 | T | 2.7 | 2.9 | 0.4 | 0.0 | 0.0 | 0.0 | 6.0 |
| 1975-76 | 0.0 | 0.0 | 0.0 | 0.0 | 0.0 | 0.0 | 0.2 | T | 1.0 | 0.0 | 0.0 | 0.0 | 1.2 |
| 1976-77 | 0.0 | 0.0 | 0.0 | 0.0 | 1.0 | 1.7 | 11.1 | T | 0.0 | 0.0 | 0.0 | 0.0 | 13.8 |
| 1977-78 | 0.0 | 0.0 | 0.0 | 0.0 | T | T | 1.3 | 5.1 | 5.0 | 0.0 | 0.0 | 0.0 | 11.4 |
| 1978-79 | 0.0 | 0.0 | 0.0 | 0.0 | 0.0 | 0.0 | 0.7 | 19.5 | T | 0.0 | 0.0 | 0.0 | 20.2 |
| 1979-80 | 0.0 | 0.0 | 0.0 | T | 0.0 | T | 16.6 | 7.0 | 15.0 | 0.0 | 0.0 | 0.0 | 38.6 |
| 1980-81 | 0.0 | 0.0 | 0.0 | 0.0 | 0.0 | 0.2 | 0.6 | 0.0 | 0.2 | 0.0 | 0.0 | 0.0 | 1.0 |
| 1981-82 | 0.0 | 0.0 | 0.0 | 0.0 | T | 1.9 | 8.3 | 10.8 | T | 0.2 | 0.0 | 0.0 | 21.2 |
| 1982-83 | 0.0 | 0.0 | 0.0 | 0.0 | 0.0 | 7.9 | 0.1 | 21.4 | 0.0 | T | 0.0 | 0.0 | 29.4 |
| 1983-84 | 0.0 | 0.0 | 0.0 | 0.0 | 0.1 | T | 1.1 | 2.8 | 0.3 | 0.0 | 0.0 | 0.0 | 4.3 |
| 1984-85 | 0.0 | 0.0 | 0.0 | 0.0 | 0.0 | T | 8.3 | T | T | 0.0 | 0.0 | 0.0 | 8.3 |
| 1985-86 | 0.0 | 0.0 | 0.0 | 0.0 | 0.0 | 1.3 | 3.3 | 4.4 | T | T | 0.0 | 0.0 | 9.0 |
| 1986-87 | 0.0 | 0.0 | 0.0 | 0.0 | 0.0 | 0.0 | 15.8 | 5.3 | 0.7 | T | 0.0 | 0.0 | 21.8 |
| 1987-88 | 0.0 | 0.0 | 0.0 | 0.0 | 4.5 | 0.0 | 8.1 | T | T | T | 0.0 | 0.0 | 12.6 |
| 1988-89 | 0.0 | 0.0 | 0.0 | 0.0 | 0.0 | 1.8 | T | 13.6 | T | T | T | 0.0 | 15.4 |
| 1989-90 | 0.0 | 0.0 | 0.0 | 0.0 | 1.1 | 9.9 | 0.0 | T | T | 0.2 | 0.0 | 0.0 | 11.2 |
| 1990-91 | 0.0 | 0.0 | 0.0 | 0.0 | 0.0 | T | | | | | | | |
| Record Mean | 0.0 | 0.0 | 0.0 | T | 0.4 | 2.0 | 5.1 | 4.2 | 2.5 | 0.1 | T | 0.0 | 14.4 |

**See Reference Notes, relative to all above tables, on preceding page.**

The climate of Roanoke is relatively mild. Roanoke is nestled among mountains which interrupt the Great Valley, extending from northernmost Virginia southwestward into east Tennessee. This location, at a point where the valley is pinched between the Blue Ridges and the Alleghenies, offers a natural barrier to the winter cold as it moves southward. It is also far enough inland that hurricanes lose much of their destructive force before reaching Roanoke. Finally, the rough terrain is an inhospitable breeding ground for tornadic activity. The elevation in the vicinity usually produces cool summer nights that make a light cover comfortable for sleeping. Although past records show extremes over 100 degrees and below zero, many years pass without either extreme being threatened.

Roanoke is located near the headwaters of the Roanoke River, which flows in a general southeasterly direction. Numerous creeks and small streams from nearby mountainous areas empty into the Roanoke River. The usual low water stage is 1 to 1.5 feet, and flood stage is 10 feet. Some low-lying streets in Roanoke and nearby Salem have to be blocked off during 7 to 8 foot stages, but damage is minor until the river overflows its banks. The highest stage on record exceeds 19 feet. Damage has been widespread on occasion and has amounted to several million dollars in the city of Roanoke alone.

The growing season averages 190 days. The average date of the last freezing temperature in spring is mid-April and the average date of the first freezing date in the fall is late October.

Rainfall is well apportioned throughout the year. Droughts are so infrequent that quoting actual records would be difficult. Snow usually falls each winter, ranging from only a trace to more than 60 inches.

**TABLE 1**          # NORMALS, MEANS AND EXTREMES

ROANOKE, VIRGINIA

LATITUDE: 37°19'N   LONGITUDE: 79°58'W   ELEVATION: FT. GRND 1149 BARO 1193   TIME ZONE: EASTERN   WBAN: 13741

| | (a) | JAN | FEB | MAR | APR | MAY | JUNE | JULY | AUG | SEP | OCT | NOV | DEC | YEAR |
|---|---|---|---|---|---|---|---|---|---|---|---|---|---|---|
| **TEMPERATURE °F:** | | | | | | | | | | | | | | |
| Normals | | | | | | | | | | | | | | |
| -Daily Maximum | | 44.8 | 48.0 | 56.9 | 68.2 | 76.4 | 83.0 | 86.7 | 85.5 | 79.4 | 68.6 | 57.4 | 47.8 | 66.9 |
| -Daily Minimum | | 26.2 | 27.8 | 35.3 | 44.3 | 53.0 | 60.1 | 64.6 | 63.8 | 57.0 | 44.9 | 36.3 | 28.7 | 45.2 |
| -Monthly | | 35.5 | 37.9 | 46.1 | 56.3 | 64.7 | 71.6 | 75.7 | 74.7 | 68.2 | 56.8 | 46.9 | 38.3 | 56.1 |
| Extremes | | | | | | | | | | | | | | |
| -Record Highest | 42 | 78 | 80 | 87 | 95 | 96 | 100 | 104 | 105 | 101 | 93 | 83 | 76 | 105 |
| -Year | | 1952 | 1985 | 1986 | 1957 | 1962 | 1959 | 1954 | 1983 | 1954 | 1951 | 1950 | 1984 | AUG 1983 |
| -Record Lowest | 42 | -11 | 1 | 10 | 20 | 31 | 39 | 47 | 42 | 34 | 22 | 9 | -4 | -11 |
| -Year | | 1985 | 1970 | 1986 | 1985 | 1966 | 1977 | 1988 | 1986 | 1983 | 1976 | 1950 | 1983 | JAN 1985 |
| **NORMAL DEGREE DAYS:** | | | | | | | | | | | | | | |
| Heating (base 65°F) | | 915 | 759 | 586 | 268 | 99 | 12 | 0 | 0 | 38 | 267 | 543 | 828 | 4315 |
| Cooling (base 65°F) | | 0 | 0 | 0 | 7 | 89 | 210 | 332 | 301 | 134 | 12 | 0 | 0 | 1085 |
| **% OF POSSIBLE SUNSHINE** | | | | | | | | | | | | | | |
| **MEAN SKY COVER (tenths)** | | | | | | | | | | | | | | |
| Sunrise - Sunset | 41 | 6.3 | 6.3 | 6.2 | 6.0 | 6.1 | 5.9 | 6.0 | 5.9 | 5.6 | 5.1 | 5.9 | 6.1 | 6.0 |
| **MEAN NUMBER OF DAYS:** | | | | | | | | | | | | | | |
| Sunrise to Sunset | | | | | | | | | | | | | | |
| -Clear | 42 | 8.4 | 7.8 | 8.0 | 8.7 | 7.5 | 7.4 | 6.7 | 7.8 | 9.6 | 12.7 | 8.8 | 8.8 | 102.1 |
| -Partly Cloudy | 42 | 7.7 | 7.0 | 8.8 | 8.6 | 10.6 | 11.6 | 12.8 | 12.5 | 9.0 | 7.3 | 8.5 | 8.0 | 112.5 |
| -Cloudy | 42 | 15.0 | 13.5 | 14.1 | 12.7 | 13.0 | 11.0 | 11.4 | 10.7 | 11.5 | 11.0 | 12.7 | 14.2 | 150.7 |
| Precipitation | | | | | | | | | | | | | | |
| .01 inches or more | 42 | 10.1 | 9.7 | 10.9 | 10.1 | 11.9 | 10.0 | 11.6 | 10.7 | 8.4 | 7.7 | 9.0 | 8.8 | 119.0 |
| Snow,Ice pellets | | | | | | | | | | | | | | |
| 1.0 inches or more | 42 | 1.8 | 2.0 | 1.0 | 0.1 | 0.0 | 0.0 | 0.0 | 0.0 | 0.0 | 0.* | 0.5 | 1.1 | 6.5 |
| Thunderstorms | 42 | 0.1 | 0.3 | 1.0 | 3.1 | 6.2 | 6.4 | 8.6 | 6.8 | 2.6 | 1.0 | 0.4 | 0.1 | 36.5 |
| Heavy Fog Visibility | | | | | | | | | | | | | | |
| 1/4 mile or less | 42 | 2.7 | 2.9 | 2.0 | 1.1 | 1.8 | 1.0 | 1.4 | 1.4 | 2.6 | 2.0 | 2.2 | 2.4 | 23.6 |
| Temperature °F | | | | | | | | | | | | | | |
| -Maximum | | | | | | | | | | | | | | |
| 90° and above | 25 | 0.0 | 0.0 | 0.0 | 0.4 | 0.6 | 5.2 | 10.2 | 8.0 | 2.3 | 0.0 | 0.0 | 0.0 | 26.8 |
| 32° and below | 25 | 5.4 | 2.9 | 0.2 | 0.0 | 0.0 | 0.0 | 0.0 | 0.0 | 0.0 | 0.0 | 0.2 | 2.6 | 11.2 |
| -Minimum | | | | | | | | | | | | | | |
| 32° and below | 25 | 23.8 | 20.4 | 12.7 | 2.6 | 0.1 | 0.0 | 0.0 | 0.0 | 0.0 | 2.8 | 10.4 | 19.6 | 92.3 |
| 0° and below | 25 | 0.4 | 0.0 | 0.0 | 0.0 | 0.0 | 0.0 | 0.0 | 0.0 | 0.0 | 0.0 | 0.0 | 0.2 | 0.6 |
| **AVG. STATION PRESS.(mb)** | 17 | 976.0 | 975.8 | 974.4 | 973.3 | 973.8 | 974.9 | 975.9 | 976.7 | 977.3 | 977.9 | 977.1 | 976.9 | 975.8 |
| **RELATIVE HUMIDITY (%)** | | | | | | | | | | | | | | |
| Hour 01 | 25 | 67 | 65 | 64 | 64 | 77 | 83 | 84 | 86 | 87 | 80 | 73 | 69 | 75 |
| Hour 07 | 25 | 70 | 69 | 70 | 70 | 79 | 81 | 83 | 87 | 88 | 84 | 76 | 72 | 77 |
| Hour 13 (Local Time) | 25 | 52 | 50 | 48 | 47 | 52 | 53 | 55 | 56 | 57 | 53 | 53 | 54 | 53 |
| Hour 19 | 25 | 57 | 55 | 50 | 49 | 58 | 62 | 64 | 67 | 69 | 64 | 61 | 61 | 60 |
| **PRECIPITATION (inches):** | | | | | | | | | | | | | | |
| Water Equivalent | | | | | | | | | | | | | | |
| -Normal | | 2.83 | 3.19 | 3.69 | 3.09 | 3.51 | 3.34 | 3.45 | 3.91 | 3.14 | 3.48 | 2.59 | 2.93 | 39.15 |
| -Maximum Monthly | 42 | 6.12 | 7.17 | 7.80 | 11.35 | 8.42 | 7.76 | 10.09 | 9.54 | 11.09 | 9.72 | 12.36 | 7.10 | 12.36 |
| -Year | | 1978 | 1960 | 1975 | 1987 | 1950 | 1989 | 1989 | 1984 | 1987 | 1976 | 1985 | 1948 | NOV 1985 |
| -Minimum Monthly | 42 | 0.29 | 0.56 | 0.43 | 0.48 | 1.27 | 0.62 | 0.45 | 1.08 | 0.44 | 0.27 | 0.44 | 0.18 | 0.18 |
| -Year | | 1981 | 1968 | 1966 | 1976 | 1951 | 1986 | 1977 | 1987 | 1968 | 1963 | 1960 | 1965 | DEC 1965 |
| -Maximum in 24 hrs | 42 | 2.71 | 2.62 | 3.02 | 5.57 | 3.99 | 3.98 | 2.74 | 5.22 | 6.60 | 6.41 | 6.63 | 3.40 | 6.63 |
| -Year | | 1968 | 1984 | 1983 | 1978 | 1973 | 1972 | 1989 | 1985 | 1987 | 1968 | 1985 | 1948 | NOV 1985 |
| Snow,Ice pellets | | | | | | | | | | | | | | |
| -Maximum Monthly | 42 | 41.2 | 27.6 | 30.3 | 7.3 | T | T | 0.0 | 0.0 | T | 1.0 | 13.8 | 22.6 | 41.2 |
| -Year | | 1966 | 1960 | 1960 | 1971 | 1989 | 1989 | | | 1953 | 1957 | 1968 | 1966 | JAN 1966 |
| -Maximum in 24 hrs | 42 | 13.7 | 18.4 | 17.4 | 7.3 | T | T | 0.0 | 0.0 | T | 1.0 | 10.0 | 16.4 | 18.4 |
| -Year | | 1966 | 1983 | 1960 | 1971 | 1989 | 1989 | | | 1953 | 1957 | 1968 | 1969 | FEB 1983 |
| **WIND:** | | | | | | | | | | | | | | |
| Mean Speed (mph) | 41 | 9.6 | 9.8 | 10.2 | 9.8 | 7.9 | 7.0 | 6.5 | 6.2 | 6.1 | 6.9 | 8.3 | 8.8 | 8.1 |
| Prevailing Direction | | | | | | | | | | | | | | |
| through 1963 | | WNW | SE | WNW | SE | SE | SE | W | SE | SE | SE | NW | NW | SE |
| Fastest Obs. 1 Min. | | | | | | | | | | | | | | |
| -Direction (!!!) | 28 | 30 | 31 | 32 | 32 | 36 | 28 | 34 | 30 | 15 | 34 | 34 | 30 | 32 |
| -Speed (MPH) | 28 | 53 | 40 | 52 | 58 | 46 | 46 | 46 | 44 | 35 | 35 | 52 | 40 | 58 |
| -Year | | 1964 | 1972 | 1967 | 1963 | 1962 | 1966 | 1980 | 1975 | 1989 | 1963 | 1963 | 1970 | APR 1963 |
| Peak Gust | | | | | | | | | | | | | | |
| -Direction (!!!) | 5 | 31 | NW | NW | NW | W | N | S | W | SE | W | W | NW | NW |
| -Speed (mph) | 5 | 56 | 59 | 52 | 77 | 48 | 43 | 38 | 37 | 54 | 39 | 46 | 52 | 77 |
| -Date | | 1989 | 1987 | 1985 | 1989 | 1989 | 1989 | 1988 | 1985 | 1989 | 1989 | 1986 | 1988 | APR 1989 |

**See reference Notes to this table on the following page.**

## PRECIPITATION (inches) — ROANOKE, VIRGINIA

**TABLE 2**

| YEAR | JAN | FEB | MAR | APR | MAY | JUNE | JULY | AUG | SEP | OCT | NOV | DEC | ANNUAL |
|---|---|---|---|---|---|---|---|---|---|---|---|---|---|
| 1961 | 1.61 | 4.50 | 4.17 | 3.86 | 2.05 | 3.79 | 1.59 | 5.14 | 1.79 | 3.35 | 3.62 | 5.07 | 40.54 |
| 1962 | 2.54 | 3.22 | 4.76 | 1.69 | 2.70 | 3.08 | 5.34 | 3.66 | 2.22 | 5.11 | 3.35 |  | 41.22 |
| 1963 | 1.10 | .97 | 3.89 | 0.87 | 1.94 | 2.61 | 2.68 | 1.81 | 2.87 | 0.27 | 3.80 | 1.86 | 25.67 |
| 1964 | 5.20 | 5.33 | 1.81 | 3.54 | 1.79 | 1.97 | 3.37 | 5.36 | 2.70 | 2.80 | 3.09 | 2.73 | 37.87 |
| 1965 | 3.72 | 3.53 | 3.93 | 1.70 | 3.83 | 1.83 | 5.50 | 1.16 | 1.97 | 3.42 | 0.95 | 0.18 | 31.72 |
| 1966 | 4.26 | 4.78 | 0.43 | 2.59 | 3.49 | 1.54 | 3.00 | 4.73 | 7.25 | 4.04 | 1.73 | 3.25 | 41.09 |
| 1967 | 1.25 | 2.51 | 4.51 | 1.67 | 3.95 | 3.19 | 4.05 | 6.36 | 1.78 | 2.42 | 1.30 | 4.84 | 37.83 |
| 1968 | 3.33 | 0.56 | 3.03 | 2.73 | 1.89 | 2.11 | 2.95 | 5.36 | 0.44 | 8.06 | 2.82 | 1.80 | 35.08 |
| 1969 | 1.86 | 2.74 | 3.35 | 1.40 | 1.58 | 4.95 | 5.35 | 5.41 | 2.79 | 2.22 | 1.40 | 5.54 | 38.59 |
| 1970 | 1.31 | 2.36 | 1.95 | 2.80 | 1.51 | 4.87 | 3.28 | 6.40 | 1.99 | 7.51 | 3.67 | 2.81 | 40.46 |
| 1971 | 1.21 | 5.13 | 2.28 | 2.55 | 7.50 | 4.84 | 5.23 | 4.46 | 3.87 | 6.75 | 2.18 | 0.83 | 46.83 |
| 1972 | 2.49 | 4.80 | 1.76 | 3.31 | 6.00 | 7.55 | 4.89 | 2.62 | 4.79 | 3.18 | 5.63 | 4.62 | 51.64 |
| 1973 | 2.60 | 2.95 | 5.92 | 5.39 | 5.58 | 3.65 | 5.10 | 3.34 | 1.84 | 4.28 | 1.79 | 5.60 | 48.04 |
| 1974 | 3.33 | 2.13 | 3.12 | 1.86 | 3.76 | 2.93 | 3.71 | 4.93 | 3.04 | 0.77 | 1.28 | 3.16 | 34.02 |
| 1975 | 3.59 | 3.05 | 7.80 | 2.04 | 6.65 | 1.54 | 5.15 | 5.68 | 6.46 | 3.01 | 1.77 | 3.67 | 50.41 |
| 1976 | 2.16 | 1.27 | 4.54 | 0.48 | 6.13 | 5.20 | 1.24 | 2.20 | 3.17 | 9.72 | 1.31 | 2.59 | 40.01 |
| 1977 | 1.46 | 0.73 | 2.61 | 3.50 | 1.52 | 2.41 | 0.45 | 2.29 | 2.71 | 4.70 | 6.46 | 2.49 | 31.33 |
| 1978 | 6.12 | 0.65 | 5.92 | 7.54 | 4.85 | 2.05 | 4.83 | 6.33 | 0.52 | 0.78 | 2.55 | 3.15 | 45.29 |
| 1979 | 5.27 | 5.37 | 3.38 | 3.99 | 2.65 | 5.78 | 3.97 | 3.37 | 9.18 | 3.56 | 3.77 | 1.13 | 51.42 |
| 1980 | 4.10 | 0.67 | 5.41 | 5.51 | 2.66 | 1.81 | 5.18 | 2.87 | 1.66 | 2.30 | 1.78 | 0.60 | 34.55 |
| 1981 | 0.29 | 2.43 | 2.30 | 1.75 | 4.56 | 2.49 | 2.86 | 1.32 | 4.52 | 3.90 | 0.68 | 3.79 | 30.89 |
| 1982 | 3.76 | 4.75 | 2.33 | 2.01 | 4.83 | 4.99 | 3.98 | 5.20 | 2.67 | 4.13 | 3.65 | 2.53 | 44.83 |
| 1983 | 1.28 | 4.12 | 6.41 | 7.95 | 3.17 | 2.38 | 1.67 | 2.23 | 1.52 | 7.73 | 4.26 | 5.61 | 48.33 |
| 1984 | 1.35 | 4.85 | 4.30 | 3.97 | 4.49 | 2.34 | 4.17 | 9.54 | 2.69 | 1.42 | 2.67 | 1.84 | 43.63 |
| 1985 | 2.45 | 3.64 | 1.80 | 1.75 | 6.89 | 2.08 | 4.18 | 8.67 | 1.26 | 3.77 | 12.36 | 0.85 | 49.70 |
| 1986 | 0.93 | 2.87 | 1.36 | 1.67 | 4.15 | 0.62 | 2.83 | 4.31 | 3.04 | 2.76 | 3.73 | 5.48 | 33.75 |
| 1987 | 4.53 | 4.55 | 4.11 | 11.35 | 2.68 | 0.71 | 3.21 | 1.08 | 11.09 | 1.10 | 5.00 | 2.16 | 51.57 |
| 1988 | 1.87 | 1.07 | 0.88 | 3.40 | 2.76 | 3.66 | 3.75 | 4.30 | 3.01 | 1.26 | 2.42 | 1.28 | 29.66 |
| 1989 | 1.31 | 2.04 | 2.96 | 2.54 | 6.46 | 7.76 | 10.09 | 1.65 | 8.94 | 4.13 | 3.86 | 2.60 | 54.34 |
| 1990 | 2.33 | 2.76 | 3.42 | 2.07 | 7.45 | 0.83 | 3.80 | 4.42 | 1.86 | 9.89 | 1.08 | 3.79 | 43.70 |
| Record Mean | 2.69 | 3.16 | 3.50 | 3.29 | 3.96 | 3.33 | 3.74 | 4.19 | 3.41 | 3.55 | 2.95 | 3.04 | 40.81 |

## AVERAGE TEMPERATURE (deg. F) — ROANOKE, VIRGINIA

**TABLE 3**

| YEAR | JAN | FEB | MAR | APR | MAY | JUNE | JULY | AUG | SEP | OCT | NOV | DEC | ANNUAL |
|---|---|---|---|---|---|---|---|---|---|---|---|---|---|
| 1961 | 33.2 | 41.1 | 50.1 | 51.0 | 61.5 | 71.3 | 76.6 | 75.6 | 71.9 | 58.3 | 49.3 | 37.2 | 56.4 |
| 1962 | 35.7 | 40.2 | 43.5 | 53.8 | 69.9 | 72.4 | 74.2 | 74.4 | 64.8 | 54.7 | 45.0 | 33.3 | 55.6 |
| 1963 | 32.9 | 32.0 | 49.7 | 58.6 | 64.4 | 72.9 | 75.0 | 73.9 | 66.0 | 60.5 | 48.6 | 30.5 | 55.4 |
| #1964 | 37.3 | 35.6 | 46.6 | 56.9 | 67.4 | 74.6 | 75.9 | 74.0 | 66.8 | 60.0 | 51.1 | 40.0 | 56.7 |
| 1965 | 36.0 | 36.4 | 41.9 | 54.9 | 69.2 | 69.7 | 73.9 | 74.2 | 69.7 | 56.0 | 47.5 | 41.5 | 55.9 |
| 1966 | 30.6 | 35.1 | 46.7 | 51.5 | 63.3 | 71.1 | 77.9 | 73.0 | 66.1 | 54.6 | 47.2 | 37.8 | 54.6 |
| 1967 | 40.8 | 34.8 | 48.5 | 59.0 | 59.0 | 70.3 | 73.4 | 72.6 | 63.2 | 54.7 | 43.4 | 41.3 | 55.1 |
| 1968 | 33.0 | 33.8 | 51.3 | 56.5 | 62.4 | 71.3 | 75.6 | 75.2 | 66.7 | 57.0 | 33.7 | 34.6 | 55.4 |
| 1969 | 32.3 | 37.2 | 40.7 | 57.3 | 65.0 | 73.1 | 76.0 | 73.5 | 66.7 | 56.6 | 44.5 | 33.6 | 54.7 |
| 1970 | 29.8 | 36.9 | 42.5 | 56.5 | 66.8 | 72.9 | 76.1 | 74.1 | 72.6 | 59.7 | 46.3 | 40.0 | 56.2 |
| 1971 | 33.9 | 39.1 | 43.6 | 55.5 | 61.5 | 72.6 | 73.5 | 69.8 | 62.1 | 45.4 | 45.3 |  | 56.3 |
| 1972 | 39.6 | 36.0 | 45.6 | 55.5 | 62.0 | 67.7 | 74.3 | 73.2 | 67.6 | 52.2 | 45.4 | 44.5 | 55.3 |
| 1973 | 37.3 | 35.8 | 51.1 | 53.8 | 61.1 | 73.8 | 75.5 | 76.0 | 70.8 | 59.2 | 49.3 | 38.2 | 56.8 |
| 1974 | 45.3 | 39.0 | 50.8 | 57.2 | 64.3 | 68.1 | 74.5 | 73.5 | 64.8 | 55.0 | 47.3 | 38.9 | 56.6 |
| 1975 | 39.6 | 40.4 | 42.2 | 52.9 | 66.5 | 71.5 | 74.5 | 77.0 | 66.6 | 60.0 | 51.1 | 38.8 | 56.8 |
| 1976 | 33.4 | 46.7 | 50.8 | 57.4 | 62.3 | 70.0 | 74.0 | 72.1 | 65.2 | 50.3 | 40.2 | 34.3 | 54.7 |
| 1977 | 23.6 | 36.6 | 52.5 | 58.9 | 68.1 | 71.1 | 79.7 | 77.8 | 70.4 | 53.6 | 48.5 | 35.9 | 56.4 |
| 1978 | 27.8 | 29.5 | 44.2 | 56.3 | 63.8 | 72.7 | 76.0 | 77.5 | 71.4 | 54.0 | 49.5 | 39.5 | 55.2 |
| 1979 | 31.4 | 29.4 | 48.6 | 55.7 | 63.8 | 69.3 | 73.5 | 74.0 | 66.3 | 54.6 | 45.6 | 40.0 | 54.8 |
| 1980 | 37.5 | 34.0 | 43.5 | 56.7 | 64.8 | 70.0 | 78.1 | 76.8 | 71.5 | 55.5 | 45.4 | 38.7 | 56.1 |
| 1981 | 32.0 | 38.2 | 43.1 | 58.6 | 60.9 | 74.0 | 76.1 | 73.4 | 66.1 | 53.7 | 45.2 | 32.8 | 54.5 |
| 1982 | 28.7 | 38.1 | 44.8 | 50.8 | 67.5 | 70.1 | 75.5 | 72.3 | 65.8 | 57.4 | 47.8 | 42.4 | 55.1 |
| 1983 | 35.6 | 36.5 | 47.0 | 52.4 | 61.0 | 70.1 | 77.9 | 77.9 | 68.0 | 57.1 | 47.1 | 34.9 | 55.4 |
| 1984 | 33.6 | 43.6 | 43.3 | 54.2 | 63.1 | 74.2 | 73.2 | 74.4 | 64.1 | 63.3 | 46.0 | 47.1 | 56.8 |
| 1985 | 31.3 | 38.6 | 50.3 | 61.9 | 67.1 | 72.7 | 76.5 | 73.8 | 68.4 | 60.3 | 55.4 | 35.1 | 57.6 |
| 1986 | 35.2 | 38.3 | 47.2 | 58.8 | 63.9 | 74.2 | 78.8 | 72.4 | 68.9 | 59.0 | 47.4 | 38.5 | 56.9 |
| 1987 | 34.2 | 36.9 | 46.6 | 53.2 | 67.1 | 75.0 | 79.3 | 77.8 | 68.9 | 51.5 | 49.6 | 41.4 | 56.8 |
| 1988 | 30.8 | 37.9 | 47.5 | 55.4 | 63.4 | 70.9 | 77.1 | 77.5 | 66.0 | 51.2 | 46.7 | 38.9 | 55.3 |
| 1989 | 41.3 | 38.2 | 47.4 | 54.3 | 61.2 | 73.7 | 75.9 | 74.1 | 68.1 | 58.5 | 46.0 | 29.6 | 55.7 |
| 1990 | 43.7 | 45.9 | 51.5 | 56.0 | 64.3 | 72.6 | 76.8 | 74.6 | 68.4 | 59.2 | 52.2 | 43.8 | 59.1 |
| Record Mean | 35.7 | 38.3 | 46.2 | 56.6 | 64.7 | 72.1 | 76.2 | 74.8 | 67.8 | 57.2 | 47.1 | 38.3 | 56.3 |
| Max | 44.8 | 48.2 | 56.9 | 67.7 | 76.2 | 83.6 | 87.1 | 85.6 | 78.7 | 68.6 | 57.5 | 47.5 | 66.9 |
| Min | 26.5 | 28.4 | 35.4 | 45.5 | 53.1 | 60.6 | 65.2 | 64.0 | 56.9 | 45.7 | 36.7 | 29.1 | 45.6 |

## REFERENCE NOTES FOR TABLES 1, 2, 3 and 6   (ROANOKE, VA)

### GENERAL

T - TRACE AMOUNT
BLANK ENTRIES DENOTE MISSING/UNREPORTED DATA.
# INDICATES A STATION OR INSTRUMENT RELOCATION.

### SPECIFIC

#### TABLE 1

(a) - LENGTH OF RECORD IN YEARS. ALTHOUGH INDIVIDUAL MONTHS MAY BE MISSING.

* LESS THAN .05

NORMALS — BASED ON THE 1951-1980 RECORD PERIOD.
EXTREMES — DATES ARE THE MOST RECENT OCCURRENCE.
WIND DIR. — NUMERALS SHOW TENS OF DEGREES CLOCKWISE FROM TRUE NORTH. "00" INDICATES CALM.
RESULTANT WIND DIRECTIONS ARE GIVEN TO WHOLE DEGREES.

#### TABLE 3

MAX AND MIN ARE LONG-TERM MEAN DAILY MAXIMUM AND MEAN DAILY MINIMUM TEMPERATURES.

### EXCEPTIONS

#### TABLES 2, 3, and 6

RECORD MEANS ARE THROUGH THE CURRENT YEAR, BEGINNING IN:
1948 FOR TEMPERATURE
1948 FOR PRECIPITATION
1948 FOR SNOWFALL

**TABLE 4**

HEATING DEGREE DAYS Base 65 deg. F          ROANOKE, VIRGINIA

| SEASON | JULY | AUG | SEP | OCT | NOV | DEC | JAN | FEB | MAR | APR | MAY | JUNE | TOTAL |
|---|---|---|---|---|---|---|---|---|---|---|---|---|---|
| 1961-62 | 0 | 0 | 36 | 211 | 485 | 856 | 904 | 688 | 658 | 354 | 34 | 1 | 4227 |
| 1962-63 | 0 | 0 | 100 | 221 | 594 | 975 | 989 | 917 | 470 | 228 | 89 | 5 | 4588 |
| 1963-64 | 0 | 1 | 64 | 150 | 485 | 1063 | 852 | 848 | 566 | 265 | 62 | 15 | 4371 |
| #1964-65 | 0 | 9 | 41 | 338 | 409 | 770 | 892 | 794 | 710 | 305 | 21 | 19 | 4308 |
| 1965-66 | 0 | 9 | 38 | 287 | 520 | 722 | 1058 | 831 | 565 | 409 | 118 | 25 | 4582 |
| 1966-67 | 0 | 0 | 51 | 317 | 527 | 837 | 740 | 838 | 505 | 202 | 206 | 28 | 4251 |
| 1967-68 | 0 | 0 | 105 | 321 | 643 | 728 | 984 | 902 | 423 | 255 | 111 | 3 | 4475 |
| 1968-69 | 0 | 12 | 11 | 244 | 502 | 963 | 1005 | 772 | 746 | 227 | 77 | 9 | 4568 |
| 1969-70 | 0 | 0 | 53 | 274 | 607 | 967 | 1087 | 783 | 691 | 269 | 66 | 2 | 4799 |
| 1970-71 | 1 | 1 | 24 | 194 | 553 | 769 | 959 | 719 | 658 | 285 | 143 | 3 | 4309 |
| 1971-72 | 0 | 0 | 12 | 117 | 595 | 603 | 780 | 837 | 594 | 305 | 99 | 31 | 3973 |
| 1972-73 | 10 | 1 | 33 | 391 | 582 | 628 | 852 | 812 | 428 | 344 | 144 | 1 | 4226 |
| 1973-74 | 0 | 0 | 12 | 196 | 461 | 826 | 607 | 722 | 440 | 255 | 96 | 14 | 3629 |
| 1974-75 | 0 | 0 | 84 | 308 | 539 | 801 | 783 | 683 | 561 | 361 | 60 | 12 | 4330 |
| 1975-76 | 0 | 0 | 59 | 173 | 415 | 809 | 973 | 523 | 438 | 271 | 126 | 22 | 3809 |
| 1976-77 | 0 | 3 | 47 | 452 | 735 | 945 | 1275 | 786 | 385 | 203 | 56 | 23 | 4910 |
| 1977-78 | 0 | 0 | 18 | 350 | 496 | 896 | 1147 | 989 | 637 | 261 | 112 | 4 | 4910 |
| 1978-79 | 0 | 0 | 29 | 335 | 461 | 784 | 1037 | 992 | 512 | 279 | 88 | 15 | 4532 |
| 1979-80 | 3 | 9 | 49 | 329 | 458 | 738 | 848 | 893 | 656 | 266 | 78 | 14 | 4341 |
| 1980-81 | 0 | 0 | 30 | 301 | 582 | 807 | 1016 | 744 | 672 | 212 | 158 | 3 | 4525 |
| 1981-82 | 0 | 0 | 58 | 357 | 589 | 991 | 1121 | 746 | 618 | 421 | 51 | 3 | 4955 |
| 1982-83 | 0 | 6 | 61 | 264 | 509 | 695 | 904 | 792 | 551 | 381 | 157 | 14 | 4334 |
| 1983-84 | 1 | 0 | 87 | 246 | 531 | 924 | 966 | 614 | 664 | 336 | 123 | 6 | 4498 |
| 1984-85 | 0 | 0 | 120 | 74 | 565 | 549 | 1041 | 734 | 471 | 168 | 39 | 11 | 3772 |
| 1985-86 | 0 | 0 | 55 | 171 | 282 | 918 | 917 | 739 | 551 | 206 | 115 | 1 | 3955 |
| 1986-87 | 0 | 22 | 22 | 231 | 523 | 813 | 950 | 782 | 562 | 352 | 58 | 0 | 4315 |
| 1987-88 | 0 | 0 | 18 | 412 | 455 | 723 | 1055 | 778 | 535 | 289 | 101 | 46 | 4412 |
| 1988-89 | 1 | 0 | 53 | 423 | 543 | 802 | 726 | 743 | 556 | 340 | 172 | 0 | 4359 |
| 1989-90 | 0 | 3 | 63 | 234 | 560 | 1091 | 654 | 528 | 441 | 297 | 77 | 3 | 3951 |
| 1990-91 | 0 | 0 | 38 | 200 | 381 | 652 | | | | | | | |

**TABLE 5**   COOLING DEGREE DAYS Base 65 deg. F          ROANOKE, VIRGINIA

| YEAR | JAN | FEB | MAR | APR | MAY | JUNE | JULY | AUG | SEP | OCT | NOV | DEC | TOTAL |
|---|---|---|---|---|---|---|---|---|---|---|---|---|---|
| 1969 | 0 | 0 | 0 | 2 | 86 | 256 | 347 | 272 | 107 | 21 | 0 | 0 | 1091 |
| 1970 | 0 | 0 | 0 | 22 | 128 | 246 | 351 | 291 | 261 | 35 | 0 | 0 | 1334 |
| 1971 | 0 | 0 | 0 | 4 | 40 | 239 | 270 | 245 | 163 | 35 | 13 | 1 | 1010 |
| 1972 | 0 | 0 | 0 | 26 | 13 | 118 | 305 | 262 | 118 | 0 | 2 | 0 | 844 |
| 1973 | 0 | 0 | 3 | 15 | 29 | 269 | 331 | 346 | 192 | 23 | 0 | 0 | 1208 |
| 1974 | 0 | 0 | 7 | 27 | 82 | 117 | 303 | 267 | 83 | 3 | 12 | 0 | 901 |
| 1975 | 0 | 0 | 0 | 5 | 108 | 213 | 301 | 379 | 114 | 27 | 5 | 0 | 1152 |
| 1976 | 0 | 0 | 8 | 53 | 49 | 179 | 285 | 230 | 58 | 1 | 0 | 0 | 863 |
| 1977 | 0 | 0 | 7 | 28 | 158 | 214 | 461 | 400 | 185 | 4 | 7 | 0 | 1464 |
| 1978 | 0 | 0 | 0 | 7 | 79 | 243 | 347 | 391 | 228 | 2 | 0 | 0 | 1297 |
| 1979 | 0 | 0 | 10 | 7 | 56 | 150 | 273 | 296 | 97 | 12 | 1 | 0 | 902 |
| 1980 | 0 | 0 | 0 | 21 | 78 | 171 | 412 | 374 | 231 | 13 | 0 | 0 | 1300 |
| 1981 | 0 | 0 | 2 | 26 | 39 | 278 | 350 | 267 | 97 | 13 | 0 | 0 | 1072 |
| 1982 | 0 | 0 | 0 | 11 | 137 | 165 | 332 | 242 | 90 | 35 | 0 | 0 | 1001 |
| 1983 | 0 | 0 | 11 | 20 | 41 | 172 | 382 | 407 | 188 | 10 | 0 | 0 | 1211 |
| 1984 | 0 | 0 | 0 | 20 | 71 | 290 | 260 | 301 | 101 | 56 | 0 | 0 | 1099 |
| 1985 | 0 | 1 | 18 | 78 | 112 | 247 | 365 | 280 | 163 | 34 | 3 | 0 | 1301 |
| 1986 | 0 | 0 | 4 | 24 | 84 | 282 | 438 | 257 | 145 | 48 | 0 | 0 | 1282 |
| 1987 | 0 | 0 | 0 | 4 | 130 | 306 | 450 | 403 | 140 | 0 | 0 | 0 | 1433 |
| 1988 | 0 | 0 | 0 | 7 | 58 | 232 | 386 | 395 | 90 | 1 | 0 | 0 | 1169 |
| 1989 | 0 | 0 | 17 | 27 | 61 | 265 | 344 | 293 | 163 | 38 | 0 | 0 | 1208 |
| 1990 | 0 | 0 | 29 | 34 | 61 | 238 | 377 | 305 | 145 | 27 | 3 | 0 | 1219 |

**TABLE 6**   SNOWFALL (inches)          ROANOKE, VIRGINIA

| SEASON | JULY | AUG | SEP | OCT | NOV | DEC | JAN | FEB | MAR | APR | MAY | JUNE | TOTAL |
|---|---|---|---|---|---|---|---|---|---|---|---|---|---|
| 1961-62 | 0.0 | 0.0 | 0.0 | 0.0 | 2.9 | 4.5 | 8.3 | 3.3 | 11.3 | T | 0.0 | 0.0 | 30.3 |
| 1962-63 | 0.0 | 0.0 | 0.0 | T | 2.4 | 14.4 | T | 12.2 | 0.7 | 0.0 | T | 0.0 | 29.7 |
| 1963-64 | 0.0 | 0.0 | 0.0 | 0.0 | T | 10.1 | 15.7 | 20.2 | 4.3 | 0.0 | 0.0 | 0.0 | 50.3 |
| 1964-65 | 0.0 | 0.0 | 0.0 | 0.0 | 0.5 | T | 12.1 | 4.0 | 4.1 | 0.0 | 0.0 | 0.0 | 20.7 |
| 1965-66 | 0.0 | 0.0 | 0.0 | 0.0 | T | 0.3 | 41.2 | 8.4 | T | 0.0 | 0.0 | 0.0 | 49.9 |
| 1966-67 | 0.0 | 0.0 | 0.0 | 0.0 | T | 22.6 | 2.7 | 15.6 | 0.8 | T | 0.0 | 0.0 | 41.7 |
| 1967-68 | 0.0 | 0.0 | 0.0 | 0.0 | T | 14.8 | 15.4 | 3.8 | T | 0.0 | 0.0 | 0.0 | 34.0 |
| 1968-69 | 0.0 | 0.0 | 0.0 | T | 13.8 | T | 0.1 | 11.4 | 13.8 | 0.0 | 0.0 | 0.0 | 39.1 |
| 1969-70 | 0.0 | 0.0 | 0.0 | 0.0 | T | 16.8 | 4.4 | 5.4 | T | 0.2 | 0.0 | 0.0 | 26.8 |
| 1970-71 | 0.0 | 0.0 | 0.0 | 0.0 | 2.0 | 10.8 | 1.1 | 3.6 | 7.3 | 7.3 | 0.0 | 0.0 | 32.1 |
| 1971-72 | 0.0 | 0.0 | 0.0 | 0.0 | 10.2 | 0.2 | T | 12.8 | T | T | 0.0 | 0.0 | 23.2 |
| 1972-73 | 0.0 | 0.0 | 0.0 | T | 0.0 | T | 2.4 | 1.4 | 5.5 | 0.2 | 0.0 | 0.0 | 9.5 |
| 1973-74 | 0.0 | 0.0 | 0.0 | T | T | 7.9 | T | 9.7 | T | 0.0 | 0.0 | 0.0 | 17.6 |
| 1974-75 | 0.0 | 0.0 | 0.0 | T | 3.3 | 6.6 | 4.6 | 6.3 | 6.2 | T | 0.0 | 0.0 | 27.0 |
| 1975-76 | 0.0 | 0.0 | 0.0 | 0.0 | T | 0.1 | T | T | 2.2 | 0.0 | 0.0 | 0.0 | 2.3 |
| 1976-77 | 0.0 | 0.0 | 0.0 | 0.0 | 2.4 | 6.4 | 8.9 | 1.5 | T | T | 0.0 | 0.0 | 19.2 |
| 1977-78 | 0.0 | 0.0 | 0.0 | T | 2.4 | 0.4 | 14.5 | 9.6 | 10.4 | 0.0 | 0.0 | 0.0 | 37.3 |
| 1978-79 | 0.0 | 0.0 | 0.0 | T | 1.6 | T | 3.0 | 19.3 | T | 0.0 | 0.0 | 0.0 | 23.9 |
| 1979-80 | 0.0 | 0.0 | 0.0 | 0.3 | T | 0.2 | 15.1 | 4.2 | 12.0 | T | 0.0 | 0.0 | 31.8 |
| 1980-81 | 0.0 | 0.0 | 0.0 | T | T | T | 1.4 | T | 10.4 | 0.0 | 0.0 | 0.0 | 11.8 |
| 1981-82 | 0.0 | 0.0 | 0.0 | 0.0 | 4.0 | 3.9 | 8.4 | 12.2 | 0.5 | 1.9 | 0.0 | 0.0 | 30.9 |
| 1982-83 | 0.0 | 0.0 | 0.0 | T | 0.0 | 6.2 | 3.8 | 24.3 | 0.3 | 0.4 | 0.0 | 0.0 | 35.0 |
| 1983-84 | 0.0 | 0.0 | 0.0 | 0.0 | T | 0.6 | 7.2 | 1.5 | 0.3 | 0.2 | 0.0 | 0.0 | 9.8 |
| 1984-85 | 0.0 | 0.0 | 0.0 | 0.0 | T | 0.8 | 2.7 | 1.2 | 1.3 | T | 0.0 | 0.0 | 6.0 |
| 1985-86 | 0.0 | 0.0 | 0.0 | 0.0 | 0.0 | 1.2 | 1.7 | 7.1 | T | T | 0.0 | 0.0 | 10.0 |
| 1986-87 | 0.0 | 0.0 | 0.0 | 0.0 | T | T | 27.9 | 19.1 | 2.7 | 6.3 | 0.0 | 0.0 | 56.0 |
| 1987-88 | 0.0 | 0.0 | 0.0 | 0.0 | 1.7 | T | 6.7 | T | T | 0.0 | 0.0 | 0.0 | 8.4 |
| 1988-89 | 0.0 | 0.0 | 0.0 | T | 0.0 | 3.8 | 0.7 | 9.1 | 0.2 | 0.2 | T | T | 14.0 |
| 1989-90 | 0.0 | 0.0 | 0.0 | 0.0 | 3.3 | 11.1 | T | 0.2 | 1.5 | 0.0 | T | 0.0 | 16.1 |
| 1990-91 | 0.0 | 0.0 | 0.0 | 0.0 | 0.0 | 0.8 | | | | | | | |
| Record Mean | 0.0 | 0.0 | T | T | 1.6 | 4.0 | 6.7 | 7.2 | 3.7 | 0.4 | T | T | 23.5 |

**See Reference Notes, relative to all above tables, on preceding page.**

The Seattle-Tacoma International Airport is located 6 miles south of the Seattle city limits and 14 miles north of Tacoma. It is situated on a low ridge lying between Puget Sound on the west and the Green River valley on the east with terrain sloping moderately to the shores of Puget Sound some 2 miles to the west. The Olympic Mountains, rising sharply from Puget Sound, are about 50 miles to the northwest. Rather steep bluffs border the Green River Valley about 2.5 miles to the east and the foothills of the Cascade Range begin 10 to 15 miles to the east of the airport.

The mild climate of the Pacific Coast is modified by the Cascade Mountains and, to a lesser extent, by the Olympic Mountains. The climate is characterized by mild temperatures, a pronounced though not sharply defined rainy season, and considerable cloudiness, particularly during the winter months. The Cascades are very effective in shielding the Seattle-Tacoma area from the cold, dry continental air during the winter and the hot, dry continental air during the summer months. The extremes of temperature that occur in western Washington are the result of the occasional pressure distributions that force the continental air into the Puget Sound area. But the prevailing southwesterly circulation keeps the average winter daytime temperatures in the 40s and the nighttime readings in the 30s. During the summer, daytime temperatures are usually in the 70s with nighttime lows in the 50s. Extremes of temperatures, both in the winter and summer, are usually of short duration. The dry season is centered around July and early August with July being the driest month of the year. The rainy season extends from October to March with December normally the wettest month, however, precipitation is rather evenly distributed through the winter and early spring months with more than 75 percent of the yearly precipitation falling during the winter wet season. Most of the rainfall in the Seattle area comes from storms common to the middle latitudes. These disturbances are most vigorous during the winter as they move through western Washington. The storm track shifts to the north during the summer and those that reach the State are not the wind and rain producers of the winter months. Local summer afternoon showers and a few thunderstorms occur in the Seattle-Tacoma area but they do not contribute materially to the precipitation.

The occurrence of snow in the Seattle-Tacoma area is extremely variable and usually melts before accumulating measurable depths. There are winters on record with only a trace of snow, but at the other extreme, over 21 inches has fallen in a 24-hour period. Usually, winter storms do not produce snow unless the storm moves in such a way to bring cold air out of Canada directly or with only a short over water trajectory.

The highest winds recorded in the Seattle-Tacoma area were associated with strong storms crossing the state from the southwest. Prevailing winds are from the southwest but occasional severe winter storms will produce strong northerly winds. Winds during the summer months are relatively light with occasional land-sea breeze effects creating afternoon northerly winds of 8 to 15 miles an hour. Fog or low clouds that form over the southern Puget Sound area in the late summer, fall, and early winter months, often dominate the weather conditions during the late night and early morning hours with visibilities occasionally lower for a few hours near sunrise. Most of the summer clouds form along the coast and move into the Seattle area from the southwest.

Based on the 1951-1980 period, the average first occurrence of 32 degrees Fahrenheit in the fall is November 11 and the average last occurrence in the spring is March 24.

## TABLE 1    NORMALS, MEANS AND EXTREMES

SEATTLE, WASHINGTON SEATTLE – TACOMA AIRPORT

LATITUDE: 47°27'N    LONGITUDE: 122°18'W    ELEVATION: FT. GRND    400 BARO    451    TIME ZONE: PACIFIC    WBAN: 24233

| | (a) | JAN | FEB | MAR | APR | MAY | JUNE | JULY | AUG | SEP | OCT | NOV | DEC | YEAR |
|---|---|---|---|---|---|---|---|---|---|---|---|---|---|---|
| **TEMPERATURE °F:** | | | | | | | | | | | | | | |
| Normals | | | | | | | | | | | | | | |
| -Daily Maximum | | 43.9 | 48.8 | 51.1 | 56.8 | 64.0 | 69.2 | 75.2 | 73.9 | 68.7 | 59.5 | 50.3 | 45.6 | 58.9 |
| -Daily Minimum | | 34.3 | 36.8 | 37.2 | 40.5 | 46.0 | 51.1 | 54.3 | 54.3 | 51.2 | 45.3 | 39.3 | 36.3 | 43.9 |
| -Monthly | | 39.1 | 42.8 | 44.2 | 48.7 | 55.0 | 60.2 | 64.8 | 64.1 | 60.0 | 52.5 | 44.8 | 41.0 | 51.4 |
| Extremes | | | | | | | | | | | | | | |
| -Record Highest | 45 | 64 | 70 | 75 | 85 | 93 | 96 | 98 | 99 | 98 | 89 | 74 | 63 | 99 |
| -Year | | 1981 | 1968 | 1987 | 1976 | 1963 | 1955 | 1979 | 1981 | 1988 | 1987 | 1949 | 1980 | AUG 1981 |
| -Record Lowest | 45 | 0 | 1 | 11 | 29 | 28 | 38 | 43 | 44 | 35 | 28 | 6 | 6 | 0 |
| -Year | | 1950 | 1950 | 1955 | 1975 | 1954 | 1952 | 1954 | 1955 | 1972 | 1949 | 1955 | 1968 | JAN 1950 |
| **NORMAL DEGREE DAYS:** | | | | | | | | | | | | | | |
| Heating (base 65°F) | | 803 | 622 | 645 | 489 | 313 | 169 | 76 | 97 | 169 | 388 | 606 | 744 | 5121 |
| Cooling (base 65°F) | | 0 | 0 | 0 | 0 | 0 | 25 | 70 | 70 | 19 | 0 | 0 | 0 | 184 |
| **% OF POSSIBLE SUNSHINE** | 23 | 25 | 38 | 48 | 52 | 56 | 56 | 65 | 64 | 60 | 43 | 28 | 21 | 46 |
| **MEAN SKY COVER (tenths)** | | | | | | | | | | | | | | |
| Sunrise - Sunset | 45 | 8.5 | 8.2 | 8.0 | 7.7 | 7.1 | 7.0 | 5.3 | 5.7 | 6.1 | 7.5 | 8.4 | 8.6 | 7.3 |
| **MEAN NUMBER OF DAYS:** | | | | | | | | | | | | | | |
| Sunrise to Sunset | | | | | | | | | | | | | | |
| -Clear | 45 | 2.5 | 2.7 | 3.1 | 2.8 | 4.4 | 5.3 | 10.4 | 9.1 | 7.9 | 4.0 | 2.5 | 2.2 | 56.7 |
| -Partly Cloudy | 45 | 3.8 | 4.1 | 5.8 | 7.2 | 8.9 | 7.6 | 9.8 | 9.7 | 8.6 | 7.4 | 4.4 | 3.7 | 81.0 |
| -Cloudy | 45 | 24.6 | 21.5 | 22.2 | 19.9 | 17.6 | 17.0 | 10.6 | 12.3 | 13.5 | 19.6 | 23.2 | 25.2 | 227.2 |
| Precipitation | | | | | | | | | | | | | | |
| .01 inches or more | 45 | 18.6 | 15.8 | 17.2 | 13.7 | 10.4 | 9.1 | 5.0 | 6.3 | 9.3 | 13.1 | 17.9 | 19.3 | 155.6 |
| Snow, Ice pellets | | | | | | | | | | | | | | |
| 1.0 inches or more | 45 | 1.7 | 0.5 | 0.5 | 0.* | 0.0 | 0.0 | 0.0 | 0.0 | 0.0 | 0.* | 0.3 | 0.9 | 4.0 |
| Thunderstorms | 45 | 0.2 | 0.3 | 0.7 | 0.9 | 0.9 | 0.7 | 0.7 | 0.7 | 0.8 | 0.3 | 0.7 | 0.3 | 7.2 |
| Heavy Fog Visibility | | | | | | | | | | | | | | |
| 1/4 mile or less | 45 | 5.6 | 3.4 | 2.2 | 1.1 | 0.8 | 0.8 | 1.7 | 2.8 | 5.3 | 7.8 | 5.8 | 6.3 | 43.4 |
| Temperature °F | | | | | | | | | | | | | | |
| -Maximum | | | | | | | | | | | | | | |
| 90° and above | 30 | 0.0 | 0.0 | 0.0 | 0.0 | 0.2 | 0.3 | 1.1 | 1.2 | 0.3 | 0.0 | 0.0 | 0.0 | 3.2 |
| 32° and below | 30 | 1.2 | 0.2 | 0.0 | 0.0 | 0.0 | 0.0 | 0.0 | 0.0 | 0.0 | 0.0 | 0.2 | 1.0 | 2.6 |
| -Minimum | | | | | | | | | | | | | | |
| 32° and below | 30 | 9.9 | 5.3 | 3.1 | 0.2 | 0.0 | 0.0 | 0.0 | 0.0 | 0.0 | 0.2 | 3.7 | 8.7 | 31.1 |
| 0° and below | 30 | 0.0 | 0.0 | 0.0 | 0.0 | 0.0 | 0.0 | 0.0 | 0.0 | 0.0 | 0.0 | 0.0 | 0.0 | 0.0 |
| **AVG. STATION PRESS. (mb)** | 17 | 1001.6 | 1000.1 | 998.9 | 1000.9 | 1001.1 | 1001.1 | 1001.6 | 1000.5 | 1000.5 | 1001.5 | 999.7 | 1001.7 | 1000.8 |
| **RELATIVE HUMIDITY (%)** | | | | | | | | | | | | | | |
| Hour 04 | 30 | 81 | 80 | 82 | 83 | 82 | 81 | 81 | 83 | 86 | 87 | 83 | 82 | 83 |
| Hour 10 | 30 | 79 | 76 | 74 | 71 | 68 | 66 | 65 | 69 | 73 | 79 | 80 | 81 | 73 |
| Hour 16 (Local Time) | 30 | 74 | 67 | 62 | 57 | 54 | 52 | 49 | 51 | 57 | 67 | 74 | 77 | 62 |
| Hour 22 | 30 | 78 | 76 | 76 | 74 | 72 | 69 | 67 | 71 | 76 | 81 | 80 | 80 | 75 |
| **PRECIPITATION (inches):** | | | | | | | | | | | | | | |
| Water Equivalent | | | | | | | | | | | | | | |
| -Normal | | 6.04 | 4.22 | 3.59 | 2.40 | 1.58 | 1.38 | 0.74 | 1.27 | 2.02 | 3.43 | 5.60 | 6.33 | 38.60 |
| -Maximum Monthly | 45 | 12.92 | 9.11 | 8.40 | 4.19 | 4.76 | 3.90 | 2.39 | 4.59 | 5.95 | 8.95 | 9.69 | 11.85 | 12.92 |
| -Year | | 1953 | 1961 | 1950 | 1978 | 1948 | 1946 | 1983 | 1975 | 1978 | 1947 | 1963 | 1979 | JAN 1953 |
| -Minimum Monthly | 45 | 0.58 | 0.71 | 0.57 | 0.33 | 0.35 | 0.13 | T | 0.01 | T | 0.31 | 0.74 | 1.37 | T |
| -Year | | 1985 | 1988 | 1965 | 1956 | 1947 | 1951 | 1960 | 1974 | 1975 | 1987 | 1976 | 1978 | SEP 1975 |
| -Maximum in 24 hrs | 45 | 3.22 | 3.41 | 2.86 | 1.85 | 1.83 | 2.08 | 0.85 | 1.75 | 2.23 | 3.74 | 3.41 | 2.61 | 3.74 |
| -Year | | 1986 | 1951 | 1972 | 1965 | 1969 | 1985 | 1981 | 1968 | 1978 | 1981 | 1959 | 1979 | OCT 1981 |
| Snow, Ice pellets | | | | | | | | | | | | | | |
| -Maximum Monthly | 45 | 57.2 | 13.1 | 18.2 | 2.3 | T | 0.0 | T | 0.0 | T | 2.0 | 17.5 | 22.1 | 57.2 |
| -Year | | 1950 | 1949 | 1951 | 1972 | 1989 | | 1980 | | 1972 | 1971 | 1985 | 1968 | JAN 1950 |
| -Maximum in 24 hrs | 45 | 21.4 | 7.2 | 7.4 | 2.3 | T | 0.0 | T | 0.0 | T | 2.0 | 9.4 | 13.0 | 21.4 |
| -Year | | 1950 | 1962 | 1989 | 1972 | 1989 | | 1980 | | 1972 | 1971 | 1946 | 1968 | JAN 1950 |
| **WIND:** | | | | | | | | | | | | | | |
| Mean Speed (mph) | 41 | 9.7 | 9.6 | 9.8 | 9.6 | 9.0 | 8.8 | 8.3 | 7.9 | 8.1 | 6.5 | 9.2 | 9.6 | 9.0 |
| Prevailing Direction through 1963 | | SSW | SW | SSW | SW | SW | SW | SW | SW | N | S | S | SSW | SW |
| Fastest Mile | | | | | | | | | | | | | | |
| -Direction (!!!) | 22 | SW | S | SW | SW | SW | SW | SW | SW | S | SW | S | S | S |
| -Speed (MPH) | 22 | 45 | 51 | 44 | 38 | 32 | 29 | 26 | 29 | 33 | 38 | 66 | 49 | 66 |
| -Year | | 1971 | 1981 | 1984 | 1972 | 1968 | 1974 | 1981 | 1977 | 1981 | 1982 | 1981 | 1982 | NOV 1981 |
| Peak Gust | | | | | | | | | | | | | | |
| -Direction (!!!) | 6 | S | S | S | SW | SW | SW | S | N | SW | S | SW | SW | S |
| -Speed (mph) | 6 | 49 | 46 | 43 | 41 | 39 | 32 | 29 | 30 | 38 | 36 | 45 | 48 | 49 |
| -Date | | 1986 | 1988 | 1986 | 1988 | 1989 | 1986 | 1988 | 1985 | 1984 | 1984 | 1986 | 1987 | JAN 1986 |

**See Reference Notes to this table on the following page.**

# SEATTLE-TACOMA, WASHINGTON

## PRECIPITATION (inches)

SEATTLE, WASHINGTON SEATTLE – TACOMA AIRPORT

**TABLE 2**

| YEAR | JAN | FEB | MAR | APR | MAY | JUNE | JULY | AUG | SEP | OCT | NOV | DEC | ANNUAL |
|---|---|---|---|---|---|---|---|---|---|---|---|---|---|
| 1961 | 7.71 | 9.11 | 4.46 | 2.35 | 3.07 | 0.54 | 0.75 | 0.82 | 0.46 | 3.27 | 4.67 | 5.32 | 42.53 |
| 1962 | 2.43 | 2.29 | 2.86 | 2.03 | 1.82 | 0.68 | 0.69 | 1.96 | 2.31 | 4.16 | 9.34 | 5.22 | 35.79 |
| 1963 | 2.25 | 4.36 | 3.43 | 3.06 | 0.90 | 1.68 | 1.18 | 0.73 | 0.59 | 5.06 | 9.69 | 5.79 | 38.72 |
| 1964 | 9.76 | 1.66 | 2.96 | 1.56 | 0.91 | 3.82 | 0.99 | 1.23 | 2.27 | 1.00 | 9.65 | 5.53 | 41.34 |
| 1965 | 5.27 | 3.88 | 0.57 | 3.73 | 1.63 | 0.59 | 0.38 | 2.18 | 0.49 | 2.76 | 4.98 | 7.10 | 33.56 |
| 1966 | 5.43 | 2.31 | 4.38 | 1.99 | 1.35 | 1.15 | 1.35 | 0.42 | 1.77 | 2.92 | 6.85 | 8.31 | 38.23 |
| 1967 | 9.32 | 2.72 | 2.50 | 2.50 | 0.38 | 2.04 | 0.01 | 0.02 | 0.94 | 6.66 | 2.56 | 4.72 | 35.58 |
| 1968 | 6.90 | 6.08 | 5.08 | 1.33 | 1.67 | 3.02 | 0.83 | 4.58 | 1.93 | 4.32 | 5.86 | 8.55 | 50.15 |
| 1969 | 5.71 | 3.16 | 2.20 | 3.45 | 2.93 | 0.91 | 0.27 | 0.45 | 5.57 | 1.19 | 2.21 | 5.68 | 33.73 |
| 1970 | 8.22 | 2.26 | 3.16 | 3.31 | 1.17 | 0.43 | 0.48 | 0.32 | 2.23 | 2.52 | 5.03 | 8.28 | 37.41 |
| 1971 | 5.32 | 4.36 | 7.12 | 2.39 | 1.43 | 2.28 | 0.68 | 0.57 | 3.51 | 3.57 | 5.31 | 6.67 | 43.21 |
| 1972 | 7.24 | 8.11 | 6.74 | 4.12 | 0.69 | 1.81 | 1.34 | 1.13 | 4.10 | 0.72 | 3.38 | 8.98 | 48.36 |
| 1973 | 4.29 | 1.89 | 1.62 | 1.35 | 1.60 | 2.50 | 0.08 | 0.27 | 1.81 | 3.31 | 7.99 | 8.33 | 35.04 |
| 1974 | 7.78 | 4.01 | 5.84 | 2.39 | 1.37 | 1.25 | 1.51 | 0.01 | 0.21 | 1.99 | 5.06 | 6.45 | 37.87 |
| 1975 | 6.01 | 5.80 | 2.87 | 2.49 | 1.13 | 0.84 | 0.27 | 4.59 | T | 7.75 | 5.07 | 7.66 | 44.48 |
| 1976 | 5.55 | 4.74 | 2.71 | 1.67 | 1.61 | 0.63 | 1.17 | 2.71 | 1.25 | 2.06 | 0.74 | 1.86 | 26.70 |
| 1977 | 1.77 | 1.58 | 3.80 | 0.55 | 3.70 | 0.54 | 0.42 | 3.59 | 2.55 | 2.60 | 5.27 | 6.47 | 32.84 |
| 1978 | 4.30 | 3.59 | 2.43 | 4.19 | 1.79 | 0.75 | 1.40 | 1.19 | 5.95 | 0.98 | 6.05 | 1.37 | 33.99 |
| 1979 | 2.25 | 5.32 | 1.55 | 0.81 | 0.88 | 0.46 | 0.73 | 1.02 | 3.38 | 1.94 | 11.85 | 32.26 | 32.26 |
| 1980 | 4.09 | 5.04 | 2.10 | 3.23 | 0.97 | 1.77 | 0.46 | 0.64 | 1.43 | 1.32 | 7.16 | 7.39 | 35.60 |
| 1981 | 2.42 | 4.45 | 2.23 | 1.58 | 1.33 | 2.31 | 1.38 | 0.25 | 3.42 | 6.40 | 4.07 | 5.56 | 35.40 |
| 1982 | 5.35 | 7.57 | 3.73 | 2.07 | 0.63 | 1.03 | 0.59 | 0.62 | 1.49 | 4.07 | 5.31 | 6.86 | 39.32 |
| 1983 | 7.07 | 4.57 | 3.81 | 1.06 | 2.10 | 1.85 | 2.39 | 1.90 | 1.85 | 1.34 | 7.97 | 5.02 | 40.93 |
| 1984 | 3.62 | 3.91 | 3.91 | 2.87 | 3.38 | 2.81 | 0.17 | 0.13 | 1.01 | 2.14 | 8.09 | 4.95 | 36.99 |
| 1985 | 0.58 | 2.63 | 2.56 | 1.30 | 0.85 | 2.80 | 0.10 | 0.55 | 1.98 | 5.74 | 4.26 | 1.78 | 25.13 |
| 1986 | 8.54 | 4.41 | 2.67 | 1.38 | 1.71 | 0.68 | 1.10 | 0.10 | 1.89 | 4.21 | 7.98 | 3.67 | 38.34 |
| 1987 | 5.98 | 2.05 | 5.53 | 2.61 | 2.38 | 0.16 | 0.39 | 0.29 | 0.91 | 0.31 | 3.21 | 6.11 | 29.93 |
| 1988 | 4.07 | 0.71 | 3.75 | 3.20 | 3.01 | 1.56 | 0.50 | 0.28 | 1.75 | 2.24 | 8.43 | 3.48 | 32.98 |
| 1989 | 2.78 | 3.43 | 5.79 | 2.80 | 2.78 | 1.14 | 0.64 | 0.89 | 0.54 | 2.98 | 6.13 | 4.79 | 34.69 |
| 1990 | 9.41 | 3.72 | 2.58 | 2.54 | 1.98 | 3.05 | 0.58 | 0.71 | 0.05 | 5.79 | 10.71 | 3.63 | 44.75 |
| Record Mean | 5.64 | 4.28 | 3.70 | 2.38 | 1.69 | 1.50 | 0.77 | 1.08 | 1.98 | 3.62 | 5.88 | 5.94 | 38.46 |

**TABLE 3**

## AVERAGE TEMPERATURE (deg. F)

SEATTLE, WASHINGTON SEATTLE – TACOMA AIRPORT

| YEAR | JAN | FEB | MAR | APR | MAY | JUNE | JULY | AUG | SEP | OCT | NOV | DEC | ANNUAL |
|---|---|---|---|---|---|---|---|---|---|---|---|---|---|
| 1961 | 43.6 | 44.4 | 45.3 | 47.0 | 53.8 | 63.5 | 67.1 | 68.4 | 58.7 | 50.8 | 41.9 | 39.3 | 52.0 |
| 1962 | 38.4 | 43.1 | 43.3 | 50.0 | 50.6 | 59.9 | 63.5 | 62.0 | 59.6 | 52.6 | 46.5 | 42.3 | 51.0 |
| 1963 | 33.9 | 48.2 | 43.8 | 48.3 | 57.7 | 59.9 | 62.4 | 64.6 | 63.5 | 54.5 | 44.0 | 40.8 | 51.8 |
| 1964 | 40.0 | 41.3 | 44.1 | 46.8 | 53.2 | 57.9 | 63.5 | 62.6 | 58.5 | 53.5 | 42.1 | 36.4 | 50.0 |
| 1965 | 40.2 | 43.0 | 47.0 | 49.5 | 51.9 | 60.8 | 67.8 | 65.7 | 58.4 | 56.4 | 40.4 | 40.4 | 52.6 |
| 1966 | 41.1 | 43.9 | 45.1 | 50.0 | 54.5 | 58.7 | 62.1 | 64.5 | 61.5 | 51.4 | 45.4 | 43.5 | 51.8 |
| 1967 | 42.4 | 42.8 | 42.2 | 46.6 | 55.4 | 62.7 | 66.5 | 71.1 | 65.7 | 54.8 | 41.6 | 53.2 | 53.2 |
| 1968 | 40.9 | 48.5 | 48.6 | 48.7 | 57.3 | 60.7 | 67.0 | 63.7 | 59.1 | 51.5 | 46.8 | 36.6 | 52.5 |
| 1969 | 33.1 | 42.3 | 46.9 | 48.9 | 58.0 | 64.3 | 64.7 | 64.0 | 61.0 | 52.4 | 46.6 | 45.2 | 52.3 |
| 1970 | 41.2 | 47.0 | 46.0 | 46.1 | 54.7 | 62.7 | 64.9 | 64.5 | 58.6 | 50.8 | 46.5 | 39.0 | 51.8 |
| 1971 | 39.7 | 42.3 | 41.3 | 48.9 | 54.5 | 55.9 | 65.5 | 67.7 | 57.6 | 51.0 | 45.7 | 37.5 | 50.6 |
| 1972 | 37.0 | 41.4 | 46.9 | 47.0 | 58.3 | 60.1 | 66.0 | 66.7 | 55.4 | 50.1 | 46.7 | 38.1 | 51.1 |
| 1973 | 38.7 | 43.9 | 44.1 | 48.6 | 56.5 | 59.3 | 64.7 | 61.6 | 61.9 | 52.2 | 43.7 | 44.4 | 51.6 |
| 1974 | 38.7 | 43.2 | 46.3 | 50.3 | 54.9 | 62.6 | 64.0 | 64.6 | 64.4 | 52.5 | 45.1 | 42.4 | 52.4 |
| 1975 | 38.8 | 40.8 | 42.9 | 45.8 | 54.6 | 60.7 | 67.5 | 63.2 | 63.0 | 51.4 | 44.9 | 41.5 | 51.3 |
| 1976 | 41.8 | 40.9 | 41.3 | 49.5 | 56.4 | 60.0 | 65.9 | 64.1 | 62.6 | 54.9 | 47.8 | 44.7 | 52.5 |
| 1977 | 39.4 | 48.7 | 45.7 | 53.6 | 54.5 | 63.0 | 65.1 | 68.5 | 58.9 | 52.2 | 43.9 | 42.2 | 53.0 |
| 1978 | 44.4 | 46.0 | 48.6 | 49.9 | 54.5 | 64.3 | 65.8 | 65.5 | 58.8 | 54.3 | 41.2 | 37.5 | 52.6 |
| 1979 | 37.8 | 42.3 | 49.3 | 50.8 | 57.2 | 62.5 | 67.4 | 64.0 | 62.6 | 54.2 | 43.9 | 44.1 | 53.0 |
| 1980 | 34.8 | 43.8 | 44.3 | 51.6 | 54.2 | 57.5 | 63.8 | 61.9 | 59.6 | 53.9 | 46.7 | 44.1 | 51.4 |
| 1981 | 44.4 | 44.2 | 48.8 | 49.6 | 54.7 | 57.5 | 63.3 | 68.1 | 61.1 | 50.9 | 41.7 | 41.7 | 52.7 |
| 1982 | 39.3 | 42.1 | 44.1 | 47.4 | 54.7 | 63.1 | 62.8 | 65.1 | 60.6 | 52.7 | 43.2 | 40.8 | 51.3 |
| 1983 | 45.0 | 46.9 | 49.4 | 50.7 | 57.7 | 59.9 | 63.3 | 65.6 | 58.3 | 51.7 | 46.8 | 36.1 | 52.7 |
| 1984 | 43.2 | 44.8 | 48.5 | 48.7 | 52.9 | 58.8 | 65.0 | 64.9 | 59.9 | 49.7 | 44.6 | 36.8 | 51.5 |
| 1985 | 37.1 | 39.0 | 43.3 | 49.2 | 54.8 | 60.0 | 68.0 | 65.2 | 58.1 | 51.4 | 35.8 | 36.2 | 49.9 |
| 1986 | 44.9 | 42.8 | 49.2 | 48.1 | 55.7 | 62.7 | 61.7 | 68.4 | 59.1 | 54.3 | 45.3 | 42.0 | 52.9 |
| 1987 | 40.5 | 46.3 | 48.9 | 52.0 | 56.9 | 62.6 | 64.2 | 66.1 | 62.3 | 55.8 | 48.5 | 39.2 | 53.6 |
| 1988 | 40.1 | 44.4 | 45.6 | 50.3 | 54.9 | 59.6 | 65.3 | 65.4 | 60.5 | 55.4 | 45.4 | 41.9 | 52.4 |
| 1989 | 40.5 | 35.9 | 43.7 | 53.4 | 56.0 | 63.2 | 64.5 | 65.3 | 64.1 | 53.1 | 47.0 | 42.9 | 52.4 |
| 1990 | 42.5 | 40.0 | 47.1 | 52.1 | 54.7 | 59.8 | 68.0 | 67.3 | 63.4 | 51.2 | 46.6 | 35.3 | 52.3 |
| Record Mean | 39.1 | 42.5 | 44.7 | 48.9 | 55.1 | 60.2 | 64.6 | 64.4 | 59.9 | 52.2 | 44.7 | 40.5 | 51.4 |
| Max | 44.1 | 48.5 | 51.8 | 57.1 | 64.2 | 69.4 | 75.0 | 74.4 | 68.9 | 59.3 | 50.2 | 45.3 | 59.0 |
| Min | 34.1 | 36.4 | 37.6 | 40.7 | 46.1 | 51.0 | 54.1 | 54.4 | 50.9 | 45.0 | 39.2 | 35.6 | 43.8 |

## REFERENCE NOTES FOR TABLES 1, 2, 3 and 6        (SEATTLE, WA)

### GENERAL

T - TRACE AMOUNT
BLANK ENTRIES DENOTE MISSING/UNREPORTED DATA.
# INDICATES A STATION OR INSTRUMENT RELOCATION.

### SPECIFIC

#### TABLE 1

(a) - LENGTH OF RECORD IN YEARS. ALTHOUGH
INDIVIDUAL MONTHS MAY BE MISSING.
* LESS THAN .05

NORMALS — BASED ON THE 1951-1980 RECORD PERIOD.
EXTREMES — DATES ARE THE MOST RECENT OCCURRENCE.
WIND DIR. — NUMERALS SHOW TENS OF DEGREES
CLOCKWISE FROM TRUE NORTH.
"00" INDICATES CALM.
RESULTANT WIND DIRECTIONS ARE GIVEN TO WHOLE DEGREES.

#### TABLE 3
MAX AND MIN ARE LONG-TERM MEAN DAILY MAXIMUM
AND MEAN DAILY MINIMUM TEMPERATURES.

### EXCEPTIONS

#### TABLES 2, 3, and 6

RECORD MEANS ARE THROUGH THE CURRENT YEAR,
BEGINNING IN        1945 FOR TEMPERATURE
1945 FOR PRECIPITATION
1945 FOR SNOWFALL

**TABLE 4** HEATING DEGREE DAYS Base 65 deg. F      SEATTLE. WASHINGTON SEATTLE – TACOMA AIRPORT

| SEASON | JULY | AUG | SEP | OCT | NOV | DEC | JAN | FEB | MAR | APR | MAY | JUNE | TOTAL |
|---|---|---|---|---|---|---|---|---|---|---|---|---|---|
| 1961-62 | 23 | 8 | 197 | 437 | 689 | 789 | 821 | 610 | 668 | 443 | 438 | 167 | 5290 |
| 1962-63 | 95 | 100 | 158 | 377 | 550 | 698 | 959 | 465 | 651 | 496 | 255 | 171 | 4975 |
| 1963-64 | 78 | 37 | 71 | 320 | 612 | 743 | 771 | 682 | 640 | 535 | 370 | 204 | 5063 |
| 1964-65 | 76 | 91 | 189 | 349 | 679 | 882 | 761 | 611 | 553 | 459 | 400 | 136 | 5186 |
| 1965-66 | 24 | 44 | 194 | 261 | 462 | 754 | 732 | 584 | 610 | 442 | 321 | 190 | 4618 |
| 1966-67 | 95 | 54 | 106 | 414 | 585 | 658 | 695 | 614 | 700 | 548 | 292 | 92 | 4853 |
| 1967-68 | 16 | 0 | 44 | 310 | 524 | 718 | 737 | 472 | 503 | 485 | 232 | 139 | 4180 |
| 1968-69 | 33 | 70 | 179 | 415 | 538 | 871 | 983 | 627 | 554 | 478 | 230 | 71 | 5049 |
| 1969-70 | 49 | 49 | 144 | 381 | 547 | 607 | 731 | 499 | 586 | 563 | 314 | 122 | 4592 |
| 1970-71 | 53 | 44 | 190 | 435 | 548 | 801 | 778 | 628 | 728 | 472 | 321 | 267 | 5265 |
| 1971-72 | 82 | 17 | 214 | 429 | 570 | 843 | 863 | 678 | 557 | 531 | 222 | 144 | 5150 |
| 1972-73 | 48 | 32 | 295 | 455 | 544 | 825 | 807 | 586 | 639 | 484 | 272 | 183 | 5170 |
| 1973-74 | 70 | 114 | 111 | 388 | 633 | 632 | 809 | 606 | 573 | 433 | 306 | 99 | 4774 |
| 1974-75 | 60 | 66 | 74 | 380 | 591 | 690 | 804 | 671 | 678 | 570 | 317 | 144 | 5045 |
| 1975-76 | 23 | 73 | 93 | 413 | 594 | 723 | 712 | 693 | 731 | 465 | 265 | 157 | 4942 |
| 1976-77 | 24 | 52 | 81 | 307 | 510 | 625 | 786 | 451 | 591 | 335 | 320 | 79 | 4161 |
| 1977-78 | 34 | 43 | 178 | 390 | 625 | 701 | 631 | 525 | 498 | 447 | 323 | 78 | 4473 |
| 1978-79 | 44 | 42 | 180 | 324 | 706 | 846 | 837 | 630 | 479 | 420 | 235 | 96 | 4839 |
| 1979-80 | 27 | 40 | 86 | 327 | 628 | 642 | 929 | 610 | 634 | 395 | 329 | 218 | 4865 |
| 1980-81 | 66 | 104 | 158 | 343 | 543 | 639 | 633 | 577 | 494 | 455 | 316 | 220 | 4548 |
| 1981-82 | 80 | 28 | 138 | 430 | 530 | 715 | 790 | 636 | 640 | 521 | 312 | 103 | 4923 |
| 1982-83 | 93 | 42 | 141 | 373 | 647 | 745 | 613 | 502 | 479 | 422 | 244 | 149 | 4450 |
| 1983-84 | 72 | 19 | 196 | 406 | 511 | 890 | 672 | 577 | 507 | 482 | 372 | 183 | 4887 |
| 1984-85 | 54 | 42 | 159 | 467 | 603 | 867 | 857 | 719 | 666 | 469 | 310 | 160 | 5373 |
| 1985-86 | 8 | 48 | 199 | 413 | 870 | 888 | 618 | 616 | 479 | 502 | 305 | 90 | 5036 |
| 1986-87 | 105 | 12 | 196 | 323 | 586 | 707 | 754 | 522 | 491 | 384 | 253 | 105 | 4438 |
| 1987-88 | 58 | 37 | 102 | 284 | 485 | 792 | 767 | 590 | 593 | 435 | 316 | 165 | 4624 |
| 1988-89 | 60 | 38 | 162 | 291 | 583 | 708 | 749 | 807 | 654 | 340 | 273 | 93 | 4758 |
| 1989-90 | 41 | 29 | 68 | 362 | 534 | 677 | 689 | 696 | 547 | 379 | 312 | 158 | 4492 |
| 1990-91 | 29 | 23 | 61 | 420 | 546 | 913 | | | | | | | |

**TABLE 5** COOLING DEGREE DAYS Base 65 deg. F      SEATTLE. WASHINGTON SEATTLE – TACOMA AIRPORT

| YEAR | JAN | FEB | MAR | APR | MAY | JUNE | JULY | AUG | SEP | OCT | NOV | DEC | TOTAL |
|---|---|---|---|---|---|---|---|---|---|---|---|---|---|
| 1969 | 0 | 0 | 0 | 0 | 19 | 55 | 44 | 25 | 28 | 0 | 0 | 0 | 171 |
| 1970 | 0 | 0 | 0 | 0 | 1 | 60 | 58 | 36 | 6 | 0 | 0 | 0 | 161 |
| 1971 | 0 | 0 | 0 | 0 | 4 | 2 | 106 | 107 | 0 | 0 | 0 | 0 | 219 |
| 1972 | 0 | 0 | 0 | 0 | 22 | 3 | 85 | 91 | 11 | 0 | 0 | 0 | 212 |
| 1973 | 0 | 0 | 0 | 0 | 16 | 19 | 67 | 17 | 21 | 0 | 0 | 0 | 140 |
| 1974 | 0 | 0 | 0 | 0 | 0 | 36 | 38 | 62 | 60 | 0 | 0 | 0 | 196 |
| 1975 | 0 | 0 | 0 | 0 | 0 | 21 | 108 | 29 | 39 | 0 | 0 | 0 | 197 |
| 1976 | 0 | 0 | 0 | 8 | 4 | 14 | 59 | 29 | 15 | 0 | 0 | 0 | 129 |
| 1977 | 0 | 0 | 0 | 0 | 0 | 26 | 44 | 158 | 4 | 0 | 0 | 0 | 232 |
| 1978 | 0 | 0 | 0 | 0 | 4 | 66 | 76 | 64 | 0 | 0 | 0 | 0 | 210 |
| 1979 | 0 | 0 | 0 | 0 | 2 | 27 | 106 | 15 | 21 | 0 | 0 | 0 | 171 |
| 1980 | 0 | 0 | 0 | 0 | 0 | 0 | 34 | 15 | 3 | 2 | 0 | 0 | 54 |
| 1981 | 0 | 0 | 0 | 0 | 1 | 3 | 35 | 131 | 24 | 0 | 0 | 0 | 194 |
| 1982 | 0 | 0 | 0 | 0 | 0 | 53 | 31 | 55 | 15 | 0 | 0 | 0 | 154 |
| 1983 | 0 | 0 | 0 | 0 | 24 | 2 | 24 | 44 | 0 | 0 | 0 | 0 | 94 |
| 1984 | 0 | 0 | 0 | 0 | 1 | 5 | 62 | 45 | 11 | 0 | 0 | 0 | 124 |
| 1985 | 0 | 0 | 0 | 0 | 3 | 17 | 125 | 59 | 0 | 0 | 0 | 0 | 204 |
| 1986 | 0 | 0 | 0 | 0 | 22 | 27 | 10 | 124 | 26 | 0 | 0 | 0 | 209 |
| 1987 | 0 | 0 | 0 | 0 | 11 | 42 | 39 | 80 | 35 | 5 | 0 | 0 | 212 |
| 1988 | 0 | 0 | 0 | 0 | 7 | 10 | 79 | 56 | 36 | 1 | 0 | 0 | 189 |
| 1989 | 0 | 0 | 0 | 0 | 2 | 47 | 32 | 45 | 46 | 0 | 0 | 0 | 172 |
| 1990 | 0 | 0 | 0 | 0 | 0 | 10 | 129 | 100 | 21 | 0 | 0 | 0 | 260 |

**TABLE 6** SNOWFALL (inches)      SEATTLE. WASHINGTON SEATTLE – TACOMA AIRPORT

| SEASON | JULY | AUG | SEP | OCT | NOV | DEC | JAN | FEB | MAR | APR | MAY | JUNE | TOTAL |
|---|---|---|---|---|---|---|---|---|---|---|---|---|---|
| 1961-62 | 0.0 | 0.0 | 0.0 | 0.0 | T | 0.9 | 1.0 | 7.0 | 1.7 | 0.0 | 0.0 | 0.0 | 10.6 |
| 1962-63 | 0.0 | 0.0 | 0.0 | 0.0 | 0.0 | T | 3.1 | 0.5 | T | 0.0 | 0.0 | 0.0 | 3.6 |
| 1963-64 | 0.0 | 0.0 | 0.0 | 0.0 | 1.0 | T | 0.5 | T | T | T | 0.0 | 0.0 | 1.5 |
| 1964-65 | 0.0 | 0.0 | 0.0 | 0.0 | 3.3 | 7.6 | 7.3 | T | 0.0 | T | 0.0 | 0.0 | 18.2 |
| 1965-66 | 0.0 | 0.0 | 0.0 | 0.0 | 0.0 | 15.3 | 2.1 | T | 5.5 | T | 0.0 | 0.0 | 22.9 |
| 1966-67 | 0.0 | 0.0 | 0.0 | 0.0 | 0.0 | 2.0 | 5.9 | T | T | T | 0.0 | 0.0 | 7.9 |
| 1967-68 | 0.0 | 0.0 | 0.0 | 0.0 | 0.0 | 3.6 | 7.5 | 0.0 | 0.0 | 0.5 | 0.0 | 0.0 | 11.6 |
| 1968-69 | 0.0 | 0.0 | 0.0 | 0.0 | 0.0 | 22.1 | 45.4 | T | 0.0 | 0.0 | 0.0 | 0.0 | 67.5 |
| 1969-70 | 0.0 | 0.0 | 0.0 | 0.0 | T | 0.0 | T | 0.0 | T | T | 0.0 | 0.0 | T |
| 1970-71 | 0.0 | 0.0 | 0.0 | 0.0 | T | 2.9 | 9.1 | 2.2 | 1.9 | T | 0.0 | 0.0 | 16.1 |
| 1971-72 | 0.0 | 0.0 | 0.0 | 2.0 | T | 10.6 | 14.0 | 0.3 | T | 2.3 | 0.0 | 0.0 | 29.2 |
| 1972-73 | 0.0 | 0.0 | T | 0.0 | T | 5.6 | 2.7 | T | 0.8 | T | 0.0 | 0.0 | 9.1 |
| 1973-74 | 0.0 | 0.0 | 0.0 | 0.0 | 0.2 | 0.3 | 3.7 | T | T | 0.0 | T | 0.0 | 4.2 |
| 1974-75 | 0.0 | 0.0 | 0.0 | 0.0 | 0.0 | 9.8 | 1.3 | T | T | 0.2 | 0.0 | 0.0 | 11.3 |
| 1975-76 | 0.0 | 0.0 | 0.0 | 0.0 | 1.6 | 2.6 | T | 0.5 | 0.2 | T | 0.0 | 0.0 | 4.9 |
| 1976-77 | 0.0 | 0.0 | 0.0 | 0.0 | 0.0 | T | 1.0 | T | 0.9 | 0.0 | 0.0 | 0.0 | 1.9 |
| 1977-78 | 0.0 | 0.0 | 0.0 | 0.0 | 0.0 | 3.5 | T | 0.0 | T | T | 0.0 | 0.0 | 3.5 |
| 1978-79 | 0.0 | 0.0 | 0.0 | 0.0 | 4.9 | 0.2 | 0.5 | 0.4 | 0.0 | 0.0 | 0.0 | 0.0 | 6.0 |
| 1979-80 | 0.0 | 0.0 | 0.0 | 0.0 | 0.0 | 1.2 | 8.8 | 2.5 | 0.1 | T | 0.0 | 0.0 | 12.6 |
| 1980-81 | T | 0.0 | 0.0 | 0.0 | T | 0.3 | 0.0 | 1.1 | 0.0 | 0.0 | 0.0 | Q.0 | 1.4 |
| 1981-82 | 0.0 | 0.0 | 0.0 | 0.0 | 0.0 | T | 7.0 | T | 2.0 | T | 0.0 | 0.0 | 9.0 |
| 1982-83 | 0.0 | 0.0 | T | 0.0 | T | 0.0 | 0.0 | 0.0 | 0.0 | 0.0 | 0.0 | 0.0 | T |
| 1983-84 | 0.0 | 0.0 | 0.0 | 0.0 | T | T | 0.3 | T | 0.0 | 0.0 | 0.0 | 0.0 | 0.3 |
| 1984-85 | 0.0 | 0.0 | 0.0 | T | T | 2.4 | T | 5.7 | T | T | 0.0 | 0.0 | 8.1 |
| 1985-86 | 0.0 | 0.0 | 0.0 | T | 17.5 | 1.7 | 0.0 | 1.1 | T | 0.0 | 0.0 | 0.0 | |
| 1986-87 | 0.0 | 0.0 | 0.0 | 0.0 | T | 0.0 | 1.4 | 0.0 | 0.0 | 0.0 | 0.0 | 0.0 | 1.4 |
| 1987-88 | 0.0 | 0.0 | 0.0 | 0.0 | 0.0 | T | T | 0.0 | T | 0.0 | 0.0 | 0.0 | T |
| 1988-89 | 0.0 | 0.0 | 0.0 | 0.0 | T | T | 1.0 | 5.8 | 7.4 | T | T | 0.0 | 14.2 |
| 1989-90 | 0.0 | 0.0 | 0.0 | 0.0 | 0.0 | 0.0 | T | 9.8 | T | 0.0 | 0.0 | 0.0 | 9.8 |
| 1990-91 | 0.0 | 0.0 | 0.0 | 0.0 | 0.0 | 3.8 | | | | | | | |
| Record Mean | T | 0.0 | T | T | 1.3 | 2.5 | 5.3 | 1.7 | 1.4 | 0.1 | T | 0.0 | 12.3 |

**See Reference Notes, relative to all above tables, on preceding page.**

Spokane lies on the eastern edge of the broad Columbia Basin area of Washington which is bounded by the Cascade Range on the west and the Rocky Mountains on the east. The elevations in eastern Washington vary from less than 400 feet above sea level near Pasco where the Columbia River flows out of Washington to over 5,000 feet in the mountain areas of the extreme eastern edge of the State. Spokane is located on the upper plateau area where the long gradual slope from the Columbia River meets the sharp rise of the Rocky Mountain Ranges.

Much of the urban area of Spokane lies along both sides of the Spokane River at an elevation of approximately 2,000 feet, but the residential areas have spread to the crests of the plateaus on either side of the river with elevations up to 2,500 feet above sea level. Spokane International Airport is situated on the plateau area 6 miles west-southwest and some 400 feet higher than the downtown business district.

The climate of Spokane combines some of the characteristics of damp coastal type weather and arid interior conditions. Most of the air masses which reach Spokane are brought in by the prevailing westerly and southwesterly circulations. Frequently, much of the moisture in the storms that move eastward and southeastward from the Gulf of Alaska and the eastern Pacific Ocean is precipitated out as the storms are lifted across the Coast and Cascade Ranges. Annual precipitation totals in the Spokane area are generally less than 20 inches and less than 50 percent of the amounts received west of the Cascades. However, the precipitation and total cloudiness in the Spokane vicinity is greater than that of the desert areas of south-central Washington. The lifting action of the air masses as they move up the east slope of the Columbia Basin frequently produces the cooling and condensation necessary for formation of clouds and precipitation.

Infrequently, the Spokane area comes under the influence of dry continental air masses from the north or east. On occasions when these air masses penetrate into eastern Washington the result is high temperatures and very low humidity in the summer and sub-zero temperatures in the winter. In the winter most of the severe arctic outbursts of cold air move southward on the east side of the Continental Divide and do not affect Spokane.

In general, Spokane weather has the characteristics of a mild, arid climate during the summer months and a cold, coastal type in the winter. Approximately 70 percent of the total annual precipitation falls between the first of October and the end of March and about half of that falls as snow. The growing season usually extends over nearly six months from mid-April to mid-October. Irrigation is required for all crops except dry-land type grains. The summer weather is ideal for full enjoyment of the many mountain and lake recreational areas in the immediate vicinity. Winter weather includes many cloudy or foggy days and below freezing temperatures with occasional snowfall of several inches in depth. Sub-zero temperatures and traffic-stopping snowfalls are infrequent.

Based on the 1951-1980 period, the average first occurrence of 32 degrees Fahrenheit in the fall is October 6 and the average last occurrence in the spring is May 4.

## TABLE 1 — NORMALS, MEANS AND EXTREMES

### SPOKANE WASHINGTON

LATITUDE: 47°38'N   LONGITUDE: 117°32'W   ELEVATION: FT. GRND 2357 BARO 2360   TIME ZONE: PACIFIC   WBAN: 24157

| | (a) | JAN | FEB | MAR | APR | MAY | JUNE | JULY | AUG | SEP | OCT | NOV | DEC | YEAR |
|---|---|---|---|---|---|---|---|---|---|---|---|---|---|---|
| **TEMPERATURE °F:** | | | | | | | | | | | | | | |
| Normals | | | | | | | | | | | | | | |
| −Daily Maximum | | 31.3 | 39.0 | 46.2 | 56.7 | 66.1 | 74.0 | 84.0 | 81.7 | 72.4 | 58.3 | 41.4 | 34.2 | 57.1 |
| −Daily Minimum | | 20.0 | 25.7 | 29.0 | 34.9 | 42.5 | 49.3 | 55.3 | 54.3 | 46.5 | 36.7 | 28.5 | 23.7 | 37.2 |
| −Monthly | | 25.7 | 32.4 | 37.6 | 45.8 | 54.3 | 61.7 | 69.7 | 68.1 | 59.4 | 47.6 | 34.9 | 29.0 | 47.2 |
| Extremes | | | | | | | | | | | | | | |
| −Record Highest | 42 | 59 | 61 | 71 | 90 | 96 | 100 | 103 | 108 | 98 | 86 | 67 | 56 | 108 |
| −Year | | 1971 | 1958 | 1960 | 1977 | 1986 | 1973 | 1967 | 1961 | 1988 | 1980 | 1975 | 1980 | AUG 1961 |
| −Record Lowest | 42 | −22 | −17 | −7 | 17 | 24 | 33 | 37 | 35 | 24 | 11 | −21 | −25 | −25 |
| −Year | | 1979 | 1979 | 1989 | 1966 | 1954 | 1984 | 1981 | 1965 | 1985 | 1984 | 1985 | 1968 | DEC 1968 |
| **NORMAL DEGREE DAYS:** | | | | | | | | | | | | | | |
| Heating (base 65°F) | | 1218 | 913 | 849 | 576 | 339 | 140 | 17 | 63 | 209 | 539 | 903 | 1116 | 6882 |
| Cooling (base 65°F) | | 0 | 0 | 0 | 0 | 8 | 41 | 162 | 159 | 41 | 0 | 0 | 0 | 411 |
| **% OF POSSIBLE SUNSHINE** | 41 | 27 | 40 | 53 | 61 | 63 | 66 | 80 | 77 | 71 | 54 | 28 | 22 | 54 |
| **MEAN SKY COVER (tenths)** | | | | | | | | | | | | | | |
| Sunrise − Sunset | 42 | 8.3 | 8.0 | 7.4 | 7.1 | 6.7 | 6.1 | 3.8 | 4.2 | 4.9 | 6.3 | 8.1 | 8.5 | 6.6 |
| **MEAN NUMBER OF DAYS:** | | | | | | | | | | | | | | |
| Sunrise to Sunset | | | | | | | | | | | | | | |
| −Clear | 42 | 3.1 | 3.2 | 4.1 | 4.5 | 5.5 | 7.3 | 16.5 | 15.3 | 12.0 | 8.0 | 3.1 | 2.8 | 85.5 |
| −Partly Cloudy | 42 | 4.2 | 5.0 | 7.7 | 8.4 | 10.2 | 10.2 | 8.4 | 8.5 | 8.2 | 7.8 | 5.1 | 3.8 | 87.5 |
| −Cloudy | 42 | 23.7 | 20.0 | 19.1 | 17.1 | 15.2 | 12.4 | 6.1 | 7.3 | 9.8 | 15.3 | 21.8 | 24.4 | 192.2 |
| Precipitation | | | | | | | | | | | | | | |
| .01 inches or more | 42 | 14.1 | 11.4 | 11.6 | 8.6 | 9.2 | 7.7 | 4.3 | 5.0 | 5.9 | 7.5 | 12.6 | 15.1 | 112.9 |
| Snow,Ice pellets | | | | | | | | | | | | | | |
| 1.0 inches or more | 42 | 5.3 | 2.9 | 1.6 | 0.2 | 0.* | 0.0 | 0.0 | 0.0 | 0.0 | 0.1 | 2.1 | 5.0 | 17.2 |
| Thunderstorms | 42 | 0.* | 0.* | 0.3 | 0.7 | 1.5 | 2.8 | 2.1 | 2.1 | 0.7 | 0.3 | 0.1 | 0.0 | 10.6 |
| Heavy Fog Visibility | | | | | | | | | | | | | | |
| 1/4 mile or less | 42 | 9.5 | 7.2 | 3.0 | 1.2 | 0.9 | 0.5 | 0.2 | 0.3 | 0.9 | 4.3 | 8.6 | 12.3 | 48.8 |
| Temperature °F | | | | | | | | | | | | | | |
| −Maximum | | | | | | | | | | | | | | |
| 90° and above | 30 | 0.0 | 0.0 | 0.0 | 0.* | 0.3 | 2.1 | 8.7 | 7.1 | 0.9 | 0.0 | 0.0 | 0.0 | 19.1 |
| 32° and below | 30 | 14.8 | 4.6 | 1.0 | 0.0 | 0.0 | 0.0 | 0.0 | 0.0 | 0.0 | 0.1 | 4.1 | 13.9 | 38.6 |
| −Minimum | | | | | | | | | | | | | | |
| 32° and below | 30 | 26.7 | 22.6 | 20.6 | 11.0 | 1.7 | 0.0 | 0.0 | 0.0 | 0.8 | 9.5 | 20.0 | 26.6 | 139.4 |
| 0° and below | 30 | 2.6 | 0.5 | 0.* | 0.0 | 0.0 | 0.0 | 0.0 | 0.0 | 0.0 | 0.0 | 0.3 | 1.8 | 5.2 |
| **AVG. STATION PRESS. (mb)** | 16 | 934.2 | 932.9 | 929.8 | 931.1 | 930.7 | 931.0 | 931.8 | 931.3 | 932.6 | 934.0 | 932.3 | 934.4 | 932.2 |
| **RELATIVE HUMIDITY (%)** | | | | | | | | | | | | | | |
| Hour 04 | 30 | 85 | 84 | 81 | 77 | 76 | 74 | 63 | 62 | 71 | 79 | 87 | 88 | 77 |
| Hour 10 (Local Time) | 30 | 83 | 80 | 69 | 57 | 53 | 49 | 40 | 43 | 52 | 66 | 83 | 86 | 63 |
| Hour 16 | 30 | 79 | 69 | 55 | 44 | 41 | 35 | 27 | 28 | 35 | 49 | 76 | 83 | 52 |
| Hour 22 | 30 | 84 | 81 | 74 | 65 | 63 | 57 | 45 | 46 | 56 | 70 | 85 | 87 | 68 |
| **PRECIPITATION (inches):** | | | | | | | | | | | | | | |
| Water Equivalent | | | | | | | | | | | | | | |
| −Normal | | 2.47 | 1.61 | 1.36 | 1.08 | 1.38 | 1.23 | 0.50 | 0.74 | 0.71 | 1.08 | 2.06 | 2.49 | 16.71 |
| −Maximum Monthly | 42 | 4.96 | 3.94 | 3.75 | 3.08 | 5.71 | 3.06 | 2.27 | 1.83 | 2.05 | 4.05 | 5.10 | 5.13 | 5.71 |
| −Year | | 1959 | 1961 | 1950 | 1948 | 1948 | 1964 | 1987 | 1976 | 1959 | 1950 | 1973 | 1964 | MAY 1948 |
| −Minimum Monthly | 42 | 0.38 | 0.35 | 0.31 | 0.08 | 0.20 | 0.16 | T | T | 0.01 | 0.03 | 0.22 | 0.60 | T |
| −Year | | 1985 | 1988 | 1965 | 1956 | 1982 | 1960 | 1973 | 1988 | 1987 | 1987 | 1976 | 1976 | AUG 1988 |
| −Maximum in 24 hrs | 42 | 1.48 | 1.11 | 0.96 | 1.01 | 1.67 | 2.07 | 1.01 | 1.09 | 1.12 | 0.98 | 1.41 | 1.60 | 2.07 |
| −Year | | 1954 | 1963 | 1989 | 1982 | 1948 | 1964 | 1987 | 1959 | 1973 | 1955 | 1960 | 1951 | JUN 1964 |
| Snow,Ice pellets | | | | | | | | | | | | | | |
| −Maximum Monthly | 42 | 56.9 | 28.5 | 15.3 | 6.6 | 3.5 | T | 0.0 | 0.0 | 0.0 | 6.1 | 24.7 | 42.0 | 56.9 |
| −Year | | 1950 | 1975 | 1962 | 1964 | 1967 | 1954 | | | | 1957 | 1955 | 1964 | JAN 1950 |
| −Maximum in 24 hrs | 42 | 13.0 | 8.9 | 6.1 | 4.9 | 3.5 | T | 0.0 | 0.0 | 0.0 | 6.1 | 9.0 | 12.1 | 13.0 |
| −Year | | 1950 | 1975 | 1989 | 1964 | 1967 | 1954 | | | | 1957 | 1973 | 1951 | JAN 1950 |
| **WIND:** | | | | | | | | | | | | | | |
| Mean Speed (mph) | 42 | 8.7 | 9.2 | 9.7 | 10.0 | 9.2 | 9.2 | 8.6 | 8.2 | 8.3 | 8.1 | 8.6 | 8.5 | 8.9 |
| Prevailing Direction through 1963 | | NE | SSW | SSW | SW | SSW | SSW | SW | SW | NE | SSW | NE | NE | SSW |
| Fastest Mile | | | | | | | | | | | | | | |
| −Direction (!!!) | 42 | SW | SW | SW | SW | W | SW | SW | SW | SW | SW | SW | SW | SW |
| −Speed (MPH) | 42 | 59 | 54 | 54 | 52 | 49 | 44 | 43 | 50 | 38 | 56 | 54 | 51 | 59 |
| −Year | | 1972 | 1949 | 1971 | 1987 | 1957 | 1986 | 1970 | 1982 | 1961 | 1950 | 1949 | 1956 | JAN 1972 |
| Peak Gust | | | | | | | | | | | | | | |
| −Direction (!!!) | 6 | SW | S | W | SW | W | SW | SW | NW | SW | SE | S | SW | SW |
| −Speed (mph) | 6 | 56 | 51 | 52 | 62 | 53 | 49 | 51 | 47 | 47 | 49 | 55 | 48 | 62 |
| −Date | 6 | 1986 | 1987 | 1988 | 1987 | 1986 | 1989 | 1989 | 1984 | 1987 | 1985 | 1986 | 1988 | APR 1987 |

**See Reference Notes to this table on the following page.**

PRECIPITATION (inches)　　　　SPOKANE WASHINGTON

**TABLE 2**

| YEAR | JAN | FEB | MAR | APR | MAY | JUNE | JULY | AUG | SEP | OCT | NOV | DEC | ANNUAL |
|------|-----|-----|-----|-----|-----|------|------|-----|-----|-----|-----|-----|--------|
| 1961 | 1.61 | 3.94 | 1.75 | 0.96 | 1.77 | 1.64 | 0.37 | 0.30 | 0.17 | 1.05 | 1.83 | 3.91 | 19.30 |
| 1962 | 1.39 | 1.72 | 2.56 | 1.02 | 1.65 | 0.78 | 0.29 | 0.63 | 0.90 | 1.62 | 1.44 | 3.02 | 17.02 |
| 1963 | 0.89 | 2.21 | 1.65 | 1.32 | 0.98 | 0.96 | 0.41 | 0.50 | 0.36 | 1.11 | 2.58 | 2.29 | 15.26 |
| 1964 | 3.15 | 0.98 | 1.53 | 0.98 | 0.45 | 3.06 | 0.39 | 1.46 | 1.03 | 0.46 | 2.89 | 5.13 | 21.51 |
| 1965 | 2.82 | 1.13 | 0.31 | 2.35 | 1.02 | 0.74 | 0.69 | 1.73 | 0.28 | 0.05 | 1.71 | 1.63 | 14.46 |
| 1966 | 1.94 | 0.50 | 2.43 | 0.13 | 0.49 | 0.70 | 0.95 | 0.15 | 0.51 | 0.36 | 3.01 | 2.96 | 14.13 |
| 1967 | 2.44 | 0.40 | 1.72 | 1.71 | 1.31 | 1.99 | 0.06 | 0.24 | T | 1.18 | 0.82 | 2.02 | 13.89 |
| 1968 | 1.57 | 2.12 | 0.71 | 0.10 | 1.16 | 0.87 | 0.23 | 1.35 | 0.63 | 2.24 | 2.35 | 2.93 | 16.26 |
| 1969 | 4.08 | 1.21 | 0.53 | 2.16 | 0.54 | 1.17 | 0.03 | T | 0.71 | 0.45 | 0.37 | 2.45 | 13.70 |
| 1970 | 4.15 | 1.83 | 1.30 | 0.93 | 0.94 | 1.60 | 0.59 | 0.10 | 0.48 | 2.13 | 2.04 | 1.43 | 17.52 |
| 1971 | 2.11 | 0.88 | 2.11 | 1.85 | 1.39 | 2.46 | 0.50 | 0.59 | 1.37 | 0.82 | 1.51 | 2.89 | 18.48 |
| 1972 | 1.74 | 1.13 | 1.05 | 1.09 | 1.99 | 1.56 | 0.25 | 0.87 | 0.86 | 0.19 | 0.88 | 1.92 | 13.53 |
| 1973 | 2.05 | 0.48 | 0.77 | 0.42 | 1.34 | 0.57 | T | 0.19 | 1.44 | 0.97 | 5.10 | 3.78 | 17.11 |
| 1974 | 3.79 | 1.79 | 2.22 | 0.80 | 1.03 | 0.23 | 0.71 | 0.04 | 0.18 | 0.12 | 2.59 | 2.54 | 16.04 |
| 1975 | 2.53 | 3.12 | 1.83 | 1.78 | 1.41 | 1.45 | 1.60 | 0.93 | 0.03 | 2.23 | 1.94 | 2.42 | 21.27 |
| 1976 | 1.28 | 2.04 | 0.83 | 0.97 | 1.24 | 0.78 | 0.79 | 1.83 | 0.05 | 0.59 | 0.22 | 0.60 | 11.22 |
| 1977 | 0.75 | 0.52 | 1.15 | 0.13 | 1.71 | 1.45 | 0.11 | 1.25 | 1.42 | 0.44 | 2.12 | 4.52 | 15.57 |
| 1978 | 2.53 | 1.64 | 0.77 | 2.62 | 2.81 | 1.22 | 1.76 | 1.71 | 0.93 | 0.13 | 2.02 | 1.05 | 19.19 |
| 1979 | 1.11 | 2.19 | 1.03 | 0.69 | 1.60 | 0.78 | 0.85 | 1.01 | 0.78 | 1.22 | 1.15 | 1.94 | 14.35 |
| 1980 | 1.96 | 1.90 | 0.91 | 1.06 | 2.34 | 0.99 | 0.21 | 0.79 | 0.84 | 0.64 | 1.67 | 3.72 | 17.03 |
| 1981 | 1.00 | 1.41 | 1.57 | 0.85 | 2.02 | 1.92 | 0.51 | 0.04 | 0.59 | 1.53 | 0.96 | 2.51 | 14.91 |
| 1982 | 1.61 | 1.67 | 1.49 | 2.23 | 0.20 | 0.85 | 1.05 | 0.25 | 1.77 | 1.48 | 1.86 | 2.79 | 17.25 |
| 1983 | 1.89 | 2.07 | 2.20 | 0.61 | 0.92 | 2.84 | 1.85 | 0.96 | 0.79 | 1.33 | 4.80 | 2.38 | 22.64 |
| 1984 | 0.99 | 1.37 | 1.80 | 1.75 | 2.01 | 1.89 | 0.07 | 0.27 | 0.56 | 0.76 | 4.26 | 2.28 | 18.01 |
| 1985 | 0.38 | 0.93 | 1.39 | 0.28 | 1.13 | 0.67 | 0.26 | 0.19 | 1.64 | 1.40 | 2.23 | 0.71 | 11.21 |
| 1986 | 3.08 | 2.02 | 1.58 | 1.33 | 1.08 | 0.48 | 0.44 | 0.15 | 1.65 | 0.46 | 2.25 | 1.03 | 15.55 |
| 1987 | 1.59 | 0.88 | 2.18 | 1.12 | 0.90 | 0.59 | 2.27 | 1.81 | 0.01 | 0.03 | 1.37 | 4.93 | 17.68 |
| 1988 | 1.76 | 0.35 | 1.57 | 2.15 | 1.50 | 1.12 | T | 0.23 | 1.63 | 0.11 | 4.35 | 1.75 | 16.52 |
| 1989 | 0.82 | 1.34 | 2.87 | 0.72 | 2.17 | 0.41 | 0.40 | 1.61 | 0.18 | 1.58 | 1.66 | 0.95 | 14.71 |
| 1990 | 2.45 | 1.01 | 0.85 | 1.34 | 3.11 | 1.91 | 2.33 | 1.03 | T | 3.05 | 0.84 | 1.69 | 19.61 |
| Record Mean | 2.05 | 1.58 | 1.36 | 1.09 | 1.37 | 1.28 | 0.55 | 0.62 | 0.83 | 1.21 | 2.05 | 2.23 | 16.22 |

**TABLE 3**　　AVERAGE TEMPERATURE (deg. F)　　　　SPOKANE WASHINGTON

| YEAR | JAN | FEB | MAR | APR | MAY | JUNE | JULY | AUG | SEP | OCT | NOV | DEC | ANNUAL |
|------|-----|-----|-----|-----|-----|------|------|-----|-----|-----|-----|-----|--------|
| 1961 | 30.3 | 37.0 | 39.9 | 45.1 | 53.0 | 66.6 | 71.9 | 74.0 | 55.9 | 45.2 | 30.7 | 26.6 | 48.0 |
| 1962 | 22.6 | 32.4 | 34.6 | 49.8 | 50.9 | 61.1 | 68.2 | 65.4 | 60.7 | 47.6 | 37.9 | 33.1 | 47.0 |
| 1963 | 19.3 | 37.4 | 40.6 | 45.0 | 54.8 | 61.7 | 66.7 | 69.1 | 66.0 | 51.1 | 26.5 |  | 48.0 |
| 1964 | 29.3 | 29.2 | 35.7 | 44.5 | 52.9 | 60.4 | 68.3 | 62.8 | 55.2 | 47.9 | 32.2 | 24.0 | 45.2 |
| 1965 | 28.6 | 32.1 | 34.4 | 47.2 | 52.4 | 61.3 | 70.1 | 67.9 | 53.8 | 52.7 | 38.0 | 30.0 | 47.4 |
| 1966 | 29.7 | 32.8 | 38.7 | 46.0 | 55.9 | 58.8 | 68.2 | 68.2 | 64.6 | 47.3 | 36.9 | 33.4 | 48.4 |
| 1967 | 33.9 | 36.2 | 37.1 | 42.3 | 52.8 | 63.5 | 70.6 | 74.5 | 65.3 | 48.4 | 35.4 | 27.8 | 49.0 |
| 1968 | 27.8 | 37.8 | 42.1 | 43.0 | 53.8 | 61.2 | 71.1 | 65.1 | 58.9 | 45.2 | 34.9 | 24.6 | 47.1 |
| 1969 | 16.3 | 26.1 | 35.6 | 46.2 | 57.4 | 65.2 | 67.4 | 67.1 | 59.8 | 43.7 | 36.3 | 29.4 | 45.9 |
| 1970 | 25.9 | 36.3 | 37.0 | 41.6 | 54.9 | 66.2 | 72.5 | 70.2 | 54.2 | 44.9 | 36.0 | 27.7 | 47.3 |
| 1971 | 31.8 | 33.6 | 35.2 | 45.3 | 56.3 | 58.2 | 74.1 | 75.2 | 55.2 | 44.2 | 35.4 | 25.8 | 47.0 |
| 1972 | 22.6 | 30.7 | 41.4 | 42.0 | 56.9 | 62.0 | 68.1 | 71.1 | 55.4 | 47.2 | 38.3 | 25.4 | 46.8 |
| 1973 | 27.0 | 34.9 | 41.1 | 46.2 | 56.5 | 62.0 | 71.2 | 69.1 | 59.7 | 47.2 | 33.7 | 33.3 | 48.5 |
| 1974 | 24.1 | 35.4 | 38.5 | 46.4 | 50.2 | 66.0 | 67.8 | 68.2 | 60.5 | 48.0 | 36.4 | 30.5 | 47.7 |
| 1975 | 23.6 | 24.7 | 34.0 | 41.7 | 52.7 | 59.2 | 72.4 | 64.1 | 61.0 | 46.9 | 33.8 | 30.9 | 45.4 |
| 1976 | 29.6 | 32.1 | 35.1 | 45.2 | 54.5 | 58.5 | 68.8 | 65.4 | 63.4 | 46.8 | 35.8 | 29.6 | 47.1 |
| 1977 | 22.0 | 35.1 | 38.2 | 50.9 | 51.1 | 65.0 | 67.0 | 71.2 | 55.1 | 46.5 | 34.0 | 26.2 | 46.9 |
| 1978 | 27.6 | 34.0 | 42.2 | 45.7 | 51.4 | 62.7 | 68.3 | 65.9 | 56.6 | 46.6 | 28.7 | 19.0 | 45.7 |
| 1979 | 10.5 | 28.8 | 40.4 | 45.5 | 54.7 | 62.7 | 70.0 | 70.0 | 63.1 | 51.1 | 35.2 | 33.2 | 46.9 |
| 1980 | 20.7 | 34.5 | 38.6 | 51.7 | 55.8 | 57.8 | 69.2 | 64.1 | 58.4 | 47.4 | 36.3 | 33.2 | 47.3 |
| 1981 | 32.8 | 33.9 | 40.9 | 45.7 | 52.0 | 57.0 | 65.1 | 71.5 | 59.7 | 45.9 | 39.9 | 29.7 | 47.8 |
| 1982 | 26.0 | 32.1 | 40.3 | 43.5 | 54.2 | 66.5 | 67.6 | 69.8 | 59.5 | 46.1 | 31.7 | 27.3 | 47.0 |
| 1983 | 35.8 | 38.1 | 43.0 | 46.3 | 57.1 | 61.9 | 65.5 | 72.3 | 57.1 | 49.7 | 35.9 | 16.2 | 48.5 |
| 1984 | 30.5 | 34.5 | 41.7 | 44.0 | 50.1 | 59.2 | 69.1 | 70.1 | 56.7 | 43.4 | 35.8 | 20.4 | 46.3 |
| 1985 | 21.4 | 24.9 | 35.9 | 48.0 | 56.2 | 61.8 | 69.0 | 64.9 | 53.3 | 44.7 | 19.5 | 19.3 | 43.7 |
| 1986 | 30.1 | 31.6 | 42.8 | 44.9 | 55.3 | 66.2 | 64.0 | 72.6 | 54.8 | 49.0 | 34.8 | 26.3 | 47.7 |
| 1987 | 26.5 | 35.1 | 41.8 | 51.1 | 57.2 | 65.1 | 66.6 | 66.2 | 62.8 | 49.5 | 38.1 | 25.9 | 48.8 |
| 1988 | 24.7 | 35.4 | 39.7 | 48.9 | 54.6 | 61.1 | 68.7 | 68.4 | 58.9 | 53.3 | 36.3 | 27.0 | 48.1 |
| 1989 | 28.8 | 21.8 | 36.6 | 48.9 | 53.1 | 64.3 | 69.7 | 64.8 | 60.1 | 47.0 | 38.0 | 31.0 | 46.9 |
| 1990 | 33.4 | 30.2 | 40.9 | 49.7 | 52.8 | 60.7 | 70.4 | 68.5 | 65.3 | 45.1 | 39.0 | 21.1 | 48.1 |
| Record Mean | 26.8 | 31.8 | 39.5 | 47.6 | 55.6 | 62.4 | 69.9 | 68.6 | 59.3 | 48.5 | 36.6 | 29.8 | 48.0 |
| Max | 32.6 | 38.8 | 48.4 | 58.5 | 67.3 | 74.5 | 84.0 | 82.7 | 72.2 | 59.2 | 43.1 | 35.0 | 58.0 |
| Min | 20.9 | 24.7 | 30.5 | 36.7 | 43.8 | 50.3 | 55.8 | 54.5 | 46.5 | 37.8 | 30.1 | 24.5 | 38.0 |

## REFERENCE NOTES FOR TABLES 1, 2, 3 and 6　　(SPOKANE, WA)

**GENERAL**

T - TRACE AMOUNT
BLANK ENTRIES DENOTE MISSING/UNREPORTED DATA.
# INDICATES A STATION OR INSTRUMENT RELOCATION.

**SPECIFIC**

**TABLE 1**

(a) - LENGTH OF RECORD IN YEARS. ALTHOUGH INDIVIDUAL MONTHS MAY BE MISSING.
* LESS THAN .05

NORMALS — BASED ON THE 1951-1980 RECORD PERIOD.
EXTREMES — DATES ARE THE MOST RECENT OCCURRENCE.
WIND DIR. — NUMERALS SHOW TENS OF DEGREES CLOCKWISE FROM TRUE NORTH.
"00" INDICATES CALM.
RESULTANT WIND DIRECTIONS ARE GIVEN TO WHOLE DEGREES.

**TABLE 3**
MAX AND MIN ARE LONG-TERM MEAN DAILY MAXIMUM AND MEAN DAILY MINIMUM TEMPERATURES.

**EXCEPTIONS**

**TABLES 2, 3, and 6**

RECORD MEANS ARE THROUGH THE CURRENT YEAR, BEGINNING IN　　1882 FOR TEMPERATURE
1882 FOR PRECIPITATION
1948 FOR SNOWFALL

## TABLE 4 — HEATING DEGREE DAYS Base 65 deg. F — SPOKANE WASHINGTON

| SEASON | JULY | AUG | SEP | OCT | NOV | DEC | JAN | FEB | MAR | APR | MAY | JUNE | TOTAL |
|---|---|---|---|---|---|---|---|---|---|---|---|---|---|
| 1961-62 | 1 | 0 | 268 | 604 | 1025 | 1180 | 1309 | 905 | 932 | 450 | 430 | 149 | 7253 |
| 1962-63 | 60 | 65 | 159 | 531 | 804 | 981 | 1411 | 768 | 748 | 593 | 318 | 145 | 6583 |
| 1963-64 | 35 | 28 | 77 | 426 | 802 | 1186 | 1098 | 1030 | 897 | 609 | 369 | 149 | 6706 |
| 1964-65 | 31 | 118 | 290 | 524 | 976 | 1268 | 1121 | 915 | 942 | 528 | 387 | 129 | 7229 |
| 1965-66 | 31 | 62 | 330 | 377 | 804 | 1078 | 1088 | 896 | 808 | 561 | 291 | 190 | 6516 |
| 1966-67 | 30 | 42 | 67 | 544 | 838 | 975 | 956 | 799 | 859 | 677 | 370 | 96 | 6253 |
| 1967-68 | 8 | 2 | 71 | 508 | 882 | 1146 | 1149 | 783 | 702 | 654 | 343 | 138 | 6386 |
| 1968-69 | 19 | 89 | 199 | 607 | 897 | 1245 | 1504 | 1080 | 905 | 559 | 236 | 88 | 7428 |
| 1969-70 | 40 | 44 | 192 | 655 | 855 | 1097 | 1208 | 797 | 859 | 696 | 305 | 101 | 6849 |
| 1970-71 | 13 | 5 | 321 | 614 | 864 | 1146 | 1022 | 873 | 918 | 584 | 270 | 215 | 6845 |
| 1971-72 | 64 | 19 | 297 | 641 | 882 | 1208 | 1308 | 991 | 726 | 684 | 274 | 127 | 7221 |
| 1972-73 | 36 | 18 | 292 | 545 | 795 | 1219 | 1171 | 838 | 734 | 558 | 286 | 152 | 6644 |
| 1973-74 | 17 | 47 | 193 | 546 | 933 | 978 | 1265 | 824 | 814 | 554 | 455 | 97 | 6723 |
| 1974-75 | 41 | 22 | 134 | 519 | 852 | 1062 | 1276 | 1122 | 953 | 694 | 375 | 173 | 7223 |
| 1975-76 | 22 | 75 | 136 | 554 | 933 | 1048 | 1091 | 946 | 922 | 588 | 317 | 213 | 6845 |
| 1976-77 | 20 | 71 | 74 | 556 | 871 | 1089 | 1324 | 832 | 824 | 436 | 409 | 66 | 6572 |
| 1977-78 | 57 | 56 | 289 | 563 | 921 | 1197 | 1154 | 862 | 701 | 576 | 412 | 101 | 6889 |
| 1978-79 | 37 | 97 | 252 | 562 | 1083 | 1424 | 1684 | 1011 | 756 | 577 | 313 | 134 | 7930 |
| 1979-80 | 41 | 4 | 91 | 423 | 1029 | 918 | 1365 | 880 | 809 | 392 | 283 | 211 | 6446 |
| 1980-81 | 19 | 77 | 195 | 543 | 854 | 977 | 992 | 867 | 741 | 570 | 395 | 243 | 6473 |
| 1981-82 | 73 | 7 | 209 | 584 | 747 | 1088 | 1202 | 912 | 761 | 639 | 328 | 76 | 6626 |
| 1982-83 | 62 | 17 | 193 | 582 | 996 | 1163 | 897 | 747 | 672 | 558 | 285 | 113 | 6285 |
| 1983-84 | 55 | 2 | 230 | 468 | 765 | 1508 | 1065 | 880 | 715 | 621 | 460 | 194 | 6963 |
| 1984-85 | 21 | 18 | 264 | 662 | 870 | 1381 | 1345 | 1117 | 895 | 501 | 280 | 128 | 7482 |
| 1985-86 | 0 | 64 | 343 | 622 | 1363 | 1409 | 1076 | 927 | 680 | 595 | 357 | 67 | 7503 |
| 1986-87 | 81 | 4 | 311 | 488 | 902 | 1193 | 1186 | 831 | 710 | 417 | 253 | 86 | 6462 |
| 1987-88 | 51 | 50 | 116 | 474 | 799 | 1206 | 1240 | 850 | 775 | 477 | 330 | 173 | 6541 |
| 1988-89 | 47 | 16 | 240 | 361 | 856 | 1171 | 1113 | 1205 | 873 | 473 | 364 | 65 | 6784 |
| 1989-90 | 22 | 76 | 149 | 554 | 805 | 1048 | 976 | 968 | 739 | 454 | 373 | 166 | 6330 |
| 1990-91 | 37 | 42 | 54 | 610 | 774 | 1356 | | | | | | | |

## TABLE 5 — COOLING DEGREE DAYS Base 65 deg. F — SPOKANE WASHINGTON

| YEAR | JAN | FEB | MAR | APR | MAY | JUNE | JULY | AUG | SEP | OCT | NOV | DEC | TOTAL |
|---|---|---|---|---|---|---|---|---|---|---|---|---|---|
| 1969 | 0 | 0 | 0 | 0 | 7 | 99 | 121 | 112 | 40 | 0 | 0 | 0 | 379 |
| 1970 | 0 | 0 | 0 | 0 | 3 | 143 | 253 | 175 | 2 | 0 | 0 | 0 | 576 |
| 1971 | 0 | 0 | 0 | 0 | 10 | 17 | 216 | 306 | 9 | 0 | 0 | 0 | 558 |
| 1972 | 0 | 0 | 0 | 0 | 28 | 41 | 138 | 213 | 10 | 0 | 0 | 0 | 430 |
| 1973 | 0 | 0 | 0 | 0 | 31 | 67 | 216 | 177 | 39 | 0 | 0 | 0 | 530 |
| 1974 | 0 | 0 | 0 | 0 | 0 | 137 | 134 | 127 | 7 | 0 | 0 | 0 | 405 |
| 1975 | 0 | 0 | 0 | 0 | 0 | 7 | 256 | 57 | 20 | 0 | 0 | 0 | 340 |
| 1976 | 0 | 0 | 0 | 0 | 0 | 24 | 143 | 93 | 33 | 0 | 0 | 0 | 293 |
| 1977 | 0 | 0 | 0 | 18 | 2 | 72 | 126 | 254 | 0 | 0 | 0 | 0 | 472 |
| 1978 | 0 | 0 | 0 | 0 | 0 | 42 | 144 | 131 | 9 | 0 | 0 | 0 | 326 |
| 1979 | 0 | 0 | 0 | 0 | 1 | 73 | 217 | 166 | 39 | 0 | 0 | 0 | 496 |
| 1980 | 0 | 0 | 0 | 1 | 3 | 2 | 156 | 56 | 6 | 3 | 0 | 0 | 227 |
| 1981 | 0 | 0 | 0 | 0 | 0 | 9 | 82 | 213 | 60 | 0 | 0 | 0 | 364 |
| 1982 | 0 | 0 | 0 | 0 | 2 | 128 | 148 | 171 | 32 | 0 | 0 | 0 | 481 |
| 1983 | 0 | 0 | 0 | 0 | 46 | 26 | 77 | 235 | 1 | 0 | 0 | 0 | 385 |
| 1984 | 0 | 0 | 0 | 0 | 3 | 28 | 155 | 181 | 23 | 1 | 0 | 0 | 391 |
| 1985 | 0 | 0 | 0 | 0 | 15 | 36 | 317 | 68 | 0 | 0 | 0 | 0 | 436 |
| 1986 | 0 | 0 | 0 | 0 | 65 | 109 | 57 | 247 | 8 | 0 | 0 | 0 | 486 |
| 1987 | 0 | 0 | 0 | 8 | 20 | 94 | 110 | 97 | 53 | 1 | 0 | 0 | 383 |
| 1988 | 0 | 0 | 0 | 0 | 12 | 63 | 169 | 128 | 67 | 0 | 0 | 0 | 439 |
| 1989 | 0 | 0 | 0 | 0 | 0 | 49 | 145 | 78 | 9 | 0 | 0 | 0 | 281 |
| 1990 | 0 | 0 | 0 | 0 | 0 | 42 | 213 | 157 | 68 | 0 | 0 | 0 | 480 |

## TABLE 6 — SNOWFALL (inches) — SPOKANE WASHINGTON

| SEASON | JULY | AUG | SEP | OCT | NOV | DEC | JAN | FEB | MAR | APR | MAY | JUNE | TOTAL |
|---|---|---|---|---|---|---|---|---|---|---|---|---|---|
| 1961-62 | 0.0 | 0.0 | 0.0 | T | 8.9 | 26.2 | 12.2 | 4.5 | 15.3 | T | 0.0 | 0.0 | 67.1 |
| 1962-63 | 0.0 | 0.0 | 0.0 | 0.0 | 4.4 | 0.5 | 8.7 | 2.7 | 1.2 | 0.5 | T | 0.0 | 18.0 |
| 1963-64 | 0.0 | 0.0 | 0.0 | 0.0 | 0.4 | 19.6 | 26.3 | 5.2 | 5.2 | 6.6 | 0.0 | 0.0 | 63.3 |
| 1964-65 | 0.0 | 0.0 | 0.0 | T | 15.2 | 42.0 | 20.1 | 2.3 | 2.0 | 0.1 | 0.0 | 0.0 | 81.7 |
| 1965-66 | 0.0 | 0.0 | 0.0 | T | 6.3 | 15.4 | 13.9 | 1.6 | 7.2 | T | T | 0.0 | 44.4 |
| 1966-67 | 0.0 | 0.0 | 0.0 | T | 0.9 | 9.0 | 6.5 | 3.1 | 6.4 | 0.8 | 3.5 | 0.0 | 30.2 |
| 1967-68 | 0.0 | 0.0 | 0.0 | T | 4.8 | 12.7 | 11.8 | 0.4 | T | T | T | 0.0 | 29.7 |
| 1968-69 | 0.0 | 0.0 | 0.0 | 0.0 | 1.2 | 19.8 | 48.7 | 5.4 | 2.0 | 0.4 | 0.0 | 0.0 | 77.5 |
| 1969-70 | 0.0 | 0.0 | 0.0 | 0.0 | T | 10.4 | 19.4 | 2.8 | 6.9 | 0.3 | 0.1 | 0.0 | 39.9 |
| 1970-71 | 0.0 | 0.0 | 0.0 | T | 6.8 | 12.0 | 6.1 | 5.5 | 1.5 | T | 0.0 | 0.0 | 31.9 |
| 1971-72 | 0.0 | 0.0 | 0.0 | 3.1 | 4.0 | 34.2 | 17.2 | 5.9 | 2.5 | 0.2 | 0.0 | 0.0 | 67.1 |
| 1972-73 | 0.0 | 0.0 | 0.0 | 0.8 | T | 4.7 | 6.5 | 3.5 | 0.5 | T | 0.0 | 0.0 | 16.0 |
| 1973-74 | 0.0 | 0.0 | 0.0 | 0.8 | 23.6 | 9.1 | 15.0 | 4.4 | 2.5 | 0.4 | 0.4 | 0.0 | 56.2 |
| 1974-75 | 0.0 | 0.0 | 0.0 | 0.0 | 0.3 | 16.6 | 30.9 | 28.5 | 7.6 | 5.1 | T | 0.0 | 89.0 |
| 1975-76 | 0.0 | 0.0 | 0.0 | 3.9 | 11.4 | 6.9 | 15.3 | 6.3 | 4.6 | 0.4 | 0.0 | 0.0 | 48.8 |
| 1976-77 | 0.0 | 0.0 | 0.0 | 0.0 | 0.1 | 4.2 | 6.8 | 2.5 | 2.7 | T | T | 0.0 | 16.3 |
| 1977-78 | 0.0 | 0.0 | 0.0 | 0.0 | 11.2 | 30.3 | 19.1 | 6.6 | 2.2 | T | T | 0.0 | 69.4 |
| 1978-79 | 0.0 | 0.0 | 0.0 | 0.0 | 15.4 | 14.8 | 16.5 | 10.6 | 3.4 | T | T | 0.0 | 60.7 |
| 1979-80 | 0.0 | 0.0 | 0.0 | 0.0 | 3.9 | 10.4 | 16.6 | 5.9 | 1.1 | 0.4 | 0.0 | 0.0 | 38.3 |
| 1980-81 | 0.0 | 0.0 | 0.0 | 0.0 | 1.2 | 6.8 | 2.6 | 3.3 | T | T | 0.3 | 0.0 | 14.2 |
| 1981-82 | 0.0 | 0.0 | 0.0 | T | 0.8 | 13.0 | 23.3 | 2.2 | 2.1 | 6.0 | T | 0.0 | 47.4 |
| 1982-83 | 0.0 | 0.0 | 0.0 | T | 5.4 | 17.4 | 8.1 | 5.5 | T | 0.2 | T | 0.0 | 36.6 |
| 1983-84 | 0.0 | 0.0 | 0.0 | 0.0 | 5.7 | 24.8 | 5.3 | 8.0 | 1.9 | 1.3 | 0.8 | 0.0 | 47.8 |
| 1984-85 | 0.0 | 0.0 | 0.0 | 1.1 | 12.0 | 24.7 | 4.6 | 14.8 | 9.6 | T | T | 0.0 | 66.8 |
| 1985-86 | 0.0 | 0.0 | 0.0 | 0.4 | 23.7 | 8.3 | 14.7 | 13.8 | T | 0.2 | T | 0.0 | 61.1 |
| 1986-87 | 0.0 | 0.0 | 0.0 | 0.0 | 5.0 | 7.9 | 11.7 | 1.1 | T | T | T | 0.0 | 25.7 |
| 1987-88 | 0.0 | 0.0 | 0.0 | 0.0 | 1.5 | 20.3 | 9.1 | 1.2 | 1.6 | T | T | 0.0 | 33.7 |
| 1988-89 | 0.0 | 0.0 | 0.0 | 0.0 | 10.9 | 16.3 | 10.5 | 19.0 | 9.4 | T | T | 0.0 | 66.1 |
| 1989-90 | 0.0 | 0.0 | 0.0 | T | 5.2 | 1.1 | 10.3 | 18.0 | 2.6 | 3.5 | T | 0.0 | 40.7 |
| 1990-91 | 0.0 | 0.0 | 0.0 | 0.0 | 1.2 | 14.3 | | | | | | | |
| Record Mean | 0.0 | 0.0 | 0.0 | 0.4 | 6.2 | 15.0 | 16.3 | 7.8 | 4.1 | 0.7 | 0.1 | T | 50.7 |

**See Reference Notes, relative to all above tables, on preceding page.**

San Juan, located on the north coast of the island of Puerto Rico, is surrounded by the waters of the Atlantic Ocean and San Juan Bay. Local custom assigns the name San Juan to the old city which lies right on the coast, but the modern metropolitan area extends inland about 12 miles. These inland sections have a temperature and rainfall regime significantly different from the coastal area. Isla Verde Airport, where weather observations are made, lies on the coast about 7 miles east of old San Juan. The surrounding terrain is level with a gradual upslope inland. Mountain ranges, with peak elevations of 4,000 feet, extend east and west through the central portion of Puerto Rico, and are located 15 to 20 miles east and south of San Juan. These mountain ranges have a decided influence on the rainfall of the San Juan metropolitan area, and on the entire island in general.

The climate is tropical maritime, characteristic of all tropical islands. The predominant easterly trade winds, modified by local effects such as the land and sea breeze and the particular island topography, are a primary feature of the climate of San Juan and have a significant influence on the temperature and rainfall. During daylight hours the wind blows almost constantly off the ocean. Usually, after sunset the wind shifts to the south or southeast, off land. This daily wind variation is a contributing factor to the delightful climate of the city. The annual temperature range is small with about a 5–6 degree difference between the temperatures of the warmest and coldest months. The inland sectors have warmer afternoons and cooler nights. In the interior mountain and valley regions even greater daily and annual ranges of temperature occur. The highest temperatures recorded in Puerto Rico have exceeded 105 degrees and the lowest have been near 40. Sea water temperatures range from 78 degrees in March to about 83 degrees in September.

Although rainfall in San Juan is nearly 60 inches, the geographical distribution of rainfall over the island shows the heaviest rainfall, of about 180 inches per year, in the Luquillo Range, only 23 miles distant from San Juan. The driest area, with annual rainfall of 30 to 35 inches, is located in the southwest corner of the island. Rain showers occur mostly in the afternoon and at night. The nocturnal showers, usually light, are a characteristic feature of the San Juan rainfall pattern. Rainfall is generally of the brief showery type except for the continuous rains occuring with the passage of tropical disturbances, or when the trailing edge of a cold front out of the United States reaches Puerto Rico. This normally occurs from about November to April.

Puerto Rico is in the tropical hurricane region of the eastern Caribbean. The hurricane season begins June 1 and ends November 30. Only a few hurricanes have passed close enough to San Juan to produce hurricane force winds or damage.

Mild temperatures, refreshing sea breezes in the daytime, plenty of sunshine, and adequate rainfall make the climate of San Juan most enjoyable for tourists and residents alike.

**TABLE 1**　　**NORMALS, MEANS AND EXTREMES**

SAN JUAN, PUERTO RICO

LATITUDE: 18°26'N　　LONGITUDE: 66°00' W　　ELEVATION: FT. GRND　　13 BARO　　69　　TIME ZONE: ATLANTIC　　WBAN: 11641

| | (a) | JAN | FEB | MAR | APR | MAY | JUNE | JULY | AUG | SEP | OCT | NOV | DEC | YEAR |
|---|---|---|---|---|---|---|---|---|---|---|---|---|---|---|
| **TEMPERATURE °F:** | | | | | | | | | | | | | | |
| Normals | | | | | | | | | | | | | | |
| -Daily Maximum | | 82.7 | 83.2 | 84.2 | 85.2 | 86.7 | 88.0 | 87.9 | 88.2 | 88.2 | 87.9 | 85.7 | 83.6 | 86.0 |
| -Daily Minimum | | 70.3 | 70.0 | 70.8 | 72.3 | 73.9 | 75.3 | 76.1 | 76.1 | 75.5 | 74.9 | 73.4 | 71.8 | 73.4 |
| -Monthly | | 76.5 | 76.6 | 77.5 | 78.8 | 80.3 | 81.7 | 82.0 | 82.2 | 81.9 | 81.4 | 79.6 | 77.7 | 79.7 |
| Extremes | | | | | | | | | | | | | | |
| -Record Highest | 35 | 92 | 96 | 96 | 97 | 96 | 97 | 95 | 97 | 97 | 98 | 96 | 94 | 98 |
| -Year | | 1983 | 1983 | 1983 | 1983 | 1980 | 1988 | 1981 | 1980 | 1981 | 1981 | 1981 | 1989 | OCT 1981 |
| -Record Lowest | 35 | 61 | 62 | 60 | 64 | 66 | 69 | 69 | 70 | 69 | 67 | 66 | 63 | 60 |
| -Year | | 1962 | 1968 | 1957 | 1968 | 1962 | 1957 | 1959 | 1956 | 1960 | 1959 | 1969 | 1964 | MAR 1957 |
| **NORMAL DEGREE DAYS:** | | | | | | | | | | | | | | |
| Heating (base 65°F) | | 0 | 0 | 0 | 0 | 0 | 0 | 0 | 0 | 0 | 0 | 0 | 0 | 0 |
| Cooling (base 65°F) | | 357 | 325 | 388 | 414 | 474 | 501 | 527 | 533 | 507 | 508 | 438 | 394 | 5366 |
| **% OF POSSIBLE SUNSHINE** | 34 | 68 | 71 | 75 | 70 | 62 | 63 | 68 | 67 | 61 | 63 | 61 | 61 | 66 |
| **MEAN SKY COVER (tenths)** | | | | | | | | | | | | | | |
| Sunrise - Sunset | 34 | 5.0 | 5.1 | 5.0 | 5.5 | 6.6 | 6.3 | 6.1 | 6.0 | 6.2 | 6.1 | 5.7 | 5.6 | 5.8 |
| **MEAN NUMBER OF DAYS:** | | | | | | | | | | | | | | |
| Sunrise to Sunset | | | | | | | | | | | | | | |
| -Clear | 34 | 8.3 | 6.9 | 8.8 | 6.6 | 3.4 | 3.7 | 4.1 | 4.6 | 3.5 | 4.1 | 5.1 | 5.9 | 64.9 |
| -Partly Cloudy | 34 | 18.6 | 17.0 | 18.0 | 17.0 | 15.7 | 16.1 | 17.7 | 17.9 | 16.9 | 17.1 | 17.9 | 18.8 | 208.7 |
| -Cloudy | 34 | 4.1 | 4.4 | 4.1 | 6.4 | 11.9 | 10.1 | 9.1 | 8.6 | 9.6 | 9.7 | 7.0 | 6.3 | 91.6 |
| Precipitation | | | | | | | | | | | | | | |
| .01 inches or more | 34 | 16.6 | 12.8 | 12.2 | 12.9 | 16.6 | 15.4 | 19.0 | 18.6 | 17.1 | 17.4 | 18.0 | 19.1 | 195.7 |
| Snow,Ice pellets | | | | | | | | | | | | | | |
| 1.0 inches or more | 34 | 0.0 | 0.0 | 0.0 | 0.0 | 0.0 | 0.0 | 0.0 | 0.0 | 0.0 | 0.0 | 0.0 | 0.0 | 0.0 |
| Thunderstorms | 34 | 0.2 | 0.3 | 0.3 | 1.0 | 4.5 | 4.9 | 5.1 | 6.1 | 8.2 | 7.3 | 3.0 | 0.7 | 41.6 |
| Heavy Fog Visibility | | | | | | | | | | | | | | |
| 1/4 mile or less | 34 | 0.0 | 0.0 | 0.0 | 0.0 | 0.0 | 0.0 | 0.0 | 0.0 | 0.0 | 0.0 | 0.0 | 0.0 | 0.0 |
| Temperature °F | | | | | | | | | | | | | | |
| -Maximum | | | | | | | | | | | | | | |
| 90° and above | 34 | 0.4 | 0.8 | 2.1 | 3.4 | 5.7 | 8.9 | 8.0 | 9.4 | 10.1 | 8.4 | 1.7 | 0.5 | 59.4 |
| 32° and below | 34 | 0.0 | 0.0 | 0.0 | 0.0 | 0.0 | 0.0 | 0.0 | 0.0 | 0.0 | 0.0 | 0.0 | 0.0 | 0.0 |
| -Minimum | | | | | | | | | | | | | | |
| 32° and below | 34 | 0.0 | 0.0 | 0.0 | 0.0 | 0.0 | 0.0 | 0.0 | 0.0 | 0.0 | 0.0 | 0.0 | 0.0 | 0.0 |
| 0° and below | 34 | 0.0 | 0.0 | 0.0 | 0.0 | 0.0 | 0.0 | 0.0 | 0.0 | 0.0 | 0.0 | 0.0 | 0.0 | 0.0 |
| **AVG. STATION PRESS.(mb)** | 17 | 1014.8 | 1014.6 | 1014.2 | 1013.2 | 1013.1 | 1014.5 | 1014.9 | 1013.6 | 1012.3 | 1011.4 | 1011.8 | 1013.9 | 1013.5 |
| **RELATIVE HUMIDITY (%)** | | | | | | | | | | | | | | |
| Hour 02 | 34 | 81 | 80 | 79 | 80 | 83 | 84 | 83 | 84 | 85 | 85 | 84 | 82 | 83 |
| Hour 08 | 34 | 81 | 80 | 77 | 75 | 77 | 78 | 79 | 80 | 79 | 80 | 81 | 81 | 79 |
| Hour 14 (Local Time) | 34 | 64 | 62 | 60 | 62 | 66 | 66 | 67 | 66 | 67 | 66 | 67 | 66 | 65 |
| Hour 20 | 34 | 75 | 74 | 73 | 73 | 77 | 77 | 78 | 78 | 78 | 79 | 78 | 77 | 76 |
| **PRECIPITATION (inches):** | | | | | | | | | | | | | | |
| Water Equivalent | | | | | | | | | | | | | | |
| -Normal | | 3.01 | 2.02 | 2.31 | 3.62 | 5.64 | 4.66 | 4.87 | 5.93 | 5.99 | 5.89 | 5.59 | 4.46 | 53.99 |
| -Maximum Monthly | 35 | 7.60 | 6.69 | 5.41 | 10.37 | 14.99 | 10.96 | 9.35 | 11.76 | 14.83 | 15.06 | 15.96 | 16.81 | 16.81 |
| -Year | | 1977 | 1982 | 1958 | 1988 | 1965 | 1965 | 1961 | 1955 | 1989 | 1979 | 1979 | 1981 | DEC 1981 |
| -Minimum Monthly | 35 | 0.61 | 0.20 | 0.72 | 0.28 | 0.44 | 0.29 | 1.12 | 1.93 | 1.73 | 1.17 | 1.91 | 0.68 | 0.20 |
| -Year | | 1978 | 1983 | 1970 | 1984 | 1972 | 1985 | 1974 | 1982 | 1987 | 1979 | 1980 | 1963 | FEB 1983 |
| -Maximum in 24 hrs | 35 | 5.08 | 2.75 | 3.91 | 7.20 | 4.74 | 3.55 | 2.28 | 5.08 | 8.84 | 5.04 | 7.07 | 8.40 | 8.84 |
| -Year | | 1969 | 1989 | 1969 | 1988 | 1986 | 1965 | 1969 | 1955 | 1989 | 1985 | 1979 | 1981 | SEP 1989 |
| Snow,Ice pellets | | | | | | | | | | | | | | |
| -Maximum Monthly | 35 | 0.0 | 0.0 | 0.0 | 0.0 | 0.0 | 0.0 | 0.0 | 0.0 | T | 0.0 | 0.0 | 0.0 | T |
| -Year | | | | | | | | | | 1989 | | | | SEP 1989 |
| -Maximum in 24 hrs | 35 | 0.0 | 0.0 | 0.0 | 0.0 | 0.0 | 0.0 | 0.0 | 0.0 | T | 0.0 | 0.0 | 0.0 | T |
| -Year | | | | | | | | | | 1989 | | | | SEP 1989 |
| **WIND:** | | | | | | | | | | | | | | |
| Mean Speed (mph) | 34 | 8.5 | 8.9 | 9.3 | 9.0 | 8.3 | 8.8 | 9.6 | 8.8 | 7.5 | 6.8 | 7.4 | 8.3 | 8.4 |
| Prevailing Direction | | | | | | | | | | | | | | |
| through 1963 | | ENE | ENE | ENE | ENE | ENE | ENE | ENE | ENE | ENE | ENE | ENE | ENE | ENE |
| Fastest Mile | | | | | | | | | | | | | | |
| -Direction (!!!) | 29 | SE | E | S | E | E | NE | E | NE | SE | NE | NE | NE | NE |
| -Speed (MPH) | 29 | 34 | 40 | 37 | 35 | 39 | 38 | 44 | 80 | 47 | 44 | 35 | 46 | 80 |
| -Year | | 1974 | 1965 | 1983 | 1970 | 1976 | 1970 | 1975 | 1956 | 1973 | 1972 | 1961 | 1970 | AUG 1956 |
| Peak Gust | | | | | | | | | | | | | | |
| -Direction (!!!) | 6 | E | ESE | E | SE | SE | SW | ESE | E | NW | SE | E | E | NW |
| -Speed (mph) | 6 | 36 | 37 | 36 | 38 | 29 | 38 | 31 | 37 | 92 | 35 | 39 | 41 | 92 |
| -Date | | 1989 | 1989 | 1989 | 1989 | 1989 | 1984 | 1984 | 1989 | 1989 | 1986 | 1985 | 1984 | SEP 1989 |

**See Reference Notes to this table on the following page.**

# SAN JUAN, P.R., WEST INDIES

## TABLE 2

PRECIPITATION (inches)  —  SAN JUAN, PUERTO RICO

| YEAR | JAN | FEB | MAR | APR | MAY | JUNE | JULY | AUG | SEP | OCT | NOV | DEC | ANNUAL |
|------|-----|-----|-----|-----|-----|------|------|-----|-----|-----|-----|-----|--------|
| 1961 | 3.51 | 1.31 | 2.64 | 2.82 | 1.77 | 5.26 | 9.35 | 5.19 | 1.93 | 8.47 | 9.26 | 10.00 | 61.51 |
| 1962 | 4.24 | 2.67 | 0.97 | 3.70 | 7.53 | 6.70 | 6.46 | 6.98 | 4.85 | 2.80 | 3.84 | 4.11 | 54.85 |
| 1963 | 3.13 | 1.39 | 4.68 | 5.21 | 6.85 | 2.74 | 5.02 | 3.43 | 10.85 | 1.63 | 3.00 | 0.68 | 48.61 |
| 1964 | 2.02 | 1.70 | 1.27 | 6.38 | 3.96 | 4.50 | 7.03 | 6.71 | 5.10 | 3.13 | 3.39 | 2.35 | 47.54 |
| 1965 | 2.62 | 0.79 | 0.86 | 2.19 | 14.99 | 10.96 | 5.88 | 8.66 | 4.80 | 5.08 | 3.93 | 5.05 | 65.81 |
| 1966 | 1.34 | 1.64 | 4.63 | 5.62 | 5.69 | 3.26 | 4.21 | 3.41 | 7.20 | 8.99 | 7.99 | 6.21 | 60.19 |
| 1967 | 3.07 | 2.93 | 1.46 | 0.85 | 4.15 | 3.38 | 4.79 | 4.20 | 5.12 | 4.47 | 5.00 | 3.13 | 42.55 |
| 1968 | 2.15 | 1.60 | 1.79 | 0.50 | 6.31 | 5.98 | 5.25 | 7.36 | 5.26 | 2.33 | 11.11 | 3.56 | 53.20 |
| 1969 | 7.49 | 3.97 | 2.89 | 2.42 | 5.79 | 4.04 | 7.49 | 6.89 | 4.86 | 6.99 | 6.70 | 2.28 | 61.81 |
| 1970 | 2.94 | 1.33 | 0.72 | 1.15 | 7.98 | 9.26 | 3.58 | 4.66 | 5.66 | 15.06 | 8.00 | 5.98 | 66.32 |
| 1971 | 2.18 | 3.67 | 1.78 | 2.93 | 3.87 | 1.24 | 1.69 | 5.18 | 2.19 | 4.61 | 2.31 | 3.93 | 35.58 |
| 1972 | 2.76 | 2.00 | 3.40 | 2.79 | 0.44 | 1.58 | 2.24 | 3.06 | 3.68 | 5.46 | 2.78 | 7.53 | 37.72 |
| 1973 | 2.27 | 0.92 | 4.66 | 8.48 | 0.48 | 4.71 | 2.44 | 7.00 | 3.13 | 3.29 | 3.01 | 4.16 | 44.55 |
| 1974 | 2.92 | 0.82 | 1.92 | 1.20 | 2.42 | 2.34 | 1.12 | 6.57 | 3.67 | 8.23 | 6.55 | 3.92 | 41.68 |
| 1975 | 2.69 | 0.71 | 1.13 | 1.01 | 1.04 | 2.64 | 3.35 | 9.29 |  | 6.60 | 10.90 | 7.82 | 51.26 |
| 1976 | 1.50 | 2.18 | 2.05 | 3.94 | 2.96 | 2.96 | 2.48 | 5.12 | 11.44 | 7.69 | 2.77 | 2.11 | 47.20 |
| 1977 | 7.60 | 1.02 | 1.73 | 0.96 | 4.04 | 1.49 | 4.64 | 4.42 | 4.71 | 5.94 | 12.44 | 3.82 | 52.81 |
| 1978 | 0.61 | 1.56 | 3.52 | 8.27 | 7.14 | 2.86 | 3.46 | 3.21 | 6.34 | 4.88 | 5.40 | 2.61 | 49.86 |
| 1979 | 1.29 | 1.80 | 2.25 | 4.28 | 12.13 | 5.76 | 6.61 | 9.38 | 10.11 | 1.17 | 15.96 | 3.81 | 74.55 |
| 1980 | 1.75 | 1.67 | 1.47 | 2.55 | 5.19 | 1.31 | 2.19 | 3.17 | 4.85 | 6.71 | 1.91 | 3.18 | 35.95 |
| 1981 | 2.55 | 2.72 | 4.39 | 11.02 | 5.48 | 7.04 | 3.32 | 2.98 | 9.32 | 4.94 | 16.81 |  | 73.46 |
| 1982 | 2.53 | 6.69 | 0.98 | 1.01 | 10.26 | 5.24 | 2.33 | 1.93 | 2.87 | 2.06 | 4.34 | 4.76 | 45.00 |
| 1983 | 0.69 | 0.20 | 1.47 | 8.54 | 3.85 | 1.91 | 6.53 | 5.15 | 2.75 | 4.06 | 3.25 | 3.50 | 41.90 |
| 1984 | 1.96 | 3.13 | 0.82 | 0.28 | 3.75 | 6.85 | 2.66 | 6.04 | 3.16 | 5.10 | 5.65 | 4.69 | 44.09 |
| 1985 | 2.80 | 2.40 | 1.84 | 1.02 | 5.95 | 0.29 |  | 2.85 | 5.44 | 11.10 | 4.54 | 2.80 | 45.36 |
| 1986 | 2.18 | 1.13 | 1.61 | 8.93 | 12.80 | 1.52 | 1.94 | 5.19 | 1.98 | 8.54 | 5.87 | 3.59 | 55.28 |
| 1987 | 2.16 | 1.20 | 5.17 | 8.88 | 12.17 | 7.07 | 3.26 | 2.48 | 1.73 | 2.70 | 7.49 | 7.69 | 62.00 |
| 1988 | 3.83 | 2.27 | 1.76 | 10.37 | 6.06 | 1.45 | 4.02 | 11.31 | 5.49 | 4.12 | 5.68 | 4.07 | 60.43 |
| 1989 | 2.96 | 6.05 | 3.39 | 2.63 | 4.88 | 2.97 | 5.54 | 7.88 | 14.83 | 2.09 | 4.95 | 2.50 | 60.67 |
| 1990 | 4.56 | 3.02 | 3.14 | 1.05 | 2.44 | 4.32 | 5.76 | 3.42 | 2.23 | 8.65 | 5.33 | 5.03 | 48.95 |
| Record Mean | 2.96 | 2.35 | 2.32 | 3.81 | 6.35 | 4.55 | 4.75 | 5.85 | 5.65 | 5.80 | 5.74 | 4.91 | 55.04 |

## TABLE 3

AVERAGE TEMPERATURE (deg. F)  —  SAN JUAN, PUERTO RICO

| YEAR | JAN | FEB | MAR | APR | MAY | JUNE | JULY | AUG | SEP | OCT | NOV | DEC | ANNUAL |
|------|-----|-----|-----|-----|-----|------|------|-----|-----|-----|-----|-----|--------|
| 1961 | 76.0 | 75.6 | 76.6 | 78.4 | 79.7 | 79.9 | 80.5 | 81.6 | 81.2 | 79.8 | 77.5 | 77.2 | 78.7 |
| 1962 | 75.2 | 74.2 | 75.7 | 77.2 | 78.5 | 80.5 | 81.7 | 81.3 | 81.0 | 80.4 | 78.9 | 77.3 | 78.5 |
| 1963 | 75.7 | 76.2 | 76.3 | 77.6 | 78.2 | 80.8 | 81.3 | 81.8 | 81.3 | 81.5 | 78.7 | 78.9 | 79.1 |
| 1964 | 76.6 | 77.5 | 78.8 | 78.5 | 80.9 | 81.6 | 81.8 | 82.2 | 82.2 | 80.6 | 79.0 | 75.7 | 79.6 |
| 1965 | 74.7 | 75.9 | 77.7 | 77.7 | 78.9 | 80.3 | 81.7 | 81.5 | 82.2 | 81.5 | 79.8 | 77.4 | 79.1 |
| 1966 | 77.4 | 76.7 | 78.1 | 78.5 | 79.5 | 81.0 | 82.1 | 82.6 | 81.1 | 80.0 | 77.5 | 77.1 | 79.3 |
| 1967 | 76.7 | 76.3 | 75.9 | 78.0 | 79.7 | 81.8 | 82.1 | 82.2 | 81.8 | 81.4 | 77.5 | 77.5 | 79.5 |
| 1968 | 76.4 | 76.5 | 76.2 | 77.0 | 79.9 | 80.4 | 81.2 | 82.0 | 81.8 | 81.6 | 79.5 | 77.5 | 79.2 |
| 1969 | 75.4 | 75.0 | 77.8 | 79.6 | 80.7 | 82.0 | 80.9 | 81.1 | 81.2 | 80.9 | 78.7 | 77.1 | 79.2 |
| 1970 | 76.5 | 76.2 | 77.9 | 80.0 | 80.6 | 81.6 | 82.4 | 82.3 | 82.2 | 81.9 | 80.2 | 78.2 | 80.0 |
| 1971 | 77.6 | 77.4 | 78.9 | 79.7 | 81.3 | 83.0 | 83.2 | 83.3 | 82.9 | 81.9 | 80.6 | 78.8 | 80.8 |
| 1972 | 77.7 | 77.8 | 78.7 | 80.1 | 81.7 | 83.8 | 83.9 | 83.4 | 82.9 | 82.6 | 81.1 | 79.2 | 81.1 |
| 1973 | 78.9 | 78.3 | 78.6 | 80.0 | 82.9 | 83.2 | 83.4 | 83.2 | 82.7 | 83.5 | 80.7 | 77.9 | 81.1 |
| 1974 | 77.3 | 78.0 | 78.5 | 79.6 | 81.4 | 83.4 | 83.7 | 83.2 | 82.9 | 82.5 | 80.0 | 78.3 | 80.7 |
| 1975 | 76.9 | 77.2 | 78.4 | 79.6 | 81.0 | 82.9 | 83.0 | 82.7 | 81.6 | 81.6 | 79.8 | 77.5 | 80.2 |
| 1976 | 76.3 | 76.6 | 76.8 | 78.5 | 80.5 | 81.7 | 83.1 | 83.5 | 83.3 | 82.5 | 80.9 | 78.3 | 80.2 |
| 1977 | 77.0 | 77.6 | 78.3 | 80.2 | 80.9 | 81.9 | 83.0 | 81.0 | 81.1 | 81.9 | 80.3 | 79.3 | 80.0 |
| 1978 | 78.3 | 79.2 | 79.8 | 80.1 | 80.8 | 82.3 | 83.1 | 83.2 | 83.9 | 82.7 | 81.8 | 79.6 | 81.2 |
| 1979 | 78.5 | 78.7 | 77.8 | 79.4 | 81.3 | 83.8 | 83.5 | 83.0 | 81.0 | 83.0 | 80.6 | 78.7 | 80.8 |
| 1980 | 78.2 | 78.6 | 79.2 | 80.8 | 83.8 | 85.1 | 85.2 | 85.1 | 84.5 | 84.4 | 82.2 | 80.7 | 82.3 |
| 1981 | 79.8 | 79.4 | 80.9 | 80.3 | 83.4 | 84.2 | 85.0 | 83.8 | 84.3 | 83.3 | 81.6 | 78.7 | 82.1 |
| 1982 | 78.5 | 77.8 | 78.0 | 80.4 | 81.0 | 82.9 | 83.3 | 84.6 | 84.6 | 83.8 | 80.2 | 78.0 | 81.1 |
| 1983 | 78.5 | 79.9 | 82.2 | 81.8 | 83.2 | 85.4 | 84.2 | 84.0 | 84.3 | 83.6 | 81.4 | 79.9 | 82.4 |
| 1984 | 78.1 | 77.8 | 80.2 | 81.8 | 81.1 | 82.4 | 82.6 | 82.6 | 82.2 | 81.3 | 78.7 | 77.3 | 80.5 |
| 1985 | 76.1 | 77.3 | 76.7 | 78.3 | 80.4 | 83.0 | 83.5 | 83.4 | 81.7 | 79.6 | 79.0 | 76.8 | 79.7 |
| 1986 | 75.5 | 76.0 | 77.4 | 79.0 | 79.1 | 81.6 | 82.0 | 82.2 | 82.5 | 81.4 | 79.1 | 77.7 | 79.5 |
| 1987 | 76.7 | 77.4 | 78.0 | 81.2 | 81.6 | 81.7 | 82.7 | 83.7 | 83.8 | 83.3 | 80.6 | 79.7 | 80.9 |
| 1988 | 76.9 | 76.6 | 77.8 | 80.4 | 82.4 | 84.3 | 83.6 | 82.8 | 82.2 | 81.6 | 79.8 | 76.9 | 80.4 |
| 1989 | 76.2 | 76.0 | 76.1 | 78.8 | 80.3 | 81.2 | 81.8 | 82.3 | 82.3 | 81.7 | 80.0 | 79.2 | 79.7 |
| 1990 | 77.1 | 76.4 | 76.5 | 79.1 | 81.8 | 82.4 | 82.6 | 82.9 | 83.4 | 82.1 | 80.7 | 77.5 | 80.2 |
| Record Mean | 76.5 | 76.6 | 77.5 | 78.9 | 80.5 | 81.8 | 82.2 | 82.3 | 82.1 | 81.5 | 79.6 | 77.7 | 79.8 |
| Max | 82.8 | 83.1 | 84.1 | 85.4 | 86.9 | 88.2 | 88.1 | 88.5 | 88.5 | 88.1 | 85.7 | 83.6 | 86.1 |
| Min | 70.2 | 70.1 | 70.9 | 72.4 | 74.1 | 75.5 | 76.2 | 76.2 | 75.7 | 74.9 | 73.5 | 71.8 | 73.5 |

## REFERENCE NOTES FOR TABLES 1, 2, 3 and 6     (SAN JUAN, PR)

### GENERAL

T - TRACE AMOUNT
BLANK ENTRIES DENOTE MISSING/UNREPORTED DATA.
# INDICATES A STATION OR INSTRUMENT RELOCATION.

### SPECIFIC

#### TABLE 1

(a) - LENGTH OF RECORD IN YEARS. ALTHOUGH INDIVIDUAL MONTHS MAY BE MISSING.

 *  LESS THAN .05

NORMALS — BASED ON THE 1951-1980 RECORD PERIOD.
EXTREMES — DATES ARE THE MOST RECENT OCCURRENCE.
WIND DIR. — NUMERALS SHOW TENS OF DEGREES
                CLOCKWISE FROM TRUE NORTH.
                "00" INDICATES CALM.
RESULTANT WIND DIRECTIONS ARE GIVEN TO WHOLE DEGREES.

#### TABLE 3

MAX AND MIN ARE LONG-TERM MEAN DAILY MAXIMUM AND MEAN DAILY MINIMUM TEMPERATURES.

### EXCEPTIONS

#### TABLE 1

1.   FASTEST MILE WINDS ARE THROUGH MAY 1983

#### TABLES 2, 3, and 6

RECORD MEANS ARE THROUGH THE CURRENT YEAR,
BEGINNING IN      1951 FOR TEMPERATURE
                        1951 FOR PRECIPITATION

**TABLE 4**

HEATING DEGREE DAYS Base 65 deg. F    SAN JUAN, PUERTO RICO

| SEASON | JULY | AUG | SEP | OCT | NOV | DEC | JAN | FEB | MAR | APR | MAY | JUNE | TOTAL |
|--------|------|-----|-----|-----|-----|-----|-----|-----|-----|-----|-----|------|-------|
| 1983-84 | 0 | 0 | 0 | 0 | 0 | 0 | 0 | 0 | 0 | 0 | 0 | 0 | 0 |
| 1984-85 | 0 | 0 | 0 | 0 | 0 | 0 | 0 | 0 | 0 | 0 | 0 | 0 | 0 |
| 1985-86 | 0 | 0 | 0 | 0 | 0 | 0 | 0 | 0 | 0 | 0 | 0 | 0 | 0 |
| 1986-87 | 0 | 0 | 0 | 0 | 0 | 0 | 0 | 0 | 0 | 0 | 0 | 0 | 0 |
| 1987-88 | 0 | 0 | 0 | 0 | 0 | 0 | 0 | 0 | 0 | 0 | 0 | 0 | 0 |
| 1988-89 | 0 | 0 | 0 | 0 | 0 | 0 | 0 | 0 | 0 | 0 | 0 | 0 | 0 |
| 1989-90 | 0 | 0 | 0 | 0 | 0 | 0 | 0 | 0 | 0 | 0 | 0 | 0 | 0 |
| 1990-91 | 0 | 0 | 0 | 0 | 0 | 0 | 0 | 0 | 0 | 0 | 0 | 0 | 0 |

**TABLE 5**

COOLING DEGREE DAYS Base 65 deg. F    SAN JUAN, PUERTO RICO

| YEAR | JAN | FEB | MAR | APR | MAY | JUNE | JULY | AUG | SEP | OCT | NOV | DEC | TOTAL |
|------|-----|-----|-----|-----|-----|------|------|-----|-----|-----|-----|-----|-------|
| 1969 | 328 | 287 | 401 | 447 | 496 | 517 | 501 | 506 | 493 | 500 | 417 | 382 | 5275 |
| 1970 | 362 | 321 | 409 | 460 | 490 | 506 | 548 | 540 | 523 | 528 | 461 | 416 | 5564 |
| 1971 | 398 | 353 | 438 | 445 | 511 | 545 | 562 | 573 | 577 | 531 | 473 | 438 | 5844 |
| 1972 | 400 | 376 | 431 | 458 | 525 | 569 | 592 | 578 | 543 | 554 | 490 | 446 | 5962 |
| 1973 | 438 | 379 | 428 | 458 | 562 | 553 | 578 | 570 | 539 | 579 | 475 | 406 | 5965 |
| 1974 | 390 | 368 | 424 | 442 | 511 | 558 | 586 | 575 | 544 | 549 | 455 | 418 | 5820 |
| 1975 | 375 | 346 | 420 | 446 | 501 | 543 | 565 | 556 | 521 | 519 | 450 | 395 | 5637 |
| 1976 | 357 | 342 | 375 | 413 | 485 | 506 | 566 | 579 | 557 | 548 | 485 | 419 | 5632 |
| 1977 | 382 | 360 | 419 | 463 | 499 | 514 | 491 | 502 | 487 | 532 | 469 | 452 | 5570 |
| 1978 | 420 | 404 | 464 | 462 | 499 | 526 | 566 | 570 | 575 | 555 | 513 | 459 | 6013 |
| 1979 | 426 | 393 | 404 | 436 | 512 | 571 | 582 | 564 | 511 | 569 | 477 | 432 | 5877 |
| 1980 | 414 | 402 | 446 | 479 | 590 | 610 | 633 | 628 | 591 | 608 | 522 | 494 | 6417 |
| 1981 | 467 | 407 | 499 | 468 | 578 | 584 | 626 | 587 | 588 | 574 | 505 | 429 | 6312 |
| 1982 | 423 | 364 | 412 | 470 | 504 | 543 | 573 | 615 | 593 | 590 | 466 | 405 | 5958 |
| 1983 | 426 | 424 | 541 | 509 | 573 | 621 | 604 | 593 | 583 | 582 | 502 | 468 | 6426 |
| 1984 | 415 | 377 | 479 | 508 | 503 | 528 | 553 | 553 | 522 | 517 | 417 | 389 | 5761 |
| 1985 | 352 | 349 | 368 | 403 | 483 | 547 | 579 | 577 | 508 | 459 | 429 | 371 | 5425 |
| 1986 | 329 | 315 | 390 | 428 | 444 | 538 | 535 | 538 | 534 | 517 | 429 | 401 | 5361 |
| 1987 | 366 | 354 | 407 | 490 | 521 | 508 | 556 | 588 | 571 | 575 | 477 | 464 | 5877 |
| 1988 | 377 | 341 | 403 | 470 | 547 | 587 | 581 | 558 | 523 | 522 | 453 | 375 | 5737 |
| 1989 | 354 | 313 | 353 | 421 | 482 | 495 | 529 | 543 | 525 | 526 | 456 | 443 | 5440 |
| 1990 | 383 | 325 | 362 | 430 | 526 | 526 | 551 | 561 | 559 | 539 | 478 | 392 | 5632 |

**TABLE 6**

SNOWFALL (inches)    SAN JUAN, PUERTO RICO

| SEASON | JULY | AUG | SEP | OCT | NOV | DEC | JAN | FEB | MAR | APR | MAY | JUNE | TOTAL |
|--------|------|-----|-----|-----|-----|-----|-----|-----|-----|-----|-----|------|-------|
| 1971-72 | 0.0 | 0.0 | 0.0 | 0.0 | 0.0 | 0.0 | 0.0 | 0.0 | 0.0 | 0.0 | 0.0 | 0.0 | 0.0 |
| 1972-73 | 0.0 | 0.0 | 0.0 | 0.0 | 0.0 | 0.0 | 0.0 | 0.0 | 0.0 | 0.0 | 0.0 | 0.0 | 0.0 |
| 1973-74 | 0.0 | 0.0 | 0.0 | 0.0 | 0.0 | 0.0 | 0.0 | 0.0 | 0.0 | 0.0 | 0.0 | 0.0 | 0.0 |
| 1974-75 | 0.0 | 0.0 | 0.0 | 0.0 | 0.0 | 0.0 | 0.0 | 0.0 | 0.0 | 0.0 | 0.0 | 0.0 | 0.0 |
| 1975-76 | 0.0 | 0.0 | 0.0 | 0.0 | 0.0 | 0.0 | 0.0 | 0.0 | 0.0 | 0.0 | 0.0 | 0.0 | 0.0 |
| 1976-77 | 0.0 | 0.0 | 0.0 | 0.0 | 0.0 | 0.0 | 0.0 | 0.0 | 0.0 | 0.0 | 0.0 | 0.0 | 0.0 |
| 1977-78 | 0.0 | 0.0 | 0.0 | 0.0 | 0.0 | 0.0 | 0.0 | 0.0 | 0.0 | 0.0 | 0.0 | 0.0 | 0.0 |
| 1978-79 | 0.0 | 0.0 | 0.0 | 0.0 | 0.0 | 0.0 | 0.0 | 0.0 | 0.0 | 0.0 | 0.0 | 0.0 | 0.0 |
| 1979-80 | 0.0 | 0.0 | 0.0 | 0.0 | 0.0 | 0.0 | 0.0 | 0.0 | 0.0 | 0.0 | 0.0 | 0.0 | 0.0 |
| 1980-81 | 0.0 | 0.0 | 0.0 | 0.0 | 0.0 | 0.0 | 0.0 | 0.0 | 0.0 | 0.0 | 0.0 | 0.0 | 0.0 |
| 1981-82 | 0.0 | 0.0 | 0.0 | 0.0 | 0.0 | 0.0 | 0.0 | 0.0 | 0.0 | 0.0 | 0.0 | 0.0 | 0.0 |
| 1982-83 | 0.0 | 0.0 | 0.0 | 0.0 | 0.0 | 0.0 | 0.0 | 0.0 | 0.0 | 0.0 | 0.0 | 0.0 | 0.0 |
| 1983-84 | 0.0 | 0.0 | 0.0 | 0.0 | 0.0 | 0.0 | 0.0 | 0.0 | 0.0 | 0.0 | 0.0 | 0.0 | 0.0 |
| 1984-85 | 0.0 | 0.0 | 0.0 | 0.0 | 0.0 | 0.0 | 0.0 | 0.0 | 0.0 | 0.0 | 0.0 | 0.0 | 0.0 |
| 1985-86 | 0.0 | 0.0 | 0.0 | 0.0 | 0.0 | 0.0 | 0.0 | 0.0 | 0.0 | 0.0 | 0.0 | 0.0 | 0.0 |
| 1986-87 | 0.0 | 0.0 | 0.0 | 0.0 | 0.0 | 0.0 | 0.0 | 0.0 | 0.0 | 0.0 | 0.0 | 0.0 | 0.0 |
| 1987-88 | 0.0 | 0.0 | 0.0 | 0.0 | 0.0 | 0.0 | 0.0 | 0.0 | 0.0 | 0.0 | 0.0 | 0.0 | 0.0 |
| 1988-89 | 0.0 | 0.0 | 0.0 | 0.0 | 0.0 | 0.0 | 0.0 | 0.0 | 0.0 | 0.0 | 0.0 | 0.0 | 0.0 |
| 1989-90 | 0.0 | 0.0 | T | 0.0 | 0.0 | 0.0 | 0.0 | 0.0 | 0.0 | 0.0 | 0.0 | 0.0 | T |
| 1990-91 | 0.0 | 0.0 | 0.0 | 0.0 | 0.0 | 0.0 | | | | | | | |
| Record Mean | 0.0 | 0.0 | T | 0.0 | 0.0 | 0.0 | 0.0 | 0.0 | 0.0 | 0.0 | 0.0 | 0.0 | T |

**See Reference Notes, relative to all above tables, on preceding page.**

Charleston lies at the junction of the Kanawha and Elk Rivers in the western foothills of the Appalachian Mountains. The main urban and business areas have developed along the two river valleys, while some residential areas are in nearby valleys and on the surrounding hills. The hilltops are around 1,100 feet above sea level, about 500 feet higher than the valleys. The Kanawha Airport is just over 2 miles northeast of the center-city area, on an artificial plateau constructed from several hilltops.

Weather records are maintained at the Kanawha Airport by National Weather Service personnel. This site tends to be slightly cooler than the river valleys during the afternoons. Conversely, the valleys can become cooler than the hilltops during clear, calm nights. The weather at Charleston is highly changeable, especially from mid-autumn through the spring.

Winters can vary greatly from one season to the next. Snow does not favor any given winter month, heavy snowstorms are infrequent, and most snowfalls are in the 4-inch or less category. Snow and ice usually do not persist on valley roads, but can linger longer on nearby hills and outlying rural roads.

Afternoon temperatures in the 40s and morning readings in the 20s are common during the winter. Yet, every winter typically has two or three extended cold spells when temperatures stay below freezing for a few consecutive days. Northwesterly winds are associated with the cold weather. Air reaching Charleston from the northwest can cause cloudiness and flurries, even when there is no nearby organized storm system. Winter conditions are much more severe over the higher mountains less than 50 miles to the northeast through the southeast. Temperatures warm rapidly in the spring and are accompanied by low daytime humidities.

Summer and early autumn have more day-to-day consistency in the weather. Sunshine is more abundant than in winter. Summer precipitation falls mostly in brief, but sometimes heavy, showers. Flash flooding can occur along small streams, but flooding is rare on the dam-controlled Kanawha and Elk Rivers.

Afternoon summer temperatures are mostly in the 80s. Readings above 95 degrees are rare. However, during a hot spell, haze and humidity can add to the unpleasantness and indoor air conditioning is recommended. Cooler and less humid air often penetrates the area from the north to end a hot spell.

Early morning fog is common from late June into October. Industrial and vehicular pollutants can contribute to limited visibility any time of the year, especially when cooler air becomes trapped in the valleys. Autumn foliage is generally at its peak during the second and third weeks of October. By the end of October, the first 32 degree temperature has usually arrived.

Ample precipitation is well distributed throughout the year. July is quite often the wettest month of the year, while October averages the least rain. Droughts severe enough to limit water use are scarce. Any dry spells during the spring or autumn can cause conditions favorable for brush fires in outlying areas.

## TABLE 1     NORMALS, MEANS AND EXTREMES

CHARLESTON, WEST VIRGINIA

LATITUDE: 38°22'N    LONGITUDE: 81°36'W    ELEVATION: FT. GRND 1016 BARO 1019    TIME ZONE: EASTERN    WBAN: 13866

| | (a) | JAN | FEB | MAR | APR | MAY | JUNE | JULY | AUG | SEP | OCT | NOV | DEC | YEAR |
|---|---|---|---|---|---|---|---|---|---|---|---|---|---|---|
| **TEMPERATURE °F:** | | | | | | | | | | | | | | |
| Normals | | | | | | | | | | | | | | |
| -Daily Maximum | | 41.8 | 45.4 | 55.4 | 67.3 | 76.0 | 82.5 | 85.2 | 84.2 | 78.7 | 67.7 | 55.6 | 45.9 | 65.5 |
| -Daily Minimum | | 23.9 | 25.8 | 34.1 | 43.3 | 51.8 | 59.4 | 63.8 | 63.1 | 56.4 | 44.0 | 35.0 | 27.8 | 44.0 |
| -Monthly | | 32.9 | 35.6 | 44.8 | 55.3 | 63.9 | 71.0 | 74.5 | 73.7 | 67.6 | 55.9 | 45.3 | 36.9 | 54.8 |
| Extremes | | | | | | | | | | | | | | |
| -Record Highest | 42 | 79 | 78 | 87 | 92 | 93 | 98 | 104 | 101 | 102 | 92 | 85 | 80 | 104 |
| -Year | | 1950 | 1977 | 1954 | 1985 | 1985 | 1988 | 1988 | 1988 | 1953 | 1951 | 1948 | 1982 | JUL 1988 |
| -Record Lowest | 42 | -15 | -6 | 0 | 19 | 26 | 33 | 46 | 41 | 34 | 17 | 6 | -12 | -15 |
| -Year | | 1985 | 1968 | 1980 | 1982 | 1966 | 1972 | 1963 | 1965 | 1983 | 1962 | 1950 | 1989 | JAN 1985 |
| **NORMAL DEGREE DAYS:** | | | | | | | | | | | | | | |
| Heating (base 65°F) | | 995 | 823 | 626 | 298 | 125 | 16 | 0 | 0 | 51 | 301 | 591 | 871 | 4697 |
| Cooling (base 65°F) | | 0 | 0 | 0 | 7 | 91 | 196 | 295 | 270 | 129 | 19 | 0 | 0 | 1007 |
| **% OF POSSIBLE SUNSHINE** | | | | | | | | | | | | | | |
| **MEAN SKY COVER (tenths)** | | | | | | | | | | | | | | |
| Sunrise - Sunset | 42 | 7.7 | 7.6 | 7.3 | 6.8 | 6.6 | 6.4 | 6.6 | 6.3 | 6.2 | 6.0 | 7.2 | 7.5 | 6.8 |
| **MEAN NUMBER OF DAYS:** | | | | | | | | | | | | | | |
| Sunrise to Sunset | | | | | | | | | | | | | | |
| -Clear | 42 | 3.8 | 4.3 | 4.8 | 5.9 | 6.1 | 4.9 | 4.4 | 5.0 | 6.7 | 8.7 | 5.1 | 4.6 | 64.5 |
| -Partly Cloudy | 42 | 6.5 | 6.0 | 7.7 | 7.7 | 10.0 | 12.9 | 13.3 | 14.3 | 11.1 | 9.2 | 7.0 | 6.5 | 112.2 |
| -Cloudy | 42 | 20.6 | 18.0 | 18.5 | 16.4 | 14.9 | 12.2 | 13.3 | 11.7 | 12.2 | 13.1 | 17.9 | 19.9 | 188.5 |
| Precipitation | | | | | | | | | | | | | | |
| .01 inches or more | 42 | 15.5 | 13.7 | 14.8 | 13.9 | 13.3 | 11.4 | 12.8 | 10.9 | 9.4 | 9.6 | 12.0 | 14.0 | 151.2 |
| Snow,Ice pellets | | | | | | | | | | | | | | |
| 1.0 inches or more | 42 | 3.4 | 2.7 | 1.5 | 0.2 | 0.0 | 0.0 | 0.0 | 0.0 | 0.0 | 0.* | 0.8 | 1.8 | 10.3 |
| Thunderstorms | 42 | 0.5 | 0.9 | 2.2 | 4.1 | 6.7 | 7.7 | 9.7 | 7.1 | 3.0 | 1.2 | 0.7 | 0.3 | 44.2 |
| Heavy Fog Visibility | | | | | | | | | | | | | | |
| 1/4 mile or less | 42 | 4.1 | 3.2 | 2.6 | 3.0 | 7.7 | 12.0 | 15.2 | 18.7 | 16.5 | 10.8 | 4.7 | 3.8 | 102.3 |
| Temperature °F | | | | | | | | | | | | | | |
| -Maximum | | | | | | | | | | | | | | |
| 90° and above | 42 | 0.0 | 0.0 | 0.0 | 0.3 | 1.1 | 4.8 | 8.0 | 5.5 | 2.2 | 0.* | 0.0 | 0.0 | 22.0 |
| 32° and below | 42 | 7.6 | 4.7 | 0.9 | 0.* | 0.0 | 0.0 | 0.0 | 0.0 | 0.0 | 0.0 | 0.5 | 4.5 | 18.3 |
| -Minimum | | | | | | | | | | | | | | |
| 32° and below | 42 | 23.4 | 20.1 | 14.6 | 4.7 | 0.4 | 0.0 | 0.0 | 0.0 | 0.0 | 3.4 | 12.8 | 21.2 | 100.5 |
| 0° and below | 42 | 1.0 | 0.3 | 0.* | 0.0 | 0.0 | 0.0 | 0.0 | 0.0 | 0.0 | 0.0 | 0.0 | 0.3 | 1.6 |
| **AVG. STATION PRESS.(mb)** | 17 | 984.3 | 983.8 | 981.7 | 980.8 | 980.9 | 981.8 | 982.9 | 983.7 | 984.3 | 985.1 | 984.3 | 984.6 | 983.2 |
| **RELATIVE HUMIDITY (%)** | | | | | | | | | | | | | | |
| Hour 01 | 42 | 74 | 72 | 68 | 67 | 80 | 87 | 90 | 91 | 89 | 83 | 75 | 75 | 79 |
| Hour 07 | 42 | 77 | 77 | 74 | 75 | 83 | 86 | 90 | 92 | 91 | 87 | 80 | 77 | 82 |
| Hour 13 (Local Time) | 42 | 62 | 59 | 52 | 47 | 50 | 54 | 60 | 58 | 56 | 53 | 56 | 61 | 56 |
| Hour 19 | 42 | 65 | 61 | 54 | 49 | 56 | 61 | 66 | 69 | 71 | 66 | 62 | 66 | 62 |
| **PRECIPITATION (inches):** | | | | | | | | | | | | | | |
| Water Equivalent | | | | | | | | | | | | | | |
| -Normal | | 3.48 | 3.11 | 4.00 | 3.52 | 3.68 | 3.32 | 5.36 | 4.15 | 3.01 | 2.63 | 2.90 | 3.27 | 42.43 |
| -Maximum Monthly | 42 | 9.11 | 6.89 | 6.80 | 6.46 | 6.79 | 7.54 | 13.54 | 10.45 | 7.61 | 6.49 | 8.45 | 8.02 | 13.54 |
| -Year | | 1950 | 1956 | 1967 | 1965 | 1989 | 1989 | 1961 | 1958 | 1971 | 1983 | 1985 | 1978 | JUL 1961 |
| -Minimum Monthly | 42 | 1.09 | 0.64 | 1.30 | 0.50 | 0.84 | 0.70 | 2.16 | 0.66 | 0.65 | 0.09 | 0.64 | 0.45 | 0.09 |
| -Year | | 1981 | 1968 | 1987 | 1976 | 1977 | 1966 | 1974 | 1957 | 1959 | 1963 | 1965 | 1965 | OCT 1963 |
| -Maximum in 24 hrs | 42 | 1.91 | 2.45 | 2.86 | 2.72 | 3.31 | 2.24 | 5.60 | 4.17 | 2.40 | 2.48 | 2.45 | 2.47 | 5.60 |
| -Year | | 1961 | 1951 | 1967 | 1948 | 1982 | 1962 | 1961 | 1958 | 1956 | 1961 | 1985 | 1978 | JUL 1961 |
| Snow,Ice pellets | | | | | | | | | | | | | | |
| -Maximum Monthly | 42 | 39.5 | 21.8 | 18.3 | 20.7 | 0.6 | 0.0 | 0.0 | T | T | 2.8 | 25.8 | 18.6 | 39.5 |
| -Year | | 1978 | 1964 | 1960 | 1987 | 1989 | | | 1989 | 1989 | 1961 | 1950 | 1962 | JAN 1978 |
| -Maximum in 24 hrs | 42 | 15.8 | 11.2 | 9.9 | 11.3 | 0.6 | 0.0 | 0.0 | T | T | 2.8 | 15.1 | 11.2 | 15.8 |
| -Year | | 1978 | 1983 | 1954 | 1987 | 1989 | | | 1989 | 1989 | 1961 | 1950 | 1967 | JAN 1978 |
| **WIND:** | | | | | | | | | | | | | | |
| Mean Speed (mph) | 42 | 7.6 | 7.6 | 8.3 | 7.7 | 6.1 | 5.6 | 5.1 | 4.5 | 4.8 | 5.2 | 6.7 | 7.1 | 6.3 |
| Prevailing Direction | | | | | | | | | | | | | | |
| through 1963 | | WSW | WSW | WSW | SW | SW | SW | S | S | S | S | SW | SW | SW |
| Fastest Obs. 1 Min. | | | | | | | | | | | | | | |
| -Direction (!!) | 40 | 25 | 19 | 32 | 27 | 25 | 32 | 29 | 29 | 20 | 25 | 29 | 25 | 25 |
| -Speed (MPH) | 40 | 45 | 40 | 46 | 45 | 55 | 50 | 46 | 50 | 35 | 45 | 40 | 55 | 55 |
| -Year | | 1951 | 1981 | 1955 | 1953 | 1953 | 1951 | 1957 | 1952 | 1956 | 1950 | 1954 | 1953 | MAY 1953 |
| Peak Gust | | | | | | | | | | | | | | |
| -Direction (!!) | 6 | W | S | NW | W | W | NW | NW | NW | N | SW | W | W | W |
| -Speed (mph) | 6 | 45 | 56 | 53 | 60 | 49 | 41 | 56 | 46 | 33 | 36 | 49 | 62 | 62 |
| -Date | | 1987 | 1986 | 1985 | 1987 | 1988 | 1987 | 1986 | 1989 | 1988 | 1988 | 1988 | 1987 | DEC 1987 |

**See Reference Notes to this table on the following page.**

PRECIPITATION (inches)  CHARLESTON, WEST VIRGINIA

**TABLE 2**

| YEAR | JAN | FEB | MAR | APR | MAY | JUNE | JULY | AUG | SEP | OCT | NOV | DEC | ANNUAL |
|---|---|---|---|---|---|---|---|---|---|---|---|---|---|
| 1961 | 3.79 | 3.63 | 4.86 | 3.22 | 4.23 | 5.22 | 13.54 | 1.19 | 1.50 | 6.11 | 2.89 | 4.74 | 54.92 |
| 1962 | 2.81 | 5.37 | 3.91 | 4.12 | 2.22 | 4.94 | 8.03 | 1.94 | 3.67 | 2.53 | 6.27 | 3.46 | 49.27 |
| 1963 | 1.85 | 2.70 | 6.37 | 1.21 | 3.48 | 2.67 | 3.06 | 2.85 | 1.34 | 0.09 | 3.19 | 1.44 | 30.25 |
| 1964 | 2.58 | 3.58 | 3.65 | 3.20 | 0.95 | 3.82 | 2.76 | 3.23 | 2.53 | 0.59 | 2.95 | 3.14 | 32.98 |
| 1965 | 4.65 | 2.02 | 4.52 | 6.46 | 1.90 | 2.18 | 2.46 | 4.38 | 3.21 | 2.09 | 0.64 | 0.45 | 34.96 |
| 1966 | 3.57 | 2.78 | 1.51 | 5.06 | 1.52 | 0.70 | 2.94 | 3.31 | 3.74 | 1.72 | 3.05 | 2.53 | 32.43 |
| 1967 | 1.21 | 2.95 | 6.80 | 3.21 | 6.45 | 1.83 | 4.59 | 1.85 | 1.68 | 2.09 | 4.30 | 4.72 | 41.68 |
| 1968 | 2.01 | 0.64 | 4.79 | 2.58 | 6.59 | 2.83 | 4.02 | 5.42 | 3.32 | 3.16 | 2.47 | 2.38 | 40.21 |
| 1969 | 1.50 | 1.27 | 1.43 | 2.35 | 1.95 | 2.43 | 6.13 | 8.20 | 3.27 | 1.52 | 2.22 | 4.85 | 37.12 |
| 1970 | 1.15 | 3.51 | 4.23 | 3.19 | 1.13 | 2.35 | 3.53 | 4.84 | 3.55 | 5.19 | 2.34 | 3.81 | 38.82 |
| 1971 | 2.35 | 3.40 | 1.97 | 1.19 | 5.17 | 2.58 | 6.59 | 2.12 | 7.61 | 1.30 | 2.83 | 1.71 | 38.82 |
| 1972 | 5.47 | 5.51 | 2.17 | 5.16 | 2.55 | 4.33 | 4.13 | 4.13 | 3.61 | 2.48 | 5.26 | 6.35 | 51.15 |
| 1973 | 1.52 | 2.41 | 3.40 | 5.44 | 5.36 | 4.48 | 6.88 | 2.07 | 3.91 | 4.75 | 5.42 | 3.68 | 49.32 |
| 1974 | 4.67 | 2.50 | 4.54 | 3.05 | 6.06 | 5.07 | 2.16 | 4.22 | 2.64 | 1.64 | 3.72 | 3.19 | 43.46 |
| 1975 | 4.84 | 3.10 | 6.01 | 4.03 | 6.44 | 4.25 | 2.71 | 5.14 | 4.99 | 3.08 | 2.66 | 3.74 | 50.99 |
| 1976 | 2.89 | 2.11 | 4.21 | 0.50 | 3.66 | 4.24 | 6.93 | 2.23 | 5.37 | 5.44 | 1.02 | 2.18 | 40.78 |
| 1977 | 1.90 | 1.08 | 3.16 | 4.06 | 0.84 | 5.93 | 4.92 | 6.58 | 1.14 | 4.16 | 3.78 | 2.07 | 39.62 |
| 1978 | 5.59 | 1.31 | 2.67 | 3.31 | 3.99 | 2.96 | 9.83 | 8.21 | 1.45 | 2.68 | 2.26 | 8.02 | 52.28 |
| #1979 | 6.48 | 3.76 | 3.00 | 3.82 | 3.87 | 3.54 | 5.17 | 4.78 | 3.95 | 3.67 | 4.02 | 2.81 | 48.87 |
| 1980 | 2.85 | 2.25 | 5.32 | 4.49 | 2.67 | 2.17 | 8.47 | 10.32 | 2.37 | 2.03 | 3.02 | 1.85 | 47.81 |
| 1981 | 1.09 | 4.59 | 1.80 | 4.04 | 3.78 | 6.46 | 3.02 | 2.24 | 2.36 | 2.43 | 1.29 | 2.71 | 35.81 |
| 1982 | 3.74 | 3.23 | 4.96 | 1.14 | 6.19 | 7.00 | 2.68 | 2.65 | 2.58 | 1.65 | 4.65 | 2.71 | 43.18 |
| 1983 | 1.24 | 2.72 | 3.15 | 3.96 | 5.98 | 2.77 | 4.19 | 2.54 | 1.33 | 6.49 | 4.80 | 3.19 | 42.36 |
| 1984 | 1.67 | 2.56 | 2.72 | 4.00 | 3.71 | 2.56 | 4.37 | 4.57 | 2.95 | 3.28 | 4.73 | 3.78 | 40.90 |
| 1985 | 3.07 | 2.32 | 4.23 | 1.84 | 5.88 | 3.07 | 3.22 | 2.02 | 0.71 | 3.65 | 8.45 | 2.71 | 41.17 |
| 1986 | 2.12 | 4.35 | 1.87 | 1.39 | 4.86 | 2.36 | 7.61 | 4.71 | 3.51 | 2.20 | 6.88 | 3.89 | 45.75 |
| 1987 | 3.23 | 3.34 | 1.30 | 4.05 | 2.49 | 3.89 | 4.23 | 3.56 | 3.89 | 1.10 | 2.71 | 4.13 | 37.41 |
| 1988 | 1.62 | 2.50 | 2.71 | 2.17 | 2.59 | 0.94 | 3.00 | 2.86 | 3.46 | 1.87 | 5.02 | 2.66 | 31.40 |
| 1989 | 2.92 | 6.05 | 5.81 | 4.13 | 6.79 | 7.54 | 3.04 | 5.62 | 7.28 | 4.09 | 2.87 | 1.83 | 57.97 |
| 1990 | 2.86 | 3.74 | 1.94 | 2.89 | 4.87 | 3.01 | 5.35 | 2.54 | 4.26 | 3.51 | 2.07 | 7.01 | 44.05 |
| Record Mean | 3.62 | 3.29 | 3.98 | 3.60 | 3.82 | 3.88 | 4.94 | 4.13 | 3.02 | 2.79 | 3.19 | 3.33 | 43.58 |

**TABLE 3**  AVERAGE TEMPERATURE (deg. F)  CHARLESTON, WEST VIRGINIA

| YEAR | JAN | FEB | MAR | APR | MAY | JUNE | JULY | AUG | SEP | OCT | NOV | DEC | ANNUAL |
|---|---|---|---|---|---|---|---|---|---|---|---|---|---|
| 1961 | 27.5 | 40.0 | 48.0 | 49.7 | 59.4 | 67.9 | 72.4 | 73.7 | 71.1 | 56.1 | 46.3 | 37.2 | 54.1 |
| 1962 | 33.6 | 40.2 | 43.6 | 51.6 | 69.8 | 73.0 | 73.0 | 74.4 | 65.0 | 57.3 | 42.9 | 30.8 | 54.6 |
| 1963 | 27.9 | 29.0 | 49.5 | 56.1 | 61.3 | 69.1 | 72.0 | 70.2 | 64.5 | 59.2 | 46.2 | 26.1 | 52.6 |
| 1964 | 35.8 | 33.2 | 46.7 | 58.5 | 67.0 | 72.9 | 75.0 | 73.1 | 67.5 | 53.2 | 49.0 | 39.2 | 55.9 |
| 1965 | 33.3 | 35.6 | 39.6 | 55.1 | 69.2 | 70.0 | 73.2 | 72.5 | 69.3 | 52.6 | 46.1 | 39.8 | 54.7 |
| 1966 | 27.1 | 36.6 | 47.7 | 54.1 | 62.1 | 72.0 | 77.3 | 73.5 | 66.5 | 55.0 | 48.2 | 35.5 | 54.6 |
| 1967 | 38.5 | 31.6 | 46.5 | 56.3 | 58.3 | 71.6 | 71.1 | 70.2 | 62.1 | 55.9 | 41.3 | 38.9 | 53.7 |
| 1968 | 29.1 | 27.1 | 47.5 | 56.4 | 61.0 | 70.6 | 74.2 | 74.1 | 66.3 | 56.0 | 46.8 | 34.2 | 53.6 |
| 1969 | 32.7 | 35.2 | 38.7 | 56.2 | 64.1 | 73.7 | 76.6 | 72.1 | 64.1 | 53.9 | 41.3 | 32.3 | 53.4 |
| 1970 | 28.5 | 36.2 | 43.3 | 58.2 | 66.9 | 73.1 | 74.6 | 73.6 | 70.0 | 57.4 | 46.0 | 38.4 | 55.5 |
| 1971 | 29.4 | 35.2 | 39.7 | 51.9 | 59.9 | 73.5 | 72.4 | 71.9 | 70.7 | 63.8 | 45.9 | 47.3 | 55.2 |
| 1972 | 38.7 | 35.2 | 43.8 | 54.5 | 63.7 | 64.9 | 73.4 | 72.7 | 68.7 | 52.5 | 43.4 | 42.1 | 54.5 |
| 1973 | 34.3 | 35.1 | 52.2 | 53.8 | 60.8 | 73.3 | 74.5 | 74.6 | 70.1 | 58.9 | 46.8 | 38.0 | 56.0 |
| 1974 | 43.5 | 37.1 | 49.1 | 56.9 | 64.2 | 67.8 | 74.2 | 73.6 | 63.2 | 52.4 | 45.2 | 36.8 | 55.3 |
| 1975 | 35.7 | 38.0 | 39.8 | 50.2 | 66.1 | 71.7 | 74.2 | 71.7 | 63.9 | 57.6 | 50.2 | 38.6 | 55.2 |
| 1976 | 31.7 | 45.8 | 51.6 | 55.2 | 61.9 | 71.9 | 72.4 | 70.2 | 63.3 | 49.5 | 37.6 | 31.0 | 53.5 |
| 1977 | 18.6 | 33.2 | 49.8 | 58.4 | 67.0 | 68.6 | 76.9 | 73.6 | 70.2 | 53.4 | 49.1 | 35.1 | 54.5 |
| 1978 | 24.4 | 24.2 | 42.6 | 56.7 | 63.1 | 70.9 | 73.8 | 74.9 | 71.0 | 53.8 | 49.4 | 39.0 | 53.6 |
| 1979 | 28.1 | 27.9 | 50.5 | 55.1 | 63.0 | 68.8 | 72.9 | 73.4 | 67.0 | 54.6 | 47.5 | 38.3 | 54.0 |
| 1980 | 34.1 | 29.7 | 42.0 | 53.3 | 63.6 | 68.8 | 76.6 | 76.3 | 69.8 | 53.6 | 43.2 | 36.3 | 54.0 |
| 1981 | 28.0 | 37.2 | 41.4 | 59.1 | 60.4 | 73.2 | 75.7 | 72.8 | 66.5 | 54.2 | 45.3 | 34.6 | 54.0 |
| 1982 | 29.8 | 36.1 | 47.2 | 51.5 | 68.6 | 68.8 | 76.2 | 71.1 | 65.9 | 57.7 | 49.0 | 44.8 | 55.6 |
| 1983 | 34.0 | 37.7 | 47.0 | 52.1 | 61.1 | 71.6 | 77.0 | 78.0 | 68.4 | 58.1 | 47.4 | 32.0 | 55.4 |
| 1984 | 30.6 | 41.5 | 41.1 | 54.2 | 61.4 | 75.3 | 73.2 | 74.9 | 65.4 | 64.4 | 44.6 | 46.9 | 56.1 |
| 1985 | 27.2 | 34.0 | 49.4 | 60.8 | 66.3 | 71.0 | 75.8 | 74.0 | 69.6 | 62.3 | 55.5 | 33.8 | 56.6 |
| 1986 | 34.1 | 40.5 | 47.1 | 57.9 | 65.3 | 72.2 | 77.2 | 71.9 | 69.5 | 57.9 | 46.4 | 36.4 | 56.4 |
| 1987 | 33.0 | 37.2 | 47.0 | 52.7 | 68.4 | 73.5 | 77.1 | 77.0 | 67.1 | 50.3 | 49.0 | 39.8 | 56.0 |
| 1988 | 31.1 | 35.2 | 46.1 | 54.1 | 63.2 | 71.0 | 78.6 | 77.4 | 66.6 | 49.3 | 47.0 | 37.4 | 54.8 |
| 1989 | 41.1 | 34.9 | 47.8 | 52.8 | 59.4 | 71.7 | 75.7 | 73.2 | 67.0 | 56.7 | 46.4 | 26.0 | 54.4 |
| 1990 | 42.3 | 45.2 | 51.7 | 55.1 | 62.9 | 72.3 | 75.8 | 74.1 | 68.7 | 58.2 | 50.7 | 43.6 | 58.4 |
| Record Mean | 35.6 | 37.6 | 46.1 | 55.8 | 64.7 | 72.1 | 75.8 | 74.7 | 69.0 | 57.5 | 46.8 | 38.0 | 56.1 |
| Max | 45.6 | 48.4 | 57.9 | 68.7 | 77.4 | 84.1 | 87.2 | 86.0 | 81.1 | 70.0 | 58.0 | 47.8 | 67.7 |
| Min | 25.6 | 26.8 | 34.3 | 43.0 | 51.9 | 60.1 | 64.5 | 63.4 | 56.9 | 45.0 | 35.5 | 28.2 | 44.6 |

## REFERENCE NOTES FOR TABLES 1, 2, 3 and 6    (CHARLESTON, WV)

**GENERAL**

T - TRACE AMOUNT
BLANK ENTRIES DENOTE MISSING/UNREPORTED DATA.
# INDICATES A STATION OR INSTRUMENT RELOCATION.

**SPECIFIC**

TABLE 1

(a) - LENGTH OF RECORD IN YEARS. ALTHOUGH
 INDIVIDUAL MONTHS MAY BE MISSING.
 * LESS THAN .05

NORMALS — BASED ON THE 1951-1980 RECORD PERIOD.
EXTREMES — DATES ARE THE MOST RECENT OCCURRENCE.
WIND DIR. — NUMERALS SHOW TENS OF DEGREES
 CLOCKWISE FROM TRUE NORTH.
 "00" INDICATES CALM.
RESULTANT WIND DIRECTIONS ARE GIVEN TO WHOLE DEGREES.

TABLE 3
MAX AND MIN ARE LONG-TERM MEAN DAILY MAXIMUM
AND MEAN DAILY MINIMUM TEMPERATURES.

**EXCEPTIONS**

TABLES 2, 3, and 6

RECORD MEANS ARE THROUGH THE CURRENT YEAR,
BEGINNING IN    1902 FOR TEMPERATURE
 1901 FOR PRECIPITATION
 1948 FOR SNOWFALL

**TABLE 4**

HEATING DEGREE DAYS Base 65 deg. F          CHARLESTON, WEST VIRGINIA

| SEASON | JULY | AUG | SEP | OCT | NOV | DEC | JAN | FEB | MAR | APR | MAY | JUNE | TOTAL |
|---|---|---|---|---|---|---|---|---|---|---|---|---|---|
| 1961-62 | 3 | 0 | 57 | 275 | 559 | 853 | 965 | 687 | 656 | 424 | 37 | 0 | 4516 |
| 1962-63 | 3 | 0 | 114 | 273 | 661 | 1052 | 1144 | 1002 | 476 | 302 | 148 | 26 | 5201 |
| 1963-64 | 10 | 6 | 81 | 177 | 558 | 1200 | 899 | 917 | 563 | 226 | 54 | 20 | 4711 |
| 1964-65 | 0 | 13 | 40 | 364 | 474 | 791 | 974 | 820 | 780 | 299 | 24 | 15 | 4594 |
| 1965-66 | 0 | 15 | 58 | 382 | 561 | 776 | 1166 | 793 | 538 | 354 | 147 | 25 | 4815 |
| 1966-67 | 0 | 1 | 44 | 315 | 507 | 910 | 815 | 932 | 517 | 275 | 217 | 17 | 4550 |
| 1967-68 | 4 | 6 | 124 | 297 | 704 | 802 | 1104 | 1095 | 539 | 263 | 141 | 15 | 5094 |
| 1968-69 | 2 | 11 | 35 | 298 | 541 | 946 | 994 | 828 | 807 | 264 | 98 | 9 | 4833 |
| 1969-70 | 0 | 0 | 95 | 352 | 703 | 1007 | 1125 | 801 | 666 | 239 | 82 | 1 | 5071 |
| 1970-71 | 3 | 0 | 40 | 246 | 563 | 817 | 1097 | 828 | 778 | 387 | 184 | 2 | 4945 |
| 1971-72 | 0 | 1 | 13 | 78 | 578 | 543 | 809 | 856 | 649 | 333 | 90 | 81 | 4031 |
| 1972-73 | 16 | 2 | 14 | 378 | 642 | 701 | 945 | 832 | 394 | 351 | 157 | 4 | 4436 |
| 1973-74 | 0 | 1 | 19 | 202 | 541 | 833 | 659 | 775 | 500 | 277 | 115 | 25 | 3947 |
| 1974-75 | 0 | 0 | 110 | 388 | 590 | 869 | 899 | 749 | 772 | 445 | 59 | 4 | 4885 |
| 1975-76 | 0 | 0 | 106 | 227 | 441 | 813 | 1025 | 549 | 427 | 342 | 142 | 4 | 4076 |
| 1976-77 | 0 | 9 | 84 | 475 | 814 | 1047 | 1432 | 888 | 482 | 242 | 81 | 52 | 5606 |
| 1977-78 | 0 | 2 | 19 | 357 | 482 | 919 | 1249 | 1138 | 691 | 258 | 137 | 23 | 5275 |
| 1978-79 | 0 | 0 | 18 | 344 | 462 | 797 | 1137 | 1031 | 456 | 308 | 125 | 19 | 4697 |
| 1979-80 | 5 | 10 | 39 | 331 | 519 | 820 | 951 | 1017 | 707 | 349 | 106 | 27 | 4881 |
| 1980-81 | 0 | 0 | 33 | 356 | 650 | 882 | 1138 | 774 | 727 | 207 | 175 | 2 | 4944 |
| 1981-82 | 0 | 1 | 76 | 335 | 585 | 936 | 1086 | 801 | 545 | 405 | 36 | 2 | 4808 |
| 1982-83 | 1 | 2 | 69 | 268 | 480 | 626 | 955 | 757 | 554 | 388 | 153 | 16 | 4269 |
| 1983-84 | 4 | 0 | 66 | 227 | 521 | 1019 | 1059 | 674 | 734 | 346 | 171 | 5 | 4826 |
| 1984-85 | 1 | 0 | 98 | 74 | 613 | 563 | 1164 | 860 | 488 | 192 | 54 | 18 | 4125 |
| 1985-86 | 0 | 0 | 51 | 127 | 294 | 960 | 954 | 679 | 554 | 249 | 83 | 7 | 3958 |
| 1986-87 | 0 | 23 | 23 | 255 | 550 | 880 | 989 | 770 | 549 | 374 | 63 | 4 | 4480 |
| 1987-88 | 0 | 0 | 37 | 447 | 473 | 774 | 1043 | 859 | 577 | 326 | 112 | 38 | 4686 |
| 1988-89 | 2 | 0 | 37 | 484 | 534 | 849 | 735 | 837 | 536 | 367 | 221 | 2 | 4604 |
| 1989-90 | 0 | 7 | 72 | 270 | 553 | 1203 | 697 | 549 | 446 | 323 | 111 | 8 | 4239 |
| 1990-91 | 0 | 0 | 59 | 230 | 428 | 655 | | | | | | | |

**TABLE 5**

COOLING DEGREE DAYS Base 65 deg. F          CHARLESTON, WEST VIRGINIA

| YEAR | JAN | FEB | MAR | APR | MAY | JUNE | JULY | AUG | SEP | OCT | NOV | DEC | TOTAL |
|---|---|---|---|---|---|---|---|---|---|---|---|---|---|
| 1969 | 0 | 0 | 0 | 7 | 79 | 277 | 368 | 227 | 75 | 15 | 0 | 0 | 1048 |
| 1970 | 0 | 0 | 0 | 40 | 147 | 251 | 310 | 273 | 197 | 18 | 0 | 0 | 1236 |
| 1971 | 0 | 0 | 0 | 0 | 32 | 265 | 237 | 219 | 190 | 49 | 11 | 5 | 1008 |
| 1972 | 0 | 0 | 0 | 24 | 56 | 85 | 283 | 247 | 132 | 0 | 0 | 0 | 827 |
| 1973 | 0 | 0 | 4 | 22 | 34 | 256 | 304 | 305 | 181 | 22 | 2 | 0 | 1130 |
| 1974 | 0 | 0 | 14 | 43 | 99 | 118 | 292 | 275 | 62 | 6 | 1 | 0 | 910 |
| 1975 | 0 | 0 | 0 | 7 | 99 | 212 | 291 | 372 | 82 | 7 | 4 | 0 | 1074 |
| 1976 | 0 | 1 | 17 | 58 | 54 | 218 | 238 | 175 | 39 | 1 | 0 | 0 | 801 |
| 1977 | 0 | 0 | 18 | 50 | 148 | 165 | 373 | 277 | 180 | 4 | 12 | 0 | 1227 |
| 1978 | 0 | 0 | 0 | 16 | 88 | 207 | 279 | 314 | 205 | 4 | 1 | 0 | 1114 |
| 1979 | 0 | 0 | 13 | 18 | 69 | 138 | 257 | 277 | 105 | 17 | 0 | 0 | 894 |
| 1980 | 0 | 0 | 0 | 6 | 71 | 147 | 370 | 358 | 182 | 9 | 0 | 0 | 1143 |
| 1981 | 0 | 0 | 2 | 38 | 41 | 256 | 340 | 251 | 126 | 5 | 0 | 0 | 1059 |
| 1982 | 0 | 0 | 0 | 6 | 154 | 122 | 355 | 196 | 101 | 47 | 5 | 6 | 992 |
| 1983 | 0 | 0 | 2 | 6 | 39 | 222 | 385 | 407 | 177 | 18 | 0 | 0 | 1256 |
| 1984 | 0 | 0 | 0 | 27 | 64 | 318 | 261 | 312 | 116 | 65 | 7 | 8 | 1178 |
| 1985 | 0 | 0 | 9 | 72 | 105 | 204 | 339 | 285 | 194 | 52 | 14 | 0 | 1274 |
| 1986 | 0 | 0 | 4 | 41 | 100 | 227 | 384 | 244 | 167 | 43 | 0 | 0 | 1210 |
| 1987 | 0 | 0 | 0 | 13 | 177 | 268 | 381 | 379 | 108 | 0 | 2 | 0 | 1328 |
| 1988 | 0 | 0 | 3 | 9 | 64 | 225 | 430 | 392 | 91 | 4 | 3 | 0 | 1221 |
| 1989 | 0 | 0 | 11 | 6 | 55 | 211 | 339 | 273 | 140 | 23 | 2 | 0 | 1060 |
| 1990 | 0 | 0 | 41 | 33 | 54 | 232 | 342 | 286 | 174 | 28 | 7 | 0 | 1197 |

**TABLE 6**

SNOWFALL (inches)          CHARLESTON, WEST VIRGINIA

| SEASON | JULY | AUG | SEP | OCT | NOV | DEC | JAN | FEB | MAR | APR | MAY | JUNE | TOTAL |
|---|---|---|---|---|---|---|---|---|---|---|---|---|---|
| 1961-62 | 0.0 | 0.0 | 0.0 | 2.8 | 0.6 | 5.6 | 3.9 | 4.8 | 8.5 | T | 0.0 | 0.0 | 26.2 |
| 1962-63 | 0.0 | 0.0 | 0.0 | 0.6 | 0.2 | 18.6 | 10.7 | 19.0 | T | T | 0.2 | 0.0 | 49.3 |
| 1963-64 | 0.0 | 0.0 | 0.0 | T | 3.6 | 12.6 | 11.3 | 21.8 | 2.2 | T | 0.0 | 0.0 | 51.5 |
| 1964-65 | 0.0 | 0.0 | 0.0 | 0.0 | 1.3 | 0.9 | 13.7 | 6.7 | 8.5 | T | 0.0 | 0.0 | 31.1 |
| 1965-66 | 0.0 | 0.0 | 0.0 | T | T | 2.7 | 19.8 | 8.0 | 1.7 | T | 0.0 | 0.0 | 32.2 |
| 1966-67 | 0.0 | 0.0 | 0.0 | T | 3.8 | 6.0 | 3.6 | 20.6 | 2.2 | 0.0 | 0.0 | 0.0 | 36.2 |
| 1967-68 | 0.0 | 0.0 | 0.0 | 0.0 | 0.2 | 16.6 | 13.3 | 9.2 | 2.0 | 0.0 | 0.0 | 0.0 | 41.3 |
| 1968-69 | 0.0 | 0.0 | 0.0 | T | 4.3 | 4.7 | 2.0 | 1.3 | 4.8 | 0.0 | 0.0 | 0.0 | 17.1 |
| 1969-70 | 0.0 | 0.0 | 0.0 | 0.0 | 4.3 | 9.5 | 12.6 | 14.2 | 2.9 | T | 0.0 | 0.0 | 43.5 |
| 1970-71 | 0.0 | 0.0 | 0.0 | 0.0 | 0.2 | 10.9 | 11.6 | 10.5 | 11.7 | T | 0.0 | 0.0 | 44.9 |
| 1971-72 | 0.0 | 0.0 | 0.0 | 0.0 | 4.2 | 0.8 | 4.0 | 9.8 | 3.5 | T | 0.0 | 0.0 | 22.3 |
| 1972-73 | 0.0 | 0.0 | 0.0 | 0.9 | 6.9 | 1.4 | 3.4 | 2.9 | 4.8 | 0.9 | 0.0 | 0.0 | 21.2 |
| 1973-74 | 0.0 | 0.0 | 0.0 | 0.0 | T | 6.5 | 0.3 | 13.0 | 0.9 | 1.2 | 0.0 | 0.0 | 21.9 |
| 1974-75 | 0.0 | 0.0 | 0.0 | 0.6 | 2.7 | 8.3 | 18.1 | 2.4 | 8.1 | 0.1 | 0.0 | 0.0 | 40.3 |
| 1975-76 | 0.0 | 0.0 | 0.0 | 0.0 | T | 4.0 | 14.3 | 2.6 | 5.4 | 0.0 | 0.0 | 0.0 | 26.3 |
| 1976-77 | 0.0 | 0.0 | 0.0 | T | 4.7 | 7.4 | 22.2 | 11.1 | 1.0 | 1.5 | 0.0 | 0.0 | 47.9 |
| 1977-78 | 0.0 | 0.0 | 0.0 | 0.0 | 4.4 | 5.4 | 39.5 | 15.6 | 11.7 | 0.0 | 0.0 | 0.0 | 76.6 |
| #1978-79 | 0.0 | 0.0 | 0.0 | 0.0 | T | 1.5 | 27.5 | 20.1 | 5.5 | T | 0.0 | 0.0 | 54.6 |
| 1979-80 | 0.0 | 0.0 | 0.0 | T | 0.9 | 0.4 | 11.7 | 12.7 | 10.5 | T | 0.0 | 0.0 | 36.2 |
| 1980-81 | 0.0 | 0.0 | 0.0 | T | 0.5 | 2.6 | 9.1 | 6.8 | 7.5 | T | 0.0 | 0.0 | 26.5 |
| 1981-82 | 0.0 | 0.0 | 0.0 | T | 0.5 | 8.2 | 12.1 | 6.4 | 7.4 | 1.0 | 0.0 | 0.0 | 35.6 |
| 1982-83 | 0.0 | 0.0 | 0.0 | 0.0 | T | 2.9 | 5.8 | 15.0 | 5.2 | 0.1 | 0.0 | 0.0 | 29.0 |
| 1983-84 | 0.0 | 0.0 | 0.0 | 0.0 | 0.3 | 3.8 | 12.8 | 9.7 | 2.4 | 0.0 | 0.0 | 0.0 | 29.0 |
| 1984-85 | 0.0 | 0.0 | 0.0 | 0.0 | T | 3.7 | 17.6 | 20.1 | 0.9 | 1.7 | 0.0 | 0.0 | 44.0 |
| 1985-86 | 0.0 | 0.0 | 0.0 | 0.0 | 0.0 | 8.9 | 13.1 | 17.7 | 3.7 | T | 0.0 | 0.0 | 43.4 |
| 1986-87 | 0.0 | 0.0 | 0.0 | 0.0 | 0.2 | 0.1 | 16.3 | 9.7 | 3.9 | 20.7 | 0.0 | 0.0 | 50.9 |
| 1987-88 | 0.0 | 0.0 | 0.0 | T | 2.4 | 5.7 | 8.3 | 7.8 | 4.6 | T | 1.4 | 0.0 | 28.8 |
| 1988-89 | 0.0 | 0.0 | 0.0 | T | T | 6.9 | 1.7 | 4.6 | T | 1.4 | 0.6 | 0.0 | 15.2 |
| 1989-90 | 0.0 | T | T | T | 2.0 | 14.1 | 11.0 | 3.8 | 6.6 | 1.1 | 0.0 | 0.0 | 38.6 |
| 1990-91 | T | 0.0 | 0.0 | 0.0 | 0.0 | 1.2 | | | | | | | |
| Record Mean | T | T | T | 0.1 | 2.2 | 5.0 | 10.6 | 8.8 | 4.6 | 0.9 | T | 0.0 | 32.3 |

See Reference Notes, relative to all above tables, on preceding page.

Madison is set on a narrow isthmus of land between Lakes Mendota and Monona. Lake Mendota (15 square miles) lies northwest of Lake Monona (5 square miles) and the lakes are only two-thirds of a mile apart at one point. Drainage at Madison is southeast through two other lakes into the Rock River, which flows south into Illinois, and then west to the Mississippi. The westward flowing Wisconsin River is only 20 miles northwest of Madison. Madison lakes are normally frozen from mid-December to early April.

Madison has the typical continental climate of interior North America with a large annual temperature range and with frequent short period temperature changes. The range of extreme temperatures is from about 110 to −40 degrees. Winter temperatures (December-February) average near 20 degrees and the summer average (June-August) is in the upper 60s. Daily temperatures average below 32 degrees about 120 days and above 40 degrees for about 210 days of the year.

Madison lies in the path of the frequent cyclones and anticyclones which move eastward over this area during fall, winter and spring. In summer, the cyclones have diminished intensity and tend to pass farther north. The most frequent air masses are of polar origin. Occasional outbreaks of arctic air affect this area during the winter months. Although northward moving tropical air masses contribute considerable cloudiness and precipitation, the true Gulf air mass does not reach this area in winter, and only occasionally at other seasons. Summers are pleasant, with only occasional periods of extreme heat or high humidity.

There are no dry and wet seasons, but about 60 percent of the annual precipitation falls in the five months of May through September. Cold season precipitation is lighter, but lasts longer. Soil moisture is usually adequate in the first part of the growing season. During July, August, and September, the crops depend on current rainfall, which is mostly from thunderstorms and tends to be erratic and variable. Average occurrence of thunderstorms is just under 7 days per month during this period.

March and November are the windiest months. Tornadoes are infrequent. Dane County has about one tornado in every three to five years.

The ground is covered with 1 inch or more of snow about 60 percent of the time from about December 10 to near February 25 in an average winter. The soil is usually frozen from the first of December through most of March with an average frost penetration of 25 to 30 inches. The growing season averages 175 days.

Farming is diversified with the main emphasis on dairying. Field crops are mainly corn, oats, clover, and alfalfa, but barley, wheat, rye, and tobacco are also raised. Canning factories pack peas, sweet corn, and lima beans. Fruits are mainly apples, strawberries, and raspberries.

## TABLE 1    NORMALS, MEANS AND EXTREMES

MADISON, WISCONSIN

LATITUDE: 43°08'N    LONGITUDE: 89°20'W    ELEVATION: FT. GRND 858 BARO 860    TIME ZONE: CENTRAL    WBAN: 14837

| | (a) | JAN | FEB | MAR | APR | MAY | JUNE | JULY | AUG | SEP | OCT | NOV | DEC | YEAR |
|---|---|---|---|---|---|---|---|---|---|---|---|---|---|---|
| **TEMPERATURE °F:** | | | | | | | | | | | | | | |
| Normals | | | | | | | | | | | | | | |
| -Daily Maximum | | 24.5 | 30.0 | 40.8 | 57.5 | 69.8 | 78.8 | 82.8 | 80.6 | 72.3 | 61.1 | 44.1 | 30.6 | 56.1 |
| -Daily Minimum | | 6.7 | 11.0 | 21.5 | 34.1 | 44.2 | 53.8 | 58.3 | 56.3 | 47.8 | 37.8 | 26.0 | 14.1 | 34.3 |
| -Monthly | | 15.6 | 20.5 | 31.2 | 45.8 | 57.0 | 66.3 | 70.6 | 68.5 | 60.1 | 49.5 | 35.1 | 22.4 | 45.2 |
| Extremes | | | | | | | | | | | | | | |
| -Record Highest | 50 | 56 | 61 | 82 | 94 | 93 | 101 | 104 | 102 | 99 | 90 | 76 | 62 | 104 |
| -Year | | 1989 | 1981 | 1986 | 1980 | 1975 | 1988 | 1976 | 1988 | 1953 | 1976 | 1964 | 1984 | JUL 1976 |
| -Record Lowest | 50 | -37 | -28 | -29 | 0 | 19 | 31 | 36 | 35 | 25 | 13 | -11 | -25 | -37 |
| -Year | | 1951 | 1985 | 1962 | 1982 | 1978 | 1972 | 1965 | 1968 | 1974 | 1988 | 1947 | 1983 | JAN 1951 |
| **NORMAL DEGREE DAYS:** | | | | | | | | | | | | | | |
| Heating (base 65°F) | | 1531 | 1246 | 1048 | 576 | 273 | 58 | 12 | 29 | 161 | 490 | 897 | 1321 | 7642 |
| Cooling (base 65°F) | | 0 | 0 | 0 | 0 | 25 | 97 | 185 | 137 | 14 | 9 | 0 | 0 | 467 |
| **% OF POSSIBLE SUNSHINE** | 43 | 48 | 52 | 53 | 52 | 58 | 64 | 68 | 65 | 60 | 54 | 40 | 40 | 55 |
| **MEAN SKY COVER (tenths)** | | | | | | | | | | | | | | |
| Sunrise - Sunset | 41 | 6.7 | 6.6 | 6.9 | 6.7 | 6.5 | 6.1 | 5.7 | 5.7 | 5.8 | 6.0 | 7.2 | 7.1 | 6.4 |
| **MEAN NUMBER OF DAYS:** | | | | | | | | | | | | | | |
| Sunrise to Sunset | | | | | | | | | | | | | | |
| -Clear | 43 | 7.5 | 7.2 | 6.3 | 6.4 | 6.8 | 7.4 | 9.2 | 9.3 | 9.6 | 9.4 | 5.6 | 6.3 | 91.1 |
| -Partly Cloudy | 43 | 6.5 | 5.9 | 7.6 | 7.8 | 9.4 | 10.1 | 11.1 | 10.4 | 8.2 | 7.5 | 6.1 | 6.1 | 96.7 |
| -Cloudy | 43 | 17.0 | 15.1 | 17.1 | 15.9 | 14.7 | 12.6 | 10.7 | 11.3 | 12.1 | 14.1 | 18.3 | 18.6 | 177.4 |
| Precipitation | | | | | | | | | | | | | | |
| .01 inches or more | 41 | 10.0 | 8.0 | 10.8 | 11.3 | 11.3 | 10.3 | 9.5 | 9.5 | 9.4 | 8.9 | 9.4 | 9.9 | 118.3 |
| Snow,Ice pellets | | | | | | | | | | | | | | |
| 1.0 inches or more | 41 | 2.8 | 2.3 | 2.5 | 0.6 | 0.0 | 0.0 | 0.0 | 0.0 | 0.0 | 0.0 | 1.2 | 3.3 | 12.9 |
| Thunderstorms | 41 | 0.2 | 0.2 | 1.9 | 3.6 | 5.3 | 7.0 | 7.4 | 6.6 | 4.7 | 2.0 | 0.9 | 0.4 | 40.1 |
| Heavy Fog Visibility | | | | | | | | | | | | | | |
| 1/4 mile or less | 43 | 2.2 | 2.0 | 2.5 | 1.3 | 1.3 | 0.9 | 1.3 | 2.1 | 1.7 | 1.8 | 2.0 | 3.0 | 22.0 |
| Temperature °F | | | | | | | | | | | | | | |
| -Maximum | | | | | | | | | | | | | | |
| 90° and above | 30 | 0.0 | 0.0 | 0.0 | 0.* | 0.3 | 3.1 | 5.3 | 2.8 | 0.6 | 0.1 | 0.0 | 0.0 | 12.3 |
| 32° and below | 30 | 21.7 | 15.6 | 6.3 | 0.4 | 0.0 | 0.0 | 0.0 | 0.0 | 0.0 | 0.* | 3.8 | 17.5 | 65.4 |
| -Minimum | | | | | | | | | | | | | | |
| 32° and below | 30 | 30.2 | 27.2 | 26.0 | 14.0 | 3.4 | 0.* | 0.0 | 0.0 | 1.2 | 10.1 | 21.4 | 29.2 | 162.7 |
| 0° and below | 30 | 11.4 | 7.0 | 1.3 | 0.* | 0.0 | 0.0 | 0.0 | 0.0 | 0.0 | 0.0 | 0.2 | 5.7 | 25.6 |
| **AVG. STATION PRESS.(mb)** | 17 | 985.8 | 986.4 | 983.6 | 982.9 | 982.6 | 982.9 | 984.5 | 985.3 | 985.7 | 986.0 | 984.7 | 985.5 | 984.7 |
| **RELATIVE HUMIDITY (%)** | | | | | | | | | | | | | | |
| Hour 00 | 30 | 78 | 78 | 78 | 76 | 77 | 80 | 84 | 87 | 88 | 82 | 82 | 82 | 81 |
| Hour 06 (Local Time) | 30 | 79 | 80 | 82 | 81 | 80 | 82 | 86 | 91 | 92 | 86 | 86 | 83 | 84 |
| Hour 12 | 30 | 69 | 66 | 63 | 55 | 53 | 55 | 57 | 59 | 61 | 59 | 68 | 72 | 61 |
| Hour 18 | 30 | 73 | 70 | 66 | 56 | 54 | 56 | 58 | 62 | 69 | 68 | 75 | 77 | 65 |
| **PRECIPITATION (inches):** | | | | | | | | | | | | | | |
| Water Equivalent | | | | | | | | | | | | | | |
| -Normal | | 1.11 | 1.02 | 2.15 | 3.10 | 3.34 | 3.89 | 3.75 | 3.82 | 3.06 | 2.24 | 1.83 | 1.53 | 30.84 |
| -Maximum Monthly | 50 | 2.45 | 2.77 | 5.04 | 7.11 | 6.26 | 9.95 | 10.93 | 9.49 | 9.51 | 5.63 | 5.13 | 4.09 | 10.93 |
| -Year | | 1974 | 1953 | 1973 | 1973 | 1960 | 1978 | 1950 | 1980 | 1941 | 1984 | 1985 | 1987 | JUL 1950 |
| -Minimum Monthly | 50 | 0.14 | 0.08 | 0.28 | 0.96 | 0.64 | 0.81 | 1.38 | 0.70 | 0.11 | 0.06 | 0.11 | 0.25 | 0.06 |
| -Year | | 1981 | 1958 | 1978 | 1946 | 1981 | 1973 | 1946 | 1948 | 1979 | 1952 | 1976 | 1960 | OCT 1952 |
| -Maximum in 24 hrs | 41 | 1.27 | 1.58 | 2.52 | 2.83 | 3.64 | 3.67 | 5.25 | 2.90 | 3.57 | 2.78 | 2.36 | 1.76 | 5.25 |
| -Year | | 1960 | 1981 | 1973 | 1975 | 1966 | 1963 | 1950 | 1965 | 1961 | 1984 | 1985 | 1985 | JUL 1950 |
| Snow,Ice pellets | | | | | | | | | | | | | | |
| -Maximum Monthly | 41 | 26.9 | 20.9 | 25.4 | 17.4 | 0.7 | T | 0.0 | 0.0 | T | 0.9 | 18.3 | 32.8 | 32.8 |
| -Year | | 1979 | 1975 | 1959 | 1973 | 1966 | 1989 | | | 1965 | 1967 | 1985 | 1987 | DEC 1987 |
| -Maximum in 24 hrs | 41 | 11.6 | 10.3 | 13.6 | 12.9 | 0.7 | T | 0.0 | 0.0 | T | 0.9 | 9.0 | 16.0 | 16.0 |
| -Year | | 1971 | 1950 | 1971 | 1973 | 1966 | 1989 | | | 1965 | 1967 | 1985 | 1970 | DEC 1970 |
| **WIND:** | | | | | | | | | | | | | | |
| Mean Speed (mph) | 43 | 10.5 | 10.4 | 11.2 | 11.4 | 10.1 | 9.2 | 8.1 | 8.0 | 8.7 | 9.6 | 10.7 | 10.3 | 9.8 |
| Prevailing Direction | | | | | | | | | | | | | | |
| through 1963 | | WNW | WNW | NW | NW | S | S | S | S | S | S | S | W | S |
| Fastest Mile | | | | | | | | | | | | | | |
| -Direction (!!!) | 42 | E | W | SW | SW | SW | W | NW | W | W | SW | SE | SW | SW |
| -Speed (MPH) | 42 | 68 | 57 | 70 | 73 | 77 | 59 | 72 | 47 | 52 | 73 | 56 | 65 | 77 |
| -Year | | 1947 | 1948 | 1954 | 1947 | 1950 | 1947 | 1951 | 1955 | 1948 | 1951 | 1947 | 1949 | MAY 1950 |
| Peak Gust | | | | | | | | | | | | | | |
| -Direction (!!!) | 6 | SW | NW | W | W | SW | W | NW | N | NW | SW | S | NE | W |
| -Speed (mph) | 6 | 46 | 62 | 61 | 53 | 63 | 70 | 49 | 64 | 64 | 59 | 52 | 58 | 70 |
| -Date | | 1988 | 1987 | 1988 | 1984 | 1988 | 1984 | 1987 | 1989 | 1985 | 1984 | 1988 | 1987 | JUN 1984 |

See reference Notes to this table on the following page.

PRECIPITATION (inches)  MADISON, WISCONSIN

**TABLE 2**

| YEAR | JAN | FEB | MAR | APR | MAY | JUNE | JULY | AUG | SEP | OCT | NOV | DEC | ANNUAL |
|------|-----|-----|-----|-----|-----|------|------|-----|-----|-----|-----|-----|--------|
| 1961 | 0.19 | 1.01 | 3.42 | 1.33 | 1.17 | 1.84 | 3.67 | 1.78 | 7.92 | 3.75 | 3.94 | 1.02 | 31.04 |
| 1962 | 1.12 | 1.39 | 1.73 | 1.43 | 3.01 | 2.09 | 4.39 | 2.04 | 1.31 | 1.68 | 0.34 | 0.90 | 21.43 |
| 1963 | 0.76 | 0.39 | 2.33 | 1.67 | 1.82 | 8.15 | 2.29 | 3.23 | 2.30 | 0.64 | 1.96 | 0.65 | 26.19 |
| 1964 | 0.93 | 0.26 | 2.12 | 3.15 | 3.87 | 2.28 | 2.52 | 2.52 | 1.85 | 0.08 | 1.94 | 0.34 | 23.62 |
| 1965 | 1.80 | 0.74 | 2.51 | 2.94 | 1.86 | 2.31 | 3.30 | 6.77 | 9.22 | 1.69 | 1.96 | 2.50 | 37.60 |
| 1966 | 1.07 | 1.36 | 2.11 | 1.54 | 4.31 | 2.91 | 3.24 | 3.83 | 0.51 | 1.65 | 1.28 | 2.62 | 26.43 |
| 1967 | 1.63 | 1.17 | 1.49 | 2.57 | 3.53 | 6.46 | 2.51 | 2.71 | 2.68 | 5.52 | 1.83 | 1.89 | 33.99 |
| 1968 | 0.56 | 0.49 | 0.59 | 4.18 | 2.02 | 7.82 | 2.54 | 2.58 | 4.45 | 0.85 | 1.74 | 2.89 | 30.71 |
| 1969 | 2.26 | 0.18 | 1.47 | 2.72 | 3.45 | 7.96 | 4.28 | 0.96 | 1.35 | 2.65 | 0.70 | 1.66 | 29.64 |
| 1970 | 0.44 | 0.16 | 1.17 | 2.53 | 6.09 | 2.26 | 2.42 | 0.97 | 8.82 | 2.65 | 1.06 | 2.12 | 30.69 |
| 1971 | 1.48 | 2.59 | 1.52 | 2.42 | 0.98 | 2.27 | 1.65 | 3.96 | 1.87 | 1.30 | 3.48 | 3.64 | 27.16 |
| 1972 | 0.40 | 0.42 | 2.23 | 2.02 | 2.83 | 1.65 | 3.49 | 7.47 | 5.26 | 2.42 | 0.86 | 1.91 | 30.96 |
| 1973 | 1.54 | 1.20 | 5.04 | 7.11 | 5.27 | 0.81 | 2.68 | 2.53 | 3.59 | 2.30 | 1.48 | 1.98 | 35.53 |
| 1974 | 2.45 | 1.17 | 3.43 | 4.24 | 5.77 | 3.86 | 4.60 | 1.08 | 3.18 | 1.79 | 1.80 | 1.80 | 36.06 |
| 1975 | 0.98 | 1.54 | 3.09 | 4.19 | 4.57 | 4.30 | 6.05 | 5.25 | 0.84 | 0.64 | 2.79 | 0.29 | 34.53 |
| 1976 | 0.56 | 1.72 | 4.75 | 4.80 | 1.95 | 1.38 | 1.46 | 1.99 | 0.50 | 1.49 | 0.11 | 0.37 | 21.08 |
| 1977 | 0.53 | 1.44 | 3.03 | 2.59 | 2.52 | 2.63 | 6.63 | 5.19 | 2.84 | 1.41 | 2.12 | 1.60 | 32.53 |
| 1978 | 1.03 | 0.24 | 0.28 | 3.50 | 3.96 | 9.95 | 4.54 | 1.63 | 5.44 | 1.11 | 3.05 | 1.71 | 36.44 |
| 1979 | 1.69 | 0.90 | 2.67 | 2.46 | 2.70 | 2.53 | 2.80 | 4.96 | 0.11 | 3.10 | 2.27 | 1.93 | 28.12 |
| 1980 | 1.11 | 0.64 | 0.68 | 2.36 | 2.08 | 3.43 | 2.67 | 9.49 | 7.84 | 1.13 | 1.33 | 1.62 | 34.38 |
| 1981 | 0.14 | 2.47 | 0.33 | 3.42 | 0.64 | 4.99 | 4.81 | 7.06 | 3.10 | 2.68 | 1.71 | 0.75 | 32.10 |
| 1982 | 1.42 | 0.17 | 2.11 | 3.26 | 4.34 | 3.40 | 3.47 | 2.67 | 1.42 | 1.46 | 4.21 | 3.65 | 31.58 |
| 1983 | 0.53 | 2.26 | 2.70 | 2.23 | 4.21 | 1.85 | 1.92 | 5.05 | 2.85 | 2.59 | 3.18 | 2.30 | 31.67 |
| 1984 | 0.36 | 1.26 | 1.15 | 3.86 | 3.32 | 7.01 | 1.96 | 1.89 | 2.79 | 5.63 | 1.83 | 2.66 | 33.72 |
| 1985 | 1.43 | 1.89 | 3.13 | 1.52 | 3.35 | 3.06 | 4.48 | 2.98 | 5.00 | 4.58 | 5.13 | 2.39 | 38.94 |
| 1986 | 1.02 | 2.72 | 1.55 | 2.27 | 1.97 | 3.24 | 4.31 | 4.38 | 6.82 | 1.85 | 1.03 | 0.69 | 31.85 |
| 1987 | 0.68 | 0.62 | 1.99 | 2.46 | 3.90 | 1.17 | 3.26 | 7.16 | 3.61 | 1.24 | 3.24 | 4.09 | 33.42 |
| 1988 | 1.82 | 0.46 | 1.20 | 2.65 | 0.92 | 2.06 | 2.44 | 2.95 | 3.33 | 1.60 | 3.58 | 1.56 | 24.57 |
| 1989 | 0.61 | 0.57 | 1.69 | 1.69 | 1.72 | 1.67 | 4.97 | 6.46 | 0.89 | 1.88 | 0.98 | 0.26 | 23.39 |
| 1990 | 1.60 | 0.99 | 4.18 | 1.90 | 5.35 | 4.88 | 2.61 | 6.03 | 1.64 | 2.25 | 1.65 | 3.46 | 36.54 |
| Record Mean | 1.17 | 1.07 | 2.07 | 2.81 | 3.28 | 3.94 | 3.65 | 3.76 | 3.19 | 2.18 | 2.05 | 1.65 | 30.81 |

**TABLE 3**  AVERAGE TEMPERATURE (deg. F)  MADISON, WISCONSIN

| YEAR | JAN | FEB | MAR | APR | MAY | JUNE | JULY | AUG | SEP | OCT | NOV | DEC | ANNUAL |
|------|-----|-----|-----|-----|-----|------|------|-----|-----|-----|-----|-----|--------|
| 1961 | 16.9 | 28.3 | 33.8 | 40.6 | 54.0 | 66.4 | 69.9 | 69.4 | 61.7 | 50.5 | 35.6 | 18.8 | 45.5 |
| 1962 | 12.4 | 17.0 | 29.5 | 45.0 | 61.4 | 66.7 | 67.3 | 69.8 | 51.9 | 51.9 | 20.4 | 44.5 | 44.5 |
| 1963 | 5.4 | 14.1 | 34.0 | 47.8 | 55.4 | 69.6 | 73.1 | 67.6 | 60.2 | 58.1 | 39.2 | 11.3 | 44.6 |
| 1964 | 24.9 | 24.9 | 30.8 | 47.5 | 62.6 | 68.5 | 73.1 | 66.9 | 59.6 | 46.9 | 38.6 | 18.8 | 46.9 |
| 1965 | 15.9 | 18.7 | 25.0 | 43.7 | 59.6 | 64.2 | 68.3 | 66.7 | 58.3 | 49.2 | 35.6 | 29.8 | 44.6 |
| 1966 | 10.0 | 21.3 | 35.4 | 42.0 | 50.3 | 66.6 | 71.1 | 66.2 | 57.1 | 47.7 | 36.0 | 23.2 | 43.9 |
| 1967 | 22.2 | 14.7 | 33.3 | 45.6 | 50.2 | 64.9 | 67.1 | 62.0 | 57.6 | 48.0 | 33.0 | 25.1 | 43.7 |
| 1968 | 19.6 | 19.0 | 39.2 | 47.8 | 54.3 | 66.2 | 68.9 | 68.8 | 60.1 | 50.7 | 35.6 | 22.6 | 46.1 |
| 1969 | 14.8 | 23.6 | 27.9 | 47.0 | 56.4 | 59.5 | 69.6 | 70.3 | 59.5 | 46.4 | 33.1 | 21.3 | 44.1 |
| 1970 | 9.9 | 20.1 | 31.1 | 47.9 | 58.5 | 66.5 | 70.6 | 68.5 | 60.0 | 51.0 | 36.3 | 22.4 | 45.2 |
| 1971 | 9.6 | 19.9 | 28.6 | 45.4 | 55.1 | 71.7 | 68.5 | 68.3 | 65.1 | 55.9 | 35.2 | 26.8 | 45.9 |
| 1972 | 12.7 | 16.5 | 28.7 | 41.3 | 59.2 | 62.8 | 68.3 | 69.2 | 59.4 | 45.8 | 34.6 | 17.3 | 43.0 |
| 1973 | 23.4 | 24.0 | 41.6 | 44.9 | 54.4 | 67.9 | 71.6 | 70.6 | 60.7 | 54.1 | 36.6 | 21.5 | 47.6 |
| 1974 | 19.2 | 18.4 | 33.1 | 48.7 | 54.1 | 64.0 | 72.1 | 66.8 | 57.4 | 50.5 | 37.1 | 26.8 | 45.7 |
| 1975 | 21.9 | 21.3 | 26.1 | 41.0 | 62.5 | 69.2 | 72.4 | 70.6 | 57.5 | 52.2 | 41.9 | 25.5 | 46.8 |
| 1976 | 15.7 | 28.4 | 36.5 | 49.3 | 54.3 | 68.3 | 73.4 | 68.8 | 58.0 | 43.7 | 28.1 | 13.2 | 44.8 |
| 1977 | 3.7 | 22.4 | 39.8 | 51.9 | 65.2 | 64.9 | 73.6 | 64.6 | 59.7 | 47.6 | 34.0 | 19.6 | 45.6 |
| 1978 | 10.5 | 12.4 | 29.4 | 44.5 | 57.9 | 65.9 | 69.7 | 69.5 | 63.8 | 47.3 | 33.5 | 21.3 | 43.8 |
| 1979 | 6.9 | 11.7 | 32.1 | 42.4 | 56.7 | 66.0 | 69.8 | 69.5 | 66.6 | 61.1 | 35.1 | 28.8 | 43.7 |
| 1980 | 17.3 | 15.7 | 28.0 | 45.5 | 57.8 | 65.3 | 73.4 | 70.3 | 59.9 | 43.7 | 35.4 | 22.6 | 44.6 |
| 1981 | 20.5 | 25.3 | 36.9 | 48.7 | 55.3 | 67.4 | 70.6 | 68.7 | 59.1 | 46.6 | 36.7 | 22.0 | 46.5 |
| 1982 | 8.0 | 19.1 | 30.6 | 41.7 | 60.8 | 59.6 | 70.9 | 66.3 | 59.0 | 50.6 | 34.2 | 28.8 | 44.1 |
| 1983 | 21.4 | 26.3 | 33.1 | 41.6 | 51.9 | 67.5 | 75.0 | 72.2 | 60.1 | 48.2 | 37.3 | 10.8 | 45.5 |
| 1984 | 14.8 | 30.2 | 26.7 | 45.6 | 53.4 | 67.5 | 70.2 | 71.3 | 59.3 | 52.0 | 33.9 | 26.4 | 45.9 |
| 1985 | 12.2 | 19.0 | 37.7 | 52.2 | 60.7 | 63.8 | 70.0 | 66.4 | 61.6 | 49.4 | 31.0 | 11.3 | 44.6 |
| 1986 | 18.2 | 19.4 | 36.2 | 49.8 | 58.4 | 65.9 | 73.2 | 68.7 | 61.6 | 49.7 | 31.2 | 25.5 | 46.2 |
| 1987 | 22.6 | 30.5 | 37.2 | 49.9 | 60.8 | 70.4 | 74.5 | 68.7 | 60.6 | 43.4 | 40.0 | 28.4 | 48.9 |
| 1988 | 13.8 | 17.4 | 34.6 | 46.0 | 60.5 | 69.5 | 74.1 | 74.5 | 63.0 | 43.5 | 38.8 | 24.6 | 46.7 |
| 1989 | 27.6 | 14.6 | 30.1 | 44.7 | 56.1 | 65.7 | 72.3 | 68.6 | 58.7 | 50.8 | 33.1 | 14.2 | 44.7 |
| 1990 | 28.6 | 25.8 | 37.7 | 48.5 | 53.6 | 67.6 | 70.6 | 69.9 | 63.7 | 48.3 | 41.0 | 21.4 | 48.1 |
| Record Mean | 17.0 | 21.1 | 32.2 | 46.3 | 57.1 | 66.8 | 71.5 | 69.5 | 60.7 | 50.0 | 35.5 | 22.4 | 45.9 |
| Max | 25.9 | 30.4 | 41.6 | 57.8 | 69.5 | 79.0 | 83.7 | 81.4 | 72.5 | 61.4 | 44.1 | 30.5 | 56.5 |
| Min | 8.2 | 11.8 | 22.7 | 34.7 | 44.7 | 54.5 | 59.3 | 57.5 | 48.8 | 38.6 | 26.8 | 14.2 | 35.2 |

## REFERENCE NOTES FOR TABLES 1, 2, 3 and 6     (MADISON, WI)

### GENERAL

T - TRACE AMOUNT
BLANK ENTRIES DENOTE MISSING/UNREPORTED DATA.
# INDICATES A STATION OR INSTRUMENT RELOCATION.

### SPECIFIC

#### TABLE 1

(a) - LENGTH OF RECORD IN YEARS. ALTHOUGH
INDIVIDUAL MONTHS MAY BE MISSING.

\* LESS THAN .05

NORMALS — BASED ON THE 1951-1980 RECORD PERIOD.
EXTREMES — DATES ARE THE MOST RECENT OCCURRENCE.
WIND DIR. — NUMERALS SHOW TENS OF DEGREES
CLOCKWISE FROM TRUE NORTH.
"00" INDICATES CALM.
RESULTANT WIND DIRECTIONS ARE GIVEN TO WHOLE DEGREES.

#### TABLE 3
MAX AND MIN ARE LONG-TERM MEAN DAILY MAXIMUM
AND MEAN DAILY MINIMUM TEMPERATURES.

### EXCEPTIONS

#### TABLES 2, 3, and 6

RECORD MEANS ARE THROUGH THE CURRENT YEAR,
BEGINNING IN    1940 FOR TEMPERATURE
1940 FOR PRECIPITATION
1949 FOR SNOWFALL

**TABLE 4**

HEATING DEGREE DAYS Base 65 deg. F          MADISON, WISCONSIN

| SEASON | JULY | AUG | SEP | OCT | NOV | DEC | JAN | FEB | MAR | APR | MAY | JUNE | TOTAL |
|---|---|---|---|---|---|---|---|---|---|---|---|---|---|
| 1961-62 | 11 | 18 | 188 | 444 | 876 | 1426 | 1630 | 1337 | 1093 | 601 | 185 | 54 | 7863 |
| 1962-63 | 23 | 11 | 252 | 414 | 884 | 1376 | 1850 | 1420 | 957 | 508 | 299 | 48 | 8042 |
| 1963-64 | 2 | 47 | 174 | 228 | 769 | 1660 | 1237 | 1156 | 1052 | 519 | 133 | 76 | 7053 |
| 1964-65 | 13 | 68 | 216 | 556 | 789 | 1427 | 1517 | 1294 | 1234 | 631 | 208 | 79 | 8032 |
| 1965-66 | 27 | 69 | 231 | 486 | 878 | 1086 | 1702 | 1220 | 911 | 684 | 454 | 83 | 7831 |
| 1966-67 | 11 | 40 | 252 | 533 | 862 | 1290 | 1321 | 1407 | 978 | 574 | 462 | 46 | 7776 |
| 1967-68 | 61 | 120 | 239 | 535 | 955 | 1229 | 1401 | 1327 | 792 | 510 | 330 | 76 | 7575 |
| 1968-69 | 34 | 66 | 159 | 460 | 873 | 1305 | 1548 | 1152 | 1143 | 535 | 282 | 197 | 7754 |
| 1969-70 | 13 | 9 | 202 | 579 | 951 | 1346 | 1705 | 1252 | 1044 | 521 | 244 | 73 | 7939 |
| 1970-71 | 28 | 18 | 196 | 431 | 853 | 1310 | 1718 | 1258 | 1124 | 582 | 312 | 22 | 7852 |
| 1971-72 | 28 | 21 | 131 | 293 | 885 | 1179 | 1616 | 1401 | 1119 | 705 | 212 | 117 | 7707 |
| 1972-73 | 44 | 42 | 188 | 587 | 905 | 1475 | 1279 | 1143 | 720 | 596 | 325 | 15 | 7319 |
| 1973-74 | 4 | 25 | 180 | 349 | 847 | 1342 | 1416 | 1298 | 979 | 494 | 347 | 90 | 7371 |
| 1974-75 | 1 | 37 | 253 | 443 | 829 | 1179 | 1329 | 1220 | 1198 | 714 | 150 | 43 | 7396 |
| 1975-76 | 18 | 11 | 236 | 412 | 687 | 1217 | 1520 | 1056 | 877 | 477 | 333 | 32 | 6876 |
| 1976-77 | 4 | 40 | 236 | 656 | 1102 | 1602 | 1898 | 1188 | 772 | 409 | 110 | 95 | 8112 |
| 1977-78 | 6 | 95 | 161 | 533 | 925 | 1404 | 1688 | 1466 | 1096 | 608 | 269 | 59 | 8310 |
| 1978-79 | 19 | 22 | 130 | 543 | 940 | 1348 | 1800 | 1489 | 1013 | 671 | 283 | 52 | 8310 |
| 1979-80 | 14 | 62 | 144 | 546 | 890 | 1112 | 1471 | 1424 | 1138 | 586 | 255 | 84 | 7726 |
| 1980-81 | 2 | 11 | 178 | 651 | 881 | 1303 | 1373 | 1107 | 864 | 482 | 307 | 30 | 7189 |
| 1981-82 | 16 | 27 | 193 | 566 | 842 | 1327 | 1765 | 1281 | 1059 | 688 | 155 | 172 | 8091 |
| 1982-83 | 5 | 66 | 230 | 444 | 918 | 1117 | 1346 | 1078 | 792 | 693 | 400 | 57 | 7332 |
| 1983-84 | 11 | 6 | 193 | 519 | 823 | 1678 | 1550 | 1006 | 1181 | 575 | 358 | 20 | 7920 |
| 1984-85 | 9 | 21 | 215 | 397 | 927 | 1191 | 1632 | 1287 | 839 | 418 | 155 | 96 | 7187 |
| 1985-86 | 12 | 36 | 198 | 475 | 1012 | 1661 | 1444 | 1272 | 888 | 462 | 220 | 73 | 7753 |
| 1986-87 | 7 | 59 | 145 | 471 | 1007 | 1218 | 1309 | 963 | 857 | 452 | 192 | 27 | 6707 |
| 1987-88 | 3 | 45 | 150 | 661 | 743 | 1127 | 1586 | 1377 | 938 | 565 | 176 | 53 | 7424 |
| 1988-89 | 4 | 18 | 107 | 661 | 777 | 1242 | 1153 | 1404 | 1076 | 602 | 290 | 68 | 7402 |
| 1989-90 | 5 | 22 | 207 | 437 | 952 | 1568 | 1122 | 1092 | 835 | 519 | 349 | 46 | 7154 |
| 1990-91 | 7 | 12 | 133 | 511 | 713 | 1349 | | | | | | | |

**TABLE 5**

COOLING DEGREE DAYS Base 65 deg. F          MADISON, WISCONSIN

| YEAR | JAN | FEB | MAR | APR | MAY | JUNE | JULY | AUG | SEP | OCT | NOV | DEC | TOTAL |
|---|---|---|---|---|---|---|---|---|---|---|---|---|---|
| 1969 | 0 | 0 | 0 | 0 | 25 | 39 | 161 | 179 | 45 | 11 | 0 | 0 | 460 |
| 1970 | 0 | 0 | 0 | 12 | 47 | 125 | 210 | 133 | 53 | 4 | 0 | 0 | 584 |
| 1971 | 0 | 0 | 0 | 0 | 13 | 229 | 144 | 131 | 140 | 20 | 0 | 0 | 677 |
| 1972 | 0 | 0 | 0 | 0 | 41 | 61 | 156 | 180 | 27 | 0 | 0 | 0 | 465 |
| 1973 | 0 | 0 | 0 | 0 | 2 | 112 | 215 | 207 | 58 | 19 | 0 | 0 | 613 |
| 1974 | 0 | 0 | 0 | 9 | 17 | 68 | 228 | 102 | 31 | 2 | 0 | 0 | 457 |
| 1975 | 0 | 0 | 0 | 0 | 81 | 176 | 256 | 190 | 18 | 21 | 0 | 0 | 742 |
| 1976 | 0 | 0 | 0 | 14 | 6 | 136 | 270 | 165 | 34 | 2 | 0 | 0 | 627 |
| 1977 | 0 | 0 | 0 | 24 | 123 | 99 | 278 | 88 | 10 | 0 | 0 | 0 | 622 |
| 1978 | 0 | 0 | 0 | 0 | 56 | 92 | 171 | 168 | 102 | 0 | 0 | 0 | 589 |
| 1979 | 0 | 0 | 0 | 0 | 33 | 88 | 168 | 115 | 33 | 13 | 0 | 0 | 450 |
| 1980 | 0 | 0 | 0 | 8 | 39 | 100 | 268 | 183 | 31 | 0 | 0 | 0 | 629 |
| 1981 | 0 | 0 | 0 | 0 | 13 | 107 | 198 | 148 | 19 | 0 | 0 | 0 | 485 |
| 1982 | 0 | 0 | 0 | 0 | 29 | 16 | 194 | 114 | 53 | 3 | 0 | 0 | 409 |
| 1983 | 0 | 0 | 0 | 0 | 0 | 138 | 327 | 237 | 52 | 6 | 0 | 0 | 760 |
| 1984 | 0 | 0 | 0 | 1 | 5 | 102 | 177 | 224 | 50 | 0 | 0 | 0 | 559 |
| 1985 | 0 | 0 | 0 | 40 | 29 | 66 | 175 | 84 | 102 | 0 | 0 | 0 | 496 |
| 1986 | 0 | 0 | 0 | 13 | 24 | 105 | 269 | 59 | 49 | 0 | 0 | 0 | 519 |
| 1987 | 0 | 0 | 0 | 0 | 8 | 69 | 194 | 304 | 165 | 26 | 0 | 0 | 766 |
| 1988 | 0 | 0 | 0 | 0 | 43 | 194 | 296 | 315 | 54 | 0 | 0 | 0 | 902 |
| 1989 | 0 | 0 | 0 | 0 | 21 | 97 | 237 | 141 | 25 | 3 | 0 | 0 | 524 |
| 1990 | 0 | 0 | 0 | 32 | 2 | 132 | 191 | 171 | 100 | 1 | 0 | 0 | 629 |

**TABLE 6**

SNOWFALL (inches)          MADISON, WISCONSIN

| SEASON | JULY | AUG | SEP | OCT | NOV | DEC | JAN | FEB | MAR | APR | MAY | JUNE | TOTAL |
|---|---|---|---|---|---|---|---|---|---|---|---|---|---|
| 1961-62 | 0.0 | 0.0 | 0.0 | 0.1 | 1.4 | 12.0 | 10.0 | 16.1 | 7.0 | 2.7 | 0.0 | 0.0 | 49.3 |
| 1962-63 | 0.0 | 0.0 | 0.0 | 0.2 | 1.0 | 6.4 | 12.0 | 4.1 | 12.8 | 0.7 | T | 0.0 | 37.2 |
| 1963-64 | 0.0 | 0.0 | 0.0 | 0.0 | 0.1 | 8.2 | 1.4 | 3.7 | 17.4 | 0.3 | 0.0 | 0.0 | 31.1 |
| 1964-65 | 0.0 | 0.0 | 0.0 | 0.5 | 3.7 | 3.5 | 18.3 | 4.7 | 19.4 | 0.8 | 0.0 | 0.0 | 50.9 |
| 1965-66 | 0.0 | 0.0 | T | 0.0 | T | 5.7 | 9.6 | 3.8 | 5.5 | 0.1 | 0.7 | 0.0 | 25.4 |
| 1966-67 | 0.0 | 0.0 | 0.0 | T | 0.1 | 10.1 | 9.4 | 13.9 | 4.5 | T | T | 0.0 | 38.0 |
| 1967-68 | 0.0 | 0.0 | 0.0 | 0.9 | 0.7 | 2.4 | 3.9 | 3.9 | 0.5 | 0.4 | 0.0 | 0.0 | 12.7 |
| 1968-69 | 0.0 | 0.0 | 0.0 | 0.0 | 11.4 | 9.7 | 1.7 | 1.7 | 10.1 | T | T | 0.0 | 33.4 |
| 1969-70 | 0.0 | 0.0 | 0.0 | 0.0 | 1.0 | 19.5 | 6.4 | 1.7 | 7.0 | 1.9 | 0.0 | 0.0 | 37.5 |
| 1970-71 | 0.0 | 0.0 | 0.0 | 0.0 | 2.0 | 20.8 | 21.9 | 3.7 | 20.1 | 0.7 | 0.0 | 0.0 | 67.4 |
| 1971-72 | 0.0 | 0.0 | 0.0 | 0.0 | 8.8 | 8.9 | 3.6 | 6.3 | 18.8 | 3.9 | 0.0 | 0.0 | 50.3 |
| 1972-73 | 0.0 | 0.0 | 0.0 | T | 1.3 | 16.3 | 1.9 | 6.0 | 1.1 | 17.4 | T | 0.0 | 44.0 |
| 1973-74 | 0.0 | 0.0 | 0.0 | 0.0 | 0.4 | 10.9 | 10.5 | 14.1 | 6.6 | 0.4 | T | 0.0 | 42.9 |
| 1974-75 | 0.0 | 0.0 | 0.0 | 0.0 | 3.0 | 15.4 | 5.2 | 20.9 | 10.0 | 5.9 | 0.0 | 0.0 | 60.4 |
| 1975-76 | 0.0 | 0.0 | 0.0 | 0.0 | 5.5 | 2.8 | 10.1 | 10.4 | 2.0 | T | 0.0 | 0.0 | 30.8 |
| 1976-77 | 0.0 | 0.0 | 0.0 | T | 1.1 | 5.8 | 8.7 | 2.6 | 5.8 | 2.3 | 0.0 | 0.0 | 26.3 |
| 1977-78 | 0.0 | 0.0 | 0.0 | 0.0 | 10.4 | 24.6 | 13.5 | 4.7 | 3.0 | 0.5 | 0.0 | 0.0 | 56.7 |
| 1978-79 | 0.0 | 0.0 | 0.0 | 0.0 | 6.2 | 23.0 | 26.9 | 8.7 | 4.0 | 7.3 | 0.0 | 0.0 | 76.1 |
| 1979-80 | 0.0 | 0.0 | 0.0 | 0.2 | 4.4 | 1.3 | 4.9 | 7.5 | 5.6 | 7.1 | 0.0 | 0.0 | 31.0 |
| 1980-81 | 0.0 | 0.0 | 0.0 | T | 3.5 | 9.2 | 2.9 | 9.2 | 1.7 | 0.0 | 0.0 | 0.0 | 26.5 |
| 1981-82 | 0.0 | 0.0 | 0.0 | 0.1 | 2.0 | 7.2 | 19.4 | 2.4 | 8.6 | 10.3 | 0.0 | 0.0 | 50.0 |
| 1982-83 | 0.0 | 0.0 | 0.0 | 0.0 | 0.3 | 3.3 | 6.5 | 13.0 | 14.1 | 4.2 | 0.0 | 0.0 | 41.4 |
| 1983-84 | 0.0 | 0.0 | 0.0 | 0.0 | 2.1 | 22.6 | 6.0 | 0.8 | 6.8 | 3.9 | 0.0 | 0.0 | 42.2 |
| 1984-85 | 0.0 | 0.0 | 0.0 | 0.0 | 0.5 | 15.8 | 19.9 | 7.4 | 8.2 | 1.9 | 0.0 | 0.0 | 53.7 |
| 1985-86 | 0.0 | 0.0 | 0.0 | 0.0 | 18.3 | 24.0 | 13.9 | 13.3 | 2.7 | 0.2 | 0.0 | 0.0 | 72.4 |
| 1986-87 | 0.0 | 0.0 | 0.0 | T | 8.6 | 8.0 | 8.7 | 0.3 | 8.9 | T | 0.0 | 0.0 | 34.5 |
| 1987-88 | 0.0 | 0.0 | 0.0 | 0.4 | 3.9 | 32.8 | 16.3 | 6.4 | 1.1 | 1.3 | 0.0 | 0.0 | 62.2 |
| 1988-89 | 0.0 | 0.0 | 0.0 | 0.2 | 5.5 | 8.2 | 2.6 | 9.7 | 9.3 | 0.2 | 0.5 | T | 36.2 |
| 1989-90 | 0.0 | 0.0 | 0.0 | 0.7 | 4.4 | 4.3 | 10.1 | 11.7 | 0.1 | 0.5 | 3.0 | T | 34.8 |
| 1990-91 | 0.0 | 0.0 | 0.0 | 3.1 | 4.5 | 23.0 | | | | | | | |
| Record Mean | 0.0 | 0.0 | T | 0.2 | 3.6 | 11.2 | 9.7 | 7.1 | 8.3 | 2.1 | 0.1 | T | 42.3 |

**See Reference Notes, relative to all above tables, on preceding page.**

Milwaukee possesses a continental climate characterized by a wide range of temperatures between summer and winter. Precipitation is moderate and occurs mostly in the spring, less in the autumn, and very little in the wintertime. Rainfall is well distributed for agricultural purposes, although spring planting is sometimes delayed by wet ground and cold weather.

Milwaukee is in a region of frequently changeable weather and its climate is influenced by general easterly–moving storms which traverse the nations midsection. The most severe winter storms, which produce in excess of 10 inches of snow, develop in the southern Great Plains and move northeast across Illinois and Indiana.

Occasionally during the cold season, frigid air masses from Canada push southeast across the Great Lakes region. These arctic air masses account for the coldest winter temperatures. Very low temperatures, zero degrees or lower, most often occur in air that flows southward to the west of Lake Superior before reaching the Milwaukee area. If northwesterly wind circulation persists, repeated incursions of arctic air will result in a period of bitterly cold weather lasting several days.

Summer temperatures, which reach into the 90s but rarely exceed 100 degrees, occur with brisk southwest winds that carry hot air from the plains and lower Mississippi River Valley across the city. A combination of high temperatures and humidity occasionally develops, usually building up over a period of several days when persistent southerly winds transport moisture from the Gulf of Mexico into the area.

The Gulf is a major source of moisture for Milwaukee in all seasons, but the type of precipitation which results is dependent upon the time of year. Cold–season precipitation (rain, snow, or a mixture) is usually of relatively long duration and low intensity, and occasionally persists for two days or more, whereas in the warm season, relatively short–duration and high–intensity showery rainfall, usually lasting a few hours or less, predominates.

The Great Lakes significantly influence the local climate. Temperature extremes are modified by Lake Michigan and, to a lesser extent, the other Great Lakes. In late autumn and winter, air masses that are initially very cold often reach the city only after being tempered by passage over one or more of the lakes. Similarly, air masses that approach from the northeast in the spring and summer are cooler because of movement over the Great Lakes.

The influence of Lake Michigan is variable and occasionally dramatic, especially when the temperature of the lake water differs strongly from the air temperature. During the spring and early summer, a wind shift from a westerly to an easterly direction frequently causes a sudden 10 to 20 degree temperature drop. When the breeze off the lake is light, this effect reaches inland only a mile or two. With stronger on–shore winds, the entire city is cooled. In the winter the relatively warm water of the lake moderates the temperature during easterly wind situations. Lake–induced snows usually occur a few times each winter, but snow accumulation is rarely heavy.

Topography does not significantly affect air flow, except that lesser frictional drag over Lake Michigan causes winds to be frequently stronger along the lake shore, and often permits air masses approaching from the north to reach shore areas one hour or more before affecting inland portions of the city.

## TABLE 1
# NORMALS, MEANS AND EXTREMES

MILWAUKEE, WISCONSIN

LATITUDE: 42°57'N   LONGITUDE: 87°54'W   ELEVATION: FT. GRND   672 BARO   691   TIME ZONE: CENTRAL   WBAN: 14839

| | (a) | JAN | FEB | MAR | APR | MAY | JUNE | JULY | AUG | SEP | OCT | NOV | DEC | YEAR |
|---|---|---|---|---|---|---|---|---|---|---|---|---|---|---|
| **TEMPERATURE °F:** | | | | | | | | | | | | | | |
| Normals | | | | | | | | | | | | | | |
| -Daily Maximum | | 26.0 | 30.1 | 39.2 | 53.5 | 64.8 | 75.0 | 79.8 | 78.4 | 71.2 | 59.9 | 44.7 | 32.0 | 54.6 |
| -Daily Minimum | | 11.3 | 15.8 | 24.9 | 35.6 | 44.7 | 54.7 | 61.1 | 60.2 | 52.5 | 41.9 | 29.9 | 18.2 | 37.6 |
| -Monthly | | 18.7 | 23.0 | 32.1 | 44.6 | 54.8 | 64.9 | 70.5 | 69.3 | 61.9 | 50.9 | 37.3 | 25.1 | 46.1 |
| Extremes | | | | | | | | | | | | | | |
| -Record Highest | 49 | 62 | 65 | 82 | 91 | 92 | 101 | 101 | 103 | 98 | 89 | 77 | 63 | 103 |
| -Year | | 1944 | 1976 | 1986 | 1980 | 1975 | 1988 | 1955 | 1988 | 1953 | 1963 | 1950 | 1982 | AUG 1988 |
| -Record Lowest | 49 | -26 | -19 | -10 | 12 | 21 | 33 | 40 | 44 | 28 | 18 | -5 | -20 | -26 |
| -Year | | 1982 | 1951 | 1962 | 1982 | 1966 | 1945 | 1965 | 1982 | 1974 | 1981 | 1950 | 1983 | JAN 1982 |
| **NORMAL DEGREE DAYS:** | | | | | | | | | | | | | | |
| Heating (base 65°F) | | 1435 | 1176 | 1020 | 612 | 334 | 84 | 11 | 25 | 117 | 444 | 831 | 1237 | 7326 |
| Cooling (base 65°F) | | 0 | 0 | 0 | 0 | 18 | 81 | 182 | 158 | 24 | 7 | 0 | 0 | 470 |
| **% OF POSSIBLE SUNSHINE** | 49 | 45 | 47 | 50 | 53 | 59 | 65 | 70 | 66 | 59 | 54 | 39 | 38 | 54 |
| **MEAN SKY COVER (tenths)** | | | | | | | | | | | | | | |
| Sunrise - Sunset | 49 | 6.8 | 6.8 | 7.0 | 6.7 | 6.3 | 6.0 | 5.3 | 5.4 | 5.6 | 5.9 | 7.2 | 7.2 | 6.3 |
| **MEAN NUMBER OF DAYS:** | | | | | | | | | | | | | | |
| Sunrise to Sunset | | | | | | | | | | | | | | |
| -Clear | 49 | 7.2 | 6.6 | 6.0 | 6.4 | 7.1 | 7.7 | 10.1 | 10.2 | 9.6 | 9.2 | 5.6 | 6.3 | 91.8 |
| -Partly Cloudy | 49 | 6.3 | 6.1 | 7.8 | 7.9 | 9.9 | 10.3 | 11.3 | 10.7 | 9.1 | 8.7 | 6.1 | 6.0 | 100.1 |
| -Cloudy | 49 | 17.5 | 15.5 | 17.2 | 15.7 | 14.0 | 12.0 | 9.6 | 10.2 | 11.3 | 13.2 | 18.4 | 18.8 | 173.3 |
| Precipitation | | | | | | | | | | | | | | |
| .01 inches or more | 49 | 11.1 | 9.6 | 11.8 | 12.0 | 11.8 | 10.7 | 9.5 | 9.2 | 9.1 | 8.9 | 10.3 | 11.0 | 125.0 |
| Snow,Ice pellets | | | | | | | | | | | | | | |
| 1.0 inches or more | 49 | 3.6 | 2.6 | 2.6 | 0.4 | 0.0 | 0.0 | 0.0 | 0.0 | 0.0 | 0.1 | 0.9 | 3.2 | 13.4 |
| Thunderstorms | 49 | 0.3 | 0.3 | 1.4 | 3.5 | 4.6 | 6.3 | 6.4 | 5.8 | 3.9 | 1.6 | 1.1 | 0.3 | 35.5 |
| Heavy Fog Visibility | | | | | | | | | | | | | | |
| 1/4 mile or less | 49 | 2.1 | 2.0 | 3.0 | 3.0 | 3.2 | 2.5 | 1.2 | 1.7 | 1.2 | 2.1 | 2.2 | 2.2 | 26.2 |
| Temperature °F | | | | | | | | | | | | | | |
| -Maximum | | | | | | | | | | | | | | |
| 90° and above | 29 | 0.0 | 0.0 | 0.0 | 0.* | 0.1 | 2.1 | 4.2 | 2.3 | 0.6 | 0.0 | 0.0 | 0.0 | 9.2 |
| 32° and below | 29 | 20.6 | 15.9 | 6.6 | 0.5 | 0.0 | 0.0 | 0.0 | 0.0 | 0.0 | 0.0 | 2.7 | 15.6 | 61.8 |
| -Minimum | | | | | | | | | | | | | | |
| 32° and below | 29 | 29.8 | 26.3 | 23.7 | 9.9 | 1.1 | 0.0 | 0.0 | 0.0 | 0.1 | 4.3 | 18.3 | 28.1 | 141.6 |
| 0° and below | 29 | 7.8 | 3.6 | 0.2 | 0.0 | 0.0 | 0.0 | 0.0 | 0.0 | 0.0 | 0.0 | 0.1 | 3.2 | 14.9 |
| **AVG. STATION PRESS.(mb)** | 17 | 992.0 | 992.8 | 990.3 | 989.5 | 989.4 | 989.3 | 990.8 | 991.6 | 992.1 | 992.5 | 991.1 | 991.9 | 991.1 |
| **RELATIVE HUMIDITY (%)** | | | | | | | | | | | | | | |
| Hour 00 | 29 | 74 | 74 | 76 | 74 | 75 | 78 | 80 | 84 | 83 | 78 | 78 | 78 | 78 |
| Hour 06 (Local Time) | 29 | 75 | 77 | 79 | 78 | 78 | 80 | 82 | 87 | 87 | 82 | 80 | 80 | 80 |
| Hour 12 | 29 | 68 | 67 | 65 | 61 | 60 | 61 | 61 | 63 | 63 | 63 | 67 | 72 | 64 |
| Hour 18 | 29 | 71 | 70 | 68 | 64 | 62 | 62 | 62 | 63 | 68 | 71 | 70 | 74 | 75 | 68 |
| **PRECIPITATION (inches):** | | | | | | | | | | | | | | |
| Water Equivalent | | | | | | | | | | | | | | |
| -Normal | | 1.64 | 1.33 | 2.58 | 3.37 | 2.66 | 3.59 | 3.54 | 3.09 | 2.88 | 2.25 | 1.98 | 2.03 | 30.94 |
| -Maximum Monthly | 49 | 4.04 | 3.94 | 6.93 | 7.31 | 5.83 | 8.28 | 7.66 | 9.05 | 9.87 | 6.42 | 7.11 | 5.42 | 9.87 |
| -Year | | 1960 | 1986 | 1976 | 1973 | 1983 | 1954 | 1964 | 1987 | 1941 | 1959 | 1985 | 1987 | SEP 1941 |
| -Minimum Monthly | 49 | 0.31 | 0.05 | 0.31 | 0.81 | 0.50 | 0.70 | 0.95 | 0.46 | 0.02 | 0.15 | 0.62 | 0.29 | 0.02 |
| -Year | | 1981 | 1969 | 1968 | 1942 | 1988 | 1988 | 1946 | 1948 | 1979 | 1956 | 1949 | 1976 | SEP 1979 |
| -Maximum in 24 hrs | 49 | 1.73 | 1.67 | 2.57 | 3.11 | 3.11 | 3.13 | 4.35 | 6.84 | 5.28 | 2.60 | 2.18 | 2.24 | 6.84 |
| -Year | | 1985 | 1960 | 1960 | 1976 | 1978 | 1950 | 1959 | 1986 | 1941 | 1959 | 1943 | 1982 | AUG 1986 |
| Snow,Ice pellets | | | | | | | | | | | | | | |
| -Maximum Monthly | 49 | 33.6 | 42.0 | 26.7 | 15.8 | 0.6 | 0.0 | T | T | T | 6.3 | 16.1 | 27.9 | 42.0 |
| -Year | | 1979 | 1974 | 1965 | 1973 | 1989 | | 1989 | 1989 | 1960 | 1989 | 1977 | 1978 | FEB 1974 |
| -Maximum in 24 hrs | 49 | 12.8 | 16.7 | 11.2 | 11.6 | 0.6 | 0.0 | T | T | T | 6.3 | 10.6 | 13.1 | 16.7 |
| -Year | | 1962 | 1960 | 1961 | 1973 | 1989 | | 1989 | 1989 | 1960 | 1989 | 1977 | 1987 | FEB 1960 |
| **WIND:** | | | | | | | | | | | | | | |
| Mean Speed (mph) | 49 | 12.7 | 12.5 | 13.0 | 12.9 | 11.6 | 10.4 | 9.6 | 9.5 | 10.5 | 11.4 | 12.5 | 12.3 | 11.6 |
| Prevailing Direction | | | | | | | | | | | | | | |
| through 1963 | | WNW | WNW | WNW | NNE | NNE | NNE | SW | SW | SSW | SSW | WNW | WNW | WNW |
| Fastest Obs. 1 Min. | | | | | | | | | | | | | | |
| -Direction (!!!) | 7 | 02 | 02 | 25 | 23 | 36 | 24 | 30 | 30 | 26 | 24 | 24 | 04 | 30 |
| -Speed (MPH) | 7 | 35 | 36 | 36 | 45 | 44 | 36 | 54 | 44 | 35 | 35 | 38 | 40 | 54 |
| -Year | | 1985 | 1984 | 1985 | 1983 | 1983 | 1983 | 1984 | 1989 | 1987 | 1984 | 1988 | 1987 | JUL 1984 |
| Peak Gust | | | | | | | | | | | | | | |
| -Direction (!!!) | 6 | SW | NW | SW | SW | SW | N | NW | NW | SW | SW | NW | NE | NW |
| -Speed (mph) | 6 | 54 | 46 | 55 | 64 | 54 | 54 | 81 | 64 | 58 | 51 | 56 | 59 | 81 |
| -Date | | 1989 | 1987 | 1985 | 1984 | 1985 | 1989 | 1984 | 1989 | 1986 | 1984 | 1989 | 1987 | JUL 1984 |

**See Reference Notes to this table on the following page.**

PRECIPITATION (inches)   MILWAUKEE, WISCONSIN

**TABLE 2**

| YEAR | JAN | FEB | MAR | APR | MAY | JUNE | JULY | AUG | SEP | OCT | NOV | DEC | ANNUAL |
|---|---|---|---|---|---|---|---|---|---|---|---|---|---|
| 1961 | 0.31 | 1.22 | 3.80 | 3.89 | 1.25 | 1.53 | 2.91 | 2.35 | 9.41 | 2.75 | 2.37 | 1.02 | 32.81 |
| 1962 | 2.48 | 2.04 | 1.69 | 1.49 | 2.17 | 1.33 | 3.74 | 1.98 | 1.49 | 2.14 | 0.81 | 0.55 | 21.91 |
| 1963 | 0.66 | 0.42 | 2.20 | 2.54 | 1.95 | 1.50 | 2.36 | 2.48 | 1.78 | 0.34 | 2.17 | 0.70 | 19.10 |
| 1964 | 1.18 | 0.41 | 3.05 | 3.81 | 2.57 | 1.70 | 7.66 | 2.62 | 1.74 | 0.17 | 2.29 | 0.98 | 28.18 |
| 1965 | 3.33 | 1.04 | 3.61 | 3.47 | 2.12 | 0.85 | 2.64 | 6.15 | 6.85 | 2.68 | 2.02 | 3.73 | 38.49 |
| 1966 | 2.06 | 1.27 | 3.61 | 2.67 | 2.00 | 1.68 | 3.32 | 3.27 | 0.48 | 1.76 | 2.70 | 2.31 | 27.13 |
| 1967 | 1.49 | 1.31 | 1.35 | 2.70 | 1.80 | 7.38 | 1.35 | 1.23 | 1.69 | 2.70 | 1.52 | 1.33 | 25.85 |
| 1968 | 0.98 | 0.56 | 0.31 | 2.90 | 3.28 | 7.79 | 3.59 | 2.59 | 3.36 | 0.94 | 2.56 | 2.65 | 31.51 |
| 1969 | 1.83 | 0.05 | 1.05 | 3.42 | 3.05 | 7.53 | 6.61 | 0.53 | 2.18 | 4.48 | 1.14 | 1.18 | 33.05 |
| 1970 | 0.41 | 0.13 | 1.62 | 2.71 | 3.41 | 3.92 | 1.93 | 0.64 | 6.94 | 2.09 | 2.03 | 3.02 | 28.85 |
| 1971 | 1.37 | 2.50 | 2.83 | 1.31 | 0.90 | 2.67 | 2.60 | 2.28 | 1.30 | 1.90 | 2.45 | 4.34 | 26.45 |
| 1972 | 0.75 | 0.86 | 2.57 | 2.76 | 2.33 | 3.33 | 4.60 | 4.82 | 7.57 | 3.28 | 1.34 | 2.47 | 36.68 |
| 1973 | 1.12 | 1.51 | 2.86 | 7.31 | 3.39 | 1.96 | 1.55 | 0.95 | 4.50 | 2.97 | 1.83 | 3.80 | 33.75 |
| 1974 | 3.61 | 3.10 | 4.29 | 3.83 | 4.10 | 3.48 | 3.51 | 2.54 | 0.50 | 1.96 | 1.86 | 2.10 | 34.88 |
| 1975 | 2.25 | 2.53 | 3.01 | 4.08 | 2.01 | 3.99 | 1.14 | 3.89 | 1.00 | 0.72 | 2.83 | 1.70 | 29.15 |
| 1976 | 1.16 | 2.65 | 6.93 | 5.01 | 3.77 | 2.27 | 2.12 | 2.05 | 1.70 | 2.82 | 0.65 | 0.29 | 31.42 |
| 1977 | 0.90 | 0.59 | 4.56 | 2.09 | 0.90 | 5.78 | 5.99 | 3.82 | 4.11 | 2.02 | 2.56 | 3.27 | 36.59 |
| 1978 | 2.03 | 0.55 | 1.08 | 4.41 | 4.66 | 4.52 | 5.98 | 3.43 | 6.81 | 2.22 | 2.13 | 2.92 | 40.74 |
| 1979 | 3.00 | 0.97 | 4.17 | 5.43 | 1.82 | 2.84 | 1.06 | 4.85 | 0.02 | 1.77 | 2.67 | 2.27 | 30.87 |
| 1980 | 1.65 | 1.75 | 0.77 | 4.02 | 1.81 | 4.67 | 3.39 | 5.06 | 3.57 | 1.63 | 1.57 | 3.52 | 33.41 |
| 1981 | 0.31 | 2.88 | 0.51 | 4.87 | 3.05 | 2.39 | 4.35 | 4.26 | 5.47 | 2.71 | 2.05 | 1.03 | 33.88 |
| 1982 | 2.92 | 0.29 | 3.20 | 4.47 | 2.76 | 3.06 | 3.88 | 3.33 | 0.64 | 3.17 | 4.74 | 4.10 | 36.56 |
| 1983 | 0.75 | 2.23 | 4.12 | 4.66 | 5.83 | 1.41 | 1.34 | 4.70 | 2.79 | 2.65 | 4.10 | 2.89 | 37.47 |
| 1984 | 0.79 | 1.20 | 2.17 | 5.04 | 4.21 | 4.07 | 3.39 | 2.93 | 2.51 | 5.30 | 3.74 | 4.25 | 39.60 |
| 1985 | 1.94 | 2.34 | 4.11 | 1.93 | 2.73 | 1.27 | 2.18 | 2.23 | 3.44 | 5.39 | 7.11 | 2.62 | 37.29 |
| 1986 | 0.91 | 3.94 | 1.85 | 1.83 | 2.74 | 4.51 | 8.82 | 7.26 | 2.24 | 0.89 |  | 1.03 | 42.17 |
| 1987 | 1.22 | 1.22 | 1.74 | 4.26 | 3.76 | 2.23 | 4.20 | 9.05 | 2.22 | 1.09 | 2.73 | 5.42 | 39.14 |
| 1988 | 3.25 | 1.29 | 1.30 | 4.12 | 0.50 | 0.70 | 1.53 | 3.25 | 4.94 | 2.97 | 5.15 | 1.43 | 30.43 |
| 1989 | 0.86 | 0.69 | 3.03 | 1.33 | 2.86 | 1.89 | 6.16 | 5.19 | 3.25 | 2.67 | 1.90 | 0.47 | 30.30 |
| 1990 | 2.57 | 1.90 | 2.75 | 2.67 | 7.56 | 4.97 | 3.02 | 4.68 | 1.89 | 2.65 | 3.54 | 2.66 | 40.86 |
| Record Mean | 1.81 | 1.58 | 2.49 | 2.90 | 3.20 | 3.47 | 2.99 | 3.01 | 3.16 | 2.33 | 2.12 | 1.86 | 30.92 |

**TABLE 3**   AVERAGE TEMPERATURE (deg. F)   MILWAUKEE, WISCONSIN

| YEAR | JAN | FEB | MAR | APR | MAY | JUNE | JULY | AUG | SEP | OCT | NOV | DEC | ANNUAL |
|---|---|---|---|---|---|---|---|---|---|---|---|---|---|
| #1961 | 19.4 | 29.8 | 35.2 | 41.2 | 50.8 | 65.3 | 69.9 | 70.3 | 64.8 | 51.2 | 37.6 | 22.8 | 46.5 |
| 1962 | 14.5 | 21.1 | 30.3 | 44.5 | 59.2 | 63.9 | 66.7 | 68.9 | 58.0 | 52.6 | 37.9 | 21.5 | 44.9 |
| 1963 | 8.7 | 15.9 | 35.2 | 45.8 | 52.3 | 65.6 | 70.8 | 67.1 | 61.2 | 58.6 | 41.7 | 13.2 | 44.7 |
| 1964 | 26.1 | 25.3 | 31.7 | 44.8 | 60.3 | 66.5 | 72.3 | 67.7 | 61.2 | 48.2 | 40.4 | 23.2 | 47.3 |
| 1965 | 19.5 | 21.2 | 25.3 | 42.7 | 58.6 | 63.1 | 68.9 | 66.8 | 61.7 | 50.8 | 38.5 | 32.9 | 45.8 |
| 1966 | 13.9 | 22.3 | 35.4 | 42.3 | 49.6 | 67.0 | 73.5 | 66.8 | 59.1 | 48.9 | 38.0 | 24.5 | 45.1 |
| 1967 | 24.5 | 17.5 | 33.2 | 44.9 | 50.2 | 66.5 | 68.6 | 66.0 | 60.8 | 50.4 | 35.2 | 28.9 | 45.6 |
| 1968 | 21.8 | 20.7 | 40.3 | 47.6 | 53.2 | 66.3 | 69.5 | 71.4 | 63.5 | 52.7 | 38.1 | 25.6 | 47.5 |
| 1969 | 18.6 | 27.3 | 29.8 | 44.9 | 55.3 | 58.9 | 67.8 | 70.9 | 62.0 | 47.5 | 34.3 | 25.1 | 45.2 |
| 1970 | 13.3 | 22.6 | 30.5 | 46.2 | 56.0 | 65.3 | 73.3 | 71.8 | 62.0 | 52.5 | 37.3 | 24.3 | 46.2 |
| 1971 | 12.7 | 21.6 | 28.6 | 40.9 | 51.1 | 67.5 | 68.0 | 67.0 | 64.9 | 55.5 | 37.3 | 29.5 | 45.4 |
| 1972 | 15.9 | 19.8 | 27.7 | 39.4 | 55.0 | 61.6 | 69.3 | 69.1 | 61.3 | 47.5 | 36.2 | 20.2 | 43.6 |
| 1973 | 24.7 | 25.4 | 39.9 | 42.7 | 51.0 | 69.2 | 71.4 | 72.5 | 63.9 | 54.6 | 38.5 | 25.5 | 48.3 |
| 1974 | 21.6 | 22.9 | 33.8 | 46.1 | 50.6 | 62.4 | 71.5 | 67.3 | 58.0 | 49.9 | 38.6 | 29.1 | 46.0 |
| 1975 | 24.0 | 23.5 | 28.6 | 37.7 | 57.1 | 65.7 | 71.7 | 71.2 | 58.5 | 54.1 | 44.5 | 27.9 | 47.0 |
| 1976 | 18.5 | 31.1 | 38.6 | 48.7 | 52.6 | 68.2 | 72.6 | 69.9 | 62.6 | 45.9 | 29.5 | 16.3 | 46.2 |
| 1977 | 8.3 | 23.7 | 39.2 | 48.9 | 61.3 | 62.5 | 73.1 | 67.2 | 61.9 | 49.0 | 37.1 | 22.8 | 46.2 |
| 1978 | 15.4 | 16.4 | 29.8 | 42.5 | 55.2 | 65.2 | 68.6 | 69.9 | 65.8 | 49.5 | 38.2 | 23.8 | 45.0 |
| 1979 | 11.6 | 15.1 | 33.2 | 42.1 | 54.9 | 64.7 | 70.9 | 68.8 | 64.7 | 51.1 | 38.2 | 31.4 | 45.6 |
| 1980 | 20.7 | 20.3 | 30.5 | 45.3 | 57.2 | 61.3 | 71.2 | 69.7 | 61.1 | 45.7 | 37.7 | 24.4 | 45.4 |
| 1981 | 18.9 | 25.3 | 35.6 | 46.5 | 51.5 | 65.2 | 67.3 | 67.8 | 59.1 | 45.8 | 37.4 | 24.2 | 45.4 |
| 1982 | 9.7 | 19.4 | 31.5 | 41.2 | 58.5 | 59.8 | 71.1 | 67.3 | 60.8 | 52.7 | 38.0 | 33.2 | 45.3 |
| 1983 | 26.4 | 29.4 | 35.0 | 41.7 | 50.2 | 66.3 | 76.2 | 74.4 | 62.9 | 52.0 | 39.9 | 14.4 | 47.4 |
| 1984 | 18.9 | 33.4 | 29.2 | 45.5 | 54.9 | 68.7 | 71.7 | 73.3 | 60.9 | 52.9 | 37.7 | 29.1 | 48.0 |
| 1985 | 15.2 | 21.3 | 37.9 | 50.8 | 58.8 | 63.8 | 72.4 | 68.4 | 64.3 | 50.7 | 36.7 | 15.7 | 46.3 |
| 1986 | 21.9 | 23.3 | 38.1 | 48.5 | 56.1 | 63.3 | 72.5 | 67.1 | 63.8 | 51.6 | 35.1 | 29.2 | 47.5 |
| 1987 | 24.8 | 32.0 | 37.8 | 48.0 | 60.1 | 72.2 | 74.8 | 69.9 | 63.3 | 46.2 | 41.9 | 31.4 | 50.2 |
| 1988 | 18.3 | 20.1 | 34.8 | 45.7 | 58.7 | 70.2 | 75.4 | 75.7 | 63.5 | 45.8 | 40.7 | 26.6 | 48.0 |
| 1989 | 30.4 | 18.0 | 32.4 | 43.2 | 54.9 | 64.4 | 71.6 | 68.8 | 60.2 | 52.7 | 35.1 | 16.7 | 45.7 |
| 1990 | 31.1 | 28.9 | 38.8 | 49.3 | 52.8 | 67.6 | 70.5 | 71.2 | 66.0 | 51.5 | 44.5 | 26.9 | 49.9 |
| Record Mean | 20.6 | 23.3 | 32.9 | 44.5 | 54.5 | 64.6 | 70.9 | 69.7 | 62.5 | 51.2 | 37.7 | 25.8 | 46.6 |
| Max | 27.9 | 30.4 | 39.9 | 52.5 | 63.6 | 73.8 | 79.5 | 77.8 | 70.7 | 59.1 | 44.5 | 32.4 | 54.4 |
| Min | 13.4 | 16.1 | 25.8 | 36.4 | 45.4 | 55.4 | 62.3 | 61.6 | 54.4 | 43.3 | 30.8 | 19.2 | 38.7 |

## REFERENCE NOTES FOR TABLES 1, 2, 3 and 6   (MILWAUKEE, WI)

**GENERAL**

T - TRACE AMOUNT
BLANK ENTRIES DENOTE MISSING/UNREPORTED DATA.
# INDICATES A STATION OR INSTRUMENT RELOCATION.

**SPECIFIC**

TABLE 1

(a) - LENGTH OF RECORD IN YEARS. ALTHOUGH
INDIVIDUAL MONTHS MAY BE MISSING.
* LESS THAN .05

NORMALS — BASED ON THE 1951-1980 RECORD PERIOD.
EXTREMES — DATES ARE THE MOST RECENT OCCURRENCE.
WIND DIR. — NUMERALS SHOW TENS OF DEGREES
CLOCKWISE FROM TRUE NORTH.
"00" INDICATES CALM.
RESULTANT WIND DIRECTIONS ARE GIVEN TO WHOLE DEGREES.

TABLE 3
MAX AND MIN ARE LONG-TERM MEAN DAILY MAXIMUM
AND MEAN DAILY MINIMUM TEMPERATURES.

**EXCEPTIONS**

TABLE 1

1. FASTEST MILE WINDS ARE THROUGH JUNE 1982.

TABLES 2, 3, and 6

RECORD MEANS ARE THROUGH THE CURRENT YEAR,
BEGINNING IN   1875 FOR TEMPERATURE
1871 FOR PRECIPITATION
1941 FOR SNOWFALL

HEATING DEGREE DAYS Base 65 deg. F        MILWAUKEE. WISCONSIN

**TABLE 4**

| SEASON | JULY | AUG | SEP | OCT | NOV | DEC | JAN | FEB | MAR | APR | MAY | JUNE | TOTAL |
|---|---|---|---|---|---|---|---|---|---|---|---|---|---|
| 1961-62 | 18 | 9 | 134 | 422 | 815 | 1303 | 1561 | 1224 | 1067 | 623 | 254 | 119 | 7549 |
| 1962-63 | 24 | 22 | 227 | 395 | 804 | 1342 | 1749 | 1372 | 915 | 570 | 388 | 82 | 7890 |
| 1963-64 | 20 | 38 | 135 | 217 | 692 | 1601 | 1199 | 1141 | 1026 | 598 | 192 | 105 | 6964 |
| 1964-65 | 7 | 47 | 177 | 515 | 730 | 1290 | 1404 | 1222 | 1226 | 664 | 232 | 123 | 7637 |
| 1965-66 | 25 | 51 | 149 | 438 | 793 | 987 | 1579 | 1189 | 915 | 674 | 473 | 88 | 7361 |
| 1966-67 | 4 | 41 | 198 | 496 | 804 | 1249 | 1249 | 1325 | 978 | 596 | 458 | 47 | 7445 |
| 1967-68 | 46 | 53 | 164 | 460 | 888 | 1112 | 1333 | 1277 | 758 | 521 | 363 | 74 | 7049 |
| 1968-69 | 31 | 23 | 82 | 403 | 799 | 1214 | 1434 | 1053 | 1087 | 596 | 317 | 215 | 7254 |
| 1969-70 | 34 | 5 | 143 | 539 | 913 | 1228 | 1180 | 1180 | 1062 | 561 | 301 | 104 | 7670 |
| 1970-71 | 7 | 7 | 145 | 383 | 823 | 1259 | 1615 | 1211 | 1122 | 716 | 421 | 65 | 7774 |
| 1971-72 | 20 | 37 | 119 | 308 | 824 | 1097 | 1518 | 1305 | 1149 | 758 | 305 | 139 | 7579 |
| 1972-73 | 40 | 32 | 133 | 534 | 859 | 1381 | 1242 | 1101 | 769 | 659 | 426 | 6 | 7182 |
| 1973-74 | 10 | 5 | 111 | 324 | 788 | 1218 | 1340 | 1173 | 959 | 560 | 448 | 106 | 7042 |
| 1974-75 | 0 | 20 | 237 | 461 | 786 | 1103 | 1260 | 1157 | 1122 | 814 | 267 | 69 | 7296 |
| 1975-76 | 17 | 4 | 203 | 353 | 610 | 1144 | 1438 | 978 | 813 | 507 | 382 | 43 | 6492 |
| 1976-77 | 2 | 21 | 124 | 589 | 1056 | 1504 | 1754 | 1152 | 790 | 490 | 173 | 151 | 7806 |
| 1977-78 | 8 | 47 | 106 | 485 | 827 | 1302 | 1531 | 1356 | 1086 | 667 | 335 | 83 | 7833 |
| 1978-79 | 21 | 5 | 76 | 473 | 796 | 1273 | 1654 | 1391 | 980 | 681 | 322 | 91 | 7763 |
| 1979-80 | 20 | 25 | 70 | 436 | 797 | 1036 | 1368 | 1290 | 1063 | 594 | 259 | 154 | 7112 |
| 1980-81 | 8 | 9 | 140 | 590 | 812 | 1250 | 1423 | 1106 | 905 | 548 | 417 | 69 | 7277 |
| 1981-82 | 44 | 21 | 187 | 590 | 820 | 1257 | 1712 | 1272 | 1032 | 707 | 215 | 172 | 8029 |
| 1982-83 | 3 | 44 | 170 | 381 | 802 | 983 | 1186 | 990 | 925 | 692 | 453 | 81 | 6710 |
| 1983-84 | 10 | 0 | 148 | 405 | 748 | 1565 | 1424 | 910 | 1103 | 579 | 318 | 35 | 7245 |
| 1984-85 | 3 | 7 | 179 | 373 | 812 | 1103 | 1542 | 1215 | 831 | 461 | 222 | 96 | 6844 |
| 1985-86 | 2 | 13 | 139 | 436 | 843 | 1523 | 1328 | 1161 | 827 | 494 | 302 | 128 | 7196 |
| 1986-87 | 13 | 34 | 98 | 407 | 891 | 1106 | 1242 | 917 | 839 | 502 | 236 | 19 | 6304 |
| 1987-88 | 12 | 28 | 91 | 576 | 686 | 1037 | 1442 | 1294 | 930 | 571 | 245 | 55 | 6967 |
| 1988-89 | 3 | 7 | 87 | 587 | 720 | 1183 | 1065 | 1307 | 1006 | 649 | 324 | 85 | 7023 |
| 1989-90 | 0 | 16 | 166 | 381 | 890 | 1493 | 1040 | 1004 | 805 | 502 | 375 | 51 | 6723 |
| 1990-91 | 21 | 9 | 93 | 418 | 612 | 1173 | | | | | | | |

**TABLE 5**     COOLING DEGREE DAYS Base 65 deg. F        MILWAUKEE. WISCONSIN

| YEAR | JAN | FEB | MAR | APR | MAY | JUNE | JULY | AUG | SEP | OCT | NOV | DEC | TOTAL |
|---|---|---|---|---|---|---|---|---|---|---|---|---|---|
| 1969 | 0 | 0 | 0 | 0 | 24 | 38 | 126 | 197 | 59 | 5 | 0 | 0 | 449 |
| 1970 | 0 | 0 | 0 | 4 | 29 | 119 | 270 | 227 | 60 | 4 | 0 | 0 | 713 |
| 1971 | 0 | 0 | 0 | 0 | 0 | 148 | 120 | 105 | 123 | 20 | 0 | 0 | 516 |
| 1972 | 0 | 0 | 0 | 0 | 3 | 42 | 180 | 166 | 26 | 0 | 0 | 0 | 417 |
| 1973 | 0 | 0 | 0 | 0 | 0 | 140 | 216 | 247 | 84 | 6 | 0 | 0 | 693 |
| 1974 | 0 | 0 | 0 | 3 | 6 | 36 | 210 | 98 | 32 | 1 | 0 | 0 | 386 |
| 1975 | 0 | 0 | 0 | 0 | 30 | 98 | 230 | 203 | 16 | 21 | 0 | 0 | 598 |
| 1976 | 0 | 0 | 0 | 24 | 5 | 144 | 247 | 181 | 62 | 4 | 0 | 0 | 667 |
| 1977 | 0 | 0 | 0 | 12 | 65 | 81 | 264 | 122 | 20 | 0 | 0 | 0 | 564 |
| 1978 | 0 | 0 | 0 | 0 | 40 | 97 | 138 | 164 | 109 | 0 | 0 | 0 | 548 |
| 1979 | 0 | 0 | 0 | 0 | 16 | 87 | 209 | 147 | 68 | 11 | 0 | 0 | 538 |
| 1980 | 0 | 0 | 0 | 9 | 25 | 50 | 207 | 164 | 29 | 0 | 0 | 0 | 484 |
| 1981 | 0 | 0 | 0 | 2 | 3 | 84 | 121 | 112 | 16 | 0 | 0 | 0 | 338 |
| 1982 | 0 | 0 | 0 | 0 | 21 | 24 | 199 | 121 | 51 | 5 | 0 | 0 | 421 |
| 1983 | 0 | 0 | 0 | 0 | 0 | 127 | 364 | 299 | 92 | 9 | 0 | 0 | 891 |
| 1984 | 0 | 0 | 0 | 1 | 11 | 152 | 216 | 270 | 63 | 3 | 0 | 0 | 716 |
| 1985 | 0 | 0 | 0 | 42 | 35 | 68 | 240 | 127 | 127 | 0 | 0 | 0 | 639 |
| 1986 | 0 | 0 | 3 | 7 | 31 | 84 | 251 | 105 | 70 | 0 | 0 | 0 | 551 |
| 1987 | 0 | 0 | 0 | 2 | 87 | 244 | 323 | 189 | 47 | 0 | 1 | 0 | 893 |
| 1988 | 0 | 0 | 0 | 0 | 57 | 215 | 333 | 344 | 48 | 0 | 0 | 0 | 997 |
| 1989 | 0 | 0 | 2 | 0 | 16 | 76 | 214 | 144 | 29 | 4 | 0 | 0 | 485 |
| 1990 | 0 | 0 | 2 | 38 | 5 | 135 | 198 | 210 | 132 | 7 | 1 | 0 | 728 |

**TABLE 6**     SNOWFALL (inches)        MILWAUKEE. WISCONSIN

| SEASON | JULY | AUG | SEP | OCT | NOV | DEC | JAN | FEB | MAR | APR | MAY | JUNE | TOTAL |
|---|---|---|---|---|---|---|---|---|---|---|---|---|---|
| 1961-62 | 0.0 | 0.0 | 0.0 | T | 2.4 | 7.7 | 22.1 | 22.2 | 11.4 | 4.0 | 0.0 | 0.0 | 69.8 |
| 1962-63 | 0.0 | 0.0 | 0.0 | 0.1 | 0.9 | 6.5 | 8.1 | 6.4 | 7.1 | T | T | 0.0 | 29.1 |
| 1963-64 | 0.0 | 0.0 | 0.0 | 0.0 | T | 12.8 | 3.8 | 5.7 | 19.8 | T | 0.0 | 0.0 | 42.1 |
| 1964-65 | 0.0 | 0.0 | 0.0 | T | 1.4 | 8.1 | 23.6 | 10.1 | 26.7 | 4.1 | 0.0 | 0.0 | 74.0 |
| 1965-66 | 0.0 | 0.0 | 0.0 | T | T | 14.5 | 24.6 | 7.7 | 2.8 | 1.3 | 0.1 | 0.0 | 51.0 |
| 1966-67 | 0.0 | 0.0 | 0.0 | 0.0 | 2.0 | 9.9 | 13.1 | 27.1 | 7.4 | T | T | 0.0 | 59.5 |
| 1967-68 | 0.0 | 0.0 | 0.0 | 0.8 | 0.4 | 1.2 | 4.6 | 3.5 | 1.2 | 0.4 | 0.0 | 0.0 | 12.1 |
| 1968-69 | 0.0 | 0.0 | 0.0 | 0.0 | 0.3 | 11.6 | 11.1 | 0.7 | 6.2 | 0.0 | T | 0.0 | 29.9 |
| 1969-70 | 0.0 | 0.0 | 0.0 | T | 0.7 | 14.9 | 6.0 | 2.0 | 10.7 | 5.2 | 0.0 | 0.0 | 39.5 |
| 1970-71 | 0.0 | 0.0 | 0.0 | 0.0 | 0.6 | 19.6 | 15.8 | 18.1 | T | 0.7 | T | 0.0 | 57.3 |
| 1971-72 | 0.0 | 0.0 | 0.0 | 0.0 | 6.1 | 2.7 | 6.8 | 10.2 | 14.9 | 1.2 | 0.0 | 0.0 | 41.9 |
| 1972-73 | 0.0 | 0.0 | 0.0 | T | 3.4 | 13.7 | 0.2 | 9.9 | 1.8 | 15.8 | T | 0.0 | 44.8 |
| 1973-74 | 0.0 | 0.0 | 0.0 | 0.0 | T | 19.6 | 14.2 | 42.0 | 7.4 | T | 0.0 | 0.0 | 83.2 |
| 1974-75 | 0.0 | 0.0 | 0.0 | T | 2.0 | 9.1 | 3.5 | 12.2 | 15.1 | 10.4 | 0.0 | 0.0 | 52.3 |
| 1975-76 | 0.0 | 0.0 | 0.0 | 0.0 | 8.4 | 12.2 | 14.8 | 7.6 | 2.1 | 0.1 | T | 0.0 | 45.2 |
| 1976-77 | 0.0 | 0.0 | 0.0 | 4.0 | 3.6 | 5.3 | 15.6 | 5.6 | 12.4 | 2.1 | 0.0 | 0.0 | 48.6 |
| 1977-78 | 0.0 | 0.0 | 0.0 | T | 16.1 | 20.8 | 25.7 | 13.3 | 4.8 | T | 0.0 | 0.0 | 80.7 |
| 1978-79 | 0.0 | 0.0 | 0.0 | 0.0 | 5.3 | 27.9 | 33.6 | 9.1 | 6.2 | 0.8 | 0.0 | 0.0 | 82.9 |
| 1979-80 | 0.0 | 0.0 | 0.0 | T | 2.1 | 0.6 | 11.6 | 22.8 | 6.3 | 3.6 | T | 0.0 | 47.0 |
| 1980-81 | 0.0 | 0.0 | 0.0 | T | 2.3 | 17.5 | 4.9 | 15.7 | 1.5 | T | 0.0 | 0.0 | 41.9 |
| 1981-82 | 0.0 | 0.0 | 0.0 | T | 2.0 | 8.3 | 29.2 | 3.0 | 13.0 | 11.7 | 0.0 | 0.0 | 67.2 |
| 1982-83 | 0.0 | 0.0 | 0.0 | T | 0.4 | 3.1 | 6.3 | 13.5 | 13.8 | 1.0 | 0.0 | 0.0 | 38.1 |
| 1983-84 | 0.0 | 0.0 | 0.0 | 0.0 | 0.3 | 13.3 | 9.6 | 1.2 | 8.2 | 0.5 | T | 0.0 | 33.1 |
| 1984-85 | 0.0 | 0.0 | 0.0 | 0.0 | T | 19.0 | 20.8 | 15.3 | 9.0 | 2.5 | 0.0 | 0.0 | 66.6 |
| 1985-86 | 0.0 | 0.0 | 0.0 | 0.0 | 3.5 | 13.5 | 10.4 | 14.0 | 0.7 | 0.3 | 0.0 | 0.0 | 42.4 |
| 1986-87 | 0.0 | 0.0 | 0.0 | T | 2.4 | 2.5 | 11.4 | T | 5.2 | 0.4 | 0.0 | 0.0 | 21.9 |
| 1987-88 | 0.0 | 0.0 | 0.0 | 0.6 | 0.4 | 19.9 | 10.2 | 20.7 | 2.9 | T | 0.0 | 0.0 | 54.7 |
| 1988-89 | 0.0 | 0.0 | 0.0 | T | 2.7 | 7.1 | 2.7 | 13.1 | 13.3 | 0.4 | 0.6 | 0.0 | 39.9 |
| 1989-90 | T | T | 0.0 | 6.3 | 11.6 | 7.4 | 19.9 | 17.9 | 0.2 | 1.2 | 3.2 | 0.0 | 67.7 |
| 1990-91 | T | 0.0 | 0.0 | 0.0 | 0.4 | 10.5 | | | | | | | |
| Record Mean | T | T | T | 0.2 | 3.0 | 10.5 | 12.9 | 9.8 | 8.7 | 1.8 | 0.1 | 0.0 | 47.0 |

**See Reference Notes, relative to all above tables, on preceding page.**

The city of Cheyenne is located on a broad plateau between the North and South Platte Rivers in the extreme southeastern corner of Wyoming at an elevation of approximately 6,100 feet. The surrounding country is mostly rolling prairie which is used primarily for grazing. The ground level rises rapidly to a ridge approximately 9,000 feet in elevation about 30 miles west of the city. This ridge is known as the Laramie Mountains, one of the ranges of the Rockies, and extends in a north–south direction. Because of this ridge, winds from the northwest through west to southwest are downslope and produce a marked chinook effect in Cheyenne which is especially noticeable during the winter months. Also, winds from the north through east to south are upslope and may cause fog or low stratus clouds in the Cheyenne area throughout the year. Because of this terrain variation, the wind direction plays an important role in controlling the local temperature and weather.

Cheyenne experiences large diurnal and annual temperature ranges. This is due to the advent of both warm and cold air masses and the relatively high elevation of the city which permits rapid incoming and outgoing radiation. The daily temperature range averages about 30 degrees in the summer and 23 degrees in the winter. Many cold air masses from the north during the winter months miss Cheyenne. Because of the downslope of land to the east and the prevailing westerlies, some of the cold air masses do move over the city, but only about 13 percent of the days in an average January, the coldest month of the year, show temperatures dropping to zero or below. Temperatures during the winter months average a few degrees higher than over the Mississippi and Missouri Valleys at the same latitude.

Windy days are quire frequent during the winter and spring months. Since the wind is usually strongest during the daytime it is a very noticeable weather element. Usually the strong winds are from a westerly direction and this tends to raise the temperature because the air is moving downslope.

Most of the air masses reaching this area move in from the Pacific and since the mountains to the west are quite effective moisture barriers the climate is semi-arid. Fortunately, about 70 percent of normal annual precipitation occurs during the growing season. In the summer months, precipitation is mostly of the shower type and occurs mainly with thunderstorms. Hail is frequent and occasionally destructive in some thunderstorms. Most of the snow falls during the late winter and early spring months. It is not uncommon to have heavy snow in May.

The growing season in Cheyenne averages about 132 days a year and extends from around May 18th to September 27th. Freezing temperatures have occurred as late in the spring as mid-June, and as early in the fall as late August.

Relative humidity averages near 50 percent on an annual basis with large daily variations. Very seldom is the relative humidity above 30 percent when the temperature is above 80 degrees.

## TABLE 1     NORMALS, MEANS AND EXTREMES

CHEYENNE, WYOMING

LATITUDE: 41°09'N    LONGITUDE: 104°49'W    ELEVATION: FT. GRND 6126 BARO 6123    TIME ZONE: MOUNTAIN    WBAN: 24018

| | (a) | JAN | FEB | MAR | APR | MAY | JUNE | JULY | AUG | SEP | OCT | NOV | DEC | YEAR |
|---|---|---|---|---|---|---|---|---|---|---|---|---|---|---|
| **TEMPERATURE °F:** | | | | | | | | | | | | | | |
| Normals | | | | | | | | | | | | | | |
|   -Daily Maximum | | 37.3 | 40.7 | 43.6 | 54.0 | 64.6 | 75.4 | 83.1 | 80.8 | 72.1 | 61.0 | 46.5 | 40.4 | 58.3 |
|   -Daily Minimum | | 14.8 | 17.9 | 20.6 | 29.6 | 39.7 | 48.5 | 54.6 | 52.8 | 43.7 | 34.0 | 23.1 | 18.2 | 33.1 |
|   -Monthly | | 26.1 | 29.3 | 32.1 | 41.8 | 52.2 | 62.0 | 68.9 | 66.8 | 57.9 | 47.5 | 34.8 | 29.3 | 45.7 |
| Extremes | | | | | | | | | | | | | | |
|   -Record Highest | 54 | 66 | 71 | 74 | 82 | 90 | 100 | 100 | 96 | 93 | 83 | 73 | 69 | 100 |
|   -Year | | 1982 | 1962 | 1986 | 1981 | 1969 | 1954 | 1954 | 1939 | 1960 | 1967 | 1954 | 1939 | JUN 1954 |
|   -Record Lowest | 54 | -29 | -34 | -21 | -8 | 16 | 25 | 38 | 36 | 8 | 2 | -14 | -28 | -34 |
|   -Year | | 1984 | 1936 | 1943 | 1975 | 1947 | 1951 | 1952 | 1952 | 1985 | 1935 | 1983 | 1989 | FEB 1936 |
| **NORMAL DEGREE DAYS:** | | | | | | | | | | | | | | |
| Heating (base 65°F) | | 1206 | 1000 | 1020 | 696 | 397 | 139 | 24 | 37 | 235 | 543 | 906 | 1107 | 7310 |
| Cooling (base 65°F) | | 0 | 0 | 0 | 0 | 0 | 49 | 145 | 93 | 22 | 0 | 0 | 0 | 309 |
| **% OF POSSIBLE SUNSHINE** | 50 | 63 | 66 | 66 | 62 | 61 | 66 | 69 | 68 | 70 | 69 | 61 | 60 | 65 |
| **MEAN SKY COVER (tenths)** | | | | | | | | | | | | | | |
| Sunrise - Sunset | 54 | 5.8 | 6.2 | 6.3 | 6.5 | 6.6 | 5.5 | 5.0 | 5.1 | 4.6 | 4.8 | 5.6 | 5.7 | 5.6 |
| **MEAN NUMBER OF DAYS:** | | | | | | | | | | | | | | |
| Sunrise to Sunset | | | | | | | | | | | | | | |
|   -Clear | 54 | 8.9 | 7.0 | 7.0 | 5.9 | 4.7 | 8.3 | 9.5 | 9.9 | 13.1 | 12.9 | 9.6 | 9.4 | 106.2 |
|   -Partly Cloudy | 54 | 9.5 | 9.1 | 9.7 | 10.3 | 12.0 | 12.4 | 15.1 | 13.2 | 8.5 | 9.0 | 9.1 | 9.1 | 127.1 |
|   -Cloudy | 54 | 13.0 | 12.2 | 14.2 | 13.8 | 14.3 | 9.2 | 6.4 | 7.9 | 8.4 | 9.1 | 11.2 | 12.7 | 132.4 |
| Precipitation | | | | | | | | | | | | | | |
| .01 inches or more | 54 | 5.7 | 6.3 | 9.4 | 9.5 | 11.9 | 10.8 | 10.7 | 9.8 | 7.4 | 5.6 | 6.0 | 5.6 | 98.6 |
| Snow,Ice pellets | | | | | | | | | | | | | | |
| 1.0 inches or more | 54 | 2.0 | 1.9 | 3.6 | 2.4 | 0.9 | 0.1 | 0.0 | 0.0 | 0.3 | 1.2 | 2.4 | 1.9 | 16.7 |
| Thunderstorms | 54 | 0.0 | 0.1 | 0.2 | 2.1 | 7.6 | 11.1 | 13.3 | 10.5 | 4.4 | 0.9 | 0.* | 0.0 | 50.2 |
| Heavy Fog Visibility | | | | | | | | | | | | | | |
| 1/4 mile or less | 54 | 0.9 | 1.8 | 3.0 | 3.0 | 2.9 | 2.0 | 1.1 | 1.4 | 2.0 | 2.0 | 1.8 | 1.3 | 23.1 |
| Temperature °F | | | | | | | | | | | | | | |
|   -Maximum | | | | | | | | | | | | | | |
|   90° and above | 30 | 0.0 | 0.0 | 0.0 | 0.0 | 0.* | 1.1 | 5.5 | 2.4 | 0.3 | 0.0 | 0.0 | 0.0 | 9.3 |
|   32° and below | 30 | 9.5 | 7.3 | 5.4 | 1.4 | 0.* | 0.0 | 0.0 | 0.0 | 0.2 | 0.6 | 4.0 | 8.7 | 37.2 |
|   -Minimum | | | | | | | | | | | | | | |
|   32° and below | 30 | 28.9 | 26.4 | 27.5 | 17.8 | 3.4 | 0.0 | 0.0 | 0.0 | 2.1 | 12.1 | 24.5 | 28.5 | 171.2 |
|   0° and below | 30 | 4.6 | 2.6 | 1.1 | 0.1 | 0.0 | 0.0 | 0.0 | 0.0 | 0.0 | 0.0 | 0.5 | 3.1 | 12.1 |
| **AVG. STATION PRESS.(mb)** | 17 | 809.0 | 809.0 | 807.0 | 809.0 | 810.2 | 813.0 | 815.4 | 815.3 | 814.3 | 813.3 | 810.0 | 809.4 | 811.2 |
| **RELATIVE HUMIDITY (%)** | | | | | | | | | | | | | | |
| Hour 05 | 30 | 57 | 61 | 65 | 67 | 71 | 71 | 69 | 69 | 66 | 61 | 60 | 59 | 65 |
| Hour 11 | 30 | 46 | 46 | 46 | 42 | 42 | 40 | 35 | 36 | 37 | 38 | 43 | 46 | 41 |
| Hour 17 (Local Time) | 30 | 50 | 48 | 46 | 41 | 43 | 41 | 38 | 38 | 38 | 41 | 50 | 53 | 44 |
| Hour 23 | 30 | 58 | 61 | 63 | 64 | 66 | 64 | 62 | 62 | 62 | 59 | 60 | 59 | 62 |
| **PRECIPITATION (inches):** | | | | | | | | | | | | | | |
| Water Equivalent | | | | | | | | | | | | | | |
|   -Normal | | 0.41 | 0.40 | 0.97 | 1.24 | 2.39 | 2.00 | 1.87 | 1.39 | 1.06 | 0.68 | 0.53 | 0.37 | 13.31 |
|   -Maximum Monthly | 54 | 2.78 | 2.16 | 2.96 | 5.04 | 5.67 | 5.32 | 5.01 | 6.64 | 4.52 | 3.57 | 2.48 | 1.68 | 6.64 |
|   -Year | | 1949 | 1953 | 1983 | 1942 | 1981 | 1955 | 1973 | 1985 | 1973 | 1942 | 1979 | 1937 | AUG 1985 |
|   -Minimum Monthly | 54 | T | T | 0.12 | 0.35 | 0.11 | 0.07 | 0.58 | 0.03 | 0.10 | 0.03 | T | 0.03 | T |
|   -Year | | 1952 | 1983 | 1966 | 1946 | 1974 | 1980 | 1969 | 1944 | 1953 | 1964 | 1965 | 1959 | FEB 1983 |
|   -Maximum in 24 hrs | 54 | 1.41 | 1.60 | 1.88 | 1.94 | 2.01 | 2.68 | 3.42 | 6.06 | 2.75 | 1.70 | 1.66 | 1.19 | 6.06 |
|   -Year | | 1949 | 1953 | 1946 | 1984 | 1987 | 1955 | 1973 | 1985 | 1973 | 1947 | 1979 | 1979 | AUG 1985 |
| Snow,Ice pellets | | | | | | | | | | | | | | |
|   -Maximum Monthly | 54 | 35.5 | 19.9 | 31.9 | 31.8 | 30.4 | 8.7 | T | T | 7.4 | 21.3 | 31.1 | 21.3 | 35.5 |
|   -Year | | 1980 | 1953 | 1983 | 1984 | 1943 | 1947 | 1989 | 1989 | 1985 | 1969 | 1979 | 1958 | JAN 1980 |
|   -Maximum in 24 hrs | 54 | 12.0 | 14.0 | 15.6 | 17.4 | 15.0 | 8.7 | T | T | 5.8 | 6.9 | 19.8 | 11.7 | 19.8 |
|   -Year | | 1980 | 1953 | 1973 | 1984 | 1942 | 1947 | 1989 | 1989 | 1985 | 1982 | 1979 | 1979 | NOV 1979 |
| **WIND:** | | | | | | | | | | | | | | |
| Mean Speed (mph) | 32 | 15.3 | 14.7 | 14.6 | 14.4 | 12.7 | 11.4 | 10.4 | 10.4 | 11.2 | 12.2 | 13.4 | 14.7 | 13.0 |
| Prevailing Direction | | | | | | | | | | | | | | |
| through 1963 | | WNW | W | WNW | WNW | WNW | WNW | WNW | W | W | W | WNW | WNW | WNW |
| Fastest Obs. 1 Min. | | | | | | | | | | | | | | |
|   -Direction (!!!) | 8 | 28 | 27 | 29 | 30 | 26 | 30 | 34 | 32 | 29 | 25 | 31 | 27 | 30 |
|   -Speed (MPH) | 8 | 49 | 48 | 51 | 58 | 48 | 41 | 44 | 42 | 40 | 41 | 46 | 46 | 58 |
|   -Year | | 1989 | 1988 | 1982 | 1982 | 1988 | 1989 | 1984 | 1983 | 1984 | 1985 | 1986 | 1987 | APR 1982 |
| Peak Gust | | | | | | | | | | | | | | |
|   -Direction (!!!) | 6 | NW | 27 | W | NW | W | NW | NW | NW | NW | SW | W | W | W |
|   -Speed (mph) | 6 | 67 | 70 | 69 | 62 | 71 | 58 | 60 | 59 | 58 | 71 | 69 | 71 | 71 |
|   -Date | | 1987 | 1986 | 1985 | 1986 | 1986 | 1989 | 1988 | 1989 | 1984 | 1985 | 1986 | 1984 | MAY 1986 |

**See Reference Notes to this table on the following page.**

PRECIPITATION (inches)          CHEYENNE, WYOMING

**TABLE 2**

| YEAR | JAN | FEB | MAR | APR | MAY | JUNE | JULY | AUG | SEP | OCT | NOV | DEC | ANNUAL |
|------|-----|-----|-----|-----|-----|------|------|-----|-----|-----|-----|-----|--------|
| 1961 | 0.06 | 0.37 | 2.08 | 0.83 | 2.92 | 2.91 | 1.53 | 3.12 | 2.17 | 0.56 | 0.35 | 0.09 | 16.99 |
| 1962 | 0.67 | 0.56 | 0.39 | 0.54 | 2.72 | 2.82 | 4.02 | 0.40 | 1.30 | 0.62 | 0.33 | 0.25 | 14.62 |
| 1963 | 0.51 | 0.17 | 0.74 | 1.66 | 1.14 | 2.84 | 0.77 | 2.28 | 3.28 | 1.06 | 0.02 | 0.42 | 14.89 |
| 1964 | 0.03 | 0.24 | 0.58 | 1.30 | 0.84 | 1.01 | 1.00 | 0.28 | 0.33 | 0.03 | 0.14 | 0.16 | 5.94 |
| 1965 | 0.57 | 0.26 | 0.76 | 0.57 | 3.11 | 4.03 | 0.89 | 1.54 | 1.32 | 0.75 | T | 0.22 | 14.02 |
| 1966 | 0.11 | 0.22 | 0.12 | 0.48 | 0.21 | 1.95 | 3.38 | 2.78 | 2.12 | 0.68 | 0.29 | 0.08 | 12.42 |
| 1967 | 0.45 | 0.54 | 0.76 | 2.15 | 4.04 | 2.63 | 1.71 | 0.99 | 0.88 | 0.46 | 0.32 | 0.46 | 15.39 |
| 1968 | 0.04 | 0.30 | 0.31 | 2.34 | 3.54 | 0.87 | 1.25 | 1.21 | 0.20 | 0.86 | 0.71 | 0.28 | 11.91 |
| 1969 | 0.23 | 0.25 | 0.27 | 0.82 | 1.77 | 2.70 | 0.58 | 0.99 | 0.84 | 2.04 | 0.23 | 0.21 | 10.93 |
| 1970 | 0.10 | 0.04 | 1.32 | 0.85 | 3.13 | 2.42 | 0.82 | 0.14 | 1.10 | 1.30 | 0.30 | 0.31 | 11.83 |
| 1971 | 0.51 | 0.62 | 1.08 | 2.81 | 2.38 | 0.97 | 1.08 | 1.41 | 1.76 | 1.16 | 0.05 | 0.07 | 13.90 |
| 1972 | 0.36 | 0.02 | 0.79 | 0.80 | 2.76 | 1.71 | 1.81 | 1.35 | 1.01 | 0.42 | 0.40 | 1.24 | 12.04 |
| 1973 | 0.23 | 0.07 | 1.85 | 1.75 | 0.31 | 1.20 | 5.01 | 0.27 | 4.52 | 0.06 | 1.25 | 1.06 | 17.58 |
| 1974 | 0.48 | 0.03 | 1.24 | 0.50 | 0.11 | 1.41 | 1.41 | 1.29 | 0.50 | 0.91 | 0.49 | 0.10 | 9.87 |
| 1975 | 0.40 | 0.17 | 1.17 | 0.47 | 2.27 | 1.49 | 2.62 | 0.39 | 0.52 | 0.49 | 0.20 | 0.52 | 10.71 |
| 1976 | 0.32 | 0.71 | 0.32 | 1.79 | 2.07 | 0.68 | 2.39 | 1.40 | 0.77 | 0.15 | 0.28 | 0.10 | 10.98 |
| 1977 | 0.14 | 0.08 | 1.21 | 1.86 | 2.50 | 2.44 | 3.49 | 1.07 | 0.19 | 0.08 | 0.35 | 0.24 | 13.65 |
| 1978 | 0.58 | 0.78 | 0.35 | 0.52 | 3.98 | 0.63 | 0.98 | 1.38 | 0.12 | 0.50 | 0.45 | 0.54 | 10.81 |
| 1979 | 0.27 | 0.14 | 1.34 | 0.77 | 2.90 | 3.32 | 1.83 | 1.86 | 0.32 | 0.46 | 2.48 | 1.50 | 17.19 |
| 1980 | 2.71 | 0.73 | 1.36 | 0.93 | 2.39 | 0.07 | 2.00 | 1.55 | 0.97 | 0.51 | 0.46 | 0.08 | 13.76 |
| 1981 | 0.30 | 0.20 | 0.70 | 0.73 | 5.67 | 1.66 | 2.85 | 2.90 | 0.31 | 0.85 | 0.09 | 0.45 | 16.71 |
| 1982 | 0.41 | 0.19 | 0.17 | 0.53 | 3.56 | 4.52 | 2.71 | 1.81 | 2.87 | 1.20 | 0.43 | 0.83 | 19.23 |
| 1983 | 0.02 | T | 2.96 | 4.45 | 2.31 | 2.81 | 2.12 | 1.95 | 0.78 | 0.49 | 2.34 | 0.46 | 20.69 |
| 1984 | 0.54 | 0.84 | 1.28 | 3.71 | 0.78 | 2.43 | 2.57 | 2.84 | 0.65 | 1.55 | 0.11 | 0.34 | 17.64 |
| 1985 | 0.66 | 0.19 | 0.36 | 1.10 | 1.05 | 1.59 | 6.64 | 3.99 | 1.78 | 0.94 | 0.84 | 0.80 | 19.94 |
| 1986 | 0.13 | 0.50 | 0.54 | 2.26 | 1.03 | 2.42 | 1.04 | 1.55 | 2.47 | 1.78 | 0.66 | 0.18 | 14.56 |
| 1987 | 0.09 | 0.90 | 1.25 | 0.68 | 4.43 | 1.80 | 2.04 | 1.23 | 0.93 | 0.33 | 0.76 | 0.85 | 15.29 |
| 1988 | 0.52 | 0.65 | 1.34 | 1.84 | 3.09 | 2.03 | 1.79 | 1.79 | 1.66 | 0.09 | 0.42 | 0.53 | 15.75 |
| 1989 | 0.27 | 1.26 | 0.49 | 0.48 | 1.37 | 2.51 | 1.70 | 1.79 | 1.62 | 0.41 | 0.14 | 0.69 | 12.73 |
| 1990 | 0.35 | 0.69 | 3.65 | 1.66 | 3.37 | 1.03 | 3.64 | 1.98 | 0.80 | 1.35 | 0.72 | 0.39 | 19.63 |
| Record Mean | 0.43 | 0.54 | 1.05 | 1.75 | 2.43 | 1.83 | 2.01 | 1.57 | 1.17 | 0.88 | 0.55 | 0.46 | 14.66 |

**TABLE 3**  AVERAGE TEMPERATURE (deg. F)          CHEYENNE, WYOMING

| YEAR | JAN | FEB | MAR | APR | MAY | JUNE | JULY | AUG | SEP | OCT | NOV | DEC | ANNUAL |
|------|-----|-----|-----|-----|-----|------|------|-----|-----|-----|-----|-----|--------|
| 1961 | 29.0 | 31.8 | 31.6 | 40.7 | 52.8 | 64.8 | 69.1 | 68.1 | 51.4 | 44.8 | 32.3 | 23.4 | 45.0 |
| 1962 | 19.0 | 27.2 | 29.0 | 45.6 | 55.1 | 59.9 | 65.6 | 67.3 | 58.9 | 51.0 | 39.8 | 31.5 | 45.8 |
| 1963 | 16.7 | 33.0 | 31.8 | 43.7 | 55.8 | 64.0 | 72.7 | 68.3 | 63.1 | 54.4 | 40.0 | 26.9 | 47.5 |
| 1964 | 26.1 | 22.3 | 27.4 | 40.8 | 54.6 | 60.5 | 70.9 | 64.3 | 56.9 | 48.7 | 35.4 | 32.1 | 44.8 |
| 1965 | 32.1 | 26.0 | 22.2 | 45.7 | 50.8 | 59.3 | 68.2 | 64.7 | 49.6 | 52.0 | 41.4 | 32.1 | 45.4 |
| 1966 | 25.8 | 26.8 | 37.7 | 39.6 | 55.6 | 61.5 | 74.5 | 66.2 | 59.9 | 47.8 | 38.8 | 31.0 | 47.1 |
| 1967 | 31.4 | 31.1 | 39.0 | 44.1 | 49.1 | 57.7 | 57.7 | 66.0 | 58.4 | 49.3 | 35.1 | 22.5 | 45.9 |
| 1968 | 28.7 | 32.6 | 38.0 | 38.9 | 49.2 | 62.6 | 68.2 | 64.5 | 57.6 | 49.2 | 34.0 | 28.0 | 46.0 |
| 1969 | 31.4 | 32.0 | 28.7 | 48.1 | 55.7 | 57.0 | 71.5 | 70.7 | 61.2 | 37.1 | 36.4 | 31.3 | 46.8 |
| 1970 | 28.7 | 34.6 | 28.9 | 37.8 | 54.3 | 60.9 | 69.5 | 70.7 | 55.0 | 41.2 | 35.7 | 29.1 | 45.5 |
| 1971 | 29.7 | 25.8 | 32.4 | 41.0 | 49.2 | 63.4 | 65.5 | 68.7 | 53.1 | 44.3 | 36.0 | 29.1 | 44.8 |
| 1972 | 25.3 | 33.2 | 39.3 | 42.5 | 51.2 | 63.2 | 64.3 | 64.6 | 55.6 | 45.5 | 29.5 | 21.0 | 44.7 |
| 1973 | 23.7 | 29.7 | 31.9 | 37.3 | 51.4 | 62.9 | 65.8 | 68.4 | 54.1 | 49.3 | 35.3 | 29.4 | 44.9 |
| 1974 | 24.1 | 31.9 | 37.1 | 43.3 | 55.0 | 64.1 | 70.1 | 65.2 | 55.3 | 48.3 | 35.6 | 26.6 | 46.4 |
| 1975 | 25.5 | 25.0 | 30.2 | 37.5 | 48.4 | 57.9 | 67.3 | 66.3 | 56.0 | 48.1 | 34.2 | 32.6 | 44.1 |
| 1976 | 26.9 | 32.9 | 30.9 | 42.7 | 51.1 | 59.7 | 69.2 | 65.0 | 57.7 | 43.4 | 33.5 | 30.6 | 45.3 |
| 1977 | 22.4 | 32.1 | 32.1 | 44.7 | 53.4 | 65.2 | 68.2 | 63.5 | 60.7 | 48.3 | 34.4 | 29.0 | 46.3 |
| 1978 | 22.1 | 25.0 | 37.7 | 43.9 | 49.0 | 61.0 | 68.7 | 64.3 | 59.6 | 47.9 | 33.5 | 21.1 | 44.5 |
| 1979 | 17.3 | 31.6 | 36.0 | 44.9 | 49.9 | 61.5 | 69.9 | 65.9 | 62.9 | 49.8 | 29.5 | 32.9 | 46.0 |
| 1980 | 22.2 | 29.4 | 33.0 | 42.3 | 51.2 | 65.5 | 71.4 | 66.5 | 60.4 | 46.7 | 36.8 | 38.5 | 47.0 |
| 1981 | 33.4 | 32.2 | 36.8 | 50.1 | 50.5 | 63.7 | 69.0 | 65.2 | 61.2 | 46.1 | 40.7 | 30.7 | 48.3 |
| 1982 | 25.5 | 28.2 | 36.1 | 41.8 | 50.5 | 57.5 | 67.7 | 69.1 | 56.7 | 45.1 | 31.4 | 28.3 | 44.8 |
| 1983 | 32.8 | 33.5 | 32.0 | 34.8 | 47.4 | 57.3 | 67.8 | 70.2 | 59.0 | 48.6 | 32.3 | 15.0 | 44.2 |
| 1984 | 24.3 | 28.4 | 32.4 | 35.7 | 53.6 | 59.4 | 68.4 | 66.6 | 53.0 | 40.0 | 35.0 | 27.0 | 43.7 |
| 1985 | 19.5 | 23.3 | 35.2 | 45.6 | 54.3 | 61.1 | 69.3 | 66.8 | 52.8 | 45.1 | 26.2 | 26.1 | 43.8 |
| 1986 | 37.0 | 30.1 | 42.2 | 43.9 | 50.6 | 64.5 | 68.5 | 67.0 | 55.3 | 44.6 | 34.3 | 28.7 | 47.2 |
| 1987 | 29.1 | 31.6 | 32.4 | 46.7 | 54.5 | 63.3 | 69.2 | 64.9 | 58.0 | 46.9 | 36.7 | 25.7 | 46.6 |
| 1988 | 21.5 | 28.4 | 32.3 | 44.4 | 53.3 | 67.4 | 69.7 | 68.7 | 57.5 | 50.3 | 35.3 | 28.7 | 46.5 |
| 1989 | 30.2 | 17.3 | 37.4 | 44.3 | 54.3 | 60.3 | 70.6 | 67.0 | 57.5 | 46.5 | 33.8 | 24.3 | 45.7 |
| 1990 | 31.5 | 28.7 | 31.9 | 42.8 | 49.3 | 64.1 | 65.0 | 66.4 | 62.2 | 46.7 | 38.7 | 20.8 | 45.7 |
| Record Mean | 26.1 | 27.9 | 32.7 | 41.5 | 51.1 | 61.1 | 67.8 | 66.3 | 57.4 | 46.4 | 35.1 | 28.4 | 45.2 |
| Max | 37.2 | 39.1 | 44.0 | 53.6 | 63.4 | 74.6 | 81.9 | 80.2 | 71.4 | 59.4 | 46.7 | 39.3 | 57.6 |
| Min | 15.0 | 16.6 | 21.3 | 29.5 | 38.7 | 47.6 | 53.8 | 52.5 | 43.3 | 33.4 | 23.5 | 17.5 | 32.7 |

## REFERENCE NOTES FOR TABLES 1, 2, 3 and 6          (CHEYENNE, WY)

### GENERAL

T - TRACE AMOUNT
BLANK ENTRIES DENOTE MISSING/UNREPORTED DATA.
# INDICATES A STATION OR INSTRUMENT RELOCATION.

### SPECIFIC

**TABLE 1**

(a) - LENGTH OF RECORD IN YEARS. ALTHOUGH INDIVIDUAL MONTHS MAY BE MISSING.

\* LESS THAN .05

NORMALS — BASED ON THE 1951-1980 RECORD PERIOD.
EXTREMES — DATES ARE THE MOST RECENT OCCURRENCE.
WIND DIR. — NUMERALS SHOW TENS OF DEGREES CLOCKWISE FROM TRUE NORTH. "00" INDICATES CALM.
RESULTANT WIND DIRECTIONS ARE GIVEN TO WHOLE DEGREES.

**TABLE 3**
MAX AND MIN ARE LONG-TERM MEAN DAILY MAXIMUM AND MEAN DAILY MINIMUM TEMPERATURES.

### EXCEPTIONS

**TABLE 1**

1. FASTEST MILE WINDS ARE THROUGH MARCH 1981.

**TABLES 2, 3, and 6**

RECORD MEANS ARE THROUGH THE CURRENT YEAR, BEGINNING IN
1871 FOR TEMPERATURE
1871 FOR PRECIPITATION
1936 FOR SNOWFALL

HEATING DEGREE DAYS Base 65 deg. F     CHEYENNE. WYOMING

**TABLE 4**

| SEASON | JULY | AUG | SEP | OCT | NOV | DEC | JAN | FEB | MAR | APR | MAY | JUNE | TOTAL |
|---|---|---|---|---|---|---|---|---|---|---|---|---|---|
| 1961-62 | 17 | 8 | 405 | 622 | 977 | 1285 | 1419 | 1056 | 1106 | 576 | 303 | 167 | 7941 |
| 1962-63 | 40 | 57 | 187 | 425 | 751 | 1031 | 1492 | 890 | 1023 | 633 | 277 | 89 | 6895 |
| 1963-64 | 3 | 10 | 76 | 323 | 742 | 1174 | 1203 | 1229 | 1160 | 720 | 340 | 166 | 7146 |
| 1964-65 | 2 | 95 | 239 | 500 | 883 | 1095 | 1012 | 1088 | 1320 | 569 | 435 | 169 | 7407 |
| 1965-66 | 11 | 47 | 454 | 397 | 702 | 1016 | 1208 | 1061 | 841 | 758 | 291 | 143 | 6929 |
| 1966-67 | 0 | 51 | 166 | 526 | 781 | 1049 | 1036 | 945 | 800 | 622 | 490 | 221 | 6687 |
| 1967-68 | 12 | 45 | 202 | 481 | 891 | 1308 | 1117 | 932 | 833 | 777 | 487 | 107 | 7192 |
| 1968-69 | 40 | 82 | 221 | 481 | 924 | 1137 | 1034 | 919 | 1118 | 498 | 297 | 248 | 6999 |
| 1969-70 | 3 | 3 | 113 | 859 | 854 | 1038 | 1115 | 846 | 1113 | 811 | 326 | 168 | 7249 |
| 1970-71 | 3 | 5 | 302 | 732 | 874 | 1108 | 1087 | 1093 | 1007 | 713 | 481 | 99 | 7504 |
| 1971-72 | 56 | 6 | 364 | 633 | 863 | 1108 | 1226 | 916 | 791 | 668 | 419 | 61 | 7111 |
| 1972-73 | 85 | 75 | 248 | 599 | 1056 | 1358 | 1275 | 980 | 1017 | 824 | 414 | 122 | 8053 |
| 1973-74 | 80 | 4 | 323 | 482 | 883 | 1098 | 1264 | 922 | 862 | 643 | 304 | 110 | 6975 |
| 1974-75 | 4 | 55 | 302 | 509 | 873 | 1180 | 1215 | 1115 | 1070 | 819 | 506 | 212 | 7860 |
| 1975-76 | 11 | 39 | 274 | 515 | 920 | 998 | 1175 | 924 | 1048 | 661 | 425 | 158 | 7148 |
| 1976-77 | 11 | 44 | 224 | 664 | 937 | 1059 | 1314 | 894 | 1014 | 602 | 352 | 44 | 7159 |
| 1977-78 | 21 | 74 | 150 | 511 | 910 | 1108 | 1324 | 1115 | 840 | 627 | 491 | 157 | 7328 |
| 1978-79 | 28 | 73 | 200 | 523 | 937 | 1358 | 1471 | 933 | 893 | 597 | 459 | 139 | 7611 |
| 1979-80 | 2 | 62 | 105 | 468 | 1058 | 990 | 1321 | 1027 | 984 | 673 | 424 | 65 | 7179 |
| 1980-81 | 0 | 41 | 151 | 558 | 840 | 812 | 974 | 913 | 868 | 440 | 445 | 95 | 6137 |
| 1981-82 | 21 | 50 | 120 | 580 | 722 | 1058 | 1216 | 1025 | 892 | 687 | 446 | 227 | 7044 |
| 1982-83 | 29 | 7 | 264 | 608 | 1002 | 1131 | 992 | 875 | 1016 | 898 | 538 | 233 | 7593 |
| 1983-84 | 23 | 0 | 202 | 502 | 974 | 1547 | 1259 | 1058 | 1002 | 870 | 348 | 177 | 7962 |
| 1984-85 | 6 | 15 | 365 | 769 | 892 | 1171 | 1403 | 1163 | 917 | 576 | 323 | 162 | 7762 |
| 1985-86 | 11 | 37 | 364 | 612 | 1158 | 1199 | 862 | 970 | 698 | 629 | 440 | 71 | 7051 |
| 1986-87 | 4 | 20 | 286 | 630 | 914 | 1121 | 1102 | 928 | 1002 | 542 | 321 | 78 | 6948 |
| 1987-88 | 27 | 79 | 214 | 554 | 841 | 1213 | 1343 | 1056 | 1008 | 611 | 361 | 42 | 7349 |
| 1988-89 | 12 | 18 | 236 | 449 | 884 | 1116 | 1075 | 1332 | 851 | 615 | 334 | 180 | 7102 |
| 1989-90 | 4 | 18 | 236 | 566 | 779 | 1257 | 1037 | 1012 | 1021 | 662 | 480 | 106 | 7178 |
| 1990-91 | 75 | 28 | 127 | 558 | 784 | 1364 | | | | | | | |

**TABLE 5**    COOLING DEGREE DAYS Base 65 deg. F     CHEYENNE. WYOMING

| YEAR | JAN | FEB | MAR | APR | MAY | JUNE | JULY | AUG | SEP | OCT | NOV | DEC | TOTAL |
|---|---|---|---|---|---|---|---|---|---|---|---|---|---|
| 1969 | 0 | 0 | 0 | 0 | 14 | 12 | 211 | 185 | 9 | 0 | 0 | 0 | 431 |
| 1970 | 0 | 0 | 0 | 0 | 2 | 52 | 149 | 189 | 11 | 0 | 0 | 0 | 403 |
| 1971 | 0 | 0 | 0 | 0 | 0 | 58 | 77 | 128 | 13 | 0 | 0 | 0 | 276 |
| 1972 | 0 | 0 | 0 | 0 | 0 | 11 | 69 | 69 | 2 | 0 | 0 | 0 | 151 |
| 1973 | 0 | 0 | 0 | 0 | 0 | 65 | 112 | 116 | 0 | 0 | 0 | 0 | 293 |
| 1974 | 0 | 0 | 0 | 0 | 4 | 88 | 173 | 67 | 17 | 0 | 0 | 0 | 349 |
| 1975 | 0 | 0 | 0 | 0 | 0 | 7 | 90 | 86 | 10 | 0 | 0 | 0 | 193 |
| 1976 | 0 | 0 | 0 | 0 | 0 | 7 | 145 | 50 | 15 | 0 | 0 | 0 | 217 |
| 1977 | 0 | 0 | 0 | 0 | 0 | 59 | 126 | 38 | 29 | 0 | 0 | 0 | 252 |
| 1978 | 0 | 0 | 0 | 0 | 1 | 43 | 150 | 59 | 44 | 0 | 0 | 0 | 297 |
| 1979 | 0 | 0 | 0 | 0 | 1 | 42 | 160 | 100 | 49 | 0 | 0 | 0 | 352 |
| 1980 | 0 | 0 | 0 | 0 | 0 | 88 | 205 | 94 | 21 | 0 | 0 | 0 | 408 |
| 1981 | 0 | 0 | 0 | 0 | 0 | 59 | 156 | 64 | 15 | 0 | 0 | 0 | 294 |
| 1982 | 0 | 0 | 0 | 0 | 0 | 8 | 120 | 140 | 21 | 0 | 0 | 0 | 289 |
| 1983 | 0 | 0 | 0 | 0 | 0 | 10 | 115 | 169 | 28 | 0 | 0 | 0 | 322 |
| 1984 | 0 | 0 | 0 | 0 | 1 | 14 | 118 | 72 | 8 | 0 | 0 | 0 | 213 |
| 1985 | 0 | 0 | 0 | 0 | 0 | 52 | 150 | 98 | 8 | 0 | 0 | 0 | 308 |
| 1986 | 0 | 0 | 0 | 0 | 0 | 62 | 118 | 89 | 0 | 0 | 0 | 0 | 269 |
| 1987 | 0 | 0 | 0 | 0 | 0 | 35 | 164 | 83 | 9 | 0 | 0 | 0 | 291 |
| 1988 | 0 | 0 | 0 | 0 | 4 | 22 | 166 | 140 | 18 | 0 | 0 | 0 | 450 |
| 1989 | 0 | 0 | 0 | 0 | 7 | 46 | 188 | 86 | 19 | 0 | 0 | 0 | 346 |
| 1990 | 0 | 0 | 0 | 0 | 0 | 86 | 84 | 79 | 49 | 0 | 0 | 0 | 298 |

**TABLE 6**    SNOWFALL (inches)     CHEYENNE. WYOMING

| SEASON | JULY | AUG | SEP | OCT | NOV | DEC | JAN | FEB | MAR | APR | MAY | JUNE | TOTAL |
|---|---|---|---|---|---|---|---|---|---|---|---|---|---|
| 1961-62 | 0.0 | 0.0 | 0.8 | 3.6 | 3.5 | 1.5 | 13.0 | 10.8 | 5.5 | 2.5 | T | 0.0 | 41.2 |
| 1962-63 | 0.0 | 0.0 | T | T | 3.8 | 3.5 | 8.9 | 3.1 | 11.8 | 3.2 | T | 0.0 | 34.3 |
| 1963-64 | 0.0 | 0.0 | 0.0 | T | 0.1 | 6.0 | 1.0 | 3.3 | 6.9 | 7.1 | 0.5 | 0.0 | 24.9 |
| 1964-65 | 0.0 | 0.0 | 0.0 | 0.0 | 2.0 | 1.6 | 8.5 | 5.5 | 10.0 | 2.5 | 1.4 | 0.0 | 31.5 |
| 1965-66 | 0.0 | 0.0 | 2.0 | T | T | 2.4 | 1.3 | 2.7 | 1.1 | 3.6 | T | 0.0 | 13.1 |
| 1966-67 | 0.0 | 0.0 | T | 4.5 | 2.3 | 0.8 | 5.4 | 8.0 | 3.4 | 15.9 | 11.0 | 0.0 | 51.3 |
| 1967-68 | 0.0 | 0.0 | 0.0 | 0.4 | 3.6 | 4.8 | 0.2 | 2.5 | 2.8 | 15.4 | 2.2 | 0.0 | 31.9 |
| 1968-69 | 0.0 | 0.0 | 0.5 | 6.0 | 5.5 | 3.0 | 4.7 | 2.9 | 3.0 | 0.0 | T | | 25.6 |
| 1969-70 | 0.0 | 0.0 | 0.0 | 21.3 | 1.8 | 2.4 | 1.2 | 1.5 | 19.4 | 8.3 | T | T | 55.9 |
| 1970-71 | 0.0 | 0.0 | T | 11.0 | 4.7 | 4.9 | 8.6 | 9.3 | 15.2 | 13.0 | 1.2 | 0.0 | 67.9 |
| 1971-72 | 0.0 | 0.0 | 7.4 | 8.1 | 0.9 | 1.4 | 7.4 | 0.4 | 10.6 | 8.5 | 0.3 | 0.0 | 45.0 |
| 1972-73 | 0.0 | 0.0 | T | 5.0 | 8.8 | 7.6 | 4.6 | 0.6 | 27.0 | 12.8 | 1.2 | 0.0 | 67.6 |
| 1973-74 | 0.0 | 0.0 | T | 0.5 | 17.4 | 13.9 | 5.0 | 0.8 | 16.3 | 8.0 | 0.0 | 0.0 | 61.9 |
| 1974-75 | 0.0 | 0.0 | 1.9 | 1.4 | 2.4 | 1.5 | 5.8 | 4.3 | 14.0 | 5.4 | 0.8 | 0.0 | 37.5 |
| 1975-76 | 0.0 | 0.0 | 0.6 | 5.5 | 4.7 | 8.4 | 6.0 | 8.5 | 9.0 | 6.7 | T | T | 49.4 |
| 1976-77 | 0.0 | 0.0 | 0.0 | 1.5 | 3.5 | 1.2 | 2.5 | 0.8 | 12.9 | 7.0 | T | 0.0 | 29.4 |
| 1977-78 | 0.0 | 0.0 | 0.0 | 0.4 | 4.3 | 5.6 | 7.0 | 12.0 | 2.5 | 1.0 | 18.3 | 0.0 | 51.1 |
| 1978-79 | 0.0 | 0.0 | 0.1 | 2.0 | 9.3 | 17.6 | 6.7 | 2.2 | 21.1 | 4.0 | 14.1 | T | 77.1 |
| 1979-80 | 0.0 | 0.0 | 0.0 | 3.6 | 31.1 | 15.6 | 35.5 | 10.7 | 17.8 | 3.4 | 3.8 | 0.0 | 121.5 |
| 1980-81 | 0.0 | 0.0 | 0.0 | 1.1 | 6.3 | 3.4 | 2.9 | 3.4 | 9.0 | 2.0 | 0.8 | 0.0 | 27.6 |
| 1981-82 | 0.0 | 0.0 | 0.0 | 4.6 | 0.8 | 5.8 | 5.6 | 2.4 | 1.7 | 2.0 | 4.0 | 0.0 | 26.9 |
| 1982-83 | 0.0 | 0.0 | 0.0 | 12.2 | 7.9 | 13.1 | 0.1 | T | 31.9 | 25.7 | 10.1 | 0.0 | 101.0 |
| 1983-84 | 0.0 | 0.0 | T | 0.2 | 27.2 | 7.0 | 7.9 | 12.1 | 13.0 | 31.8 | T | 0.0 | 99.2 |
| 1984-85 | 0.0 | 0.0 | 1.6 | 3.8 | 1.5 | 5.6 | 9.8 | 1.9 | 3.6 | 2.6 | 0.4 | 0.0 | 30.8 |
| 1985-86 | 0.0 | 0.0 | 7.4 | 6.0 | 12.4 | 13.0 | 1.3 | 4.9 | 5.6 | 11.3 | 3.8 | 0.0 | 65.7 |
| 1986-87 | 0.0 | 0.0 | 0.0 | 9.2 | 6.9 | 2.2 | 1.1 | 9.9 | 13.7 | 4.4 | T | 0.0 | 47.4 |
| 1987-88 | 0.0 | 0.0 | 0.0 | 1.3 | 4.5 | 6.1 | 9.0 | 7.5 | 16.0 | 7.5 | 2.2 | 0.0 | 64.1 |
| 1988-89 | 0.0 | 0.0 | 0.2 | 0.0 | 4.5 | 7.2 | 4.4 | 17.6 | 5.0 | 4.3 | T | T | 43.2 |
| 1989-90 | T | T | 2.6 | 3.4 | 1.9 | 9.7 | 5.6 | 11.6 | 39.2 | 5.6 | 1.3 | T | 80.9 |
| 1990-91 | T | T | T | 12.3 | 8.8 | 6.6 | | | | | | | |
| Record Mean | T | T | 0.8 | 3.6 | 6.8 | 6.2 | 6.2 | 5.9 | 12.4 | 9.0 | 3.5 | 0.2 | 54.6 |

**See Reference Notes, relative to all above tables, on preceding page.**

## QUOTES FROM WEATHER FOLKLORE–

*If three days old her face be bright and clear,*
*No rain or stormy gale the sailors fear;*
*But if she rise with bright and blushing cheek,*
*The blustering winds the bending mast will*
    *shake,*
*If dull her face and blunt her horns appear,*
*On the fourth day a breeze or rain is near.*
*If on the third she moves with horns direct,*
*Not pointing downward or to heaven erect,*
*The western wind expect; and drenching rain,*
*If on the fourth her horns direct remain.*
*If to the earth her upper horn she bend,*
*Cold Boreas from the north his blast will send;*
*If upward she extend it to the sky,*
*Loud Notus with his blustering gale is nigh.*
*When the fourth day around her orb is spread*
*A circling ring of deep and murky red,*
*Soon from his cave the God of Storms will rise,*
*Dashing with foamy waves the lowering skies.*
*And when fair Cynthia her full orb displays,*
*Or when unveiled to sight are half her rays,*
*Then mark the various hues that paint her face,*
*And thus the fickle weather's changes trace.*
*If smile her pearly face benign and fair,*
*Calm and serene will breathe the balmy air;*
*If with deep blush her maiden cheek be red,*
*Then boisterous wind the caution sailors dread;*
*If sullen blackness hang upon her brow,*
*From clouds as black will rainy torrents flow.*
*Not through the month their power these*
    *signs extend,*
*But all their influence with the quarter end.*
                  *– J. Lamb's "Aratus."*

# SPECIAL REPORT

# THE PROBLEM OF ATMOSPHERIC OZONE

For several decades scientists have sought to understand the complex interplay between the chemical, radiative, and dynamical processes that govern the structure of the Earth's atmosphere. During the last decade or so there has been particular interest in studying the processes which control atmospheric ozone since it has been predicted that man-made pollutants might cause harmful effects to the environment by modifying the total column content and vertical distribution of atmospheric ozone. Until recently most of the emphasis was directed towards understanding the stratosphere where greater than 90% of the ozone resides. However, during the last few years there has been an increasing interest in studying those factors which control ozone in the troposphere.

Changes in the total column content of atmospheric ozone would modify the amount of biologically harmful ultraviolet radiation penetrating to the Earth's surface with potential adverse effects on human health (skin cancer) and on the aquatic and terrestrial ecosytems. Changes in the vertical distribution of atmospheric ozone, along with changes in the atmospheric concentrations of other infrared active gases, could contribute to a change in climate on a regional and global scale by modifying the atmospheric temperature structure.

The ozone issue has evolved from one of the effect of individual pollutants to consideration of a multiplicity of possible pollutants the effects of which must be considered together. The man-made and natural chemicals of interest include the nitrogen oxides ($NO_x$) from subsonic and supersonic aircraft, nitrous oxide ($N_2O$) from agricultural and combustion practices, chlorofluorocarbons (CFC's) used as aerosol propellants, foam blowing agents, and refrigerants, brominated compounds used as fire retardants, carbon monoxide (CO) and carbon dioxide ($CO_2$) from combustion processes, and methane ($CH_4$) from a variety of sources including natural and agricultural wetlands, tundra, biomass burning, and enteric fermentation in ruminants. It is now clear that these same gases are also important in the climate issue.

It should be noted that there are two distinct aspects of the issue that need to be considered, i.e. understanding those processes that control the atmospheric distribution of ozone today, and those processes that need to be understood in order to be able to predict the atmospheric distribution of ozone in the future. If changes are observed in the distribution of ozone we must be able to understand how periodic and episodic natural phenomena such as solar activity and volcanic eruptions cause ozone to vary in space and time in order to isolate the impact of the changing atmospheric concentrations of gases such as the CFC's, $CO_2$, $CH_4$, and $N_2O$.

Since the scientific community first attempted to understand the chemical, radiative, and dynamical processes which control the temporal and spatial distribution of atmospheric ozone today, and to predict the distribution of ozone in the future, our recognition of the breadth of the issue has steadily increased. Originally the research emphasis was focused on understanding the physical and chemical processes occurring within the stratosphere. Now, however, we recognize that in order to be able to predict the distribution of ozone in the future we cannot be confined to simply understanding stratospheric chemistry, radiation, and dynamics but we also need to understand the processes controlling the chemical composition of the troposphere, the exchange mechanisms for energy, mass and chemical constituents across the tropopause, and the role of biospheric processes in controlling the emissions of gases into the atmosphere. This has made the ozone issue an example of how one problem requires us to bring knowledge from a variety of sources to bear on its solution and how understanding this problem contributes back to other fields such as the trace gas-climate problem and the global cycling of nitrogen and carbon.

Thus to really understand the processes which control atmospheric ozone and to predict perturbations we are drawn into a study of the complete Earth system. This requires us to study the Earth as a single coupled system which involves chemical, physical, and biological processes occurring in the atmosphere, on land, and in the oceans. This is exactly the same situation which exists if we want to understand and have some predictive capability for the climate system. This report mirrors these increasing perceptions of the coupled nature of the system and, while focusing on the stratosphere, gives more consideration to the other aspects of the issue than previous reports on the ozone issue.

(a) There is strong coupling in the stratosphere between the chemistry, radiation, and dynamics. This is because atmospheric ozone is a strong absorber of solar radiation, thus strongly influencing the temperature structure and circulation of the stratosphere, which in turn controls the distribution of atmospheric ozone and the trace gases which control ozone.

(b) Since 1930, when Chapman first proposed a simple photochemical scheme involving only odd oxygen species to explain the atmospheric concentration of ozone, our understanding of the photochemistry of the atmosphere has evolved significantly. Scientists have refined this simple scheme by invoking the importance of trace concentration (ppbv)* of hydrogen oxides ($HO_x$), $NO_x$, chlorine oxides ($ClO_x$), and to a lesser extent bromine oxides ($BrO_x$) species in catalytically controlling atmospheric ozone. In addition, we also recognize that the atmospheric concentrations of a number of carbon compounds including $CO$, $CO_2$, and $CH_4$ play a vital role in the photochemistry of ozone. In particular, we recognize that there is strong coupling between the individual members of each chemical family, and that while each of these families individually is important in controlling odd oxygen, there is strong chemical coupling between the different chemical families, thereby modifying their individual roles in controlling ozone.

(c) At different times during the last decade or so scientists have suggested that the atmospheric concentrations of one or more of the source gases of the hydrogen, carbon, nitrogen, chlorine, or bromine chemical families may be changing due to human activities, and in each case have attempted to predict the response of the ozone layer to such individual changes. We now have reliable experimental evidence that the atmospheric concentrations of several of the source gases, i.e. $CH_4$, $N_2O$, and the chlorofluorocarbons, are all currently changing at a significant rate and that their impact on atmospheric ozone must be considered collectively and not in isolation.

(d) We need to understand the role of the biosphere in regulating the emissions of gases such as $CH_4$, $CO_2$, $N_2O$, and chloromethane ($CH_3Cl$) to the atmosphere, and we need to know the most probable future industrial release rates of gases such as the CFC's, $N_2O$, $CO$, and $CO_2$ which depend upon economic, social, and political factors.

(e) Because of the fact that neither the chemical composition nor the interplay between meteorology and chemistry can be duplicated exactly in the laboratory, heavy reliance must be placed on theoretical models to describe the present and future behavior of the atmosphere. As a consequence it is necessary to define a careful strategy of investigation involving the proper balance between laboratory studies of fundamental processes, field measurements, and theoretical studies.

---

*ppbv = parts per billion by volume measure

(f) While one-dimensional photochemical models have been, and will continue to be, extensively used for assessment purposes we must place more emphasis in the future on the development of two-dimensional and three-dimensional interactive photochemical models. Such multidimensional models allow us to explore the seasonal, latitudinal, and longitudinal behavior of ozone. Also, given that they more realistically represent the real world, they are more amenable to validation using field measurements of atmospheric composition.

(g) The climate problem has broadened in scope from the $CO_2$-climate problem to the trace gas-climate problem. Changes in the atmospheric concentrations of ozone as well as $H_2O$, $CH_4$, $N_2O$, the CFC's, and other gases will all modify the thermal structure of the atmosphere.

(h) We need to improve our understanding of tropospheric chemistry because of its vital role in controlling the atmospheric lifetimes of many of the source gases such as $CH_4$ and $CH_3Cl$, which influence atmospheric ozone and the radiative balance of the atmosphere. We also recognize that changes in tropospheric ozone will influence the climate system and will affect our interpretation of trends in the total ozone column.

(i) A vital component of any atmospheric research program is the acquisition of well calibrated long-term (multiyear) measurements of atmospheric parameters in order to monitor the state of the atmosphere and to differentiate between the different scales of temporal variability.

(j) Global data sets obtained from satellites are essential to complement data obtained using ground, aircraft, balloon, and rocket based instrumentation. Such data sets are essential to more fully understand the interplay on a global scale between chemical, radiative and dynamical processes, and to validate aspects of the multidimensional models. In addition, such data are needed to check the geographical representativeness of local measurements of large scale phenomena.

Ozone is present in the earth's atmosphere at all altitudes from the surface up to at least 100 km. The bulk of the ozone resides in the *stratosphere* with a maximum ozone concentration of $5 \times 10^{12}$ molecule cm$^{-3}$ at about 25 km. Although $O_3$ concentrations in the *troposhere* are less than in the stratosphere, ozone plays a vital role in the atmospheric chemistry in this region and also affects the thermal radiation balance in the lower atmosphere.

Atmospheric ozone is formed by combination of atomic and molecular oxygen.

$$O + O_2 + M \rightarrow O_3 + M \qquad (1)$$

where M is a third body required to carry away the energy released in the combination reaction. At altitudes above approximately 20 km production of O atoms results almost exclusively from photodissociation of molecular $O_2$ by short wavelength ultraviolet radiation ($\lambda < 243$ nm):

$$O_2 + h\nu \rightarrow O + O \qquad (2)$$

At lower altitudes and particularly in the troposphere, O atom formation from the photodissociation of nitrogen dioxide by long wavelength ultraviolet radiation is more important:

$$NO_2 + h\nu \rightarrow NO + O \qquad (3)$$

Ozone itself is photodissociated by both UV and visible light:

$$O_3 + h\nu \rightarrow O_2 + O \tag{4}$$

but this reaction together with the combination reaction (1) only serves to partition the 'odd oxygen' species between O and $O_3$. The production processes (2) and (3) are balanced by chemical and physical loss processes. Until the 1950s, chemical loss of odd oxygen was attributed only to the reaction:

$$O + O_3 \rightarrow O_2 + O_2 \tag{5}$$

originally proposed by S. Chapman (1930). It is now known that ozone in the stratosphere is removed predominantly by catalytic cycles involving homogeneous gas phase reactions of active free radical species in the $HO_x$, $NO_x$, $ClO_x$ and $BrO_x$ families:

$$X + O_3 \rightarrow XO + O_2 \tag{6}$$

$$\frac{XO + O \rightarrow X + O_2}{\text{net:} \quad O + O_3 \rightarrow 2O_2} \tag{7}$$

where the catalyst X = H, OH, NO, Cl and Br. Thus these species can, with varying degrees of efficiency, control the abundance and distribution of ozone in the stratosphere. Assignment of the relative importance and the prediction of the future impact of these catalytic species is dependent on a detailed understanding of the chemical reactions which form, remove and interconvert the active components of each family. This in turn requires knowledge of the atmospheric life cycles of the hydrogen, nitrogen and halogen-containing precursor and sink molecules, which control the overall abundance of $HO_x$, $NO_x$ and $ClO_x$ species.

Physical loss of ozone from the stratosphere is mainly by dynamical transport to the troposphere where further photochemically driven sources and sinks modify the ozone concentration field. Ozone is destroyed at the surface of the earth and so there is an overall downward flux in the lower part of the atmosphere. Physical removal of ozone and other trace gaseous components can also occur in the precipitation elements and on the surface of atmospheric aerosols. Since most of the precursor and sink molecules for the species catalytically active in ozone removal in the stratosphere are derived from or removed in the troposphere, global tropospheric chemistry is a significant feature of overall atmospheric ozone behavior.

Numerical simulation techniques are used to describe and investigate the behavior of the complex chemical system controlling atmospheric composition, the models having elements of chemistry, radiation and transport. The chemistry in such models may include some 150 elementary chemical reactions and photochemical processes involving some 50 different species. Laboratory measurements of the rates of these reactions have progressed rapidly over the past decade and have given us a basic understanding of the kinetics of these elementary processes and the way they act in controlling ozone. This applies particularly in the upper stratosphere where local chemical composition is predominantly photochemically controlled.

It has proved more difficult to describe adequately both the chemistry and the dynamics in the lower stratosphere. Here the chemistry is complicated by the involvement of temporary reservoir species such as $HOCl$, $H_2O_2$, $HNO_3$, $HCl$, $HNO_4$, $N_2O_5$ and $ClONO_2$ which 'store' active radicals and which strongly couple the $HO_x$, $NO_x$ and $ClO_x$ families. The long photochemical and thermal lifetimes of ozone and the reservoir species in this region give rise to strong interaction between chemistry and dynamics (transport) in the control of the distribution of ozone and other trace gases. Moreover, seasonal variability and natural perturbations due to volcanic injections of gases and aerosol particles add further to complicate the description and interpretation of atmospheric behavior in this region. Most of the changes in the predicted effects of chlorofluoromethanes and other pollutants on ozone column density have resulted from changes in our view of the chemistry in the lower stratosphere. A great deal of importance must therefore be attached to achieving an understanding of the key factors in ozone chemistry in this region of the atmosphere.

Description of atmospheric chemistry in the troposphere is similarly complicated by dynamical influence and additionally by involvement of the precipitation elements (i.e. cloud, rain and snow) in the chemical pathways. The homogeneous chemistry of the troposphere is centered round the role of the hydroxyl radical in promoting oxidation and scavenging of trace gases released from surface terrestrial sources. Tropospheric OH is an important issue for stratospheric ozone since it controls the flux of source gases such as $CH_4$, halogenated hydrocarbons, and sulfur compounds to the stratosphere. Although the mechanisms are more complex due to the involvement of larger and more varied entities, the overall pattern of relatively rapid photochemical cycles involving a coupled carbon/hydrogen/nitrogen and oxygen chemistry is similar to that in the stratosphere. The photochemical cycles influence both the odd hydrogen budget and also, through coupling of the hydrocarbon oxidation with $NO_2$ photochemistry, the *in situ* production and removal of tropospheric ozone. The concentration and distribution of tropospheric ozone is important in respect of its significant contribution to the total ozone column, and its radiative properties in the atmospheric heat balance.

Unlike some other more localized environmental issues, e.g. acid deposition, ozone layer modification is a global phenomenon which affects the well-being of every country in the world. Many nations around the world have actively demonstrated their commitment to understand the processes which control atmospheric ozone, and its susceptibility to change because of human activities, by funding research which should reduce the uncertainties that currently exist concerning the magnitude of predicted ozone modification for different atmospheric concentrations of pollutants. In order to achieve this required greater level of understanding, national and international scientific agencies have implemented long range research programs aimed at developing an organized, reliable body of knowledge of upper atmospheric processes while providing, in the near term, assessments of potential effects of human activities on the atmosphere.

# NATIONAL WEATHER SERVICE OVERHAUL

The National Weather Service has recently begun a full-scale redevelopment of its systems and its organization. The program is described below by the National Weather Service in a text which *Weather Almanac* has digested for quicker reading and comprehension by less technical readers.

Applied research conducted over the last ten years in the National Oceanic and Atmospheric Administration's (NOAA) Environmental Research Laboratories and other Federal laboratories has demonstrated that state-of-the-art laboratory techniques for analyzing and predicting severe weather and flood phenomena can be practicably applied to Weather Service operations. Because the scientific understanding of the atmosphere and the ability to forecast large- and small-scale weather phenomena has increased dramatically over the last two decades, the Department of Commerce has set an ambitious goal for the National Oceanic and Atmospheric Administration's (NOAA's) agency, the National Weather Service (NWS). The Service is to be modernized, to take full advantage of hundreds of new technological tools for upgrading weather forecasting.

In 1988, Public law 100-685 was signed by the President which, in part, specifies conditions on the planning, reporting and accomplishment of the modernization and associated restructuring of the NWS. This Strategic Plan is the first response to the Congress required by Public law 100-685.

## Principles for the modernization and associated restructuring

The following principles will guide the planning and implementation.

Throughout the process of change, the NWS will continue to fulfill its mission which is to provide weather and flood warnings, public forecasts and advisories for all of the United States, its territories, adjacent waters and oceans areas, primarily for the protection of life and property. NWS data and products will continue to be provided to private meteorologists for the provision of all specialized services. Certain principles are essential to meet the operational mission and will be continued during the modernization and associated restructuring transition period.

## The need to implement new science and technology

The most deadly of our nation's weather events — tornadoes, severe thunderstorms, and flash floods — are also the most difficult to detect and forecast. The new systems to be installed will enable earlier detection and permit the short range prediction of destructive, violent local storms and floods. The new observational technologies planned for the next decade will provide unprecedented amounts of complex data, thereby requiring that the operational forecasters have higher levels of analytical and interpretive skills. This will require training personnel and the deployment of proven, new observational information processing, and communications technologies.

## Obsolete equipment and yesterday's methods must be replaced

At present, the vintage technologies that compose part of today's weather service infrastructure are in desperate need of being replaced. As the equipment has aged, it has become costly to maintain. By replacing the equipment with more reliable technologies that support the new scientific capabilities, the nation can move into the future with strengthened confidence in its atmospheric prediction capabilities.

New technological systems are essential in providing the opportunity to improve warning and forecast services and for replacing obsolete and increasingly unreliable existing systems. Each of the new technologies to be installed plays a unique, but complementary role in the modernization process. New observational technologies will yield high resolution, time variant, three-dimensional representations of details on the state of the atmosphere.

At Weather Forecast Offices new data processing systems will aid the forecaster in the assimilation of changing data and numerical weather prediction outputs. The meteorologist and hydrologist will be able to rapidly manipulate, display and analyze information, thus enabling them to combine scientific principles and operational experience to produce more accurate and timely warning and forecast services for the Nation. The new high-resolution data sets and derived information are an important input to business and economic decision making outside the NWS.

The NWS is joined in its acquisition of much of the major new technologies by the Department of Transportation's Federal Aviation Administration and the Department of Defense, which results in economies of scale and a reduction in purchase costs. The new geostationary meteorological satellites being procured by NOAA complement the new radars and automated surface observing systems with blanket coverage of the conterminous states. Data from these new observing systems will be shared by each participating agency and will be available in summary form throughout the nation.

Automated Surface Observing System (ASOS) automating surface observations will relieve staff personnel from the time-consuming duty of collecting surface observations manually. Over 1000 ASOS systems across the nation will provide data on pressure, temperature, wind direction and speed, runway visibility, cloud ceiling heights, and type and intensity of precipitation on a nearly continuous basis.

## Next generation weather radars (NEXRAD stations)

This is a large step forward in early warnings of tornado and severe thunderstorms. Utilizing Doppler radar technology, the NEXRAD system will observe the presence and calculate the speed and direction of motion of severe weather elements. NEXRAD will also provide quantitative area precipitation measurements so important in hydrologic forecasting of potential flooding. For example, at present, currently limited (obsolescent) radar systems, tornado warnings are usually issued *oniy when visual sightings have been reported*. The advent of NEXRAD will not oniy allow for an earlier detection of the precursors to tornadic activity, but will also provide data on the direction and speed of tornado cells once they form. The national network of 160 NEXRAD systems, when totally deployed, will sharply upgrade uniform coverage  way beyond the capability of present day radar network. The NWS will operate 121 NEXRAD systems; the remainder will be at FAA and Department of Defense locations.

## Upgrading satellites

For severe weather and flood warnings and short range forecasts, cloud imagery and atmospheric sounding data from the geostationary meteorological satellites will continue to be a major data source. The new Geostationary Operational Environmental Satellite (GOES) I-M system will have separate instrumentation that allows simultaneous image and sounding data to be observed and transmitted to ground stations. The GOES I-M system will also provide visible and infrared imagery data updates as frequently as every six minutes during severe weather warning situations over selected areas of the United States.

For longer-range forecasting, soundings from the polar orbiting satellites are a primary data input into the National Meteorological Center numerical forecast models.

## National Center advanced computer systems

Warnings and forecasts prepared by NWS offices in the next decade will rely heavily on the basic analyses and advisories provided by the National Meteorological Center (NMC), especially for periods of 36 hours and beyond. These analyses and guidance products result from numerical models of the atmosphere run on high-speed computers. These increased demands require the acquisition of dedicated next generation Class VII computer capabilities with a processing capability that is a full order of magnitude greater than the present Class VI computer.

## Advanced Weather Interactive Processing System (AWIPS)

The revised system employed by AWIPS will function as the nerve center of the National Meteorological Centers operations. AWIPS will be the data integrator receiving the high-resolution data from the observation systems, the centrally collected data and the centrally prepared analysis and guidance information developed by the National Meteorological Center. The integration of all of this data from multiple sources represents **the information base from which all warning and forecast products will be prepared**. The AWIPS system will provide fast-response interactive analysis *and display of the* data to help support the meteorologists as they make rapid decisions, prepare warnings and forecasts, and disseminate information to users.

AWIPS includes the communications network that inter-connects each Weather Forecast Office for exchange of locally generated data. NOAAPORT will provide communications support for the operational distribution of the centrally collected data and centrally produced analysis and guidance products, as well as the satellite imagery and sounding data processed by the National Environmental Satellite, Data and Information Service.

## The need to restructure

The planned restructuring involves changing the number and location of field offices, a gradual transformation of the workforce to emphasize more professionalism in its makeup, and a reallocation of operational responsibilities between field offices and the National Centers.

The need to restructure is twofold: first, the combination of new operational concepts, new data sets, and an evolving scientific understanding of the dynamic processes associated with the most dangerous weather phenomena requires an *increase in the number of meteorologists*. The percentage increase of meteorologists in the NWS workforce will improve warnings and forecasts by taking advantage of the capabilities of the new technologies. Second, productivity and efficiency gains will occur as a result of increased integration of the new technological observation, information processing and communication systems with the staff. Key tradeoffs in the restructuring process exist between human capabilities, costs, and programmatic, scientific, and technological opportunities.

## The Weather Forecast Office (WFO) and its area of responsibility

How does the new Weather Forecast Office (WFO) fit into the new scheme? Consider this analogy: think of the surface of a map of the United States...now, consider a uniform arrangement of 115 mutually adjacent cylinders, each with a radius of approximately 125 miles. The cylinders, would each extend upward from the earth's surface up through the atmosphere. The volume inside each cylinder represents the "area" of operational responsibility associated with the WFO. A WFO is located in the center of the base of the cylinder. Each section of the country and the coastal ocean area is contained in one of these cylinders, thusly the whole of the country is theoretically uniformly covered.

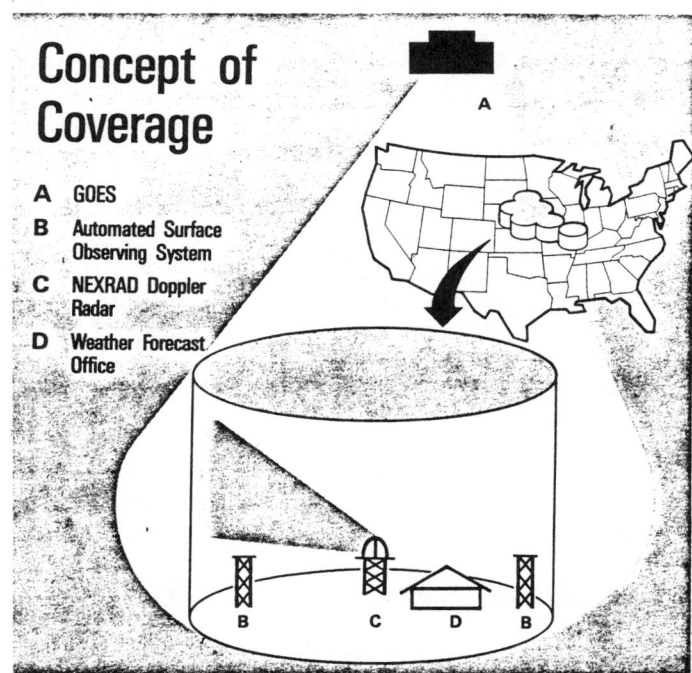

**Concept of Coverage**

A   GOES

B   Automated Surface Observing System

C   NEXRAD Doppler Radar

D   Weather Forecast Office

*The above schematic suggests how the individual weather forecast offices (WFO) will bear observation and forecast responsibility for an area which has a radius of 125 miles, and reaches to the top of the atmosphere, verically. Each office's "cylinder" of responsibility will abut cylinders around it so that 115 of these cylinders can cover the nation. Many formerly manual operations have been handed to automated gear.*

The GOES Satellite positioned over the United States is providing to each of these "cylinders" an earth image. The regularly updated image represents uniform coverage with visible and infrared imagery of each of the "cylinders." It also provides remote soundings which penetrate each cylinder from above. Associated with each WFO is one or more NEXRAD radars which scan the atmosphere from near the earth's surface to a height sufficient to detect the majority of meteorological events.

Also serving the WFOs are 1000 ASOS units. They are spread across the surface of the country and each measures surface weather parameters as fast as once every minute. All of these data within the cylinder are sent directly to the AWIPS system in each WFO. The WFO's AWIPS system is also receiving the centrally produced guidance products from the National Centers, generated from globally exchanged data. Subsets of these data are on tap for all other WFOs through the AWIPS communication network.

## Integrated operations within the WFO

The future operations will allow forecasters to comprehensively address the air-sea environment in their assigned area. The observation and analysis of current and expected weather conditions can be quickly and reliably completed, critical decisions made, and translated into immediate warnings and forecasts. This is contrasted to current operations where a number of meteorologists and technicians are required to individually evaluate a limited data base and separately derive the various warnings and forecasts.

*The concept of the local data base is central to future operations.* The high volume of data from the local NEXRAD and geostationary meteorological satellites combined with the high frequency observations from ASOS will flow directly to the Weather Forecast Office. The most complete data sets will only be available to the local WFO. However, summarized data from all NEXRADs and ASOSs in the Nation will be made available to all field offices.

The new observing systems are designed to provide data sets which can be immediately integrated into three dimensional depictions of the rapidly changing state of the environment. Each system will contribute a critical part, combining with and complementing data from all other systems to form a complete set of information about that particular cylinder of space from the earth's surface to the upper atmosphere comprising the particular WFO's area of responsibility.

AWIPS work stations will allow the forecaster to quickly update, quality control, and analyze current processes and events detailed within the area of concern. New dedicated supercomputer capabilities and high resolution models running at the National Centers will provide a stream of detailed, frequently updated guidance to forecasters, assisting in the prediction of future conditions. This represents a new, highly integrated mode of operation which greatly increases the productivity of personnel, and also holds the promise of increased accuracy and greater timeliness of forecast services for the nation.

## The new structure

The WFO will be the future weather office that will provide all warning and forecast services for its assigned area of responsibility. The forecast and warnings operations at the WFO are supported by guidance products issued from the National Centers and RFC.

## Weather Forecast Offices (WFOs)

A total of 115 WFOs will exist in the future that will provide weather and hydrologic services in four major areas:

- Watches and warnings for the general public for severe local storms, floods, flash floods and winter storms. local and zone public forecasts, and fire weather forecasts;

- local aviation watches and warnings, terminal forecasts, and domestic aviation enroute forecasts;

- Marine warnings and forecasts for coastal areas of the nation and the Great Lakes; and

- Hydrologic services which identify flash flood-prone areas and the development of community supported surveillance systems.

The foundation for the more accurate and timely warnings and forecasts will be the guidance products from the National Centers and RFCs and the data from the new observing systems: ASOS, NEXRAD, and geostationary meteorological satellites.

The basic tool for more accurate and timely warnings and forecasts from the WFO is AWIPS. It will assemble, process and display the observational data and guidance from National Centers. AWIPS will help meteorologists with the warning and forecast decision process through an interactive work station. It will pre-format warning and forecast products and disseminate these products to the users in a timely manner.

## River Forecast Centers (RFCs)

RFCs provide hydrologic forecasts and guidance information in three major categories:

- Mainstem river and flood forecasts regarding about 3000 locations.

- Flash flood and headwater guidance to WFOs for warning services.

- Long-term, seasonal forecasts providing estimates of snowmelt and water supply outlooks (from excess to drought) at approximately 1000 locations for periods up to several months in advance.

In the 1990s, the operations of RFCs are expected to change in a several ways. Each of the 13 RFCs will be co-located with a WFO. This will result in a more effective utilization of hydrological and meteorological information facilitated by a Hydrologic Analysis and Support Group in each co-located facility.

## National Meterological Center

The National Meteorological Center has the responsibility for national and international data collection. This data base is first employed for global atmospheric and oceanic analysis. The resultant analyses are distributed to international and domestic users which include the NWS, other government agencies, and private sector meteorologists. The data base is then used as initial input to global atmospheric numerical models. These models produce international aviation forecast products, high seas forecast products, long range national forecast, and forecast guidance for local WFOs and RFCs. New dedicated Class VII computer capabilities will enable increases in the resolution of the models resulting in improved forecast products and guidance. Traditionally the long range national forecasts have begun at 3 days and beyond. The new computers will reduce this threshold to beyond 36 hours. This will allow local forecasters to devote their attention to short-term weather events that are not aided by the use of centralized computer models.

## Climate Analysis Center

This Center is a specialized facility which is part of the National Meteorological Center and is colocated with it to take advantage of the facilities available there. The Center's responsibilities are national and international in scope, collecting, organizing and disseminating climate information for diagnosis of short-term climate change; the Center does research on the physical cause of short-term climate change; and issues forecasts of departures of average weather conditions from climatological means.

## The National Hurricane Center

This special facility will continue to be responsible for providing the nation its strongest measure of security from tropical storms. It functions by analyzing, predicting, and tracking     tropical weather systems, that often become  hurricanes. The Center provides leadership and coordination of storm related preparedness. It uses geostationary meteorological satellites to track and monitor tropical storms 24 hours-per-day throughout the cycle of a storm. It will utilize coastal NEXRADs radar systems which are becoming available to provide hurricane understanding well beyond that available at present. NMC's new Class VII computers will run new hurricane models which to greatly assist forecasters at the Hurricane Center. AWIPS at the National Hurricane Center will serve the Center's mission as well as NMC's.

## National Severe Storms Forecast Center

In the 1990s, the National Severe Storms Forecast Center will provide national severe weather guidance to WFOs and RFCs. It will issue more timely and specific advisories necessary to support the severe weather and flood warning activities of the WFOs.

## National Data Buoy Center

The National Data Buoy Center will continue the operation of deep sea, coastal buoys, and headland systems. Data from the buoys and these coastal systems are essential to marine warnings and forecasts, and numerical weather predictions.

## Staffing

The new observing, data processing, and display systems will provide forecasters the opportunity to sample, observe, and analyze the environment to an extent never before possible. This will mean a better product, more efficiently produced. Future field offices will have a core staff of professional scientists at each WFO and RFC to take advantage of these new capabilities. These individuals will provide all warning and forecast services across their area of responsibility. They will have far better data with which to meet these tasks, owing to the systems described.

Taking a quantum leap such as this — improving product while using fewer people — will place great emphasis on a higher level of professional skills and on retraining many technicians. NWS has strategic as well as tactical programs to effect the implied transmutation.

For instance, each WFO will operate 24 hours a day, and a certified meteorologist will be in charge at all times. Other such staffing upgrades will occur. The staffing level will be determined by peak service demands and maximum weather activity, with reduced staff requirements at selected offices during hours of lower threat and service demands.

## NWS recreates itself while carrying on busines as usual

The NWS has never undertaken a systematic modernization and associated restructuring effort of the magnitude presented in this Strategic Plan. Accomplishing the transition from today's operation to the modernized and restructured NWS of the 1990s, without disrupting ongoing services, will be a complicated process. NWS believes it has, however, made adequate provisions for achieving both aims.

# INDEX

* A multi-page report is provided for each city with asterisk designation.

*A multi-page report is provided for each city with asterisk designation.*

* A multi-page report is provided for each city with asterisk designation.

853

*A multi-page report is prded for each city with asterisk designation.*

855

Desk